National Security
Law & Policy

National Security Law & Policy

THIRD EDITION

Edited by

John Norton Moore

Guy B. Roberts

Robert F. Turner

CAROLINA ACADEMIC PRESS

Durham, North Carolina

ISBN 978-1-61163-704-5
LCCN 2015933689

Carolina Academic Press
700 Kent Street
Durham, NC 27701
Telephone (919) 489-7486
Fax (919) 493-5668
www.cap-press.com

Printed in the United States of America

Contents

A detailed table of contents is available at <http://caplaw.com/natsec3e/>.

Table of Cases

Preface

> It is "obvious and unarguable" that no governmental interest is more compelling than the security of the Nation.
>
> — U.S. Supreme Court in *Haig v. Agee*

More than a third of a century has passed since two of the editors of this book, John Norton Moore and Robert F. Turner, co-founded the Center for National Security Law (CNSL) at the University of Virginia School of Law as a nonpartisan, nonprofit research institute to promote interdisciplinary advanced scholarship and education about legal issues affecting the national security of the United States. It was the first organization focused expressly on national security law in the nation, and probably in the world. One of the Center's first projects was to design and publish a casebook in the anticipation of an exponential growth of the field of national security law and the need for other educational institutions to have the most comprehensive and up-to-date materials for use in the classroom and as a reference tool for national or homeland security professionals.

When the first edition of *National Security Law* was published in 1991, it was described as addressing "a new field in American law and legal education." Today the field of national security law is firmly established. Courses in national security law and policy are taught at the large majority of American law schools and in many other graduate and undergraduate programs, and practitioners now abound throughout the government. The Association of American Law Schools has now recognized the new field and established a Section on National Security Law. The American Bar Association (ABA) Standing Committee on Law and National Security (chaired throughout most of the 1980s and early 1990s by either Professor Moore or Turner) now publishes a book on *Careers in National Security Law*. A parallel discipline called "operational law" has developed simultaneously within the military (and a chapter on this field is included in the casebook). Indeed, the United States military leads the world in incorporation of law into military operations.

Professors and government practitioners from around the world now routinely come to the CNSL National Security Law Institute's programs, and copies of the previous edition of the casebook can be found in government libraries from Argentina and Australia to Ethiopia and Russia. The Center for National Security Law has also taken an active role in encouraging and supporting other universities to establish national security or homeland security programs. In 1994, for example, we assisted colleagues at Duke Law School establish their very excellent Center on Law, Ethics, and National Security, with which CNSL and the ABA Standing Committee annually co-sponsor a major national conference in Washington, DC. The two individuals who have served as director of the Duke center are both graduates of our National Security Law Institute, and the current director is a regular instructor at the Institute.

While there are now other casebooks titled *National Security Law*, we respectfully suggest that there is no other single volume that provides as authoritative and comprehensive review of the field. The other books, while of high quality, tend to focus on more limited areas, particularly domestic legal issues such as war powers and First and Fourth Amendment freedoms and issues of homeland security. In contrast, this volume seeks a full synergy of international law, international relations, and national law and policy related to the security of the nation, the challenge of maintaining international peace and security, and the problem of unauthorized violence in the world. With that in mind, we believe we have successfully brought together the top scholars and legal experts in the field in a single volume that we believe will be of interest to practitioners, policy makers and students for years to come. A review of the brief biographies of our contributors will confirm that we have assembled leading authorities on their respective topics, and as a result, we have produced a volume of tremendous and continuing relevance to the post-9/11 national security challenges facing this country.

This third edition is not merely a modest revision of earlier editions as evidenced by the change in title to *National Security Law & Policy*. We changed the title believing that it more accurately reflects the scope of the material contained in the casebook and the self-evident fact that policy more often than not shapes the legal constructs under which governments and societies operate, and the law likewise can shape and impact national policies. As former President of the International Court of Justice Rosalyn Higgins, and one of our authors, cogently noted:

> Policy considerations ... are integral parts of that decision making process that we call international law; the assessment of so-called extralegal considerations is part of the legal process, just as is reference to the accumulation of past decisions and current norms. There is no avoiding the essential relationship between law and politics.[1]

As the reader will quickly discern, in order to comprehensively deal with the subject matter many of the topics are addressed from both a policy and legal standpoint.

Several chapters that were of greater relevance in a Cold War setting have been deleted, other chapters have been substantially redesigned or updated, and important new chapters have been added to reflect, in part, the ever changing challenge of combatting terrorism and other national and international security threats which have only grown and diversified since the tragedy of the terrorist attacks on September 11, 2001. New chapters include: Law and Warfare in the Cyber Domain, Detention (treatment of detainees), Transnational Organized Crime (incorporating in part a chapter on counter narcotics from the second edition), "Lawfare" (the use of law as a means of struggle during armed conflict), The Foreign Intelligence Surveillance Act (FISA), and An Introduction to Economic Sanctions: A Brief History and the Basic Tools. The latter chapter is the first overview in print of the important, but highly technical, United States legal mechanisms for enforcing economic sanctions. Some chapters have been consolidated and most have been extensively revised or re-written to reflect the dynamic and constantly changing security environment.

Although the international law of conflict management is frequently presented in introductory international law courses, typically it is dealt with in cursory fashion. While it is gratifying to see more and more students taking courses on international security issues, it remains a fact that few graduates, and even surprisingly few teachers of international law, have a sophisticated knowledge and appreciation of the complexities of the international law of conflict management in all its dimensions—from initial determination of the lawfulness of coercion to efforts at arms control. Moreover, national

---

1. ROSALYN HIGGINS, PROBLEMS & PROCESS—INTERNATIONAL LAW AND HOW WE USE IT (Oxford: Clarendon Press, 1994) p. 5.

security matters are increasingly surrounded with a range of important national law issues such as the War Powers Resolution and congressional constraints on intelligence operations and arms transfers.

Indeed, one of the most dramatic trends of the past four decades in national security affairs has been the increase in congressional efforts to influence the decision-making process by the enactment of hundreds of new laws and statutory restrictions on the discretion of the Executive Branch. An illustration of the magnitude of this post-Vietnam legislative activism can be seen in the growth of the congressional publication *Legislation on Foreign Relations*. Some observers view this enhanced congressional role as a positive response to the tragedy of Vietnam and the abuses generically categorized as "Watergate," while others contend that Congress has sometimes exceeded its constitutional authority and in the process endangered the security of the nation. As this casebook is being published, Congress and the President remain at loggerheads over a number of issues of national security concern (such as the closing of the Guantanamo detention facility, alleged abuses of intelligence gathering under the Foreign Intelligence Surveillance Act, and immigration policy) which has resulted in the President taking a number of actions that the leadership in Congress believes violate the Constitution—prompting calls for additional legislation to further restrict the powers of the President. Whatever view one takes in this heated debate, the plethora of new legislation in this area has made the study of national security law essential for anyone who wishes to understand the American national security process as the U.S. Government grapples with the multi-faceted multipolar international security environment.

This casebook brings together teaching materials addressing a broad spectrum of important national security legal issues. It seeks to place such legal issues in historical and strategic context, and to acquaint the student with a wide range of recurring national security problems and issues. It is a carefully designed product integrating the expertise of the foremost authorities in each area with the editors' overall structure of the new field of national security law. While the security challenges of the 21st century know no borders, we have re-organized the casebook into two sections: one focusing on national issues and U.S. domestic responses, and the other section focused on the national responses to challenges in the international security environment.

The arena of national or homeland security law and policy has grown exponentially since the terrorist attacks of September 11, 2001, as we believe we have captured in depth and scope in these chapters. Unlike other volumes that focus strictly on the legal aspects, we included, as we did in the previous edition, chapters devoted to the theoretic bases for understanding the development of international law and the formulation of policy supporting democratic principles and rule-based government. As such, it is designed for use not just in law schools but also in graduate programs in international relations and national security, and the nation's war colleges and service academies—as well as to serve as a handy desk reference for professionals and practitioners in the field.

During our professional lifetimes the legal staff at the Central Intelligence Agency has grown from one or two lawyers to more than 120 in an explosion of litigation on national security issues. Issues once almost never raised in court are now increasingly the subject of litigation. The State Department's Office of Legal Adviser has grown even larger with more than 200 attorneys and over 100 support staff, and since the terrorist attacks of 9/11 the FBI national security law legal team has increased more than five-fold. Three decades ago there was one lawyer on the National Security Council staff who focused primarily on Freedom of Information (FOIA) requests and an occasional contracting or personnel legal issue. Today there is not only a full-time NSC Legal Adviser focused heavily upon policy issues, but a Deputy Legal Adviser and two other lawyers as well. And today's military commanders, given the many legal issues associated with deployments for peace-keeping, peace enforcement and combat operations, understands that the Staff Judge Advocate is among the most valuable resources available when planning and conducting these operations. This is amply reflected in our chapters on Operational Law and the Law of Armed Conflict and Neutrality.

The choice of *national security* as a focus for this book reflects the priority and deference generally given to this phrase in contemporary policy, and the resulting need for lawyers, social scientists, policy-makers—indeed, all citizens—to analyze and evaluate national security issues on a critical and continuing basis. We believe strongly that this effort will be enhanced by this book's comprehensive examination of the many ways in which law and national security interact. Consequently, the chapters of this book are comprehensive and often highlight the diversity of values and assumptions that underlie national policy on and current conceptions of national security. They explore the contemporary policy dilemmas and political tensions which such diversity can generate, as well as some of the traditional resolutions, tentative accommodations, and continuing contradictions embodied in the law applicable to each area.

As a principal outcome of past political accommodations, *law* is both a starting point and an end product of each new struggle by the institutions of government to balance the frequently imprecise demands of national security with the often equally vague advancement of other important values and objectives as reflected in national policies designed to meet these national security challenges. Broadly conceived as it must be, the legal process is in practice frequently the battleground on which the struggle to define and prioritize national security objectives occurs. Such struggles are seldom won or lost permanently; each generation typically feels compelled to reexamine and challenge the decisions and accommodations of earlier times as perceptions and priorities change, international realities shift, and circumstances require. It is an extraordinarily dynamic area with new challenges, such as terrorists and criminal organizations using drones to carry out their illicit activities, yet to be fully addressed by both policy and the law. We recognize, therefore, that the terrain will be a changing one in many of the areas covered in this book. Yet it is also likely that the issues posed in each area, the trade-offs that they present, and the approaches suggested for dealing with them will also be characterized by a remarkable continuity over the years. In any event, we are confident that the chapters that follow will provide a useful framework for policy analysis and decision as well as a current snapshot of the legal landscape, recognizing that the contours of the dynamic field of national security law are in constant flux, being shaped and reshaped each year in light of emerging challenges posed by globalization, the continuing threat of terrorism and the resurgence of traditional forms of state to state conflict.

The book does not propose a single grand theory or formula to assure rational choice or sound law in the realm of national security. Rather the purpose is, by the broad scope of the material covered, to expose students and practitioners to the real-world challenges and dilemmas facing decision makers and government officials in ensuring our national (and international) security. Consequently, in addition to the new chapters previously mentioned, the other chapters in the book address not only some of the central public preoccupations of our time—military force, arms control and nonproliferation, free speech, terrorism—but also a number of more esoteric corners of the law relating to national security, such as the environment and export controls, that are often ignored in public debate until, from time to time, some unexpected crisis thrusts them into the limelight and points up the need for wider discussion and understanding.

Periods of crisis can be the worst of times to consider the priorities and trade-offs that govern decisions about the making and application of law in matters of national security. As passions mount, positions tend to polarize around extremes. On the one hand, uncritical invocations of "national security" can become all-purpose justifications for disregarding or overriding values that the security of the country is in fact meant to ensure. On the other hand, skeptics of security considerations may underestimate the dangers inherent in a world that is all too frequently inhospitable to those same values. In balancing these competing considerations it is easy either to focus on the real constraints of national security or to neglect the realities of a world that is too frequently harsh in preoccupation with immediate preservation of equally real competing values. Only through an honest understanding of the realities of national security threats and competing interests can optimal and informed judgments be made about the efficacy of our national security law construct and the policies these laws are designed to implement. It should perhaps be remembered in this connection that democracies, for all their greatness, can all too easily misperceive serious totalitarian challenges and turn inward toward a more familiar and compatible world. While comforting in the short run, in a globalized multi-faceted world ignoring the many and diverse threats to international peace and security only emboldens aggressive conduct and undermines deterrence—thus increasing the risk of war.

During the last quarter-century, whether for good or for bad, the law has taken on a dramatically increased importance in the national security process. Policymakers, political scientists, historians, and citizens who seek to be informed voters all have a need to understand these changes. Members of the legal profession, in particular, have a special responsibility to understand these developments—not only because the past two decades have seen an explosion in the demand for lawyers trained in this field, but also because of the traditional role played by our profession in shaping informed public opinion about important public policy issues. Based on the reactions to previous editions, we have produced this third edition with the expectation that it will facilitate an interdisciplinary understanding of what we believe to be one of the most important public policy developments now facing the nation; and if it contributes in even a small way to that end our efforts—and those of the many scholars and practitioners who helped make this work possible—will have been justified.

In a work of this kind there will inevitably be errors. Every reasonable effort has been made to keep these to a minimum, but the breadth and dynamic nature of the subject matter—combined with the interactions of numerous contributors—virtually guarantee that there will likely be mistakes. The editors accept full responsibility for any errors, and invite readers to bring them to our attention so that future editions may be corrected.

Many of the substantive topics addressed in the volume are highly controversial and subject to legitimate differences in points of view. We believe, however, that one of the book's strengths is the diversity of viewpoints represented by the distinguished authors who have contributed individual chapters. Each contributor is of course responsible for any value judgments reflected in his or her chapter, and readers are reminded to keep in mind that many of the subjects addressed in the pages which follow involve newly developing or rapidly changing fields of law which are not without controversy and continue to be shaped as our understanding of the national and international security challenges evolves.

Finally, as the brief biographical sketches of our contributors reveal, several of our chapters have been written by individuals currently employed by the federal government. It should be emphasized that the views expressed herein and responsibility for the accuracy of facts stated are those of the contributors and should not be attributed to any department or agency of the government or any other entity with which they currently or in the past have been affiliated. Many of the chapters include lists of additional readings that will provide other insights on the subjects.

John Norton Moore, Guy B. Roberts & Robert F. Turner
Charlottesville, Virginia, March 2015

Acknowledgments

The academic field of "national security law" began at the University of Virginia School of Law more than forty-five years ago, when one of the editors (Professor John Norton Moore) offered the first American law school course on what was then called "Law and National Security." That the field began at the University of Virginia was particularly fitting, as the University was founded by one of history's greatest champions of the rule of law, Thomas Jefferson, whose personal interest in the interplay between law and national security issues while serving as U.S. Minister to France, America's first Secretary of State, and two terms as our third president, is well known.[1] "Mr. Jefferson's University" has a proud history of extraordinary scholarship and teaching in related fields and is associated with such luminaries as Permanent Court of International Justice Judge John Bassett Moore, American Political Science Association and American Society of International Law President Quincy Wright, and International Court of Justice Judge Hardy C. Dillard—who served for many years as our Law School's Dean. It is not by coincidence that the U.S. Army Judge Advocate General's Legal Center and School has since 1951 been located at the University of Virginia.

Known initially as "International Law II: Law and National Security," then as "Law and National Security," and finally as "National Security Law," the original course was supplemented over the years by more specialized seminars focusing on the separation of national security powers, foreign policy goals, intelligence, arms control, foreign trade, and other areas. To promote the teaching of national security law across the nation, in 1981 Professors Moore and Turner co-founded the Center for Law and National Security (later renamed Center for National Security Law [CNSL]) at the law school and began work on the first edition of this casebook. In the past quarter-century, the number of American law schools offering at least one course or seminar in this area has grown from four to well over 100—encompassing the large majority of the nation's accredited schools of law.

Over the decades, we have benefited greatly from the scholarship and expertise of some of the top authorities in the world on various issues related to national security law. They have traveled to Charlottesville to guest lecture in our classes or to take part in CNSL conferences, we have encountered them in our work with the American Bar Association Standing Committee on Law and National Security (to which one of us gave its current name and each of us chaired during most of the 1980s and early 1990s), they have lectured in our twenty-two past annual National Security Law Institutes, and/or we have met them

---

1. *See, e.g.,* Jefferson's *Opinion on the Treaties with France,* April 28, 1793, in 25 Papers of Thomas Jefferson 608 (John Catanzariti, ed. 1992) ("Compacts ... between nation and nation are obligatory on them by the same moral law which obliges individuals to observe their compacts.... Of these, it is true, that nations are to be judges for themselves, since no one nation has a right to sit in judgment over another. But the tribunal of our consciences remains, and that also of the opinion of the world. These will revise the sentence we pass in our own case, and as we respect these, we must see that in judging ourselves we have honestly done the part of impartial and rigorous judges.").

in other venues. Some have first come to us as students and then gone on to achieve distinction in their chosen fields.

With great sadness we note that, since the first edition of this work was published, some of the preeminent scholars and practitioners in this new field have passed from the scene. Myres S. McDougal, Sterling Professor of International Law at Yale Law School and perhaps the most able international lawyer in the world during the second half of the twentieth century, died in 1998. Thus far in this century we have lost former Yale Law School Dean Eugene V. Rostow, former State Department Legal Adviser Monroe Leigh, and other cherished scholars, practitioners, and friends. Howard S. Levie, draftsman of the Korean Armistice Agreement and former colonel in the U.S. Army's Judge Advocate General's Corps, died in 2009 at the age of 101. Ambassador Donald Mahley completed negotiation of the United Nations Arms Trade Treaty and helped update our Arms Control chapter just before his death in 2014. Each of them deserves to be recognized for their great contributions to the field of national security law, and we have all been influenced greatly by their scholarship, friendship, and wise counsel.

Rather than attempting to cover every aspect of the topic ourselves, we decided in 1981 to solicit chapters from those individuals we thought to be the leading experts in the nation—in some cases, in the world—on the specific issues being addressed. We were pleased with the result, and when we decided to produce a 2nd edition we again sought out the leading experts in each field. This same strategy was followed for our 3rd edition, again we believe with excellent results. We are deeply indebted to each of the men and women who have contributed to the 3rd edition.

Transforming chapters into a finished product required many hundreds of hours of painstaking copy editing, cite checking, and other administrative efforts. We are profoundly indebted to the casebook's project manager, our very able in-house editor Judith (Judy) Ellis. Judy labored tirelessly and without complaint for months—including many Saturdays—formatting, proofreading, updating, and corresponding with contributing authors to ensure that this new edition is as up-to-date and error-free as possible. She worked with contributors to meet tight deadlines, doing the necessary copy editing and coordinating the efforts of student assistants in checking, updating, and correcting countless details that are necessary to produce a first-quality casebook.

We are also deeply indebted to two extraordinary law students, Nathaniel (Nate) Freeman and Lauren Schwartz, who worked under Judy's supervision to check citations and assist in proofreading and other essential tasks. Both have demonstrated exceptional talents and a willingness to go far beyond the requirements with which they have been tasked, and we wish them continued success as they make the transition from law school into the professional world.

The publication of the first edition of *National Security Law* in 1991 marked our first association with Carolina Academic Press. The experience was so positive that since then we have turned to them for virtually all of our publishing needs, and with each new volume our respect and appreciation for their professionalism has risen even more. We would thus be remiss if we did not acknowledge our grateful appreciation to Dr. Keith Sipe, President of Carolina Academic Press, and to his colleagues Linda Lacy, Bob Conrow, and Tim Colton. They have made the preparation and publication of this edition a most enjoyable enterprise.

Both this project and virtually everything else our Center has done over the past thirty-four years has been made possible by the generous support of a number of philanthropic foundations and donors, to whom we owe a debt of gratitude that words cannot easily express. Without such support, this work would not be possible. We are profoundly grateful to Dr. Ingrid Gregg, Montgomery Brown, and their colleagues and board members at the Earhart Foundation, both for their generous financial support for this edition and their funding of the first edition prepared in the 1980s. Without the support of the Earhart Foundation and other philanthropic organizations, neither our Center nor this volume would exist.

We are also grateful to the following publishers, organizations, and individuals for their permission to reprint copyrighted materials in the casebook:

The American Bar Association for "The Rule of Law in Outer Space," by John Cobb Cooper, 47 *Am. Bar Ass'n J.* 23 (1961). Reprinted by permission of the *ABA Journal*; "Report of the Blue Ribbon Working Group on International Terrorism," 31 *Int'l Law News* 17 (2002). Reprinted by permission.

The *American Journal of International Law* for permission to reprint "Editorial Comments," 95 *Am. J. Int'l L.* 4, 835–43 (2001); "Memorandum by Monroe Leigh, Legal Adviser of the Department of State, to Henry Kissinger, Secretary of State, July 8, 1976," reprinted in part in 73 *Am. J. Int'l L.* 122–24 (1979); Moore, "The Secret War in Central America and the Future World Order," 80 *Am. J. Int'l L.* 43, 60–65, 80–91, 125–27 (1986); Moore, "Grenada and the International Double Standard," 78 *Am. J. Int'l L.* 153–59 (1984); Joyner, "Reflections on the Lawfulness of Invasion," 78 *Am. J. Int'l L.* 131, 134–35 (1984); Moore, "Editorial Comment: The Inter-American System Snarls in Falklands War," 76 *Am. J. Int'l L.* 830, 830–31 (1982); Moore, "Reply on the Falklands War," 77 *Am. J. Int'l L.* 610–13 (1983); Murphy, ed., "Contemporary Practice of the United States Relating to International Law," 96 *Am. J. Int'l L.* 237–255 (2002); Lobel and Ratner, "Bypassing the Security Council: Ambiguous Authorizations to Use Force, Cease-Fires and the Iraqi Inspection Regime," 93 *Am. J. Int'l L.* 124, 124–27, 144–45, 154 (1999); Matheson, "United Nations Governance of Postconflict Societies," 95 *Am. J. Int'l L.* 76, 77–83 (2001); Wilde, "From Danzig to East Timor and Beyond: the Role of International Territorial Administration," 95 *Am. J. Int'l L.* 583, 587, 591–93, 602, 605–06 (2001); Henkin, "Kosovo and the Law of 'Humanitarian Intervention', Editorial Comments: NATO's Kosovo Intervention," 93 *Am. J. Int'l L.* 824, 824–28 (1999); Wright, "The Meaning of the Pact of Paris," 27 *Am. J. Int'l L.* 39, 42–43 (1933).

The *American University International Law Review* for permission to reprint Schifter, "Human Rights at the United Nations: The South Africa Precedent," 8 *Am. U. J. Int'l L. & Pol'y* 361, 363–65, 365–69, 370–71 (1992/1993).

Aspen Publishers for the use of excerpts from Stephen Dycus' "National Security Law" chapter from National Security Law. Reprinted from National Security Law: Third Edition with the permission of Aspen Publishers.

Bloomsbury Publishing for © James Sloan, 2011, 'Militarisation of Peacekeeping in the Twenty-First Century', pp. 3–5, 282–95, Hart Publishing, used by permission of Bloomsbury Publishing Plc.

The British Institute of International and Comparative Law for permission to reprint from Christine Gray, "Regional Arrangements and the United Nations Collective Security System" in The Changing Constitution of the United Nations, 91, 101–02, 104, 107–08 (Hazel Fox ed., 1997).

The Brookings Institution Press for permission to reprint an excerpt from Paul B. Stares, Space and National Security (1987).

Cambridge University Press for permission to reprint Lauterpacht et al. eds., "The Kuwait Crisis: Basic Documents," 1 *Cambridge International Documents Series* 248 (1991);

Locke, Two Treatises of Government: A Critical Edition with an Introduction and Apparatus Criticus, section 143–48, 159–60 (P. Laslett rev. ed. 1963) (3rd ed. 1698). Reprinted with the permission of Cambridge University Press.

Carolina Academic Press for permission to reprint from Shane and Bruff, Separation of Powers Law: Cases and Materials (2011).

Columbia University Press for permission to reprint excerpts from The Development of the Law of Belligerent Occupation, 1863–1914 by Doris Graber © 1949 Columbia University Press. Reprinted with the permission of the publisher; "Pacificus No. I, Philadelphia, June 29, 1793," reprinted in 15 The Papers of Alexander Hamilton © 1969 Columbia University Press. Reprinted with the permission of the publisher.

The Continuum International Publishing Group for permission to reprint from Scharf and Schabas, Slobodan Milosevic on Trial: A Companion (2002). Reprinted by permission of The Continuum International Publishing Group.

Cornell Law Review for permission to reprint Fulbright, "American Foreign Policy in the 20th Century Under an 18th-Century Constitution," 47 *Cornell L. Q.* 1, 3 (1961).

DePaul Law Review for permission to reprint material from Stewart, "United States Ratification of the Covenant on Civil and Political Rights: The Significance of the Reservations, Understandings and Declarations," 42 *DePaul L. Rev.* 1183 (1993).

Duke Law Journal for permission to reprint from Fisher, "Congressional Access to Information: Using Legislative Will and Leverage," 52 *Duke L. J.* 323 (2002).

Duke University Press for permission to reprint material from Schifter, "The Cause of Freedom," 8 *Mediterranean Q.* 6, 7–10 (1997). Permission is granted on behalf of the publisher. © Mediterranean Affairs, Inc.

Duncker & Humblot GmbH for permission to reprint Delbruck, "The Fight Against Global Terrorism: Self-Defense or Collective Security as International Police Action? Some Comments on the International Legal Implications of the 'War Against Terror'," 44 *German Y.B. Int'l L.* 9, 13–19 (2001).

Emory Law Journal for permission to reprint from Wald, "The Freedom of Information Act: A Short Case Study in the Perils and Paybacks of Legislating Democratic Values," 33 *Emory L. J.* 649 (1984),

European Journal of International Law for permission to reprint Higgins, "Peace and Security: Achievements and Failures," 6 *Eur. J. Int'l L.* 445, 449–53, 455–60 (1995); Simma, "NATO, the UN and the Use of Force: Legal Aspects," 10 *Eur. J. Int'l L.* 1, 14–18 (1999).

The Fletcher Forum for permission to reprint an excerpt from Sheehan, "The Entebbe Raid: The Principle of Self-Help in International Law as Justification for State Use of Armed Force," 1 *Fletcher Forum* 135 (1977).

Freedom House for permission to reprint material from O'Brien, "Israel's attack on Osirak," 63 *Freedom at Issue* 3, 4 (1981); Mallison, "The Disturbing Questions," 63 *Freedom at Issue* 9, 10, 11 (1981).

The General Secretariat, Organization of American States for permission to reprint an excerpt from Farer, "Human Rights before the Second World War" in Inter-American Commission on Human Rights, Ten Years of Activities 1971–1981, at v–vi (1982).

David Graham for permission to reprint from his piece, "Operational Law—A Concept Comes of Age," in *Army Lawyer* 10 (1987).

Greenwood Publishing Group for permission to reprint material from Bowett, United Nations Forces (1965).

Harcourt, Inc. for permission to use an excerpt from The Congress of Vienna: A Study of Allied Unity, © 1946 by Harold Nicolson and renewed 1973 by Lionel Benedict Nicolson and Nigel Nicolson, reprinted by permission of Harcourt, Inc.

Harvard International Law Review for permission to reprint excerpts from Turner, "Truman, Korea, and the Constitution: Debunking the 'Imperial President' Myth," 19 *Harv. J. Int'l L.* 541–57, 563–76 © (1996) by the President and Fellows of Harvard College and the Harvard International Law Journal.

Harvard University Press for permission to reprint an excerpt from Cicero: Volume XVI. Reprinted by permission of the publisher and the Trustees of the Loeb Classical Library from Cicero: Volume XVI, Loeb Classical Library Volume L 213, translated by Clinton W. Keyes, Cambridge, Mass.: Harvard University Press, 1928. The Loeb Classical Library ® is a registered trademark of the President and Fellows of Harvard College; Casper, Separating Power. Reprinted by permission of the publisher from Separating Power: Essays on the Founding Period by Gerhard Casper, Cambridge, Mass.: Harvard University Press, Copyright © 1997 by the President and Fellows of Harvard College.

International Law Association for permission to reprint from "Fourth Interim Report of the Committee on International Terrorism," International Law Association, Report of the Sixtieth Conference (1982).

International Review of the Red Cross for permission to reprint material from Schmitt, "Wired Warfare: Computer Network Attack and Jus in Bello," 846 *International Review of the Red Cross* 365, 374 (2002).

Johns Hopkins University Press for permission to reprint Bielefeldt, Heiner, "Muslim Voices in the Human Rights Debate," *Human Rights Quarterly* 17:4 (1995), 587–617, © The Johns Hopkins University Press. Reprinted with permission of The Johns Hopkins University Press; Moore, John Norton, ed. Law and Civil War in the Modern World, pp. 13–16, 24–31, 218, 229, 235–237, 247–249, © 1974. Reprinted with permission of The Johns Hopkins University Press; Brownlie, Humanitarian Intervention in Law and Civil War in the Modern World 218 (Moore ed. 1974). Reprinted with permission of The Johns Hopkins University Press.

Kegan Paul for permission to reprint an excerpt from The Art of War 17 by Sun Tzu (Lionel Giles trans., 1910), Kegan Paul, London, New York, Bahrain 2002.

MIT Press Journals for permission to reprint an excerpt from Mearsheimer, "The False Promise of International Institutions" *International Security* 19:3 (1994–95), pp. 9, 10–12; and permission to reprint an excerpt from Krasner, "Structural Causes and Regime Consequences: Regimes as Intervening Variables" *International Organization* 36:2 (1982), pp. 186, 191–92.

The New York Times for permission to reprint Rostow, "Law 'Is Not a Suicide Pact'," © 1983, *The New York Times*.

New York University Journal of International Law & Politics for permission to reprint excerpts from Annan, "Peace-Keeping in Situations of Civil War," 26 *N.Y.U. J. Int'l L. & Pol.* 623, 623–28 (1994).

New York University Press for permission to reprint excerpts from Corwin, The President: Office and Powers, 1787–1957 (1957).

R. Richard Newcomb and Mark D. Roberts for permission to reprint "An Introduction to Economic Sanctions," copyright © 2014.

Oceana Publications, Inc. for permission to reprint excerpts from Moore, Crisis in the Gulf: Enforcing the Rule of Law, 3–11, 149–59, 420–21, 424–35 (1992).

The Orion Publishing Group Ltd. for permission to reprint material from Best, Humanity in Warfare (1980) published by Weidenfeld & Nicolson.

Oxford University Press for permission to reprint excerpts from Sieghart, The International Law of Human Rights (1983); Gray, International Law and the Use of Force (2001); Higgins, International Law and How We Use It (1994); Sarooshi, The United Nations and the Development of Collective Security (1999); Wilde, International Territorial Administration: How Trusteeship and the Civilizing Mission Never Went Away (2008); Kennedy, Freedom From Fear: the American People in Depression and War (1999); Larissa van den Herik, "Peripheral Hegemony in the Quest to Ensure Security Council Accountability for Its Individualized UN Sanctions Regimes" Journal of Conflict and Security Law (2014); and Erika de Wet "From Kadi to Nada: Judicial Techniques Favoring Human Rights Over United Nations Security Council Sanctions" Chinese Journal of International Law (2013). Used by permission of Oxford University Press.

Princeton University Press for permission to reprint material from Falk ed., "International Law and the United States Role in Vietnam: A Response to Professor Moore," in The Vietnam War and International Law (1968); Boyd ed., "Thomas Jefferson, Opinion on the Powers of the Senate Respecting Diplomatic Appointments, New York, April 24, 1790," in 3 The Papers of Thomas Jefferson (1961); Shapria, "The Six-Day War and the Right of Self-Defense," in 2 The Arab-Israeli Conflict (Moore ed., 1974); Bassiouni, "The Middle East: The misunderstood Conflict," in 2 The Arab-Israeli Conflict (Moore ed., 1974); Moore, "International Law and the United States Role in Vietnam: A Reply," in The Vietnam War and International Law (Falk ed., 1968); Moore, "The Role of Regional Arrangements in the Maintenance of World Order," in III The Future of the International Legal Order: Conflict Management (Black and Falk eds., 1971); Ely, War and Responsibility: Constitutional Lessons of Vietnam and Its Aftermath (1993).

Random House, Inc. for permission to reprint material from Swords Into Plowshares, 4th Ed by Inis L. Claude, Jr., copyright © 1956, 1959, 1964, 1971 by Inis L. Claude Jr. Used by permission of Random House, Inc.

Michael Reisman for permission to reprint excerpts from McDougal & Feliciano, Law and Minimum World Public Order (1961); McDougal & Burke, The Public Order of the Oceans (1962).

The Royal Institute of International Affairs for permission to reprint excerpts from Schwelb, "Crimes Against Humanity," 23 British Y. B. Int'l L. 178, 208–09 (1946). The work was published by Oxford University Press for the Royal Institute of International Affairs, London.

Mark J. Rozell for permission to reprint from Rozell, Executive Privilege: The Dilemma of Secrecy and Democratic Accountability 33–53 (1994).

Seven Locks Press for permission to reprint from Little, "The 'Just War' Tradition," in The Hundred Percent Challenge: Building A National Institute of Peace 7, 22–26 (Smith ed., 1985).

Simon & Schuster for permission to reprint material from The Causes of War by Geoffrey Blainey. Copyright © 1973, 1977, 1988 by Geoffrey Blainey. Reprinted with the permission of The Free Press, a Division of Simon & Schuster Adult Publishing Group. All rights reserved.

SIPRI for permission to reprint from Dwan, "Armed Conflict Prevention, Management and Resolution," in Sipri Yearbook: Armaments, Disarmament and International Security 77, 107–09 (2000).

Thomson Publishing Services for permission to reprint excerpts from Keen, The Laws of War in the Late Middle Ages 121–22 (1965); Coll, "Philosophical and Legal Dimensions of the Use of Force in the Falklands War" in The Falklands War 34, 44–46 (Coll & Arend eds., 1985); Clausewitz, On War 402, 410 (Rapoport ed., 1832).

TIME Inc. for permission to reprint an excerpt from Ruth Wedgwood, "Law in the Fog of War," TIME, May 5, © 2002 TIME Inc. Reprinted by permission.

Transnational Publishers, Inc. for permission to reprint material from Morris and Scharf, The International Criminal Tribunal for Rwanda 2–17, 29–37 (1998).

The University of Chicago Press for permission to reprint material from H. Q. Wright, A Study of War 728–31 (1942).

University of Richmond Law Review for permission to reprint material from Winchester & Zirkle, "Freedom of Information and the CIA Information Act," 21 U. Rich. L. Rev. 231 (1987). Reprinted with the permission of the University of Richmond Law Review.

University of San Francisco Law Review for permission to reprint an excerpt from Steger, "Slicing the Gordian Knot: A Proposal to Reform Military Regulation of Media Coverage of Combat Operations," 28 U.S.F.L. Rev. 957 (1994). © University of San Francisco Law Review.

University of Virginia Press for permission to reprint material from The Diaries of George Washington, Vol. 6.

Westview Press for permission to reprint an excerpt from Schachter, "Authorized Uses of Force by the United Nations and Regional Organizations" in Law and Force in the New International Order 65, 86–88 (Damrosch & Scheffer, eds., 1991).

William L. Ury for permission to reprint from Ury, "Beyond the Hotline: Meeting the Soviets Head-On to Prevent a Nuclear War," Wash. Post, Feb. 24, 1985, at 8.

Virginia Journal of International Law for permission to reprint excerpts from Joyner & Garibaldi, "The United States and Nicaragua: Reflections on the Lawfulness of Contemporary Intervention," 25 Va. J. Int'l L. (1985); Turner, "War and the Forgotten Executive Power of the Constitution," 34 Va. J. Int'l L. (1994); Moore, "Toward a New Paradigm: Enhanced Effectiveness in United Nations Peacekeeping, Collective Security, and War Avoidance," 37 Va. J. Int'l L. (1997); Zacklin, "Beyond Kosovo: The United Nations and Humanitarian Intervention," 41 Va. J. Int'l L. (2001).

The Yale Law Journal Company for permission to reprint from Taft, "The Boundaries Between the Executive, the Legislative and the Judicial Branches of the Government," reprinted by permission of The Yale Law Journal Company and William S. Hein Company from The Yale Law Journal, Vol. 25, pages 599–616; Jeffries, Jr., "Rethinking Prior Restraint," reprinted by permission of The Yale Law Journal Company and William S. Hein Company from The Yale Law Journal, Vol. 92, pages 409–437.

Yale University Press for permission to reprint excerpts from Koh, The National Security Constitution (1990) © Yale University Press; Madison, Remarks to the Constitutional Convention; July 18, 1787, 2 Records of the Federal Convention 34–35 (Ferrand ed., 1966) © Yale University Press.

Editors

John Norton Moore is the Walter L. Brown Professor of Law at the University of Virginia School of Law where he teaches numerous international and national security law courses. He also directs the University's Center for National Security Law and the Center for Oceans Law & Policy and was the Director of the Graduate Law Program at Virginia for more than twenty years. Viewed by many as the founder of the field of national security law, Professor Moore chaired the prestigious American Bar Association's Standing Committee on Law and National Security for four terms. He is the author or editor of over 45 books and over 180 scholarly articles and served for two decades on the editorial board of the *American Journal of International Law.* He is currently an honorary editor of the *Journal.* He is a member of the Council on Foreign Relations, on the Board of Directors of Freedom House, the American Law Institute, the American Society of International Law, the Order of the Coif, Phi Beta Kappa, and numerous other professional and honorary organizations. His most recent books include *Solving the War Puzzle* (2004) and *Civil Litigation Against Terrorism* (ed. 2004).

In addition to his scholarly career, Professor Moore has a distinguished record of public service. Among seven Presidential appointments, he has served two terms as the Senate-confirmed Chairman of the Board of Directors of the United States Institute of Peace and, as the first Chairman, set up this new agency. He also served as the Counselor on International Law to the Department of State, as Ambassador and Deputy Special Representative of the President to the Law of the Sea Conference, Chairman of the National Security Council Interagency Task Force on the Law of the Sea, and as a member of the United States' legal team before the International Court of Justice in the *Gulf of Maine* and *Paramilitary* cases (a Deputy Agent for the United States in the *Paramilitary* case). Professor Moore served as a Member of the Director of Central Intelligence's Historical Review Board from 1998–2002.

In the past, he has served as a Consultant to both the President's Intelligence Oversight Board and the Arms Control and Disarmament Agency. He has also been a member of the National Advisory Committee on Oceans and Atmosphere, the United States Delegation to the Conference on Security and Cooperation in Europe, the United States Delegation to the United Nations General Assembly, and the Presidential Delegation of the United States to observe the 1984 elections in El Salvador. In 1990, he served, with the Deputy Attorney-General of the United States, as the Co-Chairman of the United States-USSR talks on the Rule of Law. He also served as the legal advisor to the Kuwait Representative to the United Nations Iraq-Kuwait Boundary Demarcation Commission, and as a consultant to the OSS Society.

In 2013 he won the American Bar Association's Morris I. Liebman Award in National Security Law.

Guy B. Roberts is a senior fellow at the University's Center for National Security Law and is a consultant on national security law and policy. Previously he served as the Deputy Assistant Secretary General for Weapons of Mass Destruction Policy and Director, Nuclear Policy Planning Directorate for the North Atlantic Treaty Organization (NATO). In that capacity he is responsible for developing policy on issues related to combating the proliferation of weapons of mass destruction and overseeing NATO's nuclear deterrence posture. Prior to that he was Acting Deputy Assistant Secretary of Defense and Principal Director for Negotiations Policy in the Office of the Secretary of Defense responsible for advising senior Defense Department officials on the entire range of United States arms control and non-proliferation policies. He was also responsible for implementing policy guidance and Department positions for current and emerging proliferation issues in multilateral arms control and disarmament fora. Before that he served as the legal counsel for arms control and non-proliferation in the US Department of the Navy. He was responsible for reviewing all naval programs to ensure compliance with all arms control and nonproliferation agreements and developing policy on all arms control and nonproliferation agreements or initiatives, which could impact Departmental equities.

He also served for 25 years in the US Marine Corps before retiring with the rank of colonel. In that capacity he held a wide range of assignments in policy formulation, operations support, negotiations, management, litigation and policy/legal advisor both in the US and during overseas assignments. Positions and responsibilities included legal counsel to a four-star Combatant Commander, and military representative for disarmament and arms control issues to the United Nations, Conference on Disarmament and the International Atomic Energy Agency. He received his law degree from the University of Denver, and he holds master's degrees in international and comparative law from Georgetown University, in international relations from the University of Southern California, and in strategic studies from the Naval War College where he graduated with highest distinction and won the Stephen B. Luce Award for academic achievement. He is admitted to practice in Colorado, California, Arizona and before the Military Court of Criminal Appeals and the United States Supreme Court. Mr. Roberts has written extensively on nonproliferation, arms control, terrorism and law of war issues.

Robert F. Turner holds both professional and academic doctorates from the University of Virginia School of Law, where in 1981 he co-founded the Center for National Security Law with Professor Moore. A former Army captain who served twice in Vietnam, he left the military in 1971 to accept a position at the Hoover Institution on War, Revolution and Peace at Stanford University, where he was a Public Affairs Fellow and Associate Editor of the *Yearbook on International Communist Affairs*. His extensive federal government service includes five years as national security adviser to Senator Robert P. Griffin, a member of the Foreign Relations Committee, and subsequent assignments as Special Assistant to the Under Secretary of Defense for Policy, Counsel to the President's Intelligence Oversight Board at the White House, and Principal Deputy Assistant Secretary and Acting Assistant of State for Legislative and Intergovernmental Affairs. He served as the first President of the congressionally established U.S. Institute of Peace and during 1994–95 held the Charles H. Stockton Chair of International Law at the U.S. Naval War College. Dr. Turner has also been a Distinguished Lecturer at the U.S. Military Academy at West Point and a Silverman Lecturer at the U.S. Supreme Court Historical Society. In addition to teaching advanced national security law seminars with Professor Moore at the University of Virginia School of Law, for many years Professor Turner also taught International Law, U.S. Foreign Policy, Foreign Policy and the Law, and a seminar on the Vietnam War in what is now UVA's Woodrow Wilson Department of Politics. Each summer he runs the Center's National Security Law Institute for training law professors and government attorneys who wish to teach or practice in this growing new field. A former three-term Chairman of both the ABA Standing Committee on Law and National Security and the Committee on Executive-Congressional Relations of the ABA Section of International Law and Practice, for many years he served as editor of the ABA *National Security Law Report*. Turner has testified before more than a dozen committees of Congress, is the author or editor of more than fifteen books and has published in numerous law reviews and professional journals. He has contributed to the editorial pages of the *New York Times, Wall Street Journal, USA Today, Washington Post,* and other major American newspapers.

Contributors

John D. Altenburg Jr. is a principal with the Washington, D.C., office of the international law firm Greenberg Traurig (1750 lawyers, 36 offices). General Altenburg's experience includes service or crisis management experience in Vietnam (1969–1970), Special Operations (1974–1978), Iraq (1990–1991), Hurricane Andrew Humanitarian Relief (1992), Somalia (1992–1993), Haiti (1994), Bosnia (1995), Kosovo (1999), Guantanamo Bay, Cuba (2004–2007), Kurdistan (2006), and Kuwait and Iraq (2011). He is the only Special Forces-qualified lawyer to be promoted to general officer. He provided legal oversight of detention operations in Iraq, Haiti, and Guantanamo Bay, Cuba. He personally coordinated the release of detained persons in Baghdad and elsewhere in Iraq. He has testified numerous times before Senate and House committees in the United States Congress on a variety of legal issues.

Anthony Clark Arend is Professor of Government and Foreign Service at Georgetown University and Director of the Master of Science in Foreign Service Program (MSFS). Prior to coming to Georgetown, he was a Senior Fellow at the Center for National Security Law at the University of Virginia School of Law. Arend's publications include seven books: *Human Dignity and the Future of Global Institutions* (co-editor and contributor); *Legal Rules and International Society* (author); *International Rules: Approaches from International Law and International Relations* (co-editor and contributor)*; International Law and the Use of Force: Beyond the United Nations Charter Paradigm* (co-author); *Pursuing A Just and Durable Peace: John Foster Dulles and International Organization* (author); *The United States and the Compulsory Jurisdiction of the International Court of Justice* (editor and contributor); and *The Falklands War: Lessons for Strategy, Diplomacy, and International Law* (co-editor and contributor). Arend is a member of the Council on Foreign Relations.

James E. Baker serves as Chief Judge of the United States Court of Appeals for the Armed Forces. After serving as an infantry officer in the United States Marine Corps, Judge Baker attended Yale Law School, graduating in 1990. He began his legal career as an attorney advisor in the Office of the Legal Adviser, U.S. Department of State where he provided advice on law enforcement, intelligence, and counter-terrorism issues. He then served as Counsel to the President's Foreign Intelligence Advisory Board and Intelligence Oversight Board (1993), Deputy Legal Advisor to the National Security Council (1994–1997), and prior to his appointment to the Court in 2000, he served as Special Assistant to the President and Legal Advisor to the National Security Council (1997–2000). Judge Baker has published numerous articles on national security and is the author of, "In the Common Defense: National Security Law for Perilous Times" (Cambridge University Press, 2007). He teaches national security law at Georgetown University Law Center.

M. E. (Spike) Bowman was, most recently, Deputy, National Counterintelligence Executive. Previously he was Senior Research Fellow at the Center for Technology and National Security Policy. He is retired from the Senior Executive Service, Federal Bureau of Investigation where he served successively as Deputy General Counsel (National Security

Law) Senior Counsel for National Security Law and Director, Intelligence Issues and Policy Group (National Security Branch). He is a former intelligence officer, an international lawyer and a recognized specialist in national security law with extensive experience in espionage and terrorism investigations. In addition to national security experience he is a retired U.S. Navy Captain who has served as Head of International Law at the Naval War College, as a diplomat at the U.S. Embassy in Rome, Italy and as Chief of Litigation for the U.S. Navy.

Jeff Breinholt serves as an attorney-advisor in the Department of Justice's Office of Law and Policy, National Security Division. He previously served as deputy chief of the Counterterrorism Section and as a white-collar fraud prosecutor with the Tax Division. He also served briefly as senior fellow and director of national security law at the International Assessment and Strategy Center, a Washington D.C.-based think tank. He is the author of two books and several dozen law review and legal practitioner articles, and his legal commentary has appeared in a variety of news outlets. He is a graduate of Yale College (B.A.) and the UCLA School of Law (J.D.), and is a member of the State Bar of California.

Larry E. Christensen is a graduate of Duke Law School and a Member of Miller & Chevalier where he heads the national security, export controls, and sanctions practice. He is an Adjunct Professor of Law at Georgetown University Law Center and teaches U.S. export control and sanctions law. While in government practice, he was the primary author of the Export Administration Regulations (EAR). He practices under the International Traffic in Arms Regulations, the OFAC sanctions regulations, and the EAR. He is globally and nationally ranked by the Chambers Global and Chambers USA for International Trade: Export Controls & Economic Sanctions, among The Best Lawyers in America and Washington, DC, and Who's Who Legal for trade law.

Dr. Alberto R. Coll is Professor of Law and Director of European and Latin American Legal Studies at DePaul University College of Law. Previously, he chaired the Strategic Research Department at the U.S. Naval War College, where he also served as Dean of the Center for Naval Warfare Studies. From 1990 to 1993 he served as Principal Deputy Assistant Secretary of Defense, overseeing the Defense Department's policy, strategy and budget in the areas of special operations forces and "low-intensity" conflict, including all counterterrorism forces. For his work, he received the Secretary of Defense *Medal for Outstanding Public Service*. Professor Coll is the author of *The Wisdom of Statecraft* and editor of several books. He is the author of numerous articles on international relations, law, and U.S. foreign policy and national security. Coll is a member of the Council on Foreign Relations, the Virginia Bar, the Chicago Council on Global Affairs, and a frequent commentator on the Voice of America and National Public Radio.

Bo Cooper is a Partner in Fragomen's Washington, D.C., office and leads the firm's Government Strategies and Compliance Group. He provides strategic business immigration advice to a variety of clients, including companies, hospitals, research institutions, schools, and universities. Bo served as General Counsel of the U.S. Immigration and Naturalization Service (INS) from 1999 until February 2003, when he was responsible for the transition of immigration services to the Department of Homeland Security (DHS). He was principal legal advisor to the INS during two administrations, at a time when immigration ranked among the most sensitive issues on the national public policy agenda. Bo has testified frequently before the U.S. Congress, and has made many television, radio, and print media appearances. Bo was involved in negotiating immigration-related agreements between the U.S. and other governments, and has acted as a U.S. delegate to international organizations.

Abigail E. Cotterill of Miller & Chevalier practices in the areas of export controls, economic sanctions, and embargoes under the International Traffic in Arms Regulations (ITAR), Export Administration Regulations (EAR), and various regulations issued by the Office of Foreign Assets Control (OFAC). She has created custom economic sanctions compliance policies and filed commodity jurisdiction and classification requests. Her practice also includes Foreign Corrupt Practices Act (FCPA) and global compliance matters, for which she has conducted internal investigations and third party due diligence. A graduate of Yale University and Duke University School of Law, Ms. Cotterill served as a clerk to the Honorable Mary Ellen Coster Williams at the United States Court of Federal Claims.

When his chapter was written **John C. Cruden** was the President, Environmental Law Institute, a nationally recognized non-profit association focused on environmental law and policy. Before coming to ELI, John was the career Deputy Assistant Attorney General, Environment and Natural Resources Division, U.S. Department of Justice where he supervised all federal civil environmental enforcement and litigation involving U.S. agencies. Prior to becoming Deputy Assistant Attorney General, Mr. Cruden was Chief, Environmental Enforcement Section. Before joining the Department of Justice, he was the Chief Legislative Counsel of the Army. John has received the Presidential Rank Award from three different Presidents. He is a Past President of the District of Columbia Bar. John is also a Past Chairman, ABA Section of Environment, Energy, and Resources and a Fellow of the American Bar Foundation. In 2010, he was listed by a national magazine as one of the top 500 lawyers in America. After writing this chapter John was confirmed as the Assistant Attorney General, Environment and Natural Resources Division, U.S. Department of Justice, a position he now holds.

Robert E. Dalton received his legal training at Columbia Law School. He is Senior Adviser on Treaty Practice at the U.S. Department of State, where he previously served as the Assistant Legal Adviser for Treaty Affairs and the Counselor on International Law. He has been an Adjunct Professor of Law at Georgetown University Law Center for three decades and is a member of the American Law Institute. He has participated in various international conferences, including those that adopted the Vienna Conventions on the Law of Treaties and the General Framework Agreement for Peace in Bosnia and Herzegovina, and in bilateral negotiations on a wide range of subjects. He has also authored numerous articles and chapters on the law of treaties and U. S. treaty law and practice.

Michael L. Diakiwski serves as the Confidential Assistant to the General Counsel of the U.S. Department of Homeland Security (DHS). Prior to DHS, he was an associate at a private law firm in New York and a law clerk for a Senior Senator on the U.S. Senate Judiciary Committee. While in law school he was a White House intern and clerked for the U.S. Department of Justice and New York State Attorney General's Office, Litigation Bureau. Mr. Diakiwski holds a J.D. from Georgetown University Law Center where he was awarded the Dean's Certificate for outstanding contributions to the Law Center and earned his undergraduate degree from Providence College.

Maj. Gen. Charles J. Dunlap, Jr., USAF (Ret.) is the Executive Director of the Center on Law, Ethics and National Security at Duke Law School, where he is also a Professor of the Practice of Law. He received his undergraduate degree from St. Joseph's University (PA), and his law degree from Villanova University. Prior to retiring from the military in June of 2010, General Dunlap assisted in the supervision of more than 2,500 military and civilian attorneys worldwide. His 34-year career included tours in both the United Kingdom and Korea, and he deployed for military operations in Africa and the Middle East. A distinguished graduate of the National War College, General Dunlap is the author of more than 100 publications, and speaks frequently on a wide variety of topics including law of armed conflict issues, cyberwar, drones, civil-military relations, military justice, and a phenomenon he calls "lawfare."

Jonathan M. Fredman has held a number of legal and policy positions for the U.S. Government, including Assistant Deputy Director of National Intelligence for Special Programs, chief counsel to the Director of Central Intelligence Counterterrorist Center, and Special Assistant to the Director of Central Intelligence. He has taught national security law, the law of foreign intelligence, and the law of counterterrorism, and has been published in the *ABA National Security Law Report*, *Yale Law and Policy Review*, and *Studies in Intelligence*. Prior to entering government, Mr. Fredman was an attorney in private practice and a law clerk for U.S. District Judge Charles M. Metzner of the Southern District of New York. Mr. Fredman is a recipient of the George H.W. Bush Award for Excellence in Counterterrorism, the National Intelligence Exceptional Achievement Medal, and the Middle East Mission Manager Medallion. He is a member of the Council on Foreign Relations.

David E. Graham, a retired Army Judge Advocate Colonel, played a seminal role in developing the field of Operational Law and is currently the Executive Director of the Army Judge Advocate General's Legal Center and School (LCS). With an extensive background in international law, he had military assignments in the United States, Europe, Latin America, and the Middle East. He served as the Chief of the International/Operational Law Division, Office of The Judge Advocate General of the Army, for the last eight years of his active duty service, and as Director of the Center for Law and Military Operations, now an integral part of the LCS. Mr. Graham is a published author in multiple law journals and has lectured extensively in both domestic and international fora. He holds a J.D. from the University of Texas School of Law, and a Certificate from the Hague Academy of International Law. He is also a Distinguished Graduate of the National War College.

Richard J. "Jack" Grunawalt earned his J.D. at the University of Michigan School of Law before spending more than 25 years as a Navy JAG officer. A Vietnam veteran, his assignments included teaching at the Naval Justice School; Staff Judge Advocate, Commander in Chief, U.S. Pacific Command; Special Counsel to the Chief of Naval Operations; and Special Assistant to the Judge Advocate General of the Navy. After retiring from active duty, he became Director of the Oceans Law and Policy Department, Center for Naval Warfare Studies, U.S. Naval War College, where he also held the Charles H. Stockton Chair of International Law.

Michael O. Halas is an attorney-advisor in the Office of the General Counsel of the U.S. Department of Homeland Security (DHS), focusing on cybersecurity and infrastructure protection. He previously rotated through the legal offices of the Secret Service, DHS headquarters, the Federal Emergency Management Agency, and Customs and Border Protection as part of DHS's honors program. Before joining DHS, he was a judicial law clerk for United States District Judge Eric N. Vitaliano of the Eastern District of New York, a judicial law clerk for Justice Carolyn Berger of the Delaware Supreme Court, a patent agent and technology specialist at WilmerHale, and an engineer at IBM. Mr. Halas holds a J.D. from the Fordham University School of Law and a B.S. in electrical and computer engineering from the Rutgers University School of Engineering.

Dame Rosalyn Higgins DBE QC is President of the British Institute of International and Comparative Law. She was a Judge of the International Court of Justice (1995–2009) and its President (2006–09). Prior to being elected to the International Court, Dame Rosalyn was Professor of International Law at the University of Kent at Canterbury (1978-81) and Professor of International Law at the University of London (London School of Economics) (1981–95). She practised in public international law and petroleum law before English courts and international courts and tribunals. She was a Member of the UN Committee on Human Rights (1985–1995). Dame Rosalyn is a member of the Institut de droit international. She has published widely on United Nations law, the use of force, international legal theory, immunities, human rights and international petroleum law. Her books include: four volumes on *United Nations Peace-keeping*; *Problems and Process: International Law and How We Use It* (OUP 1994); *Themes and Theories: Selected Essays, Speeches, and Writings in International Law* (OUP 2009).

James Kraska is Professor of Oceans Law and Policy at the Stockton Center for the Study of International Law at the U.S. Naval War College. He is also a Senior Fellow at the Center for National Security Law, University of Virginia School of Law; Senior Fellow at the Center for Oceans Law and Policy, University of Virginia School of Law; and a Distinguished Fellow at the Law of the Sea Institute, University of California, Berkeley, School of Law. Professor Kraska's publications include *Maritime Power and the Law of the Sea* (Oxford University Press), which earned him the Alfred Thayer Mahan Award for Literary Achievement from the United States Navy League.

Ronald F. Lehman II chairs the DOD Threat Reduction Advisory Committee and the Governing Board of the International Science and Technology Center. He is the Counselor at Lawrence Livermore National Laboratory. Ron was Director of the U.S. Arms Control and Disarmament Agency when the Strategic Arms Reductions, Conventional Forces in Europe, Chemical Weapons, Open Skies, and other historic agreements were concluded. Ron served in DOD as Assistant Secretary, in the State Department as Ambassador and Chief Negotiator on Strategic Offensive Arms, and in the White House as Deputy Assistant to the President for National Security Affairs. He served on the NSC staff, in the Pentagon as Deputy Assistant Secretary, on the Staff of the U.S. Senate Armed Services Committee, and in Vietnam commissioned in the US Army.

Howard S. Levie, draftsman of the Korean Armistice Agreement, was a former colonel in the U.S. Army's Judge Advocate General's Corps. He was also Professor Emeritus of Law at St. Louis University Law School, and held the Stockton Chair of International Law at the Naval War College from 1971–72. His publications include the *Law of Non-International Armed Conflict* (1987); *The Code of International Armed Conflict* (1968); *The Status of Gibraltar* (1985); and the prizewinning *Prisoners of War in International Armed Conflict* (1972). He also edited *Protection of War Victims* (4 vols., 1979–1981). Mr. Levie passed away in 2009.

Ambassador Donald A. Mahley completed negotiation of the United Nations Arms Trade Treaty just before his death on March 1, 2014. Don had served in many senior positions, twice as a Deputy Assistant Secretary of State, several times as a Special Negotiator, as Deputy Assistant Director at U.S. Arms Control and Disarmament Agency (ACDA), Director on the NSC Staff, and as a member of the UN Secretary General's Disarmament Advisory Board. Don was a professor at West Point and at the National War College, a NATO Planner, commanded Army units in Europe and Vietnam and retired as a Colonel. Don was a major architect of the Chemical Weapons Convention and led the US team that inspected BW facilities in the Soviet Union and removed WMD related materials and technology from Libya.

Richard O. W. Morgan is a Senior Fellow at the Center on Law and Security at NYU School of Law, focusing on comparative intelligence oversight. For five years, Richard served as an attorney in the U.S. Intelligence Community, focusing on litigation, oversight, and operational law. An officer in the United States Navy, Richard served as a Rule of Law advisor in Ramadi, Iraq from 2008–2009. Richard clerked for Chief Judge James E. Baker of the U.S. Court of Appeals for the Armed Forces. He holds a Juris Doctorate from Yale Law School, and a degree in Philosophy, Politics, and Economics from Hertford College of Oxford University. Richard earned a Bachelor of Arts in Politics & Government from the University of Hartford, and a Bachelor of Music in Composition from the University of Hartford's Hartt School.

John F. Murphy is Professor of Law (Emeritus) at Villanova University School of Law. He has served as an attorney in the Office of the Assistant Legal Adviser in the Department of State, and has taught law at the University of Kansas, Cornell, Georgetown, and Villanova. In 1980–81, he served as the Charles H. Stockton Professor of Law at the U.S. Naval War College. A leading authority for many years on legal issues of terrorism, in 2011 the Section of International Law of the American Bar Association conferred on him the Louis B. Sohn Award "in recognition of his distinguished and long-standing contributions to the field of public international law." In 1992, the American Society of International Law awarded him a Certificate of Merit in recognition of his casebook (co-authored with Alan C. Swan), *The Regulation of International Business and Economic Relations,* " a work of great distinction, which has received this award in accordance with the regulations of the Society."

Thomas B. Nachbar is the Joseph W. Dorn Research Professor of Law at the University of Virginia School of Law and a Senior Fellow at the Center for National Security Law. He has numerous publications in the fields of constitutional law, antitrust, telecommunications, detention law and policy, and the role of legal institutions in counterinsurgency and stability operations. He also serves as a judge advocate in the U.S. Army Reserve, where he has served in a variety of capacities both in the U.S. and overseas, and is a civilian senior adviser for the U.S. Department of Defense.

R. Richard Newcomb was the Director of the U.S. Treasury Department's Office of Foreign Assets Control from 1987 to 2004 during which time he administered some 39 U.S. economic sanction programs. During this period, he played a leadership role both within the U.S. and internationally in developing economic sanctions into an effective tool of international diplomacy. He was awarded the Presidential Rank Executive Award by three U.S. Presidents—Ronald Reagan, George H.W. Bush, and William Clinton—for his "sustained extraordinary accomplishments" in this position. Upon his departure from OFAC, he was awarded the Treasury Medal recognizing that the strategies for sanctions implementation and targeting developed under his leadership are among the principal tools used to wage the war on terrorism and terrorist financing. Currently, he is a partner and chair of the International Trade Practice Group of the global law firm of DLA Piper.

Robert M. O'Neil received three degrees from Harvard including one in law and immediately clerked for U.S. Supreme Court Justice William Brennan, Jr. After teaching law for a decade at the University of California, Berkeley, he became Chancellor at Indiana University-Bloomington, followed by five years each as President of the University of Wisconsin and the University of Virginia, teaching one course each semester at each institution. He then assumed in 1990 the Directorship of the Thomas Jefferson Center for the Protection of Free Expression and is now Senior Fellow at the Association of Governing Boards of Colleges and Universities.

Robert A. Ramey is a Colonel with the United States Air Force serving as its Director of Operations and International Law. Following completion of his J.D. from the Seattle University School of Law in 1991, he received his LL.M. in Air and Space Law at McGill University, Montreal, Quebec in 1999. In 2010, Colonel Ramey completed an M.S. in

National Security Strategy with distinction from the National War College, Fort Leslie McNair, Washington, DC. He has taught at the Air Force JAG School, practiced space law at Air Force Space Command, served as Staff Judge Advocate to Air Force Global Strike Command (Provisional), served as Vice Commander, Air Force Legal Operations Agency, and led two Air Force law centers overseas.

Mark D. Roberts received a PhD and MA in Economics from the University of Maryland, an MS in National Security Studies from the National War College; and a BA in Economics and History from the University of Texas. In 30 years of Federal service, he served 17 years in the Office of Foreign Assets Control at the U.S. Department of the Treasury as Senior Policy Advisor to the Director and head of OFAC's Foreign Terrorist Asset Tracking Center. He helped develop and administer country and counter-narcotics trafficking, terrorism, and proliferation of weapons of mass destruction sanctions programs. He recently served as Deputy Director of the Office of Enforcement Analysis in the U.S. Department of Commerce's Bureau of Industry and Security.

Horace B. Robertson, Jr., is Professor of Law (Emeritus), at Duke University School of Law, where he taught from 1976 to 1990. Prior to that time he served in the U.S. Navy for 31 years, first as a surface line officer and for the final 20 years as a judge advocate. His naval career culminated in his service as Deputy Judge Advocate General and then Judge Advocate General from 1972 to 1976. Following his retirement from teaching at Duke, he served one year in the Charles H. Stockton Chair of International Law at the U.S. Naval War College, Newport, Rhode Island.

Paul Rosenzweig is the founder of Red Branch Consulting PLLC, a homeland security consulting company, and a Senior Advisor to The Chertoff Group. Mr. Rosenzweig formerly served as Deputy Assistant Secretary for Policy in the Department of Homeland Security. He is a Distinguished Visiting Fellow at the Homeland Security Studies and Analysis Institute. He is the author of *Cyber Warfare: How Conflicts in Cyberspace are Challenging America and Changing the World* and of the video lecture series, *Thinking About Cybersecurity: From Cyber Crime to Cyber Warfare* from The Great Courses. He is the coauthor (with James Jay Carafano) of *Winning the Long War: Lessons from the Cold War for Defeating Terrorism and Preserving Freedom* and co-editor (with Timothy McNulty and Ellen Shearer) of two books, *Whistleblowers, Leaks and the Media: The First Amendment and National Security,* and *National Security Law in the News: A Guide for Journalists, Scholars, and Policymakers.*

Kaiya Pontinen Sandler is an Attorney-Advisor with the Department of Homeland Security, Office of the General Counsel, Regulatory Affairs Law Division, where she handles the legal review of DHS regulatory actions. Prior to her work in the Regulatory Affairs Law Division, Ms. Sandler was an Attorney-Advisor in the Legislative Affairs Division, where she worked on legislative matters for the Department. Ms. Sandler graduated from the University of North Carolina at Chapel Hill and the American University, Washington College of Law.

Dan Sarooshi combines a leading practice as a UK Barrister in international and national courts and tribunals with his position as Professor of Public International Law at the University of Oxford and Senior Research Fellow of The Queen's College, Oxford. He was appointed by the UK Government to serve on the Attorney General's Panel of Counsel to represent the Government in public international law cases; appointed by the World Trade Organization to serve as a Member of the roster of Panellists of the WTO Dispute Settlement System; was elected in 2008 to membership of the Executive Council of the American Society of International Law; and since 2008 serves as co-General Editor of the *Oxford Monographs in International Law Series,* published by OUP.

Michael P. Scharf is Interim Dean and Joseph C. Hostetler—BakerHostetler Professor of Law at Case Western Reserve University School of Law. He is also Managing Director of the Nobel-nominated Public International Law & Policy Group. He has served as Special Assistant to the Prosecutor of the Extraordinary Chambers in the Courts of Cambodia, trained the judges who prosecuted Saddam Hussein, and was Attorney-Adviser for United Nations Affairs at the U.S. Department of State during the Bush and Clinton Administrations. He is the author of seventeen books, three of which have won national book of the year honors, and is host of the public radio program "Talking Foreign Policy."

Richard Schifter, a lawyer by profession, held from 1981 to 2001 a number of senior positions in the United States Government related to foreign affairs. They included the positions of U.S. Representative in the United Nations Human Rights Commission, Deputy U.S. Representative in the UN Security Council with the rank of Ambassador, Assistant Secretary of State for Human Rights and Humanitarian Affairs, Counselor on the staff of the National Security Council and Senior Director for East European Affairs, and Special Assistant to the Secretary of State. He was heavily involved in the negotiations leading to an end of the most serious human rights violations in the Soviet Union.

Molly Bishop Shadel is a professor at the University of Virginia School of Law and a Senior Fellow of the Center for National Security Law. She is the author of two books: *Finding Your Voice in Law School: Mastering Classroom Cold Calls, Job Interviews, and Other Verbal Challenges* (Carolina Academic Press, 2013) and *Tongue-Tied America: Reviving the Art of Verbal Persuasion* (with Robert N. Sayler, Wolters Kluwer Law & Business, 2011; 2d ed. 2014). She is a graduate of Harvard University and Columbia Law School, and formerly served as an Attorney-Advisor for the U.S. Department of Justice, Office of Intelligence Policy and Review.

Suzanne E. Spaulding serves as Under Secretary for the National Protection and Programs Directorate at the Department of Homeland Security. As Under Secretary, she oversees the coordinated operational and policy functions of the Directorate's subcomponents: Offices of Cybersecurity and Communications, Infrastructure Protection, Biometric Identity Management, Cyber and Infrastructure Analysis, and the Federal Protective Service. Ms. Spaulding has spent nearly 25 years working on national security issues for both Republican and Democratic Administrations and on both sides of the aisle of Congress. She was most recently a principal in the Bingham Consulting Group and Counsel for Bingham McCutchen LLP in Washington, D.C. Prior to joining the private sector, she served as the minority staff director for the U.S. House of Representatives Permanent Select Committee on Intelligence for Ranking Member Jane Harman (D-CA), and as general counsel for the Senate Select Committee on Intelligence. She also spent six years at the CIA, where she was an assistant general counsel, as well as a legal advisor to the Nonproliferation Center. She also served as senior counsel and legislative director for U.S. Senator Arlen Specter (PA). In addition, Ms. Spaulding served as the executive director of two congressionally mandated commissions: the National Commission on Terrorism, chaired by Amb. L. Paul Bremer III, and the Commission to Assess the Organization of the Federal Government to Combat the Proliferation of Weapons of Mass Destruction, chaired by former CIA Director John Deutch. She is the former Chair of the American Bar Association's Standing Committee on Law and National Security, and founder of the Cybersecurity Legal Task Force.

Margaret D. Stock is a member of the Alaska Bar who earned her undergraduate, graduate, and law degrees at Harvard University. A retired lieutenant colonel in the US Army Reserve Military Police Corps, she was named a 2013 MacArthur Fellow ("genius grant" recipient) by the John D. & Catherine T. MacArthur Foundation. Margaret is the author of the book, *Immigration Law & the Military*, and co-author of the fifth edition of the book, *Professionals: A Matter of Degree*, with Martin Lawler. She is the principal attorney at Cascadia Cross Border Law Group LLC in Anchorage, AK.

Michelle P. Tonelli is an Attorney-Advisor with the Department of Homeland Security, Office of General Counsel, National Protection and Programs Law Division (NPPLD). She focuses on biometrics, information sharing, privacy law, and administrative law. Prior to joining the NPPLD, Ms. Tonelli clerked for the Honorable Charles Wilson of the United States Court of Appeals for the Eleventh Circuit. She was also an Honors Attorney for the Department of Homeland Security, Office of General Counsel. As an Honors Attorney she worked for the Office of the Chief Counsel for Customs and Border Protection and the Office of Principal Legal Advisor for Immigration and Customs Enforcement. Ms. Tonelli graduated from The University of the South and from New York Law School.

Dr. Philippa Webb is Lecturer in Public International Law at King's College London. She has held visiting positions at Leiden University, Université Paris X Nanterre and Pepperdine University. She served as the Special Assistant and Legal Officer to Judge Rosalyn Higgins during her Presidency of the International Court of Justice (2006–2009) and, prior to that, as the Judicial Clerk to Judges Higgins and Owada (2004–2005). She was an Associate Legal Adviser at the International Criminal Court (2005–2006). Dr. Webb is on the International Advisory Panel for the American Law Institute's project *Restatement Fourth, Foreign Relations Law of the United States*. Her books include: *International Judicial Integration and Fragmentation* (OUP 2013) and *The Law of State Immunity* (3rd edition, OUP 2013, with Lady Hazel Fox QC).

J. Joshua Wheeler is the Director of the Thomas Jefferson Center for the Protection of Free Expression located in Charlottesville, Virginia, where he is also an adjunct faculty member at the University of Virginia School of Law. He received his Bachelor's degree from the University of North Carolina at Chapel Hill, his Master's degree from Hollins College, and his law degree from the University of Virginia. He is a member of the California, D.C., and Virginia Bars, and is admitted to practice before the United States Supreme Court. Before his work with the Thomas Jefferson Center, he practiced law in Los Angeles, California, with the law firm of Parker, Milliken, Clark, O'Hara & Samuelian.

National Security
Law & Policy

Chapter 1

Theoretical Approaches to World Order

Anthony Clark Arend

In this chapter:
Idealism
Classical Realism
Structural Realism
Neoliberal Institutionalism
Constructivism
Conclusion and Questions

When an observer considers national security law, it would not be unusual to assume that theory plays little role in the development and application of legal rules that relate to critical national security issues. In reality, however, theory affects both the manner in which decision makers develop legal rules and the way in which they apply them to concrete issues. A theory is a lens through which a person views reality. Even if he or she is not consciously aware of it, each person—whether a national security practitioner, a legal advisor or simply an average citizen—has a theoretical framework for understanding behavior in the world. This framework is based on certain assumptions about how the world works and has clear implications for expectations about the role of law and the possibility for international organization.

The purpose of this chapter is to review five of the most prominent theoretical frameworks about international relations[1] that have figured in the thought and practice of global politics: Idealism, Classical Realism, Structural Realism, Neo-Liberal Institutionalism, and Constructivism. To analyze each of these approaches, we will explore four elements of each approach: 1) The assumptions proponents of the theoretical approach make about human nature; 2) The assumptions they make about the international system; 3) Conflict management systems possible under this framework; and 4) Claims about the role of international law under this framework.

---

1. Many works have been written about different theoretical approaches to international relations. *See, e.g.,* INTERNATIONAL POLITICS: ENDURING CONCEPTS AND CONTEMPORARY ISSUES (Robert J. Art & Robert Jervis, eds., 12th ed., 2013); BACK TO BASICS: STATE POWER IN A CONTEMPORARY WORLD (Martha Finnemore and Judith Goldstein, eds., 2013); ROBERT J. LIEBER, NO COMMON POWER: UNDERSTANDING INTERNATIONAL RELATIONS (4th ed., 2001); JOSEPH S. NYE & DAVID WELCH, UNDERSTANDING GLOBAL CONFLICT AND COOPERATION: AN INTRODUCTION TO THEORY AND HISTORY (9th ed., 2012).

Before we begin this examination, several caveats need to be mentioned. First, there are, needless to say, nearly an infinite number of different theoretical frameworks. This discussion simply elaborates upon those that are featured most prominently in the contemporary international relations literature and should not be interpreted as an exhaustive explication of all possible approaches. Second, there are many nuances to each approach. In our discussion here, we will be exploring the essential contours of each approach. Any one scholar might choose to focus on, or emphasize, different aspects of the approach. Our goal here is to capture the essence of the approach and not provide an encyclopedic discussion of every aspect of the approach. Finally, it is always useful to remember that the purpose of theory is to help us understand reality. A theory is neither "right" nor "wrong," but is rather more or less useful insofar as it helps observers understand the real world.

Idealism

It may be that no thinker or public official would ever call himself or herself an "Idealist." Indeed, in most contemporary discussions of theoretical approaches to world order, there is actually very little discussion of "Idealism." This may be due to an assessment that the Idealist approach was discredited by the rise of "Realism" following the Second World War. But nonetheless, this approach forms an important framework that many still believe reflects reality. Historically, thinkers as diverse as Immanuel Kant, Karl Marx, Robert Hutchins, and Louis Sohn and statespersons from Woodrow Wilson and William Jennings Bryan to Mohandas Karamchand Gandhi have been called Idealists. But what is Idealism?

1. Human Nature

Human beings are the ultimate agents of international politics. While states, international institutions, and a variety of other non-state actors may be the international legal person that acts on the international plane, each of these actors is made up of individuals. Accordingly, Idealism asserts that understanding human nature is critical to understanding the behavior of the whole variety of international actors. In a nutshell, Idealists tend to take an optimistic view of human nature. Human beings may not be perfect, but they are essentially good and, with the proper education and guidance, can become even better.

2. The International System

While Idealists do not necessarily spend a great deal of time discussing the system as it is, as opposed to what it could become, in general, Idealists would accept that the contemporary international system consists of states as the primary actors. Moreover, while Idealists, unlike Structural Realists, would not use the term "anarchy"[2] to describe the international system, they would recognize that there is currently no "common power" that governs the international system, that the system consists of independent, sovereign states

---

2. For a discussion of the concept of "anarchy" as it applies to international politics, *see* KENNETH N. WALTZ, THEORY OF INTERNATIONAL POLITICS (1979).

and no effective world governing structure. Indeed, from the Idealist perspective this fact is part of the problem.

3. Conflict Management Systems

The term conflict management system is used here to denote a global system that seeks to promote order on the international plane.[3] While any number of such systems could be conceived, for purposes of this chapter, we will offer three systems as possible: World Government, a Collective Security System, and a Balance of Power system. A world government would be, precisely as the term indicates, a system in which there was a centralized legislature, executive, and judiciary (with compulsory jurisdiction) on the global level. It would be a "common power" at the international level. Under such a system, there could, in fact, be states as we know them, but the central government would have ultimate authority over such states.

A collective security system is one that consists of independent states. But in such a system, states enter into an international agreement in which they pledge not to commit an act of aggression—which is defined as an unjustified use of force—and further pledge that if any one of the members of this system does commit an act of aggression, all other members will unite collectively to stop that act of aggression. To implement this system, an international organization is established that has the authority to determine if aggression has occurred and what action needs to be taken to respond to this aggression. A collective security system would envision using the least amount of coercion necessary to stop the aggression. Thus, diplomatic and economic sanctions would be used before the use of military force if there were an indication that such measures might be reasonably expected to end the aggressive act. The success of this system is based on the expectation of deterrence—only an irrational state would undertake an act of aggression if it meant that the entire force of the rest of the international community would come down upon it.

A balance of power system is the most decentralized of the conflict management systems. Indeed, it is the system that exists by default in a state system. It consists of independent states that act on their own—through *ad hoc* alliances—to counter states that begin to gain overwhelming power in the system. The European State system following the Napoleonic Wars until World War I is often thought of as a classic balance of power system.

Because of a positive view of human nature, Idealists range from believing that a collective security system is possible to believing that even world government is possible. What seems to unite them is a belief that the balance of power system is destructive of world order.

4. The Role of International Law

In keeping with an optimistic view of human nature and the possibilities of the international system, Idealists tend to believe that international law has an important effect

---

3. *See,* INIS L. CLAUDE, POWER AND INTERNATIONAL RELATIONS (1962) for an outstanding discussion of systems of conflict management. This discussion draws heavily upon Claude's work.

on the behavior of international actors. Much as domestic legal rules affect the role of persons in the domestic environment, so to do international legal rules affect the behavior of states and other actors on the international plane. Accordingly, a traditional Idealist would likely see the promotion of new international legal rules—especially through formal international agreements—as an important role for public officials.

John F. Kennedy is not normally thought of as an Idealist—especially given his reactions to the Cuban Missile Crisis. But his Commencement Address at American University in 1963 can be seen as containing some elements of Idealism. What are they?

John F. Kennedy, Commencement Address at American University
June 10, 1963[4]

First: Let us examine our attitude toward peace itself. Too many of us think it is impossible. Too many think it unreal. But that is a dangerous, defeatist belief. It leads to the conclusion that war is inevitable—that mankind is doomed—that we are gripped by forces we cannot control.

We need not accept that view. Our problems are manmade—therefore, they can be solved by man. And man can be as big as he wants. No problem of human destiny is beyond human beings. Man's reason and spirit have often solved the seemingly unsolvable—and we believe they can do it again.

I am not referring to the absolute, infinite concept of peace and good will of which some fantasies and fanatics dream. I do not deny the value of hopes and dreams but we merely invite discouragement and incredulity by making that our only and immediate goal.

Let us focus instead on a more practical, more attainable peace—based not on a sudden revolution in human nature but on a gradual evolution in human institutions—on a series of concrete actions and effective agreements which are in the interest of all concerned. There is no single, simple key to this peace—no grand or magic formula to be adopted by one or two powers. Genuine peace must be the product of many nations, the sum of many acts. It must be dynamic, not static, changing to meet the challenge of each new generation. For peace is a process—a way of solving problems.

With such a peace, there will still be quarrels and conflicting interests, as there are within families and nations. World peace, like community peace, does not require that each man love his neighbor—it requires only that they live together in mutual tolerance, submitting their disputes to a just and peaceful settlement. And history teaches us that enmities between nations, as between individuals, do not last forever. However fixed our likes and dislikes may seem, the tide of time and events will often bring surprising changes in the relations between nations and neighbors.

So let us persevere. Peace need not be impracticable, and war need not be inevitable. By defining our goal more clearly, by making it seem more manageable and less remote, we can help all peoples to see it, to draw hope from it, and to move irresistibly toward it.

----

4. The text of the Address can be found online at the National Archives site: http://research.archives .gov/description/193862.

Classical Realism

During the period between the First and Second World Wars, a number of commentators were highly critical of the role played by the United States in world affairs. In his classic work, *American Diplomacy, 1900–1950*, George F. Kennan explains:

GEORGE F. KENNAN, AMERICAN DIPLOMACY

reprinted in INTERNATIONAL RULES: APPROACHES FROM INTERNATIONAL LAW AND INTERNATIONAL RELATIONS (Robert J. Beck, Anthony Clark Arend & Robert D. Vander Lugt, eds.), 101–102 (1996)

As you have no doubt surmised, I see the most serious fault of our past policy formulation to lie in something that I might call the legalistic-moralistic approach to international problems. This approach runs like a red skein through our foreign policy of the last fifty years. It has in it something of the old emphasis on arbitration treaties, something of the Hague Conferences and schemes for universal disarmament, something of the more ambitious American concepts of the role of international law, something of the League of Nations and the United Nations, something of the Kellogg Pact, something of the idea of a universal "Article 51" pact, something of the belief in world law and world government. But it is none of these, entirely. Let me try to describe it.

It is the belief that it should be possible to suppress the chaotic and dangerous aspirations of governments in the international field by the acceptance of some system of legal rules and restraints. This belief undoubtedly represents in part an attempt to transpose the Anglo-Saxon concept of individual law into the international field and to make it applicable to governments as it is applicable here at home to individuals. It must also stem in part from the memory of the origin of our own political system — from the recollection that we were able, through acceptance of a common institutional and juridical framework, to reduce to harmless dimensions the conflicts of interest and aspiration among the original thirteen colonies and to bring them all an ordered and peaceful relationship with one another. Remembering this, people are unable to understand that what might have been possible for the thirteen colonies in a given set of circumstances might not be possible in the wider international field.

It is the essence of this belief that, instead of taking the awkward conflicts of national interest and dealing with them on their merits with a view to finding solutions least unsettling to the stability of international life, it would be better to find some formal criteria of the juridical nature in which the permissible behavior states could be defined. There would then be judicial entities competent to measure the actions of governments against these criteria and to decide whether behavior was acceptable and when unacceptable. Beyond all this, of course, lies the American assumption that the things for which other people in the world are apt to contend are for the most part neither creditable nor important and might justly be expected to take second place behind the desirability of an orderly world, untroubled by international violence. To the American mind, it is implausible that people should have positive aspirations, and ones that they regard as legitimate, more important to them than the peacefulness and orderliness of international life. From this standpoint, it is not apparent why other people should not join us in accepting the rules of the game in international politics, just as we accept such rules in the competition of sport in order that the game may not become too cruel and too destructive and may not assume importance we do not mean it to have.

If they were to do this, the reasoning runs, then the troublesome and chaotic manifestations of the national ego could be contained and rendered either unsubstantial or were subject to easy disposal by some method familiar and comprehensible to our American usage. Departing from this background, the mind of American statesmanship, stemming as it does in so large a part from the legal profession in our country, gropes with unfailing persistence for some institutional framework which would be capable of fulfilling this function.

————————

Similarly, other Classical Realists, such as Hans Morgenthau,[5] E.H. Carr,[6] and Reinhold Niebuhr[7] were also quite critical of an Idealist approach to international politics. But what do the Classical Realists believe in contrast?

1. Human Nature

Unlike Idealists, Classical Realists tend to have a more negative view of human nature. The theologian, Reinhold Niebuhr, for example, would assert that while there is good in human beings, due to sin, all persons are "fallen from grace." As such, all persons will be tempted to behave in a selfish manner. Other Classical Realists, like Hans Morgenthau, would take a less theological approach, but would nonetheless claim that all human beings pursue power and that this pursuit of power would manifest itself in the behavior of the leaders of states.

2. The International System

Classical Realists tend to assume that the international system will continue to be dominated by states as the primary actors and also assume that the system will continue to be decentralized. States will continue to pursue their "national interests" as they define them.

3. Conflict Management Systems

Given the decentralized nature of the international system and the challenges posed by human nature, Classical Realists argue that only a balance of power system can exist. They would clearly reject the pursuit of world government as utopian. They would also argue that a system of collective security would be unworkable for a number of reasons. In short, states would simply not be willing to fight aggression wherever it occurred unless they perceived such fight to be in their direct national interest.

4. International Law

Classical Realists, as noted in Kennan's comments noted above, tend to be critical of international law. Their basic claim is not that international law does not matter, but

————————

5. *See, e.g.,* Hans Morgenthau, Politics Among Nations: The Struggle for Power and Peace (1948).

6. *See, e.g.,* E.H. Carr, The Twenty Years' Crisis: 1919–1939 (1939).

7. *See, e.g.,* Reinhold Niebuhr, Moral Man and Immoral Society: A Study of Ethics and Politics (1932); Reinhold Niebuhr, The Children of Light and the Children of Darkness (1944).

rather that international law should not play a significant role in foreign policy decisions. Their claim is that if state persons ignore the pursuit of their national interest in an effort to follow rules of international law, especially in areas of law relating to core security interests, their states will be endangered.

Structural Realism

During the early Cold War period, Classical Realism "won" the debate of the "isms," and Idealism was generally seen as discredited among international relations scholars. But during this period, one noted American theorist, Kenneth Waltz, began to offer a variant of Realism—what came to be known as "Neorealism" or "Structural Realism."

One of the most recent proponents of Structural Realism is John Mearsheimer. In 1994, he wrote a concise articulation of the basic principles of Structural Realism.

John Mearsheimer, *The False Promise of International Institutions*

Int'l Security, Vol. 19, No. 3 (Winter, 1994–1995), pp. 5–49 (footnotes omitted)

Realism paints a rather grim picture of world politics. The international system is portrayed as a brutal arena where states look for opportunities to take advantage of each other, and therefore have little reason to trust each other. Daily life is essentially a struggle for power, where each state strives not only to be the most powerful actor in the system, but also to ensure that no other state achieves that lofty position.

* * *

This pessimistic view of how the world works can be derived from realism's five assumptions about the international system. The first is that the international system is anarchic. This does not mean that it is chaotic or riven by disorder. It is easy to draw that conclusion, since realism depicts a world characterized by security competition and war. However, "anarchy" as employed by realists has nothing to do with conflict; rather it is an ordering principle, which says that the system comprises independent political units (states) that have no central authority above them. Sovereignty, in other words, inheres in states, because there is no higher ruling body in the international system. There is no "government over governments."

The second assumption is that states inherently possess some offensive military capability, which gives them the wherewithal to hurt and possibly to destroy each other. States are potentially dangerous to each other. A state's military power is usually identified with the particular weaponry at its disposal, although even if there were no weapons, the individuals of a state could still use their feet and hands to attack the population of another state.

The third assumption is that states can never be certain about the intentions of other states. Specifically, no state can be certain another state will not use its offensive military capability against the first. This is not to say that states necessarily have malign intentions. Another state may be reliably benign, but it is impossible to be certain of that judgment because intentions are impossible to divine with 100 percent certainty. There are many possible causes of aggression, and no state can be sure that another state is not motivated by one of them. Furthermore, intentions can change quickly, so a state's intentions can be benign one day and malign the next. Uncertainty is unavoidable when assessing intentions, which simply means that states can never be sure that other states do not have offensive intentions to go with their offensive military capability.

The fourth assumption is that the most basic motive driving states is survival. States want to maintain their sovereignty. The fifth assumption is that states think strategically about how to survive in the international system. States are instrumentally rational. Nevertheless, they may miscalculate from time to time because they operate in a world of imperfect information, where potential adversaries have incentives to misrepresent their own strength or weakness and to conceal their true aims.

None of these assumptions alone mandates that states will behave competitively. In fact, the fundamental assumption dealing with motives says that states merely aim to survive, which is a defensive goal. When taken together, however, these five assumptions can create incentives for states to think and sometimes to behave aggressively. Specifically, three main patterns of behavior result.

First, states in the international system fear each other. They regard each other with suspicion, and they worry that war might be in the offing. They anticipate danger. There is little room for trust among states. Although the level of fear varies across time and space, it can never be reduced to a trivial level. The basis of this fear is that in a world where states have the capability to offend against each other, and might have the motive to do so, any state bent on survival must be at least suspicious of other states and reluctant to trust them. Add to this the assumption that there is no central authority that a threatened state can turn to for help, and states have even greater incentive to fear each other. Moreover, there is no mechanism — other than the possible self-interest of third parties — for punishing an aggressor. Because it is often difficult to deter potential aggressors, states have ample reason to take steps to be prepared for war.

The possible consequences of falling victim to aggression further illustrate why fear is a potent force in world politics. States do not compete with each other as if international politics were simply an economic marketplace. Political competition among states is a much more dangerous business than economic intercourse; it can lead to war, and war often means mass killing on the battlefield and even mass murder of civilians. In extreme cases, war can even lead to the total destruction of a state. The horrible consequences of war sometimes cause states to view each other not just as competitors, but as potentially deadly enemies.

Second, each state in the international system aims to guarantee its own survival. Because other states are potential threats, and because there is no higher authority to rescue them when danger arises, states cannot depend on others for their security. Each state tends to see itself as vulnerable and alone, and therefore it aims to provide for its own survival. As Kenneth Waltz puts it, states operate in a "self-help" system. This emphasis on self-help does not preclude states from forming alliances. But alliances are only temporary marriages of convenience, where today's alliance partner might be tomorrow's enemy, and today's enemy might be tomorrow's alliance partner. States operating in a self-help world should always act according to their own self-interest, because it pays to be selfish in a self-help world. This is true in the short term as well as the long term, because if a state loses in the short run, it may not be around for the long haul.

Third, states in the international system aim to maximize their relative power positions over other states. The reason is simple: the greater the military advantage one state has over other states, the more secure it is. Every state would like to be the most formidable military power in the system because this is the best way to guarantee survival in a world that can be very dangerous. This logic creates strong incentives for states to take advantage of one another, including going to war if the circumstances are right and victory seems likely. The aim is to acquire more military power at the expense of potential rivals. The ideal outcome would be to end up as the hegemon in the system. Survival would then be almost guaranteed.

––––––––––

Given Mearsheimer's explication of this approach and in light of our criteria for analyzing different approaches to international politics, how can we understand the fundamental assumptions of Structural Realism?

1. Human Nature

Unlike Classical Realists, who typically base their understanding of international relations upon a philosophical conception of human nature, Structural Realisms tend to bracket the question of human nature and begin their theory with assumptions about the nature of the international system. Presumably, this is due to the fact that for Structural Realists it is less important what elements of human nature lead to a particular international structure than that there *is* a certain international system.

2. International System

It is at the systemic or structural level that Structural Realism finds its foundation. As can be seen from the excerpt from Mearsheimer, for Structural Realists, it is critical that the international system be understood as "anarchic." By anarchy, the Structural Realists do not mean that the system is utterly chaotic, but rather that there is "no common power," no centralized government on the international plan. Simply put, the system is made up of independent, sovereign states, which must rely upon themselves to maintain order in the system.

3. Conflict Management Systems

Given the assumptions that Structural Realists make about the international system, it is not surprising that they reject both the possibility of world government and a working collective security system. In the anarchic world, where each state must be concerned about the offensive capabilities of other states, no state would be willing to vest any of its decision-making on security issues to any kind of international governing institution. A true world government would be inconceivable and even a collective security system would require the kind of commitment that no state would be willing to make.

4. International Law

Because Structural Realists believe that state behavior is determined by their desire to establish their own security, they believe that international legal rules have no impact on the behavior of states. To paraphrase one commentator, international legal rules are "epiphenomenal,"[8] they may exist, but ultimately, they have no effect on the actions of international actors. States will clearly follow international legal rules when the rules are in their perceived interests, but when the requirements of international law diverge for a

––––––––––

8. Stephen D. Krasner, *Structural Causes and Regime Consequences: Regimes as Intervening Variables*, 36 INT'L ORG 185, 186, 191–92 (1982).

state's perceived interest, it will follow the dictates of that interest, feeling no compulsion to adhere to the law.

Neoliberal Institutionalism

During the 1980s, many international relations scholars became convinced that structural realism was unable to explain certain types of state behavior—in particular, the willingness of states to create international institutions and even to comply with the rules and decisions of those institutions notwithstanding that such compliance seemed to be against the immediate interests of the states. Accordingly, these scholars began developing alternative approaches to international politics. One such approach has been variously called "Rationalist Institutionalism," or "Neo-Liberal Institutionalism." Proponents of this approach include international relations scholars such as Robert Keohane[9] and Lisa Martin.[10]

As these international relations scholars began developing this approach in the early 1980s, much of the discussion revolved around the concept of a "regime." While the idea of a regime had existed for some time in international legal parlance, international relations scholars developed a very specific definition. This definition of regime provided a framework in which these scholars could hypothesize upon the role that institutions could have to affect the behavior of international actors. One of the groundbreaking works on regime theory came from a project coordinated by Stephen Krasner. This project resulted in a special edition of the journal, *International Organization*, which brought together noted international relations scholars to offer their analysis on the role regimes play in international politics.

In the excerpt that follows, Stephen Krasner provides what is the most commonly accepted definition of regimes among international relations scholars and then proceeds to sketch out the role that regimes play for Neo-Liberals characterized in his description as the "modified structural" approach.

Stephen D. Krasner, *Structural Causes and Regime Consequences: Regimes as Intervening Variables*
36 Int'l Org (1982)

Regimes can be defined as sets of implicit or explicit principles, norms, rules, and decision-making procedures around which actors' expectations converge in a given area of international relations. Principles are beliefs of fact, causation, and rectitude. Norms are standards of behavior defined in terms of rights and obligations. Rules are specific prescriptions or proscriptions for action. Decision-making procedures are prevailing practices for making and implementing collective choice.

* * *

The second orientation to regimes, modified structural, is most clearly reflected in the essays of Keohane and Stein. Both of these authors start from a conventional structural

---

9. *See, e.g.,* Robert O. Keohane, Sovereignty, interdependence and international institutions (1991).
10. *See, e.g.,* Lisa L. Martin, Coercive Cooperation: Explaining Multilateral Economic Sanctions (1992).

realist perspective, a world of sovereign states seeking to maximize their interest and power. Keohane posits that in the international system regimes derive from voluntary agreements among juridically equal actors. Stein states that the "conceptualization of regimes developed here is rooted in the classic characterization of international politics as relations between sovereign entities dedicated to their own self-preservation, ultimately able to depend only on themselves, and prepared to resort to force."

In a world of sovereign states the basic function of regimes is to coordinate state behavior to achieve desired outcomes in particular issue-areas. Such coordination is attractive under several circumstances. Stein and Keohane posit that regimes can have an impact when Pareto-optimal outcomes could not be achieved through uncoordinated individual calculations of self-interest. The prisoners' dilemma is the classic game-theoretic example. Stein also argues that regimes may have an autonomous effect on outcomes when purely autonomous behavior could lead to disastrous results for both parties. The game of chicken is the game-theoretic analog. Haas and others in this volume suggest that regimes may have significant impact in a highly complex world in which ad hoc, individualistic calculations of interest could not possibly provide the necessary level of coordination. If, as many have argued, there is a general movement toward a world of complex inter-dependence, then the number of areas in which regimes can matter is growing.

However, regimes cannot be relevant for zero-sum situations in which states act to maximize the difference between their utilities and those of others. Jervis points to the paucity of regimes in the security area, which more closely approximates zero-sum games than do most economic issue areas. Pure power motivations preclude regimes. Thus, the second orientation, modified structuralism, sees regimes emerging and having a significant impact, but only under restrictive conditions.

Krasner's work can be considered to constitute but the beginning of regime theory and an explication of Neo-Liberal Institutionalist thinking. A more recent discussion — which employs the term "rationalist institutionalist" instead of "Neo-Liberal" — can serve to encapsulate other aspects of this approach.

Anthony Clark Arend, Legal Rules and International Society
121–122 (1999) (footnotes omitted)

Throughout the rationalist literature many advantages to participation in institutional arrangements have been discussed.

* * *

First, institutions reduce transaction costs. By cooperating with other states, states can pool resources, share information, and reduce transaction time. Such benefits will encourage states to create regimes and discourage unilateralism.

Second, regimes may stabilize expectations. In order for any state to realize its goals in the international system, a high degree of predictability of the behavior of other states is optimal. As a consequence, states could find it in their interest to create institutional arrangements that regulate state behavior. Even though the states entering such arrangements may be sacrificing some autonomy, they calculate to gain in the long run by being able to anticipate how other states will behave.

Third, regimes may lengthen the "shadow of the future" and thereby promote cooperation. If a state knows that it will interact with another state only once, the shadow of the future is nonexistent. Thus, the state can pursue its short-term goals without regard to the need to interact with the other state on subsequent occasions. Institutional arrangements, however, provide for repeated interactions among states and thus lengthen the shadow of the future. If a state knows that it will be engaging in many transactions over time through such an institutional arrangement, it will need to be concerned about its long-term relationships with other states.

Fourth, institutions may also provide for decentralized enforcement of regime rules through the creation of situations of reciprocity. The following example may serve to illustrate. Let us assume that a regime regarding the admission of foreign nationals is established. Under the rules of the regime, all states will grant resident status to nationals of other regime parties. Yet, contrary to the rules, France decided not to grant such status to Sierra Leonean nationals, Sierra Leone could reciprocate and refuse to grant resident status to French nationals. This reciprocal connection may induce all parties to comply with the rules of the regime.

But even while the rationalists identify these and other benefits to be accrued from participation in international institutions, rationalist scholars argue that the interests of states remain paramount. Despite the advantages of participation in a regime, if a state believes that its interests are no longer served by a regime, it will act contrary to the rules of the regime. Indeed, many scholars of this orientation would argue that in certain areas, such as security, regimes are unlikely to be established. These scholars tend to believe that economic and resource areas are the most likely candidates for effective regimes. In these areas, they would argue, cooperative behavior is likely to be more beneficial than unilateral actions.

In light of these exemplars and other works by scholars, what is the essence of the Neo-Liberal Institutionalist approach?

1. Human Nature

Like Structural Realists, Neo-Liberal Institutionalists generally do not have a developed set of assumptions about human nature. Instead, they too begin their theoretical writings with a set of assumptions about the international system and tend to bracket claims about human nature.

2. The International System

Similarly, Neo-Liberals accept the notion that the international system is anarchic. They recognize that states are the primary actors in the international system and, despite the existence of global institutions, such as the United Nations, acknowledge that there is no true "common power."

3. Conflict Management System

Neo-Liberals would not believe that true world government were possible, and they might also be skeptical of a true collective security arrangement, because they would perceive that states would not be willing to entrust decision-making to an international organization on fundamental war-peace issues. But, as noted above, many Neo-Liberal would be willing to envision states participating in a series of "regimes" in certain issue areas.

4. International Law

Based on their understanding of the role that institutions can play, it is not surprising that many Neo-Liberals argue that international law can, in fact, affect the behavior of states. In particular, they would argue that in areas of so-called "low politics"—economic areas, resources areas, etc.—states are likely to comply with international law—even though the specific legal rules may conflict with the states' immediate interests—because in the long-term, the legal regime will produce stability and predictability and thus ultimately advance the interests of the states. Many Neo-Liberals, however, would argue that in areas of "high politics"—security, war-peace—states will be less likely to follow international legal rules where there seems to be a conflict with their perceptions of their interests.

Constructivism

The most recent approach to international relations theory that has obtained great traction in the scholarly community is Constructivism. Alexander Wendt,[11] drawing upon constructivist theory from other disciplines, has played the leading role in applying the theory to the behavior of actors in the international system. Other notable constructivist scholars include Martha Finnemore,[12] Kathleen McNamara,[13] Michael Barnett,[14] and Kathryn Sikkink.[15]

ANTHONY CLARK AREND, LEGAL RULES AND INTERNATIONAL SOCIETY
127–129 (1999) (footnotes omitted)

First, constructivists assume that the structure of the international system is a "social structure." As Wendt notes, "neorealists think it [the structure] is made only of a distribution of material capabilities, whereas constructivists think it is also made of social relationships." In other words, structural realists tend to believe that scholars can understand the structure of the system by measuring the "material resources" of states—military might, economic resources, natural and physical resources, and the like. A structural realist would thus measure power by taking account of these kinds of material resources. How much military might does a state have? What is the size of its army? How many warships does it have? How sophisticated are its weapons systems? How great is the gross national product? Does it have important natural resources like oil or strategic minerals? But for constructivists, "social structures have three elements: shared knowledge, material resources, and practices." As Wendt explains, "social structures are defined, in part, by shared understanding, expectations or knowledge." What exists "out there" depends to a degree upon how the decision-making elites in states commonly understand it. The mere existence of anarchy does not in and of itself lead to a competitive self-help system. It depends upon how states

---

11. *See, e.g.,* ALEXANDER WENDT, SOCIAL THEORY OF INTERNATIONAL POLITICS (1999).

12. *See, e.g.,* MARTHA FINNEMORE, NATIONAL INTERESTS IN INTERNATIONAL SOCIETY (1996).

13. *See, e.g.,* KATHLEEN R. MCNAMARA, THE CURRENCY OF IDEAS: MONETARY POLITICS IN THE EUROPEAN UNION (1998).

14. MICHAEL BARNETT & MARTHA FINNEMORE, RULES FOR THE WORLD: INTERNATIONAL ORGANIZATIONS IN GLOBAL POLITICS (2004).

15. *See, e.g.,* KATHRYN SIKKINK, THE JUSTICE CASCADE: HOW HUMAN RIGHTS PROSECUTIONS ARE CHANGING WORLD POLITICS (2011).

commonly understand that anarchy. The next element of "social structure" for Wendt is material resources. While constructivists recognize that things like "gold and tanks" exist, they "argue that material resources acquire meaning for human action through the structure of shared knowledge in which they are embedded." As an example, Wendt notes that "500 British nuclear weapons are less threatening to the United States than 5 North Korean nuclear weapons, because the British are friends of the United States and the North Koreans are not, and amity or enmity is a function of shared understandings." This seems to be essentially a reiteration of Wendt's first point. Reality depends to a large degree upon how states perceive the material conditions. Finally, "social structures exist, not in actors' heads nor in material capabilities, but in practices." "Social structure," Wendt contends, "exists only in process." What I believe he means here is that the social structure is not just what states "think" but rather how they behave based on what they think.

In summary, constructivists contend that the international system is socially constructed, which means two things. First, there are certain concrete, material elements of the structure—there are weapons, oceans, geographical conditions, people. Their material elements, however, take on significance as states develop shared expectations through interaction. Thus, a relationship of enmity between two states exists not merely because those states have offensive weapons systems (material element), but because they harbor ill will toward each other (shared knowledge) and they engage in activities (practices) that reflect that attitude—weapons targeting, alliance formation, etc. Second, since constructivists argue that the international system is a social structure, they would recognize certain "nonmaterial" elements also constitute part of the structure. In other words, they would acknowledge that states, through their practices, can generate certain norms of behavior (shared expectations). These norms would be just as much a part of the system as the material elements.

Second, while structural realists and rational institutionalists assume that the identity and interests of states are exogenously given, constructivists believe that the interests and identities of states are created—at least in part—through interaction and can change through interaction. In an article aptly entitled "Anarchy Is What States Make of It: The Social Construction of Power Politics," Wendt explains that "actors acquire identities—relative stable, role-specific understandings and expectations about self—by participating in … collective meanings." "Identities," Wendt continues, "are the basis of interests." Despite what other scholars might contend, "actors do not have a 'portfolio' of interests that they carry around independent of social context; instead, they define their interests in the process of defining situations." What all this means is that there is, in effect, a mutually constitutive relationship between structure and actor. States through their interactions help constitute the structure of the system, and the structure, in turn, shapes the identities and interests of states. This relationship means that participation in particular institutional arrangements can actually alter the very identity and interests of states. Describing this approach, Robert Keohane explains that "reflectivists" believe that "institutions do not merely reflect the preferences and power of the units constituting them: the institutions themselves shape those preferences and the power." "Institutions," Keohane continues, "are therefore *constitutive* of actors as well as vice versa." Consequently, "it is … not sufficient in this view to treat preferences of individuals as given exogenously: they are affected by institutional arrangements, by prevailing norms, and by historically contingent discourse among people seeking to pursue their purposes and solve their self-defined problems."

Given this assessment of constructivism, how can the fundamental tenets of this approach be summarized?

1. Human Nature

Constructivists seem to run the gamut regarding their assumptions of human nature. Whereas Idealists tend to assume the fundamental goodness of human beings and Classical Realists tend to take a less optimistic approach, Constructivists, to the extent that they even explore this question, seem to assume a malleability of human nature. Human beings can be both good and bad — depending upon human agency and the effect of interactions. A radical Constructivist might even assume that there is no fixed human nature, but rather that human interactions can change human nature in any direction. A less radical approach would suggest that there might be some "core" human characteristics that are immutable, but that a great deal of change is possible.

2. The International System

Like their Structural Realist and Neo-Liberal colleagues, most contemporary Constructivists would assert that the international system is currently anarchic, consisting of independent territorial states. Indeed, Alexander Wendt goes to great lengths to note this shared assumption with the Structural Realists. But what differentiates Constructivists from those who subscribe to other approaches is that Constructivists would assert that this state system may not have the persistence that Structural Realists and Neo-Liberals suggest. In fact, some Constructivists[16] have argued that the international system may best be understood as a "neo-medieval"[17] system. In such as system, there would be a variety of actors — states, intergovernmental organizations, supra-governmental organizations, nongovernmental organizations, multinational corporations, sub- and trans-state ethics groups (such as the Kurds, the Basques) and other trans-state political actors (such as Al-Qaeda, ISIS, Boko Haram) — that would exercise political authority and vie for the loyalty of individuals. At bottom, however, because Constructivist would argue that international actors though their behavior can "construct" the international system, any system is theoretically possible.

3. Conflict Management System

Following on the belief that actors' behavior gives rise to any type of international system, Constructivists would assert that any type of conflict management system is also possible — world government, collective security, or balance of power. Ultimately, they would say that the system of conflict management that would be likely would depend upon the nature of the relationships that the actors established. In a situation where enmities were the primary state of affairs, a balance of power system would likely obtain. If conditions of amity were created, then a collective security system or even — if a situation of extreme amity and trust were established — a world government would be possible.

---

16. Anthony Clark Arend, Legal Rules and International Society 171–85 (1999); *see also*, Human Dignity and the Future of Global Institutions 1–22 (Mark P. Lagon and Anthony Clark Arend, eds., 2014) for a discussion of the neo-medieval nature of the contemporary international system.

17. Hedley Bull described such an international system in his classic work, The Anarchical Society (1977).

4. International Law

Constructivists argue that international legal rules could have a profound impact on the behavior of international actors. Given their claim that there is a mutually-constitutive relationship between agent and structure, Constructivists would assert that states (agents) create legal rules through treaties and customary practice. These legal rules then form part of the structure of the international systems. When states create these rules, they do so with a view that these rules are in their interests. As time passes, Constructivists argue, and as states interact with each other as part of a given legal regime, the rules (structure) can actually alter the identity of the actors (states) and thus their behavior. One example of this phenomenon may be found in the nuclear non-proliferation regime:

> Following the advent of the nuclear age, possession of a nuclear weapon became a membership card to an elite club. States would clearly gain status—and thus a particular identity—in the international system by joining this club. As efforts were made to limit the proliferation of nuclear weapons, many states began to see the advantages of adhering to the non-proliferation regime. Over time, as states continued to participate in this regime, it seems reasonable to assert that they began to see themselves as "nonnuclear" states. Sweden, for example, began efforts in 1945 to establish a nuclear weapons program. After much debate, it decided such a program would not be in its interest and then went on to sign the NPT. By now, it is more than likely that Sweden sees itself as a "nonnuclear" state. Under this logic, it would not go nuclear, even though it possesses the capability, because this would be contrary to his identity. The legal regime, it would seem, played a critical role in forging this change of identity.[18]

If Constructivists are correct in their understanding of the international system, their approach to international relations would offer an important understanding of the role that international law plays. Legal rules could actually alter the very identity of states and thus their behavior.

Conclusion and Questions

The preceding discussion has reviewed five of the most discussed theoretical approaches to international relations: Idealism, Classical Realism, Structural Realism, Neo-Liberal Institutionalism, and Constructivism. Each of these approaches begins with a series of assumptions and then offers conclusions about the role legal rules play in the behavior of international actors.

As a scholar or practitioner of national security law reflects on these approaches, he or she should ask a series of questions: Which approach reflects the best understanding of the realities of international relations? What are the flaws in each approach? What are these approaches missing? Can these approaches be seen in the actions of policymakers over the past several decades? Are these approaches too Western-centric? What would policy makers from the developing world think about these approaches? Is there a better theoretical framework that would provide more explanatory power?

---

18. Anthony Clark Arend, Legal Rules and International Society 136 (1999) (footnotes omitted).

Chapter 2

Newer Theories in Understanding War: From the Democratic Peace to Incentive Theory

*John Norton Moore**

In this chapter:
The Democratic Peace
More Pieces of the Puzzle
Democracy and Deterrence
Testing the Hypothesis
Building on Other Approaches
Toward Incentive Theory
Terrorism and the Events of September 11
Consequences for Foreign Policy
Selected Bibliography

The Democratic Peace

On the eve of World War I, Norman Angell wrote in a popular bestseller that the high level of interaction among nations made war a "great illusion." Since war would not benefit the people of England or Germany, war would no longer occur. Angell's thesis, embraced by even the chairman of Britain's War Committee, died with the guns of August. It has taken almost a century for any other theory of war avoidance to gain the intellectual following enjoyed by Angell's *The Great Illusion*. Today, despite continuing protestations

---

* This chapter grew out of the author's work at the United States Institute of Peace and subsequent efforts over more than two decades to develop a more useful theory of war and peace. It has been assisted in no small measure by superb students in a seminar he teaches on War & Peace. An earlier iteration of the theme of this chapter appears in John Norton Moore, *Toward a New Paradigm: Enhanced Effectiveness in United Nations Peacekeeping, Collective Security, and War Avoidance*, 37 Va. J. Int'l L. 811 (1997). *See also*, John Norton Moore, *Enhancing Compliance with International Law*, 39 Va. J. Int'l L. 881 (1999); John Norton Moore, Comment, *Solving the War Puzzle*, 97 Am. J. Int'l L. 282 (2003); and, John Norton Moore, *Beyond the Democratic Peace: Solving the War Puzzle*, 44 Va. J. Int'l L. 341 (2004). For a more complete version, see John Norton Moore, Solving the War Puzzle (Carolina Academic Press, 2004). More recently, the author has added an additional focus on individual and group psychology of regime elites as an important missing component in understanding war, and more broadly, foreign policy.

of skeptics, the democratic peace has achieved broad support across the political spectrum. In its more cautious form, the democratic peace posits that major war will occur only rarely, if at all, between well-established democratic nations. But obviously, since major war has been occurring at a lusty rate between democratic and nondemocratic nations, the democratic peace, despite its impressive acceptance, is not an adequate theory for war avoidance. Equally, however, since the democratic peace seems to be one of the most robust correlations with war avoidance found to date, approaches that ignore it would seem themselves to be seriously incomplete. Is there a more complete approach that offers better guidance for war avoidance while incorporating the insights of the democratic peace? The answer seems to be a cautious yes. Further, the more complete approach may offer better guidance for virtually all major foreign policy goals and thus serve as a more effective foreign policy paradigm.

The democratic peace has achieved broad contemporary support because it reflects an impressive reality about war. Major international war, that is, interstate war with more than one thousand casualties, occurs at an extraordinarily low rate, if at all, among well-established democracies. This insight, postulated by Immanuel Kant more than two hundred years ago, seems powerfully supported by recent scholarship, particularly the work of Professors Rudy Rummel and Bruce Russett. According to Rummel, of 353 pairings of nations fighting in major international wars between 1816 and 1991, none occurred between democracies. And in *Grasping the Democratic Peace* published in 1993, Professor Russett, a former chairman of the Political Science Department at Yale, lends powerful support to the basic proposition, including a careful refutation of the most common counterarguments. While a few scholars still challenge the statistical reality of this seminal proposition, argue that it is principally a product of a unifying Soviet threat during the Cold War, argue that it does not apply to extended transitions to democracy, or question whether it would necessarily hold in a world of all democracies, most now accept that the democratic peace is one of the most important correlations found to date about the nature of war. The significance of this finding is powerfully supported by studies of the relationship between the type or structure of government and other widely shared goals, including human rights, economic development, environmental protection, famine avoidance, control of terrorism, corruption avoidance, and even ending mass refugee flows. On each of these major human goals, government structures rooted in democracy, the rule of law, and human freedom perform impressively better than totalitarian and authoritarian models rooted in Hegelian statist mystique.

This evidence of the relationship between government structures and performance on the principal goals of mankind, some of it initially funded and disseminated by the United States Institute of Peace, is so compelling that leaders all over the world now pepper their speeches with references to democracy and the rule of law. The Clinton administration had made democracy enlargement the core intellectual theme of its foreign policy. By itself the evidence is sufficiently compelling that democracy enlargement should be a long term goal of every nation. Indeed, the United States in the National Endowment for Democracy, the United Kingdom in the Westminster Foundation, and other of our European allies have already built into their foreign policies at least some mechanism for encouragement of democracy.

For all its power, however, the democratic peace proposition is by itself incomplete. In its most common formulations, it focuses only on the correlation between democracy and war, and this in turn fails to capture the real strength of the case for democracy, the rule of law, and human freedom across virtually all of the most commonly shared goals of mankind. Statistical quarrels with the proposition have less ability to persuade when we see that the same correlation is common across a wide variety of human goals and on some, as with the staggering twentieth century genocide, is even more conclusive. Perhaps most importantly, since democracies are all too frequently engaged in major war, as World Wars I and II and numerous limited wars since attest, the concept of the democratic peace alone has not explained war. After all, Rummel's analysis of wars between 1816 and 1991, which concludes that there were no wars between established democracies in this period, also shows 155 major war pairings between democracies and nondemocracies. How did democracies get into these wars? Are they recklessly attacking nondemocracies? Are wars between democracies and nondemocracies simply random or accidental? Or are democracies engaged in major wars with nondemocracies as a result of attacks by nondemocracies? Questions such as these caused Professors Singer and Small, who first uncovered the statistical correlation of the democratic peace in their seminal *Wages of War Statistical Handbook* in 1972, to largely dismiss the proposition in their early study of war. Further, the democratic peace proposition as yet has produced no consensus as to the mechanism accounting for the reduced rate of major war between well-established democracies. Principal competing hypotheses focus on structural or institutional checks peculiar to democracies, on broadly shared normative or cultural perspectives, or on game-theoretic models of democratic nation interactions with adversaries. Finally, there are a variety of other loose ends with the proposition, including questions of how well the proposition applies to minor coercion and to nations in transition rather than to major war and stable democracy. Given the power of the democratic peace correlation and the strongly supportive parallel correlations between government type and other major community goals, it would seem a mistake to ignore the democratic peace. But given the remaining unanswered questions with the proposition, it would seem equally necessary to formulate and test broader hypotheses if we are truly to solve the war puzzle. This chapter will suggest one such hypothesis, discuss the supporting evidence, and recommend, in general terms, actions likely to lessen the risk of war if the suggested approach is correct. But first, it may be useful to examine some additional pieces of the puzzle.

More Pieces of the Puzzle

Once we realize that the correlation with government structures holds across a wide range of the most important human goals and that nondemocratic structures and a lack of human freedom go hand in hand with a wide variety of failures, including war, terrorism, genocide, famine, poverty, environmental degradation, corruption, narcotics trafficking, infant mortality, and refugees, inquiry is pointed in the direction of a general explanation for this government failure in nondemocratic regimes. The explanation is almost certainly rooted in a broad mosaic of differences inherent in governance rooted in democracy and the rule of law versus that rooted in statist models. Indeed, it is no exaggeration to speak of competing cultures of democracy and statism.

As a core difference underlying these competing political cultures, there is yet another potentially powerful explanation for the profound difference in levels of government failure. Indeed, I believe this is likely the most important internal mechanism responsible for the democratic peace and other differences in performance between these forms of governance. This mechanism, increasingly being referred to as the theory of government failure, was the insight that won the Nobel Prize in economics for James M. Buchanan in 1986. Widely known as public choice theory, as initially developed by Professor Buchanan, it posits that government decision makers will generally act rationally in pursuit of their interests, like actors elsewhere, and that the government setting, as with markets, provides mechanisms by which elites and special interest groups may be able to externalize costs on others. While this theory of public decision making was developed primarily to explain significant government failure in democracies, the same underlying concept seems to operate off-the-scale within totalitarian and nondemocratic regimes to produce what might be characterized as massive government failure in those systems. Norman Angell was correct in *The Great Illusion* that the average citizen in a modern democracy is likely only to lose from aggressive war. But he failed to understand that regime elites in nondemocratic systems may be in a position, as was Saddam Hussein, both to personally capture the benefits of any successful aggression and to externalize the costs on others. Decision elites in nondemocratic nations may, therefore, be far more disposed to high risk aggressive actions risking major war and other disasters for their people. This conclusion is supported by the empirical work of Professors Dan Reiter and Allan C. Stam set out in their book *Democracies At War*, which indicates the greater caution of democratic leaders in war initiation as one of the principal reasons democracies have won more than three-quarters of their wars since 1815.

If this theory of government failure, and incentives for government decision makers generally, is an important part of the explanation for war, one would expect to find that democracies are, in fact, getting into major war principally, though not exclusively, as a result of aggression by nondemocratic states, either against the democracies directly or against nations or peoples on whose behalf the democracies then go to war. To test the proposition that democracies were likely to have become engaged in major war principally as defenders rather than aggressors, I recently explored these issues through an analysis of major interstate wars since the adoption of the Charter in 1945. In that time frame, and based on the totality of the historical evidence as presently understood, I believe that clear aggression by a democratic government in a major interstate war has been limited to a single instance out of approximately twenty-nine major wars studied. A further three such wars in this period might reasonably be scored as democratic aggression. That is, in this time frame there were only four wars even arguably with a democratic aggressor for 14 percent of the total wars studied, and there were twenty-five wars arguably with nondemocratic responsibility for 86 percent of the total. The one major war with a clear democratic aggressor was the Suez War of 1956 in which the United Kingdom and France jointly attacked Egypt in the wake of Nasser's nationalization of the Suez Canal. The three wars also arguably scored as democratic aggression are the Indian action in the 1971 Bangladesh War, the 1974 Turkish intervention in Cyprus, and the US/UK 2003 invasion of Iraq. The former, however, has a powerful argument that it was humanitarian intervention. Cyprus, though it went too far, was a response by a treaty guarantor to a coup against the elected Cypriot government of Archbishop Makarios in support of *enosis* with Greece, and the 2003 Iraq War was arguably lawful under Security Council Resolution 1441.[1]

Further, of these twenty-nine major wars, twenty involved democracies, and in only four of these, or 14 percent, was a democracy acting even arguably illegally as an aggressor. While this analysis of democratic versus nondemocratic aggression is certainly subject to controversy, I believe that it accurately captures a reality that, at least since the adoption of the United Nations Charter, democratic nations predominantly get into major interstate

---

1. *See, e.g.*, Nicholas Rostow, *Determining the Lawfulness of the 2003 Campaign Against Iraq*, Israel Yearbook on Human Rights, 2004.

war as a result of illegal actions of nondemocratic nations rather than the other way around or simply through random distribution of blame or accident.

Indeed, there seem to be few major interstate wars in any time frame clearly initiated by a well-established liberal democracy motivated principally by value extension. Most recently, whatever one's analysis of the legal and policy case for the United States/United Kingdom position with respect to the war in Iraq, these countries have been principally motivated by defensive considerations rather than by value extension.[2]

Summarizing the path to major interstate war of democracies since the adoption of the charter, seven involved guerrilla, terrorist, or intermittent attacks against the democracy or a treaty ally, seven involved direct invasion of the democracy or a state then assisted by the democracy, one involved a severe threat of attack against the democracy, and one involved a humanitarian intervention following a related genocide. Further, the four wars scored here arguably as democratic nation aggression under the charter were in response respectively to an illegal takeover of the Suez Canal, a severe humanitarian crisis, a military coup threatening the balance under a treaty of guarantee, and a thug committing atrocities and failing to comply with United Nations sanctions. At least since the adoption of the charter in 1945, the principal path to war for democracies seems to have been nondemocratic attack, genocide, or other illegal actions.

If democratic nations are getting into major war predominantly as a result of aggression, genocide, or other illegal actions by nondemocratic regimes, then the evidence strongly suggests, at least for purposes of continuing our search for a more comprehensive hypothesis about war, that the key missing link in democratic peace theory is the importance of external deterrence. That is, are democracies getting into war predominantly in settings where they fail to adequately deter a potential nondemocratic decision elite willing to engage in high risk behavior? Considerable evidence suggests that the answer is yes.

Before examining the evidence it is important that we define what we mean by deterrence and effective deterrence for the purposes of this hypothesis. Deterrence for our purposes is the totality of *external* incentives, that is, incentives from the international environment, which may be high or low, adequate or inadequate. Effective deterrence will be regarded as that aggregate of external incentives known to and understood by a potential aggressor as adequate to prevent the aggression. In this respect, factors affecting deterrence encompass the totality of positive and negative incentives, including potential military responses and security arrangements, power asymmetries, economic relations and trade, diplomatic actions, effects of international organizations and international law, alliances, collective security, contiguity, and other opportunity factors, or the lack thereof with respect to any of these elements. Note specifically that actions affecting incentives can be either military or non-military, either positive (offering potential benefits) or negative (offering potential costs), and either fixed (for example, contiguity) or variable (for example, effects of diplomacy), or any combination of the above. Factors affecting deterrence also include

---

2. There has been a robust legal debate about the United States/United Kingdom actions in the 2003 Iraq War and any final characterization is likely to be arguable. Defensive concerns of the United States and the United Kingdom related to Iraq's failure to adhere to its Security Council imposed sanctions to scrap its weapons of mass destruction in the broader context of Iraqi support for terrorism and its demonstrated use of chemical weapons. Further, these concerns also embraced Iraq's continuing attacks against U.S. and U.K. aircraft lawfully present on a humanitarian mission in the no-fly zones. This Iraq War is clearly a product of a post-9/11 broader war against terrorism and it likely would not have occurred but for the 9/11 attacks against the United States.

clarity of communication, past actions of the target and any potential defenders, and the perspectives and belief system of the potential aggressor. Ultimately, effective deterrence is a state of mind of the potential aggressor decision maker based on perceptions of external incentives.

As so broadly conceived, there is strong evidence that deterrence, that is, the effect of external factors on the decision to go to war, is an important missing link in the war/peace equation. An examination of the level of deterrence before the principal wars of the twentieth century shows that in every case the potential aggressor made a rational calculation that the war would be won, and won promptly. In fact, the longest period of time for victory through conventional attack seems to be the six weeks calculated by the German General Staff as the time necessary to prevail on the Western front in World War I under the Schlieffen Plan.

Democracy and Deterrence

Fitting the puzzle together, major international war seems predominantly to be a synergy between a potential aggressive nondemocratic regime and an absence of effective levels of deterrence. That is, democratic nations do not need to deter other democratic nations through external incentives even where contiguity, and thus higher risk, is present. Canada does not, and need not, fear a U.S. invasion, despite the overwhelming military superiority of the United States. And Belgium does not, and need not, fear a French invasion, despite the overwhelming military superiority of France. But NATO was certainly correct to work assiduously to deter an invasion from the then Soviet Union. Indeed, NATO may well have prevented World War III and may have been one of the most effective foreign policy initiatives in U.S. history.

The principal path to major interstate war for democracies seems to be failing to ensure adequate levels of deterrence when confronted by potential aggressors. This can occur because of an absence of adequate military forces, as was true of the U.S. entry into World War I and, in part, the Japanese attack on Pearl Harbor; lack of communication of intent (or even any advance formation of an intent to defend), as was true in the Korean and Gulf Wars; or lack of believability of the guarantee, as was true of British entry into World War II and, in part, Milosevic's decisions to defy NATO in Bosnia and Kosovo. This means, if correct, that democracies should focus on ensuring effective levels of deterrence in response to threats of aggression or genocide, considering all such factors, in settings where they would otherwise be prepared to go to war. To recognize this imperative, however, is not to supply the answers to the considerable strategic and political difficulties in meeting this challenge in settings, such as those Britain faced in Hitler's threat to Europe or those the United States faced in Hussein's initial threat to Kuwait.

A useful framework in thinking about the war puzzle is provided in the Kenneth Waltz classic *Man, the State and War*, published in 1954 for the Institute of War and Peace Studies. Waltz notes that previous thinkers about the causes of war have tended to assign responsibility at one of three levels of individual psychology, the nature of the state, or the nature of the international system. We might summarize my analysis in this popular construct by suggesting that the most critical variables are the second and third levels, or images, of analysis. Government structures, at the second level, seem to play a central role in levels of aggressiveness in high risk behavior leading to major war. In this, the democratic peace is an essential insight. The third level of analysis, the international system, or totality of external incentives influencing the decision for war, is also critical *when government structures do not restrain such high risk behavior on their own.* Quite simply, both democracy and deterrence internalize the costs to decision elites of high risk behavior leading to major war. As such, they reduce that behavior. It is also likely that image one, that of individual and group psychology of regime elites, is yet a third, and less understood but important, factor in understanding war.

Testing the Hypothesis

Hypotheses, or paradigms, are useful if they reflect the real world better than previously held paradigms. In the complex world of foreign affairs and the war puzzle, perfection is unlikely. No general construct will fit all cases even in the restricted category of major interstate war; there are simply too many variables. We should insist, however, on testing against the real world and on results that suggest that a focus on identified key variables offers enhanced usefulness over other constructs. In testing an hypothesis, we can test it for consistency with major wars. That is, in looking, for example, at major wars in the twentieth century, did they present both a nondemocratic aggressor and an absence of effective deterrence? And although it is by itself not going to prove causation, we might also want to test the hypothesis against settings of potential wars that did not occur. That is, in non-war settings, was there an absence of at least one element of the synergy? We might also ask questions about the effect of changes on the international system in either element of the synergy. That is, what, in general, happens when a totalitarian state makes a transition to stable democracy or vice versa? And what, in general, happens when levels of deterrence are dramatically increased or decreased?

Running the hypothesis for the principal wars of the twentieth century does seem to provide support. World War I began on the Eastern front with a nondemocratic Austria aggressively attacking Serbia, egged on enthusiastically by Germany. *That* aggression in turn precipitated a cascade of Russian mobilization and Germany's declaration of war against France, Russia, Luxembourg, and Belgium. World War II is a poster boy for the paradigm with both Hitler and Tojo engaged in clear aggression in the European and Pacific theaters. Similarly, the Korean and Gulf Wars reflect the same deadly mix of a nondemocratic regime initiating aggression against their neighbors.

Non-war settings, or the dogs that did not bark, also seem generally consistent with the hypothesis. Thus, neither Canada nor Switzerland seek to militarize their borders with the United States or France, respectively, despite overwhelming military (including nuclear) superiority by their large and contiguous democratic neighbors. Nor do the citizens of the United States fear the French or British nuclear deterrents, despite their ability to devastate the United States. And NATO, where substantial levels of conventional and nuclear deterrence are present, *is* a tight alliance that may well have avoided major war.

Analyses of abrupt changes in the two elements in the war synergy also lend support to the hypothesis. As examples, the ongoing shift in the former Soviet Union from totalitarianism toward democracy produced changes of enormous consequence, many of which would have been unthinkable under the former Soviet regime. These include the fall of the Berlin Wall, the reunification of Germany, the dissolution of the Warsaw Pact, the expansion of NATO to the East, dramatic reductions in military forces, and the sale by Russia to the United States of fissionable material recycled from Soviet nuclear weapons.

This quick survey, simply using historical case studies, is not presented as a full test of the hypothesis but rather as suggestive of the kinds of inquiry needed to more fully explore it. As an important point of emphasis, the reader should keep in mind that the hypothesis has been developed for *major interstate war*, not for settings of minor coercion or civil or colonial wars, although there is likely some relevance for those settings as well.

Building on Other Approaches

As we seek broader understanding of war and measures for avoiding it, we should seek to identify and incorporate the insights from other approaches that have to date served as the principal arsenal against war. Certainly neither the importance of democracy nor the importance of deterrence as measures for war avoidance are new insights. As has been seen, focus on the importance of democracy in this respect goes back at least to Kant, and there is a classic statement of deterrence in Sun Tzu's writing in *The Art of War* more than two thousand years ago. Similarly, many other approaches, including diplomacy, balance of power, collective security, arms control and peaceful mechanisms for dispute resolution, offer insights that should not be lost in the search for a more complete explanation of war. The challenge is to incorporate insights from all approaches while recognizing the limitations that may also be inherent in some.

Diplomacy is a critical tool. When done well, negotiation can not only settle longstanding disputes and promote stable expectations but it can also mobilize deterrence and in many ways reduce the risk of war. As such, diplomacy is certainly a staple in the struggle against war. But diplomacy alone is not always the answer to the problem of war. And when poorly conceived, as in the Munich debacle, it can exacerbate the risk of war and further undermine deterrence.

Balance of power theory is many things, including a useful predictive tool. Its insight that power matters is of fundamental importance. Indeed, power is an important component of deterrence and an overwhelming asymmetry in power has been shown to have an important deterrent effect. In many respects, however, a focus on government structures and on deterrence itself, including the crucial communication dimension of deterrence, may be a more important predictive focus than reliance on the distribution of power through equilibrium, bipolarity, and multipolarity, or hegemonic transitions of power in the international system. It should be noted also, as this multiplicity of theories suggests, that balance of power theory, broadly conceived, as yet has produced no consensus reconciling its own opposing approaches.

Despite lack of substantial evidence that arms races cause war, well done arms control can properly serve a variety of worthy goals. These include enhancing stability, reducing the risk of accidental or unauthorized launch, banning certain inhumane systems or practices, reducing defense expenditures, and contributing to confidence building. Further, the problem of weapons of mass destruction is a special problem requiring special attention. We should not, however, fall into the trap of focusing on arms control as the central element in war avoidance. And we should understand that poorly done arms control has the potential to undermine deterrence, as seems to have been the effect from the Japanese conclusion about the lack of real U.S. commitment to its Pacific Island possessions when the United States accepted a fortification freeze there in the 1922 Washington Agreement.

Certainly mechanisms for encouraging peaceful settlement of disputes and resolution of disputes by law rather than force are worthy additions to our arsenal against war. In the long run, encouragement of a genuine rule of law among nations is in the interest of all. Again, however, we should not confuse the development of third party dispute resolution mechanisms with an adequate answer to the problem of war. The problem with third party dispute settlement as a *core* modality for war avoidance is, quite simply, that the problem of international aggression is predominantly analogous to the problem of controlling criminal behavior, not that of resolving civil disputes. To say that Germany and Poland or Iraq and Kuwait should have resolved their disputes peacefully rather than going to war is to shockingly fail to understand that these wars were not mutual undertakings, like a contract to buy grain, but rather were the result of German and Iraqi aggression. Nor is this any different with respect to the Austrian demands made against Serbia preceding the outbreak of World War I, which were *designed* to be rejected. In this respect the aggressors are like the criminal gunman who demands your wallet. This problem of criminal behavior is not solved by dividing the wallet between the parties in court. Rather, criminal behavior is understood as requiring deterrence.

Though the conventional tool kit for war avoidance has useful tools, neither alone nor together do these tools explain war nor serve as an adequate basis for war avoidance. Sadly, the classical theories of international relations, "realism" and "idealism" as well as the newer theories operating loosely within the "realist" tradition but rejecting its rigidity with respect to international law and social context, those of "institutionalism" and "constructivism" fail not only as explanations for war but also as broader theories to guide foreign policy.

Classical "realism" and its more modern counterpart "structural realism," fail to effectively take account of individual or group psychology and regime elites, forms of government, or the more specific "deterrence" rather than "power." Their thesis that wars result from "a security dilemma" in an "anarchic world" is equivalent to saying that airplanes crash as a result of the effects of gravity. While accurate, such descriptions are of little utility in describing with greater specificity the major variables causing wars (or airplane crashes). Realism also fails to properly understand subjectivities, including law and expectations of authority, or the complex social context of the international systems.

"Idealism," in its focus on enhancing structures of deterrence and its embrace of the democratic peace, is more relevant and useful. But it too fails to provide a useful theory for more fully understanding war and a full range of foreign policy interests. As discussed above, its emphasis on third-party dispute settlement also largely misses the point in settings of aggression.

"Institutionalism," sometimes called "neoliberal institutionalism," properly focuses on the role of law and perspectives of authority, as it rejects a core rigidity of realism. But, while correct in its core thesis, it is but a scream against realism and fails to provide a broader theory either for understanding war or foreign policy generally.

Finally, "constructivism," which says that the starting point of "realism," the "anarchic" international order, is not fixed but rather "what states make of it" is again, not a real theory of international relations, nor is it an adequate basis for understanding war. Its focus on subjectivities and social context is correct, but again seems more a scream against another of the rigidities of realism than a theory of international relations.

An approach to understanding war, and more broadly to the full range of goals in foreign relations, must provide some mechanism both for identifying key variables which account for war and the foreign policy issues of importance, such as genocide, and for aggregating such factors in both understanding and enabling enhanced control. No theory that deals with these complex social realities will be perfect but we should at least expect more from theory than we get today from realism, idealism, institutionalism, or constructivism.

Toward Incentive Theory

The democratic peace emerged in the effort to solve the war puzzle. The apparent robust correlation between government type and avoidance of war, though, quickly encouraged research about the relationship between government type and other major foreign policy goals. The important findings, all pointing toward the great importance of democratic governance, human freedom, and the rule of law, are too recent to have generated any focused theoretical literature on the underlying commonalities. As has been suggested, however, there is good reason to believe that a core mechanism underlying these extraordinary correlations may be the Nobel Prize winning insight called government failure theory. Thus, war may be, at least in significant part, a product of government failure in which nondemocratic regime elites believe they can externalize costs on others while personally obtaining the benefits of any successes. As with market failure, which operates principally from a similar mechanism of externalities, when government failure occurs, it needs external checks to right the balance in incentives. With market failure, this role is performed by government. With war, absent such a central government, it must be a product of the totality of external actions creating deterrence through incentives.

Similar mechanisms related to incentives seem to underlie other correlations with government type. Thus, the principal democide seems to be generated either to capture or maintain power or in pursuit of some twisted vision of the regime elite. And the cost is paid by the millions of victims tortured or killed. The forgotten holocaust in the Congo from 1885 to 1908, which may have killed as many as ten million, was a giant forced labor camp for the personal enrichment of King Leopold II of Belgium. Pol Pot's slaughter in Cambodia seems to have been intended both to keep Pol Pot in power and in pursuit of his twisted vision of utopia.

This expansive focus suggests that the democratic peace has now evolved into a broader new paradigm in foreign relations focused on the importance of liberal democracy, the rule of law, and human freedom in achievement of virtually the full range of important goals of foreign policy. Underlying this broader approach may be a pervasive effect of incentives, particularly as they are affected for regime elites by government type.

As with war, which is not simply an internal issue within states, when terrorism or massive genocide (as in Pol Pot's Cambodia, Rwanda, or the former Yugoslavia) is taking place, it is the totality of external incentives through deterrence that is the only remaining modality of control. That is, when nondemocratic government structures massively fail, affecting the interests and commitments of other nations, the only remaining check is for other nations to structure effective external deterrence through incentives.

It is appropriate, then, that we embrace the democratic peace, while moving beyond it to a new, more complete paradigm in foreign policy that may focus our attention more effectively on the nature of the key variables and useful methods for response. That new paradigm will focus on democracy and deterrence, but its core underlying mechanism may be that of incentives. Perhaps the new paradigm, which seeks to incorporate the best insights from the full range of past approaches to foreign policy, might be termed incentive theory. Such a focus suggests that war is best explained not by any one of Waltz's three images but rather by a synergy of factors affecting incentives in the war decision. As such, the new theory blends classical realism and idealism but goes beyond both. The very breadth of the term may also offer greater insight as to the great range of relevant variables affecting incentives and, thus, the decision for war or peace. Response to incentives seems to be the core mechanism by which nature produces both biological and cultural evolution. Should we be surprised if it turns out to be of central importance for foreign policy? More specifically, incentive theory focuses on the point of decision by a regime elite to go to war and analyzes at that point correlations from images one, two, and three. That is, it envisions the role of individual and group psychology of the regime elites, internal deterrence from governmental structures exemplifying or checking these actions, and external deterrence from the international system.

Terrorism and the Events of September 11

While incentive theory has been developed for major interstate war, it seems also to have resonance for international terrorism. The most deadly international terrorism is state-sponsored or supported. Principal state sponsors of terrorism, including Afghanistan under the Taliban, Iran, Iraq under Hussein, and Libya under Gaddafi, as well as Syria, are totalitarian or authoritarian. Similarly, the private groups that undertake terrorism, with or without state support, are overwhelmingly anti-democratic. And, as with interstate war, the terrorist decision elites are able to externalize the costs of their actions on innocent civilians and even their own converts. Further, terrorism overwhelmingly occurs in settings where those initiating its use expect it, on balance, to be a strategy that will promote their objectives; that is, it occurs in settings absent effective deterrence. Indeed, until the events of September 11, the global response to terrorism had been weak, treating terrorism predominantly as a natural feature of a complex world to be dealt with largely by law enforcement. And the principal thrust of terrorism has been directed aggressively against democratic nations and governments.

The heinous attack of September 11 directed against more than 50,000 civilians and, in its financial fallout, touching literally every nation on Earth, strikingly fits this democracy/deterrence synergy. Osama bin Laden's al-Qaeda classically illustrates the anti-democratic radical regime syndrome. The Taliban government of Afghanistan, which provided sanctuary and support, was also strongly anti-democratic. With respect to levels of deterrence, the Osama bin Laden organization had been able to execute a continuing pattern of attacks against U.S. interests with little sustained response. These included attacks against U.S. Embassies in Kenya and Tanzania, following a 1998 *fatwa* virtually declaring war on America. Most recently, before what may have been their *second* attack on the World Trade Center, the organization seems to have been involved in the attack on the U.S.S. *Cole*, which produced no visible response from the United States. Newer terrorist groups, such as the so-called Islamic State of Iraq and Syria (ISIS), are both anti-democratic and exceptionally brutal.

Consequences for Foreign Policy

New slogans in foreign policy are easier to achieve than effective results. The foreign policy process is inevitably one of constrained options, inadequate information, choice among conflicting goals, and competing views as to the most appropriate actions. In that messy process, as Thomas Kuhn reminded us more than a quarter century ago in his seminal work on "The Structure of Scientific Revolutions," we are also consciously or unconsciously ruled by our prevailing paradigms. What we believe shapes what we do. It may be useful, then, to briefly examine some of the general consequences for foreign policy of a paradigm rooted in the importance of internal and external incentives.

Before examining some of the consequences for foreign policy of the new paradigm, it may be useful to begin by a brief focus on what it is not. It is emphatically not democracy building by aggressive use of force or a democratic just war or crusade for democracy. It is not an effort to impose a *Pax Americana* or to impose American cultural values alien to others. It is not a prescription that all nondemocracies are a threat to the peace; nor is it a recommendation to engage beyond our means or to naively intervene in settings where we have little ability to influence or little national interest.

Most importantly, the full range of correlations of important foreign policy goals with democracy and the rule of law suggests that an important long-term goal is support for democracy and the rule of law. With respect to long-term efforts to assist the development of democracy and the rule of law, it is particularly important that we *not* fall into the all too common trap of believing that promoting democracy is simply promoting free elections. Free elections are an essential element of genuine democracy, but, as the United States articulated for the then Soviet Union in the 1990 rule of law talks, liberal democracy is an important mix of principles, including limited government, checks and balances, free elections, freedom of speech, assembly, and the press, protections of the individual from the state, known and efficient legal rules facilitating human creativity and exchange, legal constraints on government officials, an independent judiciary, respect for economic freedom, and many others. While an electoral democracy is certainly superior to totalitarianism, the full benefits of democracy, including quite probably the very stability of democratic institutions, comes from achieving liberal democracy.

Incentive theory, with its respect for human freedom, would also strongly support efforts to remove trade barriers and broaden the parameters for human economic choice. Free trade not only benefits both sides in the trade but may also through time contribute to the network of cooperative positive incentives that are likely a factor in reducing war. Indeed, Professors Bruce Russett and John Oneal show in their book, *Triangulating Peace*, that there is a strong correlation between an important bilateral trade relationship and the reduction of war. Further, in enhancing economic growth, trade enhances the wealth of nations, which in turn tends to correlate with enhanced environmental standards. The protestors against trade and globalization in Seattle, Zurich, Quebec, Göteborg, and Genoa would seem as much "old thinkers" as the anarchists with whom they found common cause. This, of course, does not mean that we should neglect efforts to protect workers and the environment.

Just as the long run focus must be on democracy enlargement and the rule of law, we must also focus on enhancing deterrence against war, terrorism, and genocide. As long as incentives within some nations do not properly operate to control these scourges, then the incentives must be supplied externally. As with support for democracy, deterrence, in all its dimensions, must be understood as an essential element of foreign policy. Enhancing deterrence against war and terrorism in turn requires a focus on all elements of deterrence, from maintenance of a strong military to appropriate advance communication about unacceptable actions. We must also understand the complexity of deterrence and the subtlety sometimes required for effective implementation. We must never mistake deterrence for an overall foreign policy.

Finally, we should focus as well on high-risk regime elites pursuing radical ideologies and we should include ideas/subjectivities in our matrix for predicting and controlling

Figure 1. Graphic Representation of Incentive Theory in War/Peace Decisions

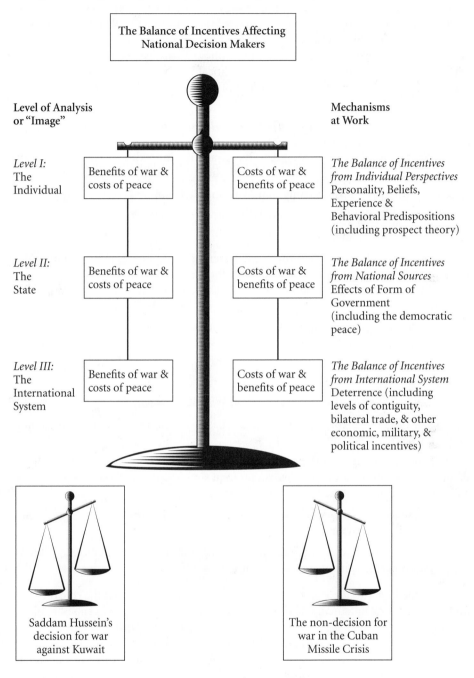

The Balance of Incentives Affecting
National Decision Makers

Level of Analysis
or "Image"

Mechanisms
at Work

Level I:
The
Individual

Benefits of war &
costs of peace

Costs of war &
benefits of peace

*The Balance of Incentives
from Individual Perspectives*
Personality, Beliefs,
Experience &
Behavioral Predispositions
(including prospect theory)

Level II:
The
State

Benefits of war &
costs of peace

Costs of war &
benefits of peace

*The Balance of Incentives
from National Sources*
Effects of Form of
Government
(including the democratic
peace)

Level III:
The
International
System

Benefits of war &
costs of peace

Costs of war &
benefits of peace

*The Balance of Incentives
from International System*
Deterrence (including
levels of contiguity,
bilateral trade, & other
economic, military, &
political incentives)

Saddam Hussein's
decision for war
against Kuwait

The non-decision for
war in the Cuban
Missile Crisis

war. Certainly there is a major need to effectively control radical ideologies supporting aggressive use of force, as we see in al-Qaeda, ISIS, and other contemporary terrorist organizations. Such unconstrained violent ideology is as dangerous for global health as virulent diseases such as Ebola. Ignoring the struggle for ideas is a glaring omission of realism, as these contemporary threats illustrate all too well.

The democratic peace has, and appropriately so, already influenced the foreign policy of democratic nations. It may be time, however, for a broader approach, which both builds on the insights of the democratic peace and seeks to go beyond it to incorporate additional insights about war and other foreign policy concerns in the interest of a more complete and operationally useful foreign policy. As always, to borrow Sir Winston Churchill's famous phrase, it is left to our political leaders to "pass ... from the tossing sea of Cause and Theory to the firm ground of Result and Fact."

Questions for Discussion

1. Do you agree that democracy, deterrence, and the individual psychology of regime elites are key variables in the effort to control war? Why or why not?

2. If so, why has it taken so long to understand their importance?

3. What do we really know about balance of power and war?

4. How do we systematically promote democracy and the rule of law?

5. How do we systematically promote deterrence? If a failure to clearly communicate what they will defend has been a pathway to war for democracies, how can this be overcome? As an example, what should the United States do today with respect to the South China Sea dispute?

6. How do we systematically tackle extreme ideologies which preach aggression and violence?

7. Can you describe incentive theory? How, if at all, is it preferable to other approaches to foreign policy?

8. Does incentive theory work for the Iraq War? Why or why not?

9. Does incentive theory also work for civil as well as interstate wars? How, if at all, might the key variables differ in civil wars?

10. Is one advantage of incentive theory that it seems to serve the principal range of democratic foreign policy objectives, rather than simply one, as might be argued against a prevailing belief in balance of power theory?

11. Does incentive theory bridge the gap between classical realism and idealism in international relations theory?

12. How important are our paradigms of thought in the actions we take to avoid war and pursue other foreign policy goals? What was your paradigm before this chapter? What is it now?

Selected Bibliography

Angell, Norman, *The Great Illusion* (1914).

Buchanan, James M., "Politics Without Romance: A Sketch of Positive Public Choice Theory and its Normative Implications," *in* II *The Theory of Public Choice* 11–22 (James M. Buchanan & Robert D. Tollison eds., 1984).

Craig, Gordon A., & Alexander L. George, *Force and Statecraft* (2d ed. 1990).

Diamond, Larry, *Developing Democracy* (1999).

Feshbach, Murray, & Alfred Friendly Jr., *Ecocide in the USSR: Health and Nature Under Siege* (1992).

Freedom House, *Freedom in the World 2001–2002* (2002).

George, Alexander L., "The Role of Force in Diplomacy," Chapter 4, *in The Use of Force After the Cold War* 78–79 (H. W. Brands ed., 2000).

Gowa, Joanne, *Ballots and Bullets: The Elusive Democratic Peace* (1999).

Gwartney, James D., & Robert A. Lawson, *Economic Freedom of the World* (1997).

Jaggers, Keith, & Ted Robert Gurr, *Polity III: Regime Change and Political Authority, 1800–1994* [computer file] (Study #6695) at <http://www.icpsr.umich.edu/icpsrweb/ICPSR/studies/06695>, 2d ICPSR version (1996), *at* <http://doi.org/10.3886/ICPSR06695.v2>.

Kagan, Donald, *On the Origins of War* (1995).

Kant, Immanuel, "Perpetual Peace: A Philosophical Sketch," *reprinted in Kant's Political Writings* (Hans Reiss ed., 1970).

Levy, Jack S., "Prospect Theory and International Relations: Theoretical Applications and Analytical Problems," *in Avoiding Losses/Taking Risks: Prospect Theory and International Conflict* (Barbara Farnham ed., 1994).

———, "War and Peace," Chapter 18, *in Handbook of International Relations* 350–68 (Carlsnaes, Risse & Simmons eds., 2002).

Mandelbaum, Michael, *The Ideas that Conquered the World: Peace, Democracy, and Free Markets in the Twenty-First Century* (2002).

Mansfield, Edward D., & Jack Snyder, "Democratic Transitions, Institutional Strength, and War," 56 *Int'l Org.* 297 (2002).

———, "Democratization and War," 74 *Foreign Aff.* 79 (1995).

de Mesquita, Bruce Bueno, et al., "An Institutional Explanation of the Democratic Peace," 93 *Am. Pol. Sci. Rev.* 791 (1999).

Owen, John M., *Liberal Peace, Liberal War* (1997).

Palmer, Mark, Destroying the Axis of Evil VI-6 (March 2002) (draft manuscript on file with the author).

Reiter, Dan, & Allan Stam, *Democracies at War* (2002).

Rummel, R. J., *Death By Government* (1994).

———, *Power Kills: Democracy as a Method of Nonviolence* (1997).

Russett, Bruce, *Grasping the Democratic Peace* (1993).

Russett, Bruce, & John Oneal, *Triangulating Peace: Democracy, Interdependence, and International Organization* (2001).

Scully, Gerald, *Constitutional Environments and Economic Growth* (1992).

Sen, Amartya, *Poverty and Famines: An Essay on Entitlement and Deprivation* (1981).

Singer, J. David, & Melvin Small, *The Wages of War, 1816–1965: A Statistical Handbook* (1972).

———, "The War-Proneness of Democratic Regimes, 1818–1965," 50 *Jerusalem J. Int'l Rel.* 50, 67–68 (1976).

Spiro, David E., "The Insignificance of the Liberal Peace," 19 *Int'l Sec.* 50 (1994).

Waltz, Kenneth N., *Theory of International Politics* (1979).

Weart, Spencer R., *Never at War: Why Democracies Will Not Fight One Another* (1998).

Zakaria, Fareed, *The Future of Freedom: Illiberal Democracy at Home and Abroad* (2003).

Zweifel, Thomas D., & Patricio Navia, "Democracy, Dictatorship, and Infant Mortality," 11:2 *J. Democracy* 99 (2000).

Chapter 3

Development of the International Law of Conflict Management

John Norton Moore

In this chapter:
Introduction
Historical Development
Selected Bibliography

Introduction

For more than two thousand years, mankind has sought to control the scourge of war. Though war has not been eliminated, those efforts have been important in reducing and controlling international violence. And whatever their success, they provide the intellectual heritage in which contemporary mankind must work to avoid thermonuclear war and reduce international violence. Where that heritage is inadequate there is no more pressing need than its successful strengthening.

Efforts to control international violence have produced nine principal intellectual approaches. These approaches are interrelated and might be usefully thought of as separate strands in a rope of increasing numbers of strands and, hopefully, strength. The first strand is *jus ad bellum,* or norms and procedures for assessing permissibility of recourse to force (see Chapter 4). That is, when is it permissible to use force in international relations? Initially, this was developed within a framework of "just war" theory. Since 1945, however, the United Nations Charter's distinction between aggression and defense has been the central focus.

Second, given a use of force, permissible or otherwise, what norms govern the *conduct* of hostilities? Conduct of hostilities, or *jus in bello,* refers to permissible weapons, practices, conduct toward neutral states, protection of noncombatants, and many other issues (see Chapters 6 and 7). Traditionally and most appropriately, this strand is referred to as "the law of war." More recently, it has been conceptualized by some as "human rights for settings of armed conflict," although in reality it serves human rights and other goals including conflict minimization.

Third, antiterrorism measures are efforts to prohibit certain violent practices of terrorist groups and governments. While terrorism has been with us throughout human history, it has been a particular threat during the twentieth century. And as the attacks on 9/11 sadly illustrate, the twenty-first century is not starting well in this respect. Typically, such measures seek to build international consensus on the impermissibility of certain acts, such as attacks on civil aviation, shipping, or diplomats. This strand has principally developed since the founding of the United Nations, and it is increasingly focused on strengthening obligations of governments not to assist terrorists and to take effective measures against terrorist threats, which has become a central concern since the 9/11 attacks with their devastating human and financial costs for, quite literally, the whole world. Many antiterrorist measures are efforts to limit targets and practices in low- and intermediate-level violence not necessarily associated with major ongoing hostilities. These measures draw heavily on the intellectual underpinnings of the laws of war and neutrality. Antiterrorism measures, however, go well beyond the laws of war. They do not simply license attacks on military targets. Thus, fuller exposition of modern antiterrorist law requires separate treatment from the laws of war and neutrality and these are treated separately in Chapters 10 and 33. More recently governments have sought to cut off funds for terrorists as is treated in Chapter 30.

Fourth, conflict management theory has long explored and encouraged procedures for dispute resolution as an alternative to violence. Typically these have included efforts at conciliation, mediation, arbitration or submission to a judicial tribunal. For the first two decades of the twentieth century, this approach was the centerpiece of international efforts at war avoidance. The modern interest in this approach is illustrated, both in its strengths and weaknesses, by the expert-level meetings between East and West as part of the Helsinki process in an effort to develop strengthened dispute settlement mechanisms during the Cold War and the creation of many new international courts, such as the International Tribunal for the Law of the Sea in Hamburg.

Fifth, we may seek to deter violation of certain conflict management norms by establishing their violation as criminal acts or civil wrongs for which there is personal responsibility (see Chapter 8). We frequently and loosely refer to this strand as the "Nuremberg principles" in reference to the war crimes trials of the Axis at Nuremberg following World War II. This strand, however, is broader than international war crimes trials and, at least for certain grave breaches of the law of war, may also be pursued through national tribunals as the "Breaker Morant" case from the Boer War and the Calley case from the Vietnam War illustrate. As theory has increasingly focused on the need to control aggressive regime elites, this strand has developed actively. New courts created in the last decade include the Yugoslav, Rwanda, and Sierra Leone Tribunals established by the United Nations and the new International Criminal Court, set up by multilateral treaty.

Sixth, we may seek institutional modes of controlling conflict through collective actions or collective security (see Chapter 5). An effectively functioning United Nations Security Council would be a paradigm of this approach. Even absent such effectively functioning collective security, however, a League of Nations or United Nations can perform a variety of roles useful for conflict avoidance and management. United Nations peacekeeping, as in the Congo and the Middle East or the United Nations Boundary Demarcation Commission following the Gulf War, illustrate the possibilities. Although both the League of Nations and the United Nations systems sought collective security, no system yet devised has fully achieved it. A challenge for the present generation is to make the existing machinery for collective security work more effectively at this central mission.

Seventh, we may seek arms control and disarmament as a way of reducing the risk of war or its destructiveness should it occur (see Chapter 13). In this respect we may seek to maintain or strengthen a strategic balance, constrain weapons testing, proliferation, area deployment, production or use, or pursue measures to reduce international tensions and lower the risk of accidental war. Arms control emerged as a major focus only after World War I. With the advent of nuclear and other weapons of mass destruction, it has, however, become an important component of conflict management efforts. Indeed, from the 1960s to about 1990, nuclear arms control between the United States and the former Soviet Union was the centerpiece, and perhaps even the preoccupation, of conflict management efforts. Today, arms control focuses more on controlling the spread of weapons of mass destruction and their delivery vehicles, and particularly on the problem of acquisition of such weapons by rogue states and terrorist groups.

Eighth, a major underpinning of some arms control, and yet an intellectual approach that may also be pursued through institutional means, alliance systems, informal relations as in the famous Nixon-Kissinger opening to China, or even unilateral actions or deployments, is the effort to enhance deterrence and to maintain or restore a central strategic or political balance. A continuing tension under the normative structure of the United Nations Charter is the extent to which certain measures to maintain a strategic balance (such as United States actions in the Cuban Missile Crisis of 1962), which may not meet traditional criteria for lawfulness, should be considered lawful, unlawful but nevertheless desirable, or unlawful and therefore undesirable. From the perspective of Tel Aviv, the Osirak raid to prevent a suspected Iraqi effort to acquire nuclear weapons may present a similar dilemma. It is difficult to reconcile the lawfulness of this raid with traditional *jus ad bellum* norms. Yet the entire world greatly benefited during the Gulf War from Iraq not having nuclear weapons to oppose the Security Council coalition.

Finally, we may look to national measures for control of use of national forces and for conflict management. Typically such measures are features of democratic as opposed to totalitarian societies. In the United States they include the neutrality acts of the 1930s passed in a misguided attempt to isolate the United States from the winds of war in Asia and Europe, and the more modern creation of the Arms Control and Disarmament Agency (subsequently phased out), the Peace Corps, and, most recently, the United States Institute of Peace.

This focus on nine principal strands is not to suggest that there are not other approaches. Balance of power theory focuses variously on balance or imbalance as the path to war. Functionalism reflects a belief in war prevention through enhancing trade, cultural, organizational and individual interactions. Some psychological approaches stress the need for greater understanding of the nature of man and his group behavior or for broad education about the folly of war. Negotiation theory seeks ways to defuse crises through better understanding of communication and negotiation techniques. And there are some theological approaches that follow the early Christian tradition of pacifism and the more recent ideas of Mahatma Gandhi, which explore nonviolent resistance as an alternative to forceful defense. Moreover the newer field of "peace studies" has developed a broad range of approaches including "second track" or private diplomacy, non-violent sanctions as opposed to pacifism, systemic theories of war, enhanced focus on negotiations theory, third party efforts at conflict management, war termination studies, and "scenario studies" of pathways into and out of war. Further, as the preceding chapter discusses, the newer approach of "incentive theory" focuses on long term efforts building democracy and the rule of law and negating extreme ideologies and, where aggressive nondemocratic leaders threaten, effective deterrence against such threats. And most broadly "incentive theory" focuses on the totality of incentives of regime elites, from the individual, state, and international systems levels. This approach would also incorporate these nine principal strands into its focus on affecting incentives of those making the decisions for war or peace.

These nine principal approaches are also not of equal importance. Norms concerning permissibility of use of force, the laws of war, the United Nations system as the principal contemporary institutional mode of conflict management, arms control, and deterrence and maintenance of the strategic balance are almost certainly the most important legal mechanisms. Collectively, however, they embody the principal intellectual heritage of over twenty centuries of human effort to control international violence. It is too early to tell whether they will be up to the apocalyptic challenge of war or peace in the modern world.

Questions for Discussion

1. To what extent do these strands reflect assumptions about the causes of war? Is war caused by social or economic injustice, disputes among nations, clashes of national interest, ideological fervor, national differences in social and political systems, arms races, incidents and accidents, competition for resources, nationalism, population pressures, the nation-state system, failure of communication processes, violence rooted in the id and superego of man, aggressive national leaders, miscalculations, national weakness, strategic imbalance, or totalitarian governments? Can you identify other factors? What are the most important causes in the contemporary international system and why? Is your conclusion scientifically supportable from the evidence? In light of the causes you believe most dangerous in the contemporary system, which existing—or new—strands do you believe most useful in preventing or controlling international violence?

2. The United States Institute of Peace—established in 1985—is charged with promoting and encouraging peace research and education. Which of these—or other—strands should be emphasized? How should behavioral knowledge and research about individual and group conflict be assimilated to the problem of war and peace? What disciplines and what lines of research should be mobilized?

3. To what extent do the principal intellectual approaches to national security discussed in previous chapters parallel any of these principal strands in the international law of conflict management? Do international law and international relations share a common intellectual heritage? What is meant by "realists" and "idealists" in international relations? Is there a counterpart in international law? What is the relation between authority and power? What is "law"?

One of the most perplexing problems facing the student of conflict management today is defining the cause(s) of war. In his *Study of War*, one of the most thorough studies of the nature of war, Quincy Wright has suggested that analyzing the cause of war is a difficult and often exasperating task.

II QUINCY WRIGHT, A STUDY OF WAR
728–31 (1942)

To some a cause of war is an event, condition, act, or personality involved only in a particular war; to others it is a general proposition applicable to many wars. To some it is a class of human motives, ideals, or values; to others it is a class of impersonal forces, conditions, processes, patterns, or relations. To some it is the entrance or injection of a disturbing factor into a stable situation; to others it is a lack of essential conditions of stability in the situation itself or the human failure to realize potentialities. These differences of opinion reflect different meanings of the word "cause." The three sentences, respectively, contrast causes of war in the historic and scientific senses, in the practical and scientific senses, and in the historic and practical senses.

In the scientific sense the cause of the changes in any variable is a change in any other variable in a proposition stating the relations of all the factors in a process or equilibrium.... A scientific statement usually asserts that if all factors can be ignored, except those observable, controllable, and presumptively measurable factors which it deals with as variables ... a specified degree of change in any variable tends to be followed immediately or in a specified time by a specified degree of change in the other variables.

In the historic sense a cause is any event or condition figuring in the description of the relevant antecedents of an effect. Such a description is usually called a history and is confined to events within a time or space sufficiently near to the effect to be presumably related to it. Proximity in time or space thus establishes a presumption of causal relation, though this presumption ought to be confirmed by other evidence to avoid the *post hoc* fallacy. Evidence may indicate that proximate events were unrelated, and it may also indicate the transmission of influence from remote times and distant places.

In the practical sense a cause is any controllable element in the statement of the origin, treatment, solution, or meaning of a problem or situation. Such statements in medicine are called diagnoses, prognoses, prophylaxes, or treatments, and in social affairs, reports, interpretations, programs, policies, or plans. Such statements of social problems usually emphasize the human actions responsible for the situation and the human actions deemed to be the most effective for realizing desired ends in the circumstances of the time and place where the statement is made.

It will be observed that in none of these cases is the word "cause" used as something which exists in phenomena but as something which exists in statements or propositions about phenomena. If one is convinced that a proposition is true, he means that he is convinced that the proposition accurately describes the phenomena. Consequently, if the truth of a proposition has been established, then the word "cause" can be considered either a term of the proposition or a phenomena designated by the term. While superficially the scientific, historic, and practical senses of the word "cause" appear to be very different, fundamentally they are merely different approaches to the same concept. A cause of an entity, an event, or a condition is a term of a true proposition capable of explaining, predicting, or controlling its existence or changes.

For Wright "[w]ars arise because of the changing relations of numerous variables — technological, psychic, social, and intellectual. There is no single cause of war. Peace is an equilibrium among many forces. Change in any particular force, trend, movement, or policy may at one time make for war, but under other conditions a similar change may make for peace."[1] Similarly Kenneth E. Boulding speaks of a war-peace cycle determined by systemic factors both leading to strain and strength in avoidance of war. At any particular time the totality of factors contributing to strain and strength determine the status of the system as stable war, unstable war, unstable peace, or stable peace.[2]

Questions for Discussion

1. Could we also conceptualize war as resulting from a mix of "motivational" and "opportunity" factors? Which of the long list of "causes" and approaches to war avoidance are exclusively or primarily "motivational" or "opportunity" factors? Is war more likely

---

1. II QUINCY WRIGHT, A STUDY OF WAR 1284 (1942).
2. See, KENNETH E. BOULDING, STABLE PEACE 31–66 (1978).

to be, by analogy to cancer, a complex multi-caused phenomenon with only incremental cures?

2. Bearing in mind the difficulties in identifying and describing the cause(s) of war, how would you characterize the nature of conflict in the twentieth century? Are there discernible factors, elements, or conditions that tend to consistently cause inter- and intrastate conflict? If so, what are they? Is deterrence, and conversely failure of deterrence, a central factor? Is it central because it is a key "opportunity" variable possibly capable of offsetting many different "motivational" factors? Is democracy a central factor? Why or why not? Is radical ideology which supports change through violence a central factor? Why or why not?

3. Have the newer theories of "the democratic peace" and now "incentive theory" gone far beyond this important initial interdisciplinary effort by Quincy Wright to understand the causes of war? Do we need to understand all historic "causes" in order to prevent war?

Historical Development

The historical development of the international law of conflict management can most usefully be divided into seven periods. The reader should bear in mind that these are divisions for heuristic purposes, that any history of thought does not come neatly divided, and that these divisions are most certainly fuzzy at the edges. These periods are: the "just war" period from approximately 335 B.C. to 1648 A.D., the "war as fact" era from approximately 1648 to 1918, the early League of Nations system from approximately 1919 to 1927, the Kellogg-Briand Pact and late League era from approximately 1928 to 1944, the early United Nations Charter system from approximately 1945 to 1959, the Charter era from approximately 1960 to the end of the Cold War in approximately 1990, and the contemporary Charter era from 1991 to the present. Table 1 illustrates this development with the bold squares reflecting the principal emphasis within each historic period.

The "Just War" Period

In criticizing Sparta for directing "all ... legislative measures ... to conquest and war," Aristotle writes in 335 B.C.:

ARISTOTLE, THE POLITICS
206, 207 (J. E. C. Welldon trans. 1883)

The object of military training should be not to enslave persons who do not deserve slavery, but firstly to secure ourselves against becoming the slaves of others, secondly to seek imperial power not with a view to a universal despotic authority, but for the benefit of the subjects whom we rule, and thirdly to exercise despotic power of those who are deserving to be slaves.

———————

Although still massively violative of human rights, in its day this approach reflected movement in conflict management theory. It was really struggling against the prevailing view of the time that "might makes right." Roman writers refined and developed this early "just war" concept. Thus, Cicero, one of the most celebrated lawyers in human history, writes:

Table 1: History of the International Law of Conflict Management

Approximate Historic Periods	Norms Concerning Permissibility of Recourse to Force: Initiation of Coercion: Jus Ad Bellum *D	Laws of War and Neutrality: Jus in Bello	Anti-Terrorism *D	Institutions for Peaceful Settlement of Disputes	Personal Responsibility for Violation of Major Conflict Norms *D
Just War 335 B.C. – …	Based on "Justice" of the cause: Aristotle, Augustine, and Aquinas	Chivalry and Early Rules	Assassination of Julius Caesar (44 B.C.)	—	—
War as Fact: Treaty of Westphalia 1648–1918	Regulation of force short of war; prohibition of force for collection of debts	Lieber Instructions (1863) Hague Conventions (1899, 1907) & Laws of Neutrality	Assassination of Archduke Franz Ferdinand (1914)	Permanent Court of Arbitration (1899) & Bryan and other Arbitration Treaties	—
World War I					
Early League of Nations 1919–1927	Largely Procedural: Arts. 10, 12, 13, & 15 of League Covenant	1925 Geneva Gas Protocol	—	Permanent Court of International Justice and Arbitration Treaties	Rudimentary Criminal Responsibility: Leipzig Trials after WWI
Kellogg-Briand Pact or "Pact of Paris" & Late League 1928–1944	Kellogg-Briand Pact of 1928: the shift to Aggression-defense	1929 Geneva Convention and continued development	League Convention for the Prevention and Punishment of Terrorists (1937)	Permanent Court of International Justice and Arbitration Treaties	—
World War II					
Early UN Charter & the Cold War 1945–1959	Continued Kellogg-Briand Shift: Charter Art. 2(4): all force incl.	1949 Geneva Conventions	—	International Court of Justice	Nuremberg & Tokyo Trials and ILC Principles
Charter Era The Cold War continues 1960–1990	UN Definition of Aggression Resolution (1973); Problems of Art. 2(4) Threshold; Intervention and Civil/Strife; Regional System Interface	1977 Protocols I & II, 1980 Conventional Weapons Convention & Protocols, 1980 ENMOD Convention	1969 Tokyo Convention & Other Functional & Regional Anti-Terrorism Conventions	International Court of Justice	Nuremberg & Tokyo Trials and ILC Principles
Contemporary Charter Era Post Cold War & 9/11 Attack 1991–present	Art. 2(4) & problems of "low intensity conflict," terrorism, international crime, scope of Security Council authority & gov't collapse	—	Functional & Regional Anti-Terrorism Conventions & Collective Action Against Terrorism	International Court of Justice & new LOS Tribunal & dispute settlement machinery	Yugoslav, Rwanda, & Sierra Leone War Crimes Tribunals & The International Criminal Court (1998)

*D Particularly relevant for the deterrence function of law.

Table 1: History of the International Law of Conflict Management *continued*

Approximate Historic Periods	Institutional Modes of Conflict Management, Including Collective Security *D	Arms Control and Disarmament	Deterrence and the Maintenance of Strategic Balance *D	National Measures for Control of Use of Force and Promotion of Peace
Just War 335 B.C. – …	—	—	201 B.C. Rome-Carthage Treaty 1139 A.D. Lateran Council Declaration	—
War as Fact: Treaty of Westphalia 1648–1918	1815 Congress of Vienna & 1899 and 1907 Hague Conf. System	1817 Rush Bagot Agreement	Concert of Europe System	—
World War I				
Early League of Nations 1919–1927	Rudimentary Collective Security: Art. 16 of League Covenant	Art. 8 of League Cov. and Washington & London Naval Conferences	The Washington (1921–22) and London (1930) Naval Conferences	—
Kellogg-Briand Pact or "Pact of Paris" & Late League 1928–1944	Rudimentary Collective Security: Art. 16 of League Covenant	1932–37 League Conference on Disarmament; America First Movement	Treaty for the Limitation of Naval Armament (1930)	Neutrality Act of 1935 (embargo on implements of war); Neutrality Act (1937); The Ludlow Amend. narrowly loses by a vote of 209–188 (1937)
World War II				
Early UN Charter & the Cold War 1945–1959	–Strengthened Collective Security –Uniting for Peace Resolution (1950)	Proposed Baruch Plan (1946) and Discussions on General Disarmament, Antarctic Treaty (1959)	–The Truman Doctrine (1947) –NSC 68 (1950) –Rio Treaty –NATO –Warsaw Pact –SEATO –CENTO –ANZUS	National Security Act of 1947 and creation of the Defense Department and the CIA
Charter Era The Cold War continues 1960–1990	Collective Security	LTBT (1963), SALT/START TNF/INF MBFR, NPT (1968), Seabed Treaty (1970), etc.	–Strategic Triad –China initiative –INF –SALT –START –Etc.	1961 Arms Control & Disarmament Agency, 1973 War Powers Resolution, 1985 United States Institute of Peace
Contemporary Charter Era Post Cold War & 9/11 Attack 1991–present	Collective Security	CFE, NPT, CWC, CTBT & MTCR & continuation of the START process, etc.	Issues of NATO enlargement, etc.	Intensive theoretical work on "The Democratic Peace" and "Incentive Theory"

*D Particularly relevant for the deterrence function of law.

21 DE OFFICIIS in CICERO IN TWENTY-EIGHT VOLUMES

37, 39 (Walter Miller trans. 1913)

The only excuse, therefore, for going to war is that we may live in peace unharmed....

[A]nd ... no war is just, unless it is entered upon after an official demand for satisfaction has been submitted or warning has been given and a formal declaration made.

16 THE REPUBLIC *in* CICERO IN TWENTY-EIGHT VOLUMES

211 (Clinton Walker Keyes trans. 1928)

[A] war is never undertaken by the ideal State, except in defence of its honour or its safety.

Although early Christian doctrine strongly reflected pacifism, subsequent writers such as St. Augustine in 412 A.D. and St. Thomas Aquinas in 1266–73 had moved to and elaborated a more complex and complete "just war" tradition.

The *Summa Theologica* of Saint Thomas Aquinas, Volume II

in 20 GREAT BOOKS OF THE WESTERN WORLD 578
(Fathers of the English Dominican province trans., revised by Daniel J. Sullivan, 1952)

In order for a war to be just, three things are necessary. First, the authority of the sovereign by whose command the war is to be waged. For it is not the business of a private person to declare war, because he can seek for redress of his rights from the tribunal of his superior. Moreover it is not the business of a private person to summon together the people, which has to be done in wartime. And as the care of the common weal is committed to those who are in authority, it is their business to watch over the common weal of the city, kingdom or province subject to them. And just as it is lawful for them to have recourse to the material sword in defending that common weal against internal disturbances, when they punish evil-doers, according to the words of the Apostle (Rom. 13.4): *He beareth not the sword in vain: for he is God's minister, an avenger to execute wrath upon him that doth evil;* so too, it is their business to have recourse to the sword of war in defending the common weal against external enemies. Hence it is said to those who are in authority (Ps. 81.4): *Rescue the poor: and deliver the needy out of the hand of the sinner;* and for this reason Augustine says (*Contra Faust.* xxii, 75): "The natural order conducive to peace among mortals demands that the power to declare and counsel war should be in the hands of those who hold the supreme authority."

Secondly, a just cause is required, namely that those who are attacked should be attacked because they deserve it on account of some fault. Therefore Augustine says (Q. X, *super Jos.*): "A just war is usually described as one that avenges wrongs, when a nation or state has to be punished, for refusing to make amends for the wrongs inflicted by its subjects, or to restore what it has seized unjustly."

Thirdly, it is necessary that the belligerents should have a right intention, so that they intend the advancement of good, or the avoidance of evil. Hence Augustine says (*De Verb. Dom.*): "True religion does not look upon as sinful those wars that are waged not for motives of aggrandizement, or cruelty, but with the object of securing peace, of punishing evil-doers, and of uplifting the good." For it may happen that the war is declared by the legitimate authority, and for a just cause, and yet be rendered unlawful through a wicked intention. Hence Augustine says (*Contra Faust.* xxii): "The passion for inflicting harm, the cruel thirst for vengeance, an unpacific and relentless spirit, the fever or revolt, the lust of power, and such things, all these are rightly condemned in war."

Subsequent "just war" theorists developed a more elaborate structure including not only norms for assessing the *initiation* of force but also (as had been present to some extent in early writers) beginning efforts at controlling the *conduct* of hostilities.

David Little, *The 'Just War' Tradition*

in The Hundred Percent Challenge: Building a National
Institute of Peace 7, 22–26 (Charles D. Smith ed., 1985)

In regard to *legitimate authority*, there is a new and stronger emphasis, [as we would expect] upon the responsibility of secular rulers in matters of war and peace[,] ... [and] a substantial reduction of the temporal role of the church. Catholics like Suarez and Vitoria still ascribed some authority to the Pope in resolving international disputes and in recommending the use of force where the church was threatened. Even Grotius, the Protestant, recommended the use of an ecumenical confederation of church leaders to arbitrate interstate disputes. But in all these proposals, the role of church authority was vestigial in comparison with the medieval perspective....

....

As to the question of *just cause*, there is, as expected, a strong emphasis upon "natural" or "moral" offenses as a warrant for using force, and again only a vestigial reference to religious causes. The writers reiterate the standard temporal just-war causes—self-defense, recovery of assets, and punishment of wrongdoing—but they also make something of the distinction between self-defense as a "defensive" war, and punishment as an "offensive" one (with recovery of assets somewhere in between). Defensive wars are direct responses to an imminent or existing unjust armed attack or seizure of property[, although] the notion also was broadened to include operations intended to "defend" foreign citizens against unjust rulers—what we might call "humanitarian intervention"—and defense of allies.

There is no unanimity among the writers concerning the question of certifying or verifying the existence of a just cause. Indeed, for obvious reasons, this was to become one of the most vexing problems for just-war theory, since belligerents are called upon, in effect, to try their own cases. Opinions [on the matter] varied sharply. Gentili's view was that, so long as both sides "aim at justice," they may legitimately fight, despite any doubts. Grotius took a harder line. If there is any doubt at all about the causes of war, then force must be foresworn. This difference produced the equally controversial doctrine of *simultaneous justice*, according to which [some writers held that] both sides in a war might ... be [equivalently] justified. While Grotius, for one, rejected the idea that from a moral point of view both sides could be equally right, he readily conceded that one or both of the belligerents might understandably, if mistakenly, *believe* themselves to be in the right. It was his sensitivity to "invincibly" biased interpretations concerning the authorizing reasons for war that led Grotius and others to counsel self-restraint and a modest and tolerant attitude in pleading the case for war. The pathology of force was always at hand.

The special, additional considerations, as loosely and somewhat informally discussed in the Middle Ages, were taken by the early-modern theorists and classified, clarified, and, in some cases, modified. The requirement of having a *peaceful intention*, so important to Augustine and Thomas, is reduced somewhat in significance, no doubt because of the preference of these writers for evaluating deeds rather than motives.

Next, all of them singled out and emphasized that force be used only as a *last resort*, which means that all other reasonable means for solving a conflict peacefully must [have been] exhausted. They also laid down the rule that any resort to force must conform to *general proportionality*. The cause, even if just, must be "grave" or "weighty" enough to warrant risking life and national treasure. In addition, the costs of using force must be proportional to the foreseeable consequences, again however just the cause. A related test requires that there be a *reasonable hope of success*. This is, of course, a counsel of prudence: It is generally irrational to undertake a costly and risky venture faced with a high probability of failure. Finally, some attention is given to requiring a *formal declaration of war*, including a statement of charges, presumably to assure full accountability.

These seven considerations—legitimate authority, just cause, peaceful intention, last resort, general proportionality, reasonable hope of success, and formal declaration—comprise a set of criteria that came to be grouped under the title, *jus ad bellum*, meaning those conditions which must be met before a decision to go to war is considered justified. Three additional conditions, present in the tradition but also somewhat revised and systematized by the early-modern theorists, make up a second category, called *jus in bello*, meaning the conditions for the permissible conduct of war.

The first of these additional criteria is the principle of *discrimination* or *noncombatant immunity*. The writers, [in] distinct[ion] from Thomas, permit the unintentional killing of innocent civilians and thereby introduce the so-called *principle of double-effect*. It works as follows: If there are two effects of an action, one good and one bad, such as attacking a military installation, but in the act unavoidably killing several innocent civilians lodged therein, then the action is permissible so long as the destruction of the installation is the only effect intended and directly and deliberately sought. The killing of civilians in that case is regarded as an unintended and indirect or "collateral" side-effect. The principle of double-effect would rule out such terroristic acts as taking hostages or directly threatening the lives of innocent civilians in order to extort compliance from the enemy.

Incidentally, all the thinkers wrestled with the problem of defining "innocent civilians." They include such groups as young children, old people, "all unable to bear arms," clerics, monastics, farmers, and so on. Moreover, [they worried] in various ways over "indiscriminate" weapons, and they offered strictures against the use of such weapons ... [whose] effects were hard to control, [such as the use of wild animals, poison, and so on].

There is some indication that, although the condition of discrimination was regarded as very important, it was not absolute for these writers, as it has become in some later just-war positions. They h[e]ld that under certain dire circumstances "military necessity" might permissibly override the prohibition against directly threatening or killing civilians. In that case, what we may call the condition of *military proportionality*—the [relation of] efficiency ... between weapons or tactics and specific military objectives—would take precedence. Such permission, incidentally, constitutes a direct violation of the principle of double-effect, though the authors do not appear to worry much about that.... [T]he writers expend considerable effort elaborating [the condition of proportionality, mentioning], as Grotius did, both qualitative and quantitative measures that ought to be applied to a prudent calculation of the costs and benefits of military actions. Nevertheless, they did not carry very far the attempt to apply this condition in practice.

The last condition concerns the *treatment of prisoners*. While the thinkers favor some measure of restraint in dealing with prisoners, their opinions vary over the degree. Grotius recommends that only those prisoners guilty of grave offenses or serious excesses in the line of duty ought to be punished. Beyond the matter of ascribing guilt and punishment, there does not appear to be much discussion of prison conditions, post-war treatment, and the host of conditions that have in more recent years been developed. Still, the beginnings of a concern to protect prisoners ... [can be] found in the writings of these theorists.

The "just war" approach was essentially a religio-philosophical doctrine that war was justified if the cause was just, subject to a variety of additional qualifications, as discussed by Professor Little. Particularly as associated with St. Augustine, St. Thomas Aquinas, and other Catholic thinkers, the focus was on the objectives motivating the use of force. If the objective was to right a wrong or punish a wrongdoer, then the war was just, again subject to other qualifications, such as proportionality. In this tradition an aggressive war can be a just war as can a defensive war. That is, it is not necessary for a just war that the other side resort to coercion first. Moreover, presumably under this tradition, if an aggressive war is just, then even defense against it would be unjust. Clearly, then, the tradition of "just war" is in a central respect fundamentally different from the aggression-defense requirements of contemporary international law and the United Nations Charter.

One strength of the "just war" approach is that it does not divorce order from justice. If force is lawfully used, it must be in the service of a just cause. In addition, it is an on-the-merits attempt at distinguishing permissible from impermissible coercion and a beginning analysis of rules for the conduct of hostilities.

Within the context of a powerful and fairly monolithic church in the Western world, which was influential in deciding the justice of a cause, the just war doctrine was not as unremarkable as it might appear today. In fact, apparently there is at least one recorded instance where Spanish authorities, before beginning a war, consulted the clergy on the question of its justice. The doctrine, then, had some foundation in actual state practice. Moreover, the sanction was said to be a real one in the hereafter, and strong religious beliefs made this a meaningful threat.

With the rise of the nation state and the coming of the Reformation, however, the power of a once-monolithic church began to wane. As it did so, the real disadvantages of the approach became even more evident. First, there were no objective criteria for distinguishing a just from an unjust war, and there was no central decision-maker to make the determination. As a result, nations were free to interpret the justness of their own cause and did so with predictable results. In fact, theorists were increasingly concerned about the problem of a war that is just on both sides. One Spanish theorist, Francisco de Vitoria, ingeniously solved this by the doctrine of "invincible ignorance," reminiscent of some of our current legal fictions. He maintained that although there could only be one objectively just side, invincible ignorance may lead one to believe that his side is just and thus excuse his conduct. Second, and most important, the just war theory failed to focus on the destructiveness of force as a strategy of change. The focus was on the justice of the cause, not on the inefficiency of coerced solutions or the injustice of widespread devastation. Third, there was little recognition of the need for procedural or institutional techniques for avoiding or controlling war, although toward the end of this period Samuel Pufendorf did exhort princes to try a conference, arbitration, or even the lot before resorting to arms.

These inherent difficulties with the rule, compounded by the Reformation and the breakup of the monolithic church drained much of its intellectual vigor and power to influence conduct. It is probably more accurate to say, however, that it was pushed aside by a more vigorous set of ideas than that it was totally abandoned. In fact, the just war tradition has continued to be the predominant approach of Catholic and Protestant theologians to problems of conflict management, although some follow the early Christian tradition of pacifism.

The Period of "War as Fact"

During the seventeenth and eighteenth centuries, the rise of the nation state and theories of absolute sovereignty began to push aside the just war notion. The *realpolitik* of Clausewitz and Machiavelli and notions of sovereignty transformed war from an instrument conceived for justice to an instrument of national policy. Simultaneously, theorists began to differentiate between moral or natural law principles and positive international law reflecting state behavior.

KARL VON CLAUSEWITZ, ON WAR
402, 410 (A. Rapoport ed., 1832)

War is only a part of political intercourse.... War is nothing but a continuation of political intercourse, with a mixture of other means.... Accordingly, [w]ar can never be separated from political intercourse....

Therefore, once more: [w]ar is an instrument of policy; it must necessarily bear its character, it must measure with its scale: the conduct of [w]ar, in its great features, is therefore policy itself, which takes up the sword in place of the pen....

―――――――

Writing in *The Law of Nations* in 1758, Vattel emphasized the distinction between natural law judgments, which distinguish just wars, and positive international law, which accounts wars just on both sides since nations are equal and independent and cannot claim a right of judgment over each other.

The central tenet of the "war as fact" period is that since each state is sovereign, international law cannot regulate the resort to war. War is a "metajuristic phenomenon," an event outside the range and control of law. The existence of war is simply a question of fact giving rise to neutral rights and duties and the law of warfare to mitigate the destructiveness of the conflict, and with which international law can properly be concerned.

This period represents a "cop-out" in making the necessary judgments between permissible and impermissible coercion. Things had moved from bad to worse. It was not all bad, however, as this period witnessed a focus of concern on the rules for conducting warfare, on the regulation of force short of war, such as reprisals, and, in the 1818–22 Concert of Europe system and Hague Conferences of 1899 and 1907, the beginning of an international conference system concerned with issues of war and peace. For the first time it began to be recognized that nation states must act in concert to promote their common interest in world order. The Hague Conferences, in fact, foreshadowed the League of Nations, as the participants promoted rules concerning the law of war, established such dispute settlement machinery as the Permanent Court of Arbitration, and, on the substantive side, even prohibited the use of force for the collection of international debts.

INIS L. CLAUDE, SWORDS INTO PLOWSHARES: THE PROBLEMS AND PROGRESS OF INTERNATIONAL ORGANIZATION

28–34 (1971)

A new sort of international conclave was instituted at the Hague in 1899 and 1907. The conscious construction of a distinctive "Hague System" of international relations was interrupted all too soon by the outbreak of World War I, but the beginning that had been made was significant enough to figure as one of the major contributions of the nineteenth century to present-day world organization.

The two "International Peace Conferences" held at the Hague, under the initial impetus provided by Czar Nicholas II of Russia, were notable as major diplomatic gatherings convoked in time of peace to deal with a variety of subjects involved in the business of international relations. Although the original motivations behind the Hague Conferences were questionable (it has been alleged that the Czar was actuated less by sincere desire to promote peace than by worry about Russia's financial disadvantage in the armaments competition), and their immediate results were not universally regarded as promising (the London *Times* held that the conference of 1907 "was a sham, and has brought forth a progeny of shams, because it was founded on a sham"), it is clear that the Hague meetings were envisaged as steps toward a more adequate organization of the state system; and it is from that point of view that they will be discussed here.

A leading feature of the Hague System was its approach toward universality. Whereas the first conference was attended by only twenty-six states and was preponderantly European in composition, the second involved representatives of forty-four states, including the bulk of the Latin American republics. Thus, the world achieved in 1907 its first General Assembly; as the president of that conference put it, "This is the first time that the representatives of all constituted States have been gathered together to discuss interests which they have in common and which contemplate the good of all mankind." This was a significant step toward broadening the focus of international diplomacy, toward escaping the increasingly unrealistic European-fixation, and toward defining more accurately the boundaries of the community of nations with whose problems statesmen had to deal.

Universality had another implication than inclusion of non-European states; it meant the acceptance at major diplomatic assemblies of the small states on equal terms with the great powers. If the Concert of Europe had been a Board of Directors of the European corporation, the Hague System, particularly in 1907 was a Stockholders Meeting of a much more extensive corporation. At the Hague the small states got a strong taste of independence and equality. The results were not uniformly good; there were some accusations that this first draught produced intoxication, evidenced by undue self-assertion and unseemly self-importance on the part of small power representatives, and angry mutterings were heard that the small states were incapable of holding the liquor of equal diplomatic status. Nevertheless, it was a foretaste of things to come. International organization got its first taste of the difficulties of solving the conflict between great and small states as to their relative status and function in the business of managing international affairs. The era of the Concert had been the period, *par excellence*, of great power hegemony; the Hague Conferences ushered in the heyday of the small states.

These conferences marked a new peak in the development of collective activity for the purpose of general, permanent reform of the system of international relations, as distinguished from the purpose of dealing with specific, temporary situations. More conspicuously than the Concert of Europe, the Hague System was divorced from the immediate problems raised by particular wars or disputes and was concerned with international problems in the abstract. In an important sense this statement justifies the contention that the conferences were a sham. The powers consented to meet largely because the original Russian initiative could not be spurned without diplomatic embarrassment and pacifistic public opinion could not be ignored without domestic embarrassment. Their willingness to consider general principles was but the reverse side of their unwillingness to submit specific issues, which were the real components of the contemporary problem of peace, to the judgment of a conference. In political terms the conference involved a considerable degree of multilateral insincerity and met in an atmosphere heavy with unreality. Nevertheless, the statesmen of the Hague, for whatever reasons, contributed to the establishment of the precedent that collective diplomacy should be oriented toward such matters as the codification and further development of important branches of international law, the formulation of standing procedures for the peaceful settlement of disputes, and the promotion of the principle that pacific solutions should be sought by disputants and might properly be urged and facilitated by disinterested states.

The Hague concepts were not revolutionary; they pointed toward encouragement of avoidance of war and mitigation of the evils and barbarities of warfare rather than recision of the legal right of states to make war, and toward the evolution of tolerable conditions of international life within the multistate system rather than drastic transformation of the system itself. But the business of the Hague was clearly the reform of the rules and methods of the system, rather than the solution of the problems arising out of particular cases of conflict within the system.

This aspect of the Hague conference was emphasized by the attention which was given to the task of institution building. For our purposes the primary historical importance of the meetings of 1899 and 1907 lies in the fact that a major concern of the participants was to create devices and agencies which would be permanently at the disposal of states.

The urge toward institutionalization was expressed first in regard to the Hague Conferences themselves. At the 1907 assembly the view clearly predominated that there should be not simply Hague Conferences, but a Hague System. The concept of regular, periodic international conferences, which had received acceptance only from 1815 to 1822 as a basic plank in the platform of the Concert of Europe, was reintroduced. The interval between the two Hague Conferences had been eight years, and the American representatives in 1907 favored the establishment of machinery by which future conferences would be regularly convened without the necessity of initiatory action by any state. This proposal was not fully accepted, but the second conference did recommend "the assembly of a Third Peace Conference, which might be held within a period corresponding to that which has elapsed since the preceding Conference, at a date to be fixed by common agreement between the Powers...." This action led Joseph H. Choate, a member of the American delegation, to comment:

> *Friends of peace, friends of arbitration, may now depend upon it that every seven or eight years there will be a similar conference, and that where the last conference left the work unfinished the new conference will take it up, and so progress from time to time be steadily made....*

The hope for a reunion at The Hague in 1915 was dashed by the outbreak of a general war, but the revitalization of the idea of a regular assembly of the nations was to prove a more significant event than the gentlemen of 1907 could have imagined.

In other important respects the Hague Conferences tended toward systematization. Their very size conduced to the adoption of innovations in conference technique.

Experimental use was made of the apparatus of chairmen, committees, and roll calls, even though "It seemed extraordinary to those not accustomed to it to see Governments, as ordinary individuals, responding to a roll-call." Although the rule of unanimity formally prevailed, this traditional practice, resting upon the fundamental respect for sovereignty which characterized international law, was mitigated to the extent that *voeux*, or recommendations of the conference, were passed by a mere majority vote. Most significantly of all, the 1907 assembly anticipated the future by proposing that a preparatory committee should be established to collect and study suggested items of business and prepare an agenda for the next meeting and to put forward a system of organization and procedure for adoption by the Third Hague Conference. The statesmen gathered at the Hague, looking forward to the completion of a permanent home for their meetings, which had been promised by Andrew Carnegie, clearly believed that they were favored to be the founding fathers of a permanently functioning, efficiently organized mechanism for the maintenance of world peace.

The Hague efforts at institutional creativity extended also to the erection of agencies which would be available for use by states involved in particular quarrels. In 1899 a Convention for the Pacific Settlement of International Disputes was adopted, containing provisions for the establishment and functioning of ad hoc International Commissions of Inquiry, at the option of the disputing parties, and for the creation of the Permanent Court of Arbitration. The latter body was misnamed, since it in fact consisted of a standing list of persons who might be selected as arbitrators whenever states wished to avail themselves of their services. Nevertheless, it was "permanent" in the sense that it was equipped with a standing professional staff and diplomatic board of control and with a set of rules for the process of arbitration. The establishment of this agency did not satisfy the ambitions of the Hague statesmen; they expended great energy in the effort to create two full-fledged judicial institutions, a Court of Arbitral Justice and an International Prize Court. These projects did not reach fruition, but the Hague Conferences nevertheless represented the climax of a century of development in which attention shifted more and more to the possibilities of international institutions as instruments of world peace.

The Hague Conferences were notable events in the history of international organization not so much because of their actual accomplishments as because of the conceptions to which they gave expression, the hopes which they dramatized, the proposals which they largely failed to put into effect, and the problems which they failed to solve but succeeded in exposing.

The abortive system of the Hague called attention to the emerging reality of a global, rather than a merely European, state system; the demands of small states for participation in the management of that system; and the need for institutionalized procedures, as well as improvised settlements, in the conduct of international relations.

The Hague approach to the problem of peace was distinctly rationalistic and legalistic. The focus on the peaceful settlement of disputes was a clear indication of the underlying assumption that war was a product of misunderstandings and emotional flurries that could be eliminated by elucidation of the facts in dispute, clarification of the applicable law, and invocation of the calmness and self-possession of reasonable men. This reliance upon rational prudence and the judicial temper may have been excessive. Postponing evaluation, let it be said here that it was, for better or for worse, a leading characteristic of the Hague approach, which was transmitted to subsequent conferences on international organization and is today a significant element in the operative theory of international organization. The Hague ideal of rationally self-restrained states submitting to a kind of Olympian judgment has not been realized but neither has it been abandoned.

The conferences of 1899 and 1907.... were devoted to building a peaceful system and preventing or controlling war in general, rather than to maintaining peace in a particular crisis or liquidating a specific war. Such an emphasis, in some degree, must characterize any system of international organization. It marks the inherent differences between systems and organizations, on the one hand, and expedients and improvisation, on the other. Nevertheless, it points to one of the standing difficulties and problems of balance in international organization.

Almost everyone is for peace in the abstract and is likely to be for war in certain specific situations; thus, international organization is likely to attract a volume of enthusiastic verbal support from public opinion when it works against *war* which may prove to be meaningless and ephemeral when it throws its influence against *wars*. On the other hand, experience shows that statesmen are unlikely to develop deep interest in the process of international organization, conceived as an approach to problems of peace in the abstract. The leaders of governments are almost by definition men who are preoccupied with the crises of the moment and the interests of their particular states; when there is a conflict between their concern for finding solutions to the problems immediately affecting their states and their commitment to improving the general workings and altering the basic characteristics of the international system, their emphasis tends to center upon the former. This problem cannot be solved simply by avowing that statesmen are selfish and short-sighted and should become world-minded and far-seeing. Some change in that direction is essential, but it is equally necessary for international organization to achieve a proper balance between the projects of building a world system and of solving current international difficulties, between transforming international relations in the long run and saving international peace in the short run. This persistent problem of international organization was foreshadowed at the Hague Conferences.

The Hague System rendered valuable service in calling attention to the fact that there are difficult problems of international organization itself — instrumental problems — which must be solved in some degree before the problems of international relations — substantive problems — can usefully be tackled by international organization. Its most significant contribution to the future of international organization lay perhaps in its identification of some of the most basic of these instrumental problems. Champions of a better world order might well reflect on the lesson of the Hague — that the most valuable support may not be enthusiastic advocacy which minimizes difficulties, but sober analysis which contributes to fuller understanding of the problems that lie ahead.

During the later years of the "war as fact" period, there was intense interest in machinery for peaceful resolution of disputes among nations as a principal intellectual underpinning of war avoidance. The First Hague Conference in 1899 established the Permanent Court of Arbitration, and it "has been estimated that between 1900 and 1914 more than 120 general arbitration treaties were concluded between pairs of States."[3] In the United States, Secretary of State William Jennings Bryan negotiated a large number of "cooling-off" treaties, beginning in August 1913, as a centerpiece of American efforts at war avoidance and strengthening international law. Even earlier, Elihu Root, an American Secretary of War and then of State, and a founder of the American Society of International Law, had actively promoted arbitration among nations for which he was awarded the Nobel Peace Prize.

---

3. Shabtai Rosenne, The World Court: What It Is and How It Works 17 (1973).

James Brown Scott, *Introduction*

to Treaties for the Advancement of Peace Between the United States and
Other Powers Negotiated by the Honorable William J. Bryan,
Secretary of State of the United States, at xxxiii–xxxv (1920)

Shortly after Mr. Wilson's inauguration, Secretary Bryan submitted to the President a written outline of the plan, and the President, after conferring with the Cabinet on the subject, authorized its presentation to the diplomatic agents of foreign nations represented at Washington, and Mr. Bryan, to remove possible misunderstanding with the other branch of the treaty making power, wisely took the precaution to confer with the Senate Committee on Foreign Relations before presenting it to the diplomats. On the 24th of April, 1913, the Ambassadors and Ministers residing at the national Capital met by invitation in the reception room of the State Department, and Mr. Bryan presented to each diplomat present a written outline of the plan, after accompanying it with explanations. The plan, as thus presented provides:

First, for the investigation of *all* disputes.

Secondly, for a permanent international commission. All of the treaties authorize the commission to act upon the request of either party and in a number of treaties the commission is empowered to act upon its own initiative, a provision which Mr. Bryan says he tried to incorporate in all of the treaties, but was unable to do so in every case. The reason for this desire and effort on his part Mr. Bryan illustrated by the following "Story" which he recounted to the diplomats, to their amusement no doubt and perhaps to their edification: "A man was complaining to a friend that he found it impossible to drink moderately, because of the numerous invitations which he received from others. The friend, to whom the complaint was made, suggested to him that the difficulty might be remedied by calling for 'sarsaparilla' whenever he found that he had all the whiskey he wanted." "But," said the complainant, "that is the trouble; when I get all the whiskey I want I can not say sarsaparilla." Upon this anecdote, given in his own words, Mr. Bryan thus comments. "The application is easily made. At the time when investigation is most needed the parties to the dispute may be restrained from asking for investigation by the fear that such a request might be construed as cowardice. It is difficult for a nation to say "investigate" when it is angry. At such a time, therefore, the commission should be authorized to tender its services, and thus relieve both parties of embarrassment."

Thirdly, for the sake of impartiality, that the commission be made up of *one subject or citizen from each nation to be chosen by that nation*, and one subject or citizen to be chosen by each nation from a foreign nation, and a fifth to be selected by agreement of the two contracting nations.

Fourthly, for a year's time for investigation and report, during which the parties are not to declare war, or resort to hostilities.

Fifthly, for the reservation by each of the nations of the right to decide for itself, at the conclusion of investigation, what action it will take.

The resemblance between this plan and the plan intended for labor troubles is, as Mr. Bryan says, very apparent. The two most important features are identical; the investigation of all disputes and the reservation of the right to act independently—the second, in Mr. Bryan's opinion, being necessary to the acceptance of the first.

The great trouble with treaties of arbitration has been and is that they leave exceptions—questions of honor, questions of independence, vital interest, and interests of the third parties. It is, however, impossible, as Mr. Bryan himself admits, to eliminate these exceptions, in the present state of public opinion, and his plan is intended to close the gap, as it were, and to leave undiscussed no dispute which may indeed become the cause of war but which should not result in war during the year allowed for investigation and report.

It is also obvious that the plan resembles that proposed for labor disputes, inasmuch as the commission is permanent and each party is allowed to select from among its citizens a member of the commission.

After sufficient time had elapsed for the diplomatic representatives to communicate with their respective countries, Mr. Bryan took up with each country the negotiation of a separate treaty along the line proposed. No attempt was made to enforce the use of any particular phraseology. On the contrary, the nations were assured that the United States stood ready to consider any changes in detail that might be suggested, as Mr. Bryan's desire was to embody in conventional form the provisions necessary to secure the submission of *all* disputes to investigation before resort to force.

The first treaty was signed with Salvador on the 7th of August, 1913, and thereafter treaties with Guatemala, Panama, Honduras, and Nicaragua in the order named....

The Netherlands was appropriately the first of the European nations to sign one of these treaties with the United States.

Only one nation, Mr. Bryan says, objected to any vital principle, and that nation finally yielded its objection to the all-inclusive character of the treaty.

On July 24, 1914, Brazil, Argentina and Chile signed simultaneously. On September 15, 1914, France, Great Britain, Spain, and China likewise signed simultaneously, thus in one day bringing, as Mr. Bryan is accustomed to say, something like nine hundred millions of people under the influence of these treaties which their negotiator believes will tend to make war a remote possibility between the contracting parties. These four treaties, Mr. Bryan adds, had been practically agreed upon for some time, but the contracting nations waited on one another, wishing to sign at the same time. The delay in this instance was apparently due to the desire and the present policy of Great Britain to submit drafts of proposed agreements to its self-governing dominions, in whose favor the treaty contained a clause permitting the withdrawal of the Imperial and the substitution of a Colonial Commissioner chosen by the colony affected.

The treaty with Russia was signed on October 1, 1914. Austria-Hungary, Belgium and Germany endorsed the plan, Mr. Bryan assures us, but they did not enter into treaties embodying it, although, to quote Mr. Bryan's exact language on this point, "the same earnest effort was put forth to negotiate treaties with them which was employed in securing treaties with the other nations, and the plan was offered to all nations alike without regard to population, extent of territory, or relative influence."

    ....

To summarize, although the "war as fact" period de-emphasized judgments concerning the initiation of major coercion, it began to develop a framework for appraisal of minor coercion, greatly accelerated development of the laws of war, introduced international machinery for peaceful settlement of disputes, began a tradition of international cooperation on issues of war and peace, and even introduced in the Concert of Europe system a concern with maintenance of the balance of power. Toward the end of the period—and on the eve of World War I—its central intellectual focus was on mechanisms and procedures for peaceful settlement of disputes.

The League of Nations

The nineteenth and early twentieth century experience with international organization combined with the worldwide revulsion at the terrible destructiveness of World War I to end the period of unlimited national discretion to resort to war. The League of Nations was founded in 1920 as an integral part of the Treaty of Versailles which concluded World War I. The Covenant of the League was essentially a response to what was believed by many to be a war by accident (this contemporary judgement about the origins of World War I is today being increasingly questioned). If, in the era of nation states, war could arise by accident without anyone really wanting war, the answer seemed to be to subject nation states to delay and procedures for peaceful settlement before permitting resort to war. Under the Covenant, then, the lawfulness of resort to war was primarily defined in procedural terms. The lawfulness of war did not depend solely on the justness of one's cause but rather on compliance with procedural standards.

Covenant of the League of Nations
Article 12

1. The members of the League agree that, if there should arise between them any dispute likely to lead to a rupture they will submit the matter either to arbitration *or judicial settlement* or to inquiry by the Council, and they agree in no case to resort to war until three months after the award by the arbitrators *or the judicial decision,* or the report of the Council.

2. In any case under this Article the award of the arbitrators *or the judicial decision* shall be made within a reasonable time, and the report of the Council shall be made within six months after the submission of the dispute.

Article 13

. . . .

4. The Members of the League agree that they will carry out in full good faith any award *or decision* that may be rendered, and that they will not resort to war against a Member of the League which complies therewith. In the event of any failure to carry out such an award *or decision,* the Council shall propose what steps should be taken to give effect thereto.

. . . .

Article 15

1. If there should arise between Members of the League any dispute likely to lead to a rupture, which is not submitted to arbitration *or judicial settlement* in accordance with Article 13, the Members of the League agree that they will submit the matter to the Council.

. . . .

6. If a report by the Council is unanimously agreed to by the members thereof other than the Representatives of one or more of the parties to the dispute, the Members of the

League agree that they will not go to war with any party to the dispute which complies with the recommendations of the report. [Emphasis added.]

The famous "gap" in the Covenant is that, although the Covenant clearly prohibited resort to war, it did so only if such action was taken prior to or without submission of the dispute to the League's procedures and principles. It is true that under Articles 12, 13, and 15, the Covenant required that states submit their disputes to arbitration, judicial settlement, or to the Council. Yet, it is unclear whether or not the Covenant inferred a legal recourse to war if a state party to the dispute failed to carry out the award. If, for example, Great Britain and Argentina had submitted their dispute over the Falklands/Malvinas Islands to arbitration for settlement under the Covenant, with the arbitral award going to Argentina, and Great Britain refused to carry out such an award, would Argentina, after the three-month waiting period, then be permitted to take the award by force?

In addition to reinstituting the distinction between lawful and unlawful war, although now defined in procedural terms, the League Covenant also instituted a rudimentary plan of collective security. Under Article 16, states which resorted to coercion in violation of their Covenant obligations would be subjected to economic and diplomatic sanctions by all of the League members and possibly to military sanctions if the Council recommended them.

The League Covenant also embodied a widespread belief that competition in arms, and particularly private arms manufacture, had contributed to the outbreak of World War I. Accordingly, Article 8 provided:

1. The Members of the League recognise that the maintenance of peace requires the reduction of national armaments to the lowest point consistent with national safety and the enforcement by common action of international obligations.

2. The Council, taking account of the geographical situation and circumstances of each State, shall formulate plans for such reduction for the consideration and action of the several Governments.

3. Such plans shall be subject to reconsideration and revision at least every ten years.

4. After these plans shall have been adopted by the several Governments, the limits of armaments therein fixed shall not be exceeded without the concurrence of the Council.

5. The members of the League agree that the manufacture by private enterprise of munitions and implements of war is open to grave objections. The Council shall advise how the evil effects attendant upon such manufacture can be prevented, due regard being had to the necessities of those Members of the League which are not able to manufacture the munitions and implements of war necessary for their safety.

6. The Members of the League undertake to interchange full and frank information as to the scale of their armaments, their military, naval and air programmes and the condition of such of their industries as are adaptable to war-like purposes.

And building on the Permanent Court of Arbitration from the Hague conferences, Article 14 of the League Covenant lays the groundwork for the first true permanent court, that of the Permanent Court of International Justice.

Article 14

The Council shall formulate and submit to the Members of the League for adoption plans for the establishment of a Permanent Court of International Justice. The Court shall be competent to hear and determine any dispute of an international character which the parties thereto submit to it. The Court may also give an advisory opinion upon any dispute or question referred to it by the Council or by the Assembly.

The major weakness of the League probably lay in the skeptical attitude of nation states toward it, their focus on balance of power as a core mechanism for security, and their continuing determination to pursue independently their own national interests as they perceived them. The failure of the United States to join despite President Wilson's leading role in creating the League was perhaps symptomatic of a deeper malaise. When William Allen White was asked to write an article for *Harper's Magazine* to be entitled "What Does Kansas Think of the League of Nations," he was reported to have replied: "Kansas does not think of the League of Nations."

Moreover, in keeping with the earlier emphasis on sovereign discretion, decisions of the Council had to be unanimous, and in practice this greatly weakened any possibility of meaningful collective security. And finally, the emphasis on procedural and institutional checks on resort to war was not clearly balanced by substantive judgment about what kinds of coercion were permissible and impermissible apart from procedural compliance. This was a matter of emphasis, as Article 10 of the Covenant did require members to respect the "territorial integrity and existing political independence" of other members. Moreover, the Fifth Assembly of the League sought to close a "gap" in the Covenant by negotiating a new protocol which would require submission of all disputes to the court, and that would declare as the aggressor any state that refused to submit a dispute to arbitration or refused to carry out an arbitral award. Ultimately, the Eighth Assembly of the League unanimously approved a resolution declaring: "All wars of aggression are, and always shall be, prohibited," but its legal effect was unclear.

Whatever the cause, the League proved incapable of stopping the deliberate aggression of Japan in China, Italy in Ethiopia, and Germany in Europe. The principal disarmament conference of the League, held in 1932, likewise proved incapable of controlling an escalating arms build-up driven by Axis determination.

The period of the League did, however, introduce important new controls on first use of lethal chemical weapons as embodied in the 1925 Geneva Protocol. This period also made further progress in regard to the laws of war—particularly the 1929 Convention on the Treatment of Prisoners of War, and it introduced, with the abortive Leipzig trials pursuant to Article 228 of the Versailles Treaty, the concept of individual criminal responsibility for violation of certain conflict management norms, and developed at the 1921-22 Washington and 1930 London Naval Conferences a model for arms control negotiations based on maintenance of the strategic balance through numerical limits on major weapons systems—in this case battleships and certain other naval ships.

The withdrawal of Japan in 1935 from the Washington-London agreements, however, reflected the same international reality that had doomed the League. It is a sad commentary on the American experience during this period that despite Wilson's lead in establishing the League and seeking to promote international relations based on law, American public opinion was strongly isolationist. As a result, America—along with the other democracies—lost an opportunity for deterrence that might have prevented World War II. Indeed, Churchill referred to World War II as "the unnecessary war." It should be recalled that

Roosevelt's famous speech in 1937, in which he called for a "quarantine" of aggressor nations, elicited a negative reaction from the American public. The winds of war were spreading flames in Asia and Europe, but American public opinion sought refuge behind the oceans.

The Kellogg-Briand Pact and the Late League Era

The lack of a normative, substantive emphasis of the League was remedied in 1928 by the controversial Treaty for the Renunciation of War. This treaty, popularly known as the Kellogg-Briand Pact, or "Pact of Paris," prohibited war for the solution of international controversies; that is, it prohibited war as an instrument of national policy. It was clear from the conference discussion that defensive use of force was excluded from this ban.

As a conflict management tool, the Pact of Paris was roundly criticized for unrealistically creating expectations that war would be controlled. But in the history of thought about permissible coercion, it was momentous. This pact filled what had become widely known as a "gap in the Covenant" (see above) that arguably permitted war. But the Kellogg-Briand Pact did far more than fill this famous "gap." It reflected a fundamental shift in the history of the international law of conflict management that may have been the single most important intellectual leap in that history. The focus was no longer whether war was "just" or whether certain procedural requirements designed to prevent accidental war had been met. Rather, the focus was squarely on whether a use of force was aggressive and thus illegal or defensive and thus lawful. A state could no longer use coercion as an instrument of national policy but rather principally only to protect against an illegal use of force.

Treaty of Paris (Kellogg-Briand Pact)

August 27, 1928

The President of the German Reich, The President of the United States of America, His Majesty the King of The Belgians, the President of The French Republic, His Majesty the King of Great Britain, Ireland and The British Dominions Beyond the Seas, Emperor of India, His Majesty the King of Italy, His Majesty the Emperor of Japan, the President of the Republic of Poland, the President of the Czechoslovak Republic,

Deeply sensible of their solemn duty to promote the welfare of mankind;

Persuaded that the time has come when a frank renunciation of war as an instrument of national policy should be made to the end that the peaceful and friendly relations now existing between their peoples may be perpetuated;

Convinced that all changes in their relations with one another should be sought only by pacific means and be the result of a peaceful and orderly process, and that any signatory Power which shall hereafter seek to promote its national interests by resort to war should be denied the benefits furnished by this Treaty;

Hopeful that, encouraged by their example, all the other nations of the world will join in this humane endeavor and by adhering to the present Treaty as soon as it comes into force bring their peoples within the scope of its beneficent provisions, thus uniting the civilized nations of the world in a common renunciation of war as an instrument of their national policy;

Have decided to conclude a Treaty ... :

....

Article I

The High Contracting Parties solemnly declare in the names of their respective peoples that they condemn recourse to war for the solution of international controversies, and renounce it as an instrument of national policy in their relations with one another.

....

Article III

The present Treaty shall be ratified by the High Contracting Parties named in the Preamble in accordance with their respective constitutional requirements, and shall take effect as between them as soon as all their several instruments of ratification shall have been deposited at Washington.

This Treaty shall, when it has come into effect as prescribed in the preceding paragraph, remain open as long as may be necessary for adherence by all the other Powers of the world. Every instrument evidencing the adherence of a Power shall be deposited at Washington and the Treaty shall immediately upon such deposit become effective as between the Powers thus adhering and the other Powers parties hereto.

The legislative history of this treaty makes it clear that the inherent right of defense was not affected. Of lesser importance, it was generally interpreted as outlawing only aggressive war and not the use of force short of war—such as reprisals—developed during the war-as-fact period.

Quincy Wright, *The Meaning of the Pact of Paris*
27 Am. J. Int'l. L. 39, 42–43 (1933)

[Correspondence exchanged by the negotiators of the Pact include the following statements on retention of the right of effective defense.]

France. "The renunciation of war, thus proclaimed, would not deprive the signatories of the right of legitimate defense."

Germany. "A Pact after (this pattern) ... would not put in question the sovereign right of any state to defend itself."

Great Britain. "Its terms (do not) exclude action which a state may be forced to take in self-defense.... Mr. Kellogg regards the right of self-defense as inalienable.... There are certain regions of the world the welfare and integrity of which constitute a special and vital interest for our peace and safety. His Majesty's Government have been at pains to make it clear in the past that interference in these regions cannot be suffered. Their protection against attack is to the British Empire a measure of self-defense. It must be clearly understood that His Majesty's Government in Great Britain accept the new treaty upon the distinct understanding that it does not prejudice their freedom of action in this respect. The government of the United States has comparable interests, any disregard of which by a foreign Power they have declared that they would regard as an unfriendly act. His Majesty's Government believe, therefore, that in defining their position they are expressing the intention and meaning of the United States Government."

Japan. "The proposal of the United States is understood to contain nothing that would refuse to independent states the right of self-defense."

SOUTH AFRICA. "It is not intended to deprive any party to the proposed treaty of any of its natural rights of legitimate self-defense."

POLAND. "The Pact does not affect in any way the right of legitimate defense inherent in each state."

CZECHOSLOVAKIA. "The right of self-defense is in no way weakened or restricted by the obligation of the new treaty and each Power is entirely free to defend itself according to its will and its necessities against attack and foreign invasion."

UNITED STATES. "There is nothing in the American draft of an anti-war treaty to restrict or impair in any way the right of self-defense. That right is inherent in every sovereign state and is implicit in every treaty. Every nation is free at all times and regardless of treaty provisions to defend its territory from attack or invasion, and it, alone, is competent to decide whether circumstances require recourse to war in self-defense. If it has a good case, the world will applaud and not condemn its action. Express recognition by treaty of this inalienable right, however, gives rise to the same difficulty encountered in any effort to define aggression. It is the identical question approached from the other side. Inasmuch as no treaty provisions can add to the natural right of self-defense, it is not in the interest of peace that a treaty should stipulate a juristic conception of self-defense since it is far too easy for the unscrupulous to mold events to accord with an agreed definition."

―――――――

The following excerpt from Professor Quincy Wright's article is particularly interesting on the question of whether, after the "Pact of Paris," "war" was any longer appropriate as a designation for defense actions:

> It has been suggested that a state of war may be legally begun because of defensive necessity or in pursuit of the League of Nations Covenant or other guaranty agreements, but it seems doubtful whether the initiation of a state of war is ever a proper defensive measure. John Bassett Moore emphasized the distinction between a state of war and an act of defense in the following words, addressed to Mr. Salmon O. Levinson, while discussions of the Pact were going on:
>
>> Do not attempt to distinguish between aggressive wars and defensive wars. The right of self-defense is inherent. It is not war.... Self-defense by a nation is not war. When once you have outlawed war, do not use the word war any more.
>
> Entry into a state of war connotes assertion of a right to bring the enemy to complete submission through employment of all the methods permitted by the law of war, while defense is necessarily limited to prevention of aggression. It seems very doubtful, therefore, whether a state could under the Pact declare war as an act of self-defense, unless another state was already in a state of war against it, in which case the other state would already have violated the Pact.
>
> ....
>
> It is believed that the legal case against war and armed violence in international affairs is complete. War cannot occur without violation of the Pact, and armed violence cannot be justified except within the legal concept of self-defense. Neutrality posited upon isolation and impartiality has lost its legal foundation. Three years of juristic and diplomatic discussion of the Pact has solidified the legal foundations of peace, but the problem of organizing that peace, to which Mr. Briand referred on August 27, 1928, remains.[4]

―――――――

4. Quincy Wright, *The Meaning of the Pact of Paris*, 27 AM. J. INT'L. L. 39, 51-61 (1933).

The Kellogg-Briand Pact was a major step in the evolution of the international law of conflict management. In the wake of World War I and its horrific casualties, the focus had shifted from the justice of the cause to the terrific destructiveness of war. The fear of catastrophic war made avoidance of war more important than achievement of justice. The League Covenant, with its focus on international organization and procedural checks on resort to war, and the Kellogg-Briand Pact outlawing war except in defense, set the stage for the United Nations. All that was needed was the catalyst of the Second World War. The open aggression of Hitler against Austria, Czechoslovakia, and Poland (no war by accident) soon provided the triggering spark. The fire spread as the Soviet Union, under cover of the nonaggression pact—or "Molotov-Ribbentrop Pact"—with Germany, invaded the Baltic states, Finland, and Poland, while in the Far East Japan pressed its attack against China and, on December 7, 1941, struck Pearl Harbor and the Philippines without warning.

The Early Period of the United Nations Charter

At the conclusion of World War II the Allies met at San Francisco, in the words of the preamble of the Charter, "to save succeeding generations from the scourge of war, which twice in our lifetime has brought untold sorrow to mankind." Thus was ushered in the period of the United Nations. Basically, the Charter built on the two great strands of the League period: first, the substantive requirements of the Kellogg-Briand Pact outlawing war except in defense and, second, the principal of collective defense from Article 16 of the League.

The Charter, however, substantially strengthened the structure of the League period. Since the Kellogg-Briand Pact had condemned "recourse to war," it was not clear that forceful reprisals and force short of war, which had been the focus of international law in the "war as fact" period, were prohibited. The Charter closed this loophole by changing the operative language from "war" to "the threat or use of force," although the permissible limits of force short of the Article 2(4) "threshold" is still debated, and this "threshold" issue was introduced by the Charter. On the procedural side, the United Nations envisioned a strengthened Security Council. Henceforth, collective security—even if only the collective security of the big five powers at the end of World War II—would be substituted for unilateral action. The Charter also greatly strengthened the role of the Secretary-General and established an International Court of Justice as an integral part of the United Nations system.

The major difficulty with the Charter structure is, of course, now history. The wartime cooperation among the major powers broke down during the Cold War—as may have been anticipated by at least some national leaders when the Charter was formally agreed upon. As a result, the agreement contemplated in Article 43 to specify national forces to be made available to the Security Council at its request was never implemented and the Security Council entered the frustrating period of the veto. It was only a result of the fortuitous absence of the Soviet Union from the Security Council in protest against the representation of China by Taiwan that the United Nations was able to recommend action in Korea against the clear aggression of North Korea in its attack on South Korea. Nevertheless, the structure of the United Nations was a major advance in conflict management, and its framework provides the starting point for analysis of the lawfulness of the use of force today. Moreover, the end of the Cold War did bring an at least limited resurgence in cooperative actions under UN authority, such as the Security Council actions in the Gulf War and the Libyan "responsibility to protect."

The Charter Structure and the Permissibility of Recourse to Force

To oversimplify somewhat, Article 2(4) of the Charter prohibits all use of armed force by one state against another except:

(1) pursuant to a decision of a competent organ of the United Nations (see UN Charter chapter VII); or

(2) in individual or collective defense against an armed attack "until the Security Council has taken measures necessary to maintain international peace and security," (Article 51); or

(3) pursuant to a decision of a regional arrangement with respect to a member as long as the use of force does not amount to enforcement action (or if it does it is authorized by the Security Council) *and* is consistent with the purposes and principles of the Charter (see chapter VIII); or

(4) where the use of force is "below the threshold" of Article 2(4); that is, not inconsistent with it; or

(5) pursuant to consent of the government of the territory in question.

It is clear that an aggressive war is illegal, no matter how just. Equally clearly, action in defense against armed aggression, whether individual or collective, is lawful provided it is necessary and proportional.

Despite a popular misconception to the contrary, there is no requirement of prior United Nations authorization before a nation may use force in defense. There is, however, an obligation to report defensive actions or actions taken pursuant to regional arrangements to the Security Council and, if the Security Council acts, to abide by any lawful decision. In most cases, when the case presented a Cold War issue or when the major powers otherwise had divergent interests, there was no Security Council action. The Indo-China, Soviet/Afghan, Central American, and Kosovo conflicts provide examples.

It should be noted that early drafts of the Charter tracked the Kellogg-Briand Treaty in outlawing aggression but saying nothing about defense. This is a strong indication that, just as was true under Kellogg-Briand, nothing in the Charter was intended to restrict the customary law right of defense. The subsequent addition of Article 51 into the Charter was at the suggestion of the Latin American States concerned to protect the developing hemispheric defense arrangement and was not motivated by a desire to restrict the scope of the customary right of defense.

There is also a general obligation under Article 33 to seek a peaceful solution by negotiation, arbitration, or judicial settlement, but this does not impair the inherent right of defense.

The Charter Period and the Law of War

Following World War II it was generally recognized that there was a major need to upgrade the protection accorded prisoners of war and other noncombatants. As a result, four conventions were concluded at Geneva in 1949. And following the Indo-China Conflict, a series of protocols sought to update these laws of war for civil and mixed civil-international settings as well as for uses of modern technology in war. (See Chapter 6 for a more detailed discussion of the Geneva Conventions and the 1977 Protocols.) The Charter period has continued to develop the laws of war and to recognize even more clearly their strong underpinnings in human rights.

The Charter Period and Norms Concerning Obligations to Terminate Hostilities

A new conflict management strand may be under development in the Charter period that would appraise conflict not solely by the lawfulness of the initiation of coercion and compliance with the laws of war but also by reference to compliance with norms concerning an obligation to seek termination of ongoing hostilities. The principal tension in this developing norm is how to encourage parties to seek negotiated solutions without sacrificing the right of effective defense. It should be clearly understood that this is, at most, an emerging norm and not one recognized even by contemporary writers.

Most recently, this strand has received considerable contemporary focus in the ad hoc Yugoslav, Rwandan, and Sierra Leone Criminal Courts and the permanent International Criminal Court. The newer incentive theory also suggests potential for this strand.

The Charter Structure and Institutions for Peaceful Settlement of Disputes

As has been seen, the Charter institutionalized the International Court of Justice as an integral part of the United Nations system. Although the Charter period has continued to regard mechanisms for peaceful resolution of disputes as a significant part of conflict management, this strand no longer receives the unique focus as the centerpiece of conflict management theory that it received during the early twentieth century at the time of the Bryan "cooling-off" treaties and the flurry of bilateral arbitration treaties. The more moderate focus, reflected in the meetings between East and West within the Helsinki process and in the creation of new functional courts, as with the Law of the Sea and GATT Tribunals, may be a more realistic focus.

The Charter Period and Personal Responsibility for Violation of Major Conflict Management Norms (the Nuremberg Principles)

In addition to building on the substantive and procedural strands of the League, the Charter period — building partly on the abortive Leipzig Trials following World War I — also made a major contribution of its own: the ascription of personal responsibility for knowing violation of the major rules of conflict management. The 1945 Charter of the Nuremberg Tribunal, since codified by the International Law Commission and the General Assembly, ascribed individual responsibility for:

(1) *Crimes against peace*: that is, the knowing participation in the planning or waging of a war of aggression in violation of international agreements;

(2) *War crimes*: that is, the knowing violation of the law of war including murder or torture of captives and devastation not justified by military necessity; and

(3) *Crimes against humanity*: that is, murder, extermination, enslavement or other inhuman acts committed against any civilian population (during the course of hostilities).

Formulation of Nürnberg Principles: Discussion in the International Law Commission

II Yearbook of the International Law Commission 181–95, at 193–95 (1950)

B. The Crimes

44. According to the Charter and the judgment, the following acts constitute crimes under international law.

(a) *Crimes against peace:* namely,

(i) *Planning, preparation, initiation or waging of a war of aggression, or a war in violation of international treaties, agreements or assurances;*

(ii) *Participation in a common plan or conspiracy for the accomplishment of any of the acts mentioned under* (i).

(i)   Both categories of crimes are characterized by the fact that they are both connected with "war of aggression or war in violation of international treaties, agreements or assurances."

(ii)   Though the Court had made a general statement to the effect that the Charter "is the expression of international law existing at the time of its creation," it also offered a certain number of arguments in order to refute the objection of the defence that aggressive war was not an international crime under international law. For this refutation the Court relied primarily on the Kellogg-Briand Pact, which in 1939 was in force between sixty-three nations. "The nations who signed the pact or adhered to it unconditionally", says the Court, "condemned recourse to war for the future as an instrument of policy, and expressly renounced it. After the signing of the pact, any nation resorting to war as an instrument of national policy breaks the pact. In the opinion of the Tribunal, the solemn renunciation of war as an instrument of national policy necessarily involves the proposition that such a war is illegal in international law; and that those who plan and wage such a war, with its inevitable and terrible consequences, are committing a crime in so doing."

(iii)   In support of its interpretation of the Kellogg-Briand Pact, the Court cited some other international documents condemning the war of aggression as an international crime. These documents were the draft of a Treaty of Mutual Assistance sponsored by the League of Nations in 1923 which in its article 1 declared "that aggressive war is an international crime", and the Preamble of the League of Nations 1924 Protocol for the Pacific Settlement of International Disputes (Geneva Protocol) which, after "recognizing the solidarity of the members of the International Community", declared that "a war of aggression constitutes a violation of this solidarity, and is an international crime", and that the contracting parties were "desirous of facilitating the complete application of the system provided in the Covenant of the League of Nations for the pacific settlement of disputes between the States and of insuring the repression of international crimes". Furthermore, the Court cited the Declaration concerning wars of aggression adopted on 24 September 1927 by the Assembly of the League of Nations, the preamble of which declared war "an international crime", and the unanimous resolution adopted on 18 February 1928 by twenty-one American Republics at the sixth (Havana) Pan-American Conference, declaring that "war of aggression constitutes an international crime against the human species".

(iv)   The Charter does not contain any definition of the term "war of aggression", nor is there any such definition in the findings of the Court. It is by evaluation of the historical events before and during the war that the Court decided that certain of the defendants planned and waged aggressive wars against ten nations and were therefore guilty of this series of crimes. According to the Court, this made it even unnecessary to discuss the subject in further detail, or to consider at any length the extent to which these aggressive wars were also "wars in violation of international treaties, agreements or assurances".

(v)   The terms "planning and preparing" of a war of aggression are considered by the Court as comprising all the stages in the bringing about of a war of aggression from the planning to the actual initiation of the war. In view of that, the Court did not make visible distinctions between planning and preparations.

(vi)   A legal notion of the Charter which was attacked by the defence is the one concerning "conspiracy" (last sentence of article 6(a) of the Charter). The Court, rejecting the objection of the defence against the adoption of this notion, applied it, though only in a restricted way. "In the opinion of the Tribunal", says the Court, "the conspiracy must be clearly outlined in its criminal purpose. It must not be too far removed from the time of decision and of action. The planning, to be criminal, must not rest merely on the declarations of a party programme, such as are found in the 25 points of the Nazi Party, announced in 1920, or the political affirmations expressed in 'Mein Kampf' in later years. The Tribunal must examine whether a concrete plan to wage war existed, and determine the participants in that concrete plan."

> (b) *War Crimes: namely, violations of the laws or customs of war. Such violations shall include, but not be limited to murder, ill-treatment or deportation to slave labour or for any other purpose of civilian population of or in occupied territory, murder or ill-treatment of prisoners of war or persons on the seas, killing of hostages, plunder of public or private property, wanton destruction of cities, towns or villages, or devastation not justified by military necessity.*

Here too the Court emphasized that the crimes defined by article 6(b) of the Charter were already recognized as war crimes under international law. "They were covered," says the Court, "by Articles 46, 50, 52 and 56 of The Hague Convention of 1907, and Articles 2, 3, 4, 46 and 51 of the Geneva Convention of 1929. That violation of these provisions constituted crimes for which the guilty individuals were punishable is too well settled to admit of argument."

> (c) *Crimes against humanity: namely murder, extermination, enslavement, deportation and other inhuman acts done against a civilian population, or persecutions on political, racial or religious grounds, when such acts are done or such persecutions are carried on in execution of or in connection with any crime against peace or any war crime.*

The above text distinguishes two categories of punishable acts: (a) murder, extermination, enslavement, deportation and other inhuman acts committed against a civilian population, before or during the war and (b) persecution on political, racial or religious ground. Both these acts, according to the Charter, constitute international crimes only inasmuch as they have been committed "in execution of or in connexion with any crime within the jurisdiction of the Tribunal". Crimes falling within the jurisdiction of the Tribunal are (a) crimes against peace; (b) war crimes. The Court applied article 6(c) in a very restrictive way. Though it admitted that "political opponents were murdered in Germany before the war, and that many of them were kept in concentration camps in circumstances of great horror and cruelty", that "the policy of persecution, repression and murder of civilians in Germany before the war of 1939, who were likely to be hostile to the Government, was most ruthlessly carried out," and that "the persecution of Jews during the same period is established beyond all doubt," the court did not consider that the acts relied on before the outbreak of war had been committed "in execution of, or in connexion with, any crime within the jurisdiction of the Tribunal". For this reason the Tribunal declared itself unable to make a general declaration to the effect that acts before 1939 "were crimes against humanity within the meaning of the Charter". Article 6(*c*) characterizes as crimes against humanity murder, extermination, enslavement, etc., committed against "any" civilian population. This means that the above acts are crimes against humanity even if they are committed by the aggressor against his own population.

As Chapter 8 will develop, war crimes trials were also held at Tokyo following World War II and in United States military commissions. These criminal principles further have relevance in trials within national military justice systems for violations as incorporated into national codes of military justice. The trial and conviction of Lieutenant Calley for the My Lai atrocities during the course of the Indo-China Conflict is a case in point. Contrary to popular mythology, individual servicemen have never been held liable under the crimes-against-peace count of the Nuremberg principles, because that category is reserved for top national leaders. Any other conclusion would expose entire armies to trial as "war criminals," since one side is by definition almost certain to be in violation of the Charter.

Within the last three decades there has been a rediscovery of the Nuremberg criminal strand in creation of the Yugoslavia, Rwanda, and Sierra Leone *ad hoc* tribunals and the creation of the new International Criminal Court.

The Charter Structure and Arms Control and Disarmament

Although it was widely believed (correctly or incorrectly) that an arms race was a major contributing factor to World War I, it was reasonably clear to most observers that the Allies had not "raced" prior to World War II, that the principal causative factor of World War II was deliberate use of force by totalitarian governments to achieve expansive national goals, and that the failure of the Allies to adequately maintain a strategic balance substantially contributed to the obvious failure of deterrence. Indeed, the Soviet Union had concluded a "nonaggression" pact with Hitler pursuant to which Communist parties around the world supported the aggressive actions of Germany and Russia joined in the conquest and division of Poland and attacked Finland. Arms control, as such, did not receive the attention in the Charter that it did in the League Covenant. Nevertheless, Article 11 (1) of the Charter provided:

> The General Assembly may consider the general principles of cooperation in the maintenance of international peace and security, including the principles governing disarmament and the regulation of armaments, and may make recommendations with regard to such principles to the Members or to the Security Council or to both.

And Article 47, which established a Military Staff Committee to assist the Security Council, briefly notes in paragraph 1 its possible advice on "the regulation of armaments, and possible disarmament."

Despite this light emphasis in the Charter, as Chapter 13 will explore, the strand of arms control has been developed and emphasized more during the Charter period than ever before in history. Indeed, it was the centerpiece of efforts at war avoidance for a thirty-year period between approximately 1960 and 1990. The new world that emerged after the first atomic bomb was dropped on Hiroshima on August 6, 1945, certainly is the principal reason for this shift in emphasis.

To summarize, the United Nations Charter structure for conflict management includes:

(1) Substantive focus on the great danger of the use of force as a strategy of change rather than the justice of the cause. Unless in defense or within another exception of the Charter, force is prohibited in international relations, no matter how just the cause. This normative emphasis on aggression-defense, taken from the Kellogg-Briand Pact, continues to be one of the most important and perceptive principles in the history of conflict management.

(2) Procedural focus on collective security. This was to be authorized by the Security Council and probably was never conceived as available against the interests of the major powers.

(3) Substantial development of a range of additional strands for conflict management including the Nuremberg principles, institutions for peaceful settlement of disputes, and, particularly, arms control.

The Charter Era to 1990

There were at least three conditions of overriding significance in conflict management development in the Charter era to 1990.

First, there was an East-West division between the "Socialist" countries led by the Soviet Union (but excluding China and a few other "Socialist" states such as Yugoslavia) and the Western democracies, loosely led by the United States. There were, of course, real intersections of interest between East and West, as in the substantial cooperation during the law of the sea negotiations. But deep divisions in national systems, goals, and interests remained even in an age of Perestroika. There is a popular temptation reinforced by constant reference to "two superpowers" to assume that the East-West rivalry simply presents a mirror image. Yet there is substantial evidence that totalitarian regimes as a class, whether of the Right or Left, are considerably more prone to resort to violence than democracies as a class. This is particularly true of those heavily motivated by an extreme ideology.[5]

Historically, this is illustrated by the aggressive behavior of Nazi Germany, Mussolini's Italy, pre-World War II Japan, the Soviet Union's actions in Eastern Europe, Finland, and Afghanistan, and Soviet support for terrorism and "wars of national liberation." Other examples include the North Korean attack on South Korea; North Vietnam's attacks against South Vietnam, Laos, and Cambodia; Syrian involvement in Lebanon; Iraq's attack on Iran; Iran's general behavior under Khomeini; Cuban sponsorship and support for subversion in Central and Latin America; Libya's attack against Chad and support for terrorism worldwide; and Argentina's unsuccessful efforts to subjugate the Falklands forcibly. These are just a few of the examples of the "radical regime" syndrome. True, India invaded Goa and the United States has sought to maintain strategic stability through interventions in Latin America and the Caribbean. On a macro scale, however, it is clear that totalitarian regimes are more willing to resort to force, while democracies — at least in the twentieth century — tend to be reluctant to use major force, sometimes to the point of isolationism.

A "radical totalitarian regime" syndrome, as illustrated by Libya, Cuba, North Korea, Iran, Iraq under Saddam Hussein, Nicaragua under the Sandinistas, and Vietnam, seems to blend together a mixture of a failing centrally planned economy, severe limitations on economic freedom, a one-party political system, an absence of an independent judiciary, a police state with minimal human rights and political freedoms at home, denials of the

---

5. On the lessened propensity of democracies to resort to violence, see particularly the work of University of Hawaii Professor R. J. Rummel, *Deadlier than War*, INST. PUB. AFFAIRS REV., Aug.–Oct. 1987, at 24. *And see,* JOHN NORTON MOORE, SOLVING THE WAR PUZZLE (2004).

right to emigrate, heavy involvement of the military in political leadership, a large percentage of GNP devoted to the military sector, a high percentage of the population in the military, leaders strongly motivated by an ideology of "true beliefs" including willingness to use force, aggressively anti-Western and antidemocratic behavior, and selective support for wars of national liberation, terrorism, and disinformation against Western or democratic interests. In 1983, Cuba, for example, had 8.4 percent of its GNP devoted to defense, as opposed to 1.2 percent for Guatemala; Libya devoted 15 percent of GNP to defense, as opposed to Niger with 4.3 percent; Nicaragua under the Sandinistas devoted at least 13.3 percent of GNP to defense (and the real figure was certainly much higher), as opposed to Honduras with 9.3 percent; Vietnam devoted an estimated — and staggering — 50 percent of its GNP to defense, as opposed to Thailand with 4.2 percent; the Soviet Union devoted 12–14 percent of GNP to defense, but in this same period the United States allocated only 6 percent to defense. These disparities between the totalitarian and democratic or nonradical regimes become even more exaggerated when one examines the percentage of the population in the armed forces.[6] In short, there is considerable evidence that for conflict management purposes the familiar bar graph depicting a continuum from Left to Right may be less informative than one in the form of a horseshoe proceeding from the totalitarian Left through the democracies to the totalitarian Right. (See Figure 1 on the next page.)[7]

Democracies are the least prone to use major force as a modality of change, while the totalitarian systems, particularly those of the "radical regime" syndrome, may be quite prone to the use of force to pursue ideological and other objectives. In short, democracies do indeed inhabit a dangerous world. This is not to suggest simplistic conclusions, such as concluding that the use of military force is the only strategy available to democracies or that democracies are incapable of the use of force as a modality of change. It is to suggest that "mirror imaging" can be dangerously simplistic. And from the standpoint of international law the democracies and the radical totalitarian regimes frequently reflect contending world order systems engaged in a struggle for law — to determine the shape of world order — as well as the traditional struggle for power.

Second, since the dawn of the atomic age in 1945, with the aptly named Trinity Test at Alamogordo by the United States, nuclear weapons have fundamentally altered the war-peace dilemma. In 1949, only four years after the American test, the Soviet Union exploded an atomic bomb and became the second nuclear power. The Allied fire bomb raids on Tokyo in the closing months of World War II killed 50,000 or more. The single uranium fission bomb exploded at Hiroshima killed over 80,000, and the subsequent plutonium fission bomb at Nagasaki killed 30,000. In 1952 the United States tested a hydrogen fusion bomb with one hundred times the power of the atomic fission bomb. One year later the Soviet Union, which had simultaneously been working on the "super" followed suit. Subsequently the nuclear arsenals of the United States and the Soviet Union numbered in the tens of thousands and were deliverable within thirty minutes by intercontinental ballistic missile. France, China, the United Kingdom, India, Israel, Pakistan, and North Korea, among possible others, are also nuclear powers today. And many other nations have the technology necessary to produce nuclear weapons in a relatively short time.

---

6. For more detailed information regarding the relation between defense expenditures and GNP, percentage of overall population in the military of the nations discussed in the text, etc., *see generally*, INTERNATIONAL INSTITUTE FOR STRATEGIC STUDIES, *Military Balance* 1982–1983 (1983), COUNTRIES OF THE WORLD AND THEIR LEADERS YEARBOOK, 1984, 2 volumes (1984), and Conference Board, CENTRALLY PLANNED ECONOMIES: ECONOMIC OVERVIEW, 1983 (1983).

7. The horseshoe chart was prepared by Dr. Ray Cline, former Assistant Secretary of State for Intelligence and Research, and Deputy Director of the Central Intelligence Agency.

Figure 1. The Political Horseshoe Spectrum

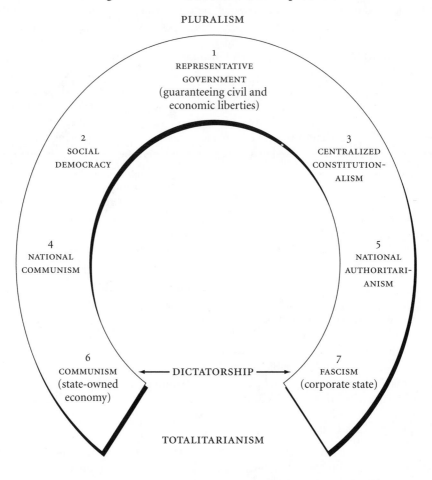

PLURALISM

1
REPRESENTATIVE
GOVERNMENT
(guaranteeing civil and
economic liberties)

2
SOCIAL
DEMOCRACY

3
CENTRALIZED
CONSTITUTION-
ALISM

4
NATIONAL
COMMUNISM

5
NATIONAL
AUTHORITARI-
ANISM

6
COMMUNISM
(state-owned
economy)

← DICTATORSHIP →

7
FASCISM
(corporate state)

TOTALITARIANISM

This "nuclear condition" has placed an enormous premium on maintenance of strategic stability and deterrence. Simultaneously, it raised arms control—particularly with respect to the large and capable international nuclear forces of the United States and the then Soviet Union—to center stage in conflict management thinking. And paradoxically, it heightened the importance of conventional weapons because of the need to maintain a conventional balance in order to keep the nuclear threshold high. Equally paradoxically, it channeled aggressive behavior predominantly toward the organization, instigation, or assistance to paramilitary and guerrilla groups, support for terrorism, covert action, disinformation, and activities that can be disguised or disavowed. Such low-intensity conflict can be profoundly dangerous and destabilizing in its totality. Subsequent to the collapse of the Soviet Union in 1990 there has, of course, been a drastic reduction in the nuclear arsenals of America and Russia.

Third, because of this channeling of conflict to low-intensity violence, terrorism, and support for wars of national liberation, the principal types of violence since World War II have not involved armies on the march, as in the Nazi invasion of Poland—although the Korean War, the final stages of the Indo-China War, and the Gulf War, among others, were characterized by such open invasions. Rather, it has been hit-and-run terrorist attacks, sustained campaigns of terrorism, sudden coups, civil strife, assistance to "wars of national liberation," and mixed civil-international incidents, all accompanied by active political warfare.

But just as the League Covenant was a response to the World War I "war by accident," so too the United Nations Charter was a response to a totalitarian threat to *all* the Allies in a war waged by armies *openly on the march* across international boundaries. The Charter has adapted less well to conflict between East and West, fostered at least in part by radical regime support for wars of national liberation, terrorism, and sustained low-intensity conflict usually waged in ambiguous social and political settings. This dilemma has given rise to the development of a significant body of scholarly writing interpreting the Charter principles for interventionary settings. To greatly oversimplify, most scholars support a principle that neither side should be externally supported in a genuinely internal conflict but that assistance to insurgents gives rise to a defensive counter-interventionary right. The debates about forceful response to sustained terrorist attacks have resulted in less consensus, but a right of response to such attacks has been broadly recognized if the response is necessary to end an ongoing series of attacks and is proportional. The fundamental principle of the Charter—that force should not be aggressively used to seek change as an instrument of national policy, but that it may be used in defense against such unlawful coercion—would seem as applicable to covert attack and sustained low-intensity terrorism as it is to armies on the march. As will be seen, the broad acceptance of United States and NATO actions against the Taliban in Afghanistan following the 2001 9/11 attacks suggests broad acceptance of a right of force against serious ongoing terrorism.

Similarly, the post-Charter setting has also given rise to a substantial debate about the limits of action by regional arrangements, acting under chapter VIII of the Charter. And it has triggered a debate about the limits of "humanitarian intervention" for the protection of human rights and newer "responsibility to protect" obligatory humanitarian actions by the UN. The debate concerning the Grenada mission at the request of the OECS, that surrounding the NATO action in Kosovo, and the UN authorized action against Gaddafi in Libya, have most recently presented these issues.

This period has witnessed an explosion in newer theories of conflict management, many loosely grouped under an emerging discipline of "peace studies." These newer approaches include negotiation theory, second track diplomacy, non-violent sanctions (as opposed to pacifism), an enhancement of interest in functionalism and rationalism, study of war termination strategies, and a study of "pathways to war" or "conflict scenarios." Not surprisingly, because of the failure of deterrence prior to World War II and the existence of the Cold War, deterrence has served as a central component of governmental policies in this contemporary Charter era, although it has been focused on nuclear and regular conventional war rather than the newer mode of "secret warfare" characteristic of the contemporary era. In addition, all of the earlier strands continue to play a role. The popular focus—as well as the focus of East-West dialogue during this era—however, because of the nuclear condition, overwhelmingly was nuclear arms control.

The Contemporary Charter Era

The world changed in 1990 with the collapse of the former Soviet Union. The end of the Cold War has had profound changes with respect to security and the development of the international law of conflict management.

While the recent agreements on strategic systems between the United States and Russia shows that arms control is still on the agenda, arms control is clearly no longer the centerpiece in efforts at war avoidance. Today, a Russia moving toward democracy is co-operatively engaged with the United States on many fronts, including the war against the al-Qaeda terrorists, and has accepted a United States interest in ABM defense against rogue state attack. In developments that would have, quite literally, been regarded during the 1970s as impossible, East and West Germany have united and NATO has enlarged to include a number of former Soviet client states. A post-Cold War Russia supported the Security Council action in rolling back Saddam Hussein's aggressive attack against Kuwait. While this coalition did not hold in the early phases of the Kosovo crisis, and recently Putin has used illegal force in Ukraine and elsewhere, there is considerably greater promise today for strengthened collective security than there was at the height of the Cold War.

Principal issues and threats in the contemporary system relate to the control of rogue states, such as Iran and North Korea, the control of terrorism as with al-Qaeda and ISIS, concern about biological, radiological, and chemical, as well as nuclear, weapons of mass destruction in the hands of such actors, the Security Council role in "failed states" such as Somalia, and uncertainties concerning the major regional powers of China and Pakistan. The world also has a greater appreciation for the problem of "democide," as was witnessed most recently in Bosnia, Rwanda, the Sudan, and Syria.

In this post-Cold War era, governments all over the world have embraced the importance of democracy and the rule of law. With a few hold-out exceptions, leaders around the globe now pepper their speeches with references to the importance of both principles. Further, subject to the usual backsliding from time to time, as we see in Venezuela under President Chavez, the thrust globally seems to be movement toward democracy and free trade. If "incentive theory" is correct, both should be helpful in lessening the risk of major war in coming years.

Following the 9/11 attacks on the World Trade Center and the Pentagon, the world also seems finally to be pulling together to combat the scourge of terrorism. The United States/NATO actions against al-Qaeda and the Taliban in Afghanistan, broadly supported internationally, suggests such an outcome in the war against terrorism. If that proves to be the case, then the world will have changed for the terrorists on September 11, 2001, rather than for those committed to human freedom.

As war/peace theory has increasingly focused on controlling aggressive national leaders, the contemporary era has also witnessed an explosion of new war crimes tribunals. These now include the Yugoslav, Rwanda, and Sierra Leone special purpose tribunals and the International Criminal Court that entered into force on July 1, 2002. It is to be hoped that differences between the United States and supporters of the new International Criminal Court can be resolved in years to come, making this new tribunal a truly effective addition to deterrence against aggression and democide.

As the at least temporary failure in the negotiation for a broadly inclusive International Criminal Court may illustrate, a world in which the United States is the principal super-power, and in which the European community has become much more cohesive in pursuit of foreign policy, may suggest both heightened similarities and heightened difficulties for the United States in pursuit of its national security policy. Ultimately, however, the com-monality of interests among a growing number of democratic nations should work to reduce the risk of major war and to serve the interests of all mankind in the quest for human freedom and dignity.

Serious challenges remain, however. Most recently, an increasingly revanchist Russia under the leadership of Putin has engaged in cyber attacks against Estonia, outright invasion of Georgia and the Crimea, and a hybrid attack against Ukraine, while rolling back democratic institutions at home. China has flouted international law in its aggressive "nine-dashed line" policy in the South China Sea and tensions with Japan and with its ASEAN neighbors are high. Of particular concern, both Russia and China are hydrogen bomb powers, permanent members of the United Nations Security Council, and non-democracies controlled by a regime elite. Most disturbingly, a violent fringe motivated by a resurgence of radical Islamic ideology has begun insurgencies in Africa and the Middle East, as well as engaging in heightened terrorism in virtually every region of the World. Terrorism and violent aggressive movements are typically a product of a violent totalitarian ideology and the violent ideology *de jure* is that of radical Islam. Al Qaeda was an early incarnation of this violent ideology but since the 9/11 attacks on the twin Trade Towers in New York such groups have proliferated both geographically and numerically, in spite of major efforts against them and optimistic pronouncements about "victory" in the misnamed "war on terror." The most serious incarnation of this threat is that from ISIL/ISIS in Iraq and Syria which now controls large swaths of both countries and which is on a quest for a new Caliphate that would transcend state boundaries. Should ISIL/ISIS establish a permanent base in Syria and Iraq it seems likely to expand its violent aggression against neighboring states. Democratic nations, as well as authoritarian leaders in the Middle East and Africa, have been much too slow in engaging this radical ideology on the battlefield of ideas which, in addition to required defensive measures, is a central front in this core contemporary struggle for peace and human dignity.

Further, other security threats also remain. Iran continues to support terrorism and secret warfare in pursuit of its radical ideology and has been flaunting IAEA safeguards in what seems a likely effort to pursue a nuclear weapons program. Hamas, an Iranian supported Palestinian group, continues a rejectionist policy toward the State of Israel and brags of its terrorist attacks against Israel. North Korea has a rogue nuclear program and continues to maintain one of the worst gulags in the world today, while engaging periodically in acts of forceful aggression against South Korea. Finally, more traditional radical movements, ostensibly hard left, continue to plague Latin America. Cuba remains a totalitarian gulag, Venezuela illustrates the dangers of a "one person, one vote, one time" transition from democracy to authoritarian thuggery, Mexico is engaged in a war with violent drug gangs and a struggle for the rule of law, and the FARC in Columbia continues to wage a brutal and destabilizing insurgency. Since the Americas broadly are our immediate neighborhood, enhanced engagement with the Organization of American States (the OAS), and against these and other threats against our Latin American neighbors, would seem a continuing priority. Likely one of the costs of the heightened Middle Eastern terrorist threats in recent years, and the War in Iraq, has been to distract the United States from greater engagement with these hemispheric threats.

Meeting these security challenges requires United States leadership. The isolationism fashionable in some political circles in America, on both the left and the right, is a false utopia. The United States cannot and need not serve as the policeman for the World, but equally the World cannot do without American leadership and engagement. The legal concepts and structures set out in this chapter can be important tools in that leadership.

Questions for Discussion

1. During the Indo-China conflict a number of divinity students petitioned then Secretary of Defense Robert McNamara on the grounds that the conflict was not in the religious tradition of a "just war." No criteria for this judgment were given. To what extent should the "just war" approach—which is in a crucial respect inconsistent with the Charter

(although it can be reinterpreted to be consistent with it) — serve as the criteria for assessing permissible and impermissible coercion in the post-Charter era? In what respect is it inconsistent with the Charter?

2. Are there any potential conflicts among strands of the international law of conflict management? Does the dilemma between the law of war principle of minimizing collateral civilian damage and the strategic stability principle of assured retaliatory destruction of counter-value targets pose a choice among important strands? Is this dilemma effectively resolved by the American Catholic bishops' conclusion that one can target nuclear weapons on counter-value targets but cannot fire them? Is there ever a dilemma between nonuse of force as a modality of change and avoidance of sudden shifts in the strategic balance? Did the 1962 Cuban Missile Crisis or the Israeli strike at the Iraqi Osirak reactor present such a dilemma? Is there a potential conflict between the right of effective defense and any new obligation to terminate ongoing hostilities? How should these and any other conflicts among strands be resolved as conflict management theory evolves?

3. Conflict management theory seems to adapt well to preventing the last great war. Is the existing framework adequate to prevent World War III? If not, how should it be changed and how can we get from here to there?

4. Once the point of nonverifiability of total fissionable materials production had been passed in the 1950s, was disarmament, as opposed to arms control, permanently precluded? How could we ever agree to destroy — as opposed to reduce — all nuclear weapons if verification is impossible? What does this suggest about efforts to radically restructure the present system? Did the Clark-Sohn Plan adequately consider this problem? Would a mutually deployed and highly effective defense against ballistic missiles potentially enable deeper cuts in nuclear arsenals?

5. Was the strong focus on arms control between 1960–1990 the equivalent of the strong 1913 focus on "cooling off" treaties and arbitration agreements as a means of war avoidance? Why or why not? Should we emphasize other — or new — strands also? Should the West seek to engage China today in a broad negotiation on "rules of the game" and world order accountability on fundamental Charter principles? Should we seek, as Ambassador Max Kampelman has urged, initial agreement on "oughts" followed by compliance discussions? Is the most effective approach one that seeks to build on all — or many — strands? Should the United States seek to promote greater cooperation among the permanent members of the UN Security Council?

6. Are mechanisms for peaceful settlement of international disputes of major importance as a strand of the international law of conflict management? Why have they not lived up to the high expectations for them in the first two decades of this century? Are judicial decisions usually zero-sum solutions? Are the outcomes on vital national issues unpredictable and how might this affect willingness of national leaders to resort to such third-party mechanisms? Have third-party mechanisms yet resolved problems of perceived bias? Most importantly, are wars more closely analogous to civil or to criminal matters in the domestic legal system?

7. Are the Nuremburg principles of major importance as a strand of the international law of conflict management? Why? Would you differentiate in your answer between violations of the laws of war and crimes against peace? Why has this strand seen such a development with new criminal tribunals in recent years?

8. What role is there in the development of conflict management techniques for national measures to control the use of force and promote peace? How do we deal with the dilemma

that democratic states, which may need them least, are the ones to adopt them rather than the totalitarian states, which may need them most?

9. How should democratic states respond if confronted with a pattern of totalitarian or terrorist state behavior at fundamental odds with the basic United Nations system? To what extent is that the case today? Is the right of effective defense always adequate in response to any such challenge, or is a broader defensive principle required? How would any broader principle be applied in a way to be even-handedly accepted as international law? How do democracies deal with the propensity for and the greater ease with which totalitarian regimes undertake covert activities?

10. To what extent do newer methodologies in the psychology of individual and group conflict, negotiations theory, scenario analysis, nonviolent sanctions, and other nontraditional approaches to conflict management offer promise in dealing with issues of war and peace? What portion of the work of the Institute of Peace should be devoted to such approaches?

11. To what extent should normative approaches to conflict management be influenced by the possibility that totalitarian and radical regime attacks against their own populations may have killed considerably more people in the twentieth century than all the century's international and domestic wars? Professor R. J. Rummel of the University of Hawaii cites 115.5 million deaths from the first cause and 35.7 million deaths from twentieth century wars, although his figure for twentieth century war deaths seems too low given the substantial World War II non-combatant casualties.

12. How would newer theories about the origin and control of war, including "incentive theory" as discussed in the last chapter, interact with the principal strands in conflict management? Which of those strands would you suggest are most important?

Selected Bibliography

The Blue Helmets: A Review of United Nations Peace-keeping (United Nations, 3d Ed., 1996).

Brierly, James L., *The Law of Nations: An Introduction to the International Law of Peace* (1963).

Claude, Inis L., *Swords into Plowshares: The Problems and Progress of International Organization* (1971).

Grotius, Hugo, *De Jure Belli ac Pacis Libre Tres* (Francis W. Kelsey trans., James B. Scott ed., 1925).

Gutman, Roy, & David Rieff eds., *Crimes of War: What the Public Should Know* (1999).

Johnson, James T., *Just War Tradition and the Restraint of War* (1981).

Little, David, "The 'Just War' Tradition and the Pursuit of Peace," Chapter 1 *in The Hundred Percent Challenge: Building A National Institute of Peace* (Charles Smith ed., 1985).

McDougal, Myres S., & Florentino P. Feliciano, *Law & Minimum World Public Order* (1961). (This is the single most important and perceptive work on the international law of conflict management.)

O'Brien, William V., *The Conduct of Just and Limited War* (1983).

Pufendorf, Samuel, *Elementorum Jurisprudentiae Universalis Libro Dua* (William A. Oldfather trans., 1931).

Rosenne, Shabtai, *The World Court: What It Is and How It Works* (1973).

Rummel, R. J., "Deadlier than War," *Inst. Pub. Affairs Rev.*, Aug.–Oct. 1987, at 24.

————, *Death by Government* (1994).

Russell, Ruth B., & Jeannette E. Muther, *A History of The United Nations Charter* (1958).

Vattel, Emer de, *The Law of Nations: or Principles of the Law of Nature Applied to the Conduct and Affairs of Nations and Sovereigns* (1883).

von Elbe, Joachim, "The Evolution of the Concept of the Just War," 33 *Am. J. Int'l L.* 665 (1939).

Wright, Quincy, "The Meaning of the Pact of Paris," 27 *Am. J. Int'l L.* 39 (1933).

————, *A Study of War* (1942). (This is a classic two volume study of war—one of the few such studies—aiming at a "scientific" approach. It is, however, dated.)

————, "The Law of the Nuremberg Trial," 41 *Am. J. Int'l. L.* 38 (1947).

Chapter 4

The Use of Force in International Relations: Norms Concerning the Initiation of Coercion

John Norton Moore

In this chapter:
Overview
The Basic Charter Framework
Continuing Problems
Illustrative Case Studies
Selected Bibliography

Overview

As discussed in Chapter 3, one of the earliest and most important strands in the development of conflict management theory is the normative structure for differentiating permissible and impermissible coercion. This is frequently referred to as *jus ad bellum*. The 1928 Pact of Paris, or Kellogg-Briand Pact, and the United Nations Charter have decisively established that the basic governing principle is that force may not be aggressively used in international relations as an instrument of national policy, but that it may be used in individual or collective defense as a response to such an aggressive use of force by others. That is, because of the destructiveness of violence in the modern world, force may not be used as a modality of major change or value extension no matter how "just" the cause is perceived to be. And in a decentralized international system lacking reliable mechanisms for community response against aggression, it is universally recognized that nations retain an "inherent" or "natural" right of defense against such an illegal use of force.

This fundamental—and dual—principle is rooted in the understanding that perceptions about justness will and do vary. Even more important, modern war is so enormously destructive that the community of nations must achieve peace or "minimum order" as a necessary precondition to enhancement of global values. An economist might add that not only is war undesirable because of the enormous transaction costs inherent in the destructiveness of modern warfare, but also that change is more likely to promote community values when freely negotiated than when coerced. The essential point, however, is that the use of force in modern warfare is so enormously destructive that, in the aggregate, the destruction resulting from the use of force under a "just war" approach would outweigh any gains in justice that might be realized. Just as in the concept of defense within domestic legal systems, however, to prohibit a nation unlawfully attacked from acting in defense would be self-defeating. Indeed, such a prohibition would encourage attacks. Moreover, in the international legal system, as the history of the Kellogg-Briand Pact illustrates, it is completely impractical to expect nations to give up a right of defense against coercion by others. The right of effective defense, then, is as essential and important a complementary principle as the ban on aggressive use of force.

Newer theory about war also tells us that for the legal system to make a difference in controlling war it must add to deterrence against aggression. If, however, it deters defensive response as powerfully as it deters the initiating aggression then an aggressor will know that whatever costs it imposes on aggression will also be imposed upon the defense. For this reason, to effectively deter, the *jus ad bellum* must robustly differentiate between aggression, which it sanctions, and defense, which it supports. Approaches, sometimes called minimalism, whose real world effect is to seek to ban all uses of force, rather than aggression, may be part of the problem of war rather than the solution to war. Sometimes this minimalism takes the form of statements that "the Charter ban on the use of force is *jus cogens*" rather than the correct statement that "the Charter ban on the aggressive use of force is *jus cogens*."

As was shown in the early development of just war theory, there are limits of contextual reasonableness placed on the lawful use of force in defense. Most important, under the modern law of the UN Charter, the defensive use of force must be both "necessary" and "proportional." That is, necessary for the preservation of the values threatened by the illegal attack and proportional to the achievement of the lawful defensive objective. Thus, in general, force should not exceed the minimum necessary to stop an illegal attack promptly and to protect the threatened values. An often-cited test of necessity is that of Secretary of State Daniel Webster in the *Caroline* incident with Canada in 1837. In an exchange of notes with Canada, Secretary Webster said there must be shown "a necessity of self-defense, instant, overwhelming, leaving no choice of means and no moment for deliberation."[1] Scholars today regard this statement of the general principle of necessity as unduly restrictive and more appropriate to the issue at stake in anticipatory defense.

Although the core Charter normative principle is to ban aggression, but permit responding defense, as will be discussed below, there are a few other bases for lawful uses of force under the Charter.

Questions for Discussion

(1)   Given the distinction between illegal aggression and lawful defensive force, is there a definition or procedure that can usefully assist in categorizing a particular use of force as one or the other?

(2)   Must an armed attack or armed aggression involve armies on the march, or does the definition include an intense covert attack, sustained terrorism, or support for an insurgent movement? Most scholars agree that the test of an armed attack is the intensity of the coercion, not the modality of overt versus covert attack. Is there a right of defense against aggressive attacks from non-governmental groups such as al-Qaeda or ISIS? Common sense and the language of the Charter would say yes but the International Court of Justice in the *Israeli Wall* Case seemed to conclude otherwise.

(3)   Is there ever a right of anticipatory defense? In the past scholars were divided on this issue but today it is generally accepted that there is a right of anticipatory defense

---

1. J.L. BRIERLY, THE LAW OF NATIONS: AN INTRODUCTION TO THE INTERNATIONAL LAW OF PEACE, 405–06 (6th ed. 1963).

provided the threat is immediate and intense. (Would the *Caroline* test be particularly appropriate as a test for anticipatory defense?) Is any claimed right of "preemption" simply anticipatory defense in the modern era or something else? Would any such claim going beyond anticipatory defense generate perverse incentives to acquire weapons of mass destruction or to attack first?

(4)   Does the prohibition against use of force in international relations extend to relations between *de facto* entities or only *de jure* entities? The fundamental Charter principle must apply to both. Any other answer would remove the Charter proscription from a host of boundary disputes, sovereignty claims, cease-fire lines, and divided-nation conflicts.

(5)   Is it lawful to provide assistance to a widely recognized government to offset external assistance provided to insurgents? Scholars differ as to whether assistance can be given to government forces in a civil-war setting, but the majority view supports the lawfulness of such assistance. The government, after all, represents the state. Further, there is substantial agreement that it is always illegal to aid insurgent forces (without armed aggression to which one is responding by assistance to insurgents) and that it is lawful to aid government forces if insurgents have received prior illegal assistance. This right of counter-intervention is the right of defense counterpart in the "norms of intervention" in applying fundamental Charter principles to civil war and mixed civil-international incidents.

(6)   Is it lawful to respond against the territory of a state willfully harboring terrorists? Was the post 9/11 response against Afghanistan in this category? Given the centrality of terrorism as a contemporary form of aggression, to not provide a right of defense would seriously undermine the Charter structure.

The following materials will seek to develop these and other issues concerning the international law of the use of force.

The Basic Charter Framework

Unlawful Aggressive Use of Force and Lawful Defense: The Complementary Structure of Articles 2(4) and 51

Article 2(4) of the United Nations Charter provides:

> All Members shall refrain in their international relations from the threat or use of force against the territorial integrity or political independence of any state, or in any other manner inconsistent with the Purposes of the United Nations.

Article 51 of the Charter provides:

> Nothing in the present Charter shall impair the inherent right of individual or collective self-defense if an armed attack occurs against a Member of the United Nations, until the Security Council has taken measures necessary to maintain international peace and security. Measures taken by Members in the exercise of this right of self-defense shall be immediately reported to the Security Council and shall not in any way affect the authority and responsibility of the Security Council under the present Charter to take at any time such action as it deems necessary in order to maintain or restore international peace and security.

Under Article 51 the right of defense is explicitly both individual and collective. That is, states may not only use force against armed attacks directed against them but also against attacks directed against third states at the request of those states or pursuant to prior defense agreements. This right of collective defense is an essential condition of an effective right of defense. Without it powerful nations would be able to attack weaker neighbors without risk. Similarly, it is the underpinning of collective defense agreements, such as the NATO and Rio treaties. "Nothing in the present Charter shall impair" this defensive right, and action under Article 51 may be taken without waiting for the Security Council—which might not act—to take action. There is an obligation to report immediately measures taken in defense to the Security Council.

Most scholars regard this defensive right in the Charter as coextensive with the pre-Charter right of defense, that is, as an inherent or natural right of defense. The French text of Article 51, which is equally authoritative with the English, speaks of the right of defense against "*agression armee*" as a "*droit natural.*" Given that the critical *jus ad bellum* distinction, both before and after the Charter, has focused on "aggression," as is reflected in the equally authentic French text of the Charter, it is preferable to use this term rather than the "armed attack" language of the English version.

Article 103 of the Charter provides:

> In the event of a conflict between the obligations of the Members of the United Nations under the present Charter and their obligations under any other international agreement, their obligations under the present Charter shall prevail.

The use-of-force obligations in the Charter, therefore, take precedence over any other agreements inconsistent with them.

John Norton Moore, *Jus ad Bellum* Before the International Court of Justice
52 Va. J. Int'l L. 903, 910–16 (2012)
The Charter *Jus ad Bellum* Framework

As a point of reference it is useful in any assessment of use of force decisions to review the lawful bases of use of force (*jus ad bellum*) under the United Nations Charter. Where there is a broad division of views it will be noted. There are five bases for lawful use of force under the Charter framework. These are:

1. Consent of a widely recognized government. The Government represents the state and its sovereignty and normally consent by a widely recognized government suffices as a basis for lawful use of force on the territory of the consenting state.[2]

2. Pursuant to a valid decision of the United Nations. This basis encompasses action authorized by the Security Council acting lawfully (*i.e.*, not in a manner *ultra vires* as specified in Article 24(2) of the Charter) under Chapter VII (Articles 39, 42 & 48), or action authorized by the General Assembly (Articles 11 & 12) in settings "[w]hile the Security Council is [not] exercising in respect of any dispute or situation the functions assigned to it in the ... Charter ... unless the Security Council so requests" *and* which is not "enforcement" action ("enforcement action" is generally understood as action directed against a government and thus General Assembly authorization

---

2. *See, e.g.*, Armed Activities on the Territory of the Congo (Dem. Rep. Congo v. Uganda), Judgment, 2005 I.C.J. 168 (Dec. 19).

normally would relate to consensual settings such as peace-keeping operations). It should be noted that when the Security Council seeks to authorize use of force the authorizing resolution will normally use the language "acting under Chapter VII" (clearly triggering Article 39) and language specifically authorizing "all necessary means," which is understood as authorizing use of force, as well as lesser measures. Contemporary United Nations practice, as opposed to an earlier time including actions under the "Uniting for Peace Resolution," rarely will authorize use of force through the General Assembly, in part because of the substantial expense involved even with peace-keeping actions.

3.   Individual or Collective Defense. Individual and collective defense in response to aggression were lawful bases for use of force under the 1928 Kellogg-Briand Pact (Pact of Paris)[3] which is the most important pre-Charter international instrument outlawing force as a modality of major change in international relations. That is, the Kellogg-Briand Pact "renounce[d] recourse to war for the solution of international controversies and … as an instrument of national policy in … [parties] relations with one another." The United Nations Charter built on Kellogg-Briand and broadened its prohibition (in Article 2(4)) to include a ban on aggression below the threshold of "war" and also banned "the threat" of aggressive use of force, as well as the actual aggressive use of force. The Charter, however, in its early draft paralleling Kellogg-Briand, and thus saying nothing about defensive use of force, and ultimately in the addition of Article 51 added at the request of Latin American nations seeking to enshrine their defensive rights under the Inter-American regional security system, was not intended to limit the pre-existing right of individual and collective defense. A careful review of the *Travaux Préparatoires* of the Charter shows only that in Commission I, Committee 1, which dealt with the general purposes and principles of the UN Charter, the final Dumbarton Oaks Charter Proposal merely incorporated an Australian proposal for Article 2(4) adding the language "against the territorial integrity or political independence of any member or state" with the declared purpose of spelling out "the most typical form of aggression…."[4] concerning forceful change of frontiers or of a state's independence.[5] The discussion also fully dealt with *jus ad bellum* issues by reference to "aggression," not "armed attack." Indeed, "aggression" has conventionally remained to this day the rubric under which countless international law scholars seek to define unlawful use of force and the parameters of *jus ad bellum*. Because, however, the English language version of Article 51, added to the Charter in Committee 4 of Commission III dealing with Chapter VIII and regional uses of force, uses the language

---

3. Treaty Between the United States and Other Powers Providing for the Renunciation of War as an Instrument of National Policy, August 27, 1928, 46 Stat. 2343 (Kellogg-Briand Pact).

4. For the Australian Proposal, see U.N. Doc. 2 G/14 (1) May 5, 1945, *in* 3 UNCIO, at 543, and for the Australian explanation of this proposal see H.V. Evatt, *The United Nations* 18, 19 (1948) (" … as the result of the above words (territorial integrity and political independence) … the most typical form of aggression would place the aggressor clearly in the wrong at the bar of the United Nations.") and 1 U.N.C.I.O. Docs. 174 (further explanation by the Deputy Prime Minister of Australia, Francis Gorde, stating "The application of this principle should ensure that no question relating to a change of frontiers or an abrogation of a state's independence could be decided other than by peaceful negotiations. It should be made clear that if any state were to follow up a claim of extended frontiers by using force or the threat of force, the claimant would be breaking a specific and solemn obligation under the Charter.").

5. Critically, this prohibition also applies to *de facto* as well as *de jure* boundaries, as was evident, for example, during the Korean and Falkland/Malvinas wars. Any other interpretation would expose the world to countless wars over disputed islands and land and ocean boundaries.

"if an armed attack occurs," and because arguably some statements of the U.S. Delegation in the Committee III discussion surrounding what became Article 51 can be interpreted as banning "anticipatory defense" (even under the pre-Charter strict standards for any such use of force), a minimalist interpretation of the Charter has urged that the "armed attack" language in Article 51 both limited the right of defense and banned anticipatory defense. Increasingly, however, scholars have accepted that the proper rubric for determining *jus ad bellum* is not "armed attack," which is never defined in the Charter, but rather the traditional "aggression" which is the phrase used in the equally authentic French language version of Article 51.[6] Moreover, today there is widespread acceptance of the right of anticipatory defense (not "preemption") provided it meets the traditional strict "imminence of attack" standard of the pre-Charter right of anticipatory defense.[7] Most importantly, for an analysis of *jus ad bellum* law under the Charter, while there is at least an arguable basis in the *travaux* and the English language version of Article 51 for minimalists to argue that anticipatory defense is no longer lawful, there is absolutely nothing in the language or the *travaux* of the Charter suggesting that the right of defense does not apply against the covert aggression spectrum, including terrorist aggression directed from non-state actors and indiscriminate mining of international waterways. Nor is there any requirement

---

6. Reasons supporting that the Charter did not limit the traditional right of individual and collective defense despite the English language version of Article 51 include:
  • The discussion in Committee 4 of Commission III concerning what became Article 51, as well as the statements of the U.S. Delegation arguably addressing anticipatory defense, were focused on the rights of regional arrangements, not on the use of force in general;
  • The discussions in Commission I, Committee 1, which dealt with the general purposes and principles of the UN Charter, including norms concerning use of force, show that the right of defense remains unimpaired. This discussion in Committee 1 of Commission I, focused on the broadest and most important questions of purposes and principles of the Charter, would seem to trump that in Committee 4 of Commission III, which was focused on rules for "regional arrangements" in Chapter VIII of the Charter;
  • The broader U.S. view on use of force (rooted in no inhibition on the traditional right of defense) was still being asserted, and accepted, on June 5 in Committee I(1) despite the earlier May 14 apparently limiting discussion and language in Committee III (4). If there was an intent to limit the right of defense generally by the "armed attack" language in the English language version of Article 51 surely there would have been a discussion about such restrictions in Commission I, which was the Commission charged globally with the general *jus ad bellum* provisions of the Charter;
  • There was no discussion reflecting an intent to write this discussion concerning regional arrangements broadly into use of force norms when a procedural committee simply moved Article 51 to Chapter VII from Chapter VIII;
  • There is no definition given in the Charter of "armed attack" as would be expected were this an important restriction on the traditional right of individual and collective defense;
  • The equally authentic French language version of the Charter uses the traditional term "aggression" in Article 51, rather than "armed attack;" and
  • There is no evidence that the cryptic discussion in Commission III by members of the U.S. Delegation, a discussion arguably supporting a limitation on the right of anticipatory defense, was accepted as a proper interpretation by any other delegation. Indeed, statements of the U.S. Delegation could not bind other delegations.

7. *See, e.g.*, Report of the High-Level Panel on Threat, Challenge, and Change, *A More Secure World: One Shared Responsibility*, U.N. Doc. A/59/565 (Dec. 2004). "Preemption," a new doctrine enunciated by the George W. Bush Administration, if it asserts a right beyond the imminence of threat standard embodied in the right of "anticipatory defense," is both illegal, and, I would urge, bad policy. During a conversation between the author and the then Legal Adviser to the National Security Council in the Bush Administration, the Legal Adviser took the position that the Bush "preemption" doctrine was not intended to go beyond the recognized right of "anticipatory defense."

in the Charter of a public or written request from a victim of aggression to trigger a right of participation in collective defense. Indeed, this latter restriction would seem counter to the core of contemporary regional defense arrangements such as the Rio and NATO Treaties, which by their terms declare that an attack against one member is an attack against all members. Actions in defense are required to be reported to the Security Council, though there is no Charter requirement of continuous reporting. Failure to report, sadly all too frequent, is to miss one of the most important opportunities to alert the world to an aggressive attack.

4. Lawful action pursuant to a regional arrangement. Such action, under Chapter VIII of the Charter, by the strict language of the Charter itself is lawful if it is "consistent with the Purposes and Principles of the United Nations" (Article 52), *and* is either not an "enforcement action," or, if an "enforcement action" is authorized by the Security Council (Article 53), *and*, by an implicit purpose of regional arrangements, the action is in relation only to a member state of the regional arrangement (Article 52 and Chapter VIII — implicit). That is, the old Warsaw Pact was not authorized to take any action concerning NATO nations under this basis and the Arab League is not authorized to take any action concerning Israel under this basis. Principal contemporary regional arrangements would certainly include the Arab League, NATO, the Rio Treaty and the Organization of Eastern Caribbean States (OECS — the English speaking countries of the Eastern Caribbean). Given the clarity under both the language and the *travaux* of the Charter for this fourth basis for lawful use of force, it remains puzzling why minimalist interpretations of the Charter never mention this basis.

5. Use of force under the threshold of Article 2(4). Article 2(4), drafted by Commission I charged with the general global rules concerning *jus ad bellum*, provides that "All Members shall refrain in their international relations from the threat or use of force against the territorial integrity or political independence of any state, or in any other manner inconsistent with the Purposes of the United Nations." This is the core prohibition in the UN Charter on use of force and the discussion in Committee 1 of Commission I makes it clear that this is the provision understood by the framers as governing the prohibition against aggression under the Charter. Thus, if a limited action such as protection of nationals or humanitarian intervention is neither inconsistent with the "Purposes of the United Nations" nor seeks to alter frontiers or remove political independence of a state it is not prohibited by the language of Article 2(4). The core actions under this basis are, of course, protection of nationals and humanitarian intervention.[8] There is a robust long-term and continuing debate as to the lawfulness of both protection of nationals and humanitarian intervention and I will not engage those debates at this point. It should be noted, however, that many states have officially recognized the right of protection of nationals under certain extreme threats to their nationals and, in the contemporary world, at least the United Kingdom recognizes the lawfulness of humanitarian intervention under appropriate conditions.[9]

---

8. Note that both protection of nationals and humanitarian intervention can also be textually argued under the Charter to be rooted in the right of individual and collective defense.

9. I, and many other scholars, have long recognized not only the lawfulness of protection of nationals but also that of humanitarian intervention. For a classic debate on humanitarian intervention, the Ian Brownlie/Richard Lillich exchange, see Chapters 10 and 11 in LAW & CIVIL WAR IN THE MODERN WORLD (John Norton Moore, ed.) (1974), and see the modern reprint of this book published in 2010 with a new introduction by the editor. And for my own long-standing support for humanitarian intervention see John Norton Moore, Chapter 1 *in* LAW & CIVIL WAR IN THE MODERN WORLD (J. N.

Uses of force as a modality of major change in the international system that do not fall under one of these five lawful bases are illegal aggression. This is so whether the aggression takes place through open invasion of tank armies across international boundaries, secret warfare, covert mining of internationally privileged straits, or terrorism, whether committed by state actors or non-state actors. The international law is so clear on the illegality of these actions that it needs no citation here.

The use of force, to be lawful, must fall under one of these five bases. But, in addition, *jus ad bellum* also requires that the action meet standards of "necessity" and "proportionality." Neither of these requirements is textually spelled out in the Charter, indicating yet again that lawful use of force cannot be simply assessed by "logic chopping" of the text of the Charter. But these requirements are generally understood to also apply to *jus ad bellum*, and in a slightly different modality to *jus in bello* law as well. Because of their general nature as basic principles these concepts are particularly subject to minimalist application in use of force decisions.

Necessity as a general proposition in *jus ad bellum* is best understood as a prohibition against use of force except in protection of major values. And proportionality as a general proposition in *jus ad bellum* is best understood as a requirement that responding coercion must be limited in intensity and magnitude to what is reasonably necessary to promptly secure the permissible objectives of defense. Emphatically, proportionality in *jus ad bellum* is not simply *tit-for-tat* application of equivalent force, such as ten tanks to respond to an attack from ten tanks, or *tit-for-tat* measurement of damages. Indeed, military doctrine calls for application of overwhelming force and history shows that failure to do so frequently results in much higher casualties on all sides.[10] As McDougal and Feliciano write in their seminal work on use of force law:

> [T]he requirements of necessity and proportionality ... can ultimately be subjected only to that most comprehensive and fundamental test of all law, reasonableness in a particular context. What remains to be stressed is that reasonableness in a particular context does not mean arbitrariness in decision but in fact its exact opposite, the disciplined ascription of policy import to varying factors in appraising their operation and functional significance for community goals in given instances of coercion.[11]

Myres S. McDougal & Florentino P. Feliciano, *Complementary Prescriptions on Permissible and Nonpermissible Coercion*

in Law and Minimum World Public Order 123, 126, 129–30 (1961)
[hereinafter McDougal & Feliciano]

States traditionally have claimed and reciprocally acknowledged a large competence to protect themselves by countering coercion with coercion. The United Nations Charter explicitly mentions and preserves this permission to resort to force in response to

---

Moore ed.) (1974). Humanitarian intervention is not the same as the "right of protection," which is limited to United Nations authorized use of force, as in the recent action in Libya.

    10. Examples of failure to effectively respond with adequate force or effective strategy necessary promptly to secure the permissible objectives of defense, with resulting higher casualties, include the limited defensive responses from the United States in the Vietnam War and Israel in the Second Lebanon War.

    11. Myres S. McDougal & Florentino P. Feliciano, Law and Minimum World Public Order: The Legal Regulation of International Coercion 242 (1961).

unauthorized coercion, describes it as an "inherent right," and recognizes that permissible coercion may be exercised by the target state individually, or by a collectivity of states, without prior authorization from the organized community (although, of course, subject to its subsequent appraisal)....

....

The Basic Postulate of Peaceful Change

The fundamental policies embodied and projected in these prescriptions are, as indicated, complementary. In formulating, interpreting, and applying the prohibition of impermissible coercion, authoritative decision-makers of the world community attempt to regulate conflicting claims by states, on the one hand, to *effect* changes, and, on the other, to *avoid* changes in the patterns of power and other value allocation among the various nation-states. The decision-makers seek to prevent coercive and violent unilateral modification and reconstruction of value patterns and, simultaneously, to encourage recourse to nonviolent, non-coercive methods of change and adjustment. This policy is instinct with a community recognition that coercion of provocative intensity and violence are not appropriate instruments for asserting and implementing claims to a reallocation of values; commonly intense coercive and violent unilateral redistribution of values in the world arena not only wastefully entails the expenditure of values for the destruction of values but also generates further value expenditure and destruction in the shape of a countering response. The basic community policy might, therefore, simply be generalized in terms of a demand for elemental public order and for the preservation of basic human values in the course of international change. In permitting, on the other hand, certain coercion as lawful authoritative decision-makers seek to utilize coercion, under appropriate conditions, for the more effective securing of such minimum public order by authorizing community enforcement action and, in deference to the still poor degree of organization obtaining in the world arena, by conceding individual and group defense against breaches of public order. The assumption which underlies the permission of lawful coercion is, like that which underlies the prohibition of unlawful coercion, not that the value distribution map and the particular configuration of the international arena existent at any given time should be immunized from change but that the common interest in minimizing the destruction of values dictates that they should not be reconstructed through intense coercion or violence.[12]

Defining Unlawful Use of Force (the Definition of Aggression)

McDougal & Feliciano

at 143–48

The Debate about Definitions

The decision of the framers of the United Nations Charter to leave such terms as "threat to the peace," "breach of the peace," and "act of aggression" ambiguous and comprehensive was a deliberate one. In recent years, however, the failure of the optimistic hopes for great power cooperation and intensifying expectations of violence have caused renewed agitation

---

12. *See generally* on the McDougal-Lasswell approach or "Yale approach," John Norton Moore, *Prolegomenon to the Jurisprudence of Myres McDougal and Harold Lasswell*, 54 Va. L. Rev. 662 (1968); Frederick Samson Tipson, *The Lasswell-McDougal Enterprise: Toward a World Public Order of Human Dignity*, 14 Va. J. Int'l L. 535 (1974).

for the clarification and elaboration of basic concepts. The continuing debates today, like those within the League of Nations, have centered principally on the question of "defining aggression." Unfortunately, the efforts of the First and Sixth Committees, the political and legal committees, of the General Assembly, the International Law Commission, and the 1953 and 1956 Special Committees on Defining Aggression to formulate a generally acceptable "definition of aggression" have not been blessed with conspicuous success. Representatives of nation-states engaged in the enterprise of defining aggression conceive of too many implications, real and unreal, for national security to permit much consensus either on any particular proposed verbalization of the conception of aggression or even on the utility of attempts at definition.

The principal formulations proposed have generally assumed one or the other, or a combination, of two [applied] forms. The first consists of a more or less lengthy catalogue of stereotypes of [aggressiveness]. The formulation vigorously propounded by the Soviet Union—a formulation which grew from the five-item closed list of overt military acts incorporated in the 1933 London Conventions for the Definition of Aggression to an open-ended fifteen-item inventory of acts of military, "indirect," "economic," and "ideological" aggression in 1956—is perhaps the best-known species of this genus of definitions. The point of such an inventory is that the state "which first commits" one of the listed acts is to be declared the aggressor. More distinctively, the Soviet formulation includes a list of negative criteria, of acts which are not to be characterized as aggression and internal conditions which do not justify the commission of any act catalogued as aggressive. The most basic defect of the Soviet and other comparable definitions is an overemphasis on material acts of coercion and on a mechanistic conception of priority; concomitantly, they fail to take into account other factors which rationally are equally relevant, factors such as the nature of the objectives of the initiating and responding participants and the character or intensity of the coercion applied.

The second major type of definition exhibits a different approach which rejects the technique of specific enumeration and seeks instead the construction of a broad and general formula that would comprehend all possible instances of aggression. Perhaps the broadest of these formulas was that submitted by Sr. Alfaro to the International Law Commission:

> Aggression is the threat or use of force by a State or Government against another State, in any manner, whatever the weapons employed and whether openly or otherwise for any reason or for any purpose other than individual or collective self-defense or in pursuance of a decision or recommendation by a competent organ of the United Nations [quoting UN Doc. No. A/CN.4/L.31, at 27].

This formulation emphasizes the complementarity of aggression on the one hand and self-defense and collective peace enforcement on the other. It is, however, little more than a posing, in highest level abstraction, of the general problem involved, and offers no index for the guidance of decision-makers who must apply it in specific cases....

    ....

A third type of definition, the so-called "mixed" definition, seeks to combine both the enumerative and "broad formula" approaches by appending an illustrative but nonexhaustive list of specific examples of aggression to a relatively abstract statement of general policy. Although the facile objection has been raised that such "mixed" definitions would only tend to cumulate the difficulties that the catalogue and abstract types of definition have individually presented, the great majority of states that support the formulation of *some* definition have favored the "mixed" kind as a possible *via media*. The draft definition submitted by Iran and Panama at the ninth session of the General Assembly is representative:

1. Aggression is the use of armed force by a State against another State for any purpose other than the exercise of the inherent right of individual or collective self-defense or in pursuance of a decision or recommendation of a competent organ of the United Nations.

2. In accordance with the foregoing definition, in addition to any other acts which such international bodies as may be called upon to determine the aggressor may declare to constitute aggression, the following are acts of aggression in all cases:

(a) Invasion by the armed forces of a State or territory belonging to another State or under the effective jurisdiction of another State;

(b) Armed attack against the territory, population or land, sea or air forces of a State by the land, sea or air forces of another State;

(c) Blockade of the coast or ports or any other part of the territory of a State by the land, sea or air forces of another State;

(d) The organization, or the encouragement of the organization, by a State, of armed bands within its territory or any other territory for incursions into the territory of another State, or the toleration of the organization of such bands in its own territory, or the toleration of the use by such armed bands of its territory as a base of operations or as a point of departure for incursions into the territory of another State, as well as direct participation in or support of such incursions [quoting Report of the 1956 Special Committee 31].

"Definition of Aggression" Resolution[13]

General Assembly of the United Nations, Dec. 14, 1974
G.A. Res. 3314, UN GAOR, 29th Sess.,
Supp. No. 31, at 142, UN Doc. A/9631 (1974)

The General Assembly,

. . . .

Deeply convinced that the adoption of the Definition of Aggression would contribute to the strengthening of international peace and security,

1. *Approves* the Definition of Aggression, the text of which is annexed to the present resolution;

. . . .

3. *Calls upon* all States to refrain from all acts of aggression and other uses of force contrary to the Charter of the United Nations and the Declaration on Principles of International Law concerning Friendly Relations and Co-operation among States in accordance with the Charter of the United Nations [G.A. Res. 2625, UN GAOR, 25th Sess., Supp. No. 28, at 121, UN Doc. A/8028 (1970).];

4. *Calls the attention* of the Security Council to the Definition of Aggression, as set out below, and recommends that it should, as appropriate, take account of that Definition as guidance in determining, in accordance with the Charter, the existence of an act of aggression.

---

13. Note that this resolution, after the Charter, seeks to define "aggression" and not "armed attack."

ANNEX
Definition of Aggression

The General Assembly,

....

Recalling that the Security Council, in accordance with Article 39 of the Charter of the United Nations, shall determine the existence of any threat to the peace, breach of the peace or act of aggression and shall make recommendations, or decide what measures shall be taken in accordance with Articles 41 and 42, to maintain or restore international peace and security,

....

Bearing in mind that nothing in this Definition shall be interpreted as in any way affecting the scope of the provisions of the Charter with respect to the functions and powers of the organs of the United Nations,

....

Believing that, although the question whether an act of aggression has been committed must be considered in the light of all the circumstances of each particular case, it is nevertheless desirable to formulate basic principles as guidance for such determination,

Adopts the following Definition of Aggression:

Article 1

Aggression is the use of armed force by a State against the sovereignty, territorial integrity or political independence of another State, or in any other manner inconsistent with the Charter of the United Nations, as set out in this Definition.

Explanatory note: In this Definition the term "State":

(a)   Is used without prejudice to questions of recognition or to whether a State is a Member of the United Nations;

(b)   Includes the concept of a "group of States" where appropriate.

Article 2

The first use of armed force by a State in contravention of the Charter shall constitute *prima facie* evidence of an act of aggression although the Security Council may, in conformity with the Charter, conclude that a determination that an act of aggression has been committed would not be justified in the light of other relevant circumstances, including the fact that the acts concerned or their consequences are not of sufficient gravity.

Article 3

Any of the following acts, regardless of a declaration of war, shall, subject to and in accordance with the provisions of article 2, qualify as an act of aggression:

(a)   The invasion or attack by the armed forces of a State of the territory of another State, or any military occupation, however temporary, resulting from such invasion or attack, or any annexation by the use of force of the territory of another State or part thereof;

(b)   Bombardment by the armed forces of a State against the territory of another State or the use of any weapons by a State against the territory of another State;

(c)   The blockade of the ports or coasts of a State by the armed forces of another State;

(d)   An attack by the armed forces of a State on the land, sea or air forces, or marine and airfleets of another State;

(e)   The use of armed forces of one State which are within the territory of another State with the agreement of the receiving State, in contravention of the conditions provided for in the agreement or any extension of their presence in such territory beyond the termination of the agreement;

(f)   The action of a State in allowing its territory, which it has placed at the disposal of another State, to be used by that other State for perpetrating an act of aggression against a third State;

(g)   The sending by or on behalf of a State of armed bands, groups, irregulars or mercenaries, which carry out acts of armed force against another State of such gravity as to amount to the acts listed above, or its substantial involvement therein.

Article 4

The acts enumerated above are not exhaustive and the Security Council may determine that other acts constitute aggression under the provisions of the Charter.

Article 5

1. No consideration of whatever nature, whether political, economic, military or otherwise, may serve as a justification for aggression.

2. A war of aggression is a crime against international peace. Aggression gives rise to international responsibility.

3. No territorial acquisition or special advantage resulting from aggression is or shall be recognized as lawful.

Article 6

Nothing in this Definition shall be construed as in any way enlarging or diminishing the scope of the Charter, including its provisions concerning cases in which the use of force is lawful.

Article 7

Nothing in this Definition, and in particular article 3, could in any way prejudice the right of self-determination, freedom and independence, as derived from the Charter, of peoples forcibly deprived of that right and referred to in the Declaration on Principles of International Law concerning Friendly Relations and Co-operation among States in accordance with the Charter of the United Nations, particularly peoples under colonial and racist regimes or other forms of alien domination; nor the right of these peoples to struggle to that end and to seek and receive support, in accordance with the principles of the Charter and in conformity with the above-mentioned Declaration.

Article 8

In their interpretation and application the above provisions are interrelated and each provision should be construed in the context of the other provisions.

———————

In voting for this "definition of aggression," the United States and certain other countries made clear their view that this resolution was intended only for guidance of the Security Council in making a decision under chapter 7 of the Charter.

Questions for Discussion

1. Since the essential condition set out in the English-language version of Article 51 for the right of defense is the occurrence of an armed attack, why should a definition purporting to delimit lawful and unlawful coercion seek to define "aggression" as opposed to "armed attack"? Is this a conceptual holdover from the pre-Charter period? Does defining "aggression" make sense only if confined to assisting the Security Council in a Chapter VII decision? Or is "armed aggression," which is used in the equally authentic French-language text of Article 51, actually the preferable terminology, particularly in a world where covert attacks have become epidemic? The fact that this resolution seeks to define "aggression" rather than "armed attack" would seem to make clear that the relevant issue to be defined is "aggression" and not "armed attack" despite the English language version of Article 51.

2. How does the provision of the resolution's preamble that "the question whether an act of aggression has been committed must be considered in the light of all the circumstances of each particular case" affect the resolution?

3. Does Article 2 of the resolution reject or recognize a right of anticipatory defense, or neither?

4. Can Article 7 of the resolution be squared with the fundamental Charter principle of nonuse of force even on behalf of "just" causes? Is this a limited post-Charter reincarnation of the "just war" theory? Is any legal effect of this article nullified by the concluding phrase "in accordance with the principles of the Charter and in conformity with the above-mentioned Declaration," as well as by Article 6? Does this legally ambiguous article reflect a "struggle-for-law" in the contemporary international system? Who would you suggest were the principal protagonists in the "struggle for law" to legitimate foreign assistance to certain wars of national liberation? Would you expect efforts to brand states as "colonial" or "racist" after this resolution?

5. Is this definition of aggression useful in separating permissible and impermissible coercion? Is it harmful? How would you approach the problem?

McDougal & Feliciano

at 151, 154–55, 167–76, 181–82, 185–92, 196, 217–18

Goal Clarification by Configurative Analysis:
An Alternative Conception

....

[E]very definition of aggression, as of any other legal term, is an abstraction; indeed, one of the principal lessons which contemporary studies on semantics and linguistics offer is that every verbalization, whether definitional or not, is an abstraction from the "unspeakable level of objective events." It does not follow from this, however, that all verbalization about aggression, of whatever order of generalization, is futile and undesirable or creates any unique risk that decision-makers may be misled in particular cases and fail to take some relevant element of the "full context" into appropriate account. Such a risk seems inherent in the application of any general concept or standard of any legal system, if not all processes of human decision-making, authoritative or otherwise. That risk is more likely to be reduced to tolerable levels, and the incidence of rational decisions (in the sense of closer approximation of community-approved value goals) is more apt to be increased, by explicit, sustained, and systematic efforts at clarifying relevant variables and policies affecting decisions about coercion. Certainly it cannot be reduced by an approach that assumes a completely utilitarian attitude toward words, views each specific case of coercion in microcosm with no more than a few terms of highest level of abstraction, and relies upon calculation of momentary expediencies and, as it were, on visceral sensitivity.

. . . .

THE ANALYSIS OF ALLEGED INITIATING COERCION

We turn now to the mode of analysis we suggest as relevant for inquiring into contextual factors that influence decisions about the lawfulness of coercion. The order in which we proceed to analysis of these factors reflects requirements of convenience in exposition rather than a posited hierarchy of intrinsic importance.

PRIORITY IN THE EXERCISE OF SUBSTANTIAL COERCION

There has been much discussion in the United Nations committees that have sought to define aggression of a purported ... "principle of the initial act." This discussion has, however, been characterized in large degree by misdirection; it has focused too much upon a reference to the chronological priority of some single, "precisely defined," physical act, divorced from the subjectivities of attack or defense accompanying the act. Much of the argument has centered about the "principle of priority" incorporated in the enumerative Soviet draft definition: the stipulation that of two contending participants, that party is the aggressor which first commits any of the acts specifically catalogued as aggressive acts. Some have urged that this particular "priority principle" furnishes the only available criterion for distinguishing a prohibited act of aggression from permissible self-defense. "None of the acts mentioned in the USSR draft resolution," the Ukrainian SSR delegate explained, "amounted to aggression *per se*. Two acts might be the same in the military sense yet from the legal point of view, one would be an act of aggression and the second legitimate retaliation [*sic*]. Aggression would inevitably be the first act, which induced or provoked the second." From an antithetical perspective, the representative of the United Kingdom asserted with equal confidence that "the question of which State was 'first' to commit a certain act was basically irrelevant and that everything depended essentially upon the circumstances." More recently, it has been appropriately emphasized that the "tasks of evaluation" involved in a determination of aggression "simply cannot be performed by limiting consideration to the occurrence of a precisely defined act, at a particular moment, in insulation from the broader context of the relations of the States concerned."

The factor of priority cannot lightly be dismissed as wholly irrelevant to judgments about permissibility or impermissibility of coercion. A conception of priority is implicit in the very notion of impermissible coercion; what community policy seeks to prohibit is resort to certain coercion, not responding coercion in necessary protection of values. Completely to reject the relevance of priority is thus, in substance, to reject the fundamental community policy of limiting permissible change to change by peaceful procedures only. It is, on the other hand, equally obvious that to assign exclusive relevance to a "principle of priority" whose reference is limited to the timing of a particular "precisely defined" operation indexed, as in the Soviet list, as aggressive, is hardly more rationally designed to secure the fundamental community policies at stake; such a unifactor test ignores the significance of subjectivities or objectives of coercion which must be considered when ascertaining responsibility for breaches of basic policy....

THE CHARACTERISTICS OF PARTICIPANTS

In considering the relevance of the character and constitution of participants for determining the lawfulness or unlawfulness of coercion, it is necessary to recall that the nation-state is still the major type of participant in world processes of coercion and ordinarily commands control of armed forces, the power base which permits the application of the most intense degree of coercion. The relative size and power of a state which is alleged to have unlawfully initiated coercion, that is, its size and power in relation to that of its opponent, may serve as indices of the real, as distinguished from the proclaimed, objectives of each participant, of the intensity of coercion exercised by each (particularly before the stage of open military violence is reached), of the realism of asserted expectations that violence is necessary for protection, and hence of the probable *situs* of responsibility. The more conspicuous the disparity in relative fighting capability, appraised in terms of both forces-in-being and potential for war, the more easily inferences of responsibility may be drawn. Both common sense and the history of such wars as the Italo-Abyssinian war, the Sino-Japanese conflicts of 1931 and 1937, and the Soviet-Finnish war of 1939 suggest that, in the ordinary course of events, a state with a low level of fighting capability is not likely to initiate highly intense coercion against a much more powerful state. A plea of self-defense has a characteristically implausible ring when uttered by a great power against a weak or disorganized or primitive state.

In weighing relative power and strength, account must be taken of the capabilities not only of the immediately contending participants but also of those defined by each participant as its allies or potential allies. The external structure of identifications that each participant projects, indeed the very configuration of the world arena, may thus be relevant. In the current world, however, the significance of an appraisal of relative capability may depend upon the extent to which the patterns of power move toward diversification rather than toward a simple, rigid bipolarity. Inquiry into such identification structures may yield a more direct indication of the character of the objectives or purposes of the respective participants by revealing the kind of world public order each demands, whether it be one which requires the subordination or destruction of independent power centers or one which seeks peaceful coordination and cooperation in a pluralistic arena.

The nature of the internal structures of authority and control in each of the contending states may also suggest relevant probabilities. A distinguished scholar has submitted that "among factors which appear to influence the war-likeness of a state are the degrees of constitutionalism, federalism, division of powers and democracy established in its political constitution." The degree to which both authoritative and effective power are shared by several organs of government and the extent to which a system of power-balancing is maintained within a state, as well as the character and composition of the ruling elite and of predominating symbols, appear in the present world to have some impact on the capacity and likelihood of a state undertaking arbitrarily to resort to force and violence. It is significant that the states which have been explicitly determined by an international organization or tribunal to have unlawfully resorted to force and violence were commonly totalitarian in internal structure: Fascist Italy, pre-war Japan, Soviet Russia, Nazi Germany, North Korea, and the People's Republic of China. Again, it does not seem unreasonable to suppose that the internal characteristics of a state, like its external identifications, reflect in certain measure the kind of public order it projects in the international arena and hence the nature of the objectives that motivate it.

THE NATURE OF PARTICIPANTS' OBJECTIVES

In the United Nations committees that sought to define aggression, certain delegations contended that the objectives or purposes or "subjective motives" of a participant charged with having unlawfully initiated coercion were not to be considered in determining the lawfulness of coercion. This view was urged principally in connection with the supposed merits of the enumerative Soviet definition. "The Soviet draft," the representative of Roumania stated, "rightly excluded the subjective element, *animo aggressionis*. The aggressor would, of course, always maintain that whatever his actions, his intention had not been to attack but merely to defend himself or to forestall aggression. Hence no opportunity should be given to the aggressor to plead alleged good intentions." A comparable view was submitted by the Iranian delegate who objected to the inclusion of a reference to "territorial integrity and political independence" in a joint Iran-Panama draft. He argued that this language introduced a "subjective element" and that "the effect of the act, rather than the intention of the aggressor, should be the decisive factor in determining aggression...."

The objectives or subjectivities of participants (or, more precisely, of the top effective decision-makers in participating states) cannot, as suggested earlier, be wholly disregarded in characterizing coercion as impermissible. Fundamental community policy does not seek to prohibit all coercion, nor even all highly intense coercion; it explicitly permits coercion for certain purposes, such as that necessary to protect certain indispensable values and to enforce certain community decisions. A participant should not, of course, be allowed to escape responsibility by simply asserting some secret legitimate intention that is belied by any reasonable construction of its acts. This is only to say that proclaimed objectives must be distinguished from objectives sought in fact, and that verbal proclamations alone do not offer conclusive indications of the purposes actually pursued. In the exercise of coercion, as in the making of agreements, the purposes or subjectivities of a participant must be "objectively" ascertained; they are, it may again be emphasized, appropriately inferred from acts and the effects of acts, the totality of a participant's operations, verbal and nonverbal, considered in detailed context. From this perspective, the dichotomy posed by the representative of Iran between the "effect of the act" and the "intention of the [actor]" or, as formulated by Dr. Pompe, between the "purport of the act" and the "purpose of the actor," appears unreal. To speak of the "purport of the act" apart from the purpose of flesh and blood actors is like, in Professor Williams' figure, "speaking of the grin without the Cheshire cat." [quoting Glanville Williams, *Language and the Law*, 61 L.Q. Rev. 71, 83 (1945)].

.....

A major category clearly discernible in the prescriptions of the Charter is that of extension or conservation; a participant charged with unlawfully initiating coercion may be seeking to expand its value resources by attacking and acquiring values held by its opponent or to conserve and maintain its own values against acquisition by its opponent. Characterizing objectives in these terms is obviously required by the fundamental policy of the community respecting permissible modes of change. International change in an arena exhibiting in high degree "position scarcity" and "resource scarcity" realistically involves a reallocation of values among the participants concerned, and reallocation commonly means expansion for the one and diminution for the other. It is perhaps just as obvious that this distinction, to be meaningful in determination of lawfulness, must be considered in conjunction with both the relative consequentiality of the values involved and the degree of coercion employed to acquire or conserve those same values.

In partial reiteration, for the overriding purpose of securing public order in its most elementary sense, basic community policy seeks to protect from destructive unilateral re-construction those patterns of value allocation that actually exist and manifest at least a minimum degree of stability. Such patterns need not entirely coincide with those which other, less critical, policies and prescriptions, or perspectives of "justice and equity," may require. It is not a theme of an international law of human dignity that our inherited dis-tribution of values among peoples accords completely with humanity's noblest conceptions of justice, nor is it an expectation of such an international law that no future wrongs against peoples will be done. The dominant theme is only that both a more just distribution of values and the revindication of future wrongs must be effected by less primitive methods than the destruction of peoples and resources. While in particular cases it may be difficult to draw lines between conservation and revindication, between defense and redress, it is necessary to continue an attempt to make a practical judgment because there is in their impact upon policy a crucial difference, a difference arising from the interposition of the community's elemental interest in minimum order.

. . . .

In a world marked by deep, continuing conflict among differing conceptions or systems of world public order, it is no longer revolutionary to suggest that the kind of public order demanded by a participant charged with unlawful coercion is a factor relevant to a decision on permissibility. The suggestion amounts to this: that decision-makers rationally should take account of the probable effects of various alternative decisions upon the values of the system of world order to which they are committed. There is growing recognition that conflict between competing conceptions or demanded systems in fact deeply affects both the prescription and application of policy on recourse to coercion, as on other problems. Clarification of fundamental policy about permissible and impermissible coercion requires clarification of the permissible and impermissible objectives of coercion. Differing conceptions of world order which incorporate different perspectives about law, human nature, and human society, and appropriate patterns for the production and sharing of values, define differently the objectives or occasions that, in terms of each system, legitimate the use of coercion and violence. The Soviet doctrine of "just" and "unjust" war offers an important illustration:

> (a) *Just* wars, wars that are not wars of conquest but wars of liberation, waged to defend the people from foreign attack and from attempts to enslave them, or to liberate the people from capitalist slavery, or lastly, to liberate colonies and dependent countries from the yoke of imperialism; and

> (b) *Unjust* wars, wars of conquest, waged to conquer and enslave foreign countries and foreign nations [quoting History of the Communist Party of the Soviet Union (Bolsheviks) Short Course 167–68 (Commission of the Central Committee of the C.P.S.U. [B] ed., 1939)].

With such differences as to the legitimate purposes of coercion and violence existing, universal consensus on any clarification of policy must seem unlikely except, perhaps, on the level of rhetoric of a sufficiently high order of generality. Furthermore, whatever the consensus achieved on an abstract verbal formulation, differences in specific interpretation and application are to be expected. In point of fact, even a cursory review of the records of the General Assembly and Security Council and of the United Nations committees on defining aggression reveals that both the draft definitions of aggression— in particular, the types of specific indices of aggression and of non-exculpating circum- stances—and the specific interpretations of broad prescription in particular cases that have been urged by states projecting totalitarian systems of world order, are constantly designed to enhance the strategies, and promote movement toward the goal values of their systems. In these circumstances, for decision-makers committed to a system of world order that seeks to honor human dignity either to dismiss as totally irrelevant the probable impact of possible alternative resolutions upon the values embodied in such system, or else to assume a nonexistent universality, may be only to engage in traumatic self-delusion. Even in today's extreme crisis, however, we do not recommend that expansion by violence be held permissible for the half-world or regions of states adhering to non-totalitarian systems of public order. Any violent expansion involves a destruction of values that is, we submit, incompatible with the overriding conception of human dignity.

Any clarification of permissible and impermissible purposes of coercion must obviously be sustained by a certain minimum community of interest and sharing of values. In last resort, all law must depend for its efficacy upon the common interest and shared values of the participants in the arena to be regulated. From the perspective of proclaimed doctrine—postulating an implacable hostility and irreconcilable conflict between the Communist world and the Western "bourgeois, capitalist" world, and explicitly envisaging the eventual liquidation of the latter at the most economic speed—a serious question arises whether the necessary community of values remains between leaders and peoples committed to such a doctrine and other peoples. From the more realistic perspective of the conditions that must eventually affect specific demand, however, there may be discernible at least an immediate mutual interest in continued survival. The fundamental import of the conditions of power which, in the contemporary global arena, manifest themselves in a precarious equilibrium of capacity for inflicting fearful destruction, is that the proponents of one system cannot destroy by violence the proponents of the other without bringing their own world to enduring radioactive ruin. As peoples dedicated to freedom maintain this last and narrow common ground, they may cherish the hope that others will recognize such common ground and that it may slowly be widened to include sharing of other values sufficient to sustain a common policy against coercion.

THE MODALITIES OF COERCION

In considering the relevance of the methods used by a participant who allegedly has initiated unlawful coercion, it may be recalled that, while armed force has for centuries been the classical instrumentality of coercion between states and still remains the ultimate means of applying the most intense coercion, it is today a commonplace that all instruments of policy—military, ideological, economic, and political—can be and are being used to achieve varying degrees of coercive effect. The burden of the experience of recent decades is that many objectives for which armed force was used in an earlier day may now frequently be realized, or at least substantially facilitated, by highly developed nonmilitary techniques of coercion without open violence. Of principal importance in this connection are the exercises of coercion emphasizing political or ideological instruments, with military instruments in a muted and background role, commonly referred to as "indirect aggression" and frequently described as more dangerous than the "direct" or military type of aggression. A chief characteristic of "indirect aggression" appears to be the vicarious commission of hostile acts by the aggressor state through the medium of third-party groups located within the target state and composed either of foreigners or nationals of the target ostensibly acting on their own initiative. The hostile acts may include the giving of aid and support and, frequently, strategic and tactical direction to rebellious internal groups. The classic postwar case is that of the Greek Communist guerrillas to whom Albania, Bulgaria, Yugoslavia, and Roumania furnished both open military aid and the use of their territory as a base for military operations against the constitutional Greek Government and also as a safe refuge in tactical defeat. The assistance given to internal groups may frequently assume more covert and subtle forms including the training, exportation, and financing of leaders and specialists in subversion, sabotage, infiltration, fomentation of civil violence, and *coups d'etat*. "Indirect aggression," disguised as a purely domestic change, presents peculiar difficulties for external decision-makers. The organized community may suddenly be confronted with a *fait accompli*, as in the case of Czechoslovakia in 1948, which may leave as an alternative to passive acquiescence only the improbable prospect of collective coercion against the victim state in an effort to dislodge the new revolutionary elite. Persuasive evidence of common fear and expectations of the effectiveness of "indirect aggression" may be found not only in the repeated proposals specifically to include condemnation of its use in a definition of aggression but also in declarations of the United Nations General Assembly. In the "Peace through Deeds" Resolution, the General Assembly did "solemnly reaffirm" that "whatever the weapons used, any aggression, whether committed openly, or by fomenting civil strife in the interests of a foreign Power, or otherwise, is the gravest of all crimes against peace and security throughout the world." In a world exhibiting in ever increasing numbers military weapons of awesome capability for destruction and in which the possibility of avoiding or limiting the use of such weapons once violence breaks out remains problematical, there is growing awareness that recourse to military force even of the "conventional" type may impose unacceptable risks of grievously exorbitant costs. Consequently, increasingly frequent resort to methods of "indirect aggression" may be anticipated since they provide more economical means of achieving unlawful objectives. The most serious problem confronting adherents to systems of world order which seek to honor freedom may thus be to devise appropriate procedures for identifying and countering unlawful attack disguised as internal change.

....

Awareness of the potentialities of all instruments of coercion may indicate that what is of particular importance for decision-makers is not the specific modality or even combinations of modalities employed, considered in typological abstraction, but rather the level and scope of intensity achieved by the employment of any one or more modalities in whatever combination or sequence. The relevance of the kinds of instruments utilized by a participant is rather limited: it lies primarily in the rough and ready indication—precise quantification not presently being practicable—which it affords, first, of the level of coercion being applied, second (in equally gross terms), of the relative proportionality of the response in coercion, and, third (though indirectly), of the nature and comprehensiveness of the participant's subjectivities.

....

THE REQUIREMENTS OF SELF-DEFENSE: NECESSITY AND PROPORTIONALITY

These preliminary distinctions make it possible now to focus more sharply upon the class of claims with which we are immediately concerned—claims to use highly intense coercion in defense against what is claimed to be impermissible initiating coercion. The principal requirements which the "customary law" of self-defense makes prerequisite to the lawful assertion of these claims are commonly summarized in terms of necessity and proportionality. For the protection of the general community against extravagant claims, the standard of required necessity has been habitually cast in language so abstractly restrictive as almost, if read literally, to impose paralysis. Such is the clear import of the classical peroration of Secretary of State Webster in the *Caroline* case—that there must be shown a "necessity of self-defense, instant, overwhelming, leaving no choice of means and no moment for deliberation." The requirement of proportionality which, as we shall develop below, is but another application of the principle of economy in coercion, is frequently expressed in equally abstract terms. One example is M. de Brouckère's formulation: "Legitimate defense implies the adoption of measures proportionate to the seriousness of the attack and justified by the imminence of the danger." There is, however, increasing recognition that the requirements of necessity and proportionality as ancillary prescriptions (in slightly lower-order generalization) of the basic community policy prohibiting change by violence, can ultimately be subjected only to that most comprehensive and fundamental test of all law, reasonableness in particular context. What remains to be stressed is that reasonableness in particular context does not mean arbitrariness in decision but in fact its exact opposite, the disciplined ascription of policy import to varying factors in appraising their operational and functional significance for community goals in given instances of coercion.

Questions for Discussion

1. Do you find this "configurative map" of the issues involved in separating permissible from impermissible coercion more helpful than the definitial approach, on the one hand, or the insistence solely on ad hoc determination, on the other? Is it more consistent with the teachings of the legal realists about legal process?

2. Could such an approach be summarized by identification and discussion of a wide variety of use-of-force claims that tend to frequently recur? Did the "just war" theorists understand some of these issues in what is really a complex matrix of use-of-force issues?

3. Does some variant of a configurative map for determining whether coercion is used for value conservation or value extension provide greater guidance in implementing the fundamental Charter principle than the General Assembly Definition of Aggression?

4. How would you recommend that the illegal use of force (aggression) be defined for purposes of the new International Criminal Court? Does the very complexity of the problem suggest that this issue should be left for Security Council determination?

5. Should any definition of *jus ad bellum* focus on unlawful use of force, lawful use of force, or both? Might it be simpler to define lawful uses of force, as previously set out in this Chapter, as opposed to defining only unlawful uses of force through the "who did what to whom first" approach of the General Assembly definition of aggression?

Necessity and Proportionality

McDougal & Feliciano
at 229, 231–44

CONDITIONS AND THE EXPECTATION OF NECESSITY

....

The structure of traditional prescription has established a standard of justifying necessity commonly referred to in exacting terms. A high degree of necessity—a "great and immediate" necessity, "direct and immediate," "compelling and instant"—was prerequisite to a characterization of coercion as "legitimate self-defense." Necessity that assumed the shape of an actual and current application of violence presented little difficulty. It was of course the purpose of high requirements of necessity to contain and restrict the assertion of claims to apply pre-emptive violence, that is when the necessity pleaded consisted of alleged expectations of an attack which had yet actually to erupt. In the *Caroline* case, it will be recalled, the British claim with which Secretary of State Webster was confronted was an assertion of anticipatory defense. There is a whole continuum of degrees of imminence or remoteness in future time, from the most imminent to the most remote, which, in the expectations of the claimant of self-defense, may characterize an expected attack. Decision-makers sought to limit lawful anticipatory defense by projecting a customary requirement that the expected attack exhibit so high a degree of imminence as to preclude effective resort by the intended victim to non-violent modalities of response.

One illustration of the application of the customary-law standard of necessity for anticipatory defense is offered in the judgment of the International Military Tribunal for the Far East in respect of the war waged by Japan against the Netherlands. Japan contended that "inasmuch as the Netherlands took the initiative in declaring war on Japan, the war which followed [could] not be described as a war of aggression by Japan." The Netherlands declared war on Japan on December 8, 1941, before the actual invasion of the Netherlands East Indies by Japanese troops and before the issuance of the Japanese declaration of war against the Netherlands, both of which took place on January 11, 1942. The evidence showed, however, that as early as November 5, 1941, the Imperial General Headquarters had issued to the Japanese Navy operational orders for the attacks upon the Netherlands East Indies, as well as the Philippines and British Malaya, and that on December 1, 1941, an Imperial Conference had formally decided that Japan would "open hostilities against the United States, Great Britain and the Netherlands." The Tribunal held that the Netherlands, "being fully apprised of the *imminence* of the attack," had declared war against Japan "in self defense." Similarly, the International Military Tribunal at Nuremberg, in rejecting a defense argument that the German invasion of Norway was "preventive" in character and designed to anticipate an Allied landing in Norway, pointed out that the German plans for invasion were not in fact made to forestall an "*imminent*" Allied landing, and that, at best, such plans could only prevent an Allied occupation "at some future time." The documentary evidence submitted to the Tribunal did indicate that there was a "definite" Allied plan to occupy harbors and airports in Norway. The Tribunal found, however, that the expectations of Germany at the time of launching the invasion did not as a matter of fact include a belief that Britain was about to land troops in Norway.

... It is against the background of the high degree of necessity required in traditional prescription that Article 51 of the United Nations Charter should be considered.... There has been considerable contention about the impact of this article upon the standard of required necessity projected in the customary law of self-defense. Some scholars have taken the view that Article 51 demands an even higher degree of necessity than customary law for the characterization of coercion as permissible defense, that it limits justifying necessity to an "armed attack" as distinguished both from an expected attack of whatever degree of imminence and from applications of nonmilitary types of intense coercion, and that it absolutely forbids any anticipatory self-defense. For instance, Professor Kunz, insisting that Article 51 provides a "clear and unambiguous text," wrote, in characteristic exegesis:

> [F]or this right [of self-defense under Article 51] does not exist against any form of aggression which does not constitute "armed attack." Secondly, this term means something that has taken place. Article 51 prohibits "preventive war." The "threat of aggression" does not justify self-defense under Article 51. Now in municipal law self-defense is justified against an actual danger, but it is sufficient that the danger is *imminent*. The "imminent" armed attack does not suffice under Article 51 [quoting Josef L. Kunz, *Individual and Collective Self-Defense in Article 51 of the Charter of the United Nations*, 41 AM. J. INT'L L. 872, 878 (1947)].

Most recently, Dr. Ninčić has argued from the canon *exceptiones sunt strictissimae interpretationis* that:

> [T]his means that nothing less than an armed attack shall constitute an *act-condition* for the exercise of the right of self-defense within the meaning of Article

51 (i.e., "subversion" and … "ideological" or "economic aggression" does not warrant armed action on the basis of Article 51). It further stipulates that *the armed attack must precede the exercise of the right of self-defense*, that only an armed attack which has actually materialized, which has "occurred" shall warrant a resort to self-defense. This clearly and explicitly rules out the permissibility of any "anticipatory" exercise of the right of self-defense, i.e., resort to armed force "in anticipation of an armed attack" [quoting Reply from Dr. Ninčić, *in* Georg Schwarzenberger, Report on Some Aspects of the Principal of Self-Defence in the Charter of the United Nations and the Topics Covered by the Dubrovnik Resolution 69 (1958)].

The major difficulties with this reading of what appears to be an inept piece of draftsmanship are twofold. In the first place, neither Article 51 nor any other word formula can have, apart from context, any single "clear and unambiguous" or "popular, natural and ordinary" meaning that predetermines decision in infinitely varying particular controversies. The task of treaty interpretation, especially the interpretation of constitutional documents devised, as was the United Nations Charter, for the developing future, is not one of discovering and extracting from isolated words some mystical pre-existent, reified meaning but rather one of giving that meaning to both words and acts, in total context, which is required by the principal, general purposes and demands projected by the parties to the agreement. For determining these major purposes and demands, a rational process of interpretation permits recourse to all available indices of shared expectation, including, in particular, that which Professor Kunz casually de-emphasized, the preparatory work on the agreement. Such a process of interpretation would, moreover, seek to bring within the attention frame of the interpreter and applier not just one element of a context suggested by one rule or principle of interpretation, such as that upon which Dr. Ninčić relied, but all the relevant variable factors of a particular context. It is of common record in the preparatory work on the Charter that Article 51 was not drafted for the purpose of deliberately narrowing the customary-law permission of self-defense against a current or imminent unlawful attack by raising the required degree of necessity. The moving purpose was, rather, to accommodate regional security organizations (most specifically the Inter-American system envisioned by the Act of Chapultepec) within the Charter's scheme of centralized, global collective security, and to preserve the functioning of these regional systems from the frustrations of vetoes cast in the Security Council. Further, in the process of formulating the prohibition of unilateral coercion contained in Article 2(4), it was made quite clear at San Francisco that the traditional permission of self-defense was not intended to be abridged and attenuated but, on the contrary, to be reserved and maintained. Committee 1/I stressed in its report, which was approved by both Commission I and the Plenary Conference, that "The unilateral use of force or similar coercive measures is not authorized or admitted. The use of arms in legitimate self defense remains admitted and unimpaired."

More comprehensively considered, the principle of restrictive interpretation, of which *exceptiones sunt strictissimae interpretationis* is but one variant, may, with at least equal cogency, be invoked against the position Dr. Ninčić has taken. "Legitimate self-defense," encompassing anticipatory defense, has long been honored in traditional authoritative myth as one of the fundamental "rights of sovereign states." In accordance with one variant of the principle of restrictive interpretation, limitations or derogations from sovereign competence are not lightly to be assumed. The view urged by Ninčić proceeds from the hypothesis that self-defense is an "exception" whose recognition tends to nullify the "general rule" of prohibition of coercion and which must therefore be confined within the narrowest of limits. Even apart from the essential complementarity of prohibited and permissible coercion to which we have so very often adverted, the permission of self-defense embodied in customary prescription cannot of itself, if appropriately applied, render ineffective or illusive either the fundamental community policy against change by destructive coercion projected in the Charter, or the peace-maintaining functions of the United Nations. As noted above, customary prescription has always required a high degree of necessity—specifically, in the case of an anticipated attack, a high degree of imminence—to support the lawfulness of intense responding coercion. One index of the required condition of necessity is precisely the degree of opportunity for effective recourse to nonviolent modes of response and adjustment, including invocation of the collective conciliation functions of the United Nations. Furthermore, permitting defense against an imminently expected attack does not, any more than permitting defense against an actual current attack, impair or dilute the "authority and responsibility" of the organized community "to maintain or restore international peace and security." Whether the events that precipitate the claim of self-defense constitute an actual, current attack or an imminently impending attack, the claim remains subject to the reviewing authority of the organized community. Finally, the continuing refusal of most of the members of the United Nations to accept the Soviet or Litvinov-Politis type of definition of aggression appears significant. If the members did concur in the narrow construction of Article 51, if their demands and expectations were that the justifying conditions of necessity for self-defense should be and have been limited to an "armed attack" and that responding coercion must in all circumstances be postponed until unlawful coercion has exploded into destructive violence, then the Soviet first-shot test of aggression would have been embraced, it might be supposed, as a matter of course.

The second major difficulty with a narrow reading of Article 51 is that it requires a serious underestimation of the potentialities both of the newer military weapons systems and of the contemporary techniques of nonmilitary coercion. If, in scholarly interpretation of authoritative myth, any operational reference is seriously intended to be made to realistically expected practice and decision, an attempt to limit permissible defense to that against an actual "armed attack," when increases in the capacity of modern weapons systems for velocity and destruction are reported almost daily in the front pages of newspapers, reflects a surpassing optimism. In these circumstances, "to cut down," Professor Waldock suggests forcefully, "the customary right of self defense beyond even the *Caroline* doctrine does not make sense …" [quoting C.H.M. Waldock, *The Regulation of the Use of Force by Individual States in International Law*, 81 Recueil des Cours 445, 498 (1952)].

. . . .

In particular connection with exercises emphasizing nonmilitary forms of attack, we have suggested that, in many contexts, the use of political, economic, and ideological instrumentalities may indeed result in no more than a modest degree of coercion, a degree which may constitute part of the ordinary coercion implicit in the power and other value processes in the world arena. To say, however, that Article 51 limits the appropriate precipitating event for lawful self-defense to an "*armed* attack" is in effect to suppose that in no possible context can applications of nonmilitary types of coercion (where armed force is kept to a background role) take on efficacy, intensity, and proportions comparable to those of an "armed attack" and thus present an analogous condition of necessity. Apart from the extreme difficulty of establishing realistic factual bases for that supposition, the conclusion places too great a strain upon the single secondary factor of modality—military violence. A rational appraisal of necessity demands much more than simple ascertainment of the modality of the initiating coercion. The expectations which the contending participants create in each other are a function not only of the simple fact that the military instrument has or has not been overtly used but also of the degree and kind of use to which all other instrumentalities of policy are being put. What must be assessed is the cumulative impact of all the means of coercion utilized; policy-oriented analysis must be *configurative* analysis. The kind, intensity, and dimension of political, economic, or ideological pressure applied may, through this analysis, serve in some contexts as relevant indices of the imminence or remoteness of an allegedly expected armed attack.

Effects and the Proportionality of Responding Coercion

We turn, finally, to appraisal of the effects of coercion claimed to be in self-defense. The principal reference here is to the degree of intensity and scope exhibited in this coercion—factors long recognized to be of special relevance in judgments about the lawfulness of particular claims to self-defense. It is primarily in terms of its magnitude and intensity—the consequentiality of its effects—that alleged responding coercion must be examined for its "proportionality." "Proportionality" which, like "necessity," is customarily established as a prerequisite for characterizing coercion as lawful defense, is sometimes described in terms of a required relation between the alleged initiating coercion and the supposed responding coercion: the (quantum of) responding coercion must, in rough approximation, be reasonably related or comparable to the (quantum of) initiating coercion. It is useful to make completely explicit that concealed in this shorthand formulation of the requirement of proportionality are references to both the permissible objectives of self-defense and the condition of necessity that evoked the response in coercion. Proportionality in coercion constitutes a requirement that responding coercion be limited in intensity and magnitude to what is reasonably necessary promptly to secure the permissible objectives of self-defense. For present purposes, these objectives may be most comprehensively generalized as the conserving of important values by compelling the opposing participant to terminate the condition which necessitates responsive coercion. Put a little differently, the objective is to cause the initiating participant to diminish its coercion to the more tolerable levels of "ordinary coercion." This is the import of Secretary of State Webster's somewhat cryptic statement that "nothing unreasonable or excessive [must be done], since the act, justified by the necessity of self-defense, must be limited by that necessity and kept clearly within it." Thus articulated, the principle of proportionality is seen as but one specific form of the more general principle of economy in coercion and as a logical corollary of the fundamental community policy against change by destructive modes. Coercion that is grossly in excess of what, in a particular context, may be reasonably required for conservation of values against a particular attack, or that is obviously irrelevant or unrelated to this purpose, itself constitutes an unlawful initiation of coercive or violent change.

From this perspective, it should be evident that an appropriate appraisal of the magnitude and intensity of an exercise of self-defense for its proportionality—a determination, in other words, of the amount of coercion reasonably necessary in a particular instance for achieving the lawful purpose of self-defense—requires functional reference to all the various factors relating to the opponent's allegedly aggressive coercion as well as to all the other factors relating to the claimant's coercion, which together comprise a detailed context. More particularly, the determination of proportionality is not, as is sometimes suggested, necessarily exhausted by ascertaining the qualitative similarity or dissimilarity of the weapons employed by one and the other contending participant. It has been urged, for instance, that a lawful defense against an attack executed with "conventional" weapons may not utilize "unconventional" or nuclear weapons; the use of nuclear arms, the argument runs, would be a disproportionate and excessive reaction. We have repeatedly indicated that modality may be useful as a quick index to intensity and scope. But, as we have just as frequently suggested, modality is no more than a prima facie rule of thumb which cannot dispense with more detailed inquiry into the consequentiality of coercion, and which must be taken in conjunction with all other relevant variable factors. Thus, in particular respect of the "conventional-nuclear" dichotomy, it would, we suggest, be an extremely hazardous prediction to say (as Dr. Singh appears in effect to be saying) that in no possible set of events will an authorized decision-maker regard the use of nuclear weapons—the "yield" of which, it should be recalled, is subject to control and may vary enormously—as reasonably necessary to stop and turn back an attack initiated with "conventional" weapons. It is perhaps symptomatic that Dr. Singh himself would concede one "possible exception": when the target state, "facing certain defeat, with a view to upholding the law and to prevent the aggressor from becoming victorious, after giving full trial to permissible weapons, uses prohibited nuclear weapons as a last resort against the law-breaker."

The Use of Force Under Regional Arrangements

Regional organizations may play a role in collective defense. In such a case their actions are assessed pursuant to the right of defense. They may, however, in some settings engage in lawful peacekeeping or other actions taken under chapter VIII of the United Nations Charter. The parameters of these actions are discussed earlier in this chapter as the fourth of five lawful bases for use of force under the Charter.

Regional arrangements may also impose procedural or substantive requirements in addition to those of the United Nations Charter. Since the oldest and one of the most important regional arrangements is that of the Organization of American States (OAS), the section below will briefly examine the principal use-of-force provisions of the OAS system.

John Norton Moore, *The Role of Regional Arrangements in the Maintenance of World Order*

in 3 THE FUTURE OF THE INTERNATIONAL LEGAL ORDER: CONFLICT MANAGEMENT
122, 140–62 (Cyril E. Black & Richard A. Falk eds., 1971)

As the United Nations ends its first quarter-century, two flaws in its normative structure have become increasingly apparent. The first and perhaps more important of these is the unresponsiveness of the Charter to the problem of control of foreign intervention in internal conflict. The second is the ambiguity surrounding the role of regional arrangements in the maintenance of world order. Unlike the problem of control of unauthorized intervention, the framers of the Charter were largely aware of the problems in the interrelation of regional arrangements and the United Nations. The clash of competing regional and universal interests, however, resulted in an ambiguous resolution of the issues. That ambiguity has been magnified as the original expectations of an effectively functioning Security Council were shattered on the rocks of the cold war. Today there is general agreement that the United Nations has the ultimate responsibility for the maintenance of international peace and security but there are major uncertainties surrounding the initial exercise of regional jurisdiction, the authority of regional arrangements to initiate coercive action, and where necessary, the procedure for United Nations authorization of regional action.

. . . .

Note

A debate about the meaning of "enforcement action" and the scope of lawful regional use of force was triggered by the 1983 Grenada Mission.[14] During that debate the Legal Adviser of the Department of State sent a letter describing the United States position on regional action in the Grenada Case to Ed Gordon, Chairman of an *Ad Hoc* Committee of the ABA Section on International Law and Practice.

Letter from Davis R. Robinson, Legal Adviser, U.S. Department of State, to Professor Edward Gordon, Reiterating U.S. Legal Position Concerning Grenada (Feb. 10, 1984)

in John Norton Moore, Law and the Grenada Mission 125–28 (1984)

The United States, both before and after the collective action, regarded three well established legal principles as providing a solid legal basis for the action: (1) the lawful governmental authorities of a State may invite the assistance in its territory of military forces of other states or collective organizations in dealing with internal disorder as well as external threats; (2) regional organizations have competence to take measures to maintain international peace and security, consistent with the purpose and principles of the UN and OAS Charters; and (3) the right of States to use force to protect their nationals. These grounds were clearly articulated in testimony of Deputy Secretary of State Kenneth W. Dam before the House Foreign Affairs Committee on November 2, 1983. I would emphasize that the United States has not taken a position as to whether any one of these grounds standing alone would have provided adequate support for the action.

. . . .

The October 21 decision by the members of the Organization of Eastern Caribbean States to take collective action provides further legal support for the U.S. action. Three principal issues have been raised in this regard: (1) Was the action consistent with the terms of the OECS Treaty? (2) Do regional organizations have the capacity to take such actions? (3) Is the OECS a competent regional organization?

With respect to the first of these issues, much of the analysis to date has focused exclusively on the language of Article 8 of the OECS Treaty. Article 8, however, defines the jurisdiction of the Defense and Security Committee of the OECS, a subordinate body under that treaty. The decision to take military action on Grenada was reached by the heads of government of the OECS nations, who — unlike the Defense and Security Committee — have plenary authority under Article 6 of that Treaty. Article 3(2) of the OECS Treaty expressly empowers the heads of government to pursue joint policies in the field of mutual defense and security, and "such other activities calculated to further the purposes of the Organization as the member States may from time to time decide."

---

14. *See generally* John Norton Moore, Law and the Grenada Mission (1984), and, for opposing views, Christopher C. Joyner, *Reflections on the Lawfulness of Invasion*, 78 Am. J. Int'l L. 131 (1984); American Bar Association Section of International Law and Practice, Report of the Committee on Grenada (1984).

It is clear from statements of the OECS Secretariat that all OECS members present at the October 21 meeting of heads of government voted in favor of collective action. The provisions of Article 6 of the OECS Treaty provide that actions may be taken without the presence of a Member State if the absent state later ratifies the decision or abstains from voting. Given the authority of the Governor General discussed above, his request for collective action manifestly constituted ratification on the part of Grenada. Perhaps the most important aspect of the debate over the OECS Treaty is that all members of the OECS regard the action taken as consistent with the treaty. We submit that the views of the members of a regional treaty on questions of treaty interpretation are entitled to a weight greater than those of third-state commentators.

An issue of far greater import for the development of international law is that of the proper scope of competence of regional organizations to act to restore internal order in a member state. This issue requires careful analysis in circumstances where an organization acts on its own initiative, absent the invitation of the lawful authorities of the State concerned. In the case of Grenada, however, this difficult issue ultimately was not posed. With the invitation of the Governor General, the member States of the OECS were doing no more collectively than they could lawfully do individually in responding to that request. Thus, the limits of what action a regional organization may properly take absent such a request were not tested in this case.

As a lawful action of a regional organization, the collective action of the OECS falls within Article 52 of the UN Charter. We are not aware of any serious contention that actions falling within the scope of Article 52 could violate Article 2(4) of the Charter, any more than actions taken at the request of lawful governmental authority could be considered to do so. Similarly, the request of lawful authority and the decision of the OECS bring the collective action within the scope of the OAS Charter. Military assistance provided at the request of lawful authority cannot be considered to violate the prohibitions of Articles 18 and 20 of that Charter, and lawful actions of a regional organization such as the OECS fall within the exceptions for regional arrangements set forth in Articles 22 and 28 of the Charter. While the *travaux preparatoire* of these articles do not indicate that the drafters consciously anticipated the development of collective security arrangements in this hemisphere apart from the Rio Treaty and the UN Charter, the *travaux* do indicate a clear decision not to refer specifically to those treaties in the Charter provisions. Accordingly, there is nothing to indicate that the drafters intended to foreclose the possibility of other similar treaties falling within the scope of Articles 22 and 28.

On a practical level, the United States has long supported the concept of dual adherences to the OAS Charter and the Rio Treaty by hemispheric countries. However, the hemispheric system has developed differently. The English speaking Caribbean countries — including the OECS states — are members of the OAS but not party to the Rio Treaty. The OECS Treaty is in effect the regional security arrangement for the Eastern Caribbean states. (And one which provides for much greater integration in the conduct of public affairs than either the OAS Charter or the Rio Treaty.) We see no principled basis for distinguishing the Rio Treaty with 23 members, from the OECS Treaty with its 7 members. Since the Rio Treaty organ of consultation may take decisions by a 2/3 vote while the OECS Treaty authority requires unanimity, in practice the difference in institutional restraints on collective action under the two systems is not significant. We attach no weight whatsoever to the relatively small size of the OECS member States. All sovereign states regardless of population or area are entitled to enjoy the benefits of regional security arrangements, which may in fact be more important to states such as the OECS members for whom maintenance of significant standing security forces is extremely burdensome. If it were the case that the OAS Charter stood as a bar to the OECS states taking collective security action, then it would seem that OAS membership would impose burdens uniquely on these states which have the greatest need for collective security.

Use-of-Force Provisions of the OAS System

Question for Discussion

It should be noted that measures taken under Articles 3 and 6 of the Rio Treaty clearly constitute "[m]easures adopted for the maintenance of peace and security in accordance with existing treaties" pursuant to Article 22 of the Revised OAS Charter. Do you see the same complementarity in the Rio Treaty and OAS Charter that are reflected in Articles 2(4) and 51 of the United Nations Charter? Which articles correspond respectively to Articles 2(4) and 51?

Problem

Early this year a guerrilla band landed in the small Latin American country of Panamala and began a military campaign to overthrow the government of Generalissimo Blanco. All available evidence indicates that the guerrillas were sent to Panamala from Cuba.

Shortly after the guerrilla attacks began, Generalissimo Blanco called upon the United States to extend military assistance to Panamala. In view of Panamala's strategic position in Latin America, the President of the United States announced in March that the United States would send 200 military advisers and a substantial amount of military equipment to Panamala. The President stated that he was acting under Article 3 of the Inter-American Treaty of Reciprocal Assistance (the Rio Treaty) and under Article 51 of the United Nations Charter, as well as under relevant U.S. legislation.

Soon after the President's announcement, the military fortunes of the Panamala regime began to decline. The guerrillas, almost all of whom were Panamalians who had been deported by the Blanco government, were warmly received by a large segment of the Panamala population, especially in the rural areas away from government strongholds. In July, Generalissimo Blanco again requested the United States to send troops to assist in the defense of Panamala from external aggression. The President refused to send more troops, but in his reply he noted that 10,000 U.S. troops would be engaged, along with Latin American forces, in Hondas, a country bordering on Panamala. (These military exercises, "Operation Joint Peace," had been organized previously by the OAS as an experiment to determine the feasibility of establishing an OAS peace force.)

Over the last few months, rumblings of discontent have multiplied within Panamala's largest cities. A large segment of the population of the cities apparently believed that the Blanco government was corrupt and was not dealing effectively with the guerrilla incursions. Leaders of this so-called City Faction urged repeatedly that the Blanco government be overturned and called for a more effective fight against the guerrillas "to wipe them from the face of the earth."

Last night, Generalissimo Blanco, his entire Cabinet, and all key legislative leaders took an airplane for Spain, announcing upon their arrival in Madrid that they wished to have nothing further to do with the situation in Panamala. Since that time, the leaders of the City Faction have begun to organize a government made up mostly of city police officials and Panamala naval officers. Most segments of the Panamala armed forces in the field have hurriedly returned to the cities, enabling guerrilla leaders to consolidate their forces and prepare for what they have called "the day of reckoning."

This morning, General Roosevelt, commander of U.S. forces taking part in Operation Joint Peace, acting on orders from the President of the United States, ordered his men across the Panamala border, ostensibly to protect the lives and property of U.S. citizens in Panamala. The U.S. troops later were joined by 100 troops from two other Latin American countries also taking part in Operation Joint Peace. At noon, this force reached the small camp in central Panamala used by the U.S. military advisers to Panamala. Roosevelt has just cabled for further orders.

This afternoon, the President of the United States convened a meeting of the National Security Council. The following proposals were put forward by various persons in attendance:

1. Order Roosevelt to withdraw U.S. troops immediately, seal off Panamala's border with Hondas, and let the City Faction and the guerrillas fight it out. Utilize U.S. ships to interdict the further shipment of men and material from Cuba and other countries.

2. Recognize the City Faction leaders as the legal government of Panamala. Commit the U.S. forces and other troops to assist the City Faction in pursuing the fight against the guerrilla forces.

3. Cordon off the cities to prevent a confrontation between the guerrillas and the City Faction. (Best military estimates indicate that given the superiority of U.S. armed forces, this option is a feasible and practicable one. However, it will require sending in 25,000 more U.S. troops.)

4. Convene the OAS and seek a resolution transforming the Operation Joint Peace force *ipso facto* into an Inter-American peace force.

5. Convene the UN Security Council or the General Assembly and seek a resolution transforming the Operation Joint Peace force *ipso facto* into a United Nations peace-keeping force.

As legal adviser to the Department of State, you have been asked to analyze the foregoing proposals under international law. You know that in addition to your legal analysis, the President would be interested in ideas on how the proposals might be altered to improve the U.S. legal position. What advice would you give? As a first stage in evaluating any national policy, the following issues should be considered in addition to the legal issues:

1. Are the goals consistent with the national interest?

2. Can the goals be realized in the context in which they are pursued?

3. If the goals are realizable, are they realizable at a cost-benefit ratio making their pursuit in the national interest?

4. Are preferable policy alternatives available to achieve the same or similar goals at a more favorable cost-benefit ratio?

It should also be noted that the legal and political issues are interrelated.

Continuing Problems

Minor Coercion and the Article 2(4) Threshold

Article 2(4) prohibits "the threat or use of force against the territorial integrity or political independence of any state, or in any other manner inconsistent with the purposes of the United Nations." Does this article leave room for lawful uses of minor or covert coercion not so directed? This question needs particularly to be examined in light of the doctrine of reprisal, which prior to the Charter unquestionably permitted certain uses of force in response to prior illegal acts of another state. It has generally been thought that when the Charter used "threat or use of force," as opposed to the term "war" in the Kellogg-Briand Pact, the intent was to prohibit reprisals as well as major coercion. Most scholars today would support the position that forceful reprisals as a justification for initiation of coercion — as opposed to a somewhat different meaning of "reprisals" in the law of war — are not sanctioned by the Charter. The language of Article 2(4), however, does not by itself require the conclusion that all forceful reprisals are unlawful.

More helpfully, analyses of the Charter in terms of its fundamental purpose, which is to prevent coercion, as a modality suggest that even minor coercion, if imposed simply as a sanction, should also be prohibited. But some actions, popularly termed reprisals, may more usefully be thought of as efforts at defense against continuing but sporadic violence. For example, should a response against a terrorist training camp be termed a reprisal or defense in a setting of continuing but intermittent attacks by terrorists trained at the camp? In the context of a particular case of continuing attacks, such an action is likely to be regarded as an exercise of the right of defense. "Minimalists," however, might argue to the contrary.

Moreover, there may be some kinds of minor coercion that are simply consistent with both the language of Article 2(4) and the purposes and principles of the Charter. Certain actions for the humanitarian protection of nationals or third-state citizens may meet this criterion.

Although controversial, there is, in post-Charter use of force analyses, always a question of whether a particular use of force — typically minor coercion — is lawful because it is not inconsistent in a doctrinal sense with Article 2(4) or in a policy sense with the principal underpinnings of the Charter — or because it is a form of lawful defense under Article 51 of the Charter.

Richard B. Lillich, *Forcible Self-Help Under International Law*

in READINGS IN INTERNATIONAL LAW FROM THE NAVAL WAR COLLEGE REVIEW, 1947–1977, at 129, 129–33, 137–38 (Richard B. Lillich & John Norton Moore eds., 1980)

[T]he general view is that the United Nations Charter permits the use of force in two areas. One of these is individual or collective self-defense, and the second is the implementation of a decision by a competent international organization. This generally, of course, would be the United Nations, but in some instances it might be a regional organization such as the Organization of American States.

Professor Lissitzyn has this to say in his book, *International Law Today and Tomorrow*, "It is generally agreed that these restrictions apply to all interstate uses of force, whether they are called war or force short of war." In other words, what I'm talking about today is covered in the same way that the actual use of warfare would be covered. He goes on to say that "forcible reprisals [and presumably other uses of self-help] are apparently no longer lawful." This quotation is an indication, of course, that we international lawyers like to avoid saying yes or no and would generally prefer to say maybe. The conclusion seems to be that they are no longer lawful. Therefore, what I want to discuss today in rather pinpointed fashion are four particular areas: retorsion, reprisal, the use of force to protect nationals, and, finally, humanitarian intervention. Hopefully, we will first determine what their standing was under customary international law, and secondly, what impact, if any, the United Nations Charter has had upon this. The interesting fact is that, despite the literature you read on the charter saying that force is restricted to the two instances that I mentioned before, all of these four doctrines are still dealt with by international law. They are obviously concepts that states deem to be necessary; at least they are invoked constantly in situations that technically, if you apply the charter rigidly, would not be deemed applicable.

I think here we have to realize that the UN Charter was originally interpreted as a rather absolutist document. The idea was that force, and particularly aggressive force, was to be eliminated except for the two instances that I have pointed out. But we are gradually beginning to realize that certain other of the sanctions that were built into the United Nations Charter, or were to be implemented through the United Nations Charter, have not actually been implemented. The charter is not wholly effective. Thus, in certain areas we may want to consider whether, in effect, some of these previous precharter doctrines could not be revised. For instance, in Professor Falk's recent book, *Legal Order in a Violent World*, he is very critical of American use of force in any of th ese less-than-warfare situations. But even he, in his book and in a recent article, has said that the elimination of violence from international life is not an absolute value. Nor is it separable from other questions at issue in international society. He points out that while the United Nations Charter does legislate against not only the use but also the threat of force, it was also designed to protect human rights and to establish and create a viable world order. Both of these are objectives which may require the use of coercion in a given instance to protect the overall objectives of the charter. If this is a valid conclusion and if the United Nations itself has not implemented all the powers that are found in the charter, then I think one has to consider whether or not some of these traditional doctrines still have validity and, if so, whether we may want to redefine them in certain ways.

The first of these foundations is retorsion. I take this doctrine first because it is generally listed as number one in all the legal literature, probably because it can be disposed of most rapidly. Retorsion consists of a legal but unfriendly act taken with a retaliatory or coercive purpose. Generally, it does not involve the use of force, but it may. Now the emphasis here is upon doing something unfriendly but legal. What would an example of this be?

Well, suppose, for instance, a country tinkers around with its tariff rate to the great detriment of the United States. The United States may respond by adopting a discriminatory tariff rate against the other country. We have done nothing illegal, we have just responded. It is certainly an unfriendly act, but it does not involve the use of force. The idea is based on the old concept of an eye for an eye. We are adopting a sanction equal to what was done against us in the hope that the first nation will relent on a quid pro quo basis. Unfortunately, it rarely operates that way, but this is the theory behind it.

Another example might be the discrimination situation. A country refuses to let certain American goods be imported. The United States might respond by revoking that country's privilege, previously granted by the United States, of fishing within the 12-mile limit.

Once again this is quite permissible, even though it may involve the use of force if that country then sent fishing boats within the particular area. This is an example of retorsion which could involve the use of force.

One of the retorsions that is of primary concern now—and very topical in respect to Peru, Bolivia, Chile, and other countries—is the reduction of foreign aid or the termination of foreign aid. We have a statute called the Hickenlooper amendment which requires the President to cut off foreign aid after 6 months if American property is taken without payment of adequate compensation. This, I would say, is an act of retorsion.

Now I just want to emphasize in ending this discussion of retorsion what I said before. It involves a legal act, something that is quite permissible and quite unfriendly, but which is not predicated upon a prior illegal act by another country such as self-defense is. You can only respond by self-defense if the other party has broken the provisions of the United Nations Charter and engaged in armed attack or otherwise committed aggression. Then it is the prior illegal act which makes your conduct legal. But in this situation, of course, your conduct is legal to start with. Because it is a legal act, it is not affected by the charter at all, so therefore, what learning we have on retorsion from before 1945 can be carried over and applied to today as well.

Now reprisals are a different matter.... [R]eprisals constitute an action involving the use of force against another state which has violated international law. The idea of reprisal in international law is not to punish the first state for the particular illegal act but to encourage it to conform to international law.

Here you have a contrast with retorsion, which is a legal act from the beginning. Reprisal is only legal in response to a prior illegal act by another country. There are also certain limitations upon reprisal, at least under traditional international law. I'll give you three of these. First of all, as I have said, there must be an illegal act by the other foreign state. Secondly, the state that is going to take the reprisal must request from the initial wrongdoing state some kind of reparation—give them an opportunity, in effect, to make right their international wrong. And then, thirdly, and this limitation is something that runs through the entire question of self-help and, indeed, of self-defense, the measures that must be adopted in carrying out a reprisal must be proportionate to the original provocation. In other words, if some infiltrator comes over your border and shoots one of your sentries, you cannot A-bomb the capital of the other country.

Classical examples of reprisals, most of which were in the area of naval warfare, would involve an embargo of the ships of an offending state, seizure of ships of the high seas, and pacific blockade. More recently it has been suggested that right of reprisal could be invoked, and indeed to some extent it was invoked, in the original response in the Gulf of Tonkin in 1964 when there was an airstrike at the oil installations immediately after the alleged attack on the American ship.

Also, during last winter, just before the release of the *Pueblo* crew, it was suggested that seizure of a North Korean fishing boat that had been built in Europe and which was being towed across the Atlantic could have been utilized as a form of reprisal. The efficacy of that is something I will leave to your speculation. In any event, it is a live doctrine and, as I am sure you are aware, it is one that the Israelis rely upon almost every day. I have not had the opportunity to see today's *New York Times*, but there was another "retaliatory raid" announced in yesterday's *New York Times*.

This brings us to the question of what is the impact of the United Nations Charter upon this doctrine of reprisal? Article 2(4) of the charter, as Professor Moore told you, prohibits the threat or the use of force. The question is, does this really mean that a state, even a state that is trying to follow the dictates of the United Nations Charter, must refrain from any use of force whatsoever when another state is violating the provisions of the charter and when the United Nations either cannot act or refuses to act in a given situation? I must say that the general view which is advanced by such people as Brownlie in his book on this subject, by Commander Harlow, by Professor Lissitzyn, and most others is that the charter prohibits all reprisals involving use of force. Professor Brierly in his book *The Law of Nations* says,

> today it is beyond argument that armed reprisals ... would be a flagrant violation of international law. Equally, it is also clear that Article 2 does not preclude a state from taking unilaterally economic or other reprisals not involving the use of armed force in retaliation for a breach of international law by another state.

There is a lot of support for this, not only among the textwriters, but also in the United Nations itself. In 1964 the Security Council censured Great Britain for carrying out a reprisal against Yemen. This was allegedly in retaliation for the Yemini support of guerrillas in Aden. You recall that the British were having great difficulty in that former colony at the time. This resolution passed the United Nations Security Council, nine votes to none, with two abstentions, and it "condemns reprisals as incompatible with the purposes and principles of the United Nations." This is a pretty general statement. It is not only condemning a specific action, as the United Nations has done in many instances with respect to Israeli retaliatory actions, but it is saying that reprisals themselves are incompatible with the purposes and principles of the United Nations Charter. Many scholars like Professor Falk go even beyond that. They conclude that the charter prohibits all forms of forcible self-help other than the exercise of self-defense within article 51 of the charter.

This raises some questions about which we may want to speculate. I am not sure it points to many answers, but at least you can see the problem. Today, most retaliatory claims are made by other states as well. Should we condemn a country like Israel merely by applying the conventional wisdom that reprisals have been outlawed by the United Nations Charter and, therefore, are no good—that Israel is engaging in acts that would have constituted reprisals and is therefore violating international law? What alternatives are available to Israel? I think it is proper to assume an unwillingness on the part of at least certain Arab governments to negotiate. Negotiations under the United Nations Charter in this situation, as you know, are required by article 33. Cannot it be read, cannot it be interpreted, that what Israel is doing is, as I suggested before, obviously taking actions that she thinks she has to take for her national security but also, in a broader sense, highlighting a defect in the operations of the United Nations or perhaps in the machinery of the United Nations? In other words, in a broader context, cannot it be argued that Israel is making, really, a plea for the cooperative type of law enforcement that the charter originally envisaged?

Professor Falk wrote his article to which I referred in the *American Journal of International Law* last July. It is an analysis of the Beirut raid and its relation to the international law of retaliation. You recall that this occurred a little over a year ago. An El Al plane had been shot up in Greece, and as retaliation, Israeli commandos in helicopters landed at the Beirut airport and destroyed all the Arab planes that were there. Unfortunately, two-thirds of those planes were not owned by anyone in Arab countries—they were owned by American businessmen. The Israelis thus destroyed about $33 million worth of property, most of which was subsequently compensated for by Lloyds of London. In any event, Professor Falk goes through a very detailed and, I think, quite correct analysis, but he comes out saying that the raid seems illegal, which is in contrast to his view that all kinds of forcible self-help are impermissible. One would expect him to say that it *definitely* was illegal. He goes on to express his dissatisfaction with this conclusion in this very interesting paragraph.

"It seems clear that on the doctrinal level Israel is not entitled to exercise a right of reprisal in modern international law. Such clarity," he goes on to say, "however, serves mainly to discredit doctrinal approaches to legal analysis." And not only in international law, I might point out, but in other areas of law as well. You just cannot read the text isolated from the complexities of certain situations. He goes on to say, "International society is not sufficiently organized to eliminate forcible self-help in either its sanctioning or its deterrent role. Therefore each reprisal claim needs to be appraised by reference to these two roles, namely sanctioning and deterrence." At the end of the article is listed a variety of criteria, and he then says that even if these criteria were being applied and even if there was a right of reprisal in international law which earlier he suggests there is not, Israel would not have met the test because its response was not proportional to the original wrong and because there was no evidence that these people who originally did the wrong to Israel came from Lebanon. They may have come from some other Arab country. But the whole question is left open, I think, at the end of the article, and the best I can do is to leave the question open today. I stated the arguments on both sides; I have indicated that there has been a valid erosion away from the original interpretation of the charter that says reprisals are entirely out; and I think perhaps we international lawyers and Government officials are rethinking the entire problem. There is a need, perhaps, for some kind of reinstitution of reprisal — if not in the most classical sense, then in a more limited sense — as some kind of sanctioning instrument under international law.

. . . .

I'd like to close by recalling a lecture given here 2 years ago by Professor McDougal in which he, in effect, admitted that he had reconsidered some of his earlier views. In particular, he said,

> I am ashamed to confess that at one time I lent my support to the suggestion that article 2(4) and the related articles did preclude the use of self-help less than self-defense. On reflection, I think that this was a very grave mistake, that article 2(4) and article 51 must be interpreted differently.

He goes on and lists his reasons, coming to the conclusion that in the absence of collective machinery to protect people against attack and deprivation, in other words in the absence of machinery as noted by Judge Jessup many years ago, the principle of major purposes requires an interpretation which would honor self-help against a prior unlawfulness.

The subsequent conduct of the parties to the UN Charter certainly confirms this. Many states of the world have used force in situations short of the requirements of self-defense to protect their national interests. That includes the United States, Great Britain, Israel, and also many other countries.

Questions for Discussion

1. Should the Israeli raid on Beirut be analyzed as a reprisal or an act of defense, whether lawful or otherwise? Why? How about the United States' raid on Libya? Why? How about the recent forceful responses by Israel against an intense terrorist attack, replete with suicide bombers, against Israel? Why? How would you differentiate a pro-active defense against a continuing pattern of terrorist attacks from reprisal?

2. What other forms of minor coercion, if any, could or should be dealt with as below the Article 2(4) threshold? Could the United States use force to prevent a Soviet trawler monitoring United States testing of an experimental torpedo from picking up the spent torpedo? What circumstances would you regard as decisive in any such hypothetical

situation? Could Sweden use force to destroy a submarine that refused to surface and identify itself in its internal waters or its territorial sea? What other "minor coercion" hypothetical situations can you construct?

3. Should the law of reprisal differentiate between forceful reprisal against a non-forceful breach of international law and a forceful breach? Should the real controlling factor be necessity and proportionality in responding to illegal coercion rather than any distinction between reprisal and defense in settings of prior forceful breach of international law?

De Facto Boundaries and Territorial Disputes

McDougal & Feliciano
at 220–22

THE CHARACTERISTICS OF PARTICIPANTS

At the outset, there may arise the problem of identifying participant groups, to whose mutual applications of coercion and violence the community policy and prescriptions distinguishing between permissible and impermissible coercion may appropriately be applicable. Allegations of impermissible coercion and accompanying claims to use intense coercion in self-defense have been made not only by officials of bodies politic universally recognized as nations-states but also by officials of territorial communities and governmental organizations not formally recognized as states by their opponents and, at times, by some members of the community of states as well. The Arab-Israeli conflict in Palestine in 1948 and the Korean war of 1950 afford familiar illustrations. The Jewish Agency for Palestine, even before issuing the proclamation on establishing an independent state of Israel, raised a charge of aggression against Trans-Jordan and Egypt before the United Nations Security Council and, at least inferentially, claimed a right to self-defense. The Arab states refused to recognize Israel as a state and indeed asserted that, with the termination of the British Mandate, Palestine had become an independent nation in which the Jews constituted a rebellious minority. In the Korean conflict, neither of the initial participants—the Republic of Korea and the North Korean People's Republic—recognized the other as a state. The Soviet Union argued to the United Nations that the exercise of violence in Korea could not be characterized as unlawful coercion since the conflict was an internal or civil one and the Charter prescriptions are not applicable to coercion between two groups within a single state. The decisions reached by the United Nations in the Palestine and Korean cases suggest that conflicts involving a newly organized territorial body politic, or conflicts between two distinct territorial units which the community expects to be relatively permanent, are, for purposes of policy about coercion, to be treated as conflicts between established states. Thus, the applicability of basic community policy about minimum public order in the world arena and competence to defend against unlawful violence are not dependent upon formal recognition of the technical statehood of the claimant-group by the opposing participant. This conclusion is but an obvious corollary of effective community policy; a contrary view would permit the thrust of fundamental policy to be avoided by the simple device of refusing to perform a ceremonial ritual. It is not the ceremony of recognition by others that constitutes a group an effective, self-directed, territorially organized community, but the facts of the world power process.

John Norton Moore, *Reply on the Falklands War*

77 Am. J. Int'l L. 610–13 (1983)

In a world drifting dangerously toward anarchy, no principle is more important than that enshrined in Article 1 of the United Nations Charter that international disputes shall be settled by peaceful means and not by armed force. This principle applies not only to clearly recognized *de jure* international boundaries but to *de facto* boundaries of whatever kind, whether they are the subject of territorial disputes between states or are lines within divided nations or cease-fire lines. Failure to recognize *de facto* boundaries would remove normative constraints on use of force from many of the most critical flash points in international life. It would mean that the basic Charter structure regulating coercion is irrelevant to attacks involving divided-nation boundaries as in the Korean War, cease-fire lines as in the Middle East, disputed territories as in the ongoing Iran-Iraq war, disputed borders as between the Soviet Union and China or overlapping Antarctic claims, the many contemporary island disputes, and over two hundred unresolved oceans boundaries.

[Original note 2: Cárdenas refers to "[a] loose reference to '15 active island disputes' and 'hundreds of [other] land and sea boundary disputes.' ..." A partial list, illustrating the extreme potential of boundary and territorial disputes for conflict, may be found in D. Downing, An Atlas Of Territorial And Border Disputes (1980). A few well-known disputes include:

— overlapping claims on the Antarctic continent and island groups south of 60° latitude — such as the South Shetlands and South Orkneys (including disputes between Great Britain, Argentina and Chile; Argentina refused to accept the referral to the ICJ by Britain in 1955 of the overlapping Antarctic claims of Great Britain and Argentina);

— the Sino-Soviet border;

— the Shikotan and Hobomai Islands (disputed between the Soviet Union and Japan);

— the Danjo Islands and the Takeshima Rocks (disputed between Japan and South Korea);

— the Senkaku/Tiao Yu Tai Islands (disputed between China and Japan);

— the Cambodia-Vietnam border;

— the Paracel Islands (disputed between China and Vietnam);

— the Spratly Islands (disputed between China, Vietnam, Taiwan, and the Philippines);

— the Jammu and Kashmir dispute (between India and Pakistan);

— the Shatt-al-Arab dispute (the subject of an ongoing war between Iran and Iraq);

— the Ogaden region (the subject of a war between Ethiopia and Somalia);

— the Beagle Channel region — including the islands of Picton, Nueva, and Lennox (disputed between Chile and Argentina);

— the El Salvador-Honduras border — including several small islands in the Gulf of Fonseca;

— oceans delimitation concerning the Islands of Saint-Pierre and Miquelon (disputed between France and Canada);

— the maritime boundary between the Soviet Union and Norway;

— the Greece-Turkey Aegean boundary;

— the continuing division between China and Taiwan (of China?);

— the continuing division of Germany;

— the continuing division of Korea; and

— continuing cease-fire lines and *de facto* boundaries in the Arab-Israeli conflict.

Unfortunately for world order, there is nothing "loose" about the existence of these and many other boundary and territorial disputes and their potential for conflict. In this respect the introduction by David Downing to his atlas of territorial and border disputes is instructive:

> Border disputes provide an all too-convenient platform for the expression of international hostility, and waving the flag and waxing lyrical about the nation's sacred soil are time-honoured methods of silencing internal opposition.... But however invidious the role of governments, it cannot be denied that the very existence of ill-drawn borders has played a major role in the fomentation of all this century's major wars.]

The principal reason why the Charter prohibition on the use of force as a means for settling disputes does and must apply in these cases is that any other answer would threaten conflict and destruction out of all proportion to any conceivable advance in "justice" from such wars. Contrary to Cárdenas's view, the United Nations has demonstrated clearly in the Korean War, the Arab-Israeli conflict, and again in the Falklands War that it fully understands the importance of this principle prohibiting the use of force as a means of settling disputes across *de facto* boundaries.

....

In sole support of his argument that the Charter prohibition on use of force does not apply to territorial disputes, Professor Cárdenas quotes from the book by Professor Jennings on *The Acquisition of Territory in International Law*. Sadly, he does not give us Jennings's full thoughts on the matter, perhaps understandably since those thoughts seem inconsistent with Cárdenas's assertion of lawful Argentinean action in the Falklands attack....

....

Most importantly, however, Jennings, writing in the context of a book on territorial acquisition, is simply wrong in implying that any degree of clarity as to legal title overcomes the Charter principle that prohibits the use of force between nations for settlement of disputes. The Charter distinction is between armed attack and defense, not between *de jure* and *de facto* settings. Indeed, the distinction made by Jennings that it might be lawful to use force to take disputed territory, contingent on willingness to submit to third-party dispute settlement, seems more in keeping with the procedural constraints of Articles 12 and 13 of the League Covenant than the substantive constraints on use of force of Articles 1 and 2 of the United Nations Charter. Would Cárdenas accept, pursuant to the Jennings distinction, that Chile has a right militarily to occupy the islands disputed with Argentina in the region of the Beagle Channel? After all, a binding arbitral award by a distinguished arbitral panel would seem "very clear" evidence of title, unlike the Falklands dispute.

Questions for Discussion

1. During the Vietnam War, should the Democratic Republic of Vietnam (North Vietnam) and the Republic of Vietnam (South Vietnam) have been regarded as entities to which the Charter prohibition of force applied? Should the two Germanies before their reunification? How about China and Taiwan? Does the Helsinki Accord reinforce your

conclusion with respect to the impermissibility of use of force across the de facto German boundary? Why has the West not sought such guarantees in dangerous de facto divisions?

2. How long does a *de facto* situation need to exist before the nonuse-of-force principle applies? Why wouldn't the Argentinean occupation of the Falklands/Malvinas Islands suffice to trigger the principle and render any subsequent British use of force illegal? Is the criterion solely a matter of time or do other factors enter in?

3. If you were looking for potentially dangerous triggers for war, in settings surrounded by ambiguity, would Taiwan be high on your list? Should the United States make clear to China that the Charter prohibition against the use of force—and the corresponding right of defense—apply fully to *de facto* as well as *de jure* boundaries? Such a statement would not be inconsistent with the Shanghai Declaration, would it?

Civil Strife and the Norms of Intervention

Since the end of World War II the predominant forms of international conflict have been revolutionary violence, terrorism, and mixed civil-international conflict. Each international organization seems primarily a response to the major breakdown in world order that triggered its creation. Thus, the League was a response to the widespread feeling that World War I arose by accident, and the United Nations was principally a response to the open aggression of the Axis. Although Charter principles are certainly useful, the syntax of the Charter is deficient both substantively and procedurally for the problem of mixed civil-international conflict, secret warfare, terrorism, and intervention, which have emerged as central public order concerns since World War II.

On the substantive side, Article 2(4) of the Charter prohibits "the threat or use of force against the territorial integrity or political independence of any state...." But is assistance at the request of a competing faction engaged in internal conflict violative of the integrity or independence of the state? The central issue in internal conflict is the question of who represents the state. Consequently, unless there is an overt external invasion, Article 2(4) of the Charter does not provide much guidance (as opposed to the underlying Charter principles that are still of fundamental importance).

Similarly, on the procedural side, the Charter is insufficiently responsive to the problems of intervention in terms of the seeming nonapplicability of reporting requirements, only limited fact-disclosure capability, and poor settlement techniques for internal authority struggles.

As a result of this major oversight of the Charter structure, international lawyers have had recourse to a parallel set of norms—the customary law norms of intervention—still in development. The newness and complexity of the problem, however, has led to significant differences of opinion about these norms.[15]

---

15. For a legal assessment of intervention, *see generally* Law and Civil War in the Modern World (John Norton Moore ed., 1974); William T. Burke, *The Legal Regulation of Minor International Coercion: A Framework of Inquiry, in* Essays on Intervention 87 (Roland J. Stranger ed., 1964); Tom Farer, *Intervention in Civil Wars: A Modest Proposal*, 67 Colum. L. Rev. 266 (1967); Wolfgang Friedmann, *Intervention, Civil War and the Rôle of International Law*, Am. Soc'y Int'l L. Proc. 67 (1965); John Norton Moore, *Legal Standards for Intervention in Internal Conflicts*, 13 Ga. J. Int'l & Comp. L. 191 (1983).

John Norton Moore, *Toward an Applied Theory for the Regulation of Intervention*

LAW AND CIVIL WAR IN THE MODERN WORLD 3, 3, 24–31
(John Norton Moore ed., 1974)

Since World War II, civil wars and mixed civil-international conflicts have replaced the more conventional international wars as the principal form of violence in the international system. Though the *threat* of large-scale nuclear exchange—or even limited nuclear war—must, in view of the enormous destructive potential of modern nuclear weapons, remain the central world-order concern, the principal *realized* violence has resulted from revolution and intervention in civil and mixed civil-international settings. In this respect, the Indo-China War has simply dramatized an already acute global problem, as evidenced by the conflicts in Greece, Palestine, Korea, the Congo (Zaire), Cyprus, Hungary, Lebanon, Cuba, the Sudan, and the Dominican Republic, among many others. Subsequent events, such as the Nigeria-Biafra and Pakistan-Bangladesh Civil Wars and the conflicts in Ceylon (Sri Lanka), Burundi, and Northern Ireland have quashed any illusion that the problem may be temporary.

With increasing realization of the problem there has been a flood of writing on the causes and conditions of revolutionary violence, the systemic causes of intervention, the interventionary activities of the principal actors, the strategies of revolution and counter-revolution, and the legal aspects of the regulation of intervention.

. . . .

… Though there is always a danger in premature formulation of standards, the present body of knowledge about civil strife and intervention suggests the utility of efforts to formulate rules and contextual thresholds for appraisal. In fact, timidity in approaching the task of recommending criteria for appraisal is a persistent shortcoming of the literature on civil strife and intervention. It is to be expected that such criteria will be rough at the edges, but it seems likely that a general theory for the regulation of intervention will develop more quickly if efforts are made at providing more specific guidance. In fact, criticisms of earlier formulations have helped greatly in the present restatement. It is in this spirit that the following standards and contextual thresholds are suggested:

Standards Concerning the Initiation of Hostilities[16]

. . . .

II. Intervention for the protection of human rights is permissible if it meets the following conditions:

  A. an immediate threat of genocide or other widespread arbitrary deprivation of human life in violation of international law;

  B. an exhaustion of diplomatic and other peaceful techniques for protecting the threatened rights to the extent possible and consistent with protection of the threatened rights;

---

16. Standard I, concerning military assistance to a widely recognized government, is omitted here. The principal modern rule seems to be simply that it is lawful to assist a widely recognized government at its request. Standard III, a "neutral non-intervention" rule has also been omitted here as it never became law.

C. the unavailability of effective action by an international agency, regional organization, or the United Nations;

D. a proportional use of force which does not threaten greater destruction of values than the human rights at stake and which does not exceed the minimum force necessary to protect the threatened rights;

E. the minimal effect on authority structures necessary to protect the threatened rights;

F. the minimal interference with self-determination necessary to protect the threatened rights;

G. a prompt disengagement, consistent with the purpose of the action; and

H. immediate full reporting to the Security Council and any appropriate regional organization and compliance with Security Council applicable regional directives.

COMMENT: There is continued controversy concerning the permissibility of humanitarian intervention and intervention for the protection of nationals. The suggested standard reflects the judgment that intervention for the protection of fundamental human rights should be permitted if carefully circumscribed. Although it is recognized that legitimating such intervention entails substantial risks, not permitting necessary actions for the prevention of genocide or other major abuse of human rights seems to present a greater risk. Opponents of any such standard should at least endeavor to weigh the risks of permitting such intervention *as carefully delimited by the suggested standard* against the risk of insulating genocidal acts and other fundamental abuse of human rights from effective response. Critical points which bear emphasis are that the standard permits unilateral action only in response to threats of genocide or other wide-spread arbitrary deprivation of human life in violation of international law, only if diplomatic and other peaceful techniques are unavailable, and only if international agencies (such as the International Committee of the Red Cross), regional organizations, or the United Nations are unable to take effective action. In earlier formulations, I sought to limit permissible intervention for the protection of human rights to interventions which would not significantly affect authority structures. Though still a close case, it now seems to me in the wake of the Bangladesh situation that the earlier formulation may have been too restrictive. The advantage of limiting such interventions to non-authority-oriented actions, however, is that it substantially reduces the risk of using humanitarian intervention as a cover for other aims.....

IV. Assistance to a widely recognized government is permissible in response to an armed attack or to offset impermissible assistance to insurgents; if the assistance to insurgents or the use of the military instrument constitutes an armed attack it is permissible to reply proportionately against the attacking State.

COMMENT: This standard embodies the right of collective defense, recognized under the United Nations Charter, as well as a related right of counter-intervention in response to impermissible assistance to insurgents. There seems little reason to prohibit assistance to a widely recognized government if impermissible assistance is being supplied to insurgents. It should also be noted that collective defense and counter-intervention tend to become indistinguishable as the level of external assistance to insurgents is increased.

V. Regional peacekeeping is permissible if it meets the following conditions:

A. Authorization by a regional arrangement acting pursuant to Chapter VIII of the Charter;

B. A genuine invitation by the widely recognized government, or, if there is none, by a major faction;

C. Neutrality among factions to the extent compatible with the peace-keeping mission;

D. Immediate full reporting to the Security Council and compliance with Security Council directives;

E. An outcome consistent with self-determination. Such an outcome is one based on internationally observed elections in which all factions are allowed freely to participate, which is freely accepted by the major competing factions, or which is endorsed by a competent body of the United Nations.

COMMENT: The greater degree of collective legitimation supplied by regional arrangements suggests a somewhat larger role for regional action than unilateral action. Thus, it seems reasonable to permit regional peacekeeping actions if carefully delimited to ensure that they are genuine peacekeeping actions and not disguised efforts at maintaining or extending hegemony. Under the United Nations Charter, regional arrangements are limited in the use of force not only by the restrictions of Article 2(4), applicable to unilateral action, but also by the article 53 requirement that "no enforcement action" shall be taken without the authorization of the Security Council. Since the suggested criteria limit regional action to that not directed against any government, such action would not constitute "enforcement action" and would be consistent with the Charter.

VI. The General Assembly or Security Council of the United Nations may authorize a peacekeeping action when requested by a widely recognized government.

COMMENT: This standard roughly reflects the existing authority of the General Assembly and the Security Council to authorize a peacekeeping force with the consent of the host government. Such actions are unlikely in the absence of extraordinary consensus that the operation will promote self-determination, human rights, and minimization of violence.

VII. The Security Council may recommend appropriate measures to restore international peace and security in situations which constitute a threat to the peace, breach of the peace, or act of aggression.

COMMENT: This standard reflects the existing authority of the Security Council under Chapter VII of the Charter. Under this authority, the Security Council can recommend assistance or withdrawal of assistance to one or another faction, or can establish a peacekeeping mission even without the consent of the government concerned.

VIII. Intervention is permissible if specifically authorized by the Security Council acting within its authority under Chapter VII of the Charter, even though in the absence of such authorization it would be impermissible. Conversely, if the Security Council specifically calls for cessation of a particular intervention, continuation is impermissible even though in the absence of such prohibition it would be permissible.

COMMENT: This standard is a corollary of standard VII. Some recommendations have tended to rely primarily on procedural standards for collective legitimation. Though collective legitimation should neither be uncritically accepted nor be the sole standard, it is certainly a highly relevant feature. In particular, the variety of viewpoints represented on the Security Council and the recognized responsibility of the Council to maintain or restore international peace and security suggest its general competence to authorize and terminate intervention when acting within its area of responsibility under Chapter VII. Moreover, Security Council recommendations, reflecting major power consensus, are not likely to lead to conflict escalation.

An earlier formulation of this rule permitted the same role for the General Assembly as for the Security Council. I am persuaded, however, that in view of the present malapportionment and politicization of the General Assembly, a more cautious approach toward a General Assembly legitimating role is in order. Accordingly, the revised standard takes no position on the effect of General Assembly authorization of assistance or request for termination. The narrowing of the earlier formulation also has the virtue of bringing the suggested standard more clearly in line with the generally recognized constitutional limits of the General Assembly and the Security Council, while not barring future developments in General Assembly competence.

Possibly, standards VI–VIII, concerning United Nations authority, should also embody careful guidelines on United Nations action. One guideline, for example, concerning authorization of assistance to insurgents under standard VIII, might be to require specification of specific insurgent movements entitled to receive assistance. One difficulty with blanket authorization of assistance to insurgents is that there is frequently a variety of competing insurgent movements. Blanket authorization then becomes an invitation to ideological competition through selected assistance.

These eight suggested standards for appraisal of interventionary conduct are policy recommendations. They do not represent an effort to describe present international law — though the extent of agreement on particular non-intervention norms and the requirements of the United Nations Charter were relevant features in suggesting what will, hopefully, approximate viable standards. Nevertheless, with the possible exception of standards II, on intervention for the protection of human rights, and V, and on regional peacekeeping, all of the suggested standards are strongly supported by present international law. And though controversial, I would urge that standards II and V also point the way to lawful action under the Charter. There is, of course, continuing disagreement whether humanitarian intervention is lawful under the Charter. For reasons which I have developed in full in an earlier article, my own view is that, if carefully circumscribed to ensure genuine promotion of human rights, such actions are presently lawful. Similarly, I would urge that standard V delimits regional peacekeeping action which is now lawful under the Charter. It is difficult to see how such carefully circumscribed regional action is either counter to Article 2(4) of the Charter or, when undertaken with the consent of the widely recognized government, if any, that it would amount to enforcement action requiring prior Security Council authorization under Article 53.

Contextual Thresholds. In addition to the standards suggested above, a number of prudential criteria or contextual thresholds have been identified, which either point the way to increased risk of escalating conflict or to increased concern for self-determination and human rights. Although for one reason or another they do not lend themselves to formulation as normative standards, they do seem useful in providing additional guidance. They concern avoidance of:

1. Intervention in a region or nation committed to an opposing bloc;

2. Participation in tactical operations;

3. Weapons of mass destruction such as nuclear, biological, or lethal and incapacitating chemical weapons;

4. Participation on behalf of a government which is not supported by its people.

COMMENT: These contextual thresholds are useful from all principal perspectives in appraising intervention, the international-legal, the national-political, and the strategic.

Though it seems unwise to create an absolute international-legal standard prohibiting intervention in a region or nation committed to an opposing bloc—a case for humanitarian intervention, for example, might be just as compelling in such a setting and, in any event, such a standard smacks of illegitimate spheres of super-power control—the threat to world order of such cross-bloc interventions would usually be high and suggests at least a "rule of the game" prohibiting such interventions. Even cross-bloc military assistance is risky, as in the case of Soviet military assistance to Cuba. In general, this seems to be a fairly well observed rule of the game, as, for example, United States avoidance of intervention in Hungary and Czechoslovakia.

Professor Tom J. Farer, in several of the most provocative articles to date on the regulation of intervention, has suggested a "flat" prohibition of participation in tactical operations, either openly or through the medium of advisors or volunteers as a single rule for the regulation of intervention. Under this rule, Farer postulates that all military assistance is permissible, except assistance involving the personnel of the assisting state in combat. This proposal is quite helpful in pointing the way toward the potential for increased escalation, psychological involvement, and increased casualties and social dis-integration which may accompany the commitment of external forces to combat operations. Moreover, as the Nixon doctrine suggests, this rule may be developing as an additional rule of the game for super-power interventions. As a policy-responsive normative standard, however, it seems undesirable, both in permitting a wide variety of activities that would now be regarded as impermissible intervention and, conversely, in overly-broadly prohibiting some forms of intervention, such as counter-intervention to offset impermissible assistance to insurgents and humanitarian intervention, which may sometimes require participation in tactical operations if they are to be effective.

Avoidance of weapons of mass destruction, such as nuclear, biological, or lethal and incapacitating chemical weapons has been a basic rule of the game in interventionary settings. It is generally recognized on all sides that such weapons may have an inordinate impact on civilian populations and may enormously increase the risk of uncontrollable and rapid escalation.

Avoidance of participation on behalf of a government which is not supported by its people has obvious relevance for the promotion of self-determination. In fact, the central tension in adopting a neutral non-intervention norm is that it may sometimes prohibit assistance to a government which *is* supported by its people, as may have been the case in the recent Ceylon (Sri Lanka) conflict, and as may be the case in the continuing conflict in Uruguay. This dilemma has led some scholars to suggest a standard of "legitimacy" based on an approximation of the authority of the government in the eyes of the people. A principal difficulty with such approaches to date is that they have not sufficiently "op-erationalized" the criteria for determining legitimacy. Until a more sensitive standard based on easily ascertainable criteria for determining legitimacy is developed, it seems preferable to retain a modified neutral non-intervention standard. Nevertheless, legitimacy, measured in terms of support by the people, is at least a useful contextual threshold for appraisal.

Questions for Discussion

1. Was Soviet support for wars of national liberation consistent with the Charter? Was the Brezhnev Doctrine consistent with the Charter? If the Soviets had been invited in by

the lawful government in Czechoslovakia, Hungary, and, most recently, Afghanistan (which seems to be factually not the case in all three instances), would their actions have been lawful under the norms of intervention?

2. Was U.S. action lawful in Vietnam? How about Central America? In each case, was its action a response in collective defense to prior assistance to insurgents amounting to an armed attack? If so, is there any legal constraint to responding proportionately against the territory of the attacking state — North Vietnam or Nicaragua? Is there any constraint on responding in kind with assistance to insurgents?

3. Was the NATO action in Kosovo lawful humanitarian intervention? If so, why didn't NATO use this legal basis for its action?

Protection of Nationals and Humanitarian Intervention

Protection of nationals may be thought of either in the context of defense or actions below the threshold of Article 2(4). If necessary and proportional, there is substantial support that such actions are lawful. Humanitarian intervention for the protection of nationals of a third state is more controversial. An increasing number of scholars, American or European, however, support the right of humanitarian intervention if carefully limited.

Richard B. Lillich, *Forcible Self-Help Under International Law*

in Readings in International Law from the Naval War College Review, 1947–1977, at 129, 134–37 (Richard B. Lillich & John Norton Moore eds., 1980)

If you go back to the first instances in which the United States sought to protect nationals by the use of contingents ashore, you will find about 188 cases in which these forces allegedly protected the lives and the property of American citizens, mostly in Latin America but in the East and the Near East as well. It was deemed to be permissible under international law, there was nothing wrong with this as states could legally use forces to protect the lives and property of their citizens abroad. It was forcible self-help, but it was a permissible sanction to protect the human rights of your citizens, including their property rights. There was no doubt that it was not deemed to be intervention under customary international law. Even those people who said it was intervention would then go on to say it was permissible intervention because it was for a permissible purpose.

Now the other concept, humanitarian intervention, is slightly different. Humanitarian intervention allows a state or a group of states to intervene in a country to protect not only its own nationals, but also to protect nationals of either third states or nationals of the country in which the intervention is made. For instance, the phrase was always stated that if the treatment of a state to its nationals shocks the conscience of mankind, as did the treatment of the Jews in Russia and various Christians in Turkey during the last century, then generally the great powers would mount some kind of expedition that would intervene and attempt to bring an end to what they deemed to be a shocking violation of human rights. Now note that here there is not a connection based upon nationality. There is a connection here based upon the need to protect individuals under a certain international law standard. So the doctrine of humanitarian intervention goes beyond the protection of nationals and actually protects not only foreigners without a country, but also the citizens of the country itself.

This is a difference not really in kind, but a difference in approach. Generally, humanitarian intervention was exercised by a group of states and not a single state as was generally the case in the protection of nationals. Humanitarian intervention was justified on the ground that although it obviously was an interference with the sovereignty of the invaded state, it was a permissible one. Sovereignty was not absolute, and when a state did reach this threshold of shocking the conscience of mankind, intervention was legal.

Now, what is the impact of the United Nations Charter on these two doctrines? If one takes a look at the discussions of the charter immediately after its adoption in 1945, for instance in Judge Jessup's excellent book, one sees quite clearly that the charter supplanted these individual measures — protection of nationals and humanitarian intervention which had been approved by customary international law. In other words, they were no longer permissible. And almost all of the writers concur in this. Some say it's very doubtful whether it still exists. Brierly, for instance, very delicately says that it is a delicate question. The Thomases, who did an excellent study in the Dominican Republic crisis, cannot effectively come to grips with the issue, but they indicate that probably only non-forcible measures, in other words, not actual force, could be used in the situation to protect human rights of either nationals or in a humanitarian context.

I do think here you have to reassess the interpretation of the charter based on the experience of the last 25 years. You need not rely exclusively upon the charter. Jessup in his book adds a very interesting caveat which, I think, has been overlooked by many people. In it he affirmed that these traditional doctrines have been replaced by the charter, but he went on to say that if the Security Council, with its Military Staff Committee, was unable to act with the requisite speed to preserve life, then forcible self-help might be allowed. And, of course, it is not a question of their acting fast enough: they do not have any contingents, they are not established, and they are unlikely to act at all. It is not a question of rapidity of the action; it is a question of getting some action initially.

It would be quite all right to forbid forcible self-help under the charter under the assumption, such as Jessup was making, that the United Nations or a regional organization such as the OAS or the Organization of African Unity had either established collective machinery to handle these situations or could act quickly on an ad hoc basis. As a matter of fact, we know that they have not. Let me give you two examples.

The first is the Congo in 1964. In the Congo situation there were several thousand foreigners and Congolese captured by the Gizenga government. It was, of course, the rebel faction that really was not a government in the legal sense, but it did occupy a portion of the country and was in rebellion against the central authority. These people were kept as hostages. There was no doubt that this constituted a violation not only of the United Nations Charter, but also of the Geneva Conventions. No one really took issue with that at all. But the United Nations got bogged down in debate upon it. They finally decided to let the Organization of African Unity attempt to do something: they tried and were very, very unsuccessful. Why should Gizenga, on his last legs, give up these hostages? He made the maximum propaganda use of them. There were broadcasts indicating they would skin these people alive and do all kinds of other horrendous things unless peace was made on his terms. These propaganda statements were not exaggerated, for it was discovered later when the United Nations did go into Stanleyville that orders had been issued and were outstanding to shoot the hostages if there was any bombing in the area. This is a violation of international law, to say the least. As a result of this, the United States, cooperating with Belgium and Britain, mounted an airdrop which, as you know, landed at Stanleyville and rescued these people. There was a tremendous sparing of life, and I think it is reasonable to assume and reasonable to conclude that this was a valid exercise, at least in the classical sense, of humanitarian intervention.

As Professor Falk points out, this really brought down the fury of the radical African governments upon the United States in the United Nations. In fact, as a result, the United States took a horrible propaganda beating. Professor Schwebel, who was here last year, was at the United Nations for the United States at that time, and he said that the United States, and Ambassador Stevenson in particular, was amazed at this fact. It was not couched in terms that this was a violation of article 2(4), it was strictly on political lines, without using legal argument except to the extent that the argument was made in very general terms that the charter forbids this type of humanitarian intervention at all.

Let me give you another example. This was the Dominican Republic in 1965. This is a lot more controversial, as I am sure many of you realize, for a variety of reasons. But at least initially, in the perception of the U.S. Government and, I think, even the strongest critics of the American action, like Professor Falk or Professor Friedmann of Columbia, the introduction of 400 or 500 marines into a crisis situation to gather, protect, and withdraw American nationals, and also the nationals of other countries that wanted to be taken out of the Dominican Republic, was allegedly a valid act of protection of nationals by the use of force overseas. Certainly this was true under customary international law. Whether it was true, of course, under the United Nations Charter and whether humanitarian intervention is valid under the charter gets us into an entirely different game.

As in the case of reprisals, certain things that were supposed to be set up have not become effective, therefore we find it necessary not to reinterpret arbitrarily the provisions of the charter but to read experience into it. I suppose, to some extent, it is like the Supreme Court, which some people feel is the Constitution by its interpretation. It is perfectly permissible to amend the charter by interpreting it differently, depending upon the expectations of the parties and the practice over the years. The argument has been made that there is no violation of the charter under article 2(4) or in its humanitarian or protection of nationals provisions because what is forbidden is the use or threat of force that would impair the territorial integrity or political independence of a state. Now in both the Congo and the Dominican Republic there was certainly nothing that impaired the territorial integrity of the states involved. The political independence of the state was not directly affected in the Congo, and, although the United States went on to introduce additional troops, it was an entirely different situation when we kept staying in the Dominican Republic under OAS authorization. At least initially, we were not attempting in any way to interfere with the political independence of the state. In fact, we were trying to find some state with which we could deal. You could also read this against the broader interpretation. It is not necessary to take a narrow reading of Article 2(4). You can say that this interpretation is consistent with the general principles of the charter. I would say that the two big things in the charter are the prevention of aggressive war and the protection of human rights. And, certainly, if a construction of one section of the charter, namely article 2(4), will further human rights, it is a proper construction. When I started out doing this research, no one supported this view. Since then I have found that Professors Reisman and McDougal of Yale now take this view. A thesis was written by, surprisingly enough, a Nepalese graduate law student in Canada last year who took this position, and I think even Professor Falk and some of the other critics of American interventionary actions are taking it as well. Now, if you can make a valid case for the right of forcible self-help in these two instances — the protection of nationals and humanitarian intervention — then I think it becomes an obligation on the part of international lawyers and the military. Let me say that this is not something that is entirely abstract because, as I'm sure some of you are aware, there will soon be exactly the same situation in Haiti that occurred in the Dominican Republic, and the United States will suffer once again an adverse political reaction if we take interventionary action. There may even be what you refer to as an Op-Order outstanding on this right now. Nobody will tell me. In any event, this type of thing will occur in the future, so we are not dealing only with the theoretical.

There are various criteria for such interventions proposed by a Professor Nanda in an article which he wrote several years ago on the Dominican Republic. For instance, he says you must have a specific limited purpose such as rescue. You cannot intervene because they are Communists or you think they are Communists or you do not like them or you want to protect your foreign investment. If possible, you should have an invitation by a recognized government. If you have an invitation, of course, it is not even a question of intervention. Thirdly, he refers to the limited duration of the mission. You cannot intervene as we did in Haiti in 1914 and stay 20 years — at least not on the rationale of protection of nationals. You also have to use a limited amount of coercion. You don't bring tanks into Santo Domingo if small arms will do the job. And fifth, you have to have no other recourse; it has to be *in extremis*, and this, of course, is pointed out quite correctly by your Navy Regulations.

I have also attempted to set some standards in my article and another piece that also was published this past summer. Of the criteria that I have stressed, one or two of them are variations on Professor Nanda's, but in addition to that, I have considered such things as the immediacy of the violation of human rights. Is a massacre really imminent, or are rumors the only source of information? For instance, the State Department said in 1965 that there was blood flowing in the streets of Santo Domingo. This was an accurate statement but in the general context in which it was issued you were left with the impression that there were rivers of blood: statements were made about heads being cut off and put on pikes. There was a lot of informal retaliation among the people in the Dominican Republic, which was revealed by the Inter-American Commission on Human Rights in its investigations after 1965. I think, however, there is a question in this instance about the immediacy of the violation of human rights. I think your Navy Regulations indicate that it has to be a very immediate and very severe human rights violation to permit this type of intervention.

I also think that it certainly helps if you have an invitation either from the recognized government or at least from some authority that appears to have a reasonable basis for making the request. Once again, the intervenor must limit the coercive measures involved and must also be relatively disinterested. Someone in the *Harvard Law Review* suggested that any state that has an interest in the outcome should not be able to intervene. Well, if you intervene to protect your nationals, how can you intervene without an interest? In fact, some of the leading advocates of the human rights aspects have suggested that it is most difficult to get people to express concern, particularly concern expressed in action, because of human rights deprivations in other countries, like the situation in Biafra and the situation several years ago in Indonesia. People are only concerned, unfortunately, when they have some interest in it themselves, and the interest, of course, is generally based upon their own nationals.

I think, in conclusion, that we can see that the Congo airdrop was a classic occasion of humanitarian intervention, and the Dominican Republic, at least initially, was a classic case of forcible self-help. I think an argument can be made for the permissibility of both these types of actions under the United Nations Charter. I think, in general, you will find that as time passes, more and more people will take a stand against an absolute prohibition of the use of force in international law in the situations that I've been discussing today.

John Norton Moore, Law and the Grenada Mission
23–24 (1984)

International law experts have long recognized that emergency protection actions where the lives of nationals are threatened are lawful under the Charter, although they differ as to whether such actions should be viewed as simply not violating Article 2(4) or as permitted defense under Article 51 of the Charter.

There is today substantial and growing support that "humanitarian intervention," which is emergency protection action where the lives of non-nationals are threatened, is also lawful under the Charter. Experts supporting the right of humanitarian intervention point out that the Charter is also intended for the protection of human rights and that such actions are thus consistent with the purposes and principles of the Charter and are not directed against "the territorial integrity or political independence of any state." Professor Richard Lillich speaks for many experts in this regard when he says:

> Surely to require a state to sit back and watch the slaughter of innocent people in order to avoid violating blanket prohibitions against the use of force is to stress black letter at the expense of far more fundamental values.

It should be noted that both actions for the protection of nationals and the broader humanitarian intervention, if undertaken at the request of lawful authority of the state on whose territory the action takes place, are lawful simply by virtue of the request and no issue of violation of the Charter even arises.

Ian Brownlie, *Humanitarian Intervention*
in Law and Civil War in the Modern World 217, 218–19
(John Norton Moore ed., 1974)[17]

It is clear to the present writer that a jurist asserting a right of forcible humanitarian intervention has a very heavy burden of proof. Few writers familiar with the modern materials of state practice and legal opinion on the use of force would support such a view. In the first place, it is significant that the very small number of writers cited in support of this view by Lillich include two, McDougal and Reisman, who lean heavily on a flexible and teleological interpretation of treaty texts. Leading modern authorities who either make no mention of humanitarian intervention and whose general position militates against its legality, or expressly deny its existence include Brierly, Castrén, Jessup, Jimenez de Arechaga, Briggs, Schwarzenberger, Goodrich, Hambro, and Simons, Skubiszewski, Friedmann, Waldock, Bishop, Sørensen, and Kelsen. In the lengthy discussions over the years in United Nations bodies of the definition of aggression and the principles of international law concerning international relations and cooperation among states, the variety of opinions canvassed has not revealed even a substantial minority in favor of the legality of humanitarian intervention. The *Repertory of Practice of United Nations Organs* provides no support; nor does the International Law Commission's Draft Declaration of the Rights and Duties of States. The voluminous materials in Whiteman's *Digest* lack even a passing reference to humanitarian intervention. Counting heads is not, of course, a sound way of resolving issues of principle. However, quite apart from the weight of the

---

17. *See also* discussion on the "responsibility to protect" in Chapter 5, Institutional Modes of Conflict Management, and Chapter 14, International Human Rights.

opinion of experts cited above, it is the writer's view that these authorities are reporting and reflecting the universal consensus of government opinion and the practice of states since 1945. Their views thus combine both policy in the sense of the reasonable expectations of states and the normative quality of rules based on *consensus*. With due respect to Lillich, it must be said that, if a new view is to be put forward, either it should be based on a much more substantial exposition of the practice, doctrine, and general development of the law relating to the use of force by states or the view should be offered *tout court* as a proposal to change the existing law.

Richard B. Lillich, *Humanitarian Intervention: A Reply to Ian Brownlie and a Plea for Constructive Alternatives*

in Law and Civil War in the Modern World 229, 235–37, 247–49
(John Norton Moore ed., 1974)

The practice of states before 1945, to quote Falk, "exhibits many instances in which intervention was prompted by humanitarian considerations that one can condemn only by waving too vigorously the banners of sovereignty." The United Nations Charter, framed as World War II drew to a close, revealing the full horrors of Nazi Germany's treatment of the Jews, sought to furl these banners where matters of basic human rights were concerned. While the Charter contains no provision authorizing unilateral or collective humanitarian intervention by States, neither does it specifically abolish the traditional doctrine. Actually, despite Dr. Brownlie's vigorous objection, it warrants reiteration that "[t]he drafters of the Charter, as Dean Huston's study shows, paid no attention to whether these doctrines [of protection of nationals and humanitarian intervention] were to survive the *Charter....*" One therefore may accept as common ground Brownlie's contention "that it is impossible to place any form of intervention in the context of the law without examining the legal regime *as a whole*," while rejecting his conclusion that the Charter and subsequent practice thereunder absolutely forbids intervention for humanitarian purposes by a state or a group of states.

Examining the United Nations Charter "as a whole," it is apparent that its two major purposes are the maintenance of peace and the protection of human rights. Article 2(4), the Charter provision relevant to both these purposes, prohibits "the threat or use of force against the territorial integrity or political independence of any State, or in any other manner inconsistent with the Purposes of the United Nations." Since humanitarian interventions by states, far from being inconsistent with Charter purposes, actually may further one of the world organization's major objectives in many situations, such interventions run afoul of Article 2(4) only if they are thought to affect the "territorial integrity" or "political independence" of the state against which they are directed....

      ....

If, as Falk has remarked, "the renunciation of intervention does not substitute a policy of nonintervention; it involves the development of some form of collective intervention," then concomitantly the failure to develop effective international machinery to facilitate humanitarian interventions arguably permits a state to intervene unilaterally in appropriate situations. Writing a decade ago, Ronning wisely observed that "it is as useless to outlaw intervention without providing a satisfactory substitute as it was to outlaw war when no satisfactory substitute was available." ... Although Brownlie does not consider this question, events during the past decade reveal a widening "credibility gap" between the absolute non-intervention approach to the Charter which he espouses and the actual practice of states. Indeed, as in the case of armed reprisals, it may be said that the law governing humanitarian intervention "is, because of its divorce from actual practice, rapidly degenerating to a stage where its normative character is in question."

If, as seems to be the case, "a simple prohibition to intervene is unable to cope with the problem of intervention," then surely, as the present writer noted some years ago, the most important task confronting international lawyers is "to clarify the various criteria by which the legitimacy of a state's use of forcible self-help in human rights situations can be judged." Nanda, taking this approach, has suggested five such criteria: (1) a specific limited purpose; (2) an invasion by the recognized government; (3) a limited duration of the mission; (4) a limited use of coercive measures; and (5) a lack of any other recourse. Occasionally overlapping these criteria but also including several additional ones, the present writer has recommended elsewhere his own five tests by which a unilateral humanitarian intervention should be judged: (1) the immediacy of the violation of human rights; (2) the extent of the violation of human rights; (3) the existence of an invitation by appropriate authorities; (4) the degree of coercive measures employed; and (5) the relative disinterestedness of the state invoking the coercive measures. Moreover, Moore has suggested three further criteria: "a minimal effect on authority structures, a prompt disengagement consistent with the purpose of the action, and immediate full reporting to the Security Council and appropriate regional organizations."

. . . .

Whether one regards humanitarian interventions as legal if they meet the various criteria recommended above, or whether one considers them illegal de jure, yet condonable de facto, if they satisfy the selfsame criteria, seems to the present writer of more jurisprudential than practical importance.

James P. Terry, *Rethinking Humanitarian Intervention After Kosovo: Legal Reality and Political Pragmatism*

(May 30, 2001) (unpublished manuscript, on file with the author)

LEGAL CONCEPTS OF HUMANITARIAN INTERVENTION

Traditionally, humanitarian intervention has referred to a forcible intervention designed to stem a large-scale human rights crisis. The late Professor Richard Lillich of the University of Virginia claimed that humanitarian intervention is normally exercised by a group of states and not by a single state as has traditionally been the case in the protection of nationals. He further stated that pre-Charter humanitarian intervention was justified on the ground that although it obviously was an interference with the sovereignty of the invaded state, it was a permissible one. "Sovereignty was not absolute and when a state did reach this threshold of shocking the conscience of mankind, intervention was legal."

Component elements of humanitarian intervention include the fact that it is executed absent the consent of the target government. In fact, this form of intervention is usually directed against the incumbent regime, although non-state actors might be the target where the state is weak or unstable. It is important that only humanitarian abuses be targeted, as addressing other political objectives and interests take an intervention out of the humanitarian category. Therefore, if intervention is approved, the objective for the use of force must be to address a human rights crisis, and more specifically, the abuses that made intervention necessary. Finally, the rule of proportionality applies to humanitarian intervention, as it would in every case of the use of force. Thus, the level of force exerted must be consistent with the magnitude of the specific crisis and must be only that required to curtail the abuse. Professor Ved Nanda explains that demanding adherence to the proportional use of force in such operations eliminates the "pretext problem" which arises when overwhelming force is used to address a situation that quite obviously does not warrant the force level committed.

Many legal experts, however, have opined that the entry into force of the United Nations Charter in 1945 has supplanted the lawfulness of humanitarian intervention, which had been approved by customary international law. The reason that humanitarian intervention would no longer apply, they claim, is that the Charter provides the exclusive authority for the use of force in such circumstances under Chapter VII. The contrary view, supported by Professors John Norton Moore and the late Richard Lillich of the University of Virginia, Professors Michael Reisman and the late Myres McDougal of Yale University, Professor Ved Nanda of the University of Denver, and Professor Christopher Green of Great Britain, to name a few, argue that humanitarian intervention is permissible in response to threats of genocide or other widespread arbitrary deprivation of human life in violation of international law, but only if diplomatic and other peaceful techniques are unavailable and the United Nations is unable to take effective action.

Legal scholars advocating the post-Charter vitality of the doctrine of humanitarian intervention have urged that a significant credibility gap exists between a strict noninterventionist policy and fulfillment of the principles of the UN Charter. Examining the UN Charter as a whole, they claim, it becomes apparent that the Charter's two major purposes are the maintenance of peace and security and the protection of human rights. Article 2(4), the Charter provision relevant to both these purposes, prohibits "the threat or use of force against the territorial integrity or political independence of any state, *or in any other manner inconsistent with the Purposes of the United Nations.*" Since humanitarian intervention by a collective of states or a regional organization, far from being inconsistent with Charter purposes, actually may further one of the world organization's major objectives if authorized, they urge that such interventions would not run afoul of Article 2(4) if they do not affect the "territorial integrity" or "political independence" of the state against which they are directed. In situations where the UN Security Council is unable to act because of a potential veto, effectuation of this doctrine by a group of concerned states, as in Kosovo, thus becomes critical to *upholding* Charter principles.

This argument is even more attractive legally when one studies the actual substance of the Charter. While the UN Charter is admittedly best known for the articles which create a minimum world order system, as represented by Articles 2(4) (prohibition on the use of force), Article 51 (exception for self-defense), and Chapter VII (Articles 39–51) addressing Security Council responsibilities, there is certainly an equal emphasis in the Charter on protection of human rights. The Preamble, in fact, focuses on the rights of individuals vice the rights of nations when it states that the purpose of the Charter is

> to save succeeding generations from the scourge of war, which twice in our lifetime have brought untold sorrow to mankind, and
>
> to reaffirm faith in fundamental human rights, in the dignity and worth of the human person, in the equal rights of men and women and of nations large and small, and
>
> to establish conditions under which justice and respect for the obligations arising from treaties and other sources of international law can be maintained, and
>
> to promote social progress and better standards of life in larger freedom * * *

Article 1(3) reinforces the Preambular language by stating that a principle purpose of the organization is "[t]o achieve international co-operation in solving international problems of an economic, social, cultural, or humanitarian character, and in promoting and encouraging respect for human rights and for fundamental freedoms for all without distinction as to race, sex, language, or religion * * *." Articles 55–60 of the Charter directly address international economic and social cooperation. Article 55, for example, emphasizes the need to promote "universal respect for, and observance of, human rights and fundamental freedoms for all without distinction as to race, sex, language, or religion." The 54 member Economic and Social Council established in Article 61 and addressed in Articles 61–72, provides the means by which the objectives set forth in Articles 55–60 are to be addressed and then reported to the General Assembly and/or to the Security Council for action. The Security Council, which alone under the Charter framework enjoys authority to authorize measures involving the use of force (in Chapter VII), can be frustrated in its decisional authority when the requirement in Article 27(3) that all permanent members support such a decision is not forthcoming. This describes the situation in March 1999 when the Chinese and Russian delegates refused to support a draft Security Council resolution authorizing NATO-led forces to intervene in the Kosovo crisis, despite the support of 12 of the 15 Council Members.

It was precisely this concern that led legal experts to debate, long prior to the Kosovo crisis, criteria which would both satisfy the need to satisfactorily address future instances of widespread human rights abuses, while at the same time preserving UN Charter principles. In 1974, Professor Lillich of the University of Virginia, anguished over the inability of the Security Council to function in matters requiring the unanimous approval of the permanent members for Chapter VII "all necessary means" operations, argued that "the most important task confronting international lawyers is to clarify the various criteria by which the legitimacy of a state's use of forcible self-help in human rights situations can be judged." Lillich suggested that consideration of the following five criteria by a state, collective of states, or regional organization prior to taking humanitarian action in a foreign state would ensure the Charter principles of the United Nations were upheld despite lack of actual Security Council approval: (1) the immediacy of the violation of human rights; (2) the extent of the violation of human rights; (3) the existence of an invitation by appropriate authority; (4) the degree of coercive measures employed; and (5) the relative disinterestedness of the state or states invoking the coercive measures. Professor Nanda has offered similar criteria in arguing for the continuing vitality of the doctrine: (1) a specific limited purpose; (2) an invasion by the recognized government; (3) a limited duration of the mission; (4) a limited use of coercive measures; and (5) a lack of any other recourse.

By far the most definitive and principled approach has been offered by Professor John Norton Moore of the University of Virginia, a former Legal Advisor to the Department of State. He suggested in 1974 that intervention for the protection of human rights is permissible if it meets the following standards: (1) an immediate threat of genocide or other widespread arbitrary deprivation of human life in violation of international law; (2) an exhaustion of diplomatic and other peaceful techniques for protecting the threatened rights to the extent possible and consistent with protection of the threatened rights; (3) the unavailability of effective action by an international agency or the United Nations; (4) a proportional use of force which does not threaten greater destruction of values than the human rights at stake and which does not exceed the minimum force necessary to protect the threatened rights; (5) the minimal effect on authority structures necessary to protect the threatened rights; (6) the minimal interference with self-determination necessary to protect the threatened rights; (7) a prompt disengagement, consistent with the purpose of the action; and (8) immediate full reporting to the Security Council and compliance with Security Council applicable regional directives.

Professor Moore urged that his suggested standard reflects the judgment that intervention for the protection of fundamental human rights should be permitted if carefully circumscribed. He explained this position by stating:

> Although it is recognized that legitimating such intervention entails substantial risks, not permitting necessary action for the prevention of genocide or other major abuse of human rights seems to present a greater risk. Opponents of any such standard should at least endeavor to weigh the risks of permitting such intervention as carefully delimited by the suggested standard against the risk of insulating genocidal acts and other fundamental abuse of human rights from effective response.

The critical point which bears emphasis with respect to the three proposed sets of criteria is that each would permit a humanitarian response involving the use of force by a regional organization such as NATO in response to threats of genocide or other widespread arbitrary deprivation of human life in violation of international law, only if diplomatic and other peaceful means are not available, and the United Nations is unable to take effective action. The other critical point is that under each of the three proposals, the territorial integrity and political independence of the target state is only temporarily affected, and then to protect other equally significant Charter values.

HUMANITARIAN INTERVENTION IN CONTEXT

The most significant post-Charter example of humanitarian intervention absent Security Council approval, other than Kosovo, occurred in the Congo in 1964. The Congo crisis in 1964 presented nearly parallel legal issues to those faced by NATO in 1999. In the 1964 Congo situation, there were several thousand foreigners and Congolese captured by the Gizenga faction in Stanleyville. The captured civilians were being held as hostages with Gizenga threatening to kill them if his demands were not met. There is no doubt that this constituted a violation not only of the UN Charter, but also of the Geneva Conventions. No one took issue that the situation presented these violations, but the Security Council was unable to agree upon a course of action. The Organization of African Unity (OAU) was thereafter ceded authority to deal with the situation. It failed miserably. The United States, seeing no alternative, much as it had in the later Kosovo crisis, cooperated with other concerned states (Britain and Belgium) in mounting an airdrop of paratroopers without the benefit of UN Security Council authority. The forces involved in the humanitarian intervention landed at Stanleyville and rescued the hostages.

It is interesting to note that while there was much political criticism of the allied intervention, led by the Russian Ambassador to the UN, there has been little scholarly legal criticism alleging a violation of Article 2(4) of the Charter in the Stanleyville operation. Not one legal commenter has found the use of limited force represented in the collective effort of Britain, Belgium and the United States to have impaired the long-term territorial integrity or political independence of the Congolese state. In fact, it can be argued that the stability of the government was enhanced once the hostage crisis was resolved.

A similar judgment can be reached in the case of Kosovo. When fighting broke out in early 1998 between FRY authorities and Kosovo Albanian paramilitary units, commonly known as the Kosovo Liberation Army (KLA), it became clear the Serb offensive was designed to eliminate all elements of Kosovar resistance. The United Nations responded to the extreme violence with Security Council Resolutions 1160, 1199 and 1203. When fighting continued, NATO leadership threatened airstrikes and this led to negotiations between U.S. Envoy Richard Holbrooke and the FRY leadership, which produced an October 12, 1998, Accord between Holbrooke and President Milosevic, leading to signed agreements on October 15, 1998, between NATO and the FRY and on October 16, 1998, between the Organization for Security and Cooperation in Europe (OSCE) and the FRY. When the follow-on peace negotiations in March 1999 at Rambuillet, France failed to reach agreement on a peace settlement the FRY was willing to sign, and the Serbs once again escalated the violence against ethnic Albanians in Kosovo, NATO forces entered Yugoslavia as part of a humanitarian intervention to force Serb forces from Kosovo and to bring an end to the violence against the ethnic Albanian citizens of this province.

The NATO determination to intervene in Kosovo under other than UN Security Council authority came after the Russian and Chinese Permanent Representatives to the Security Council advised the Council in early March 1999 that their governments would not support a draft Resolution which would authorize the use of force to stop the Serb attacks in Kosovo. This after neither Russia nor China impeded passage of earlier Security Council Resolutions 1160, 1199 and 1203. These Security Council Resolutions under Chapter VII of the UN Charter called upon both Serb and KLA forces to end the fighting, called upon Serb forces to withdraw, called upon Serb forces to cooperate with investigators and prosecutors from the War Crimes Tribunal at the Hague, and endorsed the October 15 and 16, 1998 monitoring agreements brokered by U.S. Special Envoy Richard Holbrooke, the architect of the Dayton Peace Accords in Bosnia. As noted above, when the Serbs then violated these obligations through renewed violence and refused to sign the follow-on Rambouillet Agreement in mid-March 1999 (calling for a cease-fire, Kosovo autonomy, and a NATO peacekeeping force), and commenced an offensive designed to drive all Albanian resistance from Kosovo, NATO directed execution of Operation Allied Force against Serb aggression and human rights violations on March 24, 1999. The operation continued until June 9, 1999. In the first eight days of the operation, the UN High Commissioner for Refugees (UNHCR) reported that some 220,000 persons were forcibly expelled from Kosovo to neighboring states, principally Albania, by Serbian forces. The Organization for Security and Cooperation in Europe (OSCE) Verification Mission in Kosovo estimated that over 90 per cent of the Kosovo Albanian population—some 1.45 million people—had been displaced by the conflict by the time it ended.

Although the Security Council had never authorized the intensive bombing campaign, it endorsed the political settlement that was reached and agreed to deploy an extensive 'international security presence' along with a parallel 'international civil presence.' The considerable responsibilities of each of these missions were spelled out in detail in UN Security Council Resolution 1244 of June 10, 1999.

LEGAL RATIONALE FOR THE INTERVENTION IN KOSOVO

Immediately following the start of bombing on March 24, 1999, NATO representatives of the five member states on the Security Council claimed that "NATO's action was necessary to avoid a 'humanitarian catastrophe.'" The German Foreign Minister Klaus Kinkel had earlier argued that "[u]nder these unusual circumstances of the current crisis situation in Kosovo, as it is described in Resolution 1199 of the UN Security Council, the threat of and if need be the use of force by NATO is justified." The British position on the use of force in Kosovo was stated by Foreign Office Minister Anthony Lloyd in January 1999 before the House of Commons Select Committee on Foreign Affairs. In response to a question concerning whether there was a legal right for NATO to intervene in the humanitarian crisis in Kosovo to save lives absent Security Council authorization, Minister Lloyd stated:

> Within those terms yes. International law certainly gives the legal base in the way that I have described * * * [w]e believe[ ] * * * that the humanitarian crisis was such as to warrant that intervention.

Professor Christopher Greenwood, who represented Great Britain before the International Court of Justice defending NATO's action in the Case Concerning the Legality of the Use of Force in Kosovo, explained Britain's legal position when he stated that

> * * * there is a right of humanitarian intervention when a government—or the factions in a civil war—create a human tragedy of such magnitude that it creates a threat to international peace. In such a case, if the Security Council does not take military action, then other states have a right to do so. It is from this state practice that the right of humanitarian intervention on which NATO now relies has emerged. Those who contest that right are forced to conclude that even though international law outlaws what the Yugoslav Government is doing * * * if the Security Council cannot act, the rest of the world has to stand aside. That is not what international law requires at the end of the century.

Questions for Discussion

1. Was the abortive U.S. mission to rescue the Iranian hostages lawful? If so, is it because it did not violate Article 2(4) or that it was permitted defense? How about the Israeli Entebbe raid?

2. Does Professor Brownlie sufficiently take account of the possibility of a carefully circumscribed doctrine of humanitarian intervention? Is the only alternative either a rule permitting it or proscribing it? Can it be permitted under a rule with stringent requirements? What should such requirements be?

3. Was the continuation of no-fly zones in Iraq, enforced by the United States and United Kingdom air action, lawful humanitarian intervention for the protection of Iraq's Kurds and Shi'a Muslims? Is there another legal basis for this action?

Claims to Anticipatory Defense

William V. O'Brien, *Israel's Attack on Osirak*

FREEDOM AT ISSUE, Nov.–Dec. 1981, at 3, 4

Some authorities would restrict the right of self-defense in international law to reactions to armed attacks. However, the better view is that anticipatory self-defense may be justified. As indicated at the outset, this has generally meant pre-emptive rather than preventive action. Thus, if in June 1967 Israel's apprehensions of a clear and present danger of impending attack were justified, her pre-emptive attack was an act of legitimate self-defense.

On the whole, little attention has been paid by international law authorities to the case for a preventive act of self-defense where the threat to security or vital interests is not immediate but may be predicted as the logical culmination of a clear line of events. There are obvious difficulties with anticipatory preventive self-defense. Broadly speaking, any anticipatory action can be criticized as having been premature or unnecessary since it is difficult or impossible to prove that the potential act against which the preventive measures are directed would have taken place. Even in the case of the 1967 June War it has been argued that Nasser did not really intend to attack Israel but only to profit from brinks-manship.

In the case of the Iraqi nuclear reactor it is conceivable that the facts were not as Israel saw them or that they would change with time. I have indicated my conviction that the Israeli estimate of the current situation both with regard to Iraqi intentions and capabilities was valid. As for changes, the Middle East has produced some surprises such as Sadat's 1977 initiative and Begin's responsive concessions which made possible the 1979 peace agreement. But the kinds of surprises necessary to alter the Israeli estimate of the character and intentions of Saddam Hussein's Iraq and the purpose of the Iraqi nuclear project seem so farfetched that they cannot reasonably be held as probable contingencies requiring Israeli abstention from extraordinary measures of preventive self-defense.

W. Thomas Mallison, *The Disturbing Questions*
Freedom at Issue, Nov.–Dec. 1981, at 9, 10–11

If the Israeli claim of lawful self-defense can be justified, it must be on the basis of reasonable and necessary anticipatory self-defense. Consequently, Israel must meet the stringent requirements of anticipatory self-defense rather than the less demanding requirements of self-defense in response to an actual armed attack.

Assuming for purposes of legal analysis that the government of Israel perceived an imminent danger in the Iraqi nuclear program, as it claims it did, it is clear that it undertook at most very limited peaceful procedures or diplomatic measures to deal with the threat. There is no evidence of direct contacts with the government of Iraq. Whatever inquiries or protests were made to the government of France were not deemed by Israel to result in reassurance to it. This is surprising, since the character of French nuclear assistance to foreign countries changed drastically following the intense June 1967 hostilities in the Middle East. At that time France terminated all military assistance to Israel, as it stated it would do concerning any state which commenced hostilities. Since that time, French nuclear assistance has emphasized peaceful development and excluded military uses. In view of these circumstance, it appears, in the view most favorable to Israel, to be doubtful that it has met the peaceful-purposes requirement for anticipatory self-defense.

. . . .

In evaluating the Israeli claim of actual necessity, it is decisive that the community of states has rejected the Israeli claim. So far as is known, not one single state has accepted its validity. In addition, the United Nations Security Council condemned the premeditated Israeli air attack in a unanimous resolution adopted on June 19, 1981. This stands in striking contrast to the unanimous regional approval and the substantial community of states approval which the United States received concerning its perception of the grave threat posed by the Soviet missiles in Cuba. The community of states could establish the Israeli perception of necessity, as well as its aerial attack, as lawful measures of self-defense by giving them approval. Since there has been no such approval and, on the contrary, near-unanimous condemnation, this results in the Israeli claim being rejected under the well-established customary international law process of decision.

Eugene V. Rostow, *Law 'Is Not a Suicide Pact'*
N.Y. Times, Nov. 15, 1983, at A35

The decisions of states to use force under Article 51 of the United Nations Charter is almost always a conditioned reflex under circumstances of stress. Their legality is not determined by how well they are explained, however, but by how well they correspond to the pattern of state practice deemed right by the society of nations. By that standard, the American and allied campaign in Grenada is legitimized by classic precedents in international law, notably the Cuban missile crisis of 1962.

President John F. Kennedy used armed force to prevent deployment of the Soviet Union's ground-based nuclear missiles in Cuba. The United States perceived the prospect of such a deployment as "a threat or use of force." A partial blockade was established. If the blockade had not worked, the President was prepared to invade Cuba with 250,000 troops assembled in Florida.

The American use of force, and threat to use more force, was not a response to an "armed attack" on the United States or its forces, vital interests or citizens abroad. On the contrary, it applied an established principle of the international law of self-defense: The target of an illegal use of force need not wait before defending itself until it is too late to do so. International law, after all, is not a suicide pact.

. . . .

Like the Cuban missile crisis, the invasion of Grenada must be viewed in the broader context of Soviet-Cuban Caribbean policy. The United States and many other nations have long perceived the development of the Soviet-Cuban base on Grenada with grave concern. For Grenada's island neighbors, the brutal murders of Prime Minister Maurice Bishop and some of his colleagues converted that concern into panic. They saw the course of events on Grenada as an immediate threat, and asked the United States to help them defend themselves. Their request reinforced the independent legal right of the United States to eliminate the impending deployment of a hostile force on a large scale in Grenada.

The President's action in Grenada is supported by two further elements, each of which justifies intervention under the United Nations Charter ... right of humanitarian intervention, which has long been recognized when public order disintegrates and social life sinks below minimal standards of human decency. The evidence now coming out of Grenada confirms the tentative judgments on which President Reagan acted.

The State Department has based its legal case for the invasion on the regional security treaty for the eastern Caribbean. In this the department is repeating its error of 1962, when it sought to rely on the Organization of American States treaties rather than the United Nations Charter in the mistaken belief that interpreting Article 51 to apply in Cuba would weaken the fabric of the law. But the problem of interpreting Article 51 cannot be avoided, because regional security treaties can neither modify the Charter nor authorize action which it forbids.

Questions for Discussion

1. If the doctrine of anticipatory defense is accepted, how should it be limited?

2. How would you differentiate the Israeli preemptive strike in the Six Day War from the Osirak raid? Can you differentiate Osirak from a hypothetical Soviet preemptive strike on Chinese nuclear facilities?

3. Do you agree with Professor Eugene Rostow that the Grenada mission is justified as defense? Would this also justify the Bay of Pigs Invasion? How would you answer Professor Rostow's observations that Cuba, Nicaragua, and other "radical regime" states are engaged in a continuing low-level attack on the West? Should there not be a defensive right of response in such a setting?

4. What is the legal status, if any, of the Monroe Doctrine?

5. What is the legal basis of President Kennedy's naval quarantine of the Cuban Missile Crisis? Does the Cuban Missile Crisis present a conflict between the nonuse-of-force provisions of the Charter and the requirements of strategic stability? If not defensible

under the Charter, is it one of those rare use-of-force issues posing an international equivalent of the moral dilemma underlying civil disobedience? Suppose we were—quite apart from any historic real-world case—to hypothesize an action that if undertaken would be—at least in terms of Charter syntax—illegal, but if not undertaken would result in a nuclear exchange with the death of 250 million people worldwide. Would you order the action?

6. Was the United States/NATO action against al-Qaeda and the Taliban in Afghanistan following the 9/11 attack "anticipatory defense" or simply defense?

7. What is the meaning of President Bush's doctrine of "preemptive" action against terrorists and dangerous rogue states? Under what circumstances would a preemptive use of force be lawful? Is this really the same as "anticipatory defense"? If so, was the announcement of a "new" preemption doctrine a strategic error?

Illustrative Case Studies

The Indo-China Conflict: Problems in Mixed Civil-International Settings

John Norton Moore, *International Law and the United States Role in Viet Nam: A Reply*

in The Vietnam War and International Law 401, 403–08
(Richard A. Falk ed., 1968)

Both sides in the Viet Nam debate characteristically select from the highly ambiguous context those features which reinforce their perceptions of the conflict. The "White Papers" issued by the State Department in 1961 and 1965 painted too one-sided a picture of the conflict in not recognizing the extent of indigenous support for the Viet Cong within South Viet Nam and in proclaiming a homespun view of the failure to implement the election provisions of the Geneva Accords. As a result, the White Paper model of "aggression from the North" has never captured the complex reality of the Viet Nam problem. But similarly, critics of Viet Nam policy have also engaged in this "model building." In characterizing the conflict as a "civil war" and the United States role as "intervention," they focus on the features of the context pointing to Vietnamese national unity, the ill-fated unity and election provisions in the Accords, and the instability of governments in the South. In building this "civil war-intervention" model critics characteristically do not focus on the very real ambiguities in the Geneva settlement, the more than twelve year territorial, political and ideological separation of the North and South, the existence of a cease-fire line dividing North and South, and the close relations between Hanoi and the Viet Cong. Professor Falk's model essentially reflects the critics' one-sided focus. As a result his first choice characterization of the conflict as "an internal struggle for control of a national society, the outcome of which is virtually independent of external participation [Type III conflict]," is misleading for purposes of evaluating the permissibility of United States assistance. The issues in Viet Nam are not nearly so neat and tidy and no amount of "model building" will make them so. Real-world Viet Nam combines some elements of civil strife (both within the South and between North and South) with elements of the cold war divided national problem and "aggression from the North," all complicated by an uncertain international settlement. Because of the complexity of this total context, neither the official nor critical models provides a sufficiently sensitive analytic tool for clarifying policy choices in the conflict. The starting point for selection of important contextual features must be analysis of the principal community values at stake.

A prominent feature of contemporary international law is the prohibition of coercion in international relations as a strategy of major change. The most widely accepted understanding of the requirements of both customary international law and the United Nations Charter is that force pursuant to the right of individual or collective defense or expressly authorized by the centralized peacekeeping machinery of the United Nations is lawful. Essentially all other major uses of force are unlawful. These norms reflect awareness both of the great destructiveness of war and of the necessity for the maintenance of defensive rights in a world divided between competing public order systems and with only limited expectations toward the success of existing centralized peace-keeping machinery. At a lower level of generality customary international law and the United Nations Charter outlaw major use of military force to redress grievances, however deeply felt, in the absence of major military attack on fundamental values such as political and territorial integrity. In the nuclear age it is usually better that international disputes not be settled than that they be settled by unilateral military strategies. And this is particularly true of disputes between the major contending public order systems, with their almost unlimited potential for escalation and destruction. These community norms also reflect the judgment, evident as well in national law, that when centralized peace-keeping machinery is not effectively available it is necessary to preserve the right of defense to those attacked. In a world in which power plays a large role in international affairs, this right of defense is a major source of control and sanction against aggression. As such, it may be crucial to conflict minimization that this defensive right be maintained.

In light of the critical values of world order at stake, conflict between contending governments of a nation at least de facto divided into continuing international entities and paying allegiance to contending public order systems presents a problem of major international concern. "Rational community policy must be directed to the coercive interactions of territorially organized communities of consequential size, whatever the 'lawfulness' of their origin." And this is particularly true of boundaries separating major contending public order systems. The balance of power makes the use of the military instrument across such boundaries particularly hazardous, as both Korea and Viet Nam have demonstrated. For the purposes of assessing the lawfulness of coercion across such boundaries and the lawfulness of extending assistance to the entity attacked, these real-world boundaries must be recognized as such. The label "civil strife" must not be allowed to obscure this major problem in conflict minimization. If we believe that long-run community common interest in minimization of coercion is against unilateral coercion across continuing de facto international boundaries and cease-fire lines, particularly when such boundaries separate the major cold war camps, then for purposes of policy clarification about the lawfulness of force, conflict between North and South Viet Nam is not "civil strife" regardless of other features of the context evidencing similarity with "civil strife." The ambiguous 1954 Geneva settlement certainly differentiates Viet Nam from the other divided nations of China, Germany and Korea, but the continuing and at least de facto division of Viet Nam has a substantial parallel to the cold war divided nation problem when analyzed with regard to the vital policies of minimum world public order. It is in the long run common interest not to permit change of existing and relatively permanent international divisions by unilateral military coercion however unjust the existence of the condition may seem to the protagonist of change. The Kashmir and Palestine disputes present additional contemporary examples of the importance of this principle. As applied to Viet Nam, there is substantial evidence of the at least de facto separateness of North and South, regardless of one's view of the effect of the Geneva settlement. Thus, the State of Viet Nam (the predecessor government of South Viet Nam) and the Democratic Republic of Viet Nam (North Viet Nam) were to some extent separate de facto states even prior to the Accords of 1954, and subsequent to the Accords their real separateness became much stronger. Prior to the Accords each government was recognized by a number of states as the government of Viet Nam and each carried on separate international activities. Although nations had differing expectations from the Geneva settlement, the major effect of the settlement was to consolidate territorially the existing division of Viet Nam between the two rival governments. South Viet Nam is now recognized by about 60 nations and North Viet Nam by about 24, a recognition pattern closely approximating that of North and South Korea. The substantial expectations of the separateness of North and South Viet Nam after the Accords is indicated by the January, 1957 draft resolution of the U.S.S.R., a Co-Chairman of the Geneva Conference, calling for the simultaneous admission to the United Nations of North Viet Nam, South Viet Nam, North Korea and South Korea as four separate "states." Both North and South have clearly functioned for twelve years since the Accords as separate international entities with governmental institutions of their own operating along different ideological lines. Both have long maintained separate foreign embassies and diplomatic representation, and have administered separate territories and populations. That the contending governments claim sovereignty to all of Viet Nam can hardly be decisive for purposes of conflict minimization, as the situation is parallel in this respect to that in Korea, China and Germany. Under the circumstances, this at least de facto separation can not be ignored for meaningful clarification of policy alternatives.

In addition to the continuing real-world division of Viet Nam, a factor which exists as a crucial contextual feature regardless of any interpretation of the Geneva settlement, North and South are also divided by a military cease-fire line created by that settlement. In a Special Report in 1962 the International Commission for Supervision and Control in Viet Nam found that North Vietnamese military activity across that line was a specific violation of the Accords. Some critics reply by pointing out that the Commission also found that South Viet Nam violated the Accords by accepting American defensive aid. But this neutral reporting proves little. The crucial question is whether these indicated breaches should be treated alike for purposes of community policy about maintenance of world public order. The clear answer is no. When put in context of community norms proscribing the use of force for settlement of disputes, the indicated breach of the North is exactly that kind of aggressive coercion proscribed, whereas the indicated breach of the South is permitted defensive response to such coercion. It is not at all anomalous in this context to assert that the norm, material breach of agreement justifies suspension of corresponding obligations, is available as a defense to the South but not the North. For even if the South did breach election provisions of the Accords, and there are serious questions here as to the legal position of the South with respect to these provisions of the Accords, aggressive military strategies by the North are not a permitted response to such breach. The point is that there is a major difference in character of the indicated breaches North and South which is crucial for community policies of maintenance of minimum order and which is inherent in overriding community norms as to the lawfulness of the use of force. Failure to recognize this distinction is failure to grasp the essential community policies against unilateral coercive change embodied in the United Nations Charter. Rational community policy concerned with conflict minimization must be concerned with coercion across such international cease-fire lines. This is true regardless of the merits of the dispute between North and South with respect to the Accords. Even if the underlying agreement created expectations denied by one of the participants, community policies against force as a strategy of change militate against resumption of hostilities. The existence of such an international cease-fire line in Viet Nam is another particular feature casting doubt on the utility of characterization of the conflict as an "internal struggle for control of a national society, the outcome of which is virtually independent of external participation."

Richard A. Falk, *International Law and the United States Role in Viet Nam: A Response to Professor Moore*

in THE VIETNAM WAR AND INTERNATIONAL LAW 445–47, 451–54
(Richard A. Falk ed., 1968)

My disagreement with Professor Moore centers upon the degree of discretion that international law presently accords to states with respect to the use of force in an international conflict resembling the one that has unfolded in Viet Nam in the years since 1954 and extends to the sorts of considerations (and their relative weight) that should have been taken into account in the decisions that led to the American military involvement at the various stages of its increasing magnitude. I would contend that the American military involvement resulted from a series of geo-political miscalculations, as well as from a process of decision insensitive to world order considerations.

The Viet Nam conflict demonstrates the harmful consequences for the control of international violence that can arise from contradictory national interpretations of what constitutes "aggression" and what constitutes permissible acts of "defense." Given the decentralized character of international society, it becomes more important than ever, in my view, to inhibit unilateral recourse to violence arising from contradictory and subjective national interpretations of a conflict situation. The war in Viet Nam illustrates a situation in which it is "reasonable" for each side to perceive its adversary as guilty of unprovoked aggression. The potential for military escalation that follows from each side doing whatever it deems necessary to uphold its vital interests is an alarming freedom to grant governments in the nuclear age. My approach to these world order issues presupposes the central importance of establishing binding quasi-objective limits upon state discretion in international situations in which such contradictory inferences of "aggression" are characteristic. I would argue, also, that the whole effort of international law in the area of war and peace since the end of World War I has been to deny sovereign states the kind of unilateral discretion to employ force in foreign affairs that the United States has exercised in Viet Nam.

....

The presence or absence of a consensus has considerable bearing on the legal status of a contested claim to use force in international society. The Charter of the United Nations purports to restrict the unilateral discretion of states to use force to resolve international conflicts. In cases where a claim of self-defense is made and challenged, the burden of justification falls upon the claimant. It is always possible to argue that a use of force is "defensive" and that it promotes world order by inhibiting "aggression." Therefore, fairly clear community standards would be needed to assure that what is called "defensive" is defensive; in the absence of clear community standards it becomes important to allow international institutions to determine whether recourse to "defensive force" is justified by a prior "armed attack." Where there are no generally accepted objective standards and where rivals put forward contradictory factual interpretations it becomes difficult or impossible to mobilize a consensus in the international institutions entrusted with the maintenance of peace and security. Viet Nam presents such a situation of uncertainty and institutional paralysis. What restraints upon sovereign discretion to use force remain relevant? The appraisals of disinterested international civil servants, especially the Secretary General of the United Nations, are distinctly relevant in this setting. The Secretary General contributes an impartial perspective and can, as U Thant has chosen to do with respect to Viet Nam, delineate the character of reasonable behavior by the adversary parties. Normally such an official will refrain from judging the behavior of the participants in a conflict that cannot be handled by agreement in the political organs. The persistent refusal of the United States to comply with U Thant's proposals is indicative of its unilateral approach to the determination of the legitimacy of a contested use of international force. The essence of a law-oriented approach to the use of force is to submit claims to the best available procedures for community review and to restrict force to the levels authorized.

Questions for Discussion

1. When Professor Falk's article was published in 1968, a major factual debate existed within the international legal community about the role North Vietnam and its Communist party had played, if any, in the establishment of the "National Liberation Front" (NLF) in South Vietnam. Following the "liberation" of the South in 1975, the NLF virtually disappeared, and eventually senior North Vietnamese leaders (including Defense Minister Vo Nguyen Giap and Generals Vo Bam and Van Tien Dung) openly acknowledged that the NLF had been created in and controlled by Hanoi pursuant to a 1959 decision of the Central Committee of the Vietnam Worker's [Communist] Party. Assuming these admissions to be accurate, does this help resolve any of the legal issues surrounding the U.S. commitment of combat forces to South Vietnam?

2. Five years after Professor Falk's analysis was published, a peace agreement was signed in an effort to bring an end to the conflict in Indochina. Shortly thereafter, North Vietnam deployed more than twenty divisions—nearly its entire army—in a conventional invasion of South Vietnam, leading ultimately to the military defeat of the Saigon regime and the unification of Vietnam. Is there any reasonable argument that this post-Paris Accords open invasion was not in violation of international law?

3. Apart from its role in the legal debate, the "independence" of the NLF was a central element in the argument that the United States was on the "wrong side" in Vietnam—not opposing Leninist armed aggression but standing in the way of an autonomous movement seeking peace, justice, and human rights. Following the Communist victory in 1975, the Stalinist nature of the new regime led the liberal French daily *Le Monde* to refer to "Le Vietnam Gulag," and in 1983 the Department of State rated Vietnam as the worst country in the world in which to live from the standpoint of human rights. While in the 1960s many critics had opposed the Vietnam commitment because the country lacked strategic significance, following "liberation" Vietnam's army grew to become the third largest in the world (with the United States, having more than four times its population, ranking fifth); and key naval facilities were turned over to the Soviet Pacific Fleet (which has now grown to become Moscow's largest). Another major theme of the war critics was that—whatever other values were at stake—it was essential to terminate aid to South Vietnam to "stop the killing." According to figures compiled by scholars active in the anti-war movement, approximately 1.2 million people died in the war on all sides (North Vietnamese, South Vietnamese, Laotians, Cambodians, and Americans). Following "liberation," however, estimates of the bloodbath that occurred in tiny Cambodia alone in the first two years range from one to more than two million—and at least tens if not

hundreds of thousands of others reportedly died in South Vietnam as well. In view of these developments, what judgments would you make about the conflict today?

4. Was the Vietnam War winnable? If so, how?[18]

The "Six-Day" War: Problems in Anticipatory Defense

Amos Shapira, *The Six-Day War and the Right of Self-Defence*

in 2 THE ARAB-ISRAELI CONFLICT 205, 214–16 (John Norton Moore ed., 1974)

It is granted that a conventional conception of "armed attack," as necessarily involving a massive physical frontier crossing, is out of keeping with contemporary political and military realities. Such a conception, possibly—though not probably—shared by the framers of Article 51, reflects outmoded war traditions. It is premised on the assumed ability of the United Nations, primarily the Security Council, promptly to settle all international disputes and to protect effectively all Members from all forms of aggression. This assumption, unfortunately, proved unwarranted in the Cold War (or, if you will, Cold Peace) era. A proper interpretation of the phrase "armed attack" must reckon with present-day political conditions and warfare dynamics, lest the practice of states should conspicuously drift away from the language of Article 51. Like many national constitutions, the Charter—being the Constitution of the United Nations—should be considered as a "developing instrument," adaptable to the new realities and responsive to the changing needs of the international community. Nonetheless, the rhetoric of some of the proponents of an "anticipatory" right of self-defence is ill-advised and too sweeping. An unqualified sanctioning of the institution of "preventive war" is bound to prove detrimental to an international regime established with the aim of impelling states to forego the use of force. Though some situations of "anticipated," or "imminent," or "impending" attack can realistically be regarded as an "armed attack" for the purposes of Article 51, not all— indeed, not many—such situations ought so to be regarded. The phrase "armed attack" requires a functional amplification, but a carefully structured one.

In the nature of things, the initial decision as to whether it actually faces an armed attack, justifying the use of force in self-defence, rests with the state concerned. The legitimacy of this very decision ultimately determines the lawfulness of the subsequent action taken by that state in alleged self-defence. Whether any such decision is legitimate or not depends on the circumstances of the particular case, primarily on the motivations underlying the decision and the grounds on which it is made. In passing judgment on these motivations and grounds, one ought to invoke the age-old legal concepts of good faith and reasonableness. Did the state concerned genuinely and reasonably believe, at the relevant time, that the other side was actually launching an attack, or had actually committed itself to launch an attack? Did it genuinely and reasonably believe that the other side had precipitated a process of military operations, which, if not stopped, was bound to ripen into a massive frontier crossing or could otherwise seriously endanger its territorial integrity or political independence? Did it genuinely and reasonably believe that an attack was immediately impending, and that it had to choose between either being overwhelmed by the adversary's forces or containing the attack on the adversary's own

---

18. *See* THE *REAL* LESSONS OF THE VIETNAM WAR: REFLECTIONS TWENTY-FIVE YEARS AFTER THE FALL OF SAIGON (John Norton Moore & Robert F. Turner eds., 2002). *See also* THE VIETNAM DEBATE: A FRESH LOOK AT THE ARGUMENTS (John Norton Moore ed., 1990).

soil? Did it genuinely and reasonably consider the risk as instant and formidable, and the necessity to act as urgent and compelling?

....

Turning back to the morning of June 5, 1967—can Israel establish the claim that its action was a lawful exercise of the right of self-defence in the face of an "armed attack" against it? Recalling the circumstances under which Israel decided to use force, and in light of the above criteria of good faith and reasonableness, it appears that such a claim can readily be substantiated. The snowballing Egyptian initiatives during May and the beginning of June should reasonably be expected to have convinced Israel, as in fact they clearly did, that Egypt had committed itself to launch an attack. It is irrelevant in this context whether such commitment, evident to Israel, was calmly premeditated or the inevitable (and, possibly, initially unforeseen) product of a chain of events, or a brinkmanship situation, unwittingly triggered off by Egypt. The ousting of the United Nations forces, the blockade of the port of Eilat, and the deployment of massive forces in offensive positions on its long and vulnerable frontiers were factors from which Israel could have concluded, without any reasonable doubt, that a process was set in motion by Egypt, which, if not immediately arrested, would seriously imperil Israel's very existence. The torrent of official and semi-official Arab declarations of war and threats of liquidation helped create in Israel a firm belief, that a choice had to be made between either risking the possibility of being overwhelmed by the adversary's first blow or taking the initiative to contain the attack on the adversary's own soil. Isolated, encircled and bewildered, Israel considered the risk as instant and formidable, and the necessity to act as urgent and compelling. In retrospect, one might, perhaps, contend that Israel's apprehensions were exaggerated. But, even if one indulged in hindsight wisdom and reached such a conclusion, this in itself could not detract from the validity of the considerations on which Egypt compelled Israel to make her decision early in June 1967. The good faith and reasonableness of the initial decision to act in self-defence must be examined in terms of the conditions prevailing at the time when the decision was taken, not with the wisdom of hindsight. In view of a) the particular nature and history of the Middle East dispute; b) the fact that, in terms of the professed goal of Arab-belligerence, nothing less than Israel's very survival was at stake; c) the superior arsenal at Egypt's disposal and its manifestly advantageous geographical position; d) the unreserved political backing given Egypt by the Soviet Union; and e) the conspicuous impotence of the international community, primarily the Security Council, the legitimacy of Israel's decision becomes all the more apparent.

To sum up: The Egyptian manoeuvres and operations throughout May and early June 1967 could genuinely and reasonably be regarded by Israel, as in fact they were, as amounting in their totality to an "armed attack" within the meaning of Article 51 of the United Nations Charter.

M. Cherif Bassiouni, *The "Middle East": The Misunderstood Conflict*

in 2 THE ARAB-ISRAELI CONFLICT 175, 196–97 (John Norton Moore ed., 1974)

In almost every analysis available in the United States, writers presuppose either that Israel was fully justified in 1967 in the use of force against Egypt, Syria, and Jordan or was at least sufficiently justified to attack first. Thus, on the assumption that Israel acted in self-defense, its occupation of the Arab territory becomes justifiable. It is established beyond doubt that Israel attacked Egypt first and clearly within the meaning of an "armed attack" on another sovereign state. The United Nations Charter, unlike earlier doctrines of international law, was intended to repudiate the notion that imminent threat of force authorized pre-emptive use of force in self-defense. The reason was obviously to reduce opportunities for conflict arising by "jumping the gun." Notwithstanding threats in the form of speeches, there was no "armed attack" on Israel in June 1967 by any Arab state until Israel attacked Egypt....

During and after the "six-day war," Israel consistently claimed to have been "attacked" first. Because Israel's attack was successful, however, the question of who did what to whom first was relegated until after the fact. In the meantime, there was only one witness whose proof could have been irrefutable, the U.S.S. *Liberty*. That American electronic surveillance vessel located in international waters monitored Israel's air sorties and could have provided the data that might have branded Israel as an aggressor and deprived it of the fruits of its victory. Israel destroyed that evidence as it bombed and strafed the upper decks of that vessel where the data and equipment was stored, killing 34 and wounding 166 American Navy men. A naval board of inquiry concluded shortly after the incident that it was a deliberate, unprovoked attack, that Israeli planes and torpedo boats could not have failed to identify the ship as an American vessel in international waters, and that the attack was intentional. The report of the board of inquiry was ordered to be kept secret, presumably by the White House, because of its political implications. The fact remains that Israel, with its support in Western European countries, conducted a massive propaganda campaign to indict Egypt as an aggressor before the facts were even presented. Israel at first succeeded, but in time the man-made fog lifted, and no one now questions, not even Israel, who started the *shooting*. Israel does, however, disclaim starting the *war*, which is an interesting euphemism. Israel claims that Egypt's closing of the Gulf of Aqaba, its request for withdrawal of UNEF forces from the Sinai, and the massing of 60,000 to 80,000 men on that border constituted with respect to the closing of the Gulf a *casus belli* and with respect to the troops' movement coupled with public speeches made by political leaders an imminent threat of "armed attack" that justified its preventive strike.

Central America: Case Study in Covert Attack and Response

Christopher C. Joyner & Michael A. Grimaldi, *The United States and Nicaragua: Reflections on the Lawfulness of Contemporary Intervention*
25 Va. J. Int'l L. 621, 660–63, 665–67, 680–81 (1985)

To suggest that Nicaragua currently represents a real, direct and immediate threat to the United States that warrants armed intervention in self-defense is fallacious. It is true that Nicaragua may be illegally supporting rebels in El Salvador who are engaged in civil unrest against the legitimate Duarte government. It is also true that the Sandinista regime espouses a Marxist ideology, receives aid and advice from the Soviet Union and Cuba, and may be inimical to perceived U.S. interests in the region. Nonetheless, the Nicaraguan government is not considered under international law to be an aggressor state conducting an armed attack against the sovereign territory of the United States. Interestingly enough, the Nicaraguan government has gone to the World Court with that very allegation against the United States, charging it with illegal intervention and paramilitary activities against the territorial integrity and sovereign independence of their state.

Article 2(4) of the UN Charter prohibits the use of force by member states against the territorial integrity of a member state. While the notion of "force" is left vague, it may be presumed at least to include armed force. A preeminent exception to this prohibition is the right supplied in article 51 of the Charter to use armed force—inferred to include intervention—in self-defense against an armed attack by some other state. The Reagan administration has argued recently that U.S. aid to the *contras* is justified on the basis of article 51 because the Nicaraguan government is supplying anti-government guerrillas in El Salvador with arms. In practice, therefore, article 51 of the UN Charter furnishes a convenient vehicle to legitimize U.S. assistance (i.e., lawfully requested intervention) to El Salvador in that the term "armed attack" is being interpreted broadly to encompass "indirect aggression" or illicit "interference," even when the claim of an armed attack by Nicaragua directly on El Salvador cannot be fully substantiated.

Absent an armed attack by the government of Nicaragua against the territorial integrity of El Salvador, the lawfulness of U.S. military assistance to anti-Sandinista guerrillas in Nicaragua is liable to be viewed with some doubt, especially in the Western Hemisphere. The OAS Charter and the Rio Treaty both contain specific provisions that clearly prohibit the use of force. Article 17 of the OAS Charter proclaims that "[t]he territory of a state is inviolable; it may not be the object, even temporarily, of military occupation or of other measures of force taken by another state, directly or indirectly, on any grounds whatever...." Similarly, article 6 of the Rio Treaty maintains that, "[i]f the inviolability or the integrity of the territory or the sovereignty or political independence of any American State should be affected by an aggression which is not an armed attack or by an extra-continental or intra-continental conflict, or by any other fact or situation that might endanger the peace of America, the Organ of Consultation [of the OAS] shall meet immediately in order to agree on the measures which must be taken...." Absent OAS authorization, these instruments forbid the direct or indirect use of armed force, including intervention. Moreover, not only is armed force prohibited, but other types of coercion, such as economic and political pressures on a regime or in support of a revolutionary opposition faction, are also prohibited. If Nicaragua indeed has violated the nonintervention fiats contained in both the Rio Treaty and the Charter of the OAS, then the appropriate legal response for the United States would be to turn the case over to the OAS or the Rio Treaty membership for determination of what course of action should be taken. The United States has not responded in this fashion, prompting one commentator to observe:

> The United States failure to pursue this course of action suggests an inability to muster sufficient support from parties to the Rio Treaty, possible weakness in the factual basis of United States claims regarding Nicaraguan arms shipments to El Salvador, and perhaps a reluctance to raise issues concerning "enforcement action" in the Security Council, where voting majorities are no longer as sympathetic as in the past.

Whether article 51 of the UN Charter justifies U.S. interventionary policy in Nicaragua is uncertain as well. It still remains highly questionable whether the principle of self-defense conveys the right for a third party to intervene into the affairs of the aggressor state, particularly in a situation of civil conflict. Professor Oscar Schachter noted the principle that

> counter-intervention should be limited to the territory of the state where the civil war takes place. The fact that the prior intervention was illegal (i.e., in violation of the rule of nonintervention) would not justify legally the use of armed force by a third state in the violator's territory. This territorial limitation on counter-intervention has been observed in nearly all recent civil wars.

Placed in the present legal context, even if Nicaragua were transporting significant amounts of military aid to rebels in El Salvador, international law would restrain the United States from intervening into the internal affairs of Nicaragua as a form of self-defense, either on behalf of the El Salvadoran government, or on the basis of its own anticipatory concerns. United States' intervention invites accusations that the United States has violated article

2(4) of the UN Charter, as well as the nonintervention provisions in both the OAS Charter and the Rio Treaty.

. . . .

In the Western Hemisphere, the OAS represents the preeminent inter-regional group available for performing acts of collective self-defense. As originally conceived, the OAS was constituted in large part as a pan-American continental alliance "to strengthen the peace and security of the continent ... [and] to provide for the common action on the part of those states in the event of aggression." When linked with the 1947 Rio Treaty, the OAS supplies the legal basis for the hemispheric security system, as well as a warning against potential external aggression.

For U.S. actions in Central America to qualify as legitimate collective self-defense, the United States needs to invoke the Rio Treaty, thereby activating use of the collective defense features of the regional alliance. The United States would first ascertain whether Nicaragua actually was supplying arms to El Salvadoran rebels, an action clearly violative of article 15 of the OAS Charter. If indeed illegal Nicaraguan assistance could be demonstrated, then charges could be presented to a convocation of a Meeting of Consultation under article 6 of the Rio Treaty. The case would spell out in detail Nicaragua's aggression against El Salvador, i.e., its perpetration of acts which contravene "the inviolability or the integrity of the territory or the sovereignty or political independence of [El Salvador] ... or might endanger the peace of America," inclusive of an act which "is not an armed attack." At this time also, the Organ of Consultation would assess the accuracy of the U.S. allegation that Nicaragua was violating article 15 of the OAS Charter, and decide what actions, if any, should be taken "to assist the victim of aggression or, in any case, the measures which should be taken for the common defense and for the maintenance of the peace and security of the Continent." Some might argue that the OAS was being employed to carry out the extra-continental aims of U.S. policies designed to stifle the spread of Marxist regimes in the Americas. The prospect of a negative response by the members of the OAS to such a U.S. strategy ostensibly has dissuaded the Reagan administration from heretofore pursuing such a direct course of collective defensive action. Instead, covert forms of aid to the *contras* and bilateral assistance to the Duarte government apparently have been chosen as the more effective means of countering Nicaragua's perceived threat to the region.

In an address on January 24, 1985, President Reagan declared before a group of Western Hemisphere legislators that:

> A new danger we see in Central America is the support being given the Sandinistas by Colonel Qadhafi's Libya, the PLO and, most recently, the Ayatollah Khomeini's Iran.
>
> The subversion we're talking about violates international law. The Organization of American States, in the past, has enacted sanctions against Cuba for such aggression. The Sandinistas have been attacking their neighbors through armed subversion since August of 1979. Countering this by supporting Nicaraguan freedom fighters is essentially acting in self-defense and is certainly consistent with the United Nations and OAS Charter provisions for individual and collective security.

The legal logic behind this politically attractive argument falls short, given the accepted legal content and stipulated intent of collective self-defense. The international legal potential exists for the United States to galvanize hemispheric collective self-defense into countering Nicaragua's actions against El Salvador; however, the United States has bypassed the legitimate collective self-defense mechanisms available through United Nations channels or the OAS in favor of a unilateral policy dealing with aggression in Central America.

....

The key legal facet of the Reagan Corollary as implemented in Central America turns on the rationale of U.S. self-defense, and the related need to preempt Nicaraguan-sponsored armed aggression against El Salvador. However, serious questions surface over the applicability of article 51 of the UN Charter to justify the U.S. interventionary role. Professor Oscar Schachter correctly observed that the notion of self-defense does not include the unilateral right of an outside power to intervene against the territory of an aggressor state. Thus, even if it were proven that the Sandinista government was transporting significant amounts of aid to rebels in El Salvador — patently illegal under international law — any responsive action by the United States nevertheless should neither be taken against the Sandinista government, nor conducted in Nicaraguan territory. The United States should instead limit its actions to assisting the government of El Salvador in putting down the insurgency in its own state. Though this limitation may seem inherently unjust, providing opportunities for the instigating culprit, international law sanctions neither the notion that "might makes right" nor that "two wrongs make a right."

John Norton Moore, *The Secret War in Central America and the Future of World Order*

80 Am. J. Int'l L. 43, 60–65, 80–91, 125–26 (1986)

[S]ince mid-1980 Cuba and Nicaragua have been waging a secret war against neighboring Central American states, particularly El Salvador. The attack on El Salvador is neither temporary nor small-time. It fields forces roughly one-sixth the size of the Salvadoran Army and has resulted in thousands of war casualties and over a billion dollars in direct war damage to the Salvadoran economy. Although their figures are likely to be inflated, the FMLN insurgents claim that they have inflicted more than 18,000 casualties on the Salvadoran armed forces to date, and that in the first half of 1985 they continued to kill Salvadorans at a rate of 400 per week. Cuban and Nicaraguan involvement in this serious attack includes: participation in organizing the effective insurgency; the provision of arms; the laundering of Soviet-bloc for Western arms; transshipment of arms and assistance in covert transport; assistance in military planning; financing; ammunition and explosives supply; logistics assistance; the provision of secure command and control facilities; the training of insurgents; communications assistance; intelligence and code assistance; political, propaganda and international support; and the use of Nicaraguan territory as sanctuary for attack. With the exception of some reduction in arms transport since 1982–1983, these activities are continuing today in a serious effort to overthrow the democratically elected Government of El Salvador.

The evidence of this secret attack comes from many sources, which include highly classified intelligence reviewed by both the Carter and the Reagan administrations; conclusions of the Senate and House intelligence committees after careful review of the intelligence data; conclusions of the bipartisan Kissinger Commission after careful review of the entire record and extensive inquiry in the region; statements and reports of Central American leaders and nations; reports by independent media and scholars; public statements by defectors; publicly available Cuban, Nicaraguan and FMLN positions (though to a lesser extent, for obvious reasons); and, most ironically, testimony of witnesses for Nicaragua in its pending case before the World Court.

It should be emphasized that both the Carter and the Reagan administrations, after review of the intelligence data and publicly available evidence, concluded that Cuba and

Nicaragua were engaged in a secret attack against El Salvador. The U.S. Departments of State and Defense have issued numerous detailed reports on the Cuban and Nicaraguan involvement that document repeated interception of arms and ammunition shipments. These reports, among others, were released in February 1981, March 1982, May 1983, July 1984 and April 1985. The most recent and detailed report was issued by the Department of State in September 1985. Readers are invited to review these reports and to draw their own conclusions.

Some of the relevant congressional findings appear in a report of the House Permanent Select Committee on Intelligence, dated May 13, 1983, which stated:

> The insurgents are well-trained, well-equipped with modern weapons and supplies and rely on the sites in Nicaragua for command and control and for logistical support. The intelligence supporting these judgments provided to the committee is convincing. There is further evidence that the Sandinista government of Nicaragua is helping train insurgents and is transferring arms and financial support from and through Nicaragua to the insurgents. They are further providing the insurgents bases of operations in Nicaragua. Cuban involvement, especially in providing arms, is also evident.

These findings were made by a committee with a Democratic majority that has been critical of the administration's policy in Central America and that has no incentive to arrive at such findings. Moreover, Congress as a whole found in the Intelligence Authorization Act of 1984: "By providing military support, including arms, training, logistical command and control and communication facilities, to groups seeking to overthrow the government of El Salvador and other Central American governments the Government of National Reconstruction of Nicaragua has violated Article 18 of the Charter of the Organization of American States."

Corollary evidence that the Sandinista attack against El Salvador continues to be serious was reported in March 1984 by Democratic Senator Daniel P. Moynihan, then Vice-Chairman of the Senate Select Committee on Intelligence:

> It is the judgment of the Intelligence Committee that Nicaragua's involvement in the affairs of El Salvador and, to a lesser degree, its other neighbors, continues. As such, our duty, or at the very least our right, now as it was [last November,] is to respond to these violations of international law and uphold the Charter of the OAS....
>
> In sum, the Sandinista support for the insurgency in El Salvador has not appreciatively lessened; nor, therefore, has their violation of the OAS Charter....

On August 2, 1984, the Democratic Chairman of the House Intelligence committee, Congressman Boland, in a colloquy with Congressman Coleman, made clear for the record that Nicaragua was continuing to provide "military equipment," "communications, command and control," "logistics" and "other support activities" to the insurgents in El Salvador.

The Kissinger Commission's report states that "[t]he guerrilla front [FMLN] has established a unified military command with headquarters near Managua" and that the Sandinistas, together with the Cubans and the Soviets, have given major support to the Salvadoran insurgents.

Central American leaders have reached similar conclusions. Thus, former Salvadoran President Alvaro Magaña told a Spanish newspaper on December 22, 1983, that "armed subversion has but one launching pad: Nicaragua. While Nicaragua draws the attention of the world by saying that for two years they have been on the verge of being invaded, they have not ceased for one instant to invade our country." President Duarte said in a press conference in San Salvador on July 27, 1984:

> [W]e have a problem of aggression by a nation called Nicaragua against El Salvador, that these gentlemen are sending in weapons, training people, transporting bullets and what not, and bringing all of that to El Salvador. I said that at this very minute they are using fishing boats as a disguise and are introducing weapons into El Salvador in boats at night.
>
> In view of this situation, El Salvador must stop this somehow. The contras ... are creating a sort of barrier that prevents the Nicaraguans from continuing to send arms to El Salvador by land.

In April 1984, the Foreign Minister of Honduras told the UN Security Council that his "country is the object of aggression made manifest through a number of incidents by Nicaragua against our territorial integrity and civilian population."

Similarly, the independent media and scholars have repeatedly reported evidence of the Cuban-Nicaraguan secret attack. For example, Alan Riding reported in the *New York Times* on March 18, 1982 that "the [Salvadoran] guerrillas acknowledge that, in the past, they received arms from Cuba through Nicaragua, as the Reagan Administration maintains." On September 21, 1983, the *Washington Post* carried a major article describing how reporters admitted to Nicaragua by the Sandinistas to see a "fishing cooperative" instead found a base for ferrying arms to El Salvador. On April 11, 1984, the *New York Times* reported from Managua: "Western European and Latin American diplomats here say the Nicaraguan Government is continuing to send military equipment to the Salvadoran insurgents and to operate training camps for them inside Nicaragua." In a recent study, Stephen Hosmer and Thomas Wolfe wrote of the Central American conflict: "The cooperation between members of the Soviet bloc and other radical regimes to aid the revolutionary forces in El Salvador ... is an example of a coordinated communist effort to bring about the overthrow of an established government."

Publicly available reports by defectors have further confirmed the Cuban-Nicaraguan involvement, such as an interview with the *Washington Post* and the Department of State given by Miguel Bolaños Hunter, a former member of the state security system of the Sandinista regime. He also explained that

> [t]he Sandinistas give total help, advice and direction on how to manage the war and internal politics. The guerrillas are trained in Managua, the Sandinistas help the air force, army and navy get arms through. Some arms come from Cuba via Nicaragua. They use the houses of Nicaraguan officers for safe houses and command posts. There is a heavy influx of communications giving orders. You can say the whole guerrilla effort is managed by Nicaragua.

Alejandro Montenegro, former commander in chief of the National Central Guerrilla Front of the People's Revolutionary Army in El Salvador who led the major attack against Ilopango airport, also testified to the magnitude of Nicaragua's involvement. He was reported as telling the *New York Times* "that virtually all of the arms received by the guerrilla units he led came from Nicaragua" and that "in 1981 and 1982 guerilla units under his command in San Salvador and north of the city received '99.9 percent of [their] arms' from Nicaragua." He said that the attack on the Ilopango airport was carried out by seven of his men who had returned from Nicaragua after 6 months of training in Cuba. And he told a congressional group: "What I want to make very clear is that Managua is where the command center is in every regard."

Similarly, M. López-Ariola, another former high-ranking Salvadoran insurgent, has related that representatives of the DRU from the five Salvadoran insurgent groups live in Managua and each group has a command center there. Alvaro Baldizón Aviles, the former chief investigator of the Interior Ministry's Special Investigation Committee, has recently reported the "training for guerrilla warfare" of groups of the Costa Rican Popular Vanguard Party at a site near El Castillo in southern Nicaragua. Apparently, each group would stay for 6 months of training by the Nicaraguans before returning to Costa Rica and would then be replaced by another group. Most tellingly, Edén Pastora Gómez, perhaps the principal national hero of the Sandinista revolution, recently wrote: "When the Managua government, personified by the nine top Communists, was planning the insurrection in El Salvador, I was a participant in the meetings of the National leadership...."

. . . .

III. LEGAL ISSUES IN THE CONFLICT

. . . .

It is not surprising that the commandantes deny their secret war against neighboring states. There can be no debate that the Cuban-Nicaraguan attacks are in blatant disregard of international law. Important ... norms and declarations violated by these attacks include:

- Article 2(4) of the United Nations Charter;
- Articles 3, 18, 20 and 21 of the revised Charter of the Organization of American States;
- Articles 1 and 3 of the hemispheric Rio Defense Treaty;
- Articles 1, 2, 3 and 5 of the United Nations Definition of Aggression;
- Article 3 of the 1949 General Assembly Essentials of Peace Resolution;
- Article 1 of the 1950 General Assembly Peace through Deeds Resolution;
- Article 2 of the International Law Commission's 1954 Draft Code of Offences against the Peace and Security of Mankind;
- the 1965 General Assembly Declaration on the Inadmissibility of Intervention; and
- the 1970 General Assembly Declaration on Principles of International Law Concerning Friendly Relations and Co-operation Among States.

Soviet assistance, direct or indirect, in such attacks violates not only the above Charters and declarations, but also principles intended to promote world order contained in:

- the 1972 declaration on "Basic Principles";
- Principles IV and VI of the 1975 Helsinki Final Act; and even
- the Soviet Draft Definition of Aggression.

The United States Response

The Cuban-Nicaraguan secret war against neighboring states constitutes an armed attack justifying the use of force in collective defense under Article 51 of the UN Charter and Article 3 of the Rio Treaty. Article 51 provides: "Nothing in the present Charter shall impair the inherent right of individual or collective self-defense if an armed attack occurs against a Member of the United Nations...." Article 3 of the Rio Treaty incorporates this right into the inter-American system, declares that an attack against any American state — such as El Salvador — is an attack against all American states, including the United States, and goes beyond the Charter in creating a legal obligation on the United States and all other American state parties to assist in meeting the armed attack. This obligation is parallel to that owed by the United States to NATO under Article 5 of the NATO Treaty in the event of an attack on a NATO member, or under Article 5 of the Mutual Defense Treaty with Japan in the event of an attack on Japan.

The right of individual and collective defense embodied in Article 51 of the Charter applies to secret or "indirect" armed attack as well as to open invasion. Many scholars, including Professors Bowett, McDougal and Stone, take the view that the Charter—and Article 51—was not intended to impair or restrict in any way the preexisting right of defense under customary law. These scholars note that Article 51 was added to the Charter on the initiative of the Latin American states to protect regional security organizations and that there is absolutely no evidence in the *travaux préparatoires* that it was intended to narrow the customary right of defense. Under this view, the term "armed attack" in the English-language version of Article 51 is merely illustrative of the defensive right, and thus no question even arises whether "armed attack" excludes "indirect aggression." Given the unquestioned historical basis of the customary right of defense in the drafting of the Charter, the view that it is not impaired by the Charter—absent binding Security Council action—seems correct.

But even if a more restrictive view of the Charter is accepted—that the right of defense is limited as provided by Article 51—there is no doubt that Article 51 applies to secret or "indirect" armed attacks as well as to open invasion. The French version of Article 51 speaks of "*agression armée*" ("armed aggression"), and this version is equally authentic with the English "armed attack." Moreover, neither "armed attack" nor "armed aggression" is limited by any language such as "direct," which could have been expected if the draftsmen had intended to exclude indirect attack. Rather, as we have seen, the *travaux* clearly show that Article 51 was designed to accommodate the Latin American interest in protecting the OAS system. Thus, there is no evidence, in either the text or the *travaux*, that the draftsmen of Article 51 intended to narrow the customary right of defense.

As a policy matter, it would be surprising indeed if the draftsmen of the Charter had intended to prohibit states from defending themselves against a serious secret or indirect attack on their political integrity. The insulation of attacking states from a defensive response in such settings would be a formula for the destruction of the Charter. In terms of the important Charter goal of protecting self-determination, a serious covert attack against governmental and political institutions is the functional equivalent of an open invasion. No state can be expected to forgo its defensive right against such an attack aimed at the core of its national sovereignty. Seen in terms of important Charter goals of world order, a norm insulating the aggressors in such settings would encourage these attacks, which already gravely threaten world order, and would doom the victim—and the international system as a whole—to endless war. The seriousness of indirect aggression as a challenge to world order has been clearly flagged by McDougal and Feliciano in perhaps the best scholarly treatment of the use of force under the Charter system. They observe that "[t]he most serious problem confronting adherents to systems of world order ... may thus be to devise appropriate procedures for identifying and countering unlawful attacks disguised as internal change."

Not surprisingly, even under the restrictive view of the right of defense, scholars and state practice have overwhelmingly supported the conclusion that serious and sustained assistance to insurgents is an armed attack and that Article 51 includes a right of defense against such an indirect attack. The abundant scholarly literature and state practice can only be briefly illustrated here. For example, Professor Kelsen writes:

> Since the Charter of the UN does not define the term armed attack used in Article 51, the members of the UN exercising this right of individual or collective ... defense, may interpret armed attack to mean not only an action in which a state uses its own armed forces but also a revolutionary movement which takes place in one state but which is initiated or supported by another state.

According to Professors Thomas and Thomas, experts on the OAS system:

> The force which should comprise "armed attack" ... would include not only a direct use of force whereby a state operates through regular military units, but also an indirect use of force whereby a state operates through irregular groups or terrorists who are citizens but political dissidents of the victim nation. The Inter-American system has characterized such indirect use of force as internal aggression in that it includes the aiding or influencing by another government of hostile and illegal indirect attack against the established political order or government of another country.... Since it is usually an attack against the internal order through an attempt to overthrow or harass the victim government by promoting civil strife and internal upheaval or, once civil strife has commenced, by an attempt to take over the leadership of those in rebellion, it is a vicarious armed attack.... The victim state may exercise its right of individual self-defense against the aggressor state, and, of course, may act against the subversive groups within the country.

Significantly, they add that

> the OAS has labelled assistance by a state to a revolutionary group in another state for purposes of subversion as being aggression or intervention. If this subversive intervention culminates in an armed attack by the rebel group, it can be said that an armed attack as visualized by Article 3 of the Rio Treaty has occurred.

> ....

During the Greek emergency in 1947, the United States regarded serious assistance to insurgents in Greece from Albania, Bulgaria and Yugoslavia as an armed attack. During the Algerian War, France regarded assistance to Algerian insurgents from a Tunisian rebel base at Sakiet-Sidi-Youssef as an armed attack justifying a defensive response against the base. During the 1958 Lebanon crises, the Lebanese delegate, in reserving his country's right to take defensive measures against alleged indirect aggression by the United Arab Republic, stressed to the Security Council that:

> Article 51 does not speak of a direct armed attack. It speaks of armed attack, direct or indirect, so long as it is an armed attack.... [I]s there any difference from the point of view of the effects between direct armed attack or indirect armed attack if both of them are armed and if both of them are designed to menace the independence of a country?

The record of U.S. Senate consideration of the NATO Treaty, which is based on Article 51 of the Charter and parallels the earlier Rio Treaty in its right to defense, reveals that "armed attack" may include external assistance to insurgents and is not limited to open invasion. During the 1964 Venezuelan emergency, the Ministers of Foreign Affairs of the Organization of American States adopted the view that serious indirect aggression could justify the use of force in defense under the United Nations and OAS Charters. In response to a Venezuelan request that they consider measures to be taken against Cuba for supporting subversive activities against Venezuela (activities comparable in kind but considerably less in intensity than those against El Salvador), the Ministers of Foreign Affairs adopted a resolution that concluded by warning the Government of Cuba

> that if it should persist in carrying out acts that possess characteristics of aggression and intervention against one or more of the member states of the Organization, the member states shall preserve their essential rights as sovereign states by the use of self-defense in either individual or collective form, which could go so far as resort to armed force.

Similarly, the United Nations Definition of Aggression unambiguously recognizes that aggression may include indirect aggression. Thus, Article 3(g) characterizes as acts of aggression "[t]he sending by or on behalf of a State of armed bands, groups, irregulars or mercenaries, which carry out acts of armed force against another State of such gravity as to amount to the acts listed above [invasion, military occupation, use of weapons, etc.], or its substantial involvement therein."

Even the Soviet Draft Definition of Aggression says "that State shall be declared the attacker which *first* commits … [s]upport of armed bands … which invade the territory of another State, or refusal, on being requested by the invaded State, to take in its own territory any action within its power to deny such bands any aid or protection."

As for fundamental community goals underlying the Charter, the requirement of "armed attack" under Article 51, like the requirement of "necessity" under customary law, is largely designed to restrict the right to the defensive use of intense coercion to situations that threaten fundamental values. By such verbal tests, contemporary international law establishes that minor encroachments on sovereignty, political disputes, frontier incidents, the use of noncoercive means of interference and, generally, aggression that does not threaten fundamental values such as territorial and political integrity may not be defended against by a major resort to force against another state. But where a major military assault is made against such fundamental values as self-determination and political integrity, it is irrelevant whether that assault is indirect and denied or direct and acknowledged.

The secret Cuban-Nicaraguan attack against four neighboring states is not a minor border incident or political disagreement. Nor does it consist of overenthusiastic, but minor, assistance to an insurgent faction or even isolated acts of terrorism or subversion. It is an intense and sustained secret war employing sophisticated modern weapons and inflicting thousands of casualties in an all-out assault on governmental institutions and political integrity. It has resulted in over a billion dollars in damage to El Salvador alone and in the creation of refugees and social dislocation on a massive scale. It is being contained—but not yet ended—only by a major military buildup that is stifling the development hopes of states in the region. Its success would mean loss of self-determination for the attacked states and possibly even incorporation into a greater Nicaragua. It is being pursued by an alliance that used the same formulas to take control of Nicaragua and that has openly and repeatedly pledged forcibly to install like-minded governments in neighboring states. To treat such a setting as a non-"armed attack" or one lacking any "necessity" for response would be to ignore what may well be the most serious generic threat to the contemporary Charter system—the deliberate secret or "indirect" war against territorial and political integrity.

Under the Charter, a defensive response must be not only necessary but also proportional. McDougal and Feliciano state this requirement:

> Proportionality in coercion constitutes a requirement that responding coercion be limited in intensity and magnitude to what is reasonably necessary promptly to secure the permissible objectives of self-defense…. [T]hese objectives may be most comprehensively generalized as the conserving of important values by compelling the opposing participant to terminate the condition which necessitates responsive coercion.

The values to be conserved in El Salvador and neighboring Central American states are among the most basic guaranteed to all states by the UN Charter: the rights to territorial integrity, political independence and self-determination. The Charter is not a suicide pact. It does not condemn an attacked state to perpetual attack but, instead, permits reasonable responsive coercion against the attacking state as necessary in defense. In this case, United States assistance to the contras—currently limited to nonlethal humanitarian aid—has been instrumental in reducing the level of that attack. It has certainly not been an unnecessary overreaction since the secret attack against El Salvador and neighboring states is continuing. This defensive option may also offer less risk of escalation and a greater chance for negotiated settlement than other direct military responses. As Professor Thomas Franck has recently observed:

> In counter-acting an insurgency organized and assisted substantially from another state, the victim state and its allies must respond in a fashion sufficiently effective to deter, yet not exceeding the limits of proportionality. In practical combat terms this may well argue for a strategy of assisted insurgency against the offending state, as an alternative to remedies which are either ineffective or which—as for example, is the case of large scale bombing—purchase effectiveness at a higher cost to innocent parties.

Nothing could more quickly doom the Charter to irrelevance than to limit defensive options against serious armed attack solely to those of the least military and political effectiveness. Response solely within the attacked state leaves the military advantage with the attacker. An equivalent response in kind against the attacking state, however, shifts the military multiplier effect against the aggressor, permits direct action against weapons trans-shipment points and creates a persuasive incentive not to engage in an endless secret war.

Proportionality, correctly perceived, is not so much an exercise in matching levels of force between attacker and defender as, rather, a relation between lawful objectives in using force and the effective pursuit of those objectives in the way least destructive of other values. Nevertheless, a comparison of levels of force provides one contextual feature in assessing the proportionality of the response. In its attack against El Salvador and neighboring states, Nicaragua supplies command and control, training, funding, weapons and logistical assistance. It seeks the overthrow of the democratically elected Government of El Salvador, supports terrorism and efforts to destabilize three other neighboring states and does not suffer from any apparent constraints on its activities, other than a thoroughgoing effort at concealment.

The United States, in contrast, has not responded with bombing or invasion. Its defensive response has been in kind, but currently limited by law to assistance that is not directed to overthrowing the Sandinista Government and is exclusively humanitarian. Earlier, the United States was further constrained by a complete funds cutoff and prohibitions on submarine mining and on activities of defense and intelligence agencies. It is difficult to see how the considerably more restrained U.S. response against Nicaragua can be disproportionate to Nicaragua's determined and continuing attacks against four Central American states.

There is no prohibition under the Charter—apart from the general requirement of proportionality—against covert action as part of a defensive response to an armed attack. A response in defense may lawfully be overt, covert or—as in virtually every conflict in which the United States has fought in this century—both. In World Wars I and II and the Korean War, no one regarded Allied or UN support for paramilitary forces or covert operations as illegal. Lawrence of Arabia, to mention the most famous example, led a British covert operation in World War I to create an insurgency within the Ottoman Empire as part of the Allies' overall defensive response against the Central Powers. During World War II, the Allies created and aided insurgent movements in France, Belgium, the Netherlands, Norway, Yugoslavia, Greece and China, among other countries. In Italy support was given to partisans fighting the Germans and Italian Fascists. In Germany weapons and materials were supplied to Germans and foreign workers for acts of sabotage against the Nazi war effort. The UN command itself sponsored guerrilla warfare against North Korea in response to that country's aggression in 1950–1953. With the approval of the high command, 44 teams of guerrillas were sent into North Korea to disrupt supply lines by attacking trains and truck convoys. All told, twelve hundred men were involved in this 2-year paramilitary effort against North Korea. During Sukarno's secret war against Malaysia in the 1965 "confrontation," the United Kingdom provided not only direct assistance to Malaysia but also covert assistance to guerrilla and insurgent forces operating against Sukarno within Indonesia.

The use of paramilitary forces as part of a defensive response is not unique to this century. In U.S. practice it dates at least to the presidency of Thomas Jefferson who provided arms, training and financial assistance to support an army of foreign nationals against the Bey of Tripoli as a means of ending attacks on commercial shipping in the Mediterranean. Such activities, when undertaken in defense against armed attack, have never been and are not now "state terrorism" or otherwise illegal. To make such a charge is to undermine the most important distinction in the United Nations and OAS Charters—that between aggression and defense. Moreover, the assistance to resistance forces in Nicaragua, as part of a broader defensive response against the Cuban-Nicaraguan armed attack, has been fully debated within Congress, the media and the UN Security Council and is not truly covert. The intelligence community describes such settings as "overt-covert." As we have seen, efforts to seek the peaceful settlement of disputes and to avoid escalation may make such an "overt-covert" response preferable.

The United States has not violated Articles 18 and 20 of the OAS Charter (revised in 1967) on nonintervention. Article 22 of the Charter specifically states that "measures adopted for the maintenance of peace and security in accordance with existing treaties"—in this case, Article 3 of the Rio Treaty—"do not constitute a violation of the precepts set forth in Articles 18 and 20." Under Article 21, the "American States bind themselves in their international relations not to have recourse to the use of force, except in the case of self-defense." Articles 27, 28 and 137 support the same legal point: that actions in defense under the Rio Treaty and the UN Charter are not illegal. Similarly, states faced with an armed attack are not obliged to invoke the procedural machinery of the OAS before responding. As with Article 51 of the UN Charter, Article 3 of the OAS Charter permits an immediate and continuing response against armed attack *until the procedural machinery of the UN or OAS systems concludes otherwise.* Some have confused the procedural requirements of Article 6 of the Rio Treaty, which apply to settings other than armed attacks, with those of Article 3, which govern here.

....

The secret war in Central America illustrates the danger to world order—and to the legal order itself—posed by the assaults of radical regimes. In Nicaragua three small and unrepresentative Marxist-Leninist factions came to power through focused Cuban economic and military assistance during a genuine and broad-based revolution against Somoza. Subsequently, the nine leaders of these factions joined with Cuba in a secret war against neighboring states. That war is conducted through assistance in organizing Marxist-Leninist-controlled insurgencies; the financing of such insurgencies; the provision and transshipment to them of arms and ammunition; training the insurgents; assistance in command and control, intelligence, military and logistics activities; and extensive political support. It also includes terrorist attacks and subversive activities preliminary to and supportive of an all-out covert attack.

Arrayed in support of this secret war is a diverse conglomeration of radical regimes and insurgent movements from the Soviet Union and Soviet-bloc nations such as East Germany, Bulgaria, Czechoslovakia, Cuba, Vietnam, Ethiopia and North Korea, to Libya, Iraq, Iran and the PLO. The nine comandantes have also made Nicaragua available as a more generalized sanctuary for radical terrorist attacks. Non-Central American groups currently operating from Nicaragua include: Colombia's M-19 (the terrorist group that recently took hostage the Colombian Supreme Court, which resulted in the death of 11 members of the Court), the Argentine Montoneros, the Uruguayan Tupamaros, the Basque ETA, the Palestine Liberation Organization, Italy's Red Brigades, West Germany's Baader-Meinhof gang and the Irish Republican Army.

The strategy of covert and combined political-military attack that undergirds this secret war is a particularly grave threat to world order. By denying the attack, the aggressors create doubts as to its existence; and by shielding the attack with a cloud of propaganda and misinformation, they focus world attention on alleged (and sometimes real) shortcomings of the victimized state and the permissibility of defensive response. The result is a politically "invisible attack" that avoids the normal political and legal condemnation of aggressive attack and instead diverts that moral energy to condemning the defensive response. In a real sense, the international immune system against aggressive attack becomes misdirected instead to defensive response.

Aggressive attack — particularly in its more frequent contemporary manifestation of secret guerrilla war, terrorism and low-intensity conflict — is a grave threat to world order wherever undertaken. That threat is intensified, however, when it is a form of cross-bloc attack in an area of traditional concern to an opposing alliance system. That is exactly the kind of threat presented by an activist Soviet-bloc intervention in the OAS area.

Military and Paramilitary Activities
(Nicar. v. U.S.)
1986 I.C.J. 1 (June 27) (judgment of the Court)

[In its summary:]

The Court does not believe that the concept of "armed attack" includes assistance to rebels in the form of the provision of weapons or logistical or other support. Furthermore, the Court finds that in customary international law, whether of a general kind or that particular to the inter-American legal system, there is no rule permitting the exercise of collective self-defence in the absence of a request by the State which is a victim of the alleged attack, this being additional to the requirement that the State in question should have declared itself to have been attacked.

[Specifically, the Court found that:]

195. In the case of individual self-defence, the exercise of this right is subject to the State concerned having been the victim of an armed attack. Reliance on the collective self-defence of course does not remove the need for this. There appears now to be general agreement on the nature of the acts which can be treated as constituting armed attacks. In particular, it may be considered to be agreed that an armed attack must be understood as including not merely action by regular armed forces across an international border, but also "the sending by or on behalf of a State of armed bands, groups, irregulars or mercenaries, which carry out acts of armed force against another State of such gravity as to amount to" (*inter alia*) an actual armed attack conducted by regular forces, "or its substantial involvement therein". This description, contained in Article 3, paragraph (*g*),

of the Definition of Aggression annexed to General Assembly resolution 3314 (XXIX), may be taken to reflect customary international law. The Court sees no reason to deny that, in customary law, the prohibition of armed attacks may apply to the sending by a State of armed bands to the territory of another State, if such an operation, because of its scale and effects, would have been classified as an armed attack rather than as a mere frontier incident had it been carried out by regular armed forces. But the Court does not believe that the concept of "armed attack" includes not only acts by armed bands where such acts occur on a significant scale but also assistance to rebels in the form of the provision of weapons or logistical or other support. Such assistance may be regarded as a threat or use of force, or amount to intervention in the internal or external affairs of other States. It is also clear that it is the State which is the victim of an armed attack which must form and declare the view that it has been so attacked. There is no rule in customary international law permitting another State to exercise the right of collective self-defence on the basis of its own assessment of the situation. Where collective self-defence is invoked, it is to be expected that the State for whose benefit this right is used will have declared itself to be the victim of an armed attack.

Military and Paramilitary Activities

(*Nicar. v. U.S.*) 1986 I.C.J. 1

(June 27) (dissenting opinion of Judge Schwebel)

163. In marked contrast to these approaches of "East" and "West", thirteen small and middle Powers put forward a draft definition of aggression which did not include indirect as well as direct uses of force. Their definition spoke only of "the use of armed force by a State against another State." Their list of acts of aggression conspicuously failed to include acts of force effected by indirect means. The Thirteen-Power draft further specified, in a section which did not list acts of aggression, that:

> "When a State is a victim in its own territory of subversive and/or terrorist acts by irregular, volunteer or armed bands organized or supported by another State, it may take all reasonable and adequate steps to safeguard its existence and its institutions, without having recourse to the right of individual or collective self-defence against the other State under Article 51 of the Charter."

That provision was complementary to a further proviso that:

> "The inherent right of individual or collective self-defence of a State can be exercised only in the case of the occurrence of armed attack (armed aggression) by another State ..."

. . . .

It will be observed that the essential legal rationale of the Judgment of the Court in the current case appears to be well expressed by these Thirteen-Power proposals which Professor Stone characterized as "at odds with the Charter and general international law...."

165. The Thirteen-Power proposals were not accepted by the United Nations Special Committee on the Question of Defining Aggression. They were not accepted by the General Assembly. On the contrary, the General Assembly by consensus adopted a Definition of Aggression which embraces not all, but still the essence of, the proposals of the Six Powers and the Soviet Union. Its list in Article 3 of the acts which shall "qualify as an act of aggression" includes:

> "(g) The sending by or on behalf of a State of armed bands, groups, irregulars or mercenaries, which carry out acts of armed force against another State of such

gravity as to amount to acts listed above, *or its substantial involvement therein.*" (Emphasis supplied.)

. . . .

... I wish, *ex abundanti cautela*, to make clear that, for my part, I do not agree with a construction of the United Nations Charter which would read Article 51 as if it were worded: "Nothing in the present Charter shall impair the inherent right of individual or collective self-defence if, and only if, an armed attack occurs ..." I do not agree that the terms or intent of Article 51 eliminate the right of self-defence under customary international law, or confine its entire scope to the express terms of Article 51. While I recognize that the issue is controversial and open to more than one substantial view, I find that of Sir Humphrey Waldock more convincing than contrary interpretations:

> "Does Article 51 cut down the customary right and make it applicable only to the case of resistance to armed attack by another State? This does not seem to be the case. The right of individual self-defence was regarded as automatically excepted from both the Covenant and the Pact of Paris without any mention of it. The same would have been true of the Charter, if there had been no Article 51, as indeed there was not in the original Dumbarton Oaks proposals. Article 51, as is well known, was not inserted for the purpose of defining the individual right of self-defence but of clarifying the position in regard to collective understandings for mutual self-defence, particularly the Pan-American treaty known as the Act of Chapultepec. These understandings are connected with defence against external aggression and it was natural for Article 51 to be related to defence against 'attack'. Article 51 also has to be read in the light of the fact that it is part of Chapter VII. It is concerned with defence to grave breaches of the peace which are appropriately referred to as armed attack. It would be a misreading of the whole intention of Article 51 to interpret it by mere implication as forbidding forcible self-defence in resistance to an illegal use of force not constituting an 'armed attack'. Thus, it would, in my view, be no breach of the Charter if Denmark or Sweden used armed force to prevent the illegal arrest of one of their fishing vessels on the high seas in the Baltic. The judgment in the Corfu Channel Case is entirely consistent with this view ..." [C. H. M. Waldock, "The Regulation of the Use of Force by Individual States in International Law", *Collected Courses*, The Hague (1952-II), pp. 496–497. Accord: D. W. Bowett, *Self-Defence in International Law*, 1958, pp. 182–193; Myres S. McDougal and Florentino P. Feliciano, *Law and Minimum World Public Order*, 1961, pp. 232–241; Oscar Schachter, "The Right of States to Use Armed Force", *Michigan Law Review*, 1984, Vol. 82, pp. 1620, 1634.]

John Norton Moore, Jus ad Bellum *Before the International Court of Justice*
52 Va. J. Int'l L. 903, 905–910, 946–52 (2012)

Understanding of the causes of war and aggression is still in its infancy.[19] Nevertheless, in the last century newer data about "the democratic peace," effects of high levels of bilateral trade, the importance of deterrence, and other more complete information about

---

19. The first useful data base for the study of war, the Correlates of War Project, was only completed in the 1970s.

war and aggression have greatly enhanced our understanding.[20] One of the more important newer theories in understanding war, termed "incentive theory," focuses on the incentives of regime elite decision makers from personal belief systems, key advisors or influential groups, form of government and the international system as a whole.[21] In classic international relations theory we are asking here about incentives affecting elite decision makers and militating for or against war; incentives from "image one" (the individual, including key advisors and influential interest groups), "image two" (form of government), and "image three" (effect of external incentives from the international milieu, including the effect of international law).[22] But whether we are using incentive theory or other contemporary theories in our understanding of war and aggression, it is clear that any normative system has its effect through influencing perspectives/subjectivities of, and/or costs for, regime elite decision makers as they contemplate aggression.

To achieve a deterrent effect against aggression a normative system must condemn aggression. But it must also differentiate between aggression and defense. For the totality of incentives against aggression, including the totality of defensive responses from the international milieu, are also a core deterrent against aggression. Thus, if the normative system effectively de-legitimates and imposes costs on defensive action as much as it de-legitimates and imposes costs on aggression then it will have undermined the overall normative response against aggression. And if it de-legitimates defensive action while ignoring aggression it will have effectively thrown its weight on the side of aggression. At minimum, a system treating aggression and defense without effective differentiation simply turns the normative system into a cipher, as a potential aggressor knows that the defenders will bear at least equal cost from the normative system. It is the *differential effect* between treatment by the legal system of aggression (prohibited) and defense (permitted) that generates the deterrence against aggression from the legal system.

For the most part, aggression through regular army invasion, as in Hitler's invasion of Poland starting World War II, will be quickly understood as aggression, despite propaganda efforts to initially persuade the world otherwise. The problem comes when the aggression is in the form of secret warfare (conventionally called "indirect aggression"), terrorism, clandestine laying of mines, or other covert uses of force that are not immediately understood as to their provenance. The problem is then compounded in court because of proof problems and the difficulty (indeed usually impossibility without revealing sensitive sources and methods) in relying on the intelligence sources that reveal the secret aggression. Moreover, generally the defensive responders are engaging in actions that they openly acknowledge, directly or indirectly, while the aggressors are simply lying to the world. This, in turn, plays into judicial practices weighting admissions against interest while giving lesser weight to sources of evidence consistent with a party's interest. As will be seen in the next section these problems are compounded in the contemporary international system where secret warfare and other forms of covert aggression are the norm rather than armies openly on the march.[23]

---

20. *See generally* JOHN NORTON MOORE, SOLVING THE WAR PUZZLE (2003); BRUCE RUSSETT, GRASPING THE DEMOCRATIC PEACE (1994).

21. *See* Moore, *supra* note 4.

22. *See, e.g.*, KENNETH WALTZ, MAN, THE STATE AND WAR (1954).

23. For an interesting article addressing some of these issues in maintaining an effective right of defense against contemporary forms of covert aggression, *see* Theresa Reinold, *State Weakness, Irregular Warfare, and the Right to Self-Defense Post-9/11*, 105 AM. J. INT'L L. 244 (2011) (particularly exploring "the immediacy requirement of an armed attack, the attribution standard for imputing the acts of irregulars to a state, and the twin requirements of necessity and proportionality.") (at 246). The author

. . . .

There are five principal forms of aggressive attack in the contemporary system.[24] All are in violation of the United Nations Charter and contemporary international law. These are:

- *Full scale invasion.* Examples: Hitler's 1939 invasion of Poland, North Korea's 1950 invasion of South Korea, North Vietnam's 1975 Post Paris Accords invasion of South Vietnam, Saddam Hussein's 1990 invasion of Kuwait, and the 2003 invasion of Iraq by the United States and the United Kingdom (among a coalition of other states).[25]

- *Secret warfare.* This is traditionally known in international law as "*indirect aggression.*" The covert creation, funding, training, and arming of an insurgency directed at overthrow of the government of another state. Examples: North Vietnam's opening of the Ho Chi Minh Trail with an attack against South Vietnam in the 1959–73 Phase I Vietnam War, and the Sandinistas' 1978–80's Secret War Against El-Salvador, Honduras, Guatemala and Costa Rica (with the core attack directed against El-Salvador).

- *Creation of a parallel state within a state.* The covert creation in a weak or failed state of a political party providing governmental services and a parallel army/militia (both in competition with the weak government) for the purpose of eventual takeover of the government either through the political process or military action or for the purpose of waging secret warfare against neighboring states, or both. Examples — Iranian and Syrian support for Hamas in Palestine (with parallel attacks against Israel), and Iranian and Syrian support for Hezbollah in Lebanon (with parallel attacks against Israel).

- *Terrorism.* Covert support for violence directed against governments or civilian populations for the purpose of terror and other harm against the targeted government or population. Examples: *Today,* particularly *Al Qaeda* against the United States and western nations; Iran in Iraq, Afghanistan, and elsewhere; and a range of terrorist groups in attacks against Israel. *Previously,* almost too numerous to list, such as members of the Soviet sponsored Warsaw Pact in supporting violent movements in Western Europe; Cuba in supporting violent movements in Latin and Central America; North Korea (the DRK) in covert attacks against South Korea and Japanese citizens; Libya in covert attacks against civil aviation, western democracies and African nations; a range of radical political/drug cartel groups in Colombia and more broadly Latin America in attacks against governmental and civilian interests in Colombia, Mexico and elsewhere in Latin America; and a range of radical Palestinian groups in covert attacks against Israel and Israeli interests worldwide.

- *Indiscriminate mining of international waterways.* Naval mines can be a lawful modality of warfare in settings of armed hostilities, provided their use is in compliance with Hague VIII and other applicable *jus in bello* rules. But

also notes "… the conservative pronouncements of the International Court of Justice (ICJ) on self-defense have further muddied already murky waters" (at 245).

24. There may also be other forms not directly utilizing bombs and bullets, for example a major cyber-attack intentionally resulting in substantial loss of life or destruction of economic values.

25. I believe that the evidence today suggests that the 2003 invasion of Iraq by the United States and the United Kingdom was not consistent with the Charter. I have also taken the view that it was a strategic blunder by the George W. Bush Administration. Once the action was taken, however, the strategic question was dramatically transformed into one concerning credibility, self-determination for the people of Iraq, humanitarian considerations, and other important reasons supporting the need for a successful outcome.

indiscriminate mining of straits used for international navigation and other international waterways used by neutral shipping is in violation of the Charter and is an illegal use of force. Examples include covert mining of international waterways intentionally interfering with neutral rights and navigational freedoms, as Albania in the 1946 *Corfu Channel* affair, Libya in the 1984 mining of the Red Sea approaches to the Suez Canal,[26] and Iran in the 1980–87 mining of navigational channels used by neutral shipping in the Persian Gulf.

It should be noted with particular importance that in the contemporary world covert aggression in a mixture of one or more of the last four categories of aggression is the predominant form of aggression *de jure*. Aggressive smaller regimes typically understand that they are no match for the conventional militaries of major powers and, as such, they utilize "asymmetric warfare," which typically involves concealment of their role and an effort to deny attribution. In turn, such covert actions blend in with a background of ongoing global violence and are politically less likely to generate a collective military response on behalf of those attacked. As such, these forms of covert attack present a particularly difficult problem for democratic nation responders. Indeed, for this reason Muammar al-Gaddafi lectured his war college in Libya that had Saddam Hussein simply engaged in secret warfare against Kuwait, rather than a highly visible tank attack, Kuwait might be part of Iraq today.

In addition to generally opting for covert modes of aggression, contemporary aggressors have also understood that law is important and, as such, they can leverage the ambiguity of covert attack to seek to turn the law against the defenders. Today this is widely discussed as a component of "lawfare."[27] For a healthy international legal system, efforts of an aggressor to turn the law against the defender should rebound against the aggressor. Law, and certainly *jus ad bellum*, in no way favors the aggressor—rather it is antithetical to aggression. Sadly, however, as can be seen simply by the number of aggressors filing actions in the International Court of Justice against defensive actions, "lawfare" on the part of aggressors is alive and well.[28] One of the costs to the system that such "lawfare" generates is not only undermining deterrence against aggression, but also undermining support for international law itself and important legal institutions such as the International Court of Justice. One direct cost of the *Nicaragua* decision, of course, has been the United States removal of its Article 36(2) acceptance of jurisdiction of the Court. The decision may well have also played a role in encouraging Iran to file its action against the United States in the upside down *Iran Platforms* case.

---

26. Scott C. Truver, *The Law of the Sea and the Military Use of the Oceans in 2010*, 45 La. L. Rev. 1221, 1232–33 (1985).

27. *See, e.g.* Christi Scott Bartman, *Beyond Traditional Concepts of Lawfare: Lawfare and the Definition of Aggression: What the Soviet Union and Russian Federation Can Teach Us*, 43 Case W. Res. J. Int'l L. 423 (2010). *See also* Charles J. Dunlap, Jr., Law and Military Interventions: Preserving Humanitarian Values in 21st Century Conflicts, (Carr Center for Human Rights, John F. Kennedy School of Gov't, Harvard University, Working Paper, 2001), available at http://www.ksg. harvard.edu/cchrp/Web%20Working%20Papers/Use%20of%20Force/Dunlap2001.pdf.

28. This is in no way an argument for the "Realist-Rejectionist Model" which rails against international law as a tool of weaker states seeking to tie down major powers. To the contrary, a system of international law, and particularly prohibitions against use of force as a modality of major change, as is the core of current *jus ad bellum*, is of fundamental importance to all nations, big and small. On balance, the rule of law is powerfully supportive of widely adhered goals in the interests of all nations and "lawfare," broadly conceived, should be a core modality of response against aggression and other outrages. Recently, for example, I have urged greater use of civil litigation as a tool against covert state supported terrorism. *See* J.N. Moore, *Civil Litigation Against Terrorism*, Chapter 8 *in* Legal Issues in the Struggle Against Terror 197–234 (John Norton Moore & Robert F. Turner, eds. 2010).

....

One of the basic principles of international law, a rule central to the functioning of the International Court of Justice and, more broadly, to that of the international legal system itself, is that unless the parties agree to a decision *ex aequo et bono*, the Court "is to decide in accordance with international law."[29] In this connection, Article 38 of the Statute of the Court provides specifically that the Court "shall apply," as sources of international law:

- "international conventions ... establishing rules expressly recognized by the contesting states";
- "international custom, as evidence of a general practice accepted as law";
- "the general principles of law recognized by civilized nations"; and
- " ... judicial decisions and the teachings of the most highly qualified publicists of the various nations, as subsidiary means for the determination of rules of law."[30]

International courts, and particularly the International Court of Justice, composed of some of the top international law jurists in the world, typically do an excellent job in understanding and applying the law, as rooted in the sources specified in Article 38 of the Statute. But inexplicably the legal craftsmanship of the International Court of Justice has been lacking in *jus ad bellum* decisions.

In contrast, for example, with the careful application of the interpretive provisions of the 1969 Vienna Convention on the Law of Treaties[31] by the Seabed Disputes Chamber of the International Tribunal for the Law of the Sea in its recent advisory opinion on obligations of sponsoring states with respect to activities in the area,[32] the stretched ICJ *jus ad bellum* decisions have not been rooted in careful analysis of the text of the governing Charter provisions nor in analysis of the *travaux* of the Charter. There is simply no indication from the real world, either in the text of the Charter or its *travaux*, that governing Charter principles reflect as rules "expressly recognized by the contesting states" any of the following "rules" explicitly or implicitly applied by the Court in its *jus ad bellum* decisions, including:

- That the right of defense does not include the right to sweep mines clandestinely emplaced in an international waterway and targeting neutral shipping (implicit in the *Corfu Channel* decision);
- That there is no right of individual and collective defense against ongoing "less grave" aggression or "indirect aggression" (the *Nicaragua* decision) (also, of course, factually incorrect as an assumption about the seriousness of the multi-faceted covert Sandinista attack against neighboring states);
- That there is no right of individual and collective defense against indiscriminate attacks (implicit in the *Iran Platforms* decision) (also, of course, factually incorrect as an assumption about the attacks not knowingly directed against United States shipping in the Persian Gulf);
- That there is no right of individual and collective defense against attacks from non-state actors (the *Israeli Wall* decision);
- That there is no right of individual and collective defense against insurgent or rebel attacks from the territory of a third state where that third state is simply unwilling or unable to stop the attacks (implicit in the *Congo* decision);

---

29. *See, e.g.,* articles 38(1) and 38(2) of the Statute of the International Court of Justice.
30. Article 38(1) of the Statute of the International Court of Justice.
31. *See* articles 31–33 of the Vienna Convention on the Law of Treaties (the Vienna Convention).
32. "Responsibilities and Obligations of States Sponsoring Persons and Entities with Respect to Activities in the Area" (interpretive discussion "in general" at paras 57–71).

- That there is no right of collective defense until an attacked state has first publicly declared itself to be attacked and has publicly requested assistance (the *Nicaragua* decision) (also, of course, factually incorrect as an assumption about the absence of declaration of an attack and request for assistance from El Salvador against the Sandinista attack);
- That the right of collective defense is not coterminous with the right of individual defense (implicit in the *Nicaragua* decision);
- That necessity in *jus ad bellum* law requires specific prior complaint about the role of a particular potential target of the defensive response (the *Iran Platforms* decision); and
- That proportionality in *jus ad bellum* law is a matter of weighing the damage done in an attack against the damage done in the defensive response (the *Iran Platforms* decision).

Nothing in the United Nations Charter, the governing law of *jus ad bellum*, incorporates any of the above purported rules. Indeed, most are even inconsistent with the text of Article 51 of the Charter which expressly declares "[n]othing in the present Charter shall impair the inherent right of individual or collective self-defense if an armed attack occurs...." Further, in no case in which the Court has explicitly or implicitly adopted any of the above rules has it even made an attempt to demonstrate that the rule was an agreed limitation of the pre-charter "inherent right" of defense necessary to comply with this Article 51 requirement. The policy implications of each of these "minimalist" rules is also to effectively undermine the crucial Charter prohibition against aggression by undermining the right of effective defense against such aggression.

On a case by case basis the legal craftsmanship of ICJ *jus ad bellum* decisions is just as troubling. Thus, it is at least puzzling why the Court in the *Corfu Channel* decision did not regard an illegal use of force in the clandestine laying of mines in an international waterway as triggering the use of force norms of the Charter. Instead, the Court talked of other principles such as "elementary considerations of humanity" and "every State's obligation not to allow knowingly its territory to be used for acts contrary to the rights of other States." Indeed, to this day the *Corfu Channel* decision is routinely cited in international law classrooms as announcing a core principle concerning international environmental law rather than use of force law. No doubt the Court was thrown off here by the fact that the mines were laid in the territorial sea of Albania. This "territorial sea" focus, however, as an exclusive focus, is inconsistent with the Court's own important parallel holding as to the rights of other nations to transit the strait as an international waterway. One could ask in this connection, would we analyze an aggressive shelling by Albania of neutral shipping going through the strait as simply violating "elementary considerations of humanity," or Albania "not allowing its territory to be used for acts contrary to the rights of other States," or would we regard such a setting more appropriately as aggression in violation of the Charter? And how would we analyze the right of neutral shipping through the strait responding to shore batteries with counter-battery fire? Is *Corfu Channel* not a classic setting of *jus ad bellum* as governing law, whether the illegal aggression is through covert mining or shelling by shore batteries?

If *Corfu Channel* is puzzling, the *Nicaragua* decision baldly sets aside normal international law craftsmanship. Initially, the Court deals with its jurisdictional inability to apply the United Nations Charter by simply applying customary international law of *jus ad bellum* which it declares to be identical with those of the Charter. But it is hornbook international law that the Charter will prevail over any inconsistent customary international law. Indeed, Article 103 of the Charter embodies a legal obligation that the Charter will prevail over any inconsistent international agreement.[33] How then can the Court apply customary international law of *jus ad bellum* without simultaneously interpreting the United Nations Charter, which would prevail over the customary international law rule if there were any inconsistency? The Court also fails to consider important applicable regional agreements such as the Rio Treaty, which because of the jurisdictional posture of the case the Court cannot consider, but which also would prevail over any inconsistent customary international law. Clearly if a Court cannot apply governing international law it cannot properly decide a case. Yet the Court proceeds to do just that. On this point the Dissenting Opinion of Judge Sir Robert Jennings nails the majority opinion. Judge Jennings writes:

> Article 38 of the Court's own Statute requires it first to apply "international conventions", "general" as well as "particular" ones, "establishing rules expressly recognized by the contesting States"; and the relevant provisions of the Charter—and indeed also of the Charter of the Organization of American States, and of the Rio Treaty—have at all material times been principal elements of the applicable law governing the conduct, rights and obligations of the Parties. It seems, therefore, eccentric, if not perverse, to attempt to determine the central issues of the present case, after having first abstracted these principal elements of the law applicable to the case, and which still obligate both the parties.[34]

He further notes: "[t]here is no escaping the fact that this is a decision of a dispute arising under Article 51."[35]

Adding to its sleight-of-hand in setting aside governing treaty law the *Nicaragua* decision then largely ignores the substantial body of *jus ad bellum* law supporting a right of defense against "indirect aggression," that is covert secret aggression supported by a third state for the purpose of overturning a government. In this connection, the dissenting opinion by Judge Schwebel unmistakably and correctly sets out this traditional body of *jus ad bellum* law. But the Court simply ignores this body of law despite its obvious relevance to the case.

Continuing its remarkable sleight-of-hand, the Court then seems to adopt a rule that there is no right of defense against ongoing less grave aggression (never mind for this purpose the factual inaccuracy of this characterization in the *Nicaragua* case). And the Court explicitly announces a new double-barreled *jus ad bellum* rule that for lawful collective defense a requesting state must first publicly announce that it has been attacked and then publicly announce a request for assistance. The Court creates each of these rules out of whole cloth, citing their provenance neither in pre-Charter limitations on the "inherent" right of defense, any previous pattern of state practice or *opinion juris*, any previous rules from any source "expressly recognized by the contesting states," any "general principles of law recognized by civilized nations," nor even "teachings of the most highly qualified publicists." The Court thus both ignores the textual limitation apparent from the Charter Article 51 language of "[n]othing in the present Charter shall impair the inherent right" of defense, as well as the required basis of the new rules in a recognized source of international law. This creation of new *jus ad bellum* rules, said to be rules of customary international law, is even more remarkable in that it is the United Nations Charter that is the governing international law of *jus ad bellum* and the Court jurisdictionally cannot even consider the Charter. How then can it announce new governing rules of *jus ad bellum* even if such rules were consistent with the Article 38 function of the Court?

---

33. Article 103 of the Charter of the United Nations.
34. Dissenting Opinion of Judge Sir Robert Jennings at 533.
35. *Id.* at 535.

Could it not do so only if these rules were part of the Charter *jus ad bellum* framework which it is jurisdictionally precluded from examining?

Turning to the *Iran Platforms* decision, in its insistence that the evidence show a specific Iranian intent to harm United States shipping, the Court implicitly embraces a rule that there is no right of defense against indiscriminate mining of an international waterway. Although this purported *jus ad bellum* "rule" is a key element in the decision of the Court, once again the Court announces no treaty basis for this new rule, nor any pattern of state practice demonstrating implicit state agreement for such a rule, nor any other "source" for such a rule. Nor does the Court seem to notice that its earlier *Corfu Channel* decision had not required a "specific intent" on the part of Albania that the mines be targeted at British ships.

Compounding its "minimalist" law making with respect to *jus ad bellum* law, the Court in *Iranian Platforms* goes on to apply concepts of necessity and proportionality rooted neither in treaty law, state practice nor the teachings of "the most highly qualified publicists." Thus, there is no precedent, nor any "source" of international law, cited by the Court for its assumption that "necessity" requires prior notification concerning the role of a specific defensive target, or that "proportionality" means equivalence between the aggressive attack and the defensive response. Moreover, in both respects the "rule" implicitly applied is simply not previously accepted *jus ad bellum* law and the widely accepted meanings of both "necessity" and "proportionality" are quite different.[36]

Perhaps the most shocking failure of legal craftsmanship is in the *Israeli Wall* decision. For there the Court avoids the essential review of Israel's right to construct the "wall" rooted in a right of defense against ongoing terrorist attacks by simply stating that "Israel does not claim that the attacks against it are imputable to a foreign state." The relevance of this statement, in turn, comes from the preceding statement by the Court that "Article 51 of the Charter thus recognizes *the existence of an inherent right of self-defense in the case of armed attack by one State against another State.*"[37] The Court makes this remarkable statement immediately after quoting the text of Article 51 of the Charter which, in fact, says nothing whatsoever about an attack "by one State against another State." Thus, shockingly, here in its "minimalist" quest the Court actually writes in language limiting the text of the Charter itself. Nor does the Court cite any "source" for its implicit rule, nor apparently understand the perverse policy consequences that would follow from such a rule eliminating the right of defense against aggression whenever that aggression is from non-state-sponsored actors.

Further, in its *Congo* decision the Court disregards, as a possible right of defense by Uganda, that Uganda might have a right of defense against insurgent attacks from territory of the Congo in a setting where the Congo is not involved with the attacks and thus that the attacks would not be attributable to the Congo. Once again, however, the Court neither spells out the *jus ad bellum* "rule" it is implicitly adopting nor cites any authority for such a rule. Clearly, one of the core problems of implicit assumptions as to *jus ad bellum* rules is that the Court then never provides any legal basis for the rule. As with the other "minimalist" rules generated by the Court, in fact there seems to be no such basis in the law of the Charter for this rule.

Finally, with the exception of the *Corfu Channel* case, where the Court does employ a Committee of Experts of three naval officers drawn from neutral countries to carefully develop the facts for the Court—with an opportunity for the parties to comment—the

---

36. *See, e.g.,* William H. Taft, IV, *Self-Defense and the Oil Platforms Decision,* 29 YALE J. INT'L L. 295, 304–05 (2004).

37. Emphasis added.

fact-finding in these *jus ad bellum* decisions is woefully inadequate. This is particularly true in the *Nicaragua* and *Iranian Platforms* cases. Surely fact-finding is always of critical importance, and even more so when considering vital use of force decisions.

Questions for Discussion

1. Would a rule that nations may not respond to covert aggression strengthen or weaken the fundamental Charter distinction between illegal aggression and permissible defense? Would such a rule regarding the response as just as illegal as the attack deserve moral support? Would it encourage enhanced covert attack in an international setting where such covert attack may already be a core world order threat?

2. Factual differences, or, more accurately, selection of differing facts as relevant seems crucial to the Central American legal debate. Note that again official "white papers" have had little impact on the debate. How should a democratic society inform the world of a covert attack? Are there any factors inherent in democratic societies that make it difficult for such evidence to be broadly accepted? Does this difficulty enhance the risk of totalitarian miscalculation of responses from democracies subject to attack?

3. How would you characterize the fact-finding process used by the ICJ in the Nicaragua Case? Did the Court effectively utilize its fact-finding powers under the Statute of the Court? If not, why not?

4. Even if we were to assume that no right of collective self-defense against covert action exists, why was the U.S. support for the contras in Nicaragua treated by the Court differently from the Sandinista support of the FMLN guerrillas in El Salvador? Was this issue influenced by the United States admitting assistance while the Sandinista regime totally denied it, even in sworn affidavit to the Court?

5. Where did the majority of the Court find the new rule it announced in this case that a state requesting collective defense must publicly declare that it has been attacked? After this decision, would you always recommend a public written invitation to engage in collective defense against armed aggression?

6. What is your assessment of the performance of the International Court of Justice in the Nicaragua Case? How should the United States have responded to the decision of the Court? How should the world community strengthen the Court with respect to its work concerning the use of force provisions of the U.N. Charter?

Note

For a variety of views on the *Nicaragua* case, see the January 1987 issue of the *American Journal of International Law.*

Grenada: Problems in Regional Action

John Norton Moore, *Grenada and the International Double Standard*
78 Am. J. Int'l L. 145, 153–59 (1984)

The UN Charter provides in Article 2(4) that members "shall refrain in their international relations from the threat or use of force against the territorial integrity or political independence of any state." In so doing, it seeks to end the aggressive use of force in international relations. The use of force is lawful under the Charter, however, if authorized by a competent organ of the United Nations, if in individual or collective defense, or if pursuant to action of a regional arrangement "relating to the maintenance of international peace and security," as provided in chapter VIII of the Charter.

Initially, it should be pointed out that OECS regional peacekeeping and humanitarian action was undertaken at the request of the Governor-General of Grenada—acting at the time as its only constitutional representative. On this ground alone, it was not a violation of Article 2(4) of the Charter. Moreover, the action also meets the requirements of lawful protection of nationals, humanitarian intervention and regional peacekeeping.

. . . .

Regional peacekeeping actions consistent with the purposes and principles of the United Nations are also recognized as lawful under Article 52 of the Charter. Such actions to restore order and self-determination in a setting of breakdown of authority are not enforcement actions, which would require Security Council approval, and may be undertaken at the initiative of a genuinely independent regional arrangement. Thus, to be lawful, regional action taken under Article 52 must be consistent with the purposes and principles of the Charter and, pursuant to Article 53, must not be "enforcement action" unless such enforcement action is authorized by the Security Council.

There is substantial authority both in the writings of international law scholars and in the jurisprudence of the Organization of American States that regional peacekeeping action for the purpose of restoring order and self-determination at the request of lawful authorities or in a setting of breakdown of authority is lawful under Article 52. Perhaps the clearest example is the OAS peacekeeping mission in the Dominican Republic in 1965, following the initial action by the United States.

Regional peacekeeping actions, under the conditions described above, are not directed against a government as sanctions, but instead are focused on restoring order and orderly processes of self-determination. As such, they do not amount to "enforcement action" under Article 53 of the Charter. In fact, the OAS action in the Dominican case was taken despite a Cuban argument that the "very presence of foreign military forces in a sovereign state constituted an act of coercive nature and made the measure 'an enforcement action.'"

That such regional peacekeeping actions are not "enforcement actions" is also supported by the decision of the International Court of Justice in *Certain Expenses of the United Nations*. In that case, the Court held that peacekeeping actions not directed against a state but undertaken with the permission of constitutional authorities were not "enforcement action." A major qualification is that to be consistent with the purposes and principles of the United Nations, such actions must be designed to further internationally observed elections and self-determination of the people of the nation rather than the hegemony of a foreign state or imposition of a particular government.

. . . .

Despite Soviet arguments to the contrary, there is substantial authority that regional peacekeeping actions undertaken in a setting of breakdown of authority are lawful under the UN Charter. This has been the consistent position of the United States and the OAS. It is particularly relevant in the context of the Grenada mission to note that the Article 51 defense right and the Article 52 right of regional action were included in the Charter at the insistence of Latin American states determined to maintain autonomy for regional action.

The Grenada mission by the OECS countries and Barbados, Jamaica and the United States is a paradigm of a lawful regional peacekeeping action under Article 52. It was undertaken in a context of civil strife and breakdown of government following the brutal murder of Maurice Bishop and members of his cabinet in an attempted coup. It was in response to a request for assistance in restoring human rights and self-determination from the only constitutional authority on the island, Governor-General Sir Paul Scoon. The operation resulted in only minimal casualties despite an order by Fidel Castro that the large Cuban paramilitary force fight to the last man. The OECS countries have pledged themselves to hold free elections and ensure an outcome consistent with the right of self-determination. As the lengthy OECS coexistence with the Marxist Bishop Government demonstrates, the purpose of the OECS request was not to impose a particular form of government. Finally, perhaps the best confirmation of the peacekeeping nature of the mission is the obvious relief and friendship with which the OECS forces were greeted by the people of Grenada.

The Grenada mission is also a paradigm of lawful humanitarian protection—both protection of nationals and humanitarian protection of non-nationals or "humanitarian intervention"—in conformity with Article 2(4) and 51 of the UN Charter. The context includes uncertainty as to whether any coherent group was in charge, cessation of government functions, a draconian shoot-on-sight 24-hour curfew applied to civilians, closure of the airports, reports of continued civil strife, a community of threatened non-Grenadans including about a thousand Americans as well as nationals of other OECS countries, at least 18 confirmed deaths and substantial diplomatic efforts to protect the threatened communities by measures short of force.

Although no request was necessary for this humanitarian action to be lawful, in view of the request for assistance from the Governor-General of Grenada, there can be no serious doubt that such action was lawful. It is always easy, of course, for critics to second-guess a humanitarian action and to claim that it was unnecessary. No principle of international law, however, requires delay until the taking of hostages or mass killings make such actions futile. Again, the reaction of the American students and the Grenadan people to the rescue confirms that most felt severely threatened. Indeed, that 85 percent of the population of an entire nation felt themselves or their families to be in danger prior to the mission was an extraordinary level of threat. In any event, all such speculation as to intensity of the threat seems moot in view of the request for humanitarian assistance from the Governor-General.

It is not necessary to choose among these independently sufficient legal grounds for the action: request from lawful Grenadan authority, humanitarian protection and regional peacekeeping. In reality, the mission had a combined purpose—regional peacekeeping and humanitarian protection requested by the Governor-General of Grenada—that must be judged by considering these bases together.

Jointly requested or participated in by almost one-third of the membership of the Organization of American States, the Grenada mission is also consistent with the OAS Charter. Reflecting a traditional Latin concern, Articles 18 and 20 of the revised Charter broadly prohibit intervention. These provisions have been repeatedly cited by legal critics of the OECS mission. But actions requested by lawful authority are certainly not regarded by OAS member states as "intervention." Moreover, Articles 22 and 28 of the OAS Charter make clear that regional peacekeeping or defensive action in accordance with special regional treaties do not violate the noninterventionist provisions. The OECS Treaty of 1981 is a special regional treaty within Articles 22 and 28. In fact, as the Inter-American Defense Treaty (the Rio Treaty) is applicable to other areas of Latin America, the OECS Treaty is the only applicable regional security arrangement for Grenada and the Eastern Caribbean....

[*See* Articles 22 and 28 of the revised OAS Charter.]

Despite the fact that the Rio Treaty and the United Nations Charter were the only applicable treaties in force at the time the OAS Charter was adopted in 1948 and the revised OAS Charter in 1967, the draftsmen intentionally declined to define "existing treaties" or "special treaties" for purposes of these articles by specific reference to these two treaties. Rather, they stressed that in an enduring organization charter, the citation of specific treaties was not appropriate. This deliberate action would be meaningless unless the framers intended that future treaties in force and changes in the existing treaties would automatically be included. It is also instructive that the four-nation working group that drafted the final version of Article 22 used the phrase "treaties in force" rather than the current English translation of Article 22, which reads "existing treaties." That the correct interpretation of Article 22 is "treaties in force" is conclusively demonstrated not only by this negotiating history but also by the equally authentic Spanish, Portuguese and French texts, all of which translate as "treaties in force." This reference plainly suggests that the determining factor is whether there is a regional treaty "in force" at the applicable time of action. In any event, both "existing treaties" and "treaties in force," as well as "special treaties," in no way suggest an interpretation of Articles 22 and 28 that would preclude future regional arrangements such as the OECS.

It should also be pointed out that one "treaty in force" the OAS draftsmen specifically discussed and intended under this article was the UN Charter. Therefore, OECS action taken under Articles 51 and 52 of the UN Charter would seem fully consistent with Articles 22 and 28 of the OAS Charter.

Thus, on several grounds — request by lawful authority and action under "treaties in force" and "special treaties" — the peacekeeping and humanitarian protective action of the OECS in the Grenada mission is consistent with the Charter of the OAS. Moreover, since the Grenada mission is rooted in rights recognized by the UN Charter, under Article 137 of the revised Charter of the OAS, they could not be impaired by the OAS Charter in any event. Article 137 provides: "None of the provisions of this Charter shall be construed as impairing the rights and obligations of the Member States under the Charter of the United Nations."

It is basic international law, set out in Article 103 of the UN Charter, that the "obligations" of that Charter prevail over any inconsistent treaty. The draftsmen of OAS Article 137 clearly preserved the "rights" of the parties under the UN Charter as well as these binding obligations. Consequently, lawful actions under Articles 51 and 52 of the Charter are also consistent with the OAS Charter.

The members of the OECS, as members of the OAS, are bound by the OAS Charter, but they — including Grenada — are not parties to the Rio Treaty and have not sought action under that Treaty. Therefore, the Rio Treaty does not apply to the OECS Grenada mission. Although the United States is a party to the Rio Treaty, its Article 10 preserves — parallel to Article 137 of the OAS Charter — "the rights and obligations" of parties under the UN Charter, including rights of defense and lawful regional action in accordance with other regional arrangements pursuant to Charter Articles 51 and 52. Thus, the Rio Treaty is simply not relevant to the Grenada case.

Christopher C. Joyner, *Reflections on the Lawfulness of Invasion*
78 Am. J. Int'l L. 131, 134–35 (1984)

An important legal consideration in the Grenadan case involved the proper protection of U.S. nationals on the island; indeed, this particular concern was later translated by the

U.S. Government into a principal legal justification for its action. Traditionally, intervention by a state to safeguard the well-being of its citizens in another state has been deemed legal in international law. In more recent times, however, interpretations of intervention for "limited" self-defense have been severely circumscribed and subjected to harsh legal strictures. Not surprisingly, this redirection of legal attitudes has stemmed primarily from the obvious temptation to abuse posed by such extraterritorial situations. Additionally, it is substantiated by the proliferation of international agreements that normatively sanction respect for nonintervention without exceptions or qualifications.

Plausible justification for the United States intervention in Grenada may find related grounding in the international norms pertaining to humanitarian assistance. Little real question exists that local governmental authority on Grenada had broken down, and consequently a genuine threat may have imperiled the safety and welfare of U.S. citizens there. That the lives of the U.S. nationals were actually endangered by political conditions on Grenada may be debatable; it is fair to posit, however that the invasion did indeed rescue these citizens from a volatile predicament. In the process, it also obviated the possibility of an Iranian-like hostage situation.

Yet caution should be exercised in drawing on humanitarian grounds to legitimize the U.S. intervention, either in Grenada or elsewhere. To gain legitimate currency, intervention either to protect nationals or to serve other humanitarian purposes should be severely restricted in application. Furthermore, the risk to the threatened group must be genuine, imminent and substantial. Last, the military operation undertaken should be conducted as a limited-purpose rescue mission, and not as a formidable attack against the authority structure of the internal government. These rigid qualifications are intentional and not incidental. Again, great temptation resides here for abuse — to clothe an intervention in humanitarian terms while actually carrying it out for ideological or tactical designs. If the latter consideration did prevail in the hierarchy of motives for the intervention in Grenada, then the legality of U.S. participation in the action would be impugned accordingly.

The Falklands War: Case Study in the "De Facto" Principle in Defining International Entities for Purposes of the Ban on the Aggressive Use of Force in International Relations and the Effect of Non-Compliance with Security Council Resolutions

The Cárdenas-Moore Exchange

In 1983, I wrote an editorial comment in the American Journal of International Law, which argued in part:

John Norton Moore, *Editorial Comment:*
The Inter-American System Snarls in Falklands War
76 Am. J. Int'l L. 830

The Falklands-Malvinas dispute is representative of many international conflicts concerning disputed sovereignty. In the world today there are at least 15 active island disputes and hundreds of land and sea boundary disputes. Nothing could be more fundamental under the Charter of the United Nations and the hemispheric Inter-American Treaty of Reciprocal Assistance (the Rio Treaty) than the principle that force may not be used to resolve these disputes. In the first article of the Rio Treaty the parties pledge "not to resort to the threat or use of force in any manner inconsistent with the provisions of the Charter of the United Nations or of this Treaty."

The Argentine invasion of the Falklands-Malvinas is in violation of this principle, regardless of the merits of the underlying Argentine claim. Moreover, the invasion is a use of force in disregard of the expressed preference of the peoples of the islands. International lawyers may be hard pressed to know whether Britain or Argentina would win sovereignty over the islands or how associated self-determination claims would be resolved if the dispute were submitted to an impartial arbiter. But there is no uncertainty on the more important issue of Argentine use of force in violation of the UN Charter and the Rio Treaty. If such use of force is not unequivocally condemned it could become a model for island and border wars all over the world, including many in Latin America.

———————

Shortly thereafter, Argentine Emilio J. Cárdenas wrote a letter to the Journal in which he suggested that the author's reliance upon the general prohibition against the use of force in international relations as a means of understanding this controversy was a dangerous oversimplification. Mr. Cárdenas has objected to having his letter republished in this volume.[38]

In essence, Mr. Cárdenas argued that by holding what he characterized as an overseas colonial territory which had been acquired by force, and refusing to negotiate in good faith, Great Britain had violated the "spirit" if not the letter of the UN Charter. In addition, he quoted authority for the proposition that force may be used by a State to recover its own territory without violating Article 2(4) of the UN Charter.

Although acknowledging that the inhabitants of the islands held British citizenship, and implicitly conceding the British claim that the inhabitants did not favor living under Argentine rule, Mr. Cárdenas argued that the principle of "self-determination" was an instrument of "decolonization" and could not be used to perpetuate colonial situations. Furthermore, he reasoned, the inhabitants of the islands did not properly qualify as a "people" having a right to self-determination, but were only "a population" or "a group of inhabitants." While the interests of these inhabitants deserved some consideration, he concluded that one could not forget what he termed the "legitimate rights" of the Argentine people to the islands.[39]

Alberto R. Coll, *Philosophical and Legal Dimensions of the Use of Force in the Falklands War*

in THE FALKLANDS WAR 34, 44–46
(Alberto R. Coll & Anthony C. Arend eds., 1985)

Less needs to be said about Great Britain's use of force which, regardless of whatever moral responsibility (in the Butterfieldian, existential sense of the term) the British may bear for the 1982 war, was allowed by Article 51 of the UN Charter.

. . . .

An interesting legal question is the effect which UN Security Council Resolution 502 had on the inherent right of Great Britain to self-defense. The Resolution, approved on 3 April, noted that two days earlier the President of the Security Council had requested

———————

38. *See* Emilio J. Cárdenas, *Correspondence*, 77 AM. J. INT'L L. 606 (1983).
39. For a further response by Professor Moore, *see* Response to Cárdenas, *id.* at 610, particularly on the De Facto principle.

the British and Argentine governments "to refrain from the use or threat of force in the region of the Falkland Islands." It then demanded "an immediate cessation of hostilities ... immediate withdrawal of all Argentine forces from the Falkland Islands," and called on the parties "to seek diplomatic solution to their differences and to respect fully the purposes and principles of the Charter of the United Nations."

....

It would be improper to say that in its use of force, Great Britain was carrying out the provisions of Resolution 502, as if the Security Council had empowered or authorized the British government to carry out enforcement measures on its behalf, which, of course, was not true. What can be said, however, is that, owing to Argentine noncompliance with its terms, Resolution 502 proved ineffectual. To use the analysis suggested by article 51, this was a case in which the Security Council tried but failed to take the "measures necessary to maintain international peace and security." Therefore, Great Britain's inherent right to self-defense was not preempted by any UN actions, and continued to operate in its full scope as long as the Security Council's measures were frustrated by Argentina. Thus, while Great Britain did not act as an agent of the UN, its use of force was legal, resting on a right to self-defense which, as article 51 indicates, antedates the Charter, rests on juridical foundations independent of the Charter, and is sanctioned by the Charter.

Two other legal issues related to the British use of force are, first, the level of violence required to trigger the self-defense provisions of article 51, and second, the level of violence that this article permits an offended state to use in its response to aggression. Although both issues can be highly problematical under many circumstances, they were not so in the Falkland crisis. A full-fledged armed invasion of a territory which has been administered, occupied and inhabited in its entirety by nations of a power for 150 years suffices to justify that power's exercise of its right to self-defense.

The second issue can be very difficult, and involves the connection between *ius ad bellum* and *ius in bello*. The extent of one's defensive measures must be proportional to the degree of aggression suffered. Classical just war theorists such as Vitoria and Grotius, for example, insisted that no matter how justified the use of force was, it had to be guided by the principles of proportionate objectives and proportionate means. The legality of one's cause could be tarnished or vitiated if the war's objectives and means were grossly disproportionate to the injury initially suffered. Thus proportionality linked the *ius ad bellum* and *ius in bello*. The same link is acknowledged today by most students of the problem of international violence. Argentina's taking of the Malvinas, for instance, would not have justified massive British bombings of the Argentine mainland (unless, of course, such bombings had been absolutely essential to recovering the islands). As Howard Levie has shown in this book, the British use of force was generally proportional to the degree of aggression initially carried out by Argentina. This proportionality is doubly important in the light of the legal norm outlined by Anthony Arend regarding states' obligation to pursue peaceful methods of settlement even during the course of hostilities.

The Gulf War: The Security Council Responds to Overt Invasion

JOHN NORTON MOORE, CRISIS IN THE GULF: ENFORCING THE RULE OF LAW
3–11, 149–59, 424–33 (1992)

The Challenge and the Global Stakes

Shortly after midnight, on August 2, 1990, at the direction of Iraqi President Saddam Hussein, a massive Iraqi force attacked Kuwait all along its frontier with Iraq. Within a matter of days this unprovoked attack led to the complete occupation of Kuwait—an occupation which in its brutality was an affront to all mankind—and to the seizure of thousands of international hostages in an effort to prevent a community response. Within days Saddam Hussein had begun an almost unprecedented campaign of "nationcide" against the sovereign State of Kuwait. Indeed, this brutal campaign marks the first time in history that one nation sought forceful annexation of a member State of the United Nations. And within days Saddam was in blatant disregard of what became at least nine mandatory UN Security Council directives instructing Iraq immediately to pull out of Kuwait and to comply fully with its international legal obligations and declaring the attempted annexation of Kuwait "null and void."

Following Iraq's failure to comply with these Security Council resolutions, an international coalition of thirty-three States, acting pursuant to Security Council authorization, engaged Iraqi forces to enforce the Security Council directives. Subsequently, Saddam Hussein carried out a campaign of Scud missile terror attacks against civilian population centers in Israel and Saudi Arabia (which it seems he further threatened with biological, chemical, or even nuclear weapons of mass destruction); brutally mistreated coalition force prisoners of war; further tortured, killed, and kidnapped Kuwaiti citizens in large numbers; apparently encouraged worldwide terror attacks against coalition force member States; and committed unprecedented crimes of ecocide by intentionally creating a massive oil spill in the Persian Gulf (which, at approximately 470 million gallons, is the single worst oil spill in human history, and is over 42 times larger than the 1989 *Exxon Valdez* spill) and by intentionally torching more than 600 oil wells in Kuwait. Coalition forces began a ground campaign on February 24, 1991, to force Saddam Hussein out of Kuwait, and despite Saddam's threats that the ground campaign would be "the mother of all battles," coalition forces won a more than decisive victory in only 100 hours.

With the occupation forces of Saddam Hussein driven from Kuwait after seven searing months, the people of Kuwait began the difficult struggle to control the apocalyptic fire and smoke engulfing much of their nation and to reassemble their country and their hopes. Saddam Hussein, in turn, immediately became engulfed in a bitter civil war within Iraq as the fruit of his aggression. Once again, Saddam turned his brutality inward against his own people, particularly against the Kurds, and there were shocking reports of the use of sulfuric acid and other horrors against his own population. As of December 1991, over nine months after the shooting stopped in Kuwait, Iraq was still putting pressure on the Kurds, and up to two million Kurdish refugees had fled to Iran and Turkey. During the period of April through December 1991, Saddam also systematically sought to hinder Security Council directives aimed at eliminating his chemical, biological and nuclear weapons programs. United Nations inspections revealed that he was chillingly close to atomic weapons and even had a hydrogen bomb program, all in clear violation of Iraq's obligations under the 1968 Non-Proliferation Treaty. Like earlier aggressive attacks and their aftermath, the actions of Iraq in the Gulf crisis will live in infamy.

The global stakes in the Gulf crisis were momentous, particularly for the rule of law among nations and mankind's continuing efforts to end aggressive war. For Iraq, in its aggressive attack and brutal occupation, violated the most serious fundaments of the international legal order. These were no minor technical violations or remote events. Iraq's actions:

- violated—through attacks on three neighboring States—the central underpinning of contemporary world order prohibiting the aggressive use of force in international relations, as reflected in Article 2(4) of the United Nations Charter and in article 5 of the Pact of the League of Arab States;
- violated the core obligation in the UN Charter for nations to carry out decisions made by the Security Council in the exercise of its responsibility for the maintenance of international peace and security, as reflected in Articles 2(5), 24, 25, 48, and 49 of the Charter;
- violated a central purpose of the international system to respect the self-determination of peoples, as reflected in Article 1(2) of the UN Charter;
- violated one of the most important purposes of modern international law, that of promoting and protecting human rights, as Iraq massively abridged law of war, anti-hostage-taking, and other solemn obligations for the protection of human rights in peace and war;
- violated—in a sickeningly cynical manner—the obligation not to destroy property in occupied Kuwait except as absolutely necessary for military operations, as Iraq—even after agreeing to withdraw its forces, and while under Security Council directives to comply with its obligations under the Fourth Geneva Convention—set out to systematically loot and destroy Kuwaiti property, including the destruction of public buildings and the torching of over 600 oil wells, which took over eight months to extinguish and which engulfed the nation and the region in a pall of smoke rivaling a surrealist nightmare;
- violated obligations central to peaceful discourse among nations, as Iraq violated norms and conventions for the protection of diplomatic embassies and diplomatic and consular functions;
- violated a major purpose of the international system, which is to end terrorism directed against civilian populations;
- violated major arms control regimes, including the 1968 Treaty on the Non-Proliferation of Nuclear Weapons (and Iraq's related safeguards agreement with the International Atomic Energy Agency (IAEA)) and the 1972 Convention on the Prohibition of the Development, Production and Stockpiling of Bacteriological (Biological) and Toxin Weapons, and threatened to violate the 1925 Geneva Protocol on Gas and Bacteriological Warfare; and
- violated a major purpose of contemporary international law to protect the global environment, as Iraq committed massive ecocide against the environment of the Gulf and neighboring regions.

. . . .

Rarely has there been a more serious challenge to world order and the rule of law than that presented by Iraq's invasion and brutal seven-month-long occupation of Kuwait and its barbaric response to the engagement by coalition forces. It was imperative for future peace and the rule of law in international life that the international community respond fully and effectively to the challenge. If it could not, the chances for peace for our children and our children's children would have been severely damaged. Because the international community did respond so successfully, paradoxically the Gulf crisis just might be viewed by history as a turning point in ending the tragic practice of nation at war against nation.

....

A. The General Legal Basis for the Coalition Force Response Against Iraq

There are at least two sufficient and independent legal bases for coalition nations to have assisted Kuwait in resisting and ending the illegal Iraqi aggression against Kuwait and in restoring the international rule of law.

First, such actions were authorized by the Security Council, acting pursuant to its UN Charter Chapter VII authority "with respect to threats to the peace, breaches of the peace, and acts of aggression." Thus, Security Council resolution 665 of August 25, 1990:

> 1. *Calls upon* those Member States co-operating with the Government of Kuwait which are deploying maritime forces to the area to use such measures commensurate to the specific circumstances as may be necessary under the authority of the Security Council to halt all inward and outward maritime shipping in order to inspect and verify their cargoes and destinations and to ensure strict implementation of the provisions related to such shipping laid down in resolution 661 (1990);....

And Security Council resolution 678 of November 29, 1990, authorizes "Member States co-operating with the Government of Kuwait ... to use all necessary means to uphold" the Security Council resolutions previously adopted in the Gulf crisis while providing Iraq "one final opportunity, as a pause of goodwill" to comply with those resolutions. The applicable parts of this resolution provide:

> *The Security Council,*
>
> ....
>
> *Noting that,* despite all efforts by the United Nations, Iraq refuses to comply with its obligation to implement resolution 660 (1990) and the above-mentioned subsequent relevant resolutions, in flagrant contempt of the Security Council,
>
> *Mindful* of its duties and responsibilities under the Charter of the United Nations for the maintenance and preservation of international peace and security,
>
> *Determined* to secure full compliance with its decisions,
>
> *Acting* under Chapter VII of the Charter,
>
> 1. *Demands* that Iraq comply fully with resolution 660 (1990) and all subsequent relevant resolutions, and decides, while maintaining all its decisions, to allow Iraq one final opportunity, as a pause of goodwill, to do so;
>
> 2. *Authorizes* Member States co-operating with the Government of Kuwait, unless Iraq on or before 15 January 1991 fully implements, as set forth in paragraph 1 above, the foregoing resolutions, to use all necessary means to uphold and implement resolution 660 (1990) and all subsequent relevant resolutions and to restore international peace and security in the area;
>
> 3. *Requests* all States to provide appropriate support for the actions undertaken in pursuance of paragraph 2 of the present resolution;....

It is clear from the background history of this resolution that it was intended to authorize the use of military force after January 15, 1991, if necessary to ensure Iraqi compliance with Security Council resolutions on the Gulf crisis "and to restore international peace and security in the area." It should also be noted that nothing in the UN Charter requires a prior Article 43 agreement, or that the Security Council make a responsive use of force *obligatory* as opposed to *authorizing it*, for such Security Council action to constitute valid authorization under Chapter VII of the Charter. Similarly, nothing in the Charter requires that authorized forces must be designated as United Nations forces as opposed to "forces of Members of the United Nations."

Second, the United States and other nations requested by Kuwait to assist it in repelling the Iraqi aggression could do so pursuant to the right of individual and collective defense recognized in Article 51 of the UN Charter. This right of defense, parallel to that existing under customary international law, is of fundamental importance to the UN Charter framework outlawing aggressive war. If there were no distinction between aggressive attack and defensive response, then law would not contribute to deterrence against aggression, and the Charter would be, in major part, simply irrelevant to the real world. Because of the importance to the Charter framework of this Article 51 right of defense, the English language version of Article 51 speaks of the right as "inherent," and the French language version speaks of it as "au droit naturel."

The Iraqi panzer blitzkrieg against Kuwait was a paradigm armed attack (aggression), giving rise to the right of defense under Article 51. If this attack were not an armed attack (armed aggression), then nothing would be. Moreover, in this case there can be no debate about whether the right of defense is present, because Security Council resolution 661 of August 6, 1990, expressly affirmed in the Gulf crisis "the inherent right of individual or collective self-defence, in response to the armed attack by Iraq against Kuwait, in accordance with Article 51 of the Charter." Further, Security Council resolutions 665 and 678, authorizing the use of force in response to the Iraqi aggression, both use language strongly suggesting that nations authorized are nations engaged in collective defense with Kuwait, *i.e.*, "Member States co-operating with the Government of Kuwait." These States include Egypt, France, Italy, Saudi Arabia, Syria, the United Kingdom, and, of course, the United States, among many others.

....

Although of only theoretical interest following Security Council authorization in the Gulf crisis, one seemingly plausible argument which would have restricted the defensive right under Article 51 of the UN Charter—and yet which is clearly wrong—is one presented early in the crisis by Professor Abram Chayes of the Harvard Law Faculty. Professor Chayes argued in a paper prepared for a U.S.-Soviet Conference on the Non-Use of Force, held October 4–6, 1990, that the Article 51 right of defense may have been lost in the Gulf crisis as a result of the Security Council debating and passing several resolutions concerning that crisis. To understand this argument, it is necessary to review the full language of Article 51 of the UN Charter:

> Nothing in the present Charter shall impair the inherent right of individual or collective self-defence if an armed attack occurs against a Member of the United Nations, until the Security Council has taken measures necessary to maintain international peace and security. Measures taken by Members in the exercise of this right of self-defence shall be immediately reported to the Security Council and shall not in any way affect the authority and responsibility of the Security Council under the present Charter to take at any time such action as it deems necessary in order to maintain or restore international peace and security.

Professor Chayes's apparent suggestion is that once the Security Council simply has passed resolutions on any crisis, it automatically "has taken measures necessary to maintain international peace and security." Moreover, the final sentence of Article 51 says that the measures taken by members to exert their defensive rights "shall not in any way affect the authority and responsibility of the Security Council under the present Charter to take at any time such action as it deems necessary in order to maintain or restore international peace and security." But the passing of resolutions in a crisis, as in the Gulf crisis, is *not* automatically identical either with having "taken measures necessary to maintain international peace and security" in the first sentence of Article 51, or with a decision by the Council to take action prohibiting further exercise of the right of individual or collective defense pursuant to the final sentence of Article 51.

Even assuming that the Security Council has the authority under these provisions to remove the "inherent" or "natural" right of defense—which stems from customary international law—(an assumption which is not at all clear), surely such an enormously important consequence could only result from a clear Security Council action to that effect. But during the Gulf crisis, far from clearly *removing* the right of defense, the Council has *explicitly affirmed* that right in resolution 661 of August 6, 1990, which in turn was repeatedly reaffirmed in subsequent Security Council resolutions on the crisis.

To suggest, as Professor Chayes seems to, that merely any Security Council action concerning a crisis would automatically be sufficient to remove the right of defense against aggression, is incorrect in ascribing from any such action intentions that are not only not at all identical with most Council directives but also positively unlikely, *absent explicit Council action to this effect*, given the importance to the Charter structure of the Article 51 defensive right. That the United States or the United Kingdom had such an intention in voting for Security Council resolutions concerning the Gulf crisis is simply bizarre given the importance these countries attach to the Article 51 right of defense in general, and specifically in the Gulf crisis.

In connection with Professor Chayes's argument, it should also be noted that the UN Charter was *not* so interpreted in the setting of the Falklands/Malvinas War, in which Security Council resolutions were *not* regarded as removing the defensive right of the United Kingdom. And it should be noted that the language "until the Security Council has taken measures necessary to maintain international peace and security" can most reasonably be interpreted in defensive settings as not being satisfied while the aggression continues—as it continued against Kuwait despite passage of resolution 660 and subsequent Security Council resolutions.

Moreover, that the framers of the Charter understood the difference between, on the one hand, the Security Council merely "exercising ... the functions assigned to it" in a crisis or "dealing with" such matters, as has been the case in the Gulf crisis to date, and, on the other hand, the Security Council actually prevailing in the real world so that international peace and security have been maintained, is clear from the contrast between the language of Articles 12 and 51 of the Charter. Article 12, allocating competence between the Security Council and the General Assembly, provides:

> 1. While the Security Council is exercising in respect of any dispute or situation the functions assigned to it in the present Charter, the General Assembly shall not make any recommendation with regard to that dispute or situation unless the Security Council so requests.

> 2. The Secretary-General, with the consent of the Security Council, shall notify the General Assembly at each session of any matters relative to the maintenance of international peace and security which are being dealt with by the Security Council and shall similarly notify the General Assembly, or the

Members of the United Nations if the General Assembly is not in session, immediately the Security Council ceases to deal with such matters.

But Article 51, to some extent allocating competence between the Security Council and the individual States in the exercise of their "inherent right of individual or collective" defense, uses the much higher standard of "until the Security Council has taken measures necessary to maintain international peace and security." Even more importantly, if the interpretation of the Charter suggested by Professor Chayes were adopted, it would be a formulae to destroy much of the Security Council's usefulness in response to aggression. Nations would think more than twice about going to the Security Council if doing so meant the loss of their right of individual and collective defense.

Another mistaken criticism of the coalition action has been that the United Nations authorization was not wholly self-generating but allegedly resulted from "pressure" by several Security Council members, particularly the United States and Great Britain. It is no secret that these nations, among other nations, worked hard and provided strong leadership in seeking an effective United Nations response against Iraq's aggression. At root, this criticism that the United Nations action was largely led by one or more major powers, and, thus, was "illegitimate," reflects a naivete about collective security. To date, the two major examples of effective collective security through the United Nations, in Korea and now the Gulf, depended on United States leadership. Without such leadership, there would have been no effective stand against aggression in either case. As Professor Inis L. Claude, Jr., perhaps the world's preeminent authority on collective security, has written following the Gulf conflict: "Multilateralism is not the antithesis of unilateralism. It depends upon, and starts with, unilateralism. Multilateralism is unilateralism plus." Similarly, Professor Claude cautions against the common intellectual confusion in thinking about collective security that such actions are illegitimate unless the collective security system has responded perfectly against all aggressions. Thus he says of collective security in the real world, indeed, even in a post cold-war world: "The real choice ... is not between 'sometimes' and 'always,' but between 'sometimes' and 'never.'" As has been generally conceded, neither of these essentially political criticisms reflect an even colorable legal objection to the UN action in the Gulf crisis. The reality is that the effective UN response in the Gulf crisis was in the finest tradition of the United Nations, collective security, and United States leadership. And for the future, the United Nations, collective security, and war avoidance will be strengthened.

B. The Requirements of Necessity and Proportionality

Customary international law, derived from a long history beginning with but going beyond the theologically based "just war" tradition, requires that even defensive uses of force must be both "necessary" and "proportional." The purpose of these further requirements is to minimize the use of force and to achieve economy in coercion when force must be used; that is, to limit responding coercion to the amount that is reasonably necessary for the protection of fundamental values. Necessity, however, is paradigmatically met in a setting in which aggression is aimed at the separate existence of an independent member nation of the United Nations and that entire nation is under brutal occupation.

Nothing in the UN Charter requires a nation that has been attacked, and the nations that would assist it, to engage in diplomatic efforts *prior* to a defensive response against an ongoing, intense armed aggression against the very existence of a State. Even if there were such a requirement, in the case of the Gulf crisis the parties waited five and one-half months after the initial attack before engaging the aggressor with an armed response. In the meantime, repeated diplomatic efforts at peaceful resolution were made by the UN

Security Council, the Arab League, the UN Secretary-General, the United States, the Soviet Union, France, the European Community, and many others, including repeated efforts at "second track diplomacy." In each case, Iraq simply stonewalled the diplomatic efforts made to obtain its compliance with Security Council directives. Indeed, Iraq even turned down, by rejecting the proposed dates, a United States offer for Secretary of State Baker to meet personally with President Saddam Hussein. And—in a second best exchange— when Secretary of State Baker met with Iraqi Foreign Minister Tariq Aziz in Geneva on January 9, 1991, Aziz had nothing new to offer and even rejected Baker's request that he deliver a letter written by President George Bush to President Saddam Hussein. A determined Secretary-General of the United Nations also concluded, in his final effort to avert war, that Saddam had no intention of peacefully complying with Security Council directives. Subsequently, rather than seeking a diplomatic solution to end the conflict, President Hussein even sought to embarrass the Secretary-General by demanding release of a transcript of the Secretary-General's efforts, made in talks with Saddam, to avoid war.

The requirement of "necessity" would also seem to be clearly met by the action of the Security Council in setting a January 15 "pause of goodwill" deadline in authorizing the use of force in response against the Iraqi aggression. Thus, given the history of Security Council consideration of the Gulf crisis, as well as the underlying reality of the continuing aggression against and brutal illegal occupation of Kuwait, it can hardly be persuasively argued that the customary international law requirement of "necessity" was not met. And the language in Security Council resolution 678 of November 29, 1990, authorizing "all necessary means," viewed in context and in the light of its negotiating history, clearly permitted the use of force when Iraq had not withdrawn from Kuwait by January 15, 1991.

Similarly, the requirement of "proportionality" would also seem to have been clearly met in the international coalition response against the Iraqi aggression. As stated by McDougal and Feliciano in their seminal work on the use of force under the Charter:

> Proportionality in coercion constitutes a requirement that responding coercion be limited in intensity and magnitude to what is reasonably necessary promptly to secure the permissible objectives of self-defense…. [T]hese objectives may be most comprehensively generalized as the conserving of important values by compelling the opposing participant to terminate the condition which necessitates responsive coercion.

Proportionality is emphatically *not* a requirement that the defense limit itself to weapons systems employed by the aggressor or to employ force only at levels employed by the aggressor or to employ force only at levels sufficient to be ineffectual. In the Gulf crisis, proportionality required that the coalition employ the force necessary, and only that which was necessary, promptly to ensure Iraqi compliance with the Security Council directives, to restore Kuwaiti independence and the rule of law, and, in the language of Security Council resolution 678, "to restore international peace and security in the area." That seems to be the case in describing coalition actions against Iraq. Given the tenacious refusal by President Saddam Hussein to comply with Security Council directives, even after a major coalition strategic air campaign against Iraq, it would seem ludicrous to assert that the coalition forces exceeded the bounds of proportionality in their response. Moreover, after more than three weeks of the intense air campaign, Iraq still rejected an Iranian peace initiative, apparently offering no initiative in return. Instead, the Iraqi Deputy Prime Minister Saadoun Hammadi is reported to have told the Iranians that "the current issue is not the issue of Kuwait, but that of the American, colonialist and Zionist aggression to destroy Iraq and control the region. Therefore what we have to do now is to have a united Muslim front to face this front of infidels." In the face of this hard line rejection of peace, reiteration of fake political propaganda about the conflict, and an absence of movement toward compliance with Security Council directives, it strains credulity to urge that the coalition force response exceeded the bounds of necessity or proportionality.

Finally, it should also be noted that coalition forces could lawfully have driven to Baghdad and replaced the Saddam Hussein government if necessary "to restore international peace and security in the area," and that coalition forces had a virtually unopposed opportunity to do so following the defeat of the Iraqi "Republican Guard" forces in the ground campaign. Yet the coalition forces voluntarily chose not to do so, thus making clear that coalition objectives related strictly—and even narrowly—to implementation of Security Council resolutions in the crisis.

....

Resolution 687—April 3, 1991

....

Reaffirming the need to be assured of Iraq's peaceful intentions in the light of its unlawful invasion and occupation of Kuwait,

....

Conscious of the need for demarcation of the said boundary,

Conscious also of the statements by Iraq threatening to use weapons in violation of its obligations under the Geneva Protocol for the Prohibition of the Use in War of Asphyxiating, Poisonous or Other Gases, and of Bacteriological Methods of Warfare, signed at Geneva on 17 June 1925, and of its prior use of chemical weapons and affirming that grave consequences would follow any further use by Iraq of such weapons,

....

Stressing the importance of an early conclusion by the Conference on Disarmament of its work on a Convention on the Universal Prohibition of Chemical Weapons and of universal adherence thereto,

Aware of the use by Iraq of ballistic missiles in unprovoked attacks and therefore of the need to take specific measures in regard to such missiles located in Iraq,

....

Bearing in mind its objective of restoring international peace and security in the area as set out in recent resolutions of the Security Council,

Conscious of the need to take the following measures acting under Chapter VII of the Charter,

1. *Affirms* all thirteen resolutions noted above, except as expressly changed below to achieve the goals of this resolution, including a formal cease-fire;

....

7. *Invites* Iraq to reaffirm unconditionally its obligations under the Geneva Protocol for the Prohibition of the Use in War of Asphyxiating, Poisonous or Other Gases, and of Bacteriological Methods of Warfare, signed at Geneva on 17 June 1925, and to ratify the Convention on the Prohibition of the Development, Production and Stockpiling of Bacteriological (Biological) and Toxin Weapons and on Their Destruction, of 10 April 1972;

8. *Decides* that Iraq shall unconditionally accept the destruction, removal, or rendering harmless, under international supervision, of:

(a) All chemical and biological weapons and all stocks of agents and all related subsystems and components and all research, development, support and manufacturing facilities;

(b) All ballistic missiles with a range greater than 150 kilometres and related major parts, and repair and production facilities;

9. *Decides*, for the implementation of paragraph 8 above, the following:

(a) Iraq shall submit to the Secretary-General, within fifteen days of the adoption of the present resolution, a declaration of the locations, amounts and types of all items specified in paragraph 8 and agree to urgent, on-site inspection as specified below;

. . . .

10. *Decides* that Iraq shall unconditionally undertake not to use, develop, construct or acquire any of the items specified in paragraphs 8 and 9 above and requests the Secretary-General, in consultation with the Special Commission, to develop a plan for the future ongoing monitoring and verification of Iraq's compliance with this paragraph, to be submitted to the Security Council for approval within one hundred and twenty days of the passage of this resolution;

. . . .

12. *Decides* that Iraq shall unconditionally agree not to acquire or develop nuclear weapons or nuclear-weapons-usable material or any subsystems or components or any research, development, support or manufacturing facilities related to the above; to submit to the Secretary-General and the Director-General of the International Atomic Energy Agency within fifteen days of the adoption of the present resolution a declaration of the locations, amounts, and types of all items specified above; to place all of its nuclear-weapons-usable materials under the exclusive control, for custody and removal, of the International Atomic Energy Agency, with the assistance and cooperation of the Special Commission as provided for in the plan of the Secretary-General discussed in paragraph 9 (b) above;....

. . . .

24. *Decides* that, in accordance with resolution 661 (1990) and subsequent related resolutions and until a further decision is taken by the Security Council, all States shall continue to prevent the sale or supply, or the promotion or facilitation of such sale or supply, to Iraq by their nationals, or from their territories or using their flag vessels or aircraft, of:

(a) Arms and related *matériel* of all types, specifically including the sale or transfer through other means of all forms of conventional military equipment, including for paramilitary forces, and spare parts and components and their means of production, for such equipment;

(b) Items specified and defined in paragraphs 8 and 12 above not otherwise covered above; ...

Questions for Discussion

1. Would the coalition response to Saddam Hussein's invasion of Kuwait have been lawful in the absence of Security Council Resolution 678?

2. What is the legal consequence of Saddam Hussein's violation of Security Council Resolution 687 setting the conditions for ending the coalition action against Iraq? Would a material breach of this resolution justify a forceful response to ensure compliance? Or would

lawfulness of the response to a material breach depend on whether the Security Council supported the response? Who determines a material breach in such circumstances? Is the Security Council which enacted the resolution the primary body for assessing compliance?

3. Would Security Council resolution 678 justify the use of force to remove any ongoing threats to the peace from Saddam Hussein's Iraq? What factual showing or Security Council action would be required for any such action?

4. Was the subsequent United Kingdom/United States enforcement of the "no-fly zone" in Iraq justified by resolution 678? Was it lawful humanitarian intervention? Did it have Security Council support?

The Entebbe Raid: Defense Against Terrorism

Jeffrey A. Sheehan, *The Entebbe Raid: The Principle of Self-Help in International Law as Justification for State Use of Armed Force*
1 FLETCHER F. 135, 140–42 (1977)

It is the implication of the historic evolution of the idea of reprisals that Israel's Entebbe action is not within the normal definition of peacetime reprisal. First, there are some features of Entebbe which are not covered (e.g., the measurement of the proportionality could not be made in Naulilaa terms at all). Second, the Israeli action at Entebbe does not meet certain criteria of the traditional concept of reprisal (e.g., Israel made no formal demand to the Ugandan government). United Nations activity might take the place of formal correspondence covering international disputes, but Israel did not raise the issue at the United Nations. Finally, Israel had no intention of forcing Uganda "to agree to a satisfactory settlement." The Entebbe raid was not undertaken to change Ugandan behavior, but to supplement Ugandan action which Israel considered insufficient.

More often, the principle of self-defense has been referred to as justification for the raid. It is contended that this label is not applicable and that its use is too inconsistent and too vague to provide convincing legal justification for the raid. A small sampling of the writings on self-defense reveals the difficulty of establishing a definitive interpretation of the Entebbe case. Von Glahn does not discuss the idea of self-defense. Kelson asserts:

> ... this article [United Nations Charter, Article 51] applies only in the case of an armed attack. The right of self-defense must not be exercised in case of any other violation of the legally protected interests of a Member.

The action of the PLO in hijacking the aircraft and forcing it to fly to Uganda might be construed as an armed attack. However, it is questionable that the Ugandan act can be labeled a "ratification" of the attack and therefore an act of aggression itself. Labeling Uganda an aggressor because it fails to rid itself of foreign armed bands is equally debatable.

Hyde defines self defense as " ... that form of self-protection which is directed against an aggressor or contemplated aggressor." While under certain definitions of "aggressor," this would provide legal justification for the Entebbe raid, there is much dispute over definitions of "aggression." Bowett contends that self-defense is a permissible means of protection of a wide range of substantive rights including protection of nationals. This could provide Israel with a vindication of its actions under the label of self-defense. In fact, Israeli United Nations Representative Herzog cited Bowett several times in his remarks during the Security Council debate of July 9. However, the legal issue is much more complex than Herzog acknowledged.

The criteria for judging an act of self-defense were laid down by Daniel Webster in 1842 in his note to the British on the *Caroline* case of 1837.

. . . .

Although the four criteria seem applicable in the Entebbe case, the *Caroline* affair applied to a somewhat different situation. There, Britain felt that her Canadian territory was threatened. While it is unlikely that the armed bands presented a threat to her sovereignty, Britain believed that her territorial integrity was at stake. The Entebbe situation did not involve the territorial integrity of Israel, although Israeli legal interests may have been injured in the detention of its nationals in Uganda. The threat to nationals abroad has not normally been considered to justify action in "self-defense" under the *Caroline* rule. For this reason, it is difficult to construct a convincing legal argument around self-defense.

However, in the Security Council debates, Israel invoked self-defense as justification for the raid, but neither of the scholars cited by Herzog views the issues as unequivocally as do the Israelis. Herzog quoted O'Connell: "Traditional international law has not prohibited States from protecting their nationals whose lives or property are imperilled by political conditions in another State. . . ." He did not quote another passage later in the same book which states, "Nowadays, however, the United Nations Charter would appear to limit the right of self-defence to occasions of direct attack, and to exclude the use of force altogether from the right of self-help." Likewise, Herzog's use of Bowett's analysis leaves out important passages which weaken the Israeli justification. For example:

> [This line of logic] . . . leads to a ready acceptance of the proposition that the defence of the interest of nationals is, **ipso facto**, the defence of the interests of the State. In practice it cannot be said that a threat to the safety of nationals abroad constitutes a threat to the security of the State . . . Any state invoking the right of self-defence must be prepared to justify the measures it takes in pursuance of that right before an impartial international tribunal.

Memorandum by Monroe Leigh, Legal Adviser of the Department of State, to Henry A. Kissinger, Secretary of State
(July 8, 1976), *in* 73 Am. J. Int'l L. 122–24 (1979)

Uganda's Actions Violate International Law

The apparent pattern of assistance and complicity by the Ugandan authorities with the hijackers in their continued detention of Israeli citizens, in their threats against the lives of those citizens, and in their demands for the release of terrorists detained in Israel constituted a threat and use of force against the political independence of Israel and contrary to the purposes of the United Nations in violation of Article 2, paragraph 4 of the United Nations Charter. It also constituted a flagrant violation of Uganda's obligations under the 1970 Hague Convention for the Suppression of Unlawful Seizure of Aircraft. Certainly it could not seriously be argued that a State which captured innocent travelers of another country, whether by aircraft hijacking or by other means, and held them for ransom was acting lawfully. While the Government of Uganda in this case did not itself hijack the aircraft and capture the hostages, its assistance to the terrorists and its participation with them in holding the hostages made it effectively a co-participant in the terrorist act.

Israel's Action was Consistent With International Law

Israel's action in rescuing the hostages clearly involved a temporary breach of the territorial integrity of Uganda. Normally such action would be impermissible under the

Charter of the United Nations, however well based the grievance that gave rise to it. However, there is a well-established, if narrow, right to use limited force for the protection of one's own nationals from an imminent threat of injury or death in a situation where the State in whose territory they are located either is unwilling or unable to protect them. The right, like the right of self-defense from which it flows, is limited to such use of force as is necessary and appropriate to protect the threatened nationals from injury and does not encompass acts intended to punish or exact compensation.

This theory of the right to act for the protection of one's nationals was referred to by the United States in partial justification of its interventions in the Congo in 1964, in the Dominican Republic in 1965, and in Cambodia to rescue the crew of the SS *Mayaguez* in 1975.

The requirements of this right to protect nationals seem all to have been met in the Entebbe case. Israel had good reason to believe at the time it acted that Israeli nationals were in imminent danger of execution by the hijackers, and that Ugandan authorities were unwilling to take the actions necessary to release the Israeli nationals or to prevent substantial loss of Israeli lives. The Israeli military action was apparently limited to the sole objective of extricating the passengers and crew, and terminated when that objective was accomplished. The force employed seems reasonably justifiable as necessary for the rescue of the passengers and crew: the killing of the terrorists themselves for obvious reasons; the firing on Ugandan troops because they involved themselves in the conflict; and the destruction of Ugandan aircraft to eliminate the possibility of pursuit of the Israeli force.

The fact that Israel might have secured the release of its nationals by complying with the terrorists' demands, and thus have avoided any use of force, should not alter these conclusions. No state is required to yield control over persons in lawful custody in its territory under conviction pursuant to criminal charges. Moreover, it would be a self-defeating policy to release prisoners convicted in some cases of earlier acts of terrorism in order to placate the demands of the terrorists.

It should be emphasized that this assessment of the legality of Israeli actions depends heavily on the unusual circumstances of this specific case. In particular, the strong evidence of Ugandan sympathy and complicity with the terrorists made impracticable any cooperation with or reliance on Ugandan authorities in rescuing the passengers and crew, and necessitated a surprise assault at a time when Israeli authorities had not broken off negotiations under Ugandan auspices. It is to be hoped that these unique circumstances will not arise in the future.

Questions for Discussion

1. Was the U.S. aerial strike against Libya, in response to an ongoing pattern of terrorist attacks assisted by Libya worldwide, consistent with the Charter? Should this action be discussed as lawful defensive action under Article 51 or as illegal reprisal? What pattern of attack and response is required for each such characterization?

2. Was the U.S. cruise missile strike against al-Qaeda training camps in Afghanistan in response to the bombing of U.S. embassies in Kenya and Tanzania lawful? Was the U.S. cruise missile strike against a chemical plant in the Sudan, undertaken in response to the same incident, lawful? If this latter strike was subsequently determined to be based on faulty information what are the legal consequences?

3. How should nations respond to continuing, determined state-supported terrorist attacks?

Afghanistan and the War Against Terrorism: Defense Against Terrorism Continued

Letter dated 7 October 2001 from the Permanent Representative of the United States of America to the United Nations, addressed to the President of the Security Council
UN Doc. S/2001/946 (Oct. 7, 2001)

In accordance with Article 51 of the Charter of the United Nations, I wish, on behalf of my Government, to report that the United States of America, together with other States, has initiated actions in the exercise of its inherent right of individual and collective self-defence following the armed attacks that were carried out against the United States on 11 September 2001.

On 11 September 2001, the United States was the victim of massive and brutal attacks in the states of New York, Pennsylvania and Virginia. These attacks were specifically designed to maximize the loss of life; they resulted in the death of more than 5,000 persons, including nationals of 81 countries, as well as the destruction of four civilian aircraft, the World Trade Center towers and a section of the Pentagon. Since 11 September, my Government has obtained clear and compelling information that the Al-Qaeda organization, which is supported by the Taliban regime in Afghanistan, had a central role in the attacks. There is still much we do not know. Our inquiry is in its early stages. We may find that our self-defence requires further actions with respect to other organizations and other States.

The attacks on 11 September 2001 and the ongoing threat to the United States and its nationals posed by the Al-Qaeda organization have been made possible by the decision of the Taliban regime to allow the parts of Afghanistan that it controls to be used by this organization as a base of operation. Despite every effort by the United States and the international community, the Taliban regime has refused to change its policy. From the territory of Afghanistan, the Al-Qaeda organization continues to train and support agents of terror who attack innocent people throughout the world and target United States nationals and interests in the United States and abroad.

In response to these attacks, and in accordance with the inherent right of individual and collective self-defence, United States armed forces have initiated actions designed to prevent and deter further attacks on the United States. These actions include measures against Al-Qaeda terrorist training camps and military installations of the Taliban regime in Afghanistan. In carrying out these actions, the United States is committed to minimizing civilian casualties and damage to civilian property. In addition, the United States will continue its humanitarian efforts to alleviate the suffering of the people of Afghanistan. We are providing them with food, medicine and supplies.

I ask that you circulate the text of the present letter as a document of the Security Council.

(Signed) John D. Negroponte

Jonathan I. Charney, *Editorial Comments: The Use of Force Against Terrorism and International Law*

95 Am. J. Int'l L. 835–39 (2001)

At the time of this writing, it is hard to know what international law questions will arise from the attacks of September 11, 2001, on the United States at the World Trade towers and the Pentagon. The situation is likely to change significantly between the time this Editorial is being written and its publication. Obviously, a strong response is required to suppress international terrorism, including the use of force. I support such a response but fear that the U.S. use of force without United Nations Security Council authorization under Chapter VII of the UN Charter may undermine long-term United States objectives and create an undesirable precedent damaging to the United Nations system, including world order interests shared by many.

Statements issued by the United States government to date dramatically call for a "war against terrorism" worldwide, while failing to acknowledge any formal role for the Security Council regarding the use of force in or against other states. While the U.S. administration assembled what appears to be a global alliance against international terrorism, it reserved to itself the right to decide how to use that force, including when and where it should be used. This policy was implemented by the commencement of attacks on Afghanistan on October 7, 2001. The United States claims the right to use force against other states that are associated with international terrorism. Its broad claims to use force reflect an unfortunate failure by the United States to promote the objectives of the United Nations Charter, as well as the value of maintaining and strengthening the United Nations system.

I need not restate the argument in my previous Editorial that absent actions in self-defense under Article 51 of the Charter, uses of force against the territorial integrity or political independence of another state must be authorized by the Security Council under Chapter VII. Article 2(4) otherwise forbids both the conduct of a just war and forceful reprisals. The Security Council has not adopted a decision under Chapter VII to authorize the use of force in this situation; and whether all the U.S. uses of force taken so far in response to the attacks of September 11 meet the requirements of self-defense is debatable. Military actions by the United States outside Afghanistan would be problematical if their objective is to suppress international terrorist groups generally and not to defend the United States from future attacks by those responsible for the events of September 11. They would conflict with the objectives of the self-defense exception and fall within the prohibited uses of force by reprisals or by engaging in a "just" war, in opposition to core Charter objectives to prevent states from using force in international relations to promote their policy agendas no matter how just, except for the right of self-defense or a collective decision by the Security Council.

Even the use of force in self-defense is a grave act and, thus, a limited exception to the Charter prohibition on the use of force by states. Since the use of force is irreversible and irreparable, the right should not depend merely on the credibility of conclusory statements by government officials, especially when the government has had, as in this case, sufficient time and opportunity to disclose supporting evidence.

Any state that seeks to invoke the right of self-defense should be required to furnish the international community with credible evidence that it has suffered an attack, that the entity against which the right of self-defense is exercised was the source of the attack, that the attack or threat of attack is continuing, and that the use of force is necessary to protect the state from further injury. Ordinarily, such a showing could be made easily. Sometimes it may be more difficult, as in the case of terrorist attacks when their source is not immediately self-evident. While conclusory official statements might be acceptable when the victim state has no time or opportunity to present the requisite evidence, the facts justifying its actions should otherwise be revealed prior to taking necessary defensive steps. When such disclosure is not feasible, it should be made at the earliest time thereafter.

To limit the use of force in international relations, which is the primary goal of the United Nations Charter, there must be checks on its use in self-defense. Disclosure to the international community of the basis for such action would help to serve this purpose. The alleged credibility of conclusory statements by a state's leadership should not be a sufficient basis for actions in self-defense since it would encourage abuse. When attacks on a state are so grave as to justify actions in self-defense, the supporting evidence would normally be readily available. Disclosure of that evidence should be required even if the state would wish to claim that classified information would be disclosed. The use of force in self-defense is limited to situations where the state is truly required to defend itself from serious attack. In such situations, the state must carry the burden of presenting evidence to support its actions, normally before these irreversible and irreparable measures are taken.

The United States should have disclosed the factual bases for its claim of self-defense against the terrorist attacks before engaging in military action. It had time to do so, as it waited nearly a month before initiating the use of force. In addition, it reported that it had the necessary evidence to link Afghanistan and terrorists located there to the September 11 attacks and thus should have been able to present probative support for its self-defense right. Attention had been directed to the relationship between the government of Afghanistan and terrorists operating there for some time. The United States claimed that the September 11 attacks were linked to previous attacks by the same source, some of which had led to public indictments, trials, or convictions, such as the prior bombing of the World Trade towers, the destruction of U.S. military housing in Saudi Arabia, the bombing of U.S. embassies in Africa, and the attack on the USS *Cole* in Yemen. I expect that the evidence it had collected would have enabled the United States to demonstrate a sufficient factual basis for the use of force in self-defense in response to the September 11 attacks. Its failure to do so in this situation makes it easier for others to take unjustifiable military actions based on unsupported assertions of self-defense.

Moreover, in the weeks that followed the September 11 attacks, the United States had more than sufficient time to seek the Security Council's approval for an appropriate military response, as it has done with regard to actions other than the use of force. Thus, in one subsequent resolution the Security Council declared its condemnation of the September 11 terrorist attacks and its continuing availability "to take all necessary steps in response." In a second resolution submitted by the United States and unanimously adopted on the same day, the Council acted under Chapter VII to require all member states to prevent and suppress acts of international terrorism, especially by denying terrorists the use of the states' territories and access to sources of funding. Passage of these resolutions illustrates the degree of international support at the United Nations for the U.S. opposition to terrorism. But the resolutions also clearly demonstrate that the United States decided not to seek Security Council sanction of its use of force, preferring to take its own military actions without disclosing the factual basis for them. When the United States did deliver a letter to the Security Council in support of its military actions in self-defense, as required by Article 51, it continued its unfortunate policy of providing conclusory reasons only, although the Council did discuss the issues raised by the letter.

Moreover, the U.S. policy of basing the military actions merely on a claim of self-defense in the absence of a broader Security Council authorization is counterproductive because, more than in many past situations, the United States could have benefited greatly from the direct involvement of the Security Council and the support of the United Nations system as a whole. First, international terrorism is widely condemned. The likelihood of receiving the Council's approval of broad authority for effective action against international terrorism is as great as in any prior situation in which Chapter VII authorization has been sought. Second, to the extent that the United States wishes to build a stable, long-term coalition in support of its stated objective of suppressing international terrorism worldwide, the United Nations would appear to be the preferred vehicle. It constitutes an excellent forum for the disclosure of proof of the identity of the perpetrators and the sources of future terrorist threats, and states that might be unwilling to take actions under U.S. auspices can avoid political embarrassment by casting their lot with the United Nations as the lead agency. By taking military actions without the Security Council's authorization and without legally binding other states to support such actions through Council decisions, the United States has given states freer rein to oppose long-term efforts to suppress international terrorism and military actions outside Afghanistan, especially since all the commitments of support were solely political and made only to the United States, sometimes secretly. Furthermore, by failing to use the resources of the Security Council, the United States undermines the view that the Council, and the United Nations as a whole, should be the primary vehicle to respond to threats to and breaches of the peace, which strengthens the belief that states may freely act outside the United Nations system.

....

Involvement of the Security Council in the use of force in response to the September 11 attacks would have avoided further undermining the benefits the United Nations system can provide to all. The Security Council's participation in the use of force and other actions against international terrorism could help to build durable and broadly supported defenses against this threat. Regardless of the perception by the United States of its military and economic strengths relative to those of any other state, it cannot win this "war" alone or with the uncertain support it has constructed outside the United Nations system. The world order that has benefited the United States and the international community subsequent to World War II is built on the Charter, especially its provisions on the use of force.

Over the long term the interests of the United States and the international community will be best served by the Charter-based system of world order. If international terrorists have a coherent goal, it is to undermine this system—an objective the United States is perhaps unwittingly promoting by its actions. Despite the flaws of the United Nations, no one has proposed a better system for serving the interests of peace and security in the face of the agenda of international terrorist groups. The United States should initiate a policy of strong adherence to the Charter and help make the Security Council central to the international community's response to the forces represented by the attacks of September 11. This course of action would better defend the United States than the current policy and would assure the continued strength and viability of the world order system embodied in the United Nations.

Thomas M. Franck, *Editorial Comments: Terrorism and the Right of Self-Defense*

95 Am. J. Int'l L. 839–43 (2001)

Is the United States' use of military force against the Taliban and Al Qaeda in Afghanistan lawful under the United Nations Charter? At a recent conference of primarily German international lawyers, many answered that question in the negative. This may surprise American colleagues, but their doubts need to be addressed seriously for they may be more widely shared.

The following propositions were assayed to demonstrate the alleged illegality of U.S. recourse to force:

(1) It violates the Article 2(4) of the Charter prohibition against use of force except when authorized by the Security Council under Chapter VII.

(2) Self-defense is impermissible after an attack has ended; that is, after September 11, 2001.

(3) Self-defense may be exercised only against an attack by a state. Al Qaeda is not the government of a state.

(4) Self-defense may be exercised only against an actual attacker. The Taliban are not the attacker.

(5) Self-defense maybe exercised only "until the Security Council has taken measures necessary to maintain international peace and security." Since the Council took such measures in Resolution 1373 of September 28, 2001, the right of self-defense has been superseded.

(6) The right of self-defense arises only upon proof that it is being directed against the actual attacker. The United States has failed to provide this proof.

1. *The Action Violates Article 2(4) of the Charter*

It does not.

While Charter Article 2(4) prohibits the unilateral use of force, the prohibition must be read in the context of Article 51, which recognizes "the inherent right of individual or collective self-defence if an armed attack occurs against a Member of the United Nations." This provision was included in the Charter because the drafters feared that the system of standby collective security forces envisaged in Article 43, to be deployed by the Security Council, might not come into being and that, accordingly, states would have to continue to rely on their "inherent right" of self-defense. That concern was well founded. Article 43 languished and no standby force was ever created, let alone deployed against any of the approximately two hundred armed attacks that have taken place since 1945, leaving states' security in their own hands and that of willing allies.

This interpretation accords with Charter practice. A unanimous resolution, passed the day after the attack on the United States, put the Security Council on record as "[r]ecognizing the inherent right of individual or collective self-defence in accordance with the Charter," while condemning "in the strongest terms the horrifying terrorist attacks which took place on 11 September 2001."

The resolution recognizes a right to respond in self-defense, but it does not—and legally cannot—authorize its exercise since that right is "inherent" in the victim. Under Article 51, self-defense is a right exercisable at the sole discretion of an attacked state, not a license to be granted by decision of the Security Council. How could it be otherwise? Were states prohibited from defending themselves until after the Council had agreed, assuredly there would not now be many states left in the United Nations Organization.

It is true that the International Court of Justice has ruled that the claim of a right to use force in self-defense must be supported by credible evidence of an armed attack and of the attacker's identity. However, while the production of such evidence is essential to sustaining the right, that emphatically is not a condition precedent to its exercise. This does not leave the field open for bogus self-defenders. Were a state to attack another while falsely claiming to be acting in self-defense, that would constitute an "armed attack" under Article 51 or "aggression" under Article 39, giving both the victim and the United Nations the right to respond with appropriate levels of individual or collective force (see item No. 6, below).

2. *Self-Defense Is Impermissible After an Attack Ends*

There is nothing in either the *travaux préparatoires* or the text of the Charter to justify this claim, which also defies logic. The assertion that self-defense requires "immediate" action comes from a misunderstanding of the *Caroline* decision, which deals only with *anticipatory* self-defense. In any event, Osama bin Laden has specifically promised to continue attacks on the United States.

3. *Self-Defense Is Only Exercisable Against State Acts*

Al Qaeda is not a state. Nonetheless, the actions taken against the United States on September 11 were classified by Security Council Resolution 1368 as "a threat to international peace and security." That signifies a decision to take "measures ... in accordance with Articles 41 and 42, to maintain or restore international peace and security." Such measures under Article 39 of Chapter VII were, in fact, taken sixteen days later. It is inconceivable that actions the Security Council deems itself competent to take against a nonstate actor under Articles 41 and 42 in accordance with Article 39 should be impermissible when taken against the same actor under Article 51 in exercise of a state's "inherent" right of self-defense. If the Council can act against Al Qaeda, so can an attacked state.

This intuition is supported by the language of Article 51, which, in authorizing a victim state to act in self-defense, does not limit this "inherent" right to attacks by another state. Rather, the right is expressly accorded in response to "an armed attack" and not to any particular kind of attacker. That, evidently, is why Resolution 1368 reiterates the right of self-defense by a state specifically against "terrorist attacks" (para. 3). The Council clearly identifies "international terrorism [ ] as a threat to international peace and security" against which "individual or collective self-defence" may be exercised.

4. *Self-Defense Is Only Exercisable Against an Attacker*

The September 11 attack was not launched by the Taliban. Does this make U.S. action against that faction illegal?

The question is an important one that has long exercised international lawyers. In 1944, at Dumbarton Oaks, China included the following element in the definition of aggression it proposed to the conference preparing the draft Charter articles later presented to the San Francisco Conference: "Provision of support to armed groups, formed within [a state's] territory, which have invaded the territory of another state; or refusal, notwithstanding the request of the invaded state, to take in its own territory all the measures in its power to deprive such groups of all assistance or protection."

China's proposal was not adopted. More recently, the draft articles on state responsibility prepared by the International Law Commission make it clear that a state is responsible for the consequences of permitting its territory to be used to injure another state. Security Council Resolution 1368 makes even clearer, in the context of condemning the September 11 attack on the United States, the responsibility for terrorism of "sponsors of these terrorist attacks" including those "supporting or harbouring the perpetrators" (para. 3). The Taliban clearly fit that designation.

5. *The Right of Self-Defense Is Superseded After the Security Council Invokes Collective Measures*

Article 51 provides that the right of self-defense may be exercised by any state subject to an armed attack "until the Security Council has taken measures necessary to maintain international peace and security." In Resolution 1368 the Security Council recognized the applicability of this right in the context of the September 11 attack. However, on September 28, the Council invoked Chapter VII to require states to impose mandatory controls on the financing of terrorist groups, and to prohibit states from "providing any form of support" to terrorists. Does the imposition of these measures under Chapter VII supersede the attacked state's right to use force in self-defense?

It does not. After the Iraqi invasion of Kuwait, the Security Council, as in the instant case, affirmed the inherent right to use force in individual or collective self-defense. When, almost four months later, it authorized UN members "to use all necessary means" to repel the Iraqi forces, that resolution reaffirmed the Council's earlier affirmation of the victim's right to act in self-defense, clearly implying that Chapter VII measures taken under Council authority could supplement and coexist with the "inherent" right of a state and its allies to defend against an armed attack (Art. 51). This serves to give Article 51 the sensible interpretation that a victim of an armed attack retains its autonomous right of self-defense at least until further collective measures authorized by the Council have had the effect of restoring international peace and security.

The same pattern of authorization was followed more explicitly by the Council in invoking mandatory measures under Chapter VII on September 28. This time, the resolution specifically reaffirmed "the inherent right of individual or collective self-defence as recognized by the Charter of the United Nations as reiterated in resolution 1368 (2001)." That the Council, in invoking collective measures, should ensure that these not be construed as rescinding the "inherent" right of self-defense is hardly surprising, since these new measures mandated on September 28, useful as they might be, clearly were not intended by themselves to deal decisively with the threat to international peace and security posed by Al Qaeda and its Taliban defenders.

It is a *reductio ad absurdum* of the Charter to construe it to require an attacked state automatically to cease taking whatever armed measures are lawfully available to it whenever the Security Council passes a resolution invoking economic and legal steps in support of those measures.

6. *The United States Has Not Provided Proof*

Resolution 1368, in "recognizing" the right of the United States and its allies to use force against what was deemed, clearly, to be an "armed attack" within the meaning of Article 51, and also in recognizing that those who "harbour [ ] the perpetrators, organizers and sponsors of these acts" are accountable for them, did not specify either the attacker or those who harbored them. In the absence of such clear identification of the perpetrator and sponsor, what authority is there for the exercise of Article 51's "inherent" right of self-defense? Resolution 1373, too, fails to identify the wrongdoer. It applies mandatory economic, fiscal, and diplomatic sanctions against "persons"—defined as "those who finance, plan, facilitate or commit terrorist acts"—without defining which groups are included in the category. Some critics therefore assert that neither resolution specifically authorizes action against either Al Qaeda or the Taliban.

This critique conflates two related, but separate, challenges. One is directed to the lack of factual evidence of Al Qaeda's and the Taliban's culpability. The other argues that, in law, the right to use force in self-defense arises only after the evidentiary test has been met by proof accepted as adequate by the appropriate institutions of the international system.

Critics point out that the North Atlantic Council, the governing body of NATO, on September 12 authorized invocation of Article 5 of its Charter—which states that an armed attack on one member shall be regarded as an armed attack on all—subject to the evidentiary caveat, "if it is determined that this attack was directed from abroad against the United States." Even if this condition correctly interprets the intent of NATO's September 12 decision, it is apparent that the evidentiary test has been satisfied. On October 1, NATO Secretary General Lord Robertson reported that the United States had presented to the NATO Council "compelling" and "conclusive" evidence that the attacks were the work of Al Qaeda, protected by the Taliban, and that invocation of Article 5 was therefore "confirmed." Only at this point did the U.S. military response, supported by the NATO allies, begin to be implemented.

Does this imply that the Security Council must similarly vote its acceptance of U.S. evidence? There is not a scintilla of evidence to this effect in either the *travaux* or the text of Charter Article 51. Rather, the "inherent right" being preserved in Article 51 is clearly that of a victim state and its allies, exercising their own, sole judgment in determining whether an attack has occurred and where it originated. Security Council Resolutions 1368 and 1373, while deliberately expanding the definition of what constitutes an attack and an attacker, in no way tried to take this discretion away from the victim state.

This reading of Article 51 does not mean that the question of evidence is irrelevant in law. It does mean, however, that the right of a state to defend itself against attack is not subordinated in law to a *prior* requirement to demonstrate to the satisfaction of the Security Council that it is acting against the party guilty of the attack. The law does have an evidentiary requirement, but it arises *after*, not *before*, the right of self-defense is exercised. Thus, if a state claiming to be implementing its inherent right of self-defense were to attack an innocent party, the remedy would be the same as for any other aggression in violation of Article 2(4). The innocent party would have the right of self-defense under Article 51, which is exercisable at its sole volition. It could also appeal to the Council to institute collective measures against its attacker under Chapter VII.

Any other reading of Article 51 would base the right of self-defense not on a victim state's "inherent" powers of self-preservation, but upon its ability, in the days following an attack, to convince the fifteen members of the Security Council that it has indeed correctly identified its attacker. As a matter of strategic practice, any attacked state is very likely to make an intense effort to demonstrate the culpability of its adversary, limited only by inhibitions regarding the operational effect of sharing intelligence methods. As a matter of law, however, there is no requirement whatever that a state receive the blessing of the Security Council before responding to an armed attack. Were this not so, how many states would deliberately agree to subordinate their security to the Council's assessment of the probity of the evidence on which they based their defensive strategy of self-preservation?

Sean D. Murphy, ed., *Contemporary Practice of the United States Relating to International Law*

96 Am. J. Int'l L. 237–48 (Jan. 2002)

Legal Regulation of Use of Force

Terrorist Attacks on World Trade Center and Pentagon

On September 11, 2001, nineteen persons of non-U.S. nationality boarded four U.S. commercial passenger jets in Boston, Newark, and Washington, hijacked the aircraft minutes after takeoff, and crashed them into the World Trade Center in New York, the Pentagon in northern Virginia, and the Pennsylvania countryside. All told, some three thousand persons were killed in the incidents, the worst casualties experienced in the United States in a single day since the American Civil War.

In Boston, five hijackers—Satam Al Suqami, Waleed Alshehri, Wail Alsheri, Mohamed Atta, and Abdulaziz Alomari—boarded American Airlines Flight 11, which departed from Logan Airport at 8:10 A.M. en route to Los Angeles. After takeoff, the hijackers seized the plane, flew it to New York City, and, at 8:48 A.M., crashed it into the north tower of the World Trade Center. Also in Boston, five hijackers—Marwan Al-Shehhi, Fayez Ahmed, Ahmed Alghamdi, Hamza Alghamdi, and Mohaid Alshehri—boarded United Airlines Flight 175, which departed from Logan at 7:58 A.M. en route to Los Angeles. After takeoff, the hijackers seized the plane, flew it to New York City, and, at 9:03 A.M., crashed it into the south tower of the World Trade Center.

Both 110-story towers—in which roughly 50,000 people worked—erupted into flames, forcing massive evacuations of those working on the floors below the impact sites. At 9:50 A.M., the south tower collapsed, followed by the north tower at 10:30 A.M., obliterating some 12 million square feet of office space (an amount equivalent to all the office space in Atlanta or Miami) and damaging another 18 million square feet of office space in other Manhattan buildings. Among other things, a subway station, two electrical substations, and some thirty-three miles of cables were crushed. Nearly 2,900 persons were, as of the end of 2001, confirmed dead or missing at the World Trade Center, and 157 passengers, crew, and hijackers were killed on the two planes.

Just outside of Washington, D.C., five hijackers—Khalid Almihdhar, Majed Moqed, Nawaf Al Hamzi, Salem Al Hamzi, and Hani Hanjour—boarded American Airlines Flight 77, which departed from Dulles Airport at 8:10 A.M. en route to Los Angeles. After takeoff, the hijackers seized the plane and, at 9:39 A.M., crashed it into the Pentagon, killing themselves and fifty-nine passengers and crew. On the ground, 125 persons were killed immediately or in the incinerating collapse that followed.

In Newark, four hijackers—Saeed H. Alghamdi, Ahmed Al-Haznawi, Ahmed Alnami, and Ziad Samir Jarrah—boarded United Airlines Flight 93, which departed from Newark Airport (one of the three major airports serving the New York metropolitan area) at 8:01 A.M. en route to San Francisco. After takeoff, the hijackers seized the plane, but apparently because of a revolt against the hijackers by some of the forty passengers and crew, the plane crashed into the Pennsylvania countryside at 10:10 A.M. No one survived.

In response to the terrorist attacks, the U.S. Federal Aviation Administration immediately ordered U.S. flights to land at the nearest airports, banned takeoffs from any U.S. airport for twenty-four hours, and diverted international flights to Canada. Congress passed, and President Bush signed into law on September 18, a $40 billion appropriation for emergency funds, primarily for disaster assistance and antiterrorist initiatives, needed to respond to the attacks. Because the airline industry sustained heavy losses — from the attacks themselves (including potential liability), the closure of U.S. airspace, and the reluctance of passengers to resume flying — President Bush also signed into law on September 22 a multibillion dollar aid package for the industry. This aid package includes the "September 11th Victim Compensation Fund of 2001," whose purpose is to provide monetary compensation, if necessary through a relative, to any individual who was physically injured or killed in the September 11 attacks. At the same time, the establishment of the fund was designed to help stabilize the airline industry by protecting American Airlines and United Airlines from potentially devastating lawsuits.

In the wake of the attacks, U.S. law enforcement agencies commenced the largest criminal investigation in the nation's history. The investigation revealed that the nineteen hijackers had worked as a single, integrated group for a period of eighteen months with little outside help other than funding. The six leaders of the group were well-educated, entered the United States earlier than the others, and trained as pilots. The others were younger and less educated, and served as "foot soldiers" to control the passengers. Immediately after the attacks, U.S. government officials suspected that the hijackers had been authorized and funded by a Saudi Arabian expatriate, Osama bin Laden, based in Afghanistan and working through his secretive, compartmentalized terrorist network, Al Qaeda. Bin Laden's overall objectives reportedly are to oust pro-Western governments in the Middle East, to remove U.S. military forces from the region, and to prevent an Arab-Israeli peace settlement. Even prior to September 11, Al Qaeda had been suspected of involvement in the 1993 bombing of the World Trade Center that killed 6 persons and wounded more than 1,000; the 1996 bombing of a U.S. military housing complex in Dhahran, Saudi Arabia, that killed 19 U.S. servicemen and wounded 372 other persons; the 1998 bombings of U.S. embassies in Tanzania and Kenya that killed 224 persons and wounded some 5,000 others; and the October 2000 bombing of the USS *Cole* in the harbor of Aden, Yemen, that killed 17 U.S. sailors and wounded 39. Western governments reportedly believe that once Al Qaeda terrorists are sent to a country, they are provided considerable latitude in selecting their targets and executing their plans, since doing so minimizes the likelihood of detection.

On October 4, 2001, the United Kingdom released a document entitled "Responsibility for the Terrorist Atrocities in the United States, 11 September 2001." The document provided background on bin Laden, Al Qaeda, and their relationship to the de facto government of Afghanistan, the Taliban. The document then noted:

> 21. Al Qaida virulently opposes the United States. Usama Bin Laden has urged and incited his followers to kill American citizens, in the most unequivocal terms.

> 22. On 12 October 1996 he issued a declaration of jihad as follows:

> *"The people of Islam have suffered from aggression, iniquity and injustice imposed by the Zionist-Crusader alliance and their collaborators ...*

> *It is the duty now on every tribe in the Arabian peninsula to fight jihad and cleanse the land from these Crusader occupiers. Their wealth is booty to those who kill them.*

> *My Muslim brothers: your brothers in Palestine and in the land of the two Holy Places* [i.e. Saudi Arabia] *are calling upon your help and asking you to take part in fighting against the enemy — the Americans and the Israelis. They are asking you to do whatever you can to expel the enemies out of the sanctities of Islam."*

Later in the same year he said that

"terrorising the American occupiers [of Islamic Holy Places] *is a religious and logical obligation."*

In February 1998 he issued and signed a 'fatwa' which included a decree to all Muslims:

"... the killing of Americans and their civilian and military allies is a religious duty for each and every Muslim to be carried out in whichever country they are until Al Aqsa mosque has been liberated from their grasp and until their armies have left Muslim lands."

In the same 'fatwa' he called on Muslim scholars and their leaders and their youths to

"launch an attack on the American soldiers of Satan."

and concluded:

"We—with God's help—call on every Muslim who believes in God and wishes to be rewarded to comply with God's order to kill Americans and plunder their money whenever and wherever they find it. We also call on Muslims ... to launch the raid on Satan's US troops and the devil's supporters allying with them, and to displace those who are behind them."

Further, the UK document described certain evidence that connected the hijackers to bin Laden.

61. Nineteen men have been identified as the hijackers from the passenger lists of the four planes hijacked on 11 September 2001. At least three of them have already been positively identified as associates of Al Qaida. One has been identified as playing key roles in both the East African embassy attacks and the USS *Cole* attack. Investigations continue into the backgrounds of all the hijackers.

62. From intelligence sources, the following facts have been established subsequent to 11 September; for intelligence reasons, the names of associates, though known, are not given:

- In the run-up to 11 September, Bin Laden was mounting a concerted propaganda campaign amongst like-minded groups of people—including videos and documentation—justifying attacks on Jewish and American targets; and claiming that those who died in the course of them were carrying out God's work.
- We have learned, subsequent to 11 September, that Bin Laden himself asserted shortly before 11 September that he was preparing a major attack on America.
- In August and early September close associates of Bin Laden were warned to return to Afghanistan from other parts of the world by 10 September.
- Immediately prior to 11 September some known associates of Bin Laden were naming the date for action as on or around 11 September.
- Since 11 September we have learned that one of Bin Laden's closest and most senior associates was responsible for the detailed planning of the attacks.
- There is evidence of a very specific nature relating to the guilt of Bin Laden and his associates that is too sensitive to release.

63. Usama Bin Laden remains in charge, and the mastermind, of Al Qaida. In Al Qaida, an operation on the scale of the 11 September attacks would have been approved by Usama Bin Laden himself.

64. The modus operandi of 11 September was entirely consistent with previous attacks. Al Qaida's record of atrocities is characterised by meticulous long-term

planning, a desire to inflict mass casualties, suicide bombers, and multiple si-multaneous attacks.

65. The attacks of 11 September 2001 are entirely consistent with the scale and sophistication of the planning which went into the attacks on the East African Embassies and the USS *Cole*. No warnings were given for these three attacks, just as there was none on 11 September.

66. Al Qaida operatives, in evidence given in East African Embassy bomb trials, have described how the group spends years preparing for an attack. They conduct repeated surveillance, patiently gather materials, and identify and vet operatives, who have the skills to participate in the attack and the willingness to die for their cause.

67. The operatives involved in the 11 September atrocities attended flight schools, used flight simulators to study the controls of larger aircraft and placed potential airports and routes under surveillance.

68. Al Qaida's attacks are characterised by total disregard for innocent lives, including Muslims. In an interview after the East African bombings, Usama Bin Laden insisted that the need to attack the United States excused the killing of other innocent civilians, Muslim and non-Muslim alike.

69. No other organisation has both the motivation and the capability to carry out attacks like those of 11 September—only the Al Qaida network under Usama Bin Laden.

According to UK Prime Minister Tony Blair, the evidence detailed in the document left "absolutely no doubt that bin Laden and his network are responsible" for the hijackings. Thereafter, the United States confirmed the information contained in the UK document. On October 4, Pakistan—a Muslim country—said that the evidence that the United States had compiled concerning bin Laden's responsibility for the attacks would provide a sufficient basis for an indictment in a court of law. Bin Laden himself, however, did not publicly and expressly claim responsibility for the attacks.

Some U.S. officials suspected an Iraqi role in the attacks; one of the leaders of the hijackers, Mohamed Atta, reportedly met with an Iraqi intelligence agent in Prague in June 2000. Intelligence agencies from a number of countries reportedly concluded, however, that Iraq was not involved in the attacks.

U.S. officials asserted that Al Qaeda used a web of charities, companies, and fraudulent activities (using credit cards and food stamps) to raise funds and to move those funds across the globe. On September 24, President Bush invoked his presidential authority, including that under the International Emergency Economic Powers Act (IEEPA), to issue an executive order that expanded the U.S. Treasury Department's power to target financial support for terrorist organizations worldwide. In particular, the executive order froze the assets of twenty-seven persons (including bin Laden) and groups, and blocked the U.S. transactions of those persons and of others who support them. Further, the executive order increased the ability of the Treasury Department to block U.S. assets of, and to deny access to U.S. markets by, foreign banks that refused to cooperate with U.S. authorities in identifying and freezing terrorist assets abroad. Finally, the order authorized the secretary of state and the secretary of the treasury from time-to-time to make additional designations (which occurred on November 2, when twenty-two additional groups were added). By early October, the Treasury Department reportedly had frozen more than $100 million of suspected terrorist assets in domestic and foreign banks. In early November, the United

States launched a round of domestic raids and international banking actions to shut down two financial networks that were allegedly funding Al Qaeda. In its efforts to seize terrorist assets, the United States received support from some countries, such as Saudi Arabia and the United Arab Emirates, but encountered resistance from others.

The United States regarded the September 11 incidents as comparable to a military attack. In the week following the attacks, President Bush declared a national emergency and called to active duty the reserves of the U.S. armed forces. He also signed into law a joint resolution of Congress that, after noting that "the President has authority under the Constitution to take action to deter and prevent acts of international terrorism against the United States," provided in Section 2:

> (a) IN GENERAL. That the President is authorized to use all necessary and appropriate force against those nations, organizations, or persons he determines planned, authorized, committed, or aided the terrorist attacks that occurred on September 11, 2001, or harbored such organizations or persons, in order to prevent any future acts of international terrorism against the United States by such nations, organizations or persons.
>
> (b) WAR POWERS RESOLUTION REQUIREMENTS.
>
> (1) SPECIFIC STATUTORY AUTHORIZATION. Consistent with section 8(a)(1) of the War Powers Resolution, the Congress declares that this section is intended to constitute specific statutory authorization within the meaning of section 5(b) of the War Powers Resolution.
>
> (2) APPLICABILITY OF OTHER REQUIREMENTS. Nothing in this resolution supersedes any requirement of the War Powers Resolution.

Further, in a speech to the Congress on September 20, President Bush declared: "On September 11th, enemies of freedom committed an act of war against our country." The President created an Office of Homeland Security, as well as a Homeland Security Council, charged with developing and coordinating the implementation of a comprehensive national strategy to secure the United States from terrorist threats or attacks. The potential for further attacks was confirmed when, in late September, European law enforcement authorities uncovered a fully developed plan to blow up the U.S. Embassy in Paris. Intelligence reports of possible further attacks deemed credible by U.S. authorities led the Federal Bureau of Investigation (FBI) on October 11 and 29 to issue global alerts that more terrorist attacks might be carried out against U.S. targets in the United States or abroad. Finally, during October 2001, sixteen persons in Florida, New Jersey, New York, and Washington, D.C., became infected with anthrax, either by inhalation or by contact with their skin, from contaminated letters sent through the U.S. mail system. Four persons who inhaled the virus died. As of the end of 2001, law enforcement authorities were unsure whether the anthrax letters were the work of persons linked to the September 11 incidents, of domestic extremists motivated by hatred of the U.S. government, of a disturbed loner with a personal grievance, or of someone else. When France sought to propose a UN Security Council resolution condemning the anthrax attacks, the United States responded that such a resolution was inappropriate until such time as it could be determined that they were not a domestic criminal matter.

Although the United States had never recognized the Taliban regime as the government of Afghanistan — and therefore had no diplomatic relations with that group — certain U.S. demands were communicated to the Taliban through the government of Pakistan. Further, President Bush issued the demands in a widely reported speech to a joint session of the U.S. Congress.

> [T]he United States of America makes the following demands on the Taliban: Deliver to United States authorities all the leaders of Al Qaida who hide in your land. Release all foreign nationals, including American citizens, you have unjustly imprisoned. Protect foreign journalists, diplomats, and aid workers in your country. Close immediately and permanently every terrorist training camp in Afghanistan, and hand over every terrorist and every person in their support structure to appropriate authorities. Give the United States full access to terrorist training camps, so we can make sure they are no longer operating. These demands are not open to negotiation or discussion. The Taliban must act and act immediately. They will hand over the terrorists, or they will share in their fate.

The Taliban rejected the demands, insisting that it receive proof of bin Laden's involvement in the September 11 attacks.

In describing U.S. objectives in responding to the attacks, President Bush stated in his speech to Congress:

> Our response involves far more than instant retaliation and isolated strikes. Americans should not expect one battle but a lengthy campaign, unlike any other we have ever seen. It may include dramatic strikes, visible on TV, and covert operations, secret even in success. We will starve terrorists of funding, turn them one against another, drive them from place to place, until there is no refuge or no rest. And we will pursue nations that provide aid or safe haven to terrorism. Every nation, in every region, now has a decision to make. Either you are with us, or you are with the terrorists. From this day forward, any nation that continues to harbor or support terrorism will be regarded by the United States as a hostile regime.

The reaction of the global community was largely supportive. At the United Nations, the Security Council unanimously adopted on September 12 a resolution condemning "the horrifying terrorist attacks," which the Council regarded, "like any act of international terrorism, as a threat to international peace and security." Further, on September 28, the Security Council unanimously adopted, under Chapter VII of the UN Charter, a U.S.-sponsored resolution that obligates all member states to deny financing, support, and safe haven to terrorists, that calls for expanded information-sharing among member states, and that establishes a Security Council committee for monitoring implementation of these measures on a continuous basis. While the two resolutions did not expressly authorize the use of force by the United States, they both affirmed—in the context of such incidents—the inherent right of individual and collective self-defense, as well as the need "to combat by all means" the "threats to international peace and security caused by terrorist acts." By contrast, the General Assembly condemned the "heinous acts of terrorism" but did not characterize those acts as "attacks" or recognize a right to respond in self-defense. Instead, that body called for "international cooperation to bring to justice the perpetrators, organizers and sponsors" of the incidents. The form of cooperation was not specified, but a variety of conventions are already in place that address cooperation among states in dealing with violent or terrorist offenses.

The North Atlantic Council of the North Atlantic Treaty Organization (NATO) decided on September 12 that, if it was determined that the incidents were directed from abroad against the United States, "it shall be regarded as an action covered by Article 5 of the Washington Treaty, which states that an armed attack against one or more of the Allies in Europe or North America shall be considered an attack against them all." On October 2, after being briefed on the known facts by the United States, the council determined that the facts were "clear and compelling" and that "the attack against the United States on 11 September was directed from abroad and shall therefore be regarded as an action covered by Article 5 of the Washington Treaty."

Similarly, the Organization of American States meeting of ministers of foreign affairs resolved:

> That these terrorist attacks against the United States of America are attacks against all American states and that in accordance with all the relevant provisions of the Inter-American Treaty of Reciprocal Assistance (Rio Treaty) and the principal of continental solidarity, all States Parties to the Rio Treaty shall provide effective reciprocal assistance to address such attacks and the threat of any similar attacks against any American state, and to maintain the peace and security of the continent.

Both Saudi Arabia and the United Arab Emirates broke diplomatic relations with the Taliban government. The six-member Gulf Cooperation Council issued a joint statement expressing "the willingness of its members to participate in any joint action that has clearly defined objectives. It is willing to enter into an alliance that enjoys the support of the international community to fight international terrorism and to punish its perpetrators."

With the prospect of U.S. airstrikes against Afghanistan imminent, Taliban officials acknowledged that bin Laden was being sheltered under the control of the Taliban at a secret location in Afghanistan. Further, they claimed that they were interested in negotiating with the United States and might agree to turn over bin Laden to a third country. The Bush administration maintained its position, however, that there would be no negotiations; in his weekly radio address, President Bush warned the Taliban that time was running out for them to surrender "all the terrorists in Afghanistan and to close down their camps and operations."

. . . .

After the Security Council met for two hours to hear the U.S. and UK justifications for acting in self-defense, the president of the Security Council (Ireland's UN ambassador, John Ryan) stated that the unanimity of support expressed in the Security Council's two prior resolutions "is absolutely maintained."

On the same day as the above proceedings in the Security Council, the United States and the United Kingdom launched attacks against Al Qaeda and Taliban targets in Afghanistan (twenty-six days after the September 11 incidents). In a speech to the nation, President Bush stated:

> More than 2 weeks ago, I gave Taliban leaders a series of clear and specific demands.... None of those demands were met. And now the Taliban will pay a price. By destroying camps and disrupting communications, we will make it more difficult for the terror network to train new recruits and coordinate their evil plans.
>
> . . . .
>
> Today we focus on Afghanistan, but the battle is broader. Every nation has a choice to make. In this conflict, there is no neutral ground. If any government sponsors the outlaws and killers of innocents, they have become outlaws and murderers, themselves. And they will take that lonely path at their own peril.
>
> . . . .
>
> We did not ask for this mission, but we will fulfill it. The name of today's military operation is Enduring Freedom. We defend not only our precious freedoms but

also the freedom of people everywhere to live and raise their children free from fear.

The United States used sea-based cruise missiles, long-range bombers, and carrier-based fighter aircraft to strike at antiaircraft sites, military headquarters, terrorist camps, airfields, and a concentration of Taliban tanks, principally in the Afghan cities of Kabul (the capital), Kandahar (the center of the Taliban movement), Jalalabad, and Mazar-e Sharif. At the same time, the United States began dropping food and medical supplies into Afghanistan, as well as leaflets aimed at encouraging defections from the Taliban militia. Within days, U.S. military forces controlled the skies over Afghanistan and shifted to the next phase of the campaign—bombing the barracks, garrisons, and troop encampments of Taliban military forces. Further, special forces were deployed for operations within Taliban-held territory—including a nighttime raid on the headquarters compound of the Taliban's spiritual and military leader, Mulah Muhammad Omar. Such special-operations activity, along with intelligence from foreign sources, improved the United States' ability to strike Taliban targets accurately.

Although the airstrikes were against military targets, collateral civilian casualties did occur, with bombing mistakes reported almost every day of the campaign. Thus, on October 13, a Navy jet mistakenly dropped a 2,000-pound bomb on a residential neighborhood of Kabul, reportedly killing four persons and wounding another eight. On October 14, Taliban officials took foreign journalists to a village where, the officials claimed, nearly two hundred persons had been killed. Despite the evident damage, the casualties could not be confirmed. On October 20–21, U.S. Navy jets dropped a 1,000-pound bomb near a senior-citizens home in the western city of Herat, and two 500-pound bombs in a residential area of Kabul. Two days later, a cluster bomb used on Herat left the village strewn with deadly unexploded "bomblets." Human Rights Watch documented an attack on the village of Chowkar-Karez: after bombs were dropped, slow-moving, propeller-driven aircraft gunned down civilians. In perhaps the most notorious event, U.S. planes mistakenly bombed a Red Cross complex in Kabul on October 16, and then mistakenly returned ten days later to destroy the same complex. The complex—the only one of the Red Cross in Kabul—had supplied food and blankets for fifty-five thousand disabled Afghans.

The bombing campaign was, in many ways, a difficult one for the U.S. military. In addition to the inherent difficulties of attacking targets on rugged terrain, the dispersal of Taliban forces to residential areas and civilian buildings (such as schools and mosques) complicated the ability of the United States to pursue airstrikes against those forces. Further, the U.S. targeting-approval process, while designed to help minimize civilian casualties, reportedly resulted in delays that prevented the U.S. Air Force from receiving timely clearance for air strikes against top Taliban and Al Qaeda leaders. One unexpected but fortunate outcome was that despite the expectations that the air strikes would lead to a massive flow of refugees, no such exodus occurred—probably because the journey itself was risky, and the Afghan population had become inured to living amidst warfare.

Within hours of the commencement of the air strikes on October 7, bin Laden appeared in a videotape that was broadcast worldwide. He celebrated the September 11 attacks as a "taste" of what "[o]ur Islamic nation has been tasting ... for more than 80 years, of humiliation and disgrace, its sons killed and their blood spilled, its sanctities desecrated." Further, he stated, "Every Muslim must rise to defend his religion. The wind of faith is blowing and the wind of change is blowing to remove evil from the Peninsula of Muhammad, peace be upon him." The Taliban reacted to the air strikes by reiterating its offer to hand bin Laden over to a neutral third country if the United States provided evidence connecting him to the September 11 attacks. Again, President Bush rejected the offer, stating that the U.S. demands were nonnegotiable.

In initiating its airstrikes against Afghanistan, the United States received support from various quarters that this military response was an appropriate exercise of the right of self-defense against an armed attack. The United Kingdom itself directly participated in airstrikes against Afghanistan. Access to airspace and facilities was provided not just by NATO allies, but also by nations such as Georgia, Oman, Pakistan, the Philippines, Qatar, Saudi Arabia, Tajikistan, Turkey, and Uzbekistan. Other leading nations, such as China, Egypt, Mexico, and Russia announced support for the U.S. campaign. The fifty-six nations of the Organization for the Islamic Conference called upon the United States not to extend its military response beyond Afghanistan, but made no criticism of military actions against that state. Several representatives at a League of Arab States meeting denounced bin Laden as seeking to wage a war against the world, and said that he falsely stated that he represented Muslims and Arabs. The twenty-one nations of the Asia-Pacific Economic Cooperation forum issued a statement "unequivocally" condemning the September 11 attacks and denouncing all forms of terrorism, but remained silent on the U.S.-led air strikes. Australia, Canada, the Czech Republic, Germany, Italy, Japan, the Netherlands, New Zealand, Turkey, and the United Kingdom committed the use of their ground forces if and when a military deployment occurred in Afghanistan.

Jost Delbrück, *The Fight Against Global Terrorism: Self-Defense or Collective Security as International Police Action? Some Comments on the International Legal Implications of the 'War Against Terrorism'*
44 GERMAN Y.B. INT'L L. 9, 17–19 (2001)

Although the case for the legal and legitimate exercise [of the right of self defense] appears to be waterproof, some intriguing problems remain: First, there is the problem that the military action by the United States (and obviously also by Great Britain) aimed at the destruction of the Al'Qaida strongholds in Afghanistan and at the arrest of its leader, *Osama Bin Laden*. But soon after the military actions got under way, this limited goal of the operations changed to the broader aim of deposing of the Taliban regime itself. Of course, there are many good reasons to do away with a clearly dictatorial regime that undoubtedly displayed a persistent pattern of gross violations of fundamental human rights, particularly against women and children. The question is, however, whether this goal could be legally pursued as a measure of self-defense under Art. 51 UNCh. The exercise of self-defense aims at repelling the armed attack of another state or entity and also at incapacitating the enemy to renew its attacks. To depose of the—however illegitimate— government of the enemy state is of a different quality. In the present case, the situation is complicated by the fact that the Taliban regime was not internationally recognized except by three states (Pakistan, United Arab Emirates and Saudi Arabia). It is significant that the Security Council in its Resolution 1378 only expressed its support of the "efforts of the Afghan people to replace the Taliban regime." It did not express its consent to the same efforts on the part of the United States and Great Britain. One has to admit, though, that the deposition of the Taliban regime could not be neatly separated from the fight against the Al'Qaida network. Yet, doubts remain about the soundness of stretching the concept of self-defense to the extent that it also covers the replacement of the government of the enemy state, be it only a *de facto* regime or not. This problem will be addressed later on.

Second and most importantly, there is the problem of the indeterminate character of the present measures of self-defense in terms of time and space. As already mentioned, the time frame of the actions against the Taliban regime and Al'Qaida is not objectionable as regards the time span between the attacks and the beginning of the self-defense measures if considered as an isolated event that is limited in time and space. However, given the much wider goals that have been repeatedly stated by the President of the United States and high officials of the Administration, it is indispensable to discuss the question of self-defense in the wider political and legal context. With regard to the time dimension of self-defense in the present situation, one of the most significant facts is that from the day of the attacks on the Twin Towers and the Pentagon, the United States have unequivocally proclaimed to be at *war*. After a few days this term has been replaced by the concept of a "*new war.*" Thus the use of the term 'war' or 'new war' is significant because, whether in the legal meaning of traditional or pre-UN Charter International Law or in a non-legal, non-technical or ordinary sense, war signifies an open-ended process—open-ended in the sense that its end depends on whether one of the warring parties concedes defeat or the other considers the war aims to be achieved. If—as it is the case here—the 'war' or 'new war' is carried on as a measure of self-defense—a concept that is limited in time by its very nature as a measure of self-help against an actual or clearly defined imminent attack—self-defense clandestinely becomes open-ended as well. Conflating the concept of war, which in view of the prohibition of the use of force by Art. 2(4) UNCh is not a concept legally recognized by current international law except for its role in the *ius in bello*, with the concept of self-defense amounts to nothing less than a *carte blanche* for the *unilateral* use of force, and is thus contrary to the letter and spirit of the Charter of the United Nations that was exactly designed to prohibit the unilateral use of force except within the limits of self-defense. The so-called realists will strongly disagree with this conclusion.

Questions for Discussion

1. Was the 9/11 attack an "armed attack" or "armed aggression" against the United States justifying the use of force in response? What effect does the official NATO invocation of the "armed attack" provisions of NATO have on this question?

2. Was it lawful to proceed against the Taliban in Afghanistan in response to an attack from al-Qaeda? On what basis? What kind of factual showing is required for such a response?

3. What can be done against al-Qaeda cells in other countries around the world? As a practical matter, how should the U.S. and other nations proceed against al-Qaeda, and in this war on terrorism?

4. Does Security Council Resolution 1368 of September 28, 2001, authorize the use of force in the war against terrorism? Does it recognize the inherent right of defense in that setting? What is the scope of any authorization for defense against terrorism under this resolution?

5. Even if Security Council Resolution 1368 provides an independent basis for the use of force, should the United States have sought a clearer provision?

6. What do you think of the "minimalist" arguments dispatched by Professor Thomas M. Franck? What world view or "paradigm" generates such approaches?

The Iraq War: Actions in Response to Breach of Security Council Ceasefire Conditions

Security Council Resolution 678

UN SCOR, 45th Sess., 2963d mtg., UN Doc. S/RES/678 (1990)

The Security Council,

....

Acting under Chapter VII of the Charter,

....

2. Authorizes Member States co-operating with the Government of Kuwait, unless Iraq on or before 15 January 1991 fully implements, as set forth in paragraph 1 above, the foregoing resolutions, to use all necessary means to uphold and implement resolution 660 (1990) and all subsequent relevant resolutions and to restore international peace and security in the area;

....

Security Council Resolution 687

UN SCOR, 46th mtg., 2981st mtg., UN Doc. S/RES/687 (1991)

The Security Council,

....

... acting under Chapter VII of the Charter,

....

8. Decides that Iraq shall unconditionally accept the destruction, removal, or rendering harmless, under international supervision, of:

(a) All chemical and biological weapons and all stocks of agents and all related subsystems and components and all research, development, support and manufacturing facilities;

(b) All ballistic missiles with a range greater than 150 kilometres and related major parts, and repair and production facilities;

....

33. Declares that, upon official notification by Iraq to the Secretary-General and to the Security Council of its acceptance of the provisions above, a formal cease-fire is effective between Iraq and Kuwait and the Member States cooperating with Kuwait in accordance with resolution 678 (1990);

....

Security Council Resolution 1441

UN SCOR, 57th Sess., 4644th mtg., UN Doc. S/RES/1441 (2002)

The Security Council,

....

Recognizing the threat Iraq's non-compliance with Council resolutions and proliferation of weapons of mass destruction and long-range missiles poses to international peace and security,

Recalling that its resolution 678 (1990) authorized Member States to use all necessary means to uphold and implement its resolution 660 (1990) of 2 August 1990 and all relevant resolutions subsequent to resolution 660 (1990) and to restore international peace and security in the area,

Further recalling that its resolution 687 (1991) imposed obligations on Iraq as a necessary step for achievement of its stated objective of restoring international peace and security in the area,

....

Recalling that in its resolution 687 (1991) the Council declared that a ceasefire would be based on acceptance by Iraq of the provisions of that resolution, including the obligations on Iraq contained therein,

Determined to ensure full and immediate compliance by Iraq without conditions or restrictions with its obligations under resolution 687 (1991) and other relevant resolutions and recalling that the resolutions of the Council constitute the governing standard of Iraqi compliance,

....

Determined to secure full compliance with its decisions,

Acting under Chapter VII of the Charter of the United Nations,

1.   *Decides* that Iraq has been and remains in material breach of its obligations under relevant resolutions, including resolution 687 (1991), in particular through Iraq's failure to cooperate with United Nations inspectors and the IAEA, and to complete the actions required under paragraphs 8 to 13 of resolution 687 (1991);

....

4.   *Decides* that false statements or omissions in the declarations submitted by Iraq pursuant to this resolution and failure by Iraq at any time to comply with, and cooperate fully in the implementation of, this resolution shall constitute a further material breach of Iraq's obligations and will be reported to the Council for assessment in accordance with paragraphs 11 and 12 below;

....

13.   *Recalls*, in that context, that the Council has repeatedly warned Iraq that it will face serious consequences as a result of its continued violations of its obligations;

14.   *Decides* to remain seized of the matter.

U.S. Secretary of State Colin Powell, Remarks to the United Nations Security Council (Feb. 5, 2003)

available at <http://georgewbush-whitehouse.archives.gov/news/releases/2003/02/20030205-1.html>

This is an important day for us all as we review the situation with respect to Iraq and its disarmament obligations under UN Security Council Resolution 1441.

Last November 8, this Council passed Resolution 1441 by a unanimous vote. The purpose of that resolution was to disarm Iraq of its weapons of mass destruction. Iraq had already been found guilty of material breach of its obligations stretching back over 16 previous resolutions and 12 years.

Resolution 1441 was not dealing with an innocent party, but a regime this Council has repeatedly convicted over the years.

Resolution 1441 gave Iraq one last chance, one last chance to come into compliance or to face serious consequences. No Council member present and voting on that day had any illusions about the nature and intent of the resolution or what serious consequences meant if Iraq did not comply.

And to assist in its disarmament, we called on Iraq to cooperate with returning inspectors from UNMOVIC and IAEA. We laid down tough standards for Iraq to meet to allow the inspectors to do their job.

This Council placed the burden on Iraq to comply and disarm, and not on the inspectors to find that which Iraq has gone out of its way to conceal for so long. Inspectors are inspectors; they are not detectives.

I asked for this session today for two purposes. First, to support the core assessments made by Dr. Blix and Dr. ElBaradei. As Dr. Blix reported to this Council on January 27, "Iraq appears not to have come to a genuine acceptance, not even today, of the disarmament which was demanded of it."

And as Dr. ElBaradei reported, Iraq's declaration of December 7 "did not provide any new information relevant to certain questions that have been outstanding since 1998."

My second purpose today is to provide you with additional information, to share with you what the United States knows about Iraq's weapons of mass destruction, as well as Iraq's involvement in terrorism, which is also the subject of Resolution 1441 and other earlier resolutions.

I might add at this point that we are providing all relevant information we can to the inspection teams for them to do their work.

The material I will present to you comes from a variety of sources. Some are U.S. sources and some are those of other countries. Some of the sources are technical, such as intercepted telephone conversations and photos taken by satellites. Other sources are people who have risked their lives to let the world know what Saddam Hussein is really up to.

I cannot tell you everything that we know. But what I can share with you, when combined with what all of us have learned over the years, is deeply troubling. What you will see is an accumulation of facts and disturbing patterns of behavior. The facts and … Iraq's behavior, demonstrate that Saddam Hussein and his regime have made no effort … to disarm, as required by the international community.

Indeed, the facts and Iraq's behavior show that Saddam Hussein and his regime are concealing their efforts to produce more weapons of mass destruction.

. . . .

We know that Saddam Hussein has what is called "a Higher Committee for Monitoring the Inspection Teams." Think about that. Iraq has a high-level committee to monitor the inspectors who were sent in to monitor Iraq's disarmament—not to cooperate with them, not to assist them, but to spy on them and keep them from doing their jobs.

The committee reports directly to Saddam Hussein. It is headed by Iraq's Vice President, Taha Yasin Ramadan. Its members include Saddam Hussein's son, Qusay.

This committee also includes Lieutenant General Amir al-Sa'di, an advisor to Saddam. In case that name isn't immediately familiar to you, General Sa'di has been the Iraqi regime's primary point of contact for Dr. Blix and Dr. ElBaradei. It was General Sa'di who last fall publicly pledged that Iraq was prepared to cooperate unconditionally with inspectors. Quite the contrary, Sa'di's job is not to cooperate; it is to deceive, not to disarm, but to undermine the inspectors; not to support them, but to frustrate them and to make sure they learn nothing.

We have learned a lot about the work of this special committee. We learned that just prior to the return of inspectors last November, the regime had decided to resume what we heard called, "the old game of cat-and-mouse."

For example, let me focus on the now famous declaration that Iraq submitted to this Council on December 7th. Iraq never had any intention of complying with this Council's mandate. Instead, Iraq planned to use the declaration to overwhelm us and to overwhelm the inspectors with useless information about Iraq's permitted weapons so that we would not have time to pursue Iraq's prohibited weapons. Iraq's goal was to give us in this room, to give those of us on this Council, the false impression that the inspection process was working.

You saw the result. Dr. Blix pronounced the 12,200-page declaration "rich in volume" but "poor in information and practically devoid of new evidence." Could any member of this Council honestly rise in defense of this false declaration?

Everything we have seen and heard indicates that instead of cooperating actively with the inspectors to ensure the success of their mission, Saddam Hussein and his regime are busy doing all they possibly can to ensure that inspectors succeed in finding absolutely nothing.

Following is the view of United Kingdom Attorney-General Lord Goldsmith regarding the legality of use of force in Iraq:

The Attorney-General (Lord Goldsmith): Authority to use force against Iraq exists from the combined effect of Resolutions 678, 687 and 1441. All of these resolutions were adopted under Chapter VII of the UN Charter which allows the use of force for the express purpose of restoring international peace and security:

1. In Resolutions 678, the Security Council authorised force against Iraq, to eject it from Kuwait and to restore peace and security in the area.

2. In Resolution 687, which set out the ceasefire conditions after Operation Desert Storm, the Security Council imposed continuing obligations on Iraq to eliminate its weapons of mass destruction in order to restore international peace and security in the area. Resolution 687 suspended but did not terminate the authority to use force under Resolution 678.

3. A material breach of Resolution 687 revives the authority to use force under Resolution 678.

4. In Resolution 1441, the Security Council determined that Iraq has been and remains in material breach of Resolution 687, because it has not fully complied with its obligations to disarm under that resolution.

5. The Security Council in Resolution 1441 gave Iraq "a final opportunity to comply with its disarmament obligations" and warned Iraq of the "serious consequences" if it did not.

6. The Security Council also decided in Resolution 1441 that, if Iraq failed at any time to comply with and co-operate fully in the implementation of Resolution 1441, that would constitute a further material breach.

7. It is plain that Iraq has failed so to comply and therefore Iraq was at the time of Resolution 1441 and continues to be in material breach.

8. Thus, the authority to use force under Resolution 678 has revived and so continues today.

9. Resolution 1441 would in terms have provided that a further decision of the Security Council to sanction force was required if that had been intended. Thus, all that Resolution 1441 requires is reporting to and discussion by the Security Council of Iraq's failures, but not an express further decision to authorise force.

I have lodged a copy of this Answer, together with Resolutions 678, 687 and 1441 in the Libraries of both Houses and the Vote Office of the House of Commons.[40]

Marc Weller, The Legality of the Threat of Use of Force Against Iraq
Available at <http://sites.tufts.edu/jha/archives/122> 16 Feb. 1998

It may be tempting to see in the position of the US and UK an attempt to revive the promise of the New World Order—a vision so rashly abandoned after the conclusion of the Cold War. After all, this appears to be a case where individual states are willing to make their vast military potential available to implement the will of the international community. And the aims of this operation appear laudable: to vindicate the will of the United Nations and to rid the world of a dangerous future arsenal of weapons of mass destruction.

… However, this action does in fact fundamentally challenge the presently existing structures of international order, rather than strengthening them. Here, for the first time since 1945, we see a significant example of the unilateral military enforcement of rights and obligations. The use of force by states is deemed once more acceptable for purposes other than resisting an armed attack or protecting a population in danger of extermination.

… If this operation had the backing of a formal and explicit Security Council mandate, it would appear in a different light. Then, indeed, the US and UK would need to be commended for making available the facilities necessary to make the UN system of collective security work in relation to Iraq. The international community would have determined through the appropriate mechanism that Iraq's posture represents a threat to the peace so severe that it must be addressed through forcible means, under the supervision of the Council.

… In this case, the Security Council has indeed determined that there exists a serious violation of Iraq's obligations. It has, however, not found that the violation is of a nature as to justify the application of military force. Instead, individual states take it upon themselves to identify which aims of the international community are to be pursued forcibly. The application of such force is not legally constrained, not even by the essential principle of proportionality.

… To accept that such action can be taken outside of a Security Council mandate is to embrace anarchy and to return to an acceptance of war as a means of international, if not national, policy.

… The argument of a material breach does not help to overcome this problem. It, too, locates the right to decide that force may be used in relation to Iraq away from the Council and in the hands of a coalition of the willing, who operate outside of the control

---

40. *Available at* < http://news.bbc.co.uk/2/hi/uk_news/politics/2857347.stm>.

of the UN. In addition, it undermines the stability of cease-fires elsewhere and it appears to subordinate the *jus cogens* prohibition of the use of force to misplaced analogies from the law of treaties.

... Finally, individual states are of course not legally defenceless if they are confronted with a state threatening the use of its existing arsenal of weapons of mass destruction. If the threat is manifest and unambiguous, military action can be taken to the extent strictly necessary to remove it. On the other hand, to broaden the right of self-defence beyond circumstances of instant and overwhelming necessity, leaving no choice of means and no moment of deliberation, would virtually abolish the prohibition of the use of force. All uses of force could be justified under such a loose definition of self-defence.

... The present crisis, it must be admitted, represents a difficult dilemma. Iraq must be required to comply with her obligations. However, if the states represented at the Security Council are not willing to grant a mandate for forcible action to that end, then the simple truth is that no force may be used. Instead, other avenues of pressuring the government of Iraq will need to be pursued. These might include measures to ensure that the embargo is not being undermined through uncontrolled traffic along Iraq's land borders. In parallel, it may be necessary to establish a definite catalogue of concrete requirements which Iraq must fulfill, if there is to be a lifting of the embargo. If there is no prospect of ever achieving that aim because the standard for compliance is constantly raised, there is simply no incentive for Iraq to comply with her obligations. Ironically, once the embargo has been partially lifted, the Security Council gains a threat that is at present unavailable. In order to ensure that Iraq participates in the long-term monitoring programme of her weapons, it can credibly threaten to re-impose tough measures of economic constraint. Iraq would again have something to lose.

Questions for Discussion

1. Was the coalition action lawful? If so, on what legal basis?

2. What arguments would you make in support of, and in opposition to, Attorney General Goldsmith's opinion?

3. Would anticipatory defense justify the coalition action?

4. Would humanitarian intervention justify the action? Why were humanitarian concerns not presented to the Security Council in the deliberations leading up to Resolution 1441?

5. Would the more than four hundred attacks against U.S. and U.K. aircraft in the no-fly zones justify the action? Why have the U.S. and the U.K. not asserted these attacks as a legal basis for their action?

6. Should "material breach" of Security Council imposed ceasefire conditions serve, unlike material breach of treaty generally, to authorize the use of force by revitalizing an initial Security Council authorization for the use of force? Or is this an issue for the Security Council? The U.K. position clearly is that this is an issue for the Security Council and that interpreting Resolution 1441 as to whether the Security Council did or did not authorize force in response to this breach is the key question in assessing the legality of the Iraq War.

Selected Bibliography

I. General Works on the Use of Force

Bowett, Derek, *Self-Defense in International Law* (1958).

Brownlie, Ian, *International Law and the Use of Force by States* (1963).

Falk, Richard A., *Legal Order in a Violent World* (1968).

Ferencz, Benjamin B., 2 *Defining International Aggression* (1975).

Luard, Evan, ed., *The International Regulation of Civil Wars* (1972).

McDougal, Myres S., & Florentino P. Feliciano, *Law and Minimum World Public Order* (1961). (This is the best treatment of use-of-force issues under the United Nations Charter.)

Moore, John Norton, "The Role of Regional Arrangements in the Maintenance of World Order," in 3 *The Future of the International Legal Order: Conflict Management* (Cyril E. Black & Richard A. Falk eds., 1970).

———, *Solving the War Puzzle* (2004). (See "The 'Scoring' as Lawful or Unlawful of all Major Wars Since Adoption of the U.N. Charter.")

———, ed., *Law and Civil War in the Modern World* (1974). (One of the best sources for discussion of intervention theory and the norms of intervention.)

———, *Jus ad Bellum* Before the International Court of Justice, 52 Va. J. Int'l L. 903 (2012).

O'Brien, William Vincent, *The Conduct of Just and Limited War* (1981).

Stone, Julius, *Legal Controls of International Conflict: A Treatise on the Dynamics of Disputes—and War—Law* (2d ed. 1959).

II. Works on Selected Conflicts
A. The Arab-Israeli Conflict

Moore, John Norton, ed., 1–3 *The Arab-Israeli Conflict* (1974) (An updated fourth volume of documentary materials is forthcoming.)

B. The Indo-China War

Falk, Richard A., ed., 1–4 *The Vietnam War and International Law* (1968–76).

Karnow, Stanley, *Vietnam: A History* (1983).

Moore, John Norton, *Law and the Indo-China War* (1972).

———, ed., *The Vietnam Debate: A Fresh Look at the Arguments* (1990).

C. The Cuban Missile Crisis

Allison, Graham T., *Essence of Decision* (1971).

Chayes, Abram, *The Cuban Missile Crisis* (1974).

Meeker, Leonard C., "Defensive Quarantine and the Law," 57 *Am. J. Int'l L.* 515 (1963).

Wright, Quincy, "The Cuban Quarantine," 57 *Am. J. Int'l L.* 546 (1963).

D. The Dominican Crisis

Lowenthal, Abraham F., *The Dominican Intervention* (1972).

Meeker, Leonard C., "The Dominican Situation in the Perspective of International Law," 53 *Dep't St. Bull.* 60 (1965).

Slater, Jerome, *Intervention and Negotiation: The United States and the Dominican Revolution* (1970).

Thomas, Aaron J., & Ann Thomas, *The Dominican Republic Crisis, 1965* (1967).

E. The Bangladesh War

Franck, Thomas M., & Nigel S. Rodley, "After Bangladesh: The Law of Humanitarian Intervention by Military Force," 67 *Am. J. Int'l L.* 275 (1973).

Mani, V.S., "The 1971 War on the Indian Sub-Continent and International Law," 12 *Indian J. Int'l L.* 83 (1972).

Nanda, Ved P., "Self-Determination in International Law: The Tragic Tale of Two Cities — Islamabad (West Pakistan) and Dacca (East Pakistan)," 66 *Am. J. Int'l L.* 321 (1972).

Nawaz, M.K., "Bangladesh and International Law," 11 *Indian J. Int'l L.* 251 (1971).

F. The Entebbe Raid

Green, L.C., "Humanitarian Intervention — 1976 Version," 24 *Chitty's L. J.* 217 (1976).

Knisbacher, Mitchell, "The Entebbe Operation: A Legal Analysis of Israel's Rescue Action," 12 *J. Int'l L. & Econ.* 57 (1977).

Murphy, John F., "State Self-Help and Problems of Public International Law," *in Legal Aspects of International Terrorism* 553 (Alona E. Evans & John F. Murphy eds., 1978).

Ronzitti, Natalino, *Rescuing Nationals Abroad Through Military Coercion and Intervention on the Grounds of Humanity* 37–40, 52–76 (1985).

G. Afghanistan and the Brezhnev Doctrine

Arnold, Anthony, *Afghanistan, The Soviet Invasion in Perspective* (1981).

Meissner, Boris, *The Brezhnev Doctrine* (1970).

Monks, Alfred L., *The Soviet Intervention in Afghanistan, 1979–1980* (1981).

Moore, John Norton, & Robert F. Turner, *International Law and the Brezhnev Doctrine* (1987).

Rostow, Nicholas, "Law and the Use of Force by States: The Brezhnev Doctrine," 7 *Yale J. World Public Order* 209 (1980–81).

H. The Central American Conflict

Christian, Shirley, *Nicaragua: Revolution in the Family* (1985).

Joyner, Christopher C., & Michael A. Grimaldi, "The United States and Nicaragua: Reflections on the Lawfulness of Contemporary Intervention," 25 *Va. J. Int'l L.* 621 (1985).

Moore, John Norton, "The Secret War In Central America and the Future of World Order," 80 *Am. J. Int'l L.* 43 (1986).

———, *The Secret War In Central America* (1987).

Turner, Robert F., *Nicaragua v. United States: A Look at the Facts* (1987).

Wiarda, Howard J., ed., *Rift and Revolution: The Central American Imbroglio* (1984).

Woodward, Ralph Lee, *Central America: A Nation Divided* (2d ed. 1985).

I. Exchange Between John Norton Moore and Noam Chomsky

Chomsky, Noam, "Law and Imperialism in the Central American Conflict: A Reply to John Norton Moore," 8(2) *J. Contemp. Stud.* 25 (1985).

Moore, John Norton, "Legal Issues in the Central American Conflict," 8(1) *J. Contemp. Stud.* 93 (1985).

———, "Tripping through Wonderland with Noam Chomsky: A Response," 8(2) *J. Contemp. Stud.* 47 (1985).

J. Grenada

Gilmore, William C., *The Grenada Intervention* (1984).

Joyner, Christopher C., "The United States Action in Grenada: Reflections on the Lawfulness of Invasion," 78 *Am. J. Int'l L.* 131 (1984).

Moore, John Norton, *Law and the Grenada Mission* (1984).
———, "Grenada and the International Double Standard," 78 *Am. J. Int'l L.* 145 (1984).

K. The Osirak Incident

D'Amato, Anthony, "Israel's Air Strike Upon the Iraqi Nuclear Reactor," 77 *Am. J. Int'l L.* 584 (1983).
Mallison, W.T., & Sally V. Mallison, "The Israeli Aerial Attack of June 7, 1981, Upon the Iraqi Nuclear Reactor: Aggression or Self-Defense?," 15 *Van. J. Trans. L.* 417 (1982).
Moore, John Norton, "Lessons for the Future," *Freedom at Issue*, Nov.–Dec. 1981, at 6.
Nydell, Matt S., Note, "Tensions Between International Law and Strategic Security: Implications of Israel's Preemptive Raid on Iraq's Nuclear Reactor," 24 *Va. J. Int'l L.* 459 (1984).
O'Brien, William V., "Israel's Forward Strategy," *Freedom at Issue*, Nov.–Dec. 1981, at 3.

L. The Gulf War

Moore, John Norton, *Crisis in the Gulf: Enforcing the Rule of Law* (1992).

M. Kosovo

Terry, J.P., Rethinking Humanitarian Intervention After Kosovo: Legal Reality and Political Pragmatism (May 30, 2001) (unpublished manuscript, on file with the author).

N. Afghanistan and the War Against Terrorism

Delbrück, Jost, "The Fight Against Global Terrorism: Self-Defense or Collective Security as International Police Action? Some Comments on the International Legal Implications of the 'War Against Terrorism,'" 44 *German Y.B. Int'l L.* 9, 17–19 (2001).
"Editorial Comments," 95 *Am. J. Int'l L.* 833 (2001).
Letter dated 7 October 2001 from the Permanent Representative of the United States of America to the United Nations addressed to the President of the Security Council, UN Doc. S/2001/946 (Oct. 7, 2001).
Murphy, Sean D., ed., "Contemporary Practice of the United States Relating to International Law," 96 *Am. J. Int'l L.* 237–255 (2002).

O. The Iraq War

Betts, Richard K., "Suicide From Fear of Death?," *Foreign Aff.*, Jan.–Feb. 2003.
Damrosch, Lori Fisler, & Bernard H. Oxman, "Editors' Introduction," *Am. J. Int'l L.* (July 2003).
Falk, Richard A., "What Future for the UN Charter System of War Prevention?," *Am. J. Int'l L.* (July 2003).
Farer, Tom, "The Prospect for International Law and Order in the Wake of Iraq," *Am. J. Int'l L.* (July 2003).
Franck, Thomas M., "What Happens Now? The United Nations After Iraq," *Am. J. Int'l L.* (July 2003).
Gardner, Richard N., "Neither Bush nor the 'Jurisprudes,'" *Am. J. Int'l L.* (July 2003).
Moore, John Norton, "September 11 and its Aftermath: Terrorism, Afghanistan, and the Iraq War," Ch. IX, *in Solving the War Puzzle: Beyond the Democratic Peace* (2004).
Roberts, Adam, "Use of Force," in *The United Nations Security Council Since The Cold War* (David M. Malone ed., 2004).
Rostow, Nicholas, "Determining the Lawfulness of the 2003 Campaign Against Iraq," *Israel Yearbook on Human Rights*, 2004.
Sapiro, Miriam, "Iraq: The Shifting Sands of Preemptive Self-Defense," *Am. J. Int'l L.* (July 2003).

Smock, David R., "Would an Invasion of Iraq be a 'just war'?," United States Institute of
    Peace (2003), *at* http://purl.access.gpo.gov/GPO/LPS27090.
Stromseth, Jane E., "Law and Force After Iraq: A Transitional Moment," *Am. J. Int'l L.*
    (July 2003).
Taft IV, William H., & Todd F. Buchwald, "Preemption, Iraq, and International Law,"
    Am. J. Int'l L. (July 2003).
U.S. Department of State, *Iraq: A Population Silenced* (Dec. 2002).
Wedgwood, Ruth, "The Fall of Saddam Hussein: Security Council Mandates and Preemptive
    Self-Defense," *Am. J. Int'l L.* (July 2003).
White House, *The National Security Strategy of the United States of America* (2002).
Yoo, John, "International Law and the War in Iraq," *Am. J. Int'l L.* (July 2003).

Chapter 5

Institutional Modes of Conflict Management

Rosalyn Higgins, Dan Sarooshi, and Philippa Webb

In this chapter:
Historical and Theoretical Overview
The United Nations System
The Role of Regional Arrangements
Responsibility to Protect
Selected Bibliography

Historical and Theoretical Overview

Contemporary practices in international conflict management are directly related to the evolution of the modern state system. That system resulted from the breakup of medieval European Christendom, and its historical landmarks were the 1648 Peace of Westphalia and the 1713 Treaty of Utrecht. However, it was not until the nineteenth century that a series of factors arose that enabled, and motivated, states to pursue organized means of managing international conflict. These factors included a continuing expansion and solidification of nation states, the emergence of improved communication, an increasing interdependence between states, and the recognition on the part of statesmen that some form of institutional method for conflict management was required.

The first major development in the management of international conflict was the establishment of the Council of Europe, which evolved out of a series of big power conferences in Europe beginning with the Congress of Vienna in 1815. This development, spurred by the ruinous Napoleonic Wars, changed the face of international relations by providing a forum for multilateral diplomacy rather than the traditional bilateral diplomacy. Although the European powers were unable effectively to manage their affairs within the concert system, they did, however, establish the precedent for further multilateral conferences.

The next major step in this area resulted from The Hague Peace Conferences of 1899 and 1907. These two conferences helped pave the way for the realization of the principle of universality. The 1907 Conference, for example, involved representatives from forty-four states, including most of the Latin American republics. As a result, smaller states were given the opportunity to enjoy at least superficial equality with the great powers. Perhaps the greatest achievement of the statesmen at The Hague was establishing the precedent that collective diplomacy should be oriented toward the further development and codification of international law, the formulation of procedures for the peaceful settlement of disputes, and the promotion of the principle that peaceful solutions might be urged and facilitated by disinterested states in international disputes.

The establishment of the League of Nations after World War I was a fundamental step forward in the development of a role for international organizations in the management of conflict. The founders of the League, horrified by the carnage of the war, sought to establish for the first time a system of collective security to prevent future conflict.

The concept of collective security in its ideal form institutes a system whereby a collective measure is taken against a member of a community of states that has violated certain community-defined standards. In the ideal of the system, there are three constituent elements: first, the determination by a community of states of the core standards that are sought to be maintained as part of the *status quo* of the community; second, the determination by an authorized representative of the community that a core standard has been violated in a particular case; and third, the binding determination by the authorized representative of what measures should be taken as part of the automatic response of the community to the violation by the recalcitrant state.

The system instituted by the League of Nations (LON) Covenant only contained the first two of these elements. The aim was nonetheless noble. In the words of its chief advocate, President Woodrow Wilson, the League sought to establish "not a balance of power, but a community of power; not organized rivalries, but an organized common peace."[1] To this end, Article 16 of the LON Covenant conferred on the League Council, in many ways the executive organ of the League, the right to impose economic sanctions against a member state that had resorted to an "illegal" war in violation of Articles 12, 13, and 15 of the Covenant. Accordingly, the first and second elements of our ideal collective security system — the determination by the community of states of those standards it wants to protect and the authorization, in our case, of the LON Council to determine a case of violation — were satisfied.

However, the third element was not present. The LON collective security system left to member states the decision whether to implement a recommendation of the LON Council imposing military sanctions against a recalcitrant state. The Council did not possess the authority under the LON Covenant to impose a binding obligation on member states to carry out military sanctions against a designated target state; it only had the power of recommendation. The LON Council did, however, have the competence under the Covenant to require states to apply commercial and financial measures against a state. But even where these economic sanctions were in practice imposed against an aggressor state they were only partial and thus were not effective (for example, the determination by the LON Council that Italy had resorted to an illegal war against Abyssinia, now Ethiopia, within the meaning of Article 16 of the LON Covenant led the Council only to impose temporary and partial economic sanctions against Italy, which due to their limited scope proved wholly ineffective). More generally, the collective security system of the League was not used by states in favor of a policy of appeasement and the world descended into World War II.

The League was not a total failure, however, because it laid the groundwork for the modern-day United Nations (UN). The UN learned from both the successes and failures of the League. The UN Charter not only provides disputants with a variety of mechanisms

---

1. Woodrow Wilson, address to the U.S. Senate, Jan. 22, 1917, *in* 40 THE PAPERS OF WOODROW WILSON 536 (Arthur S. Link ed., 1982).

they can use to resolve their disputes peacefully, but also establishes a modified form of collective security that in large part contains the three elements of the ideal system set out above as well as providing a role for regional arrangements as part of the global collective security system.

The United Nations System

The UN Charter was formulated against the backdrop of the devastation and suffering caused by World War II. Its terms reflect a determination to provide an international institution that could control and even prevent conflict. The latter, in particular, was to be accomplished by the UN taking the approach, reflected in the Charter, that peace, economic and social progress, and human rights are indivisible.

The way the UN was to control conflict was through specific institutional arrangements under the Charter. At the heart of it all was the requirement that the use of force by states be limited to legitimate self-defense;[2] force may not be used against the territorial integrity or political independence of a state "or in any other manner inconsistent with the Purposes of the United Nations."[3] Accordingly, the UN Charter permitted self-defense and also, in certain limited circumstances, the control of conflict through regional arrangements.[4] But central to the Charter was the resolve that it would be realistic to enjoin states not to use force save in self-defense, because collective security would be used to control interstate conflict. This collective security was to be provided by the UN itself.[5]

The pages that follow examine the institutional arrangements for the control of conflict provided by the UN Charter, and show how, in the face of the failure to establish the intended machinery, alternative institutional arrangements—often not clearly envisaged in the Charter—have developed. Also examined is the increasingly important role that regional arrangements play in managing conflict.

Membership of the United Nations

At the inception of the UN there were fifty-one members. Today there are 193, with the newest member, the Republic of South Sudan, joining in 2011. The admission of states to UN membership was in the early years of the UN the cause of great controversy. There were disputes as to whether a properly qualified applicant—a peace-loving state that accepts the obligations of the Charter and is able and willing to carry them out— could be refused admission.[6] There have also been controversies over the status of "divided" states, such as Vietnam, Korea, and Germany; difficulties with the succession of membership resulting from the dissolution of a state, such as the former Yugoslavia where there was no accepted successor state and all emergent states were required to apply for UN membership; controversy over the status of Palestine, which failed to obtain sufficient support in the Security Council to become a member state in 2011 but was granted the

---

2. *See* U.N. Charter art. 51.
3. *See id.* art. 2, para. 4. The intended complementary structure of these articles and the problems that have arisen with their interpretation and application are examined in the previous chapter.
4. *See id.* arts. 52–54.
5. *See id.* arts. 39–50.
6. *See id.* art. 4.

status of an observer by the General Assembly in 2012; and concern over whether the very small states can meet all the requirements of membership, although the general policy has been in favor of universality of membership.

The great swelling of the membership of the UN has led in turn to demands that the membership of certain non-plenary organs be enlarged. The Security Council originally consisted of eleven members, of whom five (the United States, United Kingdom, France, Russia (previously held by the former Soviet Union), and China) are permanent members.[7] In 1965, the Security Council was enlarged to fifteen members, with ten seats available for nonpermanent members, while at the same time the Economic and Social Council was enlarged from eighteen to twenty-seven members. There has continued to be some pressure both for further enlargement of the Security Council and, more controversially, for a redistribution and expansion of seats reserved for permanent members. As a consequence, the General Assembly adopted Resolution 48/26 on December 10, 1993, which established an Open-ended Working Group to "consider all aspects of the question of increase in the membership of the Security Council."[8] However, any changes in the membership of the Security Council require an amendment of the Charter, which under Article 108 can only take place with the consent of "all the permanent members of the Security Council." Such changes would significantly alter the institutional workings of the Security Council and the voting balance between permanent and nonpermanent members, and, moreover, no agreement has emerged as to the strongest claimants for special status. Thus, the impetus for change in membership has lost some momentum. Reform efforts in more recent years have focused on making the Security Council's working methods more transparent and attempts to introduce guidelines for the exercise of the veto power.

The Security Council

Security Council Decision-Making

The decisions of the Security Council were intended to be reached by formal application of the voting provision of Article 27 of the Charter, paragraph 3 of which provides for the veto power of the permanent members. Although less formal methods of decision-making have evolved, the veto has remained an important tool employed by the permanent members to achieve their own interests.

The veto power was originally given to the permanent members to ensure their unanimity in relation to the use by the Security Council of its enforcement powers under Chapter VII of the Charter. There was, however, criticism made by other states at the San Francisco Conference that there was considerable potential for abuse of the veto power in relation to non-Chapter VII decisions. In response, four of the permanent members, the United States, United Kingdom, former Soviet Union, and China adopted a non-binding statement (also subscribed to by France) that sought to provide a safeguard against the abuse of the veto.[9] This statement implied that the veto would only be used in relation to non-Chapter VII decisions when a matter was such that it may eventually lead to the use by the Council of its Chapter VII enforcement powers. This was known as the "chain-of-events" theory.

---

7. *See id.* art. 23, para. 1.

8. G.A. Res. 26, U.N. GAOR, 48th Sess., Supp. No. 28, U.N. Doc. A/Res/48/28 (1993).

9. *Statement by the Delegations of the Four Sponsoring Governments on Voting Procedure in the Security Council*, Doc. 852, III/1/37 (1), 11 U.N.C.I.O. Docs. 711 (1945).

The general question of the abuse of the veto remains, however, unresolved. The chain-of-events formula has proved to be unworkable and is not in practice applied to decisions as to whether particular votes are or are not procedural. The veto power has been used by all the permanent members in circumstances in which the chain-of-events theory is not objectively applicable (i.e., when there was no prospect, even on the basis of a possible chain-of-events, of enforcement measures being invoked). Examples here include the vetoes that have been cast in order to prevent the adoption by the Council of resolutions that were to reprimand the actions of a permanent member; to criticize a friendly power (for example, the former Soviet Union over the Indian invasion of Goa (1961) and the United States over Israel (1976, 1983, and 1995)); to reappoint the UN Secretary-General (the United States over the reappointment of Boutros Boutros-Ghali in 1996); to send military observers to a country (China over the sending of military observers to Guatemala in 1997); and to extend the duration of a UN peacekeeping force (the U.S. veto on June 30, 2002, of the proposed extension of the duration of the UN peacekeeping force in Bosnia-Herzegovina (UNMIBH) due to concerns that U.S. troops may be subject to future prosecution before the International Criminal Court).

The requirement of Article 27(3) that a party to a dispute abstain from voting (and, *a fortiori*, from casting a veto) is honored in the breach. It has not been found possible to maintain an effective distinction in practice between "situations" (where the party involved could vote) and "disputes" (where, by virtue of Article 27(3), the party involved could not). Occasional voluntary abstentions from voting—and thus, in the case of a permanent member, from the possibility of casting a veto—have been greatly outweighed by (often unchallenged) votes cast by states directly involved in disputes.

The threat or use of a veto has in a number of cases constituted a barrier to the effective use of the UN collective security system with the consequence that action has been taken by the General Assembly (in the case of Korea where the veto of the former Soviet Union prevented the Security Council from overseeing the UN authorized military action), military action has been taken by states acting outside the UN system (in the case of the NATO bombing campaign in Kosovo in 1999 after the threat of a Russian veto blocked attempts by the Security Council to respond to the humanitarian crisis, see further below), or the Security Council has been deadlocked (in the case of repeated Russian and Chinese vetoes of resolutions in 2011–2014 regarding proposed military action in Syria to respond to massive human rights violations of the civilian population).

From the late 1940s until the mid-1960s it became well accepted in UN practice that, notwithstanding the wording of Article 27(3), an abstention was not tantamount to a veto and could not prevent a resolution from being adopted. This practice introduces a degree of flexibility that promotes the effective functioning of the Council, since it allows a permanent member to express mild disapproval of, or withhold its support from, a proposed resolution without having to prevent its adoption by casting a negative vote. Controversy about the matter was resumed, however, in the late 1960s, in part as a result of the enlargement of the nonpermanent membership of the Security Council. The fact that the amended Article 27 now permitted a nonprocedural resolution to be passed by the affirmative vote of *nine* members (out of a total membership of fifteen) meant that a nonprocedural resolution could now be adopted without the positive concurrence of even a single permanent member. Some contended that this unforeseen result must mean that abstention by a permanent member was not to be treated as a "concurring vote" within the meaning of Article 27(3), since otherwise it vitiates the idea that the permanent members should act collectively to manage conflict. For example, when Rhodesia declared its unilateral declaration of independence from the United Kingdom in 1965, Portugal took the view that Council resolutions calling for mandatory economic sanctions were not validly adopted, because of the abstention of one or more of the permanent members (France and the United Kingdom). This was a view that was supported by South Africa. However, in a case that ensued before the International Court of Justice, the South African argument was effectively rejected by the Court, since it failed to regard Council resolutions adopted in the face of abstention by one or more permanent members as being invalid.[10] As such, the International Court affirmed that an abstention by a permanent member is not equivalent to a veto.

Diverse views are still held on the question of whether the absence of a permanent member is analogous to an abstention. Western States took the view that the absence of the delegate of the former Soviet Union from discussions on the complaint of aggression in Korea did not invalidate the resolutions passed. Some writers have emphasized textual problems in concluding that "concurring votes" under Article 27(3) cannot occur if a member is absent. Others have emphasized policy considerations militating against this interpretation.

> The practice that abstention is not a veto permits the United Nations to operate most effectively for the purposes of collective security for which it was designed. In contrast, a decision that absence is a veto ... would permit a single permanent member of the Security Council [to paralyze the Council] by its wilful refusal to participate in the deliberations of the Council.... [11]

Over the years attempts have been made in the UN to limit the impact of the veto. An early example, the Uniting for Peace Resolution of the General Assembly, is dealt with below. Leading up to the 2005 World Summit, the High-Level Panel on Threats, Challenges and Change called on the permanent members "in their individual capacities, to pledge themselves to refrain from the use of the veto in cases of genocide and large-scale human rights abuses".[12] In 2013, France suggested having a "code of conduct" regarding the veto, but this idea has not gained the support of the other permanent members.[13] Informal changes in practice within the Council have had more impact on the use of the veto than these formal attempts at reform. The most important change has been the increased use of decision-making by consensus. Routine decisions will sometimes be expressed by the President of the Council as having been adopted by the Council without there having been a vote. In cases of consensus decision-making, the text of a resolution, or statement made by the President on behalf of the Council, is usually worked out in informal consultations and then circulated as a written document or declared by the President in open meeting to have been approved. The defining element of a consensus decision is that no vote has been taken.

Questions for Discussion

1. What are the arguments for and against the permanent members having a veto power as provided for in Article 27(3)?

2. How was it to be determined whether a matter is or is not "procedural" within the meaning of Article 27(3)? What different method of determination has evolved in practice?

---

10. *See* Legal Consequences for States of the Continued Presence of South Africa in Namibia (South West Africa) notwithstanding Security Council Resolution 276 (1970), 1971 I.C.J. 16 (June 21).

11. Myres S. McDougal & Richard N. Gardner, *The Veto and the Charter: An Interpretation for Survival*, 60 Yale L.J. 258, 285 (1951).

12. A/56/565, 2 December 2004, para 256.

13. Laurent Fabius, *A Call for Self-Restraint at the U.N.*, New York Times (4 October 2013).

3. What is the position under Article 27(3) when one or more permanent members are absent during a nonprocedural vote? Or abstains on such a vote? Can they be deemed to have cast an affirmative vote in these circumstances? What are the policy considerations that lead you to your view in each case?

4. Should the veto power be available to permanent members when a situation concerns genocide, crimes against humanity or war crimes?

Security Council Powers

Article 24(1) of the Charter gives the Security Council the primary responsibility for the maintenance of international peace and security, and its decisions in this regard are binding on all UN members pursuant to Article 25 of the Charter. More on the secondary responsibility of the General Assembly in relation to peace and security can be found in the section on the General Assembly.

Article 24(2) leaves room for argument as to whether the Security Council, acting to maintain peace and security, must be able to base its actions on the specific powers enumerated in Chapters VI, VII, VIII, and XII, or whether the Security Council has available to it more general powers to act under Article 24(1) so long as it is acting in accordance with the Purposes and Principles of the UN. This ambiguity was apparent from the outset and arose in sharp fashion in connection with the Security Council's consideration of the Trieste question.

Oscar Schachter, *The Development of International Law through the Legal Opinions of the United Nations Secretariat*
25 BRIT. Y.B. INT'L L. 91, 96–97, 101 (1948)

Stated in general terms, the Council was faced with the following question: in carrying out its responsibility for the maintenance of international peace and security, is the authority of the Council limited to the exercise of the specific powers granted in Chapters VI, VII, VIII, and XII of the Charter?

This issue was raised as a consequence of the arrangements for a free territory of Trieste which had been agreed upon by the Council of Foreign Ministers after prolonged discussion. Under these arrangements (which were embodied in various Annexes to the draft peace treaty with Italy), the Security Council was to assume important responsibilities in regard to the Free Territory; in particular, it was to: (a) ensure the integrity and independence of the territory; (b) appoint the Governor who would be responsible to the Council and subject to its instructions; (c) determine when the Permanent Statute shall enter into force; (d) have the right to amend the Permanent Statute. The Council of Foreign Ministers (which for this purpose included the representatives of France, the USSR, the UK, and the USA) requested the Security Council to approve the instruments relating to Trieste and to accept the responsibilities which would devolve upon it under them.

At the Security Council meeting two of the representatives raised a question as to the authority of the Council to accept these responsibilities. While they did not doubt that the question of Trieste related to peace and security they maintained that the Council's responsibility could only be exercised through the specific powers granted for that purpose in Chapters VI, VII, VIII, and XII. In their opinion the specific powers did not confer upon the Council sufficient authority under the circumstances to enable it to exercise the governmental functions stipulated in the Trieste documents. In response to this contention the Secretary-General presented a brief oral statement to the Council expressing his views regarding the constitutional issue raised. In his opinion the Security Council was not limited to the specific powers laid down in the chapters mentioned; the Council had, he suggested, a power to maintain peace and security conferred upon it by Article 24 which is wide enough to enable it to assume the responsibilities arising from the agreements relating to Trieste....

....

... Article 24 is being construed as a grant of authority which is quite separate and distinct from the specific powers granted elsewhere. Moreover, it appears to have been accepted that the action taken by the Council under this residuary power may be considered as creating binding obligations under Article 25. Whether or not this interpretation is justified by the text, it seems likely, on the basis of the precedents already established, that the Council will be prepared to fall back on Article 24 as a general source of authority. But this does not mean that Article 24, broad though it is in its language, will be considered as giving the Council a *carte blanche* in matters of peace and security. In the first place it is clear from the text of paragraph 2 of this Article that the Council's power is limited by the purposes and principles set forth in Articles 1 and 2. In the second place ... Article 24 has not actually been utilized as a substitute for the more specific provisions of the Charter; it has rather been regarded as a reservoir of authority, to be invoked only in those cases which, like Trieste, relate to peace and security but which do not fall within the framework of the more detailed provisions of the Charter....

If limited in this manner, the interpretation of Article 24 as conferring residuary power would seem to be a justifiable constitutional development, in keeping with the basic principle that the Council should have broad and flexible authority, within the purposes and principles of the Organization, to act effectively in the varied circumstances which might involve threats to the peace.

These early views were confirmed by the International Court when it came to consider the UN's purported revocation of the mandate that South Africa held over South West Africa. The Security Council had adopted Resolution 276 (1970) affirming General Assembly Resolution 2145 (XXI) that had purported to terminate the mandate. Various arguments arose in the subsequent case before the International Court about the legality and legal effect of these resolutions, including the absence of specific powers in the Charter authorizing mandate revocation by the Security Council.

Legal Consequences for States of the Continued Presence of South Africa in Namibia (South West Africa) Notwithstanding Security Council Resolution 276 (1970)

1971 I.C.J. 16 (June 21)

109.... The Security Council, when it adopted these resolutions, was acting in the exercise of what it deemed to be its primary responsibility, the maintenance of peace and security, which, under the Charter, embraces situations which might lead to a breach of the peace (Art. 1, para. 1)....

110. As to the legal basis of the resolution, Article 24 of the Charter vests in the Security Council the necessary authority to take action such as that taken in the present case. The reference in paragraph 2 of this Article to specific powers of the Security Council under certain chapters of the Charter does not exclude the existence of general powers to discharge

the responsibilities conferred in paragraph 1. Reference may be made in this respect to the Secretary General's Statement presented to the Security Council on 10 January 1947, to the effect that "the powers of the Council under Article 24 are not restricted to the specific grants of authority contained in Chapters VI, VII, VIII and XII … the Members of the United Nations have conferred on the Security Council powers commensurate with its responsibility for the maintenance of peace and security. The only limitations are the fundamental principles and purposes found in Chapter I of the Charter."

Comments

1. In addition to the Council's specific powers to maintain peace and security that are referred to in Article 24(2), the Council also has specific powers relating to the establishment of UN subsidiary organs[14] and the specification of conditions for participation in its meetings by nonmembers of the Council or nonmembers of the UN.[15]

2. An important additional source of powers that the Security Council enjoys is the implied powers of the UN under the Charter. On these implied powers, the International Court of Justice, in its Advisory Opinion on the *Legality of the Use by a State of Nuclear Weapons in Armed Conflict* case, stated:

> 25.… The powers conferred on international organizations are normally the subject of an express statement in their constituent instruments. Nevertheless, the necessities of international life may point to the need for organizations, in order to achieve their objectives, to possess subsidiary powers which are not expressly provided for in the basic instruments which govern their activities. It is generally accepted that international organizations can exercise such powers, known as "implied" powers. As far as the United Nations is concerned, the [International] Court has [in the previous *Reparations* case] expressed itself in the following terms in this respect:

> 'Under international law, the Organization must be deemed to have those powers which, though not expressly provided in the Charter, are conferred upon it by necessary implication as being essential to the performance of its duties. This principle of law was applied by the Permanent Court of International Justice to the International Labour Organization in its Advisory Opinion No.13 of July 23rd, 1926 (Series B, No.13, p.18), and must be applied to the United Nations.' (*Reparation for Injuries Suffered in the Service of the United Nations* (1954).[16]

3. The concept of implied powers has in practice proved of considerable importance to the Security Council being able to maintain or restore peace and security, supplementing such provisions as Articles 24, 29, and 40 of the Charter. Examples are seen in the legal basis for the Security Council to establish UN peacekeeping forces, to delegate its Chapter VII enforcement powers to member states, to establish *ad hoc* international criminal tribunals, and to establish UN transitional administrations to govern a state or part of the territory of a state often in post-conflict situations where state institutions have collapsed and there is a widespread lack of law and order.

---

14. *See* U.N. CHARTER art. 29. This power provided in part the basis, for example, for the establishment of the UN International Criminal Tribunals for the former Yugoslavia and Rwanda as subsidiary organs of the Council.

15. *See id.* art. 32.

16. Legality of the Use by a State of Nuclear Weapons in Armed Conflict, 1966 I.C.J. 66 (July 8).

4. The issue of potential judicial review by the International Court of Justice of Security Council resolutions adopted under Chapter VII of the Charter has attained prominence since the decisions of the Court in the *Case Concerning Questions of Interpretation and Application of the 1971 Montreal Convention Arising from the Aerial Incident at Lockerbie (Libya v. U.S.), Provisional Measures,*[17] and the *Case Concerning the Application of the Genocide Convention (Bosnia and Herzegovina v. Yugoslavia), Provisional Measures.*[18] In the former case, it was asked whether the Court has the competence to review the legality of an Article 39 determination by the Council; while in the latter case the issue was whether a Council resolution imposing an arms embargo on Bosnia might be reviewed on the ground that it impaired Bosnia's right of self-defense against an alleged genocidal aggressor. As both of these Orders were issued at the provisional measures stage, there was no definitive resolution of these issues by the Court.[19] This controversial issue of potential judicial review has, nonetheless, generated considerable academic comment, much of which is in favor of some form of judicial review. For further information, see the section Judicial Review of Security Council Measures in the Selected Bibliography. In a different context, the European Court of Justice (ECJ) has reviewed the implementation of Security Council resolutions with respect to the listing of individuals (see the discussion of the *Kadi* case below).

5. Since the establishment of the International Criminal Court (ICC) in 2002, the Security Council has had a role in referring situations to the ICC Prosecutor where it believes one or more crimes (genocide, crimes against humanity or war crimes) appears to have been committed.[20] This referral is done by way of a resolution under Chapter VII of the Charter. The Security Council has referred the situation in Darfur, Sudan (Resolution 1593 of 2005) and in Libya (Resolution 1970 of 2011) to the ICC Prosecutor and investigations have commenced.

Questions for Discussion

1. What powers are available to the Security Council?

2. What is the basis for the doctrine of implied powers? Is the rationale for the existence of this doctrine cogent?

3. What are the arguments for and against the International Court of Justice being able to review the exercise by the Security Council of its Chapter VII powers? What is the essential precondition for the Court to be able to hear such a case? (In order to answer these questions, you will need to read the articles in the section Judicial Review of Security Council Measures in the Selected Bibliography.)

Security Council Enforcement Measures to Maintain or Restore Peace & Security

The collective security powers of the Security Council are contained in Chapter VII of the Charter. The Charter requires that in order to be able to use these enforcement powers, the Council must make a determination, pursuant to Article 39, that there exists "a threat

---

17. 1992 I.C.J. 3.
18. 1993 I.C.J. 3.
19. Both Orders are available from the ICJ web-site: http://www.icj-cij.org.
20. Article 13(b) of the ICC Statute. Under Article 16 of the Statute, the Security Council may suspend an investigation or prosecution for a period of 12 months by passing a resolution under Chapter VII.

to the peace, breach of the peace or act of aggression." It was not originally envisaged that these threats to the peace would come from non-state actors, but this perception has now changed and the Council has in a number of cases determined that threats to the peace are being caused by non-state actors.

Once it has made an Article 39 determination, the Council can then prescribe what measures are necessary for the restoration of peace and security. These measures will involve the Council using its other powers under Chapter VII, which include the authority to order provisional measures to be taken by a state[21] and the authority to impose economic and military sanctions against a state.[22] Although the Council usually refers to Chapter VII in express terms in a resolution that invokes Chapter VII powers, it does not, however, usually make an express reference to the specific articles of Chapter VII on which it is basing its action.

Article 39 of the Charter

Rosalyn Higgins, Problems and Process: International Law and How We Use It
255, 257 (1994)

It is clear that the envisaged sanctions provided for by Articles 41 and 42 are for the maintenance or restoration of international peace and security. It is further clear that measures under Articles 41 and 42 depend upon there having been a finding under Article 39 of the existence of any threat to the peace, breach of the peace, or act of aggression. No matter how much one may wish it otherwise, no matter how policy-directed one might wish choice between alternative meanings to be, there is simply no getting away from the fact that the Charter *could* have allowed for sanctions for gross human-rights violations, but deliberately did not do so. The only way in which economic or military sanctions for human rights purposes could lawfully be mounted under the Charter is by the legal fiction that human-rights violations are causing a threat to international peace. That was the technique introduced long ago when economic sanctions were introduced against Rhodesia; it is still the technique being used in today's ever more complex problems in Iraq and Somalia. When the Government of Ian Smith declared its Unilateral Declaration of Independence (UDI) in Rhodesia, this was regarded as the act of a racist minority government, designed at perpetuating the inferior position of the black majority. That internal act was deemed by the Security Council to constitute a threat to international peace. Thus the scene was set for the application of Chapter VII of the UN Charter. Advantage was taken of the fact that the immediate neighbours of Rhodesia were so deeply resentful of the UDI that a hostile response could have been envisaged—and so, it was said, objectively there was a threat to the peace, and economic sanctions could be mounted.

. . . .

... The fact that [in later cases such as Iraq and Somalia] the pictures of suffering appear on our television screens, rightly outraging public opinion around the world, makes more likely the possibility that such [Article 39] characterizations will occur even where the national interests of the military active Security Council members are not directly involved. Such has been the case in Somalia. In Resolution 794 (1992) the Security Council determined that the 'magnitude of the human tragedy caused by the conflict in

---

21. *See* U.N. Charter, art. 40.
22. *See id.* arts. 41–42.

Somalia' constituted a threat to international peace and security. The United Nations had already sought to provide peace-keeping support for the humanitarian operations, through the establishment of the United Nations Operation in Somalia (UNOSOM). It now declared the situation a threat to international peace and authorized 'the use of all necessary means' to establish a secure environment for humanitarian relief operations. Acting under Chapter VII of the Charter, the Council authorized the participation of states in such an effort, within a unified command. The task was essentially taken on by the United States.

Comments

1. The Charter does not itself define a threat to the peace, breach of the peace, or act of aggression. The reason for this was deliberate: to give the Council a wide discretion in making Article 39 determinations. Although in 1974 the General Assembly did adopt a resolution on the Definition of Aggression,[23] the resolution has not been used in any systematic way by the Security Council in its determinations, though individual members may invoke it in support of their claims and it has been used as the basis for the definition of aggression in the amendment to the Statute of the ICC. This was adopted at the ICC Review Conference in 2010 but will not enter into force until after 2017.

2. The Council will often make an Article 39 determination in a resolution by using the language of Article 39 (that a particular situation constitutes a threat to or breach of the peace) without making an express reference to this Charter provision in its resolution.

3. The Security Council has made Article 39 determinations in a number of cases with differing causes. These include, for example, human rights violations occurring within a state (Southern Rhodesia), large-scale human suffering occurring within a state (Somalia and Rwanda), an attack by one state against another (Korea and Iraq), the protection of the delivery of humanitarian relief supplies within a state (Somalia, Bosnia, and Albania), and the restoration of democracy in a state (Haiti). Since the terrorist attacks of September 11, 2001, the Security Council has become the focus for multilateral efforts to eradicate terrorism. The Council has discussed HIV/AIDS, climate change and sexual violence as threats to international peace and security.[24]

4. An Article 39 finding involving a state does not necessarily entail a finding that the state is a "wrongdoer." The Security Council often determines that a situation is a threat to the peace, or even that events are a breach of the peace, without characterizing any of the parties as being at fault.

Obviously, when the finding is of aggression, it is hard to avoid the incidental determination that a state is a wrongdoer. However, the Council has applied the label of aggression very sparingly in the majority of recent cases where it has made an Article 39 determination. Despite having made a number of early determinations that "aggressive acts" had been committed by Southern Rhodesia and South Africa, and a few such additional determinations in incidents concerning Benin, Tunisia, and Iraq,[25] the Security

---

23. G.A. Res. 3314, U.N. G.A.O.R., 29th Sess., Supp. No. 31, U.N. Doc. A/9631 (1974).

24. Repertoire of the Practice of the Security Council 17th Supplement 2010–2011, Part VII.

25. UN Secretariat Study, HISTORICAL REVIEW OF DEVELOPMENTS RELATING TO AGGRESSION, U.N. Doc. PCNICC/2002/WGCA/L.1, paras. 383–404, *available at* http://daccess-dds-ny.un.org/doc/UNDOC/LTD/N01/709/63/PDF/N0170963.pdf?OpenElement.

Council has not made a determination using the term aggression since 1990. The latter determination was in Resolution 667 of September 16, 1990,[26] where the Council, as part of its response to Iraq's invasion of Kuwait, strongly condemned "aggressive acts perpetrated by Iraq against diplomatic premises and personnel in Kuwait, including the abduction of foreign nationals who were present in those premises," but it failed, however, to characterize more generally Iraq's invasion of Kuwait as an act of aggression. A possible reason for this may be to avoid the long-lasting stigma that accompanies such a label being applied to a state.

Questions for Discussion

1. What role does Article 39 play in the UN collective security system?

2. How have Article 39 determinations by the Council changed over time, and, in your view, to what extent have these changes been positive?

3. To what extent can a Security Council resolution that determines a particular situation to constitute a threat to the peace be challenged before the International Court of Justice on one or both of the following grounds: (a) that the situation in question does not constitute a threat to the peace; and (b) that there has been an alleged procedural illegality by the Council in adopting the resolution? (In order to answer this question, you will need to read the articles in the section Judicial Review of Security Council Measures in the Selected Bibliography.)

Article 40 of the Charter

The Security Council can require member states to comply with provisional measure orders, since a decision made pursuant to Article 40 attracts the application of Article 25 of the Charter and as such is binding on member states. Such orders have, for example, been made by the Council in the following circumstances: to call upon a State to comply with conditions as stipulated by the International Atomic Energy Agency (IAEA) (Iran in Council Resolution 1696 (2006));[27] to require a state to withdraw its invading troops from another state (Iraq's troops from Kuwait in Council Resolution 660 (1990));[28] to call for a cease-fire between warring parties (Iran and Iraq in Council Resolution 598 (1987));[29] and to demand an end to foreign military intervention (Turkey's invasion of Cyprus in Resolution 353 (1974)).[30] With the exception of Resolution 660, the record of the Council in taking further enforcement measures to ensure compliance with its provisional measure orders has not been good.

Article 41 of the Charter: Economic and Other Sanctions

For the first four decades of the UN, the Security Council rarely imposed sanctions under Article 41 of the Charter. That situation radically changed in the 1990s, with sanctions under Article 41 becoming one of the principal tools of the Security Council

---

26. S.C. Res. 667, 55th Sess., 2940th Mtg., U.N. Doc. S/Res/667 (1990).
27. S.C. Res 1696 (2006).
28. S.C. Res. 660, 55th Sess., 2932d Mtg., U.N. Doc. S/Res/660 (1990).
29. S.C. Res. 598, 52d Sess., 2750th Mtg., U.N. Doc. S/Res/598 (1987).
30. S.C. Res. 353, U.N. SCOR, 29th Sess., Special Supp. 1-2A, at 3, U.N. Doc. S/Supplements (1974).

in its efforts to maintain international peace and security. Three developments can be identified: (1) a movement from global to targeted sanctions; (2) the growth of a 'sanctions architecture' within the UN; and (3) controversies over judicial control and review of the implementation of sanctions.

The Classic Model of Economic Sanctions: Southern Rhodesia

The first economic sanctions regime imposed by the Security Council was that employed in the wake of the Rhodesian Unilateral Declaration of Independence (UDI) from the United Kingdom in 1965.

The regime in the case of Southern Rhodesia started out in the form of a recommendation and was then changed by the Council in subsequent resolutions to become mandatory. In Security Council Resolution 217 (1965), the Council said of the UDI: "its continuance in time constitutes a threat to international peace and security," and states were urged "to do their utmost in order to break all economic relations with Southern Rhodesia, including an embargo on oil and petroleum products."[31] These terms can be contrasted with those used in the series of resolutions that followed Resolution 217 (1965):

Security Council Resolution 221

U.N. SCOR, 21st Sess., Special Supp. No. 1,
Jan.–Dec., at 5, U.N. Doc. S/Supplements (1966)

The Security Council,

    . . . .

Gravely concerned at reports that substantial supplies of oil may reach Southern Rhodesia as the result of an oil tanker having arrived at Beira and the approach of a further tanker which may lead to the resumption of pumping ... with the acquiescence of the Portuguese authorities,

Considering that such supplies will afford great assistance and encouragement to the illegal regime in Southern Rhodesia, thereby enabling it to remain longer in being,

1.   *Determines* that the resulting situation constitutes a threat to the peace;

2.   *Calls upon* the Portuguese Government not to permit oil to be pumped through the pipeline from Beira to Southern Rhodesia;

3.   *Calls upon* the Portuguese Government not to receive at ports oil destined for Southern Rhodesia;

4.   *Calls upon* all States to ensure the diversion of any of their vessels reasonably believed to be carrying oil destined for Southern Rhodesia which may be en route for Beira;

5.   *Calls upon* the Government of the United Kingdom of Great Britain and Northern Ireland to prevent, by the use of force if necessary, the arrival at Beira of vessels reasonably believed to be carrying oil destined for Southern Rhodesia, and empowers

---

31. S.C. Res. 217, U.N. SCOR, 20th Sess., Supp. Jan.–Mar., at 8, U.N. Doc. S/Supplements (1965).

the United Kingdom to arrest and detain the tanker known as the *Joanna V* upon her departure from Beira in the event her oil cargo is discharged there.

Security Council Resolution 232

U.N. SCOR, 21st Sess., Special Supp. No. 1,
Jan.–Dec., at 7, U.N. Doc. S/Supplements (1966)

The Security Council,

....

Acting in accordance with Articles 39 and 41 of the United Nations Charter,

1. *Determines* that the present situation in Southern Rhodesia constitutes a threat to international peace and security;

2. *Decides* that all States Members of the United Nations shall prevent:

   (*a*) The import into their territories of asbestos, iron ore, chrome, pig-iron, sugar, tobacco, copper, meat and meat products and hides, skins and leather originating in Southern Rhodesia ... ;

   (*b*) Any activities by their nationals or in their territories which promote or are calculated to promote the export of these commodities from Southern Rhodesia ... ;

   (*c*) Shipment in vessels or aircraft of their registration of any of these commodities originating in Southern Rhodesia and exported therefrom after the date of this resolution;

   (*d*) Any activities by their nationals or in their territories which promote or are calculated to promote the sale or shipment to Southern Rhodesia of arms, ammunition of all types, military aircraft, military vehicles, and equipment and materials for the manufacture and maintenance of arms and ammunition in Southern Rhodesia;

   (*e*) Any activities by their nationals or in their territories which promote or are calculated to promote the supply to Southern Rhodesia of all other aircraft and motor vehicles and of equipment and materials for the manufacture, assembly, or maintenance of aircraft and motor vehicles in Southern Rhodesia; the shipment in vessels and aircraft of their registration of any such goods destined for Southern Rhodesia; and any activities by their nationals or in their territories which promote or are calculated to promote the manufacture or assembly of aircraft or motor vehicles in Southern Rhodesia;

   (*f*) Participation in their territories or territories under their administration or in land or air transport facilities or by their nationals or vessels of their registration in the supply of oil or oil products to Southern Rhodesia; notwithstanding any contracts entered into or licenses granted before the date of this resolution;

3. *Reminds* Member States that the failure or refusal by any of them to implement the present resolution shall constitute a violation of Article 25 of the Charter;

....

5. *Calls upon* all States not to render financial or other economic aid to the illegal racist regime in Southern Rhodesia;

6. *Calls upon* all States Members of the United Nations to carry out this decision of the Security Council in accordance with Article 25 of the United Nations Charter; ...

Comments

1. The imposition of economic sanctions is useful in most cases since it will often provide diplomatic and other processes the time they need to try and resolve a situation before the next step of military force is ordered by the Security Council against the recalcitrant state. It may even lead a recalcitrant state to cease its offending actions that have been the cause of the threat to peace. Where, however, economic sanctions are not, or do not look as if they will be, successful then the use of military force is an important, final, collective security measure. These are the two stages that the Security Council employed against Iraq. When the economic sanctions imposed against Iraq by Resolutions 661 (1990) and 670 (1990) appeared unlikely to compel Iraq to withdraw from Kuwait,[32] the Security Council in Resolution 678 (1990) authorized UN member states to use military force against Iraq.[33]

2. Since the end of the Cold War, the Security Council has imposed mandatory economic sanctions regimes against a number of states and entities within states. These include a comprehensive regime imposed against Iraq by Council Resolutions 661 (1990) and 670 (1990) and against the Federal Republic of Yugoslavia and the Bosnian Serb Party by Resolutions 757 (1992), 787 (1992), 820 (1993), and 942 (1994).[34] However, these cases of comprehensive sanctions regimes are rare as the Security Council has moved from global to more targeted sanctions.

3. In addition to the classic type of economic sanctions regime directed at a specific state or entity within a state, the Security Council has imposed obligations on all UN member states to prevent and suppress terrorism and take action to cut off financing for international terrorism. The Council used its Article 41 power to impose such obligations on states when it adopted Resolution 1373 (2001). This Resolution also establishes a Counter-Terrorism Committee to monitor implementation by states.[35]

From Global to Targeted Sanctions

During the 1990s, controversies over the negative humanitarian consequences of global economic sanctions on civilian populations led to the increased use of targeted sanctions against a state or entities within a state. For example, consider: arms embargoes;[36] the sus-

---

32. S.C. Res. 661, 45th Sess., 2933d mtg., U.N. Doc. S/RES/661 (1990); S.C. Res. 670, 45th Sess., 2943d mtg., U.N. Doc. S/RES/670 (1990).

33. S.C. Res. 678, 45th Sess., 2963d mtg., U.N. Doc. S/RES/678 (1990).

34. S.C. Res. 757, 47th Sess., 3082d mtg., U.N. Doc. S/RES/757 (1992); S.C. Res. 787, 47th Sess., 3137 mtg., U.N. Doc. S/RES/787 (1992); S.C. Res. 820, 48th Sess., 3234th mtg., U.N. Doc. S/RES/820 (1993); S.C. Res. 942, 49th Sess., 3928th mtg., U.N. Doc. S/RES/942 (1994).

35. The ongoing work of the Counter-Terrorism Committee is *available at* http://www.un.org/en/sc/ctc/.

36. All the territories of the Former Yugoslavia: S.C. Res. 713, 46th Sess., 3009th mtg., U.N. Doc. S/RES/713 (1991); Libya: S.C. Res. 748, 47th Sess., 3063d mtg., U.N. Doc. S/RES/748 (1992); Somalia: S.C. Res. 733, 47th Sess., 3108th mtg., U.N. Doc. S/RES/733 (1992); Liberia: S.C. Res. 788, 47th Sess., 3138th mtg., U.N. Doc. S/RES/788 (1992); the military junta in Haiti: S.C. Res. 841, 48th Sess., 3238th mtg., U.N. Doc. S/RES/841 (1993); the National Union for the Total Independence of Angola (UNITA) in Angola: S.C. Res. 864, 48th Sess., 3277th mtg., U.N. Doc. S/RES/864 (1993); Rwanda: S.C. Res. 918, 49th Sess., 3377th mtg., U.N. Doc. S/RES/918 (1994); the military junta in Sierra Leone: S.C. Res. 1132, 52d Sess., 3822d mtg., U.N. Doc. S/RES/1132 (1997); the Taliban in Afghanistan: S.C. Res. 1333, 55th Sess., 4251st mtg., U.N. Doc. S/RES/1333 (2000); and Eritrea and Ethiopia: S.C. Res. 1298, 55th Sess., 4144th mtg., U.N. Doc. S/RES/1298 (2000).

pension of civil aviation links;[37] the freezing of overseas assets;[38] and bans on imports from, or exports to, the target state of key products like petroleum[39] and diamonds.[40] The Council has sought to develop "smart sanctions" that target even more specifically the members of the government whose actions have caused the imposition of the economic sanctions. This has, for example, led the Council to impose travel restrictions against senior members of UNITA and adult members of their immediate families,[41] the freezing of funds and financial resources of all officers of the Haitian military and their immediate families and those employed by or acting on their behalf,[42] and the imposition of travel restrictions on members of the military junta in Haiti and adult members of their families.[43]

Individuals may be the subject of sanctions regimes in one of two ways. First, there are individuals who are listed on the basis of their position and affiliation to a State or a faction within a State.[44] Second, individuals may be targeted because they oppose the State as rebels in an internal conflict, as designated terrorists or are otherwise associated with such designated persons.[45]

By subjecting individuals to sanctions, the Security Council has pierced the veil of the State and largely removed these individuals from the protection of their domestic legal system.[46] Criticisms of the impact of the sanctions on the rights of individuals has led the Security Council to reform its listing regime in order better to guarantee individuals rights in the implementation of sanctions.

'Sanctions Architecture' within the UN

When establishing a sanctions regime, the Security Council creates sanctions committees to monitor and oversee the implementation of the measures. In the case of a comprehensive sanctions regime, the sanctions committee is responsible for determining whether specific goods fall within the humanitarian exceptions that are provided by these regimes, and thus whether they can be lawfully exported to the target state.[47] In order to ensure that fair and clear procedures exist for listing and delisting individuals and entities on sanctions lists as well as for granting humanitarian exemptions, the Security Council adopted resolution 1730 (2006) by which it requested the Secretary-General to establish a Focal Point to receive de-listing requests. Petitioners, other than those whose names are inscribed on the list created pursuant to Resolutions 1267 (1999), 1333 (2000) and 1989 (2011)

---

37. Libya: S.C. Res. 748, 47th Sess., 3063d mtg., U.N. Doc. S/RES/748 (1992); and the Taliban in Afghanistan: S.C. Res. 1267, 49th Sess., 4051st mtg., U.N. Doc. S/RES/1267 (1999).

38. Libya: S.C. Res. 883, 48th Sess., 3312th mtg., U.N. Doc. S/RES/883 (1993); the *de facto* government in Haiti: S.C. Res. 841, 48th Sess., 3238th mtg., U.N. Doc. S/RES/841 (1993); UNITA in Angola: S.C. Res. 1173, 43d Sess., 3891st mtg., U.N. Doc. S/RES/1173 (1998); and the Taliban and Osama bin Laden in Afghanistan: S.C. Res. 1267, 49th Sess., 4051st mtg., U.N. Doc. S/RES/1267 (1999); and S.C. Res. 1333, 55th Sess., 4251st mtg., U.N. Doc. S/RES/1333 (2000), respectively.

39. Sierra Leone: S.C. Res. 1132, 52d Sess., 3822d mtg., U.N. Doc. S/RES/1132 (1997); and Haiti: S.C. Res. 841, 48th Sess., 3238th mtg., U.N. Doc. S/RES/841 (1993).

40. Angola: S.C. Res. 1173, 43d Sess., 3891st mtg., U.N. Doc. S/RES/1173 (1998).

41. S.C. Res. 1127, 42d Sess., 3814th mtg., U.N. Doc. S/RES/1127 (1997).

42. S.C. Res. 917, 39th Sess., 3376th mtg., U.N. Doc. S/RES/917 (1994).

43. S.C. Res. 1132, 52d Sess., 3822d mtg., U.N. Doc. S/RES/1132 (1997).

44. *See, e.g.*, S.C. Res 1171 (1998) (listing members of the military junta in Sierra Leone).

45. *See, e.g.*, S.C. Res 2083 (2012) (listing of individuals, groups, undertakings and other entities associated with Al-Qaida).

46. Alain Pellet and Alina Miron, 'Sanctions' (2013) MPEPIL para 38.

47. In the case, for example, of the humanitarian exceptions provided in relation to the Iraqi sanctions, see the work of the sanctions committee *available at* http://www.un.org/sc/committees/.

(the Al-Qaida Sanctions List), can submit de-listing requests either through the focal point process or through their State of residence or citizenship.[48]

In Resolution 2083 (2012) the Council authorized the Focal Point to receive travel ban and assets freeze exemption requests in relation to those individuals or entities on the Al-Qaida Sanctions List. Resolution 2161 (2014) authorized the Focal Point to receive communications from individuals removed from the Al-Qaida Sanctions List and those claiming to have been subjected to the sanctions measures mistakenly.

Another significant step has been the establishment in Resolution 1904 (2009) of the Office of the Ombudsperson.

Larissa van den Herik, 'Peripheral Hegemony in the Quest to Ensure Security Council Accountability for its Individualized UN Sanctions Regimes'

19 JOURNAL OF CONFLICT AND SECURITY LAW 427, 439–441 (2014) (footnotes omitted)

....

Initially, the institute of the Ombudsperson was primarily geared towards offering individuals a certain access and possibility to be heard. The main powers of the Ombudsperson were confined to information gathering and engaging in a dialogue. On the basis of these functions, when approached with a delisting request, the Ombudsperson would 'draft a Comprehensive Report that will exclusively: (a) summarize ... all information available to the Ombudsperson ... (b) describe the Ombudsperson's activities ... (c) based on an analysis of all information available to the Ombudsperson and the Ombudsperson's observations, lay out for the Committee the principal arguments concerning the delisting requests'. Subsequently, it remained up to the Sanctions Committee to approve or reject the delisting request through its normal decision-making procedures. The powers of the Ombudsperson were significantly expanded in Resolution 1989 when it was vested with the power to make recommendations for delisting which in principal take effect unless overturned unanimously by the Sanctions Committee or, if referred, by a majority in the Security Council. The Ombudsperson has thus contributed to greater accountability for the 1267/1989 Al Qaeda sanctions regimes by increasing the transparency of the listing process through providing better insight into the underlying reasons and, to a more limited extent, evidence for the listings. The Security Council's acceptance of independent external scrutiny over its own decisions and those of the sanctions committees was unprecedented and should therefore not be taken lightly, even if the modalities of review were still modest. In Resolution 2083, the Security Council reaffirmed its support to the Ombudsperson and it called on states to encourage individuals and entities to approach the Ombudsperson with their delisting petitions rather than regional and national courts.

The procedural reforms made in the context of the 1267/1989 Al Qaeda regime have had a certain spillover effect to other sanctions regimes, but this has generally been confined to improvements of the listing procedure and only to a much more limited extent for amendments regarding delisting. Overall, a certain trend towards greater juridification of sanctions regimes in their design can be discerned. Even if some sanctions regimes, such as the non-proliferation regimes, remain deeply political, other regimes, particularly the

---

48. Pursuant to footnote 1 of the annex to S.C. Res. 1730 (2006) a State can decide that, as a rule, its citizens or residents should address their de-listing requests directly to the Focal Point.

human rights and civil conflict regimes, are partly designed around listing criteria which are connected to international legal norms. Moreover, all sanctions committees currently operate on the basis of guidelines which prescribe some modest transparency standards in the form of notification requirements and requests to prepare narrative descriptions with reasons for the proposed listing. In contrast, the delisting innovations in the form of the Ombudsperson have been confined to the 1267/1989 Al Qaeda regime and were not extended to other regimes. In fact, when this regime was parted in two separate regimes, the Al Qaeda regime and the Taliban regime, individuals listed under the Taliban sanctions regime were henceforth excluded from the Ombudsperson's mandate.

Apart from the limited scope of her mandate, the institute of the Ombudsperson has also been criticized as being insufficient in other respects. Crucial deficiencies of the Ombudsperson from a legal perspective remained that the institute was not a judicial entity, that the mandate was too short (initially 18 months, currently 30 months), and mostly the possibility of overturn of recommendations by the sanctions committee or the Security Council. For these reasons, the Special Rapporteur for Counter Terrorism deemed the reforms unsatisfactory and criticized the absence of an effective remedy at UN level. The Rapporteur emphasized that national and regional courts had engaged with the matter as a direct consequence of this lacuna. These decentralized courts generally reviewed the Security Council implementation measures. In so doing, they ostensibly respected the Security Council prerogative and refrained from undertaking direct review of the sanctions regime or the listings at UN level. However, given the lack of any real discretion on the part of states in implementing the sanctions, a court decision which annuls the implementing measures creates a direct Article 103 conundrum for the implementing state since the primary Security Council obligation to list and implement remains in existence. Furthermore, the potential of these decentralized courts to engage in any real substantive review is curtailed by the inaccessibility of the information and evidence that underlies the decision to list at UN level.

. . . .

Judicial Review as a Form of Security Council Accountability?

The impact of targeted sanctions on the fundamental rights of individuals and the limited options for challenging the listing regime has led to litigation in European and national courts seeking to annual the domestic acts implementing Security Council sanctions. The most famous case on the human rights implications of sanctions imposed on individuals has been the *Kadi* case decided by the European Court of Justice (ECJ).[49] Mr. Kadi had spent more than a decade on the sanctions list established by SC Resolution 1267, thereby being subjected to an asset freeze and travel ban, before being delisted by the UN 1267 Sanctions Committee on 5 October 2012. His case, which went through

---

49. CFI EU, Yusuf and Al Barakaat International Foundation v Council and Commission Case T-306/01 Judgment, 21 September 2005; CFI EU, Yassin Abdullah Kadi v Council of the European Union and Commission of the European Communities Case T-315/01 Judgment, 21 September 2005; CJ EU, Yassin Abdullah Kadi, Al Barakaat International Foundation v Council of the European Union and Commission of the European Communities Joined Cases C-402/05 P and C-415/05 P Grand Chamber, Judgment, 3 September 2008; CJ EU, Yassin Abdullah Kadi v Commission Case T-85/09 General Court Judgment, 30 September 2010; CJ EU, European Commission and Others v Yassin Abdullah Kadi, Joined cases C-584/10 P, C-593/10 P and C-595/10 P Grand Chamber Judgment 18 July 2013. See also the opinions of the Advocate General (who presents a public and impartial opinion to the case before the Court), Opinion of Advocate General Poiares Maduro, Case C-415/05 (above), 23 January 2008; Opinion of Mr Advocate General Bot, Joined cases C-584/10 P, C-593/10 P and C-595/10 P (above), 19 March 2013.

various phases (*Kadi I* and *Kadi II*), was the first case in which the ECJ reviewed an EC regulation that implemented UN sanctions against a designated individual. It is also the first case in which the ECJ annulled such a regulation. The litigation triggered a re-examination of the individualized sanctions regimes and the relationship between international and European law.

Erika de Wet, *From* Kadi *to* Nada: *Judicial Techniques Favoring Human Rights Over United Nations Security Council Sanctions*

12 CHINESE JOURNAL OF INTERNATIONAL LAW 787, 790–92 (2013) (footnotes omitted)

. . . .

The Kadi dispute ... initially unfolded in 2005 before the then still Court of First Instance (currently known as the General Court) of the EU. This court considered Mr. Kadi's listing to be immune from judicial scrutiny, as it originated from a binding UNSC sanctions regime that left no discretion for implementation. From there Mr. Kadi launched a successful appeal (... Kadi CJEU I) to the Court of Justice of the European Union (CJEU). The CJEU formally separated the implementing measures at EU level from the measures taken by the UNSC and the Al Qaida sanctions committee. It applied a dualist approach in as far as it engaged in review of the implementing measures, without formally challenging the primacy of the UNSC measures at the international level. This formal separation was motivated by the fact that within the EU legal order fundamental rights (such as the right to judicial protection), formed an integral part of the general and constitutional order which could not be sacrificed. The CJEU then ordered the implementing measures to be annulled, due to the fact that the EU authorities did not communicate any reasons to Mr. Kadi regarding his listing, nor had they afforded him any opportunity to be heard.

Subsequently the EU provided Mr. Kadi with a summary of reasons that has been made available by the Al Qaida sanctions committee and allowed him a hearing, but only to dismiss his response and reinstate the sanctions on the EU level. Mr. Kadi once again turned to the General Court which—following the line of reasoning of the CJEU—determined that the reasons forwarded to Mr. Kadi were too vague to allow for meaningful review. The measures implementing the UNSC sanctions at EU level were therefore once again struck down.

This decision gave rise to another appeal to the CJEU, this time by the European Commission and Council of the EU and which was decided on 18 July 2013. Supported by several EU member states, the appellants urged the CJEU to reconsider its position that judicial immunity should not be granted to EU listings that give effect to the Al Qaida sanctions regime. According to this line of argument, the EU was under a strict obligation to give effect to these obligations and had been left with no discretion regarding the manner of implementation, as a result of which these measures should be immune from judicial review. Realizing perhaps that the CJEU was highly unlikely to reverse its position on the lack of immunity of the implementing measures (which it indeed reaffirmed rather summarily), the appellants further attempted to lower the level of scrutiny applied during judicial review. This was inspired by the fact that the EU institutions lacked any margin of discretion in relation to the manner of implementing the measures stemming from the Al Qaida sanctions regime. However, this argument failed to impress the court which retained its high level of scrutiny in reviewing and striking down the reasons submitted by the EU organs in relation to Mr. Kadi's listing.

. . . .

European Commission and Others v Yassin Abdullah Kadi,
Joined Cases C-584/10 P, C-593/10 P and C-595/10 P

Grand Chamber Judgment 18 July 2013, para 134

The essence of effective judicial protection must be that it should enable the person concerned to obtain a declaration from a court, by means of a judgment ordering annulment whereby the contested measure is retroactively erased from the legal order and is deemed never to have existed, that the listing of his name, or the continued listing of his name, on the list concerned was vitiated by illegality, the recognition of which may re-establish the reputation of that person or constitute for him a form of reparation for the non-material harm he has suffered.

Questions for Discussion

1. Does the fact that resolutions under Article 41 may be binding suffice to make UN economic sanctions legally effective? Is domestic legal action required by your country to make such a resolution internally operative? Why is this important?

2. What are the advantages and disadvantages of the Security Council's recent preference for targeted sanctions?

3. To what extent has the *Kadi* case exposed the shortcomings of the UN 'sanctions architecture'? To what extent should the Security Council strive to balance the achievement of the guaranteeing of human rights of individuals with the use of sanctions as an effective tool in the maintenance of international peace and security?

4. The Security Council's sanctions regime has led to claims that the Council suffers from a significant accountability deficit. It functions largely behind closed doors and with little transparency to the UN's general membership or to the broader public. While the Council has become increasingly active in the administration and regulation of matters that once used to be the exclusive domain of States, this shift in governance functions has not been accompanied by the creation of a meaningful mechanism to review the exercise of the Council's powers. How can the accountability of the Security Council be improved?

Article 42 of the Charter: Military Enforcement Action

The collective use of force as a military sanction does not operate in the way originally intended by the UN Charter.

The Original Charter Framework

Rosalyn Higgins, Problems and Process:
International Law and How We Use It

263–66 (1994)

It is envisaged under Chapter VII of the UN Charter that the Security Council, once it has determined the existence of a threat to the peace, breach of the peace, or act of aggression, will recommend or decide upon enforcement measures to maintain or restore international peace and security. As we have seen, Article 41 provides for economic and diplomatic sanctions; and Article 42 allows for military action by air, sea, or land forces. Article 43 then provides that all UN members undertake to make available to the Security

Council, 'on its call and in accordance with a special agreement or agreements', armed forces, assistance, and facilities. These agreements were to govern the numbers and types of forces, their location and readiness, and were to be concluded 'as soon as possible' between the Security Council and individual members of the United Nations, or groups of members. Some forty-five years later these agreements have not been concluded. The deep divisions between East and West that emerged immediately after the war made it impossible to proceed. There was no agreement upon the circumstances in which military enforcement measures would be used.

In the face of the failure of the Security Council to be able to proceed as envisaged under Article 42, the question immediately arose as to the authority of the Security Council to act under Article 42. Is the ability of the United Nations to act under Article 42 dependent upon agreements for the provision of UN forces being reached under Article 43? The Soviet Union insisted that Articles 42 and 43 have to be read together, and that, in the absence of the latter, the former was inoperative. No military action by the Security Council could be envisaged....

... For the Soviet Union, it [military action without Article 43 agreements] was not legally possible. For the West, it was a practical reality that military enforcement was not available in the absence of agreements under Article 43. The Secretary-General, after the establishment by the General Assembly of the UNEF [the UN peace-keeping force in the Middle East] in 1956, emphasized that it went to Egypt with the consent of that country, and could not operate without that consent. He continued:

> This does not exclude the possibility that the Security Council could use such a force within the wider margins provided under Chapter VII of the United Nations Charter. I would not for the present consider it necessary to elaborate on this point further, since no use of the Force under Chapter VII ... has been envisaged.

He thus left open the point as to whether enforcement action under Article 42 could, as a matter of Charter law, occur in the absence of agreements under Article 43....

....

Although the position about Article 42 action in the absence of Article 43 agreements has been left open, it has popularly been supposed that such action was not possible. It has been a short step from the practical difficulty of attempting Article 42 actions to a general assumption that such actions were legally impossible. I have never regarded that view as correct. Peace-keeping action was deemed sufficient and appropriate for the world we lived in. While this political reality was undeniable, I never understood why the legal possibilities under Article 42 were deemed unavailable. It has consistently been my view that the consequence of the failure to conclude agreements under Article 43 was that UN members could not be compelled to provide forces and assistance under Article 42. But I could see no reason of legal analysis which proscribed any member or members from volunteering forces and the Security Council being able to use them under Article 42. It would remain a matter of political judgment for the Security Council, on any given occasion, to decide if it was preferable to provide for peace-keeping (now read into Article 40) or for military enforcement (under Article 42).

What was for many years a matter of academic interest has now come back into focus in the context of the Iraqi invasion of Kuwait. Are there legal constraints upon the Security Council ordering enforcement action under Article 42? Those states who preferred to avoid UN military sanctions offered reasons other than a legal inability to rely on Article 42. This has been true both of those who wished to avoid military action altogether, and those who preferred to use collective self-defence. On 25 September 1990 Soviet Foreign Minister

Shevardnadze spoke in the Security Council on the importance of reviewing the possibilities under Article 43, of seeing whether, in the face of the improved relations between East and West, agreements could not now be reached. But it was not suggested that the absence to date of such agreements ruled out the possibility of action under Article 42. Indeed, such action was specifically envisaged in the strong speech of the Soviet Foreign Minister. The community of interest between the West and the Soviet Union conspired to put aside the common assumption of the previous forty-five years—that military sanctions could not be authorized in the absence of the agreements envisaged under Article 43. The prudence of the Secretary-General and the International Court of Justice in leaving this issue open, while focusing on peace-keeping, was apparent; and in my view the right legal answer has at last been arrived at (albeit without any apparent serious public consideration). In the absence of Article 43 agreements, no UN member can be compelled to provide military forces or assistance; but action under Article 42, by those who are willing to participate, can properly be authorized by the United Nations and carried out under UN command. It would also seem perfectly possible for such action to be authorized by the Security Council as an enforcement action under Article 42, even if it was to be carried out by UN members not under a unified UN command. And this was effectively the position achieved by Security Council Resolution 678 (1990) on the Gulf.

The Delegation by the Council of its Chapter VII Powers to UN Member States

The Security Council has in a number of different cases "authorized" member states to use military force as part of a collective security response to achieve the Council's objectives. What the Security Council is doing in substantive terms in these cases is "delegating" certain of its Chapter VII powers (including its Article 42 power) to states rather than merely "authorizing" states to use force.

Dan Sarooshi, The United Nations and the Development of Collective Security

13–15 (1999)

An authorization ... represent[s] the conferring on an entity of a very limited right to exercise a power, or part thereof; or the conferring on an entity of the right to exercise a power it already possesses, but the exercise of which is conditional on an authorization that triggers the competence of the entity to use the power. While the case of a delegation will usually represent an unencumbered right to exercise the same power as the delegator, in many cases a power of broad discretion. It is this single characteristic of a delegation of power—the transfer of a power of discretionary decision-making—that allows it to be distinguished in general terms from an authorization.

... In the case of an authorization by the Council of States to use force, the Council is not, in legal terms, simply making an authorization, but upon closer examination is in fact delegating to Member States its Chapter VII powers. The Council may be using the term 'authorization', but what it is doing in substance is delegating its Chapter VII powers to Member States. In the case where the Council 'authorises' States or a regional arrangement to use force to achieve, for example, certain humanitarian objectives and in so doing transfers certain of its own discretionary powers under Chapter VII in order to do so, then this is, applying our earlier discussion, a delegation of power from the Council since it involves a transfer of the Council's own powers of discretionary decision-making, and as such is subject to the legal framework governing a delegation of Chapter VII powers.

Even the case of what may at first seem to be an authorization by the Security Council of UN Member States to exercise their inherent right of individual or collective self-defence as provided for by Article 51 of the Charter will usually involve a delegation of power. Once there is an authorization by the Security Council of military action, it is unlikely that the Council is simply authorising individual or collective self-defence measures. Those cases where such a use of force would be justified by reference to authorized self-defence would not be many since in most cases where the Council becomes involved the stated objectives of the military action are much broader than those which would be justified under the right of self-defence of States, whether under Article 51 of the Charter or under customary international law. In this case, States may act in a way — in terms of *jus ad bellum* — which is not otherwise allowed under the law of self-defence. For example, in the case of the Security Council's authorization of Member States to use force in response to Iraq's invasion of Kuwait, the Council in resolution 678 authorized States not only to repel Iraq's armed attack but also to 'restore international peace and security in the area'. Accordingly, States were empowered to take action which went beyond what is allowed by the concept of self-defence in international law. In this way, what initially may have been the exercise by States of their right to individual or collective self-defence changed with the involvement of the Council. With the passage of resolution 678 the Council had moved past a simple authorization of collective self-defence into a delegation of its own discretionary powers to UN Member States. This provides an example then of the more general point that it is rare for there to be collective self-defence authorized by the Security Council unless it is patent from the face of the resolution that this is all the Council is authorizing and that there is no mention of States taking action to maintain or restore international peace and security. The involvement of the Council will, in most cases, necessarily confer a collective security nature on an operation. There is, accordingly, a presumption that where the Council authorises the use of force by States then this represents a delegation by the Council of its Chapter VII powers and not just a reaffirmation of States' right to use force in self-defence.

————————

The Council does not, however, possess an unconstrained competence to delegate its Chapter VII powers to UN member states. There are important limitations that exist.

Dan Sarooshi, The United Nations and the Development of Collective Security
153–58 (1999)

There are inherent dangers in the practice of the Council delegating Chapter VII powers to Member States. The main danger is that those Member States will exercise the delegated powers to achieve their own self-interest and not that of the UN.... This is contrary to the very reason for centering in the UN the responsibility for maintaining and restoring international peace and security: to regulate the use of force by States to attain their national ends.

This issue of self-interest is not, however, always antithetical to the collective security purpose for which a Chapter VII power is delegated to Member States.... The problem, as outlined above, arises however when the interests of a State are in conflict with those of the UN, as defined by the Security Council. However, the existence of limitations on the competence of the Council to delegate Chapter VII powers to Member States provides a safeguard against such a potentially negative consequence of a delegation of Chapter VII powers. There are two types of limitations on the competence of the Council to delegate Chapter VII powers to UN Member States.

The first involves a limitation on the competence of the Council to be able to delegate certain of its Chapter VII powers to Member States. These substantive limitations have already been explained in Chapter 1 and prohibit the delegation by the Council of certain of its Chapter VII powers. [The primary one being the Council's Article 39 power of determination — that a threat to, or breach of, the peace exists or has ceased to exist.]

The second — what are termed conditions for a lawful delegation — only regulate the way in which the Council should delegate its powers and do not as such prohibit the delegation of a particular power.

... [The most important of these is that] there must be a certain minimum degree of clarity in the resolution which delegates the power. Put differently, the objective for which the power is being delegated must be clearly specified. ...

... The setting by the Council of detailed objectives of the military operation and the capacity to change these objectives at any time enables the Council to exercise in an effective fashion its overall authority and control over an operation. This position has been reflected in numerous statements by Members of the Security Council and the Secretary-General. ...

....

This requirement of the Council to specify in some detail the political objectives of the operation cannot be circumvented by the provision of a vague and ambiguous objective. This consideration attains even more importance when attention is paid to the fact that the delegation by the Council of its Chapter VII powers to Member States is a 'conditional delegation'. We recall from Chapter 1 the legal position that the Council cannot delegate to another entity the competence to decide when a threat to, or breach of, international peace and security has come into existence or has ceased to exist. It thus follows that it is not for the delegate to decide when the objective which the Council has stated has been fulfilled and therefore when the delegation of powers ceases to exist. This power of decision is within the sole domain of the Council and cannot be delegated. That is, the delegation of powers continues to exist until such time as the objective which the Council has specified in the resolution which delegates powers has been fulfilled. Upon the fulfilment of this objective the delegation of powers will automatically cease. Thus the Council by specifying the objective for which the power is being delegated is in fact stipulating when the delegation of power terminates. ... This automatic termination of a delegation of powers is a necessary control on the exercise of delegated Chapter VII powers since it provides a convenient way of terminating a delegation without the requirement of another decision by the Council, which is of course subject to the veto. This guards against the use of a veto in the Council by a Permanent Member to prevent the termination of a delegation of powers and as such is a further guarantee against a Permanent Member exercising delegated powers to achieve its own interests.

Comments

1. The UN Charter does not expressly give the Security Council the competence to delegate its Chapter VII powers to UN member states such that they can carry out and command military enforcement action on behalf of the Council. As a matter of implied powers, however, the Council does possess this competence and can delegate its Chapter

VII powers to UN member states either by means of a decision or recommendation.[50] In either case there is no compulsion on states to act upon these powers potentially delegated to them, since, as set out above, the nonconclusion of Article 43 agreements means that the Council cannot obligate states to participate in military enforcement action.

2. It has been easier in the post-Cold War era for members of the Security Council to reach agreement on the existence of threats to the peace than it has been for them to agree on how to act in responding to these threats. Nonetheless, in most cases agreement has subsequently been reached to allow those states who wish to take action to deal with a threat to the peace to be able to do so. This has not meant, however, that there is no subsequent disagreement between states over the type of action that should be taken. A good example of this is the case of Iraq where, in response to its invasion of Kuwait in August 1990, there was widespread agreement among states that military action if necessary had to be taken to counter this invasion. However, after Iraqi troops were driven out of Kuwait there arose the more problematic issue of how best to deal with the continuing threat posed by Saddam Hussein to peace and security. There has been division and disagreement among states on the next course of action.

Dan Sarooshi, The United Nations and the Development of Collective Security
174, 177–80, 182–83, 185–86 (1999)

2. The case of Iraq

....

Resolution 678 was adopted by the Council acting under Chapter VII of the Charter due to the desire to take stronger measures to ensure the immediate withdrawal of Iraqi forces from Kuwait. The relevant sections of resolution 678 read as follows:

Acting under Chapter VII of the Charter [the Security Council],

1.   *Demands* that Iraq comply fully with resolution 660 (1990) and all subsequent relevant resolutions, and decides, while maintaining all its decisions, to allow Iraq one final opportunity, as a pause of goodwill, to do so;

2.   *Authorizes* Member States co-operating with the Government of Kuwait, unless Iraq on or before 15 January 1991 fully implements, as set forth in paragraph 1 above, the foregoing resolutions, to use all necessary means to uphold and implement resolution 660 (1990) and all subsequent relevant resolutions and to restore international peace and security in the area;

....

4.   *Requests* the States concerned to keep the Security Council regularly informed on the progress of action undertaken pursuant to paragraphs 2 and 3 of the present resolution;

....

(b) The powers delegated to Member States by resolution 678

The passage of resolution 678 saw the delegation to Member States of the power to use force to achieve the Council's stated objective, and the power of command and control over the forces carrying out the military enforcement action.

---

50. *See* Danesh Sarooshi, The United Nations and the Development of Collective Security 143–53 (1999).

(i) The delegation to Member States of the power to use force

Article 2(4) of the Charter proscribes the threat or actual use of force by States against the territorial integrity or political independence of any State. However, a delegation by the Council of its military enforcement powers has an empowering effect that operates to allow States to use force to achieve the Council's stated objectives. This represents a delegation by the Council to Member States of its powers under Article 42 to 'take such action by air, sea, or land forces as may be necessary to maintain or restore international peace and security. Such action may include demonstrations, blockade, and other operations by air, sea, or land forces of Members of the United Nations.'

The issue of greatest concern with respect to this delegation of Chapter VII power is that the Council is purporting to delegate to Member States a very broad power of discretion to use force without specifying clearly the objectives for which it is delegating its powers. We recall that resolution 678 states '[The Council authorizes] Member states co-operating with the Government of Kuwait ... to use all necessary means to uphold and implement resolution 660 (1990) and all subsequent relevant resolutions and to restore international peace and security in the area'. The objectives specified by the Council thus include the implementation of resolution 660 (the immediate and unconditional withdrawal by Iraq of 'all its forces to the positions in which they were located on 1 August 1990') and all subsequent resolutions; and the restoration of international peace and security in the area. The first objective is relatively clear and seems to have operated as a substantive limitation on action by Member States in their exercise of delegated powers. The decision to end hostilities was made when Iraq had been driven out of Kuwait and had agreed to accept all relevant UN resolutions.

The second objective, however, is of considerable more concern. It seems clear that the Council is purporting to delegate to Member States the competence to decide when international peace and security in the region has been restored. However, as pointed out above in Chapter 1, the Council does not possess the competence to delegate to Member States the power to decide that a threat to, or breach of, international peace and security has either started or has ceased to exist. The decision whether a particular matter constitutes a threat to the peace and the decision when to terminate military enforcement action must always rest with the Security Council.... The purported delegation by the Council of this broad power to Member States is unlawful. It is on the basis of this unrestricted character of the power delegated by resolution 678 that commentators have correctly questioned the lawfulness of the resolution. This does not, however, render the whole of resolution 678 unlawful, but only the delegation of powers to Member States for the objective of restoring international peace and security in the region.

In practice, however, the Security Council did play an important role in the termination of the delegation of powers. The success of the coalition force in expelling Iraq from Kuwait saw the US command declare a temporary cease-fire after the full retreat of Iraqi forces from Kuwait and the restoration to power of the legitimate Government of Kuwait. The Council subsequently passed resolution 686 which, *inter alia*, affirmed that all twelve prior resolutions continued to have full force and effect, and demanded that Iraq cease hostilities and designate military commanders to meet with counterparts from the coalition forces 'to arrange for the military aspects of a cessation of hostilities at the earliest possible time.' The Council continued by expressly stating in operative paragraph 4 that it '[r]ecognizes that during the period required for Iraq to comply with paragraphs 2 and 3 above, the provisions of paragraph 2 of resolution 678 (1990) remain valid'. This provision is clearly intended as an affirmation by the Council that the delegation of military enforcement powers to Member States continues to have force. It places the legality of any subsequent use of force to achieve the objectives of the Council in its previous resolutions, including resolution 678, and the conditions stated in resolution 686 beyond any doubt. However, the terms of resolution 686 were superseded by the terms of the formal cease-fire of the Council in resolution 687. The terms for a permanent cease-fire were stated by the Council in resolution 687 and these were accepted by Iraq....

... [T]he delegation of Chapter VII powers to Member States was terminated by conclusion of the formal cease-fire between Iraq and the UN, the terms of which were specified in resolution 687. Nowhere in its terms, unlike resolution 686, does resolution 687 expressly preserve the right of Member States to use force under resolution 678. In fact, the conclusion of the cease-fire, of which resolution 687 was an essential part, terminated the delegation of powers in resolution 678 to Member States of the competence to use force.... Accordingly, in the absence of a Council resolution which expressly delegates powers of military enforcement to Member States, action to enforce the terms of resolution 687, although possibly desirable, would be legally doubtful. This problem is a symptom of the deeper issue of the lack of clear specification by the Council of the goals for which it was delegating its Chapter VII powers to Member States.

. . . .

(ii) The command and control of forces in the Gulf War

It seems clear that in resolution 678 the Council delegated to Member States operational command and control over their own forces carrying out military enforcement action. The resolution does not require or envisage any form of operational command or control being exercised by the Security Council over the forces from Member States. This represents a delegation of the Council's power of command and control under Article 46 of the Charter to Member States.... Moreover, the Council did not specify in resolution 678 any form of command structure. Accordingly, the coalition forces were free to identify their own military commander and command structure. The Member States participating in the action decided to form a coalition with the United States in overall command.... This does not mean, however, that the exercise of the delegated powers is left solely to the discretion of Member States.... The Security Council will always retain overall authority and control over the exercise of Chapter VII powers it has delegated to UN Member States. Accordingly, the Council could at any time decide to terminate the delegation of powers or even decide that the powers should be exercised in another way. This has particular relevance, for example, in the context of a proportionate use of force being used to attain the Council's stated objectives. The Council could at any time have, for example, required States to change the level of force being used by Member States in the Gulf in the exercise of their delegated powers.

ROSALYN HIGGINS, PROBLEMS AND PROCESS:
INTERNATIONAL LAW AND HOW WE USE IT
259 (1994)

The military action in Iraq was undertaken under Security Council authorization, but by coalition forces acting under unified command. At the end of hostilities, Security Council Resolution 686 specified a list of requirements that had to be met for a cease-fire to come into effect. The right of the coalition forces 'to use all necessary means' remained in effect for the moment. Security Council Resolution 687 addressed matters subsequent to the cease-fire. But it was still expressly stated to be under Chapter VII of the Charter, and referred to such matters as the verified dismantling of Iraq's nuclear and offensive military capability, the provision of reparations, and (again) the repatriation of Kuwaiti and third-party nationals.

May force be used to require compliance with the terms of Resolution 687? And, if so, upon Security Council authorization only, or directly by the coalition forces? In January 1993 the Secretary-General reported violations of the Kuwait frontier by Iraq, and interferences by Iraq with UN flights being undertaken in connection with the weapons-inspection programme. Although the Security Council passed no resolution, it issued a statement read by its President demanding that the flights not be interfered with and warning of 'serious consequences which would ensue from failure to comply with its obligations'. The authorization in Resolution 678 to use 'all necessary means' was, in the context of the statements made in the Security Council, an authorization to use force. But the 'serious consequences' warning of the President of the Council in January 1993 cannot, in my view, be read as an authorization to coalition members to use force without further reference if interference with UN flights did not abate.

In the event, a series of military actions followed by some of the coalition parties— the United States, France, and the United Kingdom— in January 1993. Only one such action, directed against a target fifteen miles from Baghdad, was said by the United States to be linked to non-compliance by Iraq of its obligations under the Security Council resolutions. Other actions, taken in the no-fly zones set up to protect the Kurds and Shias, were explained in the language of self-defence. France and the United Kingdom, perhaps feeling on safer legal ground, emphasized their entitlement to patrol these zones for UN authorized purposes; and the danger to these missions when Iraq continued to fly within the zones, or to lock radar on to coalition aircraft, or to endeavour to shoot them down. Such responses are to be tested by the traditional criteria of self-defence. There is no entitlement in the hands of individual members of the United Nations to enforce prior Security Council resolutions by the use of force.

Jules Lobel & Michael Ratner, *Bypassing the Security Council: Ambiguous Authorizations to Use Force, Cease-Fires and the Iraqi Inspection Regime*

93 AM. J. INT'L L. 124, 124–27, 144–45, 154 (1999)

INTRODUCTION

In January and February 1998, various United States officials, including the President, asserted that unless Iraq permitted unconditional access to international weapons inspections, it would face a military attack. The attack was not to be, in Secretary of State Madeleine Albright's words, "a pinprick," but a "significant" military campaign. U.S. officials, citing United Nations Security Council resolutions, insisted that the United States had the authority for the contemplated attack. Representatives of other permanent members of the Security Council believed otherwise; that no resolution of the Council authorized U.S. armed action without its approval. In late February, UN Secretary-General Kofi Annan traveled to Baghdad and returned with a memorandum of understanding regarding inspections signed by himself and the Iraqi Deputy Prime Minister. On March 2, 1998, the Security Council, in Resolution 1154, unanimously endorsed this memorandum of understanding.

In the March 2 meeting, no country asserted that Resolution 1154 authorized the unilateral use of force, and a majority stated that additional Council authorization would be necessary before force could be used. Only after that meeting did U.S. officials claim otherwise; Ambassador Bill Richardson said the UN vote was a "green light" to attack Iraq if President Clinton should decide that Iraq was not living up to the agreement. This assertion in the face of the Security Council's pointed refusal to grant such authority views the Council as a source of the authority to use force, but not as an instrument for limiting its use. With at least one notable exception, however, the United States did not claim to be entitled to use force without the Council's authorization to compel Iraqi compliance with the UN inspection obligations. Rather, U.S. and British officials argued that Resolution 678 of 1990, which empowered the United States and other states to use force against Iraq, still governed and continued to provide authority to punish Iraq for cease-fire violations. This position assumed that Resolution 678's authorization to use force remained valid, albeit temporarily suspended — a loaded weapon in the hands of any member nation to use whenever it determined Iraq to be in material breach of the cease-fire. The refusal of the United States to accept limitations on its power by the Security Council thus depended on creatively interpreting the Council's resolutions to accord authority, despite the contrary positions of a majority of its members.

The U.S. and British claim highlights an important problem regarding the Security Council's method of authorizing individual member states or regional organizations to use force on behalf of the United Nations. This "contracting out" mode leaves individual states with wide discretion to use ambiguous, open-textured resolutions to exercise control over the initiation, conduct and termination of hostilities. Such states may seek to apply resolutions by the Security Council in conflict with its aims and objectives or the view of many of its members, as occurred in the 1998 Iraqi inspection crisis. This crisis thus raises questions regarding (1) whether the Security Council has authorized the use of force; (2) how the scope and extent of an authorization are determined; and (3) whether the authorization has terminated.

We argue that two fundamental values underpinning the United Nations Charter — that peaceful means be used to resolve disputes and that force be used in the interest and under the control of the international community and not individual countries — require that the Security Council retain strict control over the initiation, duration and objectives of the use of force in international relations. To ensure that UN-authorized uses of force comport with those two intertwined values, this article argues for three rules derived from Article 2(4) of the Charter: (1) explicit and not implicit Security Council authorization is necessary before a nation may use force that does not derive from the right to self-defense under Article 51; (2) authorizations should clearly articulate and limit the objectives for which force may be employed, and ambiguous authorizations should be narrowly construed; and (3) the authorization to use force should cease with the establishment of a permanent cease-fire unless explicitly extended by the Security Council.

The questions raised by the Iraqi inspection crisis of 1998 are likely to arise in the future. The claim of the U.S. Government to an ongoing UN authorization to use force against Iraq to enforce the cease-fire agreement has resurfaced often over the past seven years and is unlikely to be withdrawn. Moreover, the tendency to bypass the requirement for explicit Security Council authorization, in favor of more ambiguous sources of international authority, will probably escalate in coming years. The recent controversy over NATO's threat to intervene militarily in Kosovo raises similar issues as to the requirement for explicit authorization.

I. THE GENERAL PRINCIPLES UNDERLYING UN AUTHORIZATIONS OF FORCE

....

Problems with the authorization method surface in several related areas. First, states might use force on the basis of actions by the Security Council that could impliedly be interpreted to authorize force, but where its intent to do so was unclear. For example, in 1991 the United Kingdom, the United States and France used force to provide humanitarian aid to the Kurds and to establish safe havens and no-fly zones in northern Iraq partly on the basis of ambiguous authority in Resolution 688. That resolution made no mention of military force, nor was it intended to authorize such force. The Economic Community of West African States (ECOWAS) intervened militarily in Liberia in 1990 without any explicit authorization by the Security Council, although the Council later did issue statements and a resolution approving ECOWAS's actions.

Second, states acting under the authorization of the Council might interpret their mandate to be broader than it had intended. The potential for conflict is most pronounced where the Council has delegated wide authority to a coalition of states to address a major problem, such as the Iraqi invasion of Kuwait. For example, Resolution 678, while motivated by the goal of expelling Iraq from Kuwait, also contains broad language authorizing force "to restore international peace and security in the area." That language could mean virtually anything, depending on how one defines "peace and security" and "area." During the Persian Gulf war, a dispute arose as to whether the elimination of Iraq's war-making power, a goal asserted by some of the leaders of the coalition states, was authorized by Resolution 678. The dispute over interpretation of Resolution 678 has continued to fester. In the February 1998 crisis, the United States and the United Kingdom interpreted the broad language "to restore international peace and security" as authorizing the use of force to ensure that Iraq destroyed its biological and chemical weapons—a condition not imposed upon Iraq until after the gulf war was over. Similar questions and disputes over Security Council authorizations to use force arose during the Korean War and the Bosnian and Somalian conflicts.

Furthermore, when the authorizations are not temporally limited, questions arise about their termination. As the Iraqi inspection crisis illustrates, the states acting under Security Council authorization might want to continue to employ force after the basic goal of the mission has been achieved. Conflicts often continue to simmer after hostilities have ended. A key question is whether a permanent cease-fire or other definitive end to hostilities terminates Security Council authorizations to use force.

. . . .

To uphold the principles of the Charter, the Security Council must retain clear control over authorizations to use force (with the exception of force pursuant to Article 51), even if political and military considerations require that it delegate military command to individual nations. The difficulties of controlling the scope and extent of the use of force when its employment is delegated to individual states require, at a minimum, strict control by the Council over the initiation and termination of hostilities. Such control is achieved by the application of normative rules stipulating clear Council approval of non-Article 51 uses of force and termination of that authorization when a permanent cease-fire or other definitive end to the hostilities is reached.

. . . .

IV. Cease-Fire Agreements and Security Council Authorizations of Force

. . . .

The basic Charter principles that we have outlined—peaceful resolution of disputes and Security Council control over the use of force—require that, even where there is no termination provision in the authorization to use force, that authority expires with a permanent cease-fire unless explicitly continued. Such authorization cannot be revived by the contractees unilaterally; it is for the Security Council to consider whether a breach of that cease-fire justifies a reauthorization of force.

The Effect of the UN Charter

Pre-Charter law permitted a party to a cease-fire to treat its serious violation as a material breach, entitling it to resume fighting. The United States and the United Kingdom rely on this law to argue that Iraqi violations of the inspection regime established during the cease-fire revived the Resolution 678 authorization to use force. This view ignores the prohibition on the use of force under Article 2(4), which, properly understood, "changes a basic legal tenet of the traditional armistice." Post-Charter law holds that UN-imposed cease-fires reaffirm the basic obligation of states to refrain from using force. Therefore, a violation of the cease-fire, even a material breach, is not a ground for the other party to revive hostilities, at least short of an armed attack giving rise to an Article 51 right of self-defense. As one scholar writes, "Although terms of the armistice agreements dealing with important but collateral issues such as verification regimes or implementation mechanisms may fail, the overriding obligation not to resort to force as a means of dispute settlement is deemed severable and continues to be binding."

Strong policy interests make it advisable that Security Council authorizations to use force be terminated by the establishment of a cease-fire unless explicitly and unambiguously continued by the Council itself. The overall objectives of the Charter and the changes it has wrought in the law on the use of force mandate that disputes be settled by peaceful means, if at all possible. This suggests that the end of hostilities, however that is accomplished, reestablishes the Article 2(4) obligations on all states not to use force, including in implementing cease-fire provisions, and not to do so without a new Council authorization. For example, no one would seriously claim that member states of the UN command would have the authority to bomb North Korea pursuant to the 1950 authorization to use force if in 1999 North Korea flagrantly violated the 1953 armistice.

Moreover, that rule is especially necessary when the Security Council control consists of authorizing member states to use force, a more decentralized approach than envisioned by the Charter's framers. To permit authorizations to continue after a permanent cease-fire ends hostilities would allow individual states to use force indefinitely, a result that would undermine the Council's control—particularly when the authorized states include a permanent member that could veto any Council resolution terminating the authorization. Every authorization to use force thus far has been at the behest of a permanent member of the Security Council. This trend is likely to continue. In such situations the potential use by that permanent member of what has been termed a "reverse veto" to block the Council from terminating an authorization that no longer enjoys the support of the international community undermines the Council's legitimacy and Charter-mandated control over the use of force.

. . . .

POSTSCRIPT

On December 16, 1998, the United States and the United Kingdom launched four days of air strikes against Iraq, claiming that Iraq had failed to cooperate fully with the UN weapons inspectors [as part of their cease-fire obligations]. The United States and Great Britain acted without obtaining the Security Council's authorization to use force and, thus, as this article has argued, in violation of the Charter. The United States and Great Britain argued, as they had in February, that they had legal authority to use force to respond to Iraqi cease-fire violations. Other nations again disagreed.

The December 1998 bombing of Iraq suggests that our hopeful prediction of a strengthened role for the Security Council in controlling the use of force must be tempered by the painful reality of superpower unilateralism....

The debate over what action should be taken to require Iraq to comply with its cease-fire obligation to destroy its weapons of mass destruction reached a critical point in late 2002 when unilateral military action by the United States and United Kingdom against Iraq seemed likely. After considerable debate and disagreement as to whether another UN Security Council resolution beyond Resolution 687 (1991)[51] was required for states lawfully to use force against Iraq to require it to destroy its weapons of mass destruction, the Security Council finally adopted Resolution 1441 (2002).[52]

Security Council Resolution 1441

57th Sess., 4644th mtg., U.N. Doc. S/RES/1441 (2002)

Recalling all its previous relevant resolutions, in particular its resolutions 661 (1990) of 6 August 1990, 678 (1990) of 29 November 1990, 686 (1991) of 2 March 1991, 687 (1991) of 3 April 1991, 688 (1991) of 5 April 1991, 707 (1991) of 15 August 1991, 715 (1991) of 11 October 1991, 986 (1995) of 14 April 1995, and 1284 (1999) of 17 December 1999, and all the relevant statements of its President,

....

Recognizing the threat Iraq's noncompliance with Council resolutions and proliferation of weapons of mass destruction and long-range missiles poses to international peace and security,

Recalling that its resolution 678 (1990) authorized Member States to use all necessary means to uphold and implement its resolution 660 (1990) of 2 August 1990 and all relevant resolutions subsequent to Resolution 660 (1990) and to restore international peace and security in the area,

Further recalling that its resolution 687 (1991) imposed obligations on Iraq as a necessary step for achievement of its stated objective of restoring international peace and security in the area,

Deploring the fact that Iraq has not provided an accurate, full, final, and complete disclosure, as required by resolution 687 (1991), of all aspects of its programmes to develop weapons of mass destruction and ballistic missiles with a range greater than one hundred and fifty kilometres, and of all holdings of such weapons, their components and production facilities and locations, as well as all other nuclear programmes, including any which it claims are for purposes not related to nuclear-weapons-usable material,

Deploring further that Iraq repeatedly obstructed immediate, unconditional, and un-restricted access to sites designated by the United Nations Special Commission (UNSCOM) and the International Atomic Energy Agency (IAEA), failed to cooperate fully and un-conditionally with UNSCOM and IAEA weapons inspectors, as required by resolution 687 (1991), and ultimately ceased all cooperation with UNSCOM and the IAEA in 1998,

Deploring the absence, since December 1998, in Iraq of international monitoring, in-spection, and verification, as required by relevant resolutions, of weapons of mass

------

51. S.C. Res. 687, 46th Sess., 2981st mtg., U.N. Doc. S/RES/687 (1991).
52. S.C. Res. 1441, 57th Sess., 4644th mtg., U.N. Doc. S/RES/1441 (2002).

destruction and ballistic missiles, in spite of the Council's repeated demands that Iraq provide immediate, unconditional, and unrestricted access to the United Nations Monitoring, Verification and Inspection Commission (UNMOVIC), established in resolution 1284 (1999) as the successor organization to UNSCOM, and the IAEA, and regretting the consequent prolonging of the crisis in the region and the suffering of the Iraqi people,

Deploring also that the Government of Iraq has failed to comply with its commitments pursuant to resolution 687 (1991) with regard to terrorism, pursuant to resolution 688 (1991) to end repression of its civilian population and to provide access by international humanitarian organizations to all those in need of assistance in Iraq, and pursuant to resolutions 686 (1991), 687 (1991), and 1284 (1999) to return or cooperate in accounting for Kuwaiti and third country nationals wrongfully detained by Iraq, or to return Kuwaiti property wrongfully seized by Iraq,

Recalling that in its resolution 687 (1991) the Council declared that a ceasefire would be based on acceptance by Iraq of the provisions of that resolution, including the obligations on Iraq contained therein,

Determined to ensure full and immediate compliance by Iraq without conditions or restrictions with its obligations under resolution 687 (1991) and other relevant resolutions and recalling that the resolutions of the Council constitute the governing standard of Iraqi compliance,

Recalling that the effective operation of UNMOVIC, as the successor organization to the Special Commission, and the IAEA is essential for the implementation of resolution 687 (1991) and other relevant resolutions,

Noting the letter dated 16 September 2002 from the Minister for Foreign Affairs of Iraq addressed to the Secretary General is a necessary first step toward rectifying Iraq's continued failure to comply with relevant Council resolutions,

Noting further the letter dated 8 October 2002 from the Executive Chairman of UNMOVIC and the Director General of the IAEA to General Al-Saadi of the Government of Iraq laying out the practical arrangements, as a follow-up to their meeting in Vienna, that are prerequisites for the resumption of inspections in Iraq by UNMOVIC and the IAEA, and expressing the gravest concern at the continued failure by the Government of Iraq to provide confirmation of the arrangements as laid out in that letter,

Reaffirming the commitment of all Member States to the sovereignty and territorial integrity of Iraq, Kuwait, and the neighbouring States,

Commending the Secretary General and members of the League of Arab States and its Secretary General for their efforts in this regard,

Determined to secure full compliance with its decisions,

Acting under Chapter VII of the Charter of the United Nations,

1. *Decides* that Iraq has been and remains in material breach of its obligations under relevant resolutions, including resolution 687 (1991), in particular through Iraq's failure to cooperate with United Nations inspectors and the IAEA, and to complete the actions required under paragraphs 8 to 13 of resolution 687 (1991);

2. *Decides*, while acknowledging paragraph 1 above, to afford Iraq, by this resolution, a final opportunity to comply with its disarmament obligations under relevant resolutions of the Council; and accordingly decides to set up an enhanced inspection regime with the aim of bringing to full and verified completion the

disarmament process established by resolution 687 (1991) and subsequent resolutions of the Council;

3. *Decides* that, in order to begin to comply with its disarmament obligations, in addition to submitting the required biannual declarations, the Government of Iraq shall provide to UNMOVIC, the IAEA, and the Council, not later than 30 days from the date of this resolution, a currently accurate, full, and complete declaration of all aspects of its programmes to develop chemical, biological, and nuclear weapons, ballistic missiles, and other delivery systems such as unmanned aerial vehicles and dispersal systems designed for use on aircraft, including any holdings and precise locations of such weapons, components, sub-components, stocks of agents, and related material and equipment, the locations and work of its research, development and production facilities, as well as all other chemical, biological, and nuclear programmes, including any which it claims are for purposes not related to weapon production or material;

4. *Decides* that false statements or omissions in the declarations submitted by Iraq pursuant to this resolution and failure by Iraq at any time to comply with, and cooperate fully in the implementation of, this resolution shall constitute a further material breach of Iraq's obligations and will be reported to the Council for assessment in accordance with paragraphs 11 and 12 below;

5. *Decides* that Iraq shall provide UNMOVIC and the IAEA immediate, unimpeded, unconditional, and unrestricted access to any and all, including underground, areas, facilities, buildings, equipment, records, and means of transport which they wish to inspect, as well as immediate, unimpeded, unrestricted, and private access to all officials and other persons whom UNMOVIC or the IAEA wish to interview in the mode or location of UNMOVIC's or the IAEA's choice pursuant to any aspect of their mandates; further decides that UNMOVIC and the IAEA may at their discretion conduct interviews inside or outside of Iraq, may facilitate the travel of those interviewed and family members outside of Iraq, and that, at the sole discretion of UNMOVIC and the IAEA, such interviews may occur without the presence of observers from the Iraqi government; and instructs UNMOVIC and requests the IAEA to resume inspections no later than 45 days following adoption of this resolution and to update the Council 60 days thereafter;

6. *Endorses* the 8 October 2002 letter from the Executive Chairman of UNMOVIC and the Director General of the IAEA to General Al-Saadi of the Government of Iraq, which is annexed hereto, and decides that the contents of the letter shall be binding upon Iraq;

7. *Decides* further that, in view of the prolonged interruption by Iraq of the presence of UNMOVIC and the IAEA and in order for them to accomplish the tasks set forth in this resolution and all previous relevant resolutions and notwithstanding prior understandings, the Council hereby establishes the following revised or additional authorities, which shall be binding upon Iraq, to facilitate their work in Iraq:

   — UNMOVIC and the IAEA shall determine the composition of their inspection teams and ensure that these teams are composed of the most qualified and experienced experts available;

   ....

   — UNMOVIC and the IAEA shall have unrestricted rights of entry into and out of Iraq, the right to free, unrestricted, and immediate movement to and from inspection sites, and the right to inspect any sites and buildings, including immediate, unimpeded, unconditional, and unrestricted access to Presidential Sites equal to that at other sites, notwithstanding the provisions of resolution 1154 (1998);

— UNMOVIC and the IAEA shall have the right to be provided by Iraq the names of all personnel currently and formerly associated with Iraq's chemical, biological, nuclear, and ballistic missile programmes and the associated research, development, and production facilities;

— Security of UNMOVIC and IAEA facilities shall be ensured by sufficient UN security guards;

— UNMOVIC and the IAEA shall have the right to declare, for the purposes of freezing a site to be inspected, exclusion zones, including surrounding areas and transit corridors, in which Iraq will suspend ground and aerial movement so that nothing is changed in or taken out of a site being inspected;

....

— UNMOVIC and the IAEA shall have the right at their sole discretion verifiably to remove, destroy, or render harmless all prohibited weapons, subsystems, components, records, materials, and other related items, and the right to impound or close any facilities or equipment for the production thereof; and

— UNMOVIC and the IAEA shall have the right to free import and use of equipment or materials for inspections and to seize and export any equipment, materials, or documents taken during inspections, without search of UN-MOVIC or IAEA personnel or official or personal baggage;

8. *Decides* further that Iraq shall not take or threaten hostile acts directed against any representative or personnel of the United Nations or the IAEA or of any Member State taking action to uphold any Council resolution;

9. *Requests* the Secretary General immediately to notify Iraq of this resolution, which is binding on Iraq;.... .

11. *Directs* the Executive Chairman of UNMOVIC and the Director General of the IAEA to report immediately to the Council any interference by Iraq with inspection activities, as well as any failure by Iraq to comply with its disarmament obligations, including its obligations regarding inspections under this resolution;

12. *Decides* to convene immediately upon receipt of a report in accordance with paragraphs 4 or 11 above, in order to consider the situation and the need for full compliance with all of the relevant Council resolutions in order to secure international peace and security;

13. *Recalls*, in that context, that the Council has repeatedly warned Iraq that it will face serious consequences as a result of its continued violations of its obligations; ...

Comments

1.   The military action in Iraq in 2003 led to national inquiries into the international legal basis for the use of force. The Dutch Committee of Inquiry on Iraq established by the Prime Minister released its 550-page report in 2010. It concluded that the Security Council resolutions on Iraq passed during the 1990s did not constitute a mandate for the US-British military intervention in 2003. Despite certain ambiguities in the text, the

wording of Resolution 1441 cannot reasonably be interpreted (as the Dutch government did) as authorizing individual Member States to use military force to compel Iraq to comply with the Security Council's resolutions, without authorization from the Security Council.[53]

2.   In the UK, the then Prime Minister, Gordon Brown announced on 15 June 2009 that an Inquiry would be conducted to identify lessons that can be learned from the Iraq conflict. The Iraq Inquiry was officially launched on 30 July 2009. The Chair of the Inquiry, Sir John Chilcot, explained that the Inquiry 'will consider the period from the summer of 2001 to the end of July 2009, embracing the run-up to the conflict in Iraq, the military action and its aftermath. We will therefore be considering the UK's involvement in Iraq, including the way decisions were made and actions taken, to establish, as accurately as possible, what happened and to identify the lessons that can be learned. Those lessons will help ensure that, if we face similar situations in future, the government of the day is best equipped to respond to those situations in the most effective manner in the best interests of the country.'[54] As of October 2014, the Report had not yet been released.

Questions for Discussion

1. To what extent can military enforcement action be taken by the Council under Article 42 even if agreements under Article 43 have not been concluded?

2. How has the Council sought in practice to employ its military enforcement powers in the absence of Article 43 agreements? What is the legal basis for, and limitations on, this technique employed by the Council? To what extent has the Council complied in practice with these limitations in the case of Iraq?

3. Do collective self-defense measures need to be authorized by the Security Council? Are there collective self-defense measures that have been authorized by the Council? What differences are there between such measures and those where the Council has delegated its Chapter VII powers to member states?

4. Can UN member states use force on a unilateral basis in order to implement Security Council resolutions?

5. To what extent, if at all, does the conclusion of a permanent cease-fire or other definitive end to hostilities terminate a Security Council authorization to use force?

6. (i) Can States use force against Iraq to ensure that it comply with its obligations under Security Council Resolution 687? (ii) To what extent, if at all, would your answer in (i) change if Resolution 1441 had not been adopted by the Council?

Comments

1. In addition to the case of Iraq, the Security Council has delegated its military enforcement powers to member states in order to counter a use of force by a state or entities within a state in the cases of Korea, Somalia, and Bosnia.[55] With the exception of the case of Iraq, the enforcement action taken by member states was directed against non-state

---

53. Report of the Dutch Committee of Inquiry on Iraq, 12 January 2010.

54. http://www.iraqinquiry.org.uk/.

55. *See* Danesh Sarooshi, The United Nations and the Development of Collective Security 168–74, 187–94 (1999).

entities. As mentioned above, this practice represents a broadening of the original conception of a threat to the peace to include non-state actors.

2. The Security Council has also delegated its Chapter VII powers to member states to achieve a variety of other objectives. These include: the implementation by parties of an agreement that the Council has deemed is necessary for the maintenance or restoration of peace; the carrying out of a naval interdiction; and the achievement of humanitarian objectives.[56]

3. The Council has delegated its military enforcement powers to member states to ensure the implementation by parties of an agreement in the cases of Haiti (ensuring the implementation of the Governors Island Agreement)[57] and the Central African Republic (Resolution 1125 (1997),[58] to ensure the implementation of the Bangui Agreements). The case of Haiti, by way of example, is considered briefly in the extract below.

Dan Sarooshi, The United Nations and the Development of Collective Security
233–35, 237, 243–44 (1999)

1. The Governors Island Agreement: the restoration of democracy in Haiti

On 29 September 1991, the democratically elected government of Haiti was overthrown in a violent coup by members of the Haitian armed forces.... The OAS [Organization of American States] response to the coup saw a meeting of OAS Foreign Ministers resolve to recognise President Aristide and his government as Haiti's only 'legitimate' government and to recommend that all OAS Member States take specific action to isolate economically and diplomatically the '*de facto*' government which had seized control. The OAS imposed a non-mandatory trade embargo against Haiti which included the freezing of Haitian assets, the banning of arms sales, and the diplomatic isolation of the '*de facto*' government. With the failure of these and subsequent efforts of the OAS to dislodge the coup leaders in Haiti from political power, the matter was taken to the United Nations. Subsequently, in response to a request from the 'legitimate' government of Haiti, the UN Security Council passed resolution 841. Acting under Chapter VII, the Security Council imposed a universal arms embargo against Haiti; froze all overseas assets controlled by the '*de facto*' government; and threatened to impose a worldwide trade embargo against Haiti to come into force on 23 June 1993 unless the UN Secretary-General advised otherwise. The effect of these sanctions and growing international pressure, saw the head of the '*de facto* authorities' in Haiti conclude with President Aristide the Governors Island Agreement under the auspices of both the OAS and the United Nations. It was primarily the signing of this accord and the New York Pact of June 1993, which generated hopes for a possible peaceful transition to the restoration of democracy and prompted the Security Council in resolution 861 to suspend the economic sanctions imposed by resolution 841. The Governors Island Agreement provided for the return to Haiti of President Aristide, his designation of a Prime Minister, and the eventual return to democracy in Haiti. Subsequently, however, in the light of persistent breaches by the *de facto* authorities in Haiti of their obligations under these accords, the Secretary-General concluded that there was a serious and persistent

---

56. For analysis of Security Council delegations to achieve the latter two objectives, *see id.* at 194–232.

57. S.C. Res. 841, 48th Sess., 3238th mtg., U.N. Doc. S/RES/841 (1993).

58. S.C. Res. 1125, 52d Sess., 3808th mtg., U.N. Doc. S/RES/1125 (1997).

lack of implementation of the Governors Island Agreement, and considered, in the light of the opinions expressed also by the Secretary-General of the Organization of American States (OAS), that it was necessary to revoke the suspension of the measures set forth in resolution 841 (1993). Accordingly, the Council decided in resolution 873 to reimpose the sanctions set forth in resolution 841, unless the parties complied with their commitments. In its resolution 917 of 6 May 1994, the Council imposed additional sanctions against Haiti and decided that the sanctions regime would not be lifted until the following events had taken place: the creation of a proper environment for the deployment of UNMIH, the retirement of the Commander-in-Chief of the Armed Forces of Haiti, and the resignation or departure from Haiti of the Chief of Staff of the Armed Forces of Haiti and the Chief of the Metropolitan Zone of Port-au-Prince.

. . . .

The Council decided that economic sanctions were not sufficient to dislodge the coup leaders from Haiti when it passed resolution 940. . . .

4. *Acting* under Chapter VII of the Charter of the United Nations, [the Security Council] authorizes Member States to form a multinational force under unified command and control and, in this framework, to use all necessary means to facilitate the departure from Haiti of the military leadership, consistent with the Governors Island Agreement, the prompt return of the legitimately elected President and the restoration of the legitimate authorities of the Government of Haiti, and to establish and maintain a secure and stable environment that will permit implementation of the Governors Island Agreement, on the understanding that the cost of implementing this temporary operation will be borne by the participating Member States; . . .

6. *Requests* the Secretary-General to report on the activities of the team within thirty days of deployment of the multinational force;

. . . .

[The Security Council 8. *Decides* that the multinational force will terminate its mission and UNMIH will assume the full range of its functions described in paragraph 9 below when a secure and stable environment has been established and UNMIH has adequate force capability and structure to assume the full range of is functions; the determination will be made by the Security Council, taking into account recommendations from the Member States of the multinational force, which are based on the assessment of the commander of the multinational force, and from the Secretary-General; . . .

13. Requests the Member States acting in accordance with paragraph 4 above to report to the Council at regular intervals, the first such report to be made not later than seven days following the deployment of the multinational force.]

. . . .

In terms of the effectiveness of the exercise of these delegated Chapter VII powers, early diplomatic efforts by the US saw the '*de facto* military authorities in Haiti' agree to give up their control, thus allowing the democratically elected authorities of Haiti to resume governance of the country and the [multinational force (MNF)] to enter Haiti unopposed. These forces, spearheaded by the US, entered Haiti on 19 September 1994. Accordingly, in the majority of the reports of the MNF to the Council there are statements to the effect that the threat to the MNF was low. In fact, according to some of the reports, the gradual expansion of the MNF was 'welcomed into the outlying areas by the local population.' This is the major reason for the relative success of the operation in Haiti as compared to that which took place in Somalia. The difference being that the local population was not hostile to the foreign intervention and in fact perceived the foreign forces as carrying out desirable and legitimate objectives on behalf of the international community which were of benefit to the Haitian population as a whole. Moreover, the ability of the multinational force in Haiti to work with a government perceived as legitimate by the majority of the population in Haiti was of crucial importance.

————————

It is UN support for democracy in a more proactive manner (as a form of conflict prevention) that is, in part, the focus of Professor John N. Moore's suggested reform of the UN collective security machinery.

John Norton Moore, *Toward a New Paradigm: Enhanced Effectiveness in United Nations Peacekeeping, Collective Security, and War Avoidance*
37 Va. J. Int'l L. 811, 814–15, 855–56, 858–59, 878, 881–89 (1997)

In an age in which peacekeeping has almost become a synonym for U.N. operations, it is easy to forget that an original central purpose of the organization was collective security against aggression in order to end war. In the words of the Preamble of the Charter, the United Nations was intended:

> [T]o save succeeding generations from the scourge of war, which twice in our lifetime has brought untold sorrow to mankind ... and for these ends ... to unite our strength to maintain international peace and security....

As with the League of Nations before it, there was a belief that aggression could be ended if all the nations of the world, and particularly the major powers, would unite against any aggressor. This concept of collective security, which has an appealing and powerful logic, was to be the principal answer to war.

    ....

If the United Nations was only episodically able to directly confront aggression, it was able to develop a variety of important roles in fact finding, mediation, truce supervision, peacekeeping, and (usually, but not always constructively) the development of international law and the promotion of human rights. And following the end of the cold war, and the successful action against Iraq's aggression, there was a short period of enthusiasm for an enhanced U.N. role in maintaining world order. This euphoria, however, quickly died in the chaos of Somalia, the genocidal "ethnic cleansing" of Bosnia, and the killing fields of Rwanda. It seems to have been succeeded by a pervasive skepticism, perhaps even deeper than that at the height of the cold war.... Today, when the United Nations is considered at all, the focus seems to be on avoiding "mission creep" through careful differentiation of peacekeeping and peace enforcing missions, and on the need for organizational reform that conventional wisdom sees as the root of the U.N. malaise. Paradoxically, even in the aftermath of the cold war, with the removal of many of the barriers to effective action, the future of the United Nations is challenged as never before.

    ....

Certainly, U.N. missions should be undertaken only carefully in settings where they will be important and where they will decisively prevail. And certainly such missions should be implemented with careful attention to the precise role the United Nations is undertaking and with realistic resources and rules of engagement. Beyond these important reforms, however, I believe the root of the problem is "old thinking" in the basic paradigm with which we are approaching the United Nations, and other institutions and approaches for war avoidance. What is most needed in enhancing U.N. effectiveness is a more realistic paradigm in our thinking about the role of the United Nations, and war avoidance more generally. Perhaps, of course, there is no newer paradigm that will point the way to a more effective United Nations. If so, while we can improve certain obvious deficiencies, such as the repeated mismatch between resources and missions, we will still likely be doomed to further incrementalism and muddling through.

    ....

Recently, Professor Inis Claude has added a brilliant insight about yet another difficulty with collective security in the real world—a problem now more evident after the at least partial removal of the cold-war veto in the Security Council. That difficulty relates to the need for a major power to take the lead when a war-fighting challenge is substantial. He points out that in both Korea and the Gulf, U.S. leadership (and also U.K. leadership in the Gulf) was essential to the successful U.N. collective security operations. While after the Gulf War popular expectations were raised of UN empowerment once the cold-war impasse had ended, he notes that removing the parking brake (i.e., the veto) does not make a car climb the hill....

    ....

While all of these real-world constraints on collective security, as sought within a U.N. framework, have cogency, I believe one of the most important problems with U.N. efforts at collective security has largely been overlooked and yet stands starkly revealed in the light of the new paradigm. The new paradigm focuses clearly on the importance of deterrence in controlling aggression and democide. While collective security is theoretically a powerful form of deterrence, as it was implemented within the League, and only to a slightly lesser extent within the United Nations, it fails to provide much deterrence. Thus, as we have seen, effective deterrence must be before the fact, must have effective sanction or war fighting ability in place or credibly deliverable to the threatened theater, and must be politically credible—if not certain.

    ....

The democracy/deterrence (government structures) paradigm offers a new focus for this core role that should be vigorously explored. First, it suggests that the norm-creating and assistance roles of the United Nations should be focused on consistent long-run efforts at democracy building, in addition to the important, and I believe included, goal of human rights. By promoting a peaceful transition to democracy it is likely from current evidence that we will be reducing the incidence of major wars, reducing democide and famine, and even enhancing economic and environmental well-being. Second, it suggests that collective security should be refocused in a realistic deterrence framework. Collective security can only be effective in war and democide avoidance if it acts in advance in a certain and effective deterrence mode, rather than remaining a vague but unlikely possibility of after-the-fact action. Moreover, if the new hypothesis is right, then effective deterrence at the international system level is the key to less of the things, such as war and democide, we abhor, and more of the things we cherish and value, that is, enhanced world order and prosperity. And as a third major emphasis, a new paradigm that focuses on government structures suggests the importance of considering such structures in operations such as Somalia, rather than drawing artificial lines that may be counterproductive in the real world. That is, a government structures paradigm suggests to us the importance of focus on government structures in U.N. operations [within a particular target-state], rather than abjuring any such focus in a cloud of non-intervention political correctness....

....

IV. Some Suggestions for Strengthening the United Nations to Meet the New Challenges

....

B. Strengthening the Role of the Security Council: Toward Realistic Burden Sharing

There has always been an ambivalence about some members of the United Nations possessing a veto in the Security Council....

Rather than regarding the Security Council as suspect [because of the veto], we would more effectively serve the goals of the United Nations by focusing squarely on the responsibilities of great powers that accompany the veto and their unique Security Council role. As one example, I believe it would have been preferable to have structured the new International Criminal Court as a tool of the Security Council, initiated in specific cases at its request, rather than as yet another Court to be created by general treaty and with the usual and critical enforcement problems that go with such an arrangement. The anomalies that go with this latter way of proceeding are to not include aggression within the general jurisdiction of the Court (thus going backward from Nuremberg and the need to add deterrence to aggression), and to include a great hole in the Statute of the Court for settings in which the nation state decides to prosecute (a provision that will work reasonably in democratic countries and not at all in those non-democratic countries committing aggression and slaughtering their people).

One reality worth noting in this connection is that a strong and effective United States is required for an effective Security Council and United Nations. As the only remaining superpower, and a nation with a unique war-fighting and logistics capability, the United States is an indispensable actor for U.N. success through time. The United States has been actively involved not only in the classic collective security actions of Korea and the Gulf, but also in most major post-Gulf War peacekeeping actions of the United Nations, including Somalia, Bosnia, Haiti, Rwanda, and now possibly the Rwanda/Zaire border area. This reality in turn presents unique problems for the United States and the U.S. military. One fact that is central to more active and effective engagement is putting to rest the pervasive myths of Vietnam that disastrous foreign policy adventures inevitably result from small commitments, and that even appropriately configured and led military forces cannot prevail against small indigenous forces. My colleague, Robert F. Turner, and I teach a seminar at Virginia dedicated to exploding these and other myths of Vietnam. Such myths, however, have a powerful hold on popular culture and amplify a national fear of foreign entanglements that resonates as far back as the Administration of George Washington.

....

C. Strengthening Mechanisms for Ensuring that Operations Undertaken are Only Undertaken with Adequate Forces and Rules of Engagement to Prevail and Prevail Promptly

Settings which may require serious war-fighting, as in the Gulf, and even in Somalia and in Bosnia, must generally, with perhaps some exceptions otherwise meeting the functional requirement, be undertaken with the cooperation of a major power, such as the United States, or a major collective defense organization, such as NATO, in order to ensure adequate forces to prevail and prevail promptly. In such settings these nations or organizations will supply the command structure and must approve any rules of engagement. Similarly, collective security operations such as those in Korea and the Gulf, must be undertaken under the unitary command of the lead power. I do not propose to change that reality.

There is, however, an acute problem in settings such as the early U.N. engagement in Bosnia, where major powers in the Security Council were supporting, or even insisting on, active engagement on the ground by U.N. peacekeeping forces, without themselves being prepared to be involved in war-fighting, and in which the United Nations may be given insufficient forces to effectively carry out its mission.

To avoid such settings in which the United Nations may intervene with insufficient forces, we should seek to encourage practices and develop mechanisms which will *require* candid and careful Security Council consideration of the element of sufficiency in all of its initial deployment decisions. One simple mechanism might be to encourage a more active role for the Secretary-General, with the advice of his military advisors, in pointing out to the Council that any role for the United Nations should be undertaken only with adequate military forces and rules of engagement. We should encourage the Secretary-General, who is ordinarily a critical U.N. figure in the implementation of peacekeeping, to candidly share any specific concerns with the Security Council when he or she is asked to carry out an operation without adequate military force to prevail and prevail promptly. Perhaps a written report from the military advisor to the Secretary-General detailing the specific concerns might be made available to the Council. We might also implement a Security Council practice requiring a separate Council report, or even decision, as to the sufficiency of implementing forces and rules of engagement *prior to* any deployment decision. There are certainly other procedural possibilities for encouraging Council decisions which will ensure that deployment decisions will be taken only when the means and the will are available to carry through successfully with the mission. *Some* such procedure which the Council finds compatible should be initiated. For the underlying issue is of great importance.

In this connection, we might also note that the theory of government failure would predict that governments of states large and small may sometimes find it attractive to respond to publicity about atrocities by *seeming to* take action while not being willing to commit adequate resources to *really* take effective action. That is, national leaders may sometimes be tempted in response to domestic crosscurrents which are simultaneously urging both "action" and that "we not get involved," to seek to take cosmetic action through the United Nations, or to externalize costs of the action (for which they get political credit) on others. This tendency is exacerbated in the many real-world settings in which selecting the right course is complex and in which powerful nations are supporting different approaches. An antidote is needed to avoid these half-hearted deployment decisions that may end up undermining present and future effectiveness of both the U.N. and the national governments involved.

D. Strengthening Measures of Deterrence and Accountability for Regime Elites

This Article has earlier urged the importance of a new and creative focus of deterrence on regime elites engaged in aggression, democide, or grave breaches of the laws of war. As a specific suggestion for pursuing this important approach, I suggest that the Security Council be asked to undertake a careful and serious review of new approaches that might be taken by states individually and by the Council itself.

The Council is a useful forum to take up this initiative for three reasons. First, the very consideration of this agenda item by the Council with respect to regime elites ordering aggression or democide should have a positive effect on deterrence. Second, I believe, consistent with my earlier argument about revitalizing the role of the Council, that some of the most effective new measures in this regard would require Council involvement and approval. Finally, undertaking such a study would give the Council, and its member governments, some new ideas for action other than the full involvement of ground forces or nothing. That sadly is too often the current dilemma.

E. More Sharply Differentiating Responses to Aggression and Defense

Collective security depends heavily on the distinction between aggression and defense. Indeed, collective security assumes some behavior against which the remainder of the international community will stand. Similarly, as the new paradigm suggests, when we begin thinking of the role of international law in deterring aggression, it becomes evident that to be an effective deterrent, as opposed to a mere placebo, the law must effectively and strongly sanction aggression, and effectively and strongly support individual and collective defense against aggression. That is, the strength with which the international system differentiates between aggression and defense, sanctioning aggression, while supporting defense, becomes crucial for the very effectiveness of international law as a normative system. For if the international system responds by treating aggression and defense as equivalent, or, even worse, it largely focuses its ire on the defensive response, then the deterrent effect of law is largely lost.

In contrast with this necessity, there is at present a pervasive climate of ignoring aggression, while focusing critically on the democratic nation defensive response. Some examples from the recent Gulf War, just to cite one setting presenting this phenomenon, are:

- Arguments that the coalition forces had no right of defense once the issue had been referred to the Security Council for action,
- Arguments that if a collective defense action does not immediately respond to an armed attack (for example, it delays three months for a necessary military build-up and an effort at peacemaking as did the coalition forces in the Gulf) that the right is lost, and
- Arguments that an occupied country (for example, the State of Kuwait following the Iraqi attack) has no one that can lawfully request collective defense assistance on their behalf following a successful blitzkrieg attack.

Sadly, all of these examples are real; they were seriously advanced by well-known international law scholars and, in one case, by the then Secretary-General of the United Nations. At the same time, there was relative silence as to the illegality of the blatant Iraqi attack from these sources. This unbalanced focus on efforts to restrain effective defense against aggression I refer to as a "minimalist" approach to the important right of individual and collective defense under the Charter. It parallels a similar "minimalist" approach to deterrence within the international relations and peace studies literature.

It is important in enhancing the effectiveness of international law as a deterrent against aggression, and in turn strengthening collective security that depends in large part on the normative structure, to more sharply differentiate aggression and defense, and to more effectively and consistently sanction aggression while supporting the defensive right. To treat the two sides of this synergy as equivalent is to doom law to irrelevance in deterring aggression.

This principle may also suggest the importance of U.N. operations taking sides, and not remaining neutral, in the face of aggression or democide. While it may be attractive to hope for non-involvement in the face of outrageous behavior, in such settings it is likely that only involvement can carry out the mission. If, for example, as has recently been reported, the same Hutu militia that had engaged in democide in Rwanda was holding hundreds of thousands of Hutu civilians in refugee camps in Zaire against their will, it is hard to understand how this largely escaped notice for two years, or why the solution to the problem was a "neutral" peacekeeping force.

F. A New Democratic Caucusing Group Within the United Nations: The "Group of Democratic Nations"

If the new paradigm is correct, with its focus on the importance of government structures, then I would propose the creation within the United Nations of a new informal caucusing group that might be called the "Group of Democratic Nations." Whether or not democratic government is the most important feature correlated with the goals of the United Nations, as is strongly suggested by the evidence today, democracy, and the democratic nations, are a critically important part of the global landscape. In a world that organizes caucusing groups within the United Nations both on a regional basis and every functional basis imaginable, it seems strange that there is no democratic nation caucusing group.

Such a "Group of Democratic Nations" could be a powerful force for democracy building and the rule of law within the United Nations. It could also usefully transcend some of the regional or functional identifications now extant in the Organization.

Importantly, such a group should be begun with participation from all regional groups and should not be aimed at any nation. Rather it should be a force for peace, human rights, economic development, environmental protection, and health and well-being on a world-wide basis.

. . . .

The United Nations should become an important forum for democracy building and rule of law engagement, as a long-run strategy to promote the goals of the United Nations. In the short run, it must become more effective in deterrence, and should more systematically consider the effects of its actions on deterrence and its own credibility to carry out its missions.

There is a world of difference between theoretical collective security and effective deterrence that enables avoidance of war and democide. The latter must be the focus for future U.N. reform.

———————

No 'Group of Democratic Nations' has been formed within the UN, but the topic of the rule of law has been placed high on the UN agenda since Professor John N. Moore wrote this article. The General Assembly has adopted multiple resolutions on the rule of law.[59] The Security Council has held thematic debates on the rule of law[60] and adopted resolutions on, *inter alia*, women, peace and security (SC res 1325, SC res. 1820), children in armed conflict (e.g., SC res 1612), and the protection of civilians in armed conflict (e.g., SC res 1674).

Questions for Discussion

1. What reforms would you suggest to the way in which the Council at present employs its military enforcement powers to maintain or restore peace and security?

2. To what extent and in what ways should the UN promote democracy?

---

59. A/RES/61/39, A/RES/62/70, A/RES/63/128.
60. S/PRST/2003/15, S/PRST/2004/2, S/PRST/2004/32, S/PRST/2005/30, S/PRST/2006/28.

UN Transitional Administrations

The UN has used transitional administrations, also known as 'international territorial administrations' (ITA) to govern a state or part of the territory of a state where there has been the collapse of state institutions, a widespread paralysis of governance and the breakdown of law and order. The UN Missions in Kosovo and East Timor are the leading examples of UN transitional administrations. Subsequent UN ITAs and technical assistance missions in Sierra Leone (UNAMSIL) and the Congo (MONUC) have been less ambitious in their scope. There has also been a tendency for the UN to partner with regional organizations, as in the UN African Union Mission in Darfur (UNAMID, since 2007) and the African Union Mission to Somalia (ANISOM, since 2007).

Michael J. Matheson, *United Nations Governance of Postconflict Societies*
95 Am. J. Int'l L. 76, 77–83 (2001)

I. PREVIOUS UN INVOLVEMENT IN GOVERNANCE
OF POSTCONFLICT SOCIETIES

. . . .

The first major UN exercise in governance came with the 1991 Agreement on a Comprehensive Political Settlement of the Conflict in Cambodia. This Agreement established a Supreme National Council—composed of representatives of the contending Cambodian factions—that delegated various governmental functions to the United Nations, which were to be exercised by a UN Transitional Authority in Cambodia (UNTAC) to be created by the Security Council. Specifically, UNTAC was given direct control over Cambodian agencies in the areas of foreign affairs, national defense, finance, public security, and information; supervision over other agencies that could influence the outcome of elections; and the right to investigate various other government organs to determine whether they were undermining the accords and, if so, to take corrective measures. This authority was limited by the requirement that UNTAC follow any "advice" approved by a consensus of the factions represented in the Supreme National Council, to the extent that it did not conflict with the Agreement. All of these aspects of UNTAC's role were added to the more traditional UN functions of enforcing a cease-fire and military demobilization, and conducting elections to establish a permanent national government.

The Security Council did not authorize these UNTAC functions pursuant to its mandatory powers under Chapter VII of the Charter; rather, the Council acted under its authority to make recommendations to states for the settlement of disputes. Therefore, the consent of the Cambodian factions was an essential ingredient of the legal basis for UNTAC's mandate. In subsequent crises during the 1990s, however, the Council regularly acted under Chapter VII, which gave its decisions the force of international obligation, with or without the consent of the states in question (or other entities).

Between the signing of the 1991 Cambodian accords and the eruption of the 1999 Kosovo crisis, the Council exercised its Chapter VII authority on many occasions to end conflicts, disarm hostile forces, restore order, punish war criminals, and the like, but it did not attempt to directly govern territories affected by a conflict. For example, the mandate of the UN force introduced into Haiti included replacement of the military regime with the elected Aristide government but not UN governance of the country. The NATO-led force introduced into Bosnia with the endorsement of the Security Council was broadly authorized to enforce the cease-fire and the redeployment of forces required by the Dayton Accords, but governance was left to the Bosnian political entities. Clearly, the United Nations was reluctant to assume the functions of governing the territory of a sovereign state if indigenous institutions were available for that purpose.

II. UN Governance of Kosovo

....

On June 10, 1999, the Security Council adopted Resolution 1244, a binding decision under Chapter VII. Among other things, the resolution:

— decided on the deployment in Kosovo "under United Nations auspices, of international civil and security presences";

— authorized member states and relevant international organizations to establish the international security presence "with substantial North Atlantic Treaty Organization participation" and "under unified command and control," and empowered the security presence to use "all necessary means" to establish a safe environment and facilitate the safe return of all displaced persons;

— authorized the Secretary-General to establish "an international civil presence in Kosovo in order to provide an interim administration for Kosovo under which the people of Kosovo can enjoy substantial autonomy within the Federal Republic of Yugoslavia, and which will provide transitional administration while establishing and overseeing the development of provisional democratic self-governing institutions"; and

— enumerated the main responsibilities of the international civil presence, which included promoting the establishment, pending a final settlement, of substantial autonomy and self-government; performing basic civilian administrative functions; supporting economic reconstruction; maintaining civil law and order; and facilitating a political process designed to determine Kosovo's future status.

The mission of the international security presence—the Kosovo Force or KFOR—was similar to the traditional role of UN-authorized forces in restoring and maintaining order and removing or demilitarizing contending forces. The mission of the international civil presence, on the other hand, was unprecedented in scope and complexity.

The Secretary-General promptly created the international civil presence—known as the United Nations Interim Administration Mission in Kosovo, or UNMIK—and appointed a special representative to direct it. The special representative then assumed "all ... executive authority with respect to Kosovo," including the right to appoint "any person to perform functions in the civil administration in Kosovo, including the judiciary, or remove such person." He likewise asserted the authority to administer all funds and property of the FRY and the Republic of Serbia in the territory of Kosovo.

The structure he created for UNMIK reflected the heavy dependence of the operation on the efforts and resources of various states and international organizations. The mission was divided into four main components, each led by a different organization. First, a civil administration component, led by the UN Organization, was created to handle public administration and civil affairs (in particular, to revive health, education, and other public services); police (both to carry out police functions in the short term and to train and develop an indigenous force for the longer term); and judicial affairs (to reconstitute the law enforcement system, including by selecting and training judges, prosecutors, and prison personnel from all ethnic groups).

Second, an institution-building component, led by the Organization for Security and Cooperation in Europe (OSCE), assumed the tasks of promoting democratization and institution building (including the training of local administrators, the development of local political and professional organizations, and the creation of independent news media); elections (including voter registration and the development of provisional institutions for self-government); and human rights (particularly ensuring compliance with international norms by police, courts, and detention authorities).

Third, a humanitarian component, led by the UN High Commissioner for Refugees, took responsibility for humanitarian assistance (including coordination of efforts by various international organizations to provide food, shelter, and medical treatment for the many displaced Kosovars, as well as to revive agricultural production) and mine action (to identify and remove land mines and unexploded ordnance).

Fourth, a reconstruction component, led by the European Union (EU), was put in charge of the reconstruction of key infrastructure and other economic and social systems, including the development of a market-based economy, the coordination of international financial assistance, and the resolution of trade, currency, and banking matters.

The performance of all these functions required that UNMIK identify the law that would govern in Kosovo and make new law as needed, which was done through the promulgation by the special representative of a series of regulations. The first of these regulations asserted that "[a]ll legislative and executive authority with respect to Kosovo, including the administration of the judiciary, is vested in UNMIK and is exercised by the Special Representative of the Secretary-General." It then stated that "[t]he laws applicable in the territory of Kosovo prior to 24 March 1999"—that is, the laws imposed by the FRY prior to its withdrawal from Kosovo—"shall continue to apply in Kosovo insofar as they do not conflict with" the mandate given to UNMIK by the Security Council or any regulations issued by UNMIK.

Later the special representative specifically repealed certain FRY legislation that had been adopted in 1991 concerning property rights and housing, which he found to be discriminatory. However, this action did not go far enough for Kosovar Albanians and the newly appointed Kosovar judges, who considered FRY laws to have been "part and parcel of the revocation of Kosovo's prior autonomous status and an instrument of oppression since then." Ultimately conceding this point, the special representative decided that, in addition to his own regulations, the law applicable in Kosovo would be the law in force in Kosovo on March 22, 1989—that is, the law of Kosovo before the FRY stripped away its autonomy.

In any event, the special representative has continued to make law for Kosovo where existing law did not suffice. By regulation, he has promulgated new law on such subjects as customs duties and taxes; currency use and regulation; the importation and sale of petroleum and other products; and the regulation of telecommunications services, banks, and nongovernmental organizations. He has created new court structures, defined their jurisdiction, and provided for the appointment and duties of judges and prosecutors.

In effect, UNMIK has functioned as a general lawmaking authority over a wide range of subjects, and will undoubtedly continue to do so as further needs and gaps in existing law are discovered. This additional activity will likely include the promulgation of new codes of criminal law and procedure to fill gaps in previous law and to ensure the availability of a fully functioning legal system to control interethnic violence as well as common crimes. New law may also be needed to enable UNMIK to administer or privatize state-owned and socially owned property with a view to encouraging economic revival and development.

Finally, UNMIK's mandate from the Security Council includes "the establishment, pending a final settlement, of substantial autonomy and self-government in Kosovo," and "[f]acilitating a political process designed to determine Kosovo's future status," taking full account of the Rambouillet accords. Those accords, which had been elaborated prior to the NATO air campaign, would have adopted an "interim Constitution" for Kosovo if the FRY had been willing to sign. Although the accords recognized that Kosovo was and would continue to be part of the FRY, that constitution would have given substantial governmental powers to a Kosovar political structure, with the exception of certain reserved areas such as monetary policy, defense, and most aspects of foreign policy. It will now fall to UNMIK to implement this aspect of the Security Council's instruction to provide for an interim autonomous political structure for Kosovo, and then to pursue an undefined "political process" to reach a "final settlement." This would be no small achievement.

III. UN GOVERNANCE OF EAST TIMOR

Within months after assuming the task of pacifying and governing Kosovo, the United Nations faced a task of comparable scope and complexity in East Timor. (In some ways it was more difficult, in that the United Nations did not have the assistance of such institutions as NATO, the EU, and the OSCE.)

East Timor had been subject to Portuguese control until 1975, when Indonesian forces occupied it over the protest of the Security Council. After many years of negotiation, Portugal and Indonesia agreed in 1999 to ask the UN Secretary-General to conduct a "popular consultation" of the East Timorese to determine whether they wanted independence or autonomy within Indonesia. This consultation took the form of a direct ballot in which the East Timorese rejected such autonomy. When this result was announced, however, anti-independence militias engaged in an intense campaign of violence and intimidation that resulted in heavy destruction in East Timor and the displacement of hundreds of thousands of civilians.

In response, the Security Council acted under Chapter VII of the Charter to authorize the establishment of a multinational force empowered to use all necessary means to restore order and facilitate humanitarian assistance. This Australian-led force, known as the International Force for East Timor, quickly restored order, but the violence had already destroyed a large number of homes and other buildings, caused the collapse of the civil administration and judicial systems, and damaged or destroyed much of the waterworks and other essential public services.

As a result, the Security Council once again decided to entrust the United Nations with the burden of governance of a territory shattered by conflict. In Resolution 1272, again acting under Chapter VII, the Council established the United Nations Transitional Administration in East Timor (UNTAET), which was given "overall responsibility for the administration of East Timor" and empowered "to exercise all legislative and executive authority, including the administration of justice." The mandate of UNTAET included establishing an "effective administration," assisting in the "development of civil and social services," and supporting "capacity-building for self-government." UNTAET would be led by a special representative "who, as the Transitional Administrator, will be responsible for all aspects of the United Nations work in East Timor and will have the power to enact new laws and regulations and to amend, suspend or repeal existing ones."

Once appointed, the transitional administrator rapidly exercised his authority through the issuance of regulations in much the same manner as the special representative for Kosovo. In the first of these regulations, he decreed that "[u]ntil replaced by UNTAET regulations or subsequent legislation of democratically established institutions of East Timor, the laws applied in East Timor prior to 25 October 1999 [would] apply in East Timor" insofar as they did not conflict with Resolution 1272 or UNTAET directives. At the same time, he ordered that a series of Indonesian security laws no longer be applied in East Timor. In subsequent regulations, he promulgated rules for such matters as the appointment and removal of judges and prosecutors, the regulation of fiscal and budgetary matters, and currency transactions.

Similarly to UNMIK in Kosovo, UNTAET adopted as immediate priorities (apart from the restoration of order) facilitating the return and care of refugees and displaced persons, the restoration of public services through the reconstruction of essential infrastructure and the recruitment and training of administrators and civil servants, and the rebuilding of the judiciary and the law enforcement system. The revival of economic activity was also urgently required, since an estimated 80 percent of the population lacked any means of support.

As to the political and economic future of East Timor, the situation is substantially different from that of Kosovo. The international community never accepted that East Timor was a part of Indonesia or lawfully subject to Indonesian control. Further, under the accords concluded with Portugal and the United Nations in May 1999, if the Secretary-General determined that autonomy within Indonesia was not acceptable to the people of East Timor (as he did, following the "popular consultation"), Indonesia agreed to take the necessary steps to terminate its links with East Timor and transfer authority to the United Nations, which was to initiate the transition to independence. Accordingly, the Secretary-General has stated that "fundamental and urgent policy decisions" must now be made for the purpose of "setting the foundations of an independent East Timor."

Ralph Wilde, International Territorial Administration: How Trusteeship and the Civilizing Mission Never Went Away

(Oxford University Press, 2008) pp. 192–94, 200, 203–07, 232, 234–35
(footnotes omitted)

In order to appreciate how its policy-role is understood, it is helpful to approach international territorial administration negatively, in terms of what it is not. ITA is seen as a substitute for what is regarded as the 'normal' conduct of territorial administration: by actors whose spatial identity, as 'local', corresponds to that of the territorial unit and its population International territorial administration is being and has been used as a substitute for the involvement of 'local' actors in the activity of territorial administration, either partially or fully, because of two perceived 'problems' associated with the 'normal' model.

In the first place, the use of international territorial administration is understood as a response to what might be termed a 'sovereignty problem' relating to the presence of local actors exercising administrative control over the territory. In the second place, the use of international territorial administration is understood as a response to what might be termed a 'governance problem' relating to the conduct of territorial administration by local actors. The first perceived 'problem' concerns the identity of the local actors being substituted in the role of carrying out administration; the second perceived 'problem' concerns the quality of governance being exercised in the territory....

The First Purpose: Responding to a 'Sovereignty Problem'

... In Leticia, West Irian, Eastern Slavonia, the Saar, and Mostar, international territorial administration was used or proposed to solve what might be called a 'sovereignty problem' understood to have been caused by the identity of certain local actors who enjoyed or might have come to enjoy administrative control. The key to appreciating how the policy-role of ITA is understood here is the link between administrative control and sovereignty.... [T]he question of who exercises administrative control is a crucial issue when determining issues of sovereignty-as-ownership. Sometimes, international territorial administration has been understood as a means of interfering in this sovereignty process by calibrating the level of administrative control by certain local actors, or displacing such actors completely in the role of exercising such control. In such circumstances the value of its introduction is understood through the idea that the international actor involved is 'neutral' when compared with the local actors in relation to whom the particular sovereignty dispute relates. In being explained in terms of a 'sovereignty problem' like this, the operation of international territorial administration is understood in several different ways. In Leticia, Kosovo, West Irian, and Eastern Slavonia, it was seen as a response to a concern stemming from a wider question about the status of the territory. In the Saar and Mostar, international territorial administration was regarded as the 'response' to the status question itself.

> ....

The use of international territorial administration explained in terms of a 'sovereignty problem' implies that what might be called the 'normal' sovereignty model is considered to be in some sense 'defective'. The character of this model depends on whether the sovereignty question at issue is considered internal or external. When ITA 'solves' an internal sovereignty question—who will have administrative control—as in Mostar, the perceived defect lies in the notion that the preferred model of internal sovereignty, i.e., (more or less) unified governmental structures, is absent. Equally, when ITA used for this purpose is later discontinued, as happened in Mostar in 1996 with the introduction by the EUAM of an Interim City Statute, the preferred model of internal sovereignty is considered to have been 'restored': Mostar was supposedly 'reunified'. When the use of ITA is understood in terms of addressing an 'external' sovereignty question—what the international legal status of the territory should be—the perceived 'defect' it is understood to be remedying concerns the preferred model of external sovereignty not being adopted, whether this involves the territory being a state or part of a state. Here, ITA alone does not suffice, as it cannot resolve the status question by itself; the device of 'international territorial sovereignty' is also necessary....

The Second Purpose: Responding to a 'Governance Problem'

Unlike in the 'sovereignty problem' context, the perceived 'problem' here is not the identity of local actors acting in the role of the governmental authority but, rather, the conduct of governance by such actors. This problem can have two related features. Local actors may be considered practically incapable of conducting any governance at all. The perceived 'problem', therefore, is the supposed 'lack' of governance. Alternatively, there may be a concern that local actors will exercise their governmental powers in a manner that conflicts with certain policy objectives. Here, the perceived 'problem' concerns the supposed absence of 'good governance'....

> ....

In addition to filling a perceived 'vacuum' in local territorial governance, international territorial administration has been associated with broader and more ambitious purposes concerning governance. The perceived 'problems' here are concerned not with the existence of governance, but the quality of governance being performed. Four main policy objectives for governance can be identified in this use of ITA: first, the attainment of a certain status for the territorial unit concerned; secondly, a broad agenda concerning effectiveness, democracy, the rule of law, and liberal economic policy; thirdly, the furtherance of migration policy; and, fourthly, the exploitation of natural resources.

. . . .

As with the use of international territorial administration to respond to a perceived 'sovereignty problem', ideas about the use of ITA in relation to a perceived 'governance problem' are ultimately rooted, paradoxically, in the validity of that which ITA is understood to be the opposite of: the 'normal' and 'ideal' model of territorial governance conducted by local actors. When ITA is explained in terms of filling a vacuum that it did not create, governance itself is considered to be absent. When ITA projects are explained as means of displacing local actors in the activity of territorial administration, this is because the actors being displaced are deemed to be unwilling or unable to govern in a preferred manner. According to these ideas, if such problems with the 'normal' model were not considered to exist, there would be no need for ITA.

In 'reactive' models of ITA, local territorial administration is assumed to be the norm, to be corrected only when necessary to ensure conformity to certain policy objectives. In some of these cases, and in all the 'proactive' models of ITA, the assumption that local territorial administration is the ideal is also supported by the designation of the projects as temporary. . . .

IV. Conclusion

International territorial administration is a 'policy institution'. . . because in all cases it is understood to operate in a particular manner as a matter of policy or purposes, being used to displace local actors in the activity of territorial governance because of a perceived problem either with the identity of these actors, or with the quality of governance performed by them in the territory concerned. The exceptionalist appraisal of the Kosovo and East Timor projects ignores the place of these two projects as the latest manifestations of a rather well-established pattern of international involvement in a range of issues. In understanding ITA's future potential, one cannot focus only on the idea of altering the quality of governance carried out in the territory—the 'governance problem' category—since this takes in only half the picture. Equally, focusing exclusively on situations of plenary administration and/or ITA projects involving the United Nations arbitrarily excludes other ITA projects that have been understood to serve the same purposes in the same manner. Moreover, it would seem that labelling the projects holistically as 'temporary', 'interim', 'transitional', and so forth, . . . risks ignoring projects where the temporal duration is conceived as permanent . . . and projects which, even if they are generally understood to be a temporary, are formally constituted on an indefinite basis . . . ITA—irrespective of the particular international actor involved and despite different degrees of administrative involvement—has been used since the inception of the League as a device for certain policy ends.

Questions for Discussion

1. What is the legal basis for and status of UN transitional administrations established by the Security Council? What consequences flow from this status for: (i) the relationship between the Council and transitional administrations; and (ii) the relationship between a transitional administration and local entities within the territory being administered?

2. What are the types of governmental powers being exercised by UN international transitional administrations? What legal limitations constrain the exercise of these powers of governance?

3. What are the constraints upon a UN transitional administrator in the exercise of a general lawmaking authority within a state?

4. Does the exercise of broad powers of governance by the UN in cases such as Kosovo and East Timor represent an impermissible interference with state sovereignty?

5. In 2005, the General Assembly and Security Council jointly established a subsidiary organ called the Peacebuilding Commission with the mandate to support peace efforts in countries emerging from conflict by, *inter alia*, advising on and proposing integrated strategies for post-conflict peace building and recovery. It is not expressly authorized to exercise administrative powers in ITAs or to supervise ITAs. What role do you see the Peacebuilding Commission as playing in post-conflict zones?

The General Assembly

Comments

1. The General Assembly is the plenary body of the UN. The provision in Article 18(1) that "[e]ach member of the General Assembly shall have one vote" is based on the principle of sovereign equality set forth in Article 2 of the Charter. The main committees of the General Assembly, which are composed of all members of the Assembly, also operate by one state, one vote.

2. The required two-thirds majority for decision-making by the General Assembly in Article 18(2) is determined on the basis of those "present and voting." The Rules of Procedure explain that this means members casting an affirmative or negative vote. Thus, members who abstain are not considered as voting for purposes of identifying required majorities under Article 18.

3. The primary responsibility of the Security Council for the maintenance of international peace and security does not prevent the General Assembly from exercising a secondary responsibility in the area. Under the intended scheme of things, Articles 9–14 were not intended to provide a constitutional basis for UN military activity. Military enforcement action was undoubtedly intended to be taken by the Security Council under Articles 42 and 43. The plan of Articles 10–12 was to allow the General Assembly to discuss and make recommendations on any question arising under the Charter (Article 10) or even more specifically concerning international peace and security (Article 11), save insofar as these matters were before the Security Council and that body was exercising its Charter functions in relation to them.[61] The practice has, however, been somewhat different.

The "Uniting For Peace" Resolution

UN action in Korea was made possible by virtue of the absence of the former Soviet Union from the Security Council at the critical time. This prevented the casting of a veto, though the former Soviet Union took the view that the voting rules of the Security Council invalidated a resolution passed in the absence of a permanent member. With the rapid return of the former Soviet Union to the Security Council, it was apparent that the Council would not be able to exercise control over the enforcement action in Korea. It was against this background that General Assembly Resolution 377 (V) was passed in 1950. The effect of this Resolution was to transfer to the General Assembly authority to make certain recommendations when the Security Council was unable to carry out its responsibilities. It was through this Resolution that, in the Korean action, the initiative passed from the

---

61. *See* U.N. CHARTER art. 12.

Security Council (to which the former Soviet Union had returned) to the General Assembly—though the Unified Command had already been established by the Security Council in Resolutions 83 and 84.[62]

General Assembly Resolution 377 "Uniting for Peace"
U.N. GAOR, 5th Sess., Supp. No. 20, at 10, U.N. Doc. A/1775 (1950)

The General Assembly,

....

A

1. *Resolves* that if the Security Council, because of lack of unanimity of the permanent members, fails to exercise its primary responsibility for the maintenance of international peace and security in any case where there appears to be a threat to the peace, breach of the peace, or act of aggression, the General Assembly shall consider the matter immediately with a view to making appropriate recommendations to Members for collective measures, including in the case of a breach of the peace or act of aggression the use of armed force when necessary, to maintain or restore international peace and security. If not in session at the time, the General Assembly may meet in emergency special session within twenty-four hours of the request therefor. Such emergency special session shall be called if requested by the Security Council on the vote of any seven members, or by a majority of the Members of the United Nations; ...

D.W. BOWETT, UNITED NATIONS FORCES
290–92 (1964)

3. The Resolution on Uniting for Peace

....

The underlying assumption of ... section [A] of the Uniting for Peace Resolution is that the General Assembly may do by recommendation anything that the Security Council can do by decision under Chapter VII. The Communist States have always denied this, insisting that all matters concerning the use of force are reserved exclusively to the Security Council. They base this viewpoint on Articles 11(2), 43 and 47, and Article 24. The relationship between the Security Council and the General Assembly as revealed by Articles 11(2) and 43 has already been discussed above. It must be repeated that the International Court, during its advisory opinion on the *Expenses Case,* interpreted the term "action" in Article 11(2) to mean "enforcement action." Whereas this view indicates that the Assembly is free to take many other types of action without referring to the Security Council, it also implies that it may never, even by recommendation, undertake enforcement action. It is possible that the Court did not intend to convey this impression, and the point is not directly germane to its conclusions on the matter of expenses. It does, nevertheless, only mention the authority of the Assembly to take "action" under Article 11(2) when this involves the organization of "peace-keeping" operations, at the request, or with the consent, of the States concerned. At no time does the Court uphold the right of the Assembly to *recommend* enforcement measures (though it emphasizes repeatedly that only the Council may order coercive action), either under the Charter generally or under the Uniting for

---

62. S.C. Res. 83, U.N. SCOR, 5th Sess., 474th mtg., at 5, U.N. Doc. S/RES/83 (1950); S.C. Res. 84, U.N. SCOR, 5th Sess., 476th mtg., at 5, U.N. Doc. S/RES/84 (1950).

Peace Resolution. Moreover, the opinion of the Court studiously avoids all mention of that Resolution, even though it was much discussed in the Pleadings.

Article 24 of the Charter provides that the members of the United Nations "confer upon the Security Council primary responsibility for the maintenance of international peace and security." In support of the Uniting for Peace Resolution attention has been drawn to the fact that Article 24 gives the Security Council only "primary" responsibility, and not exclusive responsibility in matters affecting international peace. The secondary or residual responsibility of the General Assembly is apparent, as Articles 10, 11 and 14 testify. The International Court has also upheld this view of the secondary responsibility of the Assembly under Article 24(1),[63] though without seeking to relate its comments on this point to the Uniting for Peace Resolution.

Some mention must also be made at this stage of Article 12, for its guidance on the spheres of competence of the Assembly and Council is also instructive so far as the Uniting for Peace Resolution is concerned. Under the terms of this Article the General Assembly may make no recommendation on a question while the Security Council is exercising its functions in respect of that question, unless the Security Council so requests. Article 12 does not seem to prevent the General Assembly from *discussing* a situation which is being dealt with by the Security Council, nor does it specify that the Permanent Members of the Security Council all have to favour a request from that organ that the Assembly make a recommendation. The provision in Section A of the Uniting for Peace Resolution for the convening of an emergency session of the Assembly on the vote of any seven members when the Council "fails to exercise its primary responsibility for the maintenance of international peace and security" is thus compatible with the terms of the Charter. Section A also provides for the calling of an emergency session "by a majority of the Members of the United Nations"; as this would not occur until the Council had failed to act, and the residual responsibility of the Assembly implied by Article 24(1) came into play, it cannot be accepted that this is contrary to the Charter....

Christine Gray, International Law and the Use of Force
260 (3rd edition, 2008)

Article 12 has also been gradually eroded. The General Assembly has made recommendations even when the Security Council was dealing actively with an issue. If the Security Council was not actually exercising its functions at that moment, or if a resolution was blocked by a veto, the General Assembly has assumed it is free to make recommendations, provided that these did not directly contradict a Security Council resolution. The General Assembly has accordingly passed a series of resolutions condemning certain behaviour when the Security Council could not agree on a resolution or could not take measures against a wrongdoing state. Some ... states were unhappy at this; they said that the repetition of resolutions condemning states was a pointless rhetorical exercise.... [t]he General Assembly [has] regarded itself as free to call on the Security Council to lift the arms embargo on Bosnia-Herzegovina when the Security Council had been divided as to whether to do so. Technically it may be possible to make out a case on the basis of the practice of the two bodies that this did not contravene Article 12, but it seems to be precisely the type of situation that Article 12 was designed to prevent.

---

63. In the *Certain Expenses* case, see extract below.

The issue of the delimitation of powers between the Security Council and the General Assembly in relation to the maintenance of peace and security provided in part the basis for a claim in the *Expenses* case that the Assembly did not possess the competence to establish the first UN peacekeeping force in the Middle East (UNEF I). The International Court did not rely on the Uniting for Peace resolution in reaching its decision in the *Expenses* case.

Certain Expenses of the UN
1962 I.C.J. 151, 163–65 (July 20)

This argument [on expenses] leads to an examination of the respective functions of the General Assembly and of the Security Council under the Charter, particularly with respect to the maintenance of international peace and security.

    ....

The responsibility conferred [on the Council by Article 24 of the Charter] is "primary," not exclusive. This primary responsibility is conferred upon the Security Council, as stated in Article 24, "in order to ensure prompt and effective action." To this end, it is the Security Council which is given a power to impose an explicit obligation of compliance if for example it issues an order of command to an aggressor under Chapter VII. It is only the Security Council which can require enforcement by coercive action against an aggressor.

The Charter makes it abundantly clear, however, that the General Assembly is also to be concerned with international peace and security. Article 14 authorizes the General Assembly to "recommend measures for the peaceful adjustment of any situation, regardless of origin, which it deems likely to impair the general welfare or friendly relations among nations, including situations resulting from a violation of the provisions of the present Charter setting forth the purposes and principles of the United Nations". The word "measures" implies some kind of action, and the only limitation which Article 14 imposes on the General Assembly is the restriction found in Article 12, namely, that the Assembly should not recommend measures while the Security Council is dealing with the same matter unless the Council requests it to do so. Thus while it is the Security Council which, exclusively, may order coercive action, the functions and powers conferred by the Charter on the General Assembly are not confined to discussion, consideration, the initiation of studies and the making of recommendations; they are not merely hortatory.

    ....

The argument supporting a limitation on the budgetary authority of the General Assembly with respect to the maintenance of international peace and security relies especially on the reference to "action" in the last sentence of Article 11, paragraph 2. This paragraph reads [in part] as follows:

> "The General Assembly may discuss any questions relating to the maintenance of international peace and security brought before it ... and, except as provided in Article 12, may make recommendations with regard to any such question to the State or States concerned or to the Security Council, or to both. Any such question on which action is necessary shall be referred to the Security Council by the General Assembly either before or after discussion."

The Court considers that the kind of action referred to in Article 11, paragraph 2, is coercive or enforcement action. This paragraph, which applies not merely to general questions relating to peace and security, but also to specific cases brought before the General Assembly by a State under Article 35, in its first sentence empowers the General Assembly, by means of recommendations to States or to the Security Council, or to both, to organize peacekeeping operations, at the request, or with the consent, of the States concerned. This power of the General Assembly is a special power which in no way derogates from its general powers under Article 10 or Article 14, except as limited by the last sentence of Article 11, paragraph 2. This last sentence says that when "action" is necessary the General Assembly shall refer the question to the Security Council. The word "action" must mean such action as is solely within the province of the Security Council. It cannot refer to recommendations which the Security Council might make, as for instance under Article 38, because the General Assembly under Article 11 has a comparable power. The "action" which is solely within the province of the Security Council is that which is indicated by the title of Chapter VII of the Charter, namely "Action with respect to threats to the peace, breaches of the peace, and acts of aggression". If the word "action" in Article 11, paragraph 2, were interpreted to mean that the General Assembly could make recommendations only of a general character affecting peace and security in the abstract, and not in relation to specific cases, the paragraph would not have provided that the General Assembly may make recommendations on questions brought before it by States or by the Security Council. Accordingly, the last sentence of Article 11, paragraph 2, has no application where the necessary action is not enforcement action.

The practice of the Organization throughout its history bears out the foregoing elucidation of the term "action" in the last sentence of Article 11, paragraph 2. Whether the General Assembly proceeds under Article 11 or under Article 14, the implementation of its recommendations for setting up commissions or other bodies involves organizational activity—action—in connection with the maintenance of international peace and security. Such implementation is a normal feature of the functioning of the United Nations. Such committees, commissions or other bodies or individuals, constitute, in some cases, subsidiary organs established under the authority of Article 22 of the Charter. The functions of the General Assembly for which it may establish such subsidiary organs include, for example, investigation, observation and supervision, but the way in which such subsidiary organs are utilized depends on the consent of the State or States concerned.

The Court accordingly finds that the argument which seeks, by reference to Article 11, paragraph 2, to limit the budgetary authority of the General Assembly in respect of the maintenance of international peace and security, is unfounded.

Frustration with the deadlock in the Security Council over the situation in Syria in 2011–12 led the General Assembly to take the step of passing a resolution 'deploring the failure of the Security Council' to take effective action in Syria, with a large majority (133 Member States) voting in favour of the resolution.

GENERAL ASSEMBLY RESOLUTION 66/253B

U.N. GAOR, 66th Sess., 3 August 2012

The General Assembly,

Expressing its deep concern at the lack of progress towards implementation of the six-point plan, and deploring the failure of the Security Council to agree on measures to ensure the compliance of Syrian authorities with its decisions,

...

4. *Demands* that all parties immediately and visibly implement Security Council resolutions 2042 (2012) and 2043 (2012) in order to achieve a cessation of armed violence in all its forms by all parties, thereby creating an atmosphere conducive to a sustained cessation of violence ...

8. *Stresses again* the importance of ensuring accountability and the need to end impunity and hold to account those responsible for human rights violations, including those violations that may amount to crimes against humanity;

9. *Encourages* the Security Council to consider appropriate measures in this regard;

Questions for Discussion

1. What is the delimitation of powers between the Security Council and the General Assembly in relation to the maintenance or restoration of peace and security?

2. What are the arguments for and against the legality of the Uniting for Peace Resolution? Are some parts of the Resolution lawful while others are not?

3. How important is the debate about the legal status of this Resolution? What military action has the General Assembly been involved in? Does the legality of this action depend upon the Uniting for Peace Resolution? In what other ways, if any, may the General Assembly hold the Security Council accountable for its action or inaction on international peace and security?

UN Peacekeeping

Peacekeeping has become one of the most successful contributions of the UN to conflict management. These forces now carry out wide-ranging functions that include the following: observance of cease-fires, truces, and armistices; frontier control; interpositionary functions; security functions in zones placed under UN control; assistance in the restoration of law and order (including in some cases a function similar to policing); and plebiscite duties.

The main principles that govern UN peacekeeping today were established at its inception: the requirement of consent from both the host state (the state on whose territory the force is to be stationed) and the states contributing forces; and the limitation that peacekeepers should not use military force in a proactive manner.

The UN Charter does not, however, provide in express terms for peacekeeping operations, and this led to the questioning in the early years of its constitutional basis.

Constitutional Basis

ROSALYN HIGGINS, PROBLEMS AND PROCESS: INTERNATIONAL LAW AND HOW WE USE IT
174–76 (1994)

The West looked for alternatives to allow the United Nations some role in keeping the peace. It was argued that the failure of the Security Council to agree on the establishment of a UN Force meant only that the peace could therefore not be enforced; nor could UN members be *compelled* to offer troops. But if, the argument went, the peace could be kept not by enforcing it, but by policing a territory at the *request* of a state; and if other UN members *volunteered* for such a police force, then such action could be taken. While it was not what the Charter had envisaged, it was not prohibited by it, and it was directed towards a Charter objective—peace. This was the view of the United States and the West generally, and was supported by those relatively few Third World countries who were already UN members.

It was not, however, the view of the Soviet Union and its allies. They took the view that the Charter had very specific provisions for the use of force by the United Nations, exemplified by the agreements on UN forces to be agreed under Article 43, and it followed that, if those procedures could not be acted upon, alternatives *not* provided for in the Charter were necessarily unlawful. There were two further points of contention. The Charter envisaged, through the control given to the intended Military Staff Committee (i.e. the Chiefs of Staff of the Big Five), that an effective veto would obtain over the operations of a UN force. But a police force operating outside the envisaged Charter plans would avoid control by veto, and indeed would be under the day-to-day control of the Secretary-General. Was this not to move beyond what the founding instrument had intended?

Further, it was contended by supporters of the idea of UN peacekeeping that a UN police force could be ordered not only by the Security Council, but even by the General Assembly, should the operation of the veto in the Security Council make it impossible for that body to act. These ideas were acceptable to the West, which could at that time with ease command a majority in voting in UN bodies, and which had confidence in the Secretary-General. They were totally unacceptable to the Soviet Union, which, finding itself in a constant minority, needed to rely on the veto whenever possible.

It was against this background that the first UN peace-keeping force was established in 1956. After the UK-French-Israeli intervention in Suez, and the use by the United Kingdom and France of the veto to prevent a condemnatory resolution in the Security Council, Secretary-General Dag Hammarskjold proposed the establishment of a UN peace-keeping force by the General Assembly. This force would oversee a cease-fire and would monitor the withdrawal of the British, French, and Israeli forces from Egyptian territory. The invading forces and Egypt all welcomed the idea of such a force. The Soviet Union, while obviously wishing the United Kingdom and France out of Suez, was opposed to the idea of the UN Emergency Force (UNEF) for the reasons of principle that I have outlined. When the costs of UNEF were distributed among UN members, in the same proportions and way as other UN expenses, the Soviet Union and its allies refused to pay, as did France. From the outset the financing of UN peace-keeping was insecure and problematic.

The peace-keeping activity itself was successful, however. UNEF did indeed oversee the withdrawal of all foreign troops, and kept the peace in that area from 1956 to 1967. It was followed by the successful UN Observer Group in the Lebanon in 1958 (UNOGIL), and many other UN peace-keeping operations around the world—in the Congo, Indian subcontinent, Cyprus, and elsewhere. The idea of peace-keeping has taken deep roots.

Rosalyn Higgins, 1 United Nations Peacekeeping 1946–1967
262–63, 265 (1969)

The question of whether the General Assembly could legally establish a peacekeeping force was essentially interwoven with the question of the "consent" of the host state; for the majority view has been that enforcement action against a state may well be reserved to the Security Council, but UNEF represents "policing" action which, far from being carried out against a state, depends upon the specific consent of the host government. This, it has been contended, is perfectly appropriate for the Assembly to authorize. Nor, it should be added, was UNEF established in order to compel a withdrawal by the British, French, and Israeli forces.

In his second and final report on the plan for setting up of an Emergency Force, the Secretary-General touched on some of these constitutional issues:

QUESTIONS OF PRINCIPLE
....

9. Functioning, as it would, on the basis of a decision reached under the terms of the [General Assembly] resolution 337(V) "Uniting for Peace", the Force, if established, would be limited in its operations to the extent that consent of the parties concerned is required under generally recognized international law. While the General Assembly is enabled to *establish* the Force with the consent of those parties which contribute units to the Force, it could not request the Force to be *stationed* or *operate* on the territory of a given country without the consent of the Government of that country. This does not exclude the possibility that the Security Council could use such a Force within the wider margins provided under Chapter VII of the United Nations Charter. I would not for the present consider it necessary to elaborate this point further, since no use of the Force under Chapter VII, with the rights in relation to Member States that this would entail, has been envisaged.

....

30. By mid-September 1957, UNEF will have completed ten months of duty, during which it has been called upon to undertake important responsibilities involving a considerable variety of tasks. The Command for the Force, established by General Assembly resolution 1000 (ES-I), was to "secure and supervise the cessation of hostilities in accordance with all the terms of General Assembly resolution 997 (ES-I)." The General Assembly, in resolution 1001 (ES-I), approved guiding principles for the organization and functioning of the Force, as set forth in the Secretary-General's report of 6 November 1956 (A/3302), whereby, as must follow from its status under the Charter, the Force could not be stationed or operate on a country's territory without that country's consent.

31. The Force, which has an international character as a subsidiary organ of the General Assembly, as affirmed in its regulations, was not established to undertake enforcement actions. While UNEF has a military organization, it does not use all normal military methods in achieving the objectives defined for it by the General Assembly....

ROSALYN HIGGINS, PROBLEMS AND PROCESS: INTERNATIONAL LAW AND HOW WE USE IT
264–65 (1994)

[T]he International Court of Justice had in an advisory opinion in 1962 [the *Expenses* case] to address certain legal problems concerning the financing of UN peace-keeping. Dealing there with the issue of whether the expenses of the UNEF in Suez and of the UN operation in the Congo were to be considered as expenses of the organization within the meaning of Article 17(2) of the Charter, the Court felt constrained to address first the question of the lawfulness of those actions (though that was not in terms the question it was asked). It emphasized that each of the actions was lawful because it was *not* an action under Article 42 but rather a peace-keeping action, in which the UN military role was at the request of the host state, and not directed against the host state. The Court examined the effect of the failure to conclude agreements under Article 43 of the Charter. But, as it had found UNEF and ONUC not to be enforcement actions under Article 42, it only asked itself the narrower question of whether *peace-keeping* action was permissible in the absence of Article 43 agreements. Answering that in the affirmative, the Court [in the *Expenses* case] said:

> It cannot be said that the Charter has left the Security Council impotent in the face of an emergency situation when agreements under Article 43 have not been concluded ... it must lie within the power of the Security Council to police a situation even though it does not resort to enforcement action against a State....

D.W. Bowett, United Nations Forces
415 (1964)

It may ... be deduced [based on Chapter VII] that legally the Security Council may recommend or decide upon action to safeguard international peace, even on the territory of a State which is not responsible for the breach or threat thereto, much less for an aggression, and that where the Council *decides* that such action is necessary the State must accept the presence of a United Nations Force.

However, in advancing this view it has to be conceded that an alternative view is possible, namely that the requirement of consent can only be eliminated when the action taken is in the nature of an enforcement action and that *all* peace-keeping operations, whether under Chapter VI or Chapter VII of the Charter, and whether based on a decision or rec-ommendation of the Security Council, require the consent of the territorial State. It has further to be conceded that practice to date under Chapter VII has always been in situations in which such consent existed. Moreover, the International Court of Justice placed great stress on the existence of consent to the presence of ONUC when dealing with the *Expenses* Case, and this has been the approach consistently adopted by the Secretary-General. This, then, is weighty evidence which cannot be ignored. However, the fact remains that the Charter does not specifically require consent from the territorial State to any operations undertaken pursuant to a *decision* under Chapter VII, and Article 25 may on one construction be regarded as a giving of consent in advance by all Members.

See also the extract from the *Expenses* case in the section on the General Assembly, above.

Comments

1. UN peacekeeping forces are UN subsidiary organs. Moreover, all UN peacekeeping forces have been established under the authority of the Security Council, with the exception of UNSF and UNEF I that were established by the General Assembly.

2. UN peacekeeping does not, at least in theory, involve the use of military "enforcement action" against a state. This does not, however, preclude the characterization of the es-tablishment and operation of peacekeeping forces as being an exercise by the Council of its Chapter VII powers, since not every measure under Chapter VII has to involve military enforcement action. As the International Court stated when discussing the legality of UN peacekeeping operations in the *Expenses* case: "Articles of Chapter VII of the Charter speak of 'situations' as well as disputes, and it must lie within the power of the Security Council to police a situation [i.e., conduct peace-keeping] even though it does not resort to enforcement action against a State."[64] The characterization of UN peacekeeping as a

---

64. Certain Expenses of the United Nations, 1962 I.C.J. 151, at 167 (July 20).

Chapter VII measure is also supported, importantly, by the subsequent practice of the Security Council. When establishing peacekeeping forces, the Council has very often made an Article 39 determination, the prerequisite for the use of its Chapter VII powers. Examples of this practice include the following: Resolutions 425 (1978)[65] and 426 (1978)[66] in the case of the UN Force in Lebanon (UNIFIL); Resolutions 743 (1992),[67] 947 (1994),[68] and 982 (1995)[69] in the case of the UN Protection Force in the former Yugoslavia (UNPROFOR); Resolution 990 (1995)[70] in the case of the UN Confidence Restoration Operation in Croatia (UNCRO); and Resolution 998 (1995)[71] in the case of the Rapid Reaction Force (part of UNPROFOR). See further below the discussion on 'militarized peacekeeping.'

3. The requirement of consent from both host state and troop contributing states is well-established as a fundamental principle of UN peacekeeping. More difficult, however, has been the question of a state withdrawing its consent to a UN peacekeeping operation already in place. In May 1967 the Egyptian Government asked for UNEF contingents to be pulled back from their locations. Secretary-General U Thant treated this effectively as a request for withdrawal, and decided that UNEF could not remain in Egypt without its consent. From a legal perspective, this decision is difficult to justify, since the Secretary-General ordered UNEF's withdrawal from Egypt without obtaining the authorization of the General Assembly, the political organ that had established the Force. In the report of the Secretary-General on the matter, it was contended that the Secretary-General had undertaken all reasonable consultation with the Advisory Committee on UNEF and the troop-contributing states that could have been expected under the circumstances. The report points to the failure of the Advisory Committee to convene the General Assembly and the practical difficulties in so doing as a large part of the justification for the unilateral decision that was taken. However, these considerations are of a pragmatic nature and do not address the relevant issue: whether the Secretary-General had the competence to terminate a UN peacekeeping mission.[72]

4. According to the UN, as of September 1, 2002, there have been fifty-five peacekeeping operations since 1948, although it would seem that this figure includes all observer and other peacekeeping related missions.[73] UNEF I was the first UN peacekeeping force. It has been followed by a large number of other operations which include, for example: UN Security Force in West Irian (UNSF) 1962;[74] UN Operation in the Congo (ONUC) 1960;[75] UN Force in Cyprus (UNFICYP) 1964;[76] UNEF II (1973); UNIFIL (1978); UN Mission in the Central African Republic (MINURCA) 1998; UN Interim Administration Mission in Kosovo (UNMIK) 1999; UN Mission in Ethiopia and Eritrea (UNMEE) 2000; and UN Mission of Support in East Timor (UNMISET) 2002.

---

65. S.C. Res. 425, 33d Sess., 2075th mtg., U.N. Doc. S/RES/425 (1978).
66. S.C. Res. 426, 33d Sess., 2075th mtg., U.N. Doc. S/RES/426 (1978).
67. S.C. Res. 743, 47th Sess., 3055th mtg., U.N. Doc. S/RES/743 (1992).
68. S.C. Res. 947, 49th Sess., 3434th mtg., U.N. Doc. S/RES/947 (1994).
69. S.C. Res. 982, 50th Sess., 3512th mtg., U.N. Doc. S/RES/982 (1995).
70. S.C. Res. 990, 50th Sess., 3527th mtg., U.N. Doc. S/RES/990 (1995).
71. S.C. Res. 998, 50th Sess., 3543d mtg., U.N. Doc. S/RES/998 (1995).
72. *See* ROSALYN HIGGINS, 1 UNITED NATIONS PEACEKEEPING 1946–1967, 366–67 (1969); and the section Secretary-General's Role in the Conduct of UN Peacekeeping Operations, below.
73. Factual details on these and all UN peacekeeping operations are available at http://www.un.org/en/peacekeeping/.
74. ROSALYN HIGGINS, 2 UNITED NATIONS PEACEKEEPING 93–149 (1970).
75. ROSALYN HIGGINS, 3 UNITED NATIONS PEACEKEEPING 1–470 (1980).
76. ROSALYN HIGGINS, 4 UNITED NATIONS PEACEKEEPING 77–419 (1981).

5. UN military observers predated UNEF I. These observers are generally not armed and operate with the consent of the parties to report on the status of the conflict and in some cases compliance with Security Council demands (for example, UN Iraq-Kuwait Observation Mission (UNIKOM) 1991) and cease-fire obligations (for example, UN Observer Mission in Georgia (UNOMIG)), as well as in some cases the monitoring of the operations of a multinational force that is exercising delegated Chapter VII powers (for example, the UN Mission in Haiti (UNMIH) was given such a monitoring role by Council Resolution 940 (1994)[77]. The first military observer group was attached to the UN Special Committee on the Balkans (UNSCOB) in 1947.[78] Large numbers of UN military observer groups have since been used by the Council. Examples include: UN Treaty Supervision Organization, 1949;[79] UN Observer Group in Lebanon (UNOGIL) 1958;[80] UN Yemen Observation Mission (UNYOM) 1963;[81] UN Military Observer Group in India and Pakistan (UNMOGIP) 1949;[82] UN India-Pakistan Observation Mission (UNIPOM) 1965;[83] UN Angola Verification Mission (UNAVEM I) 1988; and UNCRO 1994.

6. The constitutional issues relating to UN peacekeeping and the political considerations that underlay them led to a financial crisis when the former Soviet Union and France refused to pay for UNEF I and ONUC on the basis that these operations were incorrectly funded by the General Assembly from the UN's general budget. This led to an Advisory Opinion on the matter being requested from the International Court of Justice in the *Expenses* case. As set out in the extract above, the International Court clearly dismissed the arguments of France and the former Soviet Union thereby affirming both the constitutionality of UN peacekeeping and the General Assembly's budgetary assessment.

Since that time peacekeeping finances have been raised essentially on a voluntary basis (though UNIFIL's mandate in 1978 made reference to the collective obligation to finance peacekeeping). This has proved extremely unsatisfactory. A small group of states have essentially borne the financial burden of UN peacekeeping, and successive Secretaries-General have had to operate within intolerable financial constraints and endless uncertainty.[84]

These difficulties as well as proposals for reform of the financing of peacekeeping have been highlighted in the more general UN proposals for reform of peace operations that are set out below.

7. UN forces consist of national contingents under the command of their national officers. Military discipline is a matter for these national officers, and for the military law of the troop-contributing state. The duty of these national officers is, however, to the UN and not to their national governments. These officers are responsible to the UN Force Commander, who is appointed by the Secretary-General.

8. It is standard procedure for an agreement to be entered into between the UN and the host state. This Status of Forces Agreement (which is virtually identical for all UN forces) provides for the international status of the UN force and its general immunity

77. S.C. Res. 940, 49th Sess., 3413th mtg., U.N. Doc. S/RES/940 (1994).

78. *See* ROSALYN HIGGINS, 4 UNITED NATIONS PEACEKEEPING 5–73 (1981).

79. ROSALYN HIGGINS, 1 UNITED NATIONS PEACEKEEPING 5–216 (1969).

80. *Id.* at 535–603.

81. *Id.* at 609–70.

82. ROSALYN HIGGINS, 2 UNITED NATIONS PEACEKEEPING 315–417 (1970).

83. ROSALYN HIGGINS, 3 UNITED NATIONS PEACEKEEPING 421–69 (1980).

84. For details of how a number of peacekeeping operations have in fact been financed, *see* Chapter XI in each of Volumes 1–4 of ROSALYN HIGGINS, UNITED NATIONS PEACEKEEPING.

from local jurisdiction. It seeks to provide an appropriate balance between the international mandate given to the force and the sovereignty of the host state.

Questions for Discussion

1. What is the legal basis for UN peacekeeping operations conducted under the authority of (i) the Security Council; and (ii) the General Assembly?

2. Why has nearly all UN peacekeeping emanated from the Security Council? Why have the potential powers of the Assembly, identified by the International Court in the *Expenses* case, been so little used?

3. To what extent can UN peacekeeping forces be deployed in a state that has not consented to their deployment? If a state has consented to the deployment of UN peacekeeping forces, but then subsequently withdraws its consent, must the force be withdrawn as a matter of law?

4. To what extent can UN peacekeeping forces be used to carry out military enforcement action?

The Secretary-General's Role in the Conduct of UN Peacekeeping Operations

It has to date been the consistent practice of the Council to delegate to the Secretary-General the power to determine the composition of, and exercise operational (day to day) command and control over, UN peacekeeping forces.

The Security Council, however, retains overall control over, and responsibility for, UN peacekeeping forces. The Council will often require the Secretary-General to submit periodic reports on the basis of which the Council can choose to exercise its overall control over a particular force by issuing instructions to the Secretary-General.

As the legal basis for, and mandate of, a UN peacekeeping force are rooted in a resolution of either the Council or the Assembly, it follows that the Secretary General does not possess the competence unilaterally to terminate a UN peacekeeping force—a subsidiary organ under the overall authority and control of another UN principal organ—or change its mandate unless these powers have been expressly delegated to him or her by the relevant principal organ.

The UN Secretary-General will also conclude on behalf of the UN both an agreement setting out the terms and conditions under which troops are contributed by member states to a particular peacekeeping force (Status of Forces Agreement) and an agreement between the UN and the state or states on whose territory the forces are to be stationed (Host-State Agreement).

Dan Sarooshi, *The Role of the UN Secretary-General in UN Peace-Keeping Operations*
20 Australian Y.B. Int'l L. 279, 289–94 (1999)

(b) The exercise of command and control powers over UN peace-keeping forces

. . . .

As early as 1956, in the case of UNEF, the Secretary-General exercised strategic and political control over a UN peace-keeping force. Similarly, in the second case of UN peacekeeping, in the Congo, the Secretary-General exercised authority and control over ONUC, the Secretary-General having made it clear that command and control over ONUC lay exclusively in the hands of the UN and not the host State or any contributing or other Member State. In the case of the Congo, the consequences of the delegation of command and control powers by the Council to the Secretary-General had two major consequences. First, it led to intense criticism of the role of the Secretary-General, and even led some States, notably the former Union of Soviet Socialist Republics (USSR), to call for the replacing of a single Secretary-General by a "troika", and a separate proposal to transfer operational control from the Secretary-General to a "unified African command" directly responsible to the Security Council. Both these proposals failed to gain significant support among UN Members. Second, and more serious, was the consequence that States that contributed troops to the peace-keeping force attempted to force changes in the policies of the Secretary-General. Such attempts to force changes in policy are not of course objectionable when conducted within the confines of a deliberative political organ of the UN such as the Council. However once States have contributed troops to a peace-keeping force, the attempt by States to pressure the Secretary-General either by threatening to cease to execute the orders of the UN Command, or to impose unilaterally the conditions on which their national contingents can be used, are all of dubious legality. As explained above, if a State holds a differing interpretation of the mandate of a peace-keeping force from that of the Secretary-General the appropriate forum to raise the issue is the Council. A State cannot instruct its national commander who is part of a UN peace-keeping force to disobey the orders of the Force Commander, the Secretary-General's delegate.

The absence of a legal requirement for the Secretary-General to take into consideration the views of Member States in the way that he or she exercises the command and control powers which he or she has been delegated is subject to the practical consideration that UN peace-keeping forces are consent based. Accordingly, the Secretary-General in practice will have to take into consideration, to some extent at least, the views of States that have contributed troops to such a force. This political requirement saw, in the cases of UNEF and ONUC, the establishment of "Advisory Committees" constituted of States that had contributed troops to the peace-keeping forces.... The use of Advisory Committees remains a desirable institutional innovation that the Secretary-General or Security Council should re-institute. This would help prevent the case where commanders of a national contingent receive instructions from their national command structure that are contrary to those issued by the UN Force Commander.

The Secretary-General exercises command and control over peace-keeping forces in practice by use of a Special Representative and a Force Commander. These UN Officials, as part of the UN Secretariat, are under the authority and control of the Secretary-General. The mandate of the Special Representative is usually formulated by the Secretary-General or, in exceptional cases, by the Council itself. The usual practice is that the Council simply endorses the plan put before it by the Secretary-General.

The Special Representative exercises political control over UN peace-keeping troops in the field; while the Force Commander translates the political directives emanating from the Secretary-General and the Special Representative into military commands that are given to the national commanders of each national contingent. In every peace-keeping operation the Secretary-General delegates powers—either through the Special Representative or directly—to the Force Commander. The *Summary Study* by Secretary-General Hammarskjold in respect of UNEF states that the Force Commander is the principal agent of the Secretary-General within the area of operations. These broad sub-delegations of power by the Secretary-General to a Special Representative and a Force

Commander are not *prima facie* unlawful. The reason for this derives from the status of Special Representatives and Force Commanders as part of the UN Secretariat, under the authority and control of the Secretary-General. As a result the Council, through the Secretary-General, can exercise unchallengeable authority and control over the decisions of the delegate. This position is important since, as noted above, the Council can delegate a broad power of discretion only if it retains the right to change decisions, or a policy approach to decision-making, by its delegate....

The delegation by the Secretary-General of powers of command and control over peace-keeping forces to a Special Representative and Force Commander is a necessary and important way in which the effective exercise of delegated Chapter VII powers can be carried out. This is borne out by the extensive practice of the Secretary-General in making such delegations. An important recent element of this practice has been the delegation to a Special Representative and Force Commander of the competence to order the use of force in defence of UN peace-keepers.

(c) The competence to order the use of force in defence of UN peace-keepers

It is generally accepted that the use of force by UN peace-keepers in self-defence is lawful. It is not proposed to enter into discussion here of the outer limits of this right. The present discussion is limited to examining the role of the Secretary-General when a power to use force in defence of UN peace-keepers has been given by the Council to entities external to the UN. The Council has delegated such a power to other entities in respect of the UN Protection Force (UNPROFOR) in Bosnia. The Council in resolution 836 provided:

> that ... Member States, acting nationally or through regional organizations or arrangements, may take, under the authority of the Security Council and subject to close coordination with the Secretary-General and UNPROFOR, all necessary measures, through the use of air power, in and around the safe areas in ... Bosnia ... to support UNPROFOR in the performance of its mandate....

The resolution makes clear in other provisions that Member States and regional organizations can use air power to respond to attacks on both UNPROFOR and the UN declared "safe-areas" in Bosnia. What is not so clear, however, from the terms of the resolution is who should decide when force should be used. The Secretary-General took this decision upon himself as, in effect, the representative of the UN. After noting in a report to the Council that NATO had confirmed its willingness to offer "protective air power in the case of attack against UNPROFOR in the performance of its overall mandate, if it so requests", the Secretary-General further noted: "It is of course understood that the first decision to initiate the use of air resources in this context will be taken by the Secretary-General in consultation with the members of the Security Council." This report, and thus the Secretary-General's interpretation, was expressly adopted by the Council in resolution 844 ... the adoption by the Council of a Secretary-General's report where a specific interpretation is made of a delegated mandate is taken by the Secretary-General to represent an affirmation by the Council of that interpretation. In any case the consent of the Secretary-General is required by law. The position of the Secretary-General as Commander-in-Chief of UN peace-keeping forces means that any use of force in defence of UN peace-keepers, here "close air support", would require either his or her consent or that of his or her Special Representative or Force Commander who may have been delegated this power of decision-making. The practice of the UN and NATO in the former Yugoslavia has been in accordance with this legal position....

Questions for Discussion

1. To what extent is it the Secretary-General who exercises command and control over UN peacekeeping forces?

2. To what extent is the UN Secretary-General able to exercise command and control powers over: (i) a force carrying out military action in defense of UN peacekeepers; and (ii) a UN peacekeeping force that is carrying out military enforcement action?

3. Can the Secretary-General withdraw unilaterally a UN peacekeeping force from a state where the host-state terminates its consent to the deployment of the force?

Future Mandates, Reform of UN Peacekeeping Forces and 'Militarized Peacekeeping'

Classic UN peacekeeping as set out above still continues, but it has also had to evolve in order to be effective in a number of difficult situations. UN peacekeeping forces have been deployed in situations of civil war where consent has not existed on the ground, and this has led to circumstances where peacekeeping forces have had to use force. The UN under the leadership of then Secretary-General Kofi Annan sought to incorporate lessons learned from these cases into its ongoing peacekeeping operations.

Kofi Annan, *Peace-Keeping in Situations of Civil War*
26 N.Y.U. J. Int'l L. & Pol. 623, 623–28 (1994)

Bosnia, Cambodia, Somalia: these three names alone will vividly recall the extensive relationship that has rapidly developed between peace-keeping and civil war....

....

Operations addressing situations of civil war account for nine of our seventeen current missions. Of the last eight missions deployed, seven are devoted to it. With one exception, all of these missions have come into being within the last five years.

Civil war situations are responsible for an exponential increase in our growth: where only two peace-keeping missions were deployed in our first five years, nineteen have been mounted in the last five.

Finally, the definition of peace-keeping itself has been forced to expand with the rest of the parameters. For more than forty of our forty-five years, peace-keeping was broadly understood to involve the use of multinational military personnel, armed or unarmed, under international command and with the consent of the parties, to help control and resolve conflict between hostile states and between hostile communities within a state.

In the last five years, however, hardly a single one of these parameters has remained untouched. The need for consent of the parties was overridden by humanitarian concerns. Volatile situations in the field made it necessary to expand the definitions of both self-defense and justified use of force. Even the range and nature of international command is being hotly debated.

....

Two missions offer clear and crucial lessons concerning the use of peace-keeping in situations of civil war: Somalia and Bosnia.

Somalia

Looking back over our involvement in Somalia, three points strike us immediately. First, the instability inherent in civil war makes a purely humanitarian response both dangerous and impractical. Second, all three forms of intervention open to the international community—humanitarian, security and political—must be closely and carefully coordinated if our presence is to be effective. Third, unified and unquestioned command and control is imperative if the mission is to function effectively and casualties are to be minimized.

....

Three elements have been inextricably linked in pursuing UNOSOM's [the UN peace-keeping operation in Somalia] goals—humanitarian, political, and security. Handled well, they can ensure the mission's progress; handled poorly, they constitute only a vicious circle. If security is present, humanitarian aid reaches those who need it, political instability is diminished, and restoration can move forward. If security is absent, humanitarian aid is blocked, suffering is accentuated, violence increases, political stability is weakened, and the situation is exacerbated.

....

The need for a secure environment remains an essential element in civil war peace-keeping operations. It makes the difference between a vicious circle and a constructive continuum. We must never again allow security to predominate to the point where we are seen as going to war with the people we have gone to help. But, on the other hand, we must never again subordinate security to the point where the aid we send serves only to enrich the sources of suffering and suppression. We must ensure that we are part of the solution and not part of the problem....

The stability sought in UNOSOM's mandate, however, is not dependent solely upon security, but also upon the degree of unity and cohesion within the mission itself. As long as military plans must be rearranged to accommodate national interests and egos, as long as the Force Commander does not have full authority to assign tasks or missions to subordinate commanders, and as long as home governments need to be consulted before field contingents move, the strength of the mission and the security of the people will suffer.

The most painful of all the lessons that civil war peace-keeping has taught us is that Chapter VII operations cannot be undertaken half-heartedly. A clear sense of objectives, parameters, and risks is essential at the commencement of the mission, not only because of the direction it gives, but also because of the sustained support which it provides at moments of crisis. Had legislatures and publics had to face the fact that a peace enforcement operation in Somalia might involve armed intervention and lead to casualties on both sides, they might well have been far more reluctant to intervene. But had the urgency of the appeal overridden that reluctance, it is likely that casualties, when they did occur, would not have caused the kind of exodus we are now witnessing.

Bosnia

Bosnia presents an interesting contrast to Somalia; the United Nations, having been perceived as too aggressive in the latter, is seen as too passive in the former.

Bosnia, too, raises crucial questions. What are the limits of the peace-keeper's role? How can we identify the best moment to intervene? Is a treatment that is symptomatic rather than curative plausible and justifiable in the eyes of the international community?

Peace-keepers in Bosnia have guaranteed the delivery of humanitarian aid, helped in the evacuation of displaced persons, and remained present in towns under siege to deter attacks upon them. They have not attempted to enforce peace. They have not used violence in repelling those who have interfered with their ability to carry out their mandate, except that they have, when feasible, fired back when fired upon. They have not taken up arms against those who have broken one cease-fire after another, one truce after the next. They have not been mandated to do so.

....

Peace can be neither coerced nor enforced. There must be a genuine desire for peace among the warring parties. Whether out of conviction or out of exhaustion, they must want peace. No system can achieve it when leaders use negotiation not to end conflict but merely to prolong it to advantage. And no agreement, however well-intentioned, can guarantee peace while those who sign it see greater benefit in war.

Rosalyn Higgins, *Peace and Security. Achievements and Failures*
6 Eur. J. Int'l L. 445, 449–50, 455–60 (1995)

III. The Third Phase: Developments since the End of the Cold War

....

... The Secretary-General issued his *Agenda for Peace*, a bold initiative in which specific proposals were made for new UN roles and new UN methods. In the peace and security area a remarkable new typology was offered—without ever in terms rejecting the old categories of 'enforcement' and 'peace-keeping'. The talk was now of peace-making, peace-building, peace enforcement, humanitarian assistance. In all of these, apparently, there was to be peace-keeping support. By implication, peace-keeping was thus no longer to be confined to overseeing ordered and agreed cease-fires. It could—apparently in the absence of the classic essential precondition of its deployment (along with consent), deliver humanitarian aid, provide for the introduction of democratic elections, facilitate the monitoring of human rights. UN peace-keeping had in fact already been deployed in support of some of these tasks—but with the prior agreement of the parties both for a cessation of hostilities and the achievement of the agreed outcome. The role of UNTAG in Namibia and ONUVEN in Nicaragua at the end of the decade met with a substantial success. The former operated on the basis of South Africa's consent to the Namibia peace plan; the latter on the basis of the Guatemala Agreements. But *Agenda for Peace* essentially removed the condition of prior agreements to be firmly in place.

Agenda for Peace further spoke of the need for military support of such operations, opening the way to an enforcement element *within* peace-keeping operations—thus setting aside the long-standing distinction between enforcement and peace-keeping....

....

IV. The Next Phase: A Call for Stocktaking

....

While it is, in my view, lamentable that States have failed to seize the opportunity offered by the end of the Cold War so far as effective UN enforcement is concerned, the lessons that the UN itself seems to draw from the Bosnia debacle (and indeed from the very different lessons of the failure in Somalia) are disturbing. Instead of deciding by reference to objective criteria the category of UN action required, the contemporary thinking seems to be resolutely against differentiation, with events being allowed to dictate the character of the operation, which might change from moment to moment, or have within it totally irreconcilable elements:

[T]he principles and practices which had evolved in the Cold War period suddenly seemed needlessly self-limiting. Within and outside the United Nations, there is now increasing support for 'peace-keeping with teeth'. When lightly armed peace-keepers were made to look helpless in Somalia and Bosnia, member states and public opinion supported more muscular action.... Today's conflicts in Somalia and Bosnia have fundamentally redrawn the parameters. It is no longer enough to implement agreements or separate antagonists; the international community now wants the United Nations to demarcate boundaries, control and eliminate heavy weapons, quell anarchy, and guarantee the delivery of humanitarian aid in war zones. These are clearly the tasks that call for 'teeth' and 'muscle', in addition to the less tangible qualities that we have sought in the past. In other words, there are increasing demands that the United Nations now enforce the peace, as originally envisaged in the Charter. (Kofi Annan in NATO REVIEW 4 (October 1993).)

Several observations may be made, beyond noting the tendency to conflate all experience, to reject all differentiation. Any demands that 'the United Nations now enforce the peace, as originally envisaged in the Charter', will certainly *not* be met by treating situations requiring enforcement as requiring 'muscular peace-keeping'. That is *not* what the Charter envisaged. What the Bosnia experience shows is that when States put peace-keepers in place—including those with the prime mandate to deliver humanitarian aid—then all realistic prospect of 'enforcing the peace' has gone. The enforcement of the peace of the victims of violation of Article 2(4) had already effectively been put aside by this selection of method of UN operation.

And insofar as resolutions make some later provision for protection, such as the establishing of safe havens, enforcement of these provisions also becomes intertwined with the protection of the UN personnel. Thus Resolution 836 authorized UNPROFOR '*acting in self defence*, to take the necessary measures, including the use of force, to reply to bombardments against the safe areas by any of the parties'. (Italics added). The safety of the peace-keepers becomes in effect the sole consideration. And, even then, fear of reprisals against national contingents serving in the UN operation becomes the dominant factor, and there is no realistic 'enforcement' of any sort—even when the NATO capability and the Security Council authority to act has been put in place. In February 1994 the killing of 68 civilians in Sarajevo by mortar fire led to an unprecedented response. The UNPROFOR Commander threatened to call in NATO airstrikes against Serb gun positions in the hills surrounding Sarajevo unless the guns were removed from range or placed under UN control. The ultimatum was complied with. In early April 1994 NATO executed two air support missions directed against Bosnian Serbs in the Goradze area. The request was made by UNPROFOR to protect UN military observers and liaison officers on the ground, but it also contributed to ending the Serb shelling of the city. But the UN has not followed up on that experience of the importance of credible enforcement. In later comparable circumstances of flagrant violations of the safe areas, ultimata for compliance have been indicated and ignored, with no military consequence and at the end of 1994 the siege of Bihac (another 'safe area') and associated shelling and loss of life went unpunished. The violations were instead responded to by improved UN offers on the diplomatic front.

The failure to protect the designated safe areas publicly revealed the profound disagreements within the expanded UN peace-keeping system. NATO had put in place the capacity to respond to UN requests for air strikes. But when these were asked for by the Nordic battalion in Tuzla, they received neither the support of the UN Commander in Bosnia, Sir Michael Rose, nor of Mr. Akashi, the Secretary-General's Special Representative. The UN policy was that such strikes could take place only when an attack was in progress. It hardly needs to be said that, with the sort of NATO-UN arrangement in existence, that condition will hardly if ever be met. The policy is an invitation for frequent attacks on the UN of short duration. NATO publicly expressed its disquiet at UN prevarication.

In May 1995 a negotiated truce ended, with the seizure by the Bosnian Serbs of heavy weapons that had been handed over to the UN and the use of such weapons in the Sarajevo 'safe area'. NATO airstrikes were once again ordered. The Bosnian Serbs responded by seizing 370 UN peace-keepers as hostages. This crisis was eventually resolved by diplomacy. The UN insisted that it had made no promises in order to secure the release of the hostages. But no overt promises need to be made—no one can doubt that the UN cannot in the future envisage even very occasional airstrikes while its peacekeepers are in place.

And the lesson still has not been learned. The lesson is that mixed mandate actions are doomed to failure. Rather than acknowledge this, the response was an attempt by the United Kingdom, France and the Netherlands to establish a UN Rapid Reaction Force, whose function—never entirely clear—was said to be to protect UNPROFOR from a repeat of the humiliations of May 1995 and perhaps also to be part of a NATO operation for the withdrawal of UNPROFOR, should that later be decided upon. But its role was clearly not in any direct sense to protect civilians in the various 'safe areas' or to ensure the fulfilment of UNPROFOR's mandate generally. Indeed, the Secretary-General's Special Representative was at pains to assure the Bosnian Serbs that the new UN unit would present no threat to them. If NATO's involvement already represented a mixed mandate in the former Yugoslavia, then the proposed Rapid Reaction Force constituted a further mixing of the mandate....

... Some tentative conclusions may be advanced....

6. There is little advantage, and considerable disadvantage, in setting classic peace-keeping on one side in favour of the new 'mixed function peace-keeping' enumerated in *Agenda for Peace* and since. Again, this has served to sow the seeds of uncertainty and confusion, while placing in jeopardy—perhaps irredeemably—all that had so painstakingly been built up over the years in the UN peace-keeping operations.

7. No peace-keeping force should be put in the field without prior agreement on a cease-fire and a realistic political prospect of the seriousness of that undertaking. The key peace-keeping function should remain the security of the peace on the ground. Only then should ancillary functions be added. Humanitarian assistance, electoral observation, human rights monitoring should be additional to the securing of peace, and not *in lieu* of it. Never again should the UN engage in a form of peace-keeping which endeavours to provide food while allowing the slaughter to continue.

———————

Due to criticism of the mandates and management of UN peacekeeping operations from academic, government, and other sources, the UN Department of Peacekeeping Operations established in 1995 its Lessons Learned Unit. The Unit is charged with drawing lessons from past peacekeeping efforts in order to help in the planning of future operations and the conduct of ongoing ones. An important report produced by this Unit concerned the UN Operation in Somalia (UNOSOM I & II), an operation that was given a military enforcement mandate.

THE COMPREHENSIVE REPORT ON LESSONS LEARNED FROM UNITED NATIONS OPERATION IN SOMALIA (UNOSOM)

April 1992–March 1995, *available at*
http://www.peacekeepingbestpractices.unlb.org/PBPS/Library/UNOSOM.pdf

Part II: Application of Lessons Learned from the United Nations Operation in Somalia General Framework

79. Shortly after the establishment of UNOSOM in 1992, the United Nations office responsible for peacekeeping operations was reorganized and renamed the Department of Peacekeeping Operations (DPKO). Its objective was to improve the capacity to plan, conduct and manage peacekeeping operations. The reorganization brought the political, operational, logistics, civil police, demining, training, personnel and administrative aspects of peacekeeping operations under one umbrella.

. . . .

Lesson 1. There is need for a clear and practicable mandate.

81. An effective peacekeeping operation commences with a clearly defined and practicable mandate. This lesson has been well learned in the United Nations, resulting in some successes in subsequent peacekeeping operations as well as some tragedies. In Haiti, this lesson was partially applied. The United Nations did not get involved in the operation there until it was made very clear what exactly it was required to do. This contributed in part to the effective manner in which the operation has been conducted.

. . . .

83. The formulation of a clear and practicable mandate for a peacekeeping operation remains the responsibility of the Security Council. The Secretariat regularly provides the Council with information on situations under consideration. In addition, the Council has increased the number of its own fact-finding missions to areas of conflict to assist it in determining its action.

84. These missions have enabled the Council to determine new mandates or adjust existing ones. For example, it was after the Council mission to Somalia in October 1994 that the members determined that the UNOSOM mandate must be terminated....

Lesson 2: Chapter VII and Chapter VI operations should not co-exist, and transition from Chapter VII to Chapter VI must be smooth.

85. It has been acknowledged that the United Nations is not yet capable of launching a large-scale enforcement action and that whenever in the foreseeable future it is necessary to launch such an operation under Chapter VII, it should be done by either a single State, as occurred in Rwanda in France's Operation Turquoise, or by a coalition of States, as was done early in Haiti.

86. There is wide agreement that it was a mistake in Somalia for a Chapter VII operation (UNITAF) to co-exist with a Chapter VI operation (UNOSOM I). This lesson was well applied in Haiti, where a multinational force with Chapter VII powers was phased out before a Chapter VI operation, UNMIH [UN Mission in Haiti], was deployed.

87. It was evident from Haiti that a peacekeeping operation should only follow a peace enforcement operation when conditions are secure, and that it should be granted robust rules of engagement to ensure that no party takes advantage of the change-over. Transition from peace enforcement to peacekeeping should be closely coordinated with the Secretariat

to avoid the chaotic situations which developed in the transition from UNITAF to UNOSOM II. This seems to have been done in the transition from the multinational force to UNMIH.

Lesson 3: Peacekeeping forces should not enter a conflict area if there is no political will among the parties towards reconciliation.

88. Since a peacekeeping force has no enforcement powers, it should only be deployed when the parties to a conflict have consented, as occurred with the deployment of the United Nations Operation in Mozambique (ONUMOZ) and the United Nations Angola Verification Mission (UNAVEM III)....

89. When an operation is established in a failed state, it may often be necessary to undertake civic activities and assist in repairing or developing political and economic infrastructures. This may require, as was done in Mozambique, funding for political parties to make them viable and encourage them to move from the use of arms to reconciliation.

Lesson 4: Mandates must be matched with the means to implement them.

    ....

Lesson 6: Operation in the field should be based on a fully developed, integrated structure headed by the SRSG [Special Representative of the UN Secretary-General].

    ....

Lesson 9: Command and control must be unified, and channel of command and directives clear.

116. The Secretary-General has addressed this issue in his Supplement to "An Agenda for Peace". The need for a unified command has become more apparent in the light of the UNOSOM experience. Effective command and control in peacekeeping operations demands that parallel command structures should be vigorously discouraged and that the normal unified command and control system should always apply. In order to discourage troop contingents from seeking direction from their home Governments, rules of engagement should be made as clear as possible and all operations should be within the Security Council mandate that establishes an operation.

    ....

Lesson 13: There must be clear guidelines for disarmament and demobilization, and these activities must be carried out with the agreement of the parties.

———————

On March 7, 2000, Secretary-General Annan convened a high-level panel to undertake a comprehensive review of UN peace and security activities and to present a set of recommendations to assist the UN in conducting such activities in the future. A key part of the Report of the Panel (known as the 'Brahimi Report') concerned proposals for reform of UN peacekeeping operations.

Report of the Panel on United Nations Peace Operations

55th Sess., Provisional Agenda Item 87, S/2000/809, at viii–xiii, 2–3, 10–12, 16, 20,
U.N. Doc. A/55/305 (2000)

Executive Summary

. . . .

Implications for peacekeeping: the need for robust doctrine and realistic mandates

The Panel concurs that consent of the local parties, impartiality and the use of force only in self-defence should remain the bedrock principles of peacekeeping. Experience shows, however, that in the context of intra-State/transnational conflicts, consent may be manipulated in many ways. Impartiality for United Nations operations must therefore mean adherence to the principles of the Charter: where one party to a peace agreement clearly and incontrovertibly is violating its terms, continued equal treatment of all parties by the United Nations can in the best case result in ineffectiveness and in the worst may amount to complicity with evil. No failure did more to damage the standing and credibility of United Nations peacekeeping in the 1990s than its reluctance to distinguish victim from aggressor.

In the past, the United Nations has often found itself unable to respond effectively to such challenges. It is a fundamental premise of the present report, however, that it must be able to do so. Once deployed, United Nations peacekeepers must be able to carry out their mandate professionally and successfully. This means that United Nations military units must be capable of defending themselves, other mission components and the mission's mandate. Rules of engagement should be sufficiently robust and not force United Nations contingents to cede the initiative to their attackers.

This means, in turn, that the Secretariat must not apply best-case planning assumptions to situations where the local actors have historically exhibited worst-case behaviour. It means that mandates should specify an operation's authority to use force. It means bigger forces, better equipped and more costly but able to be a credible deterrent. In particular, United Nations forces for complex operations should be afforded the field intelligence and other capabilities needed to mount an effective defence against violent challengers.

Moreover, United Nations peacekeepers — troops or police — who witness violence against civilians should be presumed to be authorized to stop it, within their means, in support of basic United Nations principles. However, operations given a broad and explicit mandate for civilian protection must be given the specific resources needed to carry out that mandate.

. . . .

Member States that do commit formed military units to an operation should be invited to consult with the members of the Security Council during mandate formulation; such advice might usefully be institutionalized via the establishment of ad hoc subsidiary organs of the Council, as provided for in Article 29 of the Charter. Troop contributors should also be invited to attend Secretariat briefings of the Security Council pertaining to crises that affect the safety and security of mission personnel or to a change or reinterpretation of the mandate regarding the use of force.

. . . .

Enhance Headquarters capacity to plan and support peace operations

The Panel recommends that Headquarters support for peacekeeping be treated as a core activity of the United Nations, and as such the majority of its resource requirements should be funded through the regular budget of the Organization. DPKO and other offices that plan and support peacekeeping are currently primarily funded by the Support Account, which is renewed each year and funds only temporary posts. That approach to funding and staff seems to confuse the temporary nature of specific operations with the evident permanence of peacekeeping and other peace operations activities as core functions of the United Nations, which is obviously an untenable state of affairs.

The total cost of DPKO and related Headquarters support offices for peacekeeping does not exceed $50 million per annum, or roughly 2 per cent of total peacekeeping costs. Additional resources for those offices are urgently needed to ensure that more than $2 billion spent on peacekeeping in 2001 are well spent. The Panel therefore recommends that the Secretary-General submit a proposal to the General Assembly outlining the Organization's requirements in full.

Following the Brahimi report, UN Member States and the UN Secretariat continued major reform efforts, including through the 'Capstone Doctrine' which set out the most important principles and guidelines for UN peacekeepers in the field (see below); Peace operations 2010 on the reform strategy of the Department of Peacekeeping Operations (DPKO); the establishment of the Peacebuilding Commission (mentioned above); and the Report of the High-level Panel on Threats, Challenges and Change on collective security for the new century.

Some of the critical operational challenges facing peacekeeping were set out in 2009 by the UN Department of Peacekeeping Operations and Department of Field Support:

The New Partnership Agenda: Charting a New Horizon for UN Peacekeeping
pp. 5–6 (2009)

The challenges facing United Nations peacekeeping are spread across five important areas of activity:

SUPPORTING A CEASEFIRE AGREEMENT BETWEEN TWO OR MORE PARTIES: Long-standing monitoring and observation missions in Cyprus, the Golan, Jammu and Kashmir, and Western Sahara continue to help deter violence. These missions are limited in size, mandate and cost. But in some cases their presence may encourage Member States to divert attention away from finding a political solution. The UN mission in Lebanon illustrates how resource-intensive and challenging such operations can be in a volatile environment.

SUPPORTING A PEACE PROCESS AND NATIONAL AUTHORITIES AFTER CIVIL CONFLICT: In some countries, UN peacekeepers face distinct challenges in helping to lay the foundations for sustainable peace. A troubled transition in the Democratic Republic of the Congo and a difficult peace process between northern and southern Sudan are straining these two large missions. These missions are struggling to strengthen political processes, which depend on regional and international support. Deterring and containing violence and protecting civilians are critical and demanding parts of their task that are complicated by both gaps in capabilities and differences of view on what robust peacekeeping can and should be expected to accomplish in the face of ongoing conflict. The large and remote territories in which these missions operate increase their difficulty as well as cost.

EXTENDING INITIAL SECURITY AND STABILITY GAINS INTO LONGER-TERM PEACEBUILDING: Many UN peacekeeping missions also serve as early peacebuilders. In Haiti, Liberia and Timor-Leste, UN peacekeepers have succeeded in establishing basic security and supporting political processes. The conditions for sustainable peacebuilding are in place. National governments, supported by the UN, international financial institutions and other partners must lead in setting strategies to deliver tangible peace dividends and economic development. UN peacekeepers must improve their ability to contribute to peacebuilding and, where called upon, to coordinate a broader effort. Peacekeeping transition and exit strategies depend on countries providing for their own security, and the UN will need to find effective ways to support this goal through better rule of law and security sector reform (SSR) assistance.

PROVIDING SECURITY AND PROTECTION IN RESPONCE TO CONFLICT: In Chad and Darfur, Sudan, UN peacekeepers are trying to minimize the effects of ongoing conflict. Their activities are focused on protecting civilians and providing security for humanitarian efforts. The willingness of major parties to these conflicts to accept and cooperate with peacekeepers is critical. The scale and remoteness of the territory make these two missions among the most expensive and difficult UN operations ever. In the absence of an agreed political solution, mitigating the conflict and preventing mission failure are the only viable strategies. These missions will likely continue to require major investment of capacity and resources for years to come.

SUPPORTING OTHER PEACE AND SECURITY ACTORS, INCLUDING THROUGH CAPACITY-BUILDING: In recent years, UN peacekeepers have been tasked to contribute to the capacity of other partners to respond to conflicts. The United Nations provides technical and capacity building support to African Union (AU) peacekeeping, which includes support to AU deployments in Darfur, Sudan and in Somalia. DPKO offers military, police, judicial, prison, disarmament, demobilization and reintegration (DDR), SSR and mine action expertise to different parts of the UN system, in particular special political missions. The 2007 creation of the Department of Field Support was designed to enhance logistics, personnel and communications support to a variety of UN field presences. UN peacekeeping is currently not configured to consistently deliver comprehensive support to others. Without viable financial arrangements and technical frameworks, its ability to fulfill a capacity-building and support role will remain limited.

LOOKING AHEAD

Taken together, the challenges described above have stretched UN peacekeeping to its limits. Yet demands could well continue to increase. Volatile commodity prices and financial markets, transnational organized crime and environmental changes may lead to political and security instability where societies lack the resources to cope with such shocks. Countries emerging from conflict are particularly vulnerable. The risk that these threats will be met with limited or partial responses is real. The global economic crisis is forcing many governments and organizations to scale back conflict management, humanitarian and development assistance. Military and police capabilities globally are in greater demand. Stretched bilateral and regional capacities increase the likelihood of UN peacekeeping being called upon to act as an instrument of last resort, yet with fewer resources and diminished support.

––––––––––

A further important challenge is the militarization of peacekeeping since 1999, which was the predictable development of 'muscular peacekeeping' referred to above and discussed below.

James Sloan, The Militarisation of Peacekeeping in the Twenty-First Century

pp. 3–5 and 282–95 (Hart, 2011) (footnotes omitted)

The term 'militarised peacekeeping' is used ... to refer to a peacekeeping operation that possesses enforcement characteristics — that is to say, is authorised, explicitly or implicitly, under Chapter VII and authorised to use force beyond self-defence. Depending on the circumstances, the consent of the host state may not be a legal prerequisite to the establishment of a militarised peacekeeping operation or to the assignment of certain tasks to it; similarly, impartiality may not be a legal requirement for some or all of its tasks....

[T]he arguments in favour of the UN reverting to militarised peacekeeping ... appear to have been animated primarily by thinking of a more wishful nature. It was considered to be so essential that peacekeepers protect those within their sphere of influence who were vulnerable in the face of a breach of security that peacekeeping mandates simply *had* to provide for this—whether or not the Organization had yet evolved such that it had the capacity to do so.... [S]ome peacekeeping operations were given the dual task of securing the restoration of peace and security in a country as well as maintaining it. Thus peacekeeping operations were, in addition to their other duties, charged with saving lives and preventing future genocide. But can such militarised peacekeeping operations work? ...

[The] UN ... is fundamentally ill-suited to conducting militarised peacekeeping operations. Although some problems certainly manifest themselves in peacekeeping operations where force is limited to self-defence, where peacekeeping operations are militarised the existing problems are generally exacerbated and new problems emerge. The problems encountered by militarised peacekeeping operations are attributable to a wide variety of factors.... : (1) difficulties of establishment; (2) management difficulties; (3) problems related to the need for host state consent or cooperation; and (4) problems relating to expectations.... .

[T]he merits of militarised peacekeeping operations need urgently to be reconsidered. Based on their performance to date, we see that such operations are under-funded, ill-equipped and poorly managed. And there is little to indicate that this is likely to change. We also see raised expectations associated with such operations are almost inevitably dashed, at considerable cost to the reputation of peacekeeping generally and the UN as a whole.

The return to a more traditional kind of peacekeeping must not be seen as an abandonment of civilians. In fact, a move away from militarised peacekeeping should lead to an improvement in the treatment of civilians, as militarised peacekeeping operations will no longer impede the establishment of quasi-enforcement operations or, where established, provide contributing states with an excuse to withdraw the quasi-enforcement operation before the security situation is well and truly restored. It must be recognised that quasi-enforcement operations are the only effective way to stop harm to civilians or restore security.... To militarise a peacekeeping operation is to ask too much of it.

Questions for Discussion

1. To what extent, if at all, do you consider that "muscular peacekeeping" by the UN is a necessary and positive development? To what extent, if at all, has the militarization of peacekeeping gone too far?

2. To what extent has the UN incorporated the lessons learned from the cases of Somalia and Bosnia into the reform proposals for UN peacekeeping?

3. Given the wide variety of challenges facing UN peacekeeping, what other reforms would you suggest to UN peacekeeping operations and why?

The UN Secretary-General

The Secretary-General is the chief administrative officer of the UN and is given certain specific powers and functions under the Charter. The original grant of powers in the sphere of peace and security was limited, but over the years successive Secretaries-General have been instrumental in developing this all-important aspect of their work. The assumption of such powers and the occasion and manner in which they have been exercised has sometimes met with hostility, especially during the Cold War from the former Soviet Union and its allies.

The power given to the Secretary-General under Article 99 of the Charter to bring matters to the attention of the Security Council was a power not enjoyed by the Secretary-General of the League of Nations. It modified considerably the classical conception of the Secretary-General as being primarily concerned with administrative matters. The Secretary-General rarely invokes Article 99 in express terms, but he does draw the attention of the Security Council to deteriorating situations that may threaten international peace and security, usually through letters to the President of the Council. For example, in 2011 Secretary-General Ban Ki-moon noted that the situation in Libya had seriously deteriorated with the disproportionate use of force by the Libyan authorities, while informing the President of the Council of his decision to appoint a Special Envoy who would offer his good offices and explore how best to resolve the crisis in Libya.[85]

ROSALYN HIGGINS, PROBLEMS AND PROCESS: INTERNATIONAL LAW AND HOW WE USE IT
170–72 (1994)

The Secretary-General may himself, under Article 99 of the Charter, bring to the attention of the Security Council any matter which in his opinion may threaten the maintenance of international peace and security....

The Security Council can investigate any dispute, and over the years some use has been made of fact-finding missions. The neutral verification of the facts is not only often necessary where the facts are in dispute, but is itself a means of containing and defusing a situation. Such missions will not be able to go into the territory without the consent of the party concerned, but it will often suit a party to show that it has nothing to hide by allowing in such a fact-finding team. The early constitutional controversy as to whether the Secretary-General may himself establish a fact-finding mission, or whether this can be done only upon authorization by the Security Council, seems to be resolved in favour of the Secretary-General so to act. The success of the fact-finding missions has been variable, depending upon the co-operation of the state concerned and the quality of the team.

A wide range of dispute-settlement possibilities is envisaged in Article 33 beyond enquiry as to the facts: negotiation, mediation, conciliation, arbitration, judicial settlement, and resort to regional agencies. Sometimes assistance in the pursuit of these measures will be suggested by the Security Council itself; sometimes assistance in respect of these

---

85. UN Doc. S/2011/126.

functions is offered by the Secretary-General, as part of his mandate. Occasionally the Secretary-General himself will put proposed solutions to the Security Council. More usually, the Security Council devises the proposals (and the tendency for initiatives to flow from the Security Council rather than, even informally, the Secretariat has become more pronounced since the improvement of East-West relations). But either way, it is often the Secretary-General who is required to make the proposals for peaceful settlement operative. This interplay is well evidenced in resolutions that have asked, in broad terms that leave maximum flexibility, the Secretary-General to use his good offices—for example, in the Netherlands-Indonesia dispute; in the enforcement of the Arab-Israeli armistice agreements; in supervising a cease-fire in Kashmir; in sending a representative to East Timor; in the Falklands dispute; the list is almost endless. The Secretary-General routinely assists in the holding of negotiations—sometimes in private, sometimes in public. He has facilitated and played an active role in direct negotiations, in a situation generally under the scrutiny of the Security Council: his role in the talks between the Turkish Cypriot and Greek Cypriot authorities is a case in point. He can equally assist in indirect negotiations, where one or more of the parties is unwilling to sit down with the other. The Arab-Israeli armistice negotiations in 1949 afford an example. The Security Council has also asked the Secretary-General to provide conciliators and mediators. In the Dutch-Indonesian disputes of 1949–1954, and in the early years of the Cyprus situation, a conciliator and mediator were respectively much relied on....

Comments

1. In the exercise of their political functions, Secretaries-General have engaged in negotiation and mediation on countless issues between and within states in order to prevent or mediate conflicts: this independent political role is known as the "good offices" of the Secretary-General. Examples are Hammarskjold's negotiations in 1955 with China that effected the release of U.S. airmen imprisoned by Beijing since the Korean War; U Thant's persuasion of the parties to the Yemeni civil war in 1963 to request the posting of UN observers in a demilitarized zone, and during the fighting between India and Pakistan in 1965 he took the lead both in starting negotiations and, when a truce was achieved, in creating a UN observer group to monitor it; Perez de Cuellar's successful mediation between Iran and Iraq that led to the end of their eight year war in 1988; and Boutros-Ghali's efforts in ensuring the implementation in Mozambique of the agreement to end the drawn out civil-war between government and rebel forces. The Secretary-General has often, however, not been able to prevent or resolve conflicts or has—for example, in the case of Cyprus—simply been drawn into ensuring that a stalemate situation does not descend into conflict. Former Secretary-General Kofi Annan resigned from his role as Joint Special Envoy of the UN and the League of Arab States in Syria on 2 August 2012, stating that a "clear lack of unity" in the Security Council had "fundamentally changed the circumstances for the effective exercise of my role ... It is impossible for me or anyone to compel the Syrian government, and also the opposition, to take the steps to bring about the political process."

2. The Secretary-General has also been involved with UN peacekeeping operations. This practice has been analyzed above in the section on UN Peacekeeping.

3. The ability of the Secretary-General to act effectively in the political sphere has depended in significant measure upon his perceived impartiality. Article 100 of the Charter seeks to ensure the impartiality of the Secretary-General and his or her staff by obliging member states not to attempt to influence the Secretary-General or his or her staff.

Members of the Secretariat are also obligated not to "seek or receive instructions from any government" or any "other authority."[86]

Questions for Discussion

1. Is the Charter description (Article 7) of the Secretariat as one of the "principal organs" of the UN justified? Which entity embodies and represents, for operational purposes, the UN Secretariat?

2. Whose interest in any situation does the Secretary-General represent? To what extent does this interest differ from that of UN member states?

3. What powers and functions can the Secretary-General exercise in relation to the maintenance of peace and security? To what extent is the Secretary-General independent in the exercise of these powers and functions from UN member states?

The Role of Regional Arrangements

The end of the Cold War has seen a Security Council that is willing to assign the roles of peace-enforcement and peacekeeping to regional arrangements. This has seen regional arrangements carry out these roles on behalf of the international community in different regions of the world. The African Union has been active in carrying out military operations in Burundi (IAMB), Sudan (AMIS, later UNAMID), Somalia (AMISOM) and the Comoros Islands (AMISEC) as well as in its efforts to deal with Chad/the Central African Republic, Côte d'Ivoire, Djibouti/Eritrea, Guinea-Bissau, Liberia, Libya, and South Sudan, including Abyei. The South African Development Community (SADC), the Central African Economic and Monetary Community (CAEMC) and the Economic Community of West African States (ECOWAS) have contributed to peacekeeping in Cote d'Ivoire, Sierra Leone, Liberia and Mali. NATO has had missions in Bosnia and Herzegovina (SFOR), Kosovo (KFOR) and Afghanistan (ISAF). The European Union has sent thousands of troops from its Member States to Bosnia and Herzegovina (EUFOR), the Former Yugoslav Republic of Macedonia (CONCORDIA), Chad and the Central African Republic (EUFOR), and the Democratic Republic of the Congo (Operation Artemis in 2003 and EUFOR in 2006).

Regional arrangements have also taken action to maintain peace on their own initiative in the Americas, Africa, and Europe. An examination of this practice by regional arrangements is carried out below. The legal parameters of action by regional arrangements to maintain peace are governed by their relationship with the Security Council, a relationship that is delineated in Chapter VIII of the Charter.

---

86. *See* Theodor Meron, *Status and Independence of the International Civil Servant*, 47 Recueil des Cours 291–384. For issues relating to the appointment of the Secretary-General, *see* Marjorie Whiteman, 13 Dig. Int'l L. 788–95 (1968).

The UN–Regional Arrangement Relationship

Oscar Schachter, *Authorized Uses of Force by the United Nations and Regional Organizations*

in Law and Force in the New International Order 65, 86–88
(Lori Damrosch & David Scheffer eds., 1991)

The U.N. Charter recognizes in its Chapter VIII that regional arrangements and agencies are appropriate means for maintaining peace and security, provided that their activities are consistent with the purposes and principles of the Charter. Indeed, Article 52 of the Charter requires states to make every effort to achieve peaceful settlement of "local disputes" through regional arrangements or agencies before referring such disputes to the U.N. Security Council. The idea that disputes and threats to the peace involving states within a region should preferably be dealt with primarily by regional bodies has been an early and persistent influence. At San Francisco the Security Council was perceived as a forum of last resort when states were unable to resolve conflicts between them through the peaceful means listed in Chapter VI or through regional instrumentalities.

. . . .

The Charter in Article 53 expressly directs the Security Council to utilize the regional arrangements or agencies covered by Chapter VIII for enforcement action where appropriate. The regional bodies are indirectly authorized to undertake enforcement action inasmuch as Article 53 states that they may not do so without the authorization of the Security Council. Thus the failure of the Council to grant permission for enforcement action would bar such action. A permanent member could therefore prevent enforcement action by a regional organization. Cases have come before the Security Council involving decisions of the Organization of American States (O.A.S.) to apply diplomatic and economic measures that were in the nature of sanctions as envisaged in Article 41 of the U.N. Charter. In these cases, the Council did not decide that those measures were covered by Article 53. The majority of members maintained that such non-forcible coercive measures were within the competence of individual states. Since states were free to sever trade or diplomatic relations, they could do so by concerted action under the aegis of a regional organization. The reasoning is not wholly compelling since concerted action by a regional body to impose sanctions of the kind contemplated in Chapter VII (Article 41) would appear to be within the meaning of enforcement action in Article 53.

. . . .

Apart from collective self-defense, regional organizations may institute peacekeeping operations that do not involve coercive measures against a state. This has been done in a number of cases. However, it has not always been agreed that the regional peacekeeping operation has actually received the consent of the territorial sovereign. Questions of this kind have come up where it was uncertain who, if anyone, may legitimately grant such consent in the absence of effective and recognized governmental authority. This emerged as a problem when U.S. forces together with troops from several Caribbean countries intervened in Grenada, claiming *inter alia* that they had been authorized to do so by a regional body (the Organization of Eastern Caribbean States) to bring peace and order to a country in a condition of anarchy. The General Assembly condemned the intervention as a violation of the Charter. However, there was no international criticism of a regional peacekeeping force of West African states that sought to bring an end to a bloody internal conflict in Liberia in 1990. This was clearly not an enforcement action or collective defense, nor was there an invitation from a government enjoying international recognition. A case of this kind would suggest an interpretation of peacekeeping by regional bodies that allows for a collective military intervention to help end an internal conflict when a government has been deposed or no longer has effective authority.

It is probable that peacekeeping actions and perhaps limited enforcement will be employed by regional organizations more frequently in the future. They are likely to be used to assist in monitoring and border patrol and perhaps to help to provide order to a country in internal conflict or near anarchy.

Comment

The use by the Security Council of regional arrangements to maintain or restore peace and security was promoted soon after the end of the Cold War by Secretary-General Boutros-Ghali.

An Agenda for Peace, Preventative Diplomacy, Peacemaking and Peace-keeping

Report of the Secretary-General pursuant to the statement adopted by the Summit Meeting of the Security Council on Jan. 31, 1992, U.N. Doc. A/47/277-S/24111, June 17, 1992

61. The Charter deliberately provides no precise definition of regional arrangements and agencies, thus allowing useful flexibility for undertakings by a group of States to deal with a matter appropriate for regional action which also could contribute to the maintenance of international peace and security..... .

62.... In Africa, three different regional groups — the Organization of African Unity, the League of Arab States and the Organization of the Islamic Conference — joined efforts with the United Nations regarding Somalia. In the Asian context, the Association of South-East Asian Nations and individual States from several regions were brought together with the parties to the Cambodian conflict at an international conference in Paris, to work with the United Nations. For El Salvador, a unique arrangement — "The Friends of the Secretary-General" — contributed to agreements reached through the mediation of the Secretary-General. The end of the war in Nicaragua involved a highly complex effort which was initiated by leaders of the region and conducted by individual States, groups of States and the Organization of American States. Efforts undertaken by the European Community and its member States, with the support of States participating in the Conference on Security and Cooperation in Europe, have been of central importance in dealing with the crisis in the Balkans and neighbouring areas.

63. In the past, regional arrangements often were created because of the absence of a universal system for collective security; thus their activities could on occasion work at cross-purposes with the sense of solidarity required for the effectiveness of the world Organization. But in this new era of opportunity, regional arrangements or agencies can render great service if their activities are undertaken in a manner consistent with the Purposes and Principles of the Charter, and if their relationship with the United Nations, and particularly the Security Council, is governed by Chapter VIII.

64.... Under the Charter, the Security Council has and will continue to have primary responsibility for maintaining international peace and security, but regional action as a matter of decentralization, delegation and cooperation with United Nations efforts could not only lighten the burden of the Council but also contribute to a deeper sense of participation, consensus and democratization in international affairs.

65. Regional arrangements and agencies have not in recent decades been considered in this light, even when originally designed in part for a role in maintaining or restoring peace within their regions of the world. Today a new sense exists that they have contributions to make....

Increasing cooperation between the UN and regional arrangements meant that the Secretary-General had enough material to provide a thematic summary of this evolving relationship three years later in his 1995 *Supplement to An Agenda for Peace* as well as being able to state the principles that should in practice govern the relationship between the UN and regional organizations when the latter are engaged in peacemaking and peacekeeping.

Supplement to an Agenda for Peace

Report of the Secretary-General on the Work of the Organization,
U.N. Doc. A/50/60-S/1995/1, Jan. 3, 1995

86. Cooperation between the United Nations and regional organizations takes a number of forms. At least five can be identified: (a) Consultation: this has been well-established for some time. In some cases it is governed by formal agreements and reports are made to the General Assembly; in other cases it is less formal. The purpose is to exchange views on conflicts that both the United Nations and the regional organization may be trying to solve; (b) Diplomatic support: the regional organization participates in the peacemaking activities of the United Nations and supports them by providing diplomatic initiatives ... and/or by providing technical input, as the Organization for Security and Cooperation in Europe (OSCE) does, for instance, on constitutional issues relating to Abkhazia. In the same way, the United Nations can support the regional organization in its efforts (as it does for OSCE over Nagorny Karabakh); (c) Operational support: the most developed example is the provision by NATO of air power to support the United Nations Protection Force (UNPROFOR) in the former Yugoslavia. For its part, the United Nations can provide technical advice to regional organizations that undertake peace-keeping operations of their own; (d) Co-deployment: United Nations field missions have been deployed in conjunction with the Economic Community of West African States (ECOWAS) in Liberia and with the Commonwealth of Independent States (CIS) in Georgia. If those experiments succeed, they may herald a new division of labour between the United Nations and regional organizations, under which the regional organization carries the main burden but a small United Nations operation supports it and verifies that it is functioning in a manner consistent with positions adopted by the Security Council. The political, operational and financial aspects of the arrangement give rise to questions of some delicacy. Member States may wish at some stage to make an assessment, in the light of experience in Liberia and Georgia, of how this model might be followed in the future; (e) Joint operations: the example is the United Nations Mission in Haiti, the staffing, direction and financing of which are shared between the United Nations and the Organization of American States (OAS). This arrangement has worked, and it too is a possible model for the future that will need careful assessment.

....

88. [The principles that should govern the relationship between the UN and regional organizations when the latter are engaged in peacemaking and peace-keeping] include: ...

(b) The primacy of the United Nations, as set out in the Charter, must be respected....
(c) The division of labour must be clearly defined and agreed in order to avoid overlap and institutional rivalry where the United Nations and a regional organization are both working on the same conflict. In such cases it is also particularly important to avoid a multiplicity of mediators; (d) Consistency by members of regional organizations who are also Member States of the United Nations is needed in dealing with a common problem of interest to both organizations, for example, standards for peace-keeping operations.

The 2005 World Summit, discussed below, the largest gathering of world leaders in history, confirmed in the Outcome Document the desire to deepen the partnership between the UN and regional organizations.

World Summit Outcome Document
U.N. Doc. A/RES/60/1, Oct. 24, 2005, paras. 93 and 170

Recognizing the important contribution to peace and security by regional organizations as provided for under Chapter VIII of the Charter and the importance of forging predictable partnerships and arrangements between the United Nations and regional organizations, and noting in particular, given the special needs of Africa, the importance of a strong African Union:

(a) We support the efforts of the European Union and other regional entities to develop capacities such as for rapid deployment, standby and bridging arrangements;

(b) We support the development and implementation of a ten-year plan for capacity-building with the African Union.

. . .

We support a stronger relationship between the United Nations and regional and sub-regional organizations, pursuant to Chapter VIII of the Charter, and therefore resolve:

(**a**) To expand consultation and cooperation between the United Nations and regional and subregional organizations through formalized agreements between the respective secretariats and, as appropriate, involvement of regional organizations in the work of the Security Council;

(**b**) To ensure that regional organizations that have a capacity for the prevention of armed conflict or peacekeeping consider the option of placing such capacity in the framework of the United Nations Standby Arrangements System;

(**c**) To strengthen cooperation in the economic, social and cultural fields.

An important way that the Security Council has used regional arrangements to maintain peace has been to delegate Chapter VII powers to these arrangements. This technique can lead to complex issues of *vires* for regional arrangements. For example, in 2008 the UN Secretary General signed a cooperation agreement with NATO's Secretary General in which both organizations pledged commitments to further collaboration and cooperation in a number of areas.[87]

---

87. *See* "NATO and the UN," Survival: Global Politics and Strategy April–May 2009, *available at*: http://www.iiss.org/en/publications/survival/sections/2009-5f8e/survival—global-politics-and-strategy-april-may-2009-9e37/51-2-02-harsch-9aad. This agreement helped paved the way for NATO

DAN SAROOSHI, THE UNITED NATIONS AND THE DEVELOPMENT OF COLLECTIVE SECURITY

250–53 (1999)

The Security Council by delegating Chapter VII powers to a regional arrangement may be authorising, depending on the terms of the delegated mandate, the use of military enforcement action against a State that is not a member of the regional community. This is consistent with the purpose of a delegation of Chapter VII powers—to maintain or restore peace by achieving the Council's stipulated objectives—and the provisions of Chapter VIII of the Charter. Article 52(1) of the Charter provides that regional arrangements can deal with 'such matters relating to the maintenance of international peace and security as [is] appropriate for regional action.' It is in this context that Article 53(1) goes on to state that the Council 'shall, where appropriate, utilize such regional arrangements or agencies for enforcement action under its authority.' The power of deciding whether it is 'appropriate' for the carrying out of enforcement action in a particular case is left to the Security Council. The Council has been given the primary responsibility for the maintenance of international peace and security. Accordingly, the Council possesses the competence to authorize a regional arrangement to carry out enforcement action against a State that is not a member of the particular regional arrangement if it deems that this is necessary for the maintenance of international peace and security. This competence of the Council to use regional arrangements with an external focus is an important feature of the delegation of powers to such arrangements. This is also of significance to the use of collective self-defence organizations such as NATO for the carrying out of military enforcement action under the auspices of the Council, since NATO has not until now been regarded as a regional arrangement for the purposes of Chapter VIII of the Charter: it has been seen as a collective self-defence pact. A major reason why NATO sought to characterize itself as a collective self-defence alliance was to avoid the obligation in Article 53(1) to seek prior permission from the Security Council before it could act in a particular case.

. . . .

... It may not always be legally possible for a regional arrangement under its constituent treaty to take up a delegation of Chapter VII powers. In such cases, a delegation of powers to a regional arrangement does not mean that the organs of that arrangement can exceed the powers they have been given by their constituent instrument. The delegation of Chapter VII powers to a regional arrangement gives the arrangement—and thus its organs—the right to exercise those powers but not in disregard of its constituent treaty. This does not of course preclude the relevant organs of a regional arrangement from deciding, according to the relevant constitutional provisions, that the arrangement will take up the delegation of Chapter VII powers. In any case, for the purposes of our current enquiry, suffice to note that the internal constitutional constraints on a regional arrangement being able to exercise delegated Chapter VII powers does not affect the lawfulness of the delegation or *the exercise of delegated powers* from the perspective of the United Nations Charter.

---

actions against Libya in support of UN Security Council Resolution 1973 (2011) imposing a "no-fly" zone over Libya.

Questions for Discussion

1. When can regional arrangements carry out military enforcement action? When should regional arrangements carry out military enforcement action?

2. To what extent is the self-characterization of a regional entity as a Chapter VIII "regional arrangement or agency" important for the entity to be used by the Council to maintain peace and security?

3. Can a regional arrangement take military action against a state that is not a member of the arrangement?

The following materials address more specifically the role that regional arrangements can and have played in the management of conflict in the Americas (the Organization of American States), Africa (the African Union and the Economic Community of West African States), and Europe (NATO).[88]

The Organization of American States

Charter of the Organization of American States

Signed at Bogotá, Columbia, Apr. 30, 1948, *amended* by the Protocol of Buenos Aires 1967, by the Protocol of Cartagena de Indias 1985, by the Protocol of Washington 1992, and by the Protocol of Managua 1993

Article 1

The American States establish by this Charter the international organization that they have developed to achieve an order of peace and justice, to promote their solidarity, to strengthen their collaboration, and to defend their sovereignty, their territorial integrity, and their independence. Within the United Nations, the Organization of American States is a regional agency.

Article 2

The Organization of American States, in order to put into practice the principles on which it is founded and to fulfill its regional obligations under the Charter of the United Nations, proclaims the following essential purposes:

    a)   To strengthen the peace and security of the continent;

    b)   To promote and consolidate representative democracy, with due respect for the principle of nonintervention;

    c)   To prevent possible causes of difficulties and to ensure the pacific settlement of disputes that may arise among the Member States;

    d)   To provide for common action on the part of those States in the event of aggression;

---

88. In terms of European-based regional arrangements, it should be noted that in addition to NATO the European Union (EU) plans to expand considerably its activities in the peace and security area. The EU has decided to establish the following decision-making political and military bodies to act on its behalf in response to international crises: a Political and Security Committee, a Military Committee, a Military Staff, a Situation Centre, and a Committee for Civilian Crisis Management. The EU has also set itself the objective of being able, by the end of 2003, to deploy within sixty days, and sustain for at least one year, forces of up to 60,000 soldiers. The EU has suggested that such a rapid reaction force could be made available to provide prompt assistance for UN peacekeeping operations.

....

Article 3

The American States reaffirm the following principles:

....

h) An act of aggression against one American State is an act of aggression against all the other American States;

....

Article 9

A Member of the Organization whose democratically constituted government has been overthrown by force may be suspended from the exercise of the right to participate in the sessions of the General Assembly, the Meeting of Consultation, the Councils of the Organization and the Specialized Conferences as well as in the commissions, working groups and any other bodies established.

John Norton Moore, *The Inter-American System Snarls in Falklands War*
76 AM. J. INT'L L. 830, 830–31 (1982)

With the end of the fighting in the Falklands war, scholars are beginning to assess the performance of the international community during the conflict. In this assessment, it is important that the actions of the Organization of American States (OAS) not be neglected. The OAS is the oldest and most successful regional organization under the United Nations system. Time and again, as in the Cuban missile crisis, it has acted to strengthen peace and freedom in this hemisphere. The core of its success is a shared belief that force shall not be used to settle disputes in international relations, that nations attacked in violation of this principle should act together in collective defense, and that peoples are entitled to self-determination. Sadly, in its actions in the Falklands-Malvinas war, and particularly in its resolution of May 29, the OAS lost sight of these great principles.

... In the first article of the Rio Treaty the parties pledge "not to resort to the threat or use of force in any manner inconsistent with the provisions of the Charter of the United Nations or of this Treaty."

The Argentine invasion of the Falklands-Malvinas is in violation of this principle, regardless of the merits of the underlying Argentine claim. Moreover, the invasion is a use of force in disregard of the expressed preference of the peoples of the islands. International lawyers may be hard pressed to know whether Britain or Argentina would win sovereignty over the islands or how associated self-determination claims would be resolved if the dispute were submitted to an impartial arbiter. But there is no uncertainty on the more important issue of Argentine use of force in violation of the UN Charter and the Rio Treaty. If such use of force is not unequivocally condemned it could become a model for island and border wars all over the world, including many in Latin America. Indeed, in the background of the South Atlantic war are the more serious disputed claims to the Antarctic continent and offshore island groups south of 60° latitude, including a major dispute among Argentina, Britain, and Chile currently frozen by the Antarctic Treaty of 1959.

Against this background the OAS might have sought to reinforce the peace initiatives of the United States or to recommend that both parties accept international arbitration or jurisdiction of a Special Chamber of the International Court of Justice as Canada and the United States have done in the *Gulf of Maine* dispute. At minimum, the Organization could have endorsed Security Council Resolution 502 calling for an immediate Argentine withdrawal, a cease-fire, and negotiations by all parties. Instead, it yielded to regional pressures, one-sidedly condemned "the unjustified and disproportionate armed attack perpetrated by the United Kingdom," and called on states parties to the Rio Treaty to give support to Argentina. It also urged the United States "to refrain" from materially aiding Britain in deference to the principle of "hemispheric solidarity." No mention was made that Argentine withdrawal was required by binding Security Council Resolution 502 or that Britain was acting under Article 51 of the Charter in defense against a prior Argentinian armed attack.

This OAS resolution of May 29 is not important for its legal effect. It is clear under Article 103 of the United Nations Charter and Article 10 of the Rio Treaty that regional actions that are inconsistent either with the obligations of the Charter or with binding action taken by the Security Council in dealing with a dispute are *ultra vires* and without a legal effect. In this case the resolution of May 29 is inconsistent both with the Charter prohibition of the use of force in international relations (and the complementary right of defense against such an illegal attack inserted in Article 51 of the Charter) and with Resolution 502, particularly in its failure to call for an immediate withdrawal of Argentine forces.

But the May 29 resolution is profoundly important for the political implications of its tilt from fundamental Charter principles to a supposed overriding regionalism. Some— indeed the conventional wisdom—may say that actions such as that of May 29 are to be expected when regional solidarity is at stake or even that under the circumstances the OAS was moderate in not putting the United States more on the spot. I believe such arguments do a disservice to the greatness of the inter-American system. It is tragic failure to place enduring Charter and regional principles—which are the real hemispheric protection— over vague calls for "hemispheric solidarity." The solidarity that counts is the willingness of the North and South Americans to stand together for enduring principles of self-determination and avoidance of the use of force as a means of settling international disputes.

The OAS did, however, in the later case of Haiti in 1991 take action, both unilaterally and in conjunction with the Security Council, which was directed at the maintenance of peace and security.[89] Apart from its involvement in Haiti, the OAS has not played a significant role in UN peacekeeping in recent years.

African Regional Arrangements

Regional arrangements have been used by states within Africa to try and maintain and restore peace with mixed results. The African Union (AU) in particular has become one of the most important players in regional peacekeeping. In 2013 the African Union Mission in Somalia (AMISOM) was expanded, a joint AU-ECOWAS mission was launched in Mali (AFISMA), operations against the Lord's Resistance Army under the AU-authorised Regional Task Force (LRA RTF) continued, and the existing MICOPAX mission of the Economic Community of Central African States (ECCAS) in the Central African Republic was re-hatted into a joint AU-ECCAS operation (AFISM-CAR2). 40,641 uniformed and civilian personnel were mandated to serve in AU peace support operations and an additional 30,424 personnel in the joint AU-UN mission in Darfur (UNAMID).[90]

---

89. *See* the section on Article 42 of the Charter, above.
90. Walter Lotze, *Strengthening African Peace Support Operations: Nine Lessons for the Future of the African Standby Force*, Center for International Peace Operations, 2 December 2013.

The African Union

The African Union was formerly known as the Organization of African Unity (OAU). The legal basis of this new organization is the Constitutive Act of the African Union, which was adopted by the African Heads of State and Government in Lome, Togo, on July 11, 2000, and which entered into force on May 26, 2001. The inaugural session of the African Union (AU) took place in Durban, South Africa, on July 10, 2002, during which there was adopted a Protocol Relating to the Establishment of the African Union Peace and Security Council (PSC) to replace the former OAU Mechanism for Conflict Prevention, Management and Resolution.

An African Peace and Security Architecture (APSA) has developed since 2002, including the PSC, an African Standby Force, a Continental Early Warning System and a Panel of the Wise. Despite the proliferation of these mechanisms, their record has been patchy: AU-deployed missions have been highly dependent on external donors; harmonization has been a significant problem; serious questions remain over AU capacity; and some of the Regional Economic Communities (RECs) are developing at a quicker pace than the AU.[91] There have also been accusations of sexual exploitation and abuse by African Union Forces in Somalia.[92]

The Economic Community of West African States (ECOWAS)

Christine Gray, *Regional Arrangements and the United Nations Collective Security System*

in THE CHANGING CONSTITUTION OF THE UNITED NATIONS 91, 101–02, 104, 107–08 (Hazel Fox ed., 1997)

In [Liberia in] December 1989 there was an uprising against President Doe who had been in power since 1980. The uprising was led by Charles Taylor (a former member of the Doe Government who had fled when charged with embezzlement) who came from the Ivory Coast with a small force (the NPFL).... By summer 1990 the rebels controlled about 90% of Liberia and were advancing on the capital, Monrovia.

It later became clear that the government had sought UN intervention in June 1990, but the Security Council did not become involved until January 1991.... In the absence of UN or US intervention the Economic Community of West African States (ECOWAS) stepped in. This was a hitherto little known organisation (like the OECS before its action in Grenada) of sixteen Member States, concerned with economic matters. In May 1990 ECOWAS established a Mediation Committee on Liberia and in August 1990 that Committee called for a ceasefire and established ECOMOG (ECOWAS Monitoring Group) with troops from Nigeria, Ghana, Gambia, Guinea and Sierra Leone. About 3,000 ECOMOG troops went to Liberia and secured Monrovia against the NPFL. Various attempts were made to reach a peaceful settlement; at one of these conferences it was agreed to establish an interim government under President Sawyer. He [sic] was established in Monrovia in December 1990, and a ceasefire held from December 1990 to August 1992. During this time attempts to produce a peaceful settlement continued and in October 1991 the Yamoussoukro IV agreement was accepted by the Doe forces, the NPFL and

---

91. Alex Vines, *A Decade of African Peace and Security Architecture*, 89 INTERNATIONAL AFFAIRS 89–109 (2013).

92. 'The Power These Men Have Over Us', Human Rights Watch Report, 8 September 2014.

Prince Johnson. This provided for a ceasefire, the disarmament of warring parties and the encampment of all forces under the supervision of ECOMOG.

But in 1992 fighting broke out again; the NPFL forces attacked Monrovia and ECOMOG not only drove them off, it went onto the offensive and took territory formerly occupied by the NPFL. In July 1993 a Peace Agreement was agreed at Contonou, Benin; however, this ceasefire broke down in 1994.

The most obvious legal question arising — a question without an obvious answer — is what was the legal basis of the ECOMOG operation? Was the intervention under ECO-MOG's own mandate, under the ECOWAS constitution and under the UN Charter and general international law?

First, ECOMOG's mandate from the ECOWAS Standing Mediation Committee was that 'ECOMOG shall assist the Committee in supervising the implementation, and ensuring strict compliance, of the ceasefire by all the parties to the conflict'. In its report to the Security Council on the establishment of ECOMOG, Nigeria said that 'ECOMOG is going to Liberia first and foremost to stop the senseless killing of innocent civilian nationals and foreigners and to help the Liberian people to restore their democratic institutions. The ECOWAS intervention is in no way designed to save one part or punish another'.

... [I]t is striking that not much attention was paid in the Security Council even to the question of the legality of the operation under the UN Charter. States in the Security Council debates simply assumed that ECOWAS had legally established peacekeeping forces. The ECOWAS communiques to the Security Council made no express reference to Chapter VIII but Nigeria spoke of 'ECOMOG as holding the fort for the UN in accordance with Chapter VIII'. The USA and China spoke simply of the peacekeeping forces set up by ECOWAS and appeared to assume their legality.

. . . .

... It [the Security Council] unanimously passed Resolution 788. This recalled Chapter VII, commended ECOWAS for its efforts to restore peace in Liberia, reaffirmed the Ya-moussoukro IV Peace Agreement, condemned violations of the ceasefire and condemned the continuing armed attacks against the peacekeeping forces of ECOWAS in Liberia by one of the parties to the conflict. It 'Requests all States to respect the measures established by ECOWAS to bring about a peaceful solution to the conflict in Liberia'. The Security Council clearly assumed the legality of ECOMOG in this resolution and in its later resolutions. The latter show the growing UN involvement in attempts to end the civil war.

In Resolution 813, also passed unanimously, the Security Council declared itself ready to consider measures against a party to the conflict if it did not implement the Yamoussoukro IV agreement. It called on the Secretary-General and ECOWAS to arrange a meeting; it was this meeting under the auspices of the UN, ECOWAS and the OAU that eventually produced the July 1993 Peace Agreement.

The Security Council subsequently established UNOMIL, a UN peacekeeping force, to complement ECOMOG. As the Secretary-General said, this was the first time the United Nations undertook a peacekeeping mission in co-operation with a force set up by another organisation. A clear understanding about the role of the different groups was crucial. Accordingly Resolution 866 provided that ECOMOG had the primary responsibility for supervising the implementation of the military provisions of the peace agreement; UNOMIL was to monitor and verify this process. The UN involvement would contribute significantly to the effective implementation of the Peace Agreement and would serve to underline the international community commitment to conflict resolution in Liberia.

The conflict in Liberia was only definitively resolved when elections were held in July 1997 with Charles Taylor emerging as the winner with 75 percent of the popular vote. This result called into question the legitimacy of the earlier enforcement action taken by ECOMOG against Taylor's forces and thereby the UN's relationship with and support for ECOMOG.

ECOWAS faced a major challenge with the situation in Mali following a *coup d'état* on 22 March 2012. The resulting political uncertainty allowed armed radical groups to gain control of northern Mali. In Resolution 2071, the Security Council accepted the principle of an international force in northern Mali. The UN gave ECOWAS 45 days from 12 October 2012 to draw up a plan for military intervention to retake the north of Mali and Resolution 2085 approved the plan in December 2012.[93]

Security Council Resolution 2085
U.N. Doc. S/RES/2085 (2012)

The Security Council,

9. Decides to authorize the deployment of an African-led International Support Mission in Mali (AFISMA) for an initial period of one year, which shall take all necessary measures, in compliance with applicable international humanitarian law and human rights law and in full respect of the sovereignty, territorial integrity and unity of Mali to carry out the following tasks:

(a) To contribute to the rebuilding of the capacity of the Malian Defence and Security Forces, in close coordination with other international partners involved in this process, including the European Union and other Member States;

(b) To support the Malian authorities in recovering the areas in the north of its territory under the control of terrorist, extremist and armed groups and in reducing the threat posed by terrorist organizations, including AQIM, MUJWA and associated extremist groups, while taking appropriate measures to reduce the impact of military action upon the civilian population;

(c) To transition to stabilisation activities to support the Malian authorities in maintaining security and consolidate State authority through appropriate capacities;

(d) To support the Malian authorities in their primary responsibility to protect the population;

(e) To support the Malian authorities to create a secure environment for the civilian-led delivery of humanitarian assistance and the voluntary return of internally displaced persons and refugees, as requested, within its capabilities and in close coordination with humanitarian actors;

(f) To protect its personnel, facilities, premises, equipment and mission and to ensure the security and movement of its personnel;

10. Requests the African Union, in close coordination with ECOWAS, the Secretary-General and other international organizations and bilateral partners involved in the Malian crisis, to report to the Security Council every 60 days on the deployment and activities of AFISMA, including, before the commencement of offensive operations in the north of Mali, on: (i) the progress in the....

---

93. Alex Vines, *A Decade of African Peace and Security Architecture*, 89 INTERNATIONAL AFFAIRS 89, 105 (2013).

11. Emphasizes that the military planning will need to be further refined before the commencement of the offensive operation and requests that the Secretary-General, in close coordination with Mali, ECOWAS, the African Union, the neighbouring countries of Mali, other countries in the region and all other interested bilateral partners and international organizations, continue to support the planning and the preparations for the deployment of AFISMA, regularly inform the Council of the progress of the process, and requests that the Secretary-General also confirm in advance the Council's satisfaction with the planned military offensive operation.... [94]

The North Atlantic Treaty Organization (NATO)

The North Atlantic Treaty

Apr. 4, 1949, arts. 1, 5–7, 5 U.S.T. 483, 34 U.N.T.S. 243

Article 1

The Parties undertake, as set forth in the Charter of the United Nations, to settle any international dispute in which they may be involved by peaceful means in such a manner that international peace and security and justice are not endangered, and to refrain in their international relations from the threat or use of force in any manner inconsistent with the purposes of the United Nations.

....

Article 5

The Parties agree that an armed attack against one or more of them in Europe or North America shall be considered an armed attack against them all and consequently they agree that, if such an armed attack occurs, each of them, in exercise of the right of individual or collective self-defence recognised by Article 51 of the Charter of the United Nations, will assist the Party or Parties so attacked by taking forthwith, individually and in concert with the other Parties, such action as it deems necessary, including the use of armed force, to restore and maintain the security of the North Atlantic area.

Any such armed attack and all measures taken as a result thereof shall immediately be reported to the Security Council. Such measures shall be terminated when the Security Council has taken the measures necessary to restore and maintain international peace and security.

Article 6

For the purpose of Article 5, an armed attack on one or more of the Parties is deemed to include an armed attack:

- on the territory of any of the Parties in Europe or North America ... ;
- on the forces, vessels, or aircraft of any of the Parties, when in or over these territories or any other area in Europe in which occupation forces of any of the Parties were stationed on the date when the Treaty entered into force....

---

94. ECOWAS had problems with rapidly deploying in Northern Mali. France launched a military operation (Operation Serval) in Mali following SC Res 2085. French officials declared that the intervention was at the request of the President of Mali and within the context of SC Res 2085.A Security Council Press Statement of 10 January 2013 'reiterate[d] [its] call to Member States to ... provide assistance to the Malian Defence and Security Forces in order to reduce the threat posed by terrorist organizations and associated groups'. The United Nations Multidimensional Integrated Stabilization Mission in Mali (MINUSMA) was established by SC Res of 25 April 2013 to support political processes and carry out security-related tasks.

Article 7

This Treaty does not affect, and shall not be interpreted as affecting in any way the rights and obligations under the Charter of the Parties which are members of the United Nations, or the primary responsibility of the Security Council for the maintenance of international peace and security.

With the end of the Cold War, NATO has sought to define a new role for itself. An important part of this new role has been to assist the Security Council in the maintenance or restoration of peace and security. This was manifested in the September 2008 UN-NATO Cooperation Agreement, discussed above, where both organizations recognized that "Further cooperation will significantly contribute to addressing the threats and challenges to which the international community is called upon to respond."…. [It underscored] "the importance of establishing a framework for consultation and dialogue and cooperation.…"

Rosalyn Higgins, *Peace and Security. Achievements and Failures*

6 Eur. J. Int'l L. 445, 452–53 (1995)

A major effort has been made to establish a working relationship between the United Nations and NATO, and it has been put into operation in the former Yugoslavia. The legal basis of this collaboration — as with so much that today happens under the new 'flexible pragmatism' — remains somewhat uncertain. Article 52 provides that nothing in the Charter 'precludes the existence of regional arrangements or agencies for dealing with such matters relating to the maintenance of international peace and security as are appropriate for regional action', provided such activities are consistent with the purposes and principles of the UN. Article 53 provides that 'The Security Council should, where appropriate, utilize such regional arrangements — or agencies for enforcement action under its authority'. NATO has never been regarded as a regional arrangement or agency, but as a collective self-defence pact. It nonetheless responded to the Security Council request to regional bodies of January 1993 to study ways and means to maintain peace and security within their areas, and ways and means to improve coordination with the United Nations. NATO's basic mandate — let alone the fact that it is not a regional organization — might have been thought to have presented a further problem. Its central mandate under Article 5 of the North Atlantic Treaty is that 'The Parties agree that an armed attack against one or more of them is considered an attack on them all'. Without formal treaty amendment to allow it either to act in circumstances other than an attack on one of the members or 'out of area', NATO has in fact systematically adopted a new role — that of 'peace support operations'. NATO had already begun its search for a new post-Cold War role, adopting its 'New Strategic Concept' at its Rome Summit in late 1992. In June 1992 NATO had determined that it would 'support peace-keeping activities under the responsibility of the Conference on Security and Cooperation in Europe'. Even before the Security Council approach of January 1993, Secretary-General Boutros Ghali had asked NATO to assist in supporting future UN resolutions in the former Yugoslavia, and had received a positive reply from NATO Secretary-General Manfred Worner, the terms of which are significant:

> We confirm the preparedness of our alliance to support, on a case by case basis and in accordance with out own procedures, peace-keeping operations under the authority of the UN Security Council, which has the primary responsibility

for peace and security. We are ready to respond positively to initiatives that the UN Secretary-General might take to seek Alliance assistance in the implementation of UN Security Council resolutions.

The commitment was thus not a generalized commitment to the UN, and it was to be done by reference to NATO's own procedures—acknowledging always the Security Council's primary responsibility. Within five months, NATO was acting out of area, in circumstances other than those envisaged in its Treaty, and in circumstances that have also to be said not to be those of Article 53 of the UN Charter. NATO has been assisting the UN in relation to (a) the naval embargoes; (b) the enforcement of the no-fly zone over Bosnia; (c) the protection of UN personnel; and (d) the protection of safe zones. It is also engaged in a variety of other related functions—including contingency planning for any possible peace plan for Bosnia.[95]

———————

NATO has, however, used military force without prior Security Council authorization. This occurred notably in the case of Kosovo where the Council was constrained from acting by the threat of a Russian veto. Nonetheless, NATO carried out extensive military air strikes against the Federal Republic of Yugoslavia, which commenced in April 1999, in order to force the Yugoslav Government to stop, *inter alia*, alleged "ethnic cleansing" in the Yugoslav province of Kosovo. The legal basis for this NATO action has been the source of considerable controversy.

Ralph Zacklin, *Beyond Kosovo: The United Nations and Humanitarian Intervention*

41 VA. J. INT'L L. 923, 924–27, 929–30 (2001)

For the United Nations, the second attempt in the twentieth century to create an international organization of universal competence and authority to maintain international peace and security, the last decade of the century proved to be tumultuous. Beginning with the end of the Cold War and the successful reversal of Iraq's aggression against Kuwait, the fulfillment of the organization's role in maintaining peace and security through an engaged and, finally, relatively cohesive Security Council appeared to be realizable. A "New World Order" was proclaimed.

Then, in swift succession, came Somalia, Bosnia and Rwanda. The Security Council's credibility and, by extension, the credibility of the United Nations as a whole, was grievously damaged. In Somalia, what began as a humanitarian mission ended in ignominious withdrawal after a succession of failed operations. The casualties sustained by the United States and other contingents blighted peacekeeping and peace-enforcement in Bosnia, and led directly to the inability to deal with the single worst crime of the second half of the century, the genocide in Rwanda. The United Nations will live with the consequences of these failures for a very long time, even as it strives to learn from them.

By the end of the last decade, with U.N. credibility hugely diminished, if not entirely destroyed, the Security Council was unable to find a working consensus on Kosovo. A NATO-led coalition undertook an enforcement action without the prior authorization of the Security Council and not in self-defense, in violation of U.N. Charter principles, including the prohibition on the use of force, thereby plunging the organization into a

———————

95. On these delegations of power, *see* DAN SAROOSHI, THE UNITED NATIONS AND THE DEVELOPMENT OF COLLECTIVE SECURITY, Ch. 6 (1999).

political, legal, institutional, and moral crisis. The decade ended with the utility and the future of the U.N. very much in doubt.

II. The Challenge of Kosovo

NATO's actions in Kosovo presented a serious threat to the United Nations and the conception that had prevailed since 1945: that as the only universal political organization, it represented the international community of states, and that the principles contained in its Charter formed the cornerstone of international relations. Quite suddenly, fundamental principles, such as the respect for sovereignty, territorial integrity and the prohibition on the use of force except in self-defense or when authorized by the Security Council, were cast into doubt. The very fabric of organized international society as we knew it appeared to have been dissolved.

What was particularly worrisome about the NATO-led action in Kosovo was that the decision to proceed with the use of force without U.N. authorization was so overt—more so than the closest precedent at the end of the Gulf War, when the coalition intervened in northern and southern Iraq on the basis of Security Council Resolution 688. Moreover, among the countries most politically and militarily engaged in Kosovo were those who historically have most consistently upheld the principles of the U.N. Charter and the importance of the authority of the United Nations as the foundation of the present system of peace and security.

The NATO-led action in Kosovo caused considerable unease not only among member states, but also among senior U.N. Secretariat officials. This unease deepened as the bombing was stepped up, as civilian installations such as the bridges across the Danube were destroyed, innocent civilians were killed and injured, and questions began to surface about the means and method of warfare and the lack of proportionality in the use of force. It was impossible for Secretary-General Kofi Annan to remain silent. He had the difficult task of trying to defend the Charter principles and its institutional framework, while at the same time recognizing that massive and systematic violations of human rights could not be permitted to unfold without an appropriate response from the United Nations. With its credibility already severely damaged in Somalia, Bosnia, and especially in Rwanda, the U.N. could not afford to be seen as indifferent to the human suffering in Kosovo. In brief press statements at the beginning of the hostilities, the Secretary-General deplored that the situation in Kosovo had not been resolved by peaceful means, and that the Security Council had not been able to fulfill its role. However, he also made it clear that, in his view, there were circumstances in which unauthorized force could legitimately be used in the defense of peace, and in the prevention of massive and systematic violations of human rights. As events in Kosovo unfolded, the need for an authoritative and more comprehensive statement on humanitarian intervention became necessary. The occasion for such an address presented itself in The Hague on May 18, 1999, during the centennial commemoration of the first International Peace Conference.

A. The Secretary-General's Address, The Hague, May 18, 1999

The Secretary-General began his address by noting that the meeting was taking place during a time of war, a reference to the then-ongoing armed intervention regarding Kosovo. He stated that a renewal of the effectiveness and relevance of the Security Council was a cornerstone in protecting and preserving the legal regime of the U.N. Charter. It was, therefore, a cause for concern that the Security Council had been disregarded on such matters as mandatory sanctions, cooperation in disarmament and non-proliferation, and the implementation of the decisions of the Yugoslav and Rwanda war crimes tribunals.

The case of Kosovo, he said, "has cast into sharp relief the fact that member states and regional organizations sometimes take enforcement action without Security Council authorization." He believed that such marginalization of the Council was regrettable. The inability of the Security Council in the case of Kosovo to unify two equally compelling interests—its primary responsibility for the maintenance of peace and the legitimacy of using force in the pursuit of peace and the defense of human rights—was a source of great danger. It was clear that "unless the Security Council is restored to its preeminent position as the sole source of legitimacy on the use of force, we are on a dangerous path to anarchy."

The core challenge of the Security Council and the United Nations as a whole was "to unite behind the principle that massive and systematic violations of human rights conducted against an entire people cannot be allowed to stand." The choice, thus, should not have been between Security Council unity and inaction in the face of genocide, as in Rwanda, and Council division and regional action, as in Kosovo.

B. The Secretary-General's Address to the General Assembly, September 20, 1999

....

Some commentators and scholars attacked the U.N. Charter system as being outmoded or irrelevant. The Secretary-General took issue with this view. The Charter's principles still defined the "aspirations of peoples everywhere." "Nothing in the Charter preclud[ed] a recognition that there are rights beyond borders." The source of the dilemma lay not in deficiencies in the U.N. Charter, but in its application—more precisely applying its principles in an era during which sovereignty and human rights had taken on new meanings in relation to one another....

....

While the events of the last several months in Kosovo, East Timor and Chechnya have focused renewed attention on the role of the United Nations and humanitarian intervention, and while the Secretary-General's address was a timely, even bold, attempt on his part to frame the debate and provoke new thinking about a doctrine of humanitarian intervention, which may or may not be evolving normatively, thus far, very little clarity has emerged. The debate has predictably given rise to much political posturing, but it has also served to highlight a number of underlying issues, such as the imperative need for reform of the Security Council, which lies at the heart of the disenchantment of a great majority of member states.

Louis Henkin, *Kosovo and the Law of "Humanitarian Intervention"*

Editorial Comments: NATO's Kosovo Intervention,
93 Am. J. Int'l L. 824, 824–28 (1999)

I.

... The terrible facts in and relating to Kosovo in 1998–1999 are known and little disputed. The need to halt horrendous crimes against humanity, massive expulsions and war crimes, was widely recognized. NATO intervention by military force was widely welcomed, but it was also sharply criticized. And it inspired much searching of soul by students of international law.

Now that the *fait* of the NATO bombing is *accompli*, and has been assimilated into a political resolution blessed by the Security Council, the legal issues of humanitarian intervention can be addressed in comparative tranquility, and the legal lessons pursued with less urgency, and with greater wisdom.

Was military intervention by NATO justified, lawful, under the UN Charter and international law? Does Kosovo suggest the need for reaffirmation, or clarification, or modification, of the law as to humanitarian intervention? What should the law be, and can the law be construed or modified to be what it ought to be?

. . . .

III.

In my view, unilateral intervention, even for what the intervening state deems to be important humanitarian ends, is and should remain unlawful. But the principles of law, and the interpretations of the Charter, that prohibit unilateral humanitarian intervention do not reflect a conclusion that the "sovereignty" of the target state stands higher in the scale of values of contemporary international society than the human rights of its inhabitants to be protected from genocide and massive crimes against humanity. The law that prohibits unilateral humanitarian intervention rather reflects the judgment of the community that the justification for humanitarian intervention is often ambiguous, involving uncertainties of fact and motive, and difficult questions of degree and "balancing" of need and costs. The law against unilateral intervention may reflect, above all, the moral-political conclusion that no individual state can be trusted with authority to judge and determine wisely.

But, as Professor Richard Falk wrote long ago: "The renunciation of [unilateral] intervention does not substitute a policy of nonintervention; it involves the development of some form of collective intervention." The need for intervention may sometimes be compelling, and the safeguard against the dangers of unilateral intervention lies in developing bona fide, responsible, collective intervention.

Serious efforts to develop "some form of collective intervention" began soon after the end of the Cold War, when it ceased to be hopeless to pursue collective intervention by authority of the UN Security Council. In 1991 and 1992, the Security Council authorized military intervention for humanitarian purposes in Iraq and Somalia. In principle, those interventions were not justified as "humanitarian" (a term that does not appear in the UN Charter); the theory supporting such actions was that some internal wars, at least when accompanied by war crimes, and massive human rights violations and other crimes against humanity even if unrelated to war, may threaten international peace and security and therefore were within the jurisdiction and were the responsibility of the Security Council under Chapters VI and VII of the Charter. Of course, under Article 27(3) of the Charter, a Security Council resolution to authorize intervention, like other "nonprocedural" matters, was subject to veto by any permanent member. Thus, by the sum (or product) of law and politics, humanitarian intervention by any state was prohibited; humanitarian intervention was permissible if authorized by the Security Council, but a single permanent member could prevent such authorization.

Kosovo surely threatened international peace and security, as the Security Council had held in several prior resolutions. And, in 1998–1999, when negotiation and political-economic pressures appeared futile, for many Kosovo begged for intervention by any states that could do so, and by any means necessary. NATO heeded the call. It did not ask leave or authorization from the Security Council.

The reason why NATO did not seek explicit authorization from the Security Council is not difficult to fathom. Even after the Cold War, geography and politics rendered unanimity by the permanent members in support of military action (especially in the

Balkans) highly unlikely. Evidently, NATO decided that not asking for authorization was preferable to having it frustrated by veto, which might have complicated diplomatic efforts to address the crisis, and would have rendered consequent military action politically more difficult.

Subsequent events confirmed that fear of the veto had not been unfounded. After the NATO action was begun, the representative of the Russian Federation proposed a resolution in the Security Council to declare the NATO action unlawful and to direct that it be terminated.

In the vote, the proposed resolution was supported by three states, including Russia and China, two of the permanent members. It was not implausible for NATO to have assumed that Russia, or China, would have vetoed a resolution authorizing military intervention by NATO.

IV.

Was the NATO action unlawful?

The Charter prohibition on intervention, even for humanitarian ends, is addressed to individual states, but what the Charter prohibits to a single state does not become permissible to several states acting together. Intervention by several states is "unilateral," i.e., "on their own authority," if not authorized by the Security Council. Was NATO intervention in Kosovo authorized? Was it a justifiable exception?

The argument for NATO might go something like this.

Human rights violations in Kosovo were horrendous; something had to be done. The Security Council was not in fact "available" to authorize intervention because of the Veto. Faced with a grave threat to international peace and security within its region, and with rampant crimes reeking of genocide, NATO had to act.

NATO intervention was not "unilateral"; it was "collective," pursuant to a decision by a responsible body, including three of the five permanent members entrusted by the UN Charter with special responsibility to respond to threats to international peace and security. NATO did not pursue narrow parochial interests, either of the organization or of any of its members; it pursued recognized, clearly compelling humanitarian purposes. Intervention by NATO at Kosovo was a "collective" humanitarian intervention "in the common interest," carrying out the responsibility of the world community to address threats to international peace and security resulting from genocide and other crimes against humanity. The collective character of the organization provided safeguards against abuse by single powerful states pursuing egoistic national interests. And action by NATO could be monitored by the Security Council and ordered to be terminated. The NATO action in Kosovo had the support of the Security Council. Twelve (out of fifteen) members of the Council voted to reject the Russian resolution of March 26, thereby agreeing in effect that the NATO intervention had been called for and should continue. And on June 10, the Security Council, in Resolution 1244 approving the Kosovo settlement, effectively ratified the NATO action and gave it the Council's support.

V.

In my view, the law is, and ought to be, that unilateral intervention by military force by a state or group of states is unlawful unless authorized by the Security Council. Some— governments and scholars—thought that NATO too needed, but had not had, such authorization, at least ab initio. But many—governments and scholars—thought that something had to be done to end the horrors of Kosovo, that NATO was the appropriate body to do it, and perhaps the only body that could do it, and that the law should not, did not, stand in the way.

....

Humanitarian intervention on the authority of the Security Council recognizes that the Charter prohibition on the use of force does not apply to the use of force "in the common interest"; it also recognizes that intervention authorized by the Security Council affords the strongest safeguard against abuse of humanitarian intervention that the contemporary political system provides. But, as Kosovo illustrated, the Council, as presently constituted and under prevailing procedures, remains seriously defective and may sometimes be unavailable for that awesome responsibility.

NATO did not seek the Council's mantle, presumably because of the fear of the veto. We are not about to see a major restructuring in the composition of the Security Council, and we are not likely soon to see an end to the veto generally. But might we pursue an exception to the veto, as regards humanitarian intervention, in practice if not in principle?

That may be what Kosovo in fact achieved, in some measure. For Kosovo, Council ratification after the fact in Resolution 1244—formal ratification by an affirmative vote of the Council—effectively ratified what earlier might have constituted unilateral action questionable as a matter of law. Unless a decision to authorize intervention in advance can be liberated from the veto, the likely lesson of Kosovo is that states, or collectivities, confident that the Security Council will acquiesce in their decision to intervene, will shift the burden of the veto: instead of seeking authorization in advance by resolution subject to veto, states or collectivities will act, and challenge the Council to terminate the action. And a permanent member favoring the intervention could frustrate the adoption of such a resolution.

VI.

Neither one state nor a collectivity of states should be encouraged to intervene on its own authority in expectation, even plausible expectation, of subsequent ratification or acquiescence by the Security Council. But that is likely to happen, as it did as regards Kosovo, unless the Security Council and the permanent members in particular are prepared to agree to adapt their procedures to permit the Council's consideration in advance, with the understanding that the veto would not be operative.

Changes in the law and in UN procedures and understandings to that end might begin with Chapter VIII of the Charter.

....

... The NATO action in Kosovo, and the proceedings in the Security Council, may reflect a step toward a change in the law, part of the quest for developing "a form of collective intervention" beyond a veto-bound Security Council. That may be a desirable change, perhaps even an inevitable change. And it might be achieved without formal amendment of the Charter (which is virtually impossible to effect), by a "gentlemen's agreement" among the permanent members, or by wise self-restraint and acquiescence. That, some might suggest, is what the law ought to be, and proponents of a "living Charter" would support an interpretation of the law and an adaptation of UN procedures that rendered them what they ought to be. That might be the lesson of Kosovo.

NATO's specific response in the case of Kosovo is part of a more general evolution that is taking place in the Alliance's own conception of its role in the management of conflict.

It adopted strategic concepts in 1999 and in 2010. In 2011, NATO answered the UN call to the international community to protect the Libyan people from the Gaddafi regime. From March to October 2011, a coalition of NATO Allies and partners enforced an arms embargo, maintained a no-fly zone and protected civilians from attack or the threat of attack in Libya under 'Operation Unified Protector'.

Bruno Simma, *NATO, the UN and the Use of Force: Legal Aspects*
10 Eur. J. Int'l L. 1, 14–18 (1999)

3. NATO's Future 'Strategic Concept': From 'Out of Area' to 'Out of Treaty'?

... NATO is hammering out a new 'strategic concept' to define its role in the 21st century. It is to be adopted on the occasion of the Alliance's 50th Anniversary Summit in Washington in late April 1999.... Nevertheless, the general direction in which the United States in particular wants the Alliance to move in the future is quite clear. For instance ... Deputy Secretary of State Strobe Talbott had, among other things, the following to say about what he referred to as the 'deepening' of NATO:

> In that project [i.e., the transformation of NATO] ... we must be ambitious. NATO was founded and designed to deal with the Soviet Union and the Warsaw Pact. That state and that alliance are gone, and so is the threat they posed.... This isn't to say that NATO's original task of collective defence is finished or that collective defence is no longer at the core of the Alliance's mission. NATO must maintain its capability, enshrined in Art.V of the Treaty of Washington, to deter and if necessary defeat what might be called classic aggression....

> However, that is not enough if NATO is to remain relevant to the times. With the end of the Cold War, new, less spectacular, but more diversified threats have arisen. Disputes over ethnicity, religion or territory, can, as we've already seen, trigger armed conflict, which in turn can generate cross-border political instability, refugee flows and humanitarian crisis that endanger European security. NATO must be able to deal with threats like these while maintaining its core function of collective defense.

> ....

> [We are not] suggesting that NATO act in splendid isolation from—or high-handed defiance of—the United Nations or the OSCE. All NATO Allies are members of both of those organizations. We believe NATO's missions and tasks must always be consistent with the purposes and principles of the UN and the OSCE. We expect NATO and its members will continue to be guided by their obligations under the UN Charter and the Helsinki Final Act.

> At the same time, we must be careful not to subordinate NATO to any other international body or compromise the integrity of its command structure. We will try to act in concert with other organizations, and with respect for their principles and purposes. But the Alliance must reserve the right and the freedom to act when its members, by consensus, deem it necessary.

The future role thus envisaged for NATO and the legal-institutional consequences which the proposed new concept implies for the relationship between NATO and the United Nations also became apparent in a 'Resolution on Recasting Euro-Atlantic Security', adopted by the North Atlantic (Parliamentary) Assembly in November 1998. In this document, the Assembly urged member governments and parliaments of the North Atlantic Alliance

...

d. to seek to ensure the widest international legitimacy for non-Article 5 missions and also to stand ready to act should the UN Security Council be prevented from discharging its purpose of maintaining international peace and security;

e. to affirm that the inherent right of individual or collective self-defence, also enshrined in Article 51 of the UN Charter, must include defence of common interests and values, including when the latter are threatened by humanitarian catastrophes, crimes against humanity, and war crimes; ...

... [T]he message which these voices carry in our context is clear: if it turns out that a Security Council mandate or authorization for future NATO 'non-Article 5' missions involving armed force cannot be obtained, NATO must still be able to go ahead with such enforcement. That the Alliance is capable of doing so is being demonstrated in the Kosovo crisis. Whether such a course is legally permissible is a different matter. In the November 1998 resolution of the North Atlantic Assembly, two different legal arguments can be identified in this regard. According to the first one, the right of self-defence 'also enshrined' in Article 51 of the UN Charter is to be interpreted so broadly as to include the defence of 'common interests and values'. This text calls for two brief observations: to start with, the wording might create the impression that self-defence in international law has a broader scope than that foreseen in Article 51, i.e., that it is justified not only against armed attacks but beyond that specific instance also against other threats. What other menaces the authors have in mind is then made clear: attacks on 'common [i.e. NATO] interests and values'. To thus widen the scope of self-defence, as a legal institution, is intolerable ... from a legal point of view and does not deserve further comment....

The second argument, contained in para. d. of the North Atlantic Assembly resolution, reads like a codification of the course that NATO is steering in the Kosovo crisis.... It is probably no coincidence that the wording chosen for para. d. is similar to that of the 'Uniting for Peace' Resolution of the UN General Assembly of 3 November 1950, considering the keenness of NATO to have its actions partake of UN legitimacy, so to speak. But of course, according to 'Uniting for Peace', it was the General Assembly, as a UN organ comprising all Member States, that was to shoulder the burden of maintaining or restoring international peace and security *in lieu* of the Security Council, not an extraneous, regional organization comprising only about 10 per cent of UN membership.

...

In view of the Russian position *vis-à-vis* the prospect of NATO 'peace missions' engaging in military enforcement out of area, a new formula has recently been put forward, according to which the necessary legal basis for non-Article 5 missions comprising the use of armed force is, 'as a rule', to be provided either by a mandate of the UN Security Council or by acting 'under the responsibility of the OSCE'....

The alternative thus offered may possibly appease the Russian Federation, but it cannot satisfy the international lawyer: the OSCE has grown into a regional organization in the sense of Chapter VIII of the Charter. As such, any military enforcement action under its responsibility will require authorization by the UN Security Council.... Thus, such peace enforcement under the aegis of the OSCE will not only require the consent of the Russian Federation but also that of the Security Council in accordance with Article 53 para.1 of the UN Charter. From the standpoint of United Nations law, therefore, the issue is not only how to obtain the consent/participation of Russia in peace enforcement but how to achieve this at the regional level in full conformity with the Charter.

The Alliance's Strategic Concept 1999

Approved by the Heads of State and Government participating in the meeting of
the North Atlantic Council in Washington DC on April 23–24, 1999

6. NATO's essential and enduring purpose, set out in the Washington Treaty, is to safeguard the freedom and security of all its members by political and military means. Based on common values of democracy, human rights and the rule of law, the Alliance has striven since its inception to secure a just and lasting peaceful order in Europe. It will continue to do so. The achievement of this aim can be put at risk by crisis and conflict affecting the security of the Euro-Atlantic area. The Alliance therefore not only ensures the defence of its members but contributes to peace and stability in this region.

. . . .

24. Any armed attack on the territory of the Allies, from whatever direction, would be covered by Articles 5 and 6 of the Washington Treaty. However, Alliance security must also take account of the global context. Alliance security interests can be affected by other risks of a wider nature, including acts of terrorism, sabotage and organised crime, and by the disruption of the flow of vital resources....

. . . .

31. In pursuit of its policy of preserving peace, preventing war, and enhancing security and stability and as set out in the fundamental security tasks, NATO will seek, in cooperation with other organisations, to prevent conflict, or, should a crisis arise, to contribute to its effective management, consistent with international law, including through the possibility of conducting non-Article 5 crisis response operations. The Alliance's preparedness to carry out such operations supports the broader objective of reinforcing and extending stability and often involves the participation of NATO's Partners. NATO recalls its offer, made in Brussels in 1994, to support on a case-by-case basis in accordance with its own procedures, peacekeeping and other operations under the authority of the UN Security Council or the responsibility of the OSCE, including by making available Alliance resources and expertise. In this context NATO recalls its subsequent decisions with respect to crisis response operations in the Balkans. Taking into account the necessity for Alliance solidarity and cohesion, participation in any such operation or mission will remain subject to decisions of member states in accordance with national constitutions.

The Alliance's Strategic Concept 2010

Adopted by Heads of State and Government at the NATO Summit in Lisbon
19–20 November 2010

1. NATO's fundamental and enduring purpose is to safeguard the freedom and security of all its members by political and military means. Today, the Alliance remains an essential source of stability in an unpredictable world.

. . .

4. The modern security environment contains a broad and evolving set of challenges to the security of NATO's territory and populations. In order to assure their security, the Alliance must and will continue fulfilling effectively three essential core tasks, all of which contribute to safeguarding Alliance members, and always in accordance with international law:

a. Collective defence. NATO members will always assist each other against attack, in accordance with Article 5 of the Washington Treaty. That commitment remains firm and binding. NATO will deter and defend against any threat of aggression, and against emerging security challenges where they threaten the fundamental security of individual Allies or the Alliance as a whole.

b. Crisis management. NATO has a unique and robust set of political and military capabilities to address the full spectrum of crises—before, during and after conflicts. NATO will actively employ an appropriate mix of those political and military tools to help manage developing crises that have the potential to affect Alliance security, before they escalate into conflicts; to stop ongoing conflicts where they affect Alliance security; and to help consolidate stability in post-conflict situations where that contributes to Euro-Atlantic security.

c.Cooperative security. The Alliance is affected by, and can affect, political and security developments beyond its borders. The Alliance will engage actively to enhance international security, through partnership with relevant countries and other international organisations; by contributing actively to arms control, non-proliferation and disarmament; and by keeping the door to membership in the Alliance open to all European democracies that meet NATO's standards

. . .

31. Cooperation between NATO and the United Nations continues to make a substantial contribution to security in operations around the world. The Alliance aims to deepen political dialogue and practical cooperation with the UN, as set out in the UN-NATO Declaration signed in 2008 . . .

Comment

This process of reflection by NATO of its changing role and its action in Libya in 2011 raise acutely the key issue of what policy considerations should be taken into account when allocating authority between universal (i.e., the UN) and regional arrangements in the management of conflict.

John Norton Moore, *The Role of Regional Arrangements in the Maintenance of World Order*

in 3 The Future of the International Legal Order, 122, 136–40
(Cyril Black & Richard Falk eds., 1971)

Policies Favoring Universalism

The principal policies favoring universalism seem to be that states affected by decisions should have an opportunity to participate in the decision-making, that effective decision may require that competing major powers be included in security decisions, that wider decision is more likely to reflect community common interest and the corollary of this principle that major power dominance of regional organizations may sometimes result in assertion of special interests.

The first of these, that states affected by decision should have an opportunity to participate in making those decisions, is a widely shared community policy. To the extent that peace and security issues affect the whole community of states, the whole community has an interest in participating in their resolution. And in the kind of interdependent world in which we live today the quality of the international peacekeeping machinery is of concern to every nation. This policy, then, strongly suggests that at least final authority for the maintenance of world order should be vested in a universal organization.

A second policy is the desirability of representation of competing major powers in security decisions. This policy reflects the importance of avoiding conflict between the competitive nuclear powers and of ensuring effective power to implement collective decisions. To the extent that world order decisions are approved by all major powers there is less likelihood of a major power clash. There is also greater likelihood that decisions will be effectively implemented. Moreover, participation in the decision process might moderate positions even if agreement is not possible.... The permanent seats for the major powers in the Security Council reflect these realities.

A third policy is that wider decision is more likely to reflect common community interest. There is, of course, no guarantee that a universal organization will always make just or rational decisions. The United Nations is a political arena with characteristics similar to other such arenas, and it is a mistake to idealize its decisions just because they are collective. Nevertheless, on a continuum from unilateral to universal decision there is greater likelihood that the wider the participation in decision the more the decision will reflect common community interest. As a corollary to this principle, since major powers exert disproportionate influence in a number of regional organizations, United Nations authority should be preferred as a check on assertion of special interests.

Policies Favoring Regionalism

Policies favoring regional authority include the principle that those with greater values at stake in decision ought to have greater participation in decision, the advantages of utilization of local expertise and interest, the principle of effectiveness and deference to consensual arrangements submitting local disputes to regional authority.

The first of these, the principle that those with greater values at stake in decision ought to have greater participation in decision, reflects the differential impact of decisions. If a decision affects only a particular region, then that region ought to participate in decision to the exclusion of nonregional participants. It is self-evident that in matters other than peace and security there are large areas of exclusive interests in which decision is and should be made unilaterally or regionally. Although few interests are that clearly exclusive if the issue is one affecting peace and security, nevertheless, even peace and security issues may have differential impact. Thus, the recent El Salvador-Honduras conflict presented a greater threat to the security of other Central American states than to the security of European or Asian states. Similarly, it may have posed a greater threat to the integrity of regional peacekeeping machinery than to the structure of the United Nations. Accordingly, it seems reasonable to accord the regional machinery of the OAS the initial competence to deal with the situation.

A second policy favoring regional authority is the desirability of taking advantage of local expertise, interest and capabilities. The inter-American system, the OAU, and to a lesser extent the Arab League embody dispute-settlement machinery which may be highly efficient in settling intraregional conflicts. The relatively quick and efficient OAS handling of the El Salvador-Honduras conflict is a case in point. Had the OAS been unsuccessful in obtaining a withdrawal of Salvadorian troops, then the greater effective power of the Security Council might have been required. But in the first instance at least, the OAS was almost certainly a more efficient forum for dealing with such a localized intraregional dispute than would have been the United Nations Security Council....

....

Summary of Criteria for Allocating Authority between Universal and Regional Arrangements

There are strong reasons for urging that a universal organization should have ultimate authority for the maintenance of peace and security. In the interdependent world in which we live, most issues of peace and security affect all of the members of the world community. Moreover, a universal forum is a more broadly based forum for the resolution of security issues, both in the sense of greater assurance that decision will reflect common community interest, and in the sense of greater effectiveness by inclusion of the major powers in the decision process. A universal security organization should encourage regional settlement of disputes, however, in situations in which the interests at stake are primarily regional, in which regional machinery offers more effective conflict management, or in which the parties to a dispute genuinely prefer a regional forum.

Questions for Discussion

1. To what extent, if at all, does the purported doctrine of humanitarian intervention provide a basis for regional arrangements to use military force to stop the commission of gross and widespread violations of human rights occurring within a state?

2. Was ECOMOG military action in Liberia lawful? Was NATO military action in Kosovo lawful? What are the similarities and differences between the military action taken by NATO in Kosovo and ECOMOG in Liberia?

3. What changes, if any, does the Kosovo case suggest should be made to decision-making by the Security Council?

4. What is NATO's evolving strategic conception of its role in the maintenance and restoration of peace and security?

5. What does the experience of the AU and ECOWAS tell us about the challenges of peacekeeping by regional organizations? To what extent should regional arrangements be a primary focus for efforts to maintain or restore international peace and security?

Responsibility to Protect

Responsibility to protect (R2P) is an emerging legal doctrine that was first developed by the International Commission on the Intervention and State Sovereignty (ICISS), established by the Canadian Foreign Minister Lloyd Axworthy and co-chaired by Gareth Evans (Australia) and Muhamed Sahnoun (Algeria). In its Report of 30 September 2001, ICISS explained basic principles of R2P as: "(A) State sovereignty implies responsibility, and the primary responsibility for the protection of the people lies with the State itself; (B) Where a population is suffering serious harm, as a result of internal war, insurgency, repression or state failure, and the state in question is unwilling or unable to halt or avert it, the principle of non-intervention yields to the international responsibility to protect."[96]

R2P was endorsed as an "emerging norm" in the 2004 Report of the High-Level Panel on Threats, Challenges and Changes.[97] The Report suggested five criteria for the determining whether an intervention based on R2P would be justified: the seriousness of the threat,

---

96. ICISS, 'The Responsibility to Protect', 30 September 2001, xi.
97. 'A More Secure World: Our Shared Responsibility', 2 December 2004, U.N. Doc. A/59/565, para 53; *see also* paras 201–205.

the proper purpose of the military action, the fact that force as a last resort, proportionality, and the balance of consequences. Secretary-General Kofi Annan expressed his strong agreement with the concept of R2P in his 2005 Report 'In Larger Freedom: Towards Development, Security and Human Rights for All', observing that "we must embrace the responsibility to protect, and, when necessary, we must act on it."[98]

The most significant expression of recognition and support for R2P came in the World Summit Outcome Document, adopted in October 2005 by an historic gathering of Heads of State and Government at the UN.[99]

World Summit Outcome Document
U.N. Doc. A/RES/60/1, Oct. 24, 2005, paras. 138–39

Responsibility to protect populations from genocide, war crimes, ethnic cleansing and crimes against humanity

138. Each individual State has the responsibility to protect its populations from genocide, war crimes, ethnic cleansing and crimes against humanity. This responsibility entails the prevention of such crimes, including their incitement, through appropriate and necessary means. We accept that responsibility and will act in accordance with it. The international community should, as appropriate, encourage and help States to exercise this responsibility and support the United Nations in establishing an early warning capability.

139. The international community, through the United Nations, also has the responsibility to use appropriate diplomatic, humanitarian and other peaceful means, in accordance with Chapters VI and VIII of the Charter, to help to protect populations from genocide, war crimes, ethnic cleansing and crimes against humanity. In this context, we are prepared to take collective action, in a timely and decisive manner, through the Security Council, in accordance with the Charter, including Chapter VII, on a case-by-case basis and in cooperation with relevant regional organizations as appropriate, should peaceful means be inadequate and national authorities are manifestly failing to protect their populations from genocide, war crimes, ethnic cleansing and crimes against humanity. We stress the need for the General Assembly to continue consideration of the responsibility to protect populations from genocide, war crimes, ethnic cleansing and crimes against humanity and its implications, bearing in mind the principles of the Charter and international law. We also intend to commit ourselves, as necessary and appropriate, to helping States build capacity to protect their populations from genocide, war crimes, ethnic cleansing and crimes against humanity and to assisting those which are under stress before crises and conflicts break out.

The Secretary-General appointed a Special Adviser on the Responsibility to Protect and the 'three pillars' of the responsibility to protect were formulated in the Secretary-General's 2009 Report (A/63/677) on Implementing the Responsibility to Protect:

1. The State carries the primary responsibility for protecting populations from genocide, war crimes, crimes against humanity and ethnic cleansing, and their incitement;

2. The international community has a responsibility to encourage and assist States in fulfilling this responsibility;

---

98. 'In Larger Freedom', 21 March 2005, U.N. Doc. A/59/2005, paras 132, 135.
99. For further discussion on R2P *see* Chapter 14, International Human Rights.

3. The international community has a responsibility to use appropriate diplomatic, humanitarian and other means to protect populations from these crimes. If a State is manifestly failing to protect its populations, the international community must be prepared to take collective action to protect populations, in accordance with the Charter of the United Nations.

Nonetheless, there has not yet been widespread and representative State practice on R2P and agreement on the specific criteria remains elusive.[100] Some of the controversies surrounding R2P were aired during a 2009 debate in the General Assembly.

Opening Statement, President of the General Assembly, Mr. Miguel d'Escoto Brockman

23 July 2009

After so much suffering, there is finally broad agreement that the international community can no longer remain silent in the face of genocide, ethnic cleansing, war crimes and crimes against humanity. This is a great progress. Yet there are currently situations, as in Gaza, which urgently need adequate and objective characterization, as well as the international community's responsibility to aid in their solution.

I would ask whether it was the absence of responsibility to protect that led to non-intervention in Gaza as recently as this year? Or was it, rather, the absence of the reform of the UN Security Council, whose veto power remains unchecked and its membership unreformed. Need I remind anyone here that we already have a Genocide Convention and various conventions on international humanitarian law, whose implementation remain erratic?

...

So why do many of us hesitate to embrace this doctrine and its aspirations? Certainly it is not out of indifference to the plight of many who suffer and who may yet be caused to suffer at the hands of their own governments.

The problem for many nations, I believe, is that our system of collective security has not yet evolved to the degree that can allow the doctrine of R2P to operate in the way its proponents intend, in view of the prevailing lack of trust from developing countries when it comes to the use of force for humanitarian reasons.

...

Member States, as I do, clearly hold strong views on this issue. I believe this morning's discussion made it clear that the most effective and just form of avoiding large-scale human suffering certainly is not by resorting to the use of military force ... the question still remains if the time for a full-fledged R2P norm has arrived, or whether as most of the panelists this morning felt, we first need to create a more just and equal world order, including in the economic and social sense, as well as a Security Council that does not create a differential system of international law geared towards the strong protecting, or not protecting, whomever they wish.

---

100. The Security Council has referred to R2P in a number of resolutions, but these have fallen short of guidelines for the implementation of the emerging norm and have been made on the premise that it is Security Council that must authorize States to use military force. *See, e.g.*, SC Res 1674 (2006), 1970 (2011), 1973 (2011), and 2150 (2014).

Comments

1. R2P does not require the Security Council or its members to put a matter on the agenda, to support a decision in the Security Council or to have a good reason for using the veto.[101] In his 2012 Report on R2P, the Secretary-General confirmed that R2P does not impose an obligation on the Security Council to act—rather, the doctrine and the Charter give the Security Council "a wide degree of latitude to determine the most appropriate course of action".[102]

2. The Council's action with regard to Libya in 2011 has highlighted the controversy over R2P. SC Resolution 1973 was hailed in certain circles as a 'successful first true test' of R2P, but the Resolution makes no express reference to the doctrine in its operative provisions.[103] In the aftermath of Gaddafi's fall some Member States have argued that non-coercive measures were not given sufficient time to have an impact on the ground and that those charged with implementing Resolution 1973 exceeded the mandate given by the Council.[104] Former Joint Envoy for Syria, Kofi Annan, has observed that Russia and China in particular feel that they were 'duped' by the Council's action on Libya in 2011: they had agreed on a resolution that they believed authorised limited measures, which was then transformed into a process of regime change.[105]

Questions for Discussion

1. To what extent is R2P a desirable development in multilateral efforts to maintain or restore international peace and security?

2. To what extent can R2P be considered as a norm of customary international law?

3. Does R2P allow a State or group of States to intervene militarily in another State if the Security Council fails to act with respect to a situation of massive human rights violations?

4. How does the concept of R2P relate to the notion of 'humanitarian intervention' and NATO's action in Kosovo discussed above?

Selected Bibliography

The United Nations System

Ian Brownlie, *The Rule of Law in International Affairs: International Law at the Fiftieth Anniversary of the United Nations* (1998).

---

101. Saira Mohamed, *Omissions, Acts, and the Security Council's (in)Actions in Syria* 31 B.U. INT'L L.J. 413, 423 (2013).

102. Responsibility to protect: timely and decisive response, Report of the Secretary-General, A/66/874, S/2012/578 (2012), para. 54.

103. Berman and Michaelsen argue that express invocation of R2P would have prevented rather than facilitated the adoption of Resolution 1973 (2011) and its authorisation of the use of force to protect civilians in Libya because China and Russia would have vetoed the resolution. David Berman and Christopher Michaelsen, *Intervention in Libya: Another Nail in the Coffin for the Responsibility-to-Protect?* 14 INT'L COMMUNITY L. REV. 337 (2012).

104. Responsibility to protect: timely and decisive response, Report of the Secretary-General, A/66/874, S/2012/578 (2012), para. 54.

105. Natalie Nougayrède, *Kofi Annan: "Sur la Syrie, à l'évidence, nous n'avons pas réussi,"* LE MONDE, 7 July 2012.

Benedetto Conforti, *The Law and Practice of the United Nations* (4th Ed. 2010).

James Crawford, "The Charter of the United Nations as a Constitution," *in The Changing Constitution of the United Nations* 3 (Hazel Fox ed., 1997).

Rosalyn Higgins, *Problems and Process: International Law and How We Use It* (1994).

Oscar Schachter, "United Nations Law: an Overview," 88 *Am. J. Int'l L.* 1 (1994).

Henry Schermers & Niels Blokker, *International Institutional Law: Unity Within Diversity* (5th Ed. 2011).

Bruno Simma, et al. (eds.), *The Charter of the United Nations: a Commentary* (3rd Ed. 2012).

Strengthening the United Nations and Enhancing War Prevention (John Norton Moore & Alex Morrison eds., 2000).

Membership of the United Nations

Georges Abi-Saab, "Membership and Voting in the United Nations," *in The Changing Constitution of the United Nations* 19–42 (Hazel Fox ed., 1997).

Vladimir-Djuro Degan, et al., "UN Membership of the Former Yugoslavia," 87 *Am. J. Int'l L.* 240–51 (1993).

Rosalyn Higgins, *The Development of International Law Through the Political Organs of the United Nations* 11–57 (1963).

Michael Wood, "Participation of the Former Yugoslav States in the United Nations," 1 *Max Planck Y.B. of UN Law* 231 (1997).

Security Council Powers and Voting

Sydney Bailey Dawson, *The Procedure of the UN Security Council* 221–73 (3d Ed. 1998).

Bardo Fassbender, *UN Security Council Reform and the Right of Veto* (1998).

Jack Garvey, "The UN Definition of Aggression: Law and Illusion in the Context of Collective Security," 17 *Va. J. Int'l L.* 177 (1976–1977).

Rosalyn Higgins, "The United Nations Security Council and the Individual State," *in The Changing Constitution of the United Nations* 43 (Hazel Fox ed., 1997).

———, "The Place of International Law in the Settlement of Disputes by the Security Council," 64 *Am. J. Int'l L.* 1 (1970).

Frederic Kirgis, "The Security Council's First Fifty Years," 89 *Am. J. Int'l L.* 506 (1995).

Susan Lamb, "Legal Limits to United Nations Security Council Powers," *in The Reality of International Law: Essays in Honour of Ian Brownlie* 361–88 (Guy Goodwin-Gill & Stefan Talmon eds., 1999).

Constantin Staviopoulos, "The Practice of Voluntary Abstentions by Permanent Members of the Security Council Under Article 25 of the Charter," 61 *Am. J. Int'l L.* 737 (1967).

Antonios Tzanakopoulos, Disobeying the Security Council (Oxford University Press, 2011).

Philippa Webb, "Deadlock or Restraint? The Security Council Veto and the Use of Force in Syria," *Journal of Conflict and Security Law*, (2014).

Michael Wood, "Security Council Working Methods and Procedures," 45 *Int'l & Comp. L.Q.* 50 (1996).

Judicial Review of Security Council Measures

Dapo Akande, "The International Court of Justice and the Security Council: Is There Room for Judicial Control of Decisions of the Political Organs of the United Nations?" 46 *Int'l & Comp. L.Q.* 309 (1997).

Jose Alvarez, Judging the Security Council, 90 *Am. J. Int'l L.* 1 (1996).

Ian Brownlie, "The Decisions of Political Organs of the United Nations and the Rule of Law," *in Essays in Honour of Wang Tieya* 91 (Ronald St. John McDonald ed., 1993).

Thomas Franck, "The 'Powers of Appreciation': Who is the Ultimate Guardian of UN Legality?" 86 *Am. J. Int'l L.* 519 (1992).

Vera Gowlland-Debbas, "The Relationship between the International Court of Justice and the Security Council in the Light of the Lockerbie Case," 88 *Am. J. Int'l L.* 643 (1994).

Robert Jennings, "The International Court of Justice after Fifty Years," 89 *Am. J. Int'l L.* 493 (1995).

Paolo Palchetti, "Judicial Review of the International Validity of UN Security Council Resolutions by the European Court of Justice" in Enzo Cannizzaro, Paolo Palchetti, Ramses A. Wesse (eds.) *International Law as Law of the European Union* (2012).

Edward McWhinney, "The International Court as Emerging Constitutional Court and the Co-ordinate UN Institutions (Especially the Security Council): Implications of the Aerial Incident at Lockerbie," 30 *Can. Y.B. Int'l L.* 261 (1992).

UN Economic and Other Sanctions

Benedetto Conforti, *The Law and Practice of the United Nations* 185–94 (2d Ed. 2000).

David Cortright & George Lopez, *The Sanctions Decade: Assessing UN Strategies in the 1990s* (2000).

Wendell Maddrey, "Economic Sanctions Against South Africa: Problems and Prospects for Enforcement of Human Rights Norms," 22 *Va. J. Int'l L.* 345 (1982).

W. Michael Reisman & Douglas Stevick, "The Applicability of International Law Standards to United Nations Economic Sanctions Programmes," 9 *Eur. J. Int'l L.* 86 (1998).

Larissa van den Herik, "Peripheral Hegemony in the Quest to Ensure Security Council Accountability for its Individualized UN Sanctions Regimes," *Journal of Conflict and Security Law* (2014).

Erika de Wet, "From Kadi To Nada: Judicial Techniques Favoring Human Rights Over United Nations Security Council Sanctions," 12 *Chinese Journal of International Law* (2013).

UN Military Enforcement Action

Yoram Dinstein, *War, Aggression and Self-Defence,* Chapter 10, (5th Ed. 2012).

Tom Farer, "Beyond the Charter Frame: Unilateralism or Condominium?" 96 *Am. J. Int'l L.* 359 (2002).

Christopher Greenwood, "International Law and the Pre-emptive Use of Force: Afghanistan, Al-Qaida, and Iraq," 4 *San Diego International Law Journal* 7–37 (2003).

———, "International Humanitarian Law and United Nations Military Operations," 1 *Y.B. Int'l Humanitarian L.* 1 (1998).

———, "New World Order or Old? The Invasion of Kuwait and the Rule of Law," 55(2) *The Modern L. Rev.* 153 (1992).

Rosalyn Higgins, *Problems and Process: International Law and How We Use It,* 254–66 (1994).

———, "Peace and Security. Achievements and Failures," 6 *Eur. J. Int'l L.* 445 (1995).

Frederic Kirgis, "The Security Council's First Fifty Years," 89 *Am. J. Int'l L.* 506 (1995).

Jules Lobel & Michael Ratner, "Bypassing the Security Council: Ambiguous Authorizations to Use Force, Cease-Fires and the Iraqi Inspection Regime," 93 *Am. J. Int'l L.* 124 (1999).

John Norton Moore, "Toward a New Paradigm: Enhanced Effectiveness in United Nations Peacekeeping, Collective Security, and War Avoidance," 37 *Va. J. Int'l L.* 811 (1997).

W. Michael Reisman, "In Defense of World Public Order," 95 *Am. J. Int'l L.* 833 (2001).

Dan Sarooshi, *The United Nations and the Development of Collective Security*, Chs. 4–5 (1999).

UN Transitional Administrations

Samuel Barnes, "The Contribution of Democracy to Rebuilding Postconflict Societies," 95 *Am. J. Int'l L.* 86 (2001).

Frederic Kirgis, "Security Council Governance of Postconflict Societies: A Plea for Good Faith and Informed Decision Making," 95 *Am. J. Int'l L.* 579 (2001).

W. Michael Matheson, "United Nations Governance of Postconflict Societies," 95 *Am. J. Int'l L.* 76 (2001).

Carsten Stahn, *The Law and Practice of International Territorial Administration: Versailles to Iraq and Beyond* (Cambridge University Press, 2008).

Hansjörg Strohmeyer, "Collapse and Reconstruction of a Judicial System: The United Nations Missions in Kosovo and East Timor," 95 *Am. J. Int'l L.* 46 (2001).

Ralph Wilde, *International Territorial Administration. How Trusteeship and the Civilizing Mission Never Went Away* (Oxford University Press, 2008).

The General Assembly

Andrew J Carswell, "Unblocking the UN Security Council: the Uniting for Peace Resolution" 18 *Journal of Conflict and Security Law* 453 (2013).

Benedetto Conforti, *The Law and Practice of the United Nations* 87–99, 210–17 (2d Ed. 2000).

Eric Suy, "The Role of the United Nations General Assembly," *in The Changing Constitution of the United Nations* 55–72 (Hazel Fox ed., 1997).

UN Peacekeeping

Kofi Annan, "Peace-Keeping in Situations of Civil War," 26 *N.Y.U. J. Int'l L. & Pol.* 623 (1994).

Antonio Cassesse, *United Nations Peacekeeping*, Chs. 1–3 (1978).

Christopher Greenwood, "Protection of Peacekeepers: The Legal Regime," 7 *Duke J. Comp. & Int'l L.* 185 (1996).

Rosalyn Higgins, *United Nations Peacekeeping* (Vols. 1–4).

John Hirsh & Robert Oakley, *Somalia and Operation Restore Hope* (1995).

F.M. Lorenz, "Rules of Engagement in Somalia: Were They Effective?" 42 *Naval L. Rev.* 62 (1995).

John Norton Moore, "Toward a New Paradigm: Enhanced Effectiveness in United Nations Peacekeeping, Collective Security, and War Avoidance," 37 *Va. J. Int'l L.* 811 (1997).

Robert Siekmann, *National Contingents in United Nations Peace-Keeping Forces* (1991).

James Sloan, *The Militarisation of Peacekeeping in the Twenty-First Century* (Hart, 2011).

Nigel White, *Keeping the Peace: The United Nations and the Maintenance of International Peace and Security* 207–76 (2d Ed. 1997).

The UN Secretary-General

Thomas Franck, "The Secretary-General's Role in Conflict Resolution: Past, Present and Pure Conjecture," 6 *Eur. J. Int'l L.* 360 (1995).

David Kennedy, "Leader, Clerk, or Policy Entrepreneur?: the Secretary-General in a Complex World," in Simon Chesterman (ed.) *Secretary or General: the UN Secretary-General in World Politics* (2007).

Dan Sarooshi, "The Role of the UN Secretary-General in UN Peace-Keeping Operations," 20 *Australian Y.B. Int'l L.* 279 (2000).

Stephen Schwebel, *The Secretary-General of the United Nations* (1952).

Paul Szasz, "The Role of the UN Secretary-General: Some Legal Aspects," 24 *N.Y.U. J. Int'l L. & Pol.* 161 (1991–1992).

The Role of Regional Arrangements

"Commentary to Chapter VIII," *in La Charte Des Nations Unies* 797 (Jean-Pierre Cot & Alain Pellet eds., 1991).

"Commentary to Chapter VIII," *in The Charter of the United Nations* (Bruno Simma ed., 2d Ed. 2002).

"Editorial Comments: NATO's Kosovo Intervention," 93 *Am. J. Int'l L.* 824–62 (1999).

Christine Gray, "Regional Arrangements and the United Nations Collective Security System," *in The Changing Constitution of the United Nations* 91 (Hazel Fox ed., 1997).

Christopher Greenwood, "Humanitarian Intervention: The Case of Kosovo," 10 *Finnish Y.B. Int'l L.* 141 (1999).

Rosalyn Higgins, "Peace and Security. Achievements and Failures," 6 *Eur. J. Int'l L.* 14 (1995).

Dino Kritsiotis, "The Kosovo Crisis and NATO's Application of Armed Force Against the Federal Republic of Yugoslavia," 49 *Int'l & Comp. L.Q.* 330 (2000).

Eric P. J. Myjer, "Peace Operations conducted by Regional Organizations and Arrangements" in Terry Gill and Dieter Fleck (eds.), *Handbook of the International Law of Military Operations* (2010).

John Norton Moore, "The Role of Regional Arrangements in the Maintenance of World Order," *in 3 The Future of the International Legal Order* 122 (Cyril Black & Richard Falk eds., 1971).

Dan Sarooshi, "The UN System for the Maintenance of International Peace: What Role For Regional Organizations such as NATO?," 52 *Current Legal Problems* 473 (1999).

Christopher Schreur, "Regionalism v. Universalism," 6 *Eur. J. Int'l L.* 477 (1995).

Bruno Simma, "NATO, the UN and the Use of Force: Legal Aspects," 10 *Eur. J. Int'l L.* 1 (1999).

Alex Vines, "A Decade of African Peace and Security Architecture," 89 *International Affairs* 89 (2013).

Ralph Zacklin, "Beyond Kosovo: The United Nations and Humanitarian Intervention," 41 *Va. J. Int'l L.* 923 (2001).

The Responsibility to Protect

A. J. Bellamy, *A Responsibility to Protect: The Global Effort to End Mass Atrocities* (Polity Press, 2009).

David Berman and Christopher Michaelsen, 'Intervention in Libya: Another Nail in the Coffin for the Responsibility-to-Protect?' 14 *International Community Law Review* 337 (2012).

E. Strauss, *The Emperor's New Clothes? The United Nations and the Implementation of the Responsibility to Protect* (Nomos, 2009).

Chapter 6

The Law of Armed Conflict and Neutrality

Howard S. Levie, Jack Grunawalt, and David E. Graham

In this chapter:
Introduction
Theoretical and Historical Overview
Scope of Application
Methods and Means of Conducting Hostilities
Naval Warfare
Air Warfare
The Law of Belligerent Occupation
Protecting Powers and Enforcement
The Law of Neutrality
Selected Bibliography

Introduction

Perhaps no other aspect of National Security Law has experienced a more dynamic evolution over the past half century than that of the Law of War. This has been the product of a period of persistent hostilities, varying substantially in their nature, scope and location. Indeed, the substance—and even the historic nomenclature of this legal regime—have undergone fundamental changes. The concept of declared "wars" has given way to the reality of any number of conflict scenarios that have failed to fall within the ambit of any given definition of traditional "warfare." Thus, the "Law of War" that purported, historically, to exclusively regulate State-on-State conflict has increasingly become referred to as "The Law of Armed Conflict" (LOAC). In turn, the international community has more recently wrestled with the matter of whether, and, if so, how even this more developed LOAC might be adapted to use of force situations that have consistently arisen between States and non-State entities. This, in turn, has resulted in the contention, by some scholars, States, and nongovernmental organizations, that con- temporary conflicts can no longer be regulated only by the LOAC, but must now be governed by "International Humanitarian Law," often defined as a blend of the LOAC and International Human Rights Law. In brief, the LOAC continues to evolve to meet the use of force challenges of the 21st century. This chapter will focus, principally, on the application of this evolving LOAC to land warfare.

Theoretical and Historical Overview

Goals

War has existed since time immemorial. In his A Study of War, Quincy Wright divides the history of war into "four very unequal stages, dominated, respectively, by animals, primitive men, civilized men, and men using modern technology."[1] It appears that we are today probably in a fifth stage, that of supertechnology. When war was fought with stones and clubs, few rules were necessary and, of course, none existed. Nevertheless, the Law of War is probably the oldest facet of international law, its evolution having begun even before that for the protection of ambassadors (now included under the rubric, "diplomatic immunity").

In Biblical days, the Law of War was still in a very embryonic state, and humanitarian rules for the protection of noncombatants, men, women, and children were yet to make their appearance, with the result that in the books of the Old Testament references will frequently be found to the victor in battle slaying all of the enemy who fell into his hands without regard to age or sex, and of the pillaging and razing of all cities taken by force. However, over centuries of almost continuous warfare, it was inevitable that mutually advantageous rules governing the conduct of war should gradually come to be recognized by all or most of the contending parties. Thus, it came about that men captured in battle were enslaved, rather than killed; women were left alive in order to breed more warriors or more slaves for the conquerors; and children were spared and were reared by the latter as slaves or as warriors in their own image. While these advances were largely the result of economic pressures and appear today to have been of dubious humanity, in the millennia before the Christian era they represented a giant step forward in the humane treatment of man by man.

Although many specific customs of war had developed, been recognized, and accepted prior to and during the Middle Ages, frequently based on the law of chivalry, records of numerous instances will still be found as late as the fifteenth century that parallel the events recorded in the Bible.

M.H. KEEN, THE LAWS OF WAR IN THE LATE MIDDLE AGES
121–22 (1965)

In a city taken by storm, almost any license was condoned by the law. Only churches and churchmen were technically secure, but even they were not often spared. Women could be raped, and men killed out of hand. All the goods of the inhabitants were regarded as forfeit. If lives were spared, it was only through the clemency of the victorious captain; and spoliation was systematic. The prospect of this free run of his lusts for blood, spoil and women was a major incentive to a soldier to persevere in the rigours which were likely to attend a protracted siege.

———————

Some four centuries later, the situation had changed considerably for the better.

———————

1. QUINCY WRIGHT, A STUDY OF WAR 30 (1942).

The Prize Cases

67 U.S. 635, 667 (1862)

The laws of war, as established among nations, have their foundation in reason, and all tend to mitigate the cruelties and misery produced by the scourge of war.

––––––––––––

The Law of War has been termed "prohibitory law" because, for the most part, it prohibits belligerents from taking specific actions that are considered to be contrary to human rights. The Law of War is humanitarian law. Even provisions that are administrative in nature have the ultimate goal of improving the lot of the victim of war, combatant or noncombatant, young or old, man, woman, or child. Restrictions on the methods and means of conducting hostilities, on the weapons that may be used and on the manner of their use, all have the single goal of making warfare more humane. Certainly, the contents of the pages that follow should not merely indicate, but should conclusively establish, that were it not for the threat of nuclear war, the application of the Law of War as it exists today would go far in attaining this goal.

As the world community of nations has recognized that the individual is entitled to benefit from more and more specific human rights and to be protected against violations of those human rights by governmental actions, whether of his own or of any other government, the humanitarian Law of War has expanded in a somewhat corresponding degree. Thus, the decade of the 1970s probably produced more humanitarian protection for individuals in all categories during time of war than has any similar period since the first decade of the twentieth century, with the possible exception of the period immediately after the end of World War II.

Historical Development

While there are currently a significant number of LOAC treaties in force, the great majority of these fall within two broad categories-the "Hague Law", regulating the means and methods of warfare (e.g., tactics, weapons, and targeting decisions), and the "Geneva Law", governing the non-derogable protections to be accorded the "victims of warfare". Whereas the Hague law regulates specific weapons and their application, the Geneva law affords protections to certain individuals and places by assigning them a legal status. A brief discussion of the development of this LOAC follows.

Opinion and Judgment of the International Military Tribunal

Nuremberg, Sept. 30, 1946
22 T.M.W.C. 411, 464

The law of war is to be found not only in treaties, but in the customs and practices of states which gradually obtained universal recognition, and from the general principles of justice applied by jurists and practiced by military courts. This law is not static, but by continual adaptation follows the needs of a changing world. Indeed, in many cases, treaties do no more than express and define for more accurate reference the principles of law already existing.

––––––––––––

Until the mid-nineteenth century, the Law of War, although increasingly well-developed, remained, with few exceptions, in the realm of customary international law. One major exception was Article XXIV of the bilateral Treaty of Amity and Commerce between the King of Prussia and the fledgling United States of America, entered into in 1785.[2] It provided rules for the treatment of prisoners of war should the two countries, then friendly, thereafter find themselves engaged in hostilities with each other. (This provision was renewed in two subsequent treaties and was considered to be still in force between Germany, as successor state to Prussia, and the United States during World War I.)[3]

In 1854, Russia and the United States entered into an agreement respecting the rights of neutrals at sea.[4] An identical agreement was signed by the Kingdom of the Two Sicilies and the United States on January 13, 1855.[5] Then, in 1856, a number of European nations entered into the Declaration of Paris, which abolished privateering, exempted certain goods from capture at sea, and specified the requirements for a valid naval blockade.

Declaration of Paris, Apr. 16, 1856

25 Martens Nouveau Recueil 791-92.

1. Privateering is, and remains, abolished;

2. The neutral flag covers enemy's goods, with the exception of contraband of war;

3. Neutral goods, with the exception of contraband of war, are not liable to capture under the enemy's flag;

4. Blockades, in order to be binding, must be effective, that is to say, maintained by a force sufficient really to prevent access to the coast of the enemy.

———————

This was the first multilateral attempt to codify, in time of peace, rules that were to be applicable in the event of war between any of the parties. Many of the other nations of the world community thereafter acceded to this declaration. The United States did not do so because of the belief that it did not go far enough in protecting the property of enemy private individuals against seizure at sea.[6]

Early in the American Civil War, General Henry W. Halleck, then the Union General in Chief, and himself a well-known expert on international law, requested Francis Lieber, a refugee German international legal scholar who had sought asylum in the United States and who was then a professor at Columbia University, to draft a code of the Law of War on land as guidance for the operations of the Union armies. Lieber did so, and his Code, promulgated on April 24, 1863, became General Orders No. 100, Instructions for the Government of the Armies of the United States in the Field.[7] This was the first official attempt to gather together in one document substantially all of the customary Law of War on land. While today we would consider some of its provisions to be rather harsh (for example, Article 17 stated that it was "lawful to starve the hostile belligerent, armed or unarmed ...";[8] Article 66 provided that a prisoner of war might "be ordered to suffer death if, within three days after the battle, it be discovered that he belongs to a corps

———————

2. Treaty of Amity and Commerce, Sept. 10, 1785, U.S.–Prussia, 8 Stat. 84 [hereinafter 1785 U.S.–Prussia Treaty].

3. *See* Documents on Prisoners of War 8, 99 (Howard S. Levie ed., 1979).

4. Convention with Russia, July 22, 1854, U.S.–Russ., 10 Stat. 1105.

5. Convention with the Two Sicilies, Jan. 13, 1855, U.S.–Two Sicilies, 11 Stat. 607.

6. *See* The Laws of Armed Conflicts 787 (Dietrich Schindler & Jiří Toman eds., 3d Ed. 1988) [hereinafter Schindler/Toman].

7. *Id.* at 3.

8. *Id.* at 6.

which gives no quarter";[9] and Article 77 makes a conspiracy by prisoners of war to escape punishable by death),[10] in its time it was considered to be extremely humanitarian. Although the Lieber Code was a unilateral action of the United States, its ultimate effect was worldwide. It was largely the basis for the 1874 Declaration of Brussels,[11] a convention on the Law of War on land drafted by a diplomatic conference of representatives from fifteen European States, which, however, never entered into force because of the 1880 Oxford Manual on the Laws of War on Land, drafted by the private, but prestigious, Institute of International Law,[12] and because of several of the 1899 and 1907 Hague Conventions mentioned below.

Meanwhile, action was also proceeding in another area of the Law of War. In 1859, Henry Dunant, a Swiss banker, was present as a spectator at the Battle of Solferino in which there were more than 40,000 dead and wounded left on the battlefield by the Austrian and Franco-Italian armies when they separated after five or six hours of engagement. Deeply moved by the lack of provision for the care of the wounded and the burial of the dead, upon his return to Switzerland, Dunant wrote a book entitled *A Memory of Solferino* in which he vividly portrayed the chaos and suffering he had witnessed.[13] He proposed steps that resulted in the creation of an organization that ultimately became the International Committee of the Red Cross (ICRC) and also in the establishment of the individual national Red Cross societies. Moreover, in 1864 a diplomatic conference held in Geneva at the invitation of the Swiss government on the initiative of Dunant's organization drafted the first Geneva Convention for the Amelioration of the Condition of the Wounded in Armies in the Field.[14] This was the beginning of a long tradition of the drafting in Geneva of humanitarian conventions for the protection of the victims of war (the wounded, sick, shipwrecked, prisoners of war, civilians, etc.). New conventions with the same title were drafted in 1906, 1929, and 1949.

A customary rule of the Law of War had evolved, prohibiting the use of weapons that caused unnecessary suffering, such as lances with barbed heads, serrated knives and bayonets, and bullets smeared with poison or other foreign substances. When a bullet that exploded on contact was invented, there was fear that, while many States would consider that such a weapon violated the foregoing prohibition, others might disagree. In order to prevent such a dispute and to ensure a general ban on the use of such weapons in war, in 1868, the Czar of Russia convened an International Military Commission at St. Petersburg that drafted such a prohibition. Although it had fewer than twenty signatories, it has been so generally recognized over the ensuing years that it is now unquestionably a part of the customary law of war.

1868 Declaration of St. Petersburg Renouncing the Use, in Time of War, Of Certain Explosive Projectiles

Nov.29/Dec. 11, 1868, Schindler/Toman 101-02

The Contracting Parties engage mutually to renounce, in case of war among themselves, the employment by their military or naval troops of any projectile of a weight below 400 grammes, which is either explosive or charged with fulminating or inflammable substances.

---

9. *Id.* at 12.

10. *Id.* at 13.

11. *Id.* at 25.

12. *Id.* at 35.

13. HENRY DUNANT, A MEMORY OF SOLFERINO (1939).

14. Geneva Convention for the Amelioration of the Condition of the Wounded in Armies in the Field, Aug. 22, 1864, 22 Stat. 940 [hereinafter 1864 Geneva Convention].

(By uniform practice, this prohibition does not preclude the use of tracer and explosive bullets fired by or against aircraft.)[15]

In 1899, a diplomatic conference called by the Czar of Russia met at The Hague, which became known as a "Peace Conference." Out of that conference came two Conventions and three Declarations pertaining to the Law of War. The two Conventions (the 1899 Hague II Convention with Respect to the Laws and Customs of War on Land [hereinafter 1899 Hague II] and the 1899 Hague III Convention for the Adaptation to Maritime Warfare of the Principles of the Geneva Convention of 22 August 1864 [hereinafter 1899 Hague III] have been totally superseded by later international instruments and therefore will not be discussed. However, it is appropriate to call attention to the so-called Martens Clause (named after the Russian international lawyer who drafted it) contained in the Preamble to the 1899 Hague II Convention.

"Martens" Clause, Preamble to the 1899 Hague II Convention
July 29, 1899, 32 Stat. 1803, 1805

Until a more complete code of the laws of war is issued, the High Contracting Parties think it right to declare that in cases not included in the Regulations adopted by them, populations and belligerents remain under the protection and empire of the principles of international law, as they result from the usages established between civilized nations, from the laws of humanity, and the requirements of the public conscience.

This statement, basic to the entire humanitarian Law of War, will be found repeated in the Preamble to the 1907 Hague IV Convention and in Article 1(2) of the 1977 Protocol I, both discussed below.

The three 1899 Declarations, all of which are arguably still in effect, were Declaration IV(1), which prohibits the launching of projectiles and explosives from balloons; Declaration IV(2), which prohibits the use of projectiles to diffuse poison gas; and Declaration IV(3), which prohibits the use of expanding ammunition.

For various reasons, the United States never ratified Declarations IV(2) or IV(3). However, it has ratified the 1925 Geneva Gas Protocol and the 1993 Chemical Weapons Convention, both of which are broader in scope than Declaration IV(2); and it does accept the illegality under the customary Law of War of the use in wartime of "irregular-shaped bullets ... and the scoring of the surface or the filing off of the ends of the hard cases of bullets."[16]

The 1907 Hague Peace Conference was considerably more prolific than its predecessor had been. Attended by forty-four of the fifty-seven then existing sovereign nations, on October 18, 1907, ten Law of War conventions were signed. These Conventions, many of which will be discussed in depth in the appropriate functional areas, were:

- Convention No. III Relative to the Opening of Hostilities, Oct. 18, 1907, 36 Stat. 2259 [hereinafter 1907 Hague III];
- Convention No. IV Respecting the Laws and Customs of War on Land [hereinafter 1907 Hague IV], with the Annexed Regulations [hereinafter 1907 Hague IV Regulations], Oct. 18, 1907, 36 Stat. 2277;

---

15. Hague Rules of Air Warfare, Dec. 1922–Feb. 1923, art. 18, Schindler/Toman 207, 210.
16. U.S. ARMY FIELD MANUAL 27-10, THE LAW OF LAND WARFARE 18 (1956) [hereinafter U.S. Army FM 27-10].

- Convention No. V Respecting the Rights and Duties of Neutral Powers and Persons in Case of War on Land, Oct. 18, 1907, 36 Stat. 2310 [hereinafter 1907 Hague V];
- Convention No. VI Relating to the Status of Enemy Merchant Ships at the Outbreak of Hostilities, Oct. 18, 1907, Schindler/Toman 791 [hereinafter 1907 Hague VI];
- Convention No. VII Relating to the Conversion of Merchant Ships into War-ships, Oct. 18, 1907, Schindler/Toman 797 [hereinafter 1907 Hague VII];
- Convention No. VIII Relative to the Laying of Automatic Submarine Contact Mines, Oct. 18, 1907, 36 Stat. 2332 [hereinafter 1907 Hague VIII];
- Convention No. IX Concerning Bombardment by Naval Forces in Time of War, Oct. 18, 1907, 36 Stat. 2351 [hereinafter 1907 Hague IX];
- Convention No. X for the Adaptation to Maritime Warfare of the Principles of the Geneva Convention, Oct. 18, 1907, 36 Stat. 2371 [hereinafter 1907 Hague X];
- Convention No. XI Relative to Certain Restrictions With Regard to the Exercise of the Right of Capture in Naval Warfare, Oct. 18, 1907, 36 Stat. 2396 [hereinafter 1907 Hague XI]; and
- Convention No. XIII Concerning the Rights and Duties of Neutral Powers in Naval War, Oct. 18, 1907, 36 Stat. 2415 [hereinafter 1907 Hague XIII].

Many of the experiences of World War I were the subjects of subsequent international activity in the diplomatic field, some successful and some unsuccessful. Thus, the 1922 Washington Conference on the Limitation of Armament drafted a Treaty Relating to the Use of Submarines and Noxious Gases,[17] which never became effective because of the failure of France to ratify it. It also created a Commission of Jurists, which, meeting at The Hague in 1922-23, produced a set of Rules for the Control of Radio in Time of War[18] and a set of Rules of Aerial Warfare.[19] While neither of these sets of rules received formal international approval, many of their provisions were based upon the practices of States and represent the customary international Law of War, except as they have been modified by later State practice and more recent conventions.

Then, in 1925, a diplomatic conference, which had been convened for the purpose of restricting the armament trade (a task at which it failed), drafted the Geneva Protocol for the Prohibition of the Use in War of Asphyxiating, Poisonous or other Gases, and of Bacteriological Methods of Warfare.[20] (Although this Protocol was originally proposed by the United States, the latter did not become a Party until 1975, when it became a Party to the 1972 Biological Weapons Convention, which prohibited the development, production, stockpiling, acquisition, or retention of biological agents or toxins, as well as weapons, equipment or means of delivery designed to use toxins for hostile purposes or in armed conflict.[21]) And on July 27, 1929, upon the initiative of the ICRC, a new Convention for the Amelioration of the Condition of the Wounded and Sick in Armies in the Field was signed at Geneva[22] (replacing a 1906 version), along with the first Geneva Convention Relative to the Treatment of Prisoners of War.[23]

---

17. Treaty Relating to the Use of Submarines and Noxious Gases, Feb. 6, 1922, 25 L.N.T.S. 202.

18. *Rules for the Control of Radio in Time of War*, 32 Am. J. Int'l L. (Supp.) 2 (1938).

19. *Rules of Aerial Warfare*, 32 Am. J. Int'l L. (Supp.) 12 (1938).

20. Geneva Protocol for the Prohibition of the Use in War of Asphyxiating, Poisonous or other Gases, and of Bacteriological Methods of Warfare, June 17, 1925, 26 U.S.T. 571, 94 L.N.T.S. 65 [hereinafter 1925 Geneva Gas Protocol].

21. *See* Chapter 13 for a detailed discussion of the Biological Weapons Convention.

22. Convention for the Amelioration of the Condition of the Wounded and Sick in Armies in the Field, July 27, 1929, 47 Stat. 2074, 118 L.N.T.S. 303.

23. Geneva Convention Relative to the Treatment of Prisoners of War, July 27, 1929, 47 Stat. 2021, 118 L.N.T.S. 343.

In 1930, a Diplomatic Conference meeting in London drafted a Treaty on the Limitation and Reduction of Naval Armaments.[24] Part IV of this Treaty set forth certain Rules of Submarine Warfare that were stated to be part of the Law of War "without limit of time."[25]

In 1949, once again on the initiative of the ICRC, a diplomatic conference met in Geneva to review and extend the coverage of the two 1929 Geneva Conventions, based upon the experiences of World War II. When that Conference ended its work on August 12, 1949, it had not only updated the two 1929 Conventions, it had also brought the 1907 Hague X Convention (Maritime Warfare) within the Geneva orbit and had drafted a completely new Convention for the protection of civilians. These four Conventions, known collectively as the 1949 Geneva Conventions for the Protection of War Victims, have now been ratified or adhered to by virtually all of the nations of the world. The Conventions are:

- Convention for the Amelioration of the Condition of the Wounded and Sick of Armed Forces in the Field, *opened for signature* Aug. 12, 1949, 6 U.S.T. 3114, 75 U.N.T.S. 31 [hereinafter First Convention];
- Convention for the Amelioration of the Condition of Wounded, Sick and Shipwrecked Members of Armed Forces at Sea, *opened for signature* Aug. 12, 1949, 6 U.S.T. 3217, 75 U.N.T.S. 85 [hereinafter Second Convention];
- Convention Relative to the Treatment of Prisoners of War, *opened for signature* Aug. 12, 1949, 6 U.S.T. 3316, 75 U.N.T.S. 135 [hereinafter Third Convention]; and
- Convention Relative to the Protection of Civilian Persons in Time of War, *opened for signature* Aug. 12, 1949, 6 U.S.T. 3516, 75 U.N.T.S. 287 [hereinafter Fourth Convention].

These Conventions advanced a change from the term, "Law of War," to that of "The Law of Armed Conflict," to emphasize that the application of their provisions did not depend upon either a formal declaration of war or a recognition by all parties concerned of the existence of a state of war.

The numerous war crimes trials that followed World War II are discussed at length in Chapter 8. They are referred to in this chapter as evidence of the existence of a substantive rule of the LOAC, as it has evolved through custom or been codified by multilateral international agreements, the violation of which is a "conventional war crime."

During World War II, as in previous conflicts, many historic monuments were accidentally or wantonly destroyed, and many art treasures representing the cultural heritage of the country in which they were located were destroyed or looted, sometimes as a matter of official policy. The efforts of UNESCO to obtain a specific agreement prohibiting such practices and providing some means of protecting such objects culminated in the drafting and adoption of the Convention (and Regulations and Protocol) for the Protection of Cultural Property in the Event of Armed Conflict.[26] While the United States always regarded this Convention's provisions as relevant to its target selection process, it was not until 2008 that it ratified this treaty.

---

24. Treaty on the Limitation and Reduction of Naval Armaments, Apr. 22, 1930, 46 Stat. 2858, 112 L.N.T.S. 65.

25. 46 Stat. at 2882. A Proce's-Verbal, Nov. 6, 1936, 173 L.N.T.S. 353, opened this portion of the Treaty to adherence by all States.

26. Convention (and Regulations and Protocol) for the Protection of Cultural Property in the Event of Armed Conflict, May 14, 1954, 249 U.N.T.S. 240 [hereinafter the 1954 Hague Cultural Property Convention].

It was recognized early that the Fourth Convention did not adequately protect civilians and that the protections that it did afford were not available to all categories of civilians. In 1956-57, the ICRC made an unsuccessful attempt to broaden its coverage with a proposed new, and perhaps too extensive, convention. Despite this setback, it continued its efforts and, after a number of preliminary conferences, in 1973 it produced a Draft Additional Protocol I to the 1949 Geneva Conventions, which not only extended the coverage of those Conventions, but also some of the aspects of the 1907 Hague IV Regulations (thus, a confluence of Geneva and Hague Law); and a Draft Additional Protocol II relating to non-international conflict. A Diplomatic Conference, which met in Geneva in 1974, required four annual sessions before it had revised these Draft Additional Protocols to the satisfaction of a sufficient majority of the many national delegations in attendance. On June 10, 1977, a Final Act was signed, to which was attached:

- Protocol Additional to the Geneva Conventions of 12 August 1949, and Relating to the Protection of Victims of International Armed Conflicts (Protocol I), *opened for signature* Dec. 12, 1977, 16 I.L.M. 1391, 1125 U.N.T.S. 3 [hereinafter 1977 Protocol I]; and

- Protocol Additional to the Geneva Conventions of 12 August 1949, and Relating to the Protection of Victims of Non-International Armed Conflicts (Protocol II), *opened for signature* Dec. 12, 1977, 16 I.L.M. 1442, 1125 U.N.T.S. 609 [hereinafter 1977 Protocol II].

Despite its many controversial provisions (for example, it makes "wars of liberation" international conflicts and gives captured members of national liberation movements prisoner-of-war status, even if they have not worn any identification, have not carried their arms openly at all times, and have not complied with the law of war), Protocol I has been widely adopted, albeit with a number of reservations and/or statements of understanding. As of this writing, it has 173 Parties. As of this same timeframe, Protocol II has 167 Parties. The United States has announced that it will not ratify Protocol I. Protocol II has been forwarded to the Senate for its advice and consent, but there is no indication that the Senate will act on this Protocol.

The Diplomatic Conference, which drafted the final versions of the two 1977 Protocols, had created an Ad Hoc Committee on Conventional Weapons tasked with studying the problems raised by the use of several of these weapons. No action was taken by the Diplomatic Conference on the work of that Committee, except to pass a resolution referring the matter to the United Nations and recommending the convening of a new Diplomatic Conference to deal with it. Thereafter, the United Nations convened two preliminary conferences, followed by two sessions of a Diplomatic Conference at Geneva, which ultimately, on October 10, 1980, produced the Convention on Prohibitions or Restrictions on the Use of Certain Conventional Weapons Which May Be Deemed to Be Excessively Injurious or to Have Indiscriminate Effects,[27] to which were attached three Protocols:

- Protocol on Non-Detectable Fragments (Protocol I) [hereinafter 1980 Protocol I];
- Protocol on Prohibitions or Restrictions on the Use of Mines, Booby-Traps and Other Devices (Protocol II) [hereinafter 1980 Protocol II]; and

---

27. Convention on Prohibitions or Restrictions on the Use of Certain Conventional Weapons Which May Be Deemed to Be Excessively Injurious or to Have Indiscriminate Effects, Oct. 10, 1980, 19 I.L.M. 1523, 1342 U.N.T.S. 137 [hereinafter the 1980 Conventional Weapons Convention].

- Protocol on Prohibitions or Restrictions on the Use of Incendiary Weapons (Protocol III) [hereinafter 1980 Protocol III].

A subsequent Review Conference called in 1995 substantially revised Protocol II and also created a new Protocol IV.[28] Finally, in 2003, a Protocol dealing with the explosive remnants of war was concluded.[29]

- Amended Protocol on Prohibitions or Restrictions on the Use of Mines, Booby-Traps and Other Devices (Amended Protocol II) [hereinafter 1996 Amended Protocol II]; and
- Protocol on Blinding Laser Weapons (Protocol IV) [hereinafter 1995 Protocol IV].
- Protocol on Explosive Remnants of War (Protocol V) [hereinafter 2003 Protocol V].

Despite the major advances in the regulation of land mines accomplished by the 1980 Protocol II and 1996 Amended Protocol II, international dismay at the continuing toll of death and disfigurement by mines irresponsibly laid by both state and non-state actors over the past several decades led to an effort to abolish antipersonnel land mines altogether. That effort, supported by the ICRC, culminated in the 1997 Ottawa Convention on the Prohibition of the Use, Stockpiling, Production and Transfer of Anti-Personnel Mines and on Their Destruction.[30] While the United States is a Party to the 1996 Amended Protocol II of the 1980 Conventional Weapons Convention, it is not a Party to the Ottawa Convention.

Two other significant LOAC treaties appeared in the 1990s. The 1993 Convention on the Prohibition of the Development, Production, Stockpiling and Use of Chemical Weapons and on Their Destruction was completed in Paris on January 13, 1993.[31] Unlike the 1925 Gas Protocol mentioned previously, the 1993 Chemical Weapons Convention mandates destruction of all chemical weapons and does not permit their employment, even in response to first use by an adversary.[32] The last significant LOAC instrument to appear in the 1990s was the 1999 Second Protocol to the Hague Convention of 1954 for the Protection of Cultural Property in the Event of Armed Conflict.[33] The principal purpose of the Second Protocol was to incorporate into the protections accorded to cultural objects by the 1954 Convention the more detailed and restrictive concepts of "military objectives" and "precautions in attack" contained in the 1977 Geneva Protocol I.

The most recent LOAC treaty, the 2008 Oslo Convention on Cluster Munitions, prohibits the development, production, stockpiling, retention or transfer of cluster munitions between signatory States. Cluster munitions are used against a variety of targets, such as air defense radars, armor, artillery, and large enemy personnel concentrations. As these bomblets

---

28. Convention on Prohibitions or Restrictions on the Use of Certain Conventional Weapons Which May Be Deemed to Be Excessively Injurious or to Have Indiscriminate Effects, as amended on Oct. 13, 1995, and May 3, 1996, 35 I.L.M. 1206, 1342 U.N.T.S. 137.

29. Protocol V (Explosive Remnants of War) to the 1980 Conventional Weapons Convention, Nov. 28, 2003.

30. 1997 Ottawa Convention on the Prohibition of the Use, Stockpiling, Production and Transfer of Anti-Personnel Mines and on Their Destruction, Sept. 18, 1997, 36 I.L.M. 1507 [hereinafter the 1997 Ottawa Convention].

31. 1993 Convention on the Prohibition of the Development, Production, Stockpiling and Use of Chemical Weapons and on Their Destruction, Jan. 13, 1993, 32 I.L.M. 800.

32. See Chapter 13 for a more complete discussion of the Chemical Weapons Convention.

33. Second Protocol to the Hague Convention of 1954 for the Protection of Cultural Property in the Event of Armed Conflict, Mar. 26, 1999, 38 I.L.M. 769.

disperse over a relatively large area and a percentage typically fail to detonate, they may create an unexploded ordinance hazard. The United States and a number of other States which manufacture and use cluster munitions are not Parties to this Convention.[34]

Questions for Discussion

1. If a new diplomatic conference were to be convened to draft another LOAC convention, with what subject matter should it be directed to concern itself?

2. As reflected in the text, the United States has chosen not to become a Party to a number of significant LOAC Conventions, while many of its past and potential coalition partners have signed on to such treaties. What effect do you believe this might have on the ability to conduct successful coalition operations in the future?

3. Do you believe that the broad extent of the coverage of the LOAC is counterproductive, making it practically impossible for members of belligerent armed forces to be acquainted with many of its provisions?

Scope of Application

1949 Geneva Conventions

Common Article I

The High Contracting Parties undertake to respect and to ensure respect for the present Convention in all circumstances.

––––––––––

The purpose of this provision, as worded, was not only to require compliance with the Conventions by the individual belligerents, but to place an obligation on all parties, including allied and neutral powers, to ensure that belligerents did comply with the provisions of these very important Conventions. It cannot be said that this provision has accomplished its purpose, as there appears to be an almost insurmountable reluctance on the part of allies and true neutrals to inform a belligerent that it is violating the LOAC. Nevertheless, perhaps in the hope that there will be a change in this attitude, this provision was repeated verbatim in Article 1(1) of the 1977 Protocol I.

The General Participation Clause

When the several 1899 and 1907 Hague Conventions and Declarations were drafted, each of them included a general participation, or *si omnes*, clause, which required that for a Convention or Declaration to be applicable in a particular conflict, all of the belligerents had to be parties thereto. During each World War, there was at least one belligerent that was not a party to those Conventions and Declarations. Technically, therefore, they were not applicable. After World War II, it was found that the rules of the Law of War on land

––––––––––

34. Oslo Convention on Cluster Munitions, May 30, 2008, 48 I.L.M. 357 (2009) [hereinafter Convention on Cluster Munitions].

set forth in the 1907 Hague IV Regulations had been applicable, without regard to the general participation clause.

Opinion and Judgment of the International Military Tribunal

Nuremberg, Sept. 30, 1946,
22 T.M.W.C. 411, 497

But it is argued that the Hague Convention does not apply in this case, because of the "general participation" clause in Article 2 of the Hague Convention of 1907. That clause provided:

> "The provisions contained in the regulations (Rules of Land Warfare) referred to in Article 1, as well as in the present convention do not apply except between contracting powers, and then only if all the belligerents are parties to the convention."

Several of the belligerents in the recent war were not parties to this convention.

In the opinion of the Tribunal it is not necessary to decide this question. The rules of land warfare expressed in the convention undoubtedly represented an advance over existing international law at the time of their adoption. But the convention expressly stated that it was an attempt "to revise the general laws and customs of war," which it thus recognized to be then existing, but by 1939 these rules laid down in the convention were recognized by all civilized nations, and were regarded as being declaratory of the laws and customs of war....

There are no general participation clauses in the 1949 Geneva Conventions. In fact, they contain a Common Article to the opposite effect, and modern doctrine rejects the principle of the general participation clause in LOAC conventions.

1949 Geneva Conventions

COMMON ARTICLE 2(3)

Although one of the Powers in conflict may not be a party to the present Convention, the Powers who are parties thereto shall remain bound by it in their mutual relations. They shall furthermore be bound by the Convention in relation to the said Power, if the latter accepts and applies the provisions thereof.

(To the same effect, see Article 96(2) of the 1977 Protocol I and Articles 7(1) and (2) of the 1980 Conventional Weapons Convention.)

Types of Hostilities

If there is compliance with the provisions of the 1907 Hague III Convention and there is a formal declaration of war or an ultimatum with an expired time limit, no questions should arise concerning the applicability of the LOAC. However, prior to World War II there were a number of international armed conflicts to which the aggressor gave some label other than "war" ("incident," "police action," "police operation," etc.) to the hostile action in which it was engaged. Then, based on that label, it would advance the contention that the Law of War was not applicable, thus attempting to excuse inhumane actions as not having fallen within the prohibitions of that law.

1949 Geneva Conventions

Common Article 2(1)

[T]he present Convention shall apply to all cases of declared war or of any other armed conflict which may arise between two or more of the High Contracting Parties, even if the state of war is not recognized by one of them.

Legal scholars have found no problems with respect to the substantive content of the foregoing provision of the 1949 Geneva Conventions, which has been reaffirmed in Article 1(3) of the 1977 Protocol I. Despite the patent intent and language of the Convention provision, however, the problem of the existence of international armed conflict and, hence, of the applicability of the LOAC has continued to exist. Major examples include the Sino-Indian conflict of 1963, in which India charged that China was not complying with the Law of War, allegedly because there had been no declaration of war;[35] and Vietnam, where the Democratic Republic of Vietnam also rejected the applicability of the Law of War in general, and of the Third Convention in particular, because there had been no declaration of war.[36]

Additionally, the first decade of the 21st century gave rise to a number of novel LOAC issues as the result of a strained attempt by the United States to apply both codified and customary LOAC to those responsible for the horrific attacks of September 11, 2001, as well as to individuals seized in the ensuing U.S.-declared "Global War on Terrorism" (GWOT). The U.S. decision to selectively apply LOAC principles to what many viewed as acts of terrorism, rather than combatant actions taken in the context of an ongoing "armed conflict", has generated significant controversy within the international community. Principal among such LOAC issues has been the manner in which the U.S. chose to accord status and treatment to those taken into U.S. custody in Afghanistan and in the subsequent GWOT. All such individuals were deemed to be "unlawful enemy combatants"-subject to detention until the termination of this "global conflict." But, as "unlawful combatants," these same individuals were said not to be entitled to Prisoner of War status and were thus denied the rights and protections of the LOAC, specifically those contained in the Third Geneva Convention.

While subsequent U.S. judicial and Executive actions have resulted in affording greater due process for, and better treatment of, such personnel, a number of these individuals remain incarcerated in a U.S. detention facility located at Guantanamo Bay, Cuba, and the U.S. has reaffirmed its right to hold certain of these detainees indefinitely.[37]

Non-International Armed Conflict (NIAC)

Sir Hersch Lauterpacht once noted that: "[I]f international law is, in some ways, at the vanishing point of law, the law of war is, perhaps even more conspicuously, at the vanishing point of international law."[38] To this, one might well add: "If the law of war is at the vanishing point of international law, then the law applicable to non-international

---

35. 2 Jerome Alan Cohen & Hungdah Chiu, People's China and International Law 1573–74 (1974).

36. Howard S. Levie, Prisoners of War in International Armed Conflict 16–17 n. 68 (1979).

37. For a detailed analysis of this issue, *see* David E. Graham, "The Legal Regime for Detainees", Chapter 1, Legal Issues in the Struggle Against Terrorism. John Norton Moore and Robert F. Turner eds. (2010). See also Chapter 9 on Detention.

38. Hersch Lauterpacht, *The Problem of the Revision of the Law of War*, 29 British Yearbook of International Law 360, 381–82 (1952).

armed conflict is surely at the vanishing point of the law of war." Why is this the case? The answer lies in the fact that, in order to apply even the rather limited provisions of the LOAC to a NIAC, it must first be determined that a NIAC exists. And, a determination as to whether certain activities do-or do not-constitute a NIAC is almost inevitably a contentious one.

Such a determination must necessarily begin with Common Article 3 of the 1949 Geneva Conventions. In 1949, the diplomatic conference that drafted the four Geneva Conventions for the Protection of War Victims broke new ground when it included, as Common Article 3 of those Conventions, a "mini-convention" providing certain minimum humanitarian protections in NIAC. "In the case of armed conflict not of an international character occurring within the territory of one of the High Contracting Parties, each Party to the conflict shall be bound to apply, as a minimum, the following provisions...."[39] The difficulty, historically, in turning to Article 3, however, has been that neither its text, nor the official Commentary on this article,[40] provides definitive guidance as to what is meant by the phrase, "conflict not of an international character." Thus, it has never been clear as to what level of violence must be reached, and how protracted such violence must be, in order for such hostilities to be deemed a NIAC—and for the humanitarian protections of Article 3 to apply. Indeed, internal situations that have reached a very high level of violence have often been viewed, certainly by the governments of the States in which such violence has occurred, as mere banditry—acts which have not reached the threshold of "armed conflict."[41] Governments have consistently resisted recognizing the

---

39. Common Article 3 of the 1949 Geneva Conventions reads as follows:

In the case of armed conflict not of an international character occurring in the territory of one of the High Contracting Parties, each Party to the conflict shall be bound to apply, as a minimum, the following provisions;

(1) Persons taking no active part in the hostilities, including members of armed forces who have laid down their arms and those placed hors de combat by sickness, wounds, detention, or any other cause, shall in all circumstances be treated humanely, without any adverse distinction founded on race, colour, religion or faith, sex, birth or wealth, or any other similar criteria.

To this end, the following acts are and shall remain prohibited at any time and in any place whatsoever with respect to the above-mentioned persons;

(a) violence to life and person, in particular murder of all kinds, mutilation, cruel treatment and torture;

(b) taking of hostages;

(c) outrages upon personal dignity, in particular, humiliating and degrading treatment;

(d) the passing of sentences and the carrying out of executions without previous judgment pronounced by a regularly constituted court affording all the judicial guarantees which are recognized as indispensable by civilized peoples.

(2) The wounded and sick shall be collected and cared for.

An impartial humanitarian body, such as the International Committee of the Red Cross, may offer its services to the Parties to the conflict.

The Parties to the conflict should further endeavour to bring into force, by means of special agreements, all or part of the other provisions of the present Convention.

The application of the preceding provisions shall not affect the legal status of the Parties to the conflict.

40. COMMENTARY TO GENEVA I FOR THE AMELIORATION OF THE CONDITION OF THE WOUNDED AND SICK IN ARMED FORCES IN THE FIELD (Jean S. Pictet ed., 1952) [hereinafter Pictet's Commentary].

41. For a discussion of State denial of the existence of a NIAC within its borders, *see* Anthony Cullen, *Key Developments Affecting the Scope of Internal Armed Conflicts in International Humanitarian Law*, MILITARY LAW REVIEW 66, 83–88 (2005).

existence of an armed conflict within their State borders for fear of according some form of de facto status or legitimacy to those fostering the violence in issue—that is, to those engaging in hostile acts in an effort to displace the de jure government. This lack of certainty and consensus regarding the scope of Article 3's applicability has led to attempts to better define Common Article 3 conflicts, as a means of more effectively triggering the LOAC relevant to them.

Both Protocols Additional to the 1949 Geneva Conventions attempted to clarify those activities that might be deemed an NIAC. Protocol I, Article 1(4), denotes certain conflicts, essentially non-international in nature, as "international" in character—that is, "armed conflicts in which peoples are fighting against colonial domination, alien occupation, or racist regimes. The ICRC Commentary on Protocol I states, however, that these specific situations constitute an "exhaustive list" of the types of internal conflicts that might be so classified.[42] Thus, Protocol I plays no defining role with respect to NIACs that do not fall within one of these three narrow categories.

Protocol II, in turn, represents the first attempt to regulate, by treaty, the methods and means of employing force in internal armed conflicts, and it seeks to confirm, clarify, and expand upon the minimal protections to be afforded under Common Article 3. This intent has largely failed, however, as Protocol II establishes a much higher threshold of application than does Common Article 3. While Common Article 3 is said to apply to all conflicts "not of an international character," Article 1(1) of Protocol II states that its provisions apply only to armed conflicts " ... which take place in the territory of a High Contracting Party between its armed forces and dissident armed forces or other organized armed groups which, under responsible command, exercise such control over a part of its territory as to enable them to carry out sustained and concerted military operations and to implement this Protocol." Triggering the application of the Protocol's provisions to these objective criteria substantially narrows the number of NIACs to which the Protocol might apply, restricting the applicability of its provisions to only internal conflicts of a high degree of intensity—essentially classic civil wars. The Protocol has rarely been deemed applicable to the great number of internal armed conflicts that have occurred since its inception, as insurgent groups simply have not met the stringent requirements of Article 1(1). Indeed, it is probable that the high bar of application established by this provision has since provided governments with a ready justification for denying the existence of a NIAC within their borders.

In October, 1995, the International Criminal Tribunal for the Former Yugoslavia (ICTY) issued the Tadic jurisdiction decision. In doing so, the Tribunal opined that: "An armed conflict exists whenever there is a resort to armed force between States or protracted armed violence between governmental authorities and organized armed groups or between such groups within a State."[43] In turn, in interpreting this definition of "armed conflict" articulated by the Tadic Appeals Chamber, the Tadic Trial Chamber stated the following:

> The test applied by the Appeals Chamber to the existence of an armed conflict for the purposes of the rules contained in Common Article 3 focuses on two aspects of a conflict; the intensity of the conflict and the organization of the parties to the conflict. In an armed conflict of an internal or mixed character, these closely related criteria are used for the sole purpose, as a minimum, of dis-

---

42. COMMENTARY ON THE ADDITIONAL PROTOCOLS OF 8 JUNE 1977 TO THE GENEVA CONVENTIONS OF 12 AUGUST 1949, 108–13 (Yves Sandoz, Christopher Swinarski & Bruno Zimmermann eds. 1987).

43. Prosecutor v. Tadic, Case No.-IT-94-1-1, Decision on Defence Motion for Interlocutory Appeal on Jurisdiction, 70 (Int'l Crim. Trib. for the Former Yugoslavia Oct. 2, 1995).

tinguishing an armed conflict from banditry, unorganized and short-lived insurrections, or terrorist activities, which are not subject to international humanitarian law.[44]

The two aspects of internal armed conflict set forth by the Tadic Trial Chamber—the "intensity" of the conflict and the degree of "organization of the parties" involved—might, arguably, now serve as a basis for the recognition of "de facto" NIACs, and thus for the application of the provisions of Common Article 3 to such conflicts. Endorsement for this reasoning is reflected in the adaptation of the "Tadic formula" in the Rome Statute of the International Criminal Court. Article 8(2)(f) of the Statute states that the Statute applies to "armed conflicts that take place in the territory of a State when there is protracted armed conflict between governmental authorities and organized armed groups or between such groups."[45] Given these developments, it would appear that an argument can be made that the Tadic formula may well have had the effect of lowering the threshold required for the recognition of a NIAC—thus triggering the application of Common Article 3 to such a conflict.

Questions for Discussion

1. Do you believe that international efforts to combat terrorism, such as, arguably, the actions of the al Qaeda network, should be governed by the LOAC? What legal and/or political considerations do you consider germane to this debate?

2. Are the provisions of Common Article 3 of the 1949 Geneva Conventions now the only "LOAC" applicable to the great majority of NIACs? Can an argument be made that international human rights law should also be applied to such conflicts?

3. Is there an agreed mechanism for determining the existence of a NIAC to which Common Article 3 applies? If so, what is it?

Methods and Means of Conducting Hostilities

General

The LOAC regulates two related aspects of combat: (1) the methods; that is, the tactics used in engaging in hostilities, and (2) the means—the weapons used in conducting hostilities. Overarching the more specific elements of the LOAC related to both the methods and means of conducting conflict, however, are the customary LOAC principles impacting all decisions made in combat. These are:

"Military Necessity": This principle "justifies those measures not forbidden by international law which are indispensable for securing the complete submission of the enemy as soon as possible." Article 23(g) of the 1907 Hague IV Regulations explicitly recognizes the validity of this principle, mandating that a belligerent not "destroy or seize an enemy's property, unless such destruction or seizure be imperatively demanded by the necessities of war." Military necessity does not authorize acts otherwise prohibited by the

---

44. Prosecutor v. Tadic, Case No.IT-94-1, Judgment, 562 (Int'l Crim. Trib. for the Former Yugoslavia May 7, 1997).

45. Rome Statute of the International Criminal Court, July 17, 1998, 2187 U.N.T.S. 90.

LOAC, to include those more specific legal constraints set forth in LOAC treaties. Nor is this principle a criminal defense for acts expressly forbidden by the LOAC. With respect to the latter, however, there exists a broader standard regarding acts undertaken on a battlefield. This standard, the Rendulic Rule, stands for the proposition that commanders and personnel should be judged based only on information reasonably available at the time that a battlefield decision was made.[46]

"Distinction": Often referred to as the principle of "discrimination", this concept requires that belligerents distinguish combatants from non-combatants and military objectives from civilian objects (i.e., protected places or property).[47]

"Proportionality": This principle requires that the anticipated loss of life and damage to property incidental to attacks must not be excessive in relation to the concrete and direct military advantage expected to be gained.[48] Rather than being a legal standard, proportionality simply provides commanders with a method by which they can balance military necessity and "collateral" civilian loss or damage that may result from an attack. Collateral damage, also referred to as "incidental" damage, consists of both unavoidable and unintentional damage to civilian personnel and (or) property resulting from an attack on a military objective.

"Unnecessary suffering": This principle, sometimes referred to as one of "superfluous injury" or "humanity", requires that military forces avoid inflicting gratuitous violence on the enemy. Arising originally from humanitarian concerns over the suffering of wounded military personnel, it was codified as a weapons limitation: "It is especially forbidden ... to employ arms, projectiles or material calculated to cause unnecessary suffering."[49] Viewed more broadly, this principle embraces the inherent intent of the Geneva Conventions to limit the effects of war on the civilian population and property. It also serves as a counterbalance to the principle of military necessity.

Regulating the Methods of Armed Conflict

Ruses

A ruse is " ... a trick of war designed to deceive an adversary, usually involving the deliberate exposure of false information to the adversary's intelligence collection system", and is intended to injure an enemy by legitimate deception.[50] Such ruses of war are lawful.[51] Examples of legitimate ruses would include: (1) the common naval tactic of disguising war ships as merchant vessels or outfitting merchant vessels with concealed armaments— then hoisting the national battle ensign before engaging the enemy; (2) the creation of fictitious units by planting false information, creating dummy installations, sending false radio transmissions, and using a small force to simulate a larger unit;[52] and (3) the use

---

46. See "Opinion and Judgment of Military Tribunal V," United States v. Wilhelm List, X Trials of War Criminals Before the Nuremberg Military Tribunals Under Control Council Law No. 10, at 1297 (Feb. 19, 1948) (Case 7).

47. Art. 48, 1977 Protocol I.

48. Art. 51, para. 5(b), 1977 Protocol I.

49. Art. 23(e), 1907 Hague IV Regulations.

50. See Joint Chiefs of Staff, Joint Pub. 1-02, U.S. Department of Defense Dictionary of Military and Associated Terms 317 (8 Nov. 2010, as amended through 31 Dec. 2010)[hereinafter JCS Joint Pub. 1-02, Dictionary of Military Terms].

51. Art. 24, 1907 Hague IV Regulations.

52. U.S. Army FM 27-10, supra note 16, at 22.

of enemy property, under certain conditions. Combatants may wear enemy uniforms (to infiltrate enemy lines, for example), but cannot fight in these uniforms with the intent to deceive. Enemy colors (flags) may be used as a ruse, but, as in the case of naval vessels, cannot be employed during actual combat.[53] Enemy equipment might be used in combat, but only after all enemy insignia has been removed. The 1977 Protocol I, art. 39 (2), prohibits virtually all use of enemy items; however, the U.S. does not consider this provision as reflective of customary LOAC. Moreover, this article expressly does not apply to naval warfare.

Treachery and Perfidy

Treachery and perfidy are prohibited under the LOAC, as such acts involve a belligerent's abuse of its protections under the LOAC in order to gain a military advantage over an adversary.[54] Such actions include: feigning surrender, incapacitation, or civilian/noncombatant status; use of a flag of truce to gain time for retreat or reinforcement; misuse of a protective symbol (such as the Red Cross or cultural property symbol); declaring no quarter or killing/injuring enemy personnel who have surrendered; and compelling enemy state nationals to take part in hostilities against their country.[55] These acts are considered to be perfidious, however, only when such an act serves as a proximate cause in the killing of enemy combatants.

Espionage

Espionage involves clandestine action (acting under false pretenses) for the purpose of obtaining information.[56] Gathering intelligence information while in uniform is not espionage. Moreover, while espionage is not a violation of the LOAC, the Geneva Conventions accord no protections for those who engage in espionage. If captured, one so engaged may be tried under the laws of the capturing State. Reaching friendly lines immunizes a spy from prosecution for past espionage activities, and, if later captured, the former spy cannot be tried for such activities.

Assassination

The hiring of assassins, placing a price on an enemy's head, or the offering of a reward for the taking of an enemy, "dead or alive", are actions prohibited as "treacherous conduct". However, the offering of a reward for information leading to the capture of an individual, or an attack on civilian personnel serving in an enemy's command and control structure do not constitute acts of assassination and are not prohibited. U.S. Government personnel are prohibited from engaging in assassination activities by Executive Order.[57]

Belligerent (Wartime) Reprisals

Reprisals refer to conduct which otherwise would be unlawful, engaged in by one belligerent against the personnel or property of another, in response to actions taken by the latter in violation of the LOAC-for the purported purpose of enforcing future compliance

---

53. *Id.* at 23.; Art. 23(f), 1907 Hague IV Regulations.
54. Art. 23(b), 1907 Hague IV Regulations.
55. Art. 37(1)(a)(b), 1977 Protocol I; Art. 23 and 23(f), 1907 Hague IV Regulations.
56. U.S. Army FM 27-10, *supra* note 16, at 31–32; 1977 Protocol I, art. 46.
57. U.S. Army FM 27-10, *supra* note 16, at 17. *See also* Exec. Order No. 12,333, 3 C.F.R. 200 (1981), as amended by Exec. Order Nos. 13,284 (2003), 13,335 (2004) and 13,470 (2008).

with the LOAC.[58] While Additional Protocol I (articles 51 and 53-56) essentially prohibits reprisals, the U.S. continues to view such actions as lawful, if they: are taken in a timely manner; respond to an enemy's act that violated the LOAC; follow an unsatisfied demand to cease and desist; and are proportionate to the precipitating illegal act. While the U.S. reserves the right to engage in such reprisals, however, actions of this nature can be taken only with the specific approval of the National Command Authority.

Combatants and Protected Persons

General Rules

The LOAC permits intentional attacks against combatants, but not civilians or non-combatants. Accordingly, the civilian population is not to be intentionally attacked. Likewise, an individual civilian is protected from direct attack, unless, and for such time, as this civilian takes a direct part in hostilities (DPH). The term, "protected person", is a more narrowly defined legal term of art, specifically referenced in Geneva Convention IV, while the term, "noncombatant" appears in Geneva Convention IV, article 15, but is not precisely defined in the LOAC. This latter term can refer to various categories of military personnel protected from attack, such as medical personnel and chaplains, as well as to those who are out of combat, such as prisoners of war (POW) and the wounded, sick, and shipwrecked. It also refers to civilians.

Combatants

Combatants are military personnel who are lawfully engaged in an armed conflict on behalf of a party to the conflict. Such personnel are lawful targets unless "hors de combat"; that is, out of combat status—captured, wounded, sick or shipwrecked personnel no longer engaged in hostilities. Combatants are also "privileged belligerents"; that is, they are authorized to use force against an enemy on behalf of a State.

Lawful Combatants

As a short-hand means of determining whether an individual is a "lawful" combatant, reference can be made to the Geneva Convention on POW (GC III), Articles 4 A. (1) and (2). These articles identify those categories of personnel who are entitled to POW status. If entitled to such status, an individual is a "lawful" combatant.

Article 4: Prisoners of war, in the sense of the present Convention, are persons belonging to one of the following categories, who have fallen into the power of the enemy:

(1) Members of the armed forces of a Party to the conflict, as well as members of militias or volunteer corps forming part of such armed forces.

(2) Members of other militias and members of other volunteer corps, including those of organized resistance movements, belonging to a Party to the conflict and operating in or outside their own territory, even if this territory is occupied, provided that such militias or volunteer corps, including such organized resistance movements, fulfill the following conditions:

    (a) that of being commanded by a person responsible for his subordinates;

---

58. U.S. Army FM 27-10, *supra* note 16, at 177.

(b) that of having a fixed distinctive sign recognizable at a distance;

(c) that of carrying arms openly;

(d) that of conducting their operations in accordance with the laws and customs of war.

Unlawful Combatants

Unlawful combatants, also referred to as "unprivileged enemy belligerents", are spies, saboteurs, or civilian personnel who directly participate in hostilities or who otherwise engage in unauthorized attacks or combatant acts. These individuals do not qualify for POW status and, thus, as unlawful combatants, they may be prosecuted for their unlawful acts. If they directly participate in hostilities, they may also become objects of attack.

Noncombatants

An individual is considered to be "hors de combat" (out of combat) and, thus, a non-combatant, if he is in the power of an adverse party, clearly evidences an intention to surrender, or is incapacitated by wounds or sickness. Such personnel may not be attacked. They must be treated humanely and, at a minimum, in accordance with the protections set forth in Common Article 3 of the Geneva Conventions.[59]

Wounded and Sick in the Field and at Sea

Members of the armed forces who are wounded, or sick and cease to fight, are to be protected, as are shipwrecked members of the armed forces at sea. "Shipwrecked persons include those in peril at sea or in other waters as a result of the sinking, grounding, or other damage to a vessel ... or of the downing or distress of an aircraft."[60] The term, "shipwrecked", includes both military and civilian personnel.[61]

Medical Personnel, Chaplains, and Personnel of Red Cross Societies and Recognized Relief Organizations

Permanent medical personnel "exclusively engaged" in medical duties, chaplains, and personnel of Red Cross Societies and other recognized relief organizations are considered noncombatants and may not be intentionally attacked.[62] To be afforded this immunity, however, these personnel must refrain from any participation-even indirectly-in hostile acts.[63] As a measure of self-defense, military medical personnel may be armed with small arms, but these may be used only for their own defense or for the protection of the wounded and sick under their care-and only if attacked in violation of the LOAC.[64] If captured, such personnel are to be accorded the status of "retained personnel". And, while they are not POWs, at a minimum, they must receive POW protections. During detention,

---

59. 1977 Protocol I, art. 41, paras. 1–2.

60. U.S. Dep't of Navy, Naval Warfare Publication (NWP 1-14), Commander's Handbook on the Law of Naval Operations (July 2007), para.11.6 [hereinafter NWP 1-14M].

61. 1977 Protocol I, art. 8, para. 2.

62. Geneva Convention I, arts. 24, 26.

63. Pictet Commentary, Geneva Convention I, p. 221.

64. U.S. Army FM 27-10, *supra* note 16, at 88.

they are to perform only medical or religious duties, and if their services are not required to minister to the needs of POW, they are to be repatriated as soon as possible.[65]

Prisoners of War

POW (noncombatant) status arises only in the context of those types of international armed conflicts referenced in Common Article 2 of the Geneva Conventions.[66] In NIAC or other types of military operations, such as peacekeeping missions, individuals who commit hostile acts or serious criminal acts resulting in their capture are not entitled to POW status and protections. These persons are often designated as "detainees". However, Common Article 3 of the Geneva Conventions serves as a useful template for the minimal treatment to be accorded such personnel. Should doubt arise as to whether captured personnel warrant POW status, Article 5 of Geneva Convention III calls for the convening of a tribunal to make such a determination.[67]

POWs are to be afforded a wide range of rights and protections, to include adequate food, facilities and medical care.[68] Additionally, they are to be protected from both physical and mental harm and are to be transported from the combat zone as quickly as circumstances permit.[69] Subject to valid security reasons, POWs must be allowed to retain their personal property, protective gear, valuables and money.

Civilians

The civilian population, as well as individual civilians, are considered noncombatants and protected, as a result of this status, from both direct (intentional) and indiscriminate attack.[70] As civilians, journalists are considered to be noncombatants-and protected as such, provided that they take no actions inconsistent with this status.[71] If captured while accompanying a military force in the field, they are to be accorded POW status.[72] The Hague Cultural Property Convention, Article 17, protects civilian personnel engaged in the protection of cultural property from direct attack. And, civilians who accompany an armed force in the field in a time of armed conflict are also protected from direct attack, provided that they do not directly participate in hostilities. These individuals, too, are entitled to POW status, if captured.[73]

Direct Participation in Hostilities (DPH)

Article 51 (3) of Protocol I to the Geneva Conventions states that: "Civilians engaging in combat or otherwise taking a direct part in combat operations, singularly or as a group, lose their protection against direct attack." While, at first glance, this concept appears to be fairly straight forward, the inherent difficulty in its practical application lies in a lack

---

65. Geneva Convention I, art. 28.
66. Geneva Convention III, art. 2.
67. *Id.* at art. 5.
68. *Id.* at arts. 24, 26, 29–32.
69. *Id.* at art. 13. These are but several of the broad range of rights, privileges, and protections to be accorded POW under the Third Geneva Convention.
70. 1977 Protocol I, arts. 48, 51(2).
71. *Id.* at art. 79.
72. Geneva Convention III, art. 4(a)(4).
73. *Id.*

of international consensus as to the scope of activities captured by the term, "direct participation in hostilities". There is a general consensus that some acts readily fall within its meaning (personally engaging in potentially lethal acts, such as firing small arms at an enemy), while extremely remote or indirect acts do not (contract factory workers far from the battlefield). Likewise, there exists general agreement that the mere presence of civilians does not immunize military objectives from direct attack. Instead, this situation presents an issue of proportionality, rather than distinction, in conducting such an attack.

The real difficulty in applying the concept of DPH centers, first, around the now common scenarios in which the actions in issue have become increasingly indirect to the existence of actual hostilities—such as activities taken by non-State transnational organized groups in locations where host States are unable or unwilling to respond. Secondly, States have increasingly turned to civilian personnel to provide support for battlefield and targeting missions.

Given these facts, there is no universally agreed definition of DPH. The ICRC has proposed a relatively narrow reading of the term, requiring (1) a threshold showing or likelihood of harm, (2) a direct causal link between the act in question and that harm, and (3) a belligerent nexus to the conflict as shown by specific intent to help or harm one or more sides. Additionally, it has proposed that individuals engaged in "continuous combat functions" be liable to attack at any time, but has also recommended that combatants attempt to capture these civilians—using deadly force only as a last resort.[74] These ICRC proposals remain a matter of intense debate within the international community and do not reflect LOAC norms.

Military Objectives and Protected Places

Military Objectives

Protocol I to the Geneva Conventions and Protocols II and III to the Conventional Weapons Convention define military objectives as ... "objects which by their nature, location, purpose, or use, make an effective contribution to military action and whose total or partial destruction, capture, or neutralization, in the circumstances ruling at the time, offers a definite military advantage."[75]

"Nature" refers to the type of object; that is, objects which, by their nature, make an effective contribution to military action, such as combatants, armored fighting vehicles, weapons, combat aircraft, supply depots, command and control centers, communication stations, etc. "Location" includes militarily important areas; that is, areas that must be captured or denied an enemy, or from which an enemy must be forced to retreat, such as a mountain pass or a bridge on a key supply route. "Purpose" speaks to the intended or possible use of objects which can make an effective contribution to military action, such as civilian trucks being moved to the front to transport military personnel from one point to another, or a factory producing ball bearings for the military. "Use" is self-explanatory. Examples would include any object which would make an effective contribution to military action—to include a school being used as a military headquarters and a supply depot located in a private residence.

---

74. *See* NILS MELZER, INT'L COMM. OF THE RED CROSS, INTERPRETATIVE GUIDANCE ON THE NOTION OF DIRECT PARTICIPATION IN HOSTILITIES UNDER INTERNATIONAL HUMANITARIAN LAW 78 (2009).

75. 1977 Protocol I, art. 52(2).

Protected Places/Property

Undefended Places

The attack or bombardment of towns or villages, which are undefended, is prohibited, unless being used by the enemy for military purposes.[76] To gain protection as an undefended place, however, a village or town must be open to physical occupation by ground forces of an adverse party.

Protected Areas

Hospital or safety zones may be established for the protection of the wounded and sick or civilians.[77] The establishment of such zones does, however, require the agreement of the Parties to a conflict. Specific provisions of the Hague Cultural Property Convention also provide for certain cultural sites to be designated in an "International Register of Cultural Property under Special Protections."[78]

Medical Units and Establishments/Hospitals

Fixed or mobile medical units must be respected and protected and cannot be intentionally attacked. Protection for such units will cease only if they are used to commit "acts harmful to the enemy."[79] A warning must be provided prior to attacking a hospital being used for such acts, and the hospital must be given a reasonable time to comply with a warning before an attack is commenced.[80] However, when receiving fire from a hospital, no warning is required prior to returning fire in self-defense.

Medical Transport

Land, sea, and air transports of the wounded and sick or of medical equipment cannot be attacked if such transports are exclusively engaged in performing this function.[81]

Civilian Property

Civilian objects are protected from intentional attack. A presumption of civilian property attaches to objects traditionally associated with civilian use, as contrasted with military objectives, such as schools and dwellings.[82] Note is made, however, that such property is still subject to incurring incidental damage from a lawful attack on a military objective.

Cultural Property

The Hague Cultural Property Convention prohibits the intentional targeting of cultural property. The Convention defines cultural property as "movable or immovable property of great importance to the cultural heritage of every people", to include, inter alia, buildings

---

76. Art. 25, Hague IV Regulations.
77. Geneva Convention I, art. 23; Geneva Convention IV, art. 14.
78. 1954 Hague Cultural Property Convention, *supra* note 25, at arts. 8,11.
79. Army FM 27-10, *supra* note 16, at 93.
80. 1977 Protocol I, art. 13.
81. Geneva Convention I, art. 35.
82. 1977 Protocol I, arts. 51(2) and 52(3).

dedicated to religion and art, as well as historic monuments. The use of such property for military purposes will, however, result in the loss of its protected status.[83]

Works and Installations Containing Dangerous Forces

Specific provisions of Protocols I and II to the Geneva Conventions prohibit an attack on dams, dikes, and nuclear electrical generating stations, even where these objects are military objectives, if such an attack will cause the release of dangerous forces and cause "severe losses" among the civilian population. Works and installations of this nature may be attacked only if they are providing "significant and direct support" to military operations, an attack is the only feasible means to terminate such support, and only after such an attack is assessed under the principle of proportionality.[84]

Objects Indispensable to the Survival of the Civilian Population

Protocol I declares that starvation, as a method of warfare, is prohibited. It is thus prohibited to attack, destroy, remove, or render useless objects indispensable for the survival of the civilian population, such as foodstuffs, crops, livestock, water installations, and irrigation works.[85] A difficulty arises in applying this concept when an overly broad interpretation of "indispensable objects" would prohibit attacking certain entities that are also used to support an enemy's forces. These so-called "dual-use targets", with both military and civilian functions, would include such objects as airfields, electric power grids, oil-refining facilities, and radio and television broadcasting sites. It also raises the question as to the circumstances under which siege warfare or blockade would be legally justifiable, as the intent of imposing a siege or blockade is to inflict a level of suffering on military forces and civilians alike that would cause them to surrender rather than continue to fight.

Protective Emblems

Objects and personnel displaying certain protective emblems are presumed to be protected under the Geneva Conventions. The recognized medical and religious emblems are the Red Cross, Red Crescent, and the Red Crystal.[86] Cultural property is identified with "[a] shield, consisting of a royal blue square ... and a royal blue triangle above the square...., the space on either side being taken up by a white triangle."[87] Works and installations containing dangerous forces are marked with "three bright orange concentric circles ... , placed on the same axis."[88]

Questions for Discussion

1. In the midst of an ongoing engagement, a Company Commander receives word that his unit is taking fire from a small group of enemy soldiers housed in a hospital. He

---

83. *See generally* 1954 Hague Cultural Property Convention, *supra* note 26.

84. 1977 Protocol I, art. 56. As in the case of many of the provisions of Protocol I, the United States Government does not consider this article authoritative in nature.

85. 1977 Protocol I, art. 54.

86. Geneva Convention I, art. 38. The Red Crystal symbol is the product of the recently concluded Protocol Additional (III) to the Geneva Conventions of 12 August 1949, and relating to the Adoption of an Additional Distinctive Emblem (Protocol III), Dec. 8, 2005, S. Treaty Doc. No. 109-10, 45 I.L.M. 558 (2006).

87. 1954 Hague Cultural Property Convention, *supra* note 26, at arts. 16–17.

88. 1977 Protocol I, annex I, art. 16.

considers the use of mortars to silence this threat. What are the LOAC principles that should impact his decision?

2. During this same engagement, several men dressed in civilian clothes are seen running from the hospital, carrying weapons. They are seized by soldiers of the Commander's company. These individuals immediately demand to be treated as Prisoners of War. Should the Commander comply with this demand?

3. Several of the Commander's personnel have been severely wounded. Their fellow soldiers are also running very low on ammunition. The Commander has one helo at his disposal; he can use this to carry ammo to his troops and then have it transport the wounded to a field hospital nearby. Should he make this call?

4. The Commander is advised that the enemy's principal supply depot is located just over a bridge from its defensive fortifications. If he can destroy this bridge, he can deprive the enemy of this essential source of supplies. He then learns that the bridge also serves as the only means by which the majority of the civilian population can gain access to the sole medical facility in the area. What would you advise him to do?

Regulating the Means of Armed Conflict

As previously noted, the principle of "unnecessary suffering", sometimes referred to as the principle of superfluous injury, originally arose from humanitarian concerns regarding the suffering of wounded soldiers- and was codified as a weapons limitation: "It is especially forbidden ... to employ arms, projectiles or material calculated to cause unnecessary suffering."[89] This principle, as now interpreted, mandates three requirements to ensure the legality of weapons and ammunitions, as well as the methods by which they are employed. Military personnel may not use weapons and ammunition deemed, by the "usage of States", as illegal, per se; i.e., that they cause unnecessary suffering (e.g, projectiles filled with glass, hollow point or soft-point small caliber ammunition, lances with barbed heads). Treaty or customary limitations on weapons use must be observed, and lawful weapons must not be unlawfully employed. That is, both the weapon and the method of its employment must be lawful under the LOAC.

There is no universally agreed definition of "unnecessary suffering", as this term is used in connection with a determination as to whether a particular weapon or munition is lawful in nature. The criterion generally utilized is whether the employment of a weapon for its normal or expected use inevitably would cause injury or suffering manifestly disproportionate to the military advantage realized by its use. Such a determination is to be made with consideration being given to comparable, lawful weapons in use on the modern battlefield. A legal review of prospective weapons is required under the 1977 Protocol I to the Geneva Conventions.[90] All U.S. weapons, weapon systems, and munitions are reviewed for legality under the LOAC by U.S. Department of Defense attorneys.[91]

---

89. Art. 23(e), Hague IV Regulations.
90. 1977 Protocol I, art. 36.
91. *See generally* DEP'T OF DEF. DIRECTIVE 5000.01, The Defense Acquisition System (12 May 2003).

Specific Weapons/Weapon Systems

Small Arms Projectiles

The 1868 Declaration of St. Petersburg prohibits exploding rounds of less than 400 grams. State practice since 1868 has limited this prohibition to projectiles weighing less than 400 grams specifically designed to detonate in the human body. Expanding military small arms ammunition—so called 'dum-dum' projectiles such as hollow point ammunition, designed to expand extensively upon impact, and frangible ammunition, designed to break apart upon impact, are prohibited by the 1899 Hague Declaration Concerning Expanding Bullets. While the U.S. is not a party to this treaty, it has taken the position that it will abide by its terms when engaged in international armed conflicts to the extent that its application is consistent with the principle of unnecessary suffering set forth in Article 23(e) of Hague Convention IV.

Certain Conventional Weapons

The 1980 United Nations Convention on Certain Conventional Weapons and its Five Protocols restrict, regulate, or prohibit the use of certain otherwise lawful conventional weapons.[92]

Protocol I prohibits any weapon whose primary effect is to injure by fragments which, when in the human body, escape detection by x-ray.

Protocol II, as amended, regulates the use of mines, booby-traps, and other devices, while prohibiting certain types of anti-personnel mines in order to enhance the protection of the civilian population. While the U.S. regards certain land mines (anti-personnel and anti-vehicle) as lawful weapons, subject to the restrictions contained in amended Protocol II, the majority of States (currently, 161) are parties to a competing treaty, the 1997 Convention on the Prohibition of the Use, Stockpiling, Production and Transfer of Anti-Personnel Mines and on Their Destruction (also known as the Ottawa Treaty on Mines).[93] As evidenced by its title, this Convention serves to ban, completely, all anti-personnel mines. The United States, as a matter of policy, no longer employs anti-personnel landmines, except in the Demilitarized Zone between North and South Korea, and has begun the destruction of such mines not required for this purpose.

Protocol III regulates the use of incendiary weapons, principally to increase the protection of the civilian population. Napalm, flame-throwers, and thermite/thermate type weapons are incendiary weapons. However, munitions with incidental incendiary effects, such as illuminants, tracers, smoke, or signaling systems are not. This Protocol also prohibits the use of air-delivered incendiaries against military objectives located within areas of concentrated civilian populations. The U.S. has reserved the right to use these munitions in such areas, however, if their use will, in fact, result in fewer civilian casualties.[94]

Protocol IV prohibits "blinding laser weapons", defined as laser weapons specifically designed to permanently blind unenhanced vision. Other types of lasers present on the battlefield are lawful, even those that may cause injuries, to include permanent blindness, if such injuries occur incidental to the legitimate military use of such lasers (range-finding, target-acquisition devices).

---

92. *See generally* 1980 Conventional Weapons Convention, *supra* note 27.
93. *See generally* 1997 Ottawa Convention, *supra* note 30.
94. INTERNATIONAL AND OPERATIONAL LAW DEP'T, THE JUDGE ADVOCATE GEN.'S LEGAL CTR. & SCH., U.S. ARMY, OPERATIONAL LAW HANDBOOK 27 (2013) [hereinafter OPLAW HANDBOOK].

Protocol V deals with explosive remnants of war and requires that parties to an armed conflict, where feasible, clear or assist the host nation or others in the clearance of unexploded or abandoned explosive ordnance following the cessation of hostilities.

Cluster Bombs or Combined Effects Munitions

These munitions are effective when used against a variety of targets, to include air defense radars, armor, artillery, and large concentrations of enemy personnel. As these bomblets dispense over a relatively large area, and a percentage typically fail to detonate, this creates an unexploded ordinance (UXO) hazard. Cluster bombs are not mines; their use is not prohibited under the LOAC, and they are not timed to detonate as anti-personnel devices. When disturbed or disassembled, however, unexploded ordinance may explode and result in civilian casualties. As a result of this fact, a significant number of States are now parties to the 2008 Oslo Convention on Cluster Munitions, which prohibits the development, production, stockpiling, retention, or transfer of such munitions between signatories.[95]

Lethal/Incapacitating Agents

Biological Weapons

The use of poison has historically been outlawed in battle as a treacherous means of warfare. While the 1925 Geneva Gas Protocol prohibited only biological (bacteriological) weapon use,[96] the 1972 Biological Weapons Convention extended this prohibition. It prohibits the development, production, stockpiling, acquisition, or retention of biological agents or toxins, weapons, equipment or means of delivery designed to use such toxins for hostile purposes or in armed conflict.[97] The U.S is a state party to both treaties and has renounced all use of biological and toxin weapons.[98]

Chemical Weapons

The 1993 Chemical Weapons Convention prohibits the production, acquisition, stockpiling, retention, and use of chemical weapons, and specifically forbids retaliatory use-a departure from the prior 1925 Geneva Gas Protocol. The Convention requires the destruction of chemical stockpiles and also prohibits the use of Riot Control Agents (RCA) as a "method of warfare."[99] The U.S. has renounced the first use of RCA in international armed conflicts, except when employed in defensive modes in order to save lives, to include: controlling riots in areas under direct and distinct U.S. control, to include rioting POWs; dispersing civilians when they are being used by the enemy to mask or screen an attack; rescuing downed pilots, passengers and escaping POWs in remote or isolated areas; and, in rear echelon areas outside a zone of immediate combat, protecting convoys from civil disturbances, terrorists, and paramilitary organizations. While the Convention prohibits the use of RCA as a "method of warfare", this term is undefined. In terms of

---

95. Convention on Cluster Munitions, *supra* note 34.

96. 1925 Geneva Gas Protocol, *supra* note 20.

97. Convention on the Prohibition of the Development, Production and Stockpiling of Bacteriological (Biological) and Toxin Weapons and on Their Destruction, April 10, 1972, 26 U.S.T. 583, T.I.A.S. 8062.

98. *See* Chapter 13.

99. (Paris) Convention on the Prohibition of the Development, Production, Stockpiling and Use of Chemical Weapons and on Their Destruction, January 13, 1993, S. Treaty Doc. No. 103-21, 1974 U.N.T.S. 3, 32 I.L.M. 800.

U.S. use of RCA, however, the President, in ratifying the Convention, was required to certify that the U.S. would not be restricted in its use of RCA in the following cases: when the U.S. is not a party to the conflict in issue, in consensual peacekeeping operations, and in U.N. peace enforcement operations. Finally, the U.S. has renounced the first use of herbicides in armed conflicts, except for the purpose of clearing vegetation around defensive positions.[100]

Nuclear Weapons[101]

In 1996, the International Court of Justice issued an advisory non-binding opinion dealing with the legality of nuclear weapons that failed to definitively address this issue. The Court opined that "[t]here is in neither customary nor international law any comprehensive and universal prohibition of the threat or use of nuclear weapons." By a divided vote, however, it then noted that "[t]he threat or use of nuclear weapons would generally be contrary to the rules of international law applicable in armed conflict." Lastly, the Court stated that it could reach no decision as to whether the threat or use of nuclear weapons would be lawful or unlawful when used by a State, acting in self-defense, to preserve its very survival.[102] In brief, nuclear weapons are not prohibited by international law. As noted previously, however, any lawful weapon system is subject to being used in an unlawful manner.

Cyber[103]

The applicability of the LOAC to the rapidly evolving concept of "cyber warfare" is a much debated topic. Initially, a determination must be made that, in applying the conflict management, use of force principles, of jus ad bellum, an "armed attack" has, in fact, occurred. If such a decision is made, it is then generally agreed that any analysis of the applicability of LOAC to cyber "attacks" must center on the four universally accepted LOAC principles of military necessity, distinction, proportionality, and unnecessary suffering (this latter principle both constraining the choice of weapons and regulating the methods through which such weapons might be employed).

The applicability of these principles to cyber attacks can best be assessed in the context of a State's ability to use two distinct approaches in responding to such attacks. They might first be examined from the standpoint of a State's decision to respond to an attack through the exclusive use of "active defense measures"—that is, electronic countermeasures designed to strike an attacking computer system, shut it down, and thus halt an attack. Secondly, a State might choose to respond to an attack, in the exercise of a legitimate right of self-defense, through the employment of kinetic weapons.

In terms of military necessity, it might be argued that active defense measures may well represent the degree of force necessary to accomplish the military mission—to shut down the attacking computer system. The use of kinetic weaponry to attack the system in issue may, generally, not only be less effective; it might well constitute a disproportionate use of force. In contrast, the traceback capabilities of active defenses may ensure that

---

100. Exec. Order No. 11850, Renunciation of Certain Uses in War of Chemical Herbicides and Riot Control Agents, 3 C.F.R., 1971–1975 Comp, p. 980 (1975). See also Chapter 13.

101. *See* Chapter 13 discussion on the legality of nuclear weapons.

102. *See* Legality of the Threat or Use of Nuclear Weapons, Advisory Opinion, 1996 I.C.J. 226, paras. 90–97 (July 8).

103. *See* Chapter 12, Law and Warfare in the Cyber Domain, for a more detailed and broader discussion.

these measures target only the source of the cyber attack. As a result, this could possibly accomplish the following: greatly reduce collateral damage relative to that which would result from the use of kinetic weaponry, thus helping to achieve proportionality; distinguish the attacking system (the military objective) from protected places, property, and civilians; and minimize the unnecessary suffering that would be the probable result of a kinetic use of force.

However, while the contention can be made that the use of active defense measures to respond to a cyber attack would better comply with the LOAC than the use of kinetic means, the use of such measures also runs a risk of triggering LOAC violations. A "surgical" strike against a computer system ostensibly at the core of a cyber attack may not be possible to achieve due to technical limitations. It is exceptionally difficult to trace an attack routed through intermediary systems. When such an attack occurs, a trace program not only requires a certain amount of time; it becomes more difficult to pinpoint the specific source of the attack once the attacker terminates the electronic connection. This may well cause either a failure to identify the attacking system or an incorrect identification of an intermediary system as the source of the attack with potentially significant LOAC implications.

Additionally, even when the source of an attack can be identified, a system administrator must then "map" the attacking system—assessing its functions and attempting to make an informed decision of the likely consequences (resulting damage) that will occur if actions are taken to shut the system down. This will also take time, and there is an inherent risk in employing active defenses against a system that has not been fully mapped. This may well lead to the accidental targeting of innocent systems, resulting in unintended and excessive collateral damage.

The contention might also be made that, in using active defenses in a particular situation, all feasible efforts have been undertaken to identify an attacking system and to evaluate the probable collateral damage that would result. However, the extent of the damage that actually occurs when a State employs such defenses, particularly in relation to innocent systems located in third States, may likely be deemed as violations of both the principles of distinction and proportionality. For example, such would be the case if the use of active defenses against an attacking system either routed through—or intricately connected with—critical national infrastructure systems of either the host or third States were to result in unanticipated and substantial damage to these systems.

In sum, given the ongoing technical challenges associated with cyber attacks, a response to such an attack by either kinetic or active defense measures leaves ample room for error and, consequently, unintended consequences. This fact mandates that carefully crafted procedures for responding to cyber attacks, to include workable Rules of Engagement, be developed in order to ensure compliance with the LOAC.[104]

Unmanned Aerial Vehicles (UAVs) and Autonomous Weaponry

Unmanned Aerial Vehicles (UAVs)

Significant attention has been focused on the U.S. employment of Unmanned Aerial Vehicles (UAVs), or drones, as a weapon system against both combatants on the battlefield

---

104. *See generally* David E. Graham, *Cyber Threats and the Law of War*, 4 J. Nat'l Security L. & Pol'y 87 (2010).

and terrorists far removed from an active zone of military operations. The most common of these UAVs are the Predator and its larger and faster cousin, the Reaper. When used for strike, versus surveillance missions, these systems are generally fitted with two types of missiles—the Hellfire and the Scorpion.[105] The use of these UAVs as weapon platforms has sparked substantial debate-with a number of commentators calling their employment "unlawful" and others demanding the negotiated conclusion of a new legal regime that would dictate when, where, and how this new technology might be deployed.[106] The reality, however, is that well-established, codified and customary international law principles, currently do just this.

The UAV, while representing new technology in terms of delivering kinetic munitions, represents nothing more than one of any number of weapon platforms available for use by the U.S. in use of force situations. Constantly under the control of an operator, it is not autonomous in nature. Moreover, just as in the case of all weapon delivery systems, the UAV, too, is subject to the above discussed LOAC targeting principles of military necessity, distinction, proportionality, and unnecessary suffering (collateral damage). Indeed, with its ability to extensively loiter over and surveil a potential target, more effectively assess the acquired target information, and more accurately deliver its munition package, the UAV might well serve as a poster child for careful compliance with such LOAC principles. Why, then, if the manner in which UAVs might be employed is dictated by an effective and proven legal regime, has their use generated controversy and a continuing demand for their enhanced regulation?

An examination of the criticisms levied against the U.S. employment of UAVs reveals that, in effect, this weapon platform has simply become the lightning rod for those who, in actuality, question the validity of the legal bases cited by the U.S. for certain use of force decisions involving the UAV, rather than the UAV itself. That is, these critics contend that the UAV, specifically, is often used by the U.S. to project force abroad in violation of recognized use of force (jus ad bellum) conflict management norms, charges that play out in the context of two distinct scenarios.

The first such scenario is an ongoing armed conflict situation, wherein a UAV might be used in a fashion similar to any other weapon platform to strike an adversary—again, in compliance with applicable LOAC targeting principles. The criticism of the use of UAVs in this scenario centers around, as of this date, the continued U.S. assertion that it remains in an "ongoing armed conflict" with Al Qaeda (AQ) and its "associated forces"— not only in Afghanistan and Pakistan, but globally. Consequently, on this basis, the U.S. has reserved the right to strike AQ and its broadly defined associated forces wherever they might be found, to include through the use of a UAV, if this is deemed to be the most effective available weapon platform.[107] And, due to its efficiency—and the most important consideration, that its use does not place U.S. personnel or aircraft at risk—the UAV has consistently proven to be the weapon platform of choice. This fact, coupled with the reality that the international community has generally rejected the U.S. contention that it remains in a global armed conflict with AQ and its associated forces and that, accordingly,

---

105. Joby Warrick & Peter Finn, *In Pakistan, CIA Refines Methods to Reduce Civilian Deaths*, Washington Post, p. A8, (April 26, 2010).

106. Pew Research Center, Global Opinion of Obama Slips, International Policies Faulted (June 13, 2012); David Ignatius, *Dazzling New Weapons Require New Rules for War*, Washington Post, p. A20 (Nov. 11, 2010).

107. Harold Koh, "The Obama Administration and International Law," speech before the American Society of International Law, Mar. 25, 2010).

it might strike such personnel wherever they might be found, has resulted in the consistent use of UAVs in this scenario being roundly criticized. Again, however, the issues at play in such a situation actually revolve around perceived unlawful uses of force by the U.S.; i.e., U.S. violations of the controlling use of force norms themselves, rather than a belief that the UAV constitutes an unlawful instrument for the projection of such force.

The second scenario of concern is the U.S. use of force in the exercise of self-defense, though not in response to an "armed attack", but, in this case, as an exercise of an inherent, customary right of self-defense against individuals posing a "continuing and imminent threat to the American people".[108] The U.S. implementation of this interpretation of the self-defense concept has led to U.S. strikes against individuals far removed from an active battlefield—actions often conducted by civilian members of the U.S. Central Intelligence Agency. And, once again, the UAV has been the weapon platform of choice in carrying out these missions. As in the previous scenario, however, the legitimacy of these U.S. "self-defense" operations has been subjected to extensive challenges. Critics have asked: "What constitutes an 'imminent threat'?" "Who determines the existence of such a threat?" "On the basis of what criteria is such a determination made?" The lack of transparency in this decision making process has also been roundly criticized.[109] Yet, here too, it is the legitimacy of the legal basis for these strikes, as well as, on occasion, the target selection process, that have been questioned, rather than the lawfulness of the UAV as a weapon system.

In sum, the legal concerns surrounding U.S. use of force actions involving UAVs actually relate to the legitimacy of the legal bases put forward for these actions, rather than to whether the UAV constitutes a lawful weapon platform. Perhaps, in the final analysis, the real issue at the center of the controversy surrounding the U.S. employment of UAVs is the probability that, due to its many operational attributes and its highly desirable, risk-averse nature, the UAV simply now makes a use of force course of action too attractive to decision makers. And, in turn, the relative ease with which such operations can be conducted has led to the need to formulate, arguably, somewhat strained and self-serving legal justifications for such activities.

Autonomous Weaponry

Autonomous weapons are those that, "once activated, can select and engage targets without further human operator involvement."[110] Currently, no such weapons exist. While opponents of such systems have argued for a preemptive ban on the development and deployment of autonomous robotic technology, such a move appears to be highly unlikely. Given the technological advances in this area, autonomous weapons may well be a relatively near-term reality. Indeed, various forms of land, sea, and air autonomous weaponry are currently undergoing testing.[111]

Given this fact, the essential issue becomes, once again, whether such weapons can be deployed in a manner that complies with the LOAC targeting principles previously discussed. In this context, it is generally agreed that, when a weapon system is adopted for use in the field, the LOAC requires that it be used in a manner that provides for dis-

---

108. President Barack Obama, Remarks by the President at the National Defense University (May 23, 2013).

109. Rosa Brooks, *Drones and the International Rule of Law*, 28 Ethics & Int'l Aff. 83 (Spring, 2014).

110. U.S. Dep't of Def., Dir. 3000.09, Autonomy in Weapon Systems 13 (Nov. 2, 2012).

111. Allyson Hauptman, *Autonomous Weapons and the Laws of Armed Conflict*, 218 Mil. L. Rev. 170 (Winter 2013).

crimination and the implementation of reasonable precautions. Thus, it would appear that a weapon might be deemed to be indiscriminate and, therefore, unlawful, per se, if it cannot be directed at a specific military objective or its effects cannot be limited.[112]

Herein resides the challenge for the future use of robotic weaponry. Such systems offer a very real military advantage and may, in many cases, improve upon the precision of target acquisition. However, given the fact that these weapons lack the reasoning capabilities of a human, will it ever be possible to program them in such a way that they might adequately meet the LOAC requirement of distinction, and, thus, the additional principles of proportionality and unnecessary collateral damage? Or will the military advantage they offer — to include greater accuracy in target acquisition and, thus, less collateral damage — serve as a proportional offset to their more limited ability to meet the principle of distinction? Suffice it to say that this is a most challenging aspect of the evolving nature of the LOAC.

Rules of Engagement (ROE)

Rules of Engagement (ROE) are not components of the LOAC or International Humanitarian Law. This term does not appear in the 1949 Geneva Conventions, nor the Additional Protocols thereto. Neither are ROE the subject of any multinational agreement relating to any aspect of armed conflict. A basic understanding of the nature of ROE is important, however, as they can play a significant role in the execution of a State's LOAC obligations and are often cited when LOAC violations are alleged.

ROE are directives issued by competent military authority that delineate the circumstances and limitations under which a State's armed forces will initiate and/or continue combat engagement with other forces encountered.[113] ROE generally perform three distinct functions. They provide guidance from a State's national command authority, as well as subordinate commanders, to deployed units on the use of force; act as a control mechanism for the transition from peacetime to combat operations; and provide a mechanism to facilitate planning. In sum, ROE provide a ready framework for reflecting national policy goals, mission requirements, and the LOAC.

ROE are a tool for ensuring that national policies and objectives are at the core of actions taken by commanders in the field. In this regard, ROE may restrict the engagement of certain targets, or the use of certain weapon systems, centered on a desire to shape world opinion, place a positive limit on the escalation of hostilities, and not unduly antagonize an enemy. ROE thus provide constraints on a commander's actions, consistent with both a State's domestic law and applicable international law. Of importance, however, is an appreciation for the fact that, for the reasons noted above, ROE often impose greater restrictions on a commander's actions than those required by the LOAC. In brief, while ROE incorporate elements of the LOAC, ROE do not constitute the LOAC.[114]

Questions for Discussion

1. While engaged in an intense battle for a key enemy position, a Battalion Commander is notified that an enemy artillery battery, located on the outskirts of a small town, has

---

112. Art. 51(4), 1977 Protocol I.
113. JCS Joint Pub. 1-02, Dictionary of Military Terms, *supra* note 50.
114. *See generally* OPLAW Handbook, *supra* note 94, at 75–78.

halted the progress of his troops. He has the ability to call for the use of combined effects munitions against this artillery emplacement. Should he?

2. A helicopter assigned to this Commander comes under enemy fire and crashes. Its crew survives, but is in imminent danger of being captured. The Commander dispatches two helos to rescue the downed crew—and authorizes their use of Riot Control Agents (RCA) in effecting this mission. The Chemical Weapons Convention prohibits the use of RCA as a "method of warfare." Given this fact, has the Commander acted unlawfully?

3. During the course of this battle, the enemy employs a laser range finding device. This device blinds two members of the Commander's staff who are forward deployed in order to better observe the enemy's positions. The Commander insists that his High Command issue a statement, charging the enemy with a violation of the LOAC by its use of laser weapons on the battlefield. Should such a charge be made?

4. "Cyber attacks" have brought a completely new dimension to warfare. Given the technical difficulties in accurately attributing such attacks to a responsible party, is it realistic to attempt to apply the traditional principles of the LOAC to "cyber warfare?"

5. In a recent military campaign, a State made extensive use of cluster bombs. Many of these failed to detonate and now pose a significant risk to the civilian population. The State in which these munitions were used has brought this matter to the United Nations—asserting that the State which employed these devices is exclusively responsible for their neutralization and removal. Is this correct? Is there law that speaks to this issue?

Naval Warfare

The 1856 Declaration of Paris provided very few fundamental rules with respect to the methods and means of conducting war at sea. While the 1899 Hague Peace Conference did not deal with this subject, except to adapt the 1864 Geneva Convention on the wounded and sick in maritime warfare, the 1907 Hague Peace Conference was quite active in this area. The following are some of the more important provisions of the numerous new conventions on war at sea drafted at this conference.

1907 Hague VIII Convention

Article 1

It is forbidden:

1. To lay unanchored automatic contact mines, except when they are so constructed as to become harmless one hour at most after the person who has laid them ceases to control them;

2. To lay anchored automatic contact mines which do not become harmless as soon as they have broken loose from their moorings;

3. To use torpedoes which do not become harmless when they have missed their mark.

Article 2

It is forbidden to lay automatic contact mines off the coasts and ports of the enemy, with the sole object of intercepting commercial shipping.

1907 Hague IX Convention

Article 1

The bombardment by naval forces of undefended ports, towns, villages, dwellings, or buildings is forbidden.

A place cannot be bombarded solely because automatic submarine contact mines are anchored off the harbor.

Article 2

Military works, military or naval establishments, depôts of arms or war matériel, workshops or plants which could be utilized for the needs of the hostile fleet or army, and the ships of war in the harbour, are not, however, included in this prohibition. The commander of a naval force may destroy them with artillery, after a summons followed by a reasonable time of waiting, if all other means are impossible, and when the local authorities have not themselves destroyed them within the time fixed.

He incurs no responsibility for any unavoidable damage which may be caused by a bombardment under such circumstances.

. . . .

Article 7

A town or place, even when taken by storm, may not be pillaged.

———————

Rules with respect to submarine warfare, not included in any of the foregoing agreements, were drafted in 1930 and reiterated in 1936.

Treaty for the Limitation and Reduction of Naval Armaments

Apr. 22, 1930,
46 Stat. 2858, 112 L.N.T.S. 65
(and the 1936 Procès-Verbal, Nov. 6, 1936, 173 L.N.T.S. 353)

Article 22. The following are accepted as established rules of International Law:

(1) In their action with regard to merchant ships, submarines must conform to the rules of international law to which surface vessels are subject.

(2) In particular, except in the case of persistent refusal to stop on being duly summoned, or of active resistance to visit or search, a warship, whether surface vessel or submarine, may not sink or render incapable of navigation a merchant vessel without having first placed passengers, crew and ship's papers in a place of safety. For this purpose the ship's boats are not regarded as a place of safety unless the safety of the passengers and crew is assured, in the existing sea and weather conditions, by the proximity of land, or the presence of another vessel which is in a position to take them on board.

. . . .

Article 23. The present Treaty shall remain in force until the 31st December, 1936, subject to the following exceptions:

(1) [Article 22] shall remain in force without limit of time. . . .

———————

An Anglo-French Declaration of September 2, 1939, at the outset of World War II, promised compliance with the foregoing rules.[115] However, given the practical realities of war at sea, unrestricted submarine warfare became the operational rule on both sides.

Opinion and Judgment of the International Military Tribunal

Nuremberg, Oct. 1, 1946,
22 T.M.W.C. 524, 559 (1948)

In view of all the facts proved, and in particular of an order of the British Admiralty announced on 8 May 1940, according to which all vessels should be sunk at night in the Skagerrak, and the answer to interrogatories by Admiral Nimitz that unrestricted submarine warfare was carried on in the Pacific Ocean by the United States from the first day that nation entered the war, the sentence of Dönitz is not assessed on the ground of his breaches of the international law of submarine warfare.

San Remo Manual on International Law Applicable to Armed Conflicts at Sea

On the initiation of the International Institute of Humanitarian Law, a Round Table on International Humanitarian Law Applicable to Armed Conflicts at Sea was convened in San Remo, Italy, in 1987 to discuss the need for the modernization of the law of naval warfare. The 1977 Additional Protocols to the 1949 Geneva Conventions addressed the law of war on land, but did not have a significant maritime dimension. During the ensuing six years, a plan of action to examine these issues and to formulate a restatement of the conventional and customary law of naval warfare was undertaken by a group of experts from around the world. The result of that effort was the adoption in June 1994, at Livorno, Italy, of the San Remo Manual on International Law Applicable to Armed Conflicts at Sea.

Hector Gros Espiell, *Foreword*

to San Remo Manual on International Law Applicable to Armed Conflicts at Sea,
at ix (Louise Doswald-Beck ed., 1995) (adopted in June 1994)

Foreword
....

This document is a contemporary restatement of the law, together with some progressive development, which takes into account recent State practice, technological developments and the effects of related areas of the law, in particular, the United Nations Charter, the 1982 Law of the Sea Convention, air law and environmental law. The last restatement of the law of armed conflict at sea was undertaken by the Institute of International Law in 1913. Developments in the law since that date have for the most part not been incorporated into treaty law, with the exception of the Second Geneva Convention which is essentially limited to protection of the wounded, sick and shipwrecked at sea, and does not address the whole question of the law on the conduct of hostilities at sea. The Manual ... represent[s] a unique effort of experts from different parts of the world to establish the present state of the law based on State practice and treaty law of continuing validity.

---

115. J.M. Spaight, Air Power and War Rights 259 (3d Ed. 1947).

The San Remo Manual is a restatement of the law and not a treaty. It therefore has no binding legal effect on states. Nonetheless, it is widely accepted as a valid expression of the current state of the LOAC at sea. International lawyers and naval experts from the United States participated actively in its creation, and the United States considers that most, but not all, of its provisions accurately reflect the customary and treaty LOAC at sea.

Air Warfare

It will have been noted that, apart from the disputed 1899 Hague Declaration IV(1) and the possible applicability by analogy of some of the 1907 Hague IV Regulations, no conventional rules relating to war in and from the air have been set forth. The 1923 Hague Rules of Aerial Warfare, which were largely a codification of then existing customary international law, although they did go beyond that in some respects, were never ratified; and for many years thereafter no official attempt was made to draft international regulations in this area.

Protection of Civilian Populations Against Bombing from the Air in Case of War, Resolution of the League of Nations Assembly

League of Nations O. J., Spec. Supp. 182, at 15 (1938)

The Assembly ...

Recognizes the following principles as a necessary basis for any subsequent regulations:

(1) The intentional bombing of civilian populations is illegal;

(2) Objectives aimed at from the air must be legitimate military objectives and must be identifiable;

(3) Any attack on legitimate military objectives must be carried out in such a way that civilian populations in the neighbourhood are not bombed through negligence....

Unfortunately, when World War II erupted, even though France, Germany, and Great Britain all replied affirmatively to an appeal by President Roosevelt against the bombardment of civilians, eventually no air force, Allied or Axis, adhered to these restrictions. The provisions of Articles 48, 49, and 51 of the 1977 Protocol I, and of Article 2(1) of the 1980 Protocol III were an attempt to establish some specific, codified restrictions on air warfare. Their viability remains to be seen. Notwithstanding the lack of a comprehensive body of treaty law applicable specifically to air warfare, as of this writing, there has not been an effort to develop a restatement of the law of air warfare similar to that achieved by the San Remo Manual dealing with naval warfare.

The Law of Belligerent Occupation

DORIS APPLE GRABER, THE DEVELOPMENT OF THE LAW OF BELLIGERENT OCCUPATION, 1863–1914

at 13 (1949)

From ancient times on, through the Middle Ages, and up to the nineteenth century, when a belligerent occupied territory belonging to his adversary, he was usually considered the absolute owner of the occupied lands. He could do what he liked with them and their inhabitants. He could devastate the country, appropriate all public and private property, kill the people, or take them prisoners, or make them swear allegiance to himself and force them to fight in his army against their old sovereign. He could even before the war was decided dispose of the territory by annexing it or ceding it to a third State.

The first thirty articles of Lieber's Code dealt with belligerent occupation. (He referred to it as "martial law," a term that has a different meaning today.) However, Articles 42-56 of the 1899 Hague II Regulations and of the 1907 Hague IV Regulations (which were substantially identical) were the first provisions of a multilateral international agreement to set out standards to guide the conduct of an Occupying Power. They were primarily concerned with property rights, but they did contain some minimal provisions for the protection of persons. These regulations remained the sole written international law with respect to belligerent occupation until the Fourth 1949 Geneva Convention became effective. (It will be found that the relevant provisions of the latter were all intended to preclude a repetition of practices followed during the course of World War II by both Germany and Japan.) Moreover, the law of belligerent occupation is one area concerning which very little is to be found in the 1977 Protocol I, apart from Article 63 thereof.

Opinion and Judgment of the International Military Tribunal Nuremberg, Sept. 30, 1946

22 T.M.W.C. 411, 486-87 (1948)

The laws relating to forced labor by the inhabitants of occupied territories are found in Article 52 of the Hague Convention [Regulations], which provides:

> "Requisition in kind and services shall not be demanded from municipalities or inhabitants except for the needs of the army of occupation. They shall be in proportion to the resources of the country, and of such a nature as not to involve the inhabitants in the obligation of taking part in military operations against their own country."

The policy of the German occupation authorities was in flagrant violation of the terms of this convention. Some idea of this policy may be gathered from the statement made by Hitler in a speech on 9 November 1941:

> "The territory which now works for us contains more than 250,000,000 men, but the territory which works indirectly for us now includes more than 350,000,000. In the measure in which it concerns German territory, the domain which we have taken under our administration, it is not doubtful that we shall succeed in harnessing the very last man to this work."

The actual results achieved were not so complete as this, but the German occupation authorities did succeed in forcing many of the inhabitants of the occupied territories to work for the German war effort, and in deporting at least 5,000,000 persons to Germany to serve German industry and agriculture.

Fourth Geneva Convention

Common Article 2

The Convention shall also apply to all cases of partial or total occupation of the territory of a High Contracting Party, even if the said occupation meets with no armed resistance.

. . . .

Article 47

Protected persons who are in occupied territory shall not be deprived, in any case or in any manner whatsoever, of the benefits of the present Convention by any change introduced, as the result of the occupation of a territory, into the institutions or government of the said territory, nor by any agreement concluded between the authorities of the occupied territories and the Occupying Power, nor by any annexation by the latter of the whole or part of the occupied territory.

. . . .

Article 49

Individual or mass forcible transfers, as well as deportations of protected persons from occupied territory to the territory of the Occupying Power or to that of any other country, occupied or not, are prohibited, regardless of their motive.

. . . .

Article 51

The Occupying Power may not compel protected persons to serve in its armed or auxiliary forces. No pressure or propaganda which aims at securing voluntary enlistment is permitted.

. . . .

Article 54

The Occupying Power may not alter the status of public officials or judges in the occupied territories, or in any way apply sanctions to or take any measures of coercion or discrimination against them, should they abstain from fulfilling their functions for reasons of conscience.

. . . .

Article 55

To the fullest extent of the means available to it, the Occupying Power has the duty of ensuring the food and medical supplies of the population; it should, in particular, bring in the necessary foodstuffs, medical stores and other articles if the resources of the occupied territory are inadequate.

. . . .

Article 78

If the Occupying Power considers it necessary, for imperative reasons of security, to take safety measures concerning protected persons, it may, at the most, subject them to assigned residence or to internment.

It is important to note that, upon a State declaring an end to active hostilities and assuming the role of an Occupying Power, while it is entitled to exercise the rights of such a Power, it must also take on the many responsibilities that such a status carries with it. In sum, the occupation of a State inevitably comes with a very real price in terms of the resources required to maintain the "actual" and "effective" occupation mandated by article 42 of the 1907 Hague IV Regulations. The recent experience of the U.S. military in Iraq is a classic example of this fact.

Protecting Powers and Enforcement

Traditionally, the Protecting Power is a State that has agreed to protect the interests of another State (called the power of origin) in the territory of a third State (called the power of residence or the detaining power) with which for some reason, such as war, the second State does not maintain diplomatic relations.[116] The selection of a Protecting Power is a consensual process, as the State that is requested by the power of origin to serve as such must agree to do so, and the State in whose territory the Protecting Power is to perform its functions must agree to accept the State proposed by its adversary. It is a fairly old institution of customary international law, dating back a number of centuries. Despite its age and its frequent use in wartime, particularly during the Franco-Prussian War and in the half century that followed, it did not find mention in any multilateral international agreement until it appeared in Article 86 of the 1929 Geneva Prisoner-of-War Convention; and that provision was completely optional and contained very little of substance.

During World War II, almost every belligerent was represented by Protecting Powers in the territories of its various enemies. However, some governments were denied the right to designate Protecting Powers; a few belligerents were not universally represented; many of the designated Protecting Powers were not actually permitted to function properly; and no provision existed for the situation that arose when a Protecting Power became a belligerent. When the 1949 Geneva Conventions were drafted, they included a number of provisions that were intended to preclude a repetition of these problems. Unfortunately, they were not particularly successful in accomplishing their purpose, so that, despite this effort, and despite the many international armed conflicts that have occurred since 1949, no real wartime Protecting Power has been designated or has functioned in any such conflict since those Conventions became effective (with the possible exception of the 1982 Falkland hostilities). Several instances of such designations are sometimes asserted, but they do not appear to represent true wartime Protecting Powers. A fully functioning Protecting Power becomes the true embodiment of the LOAC in the territory of the party to the conflict in which it is operating. The lack of a Protecting Power, or a nonfunctioning Protecting Power, will quickly become evident to the individuals, civilian and military, who require, but lack, its vigilance and its assistance.

---

116. *See* 1977 Protocol I, art. 2(c). *See also* 1961 Vienna Convention on Diplomatic Relations, April 18, 1961, art. 45, 23 U.S.T. 3227, 500 U.N.T.S. 95.

1949 Geneva Conventions

Common Article 8/8/8/9

1. The present Convention shall be applied with the cooperation and under the scrutiny of the Protecting Power whose duty it is to safeguard the interests of the Parties to the conflict....

2. The Parties to the conflict shall facilitate to the greatest extent possible, the task of the representatives or delegates of the Protecting Powers.

Common Article 10/10/10/11

1. The High Contracting Parties may at any time agree to entrust to an organization which offers all guarantees of impartiality and efficacy the duties incumbent on the Protecting Powers by virtue of the present Convention.

2. When [the persons protected by the Convention] do not benefit or cease to benefit, no matter for what reason, by the activities of a Protecting Power or of an organization provided for in the first paragraph above, the Detaining Power shall request a neutral State, or such an organization, to undertake the functions performed under the present Convention by a Protecting Power designated by the Parties to a conflict.

....

6. Whenever in the present Convention mention is made of a Protecting Power, such mention applies to substitute organizations in the sense of the present Article.

When the ICRC prepared its 1973 Draft Additional Protocol I, it included an alternative proposal that was intended to ensure the appointment of a Protecting Power in every international armed conflict. However, by the time that this proposal had been debated at the diplomatic conference that drafted the 1977 Protocol I, the value of the provisions that emerged had become highly debatable.[117]

1977 Protocol I

Article 5 — Appointment of Protecting Powers and their substitute

1. It is the duty of the Parties to a conflict from the beginning of that conflict to secure the supervision and implementation of the Conventions and of this Protocol by the applications of the System of Protecting Powers, including *inter alia* the designation and acceptance of these Powers, in accordance with the following paragraphs. Protecting Powers shall have the duty of safeguarding the interests of the Parties to the conflict.

2. From the beginning of a situation referred to in Article 1, each Party to the conflict shall without delay designate a Protecting Power for the purpose of applying the Conventions and this Protocol and shall, likewise without delay and for the same purpose, permit the activities of a Protecting Power which has been accepted by it as such after designation by the adverse Party.

3. If a Protecting Power has not been designated or accepted from the beginning of a situation referred to in Article 1, the International Committee of the Red Cross ... shall

----

117. For a discussion of the controversy regarding these provisions, *see* 1 HOWARD S. LEVIE, PRO-TECTION OF WAR VICTIMS 127–213 (1979).

offer its good offices to the Parties to the conflict with a view to the designation without delay of a Protecting Power to which the Parties to the conflict consent. . . .

4. If, despite the foregoing, there is no Protecting Power, the Parties to the conflict shall accept without delay an offer which may be made by the International Committee of the Red Cross . . . after due consultations with the said Parties . . . to act as a substitute. The functioning of such a substitute is subject to the consent of the Parties to the conflict; every effort shall be made by the Parties to the conflict to facilitate the operations of the substitute in the performance of its tasks under the Conventions and this Protocol.

. . . .

7. Any subsequent mention in this Protocol of a Protecting Power includes also a substitute.

———————

Assuming the designation of Protecting Powers for the adverse parties (and it has been found that a Protecting Power functions most effectively when the same State is the Protecting Power for both of the adverse parties, although of course this is not required), two problems remain: first, where does the Protecting Power acquire the personnel necessary to perform the functions that it has assumed; and second, what are those functions?

As regards personnel, Common Article 8/8/8/9 of the 1949 Geneva Conventions authorizes the Protecting Powers to use members of its diplomatic and consular staff, as well as "their own nationals or the nationals of other neutral powers."[118] During World War II, Switzerland, the Protecting Power for some thirty-five belligerents in anywhere from one to eighteen different territories, used only Swiss nationals. Because of the problems encountered in quickly recruiting and training the large number of persons required, Article 6 of the 1977 Protocol I provides for the peacetime recruiting and training of a pool of individuals of whom the nationals of neutral powers would be available for assignment in time of war.

Third Geneva Convention
Article 78

. . . .

2. [Prisoners of war] shall also have the unrestricted right to apply to the representatives of the Protecting Power either through their prisoners' representative or, if they consider it necessary, direct, in order to draw their attention to any points on which they may have complaints to make regarding their conditions of captivity.

. . . .

Article 126

1. Representatives or delegates of the Protecting Powers shall have permission to go to all places where prisoners of war may be, particularly to places of internment, imprisonment and labour, and shall have access to all premises occupied by prisoners of war, . . . They shall be able to interview the prisoners, and in particular the prisoners' representative, without witnesses, either personally or through an interpreter.

2. Representatives and delegates of the Protecting Powers shall have full liberty to select the places they wish to visit. . . .

———————

118. 1949 Geneva Conventions, Common Article 8/8/8/9.

....

4. The delegates of the International Committee of the Red Cross shall enjoy the same prerogatives....

————————

Article 142 of the Fourth Convention parallels Article 126 of the Third Convention for the benefit of the persons protected by that Convention.

In contemporary practice, the International Committee of the Red Cross (ICRC) now performs essentially all of those functions formerly to be undertaken by a Protecting Power.

Questions for Discussion

1. When the United States entered World War II in 1941, it was the Protecting Power for a large number of belligerents in a great many territories of adverse parties to the conflict. As a belligerent, the United States was, of course, no longer acceptable as a Protecting Power. What procedure would have to be followed by the belligerents for whom the United States had been acting as a Protecting Power?

2. During World War II, apart from putting many immovable roadblocks to impede the functioning of the Swiss as the Protecting Power for Great Britain and the United States in Japan proper, the latter country contended that the mandate of a Protecting Power did not extend to occupied territories, where the vast majority of the POWs were confined. As a result, those POWs never had access to, or the benefit of the protection of, a Protecting Power.[119] Do you consider this to be a proper interpretation of the law?

3. When the ICRC visits POWs being held by a party to an ongoing conflict-and subsequently prepares a report that may address some shortcomings in the manner in which a State is meeting its obligations under the Third Geneva Convention- it shares this report only with the State concerned, rather than issuing it publicly. What are your thoughts as to why the ICRC takes this approach? Do you agree or disagree with this policy?

4. As indicated, the ICRC has now largely assumed the responsibilities of a Protecting Power spoken to in the Third Geneva Convention and the 1977 Protocol I. Is this an abdication of this responsibility on the part of the international community? Or—is the ICRC actually better equipped/trained to take on this important mission?

The Law of Neutrality

The wartime protection of the rights of neutrals has long been a problem of major proportions, particularly because of the tendency of belligerents to feel that "if you aren't for us, then you're against us." Moreover, on the other side of the coin, there is frequently a need to ensure that neutrality is exactly that, with the neutral state treating both sides in the conflict impartially.

In the first multilateral international convention on the law of war, the 1856 Declaration of Paris, three of the four provisions dealt with matters of neutrality. While the 1899 Hague Peace Conference touched on only one small area of the subject, in one section of

————————

119. Judgment of the International Military Tribunal for the Far East, Tokyo, Nov. 4, 1948, I.M.T.F.E. 1129–32.

the 1899 Hague II Regulations (Articles 57-60), the 1907 Hague Peace Conference drafted the 1907 Hague V Convention, covering a number of the problems of neutrality in war on land, and the 1907 Hague XIII Convention, covering a number of the problems of neutrality in war at sea.

1907 Hague V Convention

Article 1

The territory of neutral Powers is inviolable.

Article 2

Belligerents are forbidden to move troops or convoys of either munitions of war or supplies across the territory of a neutral Power.

....

Article 10

The fact of a neutral Power resisting, even by force, attempts to violate its neutrality cannot be regarded as a hostile act.

....

Article 11

A neutral Power which receives on its territory troops belonging to the belligerent armies shall intern them....

....

Article 13

A neutral Power which receives escaped prisoners of war shall leave them at liberty....

1907 Hague XIII Convention

Article 1

Belligerents are bound to respect the sovereign rights of neutral Powers and to abstain, in neutral territory or neutral waters, from any act which would, if knowingly permitted by any Power, constitute a violation of neutrality.

....

Article 6

The supply, in any manner, directly or indirectly, by a neutral Power to a belligerent Power, of war-ships, ammunition, or war material of any kind whatever, is forbidden.

Article 7

A neutral Power is not bound to prevent the export or transit, for the use of either belligerent, of arms, ammunition, or, in general, of anything which could be of use to an army or fleet.

....

Article 26

The exercise by a neutral Power of the rights laid down in the present Convention can under no circumstances be considered as an unfriendly act....

Some Applications of the Law of Neutrality — and a Question

1. During the Franco-Prussian War and again during World War II, thousands of French soldiers, sometimes in fully armed and equipped units, entered Switzerland in order to escape encirclement and capture by the Germans. They were disarmed and interned.

2. In December 1939, the German pocket battleship *Graf Spee* suffered battle damage in an encounter with three enemy cruisers in the South Atlantic. It sought refuge in Montevideo, Uruguay, and its captain, Hans Langsdorff, requested that he be allowed fifteen days in which to make needed repairs to his vessel. The Uruguayan authorities determined that he required only seventy-two hours in which to render the ship seaworthy and ordered him to leave Uruguayan territory by the end of that period or have his ship and crew interned. Captain Langsdorff transferred most of his crew to a German merchant ship, which happened to be in port, took the *Graf Spee* out of the harbor, and scuttled her. His crew was thereafter interned in Argentina, to which they had been taken, and he committed suicide.

3. The *Altmark* was a German merchant vessel that acted as a supply ship for the *Graf Spee* and took aboard the crews of British merchant ships sunk by the warship. In February 1940, while the *Altmark* was en route back to Germany through neutral Norwegian waters, she was sighted by a British destroyer. The Norwegian authorities stated that, as she was unarmed and had no prisoners aboard, she had a right to pass through Norwegian waters unmolested. Nevertheless, the British boarded her by force and found and released over 300 British merchant seamen. Norway protested this violation of her neutrality. Hitler charged that Norway had connived with Great Britain in violation of her neutral status.

4. When World War II began, Spain announced her neutrality. In 1941, after Germany had invaded the Soviet Union, Spain furnished the "Blue Division" to fight on the Russian front, but without any declaration of war. Then, in 1943, the Blue Division was brought back to Spain, and Franco, the Spanish dictator, later indicated that Spain had returned to a position of neutrality.

5. After Germany had occupied Norway during World War II, she demanded that Sweden's "strict neutrality" be "pro-German neutrality." This included the right of passage of German troops and munitions by rail across Sweden. Under severe pressure, Sweden eventually agreed to such transport, with some limitations. When Germany attacked the Soviet Union in 1941, she demanded that Sweden permit the transport of a fully armed and equipped infantry division from Norway to Finland. Sweden ultimately agreed to permit this, but it did successfully refuse to permit the similar transport across its territory of a second such division.

———————

A question: You will note that all of the above examples deal with events occurring within the World War II timeframe. Can you recall any more recent conflicts that served/should have served to trigger the Law of Neutrality? Have the advent of the United Nations and the provisions of the U.N. Charter essentially voided the concept of neutrality? If not, why not?

Selected Bibliography

Aldrich, George H., "The Laws of War on Land," 94 *American Journal of International Law* 42 (2000).

Baxter, Richard R. "Modernizing the Law of War," 78 *Military Law Review* (1977).

Bothe, Michael, *et al.*, *New Rules for Victims of Armed Conflicts: Commentary on the Two 1977 Protocols Additional to the Geneva Conventions of 1949* (1982).

Dinstein,Yoram, *The Conduct of Hostilities under the Law of International Armed Conflict* (2004).

Fleck, Dieter, ed., *The Handbook of Humanitarian Law in Armed Conflicts* (2007).

Green, Leslie C., *The Contemporary Law of Armed Conflict* (2d Ed. 2000).

Helm, Anthony M., ed., *International Law Studies*, Vol. 82, "The Law of War in the 21st Century: Weaponry and the Use of Force," Naval War College (2006).

Judge Advocate General's Legal Center and School, U.S. Army, *Operational Law Handbook* (2014).

Kalshoven, Frits, *Reflections on the Law of War; Collected Essays* (2007).

Levie, Howard S., *Terrorism in War: The Law of War Crimes* (1993).

Moore, John Norton and Turner, Robert F., eds., *Legal Issues in the Struggle Against Terror* (2010).

Oppenheim, L., 2 *International Law: A Treatise: Disputes, War and Neutrality* (7th Ed., H. Lauterpacht ed., 1952).

Parks, W. Hays, "Air Law and the Law of War," 32 *Air Force Law Review* 1 (1990).

Pictet, Jean, ed., 4 *Commentaries on the Geneva Conventions of 12 August 1949* (1952-1960).

Roach, J. Ashley, "The Law of Naval Warfare at the Turn of Two Centuries", 94 *American Journal of International Law* 64 (2000).

Rogers, A.V.P., *Law on the Battlefield*, 2nd Ed. (2004).

San Remo Manual on International Law Applicable to Armed Conflicts at Sea (San Remo: International Institute of Humanitarian Law, 1994).

Solis, Gary D., *The Law of Armed Conflict* (International Humanitarian Law In War) (2010).

Spaight, J.M., *Air Power and War Rights,* 3d Ed. (1947).

von Glahn, Gerhard, *The Occupation of Enemy Territory: A Commentary on the Law and Practice of Belligerent Occupation* (1957).

Chapter 7

Operational Law

David E. Graham

In this chapter:
The Evolution of Operational Law
The Legal Framework of Operational Law
OPLAW: Selected Case Studies
OPLAW Training and Support Provided to Judge Advocates

> You can only tell the CO [Commanding Officer] that he can't shoot the prisoners so many times. You reach a point at which, when the boss has run out of beans and bullets, has certain equipment requirements, and has the locals clamoring to be paid for property damage, you have to be prepared to provide the best possible legal advice concerning these issues as well.[1]

This chapter will examine both the evolution and practice of "Operational Law" (OPLAW), that body of domestic, foreign, and international law that directly affects the conduct of military operations.[2] As such, OPLAW encompasses certain aspects of essentially all of the core military legal disciplines and thus serves as the foundation for the provision of legal advice by military attorneys to commanders and their staffs engaged in actions across the operational spectrum. A legal discipline with which military and government attorneys are familiar, OPLAW does not—for reasons readily apparent—enjoy the same degree of recognition by the civilian and academic communities. This discussion of OPLAW is designed to fill this void.

The first section of this chapter will focus on the evolution of OPLAW, tracing its origin from the days of Vietnam to its current practice by U.S. military lawyers around the world. The second section will examine the legal framework of OPLAW, demonstrating that the practice of OPLAW consists of the provision of those legal services that directly affect the command and control—and sustainment—of military operations. This section will also deal briefly with the core military law disciplines and will reflect the manner in which OPLAW serves as a transcendent mechanism that identifies and collects those specific legal issues *uniquely* associated with the command and control—and sustainment—of military operations that arise in the context of these core disciplines. The third

---

1. Quoted in David E. Graham, *Operational Law (OPLAW)—A Concept Comes of Age*, ARMY LAW. 10 (July 1987).
2. U.S. Army definition of "OPLAW," as set forth in U.S. DEP'T OF ARMY, FIELD MANUAL 1-04, LEGAL SUPPORT TO THE OPERATIONAL ARMY 5-3 (Mar. 18, 2013) [hereinafter FM 1-04, LEGAL SUPPORT TO THE OPERATIONAL ARMY]. The other U.S. military services have similar, but somewhat expanded definitions of OPLAW. These are reflected in the section of this chapter dealing with the legal framework of OPLAW.

section will focus on the actual practice of OPLAW, through an examination of a number of recent U.S. military operations, while the fourth section will speak to both OPLAW training and the broad range of OPLAW support provided to military lawyers in the field.

As a result of its evolution, development, and practice, OPLAW has become an important, and essential, companion to National Security Law. A National Security Law practitioner would be well advised to possess a working knowledge of OPLAW. This chapter should serve to facilitate that process.

The Evolution of Operational Law

In 1959, when the first Judge Advocate (military lawyer) arrived in Saigon, Vietnam, for duty, he was expected to provide legal support in the same manner as Judge Advocates (JAs) would support a commander and staff at a U.S. installation during peacetime—by administering the military justice system, advising on administrative and civil law issues, and providing counsel to soldiers needing assistance with their personal legal problems. This expectation was based on the historic concept that the role of a deployed JA was to support a mission by delivering precisely the same legal services as those offered in a peacetime garrison environment. Beginning in Vietnam, however, this concept was supplanted by a new idea: that, while a JA participating in a military operation might still prosecute and defend at courts-martial, adjudicate claims, and provide legal assistance, a military lawyer can best enhance mission success by integrating legal support into operations planning and execution at all levels of command.

What caused the abandonment of the traditional perspective that JAs involved in military operations should simply continue to engage in their same peacetime legal activities? There were at least three reasons. First, fundamental changes in the nature of warfare naturally led to changes in military doctrine and force structure, and this evolution inexorably led to a need for a different role for military lawyers. Second, the Army's experiences at My Lai, Vietnam, and the resulting establishment of the Department of Defense (DOD) Law of War Program, directly altered the role of JAs. This evolved from the fact that, in complying with this new DOD program, military lawyers were required to integrate themselves into military operations at all levels—a radical new role requiring knowledge of OPLAW. Third, and finally, the experiences of JAs deploying to Grenada as part of Operation Urgent Fury in 1983 showed conclusively that military lawyers must change the manner in which they provided legal support if they were to meet the challenges of a contingency-based military.

Change in the Nature of Warfare

The first reason underlying the evolution of OPLAW—that fundamental changes in the nature of warfare caused a change in the role of military lawyers—is easily understood. The emergence of new technology on the battlefield naturally led to changes in U.S. Army doctrine and force structure. The end of the war in Vietnam also saw an end to "attrition" as the doctrine for combat success. In its place was a contingency-oriented military characterized by an exceptionally high operational tempo. This new doctrine and force necessarily required uniformed lawyers who could do more than prosecute courts-martial and adjudicate claims. Deployments for peacekeeping, humanitarian assistance, and civil disturbance operations—in the United States and overseas—required JAs who were as adept at drafting Rules of Engagement (ROE)[3] as they were at advising on political-military matters, and who recognized that certain U.S. fiscal and environmental laws might restrict ways in which to accomplish missions. But, while changes in the nature of warfare and a corresponding reconfiguration of the military effected changes in the role played by JAs in military operations, this was only a contributing influence.

My Lai and the DOD Law of War Program

A more important second factor was a singular event that occurred on March 16, 1968, at My Lai, Vietnam. While the war crimes committed by U.S. Army personnel at My Lai caused much consternation among Americans generally, the ramifications of this tragedy for the military were even more far-reaching. The Peers Inquiry, so named because its senior member was Lieutenant General William R. Peers, thoroughly investigated the murders that occurred at My Lai. In addition to identifying those involved in the My Lai killings, the Peers Inquiry also examined the causes of the incident. For Army lawyers, in particular, one of the most significant Peers Report findings was the determination that inadequate training in the Law of War (LOW) was a contributory cause of the killings. Particularly damning was the Report's conclusion that LOW training in Lieutenant William Calley's unit was deficient with regard to the proper treatment of civilians and the responsibility for reporting war crimes.[4]

Almost immediately, senior members of the Army Judge Advocate General's Corps (JAGC) began examining ways to correct this deficiency. In May 1970, the Army regulation governing LOW training, AR 350-216, was revised in order to ensure that soldiers would receive more thorough instruction in The Hague and Geneva Conventions.[5] Of perhaps even greater importance, however, was an Army proposal to the Defense Department that it create a DOD-level Law of War Program. As a result, DOD Directive 5100.77, promulgated by the Secretary of Defense on November 5, 1974, not only established a unified Law of War Program for the Armed Forces, but also made the Army JAGC the lead organization in its implementation.[6] Moreover, while unintended, this DOD directive also played a fundamentally important role in the future development of OPLAW.

Clearly, the military legal community had responded positively to the challenge of developing and implementing an extensive LOW training program. However, with the exception of the effort to draw upon the lessons of Vietnam in crafting its approach toward providing LOW advice and training, this community did very little to capture the unique aspects of its Vietnam experience. Institutionally, it failed to view its sixteen years of JA service in Vietnam as a basis for effecting any substantial modification in the way in which it had traditionally practiced military law or in the manner in which it would approach its future delivery of legal services in a deployed environment.

It was the development of the 1974 DOD Law of War Program — a direct result of the Army's efforts to respond to the Peers Report on My Lai — that would most directly affect

---

3. Rules of Engagement (ROE) are directives issued by competent superior authority that delineate the circumstances and limitations under which U.S. forces will initiate and/or continue engagement with other forces. *See* Chairman, Joint Chiefs of Staff, Instr. 3121.01B, *Standing Rules of Engagement (SROE)/Standing Rules for the Use of Force (SRUF) for U.S. Forces* (13 June 2005).

4. United States Department of the Army, *Report of the Department of the Army Review of the Preliminary Investigations into the My Lai Incident* (Peers Inquiry) (Mar. 14, 1970).

5. Army Regulation (AR) 350-216, *Training: The Geneva Conventions of 1949 and Hague Convention No. IV of 1907* (May 28, 1970).

6. DOD Directive 5100.77, *DOD Program for Implementation of the Law of War* (Nov. 5, 1974).

the future role of JAs. In establishing this program, DOD mandated that not only must extensive LOW training be provided to armed forces personnel, but that, additionally, military lawyers must be involved in both the development and review of Operation Plans (OPLANS) in order to ensure that these plans complied with the LOW. This latter requirement was of particular significance, as it represented the first institutionally mandated involvement of military attorneys in the operational planning process. Successful implementation of the DOD Law of War Program would now require that JAs begin to communicate directly with commanders and their staff principals throughout the course of planning for an operation—identifying and resolving issues that arose during this planning process. For the first time, lawyers would be significantly involved in the manner in which military operations would be planned and conducted. It was this single factor, more than any other, that served both as the initial step in modifying the historic mindset regarding the "appropriate" role to be played by attorneys within the military and as the precursor for the later development of OPLAW.

Not until 1983, however, following the deployment of JAs to Grenada in Operation Urgent Fury, would there develop an appreciation for the need to implement and institutionalize a process by which military lawyers would be trained in and practice a newly conceived and formulated body of law directly applicable to the conduct of military operations.

Operation Urgent Fury (Grenada): Validating the Need for OPLAW

Early on October 25, 1983, U.S. Army Rangers spearheaded Operation Urgent Fury, attacking Point Salines Airport on the Caribbean Island of Grenada in a parachute assault. Initially, Army leaders anticipated that Eighty-second Airborne JAs would deal with routine types of administrative and criminal law matters normally generated by the commands that they supported at home station. Army JAs, however, had now been involved in the detailed review of OPLANs, pursuant to the My Lai generated DOD Directive 5100.77, for almost nine years and were thus far more aware of the potential for encountering legal matters impacting on the conduct of an operation. As a result of this increased awareness, JAs in Grenada sought out and became involved in numerous issues of this nature, and their resolution proved critical to the success of Urgent Fury. These issues included the preparation of ROE and related guidance for both the combat and peacekeeping phases of Urgent Fury; formulating a command policy on war trophies; advising on the treatment of captives; and assisting the Department of State (DOS) in the preparation of a Status of Forces Agreement (SOFA). JAs also created a centralized procedure for paying claims for damaged and seized property; advised the Grenadian government on drafting domestic law; and provided liaison with various U.S. government agencies and other non-U.S. organizations, such as the Caribbean Peacekeeping Force and the International Committee of the Red Cross (ICRC).

Most importantly, Grenada served as a watershed in the evolution of a formal recognition by the leadership of the Army JAGC that Army lawyers could no longer focus on performing traditional peacetime legal functions in what increasingly had become a contingency-oriented Army.[7] This conclusion was captured in the quote of the Staff Judge Advocate

---

7. David E. Graham, *My Lai and Beyond: The Evolution of Operational Law*, in The Real Lessons of the Vietnam War 367–70 (John Norton Moore & Robert F. Turner eds., 2002).

(SJA)[8] of the Eighty-second Airborne Division that opens this chapter. In sum, the experiences of JAs in Grenada functioned as a springboard to an institutional decision that JAs must be trained and resourced to provide timely and concise legal advice on a broad range of legal issues arising across the operational spectrum. The result was the development of OPLAW.

Post Grenada: Institutionalizing OPLAW Within the U.S. Armed Forces

Beginning in 1986, there began a concerted effort to reconfigure military legal assets and training for the purpose of establishing an OPLAW discipline. This effort was led by the Army's Judge Advocate General's School (TJAGSA) (now, The Judge Advocate General's Legal Center and School [TJAGLCS]), which worked to define "Operational Law," develop a curriculum for the study of OPLAW, and to write and publish a comprehensive OPLAW resource document for military attorneys in the field. The successful development and implementation of OPLAW has been the result of an unarguably valid premise. JAs who deploy on military operations are faced with a wide range of legal issues *uniquely* associated with the conduct and support of such operations. These issues cannot be neatly segregated, but instead transcend most of the legal disciplines of military law. That is, the JA will confront international law, administrative and civil law, contract and fiscal law, military justice, and claims issues that arise from and impact on the manner in which military activities are conducted and supported across the operational spectrum. It is simply a matter of identifying these issues, collecting and placing them under a common terminological umbrella, developing an extensive academic and training program dealing with these matters, and compiling comprehensive resource materials for use by military attorneys who deal with such issues in the field. Having done this, one eliminates the necessity for every deploying JA to "re-invent the wheel," the JA becomes a key member of the Commander's Staff, and the military legal community, as a whole, ensures that it plays an essential role in the contingency-oriented U.S. armed forces.

Over the course of the next several years, OPLAW was widely accepted and extensively refined. In 1987, an article in *The Army Lawyer* formally introduced the concept of OPLAW to the Army JAGC as a whole, as well as to the military legal community at large.[9] In the fall of 1987, the TJAGSA International Law faculty produced the first *Operational Law Handbook*, thus fulfilling the need for a comprehensive OPLAW resource for JAs in the field.[10] In the spring of 1990, TJAGSA hosted a first of its kind OPLAW Symposium, which served as the springboard for the development of OPLAW programs in the other military services. An OPLAW course was developed and offered to attorneys from each of the services, as well as to DOD and other U.S. government agency civilian attorneys. And, in the succeeding years, as OPLAW gained increasing credibility and recognition by both JAs and Commanders, the "International Law Divisions" within the Service JAG Schools, and at their Service Head-quarters, became the "International and Operational (or Operations) Law Divisions."

---

8. *See* Graham, *supra* note 1, at 10. The Staff Judge Advocate is the senior military legal adviser to a commander and his staff.

9. *Id.* at 9–12.

10. The *Operational Law Handbook* is updated and published annually by the International/Operational Law Department, The Judge Advocate General's Legal Center and School, U.S. Army, and is available on the Internet at www.jagcnet.army.mil, the Army JAG Corps' electronic reference library and computer network system.

Commanders, acutely sensitive to the need to conduct military operations in strict compliance with the requirements of the law, now ensure that military attorneys are fully integrated into operations at all levels of command. The next section will examine the legal framework in which these lawyers function.

The Legal Framework of Operational Law[11]

Legal Support to Operations and Warfighting Functions

Legal support to operations encompasses all legal services provided by JAs and other legal personnel in the support of units, commanders, and personnel throughout an area of operations and across the spectrum of operations. This support falls into the following warfighting functions: mission command, movement and maneuver, intelligence, fires, sustainment, and protection. JAs use the warfighting functions as a template for reviewing and analyzing operation plans for legal issues. The following are illustrative examples of the types of legal support within these functional areas.

Mission Command

Soldier discipline is an important component of the mission command function. During all operations, discipline is regulated, enhanced, and enforced through a number of means, to include orders, regulations, command policies, and the Uniform Code of Military Justice. Legal matters to consider in conjunction with this function would give rise to the following considerations:

---

11. The U.S. Army has developed doctrine dealing exclusively with the legal framework and practice of OPLAW. Accordingly, the Army model will serve as the basis for the discussion of this topic. This doctrine is set forth in FM 1-04, Legal Support to the Operational Army, *supra* note 2. Each of the other military services has, however, articulated, in a general manner, the way in which it approaches the practice of OPLAW. Legal Support to Operations, Air Force Document 1-04 (2011), provides details on legal support to operations, but does not define "operations law". Air Force policy defines "operational readiness" as the Air Force JAG Corps' core competency, encompassing the ability to provide the warfighter with a complete set of legal capabilities at any time and place, and states that the JAG Corps supports air and space operations by providing responsive legal capabilities configured to support home station and expeditionary operations. Source: International and Operations Law Division, Office of The Judge Advocate General, Headquarters, U.S. Air Force, Washington, DC. The U.S. Navy views "Navy Operational Law" as the body of law that affects the broad categories of the Law of the Sea, Law of Armed Conflict, and National Security Law. Included within these categories are all matters impacting military operations, including, but not limited to, maritime zones of the sea, air, and space; ROE/use of deadly force rules; information operations; operational support to domestic law enforcement; Homeland Security/Defense; international and domestic environmental law; counter-narcotics; counterterrorism; and arms control issues. Source: International and Operational Law Division, Office of The Judge Advocate General, Headquarters, U.S. Navy, Washington, DC. The U.S. Marine Corps definition of OPLAW is essentially the same as that of the Army's: "Operational Law is that body of international, foreign (host nation), and U.S. domestic laws, regulations, and policies that directly affect U.S. military operations across the operational spectrum — from peacetime activities to combat operations." Marine Corps Warfighting Publication 4-11.8 (Services in an Expeditionary Environment, 24 September, 2001), Chapter 3, deals specifically with the provision of legal services in an expeditionary environment. Source: International and Operational Law Branch, Judge Advocate Division, Headquarters, U.S. Marine Corps, Washington, DC. DOD Joint Publication 1-04: "Legal Support to Military Operations", 17 August, 2011, also addresses certain aspects of Operational Law.

- Are there General Orders or other Command Policies in force in the operational area that will affect any aspect of the operation plan?
- Are there any jurisdictional matters that must be resolved prior to the conduct of the operation?
- Are there provisions in place for the delivery of military justice in the operational area when an operation is commenced?

Movement and Maneuver

This warfighting function presents a unique set of legal issues which give rise to the following questions:

- Does the plan entail the movement of friendly forces into a largely civilian populated area? If so, how will these civilians be affected? If the potential exists, how does the operation plan address the possible displacement of large numbers of these civilians?
- What precautions should the commander take to minimize injuries to noncombatants and collateral damage caused by the movement of friendly forces?
- Will civilian movement be restricted or curtailed? Will roadblocks, checkpoints, or curfews be necessary? What are the applicable ROE for personnel manning roadblocks or checkpoints?
- Does the operation plan call for the use of any "countermobility" measures (such as scatterable mines) to deny enemy movement? If so, what actions should the commander consider to prevent noncombatant casualties and to minimize disruption to civilian movement? If operating with multinational partners, will the commander's ability to employ mines be affected?

Intelligence

This warfighting function involves tasks and systems enabling the commander to understand the operational environment, the enemy, the terrain, and civil considerations. The legal issues related to this function are so numerous in nature that intelligence law has become a discrete area of expertise within the field of OPLAW. When assessing intelligence-related legal issues, a JA should, at a minimum, ask the following questions:

- Does the operation plan call for the collection of information by scouts, long-range surveillance teams, or special operations forces? If so, are sufficient anti-fratricide measures in place to ensure that friendly forces do not fire upon them? Under what ROE will these teams operate?
- Does the operation plan call for the use of human intelligence, signals intelligence, or some other means of collection-such as aircraft overflights or the use of unmanned aircraft systems? What are the legal considerations, restrictions, or prohibitions relevant to the use of such systems?
- What is the plan for gathering information from enemy prisoners of war (POW) and detainees? Does this plan address tactical questioning and interrogation? What actions have been taken to ensure that U.S. personnel adhere to the proper standards for the treatment of such individuals?

Fires

This function involves the collective and coordinated use of indirect and joint fire through the targeting process. As a result of its potentially devastating effect, the use of lethal fire- particularly indirect fire-is closely regulated by ROE and other control and coordination measures in order to minimize both fratricide and collateral damage. When planning an operation or reviewing an operation plan, a JA must carefully assess all aspects of the plan that deal with the use of fire to ensure full compliance with the relevant ROE and the LOAC. In doing so, the following questions should be addressed:

- Are there provisions for the use of lethal fire contained in portions of the operation plan other than in the Fire Support Annex—such as the use of lethal fire by air defense or aviation assets? If so, are these measures consistent with the applicable ROE and the LOW?
- Are there protected places, including cultural property, in the area of operations? If so, are they designated in the operation plan or order? Are they also referenced in the ROE Annex? What steps have been taken to ensure that potential indirect fire targets, or target areas, have been deconflicted with protected places?
- What fire support coordination measures (restricted fire areas, no fire areas, or protected places) are in place to mitigate the risk of fratricide and collateral damage by lethal fire?
- Are there specific release authorities for direct and indirect fire systems in the ROE or in the unit's tactical Standard Operating Procedures? Is so, does a plan exist for delegating authority in the event that the authorizing commander is unavailable to make the necessary decision?
- What is the blast radius and accuracy of the particular weapon systems available for use? What are the fire procedures for both deliberate and hasty targeting?
- Is the use of electronic warfare contemplated and, if so, are there applicable ROE? If used, what will be the impact on host-nation communications—and what are the legal implications, if any?

Sustainment

The sustainment function is the provision of the logistics, personnel services (to include legal support), and health service support essential to the maintenance of operations until mission success is achieved. It is the very lifeblood of a military operation. Absent sustainment—to include health, legal, financial management, and all of the other sustainment functions—military forces could neither deploy, nor conduct continuous operations. The legal issues inherent in the sustainment function range from contingency contracting matters to the fiscal rules applicable to the provision of medical support to civilians and the paying of claims for property loss, injury, or death. Among the questions that should be asked are the following:

- Does the operation plan call for contracting support? If so, where, when, and how much? Will goods or services be purchased from the local economy? If so, what types? To what extent can the commander use existing contract mechanisms, to include the Logistics Civil Augmentation Program (LOGCAP) [civilian contractor support] and Acquisition and Cross-Servicing Agreements (ACSAs) [the authority to provide support to coalition forces]? Will it be necessary to lease land or facilities? Answers to these questions will dictate the types of funds to be used.
- Does the operation plan call for financial management support? If so, where will the financial management units be located? What types of funding sources will they use?
- Might it be necessary to provide medical treatment to non-U.S. personnel? If so, what are the criteria for such treatment? What are the fiscal law considerations relevant to the provision of medical treatment or humanitarian and civic assistance to non-U.S. personnel?

- Will U.S. forces be required to ensure that civilians receive medical supplies, food, and other essential services?

Protection

The protection function is the preservation of the survivability of mission-related military and non-military personnel, equipment, facilities, information, and infrastructure deployed or located within or outside a given operational area. Preserving and protecting the force enables commanders to maintain combat power. This function gives rise to multiple legal issues, many of these related to the use of force, such as ROE or Rules on the Use of Force (RUF). ROE provide guidance on the use of force in combat or other overseas military operations, while RUF govern the use of force undertaken in providing support to civil authorities. Some of the questions most relevant to legal matters associated with this warfighting function are:

- What policies, directives, or regulations deal specifically with protection issues?
- What ROE or RUF, operation orders, or procedures are in effect for personnel tasked with securing facilities, equipment, and other items valuable to U.S. forces?
- If the use of private security contractors is contemplated, under what ROE or RUF will they operate? Which organization will be responsible for prescribing and monitoring the contractors' ROE or RUF? How will they synchronize ROE or RUF with those of the U.S. military?

The Core Legal Disciplines of Military Law[12]

As has been noted, Operational Law encompasses all relevant aspects of military law that affect the conduct and sustainment of military operations. An examination of the core legal disciplines of military law follows.

International Law

Within the Army, the practice of international law includes the interpretation and application of international agreements, foreign law, comparative law, martial law, and domestic law, as this law relates to military operations and activities.

The SJA's international law responsibilities include: implementation of the DOD Law of War Program, including LOAC training, advice concerning the application of the LOAC to military operations, the determination of the status of POW, and the supervision of war crime investigations and trials; providing advice on international legal issues related to deployed U.S. forces, including the legal basis for conducting and funding operations, interpreting SOFAs and other international agreements, and assessing the impact of foreign law on Army activities, contractors, and dependents; monitoring the foreign trials and confinement of Army military and civilian personnel and their dependents; assisting with legal issues in intelligence, security assistance, counterdrug operations, and Rule of Law (ROL) and civil assistance activities; advising the command concerning the authority to negotiate and execute international agreements; and serving as the legal liaison with host or multinational legal authorities.

---

12. FM 1-04, LEGAL SUPPORT TO THE OPERATIONAL ARMY, *supra* note 2. Unless otherwise noted, the discussion dealing with specific JA OPLAW responsibilities within each of the core military law disciplines is based on material contained in this publication, at 5-1 to 5-10.

Prior to mobilization, the SJA and his staff must thoroughly understand the contingency plan and the international law affecting the operation, ensuring that the plan complies with international legal obligations, including obligations to enemy POW and civilians. They must also identify and obtain relevant international agreements (such as SOFAs, Diplomatic Notes, and ACSAs), identify requirements for additional international agreements, forward these requirements through higher headquarters to the proper negotiating authority and, when authorized, undertake the negotiation of such agreements. International law planning objectives include informing the commander and his staff of the international legal obligations of the force, protecting the legal status of unit personnel, ensuring rights of transit, and providing responsive and economical host nation support.

The SJA will also serve as the command liaison with the ICRC, DOS country team for the area of operations, legal officials of the host nation and coalition forces, and with other government, non-governmental (NGO) and international organizations, as directed by the commander. These liaison functions serve to establish working relationships that will assist in sustaining the operation, coordinating the legal aspects of deployment and entry, and confirming an understanding of agreements dealing with the status of the force and its personnel, as well as the rights of transit, basing, and host nation support. JA briefings to deploying personnel will deal with the legal basis for the operation, the legal status of deploying personnel, relevant country law, guidance on the treatment of civilians in the area of operations, and the applicability of the LOAC.

Advice to the command may involve the LOAC; the interpretation of international agreements; the treatment of civilians and/or foreign diplomats; and assistance to international organizations, U.S. or host nation government organizations, and NGOs. The SJA will also be responsible for the investigation and trial of war crimes, Article 5 Tribunal proceedings,[13] due process procedures for detainees, foreign criminal trials of U.S. personnel, foreign civil or administrative proceedings, and any proceedings that may be conducted under occupation or martial law.

Administrative and Civil Law

Administrative and Civil Law is that body of law containing the statutes, regulations, and judicial decisions that govern the establishment, functioning, and command of military organizations, as well as the duties of military organizations and installations with regard to civil authorities.

Administrative Law

DOD and Army regulations govern and regulate military command decisions and policies. The practice of administrative law involves the provision of legal support and advice to commanders in a number of specialized areas dealt with by these regulations. These subjects include military personnel law, investigations, relationships with private organizations, military installations, and government ethics. JAs advise commanders and review actions involving military personnel law, advise investigating officers, review in-

---

13. The term "Article 5 Tribunal" refers to Article 5 of the Geneva Convention Relative to the Treatment of Prisoners of War, Aug. 12, 1949, 6 U.S.T. 3316, 75 U.N.T.S. 135. This Article states, in part: "Should any doubt arise as to whether persons, having committed a belligerent act and having fallen into the hands of the enemy, belong to any of the [Prisoners of War] categories enumerated in Article 4, such persons shall enjoy the protection of the present Convention until such time as their status has been determined by a competent tribunal."

vestigations for legal sufficiency, advise authorities concerning investigative findings and recommendations, and supervise the command's financial disclosure and ethics programs.

Prior to mobilization, JAs must identify issues likely to arise in the operation and provide policy guidance in the OPLAN. Consideration of the likely legal issues takes into account the participating organizations—joint, allied or coalition, international, non-governmental, and private. For example, the plan must include policy guidance concerning access by non-DOD personnel to DOD facilities and services. During mobilization and predeployment, JAs provide guidance to commanders concerning military personnel issues that typically arise immediately prior to deployment, such as conscientious objection claims and family care plans. They also brief deploying personnel concerning issues arising in the theater, for example, the receipt of foreign gifts. During deployment and entry, these attorneys will focus on command investigations, as these may have a significant impact on the unit and mission. They will also, even in a deployed environment, supervise the government ethics program, including the filing of financial disclosure forms.

Civil Law

The practice of civil law includes those specialized areas of the law concerned with statutes and regulations applicable across all Federal government agencies, rather than those exclusively applicable to DOD and the Army. It also encompasses matters subject to civil litigation in various judicial forums. Some of the specific areas of the law that fall within this practice include environmental law, the law of federal employment, federal labor relations, government information practices, federal litigation, regulatory law, and intellectual property law. JA civil law tasks in an operational setting will include advising commanders on the following matters: the impact of host nation environmental law on a particular operation; labor relations-including certifying and negotiating with labor unions and resolving labor grievances and unfair labor practice allegations; and the recruiting, hiring, evaluating, and disciplining of employees.

Contract and Fiscal Law

Contract law is the application of domestic and international law to the acquisition of goods, services, and construction. Fiscal law is the application of domestic statutes and regulations to the funding of military operations and the provision of support to non-federal agencies and organizations.

Contract Law

The practice of contract law focuses on battlefield acquisition and contingency contracting, to include contracting for services, resolving bid protests and contract litigation disputes, exercising procurement fraud oversight, dealing with commercial activities, and negotiating/implementing ACSAs. The SJA's contract law responsibilities thus include furnishing legal advice and assistance to procurement officials during all phases of the contracting process, overseeing an effective procurement fraud abatement program, and providing legal advice to the command concerning the use of the LOGCAP program, ACSAs, and overseas real estate and construction.

Prior to deployment, JAs assist in planning for contracting by identifying the legal authorities for such contracting, obtaining relevant acquisition agreements or requesting their negotiation, assisting the contracting team in defining requirements, establishing procurement procedures for the operation, and reviewing the contracting support plan for legal sufficiency.

Fiscal Law

Fiscal law applies to the method of paying for obligations created by procurements. The SJA's fiscal law responsibilities include providing legal advice on the proper use and expenditure of funds, interagency agreements for logistic support, security assistance, and support provided to non-federal agencies and organizations. At a multinational command headquarters, a JA may be required to provide advice concerning international support agreements.

During deployment and entry, SJAs plan for additional contract and fiscal law support, as contracting and fiscal issues will increase in number and complexity. During redeployment and demobilization, contracts for subsistence, temporary lodging, or transportation will be required to allow logistics units to redeploy. As contract claims or disputes arise, JAs will assist contracting and real estate officials in resolving these matters. When these issues are not resolved, a JA will support the contracting and real estate personnel responsible for any ensuing litigation.

Claims

The Army Claims Program investigates, processes, adjudicates, and settles claims on behalf of and against the U.S., worldwide, "under the authority conferred by statutes, regulations, international and interagency agreements, and DOD Directives."[14] Categories of claims include claims for property damage of soldiers and other employees arising incident to service, torts alleged against Army or DOD personnel acting within the scope of their employment, claims for personal injury or property damage caused by non-combat military operations, and claims by the U.S. against individuals who injure Army personnel or damage Army property.

The Secretary of the Army (SA) heads the Army Claims System. The Judge Advocate General of the Army (TJAG) supervises the Army Claims Program and settles claims in accordance with delegated authority from the SA. The U.S. Army Claims Service (USARCS) administers the Army Claims Program and designates area claims offices, claims processing offices, claims attorneys, and Foreign Claims Commissions.[15] Claims must be investigated and paid in an area of operations. In multinational operations, unless otherwise specified in applicable agreements, a troop-contributing nation is generally responsible for resolving claims arising from its own operations. Foreign claims against the U.S. will normally be resolved by the military service assigned claims responsibility for a particular area under DOD Directive 5515.8, Single-Service Assignment of Responsibility for Processing of Claims. While claims are centrally processed, claims personnel will travel throughout the area of operations to investigate, negotiate, and settle such claims.

Prior to mobilization, commanders will appoint Unit Claims Officers (UCOs), who will document and report incidents to claims offices that might result in a claim by or against the U.S. The SJA and Chief of Claims develop the claims architecture for the planned operation and provide training for deployable claims JAs, legal specialists, and UCOs. The claims architecture will prescribe the technical chain of claims authority, identify additional required claims processing offices or Foreign Claims Commissions, and describe the claims procedures applicable during an operation. Claims architecture

---

14. DEP'T OF ARMY, REGULATION 27-20, CLAIMS, para. 1-1 (Feb.8, 2008).
15. The Claims Programs of the other military services function in essentially the same fashion as that of the Army's.

planning factors include the type and duration of deployment, the area of deployment, the existence of international agreements governing the presence of U.S. personnel and the processing of claims, host nation law, and the military service having claims responsibility for the area. Claims procedures will describe how claims will be received, investigated, processed, adjudicated, and paid. SJAs and their Chiefs of Claims will also coordinate with USARCS in order to facilitate the appointment of Foreign Claims Commissions or Claims Processing Offices.

During deployment and entry, claims personnel will establish the claims operation and perform claims services. When establishing the claims operation, the senior Claims JA in theater will inform host nation authorities as to how claims will be processed, provide information to the local population concerning claims procedures, and obtain translation services and local legal advice.

Military Justice

Military Justice is the administration of the Uniform Code of Military Justice (UCMJ). As a core legal discipline of Military Law, the purpose of military justice is " ... to promote justice, to assist in maintaining good order and discipline in the armed forces, to promote efficiency and effectiveness in the military establishment, and thereby strengthen the national security of the United States" (Manual for Courts-Martial). TJAG is responsible for the overall supervision and administration of military justice within the Army, while commanders oversee the administration of military justice in their units and communicate directly with their SJAs concerning military justice matters. Three organizational military justice components exist within the Army's JAGC: the SJA; the Chief, U. S. Army Trial Defense Service (USATDS); and the Chief, U.S. Army Trial Judiciary.

The SJA is responsible for providing military justice advice and services to the command and supervises the administration and prosecution of courts-martial, the preparation of records of trial, the victim-witness assistance program, and military justice training. The Chief, USATDS, exercises independent supervision, control, and direction of Army defense counsel services. The Chief Trial Judge, U.S. Army Trial Judiciary, provides military judges for general and special courts-martial, supervises these judges, promulgates rules of court, and supervises the military magistrate program. Military judges, who preside at general and special courts-martial, are not within a local commander's chain of command or the technical chain of the command's SJA.

In multinational organizations, each troop contributing country is responsible for the discipline of its military personnel. Accordingly, the U.S. element of any such organization will require military justice support during the course of a military operation. Trial defense and judiciary services will be provided on an area basis under the independent supervision and control of USATDS and the U.S. Army Trial Judiciary. The Chief, USATDS, and Chief Trial Judge supervise defense and military judge teams, respectively, and are solely responsible for their places of duty and caseloads. Under the direction of the regional and senior defense counsel, trial defense counsel travel as far forward as required throughout the area of operations to provide advice and services. Military judges are normally co-located with the Office of the SJA at a command headquarters or travel into the area of operations for periodic trial terms, depending upon judicial workloads. Military justice support transitions smoothly across the spectrum of conflict, providing continuity in jurisdictions and responsive support to commanders.

To prepare for a deployment, a military justice attorney may be called upon to perform the following tasks: aligning the convening authority structure for the deployment theater and home station; ensuring that units and personnel are assigned or attached to the appropriate organization for the administration of military justice; requesting or accomplishing required designations of home station convening authorities; transferring individual cases to new convening authorities when necessary; and publishing a General Order for the operation, when this authority is not withheld by higher headquarters.

Mission training will include briefings to deploying and home station commanders regarding military justice operations, as well as briefings to deploying personnel concerning the terms of the General Order for the operation.

Legal Assistance

Legal assistance is the provision of personal civil legal services to military personnel, their dependents, and other eligible individuals. The legal assistance mission ensures that members of the military have their personal legal affairs in order prior to deployment. Equally important, once deployed, these personnel must have their legal assistance needs resolved quickly and efficiently. The Army Legal Assistance Program serves to enhance operational efficiency by providing legal assistance to soldiers in many settings—combat readiness exercises, predeployment preparation, and in operational and deployed environments.

While each military service and each troop contributing country is responsible for the provision of legal assistance to its personnel, there may also be a requirement to provide legal assistance services at joint or multinational headquarters.

Operational Law: Synchronizing the Operational Aspects of Military Law

It is the role of the OPLAW JA to incorporate and synchronize any and all aspects of the Military Law core legal disciplines that affect the conduct and sustainment of any form of military operation. Accordingly, prior to deployment, this JA will support the military decision making process by preparing legal estimates, designing the operational legal support architecture, writing Legal Annexes, assisting in the development of and training on ROE, and reviewing Operation Plans and Orders. Additionally, the OPLAW JA will provide briefings to deploying personnel concerning the legal basis for the operation, the legal status of the deploying personnel, the relevant country law of the country concerned, the manner in which civilians should be treated in the area of operations, the content of governing General Orders, the Code of Conduct, and the applicability of the LOAC.

Upon arrival in an area of operations, the OPLAW JA will organize and coordinate the delivery of legal services in all of the core legal disciplines, in keeping with the Legal Annex to the governing Operation Plan or Operation Order. Among the operational responsibilities of this JA will be the provision of timely and accurate advice regarding lethal and nonlethal targeting- with a particular emphasis on ROE implementation- and detainee operations.

In post-conflict stability operations, OPLAW JAs will engage in activities designed to establish civil security, civil control, essential services, economic and infrastructure development, and governance. The ROL, an essential aspect of such activities, is critical to the security and stability of the civilian population and is a primary JA responsibility. Restoration of the effective and fair administration and enforcement of justice is a principal component of stability operations, a core U.S. military mission, and many ROL tasks require specialized legal expertise.

As the commander's advisor on the legal aspects of all warfighting functions, the OPLAW JA must also understand and consider intelligence law when planning and reviewing operations. Intelligence law addresses legal issues associated with intelligence activities, to include interrogation operations. In advising on interrogation matters, it is essential that the OPLAW JA be aware of the policies and national and international laws dictating the treatment and status of persons detained by U.S. forces. In supporting such detainee operations, the JA may engage in the following activities:

- Advise the commander and other personnel responsible for detention operations on all matters pertaining to the compliance with all applicable policies and law- both national and international.
- Provide legal advice on the proper composition and function of tribunals required to determine detainee status in accordance with the 1949 Geneva Convention on POW (GPW).
- Provide initial and refresher training regarding the treatment standards for detainees to all personnel involved in detainee operations, to include the detaining military personnel, interrogators, and the internment facility commander.
- Advise the appropriate commander regarding the investigation of suspected maltreatment or abuse of detainees or other suspected violations of applicable law and policy.

OPLAW: Selected Case Studies

Drawing upon this assessment of the military law legal disciplines which form the framework of OPLAW, the following section will focus on the real-world practice of OPLAW through the examination of selected OPLAW issues arising in the context of a number of U.S. military operations.

Panama — Operation Just Cause, 1989–1990[16]

In February 1988, federal grand juries in Miami and Tampa, Florida, indicted Panama's de facto leader, General Manuel A. Noriega, on numerous counts of drug trafficking. Thereafter, relations between Panama and the U.S. deteriorated steadily and, for the remainder of 1988 and into 1989, General Noriega and the National Assembly representatives whom he controlled became increasingly aggressive toward the United States and its military personnel in Panama. As Noriega's campaign of harassing U.S. citizens in Panama continued, President George H.W. Bush determined that the 30,000 Americans residing there were in danger, as was the operation of the Panama Canal. During Panamanian elections in May 1989, opposition candidates won by a three-to-one margin; Noriega, however, nullified the results and sanctioned violence against the winners.

The culmination of increasingly hostile relations between the U.S. and the Noriega regime came on December 15, 1989, when Panama's National Assembly declared that a state of war existed between Panama and the United States. The next evening, a Panama

---

16. Unless otherwise noted, the following discussion of JA involvement in Operation Just Cause — and the OPLAW issues dealt with — is based on material contained in FREDERIC L. BORCH, JUDGE ADVOCATES IN COMBAT — ARMY LAWYERS IN MILITARY OPERATIONS FROM VIETNAM TO HAITI (2001), 88–119 [hereinafter BORCH, JUDGE ADVOCATES IN COMBAT].

Defense Force soldier shot at three American officers in an automobile; one was killed. His death precipitated Operation Just Cause, authorized by President Bush on December 17, 1989. Its goals were "to create an environment safe for Americans there, ensure the integrity of the Panama Canal, provide a stable environment for the freely elected government, and bring Noriega to justice."[17]

International OPLAW Issues

Rules of Engagement

Unlike Operation Urgent Fury (Grenada), for which little JA planning was possible, Army lawyers began planning for a possible deployment to Panama almost a year and a half prior to the operation. Thus, in 1988, the United States Southern Command (SOUTH-COM) SJA had assisted in the development of the ROE for any future intervention.[18] In tailoring the SOUTHCOM ROE, Army JAs started with two basic propositions. The first was that a soldier may always exercise his right of self-defense, regardless of any restrictions on the use of force that may exist in the ROE. Thus, the rules had to be written so that a soldier would not hesitate to defend himself or others in his unit. The second basic ground rule was that the ROE would adhere strictly to the LOAC and that particular emphasis would be placed on minimizing collateral damage and casualties. In addition to these two basic ground rules, the Joint Task Force South commander raised several specific concerns and tasked his SJA to account for these in the ROE. This was a decision that was to have a significant impact on JAs (as well as on the JAGC as a whole), for the development of ROE previously had been exclusively an operations (J-3/G-3) function. JAs at that time ordinarily expected only to review operations work, not actively participate in it.

One of these ROE concerns centered on the use of indirect fire in populated areas. As such fire, by its very nature, had the potential to cause excessive collateral damage, the commander wanted its use approved at an elevated level. Another concern involved the regulation of air-to-ground attacks in populated areas, as such bombardments also ran the risk of causing extensive collateral damage. The ROE thus provided that if civilians were present, close air support, white phosphorus bombs, and incendiary weapons could not be used without the approval of the Task Force commander. Still another concern revolved around the treatment of individuals captured or detained during hostilities. To meet this concern, the SJA suggested that every soldier be instructed to initially provide every Panamanian captured or detained the full protections of the 1949 GPW. This proposal was adopted, for it ensured compliance with the LOAC, eliminated the need for an on-the-spot decision concerning the type of treatment to accord a captive, and assured maximum protection for each detainee. Under these rules, captured Panamanians would receive treatment as POW until their actual status could be determined, even following their transfer to a detainee encampment.

---

17. Thomas Donnelly, Margaret Roth & Caleb Baker, Operation Just Cause, xi (1991).

18. The U.S. Southern Command (SOUTHCOM), located in Miami and responsible for U.S. military activities in Central and South America, is one of six geographic U.S. Unified Commands. The other commands are: U.S. European Command (EUCOM), located in Stuttgart, Germany; U.S. Africa Command (AFRICOM), also located in Stuttgart; U.S. Central Command (CENTCOM), located at McDill Air Force Base, Florida—responsible for Southwest Asia; U.S. Pacific Command (PACOM), located in Honolulu, Hawaii; and the recently established Northern Command (NORTH-COM), located at Peterson Air Force Base, Colorado—and responsible for the continental United States.

By the time Operation Just Cause began on December 20, the ROE for American combat units already in or deploying to Panama were firmly in place. Their basic thrust was to use maximum firepower, but to minimize collateral damage and suffering, so that when hostilities ceased, normal life could be resumed. With this in mind, JAs provided instruction on the Task Force ROE. Some Army lawyers went even further, printing and distributing thousands of small cards containing the ROE, enabling each soldier to have a written reference that could fit into a pocket.

Law of Armed Conflict

The first Army lawyer to deploy to Panama with combat forces was the SJA of the Eighty-Second Airborne Division, who jumped into combat with the division's assault command post. Shortly thereafter, he received his first legal questions. Some of the division's M551A1 Sheridan armored reconnaissance vehicles, dropped by parachute, had landed in mud. As they were too deeply mired to be driven, the aviation brigade commander asked if his pilots could take control of Panama Defense Force helicopters and use them to extract these vehicles. Additionally, the division logistics officer (G-4) asked if civilian cars and trucks located at the airfield could be taken and used by division troops. Most of the 7,000 paratroopers on the ground were without vehicles, and transport was needed if the division was to move rapidly in the next hours and days. Knowing that the LOAC permitted the confiscation, without compensation, of enemy military equipment and that certain civilian private movable property necessary for mission success could be seized, the SJA advised that the helicopters and vehicles could be taken immediately.

At a briefing later that evening, the SJA learned that American soldiers operating two miles north of Panama City had been fired upon by enemy soldiers. The Panamanian troops had been positioned in a temple, which the U.S. paratroopers had damaged in an ensuing firefight. Now, after the fact, the SJA was asked if a cultural site could be targeted if used by the enemy. Explaining that enemy misuse of the temple had resulted in the loss of its protected status under the LOAC, he advised that firing on the structure had been lawful. Meanwhile, JAs of the Seventh Infantry Division were also providing advice on a similar LOAC matter, responding to a request from Army Rangers, who were concerned about damage done to a Panama Defense Force medical treatment clinic. The Rangers had been fired upon by persons in the clinic and had damaged it when returning fire. Recognizing that the Panamanian actions had resulted in the clinic losing its protected status, the responsible JA informed the Rangers that their return of fire — and the resulting damage — was permissible.

During the first days of Just Cause, Americans captured or otherwise took into custody some 4,100 individuals. Some detainees had no documentation, and their status was unclear. As the 1949 GPW[19] affords POW certain rights and privileges, determining the status of each person held was critical. Until such a determination occurred, the decision was made to treat each detainee as a POW. As a result, no detainee was misclassified during the fog of war, and, as every detainee was afforded the best possible treatment, such an approach demonstrated U.S. resolve to meet its responsibilities under international law.

Reaffirming that Article 5 of the GPW required that a three-person Tribunal determine the status of detainees, a JA, along with a representative of the camp commander and a military intelligence officer, began the process of classifying the individuals in question.

---

19. *See supra* note 13.

In so doing, these individuals acted as a de facto Article 5 Tribunal, examining any paperwork accompanying the detainees and questioning the individuals concerned when necessary. Within a week, all those detained had been classified. Although the Tribunal operated without being officially designated by a higher headquarters, this did not affect its value or effectiveness.

JAs also advised the camp commander on the treatment of detainees. Article 13 of the GPW Convention requires the humane treatment of POW, to include the provision of adequate housing, food, and medical care. When an ICRC delegation visited the detention center, a JA met with its members, who noted U.S. compliance with both the spirit and the letter of the law. The U.S. had, for example, taken the local diet into account by providing rice and beans as a supplement to the meals, ready-to-eat, provided each detainee. Additionally, medical care was provided to detainees on a non-discriminatory basis. Finally, Army lawyers had advised that the GPW protected the privacy of those held. Consequently, any public display of prisoners was prohibited. The media were allowed to tour the detention facility, but no roster of those in the camp was provided, and no photographs were permitted.

Claims OPLAW Issues

Although it had been thought that there would be a significant number of claims filed by Panamanians against the U.S., a major claims issue had not been anticipated: paying claims for the battlefield taking and use of private property. Under the LOAC, U.S. forces could lawfully seize private movable property when so required by military necessity. As noted earlier, acting under this authority, the Eighty-Second Airborne Division had seized scores of rental cars and privately owned vehicles in order to quickly move from Tocumen airport to Panama City. These seized vehicles were immediately "modified"—windshields kicked out, doors torn off—to make them combat ready. After the troops no longer needed the cars and trucks, they simply parked them and walked away.

Although some Eighty-Second Airborne Division officers had used 3" x 5" cards to record what had been seized and by whom, some did not. JAs thus started their claims work by gathering information on seized vehicles. Once undocumented vehicles began arriving, they also were included in the claims database. The final tally listed more than 300 seized cars, trucks, and buses, as well as three Marriott in-flight kitchen trucks. To aid in servicing commercial aircraft, a scissors-like assembly on these trucks permitted their cabs to be raised some fifteen feet off the ground. This feature had made them particularly attractive to troops, for the added height could be used as an observation point.

Complicating the issue of battlefield seizures was the question of how such claims would be paid. International law required payment for certain private property seized or requisitioned, including battlefield seizures, and the Army intended to meet this obligation. But what monies should be used? One suggested approach was to make use of the contract process to pay for the use of and damage to seized cars and trucks. Thus, for example, rental cars seized by troops at the airport and then used for the military mission would be considered an irregular procurement—a contract that could be ratified later by appropriate contracting authorities. The problem inherent in this approach was the fact that no agreement had ever existed between the property owner and the person taking the property. Similarly, an early proposal to use claims monies to pay for battlefield seizures was also abandoned. Paying monies under the Foreign Claims Act[20] requires a finding of

---

20. Foreign Claims Act (FCA), 10 U.S.C. §2734. The FCA is the most widely used claims statute in foreign deployments. Under the FCA, meritorious claims for property losses, injury, or death

negligence or some other tortuous behavior on the part of U.S. agents. A requirement also exists that the damage to or destruction of the property in question be non-combat related. As the seizures in issue were intentional in nature and combat related, payment under the Foreign Claims Act was not a viable option.

After examining the U.S. statutes governing DOD Operation and Maintenance (O&M) monies, a JA came to the conclusion that these funds could be used to pay for battlefield seizures undertaken as an operational necessity. Acting on this advice, the Joint Task Force Assistant Chief of Staff for Logistics subsequently approved the use of O&M funds for all claims related to private property seized by U.S. forces during hostilities.

Questions for Discussion

1. Why have military attorneys become increasingly involved in the drafting of Rules of Engagement (ROE)? Is this a positive development? What are the pros and cons of greater JA involvement in the ROE process?

2. Is it lawful to "confiscate" certain enemy property and to "seize" certain civilian private movable property in an operational environment? What is the difference between the "confiscation" and "seizure" of property on the battlefield?

3. Is it ever lawful to fire upon a "protected place" in the midst of combat? If so, when?

4. What is an "Article 5 Tribunal"? What purpose does it serve?

Operation Desert Storm, 1991[21]

On August 2, 1990, Iraqi tanks rolled into Kuwait, and Saddam Hussein, the Iraqi ruler, proclaimed Kuwait a province of Iraq. That same day the UN Security Council condemned the invasion, and U.S. President George H.W. Bush, joined by a large majority of the nations of the world, announced that Iraqi aggression must be opposed. Foreseeing the need for direct military action, the U.S. took the lead in developing and coordinating a multinational coalition of armed forces to liberate Kuwait and deter any possible Iraqi moves against Saudi Arabia and other Persian Gulf states.

On January 16, 1991, U.S. and coalition forces launched their air war against Iraqi forces. While aircraft and missiles attacked enemy positions in Iraq and Kuwait, the coalition prepared for the ground campaign. In late January and early February, the XVIII Airborne Corps and VII Corps met on the left of the allied front, along the Saudi-Iraqi border. On February 23, 1991, as President Bush demanded, for the last time, that Saddam Hussein comply with all UN resolutions imposed since the August 2 Iraqi invasion, coalition forces stretched inland some 300 miles from the Persian Gulf. When the Iraqi dictator refused Bush's final ultimatum on February 24, the all-out ground attack that followed took place along a broad front. With the start of Desert Storm, U.S. Central

caused by service members or the civilian component of the U.S. forces may be settled "[t]o promote and maintain friendly relations" with the receiving state. Claims that result from "noncombat activities" or negligent or wrongful acts or omissions are also compensable. Categories of claims that may not be allowed include losses from combat, contractual matters, domestic obligations, and claims that are either not in the best interest of the United States to pay or that are contrary to public policy.

21. Unless otherwise noted, the following discussion of JA involvement in Operation Desert Storm—and the OPLAW issues with which they dealt—is based on material contained in BORCH, JUDGE ADVOCATES IN COMBAT, *supra* note 22, at 122–164.

Command (CENTCOM) JAs focused almost exclusively on providing timely and accurate advice in support of combat operations.

International OPLAW Issues

ROE and the Law of Armed Conflict

During the course of Desert Storm, commanders frequently called upon JAs to address the legality of attacking a particular building, bridge, road, railroad, or other structure. In advising on such issues, CENTCOM JAs consistently, on a target-by-target basis, balanced the military necessity for attacking a target against any negative effects, such as collateral civilian damage or casualties. Pursuant to this approach, the CENTCOM staff planned the ongoing military campaign with a view toward minimizing collateral civilian casualties and damage to civilian objects. Consequently, some targets were avoided, as the value of destroying these targets was outweighed by the potential risk to nearby civilians or, in the case of certain archeological and religious sites, to civilian structures. While a policy of minimizing collateral civilian casualties and protecting civilian property furthered compliance with the LOAC and was a touchstone of CENTCOM's ROE, CENTCOM JAs discovered, nevertheless, that this policy and its implementing rules were sometimes misinterpreted. During the air war, for example, it was learned that some "pilots were pulling off legitimate targets. They thought they could not engage them because they were in civilian neighborhoods...." JAs emphasized that this unduly restrictive interpretation of the ROE was not only erroneous, but, as it increased the risk to American pilots, was a threat to the overall allied air campaign.

Other situations also illustrated how CENTCOM JAs considered the legal principles of military necessity, proportionality, and unnecessary suffering in advising on targeting. In one instance, the destruction of bridges over a river resulted in the Iraqis converting a nearby dike into a major supply route for transporting soldiers and war materiel. The targeting committee wished to destroy the dike, but recognizing that it protected the local population from flooding, asked if such an attack was lawful. Similarly, several Iraqi vehicles, identified as possibly containing chemical weapons components, were parked next to a hospital. Was it lawful to target these military vehicles, despite the risk of collateral damage to the medical facility? Using the principles of military necessity, proportionality, and unnecessary suffering, JAs concluded that both the dike and the trucks were legitimate targets under the LOAC.

With the start of the ground offensive, the VII Corps main effort in the attack was the initial breakthrough operation. To accomplish this breaching mission, the First Infantry Division moved forward and plowed through Iraqi berms and minefields. The division then assaulted the trenches containing other Iraqi soldiers. Once astride the trench lines, the division turned the plow blades of its tanks and combat earthmovers along the enemy defense line and, covered by fire from its Bradley armored infantry fighting vehicles, began filling in the trench line and its heavily bunkered fighting positions. In the process, many Iraqi soldiers surrendered to division personnel, while others died in the course of the attack and the destruction or bulldozing of their defensive positions. During the bulldozing operation, the responsible SJA was asked if burying the enemy alive in his own trenches was permitted under the LOAC. He responded by stating that the breaching operations were lawful. He advised, however, that the location where Iraqi defenders were being buried should be marked for later reporting to the ICRC.

As U.S. units continued their rapid advance, thousands of enemy soldiers were captured. The volume of prisoners was so great that it threatened to slow the American advance;

not only was transportation unavailable for moving the prisoners to rear holding areas, but there were too few soldiers to guard them. Could Iraqi prisoners simply be provided food and water and instructed to start walking south? There were minefields to the south, and Iraqi prisoners might be killed or injured if they inadvertently walked through such fields. Additionally, groups of Iraqi soldiers traveling on foot behind the front lines might be targeted by U.S. soldiers or aircraft. Were they to be killed or injured, the U.S. would bear a responsibility for violating the LOAC. The SJA advised that the requirements of the law left no alternative; prisoners must be safeguarded and moved, under escort, to the rear.

Many unusual questions surfaced in connection with Iraqi POW, all of which came to JAs for opinions. Could commanders accept offers from enemy prisoners and civilian detainees to spy for U.S. forces? Could they be utilized in psychological operations? Could captured soldiers be used as gravediggers for the enemy dead? JAs advised that Articles 49 and 52 of the 1949 GPW Convention permitted prisoner labor, as long as the work was not unhealthy, dangerous, or humiliating. Consequently, using POW volunteers as intelligence collectors, translators, and interpreters was lawful, and such service also entitled them to compensation. Furthermore, the use of prisoners for burial details was also lawful. The expeditious burial of enemy dead helped preserve a healthful environment and ensured that the burial was in accordance with Islamic religious beliefs.

Occupation Law

At the conclusion of Desert Storm, U.S. forces occupied most of southeastern Iraq. For political reasons, however, CENTCOM took the position that the U.S. was not an "occupying force." Nevertheless, as the physical seizure and control of Iraqi territory triggered the application of the 1949 Geneva Convention Relative to the Protection of Civilian Persons in Time of War (GCC),[22] CENTCOM also pledged that its forces would comply with the duties and responsibilities of an occupying force set out in that Convention. Providing legal advice on the duties of an occupier, however, proved to be a difficult task. The American Army had not occupied enemy territory since World War II, and, as a result, no commanders, staff officers, or JAs had any experience dealing with occupation law.

Under international law, military occupation does not transfer the sovereignty of an occupied territory to the occupier. Rather, it provides the Occupying Power with some of the rights of sovereignty, particularly those related to the maintenance of law and order. Thus, American forces were required to perform police functions and to establish security for Iraqi civilians in the geographic area under U.S. control. As Iraq technically retained sovereignty over the occupied area, however, restoring public order and safety did not mean a substitution of U.S. law for Iraqi law. Rather, Iraqi civil and penal laws continued in force—at least in theory. Additionally, CENTCOM JAs advised that private property could not be confiscated by the occupying force, but that, if needed for direct military use, it could be requisitioned, with payment made to the property's owner. The greatest concern to U.S. commanders in Iraq, however, was the legal requirement that civilians in the occupied area have access to sufficient food and medical supplies, particularly since the GCC required that adequate food and medical supplies be brought to the occupied territory, if local Iraqi resources proved inadequate.

---

22. Geneva Convention Relative to the Treatment of Civilian Persons in Time of War, Aug. 12, 1949, 6 U.S.T. 3516, 75 U.N.T.S. 287.

An issue related to the feeding and care of Iraqi refugees was that of political asylum. Though refugees repeatedly requested U.S. troops for asylum, JAs advised that no political asylum could be granted. Only U.S. authorities in an area over which the U.S. exercised sovereignty could grant asylum, and this was not the case in Iraq. They advised, however, that temporary refuge could be provided, but only in cases involving imminent danger to the life or safety of the person concerned — and when the person seeking refuge was not fleeing duly constituted law enforcement officials.

Just as Army lawyers had not advised on occupation law since the defeat of the Axis powers in 1945, they also had not faced issues related to liberated territory since that time. The liberation of Kuwait revealed that a major rebuilding of that nation was required. CENTCOM's Task Force Freedom, as part of its mission to assist in the restoration of Kuwait's legitimate government, was to participate in this process. But to what extent could DOD manpower, equipment, and supplies be used to provide relief to Kuwait's civilian population following their liberation from enemy forces? Could soldiers repair electrical power plants, water distribution systems, telephone exchanges, and highways? Could they engage in firefighting and control air traffic? The Task Force Freedom JA advised that a commander might properly provide life-sustaining services on a temporary basis, and otherwise maintain order, until the Kuwaiti government could be re-established. This opinion became the basis for Task Force Freedom's initial nation building efforts in Kuwait.

War Crimes

Iraqi forces retreating from Kuwait intentionally dynamited 732 producing oil wells. Over 650 of these caught fire, causing oil-laden clouds that rose as high as 22,000 feet. At the peak of destruction, the fires daily consumed approximately five million barrels of oil, valued at about $100 million, and generated more than one-half million tons of airborne pollutants. The Iraqis also intentionally polluted Kuwaiti waters by dumping great volumes of unrefined or crude oil into the Arabian Gulf. Were these wanton acts of destruction tantamount to "environmental war crimes"? CENTCOM JAs, after conferring with their counterparts at the Joint Chiefs of Staff, concluded that they were, as Article 147 of the GCC prohibits the "extensive destruction ... of property, not justified by military necessity and carried out unlawfully and wantonly." The retreat of Iraqi forces meant that the persons responsible for these environmental war crimes were unavailable for prosecution. Under international law, however, as reaffirmed by UN Security Council Resolution 687, Iraq, as a nation, incurred continuing liability for this environmental damage and the depletion of Kuwait's natural resources.

Contract OPLAW Issues

Acquisition and Contract Law

On the modern battlefield of Desert Storm, the then existing contracting system revealed serious shortcomings, particularly in the early stages of the offensive. Ordering Officer monetary authority was limited, and Ordering Officers and Contracting Officers were often unavailable to acquire urgently needed property or services. In planning for Desert Storm, American forces had anticipated that they would seize private property after crossing into Iraq and Kuwait. As earlier noted, under the LOAC, while such seizures are permitted, any private property seized during combat must later be returned to the owner and compensation paid for the use of or any damage to or loss of this property. Documentation was thus required for property accountability and to serve as a record in the event that subsequent claims were made against the U.S. for loss or damage arising out of battlefield seizures. Seizures in Grenada and Panama, particularly of privately owned automobiles and trucks, had been haphazard, hampering later efforts to pay claims for the loss of or damage to these vehicles. Determining that only a uniform system could inject discipline into the seizure process, JAs created a first-of-its-kind battlefield acquisition system, SUPCOM SJA Form 27-1, a Property Control Record Book.

Contractor vehicles represented a special contracting problem. A number of owner-operators feared that their heavy equipment transporters would be damaged. Consequently, they refused to relinquish them to U.S. military drivers without an assurance that any loss or damage to their vehicles would be compensated. JA contract attorneys immediately prepared a document entitled "U.S. Government Liability for Loss of or Damage to Leased Vehicle." It was translated into Arabic and signed by the commander of the Contracting Command of the U.S. Army component to CENTCOM. The document recited a Federal Acquisition Regulation clause, providing for liability insurance in all government contracts, and stated that the protection of the clause extended to loss of or damage to vehicles leased from their owner-operators. Significantly, the document did not commit the government to pay directly for any loss or damage, but its insurance provisions satisfied the Saudi owner-operators, and the trucks rolled.

The possible refusal of Saudi or third-country civilian drivers to operate their contract vehicles during war also posed problems. If these civilians refused to drive into an area of imminent or ongoing hostilities, the provision of fuel and ammunition to combat forces would be severely reduced. A practical solution was to have a U.S. soldier ride in each contracted vehicle headed north to Iraq and Kuwait. JAs proposed a second, complementary solution, however. The core of their idea was a printed card explaining, in both Arabic and English, that the driver was obligated to transport war materiel, as contracted. The card further notified the driver, moreover, that if he refused to proceed as dispatched, a U.S. driver would be substituted, and the vehicle would be used for the duration of the contract, with or without the presence of the contract driver. In Desert Storm, heavy reliance on contractor-furnished drivers called for unusual approaches, and the production of this card clearly demonstrated how contract law could contribute to the sustainment of the combat mission.

Administrative OPLAW Issues

As the fighting ended, the most difficult administrative law issues concerned the investigation of friendly fire incidents. The accidental killing and wounding of American soldiers from friendly, rather than hostile, fire are tragic concomitants of war. The emotional turmoil accompanying a fratricide makes its investigation more difficult than that of other incidents. Additionally, the tempo of combined arms operations on the modern battlefield made the Desert Storm friendly fire investigations more complex than those conducted in previous conflicts. It was essential to investigate fratricides, however, in order to learn the causes of the incidents and to fix responsibility. Only then could safety be improved and measures undertaken to prevent future similar incidents. JAs were key participants in all such investigations, as their education and training made them well suited to ask the right questions and to organize an investigation in a logical fashion.

Summing Up

The CENTCOM SJA called Desert Storm "the most legalistic war we've ever fought." In conducting Desert Storm, commanders consistently sought legal advice at every stage of operational planning, for they realized that JAs substantially contributed to the successful conduct of the operation through their knowledge of OPLAW.

Questions for Discussion

1. During Desert Storm, JAs focused on the LOAC principles of military necessity, proportionality, and unnecessary suffering in advising on targeting issues. How were these principles applied to such matters?

2. The taking of a large number of POWs may substantially impact the ability of U.S. forces to move quickly in an operational environment. Does operational necessity supplant the relevant Geneva POW Convention provisions in such a situation? If not, why not?

3. Did U.S. forces occupy portions of Iraq following the termination of hostilities in that country? What document contains the basic provisions of occupation law?

4. A number of combat contracting issues arose in the context of Desert Storm. Drawing upon these issues, discuss the manner in which effective JA contracting practices can contribute to the sustainment of a military operation.

Kosovo — Operation Allied Force and Task Force Hawk, 1999[23]

Operation Allied Force

In 1989, Yugoslavian President Slobodan Milosevic revoked Kosovo's status as an autonomous province of the Federal Republic of Yugoslavia (FRY), annexing Kosovo into the FRY province of Serbia. In response, the Kosovo Liberation Army (KLA), a militant group comprised of ethnic Albanians, was founded in 1993, initiating a campaign of violence against the FRY government. In 1998, Milosevic sent Yugoslav troops into KLA strongholds, and the conflict escalated. The UN Security Council called for a cease-fire in UN Security Council Resolution 1199 on September 23, 1998, and NATO authorized air strikes against Serb military targets on October 13, 1998. As a result, Milosevic agreed to withdraw troops, facilitate the return of refugees, and accept international monitors. Despite these assurances, however, the violence continued to escalate.

In 1999, the political and military leaders from Kosovo, Serbia, and the FRY agreed to attend a peace conference in Rambouillet, France. The Kosovar Albanians signed the "Rambouillet Accords," which specified that the province would remain a part of Serbia, but that it would be allowed to operate autonomously. The Serbs refused to sign the Accords, however, objecting to various provisions, most notably, elections that might potentially lead to Kosovo independence, and talks were suspended. Because the violence continued, NATO began air strikes against Serb targets in Serbia and Kosovo on March 24, 1999. The NATO air campaign, designated Operation Allied Force, lasted until June 10, 1999, when Milosevic agreed to withdraw Serb forces from Kosovo and to permit the entry of the NATO Kosovo Force (KFOR) in order to keep the peace.

International OPLAW Issues

LOAC-Targeting

Lawyers from the Army, Navy, Marine Corps, and Air Force served on the legal staff at U.S. European Command (USEUCOM) during Operation Allied Force. The USEUCOM

---

23. Unless otherwise noted, the following discussion of JA involvement in Operation Allied Force and Task Force Hawk — and the OPLAW issues with which they dealt — is based on material contained in Center for Law and Military Operations, LAW AND MILITARY OPERATIONS IN KOSOVO: 1999–2001, 44–77 (2001).

SJA (an Army JA) and Deputy SJA (an Air Force JA) both had direct involvement in the air campaign targeting process. Bombing missions concentrated on fixed targets, using high-flying, high-speed aircraft. The target selection process called for bringing all relevant staff members together in a "collaborative session" via a classified "chat room." During these sessions, all major participants were "on line" at one time, reviewing the same information, and a computer program retained a record of the discussion for future reference. The JA would access the Joint Analysis Center (JAC) classified web page prior to each session, a web page that contained files for each target, to include detailed pictures and descriptions of the target and surrounding area. The JA would then use this information to conduct a preliminary legal analysis and to develop questions and issues for discussion during the collaborative session. When the chat room convened, all participants were available electronically to analyze and discuss the various targets. Targets approved in the collaborative session would be placed on slides for the President of the United States (a "POTUS slide"). The POTUS slide was forwarded, through CINCUSEUCOM and the Joint Chiefs of Staff, to the President. As the campaign progressed, however, the authority to approve certain categories of targets was delegated down to CINCUSEUCOM.

JAs providing legal advice during Operation Allied Force were sensitive to the fact that certain participants in the target review process might misunderstand the legal implications of "collateral damage." These JAs thus worked to ensure that there was no misperception that the infliction of collateral damage was a per se violation of the LOAC and that a collateral damage analysis did not come at the expense of dismissing the "military necessity" quotient of the complete analytical process involved. Moreover, the third, and essential, component of such a process was the principle of "proportionality," thus establishing a balancing test: the loss of life and damage to property incidental to attacks [also known as collateral damage] must not be excessive in relation to the concrete and direct military advantage expected to be gained. Thus, while nothing prevented a commander from placing a high premium on minimizing collateral damage, the USEUCOM JAs pointed out that a necessary step in the equation was the effective articulation of the military advantage to be gained by striking a specific target. Disapproving targets based solely on collateral damage assessments—absent a discussion of military necessity—would raise suspicion that an overly restrictive legal standard was being applied. JAs thus emphasized to staffs and commanders that the infliction of collateral damage was only one component of the proportionality balancing test.

Task Force Hawk

International OPLAW Issues

LOAC-Targeting

Task Force Hawk was a U.S. Task Force, with an on-order NATO mission, designed to provide support to Operation Allied Force and, specifically, to address moving targets such as tanks. Potential Task Force targets were reviewed by JAs early in the targeting process in order that legal considerations might be incorporated into operational planning. JAs engaged in this review process possessed top secret clearances that enabled them to gain access to satellite imagery, and they focused on a list of 26 questions when evaluating targets. This list included questions regarding the size of the civilian population, the estimated number of civilian casualties, the importance of the target to the accomplishment of the mission, and the ability to mitigate any adverse impact on the civilian population. These JAs also monitored a protected site list and an Automated Deep Operations Coordination System (ADOCS), a system that enabled them to view engagement areas and targets, track enemy movement, anticipate the potential for collateral damage, and monitor no-fire areas.

In providing targeting advice, it was essential that JAs have an understanding of the various Army weapons systems, in-theater. For example, three types of the Army Tactical Missile System (ATACMS) exist, and Army Howitzers fire eleven types of munitions with varying burst radii and potential for collateral damage. Task Force Hawk JAs thus coordinated with the appropriate Artillery Commander in order to have his staff develop a templated "footprint" for each weapon and munition that these JAs could then apply to a map board in order to predict collateral damage when reviewing a proposed target. This information, along with intelligence concerning the presence or absence of non-combatants in the target area, provided the basis for JAs to conduct a thorough legal analysis of each potential target.

Rules of Engagement

In addition to targeting issues, Task Force Hawk JAs faced significant matters of ROE development and interpretation. NATO had not addressed rotary-wing operations when preparing for Operation Allied Force, and, while Task Force Hawk was never placed under the operational control of NATO, the training and mission rehearsals anticipated Task Force Hawk becoming a part of the larger NATO operation. The Task Force was thus unclear as to whether U.S. or NATO ROE applied to its operations. Further complicating the issue was the fact that the NATO Air ROE contemplated high-flying, fixed-wing air-craft—not low-flying helicopters. Task Force Hawk JAs eventually determined that NATO ROE would governed the U.S. Apache helicopters and that U.S. ROE would govern ground forces, reasoning that the use of Apaches for air operations in Kosovo would constitute a use of force by NATO, while U.S. ground operations in Albania would constitute solely a U.S. component of the operation.

Claims OPLAW Issues

Foreign Claims

The Department of the Army was assigned Single Service Claims Responsibility for Albania, from which the Task Force operated, and where the legal basis for the adjudication and payment of foreign claims was first derived from the claims provisions of the NATO SOFA,[24] as incorporated by the Partnership for Peace (PFP) SOFA.[25] On April 8, 1999, however, the North Atlantic Council issued a decision waiving Albania's 25 percent cost-sharing contribution required by the PFP SOFA. As a practical matter, U.S. Army adjudication of foreign claims in Albania then fell under the provisions of the Foreign Claims Act (FCA), as implemented by Army Regulation 27-20, *Claims*. However, three JA Captains were responsible for processing claims for not only the Task Force, but also for Operation Shining Hope, the Air Force humanitarian relief mission co-located at Rinas Airfield.

Reaching claimants throughout the area of operations required prior coordination and creative planning. Force protection concerns and logistical constraints limited the JAs'

---

24. Agreement Between the Parties to the North Atlantic Treaty Regarding the Status of Their Forces, June 15, 1951, 4 U.S.T. 1792, 199 U.N.T.S. 67.

25. Agreement Among the States Parties to the North Atlantic Treaty and the Other States Participating in the Partnership for Peace Regarding the Status of their Forces, June 19, 1995, T.I.A.S. No. 12,666.

ability to travel the countryside extensively, and security requirements prevented Albanian citizens from entering the camp. JAs thus coordinated with Civil Affairs (CA) personnel to share tents that had been set up adjacent to the camp and advertised the dates that claims would be received. Briefed by the JAs on claims procedures, CA personnel also agreed to receive and investigate some distant claims. Close coordination with MPs resulted in vehicle and security support when the JAs traveled outside the camp. Verifying property ownership, for claims purposes, in Albania proved to be difficult, and JAs quickly discovered the need to engage in considerable research in order to determine the governing property laws. Property records were a confusing remnant of the country's monarchical and Communist past; however, a crude system of property law and deeds registration did exist. To establish ownership and minimize fraudulent claims, JAs required claimants to either produce an official copy of a pre-existing deed or register the property under the new Albanian recordation system.

Fiscal OPLAW Issues

The most persistent fiscal law issue faced by Task Force Hawk involved the donation of Army property to the civilian population. The Purpose Statute provides that "[a]ppropriations shall be applied only to the objects for which the appropriations were made, except as otherwise provided by law."[26] Thus, expenditures must be authorized by law or be reasonably related to the purpose of an appropriation in order to be lawful. Accordingly, a military unit cannot donate property to civilians that was originally purchased for military use, unless there exists a statutory exception. One such exception is 10 U.S.C. § 2557, *Excess Nonlethal Supplies: Humanitarian Relief*, under which the Secretary of Defense may make available for humanitarian relief purposes any DOD nonlethal excess supplies. "Nonlethal excess supplies" refers to property that is in Defense Reutilization and Management Office (DRMO) channels, and may include all property except real property, weapons, ammunition, and any other equipment or materiel designed to inflict bodily harm or death. Property is "excess" if it is no longer required for the needs and the discharge of responsibilities of the relevant military service. Excess supplies furnished by the military under the authority of 10 U.S.C. § 2557 are transferred to the DOS — specifically, the U.S. Agency for International Development (AID), which is responsible for the distribution of the supplies to nations targeted for humanitarian relief.

When the mission in Kosovo ended, Task Force Hawk had on hand 80,000 gallons of aircraft fuel that were no longer needed. It first sought permission to characterize the fuel as excess and to donate it to the Albanian government, rather than incurring the transaction costs of shipping it to Task Force Falcon, the U.S.-led element of the peacekeeping forces in Kosovo (KFOR), or back to Germany. Because the fuel was still useful to the government, and not truly excess, however, JAs recommended that Task Force Hawk transport 30,000 gallons to Task Force Falcon and transfer the remainder to the Albanians as "payment-in-kind" for services provided by Albania to U.S. forces. This transfer of fuel to the Albanians was accomplished using what is commonly referred to as a "third-party transfer" under an ACSA. As previously noted, an ACSA is an agreement with a foreign government or international regional organization that allows DOD to acquire and transfer logistical support without resorting to oftentimes slow and inflexible contracting procedures. Acquisitions and transfers are effected on a replacement-in-kind, equal value exchange, or cash reimbursement basis. In the context of donating property that is not technically

---

26. 31 U.S.C. § 1301(a) (2004).

excess, the use of an ACSA also serves as a mechanism by which a violation of the Purpose Statute can be avoided.

Operation Joint Guardian, 1999[27]

The nineteen member nations of NATO, along with twenty other troop-contributing nations, combined to conduct Operation Joint Guardian, the NATO peacekeeping mission in Kosovo. Operation Joint Guardian began immediately following Operation Allied Force, the seventy-eight day NATO air campaign suspended on June 10, 1999, after the North Atlantic Council received confirmation that Yugoslav forces in Kosovo had begun to withdraw. The Yugoslav withdrawal was in accordance with the Military Technical Agreement (MTA) between NATO and the FRY, which was designed to establish a durable cessation of hostilities within Kosovo and to provide authorization for the deployment of an international security force to Kosovo. On June 10, 1999, pursuant to Chapter VII of the UN Charter, the UN Security Council passed Resolution 1244 (UNSCR 1244),[28] welcoming the FRY acceptance of the framework for a political solution to the Kosovo crisis, including a withdrawal of military police and paramilitary forces. UNSCR 1244 also authorized the deployment of an international security force under UN auspices. Synchronized with the departure of Serb forces, the first elements of the Kosovo Forces (KFOR) entered Kosovo on June 12, 1999. Thus began the peacekeeping mission in Kosovo. The U.S.-led element of KFOR was Task Force Falcon.

The initial Task Force Falcon mission was four-pronged: (1) to monitor, verify, and enforce, as necessary, the provisions of the MTA and create a safe and secure environment; (2) to provide humanitarian assistance in support of UN High Commission for Refugees (UNHCR) efforts; (3) to initially enforce basic law and order, transitioning this function to the to-be-formed designated agency as soon as possible; and (4) to establish/support the resumption of core civil functions.

International OPLAW Issues
Rules of Engagement

The ROE for Operation Joint Guardian were promulgated on June 10, 1999. ROE issues confronting Task Force Falcon JAs stemmed from the nature of coalition operations, the difficulties in training mission-specific ROE received immediately prior to executing the Task Force mission, and the matter of having to address multiple ROE.

The ROE for the Kosovo mission required the consensus of all NATO member nations through the approval of the NATO Council. 19 independent governments reaching consensus on political guidance necessary to draft the ROE was not a simple matter, as the interpretation of ROE provisions was subject to the laws and experiences of each interpreting country. JAs thus had to remain particularly aware of NATO ROE procedures and U.S. policy regarding ROE. For example, self-defense actions taken by U.S. soldiers are U.S. issues, and interpretations of such self-defense matters must remain in U.S. legal

---

27. Unless otherwise noted, the following discussion of JA involvement in Operation Joint Guardian—and the OPLAW issues with which they dealt—is based on material contained in Law and Military Operations in Kosovo: 1999-2001, *supra* note 23, at 84–163.

28. S.C. Res. 1244, U.N. SCOR, 54th Sess., 4011th Mtg., U.N. Doc. S/RES/1244 (1999).

and operational channels. This subject arose consistently in the context of out-of-sector exercises and operations.

During the planning for one out-of-sector exercise involving French and U.S. forces in the French sector of Kosovo, a member of the French staff distributed a memorandum addressing the "ROE for Attack Helicopters." The memorandum stated that to fire in self-defense, "the hostile act must have already begun (not an intention, but reality)." When pressed by U.S. representatives, including a JA, a member of the French staff explained that if an individual aimed a surface-to-air missile at a U.S. Apache helicopter, the Apache would not be able to engage the individual until he actually fired the missile. The U.S. JA explained that U.S. forces would be allowed to engage such a target under the U.S. understanding of "hostile intent." After the meeting ended, the JA drafted a letter that was ultimately sent to the Commander, KFOR, restating the U.S. position, quoting the KFOR ROE allowing for Troop Contributing Nations to follow their domestic laws when NATO ROE were inconsistent with those laws, and stating that U.S. forces would not be able to participate in exercises or operations that infringed on their right of self-defense. Ultimately, all parties agreed that U.S. soldiers and aviators would be able to defend themselves in accordance with U.S. policy.

International Agreements: Legal Framework for the Military Mission

Within Kosovo, international law provided an extremely broad area of practice. In addition to the various agreements discussed above, JAs had to remain cognizant of treaty law and fundamental human rights law. The predominant law of peace theory, that a sovereign nation retains the right to apply its own law, further complicated the issues that JAs faced when advising commanders, as they were now required to have a basic understanding of the legal codes of both the FRY and the Province of Kosovo. Commanders also expected JAs to understand the international framework for the mission in Kosovo and to provide counsel on legal issues rarely faced in previous U.S. military operations. Moreover, these commanders had to understand the international justification for the U.S. presence in Kosovo, as it drove the mission, and they had to be prepared to explain the military's task and purpose to the press, as well as to the nongovernmental and international organizations operating in Kosovo. To assist commanders, JAs conducted a program called "Leader Teach" on the framework agreements and ROE, a program designed to instruct both commanders and senior unit leaders on the key points of the framework of the Kosovo mission.

Contractor Operations and Status

JAs were consistently involved in issues concerning the status of contractors providing logistical support to the U.S. mission. To address significant delays and holdups on the route to Kosovo, NATO had negotiated a Transit Agreement for a bypass around a main border crossing between FYROM and Kosovo. The Transit Agreement, however, failed to take into consideration Brown & Root Service, the contractor that provided U.S. logistic support. JAs were thus called upon to advise coalition partners concerning the treatment of Brown & Root contract logistic personnel, and to detail the extent to which these personnel were a crucial extension of the military force.

The exercise of criminal jurisdiction over logistic personnel was also a point of concern for JAs. When civilians providing logistic support engaged in minor criminal misconduct, a contractor was quick to fire these employees and to remove them from Kosovo. The concern of the Task Force, however, was the manner in which to handle allegations of serious criminal misconduct lodged against contractor employees. Arguably, the civilians were subject to the dysfunctional Kosovo criminal system—a result that no one desired. At the same time, the prospect of returning someone suspected of a serious crime to the United States, with no possibility for prosecution due to a lack of jurisdiction in U.S. courts, was equally unpalatable. Fortunately, the Task Force never had to make this difficult decision, and the U.S. Congress subsequently passed the Military Extraterritorial Jurisdiction Act to fill this jurisdictional gap.[29]

Fiscal OPLAW Issues

Commanders and staffs deployed on peacekeeping missions face enormous pressure to act in support of numerous requests for humanitarian and civil support. U.S. law, however, may not permit such support, for, as noted previously, it requires that funds be spent in a manner consistent with congressional appropriations and authorization. While Task Force Falcon received $5 million in a two-year appropriation for urgent humanitarian assistance, the Joint Staff and EUCOM placed numerous restrictions on the use of these funds, to include project cost limitations, limits on the types of projects that the Task Force could undertake, and a requirement to use specific legal authorities for expenditures. The Task Force thus developed a system by which the CA staff section would document each potential humanitarian assistance project with cost estimates, photographs, and project details. The project was then reviewed by a group of staff officers, including a JA, prior to being forwarded to the commander for action. The JA's review would include a consideration of all fiscal restraints placed on the use of the funds in question.

Questions for Discussion

1. JAs were consistently involved in the targeting procedures associated with both Operation Allied Force and Task Force Hawk. In your view, was this JA involvement too extensive in nature? Why—or why not?

2. A significant assist to mission accomplishment in operations such as that conducted by Task Force Hawk is the ability of U.S. forces to donate military (U.S.) property to the civilian population. What rules of fiscal law are generally applicable to such property transfers?

3. The provision of civilian contractor logistic support to U.S. military operations such as Operation Joint Guardian has become essential to the success of such missions. Should such contractors—and their personnel—be accorded the same "status" privileges and immunities as those afforded U.S. military personnel under Status of Forces Agreements or similar international arrangements?

4. The ROE for Operation Joint Guardian required the consensus of all NATO states, acting through the North Atlantic Council. What were some of the more significant ROE issues encountered by JAs as a result of this ROE process?

---

29. Military Extraterritorial Jurisdiction Act of 2000, 18 U.S.C. §§ 3261-3267.

Afghanistan—Operation Enduring Freedom (OEF), 2001[30]

On September 11, 2001, terrorists hijacked four planes and flew two of these into the twin towers of the World Trade Center in New York City, one into the Pentagon, and crashed the fourth in a field in Pennsylvania. More than 3,000 civilians from over 80 countries died as a result of these actions.

On September 12, the UN Security Council issued UNSCR 1368, condemning these attacks, regarding them as threats to international peace and security and recognizing the inherent right of individual or collective self- defense in accordance with Article 51 of the UN Charter. That same day, NATO invoked Article 5 of its governing treaty for the first time in its history, also recognizing this Article 51 right of individual and collective self-defense, enabling its members to come to the assistance of the U.S., through armed force, if necessary. A short time later, the UN Security Council, in UNSCR 1373, reaffirmed the need to combat, by all means, the threats to international peace and security caused by terrorist acts.

On September 18, the U.S. Congress passed a Joint Resolution, Public Law 107-40, Authorization to Use Military Force, authorizing the President to use all necessary and appropriate force against those nations, organizations, or persons he determined to be responsible for planning, authorizing, committing, or aiding the terrorist attacks, or who harbored such organizations or persons.

The U.S. quickly identified the Al Qaeda terrorist group as being responsible for the September 11 attacks and began forming a military coalition to eliminate Al Qaeda, based in Afghanistan, and to remove the governing Taliban Afghan regime, said to be harboring and protecting Al Qaeda. Consequently, more than 14,000 troops from 27 countries eventually participated in the resulting U.S.-led operation, ENDURING FREEDOM (OEF), a military action commenced on October 7, 2001.

As U.S.-led military operations were under way in Afghanistan, a number of Afghan factions met in Bonn, Germany in December of 2001 to discuss the restoration of stability and governance in their country. The resulting Bonn Agreement included a request that the UN Security Council establish a UN-mandated military force. Accordingly, pursuant to UNSCR 1386, a security assistance force was authorized under Chapter VII of the UN Charter. This force, the NATO-led International Security Force (ISAF), undertook NATO's first mission outside the Euro Atlantic area. Eventually, 37 countries contributed forces to ISAF, and, while ISAF's original mandate was to operate in and around Kabul, its area of operations gradually expanded to include all of Afghanistan.

Unique OPLAW issues have occurred in the context of an area of operations shared by both the US-led OEF and the NATO-led ISAF. And, while the number of troops, both US and NATO, has risen and fallen over the years, both US and NATO forces remain in Afghanistan after, as of this writing, over 13 years of conflict in that country. An illustrative sampling of these OPLAW issues follows.

---

30. Unless otherwise noted, the following discussion of JA involvement in Operation ENDURING FREEDOM—and the selected OPLAW issues with which they dealt—is based on material contained in Center for Law and Military Operations, Forged in Fire: Legal Lessons Learned During Military Operations 1994–2008 (2008).

International OPLAW Issues

LOAC-Detention Operations

Status of Detainees

As the U.S. began detaining personnel in the initial stages of OEF, the most difficult and unsettled issue was that of the status to be afforded both Taliban and Al Qaeda detainees. While JAs sought guidance from higher headquarters, they advised that all detainees be treated in a manner consistent with the GPW and the GCC. The Combined Joint Task Force Chief of Operational Law dealing with this matter noted, accordingly, that, while detainees were not to be granted POW status and, thus, were not to be provided all of the rights of the GPW, they were to be treated humanely and in a manner consistent with that Convention. Then, following a period of uncertainty, President Bush issued guidance in which he determined that the GPW applied to the Taliban, but not to the Al Qaeda detainees. He went on to note, however, that even though the Convention did apply to Taliban detainees, under the terms of the GPW, these individuals did not qualify as POW. Nevertheless, he advised that, while the Taliban would not be afforded POW status, they would be provided many of the privileges of a POW- but as a matter of policy, rather than law.[31]

This rather confusing guidance proved to be difficult for JAs to apply and led to the creation of non-LOAC terms for detainees seized on the battlefield, such as Persons Under Control (PUCs) — those detainees transported to a classified location in order to establish their identities and to determine whether they met classified criteria for transfer to Guantanamo, Cuba. Such terms — and other hybrid and questionable practices dealing with OEF detainees — were eventually abandoned, however, as evolving DOD policy required, correctly, that U.S. forces comply with the controlling provisions of the LOAC.

Interrogation of Detainees

No other aspect of OEF operations generated as much controversy and legal oversight as that of the interrogation of detainees. Interrogation issues proved to be the most sensitive and difficult of those dealt with by JAs. As detainees represent a potential resource of valuable information, the possibility of extracting such information through interrogation often gives rise to the temptation to push the limits of the LOAC applicable to the interrogation process. Article 17 of the GPW prohibits the use of both mental and physical torture and coercion during interrogation, and Article 31 of the GCC contains a similar prohibition against the use of coercion in order to gain information. Moreover, torture is prohibited under all circumstances, regardless of a detainee's status. Despite these provisions, however, given the uncertainty surrounding the status of the Taliban and Al Qaeda detainees and the Presidential decision that the GPW did not apply to these individuals, JAs often fielded questions regarding the legality of certain "enhanced" interrogation techniques posed for use. While the great majority of JAs provided advice that comported with the law applicable to detainee interrogation, it is now public record that detainee abuse did occur. As a means of preventing such abuse in the future, carefully reviewed and approved interrogation techniques were eventually set forth in the 2006 Army Field Manual 2-33.3, Human Intelligence Collector Operations.

---

31. Memorandum from President George W. Bush, "Humane Treatment of Al Qaeda and Taliban Detainees", (Feb.7, 2002), reprinted in MARK DANNER, TORTURE AND TRUTH, ABU GHRAIB, AND THE WAR ON TERROR 105 (2004).

Administrative OPLAW Issues

Historical Artifacts and War Trophies

As in all operations, one of the most consistently reported OEF administrative OPLAW issues was the confusion and consternation that can arise in the absence of a clearly articulated policy on the retention of war trophies and historical artifacts. The rules on the retention of enemy property as souvenirs generally fall into two broad categories, each with its own regulatory scheme: (1) war trophies; and (2) historical artifacts. War trophies are items retained by individuals as personal property, whereas historical artifacts are items retained by armed forces museums; that is, items that may never become personal property.

SJAs scheduled for deployment to the OEF theater learned that they must ensure that their administrative law sections were familiar with-and had copies of-all theater-specific regulations, orders, and policies dealing with such matters, prior to deployment. This enabled them to publish Information Papers and to provide briefings on this subject at home station.

Once deployed, it was essential that JAs provide detailed advice and guidance on matters related to war trophies and historical artifacts, as they systematically encountered the following issues:

- Lawful Acquisition- JAs must understand the types of property that personnel and units may-and may not-seize as a war trophy or historical artifact under the LOAC.

- Customs Regulations- JAs must be familiar with U.S. customs regulations or those of the country of the unit's home station (e.g. Germany). Items that units or personnel may lawfully seize under the LOAC and service regulations may, in fact, violate such customs regulations.

- Numerous Requests- JAs must anticipate a large number of requests from units to seize and transport items as historical artifacts. Many of these items will not be eligible for such-for a variety of reasons, and JAs must be able to articulate why this is the case.

- Lengthy Delays in Processing Requests- Unit requests to redeploy with an historical artifact will always require a substantial amount of time for approval. Accordingly, JAs must be proactive in advising commanders to submit such requests very early in the deployment.

Investigations

JAs deployed to Afghanistan constantly noted the significant amount of time, effort, and resources required to process the large number of administrative investigations that arose in the context of OEF, as summarized in the following After Action Report:

> The main administrative law focus during deployment was on investigations. In one 90 day period, there were approximately 30 investigations.... Higher headquarters issued a range of policy memorandum dictating the differing incidents for which an investigation was mandatory. The primary focus was on accidents which resulted in death or serious injury, or on friendly fire or escalation of force incidents. There were also a variety of investigations involving misconduct by commanders or other senior leaders—many of which were high profile in nature. Administrative Law JAs were responsible for advising the Investigating Officers, tracking the investigation process, and conducting a legal review of the

completed investigation. The SJA was then required to brief the command on the results of the investigations and participate in any resulting disciplinary action. For investigations involving a death, Administrative Law JAs were also tasked with creating the Family Brief for the deceased's command.[32]

In order to cope with such a large number of investigations, JAs developed and implemented a systemic process for dealing with the variety of investigations involved. First, matrices were created, setting out the specific investigations required in particular circumstances. Second, more time was set aside to prepare investigatory resources prior to arriving in theater. Third, JAs focused on providing more timely legal advice to commanders regarding the type of investigation required, depending upon the circumstance involved. Fourth, JAs made a more concerted effort to more adequately prepare non-JA Investigating Officers in order to ensure that investigations were thoroughly and effectively conducted. And, fifth, JAs became increasingly skilled in the use of electronic means to track, transmit, and store investigations, both in-theater and upon return to home station.

Fiscal OPLAW Issues

Use of Operations and Maintenance (O&M) Funds for Development and Security Assistance

A dominant theme in all OEF After-Action Reports was the importance of possessing an understanding of fiscal law—the application of domestic statutes and regulations to the funding of military operations and the provision of support to non-federal agencies and organizations. Moreover, in addition to the need to fully understand fiscal law, there was a requirement to integrate this expertise into the staff planning process. Experience dictated that a JA skilled in fiscal law always be present in tactical operations centers and at every staff meeting.

The most common fiscal law issue arising during OEF operations was that of identifying the specific "pot of money" available for the funding of various operational activities. More precisely, the challenge was to avoid violating the "Purpose Statute" requirement that Congressional appropriations be applied only to the objects for which the appropriations were made-except as otherwise provided by law.[33] This issue most frequently manifested itself in the context of whether O&M dollars could be used to fund certain aspects of the operation. Tactical units generally receive only O&M appropriations, which are for day-to-day and necessary and incidental operational expenses for which another funding source does not exist. At play, however, was the fact that DOD units were often involved in two of the more common activities for which other funding sources did exist—development assistance (providing food, education, agricultural assistance, health care, environmental, and other assistance programs designed to resolve internal political unrest and poverty) and security assistance (providing supplies, training, and equipment to friendly foreign militaries). Under the Foreign Assistance Act (FAA), Congress has determined that these types of activities-development and security assistance-are DOS, rather than DOD responsibilities.

Given this statutory guidance, the question consistently posed in conducting OEF operations was whether it was appropriate to use O&M dollars to fund activities that had development or security assistance motives or effects. If the answer to this question was

---

32. 10th Mountain Division, Office of the Staff Judge Advocate, After Action Report, Operation ENDURING FREEDOM, February 2006-February 2007 10-11 (2007).
33. Purpose Statute, *supra* note 26.

that O&M funds could not be used, the issue then became whether alternative funding sources were available. Considerations concerning the proper role for DOD components to play within the FAA fiscal framework thus arose, primarily, in three areas: (1) the military provision of humanitarian assistance to the Afghan population; (2) the provision of training and support to the Afghan Army; and (3) the provision of support to other coalition partners. JAs proved to be the key players in ensuring that all proposed military activities that ostensibly appeared to be of a humanitarian or security assistance nature did, in fact, comply with the applicable fiscal rules. Often, a thorough understanding of these rules enabled JAs to craft approaches that both met the goals of their commands — and remained within the bounds of fiscal law requirements.

Claims OPLAW Issues

Solatia Payments

One of the most challenging aspects of deployed claims operations in OEF proved to be the handling of "solatia" payments made to surviving family members for the unintentional deaths of host nation personnel. These payments represent an expression of sympathy and are made without regard to liability or fault. Such payments can be made, however, only in those geographic areas where compensation of this nature is widely recognized as a customary cultural norm. Given this requirement, a November 2004 DOD Policy Memorandum recognized the norm of solatia payment in Afghanistan. Of importance, also, is the fact that payments of solatia are not made with claims funds. Nominal in nature, these payments are made with more readily available O&M funds. Both commanders and JAs were uniform in their view that the ability to make solatia payments to host nation personnel contributed to a unit's overall force protection and mission accomplishment.

Often, confusion existed regarding the use of solatia, particularly at Forward Operating Bases (FOB). Accordingly, JAs discovered that it was essential to produce written guidance, provide briefings regarding such payments, and to have claims offices closely track all solatia compensation.

Iraq—Operation Iraqi Freedom (OIF), 1993[34]

The legal basis for the U.S use of force against Iraq in 1993 was grounded on Iraq's 1990 invasion of Kuwait, in response to which the UN Security Council adopted UNSCRs 660 (demanding Iraq's withdrawal) and 678 (authorizing the use of "all necessary means" to expel Iraq from Kuwait). With the approval of the Security Council, a U.S.-led coalition launched Operation DESERT STORM in January, 1991, quickly driving Iraqi forces from Kuwait.

In April, 1991, the Security Council adopted UNSCR 687, formalizing the ceasefire between Iraqi and Coalition forces, obliging Iraq to "unconditionally accept the destruction, removal, or rendering harmless under international supervision," of its chemical and biological weapons and long-range ballistic missile capabilities, and prohibiting Iraq from acquiring or developing nuclear weapons.[35]

---

34. Unless otherwise noted, the following discussion of JA involvement in Operation IRAQI FREE-DOM — and the selected OPLAW issues with which they dealt — is based on material contained in Forged in Fire: Legal Lessons Learned During Military Operations, *supra* note 30.

35. S.C. Res. 687, U.N. Doc. S/RES/687 (Apr. 3, 1991).

While Iraq initially complied with these requirements, over the following eight years it became, incrementally, less observant of its obligations, culminating in 1998 with the cessation of all cooperation with the International Atomic Energy Agency. Moreover, the ceasefire did not result in an end to hostilities. In August, 1992, "no-fly zones" were established over Iraq in response to its attacks on the Kurdish minority and Shia Muslims, actions in violation of a UNSC mandate.[36] In 1996, Iraq again attacked Kurdish areas in Northern Iraq, drawing a U.S.-led coalition response of sea- and air-launched cruise missile attacks. Then, in 1998, in response to Iraq's termination of UN weapons inspections, the U.S. and the United Kingdom conducted four days of air strikes, an action that initiated a four year "low-profile" war of attrition against Iraqi air defense and military targets.

After continued Iraqi opposition to UN weapons inspections—and a growing concern that Iraq was reconstituting its chemical and biological weapons stockpiles and advancing its nuclear weapons program—the U.S., Spain and the United Kingdom, on February 24, 2003, requested that the Security Council authorize the use of force in order to enforce the UNSCRs applicable to Iraq. Due to strong resistance from Russia, France, and Germany, this request failed. Nevertheless, despite the absence of Security Council authorization, the U.S. made a decision to form a "coalition of the willing" and to commence combat operations against Iraq on March 19, 2003.

International OPLAW Issues

U.S. Contingency Contracting Personnel (CCP)—Weapons

The DOD utilizes contingency contracting personnel (CCP) to provide deployed U.S. forces with a wide range of support services. These include defense contractors and employees of defense contractors, as well as their subcontractors at all tiers of DOD contracts-personnel who may be U.S. citizens, U.S. legal aliens, or third and host country nationals. Services provided include communications and base operation services, interpreters, weapons systems maintenance, gate and perimeter security, intelligence analysis, and the oversight of other CCP. Accordingly, a specific DOD Instruction and Army Regulation establish the policies and responsibilities for the use of contractors in an operational setting.[37]

DOD Instruction 3020.41 governs the matter of CCP possession of weapons. While it prohibits the possession of personally-owned weapons by CCP, it provides that commanders may authorize these individuals to carry military weapons for individual self-defense. CCP acceptance of these weapons, however, must be voluntary and permitted by both the applicable contract and the responsible contractor. Importantly, also, an individual must be eligible under U.S. law to possess a firearm, and the government must ensure that those CCP issued weapons receive familiarization training and briefings on the governing rules for the use of force. JAs must thus be involved in any command decision to issue weapons to CCP, as it is their responsibility to be familiar with any limitations placed on CCP possession of weapons by SOFAs or other international agreements, host nation law—if applicable—and other regulatory schemes.

In Iraq, insurgents killed, injured, and took hostage U.S. CCP, resulting in a request by some CCP that they be authorized to carry personally-owned firearms for their protection. The U.S. Central Command (CENTCOM), however, had long prohibited the

---

36. S.C. Res. 688, U.N. Doc. S/RES/688 (Apr. 5, 1991).

37. U.S. Dep't of Defense, INSTR. 3020.41, CONTRACTOR PERSONNEL AUTHORIZED TO ACCOMPANY THE U.S. ARMED FORCES (3 Oct. 2005); U.S. Dep't of Army, REG. 715.9, CONTRACTORS ACCOMPANYING THE FORCE (29 Oct. 1999).

purchase, possession, use, or sale of privately-owned firearms and ammunition in its area of responsibility. Additionally, though some U.S. contracts included language that permitted CCP to possess weapons for their personal protection—with the authorization of the theater commander—many contracts did not.

JA legal analysis had consistently concluded that the mere possession of a weapon for self-defense neither abrogated the status of CCP as persons accompanying the force, nor transformed them into "unlawful combatants"; i.e., persons who would not be afforded the protections of the GPW. The lessons learned for JAs with respect to the authorization of DOD CCP to carry weapons in Iraq were many, nevertheless. First, it became evident that the decision to issue weapons to these individuals had to be made by a commander- or his or her delegate-on a case-by-case basis. This conclusion evolved from the fact that, under Army policy, based on international law, the responsibility for force protection resided with the armed force. Accordingly, when a request was made for CCP to carry weapons, a JA had to first review the governing contract to discern whether this was permissible-and then consider a number of other questions. For example, if a contractor had requested that all of its CCP be armed for their personal protection, would it be wise, operationally, to issue military weapons to all such employees? If not, what would constitute the basis for arming certain personnel, but not others? What limitations would be placed, if any, on the types of individuals issued weapons—U.S. citizens only, third country nationals, host country citizens? Who would be accountable for each weapon issued; would the contractor or the U.S. military exercise command and control of such weapons? Additionally, who would be responsible for providing the required weapons and use of force training? And, finally, there existed issues arising out of the potentially improper use of a weapon by a contractor. That is, if a contractor used his or her weapon, not in self-defense, but in an offensive manner-perhaps against even a fellow CCP, would the U.S. government/Army be subject to a wrongful death claim? These were but a few of the matters associated with this sensitive and, at times, highly contentious topic.

Civil OPLAW Issues

Environmental OPLAW

Conducting an early environmental survey of property used by U.S. forces overseas in an operational setting can serve to establish a baseline for the measurement of any later claims of environmental damage lodged against the U.S. Accordingly, JAs in Iraq used such surveys when operational requirements dictated the closure of particular camps. A JA was present for the physical inspection associated with the closure of every FOB and prepared a memorandum noting environmental conditions, improvements, and changes to the property that might prove to be relevant to potential claims filed against the U.S. for its use of these facilities. These inspections included the removal of hazardous materials, fuel depots, and the fill of waste burn pits.

The SJA of the 101st Airborne Division dealt with a number of environmental matters in Iraq, to include the environmental law implications of spreading fuel as a dust abatement measure at an aircraft refueling point. Citing military necessity (a recognized exception to a controlling Executive Order dealing with the environmental effects of federal actions abroad),[38] the JAs of the 101st ensured, nevertheless, that a record was made of the location of the refueling site and the type and amount of fuel dispersed.

---

38. Exec. Order No. 12,114, "Environmental Effects Abroad of Major Federal Actions", 44 Fed. Reg. 1,957 (1979).

JAs, in Iraq, were uniform in their belief that dispensing legal advice regarding environmental law in an operational context was exceptionally challenging, given the breadth and complexity of this body of law. As an example, the 101st SJA noted that the provision of advice concerning the single issue of the disposal of medical waste (e.g., needles) required a working knowledge of numerous — and extensive — documents, orders, and policy statements. Experience in the practice of this very specialized area of the law thus led to the conclusion that a single JA should receive extensive training in this discipline and be responsible for determining and promulgating the applicable environmental standards across an area of operations.

Contract OPLAW Issues

Contract Scoping

A particularly challenging contracting matter identified by JAs in Iraq was that of "contract scoping". The term, "contract scope," encompasses all work considered to be fairly and reasonably within the contemplation of the contractual parties at the time that a contract was concluded. Government procurement regulations permit Contracting Officers to effect unilateral changes to existing contracts, as long as such changes fall within the original scope of a contract. This provision is of obvious utility in a deployed environment, where evolving missions and conditions are very likely to impact contract requirements and performance. However, making a determination as to whether a change to a contract — or a Task Order placed against an existing contract — is within the scope of an original contract posed an exceptionally difficult task for reviewing JAs. Decisions of this nature have serious implications in terms of contract performance and, thus, operational effectiveness. While a Contracting Officer may order changes within the scope of an original contract by exercising the "changes clause" of this contract, changes that fall outside the scope of the original contract are deemed "cardinal changes". These latter types of changes require the formation of a new contract, often resulting in significant delay that adversely affects the operational mission. Scoping determinations were particularly demanding with respect to contracts involving interagency transfers, as the drafting and management of the Performance Work Statement (PWS) necessary to make an informed scoping determination normally occurred in the U.S.[39]

The general lack of contract oversight in Iraq, at least initially, also further exacerbated the difficulty of effecting scoping determinations. JAs were confronted with the fact that a single Contracting Officer's Representative (COR) might be expected, as an additional duty, to oversee a contract in execution in various locations all across Iraq, but report back to a Contracting Officer in the U.S. This situation made it difficult to obtain either timely or accurate information regarding a particular contract from a COR, resulting in JAs often having very little information upon which to make scoping determinations.

Given these facts, as long as contractors are relied upon to meet the deployed logistics requirements of the U.S. military, it would appear that scoping determinations will remain a frequent and challenging task. It has been proven, however, that these inherent difficulties

---

39. The Performance Work Statement (PWS) is a statement in a solicitation document that identifies the technical, functional, and performance characteristics of the agency's needs, not the specific methods for meeting those needs. U. S. OFFICE OF MANAGEMENT & BUDGET, CIRCULAR A-76, PERFORMANCE OF COMMERCIAL ACTIVITIES D-7 (29 May 2003) (C1, 31 Oct.2006). It is an essential element of government contract formation, as it serves as the baseline for measuring progress and subsequent contract changes during contract performance.

can be mitigated by JAs taking a number of preventative steps, including communicating with Contracting and Ordering Officers in order to identify and obtain copies of contracts used for repeated orders and by directly establishing contact with CORs at the earliest opportunity.

Legal Assistance OPLAW Issues

Family Law Matters—Separation and Divorce

Issues arising from separation and divorce were among those legal assistance matters most frequently encountered by JAs in Iraq. Many personnel sought advice regarding both the process involved and their rights and obligations in such situations. Some sought information regarding whether it was possible to obtain a divorce while deployed, while others requested that JAs review settlement agreements and divorce decrees, prior to returning these documents for filing with a court in the U.S.

JAs found that Separation Agreement Worksheets could often be used to determine whether a husband and wife were seriously committed to obtaining a separation or divorce while one of the two was deployed. This Worksheet also provided both the JA and the servicemember with an indication of whether it would be possible for the couple to reach agreement on the more important issues involved, to include property and asset/debt distribution, child custody—and whether the couple might be good candidates for an uncontested divorce. The latter consideration proved to be a significant one, as an agreement to such a proceeding is the only means of obtaining a divorce when one party concerned is deployed. JAs also noted that, in the case of such a divorce, it was important to be fully familiar with the applicable state law, as it varies significantly—to include the length of the required waiting periods (e.g., New York has a one-year waiting period).

Selected Case Studies: A Reflection of the Challenging Nature of OPLAW

The above sampling of the wide array of OPLAW issues dealt with by JAs across the operational spectrum serves to demonstrate the manner in which such matters arise in the context of all military law disciplines. Inherent in these case studies, then, is a validation of the need for, and the decision to define, establish, and implement the military law discipline of OPLAW. Though consistently challenging in nature, the practice of OPLAW represents the operational essence of the deployed JA. Its creation and evolution have resulted in the military attorney becoming an integral and essential component of every operational commander's staff.

Questions for Discussion

1. It is now a matter of public record that, due to confusion surrounding the status of Al Qaeda and Taliban personnel seized during OEF, certain of these individuals suffered abuse at the hands of U.S. agents. What was the basis for such confusion? Given the purported inapplicability of the GPW to these individuals, should they, nevertheless, have been afforded protections under any other provisions of international law?

2. Under the Foreign Assistance Act (FAA), Congress has determined that development and security assistance activities undertaken abroad are Department of State, vice DOD

responsibilities. In the OEF context, what are the three principal areas in which considerations arose concerning the proper role to be played by DOD within the FAA fiscal framework?

3. In providing advice as to whether to provide military weapons to contractor personnel (CCP) in Iraq, for the purpose of self-defense, what were some of the questions associated with this matter that JAs had to address?

4. "Contract scoping" proved to be a particularly challenging responsibility for JAs during OIF. Why?

OPLAW Training and Support Provided to Judge Advocates

The ability of JAs to provide timely and accurate OPLAW advice on an exceptionally broad and diverse range of legal issues arising in an operational environment, as evidenced above, is linked directly to the effectiveness of the OPLAW training and support made available to these military lawyers. The following section will focus on this training and support.

OPLAW Training

The key to the effective practice of OPLAW is an extensive and continuously updated OPLAW education and training program. Each of the military services contributes to such a program.

Army

The Army provides its classroom training in OPLAW at The Judge Advocate General's Legal Center and School (TJAGLCS), located on the grounds of the University of Virginia, in Charlottesville, Virginia. This training consists of the following courses: (1) A ten-week Basic Course, provided three times a year, to all JAs entering the Army—in which over fifty hours of international and OPLAW instruction are afforded in the form of lectures, seminars, and practical exercises. The topics covered include the means and methods of warfare, the 1949 Geneva Conventions, ROE, legal bases for the use of force, U.S. practice regarding the 1977 Additional Protocols to the Geneva Conventions, Intelligence Law, Detention Operations, Cyber Operations, and Human Rights. A one-day, interactive experience, the "Gauntlet", is the capstone event of the Basic Course. It is designed to reinforce concepts learned in the classroom through the use of scenario-based vignettes derived from lessons learned by JAs' real-world deployment experiences. The students negotiate various field Gauntlet lanes in small groups of 15 to 20, confronting scenarios that deal with such diverse matters as claims, Rule of Law, hostile act and intent situations, ROE, the use of force, public affairs, investigations, treatment of the wounded and sick, and detention and interrogation operations. Once completed, students participate in an informal After Action Review with an Observer/Controller, a faculty member; (2) A ten-month Graduate Course leading to an LLM in Military Law, attended by experienced JAs from all of the military services, in which over seventy hours of international and OPLAW instruction are provided in the form of lectures and seminars. Plenary classes focus on the Hague Regulations and Geneva Conventions; National Security Law; ROE; Rules for the Use of Force; Means and Methods of Warfare; War Crimes; International

Human Rights Law; Comparative Law; Rule of Law; Intelligence Law; Interrogation Operations; Domestic Support Operations; Cyber Operations; and Sea, Air, and Space Law. In addition, thirteen electives are offered on such subjects as Information Operations and Cyber Operations; War Crimes; Law of Sea, Air and Space; Military Operations; Intelligence Law; Advanced Topics in the Law of Armed Conflict; Human Rights; National Security Law; Rule of Law; International Agreements; History of Modern Warfare; and Current Topics in the Law of Armed Conflict; (3) A two-week Operational Law of Armed Conflict Course, offered twice, annually; one-week courses in Intelligence Law and Domestic Operational Law; and a two-day Emergent Topics in International and Operational Law Course, offered in conjunction with the OPLAW of Armed Conflict Course.[40]

In terms of ensuring that classroom OPLAW instruction is effectively utilized, in a real-world training environment, the Army JAGC has assigned JA Observer Controller/Trainers (OC/T) to each of the Army's four Combat Training Centers (CTCs).[41] These JAs are responsible for ensuring that realistic OPLAW issues are embedded in each training exercise conducted by an Army component at a CTC. Additionally, these OC/T monitor and mentor the individual JAs who rotate through these CTCs with the units to which they are assigned—ensuring that the latter are able to identify and resolve the many OPLAW matters that arise during the course of these exercises.

Air Force

The Air Force provides OPLAW training, primarily, at its Judge Advocate General's School, located on Maxwell Air Force Base, Montgomery, Alabama. This training consists of the following courses: (1) A nine-week Judge Advocate Staff Officer Course, provided three times a year, which includes thirty hours of lectures, seminars, and practical exercises dealing with International and Operations Law; (2) An Operations Law Course/Exercise—six days of classroom instruction, followed by a three-day field exercise designed to prepare JAs and paralegals to function as a team during overseas deployments—and, specifically, to support the Expeditionary Aerospace Force during joint and coalition operations. Topics include Air and Space Law, the Joint Staff and Unified Commands, Peace Operations, the Law of Armed Conflict, ROE, Intelligence Law, the Legal Aspects of Coalition Operations, Contingency Contracting, and Operational Fiscal Law; (3) A Deployed Fiscal Law and Contingency Contracting Course—three days of lectures and seminars for contracting/finance JA teams, designed to enable personnel from the legal, contracting, and finance career fields to recognize fiscal and contracting issues that arise during the deployment of U.S. armed forces overseas; (4) A one-week Cyber Law Course; and (5) A JA Functional Area Training—Joint Aerospace Command and Control Course—two days of training during a fifteen-day course, conducted five times a year, for JAs and paralegals in order to acquaint them with JA involvement in Air Operations Center activities- focusing on planning, targeting, ROE, and the impact of the Law of Armed Conflict on operations. Additionally, the major Air Force commands in Europe and the

---

40. International and Operational Law Department, The Judge Advocate General's Legal Center and School, U.S. Army, Charlottesville, Virginia.

41. The three static maneuver CTCs are: (1) the Joint Multinational Readiness Center (JMRC) in Hohenfels, Germany, (2) the Joint Readiness Training Center (JRTC) at Fort Polk, Louisiana, and (3) the National Training Center (NTC) at Fort Irwin, California. A mobile CTC, the Mission Command Training Program (MCTP), at Fort Leavenworth, Kansas, sends personnel to units to train brigade-level and more senior commanders and staffs. The realistic training and the OC/T mentoring at the CTCs supplements the formal training provided JAs at TJAGLCS. The resources provided by the OC/Ts augment the assets available through the Center for Law and Military Operations (CLAMO, an integral part of TJAGLCS).

Pacific provide OPLAW training, with theater-specific considerations, to JAs and paralegals within their commands.[42]

Navy

Basic OPLAW training, to include Law of War, Law of the Sea, and ROE, is provided to JAs entering the Navy during a 10-week Basic Lawyer Course. More extensive, maritime-oriented OPLAW training, is made available to military attorneys from all of the services through a two-week Law of Military Operations (LOMO) course. Additional courses include: a three-day course on Advanced Operational Law, a two-day course on Advanced Cyber Operational Law, and a three-day course on Information Operations Law. Navy OPLAW training occurs at the Naval Justice School, located on the Newport Naval Base, Newport, Rhode Island. Additionally, the Naval Justice School JAG Detachments in Norfolk, Virginia and San Diego, California conduct a one-week Law of Naval Operations Course at those locations, annually.[43]

Marine Corps

Marine JAs entering the Marine Corps receive six months of training in combat infantry skills and small unit leadership. These attorneys are then provided forty hours of OPLAW training during their attendance of the ten-week Basic Lawyers Course at the Naval Justice School. Many Marine JAs assigned to OPLAW positions will also attend OPLAW-oriented courses offered by both TJAGLCS and the Naval Justice School.[44]

OPLAW Support

While each of the services affords OPLAW support to its deployed JAs at various levels of command, the Army has institutionalized the OPLAW support provided to deployed Army, Marine, and Navy JAs through its establishment of the Center for Law and Military Operations (CLAMO). The Center, a directorate of The Judge Advocate General's Legal Center, is a joint, interagency, multinational entity comprised of attorneys from the Army, Marine Corps, Navy, and Coast Guard, as well as legal representatives for the United Kingdom and Germany. It is a resource organization for operational lawyers, with its mission being that of examining legal issues that arise during all phases of military operations and devising training and resource strategies for addressing these issues.

CLAMO fulfills this mission in five ways. First, it serves as the central repository for Army, Marine, and Navy information, memoranda, after-action reports, and lessons learned pertaining to the legal support provided military operations conducted across the operational spectrum, both foreign and domestic. Second, it supports Army, Marine, and Navy JAs by analyzing all data and information, developing lessons learned across all OPLAW military law disciplines, and disseminating these lessons and other operational information to the Army, Marine Corps, Navy, and joint legal communities through comprehensive publications, instruction, training, and databases- accessible, on a real-time basis, to operational forces worldwide. Third, it supports Army, Marine, and Navy JAs

---

42. International and Operations Law Division, Office of The Judge Advocate General, Headquarters, United States Air Force, Washington, DC.

43. International and Operational Law Division, Office of The Judge Advocate General, Headquarters, United States Navy, Washington, DC.

44. International and Operational Law Branch, Judge Advocate Division, Headquarters, United States Marine Corps, Washington, DC.

in the field by responding to requests for assistance, by engaging in a continuous exchange of information with JA OC/Ts at the CTCs, and by creating OPLAW training guides. Fourth, it integrates lessons learned from operations and the CTCs into emerging doctrine and into the curricula of all relevant courses, workshops, orientations, and seminars conducted at TJAGLCS. Finally, CLAMO, in conjunction with other components of TJAGLCS, sponsors conferences and symposia on topical OPLAW subjects.

CLAMO's information gathering and dissemination capability enables military attorneys to adapt quickly to emerging legal challenges and serves as a ready source for the development and implementation of timely OPLAW training. It also oversees the Army JAs assigned to the Army's CTCs.

The Center's OPLAW publications are reflected in the Bibliography that appears at the end of this chapter. In addition to these publications, CLAMO also creates and maintains both classified and unclassified databases that address a broad range of OPLAW matters.[45]

Conclusion

Since its formal inception in 1986, OPLAW has become the essence of the military legal practice. JAs now use every source of law—international, foreign, and domestic—in the operational context. The effective practice of OPLAW enables JAs to serve as "force multipliers" to commanders and their staffs. Schooled in OPLAW, provided with up-to-date OPLAW resources, and afforded support and assistance—often on a real-time basis—deployed JAs are now capable of providing advice on a wide array of legal matters, in even the most austere environments. In doing so, they function as integral and essential components of today's contingency-oriented military.

Selected Bibliography

Borch, Frederic L., Judge Advocates in Combat: Army Lawyers in Military Operations from Vietnam to Haiti (2001).

Bridge, Robert L., *Operations Law: An Overview*, 37 A.F. L. Rev. 1 (1994).

Cohen, Amichai, *Legal Operational Advice in the Israeli Defense Forces: The International Law Department and the Changing Nature of International Humanitarian Law*, 26 Conn J. Int'l L. 367 (2011).

Corn, Geoffrey S., Victor Hansen, Richard B. Jackson, Chris Jenks, Eric T. Jensen, James A. Schoettler, Jr., The Law of Armed Conflict: An Operational Perspective (2012).

DiMeglio, Richard P., *Training Army Judge Advocates To Advise Commanders As Operational Law Attorneys*, 54 B.C. L. Rev. 3 (2013).

Gent, Terrie M., *Let's Demystify Operations Law*, JAG Warrior, Dec. 1998, at 5.

Govern, Kevin H., CLAMO Report: *Paving the Road to the Warfighter: Preparing to Provide Legal Support on the Battlefield*, Army Law, March 2002, at 58.

---

45. The Center for Law and Military Operations (CLAMO): http://www.jagcnet.army.mil/CLAMO.

Graham, David E., *Operational Law—A Concept Comes of Age*, Army Law, July 1987, at 9.

———, *My Lai and Beyond: The Evolution of Operational Law*, *in* The Real Lessons of the Vietnam War: Reflections Twenty-Five Years After the Fall of Saigon (John Norton Moore & Robert F. Turner eds., 2002), 367–70.

Hammill, Barry, *Operations Law from the Viewpoint of a CINC's Lawyer*, JAG Warrior, Dec. 1998, at 1.

Lohr, Michael F., *Legal Support in War: The Role of Military Lawyers*, 4 Chi. J. Int' L. 465 (2003).

Newton, Michael A., *Modern Military Necessity: The Role & Relevance of Military Lawyers*, 12 Roger Williams U. L. Rev. 877 (2007).

Pitzul, Jerry S.T., *Operational Law and the Legal Professional: A Canadian Perspective*, 51 A.F. L. Rev. 311 (2001).

Rives, Jack L., *Expeditionary Law: Remarks on How to Succeed in the Deployed Environment*, 51 A.F. L. Rev. 345 (2001).

Ruhlmann III, Raymond E. *Legal Services Support to Operational Commanders*, Marine Corps Gazette (Nov. 2006), at 79.

Silliman, Scott L., *JAG Goes to War: The Desert Shield Deployment*, 37 A.F. L. Rev. 85 (1994).

Turner, Lisa L., *Developing Client-Ready Practitioners: Learning How to Practice National Security Law at Military Law Schools*, 7 J. Nat'l Security L. & Pol'y 1 (2014).

U.S. Air Force Judge Advocate General's School, Air Force Operations and the Law—A Guide for Air, Space, and Cyber Forces (2009).

U.S. Army, Center for Law and Military Operations (CLAMO), CLAMO *Note: Time to Train Soldier-Lawyers*, Army Law (June 2000), at 40.

———, Deployed Marine Air-Ground Task Force (MAGTF) Judge Advocate Handbook (2013).

———, Domestic Operational Law (DOPLAW) Handbook for Judge Advocates (2013).

———, Law and Military Operations in the Balkans: 1995–1998, Lessons Learned for Judge Advocates (1998).

———, Law and Military Operations in Central America: Hurricane Mitch Relief Efforts, 1998–1999: Lessons Learned for Judge Advocates (2001).

———, Law and Military Operations in Haiti, 1994–1995: Lessons Learned for Judge Advocates (1995).

———, Law and Military Operations in Kosovo, 1999–2001: Lessons Learned for Judge Advocates (2001).

———, Forged in the Fire: Legal Lessons Learned During Military Operations: 1994–2006 (2006).

———, Forged in the Fire: Legal Lessons Learned During Military Operations: 1994–2008 (2008).

———, Tip of the Spear; 2010 Supplement to Forged in the Fire: Legal Lessons Learned During Military Operations: 1994–2008 (2010).

———, Office of the Staff Judge Advocate Planning for Closing a Theater of Operations (2012).

———,Rule of Law Handbook-A Practitioner's Guide (2014).

U.S. Army, The Judge Advocate General's Legal Center and School (TJAGLCS), Operational Law Handbook (2014) (and previous editions).

U.S. Department of the Army, Field Manual 1-04, Legal Support to the Operational Army (Mar. 2013).

U.S. Navy, NWP 1-14M/MCWP 5-2.1/COMDTPUB P5800.7, The Commander's Handbook on the Law of Naval Operations (2007).

Warren, Marc L., *Operational Law—A Concept Matures*, 152 Mil. L. Rev. 33 (1996).

Zinni, Anthony C., *The SJA in Future Operations*, Marine Corps Gazette (Feb. 1996), at 15.

Chapter 8

War Crimes Tribunals

Michael P. Scharf

In this chapter:
The Nuremberg Tribunal
The Yugoslavia War Crimes Tribunal
The Debate over the Permanent International Criminal Court
Selected Bibliography

This chapter augments Chapter 6, "The Law of Armed Conflict and Neutrality," by charting the development of international tribunals for the prosecution of war criminals. It begins with a history of the creation of the Nuremberg Tribunal after World War II and an examination of the legacy of Nuremberg. It then explores the creation of the International Criminal Tribunal for the Former Yugoslavia, with emphasis placed on the question of the Security Council's authority to create such an institution. It then examines the establishment of the *ad hoc* Rwanda Tribunal, Lebanon Tribunal, Special Court for Sierra Leone, and Cambodia Tribunal. Finally, it scrutinizes the modern debate over the permanent International Criminal Court.

The Nuremberg Tribunal

Establishment of the Nuremberg Tribunal

VIRGINIA MORRIS & MICHAEL P. SCHARF, 1 THE INTERNATIONAL CRIMINAL TRIBUNAL FOR RWANDA

2–7 (1998)

The possibility of establishing an international criminal court with jurisdiction over war crimes and crimes against humanity was seriously considered for the first time in relation to the atrocities committed during the First World War. At the end of the war, the Allied Powers established the Commission on the Responsibility of the Authors of the War and on Enforcement of Penalties to investigate and recommend action on war crimes committed by the personnel of the defeated Central Powers. The Commission documented thirty categories of offenses against the laws and customs of war ranging from the deliberate bombardment of undefended places and attacks against hospital ships by the Germans to the massacre of over a million Armenians by Turkish authorities and by the Turkish populace supported by the public policy of the State.

After the war, the Treaty of Sevres and the Treaty of Versailles, respectively, provided for the prosecution of Turkish and German war criminals (including Kaiser Wilhelm II) before international tribunals. However, no international tribunals were ever established for this purpose. Instead, Kaiser Wilhelm was given sanctuary in the Netherlands and the Allied Powers consented to the trial of accused Germans before the German Supreme Court sitting at Leipzig. Of the 896 Germans accused of war crimes by the Allied Powers, only twelve were tried and of those only six were convicted (and given token sentences). The Turks fared even better by receiving amnesty for their crimes in the Treaty of Lausanne, which replaced the Treaty of Sevres.

. . . .

Despite the unsatisfactory experience with the attempt to conduct international war crimes trials after the First World War, the Allies were determined to conduct such trials at the end of the Second World War. In the midst of this worldwide conflagration, the Allies took a number of decisive measures in order to ensure that the persons who were responsible for the outbreak of the war and the atrocities that followed would be brought to justice. In 1943, the Allies set up the United Nations War Crimes Commission to collect evidence with a view to conducting trials at the end of the war. Furthermore, the Allies solemnly declared and gave full warning of their unequivocal intention to bring to justice the German political and military leaders who were responsible for the atrocities committed during the war. In 1945, the victorious Allied Governments of the United States, France, the United Kingdom and the Soviet Union concluded the London Agreement providing for the establishment of the International Military Tribunal at Nuremberg (Nuremberg Tribunal) to try the most notorious of the Germans accused of crimes against peace, war crimes and crimes against humanity. The Charter of the International Military Tribunal (Nuremberg Charter) was annexed to the London Agreement.

The Nuremberg Charter was the constitutive instrument of the Nuremberg Tribunal. Thus, the Nuremberg Charter established the structure and governed the functions of the Nuremberg Tribunal. Each State Party to the Nuremberg Charter was to appoint one of the four judges and one of their alternates. The members of the Nuremberg Tribunal were to select from among themselves a President for the first trial, with the presidency rotating among the members in successive trials. A conviction and a sentence could be imposed only by an affirmative vote of at least three members of the Nuremberg Tribunal. All other questions would be decided by majority vote, with the President having the decisive vote in the event of a tie. Each State Party was also to appoint one of the four Chief Prosecutors. The Chief Prosecutors were to act as a committee in designating the major war criminals to be tried by the Nuremberg Tribunal and in preparing the indictments. The Chief Prosecutors were also responsible for drafting the rules of procedure for the Nuremberg Tribunal, which were subject to the approval of the judges. The Nuremberg Tribunal was not bound by technical rules of evidence and was at liberty to admit any evidence which it deemed to have probative value. Moreover, the Nuremberg Tribunal was given the power to compel the presence of witnesses, to interrogate defendants, to compel the production of documents and other evidence, to administer oaths, and to appoint officers to take evidence on commission. The Nuremberg Tribunal was also authorized, upon conviction of a defendant, to impose any punishment it considered just, including the death penalty. The Nuremberg Tribunal judgments were not subject to review.

As regards jurisdiction and applicable law, the Nuremberg Charter determined the subject matter jurisdiction of the Nuremberg Tribunal and provided the definitions of the three categories of crimes with which the defendants were charged:

Crimes Against Peace: namely, planning, preparation, initiation or waging of a war of aggression, or a war in violation of international treaties, agreements or assurances, or participation in a Common Plan or Conspiracy for the accomplishment of any of the foregoing;

War Crimes: namely, violations of the laws or customs of war. Such violations shall include, but not be limited to, murder, ill-treatment or deportation to slave-labor or for any other purpose of civilian population of or in occupied territory, murder or ill-treatment of prisoners of war or persons on the seas, killing of hostages, plunder of public or private property, wanton destruction of cities, towns or villages, or devastation not justified by necessity;

Crimes Against Humanity: namely, murder, extermination, enslavement, deportation, and other inhumane acts committed against any civilian population, before or during the war, or persecutions on political, racial, or religious grounds, in execution of or in connection with any crime within the jurisdiction of the Tribunal, whether or not in violation of domestic law of the country where perpetrated.

. . . .

As regards due process, the Nuremberg Charter guaranteed certain fundamental rights of the accused in order to ensure that every accused received a fair trial, namely: (1) the right to be furnished with the indictment in a language which the accused understands at a reasonable time before trial; (2) the right to give any explanation relevant to the charges against the accused; (3) the right to translation of proceedings before the Nuremberg Tribunal in a language which the accused understands; (4) the right to have the assistance of counsel; and (5) the right to present evidence and to cross-examine any witness called by the prosecution. At the same time, the Nuremberg Charter provided for trials *in absentia*, authorized the Nuremberg Tribunal to interrogate the accused, limited the defenses available to the accused by excluding the act of State defense and the defense of superior orders; and precluded any challenges to the jurisdiction or the composition of the Nuremberg Tribunal.

In terms of procedure, the Nuremberg Charter and Rules of Procedure provided an innovative blend and balance of various elements of the Continental European inquisitorial system and the Anglo-American adversarial system in order to create a tailor-made international criminal procedure which would be generally acceptable to the States Parties representing both systems.... The Nuremberg Tribunal was governed by simplified evidentiary rules which constituted another unique feature of the Nuremberg Charter. The technical rules of evidence developed under the common law system of jury trials to prevent the jury from being influenced by improper evidence were considered to be unnecessary for trials conducted in the absence of a jury. Accordingly, the Nuremberg Charter provided that the Nuremberg Tribunal was not bound by technical rules of evidence and could admit any evidence which it deemed to have probative value. Consequently, the Nuremberg Tribunal allowed the prosecutors to introduce *ex parte* affidavits against the accused over the objections of their attorneys.

The Rationale for Creating the Nuremberg Tribunal

Michael P. Scharf & William A. Schabas, Slobodan Milosevic on Trial: A Companion

40–41 (2002)

The events that prompted the formation of the Nuremberg Tribunal in 1945 are probably more familiar to most than those which led to the creation of the Yugoslavia War Crimes Tribunal a half century later. Between 1933 and 1940, the Nazi regime established concentration camps where Jews, Communists and opponents of the regime were incarcerated without trial; it progressively prohibited Jews from engaging in employment and participating in various areas of public life, stripped them of citizenship, and made marriage or sexual intimacy between Jews and German citizens a criminal offense; it forcibly annexed Austria and Czechoslovakia; invaded and occupied Poland, Denmark, Norway, Luxembourg, Holland, Belgium, and France; and then it set in motion "the final solution to the Jewish problem" by establishing death camps such as Auschwitz and Treblinka, where six million Jews were exterminated.

. . . .

As Allied forces pressed into Germany and an end to the fighting in Europe came into sight, the Allied powers faced the challenge of deciding what to do with the surviving Nazi leaders who were responsible for these atrocities. Holding an international trial, however, was not their first preference. The British Government opposed trying the Nazi leaders on the ground that their "guilt was so black" that it was "beyond the scope of judicial process." British Prime Minister Winston Churchill, therefore, proposed the summary execution of the Nazi leaders. Soviet leader Joseph Stalin, however, urged that Nazi leaders be tried, much as he had done with dissidents in his own country during the purges of the 1930s. United States President Franklin D. Roosevelt initially appeared willing to go along with Churchill's proposal. But upon Roosevelt's death in April 1945, President Harry Truman made it clear that he opposed summary execution. Instead, at the urging of U.S. Secretary of War, Henry Stimson, Truman pushed for the establishment of an international tribunal to try the Nazi leaders.

The arguments for a judicial approach were compelling, and soon won the day. First, judicial proceedings would avert future hostilities which would likely result from the execution, absent a trial, of German leaders. Legal proceedings, moreover, would bring German atrocities to the attention of all the world, thereby legitimizing Allied conduct during and after the war. They would individualize guilt by identifying specific perpetrators instead of leaving Germany with a sense of collective guilt. Finally, such a trial would permit the Allied powers, and the world, to exact a penalty from the Nazi leadership rather than from Germany's civilian population.

The Legacy of the Nuremberg Tribunal

Virginia Morris & Michael P. Scharf, 1 The International Criminal Tribunal for Rwanda

7–17 (1998)

After a trial that lasted 284 days, the Nuremberg Tribunal convicted nineteen of the twenty-two German officials and sentenced twelve of the major war criminals to death by hanging. In the course of the lengthy trial, the Nuremberg Tribunal documented the Nazi atrocities "with such authenticity and in such detail that there can be no responsible denial of these crimes in the future and no tradition of martyrdom of the Nazi leaders can arise among informed people." The judgment of the Nuremberg Tribunal also paved the way for the trial of over a thousand other German political and military officers, businessmen, doctors, and jurists under Control Council Law No. 10 by military tribunals in occupied zones in Germany and in the liberated or Allied Nations. Moreover, the Charter and the Judgment of the Nuremberg Tribunal established the fundamental principles of individual responsibility for crimes under international law which provide the cornerstones of the legal foundation for all subsequent international criminal proceedings.

A year after the Nuremberg trial, the major Japanese war criminals were tried before the International Military Tribunal for the Far East (Tokyo Tribunal). The Charter of the International Military Tribunal for the Far East (Tokyo Charter) was based largely on the Nuremberg Charter. Nonetheless, the Charter and the Judgment of the Tokyo Tribunal are generally considered to be less authoritative than those of the Nuremberg Tribunal. Whereas the Nuremberg Charter was adopted as part of an international agreement after extensive multilateral negotiations, the Tokyo Charter was promulgated as an executive order by the Supreme Allied Commander for Japan following the war, General Douglas MacArthur, without the prior approval of the other Allied Powers. Furthermore, in contrast to the Nuremberg Tribunal whose judges and prosecutors were selected by four different countries, the prosecutor and the judges of the Tokyo Tribunal were personally selected by General MacArthur. In his dissenting opinion, the French judge of the Tokyo Tribunal, Henri Bernard, expressed the view that "so many principles of justice were violated during the trial that the Court's judgment certainly would be nullified on legal grounds in most civilized countries." Thus, the United Nations General Assembly expressly affirmed the principles of international law recognized in the Charter and the Judgment of the Nuremberg Tribunal and merely took note of the Charter and the Judgment of the Tokyo Tribunal.

Although the Nuremberg Tribunal has been hailed as one of the most important developments in international law in this century, it has also been subject to three major criticisms. While these criticisms are not entirely justified, they deserve consideration because they are also not entirely without some foundation. It is important to consider the shortcomings of the Nuremberg precedent in order to avoid them in the future. At the same time, it is important to judge the Nuremberg precedent—not by contemporary standards—but by the standards of its time.

First, the Nuremberg Tribunal has been criticized as a victor's tribunal before which only the vanquished were called to account for violations of international humanitarian law committed during the war. The victorious States created the Nuremberg Tribunal and appointed their nationals to serve as its judges. The ability of the judges to objectively perform their judicial functions was questioned due to their nationality and the various roles which they performed. In particular, two of the Nuremberg judges had earlier served on the committee of prosecutors that negotiated the Nuremberg Charter, selected the defendants for trial, and drafted the indictments against these defendants. In addition, during the Nuremberg trial the defense counsel argued that the judges were not qualified to pass judgment on the accused because the States which tried the Nuremberg defendants were guilty of many of the same crimes for which their representatives on the bench would judge their former adversaries.

The first criticism of the Nuremberg Tribunal as victor's justice is without any foundation in terms of the existing international law at the time and ignores the fact that the only other alternative that was seriously considered was far less desirable, namely, victor's vengeance. At the conclusion of the Second World War, the victorious parties to the armed conflict were fully competent as a matter of international law to try the members of the vanquished armed forces for violations of the laws and customs of war. The history of war has sadly demonstrated that vengeance often prevails on the battlefield during the war and impunity often prevails at the negotiating table after the war. It was an extraordinary triumph of justice and the rule of law that the major German war criminals were brought to trial before a court of law, rather than being summarily executed (as proposed by Winston Churchill and Joseph Stalin at the Yalta Conference in 1945) or being allowed to go unpunished (as after the First World War). As the Chief Prosecutor for the United States at Nuremberg, Supreme Court Justice Robert H. Jackson, observed in his opening remarks for the prosecution: "That four great nations, flushed with victory and stung with injury, stay the hands of vengeance and voluntarily submit their captive enemies to the judgment of the law, is one of the most significant tributes that Power has ever paid to Reason." Clearly, it would have been preferable to bring the major German war criminals before a permanent international criminal court which had been established previously by the international community and whose judiciary excluded nationals of the parties to the armed conflict. This ideal solution was quite simply not an option at the end of the Second World War. Yet few, if any, have suggested that the characteristics of the Nuremberg Tribunal as a "victor's tribunal" resulted in the conviction of a single innocent man. The documentary evidence alone was overwhelming.

The second criticism of the Nuremberg Tribunal was that the defendants were prosecuted and punished for crimes expressly defined as such for the first time in an instrument adopted by the victors at the conclusion of the war. In particular, the Nuremberg Tribunal was perceived by some as applying *ex post facto* law because it held individuals responsible for waging a war of aggression for the first time in history. Senator Robert Taft of Ohio was one of the first to voice this criticism in 1946. His views became part of the public legacy of Nuremberg when his speech was included by John F. Kennedy in his 1956 Pulitzer Prize winning book *Profiles in Courage*. To this day, articles appear in the popular press deriding Nuremberg as "a retroactive jurisprudence that would surely be unconstitutional in an American court."

This second criticism of the Nuremberg Tribunal minimizes the existing law at the time. The war crimes for which the defendants were tried and punished were violations of well established rules of law governing the conduct of war. The crimes against humanity for which the defendants were tried and punished were contrary to the national law of every civilized nation. No reasonable individual could possibly doubt the serious criminal nature of such crimes which were clearly *malum in se*. The crimes against peace for which the defendants were tried and punished were contrary to a panoply of legal instruments that prohibited aggressive warfare at the time. Nazi Germany initiated an aggressive war — not because it believed that this was permitted under international law — but because it believed that it could do so with impunity. The fact that a law has not been enforced in the past is no guarantee that it will not be enforced in the future. In this regard, there were specific warnings of individual responsibility for violations of international law at the end of the First World War and during the Second World War, as discussed previously. Furthermore, the defendants had the opportunity to raise this legal challenge which was considered and rejected by the Nuremberg Tribunal.

The third criticism of the Nuremberg Tribunal was that it functioned on the basis of limited procedural rules which did not provide sufficient protection of the rights of the accused. More specifically, the Nuremberg Charter is criticized for providing insufficient due process guarantees for the accused which were circumscribed by several rulings of the Nuremberg Tribunal in favor of the prosecution. In particular, the Nuremberg Tribunal allowed the prosecutors to introduce the *ex parte* affidavits of persons who were available to testify at trial as evidence against the defendants. As one of the Nuremberg prosecutors, Telford Taylor, wrote: "Total reliance on ... untested depositions by unseen witnesses is certainly not the most reliable road to factual accuracy.... Considering the number of deponents and the play of emotional factors, not only faulty observation but deliberate exaggeration must have warped many of the reports." The procedural rulings in favor of the prosecution were considered to be particularly troubling since the Nuremberg Charter did not provide for a right of appeal. It has further been argued that the defendants who were acquitted by the Nuremberg Tribunal did not fare much better than those who were convicted since the Nuremberg Charter failed to provide any guarantee of the *non bis in idem* principle (known in the United States as the prohibition of double jeopardy). Consequently, the defendants Schacht, von Papen and Fritzsche were acquitted by the Nuremberg Tribunal only to be subsequently tried and convicted by German national courts for similar crimes.

The third criticism of the limited procedural guarantees provided by the Nuremberg Charter ignores the fact that this was the first attempt to establish an international standard of due process and fair trial. Notwithstanding the absence of any internationally recognized standard of fair trial, the Nuremberg Charter endeavored to guarantee the minimum rights of the accused which were considered to be essential for a fair trial based on general principles of procedural fairness and due process recognized in various national criminal justice systems at the time. It is generally recognized that the defendants who were tried by the Nuremberg Tribunal were entitled to the essential procedural guarantees required for a fair trial even if there were some procedural imperfections.

The Nuremberg Tribunal was unquestionably a significant achievement for its time notwithstanding its shortcomings. Telford Taylor recognized that the Nuremberg Tribunal was not free from what he referred to as its "political warts." Even Justice Jackson acknowledged at the conclusion of the Nuremberg trial that "many mistakes have been made and many inadequacies must be confessed." But he went on to say that he was "consoled by the fact that in proceedings of this novelty, errors and missteps may also be instructive to the future." In this regard, the Nuremberg precedent provides an important benchmark for evaluating the subsequent international criminal tribunals.

Despite its shortcomings, the Nuremberg precedent has had an enduring impact on the development of international criminal law and jurisdiction. The principles of international law recognized in the Charter and the Judgment of the Nuremberg Tribunal constitute the fundamental principles of international criminal law today. The Nuremberg precedent also contributed to the further development of international criminal law after the Second World War. In 1948, the Nuremberg precedent with respect to persecution as a crime against humanity led to the adoption of the Convention on the Prevention and Punishment of the Crime of Genocide. In 1949, the Nuremberg precedent with respect to war crimes was codified and further developed in the Geneva Conventions for the protection of war victims. In terms of international criminal jurisdiction, the Nuremberg Tribunal demonstrated for the first time the feasibility of establishing an international criminal tribunal to replace the historical tradition of impunity and vengeance by a new world order based on justice and the rule of law. In doing so, the Nuremberg Tribunal laid the foundation for all subsequent international criminal jurisdictions.

Principles of the Nuremberg Charter and Judgment Formulated by the International Law Commission

and adopted by G.A. Res. 177(II)(a),
5 UN GAOR, 1st Sess., Supp. No. 12, at 11–14, para. 99, U.N. Doc. A/1316 (1946)

I. Any person who commits an act which constitutes a crime under international law is responsible therefor and liable to punishment.

II. The fact that internal law does not impose a penalty for an act which constitutes a crime under international law does not relieve the person who committed the act from responsibility under international law.

III. The fact that a person who committed an act which constitutes a crime under international law acted as Head of State or responsible Government official does not relieve him from responsibility under international law.

IV. The fact that a person acted pursuant to order of his Government or of a superior does not relieve him from responsibility under international law, provided a moral choice was in fact possible to him.

V. Any person charged with a crime under international law has the right to a fair trial on the facts and law.

VI. The crimes hereinafter set out are punishable as crimes under international law: (a) Crimes against peace, (b) War crimes, (c) Crimes against humanity....

VII. Complicity in the commission of a crime against peace, a war crime, or a crime against humanity as set forth in Principle VI is a crime under international law.

Did the Nuremberg Tribunal Exercise Universal Jurisdiction?

It is often said that the most important legacy of Nuremberg is that it extended to war crimes the concept of universal jurisdiction, which had previously been applied only to the crime of piracy. But some commentators have argued that the Nuremberg and Tokyo Tribunals should not be viewed as having been based on universal jurisdiction. Professor Madeline Morris of Duke University School of Law, for example, has written: "Both the Nuremberg and Tokyo Tribunals are more properly said to have exercised jurisdiction by virtue of the consent of the state of nationality of the defendants."[1]

Yet, in none of the judgments of the World War II international war crimes trials (the Nuremberg Tribunal and the subsequent trials conducted under the authority of Control Council Law No. 10) do the judicial opinions cite the consent of Germany as the basis for the Tribunal's jurisdiction. The absence of any reference to Germany's consent was explained by Professor Henry King, who had served as one of the junior prosecutors at Nuremberg, in the following terms: "It should be noted that the German armies surrendered unconditionally to the Allies on May 8, 1945. There was no sovereign German government which they dealt in the surrender arrangements."[2] Writing in 1945, Professor Hans Kelsen pointed out that the occupying Powers never sought to conclude a peace treaty with

---

1. Madeline Morris, *High Crimes and Misconceptions: The ICC and Non-Party States*, 64 LAW & CONTEMP. PROBS. 13 (2001).

2. Henry T. King, Jr. *The Limitations of Sovereignty from Nuremberg to Sarajevo*, 20 CAN.-U.S. L.J. 167, 168 (1994).

Germany (which could have included a provision consenting to trial of German war criminals), because at the end of the war no such government existed "since the state of peace has been de facto achieved by Germany's disappearance as a sovereign state."[3]

In this way, the legal foundation of the Nuremberg Tribunal is to be contrasted with that of the Tokyo Tribunal, which was established with the consent of the Japanese Government which continued to exist after the war. Thus, John Pritchard, the foremost expert on the Tokyo Tribunal, writes: "The legitimacy of the Tokyo Trial, unlike its Nuremberg counterpart, depended not only upon the number and variety of states that took part in the Trial but more crucially upon the express consent of the Japanese state to submit itself to the jurisdiction of such a court, relinquishing or at least sharing a degree or two of sovereignty in the process."[4]

Egon Schwelb, *Crimes Against Humanity*
23 Brit. Y.B. Int'l L. 178, 208–09 (1946)

[In his seminal article on crimes against humanity and the Nuremberg Tribunal, Professor Egon Schwelb listed the following features which evince that the Nuremberg Tribunal was not a mere occupation court applying national law, but rather an international judicial body applying universal jurisdiction over the Axis country war criminals:]

(a) the name given to the court—"The International Military Tribunal";

(b) the reference in the Preamble to the fact that the four Signatories are "acting in the interests of all the United Nations";

(c) the provision in Article 5 of the Agreement giving any Government of the United Nations the right to adhere to the Agreement … ;

(d) the provision of Article 6 of the Charter, according to which the jurisdiction of the Tribunal is not restricted to German major war criminals, but, in theory at least, comprises the right to try and punish the major war criminals of all other European Axis countries; [and]

(e) the provision of Article 10 of the Charter providing for the binding character, in proceedings before courts of the signatory States, of a declaration by the Tribunal that a group or organization is criminal.

_____

This interpretation is bolstered by the following passages from the Judgment of the Nuremberg Tribunal.

Judgment of the International Military Tribunal for the Trial of German Major War Criminals
38–42 (1945)

The Signatory Powers created this Tribunal, defined the law it was to administer, and made regulations for the proper conduct of the trial. In doing so, they have done together

_____

3. Hans Kelsen, *The Legal Status of Germany According to the Declaration of Berlin*, 39 Am. J. Int'l L. 518, 524 (1945).

4. R. John Pritchard, *The International Military Tribunal for the Far East and its Contemporary Resonances: A General Preface to the Collection*, in The Tokyo Major War Crimes Trial, at xxxi (R. John Pritchard ed., 1998).

what any one of them might have done singly; for it is not to be doubted that any nation has the right thus to set up special courts to administer law.

    ....

    ... [I]ndividuals can be punished for violations of international law. Crimes against international law are committed by men, not by abstract entities, and only by punishing individuals who commit such crimes can the provisions of international law be enforced....

    ....

    ... [T]he very essence of the Charter is that individuals have international duties which transcend the national obligations of obedience imposed by the individual state.

––––––––––––

While the Nuremberg Judgment had only the few implied references to universal jurisdiction that are quoted above, the jurisprudence of several of the subsequent war crimes trials based on the Nuremberg Charter and conducted under the international authority of Control Council Law No. 10 (CCL10) are more explicit. A prominent example was *In re List*, which involved the prosecution of German officers who had commanded the execution of hundreds of thousands of civilians in Greece, Yugoslavia, and Albania. In describing the basis of its jurisdiction to punish such offenses, the U.S. CCL10 Tribunal in Nuremberg indicated that the defendants had committed "international crimes" that were "universally recognized" under existing customary and treaty law. The Tribunal explained that "[a]n international crime is ... an act universally recognized as criminal, which is considered a grave matter of international concern and for some valid reason cannot be left within the exclusive jurisdiction of the State that would have control over it under ordinary circumstances." The Tribunal concluded that a State that captures the perpetrator of such crimes either may "surrender the alleged criminal to the State where the offense was committed, or ... retain the alleged criminal for trial under its own legal processes."

Other decisions rendered by the CCL10 Tribunals, which similarly rely on the universality principle, include the *Hadamar Trial* of 1945, the *Zyklon B Case* of 1946, and the *Einsatzgruppen Case* of 1948. Based on these precedents, the U.S. Sixth Circuit Court of Appeals noted in *Demjanjuk v. Petrovsky*[5] that "it is generally agreed that the establishment of these [World War II] tribunals and their proceedings were based on universal jurisdiction." Studies conducted by United Nations expert bodies have reached a similar conclusion:

The Charter and Judgment of the Nuremberg Tribunal: History and Analysis

80, UN Doc. A/CN.4/5, UN Sales No. 1949V.7 (1949)
(memorandum submitted by the Secretary General)

It is ... possible and perhaps ... probable, that the International Military Tribunal considered the crimes under the Charter to be, as international crimes, subject to the jurisdiction of every State. The case of piracy would then be the appropriate parallel. This interpretation seems to be supported by the fact that the Court affirmed that the signatory Powers in creating the Tribunal had made use of a right belonging to any nation.

––––––––––––

5. Demjanjuk v. Petrovsky, 776 F.2d 571, 582 (6th Circ. 1985).

Interim Report of the Independent Commission of Experts
Established Pursuant to Security Council Resolution 780 (1992)
at para. 73, UN Doc. S/25274 (1993)

States may choose to combine their jurisdictions under the universality principle and vest this combined jurisdiction in an international tribunal. The Nuremberg International Military Tribunal may be said to have derived its jurisdiction from such a combination of national jurisdiction of the States parties to the London Agreement setting up that Tribunal.

Questions for Discussion

1. The allies created the Nuremberg Tribunal to establish a historic record of atrocities, to establish individual responsibility of leaders as opposed to collective guilt of the masses, and to deter future war crimes. How well did the Nuremberg Tribunal meet those goals?

2. In what ways did the Nuremberg Tribunal contribute to the development of international law?

3. What were the criticisms of Nuremberg? Were they valid? Must an international criminal court not only be fair but also be seen as fair to accomplish its aims?

4. The United States has argued in the context of its opposition to the permanent international criminal court that an international tribunal is prohibited by international law from exercising jurisdiction without the consent of the state of nationality of the accused. In what ways does the Nuremberg precedent counter that argument? In 2012, the Special Court for Sierra Leone, an international tribunal set up by the United Nations, convicted the former President of Liberia, Charles Taylor, of aiding and abetting and planning war crimes in neighboring Sierra Leone. Does US support for the Charles Taylor trial undermine its argument about the legitimacy of the International Criminal Court's exercise of jurisdiction over the nationals of non party states who commit crimes on the territory of state parties?

The Yugoslavia War Crimes Tribunal

The Creation of the Yugoslavia Tribunal

Virginia Morris & Michael P. Scharf,
1 The International Criminal Tribunal for Rwanda
29–37 (1998)

While the General Assembly was debating the proposal to establish a permanent international criminal court, reports of Nazi-like atrocities occurring at Serbian internment camps in Bosnia prompted the Security Council to take a series of steps culminating in the establishment of an *ad hoc* international criminal tribunal for the former Yugoslavia. The Security Council adopted a number of important resolutions which laid the foundation for the eventual creation of the Yugoslavia Tribunal. In these resolutions, the Security Council expressed concern over the continuing violations of international humanitarian law in the former Yugoslavia, declared that these violations constituted a threat to international peace and security, affirmed that persons ordering or committing such violations were individually responsible therefor, and called upon States to submit substantiated information relating to these violations. On 6 October 1992, the Security Council established the Commission of Experts on the former Yugoslavia to investigate the reports of violations. The Commission concluded that serious war crimes and crimes against humanity had been committed in the former Yugoslavia. Furthermore, the Commission joined with other international bodies in recommending the creation of an *ad hoc* international tribunal to prosecute and punish the individuals who were responsible for the atrocities.

On 22 February 1993, the Security Council decided in principle to establish an international tribunal "for the prosecution of persons responsible for serious violations of international humanitarian law committed in the territory of the former Yugoslavia since 1991." In the same resolution, the Security Council requested the Secretary-General of the United Nations, Boutros Boutros-Ghali, to prepare a report "on all aspects of this matter, including specific proposals and where appropriate options for the effective and expeditious implementation of [this decision], taking into account suggestions put forward in this regard by Member States." The report of the Secretary-General was prepared on the basis of the existing rules of international law. It also took into account the views expressed by interested States and organizations on the various legal issues relating to the tribunal. The Secretary-General's report contained not only a discussion of these issues, but also a draft statute for the tribunal in response to the Security Council's request for specific proposals. The Nuremberg Charter, in particular, as well as the various proposals of States and some of the draft statutes for an international criminal court were considered in preparing the draft statute for the *ad hoc* tribunal for the former Yugoslavia. At the same time, the report clearly distinguished the Security Council's decision to establish a tribunal limited in scope and purpose to the prosecution of persons responsible for serious violations of international humanitarian law committed in the former Yugoslavia from the work of the General Assembly and the International Law Commission with respect to a permanent international criminal court of a more general character and jurisdiction.

Within three weeks of receiving the Secretary-General's report, the Security Council, acting under Chapter VII of the United Nations Charter, unanimously adopted the Statute of the Yugoslavia Tribunal, as recommended by the Secretary-General. The fact that the Security Council adopted the draft statute pursuant to Resolution 827 (1993) in a relatively short period of time was an indication of its general acceptance. While the members of the Security Council were not fully satisfied with the draft statute in every respect, there was a strong hesitancy to allow any modification of the draft statute which could have resulted in lengthy negotiations and undesirable political compromises. In an innovative approach to this dilemma, the United States persuaded France, the United Kingdom, and the Russian Federation to make similar statements interpreting certain statutory provisions during the adoption of Resolution 827. These statements addressed matters that were considered to be central to the mandate conferred on the Yugoslavia Tribunal, such as the application of Protocols I and II of the Geneva Conventions, the definition of crimes against humanity and the primacy of the Yugoslavia Tribunal over national courts.

　　. . . .

In terms of its judicial functions, the jurisdiction of the Yugoslavia Tribunal is limited to serious violations of international humanitarian law committed in the territory of the former Yugoslavia since 1 January 1991. Furthermore, the applicable law of the Yugoslavia Tribunal is limited to rules of international humanitarian law which constitute beyond any doubt customary international law. Consequently, the subject matter jurisdiction of the Yugoslavia Tribunal is limited to grave breaches of the 1949 Geneva Conventions, violations of the laws and customs of war, genocide, and crimes against humanity. In approving the Yugoslavia Tribunal Statute, several members of the Security Council emphasized that the Yugoslavia Tribunal was established for the purpose of implementing existing law rather than creating new law.

....

The first person to be tried by the Yugoslavia Tribunal was Dusko Tadic, a Bosnian Serb who was accused of raping and killing civilians in the Serbian Omarska internment camp and in several nearby towns. Dusko Tadic was initially apprehended as a suspected war criminal by the German authorities in Munich. After Tadic was transferred by Germany to The Hague, the defense counsel for Tadic filed several important preliminary motions challenging the legitimacy and the jurisdiction of the Yugoslavia Tribunal.

On October 2, 1995, the Appeals Chamber of the Yugoslavia rendered its decision on this issue, which is reproduced in relevant part below.

The Prosecutor v. Dusko Tadic

Case No. IT-94-1-AR72, Appeals Chamber,
Decision on the Defense Motion for Interlocutory Appeal on Jurisdiction,
Decision of 2 October 1995

1. The Appeals Chamber of the International Tribunal for the Prosecution of Persons Responsible for Serious Violations of International Humanitarian Law Committed in the Territory of Former Yugoslavia since 1991 (hereinafter "International Tribunal") is seized of an appeal lodged by the Defence against a judgment rendered by Trial Chamber II on 10 August 1995. By that judgment, Appellant's motion challenging the jurisdiction of the International Tribunal was denied.

2. Before the Trial Chamber, Appellant had launched a three-pronged attack:

   a) illegal foundation of the International Tribunal;

   b) wrongful primacy of the International Tribunal over national courts;

   c) lack of jurisdiction ratione materiae.

II. Unlawful Establishment of the International Tribunal

....

Meaning of Jurisdiction

....

12. In sum, if the International Tribunal were not validly constituted, it would lack the legitimate power to decide in time or space or over any person or subject-matter. The plea based on the invalidity of constitution of the International Tribunal goes to the very essence of jurisdiction as a power to exercise the judicial function within any ambit. It is more radical than, in the sense that it goes beyond and subsumes, all the other pleas concerning the scope of jurisdiction. This issue is a preliminary to and conditions all other aspects of jurisdiction.

....

18. This power, known as the principle of "*Kompetenz-Kompetenz*" in German or "*la competence de la competence*" in French, is part, and indeed a major part, of the incidental or inherent jurisdiction of any judicial or arbitral tribunal, consisting of its "jurisdiction

to determine its own jurisdiction". It is a necessary component in the exercise of the judicial function and does not need to be expressly provided for in the constitutive documents of those tribunals, although this is often done.... In international law, where there is no integrated judicial system and where every judicial or arbitral organ needs a specific constitutive instrument defining its jurisdiction, "the first obligation of the Court— as of any other judicial body—is to ascertain its own competence."

....

The Issue of Constitutionality

....

27. The Trial Chamber summarized the claims of the Appellant as follows:

> "It is said that, to be duly established by law, the International Tribunal should have been created either by treaty, the consensual act of nations, or by amendment of the Charter of the United Nations, not by resolution of the Security Council. Called in aid of this general proposition are a number of considerations: that before the creation of the International Tribunal in 1993 it was never envisaged that such an *ad hoc* criminal tribunal might be set up; that the General Assembly, whose participation would at least have guaranteed full representation of the international community, was not involved in its creation; that it was never intended by the Charter that the Security Council should, under Chapter VII, establish a judicial body, let alone a criminal tribunal; that the Security Council had been inconsistent in creating this Tribunal while not taking a similar step in the case of other areas of conflict in which violations of international humanitarian law may have occurred; that the establishment of the International Tribunal had neither promoted, nor was capable of promoting, international peace, as the current situation in the former Yugoslavia demonstrates; that the Security Council could not, in any event, create criminal liability on the part of individuals and that this is what its creation of the International Tribunal did; that there existed and exists no such international emergency as would justify the action of the Security Council; that no political organ such as the Security Council is capable of establishing an independent and impartial tribunal; that there is an inherent defect in the creation, after the event, of *ad hoc* tribunals to try particular types of offences and, finally, that to give the International Tribunal primacy over national courts is, in any event and in itself, inherently wrong." (Decision at Trial, at para. 2.)

These arguments raise a series of constitutional issues which all turn on the limits of the power of the Security Council under Chapter VII of the Charter of the United Nations and determining what action or measures can be taken under this Chapter, particularly the establishment of an international criminal tribunal. Put in the interrogative, they can be formulated as follows:

1. was there really a threat to the peace justifying the invocation of Chapter VII as a legal basis for the establishment of the International Tribunal?

2. assuming such a threat existed, was the Security Council authorized, with a view to restoring or maintaining peace, to take any measures at its own discretion, or was it bound to choose among those expressly provided for in Articles 41 and 42 (and possibly Article 40 as well)?

3. in the latter case, how can the establishment of an international criminal tribunal be justified, as it does not figure among the ones mentioned in those Articles, and is of a different nature?

The Power of the Security Council to Invoke Chapter VII

28. Article 39 opens Chapter VII of the Charter of the United Nations and determines the conditions of application of this Chapter. It provides:

> "The Security Council shall determine the existence of any threat to the peace, breach of the peace, or act of aggression and shall make recommendations, or decide what measures shall be taken in accordance with Articles 41 and 42, to maintain or restore international peace and security." (United Nations Charter, 26 June 1945, Art. 39.)

It is clear from this text that the Security Council plays a pivotal role and exercises a very wide discretion under this Article. But this does not mean that its powers are unlimited. The Security Council is an organ of an international organization, established by a treaty which serves as a constitutional framework for that organization. The Security Council is thus subjected to certain constitutional limitations, however broad its powers under the constitution may be. Those powers cannot, in any case, go beyond the limits of the jurisdiction of the Organization at large, not to mention other specific limitations or those which may derive from the internal division of power within the Organization. In any case, neither the text nor the spirit of the Charter conceives of the Security Council as legibus solutus (unbound by law).

In particular, Article 24, after declaring, in paragraph 1, that the Members of the United Nations "confer on the Security Council primary responsibility for the maintenance of international peace and security", imposes on it, in paragraph 3, the obligation to report annually (or more frequently) to the General Assembly, and provides, more importantly, in paragraph 2, that:

> "In discharging these duties the Security Council shall act in accordance with the Purposes and Principles of the United Nations. The specific powers granted to the Security Council for the discharge of these duties are laid down in Chapters VI, VII, VIII, and XII." (*Id.*, Art. 24(2).)

The Charter thus speaks the language of specific powers, not of absolute fiat.

29. What is the extent of the powers of the Security Council under Article 39 and the limits thereon, if any?

The Security Council plays the central role in the application of both parts of the Article. It is the Security Council that makes the *determination* that there exists one of the situations justifying the use of the "exceptional powers" of Chapter VII. And it is also the Security Council that chooses the reaction to such a situation: it either makes *recommendations* (i.e., opts not to use the exceptional powers but to continue to operate under Chapter VI) or decides to use the exceptional powers by ordering *measures* to be taken in accordance with Articles 41 and 42 with a view to maintaining or restoring international peace and security.

The situations justifying resort to the powers provided for in Chapter VII are a "threat to the peace", a "breach of the peace" or an "act of aggression". While the "act of aggression" is more amenable to a legal determination, the "threat to the peace" is more of a political concept. But the determination that there exists such a threat is not a totally unfettered discretion, as it has to remain, at the very least, within the limits of the Purposes and Principles of the Charter.

30. It is not necessary for the purposes of the present decision to examine any further the question of the limits of the discretion of the Security Council in determining the existence of a "threat to the peace", for two reasons.

The first is that an armed conflict (or a series of armed conflicts) has been taking place in the territory of the former Yugoslavia since long before the decision of the Security Council to establish this International Tribunal. If it is considered an international armed conflict, there is no doubt that it falls within the literal sense of the words "breach of the peace" (between the parties or, at the very least, as a "threat to the peace" of others).

But even if it were considered merely as an "internal armed conflict", it would still constitute a "threat to the peace" according to the settled practice of the Security Council and the common understanding of the United Nations membership in general. Indeed, the practice of the Security Council is rich with cases of civil war or internal strife which it classified as a "threat to the peace" and dealt with under Chapter VII, with the encouragement or even at the behest of the General Assembly, such as the Congo crisis at the beginning of the 1960s and, more recently, Liberia and Somalia. It can thus be said that there is a common understanding, manifested by the "subsequent practice" of the membership of the United Nations at large, that the "threat to the peace" of Article 39 may include, as one of its species, internal armed conflicts.

The second reason, which is more particular to the case at hand, is that Appellant has amended his position from that contained in the Brief submitted to the Trial Chamber. Appellant no longer contests the Security Council's power to determine whether the situation in the former Yugoslavia constituted a threat to the peace, nor the determination itself. He further acknowledges that the Security Council "has the power to address to [sic] such threats [...] by appropriate measures". ([Defense] Brief to Support the Notice of (Interlocutory) Appeal, 25 August 1995 (Case No. IT-94-1-AR72), at para. 5.1 (hereinafter *Defense Appeal Brief*).) But he continues to contest the legality and appropriateness of the measures chosen by the Security Council to that end.

2. The Range of Measures Envisaged Under Chapter VII

31. Once the Security Council determines that a particular situation poses a threat to the peace or that there exists a breach of the peace or an act of aggression, it enjoys a wide margin of discretion in choosing the course of action: as noted above (see para. 29) it can either continue, in spite of its determination, to act via recommendations, i.e., as if it were still within Chapter VI ("*Pacific Settlement of Disputes*") or it can exercise its exceptional powers under Chapter VII. In the words of Article 39, it would then "decide what measures shall be taken in accordance with Articles 41 and 42, to maintain or restore international peace and security". (United Nations Charter, art. 39.)

A question arises in this respect as to whether the choice of the Security Council is limited to the measures provided for in Articles 41 and 42 of the Charter (as the language of Article 39 suggests), or whether it has even larger discretion in the form of general powers to maintain and restore international peace and security under Chapter VII at large. In the latter case, one of course does not have to locate every measure decided by the Security Council under Chapter VII within the confines of Articles 41 and 42, or possibly Article 40. In any case, under both interpretations, the Security Council has a broad discretion in deciding on the course of action and evaluating the appropriateness of the measures to be taken. The language of Article 39 is quite clear as to the channeling of the very broad and exceptional powers of the Security Council under Chapter VII through Articles 41 and 42. These two Articles leave to the Security Council such a wide choice as not to warrant searching, on functional or other grounds, for even wider and more general powers than those already expressly provided for in the Charter.

These powers are *coercive* vis-à-vis the culprit State or entity. But they are also mandatory vis-à-vis the other Member States, who are under an obligation to cooperate with the

Organization (Article 2, paragraph 5, Articles 25, 48) and with one another (Article 49), in the implementation of the action or measures decided by the Security Council.

3. The Establishment of The International Tribunal As A Measure Under Chapter VII

32. As with the determination of the existence of a threat to the peace, a breach of the peace or an act of aggression, the Security Council has a very wide margin of discretion under Article 39 to choose the appropriate course of action and to evaluate the suitability of the measures chosen, as well as their potential contribution to the restoration or main-tenance of peace. But here again, this discretion is not unfettered; moreover, it is limited to the measures provided for in Articles 41 and 42. Indeed, in the case at hand, this last point serves as a basis for the Appellant's contention of invalidity of the establishment of the International Tribunal.

In its resolution 827, the Security Council considers that "in the particular circumstances of the former Yugoslavia", the establishment of the International Tribunal "would contribute to the restoration and maintenance of peace" and indicates that, in establishing it, the Security Council was acting under Chapter VII (S.C. Res. 827, U.N. Doc. S/RES/827 (1993)). However, it did not specify a particular Article as a basis for this action.

Appellant has attacked the legality of this decision at different stages before the Trial Chamber as well as before this Chamber on at least three grounds:

a) that the establishment of such a tribunal was never contemplated by the framers of the Charter as one of the measures to be taken under Chapter VII; as witnessed by the fact that it figures nowhere in the provisions of that Chapter, and more particularly in Articles 41 and 42 which detail these measures;

b) that the Security Council is constitutionally or inherently incapable of creating a judicial organ, as it is conceived in the Charter as an executive organ, hence not possessed of judicial powers which can be exercised through a subsidiary organ;

c) that the establishment of the International Tribunal has neither promoted, nor was capable of promoting, international peace, as demonstrated by the current situation in the former Yugoslavia.

(a) What Article of Chapter VII Serves As A Basis For The Establishment Of A Tribunal?

....

34. Prima facie, the International Tribunal matches perfectly the description in Article 41 of "measures not involving the use of force". Appellant, however, has argued before both the Trial Chamber and this Appeals Chamber, that:

> "... [I]t is clear that the establishment of a war crimes tribunal was not intended. The examples mentioned in this article focus upon economic and political measures and do not in any way suggest judicial measures". (Brief to Support the Motion [of the Defense] on the Jurisdiction of the Tribunal before the Trial Chamber of the International Tribunal, 23 June 1995 (Case No. IT-94-1-T), at para. 3.2.1 (hereinafter *Defense Trial Brief*).)

It has also been argued that the measures contemplated under Article 41 are all measures to be undertaken by Member States, which is not the case with the establishment of the International Tribunal.

35. The first argument does not stand by its own language. Article 41 reads as follows:

> "The Security Council may decide what measures not involving the use of armed force are to be employed to give effect to its decisions, and it may call upon the

Members of the United Nations to apply such measures. These may include complete or partial interruption of economic relations and of rail, sea, air, postal, telegraphic, radio, and other means of communication, and the severance of diplomatic relations." (United Nations Charter, art. 41.)

It is evident that the measures set out in Article 41 are merely illustrative *examples* which obviously do not exclude other measures. All the Article requires is that they do not involve "the use of force". It is a negative definition.

That the examples do not suggest judicial measures goes some way towards the other argument that the Article does not contemplate institutional measures implemented directly by the United Nations through one of its organs but, as the given examples suggest, only action by Member States, such as economic sanctions (though possibly coordinated through an organ of the Organization). However, as mentioned above, nothing in the Article suggests the limitation of the measures to those implemented by States. The Article only prescribes what these measures cannot be. Beyond that it does not say or suggest what they have to be.

Moreover, even a simple literal analysis of the Article shows that the first phrase of the first sentence carries a very general prescription which can accommodate both institutional and Member State action. The second phrase can be read as referring particularly to one species of this very large category of measures referred to in the first phrase, but not necessarily the only one, namely, measures undertaken directly by States. It is also clear that the second sentence, starting with "These [measures]" not "Those [measures]", refers to the species mentioned in the second phrase rather than to the "genus" referred to in the first phrase of this sentence.

36. Logically, if the Organization can undertake measures which have to be implemented through the intermediary of its Members, it can *a fortiori* undertake measures which it can implement directly via its organs, if it happens to have the resources to do so. It is only for want of such resources that the United Nations has to act through its Members. But it is of the essence of "collective measures" that they are collectively undertaken. Action by Member States on behalf of the Organization is but a poor substitute *faute de mieux*, or a "second best" for want of the first. This is also the pattern of Article 42 on measures involving the use of armed force.

In sum, the establishment of the International Tribunal falls squarely within the powers of the Security Council under Article 41.

(b) Can The Security Council Establish A Subsidiary Organ With Judicial Powers?

37. The argument that the Security Council, not being endowed with judicial powers, cannot establish a subsidiary organ possessed of such powers is untenable: it results from a fundamental misunderstanding of the constitutional set-up of the Charter.

Plainly, the Security Council is not a judicial organ and is not provided with judicial powers (though it may incidentally perform certain quasi-judicial activities such as effecting determinations or findings). The principal function of the Security Council is the maintenance of international peace and security, in the discharge of which the Security Council exercises both decision-making and executive powers.

38. The establishment of the International Tribunal by the Security Council does not signify, however, that the Security Council has delegated to it some of its own functions or the exercise of some of its own powers. Nor does it mean, in reverse, that the Security Council was usurping for itself part of a judicial function which does not belong to it but to other organs of the United Nations according to the Charter. The Security Council has

resorted to the establishment of a judicial organ in the form of an international criminal tribunal as an instrument for the exercise of its own principal function of maintenance of peace and security, i.e., as a measure contributing to the restoration and maintenance of peace in the former Yugoslavia.

The General Assembly did not need to have military and police functions and powers in order to be able to establish the United Nations Emergency Force in the Middle East ("UNEF") in 1956. Nor did the General Assembly have to be a judicial organ possessed of judicial functions and powers in order to be able to establish UNAT. In its advisory opinion in the Effect of Awards, the International Court of Justice, in addressing practically the same objection, declared:

> "[T]he Charter does not confer judicial functions on the General Assembly [...] By establishing the Administrative Tribunal, the General Assembly was not delegating the performance of its own functions: it was exercising a power which it had under the Charter to regulate staff relations." (Effect of Awards, at 61.)

(c) Was The Establishment Of The International Tribunal An Appropriate Measure?

39. The third argument is directed against the discretionary power of the Security Council in evaluating the appropriateness of the chosen measure and its effectiveness in achieving its objective, the restoration of peace.

Article 39 leaves the choice of means and their evaluation to the Security Council, which enjoys wide discretionary powers in this regard; and it could not have been otherwise, as such a choice involves political evaluation of highly complex and dynamic situations.

It would be a total misconception of what are the criteria of legality and validity in law to test the legality of such measures *ex post facto* by their success or failure to achieve their ends (in the present case, the restoration of peace in the former Yugoslavia, in quest of which the establishment of the International Tribunal is but one of many measures adopted by the Security Council).

40. For the aforementioned reasons, the Appeals Chamber considers that the International Tribunal has been lawfully established as a measure under Chapter VII of the Charter.

4. Was The Establishment Of The International Tribunal Contrary To The General Principle Whereby Courts Must Be "Established By Law"?

41. Appellant challenges the establishment of the International Tribunal by contending that it has not been established by law. The entitlement of an individual to have a criminal charge against him determined by a tribunal which has been established by law is provided in Article 14, paragraph 1, of the International Covenant on Civil and Political Rights. It provides:

> "In the determination of any criminal charge against him, or of his rights and obligations in a suit at law, everyone shall be entitled to a fair and public hearing by a competent, independent and impartial tribunal established by law." (ICCPR, art. 14, para. 1.)

Similar provisions can be found in Article 6(1) of the European Convention on Human Rights, which states:

> "In the determination of his civil rights and obligations or of any criminal charge against him, everyone is entitled to a fair and public hearing within a reasonable time by an independent and impartial tribunal established by law [...]" (European Convention for the Protection of Human Rights and Fundamental Freedoms, 4 November 1950, art. 6, para. 1, 213 U.N.T.S. 222 (hereinafter ECHR))

and in Article 8(1) of the American Convention on Human Rights, which provides:

> "Every person has the right to a hearing, with due guarantees and within a reasonable time, by a competent, independent and impartial tribunal, previously established by law." (American Convention on Human Rights, 22 November 1969, art. 8, para. 1, O.A.S. Treaty Series No. 36, at 1, O.A.S. Off. Rec. OEA/Ser. L/V/II.23 doc. rev. 2 (hereinafter ACHR).)

Appellant argues that the right to have a criminal charge determined by a tribunal established by law is one which forms part of international law as a "general principle of law recognized by civilized nations", one of the sources of international law in Article 38 of the Statute of the International Court of Justice. In support of this assertion, Appellant emphasizes the fundamental nature of the "fair trial" or "due process" guarantees afforded in the International Covenant on Civil and Political Rights, the European Convention on Human Rights and the American Convention on Human Rights. Appellant asserts that they are minimum requirements in international law for the administration of criminal justice.

42. For the reasons outlined below, Appellant has not satisfied this Chamber that the requirements laid down in these three conventions must apply not only in the context of national legal systems but also with respect to proceedings conducted before an international court. This Chamber is, however, satisfied that the principle that a tribunal must be established by law, as explained below, is a general principle of law imposing an international obligation which only applies to the administration of criminal justice in a municipal setting. It follows from this principle that it is incumbent on all States to organize their system of criminal justice in such a way as to ensure that all individuals are guaranteed the right to have a criminal charge determined by a tribunal established by law. This does not entail however that, by contrast, an international criminal court could be set up at the mere whim of a group of governments. Such a court ought to be rooted in the rule of law and offer all guarantees embodied in the relevant international instruments. Then the court may be said to be "established by law."

43. Indeed, there are three possible interpretations of the term "established by law". First, as Appellant argues, "established by law" could mean established by a legislature. Appellant claims that the International Tribunal is the product of a "mere executive order" and not of a "decision making process under democratic control, necessary to create a judicial organization in a democratic society". Therefore Appellant maintains that the International Tribunal not been "established by law". (Defense Appeal Brief, at para. 5.4.)

The case law applying the words "established by law" in the European Convention on Human Rights has favored this interpretation of the expression. This case law bears out the view that the relevant provision is intended to ensure that tribunals in a democratic society must not depend on the discretion of the executive; rather they should be regulated by law emanating from Parliament. (*See* Zand v. Austria, App. No. 7360/76, 15 Eur. Comm'n H.R. Dec. & Rep. 70, at 80 (1979); Piersack v. Belgium, App. No. 8692/79, 47 Eur. Ct. H.R. (ser. B) at 12 (1981); Crociani, Palmiotti, Tanassi and D'Ovidio v. Italy, App. Nos. 8603/79, 8722/79, 8723/79 & 8729/79 (joined) 22 Eur. Comm'n H.R. Dec. & Rep. 147, at 219 (1981).)

Or, put another way, the guarantee is intended to ensure that the administration of justice is not a matter of executive discretion, but is regulated by laws made by the legislature.

It is clear that the legislative, executive and judicial division of powers which is largely followed in most municipal systems does not apply to the international setting nor, more specifically, to the setting of an international organization such as the United Nations. Among the principal organs of the United Nations the divisions between judicial, executive and legislative functions are not clear cut. Regarding the judicial function, the International Court of Justice is clearly the "principal judicial organ" (*see* United Nations Charter, art. 92). There is, however, no legislature, in the technical sense of the term, in the United Nations system and, more generally, no Parliament in the world community. That is to say, there exists no corporate organ formally empowered to enact laws directly binding on international legal subjects.

It is clearly impossible to classify the organs of the United Nations into the above-discussed divisions which exist in the national law of States. Indeed, Appellant has agreed that the constitutional structure of the United Nations does not follow the division of powers often found in national constitutions. Consequently the separation of powers element of the requirement that a tribunal be "established by law" finds no application in an international law setting. The aforementioned principle can only impose an obligation on States concerning the functioning of their own national systems.

44. A second possible interpretation is that the words "established by law" refer to establishment of international courts by a body which, though not a Parliament, has a limited power to take binding decisions. In our view, one such body is the Security Council when, acting under Chapter VII of the United Nations Charter, it makes decisions binding by virtue of Article 25 of the Charter.

According to Appellant, however, there must be something more for a tribunal to be "established by law". Appellant takes the position that, given the differences between the United Nations system and national division of powers, discussed above, the conclusion must be that the United Nations system is not capable of creating the International Tribunal unless there is an amendment to the United Nations Charter. We disagree. It does not follow from the fact that the United Nations has no legislature that the Security Council is not empowered to set up this International Tribunal if it is acting pursuant to an authority found within its constitution, the United Nations Charter. As set out above (paras. 28–40) we are of the view that the Security Council was endowed with the power to create this International Tribunal as a measure under Chapter VII in the light of its determination that there exists a threat to the peace.

In addition, the establishment of the International Tribunal has been repeatedly approved and endorsed by the "representative" organ of the United Nations, the General Assembly: this body not only participated in its setting up, by electing the Judges and approving the budget, but also expressed its satisfaction with, and encouragement of the activities of the International Tribunal in various resolutions. (*See* G.A. Res. 48/88 (20 December 1993) and G.A. Res. 48/143 (20 December 1993), G.A. Res. 49/10 (8 November 1994) and G.A. Res. 49/205 (23 December 1994).)

45. The third possible interpretation of the requirement that the International Tribunal be "established by law" is that its establishment must be in accordance with the rule of law. This appears to be the most sensible and most likely meaning of the term in the context of international law. For a tribunal such as this one to be established according to the rule of law, it must be established in accordance with the proper international standards; it must provide all the guarantees of fairness, justice and even-handedness, in full conformity with internationally recognized human rights instruments.

This interpretation of the guarantee that a tribunal be "established by law" is borne out by an analysis of the International Covenant on Civil and Political Rights. As noted by the Trial Chamber, at the time Article 14 of the International Covenant on Civil and

Political Rights was being drafted, it was sought, unsuccessfully, to amend it to require that tribunals should be "preestablished" by law and not merely "established by law" (Decision at Trial, at para. 34). Two similar proposals to this effect were made (one by the representative of Lebanon and one by the representative of Chile); if adopted, their effect would have been to prevent all *ad hoc* tribunals. In response, the delegate from the Philippines noted the disadvantages of using the language of "preestablished by law":

> "If [the Chilean or Lebanese proposal was approved], a country would never be able to reorganize its tribunals. Similarly it could be claimed that the Nurnberg tribunal was not in existence at the time the war criminals had committed their crimes." (*See* E/CN.4/SR 109. United Nations Economic and Social Council, Commission on Human Rights, 5th Sess., Sum. Rec. 8 June 1949, U.N. Doc. 6.)

As noted by the Trial Chamber in its Decision, there is wide agreement that, in most respects, the International Military Tribunals at Nuremberg and Tokyo gave the accused a fair trial in a procedural sense (Decision at Trial, at para. 34). The important consideration in determining whether a tribunal has been "established by law" is not whether it was pre-established or established for a specific purpose or situation; what is important is that it be set up by a competent organ in keeping with the relevant legal procedures, and that it observes the requirements of procedural fairness.

This concern about *ad hoc* tribunals that function in such a way as not to afford the individual before them basic fair trial guarantees also underlies United Nations Human Rights Committee's interpretation of the phrase "established by law" contained in Article 14, paragraph 1, of the International Covenant on Civil and Political Rights. While the Human Rights Committee has not determined that "extraordinary" tribunals or "special" courts are incompatible with the requirement that tribunals be established by law, it has taken the position that the provision is intended to ensure that any court, be it "extraordinary" or not, should genuinely afford the accused the full guarantees of fair trial set out in Article 14 of the International Covenant on Civil and Political Rights. (*See* General Comment on Article 14, H.R. Comm. 43rd Sess., Supp. No. 40, at para. 4, U.N. Doc. A/43/40 (1988), Cariboni v. Uruguay H.R.Comm. 159/83. 39th Sess. Supp. No. 40 U.N. Doc. A/39/40.) A similar approach has been taken by the Inter-American Commission. (*See, e.g.,* Inter-Am C.H.R., Annual Report 1972, OEA/Ser. P, AG/doc. 305/73 rev. 1, 14 March 1973, at 1; Inter-Am C.H.R., Annual Report 1973, OEA/Ser. P, AG/doc. 409/174, 5 March 1974, at 2–4.) The practice of the Human Rights Committee with respect to State reporting obligations indicates its tendency to scrutinize closely "special" or "extraordinary" criminal courts in order to ascertain whether they ensure compliance with the fair trial requirements of Article 14.

46. An examination of the Statute of the International Tribunal, and of the Rules of Procedure and Evidence adopted pursuant to that Statute leads to the conclusion that it has been established in accordance with the rule of law. The fair trial guarantees in Article 14 of the International Covenant on Civil and Political Rights have been adopted almost verbatim in Article 21 of the Statute. Other fair trial guarantees appear in the Statute and the Rules of Procedure and Evidence. For example, Article 13, paragraph 1, of the Statute ensures the high moral character, impartiality, integrity and competence of the Judges of the International Tribunal, while various other provisions in the Rules ensure equality of arms and fair trial.

47. In conclusion, the Appeals Chamber finds that the International Tribunal has been established in accordance with the appropriate procedures under the United Nations Charter and provides all the necessary safeguards of a fair trial. It is thus "established by law".

48. The first ground of appeal: unlawful establishment of the International Tribunal, is accordingly dismissed.

III. Unjustified Primacy of the International Tribunal over Competent Domestic Courts

49. The second ground of appeal attacks the primacy of the International Tribunal over national courts.

50. This primacy is established by Article 9 of the Statute of the International Tribunal, which provides:

"Concurrent jurisdiction

1. The International Tribunal and national courts shall have concurrent jurisdiction to prosecute persons for serious violations of international humanitarian law committed in the territory of the former Yugoslavia since 1 January 1991.

2. *The International Tribunal shall have primacy over national courts.* At any stage of the procedure, the International Tribunal may formally request national courts to defer to the competence of the International Tribunal in accordance with the present Statute and the Rules of Procedure and Evidence of the International Tribunal." (Emphasis added.)

Appellant's submission is material to the issue, inasmuch as Appellant is expected to stand trial before this International Tribunal as a consequence of a request for deferral which the International Tribunal submitted to the Government of the Federal Republic of Germany on 8 November 1994 and which this Government, as it was bound to do, agreed to honor by surrendering Appellant to the International Tribunal. (United Nations Charter, art. 25, 48 & 49; Statute of the Tribunal, art. 29.2(e); Rules of Procedure, Rule 10.)

In relevant part, Appellant's motion alleges: "[The International Tribunal's] primacy over domestic courts constitutes an infringement upon the sovereignty of the States directly affected". ([Defense] Motion on the Jurisdiction of the Tribunal, 23 June 1995 (Case No. IT-94-1-T), at para. 2.)

. . . .

B. Sovereignty of States

55. Article 2 of the United Nations Charter provides in paragraph 1: "The Organization is based on the principle of the sovereign equality of all its Members."

In Appellant's view, no State can assume jurisdiction to prosecute crimes committed on the territory of another State, barring a universal interest "justified by a treaty or customary international law or an opinio juris on the issue." (Defense Trial Brief, at para. 6.2.)

. . . .

57. . . . .

As early as 1950, in the case of General Wagener, the Supreme Military Tribunal of Italy held:

"These norms [concerning crimes against laws and customs of war], due to their highly ethical and moral content, have a universal character, not a territorial one.... The solidarity among nations, aimed at alleviating in the best possible way the horrors of war, gave rise to the need to dictate rules which do not recognize borders, punishing criminals wherever they may be.... Crimes against the laws and customs of war cannot be considered political offences, as they do not harm a political interest of a particular State, nor a political right of a particular citizen.

They are, instead, crimes of *lese-humanite* (*reati di lesa umanita*) and, as previously demonstrated, the norms prohibiting them have a universal character, not simply a territorial one. Such crimes, therefore, due to their very subject matter and particular nature are precisely of a different and opposite kind from political offences. The latter generally, concern only the States against whom they are committed; the former concern all civilized States, and are to be opposed and punished, in the same way as the crimes of piracy, trade of women and minors, and enslavement are to be opposed and punished, wherever they may have been committed (articles 537 and 604 of the penal code)." (13 March 1950, in *Rivista Penale* 753, 757 (Sup. Mil. Trib., Italy 1950; unofficial translation.)

Twelve years later the Supreme Court of Israel in the Eichmann case could draw a similar picture:

"[T]hese crimes constitute acts which damage vital international interests; they impair the foundations and security of the international community; they violate the universal moral values and humanitarian principles that lie hidden in the criminal law systems adopted by civilized nations. The underlying principle in international law regarding such crimes is that the individual who has committed any of them and who, when doing so, may be presumed to have fully comprehended the heinous nature of his act, must account for his conduct. [...]

Those crimes entail individual criminal responsibility because they challenge the foundations of international society and affront the conscience of civilized nations.

[....]

[T]hey involve the perpetration of an international crime which all the nations of the world are interested in preventing." (Israel v. Eichmann, 36 *International Law Reports* 277, 291–93 (Isr. S. Ct. 1962).)

58. The public revulsion against similar offences in the 1990s brought about a reaction on the part of the community of nations: hence, among other remedies, the establishment of an international judicial body by an organ of an organization representing the community of nations: the Security Council. This organ is empowered and mandated, by definition, to deal with transboundary matters or matters which, though domestic in nature, may affect "international peace and security" (United Nations Charter, art 2. (1), 2.(7), 24, & 37). It would be a travesty of law and a betrayal of the universal need for justice, should the concept of State sovereignty be allowed to be raised successfully against human rights. Borders should not be considered as a shield against the reach of the law and as a protection for those who trample underfoot the most elementary rights of humanity. In the Barbie case, the Court of Cassation of France has quoted with approval the following statement of the Court of Appeal:

"[...] by reason of their nature, the crimes against humanity [...] do not simply fall within the scope of French municipal law but are subject to an international criminal order to which the notions of frontiers and extradition rules arising therefrom are completely foreign." (Federation Nationale de Deportes et Internes Resistants et Patriotes And Others v. Barbie, 78 *International Law Reports* 125, 130 (Cass. crim. 1983).)

Indeed, when an international tribunal such as the present one is created, it must be endowed with primacy over national courts. Otherwise, human nature being what it is, there would be a perennial danger of international crimes being characterized as "ordinary crimes" (Statute of the International Tribunal, art. 10, para. 2(a)), or proceedings being "designed to shield the accused", or cases not being diligently prosecuted (Statute of the International Tribunal, art. 10, para. 2(b)).

If not effectively countered by the principle of primacy, any one of those stratagems might be used to defeat the very purpose of the creation of an international criminal jurisdiction, to the benefit of the very people whom it has been designed to prosecute.

59. The principle of primacy of this International Tribunal over national courts must be affirmed; the more so since it is confined within the strict limits of Articles 9 and 10 of the Statute and Rules 9 and 10 of the Rules of Procedure of the International Tribunal.

The Trial Chamber was fully justified in writing:

> "Before leaving this question relating to the violation of the sovereignty of States, it should be noted that the crimes which the International Tribunal has been called upon to try are not crimes of a purely domestic nature. They are really crimes which are universal in nature, well recognized in international law as serious breaches of international humanitarian law, and transcending the interest of any one State. The Trial Chamber agrees that in such circumstances, the sovereign rights of States cannot and should not take precedence over the right of the international community to act appropriately as they affect the whole of mankind and shock the conscience of all nations of the world. There can therefore be no objection to an international tribunal properly constituted trying these crimes on behalf of the international community." (Decision at Trial, at para. 42.)

....

62. As a matter of fact — and of law — the principle advocated by Appellant aims at one very specific goal: to avoid the creation of special or extraordinary courts designed to try political offences in times of social unrest without guarantees of a fair trial.

This principle is not breached by the transfer of jurisdiction to an international tribunal created by the Security Council acting on behalf of the community of nations. No rights of accused are thereby infringed or threatened; quite to the contrary, they are all specifically spelt out and protected under the Statute of the International Tribunal. No accused can complain. True, he will be removed from his "natural" national forum; but he will be brought before a tribunal at least equally fair, more distanced from the facts of the case and taking a broader view of the matter.

Furthermore, one cannot but rejoice at the thought that, universal jurisdiction being nowadays acknowledged in the case of international crimes, a person suspected of such offences may finally be brought before an international judicial body for a dispassionate consideration of his indictment by impartial, independent and disinterested judges coming, as it happens here, from all continents of the world.

....

64. For these reasons the Appeals Chamber concludes that Appellant's second ground of appeal, contesting the primacy of the International Tribunal, is ill-founded and must be dismissed.

Questions for Discussion

1. Why was the Yugoslavia Tribunal created by resolution of the Security Council rather than by a treaty like the Nuremberg Tribunal and the Permanent International Criminal

Court (discussed below)? What are the legal implications that flow from the Yugoslavia Tribunal's method of establishment?

2. Why do you think the Yugoslavia Tribunal's Statute did not include the crime of aggression that was applied at Nuremberg? By its omission, did the Yugoslavia Tribunal constitute a step back or a step forward from Nuremberg?

3. Was the creation of the Yugoslavia Tribunal by the Security Council valid under international law? What arguments for the defense and prosecution did you find most compelling? Could the Yugoslavia Tribunal fairly consider these arguments, given that the judges' prestigious and lucrative jobs were at stake with the outcome?

4. On the eve of the establishment of the International Criminal Tribunal for the Former Yugoslavia in 1993, the International Committee of the Red Cross "underlined the fact that according to international humanitarian law as it stands today, the notion of war crimes is limited to situations of international armed conflict." Yet, in its first decision, on October 2, 1995, the Appeals Chamber of the Yugoslavia Tribunal held that the same principles of liability that apply to international armed conflict apply to internal armed conflicts. Despite dubious provenance, this sweeping decision has been affirmed by the Rwanda Tribunal and Special Court for Sierra Leone; it has been codified in the Military Manuals of several governments; it has been enshrined in the 1998 Statute of the International Criminal Court; and is now recognized as customary international law despite the dearth of state practice or prolonged period of development. Do International Criminal Tribunals have the ability to make new customary international law? For an analysis of this question, *see* MICHAEL P. SCHARF, CUSTOMARY INTERNATIONAL LAW IN TIMES OF FUNDAMENTAL CHANGE: RECOGNIZING GROTIAN MOMENTS (2012) (Chapter 7).

5. "In essence, with respect to 'serious offenses,' the *Tadic* decision blurred the line between international and internal armed conflict so that some of the most important rules of customary law applicable to international armed conflict would now apply to civil wars as well. According to the Appeals Chamber, these rules would include 'protection of civilians from hostilities, in particular from indiscriminate attacks, protection of civilian objects, in particular cultural property, protection of all those who do not (or no longer) take active part in the hostilities, as well as prohibition of means of warfare proscribed in international armed conflicts and ban of certain method of conducting hostilities.'... The logical outcome of this development is that war crimes other than Grave Breaches of the Geneva Conventions, whether committed in international or internal armed conflict, will now be subject to universal jurisdiction, and possibly the requirement of *aut dedere aut judicare* (the duty to prosecute or extradite) in the same way that Grave Breaches are. In addition, such war crimes will not be subject to statutes of limitations and may constitute an exception to Head of State immunity for former leaders for acts done while in office." MICHAEL P. SCHARF, CUSTOMARY INTERNATIONAL LAW IN TIMES OF FUNDAMENTAL CHANGE: RECOGNIZING GROTIAN MOMENTS (2012) (Chapter 7). How might this new rule of customary international law effect various internal armed conflicts around the world?

6. Subsequent to the establishment of the International Criminal Tribunal for the former Yugoslavia, the UN Security Council, acting under its Chapter VII authority, established the International Criminal Tribunal for Rwanda (in Arusha, Tanzania) in 1994, and the Special Tribunal for Lebanon (in The Hague) in 2009. Through agreements between the UN and domestic authorities, the Special Court for Sierra Leone (in Freetown and the Hague) was established in 2002, and the Extraordinary Chambers in the Courts of Cambodia was established (in Phnom Penh) in 2006. These five *ad hoc* international tribunals have prosecuted over 200 defendants and have produced extensive case law that

constitutes persuasive (though not binding) authority for other tribunals and domestic courts. What do you think are the pros and cons of the different types of tribunals, i.e., *ad hoc* tribunals created by Chapter VII Resolution verses *ad hoc* tribunals created by international agreement?

7. In 2002, the permanent International Criminal Court was established (at The Hague) through a treaty negotiated at the Rome Diplomatic Conference. The ICC currently has 122 State parties. The ICC Statute is available at: *http://untreaty.un.org/cod/icc/statute/romefra.htm*. The following excerpts provide background on the history of the ICC and the pros and cons related to United States support of the Institution.

The Debate over the Permanent International Criminal Court

Michael P. Scharf, *The Case for Supporting the International Criminal Court*

Washington University School of Law, Whitney R. Harris Institute for Global Legal Studies, Washington University in St. Louis, International Debate Series, No. 1 (2002).

....

Background: The Road to Rome

With the creation of the Yugoslavia and Rwanda Tribunals in the early 1990s, there was hope among U.S. policy makers that Security Council-controlled *ad hoc* tribunals would be set up for crimes against humanity elsewhere in the world. Even America's most ardent opponents of a permanent international criminal court had come to see the *ad hoc* tribunals as a useful foreign policy tool. The experience with the former Yugoslavia and Rwanda Tribunals proved that an international indictment and arrest warrant could serve to isolate offending leaders diplomatically, strengthen the hand of domestic rivals, and fortify international political will to impose economic sanctions and take more aggressive actions if necessary. Unlike a permanent international criminal court, there was no perceived risk of American personnel being prosecuted before the *ad hoc* tribunals since their subject matter, territorial and temporal jurisdiction were determined by the Security Council, which the United States could control with its veto.

But then something known in government circles as "Tribunal Fatigue" set in. The process of reaching agreement on the tribunal's statute; electing judges; selecting a prosecutor; hiring staff; negotiating headquarters agreements and judicial assistance pacts; erecting courtrooms, offices, and prisons; and appropriating funds turned out to be too time consuming and exhausting for the members of the Security Council to undertake on a repeated basis. China and other Permanent Members of the Security Council let it be known that Rwanda would be the last of the Security Council-established *ad hoc* tribunals.

Consequently, the establishment of a permanent international criminal court began to be seen by many members of the United Nations (as well as some within the U.S. government) as the solution to the impediments preventing a continuation of the *ad hoc* approach. Having successfully tackled most of the same complex legal and practical issues that U.S. diplomats had earlier identified as obstacles to a permanent international criminal court, the United States Government was left with little basis to justify continued foot-dragging with regard to the ICC. In 1994, the U.N. International Law Commission produced a draft Statute for an ICC which was largely based on the Statutes and Rules of the popular *ad hoc* tribunals. The International Law Commission's draft was subsequently refined through a series of Preparatory Conferences in which the United States played an active role. During this time, the establishment of a permanent international criminal court began to receive near unanimous support in the United Nations. The only countries that were willing to go on record as opposing the establishment of an ICC were the few states that the United States had labeled "persistent human rights violators" or "terrorist supporting states."

Thus, on the eve of the Rome Diplomatic Conference in the summer of 1998, both the U.S. Congress and the Clinton Administration indicated that they were in favor of an ICC if the right protections were built into its statute. As David Scheffer, then U.S. Ambassador-at-Large for War Crimes Issues, reminded the Senate Foreign Relations Committee on July 23, 1998: "Our experience with the establishment and operation of the International Criminal Tribunals for the former Yugoslavia and Rwanda had convinced us of the merit of creating a permanent court that could be more quickly available for investigations and prosecutions and more cost-efficient in its operation."

The Politics of Rome

The Rome Diplomatic Conference represented a tension between the United States, which sought a Security Council-controlled Court, and most of the other countries of the world which felt no country's citizens who are accused of serious war crimes or genocide should be exempt from the jurisdiction of a permanent international criminal court. These countries were concerned, moreover, about the possibility that the Security Council would once again slide into the state of paralysis that characterized the Cold War years, rendering a Security-Council controlled court a nullity. The justification for the American position was that, as the world's greatest military and economic power, more than any other country the United States is expected to intervene to halt humanitarian catastrophes around the world. The United States' unique position renders U.S. personnel uniquely vulnerable to the potential jurisdiction of an international criminal court. In sum, the U.S. Administration feared that an independent ICC Prosecutor would turn out to be (in the words of one U.S. official) an "international Ken Starr" who would bedevil U.S. military personnel and officials, and frustrate U.S. foreign policy.

Many of the countries at Rome were in fact sympathetic to the United States' concerns. Thus, what emerged from Rome was a Court with a two-track system of jurisdiction. Track one would constitute situations referred to the Court by the Security Council. This track would create binding obligations on all States to comply with orders for evidence or the surrender of indicted persons under Chapter VII of the U.N. Charter. This track would be enforced by Security Council imposed embargoes, the freezing of assets of leaders and their supporters, and/or by authorizing the use of force. It is this track that the United States favored, and would be likely to utilize in the event of a future Bosnia or Rwanda. The second track would constitute situations referred to the Court by individual countries or the ICC Prosecutor. This track would have no built in process for enforcement, but rather would rely on the good-faith cooperation of the Parties to the Court's statute. Most of the delegates in Rome recognized that the real power was in the first track. But the United States still demanded protection from the second track of the Court's jurisdiction. In order to mollify U.S. concerns, the following protective mechanisms were incorporated into the Court's Statute at the urging of the United States:

First, the Court's jurisdiction under the second track would be based on a concept known as "complementarity" which was defined as meaning the court would be a last resort which comes into play only when domestic authorities are unable or unwilling to prosecute. At the insistence of the United States, the delegates at Rome added teeth to the concept of complementarity by providing in Article 18 of the Court's Statute that the Prosecutor has to notify States with a prosecutive interest in a case of his/her intention to commence an investigation. If, within one month of notification, such a State informs the Court that it is investigating the matter, the Prosecutor must defer to the State's investigation, unless it can convince the Pre-Trial Chamber that the investigation is a sham. The decision of the Pre-Trial Chamber is subject to interlocutory appeal to the Appeals Chamber.

Second, Article 8 of the Court's Statute specifies that the Court would have jurisdiction only over "serious" war crimes that represent a "policy or plan." Thus, random acts of U.S. personnel involved in a foreign peacekeeping operation would not be subject to the Court's jurisdiction. Neither would one-time incidents such as the July 3, 1988 accidental downing of the Iran airbus by the USS *Vincinnes* or the August 20, 1998 U.S. attack on the Al Shiffa suspected chemical weapons facility in Sudan that turned out to be a pharmaceutical plant.

Third, Article 15 of the Court's Statute guards against spurious complaints by the ICC prosecutor by requiring the approval of a three-judge pre-trial chamber before the prosecution can launch an investigation. Further, the decision of the chamber is subject to interlocutory appeal to the Appeals Chamber.

Fourth, Article 16 of the Statute allows the Security Council to affirmatively vote to postpone an investigation or case for up to twelve months, on a renewable basis. While this does not amount to the individual veto the United States had sought, this does give the United States and the other members of the Security Council a collective veto over the Court.

The United States Delegation played hard ball in Rome and got just about everything it wanted, substantially weakening the ICC in the process. As Ambassador Scheffer told the Senate Foreign Relations Committee: "The U.S. delegation certainly reduced exposure to unwarranted prosecutions by the international court through our successful efforts to build into the treaty a range of safeguards that will benefit not only us but also our friends and allies." These protections proved sufficient for other major powers including the United Kingdom, France and Russia, which joined 117 other countries in voting in favor of the Rome Treaty. But without what would amount to an iron-clad veto of jurisdiction over U.S. personnel and officials, the United States felt compelled to join China, Libya, Iraq, Israel, Qatar and Yemen as the only seven countries voting in opposition to the Rome Treaty.

It is an open secret that there was substantial dissension within the U.S. Delegation (especially among Department of State and Department of Justice representatives) about whether to oppose the ICC and that the position of the Secretary of Defense ultimately carried the day. As a former Republican member of Congress, there has been conjecture that Secretary of Defense William Cohen was influenced by Senator Jesse Helms (R-NC), a vocal opponent of the ICC. President Clinton, for his part, had proven to be uniquely vulnerable on issues affecting the military due to his record as a Vietnam "draft dodger" and his unpopular stand on gays in the military. Thus, rather than focus his attention on the negotiations in Rome as they came to a head, Clinton immersed himself in a historic trip to China during the Rome Conference. And in the midst of several breaking White House scandals in the summer of 1998, there was to be no last minute rescue of the Rome Treaty by Vice President Al Gore as had been the case with the Kyoto Climate Accord a year earlier.

The Question of ICC Jurisdiction over the Nationals of Non-Party States

Once it decided that it would not sign the Court's Statute, the primary goal of the United States government (still bowing to the concerns of the Pentagon) was to prevent the ICC from being able to exercise jurisdiction over U.S. personnel and officials. As Ambassador Scheffer explained to the Senate Foreign Relations Committee: "We sought an amendment to the text that would have required ... the consent of the State of nationality of the perpetrator be obtained before the court could exercise jurisdiction. We asked for a vote on our proposal, but a motion to take no action was overwhelmingly carried by the vote of participating governments in the conference." Had the U.S. amendment been adopted, the United States could have declined to sign the Rome Statute, thereby ensuring its immunity from the second track of the court's jurisdiction, but at the same time permitting the United States to take advantage of the first track of the Court's jurisdiction (Security Council referrals) when it was in America's interest to do so.

Having lost that vote, the U.S. Administration began to argue that international law prohibits an ICC from exercising jurisdiction over the nationals of non-parties. Thus, Ambassador Scheffer told the Senate Foreign Relations Committee that "the treaty purports to establish an arrangement whereby U.S. armed forces operating overseas could be conceivably prosecuted by the international court even if the United States has not agreed to be bound by the treaty.... This is contrary to the most fundamental principles of treaty law" as set forth in the Vienna Convention on the Law of Treaties. Based on the U.S. objection to the ICC's exercise of jurisdiction over nationals of non-party States, Ambassador Scheffer expressed the "hope that on reflection governments that have signed, or are planning to sign, the Rome treaty will begin to recognize the proper limits to Article 12 and how its misuse would do great damage to international law and be very disruptive to the international political system." Senator Helms later quoted this "Vienna Convention" argument in the preamble of his anti-ICC legislation, which is discussed below.

Diplomats and scholars have been quick to point out the flaws in Scheffer's argument. First, it is a distortion to say that the Rome Statute purports to impose obligations on non-party States. Under the terms of the Rome Treaty, the Parties are obligated to provide funding to the ICC, to extradite indicted persons to the ICC, to provide evidence to the ICC, and to provide other forms of cooperation to the Court. Those are the only obligations the Rome Treaty establishes on States, and they apply only to State Parties. Thus, Ambassador Scheffer's objection is not really that the Rome Treaty imposes obligations on the United States as a non-party, but that it affects the sovereignty interests of the United States—an altogether different matter which does not come within the Vienna Convention's proscription. Moreover, although States have a sovereignty interest in their nationals, especially State officials and employees, sovereignty does not provide a basis for exclusive jurisdiction over crimes committed by a State's nationals in a foreign country. Nor does a foreign indictment of a State's nationals for acts committed in the foreign country constitute an impermissible intervention in the State's internal affairs.

Second, the exercise of the ICC's jurisdiction over nationals of non-party States who commit crimes in the territory of State parties is well grounded in both the universality principle and the territoriality principle of jurisdiction under international law. The core crimes within the ICC's jurisdiction—genocide, crimes against humanity, and war crimes— are crimes of universal jurisdiction. The negotiating record of the Rome Treaty indicates that the consent regime was layered upon the ICC's inherent universal jurisdiction over these crimes, such that with the consent of the State in whose territory the offense was committed, the Court has the authority to issue indictments over the nationals of non-party States. The Nuremberg Tribunal and the *ad hoc* Tribunal for the former Yugoslavia provide precedent for the collective delegation of universal jurisdiction to an international criminal court without the consent of the State of the nationality of the accused.

In addition, international law recognizes the authority of the State where a crime occurs to delegate its territorial-based jurisdiction to a third State or international Tribunal. Careful analysis of the European Convention on the Transfer of Proceedings indicates that the consent of the State of the nationality of the accused is not a prerequisite for the delegation of territorial jurisdiction under the Convention, and therefore that it provides a precedent for the ICC's jurisdictional regime. There are no compelling policy reasons why territorial jurisdiction cannot be delegated to an international court and the Nuremberg Tribunal provides the precedent for the collective exercise of territorial as well as universal jurisdiction.

Third, Scheffer's argument is inconsistent with past U.S. exercise of universal jurisdiction granted by anti-terrorism, anti-narcotic trafficking, torture, and war crimes treaties over the nationals of States which are not party to these treaties. In light of the past U.S. practice, the claim that a treaty cannot lawfully provide the basis of criminal jurisdiction over the nationals of non-party States, while directed against the ICC, has the potential of negatively affecting existing U.S. law enforcement authority with respect to terrorists, narco-traffickers, torturers, and war criminals.

An Effort to Modify the Rome Treaty

During hearings before the Senate Foreign Relations Committee on June 23, 1998, Senator Jesse Helms (R-N.C.) urged the Administration to take the following steps in opposition to the establishment of an international criminal court: First, that it announces that it would withdraw U.S. troops from any country that ratified the International Criminal Court Treaty. Second, that it veto any attempt by the Security Council to refer a matter to the Court's jurisdiction. Third, that it blocks any international organization in which it is a member from providing any funding to the International Criminal Court. Fourth, that it renegotiate its Status of Forces Agreements and Extradition Treaties to prohibit its treaty partners from surrendering U.S. nationals to the International Criminal Court. Finally, that it provide no U.S. soldiers to any regional or international peacekeeping operation where there is any possibility that they will come under the jurisdiction of the International Criminal Court. According to Senator Helms, these measures would ensure that the Rome Treaty will be "dead on arrival."

Ambassador Scheffer was non-committal as to the adoption of Senator Helms' proposals, saying only that "the Administration hopes that in the years ahead other governments will recognize the benefits of potential American participation in the Rome treaty and correct the flawed provisions in the treaty." In the meantime, he added, "more *ad hoc* judicial mechanisms will need to be considered." Ambassador Scheffer's testimony suggested that the U.S. response to the International Criminal Court might parallel its efforts to reform the 1982 Law of the Sea Convention. The United States refused to sign that treaty until amendments were adopted concerning its seabed mining regime. In 1994, the signatories to the Law of the Sea Convention adopted an Agreement containing the revisions sought by the United States and the United States signed the treaty, which still awaits Senate advice and consent to ratification.

In the following months, the United States tried to secure international backing for a clause to be included in the agreement that was being prepared to govern the relations between the United Nations and the ICC. Without actually amending the ICC Statute, the U.S. proposal would prevent the ICC from taking custody of official personnel of non-party States where the State has acknowledged responsibility for the act in question.

This was a major walk back from its earlier position, as this proposal would not prevent the ICC from indicting nationals of non-party States, only prosecuting them. That the Clinton Administration was willing to float this proposal indicated that it was no longer promoting Ambassador Scheffer's questionable reading of the Vienna Convention.

Prior to the Rome Diplomatic Conference, many countries felt that the success of a permanent international criminal court would be in question without U.S. support. But as it became increasingly obvious that the United States was not going to sign the Rome Treaty, the willingness to compromise began to evaporate, culminating in the overwhelming vote against the U.S. amendment requiring the consent of the State of nationality at the Rome Diplomatic Conference. The United States soon discovered that it would have no more luck with the issue through a series of bilateral negotiations than it did in the frenzied atmosphere that characterized the final days of the Rome Conference.

"If You Can't Beat 'Em, Join 'Em"

By late 2000, the Clinton Administration had come to realize that the ICC would ultimately enter into force with or without U.S. support. By December 2000, a growing number of countries had ratified the Rome Treaty, and over 120 countries had signed it, indicating their intention to ratify. Sixty ratifications are necessary to bring it into force. The Signatories included every other NATO State except for Turkey, three of the Permanent Members of the Security Council (France, Russia, and the United Kingdom), and both of the United States' closest neighbors (Mexico and Canada). Even Israel, which had been the only Western country to join the United States in voting against the ICC Treaty in Rome in 1998, later changed its position and announced that it would sign the treaty. Israel's change of position was made possible when the ICC Prep Con promulgated definitions of the crimes over which the ICC has jurisdiction, which clarified that the provision in the ICC Statute making altering the demographics of an occupied territory a war crime would be interpreted no more expansively than the existing law contained in the Geneva Conventions.

In the waning days of his presidency, William J. Clinton authorized the U.S. signature of the Rome Treaty, making the United States the 138th country to sign the treaty by the December 31st deadline. According to the ICC Statute, after December 31, 2000, States must accede to the Treaty, which requires full ratification—something that was not likely for the United States in the near term given the current level of Senate opposition to the Treaty. While signature is not the equivalent of ratification, it set the stage for U.S. support of Security Council referrals to the International Criminal Court, as well as other forms of U.S. cooperation with the Court. In addition, it put the United States in a better position to continue to seek additional provisions to protect American personnel from the court's jurisdiction.

Hostile Outsider or Influential Insider?

Clinton's last minute action drew immediate ire from Senator Jesse Helms, then Chairman of the U.S. Senate Foreign Relations Committee, who has been one of the treaty's greatest opponents. In a Press Release, Helms stated:

> Today's action is a blatant attempt by a lame-duck President to tie the hands of his successor. Well, I have a message for the outgoing President. This decision will not stand. I will make reversing this decision, and protecting America's fighting men and women from the jurisdiction of this international kangaroo court, one of my highest priorities in the new Congress.

Helms responded by pushing for passage of the "Servicemembers Protection Act," Senate Bill 2726, which would prohibit any U.S. Government cooperation with the ICC, and cut off U.S. military assistance to any country that has ratified the ICC Treaty (with the exception of major U.S. allies), as long as the United States has not ratified the Rome Treaty. Further, the proposed legislation provides that U.S. military personnel must be immunized from ICC jurisdiction before the U.S. participates in any U.N. peacekeeping operation. The proposed legislation also authorizes the President to use all means necessary to release any U.S. or allied personnel detained on behalf of the Court.

The essence of this debate, then, is whether the national security and foreign policy interests of the United States are better served by playing the role of a hostile outsider (as embodied in Senator Helms' and Lee Casey's "American Servicemembers Protection Act"), or by playing the role of an influential insider (as it has done, for example, with the Yugoslavia Tribunal). In deciding this issue, one must carefully and objectively examine the consequences that would flow from the hostile approach.

First, the hostile approach would transform American exceptionalism into unilateralism and/or isolationism by preventing the United States from participating in U.N. peacekeeping operations and cutting off aid to many countries vital to U.S. national security. This would be especially foolhardy at this moment in history when the United States is working hard to expand and hold together an international coalition against the terrorist organizations and their state supporters that were involved in the terrorist attacks of September 11, 2001.

Further, overt opposition to the ICC would erode the moral legitimacy of the United States, which has historically been as important to achieving U.S. foreign policy goals as military and economic might. A concrete example of this was the recent U.S. loss of its seat in the U.N. Commission of Human Rights, where several western countries cited current U.S. opposition to the ICC as warranting their vote against the United States.

Perversely, the approach embodied in Senator Helms' legislation could even turn the United States into a safe haven for international war criminals, since the U.S. would be prevented from surrendering them directly to the ICC or indirectly to another country which would surrender them to the ICC. And the idea that the President should use all means necessary to release any U.S. or allied personnel detained on behalf of the Court is the height of folly, as reflected in headlines describing the legislation as the "Hague Invasion Act."

Second, under the hostile approach, the United States would be prevented from being able to take advantage of the very real benefits of an ICC. The experience with the Yugoslavia Tribunal has shown that, even absent arrests, an international indictment has the effect of isolating rogue leaders, strengthening domestic opposition, and increasing international support for sanctions and even use of force. The United States has recognized these benefits in pushing for the subsequent creation of the *ad hoc* tribunals for Rwanda, Sierra Leone, and Cambodia, as well as proposing the establishment of a tribunal for Iraq. But the establishment of the ICC will signal the end of the era of Security Council-created tribunals, since even our friends and allies at the U.N. will insist that situations involving genocide, crimes against humanity, and war crimes be referred to the existing ICC rather than additional *ad hoc* tribunals. Thus, when the next Rwanda occurs, the United States will not be able to employ the very useful tool of international criminal justice unless it works through the ICC.

To bring home this point, consider that if the ICC had been in existence on September 11, 2001, the United States and the other members of the Security Council could have referred the case of Osama bin Laden and the other masterminds of the attacks on the World Trade Center and Pentagon to the ICC, rather than creating U.S.-led military tribunals which have been subject to harsh criticism in the United States and abroad. An

ICC indictment of these terrorists for their "crimes against humanity" would have strengthened foreign support for the American intervention into Afghanistan and would have deflected bin Laden's attempt to characterize the military action as an American attack against Islam. And if any of the perpetrators fell into any country's custody, an ICC would present a neutral forum for their prosecution that would have enjoyed the support of the Islamic world.

Opponents of the ICC have suggested that without U.S. support, the ICC is destined to be impotent and irrelevant because it will lack the power of the Security Council to enforce its arrest orders. But as the experience of the *ad hoc* Tribunals for Rwanda, Sierra Leone, and most recently Yugoslavia (with the surrender of Milosevic) has proven, in most cases where an ICC is needed, the perpetrators are no longer in power and are in the custody of a new government or of nearby States which are perfectly willing to hand them over to an international tribunal absent Security Council action. Moreover, the Security Council has been prevented (largely by Russian veto threats) from taking any action to impose sanctions on States that have not cooperated with the Yugoslavia Tribunal despite repeated pleas from the Tribunal's Prosecutor and Judges that it do so. Indeed, in the Yugoslavia context, where the perpetrators were still in power when the Tribunal was established, it was not action by the Security Council, but rather the threatened withholding of foreign aid and IMF loans that have induced Croatia and Serbia to hand over indictees. This indicates that, unlike the League of Nations (which United States officials have frequently referred to in this context), the ICC is likely to be a thriving institution even without United States participation. In other words, the United States may actually need the ICC more than the ICC needs the United States.

Third, the United States achieves no real protection from the ICC by remaining outside the ICC regime. This is because, as explained above, Article 12 of the Rome Statute empowers the ICC to exercise jurisdiction over nationals of non-party States who commit crimes in the territory of State Parties. Further, in its Pollyanna-ish refusal to recognize the legitimacy of the ICC's exercise of jurisdiction over the nationals of non-party States, opponents of the ICC have resorted to a questionable legal interpretation which is not only unlikely to sway the ICC or its founding members, but also has the potential of undermining important U.S. law enforcement interests.

If U.S. officials can be indicted by the ICC whether or not the U.S. is a party to the Rome Treaty, then the United States preserves very little by remaining outside the treaty regime, and could protect itself better by signing the treaty. This has been proven to be the case with the Yugoslavia Tribunal, which the U.S. has supported with contributions exceeding $15 million annually, the loan of top-ranking investigators and lawyers from the federal government, the support of troops to permit the safe exhumation of mass graves, and even the provision of U-2 surveillance photographs to locate the places where Serb authorities had tried to hide the evidence of its wrongdoing. This policy bore fruit when the International Prosecutor opened an investigation into allegations of war crimes committed by NATO during the 1999 Kosovo intervention. Despite the briefs and reports of reputable human rights organizations arguing that NATO had committed breaches of international humanitarian law, on June 8, 2000, the International Prosecutor issued a report concluding that charges against NATO personnel were not warranted. This is not to suggest that the United States co-opted the Yugoslavia Tribunal; but when dealing with close calls regarding application of international humanitarian law it is obviously better to have a sympathetic Prosecutor and Court than a hostile one.

Opponents of the ICC like to raise the specter of politicized indictments against American or Israeli officials drafted by prosecutors and confirmed by judges from countries that oppose our policies. A close examination of the list of the countries that have so far ratified the ICC, however, reveals that the ICC will be dominated not by our diplomatic opponents, but instead by our closest friends and allies. Of these 46 ratifying countries, nineteen are NATO or Western European allies, nine are Latin American and Caribbean countries with which the U.S. enjoys close relations, and four are U.S.-friendly Pacific island countries such as New Zealand and the Marshall Islands. With the possible exception of the Central African Republic, no country on the list would give a U.S. foreign policy-maker any cause for concern. On the other hand, the countries that most frequently oppose the United States in the United Nations (Asian and Middle East countries such as China, Cuba, Iraq, Libya, North Korea, Syria, and the Sudan) are the countries least likely to ratify the ICC Statute, so they will not be able to participate in the ICC Assembly of Parties or nominate judges for the ICC's bench or select the Court's Prosecutor. Consequently, even if the U.S. does not ratify the Rome Treaty, the reality is that the ICC is going to be a very U.S.-friendly tribunal, unless, that is, the United States figuratively (and literally) wages war against the institution as suggested in Senator Helms' legislation.

Rebutting the Constitutional Arguments Against the ICC

Much of argument against the ICC concerns the constitutionality of U.S. participation in the Court. But, as Yale Law School constitutional law professor Ruth Wedgwood has written, there are three reasons why we must conclude there "is no forbidding constitutional obstacle to U.S. participation in the Rome Treaty."

First, the ICC includes procedural protections negotiated by the U.S. Department of Justice representatives at Rome that closely follow the guarantees and safeguards of the American Bill of Rights. These include a *Miranda*-type warning, the right to defense counsel, reciprocal discovery, the right to exculpatory evidence, the right to a speedy and public trial, the right to confront witnesses, and a prohibition on double jeopardy.

The only significant departures from U.S. law are that the ICC employs a bench trial before three judges rather than a jury, and it permits the Prosecutor to appeal an acquittal (but not to retry a defendant after the appeals have been decided). There were good reasons for these departures: For grave international crimes, qualified judges who issue detailed written opinions should be preferred over lay persons who issue unwritten verdicts. And if the trial judges misinterpret the applicable international law, whether in favor or to the detriment of the accused, an appeal is important to foster uniform interpretation of international criminal law.

. . . .

Second, the United States has used its treaty power in the past to participate in other international tribunals that have had jurisdiction over U.S. nationals, such as the Yugoslavia Tribunal which was established by the Security Council pursuant to a treaty—the U.N. Charter. Like the ICC, the Yugoslavia Tribunal employs judges rather than a jury, and permits the Prosecutor to appeal acquittals. Moreover, the U.S. Congress has approved legislation authorizing U.S. courts to extradite indicted persons (including those of U.S. nationality) to the Yugoslavia Tribunal where there exists an order for their arrest and surrender. And this legislation has been upheld in a recent federal court case.

Third, the offenses within the ICC's jurisdiction would ordinarily be handled through military courts-martial, which do not permit jury trial, or through extradition of offenders to foreign nations, which often utilize bench trials and do not employ American notions of due process. It should be noted that U.S. federal courts have upheld the extradition of Americans to such foreign jurisdictions for actions that took place on U.S. soil but had an effect abroad.

At the conclusion of the Senate Foreign Relations Committee's hearings on the ICC in July 1998, the Committee submitted several questions about the constitutionality of U.S. participation in the ICC for the Department of Justice to answer for the record. The answers were prepared by Lee Casey's former colleagues in the Department's Office of Legal Counsel. This part of the Committee's published report should be required reading for anyone who has serious concerns about the constitutionality of the ICC. The Department of Justice specifically found that U.S. ratification of the Rome Treaty and surrender of persons including U.S. nationals to the ICC would not violate Article III, section 2 of the Constitution nor any of the provisions of the Bill of Rights.

Conclusion

Opponents of the ICC base their arguments on the assumption that it is not too late for America to prevent the ICC from coming into existence or to marginalize the Court so that it exists as a non-entity. But the spate of ratifications and the numerous powerful countries that are supporting the ICC (including virtually every other member of NATO) indicate that the ICC is a serious international institution that the United States is very soon going to have to learn to live with.

. . . .

[The risks to U.S. service members as well as the potential constitutional problems presented by the ICC have been greatly exaggerated by American opponents of the ICC, while both the practical usefulness of the ICC and the safeguards contained in the ICC Statute have been significantly undervalued. To the extent that American fears of politicized prosecutions are valid, U.S. opposition to the ICC will only increase the likelihood that the ICC will be more hostile than sympathetic to U.S. positions. And, by opposing the Court, the United States may actually engender more international hostility toward U.S. foreign policy than would have resulted from an indictment by the Court. Thus, whether or not the U.S. is able to achieve additional safeguards to prevent the ICC from exercising jurisdiction over U.S. personnel, it will be in the interests of U.S. national security and foreign policy to support, rather than oppose, the ICC.]

It is important to recognize that supporting the ICC does not require immediate U.S. ratification of the Rome Treaty. Perhaps it would be prudent for the United States to let the Court prove itself over a period of years before sending the treaty to the Senate. But in the meantime, when the next Rwanda-like situation comes along, the United States will find value in having the option of Security Council referral to the ICC in its arsenal of foreign policy responses—something the United States can do even if it does not ratify the Rome Treaty so long as it does not enact a version of Senator Helms' and Lee Casey's anti-ICC legislation.

Lee A. Casey, *The Case Against Supporting the International Criminal Court*

Washington University School of Law, Whitney R. Harris Institute for Global Legal Studies, Washington University in St. Louis, International Debate Series, No. 1 (2002)[6]

The United States should not ratify the ICC Treaty. There are two fundamental objections to American participation in the ICC regime. First, U.S. participation would violate our Constitution by subjecting Americans to trial in an international court for offenses

---

6. *See also*, Lee A. Casey, *The Case Against the International Criminal Court*, 25 FORDHAM INT'L L.J. 840 (2001–2002).

otherwise within the judicial power of the United States, and without the guarantees of the Bill of Rights. Second, our ratification of the Rome Treaty would constitute a profound surrender of American sovereignty, undercutting our right of self-government—the first human right, without which all others are simply words on paper, held by grace and favor, and no rights at all.

With respect to the Constitutional objections, by joining the ICC Treaty, the United States would subject American citizens to prosecution and trial in a court that was not established under Article III of the Constitution for criminal offenses otherwise subject to the judicial power of the United States. This, it cannot do. As the Supreme Court explained in the landmark Civil War case of *Ex parte Milligan* (1866), reversing a civilian's conviction by a military tribunal, "[e]very trial involves the exercise of judicial power," and courts not properly established under Article III can exercise "no part of the judicial power of the country."

This rationale is equally, and emphatically, applicable to the ICC, a court where neither the prosecutors nor the judges would have been appointed by the President, by and with the advice and consent of the Senate, and which would not be bound by the fundamental guarantees of the Bill of Rights. In fact, individuals brought before the ICC would only nominally enjoy the rights we in the United States take for granted.

For example, the ICC Treaty guarantees defendants the right "to be tried without undue delay." In the International Criminal Tribunal for the Former Yugoslavia (an institution widely understood to be a model for the permanent ICC), and which also guarantees this "right," defendants often wait more than a year in prison before their trial begins, and many years before a judgment actually is rendered. The Hague prosecutors actually have argued that up to five years would not be too long to wait IN PRISON for a trial, citing case law from the European Court of Human Rights supporting their position.

Such practices, admittedly, have a long pedigree, but they mock the presumption of innocence. Under U.S. law, the federal government must bring a criminal defendant to trial within three months, or let him go.

By the same token, the right of confrontation, guaranteed by the Sixth Amendment, includes the right to know the identity of hostile witnesses, and to exclude most "hearsay" evidence. In the Yugoslavia Tribunal, both anonymous witnesses and virtually unlimited hearsay evidence have been allowed at criminal trials, *large portions of which are conducted in secret*. Again, this is the model for the ICC.

Similarly, under the Constitution's guarantee against double jeopardy a judgment of acquittal cannot be appealed. Under the ICC statute, acquittals are freely appealable by the prosecution, as in the Yugoslav Tribunal, where the Prosecutor has appealed every judgment of acquittal.

In addition, the ICC would not preserve the right to a jury trial. The importance of this right cannot be overstated. Alone among the Constitution's guarantees, the right to a jury trial was stated twice, in Article III (sec. 2) and in the Sixth Amendment. It is not merely a means of determining facts in a judicial proceeding. It is a fundamental check on the abuse of power. As Justice Joseph Story explained: "The great object of a trial by jury in criminal cases is to guard against a spirit of oppression and tyranny on the part of rulers, and against a spirit of violence and vindictiveness on the part of the people." It is "part of that admirable common law, which had fenced round, and interposed barriers on every side against the approaches of arbitrary power." That said, the exclusion of jury trials from the ICC is not surprising, for that Court invites the exercise of arbitrary power by its very design.

The ICC will act as policeman, prosecutor, judge, jury, and jailor—all of these functions will be performed by its personnel, with nothing but bureaucratic divisions of authority, and no division of interest. There would be no appeal from its judgments. If the ICC abuses its power, there will be no recourse. From first to last, the ICC will be the judge in its own case. It will be more absolute than any dictator. As an institution, the ICC is fundamentally inconsistent with the political, philosophical, and legal traditions of the United States.

ICC supporters suggest that U.S. participation in this Court would not violate the Constitution because it would not be "a court of the United States," to which Article III and the Bill of Rights apply. They often point to cases in which the Supreme Court has allowed the extradition of citizens to face charges overseas. There are, however, fundamental differences between United States participation in the ICC Treaty Regime and extradition cases, where American are sought for crimes committed abroad. If the U.S. joined the ICC Treaty, the Court could try American [sic] who never have left the United States, for actions taken entirely within our borders.

A hypothetical, stripped of the emotional overlay inherent in "war crimes" issues, can best illustrate the constitutional point here: The Bill of Rights undoubtedly impedes efficient enforcement of the drug laws—also a subject of international concern. Could the federal government enter a treaty with Mexico and Canada, establishing an offshore "Special Drug Control Court," which would prosecute and try all drug offenses committed anywhere in North America, without the Bill of Rights guarantees? Could the federal government, through the device of a treaty, establish a special overseas court to try sedition cases—thus circumventing the guarantees of the First Amendment[?]

Fortunately, the Supreme Court has never faced such a case. However, in the 1998 case of *United States v. Balsys,* the Court suggested that, where a prosecution by a foreign court is, at least in part, undertaken on behalf of the United States, for example, where "the United States and its allies had enacted substantially similar criminal codes aimed at prosecuting offenses of international character …" then an argument can be made that the Bill of Rights would apply *"simply because that prosecution [would not be] fairly characterized as distinctly 'foreign[.]' The point would be that the prosecution was as much on behalf of the United States as of the prosecuting nation...."*

This would, of course, be exactly the case with the ICC. If the United States became a "State Party" to the ICC Treaty, any prosecutions undertaken by the Court would be "as much on behalf of the United States as of any other State party." Since the full and undiluted guarantees of the Bill of Rights would not be available in the ICC, the United States cannot, constitutionally, sign and ratify the ICC treaty.

ICC supporters also have argued that the U.S. should sign and ratify the Rome Treaty because the Court would be directed against people like Saddam Hussein and Slobodan Milosevic, and not against the United States. Here, as pretty much everywhere, the past is the best predictor of the future. We already have seen this particular drama staged at the Yugoslav Tribunal. Even though that Tribunal was established to investigate crimes committed during 1991–1995 Yugoslav conflict, and even though NATO's air war against Serbia was fought on entirely humanitarian grounds, and even though it was conducted with the highest level of technical proficiency in history, the Hague prosecutors nevertheless undertook a *politically motivated* investigation—motivated *by international humanitarian rights activists along with Russia and China*—of NATO's actions based upon the civilian deaths that resulted.

At the end of this investigation, the prosecutors gave NATO a pass not because, in their view, there were no violations, but because "[i]n all cases, either the law is not sufficiently clear or investigations are unlikely to result in the acquisition of sufficient evidence to substantiate charges against high level accused or against lower accused for particularly heinous offenses."

Significantly, in their report the prosecutors openly acknowledged the very elastic nature of the legal standards in this area, further highlighting the danger that the United States will be the subject of such politically motivated prosecutions in the future: "[t]he answers to these question [*sic*] [regarding allegedly excessive civilian casualties] are not simple. It may be necessary to resolve them on a case-by-case basis, *and the answers may differ depending on the background and values of the decision-maker.* It is unlikely that a human rights lawyer and an experienced combat commander would assign the same relative values to military advantage and to injury to noncombatants. Further, it is unlikely that military commanders with different doctrinal backgrounds and differing degrees of combat experience or national military histories would always agree in close cases."

These are, in fact, "will-build-to-suit" crimes. Whether prosecutions are brought against American officials will depend entirely upon the motivations and political agenda of the ICC.

In response, ICC supporters claim that we can depend upon the professionalism and good will of the Court's personnel. One of the ICC's strongest advocates, former Yugoslav Tribunal Prosecutor Louise Arbour has argued for a powerful Prosecutor and Court, suggesting that "an institution should not be constructed on the assumption that it will be run by incompetent people, acting in bad faith from improper purposes."

The Framers of our Constitution understood the fallacy of this argument probably better than any other group in history. If there is one particular American contribution to the art of statecraft, it is the principle—incorporated into the very fabric of our Constitution—that *the security of our rights cannot be trusted to the good intentions of our leaders.* By its nature, power is capable of abuse and people are, by nature, flawed. As James Madison wrote "the great difficulty lies in this: you must first enable the government to control the governed; and in the next place *oblige it to control itself.*" The ICC would not be obliged to control itself.

It is also often asserted that the principle of "complementarity," found in Article 17 of the Rome Treaty, will check the Court's ability to undertake prosecution of Americans. This is the principle that prohibits the ICC from taking up a case if the appropriate national authorities investigate and prosecute the matter. In fact, this limit on the ICC's power is, in the case of the United States, entirely illusory.

First, as with all other matters under the Rome Treaty, it will be solely within the discretion of the ICC to interpret and apply this provision.

Second, under Article 17, the Court can pursue a case wherever it determines that the responsible State was "unwilling or unable to carry out the investigation or prosecution." In determining whether a State was "unwilling" the Court will consider whether the national proceedings were conducted "independently or impartially." The United States can never meet that test as an institutional matter. Under the Constitution, the President is both the Chief Executive, i.e., the chief law enforcement officer, and the Commander-in-Chief of the armed forces. In any particular case, both the individuals investigating and prosecuting, and the individuals being investigated and prosecuted, work for the same man. Moreover, under command responsibility theories, the President is always a potential—indeed, a likely, target of any investigation. The ICC will simply note that an individual cannot "impartially" investigate himself, and it will be full steam ahead. As a check on the ICC, complementarity is meaningless.

Finally, it's important to understand exactly what is at stake here. Today, the officials of the United States are ultimately accountable for their actions to the American electorate. If the United States were to ratify the ICC Treaty this ultimate accountability would be transferred from the American people to the ICC in a very real and immediate way— through the threat of criminal prosecution and punishment. The policies implemented and actions taken by our national leaders, whether at home or abroad, could be scrutinized by the ICC and punished if, *in its opinion*, criminal violations had occurred. As Alexis de Tocqueville wrote, "[h]e who punishes the criminal is ... the real master of society." Ratification of the ICC Treaty would, in short, constitute a profound surrender of American sovereignty—our right of self-government—the first human right. Without self-government, the rest are words on paper, held by grace and favor, and not rights at all.

That surrender would be to an institution that does not share our interests or values. There is no universally recognized and accepted legal system on the international level, particularly in the area of due process, as the Rome Treaty itself recognizes in requiring that, in the selection of judges, "the principal legal systems of the world," should be represented. Moreover, although a number of Western states have signed this treaty, so have states such as Algeria, Iran, Nigeria, Sudan, Syria and Yemen. According to the U.S. State Department, each of these states has been implicated in the use of torture or extrajudicial killings, or both. Yet, each of them would have as great a voice as the United States in selecting the ICC's Prosecutor and Judges and in the Assembly of State Parties.

This is especially troubling because, as the ICTY Prosecutor conceded, who is and who is not a war criminal is very much a matter of your point of view. And I'd like to give you a fairly poignant example that I learned of, actually, while practicing before the ICTY.

In this case there was a young officer, 20 or 21 years old, who commanded a detachment of regular soldiers, along with a group of irregulars. Irregulars are, of course, always a problem. I think everyone pretty much agrees that, for example, the worst atrocities in Bosnia were committed by irregulars. At any rate, these irregulars were clearly under the officer's command when they all ran into a body of enemy troops.

There was a short, sharp firefight. A number of the enemy were killed or wounded, and the rest threw down their arms and surrendered. At that point, the officer entirely lost control of the situation. His irregulars began to kill the wounded and then the rest of the prisoners—with knives and axes actually.

After a good deal of confusion, the officer managed to form up his regulars around the remaining prisoners, but about a dozen were killed. Now, under our system of military justice, the perpetrators would be prosecuted, but the officer would very likely not be. He gave no order for the killings, and took some action to stop it.

However, under the command responsibility and "knowing presence" theories now current at the ICTY, the ICC's model, this officer is guilty of a war crime. The fact that he did make some attempt to prevent the killing would certainly be taken into account, but very likely as a matter of mitigation at sentencing.

At any rate, this is a real case. It didn't, however, happen in Central Bosnia, or Kosovo, or Eastern Slavonia, and the individuals involved were not Serbs, Croats, or Muslims. As a matter of fact, it happened in Western Pennsylvania. The soldiers were English subjects, at the time, and the irregulars were Iroquois Indians; their victims were French. The young officer was, as a matter of fact, from the county in which I live—Fairfax, Virginia. And, for those of you who are students here at the University, his name—Washington— will grace each of your diplomas.

War is, inherently, a violent affair and the discretion whether to prosecute any particular case in which Americans are involved should be kept firmly in the hands of our institutions, to be made by individuals who are accountable to us for their actions. The ICC is inconsistent with our Constitution and inimical to our national interests. It is an institution of which we should have no part.

Notes and Questions for Discussion

1. What are the potential benefits and hazards to the United States posed by the International Criminal Court?

2. On May 6, 2002, the United States sent the following diplomatic note to the Secretary-General of the United Nations:

Dear Mr. Secretary-General:

This is to inform you, in connection with the Rome Statute of the International Criminal Court adopted on July 17, 1998, that the United States does not intend to become a party to the treaty. Accordingly, the United States has no legal obligations arising from its signature on December 31, 2000. The United States requests that its intention not to become a party, as expressed in this letter, be reflected in the depositary's status lists relating to this treaty.

Sincerely,

John R. Bolton,

Under Secretary of State for Arms Control and International Security[7]

This was characterized by many commentators as "unsigning" the treaty. What was the legal effect of that action?

3. On August 3, 2002, President George W. Bush signed into law the U.S. Servicemembers Protection Act.[8] The law provides for the withdrawal of U.S. military assistance from countries ratifying the ICC treaty, and restricts U.S. participation in United Nations peacekeeping operations unless the United States obtains immunity from prosecution before the ICC. The Act did not slow the spate of ratifications. Over 60 countries have ratified the ICC Treaty since the passage of the U.S. Servicemembers Protection Act (as this book goes to press, there are currently 123 State Parties). The Act did, however, have the unintended consequence of requiring more than $89 million in anti-narcotics assistance to several Central and Latin American countries that ratified the ICC Treaty in 2003.

4. On March 31, 2005 (during the Bush Administration), the United States abstained when the UN Security Council adopted Resolution 1594, referring the Darfur situation to the International Criminal Court; and on February 26, 2011 (during the Obama Administration), the United States voted in favor of Security Council Resolution 1970, referring the Libya situation to the ICC. How do these actions undermine U.S. arguments about the illegitimacy of the ICC? Do they suggest an evolution in U.S. policy toward the ICC?

5. In addition to the Security Council referrals of the situations in Darfur and Libya to the ICC, four States Parties to the Rome Statute — Uganda, the Democratic Republic

---

7. Letter from John R. Bolton, Undersecretary of State for Arms Control and International Security, U.S., to Kofi Annan, Secretary-General, U.N. (May 6, 2002) <http://www.cnn.com/2002/US/05/06/court.letter.text>.

8. Pub. L. No. 107-206 (2002); 22 U.S.C. §§ 7401–7433 (2003).

of the Congo, the Central African Republic and Mali—have referred situations occurring on their territories to the Court. The ICC has also authorized the ICC Prosecutor to investigate the situations in Kenya and Cote d'Ivoire. To date, the ICC has confirmed charges against 25 defendants from these countries. The ICC completed its first case (Thomas Lubanga Dyilo) on December 1, 2014, sentencing him to 15 years in prison for recruitment and use of child soldiers in Congo.

6. Some of the ICC's cases have proven to be particularly controversial, such as charges issued in January 2012 against Uhuru Muigai Kenyatta, the President of Kenya for orchestrating attacks against opponents during national elections. The States of the African Union expressed displeasure that the ICC had brought charges against a sitting President of an African State and threatened to withdraw from the Court. After numerous witnesses recanted or refused to testify, on December 5, 2014, the Prosecutor withdrew the charges against Kenyatta.

Another controversial case involved the charges issued in March 2009 against Omar Hassan Ahmad Al Bashir, the sitting President of the Sudan for crimes against humanity and genocide in Darfur. Al Bashir subsequently flouted the Court (and the Security Council which had referred the matter to the ICC) by visiting several African countries, which declined to arrest and surrender him to The Hague. On February 1, 2015, the leaders of the African Union issued a statement calling on the ICC to suspend the charges against Al Bashir.

Do you think the ICC over-reached when it brought charges against the sitting Presidents of Kenya and the Sudan? Supporters of the charges against them point to the fact that the 1999 indictment by the International Criminal Tribunal for the former Yugoslavia against Serb President Slobodan Milosevic isolated him internationally and eroded support at home, eventually resulting in his ouster. How do you think the situations differ?

7. Responding to missile attacks from Hamas, Israel has conducted large scale military operations in the Gaza Strip in December 2008–January 2009, August 2011, November 2012, and July 2014. In 2009, "Palestine" lodged a declaration accepting the ICC's jurisdiction over the situation of war crimes in the Gaza Strip. After considering the matter for three years, in April 2012, Luis Moreno-Ocampo, the ICC Prosecutor, decided that his office was not the appropriate body to decide whether Palestine was a State, which is a pre-requisite to lodging a jurisdiction-accepting declaration. In November 2012, the United Nations General Assembly adopted a resolution granting Palestine "Observer State status" in the United Nations, and Palestine has subsequently acceded to a number of human rights and international humanitarian treaties over the objection of Israel and the United States. In 2013, Fatou Bensouda, the current Prosecutor of the ICC, announced that Palestine would have to submit a new declaration or instrument of accession to the Registrar of the ICC. On January 1, 2015, the Government of Palestine lodged a declaration under article 12(3) of the Rome Statute accepting the jurisdiction of the International Criminal Court over alleged crimes committed "in the occupied Palestinian territory, including East Jerusalem, since June 13, 2014." On January 2, 2015, the Government of Palestine acceded to the Rome Statute by depositing its instrument of accession with the UN Secretary General. On January 16, 2015, the Prosecutor of the ICC announced the opening of a preliminary examination into the situation of Palestine in order to establish whether the Rome Statute criteria for opening an investigation are met.

If the ICC takes up the matter of war crimes in the Gaza Strip and/or the West Bank, the Security Council can still prevent the Prosecutor and the Court from opening up an investigation by adopting a Chapter VII Resolution at twelve month intervals as provided for in Article 16 of the ICC Statute. Do you think ICC involvement would improve the Israeli-Palestinian situation, make it worse, or have no effect? What are the pros and cons of a Security Council vote requiring the ICC to defer the investigation?

8. The Security Council created the Special Tribunal for Lebanon in 2009, several years after the establishment of the ICC. Additional *ad hoc* international criminal tribunals are currently being contemplated, for example for Southern Sudan and Kosovo. Why do you think the advent of the ICC did not spell the end for new *ad hoc* international criminal tribunals?

Selected Bibliography

Appleman, John A., *Military Tribunals and International Crimes* (1971).

Bass, Gary, *Stay the Hand of Vengeance: The Politics of War Crimes Tribunals* (2000).

Clark, Roger S., & Madeleine Sann, eds., *The Prosecution of International War Crimes* (1996).

Conot, Robert, *Justice at Nuremberg* (1983).

Dinstein, Yoram, & Mala Tabory, eds., *War Crimes in International Law* (1996).

Gutman, Roy, & David Rieff, *Crimes of War: What the Public Should Know* (1999).

Morris, Virginia, & Michael P. Scharf, *An Insider's Guide to the International Criminal Tribunal for the Former Yugoslavia* (1995).

Office of the United States Chief of Counsel for Prosecution of Axis Criminality, *Nazi Conspiracy and Aggression, Opinion and Judgement* (1947).

Pictet, Jean, ed., International Committee of the Red Cross, *Commentaries on the Geneva Conventions of 12 August 1949* (4 vols.) (1952–1960).

Scharf, Michael P., *Balkan Justice: The Story Behind the First International War Crimes Tribunal since Nuremberg* (1997).

Scharf, Michael P., *Customary Internaitonal Law in Times of Fundamental Change: Recognizing Grotian Moments* (2012).

Taylor, Telford, *The Anatomy of the Nuremberg Trials* (1992).

United Nations Secretary General, *The Charter and Judgment of the Nuremberg Tribunal: History and Analysis* (1949).

United Nations War Crimes Commission, *History of the United Nations War Crimes Commission and the Development of the Laws of War* (1948).

Williams, Paul, & Michael P. Scharf, *Peace with Justice?* (2002).

Chapter 9

Detention

John D. Altenburg, Jr. and Thomas B. Nachbar

In this chapter:
Introduction
National Security Detention Determinations
Detainee Treatment
Particular Detainees
Conclusion
Selected Bibliography

Introduction

War and detention go hand-in-hand; virtually all armed conflicts involve some form of detention. Although the laws governing war itself are relatively well-developed, the same cannot be said of even the domestic (much less the international) law of government detentions related to armed conflict. Prior to the events of September 11, 2001, many observers believed detention related to armed conflict to be simple and well understood—detain until the conflict ends, then repatriate detainee. Just as changing mores altered the law of the war a century ago, the same appears to be occurring with respect to the law of armed conflict-related detention, making it an area unusually rich in uncertainty and paradoxes. This chapter highlights these uncertainties within the contemporary context within which they arose.

The focus of this inquiry is national security law, but detention is a general feature of the entire legal system, not merely national security law. Imprisonment as a punishment is itself a form of "detention" (a point obvious to those readers who have experienced that punishment at the hands of high-school assistant principals). Confinement as punishment is outside the scope of this chapter,[1] but even excluding post-conviction detention as punishment, there are many varieties of detention, some of which touch more closely on national security than others. U.S. immigration officials routinely detain thousands of suspected illegal immigrants every year. People who are mentally ill to the point of

---

1. And thus so are military commissions, which have been used to try some detainees for violations of the law of armed conflict but are instruments of punishment, not detention. Military commissions will be discussed only briefly in this chapter to the extent they overlap with detention issues. For an in depth discussion of contemporary use by the U.S. of military commissions *see* David D. Cole, *Military Commissions and the Paradigm of Prevention*, in Guantánamo and Beyond: Exceptional Courts and Military Commissions in Comparative Perspective (Oren Gross and Fionnuala Ni Aolain, eds., Cambridge: Cambridge Univ. Press, 2013) also *available at* <http://scholarship.law.georgetown.edu/cgi/viewcontent.cgi?article=2119&context=facpub>.

presenting a risk to themselves or others are detained under state mental health laws. The 2014 Ebola epidemic reminded us that those who are physically ill to the point of presenting a risk to themselves or others can be detained, or quarantined, under state and federal health laws.[2] Suspected criminals are detained by law enforcement officials on probable cause, subject to reasonable bail, but bail can be withheld if a criminal defendant poses a flight risk or a danger to the community,[3] leaving many criminal defendants languishing in jails for years prior to conviction (or exoneration). Under the law of armed conflict, enemy combatants can be detained as prisoners of war indefinitely — until the termination of hostilities[4] — which can (and frequently does) take years. Citizens of enemy nations — "enemy aliens" — have traditionally been subject to regulation and deportation (and the detention that necessarily accompanies the protracted process of deporting someone to a country at war with the deporting country).

So understood, detention is a tool of law enforcement (arrest and pretrial detention along with incarceration), civil law (in areas like immigration law, civil commitment proceedings, or public health isolation and quarantine), as well as the law of armed conflict. As the U.S. has engaged in multi-faceted campaigns against both state and non-state actors over the last three decades, it has invoked both the law-enforcement and armed-conflict paradigms, and detention has become prominent in U.S. and international debates about national security law. It is important to avoid the temptation to place too much emphasis on recent events in considering the development of detention law, but events since 2001 are a useful lens for viewing detention law, because many of the legal and practical distinctions present in detention law have been tested by the unique legal and practical considerations inherent in the series of conflicts the U.S. has found itself a party to in the last decade.

Detention raises issues that sound in both international law and domestic law. We consider both here, although we consider the international law largely through its application in U.S. domestic law. In many ways, detention is unique among war powers because the fact of detention (and the possibility of a court-ordered release) provides a rare vehicle for courts to be involved in applying the laws related to armed conflict during the conflict. Moreover, the international law of armed conflict is shaped in many ways by state practice, and in the case of detention, some U.S. domestic laws reference the international legal standard, providing a particularly close connection between international and domestic law in the field of detention. Matters of national security law frequently require careful balancing of both public security and individual rights — balancing the collective right to safety with the individual right to liberty. In this way national security detention is not unlike other governmental limits on liberty, such as state-mandated detention, isolation, and quarantine related to criminal law, health, public safety, and other civil uses of

---

2. The federal government derives its authority for isolation and quarantine from its commerce, rather than its war, powers. Under section 361 of the Public Health Service Act (42 U.S. Code § 264), the U.S. Secretary of Health and Human Services is authorized to take measures to prevent the entry and spread of communicable diseases from foreign countries into the United States and between States, an authority that has been delegated to the Centers for Disease Control and Prevention (CDC). States have general police power to protect the health, safety, and welfare of persons within their borders, and to control the spread of disease within their borders, States have laws to enforce the use of isolation and quarantine. These laws vary from State to State. In most States, breaking a quarantine order is a criminal misdemeanor.

3. United States v. Salerno, 481 U.S. 739 (1987).

4. Geneva Convention Relative to the Treatment of Prisoners of War, Aug. 12, 1949, 6 U.S.T. 3316, 75 U.N.T.S. 135 (GC III), art. 118.

detention. In all such cases, there is a balance between individual and civil rights and public safety and public health concerns.

The modern international law of armed conflict, in the form of the Geneva Conventions, provides many rules for determining not only who can be detained but also how those detained must be treated. While the applicability of the Geneva Conventions to the full range of post-2001 conflicts is itself a source of debate, the general distinction between detention determinations and detention treatment issues is valuable, and is one we retain here. Consequently, the balance of this chapter is organized along those lines: detention determinations and detainee treatment, with separate treatment of the international and domestic legal considerations of both.

National Security Detention Determinations

Little distinction was made between enemy combatants and enemy non-combatants in early recorded history; prisoners were consequently taken not only to incapacitate them as combatants but also as compensation to victors. Principles of distinction have developed considerably since then. In an international armed conflict (IAC), the Geneva Conventions (GC) authorize the routine detention of qualified combatants as prisoners of war ("POWs") and provide detailed rules for their treatment. Any person meeting specific GC criteria who has committed a belligerent act is presumed to qualify as a POW unless otherwise determined by a "competent tribunal."[5] The protections afforded to prisoners of war by the Geneva Conventions include the obligation of humane treatment,[6] the retention by POWs of their full civil capacity,[7] protections against torture or "any other form of coercion,"[8] provision of canteens (with profit-sharing to go to the prisoners)[9] and even advances of the prisoners' military pay.[10] Anywhere POWs are held must be open to the International Committee of the Red Cross (ICRC) and other "protecting powers," who have the right to access and inspect "all premises occupied by prisoners of war" and to interview POWs without witnesses. That access may be limited only in cases of "imperative military necessity."[11] Prisoners of war must be "released and repatriated without delay after the cessation of active hostilities."[12]

Civilians, on the other hand, fall into a very different classification. In an IAC, the Geneva Conventions treat civilians as "protected persons" who may not be targeted and may be detained only "if the security of the Detaining Power makes it absolutely necessary."[13] That determination is to be made by a court or administrative board and must be reconsidered twice yearly.[14] The ICRC and other "protecting powers" have similar access

---

5. GC III, art. 4. Some individuals, such as medical personnel and chaplains, while not technically POWs qualify for similar protection. *See* GC III, art. 33.
6. GC III, art. 13.
7. GC III, art. 14.
8. GC III, art. 17.
9. GC III, art. 28.
10. GC III, art. 60.
11. GC III, art. 126.
12. GC III, art. 118.
13. Geneva Convention Relative to the Protection of Civilian Persons in Time of War, Aug. 12, 1949, 6 U.S.T. 3517, 75 U.N.T.S. 287 (GC IV), art. 42.
14. GC IV, art. 43.

to internment facilities and internees as for POWs.[15] Protected persons must be detained separately from POWs[16] and, if possible, should be detained in family units,[17] which gives a very different picture of detention from that for POWs.

In a non-international armed conflict (NIAC), in which the primary guidance is likely to come from Common Article 3 of the Geneva Conventions,[18] the law is considerably less well-defined,[19] making conflict classification extremely important for determining the law applicable to detention, as we shall see in the cases below.

Many domestic laws also affect detention determinations. As an initial consideration, the President must have authority to detain someone, either a specified or inherent constitutional power or by way of a statutory grant of authority from Congress. Even then, detention must be consistent with constitutional and statutory government power. In the case of detention, courts generally retain the ultimate authority for making detention determinations, through the power to grant writs of habeas corpus, a power with constitutional significance.

Actual detention determinations require the application of all of these rules.

The recent history of combatant-related detention in the U.S. has been a story of struggle between the executive and the judiciary over the power to make detention determinations. President Bush sought to retain exclusive power to make detention determinations with a geographic solution: keep U.S. detainees outside of U.S. territory most notably at the U.S. naval base at Guantanamo Bay, Cuba, in the theatres of combat, and at several other sites (including the so-called "CIA black sites") until 2006. He asserted (with Congress's agreement) that U.S. courts did not have jurisdiction over petitions for habeas corpus from those detainees, an assertion tested through a series of cases (and statutes) culminating in *Boumediene v. Bush*.

Boumediene v. Bush

553 U.S. 723 (2008)

Justice KENNEDY delivered the opinion of the Court.

Petitioners are aliens designated as enemy combatants and detained at the United States Naval Station at Guantanamo Bay, Cuba. There are others detained there, also aliens, who are not parties to this suit.

Petitioners present a question not resolved by our earlier cases relating to the detention of aliens at Guantanamo: whether they have the constitutional privilege of habeas corpus, a privilege not to be withdrawn except in conformance with the Suspension Clause, Art. I, § 9, cl. 2. We hold these petitioners do have the habeas corpus privilege. Congress has enacted a statute, the Detainee Treatment Act of 2005 (DTA), 119 Stat. 2739, that provides certain procedures for review of the detainees' status. We hold that those procedures are

---

15. GC IV, art. 143.

16. GC IV, art. 84.

17. GC IV, art. 82.

18. Note, however, that Additional Protocol II ("AP II") of the Geneva Conventions does govern non-international armed conflicts, and provides additional guidance. The U.S. has signed, but not ratified, AP II, and so we include reference to it only where helpful.

19. The primary substantive requirement of Common Article 3 is that anyone not taking part in the conflict (including combatants out of the fight) "shall in all circumstances be treated humanely, without any adverse distinction founded on race, colour, religion or faith, sex, birth or wealth, or any other similar criteria" including some specific protections that we discuss below.

not an adequate and effective substitute for habeas corpus. Therefore § 7 of the Military Commissions Act of 2006(MCA), 28 U.S.C.A. § 2241(e) (Supp.2007), operates as an unconstitutional suspension of the writ. We do not address whether the President has authority to detain these petitioners nor do we hold that the writ must issue. These and other questions regarding the legality of the detention are to be resolved in the first instance by the District Court.* * *

I

Under the Authorization for Use of Military Force (AUMF), § 2(a), 115 Stat. 224, note following 50 U.S.C. § 1541 (2000 ed., Supp. V), the President is authorized "to use all necessary and appropriate force against those nations, organizations, or persons he determines planned, authorized, committed, or aided the terrorist attacks that occurred on September 11, 2001, or harbored such organizations or persons, in order to prevent any future acts of international terrorism against the United States by such nations, organizations or persons."

In *Hamdi v. Rumsfeld*, 542 U.S. 507, 124 S.Ct. 2633, 159 L.Ed.2d 578 (2004), five Members of the Court recognized that detention of individuals who fought against the United States in Afghanistan "for the duration of the particular conflict in which they were captured, is so fundamental and accepted an incident to war as to be an exercise of the 'necessary and appropriate force' Congress has authorized the President to use." *Id.,* at 518, 124 S.Ct. 2633 (plurality opinion of O'Connor, J.), *id.,* at 588–589, 124 S.Ct. 2633 (THOMAS, J., dissenting). After *Hamdi,* the Deputy Secretary of Defense established Combatant Status Review Tribunals (CSRTs) to determine whether individuals detained at Guantanamo were "enemy combatants," as the Department defines that term.* * *

Interpreting the AUMF, the Department of Defense ordered the detention of these petitioners, and they were transferred to Guantanamo. Some of these individuals were apprehended on the battlefield in Afghanistan, others in places as far away from there as Bosnia and Gambia. All are foreign nationals, but none is a citizen of a nation now at war with the United States. Each denies he is a member of the al Qaeda terrorist network that carried out the September 11 attacks or of the Taliban regime that provided sanctuary for al Qaeda. Each petitioner appeared before a separate CSRT; was determined to be an enemy combatant; and has sought a writ of habeas corpus in the United States District Court for the District of Columbia.

The first actions commenced in February 2002. The District Court ordered the cases dismissed for lack of jurisdiction because the naval station is outside the sovereign territory of the United States. See *Rasul v. Bush,* 215 F.Supp.2d 55 (2002). The Court of Appeals for the District of Columbia Circuit affirmed. See *Al Odah v. United States,* 321 F.3d 1134, 1145 (2003). We granted certiorari and reversed, holding that 28 U.S.C. § 2241 extended statutory habeas corpus jurisdiction to Guantanamo. See *Rasul v. Bush,* 542 U.S. 466, 473, 124 S.Ct. 2686, 159 L.Ed.2d 548 (2004). The constitutional issue presented in the instant cases was not reached in *Rasul. Id.,* at 476, 124 S.Ct. 2686.

After *Rasul,* petitioners' cases were consolidated and entertained in two separate proceedings. In the first set of cases, Judge Richard J. Leon granted the Government's motion to dismiss, holding that the detainees had no rights that could be vindicated in a habeas corpus action. In the second set of cases Judge Joyce Hens Green reached the opposite conclusion, holding the detainees had rights under the Due Process Clause of the Fifth Amendment. See *Khalid v. Bush,* 355 F.Supp.2d 311, 314 (DDC 2005); *In re Guantanamo Detainee Cases,* 355 F.Supp.2d 443, 464 (DDC 2005).

While appeals were pending from the District Court decisions, Congress passed the DTA. Subsection (e) of § 1005 of the DTA amended 28 U.S.C. § 2241 to provide that "no court, justice, or judge shall have jurisdiction to hear or consider … an application for a writ of habeas corpus filed by or on behalf of an alien detained by the Department of Defense at Guantanamo Bay, Cuba." 119 Stat. 2742. Section 1005 further provides that the Court of Appeals for the District of Columbia Circuit shall have "exclusive" jurisdiction to review decisions of the CSRTs. *Ibid.*

In *Hamdan v. Rumsfeld*, 548 U.S. 557, 576–577, 126 S.Ct. 2749, 165 L.Ed.2d 723 (2006), the Court held this provision did not apply to cases (like petitioners') pending when the DTA was enacted. Congress responded by passing the MCA, 10 U.S.C.A. § 948a *et seq.* (Supp.2007), which again amended § 2241. * * *

The Court of Appeals concluded that MCA § 7 must be read to strip from it, and all federal courts, jurisdiction to consider petitioners' habeas corpus applications, *id.,* at 987; that petitioners are not entitled to the privilege of the writ or the protections of the Suspension Clause, *id.,* at 990–991; and, as a result, that it was unnecessary to consider whether Congress provided an adequate and effective substitute for habeas corpus in the DTA.

We granted certiorari. 551 U.S. ___, 127 S.Ct. 3067, 168 L.Ed.2d 755 (2007).

* * *

III

In deciding the constitutional questions now presented we must determine whether petitioners are barred from seeking the writ or invoking the protections of the Suspension Clause either because of their status, *i.e.,* petitioners' designation by the Executive Branch as enemy combatants, or their physical location, *i.e.,* their presence at Guantanamo Bay. The Government contends that noncitizens designated as enemy combatants and detained in territory located outside our Nation's borders have no constitutional rights and no privilege of habeas corpus. Petitioners contend they do have cognizable constitutional rights and that Congress, in seeking to eliminate recourse to habeas corpus as a means to assert those rights, acted in violation of the Suspension Clause.

We begin with a brief account of the history and origins of the writ. Our account proceeds from two propositions. First, protection for the privilege of habeas corpus was one of the few safeguards of liberty specified in a Constitution that, at the outset, had no Bill of Rights. In the system conceived by the Framers the writ had a centrality that must inform proper interpretation of the Suspension Clause. Second, to the extent there were settled precedents or legal commentaries in 1789 regarding the extraterritorial scope of the writ or its application to enemy aliens, those authorities can be instructive for the present cases.

A

The Framers viewed freedom from unlawful restraint as a fundamental precept of liberty, and they understood the writ of habeas corpus as a vital instrument to secure that freedom. Experience taught, however, that the common-law writ all too often had been insufficient to guard against the abuse of monarchial power. That history counseled the necessity for specific language in the Constitution to secure the writ and ensure its place in our legal system.

Magna Carta decreed that no man would be imprisoned contrary to the law of the land. Art. 39, in Sources of Our Liberties 17 (R. Perry & J. Cooper eds. 1959) ("No free man shall be taken or imprisoned or dispossessed, or outlawed, or banished, or in any way destroyed, nor will we go upon him, nor send upon him, except by the legal judgment of his peers or by the law of the land"). Important as the principle was, the Barons at

Runnymede prescribed no specific legal process to enforce it. Holdsworth tells us, however, that gradually the writ of habeas corpus became the means by which the promise of Magna Carta was fulfilled. 9 W. Holdsworth, A History of English Law 112 (1926) (hereinafter Holdsworth).

The development was painstaking, even by the centuries-long measures of English constitutional history. The writ was known and used in some form at least as early as the reign of Edward I. *Id.*, at 108–125. Yet at the outset it was used to protect not the rights of citizens but those of the King and his courts. The early courts were considered agents of the Crown, designed to assist the King in the exercise of his power. See J. Baker, An Introduction to English Legal History 38–39 (4th ed. 2002). Thus the writ, while it would become part of the foundation of liberty for the King's subjects, was in its earliest use a mechanism for securing compliance with the King's laws. See Halliday & White, The Suspension Clause: English Text, Imperial Contexts, and American Implications, 94 Va. L. Rev. (2008) (hereinafter Halliday & White) (noting that "conceptually the writ arose from a theory of power rather than a theory of liberty")). Over time it became clear that by issuing the writ of habeas corpus common-law courts sought to enforce the King's prerogative to inquire into the authority of a jailer to hold a prisoner. See M. Hale, Prerogatives of the King 229 (D. Yale ed.1976); 2 J. Story, Commentaries on the Constitution of the United States § 1341, p. 237 (3d ed. 1858) (noting that the writ ran "into all parts of the king's dominions; for it is said, that the king is entitled, at all times, to have an account, why the liberty of any of his subjects is restrained").

Even so, from an early date it was understood that the King, too, was subject to the law. As the writers said of Magna Carta, "it means this, that the king is and shall be below the law." 1 F. Pollock & F. Maitland, History of English Law 173 (2d ed. 1909); see also 2 Bracton On the Laws and Customs of England 33 (S. Thorne transl. 1968) ("The king must not be under man but under God and under the law, because law makes the king"). And, by the 1600's, the writ was deemed less an instrument of the King's power and more a restraint upon it. See Collings, Habeas Corpus for Convicts—Constitutional Right or Legislative Grace, 40 Calif. L. Rev. 335, 336 (1952) (noting that by this point the writ was "the appropriate process for checking illegal imprisonment by public officials").

Still, the writ proved to be an imperfect check. Even when the importance of the writ was well understood in England, habeas relief often was denied by the courts or suspended by Parliament. Denial or suspension occurred in times of political unrest, to the anguish of the imprisoned and the outrage of those in sympathy with them.

A notable example from this period was *Darnel's Case,* 3 How. St. Tr. 1 (K.B. 1627). The events giving rise to the case began when, in a display of the Stuart penchant for authoritarian excess, Charles I demanded that Darnel and at least four others lend him money. Upon their refusal, they were imprisoned. The prisoners sought a writ of habeas corpus; and the King filed a return in the form of a warrant signed by the Attorney General. *Ibid.* The court held this was a sufficient answer and justified the subjects' continued imprisonment. *Id.*, at 59.

There was an immediate outcry of protest. The House of Commons promptly passed the Petition of Right, 3 Car. 1, ch. 1 (1627), 5 Statutes of the Realm 23, 24 (reprint 1963), which condemned executive "imprison[ment] without any cause" shown, and declared that "no freeman in any such manner as is before mentioned [shall] be imprisoned or detained." Yet a full legislative response was long delayed. The King soon began to abuse his authority again, and Parliament was dissolved. * * * Civil strife and the Interregnum soon followed, and not until 1679 did Parliament try once more to secure the writ, this time through the Habeas Corpus Act of 1679, 31 Car. 2, ch. 2, *id.,* at 935. The Act, which later would be described by Blackstone as the "stable bulwark of our liberties," 1 W. Blackstone, Commentaries *137 (hereinafter Blackstone), established procedures for issuing the writ; and it was the model upon which the habeas statutes of the 13 American Colonies were based, see Collings, *supra,* at 338–339.

This history was known to the Framers. It no doubt confirmed their view that pendular swings to and away from individual liberty were endemic to undivided, uncontrolled power. The Framers' inherent distrust of governmental power was the driving force behind the constitutional plan that allocated powers among three independent branches. This design serves not only to make Government accountable but also to secure individual liberty. See *Loving v. United States,* 517 U.S. 748, 756, 116 S.Ct. 1737, 135 L.Ed.2d 36 (1996) (noting that "[e]ven before the birth of this country, separation of powers was known to be a defense against tyranny"); cf. *Youngstown Sheet & Tube Co. v. Sawyer,* 343 U.S. 579, 635, 72 S.Ct. 863, 96 L.Ed. 1153 (1952) (Jackson, J., concurring) ("[T]he Constitution diffuses power the better to secure liberty"); *Clinton v. City of New York,* 524 U.S. 417, 450, 118 S.Ct. 2091, 141 L.Ed.2d 393 (1998) (KENNEDY, J., concurring) ("Liberty is always at stake when one or more of the branches seek to transgress the separation of powers"). Because the Constitution's separation-of-powers structure, like the substantive guarantees of the Fifth and Fourteenth Amendments, see *Yick Wo v. Hopkins,* 118 U.S. 356, 374, 6 S.Ct. 1064, 30 L.Ed. 220 (1886), protects persons as well as citizens, foreign nationals who have the privilege of litigating in our courts can seek to enforce separation-of-powers principles, see, *e.g., INS v. Chadha,* 462 U.S. 919, 958–959, 103 S.Ct. 2764, 77 L.Ed.2d 317 (1983).

That the Framers considered the writ a vital instrument for the protection of individual liberty is evident from the care taken to specify the limited grounds for its suspension: "The Privilege of the Writ of Habeas Corpus shall not be suspended, unless when in Cases of Rebellion or Invasion the public Safety may require it." Art. I, §9, cl. 2; see Amar, Of Sovereignty and Federalism, 96 Yale L.J. 1425, 1509, n. 329 (1987) ("[T]he non-suspension clause is the original Constitution's most explicit reference to remedies"). The word "privilege" was used, perhaps, to avoid mentioning some rights to the exclusion of others. (Indeed, the only mention of the term "right" in the Constitution, as ratified, is in its clause giving Congress the power to protect the rights of authors and inventors. See Art. I, §8, cl. 8.)

Surviving accounts of the ratification debates provide additional evidence that the Framers deemed the writ to be an essential mechanism in the separation-of-powers scheme. In a critical exchange with Patrick Henry at the Virginia ratifying convention Edmund Randolph referred to the Suspension Clause as an "exception" to the "power given to Congress to regulate courts." See 3 Debates in the Several State Conventions on the Adoption of the Federal Constitution 460–464 (J. Elliot 2d ed. 1876) (hereinafter Elliot's Debates). A resolution passed by the New York ratifying convention made clear its understanding that the Clause not only protects against arbitrary suspensions of the writ but also guarantees an affirmative right to judicial inquiry into the causes of detention. See Resolution of the New York Ratifying Convention (July 26, 1788), in 1 Elliot's Debates 328 (noting the convention's understanding "[t]hat every person restrained of his liberty is entitled to an inquiry into the lawfulness of such restraint, and to a removal thereof if unlawful; and that such inquiry or removal ought not to be denied or delayed, except when, on account of public danger, the Congress shall suspend the privilege of the writ of *habeas corpus*"). Alexander Hamilton likewise explained that by providing the detainee a judicial forum to challenge detention, the writ preserves limited government. As he explained in The Federalist No. 84:

"[T]he practice of arbitrary imprisonments, have been, in all ages, the favorite and most formidable instruments of tyranny. The observations of the judicious Blackstone ... are well worthy of recital: 'To bereave a man of life ... or by violence to confiscate his estate, without accusation or trial, would be so gross and notorious an act of despotism as must at once convey the alarm of tyranny throughout the whole nation; but confinement of the person, by secretly hurrying him to jail, where his sufferings are unknown or forgotten, is a less public, a less striking, and therefore a *more dangerous engine* of arbitrary government.' And as a remedy for this fatal evil he is everywhere peculiarly emphatical in his encomiums on the *habeas corpus* act, which in one place he calls 'the BULWARK of the British Constitution.'" C. Rossiter ed., p. 512 (1961) (quoting 1 Blackstone *136, 4 *id.*, at *438).

Post-1789 habeas developments in England, though not bearing upon the Framers' intent, do verify their foresight. Those later events would underscore the need for structural barriers against arbitrary suspensions of the writ. Just as the writ had been vulnerable to executive and parliamentary encroachment on both sides of the Atlantic before the American Revolution, despite the Habeas Corpus Act of 1679, the writ was suspended with frequency in England during times of political unrest after 1789. Parliament suspended the writ for much of the period from 1792 to 1801, resulting in rampant arbitrary imprisonment. See Hall & Albion 550. Even as late as World War I, at least one prominent English jurist complained that the Defence of the Realm Act, 1914, 4 & 5 Geo. 5, ch. 29(1)(a), effectively had suspended the privilege of habeas corpus for any person suspected of "communicating with the enemy." See *King v. Halliday*, [1917] A.C. 260, 299 (Lord Shaw, dissenting); see generally A. Simpson, In the Highest Degree Odious: Detention Without Trial in Wartime Britain 6–7, 24–25 (1992).

In our own system the Suspension Clause is designed to protect against these cyclical abuses. The Clause protects the rights of the detained by a means consistent with the essential design of the Constitution. It ensures that, except during periods of formal suspension, the Judiciary will have a time-tested device, the writ, to maintain the "delicate balance of governance" that is itself the surest safeguard of liberty. See *Hamdi*, 542 U.S., at 536, 124 S.Ct. 2633 (plurality opinion). The Clause protects the rights of the detained by affirming the duty and authority of the Judiciary to call the jailer to account. See *Preiser v. Rodriguez*, 411 U.S. 475, 484, 93 S.Ct. 1827, 36 L.Ed.2d 439 (1973) ("[T]he essence of habeas corpus is an attack by a person in custody upon the legality of that custody"); cf. *In re Jackson*, 15 Mich. 417, 439–440 (1867) (Cooley, J., concurring) ("The important fact to be observed in regard to the mode of procedure upon this [habeas] writ is, that it is directed to, and served upon, not the person confined, but his jailer"). The separation-of-powers doctrine, and the history that influenced its design, therefore must inform the reach and purpose of the Suspension Clause.

B

The broad historical narrative of the writ and its function is central to our analysis, but we seek guidance as well from founding-era authorities addressing the specific question before us: whether foreign nationals, apprehended and detained in distant countries during a time of serious threats to our Nation's security, may assert the privilege of the writ and seek its protection. The Court has been careful not to foreclose the possibility that the protections of the Suspension Clause have expanded along with post-1789 developments that define the present scope of the writ. See *INS v. St. Cyr*, 533 U.S. 289, 300–301, 121 S.Ct. 2271, 150 L.Ed.2d 347 (2001). But the analysis may begin with precedents as of 1789, for the Court has said that "at the absolute minimum" the Clause protects the writ as it existed when the Constitution was drafted and ratified. *Id.*, at 301, 121 S.Ct. 2271.

To support their arguments, the parties in these cases have examined historical sources to construct a view of the common-law writ as it existed in 1789—as have *amici* whose expertise in legal history the Court has relied upon in the past. See Brief for Legal Historians as *Amici Curiae;* see also *St. Cyr, supra,* at 302, n. 16, 121 S.Ct. 2271. The Government argues the common-law writ ran only to those territories over which the Crown was sovereign. See Brief for Respondents 27. Petitioners argue that jurisdiction followed the King's officers. See Brief for Petitioner Boumediene et al. 11. Diligent search by all parties reveals no certain conclusions. In none of the cases cited do we find that a common-law court would or would not have granted, or refused to hear for lack of jurisdiction, a petition for a writ of habeas corpus brought by a prisoner deemed an enemy combatant, under a standard like the one the Department of Defense has used in these cases, and when held in a territory, like Guantanamo, over which the Government has total military and civil control.

We know that at common law a petitioner's status as an alien was not a categorical bar to habeas corpus relief. See, *e.g., Sommersett's Case,* 20 How. St. Tr. 1, 80–82 (1772) (ordering an African slave freed upon finding the custodian's return insufficient). We know as well that common-law courts entertained habeas petitions brought by enemy aliens detained in England—"entertained" at least in the sense that the courts held hearings to determine the threshold question of entitlement to the writ. See *Case of Three Spanish Sailors,* 2 Black. W. 1324, 96 Eng. Rep. 775 (C.P. 1779); *King v. Schiever,* 2 Burr. 765, 97 Eng. Rep. 551 (K.B.1759); *Du Castro's Case,* Fort. 195, 92 Eng. Rep. 816 (K.B.1697).

* * *

We find the evidence as to the geographic scope of the writ at common law informative, but, again, not dispositive. * * *

In the end a categorical or formal conception of sovereignty does not provide a comprehensive or altogether satisfactory explanation for the general understanding that prevailed when Lord Mansfield considered issuance of the writ outside England. In 1759 the writ did not run to Scotland but did run to Ireland, even though, at that point, Scotland and England had merged under the rule of a single sovereign, whereas the Crowns of Great Britain and Ireland remained separate (at least in theory). See *Cowle, supra,* at 856–857, 97 Eng. Rep., 600; 1 Blackstone *100–101. But there was at least one major difference between Scotland's and Ireland's relationship with England during this period that might explain why the writ ran to Ireland but not to Scotland. English law did not generally apply in Scotland (even after the Act of Union) but it did apply in Ireland. Blackstone put it as follows: "[A]s Scotland and England are now one and the same kingdom, and yet differ in their municipal laws; so England and Ireland are, on the other hand, distinct kingdoms, and yet in general agree in their laws." *Id.,* at *100. This distinction, and not formal notions of sovereignty, may well explain why the writ did not run to Scotland (and Hanover) but would run to Ireland.

The prudential barriers that may have prevented the English courts from issuing the writ to Scotland and Hanover are not relevant here. We have no reason to believe an order from a federal court would be disobeyed at Guantanamo. No Cuban court has jurisdiction to hear these petitioners' claims, and no law other than the laws of the United States applies at the naval station. The modern-day relations between the United States and Guantanamo thus differ in important respects from the 18th-century relations between England and the kingdoms of Scotland and Hanover. This is reason enough for us to discount the relevance of the Government's analogy.

Each side in the present matter argues that the very lack of a precedent on point supports its position. The Government points out there is no evidence that a court sitting in England granted habeas relief to an enemy alien detained abroad; petitioners respond there is no evidence that a court refused to do so for lack of jurisdiction.

Both arguments are premised, however, upon the assumption that the historical record is complete and that the common law, if properly understood, yields a definite answer to the questions before us. There are reasons to doubt both assumptions. Recent scholarship points to the inherent shortcomings in the historical record. See Halliday & White 14–15 (noting that most reports of 18th-century habeas proceedings were not printed). And given the unique status of Guantanamo Bay and the particular dangers of terrorism in the modern age, the common-law courts simply may not have confronted cases with close parallels to this one. We decline, therefore, to infer too much, one way or the other, from the lack of historical evidence on point.

IV

Drawing from its position that at common law the writ ran only to territories over which the Crown was sovereign, the Government says the Suspension Clause affords petitioners no rights because the United States does not claim sovereignty over the place of detention.

Guantanamo Bay is not formally part of the United States. See DTA §1005(g), 119 Stat. 2743. And under the terms of the lease between the United States and Cuba, Cuba retains "ultimate sovereignty" over the territory while the United States exercises "complete jurisdiction and control." See Lease of Lands for Coaling and Naval Stations, Feb. 23, 1903, U.S.-Cuba, Art. III, T.S. No. 418 (hereinafter 1903 Lease Agreement); *Rasul*, 542 U.S., at 471, 124 S.Ct. 2686. Under the terms of the 1934 Treaty, however, Cuba effectively has no rights as a sovereign until the parties agree to modification of the 1903 Lease Agreement or the United States abandons the base. See Treaty Defining Relations with Cuba, May 29, 1934, U.S.-Cuba, Art. III, 48 Stat. 1683, T.S. No. 866.

The United States contends, nevertheless, that Guantanamo is not within its sovereign control. This was the Government's position well before the events of September 11, 2001. * * *

We [ ] do not question the Government's position that Cuba, not the United States, maintains sovereignty, in the legal and technical sense of the term, over Guantanamo Bay. But this does not end the analysis. * * * As we did in *Rasul*, however, we take notice of the obvious and uncontested fact that the United States, by virtue of its complete jurisdiction and control over the base, maintains de facto sovereignty over this territory. See 542 U.S., at 480, 124 S.Ct. 2686; *id.*, at 487, 124 S.Ct. 2686 (KENNEDY, J., concurring in judgment).

* * *

B

The Government's formal sovereignty-based test raises troubling separation-of-powers concerns as well. The political history of Guantanamo illustrates the deficiencies of this approach. The United States has maintained complete and uninterrupted control of the bay for over 100 years. At the close of the Spanish-American War, Spain ceded control over the entire island of Cuba to the United States and specifically "relinquishe[d] all claim [s] of sovereignty ... and title." See Treaty of Paris, Dec. 10, 1898, U.S.-Spain, Art. I, 30 Stat. 1755, T.S. No. 343. From the date the treaty with Spain was signed until the Cuban Republic was established on May 20, 1902, the United States governed the territory "in trust" for the benefit of the Cuban people. *Neely v. Henkel*, 180 U.S. 109, 120, 21 S.Ct. 302, 45 L.Ed. 448 (1901); H. Thomas, Cuba or The Pursuit of Freedom 436, 460 (1998).

And although it recognized, by entering into the 1903 Lease Agreement, that Cuba retained "ultimate sovereignty" over Guantanamo, the United States continued to maintain the same plenary control it had enjoyed since 1898. Yet the Government's view is that the Constitution had no effect there, at least as to noncitizens, because the United States disclaimed sovereignty in the formal sense of the term. The necessary implication of the argument is that by surrendering formal sovereignty over any unincorporated territory to a third party, while at the same time entering into a lease that grants total control over the territory back to the United States, it would be possible for the political branches to govern without legal constraint.

Our basic charter cannot be contracted away like this. The Constitution grants Congress and the President the power to acquire, dispose of, and govern territory, not the power to decide when and where its terms apply. * * *

These concerns have particular bearing upon the Suspension Clause question in the cases now before us, for the writ of habeas corpus is itself an indispensable mechanism for monitoring the separation of powers. The test for determining the scope of this provision must not be subject to manipulation by those whose power it is designed to restrain.

C

* * *

It is true that before today the Court has never held that noncitizens detained by our Government in territory over which another country maintains *de jure* sovereignty have any rights under our Constitution. But the cases before us lack any precise historical parallel. They involve individuals detained by executive order for the duration of a conflict that, if measured from September 11, 2001, to the present, is already among the longest wars in American history. See Oxford Companion to American Military History 849 (1999). The detainees, moreover, are held in a territory that, while technically not part of the United States, is under the complete and total control of our Government. Under these circumstances the lack of a precedent on point is no barrier to our holding.

We hold that Art. I, § 9, cl. 2, of the Constitution has full effect at Guantanamo Bay. If the privilege of habeas corpus is to be denied to the detainees now before us, Congress must act in accordance with the requirements of the Suspension Clause. * * * The MCA does not purport to be a formal suspension of the writ; and the Government, in its submissions to us, has not argued that it is. Petitioners, therefore, are entitled to the privilege of habeas corpus to challenge the legality of their detention.

* * *

It bears repeating that our opinion does not address the content of the law that governs petitioners' detention. That is a matter yet to be determined. We hold that petitioners may invoke the fundamental procedural protections of habeas corpus. The laws and Constitution are designed to survive, and remain in force, in extraordinary times. Liberty and security can be reconciled; and in our system they are reconciled within the framework of the law. The Framers decided that habeas corpus, a right of first importance, must be a part of that framework, a part of that law.

The determination by the Court of Appeals that the Suspension Clause and its protections are inapplicable to petitioners was in error. The judgment of the Court of Appeals is reversed. The cases are remanded to the Court of Appeals with instructions that it remand the cases to the District Court for proceedings consistent with this opinion.

It is so ordered.

Boumediene has been criticized on many levels (and inspired an impassioned dissent from Justice Scalia), but even taken on its terms, it seems to raise as many questions as it answered: Where, besides Guantanamo Bay, does federal habeas corpus jurisdiction extend? If the federal courts order a detainee released, where would he or she go? And, perhaps the largest unanswered question: What substantive standard should be applied to determine whether someone ought to be detained under this power? A series of cases following *Boumediene* answered many, but not all, of these questions.

In *Al Maqaleh v. Gates*, 605 F.3d 84 (D.C. Cir. 2010), the D.C. Circuit held that federal courts do not have habeas jurisdiction over those held by the U.S. at the Bagram detention facility in Afghanistan. Quoting *Boumediene*, the D.C. Circuit outlined the standard for determining whether habeas jurisdiction would extend to a particular petitioner:

> (1) the citizenship and status of the detainee and the adequacy of the process through which that status determination was made; (2) the nature of the sites where apprehension and then detention took place; and (3) the practical obstacles inherent in resolving the prisoner's entitlement to the writ.

The court found that, if anything, the petitioners in *Al Maqaleh* had an even stronger claim to habeas relief under the first factor. They were all foreign nationals, but so were the detainees in *Boumediene*, and the process they went through for determining their status was much less rigorous than the one used on the Guantanamo detainees. The second factor weighed strongly in favor of the U.S.: they were detained abroad (but, again, so were the detainees in *Boumediene*). Rather, it was the third factor—the practical obstacles in extending the writ—that controlled the outcome. Bagram, unlike Guantanamo, was located in a "theater of war," which distinguished many of the precedents supporting jurisdiction in *Boumediene* (specifically *Johnson v. Eisentrager*, 339 U.S. 763 (1950), which pertained to the post-war detention of a German war criminal in Landstuhl prison in Berlin). In addition, there was no reason for the court to believe that Afghan courts could not reach detention at Bagram (unlike Cuban courts in the case of Guantanamo Bay). Thus, while detention of the several hundred (at their peak) detainees at Guantanamo Bay are subject to judicial review in U.S. courts, the thousands of detainees held by U.S. forces over the course of the conflicts in Iraq and Afghanistan have remained outside the reach of U.S. courts.

Once they asserted jurisdiction over detainees at Guantanamo, the federal courts did order the release of some detainees, which raised the question of what "release" would mean, because many of the detainees could not plausibly be repatriated either to the country in which they were captured or their country of citizenship. Congress has, through a series of funding restrictions in defense appropriations bills, prohibited any Guantanamo detainee to be transferred to (much less released in) the United States. The D.C. Circuit held in *Kiyemba v. Obama*, 553 F.3d 1022 (D.C. Cir. 2009), that, while the courts could order the President to release Guantanamo detainees, they could not order him to release them in the United States, because the question whether to admit an alien to the United States is inherently up to the political branches, not the judicial branch. The result has left many Guantanamo detainees' ultimate destination unresolved, deemed by the courts (or the executive) no longer to be detainable but still held at Guantanamo pending an appropriate release location.

Finally, the question of the detention standard has been addressed several times, but almost exclusively by the executive branch. In 2004, the Deputy Secretary of Defense issued an order establishing executive-branch "Combatant Status Review Tribunals"

(CSRTs) and with them a definition of "enemy combatant," which served as the detention standard:

> an individual who was part of or supporting Taliban or al Qaida forces, or associated forces that are engaged in hostilities against the United States or its coalition partners. This includes any person who has committed a belligerent act or has directly supported hostilities in aid of enemy armed forces.[20]

Congress provided a process for courts to review such determinations in the Detainee Treatment Act of 2005, but that statute provided review based on the previously announced executive standard.[21] When Barack Obama took office, one of his very first executive orders pertained to detentions at Guantanamo; it established a standard for *continued* detention: whether detention is "consistent with the national security and foreign policy interests of the United States and the interests of justice." In court, the executive has relied on the *statutory* basis for its authority to detain: the 2001 Authorization for the Use of Military Force, which provides:

> all necessary and appropriate force against those nations, organizations, or persons he determines planned, authorized, committed, or aided the terrorist attacks that occurred on September 11, 2001, or harbored such organizations or persons, in order to prevent any future acts of international terrorism against the United States by such nations, organizations or persons.[22]

On that basis, the executive branch has asserted, and the courts have upheld, the power to detain anyone that has either carried out a belligerent act against the United States or is "part of" the Taliban, al Qaeda, or associated forces.[23]

Questions for Discussion

Although "the citizenship and status of the detainee" was specifically listed in *Boumediene* as one of the three factors for determining whether a court should extend habeas jurisdiction, the detainees at issue in both *Boumediene* and *Al Maqaleh* were all foreign nationals, with opposite results in the two cases. Should citizenship matter? There are no U.S. citizens held at Guantanamo Bay, and in a different but closely aligned context, Congress has limited the jurisdiction of military commissions to non-citizens.[24] Does providing a different standard of review for citizens and non-citizen detainees raise concerns under international law? After all, what better way to assure that non-citizen detainees receive fair process than to require that it be the same process as for citizen detainees? What would be the justification for providing a more rigorous process for citizen detainees than non-citizen detainees?

Is the U.S. legal standard (anyone who has carried out a belligerent act against the United States or is part of the Taliban, al Qaeda, or associated forces) consistent with the international detention standard? How about the current executive-branch standard (whether detention is "consistent with the national security and foreign policy interests of the United States and the interests of justice")? Is there a clear international standard for detention? Additional Protocol I to the Geneva Conventions (AP I) has been adopted

---

20. *See* Memorandum from Paul Wolfowitz, Deputy Sec'y of Defense, to the Sec'y of the Navy, Order Establishing Combatant Status Review Tribunal (July 7, 2004).

21. Detainee Treatment Act of 1995 § 1005(e)(2)(C)(i).

22. Authorization for Use of Military Force, Pub.L. No. 107-40, 115 Stat. 224 (2001).

23. Al Odah v. United States, 611 F.3d 8 (D.C. Cir. 2010).

24. Military Commissions Act of 2009, § 948b.

by many countries, but not the United States, although the U.S. accepts aspects of AP I as customary international law, including Article 75, which sets its standard in the form of a requirement for timely release: "with the minimum delay possible and in any event as soon as the circumstances justifying the arrest, detention or internment have ceased to exist."[25] The matter is complicated by questions of categorization (is the U.S. "war on terror" an armed conflict or a law enforcement action?), but even assuming an armed-conflict paradigm applies, does international law seriously constrain detention determinations made by individual nations?

Detainee Treatment

Any rational system for detention must include rules for the treatment of detainees. The Geneva Conventions provide extensive rules for the treatment of detainees (both POWs and civilian internees) but those rules only apply in "international armed conflicts"—conflicts between high contracting parties to the Geneva Conventions. Common Article 3 is the primary guidance for the treatment of detainees in "non-international" armed conflicts. And, of course, human rights law (both domestic and international) provides guidance for the treatment of detainees.

In an international armed conflict, the treatment rules are complex and detailed, as described above. Prisoners of war must be kept separately from criminals and must receive medical protection and other benefits. Moreover,

> Prisoners of war must at all times be humanely treated. Any unlawful act or omission by the Detaining Power causing death or seriously endangering the health of a prisoner of war in its custody is prohibited, and will be regarded as a serious breach of the present Convention. In particular, no prisoner of war may be subjected to physical mutilation or to medical or scientific experiments of any kind which are not justified by the medical, dental or hospital treatment of the prisoner concerned and carried out in his interest.[26]

and

> No physical or mental torture, nor any other form of coercion, may be inflicted on prisoners of war to secure from them information of any kind whatever. Prisoners of war who refuse to answer may not be threatened, insulted, or exposed to unpleasant or disadvantageous treatment of any kind.[27]

In a conflict governed by Common Article 3, the treatment requirements are much more general:

> Persons taking no active part in the hostilities, including members of armed forces who have laid down their arms and those placed hors de combat by sickness, wounds, detention, or any other cause, shall in all circumstances be treated humanely, without any adverse distinction founded on race, colour, religion or faith, sex, birth or wealth, or any other similar criteria. To this end the following

---

25. Protocol Additional to the Geneva Conventions of 12 August 1949, and Relating to the Protection of Victims of International Armed Conflicts (Protocol I), art. 48, June 8, 1977, 1125 U.N.T.S. 3 (AP I), art. 75. On the U.S. acceptance of Article 75 as customary international law, *see* CPT Thomas B. Nachbar, *Executive Branch Policy Meets International Law in the Evolution of the Domestic Law of Detention*, 53 Va. J. Int'l L. 201, 205–06 (2013).

26. GC III, art. 13.

27. GC III, art. 17.

acts are and shall remain prohibited at any time and in any place whatsoever with respect to the above-mentioned persons:

(a) violence to life and person, in particular murder of all kinds, mutilation, cruel treatment and torture;

(b) taking of hostages;

(c) outrages upon personal dignity, in particular, humiliating and degrading treatment;

(d) the passing of sentences and the carrying out of executions without previous judgment pronounced by a regularly constituted court affording all the judicial guarantees which are recognized as indispensable by civilized peoples.[28]

Of course, the fact that the law of armed conflict may require humane treatment does not mean that there is not a higher threshold imposed by another law. Domestic law, for instance, could provide broader protection for detainees as could other forms of international law. International human rights law, such as the International Covenant on Civil and Political Rights, may also impose obligations on signatories (of which the U.S. is one), such as its prohibition on "torture or to cruel, inhuman or degrading treatment or punishment"[29] and its requirement that "[a]ll persons deprived of their liberty shall be treated with humanity and with respect for the inherent dignity of the human person."[30] The Convention against Torture and Other Cruel, Inhuman or Degrading Treatment or Punishment requires states to "take effective legislative, administrative, judicial or other measures to prevent acts of torture"[31] and "to prevent in any territory under its jurisdiction other acts of cruel, inhuman or degrading treatment or punishment which do not amount to torture as defined in article I, when such acts are committed by or at the instigation of or with the consent or acquiescence of a public official or other person acting in an official capacity."[32] In the United States, the Fourth Amendment prohibits unreasonable seizures, including inhumane treatment by government officials,[33] and the obligations of the Convention Against Torture are implemented by a federal statute making torture a crime.[34]

The multitude of legal rules, though, may make it difficult to determine whether a particular form of treatment is legal with regard to a particular detainee. Further complicating the question is whether there is any remedy available to detainees who suffer mistreatment.

Forms of Treatment

Memorandum for Alberto R. Gonzales, Counsel to the President
Re: Standards of Conduct for Interrogation under
18 U.S.C. §§ 2340–2340A
August 1, 2002

You have asked for our Office's views regarding the standards of conduct under the Convention Against Torture and Other Cruel, Inhuman and Degrading Treatment or Punishment as implemented by Sections 2340-2340A of title 18 of the United States Code.

---

28. GC III, art. 3, para (1).

29. International Covenant on Civil and Political Rights, 999 U.N.T.S. 171 (1966) (ICCPR), art. 7.

30. ICCPR, art. 10.1.

31. Convention Against Torture and Other Cruel, Inhuman or Degrading Treatment or Punishment, Dec. 10, 1984, U.N.T.S. 85 (CAT), art. 2.1.

32. CAT, art. 16.

33. Graham v. Connor, 490 U.S. 386 (1989).

34. 18 U.S.C. §§ 2340–2340A.

As we understand it, this question has arisen in the context of the conduct of interrogations outside of the United States. We conclude below that Section 2340A proscribes acts inflicting, and that are specifically intended to inflict, severe pain or suffering, whether mental or physical. Those acts must be of an extreme nature to rise to the level of torture within the meaning of Section 2340A and the Convention. We further conclude that certain acts may be cruel, inhuman, or degrading, but still not produce pain and suffering of the requisite intensity to fall within Section 2340A's proscription against torture. We conclude by examining possible defenses that would negate any claim that certain interrogation methods violate the statute.

* * *

I. 18 U.S.C. §§ 2340–2340A

Section 2340A makes it a criminal offense for any person "outside the United States [to] commit[] or attempt[] to commit torture." Section 2340 defines the act of torture as an:

> act committed by a person acting under the color of law specifically intended to inflict severe physical or mental pain or suffering (other than pain or suffering incidental to lawful sanctions) upon another person within his custody or physical control.

18 U.S.C.A. § 2340(1); *see id.* § 2340A.

* * *

B. "Severe Pain or Suffering"

The key statutory phrase in the definition of torture is the statement that acts amount to torture if they cause "severe physical or mental pain or suffering." In examining the meaning of a statute, its text must be the starting point. *See INS v. Phinpathya*, 464 U.S. 183, 189 (1984) ("This Court has noted on numerous occasions that in all cases involving statutory construction, our starting point must be the language employed by Congress, ... and we assume that the legislative purpose is expressed by the ordinary meaning of the words used.") (internal quotations and citations omitted). Section 2340 makes plain that the infliction of pain or suffering per se, whether it is physical or mental, is insufficient to amount to torture. Instead, the text provides that pain or suffering must be "severe." The statute does not, however, define the term "severe." "In the absence of such a definition, we construe a statutory term in accordance with its ordinary or natural meaning." *FDIC v. Meyer*, 510 U.S. 471, 476 (1994). The dictionary defines "severe" as "[u]nsparing in exaction, punishment, or censure" or "[I]nflicting discomfort or pain hard to endure; sharp; afflictive; distressing; violent; extreme; as severe pain, anguish, torture." Webster's New International Dictionary 2295 (2d ed. 1935); see American Heritage Dictionary of the English Language 1653 (3d ed. 1992) ("extremely violent or grievous: severe pain") (emphasis in original); IX The Oxford English Dictionary 572 (1978) ("Of pain, suffering, loss, or the like: Grievous, extreme" and "of circumstances ... hard to sustain or endure"). Thus, the adjective "severe" conveys that the pain or suffering must be of such a high level of intensity that the pain is difficult for the subject to endure.

Congress's use of the phrase "severe pain" elsewhere in the United States Code can shed more light on its meaning. *See, e.g., West Va. Univ. Hasps., Inc. v. Casey*, 499 U.S. 83, 100 (1991) ("[W]e construe [a statutory term) to contain that permissible meaning which fits most logically and comfortably into the body of both previously and subsequently enacted law."). Significantly, the phrase "severe pain" appears in statutes defining an emergency medical condition for the purpose of providing health benefits. *See, e.g.,* 8 U.S.C. § 1369 (2000); 42 U.S.C § 1395w-22 (2000); *id.* § 1395x (2000); *id.* § 1395dd (2000); *id.* § 1396b (2000); *id.* § 1396u-2 (2000). These statutes define an emergency condition as one "manifesting itself by acute symptoms of sufficient severity (including severe pain) such that a prudent layperson, who possesses an average knowledge of health and medicine, could reasonably expect the absence of immediate medical attention to result in placing the health of the individual … (i) in serious jeopardy, (ii) serious impairment to bodily functions, or (iii) serious dysfunction of any bodily organ or part." *Id.* § 1395w-22(d)(3)(B) (emphasis added). Although these statutes address a substantially different subject from Section 2340, they are nonetheless helpful for understanding what constitutes severe physical pain. They treat severe pain as an indicator of ailments that are likely to result in permanent and serious physical damage in the absence of immediate medical treatment. Such damage must rise to the level of death, organ failure, or the permanent impairment of a significant body function. These statutes suggest that "severe pain," as used in Section 2340, must rise to a similarly high level—the level that would ordinarily be associated with a sufficiently serious physical condition or injury such as death, organ failure, or serious impairment of body functions—in order to constitute torture.

C. "Severe mental pain or suffering"

Section 2340 gives further guidance as to the meaning of "severe mental pain or suffering," as distinguished from severe physical pain and suffering. The statute defines "severe mental pain or suffering" as: the prolonged mental harm caused by or resulting from—

(A) the intentional infliction or threatened infliction of severe physical pain or suffering;

(B) the administration or application, or threatened administration or application, of mind-altering substances or other procedures calculated to disrupt profoundly the senses or the personality;

(C) the threat of imminent death; or

(D) the threat that another person will imminently be subjected to death, severe physical pain or suffering, or the administration or application of mind-altering substances or other procedures calculated to disrupt profoundly the senses or personality.

18 U.S.C. § 2340(2). In order to prove "severe mental pain or suffering," the statute requires proof of "prolonged mental harm" that was caused by or resulted from one of four enumerated acts. We consider each of these elements.

1. "Prolonged Mental Harm"

As an initial matter, Section 2340(2) requires that the severe mental pain must be evidenced by "prolonged mental harm." To prolong is to "lengthen in time" or to "extend the duration of, to draw out." Webster's Third New International Dictionary 1815 (1988); Webster's New International Dictionary 1980 (2d ed. 1935). Accordingly, "prolong" adds a temporal dimension to the harm to the individual, namely, that the harm must be one that is endured over some period of time. Put another way, the acts giving rise to the harm must cause some lasting, though not necessarily permanent, damage. For example, the mental strain experienced by an individual during a lengthy and intense interrogation—such as one that state or local police might conduct upon a criminal suspect— would not violate Section 2340(2). On the other hand, the development of a mental disorder such as posttraumatic stress disorder, which can last months or even years, or even chronic depression, which also can last for a considerable period of time if untreated, might satisfy the prolonged harm requirement. * * * By contrast to "severe pain," the phrase "prolonged mental harm" appears nowhere else in the U.S. Code nor does it appear in relevant medical literature or international human rights reports.

* * *

2. Harm Caused By or Resulting From Predicate Acts

Section 2340(2) sets forth four basic categories of predicate acts. First in the list is the "intentional infliction or threatened infliction of severe physical pain or suffering." This might at first appear superfluous because the statute already provides that the infliction of severe physical pain or suffering can amount to torture. This provision, however, actually captures the infliction of physical pain or suffering when the defendant inflicts physical pain or suffering with general intent rather than the specific intent that is required where severe physical pain or suffering alone is the basis for the charge. Hence, this subsection reaches the infliction of severe physical pain or suffering when it is but the means of causing prolonged mental harm. * * * Additionally, the threat of inflicting such pain is a predicate act under the statute.

Second, Section 2340(2)(B) provides that prolonged mental harm, constituting torture, can be caused by "the administration or application or threatened administration or application, of mind-altering substances or other procedures calculated to disrupt profoundly the senses or the personality." The statute provides no further definition of what constitutes a mind-altering substance. The phrase "mind-altering substances" is found nowhere else in the U.S. Code nor is it found in dictionaries. It is, however, a commonly used synonym for drugs. * * *

For drugs or procedures to rise to the level of "disrupt[ing] profoundly the senses or personality," they must produce an extreme effect. And by requiring that they be "calculated" to produce such an effect, the statute requires for liability the defendant has consciously designed the acts to produce such an effect. * * * Moreover, disruption of the senses or personality alone is insufficient to fall within the scope of this subsection; instead, that disruption must be profound. The word "profound" has a number of meanings, all of which convey a significant depth. * * *

The third predicate act listed in Section 2340(2) is threatening a prisoner with "imminent death." 18 U.S.C. § 2340(2)(C). The plain text makes clear that a threat of death alone is insufficient; the threat must indicate that death is "imminent." The "threat of imminent death" is found in the common law as an element of the defense of duress. * * * Thus, a vague threat that someday the prisoner might be killed would not suffice. Instead, subjecting a prisoner to mock executions or playing Russian roulette with him would have sufficient immediacy to constitute a threat of imminent death. Additionally, as discussed earlier, we believe that the existence of a threat must be assessed from the perspective of a reasonable person in the same circumstances.

Fourth, if the official threatens to do anything previously described to a third party, or commits such an act against a third party, that threat or action can serve as the necessary predicate for prolonged mental harm. See 18 U.S.C. § 2340(2)(D). The statute does not require any relationship between the prisoner and the third party.

* * *

4. Summary

Section 2340's definition of torture must be read as a sum of these component parts. Each component of the definition emphasizes that torture is not the mere infliction of pain or suffering on another, but is instead a step well removed. The victim must experience intense pain or suffering of the kind that is equivalent to the pain that would be associated with serious physical injury so severe that death, organ failure, or permanent damage resulting in a loss of significant body function will likely result. If that pain or suffering is psychological, that suffering must result from one of the acts set forth in the statute. In addition, these acts must cause long-term mental harm. Indeed, this view of the criminal act of torture is consistent with the term's common meaning. Torture is generally understood to involve "intense pain" or "excruciating pain," or put another way, "extreme anguish of body or mind." Black's Law Dictionary at 1498 (7th Ed. 1999); Random House Webster's Unabridged Dictionary 1999 (1999); Webster's New International Dictionary 2674 (2d ed. 1935). In short, reading the definition of torture as a whole, it is plain that the term encompasses only extreme acts.

* * *

Conclusion

For the foregoing reasons, we conclude that torture as defined in and proscribed by Sections 2340–2340A, covers only extreme acts. Severe pain is generally of the kind difficult for the victim to endure. Where the pain is physical, it must be of an intensity akin to that which accompanies serious physical injury such as death or organ failure. Severe mental pain requires suffering not just at the moment of infliction but it also requires lasting psychological harm, such as seen in mental disorders like posttraumatic stress disorder. Additionally, such severe mental pain can arise only from the predicate acts listed in Section 2340. Because the acts inflicting torture are extreme, there is significant range of acts that though they might constitute cruel, inhuman, or degrading treatment or punishment fail to rise to the level of torture.

Jay S. Bybee
Assistant Attorney General

This memo, perhaps the most famous of the "torture memos," has been the subject of much criticism. As Jack Goldsmith, who replaced Bybee as the head of the Office of Legal Counsel (OLC), has written with regard to the definition of "severe pain" as rising to "the level that would ordinarily be associated with a sufficiently serious physical condition or injury such as death, organ failure, or serious impairment of body functions": "OLC culled this definition, ironically, from a statute authorizing health benefits."[35] The memo went on to explore the possibility that § 2340 could not be applied to executive branch officials in conjunction with interrogation of al Qaeda detainees because to do so would interfere with the President's constitutional power as Commander-in-Chief of the armed forces or that defenses (such as necessity or self-defense) might preclude prosecutions.

The memo was withdrawn by the Department of Justice, Office of Legal Counsel and replaced with the following one:

Memorandum for James B. Comey, Deputy Attorney General
Re: Legal Standards Applicable Under 18 U.S.C. §§ 2340–2340A
December 30, 2004

II.

(1) The meaning of "severe."

* * *

---

35. Jack Goldsmith, The Terror Presidency 145 (2007).

Although Congress defined "torture" under sections 2340–2340A to require conduct specifically intended to cause "severe" pain or suffering, we do not believe Congress intended to reach only conduct involving "excruciating and agonizing" pain or suffering. Although there is some support for this formulation in the ratification history of the CAT, a proposed express understanding to that effect was "criticized for setting too high a threshold of pain," and was not adopted. We are not aware of any evidence suggesting that the standard was raised in the statute and we do not believe that it was."

Drawing distinctions among gradations of pain (for example, severe, mild, moderate, substantial, extreme, intense, excruciating, or agonizing) is obviously not an easy task, especially given the lack of any precise, objective scientific criteria for measuring pain. We are, however, aided in this task by judicial interpretations of the Torture Victims Protection Act ("TVPA"), 28 U.S.C. § 1350 note (2000). The TVPA, also enacted to implement the CAT, provides a civil remedy to victims of torture. The TVPA defines "torture" to include:

> any act, directed against an individual in the offender's custody or physical control, by which severe pain or suffering (other than pain or suffering arising only from or inherent in, or incidental to, lawful sanctions), whether physical or mental, is intentionally inflicted on that individual for such purposes as obtaining from that individual or a third person information or a confession, punishing that individual for an act that individual or a third person has committed or is suspected of having committed, intimidating or coercing that individual or a third person, or for any reason based on discrimination of any kind....

28 U.S.C. § 1350 note,§ 3(b)(1) (emphases added). The emphasized language is similar to section 2340's "severe physical or mental pain or suffering." As the Court of Appeals for the District of Columbia Circuit has explained:

> The severity requirement is crucial to ensuring that the conduct proscribed by the [CAT] and the TVPA is sufficiently extreme and outrageous to warrant the universal condemnation that the term "torture" both connotes and invokes. The drafters of the [CAT], as well as the Reagan Administration that signed it, the Bush Administration that submitted it to Congress, and the Senate that ultimately ratified it, therefore all sought to ensure that "only acts of a certain gravity shall be considered to constitute torture." The critical issue is the degree of pain and suffering that the alleged torturer intended to, and actually did, inflict upon the victim. The more intense, lasting, or heinous the agony, the more likely it is to be torture.

Price v. Socialist People's Libyan Arab Jamahiriya, 294 F.3d 82, 92–93 (D.C. Cir. 2002) (citations omitted). That court concluded that a complaint that alleged beatings at the hands of police but that did not provide details concerning "the severity of plaintiffs' alleged beatings, including their frequency, duration, the parts of the body at which they were aimed, and the weapons used to carry them out," did not suffice "to ensure that [it] satisf[ied] the TVPA's rigorous definition of torture."

In *Simpson v. Socialist People's Libyan Arab Jamahiriya*, 326 F.3d 230 (D.C. Cir. 2003), the D.C. Circuit again considered the types of acts that constitute torture under the TVPA definition. The plaintiff alleged, among other things, that Libyan authorities had held her incommunicado and threatened to kill her if she tried to leave. The court acknowledged that "these alleged acts certainly reflect a bent toward cruelty on the part of their perpetrators," but, reversing the district court, went on to hold that "they are not in themselves so unusually cruel or sufficiently extreme and outrageous as to constitute torture within the meaning of the [TVPA]." Cases in which courts have found torture suggest the nature of the extreme conduct that falls within the statutory definition. *See, e.g., Hilao v. Estate of Marcos*, 103 F.3d 789, 790–91, 795 (9th Cir. 1996) (concluding that a course of conduct that included, among other things, severe beatings of plaintiff, repeated threats of death and electric shock, sleep deprivation, extended shackling to a cot (at times with a towel over his nose and mouth and water poured down his nostrils), seven months of confinement in a "suffocatingly hot" and cramped cell, and eight years of solitary or near-solitary confinement, constituted torture); *Mehinovic v. Vuckovic*, 198 F. Supp. 2d 1322, 1332–40, 1345–46 (N.D. Ga. 2002) (concluding that a course of conduct that included, among other things, severe beatings to the genitals, head, and other parts of the body with metal pipes, brass knuckles, batons, a baseball bat, and various other items; removal of teeth with pliers; kicking in the face and ribs; breaking of bones and ribs and dislocation of fingers; cutting a figure into the victim's forehead; hanging the victim and beating him; extreme limitations of food and water; and subjection to games of "Russian roulette," constituted torture); *Daliberli v. Republic of Iraq*, 146 F. Supp. 2d 19, 22–23 (D.D.C. 2001) (entering default judgment against Iraq where plaintiffs alleged, among other things, threats of "physical torture, such as cutting off ... fingers, pulling out ... fingernails," and electric shocks to the testicles); *Cicippio v. Islamic Republic of Iran*, 18 F. Supp. 2d 62, 64–66 (D.D.C. 1998) (concluding that a course of conduct that included frequent beatings, pistol whipping, threats of imminent death, electric shocks, and attempts to force confessions by playing Russian roulette and pulling the trigger at each denial, constituted torture).

* * *

(3) The meaning of "severe mental pain or suffering."

An important preliminary question with respect to this definition is whether the statutory list of the four "predicate acts" in section 2340(2)(A)–(D) is exclusive. We conclude that Congress intended the list of predicate acts to be exclusive—that is, to constitute the proscribed "severe mental pain or suffering" under the statute, the prolonged mental harm must be caused by acts falling within one of the four statutory categories of predicate acts.

* * *

Turning to the question of what constitutes "prolonged mental harm caused by or resulting from" a predicate act, we believe that Congress intended this phrase to require mental "harm" that is caused by or that results from a predicate act, and that has some lasting duration. There is little guidance to draw upon in interpreting this phrase. 24 Nevertheless, our interpretation is consistent with the ordinary meaning of the statutory terms. First, the use of the word "harm"—as opposed to simply repeating "pain or suffering"—suggests some mental damage or injury. Ordinary dictionary definitions of" harm," such as "physical or mental damage: injury," Webster's Third New International Dictionary at 1034 (emphasis added), or "[p]hysical or psychological injury or damage," American Heritage Dictionary of the English Language at 825 (emphasis added), support this interpretation. Second, to "prolong" means to "lengthen in time" or to "extend in duration," or to "draw out," Webster's Third New International Dictionary at 1815, further suggesting that to be "prolonged," the mental damage must extend for some period of time. This damage need not be permanent, but it must continue for a "prolonged" period of time. Finally, under section 2340(2), the "prolonged mental harm" must be "caused by" or "resulting from" one of the enumerated predicate acts.

Although there are few judicial opinions discussing the question of "prolonged mental harm," those cases that have addressed the issue are consistent with our view. For example, in the TVPA case of *Mehinovic*, the court explained that:

[The defendant] also caused or participated in the plaintiffs' mental torture. Mental torture consists of "prolonged mental harm caused by or resulting from: the intentional infliction or threatened infliction of severe physical pain or suffering; … the threat of imminent death…," As set out above, plaintiffs noted in their testimony that they feared that they would be killed by [the defendant] during the beatings he inflicted or during games of "Russian roulette." *Each plaintiff continues to suffer long-term psychological harm as a result of the ordeals they suffered at the hands of defendant and others.*

In reaching its conclusion, the court noted that the plaintiffs were continuing to suffer serious mental harm even ten years after the events in question: "One plaintiff … suffers from anxiety, flashbacks, and nightmares and has difficulty sleeping. [He] continues to suffer thinking about what happened to him during this ordeal and has been unable to work as a result of the continuing effects of the torture he endured." Another plaintiff "suffers from anxiety, sleeps very little, and has frequent nightmares…. [He] has found it impossible to return to work." A third plaintiff "has frequent nightmares. He has had to use medication to help him sleep. His experience has made him feel depressed and reclusive, and he has not been able to work since he escaped from this ordeal." And the fourth plaintiff "has flashbacks and nightmares, suffers from nervousness, angers easily, and has difficulty trusting people. These effects directly impact and interfere with his ability to work." In each case, these mental effects were continuing years after the infliction of the predicate acts. And in *Sackie v. Ashcroft*, 270 F. Supp. 2d 596 (E.D. Pa. 2003), the individual had been kidnapped and … forcibly recruited" as a child soldier at the age of 14, and over the next three to four years had been forced to take narcotics and threatened with imminent death. The court concluded that the resulting mental harm, which continued over this three-to-four-year period, qualified as "prolonged mental harm." Conversely, in *Villeda Aldana v. Fresh Del Monte Produce, Inc.*, 305 F. Supp. 2d 1285 (S.D. Fla. 2003), the court rejected a claim under the TVPA brought by individuals who had been held at gunpoint overnight and repeatedly threatened with death. While recognizing that the plaintiffs had experienced an "ordeal," the court concluded that they had failed to show that their experience caused lasting damage, noting that "there is simply no allegation that Plaintiffs have suffered any prolonged mental harm or physical injury as a result of their alleged intimidation."

* * *

Please let us know if we can be of further assistance.

Daniel Levin
Acting Assistant Attorney General

———————

Questions for Discussion

Of the following interrogation techniques, which would be permitted under the 2002 memo but prohibited under the revised 2004 memo?

- Yelling at the detainee (not directly in his ear or to the level that it would cause physical pain or hearing problems)

- Techniques of deception (such as the interrogator falsely identifying himself as a citizen of a foreign nation or as an interrogator from a country with a reputation for harsh treatment of detainees)

- The use of stress positions (like standing), for a maximum of four hours

- The use of falsified documents or reports
- The use of an isolation facility for up to 30 days
- Interrogating the detainees in an environment other than the standard interrogation booth
- Deprivation of light and auditory stimuli
- Placing a hood over the detainee during transportation and questioning
- The use of 20 hour interrogations
- Removal of all comfort items (including religious items)
- Switching the detainee from hot food to cold, packaged food
- Removal of clothing
- Forced grooming (shaving of facial hair, etc.)
- Using detainee individual phobias (such as fear of dogs) to induce stress
- The use of scenarios designed to convince the detainee that death or severely painful consequences are imminent for him and/or his family
- Exposure to cold weather or water
- Use of a wet towel and dripping water to induce the misperception of suffocation
- Use of mild, non-injurious physical contact such as grabbing, poking in the chest with the finger, and light pushing

Would it be possible to know whether any of these acts constitute "torture" without knowing more about the detainee? Would everyone, someone, or no one suffer "prolonged mental harm" from being isolated for 30 days? Does it matter whether a particular detainee's phobia is to marshmallows or rats?

Congress addressed the subject in 2005 with the Detainee Treatment Act, which set both general and specific limits on detainee treatment. The statute directed that "no individual in the custody or under the physical control of the United States Government, regardless of nationality or physical location, shall be subject to cruel, inhuman, or degrading treatment or punishment," which it defined as "cruel, unusual, and inhumane treatment or punishment prohibited by the Fifth, Eighth, and Fourteenth Amendments to the Constitution of the United States, as defined in the United States Reservations, Declarations and Understandings to the United Nations Convention Against Torture and Other Forms of Cruel, Inhuman or Degrading Treatment or Punishment done at New York, December 10, 1984."[36] More specifically the statute pointed to an executive branch publication—the Army Field Manual on interrogations[37]—for a specific list of the permissible interrogation techniques.[38]

---

36. Detainee Treatment Act of 2005, § 1003, 42 U.S.C. § 2000dd.

37. Field Manual 34-52, Intelligence Interrogations, Headquarters, Department of the Army, Washington, D.C., 28 September 1992, *available at* http://www.loc.gov/rr/frd/Military_Law/pdf/intel_interrrogation_sept-1992.pdf.

38. *Id.* § 1002. *See also* Ensuring Lawful Detentions, Exec. Order 13491, 74 Fed. Reg. 4893 § 3(b) (Jan. 27, 2009) (referencing the Army Field Manual standard for interrogations). It raises a rather interesting (but untested) question of statutory interpretation for a federal statute to reference an executive branch-promulgated field manual as the *statutory* baseline to control conduct by the executive.

Particular Detainees

One could be excused for asking why the executive branch was analyzing the torture statute at all and not some element of the Geneva Conventions. After all, the United States had taken the stance in both domestic and international fora that it was engaged in an "armed conflict" with al Qaeda and the Taliban. If so, then the only question is whether it was an IAC (requiring the application of the full Geneva Conventions and their many, specific protections) or a NIAC (requiring the application of Common Article 3's general protections of "humane" treatment and prohibitions against not only "torture" but "violence to life and person" and "cruel treatment").

The answer lies in the Bush Administration position that al Qaeda and the Taliban detainees were covered by *neither* Common Article 2 nor Common Article 3. In order to be considered an IAC, the conflict must be between two parties to the Geneva Conventions, which excludes al Qaeda. Although the Taliban, as the government of Afghanistan might qualify, their failure to observe the requirements of the law of armed conflict meant that individual Taliban fighters would not receive the protections of the Geneva Conventions. The conflict with al Qaeda, on the other hand, while clearly not an IAC (since al Qaeda is not a party to the Geneva Conventions) was also not a NIAC, because, the argument went, Common Article 3 was intended to cover either wars between a party and a non-party *state* or conflicts that did not cross international boundaries (domestic civil wars).[39]

Thus, al Qaeda and Taliban detainees fell into a gap in the law of armed conflict, leaving only human rights treaties (such as the Convention Against Torture) and domestic law (the torture statute analysis described above) for guidance in their treatment. The statute law changed with the DTA in 2005, and the Supreme Court held in 2006 that the detainees were in fact protected at the very least by Common Article 3,[40] a view later endorsed by the executive branch.

For those who have potentially been mistreated at the hands of U.S. authorities, the options for redress are limited. Congress has expressly prohibited any claims based on the protection of the Geneva Conventions.[41] While victims of constitutional violations at the hands of U.S. officials may bring so-called *Bivens* civil claims,[42] courts have consistently held that civil suits against U.S. officials alleged to have engaged in constitutional violations related to detainees are subject to qualified immunity, which "shields government officials from civil liability to the extent their alleged misconduct 'does not violate clearly established

---

39. *See generally* GARY D. SOLIS, THE LAW OF ARMED CONFLICT: INTERNATIONAL HUMANITARIAN LAW IN WAR 214–15 (2010). Of course, either analysis would require determining whether a particular detainee was either an al Qaeda operative or Taliban fighter, and in the latter case would require a determination that the fighter had not complied with the law of armed conflict. No such system of reviews was put in place for al Qaeda or Taliban detainees until July of 2004. *See* Memorandum from Paul Wolfowitz, Deputy Sec'y of Defense, to the Sec'y of the Navy, Order Establishing Combatant Status Review Tribunal (July 7, 2004).

40. Hamdan v. Rumsfeld, 548 U.S. 557 (2006).

41. Military Commissions Act of 2006, § 5(a), 28 U.S.C. § 2241 note ("No person may invoke the Geneva Conventions or any protocols thereto in any habeas corpus or other civil action or proceeding to which the United States, or a current or former officer, employee, member of the Armed Forces, or other agent of the United States is a party as a source of rights in any court of the United States or its States or its territories.").

42. Bivens v. Six Unknown Agents of Fed. Bureau of Narcotics, 403 U.S. 388 (1971).

statutory or constitutional rights of which a reasonable person would have known.'"[43] While *Boumediene* established that some elements of the Constitution extend to locations like the detention facility in Guantanamo Bay (and fewer extend to in-theater detention facilities in Afghanistan and Iraq under the reasoning of *Al Maqaleh v. Gates*), the very fact that the line of cases leading to *Boumediene* was lengthy is itself evidence that no reasonable executive branch official would have known that any particular form of mistreatment would violate any particular constitutional prohibition for any particular detainee in any particular location.[44]

Conclusion

The American experience with detention post-9/11 has been one of rapid legal development. New theories regarding the nature of armed conflict were deployed in an attempt to cope adequately with a seemingly novel problem: how to deal with detainees who represent an armed force that does not fit our traditional understanding of a nation's military. The result was an intense legal dialogue within the executive branch and subsequently a lengthy "dialogue" between and among the executive branch, Congress, and federal courts. The solution has been subject to considerable criticism even within the executive branch as the President (at the time of this writing) still struggles to close the detention facility at Guantanamo Bay, Cuba.

What perhaps makes all of this legal development even more remarkable is that there actually was a system in place for handling detainees in 2001. At that time, it was U.S. policy that:

> (1) All persons captured, detained, interned, or otherwise held in U.S. Armed Forces custody during the course of conflict will be given humanitarian care and treatment from the moment they fall into the hands of U.S. forces until final release or repatriation.

> (2) All persons taken into custody by U.S. forces will be provided with the protections of the [the third Geneva Convention] until some other legal status is determined by competent authority.

That policy appears in Army Regulation 190-8,[45] which provides a comprehensive system of detention designed to be applied in all forms of armed conflict. And, although the focus in national security law is on the exceptional detainees—those held in Guantanamo Bay and those subjected to extreme treatment in pursuit of information— many thousands of detainees were held in Iraq and Afghanistan using procedures following a much more traditional model even as the U.S. struggled to accommodate the necessarily criminal nature of the insurgencies being fought in both countries.[46] The U.S. failure to apply this system of detention and systematically to avoid judicial oversight while establishing a new system of detention (and punishments) raises important questions about the ability of states to pre-commit themselves to policies of detention given the evolving nature of

---

43. Rasul v. Myers, 563 F.3d 527, 530–31 (D.C. Cir. 2007).

44. *Id.* at 532.

45. *See* U.S. Dep't of Army, Reg. 190-8, Enemy Prisoner of War, Retained Personnel, Civilian Internees and Other Detainees ¶¶ 1–5(a)(1–2) (Oct. 1, 1997).

46. *See generally* Robert M. Chesney, *Iraq and the Military Detention Debate: Firsthand Perspectives from the Other War, 2003–2010*, 51 Va. J. Int'l L. 549 (2011).

national security threats, particularly in regard to conflicts with non-state actors. Desperate for information about their adversaries, members of the executive branch in the days immediately following the attacks of 9/11 felt overly constrained by a system of detention designed to hold enemy fighters, not to serve as a primary source of intelligence about their enemy. After more than a decade of legal and political development (and warfighting), the U.S. government has a different understanding about the role of law and legal institutions in the conduct of detention operations than the one that motivated the decision to resist federal court oversight and to survey so closely the boundaries of torture. The question for all of us is how those understandings will endure or be altered in the conflicts to come.

Selected Bibliography

Stephanie Blum, "Preventive Detention in the War on Terror: A Comparison of How the United States, Britain, and Israel Detain and Incapacitate Terrorist Suspects," *Homeland Security Affairs Journal*, Vol. IV No. 3: October 2008, available at <http://www .hsaj.org/?fullarticle=4.3.1>.

Jennifer Elsea, *Treatment of "Battlefield Detainees" in the War on Terrorism* (2003).

Jack Goldsmith, "Detention, the AUMF, and the Bush Administration—Correcting the Record," *Lawfare*, September 14, 2010, available at <http://www.lawfareblog.com/ 2010/09/detention-the-aumf-and-the-bush-administration-correcting-the-record/>.

R.C. Hingorani, *Prisoners of War* (1982).

A.W. Brian Simpson, *In the Highest Degree Odious: Detention Without Trial in Wartime Britain* (1992).

Chapter 10

The Control of International Terrorism

John F. Murphy

In this chapter:
Introduction
Theoretical and Historical Overview
Modern Approaches
Selected Bibliography

Introduction

The first edition of this casebook was published in 1990. I had the privilege and pleasure of contributing a chapter on "The Control of International Terrorism" to the first edition. Since then, and especially after September 11, 2001, efforts to control international terrorism (no one speaks realistically anymore of eliminating it) assumed a priority status by the United States that was absent during earlier decades. Moreover, the horrific events of September 11 raised new issues, or modified old ones, regarding the appropriate steps that should be taken to combat international terrorism. A second edition of this casebook was published in 2005. I was privileged to contribute a chapter on the same subject to that edition which addressed many of these new and modified issues. Now, in 2014, shortly after being awarded emeritus status by my colleagues at the Villanova Law School, I am beginning work on a chapter for the third edition. It will be necessary, of course, to make changes and revisions to reflect developments in efforts to control terrorism that have occurred since 2005. Fortunately, however, considerable amounts of the material in my chapter for the 2005 edition are still relevant and will accordingly be incorporated into this chapter.

Even before September 11, the conventional wisdom that terrorists were not interested in killing large numbers of people—because this would undermine sympathy for their cause—had been severely challenged by, for example, the 1993 bombing of the World Trade Center and the 1998 bombings of U.S. embassies in Kenya and Tanzania. Any doubts on this score were, of course, put to rest by the events of September 11 that resulted in the deaths of approximately 3,000 people.

The severity of the September 11 attacks, and the subsequent use of military force by U.S. and select NATO forces against the Taliban and Al Qaeda in Afghanistan undertaken as part of a "war on terrorism," raised an issue as to the appropriate legal regime to apply to efforts to control international terrorism. Prior to September 11, international terrorism had been treated primarily as a criminal law matter, with emphasis placed on preventing the commission of the crime through intelligence or law enforcement means or, if prevention failed, on the apprehension, prosecution, and punishment of the perpetrators. To be sure, the United States had previously used armed force on occasion against terrorism. In 1986, the United States bombed Tripoli, Libya, in response to Libya's apparent involvement in bombing a West Berlin discotheque frequented by American soldiers, and the terrorist attack by Libyan-backed Abu Nidal on El Al airline counters that killed five Americans and wounded many others. Similarly, in 1993, the United States bombed Baghdad, Iraq, because of an assassination plot by Saddam Hussein, Iraq's president, against former President George H.W. Bush, and in 1998 it engaged in missile strikes against Afghanistan and the Sudan in response to the East African embassy bombings. But none of these actions involved military force of the magnitude and duration of the actions in Afghanistan after September 11.

At this writing, in June 2014, despite the extensive military actions in Afghanistan and elsewhere, or, as some argue, because of these military actions, "[t]he number of al Qaeda and other jihadist groups and fighters are growing, not shrinking."[1] Indeed, according to data in a Rand report,[2] from 2010 to 2013 the number of jihadist groups world-wide grew by 58%, from 31 to 49; the number of jihadist fighters doubled to 100,000; and the number of attacks by al Qaeda affiliates increased to roughly 1,000 from 392. The report also notes that the most significant terrorism threats come from groups operating in Yemen, Afghanistan, Pakistan, and Syria. Moreover, Syria in particular is proving to be a breeding ground for Jihadists.[3] Worse yet, it is estimated that 3,000 citizens from Europe have gone to fight with the rebels in Syria, and there is evidence that radical Islamist groups are encouraging these homegrown jihadists to return to their countries to engage in terrorists attacks there. French authorities recently arrested such a person in Marseille, who allegedly killed three people at a Belgian Jewish museum on May 25, 2014.[4]

By way of background, this chapter first presents a theoretical and historical overview of international terrorism, including difficulties faced in attempting to reach agreement on a definition. It then turns to an examination of so-called "modern approaches" to combating international terrorism. These include the quest for a comprehensive approach through the adoption of an international treaty that would define international terrorism and criminalize all manifestations of it; the "piecemeal" approach to combating international terrorism through the adoption of treaties and conventions criminalizing individual manifestations of terrorism, such as aircraft hijacking and hostage taking, that has in practice been followed; extradition and "informal" methods of rendition: exclusion, expulsion, and kidnapping; analogies to the law of armed conflict; fora for trying terrorists; limitations on immigration and the granting of refugee status; efforts to block the financing of international terrorism, including through money laundering; and civil suits against terrorists, terrorist organizations, and states that sponsor terrorism. The chapter concludes with a consideration of coercive measures, both against terrorists and terrorist organizations, and against states supporting international terrorism, including international claims, economic sanctions, and the use of military force.

---

1. *See* Seth G. Jones, *The Accelerating Spread of Terrorism*, WALL ST. J., June 4, 2014, at A11, col. 1.

2. *See* SETH G. JONES, A PERSISTENT THREAT: THE EVOLUTION OF AL QA'IDA AND OTHER SALAFI JIHADISTS 26–34 (Rand 2014).

3. Sam Jones, *Europe Fears "Blowback" From Conflict in Syria*, FINANCIAL TIMES, June 5, 2014, at 4, col. 1.

4. *Id.*

Theoretical and Historical Overview

International Terrorism: A Definitional Quagmire

It may come as a surprise to learn that, in spite of the considerable amount of attention devoted to the subject in recent years, there is at present no generally accepted definition of "international terrorism," as demonstrated by the cliché, "[o]ne man's terrorism is another man's heroism." Some countries believe that the causes of terrorism or the political motivation of the individual terrorists are relevant to the problem of definition. For example, the position of some governments has been that individual acts of violence can be defined as terrorism only if they are employed solely for personal gain or caprice; acts committed in connection with a political cause, especially against colonialism and for national liberation, fall outside the definition and constitute legitimate measures of self-defense. Under this approach then, the sending of bombs through the mail, hijackings of airplanes, kidnappings of, or attacks on, diplomats and international business persons, and the indiscriminate slaughter of innocent civilians by members of revolutionary groups could never constitute "terrorism" if committed on behalf of a just cause.

Another variant, but closely related approach, is to define as terrorism only the use of terror by governments, or so-called "state terrorism." Indeed, the word "terror" was first used in connection with the Jacobin "Reign of Terror" during the French Revolution. As a result of these pejorative and ideologically circumscribed uses of the term "terrorism" in international fora, no general definition has been agreed upon.

Nonetheless, for our purposes, it is necessary at a minimum to have a rough working definition of the subject we are discussing. To this end, one might consider the definition of "international terrorism" that appears in the federal crime code's chapter on terrorism. According to this definition, "international terrorism" means activities that:

> (A) involve violent acts or acts dangerous to human life that are a violation of the criminal laws of the United States or of any State, or that would be a criminal violation if committed within the jurisdiction of the United States or of any State;
>
> (B) appear to be intended—
>
> > (i) to intimidate or coerce a civilian population;
> >
> > (ii) to influence the policy of a government by intimidation or coercion; or
> >
> > (iii) to affect the conduct of a government by mass destruction, assassination, or kidnapping; and
>
> (C) occur primarily outside the territorial jurisdiction of the United States or transcend national boundaries in terms of the means by which they are accomplished, the persons they appear intended to intimidate or coerce, or the locale in which their perpetrators operate or seek asylum.[5]

Another working definition might be that of Professor Jordan Paust. Paust describes terrorism as "the intentional use of violence, or threat of violence, against an instrumental target in order to communicate to a primary target a threat of future violence so as both to coerce the primary target into behavior or attitudes through intense fear or anxiety

---

5. 18 U.S.C. § 2331(1) (2006).

and to serve a particular political end."[6] As an example where the instrumental and primary target might be the same person or group of persons, Paust cites an attack on a military headquarters in order to instill terror or intense anxiety in the military elite of that head-quarters. He notes further that "the instrumental target need not be a person since attacks on power stations can produce a terror outcome in the civilian population of the community dependent upon the station for electricity."[7] So defined, international terrorism might include—assuming the presence of a terror outcome, a political goal, and an international dimension—the explosion of bombs in the market place, the taking of hostages, attacks on international business persons and diplomats, the hijacking of airplanes, the possible use of nuclear materials or chemical and biological weapons, and attacks on energy resources such as pipelines, offshore oil rigs, and tankers carrying oil or natural gas.

Still another definitional approach and one to which we will return later is that implicit in a report of the Committee on International Terrorism of the International Law Association, a worldwide organization of scholars and international practitioners. Although the report refrains from defining terrorism, its implicit working definition covers any action in time of peace that would be a "war crime" if done by a soldier in time of war.

There are some, including myself, who believe that the term "terrorism" is inherently vague and that its indiscriminate use has seriously undermined efforts to combat those criminal acts loosely termed international terrorism. The late Richard Baxter, Professor of International Law at the Harvard University Law School and a Judge on the International Court of Justice, was among the more eminent proponents of this view.[8]

Nonetheless, despite its deficiencies, the term "international terrorism" remains with us. As such, it has been used—depending upon the particular perception—to cover three basic categories: i) *State Terrorism*. This category comprises the use of terror by governments, including, for example, torture, genocide, and the assassination of political enemies abroad by the use of diplomats or other persons enjoying special status by virtue of their governmental functions. The international dimension is supplied by the fact that these activities violate internationally recognized norms of human rights. Indeed, most commentators prefer to view state terrorism as a matter of international human rights law; ii) *Terrorism in Armed Conflict*. Included in this category are acts inflicting terror in the context of "armed conflict" covered by the law of war. Examples would include the killing of defenseless prisoners of war and the wanton slaughter of civilian noncombatants; and iii) *International Terrorism by Private Individuals*. This is the category of terrorism that will be the object of our primary focus. To be sure, governments may support some private individuals who commit terrorist acts. Indeed, as we shall see below, state support of international terrorism is a primary barrier to effective efforts to combat it. Nonetheless, this state support of private acts of international terrorism is distinguished from "state terrorism" by the nongovernmental status of the offender.

These categories are not, of course, mutually exclusive, and the line between them may be difficult to draw. For example, it may be difficult to determine whether a particular terrorist act has been committed by a private individual acting on his own or by one serving at the direction of a government. Similar difficulties may arise in determining whether a situation should be characterized as an "armed conflict" subject to the law of

---

6. Jordan Paust, *Federal Jurisdiction Over Extraterritorial Acts of Terrorism and Nonimmunity for Foreign Violators of International Law Under the FSIA and the Act of State Doctrine*, 23 Va. J. Int'l L. 191, 192–93 (1983).

7. Jordan Paust, *Terrorism and the International Law of War*, 64 Mil. L. Rev. 1, 4 (1974).

8. *See* Richard Baxter, *A Skeptical Look at the Concept of Terrorism*, 7 Akron L. Rev. 380 (1974).

war. Further, acts of state terrorism may create a political, economic, or a social milieu that precipitates acts of individual terrorism. Despite such complexities or compartmentalization, these categories are useful for present purposes, and we will employ them in our analysis of international terrorism.

To what extent, if at all, can the law and the legal process deter terrorism? When the law authorizes or commands that certain measures be taken to prevent terrorist activity, such as mandating security controls at airports and embassies or authorizing the gathering, analysis, and distribution of data by intelligence agencies, the law clearly plays a useful role.

It is debatable, however, whether the provisions and processes of criminal law regarding the prohibition of terrorist acts and the apprehension, prosecution, and punishment of those who commit them can be an effective deterrent to terrorism. The terrorist, by definition, is an ideologically motivated offender who rejects the legal characterization of his acts as criminal and who may regard the prospect of a prison term as a small price to pay for furthering his cause. Indeed, as the deaths through voluntary starvation of the Irish Republican Army (IRA) terrorists demonstrate, prison may be a milieu in which further sacrifices for the cause are undertaken.

To be sure, a prison term serves the minimal purpose of taking the terrorist off the street and preventing him from engaging in further violence against society. But, his presence in jail may stimulate additional terrorist activities by his colleagues with a view to forcing his release. The taking of hostages has been an especially effective tactic to this end.

Law may even serve as an obstacle to maximum deterrence of terrorism. Most terrorism occurs in liberal democratic societies, while the totalitarian states are relatively free of the problem. The reasons for this are manifold and complex. But, a primary reason is that the values of a democratic society, codified in positive law, prohibit the government from engaging in such antiterrorist techniques as constant surveillance of the populace, restrictions on travel, or torture. In short, democratic societies have decided not to become garrison states in the name of combating terrorism. They have decided to maintain the very values that terrorism threatens.

One should not conclude, however, that because the hardcore terrorist is unlikely to be deterred by the prospect of punishment, law and legal process have no useful role to play in deterring terrorism. Legal proscriptions against terrorism, at both the national and international levels, serve at a minimum to support the premise that terrorism is a criminal activity not justified by the particular cause the terrorist espouses. Codification of humanitarian values into legal instruments, especially if accompanied by educational efforts, may be a helpful tactic in "ideological warfare" against terrorism. Unless people of goodwill succeed in creating an atmosphere antithetical to terrorism, law on the books will be of little utility.

A Brief History of Efforts to Combat International Terrorism

The origins of individual acts of terrorism go back to the Greek and Roman Republics.[9] As Professor Friedlander points out, in its classic manifestation, the assassination of Julius Caesar on the Ides of March in 44 B.C. was an act of terrorism.

In Arabic, the word "assassin," literally translated, means "hashish-eater" or "one addicted to hashish." Acting under the influence of intoxicating drugs, and spurred on

---

9. This historical background is taken largely from ROBERT A. FRIEDLANDER, TERROR VIOLENCE 1–39 (1983).

by their leaders, a group of Muslim fanatics spread terror among prominent Christian and other religious enemies.

As noted previously, the word "terrorism" was first used during the French Revolution and the Jacobin Reign of Terror. In this manifestation, it took the form of state action designed to further political repression and social control.

The revolutionary anarchism that arose in the latter half of the nineteenth century presented a dramatic manifestation of individual acts of terrorism. The anarchists were regarded, as were pirates, as the common enemy of mankind and were suppressed by harsh government action.

Terrorism played a role in the outbreak of World War I. During the early years of the twentieth century, the Balkans became a focal point for international intrigue and revolutionary violence involving bands secretly supported by Bulgaria, Serbia, and Greece. The Serbian government supported a group known as the Black Hand against the Austro-Hungarian Empire. On June 28, 1914, a nineteen-year-old trained by the Black Hand assassinated the Archduke Franz Ferdinand, heir to the imperial throne. The assassination precipitated a series of actions and counteractions that led in a month's time to the first global conflict.

An increase in terrorist activity following World War I led to the first concerted efforts at international control of terrorism, namely, a series of meetings in the late 1920s and early 1930s under the auspices of the International Conference for the Unification of Penal Law. These meetings served to focus attention on the subject, and resulted in the revision of some extradition treaties to exclude certain terrorist acts from the category of "political offenses," thereby making them extraditable (especially attacks on heads of state, the so-called "attentat" clause first introduced by Belgium and France into all their extradition treaties). However, it was not until the assassination at Marseilles on October 9, 1934, of King Alexander of Yugoslavia, and Mr. Louis Barthou, Foreign Minister of the French Republic, that the world community began an intensive consideration at the official level of international terrorism. This concern led to the Convention for the Prevention and Punishment of Terrorism, concluded at Geneva under the auspices of the League of Nations on November 16, 1937. Under the Convention, terrorism was defined broadly to include criminal acts directed against a state and intended to create terror in the minds of a particular person, or a group of persons, or the general public. Possibly because of the breadth of this definition, only one member state of the League ratified the Convention and it never came into force.

The International Law Commission, a United Nations organ, in its 1954 Draft Code of Offenses against the Peace and Security of Mankind, took a similarly broad approach.[10] Article 2(6) of the Draft Code declares "the undertaking or encouragement by the authorities of a State of terrorist activity in another State, or the toleration by the authorities of a State of organized activities calculated to carry out terrorist acts in another State" to be an offense against the peace and security of mankind and a crime under international law. The United Nations General Assembly, however, has, at this writing, been unable to agree upon a final version of the Draft Code.

In 1974, the United Nations General Assembly adopted a resolution defining aggression.[11] Although the definition does not expressly refer to terrorism, it classifies as an act of

---

10. U.N. GAOR, 9th Sess., Supp. No. 9, U.N. Doc A/2693 at 11, (1954).
11. G.A. Res. 3314, U.N. GAOR, 29th Sess., Supp. No. 31, U.N. Doc. A/0631 at 142, (1957).

aggression actions by states in sending, organizing, or supporting "armed bands, groups, irregulars, or mercenaries, which carry out acts of armed force against another State...."

A dramatic increase in the hijackings of aircraft during the 1960s commanded the attention of the world community and led to the modern approaches to combating international terrorism. We turn now to a consideration of these.

Modern Approaches

The Quest for a Comprehensive Approach

As we shall see in the next section, in part because of its inability to agree on a definition of international terrorism, the world community has attempted to resolve the problem of definition by ignoring it and focusing instead on identifying particular criminal acts to be prevented and punished, and on particular targets to be protected. There are currently underway, however, efforts in the United Nations to draft a comprehensive convention on international terrorism. At this writing, these efforts have been unsuccessful. A major reason for this failure is the inability of member states of the United Nations to agree on the terms of an article that would set forth exclusions from the scope of the convention. As noted by an eminent commentator,

> [d]espite ... relatively promising [recent] developments ... the political positions which have retarded the development of an effective legal regime [to combat terrorism] have changed little. The Non-Aligned Movement's solidarity has been broken by a number of prominent defections, yet a substantial number of states still resist a definition of terrorism that might be applied to terrorist activities of groups that some wish to view as 'freedom fighters' or fighters in wars of 'national liberation.'[12]

There has been, moreover, considerable debate over the desirability of efforts to conclude a comprehensive convention on international terrorism.[13] The Committee on International Terrorism of the International Law Association addressed this issue and proposed a "more modest approach."

Fourth Interim Report of the Committee on International Terrorism

in INTERNATIONAL LAW ASSOCIATION,
REPORT OF THE SIXTIETH CONFERENCE 349 (1982)

1. The Committee on International Terrorism submitted an interim report to the Association at the Fifty-Sixth Conference at New Delhi. A second Interim Report was submitted at the Fifty-Seventh Conference at Madrid, and a third interim report at the Fifty-Ninth Conference at Belgrade. These reports reflected and provoked the views expressed at some length at the open meetings of the Committee during those conferences. In addition, the opinions and conclusions of many members of the Committee were presented privately to the late Professor Alona E. Evans, the distinguished and lamented Chairman-Rapporteur of the Committee from its formation until her untimely death in

---

12. W. Michael Reisman, *International Legal Responses to Terrorism*, 22 Hous. J. Int'l L. 3, 57–58 (1999).

13. *See, e.g.*, Leo Gross, *International Terrorism and International Criminal Jurisdiction*, 67 Am. J. Int'l L. 508 (1973); *Murphy-Woetzel-Lederer Correspondence* [About Professor Gross' Comments], 68 Am. J. Int'l L. 306–08, 717–19 (1974).

1980. When she died, Professor Evans was at work on revisions to a draft Single Convention on the Legal Control of International Terrorism.

2. A review of the Committee's efforts and the draft convention appearing at Part II of the Committee's third interim report showed that so many problems of both a practical and a theoretical nature remained that a reconsideration of the "single convention" approach was felt desirable. The Committee did not reject the possibility that a "Single Convention" might be feasible and useful to the international community as it seeks to coordinate its efforts to gain control over politically motivated violence that crosses national boundaries without crossing the legal threshold of "war" or "armed conflict," as envisaged by the 1949 Geneva Conventions and the 1977 Protocols to those Conventions. But without abandoning the aim of producing a comprehensive single convention, it was concluded that a more modest approach might be more useful for the purposes of this interim report and at this time.

....

19. The better course would be to develop what might be called the humanitarian law concerned with political violence in step with the humanitarian law applicable to armed conflict. There is no reason in theory or practice why a state should be willing to concede to politically motivated foreigners a license to commit atrocities while saddling their own organized armed forces with the restraints contained in the 1949 Geneva Conventions against committing the same atrocities.

20. It thus appears that general international law already contains rules which reflect a limit to politically-motivated behavior by authorized public officials, including soldiers, reflected but not necessarily fully codified in the positive law relating to "grave breaches" already adhered to by nearly all members of the international community. No reason is perceived why other equally well-motivated individuals or groups should be legally insulated by their political ideals from the punishments to which officials or soldiers are subjected for the same atrocities. Surely, the humanitarian law requiring states to cooperate in the suppression of war crimes should apply with regard to acts outside of the armed conflict classification and by persons not entitled to soldiers' privileges.

21. It would seem to follow from this that any formulation of law dealing with international terrorism should accept as a premise that: "No person shall be permitted to escape trial or extradition on the ground of his political motivation who, if he performed the same acts as a soldier engaged in an international armed conflict, would be subject to trial or extradition."

....

23. The Committee was throughout its deliberation fully conscious of the fact that states frequently differ over the qualifications of individuals and groups resorting to violence for political ends. The Report, however, makes it clear that contemporary international law imposes legal limits on the actions of such individuals and groups however they are described.

The "Piecemeal" Approach Illustrated

Regardless of its merits—and we shall return to this issue later—the "piecemeal" approach to combating international terrorism has been the one followed. It has been followed, moreover, at several different levels. That is, a number of global treaties and conventions have been adopted in the United Nations and in other fora. At the same time, several regional conventions have been drafted to reflect the particular needs and perspectives of the states in the region concerned. Finally, a number of bilateral agreements have been adopted. Some of these deal specifically with a particular manifestation of international terrorism; others are relevant to international terrorism, although they cover a wide variety of other crimes as well.

We will briefly consider these different kinds of treaties and conventions below. Then we will turn to other approaches that have been proposed, either by government officials in international organizations or by scholars. Finally, we attempt to evaluate some of these existing and proposed measures through a review of questions.

Global Treaties and Conventions

At this writing the United Nations or its specialized agencies have adopted thirteen global, multilateral antiterrorist conventions.[14] These include: Convention on Offences and Certain Other Acts Committed on Board Aircraft (1963); Convention for the Suppression of Unlawful Seizure of Aircraft (1970); Convention for the Suppression of Unlawful Acts against the Safety of Civil Aviation (1971); Convention on the Prevention and Punishment of Crimes against Internationally Protected Persons, including Diplomatic Agents (1973); International Convention against the Taking of Hostages (1979); Convention on the Physical Protection of Nuclear Material (1979); Protocol for the Suppression of Unlawful Acts of Violence at Airports Serving International Civil Aviation, supplementary to the Convention for the Suppression of Unlawful Acts against the Safety of Civil Aviation (1988); Convention for the Suppression of Unlawful Acts Against the Safety of Maritime Navigation (1988); Protocol for the Suppression of Unlawful Acts Against the Safety of Fixed Platforms Located on the Continental Shelf (1988); Convention on the Marking of Plastic Explosives for the Purpose of Detection (1991); International Convention for the Suppression of Terrorist Bombing (1997); International Convention for the Suppression of the Financing of Terrorism (1999); and International Convention for the Suppression of Acts of Nuclear Terrorism (2005).

The basic purpose of these conventions is to establish a framework for international cooperation among states to prevent and suppress international terrorism. To accomplish this goal, the Convention on the Prevention and Punishment of Crimes against Internationally Protected Persons, including Diplomatic Agents, for example, requires states parties to cooperate in order to prevent, within their territories, preparations for attacks on diplomats within or outside their territories, to exchange information, and to coordinate administrative measures against such attacks. If an attack against an internationally protected person takes place, and an alleged offender has fled the country where the attack occurred, states parties are to cooperate in the exchange of information concerning the circumstances of the crime and the alleged offender's identity and whereabouts. The state party where the alleged offender is found is obliged to take measures to ensure his presence for purposes of extradition or prosecution and to inform interested states and international organizations of the measures taken. Finally, states parties are to cooperate in assisting criminal proceedings brought for attacks on internationally protected persons, including supplying all relevant evidence at their disposal.

---

14. For a listing of these conventions with full citations, *see* Jimmy Gurule & Geoffrey S. Corn, Principles of Counter-Terrorism Law 336, fn. 34 (2011).

The key feature of these conventions requires a state party that apprehends an alleged offender in its territory either to extradite him or to submit his case to its authorities for purposes of prosecution. Strictly speaking, none of these conventions alone creates an obligation to extradite. Rather, they contain an *inducement* to extradite by requiring the submission of alleged offenders for prosecution if extradition fails. Moreover, a legal *basis* for extradition is provided either in the Convention, or through incorporation of the offenses mentioned in the Convention into existing or future extradition treaties between the parties. To varying degrees, the Conventions also obligate the parties to take the important practical step of attempting to apprehend the accused offender and hold him in custody.

The most important goal of these provisions is to ensure that the accused is prosecuted. To this end the alternative obligation to submit for prosecution is stated quite strongly in these Conventions. The obligation, however, is not to *try* the accused, much less to punish him, but to submit the case to be considered for prosecution by the appropriate national prosecuting authority. If the criminal justice system lacks integrity, the risk of political intervention in the prosecution or at trial exists. Such intervention may prevent the trial, a conviction, or the appropriate punishment of the accused.

Even if the criminal justice system functions with integrity, it may be very difficult to obtain the evidence necessary to convict when the alleged offense was committed in a foreign country. This very practical impediment to conviction can be removed between states of goodwill only by patient and sustained efforts to develop and expand "judicial assistance" and other forms of cooperation between the law enforcement and judicial systems of different countries. The conventions create an obligation to cooperate in this respect, but this obligation poses major problems for even good faith efforts among countries with different types of legal systems.

The UN Convention against the Taking of Hostages adds a new dimension to presently existing international legal measures to combat terrorism. The Convention seeks to ensure that international acts of hostage taking will be covered either by the Convention itself or by one of the applicable conventions on the law of armed conflict. For example, hostage taking is a "grave breach" of the 1949 Geneva Convention Relative to the Protection of Civilian Persons in Time of War.[15] The UN Hostages Convention also represents a partial rejection of the thesis that acts of terrorism are permissible if committed as part of a war of national liberation.

Two of the most recently adopted global antiterrorist conventions—the bombing and financing conventions—are worthy of special note. Extraordinary developments during the 1990s—including the collapse of the Soviet Union, the end of the Cold War, and the end of apartheid in South Africa—led to a less confrontational atmosphere in the United Nations and a sharp decline in support of "wars of national liberation." Bombing of civilian targets had been a favored tactic employed by national liberation movements. Article 5 of the bombing convention, however, requires states parties to adopt any measures that may be necessary to ensure that criminal acts within the scope of the convention, especially when they are intended to create a state of terror, are "under no circumstances justifiable by considerations of a political, philosophical, ideological, racial, ethnic, religious or other similar nature and are punishable by penalties consistent with their grave nature." None of the earlier antiterrorist conventions has a similar provision. Along somewhat similar lines, Article 11 expressly eliminates, for the first time in a UN antiterrorist

---

15. 1949 Geneva Convention Relative to the Protection of Civilian Persons in Time of War, *done at* Geneva, Aug. 12, 1948, Art. 147, [1956], 6 U.S.T. 3516, T.I.A.S. No. 3365, 75 U.N.T.S. 287.

convention, the political offense exception for purposes of extradition and mutual legal assistance.

For its part, the financing convention, like the bombing convention, is a "model" antiterrorist convention that incorporates what Clifton Johnson, the chief U.S. negotiator for the convention, has called:

> increasingly standard provisions of the recent counterterrorism conventions. These include provisions: 1) limiting the Convention's application to acts with an international element; 2) obligating States Parties to criminalize the covered offenses irrespective of the motivation of the perpetrators; 3) obligating States Parties to take into custody offenders found on their territory; 4) facilitating the extradition of offenders; 5) requiring States Parties to afford one another the greatest measure of assistance in connection with the criminal investigations or proceedings relating to the covered offenses; 6) prohibiting extradition or mutual legal assistance requests relating to a covered offense from being refused on political offense grounds; and 7) providing for the transfer of prisoners in order to assist the investigation or prosecution of covered offenses.[16]

Johnson goes on to point out that the financing convention adds "specific and unique provisions directed at terrorism financing."[17] We shall return to the subject of suppressing the financing of terrorism later in this chapter.

Two other multilateral conventions, while not directed expressly against terrorism, are relevant for our purposes. The Convention on the Prohibition of the Development, Production and Stockpiling of Bacteriological (Biological) and Toxin Weapons and on Their Destruction[18] applies controls on weapons that are of potential use to terrorists. To the same end, the Convention on the Prohibition of the Development, Production, Stockpiling and Use of Chemical Weapons and on Their Destruction[19] prohibits states parties from using, producing, or stockpiling poison gas or lethal chemical weapons, and requires them to dispose of existing chemical weapons by the year 2010 at the latest. It also creates rigorous verification procedures implemented through a new Organization for the Prohibition of Chemical Weapons. Several key states, however, have not ratified the convention, including Iraq, which used chemical weapons during its war with Iran, both against Iranian troops and its own Kurdish population.

Most of the multilateral conventions have relatively strong dispute settlement provisions that allow for binding arbitration or adjudication, although, in some cases, parties are allowed to "opt out" by reservation made at the time they become a party. The United States relied in part on such a provision in the UN Convention on Internationally Protected Persons as the basis for bringing its action against Iran before the International Court of Justice. None of these conventions, however, contains provisions for economic or other sanctions against states that offer safe haven or other assistance to terrorists. Efforts in September 1973 to conclude an independent enforcement convention for the International

---

16. Clifton Johnson, *Introductory Note to the International Convention for the Suppression of the Financing of Terrorism*, 39 I.L.M. 268 (2000).

17. *Id.* at 269.

18. Convention on the Prohibition of the Development, Production and Stockpiling of Bacteriological (Biological) and Toxin Weapons and on Their Destruction, *done at* Washington, London, and Moscow, Apr. 10, 1972, [1975], 26 U.S.T. 583, T.I.A.S. No. 8062.

19. Convention on the Prohibition of the Development, Production, Stockpiling and Use of Chemical Weapons and on their Destruction, *done at* Paris, Jan. 13, 1993, [1997], *reprinted in* 32 I.L.M. 800 (1993).

Civil Aviation Organization (ICAO) Conventions at the Rome Security Conference and the ICAO Extraordinary Assembly were unsuccessful.

It is unclear how effective these global conventions have been in practice. The crucial issue is the extent to which the global antiterrorist conventions have been or will be vigorously implemented. Conclusion of antiterrorist conventions is only the first step in the process. Unfortunately, many states parties seem to regard it as the last.

Vigorous implementation, moreover, encompasses more than merely ratifying the conventions and passing domestic implementing legislation. It requires the taking of active steps toward achieving the primary goals of the conventions: the prevention of the crimes covered by the conventions and the prosecution and punishment of the perpetrators of the crimes. The record of the conventions in this respect is unclear.

A major part of the problem is the lack of adequate data on the extent of successful actions to prevent terrorist acts and of successful prosecutions of terrorists. Although there appear to be adequate data available on the extradition, prosecution, and punishment of aircraft hijackers, information regarding other manifestations of terrorism is quite sparse. Most of the antiterrorist conventions contain provisions requiring the state party where the alleged offender is prosecuted to communicate the final outcome of the proceedings to the Secretary-General of the United Nations (or to the Director-General of the International Atomic Energy Agency or the Council of the ICAO), and the Secretary-General has issued reports on "Measures to Eliminate International Terrorism." But these reports focus primarily on the terrorist events that triggered the conventions and on a summary of the most important provisions of these conventions. There appears to be little information on the extent and success of efforts to prevent the acts the conventions cover or to prosecute the perpetrators of these acts.

Regional Conventions

There are now at least eight antiterrorist conventions that have been adopted at the regional level. These include: (1) Organization of American States (OAS) Convention to Prevent and Punish the Acts of Terrorism Taking the Form of Crimes Against Persons and Related Extortion that are of International Significance (1971); (2) European Convention on the Suppression of Terrorism (1977); (3) South Asian Association for Regional Cooperation (SAARC) Regional Convention on Suppression of Terrorism (1977); (4) The Arab Convention on the Suppression of Terrorism (1998); (5) Treaty on Cooperation among the States Members of the Commonwealth of Independent States in Combating Terrorism (1999); (6) Convention of the Organization of the Islamic Conference on Combating International Terrorism (1999); (7) Organization of African Unity (OAU) Convention on the Prevention and Combating of Terrorism (1999);[20] and (8) Inter-American Convention Against Terrorism (2002).[21] Five of these conventions have been adopted relatively recently, and it is therefore too early to evaluate them in terms of their operational efficiency. Some of these recently adopted regional conventions have noteworthy provisions, however, and these will be briefly explored below.

---

20. The texts of these conventions may be most conveniently found in UNITED NATIONS, INTERNATIONAL INSTRUMENTS RELATED TO THE PREVENTION AND SUPPRESSION OF INTERNATIONAL TERRORISM 134–226 (2001).

21. Adopted on June 3, 2002, text *available at* <http://www.oas.org/xxxiiga/english/docs_en/docs_items/AGres1840_02.htm>.

The OAS Convention to Prevent and Punish the Acts of Terrorism Taking the Form of Crimes Against Persons and Related Extortion that are of International Significance, which was the first antiterrorist convention adopted at the regional level, is focused narrowly on the kidnapping of diplomats, despite efforts to broaden the scope of the convention.[22] Moreover, it has only a total of nine parties, including the United States, and has not been an effective instrument for the protection of diplomats. In practice, the UN Convention on the Prevention and Punishment of Crimes against Internationally Protected Persons, including Diplomatic Agents, has in effect superceded it.

By contrast, thirty of the thirty-three nations present at the meeting of the OAS General Assembly signed the Inter-American Convention against Terrorism. And there is nothing narrow about the focus of the Inter-American Convention. On the contrary, among other things, the Convention defines "offenses" within the scope of its coverage as including the offenses covered by the UN antiterrorist conventions and requires states parties to the Inter-American Convention to make a declaration upon ratification that they are not parties to one or the other of the UN antiterrorist conventions if they wish these conventions to be inapplicable to them, thus creating a strong inducement on OAS member states to sign and ratify the UN antiterrorist conventions. Also, under Article 3 of the Convention, states parties "shall endeavor" to become parties to the UN antiterrorist conventions and "to adopt the necessary measures to effectively implement such instruments." The Convention further requires states parties to use the recommendations of the Financial Action Task Force and other specialized agencies as guidelines for measures combating the financing of terrorism, to deny safe haven to persons suspected of terrorism, and to reject application of the political offense exception to requests for extradition or mutual legal assistance.

The European Convention on the Suppression of Terrorism (European Convention) was an early attempt to deal with a primary obstacle, especially during the 1970s, in the way of efforts to combat terrorism, the political offense exception to international extradition. To this end, Article 1 of the Convention lists a series of offenses, none of which "for the purposes of extradition between Contracting States" are to be regarded "as a political offense or as an offense connected with a political motive or as an offense inspired by political motives."[23] Under Article 2, the Convention invites states parties to exclude additional acts of violence against persons or property from the political offense exception. At the same time, Article 13 of the Convention allows a state party to register a reservation permitting it to reject a request for extradition on the ground that the offense is of a political character—notwithstanding that a listed offense is involved:

> provided that it undertakes to take into consideration when evaluating the character of the offense any particularly serious aspects of the offense including:
>
> (a) that it created a collective danger to the life, physical integrity or liberty of persons; or
>
> (b) that it affected persons foreign to the motives behind it; or
>
> (c) that cruel or vicious means had been used in the commission of the offense.[24]

Under Article 5 of the Convention, a requested state may refuse to extradite an accused if it "has substantial grounds for believing that the request for extradition for an offense

---

22. UNITED NATIONS, INTERNATIONAL INSTRUMENTS RELATED TO THE PREVENTION AND SUPPRESSION OF INTERNATIONAL TERRORISM 134 (2001).
23. *Id.* at 139.
24. *Id.* at 144.

mentioned in Article 1 or 2 has been made for the purpose of prosecuting or punishing a person on account of his race, religion, nationality, or political opinion, or that the person's position may be prejudiced for any of these reasons."[25] Should a state party decide not to extradite an offender covered by the Convention, under Article 7 it must "submit the case, without exception whatsoever and without undue delay to its competent authorities for the purpose of prosecution."[26]

Although the Convention is an antiterrorism initiative, it nowhere attempts to define terrorism. In attempting to exclude a variety of common crimes as well as "terrorism" from the political offense exception to extradition, the Convention may have attempted too much, because many states, upon signing or ratifying the convention, reserved the right to refuse to extradite for an offense that they consider political. This defect, if such it be, has largely been cured, at least among states parties that are members of the European Union, by the EU's 1996 Convention Relating to Extradition between Member States.[27] Article 5 of the EU Convention eliminates the political offense exception in extradition between states parties and paragraph 4 of that article provides that reservations to the European Convention shall not apply to extradition between member states. However, a member state may limit the ambit of Article 5 of the EU Convention to the violent crimes listed in Articles 1 and 2 of the European Convention. Moreover, paragraph 3 of Article 5 preserves the right to refuse extradition if the fugitive might be persecuted or punished on account of his race, religion, nationality, or political opinion.

Adoption of the EU Convention, then, would appear to have removed, at least partially, the "internal inconsistency" of the European Convention that raised serious doubts as to its effectiveness in practice. Moreover, some early holdouts, such as Ireland and France, have become parties to the Convention, and English and French courts have applied it when surrendering fugitives. Hence, although one could wish there was more of it, there is some evidence that the European Convention has been of some use to European efforts to combat terrorism.

In sharp contrast, the Arab Convention on the Suppression of Terrorism and the OAU Convention on the Prevention and Combating of Terrorism raise the issue of the political offense exception and the exclusion for "wars of national liberation" in stark form. Both conventions contain detailed definitions of terrorism and terrorist acts. But then the Arab Convention, in Article 2(a), provides that "[a]ll cases of struggle by whatever means, including armed struggle, against foreign occupation and aggression for liberation and self-determination, in accordance with the principles of international law, shall not be regarded as an offence. This provision shall not apply to any act prejudicing territorial integrity of any Arab State."[28] To be blunt, this provision seeks to justify the commission of terrorist acts against Israel and reflects an attitude that has stymied efforts in the United Nations to reach agreement on a definition of international terrorism.

Along the same lines, in Article 3(1), the OAU Convention provides that "the struggle waged by peoples in accordance with the principles of international law for their liberation or self-determination, including armed struggle against colonialism, occupation, aggression, and domination by foreign forces shall not be considered as terrorist acts."[29] This provision

---

25. *Id.* at 141.
26. *Id.*
27. 1996 O.J. (C 313/02) 11.
28. UNITED NATIONS, INTERNATIONAL INSTRUMENTS RELATED TO THE PREVENTION AND SUPPRESSION OF INTERNATIONAL TERRORISM 152 (2001).
29. *Id.* at 103.

and the Arab Convention's provisions are incompatible with the approach taken by Article 5 of the UN bombing convention, noted above, which provides that terrorist bombings are "under no circumstances justifiable by considerations of a political, philosophical, ideological, racial, ethnic, religious or other similar nature and are punishable by penalties consistent with their grave nature."

Bilateral Agreements

In addition to the conventions on civil aviation noted above, there are at least seven bilateral agreements on aircraft hijacking. One of the more interesting examples of these bilateral agreements is the Cuban-American Memorandum of Understanding on Hijacking of Aircraft and Vessels and Other Offenses.[30] It provides that any person who hijacks an aircraft or vessel registered under the law of one party to the territory of the other party shall either be returned to the party of registry or "be brought before the courts of the party whose territory he reached for trial in conformity with its laws for the offense punishable by the most severe penalty according to the circumstances and seriousness of the acts to which this Article refers."[31] Thus, the Memorandum incorporates the extradite-or-prosecute formula, but does so in a more meaningful way than do the multilateral antiterrorist conventions. Unlike the multilateral conventions, the Cuban-American Memorandum requires that the accused actually be tried and not merely submitted "for the purpose of prosecution."

Under the Cuban-American Memorandum, each party expressly recognizes an affirmative obligation to prevent the use of its territory as a base for committing the illegal acts covered by the Memorandum. Each party must try "with a view to severe punishment" any person who, "within its territory, hereafter conspires to promote, or promotes, or prepares, or directs, or forms part of an expedition which from its territory or any other place carries out acts of violence or depredation against aircraft or vessels of any kind or registration coming from or going to the territory of the other party or … carries out such acts or other similar unlawful acts in the territory of the other party."[32]

Finally, the Cuban-American Memorandum severely limits the extent to which the prosecuting party where the hijacker arrives may take his motivation into account. It provides, in pertinent part, for taking "into consideration any extenuating or mitigating circumstances in those cases in which the persons responsible for the acts were being sought for strictly political reasons and were in real and imminent danger of death without a viable alternative for leaving the country, provided there was no financial extortion or physical injury to the members of the crew, passengers, or other persons in connection with the hijacking."[33]

In 1976, the Memorandum was denounced by Cuba on the ground that the United States had failed to control anti-Castro terrorists who had planted a bomb on a Cuban civilian aircraft. However, in practice Cuba has shown that hijackers still face imprisonment in Cuba or extradition to the United States.

Bilateral extradition agreements are also relevant to any consideration of law and the deterrence of international terrorism. These agreements normally do not contain the "ex-

---

30. Cuban-American Memorandum of Understanding on Hijacking of Aircraft and Vessels and Other Offenses, *entered into force* Feb. 15, 1973, 24 U.S.T. 737, T.I.A.S. No. 7579.

31. *Id.* art. 1.

32. *Id.* art. 2.

33. *Id.* art. 4.

tradite-or-prosecute" formula of the multilateral conventions. They do require the state party, where an alleged perpetrator of an extraditable offense is found, to extradite him for prosecution upon request to the state party in which the offense was alleged to have been committed. This obligation, however, is subject to a number of exceptions, including the one most pertinent to international terrorism: the political offense exception. By definition, terrorism involves a political dimension, and some states have therefore regarded it as a political offense *par excellence*. Even those states that reject this simplistic analysis have had trouble with the doctrine. The primary reason for this difficulty is that the precise parameters of the political offense doctrine are unclear.

As the concept has evolved, it has divided into two categories: the "pure" and the "relative" political offense. Purely political offenses are never extraditable and are limited to crimes against the state, such as treason, sedition, and espionage. The concept of a "relative" political crime has proven much more difficult because it may encompass common crimes if they are committed in connection with a political act. For example, a homicide committed in the course of a general uprising may be non-extraditable if a sufficient nexus exists between the crime and the political event.

In three cases involving members of the Irish Republican Army, U.S. courts declined to honor requests from the United Kingdom for their extradition on the ground that their alleged crimes constituted political offenses.[34] The U.S. government reacted strongly to these decisions. In the wake of the *McMullen* and *Mackin* decisions, the executive branch, in 1981, prompted the introduction of a bill in the Senate[35] that would, among other things, grant both the government and the accused the right to appeal a district court or magistrate's decision on various issues of extradition law, but reserve to the sole discretion of the Secretary of State the decision whether the political offense exception is applicable. There was general agreement on provisions granting both the government and the accused the right of appeal, as well as on a number of other changes in current extradition law the draft legislation would effect. There was, however, substantial opposition to transferring the decision-making authority regarding the political offense exception from the courts to the Secretary of State. In hearings on the legislation, it was argued that exclusion of the judiciary from the decision-making process would undermine the purpose of the political offense doctrine to protect individuals from government oppression and subject the doctrine to the political calculations of governments.

Nor was any effort made in the legislation to define the political offense exception. Rather the approach taken was to exclude explicitly certain offenses from the political offense doctrine. One version, H.R. 2643, approached the problem as follows:

> (2) For the purposes of the section, a political offense does not include —
>
> ...
>
> (C) a serious offense involving an attack against the life, physical integrity, or liberty of internationally protected persons (as defined in section 1116 of this title), including diplomatic agents;
>
> (D) an offense with respect to which a multilateral treaty obligates the United States to either extradite or prosecute a person accused of the offense;

---

34. *See In re* McMullen, Mag. No. 3-78-1099 MG (N.D. Cal. May 11, 1979) (unreported); *In re* Mackin, Mag. No. 80, Ct. Misc. 1, Aug. 13, 1981 (unreported); Matter of Doherty, 599 F. Supp. 270 (S.D.N.Y. 1984); United States v. Doherty, 786 F.2d 491 (2d Cir. 1986).

35. S. 1639, 96th Cong. (1981).

(E) an offense that consists of the manufacture, importation, distribution, or sale of narcotics or dangerous drugs;

(F) an attempt or conspiracy to commit an offense described in subparagraphs (A) through (E) of this paragraph, or participation as an accomplice of a person who commits, attempts, or conspires to commit such an offense.[36]

Neither H.R. 2643 nor any of the other bills was adopted, however, and the effort to reform the extradition laws of the United States was abandoned.

Another tactic employed by the executive branch has been to include in recent bilateral extradition treaties specific provisions reserving to the "Executive authority of the requested Party" the power to determine whether an offense for which extradition is requested is within the political offense exception. Also, on July 17, 1986, the Senate gave its advice and consent to ratification of a Supplementary Extradition Treaty between the United States and the United Kingdom. In its original form, the Supplementary Treaty would have eliminated the political offense exception as to a number of violent crimes. Because of opposition from various sources, the Senate Committee on Foreign Relations, in a highly unusual procedure, amended the treaty through negotiations among members of the Committee, representatives of the executive branch, and representatives of the British government. The most important amendments were twofold. First, two crimes—possession of firearms and conspiracy to commit any of the other offenses—were dropped from the list of crimes for which the political offense doctrine cannot be asserted. Second, and most significant, a new article was added to the treaty permitting judges to deny extradition if the accused demonstrates by a preponderance of the evidence that he is being sought "on account of his race, religion, nationality, or political opinions" or that he would be denied a fair trial because of any of these factors.[37]

In its resolution of advice and consent to ratification, the Senate declared that it "will not give its advice and consent to any treaty that would narrow the political offense exception with a totalitarian or other non-democratic regime and that nothing in the Supplementary Treaty with the United Kingdom shall be considered a precedent by the executive branch or the Senate for other treaties."

It should be noted that a new U.S./U.K. Extradition Treaty entered into force between the parties in 2007. The new extradition treaty does not contain the provision of the Supplementary Treaty that permitted judges to deny extradition if the accused demonstrated by a preponderance of the evidence that he was being sought "on account of his race, religion, nationality, or political opinions" or that he would be denied a fair trial because of any of these factors. By 2007, the situation in Northern Ireland had changed so dramatically that arguably there was no need of a so-called "humanitarian provision" along the lines of the one in the Supplementary Treaty.

Informal Methods of Rendition: Exclusion, Expulsion, and Kidnapping

Because of the many difficulties attendant to extradition, it has been resorted to less frequently than expulsion or other "informal" methods of rendition of international terrorists. Although these informal forms of rendition may be effective in returning the

---

36. H.R. 2643, 96th Cong. (1981).

37. For a decision applying this article, *see In re* Extradition of Smyth, 61 F.3d 711 (9th Cir. 1995), *cert. denied*, 518 U.S. 1022 (1996) (finding that Smyth had not carried his burden of proof, the appellate court reversed the district court's ruling that he would be subject to such discrimination and remanded for entry of an order allowing extradition).

alleged terrorist to a place where he will be prosecuted, they raise serious issues of human rights.

The *McMullen* case is illustrative. After the magistrate determined that McMullen could not be extradited to the United Kingdom because his acts fell within the political offense exception, the United States government attempted to deport him to the Republic of Ireland. The immigration judge granted McMullen's application for withholding of deportation, but the Board of Immigration Appeals reversed. On appeal, the Ninth Circuit granted McMullen's petition for the withholding of deportation, holding: (a) factual findings under the Refugee Act of 1980[38] are subject to review under the substantial evidence rule; and (b) substantial evidence did not support the Board's finding that McMullen had failed to show a sufficient likelihood of persecution for his political beliefs if he were deported to the Republic of Ireland. In his petition, McMullen alleged that the Provisional Wing of the Irish Republican Army (PIRA) would regard him as a traitor for dropping his membership, that the PIRA systematically tortured and murdered those they regarded as traitors, and that the government of the Republic of Ireland was unable to control the PIRA. He also alleged that the government of Ireland would prosecute him as a former member of the PIRA.[39]

McMullen, however, was ultimately denied withholding of deportation. Upon remand, the Board of Immigration Appeals found that McMullen was ineligible for withholding of deportation under 8 U.S.C. § 1253(H)(2)(C), which denies eligibility for withholding of deportation to "any person who ordered, incited, assisted, or otherwise participated in the persecution of any person on account of race, religion, nationality, membership in a particular social group, or political opinion." The board found that McMullen fit within these categories because of his active membership and leadership, including his training of terrorists and gunrunning, by which he knowingly furthered the PIRA's campaign of terrorist activities. This decision was affirmed upon appeal.[40]

Perhaps the most controversial use of deportation as an alternative to extradition in the United States was the case of Joseph Doherty. After unsuccessful attempts to extradite Doherty, a member of the Provisional Irish Republican Army, from the United States to the United Kingdom, where he was wanted for his role in the death of a British soldier and for his escape from prison, because of decisions by U.S. courts that his offenses fell within the political offense exception in the U.S.-U.K. extradition treaty, noted above, the United States Supreme Court upheld his deportation to Northern Ireland after long and complicated legal proceedings.[41] Although some commentators have argued that it is improper for one state to request another state to deport an individual as a means of circumventing extradition procedures, U.S. courts have repeatedly held that the existence of an extradition treaty between the United States and another country does not bar the use of other means to obtain custody over a criminal located abroad.

Unfortunately, many countries do not apply the same safeguards to the deportation process that the United States does under the Refugee Act of 1980, and these informal methods of rendition are used with little regard for protecting the fundamental human rights of the accused. Accordingly, the late Alona Evans suggested, it would be desirable to recognize expulsion or deportation as a legal method of rendition and to provide

---

38. Pub. L. No. 96-212 (1980).
39. McMullen v. Immigration and Naturalization Service, 658 F.2d 1312 (9th Cir. 1981).
40. McMullen v. Immigration and Naturalization Service, 788 F.2d 591 (9th Cir. 1986).
41. INS v. Doherty, 502 U.S. 314 (1992).

minimum standards for its use, either by a separate convention or by provision in a general convention on international terrorism.[42]

One possible method of rendition, kidnapping, is clearly illegal. Although not involving international terrorism—unless one refers to state terrorism such as, arguably, the abduction in 1960 of Adolf Eichmann from Argentina by Israeli "volunteer groups," which was condemned by the United Nations Security Council in accordance with the long standing principle of international law that abductions by one state of persons located within the territory of another violate the territorial sovereignty of the second state. However, the extent to which such a violation of international law may be raised in a United States court is unclear. In one case, *United States v. Toscanino*,[43] the Court held that the accused could raise as a defense to prosecution a claim of unlawful seizure by American agents in Uruguay, in violation of treaty as well as of American constitutional law principles, but later decisions have severely limited the scope of the *Toscanino* holding to its peculiar facts.

Moreover, the continued viability of even this limited scope of the *Toscanino* decision may be questionable after the highly controversial decision of the U.S. Supreme Court in *United States v. Alvarez-Machain*.[44] In 1990, Mexican agents paid by the U.S. Drug Enforcement Agency (DEA) apprehended Dr. Humberto Alvarez-Machain and deported him to the United States. Dr. Alvarez-Machain was a prominent Mexican gynecologist who had been indicted for the kidnap and murder of Enrique Camarena, a DEA agent stationed in Guadalajara. After strong protests by the Mexican government, and a circuit court opinion holding that the abduction violated the U.S.-Mexican extradition treaty, the Supreme Court ruled that the extradition treaty did not bar the abduction and that U.S. courts could exercise jurisdiction over the case. Although the majority opinion all but conceded by way of dicta that the abduction violated norms of customary international law, the Court did not address the issue of whether this might constitute a basis for U.S. courts to decline jurisdiction. Courts in several other countries have ruled that they have discretion in such circumstances to refuse to exercise jurisdiction.

International Judicial Assistance

The term "international judicial assistance" may be broadly defined to include arrangements between states for the exchange of information regarding criminal investigations, service of documents, interrogation of witnesses, transfer of criminal proceedings, enforcement of criminal judgments, and transfer and supervision of offenders convicted in the other country. In Western Europe, arrangements for judicial assistance in criminal matters are well developed. Until recently, however, the United States had not been involved in international agreements on judicial assistance with regard to criminal matters.

International judicial assistance takes on particular importance in connection with the extradite-or-prosecute obligation contained in the multilateral, antiterrorist conventions to which the United States is a party. If the United States decides not to extradite an alleged offender to the requesting country, it is obliged, as we have seen above, to submit the accused for the purpose of prosecution. But, this obligation lacks meaningful content if the United States has no procedural means of obtaining the evidence necessary to ensure conviction of the accused in consonance with due process and other constitutional protections afforded by United States law.

---

42. *See* Alona Evans, *Perspectives on International Terrorism*, 17 WILLAMETTE L. REV. 151 (1980).
43. 500 F.2d 267 (2d Cir. 1974).
44. 504 U.S. 655 (1992).

The first major international agreement that the United States entered into for the purpose of obtaining information and evidence needed for criminal investigations and prosecutions was the 1973 Treaty on Mutual Assistance in Criminal Matters with Switzerland, which entered into force January 23, 1977.[45] The treaty provides for assistance in locating the whereabouts of witnesses, taking of testimony, service of judicial and administrative orders, and authentication of records, and it makes special provision for assistance in uncovering organized crime. Its principal purpose is to facilitate the acquisition of relevant information about crime and the building of a case against the accused. The treaty exempts from investigation, however, any offenses that the requested state deems to be political in nature or connected therewith unless such offenses can be ascribed to an organized criminal group that uses violence as one of its techniques of action.[46] There is, accordingly, a need to ensure that no terrorist activity may be deemed by a requested state to be political in nature. As of November 15, 1997, the United States had twenty-three Mutual Legal Assistance Treaties (MLATs) in force, but the political offense exception is often available in MLATs and can be a barrier to obtaining the necessary evidence.

A landmark agreement of another type in the judicial assistance area was concluded between the United States and Mexico on November 25, 1976 — Treaty on the Execution of Penal Sentences.[47] This treaty has enabled the national of one state who is a prisoner in the other state to return to his own state to serve his sentence. No exchange is to be made, however, where a prisoner is serving time for "a political offense within the meaning of the Treaty of Extradition of 1899 between the parties, nor an offense under the immigration or the purely military laws of a party."[48] A similar treaty was concluded with Canada on March 2, 1977 — Treaty on the Execution of Penal Sentences.[49] United States courts have confirmed the constitutionality of these treaties.[50]

Despite these developments, it is safe to conclude that the United States is still insufficiently involved internationally in efforts to extend the development and use of various methods of judicial assistance. In this regard, states in Western Europe are substantially ahead of the United States, and their accomplishments may serve as a guide, although peculiar aspects of U.S. law of evidence regarding admissibility present a substantial barrier to more extended U.S. initiatives in this area.

A Proposed Convention

The 1972 United States Draft Convention on Terrorism. The kidnapping and killing at Munich on September 6, 1972, of eleven Israeli Olympic competitors by Arab terrorists, as well as a number of other spectacular acts of terrorism, resulted in United Nations General Assembly consideration of the problem of international terrorism and in the introduction by the United States on September 25 of a Draft Convention for the Prevention and Punishment of Certain Acts of International Terrorism.[51] In introducing the Convention (which was drafted by co-editor John Norton Moore when he served as Counselor on International Law to the Department of State), and in subsequent debates on it, U.S. rep-

---

45. Treaty on Mutual Assistance in Criminal Matters, May 25, 1973, U.S.–Switz., 27 U.S.T. 2019.
46. *Id.* arts. 2(1)(c)(1)(3), 6(3)(a)(b).
47. Treaty on the Execution of Penal Sentences, Nov. 25, 1976, U.S.–Mex., 28 U.S.T. 7399.
48. *Id.* art. II(4).
49. Treaty on the Execution of Penal Sentences, Mar. 2, 1977, U.S.–Can., 30 U.S.T. 6263.
50. *See* Rosado v. Civiletti, 621 F.2d 1179 (2d Cir. 1980); Pfeifer v. U.S. Bureau of Prisons, 615 F.2d 873 (9th Cir. 1980).
51. 11 I.L.M. 1383 (1972).

resentatives attempted to obviate the concern of some member states that the Convention was directed against so-called wars of national liberation. To this end, they pointed out that the Convention was limited in its coverage to "[a]ny person who unlawfully kills, causes serious bodily harm or kidnaps another person...."[52] They noted further that, even as to these acts, four separate conditions had to be met before the terms of the Convention applied. First, the act had to be committed or take effect outside the territory of a state of which an alleged offender was a national. Second, the act had to be committed or take effect outside the state against which the act was directed, unless such acts were knowingly directed against a non-national of that state. Under this provision, an armed attack in the passenger lounge of an international airport would be covered. Third, the act must not be committed either by or against a member of the armed forces of a state in the course of military hostilities. And, fourth, the act had to be intended to damage the interest of or obtain concessions from a state or an international organization. Accordingly, U.S. representatives pointed out, exceedingly controversial activities arguably terrorist in nature, such as fedayeen attacks in Israel against Israeli citizens and a wide range of activities by armed forces in Indochina and in Southern Africa, were deliberately excluded from the Convention's coverage. A particularly broad exclusion was the requirement that the act be committed or take effect outside of the country of which the alleged offender was a national. This provision would have excluded from the scope of the Convention most terrorist attacks in Latin America and elsewhere against international business personnel and facilities. As to persons allegedly committing offenses covered by the Convention and apprehended in their territories, states parties would have been required to establish severe penalties for covered acts and either to prosecute such persons or extradite them to another state party for prosecution. The decision whether to prosecute or extradite the alleged offender would have been left to the sole discretion of the state where he was apprehended.

Nonetheless, despite strenuous efforts on the part of many states to reach a compromise, the U.S. initiative was unsuccessful. On December 18, 1972, the General Assembly adopted Resolution 3034 by a roll call vote of seventy-six to thirty-five (including the United States), with seventeen abstentions. Resolution 3034, while expressing "*deep concern* over increasing acts of violence which endanger or take innocent human lives or jeopardize fundamental freedoms," and inviting states to become parties to existing conventions on international terrorism and to take appropriate measures at the national level to eliminate terrorism, focuses its primary attention on "finding just and peaceful solutions to the underlying causes which give rise to such acts of violence."[53] The resolution also "*reaffirms* the inalienable right to self-determination and independence of all peoples under the colonial and racist regimes and other forms of alien domination and upholds the legitimacy of their struggle...."[54] By way of implementation, the resolution invites states to study the problem on an urgent basis and submit their observations to the Secretary-General by April 10, 1973, and establishes an *ad hoc* committee, to be appointed by the President of the General Assembly, to study these observations and to submit a report with recommendations for elimination of the problem to the 28th session of the Assembly. The committee was appointed. However, after meeting from July 16 through August 10, 1973, the Committee reported to the General Assembly that it was unable to agree on any recommendations for dealing with the problem. Although the United Nations later adopted other measures against international terrorism, such as the Convention on Internationally

---

52. *Id.*
53. G.A. Res. 3034, GAOR 27th Sess., Supp. No. 30, U.N. Doc. A/8730 at 119, (1972).
54. *Id.*

Protected Persons and the Hostages Convention, it has taken no further action with respect to the U.S. draft convention.

This Convention is really a parallel to the Law of Neutrality for settings of low-intensity conflict; that is, generally speaking, it would prohibit waging wars of national liberation or violent revolution outside of the territory of the nation undergoing the struggle. This central feature of the draft treaty seems not to have been broadly understood.

Questions for Discussion

Section 2332 of 18 U.S.C. provides:

§ 2332. Criminal penalties

(a) HOMICIDE — Whoever kills a national of the United States, while such national is outside the United States, shall —

(1) if the killing is murder (as defined in section 1111(a)), be fined under this title, punished by death or imprisonment for any term of years or for life, or both;

(2) if the killing is a voluntary manslaughter as defined in section 1112(a) of this title, be fined under this title or imprisoned not more than ten years, or both; and

(3) if the killing is an involuntary manslaughter as defined in section 1112(a) of this title, be fined under this title or imprisoned not more than three years, or both.

(b) ATTEMPT OR CONSPIRACY WITH RESPECT TO HOMICIDE — Whoever outside the United States attempts to kill, or engages in a conspiracy to kill, a national of the United States shall —

(1) in the case of an attempt to commit a killing that is a murder as defined in this chapter, be fined under this title or imprisoned not more than 20 years, or both; and

(2) in the case of a conspiracy by two or more persons to commit a killing that is a murder as defined in section 1111(a) of this title, if one or more of such persons do any overt act to effect the object of the conspiracy, be fined under this title or imprisoned for any term of years or for life, or both so fined and so imprisoned.

(c) OTHER CONDUCT — Whoever outside the United States engages in physical violence —

(1) with intent to cause serious bodily injury to a national of the United States; or

(2) with the result that serious bodily injury is caused to a national of the United States;

shall be fined under this title or imprisoned not more than ten years, or both.

(d) LIMITATION ON PROSECUTION — No prosecution for any offense described in this section shall be undertaken by the United States except on written certification of the Attorney General or the highest ranking subordinate of the Attorney General with responsibility for criminal prosecutions that, in the judgment of the certifying official, such offense was intended to coerce, intimidate, or retaliate against a government or a civilian population.

1. The above statute is described as "antiterrorist legislation." Under the statute, is it necessary for a U.S. prosecutor to prove that the killing or serious bodily harm constituted "terrorism"? Is "terrorism" defined under the statute?

Assume that you are counsel for a foreigner charged under the statute. What arguments might you make in support of a contention that the statute violates customary international law? What responses to these arguments might you expect? How would you rule on this issue as a disinterested observer?

2. The 1972 U.S. draft convention on terrorism is at core a treaty based on the analogy to neutrality laws for settings of low-intensity conflict. What other strategies and tactics would you propose to encourage adoption of the treaty?

3. Would a new U.S. initiative to obtain international approval of this treaty under a new title of "Treaty to Prevent the Spread of Civil Conflict" be more likely to be adopted?

4. As noted above, the effort to exclude the courts from deciding whether an accused has committed a political offense was precipitated by State and Justice Department displeasure with the *McMullen* and *Mackin* decisions. In testimony before the Senate and the House, the executive branch contended that these decisions seriously undermined U.S. efforts to combat terrorism. But, in debates in international fora, the United States has not claimed that armed attacks against *military targets* constitute terrorism. To the contrary, the draft convention against terrorism that the United States introduced in the United Nations General Assembly after the murder of the Israeli Olympic competitors at Munich in 1972 would have expressly excluded any attack by or against armed forces from the scope of its coverage. Similarly, draft legislation in Congress also has expressly excluded from its definition of "international terrorism" an act "committed in the course of military or paramilitary operations directed essentially against military forces or military targets of a state or an organized armed group."[55]

Under this approach, then, *McMullen* and *Mackin* might well have been excluded from the definition of international terrorism, thus entitling them to claim protection under the political offense doctrine. Does this mean, in effect, that police and military personnel are "fair game" for would-be revolutionaries? Can you think of any approach that would avoid this implication while maintaining the values the political offense doctrine seeks to protect?

5. Review H.R. 2643's treatment of the political offense doctrine above. Is it satisfactory? What, if any, changes would you recommend?

6. Is the U.S.-U.K. Supplementary Extradition Treaty's sharp limitation of the political offense exception desirable? Does it help that under the treaty a court may be able to deny extradition if an accused proves by a preponderance of the evidence that the request for extradition has been made with a view to try or punish him on account of his race, religion, nationality, or political opinions, or that he would be denied a fair trial because of these factors? Under a rule of "non-inquiry," courts normally refrain from considering such allegations by an accused. Should they? Why? Why not? Would the provision in the U.S.-U.K. Supplementary Extradition Treaty allow a court to entertain an allegation that the courts in Northern Ireland generally do not accord an accused due process?

7. A number of states, especially in Latin America, have declined to become parties to global or regional antiterrorist conventions on the ground that they are inconsistent with the doctrine of political asylum, a doctrine sometimes enshrined in national constitutions.

---

55. S. 333, 96th Cong., 1st Sess., § 5 (1979).

Do you agree with this contention? Is the extradite-or-prosecute formula characteristic of these conventions inconsistent with granting political asylum to dissidents?

8. As noted above, Alona Evans suggested that "informal" methods of rendition of alleged offenders widely regarded by states as legal be subject to prescribed minimum standards for the protection of the accused. Are states likely to be receptive to this suggestion?

Other Approaches

Analogies to the Law of Armed Conflict

As noted above in subsection 2(a), the Fourth Interim Report of the Committee on International Terrorism of the International Law Association proposes that well-accepted norms in the Law of Armed Conflict be accepted as a limit on a government's discretion to exclude political offenders from the extradition process. On the ground that nearly all states in the world have agreed to extradite or prosecute soldiers who commit atrocities, in international armed conflicts, the Committee concludes that there is no political or legal basis for allowing persons not granted soldiers' privileges by international law a greater leeway for violence than soldiers have.

The Committee's proposal was not accepted by all of its members. In a dissenting statement, Professor L.C. Green of Canada and Dr. J. Lador-Lederer of Israel rejected "any approach to the problem of international terrorism which relates the issue in any way to the Law of Armed Conflict."[56] In their view, any attempt to compare acts of terrorism with those forbidden during armed conflict is unwarranted and confusing. Also, they contended, many states that have accepted an obligation under the treaties regulating armed conflict to seek out, punish, or extradite war criminals in their midst have failed to do so. There is, they argue, no reason to assume that such states would act any differently in the case of terrorism. Their view is influenced, of course, by the Arab-Israeli conflict and Israel's resistance to any legal or political development that might serve as support for an argument that members of the Palestine Liberation Organization are engaged in an "international armed conflict" and entitled to the status combatants under the laws of war.

Another reference to the law of armed conflict as a possible model for development of the law relating to private acts of international terrorism has been based on traditional doctrines of neutrality; that is, under the traditional approach, at least in situations where the level of conflict in a civil war had risen to the magnitude that might be termed a "belligerency" (as compared to a "rebellion" or "insurgency"), various rights and duties for both neutral states and belligerents would arise. Most particularly, neutral states were under an obligation to act towards belligerents with an impartial attitude and, conversely, belligerents had to act toward neutral states in accordance with their attitude of impartiality. A primary purpose of this law of neutrality was to limit the scope of the civil conflict and prevent it from spreading beyond the borders of the state where the conflict was taking place or from drawing outside states into the conflict.

Although there is a serious question whether the traditional law of neutrality remains extant — in light of state practice since World War II, for example, the civil wars in Algeria and Nigeria, where it was largely ignored — the basic principles underlying this law may be applicable by analogy to private acts of international terrorism. Many terrorist acts

---

56. Proceedings of the International Law Association Committee on Terrorism 379, at 380 (1986) (observations of J. Lador-Lederer, a dissenting member of the committee, arguing that terrorism is a crime against humanity).

occur in situations that would be described as rebellions or insurgencies under traditional doctrine and that are often characterized as wars of national liberation in the modern vernacular. Under a strict regime of neutrality, outside states would not intervene on the side either of the rebels or of the target government. For their part, the rebels would limit their attacks to military personnel of the government in power and would not commit even these attacks on the territory of any outside state. The concept of nonintervention by outside states is reflected in the Declaration on Principles of International Law Concerning Friendly Relations and Cooperation Among States in Accordance with the Charter of the United Nations,[57] a General Assembly Declaration that is widely regarded as an authoritative interpretation of the United Nations Charter. In its first principle, ninth paragraph, the Declaration provides:

> Every State has the duty to refrain from organizing, instigating, assisting or par-ticipating in acts of civil strife or terrorist acts in another State or acquiescing in organized activities within its territory directed towards the commission of such acts, when the acts referred to in the present paragraph involve a threat or use of force.[58]

Also, as we saw above, a primary purpose behind the 1972 United States Draft Convention on Terrorism was to limit the range of conflict in wars of national liberation to their theater of operations.

Fora for Trying Terrorists

As the previous discussion indicates, the ordinary courts of member states of the United Nations have normally been the fora for the prosecution of terrorists. September 11, however, precipitated considerable debate over the possibility of employing alternative fora. In particular, President George W. Bush's military order authorizing the creation of military commissions to try foreign terrorists, noted above, has been both challenged and defended under international law and U.S. constitutional law.[59]

There have also been proposals that the Security Council should expand the jurisdiction of the existing ad hoc international criminal tribunals, created to prosecute international crimes committed in Rwanda and the former Yugoslavia, to encompass the crimes of September 11; that new *ad hoc* tribunals for terrorism be created, either by Security Council resolution or through a multilateral agreement along the lines of the London Agreement, which established the Nuremberg Tribunal; that a special Islamic court be established to try members of Al Qaeda or the Taliban; or that a mixed tribunal, composed of judges from the Islamic and non-Islamic world, be given the task. It is worth noting that the newly created permanent International Criminal Court (ICC) has no retroactive jurisdiction and therefore the crimes of September 11, 2001, cannot be tried by the ICC— even though the crimes of September 11, acts of murder committed as part of "a widespread or systemic attack directed against any civilian population," would meet the definition of a crime against humanity under the ICC's statute.

A discussion of the merits of these various proposals or of the debate over military commissions is beyond the scope of this chapter. Suffice it for present purposes to note that an issue that is pervasive throughout this area is the need to ensure that the human

---

57. 9 I.L.M. 1292, 1294 (1970).

58. *Id.*

59. Compare, for example, the various articles contained in *Law and the War on Terrorism*, 25 HARV. J. L. & PUB. POL'Y 591 et seq. (2002). *See also* Katyal and Tribe, *Waging War, Deciding Guilt: Trying the Military Tribunals*, 111 YALE L.J. 1259 (2002).

rights of accused persons are protected, whatever kind of fora is employed to prosecute them. It seems clear that trials in federal civilian courts are likely to maximize protection of the rights of the accused. Critics contend that military commissions are the more suitable venue for terrorism trials, arguing that many of the rights afforded defendants in civilian courts, the unpredictability of juries and the challenges of handling classified evidence could lead to unjustified acquittals. But, recent convictions in federal civilian courts of high profile terrorism cases seem likely to strengthen the hand of those who want terror suspects tried in civilian courts, rather than military commissions.[60]

Limitations on Immigration and Granting of Refugee Status

In response to September 11, countries tightened immigration and asylum policies and sometimes rushed through emergency legislation. The United Nations Security Council mandated by resolution that "all States shall ... [p]revent the movement of terrorists or terrorist groups by effective border controls and controls on issuance of identity papers and travel documents."[61] For its part, the United States adopted the USA PATRIOT Act of 2001,[62] which broadened the definition of terrorist activity and added new mechanisms for the attorney general to certify noncitizens as terrorists and detain them for extended periods before removing them. The U.S. government also expanded foreign student visa monitoring and tightened visa issuance and inspection procedures.

These steps too have given rise to controversy. Again, there has been concern that they may violate the basic human rights of noncitizens. A Working Group on International Terrorism of the Section of International Law and Practice of the American Bar Association has suggested that "Special care should be taken to make sure that legislation and implementing regulations do not undermine the U.S. government's existing obligations under international refugee and human rights treaties":

> Specifically, the U.S. government should take into account the following obligations: the duty not to return a refugee to a place where he or she might experience persecution (*nonrefoulement*); maintenance of the civilian nature of refugee camps; exclusion of terrorists from refugee protection; separation of armed elements in situations of mass influx; provision of access to asylum determination procedures; avoidance of prolonged, arbitrary, and unlawful detention; meeting of the special needs of refugee women and children; and the promotion of international cooperation and responsibility sharing.[63]

Immigration and refugee issues have also come to the fore in other countries. Recent electoral successes of anti-immigration parties in Europe, especially of Le Pen in France and of similar groups in The Netherlands and Italy, have caused concern.

Efforts to Block the Financing of International Terrorism

Security Council Resolution 1373, referred to in the previous section, has as its primary focus the financing of international terrorism and is, by any measure, a landmark step by the Council. In this extraordinary resolution, acting under Chapter VII of the UN Charter,

---

60. *See* Charles Levinson and Christopher M. Matthews, *Cleric Found Guilty In Terrorism Case,* N.Y. Times, May 20, 2014.
61. S.C. Res. 1373, 56th Sess., 4385th mtg., U.N. Doc. S/RES/1373 (2001).
62. Uniting and Strengthening America by Providing Appropriate Tools Required to Intercept and Obstruct Terrorism (USA PATRIOT ACT) Act of 2001, Pub. L. No. 107-56, 115 Stat. 272 (2001).
63. *Report of the Blue Ribbon Working Group on International Terrorism*, 31 Int'l L. News 17 (Spring 2002).

the Council sets forth a plethora of steps that member states are legally *required as members of the United Nations* to take to combat terrorism. For example, the Council "[*d*]*ecides* that all States shall ... [p]revent and suppress the financing of terrorist acts" and then sets forth explicit steps that states are to take to this end. Using terms of exhortation rather than command, in Resolution 1373, the Council then "[*c*]*alls* upon all States" to take a number of actions in cooperation with other states to combat terrorism, including, among others, "intensifying and accelerating the exchange of operational information," and becoming parties to the relevant antiterrorist conventions, including the International Convention for the Suppression of Financing of Terrorism (the United States ratified the financing convention on April 19, 2002), and ensuring, "in conformity with international law," that refugee status is not abused by terrorists and that "claims of political motivation are not recognized as grounds for refusing requests for the extradition of alleged terrorists."[64]

Perhaps the most significant step the Council has taken in Resolution 1373 is to establish a committee to monitor implementation of the resolution and to call upon all states to report to the committee, no later than ninety days after the date of adoption of the resolution, on the steps they have taken to implement the resolution. The Council further "[*e*]*xpresses* its determination to take all necessary steps in order to ensure the full implementation of this resolution, in accordance with its responsibilities under the Charter." Failure to establish monitoring devices to ensure that antiterrorist measures adopted by the United Nations are effective in practice has been a major deficiency of past UN efforts.

On December 19, 2001, the United States submitted its report to the Security Council's Counter-Terrorism Committee.[65] The report notes, among other things, that even before the day Resolution 1373 was adopted (September 28, 2001), on September 23, 2001, President Bush issued an executive order[66] that froze all the assets of twenty-seven foreign individuals, groups, and entities linked to terrorist acts or supporting terrorism and authorized the freezing of assets of those who commit, or pose a significant threat of committing, acts of terrorism. The report further notes that the U.S. government continued to add names to the list of individuals and organizations linked to terrorism or terrorist financing until, as of December 4, the total was 153. On December 5, the report added, the U.S. Secretary of State designated thirty-nine groups as "terrorist organizations" under the Immigration and Nationality Act, in order to strengthen the United States' ability to exclude supporters of terrorism or to deport them if they are found within U.S. borders. The list of such designated organizations is called the "Terrorist Exclusion List."

As also noted in its report to the Counter-Terrorism Committee, the United States has been active in international forums, including the Financial Action Task Force (FATF), the International Monetary Fund, and others, in its effort to suppress the financing of terrorism. This is not an easy task, however. According to recent newspaper reports,[67] members of Al Qaeda may be turning to trade in gold, diamonds, and gems to finance their terror network in response to the freezing of their bank accounts. Also, Al Qaeda reportedly increasingly relies heavily on the Internet and on an informal money transfer system, known as "hawala" in Arabic, to move its funds. Hawala relies on trust and networks of friendship and family to move its funds and leaves no paper or electronic trails. It is, of course, impossible to monitor or freeze an account if there is no bank

---

64. S.C. Res. 1373, 56th Sess., 4385th mtg., U.N. Doc. S/RES/1373 (2001).
65. U.N. Doc. S/2001/1220 (2001).
66. Exec. Order No. 13,224, 3 C.F.R. §786 (2001).
67. *See, e.g.*, Somini Sengupta, *U.N. Report Says Al Qaeda May Be Diversifying Its Finances*, N.Y. Times, May 23, 2002, at A15, col. 1.

account or electronic movement of money. Moreover, again according to recent newspaper reports, the United States is beginning to face growing resistance among its European allies over how it identifies terrorists and their financiers.[68] European officials are reportedly questioning the listing of several individuals and organizations whose links to extremist causes are less clear than those of Al Qaeda or the Taliban. Part of the problem is that U.S. authorities can use civil proceedings to freeze assets, while the Europeans often must rely on criminal statutes, which require higher standards of evidence before action can be taken. European officials also reportedly say that the U.S.-led system is unfair because it doesn't allow for an appeal. Normally, they point out, the burden is on governments to prove guilt, not on an accused to prove innocence. Other sensitive legal issues have arisen regarding extraterritorial jurisdiction, secondary boycotts, conflicts of laws, the use of sanctions against countries or entities that do not cooperate, the role of lawyers and other professionals in assisting law enforcement officials, and the authority of the UN Security Council to mandate national laws and coordinated approaches.

On the other hand, the United States and its European allies, as well as other members of the UN Security Council, were able to agree on a resolution[69] that directs member states to freeze without delay the financial assets or other economic resources of a lengthy list of individuals, groups, undertakings and entities in the annex to the resolution. Moreover, reportedly, between September 2001 and March 2002, $103.8 million in assets had been frozen on a worldwide basis, with roughly half of the funds connected to Osama bin Laden and Al Qaeda. This amount pales, however, in comparison with the between $500 billion and $1 trillion reportedly laundered every year.

Recently, efforts to block the financing of international terrorism have encountered considerable difficulty, both in the regime developed by the UN Security Council and national law and practice. The Security Council regime has come under attack for not providing adequate procedural protections for persons whose assets are subject to asset freeze. Moreover, the apparent lack of due process in Security Council listing and delisting procedures has resulted in numerous legal challenges. Most notably, the European Court of Justice, the highest court in the European Union, handed down a decision that held that these procedures were so lacking in due process that European Union law prohibited the implementation of the Security Council decisions without the individuals and organizations whose assets were being frozen being afforded an opportunity to challenge the Council's determination that their assets should be frozen.[70]

At the national level, in the United States, there was an attack in the federal courts against the legal regime targeting the provision of material support or financing of terrorism. This regime consists of three federal statutes—18 U.S.C. sections 2339A, 2339B and 2339C—and Executive Order 13,224[71]—promulgated pursuant to the authority granted to the President under the International Emergency Economic Powers Act (IEEPA).[72] Many actions relating to the material support laws came before the lower courts and

---

68. *See, e.g.*, Ian Johnson, Christopher Cooper & Philip Shishkin, *Bush Faces Widening Gap With Europe*, WALL ST. J., May 21, 2002, at A15, col. 6.

69. S.C. Res. 1390, 57th Sess., 4452d mtg., U.N. Doc. S/RES/4452 (2002).

70. Kadi and Al Barakaat Int'l Found. V. Council of the European Union and Commission of the European Union, joined cases C-402/05 P and C-415/05 P (European Court of Justice, 3 September 2008).

71. Exec. Order No. 13224, 66 Fed. Reg. 49,079 (Sept. 2, 2001).

72. International Emergency Economic Powers Act, Pub. L. No. 95-223, 91 Stat. 1625 (1977) (codified as amended at 50 U.S.C. sections 1701–07 (2011)).

federal immigration agencies and eventually the Supreme Court was asked, for the first time, in *Holder v. Humanitarian Law Project,* to rule on several issues relating to the material support laws, in particular, section 2339B. The Court was asked to consider: first, whether the language in section 2339B prohibiting the knowing provision of "training," "expert advice or assistance," "service" and "personnel" to a designated terrorist organization was unconstitutionally vague; and second, whether the criminal prohibitions on the provision of "expert advice or assistance" "derived from scientific [or] technical ... knowledge" and "personnel" were unconstitutional with respect to speech that furthers only lawful, nonviolent activities of organizations designated as terrorist.

In a 6–3 decision,[73] authored by Chief Justice John Roberts, the Court ruled that it is not unconstitutional for the government to block speech and other forms of advocacy in support of designated terrorist organizations, even if such speech is only intended to support the group's humanitarian activities, such as feeding the poor. The Court, however, qualified its decision by holding that the activity may only be banned if it is coordinated with or controlled by the terrorist group; independent individual advocacy or speech remains protected by the First Amendment, and, therefore, may not be criminalized by the government. In support of its holding, the Court stated that:

> Congress has not ... sought to suppress ideas or opinions in the form of "pure political speech." Rather, Congress has prohibited "material support," which most often does not take the form of speech at all. And when it does, the statute is carefully drawn to cover only a narrow category of speech to, under the direction of, or in coordination with foreign groups that the speaker knows to be terrorist organizations.[74]

Questions for Discussion

1. In the lower courts, the Humanitarian Law Project (HLP) had sought pre-conviction declaratory relief to determine whether it could be prosecuted under section 2339B for training members of the PKK (Kurdistan Workers Party) — a designated terrorist organization — on how to use humanitarian and international law to peacefully resolve disputes, to obtain relief from international bodies, and to engage in peaceful international advocacy. How could this possibly constitute support for international terrorism? Wouldn't this kind of training help to induce the PKK to turn away from terroristic activity? What if the HLP had wished to provide funds for the PKK to use in its charitable giving to the poor and could provide evidence that the funds would be used for this purpose? Should this be permitted? Might the U.S. government argue that the PKK's use of such funds for charitable purposes itself causes the PKK to become a stronger terrorist organization?

2. U.S. material support for terrorism laws have been criticized as having a "chilling effect" on the provision of humanitarian assistance in both disaster and war zones.[75] It has also been argued that such laws violate international humanitarian law (also known as the law of armed conflict), especially the four Geneva Conventions, the two Additional Protocols to the Geneva Conventions, and "a body of customary law that has accumulated

---

73. Holder v. Humanitarian Law Project, 130 S. Ct. 2705 (2010).

74. Holder v. Humanitarian Law Project, 130 S. Ct. 1705, 2723 (2010).

75. *See, e.g.,* Justin A. Fraterman, *Criminalizing Humanitarian Relief: Are U.S. Material Support for Terrorism Laws Compatible with International Humanitarian Law?,* 46 N.Y.U. J. INT'L & POL. 399 (2014).

since the nineteenth century."[76] Assuming arguendo that this argument is prima facie correct, what is the effect, if any, of the International Convention for the Suppression of the Financing of Terrorism, discussed *supra*, at footnote 16, which obligates States Parties to criminalize the covered offenses irrespective of the motivation of the perpetrators? Moreover, subjection (j) of section 2339B provides that no person is to be prosecuted for the provision of "personnel," "training," or "expert advice or assistance" if the provision of such material support was approved by the Secretary of State in consultation with the Attorney General. Does this provision have any relevance to the issue of the legality of U.S. material support of terrorism laws under international law?

Civil Suits against Terrorists, Terrorist Organizations, and States that Sponsor Terrorism

Using civil lawsuits as a legal response to international terrorism has only recently been undertaken and largely only in the United States. Traditionally, the emphasis has been on punishing terrorists with criminal penalties, not on holding them civilly liable for their actions. There are, however, possible benefits to civil suits that are coming to be realized. Plaintiffs in civil suits benefit from the standard of proof in civil suits—preponderance of the evidence rather than proof beyond a reasonable doubt—and are able to use discovery devices to obtain documents and other forms of evidence unavailable in criminal proceedings. Moreover, civil suits may be more effective than criminal proceedings in establishing the full factual context in which the perpetrators committed their crimes and thereby in enhancing the prospects that the victims will have their suffering brought to the attention of the wider community and that a definitive, historically accurate account of the atrocities will be provided. Also, unlike criminal trials, civil suits provide at least the possibility that victims may be compensated for lost property, for injuries suffered, or for emotional distress caused.

To be sure, civil litigation in the United States as an alternative to criminal prosecution for the commission of international crimes or egregious human rights violations is a highly controversial subject. Subjecting foreign governments to such suits has been, if anything, even more controversial. Moreover, as we shall see below, the barriers to successful litigation in this area are formidable, and include, *inter alia*, resistance by the U.S. government, limits on the lifting of the immunity of foreign states under the Foreign Sovereign Immunities Act, difficulties in collecting judgments in the United States, and, especially, possible hostile and retaliatory reaction on the part of foreign governments.

There are several federal statutes that may provide remedies for the victims of international terrorism. First, under the Alien Tort Claims Act,[77] the plaintiff must be an alien, the complaint must allege a tort only, and the alleged tort must be in violation of "the law of nations." This ambiguous and controversial statute has been a primary basis for civil suits in federal court based on the commission of international crimes abroad. But in the one case in which the statute was invoked involving terrorism, *Tel Oren v. Libyan Arab Republic*,[78] the action was unsuccessful. The three judges in the case all wrote separate opinions and gave different reasons for their decision, but one (Judge Edwards)

---

76. *Id.* at 432. The U.S. is not a party to Additional Protocol I but has noted that many of its provisions are in accord with customary international law.
77. 28 U.S.C. § 1350 (2006).
78. 726 F.2d 774 (D.C. Cir. 1984).

found that, at least at the time of the decision, international terrorism was not clearly established as a violation of the "law of nations" (customary international law). Moreover, the Supreme Court in *Kiobel v. Royal Dutch Petroleum*,[79] held that the Alien Tort Claims Act does not allow courts to recognize a cause of action for violations of the law of nations occurring within the territory of a nation other than the United States. This has all but rendered the Act irrelevant for actions against terrorists.

Second, the Torture Victim Protection Act (TVPA)[80] authorizes suits to be brought in U.S. district courts, by aliens and U.S. citizens, for both torture and extrajudicial killing. Common acts of terrorism, such as the bombing of civilians, are regarded as examples of an "extrajudicial killing." Nonetheless, at this writing, the TVPA has not been the basis of a suit against terrorists.

Third, the Antiterrorism Act (ATA) allows any U.S. citizen who is injured "by reason of an act of international terrorism" to sue in federal court and recover treble damages. International terrorism is defined in relevant part as "violent acts ... [that] intimidate or coerce a civilian population ... to influence the policy of a government by intimidation or coercion ... [or] affect the conduct of a government by assassination or kidnapping ... [and that] occur primarily outside the territorial jurisdiction of the United States."[81] There have been more than one hundred reported decisions cited to the ATA's civil suit provision. But these decisions have recently come under sharp criticism as a misuse of the Act because of their wide interpretation of its scope.[82]

Fourth, and most significant, a state-sponsored terrorism exception to the Foreign Sovereign Immunities Act (FSIA),[83] permits jurisdiction over foreign governments sued in the United States for complicity in terrorist acts if they are on the list of states supporting international terrorism compiled by the Department of State. Under this provision, a foreign agent's actions will be imputed to the foreign state under the theory of respondent superior. Since 1996, when this provision was enacted, more than one dozen lawsuits have resulted in default judgments against foreign states.

In 1998, the FSIA was again amended to facilitate the execution of judgments obtained against state sponsors of terrorism by providing for the attachment or execution of certain property following a judicial determination of liability.[84] However, on the same day the amendment went into effect, President Clinton waived its application and nullified its impact. Since that time there has been much political intrigue involving Congress, the representatives of victims, the executive branch, and the adoption of legislation,[85] which has resulted in payments of certain antiterrorism judgments to certain persons, but not to all. The process has been sharply criticized.

Although there have been a number of suits brought under the Alien Tort Claims Act or the TVPA that have resulted in judgments in favor of plaintiffs for substantial

---

79. 133 S. Ct. 1659 (2013).

80. 28 U.S.C. §1350 Note, §3(b) (2006).

81. 18 U.S.C. §2333 (2006).

82. *See* Geoffrey Sant, *So Banks are Terrorists Now?: The Misuse of the Civil Suit Provision of the Anti-Terrorism Act*, 45 Ariz. St. L.J. 533 (2013).

83. 28 U.S.C. §1610(a)(7) (2006).

84. *Id.*

85. Victims of Trafficking and Violence Protection Act, Pub. L. No. 106-386, 114 Stat. 1464, 1541–46, §2002(a)(1)(B) (2000).

compensatory and punitive damages, these judgments seldom are collected because of the absence of assets owned by individual defendants in the United States. To the extent that the actions against terrorist organizations are successful, plaintiffs may have more success in collecting on their judgments because such organizations are more likely to have substantial assets in the United States. In many and perhaps most cases, however, the ability of plaintiffs to collect their judgments will depend upon the success (or failure) of their efforts to enforce their judgments in foreign jurisdictions. Unfortunately, even in ordinary tort and commercial cases, it may be difficult to enforce U.S. court decisions abroad. These difficulties are likely to be greatly compounded in Alien Tort Claims Act and Torture Victim Protection Act cases. Perhaps because of these difficulties, there have been very few attempts to enforce such judgments abroad.

Questions for Discussion

1. In hearings before Congress, the U.S. Departments of State and Justice strongly opposed the provisions that amended the Foreign Sovereign Immunities Act to provide a civil cause of action against state sponsors of terrorism. For example, the Department of State's representative suggested that "[f]undamental principles of sovereignty and international law are implicated in determining the extent to which foreign states should be responsible to private persons in the courts of other states."[86] She reported that the Department of State was unaware of "any instance in which a state permits jurisdiction over such tortious conduct of a foreign state without territorial limitations." On the contrary, she said, other countries limited the lifting of sovereign immunity for such acts to situations where the act occurred in the forum state. She then pronounced:

> Consistency of the FSIA with established international practice is important. If we deviate from that practice and assert jurisdiction over foreign states for acts that are generally perceived by the international community as falling within the scope of immunity, this would tend to erode the credibility of the FSIA. We have made substantial efforts over the years to persuade foreign states to participate in our judicial system—to appear and defend in actions against them under the FSIA. That kind of broad participation serves the interests of all. If we expand our jurisdiction in ways that cause other states to question our statute, this could undermine the broad participation we seek. It could also diminish our ability to influence other countries to abandon the theory of absolute immunity and adopt the restrictive view of sovereign immunity, which the United States has followed for over forty years.[87]

The Department of State's representative also contended that passage of this legislation could undermine the conduct of U.S. foreign policy and result in retaliation against the United States. In particular, she suggested that execution of judgments on foreign states' property had "always been an area of particular sensitivity."

How convincing do you find the Department of State's representative's objections? Can you think of any responses to them?

---

86. *Hearing on S. 825 Before the Subcomm. on Courts and Administrative Practice of the Senate Comm. on the Judiciary*, 103d Cong., 12 (1994) (statement of Jamison S. Borek, Deputy Legal Adviser, Department of State).

87. *Id.* at 14.

2. It is noteworthy that on September 21, 2001, following the destruction of the World Trade Center on September 11, Congress adopted legislation[88] that, for the first time in U.S. history, set up a disaster compensation system for compensating the victims of the attack on the World Trade Center and the Pentagon (both passengers on the aircraft as well as other victims of the disaster). To seek an award from the fund, claimants had to waive their right to sue over the disaster, a requirement intended to limit airline liability but, by its terms, not limited to suits against airlines. It therefore covered any lawsuits filed or to be filed against terrorists or state sponsors of terrorism based on the events of September 11.

Would it be a good idea, as some have suggested, to enact similar legislation to provide such awards for other victims of international terrorism? If so, should such legislation cover only past victims of international terrorism, or future victims as well?

3. What suggestions, if any, do you have as to steps to counteract the apparent use of "hawala" by Al Qaeda and other terrorist organizations? Should lists of financial supporters of terrorism be treated as a civil (U.S.) or criminal (European) matter? What kinds of protections should be available to persons or organizations placed on the lists?

4. Assuming that the United States and its allies' use of force in Afghanistan is justified as an exercise in self-defense under Article 51 of the UN Charter, does it follow that military action against Al Qaeda or other terrorist organizations in other countries would be? Would the legitimacy of such actions depend upon a grant of permission by the government of the country where the terrorist organizations was located? What if the terrorist group was located in one of the countries — Iran, Iraq, and North Korea — characterized by President George W. Bush as an "axis of evil"?

Coercive Measures against States Supporting International Terrorism

International Claims. A major problem facing efforts to combat international terrorism is the support given by some states to international terrorists of whom they approve. This support takes various forms. It may consist of no more than providing safe haven for terrorists who commit their acts in one state and flee to a state that is friendly toward their particular cause. In a more active manifestation of support, states may provide arms or even training and strategic direction to international terrorist groups. The Department of State has identified Syria, Libya, Iraq, Iran, Sudan, North Korea, and Cuba as states actively supporting international terrorist activities.

Unless a state has ratified an antiterrorist convention containing an extradite-or-prosecute obligation, it probably does not violate international law if it merely offers safe haven to a terrorist who commits his act in another state, although the matter is debatable. However, as reflected in the provision of the Declaration on Friendly Relations noted above, there is a well-established rule of international law forbidding states to permit their territory to be used as a base for armed bands of whatever nature to operate in the territory of another state. Accordingly, it has been urged by some that international claims should be brought against states allowing terrorists to use their territory as a base for operations, either by diplomatic protest, or, if standing exists, before an international arbitral

---

88. Air Transportation Safety and System Stabilization Act, 107 Pub. L. No. 107-42, 115 Stat. 230 (Sept. 21, 2001).

tribunal or the International Court of Justice. Claims brought might include money claims for damages caused to a state's noncombatant, innocent victims.

Economic Sanctions. As noted above, none of the multilateral antiterrorist conventions contain provisions for economic or other sanctions against states that offer safe haven or other assistance to terrorists. Also, efforts to conclude an independent enforcement convention have proven unsuccessful.

As a partial substitute for a sanctions convention, the heads of state and government of the Seven Summit countries (Canada, the United States, Great Britain, West Germany, France, Italy, and Japan), meeting in July 1978 in Bonn, issued what has become known as the Bonn Declaration.[89] Under this Declaration, which constitutes a political rather than a legal commitment, the signatories agree to halt bilateral air traffic service with countries that refuse to return the aircraft, passengers, and crews. Follow-up efforts have succeeded in obtaining more widespread support for the Declaration and in inducing additional countries to become parties to the ICAO conventions.

On December 1, 1982, the United Kingdom, the Federal Republic of Germany, and France implemented the Bonn Declaration by terminating all air traffic with Afghanistan. Scholars have questioned whether the Bonn Declaration can be implemented consistently with the obligations of the Summit countries and other states under the International Air Services Transit Agreement, the Convention on International Civil Aviation, and bilateral aviation agreements. In this instance, the bilateral aviation agreements between Afghanistan and the United Kingdom, the Federal Republic of Germany, and France posed no problem, because they were terminated in accordance with their terms. Similarly, no difficulty was likely to arise under the International Air Services Transit Agreement or the Convention on International Civil Aviation, since these agreements covered overflights and emergency landings, neither of which was involved in the case of Afghanistan. Nor is the application of the sanctions provided for in the Bonn Declaration likely to affect third states—states that are nonsignatories of the Declaration and that are not the targets of sanctions.

This happy congruence of circumstances, however, will not necessarily be present in future cases, and these legal question marks regarding the Declaration remain.

More recently, the UN Security Council has imposed economic and other sanctions against state sponsors of terrorism. Although it was its invasion of Kuwait rather than its sponsorship of terrorism that precipitated Security Council action against Iraq, in its famous Resolution 687,[90] which represents one of the most ambitious projects the Council has ever undertaken, the Council "[r]*equires* Iraq to inform the Security Council that it will not commit or support any act of international terrorism or allow any organization directed towards commission of such acts to operate within its territory and to condemn unequivocally and renounce all acts, methods and practices of terrorism." Evidence that Iraq failed to carry out this requirement was considerable.

In response to evidence of Libyan complicity in the destruction of Pan Am flight 103 over Lockerbie, Scotland, and of *Union de transports aeriens* (UTA) flight 772, the Council adopted a resolution urging the Libyan government to provide "full and effective" responses to requests made by the French, U.K., and U.S. governments concerning these catastrophes. When the Libyan government failed to do so, the Council decided that this failure constituted a threat to international peace and security. Acting under Chapter VII of the

---

89. *See* U.S. Dep't St., Bull. No. 2018, 5 (Sept. 1978).

90. S.C. Res. 687, 46th Sess., 2981st mtg., U.N. Doc. S/RES/687 (1991), *reprinted in* 30 I.L.M. 847 (1991).

Charter, the Council decided that states should adopt various sanctions against Libya unless it responded to the requests for cooperation. To avoid these measures, Libya also had to commit itself "definitely to cease all forms of terrorist action and all assistance to terrorist groups and … promptly, by concrete actions, demonstrate its renunciation of terrorism."[91] The Council applied further comprehensive sanctions against Libya in 1993.

Although they had previously strongly resisted a proposal along these lines, in 1998, the United States and the United Kingdom agreed to a trial of the two persons charged with the bombing of Pan Am flight 103 before a Scottish Court sitting in the Netherlands. The Council welcomed this initiative and decided that the Libyan government was to ensure the appearance in the Netherlands of the two accused persons. The Council also decided that it would suspend the sanctions it had imposed against Libya once the Secretary-General had reported to the Council that the two accused persons had arrived in the Netherlands for trial and the Libyan government had satisfied the French judicial authorities with regard to the bombing of UTA flight 772. Upon Libya's satisfaction of these conditions, the Council suspended the sanctions against it on April 8, 1999.

On January 31, 2001, a three-judge Scottish Court, sitting at Camp Ziest, the Netherlands, convicted one Libyan intelligence agent and acquitted the other of murdering 270 people in the bombing of Pan Am flight 103. The convicted agent was sentenced to life in prison, and this was later affirmed on appeal.

The Security Council has also imposed economic sanctions against Afghanistan (1999) and the Sudan (1996) for their support of international terrorism.

Economic sanctions in general and economic sanctions imposed by the Security Council in particular have become a highly contentious issue, with critics contending that they hurt the people but not the government of the state against which they are applied and that the Security Council actions are lacking in legitimacy because of dominance of the Council by the permanent members. Also, when sanctions imposed by the Security Council fail to induce a target state to cease its sponsorship or support of international terrorism, the controversial issue of what measures of self-help may be taken by states acting without Council authorization inevitably arises.

Armed Forces. The use of armed force by states has been subject, under the United Nations Charter, to severe limitations. In keeping with the Charter framework, the use of armed force by states is limited to action taken pursuant to Security Council authorization or as an act of self-defense in response to an "armed attack."

The use of armed force by the United States against terrorism prior to the military action against Al Qaeda and the Taliban, noted in the Introduction to this chapter, especially the bombing of Tripoli, Libya, in 1986, was criticized by some as violating the UN Charter. A discussion of these charges, however, is beyond the scope of this chapter.[92] Rather, we turn now to a brief examination of the use of armed force against Al Qaeda and the Taliban.

The drafters of the UN Charter provisions placing strict limits on the use of force by states did not envisage, of course, the kind of threat posed by a terrorist organization like Al Qaeda. They surely did not anticipate that such groups would engage in actions that would cause the kind of devastation resulting from September 11. Article 51 of the Charter provides: "Nothing in the present Charter shall impair the inherent right of individual or collective self-defense if an armed attack occurs against a Member of the United Nations,

---

91. S.C. Res. 748, 47th Sess., 3063d mtg., U.N. Doc. S/RES/748 (1992).

92. For discussion of these issues, *see, e.g.,* Jack Beard, *America's New War on Terror: The Case for Self-Defense under International Law,* 25 Harv. J. L. & Pub. Pol'y 559, 561–65 (2002).

until the Security Council has taken measures necessary to maintain international peace and security." Under Article 51, the right of self-defense envisaged is a situation in which a state has perpetrated an armed attack against another state. Accordingly, some have argued: "It is doubtful … that this conception includes an attack perpetrated by non-state actors unless their actions can be attributed to a state."[93]

The language of Article 51, however, does not support this interpretation: there is no explicit statement that an "armed attack" must be committed by a state. This interpretation is belied, moreover, by the Security Council's passage of two resolutions in the wake of September 11 that explicitly recognize "the inherent right of individual or collective self-defence in accordance with the Charter" while unequivocally condemning "in the strongest terms the horrifying terrorist attacks which took place on 11 September."[94] Most important, perhaps, an interpretation of Article 51 that would not cover an armed attack by non-state actors unless it could be attributed to a state would be exceedingly dysfunctional. It brings to mind a comment made by former U.S. Secretary of State Dean Acheson that the "law is not a suicide pact."

It is widely recognized that even when a state is lawfully engaged in the exercise of its inherent right of self-defense, it must adhere to the requirement that its use of force be necessary and proportionate. Critics had argued that the U.S. bombing of Tripoli in 1986 failed to meet this requirement. Be that as it may, there appears to be little doubt that this requirement was met in the case of the use of military force in Afghanistan against Al Qaeda and the Taliban. In light of the magnitude of the attacks on September 11 and of the continuing threat of future such attacks, it was clear that there was a need to use military force in Afghanistan to destroy the terrorist bases of Al Qaeda and remove the Taliban—a regime at the time recognized only by Pakistan—from power.

On May 29, 2014, in a commencement speech at West Point, President Obama announced a controversial new approach to foreign policy and national security threats. Having already withdrawn U.S. armed forces from Iraq, and announced that all U.S. troops would be withdrawn from Afghanistan in 2016, the President told the cadets that henceforth, the U.S. military would primarily be involved in training and equipping the forces of regional allies and turning active combat over to them.[95] In the future, President Obama said, when the United States is not directly threatened, "the threshold for military action must be higher."

The future arrived much more quickly than anticipated, however, and ironically it arrived in Iraq, on battlefields the Obama administration thought it had left behind two and a half years before when it pulled out all U.S. troops.[96] A crisis arose because Sunni militants affiliated with Al Qaeda had seized two important Iraqi cities and were in a position to threaten Baghdad. At the time of this writing (June 15, 2014) the President has a number of options he is considering, including the possibility of U.S. airstrikes to

---

93. *See, e.g.*, Muna Ndulo, *International Law and the Use of Force: America's Response to September 11*, Cornell Law Faculty Publications, Paper 56, 5 (Spring 2002).

94. The quoted language is from Security Council Resolution 1368 (56th Sess., 4370th mtg., U.N. Doc. S/RES/1368 (2001)). Using slightly different language, Security Council Resolution 1373 (56th Sess., 4385th mtg., U.N. Doc. S/RES/1373 (2001)) explicitly reaffirms "the right of individual or collective self-defence as recognized by the Charter of the United Nations."

95. Peter Baker, *Rebutting Critics, Obama Seeks Higher Bar for Military Action*, N.Y. Times, May 29, 2014, at A 13, Col. 1.

96. Mark Landler and Eric Schmitt, *U.S. Scrambles to Help Iraq Fight Off Militants: Baghdad at Risk, Obama Weighs Airstrikes*, N.Y. Times, June 13, 2014, at A1, col. 3.

aid the beleaguered Iraqi government. He has, however, ruled out the introduction into Iraq of U.S. ground troops.

Interestingly, the Rand report referred to at the beginning of this chapter[97] contains a number of criticisms of the Obama administration's policy. For example, it argues that the shift of emphasis from the Middle East to the Asia-Pacific region is "risky" because in its view: "For the near future, the most acute security threats to the U.S. homeland and its interests overseas will likely come from terrorist groups and state sponsors of terror, not countries in the Asia-Pacific" (page 49). The Rand report is also skeptical of the Obama administration's support of what it calls, "forward partnering," which involves "deploying small numbers of U.S. military forces, intelligence operatives, diplomats, and other government personnel to train local security forces, collect intelligence and undermine terrorist financing" (page 55). It doubts the efficacy of this approach and warns that "combating terrorist and insurgency groups is difficult, especially in countries with weak governments. There is no guarantee that building the capacity of local partners will weaken or defeat terrorist groups. In the absence of limited direct participation, the United States may become vulnerable to terrorist attack" (page 56). Last but not least, the Rand report contends that "a complete withdrawal from Afghanistan by 2016 could seriously jeopardize U.S. security interests because of the continuing presence of Salafi-jihadist and other terrorist groups in Afghanistan and Pakistan. U.S. forces would have little or no mandate and limited or no capabilities to assist the Afghan government if the Taliban threatened to overrun a major city or even topple the government."

What do you think of these arguments and concerns?

Selected Bibliography

I. Books

Alexander, Yonah & Edgar H. Brenner eds., Terrorism and the Law (2001).

Evans, Alona E. & John F. Murphy eds., Legal Aspects of International Terrorism (1978).

Gurulé, Jimmy & Geoffrey S. Corn, Principles of Counter-Terrorism Law (2011).

International Terrorism: Legal Challenges and Responses, Report by the International Bar Association's Task Force on International Terrorism (2003).

Lacquer, Walter, The New Terrorism: Fanaticism and the Arms of Mass Destruction (1999).

McComack, Wayne, Legal Responses to Terrorism (2nd ed. 2008) (Supplement, 2009).

Moore, John Norton, ed., Civil Litigation Against Terrorism (2004).

———, Law and Civil War in the Modern World (1974).

Murphy, John F., Punishing International Terrorists: The Legal Framework for Policy Initiatives (1985).

———, State Support of International Terrorism: Legal, Political, and Economic Dimensions (1989).

Pillar, Paul R., Terrorism and U.S. Foreign Policy (2001).

---

97. *Supra*, note 2.

Van den Wijngaert, Christine, The Political Offense Exception to Extradition: The Delicate Problem of Balancing the Rights of the Individual and the International Public Order (1980).

Wilkinson, Paul, Terrorism and the Liberal State (1977).

II. Articles

Bassiouni, M. Cherif, "Legal Control of International Terrorism: A Policy-Oriented Approach," 43 Harv. Int'l L.J. 83 (2002).

Baxter, R.R., "A Skeptical Look at the Concept of Terrorism," 7 Akron L. Rev. 380 (1974).

Benson, Jacqueline, "Send Me Your Money: Controlling International Terrorism by Restricting Fundraising in the United States," 21 Hous. J. Int'l L. 321 (1999).

Cassesse, Antonio, "Terrorism is Also Disrupting Some Crucial Legal Categories of International Law," 12 Eur. J. Int'l L. 993 (2001).

Charney, Jonathan, "The Use of Force Against Terrorism and International Law," 95 Am. J. Int'l L. 835 (2001).

Damrosch, Lori, "Sanctions Against Perpetrators of Terrorism," 22 Hous. J. Int'l L. 63 (1999).

Franck, Thomas, "Terrorism and Right of Self-Defense," 95 Am J. Int'l L. 839 (2001).

Franck, Thomas & Bert Lockwood, "Preliminary Thoughts Towards an International Convention on Terrorism," 68 Am. J. Int'l L. 69 (1974).

Fraterman, Justin A., "Criminalizing Humanitarian Relief: Are U.S. Material Support for Terrorism Laws Compatible with International Humanitarian Law?", 46 N.Y.U. J. Int'l L. & Pol. 399 (2014).

Gross, Emanuel, "Legal Aspects of Tackling Terrorism: The Balance Between the Right of a Democracy to Defend Itself and the Protection of Human Rights," 6 UCLA J. Int'l & For. Aff. 89 (2001).

Kellman, Barry, "Catastrophic Terrorism—Thinking Fearfully, Acting Legally," 20 Mich. J. Int'l L. 537 (1999).

Lillich, Richard & John Paxman, "State Responsibility for Injuries to Aliens Occasioned by Terrorist Activities," 26 Am. U. L. Rev. 217 (1977).

Moore, John Norton, "Towards Legal Restraints on International Terrorism," 67 Proc. Am. Soc'y Int'l L. 88 (1973).

Murphy, John, "Challenges of the 'New Terrorism,'" in Handbook of International Law 281–293 (ed, David Armstrong 2009).

———, "Computer Network Attacks by Terrorists: Some Legal Dimensions," in Computer Network Attack and International Law 321 (Michael N. Schmitt & Brian T. O'Donnell eds., 2002).

———, "The Future of Multilateralism and Efforts to Combat International Terrorism," 25 Colum. J. Transnat'l L. 35 (1986).

Paust, Jordan, "Antiterrorism Military Commissions: Courting Illegality," 23 Mich. J. Int'l L. 1 (2001).

Reisman, W. Michael, "International Legal Responses to Terrorism," 22 Hous. J. Int'l L. 3 (1999).

Rubin, Alfred, "Legal Responses to Terror: An International Criminal Court?," 43 Harv. J. Int'l L. 65 (2002).

Turner, Robert, "The War on Terrorism and the Modern Relevance of the Congressional Power to 'Declare War,'" 25 Harv. J. L. & Pub. Pol'y 519 (2002).

Wedgwood, Ruth, "Responding to Terrorism: The Strikes Against bin Laden," 24 Yale J. Int'l L. 559 (1999).

Chapter 11

Transnational Organized Crime: The National Security Dimension

M.E. Bowman

In this chapter:
Background
What Are the Threats?
Transnational Organized Crime: The Response

Background

Organized crime is as old as humanity but any real consideration of a transnational dimension really has to start with the Peace of Westphalia. The seminal events that ended The Thirty Years' War created the modern concept of the nation state and prompted the organization of smuggling enterprises all along the Silk Road.

Over the past few decades, transnational criminal networks have grown almost geometrically, encouraged by public corruption,[1] the drug trade, globalization and technology. The rapid growth of transnational organized crime groups (TOCs) has generated a belated concern that what were previously viewed only as criminal enterprises have now become both national and global security threats. We now live in an era in which borders no longer define security and in which the primary threats now come from non-state actors—including TOCs. Vexingly, the concept of the nation state that evolved from The Thirty Years' War is today an issue for globalized threats. Article 2, Paragraph 4 of the United Nations Charter reads:

> All members shall refrain in their international relations from the threat or use
> of force against the territorial integrity or political independence of any state,
> or in any other manner inconsistent with the purposes of the United Nations.

What this means, of course, is that transnational organized crime occurs within a political framework that still provides for unquestioned respect for sovereign borders and within which states must strive to find transnational remedies through mechanisms still national in origin. After 9/11, it was easy for the entire world to view the transnational threat of terrorism as both a national and a global security concern, but we have been

---

1. The fall of the Iron Curtain prompted enhanced corruption in the states of the former Soviet Union. *See, e.g.,* Ceccarelli, Allesandra, "Clans, politics and organized crime in Central Asia," *Trends in Organized Crime*, 2007, 10:19–36.

slower to recognize that TOCs are every bit as threatening to national and global order.[2] A natural question is whether the law of nations as we understand it today is useful or even relevant in this environment.

What we are seeing at present is TOCs becoming so powerful that they can subvert government institutions through corruption and creating governance instability. They are gaining unprecedented wealth and influence through such enterprises as the drug trade, weapons trafficking, human trafficking and even wildlife crimes. Even more concerning they extend their reach and influence by forming alliances with each other, with terrorist organizations, government officials and even state security officials.[3]

Ever evolving, organized crime threatens U.S. national security and the economy as it grows increasingly transnational as globalization has created increasingly open borders. The impact includes increased violence, taxes and social decay that threaten prosperity, security and the quality of life—even in the United States. The center of gravity for a TOC is its net profit and the center of gravity of the nation-state is governability. These are fundamentally incompatible goals.[4]

Quite naturally, after 9/11 TOCs almost fell off the radar screen. They had been on the radar screen before 9/11 but not with a sense of what globalization was creating. President Reagan started a national dialogue when he published Executive Order 12,333 which was devoted to the intelligence community, but which contained the following information collection language:

> Information obtained in the course of a lawful foreign intelligence, counterintelligence or international drug or international terrorism investigation; ...[5]

President Clinton was more definitive in 1995 when he ordered the Departments of Justice, State and Treasury, the Coast Guard, National Security Council, Intelligence Community and other federal agencies to step up and integrate their efforts against international crime syndicates and money laundering.[6] In the same year the National Security Strategy recognized that foreign criminal organizations weaken American national security and stated that:

> Not all security risks are immediate or military in nature. Transnational phenomena such as terrorism, narcotics trafficking, environmental degradation, natural resource depletion, rapid population growth and refugee flows also have security implications for both present and long term American policy. In addition, an emerging class of transnational environmental issues are increasingly affecting international stability and consequently will present new challenges to U.S. strategy.[7]

---

2. *See generally*, Levitsky, Melvyn "Transnational Criminal Networks and International Security," *Syracuse Journal of International Law and Commerce*, Summer 2003, 30:2, pp. 227–240.

3. A good explanation of how this occurs in the Russian Republic can be found in Firestone, Thomas, "What Russia Must Do to Fight Organized Crime," *Demokratizatsiya*. Winter 2006, Vol. 14 Issue 1, pp. 59–65. 7p.

4. An interesting argument for the rule of law (read governability) is in Skąpska, Grażyna, "The Rule of Law, Economic Transformation and Corruption After the Fall of the Berlin Wall," *Hague Journal of the Rule of Law*, Sept. 2009, Vol. 1 Issue 2, pp. 284–306.

5. Executive Order 12333 of Dec. 4, 1981, at 46 FR 59941, 3 CFR, 1981 Comp., p. 200.

6. Presidential Decision Directive (PDD) 42, declaring international crime a threat to the national security interest of the United States, October 21, 1995.

7. National Security Strategy of Engagement and Enlargement, 1995, http://nssarchive.us/NSSR/1995.pdf.

President Bush also noted the importance of threatening transnational networks:

> Defending our Nation against its enemies is the first and fundamental commitment of the Federal Government. Today, that task has changed dramatically. Enemies in the past needed great armies and great industrial capabilities to endanger America. Now, shadowy networks of individuals can bring great chaos and suffering to our shores for less than it costs to purchase a single tank. Terrorists are organized to penetrate open societies and to turn the power of modern technologies against us.[8]

More specific to TOCs was this language:

> Governments must fight corruption, respect basic human rights, embrace the rule of law, invest in health care and education, follow responsible economic policies, and enable entrepreneurship. The Millennium Challenge Account will reward countries that have demonstrated real policy change and challenge those that have not to implement reforms.[9]

As time passed, the threat of TOCs became increasingly apparent and recognized. President Bush continued the theme from 2002 in 2006.

> These new flows of trade, investment, information, and technology are transforming national security. Globalization has exposed us to new challenges and changed the way old challenges touch our interests and values, while also greatly enhancing our capacity to respond. Examples include:
>
> • **Illicit trade, whether in drugs, human beings, or sex, that exploits the modern era's greater ease of transport and exchange.** Such traffic corrodes social order; bolsters crime and corruption; undermines effective governance; facilitates the illicit transfer of WMD and advanced conventional weapons technology; and compromises traditional security and law enforcement.[10]

By 2009, the Intelligence Community had produced a National Intelligence Estimate (NIE)[11] relating to TOCs.[12] The NIE had been underway for two years and was originally intended to target only European TOC infiltration of energy and other strategic markets but was broadened to include a much wider swath of TOC activity, including the drug trade and Mexican cartel alignment with terrorist groups. As one Department of Justice official commented, "globalization has done great things for organized commerce, but it's also helped organized crime groups to advance as well."[13]

---

8. National Security Strategy, 2002, September 17, 2002, Introduction, http://georgewbush-whitehouse.archives.gov/nsc/nss/2002/index.html.

9. *Id.*, Section VII.

10. 2006 National Security Strategy, Section X, http://georgewbush-whitehouse.archives.gov/nsc/nss/2006/index.html.

11. National Intelligence Estimates (NIEs) are United States federal government documents that are the authoritative assessment of the Director of National Intelligence (DNI) on intelligence related to a particular national security issue. NIEs are produced by the National Intelligence Council and express the coordinated judgments of the United States Intelligence Community, the group of 16 U.S. intelligence agencies. NIEs are classified documents prepared for policymakers.

12. Palazollo, Joe, National Intelligence Estimate Targets Organized Crime, Department of Justice release, "Politics, Policy and the Law," December 28, 2009, http://www.mainjustice.com/2009/12/28/national-intelligence-estimate-targets-organized-crime/.

13. *Id.*

2010 saw the National Security Council,[14] another National Security Strategy,[15] and a Congressional Research Service publication[16] speak to the dangers of TOCs in a globalized society. By 2011, a National Security Strategy was prepared specifically for organized crime. In the President's introduction the threat is clearly expressed:

> Criminal networks are not only expanding their operations, but they are also diversifying their activities, resulting in a convergence of transnational threats that has evolved to become more complex, volatile, and destabilizing. These networks also threaten U.S. interests by forging alliances with corrupt elements of national governments and using the power and influence of those elements to further their criminal activities. In some cases, national governments exploit these relationships to further their interests to the detriment of the United States.[17]

The Executive Summary emphasizes the singular nature of the threat:

> This Strategy is organized around a single unifying principle: to build, balance, and integrate the tools of American power to combat transnational organized crime and related threats to national security—and to urge our foreign partners to do the same. The end-state we seek is to reduce transnational organized crime (TOC) from a national security threat to a manageable public safety problem in the United States and in strategic regions around the world.[18]

The Strategy also established four new initiatives designed to mitigate the TOC threat:

1) A new Executive Order will establish a sanctions program to block the property of and prohibit transactions with significant transnational criminal networks that threaten national security, foreign policy, or economic interests.

2) A proposed legislative package will enhance the authorities available to investigate, interdict, and prosecute the activities of top transnational criminal networks. A new Presidential Proclamation under the Immigration and Nationality Act (INA) will deny entry to transnational criminal aliens and others who have been targeted for financial sanctions.

3) A new rewards program will replicate the success of narcotics rewards programs in obtaining information that leads to the arrest and conviction of the leaders of transnational criminal organizations that pose the greatest threats to national security.

4) An interagency Threat Mitigation Working Group will identify those TOC networks that present a sufficiently high national security risk and will ensure the coordination of all elements of national power to combat them.

Clearly, by 2011 the government's concern had grown large. However, it is not enough to know of the concern—what was/is the real threat? As President Obama stated in the

---

14. Transnational Organized Crime: A Growing Threat to National and International Security, National Security Council, 2010, http://www.whitehouse.gov/administration/eop/nsc/transnational-crime/threat.

15. National Security Strategy, May 2010, http://www.whitehouse.gov/sites/default/files/rss_viewer/national_security_strategy.pdf.

16. Finklea, Kristin M., Organized Crime in the United States: Trends and Issues for Congress, Congressional Research Service, December 22, 2010.

17. Strategy to Combat Transnational Organized Crime, July 19, 2011, Introduction, http://www.whitehouse.gov/sites/default/files/Strategy_to_Combat_Transnational_Organized_Crime_July_2011.pdf.

18. *Id.*, Executive Summary.

introduction to the 2011 Strategy, TOCs are expanding and diversifying. It is a simple fact that globalization and technology encourage TOCs to proliferate, and there are so many weak, failing and failed states in the world that they have the luxury of selecting their home base. It is not so simple to explain to the average citizen where TOC activities become personal.

What Are the Threats?

Let's start with a few simple examples and move on to the more complex. First, who doesn't have a smartphone today? How many of us realize that to make those phones work requires minerals such as tantalum and gold—which provide a booming business for terrorists and organized criminals in conflict areas around the world? Or consider the new furniture you just bought. Organized crime is deforesting whole regions of the world at an alarming rate. Do you like avocados in your salad? More than half the avocados we eat come from Mexico where organized crime extorts millions from the avocado industry every year. Unfortunately, these brief examples don't represent the magnitude of TOC enterprises today.

Economic Espionage

Only a few years ago espionage meant spies trying to steal military and diplomatic secrets. However, with globalization came opportunities for developing nations to try to prosper as well as opportunities for organized crime to take advantage of that situation. Economic development requires research and research can be expensive. Consider how much cheaper medications might be if pharmaceutical companies did not have to recoup their research and development costs. Stealing proprietary information can result in millions of dollars of savings and a windfall as well for those who steal them. Most economic espionage today is done by individuals, but TOCs and governments are also heavily invested in the enterprise.

The thefts do not have to be eye-catching or "sexy" so long as they can save money. For example, recently a Chinese company engaged a consultant to steal a white pigment used in a wide range of products, including paper, whitening chemicals and Oreo filling.[19] In a similarly mundane case, men were spotted in a farmer's field apparently trying to steal seeds of a special strain of corn.[20] Other thefts can be more critical as in the apparent theft of U.S. F-35 designs[21] or that of the U.S. Navy's quiet drive submarine propulsion system.[22] As cyber technology has advanced, so has the capability to steal proprietary information.

Today economic and industrial espionage is so prevalent that most, if not all, major corporations have a chief security officer whose mission it is to try to prevent the activity.

---

19. Toor, Amar, "China stole the color white from DuPont, court rules," *The Verge*, March 6, 2014, http://www.theverge.com/2014/3/6/5476904/china-stole-the-color-white-from-dupont-court-rules.

20. Benci, Luke, "5 Ways China Successfully Spies On Corporate America," *Business Insider*, March 31, 2014, http://www.businessinsider.com/5-ways-china-spies-on-corporate-america-2014-3#ixzz31j6vmvjf.

21. *See*, "Theft of F-35 design data is helping U.S. adversaries–Pentagon," *Reuters*, June 19, 2013, http://www.reuters.com/article/2013/06/19/usa-fighter-hacking-idUSL2N0EV0T320130619.

22. Collins, Michael P., "Let Me Count the Ways China is Stealing Our Secrets," *M.Net*, March 14, 2012, http://www.manufacturing.net/articles/2012/03/let-me-count-the-ways-china-is-stealing-our-secrets.

In fact, it is so prevalent that corporations even try to spy on non-profits.[23] Corporate espionage has even become the latest crusade of Ralph Nader.[24] Extremely concerning was the discovery by Kaspersky labs of a global cyber espionage campaign, which may have been in existence for nearly a decade and compromised more than 350 computer systems in 40 countries. The malicious NetTraveler surveillance toolkit has been active since as early as 2004, but its activity peaked between 2010 and 2013. The initial attack begins with spear-phishing emails with malicious attachments that use vulnerabilities in Microsoft Office to compromise systems.[25]

A not-so-obvious consequence of economic and industrial espionage is the inhibiting effect it will have on research and development. Fundamental research has always been openly traded and discussed, but as technology accelerates the production of new technology there is substantial fear that there will be less openness among scientists.[26]

The end result is that economic and industrial espionage is harmful to businesses, to national prosperity and to an individual's bottom line. The rise of cyber theft has made the issues more difficult as criminals, competitors and governments are deliberately targeting advanced technologies and information assets. Additionally, many countries, including India, Singapore, Malaysia and Hong Kong, do not provide statutory protection for trade secrets or confidential information.

Some corporations have been forced out of business from these activities, others have suffered crippling financial losses, been forced to eliminate jobs, or had to scale back operations. These are problems that are exacerbated by a globalized economy because most major U.S. corporations have foreign subsidiaries and they suffer where there is weak rule of law. Nevertheless, for many companies, global sourcing is an economic imperative and a means of expanding their business in high-growth markets.

Piracy

Maritime piracy is unlike most organized crime ventures in that it is inherently violent. It is always a transnational issue because a ship is the sovereign territory of the flag nation. It is organized because commandeering a ship at sea requires considerable planning and some specialized expertise. Additionally, it is believed that there are 7–10 gangs financed by moneymen in the Persian Gulf with agents in London's shipping insurance fraternity who identify targets with the most valuable cargoes for ransom.[27]

What does piracy mean to the average person? It could mean an energy crisis if fuel does not arrive on time; it could mean humanitarian relief supplies do not arrive on time. However, it definitely means higher costs. Virtually everything moves, at some point, by ocean transport and if the costs of that transport go up, so does that gallon of milk. In

---

23. *See, e.g.,* "Spooky Business: A New Report on Corporate Espionage Against Non-Profits," Center for Corporate Policy, November 2013, http://www.corporatepolicy.org/2013/11/20/spooky-business/.

24. Nader, Ralph, "Corporate espionage undermines democracy," *Reuters*, November 26, 2013, http://blogs.reuters.com/great-debate/2013/11/26/corporate-espionage-undermines-democracy/.

25. "Kaspersky Lab Uncovers Global Cyberespionage Network," *RIA Novoski*, May 6, 2013, http://en.ria.ru/world/20130605/181515016/Kaspersky-Lab-Uncovers-Global-Cyberespionage-Network.html.

26. Rausnitz, Zach, "Economic espionage threatens openness in science and technology," *Fierce Government*, May 20, 2013, http://www.fiercegovernment.com/story/economic-espionage-threatens-openness-science-and-technology/2013-05-20.

27. "Somali Pirate Attacks Hit Record Level," *Envoy 360*, November 12, 2011, https://envoy360.com/index.php?page=news-article&nid=544.

2012 the costs of Somali piracy calculated by Oceans Beyond Piracy were some $6 billion broken out like this:

Ransoms and Recovery, $63.5 million;
Military operations, $1.09 billion;
Security Equipment and Guards, $1.65–$2.06 billion;
Ship re-routing, $290.5 million;
Increased speed, $1.53 million;
Labor, $471.6 million;
Prosecutions and Imprisonment, $14.89 million;
Insurance, $550.7 Million; and
Counter-piracy Organizations, $24.08 million.[28]

There is a further reason that piracy is a national security concern — it fosters corruption in government so that the offense is likely to continue. Of the ransom money obtained by the piratical actions, a portion will go to government officials and to armed groups that control key regions. Some portion will go to village elders and other minor officials. Of that retained by the pirates (some estimate it to be as low as 30%) they must also pay their expenses. For the pirates themselves there is seldom a pot of gold so continuing the enterprise is rather more a job than anything else. For the rest of the world, however, the simple fact remains that corrupt and unstable governments remain players on the global stage and pirate attacks will continue.[29]

Gangs, Cartels, and Organized Groups

Criminal networks linking cartels and gangs are quickly metastasizing into a new form of insurgency with tentacles that stretch increasingly into the United States. The accretion of new and augmented criminal networks in the United States spans the gamut of organized crime. In 2008 an Italian parliamentary document reported that Sicily's mafia has been sending agents to the United States to rebuild networks that had been disrupted by law enforcement activity.[30] Balkan organized crime groups, especially the Albanians, have established a solid presence in the United States.[31]

Gangs are expanding, evolving and posing an increasing threat to U.S. communities nationwide. Many are sophisticated criminal networks with members who are violent, distribute wholesale quantities of drugs, and develop and maintain close working relationships with members and associates of transnational criminal/drug trafficking organizations. There are approximately 1.4 million active street, prison, and outlaw motorcycle gang members comprising more than 33,000 gangs in the United States.[32] Gangs are responsible for an average of 48 percent of violent crime in most jurisdictions and up to

28. "The Economic Cost of Somali Piracy, 2012," *Oceans Beyond Piracy*, 2012, www.oceans beyondpiracy.org.

29. "Maritime Piracy—United Nations Office on Drugs and Crime," 2012, http://www.unodc.org/documents/data-and-analysis/tocta/9.Maritime_piracy.pdf.

30. Fraser, Christian, "Sicily Mafia 'restoring US links'" *BBC News*, February 27, 2008, http://news.bbc.co.uk/2/hi/europe/7268098.stm.

31. *See, e.g.,* Heldman, Kevin, "Anatomy of an Albanian-mob coup: The challenge, the balk, the murder," *Capital*, July 15, 2011, http://www.capitalnewyork.com/article/culture/2011/07/2654826/anatomy-albanian-mob-coup-challenge-balk-murder.

32. "Gangs in the United States," National Gang Intelligence Center, 2011, p.7, http://www.tippecanoe.in.gov/egov/documents/1319250567_366485.pdf.

90 percent in several others.[33] Gangs are increasingly engaging in non-traditional gang-related crime, such as alien smuggling, human trafficking, and prostitution.[34] U.S.-based gangs have established strong working relationships with Central American and Mexican drug trafficking organizations (DTOs) to perpetrate illicit cross-border activity, as well as with some organized crime groups in some regions of the United States.[35]

In fact the extent of the immersion of Mexican DTOs in the United States is alarming. It extends even to smaller cities.[36] A map produced by the *National Post*[37] illustrates the vast extent of the spread of those DTOs. The map makes it clear that it is not simply a south-of-the-border problem. At least 1,000 U.S. cities reported the presence of at least one of four Mexican cartels in 2010. And south of the border, drug creation and facilitation continues, generating addicts in the U.S. and more than 50,000 dead bodies in Mexico since 2006.

Moreover, the frequency of border incursions, often violent, by the DTOs is not only well known, but is a constant and deliberate threat to U.S. law enforcement.[38] The reason, of course, is the profit to be had from trafficking drugs. Between $18 billion and $39 billion flows annually from the United States across the Southwest border to enrich the Mexican drug cartels and the money is such that we find it is corrupting our own border agents.[39] Additionally, with billions of dollars in drug profits on the line, Mexican traffickers are expanding their foothold in the domestic marijuana market taking over vast swaths of U.S. public lands.[40]

Russian organized crime (ROC) is an umbrella phrase that captures a variety of crime groups and criminal activities—it does not refer exclusively to Russians. "Russian" is used generically to refer to a variety of Eurasian crime groups—many of which are not Russian. Among the active criminals in the U.S. are Armenians, Ukrainians, Lithuanians, and persons from the Caucasus region of the former Soviet Union (Chechens, Dagestanis, and Georgians). The threat and use of violence is a defining characteristic of Russian organized crime. Violence is used to gain and maintain control of criminal markets, and retributive violence is used within and between criminal groups. The common use of violence is not surprising since extortion and protection rackets are such a staple of Russian criminal activity.[41]

Russian organized crime is very adept at changing criminal activities and diversifying into new criminal markets. For example, financial markets and banks have become new

---

33. *Id.*

34. *Id.*

35. *Id.*, p. 8.

36. *See, e.g.* Howerton, Jason, "Mexican Drug Cartels Are So Deeply Embedded in Chicago, We Have to Operate Like We're 'On the Border,' " *The Blaze*, http://www.theblaze.com/stories/2012/09/27/dea-boss-mexican-drug-cartels-are-so-deeply-embedded-in-chicago-we-have-to-operate-like-were-on-the-border/.

37. Map *available at* https://nationalpostnews.files.wordpress.com/2012/07/fo0714_mexicoweb.pdf.

38. *See, e.g.,* "Armed Illegals Stalked Border Patrol," *Washington Times*, November 22, 2011, http://www.washingtontimes.com/news/2011/nov/22/armed-illegals-stalked-border-patrol/.

39. Sherman, Christopher, "US Customs: Mexican cartels corrupt border agents," *Associated Press*, March 11, 2010, http://www.boston.com/news/nation/articles/2010/03/11/us_customs_mexican_cartels_corrupt_border_agents/.

40. "Drug gangs taking over US public lands," *Associated Press*, March 1, 2010, http://www.nbcnews.com/id/35650016/ns/us_news-crime_and_courts/t/drug-gangs-taking-over-us-public-lands/#.U4ofjvldVPo.

41. Finckenauer, James, "Russian Organized Crime in the United States," International Center, National Institute of Justice, https://www.ncjrs.gov/pdffiles1/nij/218560.pdf.

targets of criminal opportunity for ROC, as witnessed by two recent prosecutions: U.S. v. Alexander Lushtak alleges a multi-million dollar investment fraud scheme and the subsequent laundering of nearly two million dollars of proceeds from that scheme by depositing monies involved in the fraud in an account at the Bank of New York, and, U.S. v. Dominick Dionisio, et al., charges two persons alleged to be associated with the LCN and an alleged member of the "Bor" Russian organized crime group with operating a multi-million dollar investment fraud and laundering the proceeds of the scheme.[42]

On October 3, 1991, William Sessions, then director of the FBI, testified at a hearing on Asian organized crime before the U.S. Senate Permanent Subcommittee on Investigations. "The Boryokudan," he said, referring to the yakuza, "have built one of the world's largest criminal organizations...."[43] The yakuza have made their presence felt in the United States principally in Hawaii, but also in California, Nevada and even New York.[44] The yakuza have also put down roots in California where they have made alliances with Korean and Vietnamese gangs and furthered their traditional partnerships with the Chinese triads. Los Angeles is particularly attractive because of the influx of young actresses desperate to get their big break in the film industry. Yakuza shills have become adept at luring these vulnerable women into porn films and prostitution. Japanese men, whether on sex tours or at home in Japan, often desire western women, particularly blondes.

The triads are underground secret societies in Chinese culture that date back centuries. In the past, like the Mafia, they were quasi-patriotic organizations dedicated to helping out the less fortunate. Eventually, however, they morphed into organized crime groups. Headquartered mainly in Hong Kong, they came to America rather later than the great Chinese immigration. Of the Chinese who originally came to America, many gathered together in Tongs for mutual support and social activities. Chinese gangsters migrated to the Tongs and later, when the Triads came they went to the Tongs for recruits. While the Triads have stayed mainly in their respective ethnic communities, they are beginning to spread out, teaming with other Asian crime groups (Korean, Vietnamese, and Cambodian) to commit ever-more sophisticated crime from credit card fraud to identity theft.[45]

Virtually every ethnic group has a place in the United States' organized crime hall of shame. Globalization and technology has made criminal enterprise easier and safer than has been the historical case. Ten years ago, the image of organized crime was of hierarchical organizations, or families, that exerted influence over criminal activities in neighborhoods, cities, or states. That image of organized crime has changed dramatically. Modern organized criminals avoid the hierarchies that previously governed more traditional organized crime groups. The fluidity of many modern organized crime groups makes it harder for law enforcement to infiltrate, disrupt, and dismantle with traditional methodologies

As with legitimate commerce, globalization has revolutionized organized crime. Trade barriers have been lowered, transportation infrastructure has broadened and the Internet and cellular telephones have permitted easy transnational movement of money, facilitated money laundering and provided platforms for fraud, cyber intrusions, theft of consumer information and permitted transnational connectivity of criminal groups which previously had to be done through physical presence.

---

42. *Id.*

43. Bruno, Anthony, "The Yakuza," *Crime Library,* http://www.crimelibrary.com/gangsters_outlaws/gang/yakuza/5.html.

44. *Id.*

45. Deitche, Scott, "Triads," *Netplaces* (Mafia), http://www.netplaces.com/mafia/the-other-mafias/triads.htm.

Today, international criminal enterprises run multi-national, multi-billion-dollar schemes from start to finish. These criminal enterprises are flat, fluid networks and have global reach. While still engaged in many of the "traditional" organized crime activities of loan-sharking, extortion, and murder, new criminal enterprises are targeting stock market fraud and manipulation, cyber-facilitated bank fraud and embezzlement, identify theft, trafficking of women and children, and other illegal activities.

Transnational Organized Crime: The Response

In the face of these enhanced criminal threats it is fair to ask what is being done to meet the modern challenge of organized crime. The answer is a complex one because it is rather like an inverted bell curve. At one time, not long ago, there was a lot being done. The CIA and the FBI were intertwined in an effort to meet the threats and the effort was a large one. Both agencies had hundreds of officers working together in a common effort. Then 9/11 happened and there was a dramatic shift in the direction of both agencies. The vast majority of those who had worked organized crime issues were shifted, almost literally overnight to counter terrorism efforts.

In time the fight against organized crime began to climb up the other side of that inverted bell curve, but the effort has not regained the momentum it once had. There is no single agency charged with investigating organized crime in the way the Federal Bureau of Investigation has been designated the lead investigative agency for terrorism. The available resources are divided among many federal agencies and the number of officers assigned to organized crime are frequently diverted and even subtracted for other purposes.[46]

Despite this, the eye has not been taken off the ball. The U.S. Department of Justice has a threefold response to international crime:

1) Investigation and prosecution
2) Creation of a network of international agreements to facilitate cooperation in the fight against international crime, and
3) Training and technical assistance programs for foreign countries striving to improve their legal infrastructure and law enforcement capabilities.[47]

In providing training, the Department focuses its resources on six core areas that are critical to the efforts of the U.S. Government in the battle against international crime.

1) Organized crime
2) Money laundering and asset forfeiture
3) Corruption
4) Narcotics trafficking

---

46. For example, in July of 2013 it was announced that, for the third time in five years, the number assigned to organized crime at the New York Field Office of the FBI had been reduced, resulting in only three dozen officers assigned to the problem.

47. The U.S. Department of State administers law enforcement training programs in several locations around the world. The curriculum is put together with the cooperation of the FBI and foreign law enforcement officers are invited to attend. Additionally, the FBI invites law enforcement officers to attend training at Quantico. One tangible advantage of these programs is that the attendees meet each other and become friends. Then, when there is a problem or question that can only be answered in another country, there is often a person who can be contacted as a personal acquaintance.

5) Trafficking in human beings
6) Intellectual property

Of course this training for other nations is not without U.S. purpose. There are several strategic objectives behind this largesse:

1) The first strategic objection is to extend the first line of defense beyond our borders so that we, too, may rely on foreign law enforcement that has been trained in things like forensics and evidence handling.

2) A second is an attempt to protect our borders by attacking smuggling and smuggling-related crimes with the help of our neighbors.

3) An extremely important objective is to deny a safe haven to international criminals. There are roughly 197 countries in the world and many of them are weak, failing and even failed states. A safe have can be found in nations that cannot control their own lands so it is our purpose to help strengthen those nations.

4) It is also our purpose to counter international financial crime. In an era of advanced technology financial crimes are extremely difficult to investigate and prosecute. It is our intention to strengthen financial criminal laws around the world and to teach other nations how to investigate them.

5) In a globalized economy we need to work with other nations to prevent criminal exploitation of international trade. Today it is possible to inspect only about 2½ percent of all the globalized trade that circles the world.

6) We need to work with other nations to be capable of responding to emerging international criminal threats. As globalization and technology enhance criminal opportunities, we need to anticipate and cooperate.

7) Of immense importance is the need to foster international cooperation and a respect for the rule of law. So many nations have emerged since World War II that were ill prepared for self-rule and a consequence has been that respect for the rule of law was not part of their cultural heritage.

8) Finally, we need to optimize the full range of national international efforts.

The effort to make all these goals become a reality is a difficult one and one that will be long in coming. However, there are inroads. We have worked hard to help create international working groups. For example, the Financial Action Task Force is an intergovernmental body established in 1989 by the Ministers of its Member jurisdictions. The objectives of the FATF are to set standards and promote effective implementation of legal, regulatory and operational measures for combating money laundering, terrorist financing and other related threats to the integrity of the international financial system. The FATF is therefore a "policy-making body" which works to generate the necessary political will to bring about national legislative and regulatory reforms in these areas.[48]

Additionally, there are several targeted working groups that meet special and/or regional needs. The Southeast European Cooperative Initiative (SECI) has been successful in providing stability in an unstable region and has found support in international organizations and countries. As of 2009, the region has found confidence in its new stability and along with the help of the SECI, has created a Regional Co-operation Council (RCC), owned and run by the countries in Southeast Europe aimed at strengthening peace, democracy and the economy in the hopes that the newfound stability can be

---

48. *See*, the FATF website at http://www.fatf-gafi.org/pages/aboutus/.

supported by those countries who not so long ago were the perpetuators of volatility.[49] In addition, also in 2009, The Southeast European Law Enforcement Center (SELEC) Convention was agreed to among the nations in the region. It established the SELEC, replacing the SECI center, whose primary purpose is to "enhance coordination in preventing and combating crime, including serious and organized crime, where such crime involves or appears to involve an element of trans-border activity."[50]

Despite the long-standing rivalry between Russia and the United States, there is an effective FBI/Russian MVD Joint working group which has successfully investigated cases leading to prosecution in one or the other countries. Of even more interest is an FBI/ Hungarian National Police Organized Crime Task Force in which FBI agents are partnered with Hungarian police in Budapest and working actual cases together.[51] Not surprisingly there is also an Italian American Working Group which has a Carabinieri officer stationed at FBI Headquarters.[52] Similar enterprises are the Pantheon Project, also for Italian organized crime issue[53] and a Central European Working group.[54]

Less well known, The FBI participates in two initiatives to bolster efforts to combat African criminal enterprises. The Department of Justice Nigerian Crime Initiative coordinates the federal investigations of Nigerian criminal enterprises by using joint task forces in six major U.S. cities. The Interpol West African Fraud annual conference brings together law enforcement agents from around the world to discuss and share information about the financial frauds perpetuated by criminal enterprises whose members are predominantly West African, and specifically Nigerian Criminal Enterprises.[55]

Finally, the United States has supported international agreements to try to meet the threats. It is not useful to list them all, but examples are the UN Convention Against Transnational Organized Crime,[56] the UN Protocol to Prevent, Suppress and Punish

---

49. A recently redesigned web site can be found at http://secinet.info/.

50. *See* Article 2, The Southeast European Law Enforcement Center Convention, available at http://www.selec.org/p521/Convention+of+the+Southeast+European+Law+Enforcement+Center+(SELEC). Other regional organizations created to fight organized criminal enterprises include the Central Asian Regional Information and Coordination Centre (CARICC), based in Kazakhstan at http://caricc.org/index.php/en/, and the Joint Interagency Task Force South based in Key West, Florida at http://www.jiatfs.southcom.mil/index.aspx.

51. *See,* Statement of former FBI agent Grant Ashley at http://www.fbi.gov/news/testimony/eurasian-italian-and-balkan-organized-crime.

52. *See* the FBI view at http://www.fbi.gov/about-us/investigate/organizedcrime/italian_mafia.

53. Director, FBI testimony found at http://www.fbi.gov/news/testimony/the-state-of-todays-fbi.

54. http://www.ceeregionalworkinggroup.net/news.php.

55. http://www.fbi.gov/about-us/investigate/organizedcrime/african.

56. The United Nations Convention against Transnational Organized Crime, adopted by General Assembly resolution 55/25 of 15 November 2000, is the main international instrument in the fight against transnational organized crime. It opened for signature by Member States at a High-level Political Conference convened for that purpose in Palermo, Italy, on 12–15 December 2000 and entered into force on 29 September 2003. The Convention is further supplemented by three Protocols, which target specific areas and manifestations of organized crime: the Protocol to Prevent, Suppress and Punish Trafficking in Persons, Especially Women and Children; the Protocol against the Smuggling of Migrants by Land, Sea and Air; and the Protocol against the Illicit Manufacturing of and Trafficking in Firearms, their Parts and Components and Ammunition. Countries must become parties to the Convention itself before they can become parties to any of the Protocols. http://www.unodc.org/unodc/en/treaties/CTOC/index.html.

trafficking in Persons,[57] and the UN Protocol Against the Smuggling of Migrants by Land, Sea and Air.[58]

All of these efforts are long term but each is a link to better policing and for international cooperation. They represent a consistent effort to combat ever cleverer and technologically improved organized criminal activity in a world where terrorism and cybercrimes have the personnel and money edge over organized crime.

---

57. The protocol can be found in its entirety at http://www.osce.org/odihr/19223?download=true.

58. The Protocol aims to criminalize the smuggling of migrants and those who practice it, while recognizing that illegal migration itself is not a crime and that migrants are often victims needing protection. Under the Protocol, governments agree to make migrant smuggling a criminal offence under national laws, adopt special measures to crack down on migrant smuggling by sea, boost international cooperation to prevent migrant smuggling, and seek out and prosecute offenders. States party to the Protocol agree to adopt domestic laws to prevent and suppress activities related to the smuggling of migrants. *See,* press release at http://www.un.org/press/en/2004/soccp280.doc.htm.

Chapter 12

Law and Warfare in the Cyber Domain

*Paul Rosenzweig**

In this chapter:
Introduction
The Basics of Cyberspace
Vulnerability on the Network
Jus ad Bellum Issues — What Is Cyber War?
Jus in Bello Requirements
Non-International Armed Conflict, Non-State Actors and Sub-War Acts
The WikiLeaks War and Beyond
Espionage or Traditional Military Activity?
Organizing to Contest Cyber Conflict

Introduction

On the day that the first draft of this chapter was outlined, *The New York Times* reported a persistent cyber threat, known by the code name "Snake," that had infiltrated the cyber systems operated by the Ukrainian government. Citing confidential U.S. government sources, the newspaper attributed Snake to Russian actors and connected the deployment of the Snake virus to both Russian intelligence collection and disruption of Ukrainian command and control systems.[1] At the same time, of course, Russian troops were on the ground in Crimea and the potential for kinetic conflict between Ukrainian and Russian military forces loomed. Just a few weeks later, Russia formally annexed the Crimea (and, by the time of this book's publication, any number of other events will have occurred).

That single episode captures, in many ways, the new reality of military operations in the cyber domain. Cyber conflict will, at a minimum, be part of combined operations against physical opponents. Cyber tools will partake of the character of both espionage activities and traditional military activities. At times, the effect of cyber tools may be

---

* Professorial Lecturer in Law, George Washington University School of Law; Distinguished Visiting Fellow, Homeland Security Studies and Analysis Institute; Principal, Red Branch Consulting, PLLC; Senior Advisor, The Chertoff Group; and former Deputy Assistant Secretary for Policy, Department of Homeland Security. Portions of this chapter first appeared in Rosenzweig, *Cyber Warfare: How Conflicts in Cyberspace are Challenging America and Changing the World* (Praeger Press, 2013).

1. Sanger and Erlanger, "Suspicion Falls on Russia as 'Snake' Cyberattacks Target Ukraine's Government," *New York Times* (March 8, 2014), <http://www.nytimes.com/2014/03/09/world/europe/suspicion-falls-on-russia-as-snake-cyberattacks-target-ukraines-government.html?_r=0>.

equivalent to kinetic weapons, while at other times they will be used in a more limited manner to degrade, disrupt, or destroy data and information. In some cases, the origin and source of the tools used in a cyber conflict will be difficult, if not impossible, to discern, rendering attribution of responsibility for an attack problematic. At other times, the origins are likely to be crystal clear but the long-term effects of the tool obscured. And all of this will occur at a time when legal norms about appropriate conduct in cyberspace are in a state of flux, without settled definition.

This chapter is about the rule of law as applied to conflict in the cyber domain. The aim is to provide an introduction to the domain of the sort that every practitioner of national security law should know. It does not purport to be either a comprehensive or an in-depth treatment. Nor does it pretend to answer the many unanswered questions. Indeed, for many of the questions there are, as yet, no definitive answers. It is hoped, however, that a review of this chapter will leave the reader with a basic understanding of the important questions and issues and provide the tools to address and formulate some thoughtful answers.[2]

The Basics of Cyberspace

It is hard to understand cyber conflict, cyber vulnerabilities, cybersecurity, and cyber warfare if you don't understand how the web is built and why it works the way it does. To a very real degree much of what we consider a vulnerability in the system is inherent in its design. Indeed, the Internet is so effective precisely because it is designed to be an open system—and while that makes the network readily accessible, it also makes it highly vulnerable.

As Temple University Professor David Post explained in his wonderful book, *In Search of Jefferson's Moose*,[3] the networks that make up cyberspace were built for ease of communication and expansion, not for security. At its core, the logic layer of the Internet (about which more in a minute) is fundamentally dumb. It is designed to do nothing more than transfer information from one place to another very quickly and very efficiently. So, even though most users tend to think of Internet connections as nothing more than a glorified telephone network the two are, in fact, fundamentally different.

The telephone networks are "hub and spoke" systems with the intelligent operation at the central switching points. Sophisticated switches route calls from one end to the other (indeed, at their inception, the intelligence at the hub of the telephone networks was human—operators making the required physical connections). By contrast, the Internet is truly a "world wide web" of interconnected servers that do nothing more than switch

---

2. And though it should be obvious from the introduction, this chapter is also limited in scope to matters relating to cyber conflict. Often cyber conflict is thought of as a component of information operations or as a subset of electromagnetic warfare. *E.g.* Department of the Air Force, *Cornerstones of Information Warfare* (1995) (cyber as information operation); Department of Army, FM-3-38, *Cyber Electromagnetic Activities* (2014) (cyber as electromagnetic warfare). Either or both of these characterizations are plausible, the first looking at the target area of a conflict while the latter looks to the cognate physical domain. For better or worse, however, the United States has chosen to characterize the domain principally based on the type of tool (or weapon, if you will) that is used— a characterization that this chapter will adhere to.

3. David Post, *In Search of Jefferson's Moose: Notes on the State of Cyberspace* (Oxford University Press, 2012). For those interested in the field generally, I highly recommend this elegant and entertaining book.

packets of information around the globe. The intelligent operations occur at the edges (in our mobile devices and laptops running various applications or "apps").

And that's what makes the Internet so successful. Access to it is not controlled at a central switching point. You don't need "permission" to add a new functionality. The way the Internet is built, anyone with a new idea can design it and add it to the network by simply purchasing a domain name and renting server space. The addressing directory (known as the Domain Name System) that allows information to be correctly routed is operated on a distributed basis that no single person really controls.[4] And, so long as the commonly accepted addressing protocols are used, virtually any function can be hooked up to the web—a store, a virtual-world game site, or a government database. Or, if you prefer, it is like the system controlling an electric generating facility or an individual's insulin pump. This flexibility is precisely what has driven the explosive growth of the Internet.

Let's consider the structure that this wild growth has given us. When we talk colloquially of the Internet, almost everyone is talking about the logical network layer where all of the information gets exchanged. If you tried to map all of these connections, it would look like a wild spaghetti web of connections.[5] Those connections change every day. A map today would look very similar to one from two years ago, but also completely different, since the connections on the network are ever-changing. What such a map would tell us is that the Internet is a vast switching system for the distribution of information at near instantaneous speeds across great distances. There are no borders on the Internet and its structure makes action across global distances, without regard for national borders, the norm rather than the exception.

But this logic layer is only a piece of the puzzle. While most people think of the Internet as the web of connections between computers, its full structure is really more complex. This schematic (derived from the strategy of U.S. Cyber Command) gives you some idea of the scope of the entire cyber domain. It is, in essence, a five-layer cake of connections:

Figure 1. Schematic of the Cyber Domain

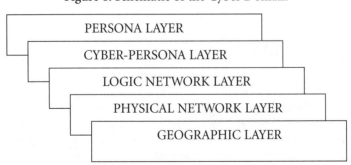

PERSONA LAYER

CYBER-PERSONA LAYER

LOGIC NETWORK LAYER

PHYSICAL NETWORK LAYER

GEOGRAPHIC LAYER

---

4. Policy regarding naming is set by a non-profit corporation known as the Internet Corporation for Assigned Names and Numbers (or ICANN) with its headquarters in California. Implementation of that policy happens through the operation of several "root servers" that maintain the authoritative list of domain names. Updates to that list are, currently, implemented by an American corporation, Verisign. For more on the topic (and current controversies relating to its evolution), *see* Rosenzweig, "Who Controls the Internet Address Book? ICANN, NTIA and IANA," *Lawfare* (March 15, 2014), <http://www.lawfareblog.com/2014/03/who-controls-the-internet-address-book-icann-ntia-and-iana/>.

5. *See*, for example, versions of the "peacock map" which illustrate how the Internet is as complex as a starry nebula, <http://www.opte.org/maps/>.

At the bottom is what we might call the "geographic layer"—that is, the physical location of elements of the network. Though cyberspace itself has no physical existence, every piece of equipment that creates it is physically located somewhere in the world. That location is often critically important for questions of law—it may define what jurisdiction's rules control and it may authorize or limit targeting decisions during a conflict.

Next is the "physical network layer." This is the place where all of the hardware and infrastructure exists and is connected together. The components of this layer include all of the wires, fiber optic cables, routers, servers, and computers linked together across geographic spaces (some of the links are through wireless connections with physical endpoints). Again, the distinction is important in the context of a conflict—all, or almost all, of this infrastructure will be dual use and that nature will affect the proportionality of any targeting decision.

Above this layer is the middle layer which is the heart of the Internet. We call it the "logic network layer." This is the virtual space where the information resides and is transmitted and routed by servers. Here packets of information—the 1's and 0's of binary code—are distributed by a switching system that operates autonomously, without human direction.

The logic layer in turn needs to be connected to the users. So, above the logic network layer is the "cyber persona layer." In this layer we see how a user is identified on the network—this could be by his e-mail address, computer IP address, or cell phone number. Most individuals have many different cyber personas. Just think of how many different email addresses and phone numbers you have.

Finally, there is the "persona layer." This is where the actual people who are using the network and have their fingers on the keyboard, so to speak, exist. While an individual can have multiple cyber personas (and, conversely, a single cyber persona can have multiple users), in the end, we need to think about uniquely identifying a particular person connected to the network. After all, in a world of conflict, the "who" of it—the identity of your conflict opponent—is often the single most critical question.

Vulnerability on the Network

Then-Deputy Secretary of Defense William Lynn summed up this structure in a speech announcing our military Strategy for Operating in Cyberspace: "The internet was designed to be open, transparent, and interoperable. Security and identity management were secondary objectives in system design. This lower emphasis on security in the internet's initial design ... gives attackers a built-in advantage."[6] And it gives rise to significant vulnerabilities that derive from six distinct, yet interrelated characteristics.

First, the network is essentially **borderless.** This is probably the place where the unusual nature of cyberspace is clearest. In the real world, a smuggler must cross the American border at some point in order to enter the United States. And that's a point where entry can be subject to governmental control. By contrast an e-mail message sent to someone in France doesn't cross the border in any single place. In travelling across the network the many packets of data are likely to cross multiple borders, some much more than once.

---

6. William J. Lynn, III, Remarks on the Department of Defense Cyber Strategy (July 11, 2011), <http://www.defense.gov/Speeches/Speech.aspx?SpeechID=1593>.

One packet might go from the U.S. to Canada, back to the U.S., then to the UK, and then on to France.

In essence, then, there are no border checkpoints on the Internet. For almost every country (China being the notable exception) there is no single landing point such as, for example, where an undersea cable comes ashore. And that means that there is no easy way to control information as it flows across national borders. There are no sovereigns on the Internet.

That's a deeply disorienting phenomenon. Since the Peace of Westphalia in 1648, sovereign nations have been defined by their ability to control territory and the transit of things and goods across that territory. Now ideas, data, and information flow across boundaries almost without limit disrupting settled expectations and threatening the status quo.

Second, the network also permits instantaneous **action at a distance**. The history of human interaction is, essentially, one of the increasing distance at which our interactions occur. Armed conflict, for example, hearkens back to the days when Romans fought at sword length with the invading Visigoths and gradually transitioned to the bows and arrows of Agincourt. Later still we developed siege cannons and artillery. Then came airplanes that were capable of projecting force across the globe. And finally we reached the point in the real world where intercontinental ballistic missiles were capable of reaching from the United States to Russia, or vice versa, in 30 minutes or less.

The cyber domain is a leap beyond all that in capability. Now action in the cyber domain occurs at the speed of light, and crosses immense distances almost instantaneously. From your desktop at the flick of a finger you can access a website in Japan, read a South American newspaper, or make reservations at a restaurant in Paris. You can also, if you wish, initiate a cyber intrusion 10,000 miles away.

This principle is best exemplified by the discovery of malware on then-Secretary of Defense Gates's unclassified Pentagon computer. In earlier times if a Chinese spy (or perhaps it was a Russian spy) had wanted to get access to the office of the Secretary of Defense, he or she would have had to pass through several checkpoints at the gates of the Pentagon and surreptitiously made their way into his inner sanctum in the E-ring of the building. By virtue of the structure of the network, in this case the malicious actor was able to penetrate Secretary Gates' computer from a distance that effectively put him or her beyond our control.

Third, the ubiquity of the Internet creates **asymmetries of power**. Where, in the kinetic world, only nation states could effectively compete against each other, in the cyber domain small nations and even non-state actors can challenge great powers. One individual with multiple, complex relationships to other levels of the environment can send anything through the network to virtually any location worldwide. And with that, we empower small groups like Anonymous (the cyber hacktivists who attacked PayPal, Amazon, and MasterCard) to, in effect, be competitors in the cyber world. To put it in more practical terms, when President Obama considers, for example, intervention in Syria he must deal with the new reality that the Syrian Electronic Army (an Assad-affiliated group) may very well be capable of effective cyber retaliation in the United States. This is a sea-change in our vulnerability analysis.[7]

The next vulnerability is the problem of **anonymity**. Given the vastness of the web it is quite possible for those who seek to do harm to do so at a distance, cloaked in the veil

---

7. I wrote more about this transformation and how it affects military operations in Rosenzweig, "The Structure of the Cyber Military Revolution," 220 *Military L. Rev.* 214 (2014).

of anonymity behind a false or ever-changing cyber persona. While we can overcome this vulnerability, doing so requires a very great investment of time and resources. It also often requires the "good guys" to use "bad guy" techniques to track the malefactors. In effect, this makes many malfeasant actors immune, for all practical purposes, from swift and sure response or retaliation.

The fifth vulnerability lies in the **difficulty of distinction**. All the 1's and 0's in the logic layer look the same. But that means that different types of activities in the logic layer are hard to distinguish. Put another way, any successful cyber attack or intrusion requires "a vulnerability, access to that vulnerability, and a payload to be executed."[8] But in practice the first two parts of that equation (identifying a vulnerability and gaining access to it in the logic layer) are the same no matter what the payload that is to be delivered.

Thus, for those on the defensive end, it is virtually impossible to distinguish *ex ante* between espionage and a full-scale cyber attack. The tools all look the same at the front end and both also often look like authorized communications. The difference arises only when the payload is executed and the effects are felt. The closest real world analogy would be never being able to tell whether the plane flying across your border was a friendly commercial aircraft, a spy plane, or a bomber.

Finally, the network is remarkably **distributed and dynamic**. Today, the globe-spanning reach of cyberspace touches the lives of more than 2.9 billion people.[9] The so-called Internet of Things controls approximately 1 trillion devices—everything ranging from cars and houses to industrial plants, elevators, and even medical devices.[10] Every day (in 2012) we created roughly 2.5 quintillion bytes of data (that is a 1 followed by 18 zeroes). Put another way, 90 percent of the data created since the dawn of human history was created (and passed through cyberspace) in the past two years.[11] As a world community our dependence upon and interdependence with the cyber domain is growing so fast that our conception of its size cannot keep up with the reality of it. And that dependence will only increase over time. It is profoundly difficult to design rule sets that scale to such a dynamic space or to create management structures that are capable of enduring application in an ever-changing environment.

Thus, the very structures that make the Internet such a powerful engine for social activity and that have allowed its explosive, world-altering growth are also the factors that give rise to the vulnerabilities in the network. We could eliminate anonymity and resolve distinction, but only at the price of changing the ease with which one can use the Internet for novel commercial and social functions. Those who want both ubiquity and security are asking to have their cake and eat it, too. So long as this Internet is The Internet, vulnerability is here to stay. It can be managed but it can't be eliminated. And that means that those who bear responsibility for defending the network have a persistent challenge of great complexity.[12]

---

8. Herbert Lin, "Offensive Cyber Operations and the Use of Force," 4 *J. Nat. Sec. Law & Plcy.* 63, 64 (2010) (footnote omitted), <http://jnslp.com/wp-content/uploads/2010/08/06_Lin.pdf>.

9. Internet World Stats, <http://www.internetworldstats.com/stats.htm>.

10. Alex Williams, <http://readwrite.com/2010/06/07/ibm-a-world-with-1-trillion-co#awesm =~oA7AYOIYdpzA6o>.

11. Data on Big Data, <http://marciaconner.com/blog/data-on-big-data/>.

12. As this description makes clear, it does seem useful to characterize the cyber domain as a separate domain if only because its characteristics are sufficiently different in degree from those of warfare in the kinetic realm that they tend over time to become differences in kind. Designation as a separate domain comes, in American usage, with a number of collateral consequences, including the creation of a separate combatant command structure. There are many who think that is a mistake—

Jus ad Bellum Issues — What Is Cyber War?

As we have already suggested, conflict in cyberspace occurs in diverse ways, ranging from traditional espionage to traditional military preparation of the battlefield to destructive activities using cyber tools with physical, kinetic effects. This proliferation of means of conflict in cyberspace raises an interesting and challenging question. How do we define weapons of war? Or are some of them of dual character, such that their use is not equivalent to an armed conflict in the physical world? Put more fundamentally, we know what war looks like in the real world — things get blown up. But what would be an "act of war" or a "use of force" in cyberspace? Consider the following hypotheticals (all of which are reasonably realistic). An adversary of the United States (known or unknown):

- Disrupts the stock exchanges for two days, preventing any trading;
- Uses cyber tools to take offline an early warning radar system;
- Introduces a latent piece of malware (that is a piece of malicious software that can be activated at a later date, sometimes called a "logic bomb") into a radar station that can disable the station when triggered, but doesn't trigger it just yet;
- Makes a nuclear centrifuge run poorly in a nuclear production plant, eventually causing physical damage to the centrifuge;[13]
- Implants a worm that slowly corrupts and degrades data on which certain military applications rely (say, for example, by degrading GPS location data);
- Adds a back door to a piece of hardware that is built into a computer system, allowing the potential for the implantation of a worm or virus that would disrupt or destroy the system;
- Takes the U.S. command and control systems offline temporarily;
- Probes a Pentagon computer to map its structure and identify its vulnerabilities;[14]
- Blockades another country's access to the Internet; or
- Disables an industrial component (say, part of the electric grid).

Some of these, like probing the Pentagon computer, are clearly analogous to espionage in the physical or kinetic world and won't be considered acts of war or the use of force. Others, like disrupting our military command and control systems, look just like acts of war in the kinetic world. But what about the middle ground? Is leaving a logic bomb behind in a radar station like espionage, or is it similar to planting a mine in another country's harbor as a preparation for war?[15] Is the blockade of Internet access like a military

---

that as a tool of warfare cyber weapons should be no different than other tools incorporated directly into the operational planning of geographic combatant commanders. Whatever the merits of that view (and, personally, I think they are quite persuasive) the U.S. government has chosen to eschew a vision of the cyber domain as a "supporting" command.

13. Public reports suggest that the United States did this to Iran. William J. Broad, John Markoff and David E. Sanger, "Israeli Test on Worm Called Crucial in Iran Nuclear Delay," *New York Times*, January 15, 2011, <http://www.nytimes.com/2011/01/16/world/middleeast/16stuxnet.html?_r=1&nl=todaysheadlines&emc=tha2>.

14. Former Deputy Secretary Lynn says this happens tens of thousands of times every day to the United States. William J. Lynn, III, "Defending a New Domain: The Pentagon's Cyberstrategy," 97 at 103 *Foreign Affairs*, Sept./Oct. 2010), <http://www.foreignaffairs.com/articles/66552/william-j-lynn-iii/defending-a-new-domain>.

15. *E.g. Republic of Nicaragua v. United States of America*, (1986 I.C.J. 14), <http://www.worldlii.org/int/cases/ICJ/1986/1.html>.

blockade in time of war? Is causing a brownout by degrading the electric grid an armed attack?

Does International Humanitarian Law Apply At All?

To begin an examination of this question, we first need to define the appropriate conflict principles for assessing whether and when a nation state can use force. The paradigm, of course, is that aggressive armed conflict is generally prohibited by international law unless authorized by an action of the Security Council of the United Nations. This does not, however, disable States from responding in self-defense when attacked. To the contrary, States may legitimately act in their own self-defense under Article 51 of the UN Charter when confronted with an armed attack.

But it is by no means mandatory, as a theoretical matter, that these rules apply in cyberspace. Indeed, for many years the proposition was contested by several nations (most notably China and Russia). It was not until June 2013 that the United Nations received a report from the so-called Group of Governmental Experts, in which that group (including all of the major nations of the world)[16] formally reached consensus that international humanitarian law applied in cyberspace.[17] As that Group said: "International law, and in particular the Charter of the United Nations, is applicable and is essential to maintaining peace and stability and promoting an open, secure, peaceful and accessible ICT [Information and Communications Technologies] environment." Though unsurprising (if not the traditional rules then which ones?) it is by no means clear how this decision will work out.

Despite the international hesitancy, American policy has been clear for some time. The Department of Defense *Strategy for Operating in Cyberspace,* in its unclassified public version, adopted generally the framework of IHL for asserting the legitimacy of self-defense (sometimes called "active defense") to authorize real time counter-attacks against incoming efforts to penetrate the Pentagon's systems.[18] More broadly, the classified version of the strategy is reported to conclude that the traditional "laws of armed conflict" apply in cyberspace just as they do in the physical world.[19]

In reaching this conclusion, the United States joins others around the globe. An independent group of experts recently published a seminal, comprehensive survey of the international law applicable to cyber conflict between nations, the *Tallin Manual.*[20] Convened by the NATO Cooperative Cyber Defense Center of Excellence, the experts sought to identify the generally applicable international law that will guide cyber conflict. They too concluded that existing international law generally applied in the cyber domain. As the

---

16. Argentina, Australia, Belarus, Canada, China, Egypt, Estonia, France, Germany, India, Indonesia, Japan, Russia, UK and U.S.A. were in the group.

17. Group of Governmental Experts on Developments in the Field of Information and Telecommunications in the Context of International Security, <http://www.un.org/ga/search/view_doc.asp?symbol=A/68/98>.

18. Department of Defense, "Strategy for Operating in Cyberspace" (July 2011), <http://www.defense.gov/news/d20110714cyber.pdf>.

19. Siobhan Gorman and Julian Barnes, "Cyber Combat: Act of War," *Wall St. Journal,* May 31, 2011 <http://online.wsj.com/article/SB10001424052702304563104576355623135782718.html>.

20. The full title is the *Tallinn Manual on the International Law Applicable to Cyber Warfare* (Cambridge Univ. Press, 2013), <www.cambridge.org/us/academic/subjects/law/humanitarian-law/tallinn-manual-international-law-applicable-cyber-warfare?format=PB>.

Manual reports: "The International Group of Experts was unanimous in its estimation that both the *jus ad bellum* and *jus in bello* apply to cyber operations."[21]

What Is an Armed Cyber Attack?

What does that imply? To begin with we must ask whether and when a cyber attack, in some form, may be characterized as an armed attack. After all, an armed attack is the hallmark of what authorizes national self-defense.

But defining a cyber "armed attack" is especially difficult, at least in part because of the indeterminate international consensus on the definition of what constitutes an armed attack, even in the physical realm. Generally, however, such an assessment looks to the scope, duration, and intensity of the use of force in question.[22] A single shot, for example, fired across the DMZ by a North Korean soldier does not mean that a state of war now exists between South Korea and North Korea.

This ambiguity in the physical arena has carried over into the cyber domain. In this domain there are three schools of thought regarding when a cyber attack might be viewed as tantamount to an armed attack (assuming always that we have been able to determine that the event was, in fact, an "attack" using cyber means).

One school looks at whether the damage caused by such an attack could previously have been **achieved only by a kinetic attack.** For example, using this model, a cyber attack conducted for the purpose of shutting down a power grid would be deemed an armed attack, inasmuch as, prior to the development of cyber capabilities, the destruction of a power grid would typically have required using some form of kinetic force.

A second school looks at the **scope and magnitude of the effects** of a cyber attack on a victim-State, rather than attempting to compare these effects to any form of kinetic attack. Here, for example, consider the disablement of a financial network. With real effects but no physical harm, this would be seen as equivalent to an armed attack, despite the fact that nothing was broken or destroyed, only some digital financial records were disrupted.

A third view is akin to a **strict liability rule.** Any attack on a State's critical national infrastructure, even if unsuccessful, would be deemed an armed attack *per se* (and thus, would cover attempted intrusions that had no consequences). It might also include any preparatory intrusions that fell short of an armed attack but could be viewed as "preparing the battlefield" for later success.

By and large, U.S. policy makers have trended toward the middle view, focusing on the overall effects of a particular cyber intrusion. But, even here, there is no consensus and hard questions lie in the grey area. If, for example, cyber agents were introduced into a system for exploitation and attack, but not yet activated, should that be considered a use of force? Or, to identify another issue, is the "mere" destruction of data a use of force? Some in the intelligence community might even deem aggressive phishing (i.e., acquiring sensitive information through fraud) a use of force. Here, we have no settled doctrine.

---

21. *Id.* at 19; *see also id.* Part A. ¶ 2.
22. *The Geneva Conventions of 12 August 1949 Commentary IV Relative to the Protection of Civilian Persons in Time of War*, 583 (Jean S. Pictet ed., 1958).

The emerging U.S. view is not universally accepted. For example, the *Tallinn Manual* takes a narrower approach. It says that an "armed attack" in the cyber domain occurs where "the effects of a cyber operation, as distinct from the means used to achieve those effects, were analogous to those that would result from an action otherwise qualifying as a kinetic armed attack."[23] This is, as you will readily see, essentially adopting the first school of thought on the definition of an armed attack and it is, perhaps, narrower than the United States is willing to accept.

Of course, there is overlap. Under either approach a cyber attack on the electric grid *would* be a military attack if the cyber assault has the same effect as a missile attack might have. But the United States might also consider the disruption of our air traffic control system as an armed attack—a view that the *Tallinn* experts would probably reject.

The Russo-Georgian War

Whichever definition we choose, however, it is clear that cyber armed attacks (and a cyber war) are a rare experience. Indeed, as of late 2014, the world has not seen a true cyber war.[24] The Russian attacks on Georgia and Ukraine are as close an approximation as we can imagine, however.

Consider the Georgian conflict. In August 2008, Russian troops came into conflict with Georgian troops regarding a disputed border area between the two countries. During the course of that conflict, a number of cyber intrusions were also made on Georgian Internet services. Among many collateral cyber effects of those attacks, a "Distributed Denial of Service" or DDoS attack (that is, one that uses multiple computers and accounts to flood a computer server with messages and overload it, preventing any legitimate efforts to connect to the server) prevented the Georgian Ministry of Foreign Affairs and other official Georgian sites from using the Internet to convey information about the attack to interested third parties. In other instances, cyber intruders corrupted the code for various official Georgian websites, defacing them with pro-Russian messages. The website of the Georgian President, for example, was attacked from 500 Internet Protocol ("IP") addresses.[25]

According to the United States Cyber-Consequences Unit,[26] these attacks were actually carried out by Russian civilians (so-called "patriotic hackers") who had advance notice of Russia's military intentions and were aware of the timing of Russia's military operations. The civilians were, in turn, aided by elements of Russian organized crime in their efforts. In particular the Russian criminal networks provided access to their own network of controlled computers (known as "botnets") for use in the attacks. In addition, the main social media chat room ("stopgeorgia.ru") that was used to organize the attacks was registered to an address located just blocks from the headquarters of the GRU, the Main Intelligence Directorate of the Russian Armed Forces, suggesting strongly (but not proving) the possibility that Russian intelligence agents may have coordinated the attacks.[27]

---

23. *Tallinn Manual* Rule 13, Commentary ¶ 4.

24. It has, however, seen many cyber intrusions, assaults and non-armed attacks. *See* Jason Healey, ed., *A Fierce Domain: Conflict in Cyberspace, 1986 to 2012* (Atlantic Council, 2013).

25. Jeffrey Carr, *Inside Cyber Warfare*, 17 (O'Reilly, 2010).

26. "Overview by the US-CCU of the Cyber Campaign Against Georgia in August of 2008," August 2009, <http://www.registan.net/wp-content/uploads/2009/08/US-CCU-Georgia-Cyber-Campaign-Overview.pdf>.

27. "Project Grey Goose, Phase II Report: The Evolving State of Cyber Warfare," 15-17 (March 20, 2009), fserror.com/pdf/GreyGoose2.pdf.

The cyber tools were effective, not only in preventing Georgia from getting its own message out to the world, but also in preventing the Georgian government from communicating with its own people in order to respond to the Russian military invasion. Thus, in some ways, the cyber tools used in Georgia represent the first use of cyber weapons in a combined operation with military forces. But notwithstanding their effectiveness, it is not clear whether the attacks met the traditional definition of an armed conflict. Though highly disruptive, it is difficult to say that their effect was equivalent to that of a kinetic attack.

Attribution and Accountability

The Russian-Georgian war also demonstrates the limits of our practical knowledge about cyber conflict between nation states. For one thing, in the cyber domain, unlike the real world, the attacker may not be so readily identified. In the end the critical question in a cyberwar may well be: "who attacked us?" For even though we have grave suspicions about Russian intent in the Georgian war, the reality is that the Internet is not designed to allow for conclusive identification of the source of an attack. As the DoD strategy puts it, in designing the Internet "identity authentication was less important than connectivity."

Here, the quasi-links between the patriotic Russian hackers and the Russian military make it difficult to draw firm conclusions about the modalities of a true cyber war. It is true, as the *Tallinn Manual* notes, that "[t]he International Court of Justice has held, in the context of military operations, that a State is responsible for the acts of non-State actors where it has 'effective control' over such actors."[28] But that rule obscures as much as it informs. How much control is necessary for it to be deemed "effective"? In the cyber domain that question is as hard (if not harder) to answer as it is with irregular forces in the kinetic domain.

The Sony Hack—An Edge Case

The late 2014 intrusion at Sony provides an instructive edge case for testing the limits of our understanding of the legal definition of war and also for demonstrating that the laws of armed conflict are not the only means of addressing cyber intrusions.[29] Recall that the intrusion, conducted by a group identified as the "Guardians of Peace," ex-filtrated terabytes of data from Sony. Some of the data involved unreleased films; other data included embarrassing internal emails and proprietary information. Beyond the damage from the release of confidential information, the hackers also demanded that Sony withhold from release *The Interview*—a movie depicting the assassination of North Korean leader Kim Jong-Un. After delaying the release for several days, Sony eventually made the movie available through several alternate outlets. The FBI (relying in part on information provided by the NSA) attributed the intrusion to North Korean government agents.[30] Estimates of

---

28. *Tallinn Manual* Rule 6, Commentary ¶ 10.

29. For a useful timeline of events related to the Sony hack, *see* Trend Micro, "The Hack of Sony Pictures: What We Know and What You Need to Know," 8 Dec. 2014, <http://www.trendmicro.com/vinfo/us/security/news/cyber-attacks/the-hack-of-sony-pictures-what-you-need-to-know>. *See also* Chapter Six for a fuller discussion of the potential applicability of the laws of arms conflict to the cyber domain.

30. *See* Schmidt, Perlroth & Goldstein, "F.B.I. Says Little Doubt North Korea Hit Sony," 7 Jan. 2015, <http://www.nytimes.com/2015/01/08/business/chief-says-fbi-has-no-doubt-that-north-korea-attacked-sony.html?_r=0>.

damage to Sony's financial interests range upward of $50 million (though, of course, Sony isn't saying).

Here we have a state actor, North Korea, using cyber means to degrade the economic interests of the citizens of another nation, the U.S. [Some, by the way, doubt the attribution to North Korea, but for now let us provisionally accept it]. How shall we characterize this action? It had no kinetic effects, nor did it significantly affect the American economy. No matter how we view it, Sony is not a "critical infrastructure" of the United States. And, so, it isn't an "armed attack" triggering the laws of armed conflict. Nor is it even an act of espionage. But, calling this a state-sponsored criminal act seems to trivialize its geopolitical context.

In the end, the Sony intrusion seems to reflect a new category of conflict—a quasi-instrumental action by a nation state (or its surrogates) that has significant but non-kinetic effects on a target nation. Such "attacks" are not a "use of force" or an "armed attack" but they are likely to generate reciprocal responses from the target state that involve a wide-array of state powers. The United States, for example, has publicly announced financial sanctions against North Korea[31] and may very well have taken other, non-public actions in response.

Legal Implications

Finally, it is worth noting that the legal conclusion (an "armed attack" has occurred) brings with it some other necessary implications. The logical consequence of applying the laws of armed conflict to the cyber domain is to authorize the United States military to use any weapon in its arsenal in response (provided it does so in a lawful manner).[32] This could include offensive cyber operations[33] against those who are deemed responsible for the attack, but it could also include the full panoply of other military options. As one wag put it, this means that "Obama reserves right to nuke hackers."[34] While that is an

---

31. Everett Rosenfeld, "US sanctions North Korea for Sony hacks," 2 Jan. 2015, http://www.cnbc.com/id/102306274.

32. Ellen Nakashima, "List of Cyber-weapons Developed by Pentagon to Streamline Computer Warfare," *Washington Post*, June 1, 2011, <http://www.washingtonpost.com/national/list-of-cyber-weapons-developed-by-pentagon-to-streamline-computer-warfare/2011/05/31/AGSublFH_story.html>.

33. Ellen Nakashima, "Pentagon: Cyber Offense Part of U.S. Strategy," *Washington Post*, Nov. 16, 2011, <http://www.washingtonpost.com/national/national-security/pentagon-cyber-offense-part-of-us-strategy/2011/11/15/gIQArEAlPN_story.html>. One interesting, and exceedingly indeterminate question is what, exactly, constitutes a cyber "weapon." Given the dual use nature of most cyber code, we are currently using an unsatisfactory *ex post* definition based upon how a particular piece of code is used. A better definition would involve an understanding *ex ante* of the characteristics that define a cyber weapon. The question is critical, both to an understanding of what weapons may lawfully be used in time of war and, relatedly, to collateral questions regarding issues such as cyber arms limitation discussions. For one proposal on resolving the question *see* Trey Herr and Paul Rosenzweig, "Cyber Weapons and Export Control: Incorporating Dual Use with the PrEP Model," ___ *J. Nat. Sec. L & P'lcy* ___ (2015) [forthcoming], http://papers.ssrn.com/sol3/papers.cfm?abstract_id=2501789.

34. <http://www.nbcnews.com/id/43081443/ns/technology_and_science-security/t/obama-reserves-right-nuke-hackers/#.VGZpM8nJ081> (*NBC News*, May 18, 2011). Of course, such a response is unlikely in the extreme—at least in part because it would violate other rules of armed conflict that require proportionality in a response. But it does emphasize the significance of the determination. When an armed attack occurs, nations are entitled to go to war.

extreme caricature, it is the case that the United States reserves the right to answer a cyber weapon with a real world weapon of proportional effect and does not limit its response to a cyber assault to the use of cyber weapons.[35]

Another legal implication derived from the analysis is that it affects our treaty obligations. In June 2014, for example, NATO updated its cyber defense policy to make it clear that a cyber attack can be treated as the equivalent of an attack with conventional weapons for purposes of NATO obligation. In other words, NATO has now expressed the view that a cyber attack on a member state is covered by Article 5, the collective defense clause of the NATO treaty. As a result, NATO members have agreed to take action against a cyber aggressor—up to and potentially including the use of armed force—to restore security.[36]

Likewise, America's analysis of what constitutes a cyber armed attack will have collateral effects on the views of other nations. After all, what is sauce for the goose is also, inevitably, sauce for the gander. If America takes an expansive view of the applicable laws of armed conflict, others may as well. Indeed, it is an interesting question (as only lawyers can define "interesting") to consider whether the Stuxnet intrusion on Iran's nuclear program met the definition of an armed attack. It certainly had the requisite physical effect. But its scope and duration were relatively narrow, modest and short-lived. Nevertheless, Iran could make a plausible argument that it was entitled to respond with armed force against the Stuxnet attacker ... if it knew who the attacker was, of course.

For this reason, some observers have argued that the Iranian attack on Saudi Aramco (known as the "Shamoon" virus) and the failed Iranian assassination attempt against the Saudi Arabian ambassador were motivated, in part, by the Iranian conclusion that Saudi Arabia was complicit in the Stuxnet virus attack.[37] This may, or may not, be factually accurate, but by some potential measures Iran might view Stuxnet as an armed attack, which allows it to use military means in self-defense. Or perhaps its judgment is ill-founded; there is precious little in the public domain connecting Saudi Arabia to the Stuxnet virus, suggesting that the Iranian response (if, in fact, it was a response) was disproportionate.[38]

Jus in Bello Requirements

Since we have accepted, as a matter of policy, the view that traditional laws of war apply to a cyber conflict, it follows that we must, perforce, make an effort to apply the *jus in bello* rules. Thus, we need to examine, *e.g.*, rules against the targeting of civilians and respecting the rights of neutrals. Yet traditional rules don't translate well to the cyber

---

35. This conclusion is by no means inevitable. Some analysts (most notably Martin Libicki of Rand) have argued that the cyber domain should be hived off from other domains as an area of conflict. *E.g.* Libicki, "Cyberspace is Not a Warfighting Domain," 8 *I/S: A Journal of Law and Policy for the Information* Society (2012) <http://moritzlaw.osu.edu/students/groups/is/files/2012/02/4.Libicki.pdf>.

36. Steve Ranger, "NATO Updates Cyber Defence Policy as Digital Attacks Become a Standard Part of Conflict," *ZDNet*, <http://www.zdnet.com/nato-updates-cyber-defence-policy-as-digital-attacks-become-a-standard-part-of-conflict-7000031064/>.

37. David E. Sanger, "America's Deadly Dynamics with Iran," *New York Times*, November 6, 2011, <http://www.nytimes.com/2011/11/06/sunday-review/the-secret-war-with-iran.html?ref=opinion>.

38. Of course, as to the assassination attempt, if this truly were an Iranian response it violated other international conventions, including the prohibition on targeting diplomats.

domain and are of problematic application. As with the application of *jus ad bello*, there are more questions than answers.[39]

The most basic requirement of *jus in bello* is that of **proportionality**. To determine proportionality, we turn (again) to a multi-factored analysis. Those advising on this matter will be obliged to determine whether a planned response is excessive when balanced against the value of the military objective sought to be gained. Consideration must also be given to whether it adequately distinguishes between military objectives and civilian property. Questions like these, about proportionality, are why the nuclear response to a hack is simply unfeasible—nobody would think that it was a proportionate response.[40]

These questions are particularly indeterminate in the cyber context. We can see the tension these uncertainties cause in the Department of Defense's 2011 report to Congress.[41] In some ways, the report is revolutionary. For the first time ever it announced that the U.S. will use cyber offensive weapons in self-defense (a policy that was conspicuously absent from earlier Defense Department policy pronouncements). But, as Jack Goldsmith of Harvard has pointed out,[42] this policy is limited to retaliation for "significant" or "crippling" cyber attacks. Small scale insurgency attacks or other forms of espionage are immune from retaliation. This might be proportionate but it also means that those forms of intrusion (which are, recall, indistinguishable from large-scale attacks before execution) are not capable of being deterred. Rather, the report seems to call for a comprehensive strategy to deal with these more frequent forms of cyber conflict. Yet no such strategy exists.

In addition, since the laws of armed conflict require a nation to **avoid collateral damage** where possible and to minimize it where it is unavoidable, the uncertainty of cyber effects from an attack make offensive cyber weapons particularly problematic. Those responses we can imagine (hacking back into an adversary's systems, for example) might cause collateral damage to civilian property or systems that is disproportionate in nature (often because, in the cyber realm, they are inextricably intertwined). More to the point, unlike kinetic weapons, where collateral damage predictions are readily calculated, in the cyber domain we have yet to develop an adequate methodology for making that sort of assessment.

It was precisely considerations of this sort that caused the Bush Administration to shelve plans to launch a cyber attack on Iraq—they had no idea what the collateral consequences of the attack might be.[43] Likewise, the same sorts of concerns were part of the

---

39. An excellent detailed early analysis of these questions that has largely withstood the changing technology with only modest need for revision is Thomas C. Wingfield, "Legal Aspects of Offensive Information Operations in Space," <http://www.au.af.mil/au/awc/awcgate/dod-io-legal/wingfield.pdf>. A nice historical oddity is that this analysis, which focuses almost exclusively on what we would today characterize as cyber operations, is nominally about "information" operations and focused on those that occur in "space" (where cyber operations were first considered).

40. Hence the *Tallinn Manual*'s conclusion that "[a] cyber attack that may be expected to cause incidental loss of civilian live, injury to civilians, damage to civilian objects, or a combination thereof, which would be excessive in relation to the concrete and direct military advantage anticipated is prohibited." *Id.* Rule 51.

41. Department of Defense Cyberspace Policy Report (November 2011), <http://www.defense.gov/home/features/2011/0411_cyberstrategy/docs/NDAA%20Section%20934%20Report_For%20webpage.pdf>.

42. Jack Goldsmith, "Can We Stop the Global Cyber Arms Race?," *Washington Post*, February 1, 2010, sec. Opinions, <http://www.washingtonpost.com/wp-dyn/content/article/2010/01/31/AR2010013101834.html>.

43. John Markoff and Thom Shanker, "Halted '03 Iraq Plan Illustrates U.S. Fear of Cyberwar Risk," *New York Times*, August 2, 2009, sec. U.S. / Politics, <http://www.nytimes.com/2009/08/02/us/politics/02cyber.html>.

calculus that led the United States to eschew a cyber attack against Libya in connection with the NATO-led military operation in 2011.[44]

As if those complexities were not enough, the lack of distinction in cyber fires and the borderless nature of the Internet can lead to a host of other almost insoluble legal issues regarding the use of cyber force. Consider the following sample of questions and issues:

- International law allows the targeting of combatants who are participants in the war. Killing armed combatants is a lawful act and is not murder. But who is a cyber combatant? Is a civilian hacker an armed combatant? How about a civilian employee with cyber responsibilities in a non-military government agency (like the CIA or its Russian equivalent)? If they are combatants then, in effect, the domain of lawful warfare is as broad and wide as the Internet itself.[45]

- Certain targets, like hospitals, are immune from attack under international law. But IP addresses don't come with labels that say "I am a hospital server," and most server systems are inextricably intertwined with one another. How can a military attack ensure that it avoids damage to privileged targets? And if it cannot, does that mean that any cyber attack is, *de jure* illegal? Surely not. But then the obligation must be (may be?) to adequately map your opponents' networks before an attack to minimize unexpected collateral consequences.[46]

- Under the laws of war, combatants must carry their arms openly and be readily identified as combatants by the uniforms they wear. The main purpose of this is to allow opposing military forces to distinguish between combatants and non-combatant civilians, and target only lawful combatants. Yet many cyber warriors do not wear uniforms. Nor, even if they do, are they readily distinguishable from civilians since the domain of conflict is a virtual one, where a combatant's "uniform" is not readily observable. Indeed, one of the principal tactics of a cyber warrior is to hide his actions behind the veneer of seemingly innocent civilian activity (an innocuous e-mail, for example). Since these cyber soldiers don't abide by the laws of war, does that mean that they (like terrorists) are not entitled to the protections of those laws when identified and/or captured?

- One of the gravest violations of the laws of armed conflict is the act of perfidy, that is, falsely surrendering or seeking a truce under a white flag and then using the cover to wage war. Yet one of the most effective tactics used in cyber conflict is the false flag — appearing to surrender or be an innocent while using that opportunity to intrude malware into an opponent's system.[47]

- The laws of armed conflict respect the rights of neutrals. World War I was, at least in part, exacerbated by the German violation of Belgium's neutrality. In the cyber domain, however, successful attacks will almost always violate neutrality by using

---

44. Eric Schmitt and Thom Shanker, "U.S. Debated Cyberwarfare Against Libya," *New York Times*, October 17, 2011, <http://www.nytimes.com/2011/10/18/world/africa/cyber-warfare-against-libya-was-debated-by-us.html?_r=1&hp>.

45. The *Tallinn Manual* concludes that all categories of persons may participate in cyber operations, *id.* Rule 25, but that civilians participating in such operations "forfeit their protection from attacks for such time as they so participate," *id.* Rule 29. The Tallinn experts were not in agreement as to how to define the temporal limits of direct participation in hostilities, *id.* Rule 29, Comment 3 — a disagreement that is echoed in the kinetic realm.

46. Here, the *Tallinn Manual*'s admonition that computer networks that form an "integral part" of medical units may not be targeted, *id.* Rule 71, seems to fly in the face of technical reality. How do we identify those networks with confidence?

47. *Compare, e.g., Tallinn Manual*, Rule 60 (narrowly defining perfidy in cyber context).

servers and computers that are located in a non-combatant country, as a means of masking an attack. Only a fool would, for example, initiate a direct attack from a U.S. server to, say, one in China. Yet, due respect for the principle of neutrality suggests that this is precisely what is required by international law. At least one report indicates that lawyers in the Department of Justice in fact believe that network attacks on servers outside of a formal war zone require the host country's permission and that, absent the permission, the attacks are unlawful.[48]

- Historically, military conflict has been confined to a relatively well-defined geographic area. To be sure, attacks on factors of production in the enemy state were also lawful, but the remainder of the globe was typically considered outside the area of conflict. Yet, now, the cyber combatant can be literally anywhere on the globe. How, if at all, should that fact limit or constrain the use of armed force? Does U.S. Cyber Command have authority to execute cyber military operations against adversaries wherever they may be? What if they are in a friendly country, like the United Kingdom? What if they are here in the U.S.? As the *Tallinn Manual* dryly puts it "[r]estrictions based on geographical limitations may be particularly difficult to implement in the context of cyber warfare."[49]

Case Study: Russia v. Ukraine

A partial list of cyber activities associated in open source media with the conflict between Russia and Ukraine over Crimea and Eastern Ukraine (as of Summer 2014) would include:

- Russian pre-attack cyber espionage and network mapping of Ukrainian systems;
- Degradation of Ukrainian telecommunications links to Crimea during the Russian invasion, followed by the severing of cross-border telecommunications connections;
- Russian social network sites blocking sites and pages with pro-Ukrainian messages;
- Russia Today (the Russian English-language website) being hacked with the word "Nazi" prominently inserted into headlines to describe Russian actors;
- An IP-telephonic attack on the mobile phones of Ukrainian parliamentarians;
- Russian forces jamming cell phones and severing Internet connections with Ukraine (and seizing telecommunications facilities in Crimea);
- Multiple hacking operations under the #OpRussia and #OpUkraine hashtags including recruitment operations among local cyber capable actors;
- A large scale DDoS attack on Russian websites (including the Kremlin and the Russian central bank) [Russia denied these were linked to the Ukrainian conflict];

---

48. Ellen Nakashima, "Pentagon Is Debating Cyber-Attacks," *Washington Post*, November 6, 2010, <http://www.washingtonpost.com/wp-dyn/content/article/2010/11/05/AR2010110507464.html>.

49. *Tallinn Manual*, Rule 21, Comment 2.

- Similar DDoS attacks on Ukrainian news sites, most noticeably during the Crimean "independence" vote, using the DirtJumper botnet; and
- Noticeable activity by hackers of Turkish, Tunisian, Albanian and Palestinian origin, more commonly attacking Russian sites in support of Ukraine.

One aspect of the conflict worthy of commentary is the evident restraint by both parties. It appears, for example, that no efforts have been made to have a kinetic, destructive effect on critical infrastructure on either side of the border. On that basis we might conclude that the cyber aspects of the Russo-Ukrainian conflict fall below the threshold of true cyber war, and reflect, more generally, only heightened cyber operations.

Non-International Armed Conflict, Non-State Actors and Sub-War Acts

Questions of *jus ad bellum* and *jus in bello* barely begin to delimit the scope of legal questions relating to the nature of cyber conflict in this new domain. Few, if any, of the conflicts we can imagine will involve actions that rise to the level of an armed attack sufficient to trigger the application of international humanitarian law. Even the pseudo-conflict in the cyber domain between Russian and Ukrainian actors seems not to have involved "armed attacks" as international humanitarian law would define them.

More to the point, even fewer of the conflicts will involve armed actions between the military of nation states. Even if the tools used rise to the level of sufficient significance to merit classification as an armed attack, the likely combatants may well be non-state actors. To be sure, a true cyber war between nation states may occur, but it is most likely to occur in the context of a kinetic armed conflict. Put colloquially, our cyber war with China will be coincident with a military confrontation over Taiwan.

As a consequence, much of the discussion of the application of international humanitarian law to cyber seems rather misfocused on events that are unlikely to occur. Instead, we can imagine any number of far more plausible conflicts that involve a nation state and a group of non-state actors (whether those actors are organized groups or *ad hoc* amalgams of individuals, and whether those groups are motivated by profit, pride, or politics) and we can equally imagine conflicts where the tools of choice involve activity that is below the level of an armed attack in international law—acts we might call "sub war" acts, involving the degradation of information, the disruption of communications, or even the destruction of capabilities.

How should we characterize these types of activities as a legal matter and what, if any, international laws govern the conduct of these activities? The answer to these questions requires, in the first instance, that we develop a taxonomy of cyber conflict, in effect scoping the domain. An effective taxonomy allows for two useful and interrelated definitional questions to be identified: First, it permits us to understand the domain of certain applicable laws and identify those domains for which applicable laws have yet to be developed. Second, it allows us to specify the boundary questions between domains—boundaries that often require legal, as well as practical definition.

To see what this means in the context of the cyber domain consider that our first effort to map international humanitarian law onto the domain of cyber conflict (through the efforts of the *Tallinn Manual* experts) has been limited to categorizing how existing international humanitarian law will apply to nation-versus-nation cyber conflicts that rise to the level of an armed conflict. These same experts have also announced their next project (helpfully called *Tallinn 2.0*) that will, when completed, attempt to characterize how international law will apply to sub-war conflicts between nations.

But that, as the chart below makes clear, barely begins to scratch the surface of the potential modalities of cyber conflict. We have no real idea (much less international agreement) as to what law applies to cyber conflicts between say, a nation and a non-state actor when the level of the conflict is equivalent to an armed attack. Put prosaically, what international law applies to a U.S. response to an attack by a hacker group that destroys a nuclear power plant (for avowed ideological reasons)?

Nor do we know what law might apply when a nation acts preemptively against a non-state actor to forestall such an armed attack. And we also have no idea how the laws might change in either of these situations when the cyber operation involves the use of tools that have less than kinetic "armed attack" effects. And, finally, international law generally applies only to States, not to individuals or non-state actors, so the domain of conflict between non-state groups is utterly *terra incognito* for the law.

Figure 2. A Taxonomy of IHL Questions

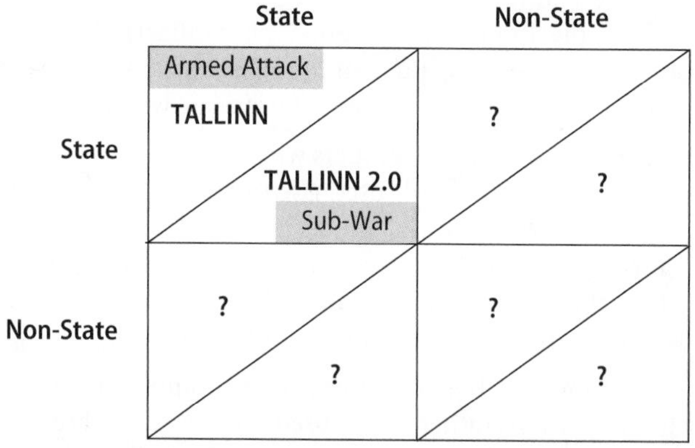

Conceptualizing the domain in this way gives us a useful theoretical framework for a broader consideration of international humanitarian law in the cyber domain. It helps us identify at least two important boundary questions that the law will need to address:

- What is the difference, in the cyber domain, between acts of armed warfare and sub-war acts?
- How do we distinguish non-state actors from state actors, and what rules of command and control allow us to attribute the acts of non-state actors to a nation state?

It also allows us to identify two important questions of the appropriate scope and jurisdiction of law in the domain:

- What international law controls cyber conflicts between a state and a non-state group?
- What international law controls cyber conflicts between two non-state groups in the cyber domain?

To be sure, these questions may have tentative answers that are derived from existing international law. There is a relatively robust doctrine of attribution, for example, that defines the degree of control necessary to impute the actions of a non-state actor to a state.[50] Likewise, norms of international humanitarian law applicable in non-international armed conflict in the kinetic context are well-known (to include, *e.g.*, the provisions of Article 3 common to the four Geneva Conventions (1949), the 1977 Second Additional Protocol to the Geneva Conventions (where the State has ratified), and norms of customary international law). But there is no international agreement that those laws are applicable in the cyber domain in the first instance. And there is even less agreement as to how they might be implemented if applicable.

Finally, virtually no law exists regarding the reciprocal obligations of the non-state actors themselves. While, for the most part, international law does not regulate the conduct of individuals and non-State actors, perhaps in the cyber domain we will need to modify that background rule. For in cyber, more so than in the physical world, individuals and groups of individuals are uniquely empowered to contest cyber conflicts against a nation state and against each other. It would be odd, indeed, if there were no law to govern such conflicts.

The WikiLeaks War and Beyond

This last scenario outlined above, of a non-state actor v. non-state actor conflict, is far from hypothetical. To see that, reflect on what we might call the "WikiLeaks War" from 2010.

With the disclosure of classified information, WikiLeaks appeared to be launching an assault on state authority (and more particularly, that of the United States, though other governments were also identified). Confronted with WikiLeaks' anti-sovereign slant, the institutions of traditional commerce soon responded. There is no evidence that any of the governments ordered any actions, but the combination of governmental displeasure and clear public disdain for Julian Assange soon led a number of major Western corporations (MasterCard, PayPal, and Amazon, to name three) to withhold services from WikiLeaks. Amazon reclaimed rented server space that WikiLeaks had used and the two financial institutions stopped processing donations made to WikiLeaks.[51]

What soon followed might well be described as the first cyber battle between non-state actors. Supporters of WikiLeaks, loosely organized in a group under the name "Anonymous" (naturally) began a series of distributed denial-of-service (DDoS) attacks on the websites of the major corporations that they thought had taken an anti-WikiLeaks stand, in order to flood the websites and prevent legitimate access to them.[52] The website of the Swedish

---

50. *E.g.*, International Law Commission, Responsibility of States for Internationally Wrongful Acts (2001 Draft), <http://legal.un.org/ilc/texts/instruments/english/draft%20articles/9_6_2001.pdf>.

51. Ashlee Vance, "WikiLeaks Struggles to Stay Online After Cyberattacks," *New York Times*, December 3, 2010, sec. World / Europe, <http://www.nytimes.com/2010/12/04/world/europe/04domain.html?_r=1&ref=world>.

52. John F. Burns and Ravi Somaiya, "Hackers Attack Those Seen as WikiLeaks Enemies," *New York Times*, December 8, 2010, sec. World, <http://www.nytimes.com/2010/12/09/world/09wiki.html?ref=todayspaper>. Joby Warrick and Rob Pegoraro, "WikiLeaks Avoids Shutdown as Supporters Worldwide Go on the Offensive," *Washington Post*, <http://www.washingtonpost.com/wp-dyn/content/article/2010/12/08/AR2010120804038.html?hpid=moreheadlines>.

prosecuting authority (who is seeking Mr. Assange's extradition to Sweden to face criminal charges) was also hacked. Some of the coordination for the DDoS attacks was done through social media, such as Facebook or Twitter.[53] Meanwhile, other supporters created hundreds of mirror sites, replicating WikiLeaks content, so that it couldn't be effectively shut down.[54] The hackers even adopted a military-style nomenclature, dubbing their efforts "Operation Payback."

And when Anonymous attacked, the other side fought back. The major sites used defensive cyber protocols to oppose Anonymous. Most attacks were relatively unsuccessful. The announced attack on Amazon, for example, was abandoned shortly after it began because the assault was ineffective. Perhaps even more tellingly, someone (no group has, to my knowledge, publicly claimed credit) began an offensive cyber operation against Anonymous itself. Anonymous ran its operations through a website, AnonOps.net, and that website was subject to DDoS counterattacks that took it offline for a number of hours.[55] In short, a conflict readily recognizable as a battle between competing forces took place in cyberspace, waged almost exclusively between non-state actors.[56]

The failure of Anonymous to effectively target corporate websites and its relative vulnerability to counter-attack are, likely, only temporary circumstances. Anonymous (and its opponents) will learn from this battle and approach the next one with a greater degree of skill and a better perspective on how to achieve their ends. Indeed, many of their more recent attacks—such as the effort to shut down the Vatican website—show a great deal more sophistication and effectiveness.[57]

Moreover, Anonymous has demonstrated that even with its limited capacity it can do significant damage to individuals and companies. When Aaron Barr, the corporate head of a security firm HB Gary, announced that his firm was investigating the identity of Anonymous participants, Anonymous retaliated. They hacked the HB Gary network (itself a significantly embarrassing development for a cybersecurity company) and took possession of internal emails that, in turn, suggested that HB Gary was engaged in some questionable business practices. As a result Barr was forced to resign his post—exactly the type of individual consequence that is sure to deter an effective counter-insurgent response.

More to the point, Anonymous has made quite clear that it intends to continue to prosecute the cyberwar against, among others, the United States. "It's a guerrilla cyberwar—that's what I call it," says Barrett Brown, 29, a self-described senior strategist and "propagandist" for Anonymous.[58] "It's sort of an unconventional asymmetrical act of

---

53. Ashlee Vance and Miguel Helft, "Hackers Give Web Companies a Test of Free Speech," *New York Times*, December 8, 2010, sec. Technology, <http://www.nytimes.com/2010/12/09/technology/09net.html?_r=1&hp>.

54. Ravi Somaiya, "Hundreds of WikiLeaks Mirror Sites Appear," *New York Times*, <http://www.nytimes.com/2010/12/06/world/europe/06wiki.html?_r=1&ref=world>.

55. Esther Addley and Josh Halliday, "Operation Payback cripples Mastercard site in revenge for WikiLeaks ban," <http://unlawflcombatnt.proboards.com/thread/8205>.

56. The sovereign states were not, of course, mere bystanders. Dutch police have arrested one suspected member of Anonymous. Tim Hwang, "WikiLeaks and the Internet's Long War," *Washington Post*, <http://www.washingtonpost.com/wp-dyn/content/article/2010/12/10/AR2010121002604.html?hpid=opinionsbox1>. And, nobody can be certain that the counterattacks on AnonOps.net were not state-authorized or state-initiated.

57. Nicole Perlroth and John Markoff, "In Attack on Vatican Web Site, a Glimpse of Hackers' Tactics," *New York Times*, February 26, 2012, sec. Technology, <https://www.nytimes.com/2012/02/27/technology/attack-on-vatican-web-site-offers-view-of-hacker-groups-tactics.html>.

58. Michael Isikoff, "Hacker Group Vows 'Cyberwar' on U.S. Government, Business," March 8, 2011, <http://www.msnbc.msn.com/id/41972190/ns/technology_and_science-security>.

warfare that we're involved in, and we didn't necessarily start it. I mean, this fire has been burning." Or, consider the manifesto posted by Anonymous, declaring cyberspace independence from world governments: "I declare the global social space we are building together to be naturally independent of the tyrannies and injustices you seek to impose on us. You have no moral right to rule us nor do you possess any real methods of enforcement we have true reason to fear."[59] In February 2012, Anonymous went further—formally declaring "war" against the United States and calling on its citizens to rise and revolt.[60]

Indeed, in many ways, Anonymous conducts itself in some of the same manner that an opposing military organization might. Also in February 2012, for example, it was disclosed that Anonymous had hacked into a telephone conversation between the FBI and Scotland Yard, the subject of which was the development of a prosecution case against Anonymous.[61] That sort of tactic—intercepting the enemy's communications—is exactly the type of tactic an insurgency might use. And by disclosing the capability, Anonymous has successfully sown uncertainty about how much *else* it might be intercepting.

In advancing their agenda, the members of Anonymous look somewhat like the anarchists who led movements in the late 19th and early 20th centuries, albeit anarchists with a vastly greater network and far more ability to advance their nihilistic agenda through individual action.[62] And, like the anarchists of old, they have their own internal disputes. In 2011 another group called "Black Hat" effectively declared war on Anonymous because it disagreed with the Anonymous agenda.[63] But even more, Anonymous and its imitators look like the non-state insurgencies we have faced in Iraq and Afghanistan—small groups of non-state actors using asymmetric means of warfare to destabilize and disrupt existing political authority.

Espionage or Traditional Military Activity?

To all of this, one must add another dimension of legal confusion; one that has bearing on cyber war both under international law and under domestic American law. The problem arises, as do so many such problems, from the fundamental nature of the Internet, in this case, the lack of any ability to distinguish between cyber espionage intrusions and cyber attacks. Our laws, however, traditionally rely on and define that distinction. Spying is spying and fighting is fighting. So much so that the actual laws that control the two

---

59. The manifesto was posted as a YouTube video: Anonymous to the Governments of the World (April 25, 2010), <http://www.youtube.com/watch?v=gbqC8BnvVHQ>.

60. The video declaration is available at: <http://planetsave.com/2012/02/28/anonymous-declares-war-on-united-states-government/>. The transcript includes the following: "Our time for democracy is here. Our time for real change is here. This is America's time, to have its own revolution. Therefore, Anonymous has decided to openly declare war on the United States government. This is a call to arms. We call upon the Citizens of the United States to stand beside us in overthrowing this corrupted body and call upon a new era. Our allegiance is to the American people, because they are us, and we are them."

61. Scott Shane, "FBI Admits Hacker Group's Eavesdropping," *The New York Times* (Feb. 3, 2012), <https://www.nytimes.com/2012/02/04/us/fbi-admits- hacker-groups-eavesdropping.html?_r=1>.

62. *See* Abe Greenwald, "The Return of Anarchism," *Commentary* at 32 (March 2011).

63. A Message to Anonymous from #Team Black Hat (December 2011), <https://www.youtube.com/watch?v=PkHhx_Hk3c0&feature=player_embedded#!>. For another report of internal divisions in Anonymous, *see* "ITAC Blog?» Blog Archive?» Trouble in Paradise for Hacker Group Anonymous?," <http://itacidentityblog.com/trouble-in-paradise-for-hacker-group-anonymous>.

activities are contained in completely different parts of the United States Code of laws. Though all practitioners know that the strict distinction is a bit of a chimera, the formalism still is of legal significance: Military matters are all regulated by Title 10 of the U.S. Code, while intelligence matters are all regulated by Title 50.[64]

Which law applies makes a great deal of difference. Domestically, it defines who is in control — a matter of both operational importance and (in the real world of Washington) a matter of some concern to those who are protecting their bureaucratic turf. It also makes a difference in determining who in Congress gets told about an operation and when. Covert intelligence operations are reported to different committees than military operations and secret military operations sometimes never get reported at all.[65] On the other hand covert operations can be, and sometimes are, publicly denied and never intended to become known, while military operations almost invariably become public at some point.

A recent example of the importance of this distinction (from the non-cyber realm) was the killing of Osama bin Laden. Though the operation was carried out by Navy Seals using military helicopters and even though it was not intended to remain secret once the operation was completed, the entire project was officially an intelligence operation run by then-CIA Director Leon Panetta.[66]

The line between the two types of activity is often indistinct (and growing more so by the day). Yet we do attempt to define the line (albeit in a rococo way, typical of how Washington writes law). We first define covert activities to be those secret operations that are intended "to influence political, economic, or military conditions abroad, where it is intended that the role of the United States Government will not be apparent or acknowledged publicly." We then say, however, that the definition does not include "traditional military activities,"[67] involving operational planning or execution and using military personnel.

In some ways this line is clear, but in the cyber realm it becomes impossibly complex. Think, for example, of the simple idea of communications. It has long been a traditional military activity to disrupt an opponent's communications. We shot down carrier pigeons and we bombed radio relay stations. Today, when the opponent will rely on Internet communications, the military sees those operations as within its zone of responsibility. But the CIA, not unreasonably, sees cyber operations that are intended to be covert as part of its own domain. That's why the CIA and the military are in a turf war over who should carry out certain types of internet operations.[68]

It also makes a difference that the cyber realm has no geographic borders. The CIA asserts that classic covert operations can occur world-wide and that traditional military activities are confined to a relatively well-defined battle space (say, the area near Afghanistan). The military sees cyber operations against al-Qaeda as a form of traditional

---

64. For those interested in an extended discussion of the Title 10/Title 50 distinction — its history and import — I recommend, Robert Chesney, "Military-Intelligence Convergence and the Law of the Title 10/Title 50 Debate" 5 *J. Nat'l Sec. Law & Plcy* 539 (2012), <http://papers.ssrn.com/sol3/papers.cfm?abstract_id=1945392>.

65. One interesting note is that an effort to mandate quarterly briefings to the House and Senate Armed Services Committees on cyber operations in the Fiscal Year 2012 National Defense Authorization Act did not survive conference, from which one may take a negative inference if one wishes.

66. "CIA Chief Panetta: Obama Made 'Gutsy' Decision on Bin Laden Raid," *PBS NewsHour* (May 3, 2011), <http://www.pbs.org/newshour/bb/terrorism/jan-june11/panetta_05-03.html>.

67. 50 U.S.C. §413b(e).

68. Ellen Nakashima, "Pentagon Is Debating Cyber-Attacks," *Washington Post*, November 6, 2010, <http://www.washingtonpost.com/wp-dyn/content/article/2010/11/05/AR2010110507464.html>.

military activity, because it is a lawful military opponent. And, they argue their activities need to be world-wide precisely because the al-Qaeda movement knows no geographic boundaries.

The distinction becomes even more complex when we consider that some of these activities might actually take place inside the United States. The Constitution and intelligence statutes delimit the nature of intelligence activity that U.S. officials may undertake, especially when operating domestically. In general, the purpose of the domestic law is to permit the exploitation of foreign intelligence sources while protecting American civil liberties. It also serves as a bedrock foundational source for the authorization of all national intelligence activity. Likewise, strict laws limit how the military may operate inside America's borders. And yet, inasmuch as cyber is borderless, it is difficult, if not impossible, to conduct an operation wholly outside American borders.

Finally, consider international law. We have already discussed the legal limitations on military activity that arise from international law. By contrast, in the context of foreign laws or international law, espionage is sometimes characterized as lawless.[69] When exploiting sources overseas the premise is that good work is all about breaking the law of some foreign jurisdiction. Without doubt any cyber espionage done by U.S. assets in, say, China, violates domestic Chinese law, but it is of little concern to American law.

The question is slightly more complex when one considers applicable customary international law. That is the part of international law that is defined by the customs of nations. Here the uncertainties are greater, both as to the content of the law and as to its binding nature. Thus, for example, it may be that if a cyber attack is a "traditional military activity" it will need to respect the neutrality of other countries and not use their servers to assist in the attack, but that if we characterize the action as a "covert intelligence action," it is lawful to use neutral countries as a transit point surreptitiously.

Organizing to Contest Cyber Conflict

The application of law to cyber conflict is also confounded by what we might call the "assumption of rapidity"—the predominant belief that things in cyberspace all happen at lightning quick speed. If that is true, then the necessity for a legal determination can be an insurmountable problem.

Decisions applying law to cyber operations are fraught with national importance. It is likely, therefore, that as a matter of policy we will want them to be made at the highest levels of government, and not at the level of, say, a Defense Department systems administrator. But, even the identity of the appropriate decision-maker is uncertain. The Commander of Strategic Command has said that he believes he can make the decision to respond to a cyber attack degrading U.S. defense capabilities. Some in the Air Force, focusing on the speed of cyber events, have suggested that there is a need to develop an

---

69. Some contest this characterization. They suggest that surveillance and espionage may transgress the provisions of the International Covenant on Civil and Political Rights ("ICCPR"), <http://www.ohchr.org/en/professionalinterest/pages/ccpr.aspx> which provides that: "No one shall be subjected to arbitrary or unlawful interference with his privacy, family, home or correspondence, nor to unlawful attacks on his honour and reputation." The International Court of Justice has, in at least one unique situation, suggested that spying on the communications between a nation and its legal advisors is unlawful. *See Timor-Leste v. Australia*, (ICJ 2014), <http://www.icj-cij.org/docket/files/156/18078.pdf>.

automated response for certain cyber scenarios. Many observers are of the view, however, that because there currently exist no definitive rules of engagement for cyber war, at least as a first approximation, all decision-making will have to be conducted at the level of the President.

This impulse for centralized control conflicts with another of the unique aspects of cyberspace that will particularly affect our organizational structures and processes—the rapidity with which cyber activities occur. When a cyber domain attack is perceived to occur at the pace of milliseconds, it may be that the deterrent or defensive response will need to occur with equal rapidity. As General Alexander, wearing his military hat as the first Commander of U.S. Cyber Command, told the Senate, "[A] commander's right to general self-defense is clearly established in both U.S. and international law. Although this right has not been specifically established by legal precedent to apply to attacks in cyberspace, it is reasonable to assume that returning fire in cyberspace, as long as it complied with the law of war principles (e.g. proportionality), would be lawful."[70] We therefore face a situation where it is possible (indeed, likely) that some subordinate commanding officer may feel compelled (and authorized) to act without higher authorization if the commander perceives that a cyber attack has begun. And what is true for the military may also be true of private actors who are protecting their own networks. They may feel the need to act instantaneously without the benefit of reflection.

This perception of the need for rapidity reflects a sea-change in conception. The physics of the Internet is believed to destroy time and space.[71] Even in the nuclear domain, the imminence of the threat was measured in minutes, allowing the development of processes (like the classic nuclear code "football") that permitted a considered, albeit hurried, human response. As General Alexander put it, some believe that the cyber domain is best characterized as one in which a near-instantaneous response is necessary.

That characterization may not, however, be accurate and its prevalence may actually be pernicious. A counter-response may be essential immediately as a purely defensive measure, but it is likely that a deterrence-based cyber response can be delayed without significant cost. As Martin Libicki pointed out in a 2009 RAND study, a cyber response is unlikely to be able to disable a cyber attacker completely. As a consequence, for deterrence policy, "[m]ore important than [the] speed [of the response] is the ability to convince the attacker not to try again. Ironically, for a medium that supposedly conducts its business at warp speed, *the urgency of retaliation is governed by the capacity of the human mind to be convinced, not the need to disable the attacking computer before it strikes again.*"[72]

The problem for cyber response is, in some ways, the same organizational challenge faced in other domains. The issue is "how to sustain human control [that is, maintain a] man-in-the-loop.... For example, control structures can have human control to unlock weapons systems, or automatic system unlock with human intervention required to override. An example of the former is the control of nuclear weapons and of the latter,

---

70. Advanced Questions for Lieutenant General Keith Alexander, USA Nominee for Commander, United States Cyber Command in Hearings Before the United States Senate Armed Services Committee at 25 (April 13, 2010), <http://www.washingtonpost.com/wp-srv/politics/documents/questions.pdf>; *see also* William J. Lynn, III, "Defending a New Domain: The Pentagon's Cyberstrategy," 97 at 103 *Foreign Affairs* (Sept./Oct. 2010) (US military must "respond to attacks as they happen or even before they arrive"), <http://www.foreignaffairs.com/articles/66552/william-j-lynn-iii/defending-a-new-domain>.

71. Remarks of Kim Taipale, Duke University Center on Law, Ethics and National Security (April 2010), <http://www.law.duke.edu/lens/conferences/2010/program>.

72. Martin Libicki, *Cyberdeterrence and Cyberwar*, at 62 (RAND, 2009) (emphasis added).

the control of a nuclear power reactor. This may be high tech, but the big questions are political and organizational."[73] Indeed, the problems associated with automated responses were demonstrated, in a more prosaic fashion, in 2010 when automated trading rules caused a 1000 point decline in the Dow Jones Industrial Average in less than 10 minutes of trading on the New York Stock Exchange.[74]

Our organizational structures and processes have not yet matured sufficiently in the cyber domain to understand this distinction, much less to enable the implementation of policies that maximize the sustainment of human control at senior policy levels. To the contrary, it would appear today that the default in response to a cyber attack is to permit critical decisions to be made at an operational level, informed only by system assurance necessity.

The conduct of cyber operations, moreover, will yield an increasing centralization of command and control. For analogies of this trend, we need not look far. One of the least-well-kept secrets in America is the CIA's operation of a covert drone campaign in the borderland between Pakistan and Afghanistan. If press reports are to be believed, the program has been successful in steadily constraining action by the core al-Qaeda leadership and slowly whittling down their numbers.

One little recognized consequence of this new practical reality has been a restructuring and centralization of command and control. Because the drone program acts at a distance, and because it is mostly operated from inside the United States, we have seen the development of a system where key targeting decisions are being taken by increasingly more responsible and senior officials. Indeed, as Professor Gregory McNeal, of Pepperdine University describes it,[75] when any significant chance of collateral damage from an attack exists the "go/no-go" decision is typically made by a general officer and is sometimes even made by the Secretary of Defense or the President.

Cyber weapons, just like drones, act at a distance. They are often deployed with forethought and are part of a pre-planned series of military actions. As such they are, like drones, far more likely to be controlled by more senior authority than is typical for a military engagement.

It is difficult to overstress how significant this change truly is. In war as we know it in the physical world, decisions are typically made by a commander on the scene in relatively close geographic proximity to events. One consequence of that situation is that legal judgments about proposed courses of action will be made by attorneys who are attached to combat units at the front and who have situational awareness of the conflict.

By contrast, with the centralization of control here at home (a policy we might well approve for other reasons) we necessarily bring with that policy an increasingly important role for lawyers. Where there is time for reflection, lawyers are far more likely to intervene. Many, of course, will see this as a good thing, but it is likely to produce some odd results. It is no surprise that, as we noted earlier in this chapter, Department of Justice lawyers have tentatively concluded that as a matter of law, U.S. cyber attacks must respect the neutrality of other countries, and that therefore, they cannot transit through servers in

---

73. Tom Blau, "War and Technology in the Age of the Electron," *Defense Security Review* 94, 100 (London 1993).

74. Nelson Schwartz & Louise Story, "When Machines Take Control," *New York Times* at B1 (May 7, 2010).

75. McNeal, Gregory S., "Targeted Killing and Accountability" (March 5, 2014) <http://ssrn.com/abstract=1819583>. 102 *Georgetown Law Journal* 681–794 (2014).

neutral countries.[76] To non-lawyer technologists, this seems to elevate form over substance. We might as well say that the United States will disarm and not conduct cyber offensive operations, for no successful operation is likely where neutrality is strictly respected. Thus, while there are benefits to centralizing command and control, the proximity to unwieldy bureaucracy also poses challenges for the management of military operations.

———————

As this brief survey makes painfully clear, the law with regard to conflict in the cyber domain is in a state of flux. We have only begun the process of defining applicable legal norms through recent agreement that traditional international humanitarian law applies, with equal force, in the cyber domain. But that agreement is only the start of a conversation. Simply asserting legal equivalence leaves for further development a host of difficult and novel questions of application. Because the cyber domain is uniquely borderless, asymmetric, and distributed, traditional IHL will require modification and/or contextualization to realize its full potential. Five years from now, when this chapter is next revised, much of that work will likely have been done. For now, however, a conscientious practitioner can best be satisfied with identifying the relevant questions, issues and the general principles that will inform a practical answer.

———————

76. Stewart Baker, "Denial of Service," <http://www.foreignpolicy.com/articles/2011/09/30/denial _of_service?page=0,1>.

Chapter 13

International Arms Restraint by Treaty, Law, and Policy

Ronald F. Lehman, Guy B. Roberts, and Donald A. Mahley

In this chapter:

The Concept and Components of International Arms Restraint
Global Regimes and the Quest for Universality
Confrontation and the Cold War Legacy
Geopolitics, Conventional Forces and Regional Arms Restraint
Cooperation and Confidence-Building
Globalization and Fragmentation: Restraint's New Look
Contemporary Dynamics of International Arms Restraint
Selected Bibliography

Weapons shape the conduct and intensity of war and peace. As military technology advanced in different civilizations, "just war" traditions and customary rules of warfare increasingly referenced specific arms. Rules of restraint for armaments and their use have long been elements of diplomacy, strategy, law, and politics. The rapid increase in the destructiveness of weapons resulting from the industrial and nuclear revolutions, however, led to the emergence of international arms restraint as its own discipline. Endeavors in arms control, disarmament, nonproliferation, and confidence building accelerated during the twentieth century and peaked as the Cold War ended. The centrality of formal bilateral arms negotiations then disappeared with the Soviet Union. International arms restraint increasingly blended back into the broader conduct of international relations. At the beginning of the new millennium, however, as the phrase "weapons of mass destruction" and the letters "WMD"[1] entered everyday vocabulary, interest in international arms restraint renewed. Powerful forces of change including globalization, networking, the fragmentation of societies, and the spread of "dual-use" technologies challenge the basic principles, priorities, and mechanisms of international arms restraint.

---

1. Weapons of Mass Destruction (WMD) may be narrowly defined to include only nuclear and biological weapons, but chemical weapons are normally included even as radiological weapons are widely excluded as weapons of mass disruption. However, there is no universally accepted definition of WMD. Most definitions include reference to nuclear, chemical, biological and radiological weapons. Strangely, the definition of a WMD in the U.S. Federal Death Penalty Act of 1994, enacted as part of the Violent Crime Control and Law Enforcement Act of 1994 (H.R. 3355, Pub. L. 103-322), includes bombs, grenades, mines, or any gun with a barrel larger than one-half inch. *See* W. Seth Carus, Defining "Weapons of Mass Destruction," Occasional Paper 8, National Defense University (2012).

The history of international arms restraints still reflects heavily the U.S.-Soviet/East-West confrontations. Many nations invested massive intellectual capital in developing policies and initiatives to deal with the bi-polar nuclear age. Many of the Cold War proposals seem archaic in today's world of global immigration, information technology, ethnic violence, and hyper-terrorism. Still, some of these approaches have new currency as interest grows in applying them to the problems of WMD proliferation and to confrontations in troubled regions such as the Middle East, South Asia, and the Korean Peninsula. This history enriches our understanding of the complexity of international arms restraint in its broader political, economic, cultural, and security contexts. Ultimately, however, efforts at arms restraint will require new approaches reflecting the changing international security environment and the rule of law within it.

The Concept and Components of International Arms Restraint

Defined comprehensively, international arms restraint includes any deliberate actions—unilateral, bilateral, or multilateral—impacting beyond the boundaries of a single nation that result in *de facto* or *de jure* quantitative, qualitative, or operational restraints on weapons, their means of delivery, the organizations or individuals that use them, and the infrastructures and activities that produce and support them. Although the selection of categories is somewhat arbitrary, the choice often carries with it a rich history of substantive debate. An examination of the most significant examples of international arms restraint will demonstrate why a strictly logical taxonomy would miss the dynamics inherent in the words we use today.[2]

Arms Control

During the Cold War, the "arms control" treaty seemed the measure of merit in international arms restraint. Mistrust between the United States and the Soviet Union resulted in ever more detailed documents. This approach reached its zenith with the bilateral strategic nuclear weapons treaties and carried over to multilateral treaties being negotiated in the same period, such as the Chemical Weapons Convention and the Treaty on Conventional Forces in Europe. The preoccupation with such treaties in the twentieth century, and the flood of such treaties as the Cold War ended, demonstrated the centrality of the concept and why "arms control" often referred to the full range of international arms restraints. The breakup of the Soviet Union and the Warsaw Pact produced greater interest in approaches in which the adversarial dimension was less central. Now "arms control" is increasingly defined as the formal negotiation of treaties limiting military forces and weapons, a more limited, and in some circles, a less enthusiastic definition. In addition, the emphasis on treaties—within the United States imposing the higher standard of a

---

2. This chapter updates Ronald F. Lehman, *International Arms Restraint by Treaty, Law and Policy*, Ch. 12, *in* NATIONAL SECURITY LAW, 2nd ed 381, 477 (John Norton Moore et al. eds., 2005), which in turn was an expansion of Ronald F. Lehman, *Nuclear Weapons: Deployment, Targeting and Deterrence*, Ch. 12, and *Measures to Reduce Tension and Prevent War*, Ch. 14, *in* NATIONAL SECURITY LAW 485, 641 (John Norton Moore et al. eds., 1990).

two-thirds vote in the U.S. Senate for consent to ratification—has diminished as less rigorous agreements are sought to deal with issues seen as less vital.[3]

Disarmament

"Disarmament" is an older term, predating the emergence of academic and professional disciplines specializing in arms and was for many years the comprehensive term for such considerations. For example, the title of the Geneva-based multilateral treaty negotiating body is the Conference on Disarmament (CD). Because the word inherently implied the elimination of "arms," in the age of nuclear deterrence the use of the word became polarized, positive for those who favored prompt abolition of nuclear weapons and negative for those who sought goals such as "strategic stability." This political dichotomy compelled the U.S. Congress to name the responsible American independent agency the "United States Arms Control and Disarmament Agency."[4] In this usage, "arms control" meant measures short of the complete elimination of weapons, "disarmament" a more ambitious end state possible only when the necessary conditions were achieved. Debate over when and how those conditions could be achieved are at the heart of political debate over arms control and disarmament.

Nonproliferation/Counterproliferation

"Proliferation" refers to the spread of weapons, primarily but not exclusively weapons of mass destruction, and their means of delivery. "Nonproliferation" as a policy increased in importance beginning in the 1950s, as many more countries acquired the knowledge, technology, and materials necessary to produce nuclear weapons. The nuclear Non-Proliferation Treaty of 1968 (NPT), an almost universal treaty, is the embodiment of this effort. The negotiation of the NPT, with its effort to reconcile the interests of the nuclear "haves" and "have-nots" highlighted a further distinction; namely between "horizontal" and "vertical" proliferation. Horizontal proliferation refers to the spread of weapons to previously non-weapons states; vertical proliferation refers to increases in the quantity or sometimes quality of the arsenals of existing weapons states. Nonproliferation has always placed a premium on prevention, but with the acquisition of weapons of mass destruction by governments such as the Democratic Peoples Republic of Korea (North Korea) and the Iraq of Saddam Hussein and the emergence of non-state, transnational supply networks such as those associated with A.Q. Khan of Pakistan, new emphasis has been placed on countering the process of proliferation and the results. Thus, nonproliferation and "counterproliferation" may be seen as the two overlapping fields of

---

3. *See* ARMS CONTROL IN A MULTI-POLAR WORLD (James Brown ed., 1996); ARMS CONTROL TOWARD THE 21ST CENTURY (Jeffrey A. Larsen & Gregory J. Rattray eds., 1996); NEW HORIZONS AND NEW STRATEGIES IN ARMS CONTROL (James Brown ed., 1998); TERENCE TAYLOR, ESCAPING THE PRISON OF THE PAST: RETHINKING ARMS CONTROL AND NON-PROLIFERATION MEASURES (1996); U.S. ARMS CONTROL AND DISARMAMENT AGENCY, ARMS CONTROL AND DISARMAMENT AGREEMENTS: TEXTS AND HISTORIES OF THE NEGOTIATIONS (1996); Lewis A. Dunn & Victor Alessi, *Arms Control by Other Means*, SURVIVAL, Winter 2000–2001, at 129; Ronald F. Lehman II, *Arms Control: Passing the Torch as Time Runs Out*, WASH. Q., Summer 1993, at 37; David Mussington, *Understanding Contemporary International Arms Transfers*, ADELPHI PAPER 1994.

4. Legislation creating the U.S. Arms Control and Disarmament Agency (ACDA) was signed by President John F. Kennedy on September 26, 1961. In April 1999, U.S. ACDA was disbanded and its functions and employees merged with the US Department of State.

prevention and response, although both terms are sometimes used to encompass the entire realm, as is "Combating WMD."[5]

Rules of Warfare

The laws of warfare, whether drawn from international law, domestic law, or canon law, place the traditional constraints of prevention, restraint, humanitarianism, proportionality, discrimination, legitimacy, and responsibility on military activities, including the use of weapons. The defense ministries and military commands of many nations also provide explicit "rules of engagement" for weapons targeting and combat operations. Indeed, most nuclear powers state their deterrence doctrines in terms consistent with international law and issue guidance designed to reduce "collateral damage." The implications of the rules of warfare, however, come into play at all levels of violence, including the use of "non-lethal" weapons. Whether one includes the rules of warfare within the realm of international arms restraints or follows the traditional consideration of them as a separate study, the interaction is significant. During negotiations of the Treaty of Rome creating the International Criminal Court (ICC), for example, proposals to include provisions aimed at the nuclear deterrent forces of the nuclear weapons states were rejected, but divisions remain about how such issues might be considered in the future.

Monitoring, Verification, and Compliance

Many treaties and agreements do not contain specifics for monitoring treaty-related activities, determining compliance, or redressing wrongs. These steps are left to the parties' own resources and to the less certain responses of other states and international bodies. The arms control and nonproliferation revolution at the end of the twentieth century, dealing with vital security interests in a climate of great distrust, began when confidence grew that "national technical means of verification" (NTM) could permit some monitoring of treaty accountable items. NTM was the term given to space-based photoreconnaissance, seismic sensors, and other essentially legal technology. Not surprisingly, the first major arms limitations were on items observable to NTM, such as atmospheric nuclear explosions, very large underground explosions, fixed land-based silo launchers for intercontinental ballistic missiles, and the number of missile submarines and missile launch tubes on

---

5. *See* Amitav Acharya & J. D. Kenneth Boutin, *Nuclear-Weapon-Free Zones in the New World Order: A Comparative Perspective, in* Non-Proliferation Agreements, Arrangements and Responses: Proceedings of the 1996 Canadian Non-Proliferation Workshop 117 (Andrew Latham ed., 1997); Arms Control and Weapons Proliferation in the Middle East and South Asia (Shelley A. Stahl & Geoffrey Kemp eds., 1992); Countering the Proliferation and Use of Weapons of Mass Destruction (Peter L. Hays et al. eds., 1998); Shai Feldman & Abdullah Toukan, Bridging the Gap: A Future Security Architecture for the Middle East (1997); Fighting Proliferation: New Concerns for the Nineties (Henry Sokolski ed., 1996); Yong-Sup Han, Nuclear Disarmament and Non-Proliferation in Northeast Asia (1995); Institute for Foreign Policy Analysis, Strategy, Force Structure, and Defense Planning for the Twenty-First Century (1997); Office of the Secretary of Defense, U.S. Department of Defense, Proliferation: Threat and Response (1996); Office of Technology Assessment, U.S. Congress, Proliferation of Weapons of Mass Destruction: Assessing the Risks (1993); Brad Roberts, Weapons Proliferation and World Order: After the Cold War (1996); Scott D. Sagan & Kenneth N. Waltz, The Spread of Nuclear Weapons: A Debate (1995); Etel Solingen, The Domestic Sources of Nuclear Postures: Influencing Fence-sitters in the Post-Cold War Era (1994); Robert Joseph, *Proliferation, Counter-Proliferation and NATO*, Survival, Spring 1996, at 111.

them. More extensive and intrusive monitoring would prove necessary to monitor more meaningful limits on nuclear forces and other activities difficult to monitor with NTM. An expanded envelope of agreed measures eventually included extensive data exchanges, displays of equipment, joint demonstration of verification instrumentation, routine visits, the exchange of telemetry tapes, and surprise on-site inspections. Monitoring, however is not the same thing as assessing the risk posed by cheating or reaching a judgment of non-compliance. To judge the risk posed by an agreement, the parties must also weigh the clarity of the agreement, the incentives to cheat, the availability of effective responses to cheating, and the likely timeliness of warning in order to enforce compliance or seek compensation or other remedy.[6]

Confidence-Building Measures (CBMs)

The idea of "confidence-building measures" seems straightforward until one surveys the diversity. Subtle differences have significance. For example, the distinction between confidence-building measures (CBMs) and more constraining confidence- and security-building measures (CSBMs) became important in European conventional arms negotiations as provisions being negotiated to insure accurate data about military units within declared locations imposed restraints on force levels and transits approaching those of more formal arms control. The term "cooperative measures" or "associated measures" originally applied specifically to steps such as site visits and equipment displays taken to facilitate the negotiation of treaties and confidence in compliance. Today, the term "cooperative measures" usually refers to broader forms of cooperation designed to reduce tensions and build bonds, particularly military-to-military or scientist-to-scientist. "Risk reduction" measures are typically CBMs seen to enhance stability in a period of crisis, for example, "hot line" communications between capitals and Nuclear Risk Reduction Centers (NRRC). Many other measures such as data exchanges, reciprocal visits, joint activities, and enhanced transparency fall under the category of confidence-building measures. At the height of the Cold War, confidence building was seen as easier to achieve than arms control treaties. Thus, CBMs were valued in their own right for reducing tensions and promoted as instrumental to other goals. Critics, however, saw them as symbolic at best and insufficient substitutes for more ambitious measures. With the end of the Cold War and as international arms restraint increasingly involves nations seeking to avoid or escape adversary relations, the term confidence building is used more as an attribute of broader cooperative activities rather than as a category of measures.[7]

---

6. *See* European Safeguards Research and Development Association and Joint Research Center, European Commission, Proceedings of Seminar on Modern Verification Regimes: Similarities, Synergies and Challenges (1998); J. Christian Kessler, Verifying Nonproliferation Treaties: Obligation, Process, and Sovereignty (1995); Verification: The Key to Arms Control in the 1990s (John G. Tower et al. eds., 1992); John Norton Moore, *Enhancing Compliance with International Law: A Neglected Remedy*, 39 Va. J. Int'l L. 881 (1999).

7. *See* Ronald F. Lehman II, *Measures to Reduce Tension and Prevent War*, *in* National Security Law 641 (John Norton Moore et al. eds., 1990); John J. Maresca, To Helsinki: The Conference on Security and Cooperation in Europe, 1973–1975 (1987); Non-Proliferation, Arms Control and Disarmament: Enhancing Existing Regimes and Exploring New Dimensions (Peter Gizewski, ed., 1997); Marie-France Desjardins, *Rethinking Confidence-Building Measures*, Adelphi Papers, 1996; *Russian Jet Flies Across U.S., Taking Photos of Military Bases*, N.Y. Times, Aug. 5, 1997, at A10; U.S. Arms Control and Disarmament Agency, Fact Sheet: Organization of American States (OAS) General Assembly Resolution on Conventional Arms Transparency and Confidence-Building in the Americas (July 30, 1997).

Unilateral and Declaratory Measures

International arms restraint operates across national boundaries, but negotiations are not always involved. Important restraints are often taken unilaterally. Among the more notable unilateral declarations were the Presidential Nuclear Initiatives (PNIs) of President George H. W. Bush in September 1991, designed to encourage nuclear reductions and consolidation of tactical nuclear weapons in the Soviet Union as its breakup seemed certain. Decisions to develop, deploy, cancel, or eliminate weapon systems can influence the behavior of other governments as can policy declarations. An announcement of policy or programmatic change is intended primarily to influence foreign behavior and may have a restraining effect with or without consultations. Such shaping of foreign decision-making is central to diplomacy and strategy. For many years the U.S. Congress required "Arms Control Impact Statements" to assess the implications of U.S. weapons research, development, or production. Decisions made primarily for domestic reasons, such as budget constraints, may not be seen as significant by foreign governments. A more certain way to insure that unilateral acts are reciprocated is to engage in prior consultations more or less linked to the decision. Joint efforts sometimes lead to "Parallel Unilateral Declarations (PUDs)"—unilateral policy declarations well-coordinated and issued so as to reinforce each other.[8]

Security Assurances

Many nations that could acquire weapons of mass destruction choose not to do so. Many factors are involved—direct and opportunity costs, regional stability, vulnerability assessments, alliances, domestic politics. Having forgone their own WMD, these nations often look to the nuclear weapons states for security assurances. When the NPT was being negotiated, numerous states sought "positive security assurances," namely, assurances that nuclear weapons states would come to their aid if they were threatened or attacked. Others sought "negative security assurances," that is, assurances that nuclear weapons states would not threaten use of nuclear weapons against them. Over the years, a number of positive and negative security assurances have been issued by the nuclear weapons states, independently and in coordination. Many of these take the form of "no use" or "no first use" pledges. Central among these are the statements issued by the five nuclear weapons states recognized under the NPT not to use nuclear weapons against non-nuclear weapons states that are compliant parties to the NPT.[9] In the 2010 Nuclear Posture Review, the United States stated that it "will not use or threaten to use nuclear weapons against non-nuclear weapons states that are party to the NPT and in compliance with their nuclear non-proliferation obligations."[10] It also made clear that there might be situations where the use or threatened use of chemical or biological weapons would result in U.S. nuclear weapons having a role to play in deterring such a threat to the United States or its allies.

---

8. *See* Rosalyn Higgins, *Institutional Modes of Conflict Management, in* NATIONAL SECURITY LAW 193 (John Norton Moore et al. eds., 1990); MODERN DIPLOMACY: THE ART AND THE ARTISANS (Elmer Plischke ed., 1979).

9. *See* George Bunn, *The Legal Status of U.S. Negative Security Assurances to Non-Nuclear Weapon States,* NONPROLIFERATION REV., Spring-Summer 1997, at 1.

10. Nuclear Posture Review Report, Department of Defense, April 2010 at http://www.defense.gov/npr/docs/2010%20nuclear%20posture%20review%20report.pdf.

Export Controls/Suppliers Regimes

Long before regulating "merchants of death" became a transnational cause in the nineteenth century, some governments had begun to regulate the shipment of arms to potential enemies. Today, the U.S. Department of State maintains a munitions list of items that must be licensed for sale to most countries and that are prohibited for sale to others. In the age of proliferation of weapons of mass destruction, regulation of the arms trade has been joined by national and multinational controls on the export of "dual-use" technology, goods and services — dual-use in the sense that, whatever their commercial application, they can be used for the development and production of WMD or their means of delivery. Most notable among these supplier regimes are the Nuclear Suppliers Group (NSG) and Zangger Committee coordinating national regulation of nuclear trade and the Australia group coordinating export controls on items that could be useful in chemical or biological weapons programs. The Missile Technology Control Regime (MTCR) focuses on potential proliferation of weapons delivery systems.[11] In addition, domestic legislation such as the Atomic Energy Act in the United States places explicit limits on who may have access to nuclear technology and information.[12]

Cooperative Threat Reduction

With the end of the Cold War and in the wake of the 9/11 terrorist attacks, the international community faced a new and complex strategic landscape. The practice of amassing nuclear, biological and chemical weapons as a means of preventing war has been joined by the threat posed by the possibility of such weapons falling into the hands of terrorists or states of proliferation concern. This new reality called for a renewed emphasis on non-proliferation financial or technical assistance initiatives variously known as Cooperative Threat Reduction (CTR), generic nonproliferation assistance or global security engagement.

These initiatives differ from treaties in that they are more flexible, allowing for swift approval or denouncement. They are politically — rather than legally — binding but agreement often carried with it financial and political costs. Since these initiatives were not legally binding the often detailed and lengthy treaty making and ratification process was by-passed. As a result, measures can be and were quickly adopted to deal with rapidly evolving situations. These non-proliferation initiatives are not limited to states and can be adopted by one or several international actors, including states or, for example, International Government Organizations (IGOs) and non-governmental organizations (NGOs).

In the non-proliferation and security realm, initiatives have been used since the early 1980s but their use accelerated after the Cold War in light of heightened concerns over "loose nukes" and a globalized economy made it easier for terrorists and international

---

11. *See* the Missile Technology Control Regime website at http://fas.org/sgp/crs/nuke/RL31559.pdf.

12. In addition to the discussion of trade and technology transfers in chapter 28 of this volume, *see*: Michael Beck et al., Strengthening Multilateral Export Controls: A Nonproliferation Priority (2002); Deltac Limited, Proliferation and Export Controls: An analysis of sensitive technologies and countries of concern (1995); Eric L. Hirschhorn, The Export Control and Embargo Handbook (2000); Restraining the Spread of the Soviet Arsenal: NIS Nonproliferation Export Controls Status Report 1996 (Gary K. Bertsch ed., 1997).

criminal organizations to engage in the trafficking of WMD materials, technology and know-how.[13] The disclosure of the A.Q. Khan network where nuclear weapons materials and design information was sold to the highest bidder further heightened concerns over non-state actors acquiring a nuclear weapons capability.[14] Each new crisis involving weapons of mass destruction (WMD) brings states, IGOs and other international actors together to devise and adopt new ways to manage the consequences of a WMD threat and the potential for further proliferation.

The most noteworthy example of this is the plethora of initiatives created since the break-up of the Soviet Union aimed at securing its massive nuclear, biological and chemical arsenals. Numerous WMD-related facilities in the Newly Independent States (NIS) of the former Soviet Union were operating in the midst of chaotic conditions. Poorly funded, many of these locations contained storage sites for fissile material, chemical weapons, or culture collections of biological warfare concern. Security was weak. Most of these installations contained technology and machinery useful for WMD programs. All had poorly paid scientists, engineers, and technicians whose knowledge and skills could be of value to the WMD programs of countries or terrorists interested in acquiring WMD. In response, the United States, many European countries, Japan, and others beyond the G-8 initiated a new approach to international arms restraint that combined features of arms control, disarmament, and nonproliferation. This approach came to be known as Cooperative Threat Reduction (CTR). The first, and most significant, of these efforts was the Nunn-Lugar program, named after the two U.S. senators who initiated the legislation.[15] Nunn-Lugar provides funding and technical assistance to countries that must eliminate nuclear delivery systems and chemical weapons under treaty commitments. Research institutes and scientists are provided funding for joint research with western scientists to discourage a "brain drain," particularly to countries of proliferation concern and to promote transparency and confidence. Efforts to develop the economies of the newly independent states through commercialization of technologies have increasingly taken on more significance, but the initial efforts at pure "defense conversion"—producing commercial goods on military production lines—has largely been abandoned as economically unworkable.[16]

The U.S. and other nations have also helped Russia secure and eliminate chemical weapons by supporting, for example, the design and construction of a chemical weapons destruction facility at Shchuch'ye. Additionally, at one point the former Soviet Union had the world's largest biological weapons program. Although admitting to having a program, the Russian Federation has subsequently refused to provide any details or allow requested access to the biological warfare complex. Consequently, CTR programs, such as the DoD's biological threat reduction program has shifted from a program to dismantle the biological weapons complex in the former Soviet Union to a world-wide initiative to promote "best practices" at biological laboratories and to develop disease surveillance systems around the world.

---

13. *See* M.B. Nikitin, P.K. Kerr, S.A. Hildreth, "Proliferation Control Regimes: Background and Status," Congressional Research Service, October 25, 2012 available at http://fas.org/sgp/crs/nuke/RL31559.pdf.

14. Christopher O. Clary, "The A.Q. Khan Network: Causes and Implications," December 2005, Federation of American Scientists, available at http://fas.org/irp/eprint/clary.pdf.

15. Former U.S. Senator Sam Nunn (D-Ga.) and U.S. Senator Richard Lugar (R-Ind.).

16. *See* Graham T. Allison et al., Avoiding Nuclear Anarchy: Containing the Threat of Loose Russian Nuclear Weapons and Fissile Material (1996); Matthew Bunn et al., Controlling Nuclear Warheads and Materials: A Report Card and Action Plan (2003).

U.S. cooperation with Russia has shrunk both as a result of Russia's economic recovery and as a product of increased tensions with the West, notably over Georgia and Ukraine, With many of the CTR projects in Russia either completed or winding down after the June 2013 expiration of the Memorandum of Understanding that governed DOD's cooperation with Russia, the two countries continue to cooperate on some areas of nuclear security including a bilateral protocol under the Multilateral Nuclear Environmental Program in the Russian Federation Agreement (MNEPR). Smaller, more diverse programs continue in other republics of the former Soviet Union.

Subsequently, the CTR effort began to shift from an emergency response former Soviet Union focused program to a broader world-wide program seeking to keep WMD from terrorist groups and states of proliferation concern. While the initial program was a DoD-centered effort with a budget of $400 million it now includes a wide variety of initiatives involving not only the DoD but also the State Department, the Department of Energy (DOE) and the Department of Homeland Security (DHS) with a combined budget approaching $1.7 billion annually. CTR programs and initiatives have been slowly expanded to the Middle East and Africa after heightened concerns that terrorist groups such as Al Qaeda and its affiliates in those areas are seeking to acquire WMD.[17]

The United States also supports global programs that are designed to prevent the smuggling or illegal export of CBRN materials and technology. For example, DOE is responsible for working with international partners under the Global Threat Reduction Initiative (GTRI), and the International Atomic Energy Agency's Action Plan to Combat Nuclear Terrorism to secure, protect, and as necessary, remove vulnerable nuclear and radiological materials at civilian facilities. The State Department, through its Nuclear Smuggling Outreach Initiative, assists nations with nuclear source materials or who pose a high-risk for nuclear smuggling to improve their capabilities in preventing, detecting and responding to incidents of nuclear smuggling. The State Department and DOE have also developed programs that are designed to reduce the risk that the weapons scientists would sell their knowledge to nations seeking their own CBRN weapons.

That over fifty CTR-related initiatives aimed at securing and eliminating these weapons, materials, delivery systems or expertise exist today is itself a testimony to the new importance placed on non-proliferation efforts in today's chaotic and uncertain security environment. Perhaps the most successful recent CTR-like initiative was the removal and destruction of chemical weapons stocks from Syria in 2014.[18]

Recognizing that one of the greatest threats to international peace and security is the prospect of terrorist groups acquiring WMD and recognizing the possible role that international criminal organizations might play in aiding and abetting such acquisition, the United Nations Security Council in 2004 passed Resolution 1540. Enacted under Chapter VII of the UN Charter, Resolution 1540 imposed a range of legally binding obligations on all UN Member States to keep their biological, chemical and nuclear weapons and the means of delivering such weapons out of the hands of non-state actors. Further, it requires all Member States, *inter alia* to adopt domestic controls and enforcement

---

17. *See* the Next Generation Cooperative Threat Reduction Act of 2013 (S. 1021) and the Cooperative Threat Reduction Modernization Act (H.R. 2314). Similar provisions are part of both the House and Senate versions of the National Defense Authorization Act of FY2014 (H.R. 1960, §1304; S. 1197, §1326).

18. For an in depth discussion of the range of and issues associated with CTR programs see Mary Beth D. Nikitin and Amy F. Woolf, "The Evolution of Cooperative Threat Reduction: Issues for Congress," Congressional Research Service, June 13, 2014.

mechanisms over WMD materials and to criminalize possession of such materials, irrespective of where the perpetrator is located. Specifically all Member States shall:

1. "refrain from providing any form of support to non-state actors that attempt to develop, acquire, manufacture, possess, transport, transfer or use nuclear, chemical or biological weapons and their means of delivery" (paragraph 1);

2. "in accordance with their national procedures ... adopt and enforce appropriate effective laws, which prohibit any non-state actor to manufacture, acquire, possess, transport, transfer or use nuclear, chemical or biological weapons and their means of delivery, in particular for terrorist purposes, as well as attempts to engage in any of the forgoing activities, participate in them as an accomplice, assist or finance them" (paragraph 2);

3. "take and enforce effective measures to establish domestic controls to prevent the proliferation of nuclear, biological and chemical weapons and their means of delivery, including by establishing controls over related materials" by developing security, physical protection and border and export controls (paragraph 3).[19]

The resolution affirms support for the multilateral treaties and other legal frameworks whose aim is to eliminate or prevent the proliferation of WMD and the importance for all States to implement them fully. The Resolution also established the 1540 Committee whose role is to facilitate the provision of technical assistance to countries that may need such assistance to fully comply with the legal obligations imposed by UNSCR 1540, and to enhance cooperation with relevant international organizations. The Committee is also mandated to engage in outreach efforts, develop assistance programs with the aid of states participating in one or more of the CTR initiatives, and to continue to institute transparency measures in order to enhance confidence.[20]

Constructive Engagement

The geo-strategic environment shapes international arms restraint and vice versa. Efforts at political and economic "constructive engagement" with potential adversaries often involve arms control and nonproliferation. Constructive engagement typically seeks step-by-step dialog and reciprocal incentives. A contemporary example of success and failure in constructive engagement is the linkage by numerous governments of their broader relations with North Korea to Pyongyang's nonproliferation compliance. At one point, the U.S., Japanese, and South Korean governments agreed to provide North Korea with fuel oil and two new nuclear reactors if it would come into compliance with the NPT, cease operations of existing reactors, end plutonium reprocessing, and bring into effect several other North-South agreements including one on de-nuclearization of the Korean Peninsula. Constructive engagement with North Korea has been disrupted numerous times because of evidence of the continuation of a covert nuclear weapons program by North Korea. Confronted with evidence of its non-compliance, North Korea withdrew from the NPT and renounced the North-South denuclearization agreement. Subsequently

---

19. *See generally* Olivia Bosch and Peter van Ham, ed., "Global Non-Proliferation and Counter-Terrorism: The Impact of UNSCR 1540" (2007); Monika Heupel, "Implementing UNSC Resolution 1540; A Division of Labor Strategy," Carnegie Papers Non-Proliferation Program 87 (2007).

20. UNSC Resolution 1977 (2011) extended the mandate of the 1540 Committee to 2021 and reaffirmed its role in monitoring compliance and providing when requested technical assistance.

North Korea conducted underground nuclear weapons tests.[21] Efforts at constructive engagement continue with North Korea, Iran, and others with mixed success.

Compulsory Inspections and Enforcement

Parties to many modern arms control and nonproliferation agreements routinely accept intrusive monitoring by inspectors and sensors, including at sensitive sites. In addition, the Chemical Weapons Convention provides for "managed access" at sensitive sites so that surprise inspections with no right of refusal could be accomplished. The infringement on sovereignty felt by governments that became parties to these intrusive regimes was possible only by a changed world reflecting the end of the Cold War and the rise of more intense globalization. The aftermath of the Gulf War of 1991, as in the days after the two World Wars, took compulsory inspections and enforcement still further. In addition to the introduction of large scale, surprise inspections by the International Atomic Energy Agency (IAEA), the United Nations Security Council created new bodies, UNSCOM and UNMOVIC to inspect for chemical and biological weapons. Some NGOs advocate armed support for inspectors.[22] Subsequent developments demonstrated the uncertainty that can continue to exist even in the context of intrusive inspections. Ultimately, the failure by Baghdad to satisfy concerns about covert WMD programs contributed to the invasion of Iraq and the removal of the regime of Saddam Hussein by a military coalition led by the United States and Great Britain. After the 2003 Iraq war, however, coalition troops occupying Iraq did not find WMD stockpiles and activities such as had been found after the 1991 war. This reinforced support for multi-national inspections and revealed weaknesses in NTM and other national intelligence. On the other hand, discovery of illegal activities in Iran, Syria, and Libya demonstrated weakness in multi-national inspections and were consistent with intelligence. The case of Libya offers an additional model for enforcement. Britain and the United States obtained detailed disclosure of the Libyan WMD programs, intrusive inspections, and the right for their nationals to remove or eliminate Libyan WMD-related equipment and materials as part of their price for lifting sanctions. Uncertainty remains as to how to respond to noncompliance or to enforce compliance, but the range of approaches taken has expanded with mixed results.

Adjuncts to Peacekeeping, Conflict Resolution, and Humanitarian Intervention

Peacekeeping and enforcement has expanded greatly throughout the world in the last fifteen years, usually under a United Nations mandate. Although these operations address issues of motivation, demand, and security that can propel trade in arms and weapons use, peacekeeping and conflict resolution are not normally considered central elements of international arms restraint. The opposite, however, is less true. Constraints on arms and the demobilization of armed forces are important tools in dealing with insurgents and terrorists involved in ethnic and internecine violence. "Disarmament" has become an essential political condition in the peace process in Northern Ireland. Removing landmines is a challenge during conflict and in reconstruction afterward, a challenge so

---

21. *See* Solving the North Korean Nuclear Puzzle (David Albright & Kevin O'Neill eds., 2000); Verifying the Agreed Framework (Michael M. May ed., 2001).
22. *See* Carnegie Endowment for International Peace, Iraq: A new Approach (2002).

great that the negotiation of a treaty banning most automatic anti-personnel landmines was placed on a fast track for humanitarian rather than arms control grounds.[23]

Vehicle for Political Reform and Regime Change

Because international arms restraints may mandate new rules, promote transparency and require accountability, policy or organizational changes necessary for implementation within the nations may be significant. For transitional governments, for example, cooperative threat reduction programs may demand adoption of internationally accepted accounting principles and best practices in administration and encourage community engagement on issues such as environmental standards associated with weapons dismantlement. During the Cold War, Western arms control approaches encouraged greater freedom of action in Eastern Europe and opened up closed societies, often reducing the national security rationale for the totalitarian state. International arms restraints did not bring down the Berlin Wall nor cause the demise of the Soviet Union, but they did help the peoples of the Soviet Union and Eastern Europe recognize that something different was possible. Not all such induced political reform blurs into "regime change." The continuation of authoritarianism in countries that do engage in arms control illustrates the limits of this tool for encouraging rapid political transformation.

Dynamics of International Arms Restraints

The sources of international arms restraint are found in customary international law, the international law of warfare, arms control treaties, other treaties, international executive agreements, parallel declarations, unilateral policy statements, domestic treaty implementation legislation, other domestic legislation, executive branch policy, legislative history, views of common sense or sound judgment, and perceptions of right and wrong. A look at international arms restraint suggests that its components can be placed along a continuum extending from measures that least involve direct engagement with a foreign entity through those that involve cooperation among governments to those that involve compelled behavior or coercion, such as the imposition of WMD disarmament on Iraq by the UN Security Council after the 1991 Gulf War. Another continuum on a different axis might run from simple, sometimes declaratory measures to intensely detailed, concrete measures. Such taxonomy based upon the degree to which approaches to arms restraint are cooperative and the degree to which they are detailed can aid analysis of existing and possible arms restraints. Greater cooperation on concrete matters in the detail that is most common among friends may prove to be the key in dealing with the future needs for international arms restraint related to proliferation and terrorism.

Fundamental to most thinking about international arms restraint are rules. In the case of formal arms control agreements, this may embody very specific measures defined in great detail in treaty text and implementing documents including domestic legislation. Yet the idea of rules is caught up in many other models for thinking about arms restraints. Approaches based upon principles of ethics, morality and justice obviously emphasize rules of right and wrong. Normative rules grow out of positive law as well. Indeed, international arms restraints often operate in ways analogous to national economic and en-

---

23. *See, e.g.,* Mats R. Berdal, *Disarmament and Demobilisation after Civil Wars,* Adelphi Papers, 1996; Marcos Mendiburu & Sarah Meek, Managing Arms in Peace Processes: Haiti (1996); Estanislao Angel Zawels et al., Managing Arms in Peace Processes: The Issues (1996).

vironmental regulatory processes, reflecting both their strengths and their weaknesses, particularly in the way they enhance the value of unregulated "gray area" activities.[24] Not all analysis of rules-based behavior, however, is so clearly normative. Studies of international arms restraints, as with the study of deterrence, draw heavily from other rules-based models such as econometrics, systems analysis, game theory, and modern social and behavioral sciences. In between the explicitly normative and more strictly analytical approaches are hybrids developed in centers for peace studies, conflict resolution, violence management, and cooperative engagement.

Goals of International Arms Restraints

Evaluation of how well approaches such as arms control or confidence-building measures operate, whether primarily normative or analytical, requires recognition of the goals and purposes sought. International arms restraint measures typically proclaim to promote security, prosperity, or freedom of action of the parties through measures that may:

(1) reduce the probability of conflict
(2) decrease the intensity of any resulting conflict
(3) deter escalation of the level of violence
(4) discourage inhumane weapons and actions during war
(5) increase opportunities for diplomatic solutions
(6) decrease reliance on military force
(7) reduce the budgetary impact of defense and diplomacy
(8) permit smaller military and defense industrial infrastructure
(9) encourage defense conversion
(10) enhance the clarity of agreements
(11) facilitate monitoring and verification
(12) increase enforcement options
(13) reinforce international norms
(14) support human rights
(15) protect the environment or resources
(16) reinforce the principle of the rule of law
(17) increase openness and transparency
(18) ease distrust
(19) encourage cooperative actions
(20) support peacekeeping or peace enforcement, and
(21) promote political reform and regime change.

Conflicts among these goals necessitate strategies of optimization. Resolving priorities is the foundation of much policy debate, especially because gain can be measured in absolute or relative terms. Much of the history of international restraints is about the evolution of cooperation in the context of competition. Unfortunately, between intense adversaries, even "win-win" strategies may be unacceptable outcomes to one or all parties.

Origins of Arms Restraint—The Early History

Modern measures of arms restraint have their parallels in ages past, long predating the emergence of the nation state system that defines international. The origins of these

---

24. *See* BRADEN R. ALLENBY ET AL., ENVIRONMENTAL THREATS AND NATIONAL SECURITY (1997).

measures are prehistoric, studied by biologists and anthropologists. Signals of peaceful or hostile intent are found in animal behavior and are well developed among primitive societies. Tradition holds that the military salute is an extension of the empty outstretched hand displayed by approaching warriors to signal peaceful intentions. Pre-Clausewitzian matching of the level of violence to the scope of the objective brought with it such ritualized restraints as surrogate battles between chieftains and the proclamation of some weapons and tactics as "taboo." By the time of recorded history, many of today's anthems of hope were well developed. "They shall beat their swords into plowshares, And their spears into pruning hooks; Nation shall not lift up sword against nation, Neither shall they learn war anymore."[25]

Similarly, in ancient China, with more of a pragmatic vision, Sun Tzu advised restraint in the conduct of war:

> In the practical art of war, the best thing of all is to take the enemy's country whole and intact; to shatter and destroy it is not so good. . . .

> Hence to fight and conquer in all your battles is not supreme excellence; supreme excellence consists in breaking the enemy's resistance without fighting.[26]

Similar themes drove evolution of the "just war" principles seen in the writings of Aristotle, Cicero, St. Augustine, and St. Thomas Aquinas, principles elaborated in the canon and international law of Hugo Grotius and others. The Medieval "Truce of God" and "Peace of God" constraints on timing and location of conflict and on technologies such as crossbows and later limitations on firearms served also to protect existing elites from revolutionary forces. Much of the subsequent history of arms restraint illuminates the efforts to limit or channel destruction while permitting violent competition between adversaries to continue.[27]

Measures to prevent surprise attack also have their origins in early rules of "proper warfare." Such codes of conduct have suffered in the century of "blitzkrieg" and "guerrilla" warfare, but the quest for legal protection against surprise attack continued. At the instigation of Russia, which had suffered from the Japanese surprise attack on Port Arthur in 1904, the 1907 Hague Conference agreed that no nation could wage war unless it had issued a formal declaration or an ultimatum. The Kellogg-Briand Pact of 1928 went further, outlawing war as "an instrument of national policy."[28]

Specific limits on arms or forces to shore up other political and legal arrangements also have a long history. The 1648 Peace of Westphalia ending the Thirty-Years War sought, but failed to achieve, the elimination of key fortifications. The U.S.-U.K. Rush-Bagot Treaty of 1817 limited naval forces on the Great Lakes, thus easing tensions along the Canadian border and avoiding the naval rivalry that had played a major role in the War of 1812. The mid-nineteenth century saw an acceleration of interest as first Britain, then France, and later Russia floated arms limitation proposals. Acting on humanitarian concerns, conventions in Geneva, beginning in 1864, and in the Hague, in 1899 and 1907, elaborated prohibitions against weapons or use "calculated to cause unnecessary

---

25. *Isaiah* 2:4 (New King James).

26. Sun Tzu, On the Art of War 17 (Lionel Giles trans., 1910).

27. *See, e.g.,* John Norton Moore, *Development of the International Law of Conflict Management,* Ch. 3, *in* National Security Law 47 (John Norton Moore et al. eds., 1990); or in this volume, chapter 3.

28. *See* State Department Historian, "The Kellogg-Briand Pact of 1928," at https://history.state.gov/milestones/1921-1936/kellogg.

suffering." Bans on asphyxiating gases and dropping bombs from balloons demonstrated growing concern that the industrial revolution had empowered unacceptable forms of military destructiveness.

The early history of negotiated arms limitations was not encouraging. The border between the United States and Canada remains the largest demilitarized boundary in the world because of the close ties of those nations, not because the Rush-Bagot Treaty remains in force. The 1919 Treaty of Versailles sought similar security through the demilitarization of the Rhineland. The Treaty of Versailles proved insufficient to secure France even with the building of the Maginot Line. Indeed, Versailles provides many examples of the real world challenges of verification and enforcement.[29] The Washington Naval Treaties of 1922 and the London Naval Treaties of 1930 and 1936 froze fortifications in the Pacific and limited the fleets of the United States, Great Britain, Japan, France and Italy. Twenty years after the process began and only five years after it collapsed, however, the surprise attack by Japan on America's key naval base in Hawaii brought the United States into World War II and made prevention of another "Pearl Harbor" a preoccupation of the post-World War II world. The Washington Naval Conference of 1921-1922 and London Naval Conference of 1935-1936 also highlighted persistent challenges to the viability of international arms restraints, including the identification of relevant categories as technology changes (battleships, aircraft carriers, submarines, etc.), the regulation of "gray area" weapons (lighter vessels with more armaments), uncertain measures of capability (numbers, tonnage, caliber), and, perhaps most important of all, the different geo-strategic context for the parties both allied and adversary (momentum and schedule for construction, geographical location, intensity of purpose, impact on domestic decision-making).[30]

Where mutually acceptable constraints could not be achieved or were not considered necessary, in the past as today, information was sought as a substitute. In rejecting the proposal of Tsar Alexander I for reductions in military forces in 1816, Lord Castlereagh noted:

> It is impossible ... not to perceive that the settlement of a scale of force for so many Powers,—under such different circumstances as to their relative means, frontiers, positions and faculties for re-arming,—presents a very complicated question for negotiation: that the means of preserving a system if once created are not without their difficulties, liable as States are to partial necessities for an increase of force: and it is further to be considered that on this, as on many subjects of a jealous character, in attempting to do much, difficulties are rather brought into view than made to disappear.[31]

---

29. *See* Richard Dean Burns & Donald Urquidi, Disarmament in Perspective: An Analysis of Selected Arms Control and Disarmament Agreements between the World Wars, 1919–1939 (1968); Georges Castellan, Le Réarmement Clandestin du Reich, 1930–1935 (1954); From Versailles to Baghdad: Post-War Armament Control of Defeated States (Fred Tanner ed., 1992).

30. *See* Raymond Aron, Peace and War: A Theory of International Relations (1966); Amos S. Hershey, The International Law and Diplomacy of the Russo-Japanese War (1906); Stanford Arms Control Group, International Arms Control: Issues and Agreements (Coit D. Blacker & Gloria Duffey eds., 2d ed. 1984); Robert Gordon Kaufman, Arms Control during the Pre-Nuclear Era (1990); Henry Kissinger, A World Restored: Metternich, Castlereagh, and the Problems of Peace, 1812–1822 (1973); Quincy Wright, A Study Of War (1942); Ellery C. Stowell, *Convention Relative to the Opening of Hostilities*, 2 Am. J. Int'l L. 50 (1908).

31. Harold Nicolson, The Congress of Vienna: A Study in Allied Unity: 1812–1822, at 255 (1946).

Following this classic statement of the fundamental tensions in international arms restraints, the British minister offered instead that each government should "explain to allied and neighboring States the extent and nature of its arrangements as a means of dispelling alarm and of rendering moderate establishments mutually convenient."[32] This early suggestion that cooperative measures might be more appropriate than strict limitations, however, was still too much for Austria's Metternich who questioned Russian motivation and intent. Again, we are reminded that issues of verification and trust are not limited only to formal treaties. Debates, in which confidence-building openness was seen as a better, or easier, substitute for binding treaty limitations rather than as primarily instrumental for such limitation raged loudly during the Cold War and reverberate today.

Global Regimes and the Quest for Universality

Two world wars, the arrival of the nuclear age, and the creation of the United Nations accelerated step-by-step approaches to international arms restraint, but also put a new spotlight on universal disarmament. Moreover, de-colonization and the breakup of larger states broadened the locus of concern beyond Europe and the Pacific as some 200 nation states and self-governing entities came into being. Proposals for universal covenants range from general and complete disarmament (GCD) to limitations on landmines and lasers. The nuclear age brought greater intensity to these efforts, but prohibitions on chemical weapons use began what has now become the effort to create universal disarmament regimes. The major universal international restraint regimes are the three treaties containing prohibitions on nuclear, biological, and chemical weapons and the conventions dealing with indiscriminate and inhumane weapons use.

The Nuclear Non-Proliferation Treaty of 1968 (NPT)

With 193 of 198 relevant sovereignties already a party or bound by the Nuclear Non-Proliferation Treaty of 1968, the NPT is the most universal arms treaty. Only India, Pakistan, Israel, South Sudan, and Kosovo have not joined.[33] Some nations do not recognize North Korea's withdrawal.[34] Phases in the negotiation and implementation of the NPT closely follow the development of post-World War international organizations and geopolitics. The seed was planted on November 15, 1945, when Canada, the United

---

32. *Id.*

33. Treaty on the Non-Proliferation of Nuclear Weapons, July 1, 1968, 21 U.S.T. 483, 729 U.N.T.S. 161. The number 198 consists of the 193 states listed in Annex 1 Pursuant to Article II, Paragraph 28 of the Comprehensive Test Ban plus Timor-Leste, Montenegro, South Sudan, Kosovo, and the Republic of China (Taiwan). [The legal status of Kosovo is disputed as are its obligations under the NPT as a former part of Yugoslovia. The current NPT obligations of the Democratic People's Republic of Korea (North Korea] are also disputed. The Republic of China (Taiwan) is considered bound by the Treaty.]

34. Here, North Korea is counted among the 193. However, on April 11, 2003, North Korea declared complete its withdrawal from the NPT. This would be the first withdrawal since the NPT entered into force in 1970. The legal obligations of North Korea under the NPT are being debated because the withdrawal took place under the cloud of accusations that Pyongyang was in material breach of the treaty. Under customary international law and the Vienna Convention on Conventions a party would not escape its obligations through withdrawal if it is in material breach. Also, the government of Japan has stated its view that the withdrawal was not in accordance with required procedures.

Kingdom, and the United States proposed "entirely eliminating the use of atomic energy for destructive purposes." This proposal was reinforced in the more famous American "Baruch Plan" of 1946 that would have placed nuclear material under international control.[35] On December 8, 1953, before the UN General Assembly, U.S. President Dwight D. Eisenhower, in his "Atoms for Peace" speech, revealed the growing destructiveness of nuclear weapons, declared that the knowledge to build them might spread, perhaps to all nations, and called for an "international atomic energy agency" to control fissile material.[36] The IAEA was created in 1957.

In 1961, the UN General Assembly unanimously approved an Irish Resolution calling for a commitment from the nuclear powers not to transfer nuclear weapons to non-nuclear weapons states and from non-nuclear weapons states not to acquire weapons. Alternative U.S. and Soviet nuclear nonproliferation language was presented over the next three years, but Soviet opposition to nuclear cooperation between the United States and its NATO allies blocked progress In 1966, however, agreement was reached on basic principles and the next year the U.S. and the Soviet Union presented separate, but identical texts. On July 1, 1968, the Nuclear Non-Proliferation Treaty was opened for signature and entered into force on March 5, 1970. In 1995, the Review Conference, meeting to consider the indefinite duration of the NPT, endorsed its continuation. Hotly debated issues raised at the NPT extension conference reflect tensions inherent in the compromises and trade-offs within the treaty and an altered international security environment.

With the end of the Cold War, concern has grown over the possible loss or theft of nuclear weapons and materials or through the unauthorized assistance of nuclear weapons scientists and engineers. A number of bilateral and multilateral Cooperative Threat Reduction (CTR) programs have been enacted to address this problem. Of equally great concern has been the fear that non-nuclear weapon states themselves are cooperating or sharing technology in support of nuclear weapons programs. In addition, the achievement of nuclear weapons capability in states like Israel, India, Pakistan, and North Korea has increased concerns that activities of their governments, institutions, or experts may intentionally or unintentionally provide assistance in support of nuclear weapons programs. Public speculation is that China aided Pakistan, which assisted North Korea which assisted Libya and Iran, which in turn might provide weapons to other regimes or terrorists.

The Article II commitment by non-NWS not to acquire nuclear weapons is also seen now in a different light. The negotiators of the NPT recognized, as had the authors of the Acheson-Lillienthal Plan within two years of the first atomic explosion, that knowledge and technology related to nuclear weapons would spread. They could not have anticipated, however, today's computers, robotics, and other technologies that greatly ease the design and construction of nuclear weapons. Nor would they have anticipated the wealth that some governments like Iran have at their disposal to finance nuclear weapons programs. Then as now, great hope was placed upon the control of weapons-useable nuclear material. The "loose nukes" and insecure storage issues have added one great concern, but the surprise appearance of uranium-enrichment in North Korea and Iran and plutonium reprocessing in North Korea demonstrates that governments can acquire such capabilities covertly.

---

35. *See* U.S. ARMS CONTROL AND DISARMAMENT AGENCY, ARMS CONTROL AND DISARMAMENT AGREEMENTS: TEXTS AND HISTORIES OF THE NEGOTIATIONS 65 (1996).

36. *See* Michael O. Wheeler, *A History of Arms Control*, ARMS CONTROL: COOPERATIVE SECURITY IN A CHANGING ENVIRONMENT 19 (Jeffrey A. Larsen, ed., 2002) and IRA CHERNUS, EISENHOWER'S ATOMS FOR PEACE (2002).

Under Article III of the NPT, all "fissionable material" in non-NWS must be safeguarded in accordance with agreements with the International Atomic Energy Agency (IAEA). Relevant materials and facilities are to be declared. Material in the NWS' weapons programs are not under IAEA safeguards, but critics argued even before the treaty was concluded that NWS' non-military facilities should also be safeguarded in order to insure political and commercial equality and to set the stage for tighter standards for accountability and protection of material and reductions in military stockpiles of weapons and material. NWS states were opposed, arguing that this would be an expensive diversion of scarce resources with little contribution to nonproliferation. Eventually, all five NWS have adopted policies to achieve safeguards agreements with the IAEA and some activities have been placed under safeguards. The greater issue today is the priority for IAEA inspections, which are primarily aimed at confirming that no diversion of safeguarded material has taken place.

Scenarios for diversion of material and strategies for countering them continue to be developed. Yet, the experiences with Iraq, Iran, Libya, Syria, and North Korea have reinforced the concern that the greatest risks come from covert facilities, assistance from outside the country, and the threat to use safeguarded material after withdrawal from the NPT rather than diversions from facilities while they are being monitored.[37] With the support of UN Security Council resolutions after the 1991 Gulf War, the IAEA was granted extensive authority to search non-declared facilities and interview Iraqi scientists. The ongoing crisis with North Korea began in 1993 because Pyongyang refused to allow a "special inspection" sought by the IAEA at an undeclared location. Control of fissile material is a necessary condition for confidence in safeguards, but IAEA safeguards may not be sufficient to deal with the danger of "breakout" posed by governments that are conducting weapons-useable activities in parallel to their safeguarded activities. This need for an "NPT plus" approach was reflected in the 1991 Agreement to Denuclearize the Korean Peninsula. The agreement between Seoul and Pyongyang banned both reprocessing and enrichment but never entered into force. The 2003 Iran crisis with the IAEA subsided when Tehran agreed to conclude the IAEA "Additional Protocol" and suspend uranium enrichment, but great breakout potential remains and Iran is now heavily sanctioned while nuclear talks are extended.

The NPT vehicle for President Eisenhower's "Atoms for Peace" is Article IV, guaranteeing to non-NWS the right to conduct peaceful research. All parties are encouraged to further the application of nuclear energy, "with due consideration for the needs of the developing areas of the world." Article V went so far as to encourage that potential benefits of "peaceful nuclear explosions" be made available to non-NWS. The NPT grand bargain that nations would give up the right to nuclear weapons in exchange for rapid economic and social advancement made possible by nuclear power and other civilian applications seemed obvious to many. Today, however, euphoria over Article IV is gone. Concern over the economics of nuclear power and the safety of all nuclear applications has stopped activity in many countries. Lengthy regulatory processes, lack of radioactive waste depositories, and non-governmental political opposition have slowed many nuclear enterprises. Demand in many countries has decreased, even as suppliers have become more concerned about the inherent proliferation risk in nuclear cooperation. Research reactors remain a proliferation issue, particularly those that use highly enriched uranium. In countries like Israel, Pakistan, India, Iran, and North Korea, the number of foreign trained scientists and engineers believed associated with nuclear weapons programs has been significant.

---

37. *See* VERIFYING THE AGREED FRAMEWORK, *supra* note 21.

Perhaps no provision of the NPT evokes more controversy than Article VI:

> Each of the Parties to the Treaty undertakes to pursue negotiations in good faith on effective measures relating to cessation of the nuclear arms race at an early date and to nuclear disarmament, and on a Treaty on general and complete disarmament under strict and effective international control.[38]

Everyone engaged in the nuclear debate parses this language in their own way. In general, the nuclear weapons states have stressed a step-by-step process built upon the prior creation of the security, political, and technical environment believed necessary for each subsequent step. For them, the goal of nuclear abolition is linked as much to "general and complete disarmament," including non-nuclear weapons, as it is to pursuing measures relating to nuclear disarmament. In short, the nuclear free world implied by Article VI is not near at hand, not time certain, and very much related to broader geopolitical and security calculations including conventional and other military arms.

Many other governments and activists, however, assert that the bargain in which non-NWS gave up their right to nuclear weapons upon adherence requires that the non-NWS not wait too long for the nuclear weapons states to give up their nuclear weapons completely. India, a non-party to the NPT, has long attacked the NPT as unequal and unjust precisely because the Treaty grandfathers for an indefinite time the five nuclear weapons states that tested a nuclear explosion prior to January 1, 1967. India found allies among the non-NWS parties to the NPT who proposed at the 1995 NPT Review and Extension Conference that the future of the NPT be conditioned on a "time-bound framework" for nuclear disarmament. Such a formal linkage was not agreed, but an action program with objectives for nonproliferation and disarmament and an enhanced review process was agreed that may prove very demanding, especially given that many non-NWS states conditioned their support for extension on achievement of a Comprehensive Test Ban on nuclear explosions that has been completed but is unlikely to enter into force soon.[39]

Article VI contains within it a further tension. Some governments joined the NPT with expectation that the NWS would disarm, but others joined with the expectation that one or more NWS would provide them with "extended deterrence," a so-called "nuclear umbrella." Both views are often voiced within a single government, reflecting a different time horizon or different element of public opinion. Japan has been a classic example of this bi-polar perspective. The NWS attempt to reconcile this dilemma has been to note that the NWS must take into account the security concerns of their allies in determining how far down the disarmament path to go and when.

The debate over Article VI underscores that the most powerful motivations for acquiring nuclear weapons have to do with security. Yet, efforts to provide security assurances directly in the text of the NPT proved impossible given disparate defense relationships and disarmament policies. In the months before the NPT was opened for signature, the United States, Great Britain, and the Soviet Union did develop and introduce a UNSC resolution in which the "tripartite" proposed that each would seek Security Council approval for immediate action if a non-NWS were "victim of an act of aggression or an object of a threat of aggression in which nuclear weapons are used."[40] The resolution passed ten to zero, with five abstentions (Algeria, Brazil, France, India, and Pakistan). India opposed the assurances on the ground that they did not cover threats against non-

---

38. U.S. Arms Control and Disarmament Agency, *supra* note 35, at 73.
39. *See* discussion of nuclear testing and nuclear reductions below.
40. S.C. Res. 255, U.N. SCOR, 1433d mtg., at 13, UN Doc. S/RES/255 (1968).

parties. France argued that it was inadequate absent nuclear disarmament. China, not a member, argued publicly that the assurance was more a threat aimed at China. The effort to provide general "positive security assurances" proved difficult for the United States after the Vietnam War and the breakup of alliances such as SEATO and CENTO. Indeed, they have paled in contrast to the security assurances inherent in the defense treaties with Japan, the Republic of Korea, and the North Atlantic Alliance.

The United States, never enthusiastic about negative security assurances, gave such an assurance in a statement by Secretary of State Cyrus Vance at the UN Special Session on Disarmament on June 12, 1978. On April 5, 1995, in reference to UNSC 984 and in language coordinated with the United Kingdom and at a time shared by all five NPT nuclear weapons states, U.S. Secretary of State Warren Christopher presented a slightly revised version of the Vance Statement:

> The United States reaffirms that it will not use nuclear weapons against non-nuclear-weapon States Parties to the Treaty on the Non-Proliferation of Nuclear Weapons except in the case of an invasion or any other attack on the United States, its territories, its armed forces or other troops, its allies, or on a State toward which it has a security commitment, carried out or sustained by such a non-nuclear-weapon States in association or alliance with a nuclear-weapon State.[41]

Russia and France issued similar statements, and China issued a broader declaration of "No-First-Use." A number of states propose that these statements be codified, clarified, or expanded.[42] More recently, as a result of a Nuclear Posture Review (NPR), the United States dropped the exception for allies of nuclear parties and declared that "the United States will not use or threaten to use nuclear weapons against non-nuclear weapons states that are party to the Nuclear Non-Proliferation Treaty (NPT) and in compliance with their nuclear non-proliferation obligations." The NPR further caveated that the United States reserved the right to revise its policy as a result of "the evolution and proliferation of the biological weapons threat and U.S. capacities to counter that threat."[43]

The NPT is often cited as a model universal regime and the keystone of the entire construct of international arms restraints in existence today. Significant treaties such as several Nuclear Weapons Free Zones (NWFZs) and limitations on nuclear weapons testing complement its restraints. Still, even if most parties strongly support the nuclear Non-Proliferation Treaty, the NPT is a troubled treaty in an uncertain environment. The withdrawal of North Korea after more than a decade of "constructive engagement" spotlights enforcement weaknesses. Iran's extensive nuclear program in an oil rich state reinforces the classic fear that the NPT provides a "fast track" for dual capable technology. Iraq illustrated the persistence of a proliferator violating a treaty to which it is a party. Libya demonstrated that nuclear weapons trade can go unnoticed. India, Israel, and Pakistan remind us that major nuclear capabilities remain outside the NPT. The unsuccessful attempt in 1995 to hold the extension of the NPT hostage to a "time bound framework" for elimination of all nuclear weapons, uniting in countries such as Japan and India

---

41. Warren Christopher, Statement (Apr. 5, 1995).

42. *See, e.g.,* George Bunn & Roland M. Timerbaev, *Security Assurances to Non-Nuclear-Weapon States,* NONPROLIFERATION REV., Fall 1993, at 11; Bob Bell, Special Assistant to the President and Senior Director for Defense Policy and Arms Control at the National Security Council (NSC), Statement Made at a White House Press Briefing (Apr. 11, 1996).

43. Nuclear Posture Review Report, Department of Defense (2010), p. 15, available at http://www.defense.gov/npr/docs/2010%20Nuclear%20Posture%20Review%20Report.pdf.

"doves" seeking abolition of nuclear weapons and "hawks" seeking an end to the NPT, which they saw as an obstacle to acquiring nuclear weapons, illustrated the confused political climate. Divisions in the UN Security Council over North Korea, Kosovo, Syria, Iran, Ukraine, and the Gulf War of 2003 reinforces uncertainty about the reliability of the existing international security architecture, especially to enforce compliance.

The Biological Weapons Convention of 1972 (BWC)

The Biological Weapons Convention of 1972 was, in the words of President Richard N. Nixon: "the first international agreement since World War II to provide for the actual elimination of an entire class of weapons from the arsenals of nations."[44] This disarmament theme, "elimination of an entire class of weapons," would reappear years later to rally support for both the Treaty on Intermediate-Range missiles (INF) and the Chemical Weapons Convention (CWC). A similar *leitmotif* was the call to act on the BWC before the momentum of technology became so strong that a "window of opportunity" might close. The history of international restraints on biological weapons goes back many years, but the challenges posed by technology are more serious today with the advent of the biotechnology revolution.

The deliberate exploitation of disease can be found in the earliest accounts of war, many centuries before the discovery of microbes. In the modern age, decades before the BWC was negotiated, general prohibitions on the use of asphyxiating gases and poisons came out of the Hague Conferences of 1899 and 1907. After the massive use of chemical weapons in World War I, these provisions were repeated in the Treaty of Versailles (1919) and in the Washington Naval Treaty of 1922, which had failed to enter into force. The 1925 Geneva Protocol did explicitly prohibit the use of bacteriological weapons in war, based upon a Polish proposal, but neither Japan nor the United States ratified the Protocol prior to World War II. President Franklin Delano Roosevelt did, however, make a no-first-use statement:

> Use of such weapons has been outlawed by the general opinion of civilized mankind. This country has not used them, and I hope that we never will be compelled to use them. I state categorically that we shall under no circumstances resort to the use of such weapons unless they are first used by our enemies.[45]

The United States ultimately ratified the Geneva Protocol in 1975 when it also ratified the BWC.

To the degree that biological weapons were considered in international negotiations prior to 1969, they were linked to chemical weapons or to general and complete disarmament, such as the U.S. and Soviet proposals of 1962 in the Eighteen-Nation Disarmament Committee (ENDC). In 1969 the United Kingdom proposed a stand-alone biological weapons treaty, and the Soviet Union proposed a combined ban on chemical and biological weapons, but most UN action was focused on the question of the legitimacy of U.S. use in Vietnam of riot control agents and herbicides, issues primarily associated at the time with chemical weapons. In an ultimately unsuccessful effort to head off the

---

44. Formally known as the Convention on the Prohibition of the Development, Production and Stockpiling of Bacteriological (Biological) and Toxin Weapons and on their Destruction, Apr. 10, 1972, 26 U.S.T. 583, 1015 U.N.T.S. 163. *See* U.S. ARMS CONTROL AND DISARMAMENT AGENCY, *supra* note 35, at 96.

45. U.S. ARMS CONTROL AND DISARMAMENT AGENCY, *supra* note 35, at 5. Japan used biological weapons in World War II in China.

use of a UNGA resolution to promulgate an interpretation of the Geneva Protocol on riot control agents and herbicides not shared by the United States, President Nixon announced on November 25, 1969, that the United States would unilaterally adopt a no-first use policy on chemical weapons including incapacitating chemicals. He then went further and announced that the United States would unilaterally eliminate its offensive biological weapons program.[46] This statement set the stage for expedited negotiation of the BWC. The next year, the United States included in its prohibition "toxins," chemical agents produced by biological organisms.

In March 1970, the Soviet Union reversed its position that any treaty on bacteriological weapons must be part of a chemical weapons ban. The United States and the Soviet Union, as co-chairs of the twenty-six nation Conference of the Committee on Disarmament (CCD), formerly the Eighteen-Nation Disarmament Committee (ENDC), developed identical texts leading to the BWC. On December 16, 1971, the UN General Assembly voted 110 to 0 for a resolution in support of the Convention. From the beginning, however, there was controversy. France abstained because verification provisions were not provided. China attacked the BWC for not including chemical weapons. Even in the United States, the U.S. Senate Foreign Relations Committee withheld action on both the BWC and the 1925 Geneva Protocol until the matter of herbicides and riot-control agents had been resolved by an Executive Order issued by President Gerald Ford that the United States would:

> [R]enounce as a matter of national policy:
>
> (1) first use of herbicides in war except use, under regulations applicable to their domestic use, for control of vegetation within U.S. bases and installations or around their immediate defensive perimeters;
>
> (2) first use of riot-control agents in war except in defensive military modes to save lives such as:
>
> (a) Use of riot-control agents in riot-control circumstances to include controlling rioting prisoners of war. This exception would permit use of riot-control agents in riot situations in areas under direct and distinct U.S. military control;
>
> (b) Use of riot-control agents in situations where civilian casualties can be reduced or avoided. This use would be restricted to situations in which civilians are used to mask or screen attacks;
>
> (c) Use of riot-control agents in rescue missions. The use of riot-control agents would be permissible in the recovery of remotely isolated personnel such as downed aircrews (and passengers);
>
> (d) Use of riot-control agents in rear echelon areas outside the combat zone to protect convoys from civil disturbances, terrorists and paramilitary organizations.[47]

Anticipating debates over the role of the executive and legislative branches in interpreting arms control treaties and, in particular, expanding the obligations undertaken by the United States as a result of its own domestic legislative process for obtaining consent for ratification, the Senate Foreign Relations Committee highlighted a statement by then U.S. ADCA Director Fred C. Ikle in response to questioning about the ease with which a future administration might change the policy presented to the U.S. Senate during consideration of the BWC:

---

46. *Id.* at 6.
47. *Id.* at 6–7.

There would be no formal legal impediment to such a decision. However, the policy which was presented to the Committee will be inextricably linked with the history of Senate consent to ratification of the Protocol with its consent dependent upon its observance. If a future administration would change this policy without Senate consent whether in practice or by a formal policy change, it would be inconsistent with the history of the ratification, and could have extremely grave political repercussions and as a result is extremely unlikely to happen.[48]

The United States deposited its instrument of ratification on March 26, 1975, and the BWC entered into effect that day. The history of the Convention since then has been one of uncertainty about the compliance of others and controversy over what should be required of those who seek to be compliant.

The BWC is not a lengthy treaty; its key provision is Article I:

Each State Party to this Convention undertakes never in any circumstances to develop, produce, stockpile or otherwise acquire or retain:

(1) Microbial or other biological agents, or toxins whatever their origin or method of production, of types and in quantities that have no justification for prophylactic, protective or other peaceful purposes;

(2) Weapons, equipment or means of delivery designed to use such agents or toxins for hostile purposes or in armed conflict.[49]

State parties are responsible for the destruction of their own stocks (Art. II), not to assist others to acquire BW (Art. III), to prevent prohibited acts on their soil (Art. IV), to consult among states parties and within the UN (Art. V); to report to the UN Security Council and to cooperate in the investigation of noncompliance (Art. VI), and to assist those threatened (Art. VII). Article VIII makes clear that nothing in the BWC limits the Geneva Protocol of 1925 banning the use of asphyxiating or poisonous gases or bacteriological methods of warfare, and Article IX commits the parties to negotiate in good faith toward a ban on chemical weapons. Article X, however, signals one of the inherent challenges in verification of the BWC in that the parties: "undertake to facilitate, and have the right to participate in, the fullest possible exchange of equipment, materials and scientific and technological information for the use of bacteriological (biological) agents and toxins for peaceful purposes."[50]

The dual-use nature of much science and technology related to biological weapons has complicated the enforcement of compliance. The amount of agent necessary to produce vaccines against BW can be greater than the amount necessary for offensive use. Many of the devices for spreading biological weapons such as aerosol sprayers are also dual-use. Proving that a particular country is engaged in an illegal offensive biological weapons program has proven very difficult. In the case of the illegal Soviet offensive BW program, numerous fatalities from accidents such as occurred at Sverdlovsk (Yekaterinburg) and extensive on-site inspection by teams from both the United States and the United Kingdom were insufficient to demonstrate to the satisfaction of many states and experts that the Soviet Union was not compliant. Only defections of key Soviet scientific personnel and the subsequent revelations after the breakup of the Soviet Union confirmed the massive nature of the Soviet offensive and defensive biological weapons programs.

---

48. *Id.* at 7.
49. *Id.* at 98.
50. *Id.* at 99.

Because demonstration of intent is difficult, some have argued that the BWC is not verifiable at all. That the Soviet Union's offensive program was finally revealed suggests that some minimal level of verifiability exists, but clearly that level is very low given that large scale activities related to the program went undiscovered for many years after the BWC went into effect. The quest for measures to achieve more meaningful verifiability for the BWC has engaged the arms control community for many years. Data exchanges have been agreed upon, but implementation is uneven, and the contributions uncertain because of the very nature of dual-use technology. A major effort to develop a Verification Protocol failed when the United States concluded that the risks to legitimate commercial and defensive programs outweighed the limited utility. Work continues on less ambitious measures to build confidence in states party compliance. In the meantime, concern over non-parties and terrorist access to biological weapons has increased greatly since the anthrax attacks in the United States in October 2001 followed the earlier efforts of the Japanese cult Aum Shinrikyo to use biological as well as chemical weapons.

The Chemical Weapons Convention (CWC)

Poison as a weapon pre-dates written history, but the industrial revolution and its huge chemical industries made possible large-scale, battlefield chemical warfare. Long before the gas attacks of World War I, however, efforts were made to ban the use of chemical weapons. The regulations against poison and poisoned weapons attached to the Hague Conventions of 1899 and 1907 did not prevent mass gas artillery strikes aimed at breaking the stalemate of World War I trench warfare, but memory of the cruel deaths on the western front dominated disarmament thinking until the nuclear age. The 1919 Treaty of Versailles repeated the ban on use, but went further, prohibiting Germany from manufacturing or possessing poisonous gases. The completion of a broad international prohibition on the production of chemical weapons would not take place for another seventy-four years, but the document seeking a universal ban on chemical weapons use was completed in 1925, the Geneva Protocol. It entered into force on February 8, 1928.[51] Extending the ban on chemical and biological weapons development, stockpiling, and production reappeared in the grand Cold War disarmament plans of the Soviet Union and the United States, as well as some others.

The entry into force of the BWC, with its call for good faith efforts to complete a Chemical Weapons Convention, increased activity in that direction in the Geneva negotiating forum, ultimately renamed the Conference on Disarmament (CD). Unlike biological weapons, which were seen primarily as weapons of indiscriminate terror, chemical weapons were proven battlefield weapons and were in the arsenals of many nations, even if primarily as a deterrent to the use of chemical weapons by others. Chemical production facilities and many chemical agents were dual-use, further complicating verification. Many nations that did not have nuclear weapons and did not want biological weapons, had great interest in chemical weapons. CW had not been used widely after World War I, but that was seen by many as underscoring their deterrent value. To give up the existing chemical option, many states insisted on a comprehensive, intrusive verification regime. Cold War secrecy and the closed societies of the Soviet Union, the Warsaw Pact countries, and China made the prospects for such a verification regime remote. The initiation of large-scale chemical weapons use, first by Iraq, and then by Iran, gave a sense of urgency to the negotiations that had been lacking previously.

---

51. *Id.* at 1–10.

Following the precedent set by NATO INF missile deployments, in the early 1980s Congress compelled the administration of President Ronald Reagan to engage in a "dual-track" approach to modernizing its chemical weapons. The price for Congressional support for the modernization track—the replacement of traditional "unitary" chemical agents with "binary" munitions[52]—was movement on the negotiating track in Geneva. In 1984, then Vice President George H. W. Bush introduced in Geneva a proposal for the elaboration of an "any time, anywhere" inspection regime. Initially, the regime was considered more than the Soviet Union could accept. As the United States and the Soviet Union, however, began to agree to ever more intrusive and cooperative approaches to verifying the Threshold Test Ban Treaty, the INF Treaty, and the Start I and II Treaties, the main obstacle became the more practical difficulty of how to protect national security and proprietary information at each and every facility that might be subject to a routine or challenge inspection. Reflecting concerns over the large Soviet chemical arsenal, the United States also pursued a parallel bilateral agreement with the Soviet Union. As the Cold War wound down, U.S. interest in retaining a chemical deterrent declined, and Soviet opposition to intrusive measures diminished. Following the Gulf War in 1991, George H. W. Bush, having become U.S. President, accelerated efforts to conclude a CW Convention. Australia, working closely with the United States, tabled a treaty text bringing together in a logical way the essential provisions contained in the "rolling text." A "friends of the Chair" group then prepared a Chairman's text that became the basis of the Convention concluded in September 1992.

In Paris on January 13, 1993, four years after the earlier Paris Conference on Chemical Weapons Use met to consider responses to chemical weapons use in the Iraq-Iran War, well over 100 nations met to sign the CWC:

1. Each State Party to this Convention undertakes never under any circumstances:
   (a) To develop, produce, otherwise acquire, stockpile or retain chemical weapons, or transfer, directly or indirectly, chemical weapons to anyone;
   (b) To use chemical weapons;
   (c) To engage in any military preparations to use chemical weapons;
   (d) To assist, encourage or induce, in any way, anyone to engage in any activity prohibited to a State Party under this Convention.

2. Each State Party undertakes to destroy chemical weapons it owns or possesses, or that are located in any place under its jurisdiction or control, in accordance with the provisions of this Convention.

3. Each State Party undertakes to destroy all chemical weapons it abandoned on the territory of another State Party, in accordance with the provisions of this Convention.

4. Each State Party undertakes to destroy any chemical weapons production facilities it owns or possesses, or that are located in any place under its jurisdiction or control, in accordance with the provisions of this Convention.

5. Each State Party undertakes not to use riot control agents as a method of warfare.[53]

---

52. Binary munitions contained two non-lethal agents that become lethal when they were combined when the projectile or missile was fired. Aging unitary stocks risk dangerous leaks and continue to be extremely expensive and controversial to eliminate. Binary components were safer to store, transport, and eliminate.

53. U.S. ARMS CONTROL AND DISARMAMENT AGENCY, CONVENTION ON THE PROHIBITION OF THE DEVELOPMENT, PRODUCTION, STOCKPILING AND USE OF CHEMICAL WEAPONS AND ON THEIR DESTRUCTION 3 (1993).

The CWC, along with its lengthy Verification Annex, was the most detailed multilateral treaty ever negotiated and provided the most intrusive inspection regime ever implemented voluntarily. In The Hague, in the Netherlands, a large, new international organization was created to oversee the treaty— the Organization for the Prevention of Chemical Weapons (OPCW). Definitions were accompanied by a schedule of agents and relevant chemicals. Parties are required to provide extensive data on stocks and facilities, including certain civilian industrial facilities engaged in related activities. Such facilities would be subject to routine inspections. Challenge inspections "any time, anywhere" were permitted with "no right of refusal," but with "managed access" procedures. Obligations were created to provide assistance and protection to parties threatened or attacked by chemical weapons. One of its far-reaching provisions was the Article VII requirement for states parties to put in place national legislation to aid enforcement.[54]

Article XXII prohibited reservations.[55] The complexity of the CWC, its intrusiveness, and demanding provisions such as in Article VII and Article XXII delayed ratification in many countries. In the United States Senate, concern was expressed over numerous issues. Large chemical manufacturers had been consulted closely during the negotiation of the Convention and were well aware of its provisions. Many small businesses, however, were surprised at the invasive possibilities and uncertain about the operation and financial burdens. The uncertainty of detecting violations, despite the intrusive regime, reinforced doubts about the wisdom of taking on those burdens. An additional problem dealt with the obligation "not to use riot control agents as a method of warfare." The Bush administration had interpreted this provision at signature as not precluding riot control agent use for the limited purposes contained in the 1974 Executive Order of President Gerald Ford; namely, in cases involving human shields, rioting prisoners of war, rescuing downed pilots, and rear area protection.[56] Subsequently, the Clinton administration submitted to the United States Senate a more narrow interpretation. After initial setbacks, the Senate consented to ratification through Senate Executive Resolution 75, which placed conditions on that consent. The CWC entered into force three days later, on April 27th.

Achievement of the objectives of the CWC has not been easy. India, South Korea, the Russian Federation, and the United States declared CW stocks that would be destroyed, but many states believed to have CW programs did not join the Convention. Membership is particularly weak among countries of the Middle East. Uncertainty accounting for the Iraqi program highlights the inherent verification difficulties, and the possibility of new technologies and "novel agents" raises concern that the challenges may grow more difficult.[57] Destruction of Russian stocks has been delayed and, as with the U.S. program, environmentally sound and politically acceptable CW destruction has become very expensive. Burdens associated with routine verification and uncertainties associated with challenge inspection have polarized assessments of the future of such control regimes.[58] Initially, many voices advocated the CWC as a model for verification of the BWC. The Aum Shinrikyo Sarin terrorist attack on the Tokyo subway has made clear that some of the most dangerous threats from chemical weapons do not come from traditional sources and may not be easily addressed by international organizations whose primary focus is

---

54. *Id.* at 19.
55. *Id.* at 45.
56. *See* U.S. ARMS CONTROL AND DISARMAMENT AGENCY, *supra* note 35, at 6–7.
57. *See* THE CHEMICAL WEAPONS CONVENTION: IMPLEMENTATION CHALLENGES AND SOLUTIONS (Jonathan B. Tucker ed., 2001).
58. *See* THE CONDUCT OF CHALLENGE INSPECTIONS UNDER THE CHEMICAL WEAPONS CONVENTION (Jonathan B. Tucker ed., 2002).

the behavior of nation states prepared to join the CWC. Nevertheless, the OPCW played a key role in the removal of chemical weapons from Syria after such weapons had been used by the government against insurgents.

Conventional Arms

Extrapolation into the future of the horrors experienced as a result of chemical warfare in World War I, Ethiopia, and the Iran-Iraq War, biological warfare by Japan in China, and the two nuclear bombs at the end World War II makes reducing the threat of weapons of mass destruction the highest priority of international arms restraint. The consequences of the large-scale use of nuclear or biological weapons could be beyond human imagination. Nevertheless, in the violent twentieth century, chemical, nuclear, and biological weapons produced only a small percentage of the casualties. If risk is a product of consequences versus probabilities, then the risk based upon past experience continues to be greatest from so-called "conventional weapons," which are in use somewhere in the world every day.

General and Complete Disarmament (GCD)

The World Disarmament Conference of 1932 failed for many reasons, including animosity among allies, disputes between France and Germany, and the withdrawal of Japan and Germany from the Conference and from the League of Nations the next year. It was, with fifty-nine nations participating, the largest such conference up to that time. In preparation for the Conference, the new Soviet Union had called for the abolition of all military forces and destruction of warships and munitions plants. During the first year of the Conference, U.S. President Herbert Hoover proposed that armies and armaments be reduced by one-third. One year later, his successor, President Franklin D. Roosevelt proposed elimination of "offensive" weapons such as aircraft, tanks, and mobile artillery. World War II was six years away.

Out of World War II emerged the United Nations. Article 26 of the United Nations Charter gave its Security Council responsibility to plan for the regulation of armaments. Article 11 gave the General Assembly responsibility to consider the principles of arms regulation and disarmament. Initially dominated by the nuclear initiatives such as the Baruch Plan for international control of atomic energy, United Nations discussion of conventional arms picked up in late 1946 when the Soviet Union proposed in the General Assembly the removal of foreign troops from all countries except former Axis powers and their satellites and the development of conventional arms limitations. In response, the Security Council established in 1947 the Commission on Conventional Armaments (CCA). The CCA accomplished little, especially after the Soviet Union walked out in 1950 to protest the exclusion of the People's Republic of China.

The U.S. placed priority on preventing the spread of nuclear weapons. The Soviet Union sought to weaken the U.S. presence in Europe. Rejecting U.S. verification proposals, the U.S.S.R also rejected a French proposal for data exchanges. Similar polarization continued when the Disarmament Commission (DC) and its five-nation subcommittee began to meet in 1952. Although both sides called for deep reductions in conventional forces, verification and the nuclear question remained obstacles. In 1955, in response to a British and French proposal the previous year for comprehensive nuclear and conventional disarmament, the Soviet Union offered a parallel plan that included fixed stations for inspections. Soviet General Secretary Nikita Khrushchev's immediate rejection of President

Eisenhower's Open Skies proposal in 1955 further stifled discussions as inspection measures advocated by the West to prevent surprise continued to be equated in Moscow with espionage. Between 1957 and 1960, both sides in the Cold War presented revised comprehensive disarmament proposals but with a greater detailing of steps and partial measures that would later become stand-alone proposals including bans on nuclear testing and production of fissile material for military purposes.

On September 25, 1961, five days after a joint U.S.-Soviet statement agreed that the goal of arms negotiations should be "general and complete disarmament" (GCD), President John F. Kennedy addressed the UN General Assembly calling for a resumption of negotiations on that basis. The United States presented its "Declaration on Disarmament: A Program for General and Complete Disarmament in a Peaceful World." Although comprehensive in nature, the actual plan called for a step-by-step implementation of both nuclear and conventional disarmament under an international disarmament organization. "General and complete disarmament" would remain a goal in the preambles of many resolutions and referenced explicitly as an obligation under Article VI of the NPT. The negotiation of a treaty on GCD, however, has never advanced. Movement toward GCD has instead been measured by the scope of partial agreements that have been concluded over the years, mostly in Europe as a result of the end of the Cold War. A few agreements constraining conventional weapons and their use, however, have been opened for universal participation.

The Convention on Prohibitions or Restrictions on the Use of Certain Conventional Weapons Which May Be Deemed to Be Excessively Injurious or to Have Indiscriminate Effects and Protocols of 1980 (CCW)

The 1980 Convention on Prohibitions or Restrictions on the Use of Certain Conventional Weapons which May Be Deemed to Be Excessively Injurious or to Have Indiscriminate Effects and Protocols (CCW)[59] extended international law to deal with the humanitarian dangers associated with particular weapons or use. The International Committee of the Red Cross (ICRC) was the catalyst for action, and the Convention with its first three protocols entered into force on December 2, 1983. The purpose of the CCW is to ban or restrict the use of specific types of weapons that are considered to cause suffering considered by the parties to be unnecessary or unjustified to combatants or to affect civilians indiscriminately. Interest in the humanitarian contributions of international arms restraint has grown significantly since then as peacekeeping and nation-building activities became primary international security endeavors. International law and arms control continue to become less separate as disciplines.

The CCW, often called the UN Convention on Inhumane Weapons (IWC), is reviewed annually and currently now contains five Protocols plus an Amended Protocol II. Protocol I was designed primarily to aid in the medical treatment of casualties. Its provisions are remarkably simple: "It is prohibited to use any weapon the primary effect of which is to injure by fragments which in the human body escape detection by X-rays."[60] Far more

---

59. Convention on Prohibitions or Restrictions on the Use of Certain Conventional Weapons Which May Be Deemed to Be Excessively Injurious or to Have Indiscriminate Effects and Protocols, Oct. 10, 1980, 1342 U.N.T.S. 137, 19 I.L.M. 1523 (as amended Oct. 13, 1995, and May 3, 1996, 35 I.L.M. 1206) [hereinafter CCW].

60. CCW, *supra* note 59, 19 I.L.M. at 1529.

complex is CCW Protocol II, prohibiting indiscriminate use of landmines and booby traps. Among the key provisions of Protocol II as amended are prohibitions dealing with designs that cause superfluous injury or detonate in the presence of non-contact mine detectors and extensive rules defining the indiscriminate use that is prohibited.[61] Protocol II goes on to require recording of minefield locations, cooperation in the protection of United Nations forces from mines and booby traps, and cooperation in removal of mines. A technical annex expands on reporting and marking. Realizing the fact that most conflicts today occur within the borders of a nation, the 1996 Amendment to Protocol II applied the provisions of the original Protocol to internal conflicts, and put a limitation on the transfer of prohibited mines to non-states parties and unauthorized entities, prohibited remotely delivered mines that did not self-deactivate and self-destruct, and required that all landmines be detectable.

Protocol III, also from 1980, restricts use of incendiary weapons, weapons that use heat or flame generated by a chemical reaction. Incendiary weapons covered include flamethrowers, fougasses, and other munitions containing incendiary substances, but not signaling and smoke making devices. Article 2 contains the provisions designed to protect civilians.[62] The United States, in ratifying this Protocol, reserved the right to use incendiaries when such use would minimize the loss of life in comparison to the use of other munitions on legitimate military targets.

The original three CCW protocols entered into force on December 2, 1983. A fourth protocol, adopted in 1995 and entered into force in 1998, banned the use of lasers specifically designed to blind adversary forces. This problem arose because of the growing use of lasers on the battlefield, and with it, the danger to eyesight, particularly to anyone using binoculars and telescopes.[63]

Finally, a Fifth Protocol was adopted in 2003 and entered into force in 2006 to address the problem of unexploded and abandoned ordnance—the explosive remnants of war (ERW)—on the fields of conflict. It is intended to commit parties to the Protocol to the eradication of the legacies of war that pose a threat to civilian populations in need of development and aid workers providing assistance to them.[64]

Greater public scrutiny of combat operations has increased the role of humanitarian law in warfare. The CCW, with its ongoing review process, has become the forum for discussion of international restraint on a wide variety of arms frequently used in conflicts. The CCW process is examining, for example, vehicular landmines, small arms, and various types of other ordnance.

Ottawa Landmine and Cluster Munitions Conventions

The Convention on the Prohibition of the Use, Stockpiling, Production and Transfer of Anti-Personnel Mines and their Destruction (Ottawa Convention)[65] is perhaps the conventional arms treaty best known to the public. With thousands of people killed or injured

---

61. CCW, *supra* note 59, 35 I.L.M. at 1210–12.

62. CCW, *supra* note 59, 19 I.L.M. at 1535.

63. CCW, *supra* note 59, 35 I.L.M. at 1218.

64. Available at http://www.unog.ch/80256EDD006B8954/(httpAssets)/5484D315570AC857C1257 1DE005D6498/$file/Protocol+on+Explosive+Remnants+of+War.pdf

65. Convention on the Prohibition of the Use, Stockpiling, Production and Transfer of Anti-Personnel Mines and their Destruction, *opened for signature* Sept. 18, 1997, 36 I.L.M. 1507.

every year by abandoned landmines or unexploded ordnance from past wars or current violence, humanitarian groups organized the "Ottawa Process "to press for the rapid negotiation of a ban on landmines that would create hazards for innocent civilians. Perhaps the most rapidly negotiated international treaty, 122 governments signed the convention after an accelerated series of diplomatic conferences. This process that was acclaimed as a model for future negotiations included the intense participation of non-governmental organizations. An umbrella organization, the International Campaign to Ban Landmines won the Nobel Peace Prize in 1997, the same year that the Convention was completed.

The key provisions are in Article 1:

> 1. Each State Party undertakes never under any circumstances:
> (a) To use anti-personnel mines;
> (b) To develop, produce, otherwise acquire, stockpile, retain or transfer to anyone, directly or indirectly, anti-personnel mines;
> (c) To assist, encourage or induce, in any way, anyone to engage in any activity prohibited to a State Party under this Convention.
> 2. Each State Party undertakes to destroy or ensure the destruction of all anti-personnel mines in accordance with the provisions of this Convention.[66]

Central to understanding issues concerning the mine ban treaty is the definition of anti-personnel mines in Article 2:

> 1. "Anti-personnel mine" means a mine designed to be exploded by the presence, proximity or contact of a person and that will incapacitate, injure or kill one or more persons. Mines designed to be detonated by the presence, proximity or contact of a vehicle as opposed to a person that are equipped with anti-handling devices, are not considered anti-personnel mines as a result of being so equipped.[67]

Despite widespread agreement on the need to prevent civilian casualties and to remove obstacles to economic reconstruction caused by unexploded ordnance left behind in war zones, perhaps no international arms restraint agreement has resulted in such political polarization as the Ottawa Convention. Strongly supported by the public, celebrities, and most nations of the world, participation has been weak in troubled regions such as South Asia and the Middle East. Major powers including the United States, Russia, China and India have not signed. Critics complained that the Ottawa process overruled the concerns of the very governments whose cooperation was most needed. These critics also argue that the Ottawa Convention does not solve the problem of mines already abandoned, but would prevent the introduction of safer new technologies with self-deactivation and self-destruct mechanisms that could prevent the problem in the future. Also, they note that the landmine production ban would not prevent common "field expedient" anti-personnel mines such as hand grenades or other munitions with trip wires or contact fuses. The critics believe that modern landmines with their self-deactivation and self-destruction features are far safer than other ordnance such as the sub-munitions of cluster bombs, and that many of the casualties attributed to landmines are caused by unexploded bombs and artillery shells with high "dud" rates. Modern self-deactivating munitions combined with the limits on landmine use of CCW Protocol II eliminate most of the future landmine problem, and, while costly, many nations, including the U.S. have adopted a 99% functioning rate requirement for all future ordnance procurement.

---

66. *Id.* art. 1.
67. *Id.* art. 2.

Advocates of the landmine ban attribute to the Ottawa Convention a number of important developments including the rapid establishment of an international norm agreed to by most nations and putting restraints on some others. Landmine production and use has been reduced, trade has declined, the search for alternatives has increased, and funding for de-mining has expanded greatly. Citing the importance of landmines to the defense of South Korea, the United States has not signed the Ottawa Convention. The U.S. has indicated that it would seek to sign the Convention if it could develop and deploy alternatives to anti-personnel mines, including those in so-called mixed systems, munitions that also have anti-vehicle components. While not a party to the Ottawa Convention, the U.S. is the largest contributor to humanitarian demining programs spending to date over $2.2 billion to eliminate landmines and other ERW.[68] Skeptical of repeating the "Ottawa Process," the U.S. has sought to deal with related issues such as unexploded ordnance or ERW in the CCW review process.

As a result of frustration over the slow decision-by-consensus process used in the CCW, coupled with the seeming success of the Ottawa Landmine Convention in achieving an outright ban on landmines, Norway launched what became known as the "Oslo Process" on cluster munitions in February 2007 by inviting all governments supporting the development of new rules prohibiting cluster munitions which cause "unacceptable suffering" to civilians to a conference in Oslo. The conference resulted in 2008 in the adoption of a legally binding international instrument prohibiting "cluster munitions that cause unacceptable harm to civilians," and the establishment of a framework for co-operation and assistance for the care and rehabilitation of survivors, the clearance of contaminated areas, risk education, and the destruction of prohibited cluster munitions. The Convention on Cluster Munitions (CCM) was adopted in 2008, and entered into force, with over 110 nations signing the CCM, on 1 August 2010. Under the Convention on Cluster Munitions, cluster munitions are defined and prohibited as a category of weapons. In Article 2 of the CCM a cluster munition is defined as "a conventional munition that is designed to disperse or release explosive sub munitions each weighing less than 20 kilograms, and includes those explosive sub munitions." Therefore the ban on cluster munitions, and all relevant Convention obligations such as stockpile destruction, applies both to the container and all the sub munitions it contains.[69] Russia, China, the United States and a number of other nations have not signed the Convention on Cluster Munitions. The United States sought to deal with the issue in the CCW process by requiring future cluster munitions to have less than a 1% failure rate. The U.S. has stated that cluster munitions produce less risk than the equivalent unitary munitions and remain essential.

United Nations Register of Conventional Arms and the Arms Trade Treaty

The nineteenth century image of "merchants of death" was one of the earliest motivators for international arms restraint, but universal approaches to limiting arms trading never gained support among nation states. Arms exports remain an important economic sector for many countries, and nearly all states rely on imports to meet their defense requirements.

---

68. Worldwide, it is estimated that there are 10 million acres of land at 1400 sites with ERW. Clean-up would cost in the tens of billions of dollars. *See* Report of the Defense Science Board Task Force on Unexploded Ordnance, at http://www.denix.osd.mil/mmrp/upload/uxo.pdf.

69. The treaty and a brief explanation of its historical antecedents can be found at http://www.icrc.org/ihl/INTRO/620?OpenDocument.

Arms export controls, therefore, were largely a matter of national or alliance policy—designed to deny specific adversaries conventional arms. After the fall of the Shah of Iran, the Falklands War, and particularly the 1991 Gulf War, however, arms exporting nations were embarrassed to see arms they had sold used against them or their allies. With the end of the Cold War, the conclusion of the Treaty on Conventional Forces in Europe (CFE), continuing turmoil in the Middle East, and the growth of international criminal organizations, concern arose also that an excess of arms production capacity would push more and better arms into the troubled Middle East. The complex calculations of regional security made formal limits on trade challenging. As a first step, nations proposed a series of transparency and openness measures with regard to arms transfers. This first step also proved challenging since, for example, prior announcement of sales would invite both competition and criticism. The accumulation of data could reveal vulnerabilities in weapons and stockpiles. The exposure of some sales might spur others. A cautious approach seemed all that would be possible even during the "window of opportunity" that presented itself in 1991.[70]

On January 1, 1992, the United Nations Register of Conventional Arms was established in accordance with UN General Assembly Resolution 46/39L (December 9, 1991). Member States are encouraged to voluntarily provide information in a standardized format on imports or exports of battle tanks, armored combat vehicles, artillery systems, combat aircraft, attack helicopters, warships, and missiles or missile launchers. Although more than three-fourths of the member states have made a submission, including "NIL" reports, reporting has never been consistent.[71] For most nations, the information provided is little different than what is available publicly.

The greatest number of war casualties produced during the decade leading to the twenty-first century were inflicted in internal wars in which small arms were the predominant weapons. Many of these small caliber arms were obtained illegally, often funded through the smuggling of drugs, diamonds, and other contraband. Vicious wars in failed states, often with children as soldiers, spotlighted the tragedies involved. In 2001, the United Nations Conference on the Illicit Trade in Small Arms and Light Weapons in All Its Aspects established a UN action program focused on securing stored arms, tracing missing weapons, destroying excess stocks, and enforcing UN embargoes. Regulating the small arms trade is a daunting task. Every nation purchases small arms, and many poor nations produce them. However, simply reporting transfer or signing on to the UN action program was universally viewed as ineffective in stopping the illicit transfer of arms to those who commit war crimes or violate international humanitarian norms. While Governments focused their efforts primarily on embargo enforcement and conflict resolution, non-governmental organizations placed a greater emphasis on a convention prohibiting sales to states violating human rights, arms treaties or other international humanitarian law and on public pressure against the major arms suppliers, both government and private.

Sustained pressure by IGOs and NGOs to stop this illicit arms trade resulted in the UN General Assembly adopting in 2013 the Arms Trade Treaty (ATT)[72] regulating the international trade in conventional arms, from small arms to battle tanks, combat aircraft

---

70. *See* Cascade of Arms: Managing Conventional Weapons Proliferation (Andrew J. Pierre ed., 1997); Stephanie G. Neuman, *Controlling the Arms Trade: Idealistic Dream or Realpolitik?*, Wash. Q., Summer 1993, at 53.

71. *See* Bureau of Political-Military Affairs, U.S. Department of State, Fact Sheet: UN Register of Conventional Arms (Apr. 15, 2002).

72. The text of the treaty can be found at https://unoda-web.s3.amazonaws.com/wp-content/uploads/2013/06/English7.pdf.

and warships. Proponents argue that the treaty will foster peace and security by thwarting uncontrolled destabilizing arms flows to conflict regions. The prohibitions contained within the ATT are intended to prevent human rights abusers and violators of the law of war from being supplied with arms, and it will make it more difficult for warlords, pirates, and gangs from acquiring these weapons. Additionally, it would establish common binding standards that must be applied to assess international weapons transfers. These standards would be based on existing international law including international human rights and humanitarian law. If fully implemented, under the ATT, a transfer of weapons will be stopped if there is compelling evidence that the weapons are likely to be used for grave violations of international human rights, humanitarian law, or will adversely affect sustainable development.

The U.S. Government was one of the first nations to sign the treaty but concerns were raised that the ATT may, despite the Obama Administration's assertions to the contrary, restrict American's Second Amendment right to bear arms. The Administration has argued that the ATT will be limited to "international transfers. Imports, exports, transit, trans-shipment, or brokering of conventional arms, whether the transfers are state-to-state, state-to-private end-user, commercial sales, leases, or loans/gifts." Domestic ownership, sales and transfers will be a matter for domestic law and will not be subject to the ATT.[73]

Environmental Modification Convention

By the late 1960s, weather modification experiments included cloud seeding to influence snowfall, rain, and the wind speed of hurricanes. In the early 1970s, congressional hearings looked at the military implications of such techniques, spurred in part by press reports of classified rainmaking by the United States in Vietnam. Administration witnesses distinguished between measures that altered the weather in temporary and limited ways and measures that might cause long-term effects. Following passage of a Senate resolution expressing concern, the Defense Department conducted a study of the issue that led the United States to take up the matter with the Soviet Union. At the July 1974 Moscow Summit, the two nations agreed to hold talks, and later that year the Soviet Union introduced a UNGA draft resolution containing broad constraints on weather, climate, and environmental modification. Although the United States abstained on the resolution, bilateral talks the next year produced an agreed approach limiting coverage to a higher "threshold" of impact. Further negotiations in the Conference of the Committee on Disarmament (CCD) in Geneva resulted in the Convention on the Prohibition of Military or Any Other Hostile Use of Environmental Modification Techniques (ENMOD).[74] Article I states:

> 1. Each State Party to this Convention undertakes not to engage in military or any other hostile use of environmental modification techniques having widespread, long-lasting or severe effects as the means of destruction, damage or injury to any other State Party.[75]

Environmental modification techniques were defined in Article II as "any technique for changing—through the deliberate manipulation of natural processes—the dynamics,

---

73. U.S. Department of State, Statement on Signing the Arms Trade Treaty, September 23, 2013 at http://www.state.gov/t/isn/armstradetreaty/.

74. Convention on the Prohibition of Military or Any Other Hostile Use of Environmental Modification Techniques (ENMOD), *opened for signature* May 18, 1977, 1108 U.N.T.S. 151, 16 I.L.M. 88.

75. *See* U.S. ARMS CONTROL AND DISARMAMENT AGENCY, *supra* note 35, at 155.

composition or structure of the Earth, including its biota, lithosphere, hydrosphere and atmosphere, or of outer space."[76] The threshold of what should be prohibited had been controversial throughout the negotiations, and an effort was made in an Understanding to the Convention to define "widespread" as several hundred square miles, "long-lasting" as several months or a season, and "severe" as "involving serious or significant disruption or harm to human life, natural and economic resources or other assets."[77] The Understanding also gave examples of techniques such as causing earthquakes, cyclones, or tsunamis (tidal waves) or changing weather patterns, the climate, ocean currents, the ozone layer, or the state of the ionosphere. Testimony on behalf of the treaty stressed the importance of heading off "environmental warfare" as a new activity, but the representatives of the Joint Chiefs of Staff also testified that options such as fog dispersal would not be constrained.

During the early 1980s debate over "nuclear winter"—the theory that dust from multiple nuclear detonations could result in a dangerous cooling of the climate—some argued that widespread use of nuclear weapons would be a form of "environmental warfare" prohibited by the Environmental Modification Convention. Prior to the 1991 Gulf War, Saddam Hussein threatened to set fire to the oil fields of Kuwait if the allied coalition sought to expel Iraq by force. Scientific studies concluded that the damage would be manageable. Thus, a form of deterrence by threat to the environment failed, but Iraq did set the oil fields on fire and also pumped large quantities of oil into the Persian Gulf. A legal analysis by the United States concluded that Iraq had not done sufficient harm to have violated ENMOD.

Confrontation and the Cold War Legacy

The world may never again see a bipolar confrontation such as that which dominated the Cold War and produced its greatest arsenals of nuclear and other weapons.[78] The immense military forces of the two sides, particularly their nuclear components were also the target of many arms control and disarmament proposals. Some of these proposals, like the Baruch Plan of 1946, were too grandiose to be negotiated. Others, like the missile launch notification agreements, seemed very small in retrospective, but were highly acclaimed at the time. All involved geo-strategic posturing and tactical negotiating maneuvers. By the end of the Cold War, however, a number of treaties and agreements with significant impact had emerged building upon the easing of tensions and, in some ways, contributing to the political change that made each next step and the end of the Cold War possible. From the perspective of nuclear disarmament and General and Complete Disarmament (GCD), they seemed far from the final goal. From the perspective of the animosity at the height of the Cold War, they would have seemed impossible. Much of the Cold War legacy of arms control seems archaic and inapplicable today. Some of the Cold War legacy, however, provides the foundation of emerging international restraint regimes.

---

76. *Id.*

77. *Id.* at 153.

78. The history of international arms restraint during the Cold War is rich and detailed, especially in nuclear arms control, European conventional force negotiations, and confidence-building measures. To keep this chapter short and to focus on contemporary issues, this section on the U.S.-Soviet and East-West experiences highlights only basic information and themes or issues of importance today. For a concise history, *see* U.S. ARMS CONTROL AND DISARMAMENT AGENCY, *supra* note 35.

From the Baruch Plan to the Nuclear Test Moratorium

The American approach to arms restraint at the end of World War II was influenced by two factors, one old and one new. The older factor was the propensity to demobilize military manpower after war. The new factor was the atomic bomb. From the U.S.-U.K.-Canadian Summit of 1945, through the Acheson-Lilienthal Report of 1946 to presentation of the Baruch Plan in June 1946, the U.S. view was that the technology for nuclear weapons would spread, that verification of national nuclear programs would be inadequate, and that only placing the entire nuclear fuel cycle under international control could prevent proliferation. Baruch proposed that the inspection regime be exempt from veto.

The Soviet approach from the beginning was to focus attention on the American nuclear advantage while rejecting on-site inspections as covers for espionage and violations of sovereignty. The Gromyko Plan presented in 1946 in response to the Baruch Plan, called simply for a ban on all nuclear weapons and for the United States to eliminate all its nuclear weapons in three months. By the end of 1946, ironically, the Soviet Union was linking nuclear disarmament to conventional force reductions aimed at the U.S. presence in Europe. The U.S.S.R. also insisted on retaining a veto over all inspections. Stalemate in the negotiations and the Korean War marked the end of the era of the Baruch Plan.

In 1952, a study done by Dr. J. Robert Oppenheimer for Secretary of State Dean Acheson concluded that an acceptable and negotiable nuclear disarmament plan was not likely and recommended that partial measures be considered to reduce the risk of a first strike. With the death of Joseph Stalin in March 1953, President Dwight Eisenhower, drawing from the Oppenheimer study in his 'Chance for Peace" speech, called for military reductions and the international control of atomic energy along with UN inspections. After the Soviet Union tested its first hydrogen bomb, President Eisenhower's "Atoms for Peace" proposal of 1953 sought a more limited approach to the nuclear question among the "powers principally involved," but with an "international atomic energy agency" receiving and controlling fissile material for peaceful purposes. A Subcommittee of Five (Britain, Canada, France, the United States, and the Soviet Union) of the UN Disarmament Commission continued to discuss nuclear disarmament, but the Atoms for Peace program was negotiated separately. No bilateral nuclear treaties were to emerge in this era in which each side competed for public opinion with grand disarmament proposals. A number of seminal developments did take place. Eisenhower's July 1955 "Open Skies" proposal for aerial verification was quickly rejected by the Soviet Union but would re-emerge years later as a multilateral confidence-building treaty that was proposed by President George H. W. Bush in 1989, concluded in 1992, and entered into force on January 1, 2002. The ten-nation (five each from the two blocs) "Conference of Experts for the Study of Possible Measures Which Might be Helpful in Preventing Surprise Attack" met in Geneva in 1958, setting the precedent of focusing on partial measures, strategic stability, and confidence-building. More dramatic, however, was the growing public concern about fallout from nuclear testing in the atmosphere.

Nuclear Testing Limitations

In 1955, the Soviet Union included a nuclear test ban in its disarmament proposals. Two years later, the U.S. responded with a proposal for a two-year test moratorium linked to a ban on the production of fissile material for nuclear weapons. After conducting a series of nuclear tests, the Soviet Union announced a unilateral test moratorium in March of 1958. During the rest of the year, a Conference of Experts was held in Geneva. In October, when negotiations on a test ban began, Great Britain and the United States announced that they also would unilaterally cease testing. When the Soviet Union insisted on a veto of investigations of seismic events and U.S. investigations indicated that verifying underground testing was more difficult than earlier believed, the United States proposed that an atmospheric test ban be negotiated, later extending the scope to the oceans and outer space. The talks made little progress and in September 1961, the Soviet Union broke out of the test moratorium with a massive series of tests including a fifty-eight megaton hydrogen bomb, the largest ever detonated. The U.S. quickly resumed testing as well. Ten months after the October 1963 Cuban missile crisis and a month after the "Hot Line" Agreement, the Soviet Union accepted the proposal to negotiate an atmospheric test ban treaty. The resulting limited test ban treaty was signed in Moscow on August 5, 1963.[79]

Limited Test Ban Treaty

The Treaty Banning Nuclear Weapon Tests in the Atmosphere, in Outer Space and Under Water, otherwise known as the Partial or Limited Test Ban Treaty (LTBT) relied on national technical means to verify the prohibitions laid out in sparse text:

> 1. Each of the Parties to this Treaty undertakes to prohibit, to prevent, and not to carry out any nuclear weapon test explosion, or any other nuclear explosion, at any place under its jurisdiction or control:
>
> (a) in the atmosphere; beyond its limits, including outer space; or under water, including territorial waters or high seas; or
>
> (b) in any other environment if such explosion causes radioactive debris to be present outside the territorial limits of the State under whose jurisdiction or control such explosion is conducted. It is understood in this connection that the provisions of this subparagraph are without prejudice to the conclusion of a Treaty resulting in the permanent banning of all nuclear test explosions, including all such explosions underground, the conclusion of which, as the Parties have stated in the Preamble to this Treaty, they seek to achieve.[80]

Although it was the most significant nuclear arms control agreement of its age and remains in effect, the LTBT was controversial. Both hawks and doves criticized it for not being disarmament, some questioned its verifiability, and the U.S. Senate held extensive hearings on the impact on U.S. nuclear weapons technology and the American deterrent. Only with assurances that the U.S. would continue underground testing and, as a "safeguard," retain the ability to test in the atmosphere did the Senate give its consent to ratification. The U.S. ratified the LTBT on October 10, 1963, and the LTBT entered into effect on that day. A month later, the UNGA passed a resolution urging other nations to adhere. Neither France nor the People's Republic of China became parties to the treaty, and the next year China conducted its first nuclear test. The LTBT has significance even today. India, Israel, and Pakistan are parties to the LTBT, but North Korea is not. The last atmospheric test was by China in 1996.

---

79. *See* U.S. ARMS CONTROL AND DISARMAMENT AGENCY, *supra* note 35, at 24–26.
80. *Id.* at 29.

Threshold Test Ban Treaty and the Peaceful Nuclear Explosions Treaty

Having eliminated the health and environmental risks associated with atmospheric nuclear testing, the LTBT also reduced the sense of urgency in the test ban negotiations. Soviet reluctance to accept intrusive inspections combined with further U.S. test data again suggesting that verification of a ban on all underground testing would be difficult discouraged progress. Arms control and disarmament talks moved in a different direction resulting in the 1968 multilateral NPT and in 1972 both the bilateral Interim Agreement on Strategic Arms Limitations (SALT I) and the Anti-Ballistic Missile (ABM) Treaty. In March 1974, Secretary of State Henry Kissinger proposed in Moscow that consideration be given to a threshold test ban treaty, one that would limit the size of each underground nuclear test. At the July 1974 Moscow Summit, President Richard Nixon signed the TTBT.

The Treaty Between the United States of America and the Union of Soviet Socialist Republics on the Limitation of Underground Nuclear Weapon Tests (TTBT) was negotiated quickly, but sixteen years would pass before it entered into force. From the beginning the TTBT was controversial, again with criticism both that it went too far and that it did not go far enough:

> 1. Each Party undertakes to prohibit, to prevent, and not to carry out any underground nuclear weapon test having a yield exceeding 150 kilotons at any place under its jurisdiction or control, beginning March 31, 1976.
>
> 2. Each Party shall limit the number of its underground nuclear weapon tests to a minimum.[81]

Because the TTBT itself did not limit so-called Peaceful Nuclear Explosions (PNEs), consideration of the TTBT would wait two more years for the completion of the Treaty on Underground Nuclear Explosions for Peaceful Purposes (PNET). Because a PNE could be the same as a weapons test, measures to bring them under the same threshold limit were necessary. Controversy over Soviet compliance with the TTBT, however, complicated ratification of the TTBT/PNET treaties and undermined confidence in the negotiation of a CTB.

The TTBT, as originally negotiated, did advance some concepts of verification. In addition to prohibiting interference with National Technical Means (NTM) of verification, the package included a Protocol providing for reciprocal data exchanges on the coordinates of test locations, the geology of test sites, and calibration data (yield, date, time, depth and coordinates) for two underground tests at each "geophysically distinct testing area."[82] The PNET went further, establishing the Joint Consultative Commission (JCC) to facilitate cooperation including access to the test site and the exchange of extensive data required in the Protocol to the PNET. In order to determine that no individual device in a cluster of detonations would violate the 150 kiloton threshold, extensive intrusiveness was necessary including advanced warning of the tests and detailed information on the placement of each explosive, the geology of the site, the depth of the water table and other such information.[83]

---

81. *Id.* at 135.
82. *Id.* at 137.
83. *Id.* at 142–43.

The TTBT/PNET Verification Protocol and the Joint Verification Experiment

In 1983, the United States proposed to the Soviet Union that an improved verification regime be negotiated for the TTBT and PNET. Moscow rejected the proposal at that time. On July 30, 1985, Soviet General Secretary Mikhail Gorbachev announced a nuclear test moratorium as the two nations prepared to resume nuclear negotiations that had been broken off by the Soviet Union after the NATO missile deployments began. At the Reagan-Gorbachev Geneva Summit at the end of the year, Gorbachev stated that verification would be not be an obstacle. Interpreting this as meaning that intrusive inspections and monitoring might be negotiable, Reagan wrote Gorbachev early the next year proposing the demonstration of an on-site hydrodynamic measurement technique known as CORRTEX, which involved drilling a hole for diagnostics near but not in the test emplacement hole. Initially, the Soviet Union rejected this approach, but with the prospect that agreement to improved verification of the TTBT and PNET would open the door for the step-by-step approach to the CTBT negotiations that the Reagan administration had negotiated with Congress, the Soviet Union agreed to join the U.S. in the Nuclear Testing Talks (NTT) that lasted from 1987 to 1990.

As the conclusion of the INF treaty in 1987 improved the political environment for negotiations, the U.S. and the Soviet Union began the Nuclear Testing Talks, turning first to the preparations for a Joint Verification Experiment (JVE) to demonstrate the monitoring proposals of the two sides. By the middle of the next year, having conducted the most detailed, technical arms negotiations ever conducted, the two sides concluded a JVE Agreement with thirty-seven highly technical annexes. On August 17, 1987, the first Soviet monitoring of a U.S. test took place at the Nevada test site. On September 14, the U.S. monitored a Soviet test at the Semipalatinsk test site.[84] The significance of these joint efforts goes beyond their role in bringing about the verification protocols to the TTBT and PNET. In many ways, the scientist-to-scientist/military-to-military problem solving undertaken in the JVE was the precursor of the later laboratory-to-laboratory, confidence-building measures and the Cooperative Threat Reduction (CTR) programs that would be put in place under the Nunn-Lugar legislation and other programs to help eliminate nuclear delivery systems and ensure the security of nuclear weapons and material. Programs such as the international science centers to prevent a "brain drain" of weapons scientists to countries of proliferation concern also had their origins in these cooperative experiments.

With the conclusion of the Joint Verification Experiments, the verification protocols were completed under the administration of President George H.W. Bush. Citing the "fly before you buy" precedent, the administration submitted the TTBT and PNET to the Senate for consent to ratification, now accompanied by the most extensive and intrusive verification regime thus far negotiated. On September 25, 1990, the U.S. Senate voted its approval for ratification by a vote of 98-0. The United States now indicated that it would continue its step-by-step movement toward a CTB by engaging the Soviet Union and by gaining experience verifying the TTBT. Rapid developments in the political environment would change all of this. With the breakup of the Soviet Union, the Russian Federation announced the termination of nuclear testing, and France joined in the moratorium. Pressure to end all testing grew rapidly.

---

84. *See* Edward Ifft, "The Threshold Test Ban Treaty," Arms Control Today, March 2009, at http://www.armscontrolorg/print/3547#14. The author was the deputy head of the U.S. delegation to the TTBT talks.

Comprehensive Test Ban Treaty (CTBT)

During the 1980s, the United States made clear that verification was only one problem Washington had with a comprehensive nuclear test ban. Washington would reserve the right to test so long as it must depend upon its nuclear deterrent for security. Opposition to this point of view was strong, at home and abroad. From 1977 to 1980, the administration of President Jimmy Carter had engaged in CTB talks with the U.K. and the Soviet Union in Geneva. Concern within the Departments of Defense and Energy and in the Senate, as well as the increasingly technical negotiations, slowed progress. The talks stopped with the Soviet invasion of Afghanistan. During the next decade, the Reagan and Bush administrations would focus primarily on verification of the TTBT and PNET. International and NGO interest in the CTBT continued.

On October 5, 1991, just two months before the end of the Soviet Union, Soviet President Gorbachev announced a one-year test moratorium. The next April, after France ceased nuclear testing and Russian President Boris Yeltsin extended the former Soviet moratorium, Congress passed the Exon-Hatfield-Mitchell bill requiring the U.S. to respect a nine-month moratorium, and then, within certain restraints, conduct up to a maximum of fifteen tests. A permanent end to testing after September 30, 1996, was mandated, unless another nation tested. The Bush administration opposed the legislation, but signed it into law when it was attached to legislation important to the Administration. The White House announced that President Bush would revisit the moratorium after the elections. President William J. Clinton changed U.S. policy, however, just as the preparations for the NPT Extension Conference was putting even more international pressure behind a CTB.

The year 1995 was pivotal for the CTBT. The NPT Extension Conference ended with agreement to conclude a CTBT no later than 1996. China, and then France, resumed nuclear testing in order to prepare for the test ban. After the United States had considered reduced thresholds between one kiloton and a few pounds, President Clinton announced on August 11, 1995, that the United States would support a zero-yield approach. The United States reserved the right to conduct so-called "subcritical" nuclear tests that might contain some nuclear material, but would not conduct weapons tests that produce nuclear yield. To maintain confidence in its nuclear stockpile, the U.S. would put in place a "science-based stockpile stewardship" program to better understand problems that might emerge.

On June 28, 1996, a Chairman's text of a zero-yield CTBT was presented in the CD, but disagreements over how to verify "zero" continued for the next two months. On August 22, India and Iran blocked consensus in the CD on the now completed text. To overcome this obstacle, Australia introduced a resolution of approval in a special session of the UNGA for a text identical to that negotiated in the CD. The resolution passed 158 to 3, with 5 abstentions. On September 24, 1996, the CTBT was opened for signature.[85]

One year after signature, President Clinton submitted the CTBT to the U.S. Senate. Indications had emerged earlier that obtaining a two-thirds approval would be difficult. In May 1998, first India and then Pakistan conducted a series of nuclear tests, prompting sanctions but also delaying action on the CTBT. Between October 6 and 8, 1999, the first conference on facilitating entry into force of the CTBT was held in Vienna, Austria. At the same time, U.S. Senate committees held hearings on the CTBT. On October 13, 1999,

---

85. Comprehensive Test Ban Treaty, *opened for signature* Sept. 24, 1996, 35 I.L.M. 1439.

after a surprise initiative by opponents of the CTBT to press for a vote, consent to ratification was denied by a vote of forty-eight to fifty-one. The test moratorium continues.

Article I provides the essential limit and creates the fundamental controversy about the treaty:

> 1. Each State Party undertakes not to carry out any nuclear weapon test explosion or any other nuclear explosion, and to prohibit and prevent any such nuclear explosion at any place under its jurisdiction or control.[86]

The CTBT does not define what is the nuclear weapon test explosion that is prohibited. In particular, it does not provide for a definition of how a "zero-yield" threshold is to be determined. Detecting small detonations and determining whether the yield is zero vastly complicates verification. The extensive International Monitoring System provided by Article IV and elaborated in Part I of the Protocol is aimed primarily at what was called the "big bang," the early focus of the negotiations.

Advocates of the CTBT argue that the United States is scientifically more advanced than other countries, especially rogue state proliferators, and that the U.S. is better able to cope with a lack of testing. They question whether testing at low yields is of value. Opponents of the CTBT counter that the first generation nuclear weapons sought by proliferators do not need to be tested to have confidence that they will work, and that levels of cheating that are difficult to detect and identify have value to nations with advanced scientific knowledge. Also, if a nation is committed to acquiring a new nuclear capability, it can simply withdraw from the treaty to conduct any tests that may be desired once those tests actually become necessary. Critics do not believe that the United States, with its transparency and democracy, will exploit these possibilities. In short, advocates see the U.S. as better positioned to live with no testing and more likely to develop new weapons if testing is permitted. Critics see other states as likely to cheat and less interested in the safety, security, and reliability concerns that often drove the U.S. to test in the past.

The internals of the CTBT such as its prohibitions and its verification measures are only part of the challenges the treaty faces. The NPT Extension was linked politically to completion of a CTBT, and this linkage was reinforced at the subsequent NPT Review Conference. The status of the CTBT is likely to be a contentious issue domestically within the United States and internationally. India, Pakistan, Israel, and North Korea are not states parties to the CTBT. Their participation and that of the United States is required for the treaty to enter into force.

Strategic Offensive Nuclear Force Limitations and Reductions

In 1964, President Lyndon B. Johnson proposed that the United States and the Soviet Union "explore a verified freeze of the number and characteristics of strategic nuclear offensive and defensive vehicles."[87] Defense Secretary Robert S. McNamara repeated that proposal in 1967 when it was announced that the United States would proceed with the Sentinel Anti-Ballistic Missile system. In July 1968, at the NPT signing ceremony, agreement was announced to begin such talks. Because of the Soviet invasion of Czechoslovakia in August 1968, however, the talks did not begin until the first year of the administration of President Richard M. Nixon. In retrospect, the SALT I negotiations would seem un-

---

86. *Id.* art. 1.
87. U.S. ARMS CONTROL AND DISARMAMENT AGENCY, *supra* note 35, at 110.

complicated, but all of the major issues of strategic arms negotiations during and after the Cold War are to be found there.

SALT I

The Strategic Arms Limitation Talks (SALT) began in Helsinki on November 17, 1969. Three years later they would conclude both the Interim Agreement on Strategic Offensive Arms, usually called SALT I, and the ABM Treaty.[88] The key issues that emerged in the SALT I talks included the definition of "strategic offensive arms," the asymmetrical size and structure of forces, measures of strategic stability, standards of verifiability, and the relationship to defensive systems, in particular ballistic missile defenses.

The difference between the Soviet Union's definition of "strategic" and that of the United States was both technical and geo-political. The United States was primarily interested in limiting intercontinental ballistic missiles. They were seen as the essential elements of surprise attack and a disarming first strike. Whether land or sea based, they were also the primary driver for the American ABM system, particularly if ballistic missiles were to be deployed with Multiple Independently-targeted Re-entry Vehicles (MIRVs). MIRVs, deployed primarily to avoid the costs associated with purchasing more launch vehicles, presented the danger that a single missile with multiple warheads could destroy a number of missiles each also having multiple warheads. The greater the number of warheads per missile on both sides, the greater the multiplier effect. Such calculations could increase the incentive to strike first in a crisis.

The Soviet approach was more explicitly geo-strategic. The Soviet Union wished to include in SALT those systems that could carry nuclear weapons and strike the homeland of the superpowers from where they are based. At various times in the Cold War talks, this included American intermediate range missiles in Europe, cruise missiles at sea or in Europe, the dual-capable aircraft of the United States on land or on aircraft carriers around the Soviet Union, and systems of U.S. allies. Comparable Soviet systems were not to be included under the Soviet definition because they were not deployed near the North American continent. The effect of the Soviet definition of "strategic" was that U.S. systems deployed to defend allies (so-called Forward Based Systems, or FBS) would count, but similar Soviet systems aimed against those allies and American forces overseas would not count. As will be seen, the U.S. approach prevailed over the years, but not without concessions to the concerns raised by the U.S.S.R, and later the Russian Federation.

Differences in the size, composition, modernization, and readiness of the strategic nuclear forces of the two sides also complicated negotiations, even after the Cold War. A sea power from the western hemisphere far from some of its vital interests and allies, the United States relied heavily on its ballistic missile submarines (SSBMs) and its heavy bombers. A Eurasian land power that had developed powerful rocket motors to lift large nuclear warheads and that could carry many smaller warheads, the U.S.S.R. favored "heavy" land-based intercontinental ballistic missiles (ICBMs). Because the concept behind SALT I was a "freeze," different levels and structures were an assumed outcome. After the "Jackson Amendment" to the resolution of ratification required future agreements to provide equality, the kinds of missiles deployed, their size, and the numbers in each category played a more important role. The Jackson Amendment reflected concern in the United States that the U.S. advantage in warheads would be quickly overtaken once the Soviet Union MIRVed its larger number of missiles, including heavy missiles with greater

---

88. In the 1970s, the ABM Treaty was also sometimes referred to as SALT I.

"throw-weight." The later addition of heavy bombers further complicated efforts to compare outcomes, especially because only a part of the bombers were on alert and an even smaller number were expected to survive a surprise attack.

Measures of merit for the quality of SALT I, like the agreements that followed, were also complex. At one level, the destructiveness of nuclear weapons suggested that small differences in capability might not matter. How large a difference would matter was a source of much political debate, a debate made even more intense when comparing asymmetrical forces structures. In SALT I, the effort to "freeze" a Soviet program rapidly surpassing the U.S. force in number of launchers was considered positive, but the future Soviet superiority in large ICBM warheads because of its "throw-weight" advantage was criticized as destabilizing. Large ICBMs had become the very symbol of first strike. On the other hand, the United States would exceed the Soviet Union in Submarine Launched Ballistic Missiles (SLBMs), which are considered more survivable. Only about half of the submarines, however, might actually be at sea. Bombers were seen by the United States as more stabilizing because they were "slow flyers" whose deployments and approach could provide significant advanced warning. In later years, the Soviet Union would argue that the deployment of difficult to detect sea launched cruise missiles (SLCMs) and air launched cruise missiles (ALCMs) constituted a "decapitating" capability, especially after "stealth" technology emerged. SALT I dealt with launchers because of the difficulty of verifying warheads by NTM alone, but subsequent agreements would limit accountable warheads and later bombs and cruise missiles.

Differences over verification, amplified in the past by the "bomber gap" and "missile gap" controversies, remained throughout all the strategic arms negotiations. SALT I was possible, however, because new space-based photo reconnaissance made it possible to count fixed silo launchers and submarines with some confidence. Non-interference with National Technical Means of verification was established as a principle, and elaborated in ever greater detail in future negotiations. Later agreements, limiting accountable missile warheads and bombs would also require greater cooperation, data exchanges, and eventually intrusive on-site inspections. In more complex agreements, confirming compliance with details was often seen as an indicator of overall compliance and intentions. Treaties established consultative bodies to review issues, over the years assessing compliance with extremely detailed and technical implementation provisions.

SALT I began as first the Soviet Union and then the United States deployed ABM systems. Both saw offensive arms limitations as a way to make their own defenses more effective or to limit the size of the defenses that would need to be deployed. The schism within the United States over the advisability of deploying ABM systems led the Johnson and Nixon administrations to seek limits on both offensive and defensive systems. Because of long-standing divisions within the United States, however, the U.S. approach has differed more than that of the Soviet Union. When ABM systems were in disfavor, the U.S. might seek to limit them, as in the original ABM Treaty and the 1974 Protocol to the ABM Treaty. Alternatively, the U.S. might offer concessions on defenses in exchange for reductions in offenses, a rationale some would give for their support of President Reagan's 1983 Strategic Defense Initiative (SDI). When ABM systems were in favor, the U.S. position was to de-link offense and defense or even to insist on a "green light" for defenses as a price for offensive arms reductions. The Soviet position on ABM changed less often, mainly because it was not the subject of intense domestic dispute. The Soviet view did undergo several modifications over the years. With the deployment of the Moscow ABM system, which still exists today, the Soviet Union favored deployments of missile defenses. Within a few years, the Soviet Union realized that American technology might surpass that of the Soviet Union. Thus, in SALT I the Soviet Union sought to limit ABM systems while trying to continue the momentum of their offensive deployments.

The Interim Agreement Between The United States of America and The Union of Soviet Socialist Republics on Certain Measures With Respect to the Limitation of Strategic Offensive Arms (SALT I) was signed in Moscow on May 26, 1972. Its operational mechanism was to prohibit new construction of ICBM silo launchers and to cap the number of SLBM launchers and ballistic missile submarines. Although the treaty did not state the number of ICBM launchers for each side, the number became 1054 for the United States and 1618 for the Soviet Union. The ceilings on SLBMs and a limit on the number of missile submarines each side could have were contained in a Protocol. The 656 SLBMs of the United States on 44 submarines could be increased to 710 SLBMs with the retirement of pre-1964 missiles. The Soviet Union, at 740 accountable SLBMs, could have no more than 950 SLBMs on 62 modern ballistic missile submarines, also requiring a one-for-one retirement of older missiles. Thus, the U.S. was permitted 1710 ballistic missiles and the Soviet Union 2358. A prohibition on the conversion of existing silo launchers for light ICBMs to launchers for heavy ICBMs capped the Soviet Heavy ICBMs at 308. Heavy bombers were not covered by the interim agreement, the United States arguing that they were slow flying, dual-use systems with low alert rates that faced unrestrained air defenses. In a short Interim Agreement text, Article V, dealing with verification, legitimized NTM, a position opposed for many years by the Soviet Union.[89] The prohibitions on interference with NTM and against deliberate concealment would provide the foundation for many more detailed provisions in later treaties.

Some of the most contentious issues were addressed in a series of Agreed Statements, Common Understandings, and Unilateral Statements that accompanied the Interim Agreement. Several were to be central in future negotiations. Concerning the provisions of the Interim Agreement limiting an increase in the size of ICBM silos, an early attempt to limit the growth of "throw-weight," Common Understanding A contained the following:

Ambassador Smith made the following statement on May 26, 1972:

The Parties agree that the term "significantly increased" means that an increase will not be greater than 10-15 percent of the present dimensions of land-based ICBM silo launchers.

Minister Semenov replied that this statement corresponded to the Soviet understanding.[90]

The failure to lock in a clear understanding of what actual dimensions would be limited and also the impact of rocket propulsion modernization and warhead miniaturization would result in a failure to achieve expectations on the effectiveness of this approach to limiting future warhead numbers. The result would be far more ambitious measures in the future.

The most difficult issues were dealt with in a series of Unilateral Statements that anticipated much of the future negotiations. The most central of these concerned withdrawal from the ABM Treaty:

On May 9, 1972, Ambassador Smith made the following statement:

The U.S. Delegation has stressed the importance the U.S. Government attaches to achieving agreement on more complete limitations on strategic offensive

---

89. *See* U.S. ARMS CONTROL AND DISARMAMENT AGENCY, *supra* note 35, at 122.
90. *Id.* at 125.

arms, following agreement on an ABM Treaty and on an Interim Agreement on certain measures with respect to the limitation of strategic offensive arms. The U.S. Delegation believes that an objective of the follow-on negotiations should be to constrain and reduce on a long-term basis threats to the survivability of our respective strategic retaliatory forces. The USSR Delegation has also indicated that the objectives of SALT would remain unfulfilled without the achievement of an agreement providing for more complete limitations on strategic offensive arms. Both sides recognize that the initial agreements would be steps toward the achievement of more complete limitations on strategic arms. If an agreement providing for more complete strategic offensive arms limitations were not achieved within five years, U.S. supreme interests could be jeopardized. Should that occur, it would constitute a basis for withdrawal from the ABM Treaty. The United States does not wish to see such a situation occur, nor do we believe that the USSR does. It is because we wish to prevent such a situation that we emphasize the importance the U.S. Government attaches to achievement of more complete limitations on strategic offensive arms. The U.S. Executive will inform the Congress, in connection with Congressional consideration of the ABM Treaty and the Interim Agreement, of this statement of the U.S. position.

Other key unilateral statements anticipating future issues concerned Land-Mobile ICBM Launchers, Covered Facilities, and "Heavy" ICBMs.[91] All of these statements help to explain why the Interim Agreement was not submitted to the United States Senate as a treaty, and why, although the ABM Treaty was of "unlimited" duration, this agreement was "interim" and only for five years. Unilateral Statement A, by U.S. Ambassador Gerard Smith made clear that Washington expected a better agreement on offensive arms to follow quickly or else the circumstances might be a threat to the supreme national interest of the United States and constitute grounds for withdrawal from the ABM Treaty. Statement B would reflect concern over the ability to verify mobile ICBMs, a serious problem in SALT II and in the Strategic Arms Reductions Talks (START) of the 1980s. The dueling nature of Statement D, reflecting U.S. frustration at its inability to capture heavy missiles more precisely and the Soviet marker on the British and French nuclear systems symbolizes the contrasting focus of the two sides, in particular crisis stability versus geo-political stability.

Not subject to a two-thirds vote of approval in the Senate, the Interim Agreement was approved with much criticism. The most significant action, however, was the September 20, 1972, amendment of Senator Henry M. Jackson of Washington:

> [T]he Congress recognizes the principle of United States-Soviet Union equality reflected in the antiballistic missile treaty, and urges and requests the President to seek a future treaty that, inter alia, would not limit the United States to levels of intercontinental strategic forces inferior to the limits provided for the Soviet Union.... [92]

The Jackson Amendment set the stage and tone for SALT II.

SALT II

At the November 1974 Vladivostok Summit, President Gerald Ford and General Secretary Leonid Brezhnev reached a framework agreement for a follow-on SALT Treaty. Introducing the concept of "nested sublimits," Vladivostok included heavy bombers for

---

91. *Id.* at 126–27.
92. Pub. L. No. 92-448, § 3, 86 Stat. 746, 747 (1972).

the first time under an aggregate ceiling of 2400 Strategic Nuclear Delivery Vehicles, of which no more than 1320 could be MIRVed launchers. The Soviet heavy ICBM launchers remained frozen at 308. The Soviet Union put down markers that it would seek limits on new strategic systems such as cruise missiles. For its part, the United States was concerned about so-called "gray area" systems such as the Soviet "Backfire" bomber that were smaller than heavy bombers, but had some capability to reach the United States. Despite a goal of completing the treaty in 1975, the resurgence of these classic issues and the fall of South Vietnam all served to delay progress until after the next American presidential election. The new President, Jimmy Carter, moved quickly to propose either an agreement deferring the most contentious issues or a "comprehensive proposal" providing for reductions in SNDVs and a 50% reduction in Soviet heavy ICBMs. The Soviet Union rejected both proposals, resulting in the SALT I Interim Agreement expiring on October 3, 1977, without a SALT II treaty to replace it. Both sides announced that they would not take actions inconsistent with the SALT I agreement of the goals of SALT II. On June 18, 1979, the SALT II Treaty was signed at the Vienna Summit.

The SALT II Treaty was the first of the lengthy, highly detailed Cold War treaties that seemed necessary to meet Senate standards for consent to ratification. It also progressed further down the path of managing the force structures of both sides in the interest of crisis stability. The SNDV ceiling of 2400 would taper down to 2250, of which in a modification of the Valdivostok Agreement no more than 1320 could be MIRVed missiles or heavy bombers with long-ranged air launched cruise missiles. The "nested sublimits" were extended further. No more than 1200 MIRVed missile launchers were permitted, and no more than 820 of them could be for ICBMs. Heavy ICBM launchers remained frozen at 308. In addition, SALT II included qualitative limits through a prohibition on more than one new type of ICBM. It also took on, indirectly, the effort of limiting the warheads deployed on ballistic missiles and heavy bombers. ICBMs were limited to a maximum of ten warheads each, and SLBMs were limited to fourteen warheads or less. Existing heavy bombers were limited to a maximum of twenty ALCMs, and future ALCM carrying fleets would be limited to an average of twenty-eight ALCMs.

Verification in particular of the ban on more than one new type of ICBM was to be enhanced by detailed information on characteristics of new types of ICBMs and a major new principle for cooperation with NTM in Article XV:

> Second Common Understanding. Each Party is free to use various methods of transmitting telemetric information during testing, including its encryption, except that, in accordance with the provisions of paragraph 3 of Article XV of the Treaty, neither Party shall engage in deliberate denial of telemetric information, such as through the use of telemetry encryption, whenever such denial impedes verification of compliance with the provisions of the Treaty.[93]

Because the number of warheads of each type of missile was to be capped at the largest number with which it had been tested, detailed provisions were provided for how to distinguish each type. Production and deployment of the SS-16, a mobile ICBM variant of the Intermediate Range SS-20, was banned. Cruise missile carriers were to be distinguished from other heavy bombers by Functionally Related Observable Differences (FRODs). An extensive data exchange was required.

SALT II seemed to have been designed with Senate consideration in mind. It provided equal numerical ceilings, although it did not reduce the number of Soviet heavy ICBMs

---

93. U.S. ARMS CONTROL AND DISARMAMENT AGENCY, *supra* note 35, at 209.

nor had it reversed the growth in capabilities of both heavy and light ICBMs. SALT II reduced the number of strategic nuclear delivery vehicles, but it did permit the number of warheads on them to continue to grow toward certain very high theoretical limits. Although heavy bombers were now limited, they were less constrained than missiles. The package included a Soviet Backfire Statement containing a promise not to give that bomber an increased radius of operations or air-to-air refueling capability. Agreed Statements and Common Understandings were included in the text of what was now a Treaty, not just an agreement. A Protocol, to expire on December 31, 1981, prohibited testing and deployment of mobile ICBMs and sea and ground launched cruise missiles with a range of more than 600 kilometers. A Joint Statement of Principles for SALT III called for deep reductions, further qualitative limitations, and resolution of the Protocol issues.

The SALT II Treaty never entered into force. Despite its lengthy, technical provisions or perhaps because of them, the Treaty came under intense scrutiny as an election year approached. Although voted out of the Senate Foreign Relations Committee (nine to six), it was opposed in the Senate Armed Services Committee by a vote of ten against and seven voting present. The failure to rein in the large increase in Soviet MIRVed ICBM warheads, the grandfathering of an even more capable Soviet heavy ICBM force, doubts that the Backfire Statement was meaningful, suspicion of loopholes in the new types rules, and the fear that the Protocol dealing with ground launched cruise missiles (GLCM) would undermine planed NATO INF deployments were the most heated criticisms. Uncertainty as to whether votes for approval would be sufficient coincided with the Soviet invasion of Afghanistan in December 1979. On January 3, 1980, President Carter withdrew the treaty from consideration.

Although SALT II was never ratified, both the United States and the Soviet Union declared they would not undercut the treaty, continuing and strengthening the practice of interim restraint in the face of unratified or expired Treaties. In 1986 the Reagan administration announced that it would no longer be bound by the treaty, citing Soviet arms control violations, but even then, the President committed the United States not to deploy more warheads than the Soviet Union.

The Intermediate-Range Nuclear Force Treaty (INF)

In 1977, the Soviet Union began to deploy a new MIRVed mobile Intermediate Range Ballistic Missile (IRBM), the SS-20, aimed at Europe. In an age of strategic parity, European defense intellectuals, including German Chancellor Helmut Schmidt, expressed concern that the purpose of the deployment was to "decouple" NATO from America's strategic nuclear umbrella. Although anti-nuclear groups welcomed the decision by President Jimmy Carter not to deploy the so-called Enhanced Radiation Weapon, or "neutron bomb" to Europe, governments expressed concern that NATO not be perceived as having lost the U.S. extended deterrent. To symbolize American commitment, NATO decided in December 1979 to deploy 108 Pershing II ballistic missiles (P II) and 464 Ground Launched Cruise Missiles (GLCM), spread among Belgium, Germany, Italy, the Netherlands, and the United Kingdom. To demonstrate a commitment to restraint, NATO agreed to a "dual track" approach in which negotiations would parallel deployments. In the last months of the Carter administration, the Soviet Union expressed a willingness to negotiate, but also included other U.S. forward based systems on their agenda.

After reaffirming the dual track decision earlier in the year, in November 1981, President Ronald Reagan surprised the world by announcing that the U.S. position in the INF talks to begin that month would be the "zero option," the elimination of all INF missiles on both sides. For the United States, this was both the PII and the GLCM. For the Soviet

Union, this would be the SS-20 and the older SS-4 and SS-5. The key element in all of the Soviet proposals was that no NATO INF missiles would be deployed, SS-20 missiles would not be reduced, and the British and French nuclear forces had to be counted. After considerable tactical maneuvering by both sides, much of it addressed to public opinion and parliaments, the Soviet Union announced on November 23, 1983, that because of the NATO missile deployments it would walk out of the INF and START talks in Geneva, and later walked out of the Mutual and Balanced Force Reductions (MBFR) talks in Vienna. The INF talks would not resume again until 1985. Two years later, the INF Treaty was signed at the December 1987 Washington Summit.

In the end, the Soviet Union agreed to the zero option. The negotiation had not been easy. Fundamentally, the negotiations were geo-political, but the most important positive factors were NATO unity and political change in the Soviet Union. NATO and the United States explored a number of options, notably equal global ceilings with the United States not deploying its full complement in Europe. A proposal for zero in Europe but deployments in Asia was negatively received by vocal critics in Japan and elsewhere in Asia, persuading Moscow finally to embrace the global zero for fear of motivating Japan to acquire nuclear weapons of its own. At heart, the entire negotiation had been about challenging NATO and increasing Soviet influence in Europe. In the end, General Secretary Mikhail Gorbachev concluded that an INF agreement might also enhance Soviet influence in Europe while facilitating internal reform at home.

There were political repercussions from the INF treaty, and not only because of its geo-strategic symbolism. Its intrusive verification provisions, including perimeter-portal monitoring and inspections at production sites, opened up a closed Soviet Union more than anyone inside or outside that country could have imagined. Both the United States and the Soviet Union began the highly public destruction of 2692 missiles.[94] With the breakup of the Soviet Union in 1991, the INF Treaty was multilateralized and relevant newly independent states continued to participate in INF Treaty implementation and inspections. The inspection regime for INF ended on May 31, 2001, but the INF Treaty is of unlimited duration. In 2014, amidst growing tensions between Russian President Vladimir Putin and the West, evidence emerged suggesting that the Russian Federation may have deployed a prohibited INF missile.

START I

With the collapse of SALT II after the Soviet invasion of Afghanistan, the Reagan administration conducted a strategic review of nuclear negotiations. The dual track of NATO took priority, but the strategic arms talks would clearly ride the same waves. In May 1982, President Reagan, having called for a new approach that would provide for reductions in warheads in addition to launchers, announced his specific proposal for Strategic Arms Reduction Talks (START). The U.S. proposed a reduction to 5000 ballistic missile warheads (a reduction of about one-third) of which no more than 2500 could be on ICBMs, along with limits on deployed ballistic missiles, particularly heavy missiles. In response, Soviet President Leonid Brezhnev proposed a freeze on all new deployments, seeking to block both the NATO INF missile deployments and the U.S. modernization program.

The START talks began in June 1982. The Soviet approach was derivative of SALT II, but with reductions to 1800 SNDVs. Assertions were made that warheads might be addressed, but the main Soviet effort was to support the "nuclear freeze" movement in the Western democracies. In this environment, four developments proved of significance

---

94. *Id.* at 255.

to START. Senator William Cohen of Maine proposed the nuclear "build-down," a requirement to reduce two nuclear warheads for every new one deployed. President Reagan announced on March 23, 1983, that he wished to pursue the Strategic Defense Initiative (SDI) to render offensive ballistic missiles "obsolete." Dubbed "Star Wars" by critics, the program challenged the Soviet Union's strength in its ICBM force and re-opened the offense-defense debate. The Scowcroft Commission, chaired by former and future National Security Advisor Brent Scowcroft concluded that the single warhead ICBM would greatly enhance stability, altering the U.S. modernization program and its negotiating position, resulting in a less negative U.S. view toward mobile missiles.

In 1985, when INF and START talks resumed in Geneva, they had a third partner, the Defense and Space Talks (D&ST). In order to obtain agreement from Moscow to return to the talks, the United States agreed to a compromise organization that had single delegations, but with three negotiations. The Soviet approach was to propose substantive linkage; the U.S. insisted on de-linkage. From the beginning, the Soviet interest was in reversing INF deployments and blocking SDI missile defense research in the United States. The new Soviet START proposal, calling for 50 percent reductions, did endorse the idea of an overall warhead ceiling. It also proposed that no more than 60 percent of the warheads be in any one leg of the triad of ICBMs, SLBMs, and bombers, thus moving in the direction of the U.S position that any treaty should protect diversity of forces and promote systems such as slow flying bombers, survivable submarines, and de-MIRVed missiles that would enhance stability. In response to the Shevardnadze proposal, the United States accepted the application of the principle of 50 percent reductions. The centerpiece of the American proposal was a limit of 4500 on accountable warheads on ballistic missiles (ICBMs and SLBMs), about 50 percent of what the two sides deployed. Splitting the difference between the two sides' proposals on ICBM warheads, the U.S. proposed a limit of 3000. A common ceiling on throw-weight would be 50 percent below the Soviet level, but a common ceiling on ALCMs would be, at 1500, about half of what the United States had planned.

At the 1985 Geneva Summit, an implied willingness by the Soviet Union to be more forthcoming on verification gave a boost to the arms talks. In January 1986, Mikhail Gorbachev proposed a phased elimination of all strategic offensive arms by the year 2000. The proposal received great public acclaim and set the stage for the famous Reykjavik Summit in October. The January statement, however, was conditioned on the early elimination of the NATO INF missiles in Europe and resulted in no change in the Soviet position in the Geneva START talks. Discussions at Reykjavik took place on two levels. Concerning negotiations underway in Geneva, movement on INF was accompanied by agreement for START that bombers not carrying ALCMs would be "discounted," in this case counted as a single warhead. This Reykjavik bomber counting rule opened the way for a common warhead ceiling that would differentiate missiles and bombers in ways the United States has always insisted upon. Discussions at Reykjavik also took place on a much higher level, with Gorbachev insisting that if the United States limited missile defense research to the laboratory, Gorbachev would agree to the elimination of all strategic offensive nuclear weapons. The US had proposed the elimination of all offensive ballistic missiles. This discussion captured the imagination of the public. President Reagan received both acclaim and blame in public opinion for refusing to agree to give up missile defense options for the future. The immediate effect of Reykjavik on the START Talks was to divert attention back toward public debate and away from the negotiations in Geneva.

In START, over the next six months, the Soviet Union withdrew some proposals made before Reykjavik, arguing that they had not been part of the discussions there. Moreover, as progress accelerated on INF, the Soviet delegation transferred delegation members from START to INF. To keep START active, the United States tabled a draft START treaty in May 1987. The Soviet delegation responded with a draft treaty of their own in July. As the INF negotiations accelerated, the United States sought to use the high level meetings to reduce the differences between the two sides in START. The result was that at the December 1987 Washington Summit at which the INF Treaty was signed, the Soviet Union and the United States reached agreement on nearly all of the major numerical ceilings of START I:

    (a) 1600 Strategic Nuclear Delivery Vehicles (ICBMs, SLBMs, and Bombers) deployed with no more than

    (b) 6000 accountable warheads, including no more than

    (c) 4900 ballistic missile warheads (ICBMs and SLBMs), including no more than

    (d) 1540 warheads on no more than 154 heavy ICBMs.

These and numerous other provisions were detailed in the Joint Summit Statement of December 10, but it would take another three and a half years for the treaty to be completed and signed.

Major remaining issues involved both highly technical matters, such as limits, verification, and counting rules for heavy ICBMs, mobile ICBMs, throw-weight, and bomber weapons, and strategic policy questions, such as linkage to Sea Launched Cruise Missiles (SLCMs) and the Defense and Space Talks. Extensive use of ministerial meetings to deal with both the technical and the policy issues proved necessary to sustain progress. The START I Treaty was signed at the Moscow Summit of July 31, 1991, just weeks before the Moscow Coup that almost toppled Gorbachev and less than six months before the demise of the Soviet Union. Concluded in a period of warming relations and political reform, the START I Treaty nevertheless was the archetypical Cold War treaty. Attention to detail resulted in a package of documents that, when published by the U.S. government, totaled 280 mostly multi-columned pages.[95] A lengthy treaty was accompanied by an Annex of thirty-eight Agreed Statements and an Annex with Definitions of 124 terms. Six lengthy Protocols dealt with Verification.[96]

The text of the START I Treaty with associated documents approximates the combined length of all previous U.S. arms control treaties including the meticulous INF treaty, which served as its model. START I went beyond INF in quantity of data exchanges, collateral commitments, and inspections. Qualitatively it expanded cooperation, particularly related to the verification of systems that would remain deployed. Perhaps the most dramatic symbol of the change in verification, reflecting also political change, was Article X on Telemetry.[97]

The telemetry cooperation provisions, with supporting documents of even greater detail, were themselves far longer than most previous treaties. Resulting from the deep distrust of the Cold War adversary relationship, telemetry cooperation to include exchange of tapes required an intimacy in cooperation that is seldom found among allies. Indeed, such provisions suggested the bilateral relationship was moving into an area in which co-operation among friends in arms restraint might become a better model than cooperation with an adversary through arms control.

---

95. *See* U.S. Arms Control and Disarmament Agency, Arms Control and Disarmament Agreements: START, Treaty Between the United States of America and the Union of Soviet Socialist Republics on the Reduction and Limitation of Strategic Offensive Arms (1991).

96. *Id.* at 11.

97. *Id.*

START I represents the classic Cold War treaty. Although both the U.S. Senate and the Russian Duma gave consent to ratification in late 1992, START I did not enter into force until December 5, 1994. The delay was primarily related to the breakup of the Soviet Union and the resulting multi-party nature of the treaty. Much of the criticism today of Cold War arms control regrets the lengthy and detailed negotiations reflecting the stalemate style of the bi-polar balance. It may be said that much post-Cold War international arms restraint seeks to avoid repeating such a process. Yet, START I, like INF, may be said to have contributed to the end of the Cold War. More significantly, the morphing into the post-Cold War process was founded in many ways on early steps that built upon START I as the Soviet Union came apart. Five major post-Cold War style initiatives were underway before START I actually entered into force: the Presidential Nuclear Initiatives (PNIs), the Global Protection System/Cooperative Early Warning Talks, the Lisbon Protocol, Co-operative Threat Reduction (Nunn-Lugar), and the simplified START II Treaty. All became highly visible components of post-Cold War arms restraint. Presidents Barack Obama and Dimitri Medvedev continued interim compliance with START I for four months after it expired while the New START agreement was negotiated.

Parallel and Unilateral Declarations

Throughout the Cold War, the Soviet Union and the United States each used unilateral statements and weapons decisions to influence political debate and the behavior of the other. Some of these actions, such as the nuclear test moratoria, had significant consequences. Others remained debating points.[98] As the end of the Soviet Union became clear, however, President George H.W. Bush began the "Presidential Nuclear Initiatives" or PNI on September 27, 1991.[99]

Coming two months after the signing of START I, one month after the Moscow Coup, and three months before the breakup of the Soviet Union, President Bush's September 1991 initiative anticipated the post-Cold War nuclear issues. Tactical nuclear weapons, long considered technically and geo-politically difficult to negotiate, were to be addressed unilaterally but with the hope of reciprocation. With growing concern over Soviet "loose nukes" and command and control, the President's initiative was designed to give Moscow an incentive to act decisively to deal with these dangers. The elimination of some strategic modernization programs and the emphasis on de-alerting portions of deployed forces signaled as much as anything an intent to stand down from the Cold War tensions. The proposal to "seek early agreement to eliminate all ICBMs with multiple warheads" anticipated the centerpiece of START II and eliminated the widespread view that it would be many years after START I implementation began before another strategic arms agreement would be sought. The call for "the Soviet leadership to join us" on initiatives on non-nuclear missile defense and early warning also anticipated a new U.S. interest in dealing with post-Cold War turmoil rather than superpower rivalry.

In Moscow, on October 5, Mikhail Gorbachev responded positively in a television broadcast. Nuclear artillery shells and nuclear warheads for tactical missiles would be destroyed. Nuclear warheads for anti-aircraft missiles would be removed from their missiles, and part would be destroyed. Nuclear weapons would be removed from surface ships and attack submarines. Gorbachev further announced that heavy bombers would be taken

---

98. *See* Controlling Non-Strategic Nuclear Weapons: Obstacles and Opportunities (Jeffrey A. Larsen & Kurt J. Klingenberger eds., 2001).

99. White House, Presidential Initiative on Nuclear Arms (Sept. 27, 1991), *available at* <http://dosfan.lib.uic.edu/acda/factshee/wmd/nuclear/unilat/sandy.htm>.

off alert and programs for new land and rail mobile ICBMs would be cancelled, and that the Soviet Union would move to 5000 accountable warheads, 1000 lower than the START I ceiling. Strategic defense nuclear warheads and strategic offensive nuclear warheads would be combined under a single command for greater security and control. He announced a willingness to discuss many issues with the United States including a fissile material cut-off, nuclear security, and cooperative strategic defense.[100]

In January 1992, President Boris Yeltsin of the now independent Russian Federation endorsed the PNIs, but Yeltsin went further calling for reductions of strategic offensive arms to about 2500 warheads. He also expressed willingness to consider a global ballistic missile defense system. This was to set the stage for the START II and START III negotiations. On January 28, 1992, President Bush, in his State of the Union address, responded by announcing that the U.S. would cancel the Midgetman single warhead ICBM development program and would cap production of the B-2 bomber at twenty aircraft. He also stopped production of additional W-88 nuclear warheads and limited advanced air-launched cruise missiles to 640. Russian President Yeltsin responded a day later with the cancellation of Blackjack and Bear-H bomber production, and he announced termination of air- and sea-launched cruise missile production. Yeltsin called for acceleration of START reductions and said that he would reduce air-delivered tactical nuclear weapons by 50 percent.

The Presidential Nuclear Initiatives were well received. Hawks saw them as being based upon changing military needs while avoiding the expense and disruption of formal verification activities. Doves saw them as cutting the "Gordian Knot" of some of the most difficult disarmament issues. The PNIs clearly facilitated closer interactions with the newly independent states formed out of the Soviet Union. And the PNIs are frequently given as examples of responsiveness to change and the value of top-down leadership. The PNIs remain popular today, but both hawks and doves have expressed some dissatisfaction at how they have played out. The meaning of a number of the Russian statements remains unclear. The status of tactical nuclear weapons returned to Russian soil is uncertain and has become a larger issue as Russia has touted those weapons as a means to compensate for its weakness in conventional forces. The call for reciprocity by President Bush had not been a demand for reciprocity, but concerns remained that the outcome over time was not balanced or was unfulfilled. Advocates of arms control expressed concern that the informal nature of the PNIs could result in the reversal of reductions. NGOs and a number of governments continue to call for a formal treaty structure for the PNIs. Several key initiatives, such as deeper reductions and the ban on MIRVed ICBMs, were included in the START II Treaty, which has itself been overtaken by events. The PNIs set the stage for continuation of the START process, but they also offered an example of an alternative process, with the 2002 Treaty of Moscow representing something of a merger of these two proposals.

Lisbon Protocol

When the START II negotiations began, START I was not yet complete. The breakup of the Soviet Union left the status of START I, negotiated as a bilateral agreement, in limbo. Fifteen newly independent states emerged out of the Soviet Republics. Only a few had major nuclear weapons facilities, but all faced difficulty determining which obligations of the former Soviet Union they should accept. The Russian Federation was most forward leaning as the successor state to the Soviet Union, but on the nuclear question, the presence

---

100. President Mikhail Gorbachev, Statement on Nuclear Weapons (televised by the TASS news agency) (Oct. 5, 1991), *in* FBIS-SOV-91-194, Oct. 7, 1991, at 2–3.

of nuclear weapons on the soil of other former Soviet Republics complicated the succession issue, particularly in the context of the nuclear Non-Proliferation Treaty.

In newly independent Ukraine, Belarus, and Kazakhstan, nuclear weapons remained in the hands of formerly Soviet troops of diverse ethnic background and in some cases uncertain citizenship or loyalty. Within each of these republics, constituencies existed that favored the retention of the weapons and the assumption of nuclear weapons state status. Even some western experts suggested that political stability would be enhanced by the emergence of additional nuclear weapons states. Some ethnic Ukrainians in the United States and Canada lobbied for nuclear weapons status for their former homeland. In the face of this confusion, the United States and many other countries nevertheless sought and obtained commitments from Belarus, Kazakhstan, and Ukraine to return existing nuclear weapons to Russia for dismantlement and to join the NPT in non-nuclear status. The Lisbon Protocol to START I of May 23, 1992, was the formal agreement implementing this agreement.[101]

In addition, each republic sent letters to President Bush reaffirming their START and NPT obligations. Implementation of this agreement proved difficult. Domestic political opposition to denuclearization grew with each passing day, aggravated by disputes among the republics over assets, resources, and relationships. Exceptional effort was required by the United States and others to bring all of the republics into the NPT and for START I to enter into force. This was not completed until 1994.

START II

START I took twelve years to negotiate. START II took less than a year and was completed almost two years before START I entered into force. The START II treaty may be considered either the last of the Cold War strategic nuclear arms treaties or the first of the post-Cold War arms control treaties. Motivated by the breakup of the Soviet Union and primed by the PNIs, the negotiations moved quickly at first, but then slowed as the euphoria in U.S.-Russian relations cooled and more traditional negotiating considerations came to the fore. A Joint Understanding on Reductions in Strategic Offensive Arms signed by Presidents Bush and Yeltsin at the June 1992 Washington Summit outlined an agreement to be nested within the START I treaty that would eliminate all MIRVed ICBMs by 2003 and reduce strategic offensive arms to no more than 3500. Reflecting both the Russian desire for a lower number and the growing American view that rigidly numerically equal forces were no longer a requirement with the end of the Cold War, the text providing the ceiling is of interest: "[F]or warheads attributed to deployed ICBMS, deployed SLBMS, and deployed heavy bombers, a number between 3000 and 3500 or such lower number as each Party shall decide for itself, but in no case shall such number exceed 3500."[102] The practice of stating the warhead ceilings as a range would continue in Helsinki with Presidents Clinton and Yeltsin and in the Treaty of Moscow with Presidents George W. Bush and Vladimir Putin.

Negotiated by small, high level interagency teams, usually operating on the margins of ministerial meetings, the START II process contrasted significantly with that of the Geneva-based START I delegations. Two issues complicated conclusion of START II. Most significant would be linkage to the ABM Treaty. The second issue grew out of the Russian

---

101. Protocol to the Treaty between the United States of America and the Union of Soviet Socialist Republics on the Reduction and Limitation of Strategic Offensive Arms, May 23, 1992, S. TREATY Doc. No. 102-32 (1992).

102. Treaty between the United States of America and the Russian Federation on Further Reduction and Limitation of Strategic Offensive Arms, Jan. 3, 1993, U.S.-Russ., S. TREATY DOC. No. 103-1, art. 1, § 3 (1993).

economic crisis and the loss of production support facilities in other former Soviet republics. The prospect that the introduction of new Russian non-MIRVed ICBMs would occur more slowly than originally planned would make it difficult for the Russian Federation to match the United States in overall numbers. This became more urgent in Russian debate because of concerns that more ballistic missile submarines would have to be retired earlier than planned. To accommodate Russian concerns, the United States agreed to let the Russian Federation keep ninety modified SS-18 heavy silos that would have been destroyed under START I, but only for use with a smaller single warhead missile. The SS-18 Heavy ICBM could not be "downloaded" to a single warhead, nor could the American MX/Peacekeeper. Also, the Russian Federation was allowed up to 105 of its SS-19 ICBMS to be downloaded from six warheads down to one warhead. A START I limit on aggregate downloading was removed. Russia also insisted that the bomber discounting rules of START I be dropped and that each bomb and cruise missile that could be carried on a heavy bomber be attributed to that bomber. In addition, to meet a long standing demand from Moscow that SLBMs be considered more like ICBMs, a ceiling of 1750 was placed upon total warheads on submarine launched ballistic missiles.

One can look to START II to see many of the characteristics that have been advocated for post-Cold War arms control. START II was impelled by top-down unilateral initiative. The text was short and negotiated quickly. It sought to save money for both sides rather than to hobble the opponent with burdensome requirements. START II established an overall warhead limit without discounting rules that were criticized by some as limiting reductions and criticized by others as a disincentive for greater "freedom to mix" strategic forces. It provided deep reductions and offered a mechanism by which further reductions could be obtained more easily. For those who favored formal agreements, START II was a treaty; for those who favored flexibility, it seemed less structured than in the detailed START I provisions to mandate crisis stability and provide effective verification. START II protected conventional military capabilities. All of this is true, but only to a degree.

For all that START II set precedents for post-Cold War arms restraint, it was grounded clearly in the architecture of START I. It was designed to co-exist with the existing START I treaty, relying on the vast verification regime that had already taken years to negotiate. The START II approach to stability achieved some of the long-standing U.S. goals, notably the elimination of all heavy ICBMs and all MIRVed ICBMs. To achieve this, the United States agreed to drop discounting bomber weapons, but it also negotiated some flexibility to remove from accountability bombers that had taken on purely conventional missions. The United States did agree to the 1750 SLBM warhead limit, which seemed at odds with the traditional American approach of nested sub-limits and "one-way freedom to mix" that were designed to encourage movement toward a balanced triad and away from highly MIRVed land-based missiles. In START II, however, the goal was the same, but achieved in a different way. Heavy and MIRVed ICBMs were simply banned. A balanced triad, however, was encouraged further by the operation of a provision that is not in START II and was only an incidental provision of START I, the 1600 limit on strategic nuclear delivery vehicles. The combination of this limit and the ICBM MIRV ban meant that the only way to achieve the maximum force levels was by diversifying away from ICBMS. An all ICBM force would permit only 1600 of the total 3500 warheads permitted, a de facto discounting of all other warheads by more than 50 percent. Both sides achieved long-term goals in START II, but the cumulative effect was to continue the Cold War evolution of agreements toward a greater formalization of restraints in the name of crisis stability.

Post-Cold War arms control was expected to be multilateral. START II was a bilateral treaty, negotiated between the Russian Federation and the United States. Yet, multilateral issues, including the delay of START I in which it was to be embedded and broader international pressure to sustain the ABM Treaty unchanged, may have determined its fate. Resolving the problems associated with the multilateralization of the START I Treaty to include non-nuclear weapons status in the NPT for all former Soviet republics except Russia delayed the implementation of START I until December 1994. By 1995, domestic political divisions in Russia turned the START II Treaty into an evaluation of Russia's status relative to the United States and a measure of the merit of Boris Yeltsin. Although the U.S. Senate acted first, giving consent to ratification on January 26, 1996, Russian opposition increased as Yeltsin's political fortunes declined. Critics charged that Yeltsin had given away Russia's most powerful missiles. Russian opponents also wanted more linkage, linkage to the ABM Treaty and to other external issues such as NATO expansion and the state of the Russian economy.

Having obtained ratification of START I, Presidents Clinton and Yeltsin met in Helsinki in March of 1997 to put together a package that might enhance ratification possibilities for START II by outlining a Start III agreement with reduced warhead ceilings that would better fit the Russian missile program. They also agreed to pursue a START II Protocol, completed seven months later, that gave four additional years for dismantlement. Drawing from precedents set in the PNIs, the two Presidents agreed in Helsinki to deactivate by December 31, 2003, all of the strategic nuclear delivery vehicles to be dismantled under the START II Protocol by December 31, 2007. On April 14, 2000, the Russian Duma passed the Federal Law on ratification of START II. The law, listing the concerns of that legislative body, was about two-thirds the length of the treaty itself. Among the key provisions were those of Article 2 describing extraordinary events giving the Russian Federation the right to withdraw from the treaty under Article VI, and including linkage to NATO expansion, the future of the ABM Treaty, and third country nuclear forces.[103] Article 9 conditioned ratification of START II to ratification by the United States of all of the agreements reached in September 1997, including those relating to the ABM Treaty.[104]

Throughout the mid-1990s two factors were to determine the fate of START II. One was the continuing difficulty the Russian Federation believed it would have maintaining forces that would reach the START II ceilings without the MIRVed ICBMs banned by START II. The second was that while the United States was divided internally over whether to withdraw from the ABM Treaty, some deployments seemed probable in time no matter which political party controlled the White House. More significantly, proponents of missile defense easily had more than enough members of the U.S. Senate to deny consent to ratification of any treaty conditioned on no withdrawal from the ABM Treaty. The decision by President George W. Bush to negotiate the Treaty of Moscow permitting MIRVed ICBMs for Russia and the decision to withdraw from the ABM Treaty and deploy ballistic missile defenses made clear that START II would be overtaken by events. On June 14, 2002, three weeks after the signing of the Treaty of Moscow and one day after the United States withdrew from the ABM Treaty, Russia announced that it would no longer be bound by its obligations to START II under international law because it did not believe that the treaty could come into effect.

---

103. Federal Bill on Ratification of the Treaty between the Russian Federation and the United States of America on Further Reduction and Limitation of Strategic Offensive Arms, art. 2 (adopted Apr. 14, 2000).

104. *Id.* art. 9.

The Anti-Ballistic Missile Treaty (ABM Treaty)

Experts debated from the beginning whether the Anti-Ballistic Missile Treaty was the primary or secondary goal of the SALT I negotiations, but the restraints of the ABM Treaty long outlived the companion SALT I Interim Agreement on Strategic Offensive Arms. Policy makers continue to debate whether the ABM Treaty was the "cornerstone of strategic stability" or a remnant of archaic strategic theology. Whatever is concluded, it remained in force for thirty years and had a significant impact on nuclear forces, arms control negotiations, international relations, and domestic politics.

The ABM Treaty was signed in Moscow on May 26, 1972, and entered into force on October 3, 1972. The ABM Treaty as negotiated did not ban ballistic missile defense systems. It explicitly permitted them. Two hundred total operational interceptors were allowed at two deployment sites, one of which would be the national capital region of each superpower. A limited number of test interceptors were allowed at other sites, but Article I explicitly prohibited a comprehensive national ballistic missile defense system.[105]

In keeping with this spirit, a Protocol to the ABM Treaty, concluded in 1974, limited each side to one deployment site with one hundred interceptors. The Soviet Union has kept its Moscow system, but Congress immediately closed down the American site built at Grand Forks, North Dakota. Forty years later, the current U.S. National Missile Defense sites in Alaska, California, and Guam are smaller than originally permitted under the ABM Treaty, but they are augmented by sea-based Aegis SM-2 and SM-3 interceptors.

Key provisions of the ABM Treaty sought to keep wide areas of the United States and the Soviet Union free of missile defenses. A number of mechanisms served this role. To minimize the utility of early warning radars for ABM systems, Article VI provided that the parties are "not to deploy in the future radars for early warning of strategic ballistic missile attack except at locations along the periphery of its national territory and oriented outward."[106]

The belief that large radars like those used in early warning would need to be deployed well back from the national boundaries in order to permit their use for ballistic missile defense was considered one of the easy-to-monitor provisions that enhanced the verifiability of the ABM Treaty. In the mid-1980s, the construction of such a radar at Krasnoyarsk, in the Soviet Far East, was declared by the United States to be a breach of the ABM Treaty and ultimately the large radar was dismantled. The advance of sensor technology and communications networking, however, increasingly blurred the distinction between what is used for ABM purposes and what is used for other purposes such as air defense or early warning. To further prevent area missile defense, the ABM Treaty also sought to limit sea-based, air-based, space-based, or mobile land-based launchers and rapid reload.[107]

Recognizing that the limiting provisions of the ABM Treaty were structured explicitly around existing technologies, Agreed Statement D was attached to the ABM Treaty:

> In order to insure fulfillment of the obligation not to deploy ABM systems and their components except as provided in Article III of the Treaty, the Parties

---

105. Treaty on the Limitation of Anti-Ballistic Missile Systems, May 26, 1972, U.S.-U.S.S.R., art. I, 23 U.S.T. 3435.

106. *Id.* art VI.

107. *Id.* art. V.

agree that in the event ABM systems based on other physical principles and including components capable of substituting for ABM interceptor missiles, ABM launchers, or ABM radars are created in the future, specific limitations on such systems and their components would be subject to discussion in accordance with Article XIII [Standing Consultative Commission] and agreement in accordance with Article XIV [amendments and five-year review] of the Treaty.[108]

Interpreting Agreed Statement D became a major issue during the Defense and Space Talks (the "Broad-Narrow Debate") and would prompt a major constitutional dispute between the legislative and executive branches over the terms and meaning of giving consent to ratification of a treaty (the "One Treaty" versus "Two Treaty") debate. In essence, the disagreement over whether the Agreed Statement D should be interpreted broadly or narrowly in limiting research, development, testing, and deployment of ABM technologies based on other physical principles expanded into a debate over whether the United States would be bound by a treaty as it was negotiated or by that treaty as the Senate believed it to be interpreted when the Senate gave consent to ratification. The debate exposing disagreement over who interprets treaties and the function of a treaty as law of the land has created the possibility that other parties to a treaty would be bound by one interpretation under international law, but the United States alone by another interpretation because of its ratification process.[109]

Article VI(a) of the ABM Treaty prohibited giving air defense systems, including defenses against theater ballistic missiles, "capabilities to counter strategic ballistic missiles or their elements in flight trajectory, and not to test them in an ABM mode; …"[110] This provision became more controversial in later years as permitted air defenses and theater missile defenses took on the physical capabilities that had once been associated with early ABM systems.

Article IX prohibited ABM deployments outside the territory of the parties.[111] Over the years, the ABM Treaty was increasingly stressed by technological and political changes related to Articles VI(a) and IX. Concern over the spread of WMD into troubled regions has generated great interest in upgraded air defenses and theater missile defenses that can exploit the latest in sensor, data processing, and propulsion technologies. The capabilities to be deployed in these regions exceed those envisioned for national ballistic missile defense when the ABM Treaty was negotiated in 1972. Moreover, many of the countries that would deploy these systems are sufficiently small that the systems defend their entire territory, embodying the very principle rejected by the ABM Treaty. With the breakup of the Soviet Union, the ABM Treaty was multilateralized. Although this reinforced broader international support for the ABM Treaty, the existence of further members exposed logical tensions within the ABM Treaty framework including the issue of international cooperation in missile defense and the question of what it means to have limited territorial defense.

---

108. *Id.* at 3456.

109. Of course, the Congress can legislate further limits on the U.S., but the issue concerns whether interpretations or misinterpretations at the time of Senate consent to ratification themselves become binding on the U.S. if they are not consistent with the international interpretation binding on others. Is the treaty that becomes part of the law of the land the same treaty that is binding under international law? *See* Robert F. Turner, The ABM Treaty and the Senate 9–15 (1999). For an extensive analysis of the constitutional question, see the unclassified volume: John Norton Moore, The "Broad-Narrow" Debate: An Appraisal of Legal Issues Concerning the Development and Testing of "Mobile" Anti-Ballistic Missile Systems or Components Based on Other Physical Principles (1989).

110. Treaty on the Limitation of Anti-Ballistic Missile Systems, art. VI *available at* http://www.state.gov/www/global/arms/treaties/abm/abm2.html.

111. *Id.* art. IX.

The Geneva Defense and Space Talks (D&ST) revisited past debates over the ABM Treaty, but also anticipated much of the controversy today. Begun in 1985 in response to Soviet insistence on linking START negotiations to negotiations on missile defenses, the talks covered a range of issues. The Soviet Union sought means to discourage or block the American Strategic Defense Initiative (SDI) announced by President Reagan in March 1983 to counter nuclear-armed ballistic missiles. The American program included research on ground-based interceptors and exotic technologies such as lasers, particle beams, and miniaturized interceptors based in space. The United States highlighted concerns about Soviet compliance with the existing ABM Treaty, but also called for a dialog on changing strategic concepts that would go beyond the ABM Treaty. The Soviet Union responded with proposals for deep reductions in offensive arms, contingent upon the United States giving up research and development on new defense and space technologies.

As the United States redirected its missile defense programs to smaller and non-Russian threats, Moscow's insistence on limiting research waned, although it has continued to maintain a policy of linkage. In 1992, the United States presented a proposal to amend the ABM Treaty to permit a limited additional number of ground-based ABM sites with several hundred interceptors while putting off the question of deployment of space-based systems. In the context of proposals for cooperative missile defense and joint early warning, a draft was tabled in the SCC in Geneva in January 1993 by the outgoing Bush administration.

The incoming Clinton administration placed priority on bringing into effect the two START treaties and was less enthusiastic about national missile defense. It eliminated significant funding for research on space-based approaches and turned to making a clearer distinction between national and theater missile defenses. On September 26, 1997, the United States and Russia concluded in the Standing Consultative Commission (SCC) two agreed statements on demarcation of national and theater missile defenses as well as an Agreement on Confidence-Building Measures. A Joint Statement on an Annual Exchange of information on the Status of Plans and Programs was also agreed.[112]

By 2000, however, the Clinton administration concluded that deployments beyond the ABM Treaty might be necessary and sought to negotiate a Protocol that would permit a limited territorial defense within the number of interceptors permitted by the ABM Treaty. Thus, the end of the Cold War did not bring about an end to the debate over the ABM Treaty. China also became more vocal that national missile defense would undermine Beijing's deterrent, and in Russia more voices expressed concern about deep reductions in the context of even limited U.S. defenses. Ultimately, however, the further spread of ballistic missile technology to countries of proliferation concern resulted in an American decision to withdraw from the ABM Treaty in order to develop and deploy systems that would have been less effective if they were ABM Treaty compliant. The withdrawal was announced on December 13, 2001, two months after the terrorist attacks on the World Trade Center and the Pentagon. On June 13, 2002, the United States withdrawal from the ABM Treaty was complete.

Space Arms Control

Sputnik and the space race prompted international concern over the militarization of space, a specter made more visible by the dual-use of rocket propulsion, satellites, and

---

112. First Agreed Statement Relating to the Treaty between the United States of America and the Union of Soviet Socialist Republics on the Limitation of Anti-Ballistic Missile Systems of May 26, 1972, *reprinted in New Start II and ABM Treaty Documents*, Arms Control Today, Sept. 1997, at 19.

even manned experiments. Many military space activities such as communications, early warning, and national technical means of verification, have become essential tools for international arms restraint. Keeping weapons of mass destruction out of space has been a more persistent theme. The Limited Test Ban Treaty of 1963 prohibited nuclear testing in outer space, and the Outer Space Treaty of 1967 prohibited orbiting or installing nuclear weapons in outer space and promulgates zones of cooperation and restraint modeled on the Antarctic Treaty of 1959. Neither of these treaties deals with the transit of intercontinental ballistic missiles or submarine launched ballistic missiles through space, but these systems are dealt with in the strategic nuclear arms negotiations. They are not, however, the only weapons that can operate in space.

As early as the 1960s, the United States had developed an anti-satellite (ASAT) capability that was retired in the mid-1970s. Interceptors or even simple ballistic missiles fired from earth could attack satellites with nuclear or conventional warheads. In the late 1970s, the Soviet Union deployed a co-orbital ASAT missile, essentially a warhead to rendezvous with the satellite it seeks to destroy. In response, President Carter initiated a dual-track program. On one track, the United States began development of a small ASAT missile that could be fired from an F-15 fighter aircraft. On the second track, it pursued negotiations with the Soviet Union. In 1978 and 1979, several discussions and negotiations were held, but no final agreement was reached before the Soviet invasion of Afghanistan in December 1979 brought about an end to the talks.

ASAT became a negotiating issue again during the Geneva Defense and Space Talks (D&ST). There the Soviet Union sought a ban on dedicated ASAT systems, but Moscow also sought prohibitions on missile defense systems such as lasers, particle beams, or interceptors, wherever based, that could attack satellites. The United States was not interested in further restrictions on research and development related to missile defenses, but much of the ASAT discussion also focused on the problem of definition and verification. Existing long-range ballistic missiles, indeed, the very systems that put satellites in space and operate them there, have inherent capabilities to operate against satellites, as do other technologies, such as electronic jamming and lasers.

Discussions of space arms control recur in multilateral fora such as the Conference on Disarmament. The United States has long been of a mixed mind about space arms control. The American military is very dependent on the use of space for communications and warning, and its civilian activity in space is intense. ASATs and weapons in space including the process of testing such systems may both endanger those activities and deter attacks against them. In many ways, the use of space is becoming more transparent, but the ability to operate against space objects may have become much easier also. The end of the Cold War neither ended the debate over outer space arms control nor made clear how negotiations might secure this fragile commons.

No First Use

"No first use" pledges and "nuclear-free zones" were contentious during the Cold War and remain so today.[113] During the 1980s controversy over deployment of LRINF missiles

---

113. *See* Alfred P. Rubin, *The Neutron Bomb Again*, 21 Va. J. Int'l L. 805, 811 (1981); Herbert Y. Schandler, U.S. Policy on the Use of Nuclear Weapons, 1945–1975 (1975); Morton H. Halperin, *A Proposal for a Ban on the First Use of Nuclear Weapons*, J. Arms Control, Apr. 1963, at 112; David Lenefsky, *No First Use of Nuclear Weapons: A Pledge*, Bull. Atom. Scientists, March 1973, at 9; Fred Charles Iklé, *NATO's "First Nuclear Use": A Deepening Trap,?* Strategic Rev., Winter 1980,

in Europe, the concept of "no first use" pledges for nuclear forces received greater attention than ever before and engendered a trans-Atlantic debate which polarized political action on both sides of the ocean. The debate went to the heart of flexible response and the "extended deterrent" provided allies.[114]

The theory behind no first use pledges during the Cold War related to the concept of the nuclear "firebreak," the need to establish clear steps in the escalatory ladder in order to control conflict and avoid or limit nuclear war. The objective would be to reduce pressures for either NATO or the Warsaw Pact to rush to the use of nuclear weapons for fear that nuclear weapons might be used immediately against them. Furthermore, extending the period of conventional conflict without the use of nuclear weapons might provide a greater opportunity to resolve the conflict short of nuclear war.

Much of the impetus for a "no first use" pledge derived from the wider context. Whereas traditional flexible response theory placed a premium on preventing war of any kind, the no first use pledge placed first priority on avoiding any use of nuclear weapons in war. Advocates of no first use pledges believed that they would ease political tensions by reassuring publics and leaders. Furthermore, they are skeptical of escalation control and fear that any use of nuclear weapons would result in quick escalation to major retaliation. Most of those who advocate "no first use" further advocate the severe reduction or even elimination of theater nuclear systems. Rather than couple the U.S. nuclear retaliatory capability directly through the escalatory ladder to conventional deterrence in Europe, their proposals tended to compartmentalize deterrence into separate nuclear and conventional rooms. Thus, some proponents of "no first use" advocated enhanced conventional forces to strengthen conventional deterrence.[115]

NATO governments have always taken a strong stand against "no first use" pledges advocated for Europe. Even at the height of anti-nuclear demonstrations in Europe and the United States, opposition to such a pledge was quick and broad based on both sides of the Atlantic. In fact, although anti-nuclear sentiment was more visible in Europe prior to the INF missile deployments in 1983, opposition to no first use was probably also most vocal within the European intelligentsia. The European fear of no first use grew out of the concern that the policy and the force structures implied by it would make Europe "safe for conventional war" and decouple Europe from the U.S. nuclear umbrella. The American opposition tended to focus on negative implications for overall deterrence through the removal of flexibility. According to this view, the possibility that NATO might

at 18; Lawrence Weiler, *No First Use: A History*, BULL. ATOM. SCIENTISTS, Nov. 1983, at 33; Bernard T. Feld, *A Pledge: No First Use*, BULL. ATOM. SCIENTISTS, May 1967, at 46; Herbert Scoville, *First Use of Nuclear Weapons*, ARMS CONTROL TODAY, July–Aug. 1975, at 1; Mason Willrich, *No First Use of Nuclear Weapons: An Assessment*, 9 ORBIS 299 (1965); Richard H. Ullman, *No First Use of Nuclear Weapons*, 50 FOREIGN AFF. 669 (1972); Bruce Russett, *No First Use of Nuclear Weapons*, WORLDVIEW, Nov. 1976, at 9; LETTER DATED 7 MAY 1984 FROM THE HEAD OF THE DELEGATION OF THE UNION OF SOVIET SOCIALIST REPUBLICS ADDRESSED TO THE CHAIRMAN OF THE DISARMAMENT COMMISSION, U.N. Doc. A/CN.10/59 (1984).

114. Michael Getler, *Laborite Reports Soviet Pledge on Missiles*, WASH. POST, Dec. 7, 1984, at A33; Karen DeYoung, *Soviets Take New Track: Guarantees Offered to Nuclear-Free Countries*, WASH. POST, Jan. 3, 1986, at A21, A24; Robert S. McNamara, *What the U.S. Can Do*, NEWSWEEK, Dec. 5, 1983, at 55; Henry Kissinger, *Issues before the Atlantic Alliance*, WASH. Q., Summer 1984, at 133.

115. *See* McGeorge Bundy, *No First Use Needs Careful Study*, BULL. ATOM. SCIENTISTS, June 1982, at 6; Jonathan Dean, *Beyond First Use*, FOREIGN POL'Y, Fall 1982, at 37; McGeorge Bundy et al., *Nuclear Weapons and the Atlantic Alliance*, 60 FOREIGN AFF. 753 (1982); Robert S. McNamara, *The Military Role of Nuclear Weapons: Perceptions and Misperceptions*, 62 FOREIGN AFF. 59 (1983); STOCKHOLM PEACE RES. INST. Y.B.

use nuclear weapons to repeal a conventional attack compelled the Warsaw Pact to disperse its forces. This aided in preventing surprise and in reducing the effect of the conventional attack. The prospect that NATO might use nuclear weapons first increased the risks that would be associated with aggression. If a conventional war broke out, Soviet nuclear forces could not move forward as freely because they would have greater reason to assume NATO might strike them with nuclear weapons.[116]

Opponents of no first use also challenged the political assumptions behind the pledge. Could NATO have confidence in a Soviet pledge not to use nuclear weapons after the Soviet Union had engaged in a major conventional attack on Western Europe? For that matter, would the Soviet Union believe that NATO would not use nuclear weapons if Western European defenses were collapsing? Even if the United States did not retaliate with nuclear weapons, would Britain and France sit by and watch the fall of Germany? Opponents also questioned the wisdom of using such pledges to "ease tensions" if the reality would be, as they believed, a weakened deterrent. Should Western publics be told that the pledge makes them more secure if NATO believes it makes them less secure?[117]

Proponents of no first use suggested that obtaining support for needed conventional and nuclear force improvements requires that the citizens of the Alliance have confidence that every step is taken to prevent nuclear war. A no first use pledge could be such a step. Opponents rejected such a bargain, noting that many who advocate no first use also advocate cuts in defense spending that, because conventional forces are predominant and costly, means cuts in conventional forces. Indeed, advocates of no first use have generally supported a less demanding standard for the adequacy of deterrence.[118] The debate continues today.[119]

Despite NATO rejection of no first use as it applied to Europe, no first use statements have found their way into the policies of the United States and its allies, particularly as negative assurances.[120] The end of the Cold War moved the no first use debate increasingly away from Europe, especially after the Russian Federation declared that it would no longer be bound by its universal no first use pledge. The core of the Russian position today is similar to that of the United States, Britain, and France. China asserts that it has made an unconditional no first use pledge to the world. Some Indian policy analysts have been

---

116. *See* Istuan Farago, No-First-Use — A Window of Opportunity (1985); James E. Goodby, *The Stockholm Conference: Negotiations on Reducing the Risk of War*, Arms Control Today, Sept. 1985, at 2.

117. Josef Joffe, The Political Role of Nuclear Weapons: No-First-Use and the Stability of the European Order (1985); Karl Kaiser et al., *Nuclear Weapons and the Preservation of Peace*, 60 Foreign Aff. 1157 (1982); Vincenzo Tornetta, *The Nuclear Strategy of Atlantic Alliance and the "No-First-Use" Debate*, NATO Rev., Dec. 1982, at 1; François de DeRose, *Inflexible Response*, 61 Foreign Aff. 136 (1982); Robert C. Tucker et al., Proposal for No First Use of Nuclear Weapons: Pros and Cons (1963); Alliance Security: NATO and the No-First-Use Question (John D. Steinbruner & Leon V. Sigal eds., 1983).

118. Richard K. Betts, *Compound Deterrence vs. No-First-Use: What's Wrong is What's Right*, 28 Orbis 697 (1985); John J. Mearsheimer *Nuclear Weapons and Deterrence in Europe*, Int'l Security, Winter 1984–85, at 19.

119. *See* Gareth Evans and Yoriko Kawaguchi, ELIMINATING NUCLEAR THREATS: A PRACTICAL AGENDA FOR GLOBAL POLICYMAKERS, Report of the International Commission on Nuclear Non-proliferation and Disarmament, 2009; Gert Krell et al., *The No-First-Use Question in West Germany*, in Alliance Security: NATO and the No-First-Use Question 147 (John D. Steinbruner & Leon V. Sigal eds., 1983); Robert E. Walters, The Nuclear Trap: An Escape Route (1974).

120. Stephen Flanagan, *Book Reviews: Strengthening Conventional Deterrence in Europe: Proposals for the 1980s*, Survival, Nov.–Dec. 1984, at 283.

skeptical of the Chinese assertion because they believe that China retains a right to use nuclear weapons if the territory of China is actually invaded. Because India and China have a border dispute, they argue that this pledge would not apply to India. The Indian government, despite these uncertainties, has joined China in pressing for universal no first use pledges. Indian hawks, however, have used India's no first use policy to legitimize its nuclear weapons development. In some cases, they also maintain that New Delhi's second-strike policy requires larger nuclear forces because of the need to ride out a first strike. India's no first use pledge puts it squarely in opposition to Pakistan, which rejects a no first use pledge on the grounds that Islamabad may need nuclear weapons to counter India's conventional superiority. Some Western experts have proposed that the U.S. pledge not to use nuclear weapons first unless the United States or its allies are attacked by weapons of mass destruction. This would help deter the threat from chemical and biological weapons but give up nuclear deterrence of conventional attack. This compromise has pleased neither traditional deterrence theorists nor those who believe that it walks back assurances already given to non-NWS parties to the NPT and various nuclear weapon free zones. The Administration of President Barack Obama has indicated in its 2010 Nuclear Posture Review that the United States would not anticipate using nuclear weapons in response to any but perhaps the largest biological weapons attacks.[121]

Nuclear Free Zones

The motivations to create "nuclear weapon free zones" (NWFZs) and the logic for them parallel those for no first use. Nuclear free zones are meant to reduce the anxieties of nations in and around the zone and to reduce the ability to use nuclear weapons in the zone if conflict escalates. Furthermore, the existence of nuclear weapons dispersed in different countries might lead to a nuclear accident or terrorist incident. Nuclear weapon free zones could be legally binding arms control treaties or politically binding confidence-building measures. During the Cold War, NWFZs were proposed widely, notably in Scandinavia, the Baltic region, the Balkans, the Mediterranean littoral, and in and around the Indian Ocean. Again, the major area for concern was Central Europe, with the Warsaw Pact favoring such zones and NATO opposed. In NATO doctrine, the presence of nuclear weapons on European soil was necessary to demonstrate the risks any aggressor might face and to symbolize commitment to forward defense. Europe was not to become a conventional "free fire zone." Nuclear weapons already in Europe were believed a more credible response and less destabilizing in a crisis than the introduction of nuclear weapons after a conflict had begun or appeared imminent. Thus, NATO viewed nuclear weapon free zones as antithetical to flexible response and dangerously decoupling the trans-Atlantic alliance.

In the face of NATO opposition, modifications to the concept were proposed, such as a "nuclear free buffer zone." Nuclear free buffer zones were no more acceptable to NATO during the Cold War than the denuclearization of Europe, and for similar reasons. NATO remained committed to forward defense in Germany and made clear that an attack on Germany could result in retaliation with nuclear weapons either on the battlefield, into the rear echelon, or even against the Soviet Union itself. Thus, the buffer zone concept might imply that the alliance was less serious about the defense of one-half of West Germany from conventional attack than it was about defending the other half. In any

---

121. *See* Department of Defense, U.S. Nuclear Posture Review Report (2010), p. 16, available at http://www.defense.gov/npr/docs/2010%20nuclear%20posture%20review%20report.pdf.

case, argued NATO military planners, the long range of many nuclear weapons negated many of the alleged military benefits of the buffer zone, and because many NATO nuclear-capable systems had shorter ranges than their Soviet counterparts, the nuclear free buffer zone was said to favor the Warsaw Pact.

The debate over the deterrence implications of nuclear free zones has quieted with the end of the Warsaw Pact and the reduced role of nuclear weapons in NATO. Indeed, Eastern Europe constitutes a partial nuclear free buffer zone between NATO and the Russian Federation, with emphasis on the word "partial" as the prospect of Russian nuclear weapons deployments to Kaliningrad is debated. The movement of nuclear forces remains a controversial subject of nuclear policy. The United States has respected the wishes of the many states that do not, as a matter of policy, allow nuclear weapons on their soil. Japan, for example, has not allowed nuclear weapons on its territory for many years.[122] At the same time, the United States has been quite adamant that, because the ultimate guarantee of all of its alliances is the American nuclear umbrella, allies under that umbrella should cooperate in making certain that deterrence is strong and credible. This becomes particularly sensitive when, for example, a non-nuclear ally acts to block transit of ships that as a part of their military mission might carry nuclear weapons. For both political and deterrence reasons, U.S. naval ships neither confirm nor deny whether they are carrying nuclear weapons.[123]

The United States has implemented policies designed to respect the wishes of nations that have prohibited the presence of nuclear weapons on their soil, but it has refused to agree to acknowledge whether any particular vessel has nuclear weapons on board. In the late 1980s, New Zealand declared itself a nuclear weapons free state and refused to allow U.S. ships to enter its ports unless they declared they did not carry nuclear weapons. They then proposed domestic legislation that would have permitted port calls by U.S. ships only if the New Zealand government first certified that the ships were not equipped with nuclear weapons. In response, the United States stopped all port calls in New Zealand, refused to participate in joint exercises, and ultimately suspended key security commitments. The strong U.S. response was motivated by concern that such actions might be copied in more troubled parts of the world. Australia has not followed New Zealand's example, but it has joined in the South Pacific Nuclear Free Zone. That zone, however, has been defined in such a way that the essential transit rights of the United States are protected.[124] In treaties to which the United States is a party, such as the Treaty of Tlatelolco, the nuclear weapons states have made provisions for transit. During the recent international conferences on the Law of the Sea, military transit rights issues were among the most important determinants of the outcome.[125]

With nuclear weapons able to transit the earth in minutes, the pressure for nuclear free zones derives its strength less from the military dimension than from the political dimension,

---

122. *See New Zealand Offers Nuclear Ban Bill: Legislation has Prompted Rift with Washington,* Wash. Post, Dec. 11, 1985, at A28; Alves, *U.S. and New Zealand: Trouble 'Down Under,'* Backgrounder, Nov. 14, 1985.

123. Given other U.S. treaty and legal obligations, the "neither confirm nor deny" policy has been adjusted to, for example, fulfill our obligations under the Treaty of Tlatelolco, the Antarctica Treaty which prohibits the presence of nuclear weapons, and the mutual defense treaty between Japan and the U.S. *See* Department of the Navy OPNAV INSTRUCTION 5721.1G, RELEASE OF INFORMATION ON NUCLEAR WEAPONS AND ON NUCLEAR CAPABILITIES OF U.S. NAVY FORCES, January 8, 2014.

124. *See* Fred Hiatt, *U.S. Nuclear Ship Uses Canal,* Wash. Post, Nov. 6, 1984, at A28; U.S. Arms Control and Disarmament Agency, *supra* note 35, at 61–62.

125. ACDA, *id.*

in particular nuclear non-proliferation.[126] The objective is to isolate and then constrict the possibilities of nuclear confrontation. The Antarctic Treaty, the Outer Space Treaty, and a number of other treaties have established areas or regions where the possession of nuclear weapons is prohibited.[127] In the context of nonproliferation, U.S. international security policy supports regional nuclear weapon free zones under the following conditions:

- The initiative for the creation of the zone should come from the states in the region concerned;
- All states whose participation is deemed important should participate in the zone;
- The zone arrangement should provide for adequate verification of compliance with its provisions;
- The establishment of the zone should not disturb existing security arrangements to the detriment of regional and international security;
- The zone arrangement should effectively prohibit its parties from developing or otherwise possessing any nuclear explosive device for whatever purpose;
- The establishment of a zone should not affect the existing rights of the participating parties under international law to grant or deny to other states transit privileges within internal waters, including port calls and over flights; and
- The zone arrangement should not seek to impose restrictions on the exercise of maritime and aerial navigation rights and freedoms recognized under international law, particularly the freedoms of navigation and over flight of the high seas, archipelagic sea lanes passage, transit through straits used for international navigation, and the right of innocent passage through territorial seas and archipelagic water.[128]

These conditions have never been satisfied to NATO satisfaction in Europe, although after the Cold War NATO issued statements indicating that it had no reason, need or intention to deploy nuclear weapons into the territory of the new member states.

Geopolitics, Conventional Forces, and Regional Arms Restraint

Negotiations over military forces served geopolitics long before weapons of mass destruction captured center stage and inevitably drew in domestic politics and economics.

---

126. Within the boundaries of nations, a more limited and often symbolic concept of the "nuclear free zone" has emerged as local communities enact legislation prohibiting nuclear power plants, materials, technologies, academic research contracts and especially the transit of nuclear forces and weapons. Moral opposition to "participation in the arms race" and a desire to make a strong political statement motivated many of these acts. Such expressions are part of a more general political, philosophical, and even religious activism on the nuclear disarmament issue. They are related to the arms control concept of international nuclear free zones, and these domestic nuclear free zones were often proposed to support political movements such as the "nuclear freeze" of the 1980s, the campaign to block deployment of the NATO INF missiles, and the more recent nuclear abolition and de-alerting campaigns. Important federal and constitutional questions can arise similar to those of other foreign policy related local ordinances.

127. See, e.g., Johan Jørgen Holst, The Pattern of Nordic Security, DAEDALUS, Spring 1984, at 195; Morton A. Kaplan, A Proposal to End the Danger of War in Europe, in GLOBAL POLICY: CHALLENGE OF THE 80S, at 101 (Morton A. Kaplan ed., 1984); NUCLEAR DISENGAGEMENT IN EUROPE (Sverre Lodgaard & Marek Thee eds., 1983); William Epstein, Nuclear-Free Zones, SCI. AM., Jan. 1965, at 48–59.

128. See U.S. ARMS CONTROL AND DISARMAMENT AGENCY, supra note 35, at 45–47.

During the Cold War, regional arms control involving the superpowers outside Europe achieved little. In some ways, the stakes were both too great and too small. An interesting case study is the bilateral Indian Ocean negotiations of 1977-1978. In 1972, after the Indo-Pakistan War in which the United States deployed a carrier task force into the Indian Ocean in support of Pakistan, the United Nations established an Ad Hoc Committee on the Indian Ocean to create an "Indian Ocean Zone of Peace." The multilateral process became mired in East-West and North-South divisions, and little progress was made.

In March 1977, President Carter went before the UN to propose bilateral Indian Ocean negotiations with the Soviet Union. Numerous motivations for the negotiations existed beyond trying to address the concerns raised by literal states in the multilateral talks. Just two years after the fall of Vietnam, the United States was reassessing its presence in Asia. The construction of an American base on the island of Diego Garcia faced considerable opposition in a Congress that had earlier called upon the Ford administration to undertake such negotiations. The Soviet Union, on the other hand, had increased the number and size of its transits in the region and had established a base in Berbera in Somalia. The growing Soviet blue-water navy, now operating out of Vietnam, and increased Soviet activity near the oil-rich Persian Gulf, led the Carter administration to seek to cap both Soviet and U.S. military activities in the region. Although limitations on the intensity of naval and air activities were less than those envisioned by the "Indian Ocean Zone of Peace," the Carter Indian Ocean initiative was seen by many as a vehicle for avoiding future superpower competition that might lead to another Vietnam War. Beginning three years after India detonated a nuclear explosive device, reducing tensions in the region had a nonproliferation objective also. Bilateral negotiations began in June 1977 and four meetings were held before the talks were cancelled in the face of a Soviet military build-up in the Horn of Africa during the Somali-Ethiopian War.[129]

The multilateral negotiations continued for many years, but Britain, France, and the United States withdrew from the Ad Hoc Committee in 1989. With the end of the Cold War, superpower naval competition disappeared from the Indian Ocean. The Gulf War of 1991, peacekeeping in Somalia, the Afghan War on the Taliban and terrorists, and the 2003 Iraq War all have since reinforced in Washington belief in the importance of Indian Ocean bases and transit rights.

If the superpowers flirted with regional and conventional arms control in the Indian Ocean, they became deadly committed to the process in Europe. Geostrategic nuclear negotiations like INF highlighted what was at stake, but the plodding negotiations on conventional arms made clear that Europe was the geopolitical battleground, and a divided Germany was the geopolitical main front. Many of the most important political differences were to be found in and among the nations of the two blocs. Within Germany, division about "Ostpolitik" interacted with the internal debates in other NATO countries over the possibilities of a real "détente" with the Soviet Union and the Warsaw Pact.

In the early 1960s, the Berlin Crisis underscored that the Wall would not easily be removed. Accepting the long-term division of Europe moved German and European thinking toward engaging the East and moved American thinking toward cutting the burden of the American troop deployments. Beginning in 1966, Senate Majority Leader Mike Mansfield introduced the first of many amendments bearing his name that called for reductions in U.S. deployments in Europe. In 1967, in its Harmel Report, NATO proposed negotiations to reduce military forces in both the eastern and western alliances. The Warsaw

---

129. *See* Honorable Leslie Gelb, Assistant Secretary of State, Statement before the House Armed Services Committee (Oct. 3, 1978).

Pact response was to propose a European security conference that would exclude the United States. The Soviet invasion of Czechoslovakia and the Vietnam War served both to heighten interest in negotiations and to stifle the initiation of action. Not until the Moscow Summit of 1972 was agreement reached by President Nixon and General Secretary Brezhnev to engage in conventional negotiations. By the end of the year, NATO and the Warsaw Pact had agreed to conduct talks on Mutual and Balanced Force Reduction (MBFR) in Vienna separate from the Conference on Security and Cooperation in Europe (CSCE).

Mutual and Balanced Force Reduction (MBFR)

The geopolitical complexity of European security negotiations was expressed immediately in basic MBFR issues including determining participants. Having withdrawn from NATO's military structure in 1966, France refused to participate in MBFR. Thus, the Soviet Union wanted Hungary excluded. Agreement was finally reached in which a Central European "reductions area" included for NATO the territory of Belgium, Germany, Luxembourg, and the Netherlands and for the Warsaw Pact the territory of Czechoslovakia, East Germany and Poland. Forces of the countries in the reductions area plus the United States, Canada, the United Kingdom, and the Soviet Union would be "direct participants." "Indirect participants" would include the other members of the two alliances, minus France, Portugal, and Iceland. Even the name of the negotiations reflected fundamental disagreement, with the Soviet Union rejecting the world "balanced" because it implied an equal numerical outcome with greater reductions for the Warsaw Pact. Rigid, formal linkage to political progress in CSCE was avoided, but success or failure in addressing human rights and transparency tempered the security negotiations overall and were reflected directly in the disagreements over verification requirements.

From its first proposal, the Soviet strategy was clear—seek equal numerical reductions in U.S. and Soviet manpower, with American troops removing their equipment as they withdraw from Europe. This would maintain the Warsaw Pact superiority in numbers of personnel and equipment, especially tanks, and would make American reinforcement in a crisis more difficult. The Western response was also clear. Seek equal numerical ceilings with an emphasis on equality in offensive equipment, especially tanks. The fundamentally different formulas were complicated by major disagreement on data. Differences in estimates of how many troops the Warsaw Pact had were sometimes larger than quantities being considered for reductions. This discrepancy became more serious as the Warsaw Pact expanded and modernized its forces in Europe even as the United States undertook post-Vietnam defense reductions. The discrepancy even became a negotiating position, with sides making their proposals contingent upon acceptance of their data.

Asymmetrical trades were considered as well. NATO's Option III of 1975 would have paired U.S. reductions in nuclear forces in Europe to Soviet reductions in tanks. Nevertheless, by the end of 1978 the two sides had agreed that reductions would take place in two phases. The first phase involved 14,000 U.S. and 30,000 Soviet troops. The second phase involved equal total manpower ceilings of 700,000 ground troops within 900,000 air and ground personnel. Issues of armament, data, verification, and individual country ceilings were not resolved. And unilateral gestures were added, with General Secretary Brezhnev announcing the withdrawal of 20,000 troops and 1,000 tanks from East Germany in 1979. The Eastern bloc would later insist that these were to be credited against any reductions later negotiated. The West responded that such reductions were lost in a band of uncertainty given the great disparity in estimates and lack of verification provisions. In response, however, the Western side proposed an initial reduction in U.S.

and Soviet forces of 13,000 and 30,000 respectively, but dropped its demand that equipment be included. This was to be accompanied by verification measures and "associated measures" to build confidence and reduce discrepancies over data.

By 1979, domestic political debate in the United States and Europe was calling for increased defense spending to counter both the Soviet conventional buildup and its deployment of the SS-20 INF missiles. Moscow was particularly concerned that this might lead to a major growth in West German military forces and successful deployment of NATO INF missiles. Picking up on an idea presented by German Chancellor Helmut Schmidt, General Secretary Brezhnev proposed initial asymmetrical reductions of 14,000 U.S. and 20,000 Soviet troops (without asking credit for earlier withdrawals) in the context of an agreement that no one state in the zone have more than 50 percent of the forces.[130] On November 18, 1981, in a speech outlining proposals for negotiations on INF, START, and nuclear risk reduction, President Reagan proposed that conventional forces in Europe be reduced to equal ceilings on both sides. The result six months later was a new Western proposal dropping NATO insistence on U.S. and Soviet reductions prior to the reductions of other forces. Instead, the common 700,000/900,000 ceilings would be phased in on all countries as the U.S. and Soviet Union undertook initial reductions of 13,000 and 30,000. Associated measures and verification would be strengthened along with provisions to insure that troops removed from the central zone did not become threats on the flanks. The East responded with a proposal for good will reductions of 13,000 U.S. and 20,000 Soviet troops with their equipment.

Posturing related to the struggle over INF deployments dominated all diplomatic interactions over the next few years, and little progress was made. In 1983, when the Soviet Union walked out of both the INF and START talks to protest the NATO missile deployments, the East left the MBFR talks refusing to set a date for renewal. A year later, the delayed talks were resumed. Little progress was made over the next two years. The West offered some flexibility on verification and eased requirements for precise data. The East offered temporary observation posts as a concession on verification. Following the resumption of INF and START negotiations in 1985 and the Reagan/Gorbachev Geneva Summit of that year, NATO offered to prime the pump with an agreement to defer resolution of data issues until after small reductions of 5,000 U.S. and 11,500 Soviet forces, but in the context of verification measures aimed at monitoring a three-year, no-increase commitment.[131]

Stalemate in MBFR only reinforced growing concerns in the West that the outcome of the negotiation was moving toward the trivial, offering little improvement in stability. Stalemate also did not help Moscow in its campaign to get the INF missiles removed or avoid a German military build-up. In an April 18, 1986, speech in East Berlin, Gorbachev proposed broad cuts in nuclear as well as conventional forces. A month later, in its Halifax

---

130. *See* Jeffrey Record, Force Reductions in Europe: Starting Over (1980); Lothar Ruehl, *MBFR: Lessons and Problems*, Adelphi Papers, 1982.

131. Ruehl, *supra* note 130. Richard F. Staar, *The MBFR Process and Its Prospects, in* Arms Control: Myth Versus Reality 47 (Richard F. Staar ed., 1984); V.L. Shvetsov, Voennaia Razriadka: Mery Doveriia (1984); Ken Scott, *MBFR: Western Initiatives Seek to End Deadlock*, NATO Rev., Sept. 1982, at 14; Center for Defense Information, War Games: The Defense Monitor (1984); Jeffrey Record, Force Reductions in Europe: Starting Over (1980); Jonathan Alford, *Confidence-Building Measures*, Adelphi Papers 1979; Richard F. Staar, Soviet Deception at MBRF: A Case Study (1986); James R. Blaker, *On-Site Inspections: The Military Significance of an Arms-control Proposal*, Survival, May–June 1984, at 98; Oleg Nikolaevich Bykov, Mery Doveriia (1983); Jeffrey Record, *MBFR: An Idea Whose Time Has Gone?*, Armed Forces J., Oct. 1980, at 26, 26–27, 30–32, 77; Michael R. Gordon, *Charges Traded at Vienna Talks*, N.Y. Times, Sept. 26, 1986, at 8; Michael Alexander, *MBFR—Verification is the Key*, NATO Rev., June 1986, at 6.

Declaration, NATO called for the development of "bold new steps" in its approach to conventional reductions, and the Warsaw Pact responded with its "Budapest Appeal" calling for reductions in troops and equipment "from the Atlantic to the Urals," an area far larger than the MBFR reductions zone. By the end of the year, NATO would call for two negotiations "from the Atlantic to the Urals" or ATTU—one on conventional arms and the other on confidence- and security-building measures. The end of MBFR was in sight, not by finishing its work, but by changing what was to be done and where. Even before MBFR came to an end on February 2, 1989, two years of Conventional Stability Talks (CST) paved the way for the new talks on Conventional Forces in Europe (CFE).

The Conventional Forces in Europe Treaty (CFE)

On January 10, 1989, all twenty-three members of NATO (including France) and the Warsaw Pact agreed on the mandate for the negotiations on Conventional Forces in Europe (CFE). CFE began in Vienna on March 9th. The political changes in the Soviet Union and Eastern Europe now evident would accelerate through the November fall of the Berlin Wall through the reunification of Germany and into the post-Soviet republics. Long-term national interests did not disappear, but numerous issues that had blocked progress on MBFR such as verification, data, and reductions in key offensive arms categories were resolved quickly in concluding a CFE Treaty by the end of the next year. Despite the momentous political changes that have seen the demise of the Warsaw Pact and the transfer of membership of some of its original parties to NATO, CFE remains in force. The negotiation of the original CFE Treaty and the additions after the initial treaty was completed give insight into the evolving European security architecture and today's sources of tension. The future of CFE is uncertain as the Russian Federation imposed a unilateral moratorium on the CFE treaty in December 2007, citing concerns over NATO's eastward expansion, U.S. missile defense plans for Europe, and the refusal of alliance members to ratify the adapted treaty. Russian officials, while arguing that the Cold War era CFE treaty is outdated and no longer reflects the political situation in Europe, have also said Russia will resume its participation in the CFE if NATO member states ratify the adapted treaty. In response, the United States and a number of its NATO allies announced in November 2011 they will no longer exchange information on conventional weapons and troops with Russia. They will, however, continue implementing the treaty and carrying out all obligations with all states other than Russia, including not exceeding the numerical limits on conventional armaments and equipment established by the Treaty.

In presenting its aggregate limits, the CFE Treaty was simple. Neither NATO nor the Warsaw Pact could have in the ATTU zone more than the following total forces:

20,000 tanks
20,000 artillery pieces
30,000 armored combat vehicles
6,800 combat aircraft, or
2,000 attack helicopters.

In implementing its limits, the CFE Treaty was not simple at all. With its eight protocols, two annexes, and thirteen agreements and statements, the CFE Treaty in many ways mirrored the START I nuclear reductions treaty with its nested sublimits, detailed definitions, extensive data exchanges, and intrusive inspections.[132]

---

132. Treaty on Conventional Armed Forces in Europe, Nov. 19, 1990, S. TREATY DOC. No. 102-8, art. 1 (1991).

Behind the complexity of the treaty could be found the fundamental desire to eliminate from military options the large-scale surprise attack. Inevitably, verification of equipment limits designed to achieve that goal would prove difficult and its codification detailed. Distinguishing tanks from self-propelled howizters and armored fighting vehicles of great diversity resulted in detailed definitions.[133]

The major issues had to do with different structures and security goals of the sides and individual countries. Removing heavy concentrations of troops from Central Europe while avoiding creating new concentrations on the flanks resulted in regional sublimits on forces, often creating very contentious negotiations. At critical moments in the negotiations, the Soviet Union rejected agreements already reached on the flanks bordering Norway and Turkey because the limitations extended deep into the heart of the Soviet Union. Ironically, one of the key issues was the Kiev military region that, a year after the conclusion of the CFE Treaty, was the heartland of a newly independent country, Ukraine. Sub-ceilings on active forces were also negotiated to reflect the different role of mobilization of reserve forces in different countries. A "sufficiency rule" provided that no more than 30 percent of the equipment of either side could be held by any one country. Because major parties such as the United States and the Soviet Union had territory outside the ATTU zone, equipment to be reduced was to be destroyed by approved means under observation. Issues of alternative approaches to paramilitary forces on the flanks also had to be resolved, an issue of significance particularly to Turkey. Indeed, the need for Turkey to have flexibility to deal with political sensitivities in Europe and security threats in the Middle East resulted in the famous, diplomatically couched "and thence to the sea" exclusion of some Turkish territory from the zone.[134]

The resolution of the manpower issue in CFE had considerable geopolitical content. On January 31, 1990, President George H.W. Bush had proposed that U.S. and Soviet manpower be limited to 195,000 each in Central Europe, a proposal quickly agreed. In addition to establishing a principle of equality, the manpower ceiling would limit the coercive effects of the Soviet military forces in Eastern Europe — a goal even members of the Warsaw Pact felt free to promote. As the "Two-Plus-Four" negotiations on the reunification of Germany proceeded,[135] the Soviet Union came under pressure to reduce and even eliminate its forces in Eastern Europe. At that point, the United States recognized that insisting on an equal ceiling would only undermine the legitimacy of an American presence that was now seen by all parties as an essential element of German reunification. The linkage was dropped. Furthermore, never having liked manpower limits because of their limited utility and difficult verification, the United States joined in proposing that manpower limits be put off until the future. That future was only 18 months away when a politically binding agreement was completed. On July 6, 1992, at the CSCE Summit, the Concluding Act of the Negotiation on Personnel Strength of Conventional Armed Forces in Europe (CFE-1A) was signed. The CFE Treaty itself entered into force on July 17, 1992.[136]

Concluded in chaos, CFE continued in turmoil for many years. The process of revising estimates of forces was so complex that the treaty gave countries ninety days in which to

---

133. *Id.* at art. II(1)(C).

134. *Id.* at art. II(1)(B).

135. The "Two-Plus-Four" negotiations on German reunification were conducted outside arms control channels, but contain significant provisions of arms restraint deemed necessary at the time to obtain political support in Europe for reunification.

136. Jeffrey D. McCausland, *Conventional Arms Control and European Security*, Adelphi Papers, 1996.

accomplish the task. By February 17, 1991, the ninety-day deadline, a dispute remained unresolved concerning the Soviet conversion of three army divisions to coastal defense units, which Moscow insisted were like naval infantry and thus should not be counted under the ceilings. This issue took several months to resolve. The major problems for CFE arose, however, from the continuation of political change. Before CFE was signed, Germany was reunited, reducing the twenty-three negotiating states to twenty-two. Before CFE entered into force, the breakup of the Soviet Union increased its membership to thirty (the Baltic States, Uzbekistan, Turkmenistan, Tajikistan, and the Kyrgyz Republic are not state parties). The Tashkent Agreement of 1992 reapportioned former Soviet equipment among newly independent states.

On September 17,1993, following a heated public debate in the Russian Federation, President Boris Yeltsin sent a letter to the CFE heads of states seeking to lift the flank ceilings so that Russia could have greater flexibility to deal with growing violence in its south. The issue became even more heated in the context of the expansion of NATO membership to include former Warsaw Pact members (and perhaps eventually even former Soviet republics). Russia failed to meet the December 31, 1995, deadline for destruction of equipment. By the end of the 1996 CFE Review Conference in May, the flank and some equipment issues were resolved. The parties were pleased to disclose the large amount of military equipment destroyed and the deep reductions in military manpower, but the Cold War structure of the treaty remained a concern. On December 1, 1996, in Lisbon, the CFE parties approved negotiations to adapt the treaty to changed circumstances. The next February, agreement was reached to negotiate dropping the regional subceilings and the two-bloc format within the overall numerical ceilings. The resulting Adaptation Agreement was signed by the thirty state-parties at the Istanbul OSCE Summit on November 19, 1999. Ratification of the Adaptation Agreement awaits Russian compliance with the May 1996 Flank agreement and its withdrawal of military forces from Moldova and Georgia. Long after the Cold War that prompted its negotiation had ended, the CFE Treaty became a vehicle for engagement on international arms restraint in regions distant from the original MBFR reduction zone and the old inter-German border. Continued turmoil in the former Soviet republics, however, has demonstrated the limits of CFE's scope and influence as the Russian Federation has occupied the Crimea and supports insurgents in Ukraine while keeping forces in a number of other former republics.

Cooperation and Confidence-Building

Proposals for advance notification of military exercises, troop movements, and missile launches, for exchanges of military information and observers, for formal declarations of military policy, and for improved communications or "hotlines" are contained in many arms control agreements. They have also been standalone measures. Negotiated or unilateral measures to reduce tension and prevent hostilities have been proposed for South Asia, the Middle East, and Korea as well as Europe. Proponents of such steps, herein referred to generally as confidence-building measures (CBMs) or cooperative measures, believe that by sharing information and avoiding certain practices, the possibility of accidental war will decline and obstacles to premeditated conflict will be increased.[137] Paradoxically,

---

137. Confidence-building measures (CBMs), and other terms describing steps to reduce the risk of conflict, often take on technical meanings in the context of specific negotiations and different names including confidence-and security-building measures (CSBMs), associated measures, measures

the serious international problems that cause nations to advocate CBMs make the achievement of concrete agreements difficult.

Theories of Confidence-Building Measures

Cooperative or confidence-building measures are closely tied to initiatives in diplomacy, defense policy, international law, and, of course, arms control, but are not limited to any of these categories. In a November 1981 speech, President Ronald Reagan cited confidence-building measures along with limitations on strategic nuclear arms, intermediate-range nuclear missiles, and conventional military forces as among the most important arms control objectives of the United States. Unlike arms control arrangements, however, CBMs generally do not place direct limitations on numbers and kinds of forces and weapons, although some proposals may constrain them. In the past, confidence-building measures focused primarily on developing political rules and procedures; today, mechanical or technological devices play an increasingly central role. A U.S. Government definition of CBMs from the Cold War illustrates their range: "[CBMs are] [m]easures designed to enhance mutual knowledge and understanding of military activities, to reduce the possibility of conflict by accident, miscalculation, or the failure of communication, and to increase stability in times of both normal circumstances and crisis."[138]

This definition also reflects the key role that reduction of uncertainty plays in these measures. Efforts at confidence-building often assume that "visibility," "transparency," or "openness" will reduce both the motivations and the opportunities for conflict. CBMs are expected to bring about greater understanding and cooperation and thereby moderate international competition and help to prevent war.

The Principle of Restraint

Central to confidence-building is the expectation that nations might restrain themselves in exchange for restraint by other nations. Because no measure of restraint would affect all nations equally, however, formulation and implementation of CBMs has been complex. Still, many political, economic, legal, and even moral constraints already confront all nations. Governments seeking to manage these constraints sometimes propose measures reducing a threat, obviating a motivation, or eliminating an opportunity for aggression.

---

to reduce the risks of war, direct communications links (DCLs), or crisis management systems. The terms CBMs and cooperative measures are generally used here to encompass the broadest formulations of measures to reduce the risks of war although "cooperative measures" in a technical sense refers to measures in an arms control agreement designed to aid verification of compliance. Typical analytical frameworks can be found in James Macinitosh, Confidence (and Security) Building Measures in the Arms Control Process: A Canadian Perspective (1985); Joseph S. Nye, Jr., *Arms Control and Prevention of War*, Wash. Q., Fall 1984, at 59; Alford, *supra* note 131; U.N. General Assembly, Comprehensive Study on Confidence Building Measures, U.N. Doc. A/34/416 (1979); Johan Jørgen Holst, *Confidence-Building Measures: A Conceptual Framework*, Survival, Jan.–Feb. 1983, at 2, 7–9; Allen Lynch, Confidence-Building in the 1980s: A Conference Report (1985); Kevin N. Lewis & Mark A. Lorell, *Confidence-Building Measures and Crisis Resolution: Historical Perspectives*, 28 Orbis 281 (1984); Barry M. Blechman, Preventing Nuclear War: A Realistic Approach (1985); Avoiding War in the Nuclear Age: Confidence-Building Measures for Crisis Stability (John Borawski ed., 1986).

138. U.S. Bureau of Public Affairs, U.S. Department of State, Security and Arms Control: The Search for a More Stable Peace 75 (1984).

Such measures can be multilateral, bilateral, or even unilateral. They can be formal or informal, binding or non-binding, explicit or implicit, or operational or declaratory. To be fully understood, however, CBMs must be viewed in the context of competition between nations, the nature of military power, and the broader causes of war.[139]

Certainty and Uncertainty

Theories of deterrence stress the value both of certainty and of uncertainty. War is believed less likely when there is uncertainty that an attack would be successful and certainty that the price of aggression would be steep.[140] Deterrence theorists, who valued the formalization of rules of conduct in the nuclear age, consider CBMs valuable when they encourage rational behavior by making clear to all the rules and realities that prevent war. Conversely, they are "destabilizing" when they expose military vulnerabilities or prevent the correction of imbalances.

Although some CBMs work through man's rationality, others address fallibility and emotion. The exchange of information or the interaction of decision-makers may eliminate groundless fears and encourage cooperation. Summits by heads of state, cultural, political, and military exchanges, even video teleconferences may address these problems. Again, however, communications can enhance fears, just as they can reduce them. Thus, the challenge to improved communications is to ease problems, not make them worse.

Buying Time to Prevent Surprise

Nowhere does the interaction of reason and emotion play more heavily in security affairs than in the concept of the surprise attack. Surprise gives the attacker such great advantage that few wars in recent history have been declared prior to the initiation of hostilities. However, surprise need not be absolute. Ambiguities, confusion, and misinformation have frequently drowned out attack indicators.[141]

Confidence-building measures that deny any aggressor surprise have long been sought. Measures preventing an unobserved military build-up or undetected access to strategic areas fall into this category. Again, however, if such measures permit the aggressor to plan his attack and target his forces more effectively, or if they deny the defender timely mobilization and key defensive terrain, then the CBMs could contribute to instability.

---

139. *See, e.g.*, Geoffrey Blainey, The Causes of War (1973); Abbott A. Brayton & Stephana J. Landwehr, The Politics of War and Peace (1981). *See also* Paul M. Kennedy, *The First World War and the International Power System*, Int'l Security, Summer 1984, at 7; Michael Howard, *Men Against Fire: The Expectations of War in 1914*, Int'l Security, Summer 1984, at 41; Stephen Van Evera, *The Cult of the Offensive and the Origins of the First World War*, Int'l Security, Summer 1984, at 58; Jack Snyder, *Civil-Military Relations and the Cult of the Offensive, 1914 and 1984*, Int'l Security, Summer 1984, at 108; Richard Ned Lebow, *Windows of Opportunity: Do States Jump Through Them?*, Int'l Security, Summer 1984, at 147.

140. *See* Thomas C. Schelling, Arms and Influence (1966); Theories of Peace and Security: A Reader in Contemporary Strategic Thought (John C. Garnett ed., 1970).

141. *See* John M. Caravelli, *The Role of Surprise and Preemption in Soviet Military Strategy*, 6 Int'l Security Rev., 209 (1981); Richard K. Betts, *Surprise Despite Warning: Why Sudden Attacks Succeed*, 95 Pol. Sci. Q. 551 (1980); Richard K. Betts, *Surprise Attack: NATO's Political Vulnerability*, 5 Int'l Security Rev., 117 (1981); Thomas C. Schelling, The Strategy of Conflict (1960); Sir John Frederick Maurice, Hostilities Without Declaration of War (1883); Michael I. Handel et al., *Forum: Intelligence and Crisis Forecasting*, 26 Orbis 817 (1983); Jiri Valenta, *Soviet Use of Surprise and Deception*, Survival, Mar.–Apr. 1982, at 50; Roberta Wohlstetter, Pearl Harbor: Warning and Decision (1962).

"Rules of the Road" and Crisis Management

Whether viewed as military brinkmanship, as sophisticated peacekeeping, or as something in between, "crisis management" attempts to control confrontation and keep conflict within bounds. Thus, it is related to confidence building and involves risk reduction in an actual crisis. In the conduct of foreign affairs and military activity—including war itself—crisis management concepts have increasingly supplemented the traditional norms of international behavior. Yet a major weakness of this approach has been to assume greater rationality in limited wars, escalation control, and obedience to rules of warfare than is warranted. Too much confidence in the control process could remove the caution that may be keeping the peace in otherwise unstable situations. Nevertheless, CBMs have been recommended to formalize some of the rules of the road in crisis management.[142]

Declaratory Restraints: Unilateral and Reciprocal

Through policy declarations, governments provide guidance to their own and other nations. Often such declarations herald future developments long before real changes take place. For that reason, confidence-building frequently involves the presentation of general principles and guidelines that, although not binding, may influence behavior. Negotiation of reciprocal agreements or concrete measures to follow through with such declarations is frequently difficult. Declarations that fail to produce the desired developments or that direct attention away from destabilizing trends can be harmful. Official statements, either unilateral or reciprocal, that energize positive efforts by realistically portraying current policies, on the other hand, may reduce both tensions and threats.

Assurances and Reassurances

Proper information sharing is important to reducing the risk of war and the concomitant issues of data exchange and verification also play an important role. Fundamental differences between open and closed societies, however, have made agreements for information sharing difficult to achieve. In the midst of the Cold War, the Eastern Bloc eventually recognized the legitimacy of National Technical Means of Verification (NTM) for arms control purposes and gradually accepted some cooperative measures for preventing interference with the normal operation of NTM. Closed societies today such as North Korea continue to view proposals for information sharing and inspection as espionage efforts, instead increasing operational security and deception practices.[143]

Exchanges of military and technical information focus on the deterrence logic of CBMs, but exchanges of officials and private citizens focus more on the psychological dimension

---

142. *See* CORAL BELL, THE CONVENTIONS OF CRISIS: A STUDY IN DIPLOMATIC MANAGEMENT (1971); Hannes Adomeit, *Soviet Risk-Taking and Crisis Behavior*, ADELPHI PAPERS, 1973; Douglas M. Hart, *Soviet Approaches to Crisis Management: The Military Dimension*, SURVIVAL, Sept.–Oct. 1984, at 214; MODERN DIPLOMACY: THE ART AND THE ARTISANS (Elmer Plischke ed., 1979); Hilliard Roderick, *Crisis Management: Preventing Accidental War*, TECH. REV., Aug.–Sept. 1985, at 50; Scott D. Sagan, *Nuclear Alerts and Crisis Management*, INT'L SECURITY, Spring 1985, at 99; GRAHAM T. ALLISON, ESSENCE OF DECISION: EXPLAINING THE CUBAN MISSILE CRISIS (1971); HAWKS, DOVES, AND OWLS: AN AGENDA FOR AVOIDING NUCLEAR WAR (Graham T. Allison et al., eds., 1985).

143. *See* SIR MICHAEL WRIGHT, DISARM AND VERIFY (1964); Blaker, *supra* note 131; Walter Slocombe, *Verification Guidelines for SALT II*, *in* NEGOTIATING SECURITY: AN ARMS CONTROL READER 33 (William H. Kincade & Jeffrey D. Porro eds., 1979); Y. Lebedev, *Concerning Washington's Speculations Over Questions of Monitoring*, PRAVDA, May 3, 1984, at 4; R.M. TIMERBAEV, CONTROL OF ARMS LIMITATION AND DISARMAMENT (1983); RICHARD L. SHEARER, ON-SITE INSPECTION FOR ARMS CONTROL: BREAKING THE VERIFICATION BARRIER (1984).

of international conflict. During the Cold War, the Western approach, illustrated in the Helsinki process, was oriented toward human rights. The Eastern approach was more structured, emphasizing solidarity with peace, scientific, political, and cultural groups in the West who might support their diplomatic endeavors. More often than not, immediate political challenges overshadow long-term understanding as the basis for such meetings. In the end, however, the fundamental question remains: "Under what circumstances is conflict more or less likely as nations come to understand each other?" Enthusiasm for contacts at all levels reflects a belief that familiarity makes conflict less likely, but history suggests limits on the restraining effects of mutual understanding. Indeed, the very members of the diplomatic, military and intelligence communities responsible for the planning and conduct of war frequently have had the most contact with, and best understanding of, their potential foe.

The Geopolitics of Confidence

That the negotiation of cooperative measures is often a form of international competition should not be surprising. Nations regard the control of military power as central to their security and see CBMs as helpful when they diffuse coercion directed against them, harmful when they prevent their own use of coercive power. Indeed, even parties not directly engaged in a confrontation can view the same confidence-building measure as either stabilizing or destabilizing, depending on the specific crisis. Pre-notification of military exercises, for example, may provide warning of, cover for, or even some protection for an attack. For example, a CBM requiring notification might reduce the deterrent effect of a show of military force. One can only speculate what effect U.S. B-52 flights had on Iran during the 1980 hostage crisis or on North Korea after the 1978 "axe murders," but clearly their impact would have been diminished had the flights been announced to the international community under terms of a formal agreement on CBMs as military exercises only.

The Cold War Experience with Confidence-Building

The United States and the Soviet Union, as the leading nuclear powers, felt great international pressure to initiate cooperative measures for avoiding military confrontation. The approaches favored by the two nations, however, most often reflected their competition rather than their cooperation. U.S. proposals tended to be specific, guided by a technical view of military stability. Soviet proposals were usually declaratory in nature and more directed at the geopolitical equation. Nevertheless, the nuclear superpowers found areas of agreement or compromise. A case can be made that the increased openness associated with cooperative measures influenced the political changes that brought about the end of the Cold War.

Basic Principles of Relations

On May 29, 1972, the United States and the Soviet Union signed the Agreement on the Basic Principles of Relations between the United States and the Union of Soviet Socialist Republics. The so-called "détente" agreement stated: "The USA and the USSR attach major importance to preventing the development of situations capable of causing a dangerous exacerbation of their relations. Therefore, they will do their utmost to avoid military confrontations and to prevent the outbreak of nuclear war,"[144] but also:

---

144. *See* Agreement on the Basic Principles of Relations Between the United States and the Union

Both sides recognize that efforts to obtain unilateral advantage at the expense of the other, directly or indirectly, are inconsistent with these objectives. The pre-requisites for maintaining and strengthening peaceful relations between the USA and the USSR are the recognition of the security interests of the Parties based on the principle of equality and the renunciation of the use or threat of force.[145]

More generally, the basis for their proposed détente was:

[To] proceed from the common determination that in the nuclear age there is no alternative to conducting their mutual relations on the basis of peaceful co-existence. Differences in ideology and in the social systems of the USA and the USSR are not obstacles to the bilateral principles of sovereignty, equality, non-interference in internal affairs and mutual advantage.[146]

Subsequent debate over the policy of détente illuminated the advantages and disadvantages of "agreements in principle" and hortatory declarations. Relations in the period immediately following the agreement were characterized by reassuring rhetoric, symbolic gestures, and some limited programs for political, economic, and cultural exchange. Optimism generated by the agreement dissipated, however, as fundamental differences in interpretation of principles such as "peaceful coexistence," as well as conflicting day-to-day objectives, challenged the assumption that significant common ground had been identified.

The Hotline

When President Kennedy presented to the UN General Assembly his September 25, 1961 comprehensive disarmament plan, he included a proposal for the formation of an international commission to study, among other things, measures to reduce the risks associated with communications failures. This subject was again mentioned in the March 15, 1962, Soviet Draft Disarmament Treaty. On April 18, 1962, in the Eighteen Nation Disarmament Conference (ENDC) at Geneva, the United States proposed that "rapid and reliable communications" be established among heads of governments and with the Secretary General of the United Nations. Following the October 1962 Cuban missile crisis, the United States urged early consideration of such improved communications by the major powers.

On June 20, 1963, the U.S. and USSR agreed to the Direct Communications Link (DCL), known as the "Hotline," providing a full-time teletype network between Moscow and Washington, D.C. Satellite circuits were added in the 1971 Protocol. On July 17, 1984, agreement was reached to apply newer technologies including facsimile transmission capability to the Hotline, thus shortening transmission time and permitting the use of maps, charts, drawings and graphics.

Parallel, lower-level direct communications circuits now exist. On April 1, 1988, the U.S. and USSR, for example, began operations of Nuclear Risk Reduction Centers (NRRC).[147] Other countries such as India and Pakistan in 2004 and Russia and China in 1996 have established hotlines, and the original hotline has seen an expansion of DCL technology and use. Although the value of the "Hotline" concept is now widely

---

of Soviet Socialist Republics, May 29, 1972, U.S.-U.S.S.R., *reprinted in* WEEKLY COMPILATION OF PRESIDENTIAL DOCUMENTS 943–44 (June 5, 1972).

145. *Id.*
146. *Id.*
147. ARMS CONTROL AND DISARMAMENT AGENCY, *supra* note 35, at 28–30.

acknowledged, the decision to create it was not easy, nor is its use without risks. The very act of initiating high-level direct communications identifies a situation as serious and could exacerbate the crisis. Both failure to use the Hotline in a crisis or transmission of an inappropriate or deceptive message might well be extremely destabilizing.

Measures to Reduce the Risks of War

The Accidents Measures Agreement (1971) and the Agreement on the Prevention of Nuclear War (1973) were declaratory in nature, but provided the U.S. and the USSR with useful policy guidance. The 1971 agreement stated that each side would take steps to prevent accidental or unauthorized use of nuclear weapons and to employ the Hotline as appropriate. This agreement also called for prior notification of missile launches outside national territory in the direction of the other party and notification of interference with early warning systems that could create risk of nuclear war. The 1973 agreement required each side to refrain from acts that might lead to military confrontations between themselves or with third parties. The USSR subsequently signed accidents agreements with the United Kingdom (1973) and France (1976).[148] Judging the success of these agreements must, of necessity, be subjective. With the possible exception of the 1973 Arab and Israeli War, they were not challenged during any Cold War crisis. The responses they called for were likely responses of the superpowers in any case. Even many missile launch notifications were already required through Notifications to Aviators and Mariners (NOTAMs).[149]

Incidents at Sea

On May 25, 1972, the day before the SALT I Summit, U.S. Secretary of the Navy John Warner and Soviet Admiral of the Fleet Sergey Gorshkov signed the Agreement on the Prevention of Incidents On and Over the High Seas (INCSEA). The Agreement, resulting from a U.S. initiative in April 1968, followed a long and troublesome history of confrontations between U.S. and Soviet naval forces. INCSEA sought observance of the spirit and letter of the International Regulations for Preventing Collisions at Sea (COLREGs), notification of dangerous situations, and avoidance of provocative acts.

Whenever an incident at sea occurred, the U.S. Navy provided information to the Soviet Naval Attaché in Washington, D.C., and the Soviet Navy provided information to the U.S. Naval Attaché in Moscow. Each year, representatives of the U.S. and Russian navies still meet privately to review implementation of the agreement, examine specific incidents for lessons learned, and propose improvements for the agreement. Although the bilateral agreement largely repeated what had been the international norm, the establishment of a regular consulting mechanism and procedures proved useful. Until the search for wreckage near the Sea of Japan crash site of the Korean Airliner 007 in late 1983, the number of U.S.-USSR at sea incidents and their seriousness had declined greatly. Incidents including the collisions between a Soviet submarine and the USS *Kitty Hawk* (March 1984) continued to be discussed at annual INCSEA meetings although the June 1985 talks were cancelled by the Soviet Union in the aftermath of U.S. responses to the

---

148. *Id.*

149. The United States and the Soviet Union cited the importance of the agreements routinely, and one study otherwise critical of Soviet compliance with arms control agreements found accident avoidance agreements as one of the "areas of apparent Soviet compliance," finding only one inadvertent violation of the Accidents Measures Agreement of 1971. *See* General Advisory Committee on Arms Control and Disarmament, U.S. Government, A Quarter Century of Soviet Compliance Practices Under Arms Control Commitments: 1958–1983: A Summary 3 (1984).

shooting death of an American military observer in East Germany.[150] Intense domestic political rhetoric in Russia following the loss of the submarine *Kursk* in 2002 demonstrated that incidents at sea are still volatile. More aggressive air and sea operations by China around disputed territory in Northeast and Southeast Asian waters has increased interest among China's neighbors in more concrete rules and processes.

Cooperative Measures: SALT/START/Treaty of Moscow

Six strategic arms limitations treaties — the SALT I Interim Agreement on Offensive Arms (1972), the SALT 11 Treaty (1979), the START I Treaty (1990), the START II Treaty (1992), the Treaty of Moscow (2002), and New START (2010) — and the Treaty on Intermediate-range Nuclear Forces (INF) have provided for cooperative measures along with data exchanges. Article XVI of SALT II required prior notification of all multiple ICBM launches (more than one missile in the air at the same time) and all single ICBM launches that impact outside national territory. Article XV contained cooperative measures prohibiting interference with national technical means of verification and prohibiting "deliberate concealment measures which impeded verification by national technical means" including in the Second Common Understanding to Article XV, "deliberate denial of telemetric information, such as through the use of telemetry encryption, whenever such denial impedes verification of compliance with the provisions of the Treaty."[151]

The SALT 11 Treaty was not ratified, but U.S. policy was not to undercut the agreement so long as the Soviet Union showed equal restraint. This policy of "interim restraint," designed to protect negotiating options for subsequent arms talks, was itself viewed as a form of tension reduction by many. Nevertheless, a major increase in the Soviet encryption of telemetry caused concern in Washington, and the U.S. Government eventually found Soviet encryption practices and the new SS-X-25 ICBM in violation of commitments with respect to the SALT II Treaty. In announcing that the provisions of SALT II after May 1986 would not bind the U.S., the U.S. Government nevertheless called upon the Soviet Union to join with it in a regime of "mutual restraint."[152]

Pre-notification of missile launches was more controversial than expected. General notification of ICBM launches that impact outside national territory and the launching of missiles from submarines have required safety notifications (NOTAMs) for many years, although the majority of Soviet ICBM tests did not go beyond the boundaries of the USSR. The Soviet Union resisted precise notification of ICBM launches in order to avoid assisting U.S. surveillance. Both sides were hesitant about detailed notification of SLBM launches in order to avoid providing information useful in ASW research or intelligence. On November 22, 1982, President Reagan proposed for the Strategic Arms Reduction Talks (START) and Intermediate-range Nuclear Force (INF) Talks in Geneva prior notification of all launches of SLBMs and long-range INF ballistic missiles along with an exchange of data on strategic and INF systems.[153] At the Moscow Summit, on June 1, 1988, President Reagan and General Secretary Gorbachev concluded an agreement requiring

---

150. *See* Sean M. Lynn-Jones, *A Quiet Success for Arms Control: Preventing Incidents at Sea*, INT'L SECURITY, Spring 1985, at 154; Leslie H. Gelb, *U.S.-Soviet Session on '72 Naval Accord Cancelled*, N.Y. TIMES, June 19, 1985, at 1A.

151. U.S. ARMS CONTROL AND DISARMAMENT AGENCY, *supra* note 35, at 266.

152. White House, The President's Unclassified Report to Congress on Soviet Noncompliance with Arms Control Agreements (Feb. 1, 1985).

153. U.S. Department of State, *Arms Control: Confidence-Building Measures*, GIST, Jan. 1985; Michael H. Mobbs, *CBMs for Stabilizing the Strategic Nuclear Competition*, *in* AVOIDING WAR IN THE NUCLEAR AGE: CONFIDENCE BUILDING MEASURES FOR CRISIS STABILITY, *supra* note 137, at 152.

advance notification of all strategic ballistic missile launches. The value of prior notification of missile launches may not be great. Launching missiles without required notification would provoke a higher state of alert, perhaps reducing the opportunities for surprise attack. A formal notification requirement may also reduce incentives to use ballistic missile test launches as geopolitical gestures, although nearly all missile tests in South Asia and Korea are interpreted in strategic terms. False notifications might conceivably be used in an actual attack to introduce hesitancy into early warning assessments. Thus, notifications do not absolve warning systems and operational procedures from the need to confirm an attack independently and issue alarm quickly without regard to notifications.

The Standing Consultative Commission (SCC), established to oversee implementation of the SALT I ABM Treaty and Interim Agreement on Offensive Arms (1972), and the Agreement on Measures to Reduce the Risk of Outbreak of Nuclear Wars (1971), negotiated a number of communications procedures related to the Hotline and to dismantlement procedures associated with arms agreements. Its sessions, however, were mainly devoted to exchanging views and data on compliance issues. In general, the SCC lacked the legal and political power necessary for resolving major issues between the U.S. and the USSR. Some interest was shown in upgrading the SCC, perhaps giving it arbitration and crisis management functions, two missions that would likely have conflicted with its compliance dispute resolution role. In 1985, the SCC negotiated two common understandings, one on obligations under the 1971 agreement on Reducing the Risks of Outbreak of Nuclear War and one on testing practices relevant to the 1972 ABM Treaty.[154]

The INF Treaty used the new Nuclear Risk Reduction Centers for notifications and established a Special Verification Commission (SVC) instead of using the SCC. Extensive on-site inspections including resident inspectors at one rocket motor production facility each in the U.S. and USSR along with extensive data exchanges and cooperative measures are all cited as steps building confidence. START I and, had it entered into force, START II use the SVC. With the U.S. withdrawal from the ABM Treaty, and with the SALT I agreement long expired and replaced by the START I Treaty, which is still in force, the activities of the SCC have been terminated. START I expanded many of the cooperative measures associated earlier agreements with the revolutionary INF Treaty. The START II decision to count non-ALCM carrying bombers "as equipped" and to exclude certain aircraft converted to conventional roles expanded the CBM potential of bomber-base displays and inspections. Although START II never entered into force, the expectation of the Treaty of Moscow was that greater transparency between the U.S. and Russian militaries would provide confidence in levels of operationally deployed forces. New START continues this process with the Bilateral Consultative Commission (BCC), which will address a number of issues left open in the treaty such as procedures for dealing with possible Russian rail mobile ICBM deployments.

Exercise Notifications

President Kennedy's comprehensive disarmament plan of 1961 cited a number of risk reduction proposals including prior notification of military movements, international inspection, and observation centers at major transportation hubs. Such proposals became a routine part of the European regional security talks, but initially found little support

---

154. *See* Colonel E. Asa Bates, Jr., USAF (Retd.), *The SALT Standing Consultative Commission: An American Analysis*, MILLENNIUM, 1975, at 132; ROBERT W. BUCHHEIM & DAN CALDWELL, THE US-USSR STANDING CONSULTATIVE COMMISSION: DESCRIPTION AND APPRAISAL (1983); William J. Perry, *Measures to Reduce the Risk of Nuclear War*, 27 ORBIS 1027 (1984).

in the bilateral negotiations. On November 22, 1982, however, President Reagan proposed bilateral advance notification of major strategic exercises that might cause concern to the other side. Subsequently, the United States voluntarily notified the Soviet Union prior to several GLOBAL SHIELD exercises, land-sea-air exercises involving both strategic and conventional forces. In 1988, then U.S. Secretary of Defense, Frank Carlucci, called upon the Soviet Union for comparable notifications. In November 1984, President Reagan proposed exchanges of observers at military exercises of the two great powers as a result of the Stockholm CDE agreement.

Prior notification of exercises mitigates some, if not all, of the coercive aspects of military movements and may also reduce the risks of attack. As with prior notification of missile launches, preparations for attack can be disguised as military exercises, but failure to announce a military movement as required could, as in the case of missiles, evoke a greater sense of alarm in the threatened country. However, even if no threat were intended, violation or perceived violation of a confidence-building rule could create a crisis.

Information Sharing and Crisis Control Systems

Nothing comes more naturally to nuclear powers than maintaining tight control over their nuclear forces and seeking a clear understanding of a potential adversary's actions. Nevertheless, despite man monitoring machine and machine monitoring man, mistakes occur. For example, in 1980 a faulty computer chip at the North American Air Defense Command (NORAD) Headquarters resulted in the transmission of information theoretically indicating that a large number of missiles were attacking the United States. The erroneous data eluded numerous mechanical safeguards in the system designed to prevent such erroneous messages. Parallel systems did not confirm the transmission, however, and military personnel on the scene immediately rejected it for its incoherence and the lack of corroboration by any other data or sensor. Although this one-in-a-million false communication was quickly identified as such, warning procedures in effect at that time resulted in extensive alert preparations by forces of the Strategic Air Command. As a Senate Armed Services Committee investigation report stated, the warning system of the United States deals effectively with numerous false alarms annually, and even in this dramatic event, the chances of accidental war were extremely remote.[155]

Still, precautions against accidental war have remained a major preoccupation of the nuclear powers, and the image of accidental war remains powerful.[156] However, war by accident may be a more remote threat to the peace than war by miscalculation or premeditation.

> The idea of 'unintentional war' and 'accidental war' seems misleading. The sudden vogue for these concepts in the nuclear age reflects not only a justifiable nervousness about war but also the backward state of knowledge about the causes of war. One may suggest that what was so often unintentional about war was not the decision to fight but the outcome of the fighting. A war was often longer and more costly than each warring nation had intended. Above all, most wars were

---

155. U.S. Senate, Committee on Armed Services, Recent False Alarms from the Nation's Missile Attack Warning System: Report of Senator Gary Hart and Senator Barry Goldwater (1980).

156. William Ury, *Beyond the Hotline*, Wash. Post, Feb. 24, 1985, at 8.

likely to end in the defeat of at least one nation that had expected victory. On the eve of each war at least one of the nations miscalculated its bargaining power. In that sense, every war comes from a misunderstanding. And in that sense every war is an accident.[157]

Whether the emphasis is on premeditation, miscalculation, or accident, communications play an essential role in reducing risk. Numerous proposals have been made for direct voice communications between world leaders or even for teleconferencing. Some proposals go further to include joint manning of crisis management or "risk reduction centers" where information could be shared, notifications exchanged, contingency planning undertaken, or, along the lines of INCSEA, concerns expressed and practices examined. Such centers might be active 24 hours a day, perhaps jointly manned, or they might simply host periodic consultations. Nuclear risk reduction centers might be energized during a nuclear accident or terrorist incident or to discuss arms reductions or nuclear proliferation. Proposals differ widely in geographical scope as well. With the end of the Cold War, troubled regions have received more attention.

Executive sectors of governments around the world have not evinced great enthusiasm for advanced teleconferencing and jointly manned crisis control centers. Many national security officials, diplomats, and military commanders fear that such mechanisms could, in fact, disrupt the decision-making process by creating symbolic bodies that could never really be given a major decision-making role. Furthermore, direct and immediate voice and television contact might work against deliberation, thereby increasing the danger of ill-considered decisions, misunderstandings, and deception.

Nevertheless, during the 1983 political confrontation with the Soviet Union over the NATO INF missile deployments, the United States proposed to the Soviet Union consideration of a technically advanced crisis prevention and control system. The initial steps delineated by Defense Secretary Weinberger included: (1) an upgrade of the Hotline, (2) a joint Military Communications Link (JMCL) for rapid transmission of lesser, perhaps highly technical information, (3) improved embassy-to-capital communications, and (4) cooperative measures related to nuclear terrorism. In modified form, all were eventually agreed. Negotiations on upgrading the hotline began in August 1983, and an agreement to include facsimile transmission to the hotline was concluded one year later. A clarification of obligations under the Accidents Measures Agreement regarding the use of immediate communications was concluded in the SCC in 1985. Initially, the Soviet Union showed little interest in discussing a broader crisis management system, in part because tension played a key role in Moscow's political campaign against NATO missile deployments. However, in the November 21, 1985, Joint Statement of President Reagan and Soviet CPSU General Secretary Mikhail Gorbachev, "The sides agreed to study the question at the expert level of centers to reduce nuclear risk, taking into account the issues and developments in the Geneva negotiations."[158] Meetings between U.S. and Soviet experts in

---

157. BLAINEY, *supra* note 139, at 144–45.

158. *Text of Joint U.S.-Soviet Joint Statement*, WASH. POST, Nov. 22, 1985, at A15; *Reagan-Gorbachev Summit Joint Statement*, NATO REV., Dec. 1985, at 25. *See also* CASPAR WEINBERGER, DIRECT COMMUNICATIONS LINKS AND OTHER MEASURES TO ENHANCE STABILITY: REPORT TO THE CONGRESS (1983); Sam Nunn & John W. Warner, *Reducing the Risk of Nuclear War*, WASH. Q., Spring 1984, at 3; DALE M. LANDI ET AL., IMPROVING THE MEANS FOR INTERGOVERNMENTAL COMMUNICATIONS IN CRISIS (1984); WILLIAM URY & RICHARD SMOKE, BEYOND THE HOTLINE: CONTROLLING A NUCLEAR CRISIS (1984); *Report of the Nunn/Warner Working Group on Nuclear Risk Reduction*, SURVIVAL, May–June 1984, at 133; PERRY, *supra* note 154; NUCLEAR RISK REDUCTION: HEARING BEFORE THE COMMITTEE

Geneva concluded in May 1987 and operations of the Nuclear Risk Reduction Centers (NRRCs) began on April 1, 1988.

Less technological approaches to information exchange—a broader diplomacy—sometimes supplement the mix of initiatives. For example, in September 1984, President Reagan proposed to the Soviet Union that regular cabinet-level discussions take place on a range of bilateral issues, that information on five-year military plans and programs be exchanged, that observers be invited to military exercises, and that experts be exchanged to measure directly the yield of underground nuclear tests. On November 1, 1985, the United States proposed to the Soviet Union an "open laboratories" measure wherein both the U.S. and the USSR would brief each other on their own strategic defense programs and invite the other side to visit their laboratories to increase confidence and cooperation."[159]

Although there were limited military-to-military contacts outside INCSEA and formal arms control negotiations early in the Cold War, meetings between national security officials, uniformed or civilian, had been few prior to 1988 and the results were usually disappointing. During 1988, however, U.S. Defense Secretary Frank Carlucci held three extensive meetings with his Soviet counterpart Defense Minister Dmitri Yazov, and visited Soviet military installations, examined military equipment, and observed military exercises. Marshall of the Soviet Union Sergei Akhromeev met twice with Chairman of the U.S. Joint Chiefs of Staff, Admiral William Crowe, in the United States and observed American military exercises.[160] Inevitably, the timing and content of such meetings are influenced by the overall political climate, but they have become a useful tool of transparency and confidence building and now include regular meetings by the military leadership of Russia, Ukraine, and several Central Asian republics. At their Geneva Summit, President Reagan and General Secretary Gorbachev also agreed to a number of exchange initiatives involving exchanges of students, professors, scientists, and athletes building upon the President's November 14, 1985, People-to-People Initiatives and also agreed to open additional consulates.[161] Today, formal exchange programs continue, but as a small percentage of the interactions of the citizens of the former Cold War adversaries as international business and tourism expand.

Earliest Warning

With strategic ballistic missiles able to span continents in 30 minutes or less, the importance of early warning was magnified immensely during the U.S.-Soviet

---

ON FOREIGN RELATIONS, UNITED STATES SENATE, NINETY-EIGHTH CONGRESS, SECOND SESSION, ON S. RES. 329 (1984); T.G. Belden, *Uses of Teleconferencing in Crisis and Warning Situations, in* PROCEEDINGS OF CONFERENCE ON TELECOMMUNICATION TECHNOLOGIES, NETWORKING, AND LIBRARIES, NATIONAL BUREAU OF STANDARDS (1977); Paul J. Bracken, *A Moscow to Peking Hotline?,* L.A. TIMES, Oct. 23, 1984, at 24; Sally K. Horn, *The Hotline, in* AVOIDING WAR IN THE NUCLEAR AGE: CONFIDENCE BUILDING MEASURES FOR CRISIS STABILITY, *supra* note 137, at 43; Richard K. Betts, *A Joint Nuclear Risk Control Center,* PARAMETERS, Spring 1985, at 39; WILLIAM URY, BEYOND THE HOTLINE: HOW CRISIS CONTROL CAN PREVENT NUCLEAR WAR (1985); Barry M. Blechman, *New Technology and Western Security Policy: Part II,* ADELPHI PAPERS, 1985; BARRY M. BLECHMAN & MICHAEL KREPON, NUCLEAR RISK REDUCTION CENTERS (1986); Joanne M. Omang, *Avoiding Armageddon,* WASH. POST, May 20, 1985, at C9.

159. Strategic defense in this case referred to ballistic missile defense. *See Text of Joint U.S.-Soviet Joint Statement, supra* note 158; *Reagan-Gorbachev Summit Joint Statement, supra* note 158.

160. *See* Edward Atkeson, *Ease Tensions in Europe: Allow Both Side's Generals to Know Each Other,* WASH. POST, May 19, 1985, at D1.

161. *Areas of Specific Bilateral Accord,* WASH. POST, Nov. 22, 1985, at A9.

thermonuclear confrontation. Fear that command, control, communications and intelligence (C3I) systems might be vulnerable increased public concern over possible "launch on warning," invoking images of a "hair trigger" controlling nuclear forces. Experts have also speculated that the detonation of one or two very large nuclear weapons high in the atmosphere could serve as the precursor to a surprise attack. Nuclear detonations can produce a powerful electromagnetic pulse (EMP) that can destroy circuits of unprotected electrical devices, in particular, modern integrated circuits. The scientific community has not reached agreement on the magnitude of the problem nor the scale of countermeasures needed. SALT II prohibited Fractional Orbital Bombardment Systems (FOBS), which attack over the South Pole rather than the Arctic—an early measure to reduce this threat, but other systems could create EMP over large regions such as in the Gulf of Arabia or over the United States.

Long after the Cold War ended, weak Russian control and early warning systems re-energized interest in cooperative measures. Most efforts at protecting C3I systems involve unilateral military programs, for example, emphasis placed on "survivability" during the Cold War. Discussion of anti-ballistic missile defenses and air defenses included debate over the confidence-building implications of defenses that might buy time for decision-makers and create greater targeting difficulties for the attacking party. In the last years of the Cold War, some called for conversion of the Strategic Defense Initiative (SDI) missile defense program into an Accidental Launch Protection Systems (ALPS).

Some experts think cooperative measures might extend warning time or provide greater clarity in a compressed decision-making process. Proposals include declaratory measures such as no-first-use of anti-satellite weapons, no-first-attack against early warning systems, and no-first-attack against national capitals or designated communications centers. Proposals also include cooperative measures such as placement of launch sensors at a potential adversary's missile base to provide more immediate and redundant warning of an attack. In addition to constraints on the operation of aircraft, ships, or submarines, such as submarine stand-off zones, proposals have included bans on the testing of submarine and air-launched ballistic missiles in a "depressed trajectory," reductions in "fast-flying" missiles as opposed to "slow-flying" "air breathing" systems, and the like. Many critics have called for a greater number of command post exercises involving actual heads of state and with officials playing their own roles in realistic scenarios. Caution has been urged, however, against revealing the actual decisions made so as not to undercut the deterrent effects that uncertainty may have on any potential attacker.

Examination of some specific proposals highlights the issues involved. Cooperative placement of "black box" missile launch sensors at the missile bases was put forward during the 1980s and received renewed interest with the collapse of the Soviet Union. For example, the United States would place its sensors in Russian missile fields along the Trans-Siberian railroad and Russia would place its sensors in the "farm belt" missile fields of the United States. Each side would be responsible for the effectiveness of its own sensors and could inspect them regularly. Continuous or regular broadcasts would confirm that missile launches had not taken place. Actual launches would trigger messages designed to corroborate other early warning reports and could confirm the size of the attack and its source. Critics of such proposals argue that on-site launch sensors are not the best way to provide further redundancy and are no quicker than space-based assets. In addition, given the difficulty of identifying the specific missile silos used during an attack, such sensors could aid an adversary by identifying which silos still contain missiles. Critics also contend that such sensors may be vulnerable to mistake or invite tampering and thus could produce false signals. A large number of sensors reduces such dangers at each ground station but does not eliminate the problem at central receiving and processing facilities.[162]

Demilitarized Areas and Stand-Off Zones

Demilitarization of regions and the creation of buffer zones have long been components of international politics. Examples abound of limited demilitarization efforts such as the Rush-Bagot Treaty of 1817 demilitarizing the Great Lakes and the Montreux Convention of 1936 limiting military activity in the Black Sea. Since the end of World War II most demilitarization efforts have focused on nuclear weapons free zones, but other, similar ideas were also explored.

One proposal, submarine stand-off zones, exemplifies the objective of many CBM proposals; namely, extension of the timeline for strategic decision-making. Such zones would prohibit missile-carrying submarines from waters within the given distance of the other nuclear power's homeland. The additional flight time required for SLBMs or cruise missiles launched from these more distant submarines would allow greater warning time and might also permit forces such as strategic bombers on alert to escape attack. Submarine stand-off zones have not been supported by the U.S. despite vast coastlines that could permit submarines to approach quite near to its capital and to some strategic bases. Interest has been even less with the end of the Cold War. ASW standoff zones would prevent U.S. submarine operations in waters adjacent to U.S. vital interests and allies overseas. Furthermore, general freedom of the seas, long a U.S. international policy, would be infringed upon.

Anti-submarine warfare free zones, advocated during the Cold War to enhance the survivability of ballistic missile submarines at sea, have again been suggested. Three NPT nuclear powers now rely heavily on such submarines, and a fourth, Russia, has sought measures to shore up the viability of its missile submarines. Anti-submarine warfare (ASW) exercises and forces would be prohibited in areas of the ocean established as sanctuaries for ballistic missile submarine. Critics of ASW free zones argue that the verification difficulties are immense, given that many ASW capabilities located outside the zones could still be used in efforts to track submarines within the zones. Aircraft and ships that would normally be expected to transit the most likely locations of ASW free zones ostensibly for other purposes could also have ASW capabilities. Given the advantages in ASW that are believed to be possessed by Western powers, they have shown little interest in negotiated submarine sanctuaries.[163]

---

162. Paul J. Bracken, The Command and Control of Nuclear Forces (1983); Brad Knickerbocker, *Military Command and Control Links*, Christian Sci. Monitor, Nov. 30, 1984, at 3; America's Hidden Vulnerabilities: Crisis Management in a Society of Networks. A Report of the Panel on Crisis Management of the CSIS Science and Technology Committee (R. James Woolsey et al., eds., 1984); Daniel Frei & Christian Catrina, Risks of Unintentional Nuclear War (1982); Walter Slocombe, *Book Review: Command and Control of Nuclear Forces*, Survival, Sept.–Oct. 1984, at 240; Bruce Blair, *Solving the Command and Control Problem*, Arms Control Today, Jan. 1985, at 1.

163. J.I. Coffey, *New Approaches to Arms Reduction in Europe*, Adelphi Papers, Summer 1974; Richard N. Haass, *Confidence-Building, Measures and Naval Arms Control*, Adelphi Papers, 1979; Harold A. Feiveson & John Duffield, *Stopping the Sea-Based Counterforce Threat*, Int'l Security, Summer 1984, at 187; The Future of the Sea-Based Deterrent (Kosta Tsipis et al., eds., 1973) (especially Bernard T. Feld & George W. Rathjens, *ASW, Arms Control and the Sea-Based Deterrent*, at 121, 136–139; Richard R. Baxter, *Legal Aspects of Arms Control Measures Concerning the Missile Carrying Submarines and Anti-Submarine Warfare*, at 209, 220–224); Joel S. Wit, *Advances in Antisubmarine Warfare*, Sci. Am., Feb. 1981, at 31; Joel S. Wit, *Are Our Boomers Vulnerable?*, U.S. Naval Inst. Proc., Nov. 1981, at 62; Joel Wit, *"Sanctuaries" and Security: Suggestions for ASW Arms Control*, Arms Control Today, Oct. 1980, at 1; Ken Booth, *Law and Strategy in Northern Waters*,

Cold War Europe: NATO and the Warsaw Pact

The concentration of military forces and the presence of four nuclear powers in Europe made avoiding confrontation between NATO and the Warsaw Pact a prime focus of CBM efforts during the Cold War. Immediate post-World War II Soviet initiatives sought elimination of U.S. overseas bases and the withdrawal of Western occupation forces in Germany. In 1956, shortly before the Hungarian Uprising and in response to the U.S. "Open Skies" proposal, the Soviet Union indicated some willingness to agree to aerial photography in a region 800 kilometers deep on each side. A year later, the "Rapacki Plan" called for denuclearization of military forces in the two Germanys, Poland, and Czechoslovakia and a non-aggression pact among the nations of NATO and the Warsaw Pact. The Conference of Experts on Surprise Attack held in Geneva in 1958 brought attention to cooperative measures that have become part of a number of proposals aimed at the security situation in Western Europe.

By the 1970s, non-binding confidence-building measures were contained in the first of the three "baskets" agreed to at the Conference on Security and Cooperation in Europe (CSCE) and had become the "Associated Measures" under negotiation at the Mutual and Balanced Force Reductions Talks (MBFR) in Vienna. On January 17, 1984, the Conference on Confidence and Security Building Measures and Disarmament in Europe (CDE) opened in Stockholm creating a forum for CBMs involving all of Europe. Nearly three years later, agreement on a number of important CBMs was reached at the Stockholm CDE Conference and the CSCE Review Conference met in Vienna to consider next steps.

Berlin and the Quadripartite Agreement

For many years geography, ideology, and differing security objectives hindered the nations of Europe in their quest for concrete measures that might diffuse the risks inherent in the military balance in Europe. Nevertheless, some useful steps were taken and contributed to the revolutionary transformation of European security with the fall of the Berlin Wall, the collapse of the Warsaw Pact, and the demise of the Communist dictatorships that had ruled the countries in the East. Berlin, the once divided city that is today the capital of a united Germany, served during the Cold War as a cause and measure of East-West tensions. In Berlin, one could see vividly the interplay of military forces, human rights, and geopolitical competition as they affected attempts to reduce the risk of conflict.

At the end of World War II, Germany and Berlin were divided into four zones administered by the United States, Great Britain, France, and the Soviet Union. In 1948, the Soviet Union withdrew from the Allied Control Council administering all of Germany, blockaded West Berlin, and subsequently withdrew from the Allied Kommandatura that administered Berlin. In 1958, the Soviet Union declared that the post-war Allied arrangements for Berlin were null and void and that all of Berlin was the capital of the German Democratic Republic (GDR). It set a six-month deadline for the creation of a demilitarized free city of West Berlin. A Four-Power Foreign Minister's Conference in 1959 failed to resolve Western differences with the Soviet Union, but a strong Western rejection of the Soviet ultimatum forced Moscow to abandon direct pressure in favor of

---

NAVAL WAR C. REV., July–Aug. 1981, at 3; KOSTA TSIPIS, TACTICAL AND STRATEGIC ANTISUBMARINE WARFARE (1974); WILLIAM EPSTEIN & BERNARD T. FELD, NEW DIRECTIONS IN DISARMAMENT (1981); John T. McNaughton, *Arms Control Measures to Protect the Sea-Based Deterrent, in* APPROACHES TO EAST-WEST ARMS CONTROL (William H. Kincade ed., 1979).

isolating East Germany and East Berlin from the West. At the Vienna Summit of June 1961, Premier Khrushchev warned President Kennedy that he intended to sign a separate peace treaty with the GDR that would negate the rights of Western powers in Berlin; on August 13, 1961, the Berlin Wall went up.

Throughout this period, the United States and the other Western powers continued to assert their right to free military access to East Berlin and to transit through and over East Germany by agreed routes. Although by agreement the Soviet Union had sovereign power over East Berlin, the continued movement of U.S. military observers in the East not only preserved legal rights and monitored Soviet military activity but also tested Soviet political attitudes and intentions.[164] If Berlin was a case study of crisis management, it was also a case study of efforts to ease tensions by expanding contacts and broadening human rights. Indeed, the U.S. détente policy in the early 1970s and West Germany's *Ostpolitik* of that period were inherently linked with the September 3, 1971, Quadripartite Agreement on Berlin, which made transit of goods to and from West Berlin and travel to East Berlin easier. Relations between the two Germanys improved, often at a price to the West but also sometimes to the visible displeasure of the Soviet Union. Still, disputes over the meaning of provisions of the agreement were a major source of tension. In particular, the Soviet Union and East Germany sought to undercut allied rights in the East, diminish the Four-Power status of Berlin, and minimize concessions on human rights.

Associated Measures in the MBFR Negotiations

Soviet forces in Eastern Europe served as forces of occupation and gave Moscow geo-strategic leverage. In contrast, American forces in Europe serve as a physical guarantee of the U.S. commitment that is at the heart of NATO. With the Atlantic Ocean as an obstacle to, and means of, reinforcement, NATO's defense planning during the Cold War placed a premium on early warning. For Moscow, whose major immediate concerns in Eastern Europe were the centrifugal political and economic pressures on its satellites, co-operative measures were explored to manage this environment.[165]

For the West, reductions in military forces were the primary stated objective in MBFR, which ceased meeting in 1989, but the history of MBFR was intimately linked to East-West relations and to the political viability of maintaining effective U.S. military forces in Europe. Beyond whatever risk reduction might be associated with the force limitations proposed at MBFR, the talks in Vienna also pressed for so-called "Associated Measures." Among the associated measures put forth by the West and incorporated into the July 1982 draft treaty were:

- prior notification of "out-of-garrison activities,"
- notification of transfer of troops into and out of the guidelines area,
- controlled entry and exit surveillance points,
- permitted aerial surveillance,

---

164. The shooting death of an American Army officer in East Germany on March 24, 1985, illustrates the dangers inherent in observer status in implementing transparency rights on the territory of hostile governments. In this case, the incident prompted high level contacts including a meeting between the military commanders-in-chief of U.S. and Soviet forces in Germany and may have contributed to decisions in Moscow to change its approach to Europe.

165. *See* Theodor H. Winkler, *Arms Control and the Politics of European Security*, ADELPHI PAPERS, 1982; ATLANTIC COUNCIL'S WORKING GROUP ON ARMS CONTROL, ARMS CONTROL, EAST-WEST RELATIONS AND THE ATLANTIC ALLIANCE: CLOSING THE GAPS (1983); Christoph Bertram, *Mutual Force Reductions in Europe: The Political Aspects*, ADELPHI PAPERS, 1972; KARL E. BIRNBAUM, CONFIDENCE BUILDING AND EAST-WEST RELATIONS (1983).

- data exchange on ground forces, and
- non-interference with NTM.

In addition, NATO advocated establishment of a consultative body, like the SALT SCC, that would meet regularly. The East accepted in principle the concept of associated measures but preferred general concepts such as "no first use" pledges, prohibitions on use of alliance territory for military action outside the region, and bans on surprise attack. In December 1985 NATO dropped its ten year insistence on an exchange of data prior to reductions in a major move designed to reach an agreement, but was disappointed when Soviet agreement to permanent entry and exit points for verification was followed by Soviet withdrawal of its agreement that troops on annual rotation should go through them. The USSR also insisted on the right to refuse on-site inspection and opposed detailed data exchanges.[166]

CSCE: Helsinki and Madrid

The Helsinki Final Act of August 1, 1975, gave the Conference on Security and Cooperation in Europe (CSCE) a document whose political nuances for human rights, freedom of movement, the flow of information, access to trade and technology, and spheres of influence were so politically sensitive that it was not made legally binding. The Helsinki process also illustrated that the quest for intercourse, openness, and exchange would not always provide a smooth path to improved relations. The Madrid CSCE Follow-up Conference (1980–1983) revealed much dissatisfaction over widely divergent interpretations and implementation of human rights commitments under the Helsinki Final Act. The concluding document at Madrid sought to clarify and expand those rights. At the same time, and as part of the overall compromise, the Madrid Conference called for the creation of the European Security Conference as an integral part of the CSCE process. This became the Stockholm-based Conference on Confidence- and Security-Building Measures and Disarmament in Europe (CDE).

The Helsinki Agreement itself contained a number of confidence-building measures including notification of maneuvers involving more than 25,000 military personnel, selective notification of smaller maneuvers (NATO provided notification for maneuvers involving between ten and twenty-five thousand troops), exchanges of observers for maneuvers, and notification of major military movements. All but the first of these measures were discretionary; the first measure obligatory within a document that was not itself legally binding. In many cases, definitions were absent or imprecise. Nevertheless, these measures were regarded as important steps even though they did not apply to all of Europe and excluded much of European USSR.

At the Madrid Follow-up Conference, however, the CDE mandate expanded the area of applicability of CBMs to the Urals. The Soviet Union had proposed that the area be extended into the Atlantic Ocean as well, but citing the international principle of free use of the high seas, the Madrid Conference retained the 1975 provisions which applied to "adjoining sea area and air space" and then only when associated with military activities in Europe itself. In a 1984 report to Congress on arms control compliance, the President of the United States found that the Soviet Union had been in violation of its CSCE political commitments with respect to prior notification of military exercises because Moscow had

---

166. Ruehl, *supra* note 130; Staar, *supra* note 131; Shvetsov, *supra* note 131; Scott, *supra* note 131; Center for Defense Information, *supra* note 131; Record, *supra* note 131; Alford, *supra* note 131; Staar, *supra* note 131; Blaker, *supra* note 131; Bykov, *supra* note 131; Record, *supra* note 131; Gordon, *supra* note 131; Alexander, *supra* note 131.

not provided advanced notification of ZAPAD 81, a large military exercise held during the 1981 Polish crisis. Failure to notify of this exercise immediately suggested that its intent was political intimidation. To have issued advanced notification of this exercise would have reduced its coercive effect on Poland. A formal CBM notification might also have created an even greater shock and backlash in Western Europe if the Soviet Union had ultimately felt it necessary to introduce large numbers of additional troops into Poland.[167]

CSCE Continued: Stockholm and Vienna

On January 17, 1984, the thirty-five nation Conference on Confidence and Security Building and Disarmament in Europe (CDE) began in Stockholm. Unlike the MBFR talks, CDE brought together neutral and non-aligned nations as well as all members of NATO and the Warsaw Pact. Based upon a 1978 French proposal and with a mandate promulgated at the final session of the Madrid CSCE review conference, the new CDE was tasked to "begin a process of which the first stage will be devoted to the negotiation and adoption of a set of mutually complementary confidence and security-building measures designed to reduce the risk of military confrontation in Europe."[168] A major accomplishment of the CDE mandate was to expand the previous area of concern for CBMs, which only extended 250 kilometers inside the border of the USSR, to the Ural Mountains, thus incorporating the more traditional definition of European Russia.

In Stockholm the NATO allies stressed that CDE should begin with the most specific measures. Speaking in Stockholm at the opening session, the U.S. Secretary of State George Shultz proposed that the conferees agree:

- To exchange Information about the organization and location of our respective military forces;
- To provide annual previews of military exercises;
- To invite observers to such military activities;
- To enhance the capacity for rapid communications among our governments in times of crisis; and
- To provide for means to verify each other's compliance with the undertakings agreed at this conference.[169]

Following by two months the 1983 Soviet walkout of the START and INF talks and involving a highly publicized meeting between U.S. Secretary of State George Shultz and Soviet Foreign Minister Andrei Gromyko, the opening CDE meeting in Stockholm drew greater attention than is normally given CBM negotiations. Thus the on-going conference was initially charged with more political rhetoric than might normally have been the case. Still, the basic differences between East and West were clear.

---

167. *See* Skjold G. Mellbin, *The Helsinki Process: Issues of Security and of Confidence-Building*, NATO Rev., Aug. 1985, at 7; F. Stephen Larrabee & Dietrich Stobbe, Confidence-Building Measures in Europe (1983); Jörg Kastl, *The CSCE Review Meeting in Madrid*, NATO Rev., Dec. 1983, 12; Max M. Kampelman, *An Assessment of the Madrid CSCE Follow Up Meeting*, Dep't of St., Current Pol'y, July 1983, at 1; The President's Unclassified Report to Congress on Soviet Non-compliance with Arms Control Agreements (Feb. 1, 1985).

168. *See* Documentation for Follow-up to the Conference on Security and Cooperation in Europe — Concluding Document, Madrid, 1983, Sept. 9, 1983, Conference on Confidence-and-Security-Building Measures and Disarmament in Europe, paragraph 2.

169. George Pratt Shultz, Building Confidence and Security in Europe: January 17, 1984, (1984).

In contrast to the West's emphasis on such specific measures as notification down to brigade level (3000 personnel) of amphibious activities, information exchange down to the brigade, regiment, and wing level, 45-day forecasts of notifiable activities, notification of mobilization down to the division level (defined as two brigades or 6000 men), and mandatory invitations to observers to significant activities, the Eastern Bloc reiterated more general themes. In May 1984, the Soviet Union put forth its proposals: a treaty on non-use of force, a declaration on no-first-use of nuclear weapons, reductions in military budgets, a chemical weapons free zone in Europe, nuclear weapons free zones for Europe, and some minor changes to the CBMs agreed to at Helsinki. At the CDE, the position of the Neutral and Non-Aligned (NNA) countries generally included the provisions of the Western position, but with an additional requirement for "constraint" proposals that would place actual limits on the size, deployment areas, and equipment of forces involved in maneuvers. Some participants also expressed interest in creating a consultative commission or even a crisis communication network among the CSCE nations.

In Dublin, Ireland, in June 1984, the President of the United States offered to enter into discussions on the Soviet non-use of force proposal if the Soviet Union would agree to negotiate on specific measures to give concrete meaning to that principle. Subsequently, the CDE, which operated by a consensus rule, agreed to form two working groups with five subgroups to consider the proposals of all parties.[170]

Progress at the CDE proved slow with major movement occurring mainly as the September 19, 1986, deadline approached. Amid threats of failure, leaks of negotiating positions, and extensive last minute maneuvering, a final agreement was concluded adopting five measures intended to reduce military risks from the Atlantic to the Urals:

(1) On November 15 of each year, parties will submit an "Annual Calendar" listing all significant military activities to be carried out during the next year;

(2) "Constraining provisions" prohibit activities involving over 75,000 troops unless they are announced two years in advance and prohibit activities involving over 40,000 troops unless one year's advanced notification is given;

(3) Data on the scope, purpose, and location and 42 days advance notice must be given on significant military activities involving more than 13,000 troops or 300 tanks organized into a division or two regiments or brigades;

(4) Observers must be invited to all notifiable activities involving over 17,000 troops; and

(5) Each party must allow up to three on-site inspections per year on its own territory if any other party desires to confirm compliance with the agreement.

The results of the Stockholm Conference were reviewed at the Vienna CSCE follow-up meeting that began on November 4, 1986, and concluded in January 1989. Agreement was reached to begin in Vienna on March 9, 1989 new 23-nation conventional arms talks to replace MBFR and new 35-nation CSBMs talks. Both proved useful to help manage the fall of the "Iron Curtain," the re-unification of Germany, and the dissolution of the Warsaw Pact. The Vienna CSCE Follow-Up Meeting, like its predecessor in Madrid,

---

170. *See* Nicole Gnesotto, *Conference on Disarmament in Europe Opens in Stockholm*, NATO Rev., Jan. 1984, at 1; U.S. Department of State, *Conference on Disarmament in Europe*, Gist, Jan. 1984; *NATO Gives Soviet Proposals on Data Exchanges*, Wash. Post, Jan. 31, 1985, at A28; Kerry S. McNamara & F. Stephen Larrabee, Approaches to Arms Control in Europe: A Conference Report (1984); Larrabee & Stobbe, *supra* note 167; Goodby, *supra* note 116; Mellbin, *supra* note 167; James Goodby, *Security for Europe*, NATO Rev., June 1984, at 9.

struggled several years over the balance between human rights and arms control, a balance fundamental to U.S. support for CSCE. Above all, the issues at stake highlighted the relationship between security and the nature of the governments involved. Indeed, Stockholm altered the dynamics of the security debate in Europe precisely because it forced the participants to focus on their individual security concerns rather than abstract common principles. As measures were considered, block behavior changed. The NNA moved to protect fundamental security interests of their own especially on the issue of mobilization of military reserves. Consequently, they often preferred the more hardnosed approaches of the West. Similarly, NATO states showed greater steadfastness than some skeptics had expected in part because of solidarity around the INF missile deployments. The Soviet Union, while retaining tight control over its Warsaw Pact allies, nevertheless found it necessary to make some moves toward greater openness that was favored by some of its Eastern European allies who expected greater freedom of action if Western observers were on their soil. This led ultimately to the 1991 and 1992 Vienna CSBMs Agreements, the 1992 Treaty of Paris, and ultimately to the Organization for Security and Cooperation in Europe (OSCE).

Multilateral Concepts and Prospects

Although most attention has been given to superpower arms control and confidence-building measures, MBFR, CSCE and CDE illustrate the multilateral dimension of cooperative measures. In the early 1990s, the United States proposed that a number of confidence-building measures be instituted between North and South Korea. These included measures to reduce further military activities in the Demilitarized Zone, to provide advanced notification of exercises, to exchange mail, to establish telephone communications, and to permit visits by divided families. The United States has provided in the past advance notification of some exercises in Korea such as TEAM SPIRIT.

Experience gained from the Nobel Prize winning United Nations peacekeeping forces in the Middle East, Cyprus, and elsewhere and the U.S. early warning system established in the Sinai between Egyptian and Israeli forces suggest that CBMs may be applicable in many more areas. The UN Disarmament Commission continues to explore regional confidence-building measures. The United Nations has, however, offered a forum for the examination of many CBM proposals. Over the years there have been a number of proposals to provide greater publicity and clarity in reporting on defense expenditures. The United Nations study and debate on this issue has shown how very difficult and controversial the mere exchange and comparison of budget data can be. Under UN auspices, an international system for standardized reporting of military expenditures has been established. The results have been disappointing. Not all nations have chosen to participate and those that do participate provide data of greatly divergent quality.[171] The UN sponsored forty-nation Conference on Disarmament (CD), based in Geneva, includes on its standing

---

171. *See generally* Barry Buzan, *The Status and Future of the Montreux Convention*, 28 SURVIVAL 242 (1983); Don Oberdorfer, *U.S. Asked China to Relay Korea Plan*, WASH. POST, June 6, 1984, at A14; Don Oberdorfer, *North Korea Says U.S. Proposals Merit Discussion*, WASH. POST, Oct. 8, 1984, at A1; Yair Evron, *Arms Control in the Middle East: Some Proposals and Their Confidence-Building Roles*, ADELPHI PAPERS 1979; GLOBAL POLICY: CHALLENGE OF THE 80's (Morton A. Kaplan ed., 1984); U.S. MISSION GENEVA, BRIEFING BOOK ON INTERNATIONAL ORGANIZATIONS IN GENEVA (1985).

agenda various collateral disarmament measures that can be considered within the category of confidence-building steps.[172]

Cooperative measures for reducing the risks of war carry with them all of the virtues and vices of law, custom, and habit. They can make cooperation easier, or they can be exploited for political and military coercion. Attitudes toward cooperative measures and CBMs do not remain constant. The weight nations give to the advantages and disadvantages of specific proposals changes with the evolving political and military climate. When tensions are high, discussion of CBMs increases but not normally the chance of acceptance. More often than not, measures that appear attractive upon first examination prove in the end to have major drawbacks. Mutually acceptable measures seldom offer the contributions to risk reduction that had been desired originally. Clearly, easing tension is not always the most immediate goal of governments, and a nation is likely to grant real additional security to potential adversaries only at a price. In the end, assessment of the value of specific measures rest on geopolitical calculations.

Globalization and Fragmentation: Restraint's New Look

Almost a quarter of a century has passed since the end of the Cold War, but the period that followed has no conventional name. Some call it the "Age of Globalization." Some call it the "New Era." Most still refer to it as the "post-Cold War Era," reflecting the transition from a period that left behind a powerful and persistent legacy to an age too uncertain to name. A resurgence of ultra-nationalism and territorial ambitions in Russia and China has led some to declare the "post-Cold War Era" over. Some believe we are in a "New Cold War." Others note the spread of nuclear weapons and call this the "Second Nuclear Age."[173] Clearly this is an age in which technological and political change will take place at rates unseen before in history.[174] International arms restraint faces new challenges and will undoubtedly take on a new look. Some elements of this new look are already evident, most notably the de-emphasis on formal arms control treaties, especially those with lengthy, complex, detailed documents. A greater emphasis is being placed on cooperation to counter potential WMD terrorism. Nevertheless, a tension remains between the relatively simple act of asserting an international norm and the more difficult task of creating the conditions under which it can be effectively implemented. Many policy divisions of the past remain vibrant today. Exactly what of the old will prove viable in the new age is not clear.

Many of the international arms restraints that helped bring the Cold War to an end anticipated approaches that may reach their zenith in the years ahead. INF Treaty verification set the stage for the U.S./Soviet Joint Verification Experiment (JVE) related to the 1974 nuclear testing treaties. The JVE, in turn, began the "lab-to-lab" cooperation between the two nations' nuclear weapons laboratories. Lab-to-lab became a catalyst for the legislation by Senators Sam Nunn and Richard Lugar to help the newly independent nations of the

---

172. *See* G.A. Res. 37/95, U.N. GAOR, 37th Sess., 101st plen. mtg., U.N. Doc. A/RES/37/95 (1982); United Nations, Report of the Working Group on the Reduction of Military Budgets, U.N. Doc. A/CM.10/1983/CRP.4 (1983).

173. *See* Paul Braken, The Second Nuclear Age (2012).

174. *See* James M. Smith & Jeffrey A. Larsen, "All our Tomorrows": A Long-Range Forecast of Global Trends Affecting Arms Control Technology (2002).

collapsed Soviet Union meet START and CWC treaty obligations to destroy weapons and to address concerns about "loose nukes" and a "brain drain" of scientists to countries of concern. Thus were born "Cooperative Threat Reduction" (CTR) and the international science centers,[175] both of which characterize a new style of cooperative arms restraint that many believe will have applications in other troubled regions of the world. The Presidential Nuclear Initiatives that followed START I and set the stage for START II were also seen as a model for how friendly governments could move more quickly. The Open Skies Treaty offered an additional tool for the greater reliance on confidence-building that many had anticipated, and European multilateral agreements such as the Treaty on Conventional Armed Forces in Europe (CFE); the 1991 and 1992 Vienna Agreements on Confidence- and Security-Building Measures (CSBMs); and the Treaty on the Final Settlement with Respect to Germany all moved Europe toward a new system focused on the fundamental causes of conflict including the nature of the governments involved. The seeds for post-Cold War arms restraint were clearly sewn during the Cold War years.

The momentum forward at the end of the Cold War also built up expectations for what was to follow. The Chemical Weapons Convention (CWC) joined the BWC in banning another class of weapons, putting a spotlight on what appeared to be only a few remaining challenges. The expulsion of Iraq from Kuwait in the Gulf War and the creation of the United Nations Special Commission on Iraq (UNSCOM) raised expectations further as to what contributions intrusive inspections might make. At the head of state level in January 1992, the UN Security Council stated that proliferation would be a threat to international security–diplomatic code for the potential use of force. In the Middle East, the Peace Process created the ACRS (Arms Control and Regional Security) sub-process. On the Korean Peninsula, bilateral inspection measures were being negotiated to implement the 1991 North South Denuclearization agreement and backup the IAEA, whose inspection procedures were also being enhanced.

This euphoria at the end of the Cold War, however, did not last. Despite the Agreed Framework for Korea in 1994, the NPT Extension in 1995, and the conclusion of the Comprehensive Test Ban Treaty in 1996, dissatisfaction is a common theme to both advocates who demand major new moves and critics who believe that existing obligations are not being met. An examination of the issues that generated this unhappiness at both ends of the policy spectrum reveals much about today's challenges to international arms restraint. This in turn exposes the international fissures and conflicts that persist and recur.

Nuclear Reductions after the Cold War

To the United States and the Russian Federation, further reductions are an immense challenge. To much of the rest of the world, the pace is seen as too slow. In the run up to the 1995 NPT Extension Conference, the call for nuclear abolition or a "time bound framework" for the achievement of that goal were demanded. These demands were not met, but additional commitments were made, including a disarmament agenda and efforts toward a Middle East free of nuclear weapons and other weapons of mass destruction.[176]

---

175. The International Science and Technology Center ("ISTC") headquartered in Moscow and Astana and the Science and Technology Center of Ukraine ("STCU") headquartered in Kiev.

176. *See* Jonathan Schell, *The Gift of Time: The Case for Abolishing Nuclear Weapons Now*, Nation, July 13, 1998; Oxford Research Group, Current Decisions Report 18: Next Steps in Nuclear Disarmament (July 1997); Avner Cohen & Joseph F. Pilat, *Assessing Virtual Nuclear Arsenals*, and Charles L. Glaser, *The Flawed Case for Nuclear Disarmament*, *in* Survival, Spring 1998, at 129 and 112; Ronald F. Lehman II, *Deterrence, Denuclearization, and Proliferation: Alternative Visions of the Next Fifty Years*,

The NPT Review Conferences

At the NPT Review Conference of 2000, a more extensive agenda for the Review Conference of 2005 was agreed, including in Paragraph 15, thirteen steps for the implementation of Article VI of the NPT:

15. The Conference agrees on the following practical steps for the systematic and progressive efforts to implement Article VI of the Treaty on the Non-Proliferation of Nuclear Weapons and paragraphs 3 and 4(c) of the 1995 Decision on "Principles and Objectives for Nuclear Non-Proliferation and Disarmament":

1. The importance and urgency of signatures and ratifications, without delay and without conditions and in accordance with constitutional processes, to achieve the early entry into force of the Comprehensive Nuclear-Test-Ban Treaty.

2. A moratorium on nuclear-weapon-test explosions or any other nuclear explosions pending entry into force of that Treaty.

3. The necessity of negotiations in the Conference on Disarmament on a non-discriminatory, multilateral and internationally and effectively verifiable treaty banning the production of fissile material for nuclear weapons or other nuclear explosive devices in accordance with the statement of the Special Coordinator in 1995 and the mandate contained therein, taking into consideration both nuclear disarmament and nuclear non-proliferation objectives. The Conference on Disarmament is urged to agree on a programme of work which includes the immediate commencement of negotiations on such a treaty with a view to their conclusion within five years.

4. The necessity of establishing in the Conference on Disarmament an appropriate subsidiary body with a mandate to deal with nuclear disarmament. The Conference on Disarmament is urged to agree on a programme of work which includes the immediate establishment of such a body.

5. The principle of irreversibility to apply to nuclear disarmament, nuclear and other related arms control and reduction measures.

6. An unequivocal undertaking by the nuclear-weapon States to accomplish the total elimination of their nuclear arsenals leading to nuclear disarmament to which all States parties are committed under Article VI.

7. The early entry into force and full implementation of START II and the conclusion of START III as soon as possible while preserving and strengthening the ABM Treaty as a cornerstone of strategic stability and as a basis for further reductions of strategic offensive weapons, in accordance with its provisions.

8. The completion and implementation of the Trilateral Initiative between the United States of America, the Russian Federation and the International Atomic Energy Agency.

9. Steps by all the nuclear-weapon States leading to nuclear disarmament in a way that promotes international stability, and based on the principle of undiminished security for all:

in FRANCINE R. FRANKEL, BRIDGING THE NONPROLIFERATION DIVIDE: THE UNITED STATES AND INDIA (1995); Oxford Research Group, Current Decisions Report 19: Proposals for a Nuclear Weapon-Free World (October 1997); Ronald F. Lehman II, *Nuclear Deterrence and Disarmament after the Cold War*, *in* OLD ISSUES AND NEW STRATEGIES IN ARMS CONTROL AND VERIFICATION (James Brown ed., 1995).

- Further efforts by the nuclear-weapon States to reduce their nuclear arsenals unilaterally.
- Increased transparency by the nuclear-weapon States with regard to the nuclear weapons capabilities and the implementation of agreements pursuant to Article VI and as a voluntary confidence-building measure to support further progress on nuclear disarmament.
- The further reduction of non-strategic nuclear weapons, based on unilateral initiatives and as an integral part of the nuclear arms reduction and disarmament process.
- Concrete agreed measures to further reduce the operational status of nuclear weapons systems.
- A diminishing role for nuclear weapons in security policies to minimize the risk that these weapons ever be used and to facilitate the process of their total elimination.
- The engagement as soon as appropriate of all the nuclear-weapon States in the process leading to the total elimination of their nuclear weapons.

10. Arrangements by all nuclear-weapon States to place, as soon as practicable, fissile material designated by each of them as no longer required for military purposes under IAEA or other relevant international verification and arrangements for the disposition of such material for peaceful purposes, to ensure that such material remains permanently outside of military programmes.

11. Reaffirmation that the ultimate objective of the efforts of States in the disarmament process is general and complete disarmament under effective international control.

12. Regular reports, within the framework of the NPT strengthened review process, by all States parties on the implementation of Article VI and paragraph 4(c) of the 1995 Decision on "Principles and Objectives for Nuclear Non-Proliferation and Disarmament," and recalling the Advisory Opinion of the International Court of Justice of 8 July 1996.

13. The further development of the verification capabilities that will be required to provide assurance of compliance with nuclear disarmament agreements for the achievement and maintenance of a nuclear-weapon-free world.[177]

The Final Document of the 2000 NPT Review Conference presents an extensive list of goals, many subject to different interpretations and some overtaken by events, such as the termination of the ABM Treaty and subsequent arms control agreements between the U.S. and Russia. Most states parties look to a step-by-step process, but clearly the expectations of many states-parties may not be met. After many delegations expressed disappointment that nuclear arms reductions still seemed far from zero and that little progress had been made toward a Middle East Nuclear Free Zone, Mexico blocked any consensus final document at the 2005 NPT Review Conference. Consensus was achieved at the 2010 NPT Review Conference and the 13 steps of the 2000 NPT Review Conference were expanded to 64 action items.[178] The upcoming 2015 NPT Review Conference may prove very difficult. Russia's difficult relations with the West including aggression against Ukraine and violation of arms control obligations, massive violence throughout the

---

177. 2000 Review Conference of the Parties to the Treaty on the Non-Proliferation of Nuclear Weapons, Final Document of the Conference, U.N. Doc. NPT/CONF.2000/28.

178. http://www.un.org/ga/search/view_doc.asp?symbol=NPT/CONF.2010/50%20(V OL.I).

Middle East, a threatening nuclear program in Iran, continued nuclear weapons testing by North Korea, growing interest in nuclear weapons in South Korea, China's territorial disputes with its neighbors, calls in Japan for a major defense buildup, and a growing tendency to return to bloc voting in the UN cast a dark shadow over what was already a difficult and challenging disarmament agenda. Likewise, as of this writing, the goal of a Middle East free of WMD does not seem achievable in the midst of the great turmoil that now characterizes that troubled region.

Helsinki/START III

The START II Treaty set the precedent that strategic arms reductions could be negotiated easily and quickly by exploiting the continuing framework and mechanisms of the START I Treaty. When START II ratification in the Russian Duma was delayed, Presidents Clinton and Yeltsin agreed at their March 20-21, 1997 Helsinki Summit to prepare for START III:

> Once START II enters into force, the United States and Russia will immediately begin negotiations on a START III agreement, which will include, among other things, the following basic components:
>
> - Establishment, by December 31, 2007, of lower aggregate levels of 2,000-2,500 strategic nuclear warheads for each of the parties.
>
> - Measures relating to the transparency of strategic nuclear warhead inventories and the destruction of strategic nuclear warheads and any other jointly agreed technical and organizational measures, to promote the irreversibility of deep reductions including prevention of a rapid increase in the number of warheads.
>
> - Resolving issues related to the goal of making the current START treaties unlimited in duration.
>
> - Placement in a deactivated status of all strategic nuclear delivery vehicles which will be eliminated under START II by December 31, 2003, by removing their nuclear warheads or taking other jointly agreed steps. The United States is providing assistance through the Nunn-Lugar program to facilitate early deactivation.
>
> The Presidents have reached an understanding that the deadline for the elimination of strategic nuclear delivery vehicles under the START II Treaty will be extended to December 31, 2007. The sides will agree on specific language to be submitted to the Duma and, following Duma approval of START II, to be submitted to the United States Senate.[179]

In the context of the Helsinki START III Framework, the two sides agreed to discuss transparency of nuclear materials and non-strategic nuclear weapons. Although the Helsinki START III ceilings follow the START II model, the related issues suggest more of an extrapolation from START I into deeper verification and transparency. Can deep reductions be undertaken with confidence without greater certainty that residual nuclear capability in warheads or nuclear material would not constitute a rapid reconstitution danger? The realm of nuclear disarmament in the context of competitor nations and adversaries has always been envisioned as requiring limitations on the entire nuclear weapons production, maintenance, and dismantlement process. In that sense, the Helsinki START III approach

---

179. *See* Office of the Press Secretary, White House, Joint Statement on Parameters on Future Reductions in Nuclear Forces (Mar. 21, 1997).

reflected the traditional link between arms control and disarmament; namely, ever more comprehensive and detailed legally binding control over the entire weapons process.

The Moscow Treaty/SORT

On May 24, 2002, President George W. Bush of the United States and President Vladimir Putin of the Russian Federation signed the Treaty of Moscow, sometimes known as the Strategic Offensive Reductions Treaty (SORT). The treaty required each side to reduce "deployed nuclear weapons" to no more than 1700 to 2200 weapons, numerical ceilings lower than those of START III.[180] The treaty had been ready for signature before the Summit. It was one page long:

> The United States of America and the Russian Federation, hereinafter referred to as the Parties,
>
> Embarking upon the path of new relations for a new century and committed to the goal of strengthening their relationship through cooperation and friendship,
>
> Believing that new global challenges and threats require the building of a qualitatively new foundation for strategic relations between the Parties,
>
> Desiring to establish a genuine partnership based on the principles of mutual security, cooperation, trust, openness, and predictability,
>
> Committed to implementing significant reductions in strategic offensive arms,
>
> Proceeding from the Joint Statements by the President of the United States of America and the President of the Russian Federation on Strategic Issues of July 22, 2001 in Genoa and on a New Relationship between the United States and Russia of November 13, 2001, in Washington,
>
> Mindful of their obligations under the Treaty Between the United States of America and the Union of Soviet Socialist Republics on the Reduction and Limitation of Strategic Offensive Arms of July 31, 1991, hereinafter referred to as the START Treaty,
>
> Mindful of their obligations under Article VI of the Treaty on the Non-Proliferation of Nuclear Weapons of July 1, 1968, and
>
> Convinced that this Treaty will help to establish more favorable conditions for actively promoting security and cooperation, and enhancing international stability,
>
> Have agreed as follows:

Article I

> Each Party shall reduce and limit strategic nuclear warheads, as stated by the President of the United States of America on November 13, 2001 and as stated by the President of the Russian Federation on November 13, 2001 and December 13, 2001 respectively, so that by December 31, 2012 the aggregate number of such warheads does not exceed 1700-2200 for each Party. Each Party shall determine for itself the composition and structure of its strategic offensive arms, based on the established aggregate limit for the number of such warheads.

---

180. Depending on the definition of "deployed weapons," the actual force level selected, the number of deployed warheads permitted under the Treaty of Moscow 1700 to 2200 overlaps the number that would have been permitted by START III 2000 to 2500.

Article II

The Parties agree that the START Treaty remains in force in accordance with its terms.

Article III

For purposes of implementing this Treaty, the Parties shall hold meetings at least twice a year of a Bilateral Implementation Commission.

Article IV

1. This Treaty shall be subject to ratification in accordance with the constitutional procedures of each Party. This Treaty shall enter into force on the date of the exchange of instruments of ratification.

2. This Treaty shall remain in force until December 31, 2012 and may be extended by agreement of the Parties or superseded earlier by a subsequent agreement.

3. Each Party, in exercising its national sovereignty, may withdraw from this Treaty upon three months written notice to the other Party.

Article V

This Treaty shall be registered pursuant to Article 102 of the Charter of the United Nations.

Done at Moscow on May 24, 2002, in two copies, each in the English and Russian languages, both texts being equally authentic.[181]

The Moscow Treaty was a surprise more because it was presented in treaty form than for what it said and did. The President had made clear in his election campaign and in his earlier policy announcements that he believed that the traditional arms control process of negotiating lengthy and detailed treaties was more appropriate to an era of adversarial relationships than to the new relationship of friendship he believed was the case with the contemporary Russian Federation. A new approach was long anticipated.[182] The President presented his arguments for the new approach in his letter submitting the Treaty to the Senate.[183] A resolution granting consent to ratification of the Treaty of Moscow was passed in the U.S. Senate on March 10, 2003 by a vote of 95 to 0. On May 14, 2003, while Secretary of State Colin Powell was meeting with Russian President Vladimir Putin in Moscow, the Russian Duma approved the Treaty by a vote of 294 to 134 despite the recent U.S. withdrawal from the ABM Treaty and Russian opposition to U.S. military action in Iraq.

The strong, rapid consent to ratification of the Treaty of Moscow did not mean that support for the approach taken was unanimous. In the Senate debate, critics argued that the definition of deployed weapons was vague and removed from counting some weapons that counted under previous START ceilings. Although the Treaty encourages new forms of bilateral transparency and cooperation, it does not provide any new formal verification commitments. Consultations substitute for a formal reductions schedule and the ceilings apply only in a point of time. As in previous strategic nuclear treaties, warheads removed

---

181. Strategic Offensive Reductions Treaty, May 24, 2002, *reprinted in* ARMS CONTROL TODAY, June 2002, at 9.

182. *See* Paul Mann, *Arms Control "Twilight": Blessing or Curse?*, AVIATION WK. & SPACE TECH., Dec. 17, 2001, at 100–103; Rose Gottemoeller, *Beyond Arms Control: How to Deal with Nuclear Weapons*, POL'Y BRIEF, Feb. 2003.

183. Moscow Treaty: Message to the Senate of the United States, *available at* <http://www.state.gov/p/eur/rls/or/2002/11347.htm>.

from systems reduced are not required to be dismantled. Indeed, the Bush administration sought to keep some warheads available as hedges against technical difficulties in deployed warheads or an unanticipated strategic threat. Advocates of the Treaty of Moscow approach believe that reductions are easier, faster, and safer if some flexibility for reconstitution is provided. Critics argue that retaining upload capability runs against the principle of irreversibility that has increasingly been enshrined in bilateral and multilateral statements on arms control in the name of arms race stability and progress under Article VI of the NPT.

Treaty between the United States of America and the Russian Federation on Measures for the Further Reduction and Limitation of Strategic Offensive Arms ("The New START Treaty")

With the START I Treaty due to expire on December 5, 2009, U.S. President Barack Obama and Russian President Dmitry Medvedev agreed in April of that year to pursue rapidly a follow-on New START Treaty. Although the Moscow Treaty (SORT) was not scheduled to expire until December 31, 2012, that treaty would lose much of its verifiability and predictability absent the coexistence of the highly detailed START I provisions. The December goal was not met, but New START was completed quickly and was signed on April 8, 2012 in Prague, entering into force on February 5, 2011 and superseding the Moscow Treaty. What resulted was something of hybrid, neither as sparse as the Moscow Treaty nor as detailed as START I.

The central provision of new START was a ceiling of 1,550 on the total of both deployed warheads on strategic ballistic missiles and accountable warheads for bombers. Whereas START I and II had used attribution rules to account for warheads on ICBMs and SLBMs so that particular missiles counted according to an agreed number for each type, New START uses an approach under which a number of operationally deployed warheads is declared. This follows the general approach of the Moscow Treaty, but, unlike the Moscow Treaty, the numbers are subject to formal sampling inspections. Under the 1550 ceiling, each operationally deployed bomber counts as one weapon only, no matter how many it can carry (the START II approach) or how many are operationally deployed at bomber bases (the US Moscow Treaty approach). As explained in the State Department's Article-by-Article Analysis:

> Paragraph 2 provides that for purposes of counting toward the 1,550 limit, one nuclear warhead is counted for each deployed heavy bomber. Counting nuclear warheads for deployed heavy bombers is thus an attribution rule. This attribution approach was adopted because on a day-to-day basis, neither the United States nor the Russian Federation maintains any nuclear armaments loaded on board its deployed heavy bombers. If the counting approach adopted for deployed ballistic missiles had been applied to deployed heavy bombers, each deployed heavy bomber equipped for nuclear armaments would have been counted with zero nuclear warheads. The New START Treaty approach strikes a balance between the fact that neither side loads nuclear armaments on its bombers on a day-to-day basis and the fact that these bombers nonetheless have the capability to deliver nuclear armaments stored on or near their air bases. The rationale for this "discounted" attribution of one weapon for each heavy bomber is based on the fact that bombers are not fast-flying, first-strike weapons, and are thus considered to be stabilizing systems.[184]

---

184. Article-By-Article Analysis of New START Treaty Documents, U.S. Department of State, Bureau of Arms Control, Verification, and Compliance, May 5, 2010.

Thus, New START continues the START I approach of directly discounting bomber weapons, going even further to give bombers carrying air launched cruise missiles the same, full discount given in START I to bombers carrying only gravity bombs. Thus, a B-52 bomber equipped for 20 weapons would have counted 10 under START I, 20 under START II, and as actually operationally deployed under the Moscow Treaty, but now counts simply as one under the New START Treaty.

Aside from the bomber discount rule, New START generally treats all strategic nuclear weapons as equal leaving it to the two sides to determine its own mix of forces. New START, like the Moscow Treaty, does not contain the many stability mechanisms of previous agreements such as nested warhead sub-limits intended to encourage diverse forces and to limit and even ban heavy and MIRVed missiles. Indeed, New START's low limit of 700 total deployed ICBMs, SLBMs, and heavy bombers encourages MIRVs. The 700 limit on deployed systems, and the 800 limit on total deployed and non-deployed missiles and bombers was agreed primarily to meet Russian concerns about U.S. breakout potential associated with possibly reversible deMIRVing.

New START also sought to retain more of the verification provisions of START I that would not have been available under the Moscow Treaty when START I expired. According to the U.S. Department of State:

> The obligations and prohibitions of New START are different than those in START, reflecting both the improved U.S.-Russian relationship and lessons learned from our experience implementing START. Accordingly, the Treaty's verification provisions are simpler and less costly to implement than those in START. The New START Treaty prohibits interference with NTM and prohibits the use of concealment measures to avoid NTM. NTM will be supplemented by: on-site inspections; periodically exchanged data on weapons systems and facilities; regular notifications and data updates; and a requirement to assign a unique alphanumeric identifier to each ICBM, SLBM, and heavy bomber. This unique identifier may be confirmed during inspections and will be included in the database and applicable notifications. To promote openness and transparency, the Parties will also conduct an annual exchange of telemetry information on up to five ICBM or SLBM launches, as chosen by the Party conducting the launches.[185]

Consideration of the New START Treaty by the United States Senate and the Russian State Duma reflected enduring issues, both procedural and substantive. Senators expressed concern about restricted access to the negotiating record in the face of pressure to give consent to ratification during a "lame duck" session.

Advocates expressed concern that the ratification failure of SALT II and START II not be repeated maintaining that a new treaty was needed to encourage predictability and restraint. Opponents feared that the letter or spirit of the treaty would undermine national security. Often the concerns in the US were the opposite of those in Russia. Critics in the US feared that limits with implications for missile defenses, conventional forces, and allied support could be troubling. In Russia, critics saw the same limits as insufficient. In the US, critics thought the low limits on delivery vehicles were one-sided and harmful to stability. In Russia, with its highly MIRVed systems, the delivery system limits were seen as too high. In both countries, opinion was divided as to whether the 1550 warhead

---

185. Comparison of the START Treaty, Moscow Treaty, and New START Treaty Fact Sheet, U.S. Department of State, Bureau of Verification, Compliance, and Implementation, April 8, 2010, *available at* http://www.state.gov/t/avc/rls/139901.htm.

limit was too high or too low. Ironically, New START was criticized both that the Treaty could result in only the US making major reductions and that under its counting rules, the US could deploy more warheads operationally than it currently had deployed and much higher than the goal of the Moscow Treaty. In both countries, a key factor in gaining support for the Treaty were political commitments to funding for nuclear weapons programs and infrastructure.

On December 22, 2010, by a vote of 71 to 26 in the lame duck session, the United States Senate approved consent to exchange the New START instruments of ratification. On January 25, 2011, the State Duma of the Russian Federation approved its ratification resolution by a vote of 350 to 96, with one abstention. The instruments of ratification were exchanged in Munich on February 11, 2011 with entry into force that day as provided by the terms of the treaty with a duration of 10 years. Extensions of up to 5 years are provided for.

The future of strategic arms negotiations after New START are both clear and uncertain. Big issues remain. How deep can reductions go while maintaining stability? Can strategic nuclear weapons be reduced further without taking into account tactical weapons, non-deployed weapons, and weapons components inside and outside official stockpiles? How would nuclear weapons reductions proceed in a world in which conventional and unconventional weapons assume similar missions? What are the implications of expanding air and missile defenses? What about the nuclear weapons of other countries? None of these issues are new; all are likely to become more intense.

De-Alerting

Concern that the breakup of the Soviet Union may have created a dysfunctional Russian early warning and command/control system for its nuclear forces increased interest in the concept of "de-alerting" nuclear forces, particularly fast-flying ballistic missiles. The fear is that missile forces on alert may be launched by accident or miscalculation through the action of a "hair trigger" system designed to launch on warning (LOW) or, after confirmation of detonations, launch under attack (LUA). Given that the superpower standoff ended with the Cold War, de-alerting is advocated to provide an additional safety buffer. A range of de-alerting proposals exist, everything from increasing the number of procedural or technical steps necessary to launch a missile all the way to taking warheads off of missiles or missiles out of launchers. The merits of de-alerting have been hotly debated despite the fact that the United States and other nuclear powers have had extensive experience with de-alerting parts of their forces.

Even during the most dangerous periods of the Cold War, much of the U.S. deterrent was not on alert. This applied to both nuclear and conventional forces. In part, this was done to permit maintenance activities, allow overhauls, reduce costs, address safety issues, and minimize manpower requirements associated with keeping forces on alert. This remains true today. Having part of the force off alert also supported deterrence doctrine, strategic presence, and the show of force. Tactical and strategic signals could be, and were, sent by placing forces back on alert. To maintain the credibility of a generated alert or other increased launch readiness, crews had to train extensively. For example, the Strategic Air Command had to re-alert regularly to avoid the creation of a political taboo against nuclear re-alerting that would undermine deterrence or survivability. The deployment of dual capable delivery systems required similar exercises. Thus, routine re-alerting was important to test readiness, minimize mistakes, avoid accidents, and demonstrate resolve. Routine re-alerting was also believed necessary to ensure that neither the U.S. nor the Soviet Union would send the wrong signal or overreact to re-alerting steps taken by the other side to improve survivability in a crisis.

De-alerting part of the nuclear deterrent was also done in the past as a symbolic political gesture to exploit budget cuts already planned and to speed reduction steps already negotiated. For example, in the Presidential Nuclear Initiatives of 1991 de-alerting was designed to encourage continued, positive political momentum in the former Soviet Union and to make it easier for the non-Russian republics to permit nuclear warheads to be removed from their soil.

Despite this history of extensive de-alerting, the United States kept key elements of its deterrent at a high level of day-to-day readiness. In part, alert status could enhance survivability as bombers escaped their bases and missiles launched through an attack. In part, this also retained some options for damage limitation during conflict in which WMD strikes against the United States or its allies might occur. During the Cold War, a substantial rationale for retaining a larger portion of the force on alert was to ensure more surviving forces after an overwhelming, disarming attack. Alert forces, however, were also expected to deter more limited strikes aimed at "escalation dominance" or "fait accompli" psychologies, just the kind of limited attacks most attractive when all or most forces are "de-alerted." Scenarios like these may be more relevant with the end of the Cold War than the all-out nuclear war model.

Precautions against the mistaken or unauthorized use of nuclear weapons have been the centerpiece of the command and control systems of the U.S. and Russia and deserve the special attention given them. Indeed, in the post-Cold War era, the standards for positive control may need to be even higher. A number of weaknesses and discrepancies in early warning and command and control were identified during the Cold War and afterwards. Stories about the breakup of Russian nuclear controls were a legitimate cause of concern, although some may have been exaggerated and others remedied. With or without de-alerting, policymakers have been insisting on improvements in weapons security, command, and control. A consensus on the need for high confidence control has not defused the de-alerting debate over whether the advantages outweigh the disadvantages. How one answers this question depends on what one believes the problem is that de-alerting is intended to solve.

Some proponents would apply de-alerting mainly to the ICBMs of Russia and the United States. The theory is that the land-based missile forces are still dominated by a "use it or lose it" concept, especially because neither the U.S. nor Russia has disavowed Launch under Attack. For the United States, which has maintained a balanced Triad and which is de-MIRVing its ICBMs, the U.S. declaratory posture is more to re-emphasize deterrence than a day-to-day survival mechanism. Launch on warning in response to the so-called "bolt out of the blue" attack is not widely seen in the U.S. as a likely event. Some Russians, on the other hand, argue that the Russian Federation's land-based missiles are vulnerable to preemption and thus, unlike the American Triad, the preponderance of Russian forces becomes vulnerable. These analysts believe that Russian silo based missiles could be successfully attacked by conventional precision guided munitions (PGMs) on B-2 stealth bombers or on missiles, nuclear armed SLCM or ALCM, and especially U.S. Trident II D-5 SLBM missiles with W-88 warheads. Despite the deeply buried Russian command centers and ABM system, decapitation is also a commonly expressed concern. In these scenarios, however, it is not U.S. ICBMs that play the most threatening role. De-alerting has not been popular with the Russians because they don't see it as solving their problem. Indeed, it may be that the only solution to Russian vulnerability concerns is a more balanced nuclear deterrent force with a greater emphasis on survivability of forces and command.

Alternatively, one could de-alert the entire nuclear force of the two sides. In theory, neither side could launch quickly, and both would be assured of warning. However, the effectiveness of such an arrangement might be compromised by the existence of conventional (or non-nuclear) PGMs and the threats posed by third parties who are not constrained by the agreement. Still, slowing down response times to prevent error or miscalculation could be of greater value than trying to enhance survivability by de-alerting, which de-alerting may not do. Every decision-maker would like more time to have more information. One could, of course, gain time simply by not launching on warning. De-alerting seeks to make that mandatory. Still, de-alerting may not always compel taking more time for decisions if de-alerting ultimately forces early decisions to mobilize. Indeed, the greatest instabilities may be associated with the twin belief that the other side is gaining advantage by re-alerting first and that violation of the de-alerting norm indicates the most threatening of intentions. And at the end of any re-alerting, the decision makers are back where they began, fully alerted and ready to go, and perhaps much more nervous if there were a race to re-alert in a climate of perceived betrayal. In many scenarios, being comfortably on alert may be the least provocative, most stable psychology.

In this age of terrorism and ethnic and sectarian violence, de-alerting has attracted support as an additional warhead security measure. Stability may be a much lower priority in the age of terrorists than preventing "loose nukes." Again, the debate continues. Preventing unauthorized access is a problem whether on alert or not. De-alerting can be a form of security for the full up missile, perhaps making unauthorized launch more difficult, but the prospects of "loose nukes" could well be increased by the separation of warheads from missiles. Even removing strategic warheads to secure storage raises questions, especially because strategic warheads are less likely to have the safety and security designs, including PALs that are put on tactical weapons. Strategic warheads, which can be smaller than some tactical warheads, may be kept under better control by retaining them on their missiles.

Other issues related to de-alerting include the impact on the American nuclear umbrella and the proliferation implications. De-alerting may involve other nations in ways that apply differently than to the United States or Russia. Whether based upon binding de-alerting agreements or not, verification remains a challenge. Even unilateral de-alerting raises the question of the ground rules for re-alerting and the stability consequences. In short, not all of the considerations weighed during the Cold War have disappeared with the end of the Cold War, although they may have become more complex.

The New Debate over Missile Defenses[186]

The end of the Cold War did not bring about an end to the debate over ballistic missile defenses, and arguments today parallel those of the previous forty years. Important differences, however, do reflect changed strategic circumstances. Although geostrategic tensions have returned, neither Russia nor China is seen today as an immediate nuclear threat. Russian force levels have declined, and projected Chinese force levels are still small. The threat from proliferation of less capable ballistic missiles elsewhere involves even smaller numbers. Both Russia and China oppose US national ballistic missile defenses, but the two Gulf Wars, missile saber-rattling from Pyongyang, proliferation of rockets and missiles around the Middle East, and the spread of WMD and missile technology

---

186. ROBERT F. TURNER, THE ABM TREATY AND THE SENATE: ISSUES OF INTERNATIONAL AND CONSTITUTIONAL LAW (1999).

have prompted a fresh examination of the relationship between offensive and defensive forces. These have implications for international arms restraint in the post-Cold War era.

Strategists and tacticians have long sought an optimal mix of offense and defense in warfare. Deterrence in the nuclear age, with its focus on stability and prevention of war, altered such priorities, placing more emphasis on the ability of one, or both sides, to inflict unacceptable destruction. In the Cold War logic, defenses became suspect. Facing defenses, one nation may fear its deterrence is weakened. With defenses, another nation might be more aggressive believing that defenses could permit it to escape the worst retaliation. Because ballistic missiles had become the symbol of mutual vulnerability, the arms race interpretation of behavior dominant during the Cold War reinforced this predisposition against ballistic missile defense. Deployment of ballistic missile defenses might incite an even greater deployment of offensive missiles in response. In U.S. and Soviet calculations, these themes influenced the debate over strategy as much as they dominated arms control thinking. They did not, however, drown out all other considerations.

In the traditional military offense-defense relationship, defense was seldom the final decisive act in a war. Thus, the offense took the lead in military thinking long before nuclear deterrence theory reigned. Defense could, however, determine the outcome. The better prepared the defense, the more offensive forces required to overwhelm it. Ratios between three-to-one and six-to-one were often the rule for planning. Of course, smaller armies could defeat larger armies by concentrating offensive forces at a critical time and place. Achieving this local numerical superiority, however, usually required going on the defensive elsewhere, building upon the military principle of "economy of force." Defenses enhanced military strength in other ways as well. They were used to delay or disrupt enemy forces to buy time. Defenses could channel attacking forces toward a desired battleground or tie them down in a specific place. They were said to shape the battle space.

Defensive operations were used extensively to provide warning, test enemy strength and intention, and in turn deny the enemy intelligence about the defender. Defenses increased the difficulty of the attack, raising the price and increasing the risk of failure. In that sense, defense also had a deterrent value. Throughout history, periods existed in which defenses in the form of fortifications and obstacles were the dominant form of military investment precisely because they were seen as preventing war or making it less destructive. Defenses also provided some sanctuary for populations and kings.

Despite the preponderance of offensive forces during the nuclear Cold War, much thinking was given to missile defense. Because the ability to strike a given number of targets determined missile force levels, planners often simply added to their forces the additional warheads necessary to replace losses to defenses. Defenses could also provide some protection for retaliatory forces against surprise attack. This option produced many "force exchange models" assessing the stability provided by different ratios of defense on two sides. Typically, opponents of missile defenses concluded they were destabilizing. Opponents of missile defenses feared that a nation striking first could overwhelm the defenses of a surprised victim whose depleted retaliatory forces would then face a fully warned and ready missile defense. This logic might encourage first strike.

Proponents of defenses argued differently. The existence of defenses complicates attack planning and provides some protection for early warning and command systems. No easy first strike would be plausible. In the face of defenses, the first strike could not be limited and could not prevent devastating retaliation. With the threshold for an attack raised to high levels, confidence in a stable balance would be enhanced especially because fear of unintended "catalytic war" caused by accidental launches, misunderstandings, or third party attacks would be reduced. Interest in limited defense raised the question in negotiations of how to make offensive and defensive forces commensurate. In the strategic arms talks linkage also became an issue. Should offensive limits require defensive limits or vice versa, or should there be no linkage at all?

The public debate, however, was more fundamental. What was the best way to reduce the danger of nuclear war? Advocates of "mutual assured deterrence" and "mutual assured survival" took opposite positions on missile and other defenses. Near total vulnerability would permit reductions to low levels of arms said the first camp. Highly effective defenses would permit reductions more safely said the other. The massive numbers of deployed nuclear weapons aimed at military targets during the Cold War often masked the security concern that would dominate thinking after the Cold War; namely, only a few nuclear weapons striking population centers could be devastating beyond human imagination.

Arguments for missile defenses today, as in the Cold War, reflect the traditional roles of the defense but with different priorities that assume any missile attack would be small and perhaps unintended. Political turmoil after the collapse of the Soviet Union raised concern that missiles might be launched by accident, misunderstanding, or renegade military officers. The spread of WMD armed missiles to so-called "rogue" states amplifies that fear. Some advocate missile defenses to discourage or counter proliferation. Existence of theater and national missile defenses may deter proliferators from acquiring missiles that may not be useful in the face of defenses. Defenses may also provide a hedge against violation of nonproliferation treaties and give more credibility to military responses to WMD proliferation. Nonproliferation coalitions may be more viable if regional members have some missile protection. Even in the U.S.-Russian context, missile defenses are seen as a potential tool of cooperative security. With the two nations working together to exploit technology on behalf of mutual defenses, some hope that missile defenses could reduce arms competition and improve relations. According to this view, the decision by the United States to withdraw from the ABM Treaty effective June 13, 2002 was justified because the treaty interfered with use of promising technologies and codified a corrosive, adversarial relationship with Russia. Still, withdrawal was widely criticized as removing a pillar of arms control. Critics believe instead that over time Russia will feel threatened with a first strike from the U.S., limiting Russian nuclear reductions. China, they believe, will have to increase its nuclear forces in order to overcome American defenses.

The great power centric debate over missile defenses, however, is currently being side-tracked by the growing importance of very advanced missile defense technology in the regional context. In every troubled region, advanced theater missile defenses are playing a prominent role both as a response to WMD proliferation and as an alternative to responding in kind. Assisting friends and allies with missile defense has become an important security and non-proliferation tool for the United States. For small countries, these are national missile defenses. In many cases, the theater systems are advanced enough to be part of a national missile defense system for a great power. Growing interest in missile defenses and the blurring of categories is presenting new challenges to deterrence, defense, and arms control policies.

NWFZs and their Role after the Cold War

During the Cold War, nearly every debate over nuclear weapon free zones reflected in some way the geopolitical jockeying of the two superpowers, particularly in Central Europe. Not all of those issues have gone away. Despite NATO statements to the contrary,

Belarus and the Russian Federation expressed concerns that nuclear weapons might someday be deployed on their borders in the former Warsaw Pact nations now entering the North Atlantic Alliance. In several other regions, however, interest in NWFZs accelerated at the end of the Cold War. In addition to their geo-strategic roles, nuclear weapon free zones are also seen as adjuncts to the NPT—strengthening non-proliferation norms, adding additional constraints, and reinforcing negative security assurances. Spreading across the globe with more than 100 members, NWFZs serve many publics as an additional measure of disarmament progress. Some believe they add little to the basic obligations nations have already undertaken, but others see in them vehicles for security cooperation within regions and as a way to influence behavior in other regions. The new nuclear weapon free zones borrow heavily from those that emerged at the heights of the Cold War, but they have added a few new features as well.[187]

The Antarctic Treaty

Almost unknown to publics and of little international security controversy, the Antarctic Treaty contains within it a number of precedents upon which many of the international arms restraint treaties and mechanisms were to build. The Treaty, however, came into being to address serious concerns arising out of territorial disputes. Seven nations, some with overlapping claims, sought sovereignty over parts of Antarctica. Eight other nations, including the U.S. and the U.S.S.R, made no claims to sovereignty but had a similar basis for asserting such claims. The foundation for the Treaty rests on the scientific interest in Antarctica and little interest in seeing it militarized. Building upon the spirit of scientific cooperation that accelerated during International Geophysical Year (1957–1958), the United States hosted the Washington Conference on Antarctica beginning on October 15, 1959 and concluded with all twelve parties in attendence signing the Antarctic Treaty on December 1, 1959 and others acceding later.

Although negotiations were completed quickly, the terms are extensive. Fundamentally, the political status quo is protected (Art. IV). Article I, Section 1, contains the most comprehensive example of international arms restraint ever negotiated:

> 1. Antarctica shall be used for peaceful purposes only. There shall be prohibited, *inter alia*, any measures of a military nature, such as the establishment of military bases and fortifications, the carrying out of military maneuvers, as well as the testing of any type of weapons.[188]

Article V, Section 1 makes one constraint even more clear: "Any nuclear explosions in Antarctica and the disposal there of radioactive waste material shall be prohibited."[189] To implement these and other provisions relating to protection of the environment and wildlife, Article VII provides for the right to routine inspections by all of the Contracting parties, the right to aerial observation "at any time over any and all areas of Antarctica," advanced notification of movements of military personnel or equipment there for peaceful purposes, and data on all locations of activities. Article III provides for exchanges of personnel and data on scientific activities, and Articles X and XI address compliance enforcement obligations and encourage alternative dispute resolution mechanisms ranging from negotiation through arbitration to the International Court of Justice.[190] The Antarctic

---

187. *See* Arms Control Association, Nuclear Weapon Free Zones at a Glance, (2012) at https://www.armscontrol.org/factsheets/nwfz.

188. U.S. Arms Control and Disarmament Agency, *supra* note 35, at 13.

189. *Id.* at 14.

190. *See id.* at 11–18.

Treaty is often said to illustrate the wisdom of prohibiting or limiting arms before they are already in place. Whatever the utility of that observation, one sees in the Antarctic Treaty the seeds of much more. In the Antarctic Treaty are the predecessors of many of the verification approaches (inspections and data exchanges) and confidence-building measures (Open Skies and personal exchanges) that would make the Cold War treaties possible. Indeed, the Antarctic Treaty established the foundation for the post-Cold War cooperation in threat reduction including the scientist-to-scientist interaction that would become so important to nonproliferation.

The Outer Space Treaty

As discussed in Chapter 16, although modeled on the Antarctic Treaty, the Treaty on Principles Governing the Activities of States in the Exploration and Use of Outer Space, including the Moon and other Celestial Bodies (the Outer Space Treaty) took six years to negotiate. Space arms control was, and remains, a controversial area. In the 1950s, both the Soviet Union and the United States had limitations on the militarization of space in their comprehensive disarmament proposals. Obstacles included the Soviet Union's preference for linkage of issues and the U.S. insistence on verification measures. In September 1960, at the UN General Assembly, President Eisenhower proposed that the approach taken the previous year for Antarctica be applied to celestial bodies. Three years later, the Soviet Union announced that it could consider a proposal to ban the orbiting of nuclear weapons separately from other issues, in particular dropping linkage to the question of U.S. missiles in Europe. Over the next few years, the positions of the two sides moved closer with the U.S. agreeing to include a ban on orbiting nuclear weapons and deciding that it could rely on its own national technical means for verification. The Treaty was completed in late 1966 and entered into force on October 10, 1967. The key arms restraint provisions are contained in Article IV:

> States Parties to the Treaty undertake not to place in orbit around the Earth any objects carrying nuclear weapons or any other kinds of weapons of mass destruction, install such weapons on celestial bodies, or station such weapons in outer space in any other manner.

> The Moon and other celestial bodies shall be used by all States Parties to the Treaty exclusively for peaceful purposes. The establishment of military bases, installations and fortifications, the testing of any type of weapons and the conduct of military maneuvers on celestial bodies shall be forbidden. The use of military personnel for scientific purposes or for any other peaceful purposes shall not be prohibited. The use of any equipment or facility necessary for peaceful exploration of the Moon and other celestial bodies shall also not be prohibited.[191]

By the time the Outer Space Treaty was negotiated, the Limited Test Ban Treaty had already banned nuclear testing in outer space, and as space is a more hostile environment even than Antarctica, cooperative exploration was only beginning. Still, provisions in the Treaty including clarification of liability have become important to joint space science.

Latin America

The Treaty for the Prohibition of Nuclear Weapons in Latin America and the Caribbean (The Treaty of Tlatelolco) predates the NPT and differs in some details, but the successful negotiation of the Treaty of Tlatelolco helped spur the NPT on to completion. Originally

---

191. *Id.* at 35–44.

proposed by Brazil in 1962, the Cuban missile crisis gave the negotiation of the Treaty a sense of urgency. Difficult issues, however, delayed its completion until February 14, 1967. Inclusion of all significant states would take a quarter of a century with Cuba itself being the last of the 33 Latin American states to submit its instrument of ratification (October 23, 2002). The Treaty provided that all eligible parties must ratify the Treaty before it would go into effect for every party, except that individual parties could waive the Treaty into effect for themselves in advance. Most countries did so within a few years, and the Agency for the Prohibition of Nuclear Weapons in Latin America (OPANAL) created by the Treaty became active very quickly. For many years after signing, however, Argentina and Brazil had nuclear weapons programs and did not waive the Treaty into effect. Chile also delayed many years. Two protocols were applied to the United States. President Nixon signed and ratified Protocol II (having to do with activities on its territories) in 1971, but Protocol I (having to do with its activities in the zone including negative security assurances) was not signed until 1977 under President Carter and not ratified until 1981 under President Reagan.

Article 1 contains the primary nonproliferation obligation, and the words differ from the NPT:

> 1. The Contracting Parties hereby undertake to use exclusively for peaceful purposes the nuclear material and facilities which are under their jurisdiction, and to prohibit and prevent in their respective territories:
>
> (a) The testing, use, manufacture, production or acquisition by any means whatsoever of any nuclear weapons, by the Parties themselves, directly or indirectly, on behalf of anyone else or in any other way, and
>
> (b) The receipt, storage, installation, deployment and any form of possession of any nuclear weapons, directly or indirectly, by the Parties themselves, by anyone on their behalf or in any other way.
>
> 2. The Contracting Parties also undertake to refrain from engaging in, encouraging or authorizing, directly or indirectly, or in any way participating in the testing, use, manufacture, production, possession or control of any nuclear weapon.[192]

The constraint on the use of nuclear materials and facilities for peaceful uses would have permitted "peaceful nuclear explosions" (PNEs). This is made clear in Article 18:

> The Contracting Parties may carry out explosions of nuclear devices for peaceful purposes—including explosions which involve devices similar to those used in nuclear weapons—or collaborate with third parties for the same purpose, provided that they do so in accordance with the provisions of this article and the other articles of the Treaty, particularly articles 1 and 5.[193]

Article 5 defines a nuclear weapon as "any device which is capable of releasing nuclear energy in an uncontrolled manner and which has a group of characteristics that are appropriate for use for warlike purposes."[194]

Complications in creating a complete Latin American nuclear weapons free zone included the status of overseas territories, the obligations of the nuclear powers, and the uncertain geo-strategic future of Cuba, but none of these was as significant as the unresolved nuclear ambitions of Argentina and Brazil. The territorial issues were defused by political

---

192. *Id.* at 50.
193. *Id.* at 55.
194. *Id.* at 51.

change including independence, amendments to the Treaty, and declarations by extra-territorial powers. The United States, as the major nuclear power, was able eventually to ratify both Protocols I and II with the promulgation of what have become traditional un-derstandings and declarations related to transits, negative security assurances (an attack by a Contracting Party assisted by a nuclear-weapons state would be inconsistent with Article 1), and that producing PNEs would be considered the same as producing a nuclear explosion.[195] The end of the Cold War deflated the significance of Cuba. Yet, the Treaty of Tlatelolco was being heralded as a model long before its viability was resolved. Much of the credit for its success rests with the persistence of those states that waived the Treaty into effect for themselves early. In the end, however, decisions by governments in Argentina and Brazil to abandon their nuclear weapons programs in favor of moving toward greater integration with the global economy and international community made possible a true Latin American NWFZ that influences approaches in other regions.[196] Whether this decision will be sustained in the years ahead is not certain, given the growing latency of nuclear weapons capability and the long-term desire of Argentina and Brazil for international status they believe is associated with nuclear technology, if not weapons or submarines, then nuclear power.

The Seabed Treaty

The Treaty on the Prohibition of the Emplacement of Nuclear Weapons and other Weapons of Mass Destruction on the Seabed and the Ocean Floor and in the Subsoil Thereof (The Seabed Treaty) of 1971 came in the same period as the NPT and Treaty of Tlatelolco, but its intellectual origins are more in the Antarctic and Outer Space Treaties. Growing scientific exploration of the ocean floor created both the prospect of militarization of the seabed and an interest in avoiding that prospect. As in the case of the Outer Space Treaty, some use of the seabed for sensors and monitoring was already taking place. And as in the case of the Antarctic Treaty, territorial disputes and unresolved issues in international law complicated matters. Moreover, differences over verification took on greater significance in the negotiation of the Seabed Treaty. Originally, the Soviet Union proposed that all military activities be covered and that reciprocal inspections be undertaken. Many small countries pressed for an international inspection regime to provide them with capabilities for verification they did not have. In the end, the concentration on the emplacement of weapons of mass destruction reduced verification demands, and provisions for assistance in verification were added. The scope presented in Article I, however, did go beyond just nuclear weapons:

> 1. The States Parties to this Treaty undertake not to implant or emplace on the seabed and the ocean floor and in the subsoil thereof beyond the outer limit of a seabed zone, as defined in article II, any nuclear weapons or any other types of weapons of mass destruction as well as structures, launching installations or any other facilities specifically designed for storing, testing or using such weapons.[197]

South Pacific

The Treaty of Rarotonga, establishing the South Pacific Nuclear Free Zone (SPNFZ) or "spinfiz," was opened for signature on August 6, 1985, forty years to the day after the

---

195. *Id.* at 46–47.

196. *See* NUCLEAR-WEAPON-FREE ZONES IN THE 21ST CENTURY (Péricles Gasparini Alves & Daiana Belinda Cipollone eds., 1997).

197. *See* U.S. ARMS CONTROL AND DISARMAMENT AGENCY, *supra* note 35, at 82.

Hiroshima bomb was dropped. Named after the largest of the Cook Islands, a newly independent nation in free association with New Zealand, the Treaty of Rarotonga entered into force on December 11, 1986. Three significant protocols were opened for signature at Suva, Fiji on August 8, 1986. Protocol 1 binds the U.S., the U.K. and France with respect to their territories in the zone. Protocol 2 prohibits the threat or use of nuclear weapons against parties or territories in the zone including territories of the U.S., U.K., and France and is open to the five NPT NWS as is Protocol 3, which prohibits all nuclear explosive testing in the zone. As a "nuclear free zone" broader than a "nuclear weapons free zone," SPNFZ was widely acclaimed for going beyond security to engage environmental issues, something of a merging of Tlatelolco and the Antarctic Treaty but with additional prohibitions on peaceful nuclear explosions (PNEs) and on dumping of radiological waste by parties in the zone or by others in the territorial seas.

From the beginning, however, tensions with the nuclear weapons states that have territories in the Pacific complicated the SPNFZ negotiations. Past atmospheric nuclear testing by the U.S. and U.K. and continuation of underground testing by France generated early interest in a nuclear weapons free zone in the Pacific, but the proposal in 1983 by Australia to press for negotiation of a treaty coincided with strong anti-nuclear protests around the world erupting because of the NATO deployments in Europe of intermediate-range nuclear missiles. The entire SPNFZ negotiation took place in the background of the INF negotiations between the U.S. and the Soviet Union. The United States sought to ensure that the Treaty was consistent with its traditional NWFZ policies on assurances and transits, but France, a European ally of the United States, was adamant on the need to continue underground testing in the Pacific. The decision by the United States and the United Kingdom to withhold signature to the protocols pending resolution of French concerns led to a major diplomatic confrontation between the United States and New Zealand, resulting in the cessation of naval ship visits between the two allies. Thus, only the Soviet Union signed its two protocols in 1986, followed by China the next year. Not until March 25, 1996, with the CTBT bringing about an end to French nuclear testing, did France, the United Kingdom, and the United States sign the three Protocols of the Treaty of Rarotonga.

Southeast Asia

The Southeast Asian Nuclear Weapons Free Zone (SEANWFZ), known as the Treaty of Bangkok, opened for signature on December 15, 1995, and entered into force on March 28, 1997 with ten members. The SEANWFZ has been described as a major step toward the Zone of Peace, Freedom and Neutrality (ZOPFAN) envisioned by the ASEAN Kuala Lumpur Declaration of November 1971, issued during the Vietnam War. Following as it did, the Korean Crisis of 1994 and coinciding with the NPT extension debate, the Treaty of Bangkok reflected ASEANs interest in strengthening its role in international security. In addition to security-related prohibitions on nuclear weapons development, testing, and deployments by the parties, the Treaty also contains prohibitions on the dumping of radioactive waste into the seas.

Although negotiations among the regional parties were completed quickly, the draft Treaty was immediately controversial due to the inclusion of continental shelves and exclusive economic zones, the exact boundaries being in dispute. Other constraints were seen as impinging on the traditional reservations of the Nuclear Weapons States having to do transits and security assurances. In particular, concerns have been raised about interpretations that may limit nuclear transits and the launching of nuclear weapons from within the zone. The history of diplomatic cooperation is uneven and confidence in the process weak. None of the 5 nuclear weapons states named have signed the Protocol,[198] but at the November 18, 2011 ASEAN leaders meeting in Bali, agreement was recorded to work toward that goal.[199]

Africa

The Treaty of Pelindaba, named for a South African nuclear facility associated with that country's nuclear weapons program, was opened for signature on April 11, 1996 and entered into force on July 15, 2009.[200] The Organization for African Unity called for an African NWFZ as early as its Cairo Summit in 1964. Three decades of major political change including the end of Apartheid and Cold War rivalries in the region were necessary before negotiations could progress. In addition to the central prohibitions against nuclear weapons acquisition and stationing, the Treaty prohibits dumping of radioactive wastes, and attacking nuclear installations; parties are to maintain high standards of physical protection at nuclear facilities. The Treaty requires full scope safeguards for all and establishes an African Commission on Atomic Energy and provides verification provisions. The Treaty included three protocols. Protocol I, signed by the five NPT nuclear weapons states, contains the commitment not to threaten with nuclear weapons the African states or territories. Under Protocol II, the same five undertake not to test nuclear explosions in the zone. Protocol III, signed by France and Spain, requires them to comply with specific relevant provisions of the Treaty in their African territories. In welcoming the Treaty of Pelindaba, the United States reflected its traditional policy concerns in highlighting that:

> The Treaty affirms the right of each party to decide for itself whether to allow visits by foreign ships and aircraft to its ports and airfields, explicitly upholds the freedom of navigation on the high seas and does not effect rights to passage through territorial waters guaranteed by international law.[201]

The Treaty of Pelindaba was an extension of an NWFZ to an entire continent, one that had seen nuclear weapons built in South Africa, tested in Algeria by an external power (France), and sought elsewhere. Coinciding with the completion of the CTBT, the African Nuclear Weapons Free Zone symbolized major movement toward denuclearization by progressive geographical exclusion. Still, fears that governments in North Africa had stocks of chemical or biological weapons caused the United States to reference the international legal principle of "belligerent reprisal" when asked if it would be totally precluded from a nuclear response if attacked by WMD, once again highlighting the difficulty of isolating one area of nonproliferation from other sources of insecurity.[202]

---

198. *See* Center for Nonproliferation Studies, Monterey Institute of International Studies, Inventory of International Nonproliferation Organizations & Regimes (2002).

199. "We welcomed the conclusion of negotiations with the Nuclear Weapons States to enable the Nuclear Weapons States to accede to the Protocol to the Southeast Asian Nuclear Weapons Free Zone (SEANWFZ) Treaty. The Nuclear Weapons States and ASEAN agreed to take the necessary steps to enable the signing of the Protocol and its entry into force at the earliest opportunity" at http://www.asean.org/news/item/joint-statement-of-the-3rd-asean-us-leaders-meeting, accessed July 27, 2014.

200. *See* A.R. Newby-Fraser, Chain Reaction (1979). Of 52 signatories, 17 of 28 required had ratified by early 2003.

201. *See* Bureau of Nonproliferation, U.S. Department of State, Fact Sheet: African Nuclear Weapons Free Zone Treaty (Jan. 20, 2001).

202. *See* Judith Miller, *Nuclear Anxieties in a New World*, N.Y. Times, Feb. 5, 2000, at A15.

Mongolia

If the Treaty of Pelindaba followed Tlatelolco in taking a continental approach to NWFZs, Mongolia demonstrated the application of NWFZs to a single country. In October 1992, in a speech before the UN General Assembly, President Ochirbat of Mongolia declared his country to be a NWFZ and proposed international recognition of this status. Mongolia's strategic location between Russia and China and near Japan and the two Koreas engendered support for this unique, single state NWFZ concept. On October 5, 2000, on behalf of the five NPT nuclear powers, the U.S. issued a statement reaffirming security assurances for Mongolia.[203] Domestic legislation was enacted in Mongolian February 4, 2000 with provisions that any subsequent treaty language would prevail. The law encourages verification agreements with international organizations and explicitly states a role for private citizens:

> 6.4 Non-governmental organizations or individuals may, within the mandate provided for by the legislation, exercise public oversight of the implementation of the legislation on the nuclear-weapon-free status and submit proposals thereon to the relevant State authority.[204]

The UN General Assembly passed a resolution in November 2000 encouraging states to help strengthen the Mongolian NWFZ.

Central Asia

To promote political stability, the foreign ministers of the five Central Asian (C5) nations announced in the Almaty Declaration on February 28, 1997 their intention to create a nuclear-weapon-free-zone. The idea had been proposed as early as 1993, citing the Mongolian precedent. The independence of Turkmenistan, Kazakhstan, Uzbekistan, Tajikistan, and the Kyrgyz Republic, all formerly part of the USSR had introduced great uncertainty into one of the world's most sensitive geo-strategic locations, the historic pathways between Russia, China, South Asia, and the Middle East. Russia removed its nuclear weapons and other WMD related materials, but significant WMD facilities and specialists remained behind. In neighboring Afghanistan, civil war and the militant Islamic Taliban regime served as a reminder of the turmoil that could spread north. Four years later, after the September 11, 2001 attacks on the United States, American, French, and other military forces moved into this region that already had attracted the political attention of Russia, China, Turkey, Iran, Japan, Korea, India, and Pakistan. Symbols of reassurance seemed as important as ever.

The process of negotiation was supported by UN General Assembly resolutions and aided by the UN Secretary General. A disagreement among the C5 over provisions related to obligations under earlier treaties (raising concern over the possible introduction of Russian nuclear weapons back into Kazakhstan, the location of the former Soviet nuclear test facility at Semipalatinsk) was resolved through compromise language reinforcing the basic intent of the Treaty. A draft of the Central Asian Nuclear-Weapon Free-Zone (CANWFZ) was completed by experts in September 2002 and immediately thereafter

---

203. *See* John D. Holum, U.S. Under Secretary of State, Statement in the First Committee of the General Assembly on Behalf of the Five Permanent Members of the Security Council on Security Assurances for Mongolia, (Oct. 5, 2000).
204. *See* http://www.opanal.org/NWFZ/Mongolia/LawMongolia.html.

meetings were held with delegations from the five nuclear weapons states concerning protocols to provide negative security assurances. The treaty entered into force in March 2009 becoming the world's first nuclear free zone located entirely in the Northern Hemisphere. All five nuclear weapon states signed the protocol to the treaty which is an integral part of the treaty providing to the Central Asian states security assurances against the use, or the threat of use, of nuclear weapons.[205]

The Korean Peninsula

On January 20, 1992, the Republic of Korea and North Korea signed the "Joint Declaration on the Denuclearization of the Korean Peninsula." The denuclearization agreement provided for a ban on reprocessing and enrichment on the entire Korean Peninsula, North and South, and provided for a bilateral inspection regime. The agreement never went into force, first because of the inability to reach agreement on implementation of inspections and finally due to the breakdown of the IAEA safeguards agreement over North Korean declarations and its covert plutonium reprocessing facility. In 2003, Pyongyang withdrew both from the NPT and the Korean Denuclearization Agreement.[206]

Other proposals have been made to expand the concept of NWFZs to Northeast Asia. Some have advocated Limited Nuclear Weapons Free-Zones build around a core of South Korea, North Korea, Japan, and perhaps Mongolia, with some proposals calling for the exclusion of tactical weapons on land or at sea within a zone around the core, to include the territory of two nuclear powers, China and Russia.[207]

Other Regions and the Future

The difficulties associated with achieving a nuclear weapon-free Korean Peninsula are matched in other regions of conflict. The long history of efforts in the Indian Ocean region and South Asia offer ideas more than fulfillment.[208] Interest in a South Asian Nuclear Weapon Free Zone increased after the Indian nuclear detonation in 1974 and was periodically referenced in UN General Assembly resolutions over the next twenty years.[209] Since the 1998 nuclear tests by India and Pakistan, interest in immediate crisis management has crowded out more long-term interests. The Middle East offers the same bleak history. Although the Arms Control and Regional Security (ACRS) discussions that grew out of the 1991 Madrid Middle East Peace Conference offered a vehicle for discussion of security and arms control measures aimed at creating conditions necessary for a Middle East free from weapons of mass destruction, the breakdown of the broader political negotiations in the context of escalating violence leaves little hope for such bold concepts soon. In each of these cases, the approach to NWFZs involves the engagement of nations with very real security threats and very serious political and strategic differences. In each of these cases, more than nuclear weapons or even weapons of mass destruction will have to be

---

205. *See* Nuclear Threat Institute, Central Asia Nuclear Weapons Free Zone, at http://www.nti.org/treaties-and-regimes/central-asia-nuclear-weapon-free-zone-canwz/.

206. Solving the North Korean Nuclear Puzzle (David Albright & Kevin O'Neill eds., 2000); Verifying the Agreed Framework (Michael M. May ed., 2001).

207. *See, e.g.,* Hiro Umebayashi, *Northeast Asia Nuclear Weapon Free Zone: Recent Developments and Analyses, in* Proceedings of INESAP 1997 Conference: Challenges and Opportunities for a Nuclear-Weapon-Free-World, Sept. 8–10, 1997.

208. *See* Shelley A. Stahl & Geoffrey Kemp, Arms Control and Weapons Proliferation in the Middle East and South Asia (1992).

209. *See, e.g., Establishment of a Nuclear-Weapon-Free Zone in South Asia,* G.A. Res. 49/72, U.N. GAOR, 49th Sess., Supp. No. 49, at 62, U.N. Doc. A/RES/49/72 (1994).

addressed by these states themselves. That in essence is what has become of the proposals in the mid-1990s by Belarus and Ukraine for Central European Nuclear Weapon Free Zones. Proposed initially as an alternative to NATO expansion eastward, ideas for a NWFZ in Central Europe were rejected by those nations preferring to join NATO. NATO, however, issued a statement that it had no reason, plans or intention to move nuclear weapons into the territory of the new NATO members. Ironically, Poland, which led much of the recent opposition to the proposal for a NWFZ was the home of the 1950s Rapacki Plan, a Cold War proposal to denuclearize Central Europe.

For many advocates, nuclear weapon free zones offer their greatest possibilities as means of enforcing global disarmament. In particular, transnational activists see local and provincial, single-nation, and sub-regional nuclear free zones as part of a major effort to spread within the northern hemisphere the nuclear free status of much of the southern hemisphere.[210] This "think globally, act locally" strategy links the disarmament issue to other economic, social, and environmental advocacy and offers nuclear abolitionists a second strategy, in addition to seeking a universal global disarmament treaty. With this strategy, nuclear weapon-free zones become a means to confine and isolate nuclear possession. This approach is incremental and requires that security concerns within regions be addressed. In this aspect, this local/regional approach overlaps with more traditional international security policy.

International Law and Nuclear Weapons

Just as World War I brought about a surge of interest in international law, with fear of gas warfare leading to a ban on the use of chemical weapons, so World War II and the nuclear age brought about a renewed interest in international organizations and efforts to control nuclear power. The relationship of international law, and also U.S. constitutional law, to nuclear weapons has taken on a special tension in the age of nuclear deterrence.[211] As with the concept of arms control, international law seeks to reduce the chance of war, and should it occur, to reduce its destructiveness. However, in the case of nuclear weapons, their destructiveness is seen as an asset in deterring war.

The uneasy relationship of international law and deterrence policy predates nuclear weapons, for example, in the consideration of conventional strategic bombardment of cities prior to and during World War II. The strong belief that nuclear deterrence has prevented war amongst the "great powers" has colored the legal debate over the legitimacy of nuclear weapons deployments, policy, and use.[212] Even as the search for more effective

---

210. *See, e.g., Nuclear Weapon-Free Zones: Crucial Steps towards a Nuclear-Free World: The Uppsala Declaration on Nuclear Weapon-Free Zones*, INESAP Info. Bull., Sept. 2001, at 84.

211. Richard A. Falk, *The Shimoda Case: A Legal Appraisal of the Atomic Attacks upon Hiroshima and Nagasaki*, 59 Am. J. Int'l L. 759 (1965); Peter B. Maggs, *The Soviet Viewpoint on Nuclear Weapons in International Law*, 29 Law & Contemp. Probs. 956 (1964); Julius Stone, Legal Controls of International Conflict 342–48 (1959); Harrop A. Freeman & Stanley Yaker, *Disarmament and Atomic Control: Legal and Non-Legal Problems*, 43 Cornell L.Q. 236 (1957); M. Nagendra Singh, *The Right of Self-Defence in Relation to the Use of Nuclear Weapons*, Indian Y.B. Int'l Aff., 1956, at 3; Ellery C. Stowell, *The Laws of War and the Atomic Bomb*, 39 Am. J. Int'l L. 784 (1945); James Warren Beebe, *Tomorrow's Weapons vs. The Constitution*, 36 S. Cal. L. Rev. 373 (1963). Charles J. Moxley Jr., John Burroughs, Jonathan Granoff, "Nuclear weapons and Compliance with International Humanitarian Law and the Nuclear Non-Proliferation Treaty, *34 Fordham International Law Journal 595*, 2011.

212. "During the 31 years leading up to the first atomic bomb, the world without nuclear weapons engaged in two global wars resulting in the deaths of an estimated 78 million to 95 million people, uniformed and civilian." *See* David Von Drehle, "Want Peace? Give a Nuke the Nobel," Time, October 11, 2009 at http://content.time.com/time/nation/article/0,8599,1929553,00.html; Alex Roland,

international law continues, the primacy of deterrence is asserted. Nevertheless, the official policy of all nuclear powers is that nuclear deterrence is consistent with international law and also that the provisions of international law apply to nuclear weapons use ... Still, issues of the morality and legality of nuclear weapons remain a central element in the consideration of nuclear policy.

In 1983 a "Pastoral Letter" on nuclear deterrence promulgated by the U.S. National Conference of Catholic Bishops demonstrated both the evolution of the "just war" tradition and its continuous relevancy, sparking a debate that continues on the moral and legal justification of U.S. nuclear weapons policy. Canon law was a major source of international law, and it remains a political factor itself. Central to the just war tradition are the themes of restraint, proportionality, discrimination, and responsibility. Even had these principles not found their way into international law, they would undoubtedly influence U.S. nuclear policy. International law is clearly guided by these considerations, and the United States has made clear to its military forces that they too must be guided by international law, morality, and practices.[213] The United States is bound to follow such law, not because a treaty requires it, but because international law imposes the obligation on all states and consistent adherence to international law is in the long term national security interests of the United States. Whatever the primacy of nuclear deterrence posture, U.S. policy is that international law is binding on the United States, its officials, and its citizens.[214] Increasingly, international law has been applied not only to broad national policies, but also to the more specific execution of military force.[215]

Combatants and Non-Combatants

Weapons of great destructive power complicate the traditional distinction between combatants and non-combatants, but international law has sought to bring further specificity to its constraints. Before nuclear weapons, nothing brought this distinction to the public mind more than aircraft. From the beginning of aviation, war from the sky, bypassing defenses and over flying armies, brought a special terror to civilian populations. Much of the international law that applies to nuclear weapons derives from the basic law of air warfare, which reflected a clear view of intent but a premature estimate of the consequences of destruction that aircraft could bring. Under the law of air warfare, the fundamental protections for civilians are to be retained in principle. "Aerial bombardment for the purpose of terrorizing the civilian population, of destroying or damaging private property not of a military character, or of injuring noncombatants is prohibited."[216]

For all of the legal constraints and pressures on aerial bombardment, international law did not prevent attacks on civilians in the World Wars of the twentieth century. These

---

"Technology and War," in American Diplomacy available at http://www.unc.edu/depts/diplomat/AD_Issues/amdipl_4/roland4.html.

213. *See* Alfred P. Rubin, *Correspondence: The Neutron Bomb Again*, 21 VA. J. INT'L L. 805, 806–08 (1981); Harry H. Almond, Jr., *Nuclear Fear Shall Make Us Free*, 11 HUM. RTS. 22 (1983); Captain Fred Bright, Jr., *Nuclear Weapons as a Lawful Means of Warfare*, 30 MIL. L. REV. 1 (1965); George Bunn, *US Law of Nuclear Weapons*, NAVAL WAR C. REV., July–Aug. 1984, at 46; Martin Feinrider, *International Law as Law of the Land: Another Constitutional Constraint on Uses of Nuclear Weapons*, 7 NOVA L.J. 103 (1982).

214. U.S. AIR FORCE, AFP 110-31, INTERNATIONAL LAW: THE CONDUCT OF ARMED CONFLICT AND AIR OPERATIONS 1–7 (1976).

215. *See generally* chapters four, The Use of Force in International Relations, and six, The Law of Armed Conflict and Neutrality.

216. *Id.*

constraints were largely ignored during World War II. Suffice it to note that an enemy's entire territory came to be considered a theater of hostilities. As Hersch Lauterpacht has stated:

> The immunity of non-combatants from direct attack was thought to be a principle of this nature. It had been recognized as such in the few instances in which international tribunals have been called upon to pronounce on the matter. In the First World War, the illegality, except by way of reprisals, of aerial bombardment directed exclusively against the civilian population for the purpose of terrorization or otherwise seems to have been generally admitted by the belligerents—although this fact did not actually prevent attacks on centres of civilian population in the form either of reprisals or of attack against military objectives situated therein.
>
> ... the practice of the Second World War reduced to the vanishing point the protection of the civilian population from aerial bombardment. That practice cannot be explained solely by reference to reprisals adopted by the Allies against Germany, on account either of her own practice of aerial warfare or the unprecedented lawlessness of her conduct in relation to the civilian population in occupied territory....[217]

Subsequently, restraints on air warfare were incorporated into the body of international law to take into account the ability of aircraft to identify some targets and their inability to identify others. In particular, the presence of military targets was not deemed sufficient to justify attacks on civilians, and certainly not targeting of populations *per se*. This principle was codified in Protocol 1, Article 51.[218] Among others, the following types of attack are to be considered as indiscriminate:

> (a) an attack by bombardment by any methods or means which treats as a single military objective a number of clearly separated and distinct military objectives located in a city, town, village, or other area containing a similar concentration of civilians or civilian objects.... [219]

Article 57 of Protocol I attempts to provide similar guidance. Specific precautions are mandated for attack planners and attacking forces emphasizing its central provision;

---

217. 2 L. OPPENHEIM, INTERNATIONAL LAW: A TREATIES: DISPUTES, WAR AND NEUTRALITY, 524–25, 529 (H. Lauterpacht ed. 7th ed. 1952).

218. Protocol Additional to the Geneva Conventions of August 12, 1949, and Relating to the Protection of Victims of International Armed Conflicts (Protocol 1), June 8, 1977, 1125 U.N.T.S. 3 [hereinafter Protocol I]. While the United States has not ratified Protocol I, many of the provisions of Protocol have been recognized by the United States as reflective of customary international law. See Statement by Gregory Nickels, U.S. Senior Advisor to the 65th General Assembly, on Agenda Item 82: Status of the Protocols Additional to the Geneva Conventions of 1949 and Relating to the Protection of Victims of Armed Conflicts, in the 6th Committee at http://usun.state.gov/briefing/statements/2010/149784.htm. Currently, 174 states have ratified Protocol I, many with reservations and understandings that dilute the rules and proscriptions contained within the Protocol. See http://www.icrc.org/applic/ihl/ihl.nsf/Treaty.xsp?documentId=D9E6B6264D7723C3C12563CD002D6CE4&action=openDocument.

219. *Id.* art. 51. *See* the 1923 Draft Hague Rules of Air Warfare, which were never ratified by any state, had elaborated this principle more fully in Article 24. *See also* Article 22 of the draft Hague Rules: "Aerial bombardment *for the **purpose of*** terrorizing the civilian population, or destroying or damaging private property not of a military character, or of injuring non-combatants is prohibited." (Emphasis supplied.)

namely that "[i]n the conduct of military operations, constant care shall be taken to spare the civilian population, civilians and civilian objects."[220]

> In the conduct of military operations at sea or in the air, each Party to the conflict shall, in conformity with its rights and duties under the rules of international law applicable in armed conflict, take all reasonable precautions to avoid losses of civilian lives and damage to civilian objects.[221]

The focus of the law has been to protect non-combatants to the extent possible especially by providing constraints and eliminating pretexts for attacks on civilians, including as a general principle, but with exceptions, reprisal. "Attacks against the civilian population or civilians by way of reprisals are prohibited."[222] Not only must efforts be made to avoid inflicting injury on non-combatants, but also steps such as advanced warning of attack are encouraged so that non-combatants can protect themselves. "Effective advance warning shall be given of attacks which may affect the civilian population, unless circumstances do not permit."[223] Again, international law has sought to create a bias toward the presumption that the correct act is the one most likely to protect non-combatants.

> In case of doubt whether an object that is normally dedicated to civilian purposes, such as a place of worship, a house or other dwelling or a school, is being used to make an effective contribution to military action, it shall be presumed not to be so used.[224]

The distinction between combatant and non-combatant remains difficult to maintain in modern warfare, often creating operational constraints on military forces attentive to their legal obligations. Still, military thinkers have not sought to dismiss this distinction, which is consistent with the post-Clausewitzian command that war have a clear political purpose and that a war limited in objective shall be limited in cost and conduct. Indeed, it is consistent with the military principles of economy of force and decisiveness in the application of military force. "This general protection of civilian objects is entirely consistent with traditional military doctrine since civilian objects are not, by definition, making an effective contribution to enemy military action, and their destruction or neutralization offers no definite military advantage."[225] Indeed, the presumption of current U.S. military policy is against any justification of mass destruction of population or property. "The mass annihilation of enemy people is neither humane, permissible, nor militarily necessary. The Hague Regulations prohibit destruction or seizure of enemy property 'unless such destruction or seizure be imperatively demanded by the necessities of war.'"[226]

Nuclear weapons have not made the protection of non-combatants by international law any easier, nor have they increased the influence of the international law on aerial bombardment. But international law has not been irrelevant, and it has become more important in the age of 24-hour news coverage. Even in the examination of nuclear war, the distinction between combatants and non-combatants remained a central theme in

---

220. Protocol I, *supra* note 218, art. 57.
221. *Id.* art. 57.
222. *Id.* art. 51. This "prohibition" on reprisals has been subject to many statements of reservations by states parties and is one of the problematic provisions that has prevented the United States from ratifying Protocol I.
223. *Id.* art. 57.
224. *Id.* art. 52.
225. U.S. Air Force, *supra* note 214.
226. *Id.* at 5–9.

deterrence theory. Indeed, the debate between those who advocate counterforce versus countervalue targeting reflects the legal, moral, and military considerations raised here. Of interest has been the degree to which the critics of doctrines of minimum deterrence and countervalue targeting have added legal arguments to their brief. With the end of the Cold War, the standards to be met will be far more stringent.[227]

Proportionality and Restraint

Those who cite international law in support of more selective nuclear weapons, greater accuracy, smaller nuclear yields, and enhanced counter-military deterrence speak not only of the need to protect non-combatants but also of the need to show proportionality. Indeed, the concept of proportionality and restraint contains the basic justification for the legal use of any nuclear force. Without some demonstration that restraint is being shown, and that escalation is at least appropriate and proportional, it is difficult to imagine that a major nuclear strike, much less countervalue targeting, would be consistent with international law. In the U.S.-Soviet confrontation, the doctrine of flexible response echoed the basic logic of international law, leaving open the question as to whether the facts of nuclear warfare could meet the legal requirements of the laws of war. In the age of American conventional military dominance, any U.S. nuclear use is seen as unlikely and unique to preventing mass casualties threatened by others. For these purposes, the U.S. has examined means to reduce the "collateral damage" associated with plausible nuclear use. These include the use of greatly reduced yields for existing warheads and earth-penetrating warheads that detonate underground.

Critics of more selective counter-military targeting have not abandoned the legal field. Even those who do not believe that mere possession of nuclear weapons is illegal argue that the inability to guarantee control of escalation means that the use of nuclear weapons could not be limited and therefore can neither discriminate between combatants and non-combatants nor be proportionate. Further, these critics argue that the intent to discriminate and be proportionate is not sufficient if there is not a reasonable prospect that the response could be limited.[228]

Current policy rejects the view that nuclear weapons must of necessity be disproportionate or indiscriminate and goes further, advocating just that both for legal and military reasons.

> We recognize that wanton destruction and unnecessary suffering are both violations
> of these military developed legal principles and counterproductive to the political

---

227. Burns H. Weston, *Nuclear Weapons Versus International Law: A Contextual Reassessment*, 28 McGill L.J. 542 (1983); Paust, *The Nuclear Decision in World War II — Truman's Ending and Avoidance Position: A Legal Appraisal and Its Ramifications*, 8 Int'l Law. 160 (1974); William G. Lee, *The United States' Nuclear First Strike Position: A Legal Appraisal of its Ramifications*, 7 Cal. W. Int'l. L.J. 508–25 (1977); W.T. Mallison, Jr., *The Laws of War and the Juridical Control of Weapons of Mass Destruction in General and Limited Wars*, 36 Geo. Wash. L. Rev. 308 (1967); William V. O'Brien, *Some Problems of the Law of War in Limited Nuclear Warfare*, 14 Mil. L. Rev. 1 (1961). *See* Morris Greenspan, The Modern Law of Land Warfare 371–72 (1959). For a general discussion of "minimum deterrence" see Keith Payne, "Minimum Deterrence: Examining the Evidence," National Institute of Public Policy, National Institute Press, 2013.

228. Richard A. Falk, *Is Nuclear Policy a War Crime?*, Hum. Rts., Winter 1983, at 18, 18–21, 54–55; Nancy Ellen Abrams, *Nuclear War and the Destruction of the World: What Can Lawyers Do?*, Cal. Law., Feb. 1983, at 24; Elliott L. Meyrowitz, *Nuclear Weapons Policy: The Ultimate Tyranny*, 7 Nova L.J. 93 (1982); Ian Brownlie, *Some Legal Aspects of the Use of Nuclear Weapons*, 14 Int'l & Comp. L.Q. 437, 446–47.

military goals of the Nation. The law of "proportionality" is simply a legal restatement of the time honored military concept of "economy of force."[229]

Deterrence, Retaliation, and Reprisals

Presumptions of the legality of nuclear deterrence under international law are continuously under attack. For example, in 1961, United Nations General Assembly passed, over the "No" votes of four of the five declared nuclear weapons states, Resolution 1653 (XVI) which declared the use of nuclear weapons a violation of the United Nations Charter and of international law.

The General Assembly ... Declares that:

1. (a) The use of nuclear and thermo-nuclear weapons is contrary to the spirit, letter and aims of the United Nations and, as such, a direct violation of the Charter of the United Nations;

(b) The use of nuclear and thermo-nuclear weapons would exceed even the scope of war and cause indiscriminate suffering and destruction to mankind and civilization and, as such, is contrary to the rules of international law and to the laws of humanity;

(c) The use of nuclear and thermo-nuclear weapons is a war directed not against an enemy or enemies alone but also against mankind in general, since the peoples of the world not involved in such a war will be subjected to all the evils generated by the use of such weapons;

(d) Any State using nuclear and thermo-nuclear weapons is to be considered as violating the Charter of the United Nations, as acting contrary to the laws of humanity and as committing a crime against mankind and civilization.... [230]

Over the years the General Assembly has passed a number of non-binding resolutions reflecting a strong aversion to the continued existence of nuclear weapons. For example, in 2013 it passed a resolution with the support of 129 states calling for the "urgent" start of multilateral negotiations to eliminate nuclear weapons and designating Sept. 26 as the international day for their "total elimination."[231] Given the strength of such political acts and the very real tension between the destructiveness of nuclear weapons and the requirements for discrimination, proportionality, and restraint, legal opinion has never felt comfortable with ruling out a judgment that the possession and use of nuclear weapons might be inconsistent with international law.

Despite strong political statements such as those of UNGA Resolution 1653, the presumption today is that, in and of themselves, neither the possession nor the use of nuclear weapons is in violation of international law. Some would argue that nuclear weapons and deterrence constitute a new category for consideration and that their possession and potential use should be judged by the higher objectives of the law of warfare; namely, to prevent war and to mitigate its consequences if it should occur. Others would argue that the possession and use of nuclear weapons are simply subject to the same limitations as exist for conventional weapons and that the manner of use determines the legality of the act. Still others would argue that first use might not be legal, but that second use would meet the standards of international law. Variations of this theme rely upon extrapolation

---

229. U.S. AIR FORCE, *supra* note 214, at 1-11, 12.
230. WILLIAM W. BISHOP, JR., INTERNATIONAL LAW: CASES AND MATERIALS 979–80 (3d ed. 1971).
231. *See* UN General Assembly Resolution GA/11463, 5 December 2013.

of legal briefs suggesting circumstances under which the act of reprisal is consistent with international law.

The nuclear powers, however, have placed special emphasis on the argument that since nuclear weapons have not been banned, they are permitted. And, if they are permitted, then there must be circumstances in which their use is legal. In this regard, the nuclear weapons states have made clear their views that nuclear weapons are legal, and these states have, as necessary, issued numerous reservations and understandings to a number of international agreements, most recently Amendments to the 1925 Geneva Protocol, to ensure that commitments made with respect to issues such as military restraint, prohibition of genocide, protection of non-combatants and the like are not permitted to add legal weight to arguments against the legality of nuclear arms.[232] For example, the United States, which was a party to the negotiations of the 1977 Protocol to the Geneva Convention of 1949, signed (but has not ratified) with the following understanding: "It is the understanding of the United States of America that the rules established by this protocol were not intended to have any effect on and do not regulate or prohibit the use of nuclear weapons." Furthermore, the United States has cited international arms control agreements and especially the Nuclear Non-Proliferation Act as expressing the recognition in international law of the legality of the possession of a nuclear deterrent. The legality of nuclear weapons is reinforced not only by limits permitting them, but also by a lack of prohibitions.[233] As explained by the U.S. Department of Defense:

> The use of explosive nuclear weapons, whether by air, sea or land forces, cannot be regarded as violative of existing international law in the absence of any international rule of law restricting their employment. Nuclear weapons can be directed against military objectives as can conventional weapons.[234]

The 1996 ICJ Advisory Opinion

On December 15, 1994 by a vote of 78 to 43, with 38 abstentions, the United Nations General Assembly passed UNGA Resolution 49/75 K requesting an advisory opinion of the International Court of Justice on the question "Is the threat or use of nuclear weapon in any circumstances permitted under international law?"[235] A year and a half later, the World Court spoke — with a divided voice. Interpretations of the opinions (all 14 judges issued separate opinions) were also divided. For the most part, the July 8, 1996 non-binding advisory ICJ opinion reaffirmed traditional interpretations of the applicability of international law to nuclear weapons. In that sense, they were constrained like other weapons. Any use must be lawful and restrained.

> A threat or use of force by means of nuclear weapons should also be compatible with the requirements of the international law applicable in armed conflict, particularly those of the principles and rules of international humanitarian law, as well as with specific obligations under treaties and other undertakings which expressly deal with nuclear weapons....[236]

---

232. *See* Rubin, *supra* note 213, at 805–06.

233. *See* Rubin, *supra* note 213, at 806; Weston, *supra* note 227; Protocol I, *supra* note 218.

234. U.S. Air Force, *supra* note 214, at 6-5. *See also* Bishop, *supra* note 230, at 804; George Schwarzenberger, The Legality of Nuclear Weapons (1958).

235. G.A. Res. 49/75 K, U.N. GAOR, 49th Sess., U.N. Doc. A/RES/49/75 (1994). An earlier request for an advisory opinion from the World Health Organization (WHO) had been denied by the ICJ on the grounds that it was not within the proper responsibilities of WHO.

236. Legality of the Threat or Use of Nuclear Weapons, 1996 I.C.J. 266 (July 8).

In its most concise statement on the question asked by the UNGA, the ICJ concluded (by an 11-3 vote), "There is in neither customary nor conventional international law any comprehensive and universal prohibition of the threat or use of nuclear weapons as such...."[237] The World Court also opined that in light of the requirements of international law the destructiveness of nuclear weapons meant that:

> "It follows from the above-mentioned requirements that the threat or use of nuclear weapons would generally be contrary to the rules of international law applicable in armed conflict, and in particular the principles and rules of humanitarian law;

> However, in view of the current state of international law, and of the elements of fact at its disposal, the Court cannot conclude definitively whether the threat or use of nuclear weapons would be lawful or unlawful in an extreme circumstance of self-defence, in which the very survival of a State would be at stake...."[238]

This judgment, reached with an equally divided court, is more controversial. In part, the ICJ seemed to be acknowledging that the elements of fact would determine legality in specific cases, the traditional view, and that it did not have at its disposal facts that would cause it to conclude that nuclear weapons never could meet those standards. The language goes further, however, suggesting that meeting the conditions for legal use would only be under extreme circumstances that are described as "self-defence, in which the very survival of a State would be at stake." Concern was raised within the World Court and by outside experts that this prejudged the issue. More importantly, concerns were raised that the ICJ opinion undermined extended deterrence and positive security assurances given to non-nuclear weapon states by nuclear weapon states. Some analysts found this extrapolation in conflict with the fundamental right of nations to collective self-defence inherent in the United Nations Charter.

Many questions have arisen about the ICJ opinion and the way in which the request for an opinion first came about. Substantive and procedural concerns have been expressed by those who believe the World Court went too far and also by those who believe it did not go far enough. These expressions were intensified by the politicized environment in which the request was made; namely, in the midst of the 1995 debate on indefinitely extending the NPT. The implications can be seen in the additional opinion of the ICJ as follows: "There exists an obligation to pursue in good faith and bring to a conclusion negotiations leading to nuclear disarmament in all its aspects under strict and effective international control."[239] The language clearly refers to Article VI of the NPT, but it is neither a complete nor an exact quotation. In particular, disagreement exists as to whether the additional language expressing an obligation to "bring to a conclusion negotiations leading to nuclear disarmament" extends the "good faith" obligations of Article VI.[240] Whether the World Court is again requested or accepts a request for an advisory opinion on these questions, the debate over the proper interpretation of Article VI will continue, especially in the enhanced review process every five years at the NPT Review Conferences.

---

237. *Id.*

238. *Id.*

239. Legality of the Threat or Use of Nuclear Weapons, 1996 I.C.J. 267 (July 8).

240. *See, e.g.,* Robert F. Turner, *Nuclear Weapons and the World Court: The ICJ's Advisory Opinion and Its Significance for U.S. Strategic Doctrine, in* THE LAW OF MILITARY OPERATIONS (Michael N. Schmitt ed., 1998). Contra John Burroughs, "The (Il)legality of Threat or Use of Nuclear Weapons," International Association of Lawyers Against Nuclear Arms, 1997.

Domestic Law and Nuclear Weapons

The United States is a land of law and lawyers, and the strategy of nuclear deterrence has brought with it an interesting legal practice. The development and deployment of nuclear weapons and their delivery systems is covered by the laws of contracts, procurement, safety, environmental protection and the like, including complex legal obligations related to the responsibility of individuals involved in maintaining deterrence. As a result, the whole field of international and national security law permeates domestic law as it relates to nuclear weapons, infrastructure, and operations. Espionage cases, congressional reporting requirements, and Environmental Impact Statements (EIS) are among numerous examples. Some issues remain relatively less active. For example, the question of personal responsibility for conduct under international law and the laws of warfare remains latent in the debate over the legality of the possession, use, or threat of use of nuclear weapons. The U.S. government has made clear that individual government officials and military personnel remain accountable for their actions under international law. In the 1980s, the legal question was raised from the moral perspective when an Archbishop of the Roman Catholic Church challenged the morality of the professions of members of the Church working in a nuclear weapons plant located within his archdiocese.[241]

In the early 1980s, a reopening of the debate over the constitutionality of the possession and use of nuclear weapons took place in the very political climate of the "nuclear freeze" campaign. Although traditional arguments on the legality of nuclear weapons were repeated, greater emphasis was placed on the evolution of a more activist judiciary and legal community to alter thinking on nuclear weapons-related legal issues and to draw more upon the United States Constitution and war powers legislation. Central in this call to political action was the assertion that the destructiveness of nuclear weapons was so great that a new approach to jurisprudence would be required, one involving greater legal intervention in the development of nuclear deterrence policy. Interestingly, despite the growth of the successor to the nuclear freeze campaign, the Global Zero movement, very few challenges have been mounted as to the nuclear weapons employment policy and deterrence posture. Inspired by President Obama's 2009 speech advocating "a world without nuclear weapons"[242] the current Global Zero movement calls for the United States and Russia—who hold more than 90% of the world's nuclear weapons—to negotiate deep cuts in their arsenals, followed by international negotiations to eliminate all nuclear weapons by 2030.[243]

Some have challenged the legality of the first use of nuclear weapons without the consent of the Congress. Advocates of such an approach do not all agree that Congressional permission would be required if the United States, or perhaps even its allies, were under nuclear attack, but some do believe that the use of nuclear weapons in response to conventional attack, especially conventional attack overseas would require congressional approval. Although the right of self-defense is acknowledged and the right of the President to order military forces to repel attack is accepted, this school argues in general that the

---

241. *See* Catholic Church, The Challenge of Peace: God's Promise and Our Response (1983); M.J. Farrell, *Roman Catholic Nuclear Pacifism, in* The Nuclear Arms Debate 353 (Phyllis Zagano ed., 1983); Bishop Roger Mahony, *The Case for Nuclear Pacifism, in* The Apocalyptic Premise: Nuclear Arms Debated 279–93 (Ernest W. Lefever & E. Stephen Hunt eds., 1982).

242. *See* http://www.whitehouse.gov/the_press_office/Remarks-By-President-Barack-Obama-In-Prague-As-Delivered.

243. *See* http://www.globalzero.org/get-the-facts/GZAP#sthash.tfljmZAP.dpuf.

decision to use nuclear weapons in and of itself is a decision to broaden the conflict in ways which, because of the destructiveness of nuclear weapons, should require a formal declaration of war. Parallel to this logic is the recommendation that Congress insert itself into the decision-making process that might consider the use of nuclear weapons at some future date. Such intervention is argued to be practical because conventional warfare is not instantaneous in the way that nuclear warfare could be. Deterrence would not be undercut, say advocates, because use of nuclear weapons, even first use, would still be possible with the consent of the Congress. Secrecy could be maintained by a secret vote. To preclude circumvention, advocates of this position would have the Congress enact legislation which would make clear the legal restraints on the use of nuclear weapons and make clear also that individuals remain responsible for their conduct under the law.[244]

Opponents of any formal Congressional veto over the use, whether first or second, of nuclear weapons generally deny a legal requirement or right and cite the potential danger that the American deterrent might appear so encumbered to an adversary that it would fail. On the legal side, many would acknowledge the power of the Congress to place limitations on the conduct of war, declared or otherwise, but believe that Congress would undercut deterrence in the process. Others believe that the powers of the President as Commander-in-Chief would still permit him to direct his forces to act in self-defense including if necessary, pre-emption by conventional and perhaps nuclear means against a WMD attack. To the extent, however, that advocates of a congressional veto desire to institutionalize a "no first use" policy, the debate becomes one of substance and policy implementation rather than one of constitutional questions. The debate over "no first use" policies also carries within it shadows of the legal debate.[245]

Contemporary Dynamics of International Arms Restraint

International arms restraints today are defined more broadly than was common during the Cold War, and the world in which they operate is more complex ranging from nuclear proliferation, through bio-terrorism, ethnic cleansing, and Al Qaeda to child soldiers and abandoned munitions. Still, the contrast with the past can be overstated even as the significance of change can be underestimated. Today, the bilateral arms control of the Cold War era regulating arms races is contrasted with the current emphasis on multilateral nonproliferation. Clearly, the U.S. and the USSR were the focus of Cold War arms control and disarmament and provided essential leadership. Cold War arms control, however, was never completely bilateral, often dealt with conventional arms, and always had nonproliferation as a central theme. Many of the Cold War era agreements such as the Antarctic Treaty, the Outer Space Treaty, the NPT, BWC, and CWC were meant to be multilateral or universal nonproliferation tools. Even nuclear arms agreements between the United States and the Soviet Union concerned the Article VI interests, and sometimes the weapons of others. The British and French nuclear deterrents were targets of Soviet negotiating demands in bilateral nuclear negotiations with the U.S. Some limitations on the expansion

---

244. Jeremy J. Stone, *Presidential First Use is Unlawful*, Foreign Pol'y, Fall 1984, at 94; Murrey Marder, *Scientists Call for an 'Additional Lock' on the Nuclear Trigger*, Wash. Post, Sept. 9, 1984, at A14. *But see*, Robert F. Turner, *Congressional Limits on the Commander in Chief: The FAS Proposal*, *in* First Use of Nuclear Weapons: Under the Constitution, Who Decides? (Peter Raven-Hansen ed., 1987).

245. *See* Rubin, *supra* note 213, at 811.

of certain patterns of allied nuclear cooperation were agreed. Destruction of West German missiles was provided for in the context of the INF treaty, and destruction of similar missiles in East Germany, Czechoslovakia, and Bulgaria undoubtedly would have been required had the West known their existence at the time the treaty was concluded.

As the recruitment of even the smallest states to sign the NPT before the 1995 NPT Extension Conference illustrated, part of the basic nonproliferation strategy has long been to seek wider international commitments not to acquire WMD in order to create international norms. By a large margin, most of the 198 treaty relevant sovereignties are a party or signatory or adhere to the three major WMD treaties, the NPT, the BWC, and the CWC. India, Israel, Pakistan, and North Korea are the only significant states currently outside the NPT, although Iran's compliance is disputed. Syria, Myanmar (Burma), Egypt, and a few other African states are non-parties to the BWC; most of the notable non-parties to the CWC are in the Middle East. Even taking into account illegal covert programs, only a few states are of immediate proliferation concern. The list, however, includes some of the most difficult regimes such as North Korea and some of the most dangerous regions such as South Asia and the Middle East. Most nations have no interest in WMD and no potential for acquiring such weapons except by gift or theft. Indeed, most of these are very small states. Many nations have some theoretical capability to develop biological weapons, but the number of concern is perhaps in the few tens.

From this perspective, nonproliferation had become an asymptotic problem, that is, a problem of dealing with the last few tough cases. To prevent the further spread of WMD, parties to the three major WMD treaties agreed to measures to prevent the transfer of critical knowledge, technology, and materials to non-parties through export controls, safeguards, sanctions, and the like. By the end of the Cold War, regimes such as the Australia Group, the Missile Technology Control Regime, the Nuclear Suppliers Group, the IAEA, Wassenaar—a modified CoCom, and the UN Arms Register were in place to manage trade in sensitive and some dual-use items internationally. The addition of France and China to the NPT in 1992 seemed to cement solidarity. Some nations including the United States adopted enhanced proliferation export controls requiring greater awareness and responsibility of the business community.

Arms control regimes among the superpowers, in Europe and globally through the CWC, promulgated very intrusive verification regimes among parties to the relevant treaties, increasing expectations for what arms control could achieve. The UNSCOM, UNMOVIC, and IAEA inspection regimes and UN Security Council sanctions imposed on Iraq suggested strong international commitment to enforce nonproliferation agreements. The January 1992 UN Security Council statement at the Head of State level that further proliferation would be viewed as a threat to international security was very strong diplomatic language. The end of the Cold War reduced the ideological fervor of a number of non-aligned factions permitting countries such as Argentina and Brazil to move toward modern economies and away from nuclear and missile programs. It also produced nuclear rollback in Ukraine, Belarus, and Kazakhstan, and facilitated rollback in South Africa. In South Asia, voices for similar economic reform were growing. Even North Korea found the need to change its relationship to the world. Pyongyang accepted the two Koreas approach to UN membership, concluded an IAEA Safeguards agreement, reached a North-South Reconciliation Agreement, and signed a de-nuclearization agreement. The agreement to de-nuclearize the Korean Peninsula, had it gone into effect, would have provided for additional bilateral inspections and banned reprocessing and enrichment.

Even as the Cold War was coming to an end, however, countervailing pressures were building that would dissipate this momentum. Some of these forces that hinder nonproliferation today are derived from the same forces that, as the Cold War came to an end, had aided international arms restraint. Key among these are:

- the information technology and telecommunications revolution,
- the globalization of the high tech market place,
- the world-wide competition for technological talent,
- the increased priority of economic competitiveness,
- the revisiting of the boundaries of sovereignty and community,
- the diminished sense of military danger,
- the great expectation for universal democracy, human rights, and the rule of law and with them peace enforcement and disarmament,
- the rapid economic growth and energy demands of the largest Asian nations,
- differing demographics within and among rich and poor nations,
- the latency of WMD technology, and
- the specter of catastrophic terrorism.

Each of these phenomena deserves detailed examination not possible here, but a number of historical developments deserve attention.

The violent breakup of Yugoslavia and subsequent ethnic violence there and elsewhere shook the credibility of important institutions that were expected to form a new security architecture through institutions such as NATO, CSCE, and the EU in Europe, and the UN globally. Over time, sanctions fatigue and the perceived ineffectiveness of punitive strikes in places like Iraq, Afghanistan, and the Sudan and divided views on the wisdom of various humanitarian interventions have created divisions that have resulted in the demise of UNSCOM, once trumpeted as proof that nonproliferation would be enforced. The controversy over the effectiveness of the IAEA and UNMOVIC in 2002-2003 upon the return to Iraq further divided governments. When, in early 2003, the UN Security Council demonstrated the difficulty it has authorizing or blocking military actions, the weakness of this important venue for nonproliferation enforcement became clear. A coalition led by the United States and the United Kingdom toppled the regime of Saddam Hussein by military force, in the face of vocal opposition from France, Germany, and the Russian Federation.

Failure of Russia to catch the new economic wave of the 1990s and of China to meet democratic expectations created international tensions that hindered emergence of anticipated strategic partnerships with the U.S., complicating cooperation on nonproliferation in Korea, South Asia, Iran, and the Middle East. U.S. efforts to sustain Chinese support for pressure on North Korea have been complicated variously by human rights, trade, and other strategic issues such as Taiwan. Russia's reaction to the Framework Agreement with North Korea was public anger. Moscow declared that the provision of reactors the U.S. proposed to a North Korea in violation of the NPT was similar to Russian nuclear reactor sales the U.S. had opposed (1) to North Korea when it was not known to be in violation, (2) to an Iran that permits IAEA inspections, and (3) to an India that is not a party to the NPT.

The complexity of interactions is not just between nations. Nationalistic backlashes, often in response to transnational forces such as the very capital, technology, labor, and culture flows that were forcing political and economic change and turmoil, hindered non-proliferation cooperation in international arms restraint. This frequently reopened divisions along the lines of economic, political, and security "haves" and "have-nots."

In developing countries, this is often a generalized anti-Western sentiment even as Western influence grows. In other cases, the resentment is focused clearly at the U.S., sometimes even within western industrial democracies. Likewise, this coexists with the adoption of significant elements of Western and American culture. In India, for example, hawkish national security positions have increasingly been associated in domestic politics with economic liberalization as the political price for change. Non-competitive state enterprises and underpaid technologists in China and the former Soviet Union and less competitive firms in the West dabble in unsavory, gray, and black market niches for military and dual-use sales, further undercutting nonproliferation and other international arms restraint. Examples include the Chinese relationship to the Pakistani nuclear effort, and other networks of technical cooperation and missile sales such as North Korea has with Iran, Pakistan, Yemen and others. Non-state trade in WMD-related technology expands the concerns in a world in which suicide bombers aspire to be technologically empowered, catastrophic terrorists.

The need to be globally competitive and the internationalization of much education and production has placed a premium in business on removing obstacles to the flow of knowledge and technology, best transferred through experts and teams. This has created dynamism in technological change and transfer that has outpaced the ability of traditional governmental bureaucracies to keep pace. Confusion exists within industry and within government over the real state of the art, true foreign availability, the actual military significance of technology, and how the licensing process should work. This confusion has created an export control system in which factions often "game the system" rather than resolve differences on the basis of policy clarity and procedural efficiency. On the international level, such dissatisfaction led to the abandonment of CoCom[246] prior to locking in a comparable nonproliferation mandate for its successor.

That the magnitude of defense-relevant trade and interactions would overwhelm national security bureaucracies should not be surprising. The entire policy structure was already experiencing an arms control fatigue syndrome expressing the summation of negotiations fatigue, verification fatigue, and compliance fatigue. Policymakers with many vital responsibilities found their time drained to struggle with complex technicalities involving increasingly less central threats that create ever more burdens on parties not of concern even as they increased conflict with nations that were not likely military adversaries. The arms control process, its cost effectiveness declining in many areas, was failing to set priorities, especially given the rise of the new terrorism.

The foreign policy community — divided along regional and functional lines — has had difficulty optimizing interests in the context of a more complex, less security centered agenda. Identifying commensurate values and even measures of merit when security, economic, human rights, environmental, and other issues must all be weighed together has proven difficult absent a good understanding of the security implications of globalization. For example, North Korea threatened to withdraw from the NPT if it were forced to submit to an IAEA suspect site inspection. Public arguments in the U.S. and in Asia over how to respond varied. Some argued Pyongyang's withdrawal would initiate a flood of withdrawals from the NPT. Better to have North Korea in the treaty and violating it than endangering it by other means, some argued. Others argued that an inability to defend Seoul meant that enforcement of the NPT against a military power was too dangerous.

---

246. CoCom stands for the *Coordinating Committee for Multilateral Export Controls,* which was established by the so-called Western bloc (today it would probably include the EU, USA and Canada) after the end of World War II. It was designed to put an arms embargo on the Warsaw Bloc and other communist dominated countries. CoCom ceased to function on March 31, 1994, and the then-current control list of embargoed goods was retained by the member nations until the successor, the Wassenar Arrangement was established.

Still others, especially in South Korea, emphasized the fear that a tough stance might cause a North Korean collapse, which, even if not violent, would impose severe reunification costs on the South and upset the economy. This fractured policy debate has continued for more than ten years.

Nation-states are increasingly exploring new balances of centralization and decentralization that have important implications for international relations. The question of whether and to what degree American local governments can enact international sanctions is before the U.S. Supreme Court. Also international, transnational, and sub-national communities, institutions, entities, groups, and organizations are increasingly acting on behalf of, in lieu of, and in opposition to functions and policies of various nation states including in areas related to international security, arms control, and disarmament. These governmental and non-governmental developments both assisted and complicated the resolution of international arms restraint issues. The Ottawa Landmine Convention bypassed existing negotiating fora, put aside the principle of consensus, abandoned many arms control standards, and ignored certain practices of constructive engagement such as negotiating with the parties of concern–all in the name of promulgating quickly a moral statement. Much of the demand for an immediate, declaratory norm, even if it meant rejecting U.S. security concerns and their nonproliferation implications in Korea was driven by modern, networked transnational activist organizations. These groups were diverse and included numerous non-governmental organizations that, in fact, actually implement or fund important humanitarian de-mining on behalf of or in lieu of governments. Human institutions are still in flux in the face of globalization.

The interaction of constructive engagement with the establishment of norms–whether they involve international security behavior, business best practices, or human decency–has been synergistic in some cases and disruptive in others. In the case of international arms restraint, the expectation that nuclear abolition could be near at hand has led many activists to focus on holding the future of the NPT hostage to dramatic commitments from the P-5. The resulting consequences were not always intended.

The complexities of Indian policymaking provide one example. Even though India was not a party to the NPT, the effect of the hostage strategy during the NPT extension conference was to build up expectations among Indian doves that their disarmament demands would be met immediately. Indian hawks, on the other hand, believed that the NPT, which they saw as a threat to India's nuclear options, would be doomed by P-5 incrementalism. In fact, most other nations favored a permanent extension of the NPT. With the extension of the NPT without a deadline for disarmament, Indian doves were damaged, and the hawks were frightened, all at a time when India seemed slowly, but inevitably heading toward nuclear testing.

The impact continued as Indian hawks and doves transferred their demands from the background of the NPT Review to the foreground of the CTBT negotiations. Many Indian hawks and doves had long been united in their support for a CTB. Either substantively or tactically, each saw it as promoting their objectives at the expense of the nuclear weapons states. Their perceived defeat in the NPT extension combined with a view that the CTBT was being forced upon India by a circumvention of the consensus rule of the Conference on Disarmament did more than increase political opposition to signing the CTBT. It created an atmosphere for foreboding that time was running out, resulting in an environment more supportive of nuclear testing and deployments. One cannot assert that India never would have tested without these unintended consequences. Domestic politics had been driving India that way more or less for some time. Still, prior to these developments, the logic of restraint carried more weight and more time seemed available to encourage a change in direction. The imposition of an immediate CTB gave legitimacy and urgency to arguments for immediate Indian nuclear testing. Each future NPT Review is likely to see a new version of the hostage strategy that may again generate unintended consequences.

Given these complexities and uncertainties, what can we say about the fundamentals that might guide positive actions? One of the most important fundamentals is to look at security concerns of other nations. This is not easy nor are generalizations always useful. Nearly all nations are party to the NPT, and that is an important fact. It is not, however, the only way to look at the problem. If one examines the WMD potential of nations by population, a somewhat different picture emerges. Half the world's population already lives in countries that have nuclear weapons. If one adds to this group those who live in countries that could develop nuclear weapons or live in alliances with nuclear weapons, the number rises to about two-thirds. With the addition of those people living in countries suspected of having covert WMD programs, the number may exceed three-fourths.

Yet, many of these nations do not seek nuclear weapons and other WMD precisely because they are part of the Western alliance structure. NATO, ANZUS, and treaties with Japan, Korea, and others have permitted these countries to increase their security, freedom, and prosperity beyond anyone's greatest expectations at the end of World War II and the beginning of the Nuclear Age. Half of the world's GNP is in NATO. Some three-fourths of the world's GNP is in nations that have defense alliances with the United States. American security commitments are a vital tool for international arms restraint in Europe and in the Asia Pacific region, and elsewhere as well.

Most of the world's population, indeed, its poorest nations, live outside reliable security architectures. And it is in many of these areas where absolute GNP is growing very large and the knowledge, technology, and materials for WMD are already widespread. If these nations do not find a way to enhance confidence in their security, additional nations in troubled regions will look to WMD as a part of their security policy. Fortunately, the number may not be great. Unfortunately, the proliferation may not be confined only to those outside the western alliance structure. A failure to deal effectively with the dangers in Northeast Asia, for example, could result in proliferation among America's friends in the region including South Korea, Taiwan, and Japan.

In this age of globalization, uncertainty exists about what is the real post-Cold War threat, balancing both probabilities and consequences. The post-Cold War proliferation threat is not only nuclear. Biological weapons are of increasing concern, and chemical threats remain. Advanced conventional weapons and information warfare capabilities are also proliferating. Although the greatest destructive power remains in the hands of the long-standing nuclear weapons states, the probability of their use of WMD against each other is very low. The greatest probability of WMD use involves other states and increasingly non-state entities such as terrorists or states other than the P-5.

Even in conventional arms, where American excellence and level of investment outpaces all others, globalization will have important leveling effects. Increasingly, the defense industrial base of the United States will look like the commercial industrial base, which will be a global industrial base, and thus increasingly a global defense industrial base. The United States should be able to maintain a comfortable overall lead for many years to come. Inevitably, however, the U.S. is going to find that, just as is happening in the high tech industry, it will not always be the best at everything or under all circumstances. The U.S. military may encounter scenarios in which U.S. forces will be vulnerable to asymmetric responses and silver bullet technologies at times and places not of its own choosing. This will be particularly telling in this age of "Roy Rogers warfare" in which "Buck Rogers" technology is expected to keep casualties small on both sides.

Given the rapidly changing strategic environment and its consequences, a better understanding of the impact of globalization on international arms restraint is needed. More efforts need to be made to bring the policy and technology communities together to understand the implications of trends already visible such as the change in human institutions and the interaction of ubiquitous supercomputing, wide-band networks, agile production, micro-manufacturing, and the like. Many issues need fresh thinking.

Renewed Challenges to International Arms Restraint

Confidence that international arms restraint will progress has always been tempered by setbacks. Interest in international arms restraint expanded with the industrial revolution as coal, steel, and chemistry made possible both unprecedented prosperity and outrageous lethality. The quest for restraint was promoted and disrupted by two world wars. Interest in arms restraints accelerated during the Cold War as dual-use nuclear technology further magnified hope and amplified fear, and it was expected to blossom in the post-Cold War era as the WMD threat was seen as shared by all nations. Instead, momentum stalled. Not only were great expectations not met, but many achievements began to erode.

Some see a "New Era" emerging as globalization and fractionation interact, complicating both cooperation and competition.[247] Some see a "second" or third or fourth nuclear age as nuclear weapons actors proliferate. Some fear a new tipping point leading if not to a new Cold War then to at least a big chill. Some see the legal and diplomatic architecture for international order coming unglued as more players stake out territorial claims from the past and mark historical grievances. Nevertheless, most of the instruments and organizations for international arms restraint remain in place. The emerging challenges of a post-post-Cold War world, however, may force changes in policy and process.

Punctuating the new instability has been Russian adventurism in opposition to Western values and interests. The populism and separatism that brought down the Soviet Union have ultimately led less to rule of law democracy than to autocratic populism, irredentism, and kleptocracy. Moscow uses tightly controlled media, modern Internet, cable television, and even Twitter at home and abroad even as opposition and non-governmental organizations are suppressed. An arms buildup and confrontation with neighbors have become central themes in Russian domestic politics. Despite considerable trade and cooperation, integration of the Russian Federation into the international system of the West has faltered. Russia has been expelled from the G-8 and focuses more now on Eurasia with its own customs union to counter the EU and its alternative collective security organization, the Commonwealth of Independent States (CIS), consisting of the original republics of the USSR minus the Baltic republics and Georgia. Moscow also seeks to co-opt as an alternative center of power the emergent Shanghai Cooperation Organization (SCO) (Russia, China, Kazakhstan, Uzbekistan, the Kyrgyz Republic, and Tajikistan as members, with Afghanistan, India, Iran, Mongolia, and Pakistan as observers and Belarus, Sri Lanka, and Turkey as dialog partners). The SCO grew out of the 1996 Treaty on Deepening Military Trust in Border Regions and the 1997 Treaty on Reduction of Military Forces in Border Regions. Its original focus was counter-terrorism, especially from Islamic

---

247. Steven L. Spiegel, Elizabeth G. Matthews, Jennifer M. Taw, and Kristen P. Williams, World Politics in a New Era, Sixth edition, USA: Oxford University Press, 2014.

extremists, but increasingly Moscow has introduced the theme of creating alternative institutions to those of the West. On the global scene, Moscow has sought to re-energize bloc activism in the NNA through interaction with other BRIC governments.

In addition to its Eurasian collective security arrangements, the Russian Federation maintains military forces or installations in Armenia, Belarus, Kazakhstan, the Kyrgyz Republic, and Tajikistan, in territories disputed with Moldova (Transnistria) and Georgia (Abkhazia and South Ossetia), and in overseas naval bases in Vietnam and Syria. Russia's annexation of Crimea, with its large Russian naval base, has shaken confidence in European security as Russia currently arms ethnic Russian separatists in other parts of Ukraine and interferes with OSCE efforts at transparency, confidence building, and investigations. To underscore its image as a regional hegemon, Moscow has violated the CFE conventional forces treaty and the INF nuclear treaty while emphasizing the Eurasian role of tactical nuclear weapons. The hollow and disjointed Russian military resulting from the breakup of the Soviet Union has now been modernized by Moscow across the board including nuclear, conventional, and unconventional forces. Considerable emphasis has also been placed on cyber operations and espionage. The focus is not simply irredentism. The two decade-long trend of growing tension between Moscow and arms restraint reflects the re-emergence of historic Russian geo-strategic aspirations in Eurasia and globally.

The challenges of the new era are not just from Russia, although Russia is both an example and a player. In other regions once dominated by great empires, boundaries of the nation states that have emerged often do not follow natural, historic, or ethnic lines, especially in Africa, the Middle East, South Asia, and parts of Europe. In 1991, broad international opposition to Iraq's invasion of Kuwait was based on a consensus that no matter what the history, boundaries should not be altered by force. Thus, turmoil in Yugoslavia and the Soviet Union initially generated opposition to partition and then opposition to further adjustment of boundaries. In the end, however, *de facto* and *de jure* boundaries were changed. Anger within the Russian population over Serbian loss of sovereignty over traditional lands such as Kosovo or over fellow Serbs in other republics was intense. Considering the fortunes of Serbia in the Yugoslav breakup only reinforced concern among Russians over the fate of ethnic Russians in other parts of the former Soviet Union. Such ethnic militancy and separatism is paralleled elsewhere, most violently in Syria, Iraq, Pakistan, and Afghanistan. One of the largest ethnic groups without a state, the Kurds, are asserting sovereign jurisdiction in significant parts of Iraq and Syria. Non-state actors, notably Islamic separatists, remain active in the Middle East, the Philippines, Thailand, China, India, etc. At the same time, governments of nations such as China, Japan, Vietnam, the Koreas, and the Philippines have also deployed military forces to stake out territorial claims. In the Pacific region, emphasis on military power has been growing in a region once characterized primarily by rapid economic growth.

The buildup of military capability in East Asia increasingly involves advanced technology. For many decades, China was slow to modernize its military forces. Now that the Chinese economy is among the world's largest, with strength in many high technology sectors, China is demonstrating great advances in dual-use science and technology. Beijing's manned space program illustrates China's great military power potential in space and on its periphery. American allies and friends in East Asia increasingly see China's anti-satellite and anti-ship programs as asymmetric responses to the very U.S. presence they value. China's association with extensive, advanced cyber-hacking only reinforces this view.

China's inevitable great military power, like that of Japan, need not be threatening, but it has become so to many governments in the region as instability grows in East Asia. Much of the concern arises from developments within China. China remains a one-party state. Great economic growth and social change have brought with them domestic issues such as inequality, corruption, stagnation, pollution, and repression that could threaten party control. Moreover, the demographics of an aging China threaten its future economic and political strength. Many fear that internal weakness may be more significant than economic and military strength in causing China to escalate revanchist claims.

China's diplomatic and military restraint in recent years may be coming to an end. In any case, China has been a reluctant participant in any international arms restraint that would require intrusive inspections or great transparency. Likewise, it has been reluctant to look at restraints that would formalize lower numbers or loss of access to capabilities that others might have. The apparent return to great power geo-politics by Russia and China as activists with ambition to change the balance of power means that the United States and its allies must now consider the possibility of not one, but two peer rivals, neither of which may be interested in international arms restraint that limits their influence on their periphery, precisely where potential competitors exist and where the United States has vital interests and allies.

Other nations such as India, Iran, Brazil, and Pakistan aspire to great power status and influence. The advance and spread of dual-use technology will enable them to achieve that status if their economies grow and to be spoilers if their economies are weak. Traditional qualitative arms control and non-proliferation such as export controls on knowledge, technology, and even WMD related materials may prove inadequate as the footprints and signatures of dual-use activities become smaller.

In sum, future international arms restraint may need to focus more on underlying causes, risk management, cross cultural perceptions, and multi-disciplinary/cross-domain threats such as cyber warfare and space attacks, all of which will require greater focus on the particulars. To deal with the new peers or with rogue states or with terrorists may require the reinvigoration of the nation state, re-engagement with coalitions of nation states, and greater accountability of nation states to both the legal and moral norms critical to fostering and maintaining international peace and security.

Questions for Discussion

1. In the 1980s revolution in arms control, the United States sought detailed, effectively verifiable formal agreements with the Soviet Union. Today, the U.S. seeks informal, co-operative openness with the Russian Federation. What are the conditions under which each approach is most valuable? What does this suggest for international arms restraint among other nations?

2. Under Article VI of the NPT nearly all nations committed to pursue a Treaty on general and complete disarmament (GCD). What is general and complete disarmament, what weapons would or should be involved, and under what conditions might it come about?

3. How does one reconcile universal international arms restraints with the different circumstances of individual nations?

4. The nuclear weapon states agreed under Article VI of the NPT to work toward the elimination of nuclear weapons. Some nations, however, signed the NPT with the expectation that nuclear weapons states would provide them extended deterrence, the so-called "nuclear umbrella." How could this dilemma be resolved?

5. How many countries will have nuclear weapons in ten years? Thirty years? Will they have conducted explosive tests of their nuclear weapons? How "latent" will nuclear weapons capability be?

6. Under what conditions, if any, would India, Israel, or Pakistan join the NPT? What nations are most likely to withdraw from the NPT? Why would they withdraw?

7. The UNSCOM and UNMOVIC inspection regimes used in Iraq have been criticized as too tough for use in the future and yet inadequate to deal with Iraq. How can we gauge the necessary and appropriate level of inspection?

8. Constructive engagement with North Korea was intended to establish greater confidence of compliance with the NPT, but the possibility that North Korea has nuclear weapons has generated great reluctance to press compliance forcefully. In the face of such a dilemma, what is to be done?

9. Iran, an oil rich country building a large nuclear establishment of nuclear reactors and a uranium enrichment facility is suspected of having a nuclear weapons program and yet welcomes IAEA inspectors. What is the significance?

10. The European CFE and CSCE treaties and agreements limit conventional forces, require great transparency, and establish conflict prevention mechanism. What has this meant in the Caucasus and the former Yugoslavia, and what might it mean in the future?

11. The Open Skies Treaty provides to many countries without space-based and other national technical means of verification certain capabilities that several of the major powers already possess. How valuable is this to those parties? Is it of much value as an adjunct to the NTM of the larger states in support of verification or is it an unnecessary expense?

12. When, where, and why would other international monitoring be an unnecessary duplication of the national capabilities? Is there a placebo effect?

13. The information superhighway and 24-hour cable news provide great amounts of information. In a crisis, when does it increase confidence and when does it add to the confusion?

14. In exchange for fuel oil and two new nuclear reactors, North Korea agreed to a step-by-step process of returning to compliance with the NPT. When do such incentives expedite compliance? How does one avoid other nations expecting payments for compliance?

15. Even in bad economic times, globalization has meant the spread of wealth to many troubled regions. Does the growing wealth of potential proliferators decrease the incentives to acquire WMD as much as it facilitates acquisition of the means to build or buy them?

16. Achievements in arms control and confidence-building were made possible by the verification enhancements of satellite reconnaissance, data exchanges, and on-site inspection. Even the most advanced capabilities of the past, however, were inadequate for timely detection of WMD programs in closed regimes, i.e., the BW program in Iraq. Now, threats to mankind come from non-state actors who may create biological weapons in a small room. What is the role of international arms restraints in dealing with sub-national threats and dual-use technologies that are readily available to all? What is the national role, and how much pressure will success place on privacy and civil liberties?

17. In what ways are verification and enforcement international or national functions? What is the role of private citizens? Private business or non-governmental organizations? Who resolves disputes over compliance assessments?

18. Despite interest in cooperative measures to reduce tensions, such measures have been criticized as being political symbols reflecting transitory improvements in relations rather than effective operational actions reducing the chances of war. In evaluating

cooperative measures, what weight should be placed on political factors and what weight placed on military factors?

19. Confidence-building measures have emphasized "transparency" and "openness" as the basis for real confidence. Dictatorships, which criticize such measures as intrusive, onerous, and potentially destabilizing efforts at espionage, prefer symbolic or limited steps. When does greater information enhance confidence and when can it undermine confidence?

20. The purpose of many CBMs, especially those involving movement of military forces, is to regularize practices and provide warning of potential military threats. Critics argue that any rigidity imposed by such measures on military operations could prevent corrective steps and strategic movements designed to signal preparedness and resolve. How does one balance the deterrent value of certainty with the deterrent value of uncertainty?

21. North and South, like East and West in the Cold War, frequently diverge on the value of "declaratory measures" such as no first use pledges and non-aggression pacts. To what degree should declaratory pledges be considered confidence-building measures? How do we measure their value? What is the significance of the Russian decision to abandon the Soviet "no first use" policy?

22. Direct communications links such as the Hotline are intended to reduce the possibility of war through accident or miscalculation. Could these same communications be used to provide misinformation as part of the cover and deception plan of an aggressor? In what situations might rapid use of direct communications links increase the risk of misunderstanding?

23. Some cooperative measures aim at improving the logic of decision-making, particularly with respect to the calculus of deterrence. Other measures aim at the emotional sources of conflict. Is it correct to suggest that some declaratory measures such as non-use of force pledges may reduce political tensions but also undercut deterrence? And can "transparency" measures designed to reduce the military threat increase political tensions?

24. Assessments of the value of individual cooperative measures and CBMs differ greatly. Will the role of cooperative measures increase or decrease in the years ahead? How significant will they be in regions like South Asia, the Korean Peninsula, and the Middle East?

25. Can all the parties to the NPT be bound to nuclear disarmament and general and complete disarmament if not all nations are parties to the NPT and the same obligations? Can they be bound if they are threatened by non-State entities?

26. What use of nuclear weapons would be legal? Does this include the use of nuclear weapons on behalf of an ally? Could this include the use of nuclear weapons on behalf of a non-nuclear weapons state that has demanded fulfillment of positive security assurances received in exchange for joining the NPT?

27. If the knowledge, technology, facilities, and material associated with WMD becomes ever more latent, how do we define "disarmament"? What is "zero" nuclear weapons? How do we know when we have achieved it?

28. In addition to treaties and other legally binding arrangements, the arms control process also includes a large number of ad hoc initiatives where like-minded states band together to address a common arms control or proliferation issue. Compare and contrast the "initiative" approach with the more traditional arms control negotiation process. Which in your view is more effective in combatting the proliferation of weapons of mass destruction?

Selected Bibliography

Albright, David, & Kevin O'Neill eds., *Solving the North Korean Nuclear Puzzle,* (2000) presents the technical issues associated with North Korea's nuclear program in understandable language in the context of the 1994 Agreed Framework.

Alford, Jonathan, "Confidence-Building Measures," *Adelphi Papers,* (1979) includes essays on the application of confidence-building measures to Europe, the Middle East, the strategic nuclear balance, and naval forces and includes some useful general analysis.

Allison, Graham T., et al., eds., *Hawks, Doves, and Owls: An Agenda for Avoiding Nuclear War,* (1985) restates basic crisis management and deterrence during the Cold War.

Blainey, Geoffrey, *The Causes of War,* (1973) provides a thorough yet colorful examination of theories about the origins of war from a historical perspective.

Bowen, Wyn Q., *The Politics of Ballistic Missile Nonproliferation,* (2000) looks at the rise of the Missile Technology Control Regime and the politics and bureaucratics of other efforts to stem proliferation.

Bull, Hedley, *The Control of the Arms Race: Disarmament and Arms Control in the Missile Age,* (1961) reflects the incorporation of arms control early in the evolution of nuclear deterrence.

Bunn, George, "U.S. Law of Nuclear Weapons," *Naval War C. Rev.,* July–Aug. 1984, at 46, pre-dates the July 8, 1996 World Court case but surveys the issues.

Cirincione, Joseph, ed., *Repairing the Regime: Preventing the Spread of Weapons of Mass Destruction,* (2000) assesses challenges to the existing nonproliferation regime and presents a number of proposals.

Desjardins, Marie-France, "Rethinking Confidence-Building Measures," *Adelphi Papers,* (1996) argues that clear mutual interest is essential to the success of CBMs.

Fairbanks, Jr., Charles H., "Arms Races: The Metaphor and the Facts," *Nat'l Interest,* Fall 1985, at 75, explores public simplification in the context of complex histories.

Glynn, Patrick, "The Sarajevo Fallacy: The Historical and Intellectual Origins of Arms Control Theology," *Nat'l Interest,* Fall 1987, at 3, critiques the theories behind many disarmament proposals.

Gray, Colin S., *House of Cards: Why Arms Control Must Fail,* (1992) argues that arms control is most successful where it is least needed.

Holst, Johan Jørgen, "Confidence-Building Measures: A Conceptual Framework," *Survival,* Jan–Feb 1983, at 7, considers the role CBMs play in international security and arms control.

Iklé, Fred Charles, "After Detection — What? 39 *Foreign Aff.* 208 (Jan. 1961), states the classic challenge of enforcement of compliance.

Kaufman, Robert Gordon, *Arms Control during the Pre-Nuclear Era,* (1990) reconsiders the Washington and London Naval Treaties in light of the U.S./Soviet strategic negotiations.

Larsen, Jeffrey A., ed., *Arms Control: Cooperative Security in a Changing Environment,* (2002) looks at evolution of arms control and emerging policies.

Lewis, Kevin N., & Mark A. Lorell, "Confidence-Building Measures and Crisis Resolution: Historical Perspectives," 28 *Orbis* 281 (Summer 1984) develops a theoretical framework for CBMs and then examines their applicability to such historical crisis as the Balkan Crisis (1912–14), the Don Pacifico Affair (1850), the Fashoda Crisis (1894) and the Anglo-French rivalry in the nineteenth century.

Macintosh, James, *Confidence (and Security) Building Measures in the Arms Control Process: a Canadian Perspective,* (1985), a study for the Canadian Department of External

Affairs, provides an outstanding survey of the history and theory of CBMs and goes beyond the mystique of CBMs to illuminate many of the real issues.

McCausland, Jeffrey D., "Conventional Arms Control and European Security," *Adelphi Papers*, 1996, examines the altered role of arms control in Europe in the context of political change in Europe.

Roberts, Guy B., *Arms Control Without Arms Control: The Failure of the Biological Weapons Convention Protocol and a New Paradigm for Fighting the Threat of Biological Weapons*, (2003).

Rostow, W.W., *Open Skies: Eisenhower's Proposal of July 21, 1955*, (1982) by a former senior political figure, recounts one of history's most famous CBM proposals.

Ruehl, Lothar, "MBFR: Lessons and Problems," *Adelphi Papers*, (1982) discusses the political and military interactions of arms control in bi-polar and alliance settings.

Taylor, Terence, *Escaping the Prison of the Past: Rethinking Arms Control and Non-Proliferation Measures*, (1996) presents new approaches to arms control based upon personal experience with inspections in Iraq.

Turner, Robert F., "Nuclear Weapons and the World Court: The ICJ's Advisory Opinion and Its Significance for U.S. Strategic Doctrine," *in The Law of Military Operations* (Michael N. Schmitt ed., 1998) stresses the importance of a detailed reading of the 1996 World Court opinion in light of divergent interpretations.

U.S. Arms Control and Disarmament Agency, *Arms Control and Disarmament Agreements: Texts and Histories of the Negotiations*, (1996) provides a brief history and text of treaties negotiated from 1961 to 1988.

Weston, Burns H., "Nuclear Weapons Versus International Law: A Contextual Reassessment," 28 *McGill L.J.* 542 (1983).

Chapter 14

International Human Rights

Richard Schifter

The Human Rights Concept

Perhaps the earliest formal iteration of the principle that the sovereign cannot reign at will but is bound by the law appears in Deuteronomy:

> When [the King] is seated on his royal throne he must write a copy of this Law on a scroll for his own use at the dictation of the levitical priests. It must never leave him and he must read it every day of his life and learn to fear the Lord his God by keeping all the words of this Law and by observing these laws. So his heart will not look down on his brothers and he will swerve neither right nor left from these commandments. If he does this, he will have long days on his throne.... [1]

The leaders of the revolt of the Netherlands against King Philip II of Spain had probably read this passage in the Old Testament. They may have concluded that when the Bible says that a king who abides by the law will have long days on his throne, it implies that a king who fails to abide by the law will see his days on the throne shortened. These Biblical words may have been on their mind when, in 1581, they proclaimed their Act of Abjuration:

> As it is apparent to all that a prince is constituted by God to be ruler of a people, to defend them from oppression and violence as the shepherd his sheep; and whereas God did not create the people slaves to their prince, to obey his commands, whether right or wrong, but rather the prince for the sake of the subjects (without which he could be no prince), to govern them according to

---

1. *Deuteronomy* 17:18–20.

equity, to love and support them as a father his children or a shepherd his flock, and even at the hazard of life to defend and preserve them. And when he does not behave thus, but, on the contrary, oppresses them, seeking opportunities to infringe their ancient customs and privileges, exacting from them slavish compliance, then he is no longer a prince, but a tyrant, and the subjects are to consider him in no other view. And particularly when this is done deliberately, unauthorized by the states, they may not only disallow his authority, but legally proceed to the choice of another prince for their defense. This is the only method left for subjects whose humble petitions and remonstrances could never soften their prince or dissuade him from his tyrannical proceedings; and this is what the law of nature dictates for the defense of liberty, which we ought to transmit to posterity, even at the hazard of our lives.[2]

Just as the authors of the Dutch Act of Abjuration may have relied on Deuteronomy, so the author of the United States Declaration of Independence may have viewed the Dutch declaration as a model. The message of human rights, the message that governments must serve the people and acquire legitimacy only with the consent of the governed was most powerfully reiterated in 1776 in a declaration that has since then inspired supporters of the cause of human rights throughout the world. In the inimitable words of Thomas Jefferson:

> We hold these truths to be self-evident, that all men are created equal, that they are endowed by their Creator with certain unalienable Rights, that among these are Life, Liberty, and the pursuit of Happiness. That to secure these rights, Governments are instituted among Men, deriving their just powers from the governed....

Marquis de Lafayette, deeply impressed by the Declaration of Independence, saw to it upon his return to France that the Constituent Assembly that convened in 1789 adopt a Declaration of the Rights of Man and of the Citizen:

1. Men are born free and remain equal in rights. Social distinctions can be based only on public utility.

2. The aim of every political association is the preservation of the natural and imprescriptable rights of man. These rights are liberty, property, security, and resistance to oppression.

3. The sources of all sovereignty reside essentially in the nation. No body nor individual may exercise any authority which does not proceed directly from the nation.

4. Liberty consists of the power to do anything that does not injure others; accordingly the exercise of the rights of each man has not limits except those that secure the enjoyment of these same rights by the other members of society. These limits can be determined only by law.

5. The law has the rights to forbid only such actions as are injurious to society. Nothing can be forbidden that is not interdicted by law, and no one can be constrained to do that which it does not order.

---

2. Ernst Kossmann, Texts Concerning the Revolt of the Netherlands 217 (1974).

6. Law is the expression of the general will. All citizens have the right to take part personally, or by their representatives, in its formation....

The Pre-Charter Era

The rights proclaimed in the foregoing documents were not characterized as the rights of only the citizens of the Netherlands, the United States, or France. The Dutch Act of Abjuration, the United States Declaration of Independence, and the French Declaration of the Rights of Man and of the Citizen used terminology of universal applicability. However, the declarations notwithstanding, the then prevailing rule in international diplomacy, that no country would interfere in the domestic affairs of another country, remained unchanged.

Paul Sieghart, The International Law of Human Rights
§§ 1.5, 1.7, at 11, 14 (1983)

Since the beginnings of the Law of Nations, one of its fundamental principles was that of national sovereignty, which reserves to each sovereign State the exclusive right to take any action it thinks fit, provided only that the action does not interfere with the rights of other States, and is not prohibited by international law on that or any other ground.

According to that principle, a sovereign State has complete freedom of action, in international law, to deal with its own nationals ('personal sovereignty') and with its own territory ('territorial sovereignty')....

It follows from this principle that, in all matters falling within the 'domestic jurisdiction' of any State, international law does not permit any interference, let alone any intervention, by any other State. Such matters do not fall within the concern of international law. Accordingly, so long as 'personal' sovereignty continued to be regarded as falling exclusively within the domestic jurisdiction of sovereign States, 'what a government did to its own citizens was its own affair and beyond the reach of international law or legal intervention by other States....[3]

Note

That the United States might ultimately support a change in the proposition that democracy and human rights were not commodities for export may have been foreshadowed in President Wilson's address to the Congress in 1917, in which he asked the Congress to declare war against Germany and stated the goal that "[t]he world must be made safe for democracy." But it took another war, World War II, and the horrors perpetrated during that war to bring about adoption of a document that recognized the international applicability of human rights standards.

---

3. Sieghart describes one exception to this legal regime, the doctrine of "humanitarian intervention." *Compare* Ian Brownlie, *Humanitarian Intervention, in* Law and Civil War in the Modern World 217 (John Norton Moore ed., 1974) *with* Richard B. Lillich, *Humanitarian Intervention: A Reply to Dr. Brownlie and a Plea for Constructive Alternatives, id.* at 229.

Tom Farer, *Human Rights Before the Second World War*

in INTER-AMERICAN COMMISSION ON HUMAN RIGHTS,
TEN YEARS OF ACTIVITIES 1971–1981, at v–vi (1982)

Before the Second World War, scholars and diplomats assumed that international law allowed each equal sovereign an equal right to be monstrous to his subjects. Summary execution, torture, conviction without due process (or any process, for that matter) were legally significant events only if the victim of such official eccentricities were the citizen of another state. In that case, international law treated him as the bearer not of personal rights but of rights belonging to his government, and ultimately to the state for which it temporarily spoke. (In effect, the individual was nothing more than a symbol and a capital asset. Assaults on his person carried out or acquiesced to by representatives of another state were deemed assaults on the dignity and material interests of his state, requiring compensation.)

Guardians of the moral realm were episodically less permissive. Virtually from the start of that bloody enterprise known as the Spanish Empire in the New World, Catholic priests struggled to restrain the awful cupidity and cruder fantasies of the Conquistadors, their secular associates in Spain's civilizing mission. In addition, both Catholic and Protestant missionaries worked to alert decent opinion in Europe to the genocidal trade in African slaves and, thereafter, to such abominations as Belgian King Leopold's personal empire in the Congo.

Even Leopold's fellow monarchs had no stomach for his methods of organizing labor, which included the mutilation of sluggards and drop-outs. And so, while completing the orderly division of Africa at the Congress of Berlin in 1885 and the Congress of Brussels four years later, they announced and Leopold nominally accepted certain standards to be followed in treating the indigenous inhabitants. Since the Conference provided no enforcement machinery, relying on the ineffable Leopold, that noble gentleman carried on business as usual. Nevertheless, the very recognition of limits on Leopold's caprice was a rare early instance of formal concern for and legal restraint on a sovereign's discretion in the disposition of his human assets.

Pogroms in Russia, the massacre of Armenians in Turkey and Maronites in Lebanon, as well as the efforts of governments to wrap raison d'etat in a higher morality (as in the Anglo-French effort during the First World War to portray the conflict as a struggle between good and evil, and the half-hearted attempt after the War to prosecute the Kaiser as a war criminal), all helped erode the long-entrenched perception that what went on within a state was not a matter of legitimate international concern unless it affected the interests of aliens. But it was not until the final stage of the Second World War that governments first took the leap from moralizing rhetoric to legal action.

They were driven by popular revulsion over Dachau and the other charnel houses operated by the Nazis, by a surge of idealism sharpened through confrontation with Nazi ideology and, perhaps, by the victors' natural desire to equate success and virtue. In succeeding decades, the community of nations, old and new, established a thicket of legal restraints.

For the first time in history, states assumed obligations to their own citizens as precisely and formally defined in many cases as the legal obligations they had hitherto owed to each other under international law (for example, with respect to the immunity of diplomats). Both through formal treaties and informal practice, they bound themselves not to torture or summarily execute their citizens, or to convict them without due process of law or to dissolve their trade unions or to discriminate among them on the basis of race or religion or to do a great number of other things that in earlier ages were matters entirely at the discretion of sovereigns.

The Charter of the United Nations was the point of departure for this unique legal development.

Shigeru Oda, *The Individual in International Law*
in Manual of Public International Law § 8.18, at 495–97 *passim*
(M. Sorensen ed., 1968)

The concept of the protection of human rights has emerged originally in the field of domestic legislation, as in the Magna Charta in England, the Bill of Rights in the United States Constitution and the Declaration of the Rights of Man in France. This domestic concept was translated into international terms only after the Second World War. The cruelties and oppression of the Nazi regime in Europe brought the conviction both during and after the Second World War that the international recognition and protection of human rights for people throughout the world is essential to the maintenance of international peace and order. This conviction was first formulated by President Roosevelt in his annual message to Congress in 1941..., and was expressed in various statements on war aims such as the Atlantic Charter of 14 August 1941..., the Declaration of the United Nations of 1 January 1942..., the Teheran Declaration of 1 December 1943..., and the Yalta Declaration on Liberated Peoples of 11 February 1945.... It was agreed at Dumbarton Oaks in the late summer of 1944 in the Proposals for the Establishment of a General International Organization to the effect that the United Nations should, *inter alia*, promote respect for human rights and fundamental freedoms.

A.H. Robertson, Human Rights in the World
2 (2d Ed. 1982)

The revolutionary nature of the concept of the international protection of human rights is shown by the fact that the classic doctrine of international law had no place for it at all. We have quoted elsewhere the statement ... that the 'so-called rights of man' not only do not but cannot enjoy any protection under international law, because that law is concerned solely with the relations between States and cannot confer rights on individuals. Traditionally it was the accepted doctrine that relations between individuals and the States of which they were nationals were questions to be determined exclusively by the national law of those States; such matters were exclusively within their domestic jurisdiction. To change this traditional attitude into a new doctrine which recognized that international standards concerning the fundamental rights of the individual have been established by international law and that international remedies are available if those standards are not respected, is a major operation requiring important modifications in the theory and practice of governments. It is not surprising if such a change takes time. We are at present in the middle of this process of transformation and, as we shall see..., much resistance is encountered and many governments seek to shelter behind the classic doctrine of international law and hide their actions behind the cloak of national sovereignty. This will appear with particular force when we come to discuss the work of the United Nations. But such obscurantist policies cannot alter the fact that the protection of human rights has found a place in international law which it never occupied in earlier times and that there is widespread recognition of the need to render the system of international protection more effective.

Human Rights Under the United Nations Charter

EIGHTEENTH REPORT OF THE COMMISSION TO STUDY THE
ORGANIZATION OF PEACE, THE UNITED NATIONS AND HUMAN RIGHTS
1–4 (1968)

1. *The Development of the Concept of International Protection of Human Rights*

The idea of international protection of human rights on a universal scale owes its origin to the tragic events accompanying the Second World War and the totalitarian excesses preceding it....

It was during one of the darkest hours of the war, when the Axis powers achieved almost complete control of the European continent, that President Roosevelt provided in his "Four Freedoms"—freedom of speech, freedom of religion, freedom from want and freedom from fear—a rallying cry for all those suffering from the ravages of war and totalitarianism. After another disaster, the Pearl Harbor attack, the Allied Governments agreed in Washington on the "Declaration by United Nations" which named as the basic goal of victory the preservation of "human rights and justice in their own lands as well as in other lands."

Encouraged by this statement, various official and unofficial groups, both in the United States and other countries, started immediately to work on an International Bill of Rights which would be proclaimed by the United Nations after their victory and which would become one of the cornerstones of the new world order to be built after the war. While the official enthusiasm for a codification of the basic principles for the protection of human rights later cooled down, active pressure of non-governmental organizations led to the inclusion in the Charter of the United Nations of several provisions on human rights.

2. *The Charter of the United Nations*

In the preamble to the Charter, the peoples of the United Nations have reaffirmed their "faith in fundamental human rights, in the dignity and worth of the human person, in the equal rights of men and women and of nations large and small," and their determination "to promote social progress and better standards of life in larger freedom." Article 1 of the Charter lists among the main purposes of the United Nations the achievement of international cooperation "in promoting and encouraging respect for human rights and for fundamental freedoms for all without distinction as to race, sex, language, or religion." Similarly, in accordance with Article 55 of the Charter, the United Nations has the duty to promote "universal respect for, and observance of, human rights and fundamental freedoms for all without distinction as to race, sex, language, or religion." In Article 56, all Members of the United Nations "pledge themselves to take joint and separate action in cooperation with the Organization for the achievement of the purposes set forth in Article 55."

The Charter of the United Nations contains also significant grants of power to various organs of the United Nations. Thus, under Article 13, the General Assembly has the duty to initiate studies and make recommendations for the purpose of "assisting in the realization of human rights and fundamental freedoms for all without distinction as to race, sex, language, or religion." Responsibility for the discharge of the functions set forth in Chapter IX of the Charter (which includes Articles 55 and 56 mentioned above) is vested by Article 60 in the General Assembly and, "under the authority of the General Assembly, in the Economic and Social Council." In discharging this responsibility the Economic and Social

Council may, according to Article 62, "make recommendations for the purpose of promoting respect for, and observance of, human rights and fundamental freedoms for all"; under Article 68, it has an obligation to set up a commission "for the promotion of human rights," which is the only functional commission expressly provided for by the Charter itself; and, under Article 64, it may make arrangements with the Members of the United Nations to obtain reports on steps taken by them to give effect to the recommendations of the General Assembly and of the Council. Finally, Article 76 lists among the basic objectives of the United Nations trusteeship system the duty "to encourage respect for human rights and for fundamental freedoms for all without distinction as to race, sex, language, or religion"; and Article 87 provides for the supervision of the administration of trust territories through a system of reports, examination of petitions and periodic visits to these territories. In a declaration regarding other non-self-governing territories embodied in Article 73 of the Charter, the Administering States accept "as a sacred trust" the obligation to promote to the utmost "the well-being of the inhabitants of these territories," and to this end to ensure "their just treatment, and their protection against abuses."

Questions for Discussion

1. The human rights provisions in the United Nations Charter described in the reading immediately above must be read against Article 2(7) of the charter, which provides: "Nothing contained in the present Charter shall authorize the United Nations to intervene in matters which are essentially within the domestic jurisdiction of any state or shall require the Members to submit such matters to settlement under the present Charter; but this principle shall not prejudice the application of enforcement measures under Chapter VII." Article 2(7) was intended to ensure that none of the human rights provisions of the charter should "be construed as giving authority to the Organization to intervene in the domestic affairs of member states."[4] A vast body of literature exists concerning this domestic jurisdiction clause and just what intervention by the United Nations it was intended to prohibit.[5] There are those who contend that over the years human rights questions—from placing them on the agenda through their investigation and debate to the adoption of specific recommendations—have come to be regarded by the United Nations as no longer essentially within the domestic jurisdiction of states. They have pointed out that where the Security Council determines a state's human rights violations to be a threat to the peace—as it has in the cases of Rhodesia in 1966 and South Africa in 1977—Article 2(7) itself renders the domestic jurisdiction clause inoperative by specifically authorizing the adoption of economic sanctions or even the use of armed force against the offending state pursuant to Articles 41 and 42 of Chapter VII. Have the cases of Rhodesia and South Africa been exceptions or do they reflect a uniform interpretation of the Charter by the United Nations Security Council?

2. One of the principal parties to the negotiation of the United Nations Charter was the Union of Soviet Socialist Republics, then under the extraordinarily brutal rule of Joseph Stalin. His agreement to the United Nations Charter did not cause Stalin to change his policies. His country became even more repressive during the remaining seven and a half years of his rule. Even though repression lessened under Stalin's successors, the Soviet Union remained a totalitarian dictatorship into the Gorbachev era. Yet, the United Nations system failed to take any action against human rights abuse in the Soviet Union, and for

---

4. 10 U.N.C.I.O. Docs. 83 (1945) (United States).
5. *See, e.g.,* Felix Ermacora, *Human Rights and Domestic Jurisdiction (Article 2, § 7, of the Charter),* 124 RECUEIL DES COURS 371 (1968-II).

about thirty years following adoption of the charter, no member of the United Nations, not even the United States, used the UN forum to criticize the Soviet Union. Given Soviet membership on the UN Security Council, what action could the UN system have taken to deal with Soviet human rights abuse? What were the reasons for the failure of the democracies, for decades, to use the UN system to criticize the Soviet Union? What does Soviet agreement to the UN Charter tell us about the effectiveness of the charter's human rights provisions at the time it was signed and in the decades immediately following? What caused the United States ultimately to use the UN as a forum for criticizing Soviet human rights violations? Can it be said that the seeds planted by the charter ultimately sprouted and brought down the totalitarian system more than forty years later?

3. Among the original fifty-one members of the United Nations were: the USSR, which was given three votes (ostensibly for the Russian Federation, Ukraine, and Belarus); China, then ruled by Chiang-Kai-Shek; Saudi Arabia, under King Ibn Saud; and white-ruled South Africa. The USSR and China were members of the United Nations Security Council, able to veto any decision taken by the council of which they disapproved. What have been the consequences of this veto authority for enforcement of the charter's human rights provisions against gross violators of human rights?

Note

Shortly after the adoption of the charter, the United Nations system started work on measures that would define the term fundamental human rights as used in the charter. That work was done by lawyers and other persons with expert knowledge who were genuinely committed to the human rights cause. Responsibility for the practical implementation of the human rights clauses of the charter was vested in such UN bodies as the General Assembly and the Security Council. Policy decisions as to what actions these bodies would take in the human rights arena, however, were left to professional diplomats, most of whom had had their training in the pre-charter era, when, as noted, it was a cardinal rule of diplomacy that foreign governments must not interfere with the actions of a sovereign toward that sovereign's citizens. As a result, the UN was for a long time quite hesitant in dealing with human rights issues, the provisions of the charter notwithstanding. While gross violations of human rights continued to be the hallmark of countries such as Joseph Stalin's Soviet Union, the UN General Assembly was willing to apply the charter provisions, ever so hesitantly, to only one country, South Africa. Even in that case the General Assembly, at the outset, considered only the treatment of persons of Indian ancestry.

Richard Schifter, *Human Rights at the United Nations: The South Africa Precedent*

8 Am. U. J. Int'l L. & Pol'y 361, 363–65 (1992/1993)

[I]t very well may have required a friendless, racist human rights violator such as South Africa to break down the barriers that stood in the way of United Nations scrutiny of a member state's abusive treatment of its own citizens.

For once the drafters of the Charter had completed their tasks and had left the scene, responsibility for creating the new international organization and making it function was vested in a group of persons committed to the traditional notions of the proper scope of diplomacy. Notably, in Article 2(7), the Charter incorporated one of the most important of these traditional notions, namely, the inviolability of domestic jurisdiction. Indeed, the representatives of South Africa would raise the issue posed by Article 2(7) every time their case came up in a United Nations forum.

The issue of racial discrimination in South Africa was indeed raised at the very first session of the UN General Assembly. But given the tradition of diplomacy, it was raised in a context that caused it to cross international borders. In this case, India claimed that South African legislation was in violation of certain human rights provisions of the Charter.

Rejecting South Africa's domestic jurisdiction argument, the General Assembly adopted Resolution 44, holding that South Africa's actions should conform with the Charter's human rights provisions. The formulation used in Resolution 44 vividly demonstrates the caution with which the General Assembly approached the human rights issue in its early years. It dealt exclusively with the concern expressed by one member over the behavior of another member toward persons who originated from the first member's country, thus limiting its action to the treatment of Indians by South Africa. The Resolution also emphasized friendly relations between member countries, adding a vague reference to the Charter without specifying that the "relevant provisions" of the Charter referred to in the Resolution were the human rights provisions. The two Governments were requested to report to the next session of the General Assembly on the measures that had been adopted to deal with the problem that had been identified. It was hardly a bold step. Yet, cautiously, and without fanfare, the United Nations General Assembly had slipped into the human rights field.

In 1947 the General Assembly entered into a full debate of the problem of the Indians of South Africa. India pointed out that South Africa had taken no steps to deal with the problem that had been the subject of Resolution 44. South Africa in turn accused India of having imposed unilateral sanctions. The General Assembly found itself unable to muster the required two-thirds to adopt a follow-up resolution, nor could it come to grips with the issue in 1948. In that year, however, India for the first time discussed South Africa's treatment of Asians and other non-whites. South Africa once again raised the "domestic jurisdiction" issue posed by Article 2(7) and presented a draft resolution stating that that the General Assembly lacked competence over the problems raised by India. The General Assembly failed to adopt the South African proposal, thus implying its rejection of the Article 2(7) argument.

Throughout these early years of the United Nations' existence, the bulk of the Organization's activities focused on the preparation of documents setting forth general human rights standards. Diplomatic tradition continued to prevent the discussion of those member states that were responsible for committing the most severe human rights violations against their citizens. A blind eye was turned toward the brutal Stalinist dictatorship of the Soviet Union. As democratically elected governments in Eastern Europe were succeeded by totalitarian dictatorships, the United Nations remained silent. In keeping with tradition, none of the Western democracies was prepared to press the cases that involved the most blatant abuses of individual human rights.

But India, perhaps inspired by diplomats not anchored to the tradition of silence, pressed on. The Dominion of India had after independence been divided into India and Pakistan. Although in disagreement on a great many issues, the two countries were united in pressing the South African discrimination issue at the United Nations. And with General Assembly Resolution 265 of May 14, 1949, India and Pakistan succeeded in prodding their colleagues to take another small step forward in the human rights arena. That resolution invited the three governments concerned — India, Pakistan, and South Africa — to meet at a conference to discuss their problem in consideration of the "purposes and principles of the Charter" and the Universal Declaration of Human Rights. A cautious General Assembly did not specify which purposes and principles it had in mind. However, the mere reference to the Universal Declaration in the context of a resolution dealing with a concrete human rights problem was significant.

Human Rights Under the International Bill of Rights

The hesitancy of the United Nations General Assembly in implementing the human rights provisions of the charter in specific cases did not prevent the United Nations system from moving forward with the preparation of documents that would spell out precisely what the term fundamental human rights, as used in the charter, meant. In February 1946 the General Assembly decided to authorize the drafting of an International Bill of Rights, and in the same month the Economic and Social Council established a Commission on Human Rights and assigned it that task. Initially, some members wanted the international bill of rights to take the form of a declaration or manifesto, while other members favored drafting it in the form of a convention or treaty. Ultimately, the commission, chaired by the United States representative, Eleanor Roosevelt, decided to prepare a draft declaration setting forth general principles, to be followed by a draft covenant that would state the legal obligations of states with respect to human rights. Measures of implementation either would be included in the covenant itself or be contained in a separate international instrument. In the event, the commission produced a Draft Declaration, two Covenants (one on civil and political rights and one on economic, social, and cultural rights), and an Optional Protocol to the Civil and Political Covenant establishing a Human Rights Committee with jurisdiction to review state reports, consider state-to-state complaints, and (in the case of states ratifying the Optional Protocol) entertain individual petitions. Together these four instruments form the International Bill of Rights.

Universal Declaration of Human Rights

The Universal Declaration of Human Rights, the product of two years of work by the Commission on Human Rights, was transmitted by the Economic and Social Council to the General Assembly in late August 1948, approved by the latter's Third Committee in the late evening/early morning of December 6-7, 1948, and adopted by the General Assembly on December 10, 1948, by a vote of forty-eight for, none against, eight abstaining, and two absent. Although the fact that no member of the United Nations had voted no was viewed as a favorable sign, it should have been clear that the eight abstainers had no intention of recognizing the declaration as a document of universal applicability. They were: the USSR (casting three votes); the other UN members then under Communist rule, namely Czechoslovakia, Poland, and Yugoslavia; Saudi Arabia; and South Africa. Close examination of the record of the forty-eight states that voted for the declaration would suggest that quite a number of them might not have taken that document very seriously either. However, there is no doubt that a majority of the UN members of December 1948 were democracies that subscribed to the principles set forth in the declaration.[6]

---

6. For an insider's account of the adoption of this important resolution, whose "impact on world public opinion has been as great as if not greater than that of any contemporary international instrument, including the Charter of the United Nations," see JOHN HUMPHREY, HUMAN RIGHTS AND THE UNITED NATIONS: A GREAT ADVENTURE 63–77 (1984).

The Universal Declaration consists of thirty articles that, as Professor Henkin correctly notes, "are in their essence American constitutional rights projected around the world."[7] More than one-half of the articles (3-18) guarantee the civil rights of individuals.[8] Another three articles (19-21) protect their political rights.[9] Finally, six articles (22-27) purport to grant individuals certain minimal economic, social, and cultural rights. Since the Universal Declaration was considered by all concerned to be a standard-setting exercise, no measures of implementation are included. How the normative impact of the standards has evolved over the years is shown by the readings that follow. They demonstrate that even though the declaration was not accompanied by an implementation mechanism, its spirit slowly but surely took hold and ultimately had the effect its authors envisioned.

Statement of Mrs. Eleanor Roosevelt,

Chairman of the Commission on Human Rights, immediately preceding
the General Assembly's vote on the Universal Declaration,
in 5 Marjorie Whiteman, Digest of International Law 243 (1965)

In giving our approval to the declaration today, it is of primary importance that we keep clearly in mind the basic character of the document. It is not a treaty; it is not an international agreement. It is not and does not purport to be a statement of law or of legal obligation. It is a declaration of basic principles of human rights and freedoms, to be stamped with the approval of the General Assembly by formal vote of its members, and to serve as a common standard of achievement for all peoples of all nations.

United Nations Action in the Field of Human Rights

at 32, UN Sales No. E.94.XIV.II (1988)

In a statement following the voting the President of the General Assembly pointed out that the adoption of the Declaration, "by a big majority, without any direct opposition, was a remarkable achievement". The Declaration, he said, only marked a first step, since it was not a convention by which States would be bound to carry out and give effect to the fundamental human rights; nor would it provide for enforcement; yet it was a step forward in the great evolutionary process. It was the first occasion on which the organized community of nations had made a declaration of human rights and fundamental freedoms. The document was backed by the authority of the body of opinion of the United Nations as a whole and millions of people — men, women and children all over the world — would turn to it for help, guidance, and inspiration.

John Humphrey, *The International Bill of Rights: Scope and Implementation*

17 Wm. & Mary L. Rev. 527, 529 (1976)

The Universal Declaration of Human Rights was not intended to be binding on states as part of positive international law; not only are resolutions of the General Assembly or-

---

7. Louis Henkin, *International Human Rights in the United States, in* 1 Human Rights in International Law: Legal and Policy Issues 25, 39 (Theodor Meron ed., 1984).

8. *See* Lillich, *supra* note 3, at 115.

9. *See* John Humphrey, *Political and Related Rights, in* 1 Human Rights in International Law: Legal and Policy Issues 171 (Theodor Meron ed., 1984).

dinarily not binding, but the Declaration was to be only one part of the International Bill of Rights which was to include a covenant having substantially the same content as the Declaration and which would be binding on those states that ratified it. If the Declaration had been intended to be binding, a covenant would have been unnecessary. Further, though some delegations attempted to breathe legal life into the Declaration by asserting that it was an authentic interpretation of the human rights provisions of the Charter or that it set forth general principles of law, others insisted more convincingly that is was not binding. In the more than a quarter of a century since its adoption, however, the Declaration has been invoked so many times both within and without the United Nations that lawyers now are saying that, whatever the intention of its authors may have been, the Declaration is now part of the customary law of nations and therefore is binding on all states. The Declaration has become what some nations wished it to be in 1948: the universally accepted interpretation and definition of the human rights left undefined by the Charter.

Comments and Questions for Discussion

The Restatement (Third) of the Foreign Relations Law of the United States includes a number of rights from the Universal Declaration in its list of rights now part of customary international law:

§ 702. Customary International Law of Human Rights

A state violates international law if, as a matter of state policy, it practices, encourages, or condones

(a) genocide,
(b) slavery or slave trade,
(c) the murder or causing the disappearance of individuals,
(d) torture or other cruel, inhuman, or degrading treatment or punishment,
(e) prolonged arbitrary detention,
(f) systematic racial discrimination, or
(g) a consistent pattern of gross violations of internationally recognized human rights.[10]

Would you agree with the *Restatement* that all of them now constitute customary international law? Of what significance is the fact that, in the case of torture, arbitrary detention, and disappearance, U.S. courts have reached this conclusion?[11]

International Covenants on Human Rights

The Universal Declaration, for all its importance, originally was intended to be no more than a statement of principles, a blueprint from which to construct a convention

---

10. The Restatement (Third) of the Foreign Relations Law of the United States § 702 (1987).

11. *See* Filartiga v. Pena-Irala, 630 F.2d 876, 882 (2d Cir. 1980) (torture); Fernandez v. Wilkinson, 505 F. Supp. 787, 798 (D. Kan. 1980), *aff'd on other grounds sub nom.* Rodriguez-Fernandez v. Wilkinson, 654 F.2d 1382 (10th Cir. 1981) (arbitrary detention); Fernandez-Roque v. Smith, 622 F. Supp. 887, 903 (N.D. Ga. 1985), *rev'd in part & aff'd in part & dismissed as moot in part sub. nom.* Garcia-Mir v. Meese, 788 F.2d 1446, 1453 (11th Cir.), *cert. denied,* 479 U.S. 889 (1986) (arbitrary detention); Forti v. Suarez-Mason, 694 F. Supp. 707 (N.D. Cal. 1988) (disappearance). On the Restatement, *see generally* Richard B. Lillich, *The Customary International Law of Human Rights in the Revised Restatement,* 79 Am. Soc'y Int'l L. Proc. 84 (1985).

or treaty laying down legal obligations for states and providing for international procedures to enforce them. The legal regime finally built by the United Nations differs somewhat from this original intention, as the reading that follows reveals.

A. H. ROBERTSON, HUMAN RIGHTS IN THE WORLD

28–33 *passim* (2d ed. 1982)

[The General Assembly on] 10 December, 1948 not only approved the text of the Universal Declaration, it also decided that work should go ahead on the other two parts of the Bill of Rights: a Covenant containing legal obligations to be assumed by States, and measures of implementation. The Commission had indeed already prepared and submitted a preliminary draft for the Covenant, but it was not yet ready for adoption and was referred back by the General Assembly....

The initial work of the Commission resulted in a text devoted to the classic civil and political rights, but when the General Assembly was consulted in 1950 for certain basic policy decisions, it decided that economic, social and cultural rights should also be included. The Commission proceeded to draft accordingly in 1951, but when the [Economic and Social] Council considered the results, and particularly the differences in the two categories of rights, it recommended that the General Assembly should reconsider its decision. As a result, the Assembly ... decided in 1952 that there should be two separate Covenants....

The articles on measures of implementation gave the Commission much more trouble than the normative provisions, principally because the views of its members were sharply divided on the basic question [of] how far governments could be expected to accept a system of international control. A number of far-reaching proposals were considered, including an Australian suggestion for an International Court of Human Rights, a proposal by Uruguay for the establishment of an Office of a United Nations High Commissioner (or Attorney-General) for Human Rights and a French proposal for an International Investigation Commission, coupled with the appointment of an Attorney-General of the Commission; India proposed that the Security Council should be seized of alleged violations, investigate them and enforce redress, while Israel suggested the creation of a new Specialized Agency for the implementation of the Covenants. The attitude of the United Kingdom and the United States was more cautious; they proposed that Human Rights Committees should be set up on an *ad hoc* basis, but only for inter-State disputes. The Soviet Union was consistently opposed to all arrangements of this sort on the ground that they would interfere in the internal affairs of States, contrary to Article 2(7) of the Charter, undermining their sovereignty and independence. The Commission finally decided by seven votes to six, with one abstention, in favour of the establishment of a permanent Human Rights Committee to consider complaints of violations of human rights on an inter-State basis; but it rejected (seven-four-three) the possibility of considering complaints by non-governmental organisations and (eight-three-three) petitions by individuals.

....

The Covenants, as revised by the Third Committee, were finally approved unanimously by the General Assembly on 16 December 1966 with more than 100 votes in favour; they required thirty-five ratifications and entered into force in 1976. The Optional Protocol was approved by majority vote (sixty-six to two, with thirty-eight abstentions) and required ten ratifications; it entered into force at the same time as the Covenant on Civil and Political Rights.

Implementing the International Bill of Rights

Note

Although ideological and political differences were behind the General Assembly's decision in 1952 to draft two separate covenants, "[t]he division has also been supported by the argument that the grant or concession of most of the rights defined in [the Covenant on Civil and Political Rights] lies in the simple power of national governments, which are able if they wish to protect or guarantee them by legislation or administrative action, whereas most of the rights described in [the Covenant on Economic, Social and Cultural Rights] are said to depend for their realization on the progressive economic development of a country, which may take many years and does not lie exclusively within the power of its government...."[12] The different phraseology used in Articles 2(1) of the respective covenants also suggests, in the view of most observers, that under the former a state must ensure the rights recognized immediately, while under the latter its obligation is only to achieve rights recognized progressively, taking into account its available resources.[13]

The rights set forth in the Universal Declaration are restated, in greater detail and with more legal precision, in Articles 6-27 of the Covenant on Civil and Political Rights and Articles 6-15 of the Covenant on Economic, Social and Cultural Rights, respectively. Take this opportunity to compare their provisions with the equivalent provisions in the declaration. A number of rights not contained in the declaration are found in the Covenant on Civil and Political Rights: the right of detained persons to be treated with humanity (Article 10); freedom from imprisonment for debt (Article 11); prohibition of propaganda for war and advocacy of hatred that constitutes incitement to discrimination, hostility, or violence (Article 20); the rights of the child (Article 24); and the rights of minorities (Article 27). On the other hand, the right to own property and not to be arbitrarily deprived of it, found in Article 17 of the declaration, is not expressly mentioned in either covenant....

The rights that an individual enjoys under the Covenant on Civil and Political Rights are not all absolute. The restrictions the Covenant allows a state to impose upon an individual's rights come in two tiers. On the first tier are a number of clawback clauses found in particular articles that permit the state to limit the rights guaranteed in those articles. Article 12(3), for instance, sanctions state restrictions on the freedom of movement when "necessary to protect national security, public order (*ordre public*), public health or morals or the rights and freedoms of others...."[14] On the second tier, Article 4(1) permits States to derogate from, that is, suspend, certain rights "[i]n time of public emergency which threatens the life of the nation...." While no derogation may be made from the rights guaranteed by Articles 6, 7, 8(1), 11, 15, 16, and 18, the fact that a wide variety of important rights—for example, the right to liberty and security of persons guaranteed by Article 9(1)—may be rendered temporarily "inoperative" by means of derogation greatly weakens the protections of this Covenant.[15] The reason for proceeding with the

---

12. Paul Sieghart, The International Law of Human Rights 25 (1983).

13. *See* A.H. Robertson, Human Rights in the World (2d ed. 1982). *Cf.* David M. Trubek, *Economic, Social, and Cultural Rights in the Third World: Human Rights Law and Human Needs Programs, in* 1 Human Rights in International Law: Legal and Policy Issues 205, 210-17 (Theodor Meron ed., 1984).

14. *See generally* Oscar M. Garibaldi, *General Limitations on Human Rights: The Principle of Legality,* 17 Harv. Int'l L.J. 503 (1976).

15. *See* Thomas Buergenthal, *To Respect and to Ensure: State Obligations and Permissible Derogations, in* The International Bill of Rights: The Covenant on Civil and Political Rights 72 (Louis

drafting and formal approval of the Covenant on Civil and Political Rights following adoption of the Universal Declaration of Human Rights was that the former, as a mere UN General Assembly resolution, was deemed nonbinding, while the Covenant, as a treaty, was considered to be legally binding on its adherents. As it is, the distinction between the nonbinding declaration and the binding Covenant has proved largely illusory. Both documents are, above all, statements of principles that have helped advocates of human rights use international fora to shame violators of these principles into modification of their behavior, and have helped other such advocates to use domestic fora to bring violators into compliance with these principles.

As of 2014, a total of 168 states have signed and ratified the International Covenant on Civil and Political Rights. Yet, only sixty of the 168 states that have signed and ratified the Covenant were rated free at the time of ratification under the country rating system of Freedom House. The remaining states were divided between forty-two that were rated partially free and thirty-nine that were rated not free. The latter group includes Saddam Hussein's Iraq and the North Korea of Kim Il Sung and Kim Jong Il. There is no generally available international enforcement mechanism in place that victims of human rights can invoke to compel a government to bring itself into compliance with the provisions of the Covenant, which that government had signed and ratified.

What the victims of human rights abuse and those who support their cause can do is use the public media to draw attention to violations of internationally recognized human rights standards. Governments that espouse international human rights principles can also use UN fora to denounce abuses and, if there is sufficient support, cause the UN system to take concrete action against the abusers. In that context, the standards set forth in the Universal Declaration are more helpful than the Covenant, whose principles are diluted by the clawback clauses.

For the UN system to take concrete action against human rights abusers, as noted, broad support for such action is necessary. Such broad support was available in three cases: those of South Africa, Southern Rhodesia/Zimbabwe, and Southwest Africa/ Namibia.

The Case of South Africa

Richard Schifter, *Human Rights at the United Nations: The South Africa Precedent*

8 Am. U. J. Int'l L. & Pol'y 361, 365–69 (1992/1993)

The real breakthrough came at the seventh session of the United Nations General Assembly. Thirteen member states made a request in September 1952 to place on the agenda of the General Assembly the conflict resulting from South Africa's *apartheid* policies. In several ways, this formulation significantly departed from those that preceded it. First, the memorandum squarely faced the issue of the treatment of the blacks. It was no longer a matter involving only Indians and the impact of their treatment on the international relations between India and South Africa. Second, the traditional effort to inject diplomatic niceties was absent. Rather, the language was condemnatory of *apartheid*

Henkin ed., 1981); Joan F. Hartman, *Derogation from Human Rights Treaties in Public Emergencies*, 22 Harv. Int'l L.J. 1 (1981); Rosalyn Higgins, *Derogations Under Human Rights Treaties*, 48 Brit. Y.B. Int'l L. 281 (1976-77). *See also Symposium: Limitation and Derogation Provisions in the International Covenant on Civil and Political Rights*, 7 Human Rights Q. 1 (1985).

practices. Third, above and beyond invoking the standard jurisdictional statement that South Africa posed a "threat to international peace," the general Assembly also stated in the memorandum that South Africa had violated the Charter's human rights provisions as well. Specifically, the memorandum called attention to: (1) a pattern of discrimination which disadvantaged 80% of South Africa's population; (2) the withholding of voting and other political rights from non-whites; and (3) the restrictions on the movement of blacks. All of these represent violations of the standards set forth in the Universal Declaration of Human Rights.

The filing of this request meant that these issues were to be raised in the context of the broader discussion concerning South Africa's discrimination against non-whites. Over the vehement objection of South Africa that the General Assembly was not competent to deal with this domestic South African problem, the item was inscribed on the agenda as requested.

The next precedent-setting step was taken on December 5, 1952, when the General Assembly passed Resolution 616 A & B. Although failing to adopt the criticisms set forth in the previously mentioned memorandum, the Resolution announced the Assembly's realization that a meeting of the interested parties would be futile. Instead, the Resolution called for the creation of a commission to study the situation in South Africa and to report its conclusions to the next session of the general Assembly.

By creating a commission to scrutinize the systemic practices of racial discrimination in South Africa, the General Assembly laid a foundation for the subjection of South Africa to public criticism of its domestic practices. Despite mentioning the Charter's non-intervention provision (Article 2 (7)), the Resolution recited the sections dealing with the UN's commitment to human rights. The Resolution assigned the task to the three-member commission to draft and submit a report to the General Assembly on how to resolve the conflict with respect to South Africa between these two seemingly mutually exclusive Charter provisions.

The commission submitted three reports to the General Assembly ... which were critical of the discriminatory practices of the Government of South Africa. In its reports, it proposed reconciliation between the two allegedly conflicting provisions of the UN Charter by deciding that the human rights provision modified the non-intervention provision. In other words, the United Nations was not to treat human rights problems as "essentially domestic." The General Assembly, however, still could not see its way clear to tackling a human rights issue without relating it to the traditional international agenda. Thus, Resolution 721 concluded that *apartheid* would "endanger friendly relations among nations." Similarly, Resolution 820 held that *apartheid* was "a grave threat to the peaceful relations among ethnic groups in the world."

In each instance the General Assembly sought to place the problem of South African race relations in a context that would suggest a threat to world peace, thus allowing UN intercession on the basis of its peacekeeping responsibilities. In large part this was due to the reluctance of traditional diplomats to assume responsibility for intruding upon South Africa's domestic legislation. In addition, member states that also engaged in human rights violations were eager to dispose of the South Africa case in a manner that would cause it to be regarded *sui generis*, thus avoiding a precedent that could haunt them. Yet, although these governments were thus preserving for themselves the option to raise technical arguments that would distinguish the case of South Africa from their own, the objective facts were that (a) *apartheid* did not pose a real threat to peace beyond the borders of South Africa; and (b) the resolutions dealing with *apartheid* challenged South

African domestic legislation on the ground that it was in conflict with the human rights provisions of the Charter.

By 1953 the United Nations had thus focused its attention on *apartheid* in South Africa. Whatever concerns there may have been that the United Nations General Assembly was involving itself in the domestic affairs of a member country had been swept aside. Although subterfuges were used in wording the resolutions, it was now clear that the United Nations had concluded that a violation of the human rights provisions of the Charter did not present an "essentially domestic" issue.

It is important to recognize that the United Nations began its work on *apartheid* prior to the massive decolonization of Africa and thus prior to the time when a large number of Black African countries joined the United Nations. After decolonization the intensity with which *apartheid* was dealt with at the United Nations increased significantly.

After years of discussion in the General Assembly concerning South Africa's policy of racial discrimination, the issue was taken to the Security Council in 1960, following the shooting of demonstrators by South African security forces. Security Council Resolution 134 of April 1, 1960, once again relying on the formula that conditions in South Africa could endanger international peace and security, called upon South Africa to abandon *apartheid*.

With its next South Africa resolution, Resolution 181 of August 7, 1963, the Security Council expressed itself more explicitly on the issue. It condemned "the policies of South Africa in its perpetuation of racial discrimination" and called upon South Africa "to liberate all persons imprisoned, interned, or subject to other restrictions for having opposed the policy of *apartheid*." The Security Council also took one other significant step by calling upon all countries "to cease forthwith the sale and shipment of arms, ammunition of all types and military vehicles to South Africa."

Resolution 182 of December 4, 1963, went one significant step further by creating a group of experts who were instructed to consider methods involving U.N. participation to resolve the dispute surrounding *apartheid*. With this resolution the Council had clearly committed itself to the application of the Charter's human rights standards to a domestic (but evidently not an *essentially* domestic) situation.

From the middle Sixties onward the issue of racial discrimination in South Africa and all its consequences became one of the major preoccupations of the entire United Nations system. Security Council Resolutions 282 (1970) and 392 (1976) emphasized the need to strengthen the arms embargo. Resolution 418 (1977) took a further step by invoking Chapter VII of the Charter and imposing a mandatory embargo on military and nuclear collaboration with South Africa. Resolution 591 (1986) urged the expansion of the embargo so as to include all items which the authorities of the exporting countries had reason to believe were destined for the military or police forces of South Africa.

The General Assembly, not restrained by a veto or the threat of a veto, went much further in its various declarations. Under Resolution 31/6 J of November 9, 1976, it adopted a comprehensive "Programme of Action against *Apartheid*." That program urged member nations: (1) to terminate diplomatic relations with South Africa; (2) to fully implement the arms embargo; (3) to terminate economic relations with South Africa; (4) to refuse to provide landing and passage facilities for South African aircraft; and (5) to suspend cultural, educational, and sporting exchanges with South Africa.

The work of the General Assembly on the subject of South Africa was paralleled by the activities of the United Nations Commission on Human Rights and the Sub-Commission on Prevention of Discrimination. Resolutions were passed and studies were undertaken on the subject of *apartheid*, which was denounced as a crime against humanity or a collective form of slavery. Other international organizations such as the International Labor Organization, the United Nations Educational, Scientific, and Cultural Organization (UNESCO), and the World Health Organization joined the effort.

[In 1989 Frederik W. de Klerk was elected State President of South Africa and promptly began to institute reforms that would end the *apartheid* policy and lead to majority rule. Majority rule came to South Africa in 1994, with the inauguration of Nelson Mandela as President.]

Looking at these decades of effort by the United Nations in dealing with the issue of racial discrimination in South Africa, what conclusions can be reached regarding the efficacy of that effort? Did it ultimately make a difference?

Although it may be difficult to demonstrate a direct relationship between a specific UN resolution and developments in South Africa, there is good reason to think that the UN's work has been effective. Those in South Africa who opposed all forms of racial discrimination had their morale boosted by the knowledge that they did not stand alone, that the international community shared their convictions and their aspirations. Ultimately the continued chorus of condemnation also appeared to have affected the thinking of a younger generation of white South Africans.

The Case of Southern Rhodesia/Zimbabwe

Southern Rhodesia posed a case quite similar to that of South Africa. The difference was that whereas South Africa was independent, white-ruled Southern Rhodesia had been a self-governing British colony, which declared itself independent in 1961. Under a constitution adopted in 1961, the black majority of the population had been effectively prevented from exercising political rights.

Because of this failure to adhere to democratic norms, the United Nations, from 1966 onward, imposed selective mandatory sanctions on Southern Rhodesia, ultimately including all imports and exports except for medical and education supplies and, in some circumstances, food. Further expansion of the sanctions regime in 1976 and 1977 interrupted communications and the transfer of funds. Under serious pressure from the United Nations and the government of the United Kingdom, the white minority government of Southern Rhodesia finally entered into negotiations with representatives of the black majority, which led to an agreement on a constitution and to free and fair elections. These elections, held in 1980, led to the creation of the independent state of Zimbabwe.

The Case of South West Africa/Namibia

A third case in this category was that of South West Africa. South West Africa had been a German colony until the end of World War I. It subsequently became a League of Nations Mandate administered by South Africa. After the United Nations had replaced the League of Nations, the General Assembly, in 1946, invited South Africa to place South West Africa under the international trusteeship system established by the United Nations. South Africa, which had originally intended to absorb South West Africa, decided not to do so, but also refused to agree to trusteeship status for the former mandate. As a result, the issue of South West Africa became from 1947 onward another point of contention between the United Nations and South Africa and one of the major issues of continuing concern to the United Nations. Increasingly, the United Nations pressed South Africa to withdraw from South West Africa, which in 1970 was renamed Namibia, and to allow free elections that would lead to the establishment of an independent state. South Africa, however, continued for many years to defy UN action.

Change came to Namibia only after the inauguration of state President de Klerk. In 1989, the UN Security Council authorized the Secretary General to send a transition assistance group, consisting of troops, to Namibia to prepare the country for independence. United Nations supervised elections of a Constituent Assembly were held in November of that year and were deemed peaceful, free, and fair. Namibia declared itself independent on March 21, 1990.

Note

The success the United Nations achieved in bringing free elections and majority rule to South Africa, Zimbabwe, and Namibia was not paralleled by similar accomplishments elsewhere. This was due to the fact that the broad agreement among member states that enabled the United Nations to move forward in those three cases could not be attained in other settings. Significantly, in this regard, when Freedom House began its annual country ratings in 1973 of the state of freedom in the world, it rated less than one-third of the United Nations' 135 members free (forty-four free, twenty-nine partially free, and sixty-two not free).

Richard Schifter, *Human Rights at the United Nations: The South Africa Precedent*
8 Am. U. J. Int'l L. & Pol'y 361, 370–71 (1992/1993)

... [W]hatever the excuse, in the case of South Africa, the UN was subjecting the laws and internal practices of a member country to review by the United Nations under the human rights provisions of the Charter. In how many other situations was it doing the same?

The answer to this question is that although the United Nations crossed the Article 2(7) Rubicon in the early 1950's by seeking to apply the Charter's human rights provisions in a specific country situation, it took more than twenty years before another country was subjected to similar treatment. That second country, Pinochet's Chile, like South Africa, also stood alone and friendless. Like South Africa, it was vehemently opposed by the Soviet Union. Even so, while resolutions directed against South Africa had by then become empathetic to the human rights cause, the initial United Nations action on Chile was quite mild. Under general Assembly Resolution 3219 of November 6, 1974, the United Nations Human Rights Commission was instructed to study human rights violations in Chile. In 1975, 1976, and 1977, the General Assembly expressed "distress" at the continuation of human rights violations in Chile. Years passed before stronger language was used.

In the meantime the United Nations system turned a blind eye toward the mass killings of Hutus in Burundi in the period 1972-1974 and to the political murders committed by President Idi Amin of Uganda. When Pol Pot killed millions of his fellow citizens, the United Nations Human Rights Commission response, in Decision 9 of March 8, 1978, was to request the Secretary General to transmit to the Cambodian Government the record of its proceedings at the 1978 session, in which there was testimony about the gross human rights violations in Cambodia. Pol Pot's Government was simply asked to send its comments and observations. By Resolution 4B of September 5, 1979, the Sub-Commission on the Prevention of Discrimination and Protection of Minorities, faced with evidence of the largest mass killing since World War II, did nothing more than to ask Cambodia to take urgent measures to restore full respect for human rights and fundamental freedoms and prevent violations from occurring in the future.

United States Ratification of the International Covenant on Civil and Political Rights

Note

Although the United States was actively engaged in the drafting of the International Covenant on Civil and Political Rights, it was not among the first thirty-five states to ratify it. It did not sign the Covenant until one year after it had taken effect and did not ratify it until another fifteen years had passed. The long interval between the signing of the Covenant by the United States and its ratification by the Senate is the result of the strong opposition by some members of the Senate to the imposition of international human rights law in the United States. The United States, these Senators emphasized, takes its legal obligations seriously; courts would enforce treaties. By 1992, these members of the Senate agreed to ratification as long as appropriate reservations were in place. The case for ratification, as presented at the initial hearings on the Covenant, and an explanation of the reservations, understandings, and declarations that accompanied ratification are set forth below.

In his testimony before the Senate Committee on Foreign Relations, Professor John Norton Moore, speaking on behalf of the American Bar Association, made it clear what the objective of ratification would be: promoting human rights in the world. A treaty that would ostensibly protect human rights within the United States was to be ratified to help reach an important foreign policy goal. Those who were concerned that the treaty-making power would here be used to supersede domestic U.S. law were told by Professor Moore that the American Bar Association believed that the package of reservations, understandings, and declarations that the Administration recommended would safeguard rights granted by the U.S. Constitution as well as the principle of federalism.

A sufficient number of Senators remained unconvinced, preventing ratification in 1979 and for years thereafter. Twelve years later, in a letter dated August 8, 1991, to Senators Pell and Helms, Chairman and Ranking Member of the Senate Committee on Foreign Relations, President George H.W. Bush reiterated the point made by Professor Moore in his 1979 testimony:

> United States ratification of the Covenant on Civil and Political Rights at this moment in history would underscore our natural commitment to fostering democratic values through international law.... U.S. ratification would also strengthen our ability to influence the development of appropriate human rights principles in the international community and provide an additional and effective tool in our efforts to improve respect for fundamental freedoms in many problem countries around the world.

This time the Senate acted on the administration's recommendation. In the article excerpted below, David Stewart of the Office of the State Department's Legal Adviser explains how the reservations, understandings, and declarations would meet the concerns that some Senators and other had expressed about the potential domestic impact of the Covenant.

Statement of Professor John Norton Moore

in International Human Rights Treaties: Hearings Before the Senate Comm. on Foreign Relations, 96th Cong., 2d Sess. 66–68 *passim* (1979)

Mr. Moore. Mr. Chairman, it is a ... special honor this morning to be testifying on behalf of the American Bar Association in support of ratification of the ... human rights treaties which are before the committee.

The American Bar Association strongly supports ratification of these ... treaties with the reservations, understandings, and declarations that have been proposed by the administration....

The points I would like briefly to discuss are these: Why the United States should ratify the ... human rights treaties; [and] why this ratification would be fully consistent with the Constitution of the United States, the Federal system and the laws of the United States....

Mr. Chairman, ratification of these treaties will be fully consistent with an important goal of the United States in promoting human rights in the world, and failure to ratify these treaties will be inconsistent with that important foreign policy goal.

I think it is important to achieve that goal for a number of reasons.

First, we want to promote minimum standards embodied in international law and it is very important to develop these uniform standards in international law guaranteeing minimum human rights. As a vice chairman of the section of international law of the American Bar Association, I would like to emphasize the importance of the development of international law in this area.

Second, as a leader in the movement to promote human rights in the world, it certainly would be inconsistent for the United States not to adhere to these agreements and it will continue to undermine the effectiveness of the United States in achieving human rights goals in failing to adhere to these treaties.

As you know, the United States has taken an active role in the past in the negotiations leading to these agreements and certainly even in the charter of the United Nations in seeking to promote respect for human rights.

In addition to that, the ratification of these ... treaties would encourage the progressive development of a variety of institutional mechanisms which would seek to protect human rights around the world. In this connection I particularly would emphasize that if we become a treaty party to the Civil and Political Covenant, we would be entitled to participate in the Human Rights Committee, and we could file state-to-state complaints in the human rights area....

Mr. Chairman, the second point I briefly want to mention is that the American Bar Association believes that the ratification of these four treaties, with the understandings, reservations, and declarations recommended, would be fully consistent with the Constitution of the United States, would be fully consistent with the State-Federal system, and would be something that would be consistent with the overall domestic law of the United States.

From time to time arguments have been raised that perhaps we ought not adhere to these treaties because of some legalism or some supposed inconsistency with the U.S. Constitution, and, provided that there is a clear understanding and reservation in those areas where there may be inconsistency, we feel that certainly there is no valid reason whatsoever not to sign the treaties on that basis. I might add that this is an area where

the American Bar Association can speak with particular authority that with these understandings and reservations it is our judgment that there is no inconsistency with the Constitution of the United States or the principle of federalism.

David P. Stewart, *United States Ratification of the Covenant on Civil and Political Rights: The Significance of the Reservations, Understandings, and Declarations*
42 DePaul L. Rev. 1183 (1993)

INTRODUCTION

The recent ratification by the United States of the International Covenant on Civil and
Political Rights (Covenant) was a very significant development in the field of international
human rights law. Considered by many to be the single most important human rights
treaty, the Covenant guarantees those basic rights and freedoms which form the cornerstones
of a democratic society. Not only does U.S. adherence reflect and reinforce a long-standing
national commitment to those values, it will also enhance the U.S. role in protecting and
promoting the rule of law and democratic ideals internationally. As President Bush stated
in August 1991, in urging renewed Senate consideration of the Covenant, ratification
strengthens the ability of the United States to influence the development of appropriate
human rights principles in the international community and provides an additional and
effective tool for efforts to improve respect for fundamental freedoms in many problem
countries.

The unanimous approval of the Covenant by the U.S. Senate also signaled an important
victory in overcoming — or at least neutralizing — a persistent thread of hostility in that
body and in the American legal community to ratification of human rights treaties. While
the United States has for years been a party to a number of such treaties, including those
relating to the political rights of women, slavery and the slave trade, slave labor, and
refugees, there is a long and contentious history to Senate consideration of the Covenant
itself, including the narrow defeat of the so-called Bricker Amendment to the U.S.
Constitution in early 1954. As a result of that debate, the United States was for decades
effectively foreclosed from becoming party to major multilateral conventions promoting
human rights, even those which it actively supported in international fora. Indeed, the
United States did not become a party to the first post-war treaty of this type, the Convention
on the Prevention and Punishment of the Crime of Genocide (Genocide Convention),
until 1988, forty years after it was written. Four other major human rights treaties submitted
to the Senate along with the Covenant during the Carter Administration received no endorsement during the Reagan and Bush Administrations. With approval of the Genocide
Convention, however, and the Senate's subsequent advice and consent to ratification of
the United Nations Torture Convention, the groundwork had been prepared for resolving
the various issues which had stood for many years in the way of ratification of the Covenant.

The elements of this accommodation are contained in the various reservations, understandings, and declarations upon which U.S. ratification was conditioned. Based largely
on proposals initially set forth in the Carter transmittal, this "package" of provisos was
proposed by the Administration after extensive inter-agency review and consultations
with various nongovernmental human rights organizations and other interested academics,
practitioners, and specialists. It also responded to the concerns of those who felt the
Covenant was a "seriously flawed" instrument, including provisions inimical to established
constitutional protections. Although during the hearings a number of witnesses criticized

the package as unnecessary, unhelpful, and proof of U.S. refusal to accept the full measure of its international obligations, it was accepted without change, or even significant debate, by the Senate.

. . . .

III. RESERVATIONS, UNDERSTANDINGS, AND DECLARATIONS

Most commentators agree that existing U.S. law generally complies with the Covenant. In fact, as indicated above, almost all of the individual rights and freedoms embodied in the Covenant have long been enjoyed by Americans by virtue of the U.S. Constitution and the constitutions and laws of the states.

Nonetheless, when the Covenant was transmitted to the Senate in February 1978, along with three other human rights treaties, it was accompanied by a number of proposed reservations, understandings, and declarations, considered necessary at the time to meet anticipated constitutional and legal objections and to make certain other adjustments in light of U.S. law. Some have criticized this as a costly tactical error on the part of the Carter Administration. The Senate Foreign Relations Committee held extensive hearings on the treaties in November 1979, including considerable debate over the necessity of the various provisos, but the Soviet invasion of Afghanistan and the hostage crisis in Iran (among other events) prevented final consideration before the change of administrations in 1981.

For its part, the Reagan Administration chose to focus its attention first on winning approval for the 1948 Genocide Convention, which had been pending before the U.S. Senate since President Truman transmitted it in 1949. When that effort proved successful in 1988, the Administration turned to the task of gaining the Senate's advice and consent to ratification of the Torture Convention, which occurred in August 1990. In each of these exercises, it proved necessary to accept a series of reservations, understandings, and declarations, generally dealing with issues of federalism, perceived conflicts with the U.S. Constitution, and differences with U.S. law.

Thus, when attention turned to consideration of the Covenant in August 1991, account had to be taken both of the proposals which the Carter Administration had made when first transmitting the Covenant to the Senate, as well as of the provisos which had been agreed to with respect to the Genocide and Torture Conventions. In substance, although it contained some modifications and new elements, the package of reservations, understandings, and declarations formally proposed by the Bush Administration in November 1991, and ultimately adopted by the U.S. Senate, was not significantly different from the one put forward some thirteen years earlier.

Some have criticized these provisos as excessive (there are five reservations, five understandings, and four declarations), unnecessary, and evidence of U.S. unwillingness to accept the international human rights regime. In fact, the United States has accepted the obligations of the Covenant with very few exceptions and limitations. While the "package" seems large, a careful reading demonstrates that each proviso addresses a legitimate issue and none is contrary to the object and purpose of the treaty. Importantly, there is no "general" reservation of the type previously attached to the Genocide Convention.

A. Reservations

1. Freedom of Speech and Expression

It is not legally possible for the United States to agree to treaty undertakings which would require action prohibited by the U.S. Constitution; even if such an international obligation were accepted, it could not be effective as a matter of domestic law. In this regard, Article 20 of the Covenant (restricting various forms of speech) was of particular concern—sufficient to lead some representatives of the press community to speak against ratification. By requiring the prohibition of propaganda for war and advocacy of national, racial, or religious hatred that constitutes incitement to discrimination, hostility, or violence, it would clearly contravene the free speech protections of the First Amendment to the Constitution.

. . . .

2. Capital Punishment

. . . .

In the United States, the citizens in a majority of states have to date determined, through the democratic process, to retain the death penalty for the most serious crimes. Moreover, recent Supreme Court decisions have upheld state laws permitting imposition of the death penalty for especially serious crimes committed by juveniles aged sixteen and seventeen, having determined that capital punishment does not in and of itself violate the Eighth Amendment's protection against cruel and unusual punishment.

Accordingly, the United States formally reserved the right, subject to its constitutional constraints, to impose capital punishment on any person (other than a pregnant woman) duly convicted under existing or future laws permitting the imposition of capital punishment, including such punishment for crimes committed by persons below eighteen years of age.

. . . .

3. Cruel, Inhuman, or Degrading Treatment or Punishment

Article 7 of the Covenant provides that no one shall be subjected to torture or cruel, inhuman, or degrading treatment or punishment, or be subjected without his free consent to medical or scientific experimentation.

In its consideration of the Torture Convention, which contains substantively similar but more detailed provisions, the United States identified a possible dissonance between these provisions and the prohibitions of the Fifth, Eighth, and/or Fourteenth Amendments to the Constitution against cruel and unusual punishment. More particularly, the Human Rights Committee, like the European Court of Human Rights in its Soering decision, has adopted the view that prolonged judicial proceedings in cases involving capital punishment could in certain circumstances constitute cruel, inhuman, or degrading treatment or punishment, even though such proceedings are entirely lawful under U.S. constitutional principles. Accordingly, the United States proposed to take a formal reservation to the Torture Convention to the effect that the United States considers itself bound by Article 7 to the extent that "cruel, inhuman or degrading treatment or punishment" means the cruel and unusual treatment or punishment prohibited by the Fifth, Eighth, and/or Fourteenth Amendments to the Constitution of the United States.

To insure uniformity of interpretation as to the obligations of the United States under the Covenant and the Torture Convention on this point, the United States took an identical reservation to the Covenant.

. . . .

4. Post-Offense Reductions in Penalty

Under U.S. law, federal as well as state, the penalty in force at the time the crime was committed generally applies to an offender. By contrast, Article 15(1) obliges States Party to give offenders the benefit of any post-offense reductions in penalty. In U.S. practice, such reductions in sentence (e.g., through legislative enactment) are in fact taken into account in sentencing decisions and are often granted in practice when there have been subsequent statutory changes.

Nonetheless, because current federal law, as well as the law of most states, does not require such relief and, in fact, contains a contrary presumption, and because upon consideration there was no disposition to effect a change in that law through adherence to the Covenant, it was considered necessary to take a reservation stating that the United States does not adhere to the third clause of paragraph 1 of Article 15.

. . . .

5. Treatment of Juveniles

United States law, policy, and practice are generally in compliance with the Covenant's requirements regarding separate treatment of juveniles in the criminal justice system. Nonetheless, close consideration of these provisions indicated that it would be prudent to retain a measure of flexibility to address exceptional circumstances in which trial or incarceration of juveniles as adults may well be appropriate. Exceptional circumstances might include prosecution of juveniles as adults based on their criminal histories or the nature of their offenses, and incarceration of particularly dangerous juveniles as adults in order to protect other juveniles in custody.

B. Understandings

1. Equal Protection and Nondiscrimination

The Constitution and laws of the United States guarantee all persons equal protection of the law and provide extensive protections against discrimination. As in most if not all legal systems, however, U.S. law does permit certain lawful distinctions to be made among individuals when those distinctions are, at minimum, rationally related to a legitimate governmental objective. By contrast, Articles 2(1) and 26 of the Covenant prohibit discrimination not only on the bases of "race, colour, sex, language, religion, political or other opinion, national or social origin, property, birth," but also on any "other status," a term which could be interpreted to prohibit even legitimate, nondiscriminatory distinctions.

Because of the central importance of the nondiscrimination obligation under the Covenant, the United States felt it appropriate to clarify, through an understanding, its interpretation that the nondiscrimination provisions of the Covenant, in particular those set forth in Article 2(1) and Article 26, which it accepts, do not prevent such distinctions when they are, at minimum, rationally related to a legitimate governmental objective. In addition, the United States stated its understanding that the prohibition in Article 4(1) on discrimination in time of emergency solely on status of race, color, sex, language, religion, or social origin does not prohibit distinctions that may have a disproportionate effect upon persons of a particular status.

. . . .

2. Right to Compensation

Articles 9(5) and 14(6) of the Covenant can be read to give every individual an absolute right in all situations to recover compensation for unlawful arrest or detention or for miscarriage of justice. While it is questionable that these provisions were in fact intended to set an international standard requiring payment of compensation in all such cases, the negotiating history on this point was considered ambiguous at best. And while it is doubtful that every state party to the Covenant accords such rights to everyone within its jurisdiction, there appears to be no authoritative interpretation limiting Article 9(5), for example, to arbitrary arrests and detentions or defining the content of "miscarriage of justice" as set forth in Article 14(6).

. . . .

... U.S. adherence was conditioned on the understanding that the proper reading of Articles 9(5) and 14(6) is that states are obliged to provide effective and enforceable mechanisms by which victims of unlawful arrest or detention or a miscarriage of justice may seek and, where justified, obtain such compensation either from the responsible individual or from the appropriate governmental entity. Moreover, the actual entitlement to compensation may be subject to reasonable requirements of domestic law.

. . . .

3. Separate Treatment of the Accused

Article 10, paragraph 2 requires that accused persons be segregated from the convicted "save in exceptional circumstances" and that juveniles who are accused of a crime be separated from adults. While, in general, federal law and prison policy conform to these requirements, some exceptions exist. For example, prison authorities are permitted to take into account such factors as a prisoner's overall dangerousness when determining treatment. Prisoners may also waive their right to segregation in order to participate in special programs. Within the military justice system, segregation of the accused from the convicted cannot always be guaranteed in light of military exigencies.

For these reasons, the United States conditioned its adherence on the understanding that the reference to "special circumstances" in Article 10(2)(a) permits the imprisonment of an accused person with convicted persons where appropriate in light of an individual's overall dangerousness and allows accused persons to waive their rights to segregation from convicts.

Paragraph 3 of Article 10 states that the essential aim of treatment of prisoners in the penitentiary system is reformation and social rehabilitation. The United States also stated its understanding that this provision does not diminish the goals of punishment, deterrence, and incapacitation (i.e., restraint) as additional legitimate purposes for a penitentiary system.

. . . .

4. Right to Counsel, Compelled Witness, Double Jeopardy

Paragraphs 3(b) and 3(d) of Article 14 provide a defendant in a criminal proceeding the right to choose his or her own counsel. Even though the right to counsel is broadly recognized and enforced within the United States, U.S. law does recognize some circumstances, such as indigence, in which a defendant may not in fact choose his own counsel but is instead furnished legal representation through the public defender's office or by court appointment. Nor does federal law recognize a right to counsel with respect to offenses for which imprisonment may not be imposed. The United States accordingly stated its understanding that these subparagraphs do not require the provision of a criminal defendant's counsel of choice when the defendant is provided with court-appointed counsel on ground of indigence, when the defendant is financially able to retain alternative counsel, or when imprisonment is not imposed.

Paragraph 3(e) of Article 14 entitles a defendant to obtain witnesses on his behalf under the same conditions as witnesses against him have been obtained. United States law permits a defendant to obtain witnesses on his own behalf to the extent necessary for his defense; absent such a showing of necessity, the defendant is not entitled to compel the attendance and examination of witnesses. Thus, the United States conditioned its acceptance of this provision on an understanding that it does not prohibit a requirement that the defendant make a showing that any witness whose attendance he seeks to compel is necessary for his defense.

Finally, paragraph 7 of Article 14 prohibits an individual from being tried or punished again for an offense for which he or she has already been finally convicted or acquitted. The prohibition against double jeopardy is well-recognized in American jurisprudence. However, under the Constitution, the prohibition attaches only to multiple prosecutions by the same sovereign and does not prohibit trial of the same defendant for the same crime in, for example, state and federal courts or in the courts of two states. The United States, therefore, stated its understanding that the Covenant's prohibition upon double jeopardy applies only when the judgment of acquittal has been rendered by a court of the same governmental unit, whether the federal government or a constituent unit, that is seeking a new trial for the same offense.

   ....

5. Federalism

One of the most difficult problems for nonunitary states to resolve in considering human rights treaties, especially when the central government is one of limited or delegated powers, is to determine when and to what extent adherence to such a treaty may properly bind the constituent units. This is not a new problem by any means, but it remains a significant one.

By expressly extending the provisions of the Covenant to all parts of federal states, Article 50 exacerbates the problem. In light of the intent behind the article (it was included precisely to prevent federal states from limiting their obligations to areas within the federal government's authority), a reservation exempting constituent units might readily be characterized as contrary to the object and purpose of the Article, if not the Covenant as a whole.

In adhering to the Covenant, the United States followed the precedent it had earlier established with respect to the Torture Convention by indicating, in an admittedly somewhat convoluted understanding, that it will carry out its obligations under the Covenant in a manner consistent with the federal nature of its form of government. More precisely, the understanding states that the Covenant "shall be implemented by the Federal Government to the extent that it exercises legislative and judicial jurisdiction over the matters covered therein, and otherwise by the State and local governments." As to matters within the jurisdiction of state and local governments, "the Federal Government shall take measures appropriate to the Federal system" to ensure that the state and local governments fulfill their obligations.

It is important to note that this provision is not a reservation and was not intended to modify or limit U.S. obligations under the Covenant, but rather concerns the steps to be taken domestically by the respective federal and state authorities....

   ....

C. Declarations

1. Not Self-Executing

As a matter of domestic law, the United States declared Articles 1 through 27 of the Covenant to be "not self-executing." As in the case of the understanding concerning federalism, this declaration does not affect the international obligations of the United States under the Covenant. Rather, it means that the Covenant does not, by itself, create private rights enforceable in U.S. courts. That can be done only by means of legislation enacted by the Congress and the president in the ordinary course. This approach reflected the view that U.S. compliance with the Covenant should be overseen through the mechanisms established by the Covenant, rather than through litigation by private parties in U.S. courts....

....

3. Human Rights Committee

The United States has made a declaration under Article 41 accepting the competence of the Human Rights Committee (Committee) to receive and consider state-to-state complaints by and against the United States on a reciprocal basis, so long as the state making or receiving the complaint has done likewise. The United States intends to participate actively in the work of the Committee, in part because of the hope that the Committee can contribute even more to the development of a generally accepted international law of human rights.

....

4. International Law

The final declaration recorded the long-standing view of the United States that the inherent right of all peoples to enjoy and utilize their natural wealth and resources fully and freely, as recognized in Article 47, may only be exercised in accordance with international law. Nothing in the Covenant permits States Party to avoid their obligations under international law or justifies arbitrary deprivation of property.

The U.S. Congress Weighs In

Note

Concerned with human rights violations in the Soviet Union and its satellites as well as in Latin America and recognizing that the United Nations had not accomplished a great deal in the human rights area outside southern Africa and that the U.S. State Department was not inclined to push for vigorous UN action in the human rights area, the U.S. Congress, in the 1970s, decided to mandate action in this field. The standards on which it was prepared to rely were the standards set forth in the International Bill of Rights, but the United States was to see to it that violations of these standards would have consequences. The Congress of the United States thus put teeth into the International Bill of Rights. Thus, a generation after the adoption of the Charter of the United Nations, a new era began in the history of the cause of international human rights; an era in which the words of UN documents were translated into action.

The first measure in this field was adoption of the so-called Jackson-Vanik Amendment to the Trade Act of 1974. It was followed by a series of additional enactments that had the effect of requiring the State Department to make the advancement of international observance of human rights a major ingredient of U.S. foreign policy. (These statutes are here set forth in the form in which they were initially enacted. Some of them have since been amended or recodified.)

The Trade Act of 1974 (Jackson-Vanik Amendment)
19 U.S.C. § 2432(a)

Sec. 2432 — Freedom of emigration in East-West trade

(a) Actions of nonmarket economy countries making them ineligible for normal trade relations, programs of credits, credit guarantees, or investment guarantees, or commercial agreements

To assure the continued dedication of the United States to fundamental human rights, and notwithstanding any other provision of law, on or after January 3, 1975, products from any nonmarket economy country shall not be eligible to receive nondiscriminatory treatment (normal trade relations), such country shall not participate in any program of the Government of the United States which extends credits or credit guarantees or investment guarantees, directly or indirectly, and the President of the United States shall not conclude any commercial agreement with any such country, during the period beginning with the date on which the President determines that such country—

(1) denies its citizens the right or opportunity to emigrate;

(2) imposes more than a nominal tax on emigration or on the visas or other documents required for emigration, for any purpose or cause whatsoever; or

(3) imposes more than a nominal tax, levy, fine, fee, or other charge on any citizen as a consequence of the desire of such citizen to emigrate to the country of his choice,

and ending on the date on which the President determines that such country is no longer in violation of paragraph (1), (2), or (3).

Foreign Assistance Act of 1961, as amended
22 U.S.C. § 2151n

(a) No assistance may be provided under subchapter I of this chapter to the government of any country which engages in a consistent pattern of gross violations of internationally recognized human rights, including torture or cruel, inhuman, or degrading treatment or punishment, prolonged detention without charges, causing the disappearance of persons by the abduction and clandestine detention of those persons, or other flagrant denial of the right to life, liberty, and the security of person, unless such assistance will directly benefit the needy people in such country.

. . . .

(d) The Secretary of State shall transmit to the Speaker of the House of Representatives and the Committeeon Foreign Relations of the Senate, by January 31 of each year, a full and complete report regarding—

(1) the status of internationally recognized human rights, within the meaning of subsection (a) of this section—

(A) in countries that receive assistance under subchapter I of this chapter, and

(B) in all other foreign countries which are members of the United Nations and which are not otherwise the subject of a human rights report under this chapter; ...

22 U.S.C. § 2304

(1) The United States shall, in accordance with its international obligations as set forth in the Charter of the United Nations and in keeping with the constitutional heritage and traditions of the United States, promote and encourage increased respect for human rights and fundamental freedoms throughout the world without distinction as to race, sex, language, or religion. Accordingly, a principal goal of the foreign

policy of the United States shall be to promote the increased observance of internationally recognized human rights by all countries.

22 U.S.C. § 2384

(f)(1) There shall be in the Department of State an Assistant Secretary of State for Human Rights and Humanitarian Affairs who shall be responsible to the Secretary of State for matters pertaining to human rights and humanitarian affairs ... in the conduct of foreign policy....

(f)(2) The Assistant Secretary of State for Human Rights and Humanitarian Affairs shall maintain continuous observation and review of all matters pertaining to human rights and humanitarian affairs ... in the conduct of foreign policy....

Agricultural Trade Development and Assistance Act of 1954, as amended
7 U.S.C. § 1712

(a) No agreement may be entered into under this title to finance the sale of agricultural commodities to the government of any country which engages in a consistent pattern of gross violations of internationally recognized human rights, including torture, or degrading treatment or punishment, prolonged detention without charges, causing the disappearance of persons by the abduction and clandestine detention of such persons, or other flagrant denial of the right to life, liberty, and the security of person, unless such agreement will directly benefit the needy people in such country....

International Financial Institutions Act of 1977
22 U.S.C. § 262d

(a) The United States Government, in connection with its voice and vote in the International Bank for Reconstruction and Development, the International Development Association, the International Finance Corporation, the Inter-American Development Bank, the African Development Fund, and the Asian Development Bank, shall advance the cause of human rights, including by channeling assistance toward countries other than those whose governments engage in—

(1) a consistent pattern of gross violations of internationally recognized human rights, such as torture or cruel, inhumane or degrading treatment or punishment, prolonged detention without charges, or other flagrant denial to life, liberty, and the security of person; ...

Richard Schifter, *America's Commitment to Human Rights*
in XIII Morality and Expediency in International and Corporate Relations
42-54 (1992)

Though the United Nations record of action regarding human rights has been inconsistent and of only marginal effectiveness, the fact that it broke the diplomatic taboo against the consideration of human rights questions at the international level was, in itself, of major significance. After all, we could not argue that Zhivkov's Bulgaria denied its citizens First Amendment rights. Nor could we easily get into disputes over what protections the Bulgarian Constitution might provide. But we could contend that internationally recognized human rights now existed and could call attention to the fact that some countries acted in contravention of internationally recognized standard-setting documents.

Though we could indeed do so, for many years we rarely did.

... Many professional diplomats continued to consider it inappropriate to use the United Nations forums to criticize the behavior of the governments of member nations toward their own citizens. Only on some occasions, when heads of United States delegations to the United Nations Human Rights Commission, who would not be professional diplomats, insisted on speaking out on the subject of human rights violations, would the United States go on record on that subject.

The climate was, however, right for the United States to do more than speechmaking. The Kennedy and Johnson administrations, responding to United Nations sanctions resolutions, acted promptly to enforce an effective arms supply cutoff against South Africa.

A few years later, in 1974, the United States Congress went one step further: Deviating from the international pattern, it took on a country that was then untouchable in the United Nations system: the Soviet Union. As the Soviet Union had increasingly followed an anti-Israel policy internationally, the country's traditional anti-Semitism had come to the fore, reflected in discrimination in the fields of education and employment. Under these circumstances, more and more Soviet Jews became interested in leaving the Soviet Union. But emigration was at best difficult, at worst impossible. Many applicants were not only turned down but lost their jobs and other benefits.

Responding to this Soviet violation of international human rights standards, which did specify that anyone should be allowed to leave any country, including his own, Senator Henry Jackson decided to add teeth to our appeals to the Soviet Union to allow those who wished to leave the country to do so. As the Congress was in 1974 considering a new trade act, Senator Jackson proposed that Communist countries would be eligible for Most Favored Nation (MFN) status only if they made significant moves toward freedom of emigration. This statutory provision, which became know as the Jackson-Vanik Amendment, was enacted into law over the strong opposition of the State Department. It sent a message to the countries subject to this restriction on MFN status, making them understand very clearly that their emigration policy mattered to the United States. It played a key role in causing the Soviet Union to change its long-standing anti-emigration policy.

Following the Jackson-Vanik Amendment, the Congress enacted a number of laws that mandated economic measures against countries that engage in "a consistent pattern of gross violations of internationally recognized human rights." Such countries would not be eligible for U.S. economic assistance. Moreover, the United States would oppose development loans to such countries from international financial institutions.

In this time frame, the middle seventies, Congress enacted another law that initially appeared to be merely a reporting requirement but had a profound impact on U.S. diplomacy. It was the law requiring the State Department to furnish the Congress annually with a country-by-country report on human rights conditions worldwide. I believe that the authors of this law did not, at the time of enactment, know how profound an impact this new statutory requirement would have on the executive branch of the United States Government.

After the reporting requirement had become law, the State Department had to decide how to discharge this new responsibility. It concluded that the embassies in the countries in question would prepare the initial drafts of the country reports on human rights. As a result, the chief of mission of every United States diplomatic post abroad would appoint a human rights officer, whose task it would be to prepare the initial draft of the annual human rights report. Though the drafting exercise would take place once a year, the officer to whom the task was assigned would necessarily have to keep track of human rights problems throughout the year, observing developments relating to human rights as they occurred and noting them down. In countries in which information about human rights violations did not appear in the official media, the human rights officer of the embassy had to reach out to opposition elements as well as look for and read clandestine publications. United States embassies thus began to deviate from normal diplomatic custom in that prominent dissidents would visit these embassies or would regularly receive American diplomats as visitors. Our embassies would as a result be the best informed about human rights conditions in countries in which opposition elements were repressed.

Diplomats are used to reporting promptly on developments in the areas of their responsibility, and human rights officers were not exceptions to this general rule. Thus, once embassies had been staffed with human rights officers, a flow of messages started notifying Washington of human rights conditions in problem countries. These messages began, in the first instance, to inform the State Department of human rights problems. But they did more. The prevailing sentiment in our American culture is that where there is a problem there must also be a solution. Thus, once Washington became aware of the details of human rights violations, we began to think of ways of dealing with those issues. Congress had mandated certain economic sanctions if the violations were particularly serious. Even if they were not serious enough to require the imposition of sanctions, the question being considered was whether our embassy should be asked to make appropriate representations to the government in question or whether the United States Government should make a public statement expressing its concern. It was in that manner that human rights factors were gradually infused into United States foreign policy formulation.

Not long after enacting the requirement to produce annual reports, Congress took another step with significant bureaucratic implications. In 1977 it established the position of Assistant Secretary of State for Human Rights and Humanitarian Affairs. Responsibility to recommend appropriate action in the human rights area was thus given to an officer of the State Department with a rank sufficiently high to make it possible for human rights issues to be presented directly to the top leadership of the State Department.

I need to explain what this means in practical terms. When the State Department prepares a policy paper dealing with a particular country, the so-called regional bureau dealing with the country in question normally writes the paper, which is signed by the Assistant Secretary who heads that bureau. But if the policy recommendation has implications involving a subject for which a so-called functional bureau is responsible, the Assistant Secretary for that functional bureau must sign off on the memorandum. Thus, if the issue concerns economic affairs, the memorandum will be co-signed by the Assistant Secretary for Economic and Business Affairs. If it involves military matters, it will be co-signed by the Assistant Secretary for Politico-Military Affairs. And if the issue posed has human rights implications, it was now to be co-signed by the Assistant Secretary for Human Rights and Humanitarian Affairs. The result of this grant of authority is that the bureau that initiates the recommendation must either get the agreement of the bureaus that must be consulted for co-signature or present the Secretary of State with alternative recommendations.

The process just described may appear to be little more than one of bureaucratic routine. To be sure, it does involve such routine, but the process is of the utmost importance in policy formulation. It does not guarantee that human rights will at all times be the dominant factor when a policy decision is made, but it assures that the human rights perspective will be presented and considered.

It took time for this fundamental reorientation of United States foreign policy to take hold. Congress would on occasion push for more stringent action than the administration was prepared to espouse, but more often than not the two branches of government were in agreement about the policy line to be adopted. What was increasingly recognized was that mere pronouncements on human rights concerns, though emotionally satisfying, would advance the human rights cause only if they were part of a thought-through strategy designed to achieve results. Our goal, we have had to keep in mind, is to improve the lot of those who have been the victims of human rights violations, not just to make ourselves feel good about having denounced the violators. This requires in each instance a careful analysis of the problem, a determination of who is responsible and what that person's or group's motivation might be, and the development of a strategy to deal with the problem. In some cases a public pronouncement might fit into the strategy. In other instances quiet diplomacy is more likely to achieve the desired goal.

At roughly the same time that human rights concerns began to be systematically injected into the making of American foreign policy, an extraordinarily important development in the content and coverage of human rights standards began unfolding through the Helsinki Process.

In the early 1970s, most European countries as well as the United States and Canada came together in what became known as the Conference on Security and Cooperation in Europe (CSCE). The Soviets under Leonid Brezhnev considered the Conference a useful tool of detente. In the absence of a post-World War II peace treaty, they looked to the Conference to ratify the status quo regarding Europe's borders. As the discussions in this Conference proceeded, the West Europeans came up with the idea of adding human rights principles to the document that was to be signed. With security cooperation known as the first basket and economic cooperation as the second basket, human rights concerns came to be identified as the third basket. The United States, with Henry Kissinger serving as Secretary of State, was initially reluctant about the injection of human rights into the agenda but went along. The Soviet bloc, well aware of the fact that it had not been adversely affected by the human rights provisions contained in the Universal Declaration on Human Rights or by its ratification of the Covenant on Civil and Political Rights, had no problem agreeing to the inclusion of human rights provisions in the document. Therefore, on August 1, 1975, Gerald Ford, Leonid Brezhnev, Helmut Schmidt of the Federal Republic of Germany, Marshal Tito of Yugoslavia, Prime Minister Olof Palme of Sweden, and thirty other heads of state or government signed the Helsinki Final Act.

This document was well publicized in many participating countries, including the Soviet Union, where it was reproduced in full in the official press. Publication there had a totally unintended and unexpected result, namely that some Soviet citizens took the document seriously. They had noted that by signing the Helsinki Final Act the Soviet Union had agreed to abide by the Universal Declaration of Human Rights, which, after all, provided for free speech, a free press, and freedom of assembly, of association, and of religion. These people decided to form the Helsinki Monitoring Committees, groups of courageous men and women who set themselves the task of publicizing Soviet transgressions against the commitments entered into at Helsinki.

As I noted earlier, the Helsinki Final Act was signed on August 1, 1975. The Helsinki Monitoring Committees began to organize themselves in early 1976. The response of the Brezhnev regime was not instantaneous. It took about a year for the apparatus of repression to move into action; but when it did, it came down hard. Beginning in early 1977, Helsinki monitors were arrested. They were then charged with anti-Soviet agitation and propaganda and were invariably convicted and sentenced to seven years of confinement and five years of internal exile. Let us keep in mind that in the Soviet Union there was no provision for time off for good behavior, only add-ons for what was deemed bad behavior.

In spite of the arrest of their leaders, the Helsinki Monitoring Committees continued their work, encouraged and, in fact, inspired by the man who had sacrificed his status of privilege in the Soviet Union for the cause of freedom, Andrey Sakharov.

The KGB was relentless: There were more arrests, more convictions, and an increasing stream of prisoners going off to the Gulag. In 1980, Sakharov and his wife, Yelena Bonner, were forcibly exiled from Moscow to Gorkiy. By then the Helsinki movement in the Soviet Union had been crushed.

The Soviet Union's Helsinki Monitoring Committees had their counterpart in Czechoslovakia in the Charter 77 Movement. Czechoslovakia's secret police responded as the KGB had done, with arrests, but Czechoslovak prison sentences were for lesser periods, four years being the maximum. Charter 77 just kept going.

What did the other signatories of the Helsinki Final Act think about these violations of commitments solemnly entered into by the Soviet Union and other Communist countries? That answer came soon after the initial arrests in the Soviet Union had begun, but it was by no means a clear response. The Helsinki Final Act had provided that the participating states would meet from time to time to review the implementation of the Accords signed at Helsinki. The first such follow-up meeting convened in Belgrade in 1977. To head the United States delegation, President Jimmy Carter had reached outside the State Department and designated a former Justice of the United States Supreme Court and former Ambassador to the United Nations, Arthur Goldberg.

We were still in the period of detente and were trying to negotiate arms control agreements with the Soviet Union. The prevailing wisdom in the State Department was that while it was all right for the Assistant Secretary of State for Human Rights and Humanitarian Affairs to go after Latin American dictators, it was unwise to pursue East European dictators with equal fervor. It is to the everlasting credit of Justice Goldberg that he did not take kindly to that approach. He insisted that the United States would have to raise the Soviet Union's serious human rights violations at the Belgrade meeting and he prevailed. And so, for the first time ever, the Soviet Union found itself in Belgrade at the receiving end of a continuing barrage of pointed criticism of its human rights record.

That record was indeed fully exposed by the United States delegation. But the United States found itself alone. Its criticism of Soviet actions had shocked not only the delegations from Eastern Europe but those from Western Europe as well. By the time the meeting adjourned, the Soviet Union certainly understood that the United States had committed itself to the principle that its representatives would vigorously discuss human rights violations at the Helsinki Process meetings. There was no indication that anyone else would join.

The next follow-up meeting convened in Madrid three years later, in the fall of 1980. In the intervening period an event had occurred that had made a good many observers understand Soviet policies much better than they had before. It was the invasion of Afghanistan in December 1979. With detente a thing of the past, the State Department fully supported vigorous discussion of Soviet human rights performance in the Helsinki Process. The head of the United States delegation, Max Kampelman, deliberately and systematically went about the task of encouraging our allies to join in these discussions. He was successful. So, for a period of three years—for the Madrid meeting lasted that long—the human rights violations for which the Soviet Union and the other East European Communist dictatorships were responsible were discussed over and over again, in substantial detail.

This was a totally unprecedented and unexpected development. The Soviet Union had signed the Helsinki Accords in the belief that the agreement would confirm its geopolitical position and strengthen its efforts to weaken the West's military preparedness. It had agreed to the human rights provisions as a sop to the West, not thinking that they had any bite in them. Yet bite they did. Over a period of three years, West Europe's media reported on the Madrid meeting and, thus, on Soviet and other East European human rights violations. Unanimous consent was required before the meeting could be adjourned, thus allowing the West to keep the meeting going as long as that was found desirable. The Soviets realized that little would be accomplished by simply walking out on a particular session.

Note

As noted above, the Conference on Security and Cooperation in Europe was assumed by its principal advocate, the Soviet Union, to be a meeting that would ratify the status quo as to the borders established in Eastern and East-Central Europe in the wake of World War II. What few, if any, of the participants in the conference anticipated was the major importance that one brief section of the Helsinki Final Act would take on. That section has become known as Principle VII:

VII. Respect for human rights and fundamental freedoms, including the freedom of thought, conscience, religion or belief

The participating States will respect human rights and fundamental freedoms, including the freedom of thought, conscience, religion or belief, for all without distinction as to race, sex, language or religion.

They will promote and encourage the effective exercise of civil, political, economic, social, cultural and other rights and freedoms all of which derive from the inherent dignity of the human person and are essential for his free and full development.

Within this framework the participating States will recognize and respect the freedom of the individual to profess and practice, alone or in community with others, religion or belief acting in accordance with the dictates of his own conscience.

The participating States on whose territory national minorities exist will respect the right of persons belonging to such minorities to equality before the law, will afford them the full opportunity for the actual enjoyment of human rights and fundamental freedoms and will, in this manner, protect their legitimate interests in this sphere.

The participating States recognize the universal significance of human rights and fundamental freedoms, respect for which is an essential factor for the peace, justice and well-being necessary to ensure the development of friendly relations and co-operation among themselves as among all States.

They will constantly respect these rights and freedoms in their mutual relations and will endeavour jointly and separately, including in co-operation with the United Nations, to promote universal and effective respect for them.

They confirm the right of the individual to know and act upon his rights and duties in this field. In the field of human rights and fundamental freedoms, the participating States will act in conformity with the purposes and principles of the Charter of the United Nations and with the Universal Declaration of Human Rights.

They will also fulfill their obligations as set forth in the international declarations and agreements in this field, including inter alia the International Covenants on Human Rights, by which they may be bound.[16]

---

16. Final Act of the Conference on Security and Co-Operation in Europe, *done at* Helsinki, Aug. 1, 1975, 73 Dept. St. Bull. 323; 14 ILM 1292.

———————

The potential of the Helsinki Final Act to advance the cause of human rights was quickly recognized by a number of members of Congress, who drafted a law that established a congressional bicameral Commission on Security and Cooperation in Europe.[17] This law brought about the rather unusual injection of the Congress into the day-to-day management of an aspect of foreign affairs, namely the Helsinki Process, particularly its engagement in the field of human rights. The human rights laws enacted by the Congress from 1974 onward were thus joined by congressional engagement in the Helsinki Process, ushering in a new and unprecedented era of U.S. activity in support of the cause of human rights.

The new approach to international human rights was reflected in the speeches delivered by representatives of the United States in international human rights fora, such as the CSCE Conference in Madrid, which lasted from 1980 to 1983, and the United Nations Human Rights Commission, which meets annually in Geneva.

Max M. Kampelman, Three Years at the East-West Divide
39–41 (1983)

Statement at the CSCE Madrid Meeting by Max Kampelman on Helsinki Monitors

May 12, 1981 Helsinki Monitors

On May 12, 1976, five years ago today, in Moscow, nine citizens of the Soviet Union met to organize the Moscow Group to Promote Observance of the Helsinki Accords. Their intent was to express their strong support for the decisions made by their government and thirty-four other governments the previous year in Helsinki. They committed themselves to strengthen the Helsinki process by monitoring its observance.

Other men and women of courage soon joined this group. They and countless others in their country, in my country, and in all the countries of Europe looked upon the Helsinki Final Act as a new impulse in man's evolution toward a higher form of civilized international behavior. The CSCE offered a means to encourage peaceful, gradual evolution away from the roots of East-West confrontation.

These men and women in Moscow were not the only ones who saw it as their duty, as well as their right, to form Helsinki monitoring groups in their own country. Similar groups were formed in other parts of the Soviet Union, in the United States, and in many other countries. Americans were particularly pleased because of the early indications that the Soviet Union would at least tolerate the formation of those groups within its borders. This seemed to us to be a sign of maturity, a concrete indication that the "détente" which the Final Act set as a goal could, in fact, be achieved. We looked with favor upon the formation of these groups in the United States. I remind the delegates to this body that members of the Helsinki monitoring groups in the United States served as public members of the American delegation during the first phase of our Madrid meeting.

But this was not to be. This delegation and others have already expressed their deep and profound regret that the Helsinki monitors in the Soviet Union were not at all tolerated. Instead, they faced repression, exile, arrest, imprisonment and ostracism in their pursuit of that which they had a right to pursue under the Final Act. The power of the Soviet state has, in these past five years, been used to oppress these men and women of compassion rather than to protect their rights.

———————

17. *See* 22 U.S.C. § 3001 (2000).

The Moscow group was not the only Helsinki monitoring group to be formed and then forcibly harassed and persecuted in the Soviet Union. A Ukrainian group, a Lithuanian group, a Georgian group, an Armenian group, the Christian Committee for the Defense of Believers, the Working Commission on Psychiatric Abuse, the Group for the Legal Struggle of the Faithful and Free Seventh Day Adventists, the Catholic Committee for the Defense of Believers—were all formed. And those who joined them found themselves punished for their conviction that the commitments of the Helsinki Final Act were to be taken seriously. They have been told that their activities, in behalf of the observance by their government of the Helsinki Final Act, are considered by the authorities to be "anti-Soviet." There are now forty-seven Soviet Helsinki monitors from this group either in prison or in internal exile, a number of them tried and sentenced during our Madrid meeting.

Moscow monitor group members imprisoned today are Vladimir Slepak, Yuri Orlov, Anatoly Shcharansky, Viktor Nekipelov, Tatyana Osipova, Leonard Ternovsky, Malva Landa, and Feliks Serebrov; and they are serving a total of fifty-seven years of labor camp and exile sentences. Many other names have here been mentioned by us and by other delegations. And they are representative of endless numbers of other nameless men and women whose rights are being violated and whom our delegation today remembers as we mark the anniversary of the founding of the Helsinki monitoring group.

In Czechoslovakia, too, a group of individuals formed what became known as the Charter 77 Human Rights Movement to engage their government in peaceful dialogue about the fulfillment of its pledges to its people and to all of us under the Helsinki Final Act. During the convening of the Belgrade CSCE meeting in the fall of 1977, the world learned to its dismay that mass arrests of this Charter 77 group had taken place. We know that these arrests in no small measure adversely affected the atmosphere of that Belgrade meeting.

Now again we note with deep regret the arrest of former Foreign Minister Jiri Hajek and about thirty other Czechoslovakian supporters of the Charter 77 human rights movement in that country, persons of distinction and courage, now charged, we understand, with "subversion." We condemn with the utmost seriousness the arrests of these Helsinki monitors by Czechoslovakian authorities.

I do not know what message the Czechoslovak authorities are seeking to convey to all of us here with these arrests. It comes at a time when many delegations believe there is a sense of heightened commitment to end our meetings constructively. The news from Prague makes us wonder how real this is. It reminds us that there is a world outside our conference hall that must be taken into account during our deliberations.

The arrests are a tangible blow to the CSCE process. We call upon the Czechoslovak authorities to consider again carefully whether, with the mass arrests they have made, they are not denying their commitment to the CSCE process and their interest in the success of this meeting.

The government of the United States, Mr. Chairman, recognizes its obligation to those monitors who took the Helsinki Final Act seriously and have been imprisoned and otherwise seriously punished for doing so. We signed the Helsinki Final Act and earnestly undertook our commitments in the belief that the other signatory nations would do the same. We cannot permit the violations of that Act to escape unnoticed by us and to be free of our most serious condemnation.

We hope that those who act against Helsinki monitors come to recognize that they are acting against the Final Act, against security and cooperation in Europe. They construct new barriers of distrust between East and West. They make agreement here in Madrid more difficult. They convince us that ambiguous verbal formulae at Madrid will not be sufficient and require us to seek clear, meaningful words as well as action, if we are to end with the substantive, balanced results which we require.

Mr. Chairman, we use this occasion of the fifth anniversary of the forming of the Moscow Helsinki Watch Group to reaffirm our commitment to the Act; our friendship and deep respect for those citizens of the Soviet Union, Czechoslovakia and elsewhere who are being punished for believing in it; and our pledge that we will not cease to express our identification with them until such time as they are once again free to pursue their rights as human beings, rights recognized by the Helsinki Final Act.

Violation of Human Rights and Fundamental Proceedings of the U.N. Human Rights Comm.

38th Sess. (1982) (Statement of Richard Schifter), *reprinted in* 2 MICHAEL NOVAK & RICHARD SCHIFTER, RETHINKING HUMAN RIGHTS 33–40 (1983)

XI. Violation of Human Rights and Fundamental Freedoms in any Part of the World

STATEMENT BY RICHARD SCHIFTER

Mr. Chairman:

As most of the delegates to this commission are aware, the United States Department of State, under provisions of law enacted by the Congress, prepares annually a report on the state of human rights throughout the world.

There are those who might think at first blush that there is an element of arrogance in one country's systematic effort to assess and judge human rights conditions in all others. We would hope, Mr. Chairman, that upon deeper analysis it will be recognized that our human rights reports reflect the genuine concern of the people of our country, of our average citizens, with the life and well-being of their fellow-men, wherever they may be. Americans genuinely and deeply believe that when the bell tolls it tolls for all of us. That belief, Mr. Chairman, underlies the act of Congress which prescribes the preparation of what have come to be known as the "country reports."

There is a close affinity between the outlook which led to preparation of the Country Reports and that which underlies the creation of this Commission and the approval of the Universal Declaration of Human Rights. The common bond is the recognition that there are some basic rights which every human being possesses and of which no government should rightfully deprive him or her. By defining internationally accepted standards of human rights, the Declaration bases itself, to paraphrase John Donne once more, on the proposition that no country is an island, entire by itself.

Does that mean that the Declaration and our activities as a Commission interfere with the domestic affairs of individual countries? To answer that question, Mr. Chairman, let us reflect on precisely what it is that we do. We pass resolutions concerning the behavior of certain countries with regard to their internal affairs. Our resolutions comment on the lack of observance of certain human rights by certain governments. When we decry apartheid we do indeed decry a domestic law. When we pronounce ourselves against religious intolerance, torture, mass arrests, or detention without trial, we are passing judgment on a country's actions toward its own citizens.

The Commission does not intervene, Mr. Chairman, in domestic affairs. We comment, in the hope that we can persuade countries to take our collective concerns to heart and effect improvements in the human condition.

What we should, of course, keep in mind is that approval of a resolution in this Commission or in any other international forum is not the ultimate goal. The ultimate goal is to help victims of human rights violations. The determination which we have to make is whether action of a particular resolution brings us nearer to that goal. It is for that reason, to accomplish results rather than merely engage in a public relations effort, that my country uses bilateral contacts and quiet diplomacy, wherever it can, to effect improvements in human rights conditions. Only when that mode of operation is unavailable or unlikely to produce useful results do we consider a public effort to constitute the right approach.

It is in this context, Mr. Chairman, that we enter the debate under agenda Item 12, Consideration of Human Rights Violations Anywhere in the World. As I indicated earlier, we are already on record on this subject. Our most recent assessment of human rights conditions in all countries, from Afghanistan to Zimbabwe was transmitted to the Congress on January 19, 1982. The volume of reports, 1142 pages in all, is now publicly available. It includes, in detail, our views of the state of human rights in each of the countries which has been expressly named for discussion under this agenda item: El Salvador, Guatemala, and the others.

What, then, can appropriately be added in this presentation? My delegation, Mr. Chairman, has concluded that those situations deserve singling out which either constitute long-standing egregious violations of human rights to which the Commission has failed to pay adequate attention in the past or those which reflect recent deteriorations in human rights conditions.

As we are all well aware, Mr. Chairman, one of this Commission's traditions, a tradition to which we have objected, is to focus its attention on the human rights problems of Latin America. We are not suggesting that there are no such problems in the region. There certainly are. What we have objected to is that a different yardstick has been applied to an analysis of conditions in that region than has been applied to the analyses of conditions in other regions of the world. It is worthy of note that all four countries which have been named for public debate under agenda Items 5 and 12 are Latin American.

Yet omitted from all debate of human rights conditions in Latin America is the region's only totalitarian tyranny, a repressive state where all individual rights are closely controlled by the communist party, where there exist no free press and freedom of speech, and where dissent and opposition are not permitted.

The thought control system instituted in Cuba, Mr. Chairman, in violation of Articles 12 and 19 of the Universal Declaration, as well as other internationally recognized human rights standards, is one of the most all-pervasive in the world.

Also, in violation of Article 12, section 2, of the Universal Declaration, Cuba generally refuses its people the right to leave the country. When the door opened a tiny crack, 125,000 slipped through in 1980. An estimated additional half million have applied to emigrate and perhaps 1 to 2 million more would be prepared to leave if given the chance to do so.

Cuba, Mr. Chairman, has a disproportionate number of people particularly creative in the arts and humanities. Before the Castro regime smothered artistic expression, Cuban writers were able to experiment with language and narrative structure free of the restraints of Soviet-style "socialist realism." But the efforts of talented Cuban writers such as the poet Herberto Padilla, the dramatist Anton Arrufat, and the short story writer Norberto Fuentes were not allowed to go unchallenged for long. The regime began what they called a "cleansing" of Cuban cultural life in the late 1960's. Trials for "ideological deviation" became frequent in the 1970's. The campaign to terrorize the intellectual community culminated in the arrest, show trial, and forced recantation of Herberto Padilla. As Padilla put it after he finally was able to leave Cuba: "During the last twenty years, I have lived in frightening laboratories of social experimentation, space walled by test tubes where the same experiment always ended with the same chemical result: tyranny."

The Stalinist character of Cuba's tyranny is underlined by the absence of what in the Soviet Union is referred to as samizdat or self-publication. Because unauthorized publication or even the possession of unauthorized publications is so severely punished, works not published by the state are not reproduced and circulated except in the most intimate circles of friends. One of the most tragic cases of repression involves Virgillo Pinera, the most highly proclaimed Cuban playwright of this century. Pinera was dismissed from his last post in 1971 for failure to conform to the 'parameters, for political culture. He was reduced to living under miserable conditions and kept under surveillance until his death in 1979. Unable to publish his works, he continued to write and seems to have left a substantial number of plays and poems. The world will remain unaware of his work, however, since all his manuscripts were confiscated by the state upon his death.

Let me add one more case, that of the internationally celebrated poet Angel Cuadra, whose works have been translated into English, Russian and German. For the offense of seeking permission to leave Cuba he was charged with conduct "against the security of the state." He was jailed from 1967 to 1976, when he was released on parole. However, after an anthology of his apolitical poems was published in the United States, his parole was revoked and he was sent to a prison "rehabilitation" program. Released again in 1979, he was rearrested for the crime of having sent a manuscript of his poems out of the country. He is still in jail.

Not only poets are held in Castro's prison. Today, 23 years after the revolution, Cuba continues to hold as many as 1000 political prisoners. As the Inter-American Human Rights Commission notes, in its 1979 report on Cuba, the exact figure is not known since international human rights organizations have not been allowed to conduct investigatory visits to Cuba.

There is one last point which I want to make on the subject of Cuba. There are those who say that following a revolution one needs to concentrate first on economic rights and only later on political rights. I have shown, Mr. Chairman, that in today's Cuba political rights are among the lowest in the whole world, 23 years after Castro came to power. But at the same time the country's economy has declined to the point where 25 percent of its gross national product consists of foreign aid, paid for by the workers and farmers of the Soviet Union. That, Mr. Chairman, is the record of Cuba, the country that imprisons its poets.

Mr. Chairman, I shall now turn to another human rights problem in our hemisphere, a problem of utmost seriousness, a problem which has worsened in recent months and weeks, yet one on which the world community has been strangely silent. I am referring to events in the Department of Zelaya, the eastern half of Nicaragua.

Zelaya, Mr. Chairman, was once a British possession. It was ceded to Nicaragua in 1894. Though it constitutes more than half of Nicaragua's territory, it contains only about 10 percent of the country's population consisting of about 100,000 Indians, mostly Miskitos, with the balance Creoles.

Having been left alone for many years, the residents of the Department of Zelaya maintained their own traditions and their own institutions. Social services in the area, including schools and hospitals were provided largely by the Moravian and Catholic churches.

All of this changed with the arrival of the Sandinistas. With the same eagerness that may have characterized colonial rulers of a different era, they have set about to bring their own brand of civilization to Zelaya. And they have run into the same kind of resistance.

The natives of Zelaya have their own traditions, their own institutions and their own pride. They have rejected the way of life that was now to be forced on them.

At the outset, in 1979, the differences between the Sandinistas and the natives of Zelaya, most particularly the Miskitos, would only occasionally result in violent confrontations. However, as the representatives of Managua increased their efforts to dismantle local institutions, destroy the structure of local communities, and replace recognized community leaders, resistance became stronger. As resistance increased, so did repression by the Sandinistas. But repression resulted in even greater resistance, which, in turn, led to violent government retribution in recent months. We have received word that Miskito villages have been bombed. Many of them have been burned to the ground. Hundreds of Miskitos have been detained and many have been killed. According to one report, the badly wounded were buried alive, with the dead, following an encounter with the Sandinista military. Thousands of Miskitos have fled to Honduras. As recently as December 1981, there were altogether 200 Miskito refugees in Honduras. Today, we are told by the High Commissioner for Refugees, there are 12,000. A total of 12,000 persons have been displaced.

Mr. Chairman, the Miskitos will undoubtedly be accused of being counter-revolutionaries, agents of the dead President Somoza. But any member of this Commission familiar with the problems of colonialism will recognize the pattern and will understand the importance of protecting an indigenous people from the efforts of outsiders to remake them in the image of these outsiders, against its own will. I submit to you, Mr. Chairman, that the Miskitos need the help of this Commission and they need it now.

I shall now turn to a discussion of recent developments in the field of human rights on another continent, the continent of Asia.

The specific situation to which I want to refer you is that of the Hmong, the largest of the highland peoples of Laos. More than 100,000 Hmong and other highlanders have been forced to flee to Thailand. Since 1976, Mr. Chairman, Hmong refugees have reported attacks on their communities in which the attackers use "rain," "gas," or "smoke." Those attacked suffer vomiting, bloody diarrhea, fever, nose bleeding and dizziness. Many Hmong have died as a result of these attacks.

Since 1981 new evidence in the form of organic samples containing unnaturally large concentrations of highly lethal mycotoxin poisons turned up from Laos, as well as Kampuchea, lending further weight to the probability that chemical and biological weapons are being used in Laos against the Hmong. The Laos Government, I regret to say, has thus far refused to cooperate with international efforts to investigate the situation which has given rise to these reports.

And now to turn to Europe: Last year, Mr. Chairman, speaking in this chamber, I called attention to the harsh measure taken by the Government of Czechoslovakia against the Charter 77 Movement, a movement whose only purpose has been to persuade the Czechoslovak Government to abide by its international commitments to respect human rights. Regrettably, in the year which has passed, the Czechoslovak authorities have stepped up their repressive measures, focusing their attention exclusively on human rights activists.

Last May, Mr. Chairman, 26 human rights activists were arrested in the Czechoslovak cities of Prague, Brno and Bratislava. Sixteen of them have been charged with large-scale subversion of the Republic. One of the leading defendants is Jirina Siklova, a sociologist. The charges against her are that she assembled and distributed on a large scale documents directed against the government. Mme. Siklova's co-defendants are mostly writers, poets, journalists and scholars. Their major offense appears to be that their works, most of them nonpolitical, have been published abroad.

It is the nature of the act which leads to a criminal indictment in a country like Czechoslovakia that deserves this Commission's attention, Mr. Chairman.

In many countries subversion means engaging in acts designed to overthrow the government by force and violence. It can also mean engaging in a conspiracy to commit such acts. But in Czechoslovakia, Mr. Chairman, it is subversion of the Republic when one exercises one's rights to freedom of opinion and expression, one's right to express one's opinions peacefully as guaranteed in Article 19 of the Universal Declaration.

Mr. Chairman, the continuing repressive measures by the Government of Czechoslovakia against the peaceful human rights activists who have formed the Charter 77 Movement represents another issue which deserves the attention of this Commission.

The Charter 77 Movement is a movement of intellectuals, students and some workers. In a neighboring country, on the other hand, the call for human rights came from a movement consisting almost entirely of workers.

It may turn out to be one of the great ironies of history, Mr. Chairman, that the first truly massive spontaneous movement of workers, as envisaged by Karl Marx, a movement without a Lenin or Trotsky, without an intellectual leadership group, the first such movement to ask for a change in the existing order, albeit for peaceful change, arose in a state which calls itself Marxist. And it has been repressed by what Milovan Djilas has called the new class, the bureaucratic apparatus which prescribes the do's and don'ts of the countries that adhere to Leninist Doctrine.

There is discussion in the corridors, Mr. Chairman, that the events of December 13, 1981, in Poland are no different from military take-overs in numerous other places throughout the world. "Why pick on the Poles?" is Moscow's message. If Poland is the subject of a resolution today, delegates are told, a great many other countries similarly situated might be the subject of Commission resolutions tomorrow.

The point I wish to make, Mr. Chairman, is that the situation in Poland is unique, on two grounds. First, military take-overs throughout the world have usually been precipitated by a break-down of law and order, by a threat to the existing social fabric from an armed minority or by the total failure of civilian government. None of these preconditions existed in Poland. What happened there was that a genuine people's organization formed itself not stimulated by political leaders, by writers or poets or persons in the academic professions. It was an organization which came straight out of the factories, the mines, as well as from the farms of the country. They came in peace, with an outstretched hand of friendship, and asked, in peace, for freedom for the right to help shape their own destiny. They spoke their mind and they wrote down their thoughts and they put together an organization of their own, Solidarnosc, with a membership of ten million people. They carried no arms. They planted no bombs. To put it in terms of our basic document, they exercised their rights under Articles 19 and 29 of the Universal Declaration.

The Government of Poland was not threatened by Solidarnosc, Mr. Chairman, not on December 13, 1981, and not at any time prior to that date. Solidarnosc, an organization led by honorable, decent men did nothing other than try to negotiate in peace for a better life for the Polish people. That activity alone was the reason for the crack-down, for the massive violations of human rights that occurred on December 13 and thereafter, the mass arrests, the imposition of martial law, the meting out of 10-year prison sentences to people who did nothing other than distribute leaflets.

Mr. Chairman. Historians may have to search far and wide to find a precedent for an action similar to that of General Jaruzelski on December 13, 1981. The head of government, of the military, and the country's ruling political party, backed by the army and the security force, by tanks, trucks, and planes had to declare a state of war to face down a totally unarmed movement of working men and women who asked for no more than a place in the sun.

In demonstrating that there was no real domestic threat to the Jaruzelski Government I have explained one point of difference between the Polish situation and that of other martial-law situations. But there would still remain some questions. If there was no real threat, why did General Jaruzelski declare a state of war in a totally peaceful setting? Why did he arrest the entire Solidarnosc leadership, who had peacefully assembled for a conference? Why did he order the detention of tens of thousands of Polish citizens? To answer these questions, I must get to the second point of difference: There was indeed a threat, but it did not come from Solidarnosc. General Jaruzelski moved as he did, Mr. Chairman, because it was made clear to him that if he did not do it, the Soviet Union would do it for him. In the parlance of this Commission, this is known as deprivation of the human right of self-determination.

For all the reasons I have stated, Mr. Chairman, Poland, too, should be on this Commission's agenda.

Let me conclude, Mr. Chairman, with a few remarks about a great man whom we mentioned earlier in this session as we did last year and the year before. It is not often in the history of the human race that a brilliant mind such as that of Andrei Sakharov comes along and the Russian people should be proud to have produced this man, who is capable of engaging in exploration along the frontiers of science. What a loss it is to all of us that another year has passed in which Dr. Sakharov's ability to function as a scientist has been severely restricted, another year in which his mind has been distracted by petty harassment, a year in which he found it necessary to engage in a hunger strike to help a person close to his family. Once again, Mr. Chairman, we urge consideration of Dr. Sakharov's case by this Commission. We urge that the Soviet Union be called upon to reverse Dr. Sakharov's banishment to Gorki, an action taken in violation of Article 13, section 1 of the Universal Declaration.

Mr. Chairman. As I stated at the beginning, my delegation did not think it would be able to cover in this statement all or most of the human rights violations in the world. If it is noted that we have concentrated on violations committed by a particular group of states, let me ask you to refer back to my initial remarks, in which I laid out the principles which guide my country's policy on human rights. I think you will agree with me that some of the situations to which we have referred are situations not frequently mentioned, yet are situations which deserve study. Let me also, at this point, reemphasize that we are concerned with *all* human rights violations, those which I have expressly mentioned and those not mentioned in this statement, in every part of the world.

Permit me also, at this point, to anticipate once again the statements that will be offered in the exercise of rights of reply. Let me note that in our dictionary an observation which is an unpleasant truth does not constitute slander. Let me further note that name-calling is not a convincing response to a charge which recites facts. Let me add that we would most assuredly welcome reasoned replies and civilized dialogue.

Note

In his history of the CSCE process, *The Promises We Keep*, William Korey reports on a "private conversation among Western diplomats at Helsinki several hours after the solemn signing ceremonies testifies to the uncertainty of how Helsinki would be viewed in history. As recorded by an American participant, one said: 'Well, they signed it.' Another said: 'And now it will be buried and forgotten.' 'No,' responded a colleague, 'you are wrong. We have started something.' "[18]

Embedded in the Helsinki Final Act was a provision for follow-up conferences "to continue the multilateral process initiated by the Conference … by proceeding to a thorough exchange of views both on the implementation of the provisions of the Final Act and of the tasks defined by the Conference."[19] The first two follow-up conferences, in Belgrade and Madrid, particularly that at Madrid, marked a turning point in U.S. policy that proved critically important for developments in Eastern Europe. The speech of Max Kampelman set out above was only one of a series of such speeches. As Korey noted:

> The repeated, continuous and precise recitation of examples of repression during the Madrid session held violators of human rights up to public scorn and contempt. Extensive media coverage, especially by the European press, and the almost daily broadcasts into Eastern Europe by Western transmitters, especially Radio Free Europe (even if jammed), magnified the negative image.

> The impact on public opinion in Europe during the three-year Madrid session cannot be underestimated.... [20]

The Madrid session adjourned in 1983 and agreed that the next session would take place in Vienna, beginning in 1986. In the interim, Mikhail Gorbachev had become the Soviet Union's new leader. In his *Memoirs*, he refers to his intention regarding the Vienna meeting: "It was our aim to fill all three 'Helsinki' baskets with fresh and useful fruits."[21] His Foreign Minister, Eduard Shevardnadze, had this to say about the Vienna meeting:

The pan-European meeting in Vienna, which concluded in January 1989, was a watershed. Europe had never known such a dialog—intense, at times dramatic, but purposeful and democratic in a way that was without precedent. The Vienna agreements were a major step in the development of the common European process, raising the continent to a new level of security and cooperation. The meeting was a turning point not only for Europe, however. Our continent is not an island. The process begun in Helsinki has become central to East-West relations. Through the United States and Canada, our multilevel dialog and versatile collaboration have entered the New World, and crossed the Urals into Asia.[22]

A Clash of Civilizations?

Samuel Huntington, *The Clash of Civilizations*

72 FOREIGN AFF. 22 (Summer 1993)

THE NEXT PATTERN OF CONFLICT

World politics is entering a new phase …

....

---

18. WILLIAM KOREY, THE PROMISES WE KEEP 2 (1993).
19. *Id.*
20. *Id.* at xxvi–xxvii.
21. MIKHAIL GORBACHEV, MEMOIRS 431 (1997).
22. EDUARD SHEVARDNADZE, THE FUTURE BELONGS TO FREEDOM 129 (1991).

It is my hypothesis that the fundamental source of conflict in this new world will not be primarily ideological or primarily economic.

. . . .

Conflict between civilizations will be the latest phase in the evolution of conflict in the modern world.

. . . .

What do we mean when we talk of a civilization? A civilization is a cultural entity. Villages, regions, ethnic groups, nationalities, religious groups, all have distinct cultures at different levels of cultural heterogeneity. The culture of a village in southern Italy may be different from that of a village in northern Italy, but both will share in a common Italian culture that distinguishes them from German villages. European communities, in turn, will share cultural features that distinguish them from Arab or Chinese communities. Arabs, Chinese and Westerners, however, are not part of any broader cultural entity. They constitute civilizations. A civilization is thus the highest cultural grouping of people and the broadest level of cultural identity people have short of that which distinguishes humans from other species. It is defined both by common objective elements, such as language, history, religion, customs, institutions, and by the subjective self-identification of people. People have levels of identity: a resident of Rome may define himself with varying degrees of intensity as a Roman, an Italian, a Catholic, a Christian, a European, a Westerner. The civilization to which he belongs is the broadest level of identification with which he intensely identifies. People can and do redefine their identities and, as a result, the composition and boundaries of civilizations change. Civilizations may involve a large number of people, as with China ("a civilization pretending to be a state," as Lucian Pye put it), or a very small number of people, such as the Anglophone Caribbean. A civilization may include several nation states, as is the case with Western, Latin American and Arab civilizations, or only one, as is the case with Japanese civilization. Civilizations obviously blend and overlap, and may include subcivilizations. Western civilization has two major variants, European and North American, and Islam has its Arab, Turkic and Malay subdivisions. Civilizations are nonetheless meaningful entities, and while the lines between them are seldom sharp, they are real. Civilizations are dynamic; they rise and fall; they divide and merge. And, as any student of history knows, civilizations disappear and are buried in the sands of time.

. . . .

Civilization identity will be increasingly important in the future, and the world will be shaped in large measure by the interactions among seven or eight major civilizations. These include Western, Confucian, Japanese, Islamic, Hindu, Slavic-Orthodox, Latin American and possibly African civilization. The most important conflicts of the future will occur along the cultural fault lines separating these civilizations from one another.

. . . .

THE WEST VERSUS THE REST

The West is now at an extraordinary peak of power in relation to other civilizations. Its superpower opponent has disappeared from the map. Military conflict among Western states is unthinkable, and Western military power is unrivaled. Apart from Japan, the West faces no economic challenge. It dominates international political and security institutions and with Japan international economic institutions. Global political and security issues are effectively settled by a directorate of the United States, Britain and France, world economic issues by a directorate of the United States, Germany and Japan, all of which maintain extraordinarily close relations with each other to the exclusion of lesser and largely non-Western countries. Decisions made at the U.N. Security Council or in the International Monetary Fund that reflect the interests of the West are presented to the world as reflecting the desires of the world community. The very phrase "the world community" has become the euphemistic collective noun (replacing "the Free World") to give global legitimacy to actions reflecting the interests of the United States and other Western powers. Through the IMF and other international economic institutions, the West promotes its economic interests and imposes on other nations the economic policies it thinks appropriate. In any poll of non-Western peoples, the IMF undoubtedly would win the support of finance ministers and a few others, but get an overwhelmingly unfavorable rating from just about everyone else, who would agree with Georgy Arbatov's characterization of IMF officials as "neo-Bolsheviks who love expropriating other people's money, imposing undemocratic and alien rules of economic and political conduct and stifling economic freedom."

Western domination of the U.N. Security Council and its decisions, tempered only by occasional abstention by China, produced U.N. legitimation of the West's use of force to drive Iraq out of Kuwait and its elimination of Iraq's sophisticated weapons and capacity to produce such weapons. It also produced the quite unprecedented action by the United States, Britain and France in getting the Security Council to demand that Libya hand over the Pan Am 103 bombing suspects and then to impose sanctions when Libya refused. After defeating the largest Arab army, the West did not hesitate to throw its weight around in the Arab world. The West in effect is using international institutions, military power and economic resources to run the world in ways that will maintain Western predominance, protect Western interests and promote Western political and economic values.

That at least is the way in which non-Westerners see the new world, and there is a significant element of truth in their view. Differences in power and struggles for military, economic and institutional power are thus one source of conflict between the West and other civilizations. Differences in culture, that is basic values and beliefs, are a second source of conflict. V. S. Naipaul has argued that Western civilization is the "universal civilization" that "fits all men." At a superficial level much of Western culture has indeed permeated the rest of the world. At a more basic level, however, Western concepts differ fundamentally from those prevalent in other civilizations. Western ideas of individualism, liberalism, constitutionalism, human rights, equality, liberty, the rule of law, democracy, free markets, the separation of church and state, often have little resonance in Islamic, Confucian, Japanese, Hindu, Buddhist or Orthodox cultures. Western efforts to propagate such ideas produce instead a reaction against "human rights imperialism" and a reaffirmation of indigenous values, as can be seen in the support for religious fundamentalism by the younger generation in non-Western cultures. The very notion that there could be a "universal civilization" is a Western idea, directly at odds with the particularism of most Asian societies and their emphasis on what distinguishes one people from another. Indeed, the author of a review of 100 comparative studies of values in different societies concluded that "the values that are most important in the West are least important worldwide." In the political realm, of course, these differences are most manifest in the efforts of the United States and other Western powers to induce other peoples to adopt Western ideas concerning democracy and human rights. Modern democratic government originated in the West. When it has developed in non-Western societies it has usually been the product of Western colonialism or imposition.

The central axis of world politics in the future is likely to be, in Kishore Mahbubani's phrase, the conflict between "the West and the Rest" and the responses of non-Western civilizations to Western power and values. Those responses generally take one or a combination of three forms. At one extreme, non-Western states can, like Burma and North Korea, attempt to pursue a course of isolation, to insulate their societies from penetration or "corruption" by the West, and, in effect, to opt out of participation in the Western-dominated global community. The costs of this course, however, are high, and few states have pursued it exclusively. A second alternative, the equivalent of "bandwagoning" in international relations theory, is to attempt to join the West and accept its values and institutions. The third alternative is to attempt to "balance" the West by developing economic and military power and cooperating with other non-Western societies against the West, while preserving indigenous values and institutions; in short, to modernize but not to Westernize.

....

THE CONFUCIAN-ISLAMIC CONNECTION

The obstacles to non-Western countries joining the West vary considerably. They are least for Latin American and East European countries. They are greater for the Orthodox countries of the former Soviet Union. They are still greater for Muslim, Confucian, Hindu and Buddhist societies. Japan has established a unique position for itself as an associate member of the West: it is in the West in some respects but clearly not of the West in important dimensions. Those countries that for reason of culture and power do not wish to, or cannot, join the West compete with the West by developing their own economic, military and political power. They do this by promoting their internal development and by cooperating with other non-Western countries. The most prominent form of this cooperation is the Confucian-Islamic connection that has emerged to challenge Western interests, values and power.

Note

In his subsequent book, *The Clash of Civilizations and the Remaking of World Order* (1996), Huntington reemphasized his thesis that democracy, the rule of law, and respect for the rights of the individual are unique attributes of Western civilization and contends that any effort to transmit these precepts to other civilizations is "misguided, arrogant, false, and dangerous." He has identified the other civilizations as consisting of Latin America, the Christian Orthodox world, and Japanese, Muslim, Confucian, Hindu, and Buddhist societies.

Freedom House, which since the early Nineteen Seventies has rated countries regarding their performance in observing human rights lists ten Latin American countries, namely Argentina, Bolivia, Chile, Costa Rica, Dominican Republic, El Salvador, Mexico, Panama, Peru, and Uruguay as "free." Eight are "partly free" and only one, Cuba, is "not free." Three predominantly Christian Orthodox countries, Bulgaria, Greece, and Romania, are "free." Most others, including Russia, Ukraine, Armenia, and Georgia, are "partly free." One Christian Orthodox country, Belarus, is "not free." Japan is "free." India, the world's largest democracy, is "free." Predominantly Buddhist countries, such as Mongolia and Thailand, are "free." In "not free" predominantly Buddhist countries such as Laos and Vietnam, Buddhist monks are in the forefront of the fight for respect for human rights, struggling against the remnants of Leninism, as is the Dalai Lama. While China, too, moves only slowly away from its Communist moorings, Taiwan, a truly Confucian country, is now classified as "free." Freedom House does not rate any Islamic country free, but Azerbaijan, Bangladesh, Djibouti, Indonesia, Jordan, Kuwait, Malaysia, Mauritania, and Morocco, are rated "partly free."

Heiner Bielefeldt, *Muslim Voices in the Human Rights Debate*

17 HUM. RTS. Q. 587, 587–617 (1995)

Human rights constitute political and legal standards. That is, they require political and legal implementation through national, regional, and international institutions including, if possible, effective monitoring mechanisms. I would like to emphasize this political and legal aspect of human rights, in order to make sure that their scope is *limited*. Unlike Islam and other religions, which claim to shape the whole lives of their adherents, human rights do not represent an all-encompassing "weltanschauung" or way of life, nor do they provide a yardstick by which to evaluate cultures and religions in general. Human rights are not necessarily the highest manifestation of ethical spirit in human history either, because they are not intended to replace, for instance, Christian demands of love, Islamic solidarity, or the Buddhist ethic of compassion. Rather, they concentrate on political justice by setting up some basic normative standards.

. . . .

The following paragraphs present some Islamic positions in the human rights debate. The distinctions between conservative, liberal, and pragmatic approaches relied on in the following paragraphs are not meant to provide an adequate structure that can do justice to the complexity of the discourse and to the individual positions within it; rather, they are only a rough way of bringing some order to the analysis.

. . . .

When the General Assembly of the United Nations had to decide on the Universal Declaration on Human Rights, in 1948, the Saudi Arabian ambassador strongly objected to religious liberty, particularly to the right to change one's religion, a right explicitly mentioned in Article 18. Saudi Arabia eventually joined South Africa and six communist states and abstained from the vote; no state rejected the declaration outright. Saudi Arabia's abstention reflects the reluctance of a conservative Islamic government to endorse the emancipatory concept of human rights, a concept that is perceived to be alien and detrimental to the Islamic tradition.

Meanwhile, different conservative approaches have arisen. Instead of rejecting human rights altogether, the emphasis is more on redefining these rights in an exclusively Islamic framework. A prominent representative of this tendency is the Pakistani author Abu l-A'la Mawdudi, an influential source of inspiration for Pakistani and international fundamentalist movements. In his book, *Human Rights in Islam*, Mawdudi blames the West for claiming human rights to be an exclusively Occidental heritage. He writes: "The people in the west have the habit of attributing every good thing to themselves and try to prove that it is because of them that the world got this blessing, otherwise the world was steeped in ignorance and completely unaware of all these benefits." This polemical criticism might be partly justified because Western arrogance often has presented an obstacle to cross-cultural discourse. Nevertheless, Mawdudi's approach deserves a similar critique, because he merely harmonizes human rights with the traditional sha'ria without addressing the possible tensions and conflicts between the two. In his view, human rights thus merely form an inherent part of the Islamic tradition.

. . . .

Some international Islamic statements on human rights also reflect this conservative disposition. This holds true for both the "Universal Islamic Declaration of Human Rights," issued by the Islamic Council for Europe in 1981, and the "Cairo Declaration on Human Rights in Islam," adopted by the Organization of the Islamic Conference in August 1990.

While the Islamic Council for Europe is a nongovernmental organization whose statements are by no means binding, the Organization of the Islamic Conference brings together representatives of the Islamic states. Hence the Cairo Declaration, albeit not legally binding, does carry some political authority.

Like Mawdudi, the authors of the Cairo Declaration seem to integrate the language of human rights into the preexisting framework of the sha'ria in such a way that the latter never is questioned critically. On the contrary, the sha'ria acts as the exclusive yardstick used to determine the scope and content of human rights. The concluding Article 25 emphasizes: "The Islamic sha'ria is the only source of reference for the explanation or clarification of any of the articles of this Declaration."

Despite the fact that Article 1 affirms the equal dignity of all human beings, "without any discrimination on the grounds of race, colour, language, sex, religious belief, political affiliation, social status or other considerations," differences in terms of basic rights continue to exist. Thus, Article 6 apparently presupposes the traditional understanding of gender relations, including the predominant role of the husband as head of the family. Article 6 states: "Woman is equal to man in human dignity, and has rights to enjoy as well as duties to perform; she has her own civil entity and financial independence, and the right to retain her name and lineage. The husband is responsible for the support and welfare of the family." Equality in dignity, which is asserted in the declaration, apparently does not amount to equal rights for women and men, as they are claimed by Muslim feminists today with reference to international standards of human rights.

Although the Cairo Declaration does not explicitly mention traditional hadd-punishments, it is revealing that Article 2, which deals with the right to life, makes a caveat on behalf of the sha'ria saying that "it is prohibited to take away life except for a sha'ria prescribed reason." The same caveat applies to "safety from bodily harm" which also is granted only by allowing exceptions on a "sha'ria prescribed reason." In any case, the legitimacy of corporal punishment is not challenged critically and might even receive reinforcement from the Cairo Declaration.

Article 5, which deals with marriage and family matters, states: "Men and women have the right to marriage, and no restrictions stemming from race, colour or nationality shall prevent them from enjoying this right." Nondiscrimination on the basis of religion is absent from this list of precluded restrictions on marriage. Accordingly, the traditional sha'ria obstacles to interreligious marriages are not addressed critically.

Even more problematic is Article 10 which unambiguously violates the principle of equality by giving Islam a privileged status above all other religions. It reads: "Islam is the religion of unspoiled nature. It is prohibited to exercise any form of compulsion on man or to exploit his poverty or ignorance in order to convert him to another religion or to atheism." The Cairo Declaration, thus, seems to ban conversion from Islam and, more clearly, all missionary work among Muslims. Undoubtedly, this is at odds with religious liberty as it has been enshrined in international legal standards within the UN framework. Hence, the Cairo Declaration actually weakens or denies some basic international human rights by claiming a general priority for the traditional sha'ria.

. . . .

Whereas conservative Islamic documents like the Cairo Declaration tend to "Islamize" human rights at the expense of their universality and their emancipatory content, liberal Muslim reformers consider human rights a genuine challenge. Liberal Muslim reformers admit that in modern circumstances a normative consensus across cultural and religious boundaries is imperative to promote international peace and cooperation. Abdullahi

Ahmed An-Na'im, a leading figure in the Islamic discourse on human rights, writes: "Under contemporary economic and political conditions, no country in the world is religiously monolithic, however traditional and 'closed' it may wish to be." Consequently, Muslims, like people of other cultures, are called upon to engage in cross-cultural dialogue on human rights.

Understanding human rights to be an international and cross-cultural demand is tantamount to the insight that these rights cannot be simply integrated into the existing normative framework of the sha'ria. It has indeed to be admitted that there are fundamental tensions between traditional sha'ria norms and the requirements of human rights. These tensions need careful assessment, rather than premature harmonization. What is at stake is a self-critical reevaluation of the sha'ria and its underlying principles: an opportunity to seek out ways to genuinely mediate between and reconcile the competing normative requirements.

. . . .

Liberal Muslim reformers advocate for an emancipated understanding of the sha'ria, stressing its original meaning as a "path" or guide, rather than a detailed legal code. They do not attempt to deny the binding character of the sha'ria. On the contrary, at stake is a critical form of obedience that seems even more demanding because it requires active efforts of interpretation by the faithful. Such active reasoning—"ijtihad"—was originally regarded as an independent source of Islamic law that, only after increasing petrification of the sha'ria, became replaced by obedience to the established teachings of the Sunna law schools. Hence, many Muslim reformers demand the recovery of ijtihad in order to do justice both to modern needs and to the original spirit of the Islamic sha'ria. Mahmasani writes: "The door of ijtihad should be thrown wide open for anyone juristically qualified. The error, all the error, lies in blind imitation and restraint of thought. What is right is to allow freedom of interpretation...." Ali Merad, a historian from Algeria, describes the task as follows: "We must therefore strive to peer through the contingencies of history, in order to discover the direction in which revelation points, to formulate normative criteria, and to find out what God's intention is. But this is a hazardous route to take."

From a liberal Islamic point of view, it seems possible that the traditional obstacles to the endorsement of human rights can be overturned critically. For many liberal Muslims, no inherent contradiction exists between Islamic principles and the emancipatory claims of human rights as embodied in the existing international standards. Moreover, the Qur'anic idea of human dignity, in the opinion of Talbi, requires a political commitment to human rights, in solidarity with people of different religious beliefs and philosophical convictions. Referring to the ongoing atrocities occurring worldwide, he insists: "In a world where giant holocausts have been perpetrated, where human rights are manipulated or blatantly ignored, our Muslim theologians must denounce all forms of discriminations as crimes strictly and explicitly condemned by the Qur'an."

. . . .

The contrast between conservative and liberal Islamic interpretations of human rights, as sketched above, does not cover the entire spectrum of the debate. Between both positions range a large number of "pragmatic" approaches that often combine liberal and conservative attitudes. Apart from fundamentalist movements that certainly do not represent the majority of Muslims today, Islam has always accommodated a pragmatic humanitarianism, in keeping with the Qur'anic promise that "God intends every facility for you; he does not want to put you to difficulties." Sura 2:185. Hence, rigidity and puritanism are atypical of the Islamic tradition as a whole. As a matter of fact, the Islamic tradition appears capable of dealing flexibly with human needs and shortcomings. Such pragmatism also has shaped the sha'ria from its very beginning. Therefore, some reconciliation between the traditional sha'ria and the modern idea of human rights conceivably could be accomplished in accordance with this well established Islamic pragmatism.

Actually, such steps already have been taken in many Islamic countries. Legal reforms, even those involving sensitive matters of family law, can be traced back to the early twentieth century. Although not breaking away from the traditional sha'ria completely, these legal reforms, nonetheless, facilitated some changes towards a better social and legal status for women. Such reforms have restricted practices such as child marriage, polygamy, and the husband's right to repudiate his wife unilaterally.

. . . .

It is noteworthy, in this context, how Muhammad Abduh, Grand Mufti of late nineteenth century Egypt, advocated restrictions on polygamy. His argument, based on the Qur'an, is as follows: Although the Qur'an allows a man to marry more than one woman, it adds the caveat that this may not be done unless the husband is able to treat all his wives with full equal justice. Sura 4:3. In another place, however, the Qur'an states that this requirement can hardly ever be satisfied: "you are never able to be fair and just as between women, even if it is your ardent desire." Sura 4:129. Muhammad Abduh and many of his Muslim followers, therefore, read the Qur'an as forbidding polygamy implicitly. Up until now, however, Tunisia is the only Arab state that has abolished polygamy completely by making reference to this interpretation of the Qur'an.

With regard to religious liberty, mainstream Islam clearly accepts religious pluralism but still seems reluctant to endorse an unrestricted right to interreligious marriage and to conversion from Islam to another religion. Thus, converts continue to face social ostracism and are viewed by some as "renegades" or "apostates." On the other hand, it is worth mentioning that Khomeini's fatwa against the novelist Salman Rushdie failed to get support from international Islamic organizations which also condemned Rushdie's *Satanic Verses*, but did not back up Khomeini's death sentence against the author. The execution of Mahmoud Muhammad Taha, leader of a liberal Islamic movement in Sudan, on the charge of heresy in January 1985, shocked most Sudanese. As Ann E. Mayer reports: "Outrage and disgust over the execution and televised heresy trial prevailed, even among Sudanese Muslims who had no personal sympathy for Taha's theological positions.... Owing to the policies of Nimeiri, Islam became associated with an act of medieval barbarism, but many Muslims considered the execution a violation of fundamental Islamic values."

While traditional sha'ria norms continue to mark family structures all over the Islamic world, the sha'ria criminal law is applied only in a few Islamic countries today. As mentioned earlier, the emphasis of the sha'ria has always been much more on family matters than on criminal law. The portrayal of the sha'ria as primarily consisting of a set of cruel punishments, as it is sometimes presented in Western media, therefore, is at least one-sided.

. . . .

In his analysis of the classical sha'ria, Joseph Schacht concludes: "There is a strong tendency to restrict the applicability of hadd-punishments as much as possible...." Narrow definitions of the crimes in question, short statutes of limitation, and extremely high evidentiary requirements ensured that those punishments would be executed only in exceptional cases.

. . . .

According to the classical sha'ria, stoning for adultery (which is not based on the Qur'an) cannot be imposed unless four male Muslim eyewitnesses with a good reputation give a detailed account of the act of penetration. (According to some law schools, one or two of the males could be replaced by a double number of female witnesses.) The question that naturally arises in that case is whether it is conceivable that people could observe such an act of sexual intercourse without thereby jeopardizing their requisite good reputation. Even a conservative author like Aly Aly Mansour has to admit: "It is nearly impossible to satisfy the prerequisite for eyewitnesses...." The only conceivable possibility is that the act of adultery is committed publicly, leading to the presumption that the people involved are insane and, consequently, cannot be punished.

Whatever the traditional sha'ria might require in theory, most contemporary Muslims will presumably feel that such a cruel punishment like stoning can never be applied in practice. This attitude seems to prevail even among conservative Muslim scholars. It might be worth mentioning, in this context, that Pakistan's Federal Sha'ria Court resisted the reintroduction of stoning in Pakistan, in the early 1980s, by repeatedly refusing to apply this form of punishment. Only by replacing some of the judges with his own allies, Prime Minister Zia ul-Haq finally succeeded in having stoning judicially confirmed as being in accordance with the sha'ria.

These examples may suggest that, not only in consciously liberal approaches, but also in moderately conservative strains of Islam, a reconciliatory mediation between tradition and modernity seems conceivable. Certainly, one should be aware of the possible mis-understandings that easily can occur in such a mediation: it can amount to a superficial harmonization between Islam and human rights, whereby the emancipatory and cosmopolitan claims of human rights get unilaterally amalgamated with the existing sha'ria tradition. In order to overcome such misunderstandings, the relationship between sha'ria and human rights needs to be further clarified. In any case, one should not un-derestimate the potential for Islam to cope with new challenges and demands in a pragmatic way. In conformity with the humane flexibility that has largely marked the sha'ria, some of the conflicts between different normative requirements might be settled.

    ....

I have tried to show that a great variety of Islamic positions in the area of human rights exist. There are conservatives who deny all conflicts between tradition and modernity, thereby simply merging the language of human rights with the classical sha'ria. Some liberal reformers, by contrast, suggest that only a self-critical reevaluation of the sha'ria, which in their view originally was intended to provide normative guidance rather than serving as a comprehensive legal code, facilitates a genuine reconciliation of the requirements of Islam and human rights. Besides the positions held by conservatives and liberals, in-termediate approaches exist as well, resulting from the pragmatic humanitarianism that has largely shaped the sha'ria.

Given the fact that democratic structures are still missing or poorly developed in many Islamic countries, it is difficult to assess the strength of the various currents in contemporary Islam. A conservative point of view, as reflected in the Cairo Declaration on Human Rights in Islam, might be representative of the convictions of a large portion of Muslims today. The militancy of fundamentalist movements, however, is basically alien to the mainstream Islamic tradition and therefore can count only on limited support. Although fundamentalist parties recently have gained ground in many Islamic countries, they are still far from rep-resenting the majority of Muslims today. Arnold Hottinger estimates that, apart from ex-ceptional political circumstances, not more than 15 percent of the Muslim population would vote in elections in favor of fundamentalist movements or parties.

Liberal critics and reformers, in turn, certainly occupy a difficult position in most parts of the Islamic world. The June 1992 assassination of Faraj Fouda, an Egyptian author who publicly proposed the adoption of secularist philosophy in Islam, shows that even physical survival of outspoken Muslim reformers is in jeopardy. It is no coincidence, therefore, that many of them have chosen to live outside their home countries. Labeling them as merely "Westernized," however, would do serious injustice to their identity as Muslims and to the complexity of the internal Islamic controversy as well.

Finally, one should take into account that many Muslims still might feel insecure about the relationship between traditional religious norms on the one hand and modern legal standards on the other. That is why many Muslims assert the validity of the traditional Islamic sha'ria in principle and, at the same time, seem prepared to accommodate pragmatically some political and legal reforms. For instance, even those who defend the legitimacy of hadd-punishment in theory, frequently prefer to avoid the actual implementation of these punishments, invoking practical obstacles to their reintroduction. Although such pragmatic accommodation is not sufficient to solve the general conflict between competing normative requirements, accommodation does provide some intermediate solutions.

What are the practical consequences of this analysis for the current debate on human rights? First, it is worth repeating that we must abandon the abstract counterpoising of universal human rights on the one hand with cultural sensitivity on the other. This is not to say that tensions and conflicts do not exist. As argued above, there are fundamental obstacles to an unconstrained and unambiguous recognition of human rights in the Islamic tradition—and in other traditions, too. However, because traditions evolve, in light of new experiences and needs, such obstacles might be overturned both by deliberate efforts on the part of intellectual reformers as well as through the pragmatic wisdom and humanitarianism of the people.

What can non-Muslims do to foster such a process? It seems clear that they should not directly engage in the internal Islamic discourse about human rights. What can be done, however, is a self-critical analysis of one's own culture in order to overcome the various forms of ideological appropriation of human rights. As people from the West, we have to detach ourselves from the idea that these rights are simply individualistic claims that are detrimental to communitarian solidarity, we should refrain from building human rights into an ideology of general progress modeled on the patterns of Western civilization, and we should not confuse human rights monitoring with demands for the introduction of a Western-style market economy. In any event, self-criticism of one's own human rights policy is a necessary precondition to any serious cross-cultural dialogue on human rights.

According to my experience, conservative Muslims frequently perceive any commitment to the implementation of human rights as a new Western "crusade." That is, they fear that human rights are part and parcel of an all-encompassing ideology or way of life that is intended to eventually replace Islamic faith and practice. In order to avoid such a misunderstanding, I have repeatedly stressed the limited scope of human rights. Their focus lies on basic political and legal institutions; and they do not pretend to serve as a transhistoric yardstick, suitable to measuring cultures and religions generally. In other words, human rights are not, and should not be presented as, an international "civil religion."

On the other hand, human rights might shed new light on the self-perception of cultural and religious communities, because the principle of human dignity, which has roots in many different cultures, serves as the foundation for human rights. Moreover, given that the recognition of human dignity under circumstances of modernity needs to become binding in terms of emancipatory political and legal claims, human rights present a challenge to authoritarian traditions in cultures and religions. However, this challenge might well open up new occasions for developing a modern religious identity, by leading, for instance, to a new awareness of some essential Islamic principles that have been over-shadowed by detailed legal casuistry.

The most desirable accomplishment of the international discourse on human rights would be an international and cross-cultural "overlapping consensus." This would be a normative consensus focusing on international political and legal standards that, at the same time, could be connected critically with the more specific perspectives of religious and cultural communities. To be sure, we are far from such an ideal situation. Human rights remain controversial across the various ideological camps throughout the world. Given that this is the case, what are we to do for the time being? Do we have to postpone the implementation of international normative standards until they are universally ac-knowledged? Does cultural sensitivity require that we refrain from monitoring human rights and first engage in cross-cultural dialogue? ...

Richard Schifter, *The Cause of Freedom*
8 MEDITERRANEAN Q. 6, 7–10 (Summer 1997)

As Huntington defines the term, *the West* traces its roots to the kingdoms and principalities established by the Germanic tribes on the ruins of the Western half of the Roman Empire. He suggests that Western civilization had its beginning around the year 800. In that year, we need to note, Charlemagne, the king of the Franks, was crowned by Pope Leo IX as the first Holy Roman Emperor.

....

For purposes of this analysis, I would like to offer a device that will help us understand the time spans of the various stages of Huntington's Western civilization since the day on which the pope placed the imperial crown on the head of the Frankish king. Let us consider a time line on which we equate the twelve hundred years from 800 to 2000 with a single day, starting at midnight and ending at midnight. An hour on this time line equals fifty years; a minute equals ten months.

At midnight, as the day begins, the Holy Roman Empire comes into existence.... Democ-racy, the rule of law, and human rights are not recognizable concepts in a system in which power is concentrated in the nobility, a system in which the highest-ranking nobleman, the emperor, usually has the final say. We know this time period as the Dark Ages.

It is noon, with half the day gone, when we see in this civilization the first glimmer of the thinking that ultimately leads to the evolution of the concepts that we identify with democracy, the rule of law, and human rights. These concepts, we need to note, do not spring as original thoughts from the minds of the residents of Western Europe.

Between noon and 3:00 P.M., some of the thinkers of the Western world reach back two thousand years to precepts written down in other civilizations in earlier days. The Renaissance looks to the writings of the classical era, of ancient Rome and ancient Greece. The Reformation places renewed emphasis on the Bible of the Ancient Hebrews, known in the Christian world as the Old Testament. An intellectual foundation is now laid in the Western world for the notions that rulers attain legitimacy only by obtaining a mandate from the people and that these rulers, too, are subject to the law. At 5:48 P.M. John Locke publishes his seminal works on democracy, the *Two Treatises of Government*.

... Between 6:00 P.M. and 8:00 P.M., other thinkers throughout the West begin to espouse the ideas that we have come to associate with the Enlightenment. However, even though the *ideology* of democracy now takes firm root, there are only a few places in the Western world where the idea is translated into practice. One such place is the West's North American offshoot, whose Declaration of Independence, promulgated at 7:31 P.M., gives life to the ideas of the Enlightenment, as does the United States Constitution and Bill of Rights, completed at 7:49 P.M.

Absolute monarchies continue to cling to power on the European continent until the democratic upsurge that shakes these monarchies just before 9:00 P.M. From 9:00 P.M. to 10:40 P.M., we witness the first flourishing throughout much of the Western world of the practices of liberal democracy, taking the form of either constitutional monarchy or democratic republic.

But then, at 10:40 P.M., the virulently antidemocratic Nazi movement arises. It is ... a Western movement that places great emphasis on the alleged racial superiority of the people of the West. It is, however, committed to wiping out the body of universalist ideas and practices that has evolved in the Western world since noon and goes to war to advance its cause. It would, if successful, return the region to a new Dark Age. By 10:50 P.M. the Anglo-Saxon countries are alone in carrying on the battle to save democracy, as most of the West is now under Nazi control. But then the fortunes of war turn. The democratic forces persevere and by 10:54 P.M. emerge victorious.

Liberal democracy now establishes itself firmly in the Western world and significantly influences political developments in Japan. The United Nations adopts a Charter and the Universal Declaration of Human Rights, which commit the organization to the cause of human rights and fundamental freedoms for all. Little is done, however, to translate these commitments into positive action in the United Nations framework.

The internal Western threat to democracy has hardly been defeated when an external antidemocratic threat arises, stemming from the Soviet Union, a country that Professor Huntington believes as belonging to another culture, that of Orthodoxy. Slightly before 11:00 P.M. the Cold War begins....

To be able to defend itself against that threat, the West prepares itself militarily. But then it takes another highly significant step. At 11:30 P.M. it commits itself, for the first time, to the pursuit of an active policy of advancing the democratic ideal worldwide, a policy that seeks to translate the promise of the Universal Declaration into reality. Communism, as practiced in the Soviet Union and its satellites, is an important target of that campaign.

After a slow start, the campaign proves successful. A trend toward greater openness in the Soviet Union is evident by 11:47 P.M. By 11:49 the Cold War is at an end. Communism, as a viable political force, is dead.

It is now 11:57 P.M., and we are told by Professor Huntington that liberal democracy, which first flourished in the Western world at 9:00 P.M. and was close to extinction at 10:50 P.M. is the unique property of the descendants of those who the previous midnight founded the Holy Roman Empire. We are further told that the ideological campaign to advance democracy, initiated by the United States twenty-seven minutes earlier in this twenty-four hour day, at 11:30 P.M., a campaign that helped end the Cold War at 11:49 P.M. and also helped bring Latin America into the democratic fold, is misguided, arrogant, false, and dangerous.

Human Rights in the Early 21st Century

As we review the state of international affairs in the second decade of the 21st century, the ideologies espoused by governments continue to play a highly significant role in international relations. What we need to note is that this is, in historic terms, a fairly recent phenomenon, a phenomenon that evolved in the 20th century. Economic and territorial ambitions played the key role in World War I. Even World War II started as a war over territory. However, European Nazism/Fascism presented, even before the outbreak of World War II, an ideological issue concerning a country's governance, an issue that caused President Roosevelt to steer U.S. policy in an "interventionist" direction in the late 1930s. Roosevelt's outlook on foreign policy was strongly influenced by the ideas of President Wilson, who had urged U.S. entry into World War I because "the world must be made safe for democracy."

It was very much in keeping with Wilson's outlook that Roosevelt saw to it that the Yalta agreement of February 1945 included the following provision: "The Premier of the Union of Soviet Socialist Republics, the Prime Minister of the United Kingdom and the President of the United States of America have consulted with each other in the common interests of the people of their countries and those of liberated Europe. They jointly declare their mutual agreement to concert during the temporary period of instability in liberated Europe the policies of their three Governments in assisting the peoples liberated from the domination of Nazi Germany and the peoples of the former Axis satellite states of Europe to solve **by democratic means** their pressing political and economic problems." (Emphasis supplied.)

The United States commitment on the international level to democracy, human rights, and the rule of law was carried on under President Truman. The United Nations Charter, signed in June 1945, committed the organization to "promoting and encouraging respect for human rights and fundamental freedoms for all without distinction as to race, sex, language, or religion." The Charter thus put on the agenda of the United Nations the task of promoting and encouraging the concept that any human being, wherever he or she may live, has personal rights which the government of the country must respect.

To follow through on this commitment, the United Nations established in 1946 the United Nations Commission on Human Rights. With former First Lady Eleanor Roosevelt, as the Representative of the United States on the Commission, in the forefront of the effort to take the next step, the Commission drafted the Universal Declaration of Human Rights, which was adopted by the United Nations General Assembly in 1948. There were no votes in opposition to the resolution, but there were eight abstentions, six of them by members of the Soviet-bloc at the UN, plus Saudi Arabia, and South Africa.

At the time of the adoption of the Universal Declaration of Human Rights the Cold War was already underway. By then the Soviet Union had clearly committed itself to a program of territorial expansion, a traditional cause for international strife, but ideology had become a major factor as well. The West, led by the United States, had come to espouse democracy and respect for human rights on the international level. The Soviet Union used its power, wherever it could, to establish Communist dictatorships, irrespective of the will of the people involved. Stalin had clearly no intention to abide by the provision in the Yalta agreement of 1945 to solve problems "by democratic means." The Soviet Union was slightly more honest in 1948 when it abstained in the UN General Assembly vote on the Universal Declaration of Human Rights. (At the UN an abstention is a polite way of indicating that a country is not in favor of a resolution.) To be sure, there was no way in which any of these human rights commitments could be legally enforced.

An additional step to have human rights standards recognized internationally was taken in 1976, when the Covenant on Civil and Political Rights took effect (with the participation of the Soviet Union, whose government had once again no intention to abide by it). But here, too, no legally enforceable rights were created. What the Covenant did do was to establish a Human Rights Committee, with which a State Party to the Covenant could file a complaint about violations of the provisions of the Covenant by another state. The Committee would seek to resolve the problem by agreement among the contending parties and if it failed to do so, file a report on that subject. Not much was accomplished under this process.

It took some years before the United States or any other country raised serious *public* questions about the totalitarianism that characterized governance in the Soviet Union and states associated with it. It was in the 1970s that Congress insisted that that be done publicly and that countries not associated with the Soviet Union also be urged to adhere to the standards set forth in the Universal Declaration. As there was no legal tribunal to which it would be possible to appeal to restrain the violators, full use came to be made of international human rights fora to "name and shame" these violators.

Thus, even in the absence of internationally legally enforceable human right standards, the basic idea that governments should respect the rights of their citizens, as set forth in the Universal Declaration, spread worldwide in the fourth quarter of the Twentieth Century. Encouraged by the position taken by the United States, citizen groups formed themselves in repressive countries and called for recognition of their rights. That included the Soviet Union, one of whose leaders, Mikhail Gorbachev, ultimately responded very positively to the concerns about human rights violations expressed to him by the United States Government.

This fundamental change in Soviet policy was marked in Gorbachev's speech to the 43rd United Nations General Assembly Session on December 7, 1988, in which he said:

> We have gone substantially and deeply into the business constructing a socialist state **based on the rule of law**. A whole series of new laws has been prepared or is at a completion stage. Many of them come into force as early as 1989, and we trust that they will correspond to the highest standards from the point of view of ensuring the rights of the individual. Soviet democracy is to acquire a firm, normative base. This means that such acts as the Law on Freedom of Conscience, on glasnost, on public associations and organizations, and on much else. **There are now no people in places of imprisonment in the country who have been sentenced for their political or religious convictions.** (Emphasis supplied.)

In the three years that followed the delivery of Gorbachev's speech to the UN General Assembly, it was possible to see the totalitarian fog lift from the streets of Moscow. It was indeed in keeping with these principles that the Soviet Union, under Gorbachev, withdrew its support from the East European dictatorships that had been under Soviet control. These countries quickly became "free" by the standards of Freedom House.

But given the series of economic problems that it faced, the Soviet Union disintegrated in 1991 and Gorbachev retired from public life. Boris Yeltsin became the leader of the principal successor state, Russia. The mismanagement of Russia under Yeltsin has now been succeeded by the authoritarianism of Vladimir Putin, which caused Freedom House to move Russia in 2005 back to being identified as "not free." Still, the basic concepts of democracy and human rights have strong support in urban areas of Russia and may very well ultimately prevail.

As we look at the world since the disintegration of the Soviet Union, we can note that most of Europe is "free" by Freedom House standards. So are most of the Latin American and Caribbean states as are most of the states in Southern Africa, as well as India, Japan, South Korea, Mongolia, and most of the South Pacific Island states. It is clear that the idea of the limits of power of government has indeed spread worldwide.

But there is a need to face another problem; massive human rights violations, such as genocide and war crimes, committed by non-state actors, violations that the governments of the states that have jurisdiction over the affected area are unwilling or unable to stop. It is in that context that the concept of the "responsibility to protect" has developed. Under Chapter VII of the UN Charter, the UN Security Council has the power to take "action with regard to threats to the peace, breaches of the peace, and acts of aggression." It is a power which, under Chapter I, Article 2 of the UN Charter, can be exercised in a manner that bypasses the sovereign rights of affected states.

But there have been situations in which breaches of the peace have occurred and the Security Council failed to take action. It is in that setting that individual states, usually led by the United States, have assumed the "responsibility to protect" and have stepped in to confront those states or non-state actors that breached the peace. They have to decide, in each instance, when and how to act in keeping with the concept of responsibility to protect, a moral concept.

The need to protect civilians against non-state actors that engage in mass killings has become a major international task in the 21st century's second decade. A new major threat to the cause of human rights has arisen. The so-called "Arab Spring" has been succeeded by the significantly increased prominence and increased influence and power of a totalitarian movement which seeks to impose its interpretation of the Islamic faith on all Muslims and which is virulently hostile to all non-Muslims. It is often referred to as militant Islam. There are some who have used the term Islamofascism to draw a line of distinction between adherents of this new movement and traditional observers of the Islamic faith.

Egypt's Muslim Brotherhood, the organization now most generally associated with the rise of the new Islamic totalitarian movement, was, at its founding in 1928, strongly committed to advancing a society based on sharia law. But beyond that it was indeed strongly opposed to Western democratic civilization. Soon after the organization got underway its leaders got in touch with Adolf Hitler, stayed in touch with him once he came to power in Germany, and collaborated with Nazi Germany during World War II.

It was after World War II, in the early 1950s, that one of the new leading personalities in the Muslim Brotherhood, Sayid Qutb, who had become one the foremost proponent of the ideology of militant Islam, added vehement anti-Americanism to the Brotherhood's platform. After having spent two years in the United States at institutions of higher education, he returned to Egypt not only as a political opponent of the United States but with a vehement hatred for American culture. He was also committed to the concept of an inferior social status for women. Qutb was a prolific writer. His books have circulated widely in the Arab world and have won believers in his ideology, which focuses principally on rejection of Western civilization. After having had initially friendly relations with Egypt's President Nasser, he subsequently had a falling out with Nasser. That led ultimately to his being charged and convicted of plotting to assassinate Nasser, ending with Qutb's execution in 1966.

As the decades have passed, Qutb's ideology has won an increasing number of adherents. His writings inspired the leaders of al-Qaeda and other groups that are committed to terrorist attacks, to jihad against Western targets. These new totalitarians do not espouse any positive program goals that they wish to achieve for their own people. Their activities in the public arena concentrate on engagement in warfare, in destruction and in killing, with the goal of world dominance of their jihad ideology, including the inferior status accorded to women.

Given the fact that much of militant Islamism stems from the Arab world, particular attention should be paid to the sharply different developments in Tunisia. It is the country where the Arab Spring started, but where, as distinct from other countries, it has effected highly significant positive change. An Associated Press story, dated January 24, 2014, reports adoption of a Tunisian Constitution and adds the following observations: "The new constitution sets out to make the North African country of 11 million people a democracy, with a civil state whose laws are not based on Islamic law, unlike many other Arab constitutions. An entire chapter of the document, some 28 articles, is dedicated to protecting citizens' rights, including protection from torture, the right to due process, and freedom of worship. It guarantees equality between men and women before the law and the state commits itself to protecting women's rights."[23] In an election held on October 24, 2014, Tunisia's largest secular party obtained a majority of the votes.

It does not require thorough research to identify the principal factor that brought about this truly unique development in Tunisia. When the country attained independence in 1956, its first President, Habib Bourguiba, emphasized the need to include *all* persons in Tunisian society. In 1957 women became eligible to vote and in 1959 to hold public office. Compulsory elementary school education for *all* children became the rule. By the 1990s a majority of the students at the University of Tunis were women. Further, under Tunisia's Code of Personal Status polygamy was abolished, women could sue for divorce, a minimum age for marriage was established, and the consent of both spouses was required for marriage.

The close interrelationship between respect for human rights and the status of equality for women cannot be more strongly underlined than by the case of Tunisia. To be sure, it has taken time for women truly to achieve equal rights in what is now viewed as the world of free countries, but it has happened, and it has strengthened the human rights cause in these countries. Yet, to this day, restrictions on human rights based on gender are in many countries the most serious obstacle to the attainment of a free society.

But even where laws are in place that should protect the rights of women, the problem is that they are often inadequately enforced. Trafficking of women against their will is in many states a serious problem, as is genital mutilation. Clear mandates to law enforcement agencies are needed to consider it to be their responsibility to see to it that these laws are adhered to. All of this is more likely to happen in countries in which women play a major role in public life.

To return to the problem posed by the deprivation of fundamental human rights to all residents of a country: although Militant Islam is a new totalitarian movement on the world scene, it is not the only such movement. While China has given up on the Leninist concept of socialism, it has retained the Stalinist system of political control of the country, which has increasingly been linked to expansionist nationalism. (President Aquino of the Philippines has drawn an analogy to Nazi Germany.)

---

23. http://www.usatoday.com/story/news/world/2014/01/26/tunisia-passes-constitution/4916489/.

What is striking in the case of China, however, is that the concept of freedom has penetrated the country in spite of continuing efforts at totalitarian control. To some extent it was brought to China by young people who had studied abroad. But there is more to it. The Internet has brought in the idea of freedom and social media have helped disseminate it. The authorities try to do their best to control the Internet in China, but have found it very difficult. There is every reason to believe that the message of the Universal Declaration has reached many people in China. It may very well lead to major changes in governance in China. But that is precisely why the country's repressive leadership does its very best to deprive citizens of online privacy.

It was in 1949 that the British writer, George Orwell published the novel *1984*. It was a novel based on Orwell's encounter with Stalinism. In it he projected how a society based on Stalinist principles could ultimately evolve. It is truly striking how North Korea to this day resembles the governmental system and the resultant culture that Orwell envisaged in *1984*. It is the world's cruelest dictatorship, a country in which about 25 million people are nothing other than mere pawns under the control of a brutal leader. Even the country's official name *Democratic People's Republic of Korea* is an outrageous lie. It is indeed a challenge to all those who believe in the principles of human rights to find a way to bring an end to this viciously repressive political system.

To be sure, in November 2014 the Third Committee of the UN General Assembly did adopt a resolution that expressed great concern regarding North Korea's truly shocking human rights violations and recommended that the Security Council refer the matter to the International Criminal Court. The vote was 111 for, 19 against, with 55 abstentions. Among those voting against were China and Russia, two members of the UN Security Council which would undoubtedly veto any resolution that would refer the case of North Korea to the ICC.

As these lines are written, almost a century has passed since Woodrow Wilson enlisted the United States in the effort to make the world safe for democracy. In the years since then the United States has certainly been engaged in the effort. Not all our goals have been reached, but progress has been made. U.S. leadership in the international effort to respect human rights remains essential.

Question for Discussion

In situations where UN Security Council approval cannot be obtained, when and under what circumstances should nations, exercising "a responsibility to protect" in order to save lives, intervene militarily in the internal affairs of another sovereign state?

Selected Bibliography

Kent, Ann, *China, the United Nations and Human Rights: The Limits of Compliance* (1999).
Korey, William, *The Promises We Keep: Human Rights, the Helsinki Process, and American Foreign Policy* (1993).
Laqueur, Walter and Barry Rubin, eds., *Human Rights Reader* (1990).
Newsom, David D., ed., *The Diplomacy of Human Rights* (1986).
Power, Samantha, *A Problem from Hell: America and the Age of Genocide* (Basic Books, 2002).
Tolley, Jr., Howard, *The U.N. Commission on Human Rights* (1987).

Chapter 15

The Law of the Sea

Horace B. Robertson, Jr. and James Kraska

In this chapter:

The Strategic Seas

Freedom of the seas is a cornerstone of American foreign policy. The first four wars that the United States fought as an independent country were largely over the principle of freedom of the seas. Soon after America's independence, for example, the new nation fought the Quasi-War with France from 1798–1800 — its first war as an independent nation — to protect the right of U.S. ships to trade freely with European states. The New Republic also fought two wars against the Barbary pirates in the Mediterranean Sea, eventually vanquishing the Ottoman principalities in 1815, and bringing to a close two hundred years of piracy against European and American seafarers. During the War of 1812, the United States freed our sailors from impressment in the British Navy.

The United States also fought World Wars I and II in part over the principle of freedom of the seas. Germany's policy of unrestricted U-boat warfare against American commercial ships drew the United States into both conflicts. President Woodrow Wilson's Fourteen Points, which outlined war aims for U.S. involvement in World War I, included the principle of freedom of the seas, in peace and in war, for all nations. Likewise, when President Franklin Delano Roosevelt and Prime Minister Winston Churchill secretly met in Argentia, Newfoundland, to outline Allied goals for the "united nations," freedom of the seas was a key element.

With the emergence of the United States as a global power following World War II and the increased awareness of interdependence among the nations of the free world, the importance of the freedom of the seas was reemphasized. During the Cold War, the U.S. alliance system was maintained through maritime links to Europe and Asia. In Europe, the North Atlantic Treaty Organization (NATO) was designed around the concept of extended deterrence, and the promise of American power to deter Soviet advancement westward. A network of five bilateral treaty commitments undergirds the security architecture in Asia. The United States is bound by defense agreements with Japan, the Republic of Korea, Thailand, the Philippines, and Australia. The links with more than fifty non-contiguous allies are critical to maintaining the sea lines of communication, as the expeditionary movement of armed forces by sea remains the most efficient, and often even the fastest, method.

Furthermore, the most secure basing mode for the U.S. strategic deterrence system is the submarine-launched ballistic missile submarine. Similarly, ballistic missile defense (BMD) technology has moved offshore, and the United States regularly commits Arleigh Burke-class guided missile destroyers to conduct BMD patrols in the waters surrounding North Korea, and in Europe. The most flexible, credible, and readily available response force for most international crises is a sea-based force. Thus, the legal regime of the oceans has a significant impact on national security. This chapter will explore the current peacetime international law of the sea that influence national security most directly, discuss how international law affects heightened military activities at sea that lie at the seam between peace and war, and examine the application of the law of naval warfare during periods of armed conflict.

Jurisdictional Claims in the Oceans

Since earliest recorded history, states have claimed the right to exercise jurisdiction and control over areas of the oceans contiguous to their shores. Territorial claims in the oceans reached their apogee at the end of the fifteenth century when Portugal and Spain received the Pope's blessing in the Papal Bull *Inter Caetera* of 1493 to divide the Atlantic Ocean between them. The following year, the division was adjusted and memorialized in the Treaty of Tordesillas, which decreed that all of the ocean and land to the east of the meridian lying 370 leagues[1] west of Portugal's Cape Verde Islands belonged to Spain. Spain's maritime and territorial claims encompassed the continents of North and South America, except for Brazil, and Portugal claimed the eastern Atlantic Ocean and Indian Ocean, which permitted it to establish colonies from Angola to India.

Over the next three centuries these pretentious claims gradually withered away. The United Provinces challenged Portugal's monopoly on the carrying trade between Europe and the Far East, and encroached on Spain's claim over North America by founding New Amsterdam in present day New York. By the early seventeenth century, the English began to emerge as the dominant maritime power, eventually displacing Spain in most of North America and ejecting Portugal from India. The Royal Navy championed the doctrine of freedom of the seas, which became the foundation of the law of the global commons. Every coastal state could claim sovereignty over a narrow coastal belt, called the territorial sea, the breadth of which was usually expressed as three nautical miles (nm), or 3.4 statute miles. From the end of the Napoleonic Wars until the end of World War II, the parallel principles of freedom of the high seas and coastal-state jurisdiction over a narrow territorial sea remained relatively stable and secure.

The end of World War II, however, brought an era of instability in which coastal states again asserted unilateral claims against the commonage of the high seas. With the adoption of the United Nations Convention on the Law of the Sea (UNCLOS or LOS Convention)

---

1. A marine league is about three nautical miles, or 5.5 kilometers.

Figure 1: Division of the Oceans in the United Nations Convention on the Law of the Sea

Kraska 2014

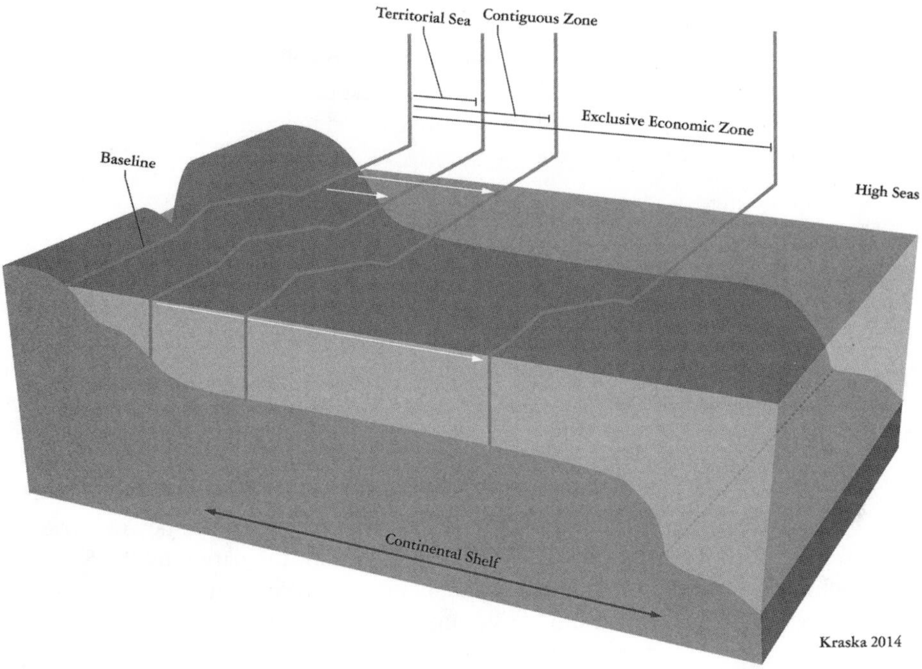

in 1982,[2] and its entry into force in 1994, the simple system of a narrow territorial sea along the coast and all waters beyond that comprising the high seas had disappeared, giving way to a complex system of broad and overlapping zones illustrated in Figure 1. On August 7, 2013, Niger became the 166th state to become a party to UNCLOS.[3]

Baselines

All coastal zones are measured outward from a line along the coast called the "baseline." The baseline is normally the low water line along the coast, following all its sinuousities, but in some cases in which the coast is deeply indented or has a fringe of islands, it may consist of a series of straight lines connecting appropriate points on the coast or fringing islands.[4] These "straight baselines," however, must "must not depart from any appreciable extent from the general direction of the coast," and the enclosed water must be "sufficiently closely linked with the land domain" to be considered internal waters.

---

2. United Nations Convention on the Law of the Sea, Dec. 10, 1982, 1833 U.N.T.S. 3.

3. Division for Ocean Affairs and the Law of the Sea, United Nations, Chronological lists of ratifications of, accessions and successions to the Convention and the related Agreements as at 29 October 2013, www.un.org.

4. Convention on the Territorial Sea and the Contiguous Zone, Apr. 29, 1958, articles 3, 4, 516 U.N.T.S. 205; LOS Convention, *supra* note 2 arts. 5, 7.

Internal Waters

Internal waters are all waters inside the baseline. Such waters may include bays, mouths of rivers, waters inside fringing islands where straight baselines have been drawn, and the like. The legal regime for internal waters is in all respects identical to that for the land territory of a state. Foreign ships and aircraft are entitled to enter the internal water of a state only with the state's permission.

Territorial Sea

The territorial sea is a band of waters outside the baseline over which the coastal state exercises full sovereignty subject to the single exception that foreign ships have the right of innocent passage. Historically, the breadth of the territorial sea was three nm. The First and Second United Nations Conferences on the Law of the Sea in 1958 and 1960 were unable to obtain agreement on a breadth, however, and broader claims proliferated. The LOS Convention, which was negotiated at the Third United Nations Conference on the Law of the Sea from 1973–82, provides that the territorial sea cannot exceed twelve nm in breadth. Consistent with that Convention, the United States extended its territorial sea to twelve nm on December 27, 1988.[5] The most recent tabulation by the Secretary General of the United Nations indicates that only nine states continue to claim territorial sea breadths greater than twelve nm.[6] Still, numerous states assert excessive competence over activities beyond the territorial sea that are inconsistent with UNCLOS.[7]

Contiguous Zone

The contiguous zone is a band of waters outside the territorial sea in which a coastal state exercises limited forms of jurisdiction for the protection of vital coastal-state interests. Prior to 1958 there was uncertainty as to the extent and nature of such jurisdiction and the distances to which it might be exercised. The 1958 Territorial Sea Convention confined the outer limit to twelve nm from the baseline and limited the controls that a state may exercise in the zone to prevent infringement of its customs, fiscal, immigration, and sanitary regulations.[8] The LOS Convention extended the outer limit to twenty-four nm from the baseline.[9]

Continental Shelf

The idea of the continental shelf as a separate legal division in the oceans originated with a proclamation issued by President Truman in 1945 in which the United States

---

5. Proclamation No. 5928, 54 Fed. Reg. 777 (Dec. 27, 1988).
6. Division for Ocean Affairs and the Law of the Sea, UN, LAW OF THE SEA BULLETIN No. 45, at 115–129 (2001).
7. James Kraska, MARITIME POWER AND LAW OF THE SEA: EXPEDITIONARY OPERATIONS IN WORLD POLITICS 114–23 (2011).
8. Territorial Sea Convention, *supra* note 4, art. 24.
9. LOS Convention, *supra* note 2, art. 33.

claimed exclusive jurisdiction and control over the "natural resources of the subsoil and sea bed of the continental shelf beneath the high seas but contiguous to the coasts of the United States."[10] No claim was made to the superjacent waters, which remained high seas. The continental shelf concept gained rapid international acceptance and was first codified in a multilateral convention in 1958.[11] Article 1 of the Convention established the outer limit as the point at which the depth of water was 200 meters or "beyond that limit to where the depth of the superjacent waters admits of the exploitation of the natural resources" of the shelf. This elastic outer boundary proved troublesome and was one of the factors leading to the convening of the Third UN Conference. The LOS Convention vastly extends the outer limit of the "legal" continental shelf. It permits all coastal states to claim 200 nm, and those with broad geological shelves to go to the edge of the continental margin, but in no case beyond either 350 nm from the baseline or 100 nm beyond the 2500 meter isobaths, whichever is farthest.[12]

Exclusive Economic Zone

The LOS Convention also adopts the concept of the Exclusive Economic Zone (EEZ), a zone that is neither territorial sea nor high seas, and extends to a distance of 200 nm from the baseline. In the EEZ the coastal state exercises sovereign rights for the exploitation of living and non-living resources of the sea, seabed and subsoil, but other states continue to enjoy the rights of navigation, overflight, cable-laying, and other non-resource-related, high-sea rights.[13]

Archipelagic Waters

The 1982 LOS Convention defines a division of the sea that was unknown to the previous law of the sea — archipelagic waters. Under the convention, certain island states, such as Indonesia and the Philippines, are entitled to draw straight "archipelagic baselines" connecting the outermost points of the outermost islands. The waters enclosed by such baselines become archipelagic waters, having some of the characteristics of the territorial sea but some that are unique to such waters. Freedom of navigation is preserved in designated sea lanes and in all normal routes used for international navigation or overflight, if the routes have not been designated. Innocent passage is permitted through all other archipelagic waters. The territorial sea, contiguous zone and exclusive economic zone extend outward from the archipelagic baselines in the same manner as from ordinary baselines.[14]

High Seas

The 1958 Convention on the High Seas, which is recognized as generally declaratory of customary international law,[15] states that the high seas shall include "all parts of the

---

10. Proclamation No. 2667, 10 Fed. Reg. 12,305 (Sept. 28, 1945).
11. Convention on the Continental Shelf, Apr. 29, 1958, 499 U.N.T.S. 311.
12. LOS Convention, *supra* note 2, article 76.
13. *Id.*, Part V.
14. *Id.*, Part IV.
15. Convention on the High Seas, Apr. 29, 1958, pmbl., 450 U.N.T.S. 82.

sea that are not included in the territorial sea or in the internal waters of a State."[16] On the high seas, ships and aircraft of all nations have equal right to conduct their lawful pursuits free from interference from any other nation. With only minor exceptions, order is preserved not by the exercise of territorial jurisdiction by states, but rather by the concept of the "flag state," by which each state exercises jurisdiction and control over vessels flying its flag and aircraft registered in the state.

Under the LOS Convention, the freedoms of the high seas are preserved essentially as they existed under the 1958 High Seas Convention, but the area in which they apply is drastically reduced. Article 86 of the LOS Convention removes from the regime of the high seas not only territorial seas and internal waters but also EEZs and archipelagic waters. Roughly 40 percent of areas formerly considered high seas are subject to some sort of coastal-state jurisdiction.

Question for Discussion

The LOS Convention was adopted by the Third United Nations Conference on the Law of the Sea (UNCLOS III) in December 1982. Although the United States was an active participant in the Conference, by 2015, it still was not a party to the Convention, primarily because of objections to provisions governing mining of the deep seabed (the "Area"). The Convention was supported by the administrations of Bill Clinton, George W. Bush, and Barack Obama. The Senate Foreign Relations Committee voted in favor of sending the Convention to the floor of the senate for consideration of advice and consent for U.S. accession in 2004, 2007, and 2012, but the full Senate has not considered the treaty due to opposition from a group of Republican senators. Nevertheless, President Reagan announced in 1983 that the United States recognizes the substantive provisions of the Convention, apart from the deep seabed provisions, as binding customary law.[17] The Convention is regarded by international law attorneys in the Department of Defense and Department of State as reflective of customary international law, and therefore binding on all states. The *Restatement (Third) of the Foreign Relations Law of the United States* also adopts this position.[18]

In light of this position, how will U.S. practice in the law of the sea be affected? Would it make a difference in your answer if the particular provision of the convention involved was identical to a provision of one of the four conventions adopted in 1958, to which the United States is a party?

Navigation and Other Internationally Lawful Uses of the Sea

The world's economic system is interdependent. Ocean commerce is its lifeblood. Interruptions in its flow would seriously undermine the well being of many states and create

---

16. *Id.* art. 1.

17. Statement of President Reagan, 19 WEEKLY COMP. PRES. DOC. 383 (Mar. 10, 1983).

18. RESTATEMENT (THIRD) OF THE FOREIGN RELATIONS LAW OF THE UNITED STATES, Part V Introductory Note (1987).

serious threats to the preservation of international peace and security. The oceans also provide areas for the deployment of national navies and air forces whose missions include the safeguarding of these international ocean highways as well as the projection of force to areas where national interests may require their presence.

Large areas of the oceans have been subjected to national jurisdiction of one sort or another. These areas of national jurisdiction often embrace many sea routes normally used for international navigation, and in some cases even a twelve-mile territorial sea will encompass the only sea links joining important ocean areas (international straits). States have exceeded their authority in making excessive maritime claims that are inconsistent with the LOS Convention and customary international law. Countries with restrictions inconsistent with the Law of the Sea Convention that would limit the exercise of high seas freedoms by foreign navies beyond 12 nautical miles from the coast include: Bangladesh, Brazil, Burma, Cambodia, Cape Verde, China, Egypt, Haiti, India, Iran, Kenya, Malaysia, Maldives, Mauritius, North Korea, Pakistan, Portugal, Saudi Arabia, Somalia, Sri Lanka, Sudan, Syria, Thailand, United Arab Emirates, Uruguay, Venezuela, and Vietnam.[19]

The United States Freedom of Navigation Program

In 1979 the United States initiated a program known as the "Freedom of Navigation Program" as a means of indicating its non-acquiescence in excessive maritime claims by other states. Recognizing that acquiescence in excessive maritime claims may allow them to develop into customary international law, the Freedom of Navigation Program consists of three elements: diplomatic protest, other representations to foreign governments, such as military-to-military engagement and exercises, and operational assertions by ships and aircraft of U.S. rights of navigation and overflight of waters and airspace over which foreign governments have made excessive claims of jurisdiction or sovereignty.

These actions by U.S. forces are a form of conventional deterrence to demonstrate tangible rejection of claims inconsistent with the LOS Convention.[20] Operations are made in a "low-key and non-threatening manner but without attempt at concealment."[21]

Innocent Passage in the Territorial Sea

The 1958 Territorial Sea Convention recognized the right of states to conduct innocent passage in the territorial sea, but the treaty did not resolve either the appropriate breadth of the territorial sea or the scope of the right of innocent passage within it. The LOS Convention, however, settled upon a 12 nm territorial sea,[22] and provided detailed provisions on the rights and duties of vessels engaged in innocent passage in article 19.

---

19. Ronald O'Rourke, Maritime Territorial and Exclusive Economic Zone (EEZ) Disputes Involving China: Issues for Congress, CRS R42784 Congressional Research Service, April 11, 2014, 4. (Reference to Navy Office of Legislative Affairs e-mail to CRS, June 15, 2012. Two additional countries—Ecuador and Peru—have restrictions inconsistent with UNCLOS that would limit the exercise of high seas freedoms by foreign navies beyond 12 nautical miles from the coast, but do so solely because they claim an extension of their territorial sea beyond 12 nautical miles.) *Id.*

20. Kraska, Maritime Power and Law of the Sea, *supra* note 7, 396–406 and 431–442.

21. J. Ashley Roach and Robert W. Smith, United States Responses to Excessive Maritime Claims 7–9 (3d Ed. 2012).

22. LOS Convention, *supra*, note 2, art. 3.

Article 19, Law of the Sea Convention (1982)

Meaning of innocent passage

1.   Passage is innocent so long as it is not prejudicial to the peace, good order or security of the coastal State. Such passage shall take place in conformity with this Convention and with other rules of international law.

2. ֵ Passage of a foreign ship shall be considered to be prejudicial to the peace, good order or security of the coastal State if in the territorial sea it engages in any of the following activities:

(a) any threat or use of force against the sovereignty, territorial integrity or political independence of the coastal State, or in any other manner in violation of the principles of international law embodied in the Charter of the United Nations;

(b) any exercise or practice with weapons of any kind;

(c) any act aimed at collecting information to the prejudice of the defence or security of the coastal State;

(d) any act of propaganda aimed at affecting the defence or security of the coastal State;

(e) the launching, landing or taking on board of any aircraft;

(f) the launching, landing or taking on board of any military device;

(g) the loading or unloading of any commodity, currency or person contrary to the customs, fiscal, immigration or sanitary laws and regulations of the coastal State;

(h) any act of wilful and serious pollution contrary to this Convention;

(i) any fishing activities;

(j) the carrying out of research or survey activities;

(k) any act aimed at interfering with any systems of communication or any other facilities or installations of the coastal State;

(l) any other activity not having a direct bearing on passage.

In at least two highly publicized incidents, the coastal state reacted forcefully against U.S. freedom of navigation challenges. The first was the encounter between U.S. and Libyan fighter planes in the Gulf of Sidra, which Libya claimed was an "historic bay" and that waters within the 115-mile straight baseline across its mouth were internal waters. The second was the "bumping" incident in 1988 between U.S. and Soviet warships in the Black Sea in an area of the territorial sea that the Soviet government purported to require prior consent for the innocent passage of warships. The latter incident, although provoking reciprocal diplomatic protests between the United States and the Soviet Union, eventually led to the Jackson Hole agreement.[23]

Joint Statement by the United States of America and the Union of Soviet Socialist Republics

September 23, 1989, Jackson Hole, Wyoming

The Governments are guided by the provisions of the 1982 United Nations Convention on the Law of the Sea ... and consider it useful to issue the attached Uniform Interpretation of the Rules of International Law Governing Innocent Passage.

---

23. *Uniform Interpretation of Rules of International Law Governing Innocent Passage*, DEP'T OF ST. BULL., Nov. 1989, at 26.

Uniform Interpretation of Rules of International Law Governing Innocent Passage

1. The relevant rules of international law governing innocent passage of ships in the territorial sea are stated in the 1982 United Nations Convention on the Law of the Sea (Convention of 1982), particularly in Part II, Section 3.

2. All ships, including warships, regardless of cargo, armament or means of propulsion, enjoy the right of innocent passage through the territorial sea in accordance with international law, for which neither prior notification nor authorization is required.

3. Article 19 of the Convention of 1982 sets out in paragraph 2 an exhaustive list of activities that would render passage not innocent. A ship passing through the territorial sea that does not engage in any of those activities is in innocent passage....

5. Ships exercising the right of innocent passage shall comply with all laws and regulations of the coastal State adopted in conformity with relevant rules of international law as reflected in Articles 21, 22, 23 and 25 of the Convention of 1982. These include the laws and regulations requiring ships exercising the right of innocent passage through its territorial sea to use such sea lanes and traffic separation schemes as it may prescribe where needed to protect safety of navigation. In areas where no such sea lanes or traffic separation schemes have been prescribed, ships nevertheless enjoy the right of innocent passage.

6. Such laws and regulations of the coastal State may not have the practical effect of denying or impairing the exercise of the right of innocent passage as set forth in Article 24 of the Convention of 1982.

7. If a warship engages in conduct which violates such laws or regulations or renders its passage not innocent and does not take corrective action upon request, the coastal State may require it to leave the territorial sea, as set forth in Article 30 of the Convention of 1982. In such case the warship shall do so immediately....

The current U.S. guidance on the Freedom of Navigation program is contained in declassified portions of Presidential Decision Directive 32:

Presidential Decision Directive 32 (1995)

in James Kraska & Raul Pedrozo, International Maritime Security Law (2013), p. 213

The United States considers the 1982 Convention on the Law of the Sea (LOS Convention) to accurately reflect the customary rules of international law concerning maritime navigation and overflight rights and freedoms.

It is U.S. policy to respect those maritime claims that are consistent with the navigational provisions of the LOS Convention. Additionally, the United States will exercise and assert its navigation and overflight rights on a worldwide basis in a manner consistent with the LOS Convention. The United States will not acquiesce in unilateral acts of other states designed to restrict the rights and freedoms of the international community in navigation and overflight and other traditional uses of the high seas.

Question for Discussion

1. Has the Freedom of Navigation program been effective in restraining excessive coastal state claims?

Straits Used for International Navigation

Corfu Channel Case (U.K. v. Alb.) (Merits)
1949 I.C.J. 4, at 28 (Apr. 9)

[Following an incident in which British warships were fired on by Albanian shore batteries while transiting the Corfu Channel, which had resulted in a protest by the British government and a reply by the Albanian government denying the right of warships to pass through the strait without prior authorization by Albanian authorities, the British Navy again sent its warships through Corfu Channel without the permission of Albania. Two destroyers struck mines. The two states agreed to take the dispute to the International Court of Justice which ruled:]

> It is, in the opinion of the Court, generally recognized and in accordance with international custom that States in time of peace have a right to send their warships through straits used for international navigation between two parts of the high seas without the previous authorization of a coastal State, provided that the passage is innocent. Unless otherwise prescribed in an international convention, there is no right for a coastal State to prohibit such passage through straits in time of peace.

> [In response to Albania's contention that passage was not authorized because Corfu was only a secondary route, the court stated:]

> [I]n the opinion of the Court the decisive criterion is rather its geographical situation as connecting two parts of the high seas and the fact of its being used for international navigation. Nor can it be decisive that this Strait is not a necessary route between two parts of the high seas, but only an alternate passage....

Reflecting the holding in the *Corfu Channel* Case, article 16, paragraph 4, of the 1958 Territorial Sea Convention adopted the principle of "nonsuspendable innocent passage" for international straits. With the adoption of the LOS Convention in 1982 and its entry into force in 1994, the territorial sea expanded from three to twelve nm in breadth, overlapping more than 100 international straits by the territorial sea. One of the concerns of naval powers during negotiations for the LOS Convention was the requirement that submarines navigate on the surface while in innocent passage. Also, there is no innocent passage regime for aircraft to overfly the territorial sea.

The right of transit passage applies to straits that connect one part of the high seas or EEZ and another part of the high seas or EEZ, including strategic straits like Gibraltar, Bab el Mandeb, Hormuz, Malacca and Singapore, Sunda, Lombok, and the Windward Passage.[24] Straits used for international navigation between one part of the high seas or an exclusive economic zone and another part of the high seas or an exclusive economic zone are subject to the legal regime of transit passage.

Transit passage is defined as the exercise of the freedoms of navigation and overflight solely for the purpose of continuous and expeditious transit in the normal modes of operation utilized by ships and aircraft for such passage. Ships and aircraft, while exercising the right of transit passage, shall: (a) proceed without delay through or over the strait; (b) refrain from any threat or use of force against the sovereignty, territorial integrity or political independence of States bordering the strait and, (c) refrain from any activities

---

24. LOS Convention, *supra* note 2, art. 37.

other than those incident to their normal modes of continuous and expeditious transit unless rendered necessary by *force majeure* or by distress. Surface warships may transit in a manner consistent with sound navigational practices and the security of the force, including the use of their electronic detection and navigational devices such as radar, sonar and depth-sounding devices, formation steaming and the launching and recovery of aircraft. Submarines are free to transit international straits submerged, since that is their normal mode of operation. Transit passage through international straits cannot be hampered or suspended by the strait states for any purpose during peacetime. This principle of international law also applies to transiting ships (including warships) of nations at peace with the bordering coastal nation but involved in armed conflict with another nation.

Questions for Discussion

1. Do the regimes of transit passage and archipelagic sea lanes passage adopted in the LOS Convention fulfill the needs of the international community for navigation through straits used for international navigation overlapped by the territorial sea?

2. Do the articles concerning transit through straits used for international navigation provide for submerged passage of submarines or overflight by aircraft? What conditions may the coastal State attach to such transit, if any? May the coastal State require its permission or consent? What arguments can be made in favor of such a right? What arguments against?[25]

Intelligence and Surveillance beyond the Territorial Sea

Since shortly after World War II, the United States and the Soviet Union have mounted significant efforts to gather electronic intelligence (ELINT) about the electronic warfare capabilities of the other state and its allies. For this effort they utilized specially equipped military aircraft and surface ships navigating near the coastline of a competitor. Although the emergence of remote sensing satellites reduced reliance on these sources of intelligence, they are to some extent still used by both states. During the fifty or so years in which these operations have been conducted, several U.S. reconnaissance planes were shot down and one U.S. warship was captured.[26] The following incident illustrates some of the legal and factual issues involved.

Capture of USS Pueblo by North Korea

On January 10, 1968, USS *Pueblo*, a lightly armed U.S. naval auxiliary, equipped specifically for passive electronic intelligence, left its base in Japan to conduct ELINT operations along the coast of North Korea. Its orders were to remain at least thirteen nm from the nearest land areas claimed by North Korea. On January 23, while on its mission, it was attacked and captured by three North Korean naval patrol craft. According to the United States, *Pueblo* never got closer than thirteen nm from North Korean land territory,

---

25. Horace B. Robertson, Jr., *Passage Through International Straits: A Right Preserved in the Third United Nations Conference on the Law of the Sea*, 20 Va. J. Int'l L. 801, 843–46 (1980).

26. In the 1967 Israeli-Egypt war, the U.S. naval intelligence ship USS *Liberty* was attacked by Israeli aircraft. Israel claimed this incident was a case of mistaken identity and paid indemnity to the United States. *See* N.Y. Times, May 29, 1968, § 1, at 4, col. 3. United States actions against Soviet ELINT vessels have been limited to ordering them out of the U.S. territorial sea when they have been detected there. *See* Meeker, *Legal Aspects of Contemporary World Problems*, 58 Dep't State Bull. 465, 468 (1968).

and at the time of seizure was at least fifteen nm away. The government of North Korea asserted that *Pueblo* was 7.6 nm from North Korean territory at the time of capture.

The United States made a two-pronged attack on the legality of the North Korean action:

> 1) *Pueblo* was on the high seas and was exercising a freedom of the high seas in performing the purely passive act of listening to North Korea's electronic emissions. As a U.S. warship *Pueblo* was entitled to complete immunity while on the high seas unless it posed a threat of armed attack on North Korea, which was clearly not the case.
>
> 2) If, contrary to the U.S. contention, *Pueblo* had strayed into North Korea's claimed territorial sea, North Korea's action should have been limited to ordering the ship to leave the territorial sea.[27]

Although North Korea's contentions were never fully articulated, since it did not take part in the Security Council debate on the incident, it would appear from the confessions it extracted from the captured crew members and the admissions it required from the United States as a condition for releasing the crew that it based its case entirely on the claimed illegal intrusion of its territorial waters.[28]

Others have suggested that North Korea could have based its action on Article 10 of the Korean Armistice Agreement, which provided that naval forces of each side "shall respect the waters contiguous to the Demilitarized Zone and to the land area of Korea under the control of the opposing side."[29]

The crew of USS *Pueblo* was released after eleven months of captivity. While in captivity they were required to sign confessions of illegal intrusion into North Korean territorial waters and espionage, which they repudiated upon their return from captivity. In a strange proceeding at Panmunjom, the United States signed a document prepared by the North Korean government which admitted the illegal intrusion into North Korean territorial waters, apologized for it, and gave assurances that it would not be repeated. At the same proceeding the U.S. spokesman read a prepared statement denying the truth of what was in the other document, saying that he was signing the North Korean government document "to free the crew and only to free the crew."[30]

Question for Discussion

If *Pueblo* had actually passed through North Korea's territorial sea, would it have been lawfully exercising the right of innocent passage under article 14 of the Territorial Sea Convention? Would the situation be changed if the LOS Convention, article 19(2) were in effect?

Military Activities in the Exclusive Economic Zone

The USS *Pueblo* incident occurred before adoption and entry into force of the LOS Convention. Since the treaty entered into force in 1994, states have worked to conform

---

27. Territorial Sea Convention, *supra* note 4, art. 23.

28. *North Korean Document Signed by U.S. at Panmunjom*, 60 DEP'T STATE BULL. 3 (1969).

29. *The 'Pueblo' Seizure: Fact, Law, Policy*, 63 PROC. AM. SOC. INT'L L. 1, 2 (1969) and *Comment, The Pueblo Seizure in a Better Ordered World*, 31 U. PITT. L. REV. 255, 268–69 (1969).

30. *Crew of USS Pueblo Released at Panmunjom: U.S. Position on Facts Unchanged*, 60 DEP'T STATE BULL. 1 (1969).

their coastal state claims to the rules set forth in the Convention. During the 1970s and 1980s, for example, most states rescinded territorial sea claims that were in excess of 12 nm. Some states, however, maintain competence or authority over offshore areas that are excessive in light of the rules of the LOS Convention.

James Kraska & Raul Pedrozo, International Maritime Security Law

278 (2013)

Worldwide, there are 18 nations that claim a security interest in the exclusive economic Zone (EEZ), typically by purporting to restrict foreign-flagged military activities. Among these nations, two are in South America (Brazil and Uruguay), two in Africa (Kenya and Cape Verde), one in the Middle East (Iran), and 13 are in Asia. Vietnam partially asserts an excessive EEZ claim by requiring warships that operate in its contiguous zone to seek and obtain permission 30 days in advance, and place weapons in an inoperative position during transit. Portugal is the only State in Europe that asserts a security interest in the EEZ, and two States making such claims are former Portuguese colonies—Brazil in South America and Cape Verde in West Africa.

In addition, the seven nations that illegally claim territorial seas in excess of 12 nm include: Benin (200 nm), Republic of Congo (200 nm), Ecuador (200 nm), Liberia (200 nm), Peru (200 nm), Somalia (200 nm) and Togo (30 nm), and there are five nations that claim security jurisdiction in their 24 nm contiguous zone: Cambodia, China, Sudan, Syria, and Vietnam.

James Kraska, Maritime Power and Law of the Sea

6 (2011)

From geostrategic and political-military perspectives, the EEZs are the most important part of the oceans. While representing a relatively small portion of the world's surface, 80 percent of the world's population lives along the littoral regions; over 80 percent of the world's capital cities are located there. Nearly all of the major global marketplaces for international trade ring the coast. Because of the concentration of people and activity, the shorelines are also the place where most of the world's important conflicts are likely to occur.[31]

Worldwide, more than one billion people depend on fish as their primary protein source.[32] Since most of the fish are located in the EEZ, the demand for food drives competition— and occasionally, conflict. Competition over other marine resources is also most acute in the EEZ. As the strip of water adjacent to the shoreline, the EEZ has acquired an undeniable element of psychological homeland security. Sovereign rights over the living and non-living resources inevitably morph into a sense of not just entitlement, but ownership over the area. The EEZ is rich in resources, crowded with people, enmeshed in vessel traffic and busy with activity. Consequently, the intersection of the political and legal status of the littoral regions and the effect of that status on expeditionary warfare has colored geopolitics for centuries and now forms the essential fabric of contemporary grand strategy.

---

31. General C. Krulak, Operational Maneuver From the Sea: A Concept for the Projection of Naval Power Ashore 1 (1999).

32. Carrie V. Kappel, et. al, *In the Zone: Comprehensive Ocean Protection*, Issues in Science & Technology 33 (2009).

On March 10, 1983, President Reagan proclaimed a U.S. 200 nm EEZ. His Proclamation confirmed that in the EEZ all states would "enjoy the high seas freedoms of navigation, overflight, the laying of submarine cables and pipelines, and other internationally lawful uses of the sea."[33] The president's statement reflects the norms contained in the LOS Convention article 58(2) and 87. Article 58 imports into the EEZ all of the high seas freedoms and other internationally lawful uses of the sea that are permitted in the high seas, including all of those identified in articles 86–115, "in so far as they are not incompatible" with Part V of the treaty that affords the coastal state certain exclusive rights to the resources of the zone. In the press release accompanying the Proclamation, the President stated:

> [T]he United States will exercise and assert its navigation and overflight rights and freedoms on a worldwide basis in a manner that is consistent with the balance of interests reflected in the [LOS] Convention. The United States will not, however, acquiesce in unilateral acts of other States designed to restrict the rights and freedoms of the international community in navigation and overflight and other related high seas uses.[34]

Question for Discussion

Is the President's statement reconcilable with the Brazilian government's statement upon ratification of the LOS Convention?

Statement of Brazil

Dec. 22, 1988, *in* Office of Legal Affairs, UN
The Law of the Sea: Declarations and Statements with Respect to the United Nations Convention on the Law of the Sea, at 22, UN Sales No. E.97.V3 (1997)

The Brazilian Government understands that the Provisions of the Convention do not authorize other States to carry out military exercises or manoeuvres, in particular those involving the use of weapons or explosives, in the exclusive economic zone without the consent of the coastal State.

At a Law of the Sea Institute conference in Hawaii in 1984, Ambassador Tommy T.B. Koh, who had represented Singapore and served as a President of the Third UN Conference on the Law of the Sea, commented on Brazil's declaration:

> The question of military activities in the exclusive economic zone is a very difficult one. Bernie Oxman will remember that the status of the exclusive economic zone was one of the last questions to be wrapped up in the negotiations in Committee Two. We finally succeeded in wrapping up this question of the status of the exclusive economic zone thanks to the personal initiative of our friend Jorge Castañeda of Mexico. Before he became foreign minister, he was the leader of the Mexican delegation. In 1977, I believe, Jorge Castañeda invited about 20 of us to dinner one evening. After dinner was over, he asked that the table be cleared and said, ... [W]e have been grappling for the last three years with the question of the status of the exclusive economic zone. I have invited you here because I

---

33. Pres. Proc. No. 5030, 48 Fed. Reg. 10,605 (Mar. 10, 1983).
34. Statement of President Reagan, *supra* note 17.

believe you represent a cross section of the points of view of the Conference and you are the leaders of the Conference. I suggest, if you all agree, that we commence informal consultations on this question. We agreed and sat down and worked, in fact, all night long. And we began to negotiate every night for two weeks and eventually wrapped up the issue.

The solution in the Convention text is very complicated. Nowhere is it clearly stated whether a third state may or may not conduct military activities in the exclusive economic zone of a coastal state. But, it was the general understanding that the text we negotiated and agreed upon would permit such activities to be conducted. I therefore would disagree with the statement made in Montego Bay by Brazil, in December 1982, that a third state may not conduct military activities in Brazil's exclusive economic zone ... [35]

No country in recent years has been more forceful in advancing excessive coastal state claims over the EEZ—and the high seas—than China. "Beijing has the most expansive security and sovereignty EEZ claim on the planet—a serial violator of the regime of high seas freedoms in the [EEZ].[36] China has pressed its claim to a security interest in the EEZ against U.S. ships and aircraft operating in the zone on numerous occasions. For example, in 2001, a Chinese fighter jet conducted an aggressive interception of a U.S. P-3C surveillance aircraft on a strategic reconnaissance operation over the South China Sea about 65 miles from Hainan Island. The jet collided with the slower propeller-driven aircraft, which caused the loss of the Chinese jet and pilot, and required an emergency landing in China by the U.S. aircraft.[37] In March 2001, September 2002, March 2009, and May 2009, Chinese ships and aircraft confronted and harassed *Bowditch*, *Impeccable*, and *Victorious*, U.S. special mission ships of the U.S. Navy, as they conducted military surveys in China's EEZ.[38] Chinese ships have also interfered with operations by Indian Navy warships, including INS *Airavat* in July 2011 and INS *Shivalik* in June 2012.[39]

The Navy EP-3 Incident in the South China Sea (2001)

In a routine electronic surveillance patrol about 65 nm off the south coast of China in 2001, a U.S. Navy EP-3 Aries II aircraft was "buzzed" by two Chinese F-8 fighter aircraft. The interception was not unusual. In this case, however, one of the Chinese aircraft approached too closely to the EP-3, and collided with it. The Chinese fighter aircraft crashed into the sea and its pilot was lost at sea. The EP-3 issued a Mayday alarm, and although badly damaged, made an emergency landing on the Chinese island of Hainan.

Mutual recriminations followed, each government asserting that the maneuvering of the other's aircraft caused the collision. The Chinese government claimed that the American aircraft violated the rules reflected in the LOS Convention by conducting intelligence, surveillance, and reconnaissance activities in its Exclusive Economic Zone. China further complained that the American aircraft violated Chinese territorial sovereignty by entering its airspace and landing at a Chinese airfield without prior entry approval.

---

35. CONSENSUS AND CONFRONTATION: THE UNITED STATES AND THE LAW OF THE SEA CONVENTION, A WORKSHOP FROM THE LAW OF THE SEA INSTITUTE, Jan. 9–13, 1984 at 303–304 (Jon M. Van Dyke, ed., Honolulu: Law of the Sea Institute, 1985).

36. Kraska and Pedrozo, *supra* note 30, p. 279.

37. Shirley A. Kan et. al, CHINA-U.S. AIRCRAFT COLLISION INCIDENT OF APRIL 2001: ASSESSMENTS AND POLICY IMPLICATIONS, CRS Report RL30946, Congressional Research Service, Oct. 10, 2001.

38. O'Rourke, MARITIME TERRITORIAL AND EXCLUSIVE ECONOMIC ZONE (EEZ) DISPUTES INVOLVING CHINA, *supra*, note 19, p. 4–5.

39. *Id.*

The U.S. government asserted, however, that the emergency landing was in accordance with "international emergency procedures." The crew of the EP-3 were released after eleven days detention when the United States expressed its "sincere regret" and was "sorry" for the loss of the Chinese plane and pilot and "sorry" that the entering of China's airspace and the landing did not have verbal clearance. The EP-3 was dismantled and returned to the United States three months later.[40]

Maritime Territorial and EEZ Disputes Involving China

Ronald O'Rourke, Congressional Research Service (April 11, 2014)

China's actions for asserting and defending its maritime territorial and exclusive EEZ claims in the East China (ECS) and South China Sea (SCS), particularly since late 2013, have heightened concerns among observers that ongoing disputes over these waters and some of the islands within them could lead to a crisis or conflict between China and a neighboring country such as Japan, the Philippines, or Vietnam, and that the United States could be drawn into such a crisis or conflict as a result of obligations the United States has under bilateral security treaties with Japan and the Philippines.

More broadly, China's actions for asserting and defending its maritime territorial and EEZ claims have led to increasing concerns among some observers that China may be seeking to dominate or gain control of its near-seas region, meaning the East China Sea, the South China Sea, and the Yellow Sea. Chinese domination over or control of this region, or Chinese actions that are perceived as being aimed at achieving such domination or control, could have major implications for the United States, including implications for U.S.-China relations, for interpreting China's rise as a major world power, for the security structure of the Asia-Pacific region, for the long-standing U.S. strategic goal of preventing the emergence of a regional hegemon in one part of Eurasia or another, and for two key elements of the U.S.-led international order that has operated since World War II — the non-use of force or coercion as a means of settling disputes between countries, and freedom of the seas.[41]

Questions for Discussion

1. Which country — the United States or China — has the most accurate understanding of the relationship between article 58 and 87 in the LOS Convention concerning military activities in the EEZ? Does the term "*inter alia*" in article 87 of the LOS Convention include the right to conduct military exercises on the high seas? What is the meaning of article 88?

2. As previously discussed, the 1982 LOS Convention creates a new legal division of the sea, the Exclusive Economic Zone.[42] Within this zone the coastal state has jurisdiction to control marine scientific research. Marine scientific research, however, is not defined. Under article 58, states other than the coastal state may exercise the high seas freedoms of navigation, overflight, laying of submarine cables and pipelines, "and other internationally lawful uses of the seas related to these freedoms, such as those associated with the operations of ships aircraft, and submarine cables and pipelines...." Does the entry into force of this Convention have any effect on the conduct of ELINT operations in the EEZ?

---

40. *Contemporary Practice of the United States Relating to International Law*, 95 Am. J. Int'l L. 626 at 630–33 (2001).

41. *See* LOS Convention, *supra* note 2, arts. 86–90 and 95.

42. LOS Convention, *supra* note 2, arts. 56, 246.

3. How do you square the rights of the coastal State in article 56 with the rights of the international community in articles 58 and 87 of the LOS Convention? What are the rights of the coastal State in the EEZ to which the international community owes "due diligence" under article 56? What rights and freedoms belong to the international community in the EEZ under articles 58 and 87?

Was it correct that the military aircraft violated international law by entering Chinese territorial airspace without prior authorization? Note that article 32 of the Convention Relating to the Regulation of Aerial Navigation of 1919[43] (Paris Convention) provides that military aircraft authorized to land or "forced to land" in another state's territory shall enjoy the privileges which are customarily accorded to foreign ships of war." The 1944 Convention on International Civil Aviation[44] (Chicago Convention), which succeeded the Paris Convention, provides that no military airplanes shall land on the territory of another state without prior permission. Do the terms of the latter Convention weaken the U.S.'s argument concerning emergency landing?

The High Seas

Weapons Exercises and Testing

Myres S. McDougal and William T. Burke,
The Public Order of the Oceans
768–70, 771–73 (1962)

Naval operations at sea during times of peace are the most common form of exclusive use considered to be in accord with international law. With the increased range of naval guns and coastal artillery, and the appearance of increasingly dangerous devices of naval warfare, states with extensive naval forces found it necessary to institutionalize some of their peacetime defensive activities in order to minimize conflict between such activities and commercial navigation and fishing. Exercises involving the use of modern weapons could not be conducted with safety except in relatively unfrequented areas, and, moreover, mariners preferred to avoid exercise areas altogether rather than to be delayed and endangered by unexpected encounters. New means of communication made it possible to supplement, if not to displace, visual signaling as a means of reducing interference between navigation and dangerous defensive activities.

Naval powers therefore began the practice of conducting their more dangerous maneuvers and defensive activities in circumscribed areas, selected with a view to the least possible interference with navigation and fishing. Mariners throughout the world were advised, through national hydrographic offices and other channels of information relating to navigation, that designated areas would be unsafe for navigation either indefinitely or at certain times. The United States has established well over 400 such areas, ranging in size from less than a square mile to the vast area surrounding Bikini and Eniwetok Atolls, and in duration from a few hours to many years. Other naval powers, including the United Kingdom, Canada, Australia, and the Soviet Union, have engaged in the same practice for similar purposes. Ordinarily, no claim is made to enforce warning areas by means of formal sanctions, and the normal responsibility for taking reasonable measures at the scene to avoid accidents is considered to rest with the authorities using the areas for

---

43. Convention Relating to the Regulation of Aerial Navigation (1919), 11 U.N.T.S. 173.
44. Convention on International Civil Aviation (1944), 15 U.N.T.S. 1180.

dangerous operations. Some danger areas are, however, announced in terms which make clear that states intend to enforce observance....

This relatively ancient practice in exclusive use, fully supported by international law, acquired a new wrinkle with the advent of rockets and missiles. Both the Soviet Union and the United States have established areas in remote parts of the ocean into which missiles are fired and have invited the ships and planes of other states to refrain from entering the area. Despite reports of radar tracking by Soviet ships of the Mercury man-in-space experimental flights, it is not likely that the United States feels obliged by international law to permit Soviet or other foreign vessels in the immediate target area. No doubt the Soviet Union also feels less than hospitable about American ships and planes intruding upon its target zone in the Central Pacific. By express pronouncement of the President, the United States regards the Soviet use of the Pacific area for missile testing as permissible under international law.

Nuclear weapons testing necessarily displaces free movement in the air and sea for thousands of square miles in the vicinity, and this activity has understandably raised controversy about limits on free navigation. Several states and writers have declared such use impermissible and have advanced in support of these contentions conceptions of freedom of the seas incorporating absolute prohibitions upon any kind of interference with the classical uses of the sea, navigation, and fishing. It is scarcely necessary to demonstrate again the manifold inadequacies which attend such misconceptions. It should suffice to note that they are quite unsatisfactory representations of the permissible exclusive authority established by the historic practice of states and ignore completely that the most relevant standard prescribed by customary international law is that of reasonableness.

Questions for Discussion

1. The standard of reasonableness, referred to by Professors McDougal and Burke, is incorporated into article 2 of the High Seas Convention, which provides in part that high seas freedoms "shall be exercised by all States with reasonable regard to the interests of other States in their exercise of the freedom of the high seas." In concluding that the U.S. nuclear tests at Bikini and Eniwetok met this standard, Professors McDougal and Burke rely on the remoteness of the areas from populations of any appreciable magnitude, minimal interference with air and sea navigation and only slight and short term interference with Japanese fishing in contrast with the vital interest at stake for the United States and the lack of any practicable alternative site. Are these arguments persuasive?[45]

2. In 1963 the United States, Great Britain, and the U.S.S.R. negotiated a treaty barring the testing of nuclear weapons in the atmosphere, outer space, and underwater. As of January 1, 1982, there were 101 parties to the treaty. France had not become a party and continued to conduct atmospheric tests in the South Pacific until 1974. In 1973, Australia and New Zealand instituted proceedings against France in the International Court of Justice seeking a declaration that atmospheric testing was contrary to international law and an order requiring France to cease testing. The Court issued an Interim Protection Order on June 22, 1973.[46] France continued to test until 1974. At that time France made unilateral declarations to the effect that it would terminate atmospheric testing. Reading these declarations as binding obligations, the I.C.J. dismissed the actions by Australia and New Zealand.[47]

---

45. *Cf.* Margolis, *The Hydrogen Bomb Experiments and International Law*, 64 Yale L.J. 629 (1955).
46. 1973 I.C.J. 99 and 135.
47. 1974 I.C.J. 253 and 457.

Blockade, Quarantine, and Defensive Declarations

Doctrine of Blockade

Prior to World War I the law of naval warfare had developed along two distinct lines with respect to belligerent measures directed to the control of maritime commerce with an enemy. One was denominated "blockade"—the maritime counterpart of siege—and was directed to the total closing of enemy ports or an entire coastline to maritime communication by ships of any nationality. The other was "contraband" and was directed to the interdiction of cargoes that might assist the enemy's war effort. Both doctrines developed rather rigid rules, particularly with respect to their effects on neutral commerce.

For blockade there were strict rules concerning such things as notification of the commencement of the blockade and the identification of areas blockaded, prohibitions against barring access to neutral ports, and the requirement that the blockade be effective and not just a "paper" blockade. The blockade was enforced by a close-in cordon of ships off the blockaded port or coast.

Contraband, on the other hand, was a measure that could be enforced anywhere on the oceans by warships of a belligerent state against neutral and enemy ships suspected of carrying goods destined for territory held by the enemy or for its armed forces. Cargoes were either subject to confiscation or "free goods" depending on whether they were or could be used to further the enemy's war efforts and their destination. Many technical rules developed from the application of these basic principles.

World War I, with its concept of "total war," as well as the emergence of the submarine, severely tested the rigid, traditional rules of blockade and contraband. Great Britain instituted a long-distance blockade in the North Sea that cut off access to neutral as well as enemy territory. Germany initiated unrestricted submarine warfare against neutral as well as enemy shipping in certain waters. Great Britain instituted a "Navicert" system by which ships and cargoes were examined in port before setting sail for blockaded areas, thus avoiding the necessity for dangerous and costly "stop-and-board" searches at sea. Since some of these measures were taken under the theory of reprisal, by which a belligerent may lawfully take an otherwise unlawful action in retaliation for an unlawful action by its enemy, there was some uncertainty as to the continuing viability of the traditional rules.

World War II saw a renewal and extension of the practices of World War I. Submarine and aircraft attacks on shipping beyond the limits of traditional rules of blockade and contraband were the rule rather than the exception. Both the Axis and Allies violated at least some aspects of the rules of submarine warfare during World War II.[48] As in World War I, many of these actions were justified on the theory of reprisal, which left the traditional law in a state of uncertainty. This uncertainty has influenced the practice of

---

48. The Nuremburg judgment held: "In view of all the facts proved and in particular of an order of the British Admiralty announced on the 8th May, 1940, according to which all vessels should be sunk at sight in the Skagerrak, and the answers to interrogatories by Admiral Nimitz stating that unrestricted submarine warfare was carried on in the Pacific Ocean by the United States from the first day that nation entered the war, the sentence of Doenitz is not assessed on the ground of his breaches of the international law of submarine warfare." The TRIAL OF THE MAJOR WAR CRIMINALS BEFORE THE INTERNATIONAL MILITARY TRIBUNAL, NUREMBURG 14 NOVEMBER 1945–1 OCTOBER 1946, Nuremburg, 1948, Vol. XXII, 558–559. *See also*, ROBERT K. WOETZEL, THE NUREMBURG TRIALS IN INTERNATIONAL LAW 14, 188–189 (London, Stevens; 1960).

states since World War II as they have attempted to use seapower to interdict or control maritime communication with an adversary in time of tension or armed conflict while attempting to minimize interference with "neutral" commerce and avoid confrontation with uninvolved states. As you examine the materials that follow, you may wish to consider whether the actions described fit within the traditional doctrines of blockade or contraband, and if they do not, why the national decision-makers chose not to rely on the traditional doctrines.

Korean War, 1950–1953

Telegram from the Joint Chiefs of Staff to the Commander in Chief, Far East (MacArthur)

in UNITED STATES DEPARTMENT OF STATE, 7 FOREIGN RELATIONS OF THE UNITED STATES, 1950, at 271 (1976)

1. In keeping with the United Nations Security Council's request for support to the Republic of Korea in repelling the Northern Korean invaders and restoring peace in Korea the President announced that he had ordered a Naval blockade of the entire Korean coast.

2. To implement this order you are authorized to use such means and forces as are available to you to deny unauthorized ingress to and egress from the Korean coast. The primary purpose is to suppress seaborne traffic to and from North Korea and to prevent movement by sea of forces and supplies for use in operations against South Korea. Care should be taken to keep well clear of the coastal waters of Manchuria and USSR.

Cuban Missile Crisis, 1962

In October 1962 the U.S. government received intelligence information from aerial reconnaissance and other means, that the U.S.S.R. was deploying offensive nuclear missiles in Cuba. While simultaneously reporting these events to the UN Security Council, the United States sought and obtained from the Organ of Consultation of the American Republics a resolution which recommended that the Member States, in accordance with Articles 6 and 8 of the Rio Treaty,[49] take all measures, individually and collectively, including the use of armed force, which they might deem necessary to prevent the missiles from becoming an active threat to the peace and security of the Continent.

Interdiction of the Delivery of Offensive Weapons to Cuba

Proc. No. 3504, 27 Fed. Reg. 10,401, (Oct. 23, 1962)

… I, JOHN F. KENNEDY, President of the United States of America, acting under and by virtue of the authority conferred upon me by the Constitution and statutes of the United States, in accordance with the aforementioned resolutions of the United States Congress and of the Organ of Consultation of the American Republics, and to defend the security of the United States, do hereby proclaim that the forces under my command are ordered, beginning at 2:00 P.M. Greenwich time October 24, 1962, to interdict, subject

---

49. Inter-American Treaty of Reciprocal Assistance, Sept. 2, 1947, 62 Stat. 1681, 121 U.N.T.S. 77. Article 6 calls for the Organ of Consultation to meet upon the happening of any event that might endanger the peace of America in order to agree on measures necessary for the common defense and maintenance of the peace and security of the Continent. Article 8 lists the measures the Organ may invoke; the list includes "use of armed force."

to the instructions herein contained, the delivery of offensive weapons and associated material to Cuba.

For the purposes of this Proclamation, the following are declared to be prohibited material:

Surface-to-surface missiles; bomber aircraft; bombs, air-to-surface rockets and guided missiles; warheads for any of the above weapons; mechanical or electronic equipment to support or operate the above items; and any other classes of materiel hereafter designated by the Secretary of Defense for the purpose of effectuating this Proclamation.

To enforce this order, the Secretary of Defense shall take appropriate measures to prevent the delivery of prohibited materiel to Cuba, employing the land, sea and air forces of the United States in cooperation with any forces that may be made available by other American States.

. . . .

Any vessel or craft which may be proceeding toward Cuba may be intercepted and may be directed to identify itself, its cargo, equipment and stores and its ports of call, to stop, to lie to, to submit to visit and search, or to proceed as directed. Any vessel or craft, which fails or refuses to respond to or comply with directions shall be subject to being taken into custody. Any vessel or craft which it is believed is en route to Cuba and may be carrying prohibited materiel or may itself constitute such materiel shall, wherever possible, be directed to proceed to another destination of its own choice and shall be taken into custody if it fails or refuses to obey such directions. All vessels or craft taken into custody shall be sent into a port of the United States for appropriate disposition.

In carrying out this order, force shall not be used except in case of failure or refusal to comply with directions, or with regulations or directives of the Secretary of Defense issued hereunder, after reasonable efforts have been made to communicate them to the vessel or craft, or in case of self-defense. In any case, force shall be used only to the extent necessary.

Vietnam War, 1964–1975

During the Vietnam War neither the Republic of Vietnam nor the United States attempted to interdict maritime commerce to North Vietnam until 1972. Rather, South Vietnamese naval forces, with U.S. assistance, concentrated on stopping the flow of war materials by sea to the Viet Cong and North Vietnamese forces operating in South Vietnam. In 1972, however, the United States and the Republic of Vietnam announced maritime interdiction measures.

U.N. Notified of New Measures against North Viet-Nam

Letter from George H. W. Bush, U.S. Representative to the United Nations,
to the President of the Security Council May 8 66 Dep't St. Bull. 750, 751 (1972)

[The] Republic of Vietnam and the United States of America have jointly decided to take the following measures of collective self-defense: The entrances to the ports of North Vietnam are being mined, commencing 0900 Saigon time May 9, and the mines are set to activate automatically beginning 1800 hours Saigon time May 11. This will permit vessels of other countries presently in North Vietnamese ports three daylight periods to depart safely. The mines will be so positioned within the internal waters and claimed territorial waters of North Vietnam as to prevent access to North Vietnamese ports and North Vietnamese naval operations from these ports. In addition, the Republic of Vietnam and the United States are advising their respective naval and air forces to take appropriate measures within the internal and claimed territorial waters of North Vietnam to prevent the delivery of seaborne supplies to North Vietnam.

Falkland Islands War, 1982

In 1982 Great Britain had been in undisturbed possession of the Falkland Islands for approximately 150 years. Britain's claim to sovereignty over the Islands, however, was disputed by Argentina, which considered the Islands rightfully Argentinian. On April 2, 1982, Argentina captured the Falkland Islands by military force. The British recaptured them on June 14, 1982. In the course of its military operations in the area, the British government took several measures to control maritime navigation and commerce in the area.

Declaration of a Maritime Exclusion Zone

TIMES (London), Apr. 8, 1982, at 6

From 0400 Greenwich Mean Time on Monday, April 12, 1982, a maritime exclusion zone will be established around the Falkland Islands. The outer limits of this zone is a circle of 200 nm radius from [point described by latitude and longitude coordinates], which is approximately the centre of the Falkland Islands.

From the time indicated, any Argentine warships and Argentine naval auxiliaries found within this zone will be treated as hostile and are liable to be attacked by British forces.

This measure is without prejudice to the right of the United Kingdom to take whatever additional measures may be needed in exercise of its right of self defense under Article 51 of the United Nations Charter.

Declaration of a Total Exclusion Zone

TIMES (London), Apr. 29, 1982, at 1

From 11 am GMT on April 30, 1982, a Total Exclusion Zone (TEZ) will be established around the Falkland Islands. The outer limit of this zone will be the same as for the MEZ established on April 12....

From the time indicated the exclusion zone will apply not only to Argentine warships and naval auxiliaries but also to any other ship, whether naval or merchant vessel, which is operating in support of the illegal occupation of the Falkland Islands by Argentine forces.

The Gulf War, 1990–1991

Special Warning No. 80
U.S. Navy (17 August 1990)

in THE KUWAIT CRISIS: BASIC DOCUMENTS 248 (E. Lauterpacht et al. eds., 1991)

1. In response to requests from the legitimate Government of Kuwait and in exercising the inherent right of collective self-defense recognized under Art. 51 of the UN Charter, United States forces will, in cooperation with regional and allied forces, conduct a maritime operation to intercept the import and export of commodities and products to and from Iraq and Kuwait that are prohibited by UN Security Council Resolution 661 [imposing an economic embargo on exports to and imports from Iraq and occupied Kuwait.]

2. Affected areas include the Strait of Hormuz, Strait of Tiran, and other choke points, key ports, and oil pipeline terminals. Specifically, Persian Gulf interception efforts will

be concentrated in international waters south of 27 degrees north latitude; Red Sea interception efforts will be conducted in international waters north of 22 degrees north latitude.

3. All merchant ships perceived to be proceeding to or from Iraqi or Kuwaiti ports, or transshipment points, and carrying embargoed material or from Iraq or Kuwait, will be intercepted and may be searched.

4. Ships which, after being intercepted, are determined to be proceeding to or from Iraqi or Kuwaiti ports, or transshipment points, and carrying embargoed material to or from Iraq or Kuwait, will not be allowed to proceed with their planned transit....

6. Failure of a ship to proceed as directed will result in the use of the minimum level of force necessary to ensure compliance.

UN Security Council Resolution 665
U.N. Doc. S/RES/665 (1990)

1. *Calls upon* those Member States co-operating with the Government of Kuwait which are deploying maritime forces to the area to use such measures commensurate to the specific circumstances as may be necessary under the authority of the Security Council to halt all inward and outward maritime shipping in order to inspect and verify their cargoes and destinations to ensure strict implementation of the provisions related to such shipping laid down in Resolution 661 (1990).

Libyan Civil War, 2011
UN Security Council Resolution 1970
U.N. Doc. S/RES/1970 (2011)

... Member States shall immediately take the necessary measures to prevent the direct or indirect supply, sale or transfer to the Libyan Arab Jamahiriya, from or through their territories or by their nationals, or using their flag vessels or aircraft, of arms and related materiel of all types, including weapons and ammunition, military vehicles and equipment, paramilitary equipment, and spare parts for the aforementioned, and technical assistance, training, financial or other assistance, related to military activities or the provision, maintenance or use of any arms and related materiel, including the provision of armed mercenary personnel.... [50]

Operative paragraph 11 called on States to inspect all cargo to and from Libya, including seaports and airports if there were reasonable grounds to believe the items were unauthorized.[51]

On March 17, 2011, the Security Council adopted Resolution 1973, which authorized member States, *inter alia*, to use all necessary measures to enforce the arms embargo imposed by Resolution 1970. Resolution 1973 replaced operative paragraph 11 of Resolution 1970 with even stronger authority to enforce an arms embargo and expand the scope of inspections of air and sea transportation into and out of Libya. The modified text called on flag States of ships and aircraft to cooperate with such inspections and it authorized

------

50. S/RES/1970 (2011), Feb. 26, 2011, para. 9.
51. *Id.*, at para. 11.

Member States to use "all measures commensurate to the specific circumstances" to conduct maritime and aviation inspections.[52]

Questions for Discussion

1. Note that in the Korean War the United States had no hesitation in calling its maritime interdiction of the Korean coast a "blockade." In all subsequent actions described above, however, the states conducting interdiction have avoided using that term. One reason for avoiding it is that blockade has traditionally been considered a "belligerent right," and in situations short of declared war, states have not wished to run the risk of bringing into play a technical state of belligerency because of the complex of relationships it might trigger with other belligerents and neutrals. Although President Kennedy's Cuban Missile Crisis Proclamation contained some of the elements of both contraband and blockade, it was not called either. A new title, *quarantine*, was coined in order, in part at least, to avoid the rigid rules applicable to these hoary doctrines.[53]

2. If the United States was not exercising a belligerent action of blockade or contraband in the Cuban Missile Crisis, on what basis was the action justified? Some publicists have suggested that the action was legally justified under the inherent right of individual and collective self-defense confirmed under Article 51 of the UN Charter.[54] Spokesmen for the United States, however, refused to rely on the right of self-defense but rather found its authority in resolutions under the Rio Treaty.[55]

If the United States relied on the authority of a regional organization (OAS), how did it avoid the stricture of Article 53, paragraph 1, of the UN Charter that, "No regional enforcement action shall be taken under regional arrangements or by regional agencies without the authorization of the Security Council?" Meeker and Chayes argue that since the resolution of the OAS was in the form of a recommendation and not binding, it was not technically an "enforcement action" and thus within the authority of a regional organization "dealing with such matters relating to the maintenance of international peace and security as are appropriate for regional action."[56] Do you find this argument convincing? Would the inherent right of self-defense be a better foundation? Note that the British government relied on the right of self-defense in the Falkland Islands declarations. Do factual differences between the two situations explain the difference?

3. Mines, unlike manned ships and aircraft, are unable to discriminate between ships based on nationality or cargo. Does their use, as in North Vietnam in 1972, upset the balance between the interest of a party to hostilities in cutting off war supplies to an enemy and the interest of non-parties in continuing maritime shipping? Does limitation of mining to "internal waters and claimed territorial waters" make the action acceptable in today's international legal order?[57]

---

52. S/RES/1973, Mar. 17, 2011, para. 13.

53. Abram Chayes, *Law and the Quarantine of Cuba*, 41 Foreign Aff. 550, 552 (1963).

54. Myres S. McDougal, *The Soviet-Cuban Quarantine and Self-Defense*, 57 Am. J. Int'l L. 597 (1962); Christol and Davis, *Maritime Quarantine: The Naval Interdiction of Offensive Weapons and Associated Material to Cuba, 1962*, 57 Am. J. Int'l L. 525 (1963).

55. Abram Chayes, *The Legal Case for U.S. Action on Cuba*, 47 Dep't State Bull. 763 (1962); Meeker, *Defensive Quarantine and the Law*, 57 Am J. Int'l L. 515 (1963). (Mr. Chayes was Legal Adviser to the Department of State and Mr. Meeker was the Deputy Legal Adviser.)

56. Charter of the United Nations, article 52, para. 1.

57. For contrasting views on the mining of North Vietnamese waters, *see* Abram Chayes, *Too Subtle for Russians? Mr. Nixon Avoids Use of "Blockade,"* Wash. Post, May 14, 1972, §B at 6, col. 5, and John Norton Moore, *A Professor on the Law of Blockade*, Wash. Post, May 20, 1972, §A at 14, cols. 3 & 4.

4. Note that U.S. interdiction of imports and exports to and from Iraq and Kuwait preceded the Security Council Resolution. Was the U.S. unilateral declaration legitimate under the inherent right of collective self-defense? Did the Security Council Resolution resolve any questions of legitimacy? Do the norms of international law (i.e., the law of war) apply to forces acting under UN authority as they would to states acting under the inherent right of self-defense recognized in Article 51 of the UN Charter?

5. In view of the almost uniform avoidance of the use of the term "blockade" by states implementing maritime commerce control measures since World War II, is the law of blockade defunct? The U.S. Navy's operational manual states, "Notwithstanding this trend in belligerent practices (during general war) away from the establishment of blockades that conform to the traditional rules, blockade continues to be a useful means to regulate the competing interests of belligerents and neutrals in more limited armed conflict."[58]

Protection of Ocean Rights

The Concept of Flag-State Jurisdiction[59]

Although recent decades have seen a proliferation of coastal-state jurisdictions over activities in the oceans, the traditional and primary means for enforcement of the public order of the oceans is the concept of the flag state. The basic elements of this concept are first, a requirement that every ship be registered in a single state, the "flag state;" second, a requirement that states granting their registration to ships exercise prescriptive and enforcement jurisdiction over them, particularly with regard to the internal order of the ships, safety at sea, and the observance of international standards for protection of the marine environment;[60] and third, the full or partial immunity of the ship from the jurisdiction of any state except the flag state.

Under all circumstances save when the crew has mutinied and is engaged in piracy, warships are fully immune from the jurisdiction of states other than the flag state in all parts of the oceans. The immunity of merchant ships depends on the part of the ocean they are in and the circumstances of their presence. On the high seas their immunity is essentially complete, the only exceptions being if the ship engages in piracy or the slave trade, is without nationality, is engaged in unauthorized broadcasting, or is pursued onto the high seas under the doctrine of "hot pursuit." In coastal zones, coastal states may be free to exercise limited jurisdiction over transiting ships under exceptional circumstances. Under the LOS Convention, for example, if a ship navigating in the territorial sea or EEZ has committed a violation of coastal state rules implementing applicable international pollution-control standards by discharging substances threatening serious damage to the coastline, the coastal state may exercise limited enforcement jurisdiction.[61] Although ships voluntarily within the territorial sea or internal waters of a foreign state other than while in innocent passage are fully subject to the jurisdiction of the coastal state, by comity most coastal states will not normally exercise jurisdiction in matters concerning the internal

---

58. A.R. Thomas and James C. Duncan, *Annotated Supplement to The Commander's Handbook on the Law of Naval Operations*, 73 U.S. NAVAL WAR COLLEGE INT'L LAW STUDIES 393 (1999).

59. LOS Convention, *supra* note 2, arts. 90–92 and 94.

60. This connection between flag state and ship is sometimes referred to as a "genuine link." LOS Convention, *supra* note 2, article 91.

61. *Id.* article 220(5).

discipline of the ship unless they affect the peace and good order of the port.[62] Details of the exceptions to the immunities of merchant ships are spelled out in the Territorial Sea Convention,[63] the High Seas Convention,[64] and the LOS Convention.[65]

In situations in which a state other than the flag state is entitled to exercise jurisdiction over a merchant ship on the high seas, the mechanism for exercising such jurisdiction is the right of visit. The right is confined to warships and is subject to a number of limiting conditions.[66]

Maritime Piracy[67]

In October 1985 four Palestinians, who had embarked as ordinary passengers, hijacked the *Achille Lauro*, an Italian-flag cruise liner, when it was some thirty miles off the coast of Egypt, taking the passengers (including a number of Americans) and crew as hostages. The hijackers demanded the release of Palestinians in Israeli jails as a condition for the release of the passengers. When Israel refused to yield, the Palestinians killed one American—a disabled Jewish man named Leon Klinghoffer—and threw his body overboard. The Palestinians forced the crew to sail the ship to Port Said, where they surrendered to Egyptian authorities, having negotiated safe passage out of Egypt. U.S. naval forces intercepted the plane carrying the hijackers over the Mediterranean, forcing it to land at a NATO base in Sicily, where the Italian authorities took them into custody. The United States brought charges against the hijackers for, *inter alia*, piracy and sought unsuccessfully to extradite them from Italy. Thereafter, there ensued a diplomatic row among the United States, Italy, and Egypt, over custody of the accused terrorists.

The hijackers were eventually tried in Italy and sentenced to long prison terms. Palestine Liberation Front (PLF) leader Muhammad Zaidan, known as Abu Abbas, however, was released by the Italian government. Abbas fled to Iraq, where he spent 17 years until he was captured by U.S. military forces in 2003. He died from heart disease while in custody. The attack on the *Achille Lauro* and the odious murder of Klinghoffer prompted the member states of the International Maritime Organization to adopt the Convention on the Suppression of Unlawful Acts against the Safety of Maritime Navigation in 1987.[68]

Definition of Piracy
Law of the Sea Convention, Article 101

Piracy consists of any of the following acts:

(a) Any illegal acts of violence or detention, or any act of depredation, committed for private ends by the crew or the passengers of a private ship or private aircraft, and directed—

---

62. Wildenhus's Case, 120 U.S. 1 (1887).
63. Territorial Sea Convention, *supra* note 4, arts. 18–22.
64. Convention on the High Seas, *supra* note 15, arts. 6 and 13–23.
65. LOS Convention, *supra* note 2, arts. 25–28, 73, 92, 99–111, and 220–221.
66. *Id.*, art. 110.
67. LOS Convention, *supra* note 2, arts. 100–110.
68. Convention for the Suppression of Unlawful Acts against the Safety of Maritime Navigation, Rome, Mar. 10, 1988, entered into force Mar. 1, 1992, 27 I.L.M. 672 (1988), UN Law of the Sea Bull. No. 11, July 1988, at 14, 1678 U.N.T.S. 221.

(i)   On the high seas, against another ship or aircraft, or against persons or property on board such ship or aircraft;

(ii) Against a ship, aircraft, persons or property in a place outside the jurisdiction of any state;

(b) Any act of voluntary participation in the operation of a ship or of an aircraft with knowledge of the facts making it a pirate ship or aircraft;

(c) Any act of inciting or intentionally facilitating an act described in subparagraph (a) or (b).

––––––––––––

Piracy is defined as any illegal act of violence, detention, or depredation committed for private (rather than governmental) ends, and committed by crew or passengers of a private ship or aircraft against another ship, persons, or crew. For a violent act to meet the definition of piracy it must be committed outside of a state's territorial waters. Inside territorial waters, such crimes constitute armed robbery at sea and are the responsibility of the coastal state. "Armed robbery at sea" in territorial waters can, a few meters away, be considered "piracy."

Subparagraph (a)(i) of article 101 requires that for an attack on the high seas to constitute piracy, it must be perpetrated against "another" ship or aircraft. Subparagraph (a)(ii) of article 101 then indicates that to be considered piracy, an attack has to be directed against a "ship or aircraft in a place outside the jurisdiction of any state." Subparagraphs (a)(i) and (a)(ii) are separated by the conjunction "and"—meaning that both elements are required to meet the definition of piracy. Piracy also includes the inchoate offenses of inciting any of the acts included in Article 101(a) or (b). Article 101(c) includes acts "inciting or intentionally facilitating" piracy.

Warships of all nations enjoy the right of visit or boarding on the high seas, even without the consent of the flag state, for the purpose of disrupting maritime piracy. If suspicion is not dispelled after inspection of the ship's registration papers, a boarding party may inspect the ship further under article 110 of the LOS Convention. Yet if suspicion proves unfounded, the state of a warship boarding a vessel flagged in another country may be liable in international law for compensation for any loss or damage that may have been sustained by the boarding or delay.[69]

Piracy encompasses all manner of unlawful depredations at sea, including theft, assault, hostage taking, and murder, and therefore is part of the human condition and cannot be completely eradicated. Piracy springs from a breakdown of civil authority and law enforcement on land, and a lack of good order at sea, so it is less prevalent where there is stable governance and the rule of law. The collapse of official authority in Somalia after 1991, for example, set off a ruinous economic depression and a shift in power from organs of the state to clan-based warlords. From 2005–2011, the incidence of maritime piracy off the coast of Somalia skyrocketed, forcing policymakers for the first time in generations to think about the origins of maritime piracy, the factors that affect its spatial distribution, and how to effectively counter it.

In the summer of 2008, at the prompting of the IMO (International Maritime Organization), the UN Security Council turned its attention toward combating piracy. Resolution 1816 was adopted on June 2, 2008 at the 5902nd meeting of the Security Council. Acting

––––––––––––

69. LOS Convention, *supra* note 2, arts. 106 and 110.

under Chapter VII of the UN Charter, the Security Council called on states to repress Somalia piracy and armed robbery. The Security Council stated it decides:

> ... States cooperating with the Transitional Federal Government (TFG) in the fight against piracy and armed robbery at sea ... may:
>
> (a) Enter the territorial waters of Somalia for the purpose of repressing acts of piracy and armed robbery at sea....
>
> (b) Use, within the territorial waters of Somalia ... all necessary means to repress acts of piracy and armed robbery.... [70]

Resolution 1816 encouraged states to increase and coordinate their efforts to deter acts of piracy in conjunction with the Somali Transitional Federal Government (TFG), Somalia's troubled legitimate authority.[71] The Somali TFG must provide notification to the UN Secretary General of states that exercise the authority. In short, the Security Council decided the situation in Somalia constituted a threat to international peace and security in the region and acted under Chapter VII to address the threat. Paragraph 7(a) of UN Security Council Resolution 1816 authorized all nations in cooperation with the Transitional Federal Government, to conduct anti-piracy naval and air maritime security operations within and beyond the territorial sea of Somalia to repress Somali piracy. Naval forces may, "in a manner consistent with action permitted on the high seas with respect to piracy under relevant international law," utilize "all necessary means to repress acts of piracy and armed robbery."[72]

The contemporary U.S. law of piracy imports verbatim the definition of piracy from the 1909 statute into Title 18 U.S. Code § 1651: "Whoever, on the high seas, commits the crime of piracy as defined by the law of nations, and is afterwards brought into or found in the United States, shall be imprisoned for life."[73] The statute imports the international law definition of piracy into U.S. law — creating a question of law for the district court in each case. The question in each case is whether the defendant committed an act of piracy, as that crime is recognized in international law and reflected in the United Nations Convention on the Law of the Sea.

Selected Bibliography

Churchill, Robin R. and A. Vaughan Lowe, *The Law of the Sea* (3d ed. 1999) is a well-respected, post-1982, one-volume treatise on the law of the sea.

Colombos, C. John, *The International Law of the Sea* (6th rev. ed. (1967)) is considered by many to be the standard reference work on the law of the sea in time of peace and war.

Fulton, T. *The Sovereignty of the Sea* (1911) provides a comprehensive historical overview of the development of the law of the sea.

Kraska, James, *Maritime Power and the Law of the Sea: Expeditionary Operations in World Politics* (2011) is a study on the relationship between expeditionary and littoral warfare and the law of the sea.

---

70. S/RES/1816 (2008), para. 7.

71. Bronwyn Bruton & J. Peter Pham, *The Splintering of Al Shabaab: A Rough Road from War to Peace*, Foreign Affairs, Feb. 2, 2012.

72. S/RES 1816, *supra* note 66, para. 7(b).

73. 18 U.S.C. § 1651 (2013).

Kraska, James and Raul Pedrozo, *International Maritime Security Law* (2013) contains legal and policy analysis of the full spectrum of maritime conflicts and security issues, from maritime law enforcement to the law of naval warfare.

McDougal, Myres and William Burke, *The Public Order of the Oceans* (1962) provides perhaps the most comprehensive and most-cited modern treatise on the law of the sea. It reflects the policy-oriented analysis of international law.

Nordquist, Myron H. ed., *United Nations Convention on the Law of the Sea 1982: A Commentary* (1985–2011) is a comprehensive, seven-volume analysis of the negotiating history of the 1982 Convention. Individual volumes were written and edited by authors who were intimately involved in the negotiation of the Convention.

O'Connell, Daniel P. *The International Law of the Sea* (Shearer, Ivan ed. 1982), a two-volume treatise, the second volume of which was completed by Professor Shearer after Professor O'Connell's death.

Pedrozo, Raul (Pete), Preserving Navigational Rights and Freedoms: The Right to Conduct Military Activities in China's Exclusive Economic Zone, 9 *Chinese Journal of International Law* 9–29 (2010).

Chapter 16

Outer Space Law

Robert A. Ramey

In this chapter:
Introduction
United Nations Space Treaties and Their Impact on U.S. Space Activities
Other Relevant International Law
Additional Issues Bearing Present or Future Implications for U.S. National Security
Selected Bibliography

Introduction

The law exists to govern human relations. The evolution of legal norms, nearly without exception, follows a preexisting need to regulate human activity. This is truest of all in cases impacting a state's national security and applies to all environments containing objects of interest—land, sea, air, cyber, and, since the middle of the twentieth century, outer space. As human interest has turned to space concerns, legal regulation has followed. With the exception of environmental protection, no major category of international law is of more recent origin than that devoted to outer space.[1]

In addition to international law, the highly commercialized and privatized U.S. space industry has precipitated growth in national legislation as well. Though the focus of this chapter is international law, both of these categories constitute the discussion of "space law" undertaken herein. Given its recent origin, and the fact that it is predominantly driven by technological advances in the exploration and use of space, space law is a discipline in transition—additional norms continue to emerge as space technology advances.

Definition and Features of Space Law

One may appropriately define space law as that law comprising "all international and national legal rules and principles which govern the exploration and use of outer space by States, international organizations, private persons and companies."[2] This broad definition reflects the rise of national legislation governing outer space activity, as well as of non-state actors in the increasingly commercialized and privatized space industry.

---

1. That space law rightfully takes its place as a major branch of international law is now beyond question.
2. Peter Malanczuk, *Space Law as a Branch of International Law*, 1994 NETH. Y.B. INT'L L. 143, 147 (1995) [hereinafter Malanczuk, *Space Law*].

Despite its relative recency, commentators have published literally thousands of articles, treatises, and reviews on the subject of space law. Indeed, several of these appeared before 1957, the year human activity within outer space began.[3] Thus, while it is a relatively recent phenomenon from the perspective of international law, space law today is a firmly established discipline resting essentially on five multilateral treaties adopted under UN auspices. From this treaty corpus, three distinctive features stand out.

First, in the continuing development of international space law, scholars, jurists, diplomats, and others make frequent use, by analogy, of norms drawn from other branches of international law. In establishing an early framework for space activities, "lawmakers were able to borrow from existing principles of international law, including analogies from international maritime law, the Antarctic Treaty, and the Partial Test Ban Treaty."[4] By use of these analogies legal experts continue to draw specific conclusions about the meaning of the regime once established. For example, one commentator has cited the legal propriety of spying from space as having emerged by reference to the law of the sea. "[S]ince outer space is beyond State sovereignty, as are the high seas, and as espionage from (or over) the latter is generally accepted as being a legal activity, it has been concluded that espionage from outer space is also legal."[5] Support for this conclusion is virtually unanimous, but the notable point is just how the commentator established it—by use of analogy. Others have accurately speculated on this basis that military spacecraft will be allowed to enter the territorial airspace of other states only upon special authorization, just as is the case with military aircraft.[6] As it has for over forty years, the principle of analogy will continue to play an important role in the evolution of space law.

Second, as a subset of public international law, and owing to continuing notions of state sovereignty, state conduct which space law does not prohibit is allowed.[7] A specific example illustrates the point. Because space law prohibits only the stationing of weapons of mass destruction in orbit around the Earth, in the absence of independent restriction

---

3. Although the United States placed a man-made object in outer space prior to this, 1957 is considered the watershed year in which the "Space Age" is most often said to have begun. On October 4 of that year, the Soviet Union launched Sputnik I, the world's first man-made satellite. For an interesting account of that event, *see* T. A. HEPPENHEIMER, COUNTDOWN: A HISTORY OF SPACE FLIGHT 122 (1997).

4. Nandasiri Jasentuliyana, *The Lawmaking Process in the United Nations*, *in* SPACE LAW: DEVELOPMENT AND SCOPE 41 (Nandasiri Jasentuliyana, ed., 1992).

5. BRUCE A. HURWITZ, THE LEGALITY OF SPACE MILITARIZATION 29, 30 (1986) [hereinafter HUR-WITZ].

6. *See* MYRES S. McDOUGAL, ET AL., LAW AND PUBLIC ORDER IN SPACE 729 (1963) [hereinafter McDOUGAL, ET AL.].

7. The general international legal proposition that that which is not forbidden is permitted is particularly relevant to space law where, though significant restrictions exist, they are few. In its advisory opinion on the threat or use of Nuclear Weapons, the International Court of Justice quoted from two previous cases for propositions of relevance to this principle. *See* The Legality of the Threat or Use of Nuclear Weapons (ICJ Advisory Opinion on Nuclear Weapons), 1996 I.C.J. 1 (referencing the *Steamship Lotus* and *Nicaragua* cases). In the *Steamship Lotus* case, the Permanent Court of International Justice (P.C.I.J.) stated that "restrictions upon the independence of States cannot ... be presumed" and that international law leaves to states "a wide measure of discretion which is only limited in certain cases by prohibitive rules." P.C.I.J. (ser. A) No. 10, at 18–19. More recently, the International Court of Justice stated that "in international law there are no rules, other than such rules as may be accepted by the State concerned, by treaty or otherwise, whereby the level of armaments of a sovereign state can be limited." Military and Paramilitary Activities (Nicar. v. U.S.) 1986 I.C.J. 4, 135. Though the latter language specifically addressed armaments, it rests on the rationale from the *Steamship Lotus* case—unless prohibited, an action is allowed.

from other sources, states may orbit weapons of lesser destructive capability for the simple reason that no specific prohibition exists.[8]

Third, international space law regulates state conduct. As sometimes distinguished from "astrolaw,"[9] and despite the widespread commercialization of space, space law is limited to "the regulation of those activities by states in outer space which are, by nature, essentially international."[10] Given the rise of private interests in space, international agreements will likely recognize the rights of non-state actors in space to an increasing degree. Nonetheless, the dominant actors, with respect to international legal rights and obligations, continue to be states.[11]

The transitional nature of space law at the beginning of the twenty-first century necessarily makes an assessment of its contribution to national security law transitional as well. Nevertheless, after several decades of legal regulation, certain implications of the legal norms governing space activity are evident. After tracing the early rise of legal regulation pertaining to space activity, this chapter will examine those current legal norms relating to human activity in space that influence national security most directly.[12]

The Human Ascent to Space

In most respects, the human development of capabilities in outer space is a history of the militarization[13] of outer space. A brief review of this history provides a helpful context from which one may proceed best to national security concerns. An early "toe in the water" toward utilization of space for military purposes came in the form of a landmark study considering the feasibility of placing man-made satellites in low Earth orbit. Project Rand[14] demonstrated the feasibility of such a feat in its report of May 2, 1946.

---

8. Prohibitions could come from a variety of sources other than space law. Customary international law could also supply the requisite prohibition on state action. Regarding conventional weapons, however, in view of the June 2002 demise of the Anti-Ballistic Missile Treaty (Treaty on the Limitation of Anti-Ballistic Missile Systems, May 26, 1972, U.S.-U.S.S.R., 23 U.S.T. 3435, 944 U.N.T.S. 13 (entered into force Oct. 3, 1972)), no such prohibition currently exists.

9. As it is sometimes conceived, astrolaw relates to the practice of law *in* outer space. Space law governs sovereign nations while the direct subjects of astrolaw are persons in space. As one source puts it, "Astrolaw focuses not upon space as a legal regime, but upon space as a place." GEORGE S. ROBINSON & HAROLD M. WHITE, JR., ENVOYS OF MANKIND: A DECLARATION OF FIRST PRINCIPLES FOR THE GOVERNANCE OF SPACE SOCIETIES 147 (1986) [hereinafter ROBINSON & WHITE].

10. Chia-Jui Cheng, *New Sources of International Space Law, in* THE USE OF AIR AND OUTER SPACE COOPERATION AND COMPETITION 209 (Chia-Jui Cheng, ed., 1998).

11. Though this is generally true as a basic tenet of international law, it is especially true of space law, which makes states internationally responsible for all national activity, whether public or private.

12. Topics related to U.S. space operations not covered in this chapter but that have implications for national security include the following: orbital slot designation and electromagnetic spectrum management by the International Telecommunications Union; U.S. participation in the International Space Station; international efforts to regulate the creation of space debris; U.S. government assistance to civil and commercial space launch activities; regulation of nuclear power sources in space; liability for civilian use of the Global Positioning System; proliferation of space tourism; and claims of private ownership over celestial bodies and other resources in space.

13. The term "militarization," as applied to outer space, should not be confused with "weaponization." The terms are conceptually distinct with weaponization best viewed as a subset of militarization. For additional discussion, *see infra* notes 85 to 95 and accompanying text.

14. Project Rand later became the Rand Corporation, a federally funded research and development corporation serving as the primary technical consultant to the U.S. Air Force.

Douglas Aircraft Co., Preliminary Design of an
Experimental World-Circling Spaceship

(1946)

If a vehicle can be accelerated to a speed of about 17,000 M.P.H. and aimed properly, it will revolve on a great circle path above the Earth's atmosphere as a new satellite. The centrifugal force will just balance the pull of gravity.... The achievement of a satellite craft by the United States would inflame the imagination of mankind, and would probably produce repercussions in the world comparable to the explosion of the atomic bomb.[15]

————————

This Report spawned numerous subsequent reports on the feasibility of satellite design, launch, and reentry. The rest is, as they say, history.

The first military satellite program, one of many that began to proliferate after the Rand Report, focused on a reconnaissance mission. In time, the mission for reconnaissance satellites in the United States would be shared between the military and the intelligence establishments. Authorities launched the venerable Corona series in early 1959 amid great secrecy and control by the U.S. Central Intelligence Agency.[16] Though the focus of public U.S. military space activity remained in the Department of Defense (DOD), decision-makers determined that reconnaissance missions from space could not be publicized.

As Corona began collecting Soviet imagery during the Eisenhower administration, the DOD established the Office of Missile and Satellite Systems with oversight for all national reconnaissance activities, later to become the National Reconnaissance Office (NRO). President Eisenhower's successor perpetuated these basic organizational changes, including the requirement to safeguard the very existence of the NRO as a state secret.[17] Indeed, from the commencement of the Kennedy administration the U.S. government refused to even acknowledge that satellites were used for reconnaissance.

While reconnaissance took priority in the early space missions, others soon followed. Almost simultaneously with the Corona program, the U.S. military was developing a missile warning system to monitor the launch of Soviet ICBMs.[18] Despite some successful test detections, the first system was replaced in the early 1970s by the highly successful Defense Support Program (DSP) satellites. DSP systems could offer the President notice

————————

15. RAND CORPORATION, PRELIMINARY DESIGN OF AN EXPERIMENTAL WORLD-CIRCLING SPACESHIP (1998) (from the abstract, and page 2; Report Number SM-11827, May 2, 1946).

16. Launched as a stopgap measure for strategic reconnaissance between the termination of U-2 high altitude reconnaissance aircraft and the WS-117L system, the Corona system remained operational from its first flight on February 28, 1959, through June 1972. The Air Force was nominally deemed a joint venture partner of the Corona program, which required mid-air recovery of film imagery taken by the orbiting camera. For a thorough account of the recently declassified Corona program, *see* CURTIS PEEBLES, THE CORONA PROJECT: AMERICA'S FIRST SPY SATELLITES (1997).

17. The National Reconnaissance Office was considered so secret that even in classified documents outside the special security controls established for satellite photos and data, the words 'National Reconnaissance Office' and 'National Reconnaissance Program' were not to be used. Instead, the phrase 'Matters under the purview of DOD TS 5105.23' would be given. (This was the directive which established the NRO.) It would be thirty-two years before the initials 'NRO' were spoken in public by a U.S. government official. *Id.* at 96.

18. MIDAS (the "Missile Detection and Alarm System") was originally designated "Subsystem G" in the WS-117L program before becoming its own separate system. *See* CURTIS PEEBLES, HIGH FRONTIER: THE U.S. AIR FORCE AND THE MILITARY SPACE PROGRAM 33 (1997). Previously, there were U.S. systems used to track space objects; however, none were focused on the distinctive heat signature left by an intercontinental ballistic missile (ICBM) or intermediate range ballistic missile (IRBM).

of a missile attack within moments of launch. In fact, in 1991, DSP satellites alerted coalition forces to the launch of Iraqi Scud missiles—the first use of U.S. missile warning satellites in combat. Though its use continues today, the follow-on system that will eventually replace it, the Space-Based Infrared System, takes the best elements of DSP into twenty-first century capabilities.[19]

Beyond these, other significant satellite systems were developed to carry military communications,[20] to provide weather intelligence,[21] and to aid navigation. Though assets supporting all three of these missions are indispensable to national security operations, the U.S. Global Positioning System has now become perhaps the best known of all U.S. space assets. Developed in the 1970s, and declared fully operational in July 1995, the Global Positioning System (GPS) currently relies on twenty-four operational satellites in medium-Earth orbits flying in six orbital planes. As advertised, the GPS provides precise navigation, timing, and velocity information.[22] International users include banks, commercial aviation and shipping, and the U.S. military. Significantly, like the Russian GLONASS and Chinese Beidou space-based navigation systems, the GPS system is operated by the military. Of the major systems, only the European Galileo system will be civilian-run, albeit this too will have a dual-use character for both military and civilian applications.

In addition to developing space payloads, the United States simultaneously developed options for access to the space environment. That access came by means of missiles and rockets, also termed "boosters" in view of their utility as launch vehicles for spacecraft. As for most other segments of space technology, rockets were first developed for use by military forces.[23] Over a dozen countries have now developed an independent launch capability, with others actively pursuing the technology to do so. And, several commercial ventures have shown the capability and market for a private launch industry.

Pre-Treaty Development of International Space Regulation

As the U.S. scientific and national security communities perfected the technologies necessary for space exploration, legal theorists began to take note. These individuals began to realize that the ascent into space would necessitate regulation. One early treatise correctly

---

19. USAF Fact Sheet: Space Based Infrared Systems (March 2013).

20. The first communications satellite, Project Score, was launched on December 18, 1958, and carried a tape-recorded Christmas message from President Eisenhower. Subsequent communications constellations have included the Defense Satellite Communications System (DSCS), supporting a wide range of national security users. USAF Fact Sheet: Defense Satellite Communications System (February 2014). Augmenting the 1990s era "Milstar" communications system, the Advanced Extremely High Frequency System consists of 4 satellites in geosynchronous orbit that provide 10 times the throughput of the Milstar satellites. USAF Fact Sheet: Advanced Extremely High Frequency System (June 2011). At the top end of the capability spectrum, just one satellite in the Wideband Global SATCOM constellation provides more SATCOM capacity than the entire DSCS constellation. USAF Fact Sheet: Wideband Global SATCOM (February 2014). Beyond these state-owned systems, the explosive growth of military dependence on commercial communications systems will only increase the legal and operational issues during times of armed conflict.

21. NASA's Tiros I satellite, launched on April 1, 1960, created a revolution in weather forecasting. However, it could not satisfy military needs for coverage, readout locations, or timeliness.

22. USAF Fact Sheet: Global Positioning System Directorate (December 2012).

23. Rockets can be distinguished from missiles essentially in that the latter possess superior navigational technology, making them more accurate for striking targets. Otherwise, the following definition of a rocket could apply to both: "A vehicle that can operate outside Earth's atmosphere, because it carries its own oxidizer, as well as fuel." JOHN M. COLLINS, MILITARY SPACE FORCES: THE NEXT 50 YEARS 159–60 (1989).

predicted that "even in the vast expanse of space it can be expected, further, that the host of participants who will in the future seek to enjoy the many different potential uses of this great resource will in countless ways, whether deliberately or inadvertently, interfere with each other."[24] In order to maximize beneficial use and minimize harmful interference, space needed a legal regime.

Because of the international interest in space, the United Nations was a logical venue for consideration of legal regulation. Although previous UN General Assembly resolutions dealt with outer space, no other international document did more to coalesce the fundamental principles that would govern state conduct in outer space than the 1963 UN General Assembly Resolution, which purported to declare "legal principles."[25] A diplomatic breakthrough when it emerged from the bilateral U.S./Soviet negotiations, the "Declaration of Legal Principles" found itself incorporated almost entirely into the 1967 Outer Space Treaty, which is discussed below.[26] Simply put, it was the first significant step in the development of space law.

Use of the terms "Declaration" and "Legal Principles" in its title attested to the resolution's importance. Because of the lengthy negotiating and drafting history predating the resolution, and its unanimous support, it practically amounted to a treaty when adopted. Though not binding on any state, the resolution read more like a treaty than a traditional resolution. As the subsequent quotations and discussion of the Outer Space Treaty will make clear, this resolution had a profound impact on the formation of legal regulation for outer space.

Importance of Governmental Organization for Space National Security

With respect to its national space activities, the way the United States has organized its organs of government makes a significant statement about its national security priorities. In a sense, the structure of relevant executive branch organizations, and their relationships to each other, is itself a facet of U.S. national security. For example, the precise relationship between the Department of Defense and the National Aeronautics and Space Administration varies from administration to administration. But the fundamental division between DOD and NASA space activities reflects a well-established policy to keep civil and military space activities distinct. Successive National Space Policies going back to the beginnings of NASA itself have perpetuated this fundamental distinction.

Questions for Discussion

1. What important implications for national security might flow from an erosion of the historic distinction between U.S. civil and national security space activities? Consider the impacts of joint technology development, launch capacity, security, and export controls.

---

24. McDOUGAL, ET AL., *supra* note 6, at 514.
25. *Declaration of Legal Principles Governing the Activities of States in the Exploration and Use of Outer Space*, Dec. 13, 1963, G.A. Res. 1962 (XVIII), UN GAOR, 18th Sess., Supp. No. 15, at 15, UN Doc. A/5515 (1964).
26. The Outer Space Treaty negotiators adopted the resolution's nine Principles practically word for word. Thus, Principle 1 became Article I, sentence 1, of the Outer Space Treaty. Principle 2, calling for the free exploration and use of space in accordance with international law, became Article I, sentence 2. Principle 3 became Article II. Principle 4, on the applicability of international law to outer space, became Article III. Principle 5, setting forth the novel requirement that states bear international responsibility for national activities in space, became Article VI. Principle 6 became Article IX. Principle 7 became Article VIII. Principle 8 became Article VII. Principle 9 became Article V.

2. As the U.S. government increasingly turns to *commercial* sources for launch and communications capacity, what might be the impacts on national security?

United Nations Space Treaties and Their Impact on U.S. Space Activities

Outer Space Treaty

It is difficult to overstate the preeminent place in space law enjoyed by the first international treaty governing outer space, commonly known as the Outer Space Treaty.[27] Even today, over four decades after its adoption, it is the authority of first resort for most questions of international law for national space operations. Pointing to its significance, the treaty is termed everything from "an ideological charter for the space age"[28] to the "*Magna Carta* of outer space law."[29] Its establishment of the free character of outer space makes it the de facto Constitution of outer space and the most important of the five UN treaties dealing specifically with space activities.[30]

Treaty on Principles Governing the Activities of States in the Exploration and Use of Outer Space, Including the Moon and Other Celestial Bodies
(1967)

Article I

. . . .

Outer space, including the moon and other celestial bodies, shall be free for exploration and use by all States without discrimination of any kind, on a basis of equality and in accordance with international law, and there shall be free access to all areas of celestial bodies.

. . . .

Article II

Outer space, including the moon and other celestial bodies, is not subject to national appropriation by claim of sovereignty, by means of use or occupation, or by any other means.

---

27. Treaty on Principles Governing the Activities of States in the Exploration and Use of Outer Space, Including the Moon and Other Celestial Bodies, Jan. 27, 1967, 18 U.S.T. 2410, 610 U.N.T.S. 205 (entered into force Oct. 10, 1967) [hereinafter Outer Space Treaty].

28. ROBINSON & WHITE, *supra* note 9, at 181.

29. Nandasiri Jasentuliyana, *The Role of Developing Countries in the Formation of Space Law*, XX: II ANNALS AIR & SPACE L. 95, 97 (1995) [hereinafter Jasentuliyana, *Developing Countries*]. *See also* Richard A. Morgan, *Military Use of Commercial Satellites: A New Look at the Outer Space Treaty and "Peaceful Purposes,"* J. AIR L. & COM., Sept.–Oct. 1994, at 296.

30. One of the 5 treaties adopted under U.N. auspices, the "Moon Agreement" discussed *infra*, is largely irrelevant. Though opened for signature in 1979, the treaty "languishes with only thirteen members and four signatories, none of which are independently space-competent." LYALL, FRANCIS & LARSEN, PAUL B., SPACE LAW: A TREATISE 178 (2009) [hereinafter LYALL & LARSEN].

Article III

States Parties to the Treaty shall carry on activities in the exploration and use of outer space, including the moon and other celestial bodies, in accordance with international law, including the Charter of the United Nations, in the interest of maintaining international peace and security and promoting international co-operation and understanding.

Article IV

States Parties to the Treaty undertake not to place in orbit around the earth any objects carrying nuclear weapons or any other kinds of weapons of mass destruction, install such weapons on celestial bodies, or station such weapons in outer space in any other manner.

The moon and other celestial bodies shall be used by all States Parties to the Treaty exclusively for peaceful purposes. The establishment of military bases, installations and fortifications, the testing of any type of weapons and the conduct of military maneuvers on celestial bodies shall be forbidden. The use of military personnel for scientific research or for any other peaceful purposes shall not be prohibited. The use of any equipment or facility necessary for peaceful exploration of the moon and other celestial bodies shall also not be prohibited.

. . . .

Article VI

States Parties to the Treaty shall bear international responsibility for national activities in outer space, including the moon and other celestial bodies, whether such activities are carried on by governmental agencies or by non-governmental entities, and for assuring that national activities are carried out in conformity with the provisions set forth in the present Treaty.

. . . .

Article VIII

A State Party to the Treaty on whose registry an object launched into outer space is carried shall retain jurisdiction and control over such object, and over any personnel thereof, while in outer space or on a celestial body.

. . . .

Article IX

States Parties to the Treaty shall be guided by the principle of co-operation and mutual assistance and shall conduct all their activities in outer space, including the moon and other celestial bodies, with due regard to the corresponding interests of all other States Parties to the Treaty.... If a State Party to the Treaty has reason to believe that an activity or experiment planned by it or its nationals in outer space, including the moon and other celestial bodies, would cause potentially harmful interference with activities of other States Parties in the peaceful exploration and use of outer space, including the moon and other celestial bodies, it shall undertake appropriate international consultations before proceeding with any such activity or experiment....

Where Is Outer Space?

The treaty repeatedly uses the phrase "outer space," yet it nowhere establishes a definition. Indeed, no authoritative definition exists anywhere in international law. While this may seem an unfortunate omission, the United States has consistently maintained that, to date, no need to define the spatial boundary between airspace and outer space exists. Similarly, in contrast to possible definitions according to physical properties, attempts to define outer space by reference to the function of selected instrumentalities have also failed to achieve a consensus. There appears to be a general international consensus that terrestrial airspace ends at some point between 80 and 120 kilometers, and that an object at its perigee in orbit around the Earth is in "outer space." Nonetheless, the boundary is nowhere authoritatively defined either by reference to location or function. Among other points raised by space-active states in support of leaving the boundary undefined, the concern that an arbitrary limit might unnecessarily restrict future national security prerogatives appears paramount.

International air law establishes state sovereignty in national airspace.[31] By contrast, Article II renders outer space beyond national appropriation by claims of sovereignty — its status approximates that of international airspace, which, under the Law of the Sea Convention and customary international law, is also beyond national appropriation by claims of sovereignty.[32] As a consequence, wherever one draws the horizontal boundary between terrestrial airspace (either international or national) and outer space, this delimitation marks the difference between complete freedom of overflight, and the prospect of complete restrictions on overflight by a subjacent state. Is it necessary to precisely define that boundary, or to define "outer space" by reference to the function of a given air or space instrumentality? Perhaps eventually it will be, but there appears little appetite at present. Until space-active states develop machines easily capable of transiting back and forth between airspace and outer space, the "delimitation" question will likely remain unresolved.[33]

The Application of International Law to State Activity in Space

Many of the excerpted provisions above raise questions of applicability to various state activities in space. At the outset, Article III's application of international law to activities in outer space stands out. Because the treaty does not qualify the phrase, it includes all international legal norms of general applicability that would restrict state conduct terrestrially. An obvious example would be those treaty and customary principles that comprise the Law of War. If a state pursued a course of action in space (or one affecting space assets) during an international armed conflict, the action would be lawful only if consistent with the Law of War. That is, the action would have to be militarily necessary, capable of sufficiently discriminating between military and purely civilian property and personnel, and the unintended collateral effects would have to be proportionate to the value of the target sought, as these terms are defined by the Law of War.

In addition, because Article III specifically references the UN Charter, the latter's use of force provisions apply to any state action in outer space. Should an adversary threaten

---

31. Convention on International Civil Aviation, Dec. 7, 1944, 15 U.N.T.S. 295, Article 1.

32. United Nations Convention on the Law of the Sea, art. 58 and 87, Dec. 10, 1982, 1833 U.N.T.S. 3 (entered into force Nov. 16, 1994; the United States has signed but not ratified).

33. "The question of the boundary grumbles on. While no space-faring state seems unduly concerned, as space activities increase and more launches take place it is anomalous that the question has not been answered. At present most launches and re-entries use either national air-space or pass over the high seas. That may diminish the present need for a solution, but at least some form of accommodation between space and air-traffic control will surely be necessary." LYALL & LARSON, *supra* note 30, at 564.

or use force in outer space, the UN Security Council could authorize a use of force in space just as it does for terrestrial threats to international peace and security. Further, any right of self-defense to which a state could lawfully lay claim would apply to conflicts involving space assets and may justify uses of force in space.[34]

"Peaceful Purposes"

Among the issues raised by Article IV, an early debate centered on the meaning of peaceful purposes, the ambiguous term operating as one of several limitations on state uses of outer space. When first used by the United States in 1957, the "peaceful and scientific purposes" of outer space activities soon became the official goal of the United Nations. On November 14, 1957, the UN General Assembly adopted Resolution 1148 (XII), which advocated an inspection system to ensure the peaceful uses of space. "This was a landmark document not only because it represented the first General Assembly resolution on outer space but also because it introduced the phrase 'exclusively for peaceful purposes' in an authoritative UN text."[35]

Though the Soviet Union and a number of other states consistently maintained the view that peaceful means non-military, the majority of the international community did not agree. Consequently, today it is a virtual tautology to assert that nonaggressive uses of space, whether military or not, are "peaceful."

> The expression 'peaceful purposes' is a legal term of art. At the beginning of the space age several views were advanced as to its meaning, with one view being that military activities in the space environment could not be and were not peaceful. The opposing position, which today has gained general acceptance, is that nonaggressive military uses are peaceful. Thus, 'peaceful' has come to mean general space activity that is beneficial to and in the interests of all countries. This is the mandate of Article 1, par. 1, of the Treaty.[36]

---

34. Every several years the U.S. re-articulates its longstanding view that principles of self-defense apply in space: "The United States will employ a variety of measures to help assure the use of space for all responsible parties, and, consistent with the inherent right of self-defense, deter others from interference and attack, defend our space systems and contribute to the defense of allied space systems ..." *National Space Policy of the United States of America* 3, June 28, 2010 [hereinafter *National Space Policy*].

35. Ivan A. Vlasic, *The Legal Aspects of Peaceful and Non-Peaceful Uses of Outer Space, in* Peaceful and Non-Peaceful Uses of Space: Problems of Definition for the Prevention of an Arms Race 37, 39 (Bhupendra Jasani, ed., 1991) [hereinafter Vlasic, *Peaceful and Non-Peaceful Uses of Outer Space*]. The 1959 Antarctic Treaty, though not a UN text, adopted the term "peaceful purposes" soon after UNGA Resolution 1148. In language reminiscent of the later Outer Space Treaty, the Antarctic Treaty asserted that "1. Antarctica shall be used for peaceful purposes only. There shall be prohibited, inter alia, any measures of a military nature, such as the establishment of military bases and fortifications, the carrying out of military maneuvers, as well as the testing of any type of weapons. 2. The present treaty shall not prevent the use of military personnel or equipment for scientific research or for any other peaceful purpose." The Antarctic Treaty, Dec. 1, 1959, 402 U.N.T.S. 71, Article I.

36. Carl Q. Christol, The Modern International Law of Outer Space 22 (1982) [hereinafter Christol, Law of Outer Space]. In addition to the textual problems associated with equating the terms peaceful and nonmilitary (indeed Article IV itself contemplates the military use of space for scientific research), the interpretation suffers from a practical difficulty. Just about any use of space can support a military purpose. Thus, even if a satellite were developed, tested, launched, and controlled by a civilian organ of state government, the information it provided could be useful for military purposes. Weather, navigation, communications, and remote sensing are just a few applications of space capabilities of great use to military forces. To say that the Outer Space Treaty forbids this activity

On this near-universal understanding, all states possess the inherent right to defend against foreign aggression in outer space, as well as within Earth's atmosphere. The current National Space Policy reiterates the original U.S. position on the meaning of peaceful purposes by stating that " 'Peaceful purposes' allows for space to be used for national and homeland security activities."[37] Despite the long debate over the term "peaceful" as used in the Outer Space Treaty, its meaning has been well-settled through the practice of states and certainly includes military activities.[38] Indeed, reference to the language of Article IV perhaps makes the point best of all. Article IV forbids military bases, installations, fortifications, and maneuvers—a meaningless partial demilitarization if peaceful simply means non-military.

Article IV limits use of celestial bodies, including the moon, to peaceful purposes. This raises the additional question of whether the peaceful purposes limitation, whatever its meaning, applies in outer space generally, away from celestial bodies. Reference solely to Article IV suggests that it does not. Indeed a former State Department Legal Advisor once advised that the omission of "outer space" on this point was no accident.[39] That this is true can be inferred by the treaty's frequent uses of outer space, "moon," and celestial bodies in various combinations elsewhere. As such, the restriction as stated in Article IV does not formally apply to space activities away from celestial bodies.

Nonetheless, non-peaceful uses of outer space away from celestial bodies are implicitly prohibited by other provisions. For example, on the assumption that non-peaceful means aggressive, such activities are already prohibited by the UN Charter. Because the Outer Space Treaty restricts state activities in space to those consistent with international law, an aggressive use of force forbidden on Earth is equally forbidden in space. Further, some states have made the peaceful uses of outer space a tenet of national policy, regardless of the location in outer space. The United States enshrined this policy in the 1958 National Aeronautics and Space Act in which it maintains, as amended, that "activities in space should be devoted to peaceful purposes for the benefit of all humankind."[40]

A further point under Article IV relates to the legal permissibility of anti-satellite weapons (ASATs), which both the United States and the former Soviet Union fielded in the 1970s and 1980s. Given more recent technology, an ASAT could find expression using one of at least four techniques:

---

seems highly dubious. Yet this is the logical extension of the claim that all uses of space must scrupulously avoid any military uses in order to be "peaceful."

37. *National Space Policy, supra* note 34. The Policy goes on to task the Secretary of Defense with developing "capabilities, plans, and options to deter, defend against, and, if necessary, defeat efforts to interfere with or attack U.S. or allied space systems." The Secretary has discharged this obligation, in part, by promulgating the *National Security Space Strategy: Unclassified Summary,* January 2011, and DoD Directive 3100.10, *Space Policy,* October 18, 2012.

38. As we have suggested, and as others have attested, the term includes the possibility of space weapons being deployed as well.

> If one chooses to ignore the controversy concerning the 'true' meaning of 'peaceful' in the Outer Space Treaty, it is safe to conclude that the treaty permits the deployment in outer space of anti-satellite weapons, directed energy weapons, or any other kind of weapon, as long as these weapons are not in conflict with the prohibitions of Article IV [such as weapons of mass destruction in orbit] of the Outer Space Treaty, or some other international agreement.

Ivan A. Vlasic, *Space Law and the Military Applications of Space Technology, in* Perspectives on International Law 397 (Nandasari Jasentuliyana, ed., 1995).

39. Vlasic, *Peaceful and Non-Peaceful Uses of Outer Space, supra* note 35, at 42. In short, the omission was clearly intentional. Christol, Law of Outer Space, *supra* note 36, at 20.

40. National Aeronautics and Space Program, 51 U.S.C. § 20102(a) (2012).

A kinetic weapon destroys or cripples a satellite by collision with either a single missile, or with a number of small objects directed towards it—the buckshot technique. Launched from the Earth or from a space platform, a kinetic weapon would have the disadvantage of producing a cloud of debris, with all its potential consequences. An alternative is the laser which could be used to knock out a satellite, again from either Earth or from space. A different possibility is the use of radio jamming to either overwhelm a satellite itself or to prevent its signals being used. Last, in a modern age dependent on electronics and the Internet, a less obvious but real possibility is cyber-attack on a perceived enemy, part of which could involve interference with command, control and use of satellite systems.[41]

ASAT weapons may appear to violate the nonaggressive mandate required of all space activities under the peaceful purposes restriction. However, regardless of their putative destabilizing character for international peace and security,[42] the Outer Space Treaty does not prohibit the transiting, or even the orbiting, of conventional weaponry in space, including ASATs. Article IV's prohibition on orbiting of weapons of mass destruction, including nuclear weapons,[43] strongly suggests a distinction between those weapons and conventional weapons of lesser destructive power, including those that may be directed at satellites. Though Article IV(1) could easily be modified to effect the de-weaponization of space, it does not do so. One expert on the national security implications of space policy helpfully summarized the pros and cons of ASATs. Though written at the height of the Cold War, substitute "Soviet Union" with "Russia," "China," or even "certain non-State actors," and the same considerations remain relevant today. The discussion also summarizes the larger positions on the relative merits of weaponizing space at all:

> [The pro-ASAT school] starts from the belief that space is just another military arena where satellites will have to adapt to new threats with new countermeasures in the same way that their counterparts on earth have adapted.... [Proponents believe the United States can] deny the Soviets the use of their space assets in wartime while simultaneously preserving the security of U.S. space systems. Moreover, they argue that any attempt to constrain the development of antisatellite systems is illogical and unfeasible; illogical because there are no such limitations on weapons capable of attacking, say, high-flying reconnaissance aircraft or early warning radars, and unfeasible because of the unavoidable presence of the residual antisatellite systems....
>
> The second school ... starts from the belief that the United States is more de-pendent on the service of military satellites than the Soviet Union is and therefore has more to lose in the event of hostilities in space. The proponents of this view remain highly skeptical of the United States' ability to defend its vital space assets in the face of unconstrained antisatellite development by the Soviet Union. In

---

41. LYALL & LARSON, *supra* note 30, at 525–526.

42. "In the case of weapons systems, there is a much broader feeling [beyond that for military support systems] that they are destabilizing and should be banned." Peter Jankowitsch, *Legal Aspects of Military Space Activities, in* SPACE LAW: DEVELOPMENT AND SCOPE 143, 150 (Nandasari Jasentuliyana, ed., 1992).

43. Because the Outer Space Treaty does not define nuclear weapon, its prohibition has stimulated debate over more recent technologies, such as the x-ray laser, which is powered by a nuclear explosion. Whether a nuclear-powered laser is a nuclear weapon will mean the difference between its lawful orbiting of Earth or not. *Id.* at 147.

addition to stimulating an expensive and in the end fruitless competition, they believe an ASAT arms race could seriously erode superpower stability during a severe crisis. Specifically, the knowledge that the other side had a highly effective ASAT weapon system capable of crippling one's own vital early warning and strategic communication satellites could become an overwhelming incentive to strike first in a major superpower crisis.[44]

A final point from Article IV pertains to the prohibition on the establishment of "military bases, installations and fortifications, the testing of any type of weapons and the conduct of military maneuvers on celestial bodies." Though this clause does not include the moon as does the one immediately preceding it, it is clear that the Outer Space Treaty uses celestial bodies as a phrase that includes the moon. Thus the first sentence of Article IV(2) speaks of the moon and *other* celestial bodies. As a result, one could logically read Article IV to prohibit both the creation of permanent military structures and weapon testing on the moon or other celestial bodies. Though non-nuclear weapon testing is not prohibited in outer space, it cannot occur on celestial bodies.[45]

State Responsibility for All National Space Activities

In addition to its other features, the treaty established an innovation in international law. Article VI requires that states bear "international responsibility for national activities in outer space ... whether such activities are carried on by governmental agencies or by non-governmental entities." Ordinarily, states bear responsibility only for state activity. By contrast, Article VI makes the contracting state liable for the offenses (or any other activity) of its citizens or private organizations with respect to space activity.[46] This provision marks the first time that such an extension of state liability occurred in a legally binding document.[47] Although this provision appears unlikely to significantly affect the ability of a state to ensure its national security, it could impact the research and development of weapons systems. For example, to the extent that a military space contractor pursues testing of space weaponry in outer space, the host state would bear international responsibility for the activity.

Further, the novel principle of state responsibility for all national activities in space could render a state liable for the unauthorized aggressive space activities of its citizens, even if carried out from foreign soil. Despite the great difficulty in regulating such activity, this could mean that the United States would bear responsibility to China, for example, should a U.S. citizen manage to destroy a Chinese satellite in space. Under Article VI, this would be true even if construction, launch, and control of the method of destruction occurred entirely outside the United States and without its authorization. As a result of the expanded responsibilities, many states have enacted a network of domestic regulations governing the space launch and on-orbit activities of its citizens.[48]

---

44. PAUL B. STARES, SPACE AND NATIONAL SECURITY 5 (1987).

45. For discussion of the prohibition on nuclear weapons tests in space, *see infra* notes 79 and 81 to 83, and accompanying text.

46. As state responsibility for national space activity has been a cornerstone of space law since 1967, it may well be a principle of customary international law binding noncontracting states as well.

47. The idea appeared previously in Principle 5 of G.A. Resolution 1962 (XVIII), *supra* note 25. However, this resolution did not legally bind any state.

48. For a brief discussion of selected U.S. regulations in this regard, *see supra* section entitled "Remote Sensing and Shutter Control."

Questions for Discussion

1. Given the no appropriation/no sovereignty status of outer space created by Articles I and II, of what effect would a state's claim to have created a "keep out" zone around its space asset be? How does the analysis differ if the zone is akin to an Air Defense Identification Zone that does not constitute a claim of sovereignty? At what point might the approach of a foreign space object to a U.S. space asset constitute a hostile act justifying use of force in self-defense? Recall that objects in orbit around Earth travel at approximately 17,000 miles per hour.

2. In 1976, eight equatorial states signed what came to be known as the "Bogotá Declaration." Among other things, the Declaration proclaimed the following: "The geostationary orbit is a scarce natural resource, whose importance and value increases rapidly together with the development of space technology and with the growing need for communication; therefore, the Equatorial countries meeting in Bogotá have decided to proclaim and defend on behalf of their peoples, the existence of their sovereignty over this natural resource." Is there any way to reconcile this language with relevant portions of the Outer Space Treaty? (At the time of signature, four of the eight states—Brazil, Ecuador, Kenya, and Zaire—were parties to the Outer Space Treaty.)

3. If a given state activity in space, during peacetime, does not violate the UN Charter, is the activity "peaceful?"

4. Article IV establishes a partial demilitarization of the moon. Some argue that this provision also effects a de-weaponization as well. For what peaceful purposes might a state wish to deploy weapons on the moon? Would such a move violate Article IV?

5. In 1967, the U.S. Secretary of Defense announced that the U.S.S.R. had been developing a Fractional Orbiting Bombing System that would enter outer space but would not circle the globe. If such a system carried nuclear warheads, would its deployment violate the Outer Space Treaty?

6. Article V labels astronauts envoys of mankind, evoking an almost diplomatic connotation. Assuming an astronaut were a member of one of the military services and were to engage in armed conflict, would this envoy status work to supercede his other status under international law, namely, a combatant subject to capture as a prisoner of war?

7. Does Article VIII prohibit the retrieval or salvage of nonfunctioning space objects? How might parallels to sunken ships illuminate the answer?

8. Article IX requires that a state enter consultations before engaging in activities in which the state "has reason to believe ... would cause potentially harmful interference with activities of other States Parties in the peaceful exploration and use of outer space...." If the United States were in armed conflict with another state party to the treaty, would it be required to consult before engaging a space-based target owned or used by the opposing belligerent? If the principle of a fundamental change of circumstances relieved the United States of compliance with the space treaties as between it and another state party with which it is engaged in armed conflict, what other targeting restrictions must the United States evaluate?

9. Should the United States ever wish to engage in the intentional jamming of a foreign satellite signal, would the provisions of article IX outlaw such behavior? Of what effect would 18 U.S.C. § 1367 be? Does your answer change if the jamming were ordered by the President to occur at an extraterritorial location in the interest of national security? Because any jamming would involve use of the radio frequency spectrum, how might the

Constitution of the International Telecommunications Union impact U.S. prerogatives? See particularly Articles 45 and 48.[49]

Rescue and Return Agreement

Agreement on the Rescue of Astronauts, the Return of Astronauts and the Return of Objects Launched into Outer Space

(1968)[50]

....

Article 2

If, owing to accident, distress, emergency or unintended landing, the personnel of a spacecraft land in territory under the jurisdiction of a Contracting Party, it shall immediately take all possible steps to rescue them and render them all necessary assistance....

....

Article 5

2. Each Contracting Party having jurisdiction over the territory on which a space object or its component parts has been discovered shall, upon the request of the launching authority and with assistance from that authority if requested, take such steps as it finds practicable to recover the object or component parts.

....

5. Expenses incurred in fulfilling obligations to recover and return a space object or its component parts under paragraphs 2 and 3 of this Article shall be borne by the launching authority.

...

As is obvious from a perusal of the few provisions quoted above, the Rescue and Return Agreement divides its concerns between astronauts on the one hand, and space objects on the other. Regarding astronauts, Article 2 requires states parties to take immediate steps to rescue and otherwise assist spacecraft personnel that have landed in the territory of another state party as a result of "accident, distress, emergency, or unintended landing." In addition, states parties must make two notifications—one to the launching authority (or make a public announcement) and one to the UN Secretary General.[51]

Regarding space objects, the Agreement imposes no affirmative duty for a state to proactively search and recover any object landing in its territory. As with the discovery of astronauts, Article 5 imposes a notification requirement on a state party finding a space object within its territory. In addition, the Agreement makes no distinction between civil and military objects and personnel. As a result, its terms apply equally to all four categories.

---

49. S. Treaty Doc. No. 104-34 (1996) (Dec. 22, 1992, as amended through 1994).

50. Agreement on the Rescue of Astronauts, the Return of Astronauts, and the Return of Objects Launched into Outer Space, Apr. 22, 1968, 19 U.S.T. 7570, 672 U.N.T.S. 119, T.I.A.S. No. 6599 (entered into force Dec. 3, 1968) [hereinafter Rescue and Return Agreement]. The widely used references to this as the astronaut agreement are unfortunate. Such references obscure the treaty's application to the return of *objects* as well as astronauts.

51. *Id.* at Article 1.

As is all too common in treaty law, the Rescue and Return Agreement employs undefined terms. Chief among them is the term space object.[52] This failure to define raises some obvious questions. For example, during the space shuttle program, would the shuttle orbiter flying piggyback on its 747 transport aircraft have constituted a "space object?" What about the 747 itself while carrying the orbiter?[53] Indeed, in the absence of definition, one could rationally determine that the solid rocket boosters needed for shuttle operations, being delivered via rail to the launch facility, constitute space objects. On the assumption that states parties will have a reasonable understanding of the concept, Article III requires that upon furnishing "identifying data," states parties "shall" return space objects found beyond the territorial limits of the launching state. However, while this provision would certainly require the return of space weaponry or satellites having landed back on Earth, it does not specify *when* such return must take place or in exactly what condition.

Intended as an elucidation of the Outer Space Treaty, the Rescue and Return Agreement seems to raise as many questions as it is meant to answer. Other questions raised by ambiguities in the Agreement include the following: "How should rescue expenses be treated? Is the launching state obligated to reimburse the rescuing state? What if a rescue attempt is bungled—will the rescuing state be liable, or does some sort of Good Samaritan principle apply? Should there be such a principle, since rescue is mandatory?"[54] Though the treaty requires rescues for astronauts, it does not specify who pays for the rescue operation or in what proportion, unlike the case respecting searches for space objects under Article 5, and the subsequent Liability Convention.[55] The answers to each of these questions could affect the evolution of regulations of national space operations as states increasingly make national security decisions in light of possible liability.

Questions for Discussion

1. Both the Outer Space Treaty (Article V) and the Rescue and Return Agreement (Article IV) require that states parties "safely and promptly" return astronauts to authorities from their state of origin. How might the United States interpret this language if it were required to entertain a request for political asylum from a foreign astronaut landing on American soil as a result of accident, distress, emergency, or unintended landing?

2. In 1979, the Soviet Cosmos 954 ocean reconnaissance satellite came down over Canada's Northwest Territories. Had the former Soviet Union requested the debris in accordance with Article V, would such request have prohibited Canada (with U.S. assistance) from reverse engineering the object prior to its return?

3. Many states are not parties to the Rescue and Return Agreement. Should an astronaut land in one of these countries under conditions of distress, would the government have

52. The Liability Convention does define space object as including the "component parts of a space object as well as its launch vehicle and parts thereof." Convention on International Liability for Damage Caused by Space Objects, Mar. 29, 1972, art. 1(d), 24 U.S.T. 2389, 961 U.N.T.S. 187 (entered into force Sept. 1, 1972) [hereinafter Liability Convention]. However, in using the very term to be defined within the definition itself, the definition is so hopelessly circular that it amounts to no definition at all.

53. Private ventures have been testing a variety of technologies that will beg similar questions. For example, Virgin Galactic's SpaceShipTwo vessel, and "mother ship" Eve, will take off mated together before separating at high altitude. Are both of these vehicles "space objects?" Just the former?

54. GLENN H. REYNOLDS & ROBERT P. MERGES, OUTER SPACE: PROBLEMS OF LAW AND POLICY 204 (2d ed., 1997) [hereinafter REYNOLDS & MERGES]. Also, although its terms suggest application to living astronauts, the treaty does not answer whether a duty exists to return the remains of expired astronauts.

55. Liability Convention, *supra* note 52.

any duty to assist? To what extent might the Rescue and Return Agreement provisions regarding the rescue and return of astronauts be rooted in customary international legal principles drawn from maritime law? Consider particularly Article 3 and the charge to assist if necessary even on the high seas or the territory of another contracting party.

Liability Convention

Convention on the International Liability for Damage Caused by Space Objects

(1972)

Article I

For the purposes of this Convention:

(a) The term damage means loss of life, personal injury or other impairment of health; or loss of or damage to property of States or of persons, natural or juridical, or property of international intergovernmental organizations;

(b) The term launching includes attempted launching;

(c) The term launching State means:

(i) a State which launches or procures the launching of a space object;

(ii) a State from whose territory or facility a space object is launched;

(d)   The term space object includes component parts of a space object as well as its launch vehicle and parts thereof.

Article II

A launching State shall be absolutely liable to pay compensation for damage caused by its space object on the surface of the earth or to aircraft in flight.

Article III

In the event of damage being caused elsewhere than on the surface of the earth to a space object of one launching State or to persons or property on board such a space object by a space object of another launching State, the latter shall be liable only if the damage is due to its fault or the fault of persons for whom it is responsible.

Article IV

. . . .

2. In all cases of joint and several liability referred to in paragraph 1 of this Article, the burden of compensation for the damage shall be apportioned between the first two States in accordance with the extent to which they were at fault; if the extent of the fault of each of these States cannot be established, the burden of compensation shall be apportioned equally between them. Such apportionment shall be without prejudice to the right of the third State to seek the entire compensation due under this Convention from any or all of the launching States which are jointly and severally liable.

Article V

1. Whenever two or more States jointly launch a space object, they shall be jointly and severally liable for any damage caused.

. . . .

The longest of the space treaties, the Liability Convention, is an expansion of the general liability provision expressed in Article VII of the Outer Space Treaty. However, while the convention establishes specific standards of liability for damage caused by space objects, it does not purport to preempt international legal principles of liability that would have otherwise applied to incidents involving space objects. Returning to the Outer Space Treaty's application of international law to outer space, the convention explicitly provides in Article XXIII that "[t]he provisions of this Convention shall not affect other international agreements in force so far as relations between the States Parties to such agreements are concerned." Thus, to the extent two or more states parties wished to negotiate between them liability schemes either more or less restrictive than the Liability Convention, those other schemes would control the resolution of damage claims as between them.[56]

Article I defines damage by reference to four categories: (1) loss of life; (2) personal injury; (3) other impairment of health; and (4) loss of or damage to property. Once such damage has been established, the convention establishes a two-tiered structure of liability. For damage caused by a space object on the surface of the Earth or to an aircraft in flight, Article II makes the launching state absolutely liable.[57] Similar to the innovation worked by Article VI of the Outer Space Treaty, Article II here appears to be an innovation as well. For the first time in 1972, an international agreement provided for the imposition of absolute liability against a state actor.

For damage occurring other than on the surface of the Earth, or to an aircraft in flight, the convention imposes fault-based liability. Perhaps another result of the lack of definition of outer space, the negotiators left fault-based liability to the space environment, without so stating, choosing rather to define space negatively — not Earth, and not air. Article III limits the potential for liability in space to a launching state's "fault or the fault of persons for whom it is responsible." In the opinion of Professor Christol, examples of compensable losses, payable in accordance with interpretations historically taken by the U.S. State Department, could include the following:

> lost time and earnings; impaired earning capacity; destruction or deprivation of use of property; rendering the property unfit for the use for which it was intended; loss of profits resulting from an interruption in business activities; loss of rents; reasonable medical, hospital, and nursing costs occasioned by harms to the person; physical impairment including impairment of mental faculties; pain and suffering; humiliation; reasonable costs for the repair of property that has been wrongfully harmed; costs incurred in mitigating existing wrongful harms; and loss of the services of a third party to which the injured party was entitled.[58]

As with the other treaties devoted to space, the Liability Convention makes no distinction between civilian and military space objects, either of which could form the basis of a claim. Thus, not only military operations short of armed conflict, but space operations

---

56. As, for example, in cases where one state launches from another state, such as Russia's practice with Kazakhstan.

57. "Launching State" under the Liability Convention is defined more expansively than "launching authority" under the Rescue and Return Agreement, though it is identical to the definition provided by the Registration Convention.

58. CHRISTOL, LAW OF OUTER SPACE, *supra* note 36, at 94.

during war itself could form the basis of monetary claims under the Convention, provided the space object[59] of the launching state caused "damage" and the act causing damage did not otherwise constitute a lawful use of force against a valid military target. Because Article I defines the term broadly to include the four categories outlined above, just about any damage directly caused by the space object of a state party will be compensable under the Convention. But again, a key factor in making this determination will be the qualification of that which caused the damage as a "space object." Some have suggested that a space object must, at a minimum, be something that is designed for travel in space.[60] On this approach, sounding rockets that fail to leave Earth's atmosphere and scientific equipment permanently left on the moon are not space objects. By contrast, a satellite in transit by truck that causes damage upon the truck's impact with another vehicle would logically subject the state of origin to absolute liability.

The Convention's best-known feature, creation of a Claims Commission process, is perhaps also its greatest failure. Though widely hailed as creating an equitable procedure for the resolution of liability claims, the Convention failed to require that its Claims Commission decisions would automatically bind litigants. Ultimately, whether the Liability Convention has succeeded in achieving its goals remains to be seen; it has never been used and thus cannot be judged effective.[61] Though the Convention does establish the international standard for compensation related to space incidents, and fixes the level of liability based on the spatial area in which the damage occurred, it is unlikely to affect a state's decision to purpose operations undertaken in the interest of national security.

Questions for Discussion

1. The Liability Convention establishes liability for the acts of states parties, not individuals. Yet, the Outer Space Treaty makes states responsible for all "national activities in outer space," interpreted to include the activity of private citizens. For these purposes, is there a meaningful difference between a state's "liability" and its "responsibility"?

2. Would the language of the Convention be sufficient to sustain a victim's claim for medical expenses incurred for a heart attack resulting from the impacting of space debris on the ground next to him? What about a creditor's losses due to the damage sustained by a debtor as a result of an errant space object? Are either of these damages "caused by" the space object of a launching state? Would the injured party's domestic law be relevant?

---

59. As stated previously, the Liability Convention's description of space object, which appears in the subsequent Registration Convention, utterly fails as a definition. Though it would appear to include nonoperational space debris, it leaves several unresolved issues. For example, it is unclear whether a space object is simply an object designed for travel in outer space. Professor Foster notes that all of the draft definitions of space object in the UN's Legal Subcommittee for the Committee on the Peaceful Use of Outer Space "contained the criterion of being designed for movement in outer space." W.F. Foster, *The Convention on International Liability for Damage Caused by Space Objects*, 1972 Can. Y.B. Int'l L. 137, 145. Because the Liability Convention definition of space object includes component parts of a space object, it is unclear whether, for example, cargo and crew of a space object also qualify themselves as space objects. They might if Christol is correct that "'component parts' is to be construed in a broad sense to include such property on board as would be conducive to the successful operation of the space object." Christol, Law of Outer Space, *supra* note 36, at 109.

60. *See* Foster, *supra* note 59.

61. The Cosmos 954 incident would have provided the first case study. Although it paid $3,000,000 of the Canadian $6,000,000 claim, and the Canadian government explicitly invoked the Convention in its claim, the Soviet Union refused to engage in legal argumentation over the convention's terms, including provisions for claim resolution.

Registration Convention

Convention on Registration of Objects Launched into Outer Space
(1974)[62]

Article I

For the purposes of this Convention:

. . . .

(c) The term "State of registry" means a launching State on whose registry a space object is carried in accordance with article II.

Article II

1. When a space object is launched into earth orbit or beyond, the launching State shall register the space object by means of an entry in an appropriate registry which it shall maintain. Each launching State shall inform the Secretary-General of the United Nations of the establishment of such a registry.

2. Where there are two or more launching States in respect of any such space object, they shall jointly determine which one of them shall register the object in accordance with paragraph 1 of this article, bearing in mind the provisions of article VIII of the Treaty on principles governing the activities of States in the exploration and use of outer space, including the moon and other celestial bodies, and without prejudice to appropriate agreements concluded or to be concluded among the launching States on jurisdiction and control over the space object and over any personnel thereof.

. . . .

Article III

1. The Secretary-General of the United Nations shall maintain a Register in which the information furnished in accordance with article IV shall be recorded.

2. There shall be full and open access to the information in this Register.

Article IV

1. Each State of registry shall furnish to the Secretary-General of the United Nations, as soon as practicable, the following information concerning each space object carried on its registry:

    (a) Name of launching State or States;

    (b) An appropriate designator of the space object or its registration number;

    (c) Date and territory or location of launch;

    (d) Basic orbital parameters, including:

        (i) Nodal period,

        (ii) Inclination,

---

62. Convention on the Registration of Objects Launched into Outer Space, Jan. 14, 1975, 28 U.S.T. 695, 1023 U.N.T.S. 15 (entered into force Sept. 15, 1976) [hereinafter Registration Convention].

(iii) Apogee,

(iv) Perigee;

(e) General function of the space object.

2. Each State of registry may, from time to time, provide the Secretary-General of the United Nations with additional information concerning a space object carried on its registry.

3. Each State of registry shall notify the Secretary-General of the United Nations, to the greatest extent feasible and as soon as practicable, of space objects concerning which it has previously transmitted information, and which have been but no longer are in earth orbit.

. . . .

––––––––––––

Professors Diederiks-Verschoor and Kopal have articulated the widespread rationale for developing a registration regime for space objects:

> (1) it is not possible to identify a spacecraft that has caused damage without an international system of registration; (2) a well-ordered, complete and informative system of registration would minimize the likelihood and even the suspicion of weapons of mass destruction being furtively put into orbit.[63]

While the second point seems overly optimistic, the first is beyond question.

That a state must maintain a registry of its space objects was never particularly controversial in the international community. The Outer Space Treaty's prior use of the phrase "State of registry" (Article V) presupposed, but did not require, that states were keeping track of their launch payloads. What the Registration Convention required, however, was entirely new. To make public reports to the United Nations of all objects launched raised the specter of a new kind of vulnerability. It was one thing for a state to keep protected records within its own government, but another thing to make reports to an international body the contents of which would be open to public inspection. As it turned out, the substantive requirements at the heart of the Convention in Article IV didn't require nearly the level of disclosure originally hoped by many.

With respect to launches containing national security assets, the convention allows registry notifications to be ambiguous, the effect of which is to mask the true nature of the mission. Two provisions from Article IV make this especially so. First, the fact that the information need only be provided as soon as practicable could legitimately be interpreted as requiring notification weeks, months, or years following the launch. Indeed, depending on the nature of the payload, it may not be practicable to reveal the contents of the launch until after the object has been deorbited. For example, during preparation for an international armed conflict, it would hardly be practicable for a state to transmit the launch of its space objects to an opposing force through the United Nations. Given the fact that Article III mandates "full and open access to the information in this [United Nations] Register," the practical result of such timing would be advance notice to the enemy. On this understanding of practicable, the launching state need not attempt to argue that the Convention's terms are suspended during armed conflict, but could appeal

––––––––––––

63. I.H.PH. DIEDERIKS-VERSCHOOR & V. KOPAL, AN INTRODUCTION TO SPACE LAW 44 (3D Rev Ed. 2008) [hereinafter DIEDERIKS-VERSCHOOR & KOPAL].

to Article IV's own terms to deny the enemy the tactical advantage of early notification of space launches.

Second, the fact that only the general function of the space object need be disclosed seems to afford additional security protection for the launching state.[64] The room for ambiguity afforded by the convention allows states to protect the identity of their military satellites, which perform an entirely legitimate function under the law. This might, for example, be used to protect the details of operational national technical means (NTM) of verification, including space reconnaissance capabilities, under various bilateral and multilateral treaties involving the United States. Because NTM are the *sine qua non* of an effective verification structure, it would appear that an expansive understanding of general function would benefit the international community as well as the launching state. Obviously, affected states must protect the secrecy of their space reconnaissance assets. The Registration Convention allows them to do this.

Some commentators euphemistically suppose that a state's disclosure of national security satellite data to the fullest possible extent could possibly allow registration to overcome the suspicion with which states traditionally approach each other.[65] Of course, this analysis overlooks the spy satellite's *raison d'etre*—acquisition of information without the sensed state's knowledge. Once its existence and characteristics are known, its effectiveness as an instrument for spying diminishes. Having exposed the implications of such suggestions for space reconnaissance activities, such positions appear tantamount to an argument that space reconnaissance should simply be outlawed. Though that position could be legitimately debated, such activities have been rightfully recognized as lawful for decades, and likely will for the foreseeable future.[66]

Beyond notifications required by the Registration Convention, the United States shares additional information with selected state and non-state actors. Pursuant to "space situational awareness" agreements, the Secretary of Defense may disclose additional information, provide services, and receive similar information and services, on a cost-reimbursable basis, from "non-United States Government entities."[67] Prior to entering such agreements, the Secretary must determine that doing so "is consistent with the national security interests of the United States."[68] Although the sharing of such sensitive information and services could risk compromises of national security data, the Secretary has determined that doing so is in the U.S. interest, at least with respect to agreements with the United Kingdom, Canada, Japan, Australia, and a variety of additional non-state actors. Obvious potential benefits could include launch support, uninterrupted coalition satellite operations, and reducing the risk of collisions.

---

64. The United Nations Office for Outer Space Affairs maintains the public register containing notifications of states parties to the Registration Convention. As the most common examples, the United States provided the following three "general function" descriptions covering numerous separate notifications in 2014: (1) "Spacecraft engaged in practical applications and uses of space technology such as weather or communications" (2) "Spent boosters, spent manoeuvring stages, shrouds and other non-functional objects" and (3) "Reusable space transportation systems" *Available at* <http://www.oosa.unvienna.org/oosa/en/Reports/docsusa.html>.

65. *See, e.g.*, Diederiks-Verschoor & Kopal, *supra* note 63, at 45.

66. In addition to reconnaissance satellites, the vague reporting requirements could easily obscure the true nature of virtually any space object of interest to the national security community.

67. 10 U.S.C. 2274(a). Such entities include (1) a State, (2) a political subdivision of a State, (3) a U.S. commercial entity, (4) the government of a foreign country, or (5) a foreign commercial entity.

68. *Id.*

Questions for Discussion

1. Do the terms of the convention require reporting the relocation of an operational space asset from its original orbital position? Put otherwise, does the convention require multiple reports?

2. How might the maritime "flag of convenience" notion, if applied to space objects, complicate the effort to keep meaningful track of all registrations?

3. How might the terms of a space situational awareness agreement more effectively accomplish the purposes of the Registration Convention than its own terms might accomplish?

Other Relevant International Law

Customary International Law for Space?

The most obvious effect of finding a body of customary international law for space would be the conclusion that it binds all states.[69] Because any such law would have been derived from the activity of relatively few states, and because of the increasing role of treaties both in international law in general and space law in particular, some conclude that customary law is of minimal importance and its significance for outer space activities has not been secured.[70] This is perhaps yet another function of the youth of space law relative to more established branches of international law—there simply has not been sufficient time and widespread uniformity for much customary law to crystallize. Nonetheless, some principles do seem to have attained the status of customary law.

Although space research and development had gone on for over a decade, it was not until the launch of Sputnik I in 1957 that international agreement emerged on basic principles that should govern outer space activity. With respect to the principle of freedom of use and exploration of space, that agreement came almost immediately following the launch of Sputnik I. Because this general agreement was largely based on the practice of only two states, many have argued that in the early days of space exploration, there could be no customary law for space. Thus, commenting in 1961, Professor Cooper asserted:

> [I]t is quite impossible to apply international legal principles in a satisfactory manner in any geographic area whose legal status is unknown. Today the legal status of outer space is as vague and uncertain as was the legal status of the high seas in the centuries before Grotius, in the *Mare Liberum*, focused attention on the need of the world to accept the doctrine of the freedom of the seas.... [N]o

---

69. As explained elsewhere in this volume, classical international legal theory views customary international law as a formal source of law. Article 38 of the Statute of the International Court of Justice charges the Court with resolving disputes in accordance with international law by applying, *inter alia*, "international custom, as evidence of a general practice accepted as law." STAT. OF THE INT'L CT. OF J., June 26, 1945, 59 Stat. 1031 (entered into force Oct. 24, 1945), at art. 38.

70. *See* Malanczuk, *Space Law*, *supra* note 2, at 159. *But see* opinion of Professors Diederiks-Verschoor and Kopal, "customary law is already playing a significant role in space law, and ... states have evidently found it necessary, or at least expedient, to abide by its rules." DIEDERIKS-VERSCHOOR & KOPAL, *supra* note 63, at 12.

general customary international law exists covering the legal status of outer space.[71]

While this was certainly true in 1961, since the late 1950s the number of states actively engaged in space activities has been steadily growing. A present listing of these states would certainly include the United States, Russia, the United Kingdom, France, China, India, Japan, and Iran.[72] The activity of these space-faring states, each of which maintains an indigenous launch capability, makes them important bellwethers for the development of customary law for outer space. To the extent these states persistently object to a would-be space norm, one could reasonably assert that the principle in question could not become customary law.[73]

On the basis of this growing activity in space, there is a general consensus that several principles of customary international law exist for outer space activities. These include the major principles codified in the Outer Space Treaty, which have been explicitly accepted by all states active in outer space. This acceptance can be shown by the practice and *opinio juris* of the ratifying states, as well as the utter lack of dissenting practice on the part of non-ratifying states.[74] At a minimum, these principles include the freedom of exploration and use of outer space by all states and the prohibition on national appropriation of outer

---

71. John Cobb Cooper, *The Rule of Law in Outer Space*, 47 Am. Bar Ass'n J. 23 (1961) (quoted in Nicholas M. Matte, Space Activities and Emerging International Law 83 (1984)). But note Professor Cheng's fascinating article in which he argues that, based on the nearly immediate consensus that emerged regarding the status of outer space, the international community had witnessed a reversal of the orthodox view of customary law—an instant customary law. Placing greater stress on the requirement that states express acceptance of a general practice (*opinio juris*), Cheng continued by noting that

[I]t may be permissible to go further and say that the role of usage in the establishment of rules of international customary law is purely evidentiary: it provides evidence on the one hand of the contents of the rule in question and on the other hand of the *opinio juris* of the States concerned. Not only is it unnecessary that the usage should be prolonged, but there need also be no usage at all in the sense of repeated practice, provided that the *opinio juris* of the States concerned can be clearly established. Consequently, international customary law has in reality only one constitutive element, the *opinio juris*. Where there is *opinio juris*, there is a rule of international customary law.

Bin Cheng, *United Nations Resolutions on Outer Space: 'Instant' International Customary Law?*, 5 Indian J. Int'l L. 23, 36 (1965).

72. While the UK previously maintained an indigenous launch capacity, it and numerous other states, including France, now exercise space activity through the intergovernmental European Space Agency. In addition to those mentioned, in 2012 North Korea successfully launched an object into orbit. However, international condemnation of this launch, and previous attempts, makes it unlikely that North Korean space contributions will affect the development of international space norms any time soon.

73. The relevance of the practice of specially affected states with respect to the formation of customary international law, in this case those most active in space activity, appears to be the method employed consistently by the International Court of Justice. For example, in the *Nicaragua* case, the Court undertook to establish the customary legal basis for the principle of nonintervention as it analyzed the dispute between the United States and Nicaragua. As part of its argument, the Court pointed out that, although the United States expressed its opinion that UN General Assembly Resolution 2131 was not a formulation of law but only a statement of political intention, the United States later accepted Resolution 2625, which purported to declare law on the same point as Resolution 2131. Military and Paramilitary Activities (Nicar. v. U.S.), 1986 I.C.J. 4, 107. The Court's attempt to resolve the apparent U.S. reservation to the principle of nonintervention makes the most sense when viewed as an attempt to show that the United States was not a persistent objector to the principle. In this light, the Court has employed a method logically flowing from its prior assertion as to the required acquiescence of specially affected states in the formation of customary international law.

74. *See* Malanczuk, *Space Law*, *supra* note 2, at 159. An exception to the lack of dissent would be the unsuccessful attempt by eight equatorial states to garner support for their "Bogotá Declaration."

space.[75] In addition, a strong case can be made that international law contains a customary right to freely observe other states from space. As Professors Diederiks-Verschoor and Kopal have noted, "[i]t is important to bear in mind that there is as yet no statutory obligation on States, in UN Resolutions or elsewhere, to ask for prior consent...."[76] Because these customary principles are codified (either explicitly or by logical extension) in the Outer Space Treaty, and because the most space-active states are parties to the treaty, customary international law seems less important in ascertaining principles applicable to state conduct in space than it might in the future.[77]

Other Sources of Treaty Law

The final UN-sponsored treaty, previously noted briefly, is the agreement commonly known as the "Moon Agreement." It is virtually irrelevant to U.S. national security law.[78] Not only is the United States neither a signatory nor a party, no other major space-active states are parties either. Of greater import are the treaties prohibiting nuclear testing and detonation in the space environment,[79] and manipulation of natural environmental processes, including those in outer space, as a method of warfare.[80] The Limited Test Ban Treaty in particular is important to national space operations for at least three reasons.

---

75. *Id.*

76. DIEDERIKS-VERSCHOOR & KOPAL, *supra* note 63, at 11. Given the generally *permissive* nature of public international law (that which is not prohibited is permitted), it is preferable to conceive the right of surveillance not as requiring authorization by customary law, but simply as a state's natural prerogative flowing from its sovereignty and the principle that space is free for peaceful purposes. *See* discussion at *infra* note 85.

77. The body of customary law pertaining to space will assume much greater importance as non-parties to the relevant space treaties become active in space activities. These might include states such as Indonesia, Colombia, Serbia, and, subject to ongoing condemnation of its launch activity, North Korea.

78. Agreement on the Activities of States on the Moon and Other Celestial Bodies, Dec. 5, 1979, G.A. Res. 34/68, UN GAOR, 34th Sess., Supp. No. 46, UN Doc. A/34/664 (1979) (entered into force July 11, 1984). Significantly, the Agreement contained a controversial "Common Heritage of Mankind" principle. Professor Christol provides instructive insight into why the Moon Agreement was likely unacceptable to the vast majority of developed states that considered

> [t]he province of mankind principle [as found in Article I of the Outer Space Treaty] ... linked to the *res communis* principle which allows for the exploration, use, exploitation, and voluntary sharing of common resources. On the other hand, the Common Heritage of Mankind principle, as contained in the Moon Agreement, may be characterized as a "*res communis* plus" principle in the sense that successful explorers, users, and exploiters of the moon and its natural resources will be obligated to conform to the decisions of the international legal regime identified in Article 11 of that agreement.... The province of mankind principle does not contemplate the formation of an international inter-governmental body or that there be an obligatory sharing of the tangible acquisitions of Moon and celestial body activity.

Carl Q. Christol, *Important Concepts for the International Law of Outer Space, in* PROCEEDINGS OF THE FORTIETH COLLOQUIUM ON THE LAW OF OUTER SPACE 73, 80 (1998).

79. Treaty Banning Nuclear Weapon Tests in the Atmosphere, in Outer Space and Underwater, Aug. 5, 1963, 14 U.S.T. 1313, 480 U.N.T.S. 43 (entered into force Oct. 10, 1963) [hereinafter Limited Test Ban Treaty]. As the title suggests, the treaty effected a "limited" ban on nuclear testing that did not restrict detonations underground. Important as its restrictions on space activities are, some scholars refer to it as a sixth space treaty. *See, e.g.,* BESS C. M. REIJNEN, THE UNITED NATIONS SPACE TREATIES ANALYZED ix (1992).

80. Convention on the Prohibition of Military or Any Other Hostile Use of Environmental Modification Techniques, May 18, 1977, 31 U.S.T. 333, 1108 U.N.T.S. 151 (entered into force Oct. 5, 1978).

First, while the treaty prohibits all nuclear detonations in space, it does not apply to detonations of a non-nuclear nature, such as those created by conventional, biological, chemical, or high energy laser weapons.[81] Second, because the treaty outlaws "any nuclear weapon test explosion, *or any other nuclear explosion*" (emphasis added), it may prohibit the use of nuclear fission as a means of space propulsion.[82] To the extent nuclear power sources operate by means other than "explosion," the treaty does not prohibit their use. Finally, the treaty prohibits the use of nuclear explosions for non-testing purposes as well. Thus, if the creation of an electromagnetic pulse in space (by means of a nuclear detonation in peacetime) were to present any strategic national security advantage for the United States (a doubtful conclusion given the heavy U.S. investment in space and drastic physical consequences of such an event), such activity is forbidden by the treaty.[83]

In addition to the foregoing authorities, which limit state activity in space to a certain extent, an additional series of bilateral launch notification agreements with the former Soviet Union further impose certain obligations on the U.S. government.[84] Drafted in order to prevent the outbreak of nuclear war, these instruments are intended to have the effect of creating transparency between the two most powerful nuclear-capable states. In sum, these agreements require advance notice of ballistic missile and space object launches under the conditions specified within each treaty.

Additional Issues Bearing Present or Future Implications for U.S. National Security

The Militarization and Weaponization of Space

The militarization of outer space does not necessarily entail its weaponization. The development of the space systems discussed at the beginning of this chapter establishes that the human ascent to space, at its outset, involved the militarization of space. Nonetheless, the possible weaponization of space is another kind of issue. Unfortunately,

---

81. REYNOLDS & MERGES, *supra* note 54, at 59.

82. *Id.* at 61. The authors note that the United States abandoned its experimentation on the ORION nuclear propulsion system, which used small atomic bombs as fuel, after ratification of the treaty. The U.S. Congressional Office of Technology Assessment opined in 1985 that existing international law prohibits "the *testing or deployment in space* of nuclear space mines or ASATs that would require a nuclear detonation as a power source." U.S. Congress, Office of Technology Assessment, *Anti-Satellite Weapons, Countermeasures, and Arms Control* 13 (1985). The basis of this conclusion is likely not the Outer Space Treaty's ban on the orbiting or stationing of nuclear weapons in space, the definition of which is reasonably open to interpretation, but the Limited Test Ban Treaty's ban on nuclear detonations in space.

83. Because electromagnetic pulses are not dissipated in space, a single two-megaton bomb exploded at 50 km or higher above the earth could affect the circuits of nearly all unshielded satellites up to the geostationary orbit. REYNOLDS & MERGES, *supra* note 54, at 59.

84. These include the following three: (1) Agreement on Measures to Reduce the Risk of Outbreak of Nuclear War, Sept. 30, 1971, U.S.-U.S.S.R., 22 U.S.T. 1590, 807 U.N.T.S. 57, (entered into force Sept. 30, 1971); (2) Agreement on Notifications of Launches of Intercontinental Ballistic Missiles and Submarine Launched Ballistic Missiles, May 31, 1988, U.S.-U.S.S.R., 27 I.L.M. 1200 (entered into force May 31, 1988); (3) Memorandum of Understanding on Notifications of Missile Launches, Dec. 16, 2000, U.S.-U.S.S.R. <http://www.state.gov/t/ac/trt/4954.htm>.

in addition to undefined terms, such as peaceful purposes[85] and outer space,[86] the law lacks basic authoritative definitions of other terms impacting any discussion of space militarization, including "space object" and "space debris." As it is generally conceived, a space object includes any artifact, manned or unmanned, that is launched into orbit. This includes objects that have ceased to function and have become debris.

But beyond terms relevant to the militarization of space are those related to the more controversial prospect of space weaponization. For example, despite the heavy militarization of space, the basic term "space weapon" lacks definition in international law. As a result, the concept it represents, which broadly speaking includes any implements of warfare in space, is difficult to isolate. Without this foundational definition, one cannot define phrases on which it might rely. The difficulty comes into particular focus by observing that any comprehensive definition of space weapon will include space systems equally used for nonmilitary, nondestructive, and nonaggressive purposes. Though space weapons may seem to include only a discrete class of armaments with easily definable characteristics, a closer examination "reveals a less obvious and more inclusive set of systems."[87]

The United States has historically resisted the prospect of fielding space weapons even as their use attracts perennial attention. Some, including a former Chief of Staff of the U.S. Air Force, view the ultimate weaponization of space as inevitable.[88] Whatever policy the United States adopts, one must immediately confront the question "what constitutes

---

85. As suggested above, the commonly accepted modern position regards peaceful purposes as synonymous with nonaggressive activity. Such operations would include not only peacetime military activity in space, but also activity involving the use of force in space during armed conflict. What makes an activity aggressive, and thus non-peaceful, is not the use or absence of armed force or its equivalent, but the larger purpose to which it is put. An aggressive act unlawfully initiated by one belligerent may trigger a lawful, though overwhelming, armed response from another in individual or collective self-defense. The latter response is not rendered aggressive even though it may involve a ferocious degree of force or even what might constitute an act of aggression. In this way, even an act of armed force may have a larger peaceful purpose. To the extent a use of force is taken in self-defense, or pursuant to a UN Security Council authorization, and is proportional to the initial aggressive act, it complies with international law and may occur in space just as elsewhere. For a discussion of the requirement that the Law of War principle of proportionality applies to acts of self-defense, see Military and Paramilitary Activities (Nicar. v. U.S.), 1986 I.C.J. 4, 103 ("The Parties also agree in holding that whether the response to the attack is lawful depends on observance of the criteria of the necessity and the proportionality of the measures taken in self-defense.").

86. Perhaps the most recurring definitional void in all of space law relates to the delimitation, or boundary, separating a state's territorial airspace and outer space.

> There is no clear answer to the question of where space begins. But equally clearly, at some point above the earth, there exists an environment completely different from the one we have here. A sort of customary law has developed ... to the effect than any object in orbit is in space, and that seems enough to satisfy everyone for the time being.

REYNOLDS & MERGES, *supra* note 54, at 12. For an excellent legal analysis of the air and space boundary question, see Elizabeth Kelly, The Spaceplane: The Catalyst for Resolution of the Boundary and 'Space Object' Issues in the Law of Outer Space? (1998) (unpublished LL.M. thesis, McGill University).

87. Paul B. Stares, *The Problem of Non-Dedicated Space Weapon Systems, in* PEACEFUL AND NON-PEACEFUL USES OF SPACE: PROBLEMS OF DEFINITION FOR THE PREVENTION OF AN ARMS RACE 147 (Bhupendra Jasani, ed., 1991).

88. David A. Fulghum, *USAF Chief Signals Key Funding Priorities*, 153:1 AV. WK. & SPACE TECH. 56 (July 3, 2000). Expanding the point, General Michael Ryan asserted that while the weaponization of space was still a ways off, "there is some inevitability that it will occur if just to protect extensive communications and navigation systems already there.... I think there will be attacks — challenges to our space capability. We will have to protect our assets in space because we're becoming much more dependent on them. So I see defense as a primary emphasis." *Id.*

a space weapon?" As one example, the meaning of "nuclear weapon" as used in the Outer Space Treaty may become less and less evident in future decades witnessing an evolution of space weaponry.[89] While some hearing the term "nuclear weapon" may immediately equate it with thermonuclear devices designed for detonation under controlled circumstances, it is certainly correct to observe that "nuclear energy may be used in different ways and may be a potential weapon even if not so designed."[90] As a result, in the absence of clear definition, one could argue that following its malfunction, the Chernobyl nuclear reactor, for example, became a nuclear weapon.

One proposed definition of space weapon illustrates the challenge:

> A space weapon is a device stationed in outer space (including the moon and other celestial bodies) or in the earth environment designed to destroy, damage, or otherwise interfere with the normal functioning of an object or being in outer space, or a device stationed in outer space designed to destroy, damage, or otherwise interfere with the normal functioning of an object or being in the earth environment. Any other device with the inherent capability to be used as defined above will be considered as a space weapon.[91]

Of particular interest is the second sentence. While acknowledging that space objects may *become* weapons if they can be used as such, it arguably leaves the definition so broad as to include just about any object at all.

A consensus among states on such a definition will at least facilitate international discussion on the advisability of imposing restrictions on weaponization. In the meantime, consideration of technologies useful for space weaponization will proceed under the principle that state action is permitted in the absence of a clear legal prohibition. Though regularly denounced by a large segment of the international community as destabilizing for the use and exploration of outer space,[92] in principle very few potential implements of space weaponization, with the exception of nuclear weapons, would violate international law.[93] Of course, the use to which these weapons are put could render them unlawful for

---

89. *See supra* note 43 for further discussion of the definition of nuclear weapons as applied to x-ray lasers.

90. Stephen Gorove, *Space Without Weapons: International Legal Aspects of Weapons and Harms, in* Space Without Weapons 29 (Nicholas M. Matte, ed., 1989) [hereinafter Gorove, *Space Without Weapons*].

91. Bhupendra Jasani, *Introduction* to Peaceful and Non-Peaceful Uses of Space: Problems of Definition for the Prevention of an Arms Race 13 (Bhupendra Jasani, ed., 1991).

92. Indeed, the Soviet Union went so far as to present a "Draft Treaty on the Prohibition of the Stationing of Weapons of Any Kind in Outer Space" to the 36th Session of the UN General Assembly on August 20, 1981. In pertinent part, the draft treaty would have required:

> States Parties ... not to place in orbit around the earth objects carrying weapons of any kind, install such weapons on celestial bodies, or station such weapons in outer space in any other manner, including on reusable manned space vehicles of an existing type or of other types which States Parties may develop in the future.

(Article 1(1)). It would have equally required states parties "not to destroy, damage, disturb the normal functioning or change the flight trajectory of space objects of other States Parties, if such objects were placed in orbit in strict accordance with Article 1, paragraph 1, of this treaty." (Article 3). Quoted in Colin S. Gray, American Military Space Policy: Information Systems, Weapon Systems and Arms Control 115 (1982). The United States dismissed the Soviet draft treaty as a hypocritical propaganda ploy. Paul B. Stares, The Militarization of Space 230 (1985). Since then, numerous similar proposals have been advanced, primarily by the Russians, Chinese, and Canadians.

93. After a discussion of the relevant provisions of the Outer Space Treaty and the Moon Agreement, Professor Christol observed in 1988:

> In the years since 1967 [Outer Space Treaty] and 1979 [Moon Agreement] science and technology have perfected new generations and families of weapons, including those

a specific objective if, for example, their use rendered them disproportionate (or indiscriminate or inhumane) under the Law of War as judged against the military objective in view. But this is an inherent possibility for any weapon, which, by itself, does not render the weapon unlawful.

Perhaps most significant to the advancement of international law relating to space weaponization, are the draft treaty proposals advanced in the United Nations Conference on Disarmament, and the U.S. response. Beginning in 2008, the draft "Treaty on Prevention of the Placement of Weapons in Outer Space and the Threat or Use of Force against Outer Space Objects" (PPWT) precipitated formal discussion on a series of related terms and concepts, including definitions of the terms "weapon in outer space," "use of force," and "threat of force."[94] The proposed text of this and related submissions in the Conference on Disarmament, followed years of dialogue, debate, and working papers on the advisability of attempts to ban space weapons.

In its response to the 2008 draft text, the United States drew some "preliminary conclusions" about significant departures from the existing legal regime for space, and regarding vague terms and troubling unanswered questions dispersed throughout the draft text related to threats and uses of force, weapons, testing compliance, treaty amendments, verification, transparency, and confidence-building measures.[95] Three points from the U.S. response merit special mention. First, the U.S. reiterated its decades-old policies against proposed legal regimes that seek prohibitions on the military or intelligence uses of space, or that fail to preserve the U.S. right to conduct research, development, testing, and

---

employing highly focused energy, such as laser weapons, and those based on sub-atomic particles, such as particle beam weapons. Pursuant to the general legal principle that which is not prohibited is permitted, it may be concluded that the more recent exotic weapons do not fall within the constraints of the foregoing treaty provisions.

Carl Q. Christol, *Outer Space: Battle-Ground of the Future?, in* SPACE LAW: PAST, PRESENT AND FUTURE 59 (Carl Q. Christol, ed., 1991) [hereinafter Christol, SPACE LAW]. The Russians have objected to the possibility of orbiting a particle beam weapon claiming that it would constitute a "weapon of mass destruction." L. B. TAYLOR, SPACE: BATTLEGROUND OF THE FUTURE? 34 (1988 ed.). However, given its presumed capacity for precision, such a weapon would not likely generate mass destruction, however lethal its effects might be for intended targets. Some authors even suggest, inexplicably, that just about all space weapons would constitute weapons of mass destruction. *See, e.g.,* Maurice N. Andem, *Implementation of Article IV of the Outer Space Treaty of 1967 During the 21st Century, in* PROCEEDINGS OF THE FORTIETH COLLOQUIUM ON THE LAW OF OUTER SPACE 338, 344 (1998).

94. *Letter Dated 12 February 2008 From the Permanent Representative of the Russian Federation and the Permanent Representative of China to the Conference on Disarmament Addressed to the Secretary-General of the Conference Transmitting the Russian and Chinese Texts of the Draft "Treaty on Prevention of the Placement of Weapons in Outer Space and of the Threat or Use of Force Against Outer Space Objects (PPWT)" Introduced by the Russian Federation and China,* CD/1839, 29 February 2008. In 2014, Russia and China submitted to the Conference on Disarmament an updated draft text (CD/1985, 12 June 2014) that provided a new proposed definition of "weapon in outer space" (" … any outer space object or its component thereof which has been produced or converted to destroy, damage or disrupt the normal functioning of objects in outer space, on the Earth's surface or in its atmosphere, or to eliminate human beings or components of biosphere which are important to human existence, or to inflict damage to them by using any principles of physics."). The updated text also defined "use of force" as " … any action intended to inflict damage on an outer space object under the jurisdiction and/or control of other States," and the term "threat of force" as " … the clear expression in written, oral or any other form of the intention to commit such an action [as the use of force]."

95. *Letter Dated 19 August 2008 From the Permanent Representative of the United States of America Addressed to the Secretary-General of the Conference Transmitting Comments on the Draft "Treaty on Prevention of the Placement of Weapons in Outer Space and of the Threat or Use of Force Against Outer Space Objects (PPWT)" As Contained in Document CD/1839 of 29 February 2008,* CD/1847, 26 August 2008.

operations in space for military, intelligence, civil, or commercial purposes. Second, the U.S. response asserted that nothing in the draft text provided grounds to change the U.S. principle that new arms control constraints or limitations on space-based systems are not in the national security interests of the United States. And third, the U.S. reasserted its long-held view that it is "not possible" to develop a verifiable agreement banning space-based weapons, or terrestrial-based anti-satellite systems. Taken together, these assertions suggest that the U.S. is largely content with the way international legal norms govern human activity related to the militarization and weaponization of outer space.

Uses of Force in Space

Beyond definitional limitations regarding what might constitute militarization or weaponization, and attempts to restrict such activity, an articulation of legal standards applicable to space activities should account for the ways most likely to trigger restrictions on the *resort* to the use of armed force under the *jus ad bellum*. One commentator has observed that space law, within which he includes the Limited Test Ban Treaty, Outer Space Treaty, Anti-Ballistic Missile Treaty, and the Moon Agreement, was developed to "permit, indeed to endorse, the arms race, including the militarization of space."[96] Though speaking with a sense of irony and regret, this scholar's comments raise questions about the law's tolerance of one state's infliction of intentional damage on another's assets and of the capture of foreign space assets.

Though the UN Charter forbids the "threat or use of force against the territorial integrity or political independence of any state, or in any other manner inconsistent with the Purposes of the United Nations,"[97] the meaning of this prohibition remains hotly contested. The traditional view is that this provision is an absolute bar to the use of force with the sole exceptions being self-defense and authorization by the Security Council.[98] The emerging view, bolstered by, among others, NATO's 1999 Operation ALLIED FORCE in Kosovo, asserts that the prohibition pertains only to the use of force for purposes inconsistent with the Charter, such as the subjugation of another state or annexation of its territory. A state's interpretation of the Charter's general prohibition on the use of force will obviously greatly impact its decision whether or not to use it. For example, if a state finds in the Charter no prohibition on uses of force in the exercise of individual or collective humanitarian intervention, it will deem such force lawful in any of the combat environments, including space.[99]

Beyond general principles under the UN Charter, one can find reference to the intentional use of force within space law itself. A careful reading of the Liability Convention discloses that it implicitly recognizes that under certain circumstances the intentional destruction of space objects might occur.[100] As previously discussed, Article II of the Liability Convention

---

96. Nicholas M. Matte, *A Treaty for 'Star Peace'*, in 2 ARMS CONTROL AND DISARMAMENT IN OUTER SPACE 190 (Nicholas M. Matte, ed., 1987).

97. UN CHARTER, art. 2, para. 4 (entered into force Oct. 24, 1945) [hereinafter UN CHARTER].

98. Ivan A. Vlasic, *Some Thoughts on Negotiating and Drafting Arms Control and Disarmament Agreements Relating to Outer Space*, in IV ARMS CONTROL AND DISARMAMENT IN OUTER SPACE: TOWARDS A NEW ORDER OF SURVIVAL 203, 211 (Nicholas M. Matte, ed., 1991) [hereinafter Vlasic, *Negotiating and Drafting Agreements Relating to Outer Space*].

99. The more narrow view of Article 2(4) is difficult to square with the UN Charter's plain language, for example Article 2(7), and the historic reticence in the UN General Assembly against foreign interventions.

100. *See* HURWITZ, *supra* note 5, at 148–50.

subjects states parties to absolute liability for damage caused by its space objects on the Earth's surface or to aircraft in flight. Article III extends liability, though based on fault, for damage by a launching state's space object to the space object of another state "being caused elsewhere than on the surface of the earth." However, Article VI provides exoneration from absolute liability in cases where either the claimant state, or the natural or juridical persons it represents, caused the damage wholly or partially by gross negligence or an act or omission done with intent to cause damage. A proper understanding of the phrase "intent to cause damage" provides insight into the convention's foresight as to the possibility of uses of force against space objects.

Under Article VI, the scope of the exoneration applies only as to absolute liability under Article II and, therefore, exoneration from liability for damage by space objects done on the surface of the Earth or to aircraft in flight. Given the purpose of space objects, that is, to launch into space, this provision for exoneration would certainly include intentional acts taken against space objects *while in space* that later cause damage on the Earth or in the air. Obviously, the exoneration for intentional damage caused by a claimant state pre-supposes the possibility that such intentional damage will occur. Thus, despite the provisions of the Outer Space Treaty prescribing the peaceful use and exploration of space, the Liability Convention pragmatically recognizes the distinct possibility that states may engage in intentional damage to space objects. While this does not imply the convention's sanction for such events,[101] it does suggest that the international community realistically expected that a claimant state might take action amounting to the intentional damaging of a space object.[102]

Legally speaking, the capture of a foreign space object is related to the question of in-tentional uses of force. Under Article VIII of the Outer Space Treaty, a state party to the treaty "on whose registry an object launched into outer space is carried shall retain jurisdiction and control over such object." At face value, this means that a satellite, for example, registered by State X belongs to State X for purposes of jurisdiction and control. Nonetheless, when State X uses its satellite to intentionally and wrongfully disable State Y's satellite, assuming that doing so amounts to an armed attack under the UN Charter, State Y may in self-defense take measures to abate the threat posed by State X's satellite, including the potential for destruction of the asset.[103] In such a circumstance, State X has

---

101. In fact, the exoneration from liability shows the very opposite. The convention purports to punish states engaging in intentional destructive acts by eliminating their remedy against the launching state. As Article VI(2) establishes, however, if the damage is caused by activities of the launching state that are inconsistent with international law, including the UN Charter and the Outer Space Treaty, there will be no exoneration from absolute liability whatever. Liability Convention, *supra* note 52, at art. VI(2). This would mean that an aggressive military operation by launching State A that causes damage on the earth or in the air to claimant State B will result in no exoneration of absolute liability for State A, even if State B contributed to the damage by acts done with an intent to cause damage.

102. After observing that the United States ratified the Liability Convention only "after being advised by the Department of State that the convention did not apply to intentional damage," Hurwitz concludes from this that "the U.S. has recognized the right to intentionally damage another State's space objects with impunity (as least as far as the 1972 Convention is concerned)." HURWITZ, *supra* note 5, at 149. Whether this overstates the U.S. position or not, it does seem clear that the convention exonerates one state from liability only as against intentional damage caused by the *claimant* state or the natural or juridical persons it represents. Liability Convention, *supra* note 52, at art. VI(1). Thus, the U.S. Department of State was certainly correct that the convention does not apply (that is, create liability) as against one state in cases where the claimant state has at least partially caused intentional damage.

103. Given the fact that Article 51 presupposes a previous customary right to self-defense (inherent right), the right to respond by State Y may not even require the occurrence of an armed attack,

violated one of the conditions assumed to exist by the Outer Space Treaty—the peaceful use of outer space. Having properly acted in self-defense, may State Y capture State X's aggressor satellite for intelligence or other purposes? It would seem that if State Y can lawfully destroy State X's satellite, it could certainly capture it, Article VIII of the Outer Space Treaty notwithstanding. Put otherwise, the only way a state may be assured the protection of its space assets is to ensure that its activities remain compliant with international law, including space law and the provisions of the UN Charter.

Questions for Discussion

1. Many space assets are jointly owned among a consortium of state and non-state actors. Assuming one has a right under the UN Charter to employ force against such an asset, how might the rights of neutral co-owners be protected? In such a scenario, would a belligerent state that lawfully targets such an asset have any obligation to non-state co-owners that hail from a neutral state?

2. During operation DESERT STORM, both the United States and Iraq leased communication time from the same satellite in the ARABSAT constellation. Assuming both sides were using the asset as an instrument of warfare, would there be any reason either side could not lawfully target the satellite?

3. Would the adoption of a treaty banning "space weapons" prevent a space arms race? Assuming it were silent on the matter, what effect would such a treaty have between states parties who are also belligerents engaged in armed conflict?

Innocent Passage for Space Objects?

An interesting principle on which debate has increasingly centered involves the potential for a customary right of innocent passage through sovereign airspace for objects headed to or from outer space. In furtherance of the point, some have pointed to the lack of objection by certain states in case of occasional violations of its airspace by space objects as evidence that the norm has crystallized. This argument is suspect. At a minimum these anecdotal occasions assume that the violated state was aware of the intrusion—unlikely in those few cases usually cited. The following analysis makes perfect sense:

> [T]he contention can hardly be sustained that the practice of space powers to launch their space objects into outer space after 1957 by crossing the air space under the sovereignty of other countries developed into custom by the acquiescence of those States. The countries affected simply often lacked the technological capacities to find out.[104]

Beyond this, even if a state knew about the violation, isolated instances of an intrusion followed by a mere failure to protest is hardly sufficient to establish a customary norm

---

depending on the nature of the customary right. State Y's act of self-defense must also be proportionate to State X's provocation.

104. PETER MALANCZUK, AKEHURST'S MODERN INTRODUCTION TO INTERNATIONAL LAW (7th ed., 1997). In at least one case, the space object in question was a disabled spacecraft in distress. While there may certainly be a right of access to foreign airspace under customary international law in these limited cases of emergency, such scenarios are distinct from the right of innocent passage described here.

binding the entire international community. More than this would be necessary to evince the requisite *opinio juris*. As Professor Wassenberg has pointed out,

> There is no a [sic] right of (instant?) *customary* international law that space objects can 'freely' transit through foreign airspace. The fact that in practice so far no objections have been raised against transit through a State's airspace by a foreign space object, is not an argument to refer to a customary right of transit, as too few States have considered to be confronted with such transit (and none have been), and no *opinio juris* with respect to such practice has been pronounced as yet.[105]

Perhaps motivating the recurring interest in exploring the innocent passage possibility is the practical problem many states face related to space access. States with geographic advantages, such as the United States, have a certain degree of independence in the launch and recovery of their space objects. Other states are entirely landlocked, however, or possess territory too small to launch objects into space using only domestic airspace or that over the high seas. In this regard, some commentators have argued that for some states to truly enjoy the free exploration and use of outer space guaranteed by the Outer Space Treaty, they must be accorded a right of innocent passage through the national airspace of other states. Some have gone even further to suggest that such a right already exists in customary international law.[106] But, as suggested previously, such a right does not currently exist in the law and is not likely to emerge in the near future given traditional state interests in territorial sovereignty.[107]

Should the notion ever catch on as more than an academic question, it is worth noting that the right would not serve the ends of belligerent states engaged in armed conflict. During such periods, passage of military assets to and from space would not be "innocent." For passage to qualify as innocent under the Law of the Sea Convention, it cannot be "prejudicial to the peace, good order or security of the coastal State."[108] It is self-evident that foreign military activity in support of armed conflict in the territory of the host state (whether territorial seas or superjacent national airspace), absent explicit permission, will be prejudicial to the peace of that state. As long as the law of the sea remains the

---

105. Henri A. Wassenbergh, Principles of Outer Space Law in Hindsight 36 (1991). By contrast, the widespread recognition of the principle of freedom of space, though it came rather quickly following the Soviet launch of Sputnik I, was accompanied not only by the lack of objection in the face of orbital overflights, but affirmative acquiescence by most states in the form of various United Nations resolutions.

106. *See* Stephen Gorove, *Legal and Policy Issues Raised by the Proposed Notion of 'Aerospace Object'*, *in* Proceedings of the Fortieth Colloquium on the Law of Outer Space 411 (1998); Christol, Space Law, *supra* note 93, at 339; Manfred Lachs, The Law of Outer Space: An Experience in Contemporary Law-Making 59, 60 (1972). As previously noted, these arguments generally rest on anecdotal evidence of spacecraft entering the national airspace of a foreign state without incident or objection.

107. In addition to arguments of those commentators previously cited, additional space law commentators cogently have made the argument that such a right does not exist, including Andrei D. Terekhov, *Passage of Space Objects Through Foreign Airspace: International Custom?*, 25:1 J. Space L. 1 (1997); Peter Haanappel, *The Aerospace Plane: Analogies with Other Modes of Transportation*, *in* Proceedings of the Thirty-Second Colloquium on the Law of Outer Space 341, 342 (1990); Bin Cheng, *The Legal Regime of Airspace and Outer Space: The Boundary Problem Functionalism Versus Spatialism: The Major Premises*, 5 Annals Air & Space L. 323, 357 (1980).

108. United Nations Convention on the Law of the Sea, art. 19, Dec. 10, 1982, 1833 U.N.T.S. 3 (entered into force Nov. 16, 1994; the United States has signed but not ratified).

controlling analogy, any future recognition of rights to innocent passage into foreign national airspace for space objects will not apply to belligerents during armed conflict.

International Code of Conduct for Space

Several very high profile events have heightened the international community's concern for the viability and safety of space activities for the future. At least two of these events focused international attention, in part, because of the large quantity of space debris they created, which will imperil space objects for years to come. The first case involved a 2007 Chinese test of an anti-satellite capability. The successful test of a kinetic kill vehicle launched atop a ballistic missile destroyed a Chinese weather satellite at an altitude of approximately 530 miles. It is thought to be the first successful ASAT test since the U.S. direct ascent ASAT launch in 1985, albeit in a much more crowded environment 22 years later. The second case involved the inadvertent 2009 collision of the Iridium 33 and Cosmos 2251 satellites in low earth orbit over Siberia. The event shocked the space community into an acute acknowledgment that there are little if any rules of the road for space, such as those, for example, that have been adopted by the International Civil Aviation Organization for international air travel.

Such occurrences have given greater urgency to the calls for a "code of conduct" for outer space. Advocates for such a code have called for a set of principles that will, with greater specificity than that afforded by the existing legal regime for space, commit state actors to conduct that is more sustainable for the future. What began as a 2008 draft code of conduct under the auspices of the European Union, and opposed by the U.S., has now expanded into a draft "International Code of Conduct" with active participation by the U.S.[109] One U.S. official has asserted that the benefits of a widely-subscribed international code (transparency and confidence-building measures, collision avoidance measures, identification of irresponsible state behavior) outweigh the potential risks. In this regard, the official stressed that the Obama Administration "would not subscribe to an International Code if it constrained or limited the inherent right of individual or collective self-defense, our intelligence community programs or operations, or our ballistic missile defense systems or capabilities."[110]

To the extent commitments in the draft code mirror existing U.S. practices and perspectives, its adoption as a "non-legally binding" document might appear consistent with U.S. interests. However, given the sweeping aspirations articulated in certain portions of the draft texts, it remains to be seen whether cooperation in the development of such standards will advance U.S. interests. At a minimum, U.S. participation will continue to

---

109. On January 17, 2012, the U.S. Secretary of State announced that the U.S. would work with the European Union and spacefaring nations to "develop and advance an International Code of Conduct for Space Activities." Her statement went on to assert that the code would be "a non-legally binding International Code of Conduct focused on the use of voluntary and pragmatic transparency and confidence-building measures to help prevent mishaps, misperceptions, and mistrust in space. An International Code of Conduct, if adopted, would establish guidelines for responsible behavior to reduce the hazards of debris-generating events and increase the transparency of operations in space to avoid the danger of collisions." Department of State Fact Sheet: An International Code of Conduct for Outer Space Activities: Strengthening Long-Term Sustainability, Stability, Safety, and Security in Space (January 17, 2012).

110. Remarks of Frank A. Rose, Deputy Assistant Secretary of State, Bureau of Arms Control, Verification and Compliance, at the National Space Symposium, Colorado Springs, CO, April 18, 2012.

invite legal scrutiny over whether state practice consistent with the code might contribute to the crystallization of customary international law. This possibility could become serious if, while the U.S. continues to develop or even adopt code of conduct standards, it failed to simultaneously emphasize with sufficient vigor, that it is *not* acting out of any sense of legal obligation.

Remote Sensing and Shutter Control

As is evident from the historical information at the beginning of this chapter, remote sensing (intelligence collection, surveillance, and reconnaissance from space) has a long and distinguished history. The very first U.S. satellite system established a space-based remote sensing capability. Perhaps not surprisingly, the notion of imaging from space has generated tremendous discussion in the international community over the years. The perceived threat to national sovereignty, particularly for more authoritarian states, was acute.

For international norms of behavior regarding remote sensing activities, the closest thing to an authoritative source is a 1986 UN General Assembly Resolution.[111] In contrast to the 1961 "Declaration of Legal Principles," the 1986 Resolution limits itself to this one specific form of outer space activity. The resolution defines remote sensing as follows in Principle I: "the sensing of the Earth's surface from space by making use of the properties of electromagnetic waves emitted, reflected or diffracted by the sensed objects, for the purpose of improving natural resources management, land use and protection of the environment."[112] In some discussions of remote sensing, the definition is broadened to include sensing for national security purposes as well, although these activities are more commonly referred to as intelligence, surveillance, and reconnaissance.[113] Given the absence of any governing treaty, the Remote Sensing Resolution is the most authoritative international document to provide not only a general definition, but also the basic parameters of permissible state activity. Passed unanimously by the General Assembly, the resolution was the culmination of previous efforts from 1968 through 1985.[114]

As Professor Christol has noted, though unanimity on the resolution was in some cases grudging, there have been no formal departures from the terms of the resolution.[115] As

---

111. *Principles Relating to Remote Sensing of the Earth from Space*, Dec. 3, 1986, G.A. Res. 41/65 (XLII), UN GAOR, 29th Sess., 95th Plen. Mtg., UN Doc. A/Res/41/65 (1987) [hereinafter *Remote Sensing Resolution*].

112. *Id.*

113. U.S. law adopts a definition of remote sensing somewhat broader than the resolution: " ... the collection of data which can be processed into imagery of surface features of the Earth from an unclassified satellite or satellites ..." 15 U.S.C. § 5602(5) (2003).

114. CHRISTOL, SPACE LAW, *supra* note 93, at 73. Professor Christol notes that in the end, even states initially hesitant to agree on freedom of surveillance from space consulted self interest and developed an expectation that the benefits to be gained by access to sensed data would outweigh any lost sovereignty to be suffered. *Id.* at 88.

115. *Id.* at 94. The author goes so far as to suggest that the resolution's principles are representative of customary international law. After considering the fact that, despite the lack of thorough agreement, there is no overwhelming demand to overturn the principles or even reduce them to a treaty, Christol concluded in 1988 that

> [f]or the moment the debate has been somewhat stilled. Even the best of agreements can become controversial or even unstuck. Perhaps the best long-term approach is to retain remote sensing on the agenda of [the Committee on the Peaceful Uses of Outer Space] so that efforts can be made to transmit the terms of the Principles into a treaty. In this manner those who wish to dissent from the Principles can opt out. In considering this approach

is generally true for UN resolutions, the longer they are used as the international standard, the stronger their authority becomes.

As military, civil, and particularly commercial space imaging capabilities have evolved, what was once an issue of little concern to the United States in the international community has now become a matter of great national security importance. Commenting in 2001, one author summarized the fundamental problem facing the U.S. government:

> The commercial availability of better than one-meter resolution imagery is a double-edged sword.... [T]he benefits for the military, agriculture, the environment, and countless other applications are immense. Such benefits include the potential commercial profit to be realized by remote sensing. Along with those benefits, however, come national security risks. Processed images taken by Space Imaging Inc.'s IKONOS satellite are available on the international market within a day of the object or area being sensed. Thus, any type of military build-up or movement is easily monitored throughout the world. Moreover, the layout of static military sites and positioning of military equipment generally unknown to the general public could soon become common knowledge for both friend and foe. For instance, IKONOS recently produced an image of a secret missile launch site in North Korea. When the image was shown to a U.S. intelligence official, the official remarked, "That's classified." Images of ... a nuclear reactor and missile base in Pakistan, and several Chinese air bases have recently become commercially available as well.[116]

The United States government has attempted several means of controlling the potential threat to national security posed by widespread access to the kinds of information mentioned above. For example, the Land Remote Sensing Policy Act gives the Commerce Department authority to promulgate regulations establishing licensing requirements for space-based commercial imagery providers.[117] Among the several licenses commercial providers must obtain before operating,[118] the remote sensing operating license imposes a few restrictions that are intended to preserve national security concerns. These include limitations on operational performance, monitoring and compliance, and limitations on foreign involvement.[119]

Among the more controversial protections afforded the government is one imposed by a Clinton-era Presidential Decision Directive (PDD). In addition to authorizing the international sale of remote sensing data to international interests, the PDD reserved a significant veto on such sales to the Secretaries of Commerce, Defense, and State.

---

they may find that they may have nowhere to go. As has been abundantly indicated, *they will not find it easy to escape the norms of customary international law.*
Id. at 95 (emphasis added). These are strong assertions regarding the legal effect of a UN General Assembly resolution. Indeed they are assertions with which many legal scholars in the U.S. national security community would likely disagree.

116. Michael R. Hoversten, *U.S. National Security and Government Regulation of Commercial Remote Sensing From Outer Space*, 50 A.F. L. REV. 253, 265 (2001) (citations omitted). The 1990 and 1991 buildup of coalition forces in the Persian Gulf region went partially undetected by Iraqi forces. The author points out that "[s]uch operations could prove to be impossible today absent some type of control over the commercial industry." *Id.* at 266.

117. 51 U.S.C. §§ 60101–60162 (2006).

118. Currently, these licenses, required by various government agencies, may include the following: (1) a remote sensing operating license; (2) a radio frequency license; (3) a launch license; and potentially (4) an export license.

119. See 15 C.F.R. § 960 (2014).

During periods when national security or international obligations and/or foreign policies may be compromised, as defined by the Secretary of Defense or the Secretary of State, respectively, the Secretary of Commerce may, after consultation with the appropriate agency(ies), require the licensee to limit data collection and/or distribution by the system to the extent necessitated by the given situation. Decisions to impose such limits only will be made by the Secretary of Commerce in consultation with the Secretary of Defense or Secretary of State, as appropriate. Disagreements between Cabinet Secretaries may be appealed to the President. The Secretaries of State, Defense and Commerce shall develop their own internal mechanisms to enable them to carry out their statutory responsibilities.[120]

For a variety of reasons, the United States government has never invoked the right of shutter control.

Questions for Discussion

1. Assuming U.S. space activities progress consistent with the draft outer space International Code of Conduct, might such activities amount to state practice supporting the emergence of customary international law? Either way, what are the risks associated with U.S. cooperation in this endeavor? In what ways might the voluntary adoption of Code of Conduct standards evolve into domestic legal standards (consider the role of Departments of Defense, Commerce, and Transportation regulatory rulemaking under the Administrative Procedures Act)?

2. What constitutional issues might the shutter control option raise?

3. Given the proliferation of remote sensing capabilities outside the United States, and recognition that a robust U.S. commercial capability undergirds U.S. national security, what will be the enduring value of the U.S. government's shutter control option?

4. With the increasing availability of high-resolution imagery in the international commercial market, what courses of action might the United States take against third country provisions of such imagery to interests hostile to the United States?

Selected Bibliography

Cheng, Bin, Studies in International Space Law (1998).
———, "United Nations Resolutions on Outer Space: 'Instant' International Customary Law?," 5 *Indian J. Int'l L.* 23 (1965).
Christol, Carl Q., ed., Space Law: Past, Present and Future (1991).
———, The Modern International Law of Outer Space (1982).
Diederiks-Verschoor, I.H.Ph. & V. Kopal, An Introduction to Space Law (3d Ed., 2008).
Gorove, Stephen, ed., United States Space Law: National and International Regulation (1982).

---

120. U.S. Policy on Foreign Access to Remote Sensing Capabilities, H.R. 6133, at 243, 103d Congress (1994) (commonly referred to as "PDD 23"). The internal mechanisms referenced in the PDD have been reduced to an interagency Memorandum of Understanding involving the Departments of State, Commerce, Defense, Interior, and the U.S. intelligence community. Fact Sheet Regarding the Memorandum of Understanding Concerning the Licensing of Private Remote Sensing Satellite Systems, Feb. 2, 2000, 15 C.F.R. §960, Appendix 2; 65 Fed. Reg. 46,836 (July 31, 2000).

HURWITZ, BRUCE A., THE LEGALITY OF SPACE MILITARIZATION (1986).

Jasani, Bhupendra, ed., PEACEFUL AND NON-PEACEFUL USES OF SPACE: PROBLEMS OF DEFINITION FOR THE PREVENTION OF AN ARMS RACE (1991).

Jasentuliyana, Nandasiri, ed., SPACE LAW: DEVELOPMENT AND SCOPE (1992).

LYALL, FRANCIS & PAUL B. LARSEN, SPACE LAW: A TREATISE (2009).

McDOUGAL, MYRES S., HAROLD D. LASSWELL & IVAN A. VLASIC, LAW AND PUBLIC ORDER IN SPACE (1963).

PEEBLES, CURTIS, THE CORONA PROJECT: AMERICA'S FIRST SPY SATELLITES (1997).

REYNOLDS, GLENN H., & ROBERT P. MERGES, OUTER SPACE: PROBLEMS OF LAW AND POLICY (2d Ed., 1998).

SPIRES, DAVID N., BEYOND HORIZONS: A HALF CENTURY OF AIR FORCE SPACE LEADERSHIP (Rev. Ed., 1998).

STARES, PAUL B., SPACE AND NATIONAL SECURITY (1987).

———, THE MILITARIZATION OF SPACE: U.S. POLICY, 1945–1984 (1985).

Chapter 17

Lawfare

Charles J. Dunlap, Jr.

In this chapter:
Introduction to the Concept of Lawfare

Introduction to the Concept of Lawfare

The concept of lawfare continues to evolve and proliferate.[1] At the time of its modern incarnation in 2001,[2] an Internet search would have revealed only a handful of references but, as noted below, that number had risen to 60,000 by 2009. Today, however, it would produce *hundreds of thousands* of results.[3] Lawfare today not only persists as a key aspect of asymmetrical conflicts involving non-state actors, but has also become the weapon of choice for the U.S. government's efforts to unwind the financial underpinnings of terrorist organizations.

And there is more: private plaintiffs are now waging a form of courtroom lawfare by using novel legal theories to sue (in U.S. courts) banks that are alleged to have helped finance terrorist operations. At the same time, in 2010 the Supreme Court endorsed what is, in reality, a *counter*-lawfare technique by sustaining the criminalization of legal advice (and legal training) if provided to designated terrorist organizations.

Technology has also impacted lawfare. As cyber incidents grow in frequency and seriousness, lawfare considerations (albeit not necessarily by that appellation) are increasingly taking center stage. Yet perhaps the most dramatic development in lawfare is the rising number of countries—to include such global powers as China and the Russian Federation—which are embracing lawfare tactics in their kinetic and non-kinetic confrontations with nation-state opponents.

The 2009 article that follows *Lawfare: A Decisive Element of 21st Century Conflicts?*[4] remains a useful primer on the modern concept of lawfare. The purpose of this introduction

---

1. Benjamin Wittes and Stephanie Leutert, *On Wikipedia, Lawfare, Blogs, and Sources*, HARV. L. NAT'L SEC. J. (May 12, 2013 at 5:55 pm), http://harvardnsj.org/2013/05/on-wikipedia-lawfare-blogs-and-sources/.

2. Charles J. Dunlap, Jr., *Law and Military Interventions: Preserving Humanitarian Values in 21st Century Conflicts* (Carr Center for Human Rights, John F. Kennedy School of Government, Harvard University, Working Paper, 2001), *available at* http://www.ksg.harvard.edu/cchrp/Web%20Working%20Papers/Use%20of%20Force/Dunlap2001.pdf.

3. Many of these cites relate to the name of a popular blog. *See, About Lawfare: A Brief History of the Term and the Site*, LAWFARE, http://www.lawfareblog.com/about/.

4. Charles J. Dunlap Jr., *Lawfare: A Decisive Element of 21st-Century Conflicts?*, 54 JOINT FORCE QUARTERLY 34–39 (2009), *available at* http://scholarship.law.duke.edu/faculty_scholarship/3347.

is to provide an overview of some of the lawfare-related issues that have arisen since that time. And, as already indicated, there have been a number of significant developments.

Among other things, the 2009 article highlighted lawfare issues arising from the conflict between Israel and Hamas in the 2008-2009 timeframe. Tragically, that conflict re-ignited in 2014, and it demonstrates that lawfare remains a central tenet of the strategy of both sides. As this writer observed in 2014:

> [I]n the present conflict, Hamas and Israel have sought to assign the other blame for the rising numbers of civilian casualties in an obvious effort to convince world opinion as to who is acting unlawfully and, therefore, gain support around the world.
>
> Hamas expertly wages lawfare by effectively publicizing the deaths of civilians as a result of deliberate Israeli attacks on them. Israelis counter by charging that Hamas is responsible since it operates amid civilians contrary to international law. In addition, Israelis insist that many civilian deaths are the result of Hamas rockets malfunctioning and falling onto Gaza.[5]

Israel clearly had superiority with respect to traditional military means, but Hamas seemed to have had the lawfare edge, at least initially.[6] However, before that contest ended, Israeli counter-lawfare techniques (and Hamas overreaching), may have re-balanced the lawfare scales Israel's way.[7] Regardless, this 2014 conflict shows that lawfare is alive and well in the 21st century.

While the description of lawfare ("the strategy of using or misusing law as a substitute for traditional military means to achieve an operational objective") used in the 2009 article still resonates, it has evolved over the years.[8] Recent developments suggest that perhaps a further adjustment is in order. One expression might be to simply identify lawfare as the use of law as a means of accomplishing what would otherwise require the application of force, or as a means of facilitating the same. So defined, the utility of the term lawfare can extend to circumstances that may not always amount to "war" or, as many prefer, "armed conflict."[9]

Indeed, the most active growth area of lawfare is not as directly associated with traditional battlefields as it might be said about the term's original formulation. For example, in his book, *Treasury's War: The Unleashing of a New Era of Financial Warfare*, Juan Zarate relates how the U.S. Treasury used a variety of laws to "attack" the financial architecture of terrorists and other 21st century adversaries.

Importantly, Professor John Norton Moore, one of the authors of this textbook, was an early advocate of using what could be characterized as a lawfare methodology—civil

---

5. Charles J. Dunlap, Jr., *Will 'lawfare' define Palestinian-Israeli conflict?*, Al-Monitor (Jul. 30, 2014), http://www.al-monitor.com/pulse/originals/2014/07/lawfare-palestine-israel-gaza-conflict-dunlap.html##ixzz 3NKTftCR4.

6. *Id.*

7. Charles J. Dunlap, Jr., *Has Hamas Overplayed Its Lawfare Strategy?*, Just Security (Aug. 5, 2014), http://justsecurity.org/13781/charles-dunlap-lawfare-hamas-gaza/.

8. There have been a variety of interpretations, to include negative characterizations. *See generally*, M. Brittany Cassell, *The Future of Lawfare: A Necessity to the United States' Strategy and Success* (2014) (unpublished manuscript, on file with author).

9. Not every use of force, even by governments, necessarily means an armed conflict is underway. *See e.g.*, Int'l Committee of the Red Cross, *How is the Term "Armed Conflict" Defined in International Humanitarian Law?*, ICRC Opinion Paper, Mar. 2008, *available at* https://www.icrc.org/eng/assets/files/other/opinion-paper-armed-conflict.pdf.

litigation—to fight terrorism.[10] That advocacy is beginning to bear fruit as the 2014 Eastern District of New York case of *Linde v. Arab Bank Plc* resulted in the first U.S. verdict holding a bank liable "in a civil suit under a broad antiterrorism statute."[11] Specifically, a New York jury found that the Arab Bank, a Jordanian institution, "helped Hamas militants carry out a wave of violence in Israel that killed and wounded hundreds of Americans."[12] Cases of this sort may become a key lawfare "tool" to "attack" the ability of terrorists to obtain financing.

Yet at the same time there also has been a disquieting development in the use of the law as a counter-terrorism weapon. In the 2010 case of *Holder v. Humanitarian Law Project*[13] the Supreme Court held, *inter alia*, that providing legal advice or even teaching law to designated terrorist organizations amounted to providing material support to terrorism in violation of 18 U.S.C § 2339. It mattered not that the intent of the Humanitarian Law Project was simply to get the designated organizations to give up violence and "use humanitarian and international law to peacefully resolve disputes."[14]

That ostensibly benign intent evidently did not sway the Court. Though they did not use the term "lawfare," the Court did illustrate how terrorists might pervert the law by explaining that:

> A foreign terrorist organization introduced to the structures of the international legal system might use the information to threaten, manipulate, and disrupt. This possibility is real, not remote.[15]

Still, this holding is troubling not just because of the Court's (and, really, Congress') evidently low opinion of the international legal system's ability to deal with persons who might attempt to abuse the law, but also because the criminalization of an effort to get a group to use the law to resolve disputes peacefully prevents the use of a well-accepted and proven means of ending otherwise intractable hostilities.[16] Moreover, most court systems have, or need to have, procedures in place to deal with *any* litigant who might seek to use the law to "threaten, manipulate, and disrupt." Denying the ability to try to use this kind of lawfare technique to defang a violent adversary is not just puzzling, it is counterproductive.

Importantly, while the article below talks mainly about the use of lawfare in situations involving non-state actors in non-international armed conflicts, it is becoming increasingly clear that nation-states either have employed lawfare, or will employ it as a means and method of warfare. For example, China has developed a rather sophisticated understanding of how law might be used in future conflict.[17]

---

10. *See, e.g.*, John Norton Moore, Civil Litigation Against Terrorism (2004).

11. Stephanie Clifford, *Arab Bank Liable for Supporting Terrorist Efforts, Jury Finds*, New York Times, Sept. 22, 2014, http://www.nytimes.com/2014/09/23/nyregion/arab-bank-found-guilty-of-supporting-terrorist.html?_r=0.

12. Erik Larson and Christie Smythe, *Arab Bank Found Liable for Hamas Terrorist Attacks*, Bloomberg (Sep 23, 2014 9:50 AM ET), http://www.bloomberg.com/news/2014-09-22/arab-bank-found-liable-for-hamas-terrorist-attacks.html.

13. *Holder v. Humanitarian Law Project*, 561 U.S. 1 (2010), *available at* http://www.supremecourt.gov/opinions/09pdf/08-1498.pdf.

14. *Id.* at 14.

15. *Id.* at 37.

16. *See, e.g.*, Kristin Archick, *Northern Ireland: The Peace Process*, U.S. Congressional Research Service (RS21333 Jan. 8, 2014), *available at* http://www.fas.org/sgp/crs/row/RS21333.pdf.

17. *See* Dean Cheng, *Winning Without Fighting: Chinese Legal Warfare*, Backgrounder #2692 on Asia and Pacific, The Heritage Foundation, May 21, 2012, *available at* http://www.heritage.org/research/reports/2012/05/winning-without-fighting-chinese-legal-warfare.

Furthermore, in the ongoing dispute over the control of maritime areas (and the resources they might contain) in the South China Sea, China has used the law to reinforce its claims, while at the same time establishing a military presence.[18] Similarly, the Philippines and other nations which are unable to challenge China militarily, are using a variety of juridical methodologies to launch their own legal attacks. It remains to be seen who will emerge as the victor in what may be the first major lawfare conflict of the 21st century.[19]

China is not alone in its effort to become a lawfare power. Although some scholars believe the Russian Federation (and the Soviets before them) have long employed lawfare strategies,[20] it is undisputed that what might be called lawfare was used in connection with several recent operations. For example, the Russians utilized "passportization" to try to establish an international law basis for their interventions in Georgia and, recently, the Ukraine. As one scholar explains, passportization is the "mass conferral of Russian citizenship to the citizens of other states" which is intended to allow Russia to then assert it was intervening simply for the lawful purpose of "protecting Russian citizens."[21]

Another commentator, Joel Harding, insists that Russia is attempting to use another form of lawfare against the Ukraine by threatening to levy genocide charges.[22] Harding contends that Russia's effort involving "the International Criminal Court at the Hague appears to be the deliberate use of the criminal system for the purpose of creating propaganda in its fight to undermine the legitimacy of the government of Ukraine."[23]

Understandably, some have argued for a kind of lawfare 'counter-attack' against Russian aggression[24] (though others challenge the wisdom of doing so[25]). Even more recently, Russian officials—reeling from sanctions initiated by the U.S. in response to the Ukraine situation—appear to be conducting lawfare by calling for an "investigation of the United States' atomic bombings of Hiroshima and Nagasaki during World War II as a 'crime against humanity.'"[26]

Obviously, lawfare is continuing to develop as a means and method of warfare in the 21st century, even though every expression of it may not be to our liking. As this writer has said before, it is useful to think of the law in the lawfare context as a weapon, which can be wielded for "good" or "bad" purposes. This is important to keep in mind as a number of emerging challenges are examined.

---

18. Zachary Keck, *China Builds Military Airstrip in Disputed South China Sea*, The Diplomat (Oct. 8, 2014), http://thediplomat.com/2014/10/china-builds-military-airstrip-in-disputed-south-china-sea/.

19. *See generally*, Richard Javad Heydarian, *The Fog of Law: China's Great South China Sea Dilemma*, The National Interest, Dec. 19, 2014, *available at* http://nationalinterest.org/feature/the-fog-law-chinas-great-south-china-sea-dilemma-11889 ("Lawfare is in full swing in the South China Sea. How will China respond to an unfavorable legal ruling?").

20. *See, e.g.,* Christi Scott Bartman, Lawfare: Use of the Definition of Aggressive War by the Soviet and Russian Governments (2010).

21. Vincent M. Artman, *Passport Annexation*, Al Jazeera America (March 14, 2014), http://america.aljazeera.com/opinions/2014/3/ukraine-russia-crimeapassportizationcitizenship.html.

22. Joel Harding, *Russia Attempting Lawfare against Ukraine*, To Inform is to Influence (blog) (Aug. 1, 2014), http://toinformistoinfluence.com/2014/08/01/russia-attempting-lawfare-against-ukraine/.

23. *Id.*

24. David B. Rivkin, Jr., and Lee A. Casey, *The Outlaw Valdmir Putin*, Wall St. J., (Apr. 8, 2014), http://www.wsj.com/news/articles/SB10001424052702304640104579485331656203834.

25. Julian Ku, *Should the U.S. Use "Lawfare" Against Russia?* Opinio Juris (April 9th, 2014), http://opiniojuris.org/2014/04/09/u-s-use-lawfare-russia/.

26. Sergei L. Loiko, *Russian leaders seek to revisit history as tension with U.S. grows*, Los Angeles Times (Dec. 26, 2014), http://www.latimes.com/world/europe/la-fg-russia-history-20141226-story.html.

For example, cyber operations present a confounding lawfare issue, mainly because state practice—so important to the evolution of international law—remains underdeveloped in the area. For a variety of reasons, many nations are reluctant to specify their reactions to various cyber events in part because of the continuing difficulty of definitive attribution,[27] and in part because they do not want to reveal their capabilities—or vulnerabilities—to a global audience.

The hack of the Sony Corporation in late 2014 attributed to North Korean operatives[28] may prove to be important for the development of international law and, consequently, lawfare. President Barack Obama very carefully characterized the event as "cyber vandalism" as opposed to an "act of war"—the latter phrase often being interpreted as equivalent to an armed attack within the meaning of Article 51 of the UN charter which could trigger authority for violent acts in self-defense.[29] The Obama Administration seems to want to temper the precedent that might emerge, while at the same time vowing a "proportional" response, a phrase that sounds in the law of self-defense.[30]

Others argue that notwithstanding the non-kinetic nature of cyber "attacks" the scale of the Sony incident should make it an "act of war" so that it can be considered "legally and politically, as an attack on the US itself."[31] Nevertheless, for the near term it is expected that many cyber events will fall below the "armed attack" threshold, and require countermeasures that are carefully crafted to conform to this complex area of international law.[32] In short, reactions to cyber incidents are much more likely to be in the lawfare realm than that historically associated with "act of war" responses. That said, if incidents persist, the law itself may be strained as victims may engage in 'cyber vigilantism' in an effort to protect themselves.[33]

That raises an important question: are contemporary challenges sapping the vitality of the law (and, necessarily, lawfare)? Besides the difficulties presented by cyber incidents, consider that the concept of reciprocity—which underpins the efficacy of the law of armed conflict (LOAC)—is becoming dangerously irrelevant in many 21st century wars.

---

27. *See, e.g.*, Jack Goldsmith, *The Consequences of Credible Doubt About the USG Attribution in the Sony Hack*, LAWFARE (Dec. 30, 2014), http://www.lawfareblog.com/2014/12/the-consequences-of-credible-doubt-about-the-usg-attribution-in-the-sony-hack/.

28. Federal Bureau of Investigation, *Update on Sony Investigation*, Dec. 19, 2014, http://www.fbi.gov/news/pressrel/press-releases/update-on-sony-investigation.

29. Article 51 of the UN Charter provides:
Nothing in the present Charter shall impair the inherent right of individual or collective self-defence if an armed attack occurs against a Member of the United Nations, until the Security Council has taken measures necessary to maintain international peace and security. Measures taken by Members in the exercise of this right of self-defence shall be immediately reported to the Security Council and shall not in any way affect the authority and responsibility of the Security Council under the present Charter to take at any time such action as it deems necessary in order to maintain or restore international peace and security.

30. *Id.*

31. Michael B. Kelley and Arin Rosen, *The US Needs To Stop Pretending The Sony Hack Is Anything Less Than An Act Of War*, BUSINESS INSIDER (Dec. 15, 2014), http://www.businessinsider.com/sony-hack-should-be-considered-an-act-of-war-2014-12#ixzz3NKQlbwpN.

32. Michael N. Schmitt, *"Below the Threshold" Cyber Operations: The Countermeasure Response Option and International Law*, 54 VA. J. OF INT'L LAW 697 (2014), *available at* http://papers.ssrn.com/sol3/papers.cfm?abstract_id=2353898.

33. Michael Riley and Jordan Robertson, *FBI Investigating Whether Companies Are Engaged in Revenge Hacking*, BLOOMBERG (Dec. 30, 2014), http://www.bloomberg.com/news/2014-12-30/fbi-probes-if-banks-hacked-back-as-firms-mull-offensives.html. For a more detailed discussion of the legal and policy issues in the cyber domain see Chapter 12.

Why? Most contemporary conflicts involve non-state actors, and most of them are not just indifferent to charges of violating LOAC, they actually revel in using brutal methods that mock the law.[34] The Islamic State in Iraq and Syria (ISIS)[35] for example, uses beheadings of prisoners and other savagery to intimidate opponents into submission. Likewise, the use of young women as sex slaves in areas ISIS occupies is employed as a recruiting tool.[36] Extremists are even making children targets as a matter of *strategy*, a stunning affront to the rule of law.[37]

Unfortunately, neither governmental nor nongovernmental actors have had much success in bringing the law to bear against such monstrous violations of the most basic tenets of international humanitarian law and international human rights law. Faced with complete impotence to influence the actions of groups like ISIS, many in the international community have focused the wrath on such nations as Israel and the United States. To be sure, neither of these countries should be exempt from scrutiny for their actions, but at the same time credit should be given for the enormous effort they have made to adhere to international law.

It does not advance the interests of the world community to demonize nations who are at least attempting to employ the rule of law, albeit imperfectly at times, just because they actually take charges seriously. The unfortunate fact is that the most egregious non-state violators simply ignore allegations and those who make them. This asymmetry in accountability and, especially, the absence of any reciprocity by non-state actors imperils the entire architecture of international law in conflict situations. Prof. Ken Anderson of American University warns:

> Obligation without reciprocity risks breakdown [of the rules of war] even faster where one side is pressed to protect the civilians of both sides put at risk because that's how the other side deliberately wages war, not merely from indifference to them. A system of formal reciprocity in the rules of war (each side has the same formal obligations), but also independence of obligation to the rules of war (each side's obligation is independent of what the other side does, including if the other side violates the rules) over time is likely either to rupture in crisis or else simply have less and less purchase as universal rules.[38]

The seriousness of this challenge to rule of law cannot be overstated. Nevertheless, as this writer has argued before, however complicated and frustrating it may be to deal to with these law and lawfare-related issues, it is surely in the best interests of the U.S. and the world community to do so.[39] Far better to employ bloodless lawfare as opposed to

---

34. Eric Schmitt, *In Battle to Defang ISIS, U.S. Targets Its Psychology*, New York Times, Dec. 28, 2014, http://mobile.nytimes.com/2014/12/29/us/politics/in-battle-to-defang-isis-us-targets-its-psychology-.html?referrer&_r=1.

35. Apparently, the U.S. Department of Defense prefers to call ISIS "Daesh." *See* Kristina Wong, *Pentagon calls ISIS 'Daesh' for first time*, The Hill (Dec. 18, 2014), http://thehill.com/policy/defense/227547-pentagon-calls-isis-daesh-for-first-time.

36. Fiona Keating, *Iraq Slave Markets Sell Women for $10 to Attract Isis Recruits*, Int'l Business Times (October 4, 2014), http://www.ibtimes.co.uk/iraq-slave-markets-sell-women-10-attract-isis-recruits-1468506.

37. Howard LaFranchi, *Why children are the targets of terror*, The Christian Science Monitor Weekly, Dec. 29, 2014, at 10.

38. Kenneth Anderson, *Laurie Blank on proportionality in the international law of targeting*, The Volokh Conspiracy (Jul. 31, 2014), http://www.washingtonpost.com/news/volokh-conspiracy/wp/2014/07/31/laurie-blank-on-proportionality-in-the-international-law-of-targeting/.

39. *Cf.* Cassell, *supra*, note 8.

bloody traditional warfare in resolving the inevitable conflicts intrinsic to the human condition. Consider now the 2009 article that follows below.

Charles J. Dunlap, Jr., *Lawfare: A Decisive Element of 21st-Century Conflicts?*

54 Joint Force Quarterly 34-39 (2009)

If anyone doubts the role of law in 21st century conflicts, one need only pose the following question: what was the U.S. military's most serious setback since 9/11? Few knowledgeable experts would say anything other than the detainee abuse scandal known as "Abu Ghraib". That this strategic military disaster did not involve force of arms, but rather centered on illegalities indicates how law has evolved to become a—and sometimes "the"—decisive element of contemporary conflicts.

It is not hard to understand why. Senior commanders readily characterized Abu Ghraib in customary military terms as "clearly a defeat" because its *effect* is indistinguishable from that imposed by traditional military clashes.[40] No one debates that the revelations energized the insurgency and profoundly undermined the ability of U.S. forces to accomplish their mission. The exploitation of the incident by adversaries allowed it to become the perfect, effects-based, asymmetrical operation that continues to present difficulties for American forces. In early 2009, a senior Iraqi official conceded that the name "Abu Ghraib" still left a "bitter feeling inside Iraqis' heart."[41]

For international lawyers and others involved in national security matters, the transformational role of law is often captured under the aegis of the term "lawfare." In fact, few concepts have arisen more quickly to prominence as than that of lawfare. As recently as 2001 there were only a handful of recorded uses of the term, and none were in today's context. By 2009, however, an internet search produces nearly 60,000 "hits." Unfortunately, "lawfare" has also generated its share of controversy.

Law in Warfare

To the best of the author's knowledge, lawfare as used in today's context first appeared in his 2001 essay for Harvard University's Carr Center.[42] At that time the term was defined to mean "the use of law as a weapon of war"[43] and, more specifically, to describe "a method of warfare where law is used as a means of realizing a military objective."[44] Today, the most refined definition, at least in this writer's view, is one that interprets lawfare as "the strategy of using—or misusing—law as a substitute for traditional military means to achieve an operational objective."[45]

The purpose of the "lawfare" conceptualization in the national security context is to provide a vehicle that resonates readily with non-lawyer audiences, particularly in the armed forces. Historically, the role of law in armed conflict was variously presented, but

---

40. Tom Brokaw, *Gen Sanchez: Abu Ghraib 'clearly a defeat'*, MSNBC.com, Jun. 30, 2004 *available at* http://www.msnbc.msn.com/id/5333895/.

41. Kim Gamel, *Iraq to Open Notorious Abu Ghraib Prison*, Associated Press (Jan. 24, 2009), *available at* http://www.huffingtonpost.com/huff-wires/20090124/ml-iraq/.

42. *See* Dunlap, note 2, *supra*.

43. *Id.* at 5.

44. *Id.* at 11.

45. Charles J. Dunlap, Jr., *Lawfare Today*, Yale Journal of International Affairs, Winter 2008, at 146, *available at* http://scholarship.law.duke.edu/cgi/viewcontent.cgi?article=5892&context=faculty_scholarship.

often simply as yet another requirement; one to which adherence was a matter of integrity and moral rectitude. As powerful as values such as "integrity" and "moral rectitude" may be as incentives, especially to the militaries of liberal democracies, conceiving of the role of law in more conventional military terms has its advantages. Understanding that the law can be wielded much like a weapon by either side in a belligerency is something to which a military member can relate. It facilitates accounting for law, and particularly the fact and perception of adherence to it, in the planning and conduct of operations.

While recognizing the ever-present ethical responsibility to comply with the law, how is it that transforming adherence to law into a strategy serves the purposes of the warfighter? The answer is to be found by recourse to the work of Baron Carl von Clausewitz, perhaps history's foremost military theorist.[46] Being a man of his times, it is true that Clausewitz had little regard for international law as a factor in war.[47] Nevertheless he was keenly aware of the political dimension, and this is the linkage to today's understanding of lawfare.

Clausewitz's famous dictum that war is a "continuation of political intercourse, carried on with other means" relates directly to the theoretical basis of lawfare.[48] Moreover, Clausewitz's analysis of the "trinity" of the people, the government, and the military whose "balance" produces success in war is likewise instructive.[49] Specifically, in modern democracies especially, maintaining the "balance" that "political intercourse" requires very much depends upon adherence to law in fact and, importantly, *perception*.

Legal experts Michael Reisman and Chris T. Antoniou put it this way in their 1994 book, *The Laws of War*:

> In modern popular democracies, even a limited armed conflict requires a substantial base of public support. That support can erode or even reverse itself rapidly, no matter how worthy the political objective, if people *believe* that the war is being conducted in an unfair, inhumane, or iniquitous way.[50]

Some adversaries see opportunity in this aspect of our political culture. Professor William Eckhart observes:

> Knowing that our society so respects the rule of law that it demands compliance with it, our enemies carefully attack our military plans as illegal and immoral and our execution of those plans as contrary to the law of war. Our vulnerability here is what philosopher of war Carl von Clausewitz would term our 'center of gravity.'[51]

In short, by anchoring lawfare in Clausewitzean logic, military personnel—and especially commanders of the militaries of democracies—are able to recognize and internalize the importance of adherence to the rule as a very *practical* and necessary element of mission accomplishment. They need not, particularly, embrace its philosophical,

---

46. *See generally*, *The Clausewitz Homepage* (Christopher Bassford, ed., Nov. 26, 2008), *available at* http://www.clausewitz.com/CWZHOME/CWZBASE.htm.

47. Clausewitz insisted that: "War is an act of force to compel our enemy to do our will ... attached to force are certain self-imposed, imperceptible limitations hardly worth mentioning, known as international law and custom, but they scarcely weaken it." CARL VON CLAUSEWITZ, ON WAR 75 (Michael Howard & Peter Paret trans., 1989).

48. *Id.* at 87.

49. *Id.* at 89.

50. W. MICHAEL REISMAN AND CHRIS T. ANTONIOU, THE LAWS OF WAR xxiv (1994) (italics added).

51. William George Eckhardt, *Lawyering for Uncle Sam When He Draws His Sword*, 4 CHI. J. INTL L. 431 (2003).

ethical, or moral foundations; they can be almost Machiavellian in their attitude towards law because adherence to it, in any event, serves wholly *pragmatic* needs. Thus, the concept of lawfare aims to insinuate law into military thinking in a new way, one that rationalizes it in terms compatible with the realities of 21st century operations.

Legal "Weaponry"

The new emphasis on law in war is something of the artifact of the larger, world-wide legal revolution. George Will recently characterized the U.S. as the "Litigation Nation" to describe how deeply legal consciousness has penetrated American society.[52] Furthermore, international commerce depends upon law, along with a variety of international fora, to operate efficiently. This, in turn, is accelerating a globalization of law.[53] As international law generally penetrates modern life it tends to influence, as other trends have, the way war is conducted.[54] Add to that the enormous impact of 21st century information mediums, from round-the-clock news sources to cell phone cameras that empower almost anyone to record events, and it is easy to understand why incidents that seemingly implicate the international law of war can rapidly have significant ramifications among the body politic.

Commanders today, keenly aware of the devastating impact on operations of incidents like Abu Ghraib, typically are willing partners in efforts to ensure that compliance with the law is part and parcel of their activities. It is no surprise, for example, that the much-heralded counterinsurgency manual[55] devotes a considerable amount of text to law and law-related considerations.[56] Counterinsurgency and other contemporary "irregular warfare" situations are especially sensitive to illegalities that can undermine the efforts to legitimize the government (and those wishing to assist it) that the insurgency is aiming to topple.

The new counterinsurgency doctrine also underlines that lawfare is more than just something that adversaries seek to use against law-abiding societies; it is something that democratic militaries can, and should, employ *affirmatively*. For example, the re-establishment of the rule of law is a well-understood component of a successful counterinsurgency strategy,[57] and has proven itself to be an important part of the success U.S. forces have enjoyed in Iraq in recent years.[58]

Of course, there are other illustrations as to how legal instruments can substitute for military means and function as an affirmative good. To illustrate: during the early stages of operations in Afghanistan, a legal "weapon"—a contract—was used to deny potentially

---

52. George Will, *Litigation Nation*, WASHINGTON POST, Jan. 11, 2009, at B07, *available at* http://www.washingtonpost.com/wp-dyn/content/article/2009/01/09/AR2009010902353.html.

53. *See, e.g., Globalization of Law*, GLOBAL POLICY FORUM, *available at* http://www.globalpolicy.org/globaliz/law/index.htm.

54. For a discussion of how the changing economic and technological environment influences war, *see generally* Alvin and Heidi Toffler, WAR AND ANTI-WAR: SURVIVAL AT THE DAWN OF THE 21ST CENTURY (Little, Brown and Company, 1993).

55. Headquarters Department of the Army, FIELD MANUAL No. 3-24, COUNTERINSURGENCY, 15 Dec. 2006, [Hereinafter FM 3-24], *also designated by* Headquarters Marine Corps Development Command, Department of the Navy, as MARINE CORPS WARFIGHTING PUBLICATION No. 3-33.5, 1 COUNTERINSURGENCY, 15 Dec 2006, *available at* http://usacac.army.mil/cac2/Repository/Materials/COIN-FM3-24.pdf.

56. *See, e.g., id.* at Chapter 7 and Appendix D.

57. *See, e.g.,* "Establishing the Rule of Law", Id., Appendix D, at D-8.

58. Michael Gordon, *In Baghdad, Justice Behind the Barricades*, NEW YORK TIMES, July 20, 2007, *available at* http://www.nytimes.com/2007/07/30/world/middleeast/30military.html?ref=world.

valuable military information (derived from commercially-available satellite imagery) from hostile forces.[59]

In addition, although strategists argue that 21st century threats emerge most frequently from nonstate actors who often operate outside of the law, they are still vulnerable to its application. Legal "weaponry," for instance, may well be the most effective means of attacking the financial networks terrorist organizations require to function.[60] Likewise, sanctions and other legal methodologies can serve to isolate insurgencies from the external support that many experts believe is essential to victory.[61]

A Tool for the Enemy?

While the employment of legal methodologies can create offensive opportunities for savvy U.S. commanders, too frequently our opponents use an exploitative form of lawfare along the lines of that arising in Abu Ghraib's aftermath. In fact, lawfare has emerged as the principle effects-based air defense methodology employed by America's adversaries today. Nowhere is this truer than in Afghanistan where the Taliban and Al Qaeda are proving themselves to be sophisticated and effective lawfare practitioners.

Specifically, the Taliban and Al Qaeda are attempting to demonize the air weapon through the manipulation of the unintended civilian casualties that airstrikes can produce. Their reason for doing so is obvious: precise air attacks are the most potent weapon they face. In June of 2008, the *Washington Times* reported a Taliban fighter's lament that "tanks and armor are not a big deal. The fighters are the killers. I can handle everything but the jet fighters."[62] More recently, *Newsweek* told of a Taliban commander who, visiting the site of an attack by a Predator,[63] marveled at how a "direct hit" was scored on the exact room an Al Qaeda operative was using, leading the publication to conclude that a "barrage of pinpoint strikes may be unsettling Al Qaeda."[64]

Yet the enemy is fighting back by mounting a massive and increasingly effective lawfare campaign. Using the media,[65] they seek to create the perception—especially among Afghanis—that the war is being waged in an "unfair, inhumane, or iniquitous way."[66] Unfortunately, some well-intended efforts at countering the adversary's lawfare blitz are proving counterproductive. For example, in June of 2007 a NATO spokesman in Afghanistan insisted that "NATO would not fire on positions if it knew there were civilians nearby."[67] A little more than a year later, another NATO spokesman went even further, stating that

59. *See* John J. Lumpkin, *Gov't. Buys Satellite War Zone Photos*, AP Online, Oct. 15, 2001, *available at* http://www.highbeam.com/doc/1P1-47533038.html.

60. *See, e.g.,* Steven R. Weisman, *World Group Tells Banks to Beware Deals With Iran*, New York Times, available at http://www.nytimes.com/2008/02/29/world/middleeast/29sanctions.html.

61. *See, e.g.,* Jeffrey Record, Beating Goliath: Why Insurgencies Win (2007) at 23–66.

62. Rowan Scarborough, *Pentagon Notebook*, Washington Times, Jun. 26, 2008, *available at* http://www.washtimes.com/news/2008/jun/26/pentagon-notebook-mcpeak-calls-mccain-too-fat/?page=2.

63. Department of the Air Force, *MQ-1B Predator Unmanned Aerial Vehicle*, July 20, 2010, *available at* http://www.af.mil/AboutUs/FactSheets/Display/tabid/224/Article/104469/mq-1b-predator.aspx.

64. Sami Yousafzai and Mark Hosenball, *Predators on the Hunt in Pakistan*, Newsweek, Feb. 9, 2009, at 85, *available at* http://www.newsweek.com/id/182653/output/print.

65. *See e.g.,* Sean D. Naylor, *Insurgents in Afghanistan Have Mastered Media Manipulation*, Armed Forces Journal, April 2008, *available at* http://www.armedforcesjournal.com/2008/04/3489740.

66. *See,* note 50, *supra*, and accompanying text.

67. Associated Press, *US Coalition Airstrikes Kill, Wound Civilians in Southern Afghanistan, Official Says*, International Herald Tribune, Jun. 30, 2007, *available at* http://www.iht.com/articles/ap/2007/06/30/asia/AS-GEN-Afghan-Violence.php (quoting Maj John Thomas, spokesman for NATO's International Security Assistance Force).

"[i]f there is the likelihood of even one civilian casualty, we will not strike, not even if we think Osama bin Laden is down there."[68] The law of war certainly does not require zero civilian casualties; rather, it only requires that they not be excessive in relation to the military advantage sought.

Regardless, NATO's pronouncements unintentionally telegraphed an opportunity for lawfare-based strategy by which the enemy could avoid—or manipulate—airstrikes. That strategy is in effect today as evidenced by a November 2008 report wherein US officers advise that the Taliban is "deliberately increasing the risk to civilians" by locating themselves among them.[69] In terms of manipulation, consider an incident where the Taliban, according to an American official, held a wedding party hostage as they fired on U.S. forces in an "attack designed to draw airstrikes on civilians and stoke anti-American sentiment."[70]

What is frustrating is the fact that revolutionary advances in aerial surveillance technologies and precision munitions have made airstrikes, in the words of Marc Garlasco of Human Rights Watch, probably "the most discriminating weapon that exists."[71] The problem is much about perceptions. Accordingly, Jaap de Hoop Scheffer, the Secretary General of NATO, correctly recognizes that perceptions are a "strategic battleground"[72] and wants to "prioritize strategic communications" to remind the world "that the Taliban remain the ruthless killers and abusers of human rights that they have always been."[73]

The Taliban are not the only adversary employing abusive lawfare tactics. In their air and ground operations in Gaza in late 2008 and early 2009 the Israelis faced a foe who, according to Israeli officials, flouted international law in an unprecedented manner. Specifically, the *New York Times* reports:

> Hamas rocket and weapons caches, including rocket launchers, have been discovered in and under mosques, schools and civilian homes, the [Israeli] army says. The Israeli intelligence chief, Yuval Diskin, in a report to the Israeli cabinet, said that the Gaza-based leadership of Hamas was in underground housing beneath the No. 2 building of Shifa Hospital, the largest in Gaza.[74]

It appears that based on its experiences in the 2006 Lebanon War,[75] the Israelis made careful and innovative counter-lawfare preparations for the Gaza operation. Besides using "meticulous technical and human intelligence" to validate targets—as well as employing low collateral damage munitions in strikes—they also subjected plans to review by military

---

68. Pamela Constable, *NATO Hopes to Undercut Taliban With Surge of Projects*, Washington Post, Sept. 27, 2008, at A12, *available at* http://www.washingtonpost.com/wp-dyn/content/article/2008/09/26/AR2008092603452_pf.html (quoting Brig. Gen. Richard Blanchette, chief spokesman for NATO forces).

69. *Inside US Hub for Air Strikes*, BBC America, Nov. 29, 2008, *available at* http://news.bbc.co.uk/2/hi/south_asia/7755969.stm.

70. Jason Stratziuso, *Official: Taliban Tricking the U.S. Into Killing Civilians*, The Arizona Republic, Nov. 8, 2008, *available at* http://www.azcentral.com/arizonarepublic/news/articles/2008/11/08/20081108afghanistan1108.html.

71. *As quoted by* Josh White, *The Man on Both Sides of Air War Debate*, Washington Post, Feb. 13, 2008, at A05, *available at* http://www.washingtonpost.com/wp-dyn/content/article/2008/02/12/AR2008021202692.html.

72. Jaap de Hoop Scheffer, *Afghanistan: We Can Do Better*, Washington Post, Jan. 18, 2009, at B7.

73. *Id.*

74. Steven Erlanger, *A Gaza War Full of Traps and Trickery*, New York Times, Jan. 11, 2009, *available at* http://www.nytimes.com/2009/01/11/world/middleeast/11hamas.html.

75. *See generally*, *Targeting of Civilian Areas in the 2006 Lebanon War*, Wikipedia, Jan. 12, 2009, *available at* http://en.wikipedia.org/wiki/Targeting_of_civilian_areas_in_the_2006_Lebanon_War.

lawyers "huddling in war rooms."[76] In addition, Israel "distributed hundreds of thousands of leaflets and used its intelligence on cell phone networks in Gaza to issue warnings to civilians, including phone calls to some families in high-risk areas."[77]

Perhaps of most interest is the implementation of a concept called "operational verification."[78] According to *Defense News*, almost every army unit has specially-trained teams equipped with video cameras, tape recorders, and other documentation gear. The aim is to "document the story in real time" while there is still a "chance to influence public opinion" about the conduct of the operation. [79]

Despite these efforts, scholar Anthony Cordesman reports that although he believes that Israel did not violate the law of war[80] and made a "systematic effort to limit collateral damage,"[81] there was, nevertheless, "almost constant negative coverage of Israel in the Arab and Islamic world, as well as in much of Europe."[82] Consequently, as the German newspaper *Der Spiegel* reports, Israeli officials are "gearing up for a wave of lawsuits from around the world" claiming violations of the law of war.[83] Other news agencies advise that the Israeli government is vowing to defend its soldiers against legal attack.[84] Interestingly, *Der Spiegel* characterized the expected legal action in lawfare terms by describing them in paraphrased Clausewitzean language as a "continuation of the war with legal means."[85]

Operationalizing Law

What does all this mean for commanders in 21st century conflicts? In the first place, it is imperative that warfighters reject interpretations of lawfare that casts the law as a villain.[86] A better, more realistic assessment is set forth by attorney Nathanial Burney:

> [Lawfare] is often misused by those who claim that there is too much law, and that the application of law to military matters is a bad thing that hamstrings commanders in the field. The fact of the matter is that lawfare is out there; it happens. It is not inherently good or bad.... It might be wiser for such critics to take it into account, and use it effectively themselves, rather than wish it didn't exist.[87]

---

76. Barbara Opall-Rome, *Israelis Document Everything to Justify Strikes*, Defense News, Jan. 12, 2009, at 8.

77. Anthony H. Cordesman, *The "Gaza War", A Strategic Analysis*, Center for Strategic and International Studies, Feb. 2, 2009, at 17, *available at* http://www.csis.org/media/csis/pubs/090202_gaza_war.pdf.

78. Opall-Rome, *supra*, note 76.

79. *Id.*

80. Cordesman, *supra*, note 77, at ii.

81. *Id.* at 17.

82. *Id.* at 70.

83. Thomas Darnstadt and Christopher Schult, *Did Israel Commit War Crimes in Gaza?*, Spiegel Online International, Jan. 26, 2009, *available at* http://www.spiegel.de/international/world/0,1518,603508,00.html.

84. *Israel Prepares Legal Defense of Soldiers*, CNN.com, Jan. 26, 2009, *available at* http://www.cnn.com/2009/WORLD/meast/01/25/gaza.legal.defense/index.html.

85. *See* Darnstadt and Schult, *supra*, note 83.

86. For example, although he does not use the term "lawfare," pundit Michael Barone complained that the "overlawyering of [the current] war" will "hamper the efforts" of the American leaders to prosecute it. *See, e.g.,* Michael Barone, *The Overlawyered War*, U.S. News & World Report, Sept. 16, 2007, *available at* http://www.usnews.com/articles/opinion/mbarone/2007/09/16/the-criminalizing-of-warfare-has-brought-the-overlawyered-war.html.

87. Nathanial Burney, *International Law Primer*, 2007, *available at* http://www.burneylawfirm.com/international_law_primer.htm#lawfare.

Besides the fact that law may sometimes offer ways of bloodlessly achieving operational objectives, it is simply historically untrue that totalitarians who operate outside of humanitarian norms the law reflects are more likely to succeed. Scholar Victor Davis Hanson points out that the basis for the enormous success of the Western militaries is their adherence to constitutional government, respect for individual freedoms, as well as constant external audit and oversight of their strategy and tactics.[88] Historian Caleb Carr goes a step further by insisting that the "strategy of terror" of waging war against civilians nearly always has proven to be a "spectacular" failure.[89] In short, adherence to the rule of law does not present the military disadvantage so many assume.

Next, the commander must be concerned with "legal preparation of the battlespace." This means that command must ensure that troops have been properly trained to understand the law applicable to the operation, and are ready to apply it under extreme stress. In this regard the 2007 Department of Defense study of soldiers and Marines in Iraq is troubling as it revealed that only "47 percent of the soldiers and 38 percent of Marines agreed that non-combatants should be treated with dignity and respect, and that well over a third of all soldiers and Marines reported that torture should be allowed to save the life of a fellow soldier or Marine."[90]

Although intensive training and strong leadership may mitigate such attitudes, experts doubt such efforts can wholly prevent incidents from occurring.[91] Furthermore, Stephen Ambrose observed that it is a "universal aspect of war" that when you put young troops "in a foreign country with weapons in their hands, sometimes terrible things happen that you wish had never happened."[92] More ground troops may mean more lawfare-exploitable events with adverse strategic consequences.

This could suggest that the best way to avoid incidents is to limit the number of troops on the ground. Supporting this conclusion is a September 2008 report by Human Rights Watch that found that civilian casualties "rarely occur during planned airstrikes on suspected Taliban targets" but rather "almost always occurred during the fluid, rapid-response strikes, *often carried out in support of ground troops*."[93] Thus, small-footprint operations can limit the risk to civilians.

Legal preparation of the battlespace also requires robust efforts to educate the media as to what the law does and does not require. As already noted,[94] adversaries today are very clever in their relations with the global media, and U.S. forces must be able to respond quickly (and, ideally, before inquiries are made) and as transparently as possible to lawfare-related incidents. Relationships with the media must be built in advance as once an

---

88. Victor Davis Hanson, Carnage and Culture (2001), at 450–51.

89. Caleb Carr, The Lessons of Terror (2002), at 11.

90. Department of Defense, *DOD News Briefing with Assistant Secretary Casscells from the Pentagon*, May 4, 2007 (news transcript) *available at* http://www.defenselink.mil/transcripts/transcript.aspx?transcriptid=3958.

91. "The extreme nature of warfare, with its inherent fear and chaos, will contribute to acts of inhuman violence against combatants and noncombatants alike. Intensive training and, perhaps more so, leadership can minimize *though not wholly prevent such acts from occurring amid the savagery of combat*." (emphasis added). *See* William Thomas Allison, Military Justice in Vietnam: The Rule of Law in American War (2007), at 92.

92. Stephen Ambrose, Americans at War (1997), at 152.

93. *"Troops in Contact" Airstrikes and Civilian Deaths in Afghanistan*, Human Rights Watch, Sept. 2008, at 4, *available at* http://hrw.org/reports/2008/afghanistan0908/afghanistan0908web.pdf (italics added).

94. *See* note 65, *supra*.

incident occurs, it is difficult to explain legal complexities or to demonstrate the efforts that are made to avoid unnecessary civilian losses on a timeline that will be meaningful.

Commanders would be wise to emulate the Israeli initiative by establishing "operational verification" teams to record activity in real time in instances where the adversary is employing an effects-based lawfare strategy centered around allegations of war crimes. In any event, multidisciplinary teams of legal, operational, intelligence, and public affairs specialists ought to be organized, trained, and equipped to rapidly investigate allegations of incidents of high collateral damage. Likewise, command and control systems ought to be evaluated for their ability to record data for the purpose of accurately reconstructing processes if required.

"Operational verification" teams could be more than simply sophisticated elements of an information operations effort. Properly organized, trained, and equipped they can fulfill legitimate public diplomacy needs, but they can also provide near real-time feedback to commanders as to how operations are being executed. Thus, commanders could rapidly adapt procedures if the empirical data such teams can gather indicates opportunities to better protect innocents.

Of course, the availability of expert legal advice is absolutely necessary in the age of lawfare. The military lawyers (judge advocates) responsible for providing advice for combat operations need to be schooled not just in the law, but also in the characteristics of the weapons, as well as the strategies for their employment. Importantly, commanders must make it unequivocally clear to their forces that they intend to conduct operations in strict adherence to the law. Helping them do so is the job of the judge advocate.

Assuring troops of the legal and moral validity of their actions adds to combat power. In discussing the role of judge advocates, Professor Richard Schragger of the University of Virginia Law School points out that:

> Instead of seeing law as a barrier to the exercise of the client's power, [military lawyers] understand the law as a prerequisite to the meaningful exercise of power.... *Law makes just wars possible by creating a well-defined legal space within which individual soldiers can act without resorting to their own personal moral codes.*[95]

That said, commanders should aim not to have a judge advocate at the elbow of every rifleman; rather, the goal should be to imbue troops with the right behaviors so that they instinctively do the right thing on the battlefield. The most effective way of doing so is to carefully explain the enemy's lawfare strategies, and to highlight the pragmatic, real-world impact of "Abu Ghraib"-type incidents on the overall success of the mission. One of the most powerful motivators of troop conduct is the desire to enhance the security and safety of fellow soldiers. Making the connection between adherence to law and that end is a critical leadership task.

Integral to defensive lawfare operations is the education of the host nation population and, in effect, the enemy themselves. In many 21st century battlespaces these audiences are not receptive to what may appear to be law imposed by the West. In 1999, for example, a Chinese colonel famously argued that China was "a weak country, so do we need to

---

95. Richard C. Schragger, *Cooler Heads: The Difference between the President's Lawyers and the Military's*, SLATE.COM, Sept. 20, 2006, *available at* http://www.slate.com/id/2150050/?nav/navoa (emphasis added).

fight according to your rules? No. War has rules, but those rules are set by the West ... if you use those rules, then weak countries have no chance."[96]

To counter such beliefs, it is an essential lawfare technique to look for touchstones within the culture of the target audience. For example, in the early 1990s the International Committee of the Red Cross produced an illustrated paperback which matched key provisions of the Geneva Convention "with bits of traditional Arab and Islamic wisdom."[97] Such innovations ought to be re-examined, along with creative ideas that would get the messages to the target audience. One way might be to provide audio cassettes in local languages that espouse what are really Geneva Convention values in a context and manner that fits with religious and cultural imperatives.

The point is to delegitimize the enemy in the eyes of the host nation populace. This is most effectively accomplished when respected indigenous authorities lead the effort. Consider Thomas Friedman's favorable assessment of the condemnation by Indian Muslim leaders of the November 2008 Mumbai attacks:

> The only effective way to stop [terrorism] is for "the village"—the Muslim community itself—to say "no more." When a culture and a faith community delegitimizes this kind of behavior, openly, loudly and consistently, it is more important than metal detectors or extra police.[98]

Moreover, it should not be forgotten that much of the success in suppressing violence in Iraq was achieved when Sunnis in Anbar Province and other areas realized that Al Qaeda operatives were acting contrary to Iraqi, and indeed Islamic sensibilities, values, and law. It also may be possible to use educational techniques to change the attitudes of enemy fighters as well.[99]

Finally, some critics believe that "lawfare" is a code to condemn anyone who attempts to use the courts to resolve national security issues. For example, lawyer-turned-journalist Scott Horton charged in the July 2007 issue of *Harper's Magazine* that "lawfare theorists" reason that lawyers who present war-related claims in court "might as well be terrorists themselves."[100] Though there are those who object to the way the courts have been used by some litigants,[101] it is legally and morally wrong to paint anyone legitimately using legal processes as the "enemy."

Indeed, the courageous use of the courts on behalf of unpopular clients, along with the insistence that even our most vile enemies must be afforded due process of law, is a deeply embedded American value, and the kind of principle the armed forces exist to preserve. To be clear, recourse to the courts and other legal processes is to be encouraged;

96. John Pomfret, *China Ponders New Rules of 'Unrestricted War,'* WASHINGTON POST, Aug. 8, 1999, at A-1.

97. Michael Ignatieff, THE WARRIOR'S HONOR (1997) at 149.

98. Thomas L. Friedman, *No Way, No How, Not Here,* NEW YORK TIMES, Feb. 17, 2009, *available at* http://www.nytimes.com/2009/02/18/opinion/18friedman.html.

99. *See, e.g.,* Andrew Woods, *The Business End,* FINANCIAL TIMES, Jun. 27, 2008, *available at* http://www.ft.com/cms/s/2/71c42ec0-40ca-11dd-bd48-0000779fd2ac.html.

100. Scott Horton, *State of exception: Bush's war on the rule of law,* HARPERS MAG, July 2007, *available at* http://www.harpers.org/archive/2007/07/0081595.

101. David B. Rivkin, Jr. and Lee A. Casey, *Lawfare,* WSJ.COM (Feb. 23, 2007), http://online.wsj.com/article/SB117220137149816987.html. *Cf., The NGO Front in the Gaza War: Lawfare Against Israel,* NGO MONITOR, Feb. 2, 2009, *available at* http://www.ngo-monitor.org/article/the_ngo_front_in_the_gaza_war_lawfare_against_israel.

if there are abuses, the courts are well-equipped to deal with them.[102] It is always better to wage legal battles, however vicious, than it is to fight battles with the lives of young Americans.

Lawfare has become such an indelible feature of 21st century conflicts that commanders dismiss it at their peril. Key leaders recognize this evolution. General James L. Jones, the nation's new national security advisor, observed several years ago that the nature of war had changed. "It's become very legalistic and very complex," he said, adding that now "you have to have a lawyer or a dozen."[103] Lawfare, of course, is about more than lawyers — it is about the rule of law and its relation to war.

While it is true, as Professor Eckhart maintains, that adherence to the rule of law is a "center of gravity" for democratic societies like ours — and certainly there are those who will try to turn that virtue into a vulnerability — we still can never forget that it is also a vital source of our great strength as a nation.[104] We can and *must* meet the challenge of lawfare as effectively and aggressively as we have met every other issue critical to our national security.

Question for Discussion

On April 1, 2015 the reputed State of Palestine joined the International Criminal Court (ICC). Under ICC rules, Palestinian membership would allow the court to exercise jurisdiction over war crimes committed by anyone on Palestinian territory, without a referral from the UN Security Council. Israel, like the United States, is not a party to the ICC, but its citizens could be tried for actions taken on Palestinian land. Is this a form of lawfare? How should Israel and the U.S. respond?

---

102. *See, e.g.,* Phillip Carter, *Legal Combat,* SLATE (Apr. 4. 2005), http://www.slate.com/id/2116169.
103. Lyric Wallwork Winik, *A Marine's Toughest Mission (Gen. James L. Jones),* PARADE MAG., Jan. 19, 2003, *available at* http://www.leatherneck.com/forums/archive/index.php/t-3618.html.
104. *See* note 51, *supra,* and accompanying text.

Chapter 18

American National Security Strategy: Continuities and Uncertainties in a Changing World

Alberto R. Coll

In this chapter:
The Nation's First Century
America's Rise as a World Power
Four Decades of Cold War and Containment
The End of the Cold War and Containment
The Uncertainties of the 1990s
National Security Strategy in the Aftermath of September 11, 2001
The Obama Years (2008–2016)

To understand the development of American national security law, it is essential to grasp the evolution of American national security strategy throughout the country's history. A number of recurrent themes emerge, shedding light on the principles and practices that have shaped national security law in the past and continue to do so today. Lord Palmerston's aphorism about Great Britain at the height of its imperial power in the mid-nineteenth century is equally applicable to the United States. "Great Britain," he said, "has no permanent friends or enemies, only permanent interests." The interests and principles behind U.S. foreign policy and its supporting national security strategy throughout different periods of the country's history reveal pronounced continuities, which in turn explain much of American national security law.

The Nation's First Century

The early republic's foreign policy and national security strategy were linked by three key interests: 1) ensuring survival in a dangerous international environment in which the young nation was highly vulnerable; 2) increasing commercial opportunities for American farmers, manufacturers, and merchants through overseas trade; and 3) expanding the country's territory. The presidencies of George Washington (1789–1797) and John Adams (1797–1801) were marked by a deliberate refusal to entangle the United States in the vortex of political and military conflicts generated by the French Revolution and the subsequent Napoleonic Wars. It would be inaccurate to describe this policy as isolationist; it was rather noninterventionist, as a mater of practical necessity. In their bitter foreign policy debates during the Washington administration, Secretary of State Thomas Jefferson's appeals to support the French Revolution lost to Treasury Secretary Alexander Hamilton's calculating arguments about the balance of power and the true nature of American national interests. The country was too weak to risk war with any of the European great powers.

At the same time, the United States sought to expand its international commerce and fought British efforts to interfere with American trade with France. The American policy tools included building a modest but not insignificant navy intended to make the British respect American rights at sea—a project that gained particular impetus during the Jefferson administration (1801–1809)—as well as vigorous recourse to diplomacy and international law. Territorial expansion also became a key priority. In 1803, taking advantage of Napoleon's troubles in Europe, President Jefferson and his Secretary of State James Madison purchased Louisiana from France for the sum of $15 million without prior congressional approval, thereby doubling the Union's territory and putting the country on a rapid course of westward expansion. Jefferson also talked about purchasing or annexing Florida, Canada, and Cuba, leaving it to his successors to implement his grand vision of what he called "an empire for liberty."

American national security strategy became more sharply defined with the enunciation in 1823 of the Monroe Doctrine, the substance of which was crafted by then Secretary of State John Quincy Adams. It stated that the United States would consider any attempt by the European powers "to extend their system to any portion of this hemisphere as dangerous to our peace and safety." In practice, the United States lacked the military power to enforce the Monroe Doctrine, but it counted on the Royal Navy to keep out other European great powers. The British themselves were not interested in new colonies, but in expanding their trade and investments, a game which the United States did not consider as threatening. The Monroe Doctrine was significant in several respects. It marked the start of the process by which the United States began to reduce European power in the Western Hemisphere and treat the region as a sphere of U.S. influence. Several generations later, President Theodore Roosevelt (1901–1909) would articulate his famous corollary to the Monroe Doctrine claiming for the United States the right to intervene militarily in the region whenever necessary to protect U.S. interests. The Monroe Doctrine also signaled that the American republic did not intend to allow its relative military weakness to relegate it to a passive role in world affairs. Henceforth, any European power contemplating fresh expansion in the Western Hemisphere would have to include American interests, and even American power (however still modest), in its calculus.

Up to the American Civil War, the three principal drivers of American foreign policy and national security strategy continued to be keeping out of war with the European great powers, increasing commercial opportunities around the world, and expanding the nation's territory. This rather ambitious three-tiered foreign policy and security agenda was backed up by a modest-sized navy, a small but highly competent army toughened up by its wars with the Native Americans, and a judicious diplomacy conducted by such able men as John Quincy Adams and Daniel Webster, who made ample use of international law in order to compensate for the country's meager military resources. During the three decades preceding the Civil War, the United States brought the huge territories of Florida and Texas into the Union, won a war with Mexico that enlarged its territory by nearly 50 percent, became a major trading partner with China and Japan as well as a sizeable commercial presence in Latin America, and successfully settled thorny boundary disputes with Great Britain and Russia while averting war with them.

Territorial expansion during this period enjoyed the added impetus of the highly popular ideology of "Manifest Destiny," which decreed that the United States was fated by destiny, history, and the will of God to control someday, if not all of North America, certainly the entire stretch between Mexico and Canada from the Atlantic to the Pacific coasts. But while Americans saw themselves as destined by God to bring the benefits of freedom and civilization to the "savage races" then occupying much of North America west of the Mississippi, only a few believed that they should extend this mission to lands outside this area. Even during his early period of unabashed expansionism, when he worked tirelessly for the annexation of Texas, Florida, and Cuba, John Quincy Adams warned against allowing pro-democratic or liberal sympathies to entangle the United States in the domestic affairs of Latin America, much less Europe, no matter how noble the cause might be. As he put it in his famous address of July 4, 1821, "[America] goes not abroad in search of monsters to destroy. She is the well-wisher to the freedom and independence of all. She is the champion and vindicator only of her own."

The four decades from the outbreak of the Civil War in 1860 to the end of the nineteenth century wrought profound transformations in American perceptions of the national interest and the country's proper role in the world. During these forty years, the United States essentially catapulted into one of the world's leading industrial and economic powers. Its population doubled to more than seventy million people, and it became a chief exporter of steel, oil, chemicals, manufactured goods, and grains. Meanwhile, the share of gross domestic product devoted to military spending remained a tiny fraction compared to that of other great powers of similar economic standing, and as late as the mid-1890s, the U.S. Navy, for example, was smaller than Chile's.

This obvious gap between the country's far-reaching economic interests and its limited capacity to defend them prompted a veritable revolution in American strategic thinking, spearheaded by such figures as Theodore Roosevelt, Alfred Thayer Mahan, John Hay, Henry Cabot Lodge, and Elihu Root. The gist of their argument was that, whether the American people liked it or not, the United States was now a global great power whose prosperity and security required a parallel ability to project military, and especially naval, power around the world. Support for American trade and the strong Navy to defend it also entailed the acquisition of colonial outposts that could serve as overseas bases. Congress and the American industrial elite came to share this way of thinking, and by the end of the 1890s, the nation had embarked on a substantial naval buildup that in a few years would place it among the world's great naval powers.

America's Rise as a World Power

The first decade of the twentieth century confirmed the United States in its new status as a great global power. Under the administration of William McKinley (1897–1901), the United States waged war against Spain, and seized for itself most of the remaining Spanish colonial empire, including the Philippines, Guam, and Puerto Rico, which became major outposts of American power in the Pacific Rim and the Caribbean. His successor Theodore Roosevelt (1901–1909) forcibly detached Panama from Colombia and secured for the United States a transoceanic canal across the Panamanian isthmus, to the great benefit of American commerce and the U.S. economy. The Canal also allowed the U.S. Navy to move its forces quickly between the Atlantic and Pacific oceans as necessary for war or crisis management. Besides intervening militarily in other parts of Latin America to advance U.S. interests, Roosevelt sent the great "White Fleet" around the world to make it clear to all that the United States was a formidable naval power to reckon with. As Henry

Kissinger has observed, Roosevelt also was the first U.S. President to recognize that the United States could not stay aloof from the operation of the world's balance of power. When war broke out between faraway Russia and Japan in 1905, Roosevelt played a leading role in mediating the conflict, thereby earning the Nobel Peace Prize. His concern was not humanitarian but hardheaded *realpolitik*: he feared that an absolute victory by either belligerent would place it in a position to threaten American interests in the Far East.

It would take World War I (1914–1918), however, to catapult the United States from great power status to the role of the preeminent industrial, financial, and military power in the world. By the war's end, the United States had supplanted British financial hegemony, its industrial capacity and trade outstripped those of Great Britain and Germany combined, and its navy was second to none. It was clear to victors and vanquished alike that American loans, industrial production, and the fresh American armies sent across the Atlantic in the winter of 1917–1918 had been the decisive factors insuring Allied victory over the Central Powers. In the immediate postwar period, it also fell to the United States, with its immense gold and dollar reserves and massive trade surpluses, to play the role of chief stabilizer for the international financial system upon which the global economy would depend for its recovery.

But the significance of World War I went well beyond this. It was under the presidency of Woodrow Wilson (1913–1921) that the United States first articulated a global vision of liberal democracy as the dominant ideological underpinning for its foreign policy and national security strategy. Wilson not only committed the United States to a major European war for the first time in its history, but he did so ostensibly in the name of "making the world safe for democracy" and spreading the liberal values enshrined in his "Fourteen Points" of national self-determination, free trade, democratic governance, and a new way of conducting international relations based on international law, transparent diplomacy, disarmament, and collective security. At the end of the war, Wilson argued that true, lasting peace could not be maintained by the traditional mechanisms of the balance of power and its accompanying arms races. What might be described today as a new "security architecture" was necessary for the whole world, a system Wilson described as "collective security" in which the whole community of nations would guarantee the safety of every state against foreign aggression, thereby rendering classical *realpolitik* and military competition unnecessary. While critics often deride Wilson's vision as highly idealistic if not downright utopian, they tend to miss a key point. The international order that Wilson wanted to create was one well suited to American interests and comparative advantages. A world of liberal democratic states, threaded together by free trade, international law, and the peaceful resolution of conflicts was one in which the United States was likely to prosper exceedingly well.

While Wilson failed to implement most of his ideas, he was far from a failure in the long run. The horrors of World War II seemed to prove his sagacity, enhancing his hold over the generations that built the post-1945 American-led international order. Since 1945, no president has been able to conduct a foreign policy or national security strategy severed from the ideological ground of liberal democratic values. Those like Richard Nixon (1968–1973) or George H.W. Bush (1989–1993), whose attachment to *realpolitik* inclined them to try to do so, paid a heavy domestic political price for it. More than anyone else, Wilson helped to integrate into the mainstream of American foreign policy and grand strategy the strands of exceptionalism and messianic liberalism present, in however attenuated a form, since the country's early beginnings. As a result of his work, in the course of the twentieth century the United States became comfortable with the notion that one of its key strategic objectives is the construction of a liberal world order based on democratic governance, individual freedoms, the rule of law, free trade, and a free market economy.

The experience of World War II and the subsequent outbreak of the Cold War were to change dramatically the substance of American foreign policy and national security strategy. In the course of fighting and winning the war, the United States emerged as one of the world's two superpowers. Moreover, the massive destruction endured by Europe and Japan meant that America's lead over the rest of the world was far more pronounced than it had been at the end of World War I. Nevertheless, as late as 1945, most, if not all, senior U.S. officials expected that in the future the United States would be able to safeguard its global security interests simply by maintaining a ring of worldwide bases for the projection of air and naval power, while the British and French Empires, Russia, and China maintained order in their respective spheres of influence. Hardly anyone believed that the United States would have to form military alliances or station large numbers of troops overseas. By 1947, the worsening U.S.-Soviet rivalry had shattered these assumptions beyond repair, and the United States found itself crafting a new grand strategy, called "containment," to deal with a world in which it was the only state capable of checking Soviet power.

Four Decades of Cold War and Containment

In the short five years between 1947 and 1952, the United States embarked on a formal policy of containment of the Soviet Union, crafted permanent alliances with the Western European powers and Japan requiring the stationing of large numbers of U.S. ground forces in Europe and Asia, increased the percentage of its gross domestic product devoted to military spending to record peacetime levels, financed the Marshall Plan for the reconstruction of Europe at a total cost of $13 billion, or 1.2 percent of GDP, and agreed to guarantee the security of such faraway places as Greece, Turkey, Iran, Korea, and Taiwan. By 1952, under the steering hand of Paul Nitze's NSC-68, containment had become an expansive strategic doctrine that committed the United States to fight Communism anywhere in the globe with every available instrument of power. Containment would remain the guiding theme of American national security policy and strategy until the collapse of Communism in Eastern Europe in 1989.

Throughout the fifties and until the late stages of the Vietnam War, containment enjoyed bipartisan support, and the great debates at home were not over whether containment should be the overall strategy, but about where and how it should be applied. Indeed, containment succeeded in fusing rather well the ideological and *realpolitik* strands of the American tradition in foreign affairs. The United States had to fight Communism because, as an ideology, it was evil, illiberal, and anti-American, and also because, in terms of pure power politics, Communism provided Soviet and Chinese power with a dynamism that enabled it to threaten important American economic and political interests around the world. The dual nature of the Communist threat as perceived by the United States—its ideological and strategic dimensions—helps to explain why containment became expansive in its outlook and costly in its implementation. Under the rubric of containment, American military spending on conventional and nuclear forces skyrocketed, as did spending on intelligence, propaganda, and covert operations. The 1947 National Security Act reorganized the United States government, and created large new security bureaucracies, such as the National Security Council and the Central Intelligence Agency, of a size and sophistication undreamed of a decade earlier, enabling the government to remain on a permanent war footing. No country around the world, regardless of how remote or seemingly insignificant, could be ignored in the zero-sum game that developed between the rival superpowers.

President Dwight Eisenhower (1953–1961) came to office convinced that the United States needed to reduce containment's expense. A hardened five-star general and veteran of two world wars, Eisenhower was skeptical of the need to spend on defense as much as his advisers claimed. Moreover, he feared that high levels of military spending would damage the American economy and harm American power in the long run. His strategic solution to the problem of containment's expense was threefold. First, he ordered a vast increase in the number and explosive yield of nuclear weapons deployed around the world, and a corresponding cut in American conventional forces. Second, in tandem with his Secretary of State, John Foster Dulles, he announced a new nuclear doctrine, "massive retaliation": an attack on American interests anywhere in the world risked a devastating nuclear response by the United States. Third, the President beefed up the CIA in order to accomplish through covert operations what otherwise might require the use of much costlier conventional military power. Eisenhower's solutions enabled him to reduce conventional military spending, as well as the share of GDP devoted to defense, but his successor, John F. Kennedy (1961–1963), thought that they created a new set of problems.

Kennedy believed that nuclear weapons were of limited utility. U.S. nuclear preponderance and threats of massive retaliation had not deterred Communist "wars of national liberation" in Southeast Asia, Soviet advances in the Middle East, or Khrushchev's dangerous saber-rattling over Berlin. Unless the United States increased its conventional capabilities in Europe, the Soviets might be tempted to move into Berlin in the belief that, faced with the stark choice of yielding the city or suffering nuclear holocaust, America never would choose the latter. Moreover, many Europeans were asking the same question: would the United States be willing to go to nuclear war with the Soviet Union in response to a Soviet conventional attack? To strengthen alliance cohesion, credibility, and deterrence, the United States needed a new strategy to replace massive retaliation. The administration named its new strategy "flexible response": the United States would respond to a threat or attack on American interests at a level, in a form, and in a place of its own choosing. The nuclear response would not be necessarily the first instrument of choice, though it could be resorted to at any point in the ladder of strategic escalation. Flexible response meant in Europe a buildup in conventional forces; in southeast Asia the development of counter-insurgency capabilities to deal with the Communist guerrillas in South Vietnam and Laos; and in Latin America a combination of covert activities against Fidel Castro, counter-insurgency assistance to friendly governments, and the Alliance for Progress, a watered-down version of the Marshall Plan, which turned out to be spectacularly unsuccessful.

In line with the new strategy, the United States further revised its nuclear doctrine. By the early 1960s, the United States had more than 10,000 nuclear warheads capable of reaching the Soviet Union, a number that in the judgment of Secretary of Defense Robert McNamara far exceeded the requirements of deterrence. A new targeting doctrine, "mutual assured destruction" (MAD), was put in place: enough U.S. nuclear warheads would be aimed deliberately at Soviet cities to insure that, even if the Soviets launched a first strike, the surviving American warheads would devastate the Soviet Union and kill much of its population. Under the tenets of mutual assured destruction, deterrence seemed perfectly assured. No leader on either side could ever hope to benefit from a first strike against the other, because the punishment on one's population would be so horrific as to throw into doubt the very survival of that society.

While the early 1960s were a highly creative period of American statecraft, the second half of the decade, under the presidency of Lyndon Johnson (1963–1969), saw the country painfully mired in the Vietnam War. This is not the place to assess fully the significance of that war or its wisdom. But some general observations can be made. First, besides being the most deeply divisive war in the nation's history since the Civil War, it also was the most unpopular. Not only was it the first time that the United States lost a major conflict, but its human and material costs seemed excessively high relative to its value to the national interest. Second, it marked the end of the bipartisan consensus on containment, especially with regard to its application in the developing world. Third, Vietnam shattered the United States' post–World War II confidence; especially among the Liberal Establishment and large sections of the Democratic Party, a growing number of Americans began to question whether the country should be as actively engaged abroad militarily or as zealous in its spread of American values.

The impact of Vietnam on the U.S. military and on U.S. strategic thinking was profound and has endured to this day. A new generation of Americans who experienced the war firsthand as young officers and then went on to occupy influential positions of political and military leadership, such as John McCain, Colin Powell, and John Kerry, concluded that never again should the United States allow itself to be drawn into conflicts where vital national interests were absent, political objectives unclear, and public support mixed. If a conflict was worth military intervention, then the United States should fight it in the classical "American way of war" that had proved so successful in the Civil War and the two World Wars: with overwhelming military force and a strong will to victory. This particular interpretation of the lessons of Vietnam later became codified into something akin to strategic dogma in the "Weinberger Doctrine," a set of principles for guiding American military intervention issued by Defense Secretary Caspar Weinberger in 1984.

Sharply aware of the ways in which the Vietnam War was eroding American power and preventing the United States from focusing on more significant strategic issues, Richard Nixon (1969–1973) came to office, along with his top foreign policy adviser Henry Kissinger, determined to disengage the United States from the conflict. The departure took far longer and was messier and less glorious than either of them expected, but in the meantime Nixon and Kissinger carried out a major reappraisal of American foreign policy and national security strategy that led to several significant accomplishments. The strategic context they faced had deteriorated from that of a decade earlier. It included an economically resurgent Europe and Japan, a militarily expansive Soviet Union that reached strategic nuclear parity with the United States in 1970 and was increasing its influence throughout the Third World, and a rising China. Meanwhile, the country was afflicted by domestic social and political unrest, and its once dominant economy was suffering from stagnation and inflation.

The Nixon-Kissinger response to what they perceived as America's relative decline was a series of initiatives that, while leaving containment in place, departed significantly from the ways it had been implemented. First, the President issued the Nixon Doctrine, moving the United States away from the expansive containment of NSC-68 and the Kennedy Inaugural Address ("we shall bear any burden, and pay any price, in the defense of freedom") to the more measured Truman Doctrine of 1947: the United States would help other countries resist aggression, but only to the extent that they were willing to help themselves and do most of the heavy lifting. American air and naval power rather than ground forces would be the preferred instrument of military support. The Nixon Doctrine set the stage for the war's "Vietnamization" program, which began to transfer combat responsibilities to the South Vietnamese, and paved the way for a complete U.S. withdrawal by 1973.

At a more significant strategic level, the Nixon-Kissinger team attempted a policy of *détente* to put the U.S.-Soviet relationship on a more predictable plane that might lead to a stabilization of the nuclear arms race and selective cooperation in regional conflicts, such as Vietnam and the Middle East. They also believed that a combination of carefully calculated incentives, matched to existing deterrent and defensive capabilities, could convince the Soviets to behave more cooperatively and even ease over time into the equivalent of a "condominium" or "Concert of Europe" relationship with the West. The ABM Treaty,[1] restricting the deployment of missile defense systems by both countries; the SALT I accords, regulating strategic nuclear weapons; and expanded U.S. agricultural sales to the Soviet Union were among the key landmarks of *détente*. The results were not all for which Nixon hoped. The Soviets refused to "link" success in arms control, which they perceived as in the interest of both parties, to reforms in domestic human rights or a more pliant posture in Vietnam or the Middle East that would redound to the West's benefit. To this day Nixon's defenders argue that *détente* would have been more successful had it not been for the Watergate crisis and its weakening of the presidency. What is clear is that, for all its shortcomings, *détente* lowered the temperature of East-West tensions, reduced to some extent the risk of nuclear war, and through the Helsinki Accords of 1975 began the gradual but inexorable weakening of Soviet power in Eastern Europe.

Much more successfully, Nixon-Kissinger reversed two decades of American isolation of China, helping to set the stage for China's gradual reintegration into international society. One of the strategic consequences of this long overdue move was the United States' improved ability to play China off against the Soviet Union, an advantage that became even more obvious during the 1980s. At least in Asia, the United States could count on China to play a helpful role in containing Soviet power.

In its substance and style, the Nixon-Kissinger approach to national security strategy was thoroughly conservative. It aimed for stabilization and predictability rather than radical transformation. It recognized what appeared to be the reality of an emerging multipolar world in which America's relative economic and military standing seemed to be shrinking. And it eschewed the ideological or crusading overtones that had long dominated containment, seeking to ground containment instead in practical *realpolitik* and balance of power thinking, the strategy toward China being the clearest example of this.

The Watergate scandal that engulfed the Nixon presidency, along with the Vietnam War, triggered a strong reaction against what critics called the "National Security State," which had grown in tandem with containment over the previous three decades. Many Americans believed that the President's national security prerogatives had expanded beyond the balance prescribed by the Constitution and that intelligence agencies, such as the FBI and the CIA, needed more stringent supervision. In 1973, over President Nixon's veto, Congress passed the controversial War Powers Resolution[2] attempting to limit the President's authority to send U.S. combat forces overseas. To this day, the legislation remains mired in legal uncertainty. In 1975, under the sponsorship of Senator Frank Church, the Senate Intelligence Committee held a series of famous hearings that exposed past CIA involvement in questionable activities, such as efforts to carry out domestic surveillance against government critics, to assassinate foreign leaders, and overthrow established governments. As a result of the "Church hearings" and the political pressures they generated, new procedures were put in place to ensure at least a modest

---

1. Treaty on the Limitation of Anti-Ballistic Missile (ABM) Systems, May 26, 1972, U.S.-U.S.S.R., 23 U.S.T. 3435.
2. Pub. L. No. 93-148, 87 Stat. 555 (1973).

level of congressional oversight of covert activities. President Ford issued an executive order prohibiting assassination,[3] and the CIA dismissed a large number of career officers with long experience in covert operations who were suspected of being out of tune with the new sensitivities. In 1978, Congress also passed the Freedom of Information Act giving ordinary citizens the right to examine government records, except in cases where the government could successfully prove that there were compelling national security reasons for not doing so. The act has served as a model for many nations attempting to develop democratic institutions and the rule of law.

The national reaction against Watergate and Vietnam also helped to bring Jimmy Carter (1977–1981) into the White House. Although Carter was eager to reintroduce into American foreign policy the Wilsonian strands that Nixon-Kissinger had sought to mute, he was not predisposed to re-launching containment in its earlier highly ideological and bellicose version — in fact, two months into his term, he even made a highly publicized reference critical of the United States' "inordinate fear of Communism." The President announced that henceforth human rights would be a major concern of U.S. foreign policy, affecting its relations with all states. In practice, the administration reserved most of its human rights sanctions for hapless Third World governments in Latin America and Africa, while employing mainly rhetorical instruments toward unsavory but valuable Middle East allies and the Soviet Union. In spite of Soviet advances in Africa, *détente* continued forward, and both countries negotiated a new round of nuclear arms control embodied in a SALT II accord signed in 1979.

By this same year, however, a series of international crises, in tandem with the domestic social and economic malaise that had been afflicting American society throughout the 1970s, had begun to shake the political and intellectual foundations of Carter's policies, including many of those inherited from Nixon-Kissinger. The resulting political earthquake would lead to a massive reorientation of American policy and strategy in the 1980s and indirectly contribute to the end of the Cold War. The first victim was *détente*.

Outwardly at least, and in spite of their massive internal economic problems that they were highly successful in hiding from the outside world, the Soviets looked unstoppable in their quest for strategic expansion. They were active in Angola and the Horn of Africa, were busy building an impressive modern blue-ocean navy with sophisticated submarines and aircraft carriers, and, in addition to their formidable conventional capabilities, were deploying a new generation of medium-range missiles (the SS-20s) in Europe threatening to undermine NATO's credibility. In late 1979, they invaded Afghanistan. In response, Carter imposed economic sanctions on the Soviet Union, started a massive military buildup such as the United States had not undergone in two decades, and backed up NATO's collective decision to deploy a new generation of Western medium-range missiles if the Soviets did not agree to withdraw their SS-20s. *Détente* was dead.

In the Middle East, the fall of the Shah of Iran (a stalwart American ally since a 1954 CIA-induced coup that returned him to power) coupled with the subsequent Iranian Revolution, the seizure of the American hostages, and the Soviet Union's threatening moves in Afghanistan prompted Carter to enunciate the Carter Doctrine: Persian Gulf oil was vital to U.S. national security and any threat to it by any outside party would be a threat to American vital interests. It was a revolutionary doctrine in ways that were immediately obvious. For the first time in its history, the United States formally committed itself to protecting with the full range of its power the Persian Gulf oil supplies on which its

---

3. Exec. Order No. 11,905, 3 C.F.R. 90 (1977).

economy and that of its allies were so highly dependent. To give teeth to this new strategic commitment, the President ordered the creation of a new Rapid Reaction Force that would deploy to the Persian Gulf in a crisis. It formed the nucleus for the future U.S. Central Command that wound up running military operations during the First Persian Gulf War of 1991, the Somalia intervention of 1992–1993, and the Afghanistan and Iraq Wars of 2001–2014.

The End of the Cold War and Containment

The death of *détente*, the massive military buildup begun in early 1980, and the enunciation of the Carter Doctrine paved the way for the more thoroughgoing reinvigoration of containment unleashed by the election of Ronald Reagan (1981–1989). The new president was what Inis L. Claude would call a "hard," as opposed to a "soft" Wilsonian. One of his favorite historical references was to John Winthrop's Biblical allegory of America as "a shining city on a hill." He believed that the future belonged to the United States and its way of life, and that the country's mission was to lead a global crusade for freedom and against communism. But whereas previous presidents had sought to contain Communism and Soviet power, Reagan expected to defeat them decisively, using every instrument short of war to increase pressure on the Soviet Union to the breaking point. In 1981, he signed a National Security directive implementing a new strategy along these lines.

The new Reagan strategy had several components. It called for a massive military buildup, including the modernization of U.S. nuclear and conventional forces. The military buildup had two objectives: to deter Soviet adventurism, and to force the Soviet Union into greater military spending and drive it into bankruptcy. Reagan also ordered a revitalization of covert operations to put greater pressure on Soviet soft spots around the world. In 1983, Reagan went further. He launched a "Strategic Defense Initiative" (SDI) to develop a missile defense shield over the United States and its allies that would protect against incoming Soviet nuclear warheads. While most American scientists doubted SDI's short-term feasibility, the Soviets took it quite seriously, believing that if it was even partly successful it could weaken the effectiveness of their nuclear deterrent. The Soviets also knew that they were technologically and financially incapable of responding to SDI.

To ratchet up pressure on the Soviet Union, in 1985 Reagan also announced the "Reagan Doctrine": the United States would do to the Soviets what they had been doing to the Americans throughout the Third World for three decades. America would give money and arms to anti-Communist "liberation" movements in Third World countries allied with the Soviet Union, such as Nicaragua, Afghanistan, Angola, and Mozambique. It put added economic and political pressure on the Soviet Union to disengage from these countries or seek a negotiated solution that would weaken Soviet influence. Under President Carter, the United States had begun to provide large amounts of money and weapons to the Afghan "freedom fighters" battling the large Soviet forces propping up that country's government. Reagan continued this policy, helping to turn Afghanistan into a Soviet Vietnam that cost the USSR billions of dollars and thousands of lives.

By 1987, the young and urbane Soviet leader who had gained power only two years earlier, Mikhail Gorbachev, had concluded that he needed to wind up the forty-year-old Cold War with the United States at all costs, if the Soviet Union was to have any chance at reforming its economy and society and surviving as a superpower. A protégé of Yuri Andropov, the head of the Soviet KGB, Gorbachev belonged to a younger generation of

Soviet technocrats and officials who by the mid-1970s had become deeply aware of their country's growing technological and economic backwardness. Faced with the Reagan strategy of heightened pressures across the board, and with the Soviet Union spending close to 20 percent of its GDP on the military, Gorbachev quickly realized that only by ending the Cold War and forming a partnership with the West could he gain the breathing space necessary for reform of the USSR. He toned down Soviet ideological rhetoric, and argued before the world that the Soviets were eager to reduce international tensions. He also agreed to withdraw all Soviet forces from Afghanistan, and in spite of his failure to persuade Reagan to give up SDI, the two superpowers engaged in a sweeping round of arms control leading to massive cuts in medium-range nuclear weapons in Europe. The key moment came in late 1989, when, in the face of popular revolutions threatening Communist governments in Poland, East Germany, and Czechoslovakia, Gorbachev refused to use military force. The Soviet empire in Eastern Europe, and its allied Communist governments, all collapsed peacefully in a few weeks. At the end of 1991, the Soviet Union itself disappeared, breaking up into a number of weaker successor states plagued by political and economic instability. The Reagan strategy had succeeded beyond anyone's wildest imagination, except perhaps the President's.

While it is an oversimplification to argue that Reagan won the Cold War, it is clear that his strategy helped to win the war by persuading the Soviet leadership, including the military that, in light of the Soviet Union's mounting troubles, the most sensible response was to seek a genuine accommodation. The U.S. military buildup and the plans to deploy SDI dismayed the Soviets because they knew they could not hope to match them. Their only viable option was to negotiate and seek an end to the struggle, even if it meant letting go of Eastern Europe and some of their other most cherished trappings of superpower status. As Gorbachev and his political allies saw it, in the new age of high technology and intellectual capital, holding on to territory or being able to deploy dozens of armored divisions was far less important than it had been in 1945. The key to power lay instead in creating the domestic conditions for innovation and the continuous enhancement of productivity, and this could not be done while fighting a prohibitively expensive Cold War with the West. While the Reagan strategy did not destroy the Soviet Union, it undoubtedly accelerated its transformation and ultimate demise.

The Uncertainties of the 1990s

The fundamental problem that plagued American national security strategy throughout the 1990s was the absence of a single, well-defined threat, such as Communism and Soviet power had provided for four decades. Like King Arthur's knights searching for the Holy Grail, American strategists and policymakers looked in vain for a coherent theme, like containment, that would enable them to construct a new strategic vision or concept. Disappointingly for many, no new Kennan or Nitze arose. Thus, the decade turned out to be one of considerable uncertainty combined with extensive improvisation, some of it highly creative. The world of the 1990s was in some ways more reassuring, but in other ways less so, than the immediate past had been.

On the positive side, the threat of U.S.-Soviet conflict virtually disappeared. The United States and Russia undertook massive reductions in nuclear weapons, while the once formidable Russian military shrank in size and capabilities. Throughout the world, military budgets declined markedly. As its economy boomed, the United States emerged more powerful in absolute and relative terms than ever before, leading some commentators to talk about America's "unipolar moment." Although the administrations of George H.W. Bush (1989–1993) and Bill Clinton (1993–2001) allowed the defense budget to decline in real dollars 35 percent below 1985 levels, U.S. military spending in 2000 still surpassed that of Russia, China, India, Japan, Germany, Great Britain, and France combined. Just as important, the American lead in military technology, including precision strike weapons and stealth capabilities, widened appreciably, leaving allies and potential rivals further behind.

There were also new security challenges. States such as Iraq and North Korea, which had been protected, as well as restrained, by their powerful Soviet ally, were now on their own. They were more vulnerable, but they also enjoyed greater freedom of action than before. Their response was to try to develop weapons of mass destruction and, in the case of Iraq, to pursue regional hegemony. The Cold War also had kept in check the dangerous rivalry between India and Pakistan, as the Soviets and Americans restrained their respective allies. With this check gone, by the end of the 1990s India and Pakistan had several dozen nuclear weapons aimed at each other, and their struggle over Kashmir brought them to the brink of nuclear war in 1997 and 2001. In the Horn of Africa, the end of the Cold War meant Russian and American indifference toward Somalia, which sank into civil war and widespread famine, forcing the United Nations in 1992 to ask the United States to lead a multinational humanitarian intervention. Throughout the Balkans, Central Asia, and the former Soviet Union, the collapse of Soviet power unleashed the revival of ancient ethnic hatreds and furious internecine wars.

Other than the successful, and militarily impressive, war to roll back Iraq's invasion of Kuwait in 1990–1991, the energies of the first Bush administration were absorbed mostly in coping with the immediate aftermath of the end of the Cold War. The administration cut the size of the military by 25 percent without shifting its Cold War emphasis on fighting large conventional wars. Wisely, the President did not push the American advantage over the Soviet Union, which had the effect of allowing the Soviet empire to disintegrate gently into its component parts, and he also supported the orderly reunification of Germany. Less wisely, the administration tried to ignore the outbreak of war in the former Yugoslavia, leaving the Clinton administration with two major conflicts in Bosnia and Croatia. Guided by the best of intentions, President Bush also began, a few weeks before leaving office, a major humanitarian intervention in Somalia, the first of several that the United States undertook later in Haiti, Bosnia, and Kosovo under his successor.

At a loss over the lack of a unifying strategic concept or vision, the Clinton administration proposed the twin themes of "engagement and enlargement." The United States was now, in the words of Secretary of State Madeleine Albright, "the indispensable nation." It would engage throughout the world with all of its instruments of power to enlarge the sway of democracy. The enlargement of democracy had several dimensions. First, the administration pursued the enlargement of NATO, with the idea of eventually bringing into the community of democratic states all of the former components of the Soviet empire and of the Soviet Union itself. Second, it worked to enhance free trade and expand the reach of multilateral institutions, such as the International Monetary Fund and the World Trade Organization, so as to strengthen the growing global network of trade, financial, and investment links supporting the global capitalist economy. It was during this decade that the term globalization came into vogue to describe the process by which much of the world seemed to be converging economically and culturally through the powerful forces of trade, technology, the demands of markets, and the influence of American culture and political power. Joseph Nye coined the term "soft power" to describe the enormous American cultural, political, and economic assets in the new international order. In spite of strong protectionist forces in Congress arrayed against him, the President used valuable political capital to ratify the NAFTA, tying the United States, Mexico, and Canada into a common market. And he helped to bring China into the World Trade Organization, creating powerful long-term incentives for the Chinese leadership to liberalize further the country's economy and integrate it more deeply into the global capitalist system.

The Clinton administration was not as creative in the area of national security strategy as it was in its economic statecraft. On the one hand, the President did not hesitate to use force judiciously to advance American interests. In Europe, he led military interventions in Bosnia and Kosovo that were successful in accomplishing their objectives. In response to Saddam Hussein's threatening moves against Kuwait in 1994 and Chinese missile tests over Taiwanese waters in 1996, he deployed American forces to the Persian Gulf and two carrier battle groups to the Taiwan Straits. Using a combination of threats and incentives, the administration also persuaded North Korea to shut down, under IAEA inspection, a nuclear reactor capable of processing plutonium in exchange for economic and technical aid to develop peaceful uses of nuclear energy. Finally, the President brought the Israelis and Palestinians closer to a comprehensive settlement of their conflict than anyone had done before. All of these accomplishments were positive, and some of them impressive. Unfortunately, they were not matched by an adjustment in military or intelligence capabilities to deal with new developing threats that were gathering just under the horizon. As in the previous Bush administration, the U.S. military remained largely a shrunken version of the Cold War institution resistant to any serious effort at reorienting its traditional emphasis on fighting large conventional wars. While outside critics called for transformation, and many of the service chiefs began to use the term frequently in their congressional testimonies, little actual change took place. In 1997, an independent commission of defense experts co-chaired by Richard Armitage warned that the nation needed to pay greater attention to what it called homeland defense and the possibility of future devastating terrorist attacks on American soil. Neither the Clinton administration nor his successor, George W. Bush (2001–2009) in his first six months in office, did anything of substance with regard to these sober warnings.

National Security Strategy in the Aftermath of September 11, 2001

The terrorist attacks that shook the United States on September 11, 2001, transformed national security strategy in several ways. While, even at the time, it was doubtful that over the long run the war against terrorism would provide the focus that containment once did, it certainly became for several years the nation's highest priority. Domestically, the events of September 11 led to the creation of a Homeland Security Department, a new cabinet agency centralizing numerous intelligence, law-enforcement, and security functions that were formerly spread out. It represented a serious effort to tackle the challenges of homeland defense. The Bush administration also pushed through Congress the USA PATRIOT Act,[4] vastly expanding the government's intelligence, investigative, and prosecutorial powers against individuals and groups suspected of terrorist activities.

---

4. Uniting and Strengthening America by Providing Appropriate Tools Required to Intercept and Obstruct Terrorism (USA PATRIOT) Act, Pub. L. No. 107-56, 115 Stat. 272 (2001).

Senior government officials also began to speak up publicly in favor of doing away with many of the restrictions placed on the CIA in the 1970s, which they alleged were hampering the fight against terrorism. The "National Security State" seemed to be coming back in strength.

During its first six years in office, the Bush administration focused its national security strategy around the core issue of terrorism, triggering many novel and far-reaching developments in the field of law and national security. In the fall of 2001, the United States successfully invaded and occupied Afghanistan, overthrowing the Taliban regime that had provided safe heaven to the Al-Qaeda terrorist network and its leader Osama bin Laden. Working with allies and friends around the world, the United States also succeeded in killing or apprehending a number of Al-Qaeda agents, although it was not until 2011 that Osama bin Laden was finally hunted down and killed. The aftermath of the Afghan intervention left the United States with serious moral and legal dilemmas on its hands. It was unclear how far the United States was willing to assume the military and economic burdens of turning war-torn Afghanistan into a stable, prosperous state in the face of powerful centrifugal forces threatening to tear the country apart again into warlord rule and chaos. Equally significant, the United States also faced the issue of what to do under international and domestic law about several thousand war captives, a mixed group of Taliban fighters and Al-Qaeda members.

By early 2002, the United States had secured at its naval base in Guantanamo, Cuba, over 700 detainees suspected of terrorism. There were several major constitutional, legal, and policy issues associated with their detention. 1) How should they be treated under international law? 2) How long could the US government hold them without either charging or trying them? 3) Were there any legal boundaries on their treatment, especially on coercive techniques to interrogate them so as to extract intelligence from them? The United States Supreme Court eventually addressed some of these issues in several landmark decisions: *Hamdi v. Rumsfeld* (2004), *Rasul v. Bush* (2004), *Hamdan v. Rumsfeld* (2006), *and Boumediene v. Bush* (2008). The Court ruled that the detainees could not be held indefinitely without some kind of hearing "by an impartial decision-maker" to determine whether they qualified for detention as "enemy combatants" (*Hamdi, Rasul*). If they were tried, they had to be tried by military commissions comporting with the rules of the Uniform Code of Military Justice (*Hamdan*). And Congress could not place the detainees out of reach of the Constitution's *habeas corpus* provisions (*Boumediene*). The issue of coercive interrogations proved far more complicated, leading to widespread bipartisan concerns that the administration was condoning techniques such as "water boarding" that amounted to torture.

Meanwhile, in September of 2002, the Bush administration issued a sweeping national security strategy articulating the bold doctrine that, with regard to dangerous regimes or rogue states supporting terrorism or developing weapons of mass destruction and the means of delivering them, the United States would take "anticipatory actions to defend ourselves, even if uncertainty remains as to the time and place of the enemy's attack. To forestall or prevent such hostile acts by our adversaries, the United States will, if necessary, act preemptively." What was novel about the new strategic doctrine was its interpretation of the well-established international law concept of preemptive force. Whereas in arbitration arising out of the 1837 *Caroline* incident, Secretary of State Daniel Webster offered the classic justification for preemption as a response to an imminent attack,[5] the Bush ad-

---

5. Webster stated that there had to be a "necessity of self-defense, instant, overwhelming, leaving no choice of means and no moment for deliberation." (Letter from Daniel Webster, Secretary of State,

ministration argued that in the era of ballistic missiles and weapons of mass destruction, the United States could not wait until an attack was imminent. In essence, the new interpretation of preemption embraced not only *preemptive* war but also *preventive* war, the use of war to prevent future threats or attacks even when they were somewhat distant. It was not clear how distant these dangers had to be to exempt a state from becoming a target of preemption. In the context of President Bush's earlier State of the Union address of January 2002, the states most likely to qualify for the new doctrine's application were the so-called "Axis of Evil": Iraq, Iran, and North Korea. In fact, throughout the fall and winter of 2002–2003, the United States undertook massive military and diplomatic preparations for a war against Iraq with the objective not only of destroying any weapons of mass destruction it might have, but also to rid the country of Saddam Hussein's dictatorial rule and establish a new democratic Iraq.

Supporters of an Iraq war argued that the establishment of a democratic Iraq would have a positive political and psychological impact on the war against terrorism. In their view, the anti-Americanism feeding the rise of terrorists was nurtured and made possible by the Arab world's undemocratic political culture, including that of American allies such as Egypt and Saudi Arabia. A democratic Iraq might pave the way for the establishment of democracy in Syria and Iran, and force Egypt and Saudi Arabia to make genuine reforms along the same lines. Off the record, many of these same advocates of an Iraqi war suggested that Iraq's defeat at the hand of the United States would provide a sharp psychological shock to the Arab world that would demoralize the radical fundamentalist forces behind terrorism and encourage more pro-Western elements.

The ensuing invasion and occupation of Iraq—undertaken against the opposition of major American allies such as France and Germany and many of the United States' democratic friends around the world—is widely recognized today as a major strategic blunder. Although Saddam Hussein was quickly overthrown in a matter of few weeks in the spring of 2003 at a small cost in American casualties, the country's ensuing occupation and reconstruction damaged American security interests in significant ways. It took a costly "surge" of American troops between 2006 and 2007 to eliminate the Sunni insurgency that consumed the country in widespread violence since late 2003. By the time President Bush left office in early 2009, the Iraq war and its aftermath had cost the United States upwards of $800 billion dollars, more than 4,000 U.S. personnel dead, and over 32,000 wounded. The weak, fragmented Iraqi state that emerged by 2006–2007 was controlled by a Shiite faction closely aligned with Iran, thereby enhancing Iran's regional power and influence. No active weapons of mass destruction programs were ever found, deeply damaging American credibility.[6] Although one of the Iraq invasion's goals was to

---

to Lord Ashburton, Aug. 6, 1842, *reprinted in* 2 John Bassett Moore, A Digest of International Law 409, 412 (1906).

6. While no active program was found there is substantial evidence to conclude that Iraq had the technical capability and the intent to reconstitute their WMD programs once sanctions were lifted. Stocks of chemical weapons were subsequently discovered and several U.S. soldiers were exposed to them suffering major injuries. See <http://eaglerising.com/10016/new-york-times-blockbuster-report-bush-didnt-lie-wmds-found-iraq/#7fGqmg05ksMrYCA8.99>. Based on the report filed with the OPCW when Iraq joined the CWC, 1,200 tons of CW were declared. See Chris Schneidmiller, *India Completes Chemical Weapons Disposal; Iraq Declares Stockpile*, Global Security Newswire, April 27, 2009. Subsequent investigation disclosed Iraq had as much as 5,000 tons and that much of it was whisked away into Syria as our troops progressed. Additionally, in the waning days of the Bush Administration the U.S. secretly transported to Canada a couple hundred tons of yellow cake and 1.7 tons of HEU which could have been used in a radiological bomb or artillery shells (Saddam's Iraq is the only known country to have actually weaponized a radiological bomb). See Brian Murphy, *AP*

demonstrate American resolve and strength to the rest of the world—especially to strategic rivals such as Iran, Russia, and China—the war had the opposite intended consequences: it left American prestige much reduced, the United States economically weaker, and the American public less inclined to support a robust global role for the country. Perhaps the most scathing verdict on the Iraqi war was given by Donald Rumsfeld's successor as President Bush's Secretary of Defense, Robert Gates. Shortly before his retirement from public office in 2011, he warned that "any future defense secretary who advises the president to again send a big American land army into Asia or into the Middle East or Africa should have his head examined."

It was only in its last two years that the Bush administration began to pull itself away from the all-consuming Iraqi imbroglio to focus, without much success, on major strategic threats that had been growing steadily, in particular the rapid progress of the North Korean and Iranian nuclear programs. It was recognition, however belated, that the fight against terrorism, necessary as it was, and largely successful as it had been, could not be the central focus of American grand strategy. While the country's energies and attention had been absorbed by the Middle East and the campaign against terrorism, the configuration of global economic and political power had been changing, with adverse strategic consequences for American interests. The doubling of world oil prices from $40 to $80 a barrel between 2003 and 2006 provided Russia's leader Vladimir Putin with the resources and self-confidence necessary to attempt to reassemble the old Soviet empire within a framework of traditional Russian nationalism. Putin aimed to recover, by force if necessary, Russia's historical position in Eurasia since the 18th century as one of the world's great powers. In spite of Vice-President Cheney's hawkish warnings, Russia fought a brief, sharp war with Georgia in 2008 that led to the independence of two independent Russian enclaves within Georgia—South Ossetia and Abkhazia—and their permanent military occupation by Russian forces as *de facto* Russian territory. On the other side of the globe, China's average annual rate of economic growth of 10% during the previous decade had turned it by 2008 into a global economic power with the resources to expand its military budget and attempt to gain hegemony over the Pacific region. All of these strategic challenges were to land on the lap of President Bush's successor, who wound up dealing with them in different ways, but with no appreciably greater success.

The Obama Years (2008–2016)

On Inauguration Day 2009, Barack Obama found himself facing the country's greatest financial crisis since the Great Depression, and a soaring unemployment rate nearing 11%. He was determined to repudiate many of his predecessor's policies and chart a new course for American national security strategy. His objectives were to withdraw the United States militarily from the Middle East, and to improve relations with major regional adversaries, allowing him to devote greater attention and resources to the United States' domestic economic and social problems. For the new administration, the fight against

---

Exclusive: U.S. Removes Uranium from Iraq, ASSOCIATED PRESS, 5 July 2008. With regard to Iraq's biological warfare program, interviews with Dr. Rihab al-Taha ("Dr. Germ") made it clear she was ready to restart their program as soon as sanctions were lifted. See James Martin, et. al., *History of Biological Weapons: From Poisoned Darts to Intentional Epidemics*, in: DEMBEK, ZYGMUNT F., ed. (2007), MEDICAL ASPECTS OF BIOLOGICAL WARFARE, (Series: Textbooks of Military Medicine), Washington, DC: The Borden Institute, p. 11).

terrorism was only an element in a larger national security strategy focused on managing relations with the major powers that might pose a strategic challenge, particularly Russia, China, and Iran. In line with these, the new president speeded up the American withdrawal from Iraq, initiated a surge in Afghanistan while simultaneously announcing that U.S. forces would leave that country by 2014, and made a series of extensive diplomatic overtures to Russia, China, and Iran with the goal of prodding them into a more cooperative relationship with the United States. The administration launched a "reset" of relations with Russia aimed at resolving rising tensions, and the president traveled to Beijing to explore the prospects for a new U.S.-Chinese strategic partnership. He also started an intense diplomatic campaign designed to persuade Iran and North Korea to give up their nuclear programs through negotiation. Across all fronts, President Obama gradually learned, as his predecessor grudgingly had done, of the intrinsic intractability of international politics and the inherent difficulty of bending the will of other powers to the objectives of U.S. national security strategy.

Although initially welcoming of the new American "reset" and the strategic arms control treaty that accompanied it in 2010, Russia eventually rebuffed it as it intensified its political and military pressures on Ukraine in 2013–2014, and subsequently annexed outright the Crimean peninsula. Fearing a Russian invasion of eastern Ukraine, the United States and the European Union imposed on Russia a set of economic sanctions rivaling those at the height of the Cold War, while talk mounted of supplying Ukraine with sophisticated weaponry. The NATO alliance, which had struck many as increasingly irrelevant at the turn of the 21st century, acquired a sharp new relevance, and the president pointedly had to reaffirm in the summer of 2014 the American commitment to go to war if necessary to defend Eastern Europe and the Baltic states against any outside aggression.

In the Pacific, China rejected U.S. efforts to draw it into a strategic partnership as it continued its push to reassert its ancient hegemony over the East and South China seas and the waters and islands within the so-called "nine-dotted line." By the end of the first decade of the 21st century, there was a growing perception in China of the United States as a declining *status quo* power that would attempt to frustrate China's inevitable rise, and yet prove ultimately unable to do so. Large swaths of China's ruling elite increasingly resented what they saw as America's implacable opposition to their country's recovering its rightful place as the dominant power in the Pacific, and China's assertions of its maritime claims in the western Pacific became stronger in tandem with the stridency of its nationalist rhetoric. As tensions rose between China and its neighbors—Vietnam, Japan, the Philippines, and Malaysia (all of them formal or *de facto* American allies)—the Obama administration announced in 2011 a strategic "pivoting" towards Asia-Pacific. The pivoting started out with little more than regular rotations of U.S. naval forces in Australia and Singapore. By 2014, in the face of China's increasingly assertive behavior towards its neighbors, the United States added to the "pivot" new arrangements to operate large naval forces out of the Subic Bay base in the Philippines, which the U.S. Navy had left in 1992, and plans not to reduce any forces in the Pacific theater.

Meanwhile, in the face of Iran's continuing efforts to develop its nuclear capabilities, the administration succeeded in putting together a near crippling set of U.N.-approved international sanctions which, however harsh, had not sufficed by late 2014 in persuading the Iranian leadership to accept Western demands. President Obama made no more headway toward North Korea and its growing array of nuclear weapons and ballistic missile capabilities than President Bush had done.

By late 2014 also, the president reluctantly had to reengage American forces in Iraq, as the new radical Sunni Islamic State of Iraq and the Levant (ISIL) threatened to take over the Shiite-controlled Iraqi state with its rich oil resources and establish its self-proclaimed caliphate. The President ordered American air strikes to stop ISIL's advance, dispatched 4,500 U.S. special operations forces to train Kurdish *peshmerga* and regular Iraqi military forces, and organized a coalition of European and Arab allies to defeat and destroy the new enemy. Simultaneously, he abandoned his three-year long attempt to stay out of Syria's raging civil war, and began a serious effort to arm and train Syrian opposition elements on Saudi military bases. Everywhere, the administration's earlier national security strategy, now in tatters, was being revised to account for a much greater willingness to project and use military force. In spite of the United States' best efforts, relations with China, Russia, and Iran were as intractable as ever, and the United States had concluded that it could not simply wash its hands of the Middle East's growing sectarian and political rivalries, and had to remain heavily involved politically and militarily.

With regard to the counter-terrorism component of his national security strategy, President Obama's policies showed a remarkable, and surprising, continuity with those of his predecessor, even to the point of expanding some of those policies considerably. Most striking was the use of "drones" in an extensive "targeted killing" program against terrorist suspects, some of them American citizens, around the world. Equally controversial was the expansion of the National Security Agency (NSA)'s surveillance programs to collect vast amounts of information worldwide, including most electronic and telephone communications in the United States, those of allied governments and heads of state, and large foreign multinational companies. The administration also did not hesitate to use special operations forces to capture or eliminate terrorist suspects overseas, most spectacularly killing Osama Bin Laden in a daring raid in Pakistan in April 2011.

As the Obama presidency entered its last two years, the United States found itself in an unprecedented situation for which it could find no historic parallels in its own history to guide it. Militarily, economically, and politically, it was the world's dominant power, with no other state coming close to matching its technological, cultural, and financial reach. Yet, in spite of its predominance, it was steadily losing its ability to shape strategic events around the world on its own. And the long-term trends did not look promising, especially in the Pacific, where China, about to become the world's largest economy, was increasingly able to finance and deploy military forces and weaponry to challenge American regional dominance and reduce the unquestioned margin of superiority that U.S. military power had enjoyed since the end of World War II.

Peering into the future, it was apparent that American national security strategy would be shaped by several major trends and strategic continuities. 1) Although the United States would remain militarily and technologically ahead of any other power, its relative dominance would be gradually eroded as other powers such as China and India became economically capable of funding and deploying larger and more sophisticated military forces. 2) The greatest single security challenge for the United States would be avoiding a major war with China, while at the same time preventing it from dominating the Pacific region. 3) Another equally steep challenge would be to create a political and diplomatic framework that might induce Iran into giving up the acquisition of nuclear weapons; there was no satisfactory long-term military solution to deal with Iran's nuclear programs, but at the same time it was not clear that the country's leadership was willing to renounce Iran's right to have nuclear weapons of its own. 4) The rise and continuing attraction of radical Islamic fundamentalism to millions, and its frequent resort to terrorism and violence, meant that the United States would remain involved in a series of seemingly never-ending military and political operations throughout the Middle East to combat and destroy movements such as ISIL and others that might threaten its security and that of regional allies. 5) In spite of the administration's announcement in 2013 that the defense budget would be reduced drastically during the following decade, it seemed unlikely that such cuts would be implemented, given the deterioration of the international security environment in Eastern Europe, the Middle East, and the Pacific. 6) However much the American people might long for reducing the nation's international commitments, faraway events, as was the case in the spring and summer of 2014 would jolt the United States recurrently into the realization that the maintenance of the existing international order needed the active, relentless exercise of American economic, political and military power. 7) Although terrorism would remain a serious issue, the core concern of American national security strategy would remain the skillful management of relations with the great powers—China, Russia, Europe, India—and a few regional powers such as Iran, Japan, and Brazil, to insure the long-term protection of American strategic interests and values.

Chapter 19

The Constitutional Framework for the Division of National Security Powers Among Congress, the President, and the Courts

Robert F. Turner

In this chapter:
The Theory of Separation of National Security Powers
The Role of the Courts
Selected Bibliography

Few areas of constitutional law are more misunderstood today than the separation of constitutional powers concerning America's relations with the external world. It is as if the Country suffered a massive hard-drive crash about the time of the Vietnam War, and constitutional understandings that had endured for nearly two centuries were suddenly forgotten by all sides in the debate. The problem has been exacerbated by some very able modern scholars who, too often, seek to understand the Constitution's textual meaning without paying adequate attention to its history and context.

Consider these brief excerpts from contemporary writers.

Harold Hongju Koh, The National Security Constitution
67, 75–76 (1990)

One cannot read the Constitution without being struck by its astonishing brevity regarding the allocation of foreign affairs authority among the branches. Nowhere does the Constitution use the words "foreign affairs" or "national security."

. . . .

[T]he first three articles of the Constitution expressly divided foreign affairs powers among the three branches of government, with *Congress*, not the president, being granted the dominant role. Article I bestowed upon Congress legislative power to "lay and collect Taxes, Duties, Imposts and Excises ... and provide for the common Defence [*sic*]"; to "regulate Commerce with foreign Nations ... and with the Indian Tribes; [t]o establish an uniform Rule of Naturalization"; to "define and punish Piracies and Felonies committed on the high Seas, and Offences against the Law of Nations; [t]o declare War, grant Letters of Marque and Reprisal, and make Rules concerning Captures on Land and Water"; plus all manner of powers regarding raising, supporting, maintaining, and regulating the army, navy, and militia, which could be exercised both domestically and abroad....

In Article II, the Framers granted the president the commander-in-chief power, the power to receive ambassadors, and the power to appoint ambassadors and make treaties with the advice and consent of the Senate.... Although the Framers also vested the "executive power" in the president, they expressly incorporated within that nebulous grant neither an exclusive power in foreign affairs nor a general war-making power. Nor, despite expansive claims later asserted by more recent advocates of presidential power, did the Framers intend apparently by that grant to bestow upon the president an unenumerated inherent authority to take external actions. Article II additionally declared that the president "shall take Care that the Laws be faithfully executed," but by its own terms that phrase more clearly imposed upon the president a duty rather than a license.

John Hart Ely, War and Responsibility: Constitutional Lessons of Vietnam and Its Aftermath

139 (1993)

Article II grants the president but four powers bearing on foreign relations — the power to receive ambassadors (which is his alone), the powers to appoint ambassadors and make treaties (each of which must be exercised jointly, with the advice and consent of the Senate), and the power to act as commander in chief (which depends on Congress's having authorized a war).

Peter M. Shane & Harold H. Bruff, Separation of Powers Law: Cases and Materials

583 (2011)

Of course, the phrases "foreign affairs" and "national security" do not appear in the constitutional text. Instead, each of the two elected branches has specific powers with obvious foreign policy relevance. For example, Article I, Section 8 of the Constitution empowers Congress to provide "for the common defense," "to regulate commerce with foreign nations," "to establish a [sic] uniform rule of naturalization," "to define and punish piracies and felonies committed on the high seas, and offenses against the Law of Nations," "to declare war, grant letters of marque and reprisal, and make rules concerning captures on land and water," "to raise and support armies," and "to provide and maintain a Navy." The potential relevance of each of these powers to foreign affairs is transparent.

For his part, the President enjoys, under Article II, the power of Commander-in-Chief, the authority to appoint ambassadors, other public ministers, and consuls, and the power, "by and with the advice and consent of the Senate," to make treaties, provided two-thirds of the Senators present concur."

These excerpts are typical of some of the most highly regarded contemporary legal scholarship in this area. As will be discussed in Chapter 20, Congress was not given the substantive power "to provide for the common Defence" of the nation, but rather the power "[t]o lay and collect Taxes, Duties, Imposts and Excises," *in order* "to pay the Debts and provide for the common Defence and general Welfare of the United States...." Nor is the President's power as Commander in Chief contingent upon "Congress's having authorized a war" — indeed, one of the President's most important military duties is to so deploy the armed forces provided by Congress as to deter aggression and *avoid* war. Chapter 20 will discuss still other common misconceptions taught to law students today about the separation of constitutional powers related to the use of armed force.

But far more fundamentally, modern scholars largely ignore the clause in Article II that the Framers understood to vest in the President of the United States the general control of the Nation's external intercourse. When they do bother to mention the grant of "executive power" to the President, it is usually done as a disparaging aside without the slightest hint of the understanding of this authority set forth in the writings of people like James Madison, Thomas Jefferson, George Washington, Alexander Hamilton, John Jay, or John Marshall. But before exploring that issue, some background may be useful.

Even the strongest champions of congressional supremacy over foreign affairs generally recognize that early presidents managed the nation's foreign intercourse with little apparent involvement by Congress beyond the Senate's enumerated constitutional responsibilities involving treaties and diplomatic appointments. But they then often try to dismiss any precedential value in this practice by suggesting it was some sort of fluke. Two excerpts illustrate this point well:

Harold Hongju Koh, The National Security Constitution
76–80 (1990)

When, in the early years of the republic, foreign sovereigns inevitably began to breach the cordon sanitaire that the British Royal Navy had imposed between the Old and New Worlds, it quickly became apparent that the Congress was poorly structured to respond. The varied tasks of nation building—recognition of and by foreign states, establishment of diplomatic relations, and conclusion of treaties—all demanded a branch of government that could react quickly and coherently to foreign initiatives. Not only was the office of the president ideally structured for such responsive action, it was filled during those early years by founding presidents of unusual personal force. For that reason, the president's constitutional authorities grew rapidly during this first era, but the growth was confined principally to expansion of his textually enumerated powers in the area of recognition, treaty making, and appointment and reception of ambassadors. Significantly, little claim was heard in those years that the president operated in foreign affairs by dint of an *inherent* unenumerated constitutional authority. The era was marked by sporadic, not steady, aggrandizement of presidential powers in foreign affairs vis-à-vis the Congress, with the presidencies of Washington, Jefferson, Jackson, and Polk marking high points amid identifiable valleys of presidential power.

. . . .

… When Washington issued the 1793 Neutrality Proclamation, his act provoked a heated exchange of letters between Hamilton (using the pen name "Pacificus") and Madison (writing under the name "Helvidius"). Foreshadowing *Curtiss-Wright*, Hamilton recited for the first time a broad argument that the president's "executive power" and duty to "take Care that the Laws be faithfully executed" in Article II of the Constitution carried within them the power unilaterally to proclaim neutrality and to prosecute private citizens who violate that proclamation. . . .

Moreover, the ensuing presidencies of Adams, Jefferson, Madison, and Monroe did not fundamentally alter the basic pattern laid down in the Washington years. Admittedly, those presidents took numerous external measures that Congress had not previously authorized.

Professor Koh's highly acclaimed volume has had a major impact upon other modern scholarship on separation of powers in the national security realm, as the following excerpt demonstrates:

PETER M. SHANE & HAROLD H. BRUFF, SEPARATION OF POWERS LAW: CASES AND MATERIALS
590 (2011)

America's original practices with respect to foreign policy and national security occurred, of course, in a context of relative weakness and isolation on the world scene. Prior to the culmination of the War of 1812, our survival was hardly taken for granted by the community of nations. Against this background, it is true that President Washington took a number of measures that appeared to bolster the case for presidential power in the foreign affairs area. Yet, it is probably also fair to say that his overriding goal was not the establishment of a particular set of interbranch relationships, but rather the pursuit of what he took to be sound policy regarding Great Britain, the hegemonic world power of the late 18th Century. These actions included rejecting Citizen Genet as a foreign emissary, withholding certain documents from the House regarding the Jay Treaty, employing special agents to conduct diplomacy on behalf of the United States, and issuing the neutrality proclamation of 1793, discussed earlier.

As related by Professor Koh, President Washington did once engage in military action against the Wabash Indians without congressional authorization. In that case, however, Congress arguably ratified his action. More generally, his separation of powers position was that the President enjoyed a sole constitutional power for *communicating* with foreign nations. It was precisely this power that John Marshall, then a member of the House of Representatives, sought to defend in an 1800 speech to the House, referring to the President as "the sole organ of the federal government in the field of international relations."

Not only did Washington not claim inherent presidential power to set the substantive terms of our foreign policy; he conceded that it was up to Congress whether to "correct, improve, or enforce" even his cherished policy of neutrality. And, indeed, Congress responded to this invitation. It enacted in 1794 the Neutrality Act, which imposed criminal penalties in the United States for persons who would assist a military expedition against any country with which the U.S. was at peace.

———————

As will be demonstrated, the assertion that the "executive power" Clause gave the President far more than merely the power "for *communicating*" with foreign governments predated by several years Hamilton's first *Pacificus* essay. Indeed, it was embraced by Washington, Jefferson, Madison, and Jay within the first year of the formation of the new American government under the Constitution.

To properly understand the original scheme of separating constitutional national security powers between the political branches of government, some historical background is necessary.

The Theory of Separation of National Security Powers

Historical Overview

Few writers dealing with the control of foreign affairs under the Constitution have been able to resist quoting the late Professor Edward S. Corwin's observation that "The Constitution, considered only for its affirmative grants of power capable of affecting the issue, is an *invitation to struggle* for the privilege of directing American foreign policy."[1] Certainly Professor Corwin is right in observing that both political branches are given significant expressed powers pertaining to foreign affairs, and that many important powers were simply not addressed directly by the Founding Fathers. However, a review of the political theory underlying the separation of powers doctrine in the national security realm suggests far less ambiguity than Professor Corwin notes is evident from a simple reading of the constitutional text.

The Influence of Locke, Montesquieu, and Blackstone

The Founding Fathers were greatly influenced by the writings of John Locke, the Baron de Montesquieu, and Sir William Blackstone concerning the separation of governmental powers[2]—and none of these writers were particularly ambiguous with respect to the control of foreign affairs.

JOHN LOCKE, TWO TREATISES OF GOVERNMENT
A CRITICAL EDITION WITH AN INTRODUCTION AND APPARATUS CRITICUS
§ 143–48, 159–60 (Peter Laslett ed., rev. ed. 1963) (3d ed. 1698)

CHAP. XII
OF THE LEGISLATIVE, EXECUTIVE, AND FEDERATIVE POWER OF THE COMMONWEALTH.

143. The *Legislative* Power is that which has a right *to direct* how the Force of the Commonwealth shall be imploy'd for preserving the Community and the Members of it....

144. But because the Laws, that are at once, and in a short time made, have a constant and lasting force, and need a *perpetual Execution*, or an attendance thereunto: Therefore 'tis necessary there should be a *Power always in being*, which should see to the *Execution* of the Laws that are made, and remain in force. And thus the *Legislative* and *Executive Power* come often to be separated.

145. There is another *Power* in every Commonwealth, which one may call *natural*, because it is that which answers to the Power every Man naturally had before he entered into Society.

---

1. EDWARD S. CORWIN, THE PRESIDENT: OFFICE AND POWERS: 1787–1957, at 171 (4th rev. ed. 1957) (emphasis added).
2. Although not a participant in the Federal Convention of 1787 (because he was representing the new nation diplomatically in Paris), Thomas Jefferson was certainly one of the preeminent thinkers in the formation of the new nation—and his letters and comments on the Constitution were directly influential on the structure and content of the document. In a letter to Thomas Mann Randolph of May 30, 1790, Jefferson recommended some books he thought would be of value to a young man entering into the study of law. He wrote: "Montesquieu's Spirit of Laws is generally recommended.... Locke's little book on Government, is perfect as far as it goes. Descending from theory to practice there is no better book than the Federalist." 8 THE WRITINGS OF THOMAS JEFFERSON 29, 31–32 (Andrew Lipscomb & Albert Bergh eds. 1904). *See also* his letter to John Norvell, 11 *id.* 222–23 (1903).

For though in a Commonwealth the Members of it are distinct Persons still in reference to one another, and as such are governed by the Laws of the Society; yet in reference to the rest of Mankind, they make one Body, which is, as every Member of it before was, still in the State of Nature with the rest of Mankind. Hence it is, that the Controversies that happen between any Man of the Society with those that are out of it, are managed by the publick; and an injury done to a Member of their Body, engages the whole in the reparation of it. So that under this Consideration, the whole Community is one Body in the State of Nature, in respect of all other States or Persons out of its Community.

146. This therefore contains the Power of War and Peace, Leagues and Alliances, and all the Transactions, with all Persons and Communities without the Commonwealth, and may be called *Federative*, if anyone pleases. So the thing be understood, I am indifferent as to the Name.

147. These two Powers, *Executive* and *Federative*, though they be really distinct in themselves, yet one comprehending the *Execution* of the Municipal Laws of the Society *within* its self, upon all that are parts of it; the other the management of the *security and interest of the publick without*, with all those that it may receive benefit or damage from, yet they are always almost united. And though this *federative Power* in the well or ill management of it be of great moment to the commonwealth, yet it is much less capable to be directed by antecedent, standing, positive Laws, than the Executive; and so must necessarily be left to the Prudence and Wisdom of those whose hands it is in, to be managed for the publick good. For the Laws that concern Subjects one amongst another, being to direct their actions, may well enough precede them. But what is to be done in reference to Foreigners, depending much upon their actions, and the variation of designs and interest, must be left in great part to the Prudence of those who have this Power committed to them, to be managed by the best of their Skill, for the advantage of the Commonwealth.

148. Though, as I said, the Executive and Federative Power of every Community be really distinct in themselves, yet they are hardly to be separated, and placed, at the same time, in the hands of distinct Persons. For both of them requiring the force of the Society for their exercise, it is almost impracticable to place the Force of the Commonwealth in distinct, and not subordinate hands; or that the Executive and Federative Power should be placed in Persons that might act separately, whereby the Force of the Publick would be under different Commands: which would be apt sometime or other to cause disorder and ruine.

....

Chap. XIV
Of Prerogative.

159. Where the Legislative and Executive Power are in distinct hands, (as they are in all ... well-framed Governments) there the good of the Society requires, that several things should be left to the discretion of him, that has the Executive Power. For the Legislators not being able to foresee, and provide, by Laws, for all, that may be useful to the Community, the Executor of the Laws, having the power in his hands, has by the common Law of Nature, a right to make use of it, for the good of the Society, in many Cases, where the municipal Law has given no direction, till the Legislative can conveniently be Assembled to provide for it. Many things there are, which the Law can by no means provide for, and those must necessarily be left to the discretion of him, that has the Executive Power in his hands, to be ordered by him, as the publick good and advantage shall require: nay, 'tis fit that the Laws themselves should in some Cases give way to the Executive Power, or rather to this Fundamental Law of Nature and Government, *viz*. That as much as may

be, *all* the Members of the Society are to *be preserved*. For since many accidents may happen, wherein a strict and rigid observation of the Laws may do harm; (as not to pull down an innocent Man's House to stop the Fire, when the next to it is burning) and a Man may come sometimes within the reach of the Law, which makes no distinction of Persons, by an action, that may deserve reward and pardon; 'tis fit, the Ruler should have a Power, in many Cases, to mitigate the severity of the Law, and pardon some Offenders: For the *end of Government* being the *preservation of all*, as much as may be, even the guilty are to be spared, where it can prove no prejudice to the innocent.

160. This Power to act according to discretion, for the publick good, without the prescription of the Law, and sometimes even against it, *is* that which is called *Prerogative*. For since in some Governments the Law-making Power is not always in being, and is usually too numerous, and so too slow, for the dispatch requisite to Execution: and because also it is impossible to foresee, and so by laws to provide for, all Accidents and Necessities, that may concern the publick; or to make such Laws, as will do no harm, if they are Executed with an inflexible rigour, on all occasions, and upon all Persons, that may come in their way, therefore there is a latitude left to the Executive power, to do many things of choice, which the Laws do not prescribe.

MONTESQUIEU, THE SPIRIT OF LAWS
151–52, 156–61 (C. T. Nugent trans. 1949)[3]

In every government there are three sorts of power: the legislative; the executive in respect to things dependent on the law of nations; and the executive in regard to matters that depend on the civil law.

By virtue of the first, the prince or magistrate enacts temporary or perpetual laws, and amends or abrogates those that have been already enacted. By the second, he makes peace or war, sends or receives embassies, establishes the public security, and provides against invasions. By the third, he punishes criminals, or determines the disputes that arise between individuals. The latter we shall call the judiciary power, and the other simply the executive power of the state.

The political liberty of the subject is a tranquility of mind arising from the opinion each person has of his safety. In order to have this liberty, it is requisite the government be so constituted as one man need not be afraid of another.

When the legislative and executive powers are united in the same person, or in the same body of magistrates, there can be no liberty; because apprehensions may arise, lest the same monarch or senate should enact tyrannical laws, to execute them in a tyrannical manner.

Again, there is no liberty, if the judiciary power be not separated from the legislative and executive. Were it joined with the legislative, the life and liberty of the subject would be exposed to arbitrary control; for the judge would be then the legislator. Were it joined to the executive power, the judge might behave with violence and oppression.

There would be an end of everything, were the same man or the same body, whether of the nobles or of the people, to exercise those three powers, that of enacting laws, that of executing the public resolutions, and of trying the causes of individuals.

---

3. *De l'Esprit des Lois* was first published in 1748. James Madison, in a discussion of separation of powers, wrote that "[t]he oracle who is always consulted and cited on this subject is the celebrated Montesquieu." THE FEDERALIST No. 47, at 324 (James Madison) (JACOB COOKE ed., 1961).

. . . .

The executive power ought to be in the hands of a monarch, because this branch of government, having need of despatch, is better administered by one than by many: on the other hand, whatever depends on the legislative power is oftentimes better regulated by many than by a single person.

But if there were no monarch, and the executive power should be committed to a certain number of persons selected from the legislative body, there would be an end then of liberty; by reason the two powers would be united, as the same persons would sometimes possess, and would be always able to possess, a share in both.

. . . .

Were the executive power not to have a right of restraining the encroachments of the legislative body, the latter would become despotic; for as it might arrogate to itself what authority it pleased, it would soon destroy all the other powers.

But it is not proper, on the other hand, that the legislative power should have a right to stay the executive. For as the execution has its natural limits, it is useless to confine it; besides, the executive power is generally employed in momentary operations. The power, therefore, of the Roman tribunes was faulty, as it put a stop not only to the legislation, but likewise to the executive part of government; which was attended with infinite mischief.

. . . .

The executive power, pursuant of what has been already said, ought to have a share in the legislature by the power of rejecting; otherwise it would soon be stripped of its prerogative. But should the legislative power usurp a share of the executive, the latter would be equally undone.

If the prince were to have a part in the legislature by the power of resolving, liberty would be lost. But as it is necessary he should have a share in the legislature for the support of his own prerogative, this share must consist in the power of rejecting.

. . . .

When once an army is established, it ought not to depend immediately on the legislative, but on the executive power; and this from the very nature of the thing, its business consisting more in action than in deliberation.

WILLIAM BLACKSTONE, 1 COMMENTARIES ON THE LAWS OF ENGLAND
230, 232–33, 242–46 (1st ed. 1765)

CHAPTER THE SEVENTH.
OF THE KING'S PREROGATIVE.

. . . .

WE are next to consider those branches of the royal prerogative, which invest this our sovereign lord, thus all-perfect and immortal in his kingly capacity, with a number of authorities and powers; in the exertion whereof consists the executive part of government. This is wisely placed in a single hand by the British constitution, for the sake of unanimity, strength and dispatch. Were it placed in many hands, it would be subject to many wills: many wills, if disunited and drawing different ways, create weakness in a government: and to unite those several wills, and reduce them to one, is a work of more time and delay than the exigencies of state will afford....

AFTER what has been premised in this chapter, I shall not (I trust) be considered as an advocate for arbitrary power, when I lay it down as a principle, that in the exertion of lawful prerogative, the king is and thought to be absolute; that is, so far absolute, that there is no legal authority that can either delay or resist him. He may reject what bills, may make what treaties, may coin what money, may create what peers, may pardon what offences he pleases: unless where the constitution hath expressly, or by evident consequence, laid down some exception or boundary; declaring, that thus far the prerogative shall go and no farther. For otherwise the power of the crown would indeed be but a name and a shadow, insufficient for the ends of government, ...

IN the exertion therefore of those prerogatives, which the law has given him, the king is irresistible and absolute, according to the forms of the constitution. And yet, if the consequence of that exertion be manifestly to the grievance or dishonour of the kingdom, the parliament will call his advisers to a just and severe account. For prerogative consisting (as Mr. Locke has well defined it) in the discretionary power of acting for the public good, where the positive laws are silent, if that discretionary power be abused to the public detriment, such prerogative is exerted in an unconstitutional manner. Thus the king may make a treaty with a foreign state, which shall irrevocably bind the nation; and yet when such treaties have been judged pernicious, impeachments have pursued those ministers, by whose agency or advice they were concluded.

THE prerogatives of the crown (in the sense under which we are now considering them) respect either this nation's intercourse with foreign nations, or it's own domestic government and civil polity.

WITH regard to foreign concerns, the king is the delegate or representative of his people. It is impossible that the individuals of a state, in their collective capacity can transact the affairs of that state with another community equally numerous as themselves. Unanimity must be wanting to their measures, and strength to the execution of their counsels. In the king therefore, as in a center, all the rays of his people are united, and form by that union a consistency, splendor, and power, that make him feared and suspected by foreign potentates; who would scruple to enter into any engagements, that must afterwards be revised and ratified by a popular assembly. What is done by the royal authority, with regard to foreign powers, is the act of the whole nation....

CHARLES THACH, CREATION OF THE PRESIDENCY

52 (1922)

State experience thus contributed, nothing more strongly, to discredit the whole idea of the sovereign legislature, to bring home the real meaning of limited government and coordinate powers. The idea, more than once utilized as the basis of the explanation of Article II of the Constitution, that the jealousy of kingship was a controlling force in the Federal Convention, is far, very far, from the truth. The majority of the delegates brought with them no far-reaching distrust of executive power, but rather a sobering consciousness that, if their new plan should succeed, it was necessary for them to put forth their best efforts to secure a strong, albeit safe, national executive.

James Madison, *Remarks to the Constitutional Convention (July 17, 1787)*

in 2 RECORDS OF THE FEDERAL CONVENTION 34–35 (Max Farrand ed., 1966)

If it be essential to the preservation of liberty that the Legislative, Executive, and Judiciary powers be separate, it is essential to a maintenance of the separation that they should be independent of each other. The Executive could not be independent of the Legislature, if dependent on the pleasure of that branch for a re-appointment. Why was it determined that the Judges should not hold their places by such a tenure? Because they might be tempted to cultivate the Legislature, by an undue complaisance, and thus render the Legislature the virtual expositer [*sic*], as well the maker of the laws. In like manner a dependence of the Executive on the Legislature, would render it the Executor as well as the maker of laws; & then according to the observations of Montesquieu, tyrannical laws may be made that they may be executed in a tyrannical manner. There was an analogy between the Executive & Judiciary departments in several respects. The latter executed the laws in certain cases as the former did in others. The former expounded & applied them for certain purposes, as the latter did for others. The difference between them seemed to consist chiefly in two circumstances — 1. the collective interest & security were much more in the power belonging to the Executive than to the Judiciary department. 2. in the administration of the former much greater latitude is left to opinion and discretion than in the administration of the latter. . . . He conceived it to be absolutely necessary to a well constituted Republic that the two first [that is, Legislative and Executive powers] sh[oul]d be kept distinct & independent of each other. Experience has proved a tendency in our governments to throw all power into the Legislative vortex. The Executives of the States are in general little more than Cyphers; the legislatures omnipotent. If no effectual check be devised for restraining the instability & encroachments of the latter, a revolution of some kind or other would be inevitable.

The Federalist Papers

The fifty-five men who gathered in Philadelphia in the summer of 1787 to draft a constitution were familiar with the writings of Locke, Montesquieu, and Blackstone, and indeed were deeply influenced by their views.[4] Since the proceedings of the Federal Convention were conducted in secret, when Congress submitted the Constitution to the states for ratification on September 28, 1787, there was no official record to explain the document. A great debate occurred between Federalist supporters of the proposed Constitution and anti-Federalist critics. During this process a series of seventy-seven essays explaining and defending the Constitution appeared in New York newspapers between October 1787 and April 1788 under the name "*Publius*." Written by Alexander Hamilton, James Madison, and John Jay, these *Federalist Papers* were instrumental in securing ratification and have become a standard reference for understanding the American system of government.[5]

THE FEDERALIST NO. 47

at 323 (James Madison) (Jacob Cooke ed. 1961)

One of the principal objections inculcated by the more respectable adversaries to the Constitution, is its supposed violation of the political maxim, that the legislative, executive, and judiciary departments ought to be separate and distinct. In the structure of the federal

---

4. LOUIS HENKIN, FOREIGN AFFAIRS AND THE CONSTITUTION 43 (1972).

5. Jefferson called them "in my opinion, the best commentary on the principles of government, which ever was written" (7 THE WRITINGS OF THOMAS JEFFERSON 183 (Andrew Lipscomb & Albert Bergh eds., 1904)). Chief Justice Marshall in *Cohens v. Virginia*, 19 U.S. 264, 418 (1821), observed: "The opinion of the Federalist has always been considered as of great authority. It is a complete commentary on our constitution; and is appealed to by all parties in the questions to which that instrument has given birth."

government, no regard, it is said, seems to have been paid to this essential precaution in favor of liberty. The several departments of power are distributed and blended in such a manner as at once to destroy all symmetry and beauty of form, and to expose some of the essential parts of the edifice to the danger of being crushed by the disproportionate weight of other parts.

No political truth is certainly of greater intrinsic value, or is stamped with the authority of more enlightened patrons of liberty, than that on which the objection is founded. The accumulation of all powers, legislative, executive, and judiciary, in the same hands, whether of one, a few, or many, and whether hereditary, self-appointed, or elective, may justly be pronounced the very definition of tyranny. Were the federal Constitution, therefore, really chargeable with the accumulation of power, or with a mixture of powers, having a dangerous tendency to such an accumulation, no further arguments would be necessary to inspire a universal reprobation of the system. I persuade myself, however, that it will be made apparent to every one, that the charge cannot be supported, and that the maxim on which it relies has been totally misconceived and misapplied. In order to form correct ideas on this important subject, it will be proper to investigate the sense in which the preservation of liberty requires that the three great departments of power should be separate and distinct.

The oracle who is always consulted and cited on this subject is the celebrated Montesquieu. If he be not the author of this invaluable precept in the science of politics, he has the merit at least of displaying and recommending it most effectually to the attention of mankind. Let us endeavor, in the first place, to ascertain his meaning on this point.

The British Constitution was to Montesquieu what Homer has been to the didactic writers on epic poetry. As the latter have considered the work of the immortal bard as the perfect model from which the principles and rules of the epic art were to be drawn, and by which all similar works were to be judged, so this great political critic appears to have viewed the Constitution of England as the standard, or to use his own expression, as the mirror of political liberty; and to have delivered, in the form of elementary truths, the several characteristic principles of that particular system. That we may be sure, then, not to mistake his meaning in this case, let us recur to the source from which the maxim was drawn.

On the slightest view of the British Constitution, we must perceive that the legislative, executive, and judiciary departments are by no means totally separate and distinct from each other. The executive magistrate forms an integral part of the legislative authority. He alone has the prerogative of making treaties with foreign sovereigns, which, when made, have, under certain limitations, the force of legislative acts. All the members of the judiciary department are appointed by him, can be removed by him on the address of the two Houses of Parliament, and form, when he pleases to consult them, one of his constitutional councils. One branch of the legislative department forms also a great constitutional council to the executive chief, as, on another hand, it is the sole depositary of judicial power in cases of impeachment, and is invested with the supreme appellate jurisdiction in all other cases. The judges, again, are so far connected with the legislative department as often to attend and participate in its deliberations, though not admitted to a legislative vote.

From these facts, by which Montesquieu was guided, it may clearly be inferred that, in saying "There can be no liberty where the legislative and executive powers are united in the same person, or body of magistrates," or, "if the power of judging be not separated from the legislative and executive powers," he did not mean that these departments ought to have no *PARTIAL AGENCY* in, or no *CONTROL* over, the acts of each other.

THE FEDERALIST NO. 70

at 471–77 (Alexander Hamilton) (Jacob Cooke ed., 1961)

There is an idea, which is not without its advocates, that a vigorous executive is inconsistent with the genius of republican government. The enlightened well wishers to this species of government must at least hope that the supposition is destitute of foundation; since they can never admit its truth, without at the same time admitting the condemnation of their own principles. Energy in the executive is a leading character in the definition of good government. It is essential to the protection of the community against foreign attacks....

....

That unity is conducive to energy will not be disputed. Decision, activity, secrecy, and dispatch will generally characterize the proceedings of one man, in a much more eminent degree, than the proceedings of any greater number; and in proportion as the number is increased, these qualities will be diminished.

This unity may be destroyed in two ways; either by vesting the power in two or more magistrats of equal dignity and authority; or by vesting it ostensibly in one man, subject in whole or in part to the control and co-operation of others, in the capacity of counsellors to him....

....

... In the legislature, promptitude of decision is oftener an evil than a benefit. The differences of opinion, and the jarrings of parties in that department of the government, though they may sometimes obstruct salutary plans, yet often promote deliberation and circumspection: and serve to check excesses in the majority. When a resolution too is once taken, the opposition must be at an end. That resolution is a law, and resistance to it punishable. But no favourable circumstances palliate or atone for the disadvantages of dissention in the executive department. Here they are pure and unmixed. There is no point at which they cease to operate. They serve to embarrass and weaken the execution of the plan or measure, to which they relate, from the first step to the final conclusion of it. They constantly counteract those qualities in the executive, which are the most necessary ingredients in its composition, vigour and expedition, and this without any counterbalancing good. In the conduct of war, in which the energy of the executive is the bulwark of the national security, every thing would be to be apprehended from its plurality....

THE FEDERALIST NO. 72

at 486–87 (Alexander Hamilton) (Jacob Cooke ed., 1961)

The administration of government, in its largest sense, comprehends all the operations of the body politic, whether legislative, executive or judiciary, but in its most usual and perhaps in its most precise signification, it is limited to executive details, and falls peculiarly within the province of the executive department. The actual conduct of foreign negotiations, the preparatory plans of finance, the application and disbursement of the public monies, in conformity to the general appropriations of the legislature, the arrangement of the army and navy, the direction of the operations of war; these and other matters of a like nature constitute what seems to be most properly understood by the administration of government.

Questions for Discussion

1. Professor Glen E. Thurow writes: "[T]he thrust of the *Federalist Papers* ... is that the great discretion required in foreign affairs can be made compatible with republican government not by dispersing the power to the greatest extent possible, but by concentrating it in the hands of the President."[6] Do you agree?

2. How did Locke, Montesquieu, Blackstone, and the Founding Fathers deal with the issue of "competence" among the branches of government? What were viewed as the strengths and weaknesses of each with respect to national security affairs?

3. Professor Richard E. Neustadt has dismissed the idea that the Constitutional Convention created a government of separation of powers, arguing: "It did nothing of the sort. Rather, it created a government of separated institutions sharing powers."[7] This has contributed to a popular paradigm of "shared powers" in the foreign policy realm, presumably with Congress having the ultimate authority to make foreign policy. But ask yourself: which powers are actually *shared* under the Constitution? To be sure, the President has a qualified negative over legislation, Congress has a negative over a Declaration of War, and the Senate has a negative over treaties and appointments. Congress also has expressed powers over foreign commerce and several other matters. But the actual role of each branch is specific. The president "nominates" and "appoints," and Congress lacks constitutional power to compel him to do either. Nor can the President interfere with the veto given to the Senate over appointments and treaties. The Senate cannot negotiate an international agreement or compel the President to do so by statute. Clearly, from their remarks and frequent references to Montesquieu, Madison and his colleagues *believed* they were adopting a system of separation of powers, blending those powers through the use of negatives placed in another branch in order to better secure liberty. While many major foreign policy initiatives ultimately require the participation of the President and the Senate (for example, through the treaty-making process) or the President and Congress (for example, whenever appropriated funds are required), the actual roles of each department are generally distinct and not "shared." Ask yourself what national security powers are "shared" in the Constitution in the sense that more than one department is empowered to take the same specific action. The problem with the "shared powers" paradigm is not that it is inaccurate to note that more than one department often must act to complete a major policy initiative, but that it may promote a blurring of the generally distinct roles of each department in this process.

The President's Special Responsibilities in Foreign Affairs

Article II, Section 1 of the Constitution provides that "The executive Power shall be vested in a President of the United States of America." It is often overlooked by those seeking to "break the code" of the separation of foreign affairs powers, as is the distinction between its broad terms and the more limited grant to Congress in Article I, Section 1, of "All legislative Powers *herein granted....*" (emphasis added.)

The Founding Fathers understood the concept of "executive power" as it has been explained by Locke, Montesquieu, and Blackstone. The late Professor Quincy Wright observed in his classic 1922 study, *The Control of American Foreign Relations*, that "when

---

6. Glen Thurow, *Presidential Discretion in Foreign Affairs*, 7 VAND. J. TRANS. L. 71, 86 (1973).
7. RICHARD E. NEUSTADT, PRESIDENTIAL POWER 26 (2d ed. 1980).

the constitutional convention gave 'executive power' to the President, the foreign relations power was the essential element in the grant, but they carefully protected this power from abuse by provision for senatorial or congressional veto."[8] This appears to have been the common understanding of all three branches of the government in the beginning. As Jefferson, Hamilton, and Madison argued,[9] exceptions to this general grant were to be construed strictly.

Executive preeminence in the field of foreign affairs was reflected in early legislation dealing with this subject, as the following excerpts illustrate:

4 GREEN HACKWORTH, DIGEST OF INTERNATIONAL LAW
642–44 (1942)
EXECUTIVE CONTROL OF FOREIGN RELATIONS
§421

In regard to the control of the foreign relations of the United States, a memorandum prepared in the Office of the Solicitor for the Department of State says:

. . . .

THE DEPARTMENT OF STATE

... The Department of State was organized July 27, 1789 by Act of Congress. (1 Stat. 28.) The act provided that the Secretary of State should perform and execute such duties as the President should intrust to him, agreeable to the Constitution relative to correspondence, commissions, and instructions to the public ministers and consuls sent out from the United States, and also pertaining to negotiations with the public ministers from foreign States. The Secretary of State is, therefore, to conduct all matters respecting foreign affairs which the President may assign to his Department, and must manage the business as the President may direct.

There was a real distinction made between this Department on the one hand, and the Treasury Department, for instance, on the other. The difference lies in the fact that the Treasury Department was created solely for the purpose of carrying out enactments of Congress. In all things concerning money the legal "impulse to action" had, from the nature of things, to come from Congress. This was not at all true of the "Foreign Department". *The sole purpose of that organization was to carry out, not orders, as expressed in legislation or resolutions, but the will of the executive.* In all cases the President could direct and control, but in the "presidential" Department he could determine *what should be done*, as well as *how it should be done.* [Emphasis in the original]

The act in question was brief and could have fit on a single page. It read in pertinent part:

Act Creating Department of Foreign Affairs
1 Stat. 28–29 (1789)

Be it enacted ... [t]hat there shall be an Executive department, to be denominated the Department of Foreign Affairs, and that there shall be a principal officer therein, to be called the Secretary for the Department of Foreign Affairs, who shall perform and execute

---

8. QUINCY WRIGHT, THE CONTROL OF AMERICAN FOREIGN RELATIONS 147 (1922).

9. *See* James Madison, Remarks to the Constitutional Convention (July 17, 1787), *in* 2 RECORDS OF THE FEDERAL CONVENTION 34–35 (Max Farrand ed., 1966); *supra* note 2.

such duties as shall from time to time be enjoined on or intrusted to him by the President of the United States, agreeable to the Constitution, relative to ... such ... matters respecting foreign affairs, as the President of the United States shall assign to the said department; and furthermore, that the said principal officer shall conduct the business of the said department in such manner as the President of the United States shall from time to time order or instruct.

Madison's Speech on the Removal Power

During the discussion in Congress over the establishment of the Department of Foreign Affairs on June 17, 1789, a debate occurred over what authority would be necessary to remove the Secretary of Foreign Affairs from office. James Madison, then a Representative from Virginia and the author of the bill under consideration, argued that this power belonged to the President under the Constitution. His reasoning provides additional insight into early thinking about the constitutional separation of powers.

James Madison, *Remarks During Debate on Establishing Department of Foreign Affairs*

in 1 ANNALS OF CONG. 515–17 (Joseph Gales ed., 1789)

The doctrine ... which seems to stand most in opposition to the principles I contend for, is, that the power to annul an appointment is, in the nature of things, incidental to the power which makes the appointment. I agree that if nothing more was said in the constitution than that the President, by and with the advice and consent of the Senate, should appoint to office, there would be a great force in saying that the power of removal resulted by a natural implication from the power of appointing. But there is another part of the Constitution no less explicit than the one on which the gentleman's doctrine is founded; it is that part which declares that the Executive power shall be vested in a President of the United States. The association of the Senate with the President in exercising that particular function, is an exception to this general rule; and exceptions to general rules, I conceive, are ever to be taken strictly....

There is another maxim which ought to direct us in expounding the Constitution, and it is of great importance. It is laid down, in most of the Constitutions or bills of rights in the republics of America; it is to be found in the political writings of the most celebrated civilians, and is every where held as essential to the preservation of liberty, that the three great departments of Government be kept separate and distinct; and if in any case they are blended, it is in order to admit a partial qualification, in order more effectually to guard against an entire consolidation. I think, therefore, when we review the several parts of this constitution, when it says that the Legislative powers shall be vested in a Congress of the United States, under certain exceptions, and the executive power vested in the President with certain exceptions, we must suppose they were intended to be kept separate in all cases in which they are not blended, and ought, consequently, to expound the Constitution so as to blend them as little as possible.

Jefferson's Advice to Washington on the Senate Role in Foreign Affairs

Thomas Jefferson began work as the new nation's first Secretary of State (initially designated "Secretary of Foreign Affairs" until the duties were increased to include such tasks as keeping the Great Seal and issuing commissions) on March 21, 1790. The Constitution was silent on many issues. As historian James Thomas Flexner has observed, the Framers left many details to be worked out among the branches and "the first session of Congress, was, in effect, a second Constitutional Convention."[10]

President Washington quickly called upon his able Secretary of State to advise him on where the Constitution had placed decisions concerning diplomacy and foreign affairs that were not specifically addressed in the instrument. For example, although it was clear by the language of Article II, Section 2, of the Constitution that the President could only appoint "Ambassadors, other public Ministers and Consuls," with the advice and consent of the Constitution, where was discretion placed to decide where diplomats ought to be dispatched, the grade appropriate for each posting, and the many other details of diplomacy and foreign relations? Jefferson's considered response is instructive:

Thomas Jefferson, *Opinion on the Powers of the Senate Respecting Diplomatic Appointments*

New York, April 24, 1790, *in* 3 THE PAPERS OF THOMAS JEFFERSON
378, 379–80, (Julian P. Boyd ed., 1961)

The constitution having declared that the President shall *nominate* and, by and with the advice and consent of the Senate, shall *appoint* ambassadors, other public ministers, and consuls, the President desired my opinion whether the Senate has a right to negative the *grade* he may think it expedient to use in a foreign mission as well as the *person* to be appointed.

I think the Senate has no right to negative the *grade*.

The constitution has divided the powers of government into three branches, Legislative, Executive and Judiciary, lodging each with a distinct magistracy. The Legislative it has given completely to the Senate and House of Representatives. It has declared that the Executive powers shall be vested in the President, submitting special articles of it to a negative by the Senate, and it has vested the Judiciary power in the courts of justice, with certain exceptions also in favor of the Senate.

The transaction of business with foreign nations is Executive altogether. It belongs, then, to the head of that department, except as to such portions of it as are specially submitted to the Senate. Exceptions are to be construed strictly.

. . . .

The Senate is not supposed by the constitution to be acquainted with the concerns of the Executive department. It was not intended that these should be communicated to them, nor can they therefore be qualified to judge of the necessity which calls for a mission to any particular place, or of the particular grade, more or less marked, which special and secret circumstances may call for. All this is left to the President. They are only to see that no unfit person be employed.

It may be objected that the Senate may by continual negatives on the *person*, do what amounts to a negative on the *grade*, and so, indirectly, defeat this right of the President. But this would be a breach of trust; an abuse of power confided to the Senate, of which that body cannot be supposed capable. So the President has a power to convoke the

---

10. JAMES THOMAS FLEXNER, WASHINGTON: THE INDISPENSABLE MAN 219 (1969).

Legislature, and the Senate might defeat that power by refusing to come. This equally amounts to a negative on the power of convoking. Yet nobody will say they possess such a negative, or would be capable of usurping it by such oblique means. If the Constitution had meant to give the Senate a negative on the grade or destination, as well as the person, it would have said so in direct terms, and not left it to be effected by a sidewind. It could never mean to give them the use of one power through the abuse of another.

———————

This view was embraced by other eminent figures of the day. Jefferson noted in the margin of his file copy of the memorandum, "endorsed by Washington,"[11] and Washington made the following notation in his Diary.

George Washington
6 PAPERS OF GEORGE WASHINGTON 68 (1979)

Had some conversation with Mr. Madison on the propriety of consulting the Senate on the places to which it would be necessary to send persons in the Diplomatic line, and Consuls; and with respect to the grade of the first—His opinion coincides with Mr. Jay's and Mr. Jefferson's—to wit—that they have no Constitutional right to interfere with either, and ... their powers extending no further than to an approbation or disapprobation of the person nominated by the President, all the rest being Executive and vested in the President by the Constitution.

The Pacificus-Helvidius *Exchange of 1793*

On April 22, 1793, President Washington issued a proclamation declaring that the United States was at peace with both France and Great Britain, and urging citizens to avoid hostile acts against either country. Although the term was not employed, the declaration is widely referred to as Washington's "neutrality proclamation." Using the pseudonym "*Pacificus*," Treasury Secretary Hamilton wrote a series of newspaper articles defending the President's conduct. Secretary of State Jefferson, who as former Minister to Paris was sympathetic to the French cause, urged Representative James Madison to take up the challenge and rebut Hamilton's essays. In so doing, Madison employed the pseudonym "*Helvidius*."

The following excerpts from the first exchange provide insight into the competing viewpoints among the Founding Fathers on the control of foreign affairs and the powers relating to war.

Alexander Hamilton, *Pacificus No. I*
Philadelphia, June 29, 1793, *reprinted in* 15 THE PAPERS OF ALEXANDER HAMILTON 33, 36–40, 41–42 (Harold Syrett ed., 1969)

It will not be disputed that the management of the affairs of this country with foreign nations is confided to the Government of the UStates.

....

———————

11. 16 PAPERS OF THOMAS JEFFERSON, at 380 n (Julian P. Boyd ed., 1961).

The Legislative Department is not the *organ* of intercourse between the UStates and foreign Nations. It is charged neither with *making* nor *interpreting* Treaties. It is therefore not naturally that Organ of the Government which is to pronounce the existing condition of the Nation, with regard to foreign Powers, or to admonish the Citizens of their obligations and duties as founded upon that condition of things. Still less is it charged with enforcing the execution and observance of these obligations and those duties.

It is equally obvious that the act in question is foreign to the Judiciary Department of the Government. The province of that Department is to decide litigations in particular cases. It is indeed charged with the interpretation of treaties; but it exercises this function only in the litigated cases; that is where contending parties bring before it a specific controversy. It has no concern with pronouncing upon the external political relations of Treaties between Government and Government. This position is too plain to need being insisted upon.

It must then of necessity belong to the Executive Department to exercise the function in Question — when a proper case for the exercise of it occurs.

It appears to be connected with that department in various capacities, as the *organ* of intercourse between the Nation and foreign Nations — as the interpreter of the National Treaties, in those cases in which the Judiciary is not competent, that is in the cases between Government and Government — as that Power, which is charged with the Execution of the Laws, of which Treaties form a part — as that Power which is charged with the command and application of the public force.

This view of the subject is so natural and obvious — so analogous to general theory and practice — that no doubt can be entertained of its justness, unless such doubt can be deduced from particular provisions of the Constitution of the UStates.

Let us see then if cause for such doubt is to be found in that Constitution.

The second Article of the Constitution of the UStates, section 1st, establishes this general Proposition, That "The EXECUTIVE POWER shall be vested in a President of the United States of America."

The same article in a succeeding Section proceeds to designate particular cases of Executive Power. It declares among other things that the President shall be Commander in Cheif [*sic*] of the army and navy of the UStates and of the Militia of the several states when called into the actual service of the UStates, that he shall have power by and with the advice of the Senate to make treaties; that it shall be his duty to receive ambassadors and other public Ministers and to take care that the laws be faithfully executed.

It would not consist with the rules of sound construction to consider this enumeration of particular authorities as derogating from the more comprehensive grant contained in the general clause, further than as it may be coupled with express restrictions or qualifications; as in regard to the cooperation of the Senate in the appointment of Officers and the making of treaties; which are qualifica[tions] of the general executive powers of appointing officers and making treaties: Because of the difficulty of a complete and perfect specification of all the cases of Executive authority would naturally dictate the use of general terms — and would render it improbable that a specification of certain particulars was designd [*sic*] as a substitute for those terms, when antecedently used. The different mode of expression employed in the constitution in regard to the two powers the Legislative and the Executive serves to confirm this inference. In the article which grants the legislative powers of the Governt. the expressions are — "*All legislative powers herein granted shall be vested in a Congress of the UStates;*" in that which grants the Executive Power the expressions are, as already quoted "The EXECUTIVE Po[WER] shall be vested in a President of the UStates of America."

The enumeration ought rather therefore to be considered as intended by way of greater caution, to specify and regulate the principal articles implied in the definition of Executive Power; leaving the rest to flow from the general grant of that power, interpreted in conformity to other parts [of] the constitution and to the principles of free government.

The general doctrine then of our constitution is, that the EXECUTIVE POWER of the Nation is vested in the President; subject only to the *exceptions* and *qu[a]lifications* which are expressed in the instrument.

Two of these have been already noticed—the participation of the Senate in the appointment of Officers and the making of Treaties. A third remains to be mentioned the right of the Legislature "to declare war and grant letters of marque and reprisal."

With these exceptions the EXECUTIVE POWER of the Union is completely lodged in the President.

. . . .

The right of the Executive to receive ambassadors and other public Ministers may serve to illustrate the relative duties of the Executive and Legislative Departments. This right includes that of judging, in the case of a Revolution of Government in a foreign Country, whether the new rulers are competent organs of the National Will and ought to [be] recognised or not: And where a treaty antecedently exists between the UStates and such nation that right involves the power of giving operation or not to such treaty. For until the new Government is *acknowledged*, the treaties between the nations, as far at least as regards *public* rights, are of course suspended.

This power of determ[in]ing virtually in the case supposed upon the operation of national Treaties as a consequence, of the power to receive ambassadors and other public Ministers, is an important instance of the right of the Executive to decide the obligations of the Nation with regard to foreign Nations.

. . . .

From the division of the Executive Power there results, in reference to it, a *concurrent* authority, in the distributed cases.

Hence in the case stated, though treaties can only be made by the President and Senate, their activity may be continued or suspended by the President alone.

No objection has been made to the Presidents [*sic*] having acknowledged the Republic of France, by the Reception of its Minister, without having consulted the Senate; though that body is connected with him in the making of Treaties, and though the consequence of his act of reception is to give operation to the Treaties heretofore made with that Country: But he is censured for having declared the UStates to be in a state of peace & neutrality, with regard to the Powers at War; because the right of *changing* that state & *declaring war* belongs to the Legislature.

It deserves to be remarked, that as the participation of the Senate in the making of Treaties and the power of the Legislature to declare war are exceptions out of the general "Executive Power" vested in the President, they are to be construed strictly—and ought to be extended no further than is essential to their execution.

While therefore the Legislature can alone declare war, can alone actually transfer the nation from a state of Peace to a state of War—it belongs to the "Executive Power," to do whatever else the laws of Nations cooperating with the Treaties of the Country enjoin, in the intercourse of the UStates with foreign Powers.

In this distribution of powers the wisdom of our Constitution is manifested. It is the province and duty of the Executive to preserve to the Nation the blessings of peace. The Legislature alone can interrupt those blessings, by placing the Nation in a state of War.

James Madison, *Letters of Helvidius, No. I*

Aug.–Sep. 1793, *reprinted in* 6 The Writings of James Madison, 138–40, 145–46, 148, 150 (Gaillard Hunt ed., 1906)

Several pieces with the signature of Pacificus were lately published, which have been read with singular pleasure and applause, by the foreigners and degenerate citizens among us, who hate our republican government, and the French revolution; whilst the publication seems to have been too little regarded, or too much despised by the steady friends to both.

. . . .

2. If we consult, for a moment, the nature and operation of the two powers to declare war and to make treaties, it will be impossible not to see, that they can never fall within a proper definition of executive powers. The natural province of the executive magistrate is to execute laws, as that of the legislature is to make laws. All his acts, therefore, properly executive, must presuppose the existence of the laws to be executed. A treaty is not an execution of laws: it does not presuppose the existence of laws. It is, on the contrary, to have itself the force of a *law*, and to be carried into *execution*, like all *other laws*, by the *executive magistrate*. To say then that the power of making treaties, which are confessedly laws, belongs naturally to the department which is to execute laws, is to say, that the executive department naturally includes a legislative power. In theory this is an absurdity—in practice a tyranny.

The power to declare war is subject to similar reasoning. A declaration that there shall be war, is not an execution of laws: it does not suppose pre-existing laws to be executed: it is not, in any respect, an act merely executive. It is, on the contrary, one of the most deliberate acts that can be performed; and when performed, has the effect of *repealing* all the *laws* operating in a state of peace, so far as they are inconsistent with a state of war; and of *enacting*, as a *rule for the executive*, a *new code* adapted to the relation between the society and its foreign enemy. In like manner, a conclusion of peace *annuls* all the *laws* peculiar to a state of war, and *revives* the general *laws* incident to a state of peace.

These remarks will be strengthened by adding, that treaties, particularly treaties of peace, have sometimes the effect of changing not only the external laws of the society, but operate also on the internal code, which is purely municipal, and to which the legislative authority of the country is of itself competent and complete.

From this view of the subject it must be evident, that although the executive may be a convenient organ of preliminary communications with foreign governments, on the subjects of treaty or war; and the proper agent for carrying into execution the final determinations of the competent authority; yet it can have no pretensions, from the nature of the powers in question compared with the nature of the executive trust, to that essential agency which gives validity to such determinations.

It must be further evident, that if these powers be not in their nature purely legislative, they partake so much more of that, than of any other quality, that under a constitution leaving them to result to their most natural department, the legislature would be without a rival in its claim.

Another important inference to be noted is, that the powers of making war and treaty being substantially of a legislative, not an executive nature, the rule of interpreting exceptions strictly must narrow, instead of enlarging, executive pretensions on those subjects.

. . . .

So far the argument from the constitution is precisely in opposition to the doctrine. As little will be gained in its favour from a comparison of the two powers, with those particularly vested m the president alone.

As there are but few, it will be most satisfactory to review them one by one.

"The president shall be commander in chief of the army and navy of the United States, and of the militia when called into actual service of the United States."

There can be no relation worth examining between this power and the general power of making treaties. And instead of being analogous to the power of declaring war, it affords a striking illustration of the incompatibility of the two powers in the same hands. Those who are to *conduct a war* cannot in the nature of things, be proper or safe judges, whether a *war ought* to be *commenced, continued,* or *concluded.* They are barred from the latter functions by a great principle in free government, analogous to that which separates the sword from the purse, or the power of executing from the power of enacting laws.

. . . .

Thus it appears that by whatever standard we try this doctrine, it must be condemned as no less vicious in theory than it would be dangerous in practice. It is countenanced neither by the writers on law; nor by the nature of the powers themselves; nor by any general arrangements, or particular expressions, or plausible analogies, to be found in the constitution.

Whence then can the writer have borrowed it?

There is but one answer to this question.

The power of making treaties and the power of declaring war, are *royal prerogatives* in the *British government,* and are accordingly treated as *executive prerogatives* by *British commentators.*

––––––––––––

Another important figure from the early days of our history to embrace the "executive Power" clause as a grant to the President of constitutional authority to manage the nation's external intercourse was John Marshall of Virginia, who went on to distinction as perhaps the most famous Chief Justice of the United States. Before being named Secretary of State by John Adams, Marshall served one term in Congress as a Federalist. A respected orator, he was tasked by his party with delivering the final summation in the lengthy debate on a Republican resolution denouncing President Adams for having surrendered a British deserter named Thomas Nast (but characterized by the Republicans as in reality an American citizen named "Jonathan Robbins" born in Danbury, Connecticut) to Great Britain under an extradition clause in the Jay Treaty without judicial authorization. Marshall's extraordinary address was regarded for decades as among the nation's finest orations and was read by generations of school children along with the words of Patrick Henry and Thomas Jefferson. As we shall see, it was also quoted by the Supreme Court in the landmark 1936 case of *United States v. Curtiss-Wright Export Corp.*[12]

––––––––––––

12. United States v. Curtiss-Wright Export Corp., 299 U.S. 304 (1936).

Representative John Marshall (Fed. Va.)

10 ANNALS OF CONG. 613–15 (1800)

The President is the sole organ of the nation in its external relations, and its sole representative with foreign nations. Of consequence, the demand of a foreign nation can only be made on him.

He possesses the whole Executive power. He holds and directs the force of the nation. Of consequence, any act to be performed by the force of the nation is to be performed through him.

He is charged to execute the laws. A treaty is declared to be a law. He must then execute a treaty, where he, and he alone, possesses the means of executing it.....

The department which is entrusted with the whole foreign intercourse of the nation, with the negotiation of all its treaties, with the power of demanding a reciprocal performance of the article, which is accountable to the nation for the violation of its engagements with foreign nations, and for the consequences resulting from such violation, seems the proper department to be entrusted with the execution of a national contract like that under consideration.....

If, at any time, *policy* may temper the strict execution of the contract, where may that *political discretion* be placed so safely as in the department whose duty it is to understand precisely the state of the political intercourse and connexion between the United States and foreign nations, to understand the manner in which the particular stipulation is explained and performed by foreign nations, and to understand completely the state of the Union? ...

It is then demonstrated, that, according to the principles of the American Government, the question whether the nation has or has not bound itself to deliver up any individual, charged with having committed murder or forgery within the jurisdiction of Britain, is a question the power to decide which rests alone with the Executive department.... *In this respect, the President expresses constitutionally the will of the nation* ... This is no interference with judicial decisions, nor any invasion of the province of a court. It is the exercise of an indubitable and a Constitutional power.[13]

Republican leader Albert Gallatin had been charged by his party with rebutting Marshall's speech, but its brilliance left the Swiss-born Pennsylvanian speechless. Historian Albert Beveridge writes: "Marshall had convinced even Gallatin himself.... When the Virginian closed, Gallatin did not come forward to answer him as his fellow partisans had expected.... 'Answer it yourself,' exclaimed the Republican leader in his quaint foreign accent; 'for my

---

13. Note the similarity between Marshall's observation that "the President expresses constitutionally the will of the nation" in this area and the earlier statement by William Blackstone that "What is done by the royal authority, with regard to foreign powers, is the act of the whole nation...." There are major differences between the powers vested in the President over foreign affairs and those of the British king at the time the Constitution was written, but beyond the expressed checks set forth in the Constitution (for example, the negative given to Congress on declaring War and that given to one-third of the Senate on treaty ratification), it is clear that Marshall believed that the President had broad authority that neither depended upon authorization by Congress nor could be controlled by simple statute. *Cf.* Marbury v. Madison, 1 Cranch 137. 165 (1803).

part, I think it unanswerable'...."[14] The Republican resolution criticizing Adams was promptly defeated in the evenly-divided House by a vote of 61 to 35.[15]

Note

From these excerpts it becomes evident that the executive power, vested by the Constitution in the President, was widely understood to include a broad grant of all powers belonging to the federal government involving relations with the outside world that were not expressly vested in another branch and that exceptions to this principle were to be construed narrowly. This was, as we have seen, the view of the first President (Washington — who had also presided over the Constitutional Convention), all three authors of the *Federalist Papers* (Jay, Madison, and Hamilton), the first Secretary of State (Jefferson — who later created the first "opposition" political party), the first and third Chief Justices, and a majority of both houses of the First Congress (who implicitly embraced Madison's argument about the breadth of the executive power clause in rejecting any Senate role in removal from office save by impeachment). It is remarkable that most modern casebooks either ignore or marginalize this source of presidential authority.

It is true that Madison argued a different position as *Helvidius*, but at the time both he and Jefferson were essentially "forum shopping" — arguing that the decision belonged properly to Congress, because they realized Hamilton had persuaded Washington and they hoped their Republican friends, whom they expected to control the new Congress, would be more sympathetic to the French cause.[16]

Professor William Goldsmith writes of the *Pacificus-Helvidius* exchanges: "Historians have generally shied away from identifying the winner of this debate, but Hamilton's theory, with all of its dangers and pitfalls, has obviously been the theory and practice which has prevailed in this country, particularly in the modern period."[17] Goldsmith argues that President Washington set the stage for subsequent developments "by leaning more towards Hamilton's advice than heeding the warnings of Jefferson and Madison." He concludes:

> Washington and his successors have demonstrated that the American Constitution is not a straightjacket, and that the President is not constricted by the absence of specific grants of power to cover all situations. Jefferson finally learned this lesson through his own travail in the office, and he was forced to reject in practice what he had so fervently supported in theory. Hamilton, a man of practical affairs and of extraordinary insight into the administrative process, understood the freedom and scope which the Chief Executive required to carry out the laws and represent the sovereign interests of the nation. It is this concept that has prevailed in the practice of the presidency in foreign affairs and in other areas. Its limits are very real, but are fundamentally political and organic to the system, not legalistic.[18]

---

14. 2 ALBERT J. BEVERIDGE, THE LIFE OF JOHN MARSHALL 474–75 (1919). *See also* HENRY ADAMS, THE LIFE OF ALBERT GALLATIN 231–32 (1879).

15. 10 ANNALS OF CONG. 619 (1800).

16. *See, e.g.,* DUMAS MALONE, JEFFERSON AND THE ORDEAL OF LIBERTY 70–71 (1962); CHARLES MARION THOMAS, AMERICAN NEUTRALITY IN 1793, at 14–15, 37 (1931).

17. 1 WILLIAM M. GOLDSMITH, THE GROWTH OF PRESIDENTIAL POWER 404 (1974). *See also* QUINCY WRIGHT, THE CONTROL OF AMERICAN FOREIGN RELATIONS 136 (1922); ABRAHAM D. SOFAER, WAR, FOREIGN AFFAIRS AND CONSTITUTIONAL POWER 114–15 (1976).

18. GOLDSMITH, *supra* note 17, at 411–12. *See also,* Myres McDougal & Asher Lans, *Treaties and*

A Tradition of Legislative Deference

Before the Vietnam War became unpopular with the American people, Congress was historically deferential to executive preeminence in foreign and national security affairs (save those areas expressly granted to Congress or to the Senate by the Constitution). For example, in 1816 the newly-established Senate standing Committee on Foreign Relations said in a report:

> The President is the constitutional representative of the United States with regard to foreign nations. He manages our concerns with foreign nations and must necessarily be most competent to determine when, how, and upon what subjects negotiation may be urged with the greatest prospect of success. For his conduct he is responsible to the Constitution. The committee considers this responsibility the surest pledge for the faithful discharge of his duty. They think the interference of the Senate in the direction of foreign negotiations calculated to diminish that responsibility and thereby to impair the best security for the national safety. The nature of transactions with foreign nations, moreover, requires caution and unity of design, and their success frequently depends on secrecy and dispatch.[19]

An 1897 Senate document provided this description of the relative powers of the political branches with respect to the nation's external relations:

Memorandum Upon the Power to Recognize the Independence of a New Foreign State
6–7, S. Doc. 54-56, 54th Cong., 2d. Sess. (1897)

It is to be remembered that effective intervention in foreign affairs sometimes requires the cooperation of other nations, while on the other hand, the expectancy of future intervention sometimes stirs up foreign governments to take preventive measures. Intervention, like other matters of diplomacy, sometimes calls for secret preparation, careful choice of the opportune moment, and swift action. It was because of these facts that *the superintendence of foreign affairs was intrusted to the executive and not to the legislative branch of the Government*.... [O]ur Constitution gave the President power to send and receive ministers ... [etc.]. These grants confirm the *executive character* of the proceedings, and indicate *an intent to give all the power to the President, which the Federal Government itself was to possess—the general control of foreign relations*.... That this is a great power is true; but it is a power which all great governments should have; and, being executive in the conception of the founders, and even from its very nature *incapable of practical exercise by deliberative assemblies*, was given to the President.

———————

There have, however, from time to time been exceptions to this deferential attitude. In 1906 Senator Augustus Bacon, of Georgia, introduced a resolution calling upon President Roosevelt to provide the Senate with negotiating instructions and other background

———————

Congressional-Executive or Presidential Agreements: Interchangeable Instruments of National Policy, 54 YALE L.J. 181, 249 (1945).

19. 299 U.S. at 319 (1936), which cites United States Senate Reports, Committee on Foreign Relations, VIII, 24, *quoted in* EDWARD S. CORWIN, THE PRESIDENT: OFFICE AND POWERS: 1787–1957, at 411.

materials pertaining to U.S. relations with Morocco. The proposal was strongly resisted by Wisconsin's Senator John Coit Spooner, a three-term Senator and member of the Foreign Relations Committee. Because Senator Spooner was regarded as one of the preeminent constitutional lawyers of his era,[20] his remarks took on an added importance.

Statement of Sen. John C. Spooner
40 Cong. Rec. 1417–20 (1906)

The Senate has nothing whatever to do with the *negotiation* of treaties or the conduct of our foreign intercourse and relations save the exercise of the one constitutional function of advice and consent which the Constitution requires as a precedent condition to the making of a treaty. Except as to the participation in the treaty-making power the Senate, under the Constitution, has obviously neither responsibilities nor power.

From the foundation of the Government it has been conceded in practice and in theory that the Constitution vests the power of negotiation and the various phases—and they are multifarious—of the conduct of our foreign relations exclusively in the President. And, Mr. President, he does not exercise that constitutional power, nor can he be made to do it, under the tutelage or guardianship of the Senate or of the House or of the Senate and House combined.

I do not deny the power of the Senate either in legislative session or in executive session—that is a question of propriety—to pass a resolution expressive of its opinion as to matters of foreign policy. But if it is passed by the Senate or by the House or by both Houses it is beyond any possible question purely advisory, and not in the slightest degree binding in law or conscience upon the President....

Mr. President, I do not stop at this moment to cite authorities in support of the proposition, that so far as the conduct of our foreign relations is concerned, excluding only the Senate's participation in the making of treaties, the President has the absolute and uncontrolled and uncontrollable authority. Under the confederation there was felt to be great weakness in a system that made the Congress the organ of communication with foreign governments; but when the Constitution was formed, it being almost everywhere else in the world a purely executive function, it was lodged with the President. He was given the power, with all other Executive functions, "to receive ambassadors and other public ministers." His exercise of that function can not, under the Constitution, be controlled by any other body in the Government.

. . . .

The President is so supreme under the Constitution in the matter of treaties, excluding only the Senate's ratification, that he may negotiate a treaty, he may send it to the Senate, it may receive by way of "advice and consent" the unanimous judgment of the Senate that it is in the highest degree for the public interest and yet the President is as free when it is sent back to the White House with resolution of ratification attached, to put it in his desk never again to see the light of day as he was free to determine in the first instance whether he would or would not negotiate it. That power is not expressly given to the President by the Constitution, but it inheres in the executive power conferred upon him to conduct our foreign relations, and it is a power which inheres in him as the sole organ under the

---

20. *See, e.g.,* Clarence Berdahl, War Powers Of The Executive In The United States 245 (1921).

Constitution through whom our foreign relations and diplomatic intercourse are conducted....

Mr. President, the three great coordinate branches of this Government are made by the Constitution independent of each other except where the Constitution provides otherwise. We have no right to assume the exercise of any executive power save under the Constitution. We can not assume judicial functions. The President may not assume judicial functions. The President may not assume legislative functions. We as the Senate, a part of the treaty making powers, have no more right under the Constitution to invade the prerogative of the President to deal with our foreign relations, to conduct them, to negotiate treaties, and that is not all — the conduct of our foreign relations is not limited to the negotiation of treaties — we have no more right under the Constitution to invade that prerogative than he has to invade the prerogative of legislation.

....

... The act creating the Department of State, in 1789, was an exception to the acts creating the other Departments of the Government. I will not stop to refer to the language of it or to any of the discussions in regard to it, but it is a Department that is not required to make any reports to Congress. It is a Department which from the beginning the Senate has never assumed the right to direct or control, except as to clearly defined matters relating to duty imposed by statute and not connected with the conduct of our foreign relations.

We *direct* all the other heads of Departments to transmit to the Senate designated papers or information. We do not address directions to the Secretary of State, nor do we direct requests, even, to the Secretary of State. We direct requests to the real head of that Department, the President of the United States, and, as a matter of courtesy, we add the qualifying words, "if in his judgment not incompatible with the public interest."

What does the conduct of our foreign relations involve? Does it involve simply, do Senators think, the negotiation of treaties? It involves keeping a watchful eye upon every point under the bending sky where an American interest is involved, where the American flag and citizens of the United States are to be found on sea and on land, every movement in foreign courts which might invade some American interest.

Senator Henry Cabot Lodge (a Harvard Law School graduate) took the floor following Senator Spooner's speech and stated: "Mr. President, I do not think that it is possible for anybody to make any addition to the masterly statement in regard to the powers of the President in treaty making ... [that] we have heard from the Senator from Wisconsin."[21] Even Senator Bacon acknowledged that the Senate's claim to the information in question was based not upon "legal right," but upon "courtesy" between the President and the Senate.[22]

Congressional deference to the President in this area continued until the Vietnam War became unpopular. Consider, for example, this lecture given at Cornell Law School on the eve of that conflict by Senate Foreign Relations Committee Chairman J. William Fulbright, who a few years later would champion a virtual revolution in Congress challenging the President's constitutional authority in foreign affairs.

---

21. 40 Cong. Rec. 1431 (1906).
22. *See* Edward S. Corwin, The President: Office and Powers: 1787–1957, at 182 (1984).

Senator J. William Fulbright, *American Foreign Policy in the 20th Century Under an 18th-Century Constitution*

47 Cornell L. Q. 1, 3 (1961) (emphasis in original)

The pre-eminent *responsibility* of the President for the formulation and conduct of American foreign policy is clear and unalterable. He has, as Alexander Hamilton defined it, all powers in international affairs "which the Constitution does not vest elsewhere in clear terms." He possesses sole authority to communicate and negotiate with foreign powers. He controls the external aspects of the Nation's power, which can be moved by his will alone — the armed forces, the diplomatic corps, the Central Intelligence Agency, and all of the vast executive apparatus. As Commander-in-Chief of the armed forces, the President has full responsibility, which cannot be shared, for military decisions in a world in which the difference between safety and cataclysm can be a matter of hours or even minutes. The President is the symbol of the nation to the external world, the leader of a vast alliance of free nations, and the prime mover in shaping a national consensus on foreign policy. It is important to note, however, that while this responsibility is indeed very broad, his authority is often infringed upon or thwarted in practice by unauthorized persons.

The war in Vietnam will be considered briefly in the next chapter. But it is important here to understand that controversies involving the war largely poisoned legislative-executive relations for many years and led to a dramatic increase in legislation designed to control the conduct of the nation's external relations. As just one example of many to illustrate this point, the congressional publication *Legislation on Foreign Relations* grew from a single volume of 658 pages in 1968 to five volumes of more than 1,000 pages *each* by 1988. Some of these laws are discussed in other chapters of this book. For present purposes, it is important to be aware that — for better or worse — the Vietnam experience produced a dramatic increase in legislation in areas traditionally recognized by Congress as being entrusted by the Constitution to the President.

Congress and "The Business of Intelligence"

As will be discussed in chapter 24, the Founding Fathers did not foresee an oversight role for Congress over intelligence programs and activities. When in 1776 the Committee of Secret Correspondence under the Second Continental Congress learned that France had agreed to provide covert support to the American Revolution, Benjamin Franklin and the other members unanimously agreed that they could not share the good news with others in Congress — because Congress had repeatedly demonstrated it could not be trusted to safeguard secrets.

Writing in *Federalist* No. 64 a dozen years later, John Jay noted that there would be valuable sources of foreign intelligence willing to confide in the secrecy of the president, but not in that of the Senate or Congress. Therefore, he explained, the Constitution had left the president "able to manage the business of intelligence as prudence may suggest." This deference to the Executive regarding intelligence, military, and diplomatic secrets was reflected in early appropriations laws, which allowed the president to account simply for the *amount* of appropriations when he felt their purpose ought not be made public.

In an 1818 debate on the floor of the House of Representatives concerning a reported diplomatic mission to South America by people who had not been confirmed as diplomats by the Senate, the legendary Henry Clay noted "[t]here was a contingent fund of $50,000 allowed to the President by law, which he was authorized to expend without rendering to Congress any account of it." Clay added that if the president had funded the mission in question from that account, "it would not have been a proper subject for inquiry" by Congress.[23]

Consistent with this background, American presidents historically held most details pertaining to sensitive intelligence matters close to the vest, and even appropriations for intelligence activities were often concealed within military appropriations with only a small number of congressional leaders even being aware of that fact. In 1968, when Congress enacted the first wiretap statute, it provided: "Nothing contained in this chapter ... shall limit the *constitutional power of the President* to take such measures as he deems necessary ... to obtain foreign intelligence information...."[24]

The courts were equally deferential to the president in this area. Thus, when the Supreme Court in 1967 held that telephone wiretaps were a constitutional "seizure" under the Fourth Amendment and thus required a judicial warrant, it included a footnote emphasizing that its holding did not address the issue of presidentially authorized wiretaps for national security purposes.[25] This exception was narrowed in the 1972 "Keith case," discussed in chapter 26, which held that a warrant was required for a search in a national security investigation in the absence of any ties to a foreign power. But, speaking for a unanimous Court, Justice Powell repeatedly emphasized that the holding did not limit the president's power to authorize wiretaps for "*foreign* intelligence" purposes.[26]

Lower courts consistently held that there was a "foreign intelligence exception"[27] to the Fourth Amendment. But in 1978, Congress enacted the Foreign Intelligence Surveillance Act (FISA)—which is the subject of chapter 27 in this book. As you read that chapter, you might give some thought to the constitutional basis for congressional control over foreign intelligence surveillance in light of prior executive, legislative, and judicial behavior. Some in Congress explained that they were merely carrying out a suggestion from the Supreme Court, noting that in 1972 Justice Powell had written for a unanimous Court:

> Given these potential distinctions between Title III criminal surveillances and those involving the *domestic* security, Congress may wish to consider protective standards for the latter which differ from those already prescribed for specified crimes in Title III. Different standards may be compatible with the Fourth Amendment if they are reasonable both in relation to the legitimate need of Government for intelligence information and the protected rights of our citizens. For the warrant application may vary according to the governmental interest to be enforced and the nature of citizen rights deserving protection.[28]

But Justice Powell was clearly talking about writing new standards for "domestic" surveillance, not setting up a congressional regime for limiting presidential control over the collection of "foreign" intelligence. When the FISA statute was enacted in 1978 it created

---

23. 32 Annals of Cong. 1466 (1818).

24. Omnibus Crime Control and Safe Streets Act of 1968, 18 U.S.C. § 2511(3)(emphasis added).

25. Katz v. United States, 389 U.S. 347 (1967), fn. 23 ("*Whether safeguards other than prior authorization by a magistrate would satisfy the Fourth Amendment in a situation involving the national security is a question not presented by this case.*").

26. United States v. United States District Court, 407 U.S. 297, 321–22 (1972)(emphasis added).

27. *See, e.g.,* United States v. Truong, 629 F.2d 908 (1980).

28. United States v. United States District Court, 407 U.S. 297 at 322–23 (emphasis added).

an appellate court known as the Foreign Intelligence Surveillance Court of Review, which in 2002 unanimously declared:

> The *Truong* court, as did all the other courts to have decided the issue, held that the President did have inherent authority to conduct warrantless searches to obtain foreign intelligence information.... We take for granted that the President does have that authority and, assuming that is so, FISA could not encroach on the President's constitutional power.[29]

Using the Power of the Purse to Constrain Executive Discretion

As Congress has sought to increase its authority over military operations and deployments, and to play a role in sensitive areas like intelligence that were historically seen as the exclusive province of the Executive,[30] presidents have understandably resisted what was often seen as a usurpation of presidential power. Lacking an explicit grant of authority over such issues as intelligence, diplomacy, and the conduct of military operations, Congress has relied upon the language in Article I, Section 9, of the Constitution providing that "[n]o Money shall be drawn from the Treasury, but in Consequence of Appropriations made by Law...." As the following summary—prepared by a scholar and national defense specialist with the Foreign Affairs and National Defense Division of the Library of Congress's Congressional Research Service—explains, in the modern era, purse-string restrictions on U.S. foreign policy have become quite commonplace.

Richard F. Grimmett, *Foreign Policy Roles of the President and Congress*
(1999), *available at* <http://fpc.state.gov/6172.htm>

....

Legislative Restrictions/Funding Denials

Congress has been most visible in its foreign policy role when it has placed legislation prohibitions or other limitations on the President's freedom of action in foreign affairs. Often these measures have been amendments to legislation authorizing or appropriating funds that the President was unlikely to veto. The use of funding restrictions or denials by Congress is a classic illustration of the "power of the purse" under the Constitution. Unlike other legislative action by Congress, its use is not subject to serious challenge by the President as an unconstitutional infringement on the President's foreign policy powers. Major legislative-executive confrontations have occurred when such restrictions have been passed despite the opposition of the President. Some examples follow.

On January 23, 1973, President Nixon announced the signing of the Paris peace accords to end U.S. involvement in the Vietnam war, but attacks by the Khmer Rouge in Cambodia continued and the United States resumed bombing in Cambodia. The Administration wanted to maintain freedom of U.S. action if North Vietnam or its Communist associates violated the accords. But Congress effectively halted such military action when it passed over the President's opposition amendments to funding legislation stating that after August

29. *In re Sealed Case*, 310 F.3d 717, 742 Foreign Int. Surv. Ct. Rev., Nov. 18, 2002 (No. 02-002, 02-001).
30. *See, e.g.*, FEDERALIST No. 64, at 432 (John Jay) (Jacob Cooke ed., 1961), in which John Jay explained that under the proposed new Constitution "the president ... will be able to manage the business of intelligence in such manner as prudence may suggest."

15, 1973, no funds under any legislation could be used to finance combat activities by United States military forces in, over, or from off the shores of North Vietnam, South Vietnam, Laos or Cambodia.

In 1974 the Nixon Administration was pursuing a policy of normalizing trade relations with the Soviet Union as part of the broader policy of detente. Against the wishes of the Administration, Congress passed amendments to the Trade Act of 1974 which limited the amount of Export-Import Bank credits to the Soviet Union to $300 million and made the granting of most-favored-nation treatment conditional upon Soviet adoption of more liberal emigration policies. Subsequently the Soviet Union stated that because of such restrictions it would not put into force the trade agreement which the United States signed in 1972.

In early 1976, when the United States was supplying covert assistance through the Central Intelligence Agency to factions in Angola against an Angolan movement supported by Cuban troops and Soviet military assistance, Congress prohibited any kind of U.S. assistance to Angola unless expressly authorized by Congress. This provision, known as the Clark amendment, forced the Administration to end U.S. aid. Congress repealed the amendment in 1985.

Throughout the Reagan Administration, Congress legislated numerous restrictions and limitations on military assistance to Central American countries. In 1983, for example, it limited the amount that could be spent on U.S. intelligence activities supporting military or paramilitary activities in Nicaragua. In 1987, after the Central American governments signed a peace accord, Congress cut off military assistance to the Nicaraguan Contras (anti-Sandinista guerillas), and in 1988 permitted only non-lethal assistance.

In 1992, Congress prohibited the testing of any nuclear weapon until July 1, 1993, and permitted using funds for nuclear tests after that time only in accord with strict guidelines and conditions, including a plan for achieving a multilateral comprehensive test ban.

In 1993, Congress established a deadline for U.S. troops to leave Somalia. No funds could be used for military action after March 31, 1994, unless the President requested an extension from Congress and received legislative authority.

On March 12, 1996, President Clinton signed into law, H.R. 927, the Cuban Liberty and Democracy Solidarity Act,[31] often referred to as the Helms Burton Act. This legislation, among other things, codifies all existing Cuban embargo Executive orders and regulations. This law does not provide for a Presidential waiver of any of these codified embargo provisions. The legislation also allows U.S. nationals to sue for money damages in U.S. Federal Court those persons that traffic in property confiscated in Cuba. The President can waive this provision for six-month periods of time. The legislation further denies admission to the U. S. of aliens involved in the confiscation of U.S. property in Cuba or in the trafficking of confiscated U.S. property in Cuba. The Helms-Burton legislation has a direct and important effect on U.S. Cuban policy and was strongly opposed by the Clinton Administration prior to its enactment.

In 1996, Congress passed H.R. 3107, legislation that would impose U.S. sanctions on foreign companies that invested in energy production in Libya or Iran, or sold certain products to Libya. The legislation, the Iran and Libya Sanctions Act of 1996, was signed into law by President Clinton on August 5, 1996 (P.L. 104172).[32]

---

31. Cuban Liberty and Democracy Solidarity Act, P.L. 104-114 (1996).
32. Iran and Libya Sanctions Act of 1996, P.L. 104172.

Some of these constraints are unremarkable because they involve expressed exceptions to the general grant of "executive Power" to the President, such as the power conferred on Congress by Article I, Section 8, of the Constitution: "[t]o regulate Commerce with foreign Nations...." But others are more problematic, as the following excerpt explains.

Robert F. Turner, *The Power of the Purse*

in The Constitution and National Security 73, 84–93
(Howard E. Shuman & Walter R. Thomas eds., 1990)

....

Some would argue that the power of the purse is "different" from other powers. People who take this position often seek authority from *Hart's Case*, an 1880 opinion in which the U.S. Court of Claims stated that "The absolute control of the moneys of the United States is in Congress, and Congress is responsible for its exercise of this great power only to the people." This is admittedly strong language, however the court itself distinguished the case from the situation we are discussing by noting that the statute in question "impinged upon no function intrusted by the Constitution to the Executive."

A far more useful precedent is the 1946 Supreme Court decision in *United States v. Lovett.* During World War II an amendment was attached to an appropriations act providing that no salary or compensation should be paid out of any appropriated funds to three named government employees—apparently thought by some to be Communists—unless they were subsequently appointed to new positions with the consent of the Senate. President Roosevelt was forced to accept the amendment in order to obtain funds to fight the war, but in signing the law he expressed the view that the provision was unconstitutional. It was challenged in the courts, and Congress responded by sending its counsel to argue "that this involved simply an exercise of congressional powers over appropriations, which are plenary and not subject to judicial control." The Court emphatically rejected this argument, reasoning:

> We ... cannot conclude, as [Counsel for Congress] urges, that [the section] is a mere appropriation measure, and that, since Congress under the Constitution has complete control over appropriations, a challenge to the measure's constitutionality does not present a justiciable question in the courts, but is merely a political issue over which Congress had final say.... We hold that [the section] falls precisely within the category of congressional actions which the Constitution barred by providing that "No Bill of Attainder or ex post facto Law shall be passed."

By vesting in Congress only those "legislative powers herein granted," and vesting in the President "the executive power," it would seem equally clear that Congress could not use its power of the purse to indirectly exercise or circumscribe Executive national security powers.

In addition to these decisions of the Supreme Court, over the years various Attorneys General have issued opinions asserting the unconstitutionality of various statutory initiatives aimed at using the "power of the purse" to infringe upon the independent powers of the President.

A Tradition of Legislative Deference

The question of using conditional appropriations to instruct or control the actions of the President or his Executive branch subordinates in the national security field is not a new one. What is different about the post-Vietnam era is that Congress has departed from the traditional legislative viewpoint that such constraints are improper. A thorough discussion of this practice is beyond the scope of this short paper, but a few examples should suffice to illustrate the traditional viewpoint.

Although the Constitution requires that "a regular Statement and Account of the Receipts and Expenditures of all public Money shall be published from time to time," when the First Congress on 1 July 1790 appropriated funds for foreign affairs the statute provided in part:

> [T]he President shall account specifically for all such expenditures of the said money as in his judgment may be made public, and also for the amount of such expenditures as he may think it advisable not to specify, and cause a regular statement and account thereof to be laid before Congress annually....

Thomas Jefferson is viewed by many as having been the champion of strong legislative authority and in principle an opponent of overly broad appropriations acts; yet Jefferson recognized that the field of foreign affairs was unique. In a 19 February 1804 letter to Secretary of the Treasury Albert Gallatin, President Jefferson wrote:

> The Constitution has made the Executive the organ for managing our intercourse with foreign nations.... The Executive being thus charged with the foreign intercourse, no law has undertaken to prescribe its specific duties.... Under ... two standing provisions there is annually a sum appropriated for the expenses of intercourse with foreign nations. The purposes of the appropriation being expressed by the law, in terms as general as the duties are by the Constitution, the application of the money is left as much to the discretion of the Executive, as the performance of the duties.... From the origin of the present government to this day, the construction of the laws, and the practice under them, has been to consider the whole fund ... as under the discretion of the President as to the persons he should commission to serve the United States in foreign parts, and all the expenses incident to the business in which they may be employed.... [I]t has been the uniform opinion and practice that the whole foreign fund was placed by the Legislature on the footing of a contingent fund, in which they undertake no specifications, but leave the whole to the discretion of the President.

One of the great early debates on the question of conditional appropriations for foreign affairs occurred in April, 1826, when Representative Louis McLane, of Delaware, proposed attaching an amendment to a bill appropriating funds for a diplomatic mission to Panama expressing the "opinion" of the House that the U.S. delegates "ought not be authorized to discuss ... any proposition of alliance ... between this country and any of the South American Governments...." Representative Daniel Webster — one of the foremost constitutional scholars of his era — spoke against this proposal on constitutional grounds:

> There is no doubt that we have the power, if we see fit to exercise it, to break up the mission, by withholding the salaries; we have power also to break up the Court, by withholding the salaries of the Judges, or to break up the office of the President, by withholding the salary provided for it by law. All these things, it is true, we have the power to do, since we hold the keys of the Treasury. But, then can we rightfully exercise this power? ... For myself, I feel bound not to step out of my own sphere, and neither to exercise nor control any authority, of which the Constitution has intended to lodge the free and unconstrained exercise in other hands....
>
> This measure comes from the Executive, and it is an appropriate exercise of Executive power. How is it, then, that we are to consider it as entirely an open question for us, as if it were a legislative measure originating with ourselves? ... The process of the gentleman's argument appears to me as singular as its

conclusion. He founds himself on the legal maxim, that he who has the power to give, may annex whatever condition or qualifications to the gift he chooses. This maxim, sir, would be applicable to the present case, if we were the sovereign of the country; if all power were in our hands; if the public money were entirely our own; if our appropriation of it were mere grace and favor; and if there were no restraints upon us, but our own sovereign will and pleasure. But the argument totally forgets that we are ourselves but public agents. . . .

The President is not our agent, but, like ourselves, the agent of the People. They have trusted to his hands the proper duties of his office; and we are not to take those duties out of his hands, from any opinion of our own that we should execute them better ourselves.

From time to time over the next 150 years efforts were made in Congress to use conditional appropriations to control the President's national security powers, and such efforts were typically defeated by voice vote following statements by more senior legislators recognizing the constitutional defects of the approach. Consider, for example, this 1928 exchange between newly elected Senator John Blaine of Wisconsin, and Senate Foreign Relations Committee Chairman William Borah:

Mr. Borah: Mr. President, the Constitution of the United States has delegated certain powers to the President; it has delegated certain powers to Congress and certain powers to the judiciary. Congress can not exercise judicial powers or take them away from the courts. Congress can not exercise executive power specifically granted or take it away from the President. The President's powers are defined by the Constitution. Whatever power belongs to the President by virtue of constitutional provisions, Congress can not take away from him. In other words, Congress can not take away from the President the power to command the Army and the Navy of the United States. . . . Those are powers delegated to the President by the Constitution of the United States, and the Congress is bound by the terms of the Constitution.

Mr. Blaine: Another question. All that the Senator has said in a general way is sound constitutional law, but before there can be any action on the part of any Government unit requiring the expenditure of funds that are in the Public Treasury, or that may be placed in the Public Treasury, Congress must first act and make an appropriation for every essential purpose. That money so appropriated can be used for no other purpose than that designated by Congress, and there is no power that can coerce Congress into making an appropriation. Therefore, Congress's power over matters respecting the making of war unlawfully, beyond the power of the President, outside of the Constitution or within the Constitution, or conducting hostilities in the nature of the war during peace time, can be limited and regulated under the power of Congress to appropriate money.

Mr. Borah: Of course, I do not disagree with the proposition that if Congress does not create an army, or does not provide for an army, or create a navy, the President can not exercise his control or command over an army or navy which does not exist. But once an army is created, once a navy is in existence, the right to command belongs to the President, and the Congress can not take the power away from him.

Modern Scholarly Opinion

Until quite recently there appeared to be a widespread consensus among constitutional scholars that Congress could not use conditional appropriations to regulate the President's conduct of foreign and national security affairs. In the interest of space, I shall mention but two examples.

Professor Quincy Wright was one of the preeminent American scholars in the field for nearly four decades. In addition to serving as President of the American Political Science Association and the International Political Science Association, Professor Wright served as President of the American Society of International Law. In his 1922 landmark study, *The Control of American Foreign Relations*, he explained:

> In foreign relations, however, the President exercises discretion, both as to the means and to the ends of policy. He exercises a discretion, very little limited by directory laws, in the method of carrying out foreign policy. He has moved the navy and the marines at will all over the world.... Though Congress has legislated on broad lines for the conduct of these services it has descended to much less detail than in the case of services operative in the territory of the United States. In foreign affairs the President, also, has a constitutional discretion as the representative organ and as commander-in-chief which cannot be taken away by Congress and because of the extraterritorial character of most of his action, his subordinates are not generally subject to judicial control.
>
> But more than this he has initiated foreign policies, even those leading to treaties and those leading to war, and has generally actively pushed these policies when the cooperation of other organs of government is necessary for their carrying out. Though Congress may by resolution suggest policies, its resolutions are not mandatory and the President has on occasion ignored them. Ultimately, however, his power is limited by the possibility of a veto upon matured policies, by the Senate in the case of treaties, by Congress in the case of war.

A more recent study by Columbia Law Professor Louis Henkin, *Foreign Affairs and the Constitution*, provides this analysis:

> *"Unconstitutional conditions"*
>
> Congress has attempted to influence the conduct of the President, and of other governments, by imposing "conditions," especially on spending and appropriations....
>
> The constitutional lawyer would distinguish between different appropriations and between different conditions. If Congress cannot properly withhold appropriations for the President's activities, it ought not be able to impose conditions on such appropriations. Even when Congress is free not to appropriate, it ought not be able to regulate Presidential action by conditions on the appropriation of funds to carry it out, if it could not regulate the action directly. So, should Congress provide that appropriated funds shall not be used to pay the salaries of State Department officials who promote a particular policy or treaty, the President would no doubt feel free to disregard the limitation, as he has "riders" purporting to instruct delegations to international conferences.

Conclusion

The architects of the Constitution understood that legislative bodies lack the unity of design, speed, and secrecy essential for the effective conduct of foreign affairs; and they intentionally gave the President the bulk of the responsibility for these activities. As Professor Quincy Wright observed: "[W]hen the constitutional convention gave 'executive power' to the President, the foreign relations power was the essential element in the grant...." To protect against Executive abuse, checks in the form of a Senate veto over proposed treaties and a legislative veto over declarations of war were incorporated in the design. As exceptions to the general grant of executive power to the President, these legislative powers were to be construed narrowly. If the recent feuding between Congress and the President over the conduct of national security policy has served no other useful purpose, it has at least affirmed the great wisdom of the Founding Fathers in their realization that legislative bodies lack the necessary attributes for successful foreign intercourse.

There is a growing realization in this country that Congress is breaking the law by some of its enactments attempting to control the President's conduct in the realm of foreign and military affairs. The post-Vietnam explosion of legislative restrictions in this critical field is unprecedented and is contrary both to the intentions of the Founding Fathers and to nearly two centuries of constitutional practice. Even when the Supreme Court has struck down as unconstitutional fundamental provisions of many of these laws — as it did by implication in the 1983 case of *I.N.S. v. Chadha* — Congress continues to leave the statutes on the books in flagrant disrespect of the oath taken by each of its members to support the Constitution.

With the recognition that Congress may not directly exercise national security powers vested by the Constitution in the President, a search has begun for indirect means of accomplishing this same end. The favored contemporary approach is by conditional appropriations. To the extent that Congress seeks through the use of conditional appropriations to exercise indirectly powers vested by the Constitution in the President, or to deny the President his constitutional discretion vis-à-vis such powers, its conduct is a threat to our constitutional system of separation of powers.

Congressional fears that the President's independent national security powers are subject to abuse are perhaps understandable, although in my view charges of Executive abuse in recent decades are generally overstated. But the Constitution includes protections against abuses of executive power. The President may not, for example, initiate an offensive "war" without formal approval of both houses of Congress. If he violates this prohibition, he is subject to impeachment. The Constitution makes no provision for anticipatory breach of its fundamental provisions by the Congress on the grounds that the President's constitutional powers might ultimately be abused.

Consider, for a moment, the frightening consequences of upholding the alleged power of Congress to use conditional appropriations to seize control over the President's commander in chief or other executive constitutional powers. Are there any limits to such a power? If Congress were permitted to tie any conditions it wished to impose on the Executive to approval of the President's salary or the basic appropriations for key government departments, would there remain any separation between the two political branches? Might not appropriations for the Defense Department be conditioned upon the President's agreement to polish the shoes of the Speaker of the House upon demand, or to nominate a designated friend of the Speaker to serve as Secretary of Defense?

Fortunately, this claimed new authority in the "power of the purse" is unlikely to withstand judicial scrutiny. The courts must recognize that if the Congress is permitted to seize control over the independent constitutional powers of the Executive branch, the independence of the Judicial branch will soon disappear as well. After all, the judiciary needs appropriated funds to pay salaries and rent, to hire marshals and publish opinions, and for numerous other purposes. If it recognizes in Congress a plenary power to use conditional appropriations to determine where troops shall be stationed or what terms shall be sought in negotiations, where lies its defense when Congress decides to destroy the power of judicial review by conditioning judicial appropriations upon certain statutes not being held unconstitutional? Put simply—under a constitutional regime of three separate, coequal, and independent branches—the courts must realize that they can not permit an assault on the independent powers of the Executive without leaving their own constitutional authority in jeopardy. Thus, the dangerous and historically discredited theory that Congress may control the President's independent national security powers by the use of conditional appropriations is highly unlikely to pass muster in the courts.

Questions for Discussion

1. What is the scope of the "power of the purse"? Does it allow Congress to exercise control over matters otherwise committed by the Constitution to the President's discretion? For example, the President's Article II, Section 3, power to "receive Ambassadors and other public Ministers" has been interpreted not only as exclusive authority to recognize foreign governments but also "to determine the policy which is to govern the question of recognition."[33] This includes not only discretion to decide which of competing "governments" to recognize as the lawful representative of a particular country, but also such issues as what boundary lines and what capital city to recognize. Under pressure from supporters of Israel, during the 1996 presidential election Congress passed the Jerusalem Embassy Act of 1995 conditioning 50 percent of appropriations for the Department of State beginning in FY 1999 upon the President's recognizing Jerusalem as the capital of Israel and moving the American Embassy from Tel Aviv to Jerusalem. Pub. L. 104-45, Sec. 6; 108 Stat. 398. Are you troubled by this?[34]

2. If Congress may use the "power of the purse" to condition funds for the conduct of foreign relations upon the President's surrendering his discretion as to where embassies are located or negotiating a particular treaty, or funds for military operations upon the President's not sending forces to a particular location, are there any limits on this power? For example, could Congress enact a "Supreme Court Neutralization Act" that prohibited the expenditure of any appropriated funds (or perhaps all funds beyond those necessary to pay the salaries of judges) by the Judiciary if any court held a particular statute—or, for that matter, *any* statute, or the practice of trying to legislate by concurrent resolution—to be unconstitutional? The Constitution makes no explicit provision for the doctrine of judicial review, which arguably results from Supreme Court *dicta* in *Marbury v. Madison*. If Congress can use its control of appropriations to usurp discretion vested in the other branches of government, can the doctrine of separation of powers survive?

The Role of the Courts

Many law students are surprised at the relative paucity of judicial opinions dealing with foreign policy. As will be discussed, many cases that are brought in this area are quickly dismissed because the plaintiffs lack standing, their alleged claims are not ripe or are moot, or the political questions doctrine persuades the courts to defer to the discretion of one or both of the political branches. But over the years the courts have provided useful guidance on issues related to this chapter.

---

33. United States. v. Pink, 315 U.S. 203, 229 (1942).

34. *See* Robert F. Turner, *Foreign Affairs Under the Constitution: Only President Can Move Embassy*, LEGAL TIMES, Jan. 22, 1996, at 46.

Separation of Powers and the Supreme Court

The Supreme Court has on numerous occasions considered the doctrine of separation of powers. The cases which follow provide a flavor of the ways in which the Court has viewed the constitutional relationship among the branches of the federal government over the years.

Marbury v. Madison
5 U.S. (1 Cranch.) 137, 165–66 (1803)

By the constitution of the United States, the President is invested with certain important political powers, in the exercise of which he is to use his own discretion, and is accountable only to his country in his political character, and to his own conscience. To aid him in the performance of these duties, he is authorized to appoint certain officers, who act by his authority and in conformity with his orders.

In such cases, their acts are his acts; and whatever opinion may be entertained of the manner in which executive discretion may be used, still there exists, and can exist, no power to control that discretion. The subjects are political. They respect the nation, not individual rights, and being intrusted to the executive, the decision of the executive is conclusive. The application of this remark will be perceived by adverting to the act of congress for establishing the department of foreign affairs. This officer, as his duties were prescribed by that act, is to conform precisely to the will of the President. He is the mere organ by whom that will is communicated. The acts of such an officer, as an officer, can never be examinable by the courts.

But when the legislature proceeds to impose on that officer other duties; when he is directed peremptorily to perform certain acts; when the rights of individuals are dependent on the performance of those acts; he is so far the officer of the law; is amenable to the laws for his conduct; and cannot at his discretion sport away the vested rights of others.

The conclusion from this reasoning is, that where the heads of departments are the political or confidential agents of the executive, merely to execute the will of the President, or rather to act in cases in which the executive possesses a constitutional or legal discretion, nothing can be more perfectly clear than that their acts are only politically examinable. But where a specific duty is assigned by law, and individual rights depend upon the performance of that duty, it seems equally clear that the individual who considers himself injured, has a right to resort to the laws of his country for a remedy.

Kendall v. United States
37 U.S. (12 Pet.) 524, 610 (1838)

The theory of the constitution undoubtedly is, that the great powers of the government are divided into separate departments; and so far as these powers are derived from the Constitution, the departments may be regarded as independent of each other. But beyond that, all are subject to regulations by law, touching the discharge of the duties required to be performed.

The executive power is vested in a President; and as far as his powers are derived from the constitution, he is beyond the reach of any other department, except in the mode prescribed by the constitution through the impeaching power.

Kilbourn v. Thompson

103 U.S. 168, 190–91 (1880)

It is believed to be one of the chief merits of the American system of written constitutional law, that all the powers intrusted to government, whether State or national, are divided into the three grand departments, the executive, the legislative, and the judicial. That the functions appropriate to each body of these branches of government shall be vested in a separate body of public servants, and that the perfection of the system requires that the lines which separate and divide these departments shall be broadly and clearly defined. It is also essential to the successful working of this system that the persons intrusted with power in any one of these branches shall not be permitted to encroach upon the powers confided to the others, but that each shall by the law of its creation be limited to the exercise of the powers appropriate to its own department and no other. To these general propositions there are in the Constitution of the United States some important exceptions. One of these is, that the President is so far made a part of the legislative power, that his assent is required to the enactment of all statutes and resolutions of Congress.

This, however, is so only to a limited extent, for a bill may become a law notwithstanding the refusal of the President to approve it, by a vote of two-thirds of each House of Congress.

So, also, the Senate is made a partaker in the functions of appointing officers and making treaties, which are supposed to be properly executive, by requiring its consent to the appointment of such officers and the ratification of treaties. The Senate also exercises the judicial power of trying impeachments, and the House of preferring articles of impeachment.

In the main, however, that instrument, the model on which are constructed the fundamental laws of the States, has blocked out with singular precision, and in bold lines, in its three primary articles, the allotment of power to the executive, the legislative, and the judicial departments of the government. It also remains true, as a general rule, that the powers confided by the Constitution to one of these departments cannot be exercised by another.

It may be said that these are truisms which need no repetition here to give them force. But while the experience of almost a century has in general shown a wise and commendable forbearance in each of these branches from encroachments upon the others, it is not to be denied that such attempts have been made, and it is believed not always without success.

Evans v. Gore

253 U.S. 245, 247, 249 (1920)

The Constitution establishes three great coordinate departments of the National Government — the legislative, the executive, and the judicial, and distributes among them the powers confided to that Government by the people. Each department is dealt with in a separate Article, the legislative in the first, the executive in the second and the judicial in the third. . . .

. . . .

The Constitution was framed on the fundamental theory that a larger measure of liberty and justice would be assured by vesting the three great powers, — the legislative, the executive, and the judicial, — in separate departments, each relatively independent of the others; and it was recognized that without this independence — if it was not made both real and enduring — the separation would fail of its purpose. All agreed that restraints and checks must be imposed to secure the requisite measure of independence; for otherwise the legislative department, inherently the strongest, might encroach on or even come to dominate the others, and the judicial, naturally the weakest, might be dwarfed or swayed by the other two, especially by the legislative.

Myers v. United States
272 U.S. 52, 106, 116–18, 127–28, 163–64 (1926)

Mr. Chief Justice Taft delivered the opinion of the Court.

. . . .

[During congressional debate, Representative James Madison said]:

"If there is a principle in our Constitution, indeed in any free Constitution, more sacred than another, it is that which separates the Legislative, Executive and Judicial powers. If there is any point in which the separation of the Legislative and Executive powers ought to be maintained with great caution, it is that which relates to officers and offices." 1 Annals of Congress, 581.

Their union under the Confederation had not worked well, as the members of the convention knew. Montesquieu's view that the maintenance of independence as between the legislative, the executive and the judicial branches was a security for the people had their full approval. Madison in the Convention, 2 Farrand, Records of the Federal Convention, 56. *Kendall v. United States*, 12 Peters 524, 610. Accordingly, the Constitution was so framed as to vest in the Congress all legislative powers therein granted, to vest in the President the executive power, and to vest in one Supreme Court and such inferior courts as Congress might establish, the judicial power. From this division on principle, the reasonable construction of the Constitution must be that the branches should be kept separate in all cases in which they were not expressly blended, and the Constitution should be expounded to blend them no more than it affirmatively requires. Madison, 1 Annals of Congress, 497. This rule of construction has been confirmed by this court in *Meriwether v. Garett*, 102 U.S. 472, 515; *Kilbourn v. Thompson*, 103 U.S. 168, 190; *Mugler v. Kansas*, 123 U.S. 623, 662.

The debates in the Constitutional Convention indicated an intention to create a strong Executive and after a controversial discussion the executive power of the Government was vested in one person and many of his important functions were specified so as to avoid the humiliating weakness of the Congress during the Revolution and under the Articles of Confederation. 1 Farrand, 66–97.

. . . .

The requirement of the second section of Article II that the Senate should advise and consent to the Presidential appointments, was to be strictly construed. The words of section 2, following the general grant of executive power under section 1, were either an enumeration and emphasis of specific functions of the Executive, not all inclusive, or were limitations upon the general grant of the executive power, and as such, being limitations, should not be enlarged beyond the words used. Madison, 1 Annals, 462, 463, 464. The executive power was given in general terms, strengthened by specific terms where emphasis was regarded as appropriate, and was limited by direct expressions where limitation was needed, and the fact that no express limit was placed on the power of removal by the Executive was convincing indication that none was intended. This is the same construction of Article II as that of Alexander Hamilton [in his first *Pacificus* letter, quoted at length in this case].

. . . .

A reference of the whole power of removal to general legislation by Congress is quite out of keeping with the plan of government devised by the framers of the Constitution. It could never have been intended to leave to Congress unlimited discretion to vary fundamentally the operation of the great independent executive branch of government and thus most seriously to weaken it. It would be a delegation by the Convention to Congress of the function of defining the primary boundaries of another of the three great divisions of government. The inclusion of removals of executive officers in the executive power vested in the President by Article II, according to its usual definition, and the implication of his power of removal of such officers from the provision of section 2 expressly recognizing in him the power of their appointment, are a much more natural and appropriate source of the removing power.

It is reasonable to suppose also that, had it been intended to give to Congress power to regulate or control removals in the manner suggested, it would have been included among the specifically enumerated legislative powers in Article I, or in the specified limitations on the executive power in Article II. The difference between the grant of legislative power under Article I to Congress, which is limited to powers therein enumerated, and the more general grant of the executive power to the President under Article II, is significant. The fact that the executive power is given in general terms strengthened by specific terms where emphasis is appropriate, and limited by direct expressions where limitation is needed and that no express limit is placed on the power of removal by the executive, is a convincing indication that none was intended.

. . . .

Our conclusion on the merits, sustained by the arguments before stated, is that Article II grants to the President the executive power of the Government, [and] ... that the provisions of the second section of Article II, which blend action by the legislative branch, or by part of it, in the work of the executive, are limitations to be strictly construed and not to be extended by implication....

United States v. Curtiss-Wright Export Corp.
299 U.S. 304, 315–21 (1936)

It will contribute to the elucidation of the question if we first consider the differences between the powers of the federal government in respect of foreign or external affairs and those in respect of domestic or internal affairs. That there are differences between them, and that these differences are fundamental, may not be doubted.

The two classes of powers are different, both in respect of their origin and their nature....

As a result of the separation from great Britain by the colonies acting as a unit, the powers of external sovereignty passed from the Crown not to the colonies severally, but to the colonies in their collective an corporate capacity as the United States of America....

Sovereignty is never held in suspense. When, therefore, the external sovereignty of Great Britain in respect of the colonies ceased, it immediately passed to the Union....

It results that the investment of the federal government with the powers of external sovereignty did not depend upon the affirmative grants of the constitution. The powers to declare and wage war, to conclude peace, to make treaties, to maintain diplomatic relations with other sovereignties, if they had never been mentioned in the constitution, would have vested in the federal government as necessary concomitants of nationality....

Not only, as we have shown, is the federal power over external affairs in origin and essential character different from that over internal affairs, but participation in the exercise of the power is significantly limited. In this vast external realm, with its important, complicated, delicate and manifold problems, the President alone has the power to speak or listen as a representative of the nation. He makes treaties with the advice and consent of the Senate; but he alone negotiates. Into the field of negotiation the Senate cannot intrude; and Congress itself is powerless to invade it....

It is important to bear in mind that we are here dealing not alone with an authority vested in the President by an exertion of legislative power, but with such an authority plus the very delicate, plenary and exclusive power of the President as the sole organ of the federal government in the field of international relations—a power which does not require as a basis for its exercise an act of Congress, but which, of course, like every other governmental power, must be exercised in subordination to the applicable provisions of the constitution. It is quite apparent that if, in the maintenance of our international relations, embarrassment—perhaps serious embarrassment—is to be avoided and success for our aims achieved, congressional legislation which is to be made effective through negotiation and inquiry within the international field must often accord to the President a degree of discretion and freedom from statutory restriction which would not be admissible were domestic affairs alone involved. Moreover, he, not Congress, has the better opportunity of knowing the conditions which prevail in foreign countries, and especially is this true in time of war. He has his confidential sources of information. He has his agents in the form of diplomatic, consular and other officials. Secrecy in respect to information gathered by them may be highly necessary, and the premature disclosure of it productive of harmful results. Indeed, so clearly is this true that the first President refused to accede to a request to lay before the House of Representatives the instructions, correspondence and documents relating to the negotiation of the Jay Treaty—a refusal the wisdom of which was recognized by the House itself and has never since been doubted....

The marked difference between foreign affairs and domestic affairs in this respect is recognized by both houses of Congress in the very form of their requisitions for information from the executive departments. In the case of every department except the Department of State, the resolution *directs* the official to furnish the information. In the case of the State Department, dealing with foreign affairs, the President is *requested* to furnish the information "if not incompatible with the public interest." A statement that to furnish the information is not compatible with the public interest rarely, if ever, is questioned.

Youngstown Sheet & Tube Co. v. Sawyer (Steel Seizure Case)

343 U.S. 579, 582, 585, 587, 589, 634–35, 637–38, 642, 644–46 (1952)

Mr. Justice Black delivered the opinion of the Court.

We are asked to decide whether the President was acting within his constitutional power when he issued an order directing the Secretary of Commerce to take possession of and operate most of the Nation's steel mills. The mill owners argue that the President's order amounts to lawmaking, a legislative function which the Constitution has expressly confided to the Congress and not to the President. The Government's position is that the order was made on findings of the President that his action was necessary to avert a national catastrophe which would inevitably result from a stoppage of steel production, and that in meeting this grave emergency the President was acting within the aggregate of his constitutional powers as the Nation's Chief Executive and the Commander in Chief of the Armed Forces of the United States....

....

The President's power, if any, to issue the order must stem either from an act of Congress or from the Constitution itself. There is no statute that expressly authorizes the President to take possession of property as he did here. Nor is there any act of Congress to which our attention has been directed from which such a power can fairly be implied. Indeed, we do not understand the Government to rely on statutory authorization for this seizure....

....

It is clear that if the President had authority to issue the order he did, it must be found in some provision of the Constitution. And it is not claimed that express constitutional language grants this power to the President. The contention is that presidential power should be implied from the aggregate of his powers under the Constitution. Particular reliance is placed on provisions in Article II which say that "The executive Power shall be vested in a President ...";that "he shall take Care that the Laws be faithfully executed"; and that he "shall be Commander in Chief of the Army and Navy of the United States."

The order cannot properly be sustained as an exercise of the President's military power as Commander in Chief of the Armed Forces. The Government attempts to do so by citing a number of cases upholding broad powers in military commanders engaged in day-to-day fighting in a theater of war. Such cases need not concern us here. Even though "theater of war" be an expanding concept, we cannot with faithfulness to our constitutional system hold that the Commander in Chief of the Armed Forces has the ultimate power as such to take possession of private property in order to keep labor disputes from stopping production. This is a job for the Nation's lawmakers, not for its military authorities.

....

The Founders of this Nation entrusted the lawmaking power to the Congress alone in both good and bad times. It would do no good to recall the historical events, the fears of power and the hopes for freedom that lay behind their choice. Such a review would but confirm our holding that this seizure order cannot stand.

The judgment of the District Court is

Affirmed.

Mr. Justice Jackson, concurring in the judgment and opinion of the Court.

....

The actual art of governing under our Constitution does not and cannot conform to judicial definitions of the power of any of its branches based on isolated clauses or even single Articles torn from context. While the Constitution diffuses power the better to secure liberty, it also contemplates that practice will integrate the dispersed powers into a workable government. It enjoins upon its branches separateness but interdependence, autonomy but reciprocity. Presidential powers are not fixed but fluctuate, depending upon their disjunction or conjunction with those of Congress. We may well begin by a somewhat over-simplified grouping of practical situations in which a President may doubt, or others may challenge, his powers, and by distinguishing roughly the legal consequences of this factor of relativity.

1. When the President acts pursuant to an express or implied authorization of Congress, his authority is at its maximum, for it includes all that he possesses in his own right plus all that Congress can delegate. In these circumstances, and in these only, may he be said (for what it may be worth) to personify the federal sovereignty. If his act is held unconstitutional under these circumstances, it usually means that the Federal Government as an undivided whole lacks power. A seizure executed by the President pursuant to an Act of Congress would be supported by the strongest of presumptions and the widest latitude of judicial interpretation, and the burden of persuasion would rest heavily upon any who might attack it.

2. When the President acts in absence of either a congressional grant or denial of authority, he can only rely upon his own independent powers, but there is a zone of twilight in which he and Congress may have concurrent authority, or in which its distribution is uncertain. Therefore, congressional inertia, indifference or quiescence may sometimes, at least as a practical matter, enable, if not invite, measures on independent presidential responsibility. In this area, any actual test of power is likely to depend on the imperatives of events and contemporary imponderables rather than on abstract theories of law.

3. When the President takes measures incompatible with the expressed or implied will of Congress, his power is at its lowest ebb, for then he can rely only upon his own constitutional powers minus any constitutional powers of Congress over the matter. Courts can sustain exclusive presidential control in such a case only by disabling the Congress from acting upon the subject. Presidential claim to a power at once so conclusive and preclusive must be scrutinized with caution, for what is at stake is the equilibrium established by our constitutional system. . . .

. . . Nothing in our Constitution is plainer than that declaration of a war is entrusted only to Congress. Of course, a state of war may in fact exist without a formal declaration. But no doctrine that the Court could promulgate would seem to me more sinister and alarming than that a President whose conduct of foreign affairs is so largely uncontrolled, and often even is unknown, can vastly enlarge his mastery over the internal affairs of the country by his own commitment of the Nation's armed forces to some foreign venture.

. . . .

That military powers of the Commander in Chief were not to supersede representative government of internal affairs seems obvious from the Constitution and from elementary American history. Time out of mind, and even now in many parts of the world, a military commander can seize private housing to shelter his troops. Not so, however, in the United States, for the Third Amendment says, "No Soldier shall, in time of peace be quartered in any house, without the consent of the Owner, nor in time of war, but in a manner to be prescribed by law." Thus, even in war time, his seizure of needed military housing must be authorized by Congress. It also was expressly left to Congress to "provide for calling forth the Militia to execute the Laws of the Union, suppress Insurrections and repel Invasions. . . ." Such a limitation on the command power, written at a time when the militia rather than a standing army was contemplated as the military weapon of the Republic, underscores the Constitution's policy that Congress, not the Executive, should control utilization of the war power as an instrument of domestic policy. . . .

. . . .

We should not use this occasion to circumscribe, much less to contract, the lawful role of the President as Commander in Chief. I should indulge the widest latitude of interpretation to sustain his exclusive function to command the instruments of national force, at least when turned against the outside world for the security of our society. But, when it is turned inward, not because of rebellion but because of a lawful economic struggle between industry and labor, it should have no such indulgence. His command power is not such an absolute as might be implied from that office in a militaristic system but is subject to limitations consistent with a constitutional Republic whose law and policy-making branch is a representative Congress. The purpose of lodging dual titles in one man was to insure that the civilian would control the military, not to enable the military to subordinate the presidential office. No penance would ever expiate the sin against free government of holding that a President can escape control of executive powers by law through assuming his military role. What the power of command may include I do not try to envision, but I think it is not a military prerogative, without support of law, to seize persons or property because they are important or even essential for the military and naval establishment.

The third clause in which the Solicitor General finds seizure powers is that "he shall take Care that the Laws be faithfully executed...." That authority must be matched against words of the Fifth Amendment that "No person shall be ... deprived of life, liberty or property, without due process of law...." (Footnotes omitted.)

Notes

Curtiss-Wright and the Origins of the Nation's Executive Power

Justice George Sutherland joined the Court after serving in the House, the Senate, and as President of the American Bar Association. In 1919 he had written *Constitutional Power and World Affairs*, setting forth the theory embraced by the Court in 1936 with but a single dissent. As noted at the start of this chapter, many modern scholars (following the lead of Yale Law School's Professor and later Dean Harold Koh) now discount the importance of *Curtiss-Wright*, contending that it has been implicitly replaced as the proper constitutional paradigm for the separation of national security powers by Justice Robert Jackson's concurring opinion in *Youngstown*. Among those who recognize that *Curtiss-Wright* remains the controlling precedent for cases involving presidential power towards the external world, there remains disagreement about the origins of this power. While Justice Sutherland saw federal control over the nation's external relations as "necessary concomitants of nationality" that required no mention in the Constitution, the prevailing view among the Framers of the Constitution seems to have been that these powers were vested in the President as part of the "executive Power" of Article II, Section 1 — subject to the important exceptions given to the Senate and Congress.

Youngstown and Foreign Affairs

Whatever the validity of Justice Jackson's analysis in the *Steel Seizure Case* in domestic matters (where it is held in high regard by scholars and courts alike), it is important to keep in mind that, as Professor Henkin notes, "*Youngstown* has not been considered a foreign affairs case."[35] Indeed, in footnote 2 of his *Youngstown* opinion, Justice Jackson expressly referred to the *Curtiss-Wright* decision, observing: "That case does not solve the present controversy. It recognized internal and external affairs as being in separate categories...."[36]

---

35. Louis Henkin, Foreign Affairs and the Constitution 341 n. 11 (1972). Henkin notes that "the majority of the Supreme Court did not treat the case as involving the reach of [the President's] foreign affairs power, and even the dissenting justices invoked only incidentally that power or the fact that the steel strike threatened important American foreign policy interest." *Id.*

36. 343 U.S. at 635.

This assessment finds support in the concurring opinion of Justice Rehnquist—joined by Chief Justice Burger and two other members of the Court—in *Goldwater v. Carter*:[37]

> The present case differs in several important respects from *Youngstown* [citation omitted] ... cited by petitioners as authority both for reaching the merits of this dispute and for reversing the Court of Appeals. In *Youngstown*, private litigants brought a suit contesting the President's authority under his war powers to seize the Nation's steel industry, an action of profound and demonstrable domestic impact.... Moreover, as in *Curtiss-Wright*, the effect of this action, as far as we can tell, is "entirely external to the United States, and [falls] within the category of foreign affairs...."[38]

Rather than being a "foreign affairs" case, as Justice Jackson observed, *Youngstown* involved a taking of private property without due process of law in violation of the Fifth Amendment.[39]

Justiciability

Although established as a coequal, independent branch of the government, the federal courts enter the national security arena under a variety of significant constraints. Some of these are mandated by the Constitution itself, while others are prudential; but taken together they have contributed to the lack of legal clarity about the precise limits of the powers of the political branches in military and foreign affairs.

Case or Controversy Problems

Article III, section 2 of the Constitution limits the jurisdiction of federal courts to "cases" and "controversies." It thus prohibits the courts from rendering hypothetical "advisory opinions," and also opinions on disputes which are not "ripe" or have already passed the stage of being a controversy and have become "moot."

These and other avoidance techniques relied upon by the courts are not unique to the national security field, but they exist there and contribute to the lack of judicial decision over many disputes involving external affairs.

In the 1979 Taiwan treaty case, which will be discussed in more detail below, Mr. Justice Powell took the position that the complaint should be dismissed because the level of conflict between the two political branches had not yet reached the stage of constituting an actual "controversy."

Goldwater v. Carter
444 U.S. 996, 997–98 (1979)

Mr. Justice Powell, concurring in the judgment.

Although I agree with the result reached by the Court, I would dismiss the complaint *as not ripe* for judicial review.

---

37. Goldwater v. Carter, 444 U.S. 996 (1979).

38. *Id.* at 1004–05.

39. Youngstown Sheet & Tube Co. v. Sawyer, 343 U.S. 646 (1952). For a discussion of this distinction, *see* Robert F. Turner, *The Supreme Court, Separation of Powers, and the Protection of Individual Rights During Periods of War or National Security Emergency,* 28 J. Sup. Ct. Hist. 323, 323–25 (2003).

I

This Court has recognized that an issue should not be decided if it is not ripe for judicial review. Prudential considerations persuade me that a dispute between Congress and the President is not ready for judicial review unless and until each branch has taken action asserting its constitutional authority. Differences between the President and the Congress are commonplace under our system. The differences should, and almost invariably do, turn on political rather than legal considerations. The Judicial Branch should not decide issues affecting the allocation of power between the President and Congress until the political branches reach a constitutional impasse. Otherwise, we would encourage small groups or even individual Members of Congress to seek judicial resolution of issues before the normal political process has the opportunity to resolve the conflict.

In this case, a few Members of Congress claim that the President's action in terminating the treaty with Taiwan has deprived them of their constitutional role with respect to a change in the supreme law of the land. Congress has taken no official action. In the present posture of this case, we do not know whether there ever will be an actual confrontation between the Legislative and Executive Branches. Although the Senate has considered a resolution declaring that Senate approval is necessary for the termination of any mutual defense treaty, *see* 125 Cong. Rec. 13672, 13695–13697 (1979), no final vote has been taken on the resolution. *See id.*, at 32522–32531. Moreover, it is unclear whether the resolution would have retroactive effect. *See id.*, at 13711–13721; *id.*, at 15210. It cannot be said that either the Senate or the House has rejected the President's claim. If the Congress chooses not to confront the President, it is not our task to do so. I therefore concur in the dismissal of this case.

The Political Question Doctrine

It has been recognized since the earliest days of our country that there are certain presidential decisions — particularly in the area of military and foreign affairs — that are unreviewable by the judiciary. An early statement of this principle occurred in the landmark judicial review case of *Marbury v. Madison*, decided by Chief Justice John Marshall during the Jefferson Administration and quoted earlier in this chapter.

Following the end of World War II, twenty-one German soldiers who had been captured by U.S. armed forces in China, and were subsequently convicted of continuing to engage in hostilities after the unconditional surrender of the German Government, sought a writ of *habeas corpus* on the grounds that their trial, conviction, and imprisonment violated provisions of the United States Bill of Rights. Speaking for the Court in rejecting their claim, Mr. Justice Jackson offered the following dicta.

Johnson v. Eisentrager

339 U.S. 763, 788–89 (1950) (Jackson, J.)

The first of the enumerated powers of the President is that he shall be Commander-in-Chief of the Army and Navy of the United States. Art. II, § 2, Const. And, of course, grant of war power includes all that is necessary and proper for carrying these powers into execution.

Certainly it is not the function of the Judiciary to entertain private litigation — even by a citizen — which challenges the legality, the wisdom, or the propriety of the Commander-in-Chief in sending our armed forces abroad or to any particular region. China appears to have fully consented to the trial within her territories and, if China had complaint at the presence of American forces there, China's grievance does not become these prisoners' right. The issue tendered by "(b)"[40] involves a challenge to *conduct of diplomatic and foreign affairs, for which the President is exclusively responsible. United States v. Curtiss-Wright Corp.*, 299 U.S. 304; *Chicago & Southern Air Lines v. Waterman Steamship Corp.*, 333 U.S. 103.

The landmark decision on the political question doctrine was the 1962 case of *Baker v. Carr*, a Tennessee apportionment controversy best known for the principle it upheld — "one man, one vote." While not a national security case, in the following, lengthy opinion, Mr. Justice Brennan addressed the doctrine's national security implications.

Baker v. Carr
369 U.S. 186, 210–14, 217 (1962)

We have said that "In determining whether a question falls within [the political question] category, the appropriateness under our system of government of attributing finality to the action of the political departments and also the lack of satisfactory criteria for a judicial determination are dominant considerations." *Coleman v. Miller*, 307 U.S. 433, 454–455. The nonjusticiability of a political question is primarily a function of the separation of powers. Much confusion results from the capacity of the "political question" label to obscure the need for case-by-case inquiry. Deciding whether a matter has in any measure been committed by the Constitution to another branch of government, or whether the action of that branch exceeds whatever authority has been committed, is itself a delicate exercise in constitutional interpretation, and is a responsibility of this Court as ultimate interpreter of the Constitution. To demonstrate this requires no less than to analyze representative cases and to infer from them the analytical threads that make up the political question doctrine. We shall then show that none of those threads catches this case.

Foreign relations: There are sweeping statements to the effect that all questions touching foreign relations are political questions. Not only does resolution of such issues frequently turn on standards that defy judicial application, or involve the exercise of a discretion demonstrably committed to the executive or legislature; but many such questions uniquely demand single-voiced statement of the Government's views. Yet it is error to suppose that every case or controversy which touches foreign relations lies beyond judicial cognizance. Our cases in this field seem invariably to show a discriminating analysis of the particular question posed, in terms of the history of its management by the political branches, of its susceptibility to judicial handling in the light of its nature and posture in the specific case, and of the possible consequences of judicial action. For example, though a court will not ordinarily inquire whether a treaty has been terminated, since on that question "governmental action.... must be regarded as of controlling importance," if there has been no conclusive "governmental action" then a court can construe a treaty and may find it provides the answer. Compare *Terlinden v. Ames*, 184 U.S. 270, 285, with *Society for the Propagation of the Gospel in Foreign Parts v. New Haven*, 8 Wheat. 464, 492–495. Though a court will not undertake to construe a treaty in a manner inconsistent with a subsequent federal statute, no similar hesitancy obtains if the asserted clash is with state law. Compare *Whitney v. Robertson*, 124 U.S. 190, with *Kolovrat v. Oregon*, 366 U.S. 187.

---

40. Contention "(b)" was that "In the absence of hostilities, martial law, or American military occupation of China, and in view of treaties between the United States and China ... the Military Commission was without jurisdiction." 339 U.S. 763, at 786 (1950).

While recognition of foreign governments so strongly defies judicial treatment that without executive recognition a foreign state has been called "a republic of whose existence we know nothing," and the judiciary ordinarily follows the executive as to which nation has sovereignty over disputed territory, once sovereignty over an area is politically determined and declared, courts may examine the resulting status and decide independently whether a statute applies to that area. Similarly, recognition of belligerency abroad is an executive responsibility, but if the executive proclamations fall short of an explicit answer, a court may construe them seeking, for example, to determine whether the situation is such that statutes designed to assure American neutrality have become operative. *The Three Friends*, 166 U.S. 1, 63, 66. Still again, though it is the executive that determines a person's status as representative of a foreign government, *Ex parte Hitz*, 111 U.S. 766, the executive's statements will be construed where necessary to determine the court's jurisdiction, *In re Baiz*, 135 U.S. 403. Similar judicial action in the absence of a recognizedly authoritative executive declaration occurs in cases involving the immunity from seizure of vessels owned by friendly foreign governments. Compare *Ex parte Peru*, 318 U.S. 578, with *Mexico v. Hoffman*, 324 U.S. 30, 34–35.

Dates of duration of hostilities: Though it has been stated broadly that "the power which declared the necessity is the power to declare its cessation, and what the cessation requires," *Commercial Trust Co. v. Miller*, 262 U.S. 51, 57, here too analysis reveals isolable reasons for the presence of political questions, underlying this Court's refusal to review the political departments' determination of when or whether a war has ended. Dominant is the need for finality in the political determination, for emergency's nature demands "A prompt and unhesitating obedience," *Martin v. Mott*, 12 Wheat. 19, 30 (calling up of militia). Moreover, "the cessation of hostilities does not necessarily end the war power. It was stated in *Hamilton v. Kentucky Distilleries & W. Co.*, 251 U.S. 146, 161, that the war power includes the power 'to remedy the evils which have arisen from its rise and progress' and continues during that emergency. *Stewart v. Kahn*, 11 Wall. 493, 507." *Fleming v. Mohawk Wrecking Co.*, 331 U.S. 111, 116. But deference rests on reason, not habit. The question in a particular case may not seriously implicate considerations of finality—*for example*, a public program of importance (rent control) yet not central to the emergency effort. Further, clearly definable criteria for decision may be available. In such cases the political question barrier falls away: "[A] Court is not at liberty to shut its eyes to an obvious mistake, when the validity of the law depends upon the truth of what is declared.... [It can] inquire whether the exigency still existed upon which the continued operation of the law depended." *Chastleton Corp. v. Sinclair*, 264 U.S. 543, 547–548. Compare *Woods v. Miller Co.*, 333 U.S. 138. On the other hand, even in private litigation which directly implicates no feature of separation of powers, lack of judicially discoverable standards and the drive for even-handed application may impel reference to the political departments' determination of dates of hostilities' beginning and ending. *The Protector*, 12 Wall. 700. (Footnotes omitted.)

. . . .

It is apparent that several formulations which vary slightly according to the settings in which the questions arise may describe a political question, although each has one or more elements which identify it as essentially a function of the separation of powers. Prominent on the surface of any case held to involve a political question is found a textually demonstrable constitutional commitment of the issue to a coordinate political department; or a lack of judicially discoverable and manageable standards for resolving it; or the impossibility of deciding without an initial policy determination of a kind clearly for nonjudicial discretion; or the impossibility of a court's undertaking independent resolution without expressing lack of the respect due coordinate branches of government; or an unusual need for unquestioning adherence to a political decision already made; or the potentiality of embarrassment from multifarious pronouncements by various departments on one question.

Unless one of these formulations is inextricable from the case at bar, there should be no dismissal for non-justiciability on the ground of a political question's presence. The doctrine of which we treat is one of "political questions," not one of "political cases." The courts cannot reject as "no law suit" a bona fide controversy as to whether some action denominated "political" exceeds constitutional authority. The cases we have reviewed show the necessity for discriminating inquiry into the precise facts and posture of the particular case, and the impossibility of resolution by any semantic cataloguing.

In May 1970 student protests at Kent State University led to the calling out of the Ohio National Guard and subsequently to a tragic confrontation during which several students were killed. Angry students brought suit in Federal District Court seeking injunctive relief to restrain the Governor from prematurely ordering the National Guard to duty in response to student protests, and also to restrain Guard leaders from violating students' rights in the future. In particular, the students sought to have the federal court supervise the "training, weaponry, and orders" of the National Guard on a continuing basis to prevent a reoccurrence of the Kent State incident. In rejecting the motion, the Supreme Court emphasized some of the considerations which constrain courts in dealing with military and national security matters.

Gilligan v. Morgan
413 U.S. 1, 5–12 (1973)

It is important to note at the outset that this is not a case in which damages are sought for injuries sustained during the tragic occurrence at Kent State. Nor is it an action seeking a restraining order against some specified and imminently threatened unlawful action. Rather, it is a broad call on judicial power to assume continuing regulatory jurisdiction over the activities of the Ohio National Guard. This far-reaching demand for relief presents important questions of justiciability.

Respondents continue to seek for the benefit of all Kent State students a judicial evaluation of the appropriateness of the "training, weaponry and orders" of the Ohio National Guard. They further demand, and the Court of Appeals' remand would require, that the District Court establish standards for the training, kind of weapons and scope and kind of orders to control the actions of the National Guard. Respondents contend that thereafter the District Court must assume and exercise a continuing judicial surveillance over the Guard to assure compliance with whatever training and operations procedures may be approved by the court. Respondents press for a remedial decree of this scope, even assuming that the recently adopted changes are deemed acceptable after an evidentiary hearing by the court. Continued judicial surveillance to assure compliance with the changed standards is what respondents demand.

In relying on the Due Process Clause of the Fourteenth Amendment, respondents seem to overlook the explicit command of Art. I, § 8, cl. 16, which vests in Congress the power:

> "To provide for organizing, arming, and disciplining the Militia, and for governing such Part of them as may be employed in the Service of the United States, reserving to the States respectively, the Appointment of the Officers, and the Au-

thority of training the Militia according to the discipline *prescribed by Congress.*" (Emphasis added.)

The majority opinion in the Court of Appeals does not mention this very relevant provision of the Constitution. Yet that provision is explicit that the Congress shall have the responsibility for organizing, arming, and disciplining the Militia (now the National Guard), with certain responsibilities being reserved to the respective States. Congress has enacted appropriate legislation pursuant to Art. I, § 8, cl. 16, and has also authorized the President—as Commander in Chief of the Armed Forces—to prescribe regulations governing organization and discipline of the National Guard. The Guard is an essential reserve component of the Armed Forces of the United States, available with regular forces in time of war. The Guard also may be federalized in addition to its role under state governments, to assist in controlling civil disorders. The relief sought by respondents, requiring initial judicial review and continuing surveillance by a federal court over the training, weaponry, and orders of the Guard, would therefore embrace critical areas of responsibility vested by the Constitution in the Legislative and Executive Branches of the Government.

. . . .

This would plainly and explicitly require a judicial evaluation of a wide range of possibly dissimilar procedures and policies approved by different law enforcement agencies or other authorities; and the examples cited may represent only a fragment of the accumulated data and experience in the various States, in the Armed Services, and in other concerned agencies of the Federal Government. Trained professionals, subject to the day-to-day control of the responsible civilian authorities, necessarily must make comparative judgments on the merits as to evolving methods of training, equipping, and controlling military forces with respect to their duties under the Constitution. It would be inappropriate for a district judge to undertake this responsibility in the unlikely event that he possessed requisite technical competence to do so.

Judge Celebrezze, in dissent, correctly read *Baker v. Carr*, 369 U.S. 186 (1962), when he said:

> "I believe that the congressional and executive authority to prescribe and regulate the training and weaponry of the National Guard, as set forth above, *clearly precludes any form of judicial regulation of the same matters.* I can envision no form of judicial relief which, if directed at the training and weaponry of the National Guard, would not involve as serious conflict with a " 'coordinate political department; … a lack of judicially discoverable and manageable standards for resolving [the question]; … the impossibility of deciding without an initial policy determination of a kind clearly for nonjudicial discretion; … the impossibility of a court's undertaking independent resolution without expressing lack of the respect due coordinate branches of government; … an unusual need for unquestioning adherence to a political decision already made; [and] the potentiality of embarrassment from multifarious pronouncements by various departments on one question.' *Baker v. Carr, supra,* 369 U.S. at 217…." *Any such relief,* whether it prescribed standards of training and weaponry or simply ordered compliance with the standards set by Congress and/or the Executive, *would necessarily draw the courts into a nonjusticiable political question, over which we have no jurisdiction.*" 456 F.2d, at 619 (emphasis added)….

. . . .

In determining justiciability, the analysis in *Flast v. Cohen* … suggests that there is no justiciable controversy (a) "when the parties are asking for an advisory opinion," (b) "when the question sought to be adjudicated has been mooted by subsequent developments," and (c) "when there is no standing to maintain the action." As we noted in *Poe v. Ullman*, 367 U.S. 497 (1961), and repeated in *Flast*, "[j]usticiability is ... not a legal concept with a fixed content or susceptible of scientific verification. Its utilization is the resultant of many subtle pressures...." 367 U.S., at 508.

In testing this case by these standards drawn specifically from *Flast*, there are serious deficiencies with respect to each. The advisory nature of the judicial declaration sought is clear from respondents' argument and, indeed, from the very language of the court's remand. Added to this is that the nature of the questions to be resolved on remand are subjects committed expressly to the political branches of government. These factors, when coupled with the uncertainties as to whether a live controversy still exists and the infirmity of the posture of respondents as to standing, render the claim and the proposed issues on remand nonjusticiable.

It would be difficult to think of a clearer example of the type of governmental action that was intended by the Constitution to be left to the political branches directly responsible—as the Judicial Branch is not—to the electoral process. Moreover, it is difficult to conceive of an area of governmental activity in which the courts have less competence....

....

In concluding that no justiciable controversy is presented, it should be clear that we neither hold nor imply that the conduct of the National Guard is always beyond judicial review or that there may not be accountability in a judicial forum for violations of law or for specific unlawful conduct by military personnel, whether by way of damages or injunctive relief. We hold only that no such questions are presented in this case. We decline to require a United States District Court to involve itself so directly and so intimately in the task assigned that court by the Court of Appeals. *Orloff v. Willoughby*, 345 U.S. 83, 93–94 (1953).

Reversed.

———————

As the following case illustrates, the Supreme Court is often divided over the precise meaning and application of the political question doctrine. The case, which has been discussed *supra*, involved a challenge by members of the legislative branch to the constitutionality of President Carter's decision to abrogate a mutual security treaty with the Republic of China (Taiwan) in connection with his decision to establish diplomatic relations with the People's Republic of China. The case was dismissed, but a majority of the Court could not agree upon the proper grounds for its decision.

Goldwater v. Carter
444 U.S. 996, 997–1007 (1979)

Mr. Justice Powell, concurring....

Mr. Justice Rehnquist suggests.... that the issue presented by this case is a nonjusticiable political question which can never be considered by this Court. I cannot agree. In my view, reliance upon the political-question doctrine is inconsistent with our precedents. As set forth in the seminal case of *Baker v. Carr*, 369 U.S. 186, 217 (1962), the doctrine incorporates three inquiries: (i) Does the issue involve resolution of questions committed by the text of the Constitution to a coordinate branch of Government? (ii) Would resolution of the question demand that a court move beyond areas of judicial expertise? (iii) Do prudential considerations counsel against judicial intervention? In my opinion the answer to each of these inquiries would require us to decide this case if it were ready for review.

First, the existence of "a textually demonstrable constitutional commitment of the issue to a coordinate political department," *ibid.*, turns on an examination of the constitutional provisions governing the exercise of the power in question. *Powell v. McCormack*, 395 U.S. 486, 519 (1969). No constitutional provision explicitly confers upon the President the power to terminate treaties. Further, Art. II § 2, of the Constitution authorizes the President to make treaties with the advice and consent of the Senate. Article VI provides that treaties shall be a part of the supreme law of the land. These provisions add support to the view that the text of the Constitution does not unquestionably commit the power to terminate treaties to the President alone. Cf. *Gilligan v. Morgan* 413 U.S. 1, 6 (1973); *Luther v. Borden*, 7 How. 1, 42 (1849).

Second, there is no "lack of judicially discoverable and manageable standards for resolving" this case; nor is a decision impossible "without an initial policy determination of a kind clearly for nonjudicial discretion." *Baker v. Carr*, *supra*, at 217. We are asked to decide whether the President may terminate a treaty under the Constitution without congressional approval. Resolution of the question may not be easy, but it only requires us to apply normal principles of interpretation to the constitutional provisions at issue. See *Powell v. McCormack*, *supra*, at 548–549. The present case involves neither review of the President's activities as Commander in Chief nor impermissible interference in the field of foreign affairs. Such a case would arise if we were asked to decide, for example, whether a treaty required the President to order troops into a foreign country. But "it is error to suppose that every case or controversy which touches foreign relations lies beyond judicial cognizance." *Baker v. Carr*, *supra*, at 211. This case "touches" foreign relations, but the question presented to us concerns only the constitutional division of power between Congress and the President.

A simple hypothetical demonstrates the confusion that I find inherent in MR. JUSTICE REHNQUIST's opinion concurring in the judgment. Assume that the President signed a mutual defense treaty with a foreign country and announced that it would go into effect despite its rejection by the Senate. Under MR. JUSTICE REHNQUIST's analysis that situation would present a political question even though Art. II § 2, clearly would resolve the dispute. Although the answer to the hypothetical case seems self-evident because it demands textual rather than interstitial analysis, the nature of the legal issue presented is no different from the issue presented in the case before us. In both cases, the Court would interpret the Constitution to decide whether congressional approval is necessary to give a Presidential decision on the validity of a treaty the force of law. Such an inquiry demands no special competence or information beyond the reach of the Judiciary. Cf. *Chicago & Southern Air Lines v. Waterman S.S. Corp.*, 333 U.S. 103, 111 (1948).[41]

Finally, the political-question doctrine rests in part on prudential concerns calling for mutual respect among the three branches of Government. Thus, the Judicial Branch

---

41. Original footnote accompanying text reads:

The Court has recognized that, in the area of foreign policy, Congress may leave the President with wide discretion that otherwise might run afoul of the nondelegation doctrine. United States v. Curtiss-Wright Export Corp., 299 U.S. 304 (1936). As stated in that case, "the President alone has the power to speak or listen as a representative of the Nation. He *makes* treaties with the advice and consent of the Senate; but he alone negotiates." *Id.* at 319 (emphasis in original). Resolution of this case would interfere with neither the President's ability to negotiate treaties nor his duty to execute their provisions. We are merely being asked to decide whether a treaty, which cannot be ratified without Senate approval, continues in effect until the Senate or perhaps the Congress takes further action.

should avoid "the potentiality of embarrassment [that would result] from multifarious pronouncements by various departments on one question." Similarly, the doctrine restrains judicial action where there is an "unusual need for unquestioning adherence to a political decision already made." *Baker v. Carr, supra*, at 217.

If this case were ripe for judicial review, ... none of these prudential considerations would be present. Interpretation of the Constitution does not imply lack of respect for a coordinate branch. *Powell v. McCormack, supra*, at 548. If the President and the Congress had reached irreconcilable positions, final disposition of the question presented by this case would eliminate, rather than create, multiple constitutional interpretations. The specter of the Federal Government brought to a halt because of the mutual intransigence of the President and the Congress would require this Court to provide a resolution pursuant to our duty " 'to say what the law is.' " *United States v. Nixon*, 418 U.S. 683, 703 (1974), quoting *Marbury v. Madison*, 1 Cranch 137, 177 (1803).

III

In my view, the suggestion that this case presents a political question is incompatible with this Court's willingness on previous occasions to decide whether one branch of our Government has impinged upon the power of another. See *Buckley v. Valeo*, 424 U.S., at 138; *United States v. Nixon, supra*, at 707; *The Pocket Veto Case*, 279 U.S. 655, 676–678 (1929); *Myers v. United States*, 272 U.S. 52 (1926). Under the criteria enunciated in *Baker v. Carr*, we have the responsibility to decide whether both the Executive and Legislative Branches have constitutional roles to play in termination of a treaty. If the Congress by appropriate formal action, had challenged the President's authority to terminate the treaty with Taiwan, the resulting uncertainty could have serious consequences for our country. In that situation, it would be the duty of this Court to resolve the issue.

Mr. Justice Rehnquist, with whom The Chief Justice, Mr. Justice Stewart, and Mr. Justice Stevens join, concurring in the judgment.

I am of the view that the basic question presented by the petitioners in this case is "political" and therefore nonjusticiable because it involves the authority of the President in the conduct of our country's foreign relations and the extent to which the Senate or the Congress is authorized to negate the action of the President. In *Coleman v. Miller*, 307 U.S. 433 (1939), a case in which members of the Kansas Legislature brought an action attacking a vote of the State Senate in favor of the ratification of the Child Labor Amendment, Mr. Chief Justice Hughes wrote in what is referred to as the "Opinion of the Court":

> "We think that ... the question of the efficacy of ratifications by state legislatures, in the light of previous rejection or attempted withdrawal, should be regarded as a political question pertaining to the political departments, with the ultimate authority in the Congress in the exercise of its control over the promulgation of the adoption of the Amendment.

> "The precise question as now raised is whether, when the legislature of the State, as we have found, has actually ratified the proposed amendment, the Court should restrain the state officers from certifying the ratification to the Secretary of State, because of an earlier rejection, and thus prevent the question from coming before the political departments. We find no basis in either Constitution or statute for such judicial action. Article V, speaking solely of ratification, contains no provision as to rejection...." *Id.*, at 450.

Thus, Mr. Chief Justice Hughes' opinion concluded that "Congress in controlling the promulgation of the adoption of a constitutional amendment has the final determination of the question whether by lapse of time its proposal of the amendment had lost its vitality prior to the required ratifications." *Id.*, at 456.

I believe it follows *a fortiori* from *Coleman* that the controversy in the instant case is a nonjusticiable political dispute that should be left for resolution by the Executive and Legislative Branches of the Government. Here, while the Constitution is express as to the manner in which the Senate shall participate in the ratification of a treaty, it is silent as to that body's participation in the abrogation of a treaty. In this respect the case is directly analogous to *Coleman, supra*. As stated in *Dyer v. Blair*, 390 F. Supp. 1291, 1302 (ND Ill 1975) (three-judge court):

> "A question that might be answered in different ways for different amendments must surely be controlled by political standards rather than standards easily characterized as judicially manageable."

In light of the absence of any constitutional provision governing the termination of a treaty, and the fact that different termination procedures may be appropriate for different treaties.... the instant case in my view also "must surely be controlled by political standards."

I think that the justifications for concluding that the question here is political in nature are even more compelling than in *Coleman* because it involves foreign relations—specifically a treaty commitment to use military force in the defense of a foreign government if attacked. In *United States v. Curtiss-Wright Corp.*, 299 U.S. 304 (1936), this Court said:

> "Whether, if the Joint Resolution had related solely to internal affairs it would be open to the challenge that it constituted an unlawful delegation of legislative power to the Executive, we find it unnecessary to determine. The whole aim of the resolution is to affect a situation entirely external to the United States, and falling within the category of foreign affairs...." *Id.*, at 315.

The present case differs in several important respects from *Youngstown Sheet & Tube Co. v. Sawyer*, 343 U.S. 579 (1952), cited by petitioners as authority both for reaching the merits of this dispute and for reversing the Court of Appeals. In *Youngstown*, private litigants brought a suit contesting the President's authority under his war powers to seize the Nation's steel industry, an action of profound and demonstrable domestic impact. Here, by contrast, we are asked to settle a dispute between coequal branches of our Government, each of which has resources not available to private litigants outside the judicial forum.[42] Moreover, as in *Curtiss-Wright*, the effect of this action, as far as we can tell, is

---

42. Original note 1 to text reads:

As observed by Chief Justice Wright in his concurring opinion below:

> Congress has initiated the termination of treaties by directing or requiring the President to give notice of termination, without any prior presidential request. Congress has annulled treaties without any prior presidential request. Congress has annulled treaties without any presidential notice. It has conferred on the President the power to terminate a particular treaty, and it has enacted statutes practically nullifying the domestic effects of a treaty and thus caused the President to carry out termination....
>
> Moreover, Congress has a variety of powerful tools for influencing foreign policy decisions that bear on treaty matters. Under Article I, Section 8 of the Constitution, it can regulate commerce with foreign nations, raise and support armies, and declare war. It has power over the appointment of ambassadors and the funding of embassies and consulates. Congress thus retains a strong influence over the President's conduct in treaty matters.
>
> As our political history demonstrates, treaty creation and termination are complex phenomena rooted in the dynamic relationship between the two political branches of our government. We thus should decline the invitation to set in concrete a particular

"entirely external to the United States, and [falls] within the category of foreign affairs." Finally, as already noted, the situation presented here is closely akin to that presented in *Coleman*, where the Constitution spoke only to the procedure for ratification of an amendment, not to its rejection.

Having decided that the question presented in this action is nonjusticiable, I believe that the appropriate disposition is for this Court to vacate the decision of the Court of Appeals and remand with instructions for the District Court to dismiss the complaint. This procedure derives support from our practice in disposing of moot actions in federal courts.[43] For more than 30 years, we have instructed lower courts to vacate any decision on the merits of an action that has become moot prior to a resolution of the case in this Court. *United States v. Munsingwear, Inc.*, 340 U.S. 36 (1950). The Court has required such decisions to be vacated in order to "prevent a judgment, unreviewable because of mootness, from spawning any legal consequences." *Id.*, at 41. It is even more imperative that this Court invoke this procedure to ensure that resolution of a "political question," which should not have been decided by a lower court, does not "spawn any legal consequences." An Art. III court's resolution of a question that is "political" in character can create far more disruption among the three coequal branches of Government than the resolution of a question presented in a moot controversy. Since the political nature of the questions presented should have precluded the lower courts from considering or deciding the merits of the controversy, the prior proceedings in the federal courts must be vacated, and the complaint dismissed.

Mr. Justice Blackmun, with whom Mr. Justice White joins, dissenting in part.

In my view, the time factor and its importance are illusory; if the President does not have the power to terminate the treaty (a substantial issue that we should address only after briefing and oral argument), the notice of intention to terminate surely has no legal effect. It is also indefensible, without further study, to pass on the issue of justiciability or on the issues of standing or ripeness. While I therefore join in the grant of the petition for certiorari, I would set the case for oral argument and give it the plenary consideration it so obviously deserves.

Mr. Justice Brennan, dissenting.

I respectfully dissent from the order directing the District Court to dismiss this case, and would affirm the judgment of the Court of Appeals insofar as it rests upon the President's well-established authority to recognize, and withdraw recognition from, foreign governments. App. to Pet. for Cert. 27A–29A.

In stating that this case presents a nonjusticiable "political question," Mr. Justice Rehnquist, in my view, profoundly misapprehends the political-question principle as it applies to matters of foreign relations. Properly understood, the political-question doctrine restrains courts from reviewing an exercise of foreign policy judgment by the coordinate political branch to which authority to make that judgment has been "constitutional[ly] commit[ted]." *Baker v. Carr*, 369 U.S. 186, 211–213, 217 (1962). But the doctrine does not pertain when a court is faced with the *antecedent* question whether a

---

constitutionally acceptable arrangement by which the President and Congress are to share treaty termination." App. to Pet. for Cert. 44A–45A (footnotes omitted).

43. Original note 2 in text reads:

This Court, of course, may not prohibit state courts from deciding political questions, any more than it may prohibit them from deciding questions that are moot, Doremus v. Board of Education, 342 U.S. 429, 434 (1952), so long as they do not trench upon exclusively federal questions of foreign policy. Zschernig v. Miller, 389 U.S. 429, 441 (1968).

particular branch has been constitutionally designated as the repository of political decision making power. Cf. *Powell v. McCormack*, 395 U.S. 486, 519–521 (1969). The issue of decision-making authority must be resolved as a matter of constitutional law, not political discretion; accordingly, it falls within the competence of the courts.

Christopher v. Harbury

536 U.S. 403 (2002)

The action alleged on the part of all the Government defendants (the State Department and NSC defendants sued for denial of access and the CIA defendants ...) was apparently taken in the conduct of foreign relations by the National Government. Thus, if there is to be judicial enquiry, it will raise concerns for the separation of powers in trenching on matters committed to the other branches. See *Department of Navy v. Egan*, 484 U.S. 518, 529, 108 S.Ct. 818, 98 L.Ed.2d 918 (1988) ("'[F]oreign policy [is] the province and responsibility of the Executive'"); *Chicago & Southern Air Lines, Inc. v. Waterman S.S. Corp.*, 333 U.S. 103, 111, 68 S.Ct. 431, 92 L.Ed. 568 (1948) ("[T]he very nature of executive decisions as to foreign policy is political, not judicial"). Since the need to resolve such constitutional issues ought to be avoided where possible, cf. *Department of Housing and Urban Development v. Rucker*, 535 U.S. 125 ... (2002) (slip op., at 9–10); *Ashwander v. TVA*, 297 U.S. 288, 345–348, ... (1936) (Brandeis, J., concurring), the trial court should be in a position as soon as possible in the litigation to know whether a potential constitutional ruling may be obviated because the allegations of denied access fail to state a claim on which relief could be granted.

In sum, the right of a defendant in a backward-looking access suit to obtain early dismissal of a hopelessly incomplete claim for relief coincides in this case with the obligation of the Judicial Branch to avoid deciding constitutional issues needlessly.

Note

Judicial Deference to Congress in Separation of Powers Disputes

Courts normally approach constitutional challenges to legislative enactments with a rebuttal presumption that Congress has acted within its legitimate powers. However, some observers argue that this rule, premised as it is on a spirit of comity and mutual respect between coordinate branches of the Government, is inapplicable when the case involves a dispute about the constitutional authority of the two political branches. Under such circumstances, the Court's duty is to remain neutral until the question has been addressed on the merits—presumptively favoring neither branch.

This position was articulated by Justice Scalia in his dissent in the "Special Prosecutor" case:

Morrison v. Olson

487 U.S. 654 (1988)

It is rare in a case dealing, as this one does, with the constitutionality of a statute passed by the Congress of the United States, not to find anywhere in the Court's opinion the usual, almost formulary caution that we owe great deference to Congress' view that what it has done is constitutional.... (citations omitted), and that we will decline to apply the statute only if the *presumption of constitutionality* can be overcome.... That caution is not recited by the Court in the present case *because it does not apply*. Where a private citizen challenges action of the Government on grounds unrelated to separation of powers, harmonious functioning of the system demands that we ordinarily give some deference, or a presumption of validity, to the actions of the political branches in what is agreed, between themselves at least, to be within their respective spheres. But where the issue pertains to separation of powers, and the political branches are (as here) in disagreement, neither can be presumed correct. The reason is stated concisely by Madison: "The several departments being perfectly co-ordinate by the terms of their common commission, neither of them, it is evident, can pretend to an exclusive or superior right of settling the boundaries between *their respective powers....*" Federalist No. 49, p. 314. The playing field for the present case, in other words, is a level one. As one of the interested and coordinate parties to the underlying constitutional dispute, Congress, no more than the President, is entitled to the benefit of the doubt.

Standing

Another important aspect of justiciability is the question of standing. A serious discussion of the topic is beyond the scope of this chapter. However, since national security disputes quite frequently do not involve specific and identifiable harm to the rights of individual citizens, the doctrine often precludes judicial resolution.

The following cases illustrate the difficulties the doctrine of standing poses for private citizens or taxpayers who believe the Government is violating the Constitution in its conduct of national security affairs. The suit involved a challenge to the constitutionality of the Central Intelligence Agency Act on the grounds that its provision allowing the CIA to account for its expenditures "solely on the certificate of the Director"[44] violated the requirement of Article I, section 9, clause 7, of the Constitution, which requires "a regular statement and account" of the expenditure of public funds.

United States v. Richardson
418 U.S. 166, 171–74, 179–80 (1974)

As far back as *Marbury v. Madison*, 1 Cranch 137 (1803), this Court held that judicial power may be exercised only in a case properly before it—a "case or controversy" not suffering any of the limitations of the political-question doctrine, not then moot or calling for an advisory opinion. In *Baker v. Carr*, 369 U.S. 186, 204 (1962), this limitation was described in terms that a federal court cannot " 'pronounce any statute, either of a State or of the United States, void because irreconcilable with the Constitution, except as it is called upon to adjudge the legal rights of litigants in actual controversies.' *Liverpool Steamship Co. v. Commissioners of Emigration*, 113 U.S. 33, 39."

Recently in *Association of Data Processing Service Organizations, Inc. v. Camp*, 397 U.S. 150 (1970), the Court, while noting that "[g]eneralizations about standing to sue are largely worthless as such," *id.*, at 151, emphasized that "[o]ne generalization is, however, necessary and that is that the question of standing in the federal courts is to be considered in the framework of Article III which restricts judicial power to 'cases' and 'controversies.'"

Although the recent holding of the Court in *Flast v. Cohen*, *supra*, is a starting point in an examination of respondent's claim to prosecute this suit as a taxpayer, that case must be read with reference to its principal predecessor, *Frothingham v. Mellon*, 262 U.S.

---

44. Central Intelligence Agency Act, 50 U.S.C. § 403 (b) (1947).

447 (1923). In *Frothingham*, the injury alleged was that the congressional enactment challenged as unconstitutional would, if implemented, increase the complainant's future federal income taxes. Denying standing, the *Frothingham* Court rested on the "comparatively minute[,] remote, fluctuating and uncertain," *id.*, at 487, impact on the taxpayer, and the failure to allege the kind of direct injury required for standing.

> "The party who invokes the [judicial] power must be able to show not only that the statute is invalid but that he has sustained or is immediately in danger of sustaining some direct injury as the result of its enforcement, and not merely that he suffers in some indefinite way in common with people generally." *Id.* at 488.

When the Court addressed the question of standing in *Flast*, Mr. Chief Justice Warren traced what he described as the "confusion" following *Frothingham* as to whether the Court had announced a constitutional doctrine barring suits by taxpayers challenging federal expenditures as unconstitutional or simply a policy rule of judicial self-restraint. In an effort to clarify the confusion and to take into account intervening developments, of which class actions and joinder under the Federal Rules of Civil Procedure were given as examples, the Court embarked on "a fresh examination of the limitations upon standing to sue in a federal court and the application of those limitations to taxpayer suits." 392 U.S., at 94. That re-examination led, however, to the holding that a "taxpayer will have standing *consistent with Article III* to invoke federal judicial power when he alleges that congressional action under the taxing and spending clause is in derogation of those constitutional provisions *which operate to restrict the exercise of the taxing and spending power.*" *Id.*, at 105–106. (Emphasis supplied.) In so holding, the Court emphasized that Art. III requirements are the threshold inquiry:

> "The 'gist of the question of standing' is whether the party seeking relief has 'alleged' such a personal stake in the outcome of the controversy as to assure that concrete adverseness ... upon which the court so largely depends for illumination of difficult constitutional questions.'" *Id.*, at 99, citing *Baker v. Carr*, 369 U.S., at 204.

The Court then announced a two-pronged standing test which requires allegations: (a) challenging an enactment under the Taxing and Spending Clause of Art. I § 8, of the Constitution; and (b) claiming that the challenged enactment exceeds specific constitutional limitations imposed on the taxing and spending power. 392 U.S., at 102–103. While the "impenetrable barrier to suits against Acts of Congress brought by individuals who can assert only the interest of federal taxpayers," *id.*, at 85, had been slightly lowered, the Court made clear it was reaffirming the principle of *Frothingham* precluding a taxpayer's use of "a federal court as a forum in which to air his generalized grievances about the conduct of government or the allocation of power in the Federal System." *Id.*, at 106. The narrowness of that holding is emphasized by the concurring opinion of MR. JUSTICE STEWART in *Flast*:

> "In concluding that the appellants therefore have standing to sue, we do not undermine the salutary principle, established by *Frothingham* and reaffirmed today, that a taxpayer may not 'employ a federal court as a forum in which to air his generalized grievances about the conduct of government or the allocation of power in the Federal System.'" *Id.*, at 114.

....

It can be argued that if respondent is not permitted to litigate this issue, no one can do so. In a very real sense, the absence of any particular individual or class to litigate these claims gives support to the argument that the subject matter is committed to the surveillance of Congress, and ultimately to the political process. Any other conclusion would mean that the Founding Fathers intended to set up something in the nature of an Athenian democracy or a New England town meeting to oversee the conduct of the National Government by means of lawsuits in federal courts. The Constitution created a *representative* Government with the representatives directly responsible to their constituents at stated periods of two, four, and six years; that the Constitution does not afford a judicial remedy does not, of course, completely disable the citizen who is not satisfied with the "ground rules" established by the Congress for reporting expenditures of the Executive Branch. Lack of standing within the narrow confines of Art. III jurisdiction does not impair the right to assert his views in the political forum or at the polls. Slow, cumbersome, and unresponsive though the traditional electoral process may be thought at times, our system provides for changing members of the political branches when dissatisfied citizens convince a sufficient number of their fellow electors that elected representatives are delinquent in performing duties committed to them.

As our society has become more complex, our numbers more vast, our lives more varied, and our resources more strained, citizens increasingly request the intervention of the courts on a greater variety of issues than at any period of our national development. The acceptance of new categories of judicially cognizable injury has not eliminated the basic principle that to invoke judicial power the claimant must have a "personal stake in the outcome," *Baker v. Carr, supra,* at 204, or a "particular, concrete injury," *Sierra Club, supra,* at 740–741, n. 16, or "a direct injury," *Ex parte Lévitt, supra,* at 634; in short, something more than "generalized grievances," *Flast, supra,* at 106. Respondent has failed to meet these fundamental tests; accordingly, the judgment of the Court of Appeals is *Reversed.*

During the same term, the Court considered a suit by an association of current and former members of the military Reserve who were opposed to U.S. involvement in the Vietnam conflict. They charged that it was unconstitutional for Members of Congress to hold positions in the Reserve, and sought to obtain standing as "citizens" of the United States.

Schlesinger v. Reservists to Stop the War

418 U.S. 208, 209–12, 216–21 (1974)

Article I, §6, cl. 2, of the Federal Constitution provides:

> "No Senator or Representative shall, during the Time for which he was elected, be appointed to any civil Office under the Authority of the United States, which shall have been created, or the Emoluments whereof shall have been increased during such time; and no Person holding any Office under the United States shall be a Member of either House during his Continuance in Office."

The Constitution thereby makes Members of Congress ineligible for appointment to certain offices through the limitation of the Ineligibility Clause, and prohibits Members of Congress from holding other offices through the latter limitation, the Incompatibility Clause.

Respondents, the Reservists Committee to Stop the War and certain named members thereof, challenged the Reserve membership of Members of Congress as being in violation of the Incompatibility Clause....

Respondents sought the above relief on behalf of four classes of persons. The Committee and the individual respondents sought to represent the interests of (1) all persons opposed to United States military involvement in Vietnam and purporting to use lawful means, including communication with and persuasion of Members of Congress, to end that involvement. The individual respondents alone sought to represent the interests of (2) all officers and enlisted members of the Reserves who were not Members of Congress, (3) all taxpayers of the United States, and (4) all citizens of the United States. The interests of these four classes were alleged to be adversely affected by the Reserve membership of Members of Congress in various ways.

As relevant here, citizens and taxpayers were alleged in respondents' complaint to have suffered injury because Members of Congress holding a Reserve position in the Executive Branch were said to be subject to the possibility of undue influence by the Executive Branch, in violation of the concept of the independence of Congress implicit in Art. I of the Constitution. Reserve membership was also said to place upon Members of Congress possible inconsistent obligations which might cause them to violate their duty faithfully to perform as reservists or as Members of Congress....

....

B
Citizen Standing

To have standing to sue as a class representative it is essential that a plaintiff must be a part of that class, that is, he must possess the same interest and suffer the same injury shared by all members of the class he represents.... In granting respondents standing to sue as representatives of the class of all United States citizens, the District Court therefore necessarily—and correctly—characterized respondent's interest as "undifferentiated" from that of all other citizens.

The only interest all citizens share in the claim advanced by respondents is one which presents injury in the abstract. Respondents seek to have the Judicial Branch compel the Executive Branch to act in conformity with the Incompatibility Clause, an interest shared by all citizens. The very language of respondent's complaint, ... reveals that it is nothing more than a matter of speculation whether the claimed nonobservance of Congress deprives citizens of the faithful discharge of the legislative duties of reservist Members of Congress. And that claimed nonobservance, standing alone, would adversely affect only the generalized interest of all citizens in constitutional governance, and that is an abstract injury. The court has previously declined to treat "generalized grievances" about the conduct of Government as a basis for taxpayer standing. *Flast v. Cohen*, 392 U.S., at 106. We consider now whether a citizen has standing to sue under such a generalized complaint.

Our analysis begins with *Baker v. Carr*, 369 U.S. 186 (1962), where the Court stated that the gist of the inquiry must be whether the complaining party has

> "alleged such a personal stake in the outcome of the controversy as to assure that concrete adverseness which sharpens the presentation of issues upon which the court so largely depends for illumination of difficult constitutional questions."
> *Id.*, at 204

Although dealing with a case of claimed taxpayer standing, *Flast v. Cohen*, ... gave further meaning to the need for a "personal stake" in noting that it was meant to assure that the complainant seeking to adjudicate his claim was the "proper party" to present the claim "in an adversary context and in a form historically viewed as capable of judicial resolution." ... While *Flast* noted that the "case or controversy" limitation on the federal judicial power found in Art. III is a "blend of constitutional requirements and policy considerations," *id.*, at 97, the Court, subsequently, in the context of judicial review of regulatory agency action held that whatever else the "case or controversy" requirement embodied, its essence is a requirement of "injury in fact." ... Although we ... noted that the categories of judicially cognizable injury were being broadened, ... we have more recently stressed that the broadening of *categories* "is a different matter from abandoning the requirement that the party seeking review must himself have suffered an injury." ... And, in defining the nature of that injury, we have only recently stated flatly: "Abstract injury is not enough." ...

Ex parte Lévitt, 302 U.S. 633 (1937), was the only other occasion in which the Court faced a question under Art. I, § 6, cl. 2, although that challenge was made under the Ineligibility Clause, not the Incompatibility Clause involved here. There a petition was filed in this Court seeking an order to show cause why one of the Justices should not be disqualified to serve as an Associate Justice. The petition asserted that the appointment and confirmation of the Justice in August 1937 was unlawful because the Act of March 1, 1937, permitting Justices to retire at full salary after a period of specified service, thereby increased the emoluments of the office and that the statute was enacted while the challenged Justice was a Senator. The appointment of the Justice by the President and his confirmation by the Senate were thus said to violate the Ineligibility Clause which provides:

> "No Senator or Representative shall, during the Time for which he was elected, be appointed to any civil Office under the Authority of the United States ... the Emoluments whereof shall have been increased during such time...."

The Court held:

> "The motion papers disclose no interest upon the part of the petitioner other than that of a citizen and a member of the bar of this Court. That is insufficient. It is an established principle that to entitle a private individual to invoke the judicial power to determine the validity of executive or legislative action he must show that he has sustained or is immediately in danger of sustaining a direct injury as the result of that action and it is not sufficient that he has merely a general interest common to all members of the public." 302 U.S., at 634.

The Court has today recognized the continued vitality of *Lévitt, United States v. Richardson, ante*, at 176–179; see also *Laird v. Tatum*, 408 U.S. 1, 13 (1972). We reaffirm *Lévitt* in holding that standing to sue may not be predicated upon an interest of the kind alleged here because of the necessarily abstract nature of the injury all citizens share. Concrete injury, whether actual or threatened, is that indispensable element of a dispute which serves in part to cast it in a form traditionally capable of judicial resolution. It adds the essential dimension of specificity to the dispute by requiring that the complaining party have suffered a particular injury caused by the action challenged as unlawful. This personal stake is what the Court has consistently held enables a complainant authoritatively to present to a court a complete perspective upon the adverse consequences flowing from the specific set of facts undergirding his grievance. Such authoritative presentations are an integral part of the judicial process, for a court must rely on the parties' treatment of the facts and claims before it to develop its rules of law. Only concrete injury presents the factual context within which a court, aided by parties who argue within the context, is capable of making decisions.

The "Unitary Executive" and Presidential Signing Statements

During the administration of President George W. Bush, major debates arose over claims that the Constitution established a "unitary executive" — in which all executive power was vested personally in the president, rather than in cabinet members and subordinate officials—and the use of "signing statements" to announce that the president would not enforce certain parts of bills as he signed them into law. When properly understood, neither issue is as controversial as the critics once alleged.

The "Unitary Executive"

The claim of a "unitary executive" was associated with a series of controversial decisions (like excluding military lawyers from decisions concerning the proper treatment of detainees believed to be associated with the terrorist group al Qaeda). Those decisions may well have been poorly made, but the underlying claim that the Constitution vests "the executive Power" in the President (rather than in the entire Executive branch) is fairly clear from the documents text. While the "legislative" and "judicial" powers are vested, respectively, in "a Congress of the United States"[45] and "one supreme Court, and in such inferior Courts as the Congress may from time to time ordain and establish"[46]; Article II, Section 1 provides: "The executive Power shall be vested in a President of the United States of America."[47] Thus, while over the years Congress has established a number of executive departments and agencies, and the Senate has consented to the appointment of nominees submitted by the president, the final decision on executive branch matters is confided by the Constitution in the president. (Because of the scope of this chapter, I am not addressing the propriety of Congress establishing "quasi-executive" entitles like the Federal Trade Commission and Federal Communications Commission, but rather such core "executive" functions as the conduct of diplomacy and military operations.)

Some critics of the theory of a "unliterary executive" have portrayed it as an unprecedented assertion of presidential "dictatorship." In 2013, American University Government Professor Chris Edelson declared in remarks to the American Constitution Society:

> In March 2009, about a month after President George W. Bush and Dick Cheney left office, Scott Horton declared that "[w]e may not have realized it, but in the period from late 2001–January 19, 2009, this country was a dictatorship. That was thanks to secret memos crafted deep inside the Justice Department that effectively trashed the Constitution." Some of the most infamous of these memos were drafted by John Yoo, an Office of Legal Counsel attorney from 2001–2003. Yoo and others—most notably, Cheney's counsel, David Addington—advanced the unitary executive theory, a theory of presidential power Cheney had personally favored for decades.[48]

Pomona College Politics Professor Amanda Hollis-Brusky notes the Unitary Executive Theory (UTE) predates the administration of Professor George W. Bush:

> The ideas and language attendant to the UET began to appear in scattered law review articles throughout the mid-to-late 1970s. However, it was not until the beginning of the Reagan Administration that the UET made its political debut.... [B]eginning in 1981 officials in the Reagan Justice Department started using the language "unitary executive" to defend and bolster presidential priorities in signing statements, OLC opinions, and legal briefs.... Reagan's Justice Department

---

45. U.S. Const, Art. I, Sec. 1.
46. *Id.*, Art. III, Sec. 1.
47. *Id.*, Art. II, Sec. 1.
48. Chris Edelson, Exploring the Limits of Presidential Power, ACS Blog, Dec. 2, 2013, https://www.acslaw.org/acsblog/exploring-the-limits-of-presidential-power.

should still be described as revolutionary for the legacy it left behind in the form of ideas and, more important, personnel who were shaped by those ideas.[49]

Writing during the first year of the Clinton Administration, Professor Lawrence Lessig of the University of Chicago Law School declared: "as should have been clear long ago, the view that the Framers embraced anything like the Unitarianism spouted by the modern unitarians is just plain myth." But he conceded: "it is not my claim that ultimately the best reading of our constitutional design is not Unitarian. Indeed, ... although ... it was not the design of the Framers, Unitarianism may be the reading most faithful to the Framers' original design today."[50]

As should be apparent from the early readings in this chapter, the Framers did embrace the idea of a unitary executive—carefully modified by the creation of certain important checks or "negatives" vested in the Senate and Congress. It is clear from the structure of Article III, Section 1, that Congress knew how to invest power in multiple components of a branch of government—as it vested the new nation's "judicial power" in "one Supreme Court, and in such inferior courts as the Congress may from time to time ordain and establish." Using the same structure, the Framers might have vested the "executive Power" in a president and such departments as Congress might establish. But the Framers elected to vest all of the nation's executive power in "a President of the United States of America," save for those exceptions spelled out in the instrument.

The principle that the President's will was to control decisions by the Secretary of Foreign Affairs (now State) was set forth clearly in the 1789 statute creating the department, in which Congress declared that officer was to "perform and execute such duties as shall from time to time be enjoined on, or intrusted to him by the President of the United States, agreeable to the Constitution...."[51] In *Marbury v. Madison*, Chief Justice John Marshall used this statute as an example of the vesting in the president of certain exclusive powers by the Constitution. Marshall explained that the President was "authorized to appoint certain officers, who act by his authority and in conformity with his orders." He explained: "their acts are his acts; and whatever opinion may be entertained of the manner in which executive discretion may be used, still there exists, and can exist, no power to control that discretion." Marshall explained that the Secretary of Foreign Affairs "is the mere organ by whom that [presidential] will is communicated."[52]

Presidential Signing Statements

Properly understood, the related principle behind presidential "signing statements" should not be constitutionally controversial. (This is not to say that some specific signing statements are not quite properly controversial.)[53] Indeed, the bipartisan practice dates back to the early nineteenth century.

---

49. Amanda Hollis-Brusky, *Helping Ideas Have Consequences: Political and Intellectual Investment in the Unitary Executive Theory, 1981–2000*, 89 Denv. U. L. Rev. 197, 201 (2011).

50. Lawrence Lessig, *Executive Branch Interpretation of the Law: Readings By our Unitary Executive*, 15 Cardozo L. Rev. 175, 176 (1993).

51. 1 Stat. 28 (1789).

52. Marbury v. Madison, 1 Cranch 137, 166 (1803).

53. For example, when Congress enacted the Detainee Treatment Act of 2005 (41 U.S.C. 21d), President Bush declared: "The executive branch shall construe ... the Act, relating to detainees, in a manner consistent with the constitutional authority of the President to supervise the unitary executive branch and as Commander in Chief and consistent with the constitutional limitations on the judicial power...." While many modern legislative acts related to war or foreign affairs do arguably conflict with the President's constitutional discretion in this area, one of the clear "exceptions" vested in

Robert F. Turner, *U.S. Constitutional Issues in the Struggle Against Terror*

in Legal Issues in the Struggle Against Terror (John Norton Moore & Robert F. Turner, eds.) 81, 106–08 (2010)

. . . .

Presidential Signing Statements

[A]nother cause of concern in recent years has been the practice of presidential "signing statements"—essentially a process by which in signing a statute into law the President declares that he will not be bound by one or more sections that he believes to be unconstitutional. An alternative version declares than an ambiguous provision of a statute will be interpreted so as to avoid violating the Constitution.

In August 2006 the American Bar Association House of Delegates approved a resolution declaring that presidential signing statements are "contrary to the rule of law and our constitutional system of separation of powers," and both indignant politicians and editorial writers have denounced the practice in similar terms. The President's constitutional duty, they remind us, is to see the laws enacted by Congress "faithfully executed," not to rewrite them or declare that certain provisions won't be enforced.

Presidential signing statements have been around since the presidency of James Monroe, and the underlying principle dates back at least to the first term of Thomas Jefferson in 1801. Shortly after assuming office, Jefferson announced that he would not enforce the Alien and Sedition Acts because they were un-constitutional, and he ordered all U.S. attorneys with pending cases to cease prosecution.

In 1942, a powerful member of the House Appropriations Committee inserted a rider in an emergency supplemental appropriations bill for World War II providing that no funds could be used to pay the salaries of three named government employees who had been identified as "subversives" by the House Committee on Un-American Activities. Some legislators compared the provision to "star chamber" proceedings and others described it as a "legislative lynching." The Senate repeatedly rejected the conference report on the bill in an effort to get the language dropped. But the money was desperately needed to fight the war, so the Senate ultimately yielded.

While signing the bill into law, President Roosevelt issued a signing statement declaring that the provision in question was unconstitutional and therefore would not bind either the executive or judicial branches. It took four years for a suit challenging the provision to make its way to the Supreme Court, which promptly struck the provision down as an unconstitutional bill of attainder.[54]

The use of signing statements has expanded dramatically since the end of the Vietnam War, and many of them have been attached to statutes that seek to control presidential discretion in foreign affairs or related areas that traditionally have been understood by all three branches to be beyond the reach of legislation. But by far the single most common reason for issuing a signing statement is the attachment by Congress of "legislative vetoes"—providing in a law that Congress or a component thereof (a single chamber, or even a single committee or chairman thereof) can reverse a decision taken by the Executive Branch without going through the constitutionally-mandated process for enacting a new law.

Congress by Article I, Section 8 is the power "To define and punish ... Offences against the Law of Nations...."

54. *United States v. Lovett*, 328 U.S. 303 (1946).

In 1974, acting pursuant to a provision of the Immigration and Nationality Act, the Attorney General suspended the deportation of a foreign exchange student named Jagdish Rai Chada on humanitarian grounds and reported the action to the Congress as required by the statute. As provided in the act, the House of Representatives then voted to overturn the Attorney General's action and ordered the immediate deportation of the alien. Article I, Section 8 of the Constitution expressly vests in Congress the power to "establish a uniform Rule of Naturalization," so there was no doubt about the power of Congress to legislate in this area. But in the summer of 1983, the Supreme Court held that, to have legal effect, actions by Congress must comply with the formalities set forth in Article I of the Constitution (*e.g.*, be approved by both chambers and be submitted to the President for signature or veto). Efforts by Congress to empower a single branch or committee to overturn executive action, or even to empower both houses to act by concurrent resolution without submitting the resolution to the President for possible veto, were held to be unconstitutional. The *Chada* decision also struck down by implication legislative vetoes in national security legislation like section 5(c) of the 1973 War Powers Resolution.

One might have expected Congress to respond to the Court's ruling by directing its staff to search the statute books to identify legislative vetoes so they could be repealed. Instead, Congress elected to ignore the Supreme Court's ruling—and since the 1983 *Chadha* decision the Congress has enacted no fewer than 500 new legislative vetoes. Presidents have tended to issue signing statements declaring that they will not be bound by these clearly unconstitutional provisions, and to refuse to enforce them in practice.

Selected Bibliography

THEORY OF SEPARATION OF POWERS

BOOKS

Calabresi Steven G., & Yoo, Christopher S., *The Unitary Executive: Presidential Power from Washington to Bush* (2008).

Cheever, Daniel, & Henry Haviland. *American Foreign Policy and the Separation of Powers* (1952).

Corwin, Edward, *The President: Office And Powers 1787–1957* (4th rev. ed. 1957).

————. *Presidential Powers and the Constitution* (1976).

Elliott, Jonathan, ed., *Debates In The Several State Conventions On Adoption of The Federal Constitution* 5 vols. (1861).

Farrand, Max, ed., *The Records of the Federal Convention Of 1787* 4 vols. (1966).

Fisher, Louis, *The Politics of Shared Power* (1998).

Goldsmith, William, *The Growth of Presidential Power*, 3 vols. (1974).

Henkin, Louis, *Foreign Affairs and the Constitution* (1972).

Koh, Harold Hongju, *The National Security Constitution* (1990).

Montesquieu, *The Spirit Of The Laws*. 2 vols. (T. Nugent trans., rev. ed. 1900).

Pomeroy, John, *An Introduction To The Constitutional Law of the United States* (9th rev. ed. 1886).

Schlesinger, Arthur, *The Imperial Presidency* (1973).

Story, Joseph, *Commentaries on the Constitution of the United States* (5th ed. 1891).

Taft, William, *Our Chief Magistrate and His Powers* (1916).

Thach, Jr., Charles, *The Creation of the Presidency: 1775–1789* (1923).

Vile, M.J.C., *Constitutionalism and Separation of Powers* (1967).

Warren, Charles, *The Making of the Constitution* (1937).

Willoughby, Westel, *Principles of the Constitutional Law of the United States* 3 vols. (2d ed. 1938).

Wilson, Bradford P., & Peter W. Schramm eds., *Separation of Powers and Good Government* (1994).

Wright, Quincy, *The Control of American Foreign Relations* (1922).

Wriston, Henry, *Executive Agents in American Foreign Relations* (1967).

ARTICLES

Bestor, Arthur, "Separation of Powers in the Domain of Foreign Affairs," 5 *Seton Hall L. Rev.* 527 (1974).

Bradley, Curtiss A. & Trevor W. Morrison, "Historical Gloss and the Separation of Powers," 126 *Harv. L. Rev.* 411 (2012).

Casper, Gerhard, "Constitutional Constraints on the Conduct of Foreign and Defense Policy," 43 *U. Chi. L. Rev.* 463 (1976).

Corwin, Edward, "The Progress of Constitutional Theory Between the Declaration of Independence and the Meeting of the Philadelphia Convention," 30 *Am. Hist. Rev.* 511 (1925).

Fisher, Louis, "The Efficiency Side of Separated Powers," *J. Am. Stud.* 119 (1971).

Henkin, Louis, "Foreign Affairs and the Constitution," 66 *Foreign Aff.* 284 (Winter 1987/88).

Levitan, David, "The Foreign Relations Power," 55 *Yale L.J.* 467 (1946).

Thurow, Glen, "Presidential Discretion in Foreign Affairs," 11 *Vand. J. Trans. L.J.* 75 (1973).

Turner, Robert F., *War and the Forgotten Executive Power Clause of the Constitution,* 34 Va. J. Int'l L. 903 (1994).

———, "Understanding the Separation of Foreign Affairs Powers Under the Constitution," 60 *N.Y. St. B. J.* 8 (1988).

———, "Separation of Powers in Foreign Policy: The Theoretical Underpinnings," 11 *Geo. Mason U. L. Rev.* 97 (1988).

———, "The Constitution and the Iran-Contra Affair," 11 *Houston J. Int'l L.* 83 (1988).

Wallace, Don, "The President's Exclusive Foreign Affairs Powers over Foreign Aid," *Duke L.J.* 293 (1970).

Wright, Quincy, "The Origins of the Separation of Powers in America," 13 *Economica* 184 (1933).

THE ROLE OF THE COURTS

BOOKS

Bickel, Alexander, *The Least Dangerous Branch* (1962).

Bland, Randall W., *The Black Robe and the Bald Eagle: The Supreme Court and the Foreign Policy of the United States 1789–1953* (1996).

Henkin, Louis, *Foreign Affairs and the Constitution* (1972).

Moore, John Norton, *Law and the Indo-China War* (1972).

Rossiter, Clinton, *The Supreme Court and the Commander in Chief* (1951).

ARTICLES

Dickinson, Todd, "The Law of Nations as Part of the National Law of the United States," 101 *U. Pa. L. Rev.* 26 (1952).

Firmage, Edwin, "The War Powers and the Political Question Doctrine," 49 *U. Colo. L. Rev.* 65 (1977).

Henkin, Louis, "The Foreign Affairs Power of the Federal Courts: Sabbatino," 64 *Colum. L. Rev.* 805 (1964).

————, "Is there a 'Political Question' Doctrine?" 85 *Yale L.J.* 597 (1976).
————, "Vietnam in the Courts of the United States: 'Political Questions,'" 63 *Am. J. Int'l L.* 284 (1969).
Moore, John Norton, "Federalism and Foreign Relations," *Duke L.J.* 248 (1965).
Scharpf, Fritz, "Judicial Review and the Political Question," 75 *Yale L.J.* 517 (1966).

Chapter 20

The Constitutional Framework for the Use of Force by the President and the Role of Congress

Robert F. Turner

In this chapter:
The Decision to Commence War
Force Short of War: Defensive Uses of Military Force by the President
Selected Bibliography

Chapter 19 began with a discussion of some of the misunderstandings that confuse much of the modern professional literature about the separation of national security powers. Once widely viewed as the primary basis for the President's special responsibilities for the making and implementation of national policy regarding the external world, the Executive Power (or "Vesting") Clause is seldom even seriously addressed in contemporary legal commentary. Similar problems exist when trying to understand the separation of powers related to the use of military force. Consider this excerpt:

STEPHEN DYCUS ET AL., NATIONAL SECURITY LAW
7–8 (2002)

How is the responsibility to "provide for the common defence" allocated among the three branches of government?

Judging simply by the proportion of words, the extensive national security powers given Congress in Article I appear to overwhelm the meager listing for the President in Article II.... Other provisions, particularly the one for impeachment of the President, also suggest legislative dominance....

By contrast, the President is provided only one obvious national security power by being designated the "Commander in Chief." Moreover, the President is directed to command the armed forces only when they are "called into the actual service of the United States."... The other Article II grants that may concern national security seem modest in comparison to powers conferred upon Congress: to appoint and receive ambassadors and ministers, and to make treaties (both powers shared with the Senate).

———

As some of the other excerpts quoted at the beginning of Chapter 19 demonstrate, this is typical of the modern "conventional wisdom" taught in American law schools today. Modern assumptions to the contrary, however, Congress was not given the substantive power "to provide for the common Defence" of the nation, but instead the power "[t]o lay and collect Taxes, Duties, Imposts and Excises," *in order* "to pay the Debts and provide for the common Defence and general Welfare of the United States...." This is evident from a lengthy 1830 letter in which James Madison carefully traced the history of the clause at the Philadelphia Convention, noting that it was added to the draft constitution on August 25, 1787, to clarify that the power to "lay & collect taxes" was to be "for payment of said debts, and for defraying the expences that shall be incurred for the common defence & general welfare." Focusing upon the "general welfare" part of the clause, which some had argued must give Congress the power to pass any legislation its members thought might promote the nation's "general welfare," Madison explained:

> That the terms in question were not suspected, in the Convention which formed the Constitution of any such meaning as has been constructively applied to them, may be pronounced with entire confidence. For it exceeds the possibility of belief, that the known advocates in the Convention for a jealous grant & cautious definition of federal powers, should have silently permitted the introduction of words or phrases in a sense rendering fruitless the restrictions & definitions elaborated by them.... The difference is equivalent to two Constitutions...."[1]

Nearly four decades earlier, in a 1791 memorandum to President Washington, Thomas Jefferson had reasoned with respect to this clause: "the laying of taxes is the *power*, and the [common defence and] general welfare the *purpose* for which the power is to be exercised.... they are not to *do anything they please* to provide for the general welfare, but only to *lay taxes* for that purpose."[2]

Nor is the President's commander-in-chief power contingent upon "Congress's having authorized a war" as alleged by former Stanford Law School Dean John Hart Ely.[3] Indeed, one of the President's most important military duties is to so deploy the armed forces provided by Congress as to deter aggression and *avoid* war. Nor, for that matter, is the President's command of the nation's armed forces contingent upon their being "called into the actual service of the United States" by Congress. (Despite the ambiguous punctuation, that clause clearly refers to the President's command "of the Militia of the several States, when called into the actual Service of the United States.")

This is not to suggest that Congress lacks critically important substantive powers related to national defense. The President has the exclusive power to "command" the nation's armed forces, but unless and until Congress "raises" those forces it is a hollow power indeed. Nor may the President expend treasury funds without prior authorization by Congress, and significant military operations are impossible without appropriations. The problem with misreading the reference in the constitutional text to "the common defense" is that it can easily be misunderstood to suggest that Congress has some role in the command of military forces or the conduct of military operations and thus blur the separation of powers that clearly exists in this area. To understand the constitutional allocation of war powers, some historical background is useful.

---

1. Letter from James Madison to Andrew Stevenson, Nov. 17, 1830, *reprinted in* 3 THE RECORDS OF THE FEDERAL CONVENTION 483, 485, 488 (Max Farrand ed., 1966).

2. *Reprinted in* 3 WRITINGS OF THOMAS JEFFERSON 145, 148 (mem. ed. 1903) (emphasis in original).

3. JOHN HART ELY, WAR AND RESPONSIBILITY: CONSTITUTIONAL LESSONS OF VIETNAM AND ITS AFTERMATH 139 n.3 (1993), quoted at the start of Chapter 19.

The Decision to Commence War

Historical Background

The theorists who most influenced the Founding Fathers in the sphere of separation of powers generally regarded the decision to initiate a war, along with other aspects of external intercourse, to be the exclusive province of the Executive.[4] This theory, however, was rejected in Philadelphia at the Constitutional Convention.

As reported by the Committee of Detail on August 6, 1787, the draft constitution empowered the legislature "to make war."[5] When this provision came up for discussion in the full convention eleven days later, concern was expressed about the slowness of legislative proceedings and it was suggested that the power in question more properly should be given to the Senate (Mr. Pinkney) or the President (Mr. Butler). James Madison, who introduced the successful amendment to reduce the power given Congress from that of making War to that of declaring War, kept the most detailed notes on the debates of the Federal Convention:

4 THE WRITINGS OF JAMES MADISON
227–28 (Gaillard Hunt ed., 1903)

M[r]. Madison and M[r]. Gerry moved to insert "*declare*," striking out "*make*" war; leaving to the Executive the power to repel sudden attacks.

M[r]. Sharman thought it stood very well. The Executive sh[d]. be able to repel and not to commence war. "Make" is better than "declare" the latter narrowing the power too much.

M[r]. Gerry never expected to hear in a republic a motion to empower the Executive alone to declare war.

M[r]. Elsworth. There is a material difference between the cases of making *war* and making *peace*. It sh[d]. be more easy to get out of war, than into it. War also is a simple and overt declaration, peace attended with intricate & secret negociations.

M[r]. Mason was ag[st]. giving the power of war to the Executive because not safely to be trusted with it; or to the Senate, because not so constructed as to be entitled to it. He was for clogging rather than facilitating war; but for facilitating peace. He preferred "*declare*" to "*make*."

On the motion to insert "*declare*" — in place of "*make*," it was agreed to.

N. H. no. Mass. abs[t]. Con[t]. no. P[a]. ay. Del. ay. M[d]. ay. V[a]. ay. N. C. ay. S. C. ay. Geo. ay.

M[r]. Pinkney's motion to strike out whole clause, disag[d]. to without call of States.

———————

As Madison recorded, the vote on the Madison-Gerry proposal was initially seven to two in favor, but a second vote was taken and Oliver Ellsworth of Connecticut changed his vote from "nay" to "ay" "[o]n the remark by Rufus King that '*make*' war might be un-

———————

4. *See* the excerpts from Locke, Montesquieu, and Blackstone in Chapter 19.
5. 2 MAX FARRAND, RECORD OF THE FEDERAL CONVENTION OF 1787, at 182 (rev. ed. 1966).

derstood to 'conduct' it which was an Executive function...."[6] Thus, the final vote in support of the Madison-Gerry amendment was eight to one.

The Eighteenth Century Meaning of "Declare War"

In trying to resolve the tension between the grant to the President of the Commander in Chief power and the vesting in Congress of the power "to declare war," most of the modern debate has focused upon the meaning of the word "war." But given the widespread understanding by the Framers that "exceptions" to the general grant of "executive Power" to the president were to be construed "strictly" or "narrowly"[7] and the fact that "declare war" was a term of art in the law of nations with an understood meaning, a more useful inquiry may be to ask what "declare war" meant to the Framers. After all, we know that they voted overwhelmingly to narrow the power being given to Congress in this area, and focusing upon the meaning of "war" ignores that reality.

Robert F. Turner, *War and the Forgotten Executive Power Clause of the Constitution*

34 Va. J. Int'l L. 903, 905–10 (1994)

III. Declarations of War

....

... Identifying clause 11 of Article I, section 8, of the Constitution as "the War Clause" may be a useful shorthand. However, it is essential to keep in mind that the operative term in this clause is not *war*, an admittedly ambiguous word, but *declare war*, which in 1789 had a well-established meaning in the law of nations. Historically, and as understood by the Founding Fathers, this was an act associated with the initiation of offensive (aggressive) hostilities.

The Founding Fathers were well-read men, and the second most common lawbook found in a study of approximately one hundred private libraries in colonial Virginia was the landmark treatise by Hugo Grotius (1583–1645), *De Jure Belli ac Pacis* (The Law of War and Peace). Among the most extensive of these libraries was that of our third president, which subsequently formed the basis of the collection of the Library of Congress. The 1983 *Catalogue of the Library of Thomas Jefferson* devotes more than 20 pages to Jefferson's books on the "Law of Nature and Nations," including multiple copies of some of the more important works.

Declarations of war were widely discussed in the leading treatises on the law of nations. Grotius, the man widely acclaimed as the "father" of modern international law, argued in 1625:

> To understand ... the declaration of war, we must draw an accurate distinction between what is required by the law of nature [which he contended was the source of international law] and what is not required by the law of nature, but is nevertheless honorable.... By the law of nature, *no declaration is required when one is repelling an invasion, or seeking to punish the actual author of some crime....* And no more

---

6. *Id.* at 319 note 1.
7. *See* Ch. 19.

necessary, by the law of nature, is any declaration when an owner wishes to lay hands on his own property [that has been wrongfully taken by another].

The eminent Dutch publicist argued further that it was superfluous for war to be "declared by both sides," and explained that "[a] declaration of war against the sovereign of a people is considered a declaration at the same time against not only all his subjects but all who will join him as allies and thereby become his accessories." It was precisely because this formal legal action by one state against another carried such a strong content that the Founding Fathers—who believed that [in Jefferson's words] "[i]f there be one principle more deeply rooted than any other in the mind of every American, it is that we should have nothing to do with conquest"—sought in the Constitution to encumber the process.

Similar observations were made by others before and after Grotius published his landmark treatise. Perhaps the most important of the earlier writers was the Italian Alberico Gentili, whose two-volume study was published in 1612. Gentili argued that it was "unjust, detestable, and savage" not to declare war properly when so required, but qualified this by noting that "when war is undertaken for the purpose of necessary *defense*, the declaration is not at all required." English scholar Richard Zouche (1590–1661) maintained the same position. Samuel von Pufendorf (1632–94) devoted but a sentence to the issue, referring his readers to Grotius. Dutchman Cornelius Van Bynkershoek (1673–1743) argued that a declaration of war was "an act of mere humanity," and that no formalities were required to defend against aggression "since all laws permit the repelling of force by force."

Another prominent authority on international law was Swiss jurist Emmerich de Vattel (1714–67). Vattel, who was frequently cited by early Americans like Jefferson, Hamilton, and John Marshall, wrote that "[h]e who is attacked and only wages *defensive* war, needs not to make any hostile declaration,—the state of warfare being sufficiently ascertained by the enemy's declaration." The German Christian Wolff (1679–1754) added in 1764, "[a] defensive war is naturally not to be announced."

Another highly respected Swiss jurist was Jean Jacques Burlamaqui (1694–1748), whose writing was also popular among educated Americans during the years leading up to the Constitutional Convention. He, too, writes about the declaration of war, concluding that "this declaration takes place only in *offensive wars.*"

One of the earliest American authorities on international law was Chancellor James Kent. He reviewed the practice of states, observing that formally declaring war had "fallen into disuse," and noted that "[t]he jurists are ... divided in opinion, in respect to the necessity or justice of some previous declaration to the enemy in the case of *offensive* war." Elsewhere, he wrote:

> It has been usual to precede hostilities by a public declaration. The ancient Romans entered on war with great solemnity.... War with them was held unlawful without a previous declaration. But the modern civilians are divided in opinion as to its necessity and it is now mostly laid aside in practice. It is essential however that some public act should announce to the people their new condition with regard to a foreign nation, and authorize their *aggression*.

————————

When trying to understand the scope of the power of Congress to "declare War," it is important to keep in mind both that this was an *exception* to the general grant of "executive" power to the President (and thus was intended by the Framers to be narrowly construed), and that declarations of war were associated only with offensive (or what we today would call "aggressive") uses of major military force.

Declarations of War in U.S. History

A review of the eleven[8] official "declarations of war" approved by the U.S. Congress reveals that most of them were not, as the term was understood by international law, true "declarations of war" at all. The declaration of war against Great Britain in 1812 was an exception, formally declaring that "War be and the same is hereby declared to exist between the United Kingdom of Great Britain and Ireland and the dependencies thereof, and the United States of America…, and that the President of the United States is hereby authorized to use the whole land and naval force of the United States to carry the same into effect.…" But the 1846 statute widely regarded as a declaration of war was actually "An Act Providing for the Prosecution of the *existing* War Between the United States and the Republic of Mexico" (emphasis added), and seems to be premised upon the theory that Mexico had begun the war by attacking the United States. The 1898 declaration of war against Spain reverted to the 1812 approach and clearly satisfied the requirements of international law. During World War I, Congress took something of a hybrid approach, asserting that "the Imperial German Government has committed repeated acts of war against the Government and the people of the United States" and then resolving "[t]hat the state of war between the United States of America and the Imperial German Government which has thus been thrust upon the United States is hereby formally declared.…" World War II followed this theme, resolving that "the state of war between the United States and the Imperial Government of Japan which has thus been thrust upon the United States is hereby formally declared.…" While eight of these joint resolutions (the Mexican-American War and various declarations during the two world wars) were arguably unnecessary under international law, they may well have served useful domestic purposes in terms of rallying public support and demonstrating national unity.

Neither the United States nor any other state has formally issued a "declaration of war" in more than half-a-century. But Congress has enacted joint resolutions authorizing the President to use military force (AUMFs) on several occasions, including Vietnam and both the 1991 and 2003 conflicts with Iraq. Whether these resolutions were strictly necessary as a matter of constitutional law, or not, they certainly satisfied any constitutional requirement for legislative sanction.

Note: The Jus Ad Bellum Meaning of "Offensive" War

A formal declaration of war was an instrument of that body of international law governing the initiation of coercion (*jus ad bellum*), not the law governing the way in which hostilities are actually conducted (*jus in bello*). Both bodies of law use the term "offensive," but with different meanings; and it is understandable that confusion sometimes results. Whether a formal declaration of war was legally necessary pertained to the reason force was being used. If two nations were at peace and one wished to resort to major war either to conquer territory or to resolve or in response to a political, diplomatic, or economic dispute—behavior that today would be described as unlawful "aggression"—most publicists contended that a formal declaration of their intentions was necessary. The term "offensive" was often used to describe such a military operation. However— just as a victim of a criminal assault under domestic law is not limited to trying to block punches, and may (consistent with requirements of necessity and proportionality) defend

---

8. The United States only "declared war" in five conflicts, but in World War I Congress declared war separately against both Germany and Austria-Hungary, and in World War II it declared war against Japan, Germany, Italy, Bulgaria, Hungary and Romania.

by striking back at the attacker—a country or its allies may lawfully respond defensively to international aggression with an "offensive" strategy. Following the North Korean invasion of South Korea in 1950, General MacArthur responded "offensively" with the Inchon landing. Four decades later, after Iraq invaded Kuwait and the UN Security Council authorized Member States to use force under Chapter VII of the Charter, General Norman Schwarzkopf brilliantly exercised an "end run" (or "left hook") that quickly led to a route of Iraqi forces. Can it reasonably be said that these "offensive" actions in defense of victims of aggression transformed the UN forces into unlawful aggressors and should have been accompanied by formal declarations of war? Keep this distinction in mind as you read the next section.

Thomas Jefferson and the Barbary Pirates

Robert F. Turner, *War and the Forgotten Executive Power Clause of the Constitution*
34 Va. J. Int'l L. 903, 910–16 (1994)

Mr. Jefferson Launches a Defensive War

An interesting debate occurred in connection with Jefferson's First Annual Message to Congress of December 8, 1801. President Jefferson essentially misrepresented the facts of an armed naval conflict with the Barbary Pirates as follows:

> I sent a small squadron of frigates into the Mediterranean, with assurances to that power [Tripoli] of our sincere desire to remain in peace, but with orders to protect our commerce against the threatened attack. The measure was seasonable and salutary. The bey had already declared war in form. His cruisers were out. Two had arrived at Gibraltar. Our commerce in the Mediterranean was blockaded, and that of the Atlantic in peril. The arrival of our squadron dispelled the danger. One of the Tripolitan cruisers having fallen in with, and engaged the small schooner Enterprise, commanded by Lieutenant Sterret, which had gone as a tender to our larger vessels, was captured, after a heavy slaughter of her men, without the loss of a single one on our part.... Unauthorized by the constitution, without the sanction of Congress, to go beyond the line of defence, the vessel being disabled from committing further hostilities, was liberated with its crew. The legislature will doubtless consider whether, by authorizing measures of offence, also, they will place our force on an equal footing with that of its adversaries.

Actually, thanks to the subsequent publication of the relevant historical documents by the Office of Naval Records and Library, by authority of the Congress, it is now established that Captain Richard Dale had been instructed by the Acting Secretary of the Navy, under direction of the President, to sail his squadron to the Mediterranean. If, upon arriving, he learned that the Barbary Pirates had declared war on the United States, he was ordered to "distribute your force in such manner, as your judgment shall direct, so as best to protect our commerce & chastise their insolence—by *sinking, burning or destroying their ships & Vessels wherever you shall find them.*"

In reality, the decision to liberate the vessel in question was made by Captain Dale, who had dispatched Lieutenant Andrew Sterret with the schooner *Enterprise* to proceed to the island of Malta to secure water for the fleet. Sterret was instructed not to be delayed by taking enemy ships as prize while en route to Malta, because "you have not much water on board." His orders provided that if Sterret engaged an enemy vessel "on your Passage to Malta you will heave all his Guns Over board Cut away his Masts, & leave him In a situation, that he can Just make out to get into some Port, but if coming back you will bring her with you if you think you can doe [sic] it with safety."

The limited character of the operation was dictated entirely by operational expedience, not constitutional principle. It is quite possible that Jefferson intentionally overstated the case in order to motivate Congress to quickly unite behind his decision to use force.

Documents contained in the Library of Congress collection of Jefferson's papers reveal that the issue had in fact been discussed during Jefferson's first cabinet meeting on May 15, 1801. The subsequent instructions to Captain Dale to sink, burn, and destroy ships of the Barbary Pirates wherever they could be found reflected the strong consensus that emerged from that meeting regarding the scope of the Commander in Chief power. Typical of the views expressed at the cabinet meeting were those of Treasury Secretary Albert Gallatin, a former member of the Pennsylvania constitutional convention, three-term congressman, and well-known champion of legislative powers. As set down in Jefferson's own hand-written notes:

> Gallatin: to declare war & to make war is synonymous. The Exve can not put us in a state of war, but if we be put into that state either by the decla of Congress or of the other nation, the command & direction of the public force then belongs to the Exve.

On the question of whether "the squadron now at Norfolk [should] be ordered to cruise in the Mediterranean" and "what shall be the object of the cruise," Jefferson noted that "all concur in the expediency of cruise." He then recorded his next inquiry:

> [W]hether the captains may be authorized, if war exists, to search for & destroy the enemy vessels wherever they can find them? All except [Attorney General Lincoln] agree they should; M[adison], G[allatin], & S[mith] think they may pursue into the harbors, but M[adison] that they may not enter but in pursuit.

As already discussed, Acting Secretary of the Navy Samuel Smith subsequently issued orders to the squadron commander including broad authority to search out and destroy the enemy if war had been declared. For reasons that are unclear but may well pertain to a perception that, as a matter of legislative strategy, this approach would get Congress quickly "on board," Jefferson subsequently misrepresented the details of the *Enterprise* encounter in his first annual message to Congress. Jefferson's inaccurate statement to Congress has become a mainstay in the scholarship of advocates of narrow presidential authority to use military force in the absence of formal congressional sanction.

Whatever Jefferson's motives, his *contention* that the Commander in Chief lacked power to use offensive force in response to a foreign attack was sharply challenged. Alexander Hamilton, for example, wrote on December 17, 1801:

> [The Constitution provides that] "[t]he Congress shall have power to declare War;" the plain meaning of which is that, it is the peculiar and exclusive province of Congress, *when the nation is at peace*, to change that state into a state of war; whether from calculations of policy or from provocations or injuries received: in other words, it belongs to Congress only, *to go to War*. But when a foreign nation declares, or openly and avowedly makes war upon the United States, they are then by the very fact, already *at war*, and any declaration on the part of Congress is nugatory: it is at least unnecessary.

A more than 2000-page analysis of the Constitution, prepared by the Congressional Research Service of the Library of Congress, concluded that "Congress apparently accept[ed]

Hamilton's view" of this dispute.[9] Hamilton's view also carried the day with the Supreme Court when President Abraham Lincoln's failure to get formal legislative sanction to attack secessionist states during the Civil War was challenged by the owners of ships seized as prizes of war, as the following excerpt reveals:

The Prize Cases
243 US 124 (1863)

By the Constitution, Congress alone has the power to declare a national or foreign war.... The Constitution confers on the President the whole Executive power. He is bound to take care that the laws be faithfully executed. He is Commander-in-chief of the Army and Navy of the United States.... He has no power to initiate or declare a war either against a foreign nation or a domestic State.... [But i]f a war be made by invasion of a foreign nation, the President is not only authorized but bound to resist force by force. He does not initiate the war, but is bound to accept the challenge without waiting for any special legislative authority. And ... it is none the less a war, although the declaration of it be "*unilateral.*".... A declaration of war by one country only, is not a mere challenge to be accepted or refused at pleasure by the other.... The President was bound to meet it in the shape it presented itself, without waiting for Congress to baptize it with a name; and no name given to it by him or them could change the fact.

Force Short of War: Defensive Uses of Military Force by the President

Protecting American Citizens Abroad

At least until the Vietnam conflict, most constitutional scholars also recognized broad presidential power to use armed force short of all-out war without formal authorization from Congress. Consider this excerpt from one of the most respected constitutional scholars of his era:

EDWARD CORWIN, THE PRESIDENT: OFFICE AND POWERS, 1787–1957
198–201 (1957)

The first question to be considered ... is whether the President may, without authorization by Congress, ever use force abroad. First and last, dozens and scores of episodes have occurred in our history in which Presidents have done this very thing and have been defended by their champions with the argument that when action of this sort is in defense of what international law itself recognizes as *rights of person and property* and is not excessive, it is not an *act of war* nor a legitimate cause for warlike retort by the country suffering from it....

---

9. CONGRESSIONAL RESEARCH SERVICE, THE CONSTITUTION OF THE UNITED STATES: ANALYSIS AND INTERPRETATION 338 (1987).

Furthermore, such action has received the highest judicial sanction. One of the precedents [*Durand v. Hollins*[10]] relied on by Justice Miller in the *Neagle* case was the outgrowth of the bombardment in 1854 by Lieutenant Hollins of the USS *Cyane*, of Greytown, Nicaragua, in default of reparation from the local authorities for an attack by a mob on the United States Consul stationed at that place. On his return to the United States Hollins was sued in a federal court by one Durand for the value of certain property which was alleged to have been destroyed in the bombardment. His defense was based on the orders of the President and the Secretary of the Navy, and was sustained by Justice Nelson in the following words:

> As the Executive head of the nation, the President is made the only legitimate organ of the General Government, to open and carry on correspondence or negotiations with foreign nations, in matters concerning the interests of the country or of its citizens. It is to him, also, that citizens abroad must look for protection of person and of property, and for the faithful execution of the laws existing and intended for their protection....
>
> Now, as respects the interposition of the Executive abroad, for the protection of the lives or property of the citizen, the duty must, of necessity, rest in the discretion of the President. Acts of lawless violence, or of threatened violence to the citizen or his property, cannot be anticipated and provided for; and the protection, to be effectual or of any avail, may, not unfrequently, require the most prompt and decided action. Under our system of Government, the citizen abroad is as much entitled to protection as the citizen at home. The great object and duty of Government is the protection of the lives, liberty, and property of the people composing it, whether abroad or at home; and any Government failing in the accomplishment of the object, or the performance of the duty is not worth preserving.

All of this serves to strengthen the argument that the power to declare war vested in Congress by the Constitution is limited in scope and pertains only to the authorization of such offensive initiation of military force as would have required a formal declaration of war at the time the Constitution was drafted. It was, in essence, an additional safeguard to prevent the Commander in Chief from endangering the lives of America's youth and the solvency of the national treasury by launching painful and costly wars over political, diplomatic, or economic grievances or from a belief that geographic expansion by military conquest would serve the people's interests. Each House of Congress was given a "veto" over such a decision as a part of our unique system of checks and balances. This was intended to be an important safeguard against abuse, but at the same time it is a narrow limitation on the President's general control of the nation's military forces. Under the constitutional scheme, the President needed no specific authorization to use force to defend against a military threat to the United States or to faithfully execute the treaties or other laws of the nation in circumstances under which the law of nations would not require a formal declaration.

———

Historically, the President has been recognized to possess independent constitutional power as Commander-in-Chief to use force short of war to protect American citizens and property abroad. Professor Quincy Wright was among the leading scholars of his generation in this field. In addition to teaching at Harvard, Chicago, Columbia, and Virginia, and

———

10. 8 F.Cas. 111, C.C.N.Y. (1860).

writing more than a dozen books, Professor Wright served as President of the American Political Science Association, the International Political Science Association, and the American Society of International Law.

QUINCY WRIGHT, THE CONTROL OF AMERICAN FOREIGN RELATIONS
306–10 (1922)

The Constitution guarantees the "privileges and immunities of citizens of the United States" and these were held in the Slaughter House cases to include the right to protection abroad. Consequently the President's duty to execute the laws includes a duty to protect citizens abroad and in pursuance of this duty he may utilize his powers as Commander-in-Chief....

[Discussion of historic incidents and Court decisions omitted.]

... In view of these incidents and judicial endorsements, we may accept Borchard's statement; with the sole qualification that "the manner" must not amount to a making of war:

> "Inasmuch as the Constitution vests in Congress authority 'to declare war' and does not empower Congress to direct the President to perform his constitutional duties of protecting American citizens on foreign soil, it is believed that the Executive has unlimited authority to use the armed forces of the United States for protective purposes abroad in any manner and on any occasion he considers expedient."

The Constitution also guarantees the States a Republican form of government and protection against invasion. Furthermore the right of national self-defense is recognized at international law and the corresponding duty of the government has been asserted by the Supreme Court:

> "To preserve its independence and give security against foreign aggression and encroachment is the highest duty of every nation, and to attain these ends nearly all other considerations are to be subordinated."

Thus, if he considers such action essential for the enforcement of acts of Congress and treaties and for the protection of the citizens and territory of the United States, the President is obliged by the Constitution itself to use his power as commander-in-chief to direct the forces abroad, and this duty resting on the Constitution itself cannot be taken away by act of Congress. Thus says President Taft:

> "The President is made Commander-in-Chief of the Army and Navy by the Constitution evidently for the purpose of enabling him to defend the country against invasion, to suppress insurrection and to take care that the laws be faithfully executed. If Congress were to attempt to prevent his use of the army for any of these purposes, the action would be void."

....

Conclusion.

Thus in practice the President has an exceedingly broad discretion to authorize the use of the forces. Under the Constitution he can use the military and naval forces to defend the territory and to protect American citizens abroad and on the high seas.... For the meeting of responsibilities under international law and treaty the President likewise has authority to use the army and navy on the high seas and in foreign territory. To meet responsibilities under inchoate international law, such as the Monroe Doctrine, the power, though often exercised, is more questionable, and for the use of forces within the territory, even to meet international responsibilities, statutory authorization is generally advisable, though apparently not strictly necessary. Finally, for the purpose of bringing pressure upon foreign governments for political objects, it is doubtful whether the President has constitutional power to use force, although he may bring diplomatic pressure. For political intervention, authorization by special resolution of Congress seems proper and has been the usual practice.

Preparing for and Conducting Military Operations

There appears to have been a strong consensus among the Founding Fathers that the actual direction of military operations should be entrusted exclusively to the discretion of the Executive.[11] As already observed, the decision to change the proposed power of Congress from "to make war" to the power "to declare war" was motivated, in part, by the concern "that 'make' war might be understood to 'conduct' it which was an Executive function...."[12] This function was already incorporated into the draft approved by the Committee on Detail, which provided that the President "shall be commander in chief of the Army and Navy of the United States, and of the Militia of the Several States"[13] — a phraseology which survived into the Constitution with only the qualification that the President's command over the Militia would take effect when the Militia was "called into the actual service of the United States."[14]

During the state ratification debates, Alexander Hamilton wrote at some length about the importance and scope of the Commander-in-Chief power.

THE FEDERALIST NO. 69

at 465 (Alexander Hamilton) (Jacob Cooke ed., 1961)

[T]he President is to be the Commander in Chief of the army and navy of the United States. In this respect his authority would be nominally the same with that of the King of Great-Britain, but in substance much inferior to it. It would amount to nothing more than the supreme command and direction of the military and naval forces, as first General and Admiral of the confederacy; while that of the British King extends to the *declaring* of war and the *raising* and *regulating* of fleets and armies; all which by the Constitution under consideration would appertain to the Legislature. The Governor of New-York, on the other hand, is by the Constitution of the State vested only with the command of its militia and navy.[15]

---

11. For example, the New Jersey Plan provided "That the Executive direct all military Operations." 2 FARRAND, RECORDS OF THE FEDERAL CONVENTION 157 (1911). The Pinckney Plan provided that the President "shall by Virtue, of his Office, be Commander-in-Chief of the Land forces of the U.S. and Admiral of the Navy...." *Id.* at 158.

12. *Id.* at 319 note 10.

13. *Id.* at 185.

14. U.S. CONST. art. II, § 2, cl. 1.

15. While this passage is often cited as evidence that the Commander in Chief power was intended to be almost a ceremonial function, it should be kept in mind that the Governor of New York was by far the strongest of all state governors at the time and had played an independent and important role in the war against Great Britain. Even by its own terms, the "supreme command and direction of the military and naval forces" is a substantial grant of power.

THE FEDERALIST NO. 72

at 486–87 (Alexander Hamilton) (Jacob Cooke ed., 1961)

The administration of government.... falls peculiarly within the province of the executive department. The actual conduct of foreign negotiations, ... the arrangement of the army and navy, the direction of the operations of war; these and other matters of a like nature constitute what seems to be most properly understood by the administration of government.

THE FEDERALIST NO. 74

at 500 (Alexander Hamilton) (Jacob Cooke ed., 1961)

The President of the United States is to be "Commander in Chief of the army and navy of the United States, and of the militia of the several States *when called into the actual service* of the United States." The propriety of this provision is so evident in itself; and it is at the same time so consonant to the precedents of the State constitutions in general, that little need be said to explain or enforce it. Even those of them, which have in other respects coupled the Chief Magistrate with a Council, have for the most part concentrated the military authority in him alone. Of all the cares or concerns of government, the direction of war most peculiarly demands those qualities which distinguish the exercise of power by a single hand. The direction of war implies the direction of the common strength; and the power of directing and employing the common strength, forms an usual and essential part of the definition of the executive authority.

The War Powers After 200 Years: Congress and the President at a Constitutional Impasse

Hearings Before the Special Subcommittee on War Powers of the Committee on Foreign Relations
100th Cong., 2d Sess. 778, 829–831 (1988) (testimony of Robert F. Turner, Associate Director, Center for Law and National Security)

During the Constitutional Convention Madison argued that "[t]he President ... would necessarily derive ... much power and importance from a state of war...." Later, during the Virginia Ratification Convention, he even used an analogy to the power of the British King in explaining the separation of "war" powers under the proposed new Constitution. On June 14, 1788, Madison argued:

> Mr. Chairman, the honorable gentleman has laid much stress on the maxim, that the purse and sword ought not to be put in the same hands, with a view of pointing out the impropriety of vesting this power in the general government. But it is totally inapplicable to this question.... The only rational meaning, is, that the sword and purse are not to be given to the same member. Apply it to the British government, which has been mentioned. The sword is in the hands of the British king, the purse in the hands of the parliament. It is so in America, as far as any analogy can exist.... [T]he president is to have the command; and, in conjunction with the senate, to appoint the officers. The means ought to be commensurate to the end. The end is general protection. This cannot be effected without a general power to use the strength of the union.... [W]here power can be safely lodged, if it be necessary, reason commands its cession. In such case it

is imprudent and unsafe to withhold it.... I can see no danger in submitting to practice an experiment which seems to be founded on the best theoretic principles. [5 THE WRITINGS OF JAMES MADISON 195–97 (G. Hunt ed. 1903)].

To give Congress—which already controls the "purse"—the power to decide ultimately upon the deployment of military forces would clearly be to *violate* the popular theory of which Madison's spoke of separating control of the "purse" from control of the "sword."

Furthermore, Madison's speeches to the Virginia Ratification Convention establish that he shared Jefferson's concern about the "tyranny of the legislatures." In proposing that the Constitution be amended by adding a Bill of Rights, Madison noted on June 8, 1789:

> In the declaration of rights which that country [Great Britain] has established, the truth is, they have gone no farther than to raise a barrier against the power of the Crown; the power of the Legislature is left altogether indefinite.... [I]t may not be thought necessary to provide limits for the legislative power in that country, yet a different opinion prevails in the United States....
>
> In our Government it is, perhaps, less necessary to guard against the abuse in the Executive Department than any other; because it is not the stronger branch of the system, but the weaker. It therefore must be leveled against the Legislative, for it is the most powerful, and most likely to be abused, because it is under the least control.[16]

As the excerpts which follow indicate, prominent constitutional scholars have recognized both the wisdom of this grant of power and its independence from legislative usurpation.

JOSEPH STORY, COMMENTARIES ON THE CONSTITUTION OF THE UNITED STATES
415–16, 546–47 (Cambridge 1833, reprinted 1987)

CHAPTER XXXVII.
EXECUTIVE—POWERS AND DUTIES.

....

§ 768. The command and application of the public force, to execute the laws, to maintain peace, and to resist foreign invasion, are powers so obviously of an executive nature, and require the exercise of qualities so peculiarly adapted to this department, that a well-organized government can scarcely exist, when they are taken away from it. Of all the cases and concerns of government, the direction of war most peculiarly demands those qualities, which distinguish the exercise of power by a single hand. Unity of plan, promptitude, activity, and decision, are indispensable to success; and these can scarcely exist, except when a single magistrate is entrusted exclusively with the power. Even the coupling of the authority of an executive council with him, in the exercise of such powers, enfeebles the system, divides the responsibility, and not unfrequently defeats every energetic measure. Timidity, indecision, obstinacy, and pride of opinion, must mingle in all such councils, and infuse a torpor and sluggishness, destructive of all military operations. Indeed, there would seem to be little reason to enforce the propriety of giving this power to the executive department, (whatever may be its actual organization,) since it is in exact

-----

16. The Madison quote is from 5 THE WRITINGS OF JAMES MADISON 380–82 (Gaillard Hunt ed., 1903).

coincidence with the provisions of our state constitutions; and therefore seems to be universally deemed safe, if not vital to the system.

William Howard Taft, *The Boundaries Between the Executive, the Legislative and the Judicial Branches of the Government*
25 Yale L.J. 599, 610–12 (1916)

When we come to the power of the President as Commander-in-Chief it seems perfectly clear that Congress could not order battles to be fought on a certain plan, and could not direct parts of the army to be moved from one part of the country to another.

The power to declare war is given to Congress. In the *Prize* cases it was held that a war might arise, creating all the legal incidents of war, from a foreign invasion or a domestic insurrection like that of our Civil War, without any declaration on the part of Congress; but it is to be inferred that our courts could not recognize or enforce rights legally incident to a war of aggression against a foreign country unless declared by Congress. This is necessarily a limitation on the power of the President to order the army and navy to commit an act of war....

... Of course the President may so use the army and navy as to involve the country in actual war and force a declaration of war by Congress. Such a use of the army and navy, however, is a usurpation of power on his part. It is likely to awaken such popular support as to compel Congress to acquiesce and register the declaration. The truth is, however, to the honor of the Executive, the instances in our history in which the jingo spirit has manifested itself in Congress and the Executive has sought to restrain it are many more in our history than those in which the Executive has sought to involve the country in war and force Congress to give it legal sanction.

Could Congress substantially restrict the President in his use of the army to take care that the laws be faithfully executed? It would seem not. This brings me to another limitation upon Congressional power over executive action. Congress in making law and achieving the object of the law through the action of the Executive may properly prescribe the form and method in which the law shall be carried out, and thus point out the path along which in enforcing the will of Congress, the Executive must proceed. But when in respect to the particular subject matter, the President is given direct power by the Constitution so that he can act without legislation, or if he is given in the Constitution, particular means with which to execute the laws and make his constitutional power effective, Congress cannot prevent exercise of the power in the former case, nor can it prevent in the latter case his use of the constitutional means for the performance of any of his constitutional duties to which it would be appropriate.

By statute, Congress has forbidden the United States marshals to call the army as a *posse comitatus*, but that is not the use of the army by direction of the President under his power as its Commander-in-Chief. Congress might refuse to vote the appropriation for an army, or might repeal the law organizing the army but it cannot provide an army of which the President must be Commander-in-Chief, and then in the law of its creation limit him in the use of the army to enforce any of the laws of the United States in accordance with his constitutional duty.[17]

---

17. Writing in Our Chief Magistrate and His Powers, 128–29 (1916), William Howard Taft added: "The President is made Commander-in-Chief of the army and navy by the Constitution evidently for the purpose of enabling him to defend the country against invasion, to suppress insurrection and to take care that the laws be faithfully executed. If Congress were to attempt to prevent his use of

————————

Throughout most of America's history the Congress has acknowledged the President's exclusive control over the actual conduct of war and the peacetime deployment of military forces,[18] and thus there is little case law on the subject. The courts, however, have not been entirely silent, as the following two cases illustrate:

Ex parte Milligan
71 U.S. (4 Wall.) 2, 139–40 (1866)
(Chase, C. J., Wayne, J., Swayne, J., & Miller, J., concurring) (emphasis added)

Congress has the power not only to raise and support and govern armies but to declare war. It has, therefore, the power to provide by law for carrying on war. This power necessarily extends to all legislation essential to the prosecution of war with vigor and success, except such as interferes with the command of the forces and the conduct of campaigns. That power and duty belong to the President as commander-in-chief. Both these powers are derived from the Constitution, but neither is defined by that instrument. Their extent must be determined by their nature, and by the principles of our institutions.

The power to make the necessary laws is in Congress; the power to execute in the President. Both powers imply many subordinate and auxiliary powers. Each includes all authorities essential to its due exercise. But neither can the President, in war more than in peace, intrude upon the proper authority of Congress, nor Congress upon the proper authority of the President. Both are servants of the people, whose will is expressed in the fundamental law. *Congress cannot direct the conduct of campaigns*, nor can the President, or any commander under him, without the sanction of Congress, institute tribunals for the trial and punishment of offences....

————————

the army for any of these purposes, the action would be void.... [I]n the carrying on of war as Commander-in-Chief, it is he who is to determine the movements of the army and navy. Congress could not take away from him that discretion and place it beyond his control in any of his subordinate, nor could they themselves, as the people of Athens attempted to, carry on campaigns by votes in the marketplace."

18. This is not to say that there have not been attempts to direct the movement of troops. For example, in the aftermath of World War I the following exchange occurred on the floor of the U.S. Senate:

> Mr. REED of Missouri. Does the Senator think and has he not thought for a long time that the American troops in Germany ought to be brought home?
> Mr. BORAH. I do.
> Mr. REED of Missouri. So do I ... Would it not be easier to bring the troops home than it would be to have the proposed conference?
> Mr. BORAH. You can not bring them home, nor can I.
> Mr. REED of Missouri. We could make the President do it.
> Mr. BORAH. We could not make the President do it. He is the Commander-in-Chief of the Army and Navy of the United States, and if in the discharge of his duty he wants to assign them there, I do not know of any power that we can exert to compel him to bring them home. We may refuse to create an Army, but when it is created he is the Commander.
> Mr. REED of Missouri. I wish to change my statement. We could not make him bring them home, because none of us want to make the President do anything, but I think if there were a resolution passed asking the President to bring the troops home where they belong, the President would recognize that request from Congress.

64 CONG. REC. 993 (1922). For a more recent example, see ROBERT F. TURNER, THE WAR POWERS RESOLUTION 28–29 (1983).

It is worth noting that, while this was but a concurring opinion joined by four members of the Court in 1866, the language was embraced by the Court majority in the 2006 case of *Hamdan v. Rumsfeld* (548 U.S. 557, 591–92 [2006]).

Swaim v. United States
28 Ct. Cl. 173, 221 (1893)

Congress may increase the Army or reduce the Army, or abolish it altogether; but so long as we have a military force Congress can not take away from the President the supreme command. It is true that the Constitution has conferred upon Congress the exclusive power "to make rules for the government and regulation of the land and naval forces;" but the two powers are distinct; neither can trench upon the other; the President can not, under the disguise of military orders, evade the legislative regulations by which he in common with the Army must be governed; and Congress can not in the disguise of "rules for the government" of the Army impair the authority of the President as commander in chief.

Congress, Declarations of War, and the United Nations Charter

Former Stanford Law School Dean John Hart Ely asserts that "[t]he oft-made observation that declarations of wars are 'outmoded' is entirely beside the point.... of any sensible constitutional argument one can imagine."[19] With due respect to Dean Ely, the argument is really quite simple. Nations generally do not issue declarations of war today because modern international law has outlawed the kinds of military actions that have historically been thought to require such an instrument under international law and which the Founding Fathers sought to limit by giving Congress a veto. By ratifying the Kellogg-Briand Treaty in 1929 and the United Nations Charter in 1945, the United States effectively surrendered its once sovereign right to commit armed aggression. However, even had it not given its consent, as a peremptory norm of modern international law (*jus cogens*), Article 2(4) of the Charter clearly prohibits the aggressive use of military force by *all* nations—at least in the absence of authorization by the U.N. Security Council. Thus, the President would violate a fundamental principle of modern international law if he initiated any use of military force that would require advance congressional authorization. (However, if he elected to do so Congress would obviously possess its constitutional negative to block the action.)

The only significant uses of force authorized for individual states today are in individual or collective defense or pursuant to the authorization of the UN Security Council.[20] While international practice admittedly has not always kept pace with legal theory, virtually all states now acknowledge that their once sovereign right to unilaterally initiate an aggressive war no longer exists. Arguably the greatest American international lawyer of the first half

---

19. John Hart Ely, War and Responsibility: Constitutional Lessons of Vietnam and its Aftermath 162 n.84 (1993).

20. For the record, lest I be misunderstood here, I should clarify that I believe the defense of human life in response to widespread and systematic Democide is also lawful under the Charter in truly egregious situations like Kosovo in 1998 and Iraq in 2003. Ideally, acts of humanitarian intervention ought to be first approved by the Security Council or conducted through other multilateral institutions rather than unilaterally. But if international law prohibits external intervention in a humanitarian crisis like the Holocaust, it is part of the problem and is unworthy of our support.

of the Twentieth Century, the late John Bassett Moore, commented upon the conclusion of the 1928 Kellogg-Briand Pact: "[s]elf-defense by a nation is not war. When once you have outlawed war, do not use the word war any more."[21]

As we have seen, the leading publicists known to the Framers were in agreement that a declaration of war was only necessary in the case of a decision to launch an "offensive" or "aggressive" war. As discussed in chapter four of this book, Articles 2(4) and 51 of the United Nations Charter essentially outlaw non-defensive uses of force by individual countries; and, under the supremacy clause of Article VI of the Constitution, this treaty obligation is part of "the supreme Law of the Land" which the President is obligated to see faithfully executed.[22]

Today, the overwhelming belief on Capitol Hill and among legal scholars is that the President must get formal statutory authorization from Congress before committing U.S. combat troops to hostilities pursuant to a decision by the Security Council to authorize the use of armed force against threats to the peace. But a review of the Senate debates on the UN Charter and subsequent debates in both Houses of Congress on the UN Participation Act suggests a surprising consensus to the contrary:

Robert F. Turner, *Truman, Korea, and the Constitution: Debunking the "Imperial President" Myth*
19 HARV. J. L. & PUB. POL'Y 541–57 (1996)

Time and again during the [UN Charter] debate, senators emphasized that ratification of the treaty [the UN Charter] would commit the United States to use military force in response to armed international aggression, and potential critics were warned not to lie "in ambush to nullify or 'submarine' this agreement" or to hold their fire "with the belief that some day when the implementing statutes and the special agreements come to us for congressional action then will be the hour to draw the military teeth from this new international agreement." For example, Senator Robert Taft—who half-a-decade later would become President Truman's leading critic on the constitutionality of the Korean commitment—asserted during the Charter ratification debate that "we commit ourselves" to make armed forces available to the United Nations "by ratifying this original treaty," and said, "If we assume certain definite obligations I am prepared to leave to the President the performance of those obligations."

. . . .

No issue received more attention, either during the Charter ratification debate or the subsequent consideration of the U.N. Participation Act, than the approval process for the agreements envisioned by Article 43 of the Charter. During the Foreign Relations Committee hearings on the Charter, John Foster Dulles suggested that these would be approved as formal treaties, but several senators argued that a joint resolution would be preferable—because the commitment involved powers expressly vested jointly in the Senate and the House of Representatives by the Constitution....

---

21. WILLIAM HARD, THE WORLD'S WORK 89 (1929).

22. Article VI, Clause 2, of the Constitution provides: "This Constitution, and the Laws of the United States which shall be made in Pursuance thereof; and all Treaties made, or which shall be made, under the Authority of the United States, shall be the supreme Law of the Land...."

What is particularly noteworthy, however, is that most of this debate over protecting the constitutional role of the House—both during the Charter ratification process and during the subsequent consideration of the U.N. Participation Act—focused not on the power of Congress "to declare war," but instead on other expressed powers of Congress. For example, Senator Lucas argued that the House should be involved because the entire Congress held the powers "to raise and support armies" and make rules for the governance and regulation of the land and naval forces. This view was reflected in the Foreign Relations Committee report on the U.N. Participation Act and in other statements by individual senators. A somewhat different theory was advanced by Senator Connally, [the Chairman of the Foreign Relations Committee and a member of the U.S. delegation that negotiated the Charter,] who reasoned:

> Since the obligation exists to furnish the forces, I think it is desirable, probably, to have the concurrence of the House of Representatives in the approval of the agreements. Appropriations will be involved for the maintenance of the armed forces. The House of Representatives always claims the right to have a hand in appropriations.

Other speakers combined both of these legislative powers as justification for involving the House of Representatives, but also did not mention the power to declare war.

. . . .

Under the Law of Nations as understood when the Constitution was written, no declaration of war was considered necessary except when what we today would call an "aggressive" war was being initiated; and the offensive-defensive distinction was made during the Philadelphia debates in drafting the Constitution and in subsequent practice and judicial interpretation. The issues arose again in this exchange during the House floor debate on the U.N. Participation Act:

> Mr. ROBSION of Kentucky. Under this bill, is there any way for our delegate to put this Nation into war?
>
> Mr. JARMAN. Absolutely not.
>
> Mr. ROBSION of Kentucky. Well, when those forces are called together and he votes for us to contribute men and ships to prevent any aggression or to stop it, would that be putting us into war?
>
> Mr. JARMAN.... [S]hould it become necessary for the Security Council to use those forces of the United Nations, it would not be a question of war but a sincere effort to prevent war, just as we ... kill a mad dog who is attacking our child.
>
> Mr. ROBSION of Kentucky. But if the other side would fight back, of course, you would have a war, would you not? ...
>
> Mr. JARMAN. If it is spread sufficiently, it would be a war, but it would not be aggressive war.

. . .

III. The U.N. Participation Act

The U.N. Charter was not fully self-executing, and was implemented through enactment of the U.N. Participation Act in December 1945. Following the unanimous recommendation of the Senate Foreign Relations Committee, the Senate approved the statute on December 4, by a vote of 65–7. Two weeks later, following a brief, two-hour debate, the House gave its approval by vote of 344–15.

It was clear from the record that both chambers believed that the basic commitment to act collectively in response to armed international aggression already had been made. The unanimous report of the House Foreign Affairs Committee, for example, recorded that:

> The basic decision of the Senate in advising and consenting to ratification of the Charter resulted in the undertaking by this country of various obligations which will actually be carried out by and under the authority of the President as the Chief Executive, diplomatic, and military officer of the Government. Among such obligations is that of supplying armed forces to the Security Council concerning which provision is made in section 6.... [T]he ratification of the Charter resulted in the vesting in the executive branch of the power and obligation to fulfill the commitments assumed by the United States thereunder....

> ....

If there was a majority view on the relationship between the President's authority under the Charter and the power of Congress to declare war, it was probably that the Declaration of War Clause was irrelevant in this context because the commitment of U.S. armed forces into hostilities pursuant to a decision of the Security Council was an act of "peace" rather than "war." Thus, the unanimous House Foreign Affairs Committee report on the U.N. Participation Act quoted at length from the earlier unanimous Senate Foreign Relations Committee's report on ratification of the U.N. Charter:

> [T]he committee is convinced that any reservation to the Charter, or any subsequent congressional limitation designed to provide, for example, that employment of the armed forces of the United States to be made available to the Security Council under special agreements referred to in article 43 could be authorized only after the Congress had passed on each individual case would clearly violate the spirit of one of the most important provisions of the Charter....

> Preventive or enforcement action by these forces upon the order of the Security Council *would not be an act of war* but would be international action for the preservation of the peace and for the purpose of preventing war. *Consequently, the provisions of the Charter do not affect the exclusive power of the Congress to declare war.*

> The committee feels that a reservation or other congressional action such as that referred to above *would also violate the spirit of the United States Constitution under which the President has well-established powers and obligations to use our armed forces without specific approval of Congress.*

Although many apparently felt that "peacekeeping" was not "war" irrespective of its magnitude, others drew a distinction between a limited use of military force in a "police" operation and the commitment of the entire U.S. military to "war." For example, one senator distinguished between spending $1 billion to send 100,000 troops into combat under the Charter as a part of "an international police force," and spending $300 billion to send 4 million troops to "war" as "an expeditionary force." He added that the President would only be able to commit "a limited force — not the whole force of all our people," saying that "when the whole force and strength of the United States is required, of course there is only one body which can make that force available through a resolution of war, and that is the Congress of the United States." Indeed, it was quite common to characterize the envisioned deployment by the Security Council of multinational troops in response to international aggression as the use of a "police force," and to argue that "throughout our history the use of a police force to enforce the laws and treaties of the United States has never been regarded as war."

IV. The Wheeler Amendment

In arguing that Congress must approve specific deployments of U.S. combat forces to implement U.N. Security Council resolutions, Dr. [Louis] Fisher relied in no small part upon the statement of Senator Burton Wheeler (R-Mont.), one of the most outspoken isolationists in the years leading up to World War II, that the American people would never support any senator or representative who embraced a policy that would allow the President to "send troops all over the world to fight battles anywhere." There is an implication that this reflected the prevailing thinking in the Senate, but it is in error; indeed, Senator Wheeler acknowledged that on the pending measure, "my voice does not carry very much weight any more in the Senate"—and he took more than a little ribbing from his colleagues because, despite his clear opposition to this aspect of the Charter, he was facing reelection in 1946 and already had announced that he would vote *for* the very popular Charter. As it turned out, Senator Wheeler suffered the fate of most of the unrepentant isolationists and failed even to obtain his party's nomination in 1946 to stand for a fifth term in the Senate.

. . . .

Ultimately, Senator Wheeler sought to resolve his problem with the Charter by proposing an amendment to the U.N. Participation Act on December 4, the final day of Senate debate, providing that:

> [T]he President shall have no authority, to make available to the Security Council any armed forces to enable the Security Council to take action under article 42 of said charter, unless the Congress has by appropriate act or joint resolution authorized the President to make such forces available ... in the specific case in which the Council proposed to take action.

Senator Wheeler's proposal took up more time than any other amendment considered by the House or Senate in connection with the United Nations, and was strongly attacked by colleagues who argued that the nation was already bound on this issue by the clear language of the Charter....

. . . .

... [T]he Wheeler Amendment was rejected by a margin of more than seven to one, receiving only nine affirmative votes. Given this overwhelming vote and the accompanying debate, it is simply not credible to contend that the Senate in 1945 expected the President to come to Congress for specific statutory authorization every time it became necessary to use armed force to uphold the Charter.

. . . .

Two weeks later, the House took up the bill. Much of the House debate focused upon charges that "the measure will involve us in every war hereafter," and that the statute violated the Constitution by giving the President the power to initiate war. For example, Representative John Robsion argued that the act would give the Security Council representative the power to decide "the extent to which the United States shall participate in policing the world," adding:

> In such proceedings the Congress does not have any say. Conditions will have developed so that we will be in the war without the consent of Congress and if this measure is adopted, Congress will not be called upon in the future to declare war as provided in the Constitution. We shall have indirectly delegated that power to our representative on the Security Council.

In response, other members asserted that such a commitment had already been made through ratification of the Charter, and argued that America's failure to join the League of Nations, and the subsequent policy of "isolation," contributed to the start of World War II. Representative James Richards (D-S.C.) responded with a "rule of law" metaphor:

> There are some here who object to the use of United States troops under the direction of the President as a contribution to the police force of this world body.…
>
> Mr. Chairman, in consideration of this bill we should remember that no chief of police in any town in the United States could effectively preserve law and order if he has to go for approval to his town council before he can use his police force to prevent a breach of the peace. Neither can the President of the United States effectively cooperate with the United Nations to preserve the peace, if his hands are tied.

Shortly thereafter, following but two hours of debate, the House approved the bill by the overwhelming vote of 344–15.

Questions for Discussion

1. Has the constitutional power of Congress to declare war been substantially constrained by the U.N. Charter? If so, does this raise any constitutional problems?

2. Might there be a useful parallel between the power granted to Congress in Article 1, Section 8, of the Constitution to declare war and the related power in the same sentence to "grant Letters of Marque and Reprisal … ?" Such letters were used at the time the Constitution was written to authorize private citizens and their vessels ("privateers") to engage in hostilities on behalf of a sovereign state. Seized enemy ships and their cargo were awarded to captain and crew by "prize courts" pursuant to statutory and/or customary standards. But the use of letters of marque and reprisal was outlawed by the 1868 Declaration of St. Petersburg. (The United States was not a signatory, but later accepted the rule.) Thus, the power of Congress to grant letters of marque and reprisal is today an anachronism. Might the same be said of the power to "declare War" granted in the same sentence? This is not to say that if the United States decided to violate international law Congress would not have its constitutional negative.

3. There has not been a clear international declaration of war anywhere in the world since the late 1940s. For the United States, such a declaration serves two separate functions. Even if the type of aggressive "total" war with which declarations of war under international law have generally been associated is now unlawful, are there still situations consistent with the U.N. Charter in which congressional authorization would be necessary for the United States to commit armed forces to hostilities? Can you think of any examples?

Comments

Not only are scholars in strong disagreement about the modern need for legislative sanction before the President may order U.S. armed forces into harm's way under various circumstances, but in some cases there may well be no "right" answer. Many modern situations may well not have even occurred to the Framers in 1787, and competing constitutional principles sometimes lead to no clear result. In such circumstances, the President is the first judge of the necessity or propriety of awaiting legislative approval. But—in the absence of an emergency setting where a failure to respond promptly may result in catastrophic consequences to the nation, its armed forces, or an ally—Alexander Hamilton was probably right when he advised, in a May 17, 1798, letter to James McHenry: "In so delicate a case, in one which involves so important a consequence as that of war — my opinion is that no doubtful authority ought to be exercised by the President."[23]

The fact that the Constitution may not *require* the President to obtain formal statutory authorization from Congress for a particular military operation does not inevitably lead to the conclusion that the President ought not seek such authority. More than 2,500 years ago, the great Chinese military genius, Sun Tzu, observed: "to win one hundred victories in one hundred battles is not the acme of skill. To subdue the enemy without fighting is the acme of skill."[24] Deterrence is a function of *perceptions* of strength and will, and just as getting authorization to use force from the UN Security Council may help persuade a threat to the peace to abandon aggressive plans or cease acts of aggression, getting Congress "on board" may both contribute to national unity and signal an adversary that the United States is determined to uphold the law. Thus, as a matter of sound *policy*, a wise President will normally welcome an expression of congressional support. In the post-Vietnam era, however, the risk has been that a highly partisan congressional debate over a resolution may actually undermine deterrence,[25] or that Congress may inadvertently achieve the same end by placing *conditions* on the resolution limiting the time period or other aspect of the operation.[26]

Modern Precedents: Korea, Vietnam, and Iraq

During and after both the wars in Korea and Vietnam, it was widely charged that American presidents had taken the nation to war without the approval of Congress in violation of the Constitution. A review of both commitments is instructive:

Robert F. Turner, *Truman, Korea, and the Constitution: Debunking the "Imperial President" Myth*
19 Harv. J. Int'l L. 563-76 (1996)

The Korean Conflict

Less than five years after its ratification, the [UN] Charter regime was put to its first major test when Kim Il sung's Democratic People's Republic of [North] Korea invaded the Republic of [South] Korea across the 38th parallel [on June 25, 1950]....

President Truman flew back to Washington on Sunday afternoon and at 7:45 that evening met for dinner at Blair House with Secretary of State Acheson, Secretary of Defense Louis Johnson ... and military leaders. During that meeting, according to Ambassador [Philip] Jessup's once highly classified summary, Truman asked the State Department "to prepare a statement for a message for him to deliver in person to Congress on Tuesday [June 27] indicating exactly what steps had been taken." Early Monday morning the United States received a formal request for assistance from the South Korean National Assembly, and shortly after 10 a.m. Secretary of State Acheson made a series of personal

---

23. *Quoted in* Robert Scigliano, *The War Powers Resolution and the War Powers*, in The Presidency in the Constitutional Order 140 (Joseph M. Bessette & Jeffrey Tulis eds., 1981).

24. Sun Tzu, The Art of War 78 (Samuel B. Griffith ed., 1963).

25. *See, e.g.*, P. X. Kelley & Robert F. Turner, *Out of Harm's War: From Beirut to Haiti, Congress Protects Itself Instead of Our Troops*, Wash. Post, Oct. 23, 1994, at C2.

26. *See, e.g.*, the discussion *infra* on congressional action authorizing Operation Desert Storm in 1991.

calls to Senator Tom Connally and other members of the Senate Foreign Relations and House Foreign Affairs Committees to update them on the crisis.

At 9:00 p.m. Monday night, President Truman again met with Acheson, Johnson, and senior military leaders, at which time he authorized limited naval and air support in defense of South Korea. During this meeting, Secretary Acheson "suggested that the President might wish to get in Senator Connally and other members of the Senate and House and tell them what had been decided," and the President responded that he already had a meeting scheduled for 10:00 a.m. Tuesday with the "Big Four," but proposed that additional congressional leaders be included and that the Secretaries of State and Defense also take part.

At some point between his return to Washington on Sunday and the meeting with congressional leaders Tuesday morning, the President also telephoned Senate Foreign Relations Committee Chairman Tom Connally, who provides this account of the conversation in his autobiography:

> He [Truman] hadn't as yet made up his mind what to do.
>
> . . . .
>
> "Do you think I'll have to ask Congress for a declaration of war if I decide to send American forces into Korea?" the President asked.
>
> "If a burglar breaks into your house," I said, "you can shoot at him without going down to the police station and getting permission. You might run into a long debate by Congress, which would tie your hands completely. You have the right to do it as commander-in-chief and under the U.N. Charter."

This account clearly refutes the conventional wisdom that Truman "ignored Congress" or merely "informed" Congress of a *fait accompli*. It may be worth mentioning that, in referring to a housebreaking burglar, Senator Connally was repeating a metaphor invoked by President Franklin D. Roosevelt in describing his vision of a United Nations and later repeated during Senate debate on ratification of the Charter. The same basic analogy was also made in the House debate over approving the U.N. Participation Act.

When the President met personally with the top congressional leaders at 11:30 a.m. on Tuesday, June 27, he began by having Secretary Acheson summarize the developments in Korea; the President then read the statement he was considering releasing to the press following the meeting and "asked for any expression of views." The congressional leaders *unanimously* supported the President's actions. . . .

This account from Ambassador Jessup's once top-secret memorandum generally is supported by other sources. Senator Connally, for example, wrote in his autobiography that, after reading his proposed press release, "[t]he President then asked each man present what he thought we should do. There was no disagreement that the United States had to help the South Koreans. Nor did anyone object to Truman's remark about the U.N." Historian David McCullough provides this account: "The congressional leaders had given the President their undivided support. No one had said a word against what he had decided. Further, he had been advised to proceed on the basis of presidential authority alone and not bother to call on Congress for a war resolution." McCullough adds:

> Cheers broke out in the House and Senate when the [President's] statement was read aloud. By a vote of 315 to 4, the House promptly voted a one-year extension of the draft law. . . .
>
> The response of the American people—by mail, telegrams, phone calls to the White House and Congress—the response of the press, of nearly everyone

whose opinion carried weight in Washington and in the country, was immediate, resounding approval—a point that would soon be forgotten.

The *Congressional Record* supports this account....

    ....

One of the most interesting Senate debates on the scope of the President's authority to use force in Korea without specific legislative sanction occurred over a period of days, commencing on June 28 with remarks by Senator Ralph Flanders, a Vermont Republican with no formal legal training. Although praising the President's actions, he asked rhetorically "whether we have here a declaration of war without consent of Congress." After some discussion of the post-World War II American commitment to South Korea, he concluded:

> So Mr. President, it seems to me that this is in no sense [a] declaration of war, but the carrying out of an existing obligation. While I do not wish to labor the point and perhaps lack the skill to do so, I would feel that any invasion of the territory north of the thirty-eighth parallel, whether in pursuit of fleeing forces, in retaliation, or for any other purpose, would constitute action of a very different sort and should be undertaken only as an act of war legally authorized by the Congress of the United States.

Shortly thereafter, Senator Taft made his attack on the constitutionality of the President's decision, followed by a sharp rebuttal from Senator Lucas. Senator Flanders then made reference to his own earlier distinction between defensive actions taken in South Korea—which he described as a "police action"—and acts taken north of the thirty-eighth parallel, which he said would require congressional authorization. Senator Lucas responded that he "wholeheartedly agree[d]" with Flanders's point, and that the key was that "in no circumstances can the United States of America be charged with being the aggressor so long as we stay within the boundaries the Senator ... has just outlined."

However, later that afternoon, Senator William Knowland (R-Cal.)—a strong conservative and anticommunist who had earlier been among the first to endorse the President's action in Korea—took the floor to express his "concern" about "some discussion on the floor of the Senate today and some statements issued by the executive branch yesterday, with particular reference to the proposal that our support of the Republic of Korea should be limited to the area south of the thirty-eighth parallel." He argued:

> The action this Government is taking is a police action against a violator of the law of nations and the Charter of the United Nations. It seems to me to be absurd to suggest that all air bombardment should be in the territory of the victim of this overt aggression.

The debate resumed the following day, after the President had announced that he was committing ground forces to the fight, with Senator Knowland arguing:

> Mr. President, I am not one of those who dispute the powers of the President of the United States to take the necessary police action. I believe that he has been authorized to do it under the terms of our obligations to the United Nations Charter. I believe he has the authority to do it under his constitutional power as Commander in Chief of the Armed Forces of the United States.
>
> Certainly the action which has been taken to date is not one which would have required ... a declaration of war, as such, by the Congress of the United States. What is being done is more in the nature of police action.

Senator John Stennis (D-Miss.) then took the floor to declare the President's stand in South Korea "the single most encouraging development in world affairs since World War

I" and he was followed by Senator Flanders, who—after quoting his own June 28 floor statement at length—remarked:

> I wish at this time to say that I am now doubtful as to the wisdom of the question which I asked or of the reply to it which was given by the distinguished Senator from Illinois. I do not want the Record to leave him committed to the answer which he gave.
>
> Further thought has convinced me that we have the right and probably the necessity for action north of the thirty-eighth parallel. . . . [T]his is an operation undertaken in behalf and under the authority of the United Nations. . . .

When Senator Flanders subsequently referred to the Korean situation as a "war," he was interrupted by Senator Eugene Millikin (R-Colo.), who suggested that it was "a police operation," to which Senator Flanders replied, "I accept the suggestion; this is a police operation, not a war."

Majority Leader Lucas then obtained the floor to recant his own earlier statement and to agree with Senator Flanders's new position, after which Senator Millikin added:

> I wish to express my satisfaction with the remarks the Senator from Vermont has been making today, and also with the remarks just made by the distinguished majority leader. I think we would be unduly clipping our wings if we were to establish any particular geographical parallel or line as the boundary of our action. The Constitution of the United States does not limit the President's powers . . . to any particular place in the world. . . . I thought the Senator was a little frugal in his remarks the other day as to the proper limits of our action.
>
> I am glad that now he has expanded our permissible field of action.

There is at least some evidence that, had the President remained silent on the issue of North Korean aggression, awaiting a "declaration of war" or other formal authorization from Congress—which might itself have involved hearings and opportunities for delay—the conquest of South Korea might have been completed before any U.S. response could occur. Indeed, the American Ambassador in Seoul reported that President Truman's press release of June 27, announcing that he had "ordered United States air and sea forces to give the Korean Government troops cover and support," was critical in shoring up South Korean morale and keeping resistance to North Korean aggression from collapsing immediately.

The military situation in Korea continued to deteriorate, and by Friday, June 30, it had become clear that U.S. ground forces would be needed if North Korea was to be stopped. The President met with congressional leaders at 11:00 that morning, and Senator Connally provided this account:

> At that meeting, Truman bluntly announced his decision to use American ground forces in the defense of South Korea. After that there was a long silence, and on almost every face I could read agreement with his decision. Only Wherry argued that the President should have consulted with the House and Senate before deciding to use ground forces. Representative Dewey Short [R-Mo.] reprimanded Wherry.

Later that day, both houses of Congress adjourned for a ten-day Fourth-of-July recess.

There are some gaps in the official records, but it is clear that on Sunday, June 25, President Truman had instructed Secretary Acheson to put the State Department's "best brains" on preparing a message to Congress on Korea. A confidential memorandum prepared by Acheson's personal secretary confirms that on July 3, Acheson spoke with Secretary of Defense Johnson seeking comments both on the draft message and on a

"Joint Resolution" on Korea (the text of which is not reprinted in the State Department collection of documents). The memorandum states that Secretary Acheson "felt that such a resolution would be helpful during the time ahead."

Later in the day, the President held a meeting with Secretaries Acheson and Johnson, several other cabinet members and military leaders, and the only member of the congressional leadership still in Washington during the recess, Senate Majority Leader Scott Lucas (who served on the Foreign Relations Committee and had played an active role during the 1945 debates on the U.N. Charter and U.N. Participation Act). Ambassador Jessup's top-secret memorandum on that meeting reports in part:

> The President asked Mr. Acheson to lead off.
>
> Mr. Acheson said the purpose of the meeting was to lay before the President and his advisors a recommendation by the Department of State that the President go before Congress some time in the near future to make a full report to a joint Session of the Congress on the Korean situation. It was proposed that this report to the Congress would be followed by the introduction of a Joint Resolution expressing approval of the action taken in Korea....
>
> The President asked Senator Lucas what was his reaction to this suggestion. He [President Truman] indicated that Congress would not reassemble until a week from today but that he wanted to consider whether he should deliver such a message when Congress reassembled.
>
> ....
>
> Senator Lucas said that he frankly questioned the desirability of this. He said that things were now going along well.... He said that the President had very properly done what he had to without consulting [sic] the Congress. He said the resolution itself was satisfactory and that it could pass. He suggested as an alternative that the President might deliver this message as a fireside chat with the people of the country.... [He] said that most of the members of Congress were sick of the attitude taken by Senators Taft and Wherry.... [T]o go up and give such a message to Congress might sound as if the President were asking for a declaration of war....
>
> The President said that it was necessary to be very careful that he would not appear to be trying to get around Congress and use extra-Constitutional powers....
>
> The President said that it was up to Congress whether such a resolution should be introduced, that he would not suggest it. He said it was not necessary to make a decision today and that he too was just thinking out loud....
>
> Senator Lucas said that he felt he knew the reactions of Congress. He thought that only Senator Wherry had voiced the view that Congress should be consulted. Many members of Congress had suggested to him that the President should keep away from Congress and avoid debate....
>
> The President said he certainly must make a report some time but he did not want to call Congress back [from recess] now. He said it was always difficult to keep 541 men informed even about legislative business. Even though he did explain matters to the leaders there were many in Congress who did not know and eventually he must report. He said.... [h]e would have further consultations with the Big Four next Monday. He said he was still just thinking out loud and if there were any better suggestion he would be glad to listen to it.
>
> Senator Lucas commented that Senator Taft was merely following his same old line. Senator Jenner's statement in Indiana was unbelievable. Senator Lucas

said if there should be a row in Congress that would not help abroad. He did not think that Congress was going to stir things up.

The President said this depends on events in Korea. He said that if this view met with the approval of those present he would wait until he had his talks with the leaders next Monday.

This was agreed.

Consistent with the advice of the Senate Majority Leader, on Wednesday, July 19, 1950, the President submitted a lengthy written message to Congress. Later that same evening, he delivered a radio and television address to the nation.

Many modern scholars criticize President Truman for agreeing that the conflict in Korea could properly be described as a United Nations "police action." Dr. Fisher, for example, argues that "the United Nations exercised no real authority over the conduct of the war" and that "[m]easured by troops, money, casualties and deaths, it remained an American war." Obviously, it was above all else a "Korean" war; but, accepting Dr. Fisher's point that most of the foreign troops under the U.N. flag were Americans, one is tempted to ask again—so what? The United States clearly gave more than its "fair share," but that did not affect the legality of the U.N.-sanctioned action.

Nor, for that matter, is the criticism of President Truman for accepting the "police action" characterization of the operation warranted. That description was used *repeatedly* in both the House and Senate during the 1945 debates, and had been in general use in the congressional floor debates for several days prior to Truman's agreement—in response to a reporter's question—that the operation could correctly be termed "a police action under the United Nations...."

The Indochina War

Like Korea, following World War II (and an eight-year struggle by Communist-led opponents of French colonialism in Indochina) Vietnam was divided into two parts, with the Communist Ho Chi Minh leading the "Democratic Republic of Vietnam" in the north and a non-Communist "Republic of Vietnam" in the south. China and the Soviet Union provided various forms of assistance to the north, while the United States supported "South Vietnam."

With the exception of the Civil War, no conflict in American history divided the country as much as the war in Indochina. After the 1975 Communist victory, North Vietnamese leaders readily acknowledged that they had made a decision in May 1959 to "liberate" South Vietnam[27] and had opened supply routes and set up the "National Liberation Front for South Vietnam," but during the 1960s many American streets were filled with protesters who sincerely believed that the NLF was an independent group of South Vietnamese "freedom fighters" who merely wanted peace, democracy, and an end to "foreign domination." State Department evidence of North Vietnamese military involvement was denounced as "lies" by indignant students and professors across the nation.[28]

---

27. For information on this decision published prior to Hanoi's admissions, *see* ROBERT F. TURNER, VIETNAMESE COMMUNISM: ITS ORIGINS AND DEVELOPMENT 180–82 (1975).

28. This is not the occasion for an in-depth discussion of the merits of the Vietnam War, but readers interested in the issue may wish to read THE *REAL* LESSONS OF THE VIETNAM WAR: REFLECTIONS TWENTY-FIVE YEARS AFTER THE FALL OF SAIGON (John Norton Moore & Robert F. Turner eds., 2002).

For our purposes, the issue of greatest concern was the accusation by war critics that President Johnson had taken the nation to war in Indochina without congressional approval. That issue is addressed in the following excerpts:

The Southeast Asia [Gulf of Tonkin] Resolution

Pub. L. No. 88-408, 78 Stat. 384 (1964)

SEC. 2. The United States regards as vital to its national interest and to world peace the maintenance of international peace and security in southeast Asia. Consonant with the Constitution of the United States and the Charter of the United Nations and in accordance with its obligations under the Southeast Asia Collective Defense Treaty, the United States is, therefore, prepared, as the President determines, to take all necessary steps, including the use of armed force, to assist any member or protocol state of the Southeast Asia Collective Defense Treaty requesting assistance in defense of its freedom.[29]

The Tonkin Gulf Resolution was approved unanimously (414–0) by the House of Representatives and by a vote of 88–2 in the Senate—a margin of 99.6%. President Johnson requested $125,000,000 in additional money to implement the resolution, a request that was more than *tripled* by Congress to $400,000,000. For several years thereafter, Congress appropriated billions and billions of dollars by margins of greater than 90 percent. It should be kept in mind that Congress could have easily brought the war to an end at any time by simply refusing to appropriate the necessary funds.

Although later—as the conflict became increasingly unpopular and critics sought to exploit the absence of a formal declaration of war—this joint resolution was to become the source of a heated controversy,[30] during the early years it was widely recognized as an act of formal congressional sanction. Senator Jacob Javits, who later became the principal

---

29. The 1955 Southeast Asia Collective Defense [SEATO] Treaty, provided in Article IV that "Each Party recognizes that aggression by means of armed attack in the treaty area against any of the Parties or against any State or territory which the Parties by unanimous agreement may hereafter designate, would endanger its own peace and safety, and agrees that it will in that event act to meet the common danger in accordance with its constitutional process." An accompanying Protocol designated South Vietnam, Laos, and Cambodia as being protected by treaty. During the Senate debate over the Gulf of Tonkin Resolution the following colloquy occurred between the Republican and Democratic floor managers of the resolution: *Mr. Cooper.* Does the Senator consider that in enacting this resolution we are satisfying the ["constitutional processes"] requirement of Article IV of the Southeast Asia Collective Defense Treaty? In other words, are we now giving the President advance authority to take whatever action he may deem necessary respecting South Vietnam and its defense, or with respect to the defense of any other country included in the treaty? *Mr. Fulbright.* I think that is correct. *Mr. Cooper.* Then, looking ahead, if the President decided that it was necessary to use such force as could lead into war, we will give that authority by this resolution? *Mr. Fulbright.* That is the way I would interpret it." 110 Cong. Rec. 18,409 (1964).

30. It was widely alleged by war critics that the North Vietnamese attacks on American warships in the Tonkin Gulf either did not occur (Hanoi now admits the August 2, 1964, attack was real) or that they were intentionally provoked by President Johnson. A wealth of evidence that has become public since the war, including tape recordings of presidential telephone calls, establishes that President Johnson felt pressured by Congress and the public to go to war in Indochina and acted in good faith on the basis of reports from the Tonkin Gulf that additional attacks on U.S. warships had occurred on the night of August 4. Many experts now believe that the *second* attacks did not occur and that the "torpedo trails" sailors reported seeing in the Gulf may have been caused by a high phosphorous content in the water and the reported sonar contacts may have been caused wake from another American ship. Since Hanoi has subsequently admitted launching a military campaign to "liberate" South Vietnam more than five years before the Tonkin incident(s), as a legal matter whether the

author of the 1973 War Powers Resolution, told his colleagues in March 1966 that "It is a fact, whether we like it or not, that by virtue of having acted on the resolution of August 1964, we are a party to present policy."[31] Senator Sam Ervin, widely regarded as the most distinguished constitutional scholar in the Senate,[32] characterized the resolution as "a declaration of war in a constitutional sense...."[33]

Similarly, in 1967 the Senate Foreign Relations Committee issued a report that stated:

> The committee does not believe that formal declarations of war are the only available means by which Congress can authorize the President to initiate limited or general hostilities. Joint resolutions such as those pertaining to Formosa, the Middle East, and *the Gulf of Tonkin* are a proper method of granting authority.... [34]

Whatever one may think of the Gulf of Tonkin Resolution itself, it is beyond serious question that Congress may authorize the President to commit U.S. armed forces to hostilities by joint resolution without formally declaring war. This has been repeatedly recognized by the Supreme Court,[35] and was acknowledged by the strongest champions of legislative prerogative during the debates on the 1973 War Powers Resolution. Indeed, section 2(c) of the War Powers Resolution provides in part:

> The constitutional powers of the President as Commander-in-Chief to introduce United States Armed Forces into hostilities, or into situations where imminent involvement in hostilities is clearly indicated by the circumstances, are exercised only pursuant to (1) a declaration of war, (2) *specific statutory authorization*, or (3) a national emergency created by attack upon the United States, its territories or possessions, or its armed forces. (Emphasis added.)[36]

Consider also the following excerpt from the writings of a former Dean of Stanford Law School, who was certainly no supporter of the Vietnam War. It also addresses the popular contention that President Nixon's 1970 decision to attack Vietnamese Communist sanctuaries in neighboring Cambodia that were being used as safe havens and to re-supply Communist forces in South Vietnam was unlawful because it had not been expressly authorized by Congress (although Cambodia was one of the "protocol states" covered by the SEATO treaty and thus incorporated by reference in the Tonkin Gulf Resolution).

John Hart Ely, War and Responsibility
32 (1993)

The defense of South Vietnam ... was a project that had been congressionally authorized by the Tonkin Gulf Resolution and other statutory provisions as well. (There is no doubt that Cambodian sanctuaries were in fact being used as bases for Communist moves into Vietnam.) Thus viewed, it is difficult to understand the theory on which the president

---

reports of August 4 were erroneous or not is of little consequence. There is no evidence it was an intentional U.S. provocation.

31. 112 Cong. Rec. 4,374 (1966). Senator Javits added: "I agree with [President Johnson's] policies [in Vietnam] to date...." *Id.*

32. *See, e.g.,* 116 Cong. Rec. 20,793 (Sen. Fulbright), 41,740 (Sen. Percy), 41,742 (Sen. Humphrey), 41,743 (Sen. Kennedy) (1970).

33. *Id.* at 15,925.

34. S. Rep. No. 797, 90th Cong. 1st Sess. 25 (1967)(emphasis added).

35. *See, e.g.,* Bas v. Tingy, 4 U.S. (4 Dall.) 37 (1800); Talbot v. Seeman, 5 U.S. (1 Cranch) 1 (1801) (Marshall, C.J.).

36. War Powers Resolution, Pub. L. No. 93-148, 87 Stat. 555, 50 U.S.C. 1541–1548 (1973)(emphasis added).

needed additional statutory authorization for the drive [into Cambodia] — any more, for example, than Franklin Roosevelt needed special congressional permission for our landings in French North Africa (at the time a neutral territory) or on various Pacific islands with which we, similarly, were not at war.

————————

The conflict in Indochina became more and more unpopular with Americans and by 1968 was a major political issue. In 1970, following the incursions into Cambodia, student protesters effectively shut down colleges and universities across the nation. Adults, too, were losing faith in the war — although it later turned out that a sizeable portion of the critics were "hawks" angry over what they saw as Defense Secretary McNamara's "no win" policies who favored more intensive military action against North Vietnam.[37] In 1972, for the first time in the entire war, President Nixon authorized the Joint Chiefs of Staff to initiate a major bombing campaign against North Vietnam that many experts believe essentially broke Hanoi's will. North Vietnam returned to the negotiating table in January 1973 and quickly signed a cease-fire agreement. But, under strong pressure from "peace" groups, in May of that year Congress enacted a statute prohibiting the expenditure of appropriated funds "to finance directly or indirectly combat activities by United States military forces in or over of from off the shores of North Vietnam, South Vietnam, Laos, or Cambodia."[38] Assured that the Americans could no longer oppose them, North Vietnam sent its entire army (minus the 325th Division, which remained to protect Hanoi) into Laos, Cambodia, and South Vietnam — where columns of Soviet-made tanks smashed through the gates of the presidential palace on April 30, 1975, in a conventional military invasion. During the three years that followed the "liberation" of non-Communist Indochina, more people were slaughtered by the new Communist regimes than had been killed in the previous fourteen years of combat. Back in Washington, Congress set about establishing a new paradigm of separation of national security powers, determined that no future president would enjoy such broad discretion in the making and implementation of policies.

The 1973 War Powers Resolution

Public dissatisfaction with the Vietnam conflict, and a widespread but false belief that Congress had been excluded from its proper constitutional role in authorizing the war, led the Congress in 1973 to enact a joint resolution to assert its proper role and ensure that Congress would be involved in future decisions to commit U.S. armed forces to hostilities. Enacted over President Nixon's veto at the height of the Watergate controversy, the most important provisions of the statute were:

————————

37. One of many "myths" surrounding the Vietnam War is that the commitment was undertaken without the support of the American people. In fact, when President Johnson first used force against North Vietnam in August 1964, his approval in the Gallup Polls shot up from 42 percent in July to 72 percent in late August. THE REAL LESSONS OF THE VIETNAM WAR, *supra* note 28 at 223. More than a year later, when there were hundreds of thousands of American troops in Vietnam, another Gallup Poll showed 60 percent of "prominent Americans" favored *escalation* of the war. *Id.* at 224. But opposition was growing, and the strong showing of anti-war candidate Eugene McCarthy during the 1968 New Hampshire Democratic political primary shocked much of the country and contributed to President Johnson's decision not to run for reelection. However, exit polls later revealed that a plurality of McCarthy voters were "super-hawks" who in the November presidential election voted for former Alabama Governor George Wallace and his vice presidential running mate, General Curtiss LeMay (who had advocated bombing North Vietnam "back to the stone age"). LESLIE H. GELB & RICHARD K. BETTS, THE IRONY OF VIETNAM: THE SYSTEM WORKED 172 (1979).

38. Pub. L. No. 93-52, 87 Stat. 130 (1973).

The War Powers Resolution

Pub. L. No. 93-148, 87 Stat. 555, 50 U.S.C. §§ 1541–1548 (1982)

JOINT RESOLUTION Concerning the war powers of Congress and the President.

Resolved by the Senate and House of Representatives of the United States of America in Congress assembled, …

....

(c) The Constitutional powers of the President as Commander-in-Chief to introduce United States Armed Forces into hostilities, or into situations where imminent involvement in hostilities is clearly indicated by the circumstances, are exercised only pursuant to (1) a declaration of war, (2) specific statutory authorization, or (3) a national emergency created by attack upon the United States, its territories or possessions, or its armed forces.

CONSULTATION

Sec. 3. The President in every possible instance shall consult with Congress before introducing the United States Armed Forces into hostilities or into situations where imminent involvement in hostilities is clearly indicated by the circumstances, and after every such introduction shall consult regularly with the Congress until the United States Armed Forces are no longer engaged in hostilities or have been removed from such situations.

REPORTING

Sec. 4. (a) In the absence of a declaration of war, in any case in which the United States Armed Forces are introduced—

(1) into hostilities or into situations where imminent involvement in hostilities is clearly indicated by the circumstances;

(2) into the territory, airspace or waters of a foreign nation, while equipped for combat, except for deployments which relate solely to supply, replacement, repair, or training of such forces; or

(3) in numbers which substantially enlarge United States Armed Forces equipped for combat already located in a foreign nation;

the President shall submit within 48 hours to the Speaker of the House of Representatives and to the President pro tempore of the Senate a report, in writing, setting forth—

(A) the circumstances necessitating the introduction of United States Armed Forces;

(B) the constitutional and legislative authority under which such introduction took place;....

....

CONGRESSIONAL ACTION

Sec. 5

....

(b) Within sixty calendar days after a report is submitted or is required to be submitted pursuant to section 4(a)(1), whichever is earlier, the President shall terminate any use of United States Armed Forces with respect to which such report was submitted (or required to be submitted), unless the Congress (1) has declared war or has enacted a specific authorization for such use of United States Armed Forces, (2) has extended by law such sixty-day period, or (3) is physically unable to meet as a result of an armed attack upon the United States. Such sixty-day period shall be extended for not more than an additional thirty days if the President determines and certifies to the Congress in writing that unavoidable military necessity respecting the safety of United States Armed Forces requires the continued use of such armed forces in the course of bringing about a prompt removal of such forces.

(c) Notwithstanding subsection (b) at any time that United States Armed Forces are engaged in hostilities outside the territory of the United States, its possessions and territories without a declaration of war or specific statutory authorization, such forces shall be removed by the President if the Congress so directs by concurrent resolution.

. . . .

SEPARABILITY CLAUSE

Sec. 9. If any provision of this joint resolution or the application thereof to any person or circumstances is held invalid, the remainder of the joint resolution and the application of such provision to any other person or circumstance shall not be affected thereby.

Questions for Discussion

1. In view of the 1964 Gulf of Tonkin Resolution, discussed *supra*, and section 2(c)(2) of the War Powers Resolution, do you believe the 1973 resolution would have prevented America's tragic involvement in Indochina?

2. Do you see any constitutional difficulties with the War Powers Resolution?

3. Assume for a moment that you are Counsel to the President of the United States, that you believe portions of the War Powers Resolution to be unconstitutional, but that you also wish to avoid if possible a constitutional confrontation with Congress and at the same time avoid acquiescing to an erosion of executive power. What advice do you give to the President in connection with reporting major military deployments to Congress?

4. Assume for a moment that you are Counsel to the Senate Committee on Foreign Relations, and the Supreme Court has held sections 2(c), 5(b) and 5(c) of the War Powers Resolution to be unconstitutional. You are asked by the Chairman whether these same results might be achieved by other means that will withstand constitutional scrutiny. What advice would you give?

The War Powers After 200 Years: Congress and the President at a Constitutional Impasse

Hearings before the Special Subcommittee on War Powers of the
Committee on Foreign Relations
100th Cong., 2d Sess. 778, 847–52, 856–57 (testimony of Robert F. Turner, Associate
Director, Center for Law and National Security)

III. The War Powers Resolution and the Constitution

Mr. Chairman, with the Committee's permission I would like at this point to take a quick look at some of the specific provisions of the current War Powers Resolution.

As you know, it consists of ten sections. In the interest of time, I shall focus upon the provisions which I find to be constitutionally suspect, and then make a general comment about the underlying standard of "imminent involvement in hostilities."

Section 2(c)

Section 2(c) appears to limit "[t]he constitutional powers of the President as Commander-in-Chief to introduce United States Armed Forces into hostilities, or into situations where imminent involvement in hostilities is clearly indicated by the circumstances," to three circumstances: "(1) a declaration of war, (2) specific statutory authorization, or (3) a national emergency created by attack upon the United States, its territories or possessions, or its armed forces."

If this provision is intended to have the effect of law—and the language would certainly suggest that—it is unquestionably *unconstitutional* as an infringement upon the independent constitutional power of the President. In December 1984 I shared a panel with Senator Javits ... in New York City under the auspices of the American Branch of the International Law Association, during which Senator Javits *acknowledged* that this language did not recognize such independent constitutional authority as the President's power to rescue endangered American citizens abroad or on the high seas. Under the Constitution, so long as Congress provides the Commander in Chief with an Army or a Navy, it is his to deploy and utilize as he deems necessary—with the single exception that if he concludes it is necessary to initiate offensive "war" against another State he must first obtain the statutory approval of both houses of Congress.

Section 3

I am a *strong* believer in the importance of "consultation," and during my service in the Department of State fought hard to replace the all too frequent practice of "informing" or "notifying" Congress of decisions already made with a policy of seeking the wisdom of congressional leaders *prior* to decisions being made. The way it is worded, I am not opposed to the principle reflected in this provision. For *political* if not legal reasons, it is essential that the President keep Congress informed about major foreign policy initiatives—consistent, of course, with the need to preserve the operational security of the mission and the safety of our military forces and other personnel.

However, consultation ought to be a process engaged in between co-equal branches of our government out of mutual self-interest and a spirit of comity. It is not a process that either branch should *impose* upon the other. As a matter of constitutional law, it is well established that Congress may not *compel* the President to provide national security information which in his judgment should be kept secret.

The President of the United States is not your "agent," but a coequal representative of the American people. It is both *unseemly* and *unconstitutional* for Congress to "direct" the President to consult about sensitive matters confided by the Constitution to his discretion—and the language of the current bill ("The President ... *shall* consult") certainly implies a legal duty. As a matter of law, of course, such language does not alter the constitutional distribution of powers and is thus without effect.

There are great benefits for the President in a cooperative, bipartisan (or nonpartisan) relationship with Congress; and the President should realize that without the understanding and approval of Congress and the American people his foreign policy initiatives are unlikely to be viable over the long run. This reality may be a political rather than a legal check, but it is just as important.

In a sense, there is a form of "checks and balances" inherent in this relationship. The President needs your understanding and support, so he has an incentive to cooperate and keep you informed. (He also, of course, needs appropriations for many activities.) The Senate and the Congress want information, and if they behave responsibly—and don't continually "leak" our nation's secrets to the world—it is in the President's *self-interest* to keep you informed. But when you word your request as a *directive*, pretending by statute to *compel* the President to comply, you provide the President with a strong *disincentive* to cooperate—lest he appear to acquiesce to the unconstitutional demand—without in the process altering in any manner the underlying constitutional realities. The simple fact is that you can't alter the constitutional separation of powers by a simple *statute*.

Section 4

Again, as a matter of political wisdom I strongly favor a responsible Congress and Senate being kept up to date about major foreign policy initiatives—to the extent consistent with operational success. The Founding Fathers clearly did not intend for Congress to be given the more sensitive secrets of military or foreign policy—and the behavior of both Houses during the past two decades has served to confirm the wisdom of the original scheme.

I haven't studied the issue, but my expectation is that few (if any) members of Congress were informed in advance about the details of the D-Day invasion during World War II. Congress has no responsibility for the operations of war, and the dangers to the lives of our troops and the success of such operations which would result from even inadvertent disclosure justify a decision to limit advanced operational information to those in the chain-of-command with a genuine "need to know."

On the basis of fifteen years of practice I think the detailed "reporting" requirement is on balance a bad provision—at least in the current political atmosphere on the Hill. If you will recall, both Jay and Locke observed that the details of war and foreign policy could not be managed effectively by antecedent "law." And yet, when you demand that the President provide you with such details as the "scope of duration" of military operations, and then treat them essentially as legally binding commitments, you require the Executive to establish precisely the sort of artificial constraints in advance of developing situations that Locke and his contemporaries recognized were incompatible with the effective conduct of military operations.

Part of the problem with section 4 may result as much from current attitudes in Congress than from the language of the provision itself. If it were understood that the details in a "war powers" report were simply good faith "estimates" which could be departed from by the President when necessary to respond to changes by other participants in the conflict or newly perceived strategic or tactical opportunities, the only serious risks would be public disclosure of the information and thus perhaps a military edge for our adversaries and an increased risk to the lives or safety of some of our forces. Those, of course, would be serious risks indeed. But in today's political environment, the President can be confident that whatever "rules of engagement" (or "scope … of the hostilities or involvement") he provides to Congress will be viewed by many in Congress as legally binding commitment—*precisely* the sort of antecedent restrictions which Locke and others were trying to avoid—and we can be reasonably certain that if a shift in strategy by our adversaries leads the President to depart from the "game plan" provided to Congress, the President will promptly be accused of "lying to Congress" or "breaking the law" by his political opposition.

But these are *policy* considerations, and there is a more fundamental *legal* problem with this section. Put simply, I don't believe you have the constitutional *power* to compel the President to provide meaningful "reports" about ongoing hostilities. If you conduct yourselves honorably, as a co-equal branch of the national government, and treat the President with the respect and dignity appropriate to such a relationship, I don't believe you will *need* a statute to receive cooperation. History demonstrates that the cooperation which characterized the early years of the Vietnam conflict broke down not because of the Executive but because members of Congress—who had played a full partnership roll in the "takeoff"—sought to find "parachutes" before there was a crash landing.

Section 5(b)

Section 5 contains in my view the most *flagrantly* unconstitutional parts of the War Powers Resolution. Section 5(b) provides that if Congress does not act to authorize the continued presence of U.S. forces within 62 (or 92) days of the initial commitment, the President must withdraw forces from any situation in which "imminent involvement in hostilities is clearly indicated by the circumstances"—even if not a single shot has been fired and the American forces are in a purely *defensive* setting and "in harms way" simply by virtue of possible foreign aggression or terrorist attack. (Deploying armed forces on your own territory, on the high seas, or on the territory of a friendly foreign country in such a manner that they may be attacked by a determined aggressor has never been viewed as an "act of war," and does not infringe the power of Congress to veto a presidential decision to initiate a "war" against another State.)

This is a direct effort by Congress to exercise the "Commander in Chief" power vested exclusively by the Constitution in the President. The situation is not in my view a close call. The way the Constitution was designed to work is clear. If the President decides that the national interests require commencing a "war" against another State, he must obtain the approval of both the House and the Senate in advance of initiating such a conflict. Like other exceptions to the President's "Executive" powers, the power "to declare war" was intended to be construed narrowly. It gives Congress a "veto" over a presidential decision to launch an offensive "war," but it does *not* empower you to seize control of the President's independent constitutional powers on the theory that the President's management of military deployments might lead another State to commit aggression against the United States.

Virtually any military deployment is accompanied by some risk—many experts believe President Truman's decision to pull U.S. combat forces out of South Korea in 1949 was a significant factor in the North Korean decision to invade the South the following year. That is precisely the kind of judgment call that the Founding Fathers left to the *uncontrolled discretion* of the President.

While it is true that the President might use his Commander in Chief powers in such a way as to increase the likelihood of involvement in war, the experience of the Neutrality Acts of the 1930s demonstrates that when his hands are tied the prospects of war from foreign aggression increase substantially. Recent history—for example the so-called "Clark Amendment" of 1975, which prohibited the President from assisting the non-communist majority in Angola to resist Soviet and Cuban intervention; and in the end led to the introduction of more than 50,000 Cuban combat troops in Angola and other parts of Africa before being repealed by a wiser Congress—confirms that lesson. Should the people elect an *evil* President who seeks to initiate offensive "war" without first consulting Congress, Congress has a "check" in the power of impeachment.

Apart from its *legal* infirmities, consider for a moment what section 5 of the War Powers Resolution actually does in practice. Consider the signal it sends to our friends and adversaries alike. Countries which might wish to associate themselves with the United States in deterring international aggression are told that the American Commander in Chief only has permission to function for sixty days. After that, he is at the mercy of a disorganized legislative establishment which has demonstrated the most incredible irresponsibility time and again in the recent past.... To make it even more outrageous, the statute tells our friends (and our enemies) that Congress has determined in advance that, in the event it can't make up its mind whether the President is right or wrong, it will assume *as a matter of law* that the President is *wrong*. Inaction by Congress means the President loses his independent constitutional power—a "silent veto" works to accomplish something otherwise achievable only through a constitutional amendment.

....

The Legal Standard Is "War," Not "Hostilities"

In an effort to make the War Powers Resolution as comprehensive as possible, the drafters came up with the basic standard that it would apply "to the introduction of United States Armed Forces into hostilities or into situations where imminent involvement in hostilities is clearly indicated by the circumstances...." This is an interesting formulation, and has led to hours of legalistic debate at both ends of Pennsylvania Avenue about whether the President was "violating the law" in the latest foreign policy crisis. Without wishing to deprive either branch of the intellectual exercise this standard promotes, I strongly believe a new standard is necessary. Put simply, this one is *illegal*.

Some may wonder how it can be "illegal" for Congress to set such a standard. After all, everyone knows that under our Constitution Congress "makes the law." And while that may be generally true, it is important from time to time to keep in mind that Congress is not the ultimate sovereign in the United States. The authority remains in the American people.

When the Founding Fathers met in Philadelphia two hundred years ago, they established a government of limited powers. To Congress they gave "[a]ll legislative powers herein granted," to the President they gave "[t]he executive power"—subject to clearly spelled out "checks" vested in Congress and the Senate—and to the courts they gave "[t]he judicial power." To establish the ultimate authority of the Constitution, they required "[t]he senators and representatives ... and all executive and judicial officers" to be "bound by oath or affirmation, to support this constitution"; and they declared that "[t]his constitution, and the laws of the United States *which shall be made in pursuance thereof*; and all treaties made ... under the authority of the United States, shall be the supreme law of the land...." It follows that statutory enactments which are contrary to the Constitution are not the "supreme law" of the land.[39]

So if you wish to be faithful to your legal duty under the Constitution and your oath of office, I would urge you to *abandon* the standard "hostilities" and return instead to the proper constitutional standard of "war." The fact that the importance of the congressional power "to declare war" has been reduced by the prohibition in the U.N. Charter of the types of war with which such declarations have historically been associated should not be viewed by you with dismay but with joy. You have "lost" nothing to the President— you have gained by developments of law which seek to provide a more peaceful world. Your diminished authority to approve "war" is hardly justification for an effort to seize other constitutional powers which were clearly denied to you by the Founding Fathers.

Finally, I would again urge you to keep in mind that the congressional role in initiating "war" was viewed by the Founding Fathers to be an "exception" to the general vesting in

---

39. Note 9 of the testimony. *See, e.g.,* Marbury v. Madison 5 U.S. 137, 180 (1803): "It is also not entirely unworthy of observation, that declaring what shall be the supreme law of the land, the constitution itself is first mentioned; and not the laws of the United States generally, but those only which shall be made in pursuance of the constitution, have that rank. Thus, the particular phraseology of the constitution of the United States confirms and strengthens the principle, supposed to be essential to all written constitutions, that a law repugnant to the constitution is void...."

the President of control over relations with other states—and thus (as Hamilton put it) was "to be construed strictly, and ought to be extended no further than is essential to [its] execution."

Omitted from the above excerpt was a lengthy discussion of the "legislative veto" in Section 5(c) of the War Powers Resolution, which clearly did not survive the Supreme Court's 1983 ruling in *I.N.S. v. Chadha*.[40] Indeed, in his dissenting remarks, Justice White observed:

> Today the Court not only invalidates § 244(c)(2) of the Immigration and Nationality Act, but also sounds the death knell for nearly 200 other statutory provisions in which Congress has reserved a "legislative veto." For this reason, the Court's decision is of surpassing importance. And it is for this reason that the Court would have been well advised to decide the cases, if possible, on the narrower grounds of separation of powers, leaving for full consideration the constitutionality of other congressional review statutes operating on such varied matters as war powers and agency rulemaking, some of which concern the independent regulatory agencies.[41]

Disenchantment with the War Powers Resolution

It is noteworthy that support for the War Powers Resolution has declined dramatically in the past two decades. One by one, strong champions of congressional checks on the President's military powers began to express their disillusionment with the 1973 statute.

In 1988, former Senator Thomas Eagleton—who had voted against the War Powers Resolution because he believed it did not go far enough in constraining the President—told the Foreign Relations Committee that he had finally come to the conclusion "that Congress really didn't want to be in on the decision-making process as to when, how, and where we go to war. I came to the conclusion that Congress really didn't want to have its fingerprints on sensitive matters pertaining to putting our Armed Forces into hostilities.... I harbor the notion that most Senators and House Members don't have the political stomach for decision-making involving war."[42]

Shortly before becoming chairman of the Foreign Relations Committee, Senator Frank Church—a key cosponsor of the War Powers Resolution in 1973—noted to his colleagues that Congress will have to confront any decision to use major military force when the President has to seek new appropriations, concluding "I wonder really whether we have done very much in furthering our purpose through the War Powers Resolution."[43]

On May 19, 1988, future Senate Majority Leader George Mitchell, former Majority Leader Robert Byrd, Armed Services Committee chairman Sam Nunn, ranking Republican (and now chairman) John Warner, and other key Senators took turns criticizing the War Powers Resolution. Senator Byrd declared that the Resolution was "unworkable" and had had "debilitating effects" on American "credibility and for America's image as a leader."[44] Senator Nunn noted that the statute "encourages confrontation rather than consultation

---

40. I.N.S. v. Chadha, 462 U.S. 919 (1983).
41. 462 U.S. at 967 (1983).
42. *Quoted in* ROBERT F. TURNER, REPEALING THE WAR POWERS RESOLUTION 160 (1991).
43. *Id.* at 161.
44. *Id.*

between the President and the Congress," and it "raises questions about the U.S. staying power in [the] midst of a crisis, thus making it harder for the United States to secure the cooperation of our friends abroad."[45]

Senator Warner denounced the Resolution because it was "unconstitutional" and "does not work." Majority Leader Mitchell added that the 1973 Resolution "oversteps the constitutional bounds on Congress' power to control the Armed Forces in situations short of war and because it potentially undermines our ability to effectively defend our national interests." He concluded: "The War Powers Resolution therefore threatens not only the delicate balance of power established by the Constitution. It potentially undermines America's ability to effectively defend our national security."[46]

During a 1991 Senate Judiciary Committee hearing on the President's authority to send U.S. forces into hostilities in Iraq, Senator Joseph Biden—who in 1988 had chaired the Foreign Relations Committee's special subcommittee that held extensive hearings on the 1973 statute—declared that "the war powers act is not practically functional; so, therefore, I think it's an academic exercise to debate that."[47]

In 1996, the Center for National Security Law set up a debate on Capitol Hill on the proposition that the War Powers Resolution ought to be repealed. Representing the negative were former House Foreign Relations Committee (and House Intelligence Committee) Chairman Lee Hamilton, and Dr. Louis Fisher of the Library of Congress' Congressional Research Service. To the surprise of many, neither Representative Hamilton nor Dr. Fisher proved willing to actually defend the War Powers Resolution. In 1998, Dr. Fisher coauthored an article in *Political Science Quarterly* concluding that it was "time to say goodbye" to the 1973 statute: "Experience under the resolution has proved to be disappointing and frustrating. It is riddled with contradictions, ambiguities, and constitutional flaws."[48] "After nearly twenty-five years of experience," they wrote, "it would be better for both branches—and for constitutional government—to repeal the War Powers Resolution and rely on traditional political pressures and the regular system of checks and balances, including impeachment."[49]

The National War Powers Commission

In 2008, the University of Virginia's Miller Center of Public Policy—in partnership with several law schools and university research centers from around the country—established the National War Powers Commission. Co-chaired by former Secretaries of State James A. Baker III and Warren Christopher, its distinguished group of ten other members included former Members of Congress like Lee Hamilton, Slade Gorton, and John O. Marsh, Jr., as well as respected scholars and former representatives of the executive and judicial branches. In announcing their conclusions, Baker noted "most legal experts consider it to be unconstitutional." The group recommended that the "impractical and ineffective" 1973 statute be repealed, and replaced by a "War Powers Consultation Act of 2009" that would promote consultation between the president and a new "Joint Congressional Consultation Committee consisting of the majority and minority leaders of both Houses of Congress as well as the chairmen and ranking members of key

---

45. *Id.* at 162.
46. *Id.* at 162–63.
47. *Id.* at 163–64.
48. Louis Fisher & David Gray Adler, *The War Powers Resolution: Time to Say Goodbye*, 113 POL. SCI. Q 1, 16 (1998).
49. *Id.* at 1.

committees." The Report emphasized that the statute it recommended was "not meant to define, circumscribe, or enhance the constitutional war powers of either the Executive or Legislative Branches of government," but rather to promote "sound public policy" and "a pragmatic approach" to the problem. It eliminated some of the clearly unconstitutional parts of the 1973 law, calling upon the President to "consult" with the proposed consultation committee prior to, or in any event within three days, of committing troops to "significant armed conflict" (military operations expected to last a week or more). Covert operations, "reprisals [sic] against terrorist groups," and such limited operations as defending an American embassy abroad would not require a report. Congress could then endorse the operation by concurrent resolution, and if that failed a joint resolution disapproving the operation could be introduced—subject to the veto of the President. In the event of a veto, a majority of either House of Congress would have (as has always been the case) the option of turning down requests for new troops, weapons, of appropriations that might be necessary to carry out the operation.

The 1991 and 2003 Conflicts with Iraq

Since the American defeat in Indochina, the United States has been involved in several relatively minor military operations (in terms of the numbers of American troops and casualties involved) in places like Grenada,[50] Central America,[51] Lebanon, and Panama. But it has also been involved in three more significant operations, two if which were directed against Iraq's President Sadam Hussein.

In August 1990 Iraq invaded neighboring Kuwait.[52] The UN Security Council promptly passed Resolution 660, condemning the invasion and demanding that Iraq withdraw all of its forces from Kuwait. Three months later, in Resolution 678, the Council authorized: "Member States co-operating with the Government of Kuwait ... to use all necessary means to uphold and implement resolution 660 (1990) and all subsequent relevant resolutions and to *restore international peace and security in the area* [emphasis added]."

President George H.W. Bush had already deployed a large American military force to the Gulf region, and his lawyers argued that he did not need authorization from Congress to assist in implementing Resolution 678. Congress insisted that the President could not act without statutory authorization, and in January 2001 the President formally requested a resolution of approval (without admitting it was constitutionally necessary). Ultimately (by a narrow and highly-partisan 52–47 vote in the Senate), Congress passed S. J. Res. 2, which authorized the President to use armed force "pursuant to United Nations Security Council Resolution 678 (1990) in order to achieve implementation of Security Council Resolutions 660, 661, 662, 664, 665, 666, 667, 669, 670, 674, and 677." By refusing to authorize the President to use force "to achieve implementation" of Resolution 678, Congress provided no authority to use force beyond ejecting Iraqi forces from Kuwait. The additional UN authorization of 678 to use force "to restore international peace and security in the area"—which might arguably have justified going all the way to Baghdad and apprehending Saddam Hussein to be tried as a war criminal—was thus not approved

---

50. *See generally,* John Norton Moore, Law & the Grenada Mission (1984).

51. *See generally,* John Norton Moore, The Secret War in Central America: Sandinista Assault on World Order (1987); and Robert F. Turner, Nicaragua v. United States: A Look at the Facts (1987).

52. *See generally,* John Norton Moore, Crisis in the Gulf: Enforcing the Rule of Law (1992).

by Congress, and during the floor debates there were references to "the lessons of Vietnam" and avoiding issuing a "blank check" to the President along the lines of the Gulf of Tonkin Resolution.[53] Operation Desert Storm began in mid-January, and in less than six weeks all Iraqi forces were ejected from Kuwait and Iraq assured the Security Council that it would obey the law and accept international supervision of the destruction of its weapons of mass destruction (WMD).

After more than a decade during which Saddam Hussein had ignored over a dozen legally-binding Security Council resolutions designed to compel Iraq to abide by its 1991 commitments regarding WMD, President George W. Bush asked Congress prior to the 2002 congressional elections to pass a resolution authorizing the use of force against Iraq. In response, Congress passed H.J. Res. 114, authorizing the President to use "the Armed Forces of the United States as he determines to be necessary to ... enforce all relevant United Nations Security Council resolutions regarding Iraq."[54] This statute clearly satisfied any constitutional requirement for congressional sanction for Operation Iraqi Freedom (OIF).

As had been the case in Korea and Vietnam, the President's political opposition subsequently claimed that "Bush lied" to trick Congress into authorizing the use of armed force against Saddam — particularly on the issue of Iraq's so-called WMD programs. Enough mistakes were made to warrant severe criticism of many people of both political parties and in the military leading up to and during OIF. But to put the allegation that President George W. Bush "lied" to Congress to persuade it to authorize a campaign to remove Saddam Hussein from power in context, two realities should be kept in mind. First of all, it is now clear that the Intelligence Community did tell the President that Iraq had WMD programs, and the same information was presented to members of congressional intelligence committees. And during the years leading up to OIF, assertions that Iraq had active WMD programs that needed to be stopped were made by President Clinton, Vice President Gore, Secretary of State Albright, National Security Adviser Berger, and such prominent Democratic members of Congress as House Speaker Nancy Pelosi, Senate Intelligence Committee Chairman Jay Rockefeller, Foreign Relations Committee Chairman John F. Kerry, as well as Senators Ted Kennedy, Hillary Clinton, and many others.[55] (They were matched as well by statements by Republican leaders.)

Indeed, more than two years before then-Texas Governor George W. Bush moved to Washington, DC, to serve as President, overwhelming majorities of both Houses of Congress enacted a statute declaring that the United States should support the removal from power of Saddam Hussein and his replacement by a democratic government. The statute provided in part: "It should be the policy of the United States to support efforts to remove the regime headed by Saddam Hussein from power in Iraq and to promote the emergence of a democratic government to replace that regime."[56]

---

53. One of the ironies of the Vietnam debate is that critics allege both that Congress gave LBJ a "blank check" and that Congress was bypassed or ignored and did not authorize the conflict. The first allegation is more accurate, but congressional authorizations for hostilities have traditionally been "blank checks" in the sense that decisions on how wars are fought are an inherent part of the Commander in Chief's power.

54. Iraq War Resolution, Pub. L. No. 107-243, 116 Stat. 1498 (2002).

55. The Internet Web site snopes.com has collected relevant quotations with links to original sources at http://www.snopes.com/politics/war/wmdquotes.asp.

56. Iraq Liberation Act of 1998, Public Law 105-338, 22 USC § 2151.

Military Intervention in Libya (2011)

In late 2010, a series of revolutions broke out in the Arab world widely referred to as the "Arab Spring." Protests spread to Libya in February of the following year, leading quickly to a civil war during which head of state Colonel Muammar Gaddafi responded ruthlessly, shelling rebels and innocent civilians as well. Later that month, the UN Security Council approved Resolution 1970 "condemning the violence and use of force against civilians" by the Gaddafi regime. When that resolution had no effect, the Security Council took action under Chapter VII of the Charter by authorizing Member States "to take all necessary measures" (i.e., to use military force) to protect Libyan civilians (expressly excluding only military occupation of Libyan territory).

UN Security Council Resolution 1973 (2011)

Adopted by the Security Council at its 6498th meeting, on 17 March 2011

The Security Council,

Recalling its resolution 1970 (2011) of 26 February 2011,

Deploring the failure of the Libyan authorities to comply with resolution 1970 (2011),

Expressing grave concern at the deteriorating situation, the escalation of violence, and the heavy civilian casualties,

Reiterating the responsibility of the Libyan authorities to protect the Libyan population and reaffirming that parties to armed conflicts bear the primary responsibility to take all feasible steps to ensure the protection of civilians,

Acting under Chapter VII of the Charter of the United Nations,

1. Demands the immediate establishment of a cease-fire and a complete end to violence and all attacks against, and abuses of, civilians;

3. Demands that the Libyan authorities comply with their obligations under international law, including international humanitarian law, human rights and refugee law and take all measures to protect civilians and meet their basic needs, and to ensure the rapid and unimpeded passage of humanitarian assistance;

Protection of civilians

4. Authorizes Member States that have notified the Secretary-General, acting nationally or through regional organizations or arrangements, and acting in cooperation with the Secretary-General, to take all necessary measures ... to protect civilians and civilian populated areas under threat of attack in the Libyan Arab Jamahiriya, including Benghazi, while excluding a foreign occupation force of any form on any part of Libyan territory....

Libya and the War Powers Resolution

As discussed above, when the Senate consented to the ratification of the UN Charter and the Congress enacted the UN Participation Act in 1945, the overwhelming viewpoint was that the president would need no additional authority to use armed force to carry out a Chapter VII decision by the Security Council. However, the text of the War Powers Resolution—which was enacted twenty-eight years later—clearly denies the president the power to commit U.S. armed forces into "hostilities" unless specifically authorized by Congress.

In the landmark 1888 Supreme Court case of *Whitney v. Robertson*, the Supreme Court decided that when a treaty provision could not be reconciled with a statute, the duty of the courts was "to construe and give effect to the latest expression of the sovereign will."[57] But that does not necessarily resolve this dispute. Clearly, if presidential authority to use force to implement a Security Council decision is derived from a 1945 treaty or statute, the courts will enforce the terms of the more recent War Powers Resolution. But if the president's authority stems from the Constitution itself, it preempts both inconsistent subsequent treaties and statutes.

In discussing possible congressional constraints on presidential use of force under the Charter, the unanimous Senate Foreign Relations Committee report advocating Senate advice and consent to the ratification of the UN Charter (in language reprinted with approval in the unanimous House Foreign Relations Committee report on the UN Participation Act) declared: "The committee feels that a reservation or other congressional action ... would also violate the spirit of the United States Constitution under which the President has well-established powers and obligations to use our armed forces without specific approval of Congress." But this history is known by few in Washington, and the modern conventional wisdom is that Congress controls when the president may use the armed forces abroad in the absence of foreign attacks.

There is an old adage that, in Washington, "where you stand often depends upon where you sit." The point is well illustrated by numerous debates about the War Powers Resolution. When Republicans hold the White House, Democrats tend to demand strict compliance with the 1973 statute while congressional Republicans declare it to be unconstitutional and irrelevant. When control of the Executive branch shifts, the parties quickly reverse roles in Congress. When legislators move to the White House, the same phenomenon can often be observed. The *New York Times* reported "President Obama rejected the views of top lawyers at the Pentagon and the Justice Department when he decided that he had the legal authority to continue American military participation in the air war in Libya without Congressional authorization, according to officials familiar with internal administration deliberations."[58]

Scholars who move in and out of government can exhibit the same phenomenon, as can be seen in this defense of presidential power to use force in Libya without congressional authorization by arguably the strongest champion of the War Powers Resolution in the academic community as a Yale law professor and dean:

Harold Hongju Koh, Legal Advisor, U.S. Department of State, Testimony Before the Senate Foreign Relations Committee, Washington, DC, June 28, 2011

Thank you, Mr. Chairman, Ranking Member Lugar, and members of the Committee, for this opportunity to testify before you on Libya and war powers. By so doing, I continue nearly four decades of dialogue between Congress and Legal Advisers of the State Department, since the War Powers Resolution was enacted, regarding the Executive Branch's legal position on war powers.

We believe that the President is acting lawfully in Libya, consistent with both the Constitution and the War Powers Resolution, as well as with international law. Our position

---

57. Whitney v. Robertson, 112 U.S. 190, 579 (1888).

58. Charlie Savage, 2 Top Lawyers Lost to Obama in Libya War Policy Debate, NY Times, June 17, 2011, http://www.nytimes.com/2011/06/18/world/africa/18powers.html?pagewanted=all&_r=0.

is carefully limited to the facts of the present operation, supported by history, and respectful of both the letter of the Resolution and the spirit of consultation and collaboration that underlies it. We recognize that our approach has been a matter of important public debate, and that reasonable minds can disagree. But surely none of us believes that the best result is for Qadhafi to wait NATO out, leaving the Libyan people again exposed to his brutality.

. . . .

Throughout the Libya episode, the President has never claimed the authority to take the nation to war without Congressional authorization, to violate the War Powers Resolution or any other statute, to violate international law, to use force abroad when doing so would not serve important national interests, or to refuse to consult with Congress on important war powers issues. The Administration recognizes that Congress has powers to regulate and terminate uses of force, and that the War Powers Resolution plays an important role in promoting interbranch dialogue and deliberation on these critical matters.

. . . .

Where, against this background, does the War Powers Resolution fit in? The legal debate has focused on the Resolution's 60-day clock, which directs the President—absent express Congressional authorization (or the applicability of other limited exceptions) and following an initial 48-hour reporting period—to remove United States Armed Forces within 60 days from "hostilities" or "situations where imminent involvement in hostilities is clearly indicated by the circumstances." But as virtually every lawyer recognizes, the operative term, "hostilities," is an ambiguous standard, which is nowhere defined in the statute. Nor has this standard ever been defined by the courts or by Congress in any subsequent war powers legislation. Indeed, the legislative history of the Resolution makes clear there was no fixed view on exactly what the term "hostilities" would encompass. Members of Congress understood that the term was vague, but specifically declined to give it more concrete meaning, in part to avoid unduly hampering future Presidents by making the Resolution a "one size fits all" straitjacket that would operate mechanically, without regard to particular circumstances.

. . . .

In the nearly forty years since the Resolution's enactment, successive Administrations have thus started from the premise that the term "hostilities" is "definable in a meaningful way only in the context of an actual set of facts." And successive Congresses and Presidents have opted for a process through which the political branches have worked together to flesh out the law's meaning over time. By adopting this approach, the two branches have sought to avoid construing the statute mechanically, divorced from the realities that face them.

. . . .

[T]he military means we are using are limited: This situation does not present the kind of "full military engagement with which the [War Powers] Resolution is primarily concerned." The violence that U.S. armed forces have directly inflicted or facilitated after the handoff to NATO has been modest in terms of its frequency, intensity, and severity. The air-to-ground strikes conducted by the United States in Libya are a far cry from the bombing campaign waged in Kosovo in 1999, which involved much more extensive and aggressive aerial strike operations led by U.S. armed forces.

. . . .

Nor are we in a "war" for purposes of Article I of the Constitution. As the Office of Legal Counsel concluded in its April 1, 2011 opinion, under longstanding precedent the President had the constitutional authority to direct the use of force in Libya, for two main reasons. First, he could reasonably determine that U.S. operations in Libya would serve important national interests in preserving regional stability and supporting the credibility and effectiveness of the U.N. Security Council. Second, the military operations that the President anticipated ordering were not sufficiently extensive in "nature, scope, and duration" to constitute a "war" requiring prior specific Congressional approval under the Declaration of War Clause.

. . . .

Scholars will certainly go on debating this issue. But that should not distract those of us in government from the most urgent question now facing us, which is not one of law but of policy: Will Congress provide its support for NATO's mission in Libya at this pivotal juncture, ensuring that Qadhafi does not regain the upper hand against the people of Libya?[59]

Defining "Hostilities"

As Dean Koh correctly notes, when Congress enacted the War Powers Resolution it did not define the central term "hostilities." University of Texas law professor Robert Chesney has provided an excellent definition: "whether U.S. forces have been authorized to use lethal force other than on a self-defense basis";[60] but it is difficult to imagine any serious definition that would not include sending U.S. aircraft over the territory of a foreign nation without that nation's consent in order to launch missiles at elements of that nation's armed forces.

Selected Bibliography

BOOKS

2 Cox, Henry Bartholomew, *War, Foreign Affairs, and Constitutional Power, 1829–1901* (1984).

Ely, John Hart, *War and Responsibility: Constitutional Lessons of Vietnam and Its Aftermath* (1993).

Fisher, Louis, *Presidential War Power* (1995).

Henkin, Louis, *Foreign Affairs and the Constitution* (1972).

Moore, John Norton, *Law and the Indo-China War* (1972).

———, *Law and Civil War in the Modern World* (1974).

Moore, John Norton, & Robert F. Turner, *The Legal Structure of Defense Organization* (1986).

Offutt, Milton, *The Protection of Citizens Abroad by the Armed Forces of the United States* (1928).

Reveley, W. Taylor, *War Powers of the President and Congress* (1981).

Rogers, James, *World Policing and the Constitution* (1945).

1 Sofaer, Abraham, *War, Foreign Affairs, and Constitutional Power: The Origins* (1976).

Turner, Robert F., *The War Powers Resolution: Its Implementation in Theory and Practice* (1983).

———, *Repealing the War Powers Resolution: Restoring the Rule of Law in U.S. Foreign Policy* (1991).

---

59. http://www.state.gov/s/l/releases/remarks/167250.htm.

60. Robert Chesney, *Will Congress Amend the WPR by Defining "Hostilities"?*, Lawfare Blog, June 16, 2011, http://www.lawfareblog.com/2011/06/will-congress-amend-the-wpr-by-defining-hostilities/.

U.S. Department of State, Office of the Solicitor, *Right to Protect Citizens in Foreign Countries by Landing Forces* (1912).

Whiting, William, *War Powers Under the Constitution of the United States* (43d ed. 1871).

Wright, Quincy, *The Control of American Foreign Relations* (1922).

———, *A Study of War* (2d ed. 1965).

ARTICLES

Carter, Stephen L., "The Constitutionality of the War Powers Resolution," 70 *Va. L. Rev.* 101 (1984).

Fisher, Louis, & David Gray Adler, "The War Powers Resolution: Time to Say Goodbye," 113 *Pol. Sci. Q.* 1 (1998).

Note, "Congress, the President, and the Power to Commit Forces to Combat," 81 *Harv. L. Rev.* 1771 (1968).

Reveley, W. Taylor, "Constitutional Allocation of the War Powers Between the President and Congress: 1787–1788," 15 *Va. J. Int'l L.* 73 (1974).

Rostow, Eugene, "Great Cases Make Bad Law: The War Powers Act," 50 *Tex. L. Rev.* 833 (1972).

Sofaer, Abraham, "The Presidency, War, and Foreign Affairs: Practice Under the Framers," 40 *Law & Contemp. Probs.* 17 (1976).

Turner, Robert F., "Truman, Korea, and the Constitution: Debunking the 'Imperial President' Myth," 19 *Harv. J.L. & Pub. Pol'y.* 533 (1996).

———, "War and the Forgotten Executive Power Clause of the Constitution," 34 *Va. J. Int'l L.* 904 (1994).

———, "Covert War and the Constitution," (debate with Jules Lobel), 5 *J. Nat'l Security L. & Pol'y* 409, 434 (2012).

U.S. Congress, The War Powers After 200 Years: Congress and the President at a Constitutional Impasse, Hearings Before the Special Subcommittee on War Powers of the Committee on Foreign Relations, United States Senate, 100th Cong., 2d Sess., 1988.

U.S. Congress, Senate Committee on Foreign Relations, Powers of the President to Send the Armed Forces Outside the United States, 82d Cong., 1st Sess., Feb. 28, 1951.

Van Alstyne, William, "Congress, the President, and the Power to Declare War: A Requiem for Vietnam," 121 *U. Pa. L. Rev.* 1 (1972).

Yoo, John C., "The Continuation of Politics by Other Means: The Original Understanding of War Powers," 84 *Cal. L. Rev.* 167 (1996).

Chapter 21

Treaties and Other International Agreements

Robert E. Dalton

Introduction

This chapter provides an overview of the law and practice applicable to treaties and other international agreements. It begins by discussing relevant definitions under both domestic and international law. It proceeds to examine the law governing the exercise of the treaty power by the United States. It also reviews the regulations applicable to treaties and other international agreements under U.S. law.

The second part of the chapter discusses the relevant international law and illustrates application of important international law rules by drawing on examples from both U.S. and general international practice. The chapter concludes with a case study of the interplay of international and domestic law in the context of the *Avena* case.

Taken as a whole, the chapter is designed to provide a framework within which a person encountering a treaty-related issue can better understand that issue and the possible interplay of the domestic and international aspects of treaty law and practice.

The Constitutional Framework

As the title of the Chapter suggests, in the United States a distinction is made between treaties in the sense of Article II, Section 2, clause 2 of the Constitution of the United

States and other international agreements. The cited provision states: "He [the President] shall have Power, by and with the Advice and Consent of the Senate, to make treaties, provided two-thirds of the Senators present concur." Other provisions of the law of the United States, including other provisions of the Constitution, serve as the legal authority for other international agreements.

While reference to the treaty clause of the Constitution set out above is the point of departure for most analyses of the treaty power of the United States, it should be noted that four of the seven articles of the Constitution pertain to treaties. Article I, Section 10, prohibits any state from entering into a "treaty, alliance, or confederation." Article II, Section l, vests executive power in the President. In addition to containing the treaty clause set out above, Article II, Section 2, provides that the President shall be Commander in Chief of the Army and Navy of the United States. Article II, Section 3, provides that he shall receive Ambassadors and other public Ministers and that he shall take care that the laws be faithfully executed. Each of those provisions of Article II has served as the basis of authority for the President to enter into international agreements other than treaties.

Article III vests the judicial power of the United States in the courts; section 2 provides "[t]he judicial power shall extend to all cases arising under … treaties made, or which shall be made" under the authority of the United States. While the text of Article III, section 2, might lead the unalerted reader to conclude that all treaty cases would be covered by that section, owing to procedural rules governing judicial jurisdiction, that conclusion would be erroneous.* Finally, Article VI, paragraph 2, contains the supremacy clause, which provides " … all treaties made, or which shall be made under the authority of the United States, shall be the supreme law of the land; and the judges in every state shall be bound thereby …"

"Treaty" or "International Agreement": Definitions and Distinctions

The distinction in United States law between treaties concluded by the President and the Senate and other international agreements is not embodied in the broader definition of treaties that is used for international purposes. For international purposes, the relevant language in the definitions—articles of the 1969 Vienna Convention on the Law of Treaties between States and the 1986 Vienna Convention on the Law of Treaties between States or between States and International Organizations or between International Organizations—could be conflated to read:

> treaty means an international agreement concluded between States, between States and international [intergovernmental] organizations or between international organizations in written form and governed by international law, whether embodied in a single instrument or in two or more related instruments and whatever its particular designation.

A number of provisions of United States law, for example those relating to reporting of international agreements and publication of the Treaties and Other International Acts

---

* *See also* "Justiciability" and "Standing" in chapter 19 (The Constitutional Framework for the Division of National Security Powers Among Congress, the President, and the Courts) of this volume.

Series, have made it necessary to develop criteria for deciding whether "any undertaking … document, set of documents, including an exchange of notes or of correspondence, constitutes an international agreement for domestic law purposes." Those criteria, which are set out in section 181.2 of Title 22 (Foreign Relations) of the Code of Federal Regulations, are consistent with the fundamental elements in the composite definition for international purposes set out in the preceding paragraph. This congruity is important. When international law is applied to a treaty or other international agreement of the United States, it will apply without regard to whether the international agreement was concluded pursuant to the treaty clause of the Constitution or on some other legal basis.[1] However, there is nothing in the definition set out above or in United States law that precludes the parties from incorporating a "conflicts of law" rule in a treaty or other international agreement.

The reason for including the "governed by international law" language in the broader definition may not be immediately clear. It is intended to distinguish between international agreements regulated by public international law and those regulated by domestic law and to include the intention of the parties to be legally bound. These two elements are specifically mentioned under the rubric "identity and intention of the parties" in section 181.2(a)(1) of the U.S. regulations:

> … The parties must intend their undertaking to be legally binding, and not merely of political or personal effect. Documents intended to have political or moral weight, but not intended to be legally binding, are not international agreements. An example of the latter is the Final Act of the Helsinki Conference on Security and Cooperation in Europe. In addition, the parties must intend their undertaking to be governed by international law … In the absence of any provision in the arrangement with respect to governing law, it will be presumed to be governed by international law.

The United Kingdom and a number of countries, such as Australia and New Zealand, which follow United Kingdom practice on the subject take the position that in addition to treaties in the international law sense, there is a class of documents called Memoranda of Understanding that lack the status of international agreements. The United Kingdom considers such instruments, which it generally refers to by the initials MOU, as non-legally binding. In addition to the title, the United Kingdom has developed terms for insertion in the text of such instruments that it considers signal the non-legally binding nature of the document.[2]

The United States does not as a matter of practice assign a subordinate role to Memoranda of Understanding. It routinely concludes international agreements that are entitled Memoranda of Understanding that it and the other party or parties consider to be legally binding. This is consistent with the general practice.[3]

---

1. For recent remarks on the subject of treaties and international agreements, see Harold Hongju Koh, *Remarks: Twenty-First-Century International Lawmaking*, 101 GEO. L.J. 725, 727–735 (2012–2013).

2. A comprehensive discussion of this subject may be found at A. AUST, THE MODERN LAW OF TREATIES, Cambridge University Press, 3rd ed. (2013), pp. 28–54. As to the signals, see ibid., Appendix G, Treaty and MOU Terminology Comparative Table, 429.

3. Shabtai Rosenne writes: "It is sometimes said that a *Memorandum of Understanding* (MOU) is not a binding agreement. As a generalization that should be avoided. The degree to which a MOU is binding is a matter for the intention of those who made it. It may be binding on the national administration of the day, leaving any future administration free to adopt whatever position it likes on it. On the other hand, it may be a treaty in the full sense of the word, at least as a matter of international law. A MOU made between two Government departments or agencies may be a binding

Several I.C.J. cases suggest that before senior officials sign documents such as communiqués, minutes, declarations, or joint statements, they should have their lawyers carefully review the documents in order to establish whether or not they might be considered as binding under international law. While the International Court of Justice in the *Aegean Sea Continental Shelf* case[4] did not see an international agreement in a joint press communiqué issued by two Prime Ministers, in the *Qatar-Bahrain* case[5] the Court found that a minute signed by the Foreign Ministers of those countries constituted a binding agreement even though the Foreign Minister of Bahrain had thought otherwise. The judgment of the I.C.J. in the Maritime Dispute case between Peru and Chile decided on January 27, 2014 finds consequences from the signature of a 1954 agreement that were likely not anticipated by its signers when they signed the agreement.

The Court was seeking to establish whether a boundary had existed between the parties. With respect to that issue, the Court found that the 1954 Special Maritime Frontier Zone Agreement between Chile, Ecuador, and Peru gave it a basis for deciding that there was a boundary. In paragraphs 90 and 91 of its opinion the Court found that the terms of the 1954 Agreement, "especially Article 1 read with the preambular paragraphs, are clear. They acknowledge in a binding international agreement that a maritime boundary already exists."[6] Continuing in paragraph 91, the Court commented: "The 1954 Special Maritime Frontier Zone Agreement does not indicate when and by what means that boundary was agreed upon. The Parties' express acknowledgment of its existence can only reflect a tacit agreement which they had reached earlier.... In this case, the Court has before it an Agreement which makes clear that the maritime boundary along a parallel line already existed between the Parties. The 1954 Agreement is decisive in this respect. That Agreement cements the tacit agreement."[7]

It should also be recognized that even a document that is not legally binding can have important political consequences. As former Secretary of State Henry Kissinger noted in testimony before the Senate Foreign Relations Committee on October 7, 1975,

> [S]tatements of our intentions ... served as a lubricant in this most recent negotiation [Egypt-Israel Sinai Agreement] ... But they must be seen in perspective and in light of historical practice ...
>
> ... [A]ssurances by the United States of our political intentions ... are often statements typical of diplomatic exchanges; in some instances they are merely reaffirmations of existing American policy. [T]o speak of memoranda of agreement as executive agreements is by no means to say that each of their individual provisions is binding on the United States. That depends entirely upon the content of the specific provisions in question ...
>
> ...
>
> The fact that many provisions are not by any standard international commitments does not mean, of course, that the United States is morally or politically free to act as if they did not exist. On the contrary, they are important statements of diplomatic policy and engage the good faith of the United States

---

treaty for the States parties to it." THE PERPLEXITIES OF MODERN INTERNATIONAL LAW, 291 Hague Academy of International Law Collected Courses 363 (2001).

4. Aegean Sea Continental Shelf (Greece v. Turkey) ICJ Rep. (1978), pp. 3, 44.

5. Qatar v. Bahrain (Jurisdiction and Admissibility) ICJ Rep. (1994), p. 112, *passim.*

6. www.icj-cij.org/Maritime Dispute (Peru v. Chile), Judgment, p. 36.

7. *Ibid.* p. 37.

so long as the circumstances that gave rise to them continue. But they are not binding commitments of the United States.[8]

Although the composite Vienna Convention definition of "treaties" is limited to agreements in writing, the law of the United States and customary international law permit oral agreements. The 1978 amendment to the Case-Zablocki Act on the reporting of international agreements to the Congress extended application of the Act to oral agreements and required all such international agreements be reduced to written form and transmitted in the same manner as written agreements. Senate Report 95-842 stated that by recommending enactment of the amendment the Foreign Relations Committee sought to eliminate "any possible incentive for entering into certain agreements orally rather than in writing" and to "require the transmission of intelligence sharing and intelligence liaison agreements, many of which are oral."

In connection with the SALT II negotiations there were several oral exchanges between President Carter and President Brezhnev relating to the Backfire Bomber. On June 16, 1979 President Brezhnev handed President Carter a written statement relating to the Backfire and stated orally that the Soviet Backfire production rate would not exceed 30 per year. President Carter then stated that the United States would enter into the SALT II agreement on the basis of commitments contained in the Soviet statement and that it would consider the carrying out of those commitments to be essential to the obligations assumed under the Treaty.

When SALT II was transmitted to the Senate it was accompanied by a document signed by Secretary of State Vance. The document included the text of President Brezhnev's written statement and reduced to writing the statements made by Presidents Brezhnev and Carter relating to the written statement.

A more recent example of an oral agreement is the telephone conversation between the Prime Ministers of Denmark and Finland during which they agreed to settle the case between the two countries concerning passage through the Great Belt that was pending in the International Court of Justice. The Danish side agreed to pay Finland 90 million Danish kroner, while the Finnish side agreed to withdraw its application in the case.[9]

Legal Basis for Treaties and Other International Agreements

Under the regulations applicable to the conclusion of treaties and other international agreements by the United States, the legal basis for any agreement must be identified prior to the opening of negotiations. The legal basis for advice and consent treaties is Article II, Section 2, clause 2 of the Constitution. The President may conclude international agreements other than treaties on any subject within his constitutional authority so long as the agreement is not inconsistent with legislation enacted by the Congress in the exercise of its constitutional authority. The constitutional sources of that authority are included in four provisions of Article II: the executive power clause (Section 1); the commander-

---

8. LXXIII Department of State Bulletin 613 (1975).
9. See paragraphs 9 and 10 of Introductory note to Order of the International Court of Justice on the discontinuance of the case by Finland and its removal from the list. XXXII INTERNATIONAL LEGAL MATERIALS 101–105 (1993).

in-chief clause (Section 2); the receive ambassadors and other public ministers clause (Section 3); and the take care that the laws be faithfully executed clause (Section 3). Courts have sustained the power of the President to conclude international agreements under each of these four provisions. Where the Constitution grants powers exclusively to the President, as in respect of the commander-in-chief power, an agreement made pursuant to that authority alone is called a sole executive agreement. An armistice agreement is the classic example of a sole executive agreement.

Where the Constitution grants power exclusively to the Congress, the Congress may authorize the President or other officials to conclude congressional-executive agreements on subjects falling within its powers. The oldest example is postal agreements, with respect to which Congress made the initial authorization in 1792. The authorizations may include special procedures for certain kinds of agreements, such as those in the Atomic Energy Act of 1954,[10] and the Bipartisan Trade Promotion Authority Act of 2002 (TPA).[11] In respect of matters not within his exclusive authority and where no existing delegations exist, the President may negotiate an international agreement subject to subsequent Congressional approval.[12] Finally, the President may conclude an international agreement pursuant to a treaty brought into force with the advice and consent of the Senate where the provisions of the treaty constitute authorization for the agreement without subsequent action by the Congress.

Authorization, Approval and Reporting Procedures: Department Circular No. 175 and the Case-Zablocki Act

For more than half a century, a State Department regulation known as Circular 175 has contained procedures on the negotiation and signature of treaties and other international agreements. The Circular 175 Procedure may be found at 11 Foreign Affairs Manual 700. In addition to ensuring that the making of treaties and other international agreements for the United States is carried out within constitutional and other appropriate limits, it requires that the objectives to be sought in a particular negotiation are approved by the Secretary or an officer authorized by him or her for that purpose and that timely and appropriate consultation is held with congressional leaders and committees. The circular also provides for public comment on treaties and other international agreements where in the opinion of the Secretary or the designee circumstances permit; that firm positions departing from authorized positions are not undertaken without approval; that authorization is obtained to sign final texts developed in the negotiating process; and that there is compliance with the Case-Zablocki Act on the transmission of the texts of international agreements other than treaties to the Congress within 60 days of their entry into force.

Drawing on his experience as both an academic and as Legal Adviser of the Department of State, Harold Koh observed:

---

10. 42 U.S.C. § 2011 et seq.
11. 19 U.S.C. § 3801(b) (2002).
12. A corollary to that rule was established in *Dames & Moore v. Regan*, 453 U.S. 654, 678, 680–82 (1981), a case in which the Supreme Court sustained a claims agreement that the Congress had not approved on the basis of Congressional acquiescence in a long-standing practice of the President in concluding such international agreements where it had known of the practice and had failed to object.

[M]ost people are unaware of the so-called "C-175" process, named after a 1955 State Department Circular setting out a standardized procedure for concluding international agreements. The few academics who have ever noticed that process often assume it is nothing more than a rubber stamp. But having now seen it from the inside, I can tell you that the process is exhaustive and designed to ensure that all proposed U.S. international agreements—even if concluded by a different agency—are subject to a rigorous legal and policy review by the State Department before being negotiated and concluded. Through this process, the State Department plays the same kind of clearinghouse role with respect to international agreements that the Office of Management and Budget (OMB) plays with regard to federal regulations. The C-175 process ensures not only that we have the legal authority to conclude the agreement in question, but also that every agency's lawyers fully understand the nature of the domestic and international legal obligations we will undertake, so that we can accurately evaluate whether the United States will be able to comply with its new international legal obligations.[13]

Congressional review of compliance with the original Case-Zablocki Act disclosed that the State Department did not have the necessary tools to carry out the statutory mandate. In 1977 and 1978, the Congress amended the Act to consolidate the Department's role as the central coordinator within the executive branch for negotiations with other countries and international organizations. The 1978 amendments included a requirement that no agreement be signed or concluded by any agency in the executive branch without prior consultation with the Secretary of State. The purpose of that requirement was to ensure that the Secretary of State was aware of agreements or classes of agreements being made by other agencies and to strengthen the Secretary's ability to coordinate negotiations between the United States and other countries. The final element addressed in the 1978 amendments required the President, through the Secretary of State, to promulgate such rules and regulations as may be necessary to carry out the provisions of the Act. Those rules and regulations, which were issued on July 13, 1981, may be found at 22 CFR Part 181.

Title 22, section 181.7(c) of the Code of Federal Regulations requires the preparation of a background statement to accompany every international agreement reported to the Congress under the Act. Each background statement includes information explaining the agreement, the negotiations, the effect of the agreement, and a precise citation of the legal authority on which it is based.

Two additional sections of Part 181 merit mention since they changed earlier practice concerning publication of treaties. The first, Section 181.8, which became effective in 2006, is entitled publication. Subsection (a) lists thirteen categories of international agreements, most of which are routine agreements dealing with matters in which there is limited public interest, that will not be published in Treaties and Other International Acts Series (TIAS). However, subsection (c) provides that, subject to a specified exception for one category of agreements, agreements falling under subsection (a) in the possession of the Department of State will be made available by the Department upon request. The second, Section 181.9, deals with Internet website publication.

Section 181.9 assigns responsibility to the Office of the Assistant Legal Adviser for Treaty Affairs, with the cooperation of other bureaus in the Department, for making publicly available on the Internet website of the Department of State each treaty or international agreement proposed to be published in the compilation entitled "United States

---

13. See H. Koh, *op. cit. supra* fn. 1, pp. 734–735 [internal footnotes omitted].

Treaties and Other International Agreements" not later than 180 days after the date on which the treaty or agreement enters into force. The bibliography at the end of this chapter will include a listing of Department of State and other Internet websites on which texts of these treaties and other international agreements may be found.

Choice between Treaty or Other International Agreement

There is no simple rule for deciding whether a particular international agreement should be concluded as an advice and consent treaty under Article II, Section 2, Clause 2 of the Constitution or as another international agreement. The Department's regulations specify that due consideration shall be given to 8 factors:

> (1) the extent to which the agreement involves commitments or risks affecting the nation as a whole; (2) whether the agreement is intended to affect State laws; (3) whether the agreement can be given effect without the enactment of subsequent legislation by the Congress; (4) past U.S. practice as to similar agreements; (5) the preference of the Congress as to a particular type of agreement; (6) the degree of formality desired for an agreement; (7) the proposed duration of the agreement, the need for prompt conclusion of an agreement, and the desirability of concluding a routine or short-term agreement; and (8) the general international practice as to similar agreements.

A review of practice shows that international agreements dealing with defense, extradition, tax, disarmament, and private international law tend to be concluded as treaties. Despite efforts by the Senate in the early 1970s to have the President submit base agreements as advice and consent treaties, base agreements are concluded as executive agreements under the President's commander-in-chief power. On the other hand, the Senate has consistently made clear that it expects the President to conclude arms control agreements as advice and consent treaties. With the exception of the SALT I Interim Agreement of May 26, 1972, which, owing to special circumstances, the United States and the Union of Soviet Socialist Republics had agreed would be approved by their legislative bodies—an exception that was acceptable to the Senate, which simultaneously gave advice and consent to a companion treaty—the author is not aware of any arms control agreement that was not concluded as an advice and consent treaty.[14]

The Congress may establish special procedures for the conclusion of international agreements relating to subjects for which the Congress has independent powers under the Constitution provided those procedures do not infringe on the President's independent Constitutional powers. Examples include the procedures specified in the Atomic Energy Act of 1954,[15] the Fishery Conservation and Management Act of 1976,[16] and the Bipartisan Trade Promotion Authority Act of 2002.[17]

In several cases plaintiffs challenged the conclusion of an international agreement on a basis other than the treaty clause. They include *Dole v. Carter*,[18] *Greater Tampa Chamber*

---

14. For a more comprehensive discussion of this topic, see TREATIES AND OTHER INTERNATIONAL AGREEMENTS: THE ROLE OF THE UNITED STATES SENATE, S. PRT. 106-71, pp. 251–265 (2001).
15. 42 U.S.C. §§ 2011, 2153.
16. 16 U.S.C. §§ 1801–1891(d) (2007).
17. 19 U.S.C. § 3801.
18. 444 F. Supp. 1065 (U.S. District Co., Kansas 1977), 569 F.2d 1109 (10th Cir. 1977).

of Commerce v. Brock Adams,[19] *Greater Tampa Chamber of Commerce v. Goldschmidt,*[20] and *Made in the USA Foundation, United Steel Workers of America v. U.S.*[21] In *Dole* and *Greater Tampa*, the district courts denied the issuance of an injunction on the grounds, respectively, that the plaintiff was unlikely to prevail on the merits and that the issue of whether the President should have submitted the "other international agreement" to the Senate for advice and consent was non-justiciable. The Court of Appeals in *Dole* found the matter non-justiciable; the Court of Appeals in *Goldschmidt* found the plaintiffs lacked standing. For a recent case concerning the amendment of an annex to MARPOL, a convention of the International Maritime Organization, see *State of Alaska v. John F. Kerry.*[22] The Court granted the Federal Government's motion to dismiss and denied the State of Alaska's motion for preliminary injunction as moot on the basis of the Court's finding that the Executive Branch had been authorized to amend the agreement without further action by the Senate. No appeal was taken within the applicable time limit.

The *Made in the USA Foundation v. United States* case challenged the constitutionality of the North American Free Trade Agreement, which was concluded pursuant to "fast track" authority, on the ground that it was not concluded as an advice and consent treaty. The district court rejected the Government's standing and jurisdictional arguments and decided the case on the merits, finding that the NAFTA Implementation Act,[23] passed by Congress as fast track legislation, was a constitutional exercise of the power of the Congress under the Commerce Clause, and NAFTA did not have to be approved under the treaty clause. On this basis, the Court granted summary judgment for the Government.

The Court of Appeals dismissed the appeal and remanded the case with instructions to dismiss the action and vacate the district court decision. While agreeing that the plaintiffs had standing, the Court of Appeals declined to reach the merits, finding that "with respect to international commercial agreements such as NAFTA, the question of just what constitutes a 'treaty' requiring Senate ratification presents a non-justiciable political question."[24]

The Senate and Treaties

Conditioning Senate Advice and Consent to Treaties

Although the words of the treaty clause of the Constitution do not address qualified or conditional advice and consent to a treaty by the Senate, the question as to whether or not this was possible arose in connection with ratification of the Treaty of Amity, Commerce and Navigation between the United States and Great Britain of November 19, 1794 (the Jay Treaty). In its resolution of advice and consent of June 24, 1795, the Senate amended the Treaty by adding an additional article providing that operation of the twelfth article of the treaty relating to trade between the United States and British islands in the West Indies would be suspended. The British accepted the amendment, which was included in the U.S. instrument of ratification, and the treaty entered into force as amended.

---

19. D.D.C. 1979 (unreported), rev'd sub nom. Greater Tampa Chamber of Commerce v. Gold-schmidt, 627 F.2d 258 (D.C. Cir. 1980).
20. 627 F.2d 258 (D.C. Cir. 1980).
21. 56 F. Supp. 2d 1226, (U.S. Dist N.D. Alabama 1999); 242 F.3d 1300 (11th Cir. 2001).
22. 971 F. Supp. 2d 1111 (D. Alaska, 2013).
23. 19 U.S.C. §§ 3301–3473.
24. 242 F.3d 1300, (11th Cir. 2001).

In addition to amendments, the Senate has developed a practice of including other kinds of conditions in resolutions of advice and consent. Most conditions fall into four general categories: reservations, understandings, declarations, and provisos. According to the definition articles of the Vienna Convention on the Law of Treaties, a reservation is "a unilateral statement, however phrased or named, made by a State when ... signing [or] ratifying ... a treaty, whereby it purports to exclude or to modify the legal effect of certain provisions of the treaty in their application to that State."[25] An understanding differs from a reservation in that it is a statement or other declaration relevant to the application or interpretation of the treaty that is not intended to exclude or modify the provisions of a treaty.[26]

In recent years the Senate has been concerned about the possibility that a United States citizen extradited to another country under an extradition treaty might be handed over to the International Criminal Court, a tribunal set up under a treaty to which the United States is not a party, for trial. It has also been concerned that evidence furnished to another country under a mutual legal assistance treaty might be used in the prosecution of a United States citizen before the Court. In response to those concerns, the Senate included understandings designed to prevent such action in its resolutions of advice and consent to a considerable number of extradition and mutual legal assistance treaties.

The following understanding appeared in the Senate's 1998 resolution of advice and consent to ratification of the Extradition Treaty with the Grand Duchy of Luxembourg:

"UNDERSTANDING. — The Senate's advice and consent to ratification is subject to the following understanding, which shall be included in the instrument of ratification:

PROHIBITION ON EXTRADITION TO THE INTERNATIONAL CRIMINAL COURT. — The United States understands that the protections contained in Article 17 concerning the Rule of Speciality would preclude the resurrender of any person from the United States to the International Criminal Court agreed to in Rome, Italy, on July 17, 1998, unless the United States consents to such resurrender; and the United States shall not consent to the transfer of any person extradited to Luxembourg by the United States to the ... Court ... unless the treaty establishing that Court has entered into force for the United States by and with the advice and consent of the Senate, as required by Article II, section 2 of the United States Constitution."

A similar prohibition was contained in the Senate's 2002 resolution of advice and consent to ratification of the Treaty with Liechtenstein on Mutual Legal Assistance in Criminal Matters. The principal difference in the Mutual Legal Assistance understanding was that the President was authorized to waive the prohibition on provision of assistance set forth in the understanding if such waiver was in accordance with applicable United States law.

While declarations are usually statements of the Senate's position, opinion or intentions on matters relating to issues raised by a particular treaty, some treaties include an article that (a) in one paragraph establishes a mechanism for the settlement of disputes relating to the application or interpretation of the treaty, e.g., reference to a tribunal, and (b) in a second paragraph permits a state to declare that it will not accept the dispute settlement mechanism. Such a declaration is not a reservation, since it does not modify the legal

---

25. 1155 U.N.T.S. 331, 333.
26. JOHN A. BOYD, DIGEST OF U.S. PRACTICE IN INTERNATIONAL LAW 1977, 375, 376 (1979).

effect of the article as a whole. In such cases, the Senate's declaration is essentially the exercise of a right provided for in the treaty. A proviso is a condition that is intended to operate solely in the domestic sphere.

The black letter law of the United States in respect of reservations made by the Senate to treaties is that if the Senate includes a reservation, the President in ratifying the treaty must include the reservation. However, it is established that "the legal effect of any matter added by the Senate depends upon its substance, not its denomination."[27] A leading case that examined this issue is *Power Authority of the State of New York v. Federal Power Commission.*[28]

On February 27, 1950, the United States and Canada concluded a Convention on Uses of the Waters of the Niagara River.[29] The Senate, uncertain as to how the U.S. share of the waters would be utilized, included in its resolution of advice and consent the following 'reservation':

> The United States on its part expressly reserves the right to provide by Act of Congress for redevelopment, for the public use and benefit, of the United States share of the waters of the Niagara River made available by the provisions of the treaty, and no project for redevelopment of the United States share of such waters shall be undertaken until it be specifically authorized by Act of Congress.

The 'reservation' was accepted by Canada and included in the President's proclamation of the treaty on October 30, 1950.[30]

In light of the failure of Congress to take the action envisaged by the 'reservation', the Power Authority of the State of New York filed an application under the Federal Power Act for a license from the Federal Power Commission to proceed with redevelopment in that state. The Federal Power Commission dismissed the application in an opinion and order declaring:

> In the absence of the treaty reservation we would act on the Power Authority's application in accordance with the provisions of the Federal Power Act. But if we are to accept the injunction of the reservation as it stands, we would have no authority to consider the application of the Power Authority on its merits ...

> Since the reservation here was intended by the Senate as part of the treaty and was intended to prevent our jurisdiction attaching to the water made available by the treaty, it is entirely authoritative with us as the Supreme Law of the Land under Article VI of the Constitution.

The New York Power Authority then sued, claiming the reservation invalid.

In its analysis of the 'reservation' the D.C. Circuit Court of Appeals noted that the reservation made no change in the treaty. "It was merely an expression of domestic policy which the Senate attached to its consent ... A true reservation which becomes a part of the treaty is one which alters 'the effect of the treaty insofar as it may apply in the relations of (the) State with the other State or States which may be parties to the treaty.'"[31]

The Court decided to "construe the reservation as an expression of the Senate's desires and not a part of the treaty." It specifically refrained from deciding the constitutional

---

27. Michael J. Glennon, Constitutional Diplomacy, Princeton University Press, 1990, 128.
28. 247 F.2d 538 (1957).
29. 1 U.S.T. 694.
30. 1 U.S.T. 694, 700.
31. Power Authority v. Federal Power Comm'n, 247 F.2d 538 (D.C. Cir. 1957).

question identified in the opinion, limiting itself to setting aside the order under review and remanding the case to the Federal Power Commission.[32] However, the Supreme Court vacated the D.C. Circuit's decision as moot after the Congress adopted the legislation called for by the Senate.[33]

There were few domestic conditions, other than ministerial provisos on such matters as not depositing the instrument of ratification until enactment of the necessary implementing legislation, in resolutions of advice and consent to treaties between 1950 and 1988, when the Senate included in its resolution of advice and consent to the Treaty between the United States and the U.S.S.R. on the Elimination of Their Intermediate-Range and Shorter-Range Missiles of December 8, 1987 (the INF Treaty) a condition known as the "Biden Condition" that addressed the interpretation of the INF Treaty by the United States:

> "That the Senate's advice and consent to ratification of the INF Treaty is subject to the condition, based on the Treaty Clauses of the Constitution, that —
>
> (1) the United States shall interpret the Treaty in accordance with the common understanding of the Treaty shared by the President and the Senate at the time the Senate gave its advice and consent to ratification;
>
> (2) such common understanding is based on:
>
>> (1) First, the text of the Treaty and the provisions of this resolution of ratification; and
>>
>> 2) Second, the authoritative representations which were provided by the President and his representatives to the Senate and its Committees, in seeking Senate consent to ratification, insofar as such representations were directed to the meaning and legal effect of the text of the Treaty; and
>
> (3) the United States shall not agree to or adopt an interpretation different from that common understanding except pursuant to Senate advice and consent to a subsequent treaty or protocol, or the enactment of a statute; and
>
> (4) if, subsequent to ratification of the Treaty, a question arises as to the interpretation of a provision of the Treaty on which no common understanding was reached in accordance with paragraph (2), that provision shall be interpreted in accordance with applicable United States law."

Although he proceeded to exchange instruments of ratification bringing the treaty into force, President Reagan issued a statement with respect to the treaty interpretation condition that stated, *inter alia*:

> The Senate condition relating to the Treaty Clause of the Constitution apparently seeks to alter the law of treaty interpretation. The accompanying report of the Committee on Foreign Relations accords primacy, second only to the treaty text, to all executive branch statements to the Senate above all other sources which international forums or even U.S. courts would consider in interpreting treaties. It subordinates fundamental and essential treaty interpretation sources such as the treaty parties' intent, the negotiating record, and the parties' subsequent practices.
>
> Treaties are agreements between sovereign states and must be interpreted in accordance with accepted principles of international law and U.S. Supreme Court

---

32. 247 F.2d 541–42 (D.C. Cir. 1957).
33. Am. Public Power Ass'n v. Power Authority, 355 U.S. 64 (1957).

jurisprudence ... Unilateral restrictions on the United States should be avoided, especially in a treaty affecting vital national security interests ...

... the principles of treaty interpretation recognized and repeatedly invoked by the courts may not be limited or changed by the Senate alone, and those principles will govern any future disputes over interpretation of this treaty.... I am compelled to state that I cannot accept the proposition that a condition in a resolution to ratification can alter the allocation of rights and duties under the Constitution ... [34]

The Biden condition, which was originally treaty specific, was incorporated in Senate resolutions of advice and consent to ratification of treaties adopted between 1988 and 1991, when the Senate gave advice and consent to the Treaty on Conventional Armed Forces in Europe (CFE). Declaration 2 of the resolution of advice and consent to the CFE extended the treaty interpretation language to all treaties.

The Treaty between the United States of America and the Russian Federation on Strategic Offensive Reductions was signed at Moscow on May 24, 2002 and transmitted to the Senate for its advice and consent on June 20, 2002.[35] The Senate held four hearings on the Treaty, which is generally referred to as "The Moscow Treaty", during the summer. On February 20, 2003, the Senate Foreign Relations Committee reported favorably on the Treaty subject to two conditions and six declarations set forth in the accompanying draft resolution of ratification.[36] Extended debate took place on the floor of the Senate on March 5 and March 6, 2003.[37] At the conclusion of the debate, the Senate adopted the resolution of ratification. The vote was 95 yeas and 0 nays.

The resolution of advice and consent to the Treaty on Strategic Offensive Reductions of May 24, 2000 describes the declarations that follow, including the declaration on treaty interpretation, as expressing "the intent of the Senate." Declaration 8 of the Senate's resolution of advice and consent to the New START Treaty in 2010 seems to be the most recent instance of the inclusion of such declarations in resolutions on arms control treaties.

There is abundant contemporary literature on the Biden Condition to the INF treaty, but limited serious attention has been given to the subject or its ramifications since 1988. The exception is John Norton Moore's Treaty Interpretation, The Constitution and the Rule of Law.[38] While he provides analysis of such intervening scholarship as Stefan A. Riesenfeld & Frederick M. Abbott, "The Scope of U.S. Senate Control Over the Conclusion and Operation of Treaties",[39] and notes that the "current blanket treaty interpretation seeks to establish that its rules of interpretation apply to all *treaties*",[40] especially important sections of the book include chapters III and IV, that deal, respectively, with the issues of the "dual" versus "unitary" standards of treaty interpretation in the foreign relations law of the United States, and whether the Senate's advice and consent power includes a general domestic lawmaking power.[41] On those two issues, his views are especially compelling.

In recent years, resolutions of advice and consent have become more diffuse and deal with matters not directly related to the treaty. For example, condition 9 of the 1997

---

34. 24 WEEKLY COMPILATION OF PRES. DOCS., No. 23, June 13, 1988, pp. 779, 780.

35. Senate Treaty Doc. 107-8, 107th Congress, 2d Session.

36. Senate Exec. Rpt. 108-1, 108th Congress, 1st Session.

37. Congressional Record-Senate, March 5, 2003, S3128–3154; Congressional Record-Senate, March 6, 2003, S 3221–3244.

38. Dobbs Ferry, N.Y.: Oceana Publications (2001).

39. 67 CHI.-KENT L. REV. 571.

40. *Id.*, p. 6 fn11.

41. *Id.*, p. 30.

resolution of advice and consent to the CFE Flank Document is entitled "Senate Prerogatives on Multilateralization of the ABM Treaty."

In the first part of the condition, the Senate found that the "accord on ABM Treaty succession, tentatively agreed to by the administration, would constitute a substantive change to the ABM Treaty, which may only be entered into pursuant to the treaty making power of the President under the Constitution". The second part of the condition required the President, prior to the deposit of the United States instrument of ratification of the Flank Document to certify to the Senate that he would submit for Senate advice and consent to ratification any international agreement –

(i) that would add one or more countries as States Parties to the ABM Treaty, or otherwise convert the ABM Treaty from a bilateral treaty to a multilateral treaty; or

(ii) that would change the geographic scope or coverage of the ABM Treaty, or otherwise modify the meaning of the term 'national territory' as used in Article VI and Article IX of the ABM Treaty.

President Clinton complied with the certification requirement but did not proceed with submittal of a succession agreement for the ABM Treaty.[42] President Bush's notice of withdrawal from the ABM treaty on December 13, 2001 mooted the matter.

Another issue addressed in Senate resolutions of advice and consent was the inclusion of no reservation clauses in the texts of treaties. For example, two of the twenty-eight conditions contained in the Senate's 1997 resolution of advice and consent to ratification of the Chemical Weapons Convention dealt with the inclusion of no reservations clauses in treaties. Condition 1 reflected the Senate's long-standing concern about this subject. That concern had been expressed when the Senate took up environmental treaties containing such clauses. For example, in presenting the Basel Convention on the Control of Trans-boundary Movements of Hazardous Wastes and Their Disposal to the Senate in 1992, the chairman of the Foreign Relations Committee stated his concern about including in treaties a provision which had the effect of inhibiting the Senate from attaching reservations it deemed necessary. In a number of similar cases, the Senate had stated that giving advice and consent to a treaty containing such a provision should not be considered a precedent for doing so in future agreements. Here, however, the Senate required "[t]he President, upon the deposit of the United States instrument of ratification, [to] certify to the Congress that the United States has informed all other States Parties to the Convention that the Senate reserves the right, pursuant to the Constitution of the United States, to give its advice and consent to ratification of the Convention subject to reservations, notwithstanding Article XXII of the Convention." The President so certified.

Condition 17 to the Chemical Weapons Convention returns to the issue raised in Condition 1 to the Senate resolution of advice and consent to that document. Under the rubric of "Constitutional Prerogatives" the Senate found that "[t]he executive branch of Government has begun a practice of negotiating and submitting to the Senate treaties

---

42. For a general discussion of practice relating to conditions in Senate resolutions of advice and consent during the 1990s *see* Philip R. Trimble and Alexander W. Koff, *All Fall Down: The Treaty Power in the Clinton Administration*, 16 Berkeley J. Int'l L. 55, 57(1998). Trimble and Koff are particularly troubled by the requirement that the President submit for advice and consent any agreement that would change the geographic scope or coverage of the ABM Treaty. "Normally such matters involving the succession of states would be settled by executive agreement and the President's constitutional foreign affairs authority. Historically, this had been an uncontroversial executive function, but Condition 9 requires the President to treat it as an Article II treaty and submit it to the Senate."

which include provisions that have the purported effect of inhibiting the Senate from attaching reservations to treaties that it considers necessary or preventing it from exercising its constitutional duty to give its advice and consent." It also included Sense of the Senate language that "United States negotiators to a treaty should not agree to any provision that has the effect of inhibiting the Senate from attaching reservations or offering amendments to the treaty." The Senate does not appear to have addressed the subject of no reservation clauses in twenty-first century resolutions of advice and consent to ratification.

Treaty Termination under U.S. Law

As a result of developments in U.S. treaty practice, the debate in the Senate on conditions proposed for the resolution of advice and consent to ratification of the Moscow Treaty, and the intervening cases of *Beacon Products Co. v. Reagan*,[43] and *Kucinich v. Bush*,[44] it is possible to speak more definitively on who has power under United States law to terminate advice and consent treaties than when the only source of authority was *Goldwater v. Carter*,[45] in which a divided Supreme Court vacated the judgment of the Court of Appeals and remanded the case with instructions to dismiss the complaint.

Although U.S. practice on termination of treaties prior to *Goldwater* had been mixed, since the decision in that case the consistent practice of the United States has been for the President to terminate treaties that have received Senate advice and consent on his own authority. The precedents are collected in a document prepared by the State Department that lists all advice and consent treaties terminated by the President since 1980. Executive Branch officials and members of the Senate referred to an earlier version of the document during the Senate's consideration of its resolution of advice and consent to ratification of the Moscow Treaty in March 2003.[46]

During hearings before the Senate Foreign Relations Committee on the Moscow Treaty, Senator Feingold explained that he thought that the Senate had a constitutional role to play in terminating treaties. He asked Secretary Powell whether it was the Administration's position that there would be no need for Senate approval of withdrawal from the Treaty. Secretary Powell replied in the affirmative. The Committee addressed the issue raised by Senator Feingold by including in its draft resolution of advice and consent a declaration urging the President to consult with the Senate prior to withdrawal. The resolution, including the aforementioned declaration, was approved by the Committee by a vote of 19 in favor to 0 against.

When the Treaty was taken up on the floor of the Senate, Senator Levin introduced an amendment to the resolution of advice and consent that would have added a condition requiring the President to give the Senate no less than 60 days advance notice of his intent to withdraw and to consult with the Senate on such action and would have deleted the declaration urging the President to consult that had been recommended by the Committee. Following an extensive debate, the amendment was defeated by a vote of 44 yeas, 50 nays, and 6 not voting. The result was consistent with the result in the only other instance in

---

43. 633 F. Supp. 1191, 1198–99 D. Mass. (1986).

44. 236 F. Supp. 2d 1 (2002).

45. 444 U.S. 996, 100 S. Ct. 533, 62 L. Ed. 2d 428 (1979).

46. *Article II, Section 2 Treaties Terminated by the President Since 1980*, Digest of U.S. Practice in International Law 2002.

which the Senate attempted to restrict the role of the President in treaty termination — condition number one in the resolution of advice and consent to the Treaty of Versailles in 1919.[47]

The third development was the decision of the United States District Court for the District of Columbia in the case of *Dennis Kucinich v. Bush*. Plaintiffs in this case, 32 members of the House of Representatives, filed an action against the President, the Secretary of State, and the Secretary of Defense challenging the President's unilateral decision to withdraw from the Anti-Ballistic Missile Treaty between the United States and the Union of Soviet Socialist Republics. Their argument was that because the Supremacy Clause of the Constitution makes treaties, like Acts of Congress, the "supreme law of the land", the President cannot terminate a treaty without Congressional consent. Lawyers for the President and his co-defendants argued that the Congressmen lacked standing, that the case raised a political question, and that termination of a treaty by the President on his own authority was consistent with the structure of the Constitution and recent historical practice.

Judge Bates dismissed the plaintiffs' complaint on two grounds. First, he concluded that because the plaintiffs had alleged only an institutional injury to Congress, not injuries that were "personal and particularized to themselves," they lacked standing to bring the case. Second, relying on the rationale of the plurality opinion in *Goldwater v. Carter* and the subsequent case of *Beacon Products Corp. v. Reagan*, which held that a constitutional challenge to President Reagan's unilateral termination of the Treaty of Friendship, Commerce, and Navigation with Nicaragua, without Congressional consent raised a political question, he concluded that the issue raised by the plaintiffs in *Kucinich* was a non-justiciable political question.

A string of earlier non-justiciable political question decisions in treaty cases, such as *Dole v. Carter*, *Greater Tampa Chamber of Commerce v. Goldschmidt*, and *Holmes v. Laird*, 459 F2d 1211, 1215 (D.C. Cir. 1972), provides a useful armory for Executive Branch briefs in future litigation.

Preemption

Even after more than two hundred years, not all questions relating to federalism and foreign relations have been resolved. However the cases discussed below, dealing respectively with treaty preemption and statutory preemption, are clarifying or have clarified the answers to some of those questions.

Treaty preemption is squarely addressed in a series of modern cases in the federal courts. In the first of these, *In re World War II Era Japanese Forced Labor Litigation*,[48] Judge Walker held that the Treaty of Peace with Japan, to which the Philippines was a party, barred Filipino plaintiffs from suing Japanese companies for damages arising out of actions taken by Japan and its nationals in the course of World War II. This was so because Article 14(b) of the Treaty waived all such claims. A California statute that purported to authorize such claims was inconsistent with Article 14(b) and thus failed to provide a basis for such a suit. In a second case involving nationals of Korea and China, countries that were not parties to the Peace Treaty, Judge Walker concluded that allowing those nationals to sue Japanese companies for reparations for forced labor during World War II would interfere with the foreign relations of the United States.

---

47. 58 Congressional Record (Part 9), 66th Cong., 1st Sess., Senate 8777 (1919).
48. 114 F. Supp. 2d 939 (N. D. Cal. 2000).

On March 3, 2003, in *Deutsch v. Turner Corp*,[49] the U.S. Court of Appeals for the Ninth Circuit held in a consolidated appeal from Judge Walker's decisions and other cases that the California statute establishing a cause of action for persons seeking to recover claims from certain corporations for actions that occurred during the course of the prosecution of World War II was unconstitutional.

The Court described the California statute, which sought to give "slave labor" and "forced labor" victims the right to redress wrongs committed in the course of World War II:

> The wrong-doers under the statute — the enslaving individuals or entities — include the Nazi regime, its allies and sympathizers, or enterprises transacting business in any of the areas occupied by or under control of the Nazi regime or its allies or sympathizers ... The governmental entities are, by definition, wartime enemies of the United States, while the "enterprises" identified in the provision, if not themselves our wartime enemies, were operating in enemy territory and presumably ... with the consent and for the benefit of our wartime enemy. Wrongs committed after the end of the war are not [covered].

Addressing the settlements after the war, the court noted that the United States exercised "its own exclusive authority to resolve the war, including claims arising out of it." After explaining how it did so with respect to Germany, the Court observed:

> [T]he Constitution allocates the power over foreign affairs to the federal government exclusively, and the power to make and resolve war, including the authority to resolve war claims, is central to the foreign affairs power in the constitutional design. In the absence of some specific action that constitutes authorization on the part of the federal government, states are prohibited from exercising foreign affairs powers, including modifying the federal government's resolution of war-related disputes.

Turning to Japan, the Court stated:

> The war with Japan ended with the Treaty of Peace, signed in San Francisco, on September 8, 1951, by the representatives of the United States and 47 other Allied powers and Japan, and ratified by the United States Senate on April 28, 1952. Treaty of Peace with Japan, Sept. 8, 1951, 3 U.S.T. 3169, T.I.A.S. No. 2490 ... Although the parties dispute whether that treaty by its own terms precludes the claims brought by any of the Appellants, that is the only dispute regarding the treaty. No party asserts that the treaty either creates — explicitly or implicitly — a private right of action against Japan or its nationals, or authorizes states of the United States to create such a right. Once again, without such authorization, states lack the power to alter the federal government's resolution of disputes relating to the war.
>
> ... The federal government, acting under its foreign affairs authority provided its own resolution to the war; California has no power to modify that resolution.

Based on the foregoing reasons the Court affirmed the district courts' dismissal of the cases before it and held the California statute "an unconstitutional intrusion on the foreign affairs power of the United States."

In *Crosby v. National Foreign Trade Council*,[50] the issue was whether the 1996 law of the Commonwealth of Massachusetts relating to the authority of its agencies to purchase goods or services from companies doing business in Burma was invalid under the Supremacy

---

49. 317 F.3d 1005 (2003).
50. 530 U.S. 363 (2000).

Clause of the Constitution. Three months later, the Congress passed a statute imposing a set of mandatory and conditional sanctions on Burma. The Council, some of whose members were affected by the Massachusetts law, sought relief against the state officials enforcing the Massachusetts law on the ground that the law unconstitutionally infringed on the federal foreign affairs power. The District Court enjoined enforcement of the state Act, holding it "unconstitutionally impinge[d] on the federal government's exclusive authority to regulate foreign affairs." The United States Court of Appeals for the First Circuit affirmed, finding that the state Act unconstitutionally interfered with the foreign affairs power of the National Government under *Zschernig v. Miller*.[51] The Supreme Court affirmed without dissent.

The Treaty Power and Federalism

Throughout our history, there has been tension between federal power and the power of the states. As we have seen, the Constitution forbids the states from concluding treaties. The most recent case dealing with aspects of federalism in the foreign relations context arose in connection with the implementing legislation for the Chemical Weapons Convention and were decided by the Supreme Court in 2011 and 2014. One result was a ruling concerning the applicability of the Tenth Amendment to the Constitution to the Chemical Weapons Convention Implementation Act. The other questioned the intention of Congress in passing implementing legislation for the Chemical Weapons Convention. But at bottom, the cases represented an attempt to overrule *Missouri v. Holland*,[52] the governing federalism case in respect of treaties.

In that case the State of Missouri sought to prevent a game warden of the United States from attempting to enforce the Migratory Bird Treaty Act passed by the Congress in 1918, as well as regulations issued by the Secretary of Agriculture in pursuance of the legislation. The challenge to the statute and regulations was based on the ground that the statute is an unconstitutional interference with the rights reserved to the States under the Tenth Amendment. The District Court sustained the Government's position that the implementing Act of Congress was constitutional. The State appealed to the Supreme Court. A decision by Justice Holmes upheld the constitutionality of the implementing Act of Congress.

After summarizing the principal points of the treaty between the United States and Great Britain (in respect of Canada), the purpose of which was to protect the birds from extermination so that they could continue to destroy insects injurious to vegetation in both countries, Holmes stated:

> (I)t is not enough to refer to the Tenth Amendment reserving powers not delegated to the United States, because by Article II, §2, the power to make treaties is delegated expressly, and by Article VI treaties made in pursuance thereof, are declared the supreme law of the land. If the treaty is valid there can be no dispute about the validity of the statute under Article I, §8, as a necessary and proper means to execute the powers of the Government.[53]

The foregoing quotation probably represents the least controversial holding of *Holland*. Yet it was to form an important element in the most recent challenge to the treaty power

51. 389 U.S. 429 (1968).
52. 252 U.S. 416 (1920).
53. *Id.* at 432.

in related cases decided by the Court of Appeals for the Third Circuit and the Supreme Court of the United States. The cases involved standing of a private individual to bring an action under the Tenth Amendment and whether the Chemical Weapons Implementation Act was a valid exercise of the law-making power of the Congress and related issues.

The first of the cases was *United States v. Bond.* Carol Anne Bond who worked for a chemical company in Pennsylvania, discovered that her friend was pregnant and that the father of the child was Bond's husband. According to the syllabus for the case, Mrs. Bond sought revenge against her friend, Myrlinda Haynes, by spreading two toxic chemicals on Haynes's car, mailbox, and door knob in hopes that Haynes would develop an uncomfortable rash. Federal prosecutors charged Mrs. Bond with violating section 229 of the Chemical Weapons Act. She moved to dismiss the chemical weapons charges on the ground that the Act violates the Tenth Amendment. When the District Court denied her motion, she pleaded guilty but reserved the right to appeal. The Third Circuit initially held that Bond lacked standing to raise her Tenth Amendment challenge, but the Supreme Court unanimously reversed.[54] The Supreme Court "expresse[d] no view on the merits" of Bond's constitutional challenge."[55] On remand, the Third Circuit rejected her 10th Amendment argument and her additional argument that section 229 did not reach her conduct.

On remand, Bond renewed her constitutional argument. She also argued that section 229 does not reach her conduct. The Court of Appeals rejected that argument.[56] The Third Circuit also rejected Bond's constitutional challenge to her conviction, holding that section 229 was "necessary and proper to carry the Convention into effect."[57] The Court of Appeals relied on the language from *Missouri v. Holland* set out above.[58]

The Supreme Court again granted certiorari, and on June 2, 2014, the Court handed down its second decision in *Bond v. United States.*[59] The Court unanimously reversed the conviction of Carol Anne Bond under the Chemical Weapons Convention Implementation Act. The Court's opinion written by Chief Justice Roberts expressed the view of six justices that, although the statutory language on its face covered Bond's use of toxic chemicals against another person, the crime was purely local and typically subject to state rather than federal jurisdiction. In that connection it also referred to several of its earlier decisions, including *United States v. Morrison,*[60] and *United States v. Bass,*[61] in which it had noted that perhaps the clearest example of traditional state authority is the punishment of local criminal activity. Thus, it said, "we will not be quick to assume that Congress has meant to effect a significant change in the sensitive relation between federal and state criminal jurisdiction."

International Law of Treaties: Introduction

International law relating to treaties is relatively well developed. The Vienna Convention on the Law of Treaties between States and the Vienna Convention on the Law of Treaties

---

54. Bond v. United States, 131 S. Ct. 2344, 2355 (2011).
55. *Id.*, at 2367.
56. 681 F.3d 149 (3d Cir. 2012).
57. *Id.*, at 162.
58. 252 U.S. 432.
59. 134 S. Ct. 2077 (2014).
60. 529 U.S. 598, 618 (2000).
61. 404 U.S. 336, 349 (1971).

between States and International Organizations or between International Organizations are codifications of the law that have been widely accepted. The former, concluded in 1969, has one hundred fourteen parties. The latter, concluded in 1986, has forty-three parties, but is not yet in force. Although the United States is not a party to either of the Conventions, it signed the 1969 Convention on April 24, 1970 and has long recognized it as generally representing customary international law. Of the two, the 1969 convention is the more important, since most of its provisions are reflected in the 1986 convention. The texts of the articles themselves are concise. They should be read in conjunction with the detailed commentaries prepared by the International Law Commission during their formulation in order to be fully understood.

The Vienna Convention on the Law of Treaties between States is divided into eight parts: I. Introduction; II. Conclusion and Entry into Force of Treaties; III. Observance, Application and Interpretation of Treaties; IV. Amendment and Modification of Treaties; V. Invalidity, Termination and Suspension of the Operation of Treaties; VI. Miscellaneous Provisions; VII. Depositaries, Notifications, Corrections and Registration; and VIII. Final Provisions.

The most important part of the introduction is the definitions article. Discussion of the terms "treaty" and "reservation" appears earlier in this chapter. A non-retroactivity provision in Article 4 makes the treaty forward looking. The Convention itself applies only to treaties which are concluded by States after the entry into force of the treaty with regard to such States.

The conclusion and entry into force part deals with technical rules relating to capacity of States to conclude treaties, full powers (documents issued by Heads of State or Government or Foreign Ministers authorizing persons to represent the State for negotiating, adopting or authenticating the text of a treaty, expressing the consent of the State to be bound by the treaty, or accomplishing any other act with respect to a treaty), and the obligation not to defeat the object and purpose of a treaty prior to its entry into force—a matter that received considerable attention in the context of the effects of signature of the Statute of the International Criminal Court by the United States and the subsequent notification to the Secretary-General of the United Nations that the United States did not intend to ratify the Statute.

Reservations

The section on reservations in part II sets out the international law rules relating to reservations to treaties. The articles on acceptance of and objection to reservations and the effects of reservations and objections, while adequate for the international practice of the 1970s and 1980s, are thought by some to be less than fully adequate to deal with the different and more complicated treaties and practices that have developed in recent years.[62] For that reason, in 1993 the General Assembly of the United Nations asked the

---

62. The proliferation of no reservations clauses in multilateral treaties seems to have prompted a number of states to look for vehicles to preserve positions that they expressed during negotiations but that were not incorporated in the text that was adopted. For examples, see the declarations by states upon becoming party to the UN Convention on the Law of the Sea. The relevant articles of that treaty are 309 and 310. The former prohibits "reservations and exceptions" unless expressly permitted by other articles of the Convention." The latter allows a State when signing or becoming a

International Law Commission to study the practice of states on reservations to treaties with the objective of developing a guide to practice on that subject. The Commission decided that its work would take the form of guidelines with commentaries which would be of assistance for the practice of States and international organizations. There is no intention to amend the reservations articles of the Vienna Convention on the Law of Treaties. The Commission finished its work on the topic in 2011. The General Assembly took note of the massive document in 2013.[63]

Reservations to bilateral treaties require acceptance by the other party. Reservations to multilateral treaties are more complicated. Reservations contrary to the object and purpose of the treaty are prohibited. Other parties may object to reservations but few objecting states reject treaty relations with the reserving state, though they are free to do so.

In order to illustrate the typical operation of reservations at the international level, there follows a communication from Pakistan to the Secretary-General of the United Nations in his role as depositary for the International Convention for the Suppression of Terrorist Bombings, done at New York December 15, 1997. The communication, which is entitled "Declaration" reads as follows:

> The Government of the Islamic Republic of Pakistan declares that nothing in this Convention shall be applicable to struggles, including armed struggle, for the re-alization of the right of self-determination launched against any alien or foreign occupation or domination, in accordance with the rules of international law. This interpretation is consistent with Article 53 of the Vienna Convention on the Law of Treaties 1969 which provides that an agreement or treaty concluded in conflict with an existing jus cogens or preemptory norm of international law is void and, the right of self-determination is universally recognized as a jus cogens.

States had twelve months after they were notified of the "declaration" to decide what position they wished to take with respect to it. As of October 12, 2014, the treaty was in force between 168 parties, 16 of which, including the United States, had filed objections to the Pakistan reservation. All chose to maintain treaty relations with Pakistan under the Convention. The Denmark objection, which is typical, stated:

> The Government of the Kingdom of Denmark considers that the declaration made by Pakistan is in fact a reservation that seeks to limit the scope of the Convention on a unilateral basis and is therefore contrary to its objective and purpose, which is the suppression of terrorist bombings, irrespective of where they take place and of who carries them out.

---

party to the Convention to make "declarations or statements, however phrased or named, with a view, *inter alia,* to the harmonization of its laws and regulations with the provisions of this Convention, provided that such declarations or statements do not purport to exclude or to modify the legal effect of the provisions of this Convention in their application to that State." Declarations (at least some of which seem not to relate to "harmonization of its laws and regulations with the provisions of the Convention") and objections to those declarations are printed at pp. 223–265 of Volume II of MULTILATERAL TREATIES DEPOSITED WITH THE SECRETARY-GENERAL STATUS AS AT 31 DECEMBER 2001. "Statements", "declarations", "interpretative declarations", "conditional interpretative declarations", "unilateral statements" and "general statements of policy" are among the labels states have attached to communications sent to depositaries of other multilateral treaties in recent years.

63. The full text of the Guide is an addendum to the 2011 Report of the International Law Commission, available at http://legal.un.org/ilc/reports2011/english/addendum.pdf. For an analysis of the main substantive issues raised by the Guide, see *Symposium: the International Law Commission's Guide to Practice on Reservations to Treaties,* 24 EUROPEAN JOURNAL OF INTERNATIONAL LAW No. 4 (2013).

The declaration is furthermore contrary to the terms of Article 5 of the Convention, according to which States Parties commit themselves to "adopt such measures as may be necessary, including, where appropriate, domestic legislation, to ensure that criminal acts within the scope of this Convention … are under no circumstances justifiable by considerations of a political, philosophical, ideological, racial, ethnic, religious or similar nature and are punished by penalties consistent with their grave nature".

The Government of the Kingdom of Denmark recalls that, according to Article 19 C of the Vienna Convention on the law of treaties, a reservation incompatible with the object and purpose of the Convention shall not be permitted.

It is in the common interest of States that all parties respect treaties to which they have chosen to become party, as to their object and purpose, and that States are prepared to undertake any legislative changes necessary to comply with their obligations under the treaties.

The Government of the Kingdom of Denmark therefore objects to the aforesaid reservation made by the Government of Pakistan to the International Convention for the suppression of terrorist bombings. This objection shall not preclude the entry into force of the Convention between the Kingdom of Denmark and Pakistan.

Provisional Application

Part II also includes Article 25 on provisional application of a treaty or a part of a treaty. The article, which represented an innovation in international law at the time of its adoption, makes clear that a treaty may be applied provisionally pending its entry into force if the treaty so provides or the negotiating States have in some other manner so agreed. The article has been relied on in a number of cases. In the bilateral context, the United States and the Union of Soviet Socialist Republics agreed in an exchange of notes dated June 1, 1990 to abide by the Agreement on the Maritime Boundary, they had also signed that day, pending its entry into force.[64] The Agreement relating to the Implementation of Part XI of the United Nations Convention on the Law of the Sea provided in Article 7 for provisional application beginning on November 16, 1994. In his letter of submittal of the Convention to President Clinton, Secretary of State Warren Christopher noted:

> Without such a provision, the Convention would enter into force on that date with its objectionable seabed mining provisions unchanged.... Provisional application by the United States will permit the advancement of U.S. seabed mining interests by U.S. participation in the International Seabed Authority from the outset to ensure that the implementation of the regime is consistent with those interests, while doing so consistent with existing laws and regulations.

In 2001, having noted that the time involved in formally bringing into force amendments approved the previous year could substantially delay the privatization of INTELSAT, the parties unanimously agreed to implement the amendments with effect from July 18, 2001, pending their entry into force. The term used to describe the effect of their decision was "rapid implementation". One of the more recent examples of provisional application with respect to U.S. treaties is the New START Treaty.

---

64. TIAS 11451.

The International Law Commission began a review of the topic of provisional application of treaties in 2012. In 2014 the United States responded to the Commission's request for information regarding practice relating to the topic by furnishing examples of practice and statements by the United States. The material was derived in large measure from the *Digest* of United States Practice over the years.[65]

A review of the Secretary-General's Depositary website indicates that as part of its instrument of accession to the Chemical Weapons Convention deposited on September 14, 2013, Syria stated that it would provisionally apply the Convention pending its entry into force for Syria in accordance with the Convention. The most recent development relating to provisional application of treaties is the Arbitral Award in *Hulley Enterprises Limited (Cyprus) v. the Russian Federation: Final Award of July 18, 2014*.[66]

Interpretation

In introducing an amendment proposed by the United States during the Vienna Conference on the Law of Treaties between States, Professor Myres McDougal, a member of the United States delegation, described the rules proposed by the International Law Commission as embodying "over-rigid and unnecessarily restrictive requirements."[67] The amendment failed, and at one time it was thought that the existence of the two articles would present an obstacle to ratification of the Convention by the United States. In fact, as indicated below, the articles seem not to have caused problems in the United States; they have increasingly been cited and followed in treaty interpretation cases before internatioinal tribunals and U.S. courts.

A Westlaw search on April 16, 2003 identified nearly fifty U.S. court cases involving references to the Vienna Convention on the Law of Treaties between 1988 and 2003. Many of them, such as *Chubb & Son v. Asiana Airlines*,[68] and *Tseng v. El Al Israel Airlines, Ltd*,[69] deal with cases under the Warsaw Convention and its progeny—a leading source of treaty interpretation cases in U.S. courts. A recent treaty interpretation case, *Abbott v. Abbott*, has generally been welcomed by commentators who follow interpretations of treaties relating to private international law.[70]

Amendment and Modification

The articles in Part IV deal with amendment and modification of treaties. Many of the multilateral treaties that were concluded in the period after World War II were designed to be difficult to amend. Those difficulties have been exacerbated by the emergence of a large number of new states, which made it even more difficult to obtain the ratification of two-thirds or three-quarters of a larger number of Parties—often within relatively

---

65. Online editions of the Digest are available beginning from 1989 at the website of the Office of the Legal Adviser <http://www.state.gov/s/l>.

66. Available on website of Permanent Court of Arbitration, http://www.pca-cpa.org/showpage .asp?pag_id=363.

67. United Nations Conference on the Law of Treaties, Official Records, First Session, 1968 p. 167. He favored combining articles 31 (general rule of interpretation) and 32 (supplementary means of interpretation) into a single article.

68. 214 F.3d 301 (2d Cir. 2002); cert. den. 533 U.S. 928 (2001).

69. 122 F.3d 99 (2d Cir. 1997).

70. 560 U.S. 1 (2010).

short time limits. An extract from Article XVII of the Agreement relating to the International Telecommunications Satellite Organization "INTELSAT" demonstrates the challenges some organizations faced:

> "Article XVI (d) An amendment which has been approved by the Assembly of Parties shall enter into force in accordance with paragraph (e) of this Article after the Depositary has received notice of approval, acceptance or ratification of the amendment from either:
>
> (i) two-thirds of the States which were Parties as of the date upon which the amendment was approved by the Assembly of Parties, provided that such two-thirds includes Parties which then held, or whose designated Signatories then held, at least two-thirds of the total investment shares; or
>
> (ii) a number of States equal to or exceeding eighty-five per cent of the total number of States which were Parties as of the date upon which the amendment was approved by the Assembly of Parties, regardless of the amount of investment shares such Parties or their designated Signatories then held.
>
> (e) The Depositary shall notify all the Parties as soon as it has received the acceptances ... required by paragraph (d) of this Article for the entry into force of an amendment. Ninety days after the date of issue of this notification, the amendment shall enter into force for all Parties ...
>
> (f) *Notwithstanding the provisions of paragraphs (d) and (e) of this Article, an amendment shall not enter into force less than eight months or more than eighteen months after the date it has been approved by the Assembly of Parties.*" (emphasis added)

While INTELSAT amended the agreement in accordance with its Constitution, a number of other organizations have sought to ignore the amendment provisions of agreements. International organizations that have decision-making powers often prefer to effect change by adopting resolutions.

Invalidity: Provisions of Internal Law Regarding Competence to Conclude Treaties

PART V of the convention deals with invalidity, termination and suspension of the operation of treaties. It presents a complete catalogue of the grounds on which a State can impeach the validity of a treaty and the consequences of invalidity, termination or suspension of the operation of treaties. It also contains four articles dealing with procedures for the peaceful settlement of disputes arising out of the application of Part V. The invalidity article that attracted the most attention in the United States Senate is Article 46 on provisions of internal law regarding competence to conclude treaties. The Article reads as follows:

> 1. A State may not invoke the fact that its consent to be bound by a treaty has been expressed in violation of a provision of its internal law regarding competence to conclude treaties as invalidating its consent unless that violation was manifest and concerned a rule of its internal law of fundamental importance.
>
> 2. A violation is manifest if it would be objectively evident to any State conducting itself in the matter in accordance with normal practice and in good faith.

In September 1972, Senator Clifford Case proposed including in the Senate's resolution of advice and consent to ratification of the Vienna Convention on the Law of Treaties an interpretation and understanding that would have read as follows:

subject to the interpretation and understanding, which understanding and interpretation are made a part and condition of the resolution of ratification, that, in accordance with Article 46 of the Convention, since Article 2, Section 2 of the United States Constitution states that the President 'shall have power, by and with the advice and consent of the Senate, to make treaties, provided two-thirds of the Senators present concur,' it is a rule of fundamental importance that no treaty (as defined by paragraph 1 (a) of Article 2 of the Convention) is valid with respect to the United States, and the consent of the United States may not be given regarding any such treaty, unless the Senate of the United States has given its advice and consent to such treaty, or the terms of such treaty have been approved by law, as the case may be.

The Executive objected to the understanding and the Vienna Convention was not reported to the full Senate at that time.

The Executive repeated its objection to the proposed interpretation and understanding set out above when it was asked by the Chairman of the Senate Foreign Relations Committee in 1986 if it had changed its views with respect to Senator Case's 1972 proposal. It took the view that the proposed language would significantly impair the ability of the President to manage foreign relations in a way that would most effectively permit protection of United States interests. Turning to its practical consequences, the Executive stated:

adoption of the proposal would seriously hamper the ability of the President to resolve international differences or provide for international cooperation by agreement. There is a wide range of unanticipated matters which require solution, frequently through a simple exchange of diplomatic notes. These exchanges often deal with problems which arise suddenly in the course of day-to-day relations and which must be solved quickly to avoid disruption of ongoing activities. The effectiveness of the United States in the realm or foreign affairs would be significantly impaired were it to deprive itself of the ability to conclude and implement agreements on short notice.

Although the Vienna Convention remains on the Senate treaty calendar, there has been no action with respect to the Convention since the 1986 hearing at which the views set out above were expressed.

Termination: Breach

Article 60 of the Vienna Convention deals with termination or suspension of the operation of a treaty as a consequence of its breach. A state is entitled to rely on the article only when the breach is material. The term "material breach" is defined in paragraph 3 as "(a) a repudiation of the treaty not sanctioned by the present Convention; or (b) the violation of a provision essential to the accomplishment of the object and purpose of the treaty."

In 1984 the Government of New Zealand decided to prohibit nuclear-armed and -powered warships and aircraft from entering New Zealand ports. The United States took the position that such action disrupted its relationship with New Zealand under the Security Treaty (ANZUS Pact), signed at San Francisco September 1, 1951, by Australia, New Zealand, and the United States.[71] On August 11, 1986, at the conclusion of bilateral

---

71. TIAS 2493; 3 UST 3420.

ministerial talks at San Francisco, Secretary of State George P. Schultz and Australian Minister for Foreign Affairs Bill Hayden issued a joint statement stressing the importance of the treaty. The U.S. side stated that it was suspending its security obligations to New Zealand under the ANZUS treaty pending adequate corrective measures. These points were repeated in an exchange of letters between Secretary Shultz and Foreign Minister Hayden dated the same day. On September 17, 1986, the United States Ambassador to New Zealand delivered to the New Zealand Foreign Minister a diplomatic note formally suspending the ANZUS treaty as between the two countries.[72]

The United States is not a party to the Vienna Convention and it did not use the expression "material breach" in setting out the basis for its action in suspending its security obligations to New Zealand under the ANZUS Treaty. However, its action seems consistent with the customary international law rule embodied in that article.

Settlement of Disputes

Article 66 of the convention establishes procedures for judicial settlement, arbitration and conciliation. Disputes concerning the application or interpretation of articles 53 or 64 (jus cogens) may be taken by any party to a dispute to the International Court of Justice unless the parties by common consent agree to submit the matter to arbitration. Any party to a dispute concerning the application or interpretation of any of the other articles in Part V may set in motion the procedure specified in the Annex to the Convention. However, there does not appear to be any case in which the procedure specified in the Annex has been invoked by a party to the Convention.

Miscellaneous Provisions

The most important article in Part VI may once have been Article 73. That article states that the provisions of the Convention shall not prejudge any question that may arise in regard to a treaty from a succession of States or from the international responsibility of a State or from the effects of armed conflicts on treaties. However, the International Law Commission subsequently developed texts on all three subjects. The 1978 Convention on Succession of States to Treaties is in force, but only among a limited number of states. While the Commission's draft conventions on state responsibility and the effects of armed conflicts on treaties have not been referred to diplomatic conferences for adoption, the texts should be consulted by anyone having a question on either of those subjects. Some of the articles on state responsibility have been applied as customary law in cases before international tribunals and cited in diplomatic correspondence. There do not seem to be similar cases with respect to the articles concerning armed conflicts.

Since Parts VII and VIII deal largely with technical matters and appear to be self-explanatory, they are not discussed in this chapter.

---

72. I CUMULATIVE DIGEST OF UNITED STATES PRACTICE IN INTERNATIONAL LAW 1981–1988, pp. 1279–81.

A Case Study of the Interplay between International and Domestic Law and the *Avena* Case

Three countries—Paraguay, Germany, and Mexico—filed cases against the United States in the International Court of Justice between 1998 and 2004. Each charged that the United States had violated its international obligations under Article 36 of the Vienna Convention on Consular Relations by not notifying certain of its nationals arrested in the United States of their rights under that Article. Jurisdiction arose in each of the cases under the Optional Protocol to the Vienna Convention on Consular Relations Concerning the Compulsory Settlement of Disputes, to which the United States and each of the three countries were parties. Each of the filings sought and obtained orders from the Court requiring the United States to stay the execution of one or more of its nationals alleged not to have been notified of their rights under Article 36, pending the I.C.J.'s final decisions in those cases.

As the introductory note to a case study on the Consular Convention indicates:

> These cases posed an unprecedented challenge to the United States as a litigant before the ICJ—and, because the ICJ concluded that the United States was violating its international obligations under the Consular Convention, to the incorporation of international law and the appropriate remedies for its violation in our federal system. One important aspect of this latter question [was] the Supreme Court's decision in *Medellín v. Texas*, 552 U.S. 491 (2008), that the obligation to comply with the ICJ judgment in *Avena* [brought against the United States by Mexico] was not self-executing ... Two additional questions [arose after] the Supreme Court in fact held in *Medellín* that the ICJ judgment in *Avena* was not self-executing. First, how should courts ensure the implementation of U.S. obligations under the Consular Convention itself (as opposed to obligations under the U.N. Charter or the Optional Protocol relating to the obligation to follow the ICJ), given state law governing procedural default remedies for violation of a defendant's treaty-based rights ... ? Second, assuming that federal law does not otherwise require states to abide by the ICJ's interpretation of the Consular Convention, may the President order them to do so?[73]

The remedies issue will be discussed later in the context of subsequent decisions of the United States Supreme Court in *Medellin v. Texas*, a case involving one of the Mexican nationals to whom the *Avena* case applied, and *Sanchez-Llamas*, domestic law cases filed by aliens in U.S. courts, that nevertheless involved one or more issues posed in the *Avena* case. But first we must examine the Supreme Court's response to the provisional measures orders of the ICJ in the Paraguay and Germany cases and the State Department's initiatives with the states concerned, Virginia and Arizona. The Supreme Court examined the provisional measures orders of the ICJ in the Paraguay and Germany cases.

The first of the provisional measures orders was issued in the Paraguay case in 1998. The Supreme Court decided that the subject of the order, Angel Breard, had not complied with the procedural rules of the State of Virginia, and declined to intervene.[74] The Secretary of State, Madeline Albright, subsequently wrote to the governor of Virginia and asked that he stay Breard's execution. The governor decided not to do so, Breard was executed, and Paraguay terminated the case.

---

73. FRANCK, THOMAS M., GLENNON, MICHAEL J., MURPHY, SEAN D., AND SWAIN, EDWARD T., FOREIGN RELATIONS AND NATIONAL SECURITY LAW, 4th ed., (Thompson/West 2012) p. 815.
74. Breard v. Greene, 523 U.S. 317, 375 (1998).

The second provisional measures order was issued in the case brought by Germany on behalf of Walter and Karl LaGrand.[75] The brothers, who had lived in the United States since infancy, had not been informed of their rights under the Vienna Convention until ten years after their convictions. They then raised their Vienna Convention rights in *habeas corpus* proceedings in the federal courts, which concluded that they were procedurally barred from doing so.[76] Following Karl's execution, Germany obtained a provisional measures order not to execute Walter similar to the order the Court had issued in the *Breard* case. The Supreme Court declined to intervene and the Governor of Arizona, whom the State Department had asked to stay Walter's execution, decided not to do so. However, in contrast to Paraguay's withdrawal of its case following Breard's execution, Germany continued its case after Walter's execution and obtained a judgment on the merits. The Court found that the United States had breached its obligations under the Convention by not immediately informing the LaGrand brothers of their right to consular notification. It also found that provisional orders are binding on States and that the United States had violated the provisional order issued in the case. Finally, the Court found that "should nationals of ... Germany be sentenced to severe penalties" without their right to consular notification having been respected, the United States "by means of its own choosing, shall allow the review and reconsideration of the conviction and sentence by taking account of the violation of the rights set forth" in the Convention.[77] The President of the Court emphasized that the language which is contained in the foregoing quotation and included as subparagraph (7) of paragraph 128 of the Court's opinion "represents a response to certain submissions by Germany and hence rules only on the obligations of the United States in cases of severe penalties imposed on German nationals."

In the *Avena* case (Mexico v. United States), Mexico claimed that the United States had violated Article 36, paragraph 1 (b), of the Vienna Convention on Consular Relations with respect to more than fifty of its nationals on death row as to whom United States arresting or interrogating authorities had sufficient information to be aware of their foreign nationality but failed to inform them of their rights under that provision. In paragraph 115 of its opinion the Court indicated that it had concluded that in most of the 52 instances there had been a failure to observe the obligations prescribed by that provision. But before proceeding to "the examination of the legal consequences of such a breach and of what legal remedies should be considered for the breach" it noted in paragraph 133 its concern that under the procedural default rule "a claim based on the violation of Article 36, paragraph 1, however meritorious in itself, could be barred in the courts of the United States."[78]

Such a result would be inconsistent with the introductory sentence of paragraph 138, the first of four paragraphs on the concept of "review and reconsideration" prescribed by the Court in the *LaGrand* case and retained in *Avena*, which begins by emphasizing that the process "should be effective." The idea continues in the next paragraph in which the Court points out that "what is crucial in the review and reconsideration process is the existence of a procedure which guarantees that full weight is given to the violation of the rights set forth in the Vienna Convention, whatever may be the actual outcome of such review and reconsideration."

---

75. Germany v. United States, 526 U.S. 111, 119 (1999).

76. LaGrand v. Stewart, 133 F.3d 1253 (9th Cir. 1998), *cert. denied* 525 U.S. 971 (1998).

77. 2001 I.C.J. Reports, 466, 516, para. 128 (7).

78. 2004 I.C.J. Reports 12, 65, para. 138. The procedural rule in U.S. law provides that a defendant who could have raised, but fails to raise, a legal issue at trial will generally not be permitted to raise it in future proceedings, on appeal or in a petition for writ of *habeas corpus*.

The holding of the case is contained in paragraph 153 of the Court's opinion, two sub-paragraphs of which follow. The more specific is subparagraph 8 in which the Court refers by name to three of the Mexicans with respect to whom the Court found that the United States breached its obligations under Article 36, paragraph 2 of the Convention.

> [B]y not permitting the review and reconsideration, in the light of the rights set forth in the Convention, of the conviction and sentences of Mr. César Roberto Fierro Reyna, Mr. Roberto Moreno Ramos, and Mr. Osvaldo Torres Aguilera, after the violations set forth in subparagraph (4) above had been established in respect of those individuals, the United States of America breached the obligations incumbent upon it under Article 36, paragraph 2, of the Convention;

In subparagraph 9, which applies to a larger group, the Court:

> Finds that the appropriate reparation in this case consists in the obligation of the United States of America to provide, by means of its own choosing, review and reconsideration of the convictions and sentences of the Mexican nationals referred to in subparagraphs (4), (5), (6) and (7) above, by taking account both of the violations set forth in Article 36 of the Convention and of paragraphs 138 to 141 of this Judgment;

As noted in subparagraph 8, one of those persons was Osvaldo Torres Aguilera. On March 2, 2004, while *Avena* was pending, the Oklahoma Court of Criminal Appeals had set May 18, 2004 as the date for Torres' execution. After the International Court of Justice issued its *Avena* decision on March 31, the Legal Adviser of the State Department wrote to the Governor informing him of the decision and asking him to give careful consideration to the fact that the United States was bound by the ICJ decision. On May 13, 2004, the Oklahoma Court of Criminal Appeals stayed the execution and remanded the case for an evidentiary hearing. Later that day, Governor Henry commuted Torres' sentence to life in prison without parole.[79] Of particular interest is the concurring opinion of Judge Chapel in *Torres*, No.PCD-442 at 3, 5.[80]

A second State case involving an individual named in the *Avena* case was decided on September 19, 2012, when the Nevada Supreme Court reversed the denial of a petition for post-conviction relief on a writ of habeas corpus for Carlos Gutierrez. In *Gutierrez v. Nevada*, the Nevada Supreme Court remanded the case, finding that he "arguably suffered actual prejudice due to [a] lack of consular assistance." A hearing has been scheduled for March 2015 in the district court to determine whether he was prejudiced by the failure to inform him of his rights under the Convention.[81]

Despite the *Torres* and *Gutierrez* cases, in which Oklahoma and Nevada were able to take action consistent with the order of the ICJ in *Avena*, several decisions of the Supreme Court of the United States posed obstacles to compliance by the United States with its obligations under the Vienna Convention on Consular Relations and the Optional Protocol on Compulsory Settlement of Disputes under that Convention. Two of those cases were brought by José Ernesto Medellín. In the first, *Medellín v. Dretke*,[82] he sought to enforce his treaty rights against the State of Texas in a claim as to which the Texas Court of Criminal

---

79. Levitt, Janet Koven, *A Tale of International Law in the Heartland: Torres and the Role of State Courts in Transnational Legal Conversation* 12 Tulsa J. Comp. & Int'l L. 163, 169–172 (2004).

80. *Id.*, at 172 n.50.

81. Gutierrez v. State, No. 53506, 2012 WL, 4355518, at *2. Excerpts from the court's opinion appear in the Digest of United States Practice in International Law, 2012, pp. 16–17. The full text of the opinion is available at <www.state.gov/s/l/c8183.htm>.

82. 544 U.S. 660 (2005).

Appeals had initially found he had defaulted as a matter of Texas procedural law because he had not raised it at trial. After the ICJ decision in *Avena*, Medellín, who was one of the named Mexicans, brought a federal *habeas*, but the lower federal courts denied relief based on *Breard*. The Supreme Court had originally agreed to hear the case, but after the issuance of President Bush's memorandum, the Court dismissed the petition to allow Medellín to seek review of his "previously unavailable" claim in Texas. The Texas Court of Criminal Appeals ruled that Medellín's claim based on *Avena*, the Optional Protocol to the Vienna Consular Convention, and the U.N. Charter did not qualify because the *Avena* judgment was not legally available as a matter of federal law.[83]

In the meantime, the Supreme Court had been considering *Sanchez-Llamas v. Oregon*,[84] which, together with *Medellín v. Texas*, "marked the conclusion of a decade-long sequence involving the effects in U.S. law of the Vienna Convention on Consular Relations, several other treaties providing for international adjudication of disputes arising under the Vienna Convention, and the application of the procedural default rule to those cases." Professor Damrosch summarizes the principal questions with which the U.S. courts had grappled during the decade as follows: [85]

- when treaties would give rise to rights and remedies for individuals in the absence of implementing legislation;
- which organ — executive or judicial; state, federal, or international — had authority to decide on the content of the treaty obligations and remedies for breach;
- what weight should be given to the conclusions of an international dispute settlement process at the International Court of Justice (ICJ) to which the United States had consented and in which it fully participated;
- whether ICJ rulings would be given effect in U.S. law; and
- how the treaty rights that had been determined at the international level would relate to procedural conditions for the exercise of such rights ("procedural default" rules) established by state or federal law.

These questions were joined in *Medellín v. Texas*, and most of them were also in play in *Sanchez-Lllamas* (although in a less dramatic form, because the petitioners in *Sanchez-Llamas* were not directly covered by the international judgment involved in *Medellín*).

While Medellin was pursuing his claim in Texas courts, the Supreme Court granted certiorari in petitions filed by two other foreign nationals, Moises Sanchez-Llamas and Mario Bustillo. Neither of those nationals had been among the persons named in the *Avena* case, but they were claiming that they had been denied their Article 36 rights by Oregon and Virginia, respectively. Bustillo had been denied relief in state court on grounds of procedural default. While Sanchez-Llamas's claim was not subject to the procedural default rule, the Oregon court denied his request for suppression of evidence on the ground that it was not an appropriate remedy for a Vienna Convention violation. The two cases were decided together in 2006, when the Supreme Court denied both claims.[86]

In 2005, President George W. Bush issued a memorandum to U.S. Attorney General Gonzalez concerning compliance with the ICJ's *Avena* decision. The memorandum stated

---

83. *Ex parte* Medellín, 223 S.W.3d 315, 352 (Tex. Crim. App. 2006).
84. 548 U.S. 331 (2006).
85. Lori F. Damrosch, *Medellin and Sanchez-Llamas: Treaties from John Jay to John Roberts* in David L. Sloss, Michael D. Ramsey, and William S. Dodge, (eds.) INTERNATIONAL LAW IN THE U.S. SUPREME COURT: CONTINUITY AND CHANGE, p. 451 Cambridge University Press (2011).
86. Sanchez-Llamas v. Oregon, 548 U.S. 331 (2006).

that the President had determined that "pursuant to the authority vested in me as President by the Constitution and the laws of the United States of America," "the United States will discharge its international obligations" under the ICJ decision in the *Avena* case "by having State courts give effect to the decision in accordance with general principles of comity."[87]

Medellín had already brought a post-*Avena* federal habeas petition, but the lower federal courts had rejected it.[88] Although the Supreme Court had agreed to hear the case, following the issuance of the President's memorandum it dismissed the petition in order to give Medellín an opportunity to pursue relief in state court.[89] The Texas Court of Criminal Appeals decided that Medellín's claim based on *Avena* and the U.N. Charter did not afford a basis for relief since the *Avena* judgment was not legally binding as a matter of federal law. In 2008, the case returned to the Supreme Court as *Medellín v. Texas*.[90] In that case, the Court decided that the Optional Protocol on Settlement of Disputes to the Vienna Convention on Consular Relations was not self-executing. It defined a non-self-executing treaty as

> one that was ratified with the understanding that it is not to have domestic effect of its own force. That understanding precludes the assertion that Congress has implicitly authorized the President — acting on his own — to achieve precisely the same result. We therefore conclude, given the absence of congressional legislation, that the non-self-executing treaties at issue here [the Optional Protocol and the U.N. Charter] did not "express[ly] or implied[ly]" vest the President with the unilateral authority to make them self-executing.[91]

Relying on *Foster v. Neilson*,[92] the Court noted:

> The President has an array of political and diplomatic means available to enforce international obligations, but unilaterally converting a non-self-executing treaty to a self-executing one is not among them. The responsibility for transforming an international obligation arising from a non-self-executing treaty into domestic law falls to Congress.[93]

The 2013 *Digest of U.S. Practice in International Law* summarizes various steps taken by the Executive to achieve that objective. They include testimony by State Department and Justice Department officials before the Senate Judiciary Committee held during the 112th Congress, together with subsequent steps taken during the 113th Congress, demonstrate the efforts being made by the executive branch to secure enactment of legislation that will enable the United States to comply with its international obligations under the Vienna Convention. For example:

Section 7085 of the Senate State, Foreign Operations, and Related Agencies Appropriations Act, Fiscal Year 2015 (S.2499), as reported by the Senate Appropriations Committee on June 19, 2014, if enacted, would have made it possible to perform the U.S. obligations to provide review and reconsideration in certain death penalty cases involving Mexican and other foreign nationals entitled to receive notification of their rights under

---

87. 44 I.L.M. 950 (2005).
88. *Medellín v. Dretke*, 371 F3d 270, 286 (5th Cir. 2004).
89. *Medellín v. Dretke*, 544 U.S. 660 (2005).
90. 552 U.S. 491 (2008).
91. *Id.* at 493, n.2.
92. 27 U.S. 2 Pet 253, 253 (1829).
93. *Id.* at 315.

Article 36 of the Vienna Consular Relations Convention or similar provisions in bilateral treaties that include parallel provisions.

Following the Supreme Court decision in *Medellín v. Texas*, the American Bar Association and the American Society of International Law established a joint task force on treaties in U.S. law to assess the implications of the decision and make recommendations for the future. The American Bar Association's Report is available at http://www.asil.org/files/TreatiesTaskForceReport.pdf.[94]

The first recommendation called for the enactment of remedial legislation with respect to existing treaties. Except for the legislation with respect to remedying the inability of the United States to implement its obligations under the consular treaties previously discussed, and earlier, separate legislation that was never brought to a vote, the author is unaware of any steps to enact remedial legislation with respect to other non-self-executing treaties.

With respect to future treaties, it is occasionally possible to identify treaties that are non-self-executing by provisions in multi-lateral treaties that require parties to enact legislation. A relatively recent example is the Chemical Weapons Convention. However, given differences in domestic law, it is exceedingly rare to find such provisions in bilateral treaties.

> The task force recommended that when a new treaty has been negotiated, the transmittal documents for sending it to the Senate—and specifically, the Secretary of State's report to the President … specifically address whether the Executive Branch considers each provision self-executing or non-self-executing and, if the latter, state specifically whether the provision is aspirational or whether implementation is needed … [95]

The task force report also favored complementary action by the Senate.

In 2008, the Senate Foreign Relations Committee changed the format of the reports on pending treaties by deciding to include in its draft resolutions of advice and consent declarations as to the self-executing or non-self-executing nature of treaty provisions. It referred expressly to the *Medellín* case in inaugurating the new practice, indicating that the case had "highlighted the utility of a clear statement regarding the self-executing nature of treaty provisions."[96] The Report continued: "The committee believes it is of great importance that the United States complies with the treaty obligations it undertakes … While situations may arise that were not contemplated when the treaty was concluded and ratified that raise questions about the authority of the United States to comply,"—a situation that some would say existed with respect to the Vienna Convention on Consular Relations—"the committee expects that such cases will be rare." The Senate Report continued further: "Accordingly, in the committee's view, a strong presumption should exist against the conclusion in any particular case that the United States lacks the necessary authority in U.S. law to implement obligations it has assumed under treaties that have received the advice and consent of the Senate."[97]

---

94. For further details, see Ronald J. Bettauer, *ABA Adopts ABA-ASIL Joint Task Force Policies on Implementing Treaties under U.S. Law*, 14 INSIGHTS (2010), *available at* http://www.asil.org/insights/volume/14/issue/10/aba-adopts-aba-asil-joint-task-force-policies-implementing-treaties.

95. ABA Report, p. 18.

96. Senate Foreign Relations Committee Report on Extradition Treaties with the European Union, Sen. Ex. Rpt. No. 110-12 (2008) p. 10.

97. *Id.*

Conclusion

While this chapter summarizes major points of law and procedure relating to treaties and other international agreements as of this writing, neither domestic nor international law is static. Fundamental changes in domestic procedures or major additional codification of the law of treaties seem unlikely, but a person faced with treaty law issues would be well-advised to check on both domestic and international law developments in order to supplement the materials herein.

Selected Bibliography

Books

Aust, Anthony, *Modern Treaty Law and Practice* (Cambridge University Press, 3rd ed., 2013).

Cannizzaro, Enzo, ed., *The Law of Treaties Beyond the Vienna Convention* (Oxford University Press, 2011).

Congressional Research Service, Library of Congress, *Treaties and Other International Agreements: The Role of the United States Senate* (Washington: GPO, 2001).

Corten, Olivier & Klein, Pierre, eds., *The Vienna Conventions on the Law of Treaties: A Commentary* (Oxford University Press, 2011).

Corwin, Edwin S., *The President: Office and Powers, 1787–1984* (New York and London: New York University Press, 5th rev. ed., Randall W. Bland, Theodore T. Hindson, Jack W. Peltason, eds., 1984).

Crandall, Samuel B., *Treaties: Their Making and Enforcement* (Washington: John Byrne & Company, 2d ed., 1916).

Dörr, Oliver & Schmalenbach, Kirsten, eds., *Vienna Convention on the Law of Treaties: A Commentary* (Springer: Berlin Heidelberg, 2012).

Henkin, Louis, *Foreign Affairs and the Constitution* (New York: Oxford University Press/Clarendon Press, 2d ed., 1997).

Hollis, Duncan B., Blakeslee, Merrit R., & Ederington, Benjamin, eds., *National Treaty Law and Practice* (Martinus Nijhoff Publishers: Leiden and Boston, 2005).

Hollis, Duncan B., ed., *Oxford Guide to Treaties* (Oxford University Press, 2012).

Moore, John Norton, *Treaty Interpretation, the Constitution and the Rule of Law* (Oceana Publications, 2001).

Nash (Leich), Marian, *Cumulative Digest of United States Practice in International Law 1981–1988* (Washington: Department of State, 1993).

Restatement (Third) of the Law of Foreign Relations (St. Paul, Minn.: American Law Institute, 1987).

Reuter, Paul, *Introduction to the Law of Treaties* (José Mico & Peter Haggenmacher, trans., Kegan Paul International: London and New York, 1995).

Riesenfeld, Stefan A., & Abbott, Frederick M., eds., *Parliamentary Participation in the Making and Operation of Treaties: A Comparative Study* (Martinus Nijhoff, Dordrecht, The Netherlands, 1994).

Rosenne, Shabtai, *Developments in the Law of Treaties 1945–1986* (Cambridge University Press, 1989).

Sinclair, Ian, *Vienna Convention on the Law of Treaties* (2nd ed., Manchester, 1984).

Sloss, David L., Ramsey, Michael D., and Dodge, William S., eds., *International Law in the Supreme Court: Continuity and Change* (Cambridge University Press, 2011).

Tams, Christian J., Tzanakopoulos, Antonios, & Zimmerman, Andreas, eds., *Research Handbook on the Law of Treaties* (Edward Elgar, 2014).

Villiger, Mark E., *Commentary on the 1969 Vienna Convention on the Law of Treaties* (Martinus Nijhoff Publishers: Leiden and Boston, 2009).

Whiteman, Marjorie M., 14 *Digest of International Law* (Washington: Department of State, 1970).

Articles

Dalton, Robert E., "International Agreements in the Revised Restatement," 25 *Va. J. Int'l L.* 153–68 (1984).

Damrosch, Lori Fisler, "The Role of the United States Senate Concerning 'Self-Executing' Treaties," in S.A. Riesenfeld & F.M. Abbott (eds.), *Parliamentary Participation in the Making and Operation of Treaties: A Comparative Study* 205–22 (Martinus Nijhoff, Dordrecht, The Netherlands, 1994).

Glennon, Michael, "The Senate Role in Treaty Ratification," 77 *Am. J. Int'l L.* 257–80 (1983).

Kearney, Richard D., "Internal Limitations on External Commitments — Article 46 of the Treaties Convention," 4 *Int'l L.* 1–21 (1969).

Kearney, Richard D., and Dalton, Robert E., "The Treaty on Treaties," 64 *Am. J. Int'l L.* 495–561 (1970).

McDougal, Myres S. & Lans, Asher, "Treaties and Congressional-Executive Agreements: Interchangeable Instruments of International Diplomacy," 54 *Yale L.J.* 181–351, 534–615 (1945), *reprinted* in Myres S. McDougal *et al.*, *Studies in World Public Order* (1st ed., 1960, reprinted 1987).

Riesenfeld, Stefan A. & Aboott, Frederick M., "The Scope of U.S. Senate Control over the Conclusion and Operation of Treaties," in S.A. Riesenfeld & F.M. Abbott (eds.), *Parliamentary Participation in the Making and Operation of Treaties: A Comparative Study* 261–327 (Martinus Nijhoff, Dordrecht, The Netherlands, 1994).

Trimble, Phillip R. & Weiss, Jack, "The Role of the President, the Senate and Congress with Respect to Arms Control Treaties Concluded by the United States," in S.A. Riesenfeld & F.M. Abbott (eds.), *Parliamentary Participation in the Making and Operation of Treaties: A Comparative Study* 329–382 (Martinus Nijhoff, Dordrecht, The Netherlands, 1994).

Vásquez, Carlos Manuel, "The Four Doctrines of Self-Executing Treaties," 89 *Am. J. Int'l L.* 695 (1995).

———, "Treaties as the Law of the Land: The Supremacy Clause and the Judicial Enforcement of Treaties," 122 *Harv. L. Rev* 599–695 (2008).

Selected Websites Providing U.S. Treaty Texts and Related Treaty Information*

Agreements Negotiated by the United States Trade Representative
    https://ustr.gov/trade-agreements
Avalon Project (Yale Law School)
    http://avalon.law.yale.edu/
Bureau of International Security and Nonproliferation (ISN) Treaties and Agreements (U.S. Dept of State)
    http://www.state.gov/t/isn/
International Judicial Assistance (U.S. Department of State)
    http://www.state.gov/1997-2001-NOPDFS///global/legal_affairs/judicial.html

---

* Adapted from Treaty Research Guide, Georgetown University Law Center.

International Tax Treaties
   http://www.intltaxlaw.com/
Private International Law Database (U.S. Dept. of State)
   http://www.state.gov/s/l/c3452.htm
Treaties in Force
   http://www.state.gov/s/l/treaty/tif/index.htm
United Nations Treaty Collection
   https://treaties.un.org/Home.aspx
U.S. Bureau of Arms Control Treaties and Agreements (U.S. Department of State)
   http://www.state.gov/t/avc/index.htm
U.S. Bilateral Investment Treaties (U.S. Department of State)
   http://www.state.gov/e/eb/ifd/bit/index.htm

Chapter 22

National Security Process: Constitutional Context, Presidential Process, and the Role of the Lawyer

James E. Baker

In this chapter:
Introduction
Defining National Security
Constitutional Framework and Process
Presidential Decision-Making
The Role of Law
The Role of the Lawyer
Duties of the National Security Lawyer

Introduction

This chapter is about national security process, with particular focus on presidential process. It begins with brief consideration of the meaning of national security; before discussing process, it is useful to define what it is we are attempting to process. The chapter then moves to the constitutional framework for national security decision-making. A brief appreciation of the role of each branch is helpful in understanding the central role of the presidency and therefore the essential role of presidential process. This constitutional context also helps to define the permits and constraints under which that process operates. Constitutional process, in the operation of the separation of powers or principles of federalism, for example, is also national security process where security is concerned. The operation of constitutional checks between the branches can also serve to generate and preserve a more effective executive decision-making process. Section three describes the normative processes presidents use to make national security decisions: the NSC, the HSC, the military chain of command, and *ad hoc* and informal process. Section four offers an assessment of national security process. Each president will define his or her own process; however, practice suggests that there are ingredients organic to good process. Administrations ignore these core ingredients at their (and perhaps our) peril. Good process is timely, contextual, and meaningful. It also addresses or accounts for the pathologies of national security decision-making like speed, secrecy, and the tendency to focus on the immediate security imperative. Finally, section five describes the role of law and of the lawyer in the national security process. In short, the law provides substantive authority to act. It provides essential process. And, it conveys and upholds essential values that contribute to U.S. security as well as liberty.

The point of departure is simple. Good process results in better decisions and better results. It ensures that the correct actors are in the room, with the best information that is available on the timeline presented. It avoids oversights. In a constitutional democracy, it also helps to ensure that decisions are made in accordance with law and by those actors either elected to make those decisions or best situated to do so. Good process also establishes accountability, which in turn improves results.

Process need not be antithetical to timely decisions, operational timelines, or to secrecy. Process must find the right balance between speed and strength, secrecy and input. But process can always meet deadlines. There is no excuse for shortcuts. Process can be made to work faster and smarter. By example, if legal review is warranted but time is short, the attorney general alone can review a matter and, if need be, do so while sitting next to the President in the Oval Office. The problem some policymakers have with process is not process but the prospect of disagreement and debate. Alternatively, it may be that the wrong operators, policymakers, and lawyers are in the room.

Process should be contextual. The military chain of command functions differently than the NSC process. Moreover, task-organized process like that used during the BP oil spill in the Gulf of Mexico or the task force established after the 2010 Haiti earthquake may work better in context than established procedures. At the same time, normative and practiced process will tend to hold up better under the pressure of crisis and speed. Process is also dependent on culture, personality, and style. Therefore, policymakers and lawyers must consciously evaluate their own process and identify any seams between formal and informal decision-making. The President can direct legal review of his decisions but if a national security adviser is not committed to such a review it will not occur in a meaningful manner, if at all.

Defining National Security

A discussion of national security process requires some understanding of the meaning of national security. Heretofore, national security has been defined broadly within the executive branch. For example, President George W. Bush's directive, "Organization of the National Security Council System," states: "National security includes the defense of the United States of America, protection of our constitutional system of government, and the advancement of United States interests around the globe. National security also depends on America's opportunity to prosper in the world economy."[1] The advancement of United States interests and the opportunity to prosper are, of course, broad statements of national security. President Clinton's comparable directive "Organization of the National Security Council" did not define United States national security, but included equally expansive language drawn from the National Security Act of 1947: "The NSC shall advise and assist me in integrating all aspects of national security policy as it affects the United States—domestic, foreign, military, intelligence and economic."[2] With such a point of

---

1. National Security Presidential Directive 1 (NSPD-1) (Feb. 13, 2001), *available at* https://www.fas.org/irp/offdocs/nspd/nspd-1.htm (last visited Dec. 1, 2013).
2. Presidential Decision Directive 2 (PDD-2) (Jan. 20, 1993).

departure, a review of national security process could encompass not only the manner in which the President determines whether to resort to military force, but also how he decides upon the use of the Exchange Stabilization Fund to shore up a foreign currency and the use of tariffs as an instrument of trade policy and domestic constituency.[3] If national security is understood to mean the protection not only of our physical safety, but the security of our way of life, then there is no limit to what might, and should, be understood to relate to national security process.

While there are good arguments why trade, the economy, public health, and the environment are, or can become, national security matters, the purpose of this chapter is to sketch the process by which core defense and foreign affairs issues are addressed within the executive branch at the presidential level. Understanding the framework of that process, readers can decide for themselves which issues should be subsumed within such a process according to their own definitions of national security. In doing so, they will have engaged in one of the first steps in the national security process—deciding which issues should be subject to national security review and decision. Of course, if the issue does not belong in one of the national security processes described below, one must ask where it belongs and is *that* process effective, timely, contextual, and meaningful.

Constitutional Framework and Process

Executive

The focus of this chapter is on presidential decision-making and the role of the lawyer within that process. This reflects the central role of the executive branch and the President in national security policy and the day-to-day management of national security. Alexander Hamilton observed: "It is of the nature of war to increase the executive at the expense of the legislative authority."[4] The "War on Terrorism" like the Cold War before has not diluted this general observation. National security process gravitates to the President in times of crisis and in times of perpetual alert. Whether this result reflects the central constitutional role of the presidency in national security, or is more accurately a reflection of the Executive's functional advantages in dealing with national security crises, or something in-between, is a topic explored elsewhere. Nonetheless, while the President's role may be paramount, as a matter of both constitutional structure and functional practice, the President remains subject to the constitutional check of the Congress and the more latent safeguard of an independent judiciary.

Of course, much of national security process is legislative in design, as presented in framework statutes like the National Security Act of 1947, as amended, the Foreign Intelligence Surveillance Act, and the Goldwater-Nichols Act.[5] And, even where presidents

---

3. Academics and commentators, less bound than executive bureaucracies by the correlation between mission statement and budget and policy reach, define national security both broadly and narrowly. *See, e.g.,* WALTER N. LIPPMAN, U.S. FOREIGN POLICY: SHIELD OF THE REPUBLIC 51 (1943); JOSEPH J. ROMM, DEFINING NATIONAL SECURITY: THE NONMILITARY ASPECTS (1993); ROBERT D. KAPLAN, THE COMING ANARCHY (2000).

4. THE FEDERALIST No. 8 (Alexander Hamilton) ("The Effects of Internal War in Producing Standing Armies and Other Institutions Unfriendly to Liberty").

5. National Security Act of 1947, Pub. L. 253, 61 Stat. 495, 498 (1947) [hereinafter National Security Act of 1947]; Foreign Intelligence Surveillance Act of 1978, Pub. L. No. 95-511, 92 Stat. 1783 (1978) [hereinafter Foreign Intelligence Surveillance Act]; Goldwater-Nichols Department of Defense

assert a right to define their own processes, such as those employed by the NSC or the military chain of command, the Executive is often influenced, guided, and spurred by congressional enactment or threat of enactment. Presidents and their lawyers are also wise to remember that sustained challenges, like those presented by terrorism, proliferation and rogue states, require sustained responses. The President acts at the zenith of his authority when he acts pursuant to his own authority as well as that provided by or delegated by the Congress.

Within the executive branch, the majority of national security decisions are taken at the department and agency level, pursuant to statutory and delegated executive authority. So too, the vast majority of presidential decisions are implemented by agency officials. Nonetheless, there is no mistaking that in terms of day-to-day impact, the President remains at the center of the national security process. This reflects the importance of the institution of the presidency not just in the United States but on the world stage. The President alone can speak on behalf of the United States in a way that congressional and other national leaders can not. As important, it is the President who holds authority over the tangible constitutional tools to shape policy and respond to crisis as Chief Executive, Commander in Chief, and pursuant to his foreign affairs powers. In addition, in times of crisis it is the President who often decides whether and how to use the national security tools that are the product of legislative authorization and appropriation. Finally, the modern presidency daily addresses modern modes of violence, which offer little opportunity for deliberation or debate both because of the consequences of their use and the rapidity of their deployment. This has been manifest with respect to nuclear weapons since World War II, but it is also true of counterterrorism and nonproliferation operations where rapid, clear, and competent decisions can save thousands, if not hundreds of thousands, of lives. This may also mean that meaningful congressional participation in the national security process, as a practical reality, must occur before the crisis in a prospective manner rather than during the crisis when executive actors and energy will focus elsewhere.

The President's role is the product of law. The Constitution, for sure, is the first source of the President's national security authority *and* process. Congress has also placed the President at the head of the national security table. The National Security Act of 1947 envisions a national security policy process revolving around the President.[6] Statutes also require the President to play a central role in implementing policy. The President alone, for example, can authorize covert action, invoke the emergency economic powers of IEEPA, or exercise the most important waiver provisions of the Foreign Assistance Act allowing for certain emergency or extraordinary expenditures and drawdowns.[7]

Congress

At the same time that the Constitution and statute empowers the President, it also delimits his authority, most notably through the formal and informal exercise of national

---

Reorganization Act of 1986, Pub. L. No. 99-433, 100 Stat. 992 (1986) [hereinafter Goldwater-Nichols Act].

6. National Security Act of 1947, Pub. L. 253, 61 Stat. 495, 498 (1947).

7. 50 U.S.C. §3093(a) (Supp. I 2013), *available at* http://uscode.house.gov/view.xhtml?req=granuleid:USC-prelim-title50-section3093&num=0&edition=prelim. This provision was previously codified as amended at 50 U.S.C. §413b (a) (2006), but was editorially reclassified to 50 U.S.C. §3093(a), effective May 20, 2013; International Emergency Economic Powers Act, 50 U.S.C.A. §1702 (2012) [hereinafter IEEPA]; Foreign Assistance Act, 22 U.S. Code §2364(a) (2012) [hereinafter Foreign Assistance Act].

security powers that are both separate and shared between the executive and the legislative branches. This constitutional structure alone dictates that national security processes account for, and provide for, the meaningful interplay between branches. This includes mechanisms to implement enumerated authorities and, as importantly, to carry out the myriad of informal contacts between the political branches that serve as the ball bearings between the political branches of government. Indeed, a national security lawyer will spend much of his or her time providing advice on just how these various powers interlock and where they are truly independent.

It is axiomatic that the process of national security includes the manner in which the Congress exercises its enumerated powers, for example, legislates in the area of national security, advises and consents on nominations and treaties, and so on. Congress's most important national security tool remains the power of the purse. While conditional funding authorizations and appropriations are subject to interpretation, funding terminations are not. The exercise of such authority can be a blunt instrument of policy removing executive opportunities for nuanced policy. However, with the exception of funding dictates precluding the President from actually exercising plenary and enumerated constitutional functions, even the most ardent adherents of executive authority recognize Congress's budget authority; thus, absolute funding cut-offs for military deployments have largely been debated on the policy merits rather than based on their legal validity.[8] Further, it is Congress's budget authority and to a lesser degree appointments authority, which ultimately underpins Congress's ability to participate as an effective partner in the informal process of consulting, signaling, and validating, which oils the gears of constitutional process between the political branches.

Congress also plays an important part in framing through statute the President's national security process. The National Security Act frames the National Security Council model of decision-making. By further illustration, the Goldwater-Nichols Act legislated a structure of command within which the President exercises his constitutional authority as Commander in Chief.[9] This structure is accepted and works, in part, because its adoption does not reflect a single constitutional perspective about the power of the President or the Congress, but accepts that both have a constitutional role to play in defining a functional command framework.

Other statutes create particular processes for addressing specific national security regimes. In the wake of the Snowden disclosures, the Foreign Intelligence Surveillance Act of 1978, as amended, is perhaps the most visible, if not transparent, such mechanism. Similarly, the Foreign Assistance Act[10] provides the basic framework and process for the administration of foreign aid. The Export Administration Act[11] (which, though lapsed,

---

8. *See* Special Foreign Assistance Act of 1971, Pub. L. No. 91-652, § 7, 84 Stat. 1942, 1942 (1971) (Prohibiting the use of any funds for the introduction of U.S. troops to Cambodia or to provide military advisors to Cambodian forces); Second Supplemental Appropriations Act of 1973, Pub. L. 103-139, § 307, 87 Stat. 99, 129 (1973) ("None of the funds herein appropriated under this Act may be expended to support directly or indirectly combat activities in or over Cambodia, Laos, North Vietnam and South Vietnam or off the shores of Cambodia, Laos, North Vietnam and South Vietnam by United States forces, and after August 15, 1973, no other funds heretofore appropriated under any other Act may be expended for such purpose."); Department of Defense Appropriations Act, Pub. L. 103-139, § 8151, 107 Stat. 1418, 1475 (1993) (Limiting the use of funding in Somalia for operations of U.S. military personnel only until March 31, 1994 after which President would have to seek Congressional authorization of additional expenditure of funds).

9. Goldwater-Nichols Act, *supra* note 5.

10. Foreign Assistance Act, *supra* note 7.

11. Export Administration Act of 1979, 50 U.S.C. App. § 2401 et seq. (2003).

has been replicated by executive order) and the Arms Export Control Act[12] do the same in the area of foreign trade. In each instance, executive regulations provide a further gloss and process upon the legislative frame. Finally, generalized grants of substantive authority like the International Emergency Economic Powers Act[13] are implemented through specific executive branch applications (i.e., a common law of actual practice).

In the day-to-day management of national security, Congress also plays an informal role in validating, testing, and ultimately holding the executive branch accountable for its national security decisions. One might be inclined to describe this as an exercise in legislative oversight. But that is too formal a term, invoking images of committee hearings, subpoenas, and a certain amount of theater, which are part of the national security process but fail to convey the extent to which the separate and shared powers are exercised through an informal process of communication between the executive branch and the legislative branch. This is an essential unwritten ingredient in the national security process. This informal process of consultation, notification, and validation occurs in all substantive areas of government, but is nowhere more important than in the area of national security where much is intended to remain out of the public eye. It is Congress that in theory, and some would say in practice, is truly representative of the public in assessing and ensuring that national security decisions are made in accordance with law, reflect national values, and are effective in reaching stated objectives. Of course, the interplay between the political branches also engages the process of politics and partisanship. Where that process begins and ends is a subject for a different chapter or perhaps a different book. Laws like the Hatch Act, which prohibit partisan political activity by certain executive employees, seek to ensure that this latter process does not begin too soon, nor take root in the federal security bureaucracy.

Judiciary

The judiciary's role in national security process has historically been perceived as intermittent. Application of prudential and legal doctrines, such as the political question doctrine, justiciability, deference, standing, and the case or controversy clause of the Constitution, delimit the judiciary's role. These doctrines of judicial restraint are reinforced by, or perhaps intertwined with, a conventional wisdom that courts are less well equipped to address questions of national security, with their deliberate and layered process of decision. The judiciary also applies a different methodology for regulating and evaluating information than that associated with the short timelines, secrecy, and incomplete information frequently associated with national security process.

The judiciary's role also reflects a well-founded judicial hesitance to decide issues not presented for resolution. The common law moves incrementally because judges are consciously careful not to advance unintended rules of law; judges often approach those statutory and constitutional questions relevant to national security with the same measure of caution. In contrast, executive and congressional actors often employ bold statements of intent reaching beyond the immediate moment to the day beyond, so that foreign and domestic actors will have no doubt as to the government's intentions. A Monroe Doctrine would not likely emanate from the judicial branch.

The limited role of courts in the national security process also bears philosophical content. Article III courts, with their lifetime tenure, are generally viewed as less democratic

---

12. Arms Export Control Act of 1976, 22 U.S.C. § 2778 (2000).
13. IEEPA, *supra* note 7.

in form than the Congress or the Office of the President. Certainly the Article III judiciary is, and should be, the least responsive to electoral influence. Therefore, as a matter of democratic theory there are good arguments for making the role of the judiciary secondary to that of the political branches in an area fraught with metaphorical and real danger.

Nonetheless, courts play a more active and continuous, albeit structured and limited, role in national security process than is generally appreciated. First, a handful of cases continue to play a defining role in shaping the structure of national security government and the arguments around which the political branches address that structure. These cases include *Youngstown, Curtiss-Wright, Nixon, Holland, Goldwater* and *Egan*.[14] However, the fact that *Totten*, an 1876 case arising out of the Civil War, remains good law, ultimately reflects the limited role precedent and courts play in the day-to-day grind of the national security process.[15]

More often, courts play a latent but continuous role in ensuring the separation of powers between branches. By example, Congress cannot effectively exercise its constitutional functions without information from within the executive branch. At the same time, the executive branch cannot effectively function without absolute control over certain information. Where there is an impasse, the risk of a defining and unfavorable judicial decision as well as the public and political consequences of litigation create important incentives to compromise. Thus, the judiciary ultimately provides an adjudicative safeguard and incentive for the informal process of constitutional interchange between political branches to work, ensuring from the public's perspective that both branches might perform their constitutional functions. In this respect, even where courts decline to decide an issue, they are nonetheless active participants in the legal outcome. As John Norton Moore and Louis Henkin have argued, justiciability might better be viewed as a deferential application of substantive law rather than a doctrine of abstinence. In declaring a matter nonjusticiable, courts are accepting the legal status quo as within constitutional bounds, without determining whether the status quo is reflective of the preferred legal outcome or most reflective of constitutional or statutory intent.

Second, courts are obviously central to the application of criminal law, which often carries national security consequences based on the subject of jurisdiction or the manner in which personal jurisdiction over the accused was obtained, through the application, or more likely potential or threatened application, of the Ker-Frisbie, Rochin, or Toscanino doctrines. Moreover, each branch of government plays a central role in extradition practice, with courts validating the identity of the subject as well as the applicability of a treaty the Senate has otherwise approved, before the Secretary of State determines whether there are foreign policy or other reasons that should bear on the extradition decision. So too, the military justice system addresses cases with national security implications as the cases involving Abu Ghraib, the Fort Hood shootings, and Chelsea Manning indicate. Indeed, the military justice system is addressed to both justice and good order and discipline, a critical component to maintaining an armed force capable of effective military action. Military commissions, as well, play a direct albeit limited role in adjudicating a select number of post-9/11 terrorism cases.

---

14. Youngstown Sheet & Tube Co. v. Sawyer, 343 U.S. 579 (1952); United States v. Curtiss-Wright Exp. Corp., 299 U.S. 304 (1936); United States v. Nixon, 418 U.S. 683 (1974); State of Missouri v. Holland, 252 U.S. 416 (1920); Goldwater v. Carter, 444 U.S. 996, 100 S. Ct. 533, 62 L. Ed. 2d 428 (1979); Dep't. of Navy v. Egan, 484 U.S. 518 (1988).

15. Totten v. United States, 92 U.S. 105, 23 L. Ed. 605 (1875).

Third, the Congress has amended the Foreign Sovereign Immunities Act[16] to provide for U.S. federal jurisdiction over suits against terrorist states and state violations of human rights. This places Article III courts in the mix of bilateral relationships between the United States government and current and past state sponsors of terrorism and torture. As the executive has taken pains to point out, judicial judgments against foreign states may carry national security implications by removing from the executive branch potentially important elements of leverage in bilateral relations. Nonetheless, this jurisdiction is exercised largely outside the reach of executive branch actors and influence.

Fourth, courts, or in particular two special courts, play an integral role in national security process in the area of foreign intelligence surveillance, where a special *ad hoc* court, the Foreign Intelligence Surveillance Court (FISC), hears government applications for electronic and physical searches for national security purposes. In turn, the Foreign Intelligence Surveillance Appeals Court may hear government appeals of FISC decisions, although from only one side, the presumption being that the target of surveillance is unaware of its existence or contemplation.

Finally, the courts are a frequent and traditional participant in the management and control over national security information. This is most apparent, and public, in the adjudication of Freedom of Information Act lawsuits, which can push the Government to disclose national security programs and documents.[17] It is also evident in the review of the increasing number of executive branch assertions of the state secrets doctrine, where courts have varied in the manner of their deference and review.[18] Less frequently, the judiciary participates in disputes between the political branches over access to specific national security information as well as the retention and/or publication of national security information by individuals invoking a First Amendment right to disclose the information. This judicial role has remained relatively static for thirty years. The benchmark national security cases about release of information still date to the 1970s and 1980s.[19]

September 11 and the U.S. response to September 11, including the advent of Guantanamo Bay as a detention facility and symbol, has tested and changed the judicial landscape in the field of national security. To start, the role of the Courts in national security has never been as central in shaping national security law and process beyond the traditional role of adjudicating cases. This is most evident in the case of the Foreign Intelligence Surveillance Court, which has seen its membership grow from seven to eleven and the number of Foreign Intelligence Surveillance Act (FISA) orders from 934 to 1,588 from 2001 to 2013.[20] However, it is also evident in the habeas review of Guantanamo detainees. The role of the military and military justice system in addressing events that

---

16. Foreign Sovereign Immunities Act of 1976, 28 U.S.C. § 1601 et seq. (2003).

17. New York Times Co. v. United States Department of Justice et al., Nos. 13-422 and 13-445, 2014 WL 2838861 (2d. Cir. June 23, 2014).

18. Laura K. Donohue, *The Shadow of State Secrets*, 159 U. Pa. L. Rev. 77-216 (2010).

19. Egan, 484 U.S. 518 (executive authority over national security information); Nixon, 418 U.S. 683 (executive privilege); New York Times Co. v. United States, 403 U.S. 713 (1971). *See also* Near v. Minnesota, 283 U.S. 697 (1931) (prior restraint and national security). Such case law suggests that constraints on the judiciary are not only legal and/or self-imposed prudential considerations, but also reflect hesitance on the part of the executive to invite an expanded role for the judiciary, notwithstanding the advantages that may accrue in a particular scenario.

20. 2001 FISA Annual Report to Congress (April 29, 2002); 2013 FISA Annual Report to Congress (April 30, 2014); *available at* http://fas.org/irp/agency/doj/fisa/#rept.

shape national security and perceptions of the United States overseas is more evident today as well. Although it is clear courts will continue to play an important role, it is less clear whether courts will continue to expand their reach into the review of operational matters as have courts in the United Kingdom and Israel, or whether traditional doctrines of restraint will prevail. The state secrets cases suggest not, with one central exception.

One area where courts will continue to play an active role in national security process is in adjudicating individual rights in homeland security context in both civil and criminal context. Whether by statutory design or inevitable constitutional process, national focus on homeland security will increase opportunity for friction between rights and protections afforded persons within the United States and necessary national security measures. This in turn will increase the opportunity for courts to adjudicate the balance between due process and the executive branch exercise of national security authority. Historically, where courts have addressed the domestic repercussions of national security decisions, they have shown less deference to the executive than when addressing decisions with primary impact abroad.[21] Moreover, at home legitimate national security measures will be evaluated in the construct of a different due process tradition and regime. The public's access to information more immediate to their lives, and even survival, may be viewed through new prisms. In any event, courts may be thrust into a more active role or, at minimum, face the justiciability bridge more often.

Other Constitutional Actors

A discussion of national security process in constitutional context must also address other governmental actors as well as non-governmental actors, including the media. The media is, of course, a significant independent source of oversight and a primary conduit by which national security information and decisions are communicated to the public. While scholars, officials, and journalists will continue to debate particular applications of the First Amendment, there is no serious debate that these traditional roles associated with the media are part of the constitutional framework of national security process.

Policymakers and observers are less likely to identify the daily influence of the media as part of the national security process itself. Nevertheless, on a given day, principals and their staff will devote a significant segment of their time to reading, digesting, and responding to the media. Thus, the national security day for many decision-makers will begin with a review of overnight intelligence product and then move to the drafting and clearing of press guidance. Throughout the day, policymakers will seek to influence the policy process through contacts with the press.

In addition, media inquiry often serves as a catalyst to decision by forcing policymakers to address issues on a timeline driven by the competition between media outlets for stories rather than considerations of policy effect. For example, a policy proposal disclosed in advance of decision may compel decision-makers to advance consideration of that proposal lest domestic and international actors respond to the proposal as if it were a decision already taken. Of course, policymakers will incorporate the media wittingly and unwittingly into their process of decision-making with just this effect in mind. Media disclosures will also generate governmental responses and the adoption of new processes either to curtail

---

21. *See, e.g.,* United States v. United States District Court (Keith), 407 U.S. 297 (1972); Zweibon v. Mitchell, 516 F.2d 594 (D.C. Cir. 1975) (en banc), *cert. denied,* 425 U.S. 944 (1976). *Compare* Curtiss-Wright, 299 U.S. 304, *with* Youngstown, 343 U.S. 579.

disclosure or respond to the loss of information. The more rapid the media play, including the play on social media, the more room there is for error and process dysfunction.

National security process recognizes that the media plays this same role worldwide, even if not pursuant to the same ground rules. This is manifest in executive decisions to form standing media "war rooms" to address the worldwide news cycle and thirst for information. However, too often the media plan is relegated to the role of annex, rather than an essential component of the decision itself. The communication of a decision can be as important as the decision itself, and good process will include the communication of decision as part of the decision itself rather than as an activity that catches up with the decision after the fact. A well-spoken, well-timed, or misspoken, statement from the President may influence events more than a hundred principals' meetings.

Finally, and most significantly for the purposes of this chapter, national security process is also driven by the desire of policymakers to control the flow of information to the press (offense) and to avoid unauthorized disclosures of information (defense). In this sense, the media may drive decision-makers to dysfunctional process. The legitimate thirst for secrecy may overwhelm the instinct for good government. Policymakers will insist on ever-smaller decision-making processes or, dangerously, move outside the process itself. Key actors may be omitted. A good process is one that acknowledges these tensions and, where essential, moves up the chain of command rather than outside the process, to ensure both a necessary exchange of views and secrecy.

In the context of homeland security, it is also evident how many additional constitutional actors or potential actors may participate in U.S. national security process. This includes, for example, the integration of state and local actors into U.S. responses to man-made and natural disasters. In context, they are constitutional actors, because their roles may be defined or delimited by the 10th Amendment and associated principles of federalism and preemption. Private actors like NGOs may not be formal participants in the national security process; however, in any given area they may play critical roles. Nowhere is this more evident than during relief operations, where NGOs often control a majority of the resources available for distribution and may have a monopoly of access to the affected area. NGOs have also played an important role in shaping the Ottawa Treaty on Land Mines and the Rome Treaty establishing an International Criminal Court. The governmental actor proceeds at his peril if he does not consider relevant NGO views and capabilities as part of the process of policy development and implementation. In homeland security context, trade associations and private health care organizations also play vital roles in shaping legislative responses and providing so called critical infrastructures. Of course, where the federal government seeks to define responsibilities through other than market mechanisms, Fifth Amendment due process issues may well arise. So too, with the advent of the TSA and USG metadata search capacities all Americans are in theory participants in the national security process.

Presidential Decision-Making

Formal Framework

Having placed the President's national security process in constitutional context, it is now time to describe that process. Presidents generally use one of three procedural mechanisms to make national security decisions: The National Security Council and process, the military chain of command, and the Homeland Security Council. In addition, Presidents will make decisions using *ad hoc* and task organized processes. Finally, decisions are often made through informal process, like a telephone call or a hallway chat. This latter "process" is really not process, but it can reflect no less a presidential decision than a written order depending on the circumstance.

Each President defines his or her own national security process within the constitutional and statutory framework of national security decision-making. This is usually accomplished at the outset of an administration by presidential directive and more importantly, the formation of practice. Foremost, such a directive will include the President's intent for the operation of the National Security Council system.

The NSC

The National Security Act of 1947, as amended, established the National Security Council (NSC). The Act provides that the "function of the [c]ouncil shall be to advise the President with respect to the integration of domestic, foreign, and military policies relating to the national security so as to enable the military services and the other departments and agencies of the Government to cooperate more effectively in matters involving the national security."[22] By statute, the council is comprised of the President, Vice President, Secretary of State, and Secretary of Defense. In 2007, The Secretary of Energy was added as a statutory member of the NSC. The Director of National Intelligence (DNI) and the Chairman of the Joint Chiefs of Staff are so-called statutorily designated advisors to the NSC, "subject to the direction of the President,"[23] in their respective areas of expertise.[24] This statutory distinction reflects actual practice as well as a tradition, founded in the culture of the armed forces and the intelligence community. The DNI and the Chairman provide professional expertise and advice to the policy process, but they do not drive that process nor set policy. The manner of application of this tradition, of course, varies on the personality of the participants and expectations of the President. In practice, Presidents include non-statutory members of their national security teams on their NSCs. Indeed, the answer to the question—who are the Members of the NSC?— is whoever the President wants. Presidents have uniformly taken the view that they can meet with and seek advice from whomever they may designate. In practice, the core members of the NSC are the President, the Vice President, the Secretary of State, the Secretary of Defense, the DNI, the Chairman of the Joint Chiefs of Staff, and the National Security Adviser. And, in the words of presidential directive as well as statute: the Council "shall be the principal forum for consideration of national security policy issues requiring presidential decision."[25]

In addition to referring specifically to the council, "the NSC" also describes the process by which the President's national security team advises the President, and by which the

---

22. National Security Act of 1947, Pub. L. No. 80-253, § 101, 61 Stat. 495, 496 (1947) (amended 1949).

23. 50 U.S.C. § 402 (2003).

24. To the extent the President is addressing the structure of his own *immediate* staff within the Executive Office of the President, as a matter of constitutional separation of powers doctrine, he is free to do so as he sees fit without congressional direction, so long as that staff is not in fact exercising statutory authority, or executive authority. So too, the President can determine with whom he meets. Thus, Congress provided that the Chairman and DCI may, subject to the direction of the President, attend and participate in meetings of the NSC.

25. Presidential Policy Directive 1, Organization of the National Security System (Feb. 13, 2009), *available at* http://fas.org/irp/offdocs/ppd/ppd-1.pdf [hereinafter PPD-1].

President makes national security decisions. "The NSC" is also used to describe the President's immediate national security staff. Therefore, lawyers must caution precision when referring to *the* NSC. Reference to "the NSC," without more, invokes the constitutional authority of the President, as well as the statutory and delegated constitutional authority that the Secretary of State and Secretary of Defense bring to bear. In contrast, the authority of the NSC *staff* extends only to advising and assisting the President in performing his duties. Of course, this advice and assistance is accompanied with all the force of persuasion one bears when one communicates the decisions and policy intentions of the President.

In addition to being driven by the President and the NSC, the national security process is driven by the Principals Committee (PC) and Deputies Committee (DC).[26] As both PPD-1 and NSPD-1 state, the NSC Principals Committee serves as "the senior interagency forum for consideration of policy issues affecting national security, as it has since 1989."[27] The Deputies are considered the senior sub-cabinet interagency forum for doing the same. Among other things, the Principals Committee and Deputies Committee frame issues for the President or resolve issues that do not require presidential decision. The Deputies Committee is also directed to "review and monitor the work of the NSC interagency process;" to "focus significant attention on policy implementation;" and, is "responsible for day-to-day crisis management, reporting to the National Security Council."[28] As the nomenclature suggests, these committees are comprised of the President's principal national security advisors, for example, the statutory members of the NSC like the Secretary of State, and designated members like the Assistant to the President for National Security Affairs (heretofore, the APNSA has been designated to chair the Principals Committee). The Deputies Committee in turn is comprised of the primary Deputies to the Principals (for example, the Deputy Secretary of Defense); however, some flexibility is provided for Deputies participation given the range of issues considered, the time commitment involved, and the role that some Deputies play in serving in effect as Chief Operating Officers of their respective agencies. This is perhaps best illustrated by the addition of a second Deputy Secretary at the State Department in 2000 largely to address the need to have both a Deputy to interact with the NSC process and a Deputy to take primary responsibility for running the Department. In contrast, it is unusual to substitute for Principals; a Principals meeting is effective, in part, because participants can immediately and definitively express the views of their respective agencies at the Cabinet level. The Principals and Deputies Committees typically meet on a biweekly basis. However, typical is atypical.

---

26. NSPD-1 lists as regular Principals Committee attendees: The Secretary of State, the Secretary of the Treasury, the Secretary of Defense, the Chief of Staff to the President, and the Assistant to the President for National Security Affairs. The DCI, Chairman of the Joint Chiefs of Staff, the Attorney General, and Director of OMB are listed as attendees for meetings pertaining to their responsibilities. The NSPD includes additional members, such as USTR and Commerce, when international economic issues are on the agenda. The directive also states that the Chief of Staff and National Security Adviser to the Vice President shall attend all meetings of the PC as will the Deputy National Security Advisor, who serves as executive secretary. The Counsel to the President shall attend any meeting, in consultation with the APNSA, he deems appropriate. PDD-2 establishing the PC for the previous administration included comparable membership, but also included the U.S. Representative to the United Nations, but did not include the Chief of Staff to the Vice President. In practice, members of the PC and DC may choose not to attend a particular meeting, and officials who are not designated members of these committees will often attend when needed. A copy of NSPD-1 is available at: http://www.fas.org/irp/offdocs/nspd/nspd-1.htm.

27. NSPD-1, *supra* note 1.

28. PPD-1, *supra* note 25.

The best of organized intentions often gives way to the reality of need, causing the Principals and Deputies to meet on a daily basis or even more frequently as events dictate.[29]

The work of the National Security Council and the Principals and the Deputies Committees is fueled by the briefing papers and issue papers generated by individual agencies and interagency working groups, who with mixed success, advance their products to the NSC executive secretary for timely dissemination to participants before meetings. By Presidential direction and longstanding practice, a meeting of the Principals or Deputies Committees can be called from above, requested by a participant, or generated at the suggestion of subordinate staff.

In addition to defining committee structure, the President will also promulgate a series of directives, which are used to review and to establish presidential policies. In contrast to executive orders, the majority of Presidential national security directives are classified and, therefore, remain unknown to the public.[30] These directives are no less binding on the executive branch than executive orders, although they are often less formal and may offer more in policy framework than declaratory direction. Moreover, in the case of closely held directives, as a practical matter, they may in reality only direct those employees with knowledge of their existence.

Among other things, national security directives are used to establish policies and create decision-making frameworks in particular areas.[31] For example, a directive may designate a lead agency responsible for a specific task, which in theory and sometimes in practice will head off in one presidential sentence thousands of hours of bureaucratic battle. Some presidential policy directives remain applicable from administration to administration;[32] however, the majority are rescinded in favor of new directives more closely tracking the policies and bureaucratic structure of each new administration. For a lawyer, trying to determine which directives have been rescinded, or rescinded in part, between administrations will make a tough title search seem routine.

Harder to define on paper are those issues that should or must come to the President for decision. Three factors weigh heavily in this determination. As a matter of constitutional and statutory law, some decisions *must* come to the President. For example, while lawyers may debate the scope of the President's authority as Commander in Chief, few lawyers seriously debate that it is the Commander in Chief and not the Secretary of Defense or a combatant commander who must in the first instance authorize the entry of U.S. forces

---

29. Put directly, it may not be an efficient use of the President's time to participate in meetings developing policy options until those options are sufficiently defined for decision. Moreover, at the policy development stage, policymakers may alter the manner of their input in the presence of the President by toning down criticism of alternate views or seeking to anticipate the President's own view and arrive there first. The President is then either briefed orally (usually by the Assistant to the President for National Security Affairs, a.k.a. the National Security Advisor) or in writing using either an information or action/decision memorandum. By volume, the majority of presidential decisions are taken in writing; however, much of the most significant work occurs in meetings with the national security team or with select members from the team.

30. The Federation of American Scientists maintains a website with a list of presidential directives and provides on-line access to publicly available directives. *See Official Intelligence-Related Documents*, FEDERATION OF AMERICAN SCIENTISTS, http://www.fas.org/irp/offdocs.

31. Known in the Obama, Bush, and Clinton administrations as Presidential Policy Directives; National Security Presidential Directives; and Presidential Decision Directives, respectively.

32. *See, e.g.*, Exec. Order No. 12,333, 46 Fed. Reg. 59,941 (Dec. 4, 1981), *amended by* Exec. Order No. 13,470, 73 Fed. Reg. 45,325 (July 30, 2008).

into combat.[33] Whether additional decisions also require the Commander in Chief's authorization will depend on the scope of the President's initial authorization and prudential factors.[34]

Certain statutes require presidential decision as a threshold for use. The National Security Act of 1947 as amended, for example, provides that only the President can authorize covert action by signing a finding. In more mundane fashion, certain statutes require that waiver authority can only be exercised by the President. At times this may seem ministerial and unduly burdensome on a Chief Executive already overextended. On the other hand, the process of generating a report for presidential signature will ensure senior agency review as well as interagency review, and therefore help to ensure that the policy proposed in fact is supported by the President's senior advisors and national security agencies and that the product itself is qualitatively appropriate for presidential signature.[35]

Second, there are matters of policy that *should* come to the President in light of their importance. For example, the Secretary of State has ample legal authority to engage in diplomacy as the Secretary of State, but it is not likely that the Secretary would table a Middle East peace initiative without the President's concurrence. In contrast, the Secretary might conclude a model extradition treaty or postal treaty of which the President may not be aware until he transmits the treaty to the Senate for advice and consent, and even then knowledge may be constructive rather than actual. In addition, there are matters for which the President will be held accountable whether or not he in fact makes the decision. For example, the President may not be involved in a particular tactical deployment of U.S. armed forces (e.g., a security patrol in Afghanistan); however, if there is a U.S. casualty the President may be asked to defend the policy that put the soldier in harm's way. Therefore, the President, or more likely his immediate staff, may insist on being kept informed of small details of policy implementation that may be perceived in the field as micromanagement rather than necessary information flow.

Finally, the President sits at the crossroads of executive branch decision-making. Where there are differences of view between agencies and/or Cabinet officers, the President alone may have the legal, moral, or policy authority to resolve those differences. (Obviously not all differences between agencies warrant or are appropriate for presidential decision.) As importantly, where many national security issues were previously perceived as issues solely for the statutory members of the NSC to address (for example, arms control), most national security matters today cut across a wide array of functional and agency disciplines (for example, homeland security). Even where there is agreement among agencies on how to proceed, the President alone may carry the authority and policy weight to quickly integrate a decision into positive bureaucratic control. Nowhere is this more evident than in the area of intelligence. While the DNI is given responsibility for leading and coordinating

---

33. The President may, of course, do this in an anticipatory manner, as in the case of authorizing U.S. forces to respond in self-defense.

34. *See* James E. Baker, *When Lawyers Advise Presidents in Wartime: Kosovo and the Law of Armed Conflict*, NAVAL WAR C. REV., Winter 2002, at 11.

35. In this way, the sometimes maligned War Powers Reports considered by some as ministerial that are required by the War Powers Resolution within 48 hours of a triggering event, can serve a useful procedural function, even if the events reported on have been carried in the media for the proceeding 48 hours with specificity. Sincerely addressed, the reporting elements cause executive officials to consider issues like the duration of stay and the potential for reinforcement at the outset of a deployment and to articulate their best judgments, at least internally, in a manner they are willing to put in writing to the President. This can result in a lowest-common denominator consensus external product, but it also can generate timely consideration of difficult policy issues within the executive branch that otherwise might initially be avoided.

the seventeen components that comprise the intelligence community, all but one of those components falls within the bureaucratic jurisdiction and control of other Cabinet officers (the Secretary of Defense (National Security Agency, National Geospatial Intelligence Agency, National Reconnaissance Office, Defense Intelligence Agency, Army Intelligence, Navy Intelligence, Marine Corps Intelligence, Coast Guard Intelligence); the Attorney General (FBI National Security Branch, Drug Enforcement Agency), or still other Cabinet agencies (Department of Homeland Security Office of Intelligence and Analysis, State Bureau of Intelligence and Research, Treasury Office of Intelligence and Analysis, Energy Office of Intelligence and Counterintelligence)). When one adds to this smorgasborg the reality that intelligence is not defined by component but as information that informs decision, prevents surprise and attack, and helps to predict the future, we are talking about information that is collected by virtually every agency of government. The coordination and leadership of this process requires a Chief Executive, and that means the President, who might be described as the "constitutional DNI."

The Military Chain of Command

A second normative mechanism by which the President makes national security decisions is the military chain of command. In fact, there are two such chains of command. The operational chain of command runs from the President, as Commander in Chief, to the Secretary of Defense, and from the Secretary of Defense to the Combatant Commander for the geographic or functional area of responsibility. There are currently nine combatant or unified commands responsible for different geographic regions of the world or for providing a functional capacity: United States Africa Command; United States European Command; United States Central Command; United States Pacific Command; United States Northern Command; United States Southern Command; United States Strategic Command; United States Special Operations Command; and United States Transportation Command.

The administrative chain of command runs from the President, as Commander in Chief, to the Secretary of Defense, to the Service Secretaries, and from the Service Secretaries to the Chiefs of Staff of each military service. It is the responsibility of the administrative chain of command to recruit, train, equip, and house each of the component services until such time as units or individuals from that service are assigned to the operational chain of command for warfighting or deployment purposes.

The Chairman of the Joint Chiefs of Staff is the principal military adviser to the President, the National Security Council, and the Homeland Security Council. Although not formally in the chain of command, as a matter of practice, operational command is usually exercised through the Chairman to the combatant commanders and from there down the chain of command. The Vice Chairman serves as the Chairman's Deputy and like the other Joint Chiefs provides both operational and administrative military advice to the President and Secretary of Defense. But there is no question in law and practice that the Chairman is the principal military adviser.[36] This is law and this is practice. But it was not always so.

The operational chain of command is a product of the Goldwater-Nichols Act of 1986, which placed in statute a normative chain of command and designated the Chairman as the President's principal military advisor. The Act recognizes the President's authority as

---

36. 10 U.S.C. § 151(b)(1) (2011).

Commander in Chief by expressly defining the chain of command, "except as otherwise directed by the President." That takes care of the constitutional concern that would arise if Congress purported to tell the Commander in Chief exactly how or through whom he or she must exercise constitutional command, for while there is room to debate what war power the President derives as Commander in Chief, there is no debate that the Constitution textually assigns to the President the role of command. However, presidents have generally adopted and operated using the chain of command as set out in the Act. It is functional and it is amenable to quick adjustment as context dictates.

As is often the case with framework national security statutes, the Goldwater-Nichols Act resulted from a confluence of historical events that spurred a parallel legislative process. In particular, the command portion of the Act responds to real and perceived failures in command and control manifest during the Iran Hostage Rescue Mission of 1980, the Beirut Barracks Bombing of 1983, and the Grenada operation of 1983. Among other things, during the Iran mission each of the services insisted on a share of the operation without there being an existing command structure to provide and allocate the capabilities required for the mission nor a single definitive military voice. Absent the presence of a Marshall or a Grant, the law at the time permitted what amounted to Command by Committee, which in turn diluted advice, responsibility, and effect. Likewise, the postmortem from Beirut revealed a chain of command that diluted responsibility and was not responsive to changes on the ground. Presidential direction flowed through multiple layers of headquarters before reaching the Marines in the field with a commensurate loss of clarity in mission purpose and responsibility between the operational and administrative elements of command. Of course, legislators also had in mind varied perspectives on how the Joint Chiefs of Staff performed during the Vietnam Conflict.

A number of recurring process questions arise in the context of the operational chain of command. First, when should or must the President, as Commander in Chief, versus the Secretary of Defense or versus a combatant commander authorize an action? Second, to what extent should the President exercise either operational or administrative command? How much is too much and how much is too little presidential involvement? In this regard, it is easy to leap, or perhaps gravitate, toward one camp or another, or as likely, one party affiliation or another. A few words of caution are warranted.

Those who would eschew presidential involvement, perhaps with images of President Johnson micromanaging the Vietnam Conflict from the basement of the White House, should recall that civilian control of the military is a bedrock constitutional principle exemplified by the designation of the President as Commander in Chief. One might also wonder what might have been had Lincoln not been an active Commander in Chief during the Civil War, spurring the Union on with such actions as the firing of General McClellan and the appointment of General Grant. Likewise, General MacArthur might well have initiated a third world war had the U.S. used nuclear weapons against China during the Korean War as MacArthur so publicly advocated. Instead, he was fired by President Truman with the support of Chairman Omar Bradley. On the administrative side, one might remember as well that it was President Truman who ordered and insisted upon the integration of the Armed Forces in 1948, not the military services. At the same time, Presidents and their staff must remember that as with all national security process, the key is timely, contextual, and meaningful process and decision.

A third process question raised by the Goldwater-Nichols framework is whether it drives the interagency process in a dysfunctional direction. Restated, does the Act encourage best practice and whole of government approaches, or does it create artificial distinctions between military actions under Title 10, intelligence actions under Title 50, and diplomatic actions under Title 22, making it harder to pool resources or establish unity of command and policy intent? In related manner, does the Act and the resulting process place too much authority in the hands of the Secretary of Defense, who rests atop both the operational and administrative chains of command? Here too, perspectives may depend in part on one's perspectives about individual secretaries of defense and the decisions with which they are associated. One might also consider whether this is a leadership issue, a resources issue, or a process issue. Where one Department controls the vast majority of personnel and financial assets that can be brought to bear in any national security context — as the saying goes, when you are a hammer, every issue may look like a nail. Is it the Secretary of Defense that has too much legal authority, or the disproportionate distribution of resources that distorts a whole of government approach?

The Homeland Security Council

The terrorist attacks on the World Trade Center and the Pentagon on September 11, 2001, brought the need for vertical as well as horizontal national security process into national and tragic prominence. Harold Lasswell in an earlier context described the sharing of danger throughout society as the socialization of danger. The socialization of danger, he wrote, was a permanent characteristic of modern violence.[37] But it was not for America, until September 11. The socialization of danger after September 11 has made ordinary citizens participants in the national security process in a way not previously experienced. In addition, it has brought federal agencies not previously associated with national security, like FEMA and the Centers for Disease Control, to the forefront of national security planning and response. September 11 has also caused the President and the Congress to look with fresh and keen eyes at the government's process for addressing homeland security, testing the manner in which information is shared, resources allocated, and perhaps the level at which fundamental decisions of life and death heretofore made by the President are taken.

Urgency was placed on finding mechanisms to coordinate the Nation's vertical response to terrorism and natural disaster from the federal government, to state government, to local government, to first responder. Over a decade later, the outlines of a lasting presidential architecture have emerged. This includes the Homeland Security Council (HSC), modeled on the National Security Council, but with domestic security and emergency focus. And, it includes the creation of multiple procedural centers, including the National Counterterrorism Center and the Joint Terrorism Task Force concept to meaningful link Washington decisions to the field and facilitate the flow of information up and down and across bureaucratic institutions.

The statutory members of the HSC are the President, the Vice President, the Attorney General, the Secretary of Homeland Security, and "such other persons as the President may direct." The Chairman of the Joint Chiefs of Staff and the DNI are so-called statutory advisors to the HSC in their respective fields of expertise and responsibility. As with the NSC, in practice, the President, which means his security staff, invite such persons to HSC meetings as they deem necessary. In this regard, it is noteworthy that with the participation of the Secretary of Homeland Security, twenty-two so called legacy agencies are represented at the table as well. Pictures of Homeland Security Council meetings

---

37. Harold D. Lasswell, *The Garrison State*, 46 Am. J. Soc. 455, 459 (1941).

reveal that the normative members of the HSC include the Attorney General, the Secretary of Homeland Security, the Assistant to the President for Homeland Security and the Director of the FBI.

A number of process questions arise in the context of the HSC. Should there be an HSC or just an NSC and, if there is an HSC, when should it rather than the NSC meet? This is more than a semantic issue as the membership of each Council is distinct. Moreover, when the NSC or the HSC meet as Principals without the President, the members are distinct indeed. Both President Bush and President Obama have opted to have both an NSC and HSC, with the HSC appearing to take the lead on matters of terrorism and domestic security and disaster, to include the protection of critical infrastructures like cyber space and the power grid. The question then becomes how to ensure a seamless policy and decision-making transition between the NSC and the HSC with respect to matters that do not recognize national boundaries and present seamless threats.

One way to do so is with the participation of overlapping Principals and Deputies, as is the case with the DNI. But this is dysfunctional because while the issues presented by terrorism, proliferation, and cyber space are geographically seamless, in bureaucratic organization they engage different policy actors and bureaucracies. Another way to ensure seamless connection between the NSC and the HSC is to link the processes at the top in the form of the overall decision-maker, the President. But this is too great a burden for one person, especially when seamless implies the fusion of intelligence, law, and resources and not just strategic policy. Another way to do so is by linking the two Councils at the bottom through the use of a common staff.

Under President Bush, the NSC and the HSC had distinct staff. Under President Obama, the staff has been combined into one, first known as the National Security Staff and as of 2014, again the NSC staff. This helps to address the seam by having one staff directorate handle intelligence, law, legislative affairs, and media relations among other functions. However, it opens the door to the risk that with a finite staff, emphasis will be placed on the traditional NSC security functions at the expense of less traditional homeland security functions. A safeguard is found in self-awareness about the risk. It is also found in making transparent the nature and membership of the NSC staff so that members of the public, the Congress, and the media can judge for themselves whether the balance is well-struck. And, there is safeguard in having an Assistant to the President distinct from the National Security Advisor who is responsible for the homeland security functions and thus has a stake in their proper and efficient staffing. Another solution, of course, is to ensure that distinct issues warranting specialized attention or *ad hoc* mechanisms have their own defined presidential processes.

Ad Hoc Presidential Process

In addition to the three normative processes of presidential decision-making identified above, the President may establish or rely on *ad hoc* decision-making processes in particular contexts. *Ad hoc* means a process that is formally established and known, but established for a limited time or purpose. By definition, if the process engaged is *ad hoc*, it is not normative in design. However, a number of common themes emerge. First, many *ad hoc* processes have as their purpose the coordination of policy or response in areas that cut across traditional national security bureaucracies and boundaries and engage new agencies and actors. Thus, presidents have found it useful to appoint senior advisors to marshal the government's efforts in such areas as climate change, energy security, nonproliferation, and trade. These advisors are known both figuratively and literally as Czars as in the case of the original and perhaps most enigmatic of such figures, the Assistant to the President for National Drug Control Policy or Drug Czar.

Second, such *ad hoc* arrangements are often addressed to matters of finite duration requiring extraordinary energy and presidential validation, such as a steering group or "war room" to advance a specialized legislative agenda or treaty, like NAFTA.

Third, there are some matters that are sui generis for which an existing process template does not exist, but necessarily involve a whole of government approach and thus the necessity of presidential leadership and control. This might occur in the context of a crisis response at home or overseas. Perhaps the most dramatic example of this is the process qua chain of command established to oversee the government's response to the BP oil spill in the Gulf of Mexico, which involved unconventional security actors such as the Secretary of Energy and the Coast Guard as lead agency.

Finally, there is a long "tradition" of presidential security process going to ground where the issues are viewed as too sensitive for normative NSC consideration. Where operational decisions are being made out of the White House, one might well look for such an *ad hoc* but routinized process. Such "process" can be hard to detect but it is there. Here one might consider the so-called "small group" for addressing counterterrorism operations during the Clinton administration, the Bush Administration's handling of detainee policy, or the "targeted killing" process during the Obama administration. Where such *ad hoc* processes are used, special attention to the elements of good process as well as the pathologies of national security decision-making is warranted.

The National Security Council Staff

The central and essential role of the President in national security decision-making necessitates the existence of a national security staff to advise and assist the President in the performance of his national security functions. Since 1947, this has meant the National Security Council staff.[38] Indeed, the National Security Act provides: "The Council shall have a staff to be headed by a civilian executive secretary...."[39] As a matter of practice, the staff functions at the direction of the National Security Adviser and Deputy National Security Advisers, with the Executive Secretary more akin to a Chief of Staff, Staff Secretary, and Jack-of-all-trades bound in one.[40] The NSC staff is organized into functional (for example, transnational threats, nonproliferation, and administration) and geographic (for example, Near East Asia, Europe, and Africa) directorates (a.k.a. offices), which largely parallel the structure at the State Department and the Office of the Secretary of Defense. With some exceptions, a Special Assistant to the President and Senior Director heads each office.[41] Subordinate policy staff members are known as directors. Directorates typically range in size from two to five persons. A directorate of ten is an empire. In

---

38. On October 8, 2001, President Bush established the Homeland Security Council (HSC) within the Executive Office of the President. Exec. Order No. 13,228, 66 Fed. Reg. 51,812 (Oct. 8, 2001).

39. 50 U.S.C. § 3021(c)(Supp. I 2013), *available at* http://uscode.house.gov/view.xhtml?req=granuleid:USC-prelim-title50-section3093&num=0&edition=prelim).

40. The statutory language is important because it precludes military officers from serving in the position of Executive Secretary. It is also a legal basis for the Executive Secretary testifying before the Congress regarding the budgetary needs of the NSC as an institution.

41. Senior Directors are, in theory, equivalent in grade to Departmental Assistant Secretaries, without of course having been through the confirmation process. But that is like saying a member of the SES is equivalent to a general. Only a general is a general, as only generals and soldiers well know.

addition, the NSC staff consists of a dedicated cadre of career and detailed support staff, an executive secretariat staff, and the situation room staff. In addition to providing the site for Principals and Deputies meetings, the situation room includes an intelligence analysis and support section and a communications capability offering the President global connection to world leaders, commanders, and officials. Traditionally about two-thirds of the policy cadre of the NSC staff is drawn from the career diplomatic and military ranks with the remainder true political appointees drawn from think tanks, academia, and campaign staffs. Of course, the President is not bound as a matter of law to fill his immediate NSC staff using a particular staff profile so long as candidates meet the necessary requirements for government service and budget constraints. In addition, there are legislative limits (usually encouraged by agencies sub silencio) on the number of detailees that can serve at the NSC at any one time.

In 1962, when McGeorge Bundy served as APNSA, the NSC staff consisted of twelve.[42] The policy staff now numbers approximately 150. The expansion in the number of NSC staff is arguably traced to the expansion in the President's national security responsibilities as well as the manner in which national security has been defined by successive administrations. For example, one would not have expected President Kennedy's staff to include a directorate dedicated to counterterrorism. However, such a directorate has existed at the NSC at least since the 1980s. Moreover, the presidency has moved from the episodic crisis and response to terrorism, to a constant state of readiness and perpetual command over the policy instruments to counter terrorism. While there may be more than one reasonable view as to when this process started, without question it was underway after the first World Trade Center attack in 1993. The NSC staff function in this area grew accordingly. The office handling terrorism became the NSC's largest policy directorate and for the first time a Senior Director for Public Health was added to the staff. After the August 1998 embassy bombings, counterterrorism became a daily, central, omnipresent feature of the national security presidency. September 11 in turn ensured that counterterrorism would remain a permanent and defining fixture of the presidency in the same way that atomic weapons permanently transformed the presidency after World War II.

As the NSC's responsibilities, and correspondingly as the NSC staff's responsibilities have grown, the functional requirements have grown as well, as reflected in the existence and size of the administrative, press, and legislative offices. The legal office is a product of the Iran-Contra affair and a recommendation by the Tower Commission; however, the office has its genesis in the longstanding recommendation of scholars like John Norton Moore, who saw the position as an essential conduit of legal advice to the President and a check, not a source of rival legal advice and bureaucracy as some agencies first saw it. Arguably, the size of the NSC staff also reflects the inherent tendency for those who seek to influence and implement policy to expand their responsibilities by expanding their capacity to work, which means more staff. However, one needs to exercise some caution in looking at numbers.[43] The critical test of numbers is not quantum but quality. Is there

---

Personality and background also play a large part in determining just where a member of the NSC staff fits into the government.

42. Under President Nixon and President Ford, the professional staff numbered fifty and under President Carter, thirty-five. JOHN TOWER, ET AL., REPORT OF THE PRESIDENT'S SPECIAL REVIEW BOARD II-4 (1987) [TOWER COMMISSION REPORT].

43. At the outset of his first administration, President Clinton announced a 25% reduction in the size of the White House staff, including the NSC staff; however, this directive was implemented with a series of lawful, but creative methods to find slots that did not count against the personnel cap, such as career training programs and certain details from agencies. In the George W. Bush Administration, some functions previously assigned to the NSC were handled by the Homeland Security Staff, also

sufficient staff to fulfill the mission promptly without creating a bureaucratic layer between Cabinet agencies and the President?[44]

Whatever the differences in style and framework between Presidents, recent manifestations of the NSC process have gravitated to certain common characteristics as well as shared tensions. The core duties are not defined in statute or by directive. They are a derivative of the Constitution and the National Security Act. NSC staff members advise and assist the President by serving as the President's eyes and ears within the policymaking bureaucracy. They write information and action memoranda to the APNSA and the President. As needed, they coordinate with other White House staff (for example, speechwriters coordinate with the Head of Communications, the press office with the Press Secretary, and so on). They prepare and coordinate input for PC and DC briefing papers. Harder to quantify is the staff's critical role in serving as an engine of government, ensuring that disparate elements of the government come together in a coordinated fashion and on a timeline that meets the President's needs and objectives.

Fundamentally, the success or failure of the NSC staff hinges on its ability to lead and coordinate the interagency process while also serving as honest brokers of policy and legal input. Policy staff may prefer to become known in their role as independent contributors to national security policy, but the process ultimately depends on a willingness to subordinate their own perspectives and accurately communicate not just their own views but those of Cabinet officers and agencies to the President. Where a Principal has dissented from a policy option, the staff must honestly communicate this dissent to the President through the APNSA.[45]

Under the Hatch Act and Hatch Act Reform Amendments of 1993, employees paid by the National Security Council, as well those employees who are paid by the State Department, Defense Department, Central Intelligence Agency, and military officers on detail to the NSC, are prohibited from engaging in partisan political activities, which are understood as activities intended to advance (or impede) the election of candidates for partisan political office.[46] Policy positions may be associated with a political party, but that does not inherently make a policy dispute subject to the Hatch Act, unless the policy positions are themselves advocated or abjured in connection with a partisan political campaign. Although the law and corresponding regulations offer little in black letter clarity, by longstanding practice and interpretation NSC staff has not assisted in writing or reviewing campaign materials and speeches, including those materials used by the

---

within the Executive Office of the President, while other functions like Public Health were relocated to agencies.

44. One test of this balance is the amount of travel performed by the NSC staff independent of the President's and National Security Advisor's own travel. An NSC staff that has time to travel apart from presidential missions may be moving away from its core mission of advising and assisting the President.

45. This is all the more essential, because in most cases it must be done on faith in those cases where the written views of Principals are not attached to presidential memos. Unlike national security agencies, the National Security Council is not subject to the Freedom of Information Act (FOIA). Armstrong v. Executive Office of the President, 90 F.3d 553 (D.C. Cir. 1996). Therefore, NSC staff are constrained in sharing drafts of presidential memoranda with agencies, which would become subject to FOIA as agency records retained by agencies. Moreover, agency documents are subject to a different quantum of constitutional review when possible claims of executive privilege are evaluated in response to congressional requests for documents. Participants in the presidential decision-making process might well be less candid if they knew their views, particularly in draft, would become public knowledge. Participants might eschew the controversial option with an eye toward the public's response.

46. Hatch Act Reform Amendments of 1993, Pub. L. No. 103-94, 107 Stat. 1001 (1993).

President. Nor have they spoken at or attended political events (except in the capacity of NSC representatives on call to the President for the briefing of national security issues that may arise during his absence from the White House). The Situation Room and facilities are not used to forward political materials to the President. What the staff can do is provide off-the-shelf policy materials to the President's staff engaged in political events applying a general rule of thumb: if it is not material that would be provided to a public requester, then it probably is not appropriate to share with campaign staff or to use at a campaign or fundraising event. Thus, NSC memoranda should not incorporate partisan political factors or considerations.

As a matter of process, application of the Hatch Act ensures that the President and his senior staff have the benefit of national security advice, free from partisan political input. It also protects career and non-political staff from being compelled to work on partisan political campaigns. In contrast, the President, who is accountable for his political and policy views through the electoral process, and employees paid by the White House Office (which would include the majority of the President's senior staff) are not legally barred from such partisan political considerations. As a longstanding tradition, most National Security Advisers and their deputies (if they are White House Office payroll employees) have refrained from any visible participation in political events, including mere attendance at political events. However, the APNSA is available (and should be available) as an interface between the policy components of the White House and the partisan political components to ensure that the President's political words both accurately track policy and do not unwittingly impact policy. Whether the APNSA's role should extend beyond this point is a question of personal style for the APNSA as well as one's view on the importance of U.S. national security policies being viewed as nonpartisan.

Assessment and Observations

White House or Cabinet Government

There are a number of inherent tensions in the President's national security process. In an age of modern communication there are few decisions, including tactical decisions, over which the President and White House might not exercise some control, should they choose to do so. This is not new. President Ford's White House communicated directly with an Air Force pilot regarding whether or not to disable the rudder of a fishing boat transporting the Mayaguez crew in the Gulf of Thailand.[47] What is new is the range of matters that the President and his immediate staff can directly influence using secure communications that can reach into almost every military rucksack or diplomat's briefcase. Moreover, the more the twenty-four-hour news cycle and the public hold the President and the White House accountable for national security events worldwide, the more the White House feels pressure to control the outcome of those events, even if such control is dysfunctional at the tactical level.

Commentators often paint White House control in broad strokes of approval or disdain. (Usually the latter as successful White House interventions are likely to go unnoticed as part of normal process or are deemed unworthy of comment absent White House efforts to get their story out.) The right measure of presidential control is contextual. An essential component of national security process is finding the right balance between operational efficacy and presidential accountability for national security decisions that reflect the

---

47. RALPH WETTERHAHN, THE LAST BATTLE 97–99 (2001).

President's policy direction. In some cases, efficacy may mean more presidential control, for example, where a definitive change in policy is warranted or commanders do not agree on how to proceed. In other cases, presidential control can delay decision or deprive a decision of the advantage in perception and immediacy afforded the actor on the ground. In addition to contextual factors specific to the issue addressed, the measure of White House control and participation will also depend on intangible and static factors like the personality and style of the President and his confidence in his subordinates.

Observers also suggest that there is a tension between Cabinet government and a strong NSC staff and process. In other words, the President must select from two models of national security government. One model posits a Cabinet government, comprised of principal agency officers like the Secretaries of State and Defense, who advise the President and implement policy using Cabinet agencies and officers. The other model is an NSC model where decision-making authority and implementation is not only exercised by the President, but is also ceded (or surrendered) by agencies to an ever expanding and powerful NSC staff. This NSC staff is viewed as moving beyond advising and assisting the President into gray areas of actual policy control, direction, and implementation.

As a matter of theory, the President might be able to ignore his Cabinet and rely exclusively on the NSC staff. In practice, there is not a zero-sum clash of models. Recall that the President gets the process he tolerates or he directs. The same is true of the Cabinet principals who serve on the NSC. What varies is the difference in tone, emphasis, and balance between administrations. Individual staff will vie for policy impact and will seek to expand their reach by expanding their staff. Some NSC staff will seek to arrogate to themselves agency (and presidential) authorities; there is risk in NSC staff stepping beyond the bounds of facilitation and coordination. But when evaluating the NSC staff and process, one needs to account for inductive reasoning. One's perspective of the process is often driven by one's reaction to a particular incident or a particular personality and not the overall process. Oliver North is not indicative of the NSC process; he is indicative of a failure in process. Individual Senior Directors may overreach. Others may not reach far enough. But absent a conspiracy of evasion, this can only be done with the concurrence, or acquiescence, of the Cabinet principals who might later be heard to complain about loss of authority. One should not lose sight of the fact that the President's principal Cabinet officers and *the* NSC are one and the same.

The President must have a staff to advise, assist, facilitate, package, and feed the Principals and Deputies Committees and the Oval Office in-box. Whether this staff goes further to exercise an independent policy voice and is allowed to challenge and not just test policy options proposed by agencies is a question of tone and leadership. As a matter of law, policy will continue to be implemented pursuant to presidential authority, or agency authority, by agency officers (unless the President directs otherwise). The key to this national security process is finding the right balance between having enough staff to assist the President and not so much staff as to create an additional layer of bureaucracy that impedes rather than facilitates decisions or that permits NSC staff to move beyond the role of advice and facilitation. This balance cannot be dictated by design alone. It must reflect the daily observation of the National Security Advisor, the President, and the Principals on how the process is working. Each administration will make different adjustments in reaching their judgment on how best to find this balance.

Informal Process

Studies of process tend to focus on formal arrangements, such as directives, structure, and numbers; however, a President's decision-making process is also defined by the nature of its informal arrangements. The majority of contact between the President's national security advisors is not at Principals' meetings but during innumerable daily conversations on secure telephone lines. Cabinet officers regularly send the President updates, sometimes called "night notes." They visit one-on-one (or more likely with the APNSA present) and regularly confer by telephone. A President who insists on *ad hoc* meetings may not receive the same quality of briefing as one that adheres to a strict schedule. At the same time, a President whose door is not figuratively open may miss the critical moment for input or decision.

The success or failure of decision-making will depend on the success or failure of this informal process as much as it depends on the formal operation of working groups, Deputies Committee meetings, Principals Committee meetings, and Presidential memoranda. Informal process raises numerous test questions. Does it involve the same rigor of analysis and requirement for agreement and dissent as formal process of briefing papers, meetings, and summaries of conclusions will generate? Are the same relevant decision-makers included in the outcome when the informal mechanism is employed as when the formal process is engaged? If not, is the President aware of who is missing and why? Does the APNSA insist on lawyers seeing all memos going to the President? Do the President and his senior advisors tolerate or encourage oral communications that may escape review, result in confusion regarding the scope of decision, and escape accountability? Does the APNSA include lawyers at the beginning of the policy process and not just at the end? Put succinctly, good national security process is as dependent on who the National Security Advisor invites to a meeting or excludes as it is on statutory framework or executive directives mandating a particular process of decision. The success or failure of the national security process depends on the style, discipline, and personality of its participants.

The value of formal process is marginalized if it is circumvented. Will the presence of a Legal Advisor at the NSC prevent an Iran/Contra? No. The presence of a President or APNSA in the White House who insists on the full integration of a legal advisor in the decision-making process will prevent an Iran/Contra. However, good process will more readily and timely identify where there is leadership weakness, or perhaps the necessity of legal change.

Good Process Is Timely, Contextual, and Meaningful

If a lawyer wants to clear a national security room, he need only mention the necessity for "process." The word invokes delay, debate, and visions of ponderous legal meetings and memos. One sometimes hears the phrase, "if you want to kill an idea, give it to the lawyers." However, the problem is not process or lawyers. Good process leads to better and more timely results. Bad process leads to delay, dysfunction, and disclosure.

A good process is timely, contextual, and meaningful. Timely process means planners, policymakers, and lawyers operate on a timeline that tees up decisions so as to influence events rather than react to them. This in turn means that often these actors will by necessity act with incomplete information and knowledge of the facts. A good process, therefore, is one that rapidly fuses information and advice from all relevant actors as well as identifies what is not known or who is not participating.

Contextual process means tailored and appropriate to the task at hand. By example, the process for handling covert action should be different than the process for handling a military operation. So too the process for handling export licenses should be different from the process for handling criminal prosecutions with national security importance. The task and the skill is to determine that mode of decision-making or conferral that will be most effective for the situation presented. That might mean a conference call, an NSC meeting, an oval office meeting, or a working group. Frank Carlucci, who served as one of President Reagan's National Security Advisors, noted the impossibility of working with feuding Cabinet officers, until he figured out that if he met privately with just the Cabinet officers over breakfast once a week, without an audience and without an agenda, animosity was swept aside. The same principle applies to national security lawyering. Not every legal question should result in a memo, not every question should be met with an oral rather than written response. The key is to find and use the appropriate means in context.

Meaningful process means a process that includes relevant actors, but not gratuitous actors and persons along for the ride. This process invites dissent. Dissent permits mitigation, by identifying policy and factual objection before decisions as opposed to "told-you-so" moments after decisions. It also identifies potential sources of bureaucratic resistance. Meaningful process is one that identifies those persons or bureaucracies accountable for the advice, the facts, or the decisions made. Accountability breeds responsibility, which in turn engenders care. Meaningful process also brings in critical actors, including lawyers, while policy is under consideration rather than after it is made. Otherwise, there is less opportunity to guide to preferred outcomes and means rather than taking yes and no positions.

Good Process Addresses the Pathologies of National Security Decision-Making

Good process also addresses the endemic pathologies of national security decision-making. There are at least four such pathologies in constant play. First, there is secrecy. Where process is secret, facts are secret, and decisions are secret, the government is more likely to miss essential arguments and facts in the making of policy. So too, one hand of government may not know what the other hand is doing. A good process is one that identifies and closes these gaps. It is also one that is honest about what or who is missing, so that decision-makers can choose to proceed or wait to close the gap.

Second, the sometime necessity of speed can lead to error and mistake. This is intuitive. A good process, therefore, builds in checks, like a requirement for a more senior official to review a matter, or an accountable process of decision, which tends to focus the attention of the persons responsible. Role-playing is also a check, by which I mean the designation of a person to play the role of devil's advocate or the inclusion of a player without a stake or hand in the outcome.

Third, as Justice Jackson noted in *Youngstown*, in Government "[t]he tendency is strong to emphasize transient results upon policies ... and lose sight of the enduring consequences, upon the balanced power structure of our Republic."[48] Although he was addressing the interpretation of law, the principle is well suited to national security generally. Where national security is concerned, especially the safety of American persons, property, and interests, the focus on solving the immediate problem or threat is fierce, as it should be. But it cannot overwhelm the capacity of decision-makers to consider the longer term consequences of the decisions and actions they take. Here too, a process that identifies this risk and invites role playing to mitigate it, is desirable.

Finally, and related, there is an inherent tendency to overreach in national security. This derives from the national security imperative. The greater the threat the more compelling is the imperative to act. For example, if the security specialist is hunting for

---

48. Youngstown, 343 U.S. 579 at 634 (Jackson, J., concurring).

a mole at the CIA he will inevitably investigate twenty innocent people too many than run the risk of falling one mole short. Similarly, the security specialist trying to prevent a terrorist attack will inevitably extend rather than curtail a wiretap, or err on the side of investigation. That is the nature of the security mission. It is also human nature to avoid the greater the risk. One should want such energy and reaching where national security is at stake. The point is to get there first with an appropriate internal or external process that identifies this risk, and through independent validation, stops and guides the deployment of finite security resources back to more effective and lawful use. If the lawyer or decision-maker never says no, it may be that the security specialist is not trying hard enough, or that the lawyer has been captured by the mission rather than the law.

The Role of Law

In a constitutional democracy, decisions are made according to law. That means that sound national security process must incorporate timely and competent legal advice. It also means that national security lawyers need to understand and articulate the role of law and how it contributes to national security.

National security law plays three critical purposes, each will advance national security if the law is wielded effectively. Law provides substantive authority to act. It facilitates process, both between branches of government and within each branch. And, it conveys fundamental legal as well as policy values, as reflected in the Constitution's commitment to the principles of liberty and the common defense. For example, the humanitarian treatment of prisoners and detainees is embedded in both domestic and international law as a legal and humanitarian value; but it is also a national security value, because such treatment is more likely to engender the gathering of intelligence and in reciprocal fashion the humane treatment of one's own captured forces.

Understanding these purposes, lawyers will be better prepared to withstand the pressures of practice and articulate to decision-makers why law can serve to advance actual national security concerns as opposed to only being followed as a matter of principle. In turn, policymakers will better understand that the law is not just a series of random obstacles. Rather, the meaningful and timely application of law leads to wiser and more enduring security results.

The Role of the Lawyer

Knowing law's mission, the lawyer might more effectively engage the national security process to provide advice. In some cases, legal review is dictated by statute, as in the case of the Foreign Intelligence Surveillance Act,[49] which requires the Attorney General, or his designee, to approve requests for electronic surveillance or physical search before they are submitted to the FISA court. In other cases, the President has directed a specific process to ensure senior legal review in areas historically prone to legal peril or inherently legal in content. For example, following the initial Iran-Contra revelations, President Reagan issued NSDD 266 (Implementation of the Recommendations of the President's

---

49. Foreign Intelligence Surveillance Act, *supra* note 5.

Special Review Board) followed by NSDD 286 (Approval and Review of Special Activities) requiring that the Attorney General concur in any proposed covert action. Subsequent Presidents have directed comparable legal review. In still other cases, a relevant Cabinet department will prescribe government wide process as in the case of the Circular 175, which describes the interagency process for obtaining authority to negotiate international agreements.[50] However, the majority of legal advice within the national security process is not required by statute or directive, but is the product of practice, custom, and the personal interchange between lawyer and client.

There is no single "best" template for such a process. Indeed, one scenario is likely to be so different from the next in terms of context that it would be dangerous to generalize—or to insist that one legal template fit all national security concerns. For example, except at the highest level of government, the lawyers that review military targets will be different than the lawyers who address funding issues. Each of these lawyers will perform under different sets of pressures, applying different legal regimes of differing clarity, subject to different measures of scrutiny and consequence. One has to maintain situational awareness to find the measure of process and approval that ensures law is applied in a manner that is faithful to constitutional, statutory, and executive dictates *and* meets operational timelines. As with the policy process, the key is timely, contextual, and meaningful process. Therefore, as with the NSC staff itself, there will always be some tension as to who should see what when. But if there is no right way to lawyer, there is a worse way, which is to exclude relevant lawyers from the process or for the lawyer to wait to be asked a question.

Lawyers are not always readily accepted into the decision-making room. This reluctance reflects concerns about secrecy, delay, and lawyer creep (the legal version of mission creep, whereby one legal question becomes seventeen, requiring not one lawyer but forty-three to answer). Of course, decision-makers may also fear that the lawyer may flatly say no to something the policymaker wants to do. So, too, there is a propensity in government to adopt smaller and smaller decision-making circles in the interest of operational security. The circle can become too small. A decision-making process limited to Cabinet principals may ask too much of too few if those principals are to address issues of policy and law on operational time lines. Similarly, a lawyer immersed in the policy outcome may subconsciously, or quite consciously, color advice working back from yes, rather than forward from the law. Good process requires an objective lawyer who calls the law as he or she sees it and is committed to upholding good process.

Each President and agency head will adopt his or her own approach to legal advice, ranging from avoidance to active engagement. As a result, the manner in which lawyers provide their advice and at what stage of the process will vary; however, the essential participants will remain the same. Traditionally, these lawyers for the President have included the Counsel to the President and the National Security Council Legal Adviser. Practice has varied as to the relative role and weight of each and the extent to which other White House lawyers, such as the Deputy White House Counsel, are involved in national security decision-making as well.

The NSC Legal Adviser should perform three basic functions: provide independent advice to the President, National Security Adviser, and NSC staff on constitutional,

---

50. For example, the Attorney General's guidelines on the handling of FOIA requests and the Department of State Circular 175 Procedures on Treaties provide for an internal executive branch process (the "Circ. 175 process") for authorizing the negotiation and signature of international agreements, including required review by the Office of the Legal Adviser, within the Department of State.

statutory, and international law; serve in the role as general counsel to the NSC, reviewing personnel actions, responding to discovery requests, and administering the NSC's ethics program; and be responsible for coordinating the interagency legal process, ensuring that presidential decisions have appropriate interagency legal review and that the Principals and Deputies Committees have timely legal input from relevant governmental lawyers. Where necessary, this is accomplished by generating interagency legal papers as background or by attending Principals and Deputies meetings to spot issues, answer questions, and guide policymakers to lawful options and preferred outcomes. (The role of the Legal Adviser in this latter function has varied from administration to administration, depending on, among other factors, the personality of participants and the extent to which the office is perceived by agencies as facilitating national security process or as a source of rival legal advice.) The Legal Adviser's relationship with the Counsel to the President has also varied from administration to administration and from Counsel to Counsel. During the Clinton administration, the Legal Adviser reported to the National Security Adviser but operated in coordination with, rather than as part of, the White House Counsel's Office. In the Bush and Obama administrations, the office has been incorporated into the office of the Counsel to the President.

Oral input, e-mails, succinct summaries and conclusions of law within larger memoranda, and bullet point papers reflecting interagency legal views remain the principal means of communication. The essential skill of the national security lawyer at the NSC is the ability to spot issues, generate timely advice through consultation with the appropriate governmental experts, and succinctly convey results to senior policymakers without losing essential nuance. In addition, the lawyer who serves as counsel, and not just attorney, will provide legal policy input and address both sides of the issue presented. How to balance the inherent tension between substantive input and speed in each context is the art of performance. Knowing above all else how much you don't know, but knowing where to find it, is the keystone to success.

Traditionally, the Office of Legal Counsel (OLC), within the Department of Justice, has taken the lead on constitutional questions in the national security arena. However, OLC's ability to provide constitutional advice is often dependent on the ability of interagency attorneys to spot the constitutional question in the first instance. OLC historically has applied a more formal process in rendering legal advice outside the Department of Justice than is the norm within the White House or Departments. Absent exigent circumstances, this usually means a written request for views and the generation of a formal memorandum reviewed by at least two deputies (and, on occasion, the Attorney General) prior to dissemination. Such a process improves accountability, where opinions are intended for public dissemination as well accountability increases. However, such a formal process does not always lend itself to national security decision-making. Therefore, the Assistant Attorney General who heads the Office of Legal Counsel, and his Deputies, who historically have alone been able to speak on behalf of the office, must find the necessary balance between a process of quasi-judicial opinion writing and meaningful input to a national security process that must keep pace with world events. One might ask, however, whether OLC places enough emphasis on presenting the arguments on each side of an issue so as to acknowledge the strengths and weaknesses of arguments and better illustrate why the better argument has been selected. Emphasis should also be placed on identifying lawful options and the legal policy pros and cons of proceeding with each.

Within the executive branch, OLC (in conjunction with the Attorney General) is also considered the penultimate arbiter of the government's legal position (short of the President) particularly where there is a difference of view between agencies. As a result, the office may come under considerable pressure from agency counsel, policymakers, and internal clients "to come out the right way." The essential test of the OLC lawyer is to honor the law at the same time that she serves the governmental client. This is, of course, true of any lawyer; however, it is particularly relevant to the Office of Legal Counsel, which can speak with government-wide authority and can be used by agency general counsel and White House Counsel to shield their own views (and efforts to push the envelope) from outside criticism.

At agencies, general counsels serve as the principal agency and departmental legal officers and ultimate arbiter of their agency's legal views. In addition to overseeing the normal legal functions of an agency, such as contracting, ethics, and litigation, the agency general counsel, in conjunction with specific managing and line attorneys, advise the department's principal policy officers on legally available options for accomplishing policy goals. Specific agency general counsel will take on additional responsibilities in substantive areas of law. For example, the State Department generally serves as the lead agency on interpreting international law, while the Department of Defense generally serves as the government's lead agency in interpreting and applying the law of armed conflict. A challenge for agency general counsel is to find the right balance between performing internal agency functions and serving the role of counselor to principal policymakers. Agency counsel also must contend with bureaucracies that rely on written input, e-mail, and personal meetings, making it challenging at times to address sensitive issues. A line attorney in an agency may have a narrower portfolio, such as responsibility for ensuring that the framework statutes and regulatory rules are applied to a particular national security regime, such as export controls. Some functions will automatically gravitate toward lawyers, whether policymakers are willing or not, such as litigation and licensing. Other lawyers must earn their access to the decision process through a steady process of trust and value added. Such is the case for an operational lawyer at the CIA.

Wherever the national security lawyer sits, the best process is the one that engages the relevant expert in the government in a timely manner, and then sifts the advice through more experienced counsel before going to the client. This process works best when, to use Dean Acheson's phrase, lawyers are "present at the creation" of a policy initiative rather than catching up and clearing on finished product.

Duties of the National Security Lawyer

It is axiomatic that the national security lawyer's duty, wherever that person might sit, is to advise decision-makers on applicable law: constitutional, statutory, international and foreign. The national security lawyer does this by guiding decision-makers toward legally available options (although some policymakers might believe the lawyer should merely cast the best legal face on whatever it is the client wants to do). In performing this function in a timely and meaningful manner, the national security lawyer provides for our physical safety and security. In doing it faithfully, based on honest belief on the application of the law, they provide for the security of our way of life, founded on the rule of law. The daily provision of national security legal advice, however, should not overshadow three additional and enduring responsibilities of today's national security lawyer.

Process. Lawyers are often the de facto guardians of national security process. In any given context, the pressure of the moment may encourage short-term thinking and the adoption of process shortcuts. Moreover, the lawyer alone may be sufficiently detached from the policy outcome to identify the enduring institutional consequences of a particular course of action. The lawyer alone may be familiar, and may feel an obligation to be familiar, with applicable written procedures. Process is substance if it means critical actors and perspectives are omitted from the discussion table. In short, lawyers serve constitutional government when they uphold executive branch process, ensuring the President has the benefit of all relevant views unvarnished, no shortcuts, *and* on a timeline that works. They do the same when they insist upon timely and meaningful congressional notification or consultation when required by law or constitutional prudence.

Education. National security lawyers also have a duty to educate. Absent a process of education, the policymaker may respond at the moment of crisis by seeing the law only as something arbitrary that allows or does not allow the policymaker to do what he wants, and thus view the lawyer as the metaphorical "speed bump" on the road to decision or a pothole to be avoided. However, if the lawyer educates on not only what the law is, but why the law is, in other words the purpose of the law and why it advances or impedes security, the decision-maker will want the lawyer in the room. Contextual advice built on a foundation already laid will be more readily absorbed and accepted by policymakers. Policymakers will internalize the parameters of the law and better understand why the law applies the way it does in a particular context. By example, a decision-maker faced with a targeting decision will not readily appreciate the overriding principles of proportionality, necessity, and discrimination if the first time he hears these terms is in a target approval briefing.

Constitutional Values. Most importantly, lawyers must be advocates for the Constitution and not just for their clients. National security lawyers have a responsibility to teach, explain, and apply the Constitution and turn it over to the next watch in as strong a position as they found it. They must be able to recognize and articulate the legitimate constitutional role of each branch in the national security process. Leon Fuerth has offered a principle for national security lawyers built around honor, that the hallmark of a successful national security lawyer is to move forward with honor, under the law, and to approach the job from the perspective of always leaving the law and Constitution intact, with the nation well taken care of.[51] This is a particularly important role, because the Constitution is opportunity and not result. The effective function of checks and balances is not automatic. Constitutional government is a daily grind of contacts and disclosure, none of which will happen without the constant effort of a few persons with the vision and commitment to meaningfully apply the process and substance of law.

National security law practice at the national level involves novel questions addressed under great time pressure involving matters of life and death. There is a natural tendency for each generation of lawyers to feel that they are the first to confront such pressures or the enormity of such pressures. But it is the nature of the practice and not an excuse or explanation for getting the law wrong or bending under pressure. As Alexander Hamilton wrote in Federalist 8:

> Safety from external danger is the most powerful director of national conduct ...
> The violent destruction of life and property incident to war, the continual effort
> and alarm attendant on a state of continual danger, will compel nations the most
> attached to liberty to resort for repose and security to institutions which have a

---

51. Email from Leon Fuerth to author (April 11, 2012) (on file with the author).

tendency to destroy their civilian and political rights. To be more safe, they at length become willing to run the risk of being less free.[52]

It is the national security lawyer's task to alert policymakers to the tension inherent in Hamilton's observation. The national security lawyer must show both sides of every coin[53] and identify the enduring consequences of governmental actions, because as Justice Jackson observed of his own government service, "[t]he tendency is strong to emphasize transient results upon policies—such as wages or stabilization—and lose sight of enduring consequences upon the balanced structure of our Republic."[54] This means not only advising the client on what legally can be done, but on the institutional and constitutional consequences of taking those legally available options.

For some this is hard to do under strong policy pressure and perhaps hardest to do when lives are at stake. But the Constitution was not designed to fail, to safeguard our security at the expense of our freedom, or celebrate freedom at the expense of security. It was designed to underpin and protect us *and* our way of life. National security lawyers must stand in the common defense of both.

It takes moral courage to participate fully and objectively as a lawyer: to say yes, to say no, and more often something in between that guides. But you cannot have law without courage. We may be a government of laws, but "[l]aws are made by men, interpreted by men, and enforced by men, and in the continuous process, which we call government, there is continuous opportunity for the human will to assert itself."[55]

Therefore, law depends on the morality of those who apply it. It depends on the moral courage of lawyers like you who will raise tough questions, who will dare to argue both sides of every issue, and who will insist upon being heard at the highest levels of decision-making and will ultimately call the legal questions as they believe the Constitution dictates and not necessarily as we may want at a moment in time.

This duty should have particular resonance with military and government lawyers who have sworn to "support and defend the Constitution of the United States..., [and to] bear true faith and allegiance to the same...." [56]

In 1916, Woodrow Wilson was asked to speak to the graduating Naval Academy class on the eve of United States entry into World War I. He arrived without a prepared speech. He closed saying:

> I congratulate you that you are going to live your lives under the most stimulating compulsion that any man can feel, the sense, not of private duty merely, but of public duty also. And then if you perform that duty, there is a reward awaiting

---

52. The Federalist No. 8 (Alexander Hamilton).

53. President Lincoln was great, the poet (and lawyer) James Russell Lowell concluded, in part because he was a lawyer *and* a lawyer who saw two sides to every issue. James Russell Lowell wrote: "His experience as a lawyer compelled him not only to see that there is a principle underlying every phenomenon in human affairs, but that there are always two sides to every question, both of which must be fully understood in order to understand either, and that it is of greater advantage to an advocate to appreciate the strength than the weakness of his antagonist's position." James Russell Lowell, *Abraham Lincoln, 1864–1865*, *in* 28 The Harvard Classics, Essays English and American, 429, 440 (Charles W. Eliot ed., 1909).

54. Youngstown 343 U.S. 579 at 634.

55. A. Whitney Griswold, *The Basis of a Rule of Law*, *in* Liberal Education and the Democratic Ideal (Greenwood Press Inc. 1976).

56. 5 U.S.C.A. § 3331.

you which is superior to any other reward in the world. That is the affectionate remembrance of your fellow men—their honor, their affection.[57]

The national security lawyers who are true to this duty will never doubt their role as part of the national security process. While they will not garner affection, they will always have the honor of having supported and defended the Constitution. That is the ultimate duty of the national security lawyer and the purpose behind national security process.

Questions for Discussion

1. Do you agree with the roles, functions and duties of the "national security" lawyer as discussed? What additional roles or duties should or can a lawyer fill in the national security arena? Is it accurate to describe the national security legal advisor as a "speed bump" or "pothole" in making and implementing national security policy?

2. The NSC Legal Adviser performs primarily three basic functions: provide independent advice to the President, National Security Adviser, and NSC staff on constitutional, statutory, and international law; serve in the role as general counsel to the NSC; and be responsible for coordinating the interagency legal process. What other roles and responsibilities would you delegate to the NSC Legal Advisor?

3. Some have argued that the national security process as described is overly complicated, too legalistic, formalistic and unrealistic since each President will choose who to consult on any given issue irrespective of the procedures and processes put in place. Do you agree? If not, what, if anything would you recommend to change the current process and procedures to make it more effective and responsive to the President in the event of a national security crisis?

---

57. Woodrow Wilson, speech to graduating class of the USNA (1916), *in* Lend Me Your Ears: Great Speeches in History 990-91 (William Safire ed., rev. ed. 1997).

Chapter 23

The Law of Foreign and National Intelligence

Richard O.W. Morgan and Jonathan M. Fredman[*]

In this chapter:
Structure of the Intelligence Community
Authorities
Covert Action
Oversight
Conclusion
Selected Bibliography
Annex

In the second decade of the 21st century, the United States Government finds itself confronting a changing international landscape. Long-term threats such as terrorism, weapons proliferation, and rogue nation states remain security challenges, while new threats emerge, including cyber attacks, transnational criminal networks, and pandemic disease. At the same time, the diffusion of information technology has allowed the masses to connect and politically organize, while highlighting the potential for conflict between the values of physical security and personal privacy. In addressing these myriad challenges, policymakers have become ever more reliant on the U.S. Intelligence Community (IC), seeking time-critical information to avoid potential attacks, long-term assessment to avoid strategic surprise, and occasionally options to influence world events in ways in which the hand of the U.S. Government will remain hidden.

However, the heightened profile of the Intelligence Community has renewed debate over the role it should play in a democratic society. The United States is founded on principles of public discourse, limited government, and the rule of law. In contrast, the business of spying must be conducted in secret, lest confidential sources of information be exposed and silenced, or methods of collection rendered useless through manipulation or avoidance. Due to this tension between democratic principles and the clandestine nature

* The authors wish to thank the New York University Center on Law and Security for its support during the drafting of this chapter, particularly Samuel Rascoff, Zachary Goldman, and Emily Baer. The authors also wish to acknowledge those who wrote the chapters on intelligence that appeared in previous editions of this casebook: Daniel B. Silver, Frederick P. Hitz, and J.E. Shreve Ariail. This article does not constitute an official release of CIA information. All statements of fact, opinion, or analysis expressed are those of the authors and do not reflect the official positions or views of the Central Intelligence Agency or any other U.S. Government agency. Nothing in the contents should be construed as asserting or implying U.S. Government authentication of information or CIA endorsement of the authors' views. This material has been reviewed solely for classification.

of espionage, it is often assumed that the intelligence services of the United States operate in a legal vacuum outside the framework of law, and in fact, U.S. intelligence agencies have in the past engaged in activities that were perhaps antithetical to American values, if not illegal.

Nonetheless, the history of U.S. intelligence activities is one of maturing institutions and improved accountability. The IC of the 21st century has become—in the words of a General Counsel of the National Intelligence Agency—a "heavily regulated industry,"[1] governed by constitutional principles, statutory laws, and executive regulations, and subject to a system of oversight involving every branch of government. This chapter provides a brief overview of that regulatory framework; while by no means comprehensive, it is designed to introduce students, academics, and practitioners to the structure of the IC, the authorities it relies on to conduct its operations, and the institutions and actors who seek to ensure that it operates consistent with the law.

Structure of the Intelligence Community

What Is Intelligence?

"Intelligence" is a broad term, with several uses in popular parlance, which may generally be broken down into the *what, how,* and *who* of intelligence. The first use (the *what*) describes those secrets that governments, groups, and individuals endeavor to acquire, and which those same actors work to preclude others from acquiring. Thus, one may refer to the "intelligence" on Chinese foreign policy regarding Taiwan, on the business dealings of an international arms trafficking syndicate, or on the physical location of a notorious terrorist leader. The second use of the term (the *how*) refers to the process by which such secrets are obtained. Accordingly, one may speak of conducting "intelligence" activities in attempting to acquire information about a reclusive regime, or the whole-of-government efforts to anticipate threats to national security. Finally, "intelligence" is often used to refer to groups and individuals that engage in clandestine or covert activities (the *who*), whether or not such activities are designed for acquiring secrets. In this manner, the term is often used as an adjective, such as "the intelligence services," or an "intelligence officer."

Because of the variety of meanings of "intelligence" in vernacular usage, it is essential to define the term, especially when discussing the legal authorities which govern it. Under United States law, the term, when used alone and without modification (as opposed to, say, the "intelligence *community*"), tends to refer to the first usage (the *what*), i.e. secret information that is relevant to national security. More specifically, the term is broken down into two categories, the first of which is "foreign intelligence," defined as "information relating to the capabilities, intentions, or activities of foreign governments or elements thereof, foreign organizations, or foreign persons, or international terrorist activities."[2] Focused on the actions and objectives of non-citizens and those outside the United States, foreign intelligence is thus limited in substantive and territorial scope. For example, foreign intelligence would not generally include primarily domestic threats to public safety, such as non-transnational criminal gang activity or wholly domestic terrorism.

---

1. Rajesh De, *The NSA and Accountability in the Era of Big Data*, 7 J. Nat'l Security L. & Pol'y 301, 310 (2014).
2. 50 U.S.C. § 3003(2).

In addition to foreign intelligence is the term "national intelligence," which includes "all intelligence, regardless of the source from which derived and including information gathered within or outside the United States" that pertains to "threats to the United States, its people, property, or interests," or the "development, proliferation, or use of weapons of mass destruction," or "any other matter bearing on national or homeland security."[3] National intelligence is more inclusive than "foreign intelligence," and potentially may include information derived from domestic law enforcement, and data collected through the normal process of government administration.[4]

The categorization of "foreign intelligence" as essentially a subset of "national intelligence" represents the first of two key conceptual distinctions that are made within the legal design of the U.S. Intelligence Community. There are several rationales for the distinction between foreign and domestic areas of interest, including that the collection of intelligence in a domestic setting is more likely to implicate constitutionally-protected individual rights, and that intelligence efforts outside the jurisdiction of the United States often cannot draw on traditional investigative tools available to law enforcement officials, such as warrants.[5] That said, in the decades since the enactment of the original National Security Act in 1947, which enshrined in statute the distinction between domestic and foreign intelligence, and indeed between law enforcement and intelligence altogether, in many instances the distinction has grown largely illusory: domestic law enforcement tools may be used to gather foreign intelligence (e.g. a grand jury information concerning foreign intelligence may be shared with the IC),[6] and foreign intelligence may lawfully be used in domestic criminal prosecutions.[7] By now, where they are still reflected in U.S. intelligence law, those distinctions usually reflect the continuing legislative and executive balancing efforts to both authorize and circumscribe intelligence activities that may implicate the civil liberties of U.S. citizens and lawful permanent residents (and, increasingly, the civil liberties of foreign nationals as well), while at the same time avoiding erecting artificial barriers to the effective sharing of information relevant to national security with other United States and foreign departments and agencies.

Beyond defining what intelligence is, it is essential to note its purpose. Put succinctly, the purpose of the *collection* of intelligence is to permit its *analysis* and *dissemination* in order to "provide the President, the National Security Council, and the Homeland Security Council with the necessary information on which to base decisions concerning the development and conduct of foreign defense, and economic policies, and the protection of United States national interests from foreign security threats."[8] Intelligence illuminates the context in which policy determinations are made, including the assessment of conditions and the potential consequences of those policy determinations. Accordingly, the *collection* of intelligence per se is only valuable to the extent that it provides the raw material for the knowledgeable *analysis* of that information and *dissemination* to the decisionmakers.

---

3. 50 U.S.C. § 3003(5).

4. *See, e.g.*, Executive Order 12,333 § 2.3(g), permitting the collection of "information arising out of a lawful personnel, physical, or security investigation."

5. *See* Jonathan M. Fredman, *Intelligence Agencies, Law Enforcement, and the Prosecution Team*, 16 Yale L. and Pol'y Rev. 331, 335–338 (1998).

6. Fed. R. Crim. P. 6(e)(3(D).

7. *See, e.g.*, Classified Information Procedures Act, 18 U.S.C. App. § 1 et. seq.

8. Executive Order 12,333, § 1.1. *See also* Office of the Dir. of Nat'l Intel., The National Intelligence Strategy of the United States of America, 2 (2014)(purpose of intelligence is to "inform decisions on national security issues and events"), available at <http://www.dni.gov/files/documents/USNI% 202013%20Overview_web.pdf>.

While it may be tempting to say that "we must have the best intelligence concerning potential terrorist attacks," what is really meant is "we have limited antiterrorism resources, and we must deploy them in the most effective manner—good intelligence will help us decide how to do so."

Furthermore, "finished intelligence" is not synonymous with "raw intelligence." This observation brings us to the second usage of the term "intelligence," i.e. the *how*. The U.S. Intelligence Community defines the production and evaluation of "finished intelligence" to be the result of a six-step cycle, wherein (1) raw information and data is collected, (2) processed into a usable format, (3) analyzed, and (4) disseminated to "consumers" (which may include policymakers, military commanders, other analysts, etc.). The consumers of this finished intelligence then (5) provide feedback to the IC, which uses the feedback to help (6) plan and direct future collection.[9] Thus, "raw intelligence" is the input to the intelligence cycle, while "finished intelligence" is the output. The value-added is a result of the analysis that contextualizes raw data and information; in other words, the process of separating useful information from irrelevant "background noise," connecting the resulting "dots," and providing analytical insight.

Complementing, and in some ways integral to, this intelligence cycle are the conduct of counterintelligence and liaison activities; when authorized by the President, the IC (normally the Central Intelligence Agency) may conduct covert action as well. Under U.S. law, the term "counterintelligence" means "information gathered and activities conducted to protect against espionage, other intelligence activities, sabotage, or assassinations conducted by or on behalf of foreign governments or elements thereof, foreign organizations, or foreign persons, or international terrorist activities."[10] Liaison activities involve IC co-operation with foreign intelligence services "on matters involving intelligence related to the national security or involving intelligence acquired through clandestine means."[11] And "the term 'covert action' means an activity or activities of the United States Government to influence political, economic, or military conditions abroad, where it is intended that the role of the United States Government will not be apparent or acknowledged publicly."[12]

It is essential to note here that effective counterintelligence is essential to the safety of intelligence officers as they collect intelligence, necessary to ensure the credibility and integrity of intelligence assessments, and a vital tool to ensure that intelligence dissemination takes place in a secure and efficacious manner. Likewise, liaison relationships are often a catalyst for collection, enabling the IC to receive information from sources and about targets that would otherwise be inaccessible. Finally, whatever else the purpose of a particular covert action may be, it is often the case that the conduct of covert action provides opportunities for intelligence collection. And the reciprocal is also true: covert action is unlikely to succeed if policy makers and those implementing the activity lack timely and accurate intelligence relevant to the activity and its objectives.

Intelligence is collected through a variety of intelligence "disciplines."[13] For example, if the IC were seeking to better understand the development of a new missile system by

---

9. Office of the Dir. of Nat'l Intel., U.S. National Intelligence: An Overview 4–6 (2013), available at <http://www.dni.gov/files/documents/USNI%202013%20Overview_web.pdf>.

10. 50 U.S.C. § 3003(3).

11. 50 U.S.C. § 3036(3).

12. 50 U.S.C. § 3093.

13. Office of the Dir. of Nat'l Intel., U.S. National Intelligence: An Overview 47 (2013), available at http://www.dni.gov/files/documents/USNI%202013%20Overview_web.pdf; *see also* Richard Morgan, *Latif v. Obama: The Epistemology of Intelligence Information and Judicial Evidence*, 22 S. Cal. Interdisc. L.J. 303, 324–326 (2013).

an adversarial state, it might draw on satellite imagery intelligence ("IMINT") of the military base where the new missiles are located.[14] Additionally, clandestine human sources ("HUMINT") might be recruited, who could provide insider details of the missile program. The IC could also attempt to collect the communications (i.e. "signals intelligence," or "SIGINT") of individuals associated with developing the missile,[15] and detailed technical information about the missile's telemetry (i.e. "measurement and signature intelligence," or "MASINT") could be acquired. Finally, the IC could scour the internet, media reports, academic journals, or trade publications to find publicly available information (i.e. "open source intelligence," or "OSINT") about the missile system. Rather than being redundant, collection on an intelligence "target" through multiple disciplines may provide the IC with a more holistic understanding of the issue, permit the validation of reporting provided through one discipline by comparison to reporting derived from another (in the words of former Director of Central Intelligence R. James Woolsey, "spies tip off satellites, and satellites tip off spies"), and reduce the impact of deception and denial by an adversarial state or group by varying the collection methodologies employed against the target.

The Intelligence Community

Having addressed the *what* and *how*, we now turn to the issue of *who* conducts intelligence. The IC currently consists of parts or all of seventeen federal agencies — and the number continues to grow. Section 3.5(h) of Executive Order 12333 provides that the U.S. Intelligence Community includes:

(1) The Office of the Director of National Intelligence;
(2) The Central Intelligence Agency;
(3) The National Security Agency;
(4) The Defense Intelligence Agency;
(5) The National Geospatial-Intelligence Agency;
(6) The National Reconnaissance Office;
(7) The other offices within the Department of Defense for the collection of specialized national foreign intelligence through reconnaissance programs;
(8) The intelligence and counterintelligence elements of the Army, the Navy, the Air Force, and the Marine Corps;
(9) The intelligence elements of the Federal Bureau of Investigation;
(10) The Office of National Security Intelligence of the Drug Enforcement Administration;
(11) The Office of Intelligence and Counterintelligence of the Department of Energy;
(12) The Bureau of Intelligence and Research of the Department of State;
(13) The Office of Intelligence and Analysis of the Department of the Treasury;
(14) The Office of Intelligence and Analysis of the Department of Homeland Security;

---

14. IMINT is a subsidiary discipline of "Geospatial Intelligence" or "GEOINT," which also includes other disciplines such as geography, topography, and cartography. *See, e.g.*, National Geospatial-Intelligence Agency, "About NGA", available at <https://www.nga.mil/About/Pages/default.aspx>.

15. More precisely, the collection of the communications of foreign actors is termed "Communications Intelligence" or "COMINT," a subsidiary discipline of SIGINT. Also included within SIGINT is "Foreign Instrumentation Signals Intelligence" or "FISINT" (a technical form of collection focusing on electromagnetic emissions), and "Electronic Intelligence" or "ELINT" (which collects non-communication electronic emissions, such as radar). Office of the Dir. of Nat'l Intel., U.S. National Intelligence: An Overview 45–47 (2013), available at <http://www.dni.gov/files/documents/USNI%202013%20Overview_web.pdf>.

Figure 1. The U.S. Intelligence Community

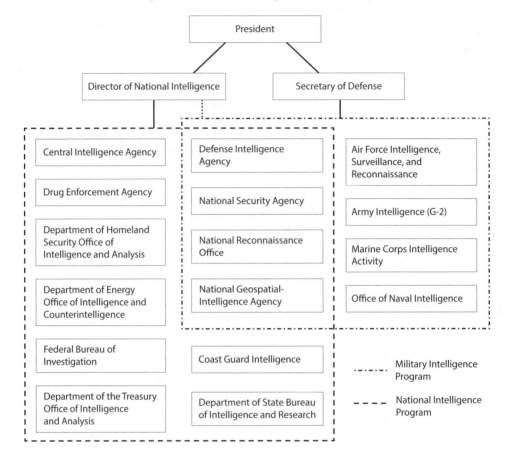

(15) The intelligence and counterintelligence elements of the Coast Guard; and

(16) Such other elements of any department or agency as may be designated by the President, or designated jointly by the Director and the head of the department or agency concerned, as an element of the IC.

The roles and specialties of the IC agencies vary greatly. Some are independent, whereas others are subordinate to cabinet-level departments; for example, the Central Intelligence Agency is an independent agency, while the National Security Agency and the Defense Intelligence Agency are subordinate to the Department of Defense. Additionally, some agencies focus on a particular intelligence discipline (e.g. the National Geospatial-Intelligence Agency, which specializes in IMINT), while others are focused on a particular issue (e.g. the Drug Enforcement Agency), or on providing support to military operations (e.g. the Office of Naval Intelligence).

Ideally, the IC utilizes its diversity of expertise to collect and analyze information in a coordinated and multidisciplinary manner, providing policymakers with the most timely and comprehensive intelligence possible. Indeed, many of the statutory and regulatory reforms of the IC over the past decade have focused on better coordinating intelligence collection resources, removing barriers to information sharing, and establishing community-wide policies regarding such issues as personnel, security, and analytic standards.

Chief among those reforms was the establishment of the Office of the Director of National Intelligence (ODNI), under the Intelligence Reform and Terrorism Prevention Act of 2004 (IRTPA).[16] An idea that had been circulated in Washington for several years, the immediate impetus for the creation of the ODNI was the Final Report of the National Commission on Terrorist Attacks Upon the United States (the "9/11 Commission Report"). The Director of National Intelligence (DNI) assumed many of the responsibilities previously exercised by the Director of Central Intelligence (DCI), who in addition to serving as the director of the CIA had also acted as the head of the IC and the principal intelligence advisor to the President. By separating the roles of Intelligence Community head and principal intelligence advisor to the President from that of directing the Central Intelligence Agency, the statute was intended to enable the Director of the Central Intelligence Agency (DCIA) to concentrate more fully on the CIA and its activities while the DNI would manage the overall IC and provide intelligence advice to the President.

Pursuant to the IRTPA, the DNI sets priorities and guidance for intelligence collection, analysis, and dissemination by IC agencies;[17] the authority to set uniform security standards and establish policies to facilitate information sharing;[18] and the ability to prescribe personnel policies,[19] and in limited circumstances to transfer personnel within the IC.[20] Furthermore, Executive Order 12,333 provides the DNI a role in the appointment or removal from office of the heads of certain intelligence agencies.[21]

Perhaps the most important authorities granted to the DNI by the IRTPA are the designation of the DNI as the "principal advisor to the President, to the National Security Council, and the Homeland Security Council for intelligence matters related to the national security,"[22] and the responsibility for the National Intelligence Program (NIP) budget. As the President's principal advisor on intelligence, the DNI has significant access to the President, and with responsibility for the consolidated NIP budget,[23] the DNI has a powerful tool for shaping IC programs.

However, the authority of the DNI over the Intelligence Community is not total, as the authority over several IC agencies is shared with other cabinet officials, such as the Secretaries of Defense and Homeland Security and the Attorney General. Most significantly, a distinction is drawn between the "National Intelligence Program" (NIP), for which the DNI is largely responsible, and the "Military Intelligence Program" (MIP), whose primary purpose is to support the "planning and conduct of tactical military operations by the United States Armed Forces,"[24] over which the Secretary of Defense exercises considerable control through the Under Secretary of Defense for Intelligence.

The boundaries between the two programs are not always clear. Although certain agencies primarily function within one category (e.g., the CIA falls under the NIP, whereas the Marine Corps Intelligence Activity falls under the MIP), other agencies may serve both national and military program requirements. For example, the NGA may collect imagery in service of both national collection requirements, as well as provide imagery in support of ongoing military operations. Although the IRTPA attempts to reconcile the

---

16. P.L. 108-458 (2004).
17. 50 U.S.C. § 3024(f)(1)(A).
18. 50 U.S.C. § 3024(g)(1).
19. 50 U.S.C. § 3024(f)(3).
20. 50 U.S.C. § 3024(e).
21. Executive Order 12,333.
22. 50 U.S.C. § 3023(b)(2).
23. 50 U.S.C. § 3024(c).
24. 50 U.S.C. § 3003(6).

overlapping responsibilities of the DNI and Secretary of Defense by stipulating roles for each official within the NIP and MIP, the language employed (the DNI "participates" in the development of the MIP budget by the Secretary of Defense, while the Secretary of Defense exercises his authorities pertaining to the NIP "consistent" with the authorities of the DNI)[25] leaves ample room for interpretation.

Questions for Discussion

1. Why does the Secretary of Defense retain control over the MIP? Are the intelligence requirements of the Department of Defense significantly different from other cabinet level departments with agencies participating in the IC? For example, should the Attorney General have primary responsibility for developing a budget for a "domestic intelligence program," with "participation" by the DNI?

2. How do you define "intelligence" for purposes of determining whether an agency should be a member of the IC? For example, considering risk to public health demonstrated by the 2001 anthrax attacks, should the Department of Health and Human Services be included? What about the Bureau of Alcohol, Tobacco, and Firearms? What are the benefits and disadvantages of a broad, inclusive conception of the IC? In contrast, what are the advantages and drawbacks of a narrow definition?

Authorities

Having outlined the structure and functions of the IC, we now turn to the authorities that enable and limit the conduct of intelligence activities.

The Constitution

Foremost among the authorities that govern the Intelligence Community is the Constitution of the United States, which defines the roles of the branches of government in national security affairs, and establishes limitations on the on the means the government may employ in seeking to "establish Justice, insure domestic Tranquillity," and "provide for the common defense."

The Constitution vests the President with significant authorities in the conduct of foreign relations. The President is the "Commander in Chief of the Army and Navy," and with the advice and consent of the Senate may "make Treaties" and "shall appoint Ambassadors, other Ministers and Consuls ... and all other Officers of the United States."[26] Broad in scope and vague in meaning, these authorities nonetheless provide the foundation for executive action for several intelligence activities, including intelligence collection overseas, the conduct of liaison activities, and covert action. However, while the President may be the "sole organ of the federal government in the field of international relations,"[27] his authority is not absolute. The President is the Chief Executive of a "government of laws, and not of men,"[28] and thus his or her authority to act is constrained by the President's

---

25. *See* 50 U.S.C. §3024(c)(3)(A); 50 U.S.C. §3038(b).
26. Art. II, Sec 2.
27. United States v. Curtiss-Wright Export Corp, 299 U.S. 304, 319 (1936).
28. John Adams, Novanglus Essays, No. 7 (1775).

duty to "take Care that the Laws be faithfully executed,"[29] and by the "Constitution, and the Laws of the United States ... and all Treaties made, or which shall be made, under the Authority of the United States," which collectively are the "supreme Law of the Land."[30]

The Constitution restrains the President's power to conduct intelligence activities primarily in two ways, the first of which is through the individual liberties secured by the Bill of Rights. As shall be discussed further in the section on oversight, the Fourth Amendment's guarantee against "unreasonable search and seizures," and the Fifth Amendment's protection from self-incrimination, each place constraints on the methods the IC may employ to collect information pertaining to "U.S. persons."[31] Likewise, the First Amendment's protection of free speech limits the activities against which intelligence collection may be pursued,[32] and the Sixth Amendment's confrontation and compulsory process clauses restrict the manner in which sensitive intelligence information may be used in domestic prosecutions.[33]

The second method by which the Constitution checks the Executive in the conduct of intelligence activities is through the tripartite division of constitutional power, which lodges certain authorities for the conduct of foreign affairs in the coordinate branches of government. As will be discussed below, the judiciary fulfills an increasingly important role in regulating the IC when appropriate matters are presented before it for decision. Affirmative authority to act, however, on its own initiative across a wide spectrum of areas reposes more strongly in the Congress. Article I of the Constitution gives Congress both general and specific authorities that relate to the conduct of foreign affairs. Of the general authorities, the Constitution first vests Congress with "[a]ll legislative Powers,"[34] and gives Congress the power to "make all Laws which shall be necessary and proper" for executing Congress's constitutional responsibilities.[35] Additionally, Congress is given the general power to "lay and collect Taxes ... to pay the Debts and provide for the common Defence,"[36] and reserves to the House of Representatives the authority to originate "[a]ll Bills for Raising Revenue."[37] When combined with the prohibition that "[n]o Money shall be drawn from the Treasury, but in Consequence of Appropriations made by Law,"[38] these collective authorities give Congress a significant ability to restrict executive intelligence activities through the power of the purse.

---

29. Art. II, Sec 3.

30. Art. VI.

31. Executive Order 12,333, section 3.5(k), provides that the term "U.S. person" means "a United States citizen, an alien known by the intelligence element concerned to be a permanent resident alien, an unincorporated association substantially composed of United States citizens or permanent resident aliens, or a corporation incorporated in the United States, except for a corporation directed and controlled by a foreign government or governments." (By common practice, the term is applied to American Samoans as well, who are nationals but not citizens of the United States.) As will be discussed below, at the time this chapter was written the United States was in the process of expanding many of these safeguards to non-U.S. persons as well, through means such as Presidential Policy Directive 28, SIGNALS INTELLIGENCE ACTIVITIES, and its implementing procedures.

32. For example, under the Foreign Intelligence Surveillance Act, the Director of the FBI may not seek an order for the production of business records, if the intent is to seek information relevant to an investigation pertaining solely to "activities protected by the first amendment to the Constitution of the United States." 50 U.S.C. § 1861(a)(2)(B).

33. 18 U.S.C. App. §§ 1–16.

34. Art. I, Sec. 1.

35. Art. I, Sec. 8.

36. *Id.*

37. Art. I, Sec. 7.

38. Art. I, Sec. 9.

Regarding powers specific to the conduct of foreign affairs, the Constitution vests Congress with the power to "regulate Commerce with foreign Nations," and "declare War."[39] Likewise, Congress is given the authority to "raise and support Armies," and "provide and maintain a Navy," as well as to "make Rules for the Government and Regulation of the land and naval Forces."[40] As noted above, the Senate is given the responsibility to "advise and consent" on international treaties, and the appointment of Ambassadors and federal officers.[41] Taken together, these constitutional powers enable Congress to influence the foreign relations of the United States, and (considering the significant proportion of the IC residing in the Department of Defense) the provisions dealing with the armed forces confer an additional ability to affect the conduct of intelligence personnel.

As Justice Jackson noted in his concurrence to *Youngstown Sheet & Tube Co. v. Sawyer,* the Constitution is "an Eighteenth Century sketch of government hoped for, not ... a blueprint for the Government that is."[42] Thus, the line of demarcation between presidential and congressional authorities in the national security arena is not always clear. Here, Justice Jackson's prescient concurrence remains instructive. Justice Jackson divided presidential action into three categories. The first category is when the President acts "pursuant to an express or implied authorization from Congress." Under such circumstances, presidential authority is at its maximum, for it "includes all that he possesses in his own right plus all that Congress can delegate." [43] In the second category, the President "acts in absence of either a congressional grant or denial of authority" and can only rely "upon his independent powers." However, Justice Jackson notes, "there is a zone of twilight in which [the President] and Congress may have concurrent authority, or in which its distribution is uncertain."[44] Finally, in the third category, "the President takes measures incompatible with the expressed or implied will of Congress." Here, the President's power "is at its lowest ebb, for then he can rely only upon his own constitutional powers minus any powers of Congress over the matter."[45]

The history of electronic surveillance is a telling example of how over time an intelligence activity may fall under all three of Justice Jackson's *Youngstown* categories. (Although the Foreign Intelligence Surveillance Act is addressed in a separate chapter of this casebook, a brief review of the subject matter is illustrative.) Early in the twentieth century, legal constraints on the government's ability to monitor citizens' communications were practically nonexistent.[46] Congress first began to legislate restraints on the use of wiretaps with the Federal Communications Act of 1934, which made it a crime "to intercept and divulge or publish the contents of wire and radio communications." And in *Katz v. United States,* 389 U.S. 347, (1967), the Supreme Court found the warrantless use of an electronic listening device in a phone booth to be a violation of the defendant's reasonable expectation of privacy under the Fourth Amendment. At the same time, the Court specifically did not address whether "safeguards other than prior authorization by a magistrate would satisfy the Fourth Amendment in a situation involving the national security."[47] The

---

39. Art. I, Sec. 8.
40. *Id.*
41. Art. II, Sec. 2.
42. 343 U.S. at 653.
43. 343 U.S. at 635–637.
44. 343 U.S. at 637.
45. 343 U.S. at 637–638.
46. *See, e.g.,* Olmstead v. United States, 277 U.S. 468, 483 (1928) (holding that wiretapping did not amount to a "search and seizure" within the meaning of the Fourth Amendment).
47. 389 U.S. at 358 n. 23.

following year, Congress passed the Omnibus Crime Control and Safe Streets Act,[48] which authorized the use of electronic surveillance for certain classes of crimes, established the procedures by which federal officers could seek a warrant for electronic surveillance, and set limits on the manner in which such surveillance could be used. However, neither law purported to restrict the President's constitutional authority to conduct domestic or foreign electronic surveillance (or physical searches) for national security purposes, including the collection of intelligence,[49] and thus for many years such surveillance was conducted without warrants—a clear example of Justice Jackson's second *Youngstown* category.[50]

In *United States v. United States District Court*, 407 U.S. 297 (1972)(*"Keith"*), the Supreme Court examined the President's authority to order surveillance without a warrant, in order to protect against purely domestic threats to national security. During pretrial proceedings, the U.S. citizen defendants (who had been charged with, amongst other things, the bombing of an office of the Central Intelligence Agency) moved to compel the government to turn over electronic surveillance that had been conducted without a warrant. Justice Powell, writing for the Court, held that the Fourth Amendment required prior judicial approval before such domestic surveillance could take place for internal security purposes. However, the Court carefully limited its holding, and did not render judgment on "the President's surveillance power with respect to the activities of foreign powers, within or without this country."[51] The Court suggested that Congress could adopt specific warrant application procedures for domestic security cases, which might differ from those employed in criminal law enforcement cases.[52]

Against the backdrop of the *Keith* case, Congress passed the Foreign Intelligence Surveillance Act of 1978 (FISA), which sought to establish exclusive procedures whereby the executive branch could conduct electronic surveillance to collect foreign intelligence within the United States.[53] The FISA statute required the executive branch to seek a warrant from a specially-designated federal judge prior to undertaking electronic surveillance for intelligence purposes. The Carter Administration supported the bill, albeit with the understanding that the bill did not strip the President of his "inherent" power under the Constitution to conduct electronic surveillance.[54]

---

48. 18 U.S.C. §§ 2510–2520.
49. The Act expressly provided that
   Nothing contained in this chapter or in section 605 of the Communications Act of 1934 (48 Stat. 1143; 47 U.S.C. 605) shall limit the constitutional power of the President to take such measures as he deems necessary to protect the Nation against actual or potential attack or other hostile acts of a foreign power, to obtain foreign intelligence information deemed essential to the security of the United States, or to protect national security information against foreign intelligence activities. Nor shall anything contained in this chapter be deemed to limit the constitutional power of the President to take such measures as he deems necessary to protect the United States against the overthrow of the Government by force or other unlawful means, or against any other clear and present danger to the structure or existence of the Government.
50. S. Rep. No. 95-604, at 9–12 (1977).
51. 407 U.S. at 308.
52. *Id.* at 322.
53. *See* S.Rep. 95-701. See Chapter 27 for a full discussion of FISA and related legislation and judicial opinions.
54. *See, e.g.*, Foreign Intelligence Electronic Surveillance Act of 1978: Hearings on H.R. 5794, H.R. 9745, H.R. 7308, and H.R. 5632 Before the Subcomm. on Legislation of the House Comm. on Intelligence, 95th Cong., 2d Sess. 15 (1978) (testimony of Att'y Gen. Griffin B. Bell) ("[T]he current bill recognizes no inherent power of the President to conduct electronic surveillance, and I want to

The FISA statute, as discussed in Chapter 27, has been amended numerous times in the intervening years, in order to bring additional surveillance methods within its scope. For example, for more than a decade after FISA was enacted the authority to conduct domestic unconsented physical searches to collect foreign intelligence continued to rest solely on the President's constitutional powers. However, following the arrest of CIA employee Aldrich Ames on charges of espionage, concerns arose as to the admissibility of evidence that had been obtained through a warrantless search of Ames's residence. Ultimately, Ames pled guilty, and the issue was avoided. However, rather than continue to rely solely upon the President's inherent constitutional authority to authorize unconsented domestic searches for the collection of foreign intelligence, the Executive and Congress agreed upon an extension of the FISA statute specifically to authorize the judicial approval of physical searches as well.[55]

FISA subsequently has been amended to authorize judicial approval of the use of pen registers (a method to record the numbers dialed by a phone) and trap and trace devices (which record numbers dialed to a phone),[56] as well as the collection of certain business records and tangible goods.[57] Following the attacks of September 11, 2001, FISA was further amended to expand the scope of business records and tangible goods that could be requested,[58] while increasing the threshold for the collection of certain materials, such as library records.[59]

Thus, with the enactment of FISA, the judicially authorized electronic surveillance for intelligence purposes became an exercise of executive authority consistent with an expressed authorization of Congress, i.e. *Youngstown* category one. Nonetheless, the possibility of a *Youngstown* category three situation may still exist: during the Clinton Administration, the Department of Justice's Office of Legal Counsel opined that when exceptional national security concerns so demand, the President may obtain electronic surveillance, even if it would be in contravention of the statute.[60]

Questions for Discussion

1. Where today does the conduct of electronic surveillance for the collection of foreign intelligence fall along the *Youngstown* spectrum?

2. As a practical matter, could the President today rely upon the Carter and Clinton Administrations' assertions that the President retains Article II powers to conduct electronic surveillance outside of the bounds of FISA?

3. In *Keith*, the Court stated "[w]e recognize ... the constitutional basis of the President's domestic security role, but we think it must be exercised in a manner consistent with the

---

interpolate here to say that this does not take away the power of the President under the Constitution").

55. *See* S. Rep. No. 103-296, at 40 (1994). *See also* NAT'L COMM'N ON TERRORIST ATTACKS UPON THE U.S., THE 9/11 COMMISSION REPORT 78 (2004) [hereinafter 9/11 Commission Report].

56. 50 U.S.C. § 1842.

57. Intelligence Authorization Act of 1999, PL 105–272 Sec. 602 (1998).

58. PL 107-56 (2001), Sec 215.

59. PL 109-177 (2006), Sec 106. Many of the reforms to FISA following the September 11th attacks were aimed at removing perceived barriers to information sharing between the Intelligence Community and domestic law enforcement. See the 9/11 Commission Report, at 78–80.

60. Department of Justice, Office of Legal Counsel, "Title III Electronic Surveillance Material and the Intelligence Community," Oct 7, 2000, available at <http://www.justice.gov/sites/default/files/olc/opinions/2000/10/31/op-olc-v024-p0261_0.pdf>.

Fourth Amendment."[61] By holding the surveillance activity in *Keith* to be unlawful, and by inviting Congress to create standards for the conduct of intelligence collection within the United States, the Court suggested that the judicial and legislative branches have a role in the conduct of intelligence activities within the United States. Considering that security threats increasingly cross divide between the foreign and domestic arenas, what does this suggest going forward about the balance of constitutional powers in the conduct of intelligence activities?

Statutory Authorities

Within the framework established by the Constitution, the conduct of intelligence activities is further regulated by statute. In the Introductory section, we discussed the two conceptual distinctions found within the design of U.S. foreign and national intelligence law, i.e. the difference between the domestic and foreign arenas, as well as between the intelligence arena itself and that of domestic law enforcement. To that, we must add a third set of conceptual distinctions that affect the development of intelligence law: those describing various methods by which the United States seeks to advance its national interests in a multipolar world.

Figure 2 provides a simplified demonstration of the division of legal authority for U.S. foreign policy, intelligence, and military activities. In the graph, the *x* axis represents the "degree of coercion" of a proposed action, by which is meant the degree to which the

Figure 2. Tripartite Statutory Division of U.S. Foreign Policy

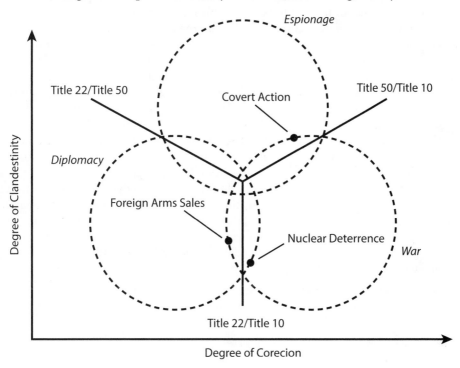

---

61. 407 U.S. at 320.

United States imposes its policies unilaterally, or with the threat or use of force. Thus, to the left on this axis would be tools of a more negotiated nature, while to the right would be tools more related to military action. The *y* axis of the graph represents the "degree of clandestinity," by which is meant the degree to which it is intended that the hand of the United States in a given act of foreign policy will remain hidden.

In charting various foreign policy options along these axes, the three general, overlapping methods become evident. The first are acts of diplomacy, which tend to involve little use of force, and—although specific details of diplomatic agreements may be secret—the fact that the United States engages in such diplomacy is usually publicly acknowledged. Thus, diplomatic methods tend to reside in the lower left corner of the graph. The second method grouping is military action, which involves the threatened or actual use of force, with the resulting effect that the hand of the United States usually cannot remain hidden. Therefore, military methods tend to fall in the lower right portion of the graph. The final method consists of acts of espionage, which by its very nature involves a high degree of clandestinity. Furthermore, because they entail individuals performing acts to which the targeted state would be unlikely to consent, espionage methods may be said to entail a certain degree of coercion. However, such coercion rarely rises to the level of the actual use of force. Espionage methods therefore tend to fall in the upper center of the graph.

The solid lines in the graph represent the division of responsibilities for foreign affairs under statutory law. Generally speaking, the lower left third consists of those authorities committed primarily to the Department of State under Title 22, while the lower right third represents the authorities granted to the Department of Defense under Title 10, and the upper third consists of the authorities committed to the IC under Title 50.

In the graph, the solid lines demarcating the statutory division of responsibilities bisect the overlapping areas of the method circles. This represents the fact that policy options that implicate one or more methods may be governed by a statutory title more aligned with one method than another. Consider, for example, a situation wherein prior to the initiation of military operations, U.S. government personnel clandestinely infiltrate a country in order to gather the support of local "resistance." Such an operation would involve both espionage and military methods. Therefore, an argument could be made that the operation is intended to "influence political, economic, or military conditions abroad" in a manner where the "role of the United States Government will not be apparent or acknowledged publicly," and therefore constitutes covert action, which is governed by 50 U.S.C. § 3093. Alternatively, depending on the personnel involved and the exact purpose of the activity, it might instead be considered military "preparation of the operational environment,"[62] which is considered a "traditional military activity." Such activities are not within the scope of covert action under Title 50,[63] and would not trigger the congressional reporting requirements contained in that Title. Instead, "traditional military activity" would likely be conducted under a congressional authorization for military force, or under the President's Article II Commander-in-Chief authority, with potential reporting requirements under Title 10.[64]

There are numerous rationales as to why a multi-method policy option may be legislated into a particular Title, such as practical necessity, historic practice, or bureaucratic "turf

---

62. *See* Joint Publication 2-01.3, "Joint Intelligence Preparation of the Operational Environment" xi (2009), available at <http://fas.org/irp/doddir/dod/jp2-01-3.pdf>.

63. 50 U.S.C. § 3093(e).

64. *See* Robert Chesney, *Military-Intelligence Convergence And The Law Of The Title 10/Title 50 Debate,* 5 J. NAT'L SECURITY L. & POL'Y 539, 599, 615 (2012).

wars." Ultimately, the decision as to how to codify policy authorities represents a political choice on the part of the political branches, rather than an inevitable distribution of power. Nonetheless, what Figure 2 demonstrates is that when speaking of "intelligence law," espionage methods, U.S. statutory codifications, and agency authorities do not perfectly align. The complexity of the issue is exponentially increased when one moves beyond the foreign arena, and considers "intelligence law" residing in the domestic arena, to include law enforcement activities under Title 18, or the role that state and municipal governments play in the conduct of intelligence collection, with the attendant issues of constitutional federalism. Any discussion of the statutes that regulate the conduct of intelligence activity is therefore likely to be either excessively narrow or overly inclusive. With this in mind, the discussion to follow sets out some of the general authorities specific to the conduct of intelligence activities. Nonetheless, practitioners and students of intelligence law must remain aware not only of intelligence authorities exclusive to the espionage "method," but also of those in the related military, diplomatic, and law enforcement methods as well.

National Security Act of 1947

The principal statutory authority for the U.S. Intelligence Community is the National Security Act of 1947. Drafted in the two years following the devastating destruction wrought by the Second World War, the act was designed by President Truman to overhaul the United States' defense establishment, in order to better prepare it to potentially confront an increasingly aggressive Soviet Union. In addition to combining the War and Navy Departments into a unified Department of Defense, Truman's plan was to create a civilian intelligence agency that would be beholden neither to the military departments, nor the State Department. Accordingly, the National Security Act transformed the presidentially-established Central Intelligence Group (successor to the war time Office of Strategic Services, or OSS) into the Central Intelligence Agency, which would be "under the direction" of the newly-created National Security Council (NSC).[65]

Drafted as a compromise bill designed to avoid controversy, the National Security Act nonetheless left unresolved many issues that would persistently dominate efforts at statutory reform in subsequent years. The first of these was the foreign/domestic arena divide. In order to avoid creating a Gestapo-like agency within the United States, Truman's National Security Act stated that the CIA would have "no police, subpoena, law-enforcement powers, or internal-security functions."[66] Furthermore, although the bill gave the DCI open access to federal agencies' intelligence related to the national security, the bill nonetheless required that the DCI make a written request in order to access intelligence held by the FBI. Finally, neither the Attorney General, the Director of the FBI, nor the Director of Central Intelligence were included as statutory members of the NSC (to this day, they are not statutory members, although they are routinely invited to participate in NSC meetings). The National Security Act may therefore be said not only to have created the Intelligence Community, but to have also begun the process of erecting the "wall" between intelligence and law enforcement that would become the focus of post-9/11 reforms.

Second, the National Security Act did not provide for a strong, centralized form of IC management. The Act provided the CIA with limited authority to fulfill its "centralized" role: the CIA would be given responsibility to (1) advise the NSC in "matters concerning

---

65. Rhodri Jeffreys-Jones, The CIA & American Democracy, 24–41 (3rd. ed., 1989).
66. National Security Act of 1947, Sec 102(d)(3), ch. 343, 61 Stat. 495.

intelligence"; (2) make recommendations for the coordination of the intelligence collection efforts of the various departments and agencies of the U.S. government; (3) correlate, evaluate, and disseminate intelligence; and (4) perform "additional services of common concern" that the NSC determined would be more efficiently accomplished centrally.[67] However, the Act did not provide the DCI the authority to direct the collection activities reserved to the State Department and military services. Critically, and in some ways reflecting the postwar military's skepticism about the ability of a civilian intelligence agency to protect sensitive information, the Act required the DCI "to protect intelligence sources and methods from unauthorized disclosure."[68]

Third, the National Security Act did not clearly delineate the CIA's authority to conduct covert action. During the Second World War, the OSS had conducted a variety of covert activities, including providing assistance and training to partisan groups combatting the Axis powers. Likewise, as the Cold War intensified in the decades following the passage of the National Security Act, the White House would increasingly turn to the CIA to conduct operations to stall the spread of communism, through covert influence campaigns, support to threatened allied governments, and actions to weaken hostile regimes. Nonetheless, as will be discussed further below, for more than forty years following the passage of the National Security Act, the only provision that the Executive could point to as a statutory authority for the conduct of covert action was the CIA's so-called "fifth function," which provided that the Agency could "perform such other activities and duties related to the national security as the National Security Council may from time to time direct."[69]

For all its initial faults, the National Security Act provides the statutory framework upon which the American intelligence enterprise is built, and for many agencies within the IC, it remains the primary (if not exclusive) statute authorizing the conduct of intelligence activities. Over the years, the Act has been dramatically modified and expanded, with its present form consisting of more than triple the number of sections contained in the original bill. Often aimed at addressing the persistent issues of the foreign/domestic divide, centralized control of the IC, and the statutory regulation of covert action, the reforms of the National Security Act have taken a variety of legislative forms, including specific reform bills, statutory charters for specific agencies, and intelligence authorization acts. We now consider each of these legislative forms in turn.

Recreating the Community: Intelligence Reform and Terrorism Prevention Act (IRPTA)

Following the September 11, 2001 attacks, Congress mandated the creation of the National Commission on the Terrorist Attacks Upon the United States, commonly referred to as the 9/11 Commission. Released in 2004, the Commission's report detailed the events leading up to the hijackings, chronicled the actions taken the day of the attack, and outlined recommendations designed to reduce the risk of another catastrophic act of terrorism in the United States. Among the reforms suggested by the Commission were significant changes to the IC aimed at increasing unity of effort across the foreign/domestic divide, promoting cooperation within the IC, enhancing information sharing, reforming the FBI's role in intelligence and national security, and improving congressional oversight.[70]

---

67. National Security Act of 1947, Sec 101(b), ch. 343, 61 Stat. 495 available at <http://research.archives.gov/description/299856>.

68. That responsibility now reposes with the DNI. 50 U.S.C. § 3024(i)(1).

69. National Security Act of 1947, Sec 101(b), ch. 343, 61 Stat. 495 available at http://research.archives.gov/description/299856.

70. 9/11 Commission Report, 399–428.

The Intelligence Reform and Terrorism Prevention Act constituted the primary legislative effort to implement the Commission's recommendations. As previously discussed, the most significant reform instituted by the IRTPA was the division of the DCI's community management, presidential intelligence advisor, and CIA director roles, creating the separate positions of DNI and DCIA. The act also created various offices subordinate to the DNI, including a Principal Deputy Director of National Intelligence, General Counsel, and Civil Liberties Protection Officer.[71] The IRPTA authorized the creation of other "offices and officials as ... the Director may establish,"[72] such as issue and country-specific Mission Managers,[73] who assist the DNI in shaping intelligence policy, prioritize and manage collection, and coordinate analysis.[74]

The IRPTA sought to address the 9/11 Commission's concerns about the dissemination of terrorism intelligence and threat information through the establishment of an Information Sharing Environment (a program which would seek to standardize how national security information was acquired, shared, accessed and used among federal, state and local agencies),[75] and created national intelligence centers, such as the National Counterterrorism Center (NCTC) and National Counterproliferation Center (NCPC). The NCTC—transformed from the presidentially-created Terrorist Threat Integration Center—reports to the DNI, and serves as the "primary organization in the United States Government for analyzing and integrating all intelligence possessed ... pertaining to terrorism and counterterrorism," as well as be responsible for conducting "strategic operational planning for counterterrorism activities." Located outside of any particular intelligence agency, the NCTC serves as the DNI's mission manager for terrorism issues, and functions as a "shared knowledge bank on known and suspected terrorists and international terror groups," distributing terrorist threat information to federal, state, and local agencies.[76] The NCPC performs similar functions in matters related to the proliferation of weapons of mass destruction, serving as the Mission Manager and central clearing house for intelligence on such weapons, their delivery systems, and related materials and technologies.

Thus, the IRPTA dramatically reshaped the structure of the Intelligence Community, based in large part upon the recommendations of the 9/11 Report, with the purpose of improving its operation and management across the board.[77] However, structure and process are not synonymous. Therefore, Congress coupled its structural reforms with sections addressing the standards and procedures used by the IC in performing its work, particularly with regard to analysis. The IRPTA requires that the DNI appoint an official to be responsible for ensuring that "finished intelligence products produced by any element

---

71. 50 U.S.C. § 3025.

72. Section 103(c)(9).

73. *See* Intelligence Community Directive 900, "Mission Management."

74. Section 102A(f)(1).

75. Section 1016. *See also* Government Accountability Office, "Information Sharing Environment," June, 2008, available at <http://www.gao.gov/new.items/d08492.pdf>.

76. <http://www.nctc.gov/overview.html>.

77. The IRTPA was not without its critics. In a departure from normal practice, the bill was drafted not by the standing intelligence committees of the House and Senate, but by the respective committees on Government Operations. Many of the proposals long sought by the Members of the intelligence committees were not included in the final version of the legislation; moreover, not all of the recommendations of the 9/11 Commission enjoyed universal approbation even at the time. *See, e.g.,* RICHARD A. POSNER, PREVENTING SURPRISE ATTACKS: INTELLIGENCE REFORM IN THE WAKE OF 9/11 (Rowman and Littlefield, 2005). The rush to enact IRPTA at the end of 2004 also precluded consideration of the then-pending recommendations of the complementary Commission on the Intelligence Capabilities of the United States Regarding Weapons of Mass Destruction, whose REPORT TO THE PRESIDENT was due and delivered on March 31, 2005.

or elements of the intelligence community are timely, objective, independent of political considerations, based on all sources of available intelligence, and employ the standards of proper analytic tradecraft."[78] The act also requires the use of alternative analysis (i.e. "red team" analysis, wherein assessments are challenged by a separate group of analysts who approach the issue from an adversarial perspective, or utilizing different assumptions),[79] stresses the importance of the IC using publicly available information as well as clandestinely collected material, and suggests the creation of an open source center.[80]

Statutory Charters: The Central Intelligence Agency Act of 1949

As noted above, the vast majority of agencies within the IC find their statutory authority to conduct intelligence activities in the various provisions of the National Security Act of 1947, combined with a hodgepodge of legislative grants found in other titles (for example, in addition to the provisions of Title 50, the FBI's intelligence authorities may be found, *inter alia,* in a note to section 532 of Title 28, which incorporates the provisions of IRTPA creating a Directorate of Intelligence within the FBI).[81] Specific statutory charters do exist for a small number of agencies, however.[82] Amongst other things, these charters define the roles of the agencies, delineate subordinate offices, establish procedures for information security and sharing, and provide unique budgetary, operational, and personnel authorities.

Demonstrative of such statutory charters is the Central Intelligence Agency Act of 1949 ("CIA Act"). Although the CIA was created through the National Security Act of 1947, the initial legislation concerning the agency had — by White House design — few substantive provisions relating to the Agency, in order to reduce potential opposition to the bill.[83] Therefore, immediately after passage of the 1947 act, work began on the CIA Act, which would provide the basic authorities perceived to be necessary for the conduct of clandestine human intelligence operations. The Act exempts the agency from any provision of law that would require the publication of the "organization, function, names, official titles, salaries, or numbers of personnel employed by the Agency";[84] gives the Director (with the agreement of the Attorney General and Commissioner of Immigration and Naturalization) the ability to admit into the United States a limited number of aliens, when in the "interest of national security or essential to the furtherance of the national intelligence mission";[85] and provides the CIA significant budgetary authorities, including the ability to transfer and receive funds, which enables the CIA to obscure its budget within the appropriations of other agencies.[86] Perhaps of most importance to the conduct of clandestine intelligence activities, section 8 of the CIA Act provides that "[n]otwithstanding any other provision of law, sums made available to the Agency by appropriation or otherwise may be expended for purposes

---

78. Section 1019(a).
79. Sec. 1017. For an explanation of alternate analysis, *see* Richard Heuer, Psychology of Intelligence Analysis, 95–110 (1999), available at <https://www.cia.gov/library/center-for-the-study-of-intellig-ence/csi-publications/books-and-monographs/psychology-of-intelligence-analysis/PsychofIntelNew.pdf>.
80. Section 1052.
81. 28 U.S.C. 532, note (incorporating P.L. 108-458 §§ 2001–2003).
82. *See, e.g.,* Central Intelligence Agency Act of 1949, P.L. 110, 63 STAT. 208; National Security Agency Act of 1959, P.L. 86-36 (1959); National Imagery and Mapping Agency Act of 1994, 10 U.S.C. § 441 *et seq.* (establishing NGA); and Homeland Security Act of 2002, 6 U.S.C. § 121 et seq.
83. L. Britt Snider, The Agency and the Hill: CIA's Relationship with Congress 1946–2004, 141–143 (2008).
84. 50 U.S.C. § 3507.
85. 50 U.S.C. § 3508.
86. 50 U.S.C. § 506.

to carry out its functions," which include "objects of a confidential, extraordinary, or emergency nature," and provides the DCIA the authority to account for such funds through a confidential certification, rather than through the usual accounting methods employed by other agencies.[87] Together, these provisions give the CIA the ability to spend its appropriations in an adaptive and atypical manner for its lawfully authorized purposes, all the while preventing the exposure of classified programs through the budget reporting procedures used by other federal agencies.

Like the National Security Act, the CIA Act has been amended and expanded over the decades in order to grant further authorities and to bring the act into conformity with the IRTPA reforms. Furthermore, many of the original and subsequent provisions of the NSA and CIA Acts have been mirrored in subsequent statutory charters and legislative authorities of other Intelligence Community agencies. For example, the NSA, NRO, NGA, and DIA possess legislative authorities similar to the protections against disclosure of internal organizational structure,[88] the performance of law enforcement and security functions at CIA installations, and the prohibition against the unauthorized use of the Agency's name, initials, and seal.[89]

Of course, intelligence agency charters (where they exist) are not uniform, and such points of divergence reveal the unique mission and roles of the agencies in question. For example, no other intelligence agency director possesses the DCIA's authorities regarding the admission into the United States of foreign nationals; such exclusivity of power is understandable considering the DCIA's responsibilities to collect HUMINT and to ensure that "appropriate account is taken of the risks to ... those involved in [human source collection]."[90] Likewise, considering the utility the public may gain from government-prepared maps and charts, the charter of the NGA has an express provision permitting that agency to engage in the public sale of its products.[91] Such an authority is not possessed (nor likely needed) by other IC members.

Authorization and Appropriations Acts

The most impactful method by which Congress exercises its supervision of the IC is through the power of the purse, which generally is effected through the sequential two-step process of authorization and appropriation. Under the rules of the House and Senate, a government agency, program, or activity must be *authorized* before funds may be *appropriated* for its purpose.[92] Prior to 1976, it was generally understood that the National Security Act of 1947 provided an ongoing authorization for intelligence activities. However, with the creation of the intelligence oversight committees, intelligence authorization

---

87. 50 U.S.C. § 3510.

88. *See, e.g.,* 10 U.S.C. § 424 ("Except as required by the President ... no provision of law shall be construed to require the disclosure of ... the organization or function" of the DIA, NRO, and NGA); Pub. L. 86-36, § 6 ("[N]othing in this Act or any other law ... shall be construed to require the disclosure of the organization or any function of the National Security Agency, or any information with respect to the activities thereof, or the names, titles, salaries, or number of the persons employed by such agency").

89. 50 U.S.C. 3513. *See also* 10 U.S.C. § 425 (prohibiting the unauthorized use of the name, initials, or seals of the DIA, NRO, and NGA); Pub. L. 86-36 § 15 (prohibiting unauthorized use of the name, initials, or seal of the NSA).

90. 50 U.S.C. § 3036.

91. 10 U.S.C § 453.

92. Congressional Research Service, Overview of the Authorization-Appropriation Process, November 26, 2012.

became an annual process,[93] with Congress passing authorization for all but five of the years between 1978 and 2014.

Through the accretion of individual provisions over the years, the Intelligence Authorization Acts have filled out the statutory framework for the IC set forth in the National Security Act and various agency charters. Primarily, the authorization acts have addressed matters related to Intelligence Community personnel and physical infrastructure—establishing employee benefits, promoting critical skill sets, as well as authorizing the construction of IC facilities.[94] However, Congress also uses the authorization acts as a vehicle to shape the conduct of intelligence activities, such as restricting intelligence cooperation and assistance to South Africa during the era of apartheid,[95] providing additional methods of collection under FISA,[96] and prohibiting the use of journalists in intelligence activities.[97] Additionally, Congress often uses the Intelligence Authorization Acts to require the IC to produce information and reports to the oversight committees, and express the sense of Congress on intelligence-related matters.[98]

The authorization process has also been used on occasion to undertake significant reforms of the IC, such as the Intelligence Authorization Act of 1991,[99] which established a statutory definition for covert action and enhanced the provisions for its oversight by the Congressional intelligence and appropriations committees. Likewise, Title VI of the Intelligence Authorization Act of 1993 codified the role the National Intelligence Council (NIC), comprised of analysts from throughout the IC. Having existed by executive authorization in various forms since the Eisenhower administration, the newly-statutory NIC would "constitute the senior intelligence advisers ... for purposes of representing the views of the intelligence community" regarding their area of substantive expertise, and jointly produce intelligence reports (the "National Intelligence Estimate") representing the collective assessment of the IC on particular national security threats. The 1993 Act also defined "intelligence" and the "intelligence community," and delineated the respective roles and responsibilities of the DCI and Secretary of Defense.[100]

Two further points bear mentioning regarding the authorization and appropriation process. First, the Intelligence Authorization Acts and the related appropriations acts routinely include classified annexes and appropriations schedules that are available to the Members but not to the public.[101] Nonetheless, the public provisions of those Acts demonstrate an iterative—if sometimes imperfect—process of Congressional oversight, where legislative regulation often reflects the regular and required reporting by the IC to the oversight committees.

Second, the Intelligence Authorization Acts are not the sole authorization process used to legislate matters related to the U.S. Intelligence Community; because funding for the

---

93. L. BRITT SNIDER, THE AGENCY AND THE HILL: CIA's RELATIONSHIP WITH CONGRESS 1946–2004, 179 (2008).

94. *See, e.g.*, P.L. 99-169 (1995).

95. P.L. 99-569 § 107.

96. P.L. 103-359 § 807.

97. P.L. 104-293 § 309.

98. *See, e.g.*, P.L. 111-259 §§ 331–349 (requiring Intelligence Community production of reports to Congress); P.L. 107-306 § 323 (expressing sense of Congress on diversity in the workforce of intelligence community agencies).

99. P.L. 102-88 §§ 501–503.

100. P.L. 102-496 §§ 701–706.

101. *See, e.g.*, P.L. 106-567 § 102.

MIP (as well as 90% of the NIP) falls under the Department of Defense budget,[102] Congress may also include provisions concerning the IC in the annual National Defense Authorization Acts and the Defense Appropriations Acts. Although such bills primarily concern military matters unconnected to the IC, they nonetheless frequently include mandates concerning IC personnel, acquisitions, and activities, and thus can significantly affect the conduct of intelligence activities.

Questions for Discussion

1. In looking at Figure 2, where would you place intelligence collection? What about liaison activities? Would these activities reside exclusively in the espionage method?

2. In many countries the conduct of foreign intelligence activities is subsumed entirely into either the diplomatic or military methods, being the responsibility of either the country's ministry of foreign affairs, or ministry of defense, respectively. What are the advantages or disadvantages of such an arrangement?

Executive Directives

In the previous section, we reviewed Congress' grants of authority to, and imposition of restraints upon, the Executive, which reflect the sharing and balancing of constitutional powers between the political branches of government. In this section, we review those orders, instructions, and policies promulgated by the executive branch to govern its own conduct of intelligence activities. This topic unavoidably raises questions as to the delineation of the Executive's power in the realm of foreign affairs. Some commentators have argued for a relatively narrow construction of executive power, such as when Justice Black noted in *Youngstown* that the President's authority to act "must either stem from an act of Congress, or from the Constitution."[103] Others have advanced a much broader conception of executive power, such as Justice Sutherland's largely discredited holding in *United States v. Curtiss-Wright*, suggesting that the President's authority in foreign affairs was premised on national sovereignty, and thus almost extra-constitutional.

Regardless of which theory is adopted, one principle is clear: the President cannot bestow on himself authorities that he does not possess; he is constrained to the powers granted to him by Congress, by the Constitution, or (under Justice Sutherland's interpretation) by the rights possessed by sovereign states. The President cannot conjure that which does not exist. Therefore, executive directives governing the conduct of intelligence activities must fall into one of three categories: (1) an exercise of authority delegated to the President by Congress; (2) an expression of the President's enumerated or inherent authority under Article II; or (3) a self-imposed restriction by the Executive of powers it possesses under the constitution or by legislative delegation. What an executive direction is not—and indeed, cannot be—is an autogenic source of executive power.

Executive directives may take on a myriad of forms, from formal Executive Orders and Presidential Proclamations to verbal instructions given from the President to his advisors during hallway conversations. Perhaps not surprisingly, there is a difference of opinion between the branches of government as to the weight and authority that various forms of executive directives possess. The Office of Legal Counsel within the Department of

---

102. Congressional Research Service, "Intelligence Spending and Appropriations," September 18, 2013.

103. 343 U.S. 579, 585.

Justice has opined that there is no legal difference between various forms of executive directives,[104] whereas the Government Accountability Office (an independent office established by, and an arm of Congress) has advised that the legal weight of a directive is dependent on a variety of factors, such as whether the directive is issued pursuant to a specific statutory delegation, whether the directive is unclassified, and whether the directive was published pursuant to the Federal Register Act of 1935 (44 U.S.C. § 1505).[105] The courts have not opined *per se* as to the legal effect of the form of executive directives, although they have (as in *Youngstown*) struck down individual directives as being unconstitutional exercises of executive power.

Executive Order 12333

For the first thirty years following the end of World War II, the functions of the U.S. Intelligence Community were largely withheld from public view. However, a series of public revelations in the early 1970s brought to light numerous activities by various federal agencies (such as the Army, the CIA, and the FBI) that appeared to violate U.S. law or were otherwise questionable or improper. The disclosures prompted investigations by both the executive and legislative branches. President Ford established an executive commission, chaired by Vice President Nelson Rockefeller, while Congress created the Senate Select Committee to Study Governmental Operations with Respect to Intelligence Activities, and the House Select Committee on Intelligence, respectively known as the "Church" and "Pike" committees, after their chairmen. The three panels varied in their size and focus, yet all three detailed further abuses, and made recommendations for an extensive reform of the IC. The reports of the Rockefeller Commission and the Church Committee were released and make for interesting reading even today; for various reasons the House of Representatives voted not to release the Pike Committee report, although portions were leaked to the *Village Voice* newspaper and published there.[106]

Although amenable to some of the congressional proposals set forth following the Rockefeller Commission and Church Committee reports, and the partial disclosure of the Pike report, President Ford attempted to preempt sweeping legislative reform of the IC through the issuance of Executive Order 11905. In part, this was because of the perceived risk of enshrining in statute procedures or methods substantively unrelated to the three reports (such as statutory limitations on the amount of rent that could be paid for clandestine locations) that would prove unworkable in practice. Ford's executive order addressed both intelligence weaknesses and abuses, through clarifying the roles and responsibilities of the IC agencies, creating an Intelligence Oversight Board, regulating the collection of information about "U.S. persons," restricting the conduct of human experimentation and undisclosed intelligence participation in U.S. organizations, prohibiting the conduct of assassinations, and making explicit that no one working for the IC would participate in, or request anyone else to undertake, any activities forbidden by that Order.[107] Ford's Executive Order was expanded upon and replaced by President Carter's issuance of Executive Order 12036, which further circumscribed collection efforts against U.S. persons, restricted the conduct of "special activities" (essentially what we now know as

---

104. Legal Effectiveness of a Presidential Directive, as Compared to an Executive Order, 24 Op. O.L.C. 29 (2000).

105. United States General Accounting Office, "Use of Presidential Directives to Make and Implement U.S. Policy," January 1992, available at: <http://fas.org/irp/offdocs/gao-nsiad-92-72.pdf>. The General Accounting Office has since been redesignated as the Government Accountability Office.

106. Rhodri Jeffreys-Jones, The CIA & American Democracy, 194–215 (3rd. ed., 1989).

107. Executive Order 11905.

covert action), and refined the rules governing undisclosed participation by the IC in U.S. organizations. The Carter Executive Order also sought to improve the coordination of intelligence collection and analysis through the creation of the Policy Review Committee (comprised of members of the National Security Council), and the National Foreign Intelligence Board (the precursor to the National Intelligence Council).[108]

The policy of continuing intelligence regulation through executive directive was continued by President Reagan, who promulgated Executive Order 12333, "United States Intelligence Activities," on December 4, 1981 in replacement of E.O. 12036. As subsequently amended by President George W. Bush in 2008, Executive Order 12333 remains in effect, and is the seminal executive document concerning intelligence matters. For intelligence agencies possessing legislative charters, Executive Order 12333 fills the regulatory gap left by lacunae in statutory provisions, while for agencies lacking a charter, it constitutes the primary governing authority for the conduct of intelligence operations.

Like its predecessors, Executive Order 12333 ("E.O. 12333") regulates the Intelligence Community in primarily three ways. First, it defines the roles and responsibilities of the DNI and the constituent intelligence agencies. Perhaps unsurprisingly, the order reiterates the structural dictates of the National Security Act of 1947. This coherency of design demonstrates not only one branch of government faithfully executing the laws established by the other, but also an iterative process of regulation: some legislative amendments to the National Security Act concerning the structure of the IC represent Congressional adoption of executive branch innovations (e.g. the National Intelligence Council), while many of the changes made to the order by President George W. Bush were undertaken to bring the order into conformity with the IRTPA. In other ways, however, E.O. 12333 is more granular than its statutory analogs. For example, whereas the National Security Act does assign some intelligence collection responsibilities (e.g. the DCIA is responsible for providing "overall direction for and coordination of the collection of national intelligence outside the United States through human sources"),[109] E.O. 12333 goes further, assigning certain agency heads the role of community mission manager for specific collection techniques (e.g. DCIA for HUMINT, Director of NSA for SIGINT, and Director of NGA for GEOINT),[110] as well as clarifying the division of labor between the CIA and FBI concerning coordinating HUMINT collection and counterintelligence inside and outside the United States.[111]

Second, E.O. 12333 establishes restrictions on the conduct of intelligence activities. The order continues the Ford and Carter regulations on assassination, undisclosed participation in organizations within the United States, and prohibits any covert action which "is intended to influence United States political processes, public opinion, policies, or media."[112] E.O. 12333 also sets forth limitations on intelligence collection, especially with regards to "United States persons." Few statutes concern the collection of intelligence *outside* the United States, and those that do tend to focus on specific collection techniques and collection directed at U.S. persons.[113] Therefore, most intelligence collection outside the United States is governed primarily (if not solely) by E.O. 12333, giving the executive order's definitions acute importance, as they delineate when additional restraints apply

---

108. Executive Order 12036.
109. 50 U.S.C. § 3036.
110. E.O. 12333 § 1.3(b)(12).
111. E.O. 12333 § 1.3(b)(20).
112. E.O. 12333 § 2.13.
113. *See, e.g.,* 50 U.S.C. §§ 1881a, 1881c.

to a particular collection target. Thus, E.O. 12333 defines a "U.S. Person" as "a United States citizen, an alien known … to be a permanent resident alien, an unincorporated association substantially composed of United States citizens or permanent resident aliens, or a corporation incorporated in the United States, except for a corporation directed and controlled by a foreign government or governments."[114]

Third, E.O. 12333 regulates the intelligence community by establishing oversight processes and requirements. The order makes clear that IC agencies are required "in accordance with applicable law" to cooperate with Congress in the "conduct of its responsibilities for oversight of intelligence activities."[115] Likewise, agencies are directed to "report to the Intelligence Oversight Board … and provide copies of all such reports to the [DNI], concerning any intelligence activities of their elements that they have reason to believe may be unlawful or contrary to executive order or presidential directive."[116] Finally, E.O. 12333 gives a significant role to the Attorney General in the conduct of oversight, mandating that he or she approve any agency directives or procedures implementing the executive order's restrictions on collection, and requiring that agencies "[r]eport to the Attorney General possible violations of Federal criminal laws by employees and of specified criminal laws by any other person."[117]

Additional Presidential and Agency Directives

For a variety of reasons — including where an executive policy may be classified, or where the White House wishes to avoid the degree of interagency coordination usually attending the drafting and promulgation of executive orders — Presidents have utilized other directives to articulate intelligence policies and regulations. These directives have been given different titles by almost every administration, including National Security Council Policy Papers (Truman and Eisenhower), National Security Action Memoranda (Kennedy and Johnson), National Security Decision Memoranda (Nixon and Ford), Presidential Directives (Carter), National Security Decision Directives (Reagan), National Security Directives (George H.W. Bush), Presidential Decision Directives (Clinton), National Security Presidential Directives (George W. Bush), and Presidential Policy Directives (Obama). An example of how such directives may be used to regulate intelligence activities is Presidential Policy Directive ("PPD") 28, which sets forth general principles and policies concerning the collection of signals intelligence activities, including limitations on the use of "bulk" signals intelligence, and provides foreign nationals essentially the same limitations on the dissemination, retention, and collection of information about them that apply to U.S. persons themselves.[118]

PPD 28, as do most Presidential Directives relating to the IC, delegates responsibility for its implementation to the DNI and the directors of the various intelligence agencies. Policies that affect the entire IC are typically articulated in Intelligence Community Directives ("ICDs"). Previously referred to as Director of Central Intelligence Directives ("DCIDs") prior to the implementation of the IRTPA, ICDs are issued by the Director

---

114. E.O. 12333 § 3.5(k).
115. E.O. 12333 § 3.1.
116. E.O. 12333 § 1.6(c).
117. E.O. 12333 § 1.6(b).
118. *See* Office of the Director of National Intelligence, "Safeguarding the Personal Information of All People: A Status Report on the Development and Implementation of Procedures Under Presidential Policy Directive 28," July 2014. The Report opens by stating that "[t]he United States is committed to protecting the personal information of all people around the world, regardless of their nationality." *Id.* at 1.

of National Intelligence, and are used to set forth IC policy on a range of issues from oversight and civil liberties, analytic standards, information security, to budgetary and appropriations matters.

In addition to Presidential Directives and ICDs, the Intelligence Community is governed by a series of agency-specific policies concerning the conduct of intelligence activities, as approved by the Attorney General pursuant to E.O. 12333. Examples of such regulations are the Department of Defense Regulation 5240.1-R "Activities of DoD Intelligence Components that Impact U.S. Persons"; the Attorney General's Consolidated Guidelines for FBI Domestic Operations; and the United States Signals Intelligence Directive 18 "Legal Compliance and U.S. Persons Minimization Procedures" (issued by the NSA). These regulations apply at the agency level the Executive Order 12333 restrictions concern the collection of intelligence concerning U.S. persons, refining those policies to meet the agencies' unique missions (e.g. the FBI conducting clandestine human intelligence collection within the United States) or collection methods (e.g. SIGINT collection by the NSA).

Questions for Discussion

1. Some commentators have argued that regulating intelligence activities through executive directives is insufficient, since subsequent administrations can simply amend or rescind previous directives; rather, restrictions on the conduct of intelligence activities should be established in statutory law. If Congress were to codify the prohibitions on assassination, or the limitations on collection established under PPD-28, would those statutory prohibitions be constitutional?

2. Under Executive Order 12333, the Attorney General must approve of any agency regulation or directive that implements the Executive Order's restrictions on collection. Assuming that a litigant could gain standing to challenge an intelligence agency's regulations, what weight, if any, should the courts give to the Attorney General's determination that regulations are lawful?

International Law

Thus far, our discussion has focused on the regulation of intelligence activities under U.S. law. Nonetheless, as espionage is primarily directed at the actions of foreign states and actors, it is natural to also consider the application of international treaties, customary international law (CIL), and implementing legislation enacted by Congress.[119] The application of international law to U.S. national security activities is addressed at length elsewhere in this casebook; however, a brief overview of the subject as applied to intelligence activities may be in order. Generally speaking, few specific provisions of treaty law or customary international law directly address the conduct of intelligence activities writ broadly, although many areas of international law may be viewed as relevant as part of a larger context (such as the conduct of diplomacy, foreign relations, and the use of military force; the rights and obligations of states and those acting on their behalf; the extent of state sovereignty and domestic prerogatives; and the like).[120]

---

119. For a more comprehensive review of this topic, *see* Ashley Deeks, *An International Legal Framework for Surveillance*, 55 VA. J. INT'L. L. ___ (2015). *See also* MICHAEL REISMAN AND JAMES E. BAKER, REGULATING COVERT ACTION (1992).

120. To be sure, specific provisions of international treaties do apply to particular situations. For example, Article 46 of Additional Protocol I to the Geneva Conventions (which the United States has signed but not ratified) provides that spies are not entitled to Prisoner of War status. However, Protocol

Certainly, multiple provisions of the United Nations Charter, the Geneva Conventions, and customary international law express the rights and obligations of states in the conduct of their foreign affairs. Nonetheless, a few examples may illustrate both the potential for and problems with looking to international law as a vehicle for regulating states' intelligence activities. Regarding customary international law, for example, some scholars have argued that espionage violates the principles of sovereignty and territorial integrity, since spying is conducted within a foreign nation's borders and likely in violation of the country's domestic laws. However, because CIL is derived from state practice, such arguments may be undermined by the fact that states routinely engage in espionage, and formal denunciations of the practice (for example, when states declare an alleged spy to be *persona non grata*) are few and infrequent.[121]

Alternatively, it has been claimed that espionage—particularly electronic surveillance—may have the effect of violating individual rights as expressed in specific treaties, such as the privacy rights guaranteed by Article 17 of the International Covenant on Civil and Political Rights ("ICCPR"). However, controversy exists as to the jurisdictional application of the ICCPR, with the United States interpreting the treaty as lacking extraterritorial application. Finally, some argue that intelligence activities may be antithetical to treaty provisions concerning state conduct. For example, some may assert that certain forms of espionage may violate the Vienna Convention on Diplomatic Relations ("VCDR"), either when sending states use their embassies and consulates for the conduct of intelligence activities, or when receiving states engage in spying on the facilities of the sending states. Once again, such arguments are vulnerable to the charge that consistent state practice—including at the time that the states party were negotiating the VCDR—undermines the inviolability of the rule or suggests that it never was intended or understood to apply to espionage activities in the first place.[122] And as a matter of domestic U.S. law, the Intelligence Authorization Act for Fiscal Year 2001 amended the National Security Act to provide that no subsequent Federal law "that implements a treaty or other international agreement shall be construed as making unlawful an otherwise lawful and authorized intelligence activity ... unless such Federal law specifically addresses such intelligence activity."[123]

Covert Action

Perhaps no area of U.S. Intelligence Community activities in the recent decades has attracted so much attention as the authorization and conduct of covert action. The National Security Act defines "covert action" as "an activity or activities of the United States Government to influence political, economic, or military conditions abroad, where it is intended that the role of the United States Government will not be apparent or acknowledged publicly."[124] Importantly, the term "covert action" does not include

---

I only applies to international armed conflicts, whereas states engage in espionage against each other every day, including during periods of peace.

121. Ashley Deeks, *An International Legal Framework for Surveillance*, 55 Va. J. Int'l. L. ___ (2015).

122. *Id.*

123. Section 1101 of the National Security Act of 1947, as amended, 50 U.S.C. § 3231.

124. 50 U.S.C. § 3093(e); *see also* Executive Order 12333, § 3.5(b). For comments on the provision that covert action is not intended to be publicly acknowledged, *see* Kenneth Anderson, *Reforming the Legal Definition of 'Covert Action'*, Volokh Conspiracy, February 2, 2014, available at <http://www.washingtonpost.com/news/volokh-conspiracy/wp/2014/02/02/reforming-the-legal-definition-of-covert-action/>; Jack Goldsmith, *Is the "Covert Action" in Syria Actually a Covert Action?*, Lawfare,

- intelligence collection activities,

- traditional counterintelligence activities,

- traditional activities to improve or maintain the operational security of United States Government programs, or

- traditional U.S. diplomatic, military, or law enforcement activities, or routine support to such activities.[125]

The term "covert action" does include activities to influence foreign political decisions, mass media, public opinion, the conduct of paramilitary operations not attributable to the U.S. Government, cyber operations to degrade and destroy the abilities of foreign adversaries to damage the United States, and similar types of activities against hostile entities abroad. Importantly, covert action must be implemented in accordance with U.S. law and the policy directives of the President.[126]

"Covert action" must be approved in advance, and in writing, by the President in a document called a Finding.[127] Significant changes to existing covert actions must be approved by the President in a written Memorandum of Notification (MoN).[128] Findings and MoNs must be notified to the Congressional intelligence committees, and to the Defense subcommittees of the appropriations committees.[129] And other U.S. departments and agencies are authorized to assist the implementing agency, normally the CIA, in the conduct of covert action so long as the respective department or agency head has approved.[130]

From 1974, when the first statutory requirement for the President to approve "special activities" was enacted as part of the Hughes-Ryan Amendment,[131] up until the enactment of the Intelligence Reform and Terrorist Prevention Act (IRTPA) of 2004, the covert action policymaking and review process was relatively straightforward. The NSC staff worked with the policy agencies (e.g., the Departments of State, Defense, Justice, and Treasury) and the implementing agency (normally the CIA), to determine whether the use of covert action would be appropriate for the accomplishment of U.S. policy objectives. If so, the NSC tasked the CIA to prepare implementation plans and draft a Presidential Finding or Memorandum of Notification for review. If the draft was approved by the President, the CIA would notify the Congressional intelligence and appropriations committees, implement the covert action, and report regularly to the NSC and the Congress.

As with any set of procedures, the actual practice of policymaking differed from time to time. In particular, the Director of Central Intelligence (DCI) served concurrently as the principal intelligence adviser to the President, the head of the U.S. Intelligence Community, and the director of one of its constituent agencies, the Central Intelligence

---

October 5, 2013, available at <http://www.lawfareblog.com/2013/10/is-the-covert-action-in-syria-actually-a-covert-action/> ; and Benjamin Wittes, *When Is a Covert Action No Longer Covert?*, Lawfare, January 21, 2012, available at <http://www.lawfareblog.com/2012/01/when-is-a-covert-action-no-longer-covert/>.

125. 50 U.S.C. § 3093(e)(1)–(4).

126. 50 U.S.C. § 3093(a)(5). For a discussion of the application of these requirements in practice *see* Jonathan M. Fredman, *Policy and Law: Covert Action, Loss of Life, and the Prohibition on Assassination*, Studies in Intelligence, semi-annual unclassified edition no. 1 (1997), at pp. 15–25.

127. 50 U.S.C. § 3093(a)(1)–(4).

128. 50 U.S.C. § 3093(d).

129. 50 U.S.C. § 3093(b), (c), (d).

130. 50 U.S.C. § 3093(a)(3).

131. P.L. 93-559 (1974). The development of Congressional oversight over covert action is described in Marshall Curtis Erwin, "Covert Action: Legislative Background and Possible Policy Questions," Congressional Research Service, April 10, 2013, at pp. 1–3.

Agency. While valuable synergies resulted from the combination of authorities entrusted to the DCI, there also were unintended consequences. CIA is not a policymaking agency, but an implementing one, and its views on certain issues may have been discounted at times; nonetheless, it remains the agency responsible for implementing covert action and often has the most comprehensive view of the operational realities that will be encountered in the course of a covert action activity.

With multiple priorities competing for attention from the former Director of Central Intelligence, as discussed above in 2004 Congress and the President separated the national level Intelligence Community responsibilities of the DCI from the responsibility to manage the Central Intelligence Agency itself, allocating the former to the Director of National Intelligence (DNI) and the latter to the Director of the Central Intelligence Agency (DCIA).[132] In 2008, the President revised the Reagan-era Executive Order 12333 to reflect the enactment of the IRTPA; as amended, E.O. 12333 provides that the DNI "shall oversee and provide advice to the President and the NSC with respect to all ongoing and proposed covert action programs."[133] CIA remains responsible for the "conduct [of] covert action activities approved by the President,"[134] and along with the DNI ensures that Congress remains fully and currently informed of covert action activities.[135]

The separation of the functions of the director of the CIA from those of the director of the IC in part reflected the tensions inherent in those dual roles with respect to the policy formulation process. The ramifications of that separation are still developing and may yet take some time to become fully apparent. It may be the case that the presence at the table of both a DNI and a DCIA, in contrast to a single Director of Central Intelligence, can contribute to a more well-rounded consideration of covert action as one among several options, each one consistent with overt U.S. policy and complementing U.S. diplomatic, military, and law enforcement activities.

Indeed, in almost all instances covert action may be most effective at the margins. By itself, covert action rarely can accomplish the fundamental national policy objectives and as such normally should be considered as part of the overall U.S. national strategy with respect to any given set of national security challenges and opportunities. Covert action should complement, and be complemented by, robust diplomatic or military activities directed toward the same national objectives. And in particular, covert action should not be undertaken in the absence of comprehensive national strategy, nor should it be contemplated as a substitute for contemporaneously conducted robust non-CA actions.[136]

Moreover, it is inherently difficult to assess the relative contribution that particular forms of covert action may produce. While one can determine the absolute number of press placements, agent recruitments, or personnel trained in the course of a paramilitary assistance program, it is much more difficult to determine the relative contribution of any of those specific activities to the achievement of our national policy objectives. For

---

132. Intelligence Reform and Terrorism Prevention Act of 2004, P.L. 108-458 (2004).

133. Executive Order 12333, § 1.3(b)(3).

134. Executive Order 12333, § 1.7(a)(4). Subsection 1.7(a)(4) further provides that "[n]o agency except the Central Intelligence Agency (or the Armed Forces of the United States in time of war declared by the Congress or during any period covered by a report from the President to the Congress consistent with the War Powers Resolution, Public Law 93-148) may conduct any covert action activity unless the President determines that another agency is more likely to achieve a particular objective."

135. Executive Order 12333, § 3.1.

136. A more detailed review of this aspect of covert action is presented in Jonathan M. Fredman, *Covert Action Policy and Procedure*, ABA NATIONAL SECURITY LAW REPORT, July–October 2009, Vol. 31, Nos. 3–4, at pp. 6–9.

example, a covert influence program may reach a given percentage of the target audience; attitudes among the target audience may have changed; but that change and its magnitude may or may not be attributable to our covert action activities. A foreign paramilitary training activity may produce a given number of trained personnel; but the capabilities represented by those personnel may or may not have been achievable through overt military or non-military support apart from covert action.

Additionally, as discussed earlier in this chapter, traditional military operations (such as operational preparation of the battlefield) are not covert action and, as such, are exempt from the Finding/MoN requirements and the covert action notification procedures to Congress.[137] The boundaries between traditional military operations and covert action, however, are not always certain,[138] and have been subject to controversy in areas such as cyber operations for decades now.[139] Importantly, in this as in so many areas, there may be a temptation to define the issue in purely legal terms and to look to the lawyers for an answer. But the issues are broader and more thematic, and require sustained policy attention to arrive at a resolution in a manner that reflects the policy considerations reflected in the statutory provisions on covert action, the national military interest, the ability of the President to manage the Executive Branch effectively, and the oversight responsibilities of the Congress.

Questions for Discussion

1. What limits are there upon the exercise by the President of his covert action authorities?

2. May the President receive funds from foreign nations to assist in covert action?

3. May the President delay or withhold notification of a covert action activity from the Congressional oversight committees?

4. Can the Congressional oversight committees take steps to prevent the implementation of a covert action?

Oversight

Executive Branch

Concentric circles of intelligence oversight exist within the executive branch.[140] The first and most immediate form of oversight is by the individual intelligence professional. Each federal employee of the IC is required by statute to swear or affirm that they will

---

137. It should be noted that notwithstanding the exclusion of traditional military, diplomatic, and law enforcement activities from the statutory definition of covert action, both the National Security Act and Executive Order 12,333 contemplate that in certain circumstances the armed forces (or some other U.S. Government department or agency) may be directed to undertake covert action operations in addition to their traditional activities. *See, e.g.,* 50 U.S.C. § 3093(a)(3) and Executive Order 12,333, § 1.7(a)(4).

138. *See* Erwin, *Covert Action: Legislative Background and Possible Policy Questions,* at 7–9.

139. *See* Robert Chesney, *Military-Intelligence Convergence and the Law of the Title 10/Title 50 Debate,* 5 J. NAT'L SECURITY L. & POL'Y 539 (2012).

140. Indeed, multiple and overlapping circles of oversight take place across the three branches of government and through the media. *See* JACK GOLDSMITH, POWER AND CONSTRAINT: THE ACCOUNTABLE PRESIDENCY AFTER 9/11, W.W. Norton and Company (2012).

"support and defend the Constitution of the United States against all enemies, foreign and domestic," that they will "bear true faith and allegiance to the same," and that they "will well and faithfully discharge the duties" of their office.[141] Likewise, such employees are bound by the IC's "Principles of Professional Ethics," which include compliance with the laws of the United States, and stewardship, which requires intelligence professionals to "report wrongdoing through appropriate channels" and to "remain accountable to ourselves, our oversight institutions, and through those institutions, ultimately to the American people."[142] When intelligence professionals become aware of malfeasance or illegal activity, statutory procedures exist permitting them to report such violations to the Intelligence Community Inspector General, Congress, or to other designated officials.[143] By statute and executive directive, retaliatory measures against individuals reporting such violations are prohibited.[144]

General Counsels and Inspectors General

Beyond the vigilance of the individual federal official, intelligence oversight at the agency level is conducted (albeit not exclusively) by General Counsels and Inspectors General. Within the IC, the DNI General Counsel and CIA General Counsel are presidentially-appointed and Senate-confirmed,[145] which may provide those offices with a degree of political independence that is conducive to reporting potential violations of the law or policy. Regardless of their manner of appointment, however, General Counsels tend to play an essential role in oversight. Often, in fulfilling their duties in advising on intelligence operations, agency lawyers tend to be among the first officials to become aware of potential violations of law. When such occurs, IC attorneys are bound by statute[146] and Executive Order 12333—as well as potentially by specific agency regulations—to report such violations to the Department of Justice and other executive branch bodies.

Nonetheless, while the reporting of malfeasance and criminal activity is a paramount duty of IC attorneys, it is not their sole function. Likewise, General Counsels do not tend to be primarily responsible for investigating violations. In contrast, Inspectors General ("IG") are mandated to investigate allegations of wrongdoing, and to conduct inspections and audits of IC programs. These officials exist at both the agency level and (as of 2010) at the community-wide level, and may be the result of legislative mandate or administrative appointment.[147] Where the office has been created through legislation (such as the

---

141. 5 U.S.C. §3331.

142. Office of the Director of National Intelligence, Principles of Professional Ethics for the Intelligence Community, available at <http://www.dni.gov/index.php/intelligence-community/principles-of-professional-ethics>.

143. *See, e.g.,* 50 U.S.C. §3033(g)(3); 50 U.S.C. §3517(d)(5).

144. *See* 42 U.S.C. §2000ee-1(e); Presidential Policy Directive 19, "Protecting Whistleblowers with Access to Classified Information," (2012), available at http://fas.org/irp/offdocs/ppd/ppd-19.pdf. *See also* Director of the Office of National Intelligence, Intelligence Community Directive 120, "Intelligence Community Whistleblower Protection (2014), available at <http://www.dni.gov/files/documents/ICD/ICD%20120.pdf>.

145. However, the General Counsels of other cabinet departments containing IC agencies (e.g. the Departments of Defense and State) are also presidentially-appointed and Senate confirmed.

146. 28 U.S.C. §535(b). *See also* "Memorandum of Understanding: Reporting of Information Concerning Federal Crimes" (1995), contained in Office of the Director of National Intelligence, Intelligence Community Legal Reference Book, 915–927 (2012); "Attorney General's Section 905(b) Guidelines Regarding Reports of Possible Criminal Activity Involving Foreign Intelligence Sources" (2002), *Id.* at 857–859.

147. It should also be noted that the IRTPA created the position of DNI Civil Liberties Protection Officer, who performs essential oversight functions by, *inter alia,* ensuring that the "protection of

Intelligence Community IG within the ODNI), IGs have been given broad authorities to fulfill their oversight function, including access to IC records and employees, the ability to take testimony under oath, and subpoena powers.[148] In turn, the Intelligence Community IG is required to report all IG investigations, inspections, and audits to the DNI, who must in turn provide the reports to the congressional intelligence oversight committees.[149] That said, the authority of the Intelligence Community IG is not total; the DNI may prohibit the Intelligence Community IG from "initiating, carrying out, or completing any investigation, inspection, audit, or review if the [DNI] determines that such prohibition is necessary to protect vital national security interests." Nonetheless, where the DNI exercises such authority, he is required to provide his rationale to Congress, and the Intelligence Community IG is provided an opportunity to likewise submit comments on the matter.[150]

Advisory Boards and Independent Oversight Agencies

Within the executive branch, agency oversight is supplemented by advisory boards within the Executive Office of the President. The President's Intelligence Advisory Board (PIAB) has existed in various forms since the Eisenhower administration, with its current structure defined in Executive Order 13462 (2008), as amended. The PIAB describes itself as a non-partisan body of 16 "distinguished citizens" drawn from outside the federal workforce, and is charged with oversight that includes not only reviewing the lawfulness of intelligence activities, but also the effectiveness of those programs as well.[151] The PIAB makes biannual reports to the President which, due to their deliberative nature, tend not to be released to the public.

One subcomponent of the PIAB is the Intelligence Oversight Board (IOB). Originally established by President Ford in Executive Order 11905, the IOB operated as an independent board until it was subsumed as a standing committee of the PIAB.[152] Under Executive Order 12333, IC agencies are required to report to the IOB "intelligence activities of their elements that they have reason to believe may be unlawful or contrary to executive order or presidential directive."[153] Based on those reports, the IOB is charged with (among other things) reviewing the "effectiveness, efficiency, and sufficiency" of agencies' intelligence oversight reporting procedures, making recommendations for corrective action, reporting potential violations of the law to the Attorney General, and reporting to the President when potential violations are not being adequately addressed, or otherwise require the President's attention.[154]

Whereas the PIAB and IOB respectively focus on the IC's efficacy and conformance to the law, the Presidential Civil Liberties Oversight Board (PCLOB) is tasked with the narrower mission of assessing the civil liberties impact of the executive branch's counterterrorism efforts. Initially created by executive order as the President's Board on Safeguarding Americans' Civil Liberties,[155] the board was renamed and given a statutory

---

privacy and civil liberties is appropriately incorporated into the policies and procedures developed for and implemented" by the ODNI, and by reviewing and assessing complaints indicating possible abuses of civil liberties. *See* 50 U.S.C. § 3029.

148. 50 U.S.C. § 3033(g).
149. 50 U.S.C. § 3033(k).
150. 50 U.S.C. § 3033(f).
151. <http://www.whitehouse.gov/administration/eop/piab>.
152. Executive Order 12863, § 2.1 (1993).
153. Executive Order 12333, § 1.6(b).
154. Executive Order 13462, § 6, as amended by Executive Order 13516 (2009).
155. Executive Order 13353 (2004).

foundation through the IRTPA in 2004. The board was reconstituted into its current form by the Implementing Recommendations of the 9/11 Commission Act of 2007, which removed the PCLOB from the Executive Office of the President, making it an independent agency with the executive branch.[156] Although authorized by legislation in 2007, the PCLOB did not begin to function until 2013, when the Senate approved the appointment of David Medine as the board's first Chairman.[157]

The PCLOB is charged with reviewing proposed and existing laws, regulations, and policies "related to efforts to protect the Nation against terrorism" to ensure that "the need for such actions is balanced with the need to protect privacy and civil liberties" and that "liberty concerns are appropriately considered" in the development of such authorities.[158] In performing its functions, the PCLOB is given broad authority to review agency records, conduct interviews, and—upon a majority vote of board members—may elect to "request" that the Attorney General issue a subpoena for the production of information. Furthermore, the 2007 act mandated the appointment of civil liberties officers within various agencies (to include DoJ, DoD, the State Department, Treasury, DNI, and CIA), who undertake civil liberties reviews within their respective agencies, and report their findings to the PCLOB.[159] In turn, both the PCLOB and agency civil liberties officers report their findings to Congress in an "unclassified form to the greatest extent possible."[160]

Questions for Discussion

1. Imagine that you are an attorney in an intelligence agency's Office of General Counsel. You become aware that officials in the agency may have inadvertently taken actions that potentially violate the law. However, the facts aren't clear. Are you required to report this information? Who are you required to report it to? Does it make a difference if the violation concerned provisions of an executive order, rather than a law?

2. Depending on the nature of the violation, it is possible that it would need to be reported to the agency Inspector General, the agency's civil liberties officer, the IOB, the PCLOB, the Department of Justice, and congressional oversight committees. Of these, who has the ultimate responsibility for determining how to handle the issue?

Congress

In the authorities section, we reviewed the primary methods by which Congress exercises oversight of the IC, namely through legislative reforms, statutory agency charters, and the process of appropriation and authorization. However, Congress possesses additional tools both to prospectively encourage IC adherence to the law, as well as to retrospectively review potential violations. On the prospective side, oversight may occur through hearings and questions for the record conducted pursuant to the Senate's "advice and consent" function in approving presidential nominees for senior positions within intelligence agencies.[161] Retrospectively, Congress may establish independent commissions (such as

---

156. 42 U.S.C. § 2000ee.
157. <http://www.pclob.gov/about-us.html>.
158. 42 U.S.C. § 2000ee(c)1.
159. 42 U.S.C. § 2000ee-1.
160. 42 U.S.C. § 2000ee(e)(1)(B)(2).
161. *See, e.g.,* Caroline Krass's written responses to the SSCI's "Questions for the Record," submitted as a part of Ms. Krass's nomination to serve as General Counsel of the CIA, available at <http://www.intelligence.senate.gov/131217/krasspost.pdf>.

the 9/11 Commission), hold public hearings concerning Intelligence activities (such as those held to investigate Iran-Contra), or prepare official reports following investigations conducted by congressional staff members.

However, a persistent issue in the conduct of congressional oversight of the IC has been access to the executive branch's classified information. In 1976, the Subcommittee on Oversight and Investigations of the House Committee on Interstate and Foreign Commerce issued a subpoena to AT&T, requiring the production of records concerning FBI phone taps initiated for the collection of foreign intelligence. The White House objected to the production of the records, fearing that the release would harm diplomatic relations, and reveal intelligence sources and methods. Attempts to reach a negotiated agreement between the House committee and the White House broke down, and the Attorney General sought and received an injunction preventing AT&T from producing the requested records. Subcommittee Chairman John Ross intervened, and sought an appeal of the injunction. The D.C. Circuit remanded the case for further negotiations, which failed to achieve a compromise.

Upon appeal following remand, Judge Leventhal declined to abstain on the basis of the political question doctrine, instead promulgating a proposed procedure designed to further negotiations between the executive and legislative branches. In doing so, Judge Leventhal noted that the framers of the Constitution

> ... rather than attempting to define and allocate all governmental power in minute detail, relied, we believe, on the expectation that where conflicts in scope of authority arose between the coordinate branches, a spirit of dynamic compromise would promote resolution of the dispute in the manner most likely to result in efficient and effective functioning of our governmental system. Under this view, the coordinate branches do not exist in an exclusively adversary relationship to one another when a conflict in authority arises. Rather, each branch should take cognizance of an implicit constitutional mandate to seek optimal accommodation through a realistic evaluation of the needs of the conflicting branches in the particular fact situation.[162]

Thus, *United States v. American Telephone & Telegraph Co.* left unresolved the question of when the executive was required to produce classified information to the legislative branch. The question was largely avoided through the creation of the Senate and House intelligence oversight committees in 1976 and 1977, which helped to effectuate the "accommodation" between the two branches, by establishment of committees with the jurisdiction to review intelligence activities, and the facilities and cleared staff necessary for the review of classified material.

However, in the ensuing decade, the Iran-Contra affair would demonstrate the accommodation to be less than "optimal." During the early 1980s, Congress mandated restrictions on the DoD and CIA provision of assistance to rebels ("Contras") fighting the leftist Sandinista government of Nicaragua. Despite this, NSC staffers—led by Marine Lieutenant Colonel Oliver North—engineered an arrangement whereby Israel sold arms to an Iranian group holding U.S. hostages in Lebanon, with the United States resupplying Israel and receiving the Iranian payment, which in turn was provided to the Nicaraguan Contras. Following public exposure of the arrangement, Congress conducted a series of hearings, resulting in the passage of the Intelligence Oversight Act of 1991, which required the President to keep the intelligence oversight committees "fully and currently informed"

---

162. United States v. American Telephone & Telegraph Co., 567 F.2d 121, 127 (D.C. Cir. 1977).

of U.S. intelligence activities, and set forth the covert action reporting mechanisms discussed above.

As currently structured, Congress oversees the Intelligence Community through the Senate Select Committee on Intelligence (SSCI)[163] and the House Permanent Select Committee on Intelligence (HPSCI).[164] The Subcommittees on Defense of the House and Senate Appropriations Committees (HAC-D and SAC-D, respectively) also review the activities of the Intelligence Community.[165] The Congressional Research Service has observed that

> The current state of affairs reflects a multi-faceted phenomenon. Not only does "intelligence" overlap both foreign and domestic areas; but it also covers a diversity of subjects, agencies, and procedures within each. Oversight of intelligence, particularly in the foreign realm, is consolidated to a large degree in the House and Senate Select Committees on Intelligence. But it is not centralized there; each panel has exclusive legislative authority over only the Central Intelligence Agency (CIA) and Director of National Intelligence (DNI). A number of other committees share oversight, including the four (Appropriations, Armed Services, Foreign Affairs/Foreign Relations, and Judiciary) that have representation on their chamber's intelligence committee. These panels also hold authorization powers over select programs or agencies or, in the case of the appropriations committees, hold appropriations authority over the entire intelligence community. Additional committees with oversight or legislative jurisdiction over parts of U.S. intelligence range across a wide variety of subjects, including civil liberties, cybersecurity, government-controlled information and access to it, government organization and reorganization, homeland security, military affairs, or individual agencies that conduct intelligence themselves or rely on other entities for it. Along with these organizational arrangements, oversight of intelligence is affected by formal reporting requirements as well as informal agreements between Members and staff in Congress and officials and staff in the executive branch. Finally, custom and tradition play a role in the oversight process.[166]

There have been proposals over the years to consolidate oversight in a joint intelligence committee, to be comprised of members of both Houses, or to combine the authorization and appropriations committees in each House, but none have yet been adopted.[167]

Questions for Discussion

1. In light of *United States v. American Telephone & Telegraph Co*, does Congress have a constitutional right to access classified information?

2. Can the Executive take actions to prevent or prosecute what it perceives to be unauthorized or unwarranted Congressional access?

---

163. The SSCI was created on May 19, 1976.

164. The HPSCI was created on July 14, 1977.

165. A detailed review of the oversight structure and proposals for reform is presented in L. Elaine Halchin and Frederick M. Kaiser, "Congressional Oversight of Intelligence: Current Structure and Alternatives," Congressional Research Service, May 14, 2012.

166. *Id.* at 1-2 (footnote omitted).

167. *See, e.g.*, Commission on the Intelligence Capabilities of the United States Regarding Weapons of Mass Destruction, REPORT TO THE PRESIDENT, at 337-340; 9/11 Commission Report, at 420.

3. Are there methods—other than political negotiation—to resolve these types of disputes?

The Courts

Several factors contribute to the relative scarcity of judicial pronouncements on intelligence matters. First, the "cases and controversies" requirement precludes the courts from proactively seeking out intelligence matters for review; the episodic opportunity to opine on intelligence activities is only triggered when a party brings a matter for judicial resolution. Likewise, because of the predominantly foreign focus and clandestine nature of intelligence activities, it is difficult for litigants to obtain the judicial standing necessary to challenge the actions of the IC. Finally, even where a litigant is able to bring a case, courts may refrain from asserting their power, either because of deference to the executive on foreign affairs, or due to abstention under the political question doctrine.

However, where courts have spoken, they have at times endorsed executive action, articulating doctrines that are essential to the conduct of intelligence collection and the protection of sources and methods. So too, courts have acted as a bulwark against encroachment on civil liberties resulting from intelligence activities, both by establishing clear principles regarding constitutional rights, and by acting as a recurring check on the executive collection and use of intelligence information.

The Courts as Balancers of Secrecy and Public Access

The ability of the executive to protect classified information from public disclosure is founded both in statute[168] and executive order.[169] However, the principle that the government may withhold information from public disclosure is in large part premised on the common-law State Secrets privilege. In the United States, the State Secrets doctrine may trace its origins to *Totten v. United States*,[170] a Supreme Court case arising out of the Civil War. The plaintiffs in the case were the executors of the estate of William Lloyd, whom the plaintiffs claimed had served President Lincoln as a spy in Confederate territory. The plaintiffs sought to recover the sums they believed Lincoln owed Lloyd for the latter's espionage services. The Court held that secret contracts like that between Lloyd and the President were non-justiciable. Writing on behalf of the Court, Justice Field noted

> It may be stated as a general principle that public policy forbids the maintenance of any suit in a court of justice the trial of which would inevitably lead to the disclosure of matters which the law itself regards as confidential and respecting which it will not allow the confidence to be violated. On this principle, suits cannot be maintained which would require a disclosure of the confidences of the confessional, or those between husband and wife, or of communications by a client to his counsel for professional advice, or of a patient to his physician for a similar purpose. Much greater reason exists for the application of the principle to cases of contract for secret services with the government, as the existence of a contract of that kind is itself a fact not to be disclosed.[171]

---

168. 18 U.S.C. §798.
169. Executive Order 13526 (2009).
170. 92 U.S. 105 (1875).
171. 92 U.S. at 107.

In the intervening years, the Supreme Court has upheld the *Totten* doctrine, both as a categorical bar against entertaining suits concerning clandestine contracts, and the more general State Secrets privilege that, when evoked, prevents the disclosure of classified information in judicial proceedings. The Court addressed the former issue in *Tenet v. Doe*,[172] a case brought by a former foreign official, who alleged that in exchange for the provision of espionage services, the CIA had promised to provide the plaintiff with "financial and personal security for life." Plaintiffs brought suit when the CIA allegedly did not subsequently provide the support plaintiffs expected. The Court held that the *Totten* doctrine applied not only to the contract between the plaintiff and the CIA, but also barred review of plaintiff's allegations that the CIA's supposed violation of plaintiff's procedural and substantive due process rights by not providing a fair internal process for reviewing plaintiff's claims.

The Court's more general articulation of the State Secrets doctrine was set forth in *United States v. Reynolds*,[173] a tort action filed by the families of Air Force civilian contractors killed in a plane crash in Georgia. The Air Force refused the plaintiffs' request for the production of the accident reports, claiming that release of such reports would harm national security. In reviewing the Air Force's refusal to provide the reports, the Supreme Court held that military secrets were privileged against disclosure in civil matters. In so holding, the Court seemed to acknowledge in *Reynolds* that need for secrecy in national security matters would sometimes trump private litigants' interests in bringing civil cases.

However, the Court set forth demanding requirements for invocation of the privilege. The Court limited invocation of the privilege to the Government (as opposed to private parties), and only when made pursuant to a formal claim of the privilege by the head of the department that has control over the matter, after actual personal consideration by that officer. Finally, the Court reserved an oversight role for the judiciary, holding that courts must determine whether the circumstances are appropriate for the claim of privilege, yet do so without forcing a disclosure of the very thing the privilege is designed to protect.[174]

The judicial role of balancing executive claims of secrecy with the interests of private litigants is replicated in suits brought under the Freedom of Information Act (FOIA). Originally passed in 1966, FOIA was designed to make the records of Federal departments and agencies available to the public, under the theory that "a democracy works best when the people have all the information that the security of the nation permits."[175] FOIA has been amended numerous times over the years, yet from its earliest incarnation, the act has excluded information that the Executive determines must be "kept secret in the interest of national defense or foreign policy," and information "specifically exempted from disclosure by statute"[176] (for example, the provision of the CIA Act exempting from disclosure the "organization, function, names, official titles, salaries, or numbers of personnel employed by the Agency").[177]

Should a FOIA requester bring suit following an agency denial of information pursuant to one of the statutory exemptions, the court may grant summary judgment to the agency when the agency's affidavits "describe the documents and the justifications for nondisclosure

---

172. 544 U.S. 1 (2005).

173. 345 U.S. 1 (1953).

174. *Id.* at 8.

175. Signing statement of President Lyndon B. Johnson, July 4, 1966, available at http://www2.gwu.edu/~nsarchiv/nsa/foia/FOIARelease66.pdf.

176. 5 U.S.C. § 552(b).

177. 50 U.S.C. § 3507.

with reasonably specific detail, demonstrate that the information withheld logically falls within the claimed exemption, and are not controverted by either contrary evidence in the record nor by evidence of agency bad faith."[178] However, while courts may give intelligence agencies' claims of risk to national security resulting from disclosure, such deference is not total. By statute, courts are required to consider government withholding of information *de novo*, and the "burden is on the agency to sustain its action."[179]

The Courts as Guarantors of Constitutional Rights

While not comprehensive, this section examines how, through a variety of court holdings and statutorily codified judicial procedures, the courts enforce and protect U.S. persons' First Amendment freedom of speech and the press, Fourth Amendment rights against unreasonable search and seizure, Fifth Amendment due process rights, and Sixth Amendment confrontation and compulsory process rights.[180]

In the context of First Amendment jurisprudence, the Court has further exercised its role as balancer of national security and the public interests. On the one hand, the Court has demonstrated great skepticism regarding Government efforts to prevent the publication of information concerning defense and intelligence matters. In *The New York Times Co. v. United States*,[181] the Supreme Court ruled against the Government's attempts to enjoin the publication of a classified study of the Vietnam War. The *per curiam* opinion included five concurring opinions, including Justice Douglas's view that there were no circumstances justifying government restraint of the press,[182] and Justice Brennan's suggestion that such restraint could only occur during times of war under circumstances where publication would "inevitably, directly, and immediately" imperil safety.[183] However, perhaps Justice Stewart phrased it best, stating that

> "[i]n the absence of the governmental checks and balances present in other areas of our national life, the only effective restraint upon executive policy and power in the areas of national defense and international affairs may lie in an enlightened citizenry—in an informed and critical public opinion which alone can here protect the values of democratic government."[184]

Although the *New York Times* case stands for the proposition that the government almost never may engage in prepublication restraint,[185] this is not to say that the courts

---

178. Military Audit Project v. Casey, 656 F.2d 724, 738 (D.C. Cir. 1981).

179. *Id.*

180. *See, e.g.*, Fred F. Manget, *Intelligence and the Rise of Judicial Intervention*, in Loch K. Johnson, ed., HANDBOOK OF INTELLIGENCE STUDIES (London: Routledge, 2007), and *Intelligence and the Criminal Law System*, STANFORD LAW & POLICY REVIEW 17:2 (2006).

181. 403 U.S. 713 (1971).

182. 403 U.S. 713 at 720 (Douglas, J., concurring).

183. 403 U.S. 713 at 726–727 (Brennan, J., concurring).

184. *Id.* at 728 (Stewart, J., concurring).

185. But see *United States v. Progressive, Inc.*, 467 F. Supp. 990 (W.D. Wisc. 1979) ("this Court concludes that publication of the technical information on the hydrogen bomb contained in the article is analogous to publication of troop movements or locations in time of war and falls within the extremely narrow exception to the rule against prior restraint."). The *Progressive* court observed that

> In *Near v. Minnesota,* 283 U.S. 697, 51 S.Ct. 625, 75 L.Ed. 1357 (1931), the Supreme Court specifically recognized an extremely narrow area, involving national security, in which interference with First Amendment rights might be tolerated and a prior restraint on publication might be appropriate. The Court stated:
>
> > When a nation is at war many things that might be said in time of peace are such a hindrance to its effort that their utterance will not be endured so long as men fight and that no Court could regard them as protected by any constitutional right." No one would

have left the IC without any legal recourse. In *Snepp v. United States*,[186] the defendant—a former CIA employee—published a memoir about CIA activities in Vietnam, without submitting the book to the CIA for prepublication classification review, as required by the defendant's employment contract.[187] The Court affirmed the Fourth Circuit's opinion that Snepp had violated his fiduciary trust in not submitting his book for review; however, the Court rejected that Circuit's ruling that the CIA was only entitled to punitive damages to the extent that the Government could show harm. The Supreme Court held that proving tortious harm would require the Government to disclose exactly the kind of secrets that the prepublication requirement was designed to protect. Thus, the Court permitted the CIA to receive all profits from the publication of Snepp's book through a constructive trust.[188]

Furthermore, under the Espionage Act,[189] the government may prosecute individuals that leak classified information to media groups.[190] Taken together, *Snepp*, the *New York Times* case, and the Espionage Act suggest that while the government may discourage the press from publishing information concerning sources and methods either through informal requests, or threats of civil damages or prosecution for leakers, the government may not outright prohibit the press from publishing.

Beyond its jurisprudence limiting IC actions with regard to the First Amendment, the judiciary also serves as an important check on executive intrusion into U.S. persons' sphere of privacy under the Fourth Amendment. As discussed previously, for many decades, the Article II authority of the Executive to conduct electronic surveillance and physical searches for the purpose of collecting foreign intelligence was an open question. With the passage of, and subsequent amendments to FISA, however, surveillance activities that had previously been the exclusive domain of the Executive became subject to external review by the judiciary. Under Title I of FISA, if intelligence agencies wish to conduct surveillance on a target inside the United States, they must make a probable cause showing

---

question but that a government might prevent actual obstruction to its recruiting service or the publication of the sailing dates of transports or the number and location of troops. *Id.* at 716, 51 S.Ct. at 631 (citation omitted).

186. 444 U.S. 507 (1980).

187. Permission to publish may be withheld solely upon the determination that the specific information is classified, regardless of whether the publication would embarrass the government or engender criticism of its leaders. *United States v. Marchetti*, 466 F.2d 1309 (4th Cir.), *cert. denied*, 409 U.S. 1063 (1972).

188. 444 U.S. at 511. The Supreme Court recognized that the First Amendment does not prohibit the limited form of prior restraint by means of prepublication review, as a condition of access to classified information, that was agreed upon by Snepp and continues to be agreed upon by the appropriate Federal employees. 444 U.S. at 509, n.3 ("this Court's cases make clear that—even in the absence of an express agreement—the CIA could have acted to protect substantial government interests by imposing reasonable restrictions on employee activities that, in other contexts, might be protected by the First Amendment. "). *See also United States v. Marchetti*, 466 F.2d 1309, (4th Cir.), *cert. denied*, 409 U.S. 1063 (1972) ("the secrecy agreement executed by Marchetti at the commencement of his employment was not in derogation of Marchetti's constitutional rights. Its provision for submission of material to the CIA for approval prior to publication is enforceable, provided the CIA acts promptly upon such submissions and withholds approval of publication only of information which is classified and which has not been placed in the public domain by prior disclosure)."

189. 18 U.S.C. §792 et seq.

190. *See, e.g.,* Spencer Hsu, *State Dept. Contractor Charged in Leak to News Organization*, Washington Post, August 28, 2010, available at <http://www.washingtonpost.com/wp-dyn/content/article/2010/08/27/AR2010082704602.html>.

to a FISA judge that the target of the surveillance is a foreign power, or agent of a foreign power; for United States persons, FISA adds the additional requirement that the "foreign power" determination cannot be premised solely on the basis of activity protected by the First Amendment.[191] Such provisions are similar, although not identical to the requirements for a criminal search warrant under Rule 41 of the Federal Rules of Criminal Procedure,[192] or for a wiretap under section 2518 of Title 18.[193] In both procedures, the relevant standard is probable cause. However, in weighing the issuance of a criminal warrant, the factual question is whether there is evidence that the subject of the warrant has committed a crime, whereas in the context of a FISA order, the question is whether the target is a foreign power, or agent thereof.

A more expansive review of FISA is conducted elsewhere in this volume.[194] Nonetheless, it suffices to make two points here. First, as the discussion above demonstrates, FISA introduced an element of separation of powers protection of Fourth Amendment rights that was perhaps missing prior to the statute's enactment. Second, FISA is but a part of a larger statutory framework making the judiciary a redoubt against potential constitutional abuses by the IC or law enforcement.

Illustrative of this latter point is the Classified Information Procedures Act (CIPA). In one sense, CIPA is merely a procedural tool designed to prevent "graymail," i.e. the threat by criminal defendants to publically reveal classified information as a part of their defense strategy. In a larger sense, however, CIPA is an important device to ensure defendants' Fourth Amendment rights against unreasonable search and seizure, Fifth Amendment rights of due process, and Sixth Amendment confrontation clause and compulsory process rights. CIPA achieves this by creating a process for both the prosecution and defense to identify and notify the opposing party of potentially classified information that may be discoverable, or used at trial.[195] If the information is relevant to the case,[196] then the United States may move to delete classified information, or provide an unclassified substitute. In turn, the judge may approve the use of the classified summary or statement if such "will provide the defendant with substantially the same ability to make his defense."[197] If

---

191. 50 U.S.C. § 1805(a)(2)(A). Similar provisions are contained in Title III for physical searches (*see* 50 U.S.C. § 1824(a)(2)). However, the standards for obtaining pen registers, trap and trace devices, business records, and for collection on persons outside the United States are lower. For example, the standard for the production of business records is that there are "reasonable grounds to believe that the tangible things sought are relevant to an authorized investigation … to obtain foreign intelligence information not concerning a United States person or to protect against international terrorism or clandestine intelligence activities, such things being presumptively relevant to an authorized investigation if the applicant shows in the statement of facts that they pertain to (i) a foreign power or agent of a foreign power; (ii) the activities of a suspected agent of a foreign power who is the subject of an authorized investigation; or (iii) an individual in contact with, or known to, a suspected agent of a foreign power who is the subject of such an authorized investigation." *See* 50 U.S.C. § 1861(b) (2).

192. Fed.R.Crim.P. 41.

193. 18 U.S.C. § 2518. An additional difference between FISA orders and criminal law enforcement warrants is that the targets of the latter are generally made aware of the fact that they have been subject to search or surveillance, *see* Fed.R.Crim.P. 41(f)(2)(C); 18 U.S.C. § 2518(8)(d), whereas the targets of intelligence surveillance under FISA usually remain unaware.

194. See Chapter 27.

195. 18 U.S.C. App. §§ 4–6. Similar provisions exist for the government disclosure of information collected through FISA. *See, e.g.,* 50 U.S.C. § 1806.

196. For example, where the information is potentially exculpatory, i.e. producible under *Brady v. Maryland,* 373 U.S. 83 (1963); the Jencks Act, 18 U.S.C. § 3500; or Federal Rule of Criminal Procedure 16.

197. 18 U.S.C. App. § 6.

the judge rejects that summary, then the United States may make an interlocutory appeal of the decision.[198] Alternatively, the judge may dismiss the indictment, dismiss specified counts, find against the United States as to any issue to which the classified information relates, or striking or precluding part of a witness's testimony.[199]

Contained within this relatively simple evidentiary procedure is a system that enforces constitutional rights, preserves the common law adversarial system, and permits the executive to weigh the protection of classified information. CIPA allows defendants to gain discovery into potentially classified exculpatory information (thus protecting the defendant's due process rights), utilize classified information where necessary to mount a defense (thereby preserving defendants' compulsory process rights), and allows defendants to challenge government witnesses, even when classified information may be at stake (thus protecting defendants' confrontation clause rights). Ultimately, when all its procedural innovations for protecting classified information have otherwise been exhausted, CIPA leaves the government with a stark choice: either proceed with the prosecution and publicly reveal the classified information, or drop the indictment or counts against the defendant. What CIPA does not permit, however, is for the government to withhold relevant information in the name of national security, all the while utilizing the courts to deny defendants of their personal liberty.

Questions for Discussion

1. Was the Court in *Totten* correct in its reasoning that permitting suits concerning espionage arrangements would be contrary to public policy? Would permitting such suits necessarily require the public disclosure of the secrets that the contract was designed to keep confidential?

2. How can you reconcile the Court's prohibiting suits such as *Totten* and *Tenet v. Doe*, yet permit the Government to sue for damages in cases such as *Snepp*?

3. Some commentators have argued for the creation of a civil evidentiary process similar to the CIPA process used in criminal proceedings. How would such a system work? What would its potential advantages and disadvantages be? How would it differ from the current practice wherein the Government must decide whether to invoke the State Secrets doctrine?

Conclusion

This chapter has provided a general outline of the laws and regulations that govern the activities of the U.S. Intelligence Community. As noted at the outset, it is not comprehensive. Nor could it be, considering the number of agencies, missions, and disciplines encompassed within the IC, as well as the vastness of the topic that the Community is charged with understanding: the security of the world in which we live.

Perhaps more importantly, the account provided is not perdurable, but rather a snapshot of the regulatory framework of the IC as it heads into the third decade of the 21st century. As intelligence is fundamentally about understanding the world as it is, and about trying to discern the world as it will be, it is a study of consistent change. Society constantly

---

198. 18 U.S.C. App. §7.
199. 18 U.S.C. App. §6(e)(2).

evolves, and new threats will inevitably arise. At the same time, certain aspects of American culture are resilient: they include our commitment to constitutional rights, desire for transparency, and democratic governance. Between these dynamic and static elements of society lies the law. The laws governing intelligence must evolve if they are to adequately provide and regulate the tools necessary to collect the information policymakers require to understand an ever-changing world. Yet laws, if they are to have any persuasive effect, must remain grounded in the timeless constitutional principles and procedures that define American society. Thus, the demand that the law of intelligence be simultaneously adaptive and constant ensures, if nothing else, that it will remain a fascinating area of study, and a professional calling for well-informed, dedicated, and principled practitioners.

Selected Bibliography

Office of the Director of National Intelligence, *IC Legal Reference Book 2012*, available at: http://www.dni.gov/index.php/about/organization/ic-legal-reference-book-2012.

ANNEX

Presidential Approval and Congressional Reporting of Covert Actions (section 503 of the National Security Act, 50 U.S.C.§ 3093)

(a) Presidential findings

The President may not authorize the conduct of a covert action by departments, agencies, or entities of the United States Government unless the President determines such an action is necessary to support identifiable foreign policy objectives of the United States and is important to the national security of the United States, which determination shall be set forth in a finding that shall meet each of the following conditions:

(1) Each finding shall be in writing, unless immediate action by the United States is required and time does not permit the preparation of a written finding, in which case a written record of the President's decision shall be contemporaneously made and shall be reduced to a written finding as soon as possible but in no event more than 48 hours after the decision is made.

(2) Except as permitted by paragraph (1), a finding may not authorize or sanction a covert action, or any aspect of any such action, which already has occurred.

(3) Each finding shall specify each department, agency, or entity of the United States Government authorized to fund or otherwise participate in any significant way in such action. Any employee, contractor, or contract agent of a department, agency, or entity of the United States Government other than the Central Intelligence Agency directed to participate in any way in a covert action shall be subject either to the policies and regulations of the Central Intelligence Agency, or to written policies or regulations adopted by such department, agency, or entity, to govern such participation.

(4) Each finding shall specify whether it is contemplated that any third party which is not an element of, or a contractor or contract agent of, the United States Government, or is not otherwise subject to United States Government policies and regulations, will be used to fund or otherwise participate in any significant way in the covert action concerned, or be used to undertake the covert action concerned on behalf of the United States.

(5) A finding may not authorize any action that would violate the Constitution or any statute of the United States.

(b) Reports to congressional intelligence committees; production of information

To the extent consistent with due regard for the protection from unauthorized disclosure of classified information relating to sensitive intelligence sources and methods or other exceptionally sensitive matters, the Director of National Intelligence and the heads of all departments, agencies, and entities of the United States Government involved in a covert action—

(1) shall keep the congressional intelligence committees fully and currently informed of all covert actions which are the responsibility of, are engaged in by, or are carried out for or on behalf of, any department, agency, or entity of the United States Government, including significant failures; and

(2) shall furnish to the congressional intelligence committees any information or material concerning covert actions (including the legal basis under which the covert action is being or was conducted) which is in the possession, custody, or control of

any department, agency, or entity of the United States Government and which is requested by either of the congressional intelligence committees in order to carry out its authorized responsibilities.

(c) Timing of reports; access to finding

(1) The President shall ensure that any finding approved pursuant to subsection (a) of this section shall be reported in writing to the congressional intelligence committees as soon as possible after such approval and before the initiation of the covert action authorized by the finding, except as otherwise provided in paragraph (2) and paragraph (3).

(2) If the President determines that it is essential to limit access to the finding to meet extraordinary circumstances affecting vital interests of the United States, the finding may be reported to the chairmen and ranking minority members of the congressional intelligence committees, the Speaker and minority leader of the House of Representatives, the majority and minority leaders of the Senate, and such other member or members of the congressional leadership as may be included by the President.

(3) Whenever a finding is not reported pursuant to paragraph (1) or (2) of this section, [1] the President shall fully inform the congressional intelligence committees in a timely fashion and shall provide a statement of the reasons for not giving prior notice.

(4) In a case under paragraph (1), (2), or (3), a copy of the finding, signed by the President, shall be provided to the chairman of each congressional intelligence committee.

(5) (A) When access to a finding, or a notification provided under subsection (d)(1), is limited to the Members of Congress specified in paragraph (2), a written statement of the reasons for limiting such access shall also be provided.

(B) Not later than 180 days after a statement of reasons is submitted in accordance with subparagraph (A) or this subparagraph, the President shall ensure that—

(i) all members of the congressional intelligence committees are provided access to the finding or notification; or

(ii) a statement of reasons that it is essential to continue to limit access to such finding or such notification to meet extraordinary circumstances affecting vital interests of the United States is submitted to the Members of Congress specified in paragraph (2).

(d) Changes in previously approved actions

(1) The President shall ensure that the congressional intelligence committees, or, if applicable, the Members of Congress specified in subsection (c)(2) of this section, are notified in writing of any significant change in a previously approved covert action, or any significant undertaking pursuant to a previously approved finding, in the same manner as findings are reported pursuant to subsection (c) of this section.

(2) In determining whether an activity constitutes a significant undertaking for purposes of paragraph (1), the President shall consider whether the activity—

(A) involves significant risk of loss of life;

(B) requires an expansion of existing authorities, including authorities relating to research, development, or operations;

(C) results in the expenditure of significant funds or other resources;

(D) requires notification under section 3094 of this title;

(E) gives rise to a significant risk of disclosing intelligence sources or methods; or

(F) presents a reasonably foreseeable risk of serious damage to the diplomatic relations of the United States if such activity were disclosed without authorization.

(e) "Covert action" defined

As used in this subchapter, the term "covert action" means an activity or activities of the United States Government to influence political, economic, or military conditions abroad, where it is intended that the role of the United States Government will not be apparent or acknowledged publicly, but does not include—

(1) activities the primary purpose of which is to acquire intelligence, traditional counterintelligence activities, traditional activities to improve or maintain the operational security of United States Government programs, or administrative activities;

(2) traditional diplomatic or military activities or routine support to such activities;

(3) traditional law enforcement activities conducted by United States Government law enforcement agencies or routine support to such activities; or

(4) activities to provide routine support to the overt activities (other than activities described in paragraph (1), (2), or (3)) of other United States Government agencies abroad.

(f) Prohibition on covert actions intended to influence United States political processes, etc.

No covert action may be conducted which is intended to influence United States political processes, public opinion, policies, or media.

(g) Notice and general description where access to finding or notification limited; maintenance of records and written statements

(1) In any case where access to a finding reported under subsection (c) or notification provided under subsection (d)(1) is not made available to all members of a congressional intelligence committee in accordance with subsection (c)(2), the President shall notify all members of such committee that such finding or such notification has been provided only to the members specified in subsection (c)(2).

(2) In any case where access to a finding reported under subsection (c) or notification provided under subsection (d)(1) is not made available to all members of a congressional intelligence committee in accordance with subsection (c)(2), the President shall provide to all members of such committee a general description regarding the finding or notification, as applicable, consistent with the reasons for not yet fully informing all members of such committee.

(3) The President shall maintain—

(A) a record of the members of Congress to whom a finding is reported under subsection (c) or notification is provided under subsection (d)(1) and the date on which each member of Congress receives such finding or notification; and

(B) each written statement provided under subsection (c)(5).

Funding of Intelligence Activities
(section 504 of the National Security Act, 50 U.S.C. § 3094)

(a) Obligations and expenditures for intelligence or intelligence-related activity; prerequisites

Appropriated funds available to an intelligence agency may be obligated or expended for an intelligence or intelligence-related activity only if—

(1) those funds were specifically authorized by the Congress for use for such activities; or

(2) in the case of funds from the Reserve for Contingencies of the Central Intelligence Agency and consistent with the provisions of section 3093 of this title concerning any significant anticipated intelligence activity, the Director of the Central Intelligence Agency has notified the appropriate congressional committees of the intent to make such funds available for such activity; or

(3) in the case of funds specifically authorized by the Congress for a different activity—

(A) the activity to be funded is a higher priority intelligence or intelligence-related activity;

(B) the use of such funds for such activity supports an emergent need, improves program effectiveness, or increases efficiency; and

(C) the Director of National Intelligence, the Secretary of Defense, or the Attorney General, as appropriate, has notified the appropriate congressional committees of the intent to make such funds available for such activity;

(4) nothing in this subsection prohibits obligation or expenditure of funds available to an intelligence agency in accordance with sections 1535 and 1536 of title 31.

(b) Activities denied funding by Congress

Funds available to an intelligence agency may not be made available for any intelligence or intelligence-related activity for which funds were denied by the Congress.

(c) Presidential finding required for expenditure of funds on covert action

No funds appropriated for, or otherwise available to, any department, agency, or entity of the United States Government may be expended, or may be directed to be expended, for any covert action, as defined in section 3093(e) of this title, unless and until a Presidential finding required by subsection (a) of section 3093 of this title has been signed or otherwise issued in accordance with that subsection.

(d) Report to Congressional committees required for expenditure of nonappropriated funds for intelligence activity

(1) Except as otherwise specifically provided by law, funds available to an intelligence agency that are not appropriated funds may be obligated or expended for an intelligence or intelligence-related activity only if those funds are used for activities reported to the appropriate congressional committees pursuant to procedures which identify—

(A) the types of activities for which nonappropriated funds may be expended; and

(B) the circumstances under which an activity must be reported as a significant anticipated intelligence activity before such funds can be expended.

(2) Procedures for purposes of paragraph (1) shall be jointly agreed upon by the congressional intelligence committees and, as appropriate, the Director of National Intelligence or the Secretary of Defense.

(e) Definitions

As used in this section —

(1) the term "intelligence agency" means any department, agency, or other entity of the United States involved in intelligence or intelligence-related activities;

(2) the term "appropriate congressional committees" means the Permanent Select Committee on Intelligence and the Committee on Appropriations of the House of Representatives and the Select Committee on Intelligence and the Committee on Appropriations of the Senate; and

(3) the term "specifically authorized by the Congress" means that —

(A) the activity and the amount of funds proposed to be used for that activity were identified in a formal budget request to the Congress, but funds shall be deemed to be specifically authorized for that activity only to the extent that the Congress both authorized the funds to be appropriated for that activity and appropriated the funds for that activity; or

(B) although the funds were not formally requested, the Congress both specifically authorized the appropriation of the funds for the activity and appropriated the funds for the activity.

Chapter 24

Access to National Security Information

Robert F. Turner

In this chapter:
Access by Congress
Access by the Courts
Access by the Public
Access by Executive Branch Employees and Contractors
Selected Bibliography

> *The necessity of procuring good intelligence, is apparent and need not be further urged. All that remains for me to add is, that you keep the whole matter as secret as possible. For upon secrecy, success depends in most Enterprises of the kind, and for want of it they are generally defeated....*
>
> —General George Washington[1]

> *The Senate is not supposed by the Constitution to be acquainted with the concerns of the Executive department. It was not intended that these should be communicated to them; nor can they therefore be qualified to judge of the necessity which ... special and secret circumstances may call for. All this is left to the President. They are only to see that no unfit person be employed.*
>
> —Thomas Jefferson[2]

> *If a nation expects to be ignorant and free, in a state of civilization, it expects what never was and never will be.*
>
> —Thomas Jefferson[3]

> *[N]o Constitution would ever have been adopted by the convention if the debates had been public.*
>
> —James Madison[4]

---

1. *Washington to Col. Elias Dayton*, July 26, 1777, *in* 8 WRITINGS OF GEORGE WASHINGTON 478–79 (John C. Fitzpatrick ed., 1933).

2. *Jefferson's Opinion on the Powers of the Senate Respecting Diplomatic Appointments*, Apr. 24, 1790, *in* 16 PAPERS OF THOMAS JEFFERSON 378, 379 (Julian P. Boyd ed., 1961). Note that in his initial draft of this document Jefferson wrote the Senate was not supposed to be acquainted with the "secrets" of the executive, but he broadened the term to "concerns" in the final version.

3. *Jefferson to Col. Charles Yancey*, Jan. 6, 1816, *in* 14 WRITINGS OF THOMAS JEFFERSON 384 (Mem. ed. 1903).

4. *Quoted in* CLINTON ROSSITER, 1787: THE GRAND CONVENTION 167 (1966).

> *A popular Government, without popular information, or the means of acquiring it, is but a Prologue to a Farce or a tragedy; or, perhaps both. Knowledge will forever govern ignorance. And a people who mean to be their own Governors, must arm themselves with the power which knowledge gives.*
>
> —James Madison[5]

> *The Government has a compelling interest in protecting both the secrecy of information important to our national security and the appearance of confidentiality so essential to the effective operation of our foreign intelligence service.*
>
> —Supreme Court of the United States[6]

The above epigrams reflect the inevitable democratic tension between the Nation's desire to keep its electorate informed and the competing objective of denying certain information to its adversaries. The inability to achieve both objectives fully—for example, by producing a newspaper or Web site that could only be read by citizens who, in turn, were denied any contact with foreign agents hostile to the United States—makes it impossible totally to reconcile both goals with full satisfaction. To understand how these competing interests have been balanced over our more than two centuries of history, some background is useful.

Robert F. Turner, *War and the Forgotten Executive Power Clause of the Constitution*

34 Va. J. Int'l L. 903, 922–29 (1994)

IV. Government Secrecy and Republican Government

. . . .

There seems to be a widespread assumption in the post-Vietnam era that the Founding Fathers viewed secrecy in government as incompatible with democratic theory. While it is true that they believed as a general principle that an informed public was essential to democratic government, they were practical men who recognized that intelligence, military, and diplomatic matters often had to be kept secret not only from the nation's enemies, but even from the American people and their elected representatives in Congress.

A. *The Committee of Secret Correspondence*

The obvious inability of legislative bodies to manage the details of foreign communication led the Continental Congress to establish a "Committee of Secret Correspondence" on November 29, 1775. Two weeks later, the Committee dispatched Thomas Story as a secret messenger to France, Holland, and England, with instructions to make contact with a network of unofficial "secret agents" serving the United States in foreign capitals, such as Silas Deane in France and Arthur Lee in England.

After meeting with Lee, Story returned to America and gave this report to the Committee, as recorded in a memorandum dated October 1, 1776, that was found among the Committee's official papers:

> On my leaving London, Arthur Lee, Esq., requested me to inform the Committee of [Secret] Correspondence that he had several conferences with the French Am-

---

5. *Madison to W. T. Barry*, Aug. 4, 1822, *in* 9 The Writings of James Madison 103 (Gaillard Hunt ed., 1910).
6. Snepp v. United States, 444 U.S. 507, 510 (1980).

bassador, who had communicated the same to the French court; that in consequence thereof the Duke de Vergennes had sent a gentleman to Mr. Lee, who informed him that the French Court could not think of entering into a war with England, but that they would assist America by sending from Holland this fall two hundred thousand pounds sterling worth of arms and ammunition to St. Eustatius, Martinico, or Cape François. That application was to be made to the Governours or Commandants of those places by inquiring for Monsieur Hortalez, and that on persons properly authorized applying, the above articles would be delivered to them.

This arguably may have been the first "covert operation" to which the United States was a party, and the secret offer of £200,000 worth of arms was welcome news in America. It was also recognized as highly sensitive news. For that reason, Benjamin Franklin and the members of the small committee he chaired agreed without dissent that it could not be shared with their colleagues in the Congress. Their memorandum explains:

> The above intelligence was communicated to the subscribers [Franklin and Robert Morris], being the only two members of the Committee of Secret Correspondence now in the city, and our considering the nature and importance of it, we agree in opinion that *it is our indispensable duty to keep it secret even from Congress*, for the following reasons:

> First, Should it get to the ears of our enemies at New York, they would undoubtedly take measures to intercept the supplies, and thereby deprive us not only of those succours, but of others expected by the same route.

> Second, as the Court of France have taken measures to negotiate this loan of succour in the most cautious and secret manner, should we divulge it immediately, we may not only lose the present benefit, but also render that Court cautious of any further connection with such unguarded people, and prevent their granting other loans and assistance that we stand in need of, and have directed Mr. Deane to ask of them. For it appears from our intelligence they are not disposed to enter into an immediate war with Britain, although disposed to support us in our contest with them. We therefore think it our duty to cultivate their favourable disposition towards us, draw from them all the support we can, and in the end their private aid must assist to establish peace, or inevitably draw them in as parties to the war.

> Third, *We find by fatal experience that Congress consists of too many members to keep secrets.*

The memorandum contained the written endorsements of Richard Henry Lee and William Hooper, to whom it had been shown some days later, with the notation that Lee "concur[red] heartily" and Hooper "sincerely approve[d]" of its contents.

B. *John Jay and* Federalist *No. 64*

One of the criticisms of American government under the Articles of Confederation was that all functions of government were entrusted to the Congress, which tended to micromanage military and diplomatic affairs and could not keep secrets. Robert R. Livingston agreed to serve as "Secretary of the United States of America for the Department of Foreign Affairs" in February 1782, but by the end of the year he had submitted his resignation in frustration. Nearly two years passed before John Jay was chosen as the successor to act as the "agent" of Congress in diplomatic intercourse. He, too, was quickly stymied by such things as the demand of Congress to receive every proposal submitted by the Spanish *Chargé* during treaty negotiations.

Jay was particularly frustrated by the demands by Congress—which, in the absence of any executive organ of government, had exclusive control over war, treaties, and other aspects of the nation's foreign communications—for access to confidential information and diplomatic letters. Professor Henry Wriston, in his classic 1929 study, explains:

> It is interesting, in connection with the submission of Lafayette's letters to Congress, to observe that Jay regarded this as a serious limitation upon the value of the correspondence. *Congress never could keep any matter strictly confidential; someone always babbled.* "These circumstances must undoubtedly be a great restraint on those public and private characters from whom you would otherwise obtain useful hints and information. I for my part have long experienced the inconvenience of it, and in some instances very sensibly."

These frustrations were widely shared. Jay went on to play a key role both in explaining the Constitution as a co-author of the *Federalist Papers* and in interpreting it as the nation's first Chief Justice. He took on the issues of secrecy and intelligence squarely in *Federalist* essay number 64, explaining the benefits of entrusting matters requiring secrecy to the executive while requiring the approval of two-thirds of the Senate before the President could ratify a completed treaty:

> There are cases where the most useful intelligence may be obtained, if the persons possessing it can be relieved from apprehensions of discovery. Those apprehensions will operate on those persons whether they are actuated by mercenary or friendly motives, and there doubtless are many of both descriptions, who would rely on the secrecy of the president, but who would not confide in that of the senate, and still less in that of a large popular assembly. The convention have done well therefore in so disposing of the power of making treaties that although *the president* must in forming them act by the advice and consent of the senate, yet *he will be able to manage the business of intelligence in such manner as prudence may suggest.*

Jay added, with an allusion to the shortcomings of the Articles of Confederation: "So often and so essentially have we heretofore suffered from the want of secrecy and dispatch, that the Constitution would have been inexcusably defective if no attention had been paid to those objects."

C. *Washington, the Senate, and Congressional Leaks*

Further contemporary insight into the Founding Fathers' perception that Congress could not be trusted to keep secrets is found in an informal note made by our first Secretary of State, Thomas Jefferson. Beginning during his service in this capacity, Jefferson made various notes, on what he called "passing transactions," to assist his memory. He later combined them into three volumes which we today know as *The Anas*. The following entry is instructive:

> *April 9th*, 1792. The President had wished to redeem our captives at Algiers, and to make peace with them on paying an annual tribute. The Senate were willing to approve this, but unwilling to have the lower House applied to previously to furnish the money; they wished the President to take the money from the treasury, or open a loan for it.... *They said ... that if the particular sum was voted by the Representatives, it would not be a secret. The President had no confidence in the secrecy of the Senate*, and did not choose to take money from the treasury or to borrow. But he agreed he would enter into provisional treaties with the Algerines, not to be binding on us till ratified here.

This is an important and largely forgotten part of our history. While certainly there was a recognition of the need for an informed public, and in most matters a presumption against government secrecy, experience had shown that secrecy was sometimes essential even beyond the scope of national security affairs, as illustrated by the Constitutional Convention of 1787.

D. *The Federal Convention of 1787*

On May 29, 1787, the fourth day of deliberation, the Constitutional Convention adopted a series of rules as part of the Standing Orders of the House. Rules three through five provided:

> That no copy be taken of any entry on the journal during the sitting of the House without the leave of the House. That members only be permitted to inspect the journal. That nothing spoken in the House be printed, or otherwise published, or communicated without leave.

The great constitutional historian Clinton Rossiter has described this so-called secrecy rule as "the most critical decision of a procedural nature the Convention was ever to make," and notes that "in later years, Madison insisted that 'no Constitution would ever have been adopted by the convention if the debates had been public.'" Indeed, at his insistence, Madison's own important notes on the convention were not published until 1840, four years after his death and more than half a century after the convention had ended.

E. *Early Congressional Practice*

Of particular value in trying to understand the original constitutional scheme are the acts of the First Congress, elected in early 1789. Two-thirds of its twenty-two senators and fifty-nine representatives had either been members of the Philadelphia Convention of 1787 or of state ratifying conventions, and only seven of them had opposed ratification. Accordingly, their actions are entitled to special weight. As Chief Justice John Marshall observed in 1821, in trying to determine the intent of the Founding Fathers, "[g]reat weight has always been attached, and very rightly attached, to contemporaneous exposition."

It is therefore noteworthy that the First Congress appropriated a "contingent fund" of $40,000, which was a considerable sum at the time, for the President to use for special diplomatic agents and other sensitive foreign affairs needs. The statute expressly provided "[t]he President shall account specifically for all such expenditures of the said money *as in his judgment may be made public,* and also *for the amount of such expenditures as he may think it advisable not to specify.*" It is significant that the President was not required to account to Congress "under injunction of secrecy" for sensitive expenditures. He was required simply to inform Congress of the sums expended so that the fund could be replenished as necessary. Congress was not to be told the details, as the Founding Fathers had learned first-hand the harm that could be done by leaks.

It is perhaps also worth noting that the contingent account was not only replenished but increased within three years to the level of one million dollars, with much of it reportedly being used for such expenditures as bribing foreign officials and ransoming hostages....

When Jefferson used his contingent account to fund a paramilitary army of Greek and Arab mercenaries to invade Tripoli and pressure its Bey to surrender American hostages, no one seems to have complained that Congress was not informed in advance of the operation. Jefferson's successor, James Madison, a man of some familiarity with the meaning of the Constitution, found that he needed additional funds to underwrite a covert action to gain control over disputed territory between Georgia and Spanish Florida in 1811, so he asked Congress to enact a "secret appropriation" of $100,000 for that purpose. The need for secrecy having passed, the secret appropriation was discretely made public years later, in 1818....

MARK J. ROZELL, EXECUTIVE PRIVILEGE: THE DILEMMA OF SECRECY AND DEMOCRATIC ACCOUNTABILITY
33–53 (1994)

[S]everal of Washington's actions established precedents for the exercise of what is now known as executive privilege. The first such action concerned a congressional request to investigate "public" information relating to the failure of a November 1791 military expedition by Gen. Arthur St. Clair against Native American Indians. The House of Representatives established an investigative committee on 27 March 1792, "to call for such persons, papers and records, as may be necessary to assist their inquiries." The investigating committee requested from the president documents regarding St. Clair's expedition.

Washington convened his cabinet to determine how to respond to this first ever request for presidential materials by a congressional committee. The president wanted to discuss whether any harm would result from public disclosure of the information and, most pertinently, whether he could rightfully refuse to submit documents to Congress. Along with Hamilton, Knox, and Edmund Randolph, Thomas Jefferson attended the 2 April 1792 cabinet meeting. He later recalled the group's determination:

> We had all considered, and were of one mind, first, that the House was an inquest, and therefore might institute inquiries. Second, that it might call for papers generally. Third, that the Executive ought to communicate such papers as the public good would permit, and ought to refuse those, the disclosure of which would injure the public: consequently were to exercise a discretion. Fourth, that neither the committees nor House has a right to call on the Head of a Department, who and whose papers were under the President alone; but that the committee should instruct their chairman to move the House to address the President.

Washington eventually determined that public disclosure of the information would not harm the national interest and that such disclosure was necessary to vindicate Gen. St. Clair. Although Washington chose to negotiate with Congress over the investigating committee's request and to turn over relevant documents to Congress, his administration had taken an affirmative position on the right of the executive branch to withhold information. Adam Breckenridge writes that "this beginning of the executive privilege indicates ... the president could refuse documents because of their secret nature, a category insisted upon by subsequent presidents ever since."

On 17 January 1794 the U.S. Senate advanced a motion directing Secretary of State Edmund Randolph "to lay before the Senate the correspondence which have been had between the Minister of the United States at the Republic of France, [Morris] and said Republic, and between said Minister and the Office of Secretary of State." The Senate later amended the motion to address the president instead of Minister Morris. Significantly, the amended version also "requested" rather than "directed" that such information be forwarded to Congress.

Believing that disclosure of the correspondence would be inappropriate, Washington sought the advice of his Cabinet as to how to handle the Senate's request. On 28 January 1794 three of Washington's cabinet members expressed their opinions:

General Knox is of the opinion, that no part of the correspondence should be sent to the Senate. Colonel Hamilton, that the correct mode of proceeding is to do what General Knox advises; but the principle is safe, by excepting such parts as the president may choose to withhold. Mr. Randolph, that all correspondence proper, from its nature, to be communicated to the Senate, should be sent; but that what the president thinks is improper, should not be sent.

Attorney General William Bradford wrote separately that "it is the duty of the Executive to withhold such parts of the said correspondence as in the judgment of the Executive shall be deemed unsafe and improper to be disclosed".

On 16 February 1794 Washington responded as follows to the Senate's request:

After an examination of [the correspondence], I directed copies and translations to be made; except in those particulars, in my judgment, for public considerations, ought not to be communicated. These copies and translations are now transmitted to the Senate; but the nature of them manifest the propriety of their being received as confidential.

Washington allowed the Senate to examine some parts of the correspondence, subject to his approval. He believed that information damaging to the "public interest" could constitutionally be withheld from Congress. The Senate never challenged the president's authority to withhold the information.

In 1796 John Jay completed U.S. negotiations with Great Britain over issues unsettled from the American Revolution. Because many considered the settlement unfavorable to the United States, Congress took a keen interest in the administration's actions in the negotiations. Not only did the Senate debate ratification of the Jay Treaty, the House set out to conduct its own investigation. On 24 March 1796 the House passed a resolution requesting from Washington information concerning his instructions to the U.S. minister to Britain regarding the treaty negotiations. That resolution raised the issue of the House's proper role in the treaty-making process. Washington refused to comply with the House request and explained his reasons for so deciding:

The nature of foreign negotiations requires caution, and their success must often depend on secrecy; and even when brought to a conclusion a full disclosure of all the measures, demands, or eventual concessions which may have been proposed or contemplated would be extremely impolitic; for this might have a pernicious influence on future negotiations, or produce immediate inconveniences, perhaps danger and mischief, in relation to other powers. The necessity of such caution and secrecy was one cogent reason for vesting the power of making treaties in the President, with the advice and consent of the Senate, the principle on which that body was formed confining it to a small number of members. To admit, then, a right in the House of Representatives to demand and to have as a matter of course all the papers respecting a negotiation with a foreign power would be to establish a dangerous precedent.

Washington explained that "the boundaries fixed by the Constitution between the different departments should be preserved, a just regard to the Constitution and to the duty of my office … forbids a compliance with your request."

Washington believed that sole authority over the substance of treaty negotiations resided constitutionally in the executive, not Congress. Alexander Hamilton also advised the president that not only did the House have no constitutional function to perform regarding the negotiation of treaties, but that it was the president's right to withhold sensitive materials from Congress.

The House of Representatives subsequently debated at length the propriety of Washington's refusal to disclose the documents. The House took no substantive action other than passing two nonbinding resolutions—one asserting that Congress need not stipulate any reason for requesting information from the executive; the other proclaiming that the House had a legitimate role in considering the speed at which a treaty was being implemented. Our chief constitutional architect, Rep. James Madison, while disagreeing in part with Washington's action, proclaimed on the House floor "that the Executive had a right, under a due responsibility, also, to withhold information, when of a nature that did not permit a disclosure of it at the time."

The Washington administration never included the Senate in the negotiation stage of the Jay Treaty. During the ratification stage, the Senate voted to keep the treaty secret, as Hamilton wrote, "because they thought it [the secrecy] the affair of the president to do as he thought fit." The Senate minority opposed to ratification listed seven objections to the treaty. None cited Washington's decision to not seek advice from the Senate.

President John Adams asserted a right to withhold information from Congress during the 1798 "XYZ Affair." . . .

Executive Privilege in the Nineteenth Century

Even the ultradefender of popular sovereignty, Thomas Jefferson, recognized the legitimacy of executive branch secrecy. As president, he classified his correspondence as either public or secret. He withheld correspondence deemed secret from both the public and Congress. . . . Most relevant to the executive privilege debate, a January 1807 House resolution requested that the president "lay before this House any information in the possession of the Executive, except such as he may deem the public welfare to require not to be disclosed." Congress had clearly acknowledged the president's right to exercise secrecy. . . .

    . . . .

The subsequent exercises of presidential secrecy in the nineteenth century are so numerous as to preclude an analysis of each one. Nonetheless, it is possible to provide a concise historical overview in order to convey the point that numerous presidents exercised what later became known as executive privilege, lending credibility to the constitutionality of that power.

The leading author of the Constitution, James Madison, withheld information from Congress during his presidency. Madison purposefully withheld information about French trade restrictions against the United States, which eventually led to widespread support for war against Great Britain. Madison, and then later President James Monroe, withheld information from Congress regarding the U.S. takeover of the Florida territory. . . .

In 1825 the House of Representatives requested from President Monroe information concerning the "Steward incident," except any details that the president determined it was not in the public interest to disclose. Monroe refused to comply and responded that submitting the requested materials "might tend to excite prejudices" and "would not comport with the public interest nor with what is due to the parties concerned."

Although President Andrew Jackson established for his time an unprecedented close relationship with the public, he did not shy away from exercising, on numerous occasions, the presidential power to withhold information. In 1832 the House requested from Jackson information pertaining to U.S. negotiations with the Republic of Buenos Aires. Jackson responded that it would "not be consistent with the public interest to communicate the correspondence and instructions requested by the House so long as the negotiation shall be pending." In 1833 he refused to divulge information to the Senate pertaining to negotiations with Great Britain over the northeastern boundary of the United States.... In 1835 the president refused to provide to the House certain requested documents pertaining to U.S.-French correspondences.... Jackson refused a Senate request for information about the removal of U.S. Surveyor General Gideon Fitz and stated that "this is another of those calls for information made upon me by the Senate which have, in my judgment, either related to the subjects exclusively belonging to the executive department or otherwise encroached on the constitutional powers of the Executive"....

President John Tyler also frequently asserted a presidential discretion to withhold information. In February 1842 he wrote to Congress that he could not divulge any details regarding the U.S.-British negotiations over the northeastern boundary because "in my judgment no communication could be made by me at this time on the subject of its resolution without detriment or danger to the public interests"....

....

President James K. Polk refused an 1846 House request for information pertaining to the foreign policy expenditures of his predecessor, John Tyler. Polk asserted his duty to uphold his predecessor's determination of confidentiality.... Furthermore, Polk maintained that his own case for protecting confidentiality was particularly compelling, given the fact that full disclosure of diplomatic correspondence during a war would have resulted in "serious embarrassment in any future negotiation between the [United States and Mexico]." Polk concluded that "I regard it to be my constitutional right and my solemn duty under the circumstances of this case to decline a compliance with the request of the House contained in their resolution"....

....

President Millard Fillmore withheld diplomatic information from the Senate on several occasions in 1851–52 when he believed that transmitting such information was not in the public interest.... President James Buchanan refused an 1859 Senate request for law enforcement documents regarding the illegal landing of a slave ship on the Georgia coast.

President Abraham Lincoln exercised the most extensive prerogative powers of any U.S. president. Given the extraordinary actions Lincoln adopted to prosecute the federal war effort, it is hardly surprising that he exercised a discretion to withhold information when deemed to be in the public interest. In 1861 Lincoln refused a House request for information about the arrests of Baltimore police commissioners at Fort McHenry. In 1862 Lincoln refused a Senate request for information pertaining to the arrest of Brig. Gen. Stone. In 1863 the House requested from the secretary of state, "if not in [his] judgment incompatible with the public interest," information on U.S. negotiations with New Grenada. Lincoln replied that it would not be in the "public interest" to comply with the request.

Lincoln's successor, Andrew Johnson, refused on several occasions in 1866 to release requested information to Congress.... In 1876 Ulysses S. Grant refused a House request for information about his presidential actions away from the nation's capital on the basis that such information had no bearing on Congress's constitutional duties.... In 1887 President Grover Cleveland refused a Senate request for information regarding the sale of an American schooner and resignation of the U.S. minister to Mexico. In April 1892 President Benjamin Harrison replied to a Senate request for information about actions regarding a proposed international conference on silver that "it would not be compatible with the public interest" to divulge the information at that time. In his second, nonconsecutive, term, President Cleveland refused an 1896 House request for all details pertaining to U.S. affairs in Cuba, but did release selected information. That same year,

Cleveland withheld from the Senate some requested information about official U.S. correspondence with the government of Spain.

Executive Privilege in the Twentieth Century

In 1901 President William McKinley refused to divulge to the Senate information on a War Department investigation of expenditures of Cuban funds. President Theodore Roosevelt replied to a January 1909 Senate resolution requesting documents from the attorney general on whether proceedings had been instituted against a company for possible Sherman Antitrust Act violations:

> I have instructed the Attorney General not to respond to that portion of the resolution which calls for a statement of his reasons for nonaction. I have done so because I do not conceive it to be within the authority of the Senate to give directions of this character to the head of an executive department, or to demand from him reasons for his action. Heads of the executive departments are subject to the Constitution, and to the laws passed by the Congress in pursuance of the Constitution, and to the directions of the President of the United States, but to no other direction whatever.

The Senate Judiciary Committee cleverly responded by issuing a subpoena for the same documents to the head of the Bureau of Corporations. Roosevelt secured the papers for himself and then told Congress that it would only get the documents by impeaching him. The president explained that "these facts ... were given to the government under the seal of secrecy and cannot be divulged, and I will see to it that the word of this government to the individual is kept sacred."

....

In July 1930 the Senate Foreign Relations Committee requested from President Herbert Hoover's secretary of state copies of correspondence concerning the London Naval Treaty. The president responded that many communications had been provided in confidence and that he had a duty not to violate the trust that negotiators had placed in him. The president did not divulge all of the requested documents.

President Franklin D. Roosevelt withheld documents requested by Congress on a number of occasions. For example, in 1941 FDR instructed his attorney general to withhold certain Federal Bureau of Investigation (FBI) papers from a House committee. In 1943 FDR's director of the Bureau of the Budget refused a House investigative committee subpoena to testify. The president had instructed that Bureau files remain confidential. That same year, the president directed the acting secretary of war not to divulge to Congress documents pertaining to the departments of War and Navy. In 1944 a House investigating committee requested information from the FBI director and issued to him a subpoena to testify. The director refused to testify and would not divulge the contents of a presidential memorandum requiring him not to testify. The attorney general wrote to the committee that communications between the president and department heads were privileged. That same year, the chairman of the Select House Committee investigating the Federal Communications Commission (FCC) acknowledged that "for over 140 years" an exemption from testifying before Congress "has been granted to the executive departments, particularly where it involves military secrets or relations with foreign nations."

President Harry S. Truman also asserted on numerous occasions a discretion to maintain secrecy.... The committee wanted to obtain information about the assistant's conversations with the president, resulting in the committee minority report assertion that "I cannot believe that any congressional committee is entitled to make that kind of investigation into the private conferences of the president with one of his principal aides." In 1950 the president directed his secretary of state, attorney general, and chairman of the Civil Service Commission not to comply with a Senate subcommittee subpoena of files pertaining to the loyalty of State Department employees. Truman cited his 1948 executive order, but eventually backed down after learning that the same documents had once before been made available to Congress. During Senate hearings in 1951 over Truman's firing of Gen. Douglas MacArthur, Gen. Omar Bradley refused a request to testify on conversations he had as an adviser to the president. Truman considered his conversations with Bradley to be confidential. The chairman of the Senate Committee on Armed Services and Foreign Relations, Sen. Richard Russell (D-Ga.), ruled that Bradley had the right to hold confidential conversations with the president. The committee subsequently upheld Russell's ruling by a vote of eighteen to eight.... Truman defended his decision to maintain the confidentiality of the activities of the Loyalty Security Program.

The Dwight D. Eisenhower administration represents an important development in the doctrine of executive privilege. The actual use of the term "executive privilege" originated in the Eisenhower administration. President Eisenhower's administration invoked that doctrine on more than forty occasions. The most important controversy over executive privilege during the Eisenhower years concerned the army-McCarthy hearings. During testimony the army counsel John Adams mentioned that he had had a conference with top White House aides in the attorney general's office. Congressional investigators sought information on what transpired in those conversations among high-ranking officials. Eisenhower intervened with a letter on 17 May 1954 to Secretary of Defense Charles Wilson instructing department employees not to testify....

Other executive branch officials used Eisenhower's letter as the justification for their refusals to testify before Congress. United Nations ambassador Henry Cabot Lodge, for example, refused to testify to Congress on the army-McCarthy affair on the basis that he was a White House adviser. Eisenhower replied affirmatively: "The position you propose to take is exactly correct. I would be astonished if any of my personal advisors would undertake to give testimony on intimate staff counsel and advice. The result would be to eliminate all such offices from the presidential staff. In turn, this would mean paralysis."

Eisenhower adopted an uncompromising stand on executive privilege. He told a group of Republican legislative leaders that "any man who testifies as to the advice he gave me won't be working for me that night." Eisenhower elaborated his position: "Those people who have a position here in this government because of me, those people who are my confidential advisors are not going to be subpoenaed.... Governor Adams's official job is really a part of me and he's not going up on the Hill." Sen. Joseph McCarthy (R-Wisc.) denounced Eisenhower's order as an "iron curtain" and exclaimed that "this is the first time I've ever seen the executive branch of government take the fifth amendment." Despite some other criticism of the president for defining executive privilege too broadly—possibly allowing every executive branch officer to assert that prerogative—the *Washington Post* agreed that the president's constitutional authority to withhold information from Congress "is altogether beyond question."

There are too many other cases of executive privilege in the Eisenhower administration to cover here. It is most important to recognize that Eisenhower's 17 May 1954 letter established a precedent for the exercise of executive privilege in the modern presidency. Indeed, Eisenhower's immediate Democratic successor, John F. Kennedy, did not shy away from executive privilege.

... Kennedy explained his view of executive privilege as follows:

Since the early days of the Republic, Americans have also recognized that the Federal Government is obliged to protect certain information which might otherwise jeopardize the security of the country. That need has become particularly acute in recent years as the United States has assumed a powerful position in world affairs, and as world peace has come to depend in large part on how that position is safeguarded. We are also moving into an era of delicate negotiations in which it will be especially important that governments be able to communicate in confidence.

Clearly, the two principles of an informed public and of confidentiality within the Government are irreconcilable in their purest forms, and a balance must be struck between them.

In 1962 a special Senate subcommittee investigated military Cold War education and speech review policies. The president wrote letters to his secretary of defense instructing the secretary not to comply with a request for the names of individuals who wrote or edited speeches. Kennedy specifically instructed the secretary "not to give testimony or produce any documents which would disclose such information." Kennedy's letter further stated that "it would not be possible for you to maintain an orderly Department and receive the candid advice and loyal respect of your subordinates if they, instead of you and your senior associates, are to be individually answerable to the Congress, as well as to you, for their internal acts and advice." The chairman of the subcommittee, Sen. John Stennis (D-Miss.), ruled in favor of Kennedy's claim of executive privilege. The subcommittee upheld that ruling.

… Kennedy used executive privilege to prevent legislative oversight of foreign policy. The president ordered his military adviser Gen. Maxwell Taylor, to refuse to testify before a congressional committee examining the Bay of Pigs fiasco.

. . . .

Although the Kennedy and Johnson administrations did not exercise executive privilege as extensively as the Eisenhower administration, they clearly accepted the validity of this presidential power. The modern exercise of executive privilege, however, reached its most expansive stage during the Nixon administration. The Nixon years also represent a major stage in the development of the executive privilege controversy. Nixon attempted to transform executive privilege from a widely accepted constitutional prerogative into an absolute, unfettered presidential power. Nixon's excesses served eventually to partially discredit the doctrine of executive privilege. Nixon's successors accordingly have been cautious about making claims to a presidential power of executive privilege.

. . . .

National Security Needs

Congress and the public's "right to know" must be balanced with the requirements of national security. Although the Constitution Framers recognized well enough the importance of secrecy, unity, and dispatch to governing, the need to enhance those values in the modern era, particularly with regard to foreign policy-making, is even more compelling than it was two centuries ago. Many, if not most, of the crises faced by modern governments cannot be dealt with through open, lengthy, national deliberations. The heightened pace of contemporary international events places a premium on rapid and decisive decision-making. The presidency possesses the institutional capacities uniquely suited to responding to crisis situations. The leading Framers recognized that, being one, rather than many, the president is much more capable than Congress of acting with unity, secrecy, dispatch, and resolve. As Paul Peterson has written, "It is the executive power that most lends itself to energy.... To speak of energy in the legislative or judicial branches would be something akin to an oxymoron." The courts have recognized the executive's preeminence in national security and foreign policy-making on a number of occasions....

The courts have generally provided broad discretionary authority to the president in national security and foreign affairs. In *Zemel v. Rusk* (1965) the Supreme Court decided that "Congress—in giving the president authority over matters of foreign affairs—must of necessity paint with a brush broader than that it customarily wields in domestic affairs." In a more recent case, *Department of Navy v. Egan* (1988), the Court offered a broad defense of presidential discretion in foreign affairs, explaining that the president's "authority to classify and control access to information bearing on national security and to determine whether an individual is sufficiently trustworthy to occupy a position in the Executive Branch ... flows primarily from [the president's commander-in-chief power] and exists quite apart from any explicit congressional grant." The courts have agreed that it is neither constitutionally proper nor prudent for Congress to tie the hands of the president in foreign affairs during an emergency situation....

    ....

... Once sensitive information is turned over to members of Congress there is no guarantee that some member will not divulge materials for policy or partisan reasons. The large majority of members are responsible public officials. Yet there may be just one who, at the wrong time, seeks to gain from his or her access to secret information. Joseph W. Bishop makes the following point: "There is no guarantee that information coming into the hands of Congress or the whole membership of one of its major committees will long remain secret.... There is no assurance ... that so large a body of men will not include a percentage, on statistical grounds, of subversives, alcoholics, psychopaths and other security risks."

Although Bishop's characterizations are less than tactful, the general point that there are, at least, a few untrustworthy individuals in any large group of persons is well taken. ABC-TV's Brit Hume reports that a member of the Senate Intelligence Committee, Sen. Joseph Biden (D-Del.), "twice threatened to go public with covert plans by the Reagan administration that were harebrained." Former speaker of the House, Jim Wright (D-Tex.), exclaimed that "the fact that a matter is classified secret, doesn't mean it's sacrosanct and immune from criticism.... It is not only my right but my responsibility to express publicly my opposition to policies I think are wrong." Former Rep. Leo Ryan (D-Calif.) told Richard Cheney in 1975 that an appropriate way for a member of Congress to block an "ill conceived operation" was to leak a state secret. In 1982 Rep. Buddy Roemer (D-La.) declared of secret information during a congressional hearing that "I will tell you as one member of this subcommittee, we ought to do and encourage you to do everything possible not just to amass the information, but to turn it over to the public." In 1974 Rep. Michael Harrington (D-Mass.) released secret testimony of CIA director William Colby, given before the House Armed Services Committee concerning the CIA's "destabilization" policy in Chile. Harrington was not a member of the committee but he was able to secure the transcript of the Colby testimony under a congressional rule that allows any member of the House or Senate access to any records of a committee of the legislative chamber in which he or she serves. The House Ethics Committee dropped the censure charges against Harrington.

    ....

There is, therefore, a compelling case that national security often requires secrecy and that the right to exercise executive privilege is a necessary precondition for the chief executive to achieve national security aims. Additionally, the chief executive needs sound staff advice, and the quality of counsel depends ultimately on the degree of candor....

Access by Congress

Prior to the Vietnam War and the controversies during the Nixon Administration, the constitutional right of the President to withhold documents and information from Congress was widely recognized. Consider these excerpts:

3 WESTEL WILLOUGHBY, THE CONSTITUTIONAL LAW OF THE UNITED STATES
1488 (2d ed. 1929)

§ 968. Information to Congress.

The constitutional obligation that the President "shall from time to time give to the Congress information of the state of the Union, and recommend to their consideration such measures as he shall judge necessary and expedient," has, upon occasion, given rise to controversy between Congress and the President as to the right of the former to compel the furnishing to it of information as to specific matters. As a result of these contests it is practically established that the President may exercise a full discretion as to what information he will furnish, and what he will withhold.

The discretionary right of the President to refuse information to Congress has been exercised from the earliest times. Thus, President Washington refused to send to the House of Representatives correspondence relating to the British treaty; Presidents Jackson and Tyler similarly refused to transmit information relating to the Maine boundary dispute; President Polk declined to send to the Senate the entire correspondence relating to the Oregon dispute with Great Britain; in 1845 President Polk refused information to the Senate regarding the pending annexation of Texas, and again, in 1848, as to the pending treaty with Mexico; President Fillmore refused the request of the Senate for information regarding negotiations with the Sandwich Islands; President Lincoln refused to transmit correspondence with regard to the slave ship Wanderer; and refused to communicate Major Anderson's dispatches from Fort Sumter.[7]

EDWARD CORWIN, THE PRESIDENT: OFFICE AND POWERS, 1787–1957
at 182–83, 211–12 (4th rev. ed. 1957)

Another precedent of great significance from Washington's administration was the first President's refusal in 1796 to comply with a call from the House of Representatives for papers relative to the negotiation of the Jay Treaty. The demand was originally fathered by

---

7. While a professor at Yale Law School, between his service as President and as Chief Justice, William Howard Taft wrote: "The President is required by the Constitution from time to time to give to Congress information on the state of the Union, and to recommend for its consideration such measures as he shall judge necessary and expedient, but this does not enable Congress or either House of Congress to elicit from him confidential information which he has acquired for the purpose of enabling him to discharge his constitutional duties, if he does not deem the disclosure of such information prudent or in the public interest." WILLIAM TAFT, OUR CHIEF MAGISTRATE AND HIS POWERS 129 (1916).

Madison and presumably reflected the theory of "Helvidius" that the President's diplomatic role is chiefly instrumental of the national legislative power in the realm of foreign relationship. Washington's declination, nevertheless, he now conceded to be proper so far as it represented the President's deliberate judgment that the papers were "of a nature that did not permit of disclosure at this time." The concession so broadened the force of the precedent that nowadays a President feels free by the same formula to decline information even to his constitutional partner in treaty-making, whereas Washington's refusal rested primarily on his denial that the House was entitled to discuss the merits of a treaty. In 1906 a debate arose in the Senate over the adventurous foreign policy of the first Roosevelt, in the course of which the entire ground that had been covered by "Pacificus" and "Helvidius" more than a century before was revisited, Senator Spooner assuming the Hamiltonian role and Senator Bacon the Madisonian. In the face of his general position Bacon conceded that "the question of the President's sending or refusing to send any communication to the Senate is not to be judged by legal rights, but [is] ... one of courtesy between the President and that body." The record of practice amply bears out this statement.

... So far as practice and weight of opinion can settle the meaning of the Constitution it is today established that the President ... is final judge of what information he shall entrust to the Senate as to our relations with other governments.[8]

The Supreme Court has recognized a constitutionally based privilege of the President to deny information to Congress—particularly in the sphere of foreign and military affairs. Consider the cases which follow.

---

8. Professor Corwin noted the role of Senator John Coit Spooner—a three-term veteran of the Senate and, by reputation, one of the preeminent constitutional lawyers of his era—in the 1906 debate. Consider this excerpt from Senator Spooner's remarks:

Always the Senate in passing resolutions of inquiry addressed to Cabinet officers, except the Secretary of State, make them in form of *direction*, not *request*. It rarely has happened that a request has been addressed to any Cabinet officer where foreign relations were involved. Where such a resolution has been adopted it has been addressed to the President, with the qualification that he is requested to furnish the information only so far as, in his judgment, the transmission of it is compatible with the public interest.

There are reasons for that, Mr. President. The State Department stands upon an entirely different basis as to the Congress from the other Departments. The conduct of our foreign relations is vested by the Constitution in the President. It would not be admissible at all that either House should have the power to force from the Secretary of State information connected with the negotiation of treaties, communications from foreign governments, and a variety of matters which, if made public, would result in very great harm in our foreign relations—matters so far within the control of the President that it has always been the practice, and it always will be the practice, to recognize the fact that there is of necessity information which it may not be compatible with the public interest should be transmitted to Congress—to the Senate or the House.

There are other cases, not especially confined, Mr. President, to the State Department, or to foreign relations, where the President would be at liberty obviously to decline to transmit information to Congress or to either House of Congress. Of course, in time of war, the President being Commander in Chief of the Army and Navy, could not, and the War Department or Navy Department could not, be required by either House to transmit plans of campaign or orders issued as to the destination of ships, or anything relating to the strategy of war, the public knowledge of which getting to the enemy would defeat the Government and its plans and enure to the benefit of an enemy.

41 CONG. REC. 97, 99–104 (1906).

United States v. Curtiss-Wright Export Corp.
299 U.S. 304 (1936)

[The President] has his confidential sources of information. He has his agents in the form of diplomatic, consular and other officials. Secrecy in respect of information gathered by them may be highly necessary, and the premature disclosure of it productive of harmful results. Indeed, so clearly is this true that the first President refused to accede to a request to lay before the House of Representatives the instructions, correspondence and documents relating to the negotiation of the Jay Treaty — a refusal the wisdom of which was recognized by the House itself and has never since been doubted....

....

The marked difference between foreign affairs and domestic affairs in this respect is recognized by both houses of Congress in the very form of their requisitions for information from the executive departments. In the case of every department except the Department of State, the resolution *directs* the official to furnish the information. In the case of the State Department, dealing with foreign affairs, the President is *requested* to furnish the information "if not incompatible with the public interest." A statement that to furnish the information is not compatible with the public interest rarely, if ever, is questioned. (Emphasis in original.)[9]

Curtiss-Wright is widely recognized to be a landmark case and has been cited by the Court more often than any other foreign affairs case in history — but the fact remains that the dispute adjudicated was a challenge by a private corporation against a statute in which the constitutional powers of the Congress and the President were combined. Thus its *dicta*, while important, were not directed at a confrontation between coordinate branches of the Federal Government.

The National Security Act of 1947 made no reference to Congress as a recipient of intelligence information, and the Director of Central Intelligence speculated after it was enacted that there would not be enough business between the CIA and Congress to justify retaining a full-time attorney.[10] Until the late 1960s, that expectation was largely born out by practice, with years passing between hearings even on the CIA budget. An historical study by the Center for the Study of Intelligence reported, for example, that "[a]s late as 1968 ... CIA records reflect only one briefing that year to the HASC [House Armed Services Committee], three to the HAC [House Appropriations Committee], and two each to the SASC [Senate Armed Services Committee] and SAC [Senate Appropriations Committee]. Attendance typically was limited to Members only, and often no record of the proceedings was kept. Sometimes, reportedly, no questions were asked at all."[11]

The situation changed dramatically during the later years of the Vietnam War, and particularly during the administration of President Richard Nixon, when "executive

---

9. Congress has often recognized the legal right of the President to withhold information. For example, a report of the Senate Foreign Relations Committee concerning the U-2 aircraft incident stated that with respect to foreign intelligence operations: "The administration has the legal right to refuse the information under the doctrine of executive privilege." S. Rep. No. 1761, 86th Cong., 2d Sess., 22 (1960).

10. Center for the Study of Intelligence, "How Intelligence-Sharing With Congress Has Evolved 1947–1974," *available at* <http://www.cia.gov/csi/monograph/lawmaker/1.htm>.

11. *Id.*

privilege" claims were increasingly relied upon as angry legislators sought greater control over military operations, foreign affairs, and intelligence—areas historically recognized by Congress as being at the core of presidential responsibility. During 1969, the CIA Office of Legislative Counsel recorded 1,400 "contacts" with Congress, including sixty substantive briefings. During the next decade, this office expanded to 32 full-time employees. By 1988, the CIA was giving more than 1,000 briefings per year to Congress and turning over more than 4,000 classified documents.[12]

Ignoring nearly two centuries of precedents, since the controversy over Vietnam Congress has made use of a variety of tools in attempts to compel presidents to abandon claims of constitutional privilege. Dr. Louis Fisher, the Senior Specialist in Separation of Powers at the Congressional Research Service of the Library of Congress—who is widely recognized to be among the most able scholars in the "pro-Congress" camp—provided a useful summary in a recent law review article.

Louis Fisher, *Congressional Access to Information: Using Legislative Will and Leverage*
52 DUKE L.J. 323 (2002)

Presidents and their advisers cite various legal principles when they withhold documents from Congress and refuse to allow executive officials to testify before congressional committees. Congress can marshal its own impressive list of legal citations to defend legislative access to information, even when presidents assert executive privilege. These legal and constitutional principles, finely-honed as they might be, are often overridden by the politics of the moment and practical considerations.

This Essay highlights the political settlements that decide most information disputes. Courts play a role, but it is a mistake to believe that handy cites from judicial opinions will win the day. Efforts to resolve interbranch disputes on purely legal grounds may have to give ground in the face of superior political muscle by a Congress determined to exercise the many coercive tools available to it. By the same token, a Congress that is internally divided or uncertain about its institutional powers will lose out in the quest for information....

   ....

I. Constitutional Principles in Conflict

No constitutional language authorizes the president to withhold documents from Congress, nor does any provision empower Congress to demand and receive information from the executive branch. The Supreme Court has recognized the constitutional power of Congress to investigate, and the president's power to withhold information, but those powers would exist with or without judicial rulings....

   ....

What informs the process of congressional access to executive branch information is the constitutional structure of separation of powers and the system of checks and balances. Neither political branch has incontestable authority to withhold information or force its disgorgement. When these executive-legislative clashes occur, they are seldom resolved judicially.... The outcome is more likely decided by the persistence of Congress and its willingness to adopt political penalties for executive noncompliance. Congress can win most of the time—if it has the will—because its political tools are formidable.

---

12. *Id.* at 5–6.

....

II. The Appropriations Power

Presidents may have to surrender documents they consider sensitive or confidential to obtain funds from Congress to implement programs important to the executive branch. This congressional leverage appears in a number of early executive-legislative confrontations over the treaty power. Although the House has no formal role in the treaty process, once a treaty is ratified and requires appropriations to carry it out, presidents must turn to the House for support, and share with it whatever documents are necessary to obtain the funds. In some cases, the administration may find it politically smart to share documents with the House while treaty negotiations are underway....

....

III. The Impeachment Power

In the struggle for information, Congress has especially strong leverage when it decides to initiate the impeachment process. This leverage exists not only when a president is personally accused of an action that may merit removal from office, but extends more broadly to malfeasance in the administration and to corruption, inefficiency, criminal activity, unethical conduct, and personal wrongdoing by agency officials.

A. Early Precedents

When President Washington denied the House the papers it requested on the Jay Treaty, he said that the only ground on which the House might have legitimately requested the documents was impeachment, "which the resolution has not expressed." The power of impeachment, said President James Polk, gives to the House of Representatives

> the right to investigate the conduct of all public officers under the Government. This is cheerfully admitted. In such a case the safety of the Republic would be the supreme law, and the power of the House in the pursuit of this object would penetrate into the most secret recesses of the Executive Department. It could command the attendance of any and every agent of the Government, and compel them to produce all papers, public or private, official or unofficial, and to testify on oath to all facts within their knowledge.

Executive privilege may also be politically imprudent in cases where lawmakers make serious charges of administrative malfeasance. President Andrew Jackson told Congress that if it could "point to any case where there is the slightest reason to suspect corruption or abuse of trust.... [t]he offices of all the departments will be opened to you, and every proper facility furnished for this purpose." The Supreme Court has noted that the power of Congress to conduct investigations "comprehends probes into departments of the Federal Government to expose corruption, inefficiency or waste."

....

C. Senate "Holds"

The informal practice of imposing "holds" allows any Senator to request that floor action on a bill or nomination be deferred. The Senate Majority Leader may then decide whether to honor the request. Although there have been objections to "secret holds" — so-called "anonymous" holds — Senators realize that holds are frequently a legitimate means of pursuing legislative interests. Efforts to place limits on holds, such as requiring Senators to make their actions known to the sponsor of a bill, have been difficult to enforce.

There are many reasons for placing a hold, but often it is to obtain information that the executive branch has refused to release to Congress. In 1993, Senator John Warner announced that he would release his hold on the intelligence authorization bill after receiving assurance from the CIA that it would search its files for information on Department of Defense nominee Morton Halperin. The CIA had previously said that it could not find the documents requested by Republican members of the Senate Armed Services Committee. CIA Director James Woolsey had planned to brief committee Republicans on this issue but apparently was ordered not to do so by White House Counsel Bernard Nussbaum.

....

V. Congressional Subpoenas

The Supreme Court has held that the congressional power of inquiry "is an essential and appropriate auxiliary to the legislative function." As a tool of this inquiry, both Houses of Congress authorize their committees and subcommittees to issue subpoenas to require the production of documents and the attendance of witnesses regarding matters within the committee's jurisdiction. If a witness from the administration refuses to testify by invoking the Fifth Amendment, Congress can vote to force testimony by granting the witness either partial or full immunity.

....

VI. The Contempt Power

When the executive branch refuses to release information or allow officials to testify, Congress may decide to invoke its contempt power. Although the legislative power of contempt is not expressly provided for in the Constitution and exists as an implied power, the Supreme Court recognized as early as 1821 that, without this power, the legislative branch would be "exposed to every indignity and interruption that rudeness, caprice, or even conspiracy, may meditate against it." If either House votes for a contempt citation, the president pro tempore of the Senate or the Speaker of the House shall certify the facts to the appropriate U.S. Attorney, "whose duty it shall be to bring the matter before the grand jury for its action." Individuals who refuse to testify or produce papers are subject to criminal contempt, leading to fines of not more than one thousand dollars and imprisonment up to one year.

....

... 2. *Henry Kissinger.* In 1975, the House Select Committee on Intelligence issued a subpoena to Secretary of State Henry Kissinger, directing him to provide documents relating to covert actions. After he refused, the committee voted ten to two to proceed to a contempt citation. President Gerald Ford invoked executive privilege to keep the material from the committee, explaining that release of the documents, which included "recommendations from previous Secretaries of State to previous Presidents," would jeopardize the internal decisionmaking process. Nevertheless, under pressure of a contempt citation, an accommodation was reached. Three committee members and two staff members visited the White House and listened to an NSC aide read verbatim from documents concerning the covert actions. The committee, stating that the White House was in "substantial compliance" with the subpoena, announced that the contempt action was "moot."

....

VII. House Resolutions of Inquiry

A House resolution of inquiry "is a simple resolution making a direct request or demand of the President or the head of an executive department to furnish the House of

Representatives with specific factual information in the possession of the executive branch." It is the practice to use the verbs "request" in asking for information from the president and "direct" when addressing department heads. "The resolution of inquiry is privileged" and "may be considered at any time after it is properly reported or discharged from committee." The privileged status applies only to requests for facts within the administration's control and not for opinions or investigations. If a resolution of inquiry "is not reported to the House within 14 legislative days after its introduction, a motion to discharge the committee" is privileged. Typically, the House debates a resolution of inquiry for no more than one hour before voting on it.

There is no counterpart in current Senate practice for resolutions of inquiry, although there are precedents dating to the end of the 19th century and an effort in 1926. Nothing prevents the Senate from passing such resolutions, but apparently the Senate is satisfied with the leverage it has through other legislative means, including the nomination process and Senate "holds." ...

House resolutions of inquiry sometimes give the administration discretion in providing factual information to Congress. For example, in 1971, the House considered a resolution directing the secretary of state to furnish certain information respecting U.S. operations in Laos, but the language of the resolution included the phrase "to the extent not incompatible with the public interest." ...

A more recent use of a resolution of inquiry occurred in 1995, after the Clinton administration offered a multibillion dollar rescue package for the Mexican peso. As initially introduced by Representative Marcy Kaptur, the resolution (House Resolution 80) did not contain discretion for the administration. It requested the president, within fourteen days after the adoption of the resolution, to submit information to the House of Representatives concerning actions taken through the exchange stabilization fund to strengthen the Mexican peso and stabilize the economy of Mexico. The House Banking Committee voted thirty-seven to five to report the resolution, but with a substitute directing the president to submit the documents "if not inconsistent with the public interest." On March 1, the House adopted the committee substitute and agreed to the resolution, 407 to 21.

Although the resolution established a deadline of fourteen days, White House Counsel Abner Mikva sent a letter to Speaker Newt Gingrich "that the Administration would not be able to provide" the documentary material until May 15, or two months after the date set in the resolution. By April 6, the Treasury Department had supplied Congress with "more than 3,200 pages of unclassified documents and 475 pages of classified documents," with additional materials promised. The White House said it was in "substantial compliance" with the resolution.

....

Conclusion

Congress depends on information from the executive branch to perform its constitutional duties. Much of the information that Congress seeks is located within executive agencies that are created, authorized, and funded by Congress. In both a legal and constitutional sense, agencies are "creatures" of Congress and must learn to serve both the executive and legislative branches. As greater portions of executive power move to the president's office, Congress has a similar need to gain access to White House documents and compel White House aides to testify.

Whether lawmakers obtain that information depends on their willingness and ability to expend the energy and time it takes to overcome bureaucratic hurdles. To do that well, members of Congress have to think of themselves as belonging to an *institution* rather than a variety of interests....

Untidy as they are, political battles between Congress and the executive branch are generally effective in resolving executive privilege disputes. Courts play a minor role, which is good for the judiciary and good for the country. There is no reason to think that greater involvement by courts would be constructive or helpful. The risk is great that the Supreme Court, in trying to settle one issue, will fashion standards and doctrines that may prove to be too broad and awkwardly drawn. For example, in the Watergate tapes case, Chief Justice Warren Burger resorted to clumsy dicta and ceded ground to presidents who claim a "need to protect military, diplomatic, or sensitive national security secrets." That issue was not before the Court, was never argued or briefed, and should not have been addressed.

Nevertheless, journalists and even academics seem to think that if the president announces that information falls within the categories of military, diplomatic, or "sensitive national security secrets," the other two branches should back off. If the courts want to do that, they may retreat in the face of such presidential claims. Congress should not. The Watergate tapes case concerned access to information by the judiciary, not Congress. Lawmakers, with specific constitutional duties over issues involving the military and national security, have no reason to defer to such presidential arguments.

....

Comments

The excerpt from Professor Rozell's book and the other readings show that, throughout most of American history, it has been widely accepted that the President has the authority to deny sensitive national security information to Congress. This is consistent as well with John Jay's discussion of the need to protect intelligence "sources" in *Federalist* No. 64,[13] which concluded that the Constitution had left the President free "to manage the business of intelligence in such manner as prudence may suggest," and with Chief Justice Marshall's observation that that certain constitutional presidential powers are unchecked by Congress or the Judiciary.[14] But, as Dr. Fisher notes, since Vietnam Congress has sought to compel the President to provide sensitive national security information and documents through the use of "political battles" using "the many coercive tools available to it," such as refusing to even take up nominations until the President agrees to provide the information demanded. In his first weeks as Secretary of State, Thomas Jefferson envisioned that Congress might theoretically usurp the President's diplomatic powers by refusing to confirm ambassadorial nominees until the President agreed to yield to Senate control. After telling President Washington that the "Executive Power" Clause had vested in the President the "transaction of business with foreign nations," including the decisions of what grade (for example, ambassador, minister, consul) to be given to diplomats and to what countries they ought to be accredited—save for strictly construed "exceptions" vested in the Senate,[15]—Jefferson speculated that the Senate might theoretically try to expand its powers improperly:

> It may be objected that the Senate may, by continual negatives on the *person*, do what amounts to a negative on the *grade*; and so indirectly defeat this right of

---

13. *See* the discussion *supra* on John Jay and *Federalist* No. 64 in TURNER, WAR AND THE FORGOTTEN EXECUTIVE POWER CLAUSE OF THE CONSTITUTION.

14. 5 U.S. 165–66, *quoted in* chapter 19.

15. See the section on "Jefferson's Advice to Washington on the Senate Role in Foreign Affairs" in Chapter 19.

the President. But this would be a breach of trust, an abuse of the power confided to the Senate, of which that body cannot be supposed capable. So the President has a power to convoke the legislature; and the Senate might defeat that power by refusing to come. This equally amounts to a negative on the power of convoking. Yet nobody will say they possess such a negative, or would be capable of usurping it by such oblique means. If the Constitution had meant to give the Senate a negative on the grade or destination, as well as the person, it would have said so in direct terms, and not left it to be effected by a sidewind. It could never mean to give them the *use* of one power thro the *abuse* of another.[16]

As discussed, Presidential claims of a right to preserve the confidentiality of information and documents in the face of legislative demands have figured prominently, though intermittently, in executive-congressional relations since at least 1792. The *Nixon* and post-Watergate cases established the broad contours of the presidential communications privilege. Under those precedents, the privilege, which is constitutionally rooted, could be invoked by the President when asked to produce documents or other materials or information that reflect presidential decision making and deliberations. In the "Fast and Furious" case congressional investigators had sought documents regarding this case for years, with the House eventually suing in federal court to force their release. The President had asserted executive privilege, claiming the documents were part of the "deliberative process" of White House decision-making and therefore didn't need to be divulged. The Department of Justice, in a letter explaining the Administration's refusal to turn over the requested documents, claimed that "Such compelled disclosure would be inconsistent with the separation of powers established in the Constitution and would potentially create an imbalance in the relationship between these two co-equal branches." DOJ further argued that a constitutionally-based "deliberative process" privilege exists and that it encompasses, at least, "pre-decisional" and "deliberative" documents. The District Court for the District of Colombia rejected the Administration's assertion of executive privilege and ordered the release of the requested documents. In November 2014 the DOJ sent Congress more than 64,000 pages of documents it had previously withheld under the claim of executive privilege. House Republicans said this was in effect an admission by President Obama that he overstepped his legal bounds. Do you agree? Can a claim of executive privilege be asserted for all documents considered "pre-decisional" and "deliberative" even if the President or his senior advisors have not seen them?

The *Nixon* and post-Watergate cases established the broad contours of executive privilege. Under those precedents, the privilege could be invoked by the President when asked to produce documents or other materials or information that reflect presidential decision making and deliberations that he believes should remain confidential. However, absent a claim that the information being sought pertains to confidential military or diplomatic secrets (*see United States v. Nixon, supra*), the privilege is a qualified one, not absolute, and can be overcome by a sufficiently compelling demonstration of need. Additionally, while reviewing courts have expressed reluctance to balance executive privilege claims against a congressional demand for information, they have demonstrated a willingness to do so if the political branches have tried in good faith but failed to reach an accommodation, as was the case here.

---

16. *Jefferson's Opinion on the Powers of the Senate Respecting Diplomatic Appointments, in* 16 PAPERS OF THOMAS JEFFERSON 378, 379–80 (Julian P. Boyd ed., 1961).

Questions

1. Does the presidential executive privilege encompass documents and information developed by, or in the possession of, officers and employees in the departments and agencies of the Executive Branch?

2. Does the privilege include all communications with respect to which the President may be interested or is it confined only to presidential decision making? If so, is it limited to any particular type of presidential decision making?

3. What kind of demonstration of need must be shown to justify release of materials that in fact qualify for the privilege?

4. Are you troubled by the separation of powers implications of the modern use of "holds"[17] on nominations, conditional appropriations riders, and the like to compel the President to release sensitive national security secrets or to control other aspects of presidential authority? Do you see any risk that this same tactic could be used to usurp vast additional areas of presidential power? Could the Senate simply refuse to consider any diplomatic or military nominations unless the President negotiated a particular treaty or nominated a particular individual favored by the Senate majority to be Secretary of State? Could conditional appropriations be used to dictate decisions of the Supreme Court? Can you think of any remedies available to other branches in response to such behavior?

5. Are you concerned about the "traditional" view that the President was the final judge of what information on military operations, diplomacy, or intelligence the executive branch would provide to Congress? While this may help safeguard sensitive informa-tion—and, as Jay explained in *Federalist* No. 64, encourage foreign intelligence sources to share information with the United States—it also reduces public accountability in these sensitive areas. Did the Framers of the Constitution draw the proper balance here? Is there a way to provide greater accountability without jeopardizing national security?

Access by the Courts

The first modern authoritative Supreme Court holding on an executive privilege dispute arose during the Watergate investigations, when the President moved to quash a subpoena *duces tecum* for the production of certain tapes and documents sought by the Special Prosecutor in connection with a criminal investigation of certain White House staff members related to the Watergate break in. While neither a "national security" case nor a dispute between Congress and the President, the case is nevertheless important as an authoritative discussion of relevant issues by a unanimous Court. In particular, note the Court's repeated distinction of the case at bar from situations involving a presidential claim of privilege based upon national security or military secrets.

---

17. For an argument that the Constitution empowers the President to make appointments subject only to a "negative" entrusted in one-half of the Senate (a simple majority vote being required to express Senate "consent"), and that a Senate rule or practice that alters the constitutional scheme by vesting this negative in a single senator, is inconsistent with the Constitution, see Robert F. Turner, *Constitutional Implications of Senate "Holds" on Treaties and Diplomatic Nominations*, 11 Tex. Rev. L. & Pol. 175 (2006).

United States v. Nixon
418 U.S. 683, 705–08, 710–13 (1974)

In support of his claim of absolute privilege, the President's counsel urges two grounds, one of which is common to all governments and one of which is peculiar to our system of separation of powers. The first ground is the valid need for protection of communications between high Government officials and those who advise and assist them in the performance of their manifold duties; the importance of this confidentiality is too plain to require further discussion....

The second ground asserted by the President's counsel in support of the claim of absolute privilege rests on the doctrine of separation of powers. Here it is argued that the independence of the Executive Branch within its own sphere, *Humphrey's Executor v. United States*, 295 U.S. 602, 629–630 (1935); *Kilbourn v. Thompson*, 103 U.S. 168, 190–91 (1881), insulates a President from a judicial subpoena in an ongoing criminal prosecution, and thereby protects confidential Presidential communications.

However, neither the doctrine of separation of powers, nor the need for confidentiality of high-level communications, without more, can sustain an absolute, unqualified Presidential privilege of immunity from judicial process under all circumstances. The President's need for complete candor and objectivity from advisers calls for great deference from the courts. However, when the privilege depends solely on the broad, undifferentiated claim of public interest in the confidentiality of such conversations, a confrontation with other values arises. Absent a claim of need to protect military, diplomatic, or sensitive national security secrets, we find it difficult to accept the argument that even the very important interest in confidentiality of Presidential communications is significantly diminished by production of such material for *in camera* inspection with all the protection that a district court will be obliged to provide.

....

To read the Art. II powers of the President as providing an absolute privilege as against a subpoena essential to enforcement of criminal statutes on no more than a generalized claim of the public interest in confidentiality of nonmilitary and nondiplomatic discussions would upset the constitutional balance of "a workable government" and gravely impair the role of the courts under Art. III.

....

In this case the President challenges a subpoena served on him as a third party requiring the production of materials for use in a criminal prosecution; he does so on the claim that he has a privilege against disclosure of confidential communications. He does not place his claim of privilege on the ground that they are military or diplomatic secrets. As to these areas of Art. II duties the courts have traditionally shown the utmost deference to Presidential responsibilities. In *C. & S. Air Lines v. Waterman S.S. Corp.*, 333 U.S. 103, 111 (1948), dealing with Presidential authority involving foreign policy considerations, the Court said:

> "The President, both as Commander-in-Chief and as the Nation's organ for foreign affairs, has available intelligence services whose reports are not and ought not to be published to the world. It would be intolerable that courts, without the relevant information, should review and perhaps nullify actions of the Executive taken on information properly held secret."

In *United States v. Reynolds*, 345 U.S. 1 (1953), dealing with a claimant's demand for evidence in a Tort Claims Act case against the Government, the Court said:

"It may be possible to satisfy the court, from all the circumstances of the case, that there is a reasonable danger that compulsion of the evidence will expose military matters which, in the interest of national security, should not be divulged. When this is the case, the occasion for the privilege is appropriate, and the court should not jeopardize the security which the privilege is meant to protect by insisting upon an examination of the evidence, even by the judge alone, in chambers." *Id.*, at 10.

No case of the Court, however, has extended this high degree of deference to a President's generalized interest in confidentiality. Nowhere in the Constitution, as we have noted earlier, is there any explicit reference to a privilege of confidentiality, yet to the extent this interest relates to the effective discharge of a President's powers, it is constitutionally based.

. . . .

We conclude that when the ground for asserting privilege as to subpoenaed materials sought for use in a criminal trial is based only on the generalized interest in confidentiality, it cannot prevail over the fundamental demands of due process of law in the fair administration of criminal justice. The generalized assertion of privilege must yield to the demonstrated, specific need for evidence in a pending criminal trial.

Access by the Public

Related to the issue of whether Congress has the constitutional right to demand sensitive national security documents from the President for its own use is the question of Congress passing laws seeking to compel the President to surrender executive branch documents to the general public and even foreign governments and their citizens.

The Freedom of Information Act

In 1966 Congress enacted the Freedom of Information Act (FOIA),[18] creating a presumptive right not only for American citizens to have access to documents and information about government activity but also for foreign nationals to receive such materials. Initially, however, both the Congress and the courts were highly deferential to the Executive with respect to national security information.

E.P.A. v. Mink
410 U.S. 73 (1973)

Mr. Justice WHITE delivered the opinion of the Court.

The Freedom of Information Act of 1966, provides that Government agencies shall make available to the public a broad spectrum of information, but exempts from its mandate certain specified categories of information, including matters that are 'specifically required by Executive order to be kept secret in the interest of the national defense or foreign policy,' s 552(b)(1), or are 'inter-agency or intra-agency memorandums or letters which would not be available by law to a party other than an agency in litigation with the agency,' s 552(b)(5). It is the construction and scope of these exemptions that are at issue here.

---

18. Freedom of Information Act (FOIA), Pub. L. No. 89-487, 80 Stat. 250 (1966).

....

Subsection (b)(1) of the Act (hereafter sometimes Exemption) exempts from forced disclosure matters 'specifically required by Executive order to be kept secret in the interest of the national defense or foreign policy.' According to the Irwin affidavit, the six documents for which Exemption 1 is now claimed were all duly classified Top Secret or Secret, pursuant to Executive Order 10501. That order was promulgated under the authority of the President in 1953, and, since that time, has served as the basis for the classification by the Executive Branch of information 'which requires protection in the interests of national defense.' We do not believe that Exemption 1 permits compelled disclosure of documents, such as the six here that were classified pursuant to this Executive Order. Nor does the Exemption permit in camera inspection of such documents to sift out so-called 'nonsecret components.' Obviously, this test was not the only alternative available. But Congress chose to follow the Executive's determination in these matters and that choice must be honored.

....

... Manifestly, Exemption 1 was intended to dispel uncertainty with respect to public access to material affecting 'national defense or foreign policy.' Rather than some vague standard, the test was to be simply whether the President has determined by Executive Order that particular documents are to be kept secret. The language of the Act itself is sufficiently clear in this respect, but the legislative history disposes of any possible argument that Congress intended the Freedom of Information Act to subject executive security classifications to judicial review at the insistence of anyone who might seek to question them. Thus, the House Report stated with respect to subsection (b)(1) that "citizens both in and out of Government can agree to restrictions on categories of information which the President has determined must be kept secret to protect the national defense or to advance foreign policy, such as matters classified pursuant to Executive Order 10501."

....

These same sources make untenable the argument that classification of material under Executive Order 10501 is somehow insufficient for Exemption 1 purposes, or that the exemption contemplates the issuance of orders, under some other authority, for each document the Executive may want protected from disclosure under the Act. Congress could certainly have provided that the Executive Branch adopt new procedures or it could have established its own procedures—*subject only to whatever limitations the Executive privilege may be held to impose upon such congressional ordering* [emphasis added]. Cf. United States v. Reynolds, 345 U.S. 1, 73 S.Ct. 528, 97 L.Ed. 727 (1953). But Exemption 1 does neither.... Congress was well aware of the Order and obviously accepted determinations pursuant to that Order as qualifying for exempt status under § (b)(1)....

....

What has been said thus far makes wholly untenable any claim that the Act intended to subject the soundness of executive security classifications to judicial review at the insistence of any objecting citizen. It also negates the proposition that Exemption 1 authorizes or permits in camera inspection of a contested document bearing a single classification so that the court may separate the secret from the supposedly nonsecret and order disclosure of the latter. The Court of Appeals was thus in error.

The following year, in the wake of the Watergate investigation and congressional anger over the war in Indochina, Congress amended the Freedom of Information Act to reverse the Court's holding in *Mink*. The amended statute is discussed in the following case.

Ray v. Turner

587 F.2d 1187 (D.C. Cir. 1978)

PER CURIAM:

This appeal presents the question whether the district court erred in dismissing a lawsuit under the Freedom of Information Act (FOIA) upon the basis of affidavits supplied by an official of the Central Intelligence Agency (CIA). We find there was error and remand.

. . . .

In 1974 Congress overrode a presidential veto and amended the FOIA for the express purpose of changing this aspect of the *Mink* case. Exemption 1 was modified to exempt only matters that are "(A) specifically authorized under criteria established by an Executive order to be kept secret in the interest of national defense or foreign policy and (B) are in fact properly classified pursuant to such Executive order."

Furthermore, the 1974 revision changed the FOIA language describing the role of a reviewing court considering any claim of exemption. It provided that "the court shall determine the matter *de novo*, and may examine the contents of such agency records in camera to determine whether such records or any part thereof shall be withheld under any of the exemptions set forth in subsection (b) of this section, and the burden is on the agency to sustain its action." The Conference Report accompanying the amendments explained that "[w]hile *in camera* examination need not be automatic, in many situations it will plainly be necessary and appropriate."

Exemption 3 originally exempted matters "specifically exempted from disclosure by statute." In *FAA Administrator v. Robertson* the Court held that a statute could "specifically exempt" matters from disclosure even if the statute gave an agency broad discretion to determine whether the information should be withheld. Concerned about excessive agency discretion, Congress in 1976 passed an amendment to change the result reached in *Robertson*. Exemption 3 now authorizes nondisclosure of matters "specifically exempted from disclosure by statute ... provided that such statute (A) requires that the matters be withheld from the public in such a manner as to leave no discretion on the issue, or (B) establishes particular criteria for withholding or refers to particular types of matters to be withheld."

B. The Nature of De Novo Review.
Procedures to be observed

In *Vaughn v. Rosen*, this court sought to cope with the difficulty of providing de novo review of exemptions claimed by the government. It initiated procedures designed to mitigate the administrative burden on the courts and ensure that the burden of justifying claimed exemptions would in fact be borne by the agencies to whom it had been assigned by Congress.

The court took its cue from a portion of the Supreme Court's *Mink* opinion that was not overruled by Congress the portion discussing how a court should proceed when there is a factual dispute concerning the nature of the materials being withheld. "Expanding" on the Supreme Court's "outline," the court established the following procedures: (1) A requirement that the agency submit a "relatively detailed analysis [of the material withheld] in manageable segments." "[C]onclusory and generalized allegations of exemptions" would no longer be accepted by reviewing courts. (2) "[A]n indexing system [that] would subdivide the document under consideration into manageable parts cross-referenced to the relevant portion of the Government's justification." This index would allow the district court and opposing counsel to locate specific areas of dispute for further examination and would be an indispensable aid to the court of appeals reviewing the district court's decision. (3) "[A]dequate adversary testing" would be ensured by opposing counsel's access to the information included in the agency's detailed and indexed justification and by *in camera* inspection, guided by the detailed affidavit and using special masters appointed by the court whenever the burden proved to be especially onerous.

In proposing the 1974 amendments, the Senate Committee outlined the ruling in *Vaughn* and added, "The committee supports this approach...."

....

The salient characteristics of *de novo* review in the national security context can be summarized as follows: (1) The government has the burden of establishing an exemption. (2) The court must make a *de novo* determination. (3) In doing this, it must first "accord substantial weight to an agency's affidavit concerning the details of the classified status of the disputed record." (4) Whether and how to conduct an *in camera* examination of the documents rests in the sound discretion of the court, in national security cases as in all other cases. To these observations should be added an excerpt from our opinion in *Weissman* (as revised): "If exemption is claimed on the basis of national security the District Court must, of course, be satisfied that proper procedures have been followed, and that by its sufficient description the contested document logically falls into the category of the exemption indicated."

———————

President Ford vetoed the 1974 FOIA amendments, arguing in his veto message:

> First, I remain concerned that our military or intelligence secrets and diplomatic relations could be adversely affected by this bill....

> I am prepared to accept those aspects of the provision which would enable courts to inspect classified documents and review the justification for their classification. However, the courts should not be forced to make what amounts to the initial classification decision in sensitive and complex areas where they have no particular expertise. As the legislation now stands, a determination by the Secretary of Defense that disclosure of a document would endanger our national security would, even though reasonable, have to be overturned by a district judge who thought the plaintiff's position just as reasonable. Such a provision would violate constitutional principles, and give less weight before the courts to an executive determination involving the protection of our most vital national defense interests than is accorded determinations involving routine regulatory matters....

> Second, I believe that confidentiality would not be maintained if many millions of pages of FBI and other investigatory law enforcement files would be subject to compulsory disclosure at the behest of any person unless the Government could prove to a court—separately for each paragraph of each document—that disclosure "would" cause a type of harm specified in the amendment. Our law enforcement agencies do not have, and could not obtain, the large number of trained and knowledgeable personnel that would be needed to make such a line-by-line examination of information requests that sometimes involve hundreds of thousands of documents, within the time constraints added to current law by this bill.[19]

———————

19. President Ford's Veto Message of Oct. 17, 1974, H. Doc. No. 93-383, reprinted in 120 CONG. REC. 36243 (1974).

However, Congress overrode the veto and the amendments became law.

Questions

In the 1948 case *C. & S. Air Lines v. Waterman*,[20] quoted in the *Nixon* case, *supra*, the Court continued:

> Nor can courts sit *in camera* in order to be taken into executive confidences. But even if courts could require full disclosure, the very nature of executive decisions as to foreign policy is political, not judicial. Such decisions are wholly confided by our Constitution to the political departments of the government, Executive and Legislative. They are delicate, complex, and involve large elements of prophecy. They are and should be undertaken only by those directly responsible to the people whose welfare they advance or imperil. They are decisions of a kind for which the Judiciary has neither aptitude, facilities nor responsibility and have long been held to belong in the domain of political power not subject to judicial intrusion or inquiry.[21]

Was it a wise decision for Congress to order that sensitive intelligence documents be provided to federal district court judges for independent *de novo* review? Would you expect the judicial branch to have the institutional competency to decide correctly whether a particular piece of information would be harmful to national security interests if disclosed? Given what you know about the Framers' understanding of separation of powers, do you see any constitutional objections to the 1974 FOIA amendments?

The Department of Justice shared the President's concerns about the constitutionality of the 1974 FOIA amendments, but concluded that the best approach would be to wait until an appropriate case or controversy presented an opportunity to take the issue to the Supreme Court. In four decades, that opportunity has not arisen, because the courts have continued to be deferential to the executive branch in national security matters.

C.I.A. v. Sims

471 U.S. 159 (1985)

Chief Justice BURGER delivered the opinion of the Court.

In No. 83-1075, we granted certiorari to decide whether § 102(d)(3) of the National Security Act of 1947, as incorporated in Exemption 3 of the Freedom of Information Act, exempts from disclosure only those sources of intelligence information to which the Central Intelligence Agency had to guarantee confidentiality in order to obtain the information. In No. 83-1249, the cross-petition, we granted certiorari to decide whether the Freedom of Information Act requires the Agency to disclose the institutional affiliations of persons whose identities are exempt from disclosure as "intelligence sources."

. . . .

Section 102(d)(3) of the National Security Act of 1947, which calls for the Director of Central Intelligence to protect "intelligence sources and methods," clearly "refers to particular types of matters," and thus qualifies as a withholding statute under Exemption 3. The "plain meaning" of the relevant statutory provisions is sufficient to resolve the question.... Moreover, the legislative history of the FOIA confirms that Congress intended § 102(d)(3)

---

20. C. & S. Air Lines v. Waterman, 333 U.S. 103 (1948).
21. *Id.*

to be a withholding statute under Exemption 3. Indeed, this is the uniform view among other federal courts.

. . . .

Respondents contend that the Court of Appeals' definition of "intelligence sources," focusing on the need to guarantee confidentiality in order to obtain the type of information desired, draws the proper line with respect to intelligence sources deserving exemption from the FOIA. The plain meaning of the statutory language, as well as the legislative history of the National Security Act, however, indicates that Congress vested in the Director of Central Intelligence very broad authority to protect all sources of intelligence information from disclosure. The Court of Appeals' narrowing of this authority not only contravenes the express intention of Congress, but also overlooks the practical necessities of modern intelligence gathering—the very reason Congress entrusted this Agency with sweeping power to protect its "intelligence sources and methods."

. . . .

The national interest sometimes makes it advisable, or even imperative, to disclose information that may lead to the identity of intelligence sources. And it is the responsibility of the Director of Central Intelligence, not that of the judiciary, to weigh the variety of complex and subtle factors in determining whether disclosure of information may lead to an unacceptable risk of compromising the Agency's intelligence-gathering process. Here Admiral Turner, as Director, decided that the benefits of disclosing the identities of institutions that had no objection to disclosure outweighed the costs of doing so. But Congress, in § 102(d)(3), entrusted this discretionary authority to the Director, and the fact that Admiral Turner made that determination in 1978 does not bind his successors to make the same determination, in a different context, with respect to institutions requesting that their identities not be disclosed. . . .

We hold that the Director of Central Intelligence properly invoked § 102(d)(3) of the National Security Act of 1947 to withhold disclosure of the identities of the individual MKULTRA researchers as protected "intelligence sources." We also hold that the FOIA does not require the Director to disclose the institutional affiliations of the exempt researchers in light of the record which supports the Agency's determination that such disclosure would lead to an unacceptable risk of disclosing the sources' identities.

Accordingly, we reverse that part of the judgment of the Court of Appeals regarding the disclosure of the individual researchers and affirm that part of the judgment pertaining to disclosure of the researchers' institutional affiliations.

Three years after *Sims* was decided, the Court made it clear that authority to control access to sensitive national security information was vested in the President by the Constitution, and thus did not require legislative authorization.

Department of the Navy v. Egan
484 U.S. 518, 526–30 (1988)

The Court of Appeals' majority stated: "The absence of any statutory provision precluding appellate review of security clearance denials in section 7512 removals creates a strong presumption in favor of appellate review," . . . One perhaps may accept this as a general proposition of administrative law, but the proposition is not without limit, and it runs aground when it encounters concerns of national security, as in this case, where the grant of security clearance to a particular employee, a sensitive and inherently discretionary judgment call, is committed by law to the appropriate agency of the Executive Branch.

The President, after all, is the "Commander in Chief of the Army and Navy of the United States." U.S. Const., Art. II, § 2. His authority to classify and control access to information bearing on national security and to determine whether an individual is sufficiently trustworthy to occupy a position in the Executive Branch that will give that person access to such information flows primarily from this constitutional investment of power in the President and exists quite apart from any explicit congressional grant. This Court has recognized the Government's "compelling interest" in withholding national security information from unauthorized persons in the course of executive business. The authority to protect such information falls on the President as head of the Executive Branch and as Commander in Chief.

Since World War I, the Executive Branch has engaged in efforts to protect national security information by means of a classification system graded according to sensitivity. After World War II, certain civilian agencies, including the Central Intelligence Agency, the National Security Agency, and the Atomic Energy Commission, were entrustedwith gathering, protecting, or creating information bearing on national security. Presidents, in a series of Executive Orders, have sought to protect sensitive information and to ensure its proper classification throughout the Executive Branch by delegating this responsibility to the heads of agencies. Pursuant to these directives, departments and agencies of the Government classify jobs in three categories: critical sensitive, noncritical sensitive, and nonsensitive. Different types and levels of clearance are required, depending upon the position sought. A Government appointment is expressly made subject to a background investigation that varies according to the degree of adverse effect the applicant could have on the national security.

It should be obvious that no one has a "right" to a security clearance. The grant of a clearance requires an affirmative act of discretion on the part of the granting official. The general standard is that a clearance may be granted only when "clearly consistent with the interests of the national security." A clearance does not equate with passing judgment upon an individual's character. Instead, it is only an attempt to predict his possible future behavior and to assess whether, under compulsion of circumstances or for other reasons, he might compromise sensitive information. It may be based, to be sure, upon past or present conduct, but it also may be based upon concerns completely unrelated to conduct, such as having close relatives residing in a country hostile to the United States. "[T]o be denied [clearance] on unspecified grounds in no way implies disloyalty or any other repugnant characteristic." The attempt to define not only the individual's future actions, but those of outside and unknown influences renders the "grant or denial of security clearances ... an inexact science at best."

Predictive judgment of this kind must be made by those with the necessary expertise in protecting classified information. For "reasons ... too obvious to call for enlarged discussion," the protection of classified information must be committed to the broad discretion of the agency responsible, and this must include broad discretion to determine who may have access to it. Certainly, it is not reasonably possible for an outside nonexpert body to review the substance of such a judgment and to decide whether the agency should have been able to make the necessary affirmative prediction with confidence. Nor can such a body determine what constitutes an acceptable margin of error in assessing the potential risk. The Court accordingly has acknowledged that with respect to employees in sensitive positions "there is a reasonable basis for the view that an agency head who must bear the responsibility for the protection of classified information committed to his custody should have the final say in deciding whether to repose his trust in an employee who has access to such information." As noted above, this must be a judgment call. The Court also has recognized "the generally accepted view that foreign policy was the province and responsibility of the Executive." "As to these areas of Art. II duties the courts have traditionally shown the utmost deference to Presidential responsibilities."

The following excerpt from an article by two experienced CIA attorneys provides a useful summary of the "*Vaughn* index" required by courts to assist them in managing the *de novo* review process mandated by the 1974 FOIA amendments and the problem presented when the CIA can neither confirm nor deny the existence of a classified covert operations without revealing classified information.

Karen A. Winchester & James W. Zirkle, *Freedom of Information and the CIA Information Act*
21 U. Rich. L. Rev. 231 (1987)

B. The 'Vaughn Index'

In *Vaughn v. Rosen*, the court of appeals addressed the courts' problem created by the necessity of *de novo* judicial review where the government seeks to withhold large quantities of information. The court in *Vaughn* defined a two-part problem. First, the in camera review of agency affidavits is *ex parte*, thereby depriving a district judge of the benefit of the views of the opposing party that would be present in a true adversarial proceeding. Since many FOIA requests involve a review of hundreds and sometimes thousands of pages of documentation, the court of appeals found that it is 'unreasonable to expect a trial judge to do as thorough a job of illumination and characterization as would a party interested in the case.' Second, the problem is made more difficult by the fact that an entire document may not be withheld where the sensitive information is segregable and may be excised, permitting release of the non-sensitive portions. Thus a judge, in making a de novo determination, is required to examine every executive justification in some detail.

The 'Vaughn Index' was the court's answer to these problems. Agencies are required to submit a 'relatively detailed analysis [of the material being withheld] in manageable segments.' Conclusory and generalized allegations of exemptions will not suffice. Further, an agency is required to provide 'an indexing system that would subdivide the document under consideration into manageable parts cross-referenced to the relevant portion of the Government's justification.' Finally, the court requires that a Vaughn Index be made available to opposing counsel to enhance the adversarial testing of the government's claimed exemptions.

It should be noted that the administrative burden to which the court referred in *Vaughn* is also of concern to agencies that are required to search and respond to what are sometimes extensive requests for materials involving sensitive national security information. It is true that an agency has at its disposal more resources than a federal district judge, but the demands on an agency are also much greater because every request must be responded to and every identifiable file must be reviewed. This would seem to raise a substantial question whether this is a wise allocation of relatively scarce resources. One should recall that a principle goal of FOIA is oversight of agency activities. In the case of the intelligence agencies, Congress has provided for designated committees of the House and Senate to fully oversee their operation.

....

III. THE GLOMAR RESPONSE

A relatively small number of FOIA requests to the CIA seek information concerning alleged intelligence activities. When the CIA receives such a request, a determination must first be made whether the fact of the existence or nonexistence of the alleged special activity is properly classifiable pursuant to the applicable Executive Order. If it is, the CIA will reply that it can neither confirm nor deny the fact of the existence or nonexistence of records responsive to the request, for to do so would indicate the existence or nonexistence of particular intelligence activities. This is the so-called 'Glomar response.' The Glomar response was first utilized in a FOIA action concerning the CIA's Glomar Explorer Project, which was undertaken, according to press reports, to raise a sunken Russian submarine believed to have been carrying nuclear weapons from the floor of the Pacific Ocean at an undisclosed location northwest of Hawaii. In May of 1977, following disclosures in the press, the government acknowledged that the CIA, operating through a contractual arrangement with Howard Hughes's SUMMA Corporation, was responsible for the project, and acknowledged the existence of 154 documents pertaining to a FOIA request initiated by a correspondent for *Rolling Stone* magazine. At that time, sixteen documents were released without deletions, 134 were released with deletions, and four were withheld in their entirety. In withholding the information, the CIA invoked the (b)(1) and (b)(3) exemptions. In the ensuing litigation, the CIA's action was upheld, based on the (b)(3) exemption and the agency's statutory requirement to protect intelligence sources and methods.

A 1982 decision upholding the Glomar response is illustrative of the problem the CIA faces in responding the FOIA requests seeking information concerning operational activities. In *Gardels v. CIA*, the CIA refused 'to confirm or deny the existence of records pertaining to covert contacts for foreign intelligence purposes between the Agency and individuals at a specific university in the United States.' Gardels, a student at the University of California at Los Angeles, had sought disclosure of past and present relationships between the CIA and individuals at the eleven campuses of that university. As the court's opinion points out, for the CIA to acknowledge that such records existed would be to assist foreign intelligence services in identifying individuals cooperating with the United States government. To deny covert contacts with the University of California would also compromise intelligence sources and methods in the same way. The CIA had received more than 125 similar FOIA requests seeking information on contacts with American colleges covering approximately one hundred schools. To indicate which schools had not been involved in covert contact would be to make the work of intelligence services much easier. They could concentrate their efforts on the remaining college campuses where their foreign nationals were located. The court in Gardels notes, in reviewing the CIA's assessment of the risk to intelligence sources and methods resulting from disclosure, that "[t]he test is not whether the court personally agrees in full with the CIA's evaluation of the danger — rather, the issue is whether on the whole record the Agency's judgment objectively survives the test of reasonableness, good faith, specificity, and plausibility in this field of foreign intelligence in which the CIA is expert and given by Congress a special role."

The court goes on to quote an earlier opinion in another case: "[T]he purpose of national security exemptions to the FOIA is to protect intelligence sources before they are compromised and harmed, not after."

The Glomar response must be used in a consistent manner to be effective. In other words, the CIA must use this response when the alleged intelligence activity does not exist, as well as when it does, or the response would be equivalent to admitting that responsive records do in fact exist. The Glomar-type response is recognized in section 3.4(f)(1) of Executive Order No. 12,356, which requires an agency to 'refuse to confirm or deny the existence or non-existence of requested information whenever the fact of its existence or nonexistence is itself classifiable under this Order.' When the CIA uses this response it does not initiate a search of its records systems, since the CIA is refusing either to confirm or deny the existence of responsive records. Therefore, in cases invoking the Glomar response, a Vaughn Index is not required.

The 1984 Central Intelligence Agency Information Act

A remarkable coalition of "strange bedfellows"—including the American Civil Liberties Union and the American Bar Association Standing Committee on Law and National Security—cooperated in 1984 to persuade Congress to enact the Central Intelligence Agency Information Act.[22] The impetus was the common realization that virtually all CIA operational files were ultimately exempt from FOIA disclosure under either Exceptions 1 or 3, and the vast amount of time being wasted by the Agency in searching through these files both wasted resources (not only money, but the time of skilled officers who had to review in some cases thousands of pages of documents) and delayed responses to FOIA requests that might produce documents.

Prior to the enactment of this statute, U.S. intelligence agencies were required by law to provide unclassified documents in their operational files in response to requests submitted from even America's acknowledged enemies. Had the Soviet KGB submitted a demand for CIA documents on its own letterhead, postmarked Moscow, the Agency was required by law to provide documents that were not protected by one of the FOIA exemptions. The writer has raised this hypothetical with CIA lawyers who have considerable experience dealing with FOIA issues, and—while they were unaware of any actual requests on "KGB letterhead"—they confirmed that the law would have required the Agency to provide any information not covered by an exemption.

With three exceptions, the 1984 statute exempted CIA operational files from FOIA searches. Those exemptions were: 1. requests from American citizens and permanent resident aliens for information in CIA files about themselves; 2. requests for information about any CIA covert operation "the existence of which is not exempt from disclosure" under FOIA—that is, operations which are no longer properly classified; and, 3. requests for information about "the specific subject matter of an investigation by the intelligence committees of the Congress, the Intelligence Oversight Board, the Department of Justice, the Office of General Counsel of the Central Intelligence Agency, the Office of Inspector General of the Central Intelligence Agency, in the conduct of an intelligence activity." This third exemption was designed to provide public access to information about alleged intelligence abuses and improprieties.

District of Columbia Circuit Court of Appeals Judge Patricia Wald provided an interesting and balanced assessment of the Freedom of Information Act while addressing students at Emory University School of Law in connection with Law Day celebrations. Her remarks were later expanded and published.

---

22. Pub. L. No. 98-477, 98 Stat. 2209 (1984).

Patricia M. Wald, *The Freedom of Information Act: A Short Case Study in the Perils and Paybacks of Legislating Democratic Values*
33 Emory L.J. 649 (1984)

I. INTRODUCTION

The theme of this year's Law Day is "Law Makes Freedom Work" — so it seems particularly appropriate to talk about a law that directly involves a fundamental freedom: the Freedom of Information Act.

The history of the Freedom of Information Act over nearly twenty years is a chronicle of the perils and problems of translating rhetoric into performance: a kind of morality play, if you will, about how to deal with the baggage that most significant "freedoms" carry with them, their costs in budgetary as well as human terms, and their vulnerability to shifts in political power and ideologies. It has been said that the Bill of Rights would not be approved by today's electorate. That may be unduly cynical, but the important point is that we do have the Bill of Rights firmly fixed in our Constitution.

. . . .

II. PASSAGE OF THE FOIA

The Freedom of Information Act was enacted in the pre-Watergate sixties. Even then, people were concerned about unaccountable bureaucrats, public officials who, in Franklin Roosevelt's words, work "with a passion for anonymity." Leading the fight for "open government" was the press, which cited numerous instances of government agencies' random, unexplained denials of access to information about crucial decisions, denials which had covered up the mistakes or irregularities of the time. Congress had its own experience with executive refusals to disclose. For 185 years it had been fencing with the executive branch over its constitutional rights to obtain executive materials for legislation and supervision. While a freedom of information act could not settle all executive privilege questions, it would establish a legal presumption in favor of disclosure to the public and consequently compel the executive to justify any nondisclosure. Lofty rhetoric, like this from Senator Edward V. Long, preceded passage of the Act:

> A government by secrecy benefits no one. It injures the people it seeks to serve; it damages its own integrity and operation. It breeds distrust, dampens the fervor of its citizens and mocks their loyalty.

. . . .

III. THE FOIA'S HISTORICAL BACKGROUND

. . . .

Despite changes in the size and complexity of our society, the need for the elimination of indiscriminate secrecy in order to preserve accountability in government has remained constant. Jefferson believed that "[t]he whole of government consists in the art of being honest." While this statement is obviously an exercise in hyperbole — government must, now as in the eighteenth century, maintain some measure of secrecy — the tone and attitude toward government embodied in Jefferson's statement reflects an important aspect of American governance. If government is indeed a public trust, then information about the deeds of the trustees — those in power — must be available to the public, except when overriding concerns necessitate confidentiality....

IV. APPLICATION OF THE ACT

The FOIA's concept is simple but revolutionary, like the Constitution itself. Any person, citizen or non-citizen — for whatever reason, good or ill — may file a request for an agency record, and the agency must disclose it unless the document falls within one of nine exemptions laid down in the law. If the agency refuses, the citizen can go to court on a priority basis, and the agency has to convince the court that the documents are exempt under the law. Most important, the court decides the issue afresh, without deference to the agency's call.

The nine exemptions are exclusive and are to be "narrowly construed." Yet they squeeze into a short subsection virtually every major dilemma, accommodation, and delicate balance that a modern democratic government faces: claims of national security in Exemption 1; trade secrets and confidential commercial information obtained from private companies in Exemption 4; confidential advice and recommendations underlying the formulation of public policy in Exemption 5; information that impermissibly invades personal privacy in Exemption 6 and investigative records compiled by law enforcement agencies in Exemption 7.

The FOIA grants a right which is virtually unprecedented anywhere else in the world: the right to obtain government documents just for the asking. However, no freedom is absolute; it must be balanced against other values, even other freedoms. This often excruciatingly difficult balancing ultimately determines the strength or impotence of the freedom in our national lives. So it is with the FOIA....

In an early ruling, the Supreme Court said that a court could not second-guess an agency classification of a document as "secret." An early decision in the D.C. Circuit said Exemption 7 authorized law enforcement agencies to withhold anything in an investigatory file, even if the investigation had been closed. As a result, in its first eight years, the number of FOIA requests was "manageable" — indeed, one might almost have written the FOIA off as a paper tiger. But in 1974, with a heavy push from history, Congress gave the statute new life.

V. THE 1974 AMENDMENT

Watergate: in 1974, the country was suffering its shock waves. High level cover-ups, agency hit lists, covert activities, and repeated invocations of executive privilege had generated a wave of indignation against closed government. The Executive's clout and credibility in Congress were at an all-time low. Watergate created a vacuum into which the demands for FOIA reform flooded.

In 1974, Congress made three basic changes in the Act. First, mandatory time limits of ten to thirty days were imposed on agencies to respond to FOIA requests. Second, courts were specifically authorized to review the propriety as well as the fact of classification of documents, and to examine relevant documents in camera when conducting such a review. Finally, the "investigatory record" exemption for law enforcement agencies was rewritten to apply only when certain harmful consequences, such as disclosing the identities of informers or the subjects of ongoing inquiries, would result from disclosure.

After 1974, the number of FOIA requests and the amount of litigation challenging agency denials increased dramatically. In 1966, the annual costs of administering FOIA requests were projected at $50,000. In 1981, the most conservative estimate of FOIA costs government-wide was $47 million; the Office of Management and Budget's figure was $250 million.

....

VI. THE COSTS OF THE ACT

Before he joined the court of appeals, my colleague Antonin Scalia referred to the FOIA as "the Taj Mahal of the Doctrine of Unanticipated Consequences, the Sistine Chapel of Cost Benefit Analysis Ignored." Of course, like all freedoms, the FOIA turned out to have its price, financially and otherwise, and some costs proved to be more unexpected than others. The Act has been used not only to gain insight into government, but also to get an inside view into the operations of private businesses and the lives of private citizens. Businesses quickly learned how to use the FOIA to get information about their competitors. Lawyers found out that they could often extract facts more quickly through FOIA requests than through the civil discovery system. In addition, the defense and intelligence agencies have been worried that their obligations under the FOIA—or even the perception of their obligations to disclose information—might compromise investigative and intelligence methods or, at best, dry up important confidential sources.

. . . .

One of the greatest surprises about the FOIA in action turned out to be the composition of its principal users. The press, historians, other "watchdogs," and, ultimately, the public—who would be served by their surrogates' increased ability to "sound the alarm"— had been envisioned as the chief beneficiaries of the Act. However, a General Accounting Office survey showed that only one out of every twenty FOIA requests was made by a journalist, scholar, or author. In contrast, four out of five requests were made by business executives or their lawyers, who astutely discerned the business value of the information which government obtains from industry while performing its licensing, inspecting, regulating, and contracting functions.

Exemption 4 of the Act protects trade secrets and commercial or financial information which is privileged or confidential. But judicial interpretation confined that protection to information which could potentially cause substantial competitive harm, or, if voluntarily submitted, impede the government's ability to obtain such information in the future. As corporations, customers, shareholders, and consumers quickly learned, that interpretation left subject to disclosure a great deal of information companies do not normally reveal. The Act has even been condemned as "a lawful tool of industrial espionage."

Lawyers also found the FOIA invaluable for litigation purposes. Information about their adversaries could often be obtained more quickly through the FOIA than through normal civil discovery channels. The Act was therefore accused of misuse as "a government subsidized discovery vehicle for the antitrust bar."

Even foreign competitors could join the game since the Act did not restrict requesters to U.S. citizens. For example, Suzuki Motor Company used the FOIA to collect Toyota submissions to the U.S. government, although Suzuki lacked comparable access to the data in Japan. According to one observer:

> The Act is being used now in a spy-counter-spy situation, where the first person will come in and ask for information and it will be logged into the agency; then the company whose information is being requested will come back and make a Freedom of Information request for the request letter and then for any information given out in response; the requester will come back and ask to see what is provided to the second company; and finally, the submitter will say not just "let me see everything you gave to the other guy, but I also want to see everything you have on him," and then it starts all over.

One major drug company reported that it sued under the FOIA to obtain copies of minutes of meetings between its own representatives and agency personnel to discover what the agency wrote down, and what information the agency was revealing about the company to others. The Act has been charged with turning agencies into information brokers between companies pursuing each other, rather than acting as a window for public assessment of how government conducts itself.

....

I relate these developments at some length to make the point that freedoms—and laws implementing freedoms—are often unpredictable in whom they help and whom they hurt; they do not always distinguish between the good guys and the bad guys....

Defense and intelligence agencies have been among the most vocal critics of the FOIA. In the 1981 hearings, the Department of Defense claimed that out of 57,000 requests annually, more than half came from businessmen or their lawyers interested in supplementing discovery in litigation over defense contracts. The CIA and the National Security Administration [sic: Agency] feared requests from foreign intelligence front organizations or even from legitimate groups who might inadvertently cause sensitive information to be revealed....

According to the CIA, two hundred high-level intelligence officers had to be assigned to FOIA to ensure that no isolated bit of information, innocent in itself but fatal when pooled with other pieces, would be unwittingly released. Sources must not be disclosed; ongoing operations must not be compromised; relations with counterpart intelligence groups in foreign governments must not be jeopardized. The CIA repeatedly invoked the spectre of egregiously far-reaching requests, citing often the $325,000 cost of processing one request from Philip Agee for all CIA records mentioning him....

Domestic intelligence agencies echoed similar complaints. Exemption 7—the most litigated exemption in the FOIA—was designed to protect their sources, their modus operandi, and the privacy of their investigations. But in 1981, the FBI said it needed more protection and requested a total exemption of at least five or ten years after closure of files dealing with counterespionage, organized crime, or terrorism. The FBI cited the following:

> —Director William H. Webster submitted 125 instances of persons who said they did not want to provide information, including information on judicial appointments, for fear their identities would be disclosed. He said the number of informants had shrunk by 25–50%.

> —The DEA said it got 40% of its requests from prisoners and 20% from known drug traders.

> —FBI and DEA informants and undercover agents claimed they risked exposure when their criminal associates submitted FOIA requests for their own files. If the government cited exemption 7 and refused to release the information, the requesters knew that they were under investigation. By pooling the information which they obtained, they could often figure out who were the informants.

....

VIII. CONCLUSION

My real message today is that passing a law like the FOIA is only the beginning. If the law fails, a piece of our freedom is chipped away. Times change—certain values, like open government, go in and out of favor. Other values may seem for the moment more consequential. The problems and risks of freedom change, too, in a modern, industrial, mass communication, high-tech society. The Founding Fathers, with uncanny wisdom, were able to define our most sacred freedoms, but they could not even begin to formulate the ways to make them work through three hundred years. History plays a critical role in the development of freedoms. Watergate reinvigorated a feeble FOIA and produced FOIA amendments more important in many respects than the original bill. Yet, again, history and political fortunes changed, and the FOIA came to be viewed as a kind of flower child of the irresponsible seventies, constantly threatened with defoliation. Proofs of its actual harm to law enforcement or national security were relatively meager—the perceptions of potential informers and allies, not concrete evidence of positive harm, were invoked to discredit it. And in truth, the FOIA, like all basic freedoms, sometimes hurts the worthy and sometimes helps the unworthy.

It takes constant vigilance, commitment, and common sense to make any law work. I hope we as citizens have all these qualities—in large measure—to keep the FOIA around for a long time and to make it work.

Comments

Judge Wald notes that the CIA once spent more than $300,000 responding to a request from Philip Agee for information in their files about him. At the time, former CIA employee Agee was actively engaged in an international campaign to expose the identities of U.S. intelligence agents around the world. In December 1975, shortly after Agee identified Richard Welch as the CIA station chief in Athens, Welch was murdered. Under the circumstances, the Supreme Court upheld the decision by the Department of State to deny Agee a U.S. passport,[23] and Congress ultimately responded by enacting the Intelligence Identities Protection Act[24] making it a felony to publish the name of such individuals. Violators are subject to a penalty of up to ten years in prison and a $50,000 fine. Following the end of the Cold War, several individuals once associated with the Soviet KGB asserted that Philip Agee had during this period been working for the KGB and the Cuban DGI.[25] After such revelations began surfacing, Agee moved to Cuba.

It is also reported that some radical political groups and individuals are using FOIA as virtually a weapon to tie up the resources of certain controversial government programs by submitting vast numbers of requests for documents that each requires searches and formal responses. One military officer recently estimated to this writer that between 15 and 20 percent of her small office staff was currently tied up primarily responding to FOIA requests from political activist groups opposed to the mission assigned to her office.

Contrary to perceptions derived from James Bond novels and movies, most of intelligence gathering does not involve secret agents breaking in to government offices but rather the collection of information from open sources. Publications like *Aviation Week & Space Technology,* the *Congressional Record,* and reports of congressional committees sometimes contain actual classified information, and far more often contain unclassified material that may be of significant assistance to foreign intelligence services in trying to collect the "missing pieces to the puzzle" of a U.S. military program or intelligence activity. Unless one knows precisely which pieces of such a puzzle a foreign intelligence service possesses, it is not easy to declare than another specific piece of information reasonably could be expected to do identifiable harm to American national security. Thus, a good deal of potentially valuable intelligence information is not eligible for classification. Under FOIA, requests for such information from foreign nationals—even if they are employed by

---

23. *Haig v. Agee,* 453 U.S. 280 (1981).
24. Intelligence Identities Protection Act of 1982, Pub. L. No. 97-200, 96 Stat. 122, June 23, 1982.
25. *See, e.g.,* CHRISTOPHER ANDREW & VASILI MITROKHIN, SWORD AND THE SHIELD 230–33 (1999).

hostile intelligence services and live in countries viewed by our government as potential enemies — must be satisfied.

In the late 1980s, this writer was told by a European diplomat that it was "common practice" for European graduate students to file FOIA requests with the U.S. government to obtain research information for their theses and dissertations — at the expense of U.S. taxpayers.

Congress finally addressed the problem of requiring the CIA and other government agencies to provide information to hostile foreign intelligence services in the Intelligence Authorization Act for Fiscal Year 2003, which amended section 552(a) of the Freedom of Information Act to prohibit an agency or part of an agency that is an element of the Intelligence Community from making any record available to a foreign government or a representative of a foreign government.[26] While commendable, a foreign intelligence service might be clever enough to submit the request in the name of an individual — perhaps an intelligence officer's spouse or child — to evade this provision.

Access by Executive Branch Employees and Contractors

Many of the most interesting questions of access to national security information pertain to demands by Congress or the courts for such documents. But most access to classified information takes place within the executive branch and by non-governmental employees of private contractors doing business with the government. Students of National Security Law should be generally familiar with the regulatory scheme within the executive branch governing classifying information and access to such information.

Throughout most of American history, military secrets were handled by each of the armed services and diplomatic secrets by the Department of State. As the Supreme Court observed in *Egan*, the President's Commander in Chief power includes "authority to classify and control access to information bearing on national security and to determine whether an individual is sufficiently trustworthy to occupy a position in the Executive Branch that will give that person access to such information...."[27] In 1857, Congress first passed legislation empowering the President to establish such regulations "as he may think conducive to the public interest" to protect diplomatic communications.[28] While presidents could enforce secrecy regulations against executive branch employees through the threat of discharge, demotion, or other punishment, only Congress can attach criminal penalties to such behavior, which Congress first did in the early twentieth century.[29]

In 1940, President Roosevelt issued Executive Order No. 8381 establishing a formal classification system for "confidential," "secret," and "top secret" information. This has been modified many times over the years, and the current version is Executive Order 13526.

Executive Order No. 13526

President Barack Obama issued Executive Order 13526 on "Classified National Security Information" in the final days of 2009. The prefatory language provides in part:

---

26. *See* 5 U.S.C. 552(a)(3)(E), as amended.
27. 484 U.S. 518, 527 (1988).
28. 11 Stat. 52 at 60 (1857).
29. 36 Stat. 1084 (1911), and 40 Stat. 217 (1917).

Our democratic principles require that the American people be informed of the activities of their Government. Also, our Nation's progress depends on the free flow of information both within the Government and to the American people. Nevertheless, throughout our history the national defense has required that certain information be maintained in confidence in order to protect our citizens, our democratic institutions, our homeland security, and our interactions with foreign nations.

Like its predecessors in recent decades, E.O. 13526 provides for three levels of classification with the same definitions: "Top Secret" for information (regardless of the form it is in) the unauthorized disclosure of which could be expected to cause "exceptionally grave danger" to U.S. national security; "Secret" to protect against "serious damage"; and "Confidential" to protect against "damage" to national security. Only eight categories of information may be classified: (a) military plans, weapons systems, or operations; (b) foreign government information; (c) intelligence activities (including sources or methods) and cryptology; (d) foreign relations; (e) scientific, technological, or economic matters relating to national security (including defense against transnational terrorism); (f) programs safeguarding nuclear materials or facilities; (g) vulnerabilities or capabilities of U.S. systems or facilities; and (h) weapons of mass destruction. The Obama order added "(including covert action) to (c) and made a few other minor alternations, but this part of the Order closely patterned those of his predecessors.

Executive Order 13526 establishes a national Declassification Center within the national Archives to streamline the declassification process (Sec. 3.7). Other additions from previous orders include the establishment of an Interagency Security Classification Appeals Panel (Sec. 5.3), to which anyone properly authorize to have access to classified materials can refer a claim that a document has been improperly classified. The new Order clarifies that "[c]lassified information shall not be declassified automatically as a result of any unauthorized disclosure of identical or similar information" (Sec. 1(4)(b)); and that previously unclassified information requested by a Freedom of Information Act request may be classified if otherwise eligible under the Order (Sec. 1.7(d)).

Once a security clearance has been granted, access to classified information is still denied unless the individual has a "need to know" the information. This provides an additional protection, limiting the information that even a fully cleared individual can access in the event they decide to betray their trust. At certain levels, cleared individuals have to submit regular disclosure reports on their financial dealings and/or undergo a polygraph examination.

Congressional staff members who have a need to know are eligible for security clearances on the same basis as employees of the Defense Department or the Intelligence Community. In the spirit of comity, Members of Congress and federal judges who have a need to know are presumed to be trustworthy, although as a constitutional matter the president would presumably have the option of denying information to a particular Member. Indeed, there are unconfirmed reports that a senior legislator was denied classified information several decades ago because of a drinking problem. In the absence of a clear justification, there might be serious consequences were the president to deny all[30] classified information to a specific legislator, but these would be primarily political rather than constitutional.

---

30. The President's constitutional authority to deny classified information to Congress as a whole, particularly if it is of a highly sensitive nature, is not doubted. The greatest political risks would presumably result if a legislator denied access to any classified information were not a member of the President's political party or otherwise a critic of the administration.

Comments
The Problem of "Leaks" of Classified Information

It is often remarked that the "Ship of State" is unique in that it is the only vessel that "leaks from the top." The unauthorized disclosure of classified information is a serious problem that sometimes threatens both lives and operational success. Imagine the consequences if Germany had learned in advance the details of the D-Day invasion, or Germany or Imperial Japan had learned the allies had broken their codes. World War II might well have been lost.

The latter half of the twentieth century witnessed a dramatic increase in "leaks," many of them attributed to Congress. While it is certainly true that more leaks come from within the Executive department, it is also true that only a tiny fraction of those individuals holding security clearances work for the Congress. Moreover, when the President or Secretary of State make a determination that the public interest would be served by making public classified information — e.g., when President Kennedy went on national television in 1962 with overhead photographs of Soviet missiles in Cuba — that is not a "leak" but rather an exercise of the discretionary powers of their high office.

The problem arises when executive branch officials (or employees) discretely transfer classified information to friendly journalists for use in a partisan way in influencing public opinion or embarrassing political opponents. When this occurs, legislators perhaps understandably want to reciprocate in kind. And after a few years of leaking on both sides of Pennsylvania Avenue, some seem to view leaking as an honored Washington pastime. The press, understandably, wants information, and few journalists seem troubled by the thought that publishing national security secrets (assuming they know the information is classified) can do serious damage to the country.

In 2000, Congress approved an amendment to the Intelligence Appropriations Act that would have attached criminal penalties to the unauthorized disclosure of classified information — including by the press (and, presumably, by Congress). Under pressure from various media and civil liberties groups, President Clinton vetoed the bill. After considering the congressionally mandated[31] report of an interagency task force chaired by the Department of Justice in the early months of the Bush Administration, Attorney General John Ashcroft announced that he was not going to push for reconsideration of such legislation at that time. Ashcroft noted that several existing statutes provided criminal penalties for the unauthorized disclosure of classified information,[32] and the real problem was usually less having statutory authority than being able to identify individuals responsible for such disclosures.[33]

Arguably the most damaging leaks in American history occurred as a result of criminal misconduct by Army Private Bradley Manning in 2010 and NSA contractor Edward Snowden beginning in 2013.[34] The public and media reaction to both acts demonstrated the degree to which attitudes have changed since Pearl Harbor. Twelve days after that attack, acting pursuant to congressional authorization, President Roosevelt established the Office of Censorship by Executive Order 8985 and appointed Associated Press Executive News Editor Byron Price as U.S. Director of Censorship. During the next four years, Price

---

31. Intelligence Authorization Act for FY 2002, Pub. L. 107-108, Sec. 310 (2001).
32. *See, e.g.,* 18 U.S.C. §§ 793, 794, and 798 (1996) and §§ 797 and 952 (1994).
33. *See* letter from Attorney General John Ashcroft to the Speaker of the House of Representatives, Oct. 15, 2002, *at* <http://www.fas.org/sgp/othergov/dojleaks.html>.
34. The Snowden case and its consequences are more fully discussed in Chapter 27.

established voluntary procedures by which American journalists could submit stories or check facts to insure they did not voluntarily aid the enemy. In those days, journalists thought of themselves as Americans first and did not conceal their desire that the allies win the war. In 1944, Price received a special Pulitzer Prize for his contributions as censorship director.

Seven decades later, few Americans—be they legislators, journalists, scholars, or member of the general public—are aware that the Founding Fathers addressed the proper balance between preserving the national security and what we today often refer to as government "transparency." Until someone finds a way to share our most sensitive secrets with the American people without risk that the information will become known to our enemies, the concept of "intelligence transparency" remains an oxymoron.

As noted earlier, in *Federalist* No. 64 John Jay explained that, because sources of valuable foreign intelligence would not confide in the secrecy of the Senate or House, the Constitution had left the president "able to manage the business of intelligence as prudence may suggest." Few Americans know that today. But the wisdom of the Founding Fathers is reaffirmed by the efforts of the American government to persuade our closest allies to share vital information that might have allowed us to prevent the terrorist attacks of September 11, 2001. The Minneapolis office of the FBI had recognized that Zacharias Moussaoui was learning to fly a large commercial airliner to use it in a terrorist attack. But when Congress enacted the 1978 Foreign Intelligence Surveillance Act (FISA), it did not consider the possibility of a "lone wolf" terrorist and required as a condition for the issuance of a FISA warrant that the government tie the target to a "foreign power"—a term that includes transnational terrorist groups like al Qaeda. Knowing very little about Moussaoui, the FBI asked help from foreign intelligence services in some of America's closest allies. But repeated inquiries of the highest priority seeking information from Great Britain were simply ignored for weeks prior to the 9/11 attacks. The following day, the British provided information tying Moussaoui to an al Qaeda training camp in Pakistan.

A nearly 400-page review of the FBI's handling of intelligence information leading up to the 9/11 attacks by the Department of Justice Inspector General's office noted: "Although the London [FBI liaison office] contacted the British authorities twice in writing, made several telephone calls, and indicated the urgency of the Moussaoui matter, the British government did not provide the FBI any information about Moussaoui until September 12." The IG report added: "It is not clear why the information from the British was not provided to the FBI until after September 11."[35] The most likely explanation is that the British intelligence information came from a very valuable source who had infiltrated al Qaeda and was providing information of tremendous value. The loss of such an asset might well deprive British intelligence of vital information that might well lead to a successful terrorist attack. Given America's inability to preserve secrets—and a media culture that often appears to view acquiring and publishing sensitive national security secrets as some sort of game that often leads to Pulitzer Prizes, promotions, and larger paychecks—one cannot blame the British or any other American ally for being reluctant to share their most sensitive intelligence secrets with a government that simply cannot guarantee they will be safeguarded.

Because of this, assertions by journalists that the classified material they published really wasn't all that vital (as if they would have all of the information necessary to make

---

35. U.S. Department of Justice (Office of the Inspector General), *A Review of the FBI's Handling of Intelligence Information Related to the September 11 Attacks* 151 (November 2004 [Released Publicly June 2006]) Available at: http://www.justice.gov/oig/special/s0606/final.pdf.

that judgment) miss the point. As Jay explained, every "leak" of classified information signals potential foreign intelligence sources as well as intelligence services in allied countries that America cannot be trusted to keep its promises that sensitive information will be protected. Without that trust, only fools will share such information with America. Without good intelligence, lives and perhaps freedom are at greater risk.

Selected Bibliography

BOOKS

Berger, Raoul, *Executive Privilege: A Constitutional Myth* (1974).
Breckenridge, Adam C., *The Executive Privilege: Presidential Control over Information* (1974).
Corwin, Edward, *The President: Office and Powers 1787–1957* (4th rev. ed. 1957).

ARTICLES

Bishop, Joseph, "The Executive's Right to Privacy," 66 *Yale L.J.* 477 (1957).
Henkin, Louis, "The Right to Know and the Duty to Withhold: The Case of the Pentagon Papers," 120 *U. Pa. L. Rev.* 271 (1971).
Kramer, Robert, & Herman Marcuse, "Executive Privilege—A Study of the Period 1953–1960," 29 *Geo. Wash. L. Rev.* 623 (1961).
Rozell, Mark J., *Executive Privilege Revived?: Secrecy and Conflict During the Bush Presidency*, 1992 *Duke L. J.* 403 (1992).
Schwartz, Bernard, "Executive Privilege and Congressional Investigatory Power," 47 *Calif. L. Rev.* 623 (1961).
Turner, Robert F., "The Constitution and the Iran-Contra Affair," *Houston J. Int'l L.* 83 (1988).
Warren, Charles, "Presidential Declarations of Independence," 10 *B.U.L. Rev.* 1 (1930).
Winchester, Karen A., & James W. Zirkle, *Freedom of Information and the CIA Information Act*, 21 *Univ. Rich. L. Rev.* 231 (1987).
Wolkinson, Herman, "Demands of Congressional Committees for Executive Papers," 10 *Fed. Bar J.* 103 (1949).
Younger, Stephen, "Congressional Investigations and Executive Secrecy," 20 *U. Pitt. L. Rev.* 755 (1959).

Chapter 25

Freedom of Expression

Robert M. O'Neil with J. Joshua Wheeler

In this chapter:
Free Expression and National Security
Restraints on National Security-Related Expression by Government Employees
Exposure of Intelligence Personnel
The Media and the Military: Press Access to Military Operations
The Road Not Taken: Possible Grounds for Future Access Claims
Guidelines for War Reporting
The News Media in Afghanistan—First Amendment Issues After September 11
The DOD's Embed Policy in Iraq: Unprecedented Access or Controlling the Message?
The First Amendment and the War on Terrorism

Free Expression and National Security

The interests of national security warrant government regulation of the flow of and access to certain types of information. Restrictions may be imposed both on the release of information in private hands (including those of the news media) and on gaining access to information which has not been released or made public. Occasionally such restrictions are challenged in court under the First Amendment's guarantees of free speech and free press. Such tensions between free expression and national security arise in a variety of situations, with results that may not seem consistent with non-security case law, or even consistent with one another as responses to national security needs. The controversy over newspaper publication of the Pentagon Papers provides an important and revealing introduction to the complex relationship between the media and the military.

The New York Times v. United States

In March 1971 Daniel Ellsberg gave to Neil Sheehan of the *New York Times* copies of a Defense Department study known popularly as the Pentagon Papers. Ellsberg had been one of thirty-six scholars employed in a Rand Corporation study of the history of American decision-making in Vietnam. Each page of the study was marked "Top Secret Sensitive," a classification designed to deny access to virtually everyone. The task force was headed by Morton Halperin and Leslie Gelb, and they were the only two persons with authorized access to the entire study.

In December 1968, as Lyndon Johnson prepared to leave office, all copies of the Pentagon Papers were placed in storage in the Rand Corporation. Ellsberg asked the president of

Rand to gain permission from Halperin and Gelb for access to the file, ostensibly in order to continue work on the study. Permission was granted. Ellsberg then contacted Anthony J. Russo, an acquaintance and former Rand employee, and copied the documents in his possession. The copies were delivered to the *New York Times*, which published three installments of the study before the United States government initiated the litigation that resulted in the following case.[1]

N.Y. Times Co. v. United States
403 U.S. 713 (1971)

PER CURIAM.

We granted certiorari in these cases in which the United States seeks to enjoin the *New York Times* and the *Washington Post* from publishing the contents of a classified study entitled "History of U.S. Decision-Making Process on Viet Nam Policy."

"Any system of prior restraints of expression comes to this Court bearing a heavy presumption against its constitutional validity." *Bantam Books, Inc. v. Sullivan,* 372 U.S. 58, 70 (1963); see also *Near v. Minnesota,* 283 U.S. 697 (1931). The Government "thus carries a heavy burden of showing justification for the imposition of such a restraint." *Organization for a Better Austin v. Keefe,* 402 U.S. 415, 419 (1971). The District Court for the Southern District of New York in the *New York Times* case and the District Court for the District of Columbia and the Court of Appeals for the District of Columbia Circuit in the *Washington Post* case held that the Government had not met that burden. We agree.

The judgment of the Court of Appeals for the District of Columbia Circuit is therefore affirmed. The order of the Court of Appeals for the Second Circuit is reversed and the case is remanded with directions to enter a judgment affirming the judgment of the District Court for the Southern District of New York. The stays entered June 25, 1971, by the Court are vacated. The judgments shall issue forthwith.

So ordered.

MR. JUSTICE BLACK, with whom MR. JUSTICE DOUGLAS joins, concurring.

I adhere to the view that the Government's case against the *Washington Post* should have been dismissed and that the injunction against the *New York Times* should have been vacated without oral argument when the cases were first presented to this Court. I believe that every moment's continuance of the injunctions against the newspapers amounts to a flagrant, indefensible, and continuing violation of the First Amendment....

  ....

In the First Amendment the Founding Fathers gave the free press the protection it must have to fulfill its essential role in our democracy. The press was to serve the governed, not the governors. The Government's power to censor the press was abolished so that the press would remain forever free to censure the Government. The press was protected so that it could bare the secrets of government and inform the people. Only a free and unrestrained press can effectively expose deception in government. And paramount among

---

1. For a general review of the Ellsberg affair, *see* PETER SCHRAG, TEST OF LOYALTY: DANIEL ELLSBURG AND THE RITUALS OF SECRET GOVERNMENT (1974).

the responsibilities of a free press is the duty to prevent any part of the government from deceiving the people and sending them off to distant lands to die of foreign fevers and foreign shot and shell. In my view, far from deserving condemnation for their courageous reporting, the *New York Times*, the *Washington Post*, and other newspapers should be commended for serving the purpose the Founding Fathers saw so clearly. In revealing the workings of government that led to the Vietnam [W]ar, the newspapers nobly did precisely that which the Founders hope and trusted they would do.

....

MR. JUSTICE DOUGLAS, with whom MR. JUSTICE BLACK joins, concurring.

....

The Government says that it has inherent powers to go into court and obtain an injunction to protect the national interest, which in this case is alleged to be national security.

Near v. Minnesota, 283 U.S. 697, repudiated that expansive doctrine in no uncertain terms.

The dominant purpose of the First Amendment was to prohibit the widespread practice of government suppression of embarrassing information. It is common knowledge that the First Amendment was adopted against the widespread use of the common law of seditious libel to punish the dissemination of material that is embarrassing to the powers-that-be. The present cases will, I think, go down in history as the most dramatic illustration of that principle. A debate of large proportions goes on in the Nation over our posture in Vietnam. That debate antedated the disclosure of the contents of the present documents. The latter are highly relevant to the debate in progress.

Secrecy in government is fundamentally anti-democratic, perpetuating bureaucratic errors. Open debate and discussion of public issues are vital to our national health. On public questions there should be "uninhibited, robust, and wide-open" debate. *New York Times Co. v. Sullivan*, 376 U.S. 254, 269–70.

I would affirm the judgment of the Court of Appeals in the *Post* case, vacate the stay of the Court of Appeals in the *Times* case and direct that it affirm the District Court.

....

MR. JUSTICE BRENNAN, concurring....

The error that has pervaded these cases from the outset was the granting of any injunctive relief whatsoever, interim or otherwise. The entire thrust of the Government's claim throughout these cases has been that publication of the material sought to be enjoined "could," or "might," or "may" prejudice the national interest in various ways. But the First Amendment tolerates absolutely no prior judicial restraints of the press predicated upon surmise or conjecture that untoward consequences may result.... [O]nly governmental allegation and proof that publication must inevitably, directly, and immediately cause the occurrence of an event kindred to imperiling the safety of a transport already at sea can support even the issuance of an interim restraining order....

[The concurring opinion of Mr. Justice Stewart, with whom Mr. Justice White joined, is omitted.]

MR. JUSTICE WHITE, with whom MR. JUSTICE STEWART joins, concurring.

I concur it today's judgments, but only because of the concededly extraordinary protection against prior restraints enjoyed by the press under our constitutional system. I do not say that in no circumstances would the First Amendment permit an injunction against publishing information about government plans or operations. Nor, after examining the material the Government characterizes as the most sensitive and destructive, can I deny that revelation of these documents will do substantial damage to public interests. Indeed, I am confident that their disclosure will have that result. But I nevertheless agree that the United States has not satisfied the very heavy burden that it must meet to warrant an injunction against publication in these cases....

....

... Prior restraints require an unusually heavy justification under the First Amendment; but failure by the Government to justify prior restraints does not measure its constitutional entitlement to a conviction for criminal publication. That the Government mistakenly chose to proceed by injunction does not mean that it could not successfully proceed in another way.

[Justice White then discussed the coverage of certain provisions of the Espionage Act, 18 U.S.C. sections 793–798, and concluded:]....

... If any of the material here at issue is of this nature, the newspapers are presumably now on full notice of the position of the United States and must face the consequences if they publish. I would have no difficulty in sustaining convictions under these sections on facts that would not justify the intervention of equity and the imposition of a prior restraint.

[Justice Marshall concurred on the ground that no act of Congress specifically authorized suits to enjoin publication of security secrets.]

[Three Justices dissented without reaching the merits of the dispute. Chief Justice Warren Burger began his dissent by noting that "so clear are the constitutional limitations on prior restraint against expression that ... we have had little occasion to be concerned with cases involving prior restraints against news reporting on matters of public interest." For him, as well as for Justices Harlan and Blackmun, the concern was one of procedure — a lament that "these cases have been conducted in unseemly haste." The dissenters suggested that it would not have been unreasonable, for example, "to give government an opportunity to review the entire collection and determine whether agreement could be reached on publication." They even ventured that "if security was not in fact jeopardized, much of the material could no doubt have been declassified." The dissenting Justices also faulted the *New York Times* ("a newspaper long regarded as a great institution in American life"), for being derelict in a presumptive "duty ... to report forthwith to responsible public officers;" the course which the *Times* followed, in contrast, "removed any possibility of orderly litigation."]

[Finally, the Chief Justice and Justices Harlan and Blackmun posed a series of questions which, in their view, the Court should have faced but because of the hasty review of the injunction, did not reach. Among those questions were "whether the First Amendment permits the federal courts to enjoin publication of stories which would present a serious threat to national security ..." and "whether the threat to publish highly secret documents is of itself a sufficient implication of national security to justify an injunction on the theory that regardless of the content of the documents harm enough results from the demonstration of such a breach of secrecy."]

[The final question listed by the dissenters that the Court never reached is especially revealing: "Whether the threatened harm to the national security or the government's possessory interest in the documents justifies the issuance of an injunction against publication in light of — (a) The strong First Amendment policy against prior restraints on publication; (b) the doctrine against enjoining conduct in violation of criminal statutes; and (c) The extent to which the materials at issue have apparently already been otherwise disseminated."]

Comments and Questions

The Pentagon Papers dissenters correctly implied that the majority's hasty disposition of the case left many important issues unresolved. For one, there was the enduring question of what standard the Court would use in reviewing a future restraint against publication. Though several members of the majority—notably Justices Brennan and Stewart—did offer standards, the *Per Curiam* opinion concluded only that, whatever might be the proper standard for barring publication of sensitive material, the government had not met it here. Only Justice Black, and possibly Justice Douglas, would have refused to countenance an injunction under any conditions, leaving four others who said, in effect, "perhaps sometime, but not now." Thus the quest for a defining standard continued well after the *New York Times* ruling, and as we shall see spawned additional litigation.

A second question left wide open in the *Pentagon Papers* case is how differently post-publication criminal sanctions would have fared, had the government sought to prosecute either of the newspapers, their editors, or the authors of the stories in issue. Justices White and Stewart strongly implied the validity of the criminal penalties for such a breach. The three dissenters would undoubtedly have accepted such sanctions. Even Justice Douglas hinted that he would view a post-publication case differently. Whatever the lineup, there were almost surely five votes at that time to sustain such charges even against a major news medium. Though First Amendment scholars are not of one mind on this issue, lawyers regularly (and properly) advise media clients that nothing in the *Pentagon Papers* case should be read as barring a post-publication prosecution for releasing such sensitive material to the public.

A third intriguing question concerns the manner in which the material had been obtained. When civil and even criminal charges arise from non-national security publications, the Supreme Court has consistently held that such sanctions are barred by the First Amendment if (but only if) the material has not been unlawfully obtained.[2] The constitutional irrelevance of the concededly larcenous origin of the Pentagon Papers marks clearly the difference between a prior restraint and a subsequent punishment. That distinction now deserves closer attention.

The Doctrine of Prior Restraint

Even the Pentagon Papers dissenters recognized that "the constitutional limits on prior restraint" were "so clear" that the high Court had seldom needed to explain the underlying doctrine. Yet the basis for our deep abhorrence to gags and injunctions, especially when imposed upon the news media, deserves closer scrutiny. In part the aversion to prior restraint is undoubtedly historical, reflecting bitter memories among the Framers of a colonial system in which injunctions were acceptable. There are important procedural differences between a prosecution after publication and a petition for a pre-publication injunction. There are also important practical differences; one never knows, or has any

---

2. *E.g.*, Florida Star v. B.J.F., 491 U.S. 524 (1989).

way to test, the potential hazards of a publication that never occurs. Even so, there may be times and conditions when interests—including but not necessarily limited to national security—would warrant a court order barring publication of sensitive material. The following excerpt thoughtfully addresses these issues:

John Jeffries, *Rethinking Prior Restraint*
92 YALE L.J. 409, 427–29 (1983)

[I]njunctions ... are also far more like subsequent punishments than conventional rhetoric would suggest. In both cases the *threat* of punishment comes before publication; in both cases the *fact* of punishment comes after. The apparent distinction in timing is in actuality only a shift in the focus of attention. The procedures in an action for criminal contempt are generally the same as those used in ordinary criminal prosecutions. Proof must be had beyond a reasonable doubt, and right to trial by jury is guaranteed where the sentence exceeds imprisonment for six months.

On examination, the chief difference between the two schemes turns out to be this: Under a system of injunctions, the adjudication of illegality precedes publication; under a system of criminal prosecution, it comes later. This is a difference, and perhaps for some purposes it matters, but why the timing of the adjudication should affect the scope of First Amendment freedoms is not at all clear....

[The reason most commonly advanced] is that an injunction deters speech more effectively than does the threat of criminal prosecution and for that reason should be specially disfavored. Arguments to this effect are found in the opinions of the Supreme Court and in the writings of leading commentators. The idea has been variously expressed but never so pithily as in Alexander Bickel's remark that, "A criminal statute chills, prior restraint freezes." Yet, with all respect to such authority, it is very hard to credit this point. It may be true, as many have asserted, that an injunction, because it is particularized, immediate, and concrete, may impinge more forcefully on the consciousness of the individual enjoined than would a more generalized and impersonal threat of criminal prosecution. But that tells only half the story, and the wrong half at that. An injunction may be more effective at stopping the activity at which it is aimed, but it is also more narrowly confined. There is less risk of deterring activities beyond the adjudicated target of suppression—activities plainly outside the injunctive ban but arguably within the necessarily more general prohibition of a penal law. And many may find even an uncertain prospect of criminal conviction and punishment sufficient incentive to steer well clear of arguably proscribed activities. In terms, therefore, of the system of free expression and of the aggregate of arguably protected First Amendment activity that might be inhibited under these regimes, it is anything but clear that injunctions are most costly. As Professor Barnett put it: "[T]he pinpointed freeze of a narrowly drawn [judicial] order might produce less refrigeration overall than the broader chill of threatened subsequent punishment...."

That point is strongly reinforced when one remembers that it is only the possibility of *erroneous* deterrence that should be the subject of concern. To the extent that the activity suppressed, whether by injunction or by criminal prosecution, is outside the protection of the First Amendment and within a legitimate sphere of legislative action, efficient inhibition is a good thing. It is only excessive deterrence, erroneous deterrence, deterrence that impinges on the substance of First Amendment freedoms, that is to be decried. In that respect, it seems entirely plausible to believe that the specifically targeted commands of an injunction are actually likely to be *less* threatening to the system of freedom of expression than the inevitably more general proscriptions of a penal statute."

United States v. Progressive

Not too many years after the Pentagon Papers decision, the government was back in court, this time seeking to enjoin a magazine from publishing an article that described the making of a hydrogen bomb. After receiving the article from its author, Howard Morland, the magazine's editor sent a copy to the U.S. Department of Energy for the purpose of verifying certain technical details. DOE officials instead concluded that the article contained "Secret Restricted Data," the publication of which was barred by the Atomic Energy Act,[3] and would threaten national security. Although DOE offered to work with the magazine to revise the article in order to make it acceptable, the editors refused to delete the targeted material, and declared their intent to publish the piece in its original form unless they were ordered not to do so.

The United States Attorney then went to federal district court, seeking a temporary restraining order against publication, under the Atomic Energy Act. Such an order was issued, and remained in effect until, some two weeks later, a hearing was held on the request for a preliminary injunction. The following opinion accompanied the later order:

United States v. The Progressive, Inc.

467 F. Supp. 990, 991, 993–96 (W.D. Wis. 1979)

WARREN, District Judge.

....

Does the article provide a "do-it-yourself" guide for the hydrogen bomb? Probably not. A number of affidavits make quite clear that a *sine qua non* to thermonuclear capability is a large, sophisticated industrial capability coupled with a coterie of imaginative, resourceful scientists and technicians. One does not build a hydrogen bomb in the basement. However, the article could possibly provide sufficient information to allow a medium size nation to move faster in developing a hydrogen weapon. It could provide a ticket to bypass blind alleys.

....

Defendants have stated that publication of the article will alert the people of this country to the false illusion of security created by the government's futile efforts at secrecy. They believe publication will provide the people with needed information to make informed decision on an urgent issue of public concern.

However, this Court can find no plausible reason why the public needs to know the technical details about hydrogen bomb construction to carry on an informed debate on this issue. Furthermore, the Court believes that the defendants' position in favor of nuclear non-proliferation would be harmed, not aided, by the publication of this article.

The defendants have also relied on the decision in the *New York Times* case. In that case, the Supreme Court refused to enjoin the *New York Times* and the *Washington Post* from publishing the contents of a classified historical study of United States decision-making in Viet Nam, the so called "Pentagon Papers."

This case is different in several important respects. In the first place, the study involved in the *New York Times* case contained historical data relating to events that occurred some three to twenty years previously. Secondly, the Supreme Court agreed with the lower

---

3. Atomic Energy Act, 42 U.S.C. § 2014 (2000).

court that no cogent reasons were advanced by the government as to why the article affected national security except that publication might cause some embarrassment to the United States.

A final and most vital difference between these two cases is the fact that a specific statute is involved here. Section 2274 of The Atomic Energy Act prohibits anyone from communicating, transmitting or disclosing any restricted data to any person "with reason to believe such data will be utilized to injure the United States or to secure an advantage to any foreign nation."

Section 2014 of the Act defines restricted data [to include] "all data concerning design, manufacture, or utilization of atomic weapons...."

....

The Court is of the opinion that the government has shown that the defendants had reason to believe that the data in the article, if published, would injure the United States or give an advantage to a foreign nation. Extensive reading and studying of the documents on file lead to the conclusion that not all the data is available in the public realm in the same fashion, if it is available at all.

What is involved here is information dealing with the most destructive weapon in the history of mankind, information of sufficient destructive potential to nullify the right to free speech and to endanger the right to life itself.

Stripped to its essence then, the question before the Court is a basic confrontation between the First Amendment right to freedom of the press and national security.

....

The Secretary of State states that publication will increase thermonuclear proliferation and that this would "irreparably impair the national security of the United States." The Secretary of Defense says that dissemination of the Morland paper will mean a substantial increase in the risk of thermonuclear proliferation and lead to use of threats that would "adversely affect the national security of the United States."

Howard Morland asserts that "if the information in my article were not in the public domain, it should be put there ... so that ordinary citizens may have informed opinions about nuclear weapons."

Erwin Knoll, the editor of *The Progressive*, states he is "totally convinced that publication of the article will be of substantial benefit to the United States because it will demonstrate that this country's security does not lie in an oppressive and ineffective system of secrecy and classification but in open, honest, and informed public debate about issues on which the people must decide."

The Court is faced with the difficult task of weighing and resolving these divergent views.

A mistake in ruling against *The Progressive* will seriously infringe cherished First Amendment rights. If a preliminary injunction is issued, it will constitute the first instance of prior restraint against a publication in this fashion in the history of this country, to this Court's knowledge. Such notoriety is not to be sought. It will curtail defendants' First Amendment rights in a drastic and substantial fashion. It will infringe upon our right to know and to be informed as well.

A mistake in ruling against the United States could pave the way for thermonuclear annihilation for us all. In that event, our right to life is extinguished and the right to publish becomes moot.

....

In light of these factors, this Court concludes that publication of the technical information on the hydrogen bomb contained in the article is analogous to publication of troop movements or locations in time of war and falls within the extremely narrow exception to the rule against prior restraint.

Post Mortem on the *Progressive* Case

If the case began with something of a roar, it ended with a whimper. To the government's eventual and considerable embarrassment, it turned out that the essential content of the Morland article could readily be found on public library shelves in Los Alamos, New Mexico. Such easy access supported Morland's claim that the "Secret Restricted Data" allegedly found in his article were not in fact "secret" but were quite public. At this point the case was dismissed as moot.[4] The Supreme Court meanwhile declined to reverse or dissolve the order as it had done in the Pentagon Papers case, *Morland v. Sprecher*.[5]

The government's initial victory against the Progressive is generally viewed as pyrrhic at best. Thomas A. Martin, who was then Deputy Assistant Attorney General for the Civil Division, later wrote: "Morland's article was published, its general accuracy had been confirmed by the government, and we had demonstrated again in the most public way possible our inability to keep the secrecy lid on."[6] Martin added, reflecting on the sobering lessons of the case, that such a fruitless quest not only requires the government to "confirm the nature and accuracy of that which it wishes to keep secret" as a prelude to any relief, but that if such a plea fails in court, "what one has is … an article that every country will pay attention to because it is certainly right." If the article is published and widely distributed, "the damage resulting is increased geometrically."

Nonetheless, clear and substantial though the government's ultimate loss may have been, the fact is that a prior restraint remained in force for several months against the publication of information that held substantial public interest, was clearly accurate (on the best and highest authority) and had not been unlawfully obtained. In any other type of proceeding, even one seeking to impose civil or criminal sanctions after publication, the convergence of those three elements would have been dispositive. The readiness of the district court to issue such an order, and the Supreme Court's reluctance to intervene, makes one wonder whether the case was an aberration or whether the Pentagon Papers doctrine had to some degree atrophied in the interim. A later case only compounds the uncertainty.

Cable News Network, Inc., et al. v. Manuel Antonio Noriega and United States

Cable News Network had obtained tapes of conversations between recently deposed Panamanian ruler General Manuel Noriega and his attorney. The conversations had been recorded in a U.S. prison in which Noriega was awaiting trial on drug-trafficking charges. Both Noriega and the government sought an order that would bar the broadcasting of the tapes on CNN. United States District Judge William M. Hoeveler did grant such an

---

4. United States v. Progressive, Inc., 610 F.2d 819 (7th Cir. 1979).
5. Morland v. Sprecher, 443 U.S. 709 (1979).
6. Thomas Martin, *National Security and the First Amendment: A Change in Perspective*, 68 A.B.A. J. 680, 683 (1983).

order.[7] The judge recognized the extraordinary nature of such intervention, barring the broadcast of material that held obvious public interest and was concededly accurate. But the court concluded that such an order was warranted in order to protect confidential attorney-client communications—at least where it could be shown that such a prior restraint offered the most effective and least restrictive means of preventing possibly irreparable harm which extensive pre-trial publicity might cause.

The Court of Appeals for the Eleventh Circuit rejected CNN's application for a stay of the restraining order. The appeals court declined to intervene at this stage of the proceeding, largely because of its view that Judge Hoeveler could not reasonably be asked to make findings on the precise nature of the potential threat to a fair trial, or on the adequacy of alternative means to preserve that right, so long as the network refused to make the tapes available to him for review.

The Supreme Court also declined to intervene when CNN sought a stay from Justice Anthony Kennedy, the relevant Circuit Justice. The prior restraint issue was referred by Justice Kennedy to the full Court, as is the practice when novel and difficult issues arise on such stay applications. Though the full Court supported Justice Kennedy's view that intervention was not appropriate at this stage, Justice Thurgood Marshall dissented, in an opinion in which Justice Sandra Day O'Connor joined. Their brief dissent is worth noting, if only because it represents the high Court's most recent encounter with prior restraint:

Cable News Network, Inc., et al. v. Manuel Antonio Noriega and United States
498 U.S. 976; 111 S. Ct. 451; 112 L. Ed. 2d 432 (1990)

MR. JUSTICE MARSHALL, with whom Ms. JUSTICE O'CONNOR joins, dissenting.

The issue raised by this petition is whether a trial court may enjoin publication of information alleged to threaten a criminal defendant's right to a fair trial without any threshold showing that the information will indeed cause such harm and that suppression is the only means of averting it. The District Court in this case entered an order enjoining petitioner Cable News Network (CNN) from broadcasting taped communications between respondent Manuel Noriega, a defendant in a pending criminal proceeding, and his counsel. The court entered this order without any finding that suppression of the broadcast was necessary to protect Noriega's right to a fair trial, reasoning that no such determination need be made unless and until CNN surrendered the tapes for the court's inspection. The Court of Appeals affirmed this conclusion.

In my view, this case is of extraordinary consequence for freedom of the press. Our precedents make unmistakably clear that "any prior restraint of expression comes to this Court bearing a "heavy presumption" against its constitutional validity,'" and that the proponent of this drastic remedy "'carries a heavy burden of showing justification for [its] imposition.'" *Nebraska Press Assn. V. Stuart,* 427 U.S. 539, 558 (1976), quoting *Organization for a Better Austin v. Keefe,* 402 U.S. 415, 419 (1971) (citations omitted); accord, *New York Times Co. v. United States,* 403 U.S. 713, 714 (1971) (per curiam). I do not see how the prior restraint imposed in this case can be reconciled with these teachings. Even more fundamentally, if the lower courts in this case are correct in their remarkable conclusion that publication can be automatically restrained pending application of the

---

7. Cable News Network v. Noriega, 752 F. Supp. 1045 (S.D. Fla. 1990).

demanding test established by Nebraska Press, then I think it is imperative that we re-examine the premises and operation of Nebraska Press itself. I would grant the stay application and the petition for certiorari.

These comments were not, however, the final word on the Noriega case. CNN eventually broadcast the first of the tapes, despite the restraining order. Judge Hoeveler did as he had warned he might do, and held the network in contempt for violating his order. The District Judge did, however, give CNN a choice between paying a "substantial" fine and broadcasting an apology, along with payment of $85,000 in court costs. The network chose the latter course, and did (some four years after the original confrontation over the tapes) express regret to its viewers. That ended the saga, about which senior First Amendment expert Floyd Abrams has noted: "The Noriega decision is an extraordinary exception [to the general pattern of refusing to enter or sustain prior restraints against the news media.]"[8]

Restraints on National Security-Related Expression by Government Employees

A former employee of the Central Intelligence Agency (CIA) named Victor Marchetti violated his signed agreement with the agency not to publish any material about his CIA service without express approval from his superiors. Although this agreement covered only classified information, Marchetti before his departure from the CIA signed another agreement in which he pledge not to disclose without agency permission "any information relating to the national defense or security." When Marchetti did take steps to publish material in breach of this provision, and was taken to court, the Fourth Circuit sustained an injunction issued by the district court to enforce the original secrecy agreement.[9] But the court of appeals cautioned that it would not have been willing to enforce a ban that went beyond protecting classified information; "to the extent that it purports to prevent disclosure of unclassified information," noted the appeals court, "to that extent, the oath would be in contravention of [Marchetti's] First Amendment rights."[10]

Several years later Frank W. Snepp raised a strikingly similar issue, which did this time reach the Supreme Court and substantially qualified the Fourth Circuit's view. Snepp had signed an agreement not to publish without agency approval information obtained during his CIA service that exceeded the classified ban by which Marchetti was bound. The ban covered "any information or material relating to the Agency, its activities or intelligence activities generally, either during or after the term of [his] employment…."[11]

Snepp then proceeded to publish a book about certain CIA activities in South Vietnam, to which he had been privy during his employment, but did not submit the manuscript for agency review as his agreement required. The government brought suit to enforce the agreement, which the district court agreed it should do because Snepp had "willfully de-liberately and surreptitiously breached his position of trust with the CIA and the secrecy agreement."[12] The court also noted that Snepp had clearly misled CIA officials into believing

---

8. Henry Weinstein, *Conflict of Free Press vs. Fair Trial*, L.A. Times, Apr. 8, 2002, at 2-1.

9. United States v. Marchetti, 466 F.2d 1309 (4th Cir.), *cert. denied*, 409 U.S. 1063 (1972).

10. *Id.* at 1317.

11. United States v. Snepp, 456 F. Supp. 176, 182 (E.D. Va. 1979).

12. *Id.*

he would submit the book for prepublication clearance.[13] The district court enjoined further breaches of Snepp's agreement, and imposed a constructive trust in the government's favor upon any royalties or profits he realized from the unauthorized publication.

The court of appeals sustained the injunction on the basis of the lower court's findings and analysis, but ruled that the record and Snepp's conduct did not warrant imposing a constructive trust on proceeds from publication in violation of the agreement.[14] The Supreme Court then granted review of the *Snepp* case, and without full briefing or oral argument summarily reinstated the judgment of the district court, reversing the Fourth Circuit on the constructive trust issue. Indeed, the high Court was unanimous on the injunction aspect of the case. Three dissenters (Justices Stevens, Brennan and Marshall) differed from the majority only on remedial issues, believing that a constructive trust was an unduly draconian sanction. They buttressed that conclusion with the government's apparent concession that the punitive damage remedy was "sufficient" to protect its interests, especially since the book contained no classified or non-public material.[15] The essence of the Court's reasoning on the permissibility of imposing a restraint on the speech of a former employee under such novel conditions is found in Part II of the opinion, as follows:

United States v. Snepp

444 U.S. 507 (1980)

Snepp's employment with the CIA involved an extremely high degree of trust. In the opening sentence of the agreement that he signed, Snepp explicitly recognized that he was entering in a trust relationship. The trust agreement specifically imposed the obligation not to publish *any* information relating to the Agency without submitting the information for clearance. Snepp stipulated at trial that—after undertaking this obligation—he had be "assigned to various positions of trust" and that he had been granted "frequent access to classified information, including information regarding intelligence sources and methods." 456 F. Supp., at 178. Snepp published his book about CIA activities on the basis of this background and exposure. He deliberately and surreptitiously violated his obligation to submit all materials for prepublication review. Thus, he exposed the classified material with which he had been entrusted to the risk of disclosure.

Whether Snepp violated his trust does not depend upon whether his book actually contained classified information. The Government does not deny—as a general principle—Snepp's right to publish unclassified information. Nor does it contend—at this stage of the litigation—that Snepp's book contains classified material. The Government simply claims that, in light of the special trust reposed in him and the agreement that he signed, Snepp should have given the CIA an opportunity to determine whether the material he proposed to publish would compromise classified information or sources. Neither of the Government's concessions undercuts its claim that Snepp's failure to submit to prepublication review was a breach of his trust.

Both the District Court and the Court of Appeals found that a former intelligence agent's publication of unreviewed material relating to intelligence activities can be detrimental to vital national interests even if the published information is unclassified. When a former agent relies on his own judgment about what information is detrimental,

---

13. *Id.* at 182
14. United States v. Snepp, 595 F.2d 926 (4th Cir. 1979).
15. Snepp v. United States, 444 U.S. 507 (1980).

he may reveal information that the CIA—with its broader understanding of what may expose classified information and confidential sources—could have identified as harmful. In addition to receiving intelligence from domestically based or controlled sources, the CIA obtains information from the intelligence services of friendly nations and from agents operating in foreign countries. The continued availability of these foreign sources depends upon the CIA's ability to guarantee the security of information that might compromise them and even endanger the personal safety of foreign agents.

Undisputed evidence in this case shows that a CIA agent's violation of his obligation to submit writings about the Agency for prepublication review impairs the CIA's ability to perform its statutory duties....

In view of this and other evidence in the record, both the District Court and the Court of Appeals recognized that Snepp's breach of explicit obligation to submit his material—classified or not—for prepublication clearance has irreparably harmed the United States Government....

The *Snepp* case posed several difficult issues apart from the remedial dispute that divided the Supreme Court. Since the rationale of all three courts was that Snepp had voluntarily relinquished, by signing the employment agreement, a citizen's free speech and press rights, one wonders how far such a waiver theory would extend to other sectors. Critics of *Snepp* have specifically questioned the soundness of the implicit rejection not only of Snepp's right to speak critically of government but also, as Harvard Professor Archibald Cox wrote soon after the decision, of "the citizenry's right to know about the conduct of its government."[16] In response, Chicago Professor (later Federal Appeals court judge) Frank Easterbrook argued that the "right to know" or the right to receive information existed only as a derivative of a First Amendment—protected right to speak. If, however, the speaker had no right to express view or convey certain information, as the *Snepp* courts ruled, then there was no corollary right to receive information. Moreover, Easterbrook argued that even if there might be an independent right to hear or learn, the authorized representatives of the people could constitutionally waive such a collective interest much as a speaker like Marchetti or Snepp could do (and had done) on an individual basis.[17]

Exposure of Intelligence Personnel

In 1974 ex-CIA agent Philip Agee declared a "campaign to fight the United States CIA wherever it is operating." Since then Agee has worked to expose the CIA agents around the world. He was joined in this effort by Louis Wolf, co-editor of *Counterspy* and subsequently of the *Covert Action Information Bulletin*, both publications devoted to disclosure of CIA operatives. Together Agee and Wolf published two books identifying hundreds of Agency personnel. These efforts proved all too successful. The CIA station chief in Greece was assassinated soon after being identified by Agee in an issue of *Counterspy*.

---

16. Archibald Cox, *Foreword: Freedom of Expression in the Burger Court*, 94 Harv. L. Rev. 1, 9–10 (1980).

17. Frank Easterbrook, *Insider Trading, Secret Agents, Evidentiary Privileges, and the Production of Information*, 1981 Sup. Ct. Rev. 309, 351–52 (1980).

The station chief in Jamaica was identified in the *Covert Action Information Bulletin,* and shortly thereafter his home was strafed with automatic fire.

Despite these events, neither Agee nor Wolf proved amenable to criminal sanctions. Many of Agee's identifications drew on classified information received by him during his employment with the CIA. It seems likely, therefore, that he could have been prosecuted under the Espionage Act[18] for disclosing classified information "relating to the national defense." The act, however, is poorly drafted and rarely invoked,[19] and in any event Agee fled the country.

Wolf's situation was different. Unlike Agee, Wolf had never been affiliated with the CIA; he gathered all his information from public sources. Since security classification has traditionally been based on the origin of the data rather than on their content, no law authorized punishment for publication of "public" data, even if the information were in fact not widely known before publication.

This perceived "gap" in the law led in 1979 and 1980 to the introduction of several bills designed to protect the identity of undercover intelligence operatives. Finally, in 1982, Congress passed the Intelligence Identities Protection Act.[20] Perhaps the most novel feature of that legislation was the extension of criminal liability to disclosure of covert intelligence operatives, even where such identification was achieved solely through research of public sources. As ultimately passed, Section 421(c) provided as follows:

> Whoever, in the course of a pattern of activities intended to identify and expose covert agents and with reason to believe that such activities would impair or impede the foreign intelligence activities of the United States, discloses any information that identifies an individual as a covert agent to any individual not authorized to receive classified information, knowing that the information disclosed so identifies such individual and that the United States is taking affirmative measures to conceal such individual's classified intelligence relationship to the United States, shall be fined not more than $15,000 or imprisoned not more than three years, or both.[21]

Thus, the act would cover not only Agee's disclosure of classified information but also Wolf's publication of identifications made from public research.

As one might expect, the bill drew fire as an infringement on First Amendment liberties. The American Civil Liberties Union, represented by Jerry Berman and Morton Halperin, opposed the bill as unconstitutional and unnecessary. In particular, they attacked the provision covering information derived from public sources. CIA Director Casey took a different view:

> Mr. Chairman, I believe it is important to emphasize that [this legislation] ... is not an assault upon the First Amendment. The "Intelligence Identities Protection Act" would not inhibit public discussion and debate about U.S. foreign policy or intelligence activities, and it would not operate to prevent the exposure of allegedly illegal activities or abuses of authority. The legislation is carefully crafted and narrowly drawn to deal with conduct which serves no useful informing function whatsoever; does not alert us to alleged abuses; does not bring clarity

---

18. Espionage Act, 18 U.S.C. § 793 (d)–(e) (1917).
19. *See generally* Harold Edgar & Benno Schmidt, *The Espionage Statutes and Publication of Defense Information,* 73 Colum L. Rev. 929 (1973).
20. Intelligence Identities Protection Act, 50 U.S.C. § 421 (1982).
21. *Id.*

to issues of national policy; does not enlighten public debate; and does not contribute to an educated and informed electorate.[22]

Casey went on to defend this view of the bill by outlining a narrow construction of that portion of the pending bill addressing identifications made from public sources:

> Disclosure of intelligence identities by persons who have not had authorized access to classified information would be punishable only under specified conditions, which have been carefully crafted and narrowly drawn so as to make the Act inapplicable to anyone not engaged in an effort or pattern of activities designed to identify and expose intelligence personnel. The proposed legislation also contains defenses and exceptions which reinforce this narrow construction. It is instructive, in this regard, to look at the elements of proof that would be required in a prosecution under [the pending bill]. Keeping in mind that the government would have to prove each of these elements beyond a reasonable doubt, the government would have to show:

> That there was an intentional disclosure of information which did in fact identify a "covert agent";

> That the person who made the disclosure knew that the information disclosed did in fact identify a covert agent;

> That the person who made the disclosure knew that the United States was taking affirmative measures to conceal the covert agent's classified intelligence affiliation;

> That the individual making the disclosure did so in the course of an effort to identify and expose covert agents with the intent to impair or impede the foreign intelligence activities of the United States; and

> That the disclosure was made *with the intent to* impair or impede the intelligence activities of the United States.

> Because of these strict conditions, [the provision] is narrowly directed at conduct which Congress has the authority and power to proscribe consistent with the First Amendment.[23]

The A.C.L.U. disagreed:

> The committee has sought to narrow the scope of the legislation by requiring proof of both a continuing effort to identify and expose covert agents and an intent to impair or impede intelligence activities. Both of these additions are commendable in that they narrow the coverage of the legislation. However, neither assures that the bill will not chill news coverage of intelligence activity or public debate on intelligence issues.

> The course of conduct required by the bill is precisely that engaged in by any enterprising investigative reporter. A reporter doing a story on U.S. intelligence activities will be engaged in an effort to uncover the identities of covert agents. Moreover, many reporters have written articles or made comments critical of some intelligence functions and would fear that a jury could be persuaded that their intent was to impair intelligence activities. Needless to say, the First

---

22. *The Intelligence Identities Protection Act: Hearing Before the Subcomm. on Legislation of the House Permanent Select Comm. on Intelligence*, 97th Cong., 1st Sess., 14 (1981).

23. *Id.* at 15.

Amendment permits any individual to use criticism to inhibit the activity of any agency of the government and to pursue that criticism by all lawful means, including publication.

Mr. Chairman, the vigorous opposition to this bill on the part of every major press organization should remove any doubt that its passage would chill public debate. We offer two of many possible scenarios in the hope that it will lead the committee to reconsider the bill's wisdom, or at the least to assure us that the bill will be drafted more narrowly than it is now.

Assume in each case a reporter who has published several articles in a weekly magazine of opinion calling for greater limits on intelligence activities. In the course of researching the reporter seeks to learn the identities of covert agents:

The reporter suspects that the new administration in its eagerness to give aid and assistance to the Savimbi-led effort in Angola has interpreted the Clark Amendment to permit aid which is used for other than military operations. He investigates and then publishes a story that Savimbi is receiving such aid. He reports also that the intelligence committees were not notified of the aid, in apparent violation of the oversight provisions of the National Security Act as amended.

The reporter suspects that the FBI has infiltrated the Catholic Church, seeking evidence that the Catholic groups opposing U.S. policy in El Salvador are part of an international network controlled by Cuba or the USSR. She consults with members of the church who search for and uncover the FBI informants in the church. The newspaper then prints the story, giving their identities.

These scenarios and a number of others make clear that the scope of the bill would often cover both legitimate newsgathering activity and public debates on important intelligence issues. We understand the committee to be saying that it has no intention of covering such situations, but the plain language of the bill remains very broad and would clearly chill public debate.[24]

The Intelligence Identities Protection Act was signed into law on June 23, 1982.[25] As will have been noted, the bill as enacted did not require an actual intent to impair or impede U.S. intelligence activities but only that the defendant have had "reason to believe that such activities would impair or impede the foreign intelligence activities of the United States."

How would this change affect the debate between Director Casey and the A.C.L.U. representatives? Are the scenarios outlined in the A.C.L.U. testimony covered by the bill as enacted? If so, does that render the law unconstitutional? Or is the scope of the law justified by a "compelling state interest"? These and other questions remain unanswered. Ultimately, of course, such issues can be resolved only by the courts.

The Media and the Military: Press Access to Military Operations

When U.S. forces briefly invaded the island of Grenada in the fall of 1983, no reporters or photographers were allowed to accompany the troops. Journalists who later made their

---

24. *Id.* at 68–69.
25. Intelligence Identities Protection Act, *supra* note 20.

own way to the island were not permitted to dispatch report. The Secretary of Defense justified such a total news blackout by citing the difficulty of ensuring the safety of journalists, and the need for secrecy during the initial phases of the landing. Two days later a small number of reporters were allowed to remain in Grenada for a few hours, and a week before the operation ended a much larger number of journalists were allowed to remain indefinitely. Media criticism of this blackout was substantial; *Washington Post* Managing Editor Howard Simons charged that "a secret war, like secret government, is antithetical to an open society ... [and is] ... absolutely outrageous."[26] Walter Cronkite added his conviction that "this is our foreign policy and we have a right to know precisely what is happening, and there can be no excuse in denying the people that right."[27] Columnist George Will, on the other hand, supported the Grenada blackout, noting that "Many journalists advocate an 'adversary' stance toward their government, denying any duty to weigh the consequences of what they print or broadcast."[28]

Several months after the Grenada invasion, a coalition of media organizations issued a comprehensive statement about news coverage of military operations. The statement urged a clearer balance between two imperatives—"the requirement that the Government conduct effective military operations and the requirement that the public, via a free press be independently informed about the actions of its Government." These media groups called for reaffirmation of the "historic principle ... that journalists should be present at U.S. military operations" to a degree consistent with "recognition of the importance of U.S. military mission security and troop safety."[29] The statement ventured, on an optimistic note, that, "when essential, both groups can agree on coverage conditions which satisfy safety and security imperatives while, in keeping with the spirit of the First Amendment, permitting independent reporting to the citizens of our free and open society, to whom our Government ultimately is accountable."[30]

The joint media statement contained harsh and sharp criticism of the Grenada blackout. Such criticism led the Chairman of the Joint Chiefs of Staff, General John W. Vessey, Jr., to create a Military-Media Relations Panel chaired by Major General Winant Sidle, USA (ret.) The panel was asked to address a single question: "How do we conduct military operations in a manner that safeguards the lives of our military and protects the security of the operation while keeping the American public informed through the media?" The panel eventually produced its report in the form of a letter to General Vessey, setting forth eight specific recommendations.

The recommendations began with a "statement of principle" that "it is essential that the U.S. news media cover U.S. military operations to the maximum degree possible consistent with mission security and the safety of U.S. forces." The specific recommendations were as follows: (1) "[t]hat public affairs planning for military operations be conducted concurrently with operational planning"; (2) that where news media pooling is necessary to provide early access to an operation, the "planning should provide for the largest possible press pool that is practical and minimize the length of time the pool will be necessary before 'full coverage' is feasible"; (3) that the Secretary of Defense should consider use of a "pre-established and constantly up-dated accreditation or notification list" for constituting such pools; (4) "[t]hat a basic tenet governing media access to military operations should

---

26. N.Y. Times, Oct. 27, 1983, at A1.
27. UPI Dispatch, Feb. 5, 1984, AM cycle.
28. The Recorder, Jan. 29, 1991, at 4.
29. *60 Minutes* (CBS television broadcast, Jan. 16, 1984).
30. *Id.*

be voluntary compliance by the media with security guidelines or ground rules established and issued by the military"; (5) that the military should provide sufficient equipment and personnel to assist correspondents in the field; (6) that "[p]lanners should carefully consider media communications requirements to assure the earliest feasible availability"; (7) that planning should include transportation support for the media; and (8) that a variety of steps should be taken to improve media-military understanding.[31]

There was one other Grenada-related development. In December 1983, the *New York Times* reported that a coalition of media organizations had sought to negotiate with the Defense Department procedures for press access to combat zones. Although the group had contemplated filing a lawsuit over the issue, analysis of the legal context convinced its members that "the suit could easily fail and might thereby set a precedent for even tighter restrictions."[32] Meanwhile, Hustler publisher Larry Flynt did file such a suit in federal court. Six months later Flynt's complaint was dismissed as moot, on the ground that the Grenada invasion was a "unique event" and that there was no "demonstrated probability" that a similar press ban would recur in the event of a future military expedition. The court went on, however, to offer its view that even if there were a live controversy the suit should still fail: "An injunction such as the one plaintiffs seek would limit the range of options available to the commanders in the field in the future, possibly jeopardizing the success of military operations and the lives of military personnel and thereby gravely damaging the national interest."[33]

Panama: A Brief Incursion with Better Coverage

In the final weeks of 1989, the United States launched a brief military foray into Panama for the purpose of displacing the country's dictatorial ruler, General Manuel Noriega. The media had been alerted to such a planned operation, and were at least in that part of the world when it occurred. During the initial phase of the campaign, however, American journalists were not allowed to accompany the troops, and remained in hotels in Panama City or at a staging area in Costa Rica. *New York Times* and Reuters reporters were detained when they sought to check on an airlift at a U.S. military base. The restrictions were eased as the operation progressed, and pools were eventually created to enable at least representative reporters and photographers to provide live coverage of later stages of the Panama operation. Even then, the extent of media access was limited. Early reports had to rely mainly on Pentagon briefings and information that journalists were able to obtain from other sources in Panama City. After this operation had ended, one network news executive observed that coverage and access were "better than Grenada" though "from our point of view, ... not good." Less than a year after Panama, another and far more intense overseas campaign would critically test the state of media-military relations.

The Persian Gulf War and Beyond

The most substantial encounter between the media and the military occurred in the early 1990s, following Iraq's invasion of Kuwait and the mobilization of U.S. forces in Saudi Arabia, first as Desert Shield, before hostilities during the late fall of 1990, and later

---

31. *Id.*

32. N.Y. TIMES, Dec. 2, 1983, at A11.

33. Flynt v. Weinberger, 588 F. Supp. 57, 60 (D.D.C. 1984), *affirmed, vacated and remanded*, 762 F.2d 134 (D.C. Cir. 1985).

as Desert Storm, when hostilities began in January, 1991. The major media organizations engaged in extensive discussions with the Defense Department (chiefly in the person of Assistant Secretary Pete Williams, a once and future NBC television news reporter). Several initial proposals from the Pentagon were ultimately withdrawn—for example, a requirement that all reporters submit to and pass a rigorous physical examination before being credentialed for the theatre of operations, and another that no journalist could interview any uniformed personnel except in the presence of a military information officer.

The rules that survived such negotiations, and went into effect at the start of hostilities early in 1991, relied chiefly on the creation of pools of reporters and photographers. Each day a small group of journalists would be selected from a group of their peers who were far too numerous to be transported to the front lines on a regular basis. The pool members would effectively constitute the eyes and ears of the media, and would upon return share their materials and their impressions with their colleagues who had remained at home base. Not surprisingly, reporters and photographers from the major print and broadcast media were disproportionately included in these pools. Partly for that reason, a group of smaller media—mainly magazines and individual writers, with *The Nation* as lead plaintiff—brought suit in federal district court to challenge on First Amendment grounds the validity of the pooling procedure and other media restrictions that had just gone into force in the Persian Gulf.

A parallel suit was filed by *Agence France Presse* on behalf of a group of non-U.S. media seeking access to the battlefield. The two cases were consolidated, and came before Judge Leonard Sand of the Southern District of New York, who initially showed much sympathy for the plaintiffs' position. As the following opinion reveals, however, Judge Sand gradually lost patience with the media challengers and, though he eventually declined to grant specific relief when hostilities ended, seized the opportunity to offer extremely important observations about the relationship between the media and the military in a foreign theatre of operations.

The Nation Magazine v. United States Department of Defense
762 F. Supp. 1558 (S.D.N.Y. 1991)

[Judge Sand began by noting that "the primary focus of plaintiff's challenge is on the question of access and not primarily on those restrictions which limit, for national security reasons, the information that pool members may publish." He also noted the Defense Department's position that the "First Amendment does not bar the government from restricting access to combat activities and that the regulations are narrowly tailored and necessitated by compelling national security concerns." Thus the case, in Judge Sand's view, presents "profound and novel questions as to the existence and scope of a First Amendment right of access." The only potential precedents were the prior restraint cases, and a few decisions upholding the exclusion of the press and the public from military bases, for example *Greer v. Spock*.[34]]

[Judge Sand then addressed several difficult procedural issues. Since hostilities had ceased in the Persian Gulf some weeks earlier, the case seemed moot, at least as far as the granting of injunctive relief. The issue of standing was also canvassed; Judge Sand concluded that the media plaintiff's were proper parties to bring such issues before a federal court. Moreover, the government had claimed but Judge Sand disagreed, that the case dealt with

---

34. *Greer v. Spock*, 424 U.S. 828 (1976).

"political questions" committed to another branch of government, and with foreign relations matters on which Executive judgment was dispositive. Finally, there was no doubt in Judge Sand's view that the plaintiffs' claims were judicially enforceable.]

[After a lengthy review of such potential barriers, and a thorough summary of the challenged media pool procedures, Judge Sand reached the substantive issues at the intersection of media access or press freedom and national security. At that level, the case seemed clearly "one of first impression, the answer to which would require charting new constitutional territory."]

The Supreme Court has on a number of occasions considered the relationship between the First Amendment and national security. *See Near*, 283 U.S. at 716; *New York Times Co.*, 403 U.S. at 722–23; *Snepp v. United States*, 444 U.S. 507, 514–15, 62 L. Ed. 2d 704, 100 S. Ct. 763 (1980). None of these cases, however, has addressed directly the role and limits of news gathering under the First Amendment in a military context abroad. Nonetheless, there is no dearth of case law on questions involving the access rights of the press and public in other circumstances. As in most cases involving novel issues, the Court must reason by analogy. It is certain that there is no right of access of the press to fora which have traditionally been characterized as private or closed to the public, such as meetings involving the internal discussions of government officials. *See United States v. Nixon*, 418 U.S. 683, 705 n. 15, 41 L. Ed. 2d 1039, 94 S. Ct. 3090 (1974). Limitations may also be placed on access to government controlled institutions, such as prisons and military bases. *See Houchins v. KQED, Inc.*, 438 U.S. 1, 16, 57 L. Ed. 2d 553, 98 S. Ct. 2588 (1978); *Greer*, 424 U.S. at 838; *Saxbe v. Washington Post Company*, 417 U.S. 843, 850, 41 L. Ed. 2d 514, 94 S. Ct. 2811 (1974); *Pell v. Procunier*, 417 U.S. 817, 828, 41 L. Ed. 2d 495, 94 S. Ct. 2800 (1974).

On the other hand, there is an almost absolute right of access to open places, including such fora as streets and parks. *See Hague v. C.I.O.*, 307 U.S. 496, 515, 83 L. Ed. 1423, 59 S. Ct. 954 (1939). In recent times the Supreme Court has been particularly generous in interpreting the scope of the public's right under the First Amendment to know about government functioning, at least in such fora as a criminal trial. *See Richmond Newspapers, Inc.*, 448 U.S. at 564. In these cases, there appears to be some indication that the basis for such a right of access could apply more broadly. *See Globe Newspaper Co. v. Superior Court for County of Norfolk*, 457 U.S. 596, 606, 73 L. Ed. 2d 248, 102 S. Ct. 2613 (1982).

A fundamental theme in *Richmond* and *Globe* was the importance of an informed American citizenry. As the Court wrote, guaranteed access of the public to occurrences in a courtroom during a criminal trial assures "freedom of communication on matters relating to the functioning of government." *Richmond Newspapers*, 448 U.S. at 575. Learning about, criticizing and evaluating government, the Supreme Court has reasoned, requires some "right to receive" information and ideas. *Martin v. City of Struthers*, 319 U.S. 141, 143, 87 L. Ed. 1313, 63 S. Ct. 862 (1943). In *Globe*, the Court devoted extensive attention to the importance of this "checking function" against abuse of government power. *See* Blasi, "The Checking Value in First Amendment Theory," 1977 Am. B. Found. Research J. 521, 593. This theme has been echoed by the Supreme Court even when the government has suggested that national security concerns were implicated. *See New York Times Co.*, 403 U.S. at 728 (Stewart, J. concurring) (" ... without an informed and free press, there can not be an enlightened people").

Given the broad grounds invoked in these holdings, the affirmative right to gather news, ideas and information is certainly strengthened by these cases. By protecting the press, the flow of information to the public is preserved. As the Supreme Court has observed, "the First Amendment goes beyond protection of the press and the self-expression of individuals to prohibit government from limiting the stock of information from which members of the public may draw." *First National Bank v. Bellotti*, 435 U.S. 765, 783, 55 L. Ed. 2d 707, 98 S. Ct. 1407 (1978). Viewing these cases collectively, it is arguable that generally there is at least some minimal constitutional right to access. *See Branzburg v. Hayes*, 408 U.S. 665, 681, 33 L. Ed. 2d 626, 92 S. Ct. 2646 (1972) ("without some protection for seeking out the news, freedom of the press could be eviscerated.").

If the reasoning of these recent access cases were followed in a military context, there is support for the proposition that the press has at least some minimal right of access to view and report about major events that affect the functioning of government, including, for example, an overt combat operation. As such, the government could not wholly exclude the press from a land area where a war is occurring that involves this country. But this conclusion is far from certain since military operations are not closely akin to a building such as a prison, nor to a park or a courtroom.

In order to decide this case on the merits, it would be necessary to define the outer constitutional boundaries of access. Pursuant to long-settled policy in the disposition of constitutional questions, courts should refrain from deciding issues presented in a highly abstract form, especially in instances where the Supreme Court has not articulated guiding standards. *See Rescue Army*, 331 U.S. at 575–85. Since the principles at stake are important and require a delicate balancing, prudence dictates that we leave the definition of the exact parameters of press access to military operations abroad for a later date when a full record is available, in the unfortunate event that there is another military operation. Accordingly, the Court declines to exercise its power to grant plaintiffs' request for declaratory relief on their right of access claim.

The second claim which this Court must determine is whether it will decide on the merits involving the question of limitations on access. Plaintiffs suggest that the government gave some members of the press preferential treatment in the form of financial assistance and more extensive access to events as they occurred. Again, the Court is being asked to provide declaratory relief that a set of regulations, though lifted, are unconstitutional on their face. It is questionable whether any inquiry would be sufficiently focused to pass muster under *Rescue Army. Id.* A brief discussion of the underlying law is useful to identify the difficulty facing this Court were it to decide this portion of the case on the merits.

In the instant case, the government chose to grant some access to the press for purposes of covering military activities in the Persian Gulf. By opening the door, albeit in a limited manner, the government created a place for expressive activity. Establishing pools for coverage of the "initial stages" of the Persian Gulf conflict, the government, in essence, determined that the war theatre was a limited public forum. *See Perry Education Ass'n v. Perry Local Educators' Assn.*, 460 U.S. 37, 48, 74 L. Ed. 2d 794, 103 S. Ct. 948 (1983). Regardless of whether the government is constitutionally required to open the battlefield to the press as representatives of the public, a question that this Court has declined to decide, once the government does so it is bound to do so in a non-discriminatory manner. *See Houchins*, 438 U.S. at 16; *Cuomo*, 570 F.2d at 1083 (2d Cir. 1977).

Once a limited public forum has been created, the government is under an obligation to insure that "access not be denied arbitrarily or for less than compelling reasons." *Sherrill v. Knight*, 186 U.S. App. D.C. 293, 569 F.2d 124, 129 (D.C. Cir. 1977); *see also Southeastern Promotions Ltd. v. Conrad*, 420 U.S. 546, 553, 43 L. Ed. 2d 448, 95 S. Ct. 1239 (1975). Restrictions on newsgathering must generally be no more "arduous than necessary, and … individual news [persons] may not be arbitrarily excluded from sources of information." *Sherrill*, 569 F.2d at 130; *see also Cox Broadcasting Corp. v. Cohn*, 420 U.S. 469, 491–92,

43 L. Ed. 2d 328, 95 S. Ct. 1029 (1975); *United States v. Associated Press*, 52 F. Supp. 362, 372 (S.D.N.Y. 1943).

The seminal case suggesting the analysis by which to determine whether regulations are discriminatory is *Police Dep't of Chicago v. Mosley*, 408 U.S. 92, 95, 33 L. Ed. 2d 212, 92 S. Ct. 2286 (1972). Above "all else," the Court wrote, "the First Amendment means that government has no power to restrict expression because of its message, its ideas, its subject matter or its content." ...

. . . .

The right of the press to be free from regulations that are discriminatory on their face or as applied, however, is not synonymous with a guaranteed right to gather news at all times and places or in any manner that may be desired. *See Heffron v. International Soc. for Krishna Consciousness, Inc.*, 452 U.S. 640, 647–48, 69 L. Ed. 2d 298, 101 S. Ct. 2559 (1981); *Cox v. Louisiana*, 379 U.S. 536, 554, 13 L. Ed. 2d 471, 85 S. Ct. 453 (1965). The activities of the press are subject to reasonable time, place, and manner restrictions. *Grayned v. Rockford*, 408 U.S. 104, 115, 33 L. Ed. 2d 222, 92 S. Ct. 2294 (1972); *Cox*, 379 U.S. at 558. In reviewing regulations, such as those that are written by DOD for use in a military operation, the Court would inquire whether they are "justified without reference to the content of the regulated speech, that they serve a significant governmental interest, and that in doing so they leave open ample alternative channels for communication of the information." *Heffron*, 452 U.S. at 648.

There is little disagreement, even from plaintiffs, that DOD may place reasonable time, place, and manner restrictions on the press upon showing that there is a significant governmental interest. Yet, when asked at oral argument about how the government may design appropriate non-content based regulations that had reasonable time, place, and manner restrictions, counsel for the NATION responded, "Fortunately, I don't have to make that decision." Transcript, March 7, 1991, at p. 46. When the Court posed a hypothetical involving an amphibious landing in a foreign land which assumed the presence of more press representatives than boats to accommodate them, counsel for the NATION had no suggestion on how to decide which members of the media should be included. Instead, arguing that no limitations whatsoever should apply, he explained, "I dare say that if NBC rented [a luxury private yacht] ... it doesn't impede the [amphibious] military operation." Transcript, March 7, 1991, at p. 53.

Of course plaintiffs' espousal of the view that any journalist wishing access to a battlefield may have such access avoids the necessity to provide for some selection process when either logistics or security concerns may mandate limitation of the number of journalists who may be present. But surely a court ruling on the possible appropriateness of such a restriction for some future military conflict must consider the possibility that at times such circumstances may be present. Who can say that during the next American overseas military operation some restriction on the number of journalists granted access at a particular time to a particular battlefield may not be a reasonable time, place, and manner restriction? Who today can even predict the manner in which the next war may be fought?

The Court, repeatedly and unsuccessfully, pressed plaintiffs to propose specific alternatives to the DOD regulations that the press believed would pass constitutional scrutiny. Except for AFP, whose request for relief is specific but moot (*i.e.* that it be admitted to the photo pool), plaintiffs' only response was that the press be allowed unlimited unilateral access. Although specifically alerted at an early pretrial conference to the Court's concern about the lack of specificity in the NATION plaintiffs' prayer for relief in the original complaint, and that the Court would carefully scrutinize the then-anticipated amended complaint for proposed specific remedial measures, the amended complaint still lacks specificity. Rather than make specific proposals, such as suggesting that any regulations must include provisions for a speedy administrative review process for those who claim they were improperly excluded from a pool, plaintiffs have adhered to an absolute "no limitation" approach.

In a case of such moment, involving significant and novel constitutional doctrines, the Court must have the benefit of a well focused controversy. *See Army Rescue*, 331 U.S. at 584. The Court should not now be evaluating a set of regulations that are currently being reviewed for probable revision, to determine their reasonableness in the context of a conflict that does not exist and the precise contours of which are unknown and unknowable. For these reasons, the Court declines to grant plaintiffs' application for declaratory relief on their First and Fifth Amendment equal access claims.

CONCLUSION

In the Court's view, the right of access claims, and particularly the equal access claims, are not sufficiently in focus at this time to meet the *Rescue Army* requirement that "the underlying constitutional issues [be presented] in a clean-cut and concrete form." *See* 331 U.S. at 584. For the reasons articulated throughout the Opinion, prudence dictates that a final determination of the important constitutional issues at stake be left for another day when the controversy is more sharply focused. Accordingly, the complaint is dismissed.

––––––––––––

One other Gulf-War related lawsuit that had been filed about the same time as the *Nation* case languished for several years, first in the district court and later in the District of Columbia Circuit. Final decision by the court of appeals did not come until the summer of 1996, more than five years after the conclusion of hostilities. The focus of this suit, brought by a group of photographers, was a Defense Department decision to deny journalists access to the mortuary at the Dover, Delaware, Air Force base, which in earlier engagements had been the site of publicized ceremonies honoring service personnel who had been killed in action. The opinion of the court of appeals, excerpted below, describes the policy and its background more fully, and sets forth the court's reasons for rejecting the photographers' First Amendment challenge.

JB Pictures, Inc. v. Department of Defense
318 U.S. App. D.C. 162; 86 F.3d 236 (D.C. Cir. 1996)

Stephen F. Williams, *Circuit Judge*

Dover Air Force Base is the site of the only mortuary operated jointly by the military services on the East Coast. For a substantial period before Operation Desert Storm, soldiers killed abroad (for instance, in Lebanon in 1983 and Panama in 1989) returned to the U.S. through Dover. These returns were events open to the public and press and were accompanied by ceremonies honoring the dead. Shortly before the start of Operation Desert Storm, the Department of Defense instituted a new policy, effectively shifting these events to sites closer to the families of the deceased and providing that the families would exercise veto power over press coverage. The Department explained that it was doing so to reduce the hardship on those of the bereaved who otherwise might have felt obliged to travel to Dover for the arrival ceremonies:

> Therefore, it is the military departments' policy that ceremonies/services be held at the service member's duty or home station and/or the interment site,

rather than at the port of entry. Media coverage of the arrival of the remains at the port of entry or at interim stops will not be permitted, but may be permitted at the service member's duty or home station or at the interment site, if the family so desires.

Public Affairs Guidance—Operation Desert Storm Casualty and Mortuary Affairs P 3 (Feb. 7, 1991), Joint Appendix ("J.A.") 123. There was no change in the pre-existing policy allowing civilians to witness other activities on the base, including outgoing transport of military personnel and supplies to the Persian Gulf, as long as such access was consistent with any other applicable restrictions.

JB Pictures and several other media and veterans' organizations and individual reporters challenged the Dover access policy on First Amendment grounds, arguing that precluding access to the war dead at Dover while permitting access to other activities—ones allegedly placing Desert Storm in a more positive light—constituted impermissible "viewpoint discrimination." The district court dismissed the complaint, finding no First Amendment violation. *JB Pictures, Inc. v. Dept. of Defense, 1993 U.S. Dist. LEXIS 6517,* No. 91-0397 (D.D.C. Apr. 22, 1993). This appeal followed.

....

On the merits, the plaintiffs recognize, as they must, that First Amendment rights to "freedom of speech, [and] of the press" do not create any per se right of access to government property or activities simply because such access might lead to more thorough or better reporting. "The prohibition of unauthorized entry into the White House diminishes the citizen's opportunities to gather information he might find relevant to his opinion of the way the country is being run, but that does not make entry into the White House a First Amendment right." *Zemel v. Rusk,* 381 U.S. 1, 17, 14 L. Ed. 2d 179, 85 S. Ct. 1271 (1965). Thus the Court has found in the First Amendment only a qualified right of access....

....

We also reject plaintiffs' effort to coax some discrimination out of the fact that the Dover access policy was adopted in contemplation of Desert Storm and represented a departure from the policy during the Panama invasion and other events in the 1980s. Surely the government is not subject to a one-way ratchet, in which any new restriction on access is automatically invalid, or even especially suspect, while any relaxation of limits becomes a new constitutional minimum (or at least a trigger of special scrutiny). Cf. *Pell,* 417 U.S. at 831 (noting that California's decision not to allow members of the press to interview prisoners designated by them reversed a former policy and brought its treatment of the press (on this point) into alignment with its treatment of the public as a whole).

We return, then, to plaintiffs' general claim of a right of access to Dover. It is obvious that military bases do not share the tradition of openness on which the Court relied in striking down restrictions on access to criminal court proceedings in *Press-Enterprise, Richmond Newspapers,* and *Globe Newspaper.* And plaintiffs fare no better under the balancing test set forth in *Branzburg* and *Pell.* The burden on their news gathering activity imposed by the Dover access policy is relatively modest. Plaintiffs do not allege that greater access to Dover will reveal new information about the occurrence or magnitude of casualties in military conflict. Thus, unlike the restrictions upheld in *Saxbe* and *Pell,* the Dover policy does not impede acquisition of basic facts, the raw material of a story.

Further, as noted above, the Dover policy allows public and press access to interment ceremonies if the relevant family members consent, and also to any arrival ceremonies held at the soldiers' home bases, again with the family's consent. See Public Affairs Guidance—Operation Desert Storm Casualty and Mortuary Affairs P 3, J.A. 123. This may not be a perfect substitute for general access to Dover, of course; among other things, access depends on the decision of the bereaved. But it surely lessens the bite of the restriction at Dover, much as the breadth of the opportunity for press-prisoner contact in *Saxbe* and *Pell* led the Court to conclude that the press enjoyed "substantial," though not complete, access to inmates. *Saxbe*, 417 U.S. at 846; *Pell*, 417 U.S. at 833.

The government points to a number of interests in support of the Dover policy, of which we think two amply suffice. First, as the government stated in announcing the policy, the limitation on access is intended to reduce the hardship on the families and friends of the war dead, who "may feel obligated to travel great distances" to attend arrival ceremonies at Dover if such ceremonies are held. Public Affairs Guidance—Operation Desert Storm Casualty and Mortuary Affairs P 3, J.A. 123. Plaintiffs respond that families and friends would not feel obliged to come if arrival ceremonies were not held and that the government can therefore avoid the problem by simply not holding arrival ceremonies. We are unsure whether the family and friends of a deceased soldier would cease to feel any obligation to be present at a *public* transit through Dover just because it was not to be accompanied by an "arrival ceremony." In any event, we do not see how the Constitution can be said to put the government to such a choice—public arrival at Dover without a ceremony (exposing the government to a probably justifiable charge of callous indifference) or public arrival with a ceremony (actually inflicting burdens on the bereaved, and thus exposing it to a charge of callousness).

The government also asserts an interest in protecting the privacy of families and friends of the dead, who may not want media coverage of the unloading of caskets at Dover. The strength of the interest will of course vary with the pattern of use of Dover: the smaller the number arriving at any given time, and the smaller the number of occasions of arrival, the easier it is for outsiders to infer the identity of an individual soldier. In any event we do not think the government hypersensitive in thinking that the bereaved may be upset at public display of the caskets of their loved ones. We note that the government's policy of allowing the family the right to deny access to services at the home base is consistent with its assertion of this interest behind the policy at Dover. Accordingly, we have no hesitation in concluding that there was nothing impermissible about the access restrictions imposed at Dover Air Force Base.

Apart from their access claim, plaintiffs invoke a theory that their exclusion from Dover when war dead are present unconstitutionally denies them a right to the opportunity to *speak* in that setting. The district court found that the plaintiffs' allegations did not embrace a claim based on the right to engage in speech on the base. *JB Pictures*, Mem. op. at 6 n.6. We agree.

To support the view that their complaint raised such a claim, plaintiffs point to a single allegation—that members of plaintiff Veterans for Peace ("VFP") intended to "witness and pay their respects to the war dead as they arrived in the United States." Complaint P 7. In some contexts, of course—e.g., "bear witness"—the word "witness" connotes expressive activity, indeed, commonly speech. But in the context used here, the "witness" component of this isolated phrase suggests mere seeing, i.e., an aspect of the overall access claim. The paragraph in which the phrase appears further undermines the idea that it asserts a right to speak at Dover. The two preceding sentences introduce and describe the functions of the VFP organization in the following terms:

> [VFP] is a non-profit *educational* organization of over 2,600 veterans of U.S.
> wars with 53 chapters that is *dedicated to abolishing war as an instrument of in-*

ternational policy. VFP provides *public information about the costs of war,* establishes relations with peace-seeking veterans of other nations, and participates in international fact-finding and monitoring missions.

Id. (emphasis added). Thus, VFP is an organization primarily concerned with carrying a message *from* Dover. In context, then, the isolated allegation of a desire to witness and pay tribute to the war dead does not discernibly constitute a claim to a right to speak on the base.

The other plaintiffs before us echo VFP in describing themselves in the complaint entirely in terms of their interests in such matters as reporting news and educating the American people, i.e., in carrying messages from Dover to a broad national (or international) audience. We see no error in the district court's failure to discern in their allegations something besides what they plainly focused on — the right to access for news gathering. Plaintiffs were, of course, free to seek the court's permission to amend their complaint (perhaps after filing a motion to set aside the court's judgment under Rule 59(e) or 60(b) of the Federal Rules of Civil Procedure, see *Vicom, Inc. v. Harbridge Merchant Services, Inc.,* 20 F.3d 771, 784–85 (7th Cir. 1994)), but they chose not to avail themselves of that opportunity.

Because the access policy at Dover does not violate the First Amendment's guarantees of freedom of speech and of the press, and because the complaint does not embrace a claim based on the right to engage in on-base speech, the judgment of the district court is *Affirmed.*

———————

After the *JB Pictures* decision, and long after the end of Persian Gulf military activities, the time seemed ripe to review what had happened in the courts, and to speculate about possible future tensions or conflicts between the news media and the military. The excerpt below concludes by noting (and quoting in full) a remarkable set of guidelines, which the Defense Department and the major media organizations negotiated with an eye to possible future overseas engagements.

Robert M. O'Neil, *The Media and the Military: The Persian Gulf War and Beyond*
1 J. Nat'l Sec. L. 10–15 (1997)

By the fall of 1996, the Gulf War litigation had finally run its course. Several general observations seem appropriate: First, only one of the three cases, *Agence France Presse,* was dismissed as moot, and only when the avenue of access it had sought literally ceased to exist.[35] Moreover, Judge Sand referred at several points to the surviving interests of such a foreign news service, suggesting that technical mootness did not preclude consideration of the substantive issues AFP had raised during the Gulf operation.[36] By ruling on the government's hard-pressed mootness claims, courts in both surviving cases recognized the degree to which similar, indeed identical, disputes might well arise in the event of future overseas military engagements. In this regard, Gulf War litigation contrasts

———————

35. *Nation Magazine,* 762 F. Supp. at 1558 (1991). Originally, the district court held that Agence France Presse had standing to bring its suit. *Id.* at 1565–69.

36. *Id.* at 1568–69. The court said that it was reasonable to conclude that these "same parties" would be "litigating the same issues" the next time the United States engaged in military initiative overseas. *Id.* at 1569.

with its most recent antecedent; a case challenging the legality of the Grenada invasion. That case was dismissed as moot because the court saw "no reasonable expectation" that media-military disputes would recur.[37]

Second, the two surviving cases received a far more congenial hearing than most observers would have expected when they were filed. Judge Sand's opinion was striking for its receptivity to novel claims of access to military activity and information, even where such access would not clearly exist in the closest civilian counterpart. While the court of appeals in the Dover case was less sympathetic, it did not reject such claims out of hand. Rather, Judge Williams stressed the special government interest in the new policy, and the alternative open to those who wished to cover military casualties at a different time and place. Perhaps most significant, the appeals court also gave modest credence to the claim that the government engaged in viewpoint discrimination by permitting, indeed encouraging, coverage of troops departing for combat, but denying coverage of casualties returning home from combat.[38]

Finally, both the *Nation* and the Dover cases are notable for their receptiveness to civilian analogies in the First Amendment area. All three courts could have ruled that access to military locations and information was so unique that non-military precedents were of no help; or, alternatively, that prison cases might be pertinent, but not cases involving access to more benign civilian sites. Yet all three courts assumed the potential pertinence of a range of cases from various sites, courtrooms, the White House, legislative chambers, etc.[39] That none of these judges found strong support for claims of Gulf War access in such analogies is hardly surprising. Even in purely stateside civilian settings, no court has gone further than Judge Sand in defining the rights of U.S. journalists in Saudi Arabia.

The Road Not Taken: Possible Grounds for Future Access Claims

Despite relevant litigation, the issue of media access to military operations remains largely unresolved. Before the next major engagement, it might be useful to speculate about grounds for access not yet fully developed, and their future potential. Several areas of law and policy contribute potentially useful arguments.

First is the one area in which claims of access most clearly apply, the criminal court room.[40] In recognizing a public right of access for the first time, and not simply a right of

---

37. Flynt v. Weinberger, 762 F.2d 134, 135 (D.C. Cir. 1985). *See Conyers v. Reagan,* 765 F.2d 1124 (D.C. Cir. 1985), for a similar post-combat disposition of a suit brought by members of Congress to challenge the legality of the Grenada campaign.

38. *See* JB Pictures, Inc., 86 F.3d at 239 (conceding that there is "some truth in [plaintiff's] observation" that visual images of arriving caskets conveys contrasting message to soldiers being loaded onto transport plane).

39. *See, e.g., id.* at 238 (citing Zemel v. Rusk, 381 U.S. 1, 17 (1965), which held that entry into White House was not First Amendment right); Nation Magazine, 762 F. Supp. at 1572 (citing Richmond Newspapers, Inc., 448 U.S. at 575, where U.S. Supreme Court struck down ban on access to criminal court proceedings).

40. *See, e.g.,* Richmond Newspapers, Inc., 448 U.S. at 581 (1980). The right to free speech entails the freedom to listen which grants both the public and the media equal access to attend a criminal trial. *Id.* at 576. A criminal trial must be open to the public unless there is an overriding interest to the contrary. *Id.* at 581.

the media, the Supreme Court did not limit the scope of that right to the criminal trial.[41] Rather, Chief Justice Burger's opinion clearly identified "access to places traditionally open to the public" as the general determinant, of which the criminal court was simply an example, albeit one of special clarity and importance.[42] In a footnote, the Court left open the related issue of access to civil trials, adding, "we note that historically both civil and criminal trials have been presumptively open."[43] Thus a California Court of Appeals recently, and for the first time, recognized a First Amendment right of access to civil proceedings, derived entirely by applying *Richmond Newspapers'* canon of "[places traditionally] open to the public."[44]

Since this is the criterion that should be applied to access issues at any site, not just criminal court, the central question to ask is what facets of military activity have been "traditionally open to the public." One thoughtful commentator finds the historical precedent quite helpful:

> [T]he first two hundred years of the use of American military force saw the media enjoy broad access to theatres of operations. Only in certain instances in the Civil War and the Spanish-American War were American reporters excluded from the front lines. In World War I, World War II, and the Korean War, the press received wide access to most aspects of combat. Likewise, in Vietnam, the media enjoyed unparalleled access to virtually every aspect of the conflict.[45]

Given this "long tradition of coverage of military combat," Steger argues that "the American media does enjoy a historical right of access to military operations" under *Richmond Newspapers* and the criminal court access cases that followed.[46]

The claim of access based on history may in fact have two dimensions arising from the criminal trial access cases. One, the major focus of the foregoing discussion, involves access to physical sites or places the record of history demonstrates have, more often than not, been open to the media, if not to the general public. The other dimension focuses on access to information about military operations, and would note that such information is most readily and naturally gathered by reporters observing the events in person rather than relying on secondary accounts.

In fact, access to information, as a vital element in our democratic governmental system, has deep and reputable roots. James Madison recognized the importance to citizenship of the receipt of information about government when he said, "[a] popular [g]overnment, without popular information, or the means of acquiring it, is but a [p]rologue to a [f]arce or a [t]radegy; or, perhaps both. Knowledge will forever govern ignorance: [a]nd a people who mean to be their own [g]overnors, must arm themselves with the power which knowledge gives."[47]

Successive Supreme Court decisions reaffirmed Madison's emphasis on the flow of information as a key to citizenship and democratic government. In so doing, the Court often recognized quite specifically the mass media's role in gaining and disseminating

---

41. *Id.* at 577.

42. *Id.*

43. Richmond Newspapers, Inc., 448 U.S. at 580 n.17 (1980).

44. NBC Subsidiary (KNBC-TV), Inc. v. Superior Court, 56 Cal. Rptr. 2d 645, 650 (Ca. Ct. App. 1996).

45. Michael Steger, *Slicing the Gordian Knot: A Proposal to Reform Military Regulation of Media Coverage of Combat Operations*, 28 U.S.F. L. Rev. 957, 992–93 (1994).

46. *Id.* at 993.

47. 9 Writings of James Madison 103 (G. Hunt ed. 1910), *quoted in* Board of Education v. Pico, 457 U.S. 853, 867 (1982).

such information. For example, in the case that rejected a journalist's plea for First Amendment protection of confidential sources, the majority disclaimed any suggestion "that news gathering does not qualify for First Amendment protection [and added] without some protection for seeking out the news, freedom of the press could be eviscerated."[48] Later, in cases denying media access to prisoners for interviews, the Court stressed that the media had ample alternative channels by which to obtain information and inform the public about the conditions in prisons and jails.[49] Justice Stewart, author of the prison cases, concurred in the Court's later decision to deny a TV camera crew access to a county detention facility, but added his warning that "terms of access that are reasonably imposed on individual members of the public may, if they impede effective reporting without sufficient justification, be unreasonable as applied to journalists who are there to convey to the general public what the visitors see."[50] Statements such as these, accompanying a rejection by the Supreme Court of certain media access claims, may nonetheless prove extremely useful in advancing the access issue beyond where Gulf War litigation left it.

Closely related in origin, though quite different in evolution, is the citizen's First Amendment right to receive information. In a plurality opinion which imposed constitutional standards on book removal by public and school library boards, Justice Brennan gave clear and explicit recognition to such a right stating "we have held that in a variety of contexts 'the Constitution protects the right to receive information and ideas.'... [T]he right to receive ideas is a necessary predicate to the recipient's meaningful exercise of his own rights of speech, press, and political freedom."[51]

In the spirit of that case, a number of lower court decisions also recognized a right to receive information, mainly, through not exclusively, in the library context.[52] The potential of this well settled right to receive information, as a basis for claims of access to combat activities and defense operations, remains to be tested in the military setting. Yet it has much potential, especially in tandem with claims reflecting the historic openness of battlefields and other sectors.

Yet a different basis for access recognizes certain respects in which seemingly uniform bans of military access could be considered selective. There was, for example, the rather ingenious claim advanced by the plaintiffs in the Dover mortuary case, that a ban on covering bodies as they *returned* to the United States, with no comparable ban against covering troops *headed for combat* did, in a sense, impose viewpoint discrimination of a kind the Court recently disfavored.[53] The point is that the Defense Department welcomes dissemination of "good news" but, at least in this instance, disfavored dissemination of "bad news." The option to cover graveside ceremonies in the hometowns of the deceased was somewhat illusory; not only because the news value would largely have ebbed, but because any family could block such coverage if it wished.

There may be evidence of selectivity on an even broader scale. Since media coverage of military engagements has been permitted throughout most of American history, and at times (for example, the early years in Vietnam) facilitated, it could be argued that limiting access of the media to a *particular* engagement is the power to ensure readers

48. Branzburg v. Hayes, 408 U.S. 665, 681 (1972).
49. Procunier, 417 U.S. at 824–28; Saxbe, 417 U.S. at 846–50.
50. Houchins, 438 U.S. at 17.
51. Pico, 457 U.S. at 867 (citing Stanley v. Georgia, 394 U.S. 557, 564 (1969)).
52. *E.g.*, Minarcini v. Strongsville City Sch. Dist., 541 F.2d 577 (6th Cir. 1976); Right to Read Defense Comm. v. School Comm., 454 F. Supp. 703 (D. Mass. 1978).
53. *See, e.g.*, R.A.V. v. City of St. Paul, 505 U.S. 377 (1992); Texas v. Johnson, 491 U.S. 397 (1989).

and viewers know only about "good wars" and not about what the Pentagon may deem "bad wars". This is not to suggest the Defense Department has in fact been so selective in its coverage, for the record would not support such a claim. Indeed, had the only goal been to maximize favorable coverage, the Panama[54] and Grenada[55] incursions would presumably have been as open to the media as the search-lighted and media-saturated midnight landing on the beach at Mogadishu.[56]

Mention of publicity, however, suggests another promising line of analysis. The Pentagon has never been bashful about its achievements or role in national security. While some of the claims advanced in the inflammatory "Selling of the Pentagon" television special were exaggerated, there is little doubt that the armed forces devote substantial energy and expense to presenting a positive image to American readers and viewers. The claim of access to those military operations the Pentagon may *not* wish the media, or their viewers and readers, to see gains considerable force from the Pentagon's substantial effort to put its best foot forward. An agency which hides its light under a bushel basket may be able to hide its faults in the same way; the case is far less convincing for a branch of government that flaunts its virtues.

Finally, there remains one other component of the case to be made in support of future access claims. The Supreme Court consistently requires government to choose means of regulation that are "no more extensive than necessary"[57] or which "burden no more speech than necessary."[58] While the "least restrictive alternative" doctrine has not been invoked directly to support claims of access to, rather than dissemination of information, one might recall Justice Stewart's concurring caveat that restraints on access to areas of public interest might be unreasonable "if they impede effective reporting without sufficient justification."[59] Even more useful, perhaps, are the standards the Court developed for determining access to disputed portions of the criminal trial. Given the general presumption of openness that derives from the historical status of criminal law, disclosing certain parts of a trial was not *per se* unconstitutional.[60] But the government could deny access only when such a step is "necessitated by a compelling governmental interest, and is narrowly tailored to serve that interest."[61] The inference that naturally arises is that access restrictions should, where history creates a presumption of access, be tested by the same "no broader than necessary" test that applies to curbs on expression.

To the extent that criterion governs limits on access to military sites or information, it sets in motion a quest for less restrictive alternatives that would meet the government's demonstrated needs. This is not the time or the place to canvass the full range of interests or options. That has been done elsewhere and by persons far more expert in military matters. For this purpose, it should suffice to describe one unusually productive option

---

54. *See* Michael Linfield, *Hear No Evil, See No Evil, Speak No Evil: The Press and the Persian Gulf War*, 25 Beverly Hills B. Ass'n J. 142 (1991) (discussing press access during December 20, 1989, Panama invasion).

55. *See* Paul G. Cassell, *Restrictions on Press Coverage of Military Operations: The Right of Access, Grenada, and 'Off-the-Record Wars'*, 73 Geo. L.J. 931 (1985) (discussing media access during October 25, 1983 Grenada invasion).

56. *See* Jan Perlez, *U.S. Forces Arrive in Somalia on Mission to Aid the Starving*, N.Y. Times, Dec. 9, 1992, at A1, A16 (describing media presence at landing).

57. 44 Liquormart, Inc. v. Rhode Island, 116 S. Ct. 1495, 1510 (1996).

58. Madsen v. Women's Health Ctr., 512 U.S. 753, 765 (1994).

59. Houchins, 438 U.S. at 17.

60. Globe Newspaper Co. v. Superior Court, 457 U.S. 596, 606 (1982) (stating the "[public] scrutiny of a criminal trial enhances the quality and safeguards the integrity of the fact finding process....").

61. *Id.* at 606–07.

that did emerge from the Gulf War, though it remains to be tested with regard to practicality and constitutionality.

Guidelines for War Reporting

Roughly a year after the conclusion of the hostilities in the Persian Gulf, the Defense Department reopened discussions with the major news organizations about coverage of overseas military operations. Those discussions proved remarkably productive. By the summer of 1992, they yielded a set of Guidelines that embodied a consensus between the media and the military on virtually every issue that had divided them during previous engagements. The only issue on which the parties effectively agreed to disagree was the handling of battlefield disputes about the dispatch of a news item or photograph which the field commander or other responsible officer felt could jeopardize national security. The full text of the Guidelines deserves inclusion in any such comprehensive treatment.

Open and independent reporting will be the principle means of coverage of U.S. military operations.

Pools are not to serve as the standard means of covering U.S. military operations. Pools may sometimes provide the only feasible means of early access to a military operation. Pools should be as large as possible and disbanded at the earliest opportunity—within 24 hours to 36 hours when possible. Early-access pools will not cancel the principle of independent coverage for journalist already in the area.

Even under conditions of open coverage, pools may be appropriate for specific events, such as those at extremely remote locations or where space is limited.

Journalists in a combat zone will be credentialed by the U.S. military and will be required to abide by a dear set of military security ground rules that protect U.S. forces and their operations. Violations of the ground rules can result in suspension of credentials and expulsion from the combat zone.

Journalists will be provided access to all major military units. Special operations restrictions may limit access in some cases.

Military public affairs officers should act as liaisons but should not interfere with the reporting process.

Field commanders will permit journalists to ride on military vehicles and aircraft whenever possible. The military will be responsible for the transportation of pools.

Consistent with its capabilities, the military will supply public affairs officer with facilities to enable timely, secure, compatible transmission of pool material and will make these facilities available whenever possible for filing independent coverage. The military will not ban communications systems operated by news organizations, but security in some battlefield situations may require limited restrictions on equipment.

These principles will apply as well to the operations of the standing Department of Defense National Media Pool system.[62]

---

62. Howard Kurtz & Barton Gellman, *Guidelines Set for News Coverage of Wars*, Wash. Post, May 22, 1992, at A23.

The News Media in Afghanistan — First Amendment Issues After September 11

While the 1990s saw brief skirmishes between the media and the military in the Balkan countries and in Haiti, there were few tests for the new guidelines until the major military initiative in Afghanistan, which followed the September 11 attacks on the World Trade Center and the Pentagon. Although war was not declared in the fall and winter of 2001– 02, the stakes were clearly far higher for the United States and its armed forces than they had been at any time since Vietnam, and perhaps even earlier. Before troops were sent to Afghanistan, discussions occurred between media representatives and Assistant Secretary of Defense Victoria Clarke, the content of which was open, widely reported and generally reassuring to the press. Once planes were in the air and troops were on the ground, however, media access proved more limited than had been expected. The restrictions that were actually put in place seemed to some observers to be unprecedented. Indeed, the lead article in the January–February 2002 issue of the *Columbia Journalism Review* opened with this charge: "Journalists have been denied access to American troops in the field in Afghanistan to a greater degree than in any previous war involving U.S. military forces."

The article cited one especially troubling incident. In early December, the first casualties occurred on the ground; several service personnel were killed and others wounded by a stray B-52 bomb. The reporters and photographers closest to the scene not only were not allowed to cover the event, but were actually confined to a warehouse throughout the day. Assistant Secretary Clarke, responding to media protest, apologized to the Washington media bureau chiefs and promised there would be no recurrence of such restraint. The ensuing months brought no comparable confinement, and in fact media access to activities in Afghanistan was widened somewhat as the success of U.S. forces became increasingly apparent.

Despite persistent accusations that the post-September 11 rules were not fully compatible with the media-military accord of a decade earlier, only one challenge actually found its way to court. The plaintiff was the irrepressible Larry Flynt, erstwhile challenger of the Grenada press restrictions. Flynt's suit sought an order restraining Defense Secretary Donald Rumsfeld from "prohibiting or interfering with plaintiffs' asserted First Amendment rights to have Hustler magazine correspondents accompany American troops on the ground in Afghanistan." In February 2004, the U.S. Court of Appeals for the District of Columbia affirmed a lower court's denial of Flynt's request using language that essentially foreclosed a constitutional right of the press to accompany military forces in combat.

Flynt v. Rumsfeld

355 F.3d 697 (D.C. Cir. 2004).

SENTELLE, Circuit Judge:

. . . .

The facial challenge is premised on the assertion that there is a First Amendment right for legitimate press representatives to travel with the military, and to be accommodated and otherwise facilitated by the military in their reporting efforts during combat, subject only to reasonable security and safety restrictions. There is nothing we have found in the Constitution, American history, or our case law to support this claim.

To support the position that there is such a constitutional right, appellants first point to cases that discuss the general purposes underlying the First Amendment. See *New York Times Co. v. United States*, 403 U.S. 713, 717, 91 S.Ct. 2140, 29 L.Ed.2d 822 (1971) ("[t]he press was protected so that it could bare the secrets of government and inform the people.") (Black, J., concurring); *Mills v. Alabama*, 384 U.S. 214, 218, 86 S.Ct. 1434, 16 L.Ed.2d 484 (1966) (the First Amendment supports the "free discussion of governmental affairs."). These cases, however, say nothing about media access to the U.S. combat units engaged in battle.

....

[T]his Court has held that "freedom of speech [and] of the press do not create any per se right of access to government ... activities simply because such access might lead to more thorough or better reporting." *JB Pictures, Inc. v. Dep't of Defense*, 86 F.3d 236, 238 (D.C.Cir.1996). Appellants admit they face a "dearth of case law concerning press access to battles." From this unenviable position, they ask us to look to *Richmond Newspapers, Inc. v. Virginia*, 448 U.S. 555, 100 S.Ct. 2814, 65 L.Ed.2d 973 (1980), for guidance.

In *Richmond Newspapers*, a plurality of the Supreme Court held that a constitutional right of public access to criminal trials existed based on a long history of such access in the United States and in England at the time our organic laws were created. *Id.* at 581, 100 S.Ct. 2814. According to appellants, *Richmond Newspapers* established that the First Amendment may be interpreted to provide for a right of access to government operations, and that access is not limited to criminal trials. They assert that we must apply a *Richmond Newspapers* analysis to the facts of this case. We disagree.

In *Center for National Security Studies v. Department of Justice*, 331 F.3d 918 (D.C.Cir.2003), cert. denied, 2004 WL 46645 (Jan. 12, 2004), we held that there was no First Amendment right for plaintiffs to receive the identities of INS detainees and material witnesses who were detained in the wake of the September 11 attacks. Indeed, we made it clear that "[n]either the Supreme Court nor this Court has applied the Richmond Newspapers test outside the context of criminal judicial proceedings or the transcripts of such proceedings." *Id.* at 934. For emphasis, we added that "neither this Court nor the Supreme Court has ever indicated that it would" do so. *Id.* (emphasis in original). Instead, we noted that in all areas other than criminal proceedings, the Supreme Court has applied the general rule of *Houchins v. KQED*, 438 U.S. 1, 98 S.Ct. 2588, 57 L.Ed.2d 553 (1978) (plurality opinion), not the exception of *Richmond Newspapers*. *Ctr. for Nat'l Sec. Studies*, 331 F.3d at 935. *Houchins* held that the press have no First Amendment right of access to prisons, and in doing so stated that the First Amendment does not "mandate[ ] a right of access to government information or sources of information within the government's control." *Houchins*, 438 U.S. at 15, 98 S.Ct. 2588. To summarize, neither this Court nor the Supreme Court has ever applied *Richmond Newspapers* outside the context of criminal proceedings, and we will not do so today.

Appellants argue that we did, however, use the analysis underlying the *Richmond Newspapers* decision in *JB Pictures Inc. v. Department of Defense*, 86 F.3d 236, 240 (D.C.Cir.1996). In that case, several media and veterans organizations challenged a Department of Defense policy. That policy shifted ceremonies for deceased service members arriving from overseas from Dover Air Force base to locations closer to the service members' homes. It also gave the families of deceased military personnel the authority to limit press access to those ceremonies. Contrary to appellants' assertion, the extent of our *Richmond Newspapers* discussion in that case is contained in one sentence: "[i]t is obvious that military bases do not share the tradition of openness on which the Court relied in striking down restrictions on access to criminal court proceedings in ... *Richmond Newspapers*." *Id.* Thus J.B. Pictures not only does not support wholesale adoption of a *Richmond Newspapers* analysis in every case involving requests for access to government activities or information, it rejects such a rule.

Even if we were to apply a *Richmond Newspapers* test, which again, we do not, it would not support appellants' facial challenge to the Directive. As an initial matter, the history of press access to military units is not remotely as extensive as public access to criminal trials. Without going into great historic detail, it is sufficient that in *Richmond Newspapers* the Supreme Court relied on the "unbroken, uncontradicted history" of public access to criminal trials. *Id.* at 573. This includes the time when "our organic laws were adopted." *Id.* at 569, 100 S.Ct. 2814. Indeed, even since "the ancient town meeting form of trial," the "people retained a 'right of visitation' which enabled them to satisfy themselves that justice was in fact being done." *Id.* at 572, 100 S.Ct. 2814 (internal citations omitted).

No comparable history exists to support a right of media access to U.S. military units in combat. The very article cited by appellants for the proposition that media have traditionally had broad access to soldiers in combat does not support this position. *See* John E. Smith, *From the Front Lines to the Front Page: Media Access to War in the Persian Gulf and Beyond*, 26 Colum. J.L. & Soc. Probs. 291, 292–305 (1993). Beginning with the American Revolution, war reporting was primarily in the form of private letters from soldiers and official reports that were sent home and published in newspapers. *Id.* at 293. Indeed, the rise of the professional war correspondent did not begin until at least the time of the Civil War. *Id.* In addition, it is not entirely clear that in any of our early wars the media was actively embedded into units, which is the right appellants seek. In sum, even if we were to attempt a Richmond Newspapers analysis and consider the historical foundations of a right of media access to combat units, appellants' claim would fail miserably.

Even if *Richmond Newspapers* applied in this context, and even if there was a historical basis for media access to troops in combat, the Directive would still not violate the First Amendment. *Richmond Newspapers* expressly stated that "[j]ust as a government may impose reasonable time, place, and manner restrictions" in granting access to public streets, "so may a trial judge … impose reasonable limitations on access to a trial." 448 U.S. at 581 n. 18, 100 S.Ct. 2814. These limitations could be based on the need to maintain a "quiet and orderly setting," or "courtrooms'… limited capacity." *Id.* The Directive appellants challenge is incredibly supportive of media access to the military with only a few limitations. The Directive begins with the command that "[o]pen and independent reporting shall be the principal means of coverage of U.S. military operations." DOD Directive 5122.5 ¶ E3.1.1. It further orders military public affairs officers to "act as liaisons, but [ ] not [to] interfere with the reporting process." *Id.* at ¶ E3.1.6. Additionally, "field commanders should be instructed to permit journalists to ride on military vehicles and aircraft when possible." *Id.* at ¶ E3.1.7. The restrictions contained in the Directive are few, including: special operations restrictions; limited restrictions on media communications owing to electromagnetic operational security concerns; use of media pools when the sheer size of interested media is unworkable, such as at the beginning of an operation; and expulsion for members of the media who violate the ground rules. *Id.* at ¶¶ E3.1.2.– E3.1.8. Appellants have offered no reason to conclude that these restrictions are unreasonable. Even if *Richmond Newspapers* did apply, appellants' argument would fail.

   ….

Because we hold that there is no constitutionally based right for the media to embed with U.S. military forces in combat, and because we further hold that the Directive was not applied to Flynt or *Hustler* magazine in any unconstitutional manner, the District Court's judgment is affirmed.

The DOD's Embed Policy in Iraq: Unprecedented Access or Controlling the Message?

The Court of Appeals determination that there was no *constitutional* right of the press to accompany military forces in combat did not prohibit the Defense Department from choosing to implement a policy allowing journalists from a pool of media organizations to be embedded with the troops. Under the program, which was announced in 2002 and debuted during the invasion of Iraq, reporters not only accompany the troops on combat missions but also live alongside them. The military has hailed the program as granting unprecedented access to the media while also being strategically beneficial by combating false narratives about the war. In exchange for this access, embedded reporters have to abide by military regulations limiting the publication of confidential national security information. The military maintains these restrictions are "in no way intended to prevent release of derogatory, embarrassing, negative or uncomplimentary information." Embeds can publish approximate friendly force numbers, generalized mission results, generic descriptions of military operations (like "land-based maneuvers"), and service members names and hometowns (with their consent). They are not permitted to publish information about specific troop numbers, equipment or vehicles, future operations, security levels, intelligence collection, or the effectiveness of an enemy action, or the identifying features of enemy prisoners of war or detainees. Journalists may report American casualties but cannot disclose their identities for 72 hours, or at least until the deceased's next of kin are notified.

Commanders in the field may grant the media more access to confidential information on a discretionary basis provided they agree to military inspection of any resulting stories before publication. The review would not be of the editorial content, but only to see if there was sensitive information that should be removed or the publication of which should be delayed. The military has stressed that this process is "voluntary," but failure to comply with requests to remove content can lead to removal of embedded status.[63] Many other members of the press have covered the war as "unilaterals," outside of the embed structure. These journalists had the advantage of being free of the restrictions of the embed program, but they have faced significant obstacles in obtaining transportation, shelter, and contact with military sources.

The embed policy has been criticized for skewing the coverage of the war.[64] The concerns raised were that the publication restrictions combined with the unconscious psychological effects on reporters of living alongside and entrusting their lives to the subjects they were reporting on, would cause the coverage to be overly positive. Some have even suggested that these issues could rise to the level of constitutional claims. They argued that the prepublication requirements were prior restraints on speech, and furthermore, that by establishing the embed program, the military had created a limited public forum and

---

63. In 2013, a reporter whose embed status was terminated for publishing a story in violation of the regulations sued the military for damages claiming his First Amendment rights had been violated. The D.C. District Court dismissed his claim, finding the military officials had qualified immunity. The Court, extending the logic of *Flynt*, concluded that a right of access to embed with the embed program was not clearly established. Anderson v. Gates, ___ F. Supp.2d ___ (D.D.C. 2013).

64. For a detailed analysis of the embed program *see* Richard K. Wright, *Assessment of the DoD Embedded Media Program*, Institute for Defense Analysis, IDA Paper P-3931 (September 2004) *available at* <www.dtic.mil/cgi-bin/GetTRDoc?AD=ADA441268>.

then engaged in viewpoint discrimination by creating an environment that favored pro-military speech. However, courts have yet to weigh in on these issues.[65]

The First Amendment and the War on Terrorism

In 1968, the Supreme Court provided a clear answer to a question it had struggled with many times before: when may the State criminalize *speech* on the ground that it might further an illegal end? In *Brandenburg v. Ohio*, the Court held that the First Amendment "do[es] not permit a State to forbid or proscribe advocacy of the use of force or of law violation except where such advocacy is directed to inciting or producing imminent lawless action and is likely to incite or produce such action."[66] With respect to *association*, the Court held in *Scales v. United States*[67] and its progeny that Congress could not punish membership in the Communist Party absent proof that an individual specifically intended to further the party's unlawful ends.[68] In 2010, however, the Supreme Court called into question the continued viability of these highly protective speech and association principles.

In *Holder v. Humanitarian Law Project*,[69] the Court addressed the constitutionality of 18 U.S.C. § 2339, a counterterrorism statute criminalizing the provision of "service" or "material support" to designated "foreign terrorist organizations."[70] With respect to "service," the Court declined to rule on plaintiffs' pre-enforcement challenge, stating that "adjudication of the reach and constitutionality of the statute['s service provision] must await a concrete fact situation."[71] The Court did, however, discuss the plaintiffs' as-applied challenge to the statute's ban on "material support."[72] Although the case involved application of 18 U.S.C. § 2339 to plaintiffs' advocacy, the Court did not consider *Brandenburg* in its analysis. Instead, the Court applied strict scrutiny.[73] To the surprise of many, the Court then held the statute to be constitutional as-applied, despite the fact that regulations subject to strict scrutiny almost always violate the First Amendment.[74]

---

65. For a view that the embed program on its face does not violate the First Amendment and that it is better for free speech than the alternatives *see* Elana Zeide, *In Bed With the Military: First Amendment Implications of Embedded Journalism* 80 N.Y.U. L. REV. 1309 (2005).

66. 395 U.S. 444, 447 (1968) (*per curiam*); *see also* Hess v. Indiana, 414 U.S. 105 (1973).

67. 367 U.S. 203 (1961).

68. In *Scales*, the Court interpreted a statute criminalizing membership in the Communist Party to require proof of "specific[ ] inten[t] to accomplish [the aims of the organization] by resort to violence." 367 U.S. at 229 (quoting *Noto v. United States*, 367 U.S. 290, 299 (1961)). This principle was subsequently applied to a variety of noncriminal sanctions, including the denial of a security clearance, *United States v. Robel*, 389 U.S. 259, 262 (1967) (holding that the government could not ban Communist Party members from working in defense facilities absent proof that they had specific intent to further the party's unlawful ends); state employment, *Keyishian v. Bd. of Regents*, 385 U.S. 589, 606 (1967) ("[m]ere knowing membership without a specific intent to further the unlawful aims of an organization is not a constitutionally adequate basis" for barring Communist Party members from employment in a state university system); denial of access to school meeting rooms, *Healy v. James*, 408 U.S. 169, 188–89 (1972); and civil damages, *NAACP v. Claiborne Hardware, Co.*, 458 U.S. 886, 920 (1982).

69. 566 U.S. 1 (2010).

70. 18 U.S.C. § 2339B(a)(1) (2006).

71. 566 U.S. at 25.

72. *Id.* at 25–26.

73. *Id.* at 28–29. Although the Court did not explicitly use the term "strict scrutiny," it did require "a more demanding standard" than intermediate. Strict scrutiny is the only standard that meets this criterion.

74. *Id.* at 28.

Humanitarian Law Project marked the first time in the Court's history that it upheld the criminalization of speech advocating only nonviolent, lawful ends on the ground that such speech might unintentionally assist a third party in criminal wrongdoing.[75] The plaintiffs in *Humanitarian Law Project* sought to work with two groups designated by the Secretary of State as "foreign terrorist organizations."[76] Rather than further the organizations' illegal ends, however, the plaintiffs sought to dissuade them from violence, and to urge them to pursue lawful ends through peaceful means.[77] Yet, by a vote of 6–3, the Court held that the First Amendment permitted criminal prosecution of such speech. The Court reasoned that even if the plaintiffs' speech was intended to promote peaceable, lawful conduct, it "frees up other resources within the [terrorist] organization that may be put to violent ends. It also importantly helps lend legitimacy to foreign terrorist organizations—legitimacy that makes it easier for those groups to persist, to recruit members, and to raise funds—all of which facilitate more terrorist attacks."[78] The Court additionally found that "providing foreign terrorists groups with material support in any form also furthers terrorism by straining the United States' relationships with its allies and undermining cooperative efforts between nations to prevent terrorist attacks."[79]

Humanitarian Law Project left unanswered at least two important questions. First, why did the Court not apply its longstanding *Brandenburg* incitement test for speech advocating unlawful action? Second, what future cases might also fall outside *Brandenburg*? The Court did note three distinguishing factors to stress the narrowness of its holding in *Humanitarian Law Project*: (1) the law leaves unregulated independent advocacy; (2) the speech in question related to foreign affairs and national security; and (3) the law governed only speech in coordination with foreign organizations, not domestic groups.[80] Left unexplained, however, was what impact, if any, these factors might have on future cases.

This uncertainty has already manifested itself in the recent holdings of at least two United States Circuit Courts. Despite Chief Justice Roberts' assurance that the Court's holding in *Humanitarian Law Project* applied only to "advocacy performed in coordination with, or at the direction of, a foreign terrorist organization,"[81] the First Circuit, in *United States v. Mehanna*, nevertheless upheld a material support conviction based solely on independent advocacy.[82] Tarek Mehanna, a U.S. citizen, was convicted and sentenced to serve 17 years in federal prison after prosecutors argued that Mehanna's independent translation of jihadist texts, his promotion of such speech and ideas online, and his association with individuals who were themselves al-Qaida associates, constituted unlawful coordinated material support of terrorists. The Supreme Court denied cert in October 2014.[83] In comparison, the Ninth Circuit Court of Appeals in *Al-Haramain Islamic Foundation, Inc. v. U.S. Dept. of Treasury*,[84] held that the government could not ban coordinated advocacy with a domestic group deemed by the United States to be "specially designated global terrorist[s]."[85] The Ninth Circuit applied *Humanitarian Law Project*,

---

75. *See* David Cole, *The First Amendment's Borders: The Place of Holder v. Humanitarian Law Project in First Amendment Doctrine*, 6 HARV. L. & POL'Y REV. 147, 149 (2012).
76. 566 U.S. at 36–37.
77. *Id.* at 36–39.
78. *Id.* at 30.
79. *Id.* at 32.
80. Cole, *supra*, at 149.
81. 566 U.S. at 24.
82. 735 F.3d 32 (2013).
83. 135 S.Ct. 49.
84. 686 F.3d 965 (2012).
85. *Id.* at 998–1001.

"but reasoned that the government had not shown that banning speech coordinated with a domestic entity whose assets the government had already frozen was necessary to further the compelling interest in preventing terrorism. That decision points the way to an understanding of *Humanitarian Law Project* that takes the Supreme Court at its word, and limits its reasoning to the very particular facts presented."[86]

However one assesses the result of *Holder v. Humanitarian Law Project*, the language and analysis employed by the Court makes it far more difficult to predict the outcome of future conflicts between free speech rights and national security concerns.[87]

---

86. Cole, *supra*, at 150.

87. *See* Robert Chesney, *The Supreme Court, Material Support, and the Lasting Impact of Holder v. Humanitarian Law Project*, 1 Wake Forest L. Rev. Forum 13–19 (2011); Owen Fiss, *The World We Live In*, 83 Temp L. Rev. 295 (2011); Wadie E. Said, *Humanitarian Law Project and the Supreme Court's Construction of Terrorism*, 2011 BYU L. Rev. 1455 (2011).

Chapter 26

National Security and the Fourth and Fifth Amendments

M.E. Bowman

In this chapter:
Introduction
National Security and the Warrant Requirement
The Foreign Intelligence Surveillance Act (FISA)
Conclusions
Selected Bibliography

Introduction

When the Bill of Rights was ratified, it was with a twofold purpose. First, it was to guarantee the rights of the people, and, second, it was to restrain the power of the government to intrude on the people. The Bill of Rights was not intended to function as a mechanism for, or even to be a player in, issues of national security.[1] Still, it cannot be surprising that, in a world of constant tension, security of the nation as a whole would, from time to time, challenge the personal liberties that the Bill of Rights was intended to protect. In that context, the Fourth and Fifth Amendments to the Constitution occasionally have been interpreted differently in times of crisis than in times of calm. In more recent years, a certain degree of stability has evolved when applying these rights to national security issues, but consistency of application remains elusive when personal liberties and national security collide.

National security threats normally are recognized well in advance of actual criminal activity, which means that surveillance needs often arise outside any criminal context. Additionally, they often arise in the context of a vexing convergence of First and Fourth, and occasionally Fifth, Amendment values not present in the criminal case. The practical consequence of this has become recognition of a fact not considered in 1789—that the probable cause requirements for obtaining surveillance authority for the two threats must be fundamentally distinct. For criminal investigations, the probable cause requirement

---

1. Although the text of the Bill of Rights does not incorporate a right of privacy, contextual evidence indicates that the Fourth Amendment was designed to protect individual privacy. In advocating the adoption of the Bill of Rights, Patrick Henry claimed that officials "may, unless the government be restrained by a bill of rights ... go into your cellars and rooms, and search, ransack, and measure, everything you eat, drink, and wear." III The Debates in the Several Conventions on the Adoption of the Federal Constitution 448–49 (Jonathan Elliot ed., 1836).

is "a fair probability that contraband or evidence of a crime will be found in a particular place."[2] For national security investigations, the predicate is an external threat to the security of the nation. The Bill of Rights, and particularly the Fourth Amendment, cannot, and does not, provide evenhanded guidance to both types of probable cause.

The consequence of reaction to crisis, whether real or perceived, is that constitutional guarantees occasionally bend to the threat. Not unexpectedly, retrospective analysis often finds that reaction to a national security threat has been overreaching. Through the years we've seen wholesale abuses predicated solely on ethnicity,[3] abuses that struck at fundamental values such as freedom of speech,[4] and the sanctity of personal mail.[5] Also not unexpectedly, concern over the government activities that led to abuse normally arose only when the crisis was past and one could look at the situation from a distance. The very nature of crisis is the unexpected event for which there is little, no, or infrequent experience; in consequence, reaction easily can be overbroad.

If the past is prologue, it is clear that no template can be created against which national security threats can be balanced with constitutional interests in a preconceived or mechanical fashion. Still, it is necessary to understand how national security interests have, can, and certainly will in the future shape, bend, or even side-step the application of constitutional standards. In this chapter, we look briefly at the authority of the executive branch to conduct electronic surveillance, physical searches, and seizures without satisfying customary warrant requirements. The reaction and occasional support of Congress and the federal judiciary are also examined. The Fifth Amendment's privilege against self-incrimination and its relation to national security is discussed as well, although it will become clear that it is of less concern in national security matters than is the Fourth Amendment.

National Security and the Warrant Requirement

Americans greatly cherish their privacy—the right to be left alone. This "right" stems from our heritage and, in part, grew out of a perceived evil of British law applied to the colonial experiment, the general warrant. The British general warrant was a search tool employed without limitation on location and without any necessity precisely to describe the object or person sought. British authorities were simply given license to "search diligently" wherever they chose. With that kind of unfettered discretion, the general warrant could be, and often was, used to intimidate. General warrants executed during the reign of Charles I sought to intimidate dissidents and authors and printers of seditious material by ransacking homes and seizing personal papers.[6]

---

2. Illinois v. Gates, 462 U.S. 213, 238 (1983).

3. *See, e.g.*, Korematsu v. United States, 323 U.S. 214 (1944) (sustaining conviction for violating military order during World War II excluding all persons of Japanese ancestry from designated areas on the West Coast). *See also* Hirabayashi v. United States, 320 U.S. 81 (1943) (sustaining curfew orders covering West Coast areas).

4. The Alien and Sedition Acts, for example, made it a crime to write or publish any false, scandalous, or malicious writing against the government, Congress, or the President. These included the Naturalization Act, 1 Stat. 566 (1798); the Alien Act, 1 Stat. 570 (1798); the Alien Enemies Act, 1 Stat. 577 (1798) and the Sedition Act, 1 Stat. 596 (1798).

5. In *Ex parte Jackson*, 96 U.S. 727 (1877), Fourth Amendment warrant requirements were held applicable to a sealed letter entrusted to the mail.

6. *See* David M. O'Brien, Privacy, Law, and Public Policy 38 (1979).

The abusive nature of the general warrant was easily recognized, and in 1765, general warrants were declared illegal by the courts, and by the Parliament a year later.[7] One might have thought that to be the end of the matter, but it was not so in the colonies. In the colonies there were growing complaints that royal officials were violating the privacy of colonists through the use of writs of assistance — equivalent to general warrants.[8] Because English law did not as yet recognize a right of personal privacy, the crown's abuses in the colonies were not remediable at law. It was thus no surprise that the new American Constitution and the government it created would respect a series of individual freedoms.

James Madison authored what would become the Fourth Amendment and proposed it to the Congress on June 8, 1789. For the new nation, warrants would require specificity to physically invade the privacy of its citizenry. Today, that same specificity is required to authorize both electronic and physical invasions of privacy. Although the Fourth Amendment eliminated the abuses of general warrants, its commands have often proved to be ambiguous, especially in the face of technological progress. Moreover, the Fourth Amendment was designed to protect against overreaching in investigations of criminal enterprises. Investigations of politically motivated threats to our national security, such as terrorism or espionage, were simply not contemplated. However, contemplated or not, the Fourth Amendment has played a critical role in intelligence investigations in this century. Leaving traditional analysis of the Amendment aside, it is worthwhile to focus specifically on the intersection of this very important part of our law and national security.

The Fourth Amendment reads as follows:

> The right of the people[[9]] to be secure in their persons, houses, papers and effects, against unreasonable searches and seizures shall not be violated, and no Warrants shall issue, but upon probable cause, supported by Oath or affirmation, and particularly describing the place to be searched, and the persons or things to be seized.

The Amendment has two principal clauses: the first is the reasonableness clause, which protects against all unreasonable searches and seizures; and the second is the warrant clause, which states the controlling principles for the issuance of warrants. For many years, the Supreme Court struggled to decide which clause was predominant. After many cases and much vacillation, the Court seized on the warrant clause as the most defining part of the Amendment's guarantees, although it has recognized some exceptions to the warrant requirement. The Court describes its decisions as follows:

> "Over and again this Court has emphasized that the mandate of the [Fourth] Amendment requires adherence to judicial processes," *United States v. Jeffers*, 342 U.S. 48, 51, and that searches conducted outside the judicial process, without prior approval by judge or magistrate, are *per se* unreasonable under the Fourth Amendment — subject only to a few specifically established and well-delineated exceptions.[10]

It is, perhaps, unfortunate that the Supreme Court confronted this issue before ever having had to seriously consider the potential for a national security exception to the warrant clause. In subsequent years it has become increasingly clear that there is an

---

7. *See* Entrick v. Carrington, 95 Eng. Rep. 807 (K.B. 1765). *See also* O'Brien, *id.*

8. *See* O'Brien, *supra* note 6, at 38–39.

9. It is worthy of note that several amendments refer to "the people" rather than to any "person" as others, and most statutes, would do. This is generally considered to mean that the guarantees awarded to "the people" do not apply, or do not apply in full force, to aliens.

10. Katz v. United States, 389 U.S. 347, 357 (1967).

exception and that it rests for its legitimacy on the reasonableness clause. The difficulty with an exception, however, is that, without more, it is unbounded. Therefore, it is not surprising that in a nation founded on principles of law rather than power, there has always been a preference for the check of the independent judiciary on government power. That is the focus of this chapter, but not in the context in which the Fourth Amendment is most commonly addressed.

Introduction to Fourth Amendment Issues

The Fourth Amendment regulates a host of governmental actions, and the most common analysis of the Amendment proceeds from reaction to criminal activity. Some actions—for example, stop and frisk and automobile searches—have been so often examined that the rules for them are very clear. Other actions not usually thought of as involving enforcement of the criminal law—for example, occupational and safety inspections and health inspections—also have discernible rules. These are of no concern for this chapter. Herein we are interested only in the far more ephemeral intersection between national security interests and the constitutional interests of "the people."

From the vantage point of the twenty-first century, we see clearly that the Fourth Amendment is all about the privacy of U.S. citizens, but it was not always so clear. Not until the government had the ability to be greatly intrusive into the private lives of the citizenry was there cause to be concerned about widespread abuse. Technology is what has driven increasingly sharper analysis and interpretation of the Fourth Amendment—primarily technology associated with private communications and, most particularly, the telephone.

The genesis of a long and tortuous path to relevant law in this arena began in 1928 when the wiretap technique was considered in the context of the Fourth Amendment. It was a wooden application of the property-based conception of Fourth Amendment principles to electronic surveillance that caused the Supreme Court, in *Olmstead v. United States*, to hold that conversations over the telephone were unprotected because there was no entry, no search, and no seizure involved in intercepting them, a decision so markedly different from contemporary holdings that a law student today might wonder if we are using the same Constitution.[11] However, one justice did recognize the fundamental issue. In a scathing dissent, Justice Brandeis paved the way for the inclusion, indeed, the dominance, of privacy in future decisions. Brandeis presciently noted that technological changes continued to permit the government to employ ever more subtle and more expansive means of invading privacy.[12]

It would still be many years before judicial analysis emerged with mature concepts of constitutionally-based privacy, but they did emerge. This began with associational privacy issues that ranged from the NAACP[13] to the Communist Party.[14] Political privacy followed[15] and continued in 1965 with what many see as modern privacy law in its widest manifestations when the Court decided the Connecticut contraceptives case *Griswold v. Connecticut*.[16] These set the stage for the cases that lead us to present day Fourth Amendment

---

11. Olmstead v. United States, 277 U.S. 438 (1928).
12. *Id.* at 478.
13. *NAACP v. Alabama*, 357 U.S. 449 (1958).
14. Konigsberg v. State Bar of California, 353 U.S. 252 (1961); Communist Party v. Subversive Activities Control Board, 367 U.S. 1 (1961).
15. *See, e.g.*, Watkins v. United States, 354 U.S. 178 (1957).
16. Griswold v. Connecticut, 381 U.S. 479 (1965).

law in the context of the national security. *Katz v. United States*, quoted above, broke new ground for the Court, as the Court said that Katz's Fourth Amendment rights were violated when FBI agents listened in on his calls from a public telephone booth by means of an eavesdropping and recording device attached to the outside of the booth.

Katz was a routine criminal case, but it is vital to any analysis of national security interests because the majority opinion by Justice Stewart, with a concurring opinion by Justice White, states that the Court was not deciding "whether safeguards other than prior authorization by a magistrate would satisfy the Fourth Amendment in a situation involving national security...."[17] *Katz* is also a critical element in the law because when, in 1968, Congress regulated the warrant requirements for electronic surveillance in the Crime Control Act,[18] it took into account these views and inserted in the statute a neutral clause recognizing that the President has, or at least has a claim to have, alternative authorities for national security purposes.[19] However, judicial interpretation of privacy interests of the Fourth Amendment would remain fractured for many more years. More importantly, just what the national security means, and how it might be threatened, were yet to be addressed. That would come in 1972 when Justice Powell wrote the opinion for the most important of this line of cases.

United States v. United States District Court (Keith)[20] arose from a criminal proceeding in which the United States charged three defendants with conspiracy to destroy government property. One defendant was also charged with the dynamite bombing of a CIA office in Ann Arbor, Michigan. The Attorney General admitted that a warrantless wiretap had intercepted conversations involving the defendants but defended the surveillance on grounds of national security. After an *in camera* review of the surveillance logs and review of an affidavit, District Court Judge Keith was not persuaded that the surveillance was a "reasonable exercise" of the President's national security powers. He found that the surveillance violated the Fourth Amendment, and he ordered disclosure of the overheard conversations to defendant Plamondon.[21] The Sixth Circuit Court of Appeals affirmed and the stage was set for constitutional challenge.[22]

As would be expected, the government argument was based on constitutional principles of protection of the national security and on the disclaimer in the Crime Control Act. Justice Powell, who, prior to ascendancy to the Court, had been a champion of governmental right and obligations to protect the national security was forced into a difficult decision. Conceding that the statutory provision may constitute "an implicit recognition" that the President has constitutional authority to engage in surveillance in furtherance of the nation's security, Justice Powell concluded that the "language is essentially

---

17. Katz v. United States, 389 U.S. 347, 358 n. 23 (1967).

18. Title III of the 1968 Omnibus Crime Control and Safe Streets Act, 18 U.S.C.A. §§ 2510–20. The statute established the conditions under which an order, equivalent to a warrant, could be issued to approve electronic surveillance. It limited the use of electronic surveillance to situations in which more traditional searches were ineffective and it required elaborate findings to justify any surveillance order. The statute provided, however, that it did not limit certain constitutional powers of the President.

19. Nothing in Title III shall "be deemed to limit the constitutional power of the President to take such measures as he deems necessary to protect the United States against the overthrow of the Government by force or other unlawful means, or against any other clear and present danger to the structure or existence of the Government." 407 U.S. 297 (1972).

20. United States v. United States District Court (Keith), 407 U.S. 297 (1972).

21. *See* United States v. United States District Court for the Eastern District of Michigan, 444 F.2d 651, 654 (1971).

22. *Id.*

neutral" concerning the President's electronic surveillance power: "Congress ... simply did not legislate with respect to national security surveillances."[23]

There were, however, two additional, and critical, parts of the decision. The first expressed a distinction between domestic and foreign threats to the national security. Justice Powell emphasized that the Court was deciding only the right of the government to engage in warrantless electronic surveillance of a domestic organization with no alleged connection to a foreign government.[24] In the second, Justice Powell framed the constitutional inquiry as a determination of the "reasonableness" of the surveillance in light of the Fourth Amendment Warrant Clause.[25] He found authority implicit in the President's Article II Oath Clause "to protect our Government against those who could subvert or overthrow it by unlawful means" sufficient to justify electronic surveillance of would-be subversives. But the "broader spirit" of the Fourth Amendment, as expressed in *Katz*, and "the convergence of First and Fourth Amendment values" in national security wiretapping cases made the Court especially wary of possible abuses of the national security power.

In affirming the courts below, Justice Powell was careful to state that this case involves only the *domestic* aspects of national security: "We ... express no opinion as to, the issues which may be involved with respect to activities of foreign powers or their agents."[26] Justice Powell clearly suggested the possibility that different warrant standards and procedures than those required in a normal criminal investigation might be applicable in a national security investigation. Congress was thus implicitly invited — in context, it might even be seen as a demand — to promulgate a set of standards for such surveillance.

Case Law after *Keith*

Keith sharpened the issues but did not resolve them. It left unresolved the proper approach to the warrant question when the origins of the threat cannot be determined in advance. For example, a primary objective of investigation might well be to determine whether a domestic organization has any significant connection with a foreign power. Nor were searches and seizures addressed. What *Keith* did do, helpfully, was to hold that in the foreign intelligence arena the needs of the executive are so compelling that a uniform warrant requirement would "unduly frustrate" the President in carrying out his foreign affairs duties.[27]

Following *Keith*, a handful of cases were decided that eventually led Congress to promulgate a statutory "fix" that addressed at least most of this arena of decidedly "gray" jurisprudence. One of the first was *United States v. Brown*, in which the Fifth Circuit upheld the legality of surveillance of an American citizen who was incidentally overheard as a result of a warrantless wiretap authorized by the Attorney General for foreign intelligence purposes.[28] The court considered Fourth Amendment challenges, but found that on the basis of "the President's constitutional duty to act for the United States in the field of foreign affairs, and his inherent power to protect national security in the conduct of foreign affairs ... the President may constitutionally authorize warrantless wiretaps for the purpose of gathering foreign intelligence."[29]

---

23. Keith, 407 U.S. at 306.
24. *Id.* at 321.
25. *Id.*
26. *Id.*
27. *Id.* at 297.
28. United States v. Brown, 484 F.2d 418 (5th Cir. 1973).
29. *Id.* at 426.

A similar result was obtained in *United States v. Butenko*, where the Third Circuit upheld electronic surveillance conducted without a warrant after finding that the primary purpose of the surveillance was to obtain foreign intelligence information.[30] The few courts that addressed these national security issues were generally very supportive. "[N]o one would seriously doubt in this time of serious international insecurity and peril that there is an imperative necessity for obtaining foreign intelligence information, and we do not believe such gathering is forbidden by the Constitution or by statutory provision...."[31]

However, the seminal decision that moved this issue forward was *United States v. Humphrey and Truong Dinh Hung*.[32] This was an espionage case arising from the Vietnam conflict. It was known that the North Vietnamese peace delegation in Paris was receiving information concerning the U.S. negotiating positions and the Federal Bureau of Investigation was charged with investigating. During the course of investigation, the Attorney General authorized a warrantless wiretap for national security reasons. When the case eventually came to trial, defendants Humphrey and Truong challenged the warrantless surveillance, alleging the purpose of the surveillance was to gather criminal evidence, rather than foreign intelligence.

The government had three burdens to overcome. First was the warrantless surveillance of a U. S. citizen, a factor that had played into the *Keith* decision. Second was the fact that espionage is a criminal offense and there could be little doubt that the government would prosecute if it could gather and introduce evidence of the crime. Third, and what proved to be the most problematic, was the fact that during the course of the investigation, the Department of Justice wrote a memorandum that acknowledged it was assembling a criminal prosecution.

Accepting the reasoning of the Third and Fifth Circuits, Judge Bryan analyzed the facts of this case. After consideration, he rejected one aspect of the *Butenko* holding. *Butenko* had approved a warrantless national security wiretap, but had held that the technique must be used "solely" to gather foreign intelligence. Judge Bryan specifically found that qualifier overbroad and applied instead a "primary purpose" test. His rejection of this qualifier was, apparently, based at least in part on his finding that all intelligence cases normally have an imbedded criminal element.[33]

Judge Bryan ruled that it is appropriate to balance the interests of the government in the conduct of foreign affairs with the defendant's otherwise constitutional rights under the Fourth Amendment. The court turned to the facts of the case asking the predicate question, "was the primary purpose of this surveillance on this day to gather foreign intelligence information?"[34] Reacting to defense challenge, the court was "not convinced that the primary purpose of the surveillance remained foreign intelligence gathering throughout the life of the surveillance."[35] With that in mind, he suppressed the information

---

30. United States v. Butenko, 494 F.2d 593 (3d Cir. 1974) (*en banc*), *cert. denied sub nom.* Ivanov v. United States, 419 U.S. 881 (1974).

31. United States v. Clay, 430 F.2d 165, 172 (5th Cir. 1970).

32. United States v. Humphrey and Truong Dinh Hung, 456 F. Supp. 51 (E.D. Va. 1978), *aff'd sub nom.* United States v. Truong Dinh Hung, 629 F.2d 908 (4th Cir. 1980), *cert. denied,* 454 U.S. 1144 (1982).

33. This rationale figured prominently in the adoption of the Foreign Intelligence Surveillance Act adopted a few years later.

34. Humphrey and Truong, 456 F. Supp.at 58 (emphasis added). Notably, the court's focus was on the technique, not on the investigation. That is a critical element of this portion of national securitiy authority, but one often overlooked.

35. *Id.*

gathered pursuant to the warrantless wiretap, but only for the time after which the Criminal Division of the Department of Justice had begun to assemble the criminal case.

Not unexpectedly, the case was appealed to the Fourth Circuit Court of Appeals and it is here that contemporary analysis for "primary purpose" picks up.[36] The Fourth Circuit approved the District Court's treatment of the issues, making the requirements even more explicit. Thus, the warrantless surveillance would be approved only where the object of the surveillance is a foreign power, its agent or collaborators.[37] Echoing the initial tests proposed by Judge Bryan, the court ruled that the surveillance could be conducted only when it is "primarily" for foreign intelligence reasons. As did the District Court, it explicitly rejected the argument that the test should be whether the surveillance is "solely" for foreign policy reasons, noting that almost all foreign intelligence investigations are in part criminal investigations.[38] Then, adopting the words of the District Court, the Fourth Circuit concluded its analysis by citing the lower court's finding that "on July 20, 1977, the investigation of Truong had become primarily a criminal investigation because 'the government had begun to assemble a criminal investigation'... and the Criminal Division of the Justice Department had 'taken a central role in the investigation.'"[39]

Subsequent cases would add to the "lore" of this somewhat arcane arena of law. In *Zweibon v. Mitchell*,[40] a far less sympathetic court questioned any electronic surveillance without a warrant, but held its opinion to a requirement that a warrant be obtained before a wiretap can be installed on a domestic organization that has no arguable connection with a foreign power. That court also rejected arguments concerning "leaks" of classified information. The government argued that the standard of probable cause might be more difficult to meet in a prior judicial proceeding and that a judge's error before surveillance occurs would more likely harm the national security than an error in post-surveillance proceedings.[41] A similar result was reached in *Berlin Democratic Club v. Rumsfeld*, where a warrant was required to wiretap Americans living in West Germany despite Department of Defense arguments about dangers to U.S. forces and to American foreign policy.[42]

Physical Searches

Another aspect of Fourth Amendment law that must be considered is physical search. Before 1966, the FBI conducted over two hundred warrantless surreptitious entries for intelligence purposes other than microphone installation, such as physical search and photographing or seizing documents. These operations were authorized, in writing, by the FBI Director or his deputy, although the Attorney General was apparently not informed. Most records of surreptitious entries were destroyed soon after an entry was accomplished. The use of warrantless searches against domestic targets declined radically after J. Edgar Hoover banned such "black bag jobs" in 1966.[43]

---

36. United States v. Truong Dinh Hung, 629 F.2d 908 (4th Cir. 1980), *cert. denied*, 454 U.S. 1144 (1982).

37. *Id.* at 915.

38. *Id.*

39. *Id.* at 916.

40. Zweibon v. Mitchell, 516 F.2d 594 (D.C. Cir. 1975), *cert. denied*, 425 U.S. 944 (1976).

41. *Id.* at 646

42. Berlin Democratic Club v. Rumsfeld, 410 F. Supp. 144 (D.D.C. 1976).

43. 3 Final Report of the Select Committee to Study Governmental Operations with Respect to Intelligence Activities, S. Rep. No. 94-755, at 355 (1976).

Unlike electronic surveillance, the Supreme Court has never recognized a national security exception to the warrant clause for physical searches. In part, this is probably because it has never had a physical search parallel to *Keith*, where it could begin to sort the law of national security searches on the basis of the origins of the surveillance target. The possibility of a national security exception to the warrant requirements for a search was briefly considered in 1960 by the Supreme Court in *Abel v. United States*, but the case did not lend itself to any real consideration of the issue.[44] In the course of an opinion upholding the espionage conviction of a KGB agent, based in part on a warrantless search incident to a valid deportation arrest, the Court parenthetically rejected the notion that national security justified an exception to Fourth Amendment requirements.[45]

The government has twice argued for a national security exception to a warrant for a physical search. The first stemmed from the infamous Pentagon Papers fiasco in the summer of 1971. After his doctor refused to yield medical information about Daniel Ellsberg, then under indictment for disclosing the Papers, an attempt was made to obtain them through a covert search. In *United States v. Ehrlichman*,[46] District Court Judge Gesell found the warrantless search "clearly illegal under the unambiguous mandate of the Fourth Amendment."[47] Judge Gesell rejected the assertion that the President may suspend Fourth Amendment requirements when exercising his "special responsibilities" concerning national security, holding that Fourth Amendment rules apply "except under the most exigent circumstances ... even when known foreign agents are involved." If there is an exception to Fourth Amendment rules for intelligence collection, according to Judge Gesell, the exception is limited to wiretapping, "a relatively nonintrusive search." To expand this exception to physical searches "would give the Executive a blank check to disregard the very heart and core of the Fourth Amendment...."[48] Of interest however, the court found that the President had not authorized the search.[49] The D.C. Circuit, on appeal, even more cautiously found that no "national security" exception to the warrant requirement could be invoked without specific authorization by the President or Attorney General.[50]

The second judicial review of warrantless physical searches carried out for national security purposes harkens back to the criminal convictions of Ronald Humphrey and Truong Dinh Hung. As noted previously, Humphrey and Dinh Hung were convicted of several espionage-related offenses for transmitting classified U.S. government information to representatives of the government of North Vietnam. Letters and packages entrusted to an FBI asset to courier to the North Vietnamese in Paris had been opened and searched, revealing clear evidence of criminal wrongdoing.

The courts addressed the searches independently, but consistently with their consideration of the electronic surveillance, finding either that the warrant exception for national security applied or that there was no reasonable expectation of privacy. The courts paid considerable deference to the proposition that the executive branch is in a superior position to assess

---

44. Abel v. United States, 362 U.S. 217 (1960).
45. Agents found the evidence of espionage in a hollow pencil in a trash basket after Abel had paid his bill and left his hotel room. The court thus ruled that Abel had no reasonable expectation of privacy in the room or the pencil after he had left them. *Id.* at 241.
46. United States v. Ehrlichman, 376 F. Supp. 29 (D.D.C. 1974), *aff'd*, 546 F.2d 910 (D.C. Cir. 1976), *cert. denied*, 429 U.S. 1120 (1977).
47. *Id.* at 32.
48. *Id.* at 33.
49. *Id.* at 34.
50. United States v. Ehrlichman, 546 F.2d 910, 925 (1976).

threats to the national security. It was only when the issues devolved to criminal process, the arena of courts and judges, that they were willing to interfere.

> We think that the district court adopted the proper test, because once surveillance becomes primarily a criminal investigation, the courts are entirely competent to make the usual probable cause determination, and because, importantly, individual privacy interests come to the fore and government foreign policy concerns recede when the government is primarily attempting to form the basis for a criminal prosecution.[51]

An Evolving Rule

In retrospect, it seems clear that the *Keith* rejection of the theory that a wiretap is a form of "search" was influenced by the "convergence of First and Fourth Amendment values,"[52] but it probably reflects even more an evolution of societal values. When the nation was young, when it was at war, when it was threatened, privacy was less important than security. In a more secure environment, privacy clearly became increasingly important to "the people" and court decisions reflected the concerns. Additionally, the law that emerges from *Keith* and subsequent decisions of lower courts also reflects the importance of knowing the origins of the threats to national security. However, it does not provide guidance when the threat is known, but the origin is not. Nor does it address the need for urgent, immediate preventive measures when a threat looms.

Some guidance has arisen in other contexts. The term "the people" appears to have been given meaning by default. In *United States v. Verdugo-Urquidez*,[53] the Court considered whether the Fourth Amendment applies to searches and seizures by U.S. agents of property owned by a nonresident alien and located in a foreign country. The Court concluded that it does not. Noting that the Court had previously held that aliens outside the sovereign territory of the United States have no claim on the Fifth Amendment, which speaks only of "persons," the Court concluded that it cannot be that the Fourth Amendment, referring to "the people," could afford greater rights.[54]

With a predictable symmetry, it also appears that the Fourth Amendment travels abroad with "the people," although it is not clear what the extent of the right is. For example, federal magistrates have no jurisdiction to issue warrants for overseas locales so normal judicial protection of citizen rights does not exist abroad.[55] However, if there is a warrant exception for national security reasons within the United States, clearly it must apply abroad as well.[56] There is, however, an unsatisfying quality to a lack of firm standards.

---

51. United States v. Truong Dinh Hung, 629 F.2d 908, 915 (4th Cir. 1980), *cert. denied*, 454 U.S. 1144 (1982).

52. *See* United States v. United States District Court (Keith), 407 U.S. 297, 313 (1972).

53. United States v. Verdugo-Urquidez, 494 U.S. 259 (1990).

54. *Id.* at 268–69. In Johnson v. Eisentrager, 339 U.S. 763, 784 (1950), the Court held that enemy aliens arrested in China and imprisoned in Germany after World War II could not obtain writs of habeas corpus in federal courts on the ground that their convictions for war crimes had violated the Fifth Amendment.

55. A line of cases beginning with Reid v. Covert, 354 U.S. 1 (1957), make clear that the Constitution does travel with U.S. citizens with respect to governmental actions. As for aliens, a substantial connection to the United States would be required for similar treatment.

56. United States v. Bin Laden, 126 F. Supp. 2d 264 (N.D.N.Y. 2000) held that the normal requirements of primary purpose, foreign agency, and authorization by the President or Attorney General applied.

This became apparent in the mid-1970s when abuses, or perceived abuses of law enforcement and intelligence agencies were made public by the Senate Select Committee to Study Governmental Operations with Respect to Intelligence Activities, better known as the Church Committee.

In a multi-volume report, the Committee found that the intelligence community was largely unregulated, inefficient and out of step with evolving social values of the American people. There was clear evidence, they said, of unlawful and inappropriate activity in virtually every aspect of the community, both civilian and military. The Committee found multiple shortcomings in intelligence operations, harmful effects of secrecy, and, what should have come as no surprise, failure by Congress to oversee intelligence activities. They found duplication, waste, and inertia. Most commonly, however, they found that activities of the intelligence community had violated individual privacy.

Although the Committee acknowledged that secret government activities are necessary to the effectiveness of government, they nevertheless concluded secrecy could be a threat to democratic society. The Committee believed control and accountability were lacking and that covert actions had been both excessive and a means of circumventing the democratic process. With a certain deterministic ring to it, the Committee concluded that intelligence efforts had violated the Constitution *and that the reason was lack of legislation*. The remedy, they asserted, was to have Congress prescribe rules for intelligence activities, a draconian measure that was narrowly avoided when President Ford issued the first Executive Order regulating the intelligence community and adopting most of what the legislation would have provided.[57]

Not all the remedial measures of the era can be traced to the Church Committee, but there is a clear consistency of thought process in the Privacy Act, the Freedom of Information Act, the Foreign Intelligence Surveillance Act and similar legislation. There is also consistency in executive branch actions, notably the Ford, Carter, and Reagan Executive Orders regulating the intelligence community, and in implementing regulations of the affected agencies.[58] Acting separately, but with a similar focus, all the branches of government embarked on a mission to ensure an open government, protection of the privacy of its citizens and adequate, measured tools to protect the national security. In accord with executive order requirements, the military and intelligence communities adopted new measures to protect the rights of U.S. persons.

By trial and error, both the Executive and Congress sought to find a legislative solution to the issue of warrantless search and surveillance. In 1976, President Ford submitted a bill to the Senate that would have codified existing executive branch practices, and Attorneys General William Saxbe and Edward Levi pledged their cooperation to work with the Congress to create legislation to regulate electronic surveillance. Debate and discussion concerned the questions of inherent executive authority and whether the traditional criminal law standard should be included in the legislation.[59]

---

57. 2 FINAL REPORT OF THE SELECT COMMITTEE TO STUDY GOVERNMENTAL OPERATIONS WITH RESPECT TO INTELLIGENCE ACTIVITIES, S. REP. NO. 94-755, at 1–14, 423–74 (1976).

58. Exec. Order No. 11,905, 41 Fed. Reg. 7707 (1976), issued by President Ford, was the first. The Ford Executive Order was a template for future executive orders that would regulate the intelligence community. President Carter replaced Exec. Order No. 11,905 with Exec. Order No. 12,036, 43 Fed. Reg. 3678 (1978), and President Reagan replaced Exec. Order No. 12,036 with the still current Exec. Order No. 12,333, 46 Fed. Reg. 59,941 (1981). By Order, each affected agency was to issue implementing regulations approved by the Attorney General.

59. *See* Americo R. Cinquegrana, *The Walls (and Wires) Have Ears: The Background and First Ten Years of the Foreign Intelligence Surveillance Act of 1978*, 137 U. PA. L. REV. 793, 809–811 (1989).

Senator Kennedy initially proposed restrictive legislation that would have expressly eliminated congressional recognition of inherent executive power in this sphere. Predictably, most controversy centered on the standards for targeting Americans who were not accused of criminal acts. The Carter administration supported the legislation in principle, and eventually both chambers approved the Kennedy proposal, as amended, dropping the disclaimer and including a "quasi-criminal" targeting standard for U.S. persons and lesser protections for aliens.[60] Justice Powell's invitation was finally accepted when Congress passed and President Carter signed into law the Foreign Intelligence Surveillance Act of 1978 (FISA) in October 1978.[61] It is probably important to understand, however, that the impetus for this law was as much a response to social issues as to legal ones. To understand this law, and the reason for its existence, one has to understand the practices that preceded it, not merely those few court cases that reported the legal issues.

The Foreign Intelligence Surveillance Act (FISA)[62]

Even a casual perusal of the Fourth Amendment yields the inescapable conclusion that electronic surveillance has been the heart of the national security issues in the past fifty years. In the national security context it had been approved frequently through the years. In 1915, President Wilson instructed the Secretary of the Treasury to put German and Austro-Hungarian legations under surveillance. Acting in furtherance of Wilson's instructions, the Secret Service also installed wiretaps on the German and Austro-Hungarian legations.[63] The specter of German subversion far surpassed reality, but the result, nevertheless, was reminiscent of the Alien and Sedition Acts. Enacted on June 15, 1917, the Espionage Act authorized the government to confiscate property, wiretap, search and seize private property, censure writings, open mail, and restrict the right of assembly.[64]

Subsequently, throughout the 1930s the Justice Department utilized telephone wiretaps for intelligence investigations. Authority for the use of those wiretaps was based solely on the personal approval of bureau chiefs. This authority was employed in "exceptional cases where the crimes are substantial and serious, and the necessity is great and [Department of Justice officials] are satisfied that the persons whose wires are to be tapped are of the criminal type."[65]

Beginning in 1940, President Roosevelt authorized the Attorney General to approve electronic surveillance where "grave matters involving defense of the nation" were at stake.[66] The President authorized and directed the Attorney General "to secure information

---

60. *Id.*

61. Foreign Intelligence Surveillance Act of 1978 (FISA), 50 U.S.C. §§ 1801–1863 (1998), amended by Pub. L. No. 106-120, Dec. 3, 1999, 113 Stat. 1606.

62. See Chapter 27 for a detailed and comprehensive discussion of the FISA and additional issues in using FISA procedures and process in collecting intelligence on terrorist groups and their activities.

63. *See* Barbara Tuchman, The Zimmerman Telegram 74–78 (1958). *See also* Arthur Link, Wilson: The Struggle for Neutrality 563 (1960). Wilson was never comfortable with the clandestine arts, but he was convinced, even in advance of the proof that soon was to come, that the Germans had thoroughly infiltrated the United States with agents of all kinds.

64. *See* Espionage Act, 18 U.S.C. § 793 (2000). The espionage statutes have changed little from the 1917 Act and have a recognizable antecedent in the earlier acts of the Continental Congress.

65. Foreign Intelligence Surveillance Act of 1977, S. Rep. No. 95-604, at 9 (1977).

66. *Id. See also Report 95-1283, Pt. I, Foreign Intelligence Surveillance Act of 1978*, 50 U.S.C. § 1862 (2000).

by listening devices [directed at] the conversation or other communications of persons suspected of subversive activities against the Government of the United States, including suspected spies."[67] The Attorney General was requested "to limit these investigations so conducted to a minimum and to limit them insofar as possible to aliens."[68] By 1954, J. Edgar Hoover announced to the FBI that the Bureau was authorized to enter private property for the purpose of installing electronic surveillance devices, without regard for surreptitious entry and without prior authorization from the Attorney General. According to FBI policy, such surveillance was authorized whenever the Bureau concluded that the "national interest" so required.[69]

After the war, electronic surveillance continued to play a major role in government affairs, though not necessarily a savory one. Similar to the era of the Alien and Sedition Acts, and the hysteria in World War I, things foreign became suspect. For example, congressmen called on constituents to hunt down "internal enemies," while the state of Georgia issued a declaration of war against aliens.[70] By the early 1950s, several Soviet spy rings had been uncovered in the United States, the Communists had overrun China and Americans were dying in Korea. During this time, the now infamous House Un-American Affairs Committee and the Smith Act emerged.[71] Once again the nation was willing to accept extraordinary measures in the name of national security. Foreign threats were targeted, but so were a domestic fifth column of Americans who might be a domestic threat to the national security.

An extremely ambitious project, code-named Operation Shamrock, was designed to gain access to all overseas cables (then in paper form) to, and from, foreign embassies and consulates, and from U.S. persons and commercial firms.[72] Then, with technological advances, it soon became possible to put all such communications on magnetic media. This permitted leaving the paper trail behind in favor of "watch lists" of names that could be developed and electronically searched without reference to foreign or domestic interests. This was so efficient that, as Attorney General, Robert Kennedy employed the watch lists against major crime figures to capture their communications, thereby casting aside entirely the national security predicate.[73] A spin-off called Operation Minaret specifically targeted both cables and telephone calls for information about possible foreign influence on civil disturbances in the United States related to the Vietnam conflict.[74] The possibilities for the new technologies were virtually endless. The expansive nature of these operations came to an end only when congressional interest in intelligence activities began to focus on privacy issues. One result of this was the Foreign Intelligence Surveillance Act (FISA).

FISA is often interpreted as a legislative response to intelligence abuse. That is probably a fair analysis, but it falls short of the complete picture. FISA represents a political compromise. The overreaching of intelligence agencies can be controlled by statute and penalties, but the mere fact that it took several years and many different drafts of legislation

---

67. S. Rep. No. 95-604, *supra* note 65, at 11.

68. *Id. See also* From the Secret Files of J. Edgar Hoover 134–135 (Athan Theoharis ed., 1991).

69. *See* S. Rep. No. 95-604, *supra* note 65, at 9.

70. Ernest Volkman & Blaine Baggett, Secret Intelligence: The Inside Story of America's Espionage Empire 33 (1989).

71. Smith Act, 18 U.S.C. § 2385 (1940) (making it illegal to advocate the overthrow of the government or to belong to a group that did).

72. *See generally*, James Bamford, The Puzzle Palace 302–08, 350, 369, 372, 380–90 (1982) (describing Operation Shamrock).

73. *Id.* at 315–17.

74. *Id.* at 320–24.

before passage reflects the fact that the inherent power of the President cannot merely be shunted aside. On the one hand regularity and visible process for government actions is highly desirable—especially for a nation that was born in mistrust of government. On the other, the hands that protect "the people" cannot be tied beyond their capability to react and protect. Moreover, if the President does have inherent powers, and it now seems clear that he does, even though their extent is seldom clear, then Congress cannot, by statute, negate a constitutional power. That was made clear by successive presidents by the manner in which they gave their support for the FISA legislation.[75]

FISA was intended by Congress to provide the exclusive means for authorizing some categories of foreign intelligence surveillance, including the interception of "international radio or wire communications to or from a particular United States person in the United States in circumstances where that person has a reasonable expectation of privacy and a warrant would be required if the interception or monitoring were undertaken for law enforcement purposes."[76] The same rule applies to "a wholly domestic radio communication, and the installation or use of any monitoring device (such as a television camera or pen register) to acquire information about a person's activities other than the contents of the communications," and to the interception of wire communication "from any person in the United States without the consent of the party to the communication."[77] A question unanswered, but not often asked, is whether, after Congress has legislated the field of electronic surveillance with both criminal and intelligence procedural statutes, there remains any unaddressed authority of the President. The answer to that undoubtedly lies in future threats and the way technology addresses them.

Interestingly, when FISA was enacted it focused solely on electronic surveillance. The primary Fourth Amendment "issues" arising from the Church Committee stemmed from electronic surveillance. Accordingly, search was not considered in the original version of the Act. Nor was the Department of Justice particularly interested in including searches. There remained some residual skepticism in the executive branch concerning the potential for judicial interference in national security matters. Nevertheless, and while maintaining the President's constitutional authority to approve a national security-related search, in 1980, Attorney General Civiletti sought Foreign Intelligence Surveillance Court (FISC) authority for national security-related physical searches.[78] The ostensible reason for the Attorney General's decision was the security and expertise of the newly created FISC, but it was also a little bit more. The Justice Department had already obtained three FISA searches from the FISC arguing that authority was available through the All Writs Act.[79]

---

75. Attorney General Griffin Bell testified before the House Select Committee on Intelligence:
The current bill recognizes no inherent power of the president to conduct electronic surveillance, and I want to interpolate here to say that this does not take away the power of the president under the Constitution. It simply, in my view, is not necessary to state that power, not so there is no reason to reiterate it or iterate it as the case may be. It is in the Constitution, whatever it is. The president, by offering this legislation, is agreeing to follow the statutory procedure.
(*Foreign Intelligence Surveillance Act of 1977: Hearings before the Subcomm. on Legislation of the House Permanent Select Comm. on Intelligence*, 95th Cong., 2d Sess. (1978), at 15. *See generally* Philip Lacovara, *Presidential Power to Gather Intelligence: The Tension Between Article II and Amendment IV*, 40 L. & CONTEMP. PROBS. 106 (1976).)

76. Foreign Intelligence Surveillance Act of 1978, 50 U.S.C. § 1801(f)(1) (2000).

77. *Id.* at § 1801(f)(2).

78. *See* Americo R. Cinquegrana, *The Walls (and Wires) Have Ears: The Background and First Ten Years of the Foreign Intelligence Surveillance Act of 1978*, 137 U. PA. L. REV. 793, 809–11, 820 (1989).

79. *Id.* at 821. The All Writs Act provides: "Except as otherwise provided by an Act of Congress, the district courts shall have original jurisdiction of all civil actions, suits or proceedings commenced

Subsequently, the FISC determined that the All Writs Act was not a basis for the FISC to authorize physical search, so in 1981, President Reagan's new Attorney General, William French Smith, submitted a fourth application to the FISC for a national security physical search, but with a twist. This time the Department asked that the application be rejected on grounds that the FISC had no jurisdiction to approve such an application.[80] Until recently, that was the only published opinion of the FISC. Not surprisingly, the court held that the FISC had no jurisdiction over physical searches.[81]

While the Smith application clarified FISC authority, it did nothing more; search was still not authorized except under executive authority. However, after CIA spy Aldrich Ames pled guilty to espionage charges in April 1994, the Clinton administration actively sought to extend the FISA to such searches. A warrantless search of Ames' office was used to develop the government's case against him, and, according to Ames' lawyer, a challenge was planned to the constitutionality of this particular warrantless search.[82] Although Ames' guilty plea mooted the constitutional challenge, the threat prompted the change of stance by the Justice Department. According to Associate Attorney General Jamie Gorelick, "Our seeking legislation in no way should suggest that we do not believe we have inherent authority.... We do ... but as a policy matter, we thought it was better to have Congress and the judiciary involved."[83]

After the *Ames* case, virtually everyone appeared to believe that these type of searches should be regulated under FISA. Therefore, in 1994, as part of the Intelligence Authorization Act for Fiscal Year 1995, Congress amended FISA to authorize submission of applications to the FISC for an order approving a physical search in the United States, for the purpose of collecting "foreign intelligence information," of the "premises, property, information or material of a foreign power or agent of a foreign power."[84] The prerequisites for a FISA search thus parallel those for electronic surveillance.

The utility of FISA was not only apparent by this time, but its value was increasing as instability began to grip much of the world. In 1998, Congress again amended FISA to permit FBI use of pen register and trap and trace devices[85] in counterintelligence and international terrorism investigations, following FISA procedures.[86] The same act authorized FISA surveillance procedures for government access to hotel, car rental, bus, airline, and other business records.[87] The authorities were not altogether freely given. There remained

---

by the United States, or by any agency or officer thereof expressly authorized to sue by Act of Congress." 28 U.S.C. § 1345 (1998).

80. Cinquegrana, *supra* note 78, at 822.

81. *In the Matter of the Application of the United States for an Order Authorizing the Physical Search of Nonresidential Premises and Personal Property* (1981) (*reproduced in* Dycus, *et al.* National Security Law 469 (1st ed. 1990)).

82. *See* Peter Maas, Killer Spy: The Inside Story of the FBI's Pursuit and Capture of Aldrich Ames, America's Deadliest Spy 224–34 (1995).

83. Benjamin Wittes, *Surveillance Court Gets New Powers*, 27 Legal Times No. 25, Nov. 7, 1994, at 22.

84. Intelligence Authorization Act for Fiscal Year 1995, 50 U.S.C. §§ 1821–1829 (2000). Pursuant to the 1994 amendment, applications may be submitted only if the President has, by prior written authorization, empowered the Attorney General to approve such submissions. *Id.* at § 807. Written authorization was subsequently supplied by Exec. Order No. 12,949 in February 1995. Exec. Order No. 12,949, 60 Fed. Reg. 8169, Feb. 13, 1995.

85. A pen register records the dialed numbers identifying outgoing calls on a surveilled line. A trap and trace device records the number of origin for incoming calls.

86. Intelligence Authorization Act, Fiscal Year 1999, Pub. L. No. 105-272, § 601, 112 Stat. 2396, 50 U.S.C. §§ 1841–1846 (adding Title IV to FISA).

87. *Id.* at § 602, 112 Stat. 2404, adding Title V to the Foreign Intelligence Surveillance Act.

a visceral distrust of secret proceedings, so Congress, in granting the authority, also restricted them substantially more than was asked of the same authorities exercised for law enforcement purposes. The law enforcement officer need only certify that the information expected to be obtained is relevant to an authorized investigation. For intelligence purposes it had to be demonstrated that the target of the technique *was* an agent of a foreign power. Similarly, the government asked Congress to grant the equivalent of an administrative subpoena, allowing FBI officials to demand business records without judicial intervention as can be done through a grand jury process for criminal investigative purposes. The 1998 amendment to FISA instead requires that business records requests obtain approval from the FISC, thereby making the process far slower and more cumbersome for intelligence investigators than it is for criminal investigators.[88]

Using FISA

Unlike the criminal process, FISA focuses not on criminality for probable cause, but on foreign agency. If the target is a "U.S. Person" (citizen or alien admitted for permanent residency), an additional burden of knowing culpability related to national security crimes must be shown, but not to the extent of showing that the target actually is breaking the law.[89] It remains unclear (but largely unchallenged) whether substitution of the FISA review process assures satisfaction of the *Keith* court's first measure of the reasonableness of warrantless surveillance—that is, whether rights of privacy and free expression are adequately served without a warrant requirement. The second element of the reasonableness inquiry framed in *Keith*—whether a judicially imposed law enforcement warrant requirement would "unduly frustrate the efforts of Government to protect itself"—is much more easily met in the foreign intelligence setting because without secrecy the target is more likely to learn of the surveillance and could alter its activities, likely rendering the intelligence useless.

One perpetually vexing question has been the extent to which the government can use FISA surveillance to obtain evidence for criminal prosecution. Ordinarily, law enforcement investigations have a criminal prosecution purpose from the start. In contrast, FISA surveillances must have an intelligence purpose. The very few courts that have allowed evidence gathered during the surveillance to support a criminal conviction appear to have done so only after having been assured that intelligence was the "primary" purpose of the surveillance,[90] or at least a purpose (not necessarily primary).[91]

A poignant example of the "purpose" issue stems from the *Ames* espionage case. During the course of the investigation of Ames, an Attorney General-authorized physical search of his house turned up significantly incriminating information. That presented the defense with a critical defense issue. The issue was significant enough that his attorney strongly recommended that Ames enter a plea of not guilty and defend on the basis of illegal search. In the end, Ames rejected his attorney's advice and entered a plea of guilty in return for a more lenient sentence for his spouse. Had Aldrich Ames gone forward with the claim that the search of his office was unconstitutional, his argument would have been based on the primary purpose standard from *Truong*. The defense would have been that the investigation had evolved to the point where its primary purpose was no longer

---

88. Foreign Intelligence Surveillance Act of 1978 (FISA), 50 U.S.C. §§ 1801–1863, 1861 (2000), amended by Pub. L. No. 106-120, Dec. 3, 1999, 113 Stat. 1606.

89. *See id.* at § 1801 (b)(2).

90. United States v. Megahey, 553 F. Supp. 1180, 1189–90 (E.D.N.Y. 1982).

91. United States v. Falvey, 540 F. Supp. 1306, 1314 (E.D.N.Y. 1982).

foreign counterintelligence, but was instead designed specifically to gather evidence of a crime. One can readily believe that Ms. Gorelick was correct that "it was better to have Congress and the judiciary involved" in such searches, although the constitutional question remained unresolved, notwithstanding the amendment to FISA. More recent events have shed new light on the critical issue of "purpose."

Congress Speaks Again — The USA PATRIOT Act[92]

Due to uncertainty or misunderstood legal theory of "purpose" or "primary purpose," the Department of Justice traditionally imposed severe restrictions on the exposure of intelligence information, particularly that obtained by FISA techniques, to criminal investigators or prosecutors. The USA PATRIOT Act[93] was a congressional vehicle to address at least some of the issues associated with the artificial wall built between intelligence and criminal investigators. One profound change was to modify the language of the statute from "purpose" to "significant purpose" for the utilization of FISA, thereby acknowledging more clearly what had previously been perhaps too subtle — that a FISA technique may be used for intelligence purposes even if there is an intent to prosecute.[94] That change also highlighted the often misunderstood fact that FISA is about a technique (that is, electronic surveillance or search) and not about the broader investigation. Other provisions brought many of the intelligence techniques, such as National Security Letters, Pen Register/Trap and Trace, and roving wiretaps into conformity with criminal law standards (that the technique sought would provide information relevant to an authorized investigation).

As significant as the USA PATRIOT Act was, however, it may be that a shift in views at the Department of Justice was even more important. By 2002, it had become apparent that greater sharing of information was needed effectively to combat the post-9/11 terrorist threat. That began a tug-of-war between the Department and the FISC. The Department, now faced with a daunting increase in the number of surveillances authorized to prevent terrorism, wanted to tear down walls and make complete sharing possible. The FISC, on the other hand, continued to impose walls in their orders, insisting that intelligence and criminal purposes be kept both separate and distant. A key FISC order stated:

> Law enforcement officials shall not make recommendations to intelligence officials concerning the initiation, operation, continuation or expansion of FISA searches or surveillances. Additionally, the FBI and the Criminal Division [of the Department of Justice] shall ensure that law enforcement officials do not direct or control the use of the FISA procedures to enhance criminal prosecution, and that advice intended to preserve the option of a criminal prosecution does not inadvertently result in the Criminal Division's directing or controlling the investigation using FISA searches and surveillances toward law enforcement objectives.[95]

This was directly contrary to the perceived need to put as many eyes "on target" as possible, and to bring all relevant experience to bear, in the mission to prevent terrorism.

---

92. *See also* Chapter 27 for a comprehensive discussion on the changes made by the USA PATRIOT ACT to FISA and other relevant statutes applicable to gathering intelligence/information to prevent terrorism.

93. Uniting and Strengthening America by Providing Appropriate Tools Required to Intercept and Obstruct Terrorism (USA PATRIOT) Act of 2001, HR 3162, Pub. L. No. 107-56, 115 Stat. 291, Oct. 26, 2001.

94. *See id.*

95. *In re Sealed Case* No. 02-001, 310 F.3d 717, 720 (2002).

The question was whether the FISC ruling was compelled by Constitution, statute, or inertia. The FISC order prompted the first-ever convening of the Foreign Intelligence Appellate Court. That court found no predicate in either statute or the judicial law of "primary purpose" for the proposition that criminal purpose was incompatible with intelligence techniques. "It is [thus] virtually impossible to read the 1978 FISA to exclude from its purpose the prosecution of foreign intelligence crimes, most importantly because, as we have noted, the definition of an agent of a foreign power—if he or she is a U.S. person—is grounded on criminal conduct."[96]

The FISA Appellate Court cited persuasive legislative history to indicate that a "wall" was neither required nor appropriate. The House had stated "obviously, use of 'foreign intelligence information' as evidence in a criminal trial is one way the government can lawfully protect against clandestine intelligence activities, sabotage, and international terrorism,"[97] and the Senate similarly reported that "intelligence and criminal law enforcement tend to merge in this area. Surveillances conducted under [FISA] need not stop once conclusive evidence of a crime is obtained, but instead may be extended longer where protective measures other than arrest and prosecution are more appropriate."[98]

As if to drive a final nail in the coffin, the court went on to note that in any case, the USA PATRIOT Act clearly expressed a congressional repudiation of the "wall" interpretation of FISA. Congress changed the "purpose" requirement to "significant purpose,"[99] permitted intelligence agents to consult with law enforcement officers,[100] and stipulated that no such consultation or coordination would negate the "significant purpose" of gathering foreign intelligence information.[101] This essentially eviscerated both the FISC ruling as well as the former Department of Justice practice that mandated walls going back for many years and validated both the 1978 Foreign Intelligence Surveillance Act and the USA PATRIOT Act in terms of the Fourth Amendment.[102]

This ruling provides a certain symmetry to prior holdings of the court that had challenged the FISA process on grounds of separation of powers and/or principles of judicial independence in Article III because the FISC judges' appointments may be revoked during their seven-year terms, thus potentially influencing a judge's conduct on the FISC.[103] The rejection actually affirmed the constitutional separation of powers doctrine, acknowledging that the surveillance decision is for the President alone to make while the FISC engages in day-to-day fact-finding like that performed regularly by judges.[104]

The Fourth Amendment in Retrospect

The Fourth Amendment existed for more than a hundred years without generating appreciable controversy. It was, after all, a reaction to perceived abuses of British soldiers

---

96. *Id.* at 723.
97. *Id.* at 724.
98. *Id.* at 725.
99. USA PATRIOT Act, 50 U.S.C. § 1804(a)(7)(B) (Supp. 2002).
100. *Id.* at § 1806(k)(1).
101. *Id.* at § 1806(k)(2).
102. *In re Sealed Case*, 310 F.3d, at 746.
103. United States v. Cavanaugh, 807 F.2d 787, 792 (stating that temporary assignment within the federal judicial system is common and does not undermine judicial independence).
104. *See* United States v. Duggan, 743 F.2d 59, 74–75 (2d Cir. 1984) (limited judicial role in determining whether the target of a warrant is properly subject to the prescribed procedure is not a political question and does not inject courts into the making of foreign policy).

invading the sanctity of the home that drove its creation. In consequence, it was born with physical trespass in mind, and it was that theory that carried the law of the Amendment into the twentieth century. The technology of communications, specifically the telephone, changed that. Trespass theory simply didn't provide the privacy that Americans demanded and the law began to evolve. However, technology developed alongside world politics. Over time, the oceans appeared to offer less and less protection, so the security of the nation became periodically a concern.

From the era of World War I forward, presidents have felt the need to know what suspect individuals were up to, and the telephone, which provided ease of communications to all, offered as well a means to hear the words of the suspects. The wiretap was a perfect technique for that, and, after all, it couldn't be illegal—it wasn't a trespass. As we've seen, though, that theory yielded to new thinking, although it still took many years for privacy concerns and the necessity to obtain a warrant to become settled law.

The national security dimension of the problem arose because national security issues were not always germane to criminal conduct, without which it seemed a warrant was unobtainable. Could there be a national security exception to the warrant requirement? Whether there was or not, presidents acted as though there was and ordered electronic surveillance frequently. When cases came to courts, most were deferential to the executive branch. Without actually passing judgment, courts assumed that the exception existed and proceeded from that point. Congress also left the authority untested, preferring to legislate procedures and leave any constitutional authorities to be defined elsewhere.

The fundamental issues boiled over when the exception was claimed for a domestic crime. The Supreme Court was forced to confront the issue, and while they did not address it head on, they did focus on reasonableness rather than warrant for any presidential authority that might exist. They also noted that foreign intelligence requirements were such that flexibility of the Executive was a necessity, thereby negating any uniform formula for authorizing a surveillance. Then, in the span of only a few years, the Fourth Amendment was addressed with sufficiently varied fact patterns, in enough different jurisdictions, to give substantial definition to the national security issues.

Although the Supreme Court has never directly confirmed presidential authority in this area, the Court, Congress, and successive Presidents all, at various times, have assumed or acquiesced to the claim. In consequence, today, we know that reasonableness is the relevant Fourth Amendment standard for search and surveillance actions taken in the name of national security. The technique, whether search or surveillance, must have an intelligence purpose, but we may have a goal of prosecution nonetheless. We know also that the intelligence purpose must be one of foreign intelligence, not domestic, for which standard criminal law and the normal court system are competent. We know that Congress believes it has occupied the field with FISA and the criminal procedures for surveillance and search; whether they have is probably fact dependent—that is, whether a national security requirement arises that cannot be addressed by these two procedures. Clearly, if the national security exception is a constitutional power of the President, statute may regulate procedure, but it cannot negate the authority.

As we move forward into the 21st Century, we are finding that the Fourth Amendment has still more surprises for us. In the years following *Olmstead*, the Court continued to cling to a property-based theory of the Fourth Amendment. In a 1942 case, *Goldman v. United States*[105] law enforcement had placed a listening device on the wall adjacent to a

---

105. Goldman v. United States, 316 U.S. 129 (1942).

telephone the defendant was using and had listened to one half of a conversation. It was enough to convict and when the Fourth Amendment challenge came to the Court it was held that divulgence of a person's telephone conversation, overheard as it was spoken into the telephone receiver, does not violate § 605 of the Federal Communications Act, as in such case there is neither a "communication" nor an "interception" within the meaning of the Act.[106] It was further held that the use by federal agents of a detectaphone, whereby conversations in the office of a defendant were overheard through contact on the wall of an adjoining room, did not violate the Fourth Amendment, and evidence thus obtained was admissible in a federal court.[107]

A similar case occurred in 1961 when a listening device was implanted in the adjacent wall and one-half a conversation was overheard. The case was similar, but the result was different. In Silverman v. United States,[108] the Court found that the act of implanting the device constituted a trespass—"a fair reading of the record in this case shows that the eavesdropping was accomplished by an unauthorized physical penetration of the premises occupied by the petitiioners."[109]

For the logical progeny of *Goldman* and *Silverman* the reader should reflect back on the *Griswold*, *Katz* and *Keith* cases. However, the import is more current. By way of background *Goldman* and *Silverman* set the standard for placing tracking devices on vehicles. Placed *on* the car the Goldman standard applied. Placed more securely *in* the car the Silverman standard applied. However, technology has a way of changing social standards. The original trackers were capable of yielding a limited amount of information. Modern GPS devices are capable of recording every moment of driving activity. In *Jones v. United States*[110] a GPS device had been placed without a warrant *on* a car pursuant to investigation of and the subsequent conviction of illegal drug smugglers. The conviction was appealed and the D.C. Circuit Court overturned the conviction recognizing how much more intrusive modern technology can be explaining that:

> Prolonged surveillance reveals types of information not revealed by short-term surveillance, such as what a person does repeatedly, what he does not do, and what he does ensemble. These types of information can each reveal more about a person than does any individual trip viewed in isolation. Repeated visits to a church, a gym, a bar, or a bookie tell a story not told by any single visit, as does one's not visiting any of these places over the course of a month. The sequence of a person's movements can reveal still more; a single trip to a gynecologist's office tells little about a woman, but that trip followed a few weeks later by a visit to a baby supply store tells a different story. A person who knows all of another's travels can deduce whether he is a weekly church goer, a heavy drinker, a regular at the gym, an unfaithful husband, an outpatient receiving medical treatment, an associate of particular individuals or political groups—and not just one such fact about a person, but all such facts.[111]

The unanimous opinion of the Court was that the effect of placing a GPS device on defendant's car was a search within the meaning of the Fourth Amendment. The government argued that if it were a search it was nevertheless a reasonable one. The Court

---

106. *Id.* at 133.
107. *Id.* at 135.
108. Silverman v. United States, 365 U.S. 505 (1961).
109. *Id.* at p. 364.
110. United States v. Jones, 132 S. Ct. 945, 565 U.S. ___ (2012).
111. United States v. Maynard, 615 F.3d 544, 562 (D.C. Cir. 2010).

did not consider the argument because it had not been raised below so that issue remains open.[112]

This case could portend a fundamental transformation of law enforcement work for the future. Not only does it threaten, significantly, a half-century of practice, but the government also wanted a remand so they could argue that all the data the GPS device collected was essentially third party data in accord with *Smith v. Maryland* because it was visible to the public. This argument was met head-on in a concurring opinion by Justice Sotomayor:

> More fundamentally, it may be necessary to reconsider the premise that an individual has no reasonable expectation of privacy in information voluntarily disclosed to third parties. E.g., Smith, 442 U. S., at 742;United States v. Miller, 425 U. S. 435, 443 (1976). This approach is ill suited to the digital age, in which people reveal a great deal of information about themselves to third parties in the course of carrying out mundane tasks. People disclose the phone numbers that they dial or text to their cellular providers; the URLs that they visit and the e-mail addresses with which they correspond to their Internet service providers; and the books, groceries, and medications they purchase to online retailers.[113]

This, too, portends a sea change in the business of law enforcement. Since the 1979 decision of *Smith v. Maryland* third party data has been constitutionally unprotected and subject to seizure by law enforcement through administrative means. A change to this would mean extraordinary difficulty for law enforcement. However, two other circuits are of an opinion similar to Justice Sotomayor. In *United States v. Warshalk,*[114] government officials, relying on *Smith v. Maryland* and the Stored Communications Act[115] compelled the production of defendant's e-mails. In a cogent opinion the Sixth Circuit held that e-mails should be protected just as the U.S. mail service is:

> Given the fundamental similarities between email and traditional forms of communication, it would defy common sense to afford emails lesser Fourth Amendment protection.[116]

The Second Case is *United States v. Cotterman*[117] in which the defendant, a United States citizen, was entering the United States carrying a laptop. There was an alert on Mr. Cotterman based on a 15-year-old conviction for child molestation so a customs agent asked to inspect the computer. It was partially inspected and Mr. Cotterman claimed it was a shared computer and he did not have the password but promised to get it and come back. Instead, Mr. Cotterman left the country and when Customs eventually managed to open the passworded part of the computer child pornography was found. Eventually Mr. Cotterman was returned to the United States and indicted but the District Court suppressed the evidence and the government appealed.

The Ninth Circuit reversed. The issue considered by the Ninth Circuit is instructive:

> This watershed case implicates both the scope of the narrow border search exception to the Fourth Amendment's warrant requirement and privacy rights

---

112. *Supra* note 110, at 954.

113. *Supra* note 110, Sotomayor Concurrence at 957.

114. United States v. Warshalk, United States Court of Appeals for the Sixth Circuit, Nos. 08-3997/4085/4087/4212/4429; 09-3176, Argued: June 16, 2010, Decided and Filed: December 14, 2010, recommended for full publication.

115. The Stored Communications Act ("SCA"), 18 U.S.C. §§ 2701 et seq.

116. Warshalk, *supra* n. 114 at 9.

117. United States v. Cotterman, United States Court of Appeals for the Ninth Circuit, No. 09–10139. Decided: March 8, 2013.

in commonly used electronic devices. The question we confront "is what limits there are upon this power of technology to shrink the realm of guaranteed privacy." Kyllo v. United States, 533 U.S. 27, 34, 121 S.Ct. 2038, 150 L.Ed.2d 94 (2001). More specifically, we consider the reasonableness of a computer search that began as a cursory review at the border but transformed into a forensic examination of Cotterman's hard drive.[118]

The Court considered some three decades of Supreme Court affirmation of the extended border search exception to the Fourth Amendment but also considered that technology has provided us with the tools to put our lives on small devices and most of us do just that. Accordingly, the *en banc* court followed other decisions holding that a reasonable suspicion must predicate a forensic border search of things like laptops and smart phones, noting how much information we put on these devices — an alert of a 15-year-old offense was not sufficient but the totality of the circumstances afforded the reasonable suspicion.[119] Clearly the Ninth, Sixth and D.C. Circuits, and Justice Sotomayor, believe that technology is changing what is socially acceptable in the United States. As of this writing the National Security Agency's collection of third party data has begun to accelerate the issue social acceptance and what is a reasonable expectation of privacy.[120]

In sum, Fourth Amendment law in the arena of national security has been sharpened considerably since the 1980s, and it is likely that, as technology modifies the way Americans live, it will undergo further analysis and modification. In that respect, Justice Powell's analysis of *Keith*, which made clear the need for flexibility of process to meet the exigencies of national security, will likely continue to serve as the departure point for future, presently unknown issues.

The Fifth Amendment

Unlike the Fourth Amendment, the Fifth has had only marginal impact on national security issues. However, the limited impact that it has includes personnel security in a way that affects directly a great many persons — primarily those employed by or contracting with the federal government. The Fifth Amendment reads as follows:

> No person shall be held to answer for a capital or otherwise infamous crime, unless on a presentment or indictment of a Grand Jury, except in cases arising in the land or naval forces, or in the Militia, when in actual service in time of war or public danger; nor shall any person be subject for the same offence to be twice put in jeopardy of life or limb; nor shall be compelled in any criminal case to be a witness against himself, nor be deprived of life, liberty, or property,

---

118. *Id.* at 2.

119. The en banc court held that the border agents had reasonable suspicion to conduct an initial search at the border (which turned up no incriminating material) and the forensic examination. The en banc court wrote that the defendant's Treasury Enforcement Communication System alert, prior child-related conviction, frequent travels, crossing from a country known for sex tourism, and collection of electronic equipment, plus the parameters of the Operation Angel Watch program aimed at combating child sex tourism, taken collectively, gave rise to reasonable suspicion of criminal activity. *Id.* at 3.

120. Not particularly germane to this article, but of interest also, the en banc court explained that a border search of a computer is not transformed into an "extended border search" requiring particularized suspicion simply because the device is transported and examined beyond the border. *Id.* at 2.

without due process of law; nor shall private property be taken for public use, without just compensation.

The Federal Employee and the Fifth Amendment

Personnel security is a vexing part of much federal employment law and procedure. A great many persons must have access to information that is classified in the interests of national security. This requires background investigations to probe for loyalty or instability, the physical means to protect information, limitation of access to those with a "need to know," and training of personnel on their personal responsibilities. It was the post-World War II era, and bi-polar nuclear threats, that generated much of the perceived need, as well as the procedure to govern this somewhat arcane area of national security law.

In 1953, President Eisenhower issued Executive Order 10,450,[121] which mandates that employment in the federal work force be "clearly consistent with the interests of the national security." Subsequently, the clearance of an aeronautical engineer employed by a contractor of defense equipment was summarily revoked and, in consequence, he lost his job because he was unable, then, to perform his work. He challenged his discharge on Fifth Amendment grounds, claiming that the action of the Defense Department, based on informant statements, deprived him of Fifth Amendment "property" and "due process." The issues worked their way to the Supreme Court in 1959, where Chief Justice Warren, writing for the Court, eschewed the substantive issues but held that the petitioner had been denied his right to a confrontational hearing and remanded on due process grounds.[122] It is, of course, obvious that the Court did not hold that Mr. Green had a right to a security clearance, only that it could not be removed without notice and opportunity to be heard.

From that point on, there were a great many security clearance issues that gave birth to both regulatory schematics and judicial reviews. Civil Service law and regulations were enacted that permitted adverse actions only for the efficiency of the service[123] and only after a hearing and a decision based on a preponderance of the evidence.[124] Congress also enacted a separate law that would give agency heads summary dismissal power to be used when removal is necessary or advisable in the interest of national security (that is, when a confrontational hearing would, itself, cause harm to national security).[125]

This scheme was tested in 1988 when a security clearance was revoked based on a criminal conviction and being a felon in possession of a firearm. The U.S. Navy revoked a security clearance pursuant to Civil Service law and regulations, causing Egan to lose his job as a welder aboard Navy vessels. Mr. Egan challenged the standard of review, initiating a checkered history of decision-making from the initial hearing level of the Merit Systems Protection Board, through the Federal Circuit, and finally to the Supreme Court. Justice Blackman wrote the Court's opinion, laying to rest many issues that had persisted since *Green v. McElroy.*

In *Department of the Navy v. Egan,*[126] the Court concurred with the statement of the Federal Circuit which had held that the traditional presumption of appellate review is

---

121. Exec. Order No. 10,450, 18 Fed. Reg. 2489 (1953).
122. *See* Green v. McElroy, 360 U.S. 474 (1959).
123. 5 U.S.C. § 7513(a) (1994).
124. *Id.* at § 7501(c)(1).
125. *Id.* at § 7532.
126. Department of the Navy v. Egan, 484 U.S. 518 (1988).

strong, but Justice Blackman, perhaps in reference to the nautical origins of the case, then noted that this presumption "runs aground" when it encounters concerns of national security. Noting that the Court previously had confirmed the President's compelling need to withhold national security information from unauthorized persons,[127] and that no one has a right to a security clearance, the Court affirmed the discretionary nature of granting clearance through predictive judgment made by those with expertise in protecting classified information. In the final analysis, reversing the Federal Circuit, the Court held that the "preponderance of the evidence" standard used by the Merit Systems Protection Board pursuant to 5 U.S.C. § 7701(c)(1)(B) is inconsistent with the principle that security clearances will be granted only if "clearly consistent with the interest of the national security."[128]

Egan is a powerful tool for national security, but it does not answer all the issues, and the actual holding is based on a finding that there was no evidence that Congress, in enacting legislation, had any intent to change the discretion of the executive branch in granting or denying security clearances. One difficult issue concerns the Amendment's guarantee against compelled self-incrimination, which backs up into one frequently used tool for assessing suitability for access to classified information, the polygraph.

In 1983, President Reagan issued National Security Decision Directive 84,[129] which required agencies who had employees with access to classified information to revise regulations that would require employees with that access to submit to polygraph examinations when appropriate, in the course of investigations of unauthorized disclosures of classified information. That NSDD was soon withdrawn, but use of the polygraph is extensive at CIA, NSA, and FBI, and to a lesser extent in Department of Defense elements. In a case that combined both Fourth and Fifth Amendment challenges, Ann Stehney, a contract employee working on NSA tasks, brought suit for loss of clearance and termination when she refused to take a polygraph.

The plaintiff in *Stehney v. Perry*[130] argued that the polygraph was a search not based on probable cause. The case turned primarily on the Fourth Amendment, for which the Court provided extensive citations to deny the search claim. Fifth Amendment issues, although argued, were not directly addressed. However, there are issues to keep in mind. For example, not all employees are subject to a polygraph, so one might claim denial of the Amendment's clause on equal protection. That was rejected in 1986 in *Anderson v. City of Philadelphia*.[131] A more serious concern is the holding of *Green v. McElroy* that "the right to hold specific private employment and to follow a chosen profession free from unreasonable governmental interference comes within the 'liberty' and 'property' concepts of the Fifth Amendment."[132]

In any case, this District Court opinion, which upheld mandatory polygraph testing, remains suspect for its breadth — if for no other reason than that the technique has never been judicially tested for its invasive nature. For example, mandatory blood tests are not considered "uniquely" invasive and are therefore routinely upheld. Could a polygraph be

---

127. Snepp v. United States, 444 U.S. 507, 509 n. 3 (1980).

128. The Eisenhower standard has been carried forward in subsequent executive orders prescribing conditions for eligibility for access to classified information. As of this writing, the current Executive Order is 12,968, 60 Fed. Reg. 40,245 (1955).

129. *Reprinted in Review of the President's National Security Directive 84 and Proposed Dept. of Defense Directive on Polygraph Use: Hearings before the Legislation and National Security Subcomm. of the House Comm. on Government Operations*, 98th Cong., 1st Sess. 222 (1984).

130. Stehney v. Perry, 907 F. Supp. 806 (D. N.J. 1995).

131. Anderson v. City of Philadelphia, 845 F.2d 1216 (3d Cir. 1986).

132. Green v. McElroy, 360 U.S. 474, 492 (1959).

more intrusive that physically invading the body? Well, perhaps! A polygraph might be considered uniquely invasive because, depending on the questions asked, it could be likened to a mental "strip search." Perhaps more to the point, it might be considered testimonial in nature, which, of course, would invoke directly the Fifth Amendment. As time passes and as polygraphs continue to be used routinely, that becomes less and less likely, but some issues, possibly approaching a constitutional dimension, have never been concretely addressed.

Another issue approaching Fifth Amendment guarantees concerns discretionary authority to terminate an employee. *Webster v. Doe*[133] arose from the decision of the Director of the CIA to fire Doe. That action was taken pursuant to a statutory grant of authority to the Director to terminate an employee when he deemed it "necessary or advisable in the interests of the United States."[134] Doe then claimed various constitutional and statutory violations, including a due process argument for arbitrary and capricious decision-making. The District Court had granted partial summary judgment. The Court of Appeals vacated that decision but affirmed that the arbitrary and capricious due process claim was reviewable. On certiorari, a divided Supreme Court held that the discretion of the Director was statutorily unreviewable but that constitutional challenges could still be made. At least two justices dissented on the grounds that a matter may not be both reviewable and unreviewable, prompting a question as to where the law actually is.

Assuming that one is looking for firm answers, this brief overview of Fifth Amendment issues in personnel law leads to somewhat unsatisfying conclusions. *Green v. McElroy* had no difficulty in finding that the plaintiff had a Fifth Amendment interest in his job that, at least under the procedures enacted by the Department of Defense, required the safeguards of confrontation and cross examination to terminate. That decision was based on regulations in effect and avoided the fundamental national security issue of whether a departure from the norm of fair procedures might be available, or even what limits might exist for either congressional or executive authority.

Egan answered many of the outstanding questions and took a step that *Green* had declined to do. *Egan* ruled explicitly that the presumption of reviewability did not apply to "concerns of national security." At bottom, however, *Egan* merely holds that Congress did not intend to authorize the Merit Systems Protection Board to review the merits of security clearance decisions. Still, *Egan* may have an effect larger than its holding. In *dicta*, it strongly approves the President's plenary constitutional classification and clearance authority and notes that courts owe deference to that authority. Not only is this clear guidance, but the difference in approach between the two decisions is stark. *Green* requires the government to accept the full burden and focuses on the effect of adverse decision on the employee. *Egan* barely pauses for employee rights—except to note the lack of them and foreclose administrative (perhaps even judicial) review of the discretionary, predictive judgment of the Executive as to a person's suitability for access to national security information.

When the issue arose again in *Doe v. Webster*, the effect of *Egan* was immediately apparent as the presumption of reviewability, at least for nonconstitutional claims, was unavailable. What is left is the question of reviewability for constitutional claims. An earlier case, *United States v. Robel*,[135] provides some guidance. In that case, Congress had enacted legislation prohibiting any member of a Communist-action organization to engage

---

133. Webster v. Doe, 486 U.S. 592 (1988).
134. 50 U.S.C. § 403-4(g) (2000).
135. United States v. Robel, 389 U.S. 258 (1967).

in any employment in any defense facility.[136] Although it took pains to acknowledge national security concerns, the Court found too great a burden on First Amendment activities to sustain the law or its effect. It did not completely reject the concept, but it did insist on a more narrowly drawn statute that would not so drastically impact First Amendment freedoms. If nothing else, however, this decision confirms what many federal and contractor employees already know—that they have a diminished expectation of rights if employed in the heavily-regulated, security apparatus of government. However, the problem for the government is obvious. The disgruntled employee will always claim constitutional infringement as the means to get to court.

Liberty and Property

In 1986, the International Court of Justice held that U.S. financial support of Contra paramilitary activities against the Sandinista government in Nicaragua was a violation of both treaty and customary international law. Soon thereafter, the *Committee of U.S. Citizens Living in Nicaragua v. Reagan*[137] used that judgment to seek injunctive and declaratory relief on a variety of grounds. One argument they proposed was based on the Fifth Amendment. Plaintiffs alleged that the Contras had deprived them of liberty and property and that since they were partly funded by the U.S. government, the government should be liable.

The government, in argument at trial, did not dispute the merits of the ICJ opinion, rather it was argued that Congress was aware of the decision and chose to ignore it. On that basis, the Court held that not every violation of a legal norm constitutes a justiciable injury, that Congress could not be held to have acted arbitrarily since they consciously ignored the opinion and that, in any case, the ICJ holding reflected a breach of duty between two sovereigns without reference to individuals. The attempt to turn a violation of international law into a Fifth Amendment claim was soundly rejected.

Although it was never adjudicated, a similar issue arose in a domestic context. During the Vietnam War, the CIA instituted Operation CHAOS, which was designed to identify and monitor domestic critics of the war. Some of the individuals monitored eventually brought suit on various constitutional grounds, including denial of due process under the Fifth Amendment.

A claim of state secrets[138] precluded litigation, but a question remains. Suppose the plaintiffs had otherwise been entitled to damages under the Federal Tort Claims Act; might this not be an instance of uncompensated injury without due process? A partial answer might arise from an FBI case.

Hobson v. Wilson[139] arose from Operation COINTELPRO, in which the FBI engaged in a number of activities that interfered with lawful political activities of "Black Nationalist" and "New Left" organizations and individual members. At trial, the Court found violations of First Amendment associational rights and Fifth Amendment rights affording protection from emotional distress and impairment of reputation and earning capacity. The Appellate Court found that the plaintiffs were entitled to relief under a variety of theories, to include

---

136. Subversive Activities Control Act of 1950, 64 Stat. 992, 50 U.S.C. § 784(a)(1)(D) (2000).
137. Committee of U.S. Citizens Living in Nicaragua v. Reagan, 859 F.2d 929 (D.C. Cir. 1988).
138. *See* Halkin v. Helms, 690 F.2d 977 (D.C. Cir. 1982).
139. *See* Hobson v. Wilson, 737 F.2d 1 (D.C. Cir. 1984), *cert. denied sub nom.* Brennan v. Hobson, 470 U.S. 1084 (1985).

under the Constitution alone. Assuming the injuries in *Hobson* and *Halkin* were similar, it would appear that the extraordinary exercise of State Secrets Privilege is available to trump even a constitutionally-based claim.

Another niche of Fifth Amendment law and lore is one that needs little explanation. Fred Korematsu was an American of Japanese ancestry who, during World War II, was convicted for remaining in California after a military order prescribed internment at inland locations for all persons of Japanese descent. Presumably the authority flowed from Executive Order 9,066, which authorized military commanders to prescribe "military areas" from which any or all persons could be excluded. As a matter of law, however, analysis isn't so easy.

The Supreme Court upheld the conviction based on military necessity, but the decision was less than satisfying. The Court refused to consider racial prejudice but opinions were spread across the landscape. Justice Jackson, in what amounts to an extraordinary commentary on the perceived crisis, dissented on the law but suggested that judicial interference would have been inappropriate anyway. The footnote to the personal aspect of the case came from a writ of *coram nobis* in 1984 when Judge Patel vacated the conviction based on recently discovered evidence of prosecutorial misconduct. The larger issue came to a head a year earlier when survivors and descendants filed claims based on several constitutional rights, with the Fifth Amendment claim for equal protection and forfeiture of liberty and property without due process figuring prominently. At trial it was held that all but the real and personal property and contract rights of the Fifth Amendment claim was barred by sovereign immunity and that was barred by the statute of limitations. Nevertheless, presumably because constitutional values had been breached, in 1988 Congress appropriated $1.2 billion in compensation. It is difficult to square the State Secrets result of *Halkin* with the sovereign immunity consideration of this case, except to note that the *Halkin* decision was based on a common law privilege that precluded evaluation of the case on the merits.

The Japanese resettlement cases dealt with both immigrant aliens and citizens but treated the two classes equally shamefully. Recently, the immigrant alien has again become a matter of national attention. September 11, 2001, prompted an uncomfortable awareness that even small groups of aliens could cause catastrophic events. This inspired a dedicated effort to remove those who were not entitled to be here. In the course of alien immigration proceedings, it has not been unusual to find that classified intelligence information would be presented, *ex parte* and *in camera*, to the immigration court. This generates a poignant tension between the needs of national security and due process rights of the respondent alien.

It is not hard to find competing opinions on the fundamental issues — whether in the national media or in academia. One finds substantial numbers of commentaries to the effect that secret evidence produced in immigration proceedings denies the Sixth Amendment right to confrontation and the Fifth Amendment right to due process. More generous, but equally off the mark, are articles that analyze the issues in terms of federal court cases, the Alien Terrorist Removal Court procedures, and/or the Classified Information Procedures Act. Some of the latter category argue that the executive branch simply needs to construct better procedures.

What these arguments, as a rule, fail to recognize is fundamental to the process. First, immigration proceedings are administrative hearings that consider information, not evidence. Second, the right of confrontation is a criminal standard, not an administrative one. Third, an immigration decison does not award punishment. It might cause hardship, deportation or detention, but administering the rules that permit, or deny, the presence in the United States of an alien is not administration of punishment.[140] Finally, and perhaps most importantly, due process is not an absolute value. Tritely put, due process is whatever process is due. Certainly due process is heightened in a criminal trial, but it is less demanding in an administrative hearing because the results are not of equal merit. Criminal punishment and administrative rulings are not equivalent, and the courts have made that clear.

The Supreme Court has had a long struggle with these issues. In 2001, the Court was faced with a situation in which a large number of aliens were, pursuant to law and regulation, being held in detention after having been found deportable. The problem the Court addressed, however, was that there was no place to which they could be deported. In that circumstance of indefinite detention, the Court held that due process required them to be released.[141] When they addressed a related issue in 2003, the holding was substantively different. Hyung Joon Kim was a lawful permanent resident, with significantly more rights than the aliens the court freed two years earlier, but as a convicted felon, Kim also was deportable. He was detained by the Immigration and Naturalization Service pending deportation as provided by statute and regulation. Considering his substantial contacts in the country, and with no information presented that he was a danger to the community or a flight risk, both District and Circuit Courts found his detention a violation of the Fifth Amendment. Other Circuits had reached similar holdings in immigration cases.[142]

The Supreme Court disagreed. Chief Justice Rehnquist, writing for the majority made clear one issue that is often overlooked in these administrative hearings—that any policy toward aliens is interwoven with contemporaneous policies of foreign relations, the war power, and the maintenance of a republican form of government.[143] The Court also repeated an assertion made previously that Congress may make rules for aliens that would be unacceptable if applied to citizens. While they recognized that the Fifth Amedment entitles aliens to due process of law in deportation proceedings,[144] it also recognized that detention is a constitutionally valid aspect of deportation proceedings. Deportation proceedings "would be in vain if those accused could not be held in custody pending the inquiry into their true character."[145] The Court drew upon a number of disparate but related holdings, some with vintage labels, to cobble together a more coherent concept of Fifth Amendment guarantees at the intersection of national security and immigration issues. At bottom it was a reasonableness holding—due process is the process that is due under the circumstances, taking into account the status of the individual.

For aliens who have no substantial nexus to the United States, such as domicile or residence, the decision of an administrative officer, acting under powers granted by Congress, to admit or exclude *is* due process.[146] Even an alien who is returning to the United States from abroad gains no status superior to an entering alien and may be excluded by the Attorney General without a hearing on the basis of secret and undisclosed information,[147] but secrecy in the hearing is a subject on which we have not yet heard the last word.[148] The most that may be said in favor of the alien is that notice and opportunity

---

140. *See* Harisiades v. Shaughnessy, 342 U.S. 580 (1952).

141. Zadvydas v. Davis, 533 U.S. 678, 699 (2001).

142. *See* Demore v. Yyung Joon Kim, 538 U.S. 510 (2003)

143. *Id.* citing Matthews v. Diaz, 426 U.S. 67, at 81 n. 17.

144. Reno v. Flores, 507 U.S. 292, 306 (1993).

145. Wong Wing v. United States, 163 U.S. 228, 235 (1896).

146. United States v. Ju Toy, 198 U.S. 353, 263 (1905).

147. Shaughnessy v. United States, *ex rel.* Mezel, 345 U.S. 206 (1953).

148. Regarding the post-9/11 detention hearing, there has now been a split in the Circuits, though not precisely on the same issues. *Detroit Free Press, Inc. v. Ashcroft,* 303 F.3d 681 (6th Cir. 2002), and

to be heard are required,[149] but the hearing need not be a full disclosure of the considerations, particularly if information pertaining to national security forms the basis for the cause of exclusion, removal, or deportation.[150] The angst over ethical treatment of aliens in the post-9/11 era probably means that the final chapter for administrative hearings is yet to be written, but comparing these hearings to actual criminal process yields some guidance for the processes that merit a lesser standard of review.

The final issue arises in the context with which the public is most familiar—the criminal process. In the context of national security, this generally arises when a defendant contends that classified information is necessary for his/her defense. It will come as no surprise to anyone that claims of need are often greatly exaggerated in an effort to persuade the government to drop criminal charges. Through the years, this tactic was relatively successful and many prosecutions were withheld in the interest of protecting national security. The reason is a simple one. Criminal charges simply cannot be pursued if the government refuses to cooperate in the discovery of all relevant information, or to let all admissible information be introduced into evidence.[151] "[I]t is unconscionable to allow [the government] to undertake prosecution and then invoke its governmental privileges to deprive the accused of anything which might be material to his defense."[152] Hence, if a colorable claim of need could be sustained, the government was often forced to choose between maintaining secrets and prosecution.

This rule represents fundamental fairness, but it also enabled a great many defendants to escape prosecution through what came to be known as "graymail." Threatened exposure of government secrets was a powerful lever for many years. Then, in 1980, the Congress passed the Classified Information Procedures Act (CIPA).[153] CIPA did not eliminate graymail, but it does permit the government, well in advance, to present and litigate issues of relevance and admissibility *in camera* and, if necessary, *ex parte*. Basically, the statute permits the government to make decisions in stages rather than, as before, to place all the eggs in one basket and guess where the rulings and the evidence might lead. It permits substitutions of evidence, and similar alternatives, so long as the defendant is not prejudiced thereby. CIPA does not modify rules of evidence, but it advances the time in which decisions may be made.

CIPA was enacted with the primary purpose of easing the problem of graymail, but it also recognizes the right of the defendant to all relevant and admissible evidence—even if it is classified. This would obviously be necessary if the charged conduct is classified, but it might also be necessary to obtain information about the defendant that is in the possession of the government or to help explain material facts about the charged conduct. The other side of the coin is that defendants have claimed that the notice requirements of CIPA *per se* violate Fifth Amendment rights because defendants are required to disclose much of the defense case in the early *in camera* relevancy and admissibility hearings. Those arguments have been rejected by the courts.[154]

North Jersey Media Group Inc. v. Ashcroft, 308 F.3d 198 (3d Cir. 2002), have taken different approaches to secret proceedings. As of this writing, it is not yet known if the issues are sufficiently concrete that they will be the subject of a petition for certiorari.

149. *See* Kwong Hai Chew v. Colding, 344 U.S. 590, 596 (1953).

150. Jay v. Boyd, 351 U.S. 345 (1956). Suspension of deportation is not a matter of right, but of grace.

151. *See* United States v. Nixon, 418 U.S. 683, 711 (1974); Jencks v. United States, 353 U.S. 657, 670–72 (1957).

152. United States v. Reynolds, 345 U.S. 1, 12 (1953).

153. Classified Information Procedures Act (CIPA), 18 U.S.C. App. §§ 1 et seq. (1982).

154. *See, e.g.*, United States v. Collins, 720 F.2d 1195, 1200 (11th Cir. 1983).

Conclusions

The law relating to matters of national security remains today a work in progress. Its development has been uncertain because the law depends for its content and focus on actions that sometimes have little, if any, counterpart to normal, substantive law. At other times there is a considerable overlap, but even with two centuries of experience, settled law offers scant guidance when personal liberties and national security collide. In a simpler era, when national security meant fending off foreign aggression, the President was free to engage espionage agents, send military forces into harm's way, and even take extraordinary measures within national borders without challenge. Congress provided funding, but little else, and was content to leave the national security arena to the Executive.

Today, national security is far more complex than even a few decades ago. To the extent that the problems of investigating national security issues in the United States are similar to those of standard criminal investigations, including those we label domestic security investigations, we have had to struggle to honor constitutional safeguards. However, through the years we have learned that the distinctions, when they are drawn, emanate from the origin of the threat. The rules are thus more relaxed when it can be shown that surveillance is designed to target one or more foreign powers or their agents. Yet experience demonstrates that "U.S. Persons" are as capable of serving a foreign master or wreaking catastrophic damage as any other. Witness, for example, Aldrich Ames and Timothy McVeigh.

The trial-and-error method has, to date, shown us that it is reasonable for the President to exercise extraordinary powers to protect the national security so long as the threat is of foreign origin. Procedurally, the Congress has taken some steps both to aid and to regulate the Executive, but has not sought to displace the claim of executive authority in this arena. The Fourth Amendment has shaped national security law primarily through restricting unfettered discretion for search and surveillance. Although quantitatively limited in application, the resultant law that has developed around application of the Fourth Amendment to national security issues has been high profile and sharply scrutinized, but a body of law, both judicial and legislative, has emerged that offers fair guidance.

By contrast, the application of Fifth Amendment values to national security issues has occupied a significantly lower profile, but has affected a great many more people. While great deference has been shown to the Executive by both the Legislature and Judiciary in Fourth Amendment law, they have shown perhaps even more deference with respect to Fifth Amendment issues. One reason for this is that the exposure of privacy interests is both more regulated (that is, more formatted) and more protected (by law and regulation) than is the case with search and seizure issues. Polygraph and security questionnaires, for example, may lay bare significant privacy concerns, but their exposure is likely limited to a select handful of persons whose job it is to evaluate and then to protect the information developed.

For either Amendment, however, the lesson to be drawn for analysis of permissible executive branch responses to national security threats seems to stem directly from the *Keith* case. Justice Powell presented the issue this way:

> Our present inquiry, though important, is therefore a narrow one.... Whether safeguards other than prior authorization by a magistrate would satisfy the Fourth Amendment in a situation involving the national security.... The determination of this question requires the essential Fourth Amendment inquiry into the 'reasonableness' of the search and seizure in question, and the way in which that

'reasonableness' derives content and meaning through reference to the warrant clause.[155]

Although *Keith* addressed only the Fourth Amendment issues, case law such as *Kim* seems to indicate that it is the standard Justice Powell applied that is relevant to the intersection of personal liberties and national security issues. If the government is "reasonable" in its approach to national security threats, constitutional standards may be different from (such as, warrantless surveillance or surveillance with different standards) or additional to (for example, security clearances) those we would demand in a "normal" situation.

Selected Bibliography

Schulhofer, Stephen, *More Essential than Ever: The Fourth Amendment in the Twenty First Century (Inalienable Rights)* (2012).

Musch, Donald, *Civil Liberties and the Foreign Intelligence Surveillance Act* (2003).

Atkin, Michelle Louise, *Balancing Liberty and Security: An Ethical Study of U.S. Foreign Intelligence Surveillance, 2001–2009* (2011).

Yoo, John,*Confronting Terror: 9/11 and the Future of American National Security* (2011).

Sulmasy, Glenn, *The National Security Court System: A Natural Evolution of Justice in an Age of Terror* (2009).

---

155. United States v. U.S. Dist. Court for Eastern Dist. of Mich., Southern Division, 92 S.Ct. 2125, 2133 (1972).

Chapter 27

The Foreign Intelligence Surveillance Act

Molly Bishop Shadel

In this chapter:

Introduction

The Foreign Intelligence Surveillance Act (FISA)[1] enables the government to conduct electronic surveillances and physical searches of property being used in the United States by foreign powers or agents of a foreign power. It differs from the surveillance and search powers granted to the government in criminal cases under Title III of the U.S. criminal code[2] in that it does not require a showing of criminal activity; instead, a FISA warrant is issued upon showing that the target is a foreign power or an agent of a foreign power. This once-obscure statute catapulted to national prominence after the September 11, 2001 terrorist attacks on the World Trade Center and the Pentagon, proving a powerful tool to enable the intelligence community to fight foreign national security threats. It gained notoriety after Edward Snowden's disclosure of thousands of classified documents in 2013, which he obtained while working as a contractor for the National Security Agency (NSA). These documents revealed the existence of NSA surveillance activities authorized under FISA, causing a national debate about the wisdom and legality of mass surveillance programs.

This chapter will discuss the history of FISA; the authorities available under FISA; oversight mechanisms; challenges to FISA; and how FISA has changed as a result of the September 11 attacks.

---

1. 50 U.S.C.A. §§ 1801–1871.
2. 18 U.S.C.A. § 2518.

Historical Overview: Intelligence Abuses
in the 20th Century

Before FISA was enacted, the FBI conducted domestic surveillance related to national security threats without first obtaining a warrant, believing that the President possessed inherent Constitutional authority to conduct warrantless electronic surveillance for national security purposes.[3]

In the wake of the Watergate scandal and Congressional proceedings considering the impeachment of President Nixon in 1974, the Senate became alarmed by allegations of intelligence service misdeeds. Therefore, it established an investigating body, called the Church Committee, headed by Senator Frank Church of Idaho.[4] During 1975, the Church Committee interviewed over 800 officials and conducted numerous hearings probing intelligence abuses by the Central Intelligence Agency (CIA), the Federal Bureau of Investigation (FBI), and the NSA. The Committee detailed many executive branch abuses in a multi-volume report issued in 1976.[5]

The Church Committee determined that, for decades, presidents had been authorizing the FBI to conduct electronic surveillance on United States citizens whose views might be politically disruptive. For example, in 1946, President Truman issued an authorization for the Attorney General to approve wiretaps to investigate "subversive activity" and to protect "domestic security."[6] During the Eisenhower, Kennedy and Johnson administrations, the FBI wiretapped the Nation of Islam. During the Johnson administration, Attorney General Robert Kennedy approved FBI requests for wiretaps on the Ku Klux Klan, Malcom X, and Dr. Martin Luther King.[7] During the Johnson and Nixon eras, the FBI conducted electronic surveillance on Vietnam War protestors, "accumulate[ing] massive information on lawful activity and law-abiding citizens for vaguely defined 'pure intelligence' and 'preventive intelligence' purposes related only remotely or not at all to law enforcement or the prevention of violence."[8] The FBI also developed a covert program known as COINTELPRO to harass and disrupt the activities of dissenters and anti-war protestors.[9] Warrantless surveillance by the FBI of purely domestic activity — that is, activity of domestic rather than foreign groups — was declared illegal in 1972 by the Supreme Court in *United States v. United States Court for the Eastern District of Michigan,*[10] commonly known as the *Keith* case (after the district court judge named as the respondent), but prior to this decision, the activity was commonplace.

The Church Committee also learned that the executive branch was collecting domestic political information incidentally during the course of investigations that were launched

---

3. *See* U.S. v. U.S. Dist. Court for Eastern Dist. of Mich., Southern Division, 407 U.S. 297, 92 S. Ct. 2125, 32 L. Ed. 2d 752 (1972) (in a case of the wiretap of a domestic organization, the Supreme Court rejected government's arguments that the President had inherent authority to conduct electronic surveillance to protect the national security, but left unresolved the question of whether the President could conduct warrantless electronic surveillance for foreign intelligence purposes).

4. *See* S. Res. 21 (Jan. 27, 1975) (establishing the Senate Select Committee to Study Governmental Operations with Respect to Intelligence Authorities).

5. Senate Select Committee to Study Governmental Operations With Respect to Intelligence Activities, S. Rep. No. 94-755 (1976) (available at http://www.intelligence.senate.gov/pdfs94th/94755_II.pdf) [hereinafter Church Report].

6. Church Report Book II at 62.

7. *Id.* at 63.

8. *Id.* at 68.

9. *Id.* at 69.

10. 407 U.S. at 297, 92 S. Ct. at 2125, 32 L. Ed. 2d at 752 (1972).

initially to investigate foreign activity. For example, in 1961 and 1962, the Kennedy Administration was concerned that a sugar bill might be enacted containing quotas favorable to the Dominican Republic. Attorney General Robert Kennedy therefore authorized a number of wiretaps on three executive branch officials, two American lobbyists working on behalf of the Dominican Republic, a staff member of a House of Representatives Committee, and on U.S. Congressman Harold D. Cooley, the Chairman of the House Agricultural Committee. While the investigation initially began because of concerns about the activities of a foreign power, the Kennedy administration was also interested in the political outcome of the legislative wrangling, the Church Committee concluded.[11] Presidents Johnson and Nixon also used FBI foreign intelligence wiretaps to acquire domestic political intelligence for the White House.[12]

The Church Committee found one instance of the FBI instituting an electronic surveillance of a foreign target for the purpose of intercepting the communications of an American citizen, a process known as "reverse targeting." According to an FBI memorandum, President Johnson was concerned that the South Vietnamese were attempting to sabotage peace negotiations in the hope that it would cause Richard Nixon to be elected president and take a harder line with North Vietnam. The FBI therefore began surveillance of Anna Chennault, a prominent Republican and an "American citizen who could not be legitimately surveilled directly."[13]

The Church Committee reported that the FBI was not the only agency engaged in warrantless electronic surveillance. The NSA was created in 1952 to conduct "signals intelligence," or communications by electronic means. The NSA is limited to collecting foreign communications, which it has interpreted to include communications between the United States and a foreign country.[14] The Church Committee found that the NSA, under a secret arrangement with three United States telegraph companies, intercepted millions of private telegrams sent from, to, or through the United States between 1947 and 1975 in a program called Operation Shamrock.[15] The NSA in the 1960s and 1970s also began intercepting information on American individuals and organizations who might cause "civil disturbances or otherwise subvert the national security of the United States," under a program called Operation Minaret.[16]

Similarly, the Church Committee reported that the CIA undertook an extensive program of domestic spying on Americans from 1967–1974, called the CHAOS program. Operation CHAOS was designed to investigate racial, antiwar and other protest activity in the United States to look for foreign influence over these activities.[17] The CIA's actions were particularly controversial because the CIA's statutory charter directs it to focus on foreign intelligence matters, not domestic matters.[18]

---

11. Church Report Book II at 200–201.
12. *Id.* at 70.
13. *Id.* at 120.
14. *Id.* at 104.
15. *Id.* at 6.
16. *Id.* at 104–105.
17. Church Report Book III at 681.
18. *Id.*

Congress' Reaction: The Enactment of FISA in 1978

In response to the Church Committee's report, Congress enacted the Foreign Intelligence Surveillance Act in 1978.[19] FISA is designed to provide a check on the government's power by limiting when it can conduct electronic surveillance and physical searches in the United States for foreign intelligence purposes. Warrantless searches and electronic surveillances are prohibited; instead, the government must obtain a warrant from the Foreign Intelligence Surveillance Court before undertaking electronic surveillance or physical searches of agents of foreign powers within the United States. The statute limits the targeting of "United States persons" (American citizens, permanent resident aliens, associations comprised substantially of U.S. citizens or permanent resident aliens, or corporations in-corporated in the U.S.).[20] It prohibits "reverse targeting" of the kind that was done on Anna Chennault, described above (that is, targeting an agent of a foreign power in the hope of acquiring communications of a U.S. citizen against whom there is no probable cause sufficient to obtain a warrant). It also requires that the government take certain steps to reduce its intrusion on the privacy of U.S. persons by redacting ("minimizing") information acquired during its foreign intelligence collections.

FISA Today: How to Obtain a FISA Warrant

Requests for FISA warrants usually originate with the FBI or NSA, which are the only two executive agencies that have publicly disclosed using FISA (and are the only executive agencies authorized to engage in the kind of activities that would require a FISA order).[21] Imagine, then, that the FBI has been investigating a target that it believes is a spy or a terrorist, and wants to tap that person's cellphone, read his e-mail, and search his home.

Elements of the Application

The FBI gathers the information necessary to show the following:

(1) *The application must show probable cause to believe that the target is a foreign power or an agent of a foreign power.*[22]

The application must specify who is being searched or electronically surveilled, and why the target may be searched or surveilled. This requires a showing that the target is a foreign power or an agent of a foreign power.

---

19. In 1978, the statute authorized electronic surveillance only. Pub. L. No. 95-511, 92 Stat. 1783 (1978); 50 U.S.C.A. §§ 1801–1811. In 1994, the statute was broadened to permit physical searches. Pub. L. No. 103-359 (1994); 50 U.S.C.A. §§ 1821–1829. In 1998, pen/trap surveillance and the production of business records were added. Pub. L. No. 105-272 (1998), 50 U.S.C.A. §§ 1841–1846, 1861–1862.

20. 50 U.S.C.A. § 1801(i).

21. Under Exec. Order No. 12333 § 2.4(a) (1981), the CIA may not "engage in electronic surveillance within the United States except for the purpose of training, testing, or conducting countermeasures to hostile electronic surveillance." That same Executive Order prohibits the NSA and the CIA from engaging in "[u]nconsented physical searches" in the United States. Exec. Order No. 12333 § 2.4(b). The FBI may obtain information from any lawful source, including the CIA, and can use that information to apply for a FISA order, but under Exec. Order No. 12333, only the FBI or the NSA would be authorized to conduct the activities that would require a FISA order.

22. *See* 50 U.S.C.A. §§ 1805(a)(2)(A) (electronic surveillance), 1824(a)(2)(A) (physical search).

FISA's definition of "foreign power" includes a foreign government, a group of nations, a foreign political faction, an entity controlled by a foreign government, or a terrorist group.[23] That means the FBI might show, for example, that the target is working for al Qaeda, or is an employee of a foreign embassy, or works for a bank wholly owned by a foreign country.

"Probable cause" is determined considering all the circumstances known about the target; if there is a fair probability that the target is a foreign power or an agent of a foreign power, then this part of the statute is satisfied. FISA provides that in determining probable cause, a judge "may consider past activities of the target, as well as facts and circumstances relating to current or future activities of the target."[24] This is similar to the standard for probable cause required in the criminal context, though the object of the probable cause is different. In a criminal warrant, an applicant must show probable cause that a crime is being committed; under FISA, the showing required is probable cause that the target is a foreign power or an agent of a foreign power.[25]

When the target is a United States person (defined above), the government has a higher probable cause standard to meet: it must show that the target is "knowingly" violating or about to violate criminal law. To be a FISA target, a U.S. person must be "knowingly" engaged in international terrorism;[26] "knowingly" engaged in clandestine intelligence gathering activities that "involved or are about to involve" a crime; knowingly engaged in criminal sabotage; or knowingly engaged in assuming a false or fraudulent identity while entering or within the United States.[27] So, for example, if a U.S. person donated money to a charitable organization that is actually a front for al Qaeda, but did not know about that connection, then the "knowingly" requirement of the statute has not been satisfied and the warrant will not be issued. A non-U.S. person can be a target under FISA simply for being an employee of a foreign government without engaging any wrongdoing, but a U.S. person must be knowingly breaking or about to break the law.

A U.S. person also cannot be found to be the agent of a foreign power solely on the basis of activities protected by the First Amendment.[28] A U.S. person's membership in a particular political or religious group, attendance at a controversial mosque, and statements

---

23. *See* 50 U.S.C.A. § 1801 (a) :
'Foreign power' means—
    (1) a foreign government or any component thereof, whether or not recognized by the United States;
    (2) a faction of a foreign nation or nations, not substantially composed of United States persons;
    (3) an entity that is openly acknowledged by a foreign government or governments to be directed and controlled by such foreign government or governments;
    (4) a group engaged in international terrorism or activities in preparation therefor;
    (5) a foreign-based political organization, not substantially composed of United States persons;
    (6) an entity that is directed and controlled by a foreign government or governments; or
    (7) an entity not substantially composed of United States persons that is engaged in the international proliferation of weapons of mass destruction.
24. 50 U.S.C.A. § 1805(c).
25. *See* David S. Kris & J. Douglas Wilson, National Security Investigations & Prosecutions § 11:5 2d, Vol. 1, (2012) [hereinafter Kris & Wilson].
26. 50 U.S.C.A. § 1801(b)(2)(C).
27. 50 U.S.C.A. § 1801(b)(2)(A)–(E).
28. 50 U.S.C.A. § 1805(a)(2)(A) and § 1824(a)(2)(A).

of dissatisfaction with the government will not suffice to establish him as an agent of a foreign power, while the same circumstances could give rise to a FISA on a non-U.S. person, depending on the totality of the circumstances.

If the target is engaged in terrorism, that terrorism must have an international tie. Some part of the activity must occur outside of the United States or must transcend national boundaries. Purely domestic terrorists like Timothy McVeigh, who bombed the federal building in Oklahoma City, are not within the reach of the FISA statute; instead, the government must use criminal law authorities.[29] The terrorist does not have to be formally recognized in order to qualify as an international terrorist group.[30] The group can have as few as two members to qualify as an international terrorist organization.[31] A terrorist operating alone (known as a "lone wolf" terrorist) and not working on behalf of a particular foreign power can also be subject to a FISA warrant, but only if he is a non-U.S. person and is engaged in international terrorism (requiring activities that occur outside the United States or transcend national boundaries).[32]

(2) *The application must contain a description of what is to be surveilled or searched and its connection to the target.*[33]

An application for electronic surveillance must describe "the type of communications or activities to be subjected to the surveillance"[34] and must establish that "each of the facilities or places at which the electronic surveillance is directed is being used, or is about to be used, by a foreign power or an agent of a foreign power."[35] For example, the FBI agent might show that the target has ordered a new telephone line, which will be activated tomorrow—that phone is "about to be used" by the target and therefore could be the subject of a FISA surveillance. Similarly, the agent could request a warrant to surveil the cellphone of the target's teenage daughter if he can show that the target also uses that phone, even though the contract for the phone is in the daughter's name. (This surveillance might therefore collect conversations between the daughter and her U.S. boyfriend unrelated to the foreign intelligence investigation, and those conversations would have to be minimized to protect their privacy—see "FISA's Minimization Requirements," below.) The statute also permits "roving" surveillance, which allows surveillance of targets to continue if they switch cellphones.[36]

Similarly, an application for a physical search must describe the premises or property to be searched, and must state that "the premises or property to be searched contains foreign intelligence information" and "is or is about to be owned, used, possessed by, or is in transit to or from a foreign power or an agent of a foreign power."[37] This might mean that the FBI agent could request a warrant to search the target's mail, or the house of his neighbor if he can show that the target stores his belongings there.

---

29. *See* FISA House Report at 30 (a group engaged in "terrorism of a purely domestic nature" is not an international terrorist group under the FISA statute).
30. *See* U.S. v. Benkahla, 437 F. Supp. 2d 541, 555 (E.D. Va. 2006).
31. *See* FISA House Report at 74.
32. *See* 50 U.S.C.A. § 1801(b)(1(C).
33. *See* 50 U.S.C.A. §§ 1805(a)(2)A) (electronic surveillance), 1824(a)(2)(A) (physical search).
34. 50 U.S.C.A. § 1804(a)(5).
35. 50 U.S.C.A. § 1804(a)(3)(B).
36. 50 U.S.C.A. § 1808(c)(2)(B).
37. 50 U.S.C.A. § 1823(a)(3)(C).

(3) *The application must contain a description of the information sought by search or surveillance.*[38]

FISA requires that the application for a warrant contain "a description of the nature of the foreign intelligence sought."[39] The application must certify that the information sought is "foreign intelligence information," which is defined as "information that relates to, and if concerning a United States person is necessary to, the ability of the United States to protect against" acts by a foreign power.[40] The FISA House Report states that "necessary" means that the information is "important and required," not merely "useful and convenient."[41] If the target is a non-U.S. Person, then the government need only show that the information is "relevant"; if a U.S. Person, the required showing is "necessary."

From the FBI to the U.S. Department of Justice, Office of Intelligence

Once the FBI has amassed the information required by the statute, it provides this information to the U.S. Department of Justice's Office of Intelligence.[42] The Office of Intelligence presents FISA applications to the Foreign Intelligence Surveillance Court (FISC),[43] and also serves a gatekeeping function. Before the Office of Intelligence will submit an application to the court, it puts the request through a vigorous review process to make sure that the requirements of the FISA statute are satisfied. As a 2008 press release from this office explains, "Justice Department attorneys ... have been given comprehensive authority to examine the FBI's national security program for adherence to all applicable laws, regulations, and guidelines."[44]

Typically, the Department of Justice attorneys ask questions of the FBI agent handling the case to make sure that the requirements of the statute are satisfied, and sometimes the FBI must acquire additional information before the Office of Intelligence will present the application. The draft application is then reviewed for accuracy by senior attorneys at the Office of Intelligence, agents at FBI Headquarters and in the field office where the request originated, and lawyers at the FBI's National Security Law Branch. Law clerks of the FISC also review the draft application to let the Department of Justice know if there are issues that are likely to cause the application to be denied. Once the application is in final form, it must be approved and signed by the Attorney General of the United States,

---

38. *See* 50 U.S.C.A. §§ 1804(a)(2)A) (electronic surveillance), 1823(a)(5) (physical search).

39. 50 U.S.C.A. § 1823(a)(5) (physical search); the language for electronic surveillance ("the nature of the information sought") is similar.

40. 50 U.S.C.A. § 1801(e).

41. Permanent Select Comm. on Intelligence, Foreign Intelligence Surveillance Act of 1978, H.R. Doc. No. 95-1283, at 47 (2d Sess. 1978) (available at http://www.fas.org/irp/agency/doj/fisa/hspci1978.pdf [*hereinafter* FISA House Report].

42. The Office of Intelligence was formerly known as the Office of Intelligence Policy and Review. It was renamed the Office of Intelligence in the USA Patriot Improvement and Reauthorization Act of 2005, 28 U.S.C.A. § 509A.

43. 50 U.S.C.A. § 1803(a) & (b) establish both the Foreign Intelligence Surveillance Court (FISC) and the Foreign Intelligence Surveillance Court of Review, to which orders by the FISC can be appealed.

44. Office of Intelligence April 2008 Press Release (available at http://www.justice.gov/opa/pr/2008/April/08_nsd_360.html).

stating that he finds that the application satisfies the statutory requirements.[45] The application must also be signed by the deputy director of the FBI, who must certify that the information to be sought is foreign intelligence information and describing the type of foreign intelligence information; that a "significant purpose" of the electronic surveillance or physical search is to obtain foreign intelligence information; and that the information cannot reasonably be obtained by normal investigative techniques.[46] The application is then presented to the FISC.

The Foreign Intelligence Surveillance Court (FISC) and the Foreign Intelligence Surveillance Court of Review

The FISC is comprised of 11 federal district court judges chosen by the chief justice of the Supreme Court. A FISC judge serves for a term of seven years, while also continuing his or her duties as a federal judge in his home district. At least three of the 11 judges must reside within 20 miles of the District of Columbia, while the others may hail from all over the country.[47] The court meets in a top-secret, secure facility to hear applications. Also present are the attorney from the Office of Intelligence and the FBI agent requesting the warrant. FISA also provides for emergency applications; hearings on those applications can take place in odd locations. For example, Judge Royce Lamberth, who was the presiding judge of the FISC in 1998 when al Qaeda bombed the U.S. embassies in Africa, said, "On the night of the bombings of the U.S. embassy in Africa, I started the first emergency hearings in my living room at 3:00 a.m."[48]

The hearings of the FISC take place *ex parte*; that is, there is no attorney for the target present because the target rarely will ever know that he or she was being investigated.[49] This is why the Office of Intelligence's gatekeeping function is critical to the integrity of the FISA process, and also why the FISC actively questions the attorney and the FBI before approving a warrant. Occasionally it is reported that the FISC rubber stamps FISA applications, because request for FISA warrants are so rarely denied. Judge Reggie Walton, presiding judge of the FISC in 2013, addressed this criticism in a letter to the Committee of the Judiciary of the United States Senate:

> If after receiving a final application, the judge is inclined to deny it, the Court will prepare a statement of reason(s) pursuant to 50 U.S.C. § 1803(a)(1). In some cases, the government may decide not to submit a final application, or to withdraw one that has been submitted, after learning that the judge does not intend to approve it. The annual statistics provided to Congress by the Attorney General pursuant to 50 U.S.C. §§ 1807 and 1862(b) — frequently cited to in press reports as a suggestion that the Court's approval rate of applications is over 99% — reflect only the number of *final* applications submitted to and acted on by the Court. These statistics do not reflect the fact that many applications are altered prior to

---

45. If the Attorney General is not available, the application can be signed by the Acting Attorney General, the Deputy Attorney General, or the Assistant Attorney General for National Security (if so designated by the Attorney General). 50 U.S.C.A. §§ 1801 (g), 1804, 1823.

46. 50 U.S.C.A §§ 1804(a)(6), 1823(a)(6).

47. 50 U.S.C.A. § 1803(a)(1).

48. Kris & Wilson, *supra* note 25, at 136.

49. 50 U.S.C.A. §§ 1805(a)(electronic surveillance), 1824(a)(physical search), 1842(d)(1)(pen/trap), 1861(c)(1)(tangible things).

final submission or even withheld from final submission entirely, often after an indication that a judge would not approve them.[50]

James Baker, then the Counsel for Intelligence Policy, offered a similar explanation in an interview on *Frontline*:

> I just want to say that the idea that the FISA court is a rubber stamp is to my mind ridiculous, and I think the American people need to know that. I think folks really don't understand the process. They don't understand the give-and-take.... [W]e have an interactive process with the FISA court. So if they have questions—they don't understand something about the application, they have a concern ... they'll ask us about it.... We'll say: 'We don't know, Judge. We'll go back and find out. We'll go back to an FBI field office, let's say, and ask them. They'll say, 'Well, actually we do have some additional information.' So we'll file a supplemental document, submit that to the court, and then the court might be satisfied, and then the matter is resolved; the application is approved. So could the court, when it first got the application ... denied it or issued some kind of order? I guess they could have in that kind of a scenario, but that's not how the process works. The process is more interactive than that.[51]

If the FISC denies an application for FISA electronic surveillance or physical search, the government's only recourse is to appeal to the Foreign Intelligence Surveillance Court of Review. This court consists of three federal district or court of appeals judges designated by the chief justice of the Supreme Court to hear appeals of denials by the FISC.[52] The court has rarely been convened. Only two decisions of the court have been made public, one from 2002,[53] and a second from 2008.[54]

Other Authorities Available under FISA

The preceding section described applications for electronic surveillances and physical searches under FISA, which are the activities that FISA traditionally permitted. The current version of the statute also provides for several additional investigative tools.

Pen Register/Trap-and-Trace Surveillance

FISA permits pen register/trap-and-trace surveillance.[55] This type of surveillance does not acquire the contents of a communication; instead, the surveillance gathers routing and addressing information (telephone numbers or e-mail addresses sending or receiving the communication). The Supreme Court has held that a caller does not expect the phone number that he calls to remain private, and therefore has no Fourth Amendment right

---

50. Letter from Hon. Reggie B. Walton to Hon. Patrick J. Leahy, Chairman, Committee on the Judiciary, U.S. Senate (July 29, 2013) (available at http://www.leahy.senate.gov/download/honorable-patrick-j-leahy).

51. Interview with James Baker, quoted in Kris & Wilson, *supra* note 25, at 140.

52. 50 U.S.C.A. § 1803(b).

53. *See* In re Sealed Case, 310 F.3d 717, 190 A.L.R. Fed 725 (Foreign Intel. Surv. Ct. Rev. 2002).

54. *See* In re Directives Pursuant to Section 105B of Foreign Intelligence Surveillance Act, 551 F.3d 1004 (Foreign Intel. Surv. Ct. Rev. 2008).

55. 50 U.S.C.A. § 1842.

to privacy in the call logs obtained in a pen register.[56] FISA does not regulate pen/trap surveillance of facilities located outside the United States. The requirements for pen/trap surveillance are less demanding than those of a traditional electronic surveillance under FISA because no certification from a high-ranking executive branch official is required.[57]

Emergency FISAs

FISA permits the Attorney General to authorize electronic surveillance, physical searches, or pen/trap surveillance without first obtaining a warrant from the FISC in the case of an emergency.[58] The Attorney General must notify the FISC of the emergency, and must apply to the FISC for a warrant not more than seven days after the emergency authorization. If the FISC denies the application, the FISA search or surveillance must cease immediately; the information cannot be used in any proceeding; and the FISC has the discretion to notify the target of the search or surveillance if the target is a U.S. person.[59]

Electronic Surveillance and Physical Search of Foreign Powers without Judicial Approval

The Attorney General may authorize electronic surveillance and physical searches for up to a year without a court order on communications channels used exclusively by foreign powers if there is no substantial likelihood that the search or surveillance will infringe on a U.S. person's privacy.[60] The search or surveillance must also be subject to minimization procedures (discussed more fully below). This provision might be used to surveil an embassy, for example, though such surveillance might also run afoul of the Vienna Convention on Diplomatic Relations.

Surveillance and Searches Abroad

Traditionally, no FISA warrant was required for surveillance and searches conducted overseas; instead, NSA collected foreign-to-foreign communications under the President's Article II national security powers. This collection of purely foreign communications did not violate the Fourth Amendment because the Supreme Court has established that the Fourth Amendment does not protect foreigners abroad against searches and seizures by the U.S. government.[61] Some federal courts have also found that the Warrant Clause does not apply to intelligence searches of U.S. citizens conducted abroad, holding instead that the search need only be "reasonable" to satisfy the Fourth Amendment, though this question has not been addressed by the Supreme Court.[62] Consistent with this line of

---

56. Smith v. Maryland, 442 U.S. 735, 99, S. Ct. 2577, 61 L. Ed. 2d 220 (1979).
57. 50 U.S.C.A. § 1842(a)(1)(c).
58. 50 U.S.C.A. § 1805(e)(1)(A) (electronic surveillance); § 1821(e)(1)(A) (physical search).
59. 50 U.S.C.A. § 1805(j) (electronic surveillance); § 1821(j) (physical search).
60. 50 U.S.C.A. § 1802(a)(1)(A)(1).
61. *See* United States v. Verdugo-Urquidez, 494 U.S. 259, 265–66, 110 S. Ct. 1056, 108 L. Ed. 2d 222 (1990).
62. *See, e.g.*, United States v. Bin Laden, 126 F. Supp. 2d 264 (S.D.N.Y. 2000), *aff'd*, 552 F.3d 157 (2d Cir. 2008), *cert. denied*, 130 S. Ct., 1050, 175, L.Ed.2d 928 (2010); *In re* Terrorist Bombings of U.S. Embassies in East Africa, 552 F.3d 157 (2d Cir. 2008), *cert. denied*, 130 S. Ct. 1050, 175 L. Ed. 2d 928 (2010).

thought, when FISA was first enacted, Congress intentionally and carefully excluded foreign-to-foreign communications from its scope in order not to interfere with these overseas operations. The 1978 version of FISA did not regulate wire surveillance of international communications conducted outside the United States, or radio surveillance of international communications in any location, including communications to or from Americans, so long as no known American was targeted.[63]

Technology has changed. NSA now can collect international telephone calls more easily within the United States, though it needs the help of communications providers to do so.[64] The advent of e-mail poses a similar difficulty. Today, even when both senders and recipients of emails are foreign, their emails land in America for a moment because they travel through U.S. servers. As then-NSA Director Michael Hayden explained, "A single communication can transit the world even if the communicants are only a few miles apart. And in that transit NSA may have multiple opportunities to intercept it as it moves and changes medium. As long as a communication is otherwise lawfully targeted, we should be indifferent to where the intercept is achieved.... We need to be able to use all the technological tools we have."[65] In other words, the NSA wanted the ability to collect foreign-to-foreign communications from within the U.S., and it needed approval to present to the communications providers to obtain their help.

The FISA Amendments Act of 2008 added a provision to the statute commonly called Section 702, which permits the intelligence community to acquire information by targeting persons it reasonably believes are located abroad.[66] Under Section 702, the Attorney General and the Director of National Intelligence may authorize jointly the targeting of persons reasonably believed to be outside the United States to acquire foreign intelligence information. The target has to be overseas; the collection must comply with the Fourth Amendment; and the collection is subject to minimization procedures. For non-U.S. persons, there is no probable cause requirement; so long as the government reasonably believes that the target is located outside of the United States, the surveillance is permissible. The Attorney General and the Director of National Intelligence must supply a written certification and supporting affidavit to the FISC before beginning the operation (or within 7 days of beginning the surveillance, in the case of an emergency). The FISC reviews the certification, and if it finds that it complies with FISA, an order must be entered approving the certification. If the FISC finds that it does not satisfy FISA, it can order the government to correct the deficiency or cease the surveillance. If the target is a U.S. person, the government must show probable cause that the target is an agent of a foreign power, and must cease the collection if the target returns to the United States.[67]

Section 702 also enables the government to issue a "directive" to get access to an American service provider's systems. If the communications provider does not wish to comply, it may challenge the directive before the FISC. FISA also releases the communications provider from liability for complying with the directive.[68]

---

63. *See* Kris & Wilson, *supra* note 25, at § 16:5.
64. *See* Kris & Wilson, *supra* note 25, at § 16:5, quoting then-Assistant Attorney General Ken Wainstein ("[W]e rely on the communications providers to do our intelligence surveillance. We can't do [the surveillance] without them because ... we ... don't own the communications systems. We need to rely on their assistance.").
65. *See* Kris & Wilson, *supra* note 25, at § 16:5.
66. 50 U.S.C.A. §§ 1881a–1881c.
67. 50 U.S.C.A. § 1881a(i)(3).
68. 50 U.S.C.A. § 1881a(h).

Business Records and Tangible Things

In 1998, FISA was amended to permit the government to obtain "records" from a "common carrier" (a telephone company), a "public accommodation facility" (like a hotel), and a "physical storage facility or a vehicle rental facility."[69] The business records provision originally required a showing that the sought-after record pertained to a target who was a foreign power or an agent of a foreign power. But that authority did not prove to be terribly useful to the government—between 1998 and 2001, the government obtained only one FISA order for business records.[70]

After September 11, Congress amended FISA several times to make it more useful. In 2001, the USA PATRIOT Act amended this part of the statute (now commonly referred to as Section 215 of the PATRIOT Act) to expand the type of information that could be sought to include "any tangible things" (including books, records, papers, documents, and other items).[71] These tangible things could now be obtained from any person or entity, not just phone companies. When the amendment was enacted, there was public concern that the government would use the statute to collect information like lists of books people borrowed from the library. Despite this outcry, the statute still was not used much by the government, and was considered a "tool of last resort."[72]

The statute was amended again in 2006 by the USA PATRIOT Act Reauthorization Act, and this time the change proved to be significant. Under this version of the statute, the government needn't show that the sought-after records pertained to terrorists or other agents of foreign powers; instead, it only needed to show that the records are "relevant" to a foreign intelligence investigation.[73] "Relevant" is a term used throughout FISA, and is distinguished from a more-demanding showing of being "necessary." According to a U.S. House of Representatives report on FISA, "necessary" is "important and required," not just "useful and convenient."[74] "Relevant," in FISA terms, is something less than that. This revision permits the government to collect a greater universe of materials, and led to the collection of Verizon telephone metadata, discussed below.

The recipient of a tangible things order may challenge the order by filing a petition with the FISC.[75]

FISA's "Minimization" Requirements

During a national security investigation, it is likely that a FISA search or electronic surveillance will collect irrelevant information—conversations between the target's teenage daughter and her American boyfriend, in the cellphone example described above, or innocent e-mails from a business acquaintance unrelated to the target's activities on behalf of a foreign power. FISA requires the government to "minimize" this irrelevant information in order to protect the privacy of U.S. persons who are not targets of the investigation.

---

69. 50 U.S.C.A. § 1862(a) (1998).
70. 2007 OIG Section 215 Report at 7 (available at http://www.justice.gov/oig/special/s0703a/final.pdf).
71. 50 U.S.C.A. § 1861(a)(1).
72. 2007 OIG Section 215 Report at 75.
73. 50 U.S.C.A. § 1861(b)(2)(A).
74. FISA House Report at 47.
75. 50 U.S.C.A. § 1861(f)(2)(A)(i).

FISA requires that the Attorney General adopt "specific procedures … that are reasonably designed in light of the purpose and technique" of the surveillance or search "to minimize the acquisition and retention, and prohibit the dissemination, of nonpublicly available information concerning unconsenting United States persons consistent with the need of the United States to obtain, produce, and disseminate foreign intelligence information."[76] The statute prohibits the government from disseminating this information in a manner that would identify the U.S. person unless the person's identity "is necessary to understand such foreign intelligence information or assess its importance."[77] However, if the information shows criminal activity, then the information can be disseminated for law enforcement purposes.[78]

The limits on retention and dissemination of information often play a more significant role in protecting privacy interests than do limits on acquisition. While the legislative history of FISA suggests that Congress imagined that recording devices might be temporarily turned off to avoid collecting irrelevant information,[79] it is often impracticable in modern surveillance for this to occur as much of this collection is done automatically rather than by an agent listening in real time. The FISC has explained that when the FBI is monitoring communications under FISA, it often will collect "large amounts of communication … by automatic recording to be minimized after the fact."[80] The communications may be taking place in a foreign language; they may be coded; and it may take time for the government to analyze the information to detect patterns of innocent conversations.[81] Consequently, minimization is frequently accomplished at the retention phase, rather than at the time of acquisition.

What, then, is the government allowed to retain under minimization requirements? The FISC has stated that the government can retain the information obtained unless "the information 'could not be' foreign intelligence."[82] Information that is clearly irrelevant cannot be retained, but in a national security investigation, it can take time to determine what is or is not relevant. According to the FISC, once acquired information is made intelligible (translated if in a foreign language, or transcribed if in audio form), it is reviewed by an official, usually an FBI case agent. That agent logs any foreign intelligence information into the FBI's records. Information that is not foreign intelligence information is then minimized (erased, discarded, destroyed, or not indexed and therefore made irretrievable).[83]

Oversight of FISA

When Congress enacted FISA, it realized that the powers it was authorizing could be abused. The statute itself was designed to cabin executive branch actions related to national security investigations by providing a check in the form of judicial oversight via the FISC, as well as through the gatekeeping function of the Office of Intelligence. Congress also

---

76. 50 U.S.C.A. § 1801(h)(1) (electronic surveillance); § 1821(4)(A) (physical search).

77. 50 U.S.C.A. § 1801(h)(2) (electronic surveillance); § 1821(4)(B) (physical search).

78. 50 U.S.C.A. § 1801(h)(3) (electronic surveillance); § 1821(4)(C) (physical search).

79. FISA House Report at 55.

80. *In re* All Matters Submitted to Foreign Intelligence Surveillance Court, 218 F. Supp. 2d 611, 617 (Foreign Intel. Surv. Ct. 2002) (abrogated on other grounds by *In re* Sealed Case, *supra* note 53).

81. *See* United States v. Rahman, 861 F. Supp. 247, 252–53 (S.D.N.Y. 1994), *aff'd*, 189 F.3d 88, 52 Fed. R. Evid. Serv. 425 (2d Cir. 1999).

82. *In re* All Matters Submitted to Foreign Intelligence Surveillance Court, *supra* note 78, at 618.

83. *Id.*

mandated that the Attorney General "fully inform" the House and Senate Intelligence Committees about the government's activities under FISA.[84] The legislative history of the statute explains that "the word 'fully' means that the committee must be given enough information to understand the activities of, but does not mean that the Attorney General must set forth each and every detailed item of information relating to" the government's use of FISA.[85] The statute also requires periodic reporting to the Intelligence Committees and the Senate Judiciary Committee about the government's use of FISA, including the number of emergency FISA applications,[86] the number of "roving" FISA surveillances,[87] and a description of the criminal cases in which information obtained via FISA will be used at trial,[88] among numerous other statistics related to the use of FISA.[89]

Challenging a FISA Warrant

How can a FISA warrant be challenged?

Suit by Target or Those Communicating with Target

In most circumstances, a target and those with whom he communicates will never know that they were under FISA surveillance. FISA warrants are classified, and are issued in secret and on an *ex parte* basis.[90] The FISA statute contains provisions that seem to imply that a suit could be brought if the statute has been violated. Under 50 U.S.C.A. § 1810, an "aggrieved party" who is not a foreign power or an agent of a foreign power can sue if he can show that he was "subjected to an electronic surveillance." 50 U.S.C.A. § 1828 provides for a similar suit in the case of a physical search. If a party cannot prove that he was the subject of FISA surveillance or search, then he will not have standing to challenge the warrant in court, no matter how likely it is that FISA was used. Such was the case in *Clapper v. Amnesty International*,[91] in which a group of lawyers, journalists and human rights advocates who regularly communicate with known terrorists sued because of the likelihood that their communications were being monitored under FISA. The Supreme Court ruled that the plaintiffs could not prove that the surveillance was taking place, and therefore did not have standing to challenge FISA's constitutionality.

FISA also provides for criminal penalties for unauthorized electronic surveillance and physical searches.[92] To date, no one has been prosecuted under these provisions.[93]

---

84. 50 U.S.C.A. §§ 1801(a)(1) (electronic surveillance), 1826 (physical search), 1846(a)(pen/trap surveillance), 1862(a)(tangible things).

85. FISA House Report at 96.

86. 50 U.S.C.A § 1808(a)(2)(C).

87. 50 U.S.C.A. § 1808(a)(2)(A). A "roving" surveillance means that the location of the electronic surveillance is unknown, such as when a target uses multiple cellphones.

88. 50 U.S.C.A. § 1808(a)(2)(B).

89. *See* 50 U.S.C.A. §§ 1846 (pen register/trap and trace), 1862 (business records), 1871 (semiannual report of the Attorney General), 1881(f) (foreign communications outside the United States acquired in the United States), 1885c (protection of persons assisting the government).

90. 50 U.S.C.A. §§ 1805(a)(electronic surveillance), 1824(a)(physical search), 1842(d)(1)(pen/trap), 1861(c)(1)(tangible things).

91. *Clapper v. Amnesty,* 133 S. Ct. 1138 (2013).

92. 50 U.S.C.A. §§ 1809, 1827.

93. *See* Kris & Wilson, *supra* note 25, at 14:3.

Use of FISA Information in Criminal Cases

Information derived from a FISA search or surveillance can be used in a criminal prosecution "with the advance authorization of the Attorney General."[94] The person against whom the evidence is being introduced may file a motion to suppress on the grounds that "the information was lawfully acquired" or "the surveillance was not made in conformity with an order of authorization or approval."[95] If such a motion is made, the criminal court will review "in camera and ex parte" the FISA application in order to determine its legality.[96] Neither the defendant nor the defendant's lawyer is likely to be permitted to actually see the FISA application or order. The court may disclose portions of the application and order to the aggrieved person if the disclosure is necessary to make an accurate determination of the legality of the FISA surveillance or search;[97] however, to date, no court has ever ordered the disclosure of a FISA application or order to a defendant.[98]

Challenges by Communications Providers

As discussed above, a telecommunications provider receiving a directive under Section 702 of FISA can appear before the FISC to challenge that directive.[99] Similarly, anyone receiving an order under 50 U.S.C.A. § 1861 to produce business records may challenge that order before the FISC.[100] Communications providers and others who comply with FISA are immune from liability and cannot be sued for their cooperation.[101]

Appeals to the Foreign Intelligence Court of Appeals

Only the government can lodge an appeal to a ruling by the FISC with the Foreign Intelligence Court of Appeals.[102] However, during one of the rare times that that court has been convened, the American Civil Liberties Union and the National Association of Criminal Defense Lawyers were permitted to file *amicus* briefs with the court.[103]

FISA and the September 11, 2001 Terrorist Attacks

Between its original enactment in 1978 and the September 11, 2001 terrorist attacks on the United States, FISA was used primarily to investigate and prevent espionage. After September 11, FISA became a useful tool to combat terrorism, and applications for FISA warrants grew exponentially. For example, in the 23 years between 1978 and September

---

94. 50 U.S.C.A. § 1806(b).
95. 50 U.S.C.A. § 1806(e).
96. 50 U.S.C.A. § 1806(f).
97. 50 U.S.C.A. § 1806(g).
98. *See* Kris & Wilson, *supra* note 25, at § 31:3.
99. 50 U.S.C.A. § 1881(a)(h)(4).
100. 50 U.S.C.A. § 1861 (f)(2)(A)(i).
101. *See* 50 U.S.C.A. § 1805 (electronic surveillance), 50 U.S.C.A. § 1842 (pen register/trap-and-trace), 50 U.S.C.A. § 1861 (business records), 50 U.S.C.A. § 1881(a) (foreign communications/Section 702), 50 U.S.C.A. § 1881(b) (foreign communications outside the United States acquired in the United States).
102. 50 U.S.C.A. § 1803(b).
103. *See In re* Sealed Case, 310 F.3d 717, 190 A.L.R. Fed. 725 (Foreign Intel. Surv. Ct. Rev. 2002).

10, 2001, there were a total of 46 emergency authorizations under FISA; in the single year after the September 11 attacks, there were 113 emergency authorizations.[104] The Office of Intelligence was comprised of 20 lawyers in 2000; by 2008, because of the increased demand for FISA warrants, there were almost 100 lawyers working there.[105]

As FISA warrants became more commonplace, the statute gained some notoriety. The statute received significant press after September 11 because of the "FISA Wall," which curtailed sharing of information between the intelligence and law enforcement communities. It came into the spotlight again at the end of 2005, when revelations of warrantless surveillance by the NSA were published by the *New York Times*. And in 2013, FISA received significant attention as a result of the disclosure of information about NSA activity by Edward Snowden.

The "FISA Wall"

As originally enacted, FISA required that the "primary purpose" of the electronic surveillance (and later, physical searches) be to obtain foreign intelligence information. Courts and the intelligence community took this to mean that prosecution of a spy or terrorist could be a secondary purpose of FISA surveillance, but not the primary purpose. If criminal prosecution became the goal of the surveillance, the government believed that the surveillance would have to be stopped and any evidence obtained via FISA suppressed. [106] This resulted in the "FISA Wall"—a separation of the intelligence community from the law enforcement community, in an effort to avoid violating FISA.

After the September 11, 2001 attacks, the Department of Justice asked Congress to amend FISA to permit greater coordination between the intelligence and law enforcement communities. Congress revised FISA to state that a "significant purpose" of the search or surveillance must be to protect national security, but no longer required that this be the only purpose.[107] As a result, Attorney General John Ashcroft adopted new procedures to permit the exchange of information between the intelligence and law enforcement worlds, but the FISC rejected some of these procedures in a 2002 ruling.[108] The Department of Justice appealed the FISC's ruling, thereby causing the Foreign Intelligence Court of Review to be convened for the first time in history. The Court of Review reversed the FISC's decision and upheld the information sharing procedures, ushering in a new era of collaboration between intelligence and law enforcement.[109]

The NSA "Special Collection Program"

In the period following the September 11 attacks, the intelligence world came under intense pressure to investigate and thwart the activities of al Qaeda, and was also the

---

104. *See* Kris & Wilson, *supra* note 25, at § 5:3 (citing a Letter from Daniel Bryant, Assistant Attorney General, Office of Legislative Affairs, to Senator Joseph Biden (Oct. 7, 2002)).

105. Office of Intelligence April 2008 Press Release, *supra* note 44. For a detailed discussion of the history of the Office of Intelligence, *see* Kris & Wilson, *supra* note 25, at 1:8.

106. *See* Kris & Wilson, *supra* note 25, at § 10:3.

107. In 2001, the USA PATRIOT Act (*hereinafter* PATRIOT Act) amended the statute to amend the "purpose" for which FISA warrants can be sought (Patriot Act § 216), and to allow coordination between intelligence and law enforcement communities (Patriot Act § 504).

108. *In re* All Matters Submitted to Foreign Intelligence Surveillance Court, 218 F. Supp. 2d 611 (Foreign Intel. Surv. Ct. 2002).

109. *In re* Sealed Case, 310 F.3d 717, 190 A.L.R. Fed. 725 (Foreign Intel. Surv. Ct. Rev. 2002).

subject of much criticism (because of the FISA Wall) for being too risk averse. In reaction to concerns that the intelligence world was hampered by legal restrictions that would keep it from fighting terrorism effectively, President Bush authorized the NSA to monitor international telephone calls and e-mail messages of "hundreds, perhaps thousands, of people inside the United States without warrants."[110] While the NSA reportedly sought FISA warrants to monitor entirely domestic communications, it eavesdropped without warrants on others in the United States as part of a "special collection program," which the White House concluded could be authorized as part of the President's wartime powers. FISA allows for warrantless wartime domestic electronic surveillance, but only for the first 15 days of war,[111] making the continuation of this program for longer than 15 days problematic. Electronic surveillance conducted by the federal government must comport either with FISA or Title 18 of the criminal code; otherwise, that surveillance is illegal.[112]

The *New York Times* broke the story on December 16, 2005, reporting that the program began soon after the September 11 attacks, and grew exponentially after the CIA began capturing top al Qaeda operatives overseas. The CIA reportedly seized the computers, cellphones, and personal phone directories of these terrorists, and provided that information to the NSA. The NSA monitored those numbers and e-mail messages, as well as others linked to them, including many in the United States, without going through the FISA process. Congressional leaders from both parties were reportedly briefed about the program, although the extent of their knowledge is unclear.[113] The *New York Times* reported:

> Some of those who object to the operation argue that it is unnecessary. By getting warrants through the foreign intelligence court, the N.S.A. and F.B.I. could eavesdrop on people inside the United States who might be tied to terrorist groups without skirting longstanding rules, they say.... Administration officials counter that they sometimes need to move more urgently, the officials said. Those involved in the program also said that the N.S.A.'s eavesdroppers might need to start monitoring large batches of numbers all at once, and that it would be impractical to seek permission from the Foreign Intelligence Surveillance Court first, according to the officials.[114]

Interestingly, the *New York Times* was first alerted to the existence of the Special Collection Program by Thomas Tamm, a Department of Justice lawyer in the Office of Intelligence Policy and Review (which was later renamed the Office of Intelligence). Tamm reportedly learned of the program in 2004 and attempted to raise the issue with supervisors and a colleague working for the Senate Judiciary Committee, but was told to drop the subject. He then called the *New York Times* and told them about the warrantless surveillance, while refusing to reveal "sources and methods" or any operational details about the program to the reporters. The *New York Times* won a Pulitzer Prize for its story.[115]

Around the same time that Thomas Tamm was asking questions about the Special Collection Program, others within the Justice Department were raising similar concerns. Attorney General John Ashcroft had fallen ill and was in the hospital in March 2004. James Comey, then the Deputy Attorney General (and later the director of the FBI),

---

110. James Risen & Eric Lichtblau, *Bush Lets U.S. Spy on Callers Without Courts*, N.Y. TIMES, December 16, 2005.

111. 50 U.S.C.A § 1811.

112. 50 U.S.C.A § 1809.

113. *Id.*

114. *Id.*

115. Michael Isikoff, *The Whistleblower Who Exposed Warrantless Wiretaps*, NEWSWEEK, December 12, 2008.

became the Acting Attorney General in Ashcroft's place and refused to renew the NSA Special Collection Program, believing it to be illegal. Andrew Card, the White House Chief of Staff, and Alberto Gonzales, then White House Counsel and later the Attorney General, rushed to Ashcroft's hospital room to pressure Ashcroft into overriding Comey's decision.[116] Ashcroft refused to do this, though President Bush ordered the program to continue anyway.[117]

Despite the seeming illegality of the NSA Special Collection Program, no action was ever taken to sanction the actors involved. Instead, Congress enacted the FISA Amendments Act of 2008. As described above, this amendment added Section 702 to the statute, which permits the Director of National Intelligence and the Attorney General to jointly authorize electronic surveillance, for 1-year periods, targeted at a foreigner who is abroad. [118] The FISC must approve this surveillance if it comports with the requirements of FISA. Section 702 also provides legal immunity to telecommunications providers for complying with FISA directives from the government.[119]

Edward Snowden

In May 2013, FISA once again took the spotlight when Edward Snowden, an NSA contractor, released thousands of classified documents about the United States' intelligence activities. Unlike Thomas Tamm, Snowden disclosed information about operations, sources and methods, and was charged with espionage for his activities.[120] Among the information disclosed by Snowden were two NSA bulk surveillance programs operating under FISA: the PRISM program, and the bulk collection of telephone metadata from Verizon.

PRISM was an electronic surveillance data mining program begun in 2007 under the authorities granted by Section 702 (discussed above) to collect communications of foreigners abroad. The NSA reportedly tapped directly into the servers of U.S. service providers Microsoft, Yahoo, Google, Facebook, PalTalk, AOL, Skype, YouTube, and Apple to obtain the information.[121]

The Verizon metadata collection took place under Section 215 of the PATRIOT Act of 2006 (discussed above), which governs the collection of "business records." The statute permits the government to collect business records, such as Verizon call logs (similar to information gathered by a pen register/trap-and-trace, discussed above), even if it does not know whether the phone number is being used by a terrorist, so long as it can show that the information is "relevant" to a foreign intelligence investigation. The FISC reportedly authorized the NSA to collect the metadata of calls made by millions of Verizon customers

---

116. Eric Lichtblau & James Risen, *Justice Deputy Resisted Parts of Spy Program*, N.Y. Times, January 1, 2006.

117. Michael Isikoff, *The Whistleblower Who Exposed Warrantless Wiretaps*, Newsweek, December 12, 2008.

118. 50 U.S.C.A. §§ 1881a–1881c.

119. 50 U.S.C.A. § 1881a(h).

120. *See* Peter Finn & Sari Horwitz, *U.S. Charges Snowden With Espionage*, Wash. Post, June 21, 2013.

121. *See* Barton Gellman & Laura Poitras, *US Intelligence Mining Data From Nine U.S. Internet Companies in Broad Secret Program*, Wash. Post, June 6, 2013.

under this authority.[122] Federal courts have disagreed about whether the program passes muster under the Fourth Amendment of the Constitution.[123] While Supreme Court precedent indicates that there is no Fourth Amendment privacy interest in phone logs, advances in technology and the sheer bulk of the data collection may implicate greater privacy concerns today.

It is interesting to note that both of these bulk collections were made possible by amendments to FISA that Congress made after learning of the NSA warrantless surveillance disclosed by Thomas Tamm in 2005. While the details of the programs remain classified, they appear to be legal under the terms of the FISA statute. Nevertheless, even though the collections programs were run with the approval of the FISC and were disclosed through a data dump of numerous classified documents, the public outrage over the existence of these programs was markedly higher than the reaction to Tamm's more careful disclosure of unlawful surveillance.

Conclusion

FISA provides the government with a necessary and powerful tool that has proved instrumental in defending the country against the threat of international terrorism. As Judge Pauley wrote in *American Civil Liberties Union v. Clapper*:

> The September 11th terrorist attacks revealed, in the starkest terms, just how dangerous and interconnected the world is. While Americans depended on technology for the conveniences of modernity, al-Qaeda plotted in a seventh-century milieu to use that technology against us. It was a bold jujitsu. And it succeeded because conventional intelligence gathering could not detect diffuse filaments connecting al-Qaeda.

> Prior to the September 11th attacks, the National Security Agency ("NSA") intercepted seven calls made by hijacker Khalid al-Mihdhar, who was living in San Diego, California, to an al-Qaeda safe house in Yemen. The NSA intercepted those calls using overseas signals intelligence capabilities that could not capture al-Mihdhar's telephone number identifier. Without that identifier, NSA analysts concluded mistakenly that al-Mihdhar was overseas and not in the United States. Telephony metadata would have furnished the missing information and might have permitted the NSA to notify the Federal Bureau of Investigation ("FBI") of the fact that al-Mihdhar was calling the Yemeni safe house from inside the United States.

> The Government learned from its mistake and adapted to confront a new enemy: a terror network capable of orchestrating attacks across the world. It launched a number of counter-measures, including a bulk telephony metadata collection program—a wide net that could find and isolate gossamer contacts

---

122. *See* Glenn Greenwald, *NSA Collecting Phone Records of Millions of Verizon Customers Daily*, The Guardian, June 5, 2013.

123. *Compare* Klayman v. Obama, 947 F. Supp. 2d 1 (D.D.C. 2013) (program is unconstitutional) *with* American Civil Liberties Union v. Clapper, 959 F. Supp. 2d 724 (S.D.N.Y. 2013) (program is constitutional).

among suspected terrorists in an ocean of seemingly disconnected data. This blunt tool only works because it collects everything.[124]

At the same time, secret activities by the government such as those enabled by FISA can be dangerous and are vulnerable to abuse if not properly checked. As Attorney General Harlan Fisk Stone warned in 1924 when the FBI was created:

> There is always the possibility that a secret police system may become a menace to free government and free institutions because it carries with it the possibility of abuses of power which are not always quickly apprehended or understood. The enormous expansion of federal legislation ... has made a federal bureau of investigation a necessary instrument of law enforcement. But it is important that its activities be strictly limited to those functions for which it was created and that its agents themselves be not above the law or beyond its reach.[125]

FISA is essential to the national self-defense. But the checks imposed by FISA on the government's power are equally vital to protecting the civil liberties necessary to a functioning democracy.

Questions for Discussion

1. In an unprecedented concentration of power, the judges of the FISC are appointed solely by the Chief Justice of the United States—with no advice or consent from Congress. Judges are chosen from among those currently serving on the federal bench. The Chief Justice has used this power to name almost exclusively judges initially appointed by Republican presidents, many of whom have a history of working as prosecutors or for the executive branch. Should the way judges on FISC are appointed be changed?

2. As noted, there is no true adversarial process in cases before the FISC. The judges hear only the government's side of the story. What changes would you impose, while protecting "methods and means" and sources, to create a more adversarial process and give plaintiffs a reasonable opportunity to defend against warrantless searches and seizures?

---

124. 959 F. Supp. 2d at 729–730.

125. Alpheus Thomas Mason, Harlan Fiske Stone: PILLAR OF THE LAW 153 (1956) (quoting N.Y. TIMES, May 10, 1924).

Chapter 28

National Security Violations

Jeff Breinholt

In this chapter:

Introduction[1]

This chapter focuses on the main national security criminal violations. What constitutes a national security violation? Are they the crimes that are typically investigated by the expedient tools carved out in the name of national security? If so, it would sweep in all terrorism offenses. This chapter instead is limited to domestic behavior which has the tendency to adversely impact United States military operations and foreign policy: treason, seditious conspiracy, material support to Al Qaida, the Neutrality Act, and disclosure of government secrets.

Treason

Treason is a big deal. The crime—currently codified at 18 U.S.C. § 2381—is rarely used by prosecutors, in part because is it so difficult to prove. One of the reasons for this is that treason, by virtue of the U.S. Constitution (art. III, § 3) requires two witnesses for every overt act: "Treason against the United States, shall consist only in levying War against them, or in adhering to their Enemies, giving them Aid and Comfort. No person shall be convicted of Treason unless on the Testimony of two Witnesses to the same overt Act, or on Confession in open Court."

The Framers no doubt mandated this requirement because of the heavy stigma attached to the crime of treason. As the Supreme Court noted a few years after the ratification of the Constitution:

---

1. *The views expressed in this chapter are the author's own and do not represent those of the Department of Justice.*

As there is no crime which can more excite and agitate the passions of men than treason, no charge demands more from the tribunal before which it is made, a deliberate and temperate inquiry. Whether this inquiry be directed to the fact or to the law, none can be more, solemn, none more important to the citizen or to the government; none can more affect the safety of both.... It is therefore more safe as well as more consonant to the principles of our constitution, that the crime of treason should not be extended by construction to doubtful cases; and that crimes not clearly within the constitutional definition, should receive such punishment as the legislature in its wisdom may provide.

Ex parte Bollman, 4 Cranch 75, 125, 127 (1807).

Cramer v. United States
325 U.S. 1 (1945)

Anthony Cramer was convicted of treason under Criminal Code § 1, 18 U.S.C.A. § 1, and to review a judgment of the Circuit Court of Appeals, 137 F.2d 888, which affirmed the conviction, he brings certiorari.

Reversed.

Mr. Justice DOUGLAS, Mr. Chief Justice STONE, Mr. Justice BLACK, and Mr. Justice REED dissenting.

On Writ of Certiorari to the United States Circuit Court of Appeals for the Second Circuit.

Mr. Justice JACKSON delivered the opinion of the Court.

Anthony Cramer, the petitioner, stands convicted of violating Section 1 of the Criminal Code, which provides: 'Whoever, owing allegiance to the United States, levies war against them or adheres to their enemies, giving them aid and comfort within the United States or elsewhere, is guilty of treason.'

. . . .

Cramer owed allegiance to the United States. A German by birth, he had been a resident of the United States since 1925 and was naturalized in 1936. Prosecution resulted from his association with two of the German saboteurs who in June 1942 landed on our shores from enemy submarines to disrupt industry in the United States and whose cases we considered in Ex parte Quirin, 317 U.S. 1. One of those, spared from execution, appeared as a government witness on the trial of Cramer. He testified that Werner Thiel and Edward Kerling were members of that sabotage crew, detailed their plot, and described their preparations for its consummation.

Cramer was conscripted into and served in the German Army against the United States in 1918. After the war he came to this country, intending to remain permanently. So far as appears, he has been of good behavior, never before in trouble with the law. He was studious and intelligent, earning $45 a week for work in a boiler room and living accordingly.

There was no evidence, and the Government makes no claim, that he had foreknowledge that the saboteurs were coming to this country or that he came into association with them by prearrangement. Cramer, however, had known intimately the saboteur Werner Thiel while the latter lived in this country. They had worked together, roomed together, and jointly had ventured in a small and luckless delicatessen enterprise. Thiel early and frankly avowed adherence to the National Socialist movement in Germany; he foresaw the war and returned in 1941 for the purpose of helping Germany. Cramer did not do so. How much he sympathized with the doctrines of the Nazi Party is not clear. He became at one time, in Indiana, a member and officer of the Friends of New Germany, which was a predecessor of the Bund. However, he withdrew in 1935 before it became the Bund. He says there was some swindle about it that he did not like and also that he did not like their drilling and 'radical activities.' In 1936 he made a trip to Germany, attended the Olympic Games, and saw some of the Bundsmen from this country who went there at that time for conferences with Nazi Party officials. There is no suggestion that Cramer while there had any such associations. He does not appear to have been regarded as a person of that consequence. His friends and associates in this country were largely German. His social life in New York City, where he recently had lived, seems to have been centered around Kolping House, a German-Catholic recreational center.

Cramer retained a strong affection for his fatherland. He corresponded in German with his family and friends there. Before the United States entered the war he expressed strong sympathy with Germany in its conflict with other European powers. Before the attack upon Pearl Harbor, Cramer openly opposed participation by this country in the war against Germany. He refused to work on war materials. He expressed concern about being drafted into our army and 'misused' for purposes of 'world conquest.' There is no proof, however, except for the matter charged in the indictment, of any act or utterance disloyal to this country after we entered the war.

Coming down to the time of the alleged treason, the main facts, as related on the witness stand by Cramer, are not seriously in dispute. He was living in New York and in response to a cryptic note left under his door, which did not mention Thiel, he went to the Grand Central Station. There Thiel appeared. Cramer had supposed that Thiel was in Germany, knowing that he had left the United States shortly before the war to go there. Together they went to public places and had some drinks. Cramer denies that Thiel revealed his mission of sabotage. Cramer said to Thiel that he must have come to America by submarine, but Thiel refused to confirm it, although his attitude increased Cramer's suspicion. Thiel promised to tell later how he came to this country. Thiel asked about a girl who was a mutual acquaintance and whom Thiel had engaged to marry previous to his going to Germany. Cramer knew where she was, and offered to and did write to her to come to New York, without disclosing in the letter that Thiel had arrived. Thiel said that he had in his possession about $3600, but did not disclose that it was provided by the German Government, saying only that one could get money in Germany if he had the right connections. Thiel owed Cramer an old debt of $200. He gave Cramer his money belt containing some $3600, from which Cramer was to be paid. Cramer agreed to and did place the rest in his own safe deposit box, except a sum which he kept in his room in case Thiel should want it quickly.

After the second of these meetings Thiel and Kerling, who was present briefly at one meeting, were arrested. Cramer's expectation of meeting Thiel later and of bringing him and his fiancée together was foiled. Shortly thereafter Cramer was arrested, tried, and found guilty.

. . . .

Cramer's contention may be well stated in words of Judge Learned Hand in United States v. Robinson: . . .

> Nevertheless a question may indeed be raised whether the prosecution may lay as an overt act a step taken in execution of the traitorous design, innocent in itself, and getting its treasonable character only from some covert and undeclared intent. It is true that in prosecutions for conspiracy under our federal statute it is well settled that any step in performance of the conspiracy is enough, though

it is innocent except for its relations to the agreement. I doubt very much whether that rule has any application to the case of treason, where the requirement affected the character of the pleading and proof, rather than accorded a season of repentance before the crime should be complete. Lord Reading in his charge in Casement's Case uses language which accords with my understanding: "Overt acts are such acts as manifest a criminal intention and tend towards the accomplishment of the criminal object. They are acts by which the purpose is manifested and the means by which it is intended to be fulfilled."

The Government, however, contends for, and the court below has affirmed, this conviction upon a contrary principle.... It said 'We believe in short that no more need be laid for an overt act of treason than for an overt act of conspiracy.... Hence we hold the overt acts relied on were sufficient to be submitted to the jury, even though they perhaps may have appeared as innocent on their face.' A similar conclusion was reached in United States v. Fricke; ... it is: 'An overt act in itself may be a perfectly innocent act standing by itself; it must be in some manner in furtherance of the crime.'

   ....

III.

Historical materials aid interpretation chiefly in that they show two kinds of dangers against which the framers were concerned to guard the treason offense: (1) Perversion by established authority to repress peaceful political opposition; and (2) conviction of the innocent as a result of perjury, passion, or inadequate evidence. The first danger could be diminished by closely circumscribing the kind of conduct which should be treason— making the constitutional definition exclusive, making it clear, and making the offense one not susceptible of being inferred from all sorts of insubordinations. The second danger lay in the manner of trial and was one which would be diminished mainly by procedural requirements—mainly but not wholly, for the hazards of trial also would be diminished by confining the treason offense to kinds of conduct susceptible of reasonably sure proof. The concern uppermost in the framers' minds, that mere mental attitudes or expressions should not be treason, influenced both definition of the crime and procedure for its trial. In the proposed Constitution the first sentence of the treason article undertook to define the offense; the second, to surround its trial with procedural safeguards.

'Compassing' and like loose concepts of the substance of the offense had been useful tools for tyranny. So one of the obvious things to be put into the definition of treason not consisting of actual levying of war was that it must consist of doing something. This the draft Constitution failed to provide, for, as we have pointed out, it defined treason as merely 'adhering to the enemies of the United States, or any of them.'

Treason of adherence to an enemy was old in the law. It consisted of breaking allegiance to one's own King by forming an attachment to his enemy. Its scope was comprehensive, its requirements indeterminate. It might be predicated on intellectual or emotional sympathy with the foe, or merely lack of zeal in the cause of one's own country. That was not the kind of disloyalty the framers thought should constitute treason. They promptly accepted the proposal to restrict it to cases where also there was conduct which was 'giving them aid and comfort.'

'Aid and comfort' was defined by Lord Reading in the Casement trial comprehensively, as it should be, and yet probably with as much precision as the nature of the matter will permit: '... an act which strengthens or tends to strengthen the enemies of the King in the conduct of a war against the King, that is in law the giving of aid and comfort' and 'an act which weakens or tends to weaken the power of the King and of the country to resist or to attack the enemies of the King and the country ... is ... giving of aid and comfort.' Lord Reading explained it, as we think one must, in terms of an 'act.' It is not easy, if indeed possible, to think of a way in which 'aid and comfort' and be 'given' to an enemy except by some kind of action. Its very nature partakes of a deed or physical activity as opposed to a mental operation.

Thus the crime of treason consists of two elements: adherence to the enemy; and rendering him aid and comfort. A citizen intellectually or emotionally may favor the enemy and harbor sympathies or convictions disloyal to this country's policy or interest, but so long as he commits no act of aid and comfort to the enemy, there is no treason. On the other hand, a citizen may take actions, which do aid and comfort the enemy — making a speech critical of the government or opposing its measures, profiteering, striking in defense plants or essential work, and the hundred other things which impair our cohesion and diminish our strength — but if there is no adherence to the enemy in this, if there is no intent to betray, there is no treason.

Having thus by definition made treason consist of something outward and visible and capable of direct proof, the framers turned to safeguarding procedures of trial and ordained that 'No Person shall be convicted of Treason unless on the Testimony of two Witnesses to the same overt Act, or on Confession in open Court.' This repeats in procedural terms the concept that thoughts and attitudes alone cannot make a treason. It need not trouble us that we find so dominant a purpose emphasized in two different ways. But does the procedural requirement add some limitation not already present in the definition of the crime, and if so, what?

While to prove giving of aid and comfort would require the prosecution to show actions and deeds, if the Constitution stopped there, such acts could be inferred from circumstantial evidence. This the framers thought would not do.... So they added what in effect is a command that the overt acts must be established by direct evidence, and the direct testimony must be that of two witnesses instead of one. In this sense the overt act procedural provision adds something, and something important, to the definition.

Our problem begins where the Constitution ends. That instrument omits to specify what relation the indispensable overt act must sustain to the two elements of the offense as defined: viz., adherence and giving aid and comfort. It requires that two witnesses testify to the same overt act, and clearly enough the act must show something toward treason, but what? Must the act be one of giving aid and comfort? If so, how must adherence to the enemy, the disloyal state of mind, be shown?

The defendant especially challenges the sufficiency of the overt acts to prove treasonable intention. Questions of intent in a treason case are even more complicated than in most criminal cases because of the peculiarity of the two different elements which together make the offense. Of course the overt acts of aid and comfort must be intentional as distinguished from merely negligent or undesigned ones. Intent in that limited sense is not in issue here. But to make treason the defendant not only must intend the act, but he must intend to betray his country by means of the act. It is here that Cramer defends. The issue is joined between conflicting theories as to how this treacherous intention and treasonable purpose must be made to appear.

Bearing in mind that the constitutional requirement in effect in one of direct rather than circumstantial evidence, we must give it a reasonable effect in the light of its purpose both to preserve the offense and to protect citizens from its abuse. What is designed in the mind of an accused never is susceptible of proof by direct testimony. If we were to hold that the disloyal and treacherous intention must be proved by the direct testimony of two witnesses, it would be to hold that it is never provable. It seems obvious that adherence to the enemy, in the sense of a disloyal state of mind, cannot be, and is not required to be, proved by deposition of two witnesses.

Since intent must be inferred from conduct of some sort, we think it is permissible to draw usual reasonable inferences as to intent from the overt acts. The law of treason, like the law of lesser crimes, assumes every man to intend the natural consequences which one standing in his circumstances and possessing his knowledge would reasonably expect to result from his acts. Proof that a citizen did give aid and comfort to an enemy may well be in the circumstances sufficient evidence that he adhered to that enemy and intended and purposed to strike at his own country. It may be doubted whether it would be what the founders intended, or whether it would well serve any of the ends they cherished, to hold the treason offense available to punish only those who make their treacherous intentions more evident than may be done by rendering aid and comfort to an enemy. Treason — insidious and dangerous treason — is the work of the shrewd and crafty more often than of the simple and impulsive.

While of course it must be proved that the accused acted with an intention and purpose to betray or there is no treason, we think that in some circumstances at least the overt act itself will be evidence of the treasonable purpose and intent. But that still leaves us with exceedingly difficult problems. How decisively must treacherous intention be made manifest in the act itself? Will a scintilla of evidence of traitorous intent suffice? Or must it be sufficient to convince beyond reasonable doubt? Or need it show only that treasonable intent was more probable than not? Must the overt act be appraised for legal sufficiency only as supported by the testimony of two witnesses, or may other evidence be thrown into the scales to create inferences not otherwise reasonably to be drawn or to reinforce those which might be drawn from the act itself?

It is only overt acts by the accused which the Constitution explicitly requires to be proved by the testimony of two witnesses. It does not make other common-law evidence inadmissible nor deny its inherent powers of persuasion. It does not forbid judging by the usual process by which the significance of conduct often will be determined by facts which are not acts. Actions of the accused are set in time and place in many relationships. Environment illuminates the meaning of acts, as context does that of words. What a man is up to may be clear from considering his bare acts by themselves; often it is made clear when we know the reciprocity and sequence of his acts with those of others, the interchange between him and another, the give and take of the situation.

It would be no contribution to certainty of judgment, which is the object of the provision, to construe it to deprive a trial court of the aid of testimony under the ordinary sanctions of verity, provided, of course, resort is not had to evidence of less than the constitutional standard to supply deficiencies in the constitutional measure of proof of overt acts. For it must be remembered that the constitutional provision establishes a minimum of proof of incriminating acts, without which there can be no conviction, but it is not otherwise a limitation on the evidence with which a jury may be persuaded that it ought to convict. The Constitution does not exclude or set up standards to test evidence which will show the relevant acts of persons other than the accused or their identity or enemy character or other surrounding circumstances. Nor does it preclude any proper evidence, of non-incriminating facts about a defendant, such for example as his nationality, naturalization, and residence.

From duly proven overt acts of aid and comfort to the enemy in their setting, it may well be that the natural and reasonable inference of intention to betray will be warranted. The two-witness evidence of the acts accused, together with common-law evidence of acts of others and of facts which are not acts, will help to determine which among possible inferences as to the actor's knowledge, motivation, or intent are the true ones. But the protection of the two-witness rule extends at least to all acts of the defendant which are used to draw incriminating inferences that aid and comfort have been given.

The controversy before us has been waged in terms of intentions, but this, we think, is the reflection of a more fundamental issue as to what is the real function of the overt act in convicting of treason. The prisoner's contention that it alone and on its face must manifest a traitorous intention, apart from an intention to do the act itself, would place on the overt act the whole burden of establishing a complete treason. On the other hand, the Government's contention that it may prove by two witnesses an apparently commonplace and insignificant act and from other circumstances create an inference that the act was a step in treason and was done with treasonable intent really is a contention that the function of the overt act in a treason prosecution is almost zero. It is obvious that the function we ascribe to the overt act is significant chiefly because it measures the two-witness rule protection to the accused and its handicap to the prosecution. If the over act or acts must go all the way to make out the complete treason, the defendant is protected at all points by the two-witness requirement. If the act may be an insignificant one, then the constitutional safeguards are shrunken so as to be applicable only at a point where they are least needed.

The very minimum function that an overt act must perform in a treason prosecution is that it show sufficient action by the accused, in its setting, to sustain a finding that the accused actually gave aid and comfort to the enemy. Every act, movement, deed, and word of the defendant charged to constitute treason must be supported by the testimony of two witnesses. The two-witness principle is to interdict imputation of incriminating acts to the accused by circumstantial evidence or by the testimony of a single witness. The prosecution cannot rely on evidence which does not meet the constitutional test for overt acts to create any inference that the accused did other acts or did something more than was shown in the overt act, in order to make a giving of aid and comfort to the enemy. The words of the Constitution were chosen, not to make it hard to prove merely routine and everyday acts, but to make the proof of acts that convict of treason as sure as trial processes may. When the prosecution's case is thus established, the Constitution does not prevent presentation of corroborative or cumulative evidence of any admissible character either to strengthen a direct case or to rebut the testimony or inferences on behalf of defendant. The Government is not prevented from making a strong case; it is denied a conviction on a weak one.

It may be that in some cases the overt acts, sufficient to prove giving of aid and comfort, will fall short of showing intent to betray and that questions will then be raised as to permissible methods of proof that we do not reach in this case. But in this and some cases we have cited where the sufficiency of the overt acts has been challenged because they were colorless as to intent, we are persuaded the reason intent was left in question was that the acts were really indecisive as a giving of aid and comfort. When we deal with acts that are trivial and commonplace and hence are doubtful as to whether they gave aid and comfort to the enemy, we are most put to it to find in other evidence a treacherous intent.

We proceed to consider the application of these principles to Cramer's case.

IV.

The indictment charged Cramer with adhering to the enemies of the United States, giving them aid and comfort, and set forth ten overt acts. The prosecution withdrew seven, and three were submitted to the jury. The overt acts which present the principal issue ... are alleged in the following language:

'1. Anthony Cramer, the defendant herein, on or about June 23, 1942, at the Southern District of New York and within the jurisdiction of this Court, did meet with Werner Thiel and Edward John Kerling, enemies of the United States, at the Twin Oaks Inn at Lexington Avenue and 44th Street, in the City and State of New York, and did confer, treat, and counsel with said Werner Thiel and Edward John Kerling for a period of time for the purpose of giving and with intent to give aid and comfort to said enemies, Werner Thiel and Edward John Kerling.'

'2. Anthony Cramer, the defendant herein, on or about June 23, 1942, at the Southern District of New York and within the jurisdiction of this Court, did accompany, confer, treat, and counsel with Werner Thiel, an enemy of the United States, for a period of time at the Twin Oaks Inn at Lexington Avenue and 44th Street, and at Thompson's Cafeteria on 42nd Street between Lexington and Vanderbilt Avenues, both in the City and State of New York, for the purpose of giving and with intent to give aid and comfort to said enemy, Werner Thiel.'

At the present stage of the case we need not weight their sufficiency as a matter of pleading. Whatever the averments might have permitted the Government to prove, we now consider their adequacy on the proof as made.

It appeared upon the trial that at all times involved in these acts Kerling and Thiel were under surveillance of the Federal Bureau of Investigation. By direct testimony of two or more agents it was established that Cramer met Thiel and Kerling on the occasions and at the places charged and that they drank together and engaged long and earnestly in conversation. This is the sum of the overt acts as established by the testimony of two witnesses. There is no two-witness proof of what they said nor in what language they conversed. There is no showing that Cramer gave them any information whatever of value to their mission or indeed that he had any to give. No effort at secrecy is shown, for they met in public places. Cramer furnished them no shelter, nothing that can be called sustenance or supplies, and there is no evidence that he gave them encouragement or counsel, or even paid for their drinks.

The Government recognizes the weakness of its proof of aid and comfort, but on this scope it urges: 'Little imagination is required to perceive the advantage such meeting would afford to enemy spies not yet detected. Even apart from the psychological comfort which the meetings furnished Thiel and Kerling by way of social intercourse with one who they were confident would not report them to the authorities, as a loyal citizen should, the meetings gave them a source of information and an avenue for contact. It enabled them to be seen in public with a citizen above suspicion and thereby to be mingling normally with the citizens of the country with which they were at war.' The difficulty with this argument is that the whole purpose of the constitutional provision is to make sure that treason conviction shall rest on direct proof of two witnesses and not on even a little imagination. And without the use of some imagination it is difficult to perceive any advantage which this meeting afforded to Thiel and Kerling as enemies or how it strengthened Germany or weakened the United States in any way whatever. It may be true that the saboteurs were cultivating Cramer as a potential 'source of information and an avenue for contact.' But there is no proof either by two witnesses or by even one witness or by any circumstance that Cramer gave them information or established any 'contact' for them with any person other than an attempt to bring about a rendezvous between Thiel and a girl, or that being 'seen in public with a citizen above suspicion' was of any assistance to the enemy. Meeting with Cramer in public drinking places to tipple and trifle was no part of the saboteurs' mission and did not advance it. It may well have been a digression which jeopardized its success.

. . . .

The Government contends that outside of the overt acts, and by lesser degree of proof, it has shown a treasonable intent on Cramer's part in meeting and talking with Thiel and Kerling. But if it showed him disposed to betray, and showed that he had opportunity to do so, it still has not proved in the manner required that he did any acts submitted to the jury as a basis for conviction which had the effect of betraying by giving aid and comfort. To take the intent for the deed would carry us back to constructive treasons.

It is outside of the commonplace overt acts as proved that we must find all that convicts or convinces either that Cramer gave aid and comfort or that he had a traitorous intention. The prosecution relied chiefly upon the testimony of Norma Kopp, the fiancée of Thiel, as to incriminating statements made by Cramer to her ... upon admissions made by Cramer after his arrest to agents of the Federal Bureau of Investigation ... upon letters and documents found on search of his room by permission after his arrest ... and upon testimony that Cramer had curtly refused to buy Government bonds.... After denial of defendant's motion to dismiss at the close of the prosecution's case, defendant became a witness in his own behalf and the Government obtained on cross-examination some admissions of which it had the benefit on submission....

It is not relevant to our issue to appraise weight or credibility of the evidence apart from determining its constitutional sufficiency. Nor is it necessary in the view we take of the more fundamental issues, to discuss the reservations which all of us entertain as to the admissibility of some of it or those which some entertain as to other of it. We could conclude in favor of affirmance only if all questions of admissibility were resolved against the prisoner. At all events much of the evidence is of the general character whose infirmities were feared by the framers and sought to be safeguarded against.

Most damaging is the testimony of Norma Kopp, a friend of Cramer's and one with whom, if she is to be believed, he had been most indiscreetly confidential. Her testimony went considerably beyond that of the agents of the Federal Bureau of Investigation as to admissions of guilty knowledge of Thiel's hostile mission and of Cramer's sympathy with it. To the extent that his conviction rests upon such evidence, and it does to an unknown but considerable extent, it rests upon the uncorroborated testimony of one witness not without strong emotional interest in the drama of which Cramer's trial was a part. Other evidence relates statements by Cramer before the United States was at war with Germany. At the time they were uttered, however, they were not treasonable. To use pre-war expressions of opposition to entering a war to convict of treason during the war is a dangerous procedure at best. The same may be said about the inference of disloyal attitude created by showing that he refused to buy bonds and closed the door in the salesman's face. Another class of evidence consists of admissions to agents of the Federal Bureau of Investigation. They are of course, not 'confession in open court.' The Government does not contend and could not well contend that admissions made out of court, if otherwise admissible, can supply a deficiency in proof of the overt act itself.

V.

The Government has urged that our initial interpretation of the treason clause should be less exacting, lest treason be too hard to prove and the Government disabled from adequately combating the techniques of modern warfare. But the treason offense is not the only nor can it well serve as the principal legal weapon to vindicate our national cohesion and security. In debating this provision, Rufus King observed to the Convention that the 'controversy relating to Treason might be of less magnitude than was supposed; as the legislature might punish capitally under other names than Treason.'... His statement holds good today. Of course we do not intimate that Congress could dispense with the two-witness rule merely by giving the same offense another name. But the power of Congress is in no way limited to enact prohibitions of specified acts thought detrimental to our wartime safety. The loyal and the disloyal alike may be forbidden to do acts which place our security in peril, and the trial thereof may be focused upon defendant's specific intent to do those particular acts ... thus eliminating the accusation of treachery and of general intent to betray which have such passion-rousing potentialities. Congress repeatedly has enacted prohibitions of specific acts thought to endanger our security ... and the practice of foreign nations with defense problems more acute than our own affords examples of others....

The framers' effort to compress into two sentences the law of one of the most intricate of crimes gives a superficial appearance of clarity and simplicity which proves illusory when it is put to practical application. There are few subjects on which the temptation to utter abstract interpretative generalizations is greater or on which they are more to be distrusted. The little clause is packed with controversy and difficulty. The offense is one of subtlety, and it is easy to demonstrate lack of logic in almost any interpretation by hypothetical cases, to which real treasons rarely will conform. The protection of the two-witness requirement, limited as it is to overt acts, may be wholly unrelated to the real controversial factors in a case. We would be understood as speaking only in the light of the facts and of the issues raised in the case under consideration, although that leaves many undetermined grounds of dispute which, after the method of the common law, we may defer until they are presented by facts which may throw greater light on their significance. Although nothing in the conduct of Cramer's trial evokes it, a repetition of Chief Justice Marshall's warning can never be untimely:

> 'As there is no crime which can more excite and agitate the passions of men than treason, no charge demands more from the tribunal before which it is made, a deliberate and temperate inquiry. Whether this inquiry be directed to the fact or to the law, none can be more solemn, none more important to the citizen or to the government; none can more affect the safety of both.... It is therefore more safe as well as more consonant to the principles of our constitution, that the crime of treason should not be extended by construction to doubtful cases; and that crimes not clearly within the constitutional definition, should receive such punishment as the legislature in its wisdom may provide.' Ex parte Bollman, 4 Cranch 75, 125, 127.

It is not difficult to find grounds upon which to quarrel with this Constitutional provision. Perhaps the framers placed rather more reliance on direct testimony than modern researches in psychology warrant. Or it may be considered that such a quantitative measure of proof, such a mechanical calibration of evidence is a crude device at best or that its protection of innocence is too fortuitous to warrant so unselective an obstacle to conviction. Certainly the treason rule, whether wisely or not, is severely restrictive. It must be remembered, however, that the Constitutional Convention was warned by James Wilson that 'Treason may sometimes be practiced in such a manner, as to render proof extremely difficult—as in a traitorous correspondence with an Enemy.' The provision was adopted not merely in spite of the difficulties it put in the way of prosecution but because of them. And it was not by whim or by accident, but because one of the most venerated of that venerated group considered that 'prosecutions for treason were generally virulent.' Time has not made the accusation of treachery less poisonous, nor the task of judging one charged with betraying the country, including his triers, less susceptible to the influence of suspicion and rancor. The innovations made by the forefathers in the law of treason were conceived in a faith such as Paine put in the maxim that 'He that would make his own liberty secure must guard even his enemy from oppression; for if he violates this duty he establishes a precedent that will reach himself.'... We still put trust in it.

We hold that overt acts 1 and 2 are insufficient as proved to support the judgment of conviction, which accordingly is

Reversed.

Comments and Questions for Discussion

1. The constitutional requirement for proving treason does not make the crime dead letter. Indeed, in another World War II-era case, the government had better success. Hans Max Haupt, an American citizen, was the father of Herbert Haupt, one of the eight German saboteurs convicted by a military tribunal. *Ex Parte Quirin*, 317 U.S. 1. The Supreme Court affirmed Hans' treason conviction, finding that his overt acts—sheltering his son, assisting him with getting a job and in buying a car, all alleged to be with knowledge of his son's mission—were sufficiently different than the "aid and comfort" acts found lacking in *Cramer*. "We hold, therefore, that the overt acts laid in the indictment and submitted to the jury do perform the functions assigned to overt acts in treason cases and are sufficient to support the indictment...." *Haupt v. United States*, 330 U.S. 631(1947)(Jackson, J.).

2. The United States has obtained an indictment of American citizen Adam Gadahn for treason, for his conduct in assisting al Qaida by serving as its public spokesman. If Gadahn is ever arrested, will the government be able to fulfill the two-witness rule in his U.S. prosecution?

3. In *Cramer*, the Court suggested there would be constitutional problems if Congress enacted a statute that punished treason "by giving the same offense another name," and did not have the two-witness rule or overt act requirements. Does the Treason Clause place any significant limitation on Congress's ability to enact statutory penalties against what is clearly traitorous activity?

4. Seditious conspiracy, linguistically, comes very close to treason. By its terms, treason is levying war against the United States, while seditious conspiracy is conspiracy to levy war against the United States. Conspiracy crimes, of course, often require overt acts in furtherance of the conspiracy. Is there a two-witness rule for seditious conspiracy? See 18 U.S. Code § 2384.

Seditious Conspiracy

United States v. Rahman

189 F.3d 88 (2d. Cir. 1999)

Affirmed in part; remanded in part.

Before: NEWMAN, LEVAL, and PARKER, Circuit Judges.

PER CURIAM:

INTRODUCTION

These are appeals by ten defendants convicted of seditious conspiracy and other offenses arising out of a wide-ranging plot to conduct a campaign of urban terrorism. Among the activities of some or all of the defendants were rendering assistance to those who bombed the World Trade Center, *see* United States v. Salameh, 152 F.3d 88 (2d. Cir. 1998) (affirming convictions of all four defendants), planning to bomb bridges and tunnels in New York City, murdering Rabbi Meir Kahane, and planning to murder the President of Egypt. We affirm the convictions of all the defendants. We also affirm all of the sentences, with the exception of the sentence of Ibrahim El-Gabrowny, which we remand for further consideration.

> ....

Defendant Nosair (joined by other defendants) contends that his conviction for seditious conspiracy, in violation of 18 U.S.C. § 2384, was illegal because it failed to satisfy the requirements of the Treason Clause of the U.S. Constitution, Art. III, § 3....

Article III, Section 3 provides, in relevant part:

> Treason against the United States, shall consist only in levying War against them, or in adhering to their Enemies, giving them Aid and Comfort. No Person shall be convicted of Treason unless on the Testimony of two Witnesses to the same overt Act, or on Confession in open Court.

The seditious conspiracy statute provides:

> If two or more persons in any State or Territory, or in any place subject to the jurisdiction of the United States, conspire to overthrow, put down or to destroy by force the Government of the United States, or to levy war against them, or to oppose by force the authority thereof, or by force to prevent, hinder or delay the execution of any law of the United States, or by force to seize, take, or possess any property of the United States contrary to the authority thereof, they shall each be fined under this title or imprisoned not more than twenty years, or both.

18 U.S.C. § 2384.

Nosair contends that because the seditious conspiracy statute punishes conspiracy to "levy war" against the United States without a conforming two-witness requirement, the statute is unconstitutional. He further claims that because his conviction for conspiracy to levy war against the United States was not based on the testimony of two witnesses to the same overt act, the conviction violates constitutional standards.

It is undisputed that Nosair's conviction was not supported by two witnesses to the same overt act. Accordingly the conviction must be overturned if the requirement of the Treason Clause applies to this prosecution for seditious conspiracy.

The plain answer is that the Treason Clause does not apply to the prosecution. The provisions of Article III, Section 3 apply to prosecutions for "treason." Nosair and his co-appellants were not charged with treason. Their offense of conviction, seditious conspiracy under Section 2384, differs from treason not only in name and associated stigma, but also in its essential elements and punishment.

In the late colonial period, as today, the charge of treason carried a "peculiar intimidation and stigma" with considerable "potentialities ... as a political epithet." *See* William Hurst, *Treason in the United States* (Pt. II), 58 HARV. L. REV. 395, 424–25 (1945).

At the time of the drafting of the Constitution, furthermore, treason was punishable not only by death, but by an exceptionally cruel method of execution designed to enhance the suffering of the traitor....

In recognition of the potential for political manipulation of the treason charge, the Framers may have formulated the Treason Clause as a protection against promiscuous resort to this particularly stigmatizing label, which carries such harsh consequences. It is thus possible to interpret the Treason Clause as applying only to charges denominated as "treason."

The Supreme Court has identified but not resolved the question whether the clause applies to offenses that include all the elements of treason but are not branded as such. Compare Ex Parte Quirin, 317 U.S. 1, 38, 63 S. Ct. 2, 87 L. Ed. 3 (1942) (suggesting, in dictum, that citizens could be tried for an offense against the law of war that included all the elements of treason), with Cramer v. United States, 325 U.S. 1, 45, 65 S. Ct. 918, 89 L. Ed. 1441 (1945) (noting in dictum that it did not "intimate that Congress could dispense with [the] two-witness rule merely by giving the same offense [of treason] another name."). The question whether a defendant who engaged in subversive conduct might be tried for a crime involving all the elements of treason, but under a different name and without the constitutional protection of the Treason Clause, therefore remains open. And we need not decide it in this case, because the crime of which Nosair was convicted differs significantly from treason, not only in name and punishment, but also in definition.

Seditious conspiracy by levying war includes no requirement that the defendant owe allegiance to the United States, an element necessary to conviction of treason. See 18 U.S.C. § 2381 (defining "allegiance to United States" as an element of treason). Nosair nevertheless maintains that "[t]he only distinction between the elements of seditious conspiracy under the levy war prong and treason by levying war is that the former requires proof of a conspiracy while the latter requires proof of the substantive crime." Reply Brief for Nosair at 9. Noting that the requirement of allegiance appears explicitly in the treason statute, but not in the Treason Clause, Nosair suggests that allegiance to the United States is not an element of treason within the contemplation of the Constitution. He concludes that, for constitutional purposes, the elements constituting seditious conspiracy by levying war and treason by levying war are identical, and consequently that prosecutions for seditious conspiracy by levying war must conform to the requirements of the Treason Clause.

The argument rests on a false premise. The Treason Clause does not, as Nosair supposes, purport to specify the elements of the crime of treason. Instead, in addition to providing evidentiary safeguards, the Clause restricts the conduct that may be deemed treason to "levying war" against the United States and "adhering to their Enemies, giving them Aid and Comfort." It does not undertake to define the constituent elements of the substantive crime.

Moreover, any acceptable recitation of the elements of treason must include the breach of allegiance. The concept of allegiance betrayed is integral to the term "treason," and has been since well before the drafting of the Constitution. See 3 Holdsworth, History of English Law 287 (noting that "the idea of treachery" has been part of the treason offense since the reign of Edward III). In both "its common-law and constitutional definitions the term 'treason' imports a breach of allegiance." Green's Case, 8 Ct. Cl. 412, 1872 WL 5731 (1872). Treason "imports a betraying." Id. (quoting 3 Tomlin's Law Dictionary 637). Blackstone, too, noted that treason, "in it's [sic] very name ... imports a betraying, treachery or breach of faith." 4 Blackstone, supra, at *75. Early on, our Supreme Court recognized that "[t]reason is a breach of allegiance, and can be committed by him only who owes allegiance." United States v. Wiltberger, 18 U.S. (5 Wheat.) 76, 97, 5 L. Ed. 37 (1820) (Marshall, C.J.). Nor is there any doubt that the delegates to the Constitutional Convention "used [the term 'treason'] to express the central concept of betrayal of allegiance." Hurst, supra, at 415.

Nosair's suggestion that the statutory definition of treason added the requirement of allegiance is mistaken. The reference to treason in the constitutional clause necessarily incorporates the elements of allegiance and betrayal that are essential to the concept of treason. Cf. Wiltberger, 18 U.S. at 97 (noting that the inclusion of the words "owing allegiance" in a statute punishing treason are surplusage because the concept is implicit in the term). The functions of the Clause are to limit the crime of treason to betrayals of allegiance that are substantial, amounting to levying war or giving comfort to enemies, and to require sufficiently reliable evidence. Treason, in other words, may not be found on the basis of mere mutterings of discontent, or relatively innocuous opposition. The fact that the Treason Clause imposes its requirements without mentioning the requirement of allegiance is not a basis for concluding that treason may be prosecuted without allegiance being proved. That any conviction for treason under the laws of the United States requires a betrayal of allegiance is simply implicit in the term "treason." Nosair was thus tried for a different, and lesser, offense than treason. We therefore see no reasonable basis to maintain that the requirements of the Treason Clause should apply to Nosair's prosecution. Cf. United States v. Rodriguez, 803 F.2d 318, 320 (7th Cir. 1986) (rejecting argument that "oppose by force" prong of Section 2384 conflicts with Treason Clause.

. . . .

We have considered all of the other claims raised on appeal by all of the defendants, beyond those discussed in this opinion, and conclude that they are without merit. The convictions of all ten defendants are affirmed. With the exception of the sentence of defendant El-Gabrowny, which is remanded for further proceedings as set forth in this opinion, the sentences of all the other defendants are affirmed.

Questions for Discussion

1. The *Rahman* court suggests that the protections in the Treason Clause are reserved only for a crime labeled as "treason" because of the extreme opprobrium associated with that crime, notwithstanding that the Treason Clause defines the crime as including "levying war against them [the United States]" while the seditious conspiracy statute penalizes, among other things, conspiracies to "levy war against them." Does such an interpretation essentially nullify the protections in the Clause?

2. The court also distinguishes the two offenses because treason requires proof of allegiance to the United States, while seditious conspiracy does not, and upholds the convictions notwithstanding the possibility that one or more of the defendants may in fact have owed allegiance to the United States (was an American citizen), a fact easily provable by a birth certificate, among other things. If it were publicly known that a defendant convicted of conspiring to levy war against the United States was a native U.S. citizen and a long-time resident of the country, would the fact that he was not convicted of "treason" per se alter the lay public's perception that he was a traitor?

Providing Material Support

One of the things prohibited by the treason statute is giving "aid and comfort to the enemy." For the last few decades, at least in Afghanistan, the enemy was not a country but rather a subnational terrorist organization—al Qaeda and its affiliates. During this period, prosecutors started taking advantage of a 1996 crime that prohibits anyone from knowingly providing "material support or resources" to designated foreign terrorist organizations. Al Qaeda was first designated in 1999, shortly after the 1998 East Africa

Embassy Bombings. Since then, this statute—18 U.S.C. §2339B—has proven to be a very robust tool for redressing the phenomenon of Americans helping al Qaeda.

U.S. v. Lindh

212 F. Supp. 2d 541 (E.D. Va. 2002)

JUDGE LEE:

John Phillip Walker Lindh ("Lindh") is an American citizen who, according to the ten-count Indictment filed against him in February 2002, joined certain foreign terrorist organizations in Afghanistan and served these organizations there in combat against Northern Alliance and American forces until his capture in November 2001. In seven threshold motions, Lindh sought dismissal of certain counts of the Indictment on a variety of grounds....

I.

The Indictment's allegations may be succinctly summarized. In mid-2001, Lindh attended a military training camp in Pakistan run by Harakat ul-Mujahideen ("HUM"), a terrorist group dedicated to an extremist view of Islam.[2] After receiving several weeks of training, Lindh informed HUM officials that "he wished to fight with the Taliban[3] in Afghanistan." Indictment. p. 6, ¶5. Thus, in May or June 2001, he traveled from Pakistan into Afghanistan "for the purpose of taking up arms with the Taliban," eventually arriving at a Taliban recruiting center in Kabul, Afghanistan—the Dar ul-Anan Headquarters of the Mujahideen. Indictment, p. 7, ¶6. On his arrival, Lindh presented a letter of introduction from HUM and advised Taliban personnel "that he was an American and that he wanted to go to the front lines to fight." Indictment, p. 7, ¶7.

While at the Dar ul-Anan Headquarters, Lindh agreed to receive additional and extensive military training at an al Qaeda[4] training camp. He made this decision "knowing that America and its citizens were the enemies of Bin Laden and al-Qaeda and that a principal purpose of al-Qaeda was to fight and kill Americans." Indictment, p. 7, ¶8. In late May or June 2001, Lindh traveled to a bin Laden guest house in Kandahar, Afghanistan, where he stayed for several days, and then traveled to the al Farooq training camp, "an al Qaeda facility located several hours west of Kandahar." Indictment, p. 7 ¶10. He reported to the camp with approximately twenty other trainees, mostly Saudis, and remained there throughout June and July. During this period, he participated fully in the camp's training activities, despite being told early in his stay that "Bin Laden had sent forth some fifty people to carry out twenty suicide terrorist operations against the United States and Israel." Indictment, p. 7, ¶11. As part of his al Qaeda training, Lindh participated in "terrorist

---

2. On October 8, 1997, HUM was designated by the Secretary of State as a foreign terrorist organization, pursuant to Section 219 of the Immigration and Nationality Act. *See* 62 Fed. Reg. 52650 (1997).

3. According to the Indictment, the Taliban is Afghanistan's dominant political force and its members, like the members of HUM, practice an extremist form of Islam. Specifically, members of the Taliban believe in conducting "jihad," or holy war, against those whom they believe threaten their form of Islam, including the United States.

4. The Indictment alleges that al Qaeda is an organization, founded by Osama bin Laden and others; that is, dedicated to opposing non-Islamic governments with force and violence. On October 8, 1999, al Qaeda was designated by the Secretary of State as a foreign terrorist organization, pursuant to Section 219 of the Immigration and Nationality Act. See 64 Fed. Reg. 55112 (1999). The Secretary of State has also declared al Qaeda a "specially designated terrorist," pursuant to the International Emergency Economic Powers Act. *See* 66 Fed. Reg. 54404 (2001).

training courses in, among other things, weapons, orienteering, navigation, explosives and battlefield combat." Indictment, pp. 7–8, ¶ 12. This training included the use of "shoulder weapons, pistols and rocket-propelled grenades, and the construction of Molotov cocktails." Indictment, p. 8, ¶ 12. During his stay at al Farooq, Lindh met personally with bin Laden, "who thanked him and other trainees for taking part in jihad." Indictment, p. 8, ¶ 13. He also met with a senior al Qaeda official. Abu Mohammad Al-Masri, who inquired whether Lindh was interested in traveling outside Afghanistan to conduct operations against the United States and Israel. Lindh declined Al-Masri's offer in favor of going to the front lines to fight. It is specifically alleged that Lindh swore allegiance to jihad in June or July 2001.

When Lindh completed his training at al Farooq in July or August 2001, he traveled to Kabul, Afghanistan, where he was issued an AKM rifle "with a barrel suitable for long range shooting." Indictment, p. 8, ¶ 16. Armed with this rifle, Lindh, together with approximately 150 non-Afghani fighters, traveled from Kabul to the front line at Takhar, located in Northeastern Afghanistan, where the entire unit was placed under the command of an Iraqi named Abdul Hady. Lindh's group was eventually divided into smaller groups that fought in shifts against Northern Alliance troops in the Takhar trenches, rotating every one to two weeks. During this period, Lindh "carried various weapons with him, including the AKM rifle, an RPK rifle he was issued after the AKM rifle malfunctioned, and at least two grenades." Indictment, p. 8, ¶ 19. He remained with his fighting group following the September 11, 2001 terrorist attacks, "despite having been told that Bin Laden had ordered the [September 11] attacks, that additional terrorist attacks were planned, and that additional al Qaeda personnel were being sent from the front lines to protect Bin Laden and defend against an anticipated military response from the United States." Indictment. p. 9, ¶ 20. Indeed, it is specifically alleged that Lindh remained with his fighting group from October to December 2001, "after learning that United States military forces and United States nationals had become directly engaged in support of the Northern Alliance in its military conflict with Taliban and al Qaeda forces." Indictment, p. 9, ¶ 21.

In November 2001, Lindh and his fighting group retreated from Takhar to the area of Kunduz, Afghanistan, where they ultimately surrendered to Northern Alliance troops. On November 24, 2001, he and the other captured Taliban fighters were transported to Mazar-e-Sharif, and then to the nearby Qala-i-Janghi (QIJ) prison compound. The following day, November 25, Lindh was interviewed by two Americans—Agent Johnny Micheal Spann from the Central Intelligence Agency (CIA) and another government employee. Later that day, it is alleged that Taliban detainees in the QIJ compound attacked Spann and the other employee, overpowered the guards, and armed themselves. Spann was shot and killed in the course of the uprising and Lindh, after being wounded, retreated with other detainees to a basement area of the QIJ compound. The uprising at QIJ was eventually suppressed on December 1, 2001, at which time Lindh and other Taliban and al Qaeda fighters were taken into custody by Northern Alliance and American forces.

Following his capture, Lindh was interrogated, transported to the United States, and ultimately charged in this district with the following offenses in a ten-count Indictment:

(i) conspiracy to murder nationals of the United States, including American military personnel and other governmental employees serving in Afghanistan following the September 11, 2001 terrorist attacks, in violation of 18 U.S.C. § 2332(b)(2) (Count One);

(ii) conspiracy to provide material support and resources to HUM, a foreign terrorist organization, in violation of 18 U.S.C. § 2339B (Count Two);

(iii) providing material support and resources to HUM, in violation of 18 U.S.C. § 2339B and 2 (Count Three);

(iv) conspiracy to provide material support and resources to al Qaeda, a foreign terrorist organization, in violation of 18 U.S.C. § 2339B (Count Four);

(v) providing material support and resources to al Qaeda, in violation of 18 U.S.C. § 2339B and 2 (Count Five);

(vi) conspiracy to contribute services to al Qaeda, in violation of 31 §§ C.F.R. 595.205 and 595.204 and 50 U.S.C. § 1705(b) (Count Six);

(vii) contributing services to al Qaeda, in violation of 31 C.F.R. §§ 595.204 595.204 and 595.205 and 50 U.S.C. § 1705(b) and 18 U.S.C. § 2 (Count Seven);

(viii) conspiracy to supply services to the Taliban, in violation of 31 C.F.R. §§ 545.206(b) and 545.204 and 50 U.S.C. § 1705(b) (Count Eight);

(ix) supplying services to the Taliban, in violation of 31 C.F.R. §§ 545.204 and 545.206(a) and 50 U.S.C. § 1705(b) and 18 U.S.C. § 2 (Count Nine); and

(x) using and carrying firearms and destructive devices during crimes of violence, in violation of 18 U.S.C. §§ 924(c)(1)(A), 924(c)(1)(B)(ii) and 2 (Count Ten).

. . . .

Lindh[ ] ... seeks dismissal of Counts Two through Five of the Indictment, pursuant to Rule 12, Fed.R.Crim.P. These counts charge Lindh with four distinct violations of 18 U.S.C. § 2339B, which, in pertinent part, provides criminal penalties for "[w]hoever within the United States or subject to the jurisdiction of the United States, knowingly provides material support or resources[5] to a foreign terrorist organization,[6] or attempts or conspires to do so." Lindh argues for dismissal of these counts on grounds (i) that the

---

5. Section 2339B incorporates the definition of "material support or resources" provided in 18 U.S.C. § 2339A, which prohibits the provision of material support or resources for use in connection with a terrorist act. *Id.* § 2339B(g)(4). As defined in that section, "material support or resources" means "currency or monetary instruments or financial securities, financial services, lodging, training, expert advice or assistance, safe houses, false documentation or identification, communications equipment, facilities, weapons, lethal substances, explosives, personnel, transportation, and other physical assets, except medicine or religious materials." *Id.* § 2339A(b). This section was amended by the USA Patriot Act so that the phrase "currency or monetary instruments or financial securities" replaced "currency or other financial securities" in the definition, and the term "expert advice or assistance" was added. *See* USA Patriot Act, Pub. L. No. 107–56, § 805(a)(2), 115 Stat. 272, 377 (Oct. 26, 2001). These amendments are not at issue in this motion. The Antiterrorism and Effective Death Penalty Act of 1996 (AEDPA), codified at 18 U.S.C. § 2339B, also modified the existing definition of "material support or resources" in Section 2339A to reflect the findings and purpose of the legislation. The definition previously excluded "humanitarian assistance to persons not directly involved in such violations" from the list of items defined as constituting "material support or resources." *See* Violent Crime Control and Law Enforcement Act of 1994, Pub. L. No. 103–322, § 120005, 108 Stat. 1796, 2022 (Sept. 13, 1994) (original version of statute). The AEDPA eliminated this exclusion in favor of a narrower exemption for "medicine and religious materials." AEDPA, § 322, 110 Stat. at 1255. The House Conference Report emphasized that "medicine" was "limited to medicine itself, and does not include the vast array of medical supplies," and that "religious materials" did not include "anything that could be used to cause physical injury to any person." H.R. Conf. Rep. No. 104–518, at 114 (1996), reprinted in 1996 U.S.C.C.A.N. 924, 947.

6. A "foreign terrorist organization" for purposes of the statute is one so designated by the Secretary of State pursuant to the provisions of Section 219 of the Immigration and Nationality Act. 18 U.S.C. § 2339B(g)(6).

Indictment is insufficient on its face; and (ii) that his alleged conduct does not violate Section 2339B.

A motion to dismiss an indictment "tests whether the indictment sufficiently charges the offense set forth against defendant." United States v. Brandon, 150 F. Supp. 2d 883, 884 (E.D. Va. 2001); *see also* United States v. Sampson, 371 U.S. 75, 78–79, 83 S. Ct. 173, 9 L. Ed. 2d 136 (1962). In this respect, the standard an indictment must meet is found in Rule 7(c)(1), Fed. R. Crim. P., which provides that "[t]he indictment or the information shall be a plain, concise and definite written statement of the essential facts constituting the offense charged.... It need not contain a formal commencement, a formal conclusion or any other matter not necessary to such a statement." More particularly, it is generally settled that "if an indictment sets forth the essential elements of [an] offense in sufficient detail so as fairly to inform the defendant of the nature of the charge, then it is immune from attack on a motion to dismiss." Brandon, 150 F. Supp. 2d at 884; *see also* United States v. Darby, 37 F.3d 1059, 1063 (4th Cir. 1994). And, to give a defendant sufficient notice of the charges against him, the indictment need only track the language of the statute at issue. See United States v. Wicks, 187 F.3d 426, 427 (4th Cir. 1999); United States v. Smith, 44 F.3d 1259, 1264 (4th Cir. 1995); United States v. Fogel, 901 F.2d 23, 25 (4th Cir. 1990). An indictment satisfies the constitutional guarantees of the Fifth and Sixth Amendments "if it, first, contains the elements of the offense charged and fairly informs a defendant of the charge against which he must defend, and, second, enables him to plead an acquittal or conviction in bar of future prosecutions for the same offense." Wicks, 187 F.3d at 427 (quoting Hamling v. United States, 418 U.S. 87, 117, 94 S. Ct. 2887, 41 L. Ed. 2d 590 (1974)).

These principles, applied here, compel the conclusion that Lindh's motion to dismiss Counts Two through Five of the Indictment as insufficient must fail. Each two-paragraph count of the Indictment begins by realleging and incorporating by reference all ten paragraphs of the general allegations and all 21 overt acts alleged in Count One.[7] In the second paragraph of each Count may be found all the essential elements of the Section 2339B offenses, the approximate dates on which Lindh allegedly committed the offenses, and the foreign terrorist organization he is alleged to have assisted. These general allegations describe HUM and al Qaeda in some detail, and specifically allege their respective designations as foreign terrorist organizations. Thus, "on its face, the Indictment clearly

---

7. The second paragraph of each count then tracks the statutory or regulatory language, with variations concerning the dates, the nature of the charge (substantive or conspiracy), and the foreign organization involved. Thus, paragraph two of Count Two reads as follows:

> From in or about May 2001 through in or about June 2001, the defendant, JOHN PHILLIP WALKER LINDH, subject to the jurisdiction of the United States, but outside of the jurisdiction of any particular state or district, with other persons known and unknown to the Grand Jury, did knowingly conspire to knowingly provide material support and resources, as that term is defined in 18 U.S.C. § 2339A(b), to a foreign terrorist organization, namely Harakat ul-Mujahideen ("HUM"). (In violation of 18 U.S.C. § 2339B.)

Indictment, p. 10. Count Three reads the same as Count Two, except that the second paragraph alleges that Lindh "did knowingly provide and attempt to provide material support and resources," rather than conspire with others to do so. *Id.* Count Four, like Count Two, is a conspiracy provision, except that it charges Lindh with conspiring with others over the period from May 2001 through December 2001 to provide material support and resources to al Qaeda. *See* Indictment, p. 11. Finally, Count Five charges that Lindh committed the substantive offense of providing and attempting to provide material support and resources to al Qaeda during the same time period as alleged in Count Four. *See id.*

passes muster under the applicable legal standard, as it sets forth the essential elements of the offenses in a manner that fairly informs [defendant] of the nature of the charges against [him]." Brandon, 150 F. Supp. 2d at 885; *see also* United States v. American Waste Fibers Co., 809 F.2d 1044, 1046–47 (4th Cir. 1987) (holding that the indictment was sufficiently detailed as it "alert[ed] [defendant] to the elements of the offenses by following the language of the statute" and listed several overt acts "together with locations and dates").

A second argument in support of Lindh's motion to dismiss is that his alleged conduct does not violate Section 2339B. There are two conclusive responses to this contention. First, the Indictment plainly and adequately charges a violation of Section 2339B. And, as noted above, it does so in the required degree of detail so as fairly to apprise Lindh of the nature of the charges against him. There is no requirement for the government to detail its evidence in the Indictment. Lindh's argument is essentially that the evidence will not bear out the charges. This argument is premature; a pre-trial motion to dismiss under Rule 12(b). Fed. R. Crim. P., "cannot be based on a sufficiency of the evidence argument because such an argument raises factual questions embraced in the general issue." United States v. Ayarza-Garcia, 819 F.2d 1043, 1048 (11th Cir. 1987).

The second conclusive response is that Section 2339B's plain language covers Lindh's alleged conduct ... As noted previously, this plain language trumps any suggestion in the legislative history that the provision is limited to proscribing commercial transactions.... Lindh contends his conduct does not, as a matter of law, amount to providing "material support and resources," including "training" and "personnel," because he provided no training and that merely enlisting in an armed force—rather than recruiting for such a force—does not constitute providing personnel. Lindh is incorrect on both arguments.

First, the government has indicated that it may well attempt to show that Lindh provided training. Second, assuming the government fails in this respect, Lindh's conduct as a participant in the training camp and battlefield falls squarely within Section 2339B's proscription against providing support and services, including "personnel." There is little doubt, given the plain meaning of "Personnel"[8] that Lindh provided such support and services. Citing the legislative history, Lindh contends that the term "personnel" is limited to recruitment. This contention is flatly controverted by the term's plain meaning. Indeed, under any reasonable construction of Section 2339B's statutory language, a person who joins the armed force of a foreign terrorist organization, receives combat training from that organization, and serves in a combat unit to protect the organization and advance its goals has provided material support and resources—including, specifically, "personnel"—to

---

8. The dictionary definition of the term "personnel" is "a body of persons usually employed (as in a factory, office, or organization)" or "a body of persons employed in some service." *See supra* Part VI; *see also* United States v. Maxwell, 285 F.3d 336, 341 (4th Cir. 2002) (holding that where a particular term is undefined within a statute, "we turn to its dictionary definition for its common meaning".) These definitions are consistent with the interpretation provided by the United States Attorney's Manual: "There are two different ways of providing 'personnel' to a designated foreign terrorist organization: 1) by working under the direction or control of the organization: or 2) by recruiting another to work under its direction or control. The statute encompasses both methods, so long as the requisite direction or control is present." U.S.A.M. §9–9–91.100 (2001). The broad reading of the term "personnel" is also consistent with the Findings and Purpose of AEDPA, which provide that the statute is to be interpreted broadly, "to provide the Federal Government the fullest possible basis, consistent with the Constitution, to prevent persons within the United States, or subject to the jurisdiction of the United States, from providing material support or resources to foreign organizations that engage in terrorist activities." AEDPA §301(b), 110 Stat. at 1247.

that group. By any measure, Lindh provided personnel, i.e., himself, to al Qaeda and HUM when he allegedly joined these organizations and engaged in a variety of conduct, including combat, to further the goals of these organizations. Thus, to provide personnel is to provide people who become affiliated with the organization and work under its direction: the individual or individuals provided could be the provider himself, or others, or both.

Finally, Lindh asks the Court to construe Section 2339B narrowly, given the constitutional doubt doctrine and the rule of lenity. Neither doctrine applies in this case, however, because the statute is not ambiguous. *See* United States v. Photogrammetric Data Services, 259 F.3d 229, 252 (4th Cir. 2001) ("Because we find the language of the[ ] statute to be unambiguous, ... the rule of constitutional doubt raised by appellants is likewise inapplicable."), cert. denied, 535 U.S. 926, 122 S. Ct. 1295, 152 L. Ed. 2d 208 (2002); Clifford, 197 F. Supp. 2d at 522 (holding that the rule of lenity will not apply unless a statute's plain language is ambiguous).

Comments

1. John Walker Lindh ultimately pled guilty to illegal transactions with the al Qaida in violation of the International Emergency Economic Powers Act (50 U.S.C. § 1705) and was sentenced to 17 years imprisonment.

2. The principle established in *Lindh*, that providing your own body to a foreign terrorist organization constitutes the provision of "personnel" for purposes of 2339B, was a watershed event. It allowed prosecutors to seek indictments of similar people in Portland (Oregon) and Lackawanna (New York) and initiate the *Khan* case in Virginia (page 572). Congress thereafter amended the definition of "material support" to make clear that personnel means "one of more persons, who may be or include oneself." 18 U.S.C. § 2339A(a). It also created the new crime of receiving military-style training from a foreign terrorist organization. 18 U.S.C. § 2339D.

3. The similarity between "material support" and treason, noted above, is illustrated by the fact that, in the most recent treason indictment—involving Adam Gadahn—prosecutors added "material support" charges to the indictment. Consider also the remarkably similar excerpts from judicial opinions outlining the breadth of the two crimes (in the face of challenges that they unconstitutionally criminalize advocacy and association):

From *Humanitarian Law Project v. Reno*, 205 F.3d 1130, 1133–34 (9th Cir. 2000), *cert. denied*, 532 U.S. 904, 121 S. Ct. 1226, 149 L. Ed. 2d 136 (2001):

> The statute does not prohibit being a member of one of the designated groups or vigorously promoting and supporting the political goals of the group. Plaintiffs are even free to praise the groups for using terrorism as a means of achieving their ends. What AEDPA prohibits is the act of giving material support, and there is no constitutional right to facilitate terrorism by giving terrorists the weapons and explosives with which to carry out their grisly missions. Nor, of course, is there a right to provide resources with which terrorists can buy weapons and explosives.

From *Cramer v. United States*, 325 U.S. 1 (1945):

> A citizen intellectually or emotionally may favor the enemy and harbor sympathies or convictions disloyal to this country's policy or interest, but so long as he commits no act of aid and comfort to the enemy, there is no treason. On the other hand, a citizen may take actions, which do aid and comfort the enemy—

making a speech critical of the government or opposing its measures, profiteering, striking in defense plants or essential work, and the hundred other things which impair our cohesion and diminish our strength — but if there is no adherence to the enemy in this, if there is no intent to betray, there is no treason.

Question for Discussion

1. Why was John Walker Lindh not charged with treason?

Neutrality Act

Americans helping to kill other Americans in wartime is a particularly pernicious thing, which is why most people can appreciate the wisdom of the treason and material support statutes. What about Americans fighting in wars to which the United States is not party?

Foreign fighters from Western states traveling to Syria has been described as a major national security challenge. The fear is that the fighters' experience in Syria (and now Iraq) will leave them militantly radicalized, and that they will eventually return home and turn their sights on their home countries as targets.

Are there any American criminal statutes that could incapacitate foreign fighters before they go abroad?

Tucked into the middle of Title 18 (Chapter 45, Foreign Relations) is a grab-bag of criminal offenses that are collectively known as the Neutrality Act, which could be harnessed against this particular brand of conduct. Although they are not the crimes of the century, they reach such conduct as being an unregistered agent of a foreign government (§ 951), conspiracy to kill maim or injure person or damage property in a foreign country (§ 956), commission to serve against a friendly nation (§ 958), enlistment in a foreign service (§ 959) and expedition against friendly nation (§ 960).

The following case shows the occasional interplay between the Neutrality Act, seditious conspiracy, and material support.

U.S. v. Khan

461 F.3d 477 (4th Cir. 2006)

Before WIDENER and DUNCAN, Circuit Judges, and JOSEPH R. GOODWIN, United States District Judge for the Southern District of West Virginia, sitting by designation.

DUNCAN, Circuit Judge

Defendants Masoud Khan ("Khan"), Seifullah Chapman ("Chapman"), and Hammad Abdur-Raheem ("Hammad") appeal their convictions after a bench trial on various counts related to a conspiracy to wage armed conflict against the United States and a conspiracy to wage armed conflict against a country with whom the United States is at peace....

Because of the lengthy and complex background of this case, we initially describe the facts and procedural history generally applicable to all of the defendants. Facts specific to each defendant will be set forth in the discussion of the arguments of each.

I.

Between 1999 and September 11, 2001, Khan, Chapman and Hammad attended the Dar al Arqam Islamic Center in Falls Church, Virginia where Ali Timimi ("Timimi"), a primary lecturer, spoke of the necessity to engage in violent jihad[9] against the enemies of Islam and the "end of time" battle between Muslims and non-Muslims. Several of the attendees, including Chapman and Hammad, organized a group to engage in activities in preparation for jihad.

In the spring of 2000, members of the group began simulating combat through paintball exercises[10] and practices at firing ranges. By early summer, the group was meeting every other weekend. Chapman, Hammad, and others brought AK-47 style rifles to paintball training and also practiced marksmanship. Members were required to follow three rules: don't tell anyone, don't bring anyone, and invoke the Fifth Amendment right against self-incrimination if questioned by the police.

Because Hammad and Chapman had prior military experience, they assisted in leading the paintball drills and conducting the training. Chapman eventually took over and increased the drills' intensity. Chapman told the group that members were going to learn to fight; he enforced Draconian training and imposed physical punishment for infractions of rules that were out-of-character for a recreational paintball pastime. For example, being made to push a car in neutral was the punishment meted out for tardiness. The group also learned combat skills, such as how to avoid a helicopter attack, that appear inconsistent with a recreational pursuit.

Members of the group had ties to Lashkar-e-Taiba ("LET"), the military wing of a Pakistani organization initially founded to conduct jihad against Russians in Afghanistan. Between 1999 and 2003, LET primarily focused on expelling India from Kashmir. Both through its website and through other means, LET proclaimed its support for and involvement in a number of violent acts, particularly against India. In addition, LET advertised that it provided free jihad training camps in Pakistan.

One member of the paintball group, Mr. Hamdi, openly discussed wanting to go to fight in Kashmir and ultimately die as a martyr in combat. Hamdi traveled to Pakistan in August 2000 and was admitted to the LET camps. While there, he fired on Indian positions in Kashmir. Upon his return, he rejoined the paintball group and informed the others about LET's mission to destroy India, Israel, and the United States.

In September 2000, FBI agents visited Chapman and asked him about the paintball activities. After this interview, members of the group discussed whether they should continue in light of the government's knowledge of their activities. They decided to do so, but with heightened secrecy.

Seeking more intense and realistic fighting experience in the summer of 2001, Chapman traveled to the LET camps in Pakistan. While there, he participated in training and fired various rifles and handguns, including at least one automatic weapon. During that time, Chapman also met an LET official in Pakistan by the name of Singh. In 2002, Singh tried to purchase over the internet a wireless video module and a control module for use in an

---

9. Jihad is "a holy war undertaken as a sacred duty by Muslims." WEBSTER'S UNABRIDGED DICTIONARY 1029 (2nd. Ed. 2001).

10. Paintball is a game that simulates military combat in which players on one team try to eliminate players on the opposing team by shooting capsules of water-soluble dye at them from air powered rifles.

unmanned aerial vehicle ("UAV"). Singh selected an airborne video system with a camera and transmitter able to transmit video images from a UAV back to a receiver from as far as 15 miles away. The video camera could be used in military reconnaissance and in helping aim artillery and other weaponry across enemy lines. Singh placed his order from England, but the vendor was unable to confirm the overseas credit card. Chapman and Khan assisted Singh in completing the purchases. In the summer of 2002, Singh visited Virginia, staying first with Chapman and then with Khan.

The terrorist attacks of September 11, 2001, affected both the focus of the paintball group and the relationship of its members to the Dar al Arqam Islamic Center. That night, Timimi argued that the attacks should not be condemned. He was thereafter not invited to lecture at Dar al Arqam, and the tapes of his speeches were destroyed. However, on September 16, 2001, Timimi met with the paintball group, including Khan and Hammad, at a member's house. Chapman, still at the LET camps, was not present. Timimi said that the September 11 attacks were justified and that it was the obligatory religious duty of those present to defend the Taliban against the American troops that were expected to invade Afghanistan in pursuit of Al-Qaeda. The discussion focused on training at the LET camps as necessary preparation to fight with the Taliban against the United States. Several of the members, including Khan, expressed their intent to train at the LET camps and to fight in Afghanistan after their training was complete. For purposes of their travel, they agreed that Khan would be their "emir," or leader.

Khan trained at the LET camps for approximately six weeks. During that time, he traveled through four different camps and received training in commando tactics, reconnaissance, hand-to-hand combat, and survival skills. He received instructions on and used weapons, including AK-47 automatic rifles, machine guns, anti-aircraft guns, rocket-propelled grenades, and mines. He performed sentry duty and routine maintenance tasks for LET. During this time, Khan left the camps on personal business at least once and returned shortly thereafter.

American troops began a ground war against the Taliban on or about October 20, 2001. By mid-November 2001, American and allied troops were defeating Taliban forces throughout northern Afghanistan. On November 13, 2001, the Taliban withdrew from the Afghan capital of Kabul, and forces allied with the United States took control of the city. By November 15, Taliban forces had retreated to Kandahar. In November 2001, while at LET camp, Khan learned through radio reports that American forces were quickly defeating the Taliban in Afghanistan. Further, he learned that Pakistan had closed its border with Afghanistan and that LET would not facilitate his travel there. Moreover, Pakistani authorities were aggressively removing foreigners from the camps. As a result, Khan left the camps in the fall of 2001 without ever having reached Afghanistan.

The government's investigation into the activities of Khan, Chapman, Hammad, and their colleagues became public in February 2003, when a search warrant was executed at Timimi's house. On March 24, 2003, the FBI approached Caliph Abdur Raheem ("Caliph"), one of the paintball members who was tried with defendants in this case and acquitted, and obtained a statement from him. Caliph told the FBI that paintball was used for jihad training and that the reason the trainees had acquired AK-47–style rifles was that they were the type of weapon used overseas. When Hammad learned of the admissions, he called a colleague with the "bad news" that Caliph had "cracked."

As a result of the government's investigation, Hammad, Chapman, and Khan, along with eight others—Caliph, Donald Surratt II, Yong Ki Kwon, Muhammed Aatique, Khwaja Hasan, Randall Todd Royer, Ibrahim Ahmed Al-Hamdi, and Sabri Benkhala—

were indicted in June 2003 for various offenses concerning a conspiracy to engage in military expeditions against India and the United States.

Surratt, Kwon, Aatique, and Hasan all pleaded guilty before trial and cooperated with the government. As a result of their assistance, a superseding indictment was returned against the remaining seven defendants in September 2003. Because of his attempts to fight with the Taliban, Khan was charged with a conspiracy to levy war against the United States, a conspiracy to provide material support to Al-Qaeda, and a conspiracy to contribute services to the Taliban. Neither Chapman nor Hammad was charged with these conspiracies.

In January 2004, Royer and Hamdi pleaded guilty. Benkhala was tried separately and acquitted. The government proceeded against Caliph, Chapman, Hammad, and Khan. Chapman and Hammad moved to have their trial severed from Khan's, arguing that evidence that would be presented against Khan would prejudice their right to a fair trial. The district court denied the motion for severance. Chapman, Hammad, and Khan then moved for a bench trial, which the district court granted.

At trial, the government presented the statements made by Caliph to the FBI that the paintball activities were intended to be training for jihad, and that the trainees had obtained AK-47 style weapons because that was the type of weapon used in combat overseas. After the government's presentation of evidence against him, Caliph moved for an acquittal pursuant to Federal Rule of Criminal Procedure 29. The district court granted that motion. As a result, Caliph never testified, and his co-defendants had no opportunity to cross-examine him concerning his statements.

At the conclusion of the bench trial, the district court wrote a comprehensive opinion detailing the evidence against the three remaining defendants and referencing the wealth of cumulative evidence of record. Khan was acquitted on four counts and convicted on the following eight counts: (1) one count of conspiracy to enlist in armed conflict against the United States in violation of 18 U.S.C. §§ 371, 2390; (2) one count of conspiracy to levy war against the United States in violation of 18 U.S.C. § 2384; (3) one count of conspiracy to contribute services to the Taliban in violation of 50 U.S.C. § 1705; (4) one count of conspiracy to contribute material support to LET, knowing and intending that it was to be used in preparation for and in carrying out a conspiracy to kill or injure persons in a foreign country with which the United States is at peace in violation of 18 U.S.C. § 2339A; and (5) four counts of conspiracy to use firearms in relation to a crime of violence in violation of 18 U.S.C. § 924. Chapman was acquitted on two counts, but convicted on the following five counts: (1) one count of conspiracy to violate the Neutrality Act (18 U.S.C § 960); (2) one count of conspiracy to contribute material support to LET, knowing and intending that it was to be used in preparation for and in carrying out a conspiracy to kill or injure persons in a foreign country with which the United States is at peace in violation of 18 U.S.C. § 2339A; and (3) three counts of conspiracy to use firearms in relation to a crime of violence in violation of 18 U.S.C. § 924. Hammad was acquitted on four counts, but convicted on the following three counts: (1) one count of conspiracy to violate the Neutrality Act (18 U.S.C § 960); (2) one count of conspiracy to contribute material support to LET, knowing and intending that it was to be used in preparation for and in carrying out a conspiracy to kill or injure persons in a foreign country with which the United States is at peace in violation of 18 U.S.C. § 2339A; and (3) one count of conspiracy to use firearms in relation to a crime of violence in violation of 18 U.S.C. § 924. The district court noted that it included in its opinion only a fraction of the facts supporting the convictions and that it could have, with time, included four times as many facts in its opinion in support of its conclusions.

. . . .

Each of the defendants first challenges his convictions, arguing that they were not supported by sufficient evidence. When we assess the sufficiency of the evidence of a criminal conviction on direct review, "[t]he verdict of [the] jury must be sustained if there is substantial evidence, taking the view most favorable to the Government, to support it." Glasser v. United States, 315 U.S. 60, 80, 62 S. Ct. 457, 86 L. Ed. 680 (1942). We address each argument in turn.

A. Khan's Convictions

Khan argues that there was insufficient evidence presented at trial to support his convictions for (1) Count One, conspiracy to enlist in armed conflict against the United States in violation of 18 U.S.C. §§ 371, 2390; (2) Count Two, conspiracy to levy war against the United States in violation of 18 U.S.C. § 2384 and (3) Count Four, conspiracy to contribute services to the Taliban in violation of 50 U.S.C. § 1705(b). We disagree.

The essential elements of Count One, as applied to Khan, are (1) a conspiracy (2) to enlist or engage within the United States or any place subject to the jurisdiction thereof, (3) with intent to serve in armed hostility against the United States. 18 U.S.C. §§ 371, 2390. The essential elements of Count Two are (1) a conspiracy (2) to overthrow, put down, or to destroy by force the Government of the United States, or to levy war against them, or to oppose by force the authority thereof, or by force to prevent, hinder, or delay the execution of any law of the United States, or by force to seize, take, or possess any property of the United States contrary to the authority thereof. 18 U.S.C. § 2384. The essential elements of Count Four are (1) a conspiracy (2) to willfully make or receive any contribution of funds, goods, or services, to or for the benefit of the Taliban. 50 U.S.C. § 1705(b); 31 C.F.R. § 545.201–545.208.

There was sufficient evidence to support the district court's findings of guilt on all of these counts. When the group members were meeting and discussing going to Afghanistan to aid the Taliban against the United States, Khan exhorted the others to go with him to Afghanistan because "the cowards and the weak hearted are the first to run away." J.A. 1013. Khan did, in fact, travel to Pakistan to engage in training in the LET camps, and there was evidence that Khan intended to go to Afghanistan to fight with the Taliban against the United States after training. Khan was also selected as the leader of the group when they arrived in Pakistan. All of the group members that Khan led directly testified that they intended to engage in armed hostilities against the United States. The district court found their testimony to be credible; indeed, it was unrebutted. We conclude that this evidence amply supports the finding that Khan was guilty of Counts One, Two, and Four.

Khan next argues that there was insufficient evidence to support his conviction under Count Five, conspiracy to contribute material support to LET, knowing and intending that it was to be used in preparation for and in carrying out a conspiracy to kill or injure persons in a foreign country with which the United States is at peace, in violation of 18 U.S.C. § 2339A. While he concedes that he provided material support to LET, Khan contests that there was sufficient evidence to demonstrate that he knew that LET was intent on committing acts of murder or injury to others. We disagree.

The evidence reflects that LET broadly disseminated its goals for the destruction of India, America, and Israel on its web site and elsewhere. Khan was personally acquainted with Singh, an LET official, whom he assisted in purchasing paramilitary equipment. Even if Khan remained unaware of the nature of LET's activities before training in its camps, he was certainly aware of it by the time he returned to them after leaving temporarily because the LET camps were full of descriptions of LET's violent exploits. We therefore conclude that sufficient evidence was introduced for a rational trier of fact to find the essential elements necessary for Khan's conviction under Count Five....

B. Chapman's Convictions

The district court found Chapman guilty of Count One, conspiracy to violate the Neutrality Act, which makes it a crime to

> knowingly begin[ ] or set[ ] on foot or provide[ ] or prepare[ ] a means for or furnish[ ] the money for, or take[ ] part in, any military or naval expedition or enterprise to be carried on from thence against the territory or dominion of any foreign prince or state, or of any colony, district, or people with whom the United States is at peace.

18 U.S.C. § 960. The district court found that "Chapman and [Hammad] furthered the conspiracy by training co-conspirators in combat skills through paintball games and the acquisition of weapons, with the knowledge that some co-conspirators had already traveled to Kashmir and fired on Indian positions, and with the expectation that other co-conspirators would do the same, using the training that Chapman and [Hammad] provided."

Chapman argues that, even assuming that paintball was a form of jihad training, the evidence does not reveal any specific intent to join LET attacks in India. We cannot agree. The record contains evidence that Chapman continued to provide support to two members of the group who expressly acknowledged going to Pakistan and firing on Indian troops while there. Sufficient evidence, therefore, supports the district court's factual findings and, accordingly, the conspiracy conviction.

Chapman next challenges his conviction under Count Five for conspiracy to provide material support to LET, a terrorist organization, in violation of 18 U.S.C. § 2339A. The thrust of Chapman's challenge in this regard is that much of the evidence the government relies upon to support his conviction on this count predates the statute criminalizing such conduct. Conspiracy to provide material support to terrorists was not made a crime until October 26, 2001; until that date, § 2339A was a substantive crime only.

Chapman's argument, however, overlooks the fact that, like Khan, he assisted Singh in purchasing parts for a UAV with video surveillance equipment designed primarily for military and scientific use. He provided this assistance after October 26, 2001. Export of this equipment was controlled by law; its uses as a "Military Unmanned Aerial Vehicle" include reconnaissance, weapons targeting, and similar military purposes. Even assuming that Chapman's ongoing training activities with the paintball group did not qualify as a conspiracy for purposes of § 2339A, the district court specifically found that providing paramilitary equipment to a known LET official certainly did, and we agree.

. . . . .

C. Hammad's Conviction

Hammad was convicted under Count Five of conspiring to contribute material support to LET in violation of 18 U.S.C. § 2339A because he knowingly trained individuals through the paintball exercises in military techniques for use with LET. Hammad argues that he did not do so knowingly. Instead, he argues, he trained members of the group for recreation and physical fitness and did not train members of the group for LET after he learned that LET was engaged in armed conflict with India. This assertion, however, is belied by the record. Ample evidence demonstrates that Hammad continued to train people in his paintball group after he learned that some members of the group were going to work with LET in the fight against India. In light of the overwhelming evidence to the contrary, the district court expressly declined to "credit [Hammad's] testimony that paintball was strictly for recreation and physical fitness." ... We conclude that sufficient evidence supports Hammad's conviction for knowingly providing material support to LET in the form of trained personnel.

In short, we conclude that sufficient evidence supported all convictions for all defendants.

. . . . .

C. The Validity of Counts Five and Eleven

All three defendants contend that Counts Five and Eleven are invalid because they constitute "conspiracies to conspire." Specifically, Count Five alleged a conspiracy to provide material support in carrying out a violation of 18 U.S.C. § 956, which criminalizes conspiracy to kill or injure persons or damage property in a foreign country. Count Eleven alleged a conspiracy to use firearms in connection with a conspiracy to commit a crime of violence. Because one cannot "conspire to conspire," defendants argue, these Counts should be dismissed. We disagree.

The facial validity of the statutes under which the defendants were charged presents a question of law which we review de novo. Multi-Channel TV Cable Co. v. Charlottesville Quality Cable Corp., 65 F.3d 1113, 1123 (4th Cir. 1995).

Under Count Five, defendants were convicted of "conspir[ing] to," 18 U.S.C. § 2339A(a), "provide[ ] material support ... intending that [it] be used ... in carrying out ... a violation of ... [18 U.S.C. § 956]." J.A. 3220. Section 956, in turn, criminalizes "[c]onspiracy to kill, kidnap, maim, or injure persons or damage property in a foreign country." 18 U.S.C. § 956. Under Count Eleven, defendants were convicted of conspiring to use, carry, or possess a firearm in furtherance of, inter alia, a conspiracy to violate the Neutrality Act and a conspiracy to provide services to the Taliban. 18 U.S.C. §§ 924(c),(o).... Both Count Five and Count Eleven, in other words, expressly allow one conspiracy to serve as the predicate for another conspiracy. Nothing about this statutory framework is unconstitutional, improper, or even unusual.

Courts have recognized that one conspiracy can serve as the predicate for another conspiracy when the "[overarching] conspiracy and the predicate conspiracy are distinct offenses with entirely different objectives." United States v. Pungitore, 910 F.2d 1084, 1135 (3rd Cir. 1990); see also United States v. Ruggiero, 726 F.2d 913, 918 (2nd Cir. 1984) (holding that conspiracies can serve as predicate acts for a RICO conspiracy); United States v. Brooklier, 685 F.2d 1208, 1216 (9th Cir. 1982) (same). In Count Five, the conspiracy to provide material support to terrorism represents a distinct offense with different objectives from the predicate conspiracy to kill a person. In Count Eleven, the conspiracy to use or possess a firearm represents a distinct offense with different objectives from the predicate conspiracy to violate the Neutrality Act or provide services to the Taliban. Therefore, the underlying conspiracies may properly serve as predicates for the overarching conspiracies alleged.

More fundamentally, the statutes in question expressly contemplate allowing one conspiracy to serve as the predicate offense for another conspiracy. Defendants point to no constitutional or other reason why these statutes should be struck down as invalid, and we find none.

Affirmed in part, reversed in part.

Comments

1. The lower court proceedings consisted of a bench trial before Judge Brinkema, which resulted in a rare phenomenon: a detailed, lengthy opinion on her findings of fact, where

the specific evidence is marshaled with regard to each defendant. *U.S. v. Khan*, 309 F. Supp. 2d 789 (E.D. Va. 2004).

2. *Khan* makes reference to the fact that Sabri Benkahla was tried separately and acquitted. There was a reason for this: he took the stand and lied in his own defense. Benkahla was thereafter indicted and convicted of perjury, and sentenced to 10 years imprisonment. *U.S. v. Benkahla*, 530 F.3d 300 (4th Cir. 2008).

3. Ali Al-Timimi, a religious leader, seems in the *Khan* opinion to be the driving force behind the conspiracy, based on words he uttered in what was arguably a religious context shortly after 9/11. What happened to Al-Timimi? Following Judge Brinkema's opinion, prosecutors in Virginia obtained an indictment of him for seditious conspiracy. At trial, the court gave the jury an instruction under *Brandenburg v. Ohio*, 395 U.S. 444 (1969), that the government cannot punish inflammatory speech unless that speech is directed to "inciting, and is likely to incite, imminent lawless action." The jury convicted him. He was sentenced to life imprisonment.

4. LET was later officially designated as a Foreign Terrorist Organization by the State Department. Had it been designated before, prosecutors would have had an easier job of convicting some of the Virginia Paintball conspirators, because they could have relied on 18 U.S.C. § 2339B rather than the more exacting § 2339A.

Question for Discussion

There is arguably a great American tradition of fighting in foreign wars—think of the Americans who have joined the French Foreign Legion, or Ernest Hemingway in the Spanish Civil War. Do the foregoing Neutrality Act violations run in the face of this tradition?

Espionage

Espionage and its primary criminal statutes, 18 USC § 793 and § 794, has a long judicial history. With the end of the Cold War, however, the cases involving state-sponsored espionage (like Aldrich Ames and Robert Hanssen) have slowed to a trickle. Many espionage investigations today involve leaks of classified information to journalists, generally by self-styled whistleblowers. The last few years have seen high-profile investigations of employees of the National Security Agency, the Justice and State Departments, the Pentagon and the Central Intelligence Agency, suspected of leaking classified information to the press.

United States v. Hitselberger

___ F. Supp. 2d ___, 2013 WL 6238863 (D.D.C. 2013)

RUDOLPH CONTRERAS, United States District Judge

I. INTRODUCTION

Defendant, Mr. Hitselberger, has been charged by the United States of America on three counts of violating 18 U.S.C. § 793(e), for willfully removing and retaining documents relating to the national defense. He has also been charged on three counts of violating 18 U.S.C. § 2071(a), for willfully and unlawfully removing public documents from their secured location. Count one charges Mr. Hitselberger for the unlawful retention of two documents containing information relating to the national defense, found in his backpack on April 11, 2012. Count two charges Mr. Hitselberger for the unlawful retention of a third document containing information relating to the national defense, found in Mr. Hitselberger's room on April 11, 2012 and dated March 8, 2012. Count three charges Mr. Hitselberger for the unlawful retention of a fourth document containing information relating to the national defense, dated February 13, 2012. Defendant now argues that 18 U.S.C. § 793(e) is unconstitutionally vague as applied. Specifically, Mr. Hitselberger argues (1) that the phrase "relating to the national defense" covers too much information to draw a clear line between criminal and non-criminal conduct, (2) that the statute fails to specify what constitutes a culpable mens rea, and (3) that the phrase "used to the injury of the United States" has no judicial gloss and is unconstitutionally vague.

II. FACTUAL BACKGROUND

James Hitselberger is a 56-year-old linguist. He is fluent in Arabic, Farsi, and Russian. In June 2011, he was hired by Global Linguist Solutions, which assigned him to work for the United States Navy at a base in Bahrain. Mr. Hitselberger regularly worked with classified information. After being hired as a linguist, Mr. Hitselberger underwent training on the different types of classified information and the proper handling of such materials. Govt's Mem. in Supp. of Detention, 4, Dec. 12, 2012, ECF No. 13. At that time, Mr. Hitselberger was instructed that information classified at the Confidential level or higher could cause grave damage to the United States. *Id.* at Ex. 1.

At the end of his training, Mr. Hitselberger signed a non-disclosure agreement, which acknowledged in relevant part, "I agree that I shall return all classified materials which have or may come into my possession or for which I am responsible because of such access." Govt's Mem. in Supp. of Detention, Ex. 4, at ¶ 7. Since his initial training, Mr. Hitselberger attended regularly scheduled security briefings in the Restricted Access Area. Govt's Mem. in Opp'n to Def's Mot. for Vagueness, 3, April 5, 2013, ECF No. 51. These sessions reiterated that classified information must not be removed from Restricted Access Areas. *Id.*; Govt's Mem. in Supp. of Detention, Exs. 4–6. As of September 2011, Mr. Hitselberger worked as a linguist for the Joint Special Operations Task Force in Bahrain. Tr. of Mot. Hr'g, Morning Session, 105, Sept. 6, 2013. His workplace was located in a Restricted Access Area. Hr'g Tr. 10.

The Government alleges that on April 11, 2012, two supervisors observed Mr. Hitselberger checking his email in a Restricted Access Area and then printing multiple pages clearly marked as SECRET from a SECRET printer. Compl. ¶¶ 12–13, Aug. 6, 2012, ECF No. 1. The Government contends that Mr. Hitselberger was observed taking the classified documents from the printer, placing them into an Arabic-English Dictionary, and attempting to leave the building with the SECRET documents. *Id.* at ¶ 12. Mr. Hitselberger was stopped by his supervisor and his commanding officer after exiting the building and was asked to produce the documents he just printed. *Id.* The documents recovered from Mr. Hitselberger's backpack were marked as SECRET in red, bold type in the header and footer of each page. Tr. of Mot. Hr'g, Morning Session, 24–25. The documents contained the availability of improvised explosive devices in Bahrain, schedule for the monthly travel of a high-ranking commander in Bahrain and information about the locations of U.S. armed forces in the region and their activities. Govt's Mem. in Supp. of Detention, 7, Ex. 7.

On April 11, 2012, NCIS Special Agents conducted a Command Authorized Search and Seizure of Mr. Hitselberger's living quarters in Bahrain. Compl. ¶ 14. Inside, Special Agents found documents classified as SECRET with the SECRET warning label cut off the top and bottom of the pages. Compl. ¶ 14. This document contained information about the location of U.S. forces and their undisclosed activities in the region. Govt's

Mem. in Supp. of Detention, at 8, Exs. 10–11. The last document, located in the Hoover Institute's public library, was originally classified as SECRET. Govt's Mem. in Supp. of Detention at 10–11, Ex. 13. This document discusses gaps in U.S. intelligence with respect to the political situation in Bahrain. *Id.* at 10–11, Ex. 14. After investigation, it was determined that Mr. Hitselberger received the documents as an e-mail attachment sent to several persons on a distribution list. Compl. ¶ 14.

Defendant now asks this Court to dismiss Counts One through Three, arguing that 18 U.S.C. § 793(e), is unconstitutionally vague as applied. Specifically, Mr. Hitselberger argues that (1) the phrase "relating to the national defense" covers too much information to draw a clear line between criminal and non-criminal conduct, (2) the statute fails to specify what constitutes a culpable mens rea, and (3) the phrase "used to the injury of the United States" has no judicial gloss and is unconstitutionally vague.

III. ANALYSIS

Mr. Hitselberger argues that 18 U.S.C. § 793(e) violates the fair warning requirement under the Due Process Clause of the Fifth Amendment because the clauses are vague, and thus do not provide him notice as to what conduct is criminalized under the statute. *See* United States v. Lanier, 520 U.S. 259, 266, 117 S.Ct. 1219, 137 L. Ed. 2d 432 (1997). The Fifth Amendment imposes a clarity requirement on criminal statutes, requiring the legislature to set "reasonably clear guidelines for law enforcement officials and triers of fact in order to prevent 'arbitrary and discriminatory enforcement.' " Smith v. Goguen, 415 U.S. 566, 572–3, 94 S.Ct. 1242, 39 L. Ed. 2d 605 (1974) (citations omitted). "[T]he touchstone is whether the statute, either standing alone or as construed, made it reasonably clear at the relevant time that the defendant's conduct was criminal." Lanier, 520 U.S. at 267, 117 S.Ct. 1219. This clarity, however, does not need to come from the statutory language alone. "[C]larity at the requisite level may be supplied by judicial gloss on an otherwise uncertain statute." Lanier, 520 U.S. at 266, 117 S.Ct. 1219; *see also* United States v. Morison, 844 F.2d 1057, 1071 (4th Cir. 1988) ("[A]ll vagueness may be corrected by judicial construction which narrows the sweep of the statute within the range of reasonable certainty.").

18 U.S.C. Section 793(e) states:

> Whoever having unauthorized possession of, access to, or control over any document, writing, code book, signal book, sketch, photograph, photograph negative, blueprint, plan, map, model, instrument, appliance, or note relating to the national defense, or information relating to the national defense which information the possessor has reason to believe could be used to the injury of the United States or to the advantage of any foreign nation, willfully communicates ... or willfully retains the same and fails to deliver it to the officer of employer of the United States entitled to receive it ... Shall be fined under this title or imprisoned not more than ten years, or both.

Mr. Hitselberger takes particular issue with the clauses: "relating to the national defense," "reason to believe could be used to the injury of the United States," and "willfully retains." As is discussed further below, courts have uniformly held that the judicial gloss on these clauses provides sufficient notice of what conduct is criminalized under 18 U.S.C. § 793(e). *See generally*, United States v. Morison, 844 F.2d 1057 (4th Cir. 1988); United States v. Kiriakou, 898 F. Supp. 2d 921 (E.D. Va. 2012); United States v. Drake, 818 F. Supp. 2d 909 (D. Md. 2011); United States v. Kim, 808 F. Supp. 2d 44 (D.D.C. 2011); United States v. Abu-Jihaad, 600 F. Supp. 2d 362 (D. Conn. 2009); United States v. Rosen, 445 F. Supp. 2d 602 (E.D. Va. 2006); United States v. Morison, 622 F. Supp. 1009 (D. Md. 1985).

This court easily dismisses Mr. Hitselberger's challenge of the phrase "used to the injury of the United States." As numerous other courts have recognized, 18 U.S.C. § 793(e) criminalizes retention of two types of information: tangible items and intangible information. United States v. Aquino, 555 F.3d 124, 128 (3rd Cir. 2009); United States v. Kiriakou, 898 F. Supp. 2d at 923; United States v. Kim, 808 F. Supp. 2d at 51–52; United States v. Drake, 818 F. Supp. 2d at 916–917. The "document" clause criminalizes a defendant's willful retention of tangible items "relating to the national defense" while the "information" clause criminalizes a defendant's willful communication of intangible information "relating to the national defense which information the possessor has reason to believe could be used to the injury of the United States, or to the advantage of any foreign nation" to a person not entitled to receive it. In essence, the "information" clause imposes an additional mens rea requirement on the defendant, requiring that the defendant know that the information could be used to injure the United States or advantage a foreign nation.

Mr. Hitselberger has been charged under the "document" clause of 18 U.S.C. § 793(e). Govt's Opp'n to Def's Mot. for Vagueness, at 8; Superseding Indictment, ECF No. 30 at 1–3. As such, the additional mens rea clause "which information the possessor has reason to believe could be used to the injury of the United States" is inapplicable to Mr. Hitselberger's prosecution. "The usual rule is that the alleged vagueness of a criminal statute must be judged in light of the conduct that is charged to be violative of the statute." Kolender v. Lawson, 461 U.S. 352, 369, 103 S.Ct. 1855, 75 L. Ed. 2d 903 (1983) (J., White, dissenting). See also, United States v. Mazurie, 419 U.S. 544, 550, 95 S.Ct. 710, 42 L. Ed. 2d 706 (1975); United States v. Powell, 423 U.S. 87, 92–93, 96 S. Ct. 316, 46 L. Ed. 2d 228 (1975). Because Mr. Hitselberger is not charged under the "information" clause here, he has no standing to challenge the phrase "used to the injury of the United States" as vague.[11]

Mr. Hitselberger next argues that the clause "relating to the national defense" is impermissibly vague, as it does not give defendants enough notice of the substantive content that cannot be retained. He first notes that "relating to the national defense" has "consistently been construed broadly," United States v. Rosen, 445 F. Supp. 2d 602, 620 (2006), and that this definition includes innocuous information of alarming breadth. United States v. Heine, 151 F.2d 813, 815 (2d Cir. 1945) (explaining that the accepted definition includes information about supplies collected for the armed services such as food, water, and clothing). While this might be true, the Supreme Court has found the phrase "relating to the national defense" to be sufficiently definite "to apprise the public of prohibited activities" and to be "consonant with due process." Gorin v. United States, 312 U.S. 19, 28, 61 S. Ct. 429, 85 L. Ed. 488 (1941). As Gorin notes, "from the standpoint of military or naval strategy it might ... be dangerous to us for a foreign power to know our weaknesses and our limitations." Id. at 31, 61 S.Ct. 429. And every court to consider this issue has consistently rejected a constitutional vagueness challenge to this phrase. United States v. Squillacote, 221 F.3d 542, 580 n.23 (4th Cir. 2000); United States v. Boyce, 594 F.2d 1246, 1252 n. 2 (9th Cir. 1979) (upholding the language of 18 U.S.C. §§ 793 and 794); Morison, 844 F.2d at 1070–1073; Kim, 808 F. Supp. 2d at 52–55; Drake, 818 F. Supp. 2d at 918–19; Dedeyan, 584 F.2d at 39; United States v. Abu-Jihaad, 600 F. Supp. 2d 362, 385 (D.

---

11. Mr. Hitselberger also argues that the phrase "used to the injury of the United States" does not clearly define how significant the injury must be, thus running afoul of First Amendment freedom of speech protections. This court does not address this First Amendment argument as Mr. Hitselberger does not have standing to challenge this phrase.

Conn. 2009); Rosen, 445 F. Supp. 2d at 617–22. Certainly defendant cites no cases to the contrary.

Mr. Hitselberger's vagueness challenge is particularly unpersuasive in light of the alleged content of the documents he retained. The documents contained highly sensitive information, including information about U.S. troop movements, activities in the region, the availability of improvised explosive devices, and gaps in U.S. intelligence of the political situation in Bahrain. These documents were marked as SECRET, a classification level that applied to information that, "if lost or compromised, would cause serious damage to the security of the United States."

Even if the classification system is not 100% accurate, as Mr. Hitselberger claims, his training places him on notice that the government considers information contained in classified documents important to national security. *See* United States v. Dedeyan, 584 F.2d 36, 41 (4th Cir. 1978) (finding that a document related to the national defense based on its content, notwithstanding its improper classification); United States v. Kiriakou, 898 F. Supp. 2d 921, 925 (E.D. Va. 2012) (finding that defendant, "a government employee trained in the classification system ... could appreciate the significance of the information" within the documents and was thus sufficiently placed on notice for purposes of a vagueness challenge); United States v. Rosen, 445 F. Supp. 2d 602, 623 (E.D. Va. 2006) ("[W]hile the language of the statute, by itself, may lack precision, the gloss of judicial precedent has clarified that the statute incorporates the executive branch's classification regulations, which provide the requisite constitutional clarity."). Given the record before the Court, it appears that the documents here would comfortably qualify as "relating to the national defense." *See generally*, Morison, 844 F.2d at 1074 (rejecting vagueness challenge to §793(d) based in part on defendant's knowledge that information was classified as "Secret"); Kim, 808 F. Supp. 2d at 53 (rejecting vagueness challenge to §793(e) in an almost identical scenario).

Mr. Hitselberger argues, finally, that the mens rea element of §793(e) is unconstitutionally vague. Section 793(e) proscribes the "willful" retention of certain documents. Mr. Hitselberger argues that the term "willful" can take on different meanings in different contexts, thus allowing courts to reach disparate conclusions as to the requisite mens rea necessary to violate the Act. Mr. Hitselberger relies on United States v. Rosen and Gorin v. United States to argue that courts must impose an "additional and significant scienter requirement" above the standard definition of "willfulness," such as a showing of evil purpose. Rosen, 445 F. Supp. 2d at 625; Gorin v. United States, 312 U.S. 19, 27–28, 61 S. Ct. 429, 85 L. Ed. 488 (1941).

Mr. Hitselberger incorrectly relies on these cases, which interpret a different scienter requirement. In Gorin, the Court interpreted a predecessor statute that required the defendant to act with "intent or reason to believe that the information to be obtained is to be used to the injury of the United States or to the advantage of any foreign nation." Gorin, 312 U.S. at 21, n. 1, 61 S.Ct. 429. Rosen interpreted the mens rea requirement in the "information" clause, which similarly requires the defendant to "have reason to believe that [the information] could be used to the injury of the United States, or to the advantage of any foreign nation." Rosen, 445 F. Supp. 2d at 625–7. As already noted above, this additional scienter language is not applicable to the willfulness standard in the "documents" clause, under which Mr. Hitselberger has been charged.

Although "willfulness" may be considered a "word of many meanings" Bryan v. United States, 524 U.S. 184, 191, 118 S. Ct. 1939, 141 L. Ed. 2d 197 (1998), even a simple scienter requirement may mitigate a statute's vagueness, "especially with respect to the adequacy of notice to the complainant that his conduct is proscribed." Village of Hoffman Estates

v. Flipside, Hoffman Estates, Inc., 455 U.S. 489, 499, 102 S. Ct. 1186, 71 L. Ed. 2d 362 (1982). "[W]here the punishment imposed is only for an act knowingly done with the purpose of doing that which the statute prohibits, the accused cannot be said to suffer from lack of warning or knowledge that the act which he does is a violation of law." Screws v. United States, 325 U.S. 91, 102, 65 S. Ct. 1031, 89 L.Ed. 1495 (1945).

In cases involving the "documents" clause, a simple "willfulness" standard is sensible, as "a defendant will more readily recognize a document relating to the national defense based on its content, markings or design than it would intangible or oral 'information.'" United States v. Drake, 818 F. Supp. 2d 909, 917 (D. Md. 2011); see also S. Rep. No. 2369, pt.1, 81st Congress, 2nd Sess., 8–9 (1950); New York Times Company v. United States, 403 U.S. 713, 738, n. 9, 91 S. Ct. 2140, 29 L. Ed. 2d 822 (1971) (J., Stewart, Concurring) (comparing §793(e) to §793(d) and finding that "in prosecuting for communicating or withholding a 'document' as contrasted with similar action with respect to 'information' the Government need not prove an intent to injure the United States or benefit a foreign nation" but instead only needs to prove "willful and knowing conduct"); Rosen, 445 F. Supp. 2d at 626 ("[I]f a person transmitted classified documents relating to the national defense to a member of the media despite knowing that such an act was a violation of the statute, he could be convicted for 'willfully' committing the prohibited acts even if he viewed the disclosure as an act of patriotism.") (emphasis omitted).

Moreover, simple willfulness has never been held to be unconstitutionally vague. The Supreme Court interpreted "willfulness" in Bryan v. United States, 524 U.S. 184, 118 S. Ct. 1939, 141 L. Ed. 2d 197 (1998) and held that "in order to establish a 'willful' violation of a statute, 'the Government must prove that the defendant acted with knowledge that his conduct was unlawful.'" Bryan, 524 U.S. at 191–2, 118 S. Ct. 1939 (quoting Ratzlaf v. United States, 510 U.S. 135, 137, 114 S. Ct. 655, 126 L. Ed. 2d 615 (1994)). The Bryan Court accepted jury instructions, which explained "willfulness" as follows:

> A person acts willfully if he acts intentionally and purposely and with the intent to do something the law forbids, that is, with the bad purpose to disobey or to disregard the law. Now, the person need not be aware of the specific law or rule that his conduct may be violating. But he must act with the intent to do something that the law forbids.

Bryan, 524 U.S. at 190, 118 S. Ct. 1939. Thus, the core of "willful" misconduct is to act with the knowledge or intent to disregard the law, not an evil intent to injure the United States.

And courts have consistently interpreted the "willful" mens rea standard in 18 U.S.C. §793(e) as acting with a bad purpose, refusing to find the term unconstitutionally vague. See United States v. Truong Dinh Hung, 629 F.2d 908, 919 (4th Cir. 1980); United States v. Kiriakou, 898 F. Supp. 2d 921, 923 (E.D.Va. 2012); United States v. Kim, 808 F. Supp. 2d 44, 53–4 (D.D.C. 2011) (adopting the Bryan standard and noting that "[b]ecause the Government must prove that Defendant knew his conduct was unlawful, he cannot complain that he did not have fair warning that he could be criminally prosecuted for his actions."); United States v. Morison, 622 F. Supp. 1009, 1010 (D.Md. 1985) (holding that it is irrelevant under the documents clause whether the defendant believed the items to relate to the national defense). This court joins the weight of authority to find that the "willful" mens rea standard in 18 U.S.C. §793(e) is not unconstitutionally vague.

IV. CONCLUSION

For the foregoing reasons, Defendant's motion to find 18 U.S.C. §793(e) unconstitutionally vague is DENIED. Although Mr. Hitselberger has requested that the

Court provide limiting instructions that define the terms he claims are vague, this court will wait until a later date to consider jury instructions. An order consistent with this Memorandum Opinion is separately and contemporaneously issued.

Comment

1. Hitselberger ultimately negotiated a plea to one count of unauthorized removal and retention of classified information, in violation of 18 U.S.C. § 1924. He was sentenced in July 2014 to time served.

U.S. v. Kim

808 F. Supp. 2d 44 (D.D.C. 2011)

COLLEEN KOLLAR-KOTELLY, District Judge.

Defendant Stephen Jin-Woo Kim ("Defendant" or "Kim") has been charged by indictment with unlawfully disclosing national defense information to a person not entitled to receive it in violation of 18 U.S.C. § 793(d) and making a false statement to agents of the Federal Bureau of Investigation ("FBI") in violation of 18 U.S.C. § 1001(a)(2). Presently pending before the Court are: Defendant's Motion to Dismiss Count One of the Indictment Under the Treason Clause of the Constitution [and] Defendant's Motion to Dismiss Count One of the Indictment on Due Process and First Amendment Grounds.... The Government has filed a consolidated opposition to these motions, and Defendant has filed a consolidated reply. Accordingly, the motions are ripe for the Court's resolution. For the reasons explained below, the Court shall deny Defendant's motions.

. . . .

I. BACKGROUND

Defendant was charged in a two-count indictment on August 19, 2010 and arraigned on August 27, 2010. Count One of the Indictment alleges that Kim had lawful possession of, access to, control over, or was entrusted with information relating to national defense—specifically, the contents of an intelligence report marked TOP SECRET/SENSITIVE COMPARTMENTED INFORMATION concerning intelligence sources and/or methods and intelligence about the military capabilities and preparedness of a particular foreign nation. The indictment charges that Kim had a reason to believe that this information could be used to the injury of the United States and to the advantage of a foreign nation and that Kim knowingly and willfully communicated, delivered or transmitted that information to a reporter for a national news organization, who was not entitled to receive that information. The indictment charges this conduct was a violation of 18 U.S.C. § 793(d), part of the Espionage Act of 1917, as amended. Section 793(d) reads as follows:

> Whoever, lawfully having possession of, access to, control over, or being entrusted with any document, writing, code book, signal book, sketch, photograph, photographic negative, blueprint, plan, map, model, instrument, appliance, or note relating to the national defense, or information relating to the national defense which information the possessor has reason to believe could be used to the injury of the United States or to the advantage of any foreign nation, willfully communicates, delivers, transmits or causes to be communicated, delivered, or transmitted or attempts to communicate, deliver, transmit or cause to be communicated, delivered or transmitted the same to any person not entitled to receive it, or willfully retains the same and fails to deliver it on demand to the officer or

employee of the United States entitled to receive it ... [s]hall be fined ... or imprisoned not more than ten years, or both.

18 U.S.C. §793(d).

. . . .

II. DISCUSSION

A. Motion to Dismiss Count One Under the Treason Clause

Defendant's first motion to dismiss Count One of the indictment is based on his view that the Treason Clause, Article III, Section 3 of the United States Constitution, precludes Congress from imposing criminal liability for the conduct charged in Count One. Defendant argues that the Framers intended to limit the power of Congress to prosecute persons for "political" offenses against the United States, and they did so by enshrining in the Constitution a limited definition of treason with heightened evidentiary requirements. The Treason Clause provides in full:

> Treason against the United States, shall consist only in levying War against them, or in adhering to their Enemies, giving them Aid and Comfort. No Person shall be convicted of Treason unless on the Testimony of two Witnesses to the same overt Act, or on Confession in open Court. The Congress shall have Power to declare the Punishment of Treason, but no Attainder of Treason shall work Corruption of Blood, or Forfeiture except during the Life of the Person attained.

U.S. Const., art. III, §3.

Defendant argues that the Framers intended treason to be the exclusive mechanism for prosecuting crimes against the United States, and therefore he contends that the Government cannot prosecute him under the Espionage Act for speech-based conduct against the United States. Defendant's argument, essentially, is that he must be charged with treason or nothing at all.

Defendant makes a compelling and eloquent argument based on the history of treason in England and America and the debate among the Framers regarding the Treason Clause. However, Defendant's interpretation of the Treason Clause has been rejected by the Supreme Court. In Cramer v. United States, 325 U.S. 1, 65 S.Ct. 918, 89 L.Ed. 1441 (1945), the Supreme Court reviewed a conviction for treason. In doing so, the Court rejected the government's argument that the Treason Clause should be interpreted broadly, noting that "the treason offense is not the only nor can it well serve as the principal legal weapon to vindicate our national cohesion and security." *Id.* at 45, 65 S.Ct. 918. The Court elaborated:

> Of course we do not intimate that Congress could dispense with the two-witness rule merely by giving the same offense another name. But the power of Congress is in no way limited to enact prohibitions of specified acts thought detrimental to our wartime safety. The loyal and the disloyal alike may be forbidden to do acts which place our security in peril, and the trial thereof may be focussed [sic] upon defendant's specific intent to do those particular acts thus eliminating the accusation of treachery and general intent to betray which have such passion-rousing potentialities. Congress repeatedly has enacted prohibitions of specific acts thought to endanger our security and the practice of foreign nations with defense problems more acute than our own affords examples of others.

Id. at 45–46, 65 S.Ct. 918 (footnote omitted).

Following the word "security" in this passage, the Court included a footnote referencing the prior version of the Espionage Act provision with which Kim is charged in Count One. *See id.* at 45 n. 53, 65 S.Ct. 918. The Second Circuit has ruled, based on Cramer, that prosecutions for Espionage Act violations are not subject to the requirements of the Treason Clause and are properly prosecuted as separate offenses. *See* United States v. Rahman, 189 F.3d 88, 111–14 (2d Cir. 1999); United States v. Drummond, 354 F.2d 132, 152 (2d Cir. 1965). If Defendant's interpretation of the Treason Clause were correct, the prosecutions in these cases would have been declared unconstitutional.

In fact, in Frohwerk v. United States, 249 U.S. 204, 39 S.Ct. 249, 63 L.Ed. 561 (1919) — a case not cited by the parties in their discussion of this issue — the Supreme Court essentially rejected Defendant's argument without discussion. Frohwerk involved review of convictions under the Espionage Act shortly after its passage in 1917. Writing for the majority, Justice Oliver Wendell Holmes wrote,

> Some reference was made in the proceedings and in argument to the provision in the Constitution concerning treason, and it was suggested on the one hand that some of the matters dealt with in the Act of 1917 were treasonable and punishable as treason or not at all, and on the other that the acts complained of not being treason could not be punished. These suggestions seem to us to need no more than to be stated.

249 U.S. at 210, 39 S. Ct. 249. The Court upheld the indictment. Other courts have recognized this holding of Frohwerk and rejected similar arguments. For example, in Wimmer v. United States, 264 F. 11 (6th Cir. 1920), a case involving the Espionage Act, the court noted:

> Wimmer's first position is that the act is unconstitutional, because it punishes treasonable conduct, without proof of the overt act and without the two witnesses thereto required by the Constitution. As we understand the argument, it is, in substance, that adhering to and giving aid and comfort to the enemy is treason, according to the constitutional definition; that to support the cause of the enemy, or oppose that of the United States, against the prohibition of the Espionage Act, is adhering to and giving aid and comfort to the enemy, and is therefore treason; and hence that it cannot be punished unless shown by the degree of proof required by the Constitution. A very similar contention was summarily overruled by the Supreme Court in Frohwerk....

264 F. at 12; accord Berg v. State, 29 Okla. Crim. 112, 233 P. 497 (Okla. Crim. App. 1925) (rejecting challenge to criminal syndicalism statute based on Treason Clause).

Both Frohwerk and Cramer make clear that conduct which is not equivalent to treason as defined in the Treason Clause may be otherwise proscribed by Congress. Accordingly, the Court finds that Defendant's prosecution under § 793(d) does not violate the Treason Clause.

B. Motion to Dismiss Count One on Due Process and First Amendment Grounds

In his second motion to dismiss Count One of the indictment, Defendant raises challenges under both the First and Fifth Amendments to the U.S. Constitution. First, Defendant argues that his prosecution under § 793(d) violates his right to due process under the Fifth Amendment because the statute fails to provide him constitutionally adequate notice that it was unlawful for him to verbally communicate information contained in or derived from a classified report to the news media. Second, Defendant argues that his prosecution under § 793(d) violates the First Amendment. The Court shall review each challenge in turn.

1. Defendant's Due Process Challenge

At the beginning of his motion to dismiss Count One on due process grounds, Defendant briefly discusses the history of government leaks and essentially argues that the practice has become so commonplace in the modern era that he could not have had fair warning that the conduct charged in the indictment—which reaches the verbal disclosure of information obtained from a classified report—was unlawful. Defendant's argument is based on the void-for-vagueness doctrine, which generally holds that criminal statutes must be sufficiently specific that they provide "fair warning" of the conduct that is proscribed. *See* United States v. Lanier, 520 U.S. 259, 266, 117 S. Ct. 1219, 137 L. Ed. 2d 432 (1997). The Fifth Amendment's guarantee of due process "bars enforcement of 'a statute which either forbids or requires the doing of an act in terms so vague that men of common intelligence must necessarily guess at its meaning and differ as to its application.' " *Id.* at 266, 117 S. Ct. 1219 (quoting *51 Connally v. Gen. Constr. Co., 269 U.S. 385, 391, 46 S. Ct. 126, 70 L. Ed. 322 (1926)). This guarantee is also enforced through the rule of lenity, which "ensures fair warning by so resolving ambiguity in a criminal statute so as to apply it only to conduct clearly covered." *Id.* "[A]lthough clarity at the requisite level may be supplied by judicial gloss on an otherwise uncertain statute, due process bars courts from applying a novel construction of a criminal statute to conduct that neither the statute nor any prior judicial decision has fairly disclosed to be within its scope." *Id.* (internal citations omitted). The void-for-vagueness doctrine "requires legislatures to set reasonably clear guidelines for law enforcement officials and triers of fact in order to prevent 'arbitrary and discriminatory enforcement.' " Smith v. Goguen, 415 U.S. 566, 572–73, 94 S. Ct. 1242, 39 L. Ed. 2d 605 (1974) (citations omitted). Where a statute criminalizes activity that would otherwise be protected by the First Amendment, "the doctrine demands a greater degree of specificity than in other contexts." *Id.* at 573, 94 S. Ct. 1242; *see also* Grayned v. City of Rockford, 408 U.S. 104, 109, 92 S. Ct. 2294, 33 L. Ed. 2d 222 (1972). "[T]he touchstone is whether the statute, either standing alone or as construed, made it reasonably clear at the relevant time that the defendant's conduct was criminal." Lanier, 520 U.S. at 267, 117 S. Ct. 1219.

Defendant argues that 18 U.S.C. § 793(d) is vague as applied to him in Count One because it is not clear that the phrase "information relating to the national defense" encompasses intangible information that might be gleaned from classified documents. Defendant points to the fact that this phrase follows a series of tangible items (document, writing, code book, signal book, sketch, photograph, photographic negative, blueprint, plan, map, model, instrument, appliance, or note) and asks the Court to apply the doctrine of noscitur a sociis, a canon of statutory construction that says that "words are generally known by the company they keep." FTC v. Ken Roberts Co., 276 F.3d 583, 590 (D.C. Cir. 2001). This canon is applied "to avoid ascribing to one word a meaning so broad that it is inconsistent with its accompanying words, thus giving 'unintended breadth to the Acts of Congress.' " Gustafson v. Alloyd Co., 513 U.S. 561, 575, 115 S. Ct. 1061, 131 L. Ed. 2d 1 (1995) (quoting Jarecki v. G.D. Searle & Co., 367 U.S. 303, 307, 81 S. Ct. 1579, 6 L. Ed. 2d 859 (1961)). However, it is reasonably clear from the text and the structure of § 793(d) that Congress intended the phrase "information relating to the national defense" to encompass both physical and intangible forms of information.

Firstly, the word "information" is usually defined so as to include intangible forms of data or knowledge. See *Merriam-Webster's Collegiate Dictionary* 599 (10th ed. 1997) (defining information as "the communication or reception of knowledge or intelligence"). "It is well established that, when the statutory language is plain, we must enforce it according to its terms." Jimenez v. Quarterman, 555 U.S. 113, 118, 129 S. Ct. 681, 172

L. Ed. 2d 475 (2009). Given this ordinary definition of the term, it would be unusual to construe the word "information" to refer only to information in tangible forms. This is particularly so in light of the fact that the list of tangible items in §793(d) is structurally separated from the phrase "information relating to the national defense," which alone is modified by the requirement that "the possessor has reason to believe [the information] could be used to the injury of the United States or to the advantage of any foreign nation." 18 U.S.C. §793(d). Congress's decision to impose a mens rea requirement for the communication, delivery, or transmission of "information" but not for tangible items demonstrates that Congress understood and embraced the distinction between the tangible items listed in the statute and intangible "information." See United States v. Aquino, 555 F.3d 124, 131 n. 13 (3d Cir. 2009) ("Section 793(e) differentiates between 'tangible' information, i.e., the laundry list of items in the statute, and 'intangible' information, i.e., knowledge.")[12] FN2; United States v. Morison, 622 F. Supp. 1009, 1011 (D. Md.), appeal dismissed, 774 F.2d 1156 (4th Cir. 1985).

Defendant argues that construing the word "information" as "knowledge" will lead to absurd results because §793(d) makes it unlawful to "willfully retain[ ]" such information and "fail[ ] to deliver it on demand to the officer or employee of the United States entitled to receive it." 18 U.S.C. §793(d). Defendant argues that it makes no sense to criminalize the retention of intangible information, as a person cannot relinquish knowledge he has acquired, voluntarily or otherwise. See United States v. Rosen, 444 F. Supp. 2d 664, 669 n. 6 (E.D. Va. 2006) ("Because punishing someone for the willful retention of intangible information, i.e., knowledge, is absurd, this clause could not apply to the information alleged to have been disclosed orally to [defendants]."). However, as Judge T.S. Ellis III recently explained in a thorough and thoughtful opinion, "[a] closer look at §793's history reveals that th[is] absurdity … is a result of inadvertence and careless drafting, and not an indication that the drafters intended to restrict the prohibition of the first clause to tangible items." United States v. Rosen, 445 F. Supp. 2d 602, 615–17 (E.D. Va. 2006), aff'd in part on other grounds, 557 F.3d 192 (4th Cir. 2009). Therefore, the fact that the retention clause in §793(d) might apply only to tangible items does not provide a basis for narrowing the plain meaning of "information" with respect to the communication clause. Furthermore, Defendant was not charged under the retention clause and therefore he lacks standing to challenge it on vagueness grounds. See Vill. of Hoffman Estates v. Flipside, Hoffman Estates, Inc., 455 U.S. 489, 495, 102 S. Ct. 1186, 71 L. Ed. 2d 362 (1982) ("A [party] who engages in some conduct that is clearly proscribed cannot complain of the vagueness of the law as applied to the conduct of others."); Parker v. Levy, 417 U.S. 733, 756, 94 S. Ct. 2547, 41 L. Ed. 2d 439 (1974) ("One to whose conduct a statute clearly applies may not successfully challenge it for vagueness.").

Defendant also argues that the phrase "relating to the national defense" is unconstitutionally vague. However, the Supreme Court rejected this argument in Gorin v. United States, 312 U.S. 19, 61 S.Ct. 429, 85 L.Ed. 488 (1941), which involved a challenge to the same language in §2(a) of the Espionage Act. FN3 The Court found that the term "national defense" has "a well understood connotation" and held that "[f]he language employed appears sufficiently definite to apprise the public of prohibited activities and is consonant with due process." 312 U.S. at 28, 61 S. Ct. 429. "The question of the connection of the information with national defense is a question of fact to be determined by the jury

---

12. Section 793(e) contains the same language at issue as §793(d), but it applies to persons who have unauthorized rather than lawful access to information relating to national defense. See 18 U.S.C. §793(e).

as negligence upon undisputed facts is determined." *Id.* at 32, 61 S. Ct. 429. Other courts have also recognized that the phrase "relating to the national defense" in § 793(d) is not unconstitutionally vague. *See* United States v. Morison, 844 F.2d 1057, 1071–74 (4th Cir. 1988); Rosen, 445 F. Supp. 2d at 618–22. Defendant's vagueness challenge is particularly unpersuasive in light of the fact that he is charged with disclosing the contents of an intelligence report concerning intelligence sources and/or methods and intelligence about the military capabilities and preparedness of a foreign nation and which was marked TOP SECRET/SENSITIVE COMPARTMENTED INFORMATION, a classification level that was applied to information, "the unauthorized disclosure of which reasonably could be expected to cause exceptionally grave damage to the national security." Exec. Order No. 12958 § 1.2, as amended by Exec. Order No. 13,292, 3 C.F.R. 196 (2004), reprinted, 50 U.S.C. § 435 note (2006). Furthermore, "[t]he unauthorized disclosure of foreign government information is presumed to cause damage to national security." *Id.* § 1.1. There can be no reasonable doubt that such information qualifies as "relating to the national defense." Accord Morison, 844 F.2d at 1074 (rejecting vagueness challenge to § 793(d) based in part on defendant's knowledge that information was classified as "Secret").

Defendant may dislike the breadth of the phrase "information relating to the national defense," but breadth and vagueness are not congruent concepts. To sustain a vagueness challenge, "the complainant must prove that the enactment is vague 'not in the sense that it requires a person to conform his conduct to an imprecise but comprehensible normative standard, but rather in the sense that no standard of conduct is specified at all.'" Vill. of Hoffman Estates v. Flipside, Hoffman Estates, Inc., 455 U.S. 489, 495 n. 7, 102 S. Ct. 1186, 71 L. Ed. 2d 362 (1982) (quoting Coates v. City of Cincinnati, 402 U.S. 611, 614, 91 S. Ct. 1686, 29 L. Ed. 2d 214). The Due Process Clause does not require "that a person contemplating a course of behavior know with certainty whether his or her act will be found to violate the [statute]. Rather, ... [it] requires that the enactment be drafted with reasonable specificity sufficient to provide fair notice." United States v. Thomas, 864 F.2d 188, 195 (D.C. Cir. 1988). The Court finds that the ordinary meaning of "information relating to national defense" is sufficiently specific to put Defendant on notice that it includes intangible information.

Secondly, any vagueness concerns about the meaning of "information relating to national defense" are eliminated by the other limitations in the statute, most importantly the willfulness requirement. The Supreme Court has recognized that "a scienter requirement may mitigate a law's vagueness, especially with respect to the adequacy of notice to the complainant that his conduct is proscribed." Vill. of Hoffman Estates, 455 U.S. at 499, 102 S. Ct. 1186. In this case, the Government must prove not only that Defendant had a reasonable belief that the information he possessed could be used to the injury of the United States or to the advantage of any foreign nation but also that Defendant willfully communicated that information to a person not entitled to receive it. "[I]n order to establish a willful violation of a statute, the Government must prove that the defendant acted with knowledge that his conduct was unlawful." Bryan v. United States, 524 U.S. 184, 191–92, 118 S. Ct. 1939, 141 L. Ed. 2d 197 (1998) (internal quotation marks omitted). Because the Government must prove that Defendant knew his conduct was unlawful, he cannot complain that he did not have fair warning that he could be criminally prosecuted for his actions. *See* Screws v. United States, 325 U.S. 91, 102, 65 S. Ct. 1031, 89 L. Ed. 1495 (1945) (plurality opinion) ("[W]here the punishment imposed is only for an act knowingly done with the purpose of doing that which the statute prohibits, the accused cannot be said to suffer from lack of warning or knowledge that the act which he does is a violation of law."); Gorin, 312 U.S. at 27–28, 61 S. Ct. 429 (rejecting vagueness challenge based on scienter requirement in statute).

Defendant also argues that § 793(d) is unconstitutionally vague because it does not specify who is "not entitled to receive" such information. Defendant is correct that the statute does not define this phrase. However, courts interpreting similar language have generally construed the statute harmoniously with applicable regulatory restrictions on the disclosure of protected information. For example, in United States v. Girard, 601 F.2d 69 (2d Cir. 1979), the court affirmed the defendants' convictions under 18 U.S.C. § 641[13] FN4 for selling confidential law enforcement records; the court held that the law enforcement agency's own "rules and regulations forbidding such disclosure may be considered as both a delimitation and a clarification of the conduct proscribed by the statute." *Id.* at 71; *see also* McGehee v. Casey, 718 F.2d 1137, 1143–44 (D.C. Cir. 1983) (construing the term "national security" with reference to the classification system). As the district court explained in United States v. Morison, "[t]he phrase 'not entitled to receive' is not at all vague when discussed in reference with the classification system, which clearly sets out who is entitled to receive (those with proper security clearances and the 'need to know') and [defendant] was certainly aware of the prescripts of the classification system." 604 F. Supp. at 662; accord Morison, 844 F.2d at 1075 ("We ... hold that the words 'entitled to receive' in the statute in this case can be limited and clarified by the Classification Regulations and, as so limited and clarified, are not vague."); "[W]hile the language of the statute, by itself, may lack precision, the gloss of judicial precedent has clarified that the statute incorporates the executive branch's classification regulations, which provide the requisite constitutional clarity." Rosen, 445 F. Supp. 2d at 623.

Defendant argues that incorporating the classification regulations does not resolve the ambiguity in the statute with respect to oral disclosures of information. Defendant proffers a hypothetical situation in which a government official has access to classified information that is also published in a newspaper. Because classification regulations dictate that "[c]lassified information shall not be declassified automatically as a result of any unauthorized disclosure of identical or similar information," Exec. Order No. 13292 § 1.1(b), Defendant argues that the hypothetical government official might be prosecuted for orally discussing the contents of the newspaper article with a member of the press, whereas another government official who did not have access to the classified information could discuss the same article without fear of prosecution. Defendant also argues that applying § 793(d) to oral disclosures is problematic because not all information contained within a classified document is necessarily classified, and therefore government officials are not given fair notice as to what information can or cannot be revealed. The Court fails to see a vagueness problem with Defendant's hypothetical. First of all, it is far from clear that the hypothetical defendant would be found to have "communicated, delivered, or transmitted" information if he did not explicitly or implicitly confirm the validity of the newspaper article. Second of all, the hypothetical defendant might be able to persuade a jury that based on the public disclosure of the information, he did not act "willfully." Ultimately, these are factual issues that must be decided by the jury in a particular case; they do not indicate unconstitutional vagueness in the statute. To the extent that Defendant intends to argue that the information he is charged with leaking was previously disclosed or was not properly classified, he may do so as part of his defense, but such arguments do not render the statute vague.

Finally, Defendant argues that his prosecution for Count One violates the "arbitrary enforcement" aspect of the vagueness doctrine, which "require[s] that a legislature establish

---

13. The statute provides in pertinent part that "[w]hoever ... without authority, sells, conveys or disposes of any record ... of the United States" shall be subject to criminal sanction. 18 U.S.C. § 641.

minimal guidelines to govern law enforcement." Smith, 415 U.S. at 574, 94 S. Ct. 1242. Defendant argues that government leaking is commonplace but rarely prosecuted, and therefore it is nearly impossible to determine the circumstances under which §793 will be enforced. Again, however, the willfulness requirement in the statute effectively eliminates any concerns that Defendant may have been subject to arbitrary enforcement. *See* United States v. Klecker, 348 F.3d 69, 71 (4th Cir. 2003) ("The intent requirement alone tends to defeat any vagueness challenge based on the potential for arbitrary enforcement."). The fact that the government infrequently prosecutes leakers under §793(d) does not necessarily suggest that enforcement is arbitrary. To the contrary, the statute requires the Government to prove: (1) that the defendant lawfully had possession of, access to, control over, or was entrusted with (2) information relating to the national defense (3) that the defendant reasonably believed could be used to the injury of the United States or to the advantage of a foreign nation and (4) that the defendant willfully communicated, delivered, or transmitted such information to a person not entitled to receive it. 18 U.S.C. §793(d). The difficulty in establishing such a violation, combined with the sensitive nature of classified information and the procedures that must be followed in using such information in a trial, *see* 18 U.S.C. App. 3, are the most likely reasons for the dearth of prosecutions. Our justice system's reliance on prosecutorial discretion means that Defendant cannot be set free merely because others have escaped prosecution for similar acts. The Court is not persuaded that §793(d) is so vague as to permit arbitrary enforcement. Therefore, the Court shall deny Defendant's motion to dismiss Count One on due process grounds.

2. Defendant's First Amendment Challenge

Defendant argues that §793(d), when applied to information communicated orally, amounts to a content-based restriction on his First Amendment right to free speech that cannot survive strict scrutiny. The Government argues that the conduct charged in the indictment is not protected by the First Amendment; alternatively, it argues that §793(d) can withstand any level of First Amendment scrutiny.

Although oral disclosures of national security information do qualify as "speech," the Supreme Court has made clear that not all categories of speech are protected by the First Amendment. "From 1791 to the present, ... the First Amendment has permitted restrictions upon the content of speech in a few limited areas." United States v. Stevens, ___ U.S. ___, 130 S.Ct. 1577, 1584, 176 L. Ed. 2d 435 (2010) (quotation marks and citation omitted). "These historic and traditional categories ... includ[e] obscenity, defamation, fraud, incitement, and speech integral to criminal conduct." *Id.* (quotation marks and internal citations omitted). With respect to the latter category, the Supreme Court has said, "It rarely has been suggested that the constitutional freedom for speech and press extends its immunity to speech or writing used as an integral part of conduct in violation of a valid criminal statute. We reject the contention now." Giboney v. Empire Storage & Ice Co., 336 U.S. 490, 498, 69 S. Ct. 684, 93 L. Ed. 834 (1949); accord United States v. Freeman, 761 F.2d 549, 552 (9th Cir.1985) ("[W]here speech becomes an integral part of the crime, a First Amendment defense is foreclosed even if the prosecution rests on words alone."). Because §793(d) makes it unlawful to communicate national defense information to those not entitled to receive it, courts have held that the First Amendment affords no protection for this type of conduct even though it clearly involves speech. *See, e.g.,* Haig v. Agee, 453 U.S. 280, 308–09, 101 S. Ct. 2766, 69 L. Ed. 2d 640 (1981) (holding that defendant's "repeated disclosures of intelligence operations and names of intelligence personnel" are "clearly not protected by the Constitution"); Frohwerk, 249 U.S. at 205–06, 39 S. Ct. 249 (holding that defendants' attempts to cause disloyalty and mutiny in the military through the publication of newspaper articles in violation of the Espionage

Act were not protected by the First Amendment); Morison, 844 F.2d at 1069 ("[I]t seems beyond controversy that a recreant intelligence department employee who had abstracted from the government files secret intelligence information and had wilfully transmitted or given it to one 'not entitled to receive it' as did the defendant in this case, is not entitled to invoke the First Amendment as a shield to immunize his act of thievery.").

Defendant acknowledges that "the First Amendment does not confer on a government official a right to violate the law in order to disseminate information to the public," Def.'s Br. at 30, but he contends that purely oral dissemination of information is somehow protected. The Supreme Court, however, has made clear that the First Amendment protects expressive conduct whether it is oral, written, or symbolic. *See* Texas v. Johnson, 491 U.S. 397, 404, 109 S. Ct. 2533, 105 L. Ed.2d 342 (1989) ("The First Amendment literally forbids the abridgment only of 'speech,' but we have long recognized that its protection does not end at the spoken or written word."). There is no authority for Defendant's proposition that the First Amendment protects his ability to orally disclose the contents of a classified document but not his transmission of that document in writing.

Recently, the U.S. Court of Appeals for the D.C. Circuit, sitting en banc, noted that "there are many federal provisions that forbid individuals from disclosing information they have lawfully obtained," including § 793(d), and that "[t]he validity of these provisions has long been assumed." Boehner v. McDermott, 484 F.3d 573, 578 (D.C. Cir. 2007) (en banc). Relying on the Supreme Court's decision in United States v. Aguilar, 515 U.S. 593, 115 S. Ct. 2357, 132 L. Ed.2d 520 (1995), the D.C. Circuit explained that "those who accept positions of trust involving a duty not to disclose information they lawfully acquire while performing their responsibilities have no First Amendment right to disclose that information." 484 F.3d at 579. Under that standard, it seems clear that Defendant's prosecution under § 793(d) does not run afoul of the First Amendment. By virtue of his security clearance, Defendant was entrusted with access to classified national security information and had a duty not to disclose that information. He cannot use the First Amendment to cloak his breach of that duty. The Government also notes that Defendant expressly waived in writing his right to disclose the national security information he obtained while in his government position. Courts have uniformly held that government employees who sign such nondisclosure agreements lack protection under the First Amendment. *See* McGehee, 718 F.2d at 1143 (holding that CIA's enforcement of secrecy agreement signed by former employee does not violate the First Amendment); Berntsen v. CIA, 618 F. Supp. 2d 27, 29 (D.D.C. 2009) ("[T]he CIA's enforcement of its secrecy agreement, and the corresponding prohibition on [defendant's] publication of classified information, do not implicate the first amendment.").

Accordingly, the Court finds that Defendant's First Amendment challenge lacks merit.

III. CONCLUSION

For the foregoing reasons, the Court finds that Defendant's prosecution under 18 U.S.C. § 793(d) does not violate the Treason Clause, the Due Process Clause, or the First Amendment to the United States Constitution..... .

SO ORDERED.

Comments

1. If the old form of espionage has given way to one that focuses on classified information provided to news outlets, as in *Kim*, the courts will increasingly face the argument that there is a journalist privilege which bars reporters from being compelled by the government

to provide information about their sources. The Fourth Circuit recently faced this issue in the case of Jeffrey Sterling, a former CIA case officer indicted under 793(d) and (e) for allegedly providing classified information about Iran to New York Times reporter James Risen, who published it in his 2006 book *State of War*. There, the Fourth Circuit rejected Risen's argument that the First Amendment necessitates a reporter's privilege that entitles him to refuse to testify at a criminal trial concerning the source and scope of classified national defense information disclosed to him. *United States v. Sterling*, 724 F.3d 482 (4th Cir. 2013). The lengthy opinion bases this conclusion on the Supreme Court's opinion in *Branzberg v. Hayes*, 408 U.S. 665, 92 S. Ct. 2646 (1972). The Fourth Circuit also rejected Risen's argument that a reporter's privilege exists in federal common law. The Supreme Court declined to review the 4th Circuit's Sterling opinion. 134 S. Ct. 2696 (Mem)(2014). Other circuits have reached the same conclusion. *United States v. Moloney (In re Price)*, 685 F.3d 1 (1st Cir. 2012), *ACLU v. Alvarez*, 679 F.3d 583 (7th Cir. 2012), *In re Grand Jury Subpoena, Judith Miller*, 438 F.3d 1141 (D.C. Cir. 2006).

2. *Kim* involved the arguable connection between espionage and treason. We saw in *Khan* how defendants can be charged with seditious conspiracy, material support, and the Neutrality Act based on a common scheme. Do the espionage statutes lend themselves to the same treatment with these other crimes? There has been only one case so far in which the espionage statute, specifically § 793, has been used in tandem with a material support offense, and the government's success was mixed. Hassan Abujihaad, a U.S. Navy signalman, was indicted and convicted in Connecticut of disclosing national security information and of providing material support to terrorists, in violation of § 2339A. A British investigation in the U.K. into an entity known as Azzam Publications—a website which glorified Al Qaida-inspired jihad—included a raid on the Azzam offices and the discovery of a computer document that detailed sensitive location information about the USS Belfield. It also uncovered 11 emails between Abu Jihaad and the Azzam leadership, where he wrote approvingly about jihad. The government indicted Abu Jihaad for providing classified information to Azzam, in violation of § 793, and for providing material support knowing it would be used to kill people, in violation of § 2339A. The jury convicted him of both. However, the district court granted Abu-Jihaad's post-trial motion to dismiss the material support charge based on lack of sufficient evidence, writing:

> To be sure, context and facts matter. Yet, it is context and facts that are entirely missing in this case. For we do not know how Mr. Abu-Jihaad conveyed the defense information to Azzam or what arrangements, if any, they had with each other. It could well be that Mr. Abu-Jihaad asked Azzam how he could help in supporting jihad, they told him to send defense information about the movements of the battle group so terrorists could attack the battle group, and Mr. Abu-Jihaad did as requested. In those circumstances, the Court would have little difficulty concluding that Mr. Abu-Jihaad had volunteered himself as personnel, acting in coordination with Azzam to kill U.S. nationals. On the other hand, perhaps Mr. Abu-Jihaad on a whim simply sent defense information to Azzam on one occasion, not knowing if Azzam wanted it and without any pre-disclosure or post-disclosure communication with Azzam about the information. In those circumstances, he surely provided defense information to someone not entitled to receive it, as the Court has previously found, but it would be linguistically odd to describe that lone, voluntary act as making personnel available to Azzam.

The Government recognizes this gap in the evidence and seeks to get around it by pointing to a general request by Azzam to its readership in November 2000, in which it sought aid for the Taliban by requesting money, gas masks, or battlefield medical services. Of course, Azzam also exhorted its readers to assist in violent jihad. But to build a quid pro quo or understanding from these generalized requests for assistance is more than the evidence will bear, even taking all reasonable inferences in the light most favorable to the Government. In short, the evidence showed beyond a reasonable doubt that Mr. Abu-Jihaad provided classified defense information to Azzam. He may also have made himself available to assist Azzam in violent jihad. However, we simply do not know that from the evidence presented, even viewing the evidence in the light most favorable to the Government. Therefore, the Court will grant the Motion for Judgment of Acquittal on the material support charge under 18 U.S.C. § 2339A.

United States v. Abu-Jihaad, 600 F. Supp. 2d 362, 401–2 (D. Conn. 2009).

Selected Bibliography

Norman Pearlstine, *Off the Record: The Press, The Government and The War Over Anonymous Sources* (2007).
Jonathan R. White, *Defending the Homeland: Domestic Intelligence, Law Enforcement, and Security* (Contemporary Issues in Crime and Justice Series) (2003).

Chapter 29

Immigration Law and National Security

Bo Cooper and Margaret D. Stock

In this chapter:
U.S. Immigration Law Overview
The Security-Related Grounds of Inadmissibility and Removability
Procedures for Removal Affecting National Security Cases
Post 9/11 Restrictions on Access to Unclassified Information in the Immigration Process
Detention Principles and Practices Affecting National Security Cases
General Measures to Improve the Security of the Immigration System
International Protection Treaties and National Security
National Security Immigration Benefits
A Final Note
Selected Bibliography

To a great extent, immigration law has been considered a part of the country's national security apparatus since there was such a thing as United States immigration law. Throughout America's history, Congress has passed laws effectively excluding entire nationalities, courts have spoken of plenary powers and the duty to "give security against foreign aggression," and all three branches of the federal government have grappled with questions surrounding the legitimacy of undisclosed national security information as the basis for individual immigration decisions. But since the September 11, 2001, attacks on New York and Washington, immigration issues have become a matter of national security with a level of clarity—or at least of force—like never before. The executive branch has asked for, and received, expanded statutory powers to detain and deport suspected terrorists. Traditional detention authorities have been invoked in new and controversial ways. Aliens within broad categories thought to pose security risks have been subjected to special registration and reporting requirements. Processes for granting visas abroad to persons seeking to enter the United States and for resettling refugees seeking protection from persecution have been revised to allow for much more thorough, but much more time-consuming, background checks. The Immigration and Naturalization Service, the government agency with the greatest share of responsibility for administering the immigration laws, was also dismantled amid the most bitter criticism of its often troubled history, and its functions transferred to the new Department of Homeland Security as part of the largest structural change to the federal government in more than a half-century.

At the same time, a few measures were implemented after the 9/11 terrorist attacks to allow certain foreigners who might benefit U.S. national security, or who had helped the U.S. in the post 9/11 conflicts, to enter the United States or become United States citizens.

These national security benefits programs should not be overlooked in any discussion of how immigration law intersects with other national security laws.

This chapter will offer a brief introduction to the issues surrounding immigration law as a function of national security. It will begin with a short tour of the immigration law structure and its basic terms. It will then address procedures for removal of persons thought to pose threats to the national security, the grounds for excluding or deporting such persons, questions involving the use of national security information that the alien whose interests are at stake is not permitted to see, other measures for controlling public disclosure of information deemed sensitive by the government, and matters surrounding the custody of aliens during and after immigration proceedings. It will then provide a short look at the ways in which international protection principles intersect with security issues. Finally, it will conclude with a brief discussion of immigration benefits that are available to immigrants who benefit U.S. national security by working for the United States Government or providing assistance in national security matters.

Immigration issues in general have divided the country deeply and fairly steadily throughout its history, but those divisions have come into particularly sharp focus at the beginning of the twenty-first century. This chapter will also introduce the ways in which those divisions have reappeared, and perhaps deepened, in the national debate over immigration policy and national security in the years leading up to and following the September 11 attacks.

U.S. Immigration Law Overview

This section will provide a brief overview of the major aspects of American immigration law: the avenues that are available to aliens who wish to acquire lawful permanent resident status in the United States; the avenues that are available to aliens who wish to acquire nonimmigrant, or temporary, status in the United States; and the rules establishing categories of aliens not entitled to enter or remain.

Immigration is a complex field, and this overview can only provide the most fundamental introduction to its general architecture and its basic terms. Each of the topics touched on below — naturalization, asylum and refugee law, business immigration, and others — could easily fill an entire course. Relatively new statutory limits on judicial review have undergone intense judicial testing and are nowhere near having assumed their final shape, more than a decade after passage. The constitutional limits, which we will touch on very briefly later in the chapter, have been a constant source of judicial and scholarly attention since Congress first began to regulate immigration, and have been the focus of renewed Supreme Court attention on a regular basis.

To consider how immigration law fits in as part of the national security regime, though, it is important to have a basic sense of how far-reaching the topics of concern to the immigration law are: An immigration officer might in the course of a day be considering whether a person holding a visitor's visa in fact intends not to work while in the country; whether a student has maintained a full course of study; whether a senior production assistant at a television network qualifies as a "specialty occupation" worker; whether a person is at risk for political persecution in a distant country; whether a marriage is real; whether a naturalization applicant has maintained "good moral character"; whether a conviction for theft with a one-year suspended sentence expunged on completion of probation is a deportable criminal offense; or whether a person has participated in fundraising for a terrorist organization. It is also critical to realize how many millions of people come into this country legally each year, for purposes as diverse as tourism, business, study, scientific exchange, and family reunification. September 11 showed in the cruelest way how gaps in the day-to-day immigration system can be exploited by those wishing to do harm in this country. It is essential to fill those gaps, and to reorder immigration policy priorities to better safeguard national security. Much of that work has been underway since the attacks. But there is also a debate that goes far beyond what has been so far undertaken in this country over the extent to which this country should, or even could, clamp shut its immigration process to the extent necessary to truly guard against the possibility that persons from other countries could come into this one to cause harm. Creating a large security apparatus and the means to keep people out of the United States can also harm national security if such measures damage the economy or the underlying principles of freedom that are also essential to America's security. In order to provide a basis for considering these sorts of questions, and to provide a foundation for the more specifically security-related topics that this chapter will explore, what follows is a much-abbreviated introduction to the United States immigration regime.

The principal U.S. immigration law is the Immigration and Nationality Act ("INA"), originally enacted in 1952, but amended many times since. It occupies Title 8 of the United States Code. The fundamental statutory distinction is that between "aliens" and "nationals." A "national" is any person who owes permanent allegiance to the United States. Most U.S. nationals are also citizens,[1] enjoying full political membership in civil society. Almost everyone born in the United States is born a citizen, and certain persons born outside the United States may derive citizenship from one or both parents.

An alien, by definition, is any person who is not a national of the United States. The chief purpose of the INA is to regulate the circumstances under which persons who owe no allegiance to the United States may come to the United States to visit, work, and live, and under which they may become citizens. Only an alien must comply with the requirements of the INA in order to come into the United States. Only an alien can be forcibly removed from the United States under the INA.

Many government agencies play a role in carrying out the immigration laws. The Department of State is responsible for overseas refugee processing and for processing the immigrant and nonimmigrant visas that aliens must acquire before applying for admission into the United States from abroad. The Department of Labor oversees the labor market evaluations, and determinations of the availability of U.S. workers for particular jobs, that are required as part of the approval process for many of the employment-based visa categories. Until 2003, the Immigration and Naturalization Service (INS), which had been housed within the Department of Justice and exercised statutory authority given to the Attorney General, played the most central role in the American immigration system. The INS was primarily responsible for administering a broad share of the INA's authorities, from deciding the petitions that form the basis for most admissions in the family- and employment-based immigrant and nonimmigrant categories, to adjudicating applications from people seeking refuge from persecution, to making decisions on petitions to gain citizenship in the United States, to initiating and prosecuting removal proceedings against those it believes are not entitled to enter or remain in the country, to detaining aliens at various stages of the removal process, to carrying out the deportation of those ordered removed. Most of those functions were transferred to the newly created Department of

---

1. Today, the only U.S. nationals who are not also U.S. citizens are persons born in American Samoa and Swain's Island, the only two remaining "unincorporated" territories of the United States.

Homeland Security in March 2003, as part of the largest reorganization of the federal government in half a century. As a part of that same reorganization, a substantial share of responsibility for the overseas visa issuance process was transferred from the Department of State to the Department of Homeland Security. Within DHS, three new immigration agencies were created—United States Citizenship & Immigration Services (USCIS), which is primarily a benefits agency; Immigration & Customs Enforcement (ICE), which is responsible for immigration enforcement functions within the United States; and Customs & Border Protection (CBP), which guards the borders and inspects and admits people to the United States (and turns many away).

The Executive Office for Immigration Review (EOIR) is an independent DOJ agency that bears primary responsibility for the adjudication of all removal cases formerly brought by the INS, now brought by the Department of Homeland Security. EOIR includes the immigration judges nationwide who adjudicate the removal cases in the first instance, and the Board of Immigration Appeals (BIA), an administrative appellate body that reviews appealed immigration judge decisions and has the authority to issue precedents that bind immigration judges and DHS officers in future similar cases.

Aliens are admitted into the country either as immigrants or nonimmigrants. Immigrants are given lawful permanent residence, or "green cards." Immigrants may remain in the United States indefinitely, so long as they do not abandon their permanent resident status or engage in conduct that would make them deportable. They may become eligible to gain citizenship through naturalization after remaining in the country for a certain number of years. Nonimmigrants are generally admitted temporarily, usually on the basis partly of a determination that they have a residence abroad that they intend to return to at the end of their sojourn in the United States. That temporary stay may be as short as a brief admission for those coming to visit the country as tourists, or for many years, as for some students or workers in a specialty occupation such as information technology. Roughly a million people are given permanent residence in this country each year, with more than forty million admitted as nonimmigrants.

Aliens are generally given permanent residence in the United States on the basis of family relationships, employment capabilities, humanitarian needs, or as winners of a special "Diversity Visa" lottery. There are also certain "special immigrants"; a familiar national security category of "special immigrant" includes persons who have worked as overseas interpreters for the U.S. government during the wars in Iraq and Afghanistan. Family-based immigration generally includes immediate relatives of United States citizens, who are not subject to numerical limits, and other close family of citizens or permanent residents.

The employment-based immigrant classifications include: "priority workers," which are described as "aliens of extraordinary ability," "outstanding professors and researchers," or "multinational executives or managers"; aliens who hold advanced degrees and those of "exceptional ability"; "skilled workers"; "special immigrants," such as ministers and other religious workers; and aliens who make qualifying, job-creating investments in a new business in the United States.

Acquisition of permanent residence is the result of a multi-step process that often involves the Department of State and, for employment-based immigrants, the Department of Labor. Generally, the alien himself or herself cannot begin the process, but must depend on the initiative of the relative or employer in the United States. Typically, there are three basic steps in the process: the relative or employer will file and the USCIS will approve an immigrant visa petition; the alien will apply for an immigrant visa from the Department of State abroad (or for "adjustment of status," if already in the U.S.); and CBP will admit the person at a port of entry (or USCIS will adjust the person's status if the person is already in the United States). The difference between gaining permanent residence through consular processing abroad or through adjusting status in the United States is explained in the following paragraphs.

Once USCIS has approved the appropriate immigrant visa petition, there are two different ways to become a resident alien. The theoretically more normative way is for the alien to apply for an immigrant visa at a U.S. consulate outside the U.S. If the consul finds that the alien qualifies — that is, falls within a category of aliens that Congress has determined can be admitted to this country for permanent residence — the consul issues an immigrant visa. The visa permits the alien to travel to the U.S. and seek admission, but does not guarantee admission. At the port of entry, an immigration inspector again examines the alien's case. If the inspector finds that the alien is admissible in the classification shown on the visa, the inspector admits the alien. The alien is then a resident alien.

If the alien is in the U.S. in a lawful status (or qualifies for an exemption from the lawful status requirement), the alien may apply to USCIS to "adjust" his or her status to lawful permanent residence, without having to leave the U.S. If USCIS finds that the alien qualifies for the immigrant visa classification and is admissible, USCIS may adjust the alien from whatever status the alien has to that of a resident alien. Although this means of acquiring permanent residence is theoretically exceptional, in fact today the majority of aliens acquire permanent residence by adjusting status inside the United States.

As noted above, the INA allocates only a certain number of immigrant visas for each fiscal year. Unless an alien qualifies as an immediate relative, the alien must "wait in line" until those who qualified ahead of the alien are able to seek resident alien status. Each immigrant who is subject to the numerical limits has a "priority date," based on when the relative or employer first filed the papers needed to facilitate the immigrant's immigration. Each month, the U.S. Department of State publishes the priority date cut-off for each classification. An immigrant may actually apply for an immigrant visa or for adjustment of status only when this publication shows a cut-off date that is later than the date on which the relative or employer filed the petition.

In addition to regulating the admission of aliens who seek to live in the United States as permanent residents, the INA also governs the admission of aliens seeking to come here on a temporary basis. These aliens are called nonimmigrants. There are many categories of nonimmigrants, and in some categories the alien is permitted to remain for an extended period. In fact, some nonimmigrant classifications are designed specifically as "stepping stones" to permanent residence. Thus, the chief defining characteristic of nonimmigrant status is not so much how long the person may remain, but the fact that he or she is admitted to the United States lawfully but not as a permanent resident.

Under INA section 214, every alien applying for admission is presumed to be intending to remain permanently as an immigrant. The alien may overcome this presumption only by establishing that he or she qualifies for one of the nonimmigrant classifications. There are twenty-seven nonimmigrant classifications. The letter assigned to each classification is based on the subparagraph in INA section 101(a)(15) that defines the classification. Except for the visitor, alien in transit, and crewman classifications, a nonimmigrant's spouse and children also qualify for the nonimmigrant classification if accompanying or following to join the principal alien.

As with immigrants, acquiring nonimmigrant status is often a multi-step process. Typically, the alien must obtain a nonimmigrant visa from a U.S. consular officer. To do so, the alien must prove that he or she qualifies for the classification. There is no judicial review of the consular officer's decision.

If the alien obtains a visa, the visa does not necessarily guarantee admission to the United States. Nor does the visa determine the length of the alien's sojourn. The visa simply permits the alien to travel to a port of entry in the United States to seek admission. At the port of entry, the alien must again prove to the CBP inspector that the alien actually qualifies for the nonimmigrant status. If the alien does qualify, then the inspector admits him or her. The inspector also determines the duration of the alien's authorized stay, in accordance with the regulations governing the specific nonimmigrant classification. If the inspector denies admission, CBP will either permit the alien to withdraw the application for admission and leave immediately or initiate a removal proceeding.

For some nonimmigrant classifications, there are special requirements that must be met before the alien can apply for a visa. For example, students and exchange visitors must obtain documents from their respective programs that establish their eligibility. For those coming to work temporarily, such as treaty traders, specialty occupation workers, or executives being transferred within multinational corporations, or scientists, artists, athletes, and others having extraordinary ability, USCIS must approve a nonimmigrant visa petition before the alien can apply for a visa.

In addition to the family and work-related avenues to immigrate to the United States, and the various categories for those coming temporarily to visit or work, U.S. immigration law provides several humanitarian-based means by which persons may travel to or remain in the United States, either permanently or temporarily.

Section 207 of the INA provides for the direct admission into the United States of aliens who, while still abroad, seek refugee status. The President sets the number of refugees who may be admitted under section 207 of the INA annually after consultation with Congress. In FY 2014, the refugee admission cap was 70,000. While refugee applicants apply from abroad for admission into the United States, asylum-seekers apply for protection from within the United States. Unlike refugee admissions, asylum is not subject to numerical limitations.[2]

The definition of a "refugee" governs determinations made for both refugee processing abroad and asylum processing within the United States. Section 101(a)(42) of the INA defines a refugee as a person "who is unable or unwilling to return to, and is unable or unwilling to avail himself or herself of the protection of, that country because of persecution or a well-founded fear of persecution on account of race, religion, nationality, membership in a particular social group, or political opinion...." After one year, refugees and asylees may be eligible to adjust their status to that of a permanent resident.

Temporary Protected Status (TPS) is a temporary immigration status granted to eligible nationals of designated countries. The Attorney General may provide TPS to aliens in the United States who are temporarily unable to return to their homeland because of armed conflict, environmental disaster, or other extraordinary and temporary conditions. Thus, while asylum or refugee status depends upon a determination that, for reasons particular to him or her, a person cannot safely return home, TPS is given where temporary conditions in a particular country make return generally unsafe. During a period of TPS,

---

2. Statistical Information on the number of refugees and the number of persons granted asylum in the United States during a given fiscal year can be found at the DHS website <http://www.dhs.gov/data-statistics>.

beneficiaries may remain and work in the United States. However, TPS does not lead to permanent resident status.

There is no requirement that a lawful permanent resident alien must seek to become a U.S. citizen. If an alien desires to do so, the alien may apply when he or she becomes eligible. Most aliens must reside in the United States for at least five years before seeking naturalization. The spouse of a citizen, however, may apply after three years' residence if the alien spouse and citizen spouse have lived together as a married couple for three years. Persons serving in the military may apply after one day of honorable military service on active duty or in the Selected Reserve of the Ready Reserve (including the National Guard) if they have served after September 11, 2001 or during another specified "wartime" period. All applicants must be persons of good moral character, must have a sufficient understanding of American history and our system of government, and, unless exempt by age or other factor, must be able to read, write, and speak English. If USCIS approves the naturalization application, the alien becomes a citizen when the alien takes the statutory oath of allegiance at a public ceremony. Once naturalized, the person enjoys all the political rights of natural born citizens, except that a naturalized citizen may not serve as President or Vice President.

Congress has prescribed specific classes of aliens who may not be admitted to the United States.[3] Congress has also specified classes of aliens who, if admitted, are to be expelled.[4] The provisions forbidding admission are called grounds of inadmissibility. The provisions for expulsion are called grounds of removal, which are also colloquially referred to as grounds of "deportation."

The grounds of inadmissibility apply to aliens actually seeking admission at a port of entry and to aliens who have come into the interior of the United States without having been admitted by CBP. There are ten broad categories of inadmissibility. These are more extensive (and more colorful) than the grounds of removability. The most prominent categories cover aliens convicted of certain categories of crimes and those who admit to having committed the essential elements of those crimes, ranging from "crimes involving moral turpitude" through trafficking in controlled substances to prostitution and commercialized vice; aliens whose admission is contrary to the national security, which will be examined in much greater detail below; aliens lacking valid entry documents; and aliens who are present without having been admitted or who seek admission fraudulently. Additional grounds cover aliens with a "communicable disease of public health significance,"; foreign government officials who have committed "particularly severe violations of religious freedom;" aliens likely to become a public charge; aliens who have accrued sufficient previous periods of unlawful presence in this country; illegal voters; stowaways; and practicing polygamists.

The grounds of removal apply to aliens who have been admitted by CBP and other aliens found inside the United States. There are several broad categories of removable aliens. These include aliens convicted of specified crimes; aliens who were lawfully admitted but who have violated the terms of their admission; aliens who have committed some other sort of immigration-related violation, such as marriage fraud, alien smuggling, or document fraud; aliens whose continued presence is contrary to foreign policy interests or national security, including those who can be shown to have engaged in terrorist activity; aliens who vote illegally; and even aliens who fail to report promptly their changes of address.

---

3. Immigration and Nationality Act, § 212(a) (2014) [hereinafter INA].
4. *Id.* § 237(a).

If an alien is placed into removal proceedings, there are various forms of relief from deportation that he or she may seek: asylum, adjustment of status, cancellation of removal, voluntary departure, or other forms of relief. Some persons, however, are not eligible for any form of relief from removal.

The Security-Related Grounds of Inadmissibility and Removability

Regulation of immigration for the sake of national security can be traced to the earliest stages of the country's existence. In the late eighteenth century, for example, the Alien Enemies Act and the Alien Friends Act gave the President power to deport any alien whom he considered dangerous to the welfare of the nation. One rationale advanced at the time invokes the concept of sovereignty, and of the government's duty to provide security to its citizenry, that underlie the security function of immigration regulation even today: "If no law of this kind was passed, it would be in the power of an individual state to introduce such a number of aliens into the country, as might not only be dangerous, but as might be sufficient to overturn the government, and introduce the greatest confusion in the country."[5]

Later developments in security-related immigration law are apparent in the following passage from a 1972 Supreme Court decision involving the denial of a visa on ideological grounds to a Marxist writer from Belgium.

> Until 1875 alien migration to the United States was unrestricted. The Act of March 3, 1875, 18 Stat. 477, barred convicts and prostitutes. Seven years later Congress passed the first general immigration statute.[6] Act of Aug. 3, 1882, 22 Stat. 214. Other legislation followed. A general revision of the immigration laws was effected by the Act of March 3, 1903, 32 Stat. 1213. Section 2 of that Act made ineligible for admission "anarchists, or persons who believe in or advocate the overthrow by force or violence of the Government of the United States or of all government or of all forms of law." By the Act of Oct. 16, 1918, 40 Stat. 1012, Congress expanded the provisions for the exclusion of subversive aliens. Title II of the Alien Registration Act of 1940, 54 Stat. 671, amended the 1918 Act to bar aliens who, at any time, had advocated violent overthrow of the United States Government.
>
> In the years that followed, after extensive investigation and numerous reports by congressional committees, *see* Communist Party v. Subversive Activities Control Board, 367 U.S. 1, 94 n. 37..., Congress passed the Internal Security Act of 1950, 64 Stat. 987. This Act dispensed with the requirement of the 1940 Act of a finding in each case, with respect to members of the Communist Party, that the party did in fact advocate violent overthrow of the Government. These provisions were carried forward into the Immigration and Nationality Act of 1952.[7]

As enacted in 1952, the INA contained several provisions dealing with the expulsion of aliens deemed to pose a threat to national security. These broadly worded provisions

---

5. *See* Select Commission on Immigration and Refugee Policy, U.S. Immigration Policy and the National Interest, Staff Report at 161.
6. Act of Aug. 3, 1882, 22 Stat. 214.
7. Kleindienst v. Mandel, 408 U.S. 753, 761 (1972).

included aliens who were coming to the United States "to engage in activities which would be prejudicial to the public interest, or to endanger the welfare, safety, or security of the United States."[8] Former INA section 212(a)(28) set forth detailed categories of such excludable aliens as "anarchists," "those who advocate or teach ... opposition to all organized government," members of the Communist Party, other aliens who "advocate ... the establishment in the United States of a totalitarian dictatorship." No provisions dealt specifically in terms of terrorism, terrorists or persons who were associated with terrorist organizations. By the 1980s the application of the 1952 provisions had led to considerable controversy in both political and judicial forums.

In 1990, Congress significantly revised the immigration statute's deportation and exclusion provisions, aiming with greater particularity at national security and post-Cold War foreign policy interests. Membership in the Communist or other totalitarian party remains a ground of inadmissibility today, although under much narrower circumstances than those set out in prior law.[9] The Immigration Act of 1990 incorporated into the INA the first specific provisions for the exclusion or deportation of an alien who has engaged or is likely to engage after entry in terrorist activity.[10] The 1990 enactment also included detailed definitions of certain key terms, and those definitions were later expanded. On April 24, 1996, Congress enacted the Antiterrorism and Effective Death Penalty Act (AEDPA), which contained important changes to the security-related (and other) provisions of the INA. The AEDPA created a mechanism for the Secretary of State to designate "foreign terrorist organizations," with such designations permitting the Secretary of the Treasury to freeze assets of the organization,[11] and rendering the organizations' representatives and members inadmissible.[12] The AEDPA also expanded the bars to most forms of relief from removal to cover those who have "engaged in terrorist activity."

A short five months later, Congress again amended these provisions. As part of the Illegal Immigration Reform and Immigrant Responsibility Act (IIRIRA), with its wide-ranging changes to the INA, Congress amended the "terrorist activities" provision to reach an alien who has "under circumstances indicating an intention to cause death or serious bodily harm, incited terrorist activity."[13] IIRIRA also provided that a member of a foreign terrorist organization designated by the Secretary of State would be inadmissible only if that person knew or should have known that the organization is a terrorist organization.[14]

On October 26, 2001, just six weeks after the September 11 attacks, the President signed into law the Uniting and Strengthening America by Providing Appropriate Tools Required to Intercept and Obstruct Terrorism (USA PATRIOT) Act of 2001. This act, as part of a broad package of amendments designed to enable the government to combat more effectively the threat of terrorism, made yet further amendments to INA section 212(a)(3). First, the USA PATRIOT Act broadened the definition of "terrorist activity" to include the use of any dangerous device, rather than just explosives or firearms, to endanger the safety of others or to cause substantial property damage.[15] Second, Congress

---

8. *See* former INA § 212(a)(27).

9. INA § 212(a)(3)(D) (2014).

10. INA § 212(a)(3)(B)(i) (then for exclusion, now for inadmissibility), § 241(a)(4)(B) (moved in 1996 to § 237(a)(4)(B), for deportability).

11. INA § 219 (2014).

12. INA § 212(a)(3)(B)(i) (2014).

13. Illegal Immigration Reform and Immigrant Responsibility Act, § 342, adding INA § 212(a)(3)(B)(i)(II) (2014) [hereinafter IIRIRA].

14. IIRIRA § 355, amending INA § 212(a)(3)(B)(i)(V) (2014).

15. INA § 212(a)(3)(B)(iii)(V)(b) (Supp. I 2002).

amended the definition of "engage in terrorist activity" to impose stricter consequences on fundraising and other supporting activities.[16] Third, Congress added a much-broadened definition of "terrorist organization" that includes: (a) any organization designated under INA § 219; (b) any organization otherwise designated upon publication in the Federal Register, by the Secretary of State (after consultation with or at the request of the Attorney General) as a terrorist organization after a finding that the organization commits or incites to commit terrorist activity, prepares or plans a terrorist activity, or gathers information on potential targets for terrorist activity, or that the organization provides material support to further terrorist activity; and (c) a group of two or more individuals, whether organized or not, that commits or incites to commit terrorist activity, prepares or plans a terrorist activity, or gathers information on potential targets for terrorist activity. National security lawyers today refer to these three designations as tiers, so that today there are Tier I, Tier II, and Tier III terrorist organizations ; the latter group includes hundreds of named and unnamed groups (indeed, it includes any group of two or more persons that has tried to forcibly overthrow a government at any time).

As the preceding paragraphs might suggest, the security-related provisions of the INA have been among the most complex parts of an already complex statute since they were added in 1990. These provisions have become even more complicated with the series of amendments made by AEDPA, IIRIRA, and the USA PATRIOT Act. Today, the term "terrorist activity" has been broadened to include some behaviors that were formerly thought to be ordinary criminal acts. For example, the term today includes not only activities such as hijacking or sabotage of any conveyance; seizing or detaining, and threatening to kill, injure, or continue to detain, someone in order to compel a third person or governmental organization to take or refrain from taking an action; violently attacking an "internationally protected person;" assassination; using a biological, chemical, or nuclear device with intent to endanger an individual or cause substantial damage to property; using an explosive device or firearm (other than for personal monetary gain) with intent to endanger others or cause substantial property damage; but also the use of any weapon with intent to endanger one or more individuals.[17] Many commentators have said that the definition is overly broad and can turn even an ordinary knife fight into a "terrorist activity."

The phrase "engage in terrorist activity" is also now broadly defined to mean "in an individual capacity or as a member of an organization, ... to commit or to incite to commit ... a terrorist activity; to prepare or plan a terrorist activity; to gather information on potential targets for terrorist activity; to solicit funds or other things of value for" a terrorist activity or organization, and to solicit others or provide "material support" to a terrorist activity or terrorist organization."[18] Thus, an alien will be inadmissible for such activities as engaging in the preparation or planning of a terrorist activity, the gathering of information on potential targets for terrorist activity, providing to terrorists such material support as a safe house, transportation, communications, funds, false identification, weapons, explosives, or training; soliciting funds or other things of value for terrorist activity or a terrorist organization, or soliciting persons for membership in a terrorist organization, terrorist government, or to engage in a terrorist activity.

Notwithstanding the detailed congressional and executive branch attention to the security-related removal grounds, however, they have seldom been put to use to remove

---

16. INA §§ 212(a)(3)(B)(iii)(iv)(IV)–(VI) (Supp. I 2002).
17. INA § 212(a)(3)(B)(iii) (2014).
18. INA § 212(a)(3)(B)(iv) (2014).

aliens from the United States. Immigration removal cases in which the national security has been invoked have tended often instead to be cases in which evidence relating to the threat a person is believed to pose to national security has been introduced not to show that the person is unlawfully in the country in the first place, but instead to contest a request to be released from custody or to receive some sort of relief from removal such as asylum or lawful permanent resident status.

Thus, rather than causing the removals of large numbers of aliens from the United States, the post-9/11 expansion of the definitions of "terrorist activity" and a "terrorist organization" have much more often resulted in denials of refugee or asylee or lawful permanent resident status, typically to aliens who are alleged to have provided "material support" to a terrorist organization or to have engaged in "terrorist activity." In some cases, the use of the "material support to terrorism" bar has led to absurd results, such as the inability of some US allies to immigrate to the United States because pro-democracy activities have now been inadvertently defined as "terrorist activities" under the immigration laws:

> The definition of "material support" is directly tied to characterizations of "terrorist organization" and "terrorist activity," both of which were significantly expanded after September 11, 2001.
>
> The Patriot Act, which became law in October 2001, created a three-tier terrorist group classification system. The State Department was designated the responsibility (which it already held in a smaller capacity) of maintaining lists of Tier I (most dangerous) and Tier II organizations.
>
> The act also defined a terrorist organization as any "group of two or more individuals, whether organized or not, which engages in, or has a subgroup which engages in, terrorist activity." This last category gives particular latitude to individual DHS case managers and immigration judges to classify groups as "nondesignated Tier III" terrorist organizations, and to bar or expel a material-support provider from the United States on that basis.
>
> The availability of the Tier III designation has affected many individuals belonging to minority groups that have assisted prodemocracy antiauthoritarian organizations. For example, the Karen National Union and the Chin National Front have fought for the rights of minority refugees in Burma. Individuals who supported their causes are found to have provided material support to groups that qualify as nondesignated Tier III organizations, and have had significant difficulties entering the United States as refugees.
>
> Paradoxically, affiliates of groups that have actively assisted the U.S. government have also been stigmatized. The material-support bar has excluded many relatives of the Cuban Alzados, an anti-Castro group that sided and fought with U.S. troops in the Bay of Pigs invasion.
>
> The Hmong, an ethnic minority group in Southeast Asia, fought with U.S. and South Vietnamese troops during the Vietnam War. Though large numbers of Hmong were resettled in the United States immediately after the conflict, they faced restrictions in applying for refugee status after September 11, as their antigovernmental stance in Laos fell under the new definition of terrorist activity. The secretaries of State and Homeland Security waived the ban against material supporters of Hmong organizations in October 2006.[19]

---

19. *See, e.g.,* Swetha Sridharan, "Material Support to Terrorism—Consequences for Refugee and Asylum Seekers in the United States," Migration Policy Institute Feature, Jan. 30, 2008, *available at*

A significant problem with the "material support" bar has been that there is no "*de minimis*" threshold to the support, and even support that is involuntary or coerced can cause an alien to be denied U.S. immigration benefits. In a 2004 Third Circuit case, for example, the court held that the magnitude of the support provided was irrelevant in determining whether the material support bar applied; the alien in that case was a Sikh who had provided food and set up tents for a religious organization that had some members who were part of a group that could have been designated as a Tier III terrorist organization.[20] The court denied adjustment of status and upheld a removal order against the alien.

Under INA § 212(d)(3)(B)(i), the DHS has discretion to waive most of the terrorism grounds of inadmissibility in the case of asylum and withholding of removal cases. DHS, however, rarely exercises this discretion, and such discretion can only be sought when a person is subject to a final order of removal. DHS has, however, announced that certain persons who are inadmissible under INA § 212(a)(3)(B) may be eligible for a "blanket" waiver; to be eligible, they must have received military-type training from terrorist organizations under duress; solicited funds for a terrorist organization or individual under duress; voluntarily provided medical care to persons associated with terrorist activities or organizations; or they are the spouses and children of such individuals. The criteria for the blanket exemptions were described in two DHS policy memoranda, both issued on November 20, 2011.[21] On August 10, 2012, DHS Secretary Janet Napolitano announced yet further exemptions for certain aliens who had been granted immigration benefits before DHS realized that the terrorism-related inadmissibility grounds applied to them. To obtain this exemption, the alien must have solicited funds or things of value, solicited individuals to be members, provided material support, or received training from or on behalf of a terrorist organization not otherwise designated as being associated with Al Qaeda or the Taliban.[22]

The INA also bars the admission of aliens whose entry or proposed activities in the United States the Secretary of State has reasonable grounds to believe would have potentially serious adverse consequences for the country's foreign policy.[23] A parallel ground of deportability exists at INA section 237(a)(4)(C). These provisions are subject to a pair of exceptions. Under the first, seemingly drawn to incorporate First Amendment principles, an official of a foreign government or a candidate for office in a foreign government cannot be subject to removal for beliefs, statements, or associations that would be lawful in this country. The second excepts any alien, not just foreign government officials or candidates, from removal on the basis of such beliefs, but allows for the Secretary of State to override the exception if he or she personally determines that the alien's admission or presence would compromise a compelling Unites States foreign policy interest.

<http://www.migrationpolicy.org/article/material-support-terrorism-%E2%80%94-consequences-refugees-and-asylum-seekers-united-states>.

20. Singh-Kaur v. Ashcroft, 385 F.3d 293 (3d Cir. 2004).

21. *See* U.S. Dep't of Homeland Security, Policy Memorandum PM-602-0051, "Revised Guidance on the Adjudication of Cases Involving Terrorism-Related Inadmissibility Grounds (TRIG) and Further Amendment to the Hold Policy for Such Cases," Nov. 20, 2011, available at <http://www.ilw.com/immigrationdaily/news/2011,1128-trig.pdf > and U.S. Dep't of Homeland Security, Policy Memorandum PM-602-0052, "Implementation of New Exemption Under INA Section 212(d)(3)(B)(i) for the Provision of Material Support in the Form of Medical Care," Nov. 20, 2011, *available at* <http://www.uscis.gov/sites/default/files/USCIS/Laws/Memoranda/Static_Files_Memoranda/Voluntary-Medical-Care-PM-602-0052.pdf>.

22. *See* 77 Fed. Reg. 49821–49822 (Aug. 17, 2012).

23. INA § 212(a)(3)(C) (2014).

Procedures for Removal Affecting National Security Cases

After having examined the security-related grounds of inadmissibility and deportability, this section will turn to the removal procedures affected national security cases. While a full evaluation of the constitutional issues lies beyond the scope of this chapter, it will become evident in the following discussion and elsewhere that the constitutional protections afforded an alien in the removal process differ depending on the degree of the person's connection with this country. That is, a person who is literally standing at a port of entry seeking admission is afforded the lowest level of constitutional protections; a person admitted to permanent residence enjoys a great deal more protection; and a complex and unsettled constitutional structure exists in between. This section will focus on three removal processes, going from the most specialized to the most general. We start with the Alien Terrorist Removal Court, move to expedited removal procedures for arriving aliens suspected to pose a security risk, and finally discuss "normal" removal procedures in immigration court.

The Alien Terrorist Removal Court

With the passage of AEDPA in 1996, Congress established the Alien Terrorist Removal Court (ATRC) through the addition of Title V to the INA. Title V of the INA provides for the removal of aliens believed to be deportable on terrorism grounds on the basis of classified evidence in proceedings before the ATRC.[24] This special removal court is made up of five federal district judges appointed by the Chief Justice of the United States for fixed terms. As of 2014, as discussed further below, this court has never been used.[25]

In proceedings before the ATRC, the Department of Justice may present classified evidence *in camera* and *ex parte* to prove that the alien is deportable under section 237(a)(4) of the INA, in that the alien "has engaged, is engaged, or at any time after admission engages in any terrorist activity." As discussed above, this ground of deportation refers back to the complex definition of "engaging in terrorist activity" contained in the comparable inadmissibility ground.[26] To initiate a case in this special court, the Attorney General must certify that probable cause exists that the alien's removal in conventional removal proceedings "would pose a risk to the national security of the United States."[27] The court is designed for use only where the government intends to rely on classified information and only where the alien is not an arriving alien. In that case, the expedited procedures discussed above for arriving aliens inadmissible on security grounds would apply.[28]

The ATRC is noteworthy for certain key features that set it apart from conventional removal proceedings. First, it would permit the government to use classified information *ex parte* and *in camera* to show that an alien—even one who is a lawful permanent resident—is deportable, as opposed to inadmissible or ineligible for some discretionary

---

24. *See* INA §§ 502, 503 (2014).
25. Andrew Becker, "Terrorist Court Unused 16 Years After Creation," California Watch (Apr. 12, 2013).
26. INA § 212(a)(3)(B)(iii) (2014).
27. INA § 503(a)(1)(D)(iii) (2014).
28. INA § 235(c) (2014).

remedy. Second, in the public hearing that takes place, the alien has a right to be represented by counsel, including appointed counsel if the alien is in financial need. Third, there are special provisions for the use of classified information. Where removal is to be based on information whose disclosure would "present a risk to the national security of the United States, the judge must examine it *ex parte* and *in camera*, and the alien would receive generally an unclassified summary of the classified information. Even that summary, though, is not available if the judge finds that "(I) the continued presence of the alien in the United States would likely cause serious and irreparable harm to the national security or serious bodily injury or death to any person, and (II) the provision of the summary would likely cause serious and irreparable harm to the national security or death or serious bodily injury to any person."[29] In that event, if the alien is a lawful permanent resident, a "special attorney" designated to assist the alien may review the classified evidence on the alien's behalf and contest its veracity in an *in camera* proceeding, but may not disclose the information to the alien or to other counsel for the alien.[30]

The ATRC is also noteworthy for the fact that it has never been used. In the wake of its passage it was criticized as a "Star Chamber." In the controversies surrounding the use of classified evidence in conventional removal proceedings, by contrast, it was often cited as process whose use the government chose to avoid because of its enhanced procedural protections. Its disuse might instead be traced to other factors.

First, the ATRC legislation effectively requires that conventional immigration proceedings be considered before resort to the ATRC, as a determination that removal proceedings under Title II of the INA "would pose a risk to the national security of the United States" is a jurisdictional prerequisite to invoking the ATRC.[31] If a suspected alien terrorist is a non-resident alien removable in conventional proceedings for a conventional immigration violation (such as overstaying a visa) that can be easily proven without the use of classified evidence, there is no need to resort to classified evidence for the purpose envisioned in the ATRC process. Litigation in that context will generally focus not on removability, but on an application for relief from removal. In such cases, the statute authorizes the government to present classified information *ex parte* and *in camera* to the immigration judge to oppose an alien's request for discretionary relief from removal.[32] Thus, Title II proceedings would not apparently be unavailable for purposes of invoking ATRC procedures.

Second, the universe of potential ATRC cases decreased five months after the enactment of the AEDPA, with the passage of IIRIRA. The ATRC was enacted in order to remove only aliens who are deportable (as opposed to in admissible) without compromising national security. Pursuant to IIRIRA, aliens who may have entered the United States without inspection are no longer considered "deportable" aliens. Here again, at least as a statutory matter, the government can use undisclosed classified evidence against them in conventional Title II proceedings to oppose their formal admission into the United States.[33]

Finally, in some cases intelligence objectives or prospects for criminal prosecution will take precedence over any type of immigration action, including the ATRC. Whatever the reasons it has never been used, the ATRC is an interesting part of the national security arsenal. As a means of using undisclosed classified evidence to prove deportability of even

---

29. INA § 504(e)(3) (2014).
30. INA § 504(e)(3)(F) (2014).
31. INA § 503 (2014).
32. INA § 240(b)(4) (2014).
33. *See* INA §§ 235(c), 240 (2014), discussed below.

those aliens with the most heightened constitutional protections, lawful permanent residents, it poses significant untested constitutional issues. But it also offers a number of procedural safeguards—such as the fairly strict requirement that an unclassified summary be produced, and the mechanism for cleared counsel who can see and contest the classified information on the alien's behalf—that might provoke the interest of those favoring a different balance in conventional immigration proceedings between security interests and fuller process.

Expedited Removal in Security Cases

In 1952, Congress provided statutory authority for the Attorney General to order the removal, without a hearing under what is now section 240, of an arriving alien under most of the national security-related grounds of inadmissibility.[34] The Attorney General may do so on the basis of undisclosed classified evidence if he concludes, after consultation with appropriate security agencies, that disclosure of the evidence would be "prejudicial to the public interest, safety, or security." In *United States ex rel. Knauff v. Shaughnessy*,[35] the Supreme Court considered the summary exclusion of a woman seeking to enter the United States to join her citizen husband, under a regulation that was in key ways the predecessor for today's section 235(c). In the absence of an express statutory grant of authority, the Attorney General had provided by regulation for the exclusion without a hearing of aliens considered to be excludable on the basis of information whose disclosure would be prejudicial to the public interest.[36] Noting Congress's inherent power to govern entry into the country, or to authorize broadly the executive branch to exercise that power "in the best interests of the country during a time of national emergency," the Supreme Court gave this often-cited explanation for rejecting Ms. Knauff's constitutional arguments: "Whatever the procedure authorized by Congress is, it is due process as far as an alien denied entry is concerned."[37]

Three years later, the Court again examined the Attorney General's summary exclusion regulation in *Kwong Hai Chew v. Colding*.[38] It held that the regulation could not constitutionally be applied to a resident alien returning from a four-month absence from the country in the merchant marines. Weeks later, though, the Court upheld the application of the regulation to another resident alien, named Mezei, who had "remained behind the Iron Curtain for nineteen months."[39]

> It is true that aliens who have once passed through our gates, even illegally, may be expelled only after proceedings conforming to traditional standards of fairness encompassed in due process of law.... But an alien on the threshold of initial entry stands on a different footing: "Whatever the procedure authorized by Congress is, it is due process as far as an alien denied entry is concerned." [citing *Knauff*]. And because the action of the executive officer under such authority is final and conclusive, the Attorney General cannot be compelled to disclose the evidence underlying his determinations in an exclusion case; "it is not within the province of any court, unless expressly authorized by law, to review the de-

---

34. INA § 235(c) (2014).
35. United States ex rel. Knauff v. Shaughnessy, 338 U.S. 537 (1950).
36. *See* 8 C.F.R. § 175.57(b) (1945 Supp.).
37. 338 U.S. at 543.
38. Kwong Hai Chew v. Colding, 344 U.S. 590 (1953).
39. Shaughnessy v. United States ex rel. Mezei, 345 U.S. 206, 214 (1953).

termination of the political branch of Government." [citing *Knauff*]. In such a case as this, courts cannot retry the determination of the Attorney General.[40]

The availability of expedited proceedings under section 235(c) was sharply limited in *Rafeedie v. INS*.[41] There the immigration agency had sought to apply section 235(c) procedures to a person who had been a lawful permanent resident for fourteen years. He left the United States bearing a reentry permit, ostensibly to be with his mother in Cyprus during major heart surgery. In truth, his mother was in Youngstown, Ohio, and he traveled to Syria instead. The government suspected him of involvement there with a terrorist organization, and sought to exclude him upon his return. The court struck down the use of the section 235(c) process in that context, finding his situation as a permanent resident returning from a brief visit abroad far distinct from those of Chew and Mezei. Instead, the court found Rafeedie entitled to due process of law as measured by the test set out in *Mathews v. Eldridge*.[42] That test calls for an analysis of three factors:

> First, the private interest that will be affected by the official action; second, the risk of an erroneous deprivation of such interest through the procedures used, and the probable value, if any, of additional or substitute procedural safeguards; and finally, the Government's interest, including the function involved and the fiscal and administrative burdens that the additional or substitute procedural requirements would entail.[43]

The court stated that "Rafeedie — like Joseph K in *The Trial* — can prevail ... only if he can rebut the undisclosed evidence against him, that is, prove that he is not a terrorist regardless of what might be implied by the government's confidential information. It is difficult to imagine how even someone innocent of all wrongdoing could meet such a burden."[44] (When courts begin mentioning Joseph K., government lawyers defending the use of classified evidence always know they are on the ropes.)

Standard Removal Proceedings and Classified Evidence

Removal proceedings normally take place in an administrative setting that operates in many ways according to the standard adversarial model that prevails in American courtrooms. The procedures are set out in INA § 240. An immigration judge, who works for the Department of Justice as an executive branch employee, but who is independent of DHS agency that initiated the case, presides. The case is initiated through the service and filing of a "notice to appear," which specifies the nature of the proceedings against the alien, the legal authority under which they are being conducted, the acts or conduct at issue, and the charges against the alien.[45] The alien may be represented by counsel, though not at government expense.[46] (As one might imagine, many persons in removal proceedings have no lawyer.) The judge may administer oaths, receive evidence, and may question the alien and any witnesses, and the alien must have a reasonable opportunity to examine the evidence against him, present evidence on his own behalf, and cross-

---

40. 345 U.S. at 212.
41. Rafeedie v. INS, 880 F.2d 506 (D.C. Cir. 1989).
42. Mathews v. Eldridge, 424 U.S. 319 (1976).
43. 880 F.2d. at 524.
44. 880 F.2d at 516.
45. INA § 239 (2014).
46. INA § 240(4)(A) (2014).

examine government witnesses. (There is an exception, discussed below, for classified evidence.)

The burden of proof varies, depending upon the alien's immigration status or the type of charge. An applicant for admission bears the burden of proving that he or she is "clearly and beyond a doubt entitled to be admitted" or of proving by clear and convincing evidence that he or she has in fact already been admitted.[47] If the alien has already been admitted, the government bears the burden of proving by clear and convincing evidence that the alien is removable.[48]

During the 1990s and at the turn of this century, perhaps the most pressing and controversial issue surrounding immigration law as an instrument of national security involved the propriety of the government's use of classified information, *in camera* and *ex parte*, in these standard removal proceedings. In defending this practice, the government pointed to the judicial decisions spanning a period of more than fifty years that sustained the INS's use of classified information in immigration proceedings, such as *Knauff* and *Mezei*. As discussed above, in both of these cases the Supreme Court upheld exclusion orders entered without a hearing and on the basis of undisclosed classified information against persons considered to be seeking initial admission; that is, in a posture where aliens have the lowest level of constitutional due process protection.

Building on those decisions, the Supreme Court concluded in *Jay v. Boyd*[49] that the INS could use classified information to oppose an application for discretionary relief from deportation. The case involved a sixty-five year old citizen of Great Britain who had been resident in the United States for *more than* forty years. The petitioner had been found deportable under a section of the immigration statute providing for the deportation of any alien "who was at the time of entering the United States, or has been at any time thereafter," a member of the Communist Party of the United States. The petitioner acknowledged having been a member of the Communist Party from 1935 to 1940 (before such membership was made a basis for deportability). He sought a form of discretionary relief known as suspension of deportation. This remedy was available under former INA section 244(a)(5), in the Attorney General's discretion, to persons who were deportable, but who had been in the United States for more than ten years since becoming deportable, had maintained good moral character during that time, and whose deportation would result in "exceptional and extremely unusual hardship." (A much-contracted version now exists in the INA under the name "cancellation of removal.")

The petitioner's eligibility for suspension was not at issue in the litigation; the controversy turned instead on whether the Attorney General's delegate could exercise his discretion against granting the remedy on the basis of undisclosed confidential evidence. The Board of Immigration Appeals had acted under a regulation permitting it, when considering the suspension application of an applicant who had met the basic eligibility requirements, to make the separate discretionary decision on the basis of undisclosed confidential information where its disclosure would be "prejudicial to the public interest, safety, or security."[50] Noting that Congress empowered the Attorney General to grant or deny suspension to eligible applicants in his unfettered discretion, the Court upheld the exclusion order, finding that the statute did not entitle an applicant to full disclosure of the information underlying the *discretionary* aspect of the decision. Moreover, though constitutionality

---

47. INA § 240(c)(2) (2014).
48. INA § 240(c)(3) (2014).
49. Jay v. Boyd, 351 U.S. 345 (1956).
50. 8 C.F.R. § 244.3 (1952).

was not litigated, the Court stated that it would have "no difficulty" with this interpretation as a constitutional matter.[51]

Jay v. Boyd, a 5–4 decision, provoked dissenting views that illustrate well the basic tension involved in the use of undisclosed classified information and that foreshadowed the sorts of conflicting judicial and public viewpoints that have characterized more recent consideration of immigration and security matters. Chief Justice Warren began his dissent with the statement that, "[i]n conscience, I cannot agree with the opinion of the majority. It sacrifices to form too much of the American spirit of fair play both in our judicial and administrative processes."[52] Justice Black's dissent began, "This is a strange case in a country dedicated by its founders to the maintenance of liberty under law."[53] Justice Frankfurter invoked a particularly colorful statement made by President Eisenhower, in the fall of 1953 at a B'nai B'rith dinner in Washington, D.C.:

> Why are we proud? We are proud, first of all, because from the beginning of this Nation, a man can walk upright, no matter who he is, or who she is. He can walk upright and meet his friend—or his enemy; and he does not feel that because that enemy may be in a position of great power that he can be suddenly thrown in jail to rot there without charges and with no recourse to justice. We have the habeas corpus act, and we respect it.

> I was raised in a little town of which most of you have never heard. But in the West it is a famous place. It is called Abilene, Kansas. We had as our Marshal for a long time a man named Wild Bill Hickock. If you don't know anything about him, read your Westerns more. Now that town had a code, and I was raised as a boy to prize that code.

> It was: meet anyone face to face with whom you disagree. You could not sneak up on him from behind, or do any damage to him, without suffering the penalty of an outraged citizenry. If you met him face to face and took the same risks he did, you could get away with almost anything, as long as the bullet was in the front.

> And today, although none of you has the great fortune, I think, of being from Abilene, Kansas, you live after all by that same code, in your ideals and in the respect you give to certain qualities. In this country, if someone dislikes you, or accuses you, he must come up in front. He cannot hide behind the shadow. He cannot assassinate you or your character from behind, without suffering the penalties an outraged citizenry will impose.[54]

Other cases held the use of classified information. In the case *United States ex rel. Barbour v. District Director of INS*,[55] for example, the court affirmed (in the case of a person who had been admitted as a nonimmigrant) the government's ability to rely on classified evidence *in camera* and *ex parte* in opposing release on bond. The court relied specifically on *Jay v. Boyd*. In *Ali v. Reno*,[56] involving Sheikh Omar Abdel Rahman, who is serving a criminal sentence for seditious conspiracy in connection with the first World Trade Center bombing in 1993, the court allowed the introduction of classified evidence in opposition to applications for asylum and withholding from an immigrant whose permanent residence was being rescinded.

---

51. 351 U.S. at 356–58, 358 n.21.
52. 351 U.S. at 361.
53. 351 U.S. at 362.
54. 351 U.S. at 374 n.1.
55. United States ex rel. Barbour v. District Director of INS, 491 F.2d 573 (5th Cir. 1974).
56. Ali v. Reno, 829 F. Supp. 1415 (S.D.N.Y. 1993), *aff'd*, 22 F.3d 442 (2d Cir. 1994).

For decades, various regulations contemplated the use of undisclosed classified evidence for certain purposes in conventional immigration proceedings. The government's authority to act on such regulations was the central issue in the cases discussed above. Yet the statute itself did not provide any such express authority until 1996. Under the INA, as amended by IIRIRA, the government generally cannot use classified evidence in proceedings under INA § 240 to prove a charge of deportability, because the alien must have a "reasonable opportunity to examine the evidence" presented to support the charge.[57] The alien is not, however, "entitled to examine such national security information as the government may proffer in opposition to the alien's admission to the United States or an application by the alien for discretionary relief."[58]

Certain points about the use of classified evidence in immigration proceedings under section 240 bear emphasis. First, as noted above, it cannot be used to prove that an alien is deportable. In practice, it has typically been introduced to support continued custody of a person whose deportability was established, or to oppose an application for a discretionary remedy, such as asylum, cancellation of removal, or adjustment of status to permanent residence. Thus, the legal question that such evidence is typically introduced to help answer is whether an alien who is in the United States illegally—and who the government believes to pose some degree of threat to the national security—should nevertheless remain in the United States by virtue of a form of relief from deportation that is purely discretionary, or whether such a person should be released from detention while his or her immigration proceeding moves forward. Second, the use of classified evidence in immigration proceedings is quite rare. In early 2000, for example, the immigration agency indicated in congressional hearings on the issue that, of about 300,000 immigration cases that go before the Executive Office for Immigration Review each year, only eleven then-pending cases involved undisclosed classified information, and in only four of those was the alien in custody. Third, the information at issue can only be classified in the first place if the original classifying authority "determines that the unauthorized disclosure of the information reasonably could be expected to result in damage to the national security and the original classifying authority is able to identify or describe the damage."[59] Nearly always the FBI or some other intelligence or law enforcement agency, rather than the immigration agency using it in court, is the "original classifying authority" for the evidence at issue.

Despite the explicit congressional endorsement in 1996 of the use of classified evidence in immigration proceedings to oppose admission or to contest an application for a discretionary remedy, that practice did not fare well in the courts in the following years. In *Kiareldeen v. Reno*,[60] for example, the court held unconstitutional on due process grounds the government's reliance on undisclosed classified evidence to detain the petitioner. Hany Kiareldeen had come to the United States as a student in 1990, and then violated the terms of his admission by remaining beyond the completion of his studies four years later. The INS ordered him detained without bond while his deportation hearing went forward. Before the immigration judge, Mr. Kiareldeen admitted his deportability, but sought a form of discretionary relief called adjustment of status to permanent residence, on the basis of his marriage to a United States citizen. The INS submitted classified evidence *in camera* and *ex parte*, alleging that (1) Kiareldeen was a member of a foreign terrorist organization; (2) that he was involved in a meeting planning the 1993 World

---

57. INA § 240(b)(4)(B).
58. *Id.*
59. Exec. Order No. 12,958 at § 1.2(a)(4), 60 Fed. Reg. 19 (1995).
60. Kiareldeen v. Reno, 71 F. Supp. 2d 402 (D.N.J. 1999).

Trade Center attack one week before the actual attack; and (3) that he later threatened to kill then-Attorney General Janet Reno for her role in the conviction of those responsible for that attack. The INS also introduced evidence that Mr. Kiareldeen had submitted a false birth certificate, underscoring the uncertainties that surround the possibility of false identities in the immigration context.

Mr. Kiareldeen was presented with a series of unclassified summaries of the classified information. These summaries indicated that the information came from a Joint Terrorism Task Force, one of a series of interagency counterterrorism operations around the country led by the FBI and including representatives from a number of law enforcement agencies. The summaries indicated that the information had come from multiple foreign intelligence sources, that the FBI considered it to be reliable, and that such information is classified "to protect against disclosure that would permit a terrorist or suspected terrorist organization, group, or individual to avoid preventive or detection measures, or would reveal FBI or other intelligence agency sources and methods by which such information is obtained."[61] Mr. Kiareldeen speculated, however, that one likely source of these allegations was his former wife, who he claimed wished to take revenge for a bitter divorce. He produced evidence that he was arrested on a series of occasions when she accused him of domestic violence, and that none of these arrests ever led to a prosecution because of a lack of reliable evidence (and indeed that the police reports and other background documents cast doubt on the veracity of her allegations against him), and that a state court considering a request for a restraining order had specifically found her allegations to be unbelievable.[62]

Relying on *Rafeedie, Matthews v. Eldridge,* and *AADC*,[63] the court found the government's reliance on undisclosed classified information to violate the Constitution's Due Process requirements. The focus of the decision was the difficulty of assessing the reliability of evidence that is not made to stand up to the test of the adversary process. This concern has driven opponents of the use of undisclosed classified evidence in immigration proceedings, from the dissenting Supreme Court Justices in *Jay v. Boyd* in 1956 through the most recent judicial decisions striking down the practice. *Kiareldeen* is illuminating because it lays bare the arguments that come into tension on this issue. Opponents of the use of undisclosed classified evidence urge that it can result in innocent people suffering serious consequences because of its inherent unreliability (or even, as the allegations sometimes go, knowing misuse). The government argues that, given the stakes involved in matters of national security, and the damage to intelligence gathering that results when intelligence information is publicly disclosed, it is both possible and necessary to forego the enhanced procedural protections that the adversarial system provides. That tension appears particularly acute in the *Kiareldeen* context, where Mr. Kiareldeen was able to guess at the source of the allegations and discredit that source quite compellingly. The evidence thus seemed the most vivid example of the unreliability of evidence kept secret and untested. The government was not in a position even to confirm whether the disgruntled ex-wife was in fact the source of the allegations, or if so to explain why it nonetheless credited her allegations, or to explain whether there was other information that caused it to be concerned that Mr. Kiareldeen posed a threat to the national security. Quite understandably, therefore, many observers considered this case to exemplify why the government should not have authority to use undisclosed classified information.

---

61. *See id.*; Kiareldeen v. Ashcroft, 273 F.3d 542, 545–46 (3d Cir. 2001).
62. 71 F. Supp. 2d at 416–17.
63. Reno v. American-Arab Anti-Discrimination Comm., 525 U.S. 471 (1999).

Kiareldeen is also illuminating for the hints that a decision at a later stage in the case offers to the possibility that it, and other cases striking down the practice, might have come to a quite different conclusion if decided after the September 11 attacks. In a decision three months after those attacks, the Third Circuit held that the government's position was "substantially justified," so that Kiareldeen was not entitled to attorney fees under the Equal Access to Justice Act. While the court emphasized repeatedly that it was not reaching conclusions on the merits of the administrative proceedings or the district court litigation, it spoke on the issues in unusually strong terms: "That the FBI would be unwilling to compromise national security by revealing its undercover sources, is both understandable and comforting. That a court would then choose to criticize the FBI for being unwilling to risk undermining its covert operations against terrorists is somewhat unnerving."[64] The court went further, well beyond what would have been necessary to reverse the fee-shifting decision of the district court:

....

We are not inclined to impede investigators in their efforts to cast out, root and branch, all vestiges of terrorism both in our homeland and in far off lands. As the Court has stated:

Few interests can be more compelling than a nation's need to ensure its own security. It is well to remember that freedom as we know it has been suppressed in many countries. Unless a society has the capability and will to defend itself from the aggressions of others, constitutional protections of any sort have little meaning.

Wayte v. United States, 470 U.S. 598, 611–12 ... (1985).

....

The eerie, if not prescient, information that the Joint Terrorism Task Force assembled from sources, must be evaluated in light of "the degree of suspicion that attaches to particular types of [activities]" [quoting *Illinois v. Gates*, 462 U.S. 213, 243–44 n.13 (1983)]. In light of the pummeling that the FBI received following the September 11th tragedy for not possessing sufficient intelligence materials, consider the following information revealed by its sources in 1998, dealing with a meeting at which Kiareldeen was allegedly present:

A source advised that approximately one week before the bombing of the World Trade Center (WTC) in New York [in 1993], Kiareldeen was present at a meeting with several individuals who were talking about plans to bomb the WTC. The meeting took place at Kiareldeen's residence in Nutley, New Jersey. According to a source, Nidal Ayyad (Ayyad) was present at the meeting (Ayyad is a convicted co-conspirator in the WTC bombing). Ayyad did most of the talking about bombing the WTC as others listened. Ayyad stated that he suggested to Sheikh Omsar Abdel Rahman (Rahman) that a suicide bombing should be attempted on the WTC. According to Ayyad, Rahman had another idea about bombing the WTC and stated that a suicide bombing was not appropriate [citing to record evidence].

On July 29, 1998, the Joint Terrorism Task Force had information that Ayyad, the convicted terrorist in the 1993 bombing of the World Trade Center, suggested a suicide bombing of the Center. This understandably created apprehension on

---

64. 273 F. 3d at 552.

the part of the Joint Terrorism Task Force, alerting the government to take all necessary action to investigate all leads and assure the defense of our nation. On September 11, 2001, slightly *more than* two years after the government supplied this information to both the INS and the district court in this case, the convicted terrorist's suggestion became a reality. It is impossible to conjure up a "particular type[]" of activity, as mentioned in *Gates*, that would be more nefarious than that which happened on Black Tuesday.[65]

As an aside, these instances in which the government is seeking to support its removal efforts with information that an alien poses a security threat raise an important issue involving the nature of immigration law as a national security tool. The district court articulated this question in *Kiareldeen*: "even the government does not find its own allegations sufficiently serious to commence criminal proceedings."[66] This is a criticism commonly leveled against the government's immigration practices when national security issues are at stake. Why, it is asked, is the government taking such extreme steps as extended custody or using classified evidence to which the alien has no access, and invoking such solemn justifications as the protection of the nation's security, when it charges only a garden variety immigration violation? Where is the criminal charge? The circuit court in Kiareldeen disagreed with the district court's criticism of the government on this point, finding it:

> a simplistic and entirely uninformed view of the processes by which the Justice Department investigates and deals with suspected terrorists within our borders. It completely disregards the often complex determinations involved in releasing confidential counter-terrorism intelligence into the public arena through its introduction into both administrative hearings and court proceedings. Such a criticism implies that the government may only utilize information against an individual in a civil context, such as in deportation proceedings, if it also intends to commence criminal proceedings against that same individual. Such a fettering of the Executive Branch has no support either in case law or statute.[67]

Clearly criminal prosecution sits higher on the hierarchy of law enforcement preferences surrounding suspected terrorists. Often the government's decision to enforce the immigration laws rather than the criminal laws against a person suspected to pose a national security threat is precisely because the government's suspicion is based on evidence that it believes sufficient to satisfy the lower standards applicable to many of the relevant immigration decisions, but not sufficient to fulfill the requirement in criminal cases to prove guilt "beyond a reasonable doubt." The law quite clearly contemplates that immigration decisions may be made on the basis of lower standards than those that would be acceptable in the criminal context. (As discussed above, for example, the law denies asylum to a person who, based on reasonable grounds, may be regarded as a threat to the national security.) Nevertheless, it does seem fair to ask whether the simple removal of a person believed to be a terrorist, even if it is the best legal alternative, still leaves important security vulnerabilities.

In any case, the seemingly more accepting view evidenced by the *Kiareldeen* appeals court of the use in immigration proceedings of undisclosed classified information contrasts sharply with what had been strong momentum against the practice prior to the attacks. In addition to the strongly worded district court decision quoted above in *Kiareldeen*, for example, a Miami district court struck down on due process grounds the government's

---

65. 273 F.3d at 555–57.
66. 71 F. Supp. 2d at 414.
67. 273 F.3d at 553.

use of undisclosed classified evidence to support the detention of Mazen Al Najjar. Mr. Al Najjar is a Palestinian whom the government accused of fundraising in this country for the Palestinian Islamic Jihad.[68]

On the legislative front, in 1999 and again in 2001, Congress considered the "Secret Evidence Repeal Act." This bill would have repealed most of the statutory authority to present classified evidence *in camera* and *ex parte* in any sort of immigration proceeding. In particular, it would have eliminated the provisions in the INA for a special Alien Terrorist Removal Court, discussed above. It would also have removed from INA section 240(4)(B) the limit on an alien's right of access to national security information presented by the government to oppose the alien's admission into the United States or application for discretionary relief under the INA. It would have specifically granted aliens in regular removal proceedings access to all information pertaining to their admission or presence in the country, and prohibited any decision on an immigration benefit, including release from custody, on the basis of evidence not shared with the alien. Finally, it would have prohibited the use of classified evidence in section 235(c) cases against lawful permanent residents, aliens given permission to be in the country without a formal immigration status under what is known as the "parole" authority, and aliens seeking asylum.

A Senate bill would have applied the Classified Information Procedures Act (CIPA), which governs the use of classified information in the criminal context, to immigration cases. Among other things, CIPA requires a record of all proceedings involving the use of classified information, including those held *in camera*, and provides the option of substituting a stipulation of the facts the classified evidence would tend to prove.[69]

Even within the executive branch there was building momentum against the use of classified evidence in immigration court proceedings. Efforts in the Justice Department at the end of the Clinton administration to promulgate a stricter process for approving the use of classified information—but one that would still have sanctioned its use—was never approved by the White House, and the issue was left unresolved. In the campaign leading up to his election, President George W. Bush noted substantial misgivings about the practice and indicated that his administration would reconsider its appropriateness. This reconsideration was underway at the staff level of the Justice Department and the White House before the September 11 attacks.

After the attacks, perhaps predictably, the momentum subsided. The *Kiareldeen* appeals court issued the aggressive opinion described above. Mr. Al Najjar was deported after an order finding him deportable for having overstayed his student visa became final and enforceable, his continued detention was no longer based on any alleged security threat, and the litigation over that basis for his detention thus became moot.[70] While it concluded that no case or controversy remained for it to adjudicate, the court noted the "compelling" issues raised by the government in its appeal of the district court's constitutional holding.[71] Neither of the bills previously at play in Congress was passed, and neither those nor any other proposed restrictions on the use of classified information in immigration cases have come before the Congress since the September 11 attacks. Interestingly, though, while it did rely on classified information in a small number of cases involving arriving aliens under the terms of section 235(c), the Bush administration did not initiate any new traditional removal proceedings involving the use of classified evidence. This controversy,

---

68. Al Najjar v. Reno, 97 F. Supp.2d 1329 (S.D. Fla. 2000).
69. *See* 18 U.S.C. App. 3, §§ 4, 6 (2000).
70. *See* Al Najjar v. Ashcroft, 273 F.3d 1330 (11th Cir. 2001).
71. 273 F.3d at 1340–41.

which had flared so bright in the years before the September 11 attacks, was not among the key issues surrounding immigration as a national security matter in the wake of those attacks.

Post-9/11 Restrictions on Access to Unclassified Information in the Immigration Process

After the September 11, 2001 attacks, a different set of issues involving the flow of information in national security cases arose instead. As discussed in the paragraphs above, before the Bush administration, the government's strategy to enforce the immigration laws against those it considered national security threats rested in large part on the introduction, *in camera* and *ex parte*, of evidence bearing on the perceived security threat itself. After the September 11 terrorist attacks, however, the government adopted a different strategy, relying still on the control of access to potentially sensitive information, but with a different set of information flow rules covering an exponentially larger category of information. Where the government believed an alien to be in the country and to pose national security issues–either because of potential connections to terrorist activities or possession of information about such activities–the government proceeded with removal proceedings under the authority of section 240 of the INA. Special measures were taken, however, to ensure that information relating to the proceeding would not be known beyond the immigration agency, the immigration court, and the alien himself. Media organizations and others challenged these policies on first amendment grounds in *Detroit Free Press v. Ashcroft*,[72] and *North Jersey Media Group, Inc. v. Ashcroft*.[73]

The case closure policy was set out in what has come to be known as the "Creppy Memorandum," issued by Chief Immigration Judge Michael Creppy to the national corps of immigration judges under his supervision.[74] Cases implicating the sensitivities described above, designated "special interest" cases, fell subject to heightened security measures. Those measures required the immigration judges "to close the hearings to the public, and to avoid discussing the cases or otherwise disclosing any information about the cases to anyone outside the Immigration Court."[75] Immigration judges were further instructed that "the courtroom must be closed for these cases—no visitors, no family, and no press."[76] Nor were judges or court personnel to "confirm[ ] or deny[ ] whether such a case is on the docket or scheduled for a hearing."[77] These instructions were issued under the authority of 8 C.F.R. § 3.27, which permits immigration judges to order closed hearings to protect "witnesses, parties, or the public interest."

The government asserted a security interest in protecting the integrity of its efforts to investigate the September 11 attacks and to prevent further acts of terrorism. The case closure policy was based on the "mosaic theory," described in another context by the court in *McGehee v. Casey*: "Due to the 'mosaic-like nature of intelligence gathering,' ... 'what may seem trivial to the uninformed[ ] may appear of great moment to one who has a

---

72. Detroit Free Press v. Ashcroft, 303 F.3d 681 (6th Cir. 2002).
73. North Jersey Media Group, Inc. v. Ashcroft, 308 F.3d 198 (3d Cir. 2002).
74. The text of the memorandum is available at <http://news.findlaw.com/hdocs/docs/aclu/creppy092101memo.pdf>.
75. 308 F.3d at 202–03.
76. *Id.*
77. *Id.*

broad view of the scene and may put the questioned item of information in context.' "[78] According to the FBI, the aliens whose cases posed "special interest" might have "connections with, or possess information pertaining to, terrorist activities against the United States."[79] Public disclosure of information about their cases could therefore communicate sensitive information to others who might pose a continuing threat to the security of the United States. For example, " 'if evidence is offered about a particular phone number link between a detainee and a number connected to a terrorist organization or member,' the terrorists 'will be on notice that the United States is now aware of the link,' and 'may even be able to determine what sources and methods the United States used to become aware of that link.' "[80] According to the FBI, "information that might appear innocuous in isolation ... can be fit into a bigger picture by terrorist groups in order to thwart the government's efforts to investigate and prevent terrorism."[81] Such groups might, for example, alter future attack plans, destroy evidence, or tailor their methods of entry into the country on the basis of government enforcement patterns they might discern from open hearings.[82]

The two appellate courts reached dramatically different conclusions. The Sixth Circuit found the closure policy unconstitutional in *Detroit Free Press*, and the Third Circuit upheld the policy in *North Jersey Media Group*. Because they capture eloquently the opposing viewpoints toward the balance between constitutional protections and security needs in the wake of September 11, it is worthwhile to compare passages from the decisions.

In striking down the case closure policy, the Sixth Circuit in *Detroit Free Press* emphasized the role of public debate in democratic society:

> Today, the Executive Branch seeks to take this safeguard [of press access] away from the public by placing its actions beyond public scrutiny. Against non-citizens, it seeks the power to secretly deport a class if it unilaterally calls them "special interest" cases. The Executive Branch seeks to uproot people's lives, outside the public eye, and behind a closed door. Democracies die behind closed doors. The First Amendment, through a free press, protects the people's right to know that their government acts fairly, lawfully, and accurately in deportation proceedings. When government begins closing doors, it selectively controls information rightfully belonging to the people. Selective information is misinformation.[83]
>
> ....
>
> ... [T]he public's interests are best served by open proceedings. A true democracy is one that operates on faith — faith that government officials are forthcoming and honest, and faith that informed citizens will arrive at logical conclusions. This is a vital reciprocity that America should not discard in these troubling times. Without question, the events of September 11, 2001, left an indelible mark on our nation, but we as a people are united in the wake of the destruction to demonstrate to the world that we are a country deeply committed to preserving the rights and freedoms guaranteed by our democracy. Today, we reflect our commitment to those democratic values by ensuring that our government is held accountable to the people and that First Amendment rights are not impermissibly

---

78. McGehee v. Casey, 718 F.2d 1137, 1149 (D.C. Cir. 1983).

79. 308 F.3d at 202–03 (discussing declaration of Dale L. Watson, then the FBI's Executive Assistant Director for Counterterrorism and Counterintelligence).

80. 308 F.3d at 202–03.

81. *Id.*

82. *Id.*

83. 303 F.3d at 683.

compromised. Open proceedings, with a vigorous and scrutinizing press, serve to ensure the durability of our democracy.[84]

In *North Jersey Media Group*, the Third Circuit emphasized instead the duty of government to secure the nation.

> This case arises in the wake of September 11, 2001, a day on which American life changed drastically and dramatically. The era that dawned on September 11th, and the war against terrorism that has pervaded the sinews of our national life since that day, are reflected in thousands of ways in legislative and national policy, the habits of daily living, and our collective psyches. Since the primary national policy must be self-preservation, it seems elementary that, to the extent open deportation hearings might impair national security, that security is implicated in [the "logic" prong of the First Amendment analysis].[85]

In finding that the government could constitutionally close the "special interest" cases, the court quoted from a commentary critical of the *Detroit Free Press* decision that appeared in the *Washington Post*:

> *"Democracies die behind closed doors."* So they do, sometimes. But far more democracies have succumbed to open assaults of one sort or another — invasions from without, military coups and totalitarian revolutions from within — than from the usurpation-by-in-camera-incrementalism that Judge Keith fears.
>
> Democracy in America does at this moment face a serious threat. But it is not the threat the judge has in mind, at least not directly. It is true that last September's unprecedented mass-slaughter of American citizens on American soil inevitably forced the government to take security measures that infringed on some rights and privileges. But these do not in themselves represent any real threat to democracy. A real threat could arise, however, should the government fail in its mission to prevent another September 11. If that happens, the public will demand, and will get, immense restrictions on liberties.[86]

The constitutional issue is likely to remain unresolved for the foreseeable future, as the Supreme Court declined in May 2003, at the urging of the Solicitor General, to accept certiorari.

Between *North Jersey Media Group* and *Detroit Free Press*, which reasoning do you find more compelling as a matter of legal analysis? As a policy approach? Does your answer depend on how a case gets into the category of "special interest" cases about which information cannot be disclosed?

One of the central objections underlying the challenges to the case closure policy was that the policy applied as a blanket matter, to all cases designated as holding "special interest" to the government, without standards subject to independent application to govern individual cases. In the late spring following the attacks, the Department of Justice issued a regulation creating a mechanism for immigration courts to issue protective orders against the disclosure of information presented in removal proceedings.[87] The preamble to the rule noted that, "[I]n this post-September 11, 2001, era, the highest priority of the Department of Justice is to prevent, detect, disrupt, and dismantle terrorism while preserving constitutional liberties," and offered a detailed invocation of the mosaic theory.

---

84. *Id.* at 711.
85. 308 F.3d at 202.
86. 308 F.3d at 220–21.
87. 67 Fed. Reg. 36799 (May 28, 2002), adding 8 C.F.R. § 3.46.

The regulation gives immigration judges the authority to issue a protective order barring disclosure of information presented by the government that would, if disclosed, harm the national security or law enforcement interests of the United States. This standard is meant to permit protective orders against the disclosure of information that would not justify classification under the standards set out in Executive Order No. 12,958, discussed above. Violation of a protective order can result in the denial of any form of discretionary relief from removal, or loss of the ability to appear in future immigration matters in the case of an attorney found to have disclosed protected information. There is no parallel provision for information the respondent in immigration proceedings seeks to keep confidential. In the preamble, the Attorney General characterized the regulation as "a prudent and balanced acknowledgment of the reality that the government's efforts against terrorism require the Department to treat information collected by the law enforcement and intelligence communities as vital national assets."[88]

Shortly before issuing the protective order regulation, the Department of Justice issued, though the immigration agency, another regulation designed to afford greater control over the release of information about aliens detained in state or local detention facilities. These sorts of contractual arrangements account for an increasing percentage of immigration detention. A New Jersey state court had ordered county officials to release information about federal immigration detainees in local custody under state law. In order to protect against the disclosure of information under state law, and for the same reasons as those underlying the case closure policy, the Department's regulation provides that public disclosure of information about immigration detainees is governed under federal law, including the Freedom of Information Act, regardless of whether the persons are detained in federal, state, or local facilities.[89] As with the case closure policy and the protective order regulation, this rule invoked the mosaic theory: "[I]t requires little reflection to understand that the business of foreign intelligence gathering in this age of computer technology is more akin to the construction of a mosaic than it is to the management of a cloak and dagger affair. Thousands of pieces of seemingly innocuous information can be analyzed and fitted into place to reveal with startling clarity how the unseen whole must operate."[90] The preamble to the regulation also noted "the primacy of Federal law in matters related to aliens and immigration."[91]

Detention Principles and Practices Affecting National Security Cases

Detention has long been a source of great controversy in the immigration system generally. Critics in the field, and many more casual observers, are astonished that a person who may have committed a fairly routine immigration violation can wind up in immigration custody—in most respects, indistinguishable to the naked eye from criminal jail time—for periods longer than many criminal sentences. Others point to the relative ease with which it has been possible for a person not in custody to simply decline to comply with removal orders at the end of what can be a long process, and decry the

---

88. 67 Fed. Reg. at 36800 (2002).
89. 67 Fed. Reg. 19508 (April 22, 2002), amending 8 C.F.R. §§ 236, 241.
90. 67 Fed. Reg. at 19509 (2002).
91. *Id.* (citing Toll v. Moreno, 458 U.S. 1 (1982)).

significant expenditure of public resources in a system in which so few people who are ordered removed actually leave. The question is of course more complex than either of these viewpoints might account for. It is made more complex yet by the fact that the statute sets out a somewhat complicated framework of detention rules, depending on the alien's status and stage of the immigration process, as well as by the fact that the limits and safeguards of the Constitution differ dramatically depending on those same sorts of factors. It is clear, though, that the government possesses broad detention authorities, and that the use of those authorities has been a critical part of its strategy to minimize risks to public safety from removable aliens who may pose such risks.

The basic custody rules work as follows. Arriving aliens — those appearing at ports of entry and seeking admission — in general "shall be detained" while their admissibility is determined, according to section 235(b)(2), though they may be released on parole under certain circumstances, including where "continued detention is not in the public interest."[92] Aliens other than arriving aliens may be detained or released on bond. INA section 236(a), and the regulations set up a mechanism for them to seek a different custody decision from the immigration judge in the course of their proceedings. Certain groups of aliens in proceedings must, however, be detained, with no discretion on the part of any administrative officer to release them. Mandatory detention provisions had been a part of the INA since the 1980s but were significantly broadened by both AEDPA and IIRIRA in 1996. These mandatory detention categories include aliens covered by the terrorist removal grounds, as well as broad groups of aliens who have been convicted of crimes.[93]

For aliens not subject to mandatory custody, the presumption before 1996 was that deportable aliens should be released without bond during their proceedings, unless shown to be a threat to the national security or a poor bail risk.[94] The regulations now provide that the "alien must first demonstrate, by clear and convincing evidence, that release would not pose a danger to the safety of other persons or of property [and] ... that the alien is likely to appear for any scheduled proceeding ..."[95]

Once the immigration court has issued a removal order, the statutory detention authority shifts to INA section 241. That section provides that removal must normally take place within a ninety-day "removal period," during which the immigration authority "shall detain" the alien.[96] While this seemingly broad requirement apparently leaves some administrative flexibility with respect to certain categories of aliens ordered removed, "under no circumstances" shall an alien within this category be released if that person has been found inadmissible or deportable under the grounds relating to criminal or terrorist activity. If removal is not accomplished within the ninety-day removal period, the government may release the person under supervision, or detention may extend beyond the removal period for those found inadmissible, those found deportable under criminal or security grounds, and those determined to pose a risk to the community or a risk of flight.[97] (Yet a separate set of rules governs the post-order custody of aliens who were put into proceedings upon arrival at a port of entry, who "shall be removed immediately," subject to rules permitting the government to stay such removal, set bonds during periods of stay, and so forth.[98])

---

92. 8 C.F.R. §212.5 (2002).
93. *See* INA §236(c) (2014).
94. *See* Matter of Patel, 15 I. & N. Dec. 666 (B.I.A. 1976).
95. 8 C.F.R. §236.1(c)(3) (2014).
96. INA §241(a)(2) (2014).
97. INA §241(a)(3), (6) (2014).
98. *See* INA §241(c) (2014).

Significant uncertainty and extensive litigation have surrounded questions over the scope of the detention authority at the various points along the immigration spectrum, and the extent of the statutory and constitutional limitations on such authority. In 2003, for example, the Supreme Court upheld the mandatory detention provisions of section 236(c), even as to lawful permanent residents.[99] Issues surrounding the detention authority warrant far more attention than the scope of this chapter permits.

One question deserving particular mention here, though, concerns the length of time that post-order custody, discussed above, can extend where removal cannot be accomplished, such as where the country of nationality will not accept the alien's return. In the context of excludable Mariel Cubans, and citing to security and foreign policy implications, the courts had sustained the government's statutory and constitutional authority to detain such persons for years, so long as there were periodic reviews to determine whether continued detention was justified.[100] Different results began to appear, however, even in the context of exclusion,[101] but especially in the context of persons who had been lawful permanent residents.[102] The Supreme Court addressed this dispute in *Zadvydas v. Davis*.[103] There a narrow majority concluded that indefinite post-order custody of deportable aliens would raise serious constitutional questions but, in an act of constitutional avoidance that is often regarded even by supporters of its result as a stretched reading of the statute, held that the INA does not permit such detention. The court held instead that, the government could detain even beyond the ninety-day removal period, but only for so long as reasonably necessary to secure the alien's removal. The Court adopted a "presumptively reasonable period of detention … for the sake of uniform administration in the federal courts" of six months from the date of a final removal order.[104] Custody may continue beyond that period if the government produces evidence sufficient to rebut the presumption after six months that there is "no significant likelihood of removal in the reasonably foreseeable future."[105]

Two points from *Zadvydas* seem to stand out in the national security context. First, the Court appears to rest its holding on the basic point that the immigration detention authority exists in aid of removal. Post-order detention that is not linked to "the statute's basic purpose, namely, assuring the alien's presence at the moment of removal,"[106] will generally not be sustained, even if designed to protect the safety of the community. (Both aliens at issue in the case had robust criminal histories, including for one a conviction for gang-related manslaughter.) Second, though, the Court was careful to leave open the context of cases involving "terrorism or other special circumstances where special arguments might be made for forms of preventive detention and for heightened deference to the judgments of the political branches with respect to matters of national security."[107] The Court noted that, in the ATRC context, the statute specifically accounts for the long-term post-order detention of a terrorist who cannot be removed, so long as the government continues its efforts to bring about removal.[108] In November 2001, the Attorney General

---

99. *See* Demore v. Hyung Joon Kim, 123 S. Ct. 1708 (2003).

100. *See, e.g.*, Barrera-Echavarria v. Rison, 44 F.3d 1441 (9th Cir. 1995), *cert. denied*, 516 U.S. 976 (1995).

101. *See* Rosales-Garcia v. Holland, 238 F.3d 704 (6th Cir. 2001).

102. *See, e.g.*, Ma v. Reno, 208 F.3d 815 (9th Cir. 2000); Zadvydas v. Underdown, 185 F.3d 279 (5th Cir. 1999).

103. Zadvydas. V. Davis, 533 U.S. 678 (2001).

104. 533 U.S. at 680.

105. 533 U.S. at 677.

106. 533 U.S. at 699.

107. 533 U.S. at 696.

108. *See* INA § 507(b)(2)(c) (2014).

revised the regulations to account specifically for the possibility of continued detention where the government determines that the alien is described in the security-related removal grounds (without regard to whether such ground was the actual basis for the removal order), the alien's release would present a significant threat to the national security or a significant risk of terrorism, and no conditions of release can reasonably be expected to avoid the risk of terrorism or other security threat.[109]

In addition to expanding the security related grounds of inadmissibility and deportability, as discussed above, the USA PATRIOT Act altered as well the statutory provisions for detention of suspected terrorists, from the time before immigration proceedings are begun through the post-order period. Under section 412(a) of the USA PATRIOT Act, an alien will be subject to mandatory custody where the Attorney General certifies his belief that the alien is engaged in terrorism or activity that endangers the security of the United States. The alien must within seven days be criminally charged, placed into removal proceedings, or released. Such an alien, if ordered removed, may be detained for an unlimited number of additional six-month periods, even if removal is not reasonably foreseeable, where release would threaten the national security or the safety of the community. The initial certification is subject to immediate federal court review. It does not appear, however, that this mandatory custody authority for terrorists has been invoked.

As part of its urgent efforts after the September 11 attacks to discover their sources and to prevent any further attacks, the Department of Justice adopted a strategy involving the aggressive use of all the law enforcement tools available to it, including the removal authority and the authority to detain those in the various stages of the removal process. In the months following September 11, the INS, working with the FBI and other Department of Justice components, initiated removal proceedings against and placed into custody hundreds of persons who were thought in varying degrees to have some connection with terrorist organizations or to have information that might be important to the investigation. All were persons alleged by the government not to have a valid immigration status in the United States. This was the same group of aliens whose proceedings were designated "special interest" cases and closed under the terms described above.

The detention policy for these "special interest" cases involved exercising the INS detention authority by holding such persons in custody without bond, opposing release on bond when it was requested before the immigration judge, appealing any immigration judge decisions to release a "special interest" alien on bond, and invoking a stay of such decisions while the appeal was pending. If the FBI determined in the meantime that the person was no longer "of interest," then the immigration agency would take whatever position on release the person's circumstances otherwise dictated, including acceding to release on a reasonable bond. As a practical matter, however, these decisions were often very slow in coming, given the breadth and urgency of the investigative effort, and the FBI often prioritized the investigation of new leads over the completion of its investigation into those already designated "special interest" cases. As a result, the aliens who had provoked suspicions leading to special designation of their cases often remained in detention throughout their cases.

This policy generated significant disagreement. Many considered it to amount to invidious profiling against aliens who were Muslim from the Middle East, and to tolerate disproportionate law enforcement steps against aliens about whom there might be little to justify suspicion on correspondingly serious national security grounds. The routine

---

109. 8 C.F.R. § 241.14(d) (2002).

immigration charges common in most of the cases were decried as pretextual. Serious allegations arose as well about the conditions of confinement. The government countered that the immigration charges were correct in the cases and the aliens here unlawfully, and that the detention policy was fully justified given the security imperatives in play.

A number of complicated questions arose, however, involving the detention authorities discussed above. For example, in addition to declining to release persons who had not been cleared by the FBI or other intelligence agencies, the government also refrained from removing such aliens from the United States, when their removal orders became final, until the FBI had concluded its evaluation whether they were involved in terrorist activity. This juncture often arrived early in the case, as it was not uncommon in these "special interest" cases for the alien involved to acknowledge deportability and accept an order at the early stages of the removal proceeding. This raised questions over whether the government could continue detaining but refrain from removing an alien whom it had both the authority and the ability to remove, both during the ninety-day removal period and beyond, until it had resolved any security concerns. (Remember that *Zadvydas* involved the government's authority to detain beyond the removal period where it had the authority to remove the alien but not the ability, because the country of removal would not accept the alien's deportation.)

An interesting glimpse into the complexities involved in this policy, and in the interagency discussions that surrounded it, can be gained from a report of the Department of Justice's Inspector General, released in June 2003. The report, undertaken at the request of the Attorney General, found significant problems with various aspects of the post 9/11 detention practices, involving the immigration agencies, FBI, and the Department of Justice, as well as with the conditions of confinement for certain members of this group of detainees. These issues were also addressed in the courts. For example, *Turkmen v. Ashcroft*, a class action initiated in the Eastern District of New York in April 2002, more than a decade later resulted in a 2013 memorandum and order from a federal judge in which the judge allowed certain tort claims to go forward, and described the treatment of the detained immigrants as follows:

> The plaintiffs are eight male, non-United States citizens who were arrested on immigration charges following the terrorist attacks on September 11, 2001 ("9/11 attacks"). They were held in immigration custody for periods ranging from three to eight months after receiving final orders of removal or grants of voluntary departure. All but two are Muslims of Middle Eastern, North African, or South Asian origin; the others, natives of India and Nepal, are Hindu. Plaintiffs bring this putative class action on behalf of themselves and a class of male non-citizens who are Arab or Muslim, or were perceived by the defendants to be Arab or Muslim,2 and were (1) arrested by the Immigration and Naturalization Service ("INS") or the Federal Bureau of Investigation ("FBI") after September 11, 2001, and charged with immigration violations; (2) treated as "of interest" to the government's terrorism investigation; (3) detained under a blanket "hold-until-cleared" policy, pursuant to which they were held without bond until cleared of terrorist ties by the FBI; and (4) confined in the Metropolitan Detention Center ("MDC") or the Passaic County Jail ("Passaic Jail")....

> The MDC Detainees also were subjected to frequent physical and verbal abuse by many of the officers.... The physical abuse included slamming the MDC Detainees into walls; bending or twisting their arms, hands, wrists, and fingers; lifting them off the ground by their arms; pulling on their arms and handcuffs; stepping on their leg restraints; restraining them with handcuffs and/or shackles even while in their cells; and handling them in other rough and inappropriate

ways. The use of such force was unnecessary because the MDC Detainees were always fully compliant with orders and rarely engaged in misconduct. The verbal abuse included referring to the MDC Detainees as "terrorists" and other offensive names, threatening them with violence, cursing at them, insulting their religion, and making humiliating sexual comments during strip-searches.

Both the MDC Detainees and the Detainees held at the Passaic Jail (the "Passaic Detainees") were subjected to unreasonable and punitive strip-searches. The MDC Detainees were strip-searched every time they were removed from or returned to their cells, including before and after visiting with their attorneys, receiving medical care, using the recreation area, attending a court hearing, and being transferred to another cell. They were strip-searched upon each arrival at the MDC in the receiving and discharge area and again after they had been escorted—shackled and under continuous guard—to the ADMAX SHU. These strip-searches occurred even when they had no conceivable opportunity to obtain contraband, such as before and after non-contact attorney visits (to and from which they were escorted—handcuffed and shackled—by a four-man guard). Supp. OIG Rep. at 3. The MDC had no written policy governing when to conduct strip-searches, and they were conducted inconsistently.

The strip-searches were unnecessary to security within the MDC. Rather, they were conducted to punish and humiliate the detainees. Female officers were often present during the strip-searches; the strip-searches were regularly videotaped in their entirety (contrary to BOP policy ...); and MDC officers routinely laughed and made inappropriate sexual comments during the strip-searches.

Officers at the MDC and the Passaic Jail also interfered with the Detainees' ability to practice and observe their Muslim faith....

In addition, most of the MDC Detainees were held incommunicado during the first weeks of their detention (the "communications blackout"). MDC staff repeatedly turned away everyone, including lawyers and relatives, who came to the MDC looking for the MDC Detainees, and thus the MDC Detainees had neither legal nor social visits during this period. This communications blackout lasted until mid-October 2011.

After the initial communications blackout, the MDC Detainees were nominally permitted one call per week to an attorney. However, MDC officers obstructed Detainees' efforts to telephone and retain lawyers in multiple ways. They were denied sufficient information to obtain legal counsel; although they were given a list of organizations that provide free legal services, the contact information for these organizations was outdated and inaccurate. Legal calls that resulted in a wrong number or busy signal were counted against their quota of calls, as were calls answered by voicemail. Officers frequently asked the MDC Detainees, "Are you okay?," and if the MDC Detainees responded affirmatively, the officers construed this as a waiver of their already-limited privilege to make legal calls. The officers also often brought the phone to the MDC Detainees early in the morning before law offices opened for the day. And they frequently pretended to dial a requested number or deliberately dialed a wrong number and then claimed the line was dead or busy. They then refused to dial again, saying that the Detainee had exhausted his quota.

When the MDC Detainees managed to reach their attorneys by phone, the officers frequently stood within hearing distance of conversations that should have been treated as privileged. Legal visits were non-contact and the MDC Detainees were handcuffed and shackled during the entirety of the visits. The MDC video- and audio-recorded the MDC Detainees' legal visits until April 2002 or later.

The MDC Detainees were nominally permitted one social call per month after the initial communications blackout. However, these calls were just as severely restricted as the legal calls. Social visits were restricted to immediate family, yet even immediate family members were sometimes turned away. As with their legal visits, social visits were non-contact and the MDC Detainees were handcuffed and shackled during the entirety of the visits.[110]

A similar case, *Omar v. Casterline*, an individual suit brought in the Eastern District of Louisiana in September 2002, ended in 2006 when the court granted summary judgment in favor of the federal defendants.[111]

General Measures to Improve the Security of the Immigration System

When it became apparent that many of the September 11 hijackers had fairly easily used the immigration process to gain entry to the country, sometimes repeatedly, Americans were outraged. Two of the hijackers, for example, were in the United States with student visas that enabled them to take flight training. Another had a student visa but never attended school, without enforcement consequences. Some among them had entered in one category and changed status with relative ease and had been readmitted under circumstances where prior stays and overstays in the country made their admissibility questionable. It became quite clear that the immigration system in many ways lacked the discipline and the tools necessary to manage promptly the information necessary to track and make decisions about the entries, exits, stays, and subsequent visits of aliens admitted to the country, particularly the millions admitted each year as nonimmigrants.

As one set of corrective measures, Congress enacted the Enhanced Border Security and Visa Entry Reform Act of 2002. This legislation contained a number of requirements aimed at better control over the process for lawful admissions to the country. It called, for example, for increased staffing at the borders, and for enhanced training of consular officers overseas. It called for the accelerated establishment of an integrated entry and exit data system, first mandated by section 110 of IIRIRA but repeatedly postponed. It called for the government to begin issuing machine-readable, tamper-resistant travel documents with biometric identifiers by October 26, 2004. It contained a number of provisions designed to result in improved data systems and better coordination of law enforcement and other information.

The Enhanced Border Security Act also altered and continued requirements originating in section 641 of IIRIRA and section 416 of the USA PATRIOT Act to put into place an electronically based program to monitor foreign students. The Student and Exchange Visitor Program, which went into place January 30, 2003, replaced a previous manual

---

110. Turkmen v. Ashcroft, 915 F. Supp. 2d 314 (E.D.N.Y. 2013) (Memorandum and Order granting in part and denying in part the defendants' motion to dismiss).

111. Omar v. Casterline, 414 F. Supp. 2d 582 (W.D. La. 2006).

(and largely ineffectual) process with an automated system called the Student and Exchange Visitor Information System (SEVIS). Under the new student-monitoring program, DHS notifies sponsoring educational institutions when aliens enter on student visas, and the institutions in turn report whether the students arrive at the school. The schools provide extensive information, electronically, on students' addresses, major courses of study, maintenance of course loads, and other relevant matters.

The agencies involved in the immigration system have, independent of statutory mandates, taken numerous other steps designed to make the process more secure. For example, on November 14, 2001, the Department of State issued a cable to its embassies and consular posts worldwide, classified but publicly reported, calling for new visa security check procedures in connection with visa issuance. These new processes were to apply to nationals of Afghanistan, Algeria, Bahrain, Djibouti, Egypt, Eritrea, Indonesia, Iran, Iraq, Jordan, Kuwait, Lebanon, Libya, Malaysia, Morocco, Oman, Pakistan, Qatar, Saudi Arabia, Somalia, Sudan, Syria, Tunisia, Turkey, the United Arab Emirates, and Yemen. Processes for increased security checks at visa issuance posts and within the United States have evolved steadily since, and can be expected to evolve further as requirements from the Homeland Security Act are implemented that will involve the Department of Homeland Security more closely in the visa issuance process.

Another example of a major security-based agency initiative was a controversial "special registration" program. In June 2002, the Department of Justice instituted a special registration program for nonimmigrants, formally known as the National Security Entry-Exit Registration System (NSEERS) and initially considered by the Department to be a "vital line of defense in the war against terrorism." The program involved fingerprinting and photographing covered aliens at ports of entry into the country, periodic registration of those staying more than thirty days (and certain categories of aliens already in the country), and exit controls designed to monitor whether those admitted temporarily in fact left on time.

These measures had antecedents in 1996, when the INS published a notice providing for the fingerprinting and registration of nonimmigrants using Libyan or Iranian travel documents. The action was based on "concern for national security resulting from terrorist attacks and uncovered plots directed by nationals of Iran and Libya."[112] Earlier in that decade, in the wake of the Iraqi invasion of Kuwait, a similar program was in place for nonimmigrants using Iraqi or Kuwaiti travel documents.

Attorney General John Ashcroft announced the special registration program in June 2002:

> On September 11, the American definition of national security was changed forever. A band of men entered our country under false pretenses in order to plan and execute a murderous act of war. Some entered the country several years in advance; others entered several months in advance. Once inside the United States they were easily able to avoid contact with the immigration authorities and violate the terms of their visas with impunity.
>
> In this new war, the enemy's platoons infiltrate our borders, quietly blending in with visiting tourists, students, and workers. They move unnoticed through our cities, neighborhoods, and public spaces. They wear no uniforms. Their camouflage is not forest green, but rather it is the color of common street clothing. Their tactics rely on evading recognition at the border and escaping detection

---

112. 61 Fed. Reg. 46829 (1996).

within the United States. Their terrorist mission is to defeat America, destroy our values, and kill innocent people.

The vulnerabilities of our immigration system became starkly clear on September 11. About a quarter century ago, the United States stopped asking international visitors to register periodically with immigration authorities, and stopped keeping track of our visitors' activities and whereabouts.[113]

The new program was proposed in the Federal Register on June 13, 2002,[114] and the proposed rule was adopted without substantial modifications sixty days later.[115] The regulation broadened existing registration requirements for nonimmigrant aliens from certain designated countries, and other nonimmigrant aliens whose presence in the United States the government deemed to require closer monitoring, to require that they provide specific information at regular intervals to ensure their compliance with the terms of their visas and admission, and to ensure that they depart the United States at the conclusion of their authorized stay. Such reports were required upon arrival; again thirty days after arrival; upon such events as a change of address, employment or school; annually after arrival; and at the time of departure from the country. The requirements applied to non-immigrants from selected countries specified in notices published in the Federal Register, and nonimmigrants meeting certain pre-existing—but unspecified—criteria determined by the Attorney General or the Secretary of State to indicate a heightened need for monitoring while in the country for law enforcement or national security reasons.[116] Persons who failed willfully to comply with the registration requirements were considered to have failed to maintain their nonimmigrant status and thus were deportable under INA section 237(a)(1)(C)(i). Those failing to report to an inspector upon departure were presumed, if they sought to return to the United States, to be inadmissible under section 212(a)(3)(A)(ii) as persons seeking to enter the United States to engage in unlawful activity. Over the succeeding months, the Department of Justice published notices in the Federal Register applying the special registration requirements to male nonimmigrants between sixteen and forty-five who were already in the country and who were nationals or citizens of Afghanistan, Algeria, Bahrain, Eritrea, Iran, Iraq, Lebanon, Libya, Morocco, North Korea, Oman, Qatar, Somalia, Sudan, Syria, Tunisia, United Arab Emirates, or Yemen.

The new requirements were based on longstanding, but not rigorously enforced, statutory provisions governing registration. INA section 262(a) provides that all aliens who have not been previously registered and fingerprinted must apply for registration and be fingerprinted if they remain the United States for thirty days or longer. Registration had taken place through the use of a paper arrival-departure record that was given to nonimmigrants at admission, and in principle (despite spotty practice) collected at the time of departure.[117] As authorized by INA section 262(c), however, INS regulations waived the fingerprint requirement for many nonimmigrants.[118] Thus, most nonimmigrants were admitted without being photographed and fingerprinted.[119] INA section 263(a) also

---

113. Attorney General Prepared Remarks on the National Security Entry-Exit Registration System (June 6, 2002), *available at* <http://www.usdoj.gov/ag/speeches/2002/060502agpreparedremarks.htm>.

114. 67 Fed. Reg. 40581 (2002).

115. 67 Fed. Reg. 52583 (Aug. 12, 2002).

116. 8 C.F.R. § 264.1(f) (2002).

117. The arrival-departure record system became mostly electronic in 2013. *See* Factsheet, US Customs & Border Protection, I-94 Automation, March 2013, *available at* <http://www.cbp.gov/sites/default/files/documents/i94_factsheet_2.pdf>.

118. 8 C.F.R. § 264.1(a) (2002).

119. 67 Fed. Reg. at 52586 (2002).

authorizes the Attorney General to apply special regulations and forms for the registration of "aliens of any … class not lawfully admitted to the United States for permanent residence." INA section 214 authorizes the Attorney General to prescribe conditions for the admission of nonimmigrant aliens. Finally, INA section 265 requires most aliens who remain in the United States for thirty days or longer to notify the Attorney General within ten days of any change of address. As noted above, willful failure to fulfill the change of address notification requirements can result in deportability.

On the day he announced the program, at the end of his remarks, the Attorney General made reference to a remarkable legal conclusion. He explained that persons who violated the registration program rules would be identified in the National Crime Information Center (NCIC) system, which is checked by hundreds of thousands of police officers nationwide in the regular course of traffic stops and other routine encounters. Police officers encountering special registration program violators would arrest and transfer them to the custody of the immigration agency. According to the Attorney General, the Justice Department's Office of Legal Counsel (OLC) had concluded that the power to arrest for such violations of even the civil provisions of the immigration laws lies "within the inherent authority of the United States." This conclusion, stood in contrast to a previous opinion of that Office, which reached the conclusion that state and local law enforcement authorities lack the power to make arrests for civil, as opposed to criminal, immigration violations.[120] If the new OLC opinion were determined to be correct, the states' inherent authority would seem to make unnecessary Congress's action in enacting INA section 287(g), which empowers the Attorney General to delegate to the states the authority to enforce the federal civil immigration provisions, but seems to require, or at least to provide for, a fairly complex arrangement involving written agreements, training of state officers, federal acceptance of civil tort liability, and other features. The Department of Justice's reversal of its earlier position on state authority to enforce the civil immigration laws provoked considerable public controversy, including by some police authorities around the country who did not want to engage in enforcement of the federal civil immigration laws.[121]

The special registration program itself sparked a great deal of public criticism. Critics charged that it amounted to unfair profiling of those from Arab or Muslim countries, and that it would not further the country's national security interests.[122] As of April 2003, more than 129,000 aliens had registered, of which more than 2,310 had been detained and 9,888 placed into removal proceedings.[123] The Senate in early 2003 passed a budget bill that included a provision to suspend funding for the program, although this provision was eliminated from the final bill.[124] The program also created a certain amount of diplomatic friction with the countries whose nationals were affected. The government of Canada even took the extraordinary step of issuing a travel advisory warning its citizens

120. *See* 1996 Opinion on OLC web site *available at* <http://www.usdoj.gov/olc/immstopo1a.htm>.

121. For a thorough discussion of the issues surrounding the role of state and local law enforcement agencies in enforcing U.S. immigration law, *see* Michael John Garcia & Kate M.Manuel, "Authority of State and Local Police to Enforce Federal Immigration Law," Congressional Research Service, Sept. 10, 2012, *available at* < http://fas.org/sgp/crs/homesec/R41423.pdf>. In Arizona v. United States, 132 S. Ct. 2492 (2012), the United States Supreme Court held that states are generally preempted from arresting or detaining aliens for immigration violations, thus calling into question the validity of the OLC opinion.

122. *See* 67 Fed. Reg. at 52585 (2002), addressing comments to the proposed rule; Mathew Barakat, *Immigration Advocates: Program is Catch-22*, ASSOCIATED PRESS, April 25, 2003.

123. Barakat, *supra* note 122.

124. *See* Edward Walsh, "Senate Votes to Halt INS Registration Program," WASH. POST, January 25, 2003.

who might have dual nationality with a covered country of the consequences of the registration requirements.

In April 2003, the Secretary of Homeland Security announced plans for a new, broader compliance-monitoring program called the United States Visitor and Immigration Status Indicator Technology (US VISIT) system. US VISIT was conceived as the means to fulfill the integrated entry-exit system called for in the various legislative enactments discussed above and would, according to the Department of Homeland Security, entirely supersede NSEERS; it would also apply to almost all aliens entering and leaving the United States, not just aliens from certain countries. In April 2011, after years of criticism of the program, DHS mostly ended NSEERS by "de-listing" all the countries whose citizens were subject to the program.[125] Critics pointed out that NSEERS had failed to identify anyone suspected of involvement in terrorism-related crimes and had cost more than $10 million annually. In February 2012, DHS's Office of the Inspector General recommended fully terminating NSEERS.[126] US VISIT continued to operate and to improve its ability to record the entries and exits of aliens. In March 2013, DHS established the Office of Biometric Identity Management (OBIM) to replace the US VISIT program. OBIM works with federal, state, and local law enforcement and other agencies to support the identification of aliens who enter and leave the United States.

International Protection Treaties and National Security

While immigration is in most respects a domestic law issue, there are key areas in which it intersects with or derives from principles of international law. These areas, like any other in immigration law, can have important national security implications. One obvious example is the area involving refugee and asylum law, discussed above. The statutory provisions governing the U.S. refugee and asylum programs derive from the 1951 U.S. Convention relating to the Status of Refugees, to which the United States became a party in 1968. These programs are critical humanitarian elements of U.S. immigration policy. They can be sensitive from a security standpoint, however, since they revolve around complex judgments involving predictions about the likelihood that a person may face persecution in a political situation about which the adjudicator's information is at best imperfect. Moreover, these judgments are made after interactions in which language differences often pose a significant barrier to the free flow of important evidentiary information, and in which the adjudicator often will have access to nothing more than the applicant's own testimony.

From a legal standpoint at least, there are mechanisms to meet the country's treaty-based protection obligations while safeguarding the national security. Asylum, for example, which is available only at the discretion of the Attorney General or the Secretary of Homeland Security, is forbidden to those who may reasonably be regarded as a danger to the national security or who fall within the security-related grounds of inadmissibility or deportability.[127] Likewise withholding of removal, a mandatory remedy based on Article

---

125. Removing Designated Countries From the National Security Entry-Exit Registration System (NSEERS), 76 Fed. Reg. 23830 (Apr. 28, 2011).

126. Dep't of Homeland Security—Office of Inspector General, Information Sharing on Foreign Nationals: Border Security (Redacted), at 15, available at <http://www.oig.dhs.gov/assets/Mgmt/2012/OIGr_12-39_Feb12.pdf>.

127. INA § 208(b)(2)(A)(iv), (v) (Supp. I 2002).

33 of the Refugee Convention, which provides that "[n]o Contracting State shall expel or return ('refouler') a refugee in any manner whatsoever to the frontiers of a territory where his life or freedom would be threatened on account of race, religion, nationality, membership of a particular social group or political opinion."[128] The 1951 Convention, both in Article 33 and in connection with the definition of "refugee" contained in Article 1, provide for the exclusion from protection of persons who because of criminal and other conduct are not deserving of international protection, including those creating a security threat to the would-be host country. There are similar grounds for denying refugee status to persons applying from abroad.

A more complex situation arises, however, in the context of U.S. obligations under a more recent international protection instrument, the UN Convention Against Torture and Other Cruel, Inhuman, and Degrading Treatment or Punishment. The Convention Against Torture, under which the United States has borne obligations since November 1994, includes a provision similar to the nonrefoulement provision of Article 33 of the Refugee Convention. Article 3 of the Convention against Torture requires contracting states not to "expel, return (refouler), or extradite" a person to another state where he or she would be tortured. The Convention against Torture does not, however, contain exclusions from its nonrefoulement obligation parallel to those included in the Refugee Convention. This presented a difficult implementation issue: how was the United States to deal with persons who would face torture if returning home, but who might pose a danger to the security of the United States? Did the Convention leave room for states to apply national security, criminal and other exclusions similar to those in effect under the Refugee Convention?

In legislation implementing the Convention against Torture's nonrefoulement obligation in U.S. domestic law, Congress posed this question squarely to the executive branch. That implementing legislation was contained in section 2242 of the Foreign Affairs Reform and Restructuring Act of 1998. Section 2242(c) instructed executive branch authorities that, "[t]o the maximum extent consistent with the obligations of the United States under the Convention, the regulations [to implement the Article 3 nonrefoulement obligation] shall exclude from the protection of such regulations aliens described in" the statutory provisions that set out the Refugee Convention-based exclusion grounds. Because the Convention against Torture did not explicitly authorize any exclusions from the prohibition on return of those facing torture, this statutory language left it to the executive branch, in the rulemaking process, to determine to what extent any such exclusions might be consistent with the Convention. Given the absence of any such Convention-based exclusion, the Department of Justice concluded that such protection was absolute: "[a]rticle 3 prohibits returning any person to a country where he or she would be tortured, and contains no exceptions to this mandate."[129] The Department of Justice pointed to the principle that, "[w]herever possible, subsequent acts of Congress must be construed as consistent with treaty obligations."[130]

In order to comply with Congress's instruction to exclude to the maximum extent possible persons who would have been excluded under the Refugee Convention, the Department of Justice created a two-tiered protection system. Nonrefoulement, under either the Refugee Convention or Convention against Torture, does not require granting any

---

128. INA § 241(b)(3) (Supp. I 2002).

129. 64 Fed. Reg. at 8481 (Feb. 10, 1999).

130. *Id.* (citing *Cook v. United States*, 288 U.S. 102, 120 (1933) ("[a] treaty will not be deemed to have been abrogated or modified by a later statute unless such purpose on the part of Congress has been clearly expressed")).

sort of long-term immigration status, such as is granted with asylum, where the recipient can gain permanent residence. Instead, it simply requires that the person not be returned to the country where the risk exists. Therefore, the primary means of protection under the Convention against Torture is called withholding of removal, and the parallel provision implementing the Refugee Convention is called the nonrefoulement provision.[131] For those who would have been excluded under the Refugee Convention, including those posing a risk to national security, a lesser form of protection called deferral of removal is provided, in essence permitting the grant to be rescinded more easily upon a change in the conditions that created the risk of torture in the first instance.[132]

This, of course, presents the question what the government can do when a terrorist or other security risk cannot be returned because of a risk of torture. As with withholding of removal under either Convention, the government remains free to return the alien to any country where no qualifying threat of torture exists. This of course, is not often practicable. Few countries are willing to accept another country's terrorist deportees. It also remains possible to return an alien to a country where the risk of torture has subsided below the qualifying level of likelihood. This, though, is not always an available solution to the security problem. The regulation also sought specifically to invoke whatever detention authority the government holds, even if indefinite.[133] Indeed, the implementing legislation appeared specifically to contemplate this avenue: "[n]othing in this section shall be construed as limiting the authority of the Attorney General to detain any person under any provision of law, including, but not limited to, any provision of the Immigration and Nationality Act." Section 2242(e) of the Foreign Affairs Reform and Restructuring Act of 1998. Both the statutory provision and the implementing regulation predated the Supreme Court's decision limiting post-removal period detention in *Zadvydas*. That decision, though, as discussed above, expressly did not address circumstances where such detention might be justified by national security concerns. Finally, the regulation created a final mechanism apparently designed to account for extraordinary circumstances such as the inability to remove a terrorist or other security threat. Section 208.18(c) sets out procedures under which the Attorney General (now the Secretary of Homeland Security) can determine, on the basis of advice from the Secretary of State, that diplomatic assurances from the would-be torturing state that a particular alien would in fact not be tortured have eliminated the risk sufficient to return the alien. The Department of Justice declared its view that such cases "will be rare,"[134] and they have been. Nevertheless, returns have taken place with these kinds of diplomatic assurances in a small number of cases and, as might be anticipated, the use of this mechanism has sparked opposition from outside the government.

Even if the Department of Justice is correct that the Convention against Torture admits of no exceptions in the case of terrorists or other threats to the national security or public safety, Congress always remains free to recede from the Convention obligation, and it considered such legislation in 2000. No changes to the statute resulted. Nor is the interpretation that the Convention against Torture admits of no exceptions in security cases universally shared. A Canadian court has concluded, for example, that under Canadian law it is permissible to balance the risk of torture against competing national security issues.[135]

---

131. 8 C.F.R. § 208.16(c) (2002).
132. 8 C.F.R. § 208.17(a) (2002).
133. *See* 64 Fed. Reg. at 8481 (1999), 8 C.F.R. § 208.17(c) (2002).
134. 64 Fed. Reg. at 8484 (1999).
135. *See* Suresh v. Canada (Minister of Citizenship and Immigration) [2002], 1 S.C.R. 3.

National Security Immigration Benefits

Until now, this chapter has mainly discussed methods for keeping aliens out of the United States if they are thought to be threatening to national security, or removing them once they have arrived here. But another side of immigration law recognizes that certain aliens may benefit U.S. national security. America often describes itself as a "nation of immigrants," and historically, immigrants have benefitted the United States far more than they have threatened our national security. Recognizing this, US immigration law grants benefits to aliens who have improved US. national security, providing them in some cases with immigrant visas and in other cases, expediting their naturalization as United States citizens. This part of the chapter will briefly discuss immigration benefits for those aliens who enlist in the military; special visas and naturalization rules for aliens who benefit U.S. national security; and special immigrant visas for certain aliens who have worked for the U.S. military or the U.S. Government in Iraq and Afghanistan.

Before September 11, 2001, enlistment in the different branches of the military was governed by different statutes and regulations. No statute prohibited the U.S. Navy and Marine Corps from enlisting noncitizens generally, but the U.S. Army and Air Force were not permitted to accept peacetime recruits who were not U.S. citizens or lawful permanent residents ("green card holders"). For example, the 2001 Army enlistment statute stated: "In time of peace, no person may be accepted for original enlistment in the Army unless he is a citizen of the United States or has been lawfully admitted to the United States for permanent residence ..."[136] After September 11, 2001, citizenship-related requirements for enlistment were tightened. In January 2006, Congress substantially changed military enlistment law, repealing the separate statutes that had previously governed enlistment in each of the services and replacing them with a single unified statute that applies to all the armed services. Congress also eliminated the wartime/peacetime distinction that had previously allowed virtually unlimited enlistment of aliens in wartime. The new statute, 10 USC § 504(b)(1), which applies in both wartime and peacetime, provides that enlistment in the U.S. military is limited to:

(A) A national of the United States, as defined in section 101(a)(22) of the Immigration and Nationality Act.[137]

(B) An alien who is lawfully admitted for permanent residence, as defined in section 101(a)(20) of the Immigration and Nationality Act.[138]

(C) A person described in section 341 of one of the following compacts:

(i) The Compact of Free Association between the Federated States of Micronesia and the United States....[139]

(ii) The Compact of Free Association between the Republic of the Marshall Islands and the United States....[140]

---

136. 10 USC § 3253 (2001) (repealed).

137. Immigration and Nationality Act (INA) § 101(a)(22), 8 USC § 1101(a)(22). Note that all U.S. citizens are also U.S. nationals, but not all U.S. nationals are U.S. citizens. U.S. nationals from American Samoa and Swain's Island are permitted to enlist in the U.S. Armed Forces under this statute, but they must naturalize as U.S. citizens to have all the rights and privileges of U.S. citizens. INA § 325 (8 USC § 1436) permits them to naturalize under certain relaxed conditions.

138. INA § 101(a)(20), 8 USC § 1101(a)(20).

139. 117 Stat. 2784; 48 USC § 1921 note.

140. 117 Stat. 2823; 48 USC § 1921 note.

(iii) The Compact of Free Association between Palau and the United States....[141]

The statute does contain an exception, however:

(2) Notwithstanding paragraph (1), the Secretary concerned may authorize the enlistment of a person not described in paragraph (1) if the Secretary determines that such enlistment is vital to the national interest.[142]

This exception, subsection (b)(2) of the new enlistment statute, gives the secretaries of the military services authority to waive the requirement that a person seeking to enlist have U.S. citizenship, nationality, or a green card if the secretary concerned determines "that such enlistment is vital to the national interest."[143] Green card holders are authorized by the above statute to enlist in all branches of the military, but they can serve only in jobs that do not require U.S. citizenship or a security clearance. The enlistment statute provides that certain Pacific Islanders—citizens of the Federated States of Micronesia, the Republic of the Marshall Islands, and Palau—also may enlist in the U.S. Armed Forces. By treaty, the United States is obligated to defend these countries, which do not maintain armed forces—so citizens of those countries are permitted to serve in the U.S. Armed Forces instead of their own armed forces.[144] The enlistment statute conforms to the treaty obligations of the United States to accept voluntary enlistments from citizens of those countries.

Early in 2011, the U.S. Army issued a revised personnel regulation with far-reaching consequences for U.S. citizens who also hold citizenship in another country.[145] Under Army Regulation 601-210, persons who are dual citizens of the United States and another country are not permitted to enlist in the Army, Army Reserve, or Army National Guard for jobs that require a security clearance "unless they already possess a security clearance."[146] This regulation potentially bars millions of Americans from most Army jobs because the vast majority of Army jobs require a security clearance—including officer appointments, Special Forces, military intelligence, and military police jobs, among others. Dual citizenship is a status that millions of Americans possess, often inadvertently, but other times because dual citizenship allows them to travel more freely, or live and work easily in other countries.[147]

Whether a person holds citizenship in a particular country is a matter of that country's law, not of U.S. law. One's citizenship is thus not always within the control of either the individual or the U.S. government. Although some countries allow their citizens to expatriate, others do not. Some people are dual citizens because their parents or

---

141. 100 Stat. 3678; 48 USC § 1931 note.

142. 10 USC § 504(b) (2006).

143. 10 USC § 504(b)(2) (2006).

144. *See* section 341 of the following treaties: Compact of Free Association between the Federated States of Micronesia and the United States, Pub. L. No. 108-188, sec. 201(a), 117 Stat. 2784 (48 USC § 1921 note); Compact of Free Association between the Republic of the Marshall Islands and the United States, sec. 201(b), 117 Stat. 2823 (48 USC § 1921 note); and Compact of Free Association between Palau and the United States, Pub. L. No. 99-658, sec. 201, 100 Stat. 3678 (48 USC § 1931 note). *See also* Dep't of the Army, Regular Army and Army Reserve Enlistment Program, Army Reg. 601-210, ¶ 2–4.a(4) (June 7, 2007).

145. *See also* Selective Service System: Fast Facts: Aliens and Dual Nationals, *available at* <www. sss.gov/FSaliens.html>.

146. *See* Army Regulation 601-210, Active and Reserve Components Enlistment Program (Feb. 8, 2011, revised Mar. 12, 2013), *available at* <www.apd.army.mil/jw2/xmldemo/r601_210/main.asp>.

147. *See* M. T. Luongo, "Carrying Several Passports? It's Not Just for Spies," *New York Times* (Jan. 20, 2009), at B6 (describing how millions of Americans hold dual citizenship in the United States and other countries).

grandparents hold citizenship in a foreign country; others are dual citizens because they were born in another country. The U.S. Office of Personnel Management (OPM) has published *Citizenship Laws of the World*,[148] a publication that explains the wide variety of rules regarding citizenship. Although this reference is not up to date (some countries have changed their laws since it was published), it can give one a good idea of the potential problems posed by the Army's personnel regulation. According to OPM, for example, the country of Iran considers the children of male Iranian citizens to be Iranian citizens as well, and prevents them from renouncing Iranian citizenship — so any U.S.-born child of an Iranian male citizen is necessarily a dual citizen of the United States and Iran, and can't rid himself of Iranian citizenship. The Army's regulation preventing all dual U.S. citizens from enlisting in most Army jobs is a much broader bar than the military has previously applied. Previously, dual citizenship did not prevent enlistment into any job and did not automatically bar a person from holding a security clearance; instead, security officials would evaluate each person's case individually.[149] It is unclear whether Army officials understood the impact of the new personnel regulation when they published it, so it may be revised in the future. New military regulations also now bar American citizens and immigrants from enlisting altogether if their spouses and children are not authorized to be in the United States.

In the past, the United States has occasionally had overseas enlistment programs. Under the Lodge-Philbin Act[150] and the United States–Philippines Military Bases Agreement of 1947,[151] certain noncitizens living overseas were permitted to enlist in the U.S. military. Today, no such programs exist — with the exception of programs to recruit persons from Micronesia, Palau, and the Marshall Islands, as noted earlier — and U.S. military recruiters are generally prohibited from recruiting persons who are outside the United States and its possessions.[152]

Although no service secretary has yet approved the enlistment of any unauthorized immigrants, the service secretaries have authorized the enlistment of a small number of lawfully present aliens who are not green card holders under the "vital to the national interest" prong of the enlistment statute. In November 2008, Defense Secretary Robert Gates authorized the services to conduct a new pilot enlistment program, Military Accessions

---

148. U.S. Office of Personnel Management, *Citizenship Laws of the World* (stating that the U.S. government recognizes dual citizenship).

149. The Marine Corps, for example, apparently still allows dual citizens to enlist into any job but requires such persons to state their "willingness" to renounce their other citizenship, and to destroy their foreign passport. *See* MCRCO 1100.1, Nov. 9, 2011, *available at* <www.hqmc.marines.mil/ Portals/61/Docs/FOIA/MCRCO1100.1EPM.pdf>, at 3–17.

150. The Lodge Act allowed certain foreign nationals overseas to join the U.S. Armed Forces. *See* Act of June 30, 1950, Pub. L. No. 81-597, 64 Stat. 316. The Lodge Act permitted up to 2,500 nonresident aliens (later expanded to allow up to 12,500) to enlist. If they successfully served for five years, they could apply for U.S. citizenship. Members of this force who died during active service or from injuries or illness during active service could obtain posthumous citizenship.

151. In the United States–Philippines Military Bases Agreement of 1947, the parties agreed that the United States could recruit Filipinos for voluntary service in the U.S. military. This agreement was renegotiated in 1952 to provide that 1,000 Filipinos could be recruited for the U.S. Navy each year, and the number was revised upward to 2,000 per year in 1954. The agreement was renewed periodically until the Military Bases Agreement was terminated in 1992, which ended overseas Filipino enlistment in the U.S. Armed Forces. Some Filipinos who enlisted under the terms of the agreement are still serving in the Navy today.

152. *See, e.g.,* Army Regulation 601-210, Active and Reserve Components Enlistment Program (Feb. 8, 2011, with Rapid Action Revision dated Aug. 4, 2011), *available at* http://armypubs.army.mil/ epubs/pdf/R601_210.PDF, ¶ 2–4(a)(6) ("Conducting recruiting activities in foreign countries, including Canada, is prohibited, however, unless such activities are specifically authorized").

Vital to the National Interest (MAVNI), where almost 3000 persons who were lawfully present in the United States (but who did not yet have green cards) and possessed critical skills were allowed to join the U.S. Armed Forces despite their lack of a green card.[153] Under the MAVNI program, the U.S. Army, Navy, and Air Force began recruiting certain lawfully present aliens who were U.S.-licensed health care professionals or fluent in one of more than 30 strategic languages. These new enlistees were permitted to naturalize almost immediately under INA § 329, which allows the naturalization of non-LPRs in wartime. The pilot program was judged to be highly successful. The program stopped enlisting people in mid-2010, but the U.S. Department of Defense (DOD) restarted the program in 2012 and it is currently operating with an increased quota of 1,500 recruits per year. Enlistments are permitted for both active-duty and reserve assignments (but not in the National Guard).

It is commonly believed that the U.S. military accepts enlistments from undocumented immigrants, but no branch of the military knowingly allows undocumented immigrants to enlist. Although unauthorized or undocumented immigrants are required to register for Selective Service, they cannot lawfully enlist in the military unless a service secretary determines that their enlistment is "vital to the national interest," as required in 10 USC § 504(b)(2). No service secretary has to date authorized any undocumented immigrant to enlist, and since at least 2004, the U.S. Armed Forces have checked every noncitizen recruit's immigration status by querying a U.S. government database,[154] so that undocumented immigrants with false green cards or invalid Social Security numbers can no longer enlist as they once did. News reports and anecdotal accounts indicate that undocumented immigrants who have attempted to enlist have been turned away, or, in some cases, have been arrested and removed. Undocumented immigrants who enlist or attempt to enlist using fraudulent documents can face criminal charges and discharge from the military.[155] If an undocumented immigrant manages to enlist and serve honorably, however, wartime naturalization authority can allow the person to naturalize through his or her honorable military service.

On September 25, 2014, the Undersecretary of Defense for Personnel and Readiness issued a memorandum authorizing the US Armed Forces to enlist certain aliens with "deferred action" status, but only if they could qualify for the MAVNI (Military Accessions Vital to the National Interest) program.[156] As of this writing, none of the Services had agreed to allow these enlistments and none of them had any procedures for enlisting people with "deferred action."

Noncitizens who are serving in or who are veterans of the United States Armed Forces— which include the US Army, Air Force, Navy, Marine Corps, and Coast Guard, along with their Reserve Components and the National Guard—have traditionally been permitted to obtain U.S. citizenship more quickly than other noncitizens; laws providing for such expedited citizenship date back to the Civil War era.[157] Expedited citizenship benefits not

---

153. *See* DOD News, Fact Sheet: "Military Accessions Vital to the National Interest," *available at* <www.defenselink.mil/news/mavni-fact-sheet.pdf>.

154. USCIS operates a system called Systematic Alien Verification for Entitlements (SAVE), which is used to verify the documents submitted by potential enlistees. Military recruiting personnel use an automated system, or submit Form G-845, Document Verification Request, via fax to a special USCIS office, which verifies the person's status and replies to the military, which then determines whether the person is eligible for enlistment, based on the information provided by USCIS.

155. *Id.*

156. *See* Memorandum, Military Accessions Vital to the National Interest Program Changes, Sept. 25, 2014.

157. Act of July 17, 1862, (sec. 2166, R.S., 1878) (making special naturalization benefits available to those with service in the "armies" of the United States).

only the noncitizens; rapid naturalization also benefits the government by reducing or eliminating legal problems relating to military service by noncitizens[158] and allowing them to be used fully in more jobs and duty assignments. Although most lawful permanent residents are required to wait three to five years before applying for U.S. citizenship, two special military-related immigration statutes provide that qualified members of the U.S. Armed Forces are permitted to apply for U.S. citizenship after one year of service (when no presidential order regarding ongoing hostilities is in effect)[159] or immediately (when a presidential executive order regarding wartime hostilities is in effect).[160] Another statute provides for posthumous naturalization of a person who was serving or previously served in the military; this statute allows the person's bereaved relatives to obtain immigration and citizenship benefits after the person's death.

The two military naturalization statutes—Immigration and Nationality Act (INA) § 328, the peacetime military naturalization statute, and INA § 329, the wartime military naturalization statute—contain significant differences from naturalization statutes that apply to civilians. These differences make them attractive options for many noncitizens. For example, during wartime, military personnel may naturalize without obtaining lawful permanent resident status first. Under INA § 329, immigrants who are serving honorably in the U.S. Armed Forces may naturalize regardless of their length of time in service or their immigration status.[161] This statute applies during specified statutory periods, or when a presidential executive order exists that has invoked the statute. Presidents have long used this statute to bestow citizenship benefits on immigrants in the military and President George W. Bush did so on July 3, 2002, proclaiming that all immigrants who have served honorably on active duty in the armed forces after September 11, 2001, shall be eligible to apply for expedited U.S. citizenship.[162] Not every overseas deployment of U.S. forces into combat is covered by this statute or by an executive order invoking this statute; for example, as of this writing, no president has issued an executive order to naturalize military personnel who served between 1991 and 2001, when the U.S. military engaged in numerous combat operations in places such as Bosnia, Haiti, Panama, and Somalia, among others. People who served in the military during those periods may naturalize under INA § 328, if they qualify, but not under INA § 329.

A significant, potential, new disability also attaches to military naturalizations: Persons naturalized through military service after November 24, 2003, may face possible revocation of their U.S. citizenship based on post-naturalization misconduct or failure to serve honorably for a period or periods aggregating five years.[163]

The U.S. Government has also provided avenues for some aliens not in the U.S. Armed Forces to immigrate to the United States if they have worked for the United States Government overseas. For example, since September 11, 2001, Congress has created three different programs that apply to Iraqi and Afghan nationals who have worked with the

---

158. Such legal problems can include claims by foreign countries that those of their citizens who serve in the U.S. military are under the jurisdiction of the foreign government for various purposes. These problems are often lessened when noncitizen service members naturalize in the United States, because the naturalization can sometimes work as a renunciation of the foreign citizenship. Once a noncitizen naturalizes through military service, the United States may also require that noncitizen to renounce his or her foreign citizenship as a condition of service; the United States cannot require such a renunciation when the person does not yet have U.S. citizenship.

159. *See* Immigration and Nationality Act (INA) § 328, 8 USC § 1439.

160. *See* INA § 329, 8 USC § 1440.

161. INA § 329, 8 USC § 1440.

162. Executive Order No. 13269 of July 3, 2002, 67 Fed. Reg. 45287 (July 8, 2002).

163. INA §§ 328(f), 329(c); 8 USC §§ 1439(f), 1440(c).

U.S. Armed Forces or the U.S. Department of State (DOS) in Iraq or Afghanistan. These programs, which do not cover nationals of other countries who have worked for the United States in those areas, allow certain Iraqis and Afghans to obtain special immigrant visas (SIVs) that allow them to enter the United States as immigrants or adjust status to that of a lawful permanent resident while legally present in the United States. These three different programs have been extended and changed repeatedly by Congress.[164]

The requirements of the three SIV programs are somewhat different, and eligible persons may file under more than one program. Iraqis and Afghans also often seek classification as refugees through the regular U.S. refugee programs; the SIV and refugee programs are not mutually exclusive, and Iraqis and Afghans are permitted to seek a SIV at the same time that they seek refugee status through the United Nations High Commissioner for Refugees or the U.S. Refugee Admissions Program. Like refugees, Iraqis and Afghans who immigrate under SIV programs are eligible for certain resettlement assistance, entitlement programs, and other benefits after they are admitted to the United States.

Because of controversy over problems with DOS's processing of visas for Iraqis and Afghans who have worked for the U.S. government, Congress has added more protections for SIV applicants in amendments to the original laws. Both laws now contain provisions for consideration of a credible sworn statement depicting dangerous country conditions, together with official evidence of such country conditions from the U.S government, as a factor in a determination of whether an applicant has experienced or is experiencing an ongoing serious threat as a consequence of employment by the U.S. government. An applicant now may also appeal a denial by the chief of mission within 120 days of receiving the denial letter, and obtain legal representation by an attorney or other accredited representative during the application process, including at relevant interviews and examinations. Congress has also regularly changed the quotas and filing deadlines for these programs.

For aliens who have not been employed by the U.S. Government, but who have provided "critical reliable information" regarding a terrorist or criminal organization or enterprise, the law provides for a non-immigrant "S" status that can eventually result in permanent residents for an eligible alien.[165] Created by law in 1994, the S visa can be given to an alien and the alien's spouse and children if the alien is in possession of critical reliable information concerning a terrorist organization, enterprise, or operation; is willing to provide this information to federal authorities or the federal courts; and will be or has been placed in danger as a result of cooperating with the terrorism investigation. The alien must also be eligible to receive a reward under section 36(a) of the State Department's Basic Authorities Act of 1956.[166] The S visa can only be accorded to 200 persons per fiscal year, but may eventually allow the person to adjust status to that of a lawful permanent resident. Essentially, the S visa operates as a reward for key terrorism prosecution witnesses.

Finally, a little-used provision of the Immigration & Nationality Act provides for the naturalization of aliens who have made an extraordinary contribution to the national

---

164. For example, as this chapter was going to press, the Carl Levin and Howard P. 'Buck' McKeon National Defense Authorization Act for Fiscal Year 2015 (NDAA 2015) had just been signed into law. Section 1227 of that bill extended the Afghan Special Immigrant Visa (SIV) Program through March 31, 2017; allowed Afghans to begin the process to apply for such visas through the end of 2015; and expanded eligibility for SIVs to certain Afghans who had not previously been eligible. *See* Carl Levin and Howard P. 'Buck' McKeon, National Defense Authorization Act for Fiscal Year 2015 (NDAA 2015), Public Law (PL) 113-291, § 1227 (2014). Congress may pass additional extensions in the future.

165. INA § 101(a)(15)(S), 8 USC § 1101(a)(15)(S) and § 214(k)(1), 8 USC § 1184(k)(1) (2014).

166. 22 USC § 2708(a).

security of the United States or to the conduct of U.S. intelligence gathering activities.[167] The provision may only benefit five persons each fiscal year, and the Central Intelligence Agency director must notify Congressional intelligence and judiciary committees within a reasonable time before anyone files an application under this law. A person who applies under this law must have the approval of the CIA director, the Attorney General, and head of the immigration agency. Applicants for naturalization under this provision cannot be persecutors of others, cannot have committed serious nonpolitical crimes outside the United States or particularly serious crimes in the United States, cannot be a danger to the security of the United States, and cannot be inadmissible under the terrorism ground of inadmissibility.[168]

In conclusion, U.S. immigration law is not only about turning aliens away or removing them from the United States when they are deemed a threat to U.S. national security. It also provides significant benefits to those who are willing to work for the United States Government in the military or in national security related areas.

A Final Note

A sign of the extent to which national security has affected the calculus in immigration legal and policy decisions since the September 11 terrorist attacks can be seen in a return to the detention context, in the decision of the Attorney General in *In re D-J-*.[169] That decision concerned what many might regard as an issue somewhat removed from core national security concerns, at least in the counterterrorism sense. *In re D-J-* was a bond decision arising from the immigration custody of a Haitian national caught trying to enter the United States unlawfully. On October 29, 2002, he was among a group of more than 200 undocumented Haitians (and some Dominicans as well) aboard a vessel that sailed into Biscayne Bay, Florida. After the vessel apparently ran aground just offshore while trying to evade coastal interdiction by the United States Coast Guard, with news helicopters circling overhead, many of its passengers began jumping overboard and coming ashore. In an extraordinary sequence of events, CNN broadcast the episode live, as law enforcement officers sought to apprehend the boat's passengers and the passengers in turn sought to escape apprehension, some even seeking to hail taxis on Brickel Bridge. The INS detained the passengers as a group, asserting that declining to detain such aliens while their removal proceedings were underway would encourage further surges of mass migration from Haiti by sea, with "attendant strains on national and homeland security resources."[170]

The respondent was among those put into regular removal proceedings under INA section 240 and charged as inadmissible for being present without admission or parole under section 212(a)(6)(A)(i). He sought asylum and asked to be released on bond while his claim was in process. After an immigration judge ordered his release and the INS appealed, the Board of Immigration Appeals dismissed the appeal, concluding that such custody decisions must rest on factors specific to the alien himself rather than on the broad and more generalized national interests asserted by the INS. The Attorney General

---

167. INA § 316(f), 8 U.S.C. § 1427(f) (2014).
168. INA § 316(f)(1).
169. *In re* D-J-, 23 I. & N. Dec. 572 (B.I.A. 2003).
170. 23 I. & N. Dec. at 577.

overturned the BIA's decision, concluding that "[e]ncouraging such unlawful mass migrations is inconsistent with sound immigration policy and important national security interests.... [S]urges in such illegal immigration by sea injure national security by diverting valuable Coast Guard and [Department of Defense resources involved in U.S. migrant interdiction efforts] from counterterrorism and homeland security responsibilities."[171] These broad national security concerns, the Attorney General held, were sufficient to support a decision to hold D-J- in custody while his proceedings went forward. This decision was resurrected in the summer of 2014, when large numbers of unauthorized migrants began arriving on the southern U.S. border, mainly from El Salvador, Guatemala, and Honduras. Government attorneys began citing this decision as a basis for detaining the migrants, who were mostly women and children, and denying them bond.

This decision raises the question where the limiting principle might lie in basing immigration, or other, policy decisions on national security considerations. If, on the one hand, there were demonstrable security-based needs for the limited number of Coast Guard vessels, then why shouldn't the government shape its policies in other areas so as to avoid the unnecessary expenditure of those resources? On the other hand, could any policy step designed to conserve law enforcement, intelligence, or other governmental resources be justified as a means to conserve assets for the war on terror?

It would be difficult to overestimate how much the September 11 attacks and the attendant national security issues have divided the national public and lawmaking psyche on immigration issues—already the subject of intense polarity even before the terrorist threat in this country reached such proportions. Those divisions continue to show themselves starkly in nearly every context involving public substantive debate. As a final example, consider a judicial decision reached just before this text went to press, involving not this country's immigration law itself but a decision concerning the Freedom of Information Act, and the extent to which it provides public access to information about the persons detained by the government as part of the law enforcement measures taken in the weeks and months after the attacks. The following account comes from coverage in the *New York Times* of the decision of the D.C. Circuit in *Center for National Security Studies v. U.S. Department of Justice,*[172] overturning the decision of a district court requiring the Justice Department to disclose under FOIA the names of the post 9/11 detainees and their counsels:

> A federal appeals court, reversing a lower-court decision, ruled today that the government did not have to disclose the names of more than 700 people detained in the aftermath of Sept. 11, 2001, agreeing with the Justice Department that making that information public could "allow Al Qaeda and other terrorist groups to map the course of the investigation."

> The 2-to-1 decision by a panel of the United States Court of Appeals for the District of Columbia was a rebuff to the civil liberties and other groups that were challenging the Bush administration's refusal to provide the names and other information about people, mostly immigrants, held in connection with the 9/11 terrorism investigation, on the ground of national security.

> The court said the government could withhold the dates and locations of arrest, detention and release of all detainees, including those charged with federal crimes, and the names of lawyers representing them.

---

171. 23 I. & N. Dec. at 579.
172. Center for Nat'l Sec. Studies v. United States Dep't of Justice, 331 F.3d 918 (D.C. Cir. 2003).

"A complete list of names informing terrorists of every suspect detained by the government at any point during the Sept. 11 investigation would give terrorist organizations a composite picture of the government investigation," the majority wrote today. "Disclosure would inform terrorists of both the substantive and geographic focus of the investigation. Moreover, disclosure would inform terrorists which of their members were compromised by the investigation, and which were not."

But in a sharply worded dissent, Judge David S. Tatel faulted his two colleagues, David B. Sentelle and Karen Lecraft Henderson, for showing "uncritical deference to the government's vague, poorly explained arguments for withholding broad categories of information about the detainees."

While noting that the government had a legitimate basis for keeping some information secret, Judge Tatel cited "another compelling public interest," which he defined as "knowing whether the government, in responding to the attacks, is violating the constitutional rights of the hundreds of persons whom it has detained in connection with its terrorism investigation."

"Citizens have a compelling interest in ensuring that their government does not, in discharging its duties, abuse one of its most awesome powers, the power to arrest and jail," Judge Tatel wrote in arguing that the government had overextended its use of an exemption under the Freedom of Information Act.

Judge Tatel said fuller disclosure concerning the detainees would help the public determine whether people had been detained "mainly because of their religion or ethnicity" and whether the government was "holding them in custody for extended periods without charge or preventing them from seeking or communicating with legal counsel."

But Judges Sentelle and Henderson said the judiciary owed a certain amount of deference to the government in determining what would and would not harm national security interests in the campaign against terrorism.

"America faces an enemy just as real as its former Cold War foes, with capabilities beyond the capacity of the judiciary to explore," the judges wrote. "It is abundantly clear that the government's top counterterrorism officials are well-suited to make this predictive judgment. Conversely, the judiciary is in an extremely poor position to second-guess the executive's judgment in this area of national security."[173]

This colloquy between majority and dissenting judges, as with the others noted in this chapter, captures well the gaping questions facing U.S. immigration law and policy. Is immigration a system that can work principally as an encounter in which the government can apply security information it might gain about a particular alien? And is there a risk that trying to make the system function more broadly as a national security enforcement mechanism would cause damage to the ability of this country to benefit from robust immigration? Or is it a reality the nation must face that the terrorist threat to this country has reached such dimensions, and the immigration system such a clear vulnerability, that the government would be failing its citizens not to tighten access to immigration significantly, even if that comes at some expense to the ease of coming to this country from abroad? The country is yet nowhere near to its answer on these questions, or to a

---

173. 331 F.3d at 928.

carefully devised balance between the two. But clearly they will occupy a prominent place on the policy agenda for years to come.

Selected Bibliography

ALEINIKOFF, T. ALEXANDER, DAVID A. MARTIN, HIROSHI MOTOMURA, MARYELLEN FULLERTON, IMMIGRATION AND CITIZENSHIP — PROCESS AND POLICY (West, 7th Ed., 2011).

Chishti, Muzaffar, Doris Meissner, Demetrios Papademetriou, Jay Peterzell, Michael Wishnie, and Stephen Yale-Loehr, "America's Challenge: Domestic Security, Civil Liberties, and National Unity after September 11," Migration Policy Institute, June 2003.

COLE, DAVID, ENEMY ALIENS: DOUBLE STANDARDS AND CONSTITUTIONAL FREEDOMS IN THE WAR ON TERRORISM (New Press 2003).

Dinh,Viet, "Law and the War on Terrorism: Freedom and Security After September 11," 25 HARV. J.L. & PUB. POL'Y 399 (2002).

Gorman, S., "National Security — The Ashcroft Doctrine," NATIONAL JOURNAL (Dec. 21, 2002).

Gross, S., & D. Livingston, "Racial Profiling Under Attack," 102 COLUM. L. REV. 1413 (2002).

Kerwin, Donald & Margaret D. Stock, "The Role of Immigration in a Coordinated National Security Policy," 21 GEO. IMMIGR. L. J. 383 (2007).

KNAUFF, E., THE ELLEN KNAUFF STORY (Norton 1952).

Rights Working Group, The NSEERS Effect: A Decade of Racial Profiling, Fear, & Secrecy, Pennsylvania State University, May 2012, *available at* https://pennstatelaw.psu.edu/_file/clinics/NSEERS_report.pdf.

STOCK, MARGARET D., IMMIGRATION LAW & THE MILITARY (American Immigration Lawyers Association, 2d. ed. 2014).

U.S. Department of Justice, Office of the Inspector General, "The September 11 Detainees: A Review of the Treatment of Aliens Held on Immigration Charges in Connection with the Investigation of the September 11 Attacks" (April 2003), *available at* <http://www.usdoj.gov/oig/special/0306/full.pdf>.

Wadhia, Shoba Sivasprasad *et al.*, The 9/11 Effect and Its Legacy on U.S. Immigration Laws: Essays, Remarks, and Photographs, Pennsylvania State University, September 16, 2011, *available at* <https://pennstatelaw.psu.edu/_file/Immigrants/9_11_Effect_Online_Publication.pdf>.

Chapter 30

An Introduction to Economic Sanctions: A Brief History and the Basic Tools[1]

R. Richard Newcomb and Mark D. Roberts[2]

In this chapter:

An Overview of U.S. Economic Sanctions Programs Since 1940

Development of Economic Sanctions Under the International Emergency Economic Powers Act

General Sanctions Authorities and Strategic Considerations Concerning the Implementation of Sanctions

Sanctions Implementation Practices

In recent years, in response to threats to the national security, foreign policy and economy of the United States, economic sanctions have become a foreign policy tool of choice. Economic sanctions are a very powerful instrument for use in the conduct of U.S. national security and foreign policy and for use by multilateral organizations such as the United Nations and the European Union ("EU") when international peace and security is threatened by rogue regimes or by acts of dictators that occur in repressive regimes in countries around the world. When economic sanctions are employed by the United States and often later multilaterally, it is when the traditional norms and methods of diplomacy have failed and more coercive measures are looked to as the last step before some form

---

1. This chapter contains excerpts from a number of sources. These excerpts include the footnotes as they were in the original source documents. However on certain occasions, the numbering of these footnotes are not the same as in the original source documents. The footnotes throughout this chapter, whether a footnote to the text written by the authors, or a footnote that is part of an excerpt, run sequentially from the beginning of the chapter to the end so as to avoid the confusion of having more than one footnote with the same number. For a related discussion see chapter 31 in this book "Export Controls and Economic Sanctions."

The views expressed in this chapter are those of the authors and do not purport to reflect the official policy or views of the Department of the Treasury, the U.S. Government, or the views of any of the authors of works cited in this chapter.

2. Mr. Newcomb served as Director of the Office of Foreign Assets Control of the U.S. Department of Treasury from 1987–2004. He is currently a partner at the Law Firm, DLA Piper, where he is the Chair of the International Trade Practice Group.

Mr. Roberts, a Ph.D. in Economics, was the Senior Policy Advisor to the OFAC director and the head of OFAC's Foreign Terrorist Asset Tracking Center. He also served as Deputy Director of the Office of Enforcement Analysis in the U.S. Department of Commerce Bureau of Industry and Security.

of military or other coercive method is adopted. It doesn't always work like that, but it is more often the case than not.

Economic sanctions are administered by the Office of Foreign Assets Control (OFAC). The OFAC website describes its mission: " ... (OFAC) of the US Department of the Treasury administers and enforces economic and trade sanctions based on US foreign policy and national security goals against targeted foreign countries and regimes, terrorists, international narcotics traffickers, those engaged in activities related to the proliferation of weapons of mass destruction, and other threats to the national security, foreign policy or economy of the United States. OFAC acts under Presidential national emergency powers, as well as authority granted by specific legislation, to impose controls on transactions and freeze assets under US jurisdiction. Many of the sanctions are based on United Nations and other international mandates, are multilateral in scope, and involve close cooperation with allied governments."[3]

The ever expanding role that economic sanctions plays is reflected by the current use of economic sanctions in national security policy, and the concurrent posture that enforcement authorities have been taking in recent years with regard to U.S. dollar-denominated financial transactions that involve sanctioned countries, groups, entities, and persons. This is especially true with Iran, but also with sanctions against Syria, Sudan, and Russia.

The President has imposed economic sanctions pursuant to broad delegations of authority from Congress in the International Emergency Economic Powers Act, 50 U.S.C. 1701–1706 ("IEEPA"), and the Trading with the Enemy Act, 50 U.S.C. App. 5(b) ("TWEA"). Sanctions have also been imposed, especially more recently, pursuant to specific legislation targeting particular threats. Before 1977, TWEA authorized the President to impose sanctions during both times of war and times of national emergency. With the passage of IEEPA in 1977, TWEA was limited to times of war and certain grandfathered sanctions programs, and IEEPA became the authority for sanctions to deal with national emergencies declared pursuant to the National Emergencies Act, 50 U.S.C. 1601–51.

This chapter focuses primarily, but not exclusively, upon economic sanctions administered by OFAC. Section I provides a comprehensive overview of many of these programs to acquaint the reader with both the wide variety of situations in which sanctions have been employed and the often complicated political context and historical factors that have shaped them. The summary is intended to provide the reader with prologue to the later discussions in Sections II through IV that discuss the developmental stages of sanctions, the underlying legal authorities and strategic considerations involved, and the implementation practices and certain court challenges that have helped to shape the legal environment in which these programs now operate. This presentation is intended as an introduction to economic sanctions for the law student.

---

3. http://www.treasury.gov/about/organizational-structure/offices/Pages/Office-of-Foreign-Assets-Control.aspx.

I
An Overview of U.S. Economic Sanctions Programs Since 1940

Economic sanctions are a foreign policy and national security instrument used by the President. Pursuant to delegated authority from the President, the U.S. Department of the Treasury ("the U.S. Treasury") has traditionally administered sanctions—whether protectively or punitively—in consultation and coordination with the U.S. Department of State which provides foreign policy advice. While sanctions and the Secretary of the Treasury's involvement with sanctions goes back to the War of 1812, and economic sanctions were used by the United States during both the Civil War and World War I, modern economic sanctions since 1940 have been administered primarily by the Office of Foreign Assets Control and by its predecessor office, during the World War II, known as the Office of Foreign Funds Control.

World War II and Foreign Funds Control.[4] The Foreign Funds Control (FFC) was established at Treasury to administer asset blocking controls instituted under authority of Executive Order 8389 and the Trading With the Enemy Act of 1917 ("TWEA"),[5] after the German invasion of *Norway* and *Denmark* in April of 1940. The program's initial purpose was to prevent Nazi use of the occupied countries' holdings of foreign exchange and to prevent forced repatriation of funds belonging to nationals of those countries. The controls eventually involved punitive measures, as they were applied to other occupied countries and extended to *Germany, Japan, Italy* and the *whole of Europe* in 1941, and as a protective measure to prevent looting of U.S. deposits of *Nazi opponents in occupied countries in Europe*. After the formal entry of the United States into the war, the program became the major American instrument of economic warfare against the Axis powers with activities ranging from the control of most enemy property in the United States to restriction of foreign trade and financial operations and related activities.[6]

The Creation of OFAC and Sanctions in the 1950–1970s. After the FFC was disbanded in late 1948, the sanctions administration function was reformulated and placed in the

---

4. This paragraph and part of the next paragraph are edited excerpts of an unpublished history of sanctions drafted by former OFAC and Treasury personnel and also of a short history of the FFC found on the OFAC website at http://www.treasury.gov/resource-center/faqs/Sanctions/Pages/answer.aspx#2.

5. Trading With the Enemy Act (TWEA), 50 U.S.C. App.§§ 5, 16.

6. The Foreign Funds Control program was concluded in June 1995 after OFAC unblocked the assets, frozen since 1940, of the newly liberated countries of Latvia, Lithuania, and Estonia and removed the regulations (31 CFR 520). *See* http://www.gpo.gov/fdsys/pkg/FR-1995-06-29/pdf/95-15927.pdf. The United States had never recognized Stalin's forced incorporation of these Baltic countries in 1940 into the Soviet Union. In addition to the phased unblocking of assets in the decades after World War II, OFAC also administered restrictions on the trading of U.S. dollar- denominated bearer securities believed to have been looted during the war by Germany. *See* http://webcache.googleusercontent.com/search?q=cache:BYy7kIekZtwJ:www.clintonlibrary.gov/assets/storage/Research%2520-%2520Digital%2520Library/holocaust/theft/Box%2520186/6997222-defrosting-foreign-funds-control.pdf+&cd=5&hl=en&ct=clnk&gl=us&client=firefox-a, and http://webcache.google usercontent.com/search?q=cache:vHv6RUILv4sJ:www.clintonlibrary.gov/assets/storage/Research%2520-%2520Digital%2520Library/holocaust/theft/Box%2520197/6997222-blocked-foreign-assets-in-the-us-1983-1984.pdf+&cd=7&hl=en&ct=clnk&gl=us&client=firefox-a.

Office of Foreign Assets Control in December 1950, following the entry of China into the Korean War and the declaration of a national emergency by President Truman, under authority of TWEA. The Foreign Asset Control Regulations issued shortly thereafter, blocked all *Chinese* and *North Korean* property under U.S. jurisdiction and banned all transactions with China and North Korea and nationals thereof.[7] Chinese assets in the United States were unblocked in 1980 as a part of an overall financial claims settlement between the two countries.[8]

Sanctions imposed against North Korea, under TWEA, and subsequently under the International Emergency Economic Powers Act ("IEEPA"),[9] have continued for over 60 years.[10] More recently, certain North Korean institutions have also been named by OFAC as Specially Designated Nationals[11] and have had assets blocked and transactions prohibited under counter-proliferation programs for alleged money laundering pursuant to assisting North Korea in its nuclear proliferation procurement activities. Import of goods, services, or technology from North Korea to the United States are prohibited currently without a license from OFAC.

Economic sanctions also were imposed under TWEA against *Vietnam* (1964) and *Cambodia* (1975) in response to the Communist takeovers[12] and remained in effect until terminated on February 3, 1994, by President Bill Clinton, and some follow-on actions into 1995.[13]

---

7. *See* Peterson Institute website: http://www.iie.com/research/topics/sanctions/nk.cfm.

8. *See* Department of State website http://history.state.gov/historicaldocuments/frus1977-80v13/d222 and 45 Fed. Reg. 7224, January 31, 1980. 64.

9. International Emergency Economic Powers Act (IEEPA), 50 U.S.C. §§ 1701–1706.

10. Sanctions against North Korea were originally imposed under the Trading with the Enemy Act and were implemented under the Foreign Assets Control Regulations, 31 C.F.R. part 500. On June 26, 2008, the President signed Proclamation 8271 terminating the application of TWEA authorities with respect to North Korea (effective June 27, 2008) and issued Executive Order 13466, The Foreign Assets Control Regulations, 31 C.F.R. part 500, to the extent they were promulgated under TWEA authority were no longer in force with respect to North Korea. Any North Korean sanctions in the future would be implemented under IEEPA. Subsequently, the President on August 30, 2010, issued Executive Order 13551 with respect to sanctions against North Korea. OFAC issued the North Korea Sanctions Regulations, 31 C.F.R. part 510 (the "NKSR") (75 Fed. Reg. 67912, November 4, 2010), to implement E.O. 13466 and E.O. 13551. On April 18, 2011, the President further modified economic sanctions against North Korea by issuing Executive Order 13570. This information was edited and excerpted from the OFAC website: http://www.treasury.gov/resource-center/sanctions/Programs/Documents/nkorea.pdf.

11. A "specially designated national" is a person (entity or individual) who is owned or controlled by or acting for or on behalf of a sanctioned country or group. In later years, when sanctions programs began targeting narcotics traffickers, terrorist groups, and proliferators of weapons of mass destruction, additional designation criteria were added for those programs to include persons providing material, financial, or technological support to the targeted group or individuals. Persons determined to be SDNs by the US government are placed on the SDN List. Because prohibitions may differ from sanctions program to sanctions program, names on the SDN List indicate which program(s) under which an entity or individual is named.

12. President Gerald R. Ford extended the 1964 sanctions on North Vietnam to cover the reunified nation after the U.S. withdrawal from South Vietnam. (Office of Foreign Assets Control, Department of Treasury, "Foreign Assets Control Regulations," 40 Federal Register 19202–3, May 2, 1975). Source: Michael F. Martin, *U.S.-Vietnam Economic and Trade Relations: Issues for the 113th Congress,*" Congressional Research Service, August 13, 2014.

13. The termination of the embargo followed a series of negotiations over several administrations to resolve wartime issues, and after Vietnam's withdrawal from Cambodia. On March 9, 1995, 60 FR 12885, "Foreign Assets Control Regulations; North Korean Travel and Financial Transactions; Information and Informational Materials," was issued pursuant to The Treasury Department's Office of Foreign Assets Control unblocking assets in which Vietnam or a national thereof has an interest,

Cuba: 1963 to the present. *Cuba* was sanctioned under TWEA with the issuance of the Cuban Assets Control Regulations ("CACR") on July 8, 1963, for its alignment with Soviet-Sino Communism and its related hostile actions. The CACR prohibit all economic transactions and dealings in property in which Cuba[14] has an interest by persons subject to the jurisdiction of the United States. This included by definition foreign subsidiaries of U.S. companies. In 1982, in response to the adventurism and interference by Cuba in the internal affairs of countries in Central and South America and attempts to spread Communism in emerging states in Africa, the Reagan Administration took steps to significantly tighten the embargo, including much more restrictive rules on travel to the island country by U.S. persons to further deprive Cuba of U.S. dollars that could be used to implement its goals.

Congress, witnessing the new potential for sanctions, responded to the calls of the politically powerful Cuban-American community by the passage of the Cuba Democracy Act—enhancing the already comprehensive TWEA-based sanctions against Cuba. Cuba has continued to be sanctioned, in addition to TWEA, by Congress under the Cuban Democracy Act of 1992,[15] the so-called Helms–Burton Act of 1996,[16] the provision for naming terrorist-supporting states under the Export Administration Act (EAA) of 1979 and its implementing regulations (the Export Administration Regulations (EAR)).[17]

In sum, sanctions imposed over the years have been in response to the Castro regime's continued politically repressive actions against the Cuban people, the expropriation of private property, and their numerous continued hostile actions toward the United States. These hostile actions have included Cuba's alignment with the Cold War international communist movement and attempts to politically destabilize regions in the Caribbean, Central and South America, and Africa.

Although the Trade Sanctions Reform and Export Enhancement Act of 2000 permitted some liberalization of agricultural and medical exports to Cuba—under a number of conditions and restrictions—it has left other sanctions largely intact[18] with little licensing discretion accorded to OFAC in certain areas. In recent years, there has been a relaxation of the strict prohibition of travel by U.S. persons to Cuba. However, this activity is still subject to comprehensive regulatory rules administered by OFAC.[19]

Iran: 1979 to the present. Economic sanctions have been imposed against *Iran* on multiple occasions. The first sanctions were imposed upon Iran for the taking of 52 U.S. nationals

---

pursuant to an agreement entered into on January 28, 1995, between the U.S. Government and the Government of the Socialist Republic of Vietnam. Subsequently, the United States and Vietnam signed a bilateral trade agreement (BTA) on July 13, 2000, which went into force on December 10, 2001. Source: Michael F. Martin, *U.S.-Vietnam Economic and Trade Relations: Issues for the 113th Congress*, Congressional Research Service, August 13, 2014.

14. This includes the Cuban Government, Cuban nationals, any person ordinarily resident in Cuba, or any person or entity owned or controlled by or acting for or on behalf of Cuba, wherever in the world located. *See* 31 CFR 515.201; 515.301–515.308.

15. Cuban Democracy Act ("CDA"), USC Title 22. Foreign Relations and Intercourse, Chapter 69. The CDA was implemented by Executive Order (E.O.) 12854 (July 4, 1993) "Implementation of the Cuban Democracy Act." *See also*, http://www.treasury.gov/resource-center/sanctions/Documents/cda.pdf.

16. Cuban Liberty and Democratic Solidarity (Libertad) Act of 1996 (Codified in Title 22, Sections 6021–6091 of the U.S. Code) P.L. 104-114.

17. Export Administration Act (EAA) of 1979 (P.L. 96-72). The EAA has lapsed, and the EAR and the provisions for naming state sponsors of terrorism is now upheld under an Executive Order issued under IEEPA.

18. The Trade Sanctions Reform and Export Enhancement Act of 2000 ("TSRA"), Title IX of Public Law 106 387 (October 28, 2000).

19. *See* 31 CFR 515.560.

as hostages in 1979. Iran's considerable assets in the United States and offshore branches of U.S. banks, amounting at the time to nearly $12 billion, were frozen.[20] The hostages were released after 444 days of captivity with the signing in January 1981 of the Algiers Accords. Following the landmark decision of the Supreme Court in Dames and Moore v. Donald T. Regan, 453 U.S. 654 (1981) issued on July 2, 1981 — recognizing the President's authority to transfer assets and settle claims — the Iran-U.S. Claims Tribunal was established in The Hague to arbitrate pre-1981 disputes between the United States and Iran and to settle claims of certain U.S. nationals against the Government of Iran.[21]

---

20. Sanctions were imposed against Iran in a series of Executive orders (all dates are the effective dates of the orders):
- E.O. 12170 (November 14, 1979), "Blocking Iranian Government Property;
- E.O. 12205 (April 17, 1980), "Prohibiting Certain Transactions With Iran;" and
- E.O. 12211 (April 17, 1980), "Prohibiting Certain Transactions With Iran."

21. The Executive orders to unwind the Iranian Sanctions are:
- E.O. 12276 (January 23, 1981), "Direction Relating to Establishment of Escrow Accounts;"
- E.O. 12277 (January 23, 1981), "Direction To Transfer Iranian Government Assets;"
- E.O. 12278 (January 23, 1981), "Direction To Transfer Iranian Government Assets Overseas;"
- E.O. 12279 (January 23, 1981), "Direction To Transfer Iranian Govt. Assets Held By Domestic Banks;"
- E.O. 12280 (January 23, 1981), "Direction To Transfer Iranian Government Financial Assets Held By Non-Banking Institutions;"
- E.O. 12281 (January 23, 1981), "Direction To Transfer Certain Iranian Government Assets;"
- E.O. 12282 (January 23, 1981), "Revocation of Prohibitions Against Transactions Involving Iran;"
- E.O. 12283 (January 23, 1981), "Non-Prosecution of Claims of Hostages and for Actions at the United States Embassy and Elsewhere;"
- E.O. 12284 (January 23, 1981), "Restrictions on the Transfer of Property of the Former Shah of Iran;" and
- E.O. 12294 (February 26, 1981), "Suspension of Litigation Against Iran."

The implementing regulations were the Iranian Assets Control Regulations (IACR), 31 C.F.R Part 535.

The U.S. Department of State website (http://www.state.gov/documents/organization/153979.pdf) provides the following background to the Algiers Accord and the Iran-U.S. Claims Tribunal at The Hague:

> On January 19, 1981, the United States and Iran entered into an international executive agreement embodied in two declarations of the Government of Algeria, known as the Algiers Accords. Declaration of the Government of the Democratic and Popular Republic of Algeria Relating to the Commitments Made by Iran and the United States ("General Declaration") and Declaration of the Democratic and Popular Republic of Algeria Concerning the Settlement of Claims by the Government of the United States of America and the Government of the Islamic Republic of Iran ("Claims Settlement Declaration") 20 I.L.M. 223 (1981). The Algiers Accords brought about the release of the American hostages and established the Iran U.S. Claims Tribunal ("Tribunal") at The Hague, the Netherlands, to resolve existing disputes between the two countries and their nationals. Under the Algiers Accords, the United States released the vast majority of Iran's blocked assets and transferred them directly to Iran or to various accounts to pay outstanding claims. The claims addressed by the Tribunal include claims of U.S. nationals against the Government of Iran, and government to government claims between the United States and Iran.
>
> After the Accords were concluded, the United States unblocked [and transferred certain] Iranian assets located in the United States, but on March 26, 1981, the United States informed Iran, through the Government of Algeria, that the United States would not approve licenses for the export of Iranian military equipment located in the United States because of the export controls imposed by the Arms Export Control Act and its implementing regulations. Iran sought the return of these items, or in the alternative, their alleged replacement value.
>
> The Tribunal dismissed Iran's claim for compensation based on the U.S. refusal to license the export of Iran's export controlled properties, concluding that Iran had failed to establish that U.S. action resulted in any compensable loss to Iran's pre-November 14, 1979 financial

Sanctions were imposed again on Iran:

- In 1987, in the form of an import embargo[22] because of its threat to international shipping in the Persian Gulf;
- In 1995 and 1997 because of its support for terrorism and terrorist groups and active pursuit of weapons of mass destruction;[23] and
- Again, in recent years because of its efforts to build nuclear weapons and other weapons of mass destruction.

The sanctions imposed in 1995 did not include a blocking of Iranian assets—primarily as a result of certain provisions in the Algiers Accord and a desire to keep the Iran-U.S. Claims Tribunal continuing to function effectively (as it has to this day). Sanctions were imposed without blocking, primarily by the prohibition of import and export transactions involving goods, services, and technology, and dealing in Iranian properties (see especially 31 CFR 560.201–.206). These regulations and sanctions program were aptly titled, the "Iranian Transactions Regulations." ("ITR")[24]

To prevent foreign oil exploration and production companies from inheriting a windfall by stepping into the shoes of U.S. companies that were now prohibited from developing the rich South Pars oil field in Iran, the U.S. Congress passed a series of laws pressing for stronger Executive action against non-U.S. oil companies for certain of their more economically significant activities in Iran. The new laws began to lay the groundwork for the extraterritorial reach of U.S. sanctions, that sought to prevent non-U.S. companies from participating in the development of Iran's vast oil reserves above certain specified

---

position with respect to those properties. Accordingly, the Tribunal did not award any damages to Iran. However, the Tribunal deferred to further proceedings the question of whether certain provisions of the Treasury Department's regulations issued on February 26, 1981 had caused Iran to suffer any harm in connection with its export controlled properties. In a related case, Case A/15 (II:A), the Tribunal had determined that these regulations were improper.

On August 3, 2009, Iran requested that the Tribunal reconsider the decision to dismiss Iran's claim to compensation based on the U.S. refusal to license the export of Iran's export controlled properties. On August 14, 2009, the United States objected to this request because the Tribunal's Rules of Procedure provide no basis for such a review. The United States also requested that the Tribunal issue an additional award dismissing any Iranian claim with respect to the Treasury Department's regulations.

The Algiers Accords, January 19, 1981 can be found at http://www.parstimes.com/history/algiers_accords.pdf.

22. The OFAC "Iran: What You Need to Know About U.S. Sanctions" information sheet found at http://www.treasury.gov/resource-center/sanctions/Programs/Documents/iran.pdf provides the following background:

As a result of Iran's support for international terrorism and its aggressive actions against non-belligerent shipping in the Persian Gulf, President Reagan, on October 29, 1987, issued Executive Order 12613 imposing a new import embargo on Iranian-origin goods and services. Section 505 of the International Security and Development Cooperation Act of 1985 ("ISDCA") was utilized as the statutory authority for the embargo, which gave rise to the Iranian Transactions Regulations, Title 31, Part 560 of the U.S. Code of Federal Regulations (the "ITR").

23. The Executive Orders are:

- E.O. 12957 (March 16, 1995), "Prohibiting Certain Transactions With Respect to the Development of Iranian Petroleum Resources;"
- E.O. 12959 (May 7, 1995), "Prohibiting Certain Transactions With Respect to Iran;" and
- E.O. 13059 (August 20, 1997), "Prohibiting Certain Transactions With Respect to Iran."

24. Iranian Transactions Regulations (ITR), 31 CFR 560 of the U.S. Code of Federal Regulations. These regulations were revised, renamed and reissued in their entirety on October 22, 2012 as the Iranian Transactions and Sanctions Regulations (ITSR).

levels. Foreign companies violating certain parameters in their dealings with Iran were subject to sanctions from a menu of possible financial and commercial prohibitions on their dealings with the U.S. government and U.S. persons.

The Iran and Libya Sanctions Act of 1996 ("ILSA") and later, after sanctions on Libya were removed, called the Iran Sanctions Act ("ISA"), the first in a series of Congressional acts; directed the selection and imposition of sanctions from a menu of specific actions — that included certain transactions prohibitions — against non-U.S. companies if they assisted Iran in the development and production of its oil assets, its refining capabilities and import of refined oil products beyond a certain level.[25]

However, because of the irritation ISA caused to bilateral relations with some of the United States' closest allies, and what seemed to many U.S. policymakers at the time to be an overreaching assertion of U.S. extraterritorial jurisdiction over non-U.S. companies' otherwise lawful activities, the penalties available under the ISA were not employed. In fact, successive Administrations between 1995 and 2010 declined to take action against any non-U.S. companies that raised ISA sanctions issues.

Congress addressed this situation when it passed the Comprehensive Iran Sanctions, Accountability, and Divestment Act of 2010 ("CISADA")[26] and then the Iran Threat Reduction and Syria Human Rights Act of 2012 ("ITRA").[27] Both Acts, among other things, added additional causes for sanctions and both amended ISA to provide new sanctions options under that statute. Additionally, CISADA, the National Defense Authorization Act for Fiscal Year 2012 (NDAA)[28] and the Iran Freedom and Counter-proliferation Act of 2012 (IFCA)[29] added their own new sets of sanctions.[30,31]

By 2010, Congressional demands and Iran's continuing support for terrorism and its potential for development of a nuclear threat led to a series of enforcement actions against third country companies involved in activity proscribed by ISA as amended by CISADA and over time to new more broadly constructed Executive Orders to implement the

---

25. P.L. 104-172 104th Congress August 5, 1996, Iran and Libya Sanctions Act of 1996 (referred to as ILSA, and later when it was amended and Libya was dropped, ISA).

26. Comprehensive Iran Sanctions, Accountability, and Divestment Act of 2010 (CISADA), (P.L. 111-195; 22 U.S.C. 8501 et seq.

27. Iran Threat Reduction and Syria Human Rights Act of 2012 ("ITRA") (P.L. 112-158; 22 U.S.C. 8701 et seq.).

28. National Defense Authorization Act for Fiscal Year 2012 (NDAA) (Sec. 1245 of P.L. 112-81; 22 U.S.C. 8513a; as amended).

29. Iran Freedom and Counter-proliferation Act of 2012 (IFCA); (Title XII, subtitle D, of National Defense Authorization Act for Fiscal Year 2013; NDAA 2013; P.L. 112-239; 22 U.S.C. 8801 et seq.).

30. The Iranian related laws have given rise to new Iranian sanctions programs and prompted changes to the ITR. The Iranian Financial Regulations (31 CFR Part 561) implement parts of Comprehensive Iran Sanctions, Accountability, and Divestment Act of 2010 (CISADA) (subsections 104(c) and (d)), the National Defense Authorization Act of Fiscal Year 2012 (NDAA) (subsections 1245(d)(1), (d)(2), (d)(3), (d)(4)(C),(h), and (g)), (Section 504(a)(1)(B) of the Iran Threat Reduction and Syria Human Rights Act of 2012 (TRA) amends section 1245(d)(4)(D) of the NDAA sections 503 and 504), and the Iran Freedom and Counter-Proliferation Act of 2012 (IFCA) as they relate to foreign financial institutions (section 1247). The Iranian Transactions and Sanctions Regulations (31 CFR Part 560) — which implements ISA, parts of CISADA, NDAA section 1245(c), (d)(1)(B) and (g), TRA sections 218, 602, and 604, and TSRA) is a revision to the ITR. Some sanctions provisions in the recent statutes, such as CISADA, that are related to human rights violations, are covered in the Iranian Human Rights Abuses Sanctions Regulations (31 CFR Part 562).

31. See 50 U.S.C. 1701 note and 22 U.S.C. 8501–8811 for statutory requirements for causes for sanctions and sanctions options.

sanctions provisions of CISADA, ITRA, NDAA and IFCA.[32] Subsequently, this led to amendments to the ITR sanctions program (31 CFR Part 560), since re-named the "Iranian Transactions and Sanctions Regulations" ("ITSR"). The ITSR sanctions, in contrast to the ITR sanctions, along with other amendments block the assets of the Government of Iran, Iranian financial institutions, and other designated parties.[33] Some of the ITSR-designated entities and individuals are also designated under counter-terrorism and counter-proliferation sanctions programs, which have counterpart programs promulgated at the United Nations.[34]

In addition to the ITSR, two other sanctions regulatory programs were developed from this legislation: one imposed sanctions, pursuant to CISADA, on foreign financial institutions engaging in specified transactions involving Iran,[35] and the other dealing with human rights violations.[36] The Congressional statutes directing sanctions against persons in third countries conducting business with Iran, its matrix of targets and provisions, and their integration

---

32. The E.O.s that that underlie these programs and the Iran-specific legislation that they implement are:
- EO. 13553 (September 28, 2010), "Blocking Property of Certain Persons With Respect to Serious Human Rights Abuses By The Government of Iran and Taking Certain Other Actions" (CISADA, IEEPA/NEA);
- EO. 13574 (May 23, 2011), "Authorizing the Implementation of Certain Sanctions Set Forth in the Iran Sanctions Act of 1996, as Amended" (ISA 1996, CISADA, IEEPA/NEA);
- E.O. 13590 (November 20, 2011), "Authorizing the Imposition of Certain Sanctions With Respect to the Provision of Goods, Services, Technology, or Support for Iran's Energy and Petrochemical Sections;"
- E.O. 13599 (February 6, 2012), "Blocking Property of the Government of Iran and Iranian Financial Institutions" (NDAA 2012, IEEPA/NEA);
- E.O. 13606 (April 23, 2012), "Blocking the Property and Suspending Entry Into the United States of Certain Persons With Respect to Grave Human Rights Abuses by the Governments of Iran and Syria via Information Technology;"
- E.O. 13608 (May 1, 2012), "Prohibiting Certain Transactions With and Suspending Entry Into the United States of Foreign Sanctions Evaders With Respect to Iran Syria;"
- E.O. 13622 (July 30, 2012), "Authorizing Additional Sanctions With Respect to Iran" (NDAA 2012, IEEPA/NEA);
- E.O. 13628 (October 9, 2012), "Authorizing the Implementation of Certain Sanctions Set Forth in the Iran Threat Reduction and Syria Human Rights Act of 2012 and Additional Sanctions with Respect to Iran" (ISA 1996, CISADA, ITRA, INA, IEEPA/NEA);
- E.O. 13645 (June 3, 2013), "Authorizing the Implementation of Certain Sanctions Set Forth in the Iran Freedom and Counter-Proliferation Act of 2012 and Additional Sanctions With Respect To Iran" (CISADA, IFCA, INA, IEEPA/NEA).

33. A comprehensive description of the Iranian-related sanctions legislation and how it relates to subsequent Executive Orders can be found at:
- "Iran: U.S. Concerns and Policy Responses," by Kenneth Katzman, Congressional Research Service, December 17, 2014 http://www.fas.org/sgp/crS/Mideast/RL32048.pdf;
- "Iran: U.S. Economic Sanctions and the Authority to Lift Restrictions" by Dianne E. Rennack, Congressional Research Service, December 11, 2014, http://fas.org/sgp/crS/Mideast/R43311.pdf; and
- "Overview of U.S. Sanctions on Iran Pertaining to Activities and Transactions by non-U.S. Individuals and Entities," March 28, 2014, U.S. Department of State, http://www.state.gov/documents/organization/224453.pdf.

34. Some examples of the UN Security Council Resolutions ("UNSCRs) with relevance to Iran and counter-proliferation are UNSCR 1540, 1673, 1696, 1737, 1747, 1803, and 1929.

35. Implemented in regulations at 31 CFR Part 561 by OFAC and named the "Iranian Financial Sanction Regulations," containing CISADA and NDAA-based sanctions on certain financial institutions for knowingly engaging in or facilitating certain activities for or on behalf of Iran.

36. Implemented in regulations at 31 CFR Part 562 by OFAC and named the "Iranian Human Rights Abuses Sanctions Regulations."

into IEEPA-based programs presents one of the most, if not the most, complex implementation and administration of sanctions in the history of sanctions.

South Africa. Sanctions were imposed against *South Africa* as directed by Congress under the Comprehensive Anti-Apartheid Act of 1986[37] prohibiting new investment in South Africa[38] and certain other specific measures to pressure the government to abandon the apartheid regime. This led some U.S. companies to disinvest altogether from South Africa. Over the next several years, these sanctions had their intended effect. Prime Minister "F. W. de Klerk, in a move that surprised observers, announced in his opening address to Parliament in February 1990 that he was lifting the ban on the ANC and other black liberation parties, allowing freedom of the press, and releasing political prisoners.... After Prime Minister de Klerk agreed to democratic elections for the country, the United States lifted sanctions and increased foreign aid.... In April 1994, Nelson Mandela was elected as South Africa's first black president." [39]

Nicaragua, Panama and Haiti. In Central America, certain economic and trade sanctions were imposed against *Nicaragua* because of the policies of the Sandinista regime of Daniel Ortega,[40] and sanctions against *Panama* prohibiting payments, including especially tax payments, to the Government following the coup-d'état and narcotics trafficking by its leader, Manuel Noriega.[41] Sanctions were imposed against *Haiti* in 1992 following the stolen election involving then President-elect Aristide.[42]

Serbia and Montenegro. In the Balkans, sanctions were imposed against *Serbia by both the United States and the UN* in 1992[43] and were enhanced as the Serbs resisted. Jeffrey Johnson in his dissertation writes:[44]

> In April 1993, after the Bosnian Serbs failed to support the Vance Owen Peace Plan, the UNSC issued UNSCR 820 against FRY (S/M) [the Federal Republic of Yugoslavia (Serbia/Montenegro)]. This resolution tightens the sanctions and calls for stronger enforcement measures on the Danube River and in the Adriatic Sea. In addition, the United States has helped block FRY (S/M) membership in

---

37. President Reagan implemented the Comprehensive Anti-Apartheid Act of 1986 by issuing, "Executive Order 12571 (October 27, 1986) "Implementation of the Comprehensive Anti-Apartheid Act," and codified at 31 CFR 545 by OFAC and named the "South African Transactions Regulations."

38. Pub. L. 99–440 Section 310 (a), "No national of the United States may, directly or through another person, make any new investment in South Africa."

39. Quote from Department of State website, http://2001-2009.state.gov/r/pa/ho/time/pcw/98678.htm.

40. President Reagan issued Executive Order 12513 (May 1, 1985) "Prohibiting trade and certain other transactions involving Nicaragua," implementing sanctions against Nicaragua under IEEPA and codified in regulations at 31 CFR 540 by OFAC.

41. President Reagan issued Executive Order 12635 (April 8, 1988), "Prohibiting certain transactions with respect to Panama" and codified in regulations at 31 CFR 565 by OFAC.

42. President Bush issued Executive Order 12775 (October 4, 1991), "Prohibiting Certain transactions with respect to Haiti" and codified in regulations at 31 CFR 580 by OFAC.

43. President Bush issued Executive Order 12808 (May 30, 1992), "Blocking "Yugoslav Government" Property and Property of the Governments of Serbia and Montenegro." Other E.O.s were issued for these sanctions. President Clinton issued Executive Order 13088 (June 9, 1998), "Blocking Property of the Governments of the Federal Republic of Yugoslavia (Serbia and Montenegro), the Republic of Serbia, and the Republic of Montenegro, and Prohibiting New Investment in the Republic of Serbia in Response to the Situation in Kosovo." Other orders related to these were Executive Orders 12810 of June 5, 1992, E.O. 12831 of January 15, 1993, E.O. 12846 of April 25, 1993, 12934 of October 25, 1994, E.O. 13121 of April 30, 1999.

44. "Economic Sanctions: Effectiveness as a Foreign Policy Tool in the Case of the Former Yugoslavia" by Jeffrey L. Johnson, December 1998, Naval Postgraduate School, Monterey, California, p. 18.

financial institutions such as the IMF, World Bank, and the European Bank for Reconstruction and Development. Further, the United States froze all foreign assets of FRY (S/M) and their proxies in Bosnia, the Bosnian Serbs.

Johnson explains how devastating these sanctions were to Serbia:[45]

> According to FRY (S/M) Vice-Premier Dragan Tomic, the cumulative losses caused by the sanctions amounted to between $100 billion and $150 billion.[46] Along with destroying FRY (S/M)'s industrial export markets, the sanctions caused a severe shortages of imported spare parts and raw materials. In 1993 alone, FRY (S/M)'s industrial output fell by 40 percent and retail sales dropped 70 percent from 1992 figures. Because of the drop in sales, approximately 60 percent of the industrial labor force was laid off.[47] Inflation that became hyper-inflation undermined the integrity of FRY (S/M)'s currency and eliminated the value of savings. Inflation was 122 percent in 1991; 9,000 percent in 1992; and was more than 100 trillion percent in 1993.[48]

Ultimately, the sanctions had their intended policy effect:[49]

> … from the outbreak of hostilities to the failed Vance-Owen Peace Plan, the one stumbling block was a Bosnian-Serb endorsement to any given peace plan. Thus, the tactic of the European negotiators, and later the U.S. negotiation team led by Richard Holbrooke, was to force Milosevic to not only represent the FRY (S/M), but the Bosnian Serbs as well. This tactic of "splitting the Serbs" circumvented the ultra-nationalist Bosnian-Serb leadership (Radovan Karadzic and BSA General Ratko Mladic), thereby eliminating them as a blocking force to any future peace proposals. David Owen states: "I had no doubt then, and have never doubted since, that it was the prospect of financial sanctions which Milosevic most feared: the chance of avoiding any further economic misery was too attractive domestically for him to go on humoring Karadzic as he obstructed virtually any deal."[50]

Getting Milosevic to negotiate on behalf of the Bosnian Serbs ran counter to a major FRY (S/M) policy goal; that being a Greater Serbia. Milosevic rose to power on a nationalist platform. Once it became evident that the former Yugoslavia would break apart, Milosevic espoused the policy of uniting all the Serbs under the FRY (S/M) umbrella of a "Greater Serbia." If the west wanted to "split the Serbs" and have Milosevic sign a peace accord that included UN Security Council Resolution goals, then the west had to force Milosevic to abandon the "Greater Serbia" concept. Owen states that sanctions had an effect in forcing Milosevic to abandon this ideal: "From this point, 25 April 1993, onwards Milosevic formally

---

45. "Economic Sanctions: Effectiveness as a Foreign Policy Tool in the Case of the Former Yugoslavia" by Jeffrey L. Johnson, December 1998, Naval Postgraduate School, Monterey, California, p. 86.

46. "Analysis: Moves to Lift Sanctions are Reward for Serbian Leader [on line]," Reuters Information Service, 21 November 1995 (accessed 19 April 1998); available from http://www2.nando.netinewsroomintrilworld/112195/world1901side3.html; Internet.

47. American University, Serbia Sanctions and the Environment [on line] (Washington D.C.: American University, July 1995, accessed 28 April 1998; available from http://gurukul.ucc.american.edu/TED/SERBSANC.htm; Internet.

48. Department of State, Inter-Agency Task Force on Serbian Sanctions, UN Sanctions Against Belgrade: Lessons Learned for Future Regimes (Washington, D.C., June 1996), 3.

49. "Economic Sanctions: Effectiveness as a Foreign Policy Tool in the Case of the Former Yugoslavia" by Jeffrey L. Johnson, December 1998, Naval Postgraduate School, Monterey, California, pp. 60–61.

50. David Owen, *Balkan Odyssey*, 153.

gave up Greater Serbia and argued for a settlement on terms a majority in the Security Council could have accepted, and throughout the next two years he did not waver in seeking such a solution."[51]

After the Serbian sanctions had concluded, sanctions were continued against the *Balkans War Criminals* in 2001[52] in response to the earlier military and genocidal acts of Slobodan Milosevic and Radovan Karadžić.

Sudan. On November 3, 1997, the President imposed a trade embargo against the territory of Sudan and a comprehensive blocking of the Government of Sudan[53] due to the policies and actions of the Government of Sudan, including continued support for international terrorism, ongoing efforts to destabilize neighboring governments, and the prevalence of human rights violations, including slavery and the denial of religious freedom. "Later, in response to United Nations Security Council Resolution 1591 of March 29, 2005, which condemned the continued violations of human rights and international humanitarian law in Sudan's Darfur region, the President on April 26, 2006 found ..." there to be a "....persistence of violence in *Sudan's Darfur region*, particularly against civilians and including sexual violence against women and girls, and by the deterioration of the security situation and its negative impact on humanitarian assistance efforts" and blocked "....the property of certain persons in connection with the conflict in Darfur."[54]

Subsequently, in 2011, in recognition of the newly established state of *South Sudan*, OFAC made clear that the Sudan sanctions did not apply to that new country, except for transactions that also involved Sudan (such as South Sudanese oil being shipped through a Sudanese pipeline to Khartoum). An OFAC Fact Sheet at that time explained:[55]

> On January 9, 2011, in a popular referendum, the people of Southern Sudan voted in favor of independence. On July 9, 2011, Southern Sudan gained its independence, becoming the new Republic of South Sudan, and was formally recognized by the United States Government. Since July 9, 2011, the Republic of South Sudan has been an independent state. As such, it is no longer subject to the Sudanese Sanctions Regulations (SSR) administered by the U.S. Department of the Treasury's Office of Foreign Assets Control (OFAC).

> While the Republic of South Sudan is no longer subject to the SSR, certain activities in or involving the Republic of South Sudan continue to be prohibited by the SSR, absent authorization from OFAC, given the interdependence between certain sectors of the economies of the Republic of South Sudan and Sudan. In order to encourage U.S. investment in the Republic of South Sudan, OFAC has today issued two general licenses (GLs) that authorize, to the extent otherwise prohibited by the SSR, (1) activities and transactions relating to the petroleum and petrochemical industries in the Republic of South Sudan and related financial transactions and (2) the transshipment of goods, technology, and services through Sudan to and from the Republic of South Sudan and related financial transactions.

---

51. *Id.*

52. President Bush issued Executive Order 13219 (June 27, 2001), "Blocking Property of Persons Who Threaten International Stabilization Efforts in the Western Balkans."

53. E.O. 13067, *see* http://www.treasury.gov/resource-center/sanctions/Programs/Documents/sudan.txt.

54. E.O. 13400, on April 26, 2006. *See* http://www.treasury.gov/resource-center/sanctions/Programs/Documents/sudan.txt.

55. "Office of Foreign Assets Control Fact Sheet Regarding Activities in the Republic of South Sudan," Date: December 8, 2011, http://www.treasury.gov/resource-center/sanctions/Programs/Documents/south_sudan_12082011.pdf.

Subsequently, because of violence in South Sudan between competing political factions of the newly independent state, President Obama, on April 3, 2014, issued Executive Order 13664 targeting sanctions against certain persons determined to be fostering such violent activity.[56]

Syria. *Syrian* sanctions began pursuant to the Syria Accountability Act of 2003 ("SAA") and later expanded by successive Executive Orders.[57] The SAA prohibited exports to Syria of products of the United States except for food and medicine, which were exempted.[58] Successive Executive orders prohibited, *inter alia*, new investment and the export of services by U.S. persons to Syria and the targeting with sanctions of persons in the leadership and principal supporters of the Assad regime.[59]

Burma. *Myanmar (Burma)* sanctions began pursuant to Section 570 of the Foreign Operations, Export Financing, and Related Programs Appropriations Act, 1997 and later pursuant to the Burma Freedom and Democracy Act of 2003. They were subsequently expanded and implemented by successive laws and Executive Orders.[60] The primary focus

---

56. E.O. 13664 (April 3, 2014), "Blocking Property of Certain Persons With Respect to South Sudan."

57. Syria Accountability and Lebanese Sovereignty Act of 2003 (Pub. L. 108-175). The follow-on Executive orders relating to sanctions against Syria are:
- E.O. 13338 (May 12, 2004), "Blocking Property of Certain Persons and Prohibiting the Export of Certain Goods to Syria;"
- E.O. 13399 (April 26, 2006), "Blocking Property of Additional Persons in Connection With the National Emergency With Respect to Syria;"
- E.O. 13460 (February 15, 2008), "Blocking Property of Additional Persons in Connection With the National Emergency With Respect to Syria;"
- E.O. 13572 (April 29, 2011), "Blocking Property of Certain Persons with Respect to Human Rights Abuses in Syria;"
- E.O. 13573 (May 18, 2011), "Blocking Property Of Senior Officials Of The Government Of Syria;"
- E.O. 13582 (August 18, 2011), "Blocking Property of the Government of Syria and Prohibiting Certain Transactions with Respect to Syria;"
- E.O. 13606 (April 23, 2012), "Blocking the Property and Suspending Entry Into the United States of Certain Persons With Respect to Grave Human Rights Abuses by the Governments of Iran and Syria via Information Technology;" and
- E.O. 13608 (May 1, 2012), "Prohibiting Certain Transactions With and Suspending Entry Into the United States of Foreign Sanctions Evaders With Respect to Iran and Syria."

58. Implemented by U.S. Department of Commerce, Bureau of Industry and Security in General Order 2 to Supplement No. 1 to 15 CFR Part 736 of the Export Administration Regulations (May 14, 2004).

59. The E.O.s were implemented and codified in regulations at 31 CFR Part 542 by OFAC.

60. Section 570 of the Foreign Operations, Export Financing, and Related Programs Appropriations Act, 1997 (Public Law 104–208), Burma Freedom and Democracy Act of 2003, PL 108-61 (50 U.S.C. § 1701 note). The initiating and follow-on Executive orders related to sanctions against Burma are:
- E.O. 13047 (May 21, 1997), "Prohibiting New Investment in Burma;"
- E.O. 13310 (July 29, 2003), "Blocking Property of the Government of Burma and Prohibiting Certain Transactions;"
- E.O. 13448 (October 19, 2007), "Blocking Property and Prohibiting Certain Transactions Related to Burma;"
- E.O. 13464 (May 1, 2008), "Blocking Property and Prohibiting Certain Transactions Related To Burma."

On July 29, 2008, the President signed into law the Tom Lantos Block Burmese JADE (Junta's Anti-Democratic Efforts) Act of 2008 (Public Law 110-286) ("JADE Act") which, among other things, imposed sanctions on certain categories of persons enumerated in the JADE Act, and amended the BFDA importation ban to prohibit the importation into the United States of any jadeite or rubies mined or extracted from Burma and any articles of jewelry containing jadeite or rubies mined or extracted from Burma.

of successive sanctions Executive orders was to prohibit new investment, the export of financial services, and the import into the United States of products of Burma. On July 11, 2012 and August 7, 2013, sanctions were modified by President Obama to remove several sanctions.[61] Other financial and trade restrictions were suspended by the issuance of general licenses. However, certain military leadership and entities targeted and named on the OFAC SDN List remain blocked. This includes most major Burmese international banks with certain exceptions.[62]

Libya. *Libya* was the target of various sanctions in the 1980s and 1990s for its terrorist activities—first an asset blocking and trade embargo imposed by the United States in 1986 for a night club bombing in Italy and then later in the early 1990s pursuant to a United Nations Security Council Resolution promulgated in response to the 1988 bombing of Pan Am Flight 103 over Lockerbie, Scotland.[63] A lifting of these sanctions[64] in 2004 was a result of a partial settlement of these issues with Libyan President Muammar Gaddafi and Libya's disclosure and renunciation of its secret nuclear program. According to an article on the Arms Control Association website:[65]

> On December 19, 2003, long-time Libyan President Moammar Gaddafi stunned much of the world by renouncing Tripoli's weapons of mass destruction (WMD) programs and welcoming international inspectors to verify that Tripoli would follow through on its commitment.

---

61. The Executive orders that removed many of the restrictions imposed in previous Burma-related E.O.s were:
- E.O. 13619 (July 11, 2012), "Executive Order Blocking Property of Persons Threatening the Peace, Security, or Stability Of Burma;" and
- E.O. 13651 (August 7, 2013), "Prohibiting Certain Imports of Burmese Jadeite and Rubies."

"On August 6, 2013, in light of the expiration of the BFDA and the importation ban contained therein, as amended by the JADE Act, the President issued E.O. 13651, revoking the provisions of E.O. 13310 implementing the broad BFDA importation ban on products of Burma. However, E.O. 13651 continued the prohibition on the importation into the United States of any jadeite or rubies mined or extracted from Burma and any articles of jewelry containing jadeite or rubies mined or extracted from Burma that was originally imposed by the JADE Act amendments to the BFDA. Also in E.O. 13651, the President waived the sanctions described in section 5(b) of the JADE Act."

62. Some of the sanctions imposed were suspended by the issuance of a series of General Licenses. For example, *see* Burma General Licenses16 and 17 on July 11, 2012 authorizing some exportation and reexportation of financial services and investment, and Burma General License 19 on February 22, 2013, "authorizing most transactions, including opening and maintaining accounts and conducting a range of other financial services, with four of Burma's major blocked financial institutions: Asia Green Development Bank, Ayeyarwady Bank, Myanma Economic Bank, and Myanma Investment and Commercial Bank."

All of the above quotes from "Burma Sanctions Program, Department of Treasury, Office of Foreign Assets Control," http://www.treasury.gov/resource-center/sanctions/Documents/burma.pdf.

63. President Reagan signed Executive Order 12543 (January 7. 1986), "Prohibiting trade and certain transactions involving Libya, and the next day he signed Executive Order 12544 (January 8, 1986), "Blocking Libyan Government property in the United States or held by U.S. persons." After learning of Libya's role in the PanAm 103 bombing, President Clinton signed the Iran and Libya Sanctions Act of 1996, 60 U.S.C. §1701 on August 5, 1996. The United Nations passed several UN Security Council Resolutions imposing economic sanctions, they were 731 (January 21, 1992), 749 (March 31, 1992), and 883 (November 11, 1993).

64. E.O. 13357 (September 20, 2004), "Termination of Emergency Declared in Executive Order 12543 with Respect to the Policies and Actions of the Government of Libya and Revocation of Related Executive Orders."

65. "Chronology of Libya's Disarmament and Relations with the United States," by Kelsey Davenport on the Arms Control Association website http://www.armscontrol.org/factsheets/LibyaChronology.

Following Gaddafi's announcement, inspectors from the United States, United Kingdom, and international organizations worked to dismantle Libya's chemical and nuclear weapons programs, as well as its longest-range ballistic missiles. Washington also took steps toward normalizing its bilateral relations with Tripoli, which had essentially been cut off in 1981....

The factors that induced Libya to give up its weapons programs are debatable. Many Bush administration officials have emphasized the U.S.-led 2003 invasion of Iraq, as well as the October 2003 interdiction of a ship containing nuclear-related components destined for Libya, as key factors in Tripoli's decision. But outside experts argue that years of sanctions and diplomatic efforts were more important.

A sanctions program was imposed in 2011 relating to the Qaddafi regime's brutal suppression of public protests against his government during the Arab Spring uprisings.[66] His regime was subsequently overthrown and the country is now engaged in sectarian conflict.

Iraq: 1990, The First Gulf War. Comprehensive sanctions were used by the United States against *Iraq* immediately following its invasion of Kuwait in August 2, 1990 as a key component of what was called Operation Desert Shield,[67] and a key first step in the military action called Operation Desert Storm. Also the *Government of Kuwait*'s vast direct and portfolio investments in the United States and in countries around the world were blocked to protect them from being looted by Iraq.[68] Sanctions quickly became an international effort. The United Kingdom and France froze Iraqi assets, and Russia suspended delivery of military equipment also on August 2, 1990, and the UN passed UNSCR 660 condemning the Iraqi invasion. The following day, Germany, Belgium, Netherlands, Luxembourg,

---

66. Sanctions were also imposed again in a new program in 2011 for the Qadaffi regime's brutal suppression of public protests against his government when President Obama issued Executive Order 13566 (February 25, 2011). "Blocking Property and Prohibiting Certain Transactions Related to Libya."

67. Iraq-related Executive orders were as follows:
- E.O. 12722 (August 2, 1990), "Blocking Iraqi Government Property And Prohibiting Transactions With Iraq;"
- E.O. 12724 (August 9, 1990), "Blocking Iraqi Government Property And Prohibiting Transactions With Iraq;"
- E.O. 12817 (October 23, 1992), "Transfer Of Certain Iraqi Government Assets Held By Domestic Banks;"
- E.O. 13290 (March 20, 2003), "Confiscating and Vesting Certain Iraqi Property;"
- E.O. 13303 (May 22, 2003), "Protecting the Development Fund for Iraq and Certain Other Property in Which Iraq Has an Interest;"
- E.O. 13315 (August 29, 2003), "Blocking Property of the Former Iraqi Regime, Its Senior Officials and Their Family Members, and Taking Certain Other Actions;"
- E.O. 13350 (July 30, 2004), "Termination of Emergency Declared in Executive Order 12722 With Respect to Iraq and Modification of Executive Order 13290, Executive Order 13303, and Executive Order 13315;"
- E.O. 13364 (November 29, 2004), "Modifying the Protection Granted to the Development Fund for Iraq;"
- E.O. 13438 (July 17, 2007) "Blocking Property of Certain Persons Who Threaten Stabilization Efforts in Iraq."

68. The Kuwait-related Executive Orders were:
- E.O. 12723 (August 2, 1990), "Blocking Kuwaiti Government Property;"
- E.O. 12725 (August 13, 1990), "Blocking Kuwaiti Government Property and Prohibiting Trans-actions With Kuwait." And the Executive Order removing these sanctions was:
- Executive Order 12771 (July 29, 1991), "Revoking Earlier Orders With Respect to Kuwait."

and Norway froze Kuwaiti assets. On August 4, the EU imposed economic sanctions. On August 5, China imposed an arms embargo, and Japan imposed trade restrictions. On August 6, the United Nations passed UN Security Council Resolution 661, calling upon and directing member states to impose comprehensive trade and financial sanctions.[69]

Prior to this first Gulf War, sanctions made Iraq's access to war materiel more difficult. At the end of the war, sanctions remained on Iraq, and did not end until 2003, after the end of the second Gulf War. In between the two wars the sanctions program substantially reduced Iraqi trade and access to foreign funds. In response to cries for humanitarian relief for Iraq, the so-called UN "Oil-for-Food" program was established. The program was intended to allow Iraq to earn money to buy food and medicine by selling oil under the auspices of the United Nations, and, by implementing a licensing program, to permit the purchase of food and medicine with payment from the escrowed oil sales fund. The intent was to provide humanitarian relief while preventing Iraq from earning and using funds to obtain weapons of mass destructions.

Under the program, Iraq would identify desired food and medicine purchases from vendors it chose, and a UN committee would decide whether to license the vendors. This program was one of the first programs in which the UN itself directly supervised a sanctions licensing effort. However, because there were many charges of fraud and abuse in the deals that Iraq had made with its oil buyers, and the vendors from whom Iraq purchased food and medicine, and the subsequent diversion and misuse of funds, a UN commission was established on April 21, 2004, under Paul Volcker, a former head of the U.S. Federal Reserve, to investigate.[70] This Commission subsequently alleged that there were a number of abuses— estimating that at least $2 billion worth of funds were diverted. The Commission advocated better UN oversight and controls for any such future UN-run sanctions program.[71]

Since the 1990s, sanctions have been employed against non-state actors, as well as state actors:

Counter-Terrorism: A variety of sanctions have been imposed against terrorists and terrorist groups around the globe who seek to use terror to forward their political goals. The first counter-terrorism sanctions were imposed in 1979 against terrorism-supporting countries, under the Export Administration Act (EAA) of 1979, which required the Department of State to identify terrorism-supporting countries—countries determined to have provided support for repeated acts of international terrorism.[72] The names of these State-identified countries, as they are designated, are incorporated into the Export Administration Regulations (EAR) and the items controlled for sale and export to these countries under EAA section 6(j) are described in 15 CFR Chapter VII Supplement 2 to part 742. Due to the lapse of the EAA and the reluctance of Congress to renew this authority, IEEPA has been used as the substitute authority to support the provisions of

---

69. *Economic Sanctions Reconsidered: History and Current Policy*, Vol. 2, 2nd ed., by Gary Clyde Hufbauer, Jeffrey J. Schott, Kimberly Ann Elliott, November 1990, Institution for International Economics, pp. 283–284.

70. UNSCR 1538 (April 21, 2004) calls for cooperation with the newly established Commission.

71. *See* "Head of Oil-for-Food Inquiry Calls for Wide-Ranging Reform within United Nations" at the UN website http://www.un.org/News/Press/docs/2005/ik524.doc.htm.

72. Export Administration Act (EAA) of 1979 (P.L. 96-72) 6(j) provision. The sanctions that result from a 6(j) designation involve restrictions on sales of U.S. dual use items, a ban on direct U.S. financial assistance and arms sales, a requirement that the United States vote to oppose multilateral lending, a withholding of U.S. foreign assistance to Suppliers [to] Terrorism List Countries, and withholding of U.S. aid to organizations that assist a 6(j) country. Kenneth Katzman, *Iran Sanctions*, Congressional Research Service, October 23, 2014, pp 3–4.

the EAA as implemented in the EAR.[73] Currently *Syria, Cuba, Iran,* and *Sudan* are listed, and in the past *South Yemen, Libya, North Korea,* and *Iraq* were listed, but have since been removed. Those named are referred to as 6(j) countries, after the section in the EAA.[74] OFAC promulgated the "Terrorism List Governments Sanctions Regulations," 31 CFR 596 to address some of the sanctions prohibitions related to 6(j) countries.

The second set of economic sanctions against terrorists was imposed by President Clinton on January 23, 1995, when he issued Executive Order 12947, "Prohibiting Transactions with Terrorists Who Threaten to Disrupt the Middle East Peace Process."[75] Persons (entities and individuals) named under these sanctions are referred to as Specially Designated Terrorists (SDTs) and are included on the OFAC SDN List, resulting in the blocking of their assets in the United States and the prohibition on U.S. persons to engage in transactions of any nature with a person so-named. Osama bin Laden was first designated as a terrorist in 1998 under these sanctions with the issuance of E.O. 13099 (August 20, 1998) — a revision of E.O. 12947.

The third set of sanctions was against foreign terrorist organizations. On April 24, 1996, President Clinton signed the Antiterrorism and Effective Death Penalty Act of 1996 ("AEDPA"),[76] which requires the Department of State to name, in consultation with Treasury and Justice, and include on the OFAC SDN List, terrorist groups, to whom U.S. persons are prohibited from providing material support and fundraising. U.S. financial institutions are required to block their funds. These designations must be renewed every two years documenting their continued involvement in terrorist activity over the previous two year period, or they lapse with regard to that named terrorist group.[77] The AEDPA made it a criminal offense for U.S. persons to engage in financial transactions with a designated foreign terrorist organization.

The fourth set of sanctions against *terrorist groups,* "The Global War on Terrorism" sanctions program was initiated by President Bush on September 23, 2001, in response to the terrorist acts of September 11, 2001, when he issued E.O. 13224, "Blocking Property and Prohibiting Transactions with Persons who Commit, Threaten to Commit, or Support Terrorism." The groups, entities and individuals named under these sanctions are called Specially Designated Global Terrorists (SDGTs).[78]

For slightly more than two years, the *Taliban* was sanctioned as a terrorist-supporting group under its own sanctions program initiated by Executive Order 13129 on July 4,

---

73. E.O. 12924 (August 19, 1994).

74. Syria was designated in 1979, Cuba in 1982, Iran in 1984, and Sudan in 1993. http://www.state.gov/j/ct/list/c14151.htm. The following countries had been designated and removed as follows: South Yemen (1979–1990), Libya (1979–2006), North Korea (1988–2008), and Iraq (on and off the list, 1979–1982; and 1990–2004) (*See* Mark P. Sullivan, "Cuba and the State Sponsors of Terrorism List," Congressional Research Service Report for Congress, Updated May 13, 2005. As noted in 74 FR 23112, May 18, 2009, Section 321 of the Antiterrorism and Effective Death Penalty Act of 1996, 18 U.S.C. 2332d (the "Act"), it is a criminal offense for United States persons, except as provided in regulations issued by the Secretary of the Treasury in consultation with the Secretary of State, to engage in financial transactions with the governments of countries designated under section 6(j) of the Export Administration Act of 1979, 50 U.S.C. App. 2405(j) (the "EAA"), as supporting international terrorism. To implement section 321 of the Act, OFAC promulgated the Terrorism List Governments Sanctions Regulations, 31 CFR part 596.

75. *See* Terrorism Sanctions Regulations, 31 CFR part 595.

76. Antiterrorism and Effective Death Penalty Act of 1996, Pub. L. No. 104-132, 110 Stat. 1214.

77. Those groups named under these sanctions are called Foreign Terrorist Organizations. *See* Foreign Terrorist Organizations Sanctions Regulations, 31 CFR part 597.

78. *See* Global Terrorism Sanctions Regulations, 31 CFR part 594.

1999, "Blocking Property and Prohibiting Transactions With the Taliban." There were some difficulties in establishing this program, largely because of the difficulty in correctly identifying such persons by name and with accurate personal identifying information. President Bush terminated it as a separate sanctions program and moved the Taliban as a named group under the "Global War on Terrorism" sanctions program by issuing Executive Order 13268 on July 2, 2002, "Termination of Emergency With Respect to the Taliban and Amendment of Executive Order 13224 of September 23, 2001."

Collectively these programs have imposed sanctions against terrorist groups, but more importantly they have aimed at the terrorist groups' underlying operational viability—their financial and support networks—especially those of *Al Qaeda, Hezbollah, Hamas, the Taliban*, the Islamic State of Iraq and the Levant ("ISIL"), and against dozens of others.

Counter-Narcotics: President Clinton in October 1995, at the 50th anniversary ceremony commemorating the founding and establishment of the United Nations, announced, as part of the War on Drugs, sanctions against *significant narcotics traffickers in Colombia* located primarily in and around the city of Cali.[79]

The success of the sanctions against *significant narcotics traffickers in Colombia*[80] was recognized by Congress when it passed, the Foreign Narcotics Traffickers Kingpin Act,[81] which provides authority to impose sanctions on narcotics kingpins in *Mexico* and *throughout the world*, and against those that act on behalf of or who assist them. President Clinton signed the Act into law on December 3, 1999. The sanctions do not rely upon IEEPA or the issuance of an Executive order. Like TWEA sanctions, these sanctions are implemented by issuing a regulation and then identifying the names of Kingpins and their subordinates who act on their behalf in a two-tier process.

On July 5, 2000, OFAC issued the Foreign Narcotics Kingpin Sanctions Regulations, 31 CFR Part 598 to implement the law. "The President's designation of kingpins under the Act is based on information provided to him by the Secretary of the Treasury, the Attorney General, the Secretary of Defense, the Secretary of State, and the Director of Central Intelligence following an interagency consultative process. The entities designated by the President, and thereby subject to sanctions under the Act, are referred to as "Tier I" designees.... Although the Kingpin Act does not mandate that secondary (i.e., Tier II) targets be identified, the Act is designed to be implemented like the IEEPA-Colombia program where secondary targets are publicly identified and their assets in the United States blocked."[82] OFAC identifies these secondary targets, puts them on the SDN List and transactions with such named persons by U.S. persons are prohibited.

Blood Diamonds: On April 25, 2003, the President signed the Clean Diamond Trade Act (Pub. L. 108-19) (the "Act"). The Act requires the President to take steps to implement the Kimberley Process Certification Scheme for rough diamonds (KPCS) in the United

---

79. President Clinton on October 21, 1995 signed Executive Order 12978 (October 21, 1995), "Blocking Assets and Prohibiting Transactions With Significant Narcotics Traffickers."

80. OFAC several years later published a report on the impact of the sanctions program on the Colombian Drug Cartels entitled, "Impact Report March 2007: Economic Sanctions Against Colombian Drug Cartels," Office of Foreign Assets Control.

This report can be found at http://www.treasury.gov/resource-center/sanctions/Documents/narco_impact_report_05042007.pdf.

81. Kingpin Act (21 U.S.C. §§ 1901–1908 and 8 U.S.C § 1182.

82. The Judicial Review Commission on Foreign Asset Control ("JRC"), p. 45, 49.

States. On July 29, 2003, the President issued Executive Order 13312, "Implementing the Clean Diamond Trade Act."

Counter-Proliferation: Specifically-named Traffickers in Weapons of Mass Destruction and nuclear materials[83] from and on behalf of *China, North Korea, Pakistan,* and *Syria,* in addition to *Iran,* and those that provide support and financing for proliferation activities face sanctions by being identified and listed on the OFAC SDN List. Additionally, the United States has implemented a protective sanctions program that blocks U.S. payments to *Russia* for their sales of Highly Enriched Uranium to the United States to prevent these funds from being attached by Russia's creditors. The blocked payments are then licensed for release only to Russia.[84]

Repression, Thwarting the Democratic Process, War Criminals, Transnational Crime, Human Rights Violators, Kleptocracy, Infringing on National Sovereignty, etc.: During the last 30 years, economic sanctions have also been imposed on other countries, groups, and individuals, such as *Belarus,*[85] the *Palestinian Authority,*[86] *Western Balkans War Criminals, Cote d'Ivoire,*[87] *Democratic Republic of the Congo,*[88] *Liberia (Former Regime of Charles Taylor),*[89] *Persons Undermining the Sovereignty of Lebanon or Its Democratic Processes and*

---

83. The Executive orders related to counter-proliferation sanctions are:
- E.O. 12938 (November 14, 1994), "Proliferation of Weapons of Mass Destruction;"
- E.O. 13094 (July 29, 1998), "Proliferation of Weapons of Mass Destruction;" and
- E.O. 13382 (June 29, 2005), "Blocking Property of Weapons of Mass Destruction Proliferators and Their Supporters;"

These are codified in regulations at 31 CFR 544 by OFAC.

84. The Executive orders related to protective sanctions for Russian HEU sales to the United States are:
- E.O. 13159 (June 22, 2000), "Blocking Property of the Government of the Russian Federation Relating to the Disposition of Highly Enriched Uranium Extracted From Nuclear Weapons;"
- E.O. 13617 (June 25, 2012), "Blocking Property of the Government of the Russian Federation Relating to the Disposition of Highly Enriched Uranium Extracted From Nuclear Weapons."

These are codified in regulations at 31 CFR 540 by OFAC.

85. Executive Order 13405 (June 16, 2006), "Blocking Property of Certain Persons Undermining Democratic Processes or Institutions in Belarus," and codified in regulations at 31 CFR 548 by OFAC.

86. Hamas is a Foreign Terrorist Organization and is listed as an SDT and an SDGT. Hamas' influence over the government in 2006 led to a freezing of PLA assets. Subsequently, Hamas influence in the PLA-run government in the West Bank has diminished and a General License was issued in 2007 to again permit dealings with the PLA.

87. Executive Order 13396 (February 7, 2006), "Blocking Property of Certain Persons Contributing to the Conflict in Cote d'Ivoire," and codified in regulations at 31 CFR 543 by OFAC.

88. The President issued Executive Order 13413 "Blocking Property of Certain Persons Contributing to the Conflict in the Democratic Republic of Congo" on October 27, 2006, to address the widespread violence and atrocities in the DRC that threatened regional stability, codified in regulations at 31 CFR 547 by OFAC. The United Nations Security Council passed several resolutions:
- UNSCR 1596 (18 April 2005), "Reiterating its serious concern regarding the presence of armed groups and militias in the Eastern part of the Democratic Republic of the Congo, particularly in the provinces of North and South Kivu and in the Ituri district, which perpetuate a climate of insecurity in the whole region;"
- UNSCR1649 (21 December 2005), "Reiterating its serious concern regarding the continuation of hostilities by militias and foreign armed groups in the eastern part of the Democratic Republic of the Congo;"
- UNSCR 1698 (31 July 2006), "Condemning the continuing illicit flow of weapons within and into the Democratic Republic of the Congo."

89. Executive Order 13348 (July 22, 2004), "Blocking Property of Certain Persons and Prohibiting the Importation of Certain Goods from Liberia," and codified in regulations at 31 CFR 593 by OFAC.

Institutions,[90] *Zimbabwe,*[91] *Somalia,*[92] *Angola,*[93] *transnational criminal organizations,*[94] *human rights violators,*[95] *Individuals Responsible for Undermining the Sovereignty, Territorial Integrity and Government of Ukraine,*[96] and *Certain Person with Respect to South Sudan.*[97] These programs are often referred to as "list based" programs as the names of persons and entities sanctioned are contained on the OFAC List of Specially Designated Nationals (the "OFAC SDN List"). In addition, no transactions of any nature can be conducted with any person or entity whose name appears on the OFAC SDN List or with any person or entity owned 50% or more by such named persons.

In addition to the OFAC SDN List, OFAC has created another targeting mechanism called Sectoral Sanction Identifications ("SSI") to implement one part of the *Individuals Responsible for Undermining the Sovereignty, Territorial Integrity and Government of Ukraine* sanctions program. E.O. 13662 identified sectors of the Russian economy to be targeted, such as financial services, energy, metals and mining, engineering, and defense and related material. OFAC has implemented this part of the Executive Order by identifying persons (corporate entities) in these sectors in a set of directives which impose specific restrictions on the dealings U.S. persons may have with them, while still permitting other types of

---

90. E.O. 13441 (August 1, 2007), "Blocking Property Of Persons Undermining The Sovereignty Of Lebanon Or Its Democratic Processes And Institutions," and codified in regulations at 31 CFR 549 by OFAC.
91. The executive orders relating to sanctions against persons in Zimbabwe are:
- E.O. 13288 (March 7, 2003), "Blocking Property of Persons Undermining Democratic Processes or Institutions in Zimbabwe;"
- E.O. 13391 (November 23, 2005), "Blocking Property of Additional Persons Undermining Democratic Processes or Institutions in Zimbabwe;"
- E.O. 13469 (July 25, 2008), "Blocking Property of Additional Persons Undermining Democratic Processes or Institutions in Zimbabwe."
These are codified in regulations at 31 CFR 541 by OFAC.
92. The executive orders relating to sanctions against persons in Somalia are:
- E.O. 13536 (April 13, 2010), "Blocking Property of Certain Persons Contributing to the Conflict in Somalia;"
- E.O. 13620 (July 20, 2012), "Taking Additional Steps to Address the National Emergency With Respect to Somalia."
These are codified in regulations at 31 CFR 551 by OFAC.
93. The executive orders relating to sanctions against UNITA in Angola are:
- E.O. 13069 (December 12, 1997), "Prohibiting Certain Transactions With Respect to UNITA;"
- E.O. 13098 (August 19, 1998), "Blocking Property of UNITA and Prohibiting Certain Transactions with Respect to UNITA."
These are codified in regulations at 31 CFR 553 by OFAC.
94. E.O. 13581 (July 25, 2011), "Blocking Property of Transnational Criminal Organizations," codified in regulations at 31 CFR 590 by OFAC.
95. Sergei Magnitsky Rule of Law Accountability Act of 2012—Public Law 112-208 (Approved December 14, 2012). The sanctions in this act are administered by OFAC. *Also see* Iran Threat Reduction and Syria Human Rights Act of 2012 ("ITRA") (P.L. 112-158; 22 U.S.C. 8701 et seq.) and "Iranian Human Rights Abuses Sanctions Regulation," 31 CFR 562.
96. The executive orders relating to sanctions against persons contributing to the situation in Ukraine are:
- E.O. 13660 (March 6, 2014), "Blocking Property of Certain Persons Contributing to the Situation in Ukraine;"
- E.O. 13661 (March 17, 2014), "Blocking Property of Additional Persons Contributing to the Situation in Ukraine;"
- E.O. 13662 (March 20, 2014), "Blocking Property of Additional Persons Contributing to the Situation in Ukraine."
These are codified in regulations at 31 CFR 589 by OFAC.
97. Executive Order 13664 (April 3, 2014), "Blocking Property of Certain Persons With Respect to South Sudan," codified in regulations at 31 CFR 558.

transactions. SSI directives and the types and range of restrictions found in them may be and have been amended to address the evolving emergency.

Do Sanctions Work?

Economic sanctions are frequently employed, but are often criticized and a misunderstood instrument used for the protection and advancement of U.S. national security and foreign policy goals. Sanctions are not an end in themselves. They are instruments that can be effectively used as a part of, and in the context of, a larger coordinated U.S. and/or international diplomatic and enforcement effort. They can and do provide significant leverage, but they are not a panacea and cannot operate in a vacuum.

Economic sanctions have sometimes been called economic warfare. The analogy between sanctions, or economic warfare, and military actions, or conventional warfare, is a close one. Both come after more moderate measures, such as normal diplomatic efforts, have failed. But like any concerted diplomatic or military initiative, sanctions do not come free. Both involve elevating the interests of the nation-state over the normal commercial activities and interaction of citizens. Both risk unintended casualties in some form and, to many of the individuals and institutions affected, sanctions seem blunt and destructive with high and real costs.

Like any military campaign, to take the analogy one step further, there should be clearly defined, realistic goals and objectives before taking action. Otherwise, it will not be possible to determine how success will be measured.

Some programs have yielded more dramatic or successful results than others. In assessing a sanctions program, the first questions that come to mind for a program are whether it was a good idea or a bad idea, and, the second, was it successful in achieving its goal?[98] Below are some considerations to take into account when addressing these questions; the answer has most often been that economic sanctions have been effective and had greater leverage when the following elements are present:

First: when the sanctions target has substantial dependence upon the international financial and commercial system, such as, external assets that are subject to blocking action, it conducts transactions in U.S. dollars, and/or has a high dependence on imports or exports which can be embargoed. A good example of this was the leverage provided by the unilateral U.S. blocking of Iranian assets in 1979. Iran's dependence on the U.S. financial system, the high dependence at the time on U.S. commerce, and the leverage provided by the $12 billion in Iranian government assets caught by the U.S. blocking action provided the principal lever in the release of the American hostages and negotiating what has proven to be one of the most favorable bilateral claims settlement agreements in U.S. history.

Second: when the United States is able to generate a consensus with other nations, which includes:

- agreeing that a threat is serious;
- obtaining a commitment to absorb the economic and political costs;
- identifying the specific targets of sanctions; and
- developing a common strategy with uniform goals and objectives.

---

98. Over the course of sanctions, critics often claim a program has failed because it has not achieved its purpose quickly, or it has been measured against a purpose for which it was not designed. Any assessment should be made against the policy purposes for which it was imposed, and the changes in the behavior thereafter of the target.

International consensus allows for the imposition of multilateral sanctions, which in recent years have worked better than unilateral sanctions as there are fewer avenues for evasion or sanctions busting.

Third: when there is a fairly uniform and realistic implementation plan so that some countries are not able to shift the burden of sanctions enforcement onto other countries.

Problems arise when there are disparities between nations in:

- the interpretation of permissible business activity with a sanctioned country. Countries with less strict standards gain at the expense of others. Such "free rider" behavior leads to the deterioration of any sanctions regime.
- the granting of licenses to permit otherwise prohibited transactions. When members of an international licensing body take an "if you'll scratch my back, I'll scratch yours" approach, this politicization will ultimately lead to the deterioration of an entire sanctions program.
- enforcing sanctions against violators. Sanctions can have the unfortunate side effect of creating enormous opportunities for profit for those who engage in sanctions-busting activity. Past experience demonstrates these opportunities surface and become known almost immediately to a certain class of unscrupulous profiteers. Strong and coordinated enforcement has proven to be a significant deterrent to sanctions busting and evasion.

The chain is only as strong as the weakest link. Unless nations are willing and able to maintain a united front in interpretation, licensing, and enforcement, not only is the sanctions effort less likely to succeed, but also opportunities emerge for international organized criminal activity to flourish uninhibited.

Fourth: when there is a strong legal and regulatory foundation for domestic enforcement in all countries. This involves enacting laws and regulations specifically designed to implement sanctions. Some countries have implemented sanctions through a combination of laws and regulations—criminal, civil, money laundering and foreign exchange controls—that are already on the books, but these laws have loopholes and are administered by a variety of agencies whose primary focus is elsewhere. Nevertheless, since the September 11, 2001 terrorist attacks, the EU and other countries have been developing better and more coherent sanctions laws and regulations. The United States has long had the legal foundation for effective sanctions programs based on the broad powers granted to the President under the constitution, enabling legislation, such as IEEPA, and a history of case law supporting sanctions enforcement by OFAC.

Fifth: when a professional sanctions apparatus is able to carry out implementation functions. This means devoting sufficient administrative resources to actively implement and enforce the sanctions and manage the domestic sanctions. Authorities must do more than issue regulations. There must be a program to actively assess compliance by regulated parties, coordinate activities with banking regulators and foreign sanctions authorities, and integrate financial sanctions with trade embargo enforcement. Sanctions administrators should not have responsibilities which compete or conflict with sanctions enforcement.

Sixth: when persons (entities and individuals) with a direct commercial involvement with the sanctions' targets—banks, oil companies, and other commercial enterprises—have an effective compliance program to ensure that they do not engage in proscribed conduct. They are on the front lines and must be the first line of defense

Seventh: when speed and discretion are employed in implementation. The imposition of sanctions, carried out with speed and with minimal warning, enables the United States and its allies to exert maximum economic leverage over the target, for example, by capturing as many assets as possible through blocking. Trying to freeze assets after the target has been alerted usually yields disappointing results.

Sanctions are not an end in themselves. They must be part of a coordinated diplomatic and enforcement strategy where all parts of the government and business and financial communities are carefully working together, without delay, to achieve the stated foreign policy goal. Sanctions can prove to be an inadequate, or even counterproductive, policy tool if not planned, implemented, and understood and coordinated by those involved in their implementation.

An Example of How Sanctions Can Go Wrong

David M. Kennedy, author of *Freedom from Fear*, who, among other historians of this time tells the story of how economic sanctions had been imposed by President Roosevelt in the summer of 1940 against Japan and then not implemented as directed and the disastrous results that followed. The following is based upon excerpts from his book:[99]

> The events that eventually led to war between Japan and the United States could be summed up in a single word—China. Washington had two means of restraining Japan, either by bolstering China, as it was bolstering Britain, or by imposing economic sanctions on Japan—potentially highly effective against import-dependent Japan. As for direct aid to China, China was not Britain and Chiang Kai-Shek was not Winston Churchill. Thus, Washington's principal tool for restraining Tokyo was economic sanctions against Japan.

> In 1940, Japan was dependent on the United States for a long list of indispensable strategic materials including, most significantly, oil. Eighty percent of Japan's fuel supplies came from the United States. Roosevelt knew it was a powerful club and a potentially dangerous weapon. It was recognized that it may conceivably lead to war. If the United States were to cut off oil supplies to the Japanese, Japan would, in all probability, send her fleets down to take the Dutch East Indies.

> On July 26, 1940, FDR began an important link in the chain of events.

> Seeking to restrain Japanese pressure on Southeast Asia, Roosevelt declared an embargo on the shipment to Japan of premium grades of scrap iron and steel and high octane aviation gas. Although irritating to Japan it did not deter them. Japan moved into French Indochina and officially joined the Axis by signing the Tripartite Pact with Germany and Italy, sending the message that if the United States got involved in either the European or Sino-Japanese Conflicts that it would face a two-ocean war.

> Washington responded with a further turn of the economic screw by extending the list of embargoed items to include all iron and steel shipments. The standoff continued for the next year with the delicate balance of a rhythm of escalating moves. The United States gambled that it could pressure Japan by economic sanctions without driving Japan to war.

---

99. This is a collection of excerpts, that have been edited and paraphrased, from David M. Kennedy, *Freedom From Fear: The American People in Depression and War, 1929–1945*, Oxford University Press, 1999, pp. 504–512.

In December 1940, Washington added iron ore and pig iron to the prohibited list; the following month, copper and brass, and other materials were added on a regular basis thereafter, but still not oil.

Through 1941, Japan's Ambassador Nomura indicated that Japan would back off Southeast Asia if the U.S. would stop aiding China and lift the trade sanctions.

The wild card came when Hitler invaded the USSR without forewarning its "ally" Japan. This triggered a fateful debate within the Japanese government, pitting the "northerners" who favored joining Hitler's attack on the Soviet Union against the "southerners" who argued that now was the time, while the Soviet-German death struggle secured the Siberian front, to move into Indochina, Malaysia and the Dutch East Indies, thus encircling China and cutting off Chiang. Moreover, Japan had only an 18-month supply of oil under wartime conditions and the United States could turn off the spigot at any time, a humiliating dependence on the Americans for essential fuel supplies. On July 2, 1941, the "southern" strategy carried the day.

For good reason, Roosevelt still wanted peace in the Pacific. On July 26, 1941, Roosevelt announced an immediate freeze on all Japanese assets in the United States, requiring any further Japanese purchases to be cleared through a government committee that would unblock dollars to pay for the exports. But, although much misunderstood, it still was not a total embargo on trade with Japan. Roosevelt conceived of the freeze on assets as a temporary device, one more click in the trade sanctions ratchet, a carefully calibrated policy consistent with the slowly escalating sanctions. Roosevelt's goal was to cultivate uncertainty, thus stalling for more time. Certainly, Roosevelt did not envision the freeze as a provocation to war, but rather to avoid it, or at least prolong the time until the inevitable.

In sum, in one of those striking vignettes that illustrate the contingent character of history, the asset freeze was promulgated on the eve of Roosevelt's departure for Argentina (to meet with Churchill) and in his absence, poorly instructed and temperamentally aggressive government officials refused to thaw any Japanese assets at all, for any purchases whatsoever. Roosevelt learned only in September 1941, after his return [from Newfoundland], that his intended temporary freeze had congealed into the glacial burdens of a total embargo. By then, it would have been a sign of weakness to back down. Contrary to the President's original intention, all American trade with Japan was cut off.... the Americans had thrown down the gauntlet. The challenge would have to be accepted soon. In September a Japanese Imperial Conference stipulated that if a reversal of American policy was not achieved through diplomatic means by early October, Japan would launch the Southern Operation with the main objective.... the oil in the Dutch East Indies. But for that to be successful, Japan would first need to knock the American Pacific fleet at Pearl Harbor. Successive efforts by Japan to end the trade embargo were unsuccessful.

As this story demonstrates economic sanctions can be a very powerful and effective diplomatic weapon. But they can be dangerous if not deftly handled and carefully coordinated to support the President's policy objectives.[100]

---

100. For another excellent treatment of the handling and impact of sanctions imposed upon Japan, *see* Edward S. Miller, Bankrupting the Enemy: The U.S. Financial Siege of Japan before Pearl Harbor. Annapolis: Naval Institute Press, 2007.

II

Development of Economic Sanctions under the International Emergency Economic Powers Act

Many of the issues related to modern economic sanctions were first tested under TWEA—with programs targeting Cuba, North Korea, Vietnam, Cambodia, China and the Germany/Japan Axis in World War II. The courts established deference to the Executive in carrying out U.S. foreign policy and national security with respect to the use of economic sanctions. Sanctions have since evolved, developed and expanded under IEEPA.

Phase I: Testing IEEPA, 1979–1990

IEEPA was enacted in 1977 for use in national emergencies during peacetime. The first test of IEEPA occurred with the Iranian hostage crisis of 1979 when fifty-two U.S. Nationals were taken hostage and the Iranian Finance Minister threatened to withdraw Iran's deposits from U.S. banks and attack the U.S. dollar in foreign exchange markets. The United States responded with a freeze of Iran's assets which ultimately proved to be some 12 billion dollars of funds and other property. On January 20, 1981, upon the inauguration of Ronald Reagan as President, and following the signing of the Algiers Accords, the hostages were freed and a process was initiated to unfreeze the assets and address U.S. and Iranian financial and commercial claims and counterclaims. Robert Carswell, who served as Deputy Secretary of Treasury from 1977–1981 says of these sanctions:[101]

> The blocked assets proved a key bargaining chip in obtaining the hostage release. The Iran-Iraq war, the increasing isolation of Iran, a growing need for the blocked assets and the prospect of dealing with a hostile-sounding new Administration combined to force Iran to negotiate. The ensuing settlement not only freed the hostages but also put virtually all U.S. lenders and claimants against Iran in a much more favorable position than they had been prior to the seizure of the hostages.

Over the next several years, U.S. private, corporate and bank claims against Iran were settled, many, especially U.S. bank claims, at or near 100 cents on the dollar. The Algiers Accords between the United States and Iran, *inter alia*, provided for the establishment of the Iran-U.S. Claims Tribunal. The Tribunal continues to this day to hear government-to-government claims between Iran and the United States and is the largest and most successful program of its kind.[102]

Flush on the success of the first Iran sanctions effort, there followed a series of other IEEPA-based programs, some with varying degrees of success—Libya, Nicaragua, South Africa, and Panama.

During the late 1980s to mid-1990s, sanctions programs involving Vietnam, South Africa, Panama and Nicaragua were winding down. The Soviet Union had fallen peacefully. There was speculation that the United States would lift sanctions on Cuba when suddenly on August 1, 1990, Iraq invaded Kuwait.

---

101. Robert Caswell, "Economic Sanctions and the Iran Experience," *Foreign Affairs*, Winter 1981/2. *Available at* http://www.foreignaffairs.com/articles/35846/robert-caswell/economic-sanctions-and-the-iran-experience.

102. The Iran-United States Claims Tribunal has a website (*see* http://www.iusct.net/), which provides information on its decisions and cases.

Phase II: The Internationalization of Sanctions, 1990–1995

An important new phase of economic sanctions emerged in August of 1990 when Iraq invaded Kuwait. The lead that President George H. W. Bush took on the morning of August 2 to impose sanctions against Iraq was immediately followed within two days by the United Kingdom and France. Since the former Soviet Union was not present at the United Nations to veto proposed multilateral sanctions, a week later the United Nations followed with the passage of United Nations Security Council Resolution (UNSCR) 661 — a watershed event for multilateral sanctions. Not since World War II was there a truly comprehensive coordinated multilateral embargo, in this case against Iraq, as a punitive measure, and for Kuwait, as a protective measure. UNSCR 661 began the process for a broad coalition using sanctions as a diplomatic tool.

The United Nations, largely at the United States' urging, continued to use sanctions to achieve diplomatic objectives. It developed programs targeting Haiti, and Libya (when its involvement in the bombing of Pan Am Flight 103 became clear) and perhaps most significantly Serbia (the Federal Republic of Yugoslavia (Serbia and Montenegro)) and its leader, Slobodan Milosevic, because, in part, for what has been termed "ethnic cleansing by Serbia."[103]

At least in the initial phases of these programs, the UN was new to the complicated task of administering and enforcing sanctions. Quickly, the UN Sanctions Committee took on the role of a licensing body and its efforts soon became bogged down in the politics and concerns such a body must address with so many member states, each of whom wished to support their companies seeking licenses to be able to sell products to Iraq. The so-called Oil for Food scandal involving Iraq prompted several member states to raise serious concerns as to the efficacy and wisdom of using sanctions at all,[104] charging that the program had hurt mainly the domestic population (*see* the discussion of the international smart sanctions movement in Phase III below). The actual impact of sanctions on Iraq and its weapons of mass destruction programs would take years to assess, and is still debated by some.

The program involving Serbia, also a UN-mandated program, however proved to be a greater success. The Bush Administration in Executive Order 12808 of May 30, 1992, "Blocking "Yugoslav Government" Property and Property of the Governments of Serbia and Montenegro" targeted the Milosevic regime, but unilateral sanctions by the United States were not sufficient to stop the bloodshed. A multi-lateral approach was clearly required.

The UN Security Council after passing a series of resolutions calling for an arms embargo against the Federal Republic of Yugoslavia in 1991 and 1992, passed UNSCR

---

103. U.S. and UN sanctions were imposed for a number of reasons, among what has been termed "ethnic cleansing." In response to actions taken by Serbia, Milosevic, and his allies in Bosnia against the Muslim population in Bosnia, the 1992 UN Security Council Resolution 757 affirmed the need for sanctions to stop the ethnic cleansing by: "Deploring further that its [the UN's] call for the immediate cessation of forcible expulsions and attempts to change the ethnic composition of that population has not been heeded, and reaffirming in this context the need for the effective protection of human rights and fundamental freedoms, including those of ethnic minorities."

104. The UN appointed Paul A. Volcker, former Chairman of the U.S. Federal Reserve Board of Governors, to investigate the corruption of the Oil for Food program, and the report was referred to as the Volcker report. A description of the report can be found on the UN website at http://www.un.org/News/dh/iraq/oip/facts-oilforfood.htm.

757 on May 30, 1992, calling on member states to implement sanctions against Serbia and Montenegro. Because sanctions were now multilateral, and because the new states of the former Yugoslavia were part of Europe, the United States had leverage with the Europeans to do something jointly to prevent these new Yugoslav states from attacking each other and engaging in their own versions of ethnic cleansing.[105,106] UNSCR 757 was later clarified and enhanced by UNSCR 787 (November 16, 1992) and UNSCR 820 (April 17, 1993) to provide needed authority for enhanced multi-lateral sanctions enforcement. The strong and active political leadership of the White House helped to provide the leverage needed to coordinate economic sanctions efforts with key EU allies in Europe and greatly enhanced the effectiveness and ultimate success of the sanctions. As previously noted in Section I, sanctions were a significant factor in what ultimately brought Slobodan Milosevic to the table at the Dayton Peace Conference and to negotiate the Accords[107] in November 1995.

Phase III: Financial Sanctions Reform — Smarter Targeting, 1995–2001

In 1995, the President again imposed economic sanctions on Iran for its support of terrorism and terrorist activities. The triggering event for the 1995 Iranian sanctions was the need to prevent a U.S. oil company from completing its then lawful contract with Iran to develop Iran's rich South Pars oil field.

When the U.S. oil company was ousted from Iran by Executive Order 12957, other non-U.S. oil companies were poised to fill the vacuum and reap the windfall. In response, Congress decided in 1996 that extraterritorial U.S. sanctions could help ensure that no other foreign company could do this and passed the Iran Libya Sanctions Act ("ILSA" and later renamed "ISA" after the law was amended and Libya was dropped as a target). The

---

105. Additional Executive orders were issued extending and strengthening U.S. sanctions against the FRY and matching provisions in the subsequent UNSCRs as well. The E.O.s were:
- Executive Order 12810, June 5, 1992;
- Executive Order 12831, January 15, 1993;
- Executive Order 12846, April 25, 1993;
- Executive Order 12934, October 25, 1994.

Follow-on UNSCRs renewed and extended the sanctions, such as UNSCR 787, November 16, 1992; and UNSCR 820; April 17. 1993.

106. The European Community and its Member States in the first few years of sanctions against Yugoslavia implemented UNSCR No 757 (1992) and related resolutions by issuing:
- Regulations (EEC) No 1432/92 (OJ No L 151, 3. 6. 1992, p. 1, (Regulation repealed by Regulation (EEC) No 990/93 (OJ No L 102, 28. 4. 1993, p. 14);
- Regulation (EEC) No 2656/92 (OJ No L 266, 12. 9. 1992, p. 27, (Regulation repealed by Regulation (EEC) No 990/93 (OJ No L 102, 28. 4. 1993, p. 14));
- Regulation (EEC) No 990/93 of 26 April 1993; and
- Council Regulation (EC) No 1733/94 of 11 July 1994 (prohibiting the satisfying of claims with regard to contracts and transactions the performance of which was affected by the United Nations Security Council Resolution No 757 (1992) and related resolutions).

A number of other regulations were issued in later years as the sanctions regime changed.

107. The agreement in Dayton talks resulted in what is commonly referred to as the "Dayton Accords." See http://www.state.gov/p/eur/rls/or/dayton/. The talks resulted in what is referred to more formally as the "General Framework Agreement for Peace in Bosnia and Herzegovina of November 21, 1995," and the resulting documents are entitled the "Dayton Peace Agreement Documents" which were initialed in Dayton, Ohio on November 21, 1995. See http://www.state.gov/p/eur/rls/or/dayton/52577.htm.

law was perceived by foreign oil companies and their host governments as an overreaching extraterritorial assertion of U.S. economic power.

Foreign frustration over the extraterritorial reach of U.S. sanctions probably hit its apogee with the Helms Burton Act[108] enacted after the shoot down of the Brothers to the Rescue plane over international waters by the Government of Cuba in 1996.[109] Under this Act, a private right of action was established under U.S. law allowing U.S. nationals to recover treble damages against foreign entities and individuals who "traffic" in the property that was confiscated from U.S. nationals by Fidel Castro. Additionally, the State Department was required to deny a visa to any trafficker in such confiscated property.

By 1996, the U.S. business community was starting to push back against the seemingly unrelenting and unstoppable pace of ever-new sanctions programs from the Executive and Legislative Branches of the United States and international bodies. Sanctions entered a third phase in development, "Sanctions Reform," and a new idea emerged, "targeted financial sanctions," an idea with strong and growing support that lasted until the terrorist attacks on the United States on September 11, 2001. Dozens of think tanks, study groups and Congressional committees looked at how sanctions could be reformed and shaped so that they would not proliferate at such a feverish pace and would be more targeted and less devastating to the civilian population of the targeted country and the business communities of the United States and its allies.

A multitude of domestic and international conferences were held, termed "Smart Sanctions" dialogues, with scholars and government officials from around the world to address the question of how sanctions could be more focused and targeted with less collateral damage to the innocent population at large. Everyone agreed that "Smart Sanctions" was the best way forward but there was a clear lack of consensus on the way forward and how to do it.

The Swiss Government played a leadership role by the establishment of a series of international meetings held in Interlaken, Switzerland with political leaders and sanctions administrators from around the world to discuss how sanctions could be more tailored to target more narrowly the political leadership, its support structures and the elite community, not the broader population as had suffered during the sanctions on Iraq. The Interlaken Process, as it came to be called, resulted in a report with a series of recommendations to strengthen multilateral issues with smarter and more targeted sanctions.[110] The targeting recommendations from the first conference included:

---

108. Public Law 104-114, Cuban Liberty and Democratic Solidarity (LIBERTAD) Act of 1996, http://thomas.loc.gov/cgi-bin/query/z?c104:H.R.927.ENR:.

109. http://www.cnn.com/US/9603/cuba_shootdown/05/military/.

110. In 1998, the Swiss, under the Interlaken initiative, assembled government sanctions experts to discuss how to better target sanctions while still making them effective. The findings from this conference were to inform the United Nations sanctions effort. The Swiss Federal Office for Economic Affairs published the findings, entitled:

- Swiss Federal Office for Foreign Economic Affairs, Department of Economy, "Expert Seminar on Targeting UN Financial Sanctions," March 17–19, 1998, Interlaken, Switzerland.

In 1999, the Swiss held a second Interlaken conference and published a report from the conference entitled:

- Swiss Federal Office for Foreign Economic Affairs, "2nd Interlaken Seminar on Targeting United Nations Financial Sanctions," 29–31 March, 1999, in cooperation with the United Nations Secretariat.

In 2001, the Swiss published a paper in conjunction with the Brown University Watson Institute entitled:

- "Targeted Financial Sanctions: A Manual for Design and Implementation," Contributions from the Interlaken Process, The Swiss Confederation in cooperation with the United Nations Secretariat and the Watson Institute for International Studies, Brown University.

1. A targeted financial sanctions regime should have certain commonly understood elements. These are:

    a) clear understanding of the targeted entities, assets, and transactions,

    b) a clear understanding of the extent of coverage of the program (i.e., exactly who and what are covered by the program),

    c) information on financial leverage that can be brought against the target,

    d) whether the multilateral enforcement regime is adequate to ensure the consistency of its application, and

    e) whether information gathering or sharing mechanisms are adequate to maintain a strong sanctions regime.

2. Uniformity in interpretation and enforcement are seen as necessary to avoid exploitation of ambiguities and forum shopping by the potential targets of sanctions regimes.

3. There was a recognition that implementing states need as much advance notice as possible to implement financial sanctions. It was, however, widely recognized that assets move quickly when public discussions begin and that both speed and discretion in application of these regimes are critical to their success.

4. Prior analysis of the vulnerability of targeted governments and elites are needed to ensure the efficiency of financial sanctions regimes. Among the elements to be considered are:

    a) the sophistication of the national economy

    b) description of the fortunes of the ruling class

    c) the tailoring of the sanctions to have the greatest effect on those to be targeted

    d) what positive elements can be built into the regime to motivate compliance by targeted individuals.

5. There was general agreement that states depend on lists containing the names of the targets in order to be in a position to implement targeted sanctions. Whenever possible, such lists should emanate from the UN Security Council.

The call for targeted sanctions was partly answered by the sanctions model developed and successfully used in 1995 by the United States, first against terrorist groups disrupting the Middle East peace process[111] and then against the Cali Cartel in Colombia.[112] The latter program began with a call to OFAC by senior U.S. Justice Department officials, who asked OFAC to develop a program to target narcotics trafficking in Colombia. OFAC developed a program that targeted narcotics traffickers and the companies owned and controlled by them. It was announced by President Clinton at the 50th anniversary celebration of the United Nations. The Specially Designated Narcotics Trafficker (SDNT)

In 2006, Germany, Sweden, and Switzerland sponsored their own study for submission to the United Nations, under the targeted sanctions effort entitled:

- "Strengthening Targeted Sanctions Through Fair and Clear Procedures," White Paper prepared by the Watson Institute Targeted Sanctions Project, Brown University, 30 March 2006.

All of these reports can be found on the Swiss website: http://www.seco.admin.ch/themen/00513/00620/00639/00641/index.html?lang=en.

111. Executive Order 12947, "Prohibiting Transactions with Terrorists Who Threaten to Disrupt the Middle East Peace Process." The regulations for these sanctions are found in Terrorism Sanctions Regulations, 31 CFR part 595. Persons named under these sanctions are referred to as Specially Designated Terrorist (SDT).

112. Executive Order 12978 (October 21, 1995), "Blocking Assets and Prohibiting Transactions With Significant Narcotics Traffickers."

program was very successful[113] and was the model for the Foreign Narcotics Kingpin Designation Act of 2000,[114] which targets narcotics traffickers and drug kingpins from around the world and blocks their assets in the U.S. and bars U.S. persons from any dealings with their enterprises, by adding their names and entities to the OFAC SDN list. But more important, as with all persons and entities named on the OFAC SDN List, it prohibits U.S. persons from having any financial transactions whatsoever.[115]

This same type of program was also adopted against foreign terrorist organizations in the Anti-terrorism and Effective Death Penalty Act passed by Congress in 1996 (AEDPA).[116] Under this law the Departments of Justice (DOJ), State and Treasury, name and publish on a biennial basis the worldwide Foreign Terrorist Organizations (FTOs) currently involved in terrorist activity and thus prohibit fundraising on their behalf and freeze their funds in the United States.[117] The FTOs currently listed by this process have been steady at approximately 57 in number.[118] There have been several cases prosecuted in the United States for violations of the prohibitions. For example, on April 30, 2009, a person pled guilty to the charge of conspiracy to provide material support to al-Qaeda, a banned Foreign Terrorist Organization (FTO), in violation of 18 U.S.C. § 2339B ("§ 2339B"). Also in 2009, officers of the Holy Land Foundation for Relief and Development (HLF) in Richardson, Texas were convicted for providing financial support to Hamas, an FTO.[119]

The U.S. Government was moving more and more by this time into the counter-terrorism arena, especially in the wake of the embassy bombings in Nairobi, Kenya and Dar-es-Salam, Tanzania. Osama bin Laden and Al Qaeda were named in 1998 as a Specially Designated Terrorist (SDT) under the 1995 sanctions program that targets terrorist groups disrupting the Middle East Peace Process. During this period, OFAC began direct consulting with the central banks and enforcement authorities in Saudi Arabia, U.A.E, Kuwait, and Bahrain about steps to be taken to disrupt the flow of funds to Al-Qaeda, Osama bin Laden and terrorist groups, the funding of terror, and to create a more systematic approach to target terrorist activity and terrorist finance.

Phase IV: Attacking Support Structures of Groups and Individuals, 2001–2014

A fourth phase in sanctions development under IEEPA followed on the heels of the terrorist attacks on U.S. soil on September 11, 2001. The world changed dramatically as a result of those attacks. President George W. Bush signed Executive Order 13224 imposing

---

113. OFAC published a report on the impact of the sanctions program on the Colombian Drug Cartels entitled, "Impact Report March 2007: Economic Sanctions Against Colombian Drug Cartels," Office of Foreign Assets Control.

This report can be found at http://www.treasury.gov/resource-center/sanctions/Documents/narco_impact_report_05042007.pdf.

114. The Judicial Review Commission on Foreign Asset Control, p. 4.

115. U.S.C. Title 21 Chapter 24. International Narcotics Trafficking, Section 1904.

116. The Antiterrorism and Effective Death Penalty Act of 1996, Pub. L. No. 104-132, 110 Stat. 1214, ("AEDPA"), signed into law on April 24, 1996.

117. AEDPA Sec. 302. Describes the designation process of foreign terrorist organizations and the prohibition of fundraising and freezing of funds in the United States.

118. The State website page http://www.state.gov/j/ct/rls/other/des/123085.htm provides a current list of FTOs, and a list of FTOs that have been removed.

119. Two FTO cases are described by Wadie E. Said, "The Material Support Prosecution and Foreign Policy" *Indiana Law Journal* Volume 86, Iss. 2 (2011) *available at* http://ilj.law.indiana.edu/articles/86/86_2_Said.pdf.

comprehensive economic sanctions (along with other UN member states) against a new kind of target—Osama bin Laden, Al Qaeda and other terrorist groups acting worldwide in what was soon thereafter described as the Global War on Terrorism, and called upon the Treasury Department and OFAC to administer them. Working with other key elements of the U.S. government—law enforcement, intelligence, the diplomatic, and the military communities—and very closely with U.S. allies, the financial war on terror has sought to disrupt the flow of funds to, and business relationships and transactions of any nature whatsoever with, terrorist groups, their members and support structure. These terms are very broadly defined and are intended to affect any and all business relationships by U.S. persons with these persons. The United States maintains lists of these persons and puts them on the OFAC SDN list, whenever appropriate, when sufficient evidence has been developed. In turn, OFAC submits these names to the UN for inclusion on the UN list and consequent multi-lateral sanctions implementation and enforcement action.

When members of the Congressionally-mandated 9-11 Commission issued a follow-up report in 2005 on the U.S. response to the attacks of September 11, 2001 and its Global War on Terror, it graded the five government elements—Military, Law Enforcement, Intelligence, Diplomatic, and Finance. Of these five elements, the Financial War on Terror got the highest grade, an A-. The other four received scores ranging from B to a failing grade.[120]

The Bush Administration became particularly aggressive in the use of economic sanctions as a tool of national security and foreign policy, especially in the wake of the events of September 11, 2001, and the high marks from the 9-11 Commission.[121] Similarly, the Obama Administration has been aggressive in the use of economic sanctions.

The focus of economic sanctions on terrorism is typically aimed at groups and individuals that provide material support for terrorist groups. The terrorist support structure—that educates, indoctrinates, recruits, trains, provides logistical support to terrorists, and helps terrorists plot, plan and prepare for an attack—can require considerable resources. Those providing fundraising, financial support, and helping build and participate in the terrorist support structure often depend on the international financial and commercial systems and, if designated, could suffer substantial financial loss by being excluded from it.

Sanctions are a powerful deterrent to those who provide financial and logistical support for terrorism, if they are named or fear exposure. Although a terrorist act of buying a plane ticket and hijacking a flight may be a low budget activity, and the hijacker may not care about financial sanctions, those funding and providing substantial resources to the support structure for that act are vulnerable, and the naming or threat of naming such persons on the OFAC SDN List can have a significant deterrent effect.

Additionally, in countries whose laws are lax in tracking the receipt of charitable contributions and the disposition of those funds, terrorists can exploit this laxness by setting up a charity as a front to raise funds and funnel resources to their organization. Sanctions and the threat of naming their institutions can spur participating countries to close these

---

120. This scorecard is on p. 5 of the "9/11 Public Discourse Project: Final Report on 9/11 Commission Recommendations, December 5, 2005." The report can be found on the website location http://i.a.cnn.net/cnn/2005/images/12/05/2005-12-05_report.pdf.

121. *The 9-11 Commission Report* can be found at http://www.9-11commission.gov/report/911Report.pdf. *Also see* the "National Commission on Terrorist Attacks Upon the United States: Monograph on Terrorist Financing," Staff Report to the Commission, by John Roth, Douglas Greenburg, and Serena Wills. This report can be found at the website http://www.9-11commission.gov/staff_statements/.

loopholes and put their charities on a sound anti-money laundering ("AML")/sanctions compliance ("SC")/anti-terrorist financing ("ATF") footing.

The focus of such targeted sanctions is not generally or necessarily upon the non-state actor who commits the terrorist attack *per se* as he is typically a person without blockable resources. More significantly, counter-terrorism economic sanctions are a leverage tool against those who have investment in and some dependency upon the international financial and commercial systems. Terrorist bomb throwers normally do not fit into this profile. Putting terrorist bomb throwers on the SDN List has its limits for effectiveness, and can unnecessarily complicate the process that financial institutions and corporate entities must follow in their sanctions compliance programs. Other than a visa or travel ban, which is critically important to keep terrorists out of the United States and other allied countries, a listing of a terrorist on the SDN List may be largely symbolic, because such persons and their families do not directly depend on the international financial system for their livelihood or for their economic transactions.[122]

What is common to terrorists, terrorist groups and financial supporters is that they generally do not open accounts or transfer money in their own name, but use front companies and assumed names when engaging in activities related to or supporting terrorism. When moving money across borders they often rely upon trusted cash couriers or other informal cash transfer systems that are inexpensive and convenient. The money normally returns back into the formal financial system. This has shifted a considerable burden onto the banking sector for enhanced risk-based internal procedures for better AML/SC/ATF customer identification procedures, suspicious activity reporting, "know your customer," "know your customer's customer," and know who may have a greater than 50 percent ownership interest in your customer. Banks truly have become the first line of defense and often are not sufficiently appreciated for what they are required to do.

Sanctions that counter proliferation of weapons of mass destruction (e.g., E.O. 12938, November 14, 1994) and E.O. 13382 (June 29, 2005)—made multilateral by UN Security Council Resolutions (e.g. UNSCR 1540 (April 28, 2004) and UNSCR 1673 (April 27, 2006))—over the last 15 years have also focused on support structures which included the designation and naming on the OFAC SDN list of persons providing the financing, component parts and expertise to Iran, Syria, and North Korea to develop weapons of mass destruction (including nuclear, chemical, and biological) and delivery systems for these weapons.

In addition to the counter-terrorism and counter-proliferation sanctions programs, specific legislation, previously described, related to Iran and Syria, *et al* has called for additional sanctions against elements of these governments (involved in the promotion of terrorism, development of weapons of mass destruction and their delivery systems, and human rights violations) and against persons within and outside of these countries who facilitate their procurement activities through investments, trade financing, financial services, trade, and expertise. Three Iranian sanctions programs have been either revised or initiated at the instigation of these laws.[123]

---

122. Terrorism sanctions also involve a prohibition on issuing visas (*see* Proclamation 8693 (July 24, 2011), "Suspension of Entry of Aliens Subject to United Nations Security Council Travel Bans and International Emergency Economic Powers Act Sanctions." So naming a terrorist bomb thrower may prevent them from moving between countries, which they frequently do, provided they travel in their true name.

123. As previously noted, the Iranian Transactions Regulations ("ITR") (31 CFR Part 560) were changed and re-named the "Iranian Transactions and Sanctions Regulations" ("ITSR"), and the two more sanctions programs were added with the issuing of the Iranian Financial Sanctions Regulations" (31 CFR Part 561) and the Iranian Human Rights Abuses Sanctions Regulations (31 CFR Part 562).

The overlay of Iran sanctions, counter-terrorism, counter-proliferation, counter-human rights violations, and sanctions aimed at elements of the Iran government and those who assist them in supporting terrorism, proliferation and human rights violations have added significant levels of complexity to the sanctions effort, both for the regulators and for those trying to comply. A person or a government entity may be designated under more than one sanctions program, and the prohibitions of dealings may differ between programs. If a person is removed from being named under one program, this does not mean they are necessarily removed from another.

The Obama Administration has followed suit with the Bush Administration in attacking support structures of threats to the United States. It has significantly enhanced this effort at the urging of the U.S. Congress. Economic sanctions have become a prime weapon for the Obama administration—especially in the War on Terror—in dissuading Iran from the pursuit of nuclear weapons; and stopping Russia from further incursions into Ukraine and other nations, following the abdication of former Ukrainian President Yanekovich and Russia's annexation of the Crimea.

For example, under the "Blocking Property of Certain Persons Contributing to the Situation in Ukraine" sanctions, each subsequent Executive Order[124] expands primarily

---

124. E.O. 13660 (March 6, 2014), "Blocking Property of Certain Persons Contributing to the Situation in Ukraine" provides for the designation of persons who are determined:
    (a)(i) to be responsible for or complicit in, or to have engaged in, directly or indirectly, any of the following:
        (A) actions or policies that undermine democratic processes or institutions in Ukraine;
        (B) actions or policies that threaten the peace, security, stability, sovereignty, or territorial integrity of Ukraine; or
        (C) misappropriation of state assets of Ukraine or of an economically significant entity in Ukraine;
    (a)(ii) to have asserted governmental authority over any part or region of Ukraine without the authorization of the Government of Ukraine;
    (a)(iii) to be a leader of an entity that has, or whose members have, engaged in any activity described in subsection (a)(i) or (a)(ii) of this section or of an entity whose property and interests in property are blocked pursuant to this order;
    (a)(iv) to have materially assisted, sponsored, or provided financial, material, or technological support for, or goods or services to or in support of, any activity described in subsection (a)(i) or (a)(ii) of this section or any person whose property and interests in property are blocked pursuant to this order; or
    (a)(v) to be owned or controlled by, or to have acted or purported to act for or on behalf of, directly or indirectly, any person whose property and interests in property are blocked pursuant to this order.
E.O. 13661 (March 16, 2014), "Blocking Property of Additional Persons Contributing to the Situation in Ukraine.; in addition to persons listed in the Annex added persons determined:
    (A) to be an official of the Government of the Russian Federation;
    (B) to operate in the arms or related materiel sector in the Russian Federation;
    (C) to be owned or controlled by, or to have acted or purported to act for or on behalf of, directly or indirectly:
        (1) a senior official of the Government of the Russian Federation; or
        (2) a person whose property and interests in property are blocked pursuant to this order;
or
    (D) to have materially assisted, sponsored, or provided financial, material, or technological support for, or goods or services to or in support of: Executive Order 13662—
        (1) a senior official of the Government of the Russian Federation; or
        (2) a person whose property and interests in property are blocked pursuant to this order.

upon attacking the network of persons, often referred to as "cronies of Vladimir Putin," who constitute the support structure for destabilizing Ukraine and on specific sectors of the economy—banking, energy, metals and mining, engineering, and defense-related material—for specific targeting.[125] At this writing, the architecture of this program is still developing, unfolding and expanding.

III
General Sanctions Authorities and Strategic Considerations Concerning the Implementation of Sanctions

The OFAC Judicial Review Commission

As discussed above, IEEPA was first tested with the Iran sanctions promulgated in 1979 in response to the taking of 52 U.S. nationals hostage. In the years that followed with a flood of new economic sanctions programs, it was perceived by the business and legal community that sanctions required additional procedures and processes to protect property and rights under the constitution.

After the Foreign Narcotics Kingpin Designation Act was enacted to use economic sanctions against narcotics traffickers around the world—and patterned after the successful Colombia Narcotics Traffickers sanctions program—Congress established The Judicial Review Commission on Foreign Asset Control ("JRC"). Although the JRC was asked primarily to look at certain provisions of the Kingpin Act and their constitutionality, it received a broad mandate that permitted it to look at the administration of economic sanctions programs.[126,127]

---

125. E.O. 13662 (March 20, 2014), "Blocking Property of Additional Persons Contributing to the Situation in Ukraine," added persons determined:

    (i) to operate in such sectors of the Russian Federation economy as may be determined by the Secretary of the Treasury, in consultation with the Secretary of State, such as financial services, energy, metals and mining, engineering, and defense and related materiel;

    (ii) to have materially assisted, sponsored, or provided financial, material, or technological support for, or goods or services to or in support of, any person whose property and interests in property are blocked pursuant to this order; or

    (iii) to be owned or controlled by, or to have acted or purported to act for or on behalf of, directly or indirectly, any person whose property and interests in property are blocked pursuant to this order.

126. The Judicial Review Commission on Foreign Asset Control ("JRC"), "Scope of the Commission's Mandate," pp. 8–10.

127. The JRC Report's Conclusion was favorable to the Kingpin program, but the Kingpin legislation had barred judicial review of designations made by OFAC. The JRC Report recommended permitting judicial review of the designation process to enhance the public faith in the process. Judicial review is permitted under IEEPA, so this was not an issue for IEEPA programs. The JRC Report Recommendations, in regard to IEEPA programs called upon OFAC to modify licensing procedures to be more responsive to blockings that affect U.S. persons, to promulgate regulations that reflect internal policies regarding civil penalties and to establish safe harbors, allow public comment on regulations unless exigent circumstances do not allow it, to provide more transparency regarding decision-making standards, and to encourage OFAC-business dialogue. OFAC has taken steps since to address these issues.

The JRC performed "an extensive assessment of the impact of U.S. economic sanctions programs on U.S. citizens and businesses ("U.S. persons"), and the relief available to U.S. persons adversely affected by the administration and enforcement of such programs."[128] In so doing, the JRC looked at sanctions laws—more particularly at TWEA, IEEPA, and the Kingpin Act—and the court challenges and views to various aspects of the implementation and administration of TWEA and IEEPA. The JRC's mandate from Congress gave it broad authority to conduct hearings and collect considerable amounts of material from the U.S. agencies involved with the implementation and administration of sanctions programs, and to receive expert comments and testimony—information and material that had not been assembled so comprehensively to that date. In 2001, the JRC issued its report.

Excerpts of the JRC Conclusion and Recommendations are quoted below along with the page number where they are found:

Conclusion (p. 148).

The Kingpin Act's expansion world-wide of the highly successful Colombian sanctions program was a bold and aggressive step by Congress to strike at the heart of the multi-faceted financial enterprises that the modern breed of narcotics traffickers are surreptitiously operating. Balancing the needs of law enforcement in combating these forces with the due process protections of U.S. businesses and citizens who may unwittingly do business with them is a delicate and never-ending challenge. By allowing judicial review of Tier II designations by the Secretary of the Treasury in the manner the Commission recommends, Congress would strengthen the domestic and international business communities' faith in the integrity and fairness of the process. That enhanced faith in the system will be critical to OFAC as it faces the daunting challenge of administering this program on a global scale with the limited resources it has been allotted. The Commission trusts that Congress will vigilantly monitor this program and strongly support OFAC's needs in the years to come.

JRC Report Recommendations (pp. v–vi; and 125–147):

- Congress should amend the Kingpin Act to eliminate the preclusion of judicial review codified at 21 U.S.C. 5 1904(f).
- Congress should enact legislation to establish a system of administrative review with respect to actions by the Secretary of the Treasury, or the Secretary's designee, concerning the administration and enforcement of sanctions programs instituted under the Kingpin Act and IEEPA.
- Congress should amend the Kingpin Act to clarify the standards for designations by the Secretary of the Treasury ("Tier II designations").
- Congress should consider whether to amend the Kingpin Act to eliminate OFAC's authority to "block [assets] during the pendency of an investigation".
- Congress should require OFAC to make certain revisions to its licensing procedures so that those procedures are more responsive to the legitimate needs of U.S. persons affected by the blocking of assets of foreign persons.
- Congress should amend the Kingpin Act's civil penalty provisions to conform more closely to the civil penalty provisions in IEEPA.
- OFAC should promulgate regulations that both reflect current internal policies regarding civil penalties and establish "safe harbors".
- Congress should amend the criminal penalty provisions of the Kingpin Act.
- OFAC should publish proposed sanctions regulations for public notice and comment unless exigent circumstances are present.
- OFAC should take steps to expand and enhance the "transparency" of its operations and decision-making standards in order to facilitate greater understanding of, and compliance with, the sanctions laws it administers.
- Congress should establish an advisory committee to provide a forum for dialogue between OFAC and the U.S. business community affected by sanctions laws.
- Congress should appropriate such additional funds for OFAC as may be necessary to implement the recommendations of the Commission, if adopted, and to facilitate the successful administration of the Kingpin Act.

128. The Judicial Review Commission on Foreign Asset Control, p.1.

The JRC report now is a repository of information regarding TWEA and IEEPA, an analysis of sanctions law, a review of court challenges, and a description of sanctions implementation and administrative processes that previously were not available to the public.

Judicial Review Commission on Foreign Asset Control[129]

1. Trading with the Enemy Act

2. International Emergency Economics Power Act

TWEA is the oldest statute under which U.S. sanctions programs are currently operating.[130] Enacted in 1917 shortly after the United States entered World War I, TWEA was intended to "define, regulate, and punish trading with the enemy."[131] Section 5(b) of TWEA granted the President broad powers to regulate or prohibit commerce during wartime. Congress amended TWEA in 1933 to give the President additional authority to exercise his powers under section 5(b) when he declared a "national emergency" during peacetime.[132] TWEA was amended again in 1977 in conjunction with the enactment of IEEPA to limit the application of TWEA to wartime (its original purpose) and pre-existing declared emergencies.[133] IEEPA was enacted as the sanctions mechanism for responding to new national emergencies.[134]

.... TWEA is directed against an "enemy" and an "ally of [an] enemy" of the United States, which is statutorily defined to include, *inter alia*, "[a]ny individual, partnership ... of any nationality, resident within the territory ... of any nation with which the United States is at war ... and any corporation incorporated within such territory of any nation with which the United States is at war ...,"[135] as well as "[t]he government of any nation with which the United States is at war, or any ... subdivision thereof, or any officer, official, agent, or agency thereof."[136]....

Section 5(b) of TWEA grants the President broad powers to "investigate, regulate, or prohibit" a wide range of financial transactions and to "investigate, regulate ... prevent

---

129. Excerpts from the JRC pp. 20–28.

130. *See* Cuban Assets Control Regulations, 31 C.F.R, pt. 515; Foreign Assets Control Regulations (North Korea), 31 C.F.R. pt. 500.

131. *See* Act of Oct. 6, 1917, ch. 106, 40 Stat 411 (1917). For a discussion of TWEA's history, *see* BARRY C. CARTER, INTERNATIONAL ECONOMIC SANCTIONS: IMPROVING THE HAPHAZARD U.S. LEGAL REGIME (1988), at 186; Alexewicz v. General Analine & Film Corp., 43 N.Y.S. 2d 713, 718–20 (N.Y. Sup. Ct. 1943).

132. *See* Emergency Banking and Bank Conservation Act of 1933, ch. I, §2, 48 Stat. 1-2 (codified as amended at 50 U.S.C. §5(b) (1982)).

133. Title I, §101, of Pub. L. 95-223, 91 Stat. 1625 (1977), amended §5(b) of TWEA "by striking out 'or during another period of national emergency declared by the President' in the text preceding subparagraph (A)." *See* Barry C. Carter, *supra* note 131, at 189. At the time of the 1977 amendment, existing TWEA sanctions, such as those against Cuba and Vietnam, were grandfathered in the legislation. *See* Pub. L. No. 95-223, §101(b), 91 Stat. 1625 (1977), *reprinted in* 50 U.S.C. app. §5 note (1982). *See* Regan v. Wald, 468 U.S. 222, 228–29 (1984) (discussing grandfather provision); *see also* Carter, *supra*, at 190.

134. *See* Carter, *supra* note 131, at 189; *see also* Stanley J. Marcuss, *Grist for the Litigation Mill in U.S. Economic Sanction Programs*, 30 LAW & POLICY INT'L BUS. (1999), at 502.

135. 50 U.S.C. app. §2(a).

136. 50 U.S.C. app. §2(b). In implementing an Executive Order pursuant to TWEA, OFAC identifies additional, specific "targets" of the sanctions. For example, in regulations implementing the TWEA-based Cuban sanctions, OFAC has designated specific individuals and organizations that act on behalf of Cuba, and therefore are subject to sanctions. *See* 31 C.F.R. ch. V, App. A ("Specially Designated Nationals of Cuba").

or prohibit ... transactions involving, any property in which any foreign country or a national thereof has any interest."[137] Although the statute does not use the term "block," the Presidential authority to "regulate ... transactions involving, any property" has been interpreted to encompass the power to block or "freeze" a target's property.[138] Once assets are frozen under TWEA, what is perhaps the most significant power afforded to the President under TWEA—the authority to "vest ... property"—comes into play.[139] TWEA specifically allows the federal government to take title to the "frozen" assets of designated targets, and to use those assets "for prosecution of threatened war or to compensate our citizens or ourselves for the damages done by the government of the national affected."[140]

The statute authorizes the President to act through "any agency he may designate, and under such rules and regulations as he may proscribe ..."[141]

... the Cuban Asset Control Regulations,[142] originally promulgated in 1963 pursuant to TWEA, continue to be challenged on a variety of grounds.[143] In considering challenges to TWEA-based sanctions programs, the courts have afforded significant deference to the Executive Branch.[144]

.... Congress amended TWEA in 1977 to restrict its use to wartime and enacted IEEPA to serve as the mechanism for imposing economic sanctions in response to peacetime crises. IEEPA authorizes the President to impose economic sanctions "to deal with any unusual and extraordinary threat, which has its source in whole or substantial part outside

---

137. 50 U.S.C. app. § 5(b)(1)(B).

138. *See* Propper v. Clark, 337 U.S. 472, 484 (1949) (stating that Executive Order No. 8785 "immobilized the assets covered by its terms so that title to them might not shift from person to person except by license....."); Orvis v. Brownell, 345 U.S. 183 (1953). The courts referred to Executive Orders issued pursuant to TWEA during the Second World War as "freeze orders." *See Propper,* 337 U.S. at 475; *Orvis,* 345 U.S. at 186.

139. 50 U.S.C. app. § 5(b)(1).

140. *Propper,* 337 U.S. at 484.

141. 50 U.S.C. app. § 5(b)(1).

142. 31 C.F.R. pt. 515.

143. *See* Richardson v. Simon, 560 F.2d 500 (2d Cir. 1977) (challenging Cuban asset control regulation governing transfers of designated person's property by succession on due process grounds); Sardino v. Federal Reserve Bank of New York, 361 F.2d 106 (2d Cir. 1966), *cert. denied,* 385 U.S. 898 (1966) (challenging Cuban asset control regulations' prohibitions on property transfers on grounds that they constitute an unconstitutional delegation of authority and Fifth Amendment due process grounds); Freedom to Travel Campaign v. Newcomb, 82 F.3d 1431 (9th Cir. 1996) (challenging Cuban asset control regulations travel restrictions as an unconstitutional delegation of authority and as unconstitutionally vague on First and Fifth Amendment grounds).

144. *See Regan [v. Wald, 468 U.S.] 244 [(1984])* (confirming the deference due to the Executive Branch's implementation of TWEA-based sanctions programs); *see also Richardson,* 560 F.2d at 504 (upholding Secretary of the Treasury's application of Cuban asset control regulations and stating that "[s]ince decisions in these matters may implicate our relations with foreign powers, and since a wide variety of classifications must be defined in the light of changing political and economic circumstances, such decisions are frequently of a character more appropriate to either the Legislature or the Executive than to the Judiciary."); *Freedom to Travel,* 82 F. 2d at 1439 (declining to examine the policy reasons underlying the Cuban travel ban and citing the "history of judicial deference" to executive decision making in the foreign policy area); *DeCuellar v. Brady,* 881 F. 2d 1561, 1596 (11th Cir. 1989) (affirming OFAC's application of Cuban asset control regulations to plaintiffs, assets as well as the agency's denial of a specific license and stating that the agency's decision is "entitled to great deference from this court"); *United States v. Fernandez-Pertierra,* 523 F. Supp. 1135, 1140–42 (S.D. Fla. 1981) (affirming a conviction for violation of the Cuban asset control regulations and declining "to abandon [the] general judicial policy of deference to the executive in the area of foreign relations for purposes of this particular case").

the United States, to the national security, foreign policy, or economy of the United States, if the President declares a national emergency with respect to such threat."[145]. ...

IEEPA itself does not specifically identify the sanctions target; instead, the "unusual and extraordinary threat" is identified in the Executive Order declaring the national emergency. The source of the "threat" is the primary target of the sanctions.[146] Foreign entities or individuals related to the primary target are later identified by OFAC as secondary targets, which, in turn, are subject to sanctions because of their relationship to the primary target. ...

The powers granted to the President pursuant to IEEPA mirror those granted under TWEA,[147] with certain particular exceptions.[148] Most IEEPA-based programs contain authority to block assets and to prohibit any transaction or dealing by a U.S. person or within the United States, in the property or interests in property of a target of the sanctions. ... [149]

IEEPA permits the President to "regulate" specified commercial activities "under such regulations as he may prescribe, by means of instructions, licenses or otherwise ..."[150] Pursuant to this power, as delegated, OFAC promulgates regulations governing each IEEPA-based sanctions program. These regulatory schemes reflect the basic provisions of IEEPA and the applicable Executive Order and, among other things, establish specific exceptions to prohibitions (in the form of general licenses), procedures by which persons

---

145. 50 U.S.C. § 1701(a).

146. Utilizing his authority under IEEPA, the President has imposed sanctions on sovereign nations (Iran, Iraq, Burma, Libya, Sudan, Federal Republic of Yugoslavia), particular organizations (specially designated terrorists, significant narcotics traffickers centered in Colombia, the Taliban in Afghanistan, UNITA), and both countries and entities engaged in spreading "weapons of mass destruction." *See, e.g.,* Exec. Order No. 12,722, 55 Fed. Reg. 31,803 (1990) (blocking Iraqi government property and prohibiting transactions with Iraq); Exec. Order 12,543, 51 Fed. Reg. 875 (1986) (Libyan sanctions); Exec. Order No. 12,170, 44 Fed. Reg. 65,729 (1979) (blocking Iranian government property).

147. Section 1702(a)(1) of IEEPA provides:
At the times and to the extent specified in section 1701 of this title, the President may ... (A) investigate, regulate, or prohibit—(i) any transactions in foreign exchange, (ii) transfers of credit or payments between, by, through, or to any banking institution, to the extent that such transfers or payments involve any interest of any foreign country or a national thereof, (iii) the importing or exporting of currency or securities; and (b) investigate, regulate, direct and compel, nullify, void, prevent or prohibit, any acquisition, holding, withholding, use, transfer, withdrawal, transportation, importation or exportation of, or dealing in, or exercising any right, power, or privilege with respect to, or transactions involving any property in which any foreign country or national thereof has any interest; by any person or with respect to any property, subject to the jurisdiction of the United States.

148. According to the Supreme Court, "[t]he authorities granted to the President by § 203 of IEEPA are essentially the same as those in § 5(b) of TWEA, but the conditions and procedures for their exercise are different." *Regan,* 468 U.S. at 228.

149. From its study of Presidential emergency powers, Congress concluded that it was necessary to "revise and delimit the President's authority to regulate international economic transactions during wars or national emergencies." S. Rep. No. 95-466 (1976) *reprinted* in 1976 U.S.C.C.A.N. 2288, 4541. Thus, IEEPA includes procedures governing the exercise of Presidential powers during a declared "national emergency," which are designed to delimit the President's exercise of powers. To this end, section 1701(b) of IEEPA requires that the President follow procedures for declaring national emergencies specified in the National Emergencies Act. Section 1702(b) of IEEPA prohibits the President from exercising his emergency authority to regulate certain communications, types of humanitarian aid, publications and media, and transactions "ordinarily incident to travel to or from any country." IEEPA also contains guidelines for mandatory consultation with Congress, as well as providing the authority for Congress to terminate the declared "emergency" on its own. *See* 50 U.S.C. § 1703; H. Rep. No. 95-459 (1977).

150. 50 U.S.C. § 1702(a)(1).

may apply for specific exceptions to the prohibitions (in the form of specific licenses), and procedures for civil enforcement of the prohibitions.

.... IEEPA does not contain a statutory provision prohibiting judicial review. Thus, persons and entities designated for sanctions by the Secretary of the Treasury may challenge their designation in the federal courts on a variety of bases, including the APA [Administrative Procedures Act] and constitutional grounds. Foreign persons designated by the President, however, may not challenge their designation under the APA. Challenges under the APA must be made to "final action" by an "agency," and the President is not an "agency" for purposes of the APA.[151] Instead, foreign persons designated by the President may challenge their designations only on constitutional grounds, provided they have sufficient ties to the United States.[152]

The consistent theme in the courts' review of OFAC actions in IEEPA-based sanctions programs is judicial deference to the agency. In reviewing OFAC decision making under the APA, the courts have emphasized that they are obligated to "show substantial deference to the administrative determination."[153] In particular, when the case involves "a contemporaneous application of OFAC's own regulations," the courts afford OFAC a great degree of deference and OFAC's interpretation "must prevail unless plainly inconsistent with the regulation."[154] In fact, some courts have stated that OFAC's decision is entitled to "a presumption" of validity, and place the burden on the plaintiff to provide evidence to overcome that presumption.[155] Because challenges to agency decisionmaking in IEEPA-based sanctions programs involve matters of foreign policy and national security, the courts consider that they are "particularly obliged to defer to the discretion of the executive agencies interpreting their governing law and regulations."[156]

———————————

As noted above, there are several differences between the IEEPA and TWEA, but as a practical matter the principal difference is in the way these sanctions have been applied — the Cuban Assets Control Regulations promulgated under TWEA had been applied extraterritorially to include all persons "subject to the jurisdiction of the United States" including foreign subsidiaries of U.S. companies incorporated and operating outside of the United States. This has been an issue of irritation to several of the United States' closest allies, particularly the European Union, Canada, the United Kingdom and Switzerland. Some countries, such as the United Kingdom, Canada, Mexico and the European Union have laws against U.S.-owned subsidiaries — incorporated under their laws — complying with U.S. sanctions.[157] Issues arising over U.S. extraterritorial reach with U.S. allies

———————————

151. *See Franklin v. Massachusetts*, 505 U.S. 788, 800 (1992) (President may not be subjected to provisions of APA because not an "agency" as defined in the act).

152. *See* Section VI of this Final Report.

153. *Beobanka d.d. Belgrade v. United States*, 1997 U.S Dist. LEXIS 424, (S.D.N.Y. 1997) *(citing Citizens to Preserve Overton Park, Inc. v. Volpe*, 401 U.S. 402 (1971)).

154. *Consarc Corp. v. Iraqi Ministry ("Consarc I")*, 27 F.3d 695, 702 (D.C. Cir. 1994) *(citing Stinson v. United States*, 508 U.S. 36, 44–45 (1993)).

155. *See Sage Realty Corp. v. Department of Treasury*, 2000 WL 272192 (S.D.N.Y. Mar. 10, 2000); *Milena Ship Management Co. v. Newcomb*, 804 F. Supp. 859, 861 (E.D. La. 1992), *aff'd,* 995 F.2d 620 (1993) ("Inherent in the standard is a high degree of deference to the agency's decision, bordering on a presumption that the action taken is valid.").

156. *Paradissiotis v. Rubin*, 171 F.3d 983, 988 (5th Cir. 1999) *(citing Haig v. Agee*, 453 U.S. 280, 292 (1981)).

157. Some examples of laws and regulations used to address extraterritorial concerns with Helms-Burton and ILSA are, regarding:

traditionally have been resolved, more or less quietly, between the respective regulators, but because of the recent expanded extraterritorial reach of U.S. sanctions against Iran in particular, this has become an issue once again.

The extraterritorial application of the IEEPA sanctions in the case of Iran was addressed in a provision of the Iran Threat Reduction Act signed into law in August 2012 ("ITRA").[158] Under this law, U.S. parent companies are now by statutory definition held responsible and subject to penalties for actions by their foreign subsidiaries involving Iran.[159] A U.S. foreign subsidiary is an entity incorporated under the laws of another nation. The ITRA requires OFAC to assert jurisdiction based on ownership or control by the U.S. parent of the foreign subsidiary. ITRA section 218 defines "own or control" to mean, with respect to an entity (A) to hold more than 50 percent of the equity interest by vote or value in the entity; (B) to hold a majority of seats on the board of directors of the entity; or (C) to otherwise control the actions, policies, or personnel decisions of the entity.

Strategic Considerations Concerning the Implementation of Sanctions

Clearly there are many differences with the strategies targeting Iran, Russia and other current and former sanctions targets, such as Iraq and Libya. There also are striking parallels and similarities. No military tactician would ever unleash the full might of war without carefully choosing targets and without an understanding and concern for the possible collateral damage and the ramifications of decisions to act or for failure to act. Economic sanctions are not an end in themselves. Rather, they are among the many tools of national security and diplomacy, and must be used as such. Yet, it has sometimes been the case that because economic sanctions are relatively easy to impose, and often the least costly for the U.S. Government to implement, they have often become a first choice of political leaders, policymakers and Members of Congress who sometimes later complain that "economic sanctions don't work." Sanctions can work if correctly applied, planned, deployed, implemented and enforced.

There are many options in the President's tool kit of possible actions short of military force, sometimes referred to as "carrots and sticks." Carrots are used to encourage and reward proper state behavior, a diplomatic concession of some sort or somehow fulfilling a need with financial or trade assistance, for example. Sticks are used when carrots have

---

- The EC: Council Regulation 2271/96, 1996 O.J. (L 309) 1;
- The United Kingdom: Protection of Trading Interests Act 1980; 1980 Chapter 11 [20th March 1980]; http://www.legislation.gov.uk/ukpga/1980/11/pdfs/ukpga_19800011_en.pdf;
- Canada: Foreign Extraterritorial Measures Act, R.S.C., ch. F-29, §5(1) (1985) (Can.) ("FEMA"); and
- Mexico: Ley de Protección al Comercio y la Inversión de Normas Extranjeras que Contravengan el Derecho Internacional, D.O., 22 de Octubre de 1996.

158. Iran Threat Reduction and Syria Human Rights Act of 2012 H.R. 1905 (PL 112-158), Section 218.

159. Prior to the passage of Section 218 of the ITRA, a U.S. firm's controlled foreign subsidiary could subject the U.S. parent company to liability for its actions with a sanctioned country or person if as a practical matter its U.S. parent was active in day-to-day decision-making and consultation and approval was required on such matters as risk-taking, operational activities; and the extent to which the foreign subsidiary is subject to the day-to-day direction and control of the U.S. parent.

failed to work. There can be a small stick applied for more gentle persuasion or there can be a big stick, such as punitive sanctions of the kind implemented by OFAC at the U.S. Treasury.

The United States takes economic sanctions enforcement very seriously. In recent years OFAC has had a staff of between one hundred fifty to two hundred employees — developing sanctions programs and regulations, designating specific persons for the SDN List, issuing licenses, enhancing compliance, and taking enforcement actions — and is supported by hundreds more in various Departments — Treasury, Justice, State and other agencies. No other government has anything like it and it has long been looked to as a primary leader in this area.

Until recently, countries from the EU and elsewhere had only a handful of employees dedicated to working on sanctions implementation and enforcement — many had maybe one or two employees. Placement of the responsibilities for the sanctions effort varied by member state. The seriousness with which multilateral sanctions were implemented and enforced by member states was also varied. These inconsistencies lessen the effectiveness of the multilateral sanctions programs as the chain is only as strong as its weakest link. For example, the Iraq program from 1990 to 2003 had a multitude of conflicting requirements across the various UN member countries.

After September 11, 2001, the EU has provided enhanced guidance to member states for implementing the sanctions effort — which parallels in many ways U.S. sanctions — and for coordinating efforts between member states. And, in recent years EU member states have expanded significantly their sanctions regimes and enforcement efforts. However, each member state still implements sanctions according to its own national laws and decides which institutions to invest the administrative and enforcement responsibilities.[160]

Authorities. The United States is unique, most notably because it has OFAC as the administrative and enforcement body and the broad authority of the International Emergency Economic Powers Act,[161] also known as IEEPA, as the basic implementing statute. As previously noted, the Trading With the Enemy Act ("TWEA"), which dates back to World War I, was used against Japan and Germany during World War II, China after the Communist takeover, and during the Cold War against North Korea, Cuba, and Vietnam. However, since IEEPA was enacted in 1977, it is now the primary statutory authority used by the President to promulgate sanctions under a national emergency during peacetime, at his own behest or spurred by or in conjunction with specific legislation.[162,163]

---

160. *See* European Union website http://eeas.europa.eu/cfsp/sanctions/index_en.htm for a description of EU restrictive measures and http://eeas.europa.eu/cfsp/sanctions/docs/index_en.pdf#5 and http://register.consilium.europa.eu/doc/srv?l=EN&f=ST%208666%202008%20REV%201 for guidance to member states on how restrictive measures should be implemented.

161. International Emergency Economic Powers Act (IEEPA), 50 U.S.C. §§ 1701–1706.

162. A current list of sanctions enabling statutes of general application are: Sections 5 and 16 of the Trading With the Enemy Act (TWEA), 50 U.S.C. App.§§ 5, 16; International Emergency Economic Powers Act (IEEPA), 50 U.S.C. §§ 1701–1706; National Emergencies Act (NEA), 50 U.S.C. §§ 1601–1651; Section 5 of the United Nations Participation Act of 1945 (UNPA), 22 U.S.C. § 287c; USAPATRIOT ACT, P.L. 107–56 — Oct. 26, 2001.

163. In recent years, the Congress has enacted legislation that either reinforces the action of the President, or expands upon it or substitutes its vision of what U.S. foreign policy should be with regard to the use of economic sanctions to achieve a particular foreign policy goal. A partial list of specific sanctions statutes include: Burma Freedom and Democracy Act of 2003, PL 108-61 (50 U.S.C. § 1701 note)(as originally enacted, without subsequent amendments, including by the JADE Act);

Under IEEPA, the President has very broadly delegated authority from the Congress to regulate economic transactions of any nature whatsoever by U.S. persons (individuals and entities) wherever in the world located in times of national emergency. IEEPA also provides powerful implementing tools. Importantly, the United States has had a long history of using economic sanctions, providing decades of experience to test and define its economic sanctions program requirements and laws in practice and in court. IEEPA has benefited from the many precedents set by court challenges to it and its predecessor sanctions statute, TWEA, as well as by court cases related to national security issues in general.

Under IEEPA, the President is required to make a declaration of a national emergency, under the National Emergencies Act, because of a threat in whole or substantial part from outside of the United States to the national security, foreign policy or economy. Simultaneous with the national emergency declaration, the President issues an Executive Order which spells out the specific terms and requirements that all U.S. persons, as a matter of the law, must follow with regard to the subject or target of the order, whether it be a nation, a terrorist group, narcotics kingpin, or any person or entity determined to be an agent of (e.g., owned or controlled by or acting for or on behalf of), or affiliated with (e.g. materially, financially, or technologically assisting) the target. The basis for the national emergency is typically described (e.g. support for terrorism, nuclear proliferation, interference with the democratically elected government, invasion of another country, etc.) in the Executive Order and becomes the standard to expand the scope, coverage and application of the Executive Order.

Under this authority, the President and his National Security team (primarily the Departments of State, Justice, Treasury, Defense, and the Intelligence agencies and other government agencies when additional specialized expertise is required) can then shape a program to meet the particular needs of the national security crisis that the President believes the country faces. The President can choose from one or more of a number of options, which can include the following examples among others:

- A freezing of assets of the targeted country or of specific persons within the leadership circle of the targeted country (i.e., cronies, elites, etc.), or of a target group and persons.
- Import and export prohibitions.
- Transportation and travel bans.

Section 570 of the Foreign Operations, Export Financing, and Related Programs Appropriations Act, 1997, PL 104-208, §§ 570 Tom Lantos Block Burmese Jade (Junta's Anti-Democratic Efforts) Act Of 2008, PL 110-286 (50 U.S.C. § 1701 note); Foreign Narcotics Kingpin Designation Act, 21 U.S.C. §§ 1901–1908; Antiterrorism and Effective Death Penalty Act of 1996 (AEDPA), 8 U.S.C. § 1189, 18 U.S.C. § 2339B; Cuban Democracy Act of 1992 (CDA), 22 U.S.C. §§ 6001–6010; Cuban Liberty and Democratic Solidarity (Libertad) Act of 1996, 22 U.S.C. §§ 6021–6091; Comprehensive Iran Sanctions, Accountability, and Divestment Act of 2010 (CISADA), PL 111-195; Iran Freedom and Counter-Proliferation Act of 2012 (IFCA) (PL 112-239); Iran Sanctions Act of 1996, as Amended, 50 U.S.C. § 1701 note; International Security and Development Cooperation Act of 1985 (ISDCA), 22 U.S.C. § 2349aa-9; Iran Threat Reduction and Syria Human Rights Act of 2012 H.R. 1905 (PL 112-158); National Defense Authorization Act For Fiscal Year 2012 PL 112-81; Trade Sanctions Reform and Export Enhancement Act of 2000 (TSRA), 22 U.S.C. §§ 7201–7211; Sergei Magnitsky Rule of Law Accountability Act of 2012—Public Law 112-208 (Approved December 14, 2012); Clean Diamond Trade Act, 19 U.S.C. §§ 3901–3913; Darfur Peace and Accountability Act of 2006 (DPAA), PL 109-344 (50 U.S.C. § 1701 note).

- Payment prohibitions.
- Mandatory disinvestment.
- Prohibited investments, loan financing, trade financing or dealings.
- Prohibition on any type of transaction whatsoever involving goods, services, or technology with the targeted country or a defined class of persons or entities.
- Prohibition of economic transactions of any nature whatsoever by persons covered by the Executive Order, unless there is an authorization in the form of a license from OFAC.

Put them all together and there are comprehensive economic sanctions. As each sanctions program is shaped at different times by different people to address different national security problems and foreign policy concerns, no two sanctions programs are ever exactly the same. Considering that a dozen or more sanctions programs may be in place at any given time, there are many things that companies and financial institutions need to know and do to comply with these programs, especially in the post-9-11 environment and since the passage of the USA PATRIOT Act.[164]

In addition, the United States has taken other extraordinary steps to exert its authority and expand jurisdiction to the international non-U.S. banking sector, which relies upon the U.S. banking system for the ability to conduct U.S. dollar denominated transactions — which is the currency most widely used in the world's international financial transactions — and the related correspondent banking relationships upon which these transactions depend and without which they cannot function. Simply put, the U.S. dollar is the primary currency of the international financial system. Non-U.S. banks maintain correspondent accounts with U.S. banks to conduct international financial transactions in U.S. dollars. Without this correspondent bank relationship or some other type of access to the U.S. banking sector, non-U.S. banks that conduct U.S. dollars-denominated transactions cannot effectively serve their customers involved in international commerce. Without access to U.S. correspondent banks, most international banks would not be able to continue in business.

U.S. foreign policy often dictates that only a few of the prohibitions outlined above are to apply or that only certain designated persons are to be targeted. Sometimes under a sanctions program the threat situation changes. For example, if an adversary changes its behavior in exchange for a lessening or removal of sanctions, the sanctions may be decreased. Alternatively, if an adversary commits additional provocative acts, sanctions may be increased. Either way as a tool to implement foreign policy, sanctions need to be flexible. Sanctions prohibitions and their application need to change as the threat and the policy toward the threat changes:

- If more economic activity is to be permitted under a given Executive Order, general and specific licenses may be issued.
- If there is a need to increase the prohibitions, a new Executive Order may be issued.

A single sanctions program may undergo many transformations over the course of a national emergency. Some programs have involved a dozen or more Executive Orders. When sanctions are lifted, an Executive Order or a series of Executive Orders are issued to terminate the national emergency and revoke the sanctions prohibitions.

---

164. "Uniting and Strengthening America by Providing Appropriate Tools Required to Intercept and Obstruct Terrorism Act of 2001, (USA PATRIOT Act)," P.L. 107–56 — Oct. 26, 2001.

IV
Sanctions Implementation Practices

OFAC's sanctions implementation practices and certain court decisions provide the basis for imposing strong economic sanctions programs. Among the more significant of these sanctions implementation practices involve:

1. Court deference to the Executive Branch in conducting foreign policy, especially in imposing sanctions where the constitutional authority of the President is augmented by legislation.
2. Broadly defining a foreign threat.
3. Blocking property and property interests and prohibiting transactions with a sanctions target.[165]
4. Broadly defining property and property interests.[166]
5. Broadly defining prohibited transactions or dealings.
6. Using licensing authority to fine tune or target sanctions policy.
7. Prohibiting evasions, causing violations, conspiracies, and facilitation to prevent sanctions busting.[167,168]
8. Establishing a strict liability standard, encouraging compliance, and imposing stiff penalties for willful and egregious violations of sanctions.
9. Authority to issue administrative subpoenas for information collection.
10. Jurisdictional reach — to U.S. foreign subsidiaries and foreign persons.

What follows is a description of the importance of these sanctions implementation practices and selected court cases that have helped clarify and uphold their use.

1. Court Deference to the Executive Branch in Conducting Foreign Policy

Four cases of note in which the courts have given wide deference to the Executive to take economic measures in conducting foreign policy and national security are in:

- Youngstown Sheet & Tube Co. v. Sawyer, 343 U.S. 579, 637 (1952), action by the President pursuant to an Act of Congress "would be supported by the strongest of presumptions and the widest latitude of judicial interpretation, and the burden of persuasion would rest heavily upon any who might attack it."[169]
- Dames and Moore v. Regan, 453 U.S 654, 673 (1981), which recognizes the President's ability to control foreign assets as a foreign policy tool, "The frozen assets serve as a "bargaining chip" to be used by the President when dealing with a hostile country."
- Regan v. Wald, 468 U.S. 222, 242 (1984) the courts refused to scrutinize asserted foreign policy rationale for the Cuban embargo.[170]
- Freedom to Travel Campaign v. Newcomb, 82 F.3d 1431, 1439 (9th Cir. 1996) the courts noted "history of judicial deference" to decisions by the political branches

---

165. *See* example in 31 CFR 560:204–208, 211 under the ITSR.
166. *See* example in 31 CFR 560:323,325 under the ITSR.
167. *See* example in 31 CFR 560:203 under the ITSR.
168. *See* example in 31 CFR 560:417 under the ITSR.
169. JRC p. 62.
170. JRC p. 23.

of government as to whether an "adequate foreign policy rationale" exists in a particular context).[171]

2. Broadly Defining a Foreign Threat

Under an IEEPA sanctions program, the initiating Executive Order ("E.O.") identifies the country and government or group that is considered a threat and describes the threatening conduct. It also frequently identifies the names of persons (entities and individuals) whose property is blocked because they have been determined to be engaged in the activities that contribute to the described threat and with whom U.S. persons are prohibited from having transactions or dealings. Persons specifically named in the E.O. are considered named by the President.

The E.O. also typically provides that sanctions apply to persons who have not been named in the E.O., but fall under a set of specific criteria provided in the E.O., that meet the defined specific threat criteria. OFAC is delegated authority to identify and publish the names of such persons acting for or on behalf of, or owned or controlled by the sanctioned country, group or person. OFAC, in consultation with the U.S. State Department and other Federal agencies, identifies persons who meet the criteria and publishes them on its Specially Designated Nationals and Blocked Entities (SDN) List.

OFAC considers all sources of information when making a designation determination under an administrative standard of "reasonable cause to believe." Non-U.S. persons who feel they are improperly designated because of mistake of fact, or who wish to have their designation rescinded by changing their behavior, can seek removal by cooperating with OFAC, for example, by providing information and assurances sufficient to obtain their removal.[172]

The OFAC SDN List is not an exhaustive list of persons that meet the primary or derivative designation criteria. In 2008, OFAC issued a bright-line simplified "50% rule."[173] This applies to any entity in which an SDN-listed person has a 50% or greater direct or indirect ownership interest and thus considered to be a prohibited person, whether that entity is named on the OFAC SDN List or not. Its property and property interests are considered by OFAC as blocked as if its name was listed on the OFAC SDN List.[174] This rule requires a higher compliance standard, making affected persons responsible to determine the ownership composition of the foreign entities with which they transact business, even when there are no red flags or when the ownership of their customer or counter party is not easily knowable. This is a significant responsibility. Now, U.S. and non-U.S. persons who are engaged in commercial and financial transactions in U.S. dollars must engage in greater research about their customers and counterparties lest they face penalties and substantial reputational damage."[175]

---

171. JRC p. 23, 81.

172. 31 CFR 501.807.

173. http://www.treasury.gov/resource-center/sanctions/Documents/licensing_guidance.pdf.

174. For example, a Final Rule for amending the terrorism regulations 31 CFR 594 and 31 CFR 595 establishes the 50 percent rule, is found in the Federal Register 78 FR 38574 Page 38574 -38577 CFR: Document Number: 2013-15424 at https://federalregister.gov/a/2013-15424. OFAC in its guidance document on the 50% rule noted that it would incorporate the 50% rule into new sanctions program regulations as they were issued and into old regulations as they were came up for revision. *See* http://www.treasury.gov/resource-center/sanctions/Documents/licensing_guidance.pdf.

175. As stated in 31 CFR 594 the new rule reads "A person whose property and interests in property are blocked pursuant to § 594.201(a) has an interest in all property and interests in property of an

Further, in an effort to more carefully target sanctions, declared threats to the United States have shifted from entire countries and their governments and persons ordinarily resident in that country to more specifically targeted groups, entities, individuals, and persons or groups tied to, or identified to be closely connected with part of a government, or elements of a government. The designation criteria "acting for or on behalf of, or owned or controlled by" the target—has expanded in recent programs to now include material, financial or technological assistance to the threat. The possibility of being named by OFAC on its SDN List acts as a powerful incentive to both U.S. and non-U.S. persons engaged in international commerce to have effective compliance programs with sufficient routine due diligence to ensure they do not engage in transactions with persons or entities named by OFAC on its SDN List or with whom they might reasonably consider may be named on the SDN List or with persons or entities owned 50% or more by persons or entities named on the OFAC SDN List.

Designating Foreign Persons on the OFAC SDN List

A person derivatively designated as an SDN by OFAC under the Libya sanctions program challenged his naming in Paradissiotis v. Rubin (1999).

Paradissiotis v. Rubin
171 F.3d 983, 986–987 (1999)

In 1991, OFAC labeled Paradissiotis a Specially Designated National of Libya pursuant to 31 C.F.R. § 550.304(c). See 56 Fed.Reg. 37156 (1991). This designation was based on his service as president and member on the Boards of Directors of Holborn Investment Company Limited ("HICL") and Holborn European Marketing Company Limited ("HEMCL"). Both HICL and HEMCL are subsidiaries of Oilinvest (Netherlands) B.V., which, in turn, is a wholly owned subsidiary of Oilinvest International, N.V., a Libyan state-controlled holding company. By virtue of his connection to these and other Libyan-related entities and, therefore, his direct or indirect actions taken on behalf of Libya, OFAC found that Paradissiotis constituted the Government of Libya ("GOL") for purposes of the sanctions regulations. See 31 C.F.R. § 550.304(c). As a specially designated national, Paradissiotis's United States assets were frozen.

From January 1993 through December 1996, Paradissiotis applied repeatedly to OFAC for a license under 31 C.F.R. § 501.801(b)(2) so that he could sell stock and exercise stock options in the Coastal Corporation ("Coastal") and receive the proceeds. Paradissiotis had received this property as President of HOTL, a downstream and offshore subsidiary of Coastal, a Delaware corporation, before the Libyan sanctions went into effect. OFAC permitted Paradissiotis to retain counsel in this country but denied his requests to conduct any other prohibited transaction.

Paradissiotis then filed suit seeking declaratory, injunctive, and monetary relief for being categorized as a Specially Designated National under the regulations. The district

---

entity in which it owns, directly or indirectly, a 50 percent or greater interest. The property and interests in property of such an entity, therefore, are blocked, and such an entity is a person whose property and interests in property are blocked pursuant to § 594.201(a), *regardless of whether the entity itself is listed in the Annex to Executive Order 13224, as amended, or designated pursuant to § 594.201(a)."* *(Italics added.)* On August 13, 2014, OFAC provided further guidance regarding the 50 percent rule, which says, "any entity owned in the aggregate, directly or indirectly, 50 percent or more by one or more blocked persons is itself considered to be a blocked person." *See* http://www.treasury.gov/resource-center/sanctions/Documents/licensing_guidance.pdf.

court denied Paradissiotis's request for a preliminary injunction and granted the government's motion for summary judgment. Paradissiotis timely appealed.

. . . .

The federal courts' role in this controversy is circumscribed at two levels. First, OFAC's designation of Paradissiotis as a specially designated national of Libya, being "an agency's application of its own regulations, receives an even greater degree of deference than the *Chevron* standard, and must prevail unless plainly inconsistent with the regulation." *Consarc Corp. v. United States Treasury Dept., Office of Foreign Assets Control,* 71 F.3d 909, 914 (D.C.Cir.1995) (internal quotation omitted). *See also, Thomas Jefferson University v. Shalala,* 512 U.S. 504, 512, 114 S. Ct. 2381, 2386–87, 129 L.Ed.2d 405 (1994). Second, a challenge to OFAC's regulation must either demonstrate that the statute clearly forbids the statute's interpretation or that the interpretation is unreasonable. *Chevron U.S.A., Inc. v. Natural Resources Defense Council, Inc.,* 467 U.S. 837, 843–44, 104 S.Ct. 2778, 2781–83, 81 L.Ed.2d 694 (1984).

---

3. Blocking Property and Property Interests and Prohibiting Transactions with a Sanctions Target

The principle that a blocking of an asset is not a taking permits OFAC to rapidly immobilize assets of an adversary and at the appropriate time in the future, if necessary, use unblocking of assets as a bargaining chip in a negotiated diplomatic or claims settlement with the sanctions target. Meanwhile, the target of sanctions is deprived of resources that otherwise might be used against the United States. Even if an adversary claims that unblocked frozen funds would be used for a benign purpose, since property is fungible, releasing blocked funds may permit an adversary to use more of its other resources outside of U.S. jurisdiction to continue to threaten the United States or otherwise benefit from the use of its assets.

OFAC regulations define property and property interests broadly. OFAC regulations direct U.S. persons to block and report these holdings in property and interests in property[176]—OFAC does not take possession of or title to blocked property. The regulations provide authority for licensing of transactions, including the unblocking of blocked property.

When a freeze or blocking of property is directed by an Executive Order, there is no vesting or seizure by the U.S. Government. The property is not held by the U.S. Government, but rather it is the responsibility of U.S. persons in possession of such property to maintain possession and freeze the foreign-owned property in the United States that is within their custody and within ten days make a report to OFAC. The owner still holds title, but is deprived of the use of the property. The sanctions regulations guide and direct U.S. persons in their responsibilities for blocking, holding, reporting to OFAC, and maintaining the value of the blocked property.[177,178]

---

176. *See* 31 CFR 501.603, "Reports on blocked property."

177. *See* as an example 31 CFR 560.213, "Holding of funds in interest-bearing accounts; investment and Reinvestment," and 31 CFR 560.214, "Expenses of maintaining blocked physical property; liquidation of blocked property." [ITSR] *Also see* 31 CFR 501.603, "Reports on blocked property."

178. The U.S. government's designation of foreign terrorist groups has led to the designation of their affiliated organizations within the United States, such as the Holy Land Foundation of Texas, Al Haramain of Oregon, and KindHearts for Charitable Humanitarian Development, Inc. of Ohio. Al Haramain and KindHearts, as U.S. persons with constitutional rights, challenged their designation

A Blocking Is Not a Taking
OFAC Judicial Review Commission Report
Takings Clause[179]

Another constitutional issue presented by the Kingpin Act, and by sanctions programs instituted under other statutory authority, is whether asset-blocking produces an uncompensated "taking" of private property in violation of the Fifth Amendment.[180] From the perspective of the individual or entity whose assets are blocked, blocking may seem functionally equivalent to an outright taking because, during the time assets remain blocked, they may not be transferred, sold, or used in any manner without prior OFAC approval.[181] The adverse effects may be exacerbated in cases where the blocking remains in effect for years, as in many cases under the Cuban sanctions program.[182] In such cases, blocking is no different in kind, from the blocked person's perspective, than if the blocked assets were declared forfeited to the United States and physically seized by Treasury agents.

The Department of Justice takes a contrary view. According to the Department, blocking actions do not constitute unconstitutional takings because they "do not effect a forfeiture of property ... and [do not] vest title in favor of the Government...."[183] In support of that view, the Department observes that

> individuals or companies who can show that they are no longer owned or controlled by, or act for or on behalf of, a designated individual or entity, for example, can have blocking orders rescinded and blocked property unblocked. Similarly, assets and property may be unblocked if the President determines that the national emergency no longer exists under IEEPA, or that an individual or entity named under the Kingpin Act no longer engages in narcotics trafficking activities.[184]

Based on judicial precedent to date, the courts would be unlikely to hold that blocking produces a "taking" requiring just compensation. The purpose of the Takings Clause is simple enough—"to bar Government from forcing some people alone to bear public burdens which, in all fairness and justice, should be borne by the public as a whole."[185]

---

and the blocking of their funds. Court rulings regarding Al Haramain's suit led OFAC to modify its pre-designation processes for U.S. persons. (For example, the most recent Al Haramain Islamic Foundation v Obama, No. 11-15535 D.C. No 3:07-cv-00109-VRW Opinion, found at http://cdn.ca9. uscourts.gov/datastore/opinions/2012/08/07/11-15468.pdf; and earlier court ruling Al Haramain Islamic Foundation v Bush, US District Court, Case No. 06-274-KI, Opinion and Order https://www.fas.org/sgp/jud/statesec/ahif090706.pdf.) A proposed U.S. designee may be provided with the non-classified information being used to make the proposed designation determination and given an opportunity to respond. (*See* KindHearts for Charitable Humanitarian Development, Inc. v. Geithner et al.)

In the case by KindHearts challenging its blocking, after a court ruling favorable to KindHearts, the U.S. government and KindHearts negotiated a settlement agreement rather than pursue their respective positions further. In the agreement, KindHearts agreed to dissolve and close down, and the government agreed to delist KindHearts and permit its assets to be unblocked by OFAC license, and donated to specified approved charitable organizations. (*See* the settlement agreement with Kindhearts can be found at https://www.aclu.org/files/assets/kindhearts_v__geithner_-_settlement.pdf.)

179. JRC pp. 89–91.

180. *See* U.S. Const. amend. V (providing that "private property" shall not "be taken for public use without just compensation").

181. *See* 21 U.S.C. § 1904(c) (listing "prohibited transactions" for blocked assets).

182. The first Cuban Asset Control Regulations were promulgated in 1963. *See* 31 C.F.R. pt. 515.

183. Written Statement of Deputy Assistant Attorney General Thomas J. Perrelli at 4–5 (citations omitted) [App. E at 309–10].

184. *Id.* at 5 [App. Eat 310].

185. Armstrong v. United States, 364 U.S. 40, 49 (1960).

The Clause is designed "not to limit the governmental interference with property rights *per se,* but rather to secure compensation in the event of otherwise proper interference amounting to a taking."[186]

The fact that asset-blocking does not transfer title or possession of blocked assets to the government, standing alone, does not preclude a finding that blocking produces a taking. Since Pennsylvania Coal Co. v. Mahon,[187] the Supreme Court has recognized that "if the protection against physical appropriations of private property was to be meaningfully enforced, the government's power to redefine the range of interests included in the ownership of property was necessarily constrained by constitutional limits."[188] As a result, the Court has cautioned, "while property may be regulated to a certain extent, if regulation goes too far it will be recognized as a taking."[189]

At the other extreme, economic harm resulting from government regulatory action does not necessarily transform it into a taking requiring payment of just compensation. The Court recognized this principle in Pennsylvania Coal., stating that "[government] hardly could go on if to some extent values incident to property could not be diminished without paying for every such change in the general law."[190] Consistent with this recognition, the Supreme Court has held, "in a wide variety of contexts, that government may execute laws or programs that adversely affect recognized economic values" without compensating adversely affected property owners.[191] Thus, "the Court has often upheld substantial regulation of an owner's use of his own property where deemed necessary to promote the public interest."[192]

In determining whether the government has infringed property rights without adequate justification—in other words, when "regulation goes too far"[193]— "essentially ad hoc, factual inquiries are required" where, as here, *per se* takings are not at issue.[194] These

---

186. First English Evangelical Lutheran Church of Glendale v. County of Los Angeles, 482 U.S. 304, 314 (1987). The Constitution "does not require that just compensation be paid in advance of or even contemporaneously with the taking," and the existence of an after-the-fact legal mechanism for obtaining just compensation (such as the Tucker Act, 28 U.S.C. § 1491, for takings by the federal government) satisfies the constitutional mandate. Preseault v. Interstate Commerce Comm' n, 494 U.S. I, 11 (1990). *See generally* 28 U.S.C. § 1491 (conferring exclusive jurisdiction on Court of Federal Claims over damages suits for uncompensated takings or other violations of federal law by the federal government); *id.* § 1346(a)(2) (conferring concurrent jurisdiction on Court of Federal Claims and U.S. District Courts for such suits seeking $10,000 or less); *see also Preseault,* 494 U.S. at 13 ("[W]e have always assumed that the Tucker Act is an 'implie[d] promis[e]' to pay just compensation which individual laws need not reiterate.").

187. 260 U.S. 393 (1922).

188. Lucas v. South Carolina Coastal Council, 505 U.S. 1003, 1014 (1992).

189. *Pennsylvania Coal,* 260 U.S. at 415 (Holmes, J.) (prohibition on subsurface mining a taking because it essentially destroyed the plaintiff's reserved mineral rights); *see also* United States v. Pewee Coal Co., 341 U.S. 114 (1951) (wartime seizure and operation of coal mine to prevent a national strike constituted a taking).

190. *Pennsylvania Coal,* 260 U.S. at 413.

191. Penn Central Transp. Co. v. City of New York, 438 U.S. 104, 124 (1978); *see also id.* at 131 (noting that the Supreme Court has "uniformly reject[ed] the proposition that diminution in property value, standing alone, can establish a 'taking') (citations omitted). Examples include municipal preservation programs prohibiting development of historic landmarks, *see id.* at 138, and a government order closing gold mines to make skilled miners available for other types of mining more useful to the war effort, *see* United States v. Central Eureka Mining Co., 357 U.S. 155 (1958).

192. Loretto v. Teleprompter Manhattan CATV Corp., 458 U.S. 419, 426 (1982).

193. *Pennsylvania Coal,* 260 U.S. at 415.

194. *See generally Lucas,* 505 U.S. at 1015 ("We have ... described at least two discrete categories of regulatory action as compensable without case-specific inquiry into the public interest advanced

inquiries are captured by "several factors that have particular significance" in the takings calculus: (1) the "economic impact of the regulation on the claimant"; (2) "the extent to which the regulation has interfered with distinct investment-backed expectations"; and (3) "the character of the governmental action."[195]

There has been a significant amount of litigation over whether blockings under the Kingpin Act's statutory antecedents—TWEA and IEEPA—constitute takings requiring just compensation. Without exception, the precedent to date holds that governmental actions to block or "freeze" assets in the United States pursuant to economic sanctions programs do not constitute takings requiring just compensation.[196]

The OFAC Judicial Review Commission Report Describes Tran Qui Than v. Regan — Challenging a Blocking under TWEA — As a Taking

... the Ninth Circuit addressed a takings challenge to an order of the Treasury Department freezing a South Vietnamese bank's assets under TWEA. A resident alien shareholder in the foreign bank sought to have the blocking lifted so that he could collect on the bank's right to obtain payment from the U.S. Army for goods and services rendered by the bank's assignor. The court concluded that "the blocking program ... does not constitute a constitutionally cognizable taking."[197]

Tran Qui Than v. Regan

658 F.2d 1296 1304 (1981)

Than's arguments that the blocking of the Bank's United States assets constitutes an unconstitutional taking without just compensation and violates his right to equal protection of the laws are unpersuasive. The Trading with the Enemy Act and the Regulations promulgated pursuant thereto with respect to "blocking" received the constitutional imprimatur of the Supreme Court in Propper v. Clark, 337 U.S. 472, 69 S.Ct. 1333, 93 L.Ed. 1480 (1949). In Propper the Court upheld the President's "freezing" order issued pursuant to s 5(b) of the TWEA which prohibited certain transactions involving Austrian property except as they were specifically licensed by the Secretary of the Treasury.

---

in support of the restraint. The first encompasses regulations that compel the property owner to suffer a physical 'invasion' of his property.... The second situation in which we have found categorical treatment appropriate is where regulation denies all economically beneficial or productive use of land."); see also Penn Central, 438 U.S. at 124.

195. Penn Central, 438 U.S. at 124. The latter factor is significant because "[a] 'taking' may more readily be found when the interference with property can be characterized as a physical invasion by government than when interference arises from some public program adjusting the benefits and burdens of economic life to promote the common good." Id.

196. See 767 Third Avenue Assoc. v. United States, 30 Fed. Cl. 216, 223 (1993) (rejecting takings claim and holding that the government's action "under the authority of the Constitution and the IEEPA [was] fully within its sovereign rights to conduct foreign affairs and [the government] took no property interests owned by [plaintiff] for which [it] would be entitled to just compensation"), aff'd, 48 F.3d 1575 (Fed. Cir. 1995); Rockefeller Center Properties v. United States, 32 Fed. Cl. 586, 594 (Ct. Cl. 1995) (holding that "no compensable taking was effected when the OFAC..denied [plaintiff] its contract rights to evict [designated entity] and to draw upon [a] letter of credit"); Chang v. United States, 859 F.2d 893 (Fed. Cir. 1988) (affirming Court of Claims dismissal on grounds that plaintiffs' loss of employment contracts with Libyan oil company due to prohibitions of Libyan Sanctions Regulations did not constitute a "taking"); see generally Tole S.A. v. Miller, 530 F. Supp. 999, 1004 (S.D.N.Y. 1981) (noting that a taking's challenge "to the government's freezing of assets has been rejected by every court that has previously considered this issue"), aff'd, 697 F.2d 298 (2d Cir. 1982).

197. JRC p. 92.

....

We recognize that blocking involves a deprivation of the enjoyment of a property interest. That deprivation is temporary, however, and is not equivalent to vesting. Vesting occurs when title to assets is transferred to the government; blocking does not transfer title but rather prohibits, temporarily, transactions involving those assets. We also recognize that an action intended by the government to be a temporary block on any transactions involving those assets may amount to an interminable denial of property to the individual who must await the often slow and labyrinthian course of international relations. The possibility remains, however, that the President and the Congress may decide that resumption of diplomatic and economic intercourse with the South Vietnamese government would be in our national interest.

....

We conclude that the blocking program with respect to the assets at issue does not constitute a constitutionally cognizable taking without just compensation.

Dames & Moore v. Regan

453 U.S. 654, 101 S. Ct. 2972 2977, 2983, 69 L.Ed.2d 918 (1981)

[p 2977].... [This] dispute involves various Executive Orders and regulations by which the President nullified attachments and liens on Iranian assets in the United States, directed that these assets be transferred to Iran, and suspended claims against Iran that may be presented to an International Claims Tribunal. This action was taken in an effort to comply with an Executive Agreement between the United States and Iran.

....

[p 2983].... we think both the legislative history and cases interpreting the TWEA fully sustain the broad authority of the Executive when acting under this congressional grant of power. *See, e. g.,* Orvis v. Brownell, 345 U.S. 183, 73 S. Ct. 596, 97 L.Ed. 938 (1953).FN5 Although Congress intended to limit the President's emergency power in peacetime, we do not think the changes brought about by the enactment of the IEEPA in any way affected the authority of the President to take the specific actions taken here.

....

[p 2983] This Court has previously recognized that the congressional purpose in authorizing blocking orders is "to put control of foreign assets in the hands of the President...." *Propper v. Clark,* 337 U.S. 472, 493, 69 S.Ct. 1333, 1345, 93 L.Ed. 1480 (1949). Such orders permit the President to maintain the foreign assets at his disposal for use in negotiating the resolution of a declared national emergency. The frozen assets serve as a "bargaining chip" to be used by the President when dealing with a hostile country. Accordingly, it is difficult to accept petitioner's argument because the practical effect of it is to allow individual claimants throughout the country to minimize or wholly eliminate this "bargaining chip" through attachments, garnishments, or similar encumbrances on property. Neither the purpose the statute was enacted to serve nor its plain language supports such a result.

Any question of redress against the United States only comes up with respect to the suspension of claims. The nullification of attachments and transfer of blocked property were held to be proper exercises of the President's authority under IEEPA—thus they were supported both by delegated authority from Congress plus the President's constitutional foreign affairs powers. The Court therefore held that the nullification of attachment and transfer of property were constitutional and did not constitute a taking of property. Where it left an open question as to future redress was with respect to the suspension of claims in U.S. courts. The Court said this was not an exercise of IEEPA powers. Thus it was only supported by the President's constitutional foreign affairs powers. The Court upheld the suspension of claims but left open the question as to whether it constituted a taking of property. It said this question could be decided in the future through a Tucker Act action should the Tribunal turn out not to provide just compensation.[198]

4. Broadly Defining Property and Property Interests

Property and property interests are broadly defined for the purpose of blocking. A narrower definition of property and property interests might permit a sanctions loophole through the use of financial and commercial instruments and types of property that are not covered. The Iranian Transactions and Sanctions Regulations' definitions of interest, property and property interests are examples of the broad definitions traditionally used by OFAC for this purpose:

> § 560.323 Interest. Except as otherwise provided in this part, the term interest, when used with respect to property (e.g., "an interest in property"), means an interest of any nature whatsoever, direct or indirect.

> § 560.325 Property; property interest. The terms property and property interest include, but are not limited to, money, checks, drafts, bullion, bank deposits, savings accounts, debts, indebtedness, obligations, notes, guarantees, debentures, stocks, bonds, coupons, any other financial instruments, bankers acceptances, mortgages, pledges, liens or other rights in the nature of security, warehouse receipts, bills of lading, trust receipts, bills of sale, any other evidences of title, ownership or indebtedness, letters of credit and any documents relating to any rights or obligations thereunder, powers of attorney, goods, wares, merchandise, chattels, stocks on hand, ships, goods on ships, real estate mortgages, deeds of trust, vendors' sales agreements, land contracts, leaseholds, ground rents, real estate and any other interest therein, options, negotiable instruments, trade acceptances, royalties, book accounts, accounts payable, judgments, patents, trademarks or copyrights, insurance policies, safe deposit boxes and their contents, annuities, pooling agreements, services of any nature whatsoever, contracts of any nature whatsoever, and any other property, real, personal, or mixed, tangible or intangible, or interest or interests therein, present, future, or contingent.[199]

The definition of property and interest in property may expand over time as new financial and commercial instruments and products are developed or transformed. Currently, property is construed to mean property and property interest of any nature whatsoever whether present, future, or contingent.

OFAC's broad definition of blockable property interests under the Iraq sanctions regulations and its actions based upon this definition were challenged in Consarc Corp. v. Iraqi Ministry.

---

198. Tucker Act, 28 U.S.C. § 1491.

199. *See* for example § 560.323 Interest; § 560.325 Property; property interest. [ITSR]. *See* another example, 31 CFR 576.312 Property; property interests [Iraq].

Consarc Corp. v. Iraqi Ministry

27 F.3d 695, 697, 701 (1994)

Consarc Corporation, a New Jersey furnace manufacturer, brought suit in the United States District Court for the District of Columbia against the Iraqi Ministry of Industry and Minerals ("IMIM") and the Rafidain Bank of Iraq (a governmental entity), alleging breach of contract and fraud arising from a sales contract between Consarc and IMIM. After Consarc obtained a default judgment against the Iraqi defendants, the Treasury Department's Office of Foreign Assets Control ("OFAC") intervened, arguing that the assets against which the judgment would be satisfied were frozen by Presidential order. Consarc filed a "supplemental" complaint that added OFAC as a defendant.

. . . .

. . . . OFAC may choose and apply its own definition of property interests, subject to deferential judicial review. By section 1704 of the Emergency Powers Act the President may "issue such regulations, including regulations prescribing definitions, as may be necessary for the exercise of the authorities granted by this chapter." 50 U.S.C. § 1704. Among those authorities is the power to "prohibit any ... transfer [of] ... any property in which any foreign country or a national thereof has any interest." *Id.* § 1702(a)(1)(B). The President delegated his power to define the statutory terms to the Secretary of the Treasury, *see Exec. Order No. 12724*, 55 Fed.Reg. 33089 (1990), and OFAC exercises the delegated power on the Secretary's behalf. By these provisions OFAC has received the authority to administer the statute, *cf. Wagner Seed Co. v. Bush*, 946 F.2d 918, 920 (D.C.Cir.1991), *cert. denied*, 503 U.S. 970, 112 S. Ct. 1584, 118 L.Ed.2d 304 (1992), so that we must give effect to OFAC's regulations unless they contradict express statutory language or prove unreasonable. *See Chevron U.S.A. Inc. v. NRDC*, 467 U.S. 837, 844–45, 104 S. Ct. 2778, 2782–83, 81 L.Ed.2d 694 (1984).

OFAC Judicial Review Commission Report's Commentary on Consarc

The courts have upheld OFAC's interpretation and application of this expansive regulatory definition. In Consarc I, the court of appeals upheld OFAC's determination that a "contingent reversionary interest" in a letter of credit constituted an interest in property within the meaning of the IEEPA-based Iraqi Sanctions Regulations, 31 C.F.R. § 575.315. In reaching its conclusion, the court in Consarc I observed that "OFAC may choose and apply its own definition of property interests, subject to deferential judicial review." 27 F.3d at 701.[200]

Courts reviewing OFAC actions under the APA [Administrative Procedures Act][201] will consider only whether OFAC's action is "arbitrary and capricious," and will not consider whether the decision is the "best" decision possible. . . . [202]

Blocking Property

As the number of sanctions programs have increased, the management of blocked assets has grown more complex and become an issue for a wider number of U.S. persons. The OFAC JRC Report describes how blockable property and interest in property are blocked and managed:

---

200. JRC p. 34.
201. Pub. L. 89-554, 80 Stat. 381 (codified at 5 U.S.C. § 551 *et seq.* (1996 & 2000 Supp.)).
202. JRC p. 62.

OFAC Judicial Review Commission Report

1. Blocking of Assets of Designated Foreign Persons

a. Blocking of Funds

b. Blocking of Tangible and "Other" Property

2. Prohibition on Dealing by United States Persons [203]

Assets of foreign persons who are designated as targets under any of the IEEPA-based sanctions programs are "blocked" by operation of law immediately upon the designation of the person or entity.[204] OFAC does not provide any advance notice to foreign persons prior to their designation that their property will be blocked.[205] Similarly, no prior notice is given to U.S. persons who have an interest in the property that will be blocked, or who may be adversely affected by the blocking.[206]

U.S. persons (either individuals or business entities) effectuate the blocking of assets of designated foreign persons. It is a legal obligation of U.S. persons or persons within the jurisdiction of the United States to block the assets of designated foreign persons and to report such blocking to OFAC.[207] Failure to block the assets of designated foreign persons, when such assets are in the custody or control of U.S. persons, constitutes a violation of the particular sanctions regime, and may be the basis for civil or criminal penalties.[208]

. . . .

According to OFAC, "any U.S. person holding funds, such as currency, bank deposits, or liquidated financial obligations" which are subject to blocking "must hold or place such funds in a blocked interest-bearing account, earning interest at rates which are commercially reasonable, in a federally-insured U.S. bank, thrift institution, or credit union, located in the United States.[209] Not only must funds belonging to an SDNT that are within the

---

203. JRC p. 33, 35, 36.

204. *See id.* at 4 [App. B at 49]. There is no separate order issued by the government directing that particular assets be blocked.

205. *See id.* at 21 [App. B at 66].

206. *See id.*

207. *See* 31 C.F.R. § 501.601 ("Records and Record-Keeping Requirements"). Part 501 of OFAC regulations (title 31 of the Code of Federal Regulations) sets forth standard procedures applicable to all OFAC-administered sanctions programs.

208. OFAC reported to the Commission that when it "discovers that blocked assets are not being held in accordance with law, [it] can issue an administrative order or directive requiring compliance with the law." OFAC Responses to Written Questions at 18 [App. B at 63]. The Commission has not been apprised of the circumstances in which OFAC would proceed by "administrative order or directive" rather than seeking civil penalties for the failure by a U.S. person to block the assets of a designated foreign person.

In its publication for financial institutions, OFAC states that it has imposed "millions of dollars in civil penalties" on U.S. banks, and that the "majority of the fines resulted from banks' failure to block illicit transfers...." Office of Foreign Assets Control, U.S. Dep't of the Treasury, "Foreign Asset Control Regulations for the Financial Community," at 2 (Aug. 18, 2000) (hereinafter "Foreign Asset Control Regulations for the Financial Community") [App. C at 19]. OFAC cautions banks:

    If your bank does not block and report a transfer and another bank does, then your bank
    is in trouble. A bank in non-compliance may be opening itself to adverse publicity, fines,
    and even criminal penalties (if violations are other than inadvertent).

Foreign Asset Control Regulations for the Financial Community at 3 [App. C at 20].

209. Newcomb, *Coping with U.S Export Controls 1999, supra,* at 126. Alternatively, OFAC allows blocked funds to be "placed with a broker or dealer registered with the Securities and Exchange Commission under the Securities Exchange Act of 1934, provided the funds are invested in a money market fund or in U.S. Treasury bills." *Id.*

jurisdiction of the United States or within the "possession or control of U.S. persons" at the time of the designation be blocked, but funds that subsequently "come within the United States, or ... within the possession or control of U.S. persons" also must be blocked.[210] For financial institutions, the practical effect of this requirement is that the institution must monitor all transactions routed through it so as to block, and place into a blocked account, funds in which an SDNT has any "interest."[211] For example, U.S. banks (and foreign branches of U.S. banks) are required to block "funds transfers" even though the funds "merely pass through a bank that is associated with a target," when neither the originator nor the beneficiary has any association with the target.[212] Once such funds are blocked, neither the originator nor the beneficiary can access the funds without a license from OFAC.[213]

    ....

In addition to obligating U.S. persons to block the property of designated sanctions targets, Executive Orders issued pursuant to IEEPA usually prohibit U.S. persons from engaging in "any transaction or dealing" in the "property or interests in property of the persons designated" as targets in the sanctions program.[214] It is OFAC's general practice to issue "alert letters" to U.S. companies to "advise them of the existence of economic sanctions and request compliance."[215]

Authorizations that permit otherwise prohibited transactions, and which are of general applicability, are set forth in the regulations. These authorizations or "general" licenses are categorical exceptions to the prohibition on "dealing."

5. Broadly Defining Prohibited Transactions or Dealings

OFAC asserts broad prohibitions on different types of economic transactions or dealings with prohibited parties. The types of economic prohibitions which are imposed depends upon the nature of the national security threat and upon the President's foreign policy purposes. Some economic sanctions programs apply several of the prohibitions on transactions or dealings listed below; whereas, other sanctions programs may impose all of the prohibitions on transactions or dealings listed below (the list below is fairly

---

210. 31 C.F.R. § 536.201(a).

211. Written Submission of the New York Clearing House Ass'n at 3–5 [App. D at 54–56].

212. *Id.* at 5 [App. D at 56].

213. *See* Newcomb, *Coping with U.S. Export Controls 1999, supra,* at 111 ("Frozen [blocked] assets (*e.g,* bank deposits and other forms of property) cannot be paid out, withdrawn, set off, transferred or dealt in in [sic] any manner without a Treasury license.").

214. In Section 2 of Executive Order 12978, "Blocking Assets and Prohibiting Transactions with Significant Narcotics Traffickers," the President stated that:

    Further, except to the extent provided in section 203(b) of IEEPA and in regulations, orders, directives, or licenses that may be issued pursuant to this order, and notwithstanding any contract entered into or any license or permit granted prior to the effective date, I hereby prohibit the following:

    (a) any transaction or dealing by United States persons or within the United States in property or interests in property of the persons designated in or pursuant to this order;

    (b) any transaction by any United States person or within the United States that evades or avoids, or has the purpose of evading or avoiding, or attempts to violate, any of the prohibitions set forth in this order.

215. OFAC Responses to Written Questions at 31 [App. B at 76]. Examples of alert letters, as redacted by OFAC, may be found in Appendix C to this Final Report, at 55–63.

comprehensive, but there may be other possible prohibitions in current or future programs that are not listed).

- Importing directly or indirectly.
- Exporting directly or indirectly.
- Brokering.
- Trade financing.
- New Investment.
- Mandatory disinvestment.
- Payments.
- Dollar clearing.
- Asset freeze or blocking.
- Contract performance.
- Grant or extension of credit or loan.
- Transport of goods.
- Transportation transactions.
- Travel transactions.
- Any other type of transaction or dealing whatsoever.
- Transactions which evade or avoid or cause violations.

How these prohibited transactions are interpreted and what transactions are licensed or permitted may differ between programs. Each part of 31 CFR that addresses a specific sanctions program has language in subpart 101 to make this point clear. An example of the type of language that makes these points in subpart 101 is:

> This part is separate from, and independent of, the other parts of this chapter, with the exception of part 501of this chapter, the recordkeeping and reporting requirements and license application and other procedures of which apply to this part. Actions taken pursuant to part 501 of this chapter with respect to the prohibitions contained in this part are considered actions taken pursuant to this part. Differing foreign policy and national security circumstances may result in differing interpretations of similar language among the parts of this chapter. No license or authorization contained in or issued pursuant to those other parts authorizes any transaction prohibited by this part. No license or authorization contained in or issued pursuant to any other provision of law or regulation authorizes any transaction prohibited by this part. No license or authorization contained in or issued pursuant to this part relieves the involved parties from complying with any other applicable laws or regulations.[216]

6. Using Licensing Authority to Fine Tune or Target Sanctions Policy

When sanctions are imposed by Executive order, they are designed to have broad application and significant impact on the sanctions targets' financial or commercial interests. However, sanctions by their very nature are a blunt instrument. Some prohibited activity may unintentionally stop what U.S. foreign policy might otherwise want to permit and in which case can be authorized by license. OFAC issues the license and, in consultation

---

216. 31 CFR 594.101.

with State and Treasury Department policymakers, determines the conditions of the license. OFAC also can withdraw it if the U.S. foreign policy toward the licensed activity or the target changes or if it believes the license has been or may be misapplied. The license is not open to creative interpretation by the license holder; OFAC determines the meaning of the license, not its holder. OFAC can and often does require reporting on how the license holder uses the license. This licensing approach helps prevent evasion of sanctions, and permits the flexible administration of sanctions to meet changing policy demands.

There are two types of licenses — a general license and a specific license. A general license provides broad regulatory authorization to all persons meeting the conditions contained in the license. It can be used without further communication with or authorization from OFAC. A specific license is sought by making a written request outlining the proposed activity. It is granted on a case-by-case basis. OFAC often defines those categories of specific licenses it will consider by issuance of a "Statement of Licensing Policy." As the determination to issue such a license is very fact dependent, the applicant must describe in sufficient detail the context, background, need and all other relevant facts involved. Whether a transaction is authorized by general or specific license, OFAC has for all of the programs it administers a five year recordkeeping requirement for all transactions or activities authorized by license.[217]

OFAC Has Broad Discretion in Licensing Transactions

Under the Federal Republic of Yugoslavia (Serbia and Montenegro) economic sanctions program, OFAC had issued a license to Sage Realty Corp to collect rent from a Yugoslav tenant from blocked funds, but once the Yugoslav tenant's property had been removed, OFAC withdrew the license that permitted the drawing upon blocked funds. In response, Sage Realty brought a lawsuit against the Department of Treasury.

Sage Realty Corp. v. Department of Treasury
2000 WL 272192 (S.D.N.Y.) 1–3, 7 (2000)

Plaintiff Sage Realty Corp. ("Sage") challenges the determination of the Office of Foreign Assets Control ("OFAC") denying Sage a license to receive blocked funds from a Yugoslav bank in order to enforce a judgment obtained by plaintiff.

The present case arises out of Sage's inability to enforce a judgment in a lease dispute between Sage and Jugobanka, D.D. New York Agency ("Jugobanka"), one of Sage's former tenants. On June 25, 1991, Jugobanka, a Yugoslav banking corporation, entered into a lease agreement with Sage to rent a portion of the third floor at 437 Madison Avenue, New York, a building for which Sage is the managing agent. In June 1993, acting pursuant to President Clinton's Executive Order, OFAC agents revoked Jugobanka's license to conduct

---

217. 31 CFR 501.601, "Records and recordkeeping requirements. Except as otherwise provided, every person engaging in any transaction subject to the provisions of this chapter shall keep a full and accurate record of each such transaction engaged in, regardless of whether such transaction is effected pursuant to license or otherwise, and such record shall be available for examination for at least 5 years after the date of such transaction. Except as otherwise provided, every person holding property blocked pursuant to the provisions of this chapter or funds transfers retained pursuant to § 596.504(b) of this chapter shall keep a full and accurate record of such property, and such record shall be available for examination for the period of time that such property is blocked and for at least 5 years after the date such property is unblocked."

business in the United States, directed Jugobanka to vacate the premises at 437 Madison Avenue, and blocked all of Jugobanka's assets located in the United States. OFAC then issued a license to Sage permitting the release of funds from Jugobanka's blocked account at the Bank of New York and directing that those funds be used to pay rent to Sage.

. . . .

In August 1994, OFAC notified Sage that the leased space was being vacated and that Sage's license was being revoked, thereby preventing Sage from continuing to receive funds from Jugobanka's blocked account to satisfy future rent obligations. At the same time, however, OFAC issued a new license to Sage, authorizing Sage to receive rent from "fresh funds." [Funds from outside the jurisdiction of the United States, thus preserving the pool of blocked funds in the United States.] On August 29, 1994, Jugobanka's belongings were removed from 437 Madison Avenue by OFAC.

Sage stopped receiving rental payments from Jugobanka in September 1994. It then brought an action for breach of contract against Jugobanka in this Court.

. . . .

Under the APA [Administrative Procedures Act.], this Court must decide whether OFAC's decision denying Sage a license was "arbitrary, capricious, an abuse of discretion, or otherwise not in accordance with law." 5 U.S.C. § 706(2)(A). Substantial deference must be accorded to the agency. In fact, a presumption of validity attaches to agency action, and the burden of proving that OFAC's decision was arbitrary or capricious rests with plaintiff. *Mississippi Hosp. Ass'n, Inc. v. Heckler,* 701 F.2d 511, 516 (5th Cir.1983) (citing *Alabama Nursing Home Ass'n v. Harris,* 617 F.2d 388, 393 (5th Cir.1980)); *accord Friedman v. Perales,* 668 F.Supp. 216, 221 (S.D.N.Y.1987), *aff'd,* 841 F.2d 47 (2d Cir.1988); *see also Milena Ship Management Co. v. Newcomb,* 804 F.Supp. 859, 861 (E.D.La.1992) (addressing a challenge to a decision by OFAC refusing to unblock vessels owned by Yugoslav entities and stating that "[i]nherent in the standard is a high degree of deference to the agency's decision, bordering on a presumption that the action taken is valid."), *aff'd,* 995 F.2d 620 (1993) (citations omitted).

OFAC's decision may be deemed arbitrary or capricious, or an abuse of discretion

> "if the agency has relied on factors which Congress has not intended it to consider, entirely failed to consider an important aspect of the problem, offered an explanation for its decision that runs counter to the evidence before the agency, or is so implausible that it could not be ascribed to a difference in view or the product of agency expertise." *Henley v. Food and Drug Admin.,* 77 F.3d 616, 620 (2d Cir. 1996) (quoting *Motor Vehicle Mfrs. Assoc. of the United States, Inc. v. State Farm Mut. Auto. Ins. Co.,* 463 U.S. 29, 43 (1983)).

In determining whether OFAC's decision was arbitrary or capricious, " 'the focal point for judicial review should be the administrative record already in existence, not some new record made initially in the reviewing court.'" *Florida Power & Light Co. v. Lorion, et al.,* 470 U.S. 729, 743 (1985) (quoting *Camp v. Pitts,* 411 U.S. 138, 142 (1973) (per curiam)). The Court's review of the administrative record must be "searching and careful," but it is also narrow, and the Court must not substitute its judgment for that of OFAC. *Citizens to Preserve Overton Park v. Volpe,* 401 U.S. 402, 416 (1971).

. . . .

Because Sage cannot show that OFAC's decision to deny Sage a license to enforce the judgment was arbitrary or capricious, an abuse of discretion, or otherwise not in accordance with the law, the Court awards summary judgment to OFAC on Sage's claim under the APA.

7. Prohibiting Evasions, Causing Violations, Conspiracies, and Facilitation to Prevent Sanctions Busting[218]

OFAC regulations specifically prohibit U.S. persons from engaging in any activities that would have the result of evading sanctions prohibitions, facilitation, conspiracy, and causing violations by U.S. persons.

Several sections in the Iran Transactions and Sanctions Regulations (31 CFR 560) and Sudanese Sanctions Regulations (31 CFR 538) illustrate this point by specifying what constitutes an evasion or facilitation to evade a sanctions program prohibitions of dealings. For example, in 31 CFR Part 560, §§.203, .208, and .417:

§ 560.203 Evasions; attempts; causing violations; conspiracies.

(a) Any transaction on or after the effective date that evades or avoids, has the purpose of evading or avoiding, causes a violation of, or attempts to violate any of the prohibitions set forth in this part is prohibited.

(b) Any conspiracy formed to violate any of the prohibitions set forth in this part is prohibited.

§ 560.208 Prohibited facilitation by United States persons of transactions by foreign persons.

Except as otherwise authorized pursuant to this part, and notwithstanding any contract entered into or any license or permit granted prior to May 7, 1995, no United States person, wherever located, may approve, finance, facilitate, or guarantee any transaction by a foreign person where the transaction by that foreign person would be prohibited by this part if performed by a United States person or within the United States.

§ 560.417 Facilitation; change of policies and procedures; referral of business opportunities offshore.

With respect to § 560.208, a prohibited facilitation or approval of a transaction by a foreign person occurs, among other instances, when a United States person:

(a) Alters its operating policies or procedures, or those of a foreign affiliate, to permit a foreign affiliate to accept or perform a specific contract, engagement or transaction involving Iran or the Government of Iran without the approval of the United States person, where such transaction previously required approval by the United States person and such transaction by the foreign affiliate would be prohibited by this part if performed directly by a United States person or from the United States;

(b) Refers to a foreign person purchase orders, requests for bids, or similar business opportunities involving Iran or the Government of Iran to which the United States person could not directly respond as a result of the prohibitions contained in this part; or

---

218. United States Code Annotated, Title 50. War and National Defense, Chapter 35. International Emergency Economic Powers, § 1702. Presidential authorities.

(c) Changes the operating policies and procedures of a particular affiliate with the specific purpose of facilitating transactions that would be prohibited by this part if performed by a United States person or from the United States.

The prohibitions on evasion and facilitation are critical elements of OFAC programs as they prohibit U.S. persons from structuring transactions that would frustrate the intent of a sanctions program, while preserving markets for themselves at the expense of their U.S. competitors who are complying.

Also considered as a sanctions violation are transactions that "cause a violation." This occurs, for example, when a non-U.S. bank performs a U.S. dollar clearing transaction or any other transaction on behalf of a designated person or sanctioned country through its U.S. correspondent bank account by stripping the message traffic directing and supporting the transfer of any information that would identify the prohibited parties for whom they are acting. When this occurs the U.S. correspondent bank is unaware that it is processing a transaction on behalf of a sanctions target because its foreign correspondent customer has removed identifying information about its customer, thus "causing" the U.S. bank unknowingly to commit a violation. But as it was not aware of the party on whose behalf it was processing the transaction it cannot be held liable. When this occurs the non-U.S. bank has "caused" such a violation and will be held accountable.

8. Establishing a Strict Liability Standard, Encouraging Compliance, and Imposing Stiff Penalties for Willful and Egregious Violations of Sanctions

IEEPA authorizes significant penalties to be assessed against sanctions violators, and does this under a strict liability standard:

United States Code Annotated, Title 50. War and National Defense, Chapter 35. International Emergency Economic Powers, § 1705. Penalties

(a) Unlawful acts

It shall be unlawful for a person to violate, attempt to violate, conspire to violate, or cause a violation of any license, order, regulation, or prohibition issued under this chapter.

(b) Civil penalty

A civil penalty may be imposed on any person who commits an unlawful act described in subsection (a) of this section in an amount not to exceed the greater of—

(1) $250,000; or

(2) an amount that is twice the amount of the transaction that is the basis of the violation with respect to which the penalty is imposed.

(c) Criminal penalty

A person who willfully commits, willfully attempts to commit, or willfully conspires to commit, or aids or abets in the commission of, an unlawful act described in subsection (a) of this section shall, upon conviction, be fined not more than $1,000,000, or if a natural person, may be imprisoned for not more than 20 years, or both.

The penalties can rapidly build with each count, and some recent fines have reached into the billions of dollars. That has received the attention of the financial and commercial communities.[219]

Although OFAC's recent civil penalty actions have been substantial and there have been significant criminal cases, the focus of OFAC's efforts is to encourage U.S. persons to comply fully and effectively with sanctions prohibitions and requirements. However, OFAC has enforcement options to spur compliance that extend beyond civil and criminal penalties, to include: a proactive outreach to facilitate a compliance effort; issuance of a cautionary or warning letter, revocation of a license, issuing a cease and desist order, or a decision to take no action.

Sanctions are administered on a strict liability standard. OFAC does not direct how U.S. persons should comply with its requirements. But failure to comply likely will result in adverse action depending on the facts of the particular situation. OFAC does provide information regarding known risks that financial and commercial institutions face,[220] including publishing a "risk matrix" that may help institutions shape and determine where to focus the resources of their compliance programs. OFAC also maintains a hotline to answer public questions,[221] performs outreach to the U.S. financial and business communities and foreign counterparts, and maintains a website that provides an abundance of sanctions program information.[222]

OFAC has published guidelines that provide very significant incentives to the voluntary disclosure of possible violations and promote making a serious effort to maintain an effective compliance program.[223] Penalties can be very significantly reduced by knowing the law and demonstrating a good faith effort to follow it with an effective risk-based compliance program.

However, for willful and egregious violations, civil penalties have become much stiffer over the recent years. In 2004, the civil penalties for a violation of IEEPA were $11,000

---

219. The Department of Justice ("DOJ") has become much more aggressive in investigating these crimes for possible prosecution. In recent years, there have been such high-profile enforcement actions resulting in deferred prosecution agreements and the payment of fines in the hundreds of millions to billions of dollars by non-U.S. (foreign) banks for having used the U.S. banking system to provide dollar account banking services to banks in sanctioned countries. For example, Lloyds Bank TSB of London, in a deferred prosecution agreement, paid a fine of more than $340 million dollars to the Manhattan District Attorney and DOJ for its sanctions busting activities. Credit Suisse agreed to pay more than $500 million in settlement. ING Bank agreed to forfeit $619 million to settle OFAC violations. Standard Chartered Bank agreed to pay $340 million to the New York State regulator to settle claims for such violations. BNP Paribas SA agreed to pay nearly $963 million in settlement for apparent violations of multiple sanctions programs.

220. For example, Office of Foreign Assets Control—Overview in the FFIEC BSA/AML Examination Manual pp 137–148 at http://www.treasury.gov/resource-center/sanctions/Documents/ofac_sec_frb _080106.pdf; See OFAC-provided general compliance risk matrix at http://www.treasury.gov/resource-center/sanctions/DocumentS/Matrix.pdf. See "Risk Factors for OFAC Compliance in the Securities Industry" at http://www.treasury.gov/sanctions/Documents/securities_risk_11052008.pdf, and see "Risk Factors for Charities Disbursing Funds or Resources to Grantees" at http:// www.treasury.gov/resource-center/sanctions/Documents/charity_risk_matrix.pdf.

221. Toll Free Hotline: 1-800-540-6322; Local Hotline: 1-202-622-2490; OFAC Licensing Division (Direct): 1-202-622-2480; OFAC Fax-on-demand document service: 1-202-622-0077, see http:// www.treasury.gov/about/organizational-structure/offices/Pages/Office-of-Foreign-Assets-Control.aspx# fragment-7.

222. See OFAC website at http://www.treasury.gov/resource-center/sanctions/Pages/default.aspx.

223. Appendix A to Part 501—Economic Sanctions Enforcement Guidelines. This rule was first published in the Federal Register / Vol. 74, No. 215 / Monday, November 9, 2009 / Rules and Regulations, with a description and explanation for the Final Rule starting at page 57593.

per count. This went to $50,000 per count in 2006. And in 2008, it went to $250,000 per count or two times the value of the transaction in question, whichever is the greater amount.

Mitigating and Aggravating Factors in OFAC Sanctions Compliance and Enforcement Actions

Although there is a strict liability standard under IEEPA, OFAC sanctions regulations provide for consideration of mitigating and aggravating circumstances when assessing civil penalties. Among the most significant mitigation factors are whether the violation was egregious and whether a voluntary disclosure is made to OFAC upon learning that a violation may have occurred.

III. General Factors Affecting Administrative Action

(Edited and excerpted from 31 CFR 501 Appendix A. III.
GPO website: current as of June 12, 2014)

A. Willful or Reckless Violation of Law: 1. Willfulness; 2. Recklessness; 3. Concealment; 4. Pattern of Conduct; 5. Prior Notice; 6. Management Involvement.

B. Awareness of Conduct at Issue: 1. Actual Knowledge; 2. Reason to Know; 3. Management Involvement. C. Harm to Sanctions.

C. Harm to Sanctions Program Objectives: 1. Economic or Other Benefit to the Sanctioned Individual, Entity, or Country; 2. Implications for U.S. Policy; 3. License Eligibility; 4. Humanitarian activity.

D. Individual Characteristics: 1. Commercial Sophistication; 2. Size of Operations and Financial Condition; 3. Volume of Transactions; 4. Sanctions History.

E. Compliance Program.

F. Remedial Response: 1. The steps taken by the Subject Person upon learning of the apparent violation; 2. In the case of an entity, the processes followed to resolve issues related to the apparent violation; 3. In the case of an entity, whether the Subject Person adopted new and more effective internal controls and procedures to prevent a recurrence of the apparent violation; 4. Where applicable, whether the Subject Person undertook a thorough review to identify other possible violations.

G. Cooperation with OFAC: 1. Did the Subject Person voluntarily self-disclose the apparent violation to OFAC? 2. Did the Subject Person provide OFAC with all relevant information regarding an apparent violation (whether or not voluntarily self-disclosed)? 3. Did the Subject Person research and disclose to OFAC relevant information regarding any other apparent violations caused by the same course of conduct? 4. Was information provided voluntarily or in response to an administrative subpoena? 5. Did the Subject Person cooperate with, and promptly respond to, all requests for information? 6. Did the Subject Person enter into a statute of limitations tolling agreement, if requested by OFAC?

H. Timing of apparent violation in relation to imposition of sanctions.

I. Other enforcement action.

J. Future Compliance/Deterrence Effect.

K. Other relevant factors on a case-by-case basis.

V. Civil Penalties

(Edited and excerpted from 31 CFR 501 Appendix A. V.
GPO website: current as of June 12, 2014)

B. Amount of Civil Penalty

1. Egregious case. In those cases in which a civil monetary penalty is deemed appropriate, OFAC will make a determination as to whether a case is deemed "egregious" for purposes of the base penalty calculation. This determination will be based on an analysis of the applicable General Factors. In making the egregiousness determination, OFAC generally will give substantial weight to General Factors A ("willful or reckless violation of law"), B ("awareness of conduct at issue"), C ("harm to sanctions program objectives") and D ("individual characteristics"), with particular emphasis on General Factors A and B. A case will be considered an "egregious case" where the analysis of the applicable General Factors, with a focus on those General Factors identified above, indicates that the case represents a particularly serious violation of the law calling for a strong enforcement response. A determination that a case is "egregious" will be made by the Director or Deputy Director.

Examples that Illustrate the Application of Aggravating and Mitigating Factors in IEEPA Civil Penalties Cases

Clearstream Banking, S.A. Settles Potential Liability for Apparent Violations of Iranian Sanctions

January 23 2014[224]

Clearstream Banking, S.A. ("Clearstream"), Luxembourg, has agreed to remit $151,902,000 to settle potential civil liability for apparent violations of the Iranian Transactions and Sanctions Regulations ("ITSR"), 31 C.F.R. part 560.1 From at least December 2007 through June 2008, Clearstream maintained an account at a U.S. financial institution in New York through which the Central Bank of Iran ("CBI") maintained a beneficial ownership interest in 26 securities, with a nominal value of $2.813 billion, held in custody at a central securities depository in the United States. Due to the omnibus nature of Clearstream's account in New York, the CBI's beneficial ownership interest in the 26 securities was not transparent to the U.S. financial institution. Clearstream, as intermediary, served as the channel through which the CBI held an interest in these securities. Clearstream exported custody and related services from the United States to the CBI in apparent violation of the ITSR.

OFAC officials met with Clearstream in late 2007 and early 2008 to discuss Clearstream's business with Iranian clients, including implementing its decision to terminate this business. In February 2008, Clearstream, acting on instructions from the CBI, transferred the securities entitlements free-of-payment ("FOP") from the CBI's account with Clearstream to a European bank's newly opened custody account at Clearstream, an account which allowed the CBI to continue holding its interest in the securities through Clearstream. As a result of the FOP transfers, the record ownership of the securities en-

---

224. According to OFAC, "The Economic Sanctions Enforcement Guidelines, as well as recent final civil penalties and enforcement information, can be found on OFAC's Web site at http://www.treasury.gov/resource-center/sanctions/CivPen/Pages/civpen-index2.aspx." The case write-up quoted above is found at: http://www.treasury.gov/resource-center/sanctions/CivPen/Documents/20140123_clearstream.pdf.

titlements on Clearstream's books changed, but the beneficial ownership did not, resulting in the CBI's interest being buried one layer deeper in the custodial chain. Following the FOP transfers, the ultimate place of custody for the securities remained the United States, and the CBI's interest continued to be held through Clearstream's omnibus account in New York. Given the totality of facts and circumstances surrounding the transfers, Clearstream had reason to know that the CBI was retaining beneficial ownership of the securities. Clearstream's exportation of services from the United States to the CBI continued after the securities entitlements were moved to the European bank's custody account.

OFAC has determined that Clearstream did not voluntarily self-disclose the apparent violations, and that the apparent violations were reckless and constitute an egregious case. The total base penalty amount for the apparent violations was $5.626 billion.

The settlement amount reflects OFAC's consideration of facts and circumstances pursuant to the General Factors under OFAC's Economic Sanctions Enforcement Guidelines, 31 C.F.R. part 501, app. A. The following were considered aggravating factors: Clearstream acted recklessly in failing to perform sufficient due diligence transferring the securities entitlements FOP to another financial institution's custody account with Clearstream in February 2008; several Clearstream employees, including at least one supervisor and a senior executive, had reason to know that the CBI's beneficial ownership of the securities would not change following their transfer; and Clearstream's actions caused significant harm to U.S. sanctions program objectives. This enforcement action highlights the particular sanctions risks faced by intermediaries, custodians, and other firms operating in the international securities markets. The following were considered mitigating factors: Clearstream has undertaken significant remedial action by enhancing its controls to prevent a recurrence of the apparent violations and has adopted new best practices in an effort to position itself as an industry leader in sanctions compliance standards; Clearstream demonstrated substantial cooperation with OFAC during its investigation of the apparent violations, including by signing a statute of limitations tolling agreement; Clearstream has not been the subject of an OFAC enforcement action in the five years preceding the earliest date of the transactions giving rise to the apparent violations; and, OFAC considered the totality of the circumstances to ensure that the enforcement response was proportionate to the nature of the apparent violations.

ING Bank N.V. Settles Potential Liability for Apparent Violations of Multiple Sanctions Programs:

June 12, 2012[225]

ING Bank N.V. ("ING") has agreed to settle potential civil liability for apparent violations of: the Cuban Assets Control Regulations ("CACR"), 31 C.F.R. part 515; the Burmese Sanctions Regulations ("BSR"), 31 C.F.R. part 537; the Sudanese Sanctions Regulations ("SSR"), 31 C.F.R. part 538; the now-repealed Libyan Sanctions Regulations ("LSR"), 31 C.F.R. part 550; and the Iranian Transactions Regulations ("ITR"), 31 C.F.R. part 560. ING's settlement with the Office of Foreign Assets Control ("OFAC") is part of a global

-----

225. The two civil case descriptions that follow are from: http://www.treasury.gov/resource-center/sanctions/CivPen/Documents/06122012_ing.pdf and http://www.treasury.gov/resource-center/sanctions/CivPen/Documents/20140630_bnp.pdf.

settlement among ING, OFAC, the U.S. Department of Justice, and the New York County District Attorney's Office. The bank agreed to settle with OFAC the apparent violations of OFAC regulations, which OFAC determined were egregious, for $619,000,000, with the obligation deemed satisfied by a payment of $619,000,000 to the Department of Justice and the New York County District Attorney's Office.

ING processed 20,452 wire transfers, trade finance transactions, or travelers checks totaling approximately $1,654,657,318 between October 22, 2002, and July 6, 2007, involving Cuba in apparent violation of the CACR. The total base penalty for this set of apparent violations was $636,450,000. ING processed 41 wire transfers and trade finance transactions totaling approximately $15,469,938 between December 26, 2003, and September 6, 2007, in apparent violation of the BSR. The total base penalty for this set of apparent violations was $19,919,545. ING processed 44 wire transfers and trade finance transactions totaling approximately $1,976,483 between January 14, 2004, and December 11, 2006, in apparent violation of the SSR. The total base penalty for this set of apparent violations was $6,531,899. ING processed three wire transfers totaling approximately $26,803 between January 13, 2004, and April 27, 2004, involving the Government of Libya or Libyan persons in apparent violation of the now-repealed LSR. The total base penalty for these apparent violations was $375,000. On or about February to March, 2004 and on October 27, 2004, ING processed two trade finance transactions in the aggregate amount of $1,358,000, in apparent violation of the ITR. The total base penalty for these apparent violations was $2,716,000.

The above-referenced apparent violations involved ING's commercial banking offices in The Netherlands, Belgium, France, Curacao, and Cuba, and did not involve ING's insurance or banking operations in the United States. ING voluntarily self-disclosed all of these apparent violations under the terms of OFAC's Economic Sanctions Enforcement Guidelines ("the Guidelines") except for the February to March, 2004, apparent violation of the ITR, which ING did not voluntarily self-disclose. The statutory maximum penalty in this case was $1,329,268,888. The total base penalty amount under the Guidelines for all apparent violations was $665,992,444.

In reaching its determination that the above-referenced apparent violations were egregious OFAC determined that ING's conduct was marked by willfulness and recklessness; several ING employees, including senior management, were aware of the conduct that led to the apparent violations; the apparent violations resulted in significant harm to U.S. sanctions programs objectives; and ING is a highly sophisticated global financial institution. OFAC further aggravated the base penalty because ING did not consistently cooperate with OFAC early in its investigation with regard to explicit requests for information. Mitigation was extended because some of the apparent violations processed by ING (relating to agricultural or medical transactions or large personal remittances) may have been eligible for an OFAC license; ING has not received a penalty notice, finding of violation, cautionary letter, warning letter, or other administrative action from OFAC in the five years preceding the date of the transactions giving rise to the apparent violations; ING voluntarily self-disclosed all of the apparent violations except the apparent ITR violation processed by ING Bucharest; ING provided some cooperation to OFAC during the later stages of its investigation by providing substantial and well organized information for OFAC's assessment, by signing a tolling agreement and multiple extensions of that agreement, and by responding to multiple inquiries and requests for information; and ING took appropriate remedial action in response to matters described above. Mitigation was further extended because ING agreed to settle these apparent violations.

BNP Paribas SA Settles Potential Civil Liability for Apparent Violations of Multiple Sanctions Programs

June 30, 2014

BNP Paribas SA ("BNPP") has agreed to settle potential civil liability for 3,897 apparent violations of: the Sudanese Sanctions Regulations (the "SSR"), 31 C.F.R. part 538; the Iranian Transactions and Sanctions Regulations (the "ITSR"),1 31 C.F.R. part 560; the Cuban Assets Control Regulations (the "CACR"), 31 C.F.R. part 515; and the Burmese Sanctions Regulations (the "BSR"), 31 C.F.R. part 537. BNPP's settlement with the Office of Foreign Assets Control ("OFAC") is part of a global settlement among BNPP, OFAC, the U.S. Department of Justice, the New York County District Attorney's Office, the Federal Reserve Board of Governors, and the Department of Financial Services of the State of New York. BNPP agreed to settle with OFAC the apparent violations of OFAC regulations for $963,619,900, with the obligation deemed satisfied by payment of an equal or greater amount in satisfaction of penalties by the Department of Justice and the New York County District Attorney's Office arising out of the same pattern of conduct.

OFAC determined that BNPP did not voluntarily self-disclose these apparent violations, and that the apparent violations constitute an egregious case. Both the statutory maximum and base civil monetary penalties in this case were $19,272,380,006.

For a number of years, up to and including 2012, BNPP processed thousands of transactions to or through U.S. financial institutions that involved countries, entities, and/or individuals subject to the sanctions programs listed above. BNPP appears to have engaged in a systematic practice, spanning many years and involving multiple BNPP branches and business lines, that concealed, removed, omitted, or obscured references to, or the interest or involvement of, sanctioned parties in U.S. Dollar Society for Worldwide Interbank Financial Telecommunication payment messages sent to U.S. financial institutions. The specific payment practices the bank utilized in order to process certain sanctions-related payments to or through the United States included omitting references to sanctioned parties; replacing the names of sanctioned parties with BNPP's name or a code word; and structuring payments in a manner that did not identify the involvement of sanctioned parties in payments sent to U.S. financial institutions....

BNPP processed 2,663 wire transfers totaling approximately $8,370,372,624 between September 6, 2005, and July 24, 2009, involving Sudan in apparent violation of the SSR. The total base penalty for this set of apparent violations was $16,826,707,625. BNPP processed 318 wire transfers totaling approximately $1,182,075,543 between July 15, 2005, and November 27, 2012, involving Iran in apparent violation of the ITSR. The total base penalty for this set of apparent violations was $2,382,634,677. BNPP processed 909 wire transfers totaling approximately $689,237,183 between July 18, 2005, and September 10, 2012, involving Cuba in apparent violation of the CACR. The total base penalty for this set of apparent violations was $59,085,000. BNPP processed seven wire transfers totaling approximately $1,478,371 between November 3, 2005, and approximately May 2009, involving Burma in apparent violation of the BSR. The total base penalty for this set of apparent violations was $3,952,704.

The settlement amount reflects OFAC's consideration of the following facts and circumstances, pursuant to the General Factors Affecting Administrative Action under OFAC's Economic Sanctions Enforcement Guidelines, 31 C.F.R. part 501, app. A. The following were found to be aggravating factors: BNPP had indications that its conduct might have constituted violations of U.S. law, and therefore BNPP acted with reckless disregard for U.S. sanctions regulations; at least one member of BNPP's senior management was aware of the conduct leading to the apparent violations; BNPP's business line management and supervisors were aware, and/or had reason to know, of the conduct leading to the apparent violations; the conduct described above resulted from a pattern or practice that spanned many years and multiple BNPP branches and product lines; the conduct described above conferred significant economic benefit to persons subject to U.S. sanctions and undermined the integrity of multiple U.S. sanctions programs; BNPP is a large and commercially sophisticated financial institution; and BNPP did not maintain adequate policies, procedures, or internal controls to ensure compliance with the sanctions programs administered by OFAC. Mitigation was extended because BNPP has not received a penalty notice or Finding of Violation from OFAC in the five years preceding the date of the earliest transaction giving rise to the apparent violations; BNPP cooperated with OFAC's investigation of the apparent violations by conducting an extensive internal investigation and executing a statute of limitations tolling agreement with multiple extensions; BNPP took remedial action in response to the apparent violations described above; and a consideration of the totality of the circumstances warrants further mitigation to ensure an enforcement response that is proportionate to the nature of the violations.

Example of an IEEPA Criminal Case and a Civil Forfeiture Case
Embargo Violations by Alleged Arms Dealer
December 13, 2013[226]

On December 13, 2013, Richard Ammar Chichakli, an associate of international arms dealer Viktor Bout, was found guilty by jury in the Southern District of New York, of conspiring with Bout and others to violate the International Emergency Economic Powers Act ("IEEPA") by attempting to purchase commercial airplanes from American companies, in violation of U.S. sanctions. Chichakli, a citizen of Syria and the United States, was also found guilty of money laundering conspiracy, wire fraud conspiracy, and six counts of wire fraud, in connection with the attempted aircraft purchases. According to evidence at trial and documents previously filed in Manhattan federal court, Chichakli conspired with Bout and others to violate IEEPA by engaging in prohibited business transactions with companies based in the United States. The focus of these transactions was the purchase of commercial airplanes for a company that Bout and Chichakli controlled, and the ferrying of those aircraft to Tajikistan. At the time of these unlawful transactions, both Chichakli and Bout had been designated by the U.S. Treasury Department as Specially Designated Nationals ("SDNs"), which meant that individuals and businesses in the United States were prohibited from engaging in financial transactions with them. Chichakli sought to evade these SDN sanctions by, among other things, concealing his identity and his SDN listing, and by concealing Bout's involvement in the airplane transactions. In connection with this fraudulent scheme, Chichakli helped to make a series of wire transfer payments, totaling more than $1.7 million. These payments were sent from overseas bank accounts into accounts in the United States. Chichakli faces a maximum sentence of five years in prison on the IEEPA conspiracy count, and a maximum of 20 years in prison on each of the other eight counts. Chichakli's co-conspirator, Bout, is currently serving a 25-year prison term as a result of his November 2011 conviction in the Southern District

---

226. The description of the two criminal cases cited here are found in the Department of Justice's, "Summary of Major U.S. Export Enforcement, Economic Espionage, Trade Secret and Embargo-Related Criminal Cases (January 2008 to present: updated March 26, 2014)," March 2014, NSD, www.justice.gov.

of New York in connection with his conspiring to sell millions of dollars of weapons to a designated foreign terrorist organization. This case was investigated by the DEA-Special Operations Division.

Manhattan Office Building Secretly Owned and Controlled by Government of Iran

September 17, 2013

On September 17, 2013, in the Southern District of New York, a decision was issued granting summary judgment in favor of the United States' claims for forfeiture of the 36-story Midtown Manhattan office building located at 650 Fifth Avenue, New York, New York ("the Building"), as the result of violations of the Iranian Transactions Regulations promulgated under the International Emergency Economic Powers Act ("IEEPA"), and the federal money laundering statutes. The Court found that the partners of the Building's owner, the Alavi Foundation and Assa Corp., committed the IEEPA violations and money laundering offenses. According to the amended civil forfeiture Complaint and the oral and written opinions issued by Judge Forrest in this case: The Alavi Foundation has been providing numerous services to the Iranian Government, including managing the Building for the Iranian Government, running a charitable organization for the Iranian Government, and transferring funds from 650 Fifth Avenue Company to Bank Melli Iran ("Bank Melli"), a bank wholly owned and controlled by the Government of Iran. Likewise, Assa Corporation and Assa Company Limited ("Assa Co. Ltd.") have been providing numerous services to Bank Melli in contravention of IEEPA and the Iranian Transactions Regulations promulgated thereunder, including transferring rental income generated from 650 Fifth Avenue Company to Bank Melli, following Bank Melli's instructions with regard to Assa Corporation's affairs, reporting back to Bank Melli on Assa Corporation's financial situation and business dealings, and managing the affairs of Assa Corporation for the benefit of Bank Melli. The Alavi Foundation owns 60 percent of 650 Fifth Avenue Company, and Bank Melli owns 40 percent of 650 Fifth Avenue Company, through Assa Corp. and Assa Co. Ltd. On December 17, 2008, a civil Complaint was filed seeking forfeiture of the 40 percent interest held by Assa Corporation in 650 Fifth Avenue Company. In the Amended Complaint, the United States seeks to forfeit all right, title and interest in 650 Fifth Avenue Company, including the Alavi Foundation's 60 percent interest in the company. The United States also seeks to forfeit the contents of bank accounts held by 650 Fifth Avenue Company, the Alavi Foundation, and Assa Corporation, as well as other real properties owned by the Alavi Foundation. Claims against the building in this consolidated action by private parties holding judgments against the Government of Iran remain pending. The investigation was conducted by the FBI, IRS, CID, and the Joint Terrorism Task Force.

9. Authority to Issue Administrative Subpoenas for Information Collection

Under OFAC regulations, 31 CFR 501.602 "Reports to be furnished on demand," the Director of OFAC can directly issue administrative subpoenas for information related to its sanctions programs:

> Every person is required to furnish under oath, in the form of reports or otherwise, from time to time and at any time as may be required by the Director, Office of

Foreign Assets Control, complete information relative to any transaction, regardless of whether such transaction is effected pursuant to license or otherwise, subject to the provisions of this chapter or relative to any property in which any foreign country or any national thereof has any interest of any nature whatsoever, direct or indirect. The Director may require that such reports include the production of any books of account, contracts, letters or other papers connected with any such transaction or property, in the custody or control of the persons required to make such reports. Reports with respect to transactions may be required either before or after such transactions are completed . . .

The administrative subpoena is a powerful authority for the collection of information pursuant to administering sanctions. The administrative subpoena can be issued directly by the OFAC Director to U.S. persons to produce information related to a foreign prohibited person.

Further, under 31 CFR 501.601 U.S. persons are required to maintain records for five years related to transactions covered by the sanctions program and provide reports on: blocked property (.603); rejected transactions (.604); litigation, arbitration and dispute resolutions (.605); in addition to those under demand (.602).[227] These requirements provide for a robust collection of information regarding sanctions-related transactions and activity.

10a. Jurisdictional reach to U.S. foreign subsidiaries

Both IEEPA and TWEA authorize the President to regulate or prohibit, direct and compel, investigate, void, nullify, etc., transactions "by any person, or with respect to any property, subject to the jurisdiction of the United States. . . ."[228] This language authorizes the President to impose sanctions requirements to the extent of U.S. jurisdiction, including on foreign subsidiaries of U.S. persons. Using this authority in TWEA, the President required compliance by foreign subsidiaries of U.S. persons when he imposed sanctions on countries such as China, North Korea, Vietnam, Cambodia and Cuba. Yet, as a matter of policy, nearly all IEEPA sanctions that have been imposed by the United States[229] require compliance by U.S. persons, a term that is defined in the relevant Executive orders and OFAC regulations to mean any United States citizen or permanent resident alien, any juridical entity organized under the laws of the United States or any jurisdiction within the United States, including foreign branches, or any person in the United States. Foreign subsidiaries of U.S. companies, because they are established under the laws of another nation, by definition are not U.S. persons and, therefore, are not themselves subject to sanctions programs requiring compliance by U.S. persons.

---

227. For example, see 31 CFR 501.601 "Records and recordkeeping requirements. Except as otherwise provided, every person engaging in any transaction subject to the provisions of this chapter shall keep a full and accurate record of each such transaction engaged in, regardless of whether such transaction is effected pursuant to license or otherwise, and such record shall be available for examination for at least 5 years after the date of such transaction. Except as otherwise provided, every person holding property blocked pursuant to the provisions of this chapter or funds transfers retained pursuant to § 596.504(b) of this chapter shall keep a full and accurate record of such property, and such record shall be available for examination for the period of time that such property is blocked and for at least 5 years after the date such property is unblocked."

228. TWEA, § 5(b); IEEPA, § 203, 50 U.S.C. 1702.

229. The one exception is the first Iran sanctions program, which was imposed in response to the taking of the hostages in 1979 and was the very first exercise of IEEPA authority.

Nevertheless, in all OFAC sanctions programs, the foreign subsidiary's business within a sanctioned country could subject the U.S. parent to liability for sanctions violations. U.S. parent companies have always been liable for their foreign subsidiaries' economic transactions with a sanctioned country when those foreign subsidiaries were not operating independently of the U.S. parent or when the U.S. parent facilitated the transaction in some way.

Other than the Iranian program, where the prohibition on the foreign subsidiary and the U.S. parent liability for violations by the foreign subsidiary now are established by statute,[230] a determination of U.S. parent liability for transactions by its foreign subsidiary that would be violations of the sanctions program if engaged in by a U.S. person are based upon the independence of the foreign subsidiary and whether the transaction is facilitated by the U. S. parent:

First: Independence vs Control. For a foreign subsidiary of a U.S. company to engage in transactions with a sanctioned country that would be prohibited for the parent, that foreign subsidiary must operate independently of the U.S. parent. Otherwise, the prohibited transactions in which the foreign subsidiary engages will be attributed to the U.S. parent.

Whether a foreign subsidiary is indeed independent will be determined from the totality of the facts and circumstances, such as:

- Who directs the operations of the subsidiary?
  - How does the subsidiary do business in terms of decision-making, risk taking, approvals, day-to-day operations, financing, etc.? Are approvals by the parent required and, if so, for what decisions?
  - What is the makeup of the management and board of directors?
  - Which national entity, the U.S. or foreign corporation, has the majority of appointed directors, and what is the nationality of each director?
  - Does the U.S. parent or joint venture partner have veto authority over the decisions of the subsidiary management or board?
- What is the percentage of ownership?
- When and how was the subsidiary established or acquired?
- What is the corporate structure of subsidiary and parent?
- What is the volume of business with the sanctioned country?
- What other business does the subsidiary conduct?
- What is the relationship of the subsidiary's business to the parent's business? and so on.

This is a very fact-based analysis that includes consideration of intent and purpose of the elements identified above and any other factors that may be relevant to the parent/subsidiary relationship.

Second: Facilitation. The U.S. parent must not in any way facilitate or approve the foreign subsidiary's transactions with the sanctioned country or entity. A prohibited facilitation or approval of a transaction by a foreign person occurs, among other instances, when a U.S. person:[231]

- Alters its operating procedures, or those of a foreign affiliate, to permit a foreign affiliate to accept or perform a specific contract, engagement or transaction involving a sanctioned country that is otherwise prohibited to it.

- Refers to foreign affiliate purchase orders, requests for bids or similar business opportunities involving the sanctioned country or its government to which the U.S.

---

230. Section 218 of the Iranian Threat Reduction Act.
231. *See* for example, 31 CFR 560.208 and 560.417.

person could not itself respond as a result of the applicable OFAC-administered sanctions.

- Changes the operating policies and procedures of a particular affiliate with the specific purpose of facilitating prohibited transactions with the sanctioned country or its government.

The prohibition against facilitation also means that the U.S. person must not engage in any action that assists or supports the foreign affiliate's trading activity or financial transactions with the sanctioned country, entity or person.

Third: Ownership. What is the percentage ownership of the U.S. parent in the subsidiary? What is the level of ownership to other shareholders?

With regard to Iran, Section 218 of the Iran Threat Reduction Act requires the President, within 60 days of the date of enactment of the ITRA, to prohibit an entity owned or controlled by a United States person and established or maintained outside the United States from knowingly engaging in any transaction directly or indirectly with the Government of Iran or any person subject to the jurisdiction of the Government of Iran that would be prohibited by any order or regulation issued pursuant to IEEPA if the transaction were engaged in by a United States person or in the United States. The civil penalties provided for in IEEPA apply to the United States person if an entity owned or controlled by the United States person and established or maintained outside the United States violates, attempts to violate, conspires to violate, or causes a violation of any such order or regulation. The term "own or control" is defined in § 218 as follows:

(2) OWN OR CONTROL. — The term "own or control" means, with respect to an entity —

(A) to hold more than 50 percent of the equity interest by vote or value in the entity;

(B) to hold a majority of seats on the board of directors of the entity; or

(C) to otherwise control the actions, policies, or personnel decisions of the entity.

Thus, a foreign subsidiary of a U.S. corporation that meets any one of the three criteria set out in the statute will expose the U.S. parent to penalties if it deals with Iran. The prohibitions apply also to the foreign subsidiary. The long-held OFAC enforcement considerations focus in regard to two of these criteria — whether the U.S. parent is controlling and facilitating the actions of its foreign subsidiary — the statutory considerations now applied to Iran programs are similar. However, ITRA goes further. If a U.S. parent owns more than 50% of a foreign subsidiary, the parent becomes responsible for the dealings of its subsidiary with sanctioned parties.

Thus, in all sanctions programs, U.S. firms have a high bar to avoid charges of control and facilitation and to ensure their subsidiaries are truly independent. One misstep and the U.S. parent could be charged with a violation of sanctions. Alternatively, if the subsidiary is indeed independent and avoids facilitation, having a subsidiary conduct business with an adversary of the United States, could severely damage the reputation of the U.S. parent. For this reason, many U.S. firms direct their subsidiaries to forgo all dealings with U.S. sanctioned countries, entities, and prohibited parties. In the Iran sanctions program, the bar is set even higher, as, in addition to control and facilitation, the prohibitions also apply to any foreign entity that is "owned" by a U.S. person. The U.S. person could be subject to civil penalties for violations by its foreign subsidiary, even if the foreign subsidiary operates independently and the transaction is not facilitated by the U.S. person.

Further Section 219 of the ITRA requires U.S. companies to report to the Securities and Exchange Commission any activities it or its affiliates engage in that could be sanctionable under ISA and CISADA and ITRA itself, and any dealings with listed persons under counter-terrorism (E.O. 13224) and counter-proliferation sanctions (E.O. 13382) programs.[232]

10b. U.S. Sanctions Reach to Foreign Persons

U.S. sanctions reach, with regard, for example, to the ever tightening sanctions on Iran, have expanded dramatically, involving greater initiatives focusing especially on one of the most significant economic levers the U.S. Treasury has—and for that matter that the U.S. Government has available to itself outside of diplomatic, military and law enforcement channels—the U.S. dollar. And now, as a condition of using the U.S. financial system, the United States is imposing through U.S. law and regulations restrictions on foreign financial institution in their use of the U.S. financial system for their dollar de-nominated transactions—particularly with regard to Iran. Non-compliance could be considered a violation of U.S. financial sanctions and anti-money laundering laws, and result in the loss of U.S. correspondent banking privileges and resulting in the non-complying institution being shutout of the U.S. financial market.[233,234,235] This lever will

---

232. Iran Threat Reduction and Syria Human Rights Act of 2012 ("ITRA,") (P.L. 112-158; 22 U.S.C. 8701 et seq.), Section 219.

233. USA PATRIOT Act, Sections 311 and 319 of P.L. 107-56—Oct. 26, 2001.

234. In regard to the NDAA, the State Department website (http://www.state.gov/e/eb/tfs/spi/iran/fs/200286.htm) explains that:

> On December 31, 2011, President Obama signed into law the National Defense Authorization Act for Fiscal Year 2012. Under Section 1245 of the Act, foreign financial institutions that knowingly facilitate significant financial transactions with the Central Bank of Iran ("CBI") or with Iranian financial institutions designated by Treasury risk being cut off from direct access to the U.S. financial system. The provisions of the Comprehensive Iran Sanctions, Accountability, and Divestment Act of 2010 ("CISADA") remain in effect ...
> **Non-Petroleum Banking Sanctions.**
> The Act mandates that the President sanction private foreign financial institutions that are found to knowingly conduct or facilitate significant non-petroleum transactions (except transactions for the sale of food, medicine, or medical devices to Iran) with the CBI or with a U.S.-designated Iranian financial institution. This provision takes effect 60 days after the enactment of the Act. **Non-petroleum banking sanctions do not apply to foreign central banks or state-owned or controlled foreign financial institutions, although these financial institutions remain subject to section 104 of CISADA,** which provides authority for sanctions on foreign financial institutions that are found to have knowingly engaged in facilitating significant transactions for specific Iranian-linked individuals and entities.
> **Petroleum-Related Banking Sanctions**
> The Act also mandates that the President impose banking sanctions on all foreign financial institutions, including foreign central banks or foreign state-owned or controlled banks, that are found to knowingly conduct or facilitate significant financial transactions for the purchase of Iranian petroleum or petroleum products with either the CBI or any U.S.-designated Iranian financial institution. Foreign central and foreign state-owned or controlled banks are also subject to these sanctions if the transactions are for the sale of petroleum or petroleum products to Iran. This provision does not apply to transactions for the purchase of petroleum and petroleum products from Iran for 180 days after enactment, or longer depending on the President's determination on the availability of price and alternative supplies ...

235. EO 13645 (June 3, 2013), "Authorizing the Implementation of Certain Sanctions Set Forth in the Iran Freedom and Counter-Proliferation Act of 2012 and Additional Sanctions With Respect To Iran." *See also*, Department of State "Fact Sheet: Iran Freedom and Counter Proliferation Act of 2012," http://www.state.gov/documents/organization/208111.pdf.

continue to be very effective for the U.S. Government as long as the dollar maintains its strength, value and worldwide use—as commodities, goods and especially oil continue to trade in dollars. For now, many third-country banks in Europe and the Gulf will not do a dollar transaction without near certainty that it won't be blocked or rejected in the United States, which would possibly subject it to an investigation and having to defend itself against suspicion of sanctions violations.

The NDAA requirements on foreign banks correspondent accounts with U.S. banks for dollar transactions and E.O. 13645 are important in two very significant ways—it was the broadest extension of extraterritorial application of U.S. law to non-U.S. persons. It has been suggested that these two measures are likely what brought Iran to the table under the Joint Plan of Action (JPOA).[236]

The authors wish to acknowledge the review and thoughtful comments on this chapter provided to the authors by Mr. Loren Dohm, former Deputy Director of OFAC, and Ms. Rochelle Stern, a former Assistant Director of OFAC. They reviewed and provided comments to the original draft and applied their wealth of knowledge and experience to hone the presentation, and add further detail and technical advice to this complex area of national security law. The authors also wish to acknowledge Mr. Thomas Prevas, an associate of DLA Piper, for his assistance. Notwithstanding their review and contributions, any mistakes that may remain are the responsibility of the authors.

---

236. In the JPOA the U.S. government (USG) has committed to suspend temporarily certain sanctions involving Iran's purchase and sale of gold and other precious metals, Iran's export of petrochemical products, Iran's automotive industry, and certain associated services regarding each of the foregoing. The JPOA also includes a commitment to establish financial channels to facilitate Iran's import of certain humanitarian goods to Iran, payment of medical expenses incurred by Iranians abroad, payments of Iran's UN obligations, and payments of $400 million in governmental tuition assistance for Iranian students studying abroad. In addition, the JPOA includes a commitment to license certain transactions related to the safety of Iran's civil aviation industry. Finally, in the JPOA the USG has committed to pause efforts to further reduce Iran's crude oil exports and to enable Iran to access $4.2 billion in Restricted Funds in installments over the course of the six month period beginning January 20, 2014, and ending July 20, 2014 (the JPOA Period). Unless otherwise noted, these relief measures do not include transactions with persons on the U.S. Treasury Department's Office of Foreign Assets Control's (OFAC) List of Specially Designated Nationals and Blocked Persons (the SDN List).

The USG will continue to vigorously enforce our sanctions against Iran that are not subject to the limited relief provided pursuant to the JPOA, including by taking action against those who seek to evade or circumvent our sanctions. The USG also retains the authority to revoke this limited sanctions relief at any time if Iran fails to meet its commitments under the JPOA.

Source: http://www.treasury.gov/resource-center/sanctions/Programs/Documents/jpoa_faqs.pdf.

Chapter 31

Export Controls and Economic Sanctions: Counterterrorism, Nonproliferation, National Security, and the Foreign Policy of the United States

Larry E. Christensen and Abigail E. Cotterill

In this chapter:
Introduction
Jurisdictional Reach of U.S. Export Controls and Economic Sanctions
Export Controls
Economic Sanctions
Multilateral Export Control Regimes
Enforcement Authority
Limits on the Reach of Certain Reexport Controls and Economic Sanctions

1. Introduction

The export controls and economic sanctions of the United States operate at the intersection of commerce, national security, and foreign policy. On the spectrum of the U.S. Government's national security and foreign policy tools, export controls and economic sanctions occupy the space between diplomacy and use of force. Oftentimes, the U.S. Government employs several such tools at once to implement a specific policy goal. For this reason, no discussion of the United States' response to hostilities and military threats, counter-terrorism, proliferation of chemical, biological or nuclear weapons of mass destruction, despotism, or regional instability is complete without consideration of export controls and economic sanctions. Export controls and economic sanctions are similarly critical to other issues, including security from cyber-attacks and efforts to prevent the transfer of sensitive technology to blacklisted or blocked parties.

As regulations on trade and finance, export controls and economic sanctions affect the day-to-day operations of American businesses and their foreign partners. The U.S. Government agencies with primary jurisdiction over export controls and economic sanctions include the U.S. Department of State ("State"), the U.S. Department of Commerce ("Commerce"), and the U.S. Department of the Treasury ("Treasury"). The central goal of these agencies' export controls and economic sanctions programs is to balance the United States' interests in national security, nonproliferation of weapons of mass destruction, and counterterrorism with ongoing efforts to strengthen the U.S. industrial base through the export of products into the global economy. This balance, executed through a network of executive orders, statutes, regulations and interpretive guidance, was born from the foreign policy of the Cold War and refined to reflect modern threats including terrorism.

In 2009, the Obama Administration launched the Export Control Reform ("ECR") initiative.[1] ECR represents a systematic effort to recalibrate the level of control for various goods, services, and technologies, especially parts and components, to provide for more flexible controls consistent with national security. In phases designed to bring the United States' regulatory landscape into harmony with current international threats and economic challenges, many of the items previously controlled by State as "defense articles" have shifted to the jurisdiction of Commerce. As discussed in greater detail below, the creation of the "600 series" of items on the Commerce Control List ("CCL") embodies this policy shift. The many economic sanctions programs of the U.S. Government, with their differing scope and application, demonstrate the practical contours of the U.S. Government's approach to national security in recent years.

This chapter will address the regulation of defense articles and defense services by the International Traffic in Arms Regulations ("ITAR") of State. It will then explain the so-called dual-use regulations of the United States, namely, the Export Administration Regulations ("EAR") of Commerce and its Bureau of Industry and Security ("BIS"). The export control and economic sanctions practitioner will find the U.S. Government regulations relevant to virtually every export control question and the statutory authority relevant to a tiny number of export control questions.[2] For this reason, this Chapter will discuss the statutory authority for export controls in brief and concentrate on the structure of the ITAR and EAR, and certain key areas such as the jurisdictional line between the United States Munitions List ("USML") and the CCL.

Our focus will then shift to the regulatory programs implemented by Treasury's Office of Foreign Assets Control ("OFAC"). In general, these programs can be divided into three categories: List-Based Programs, Limited Programs, and Comprehensive Programs. Each program is tailored to include elements such as partial and comprehensive embargoes on certain target nations, blacklists of specially designated persons and corporations who are fronts for embargoed governments, prohibitions on dealings including importing and exporting, and requirements for asset blocking and reporting to enforcement authorities at OFAC.

We will then consider how reexport controls on the transfer of goods, services and technology from one non-U.S. country to another are at the very heart of both the export controls and economic sanctions of the United States. These controls reach into the economies of other countries and extend to corporations and natural persons who are not in the territory of the United States, or U.S. Citizens. One of the United States' largest

---

1. INTERNATIONAL TRADE ADMINISTRATION, "The President's Export Control Reform Initiative," <http://export.gov/%5C%5C/ecr/index.asp>.

2. The reader should note that this chapter was written in August 2014, and the ITAR, the EAR and the various regulations issued by OFAC change often, sometimes as often as dozens of times in a given calendar year. For this reason, the reader must be mindful that to comply with these rules, it is essential to have a means to follow the Federal Register each day to identify changes in export control regulations and policy. Additionally, the Code of Federal Regulations (CFR), which contains the full and current text of the ITAR, the EAR, and the various economic sanctions program regulations, can be found online in its most up-to-date form, the "e-CFR."

diplomatic challenges is the negotiation and formation of multilateral export controls and economic sanctions policies supported by all nations that are sources of goods, technology or services to which the United States seeks to deny access for specific parties and nations. The multilateral regimes and treaties that underpin the U.S. export controls and economic sanctions are relevant to practitioners, and are described briefly. The Chapter concludes with a discussion of limits on the extraterritorial reach of export controls and economic sanctions.

2. Jurisdictional Reach of U.S. Export Controls and Economic Sanctions

Before engaging in any regulatory analysis, students and practitioners alike must answer a critical threshold question: To whom do the export controls and economic sanctions of the United States apply? The export controls and economic sanctions of the United States apply to persons, goods, services and technology under five theories of jurisdiction. These theories of jurisdiction are citizenship jurisdiction, territorial prescription, territorial remedies and penalties, *quasi in rem* or reexport control list-based jurisdiction, and prescriptive jurisdiction that meets the effects test and the factors described in the rule of reason under the Restatement (Third) of the Foreign Relations Law of the United States ("Restatement (Third)"). The only one of these theories that is limited to U.S. persons is citizenship jurisdiction.

The U.S. Government may exercise jurisdiction over its citizens, wherever located. This exercise of jurisdiction reaches both natural and legal persons. Natural persons include passport holders and permanent lawful residents. Legal persons include corporations organized under the laws of any jurisdiction within the United States, juridical bodies, and foreign branches of U.S. corporations.[3] Such jurisdiction over legal persons is widely accepted by other nations. The U.S. Government also exercises jurisdiction within the territory of the United States, and through territorial remedies and penalties. Jurisdiction over goods, services and technologies exported and reexported from the United States exists under a *quasi in rem* theory.

The U.S. Government also exercises extraterritorial jurisdiction over non-U.S. persons and corporations. The Commerce Clause of the Constitution authorizes Congress to pass statutes that regulate foreign commerce of the United States. Congress has delegated broad powers to the President under statutes such as the Arms Export Control Act ("AECA"),[4] the International Economic Emergencies Powers Act ("IEEPA"),[5] and the United Nations Participation Act.[6] Under the various export controls and trade sanctions of the United States, the extraterritorial reach of such regulations, statutes, and theories of prosecution have long prescribed restrictions on the trade and financial transactions of other countries, and have created tensions between the United States and other countries, including its allies. At the beginning of the Cold War, U.S. reexport controls became the essence of

---

3. For example, under the Iran Transactions and Sanctions Regulations (ITSR), a U.S. person "means any United States citizen, permanent resident alien, entity organized under the laws of the United States or any jurisdiction within the United States (including foreign branches), or any person in the United States." Iranian Transactions and Sanctions Regulations, 31 C.F.R. § 560.314 (2014).

4. AECA (Arms Export Control Act), 22 U.S.C. § 2778 (2000).

5. International Emergency Economic Powers Act (IEEPA), 50 U.S.C. §§ 1701–1706 (2000).

6. United Nations Participation Act, 22 U.S.C. § 287c (2000).

the U.S. export controls and economic sanctions system; the centrality of reexport controls still holds true today. Using all five of the jurisdictional theories above, the U.S. export control agencies claim extraterritorial reach into the economies of foreign countries.

In addition to the five types of jurisdiction exercised by policy makers and rule writers, prosecutors use five types of charging strategies and procedures: causing, conspiracy, aiding and abetting, extradition and other means to obtain jurisdiction over the body, and enforcement of fines and forfeiture orders against assets in the United States. These prosecutorial theories also extend the extraterritorial reach of U.S. export controls and economic sanctions. The limits on the reach of extraterritorial jurisdiction are discussed in greater detail at the end of this chapter.

3. Export Controls

Export Controls and Agency Jurisdiction: Drawing the Line between the ITAR and the EAR

An export is an actual shipment or transmission of goods, services or technology out of the United States, or the release of government-controlled technology or software to a foreign national in the United States. The latter scenario is referred to as a "deemed export," and extends the reach of export controls to interactions on U.S. soil. After determining that a good, service or technology will be exported or reexported from the United States, the next question for consideration is which U.S. Government agency has jurisdiction over this good, service or technology. For the most part, the challenge is one of drawing a line between the jurisdiction of State as articulated in the ITAR and that of Commerce as described in the EAR. More specifically, the USML of the ITAR and the CCL of the EAR contain detailed descriptions of the goods, services and technology controlled by each agency. Under ECR, the jurisdictional line between the two agencies has changed significantly in recent years.

As an initial matter, the USML takes precedence over the CCL. The EAR provides that an item is not subject to the EAR if it is subject to the exclusive jurisdiction of another federal agency.[7] The USML covers lethal weapons, but it also captures many items that have commercial application. If an item is captured by the USML, then State's Directorate of Defense Trade Controls (DDTC) has exclusive jurisdiction over the export and reexport of that item under the ITAR. 22 C.F.R. § 121. DDTC retains exclusive jurisdiction over the item on the USML even if the CCL specifies the same item. For these reasons, an EAR export controls practitioner must also be an expert in the USML.

The International Traffic in Arms Regulations

The ITAR are promulgated under the authority of Section 38 of the AECA, which authorizes the President to control the export and import of defense articles and services. A defense article is any item or technical data designated on the USML. 22 C.F.R. § 120.6. Under the ITAR, defense service means:

(1) The furnishing of assistance (including training) to foreign persons, whether in the United States or abroad in the design, development, engineering, manufacture,

---

7. 15 C.F.R. § 734.3(b)(1)(i) (2002).

production, assembly, testing, repair, maintenance, modification, operation, demilitarization, destruction, processing or use of defense articles;

(2) The furnishing to foreign persons of any technical data controlled under this subchapter (*see* § 120.10), whether in the United States or abroad; or

(3) Military training of foreign units and forces, regular and irregular, including formal or informal instruction of foreign persons in the United States or abroad or by correspondence courses, technical, educational, or information publications and media of all kinds, training aid, orientation, training exercise, and military advice. (*See also* § 124.1.)[8]

Classification of Defense Articles and Services: The USML

The USML is found at Part 121.1 of the ITAR.[9] It is comprised of twenty-one categories of defense articles and services. For example, Category I contains Firearms, Close Assault Weapons and Combat Shotguns; Category II contains Guns and Armament; Category V contains Explosives and Energetic Materials, Propellants, Incendiary Agents, and their Constituents; and Category VI contains Surface Vessels of War and Special Naval Equipment.

Scope of List-Based Jurisdiction of the ITAR and "Catch" and "Release"

In performing agency jurisdiction and classification of a given item, you must review the ITAR's USML before considering the EAR, because items subject to the ITAR are not subject to the EAR. An item is not subject to the ITAR unless the commodity, software, technology, or service is described on the USML. If an item or service is not described on the USML, it is subject to the EAR. Items and services are described on the USML in two fundamentally different types of clauses: enumerated clauses and catchall clauses.

First, if an item or service is described in an "enumerated" clause of the USML, it is subject to the ITAR regardless of its use. An item described in an enumerated clause may not be released under any of the five release subparagraphs of ITAR Section 120.41(b) described below. Second, a "catchall" clause is a clause that is modified by either the phrase "specially designed" or similar language. If a clause or phrase is not modified by such specially designed language, then it is an enumerated clause and not a catchall clause. The existence of catchall clauses on the USML (and, as discussed below, on the EAR's CCL) gives rise to the concept of "catch" and "release."

Catch

To say that an item is "caught" at a particular clause means that, by interpreting both the language that follows the phrase "specially designed" and the definition of specially designed at ITAR Section 120.41(a), the item is in fact "caught" in that USML clause. For example, USML Category VIII(a)(16) includes aircraft that "are armed or specially designed to be used as a platform to deliver munitions or otherwise destroy targets (*e.g.,* firing lasers, launching rockets, firing missiles, dropping bombs, or strafing)." To understand whether a particular item is "caught" in Category VIII(a)(16), one must determine if it is "specially designed" to be used in any of the applications described following this clause. This exercise

---

8. 22 C.F.R. § 120.9.

9. 22 C.F.R. § 121.1. Available at http://www.ecfr.gov/cgi-bin/text-idx?rgn=div5&node=22:1.0.1.13.58.

requires one to turn to Section 120.41(a) for a full review of the ways to be "caught" under this catchall clause. Any item is caught under Section 120.41(a)(1) if it "has properties peculiarly responsible for achieving or exceeding the controlled performance levels, characteristics, or functions described in the relevant USML paragraph." In practical terms, the "peculiarly responsible" standard means the item being classified is both necessary and sufficient to achieve or exceed the stated performance levels. In seminars and training presentations, the Administration has made clear that it interprets the "peculiarly responsible" standard to cast a broad net. If the item being classified is not caught by the description in Section 120.41, then it is not subject to the clause or the ITAR.

One of the objectives of ECR was to move parts and components common to use in both defense end items and commercial end items to the more flexible control procedures of the EAR and its CCL. Another objective of the revision of the scope of the ITAR was to eliminate DDTC's discretion to determine that a part or component is on the USML if it is not "predominantly" used in commercial items or was first used in a military item. *See* 78 Fed. Reg. 22740, 22745 (April 16, 2013). To achieve this goal, the Administration adopted a structure in which a single use in a defense article captures a part or component, and a single use in or with the production of an item not described on the USML releases the item from the ITAR. A majority of parts and components common to items on the USML and CCL or EAR99[10] are released from the ITAR catchall clauses under the procedure described below, and are instead controlled under the standards of the EAR.

Release

If an item is in fact "caught" by the language of the USML category read in combination with the "catch" provisions at Section 120.41(a), one must then analyze whether that item is "released" by the "release" provisions of Section 120.41(b). Items described in a USML catchall clause or phrase may be released from the agency jurisdiction of the ITAR if the item or service meets any of the five regulatory criteria at Section 120.41(b) of the ITAR. Items described in a CCL catchall clause or phrase may be released from such a clause to a less restrictive ECCN or EAR99 as provided in the EAR definition of "specially designed" at Part 772 of the EAR. A complete description of the catch and release provisions is beyond the scope of this chapter. The mastery of catch and release provisions of both the ITAR and the EAR are essential skills sets for determination of jurisdiction under the ITAR, which trumps the EAR, and the proper classification under the USML, the CCL, and the commonly-applicable classification known as EAR99, discussed in greater detail later in this chapter.

DDTC Licensing

The license requirements of the ITAR relate both to licenses issued by DDTC and agreements approved by DDTC. These include licenses for export and temporary import of defense articles and services under Part 123, agreements such as Technical Assistance Agreements and Manufacturing Agreements under Part 124, and licenses for the export of technical data and classified defense articles under Part 125. Guidance regularly published on the DDTC website is important for the practitioner to create applications that meet the U.S. Government's expectations, of which the most important are the Guidelines for

---

10. Many commercial goods are not on the Commerce Control List and do not have an ECCN. These goods are designated as EAR99. EAR99 items generally consist of low-level technology, consumer goods, etc. and do not require a license in most situations.

Preparing Electronic Agreements.[11] The various license application forms are described at and may be downloaded from <http://www.pmddtc.state.gov/licensing/forms.html>.

Brokering under the ITAR

Part 129 of the ITAR defines brokering activity and requires registration, license approvals and reporting on brokering activity. The regulation of brokering activity is distinct from controls on exports, reexports, and transfers. Persons subject to Part 129 include a U.S. person anywhere in the world, a foreign person located in the United States, and a foreign person located outside the United States owned or controlled by a U.S. person. (Remember that the definition of U.S. persons includes legal persons.) Ownership of a foreign person by a U.S. person means owning 50% or more of the equity of the foreign person. Control means holding *de facto* control over the day-to-day operations of the foreign person. ITAR Section 129.2(a), 22 C.F.R. § 129.2(a) (2014). The brokering rules do not apply to a foreign person when outside the United States if no U.S. person owns or controls the foreign person.

Brokering activity is "any action on behalf of another to facilitate the manufacture, export, permanent import, transfer, reexport, or retransfer of a U.S. or foreign defense article or defense service, regardless of its origin." The term "brokering activity" is broad and includes, but is not limited to, "financing, insuring, transporting, or freight forwarding defense articles and defense services" or "soliciting, promoting, negotiating, contracting for, arranging, or otherwise assisting in the purchase, sale, transfer, loan, or lease of a defense article or defense service." ITAR Section 129.2(b), 22 C.F.R. § 129.2(b). Brokering activity does not capture activity related to an article or service that is not described on the USML. Moreover, a corporation that performs a described activity for itself is not taking an action "on behalf of another," and is therefore not within the scope of brokering activity.

Part 129 requires brokering registration by a person defined above who engages in brokering activities. Registration is required for one or more instances of brokering activity. Part 129 also contains complex exemptions. For example, there is an exemption to this registration requirement that applies to air carriers and freight forwarders who only transport or arrange transportation for defense articles licensed for export or reexport by the owner of the articles. Another example is the registration exemption for provision of commercially available lines of credit or letters of credit to persons registered with DDTC as an exporter or broker, so long as the lender is not directly involved in arranging transactions involving defense articles or defense services or holding title to defense articles, even when no physical custody of defense articles is involved. ITAR Section 129.3(a) and (b), 22 C.F.R. § 129.2(a)–(b).

Section 129.3(c) provides that parties exempt from registration, approval, record keeping and reporting are subject to the ITAR policy on embargoes and other proscriptions at Section 129.7. This includes the obligation to obtain DDTC approval before engaging in or making a proposal to engage in brokering activity involving "any country, area, or person" referred to in Section 126.1 and persons subject to debarment pursuant to Section 127.7. These lists change from time to time. As of this writing, Section 126.1 most notably includes China as well as countries subject to U.S. multilateral and unilateral arms embargoes and certain other sensitive destinations.

---

11. *See* U.S. Department of State Directorate of Defense Trade Controls, <http://www.pmddtc.state.gov/licensing/agreement.html>.

A person required to be registered as a broker requires prior approval from DDTC to engage in a given brokering service, and the prior approval is in the form of a license. Approval is required for brokering of any foreign defense article or defense service,[12] and certain specifically defined U.S. origin defense articles or defense services. ITAR Section 129.4(a). Part 129 requires brokering registration by a person defined above who engages in brokering activities and contains complex exemptions.

Commodity Jurisdiction Requests to DDTC

DDTC provides a procedure, called the commodity jurisdiction process, under which an exporter may ask whether DDTC has jurisdiction over a given item. 22 C.F.R. § 120.4. Despite its name, the process applies to commodities, software, and technology. If in doubt about whether an item is subject to the ITAR, you must either refrain from making an export or refrain from making an export until you submit a commodity jurisdiction request to DDTC, receive DDTC's determination, and then obtain appropriate export authority under the regulatory scheme specified by DDTC. Even rather straightforward commodity jurisdiction requests require considerable expertise to prepare and often months to resolve.

In the case of nuclear materials, certain items are subject to the exclusive jurisdiction of the Nuclear Regulatory Commission ("NRC") or the Department of Energy ("DOE"), and are not subject to the EAR.[13] The jurisdictional lines between the NRC, DOE, and the CCL (administered by the Bureau of Industry and Security) are quite clear. Jurisdictional disputes and risks to exporters are relatively rare. This chapter therefore does not contain a further discussion of the export control rules of the NRC and DOE.

The Department of Commerce and the EAR

The Department of Commerce implements export controls under the EAR.[14] The EAR are implemented, administered and enforced by BIS.[15] Commerce implements the EAR under the authority of IEEPA. Normally, the statutory basis for the EAR is found in the Export Administration Act of 1979 as amended ("EAA").[16] However, the EAA is not permanent legislation. Congress has let it expire on several occasions. At this writing, Congress has failed to renew the EAA for several years. During these periods of lapse in the EAA, the President has maintained the EAR by means of emergency declarations under IEEPA.[17]

The presidential exercise of authority under IEEPA includes incorporation by reference of the text of the EAA and makes the EAA effective to the extent permitted by law.[18] The

---

12. *See* § 120.44 for definition of foreign defense articles and foreign services and § 129.5 for exemptions.
13. 15 C.F.R. § 734.3(b)(1)(iii) and (iv).
14. Export Administration Regulations (EAR), 15 C.F.R. § 730 (2002).
15. Additional information about the Bureau of Industry and Security's programs and regulations is available at <http://www.bis.doc.gov>.
16. Export Administration Act of 1979, 50 U.S.C. app. §§ 2401–20 (2000).
17. Executive Order 13222 of August 17, 2001 continued the EAR under IEPPA, and successive Presidential Notices have extended the EAR since.
18. 50 U.S.C. §§ 1701–1706 (2000); *see* Exec. Order No. 13,222, 66 Fed. Reg. 44025, (2001), as extended by the Notice of August 14, 2002, 67 Fed. Reg. 5371 (2002).

text of the EAA so incorporated is considered by many, including the authors of this chapter, to have the weight of a regulation. Consistent with such a view, Commerce takes the position that it has the authority to amend the EAA in a manner that is inconsistent with the EAA, and that the penalty provisions of IEEPA apply to violations of the EAR but the EAA penalty provisions do not.

The purposes of the EAR are to further the national security, non-proliferation, and counterterrorism goals of the United States. Other objectives include crime control, regional stability, encryption policy, and other foreign policies of the United States.

The EAR contain four major parts—scope, general prohibitions, license exceptions, and license review. These four major parts must be taken in order. If they are reviewed out of order, the practitioner often reaches an incorrect answer to the basic question: Must I obtain prior government permission for my export or activity? Part 732[19] of the EAR contains steps and flow charts that direct the reader to consider the parts of the EAR in order.

Scope of the EAR

Part 734 of the EAR defines its scope with use of the term of art "subject to the EAR."[20] An item is subject to the EAR if the item: (1) is of U.S. origin (wherever located); (2) is in the United States (regardless of origin); (3) has incorporated more than the so-called *de minimis* level of controlled U.S. parts, components, or materials; or (4) is a foreign-produced direct product of U.S. technology controlled for national security reasons and when the technology requires a written assurance as a precondition to its export or certain components of plants.

Section 734.3(b)(1)(i) of the EAR provides that, regardless of the above, an item is not subject to the EAR if it is subject to the exclusive jurisdiction of another federal agency such as State under the ITAR. 22 C.F.R. § 121. Of course, such items are subject to the export requirements of the ITAR.

Technology and software that is publicly available is not subject to the EAR.[21] To qualify as publicly available technology, technology must be: (1) published or in a library open to the public; (2) available on the public record (for example a patent office or copyright office); (3) taught in a college or university catalogue course or laboratory; (4) fundamental research that will be published, (5) released or to be released at an open conference; or (6) given away at no more than the cost of reproduction and distribution.

Software may qualify for publicly available treatment in only one way: it must be given away at no more than the cost of reproduction and distribution. 15 C.F.R. § 734.7(b). The significance of publicly available treatment is that the information or software is not subject to the EAR. It does not require a license for export to any destination, it is not subject to the EAR end use restrictions on items, and it is not subject to end user or blacklists of the EAR. However, be mindful that the activity restrictions on U.S. persons apply to a U.S. person giving any type of support to prohibited proliferation. 15 C.F.R. § 734.5. Moreover, certain prohibitions against dealing with restricted parties or entities under rules issued by Treasury's OFAC may apply.

---

19. All referenced Sections of the EAR are found in Title 15 of the C.F.R. (and the "e-CFR").
20. 15 C.F.R. § 734.3(a).
21. *See* 15 C.F.R. §§ 734.7–11.

Classification of Commodities, Software and Technology: The CCL

The CCL is Commerce's equivalent to State's USML. As it covers a much greater percentage of the goods, services and technology in the economy, however, it is significantly longer than the USML. Found at Supplement 1 to Part 774 of the EAR, the CCL contains ten categories of Export Control Classification Numbers, or "ECCNs." ECCNs are five-letter alphanumeric codes used to identify items controlled on the CCL.[22] EAR99 is a special code used to describe those items that are subject to the EAR under the above definition, but not otherwise classified at a specific ECCN. Proper classification under the CCL or EAR99 is an essential process and skill set. For any commodity, software or technology (collectively, "items"), one correct classification exists under the CCL. The rules of interpretation or use of the CCL are as follows: First, gather the description, performance level, and specification of the item you will export, reexport, or release as a deemed export or deemed reexport. An effective classification process at a company requires collaboration between an employee with technical expertise who understands the technical characteristics of the item for export, and a regulatory expert who understands the structure of the CCL.

Second, examine the CCL in the following order until you find an entry or clause that captures the item: Starting from the beginning of the CCL: (1) compare your item to all the 600 series entries; (2) review all the multilateral ECCN entries from the beginning of the CCL. Multilateral entries are those subject to multilateral regimes such as the Wassenaar Arrangement, the Missile Technology Control Regime, the Australia Group, and the Chemical Weapons Convention; (3) compare your item to unilateral entries. The ECCNs contain the number "9" in the third or fourth digit of a five digit ECCN. See Supplement No. 4 to Part 744 Commerce Control List Order of Review and the description of the structure of an ECCN number at <http://www.bis.doc.gov/index.php/regulations/com-merce-control-list-ccl>. The alphanumeric index to the CCL at Part 774, key word searches on the CCL, and a process of elimination combine to provide an effective review of the CCL. While this description provides a starting point, there is no perfect substitute for experience working with the CCL itself.

In the classification of technology, the term "required" narrows the type of information that rises to the level of technology controlled by the CCL and the EAR. This multilateral term generally means development, production, and use information necessary and sufficient to achieve a describe control parameter. 15 C.F.R. §772. The example contained in the definition illustrates the proper use of the term. Also see the definitions of development, production, and use technology. The alphanumeric index, key work searches on the CCL, and a process of elimination combine to provide an effective review of the CCL; again, however, experience with the CCL is necessary. Classification of items that have data security or encryption capabilities require reference to guidance at http://www.bis.doc.gov/index.php/policy-guidance/encryption and the regulations described there.

If and only if (a) your item is not subject to the ITAR and (b) you cannot find your item on the CCL after this review or classification exercise, is your item then classified as EAR99. You cannot know whether you require a license from BIS unless you know the

---

22. For more information on ECCNs and the CCL structure, visit the BIS website at <http://www.bis.doc.gov/index.php/licensing/commerce-control-list-classification/export-control-classifica-tion-number-eccn>.

proper classification, as well as the destination, end use, and end user of the item. With ECR, classification has also become an important skill set and compliance process under the USML.

ECR and the 600 Series

As a result of ECR, the Administration removed many items from the USML at State and transferred them to the CCL at Commerce. Many, but not all, of these items were placed in new ECCNs under what is known as the "600 series" of each category of the CCL. The items are subject to rigorous control requirements but with more flexibility than the ITAR affords. Certain 600 series items are referred to as CCL-military items. The catch and release provisions of the EAR typically apply to end items in a 600 series entry and to specially designed parts and components under subparagraph ".x" of a 600 series. BIS has provided a decision tool for application of the catch and release provisions of the EAR. A full discussion of the catch and release provisions is beyond the scope of this chapter; however mastering the concepts of catch and release are essential for the practitioner to make correct classification determinations under the CCL.

The items properly classified under a 600 series CCL entry are typically not eligible for most license exceptions of the EAR. Rather, 600 series end items and parts, components accessories, and attachments at subparagraph ".x" items are eligible for License Exception STA. License exceptions exempt products that would otherwise require a BIS license for export or reexport from that requirement. License Exception STA requires substantial documentation and notifications to export and reexport consignees to assure against diversion to unauthorized destinations. BIS has provided a decision tool for application of License Exception STA at <http://www.bis.doc.gov/index.php/statool>.

Catch and Release under the EAR and CCL

Classification decisions for goods, services and technology are highly fact-specific, a reality that comes into play in cases brought by the U.S. Government for violations of the export control laws.[23] Like the USML, the CCL contains both enumerated clauses and catchall clauses. If an item is described in an "enumerated" clause of the CCL, the clause or that entry is the proper classification. Under any of the six release subparagraphs of the definition of "specially designed" at Part 772 of the EAR, an item may be released to a lesser control within the CCL or to EAR99.

If an article is described in a catchall clause under the CCL, you must then evaluate the catch and release provisions of the EAR. The catch provisions are broad. Many of the release provisions of the EAR are similar but not always identical to the ITAR. The preamble to the BIS Federal Register notice provides a detailed regulatory history and the regulatory intent of the BIS catch and release provisions.[24] BIS has provided a useful tool for application of its catch and release provisions at http://www.bis.doc.gov/index.php/specially-designed-tool. An understanding of the catch and release provisions of the EAR is essential to proper commodity classification.

---

23. *United States v. Spawr Optical Research, Inc.*, 864 F.2d 1467 (9th Cir. 1988), *cert. denied*, 493 U.S. 809 (1989).
24. See 78 Fed. Reg. 22740, 22660 (April 16, 2013).

Ten General Prohibitions of the EAR[25]

Determination of a product's classification on the CCL is an important step in identifying a party's legal obligations under the export controls laws of the United States. However, the ten General Prohibitions of EAR Part 736 demonstrate that classification is, on its own, insufficient to determine the full extent of those obligations. General Prohibitions 1, 2, and 3 of the EAR require a license for export or reexport of items on the CCL for countries with an "X" in the appropriate box on the Country Chart at Supplement No. 1 to Part 738 of the EAR. These are list-based prohibitions, in that the product/country pairing defines a requirement to seek a license from the Commerce Department unless a license exception is available. As noted further below, the determination of where an item falls on the CCL and whether an item is on the CCL is critical in the determination of whether the three list-based general prohibitions apply. The CCL is Supplement No. 1 to Part 774 of the EAR. It contains in each entry the reasons for control and columns that one must check on the Country Chart of Part 738 to determine whether most list-based requirements apply.

General Prohibition 4 prohibits any party from dealing with a denied party in any item subject to the EAR. Denied parties are those that have been temporarily or permanently made subject to an order that denies them export privileges and prohibits other parties from dealing with them. This is in effect a blacklist. It is the primary enforcement method Commerce takes against parties that it may not bring under the jurisdiction of the criminal courts of the United States, and it is an administrative enforcement tool that Commerce may also apply to parties in the United States. General Prohibition 5 imposes license requirements for exports or reexports with knowledge the item will be used for nuclear, missile, or chemical and biological end uses. This incorporates the detailed provisions of Part 744 of the EAR.

General Prohibition 6 refers to certain country embargoes in Part 746 of the EAR. General embargoes, such as the embargoes on Cuba,[26] Libya, and Iran, apply to all items subject to the EAR. That includes common items such as basketballs and refrigerators, which of course are not on the CCL. The CCL describes only about four percent of items in the U.S. economy, whereas, the embargo rules apply to all items subject to the EAR (100% of items in the U.S. economy).

General Prohibition 7 prohibits a U.S. person from supporting proliferation activity in certain countries unless that person first obtains a license. General Prohibition 8 prohibits certain in-transit shipments and unlading, primarily in specific former Soviet states absent a license. General Prohibition 9 prohibits the violation of any order, term or license condition issued by BIS. General Prohibition 10 provides that no one may:

> [S]ell, transfer, export, reexport, finance, order, buy, remove, conceal, store, use, loan, dispose of, transport, forward, or otherwise service, in whole or in

---

25. *Id.* at §736.2(b).

26. As of this writing in August 2014, the Obama Administration announced its intention to begin normalizing relations with Cuba to include the lifting of sanctions. It has asked the State Department to re-evaluate Cuba's designation as a state sponsor of terror and announced plans to open an embassy there. However, in order to lift sanctions Congress would have to repeal the 2000 Trade Sanctions Reform and Export Enhancement Act (Title IX of Public Law 106-387, October 28, 2999) to allow tourist travel and the 1996 Helms Burton Act (Pub.L. 104-114, 110 Stat. 785, 22 U.S.C. §§6021–6091) which imposed the embargo against Cuba. Establishing an embassy would also require Congressional funding and Senate confirmation of an ambassador.

part, any item subject to the EAR and exported or to be exported with knowledge that a violation of the Export Administration Regulations ... has occurred, is about to occur, or is intended to occur in connection with the item.

If none of the ten General Prohibitions apply, the export may be made under an authority called No License Required (NLR). Even if an item is classified as EAR99, if any of the above General Prohibitions apply the item is not in fact automatically qualified for export under NLR authority. Rather, you must follow the steps at EAR Part 732.3 to properly address and potentially overcome the General Prohibition and, if it cannot be overcome and a license exception is not available, apply for a license from BIS. Moreover, NLR is the authorization to export an item classified in an ECCN when there is no "X" in the box under the relevant reasons for control and across from the ultimate destination on the Country Chart at Supplement No. 1 to Part 738 of the EAR. The difference between an EAR99 classification and the ability to legally export or reexport an item under NLR authority is an important one that eludes even experienced practitioners.

License Exceptions

License Exceptions are described in Part 742 of the EAR. If General Prohibitions 1, 2, and 3 apply, the next step under the EAR is to determine whether one or more license exceptions overcome that list-based prohibition. There are many License Exceptions, and a complete discussion of License Exceptions is beyond the scope of this chapter. However, it is important to note a few principles concerning the use of License Exceptions.

First, certain list-based License Exceptions such as "Shipment to Country Group B Countries" ("GBS") and "Civil End Users" ("CIV") are identified on the CCL. Once you properly classify your item and determine that a license is required for export of that item following all relevant EAR guidance (including review of the General Prohibitions and use of the EAR Part 738 Country Chart), the relevant entry on the CCL will indicate which list-based License Exceptions are or may be available. It is critical to understand that the notation on the CCL for availability of a License Exception is only the first step in the analysis to determine if a list-based License Exception authorizes a given export or reexport. The second step is to read and understand the terms and conditions of each potential License Exception as described in Part 742 of the EAR. The EAR also contains certain transaction-based License Exceptions. An example is License Exception TMP.[27] TMP stands for temporary exports, reexports, and imports. One of the sub-authorities under License Exception TMP is for tools of the trade. Note that the terms and conditions require control over the item and return within one year. This is just one example of the numerous and complex License Exceptions available for use under the EAR.

License Review

If a General Prohibition applies, and a License Exception is not available to overcome that requirement, the exporter or reexporter must submit a license application on Multipurpose Form 748 or electronically to BIS for review. The review process can be time consuming. The application and review processes are described at Parts 748 and 750 of the EAR. The review standards applied by Commerce and the reviewing agencies are

---

27. 15 C.F.R. § 740.9.

described at 744 of the EAR. In addition, the Departments of Defense and State may review all license applications submitted to Commerce.

Three Types of License Requirements under the Export Administration Regulations — List-Based, End-Use-Based, and End User-Based

Three distinct types of license requirements exist under the EAR. The first are the list-based requirements of General Prohibitions 1, 2, and 3. The second type of license requirement relates to transfers, exports, and reexports to prohibited end uses such as nuclear, missile and chemical and biological end uses. The product scope for such end-use controls extends to all items subject to the EAR, not just items on the CCL. This license requirement is triggered only if the exporter or reexporter knows or has reason to know the item will be put to the prohibited end use. The standard of care required under this provision is discussed below in connection with the Know Your Customer Guidance of BIS.

The third type of license requirement is based upon published names of blacklisted parties, known as denied persons.[28] In addition, the EAR contains a so-called Entity List, which includes names of parties that BIS believes are engaged in proliferation activities. For such parties, a license is required for all items subject to the EAR, including items not on the CCL in addition to items captured on the CCL.[29] BIS also publishes a list of unverified parties, or parties that BIS cannot verify have received and put licensed items to only that end use authorized on a license, in the location authorized on the same license. For the exporter and reexporter, a consignee on the Unverified List raises a so-called red flag and requires the exporter and reexporter to make affirmative inquiries regarding the actual end use, end user and ultimate destination of the proposed export or reexport. See the below discussion regarding dozens of additional lists of restricted parties issued by OFAC, State, and other agencies and countries.

Per se Violations

It is a *per se* violation of the EAR to export or reexport without a license required by the list-based rules or to deal with a denied person or party on the Entity List. Prosecutors in administrative cases need not prove knowledge, malice or willfulness to establish such a violation by an exporter in the United States or a reexporter abroad.

In *Iran Air v. Kugelman*,[30] then Circuit Judge Ruth Bader Ginsburg held that the EAR does not require knowledge to be an element of the administrative action. In this case, Iran Air submitted a purchase order in Germany for certain signal generators (civil aircraft parts) to be forwarded from Frankfurt to Tehran. Its supplier in Germany transferred U.S.-origin parts, but did not inform Iran Air the parts were of U.S.-origin. Moreover, the supplier failed to include on the commercial invoices a required destination control statement, such as "for ultimate destination" Germany and "diversion contrary to United States Law is prohibited." Despite the failure of the supplier to give Iran Air such actual notice, the court concluded that Commerce proved a *per se* violation of the EAR even

---

28. 15 C.F.R. §§ 736.2(b)(4) and 764.
29. 15 C.F.R. § 774 (2002).
30. *Iran Air v. Kugelman*, 996 F.2d 1253 (D.C. Cir. 1993).

though Iran Air did not know a reexport license was required. Criminal charges for violations of the EAR do require proof of criminal intent.

The Standard of Care for End-Use Controls and Other Knowledge-Based Prohibitions

The EAR's knowledge-based end-use prohibitions drive some of the most difficult decisions facing practitioners and compliance officers. Similar challenges are presented by General Prohibition 10, which prohibits a wide variety of activities taken with the knowledge that a diversion is about to occur or has occurred. What, then, is knowledge? More specifically, what type of information is sufficient to constitute a violation of the EAR's knowledge-based prohibitions?

The Know Your Customer Guidance and related "Red Flags" of the EAR provide some answers to these persistent and demanding questions.[31] Commerce takes the position that a corporation knows that which its employees know. Thus, companies must train the sales force on end-use prohibitions, because the sales force will likely know more about the customer's end use than any other part of the selling entity. The Know Your Customer Guidance provides for six steps:

1. Decide whether there are red flags or abnormal business circumstances;
2. If there are red flags, then inquire about the ultimate end use, end user, and destination;
3. Do not self-blind your organization but consider information that flows to the organization in the normal course of business;
4. Provide employees a procedure to refer red flags to compliance officers;
5. Reevaluate the information after the inquiry to determine whether the original cause for concern remains; and
6. If it does, then refrain from the transaction or advise BIS and await decision.

Reexport Controls

Reexport controls are central to the U.S. export control system. The list-based requirements of the EAR and the ITAR in effect attach the American flag to an item as it travels around the world and is reexported from one foreign nation to another. It is this *quasi in rem* theory of jurisdiction that prescribes the conduct of non-U.S. persons. Exercising reexport controls over items is the top pillar of the U.S. export control system, although other nations have complained about U.S. reexport controls and their extraterritorial impact. The U.S. policy reason for reexport controls results from the belief that unfettered reexports of U.S. items would quickly undermine the goal of export controls — to deny adversaries and proliferators access to critical items. The common law prohibition that a person may not do indirectly that which he may not do directly also justifies reexport controls.

What then is a reexport? It is "an actual shipment or transmission of items subject to the EAR from one foreign country to another foreign country."[32] Note that a foreign person with no U.S. citizenship or visa becomes subject to reexport controls by exporting

---

31. 15 C.F.R. §732.
32. 15 C.F.R. §772.

a listed item from one foreign country to another. The application of reexport controls under the EAR is not limited to U.S. persons.

Deemed Exports and Deemed Reexports

Under the EAR, an export includes, among other things, release of technology or source code subject to the EAR to certain foreign nationals.[33] This is often referred to as the deemed export rule. The deemed export rule presents a significant compliance challenge for companies that hire foreign nationals such as Indian, Chinese, and Russian nationals in certain high-tech industries. It also presents challenges in low-tech industries such as chemicals. The EAR may also control deemed exports.[34] The deemed export and reexport rules apply to both technology and source code but do not apply to software in machine code form or the use of commodities.

These rules define one type of export and one type of reexport. The EAR rules for physical exports and reexports apply to deemed exports and reexports. Thus, a License Exception that authorizes the physical export or intangible transmission of controlled software to China, for example, will also authorize release to a national of China in the United States or any other country. Note that, in the EAR, nationality is defined not by the passport of the person but by permanent resident status. Thus, a Chinese passport holder is not subject to the deemed export rule if he or she is a permanent resident of the United States. [35] A similar exclusion applies to the deemed reexport rule for persons with a right to permanently reside in another country.[36]

Computer Server Access

In the typical, modern multinational corporation, server access presents perhaps the biggest challenge to export controls involving technology. An export includes an actual shipment or transmission or "release of technology or software in a foreign country." "Release" includes oral exchanges and applications abroad.[37] When an employee of a firm in India downloads information from the server owned by the U.S. parent corporation, an export to India occurs. This is true even though the transfer occurs from one part of an enterprise to another part of the same enterprise. This is not a deemed export, but rather, it is treated as a transmission.

Is it an export for a chief information officer of a company to merely give a person outside the United States access to information and software on a server in the United States? Must prosecutors prove a person in another country actually downloaded or read the information that is the subject of an alleged violation? BIS has not yet answered these questions. In the view of the authors of this chapter, the rules may be reasonably interpreted to mean a violation has not occurred if the company can establish the individual has not downloaded or read the information. Consider a scenario where a corporation provides access to its server and a Russian national downloads information while working in the United States, while a Pakistani national downloads the information while in Pakistan. BIS considers the first download to be a deemed export to Russia and the second download

---

33. 15 C.F.R. § 734.2(b)(2)(ii).
34. 15 C.F.R. § 734.2(b)(5).
35. 15 C.F.R. § 734.2(b)(2)(ii).
36. 15 C.F.R. § 734.2(b)(5).
37. 15 C.F.R. § 734.2(b)((1)–(5).

to be a physical export or transmission to Pakistan. A separate issue involves internal trade secrets: EAR compliance requires corporations to list and classify their internal trade secrets, despite the difficulties that doing so poses for companies.

Data Encryption

Items that incorporate data security or encryption features exist throughout the economy. The U.S. encryption export control policy is highly complex. The general principles of the EAR almost never apply to encryption controls. Often, a one-time review is required before an exporter or reexporter may use one of the various authorities of License Exception ENC. BIS also requires certain reports.[38]

4. Economic Sanctions

Regulations of the Department of the Treasury's Office of Foreign Assets Control

OFAC plays a significant role in the imposition of sanctions and embargoes. OFAC also implements regulations that block funds to terrorists, narcotics traffickers, and fronts for embargoed governments. OFAC issues its regulations primarily under IEEPA, though it also relies on the United Nations Participation Act and the Trading with the Enemy Act ("TWEA").[39]

At the time of this writing in August 2014, OFAC administers and enforces 26 sanctions and embargo programs,[40] which can be divided into three categories: List-Based Sanctions Programs, Limited Sanctions Programs, and Comprehensive Sanctions Programs. "List-based" refers to lists of blacklisted names of natural persons, legal persons, and vessels. OFAC's List-Based Sanctions Programs prohibit the provision of services to Specially-Designated Nationals ("SDNs"), persons on Sectoral Sanctions Identifications Lists or the Foreign Sanctions Evaders List, and other blocked parties. OFAC's Limited Sanctions Programs also prohibit providing services to SDNs but bar additional defined activities based on the United States' foreign policy toward the sanctioned country. Comprehensive Sanctions Programs prohibit doing almost any business with a sanctioned country.

The 26 OFAC sanctions programs apply to all U.S. persons, a term specifically defined in each sanctions program. The most common definition includes all natural persons, legal persons, and other persons, both natural and legal, when in the territory of the

---

38. 15 C.F.R. §§740.17 and 742.15.

39. Trading with the Enemy Act (TWEA), 50 U.S.C. app. §§1–44 (imposing sanctions on Cuba and North Korea).

40. For examples of the regulations associated with some of these programs, *see, e.g.,* the Cuban Assets Control Regulations, 31 C.F.R. §515 (2011); Iranian Transaction Regulations, 31 C.F.R. §560 (2012); Iranian Assets Control Regulations, 31 C.F.R. §535 (2012); Libyan Sanctions Regulations, 31 C.F.R. §550 (2004); Foreign Assets Control Regulations, 31 C.F.R. §500 (2004) (applicable to North Korea); South Sudanese Sanctions Regulations, 31 C.F.R. §538 (See 79 FED REG 37190, July 1, 2014) (2014); Narcotics Trafficking Sanctions Regulations, 31 C.F.R. §536 (2002); Terrorism Sanctions Regulations (61 FED. REG. 3805, February 2, 1996); Foreign Terrorist Organizations Sanctions Regulations, 31 C.F.R. §597 (2002). Note this is not a complete list of OFAC regulations. *See* the OFAC web site at <http://www.ustreas.gov/ofac/>.

United States. Thus, a Mexican citizen, when in the United States territory, is a U.S. person, as is the CEO of a French company when visiting New York City.

List-Based Sanctions Programs

List-Based Sanctions Programs prohibit U.S. persons, wherever located, from dealing in the property and interests in property of all individuals, entities, vessels, and aircraft appearing on OFAC's SDN List. Examples of List-Based Sanctions Programs include the Lebanon, Libya, and Somalia Sanctions Programs. OFAC defines the terms *property* and *property interest* very broadly.[41] OFAC interprets property interests to include products set aside in the United States for shipment to a blocked party, and funds received by a U.S. person in payment from a blocked person for a completed contract. These broad definitions effectively prohibit U.S. persons from engaging in any trade or financial transactions involving, in any manner, an SDN[42] or other party blacklisted by any agency.

Fifty Percent Rule Affecting SDN-Owned Entities

OFAC rules also prohibit U.S. persons, wherever located, from engaging in any transactions involving entities that are 50 percent or more owned by SDNs, even if those owned entities do not themselves appear on the OFAC SDN List. These owned entities are "blocked parties," as are the SDNs on the OFAC List. The OFAC prohibitions are the same for both published SDNs and parties that are blocked by operation of law via ownership by a published SDN or other blocked parties (which parties may not appear on the SDN List). U.S. persons have an obligation to conduct due diligence on the individuals and entities with whom they plan to conduct business. It can be difficult to investigate the ownership of an unfamiliar entity and this so-called "Fifty Percent Rule" can therefore pose significant compliance challenges.

Blocking of Funds

Any property or interest in property of an SDN or blocked party that comes into the control of a U.S. person must be "blocked" or frozen. Accordingly, U.S. financial institutions or other U.S. persons who receive funds in which an SDN or a blocked party has an

---

41. *See, e.g.,* Weapons of Mass Destruction Proliferators Sanctions Regulations ("WMDPSR"), 31 C.F.R. §594.309. The terms *property* and *property interest* "include, but are not limited to, money, checks, drafts, bullion, bank deposits, savings accounts, debts, indebtedness, obligations, notes, guarantees, debentures, stocks, bonds, coupons, any other financial instruments, bankers acceptances, mortgages, pledges, liens or other rights in the nature of security, warehouse receipts, bills of lading, trust receipts, bills of sale, any other evidences of title, ownership or indebtedness, letters of credit and any documents relating to any rights or obligations thereunder, powers of attorney, goods, wares, merchandise, chattels, stocks on hand, ships, goods on ships, real estate mortgages, deeds of trust, vendors' sales agreements, land contracts, leaseholds, ground rents, real estate and any other interest therein, options, negotiable instruments, trade acceptances, royalties, book accounts, accounts payable, judgments, patents, trademarks or copyrights, insurance policies, safe deposit boxes and their contents, annuities, pooling agreements, services of any nature whatsoever, contracts of any nature whatsoever, and any other property, real, personal, or mixed, tangible or intangible, or interest or interests therein, present, future or contingent." Other list-based sanctions programs apply the same or similar definitions of *property* and *property interest.*

42. U.S. persons may request specific authorization from OFAC to deal with SDNs in limited circumstances. OFAC issues specific authorization on a case-by-case basis.

interest must place those funds in a blocked account. This obligation applies even when U.S. financial institutions: (1) are operating solely as an intermediary; (2) do not have any direct relationship with a blocked party; and (3) do not know or have reason to know the entity's ownership or other information demonstrating the entity's blocked status.[43]

For example, many non-U.S. financial institutions appear on the SDN List. Any payment destined for or coming from an SDN financial institution, but transiting the United States, must be blocked by any U.S. bank, its branch abroad, and a branch in the United States of a non-U.S. bank that is involved in the transfer. If a U.S. person effects payments originating from or transiting through the United States, those payments should not involve any SDNs or blocked parties because those payments would be blocked by the bank. The funds would not be forwarded to the beneficiary or returned to the remitter. Moreover, U.S. financial institutions are required to report blocked funds, including remitter and beneficiary information, to OFAC in a Suspicious Activity Report ("SAR") and may not inform the remitter or beneficiary that information regarding their transfer has been reported to OFAC in an SAR.

Prohibited Facilitation and Approval

The OFAC List-Based Sanctions Programs prohibit U.S. persons from facilitating transactions by non-U.S. persons that would be prohibited if conducted by a U.S. person or within the territory of the United States. The best OFAC explanation of "facilitation" is under the Sudan Sanctions Program. Under Section 538.206 of the SSR, "the facilitation by a United States person, including but not limited to brokering activities, of the exportation or reexportation of goods, technology, or services from Sudan to any destination, or to Sudan from any location, is prohibited."[44] The most comprehensive definition of "facilitation" in OFAC regulation is at Section 538.407 of the SSR. OFAC applies this standard when it interprets the term "facilitation" in other Sanctions Programs as well. OFAC has not issued comprehensive guidance on the full spectrum of activities that qualify as prohibited facilitation, but instead considers facilitation on a case-by-case basis. OFAC's regulations also prohibit attempts to evade the Sanctions Program rules:

> [A]ny transaction for the purpose of, or which has the effect of, evading or avoiding, or which facilitates the evasion or avoidance of, any of the [other] prohibitions set forth in [the regulations, as well as ...] [a]ny attempt to violate the prohibitions set forth in [the regulations, or] ... [a]ny conspiracy formed for the purpose of engaging in a transaction prohibited by [the regulations].[45]

Moreover, a U.S. person may not change its business procedures for the purpose of evading OFAC sanctions.[46]

Vicarious Liability of Non-U.S. Entities

Non-U.S. entities may be liable for the sanctions violations of its U.S. person employees. This "vicarious liability" expands the extraterritorial scope of the OFAC Sanctions Programs. OFAC's *Enforcement Guidelines* reject the idea that employers should not be held liable

---

43. OFAC FAQ 116, available at: http://www.treasury.gov/resource-center/faqs/Sanctions/Pages/answer.aspx#60.

44. 31 C.F.R. §538.206.

45. *See, e.g.*, the Narcotics Trafficking Sanctions Regulations, 31 C.F.R. §536.204. Other list-based programs have the same or similar prohibitions.

46. 31 C.F.R. §560.417.

for the acts of their employees.[47] In particular, OFAC states, "The actions of employees may be properly attributable to their organizations depending on the facts and circumstances of the particular case." Generally, OFAC does not impose vicarious liability upon non-U.S. legal persons for clerical functions of a non-U.S. natural person. OFAC considers several factors when determining whether to hold an employer liable for the acts of its employee: the position of the employee in question, the nature of the conduct and how long it lasted; who else was or should have been aware of the conduct; and the existence and nature of a compliance program intended to identify and stop such conduct. OFAC decides to hold an employer liable at its own discretion and will make that decision based on its own calculations and internal policy.

Limited Sanctions Programs

Limited Sanctions Programs include all the prohibitions of List-Based Sanctions Programs (*i.e.*, prohibited dealings with SDNs and blocked parties), but also include broader proscriptions on other activities. The Limited Sanctions Programs apply to U.S. persons. Each Limited Sanctions Program responds to unique foreign policy goals, so the rules differ from program to program. U.S. persons must understand the scope of each program's prohibitions to do business in those countries safely.

Example: The Burma Sanctions Program

The prohibitions of the Burma Sanctions Program apply to U.S. persons.[48] In addition to prohibiting dealings in blocked property and facilitation, the Burmese sanctions rules prohibit the importation of jadeite or rubies mined or extracted from Burma (also referred to as Myanmar).[49]

The Burma Sanctions Program also prohibits two other kinds of transactions: (1) the exportation and reexportation of "financial services" to Burma (where the term "financial services" includes the transfers of funds);[50] and (2) new investment in Burma, which are defined as the economic development of resources, including the extraction of oil and gas, timbering, or the acquisition of land.[51] However, OFAC has issued general licenses that largely overcome these two prohibitions. As is the case for any of OFAC's general licenses, the general licenses for Burma apply only under certain circumstances and are subject to record-keeping requirements.

The Burmese sanctions rules exempt transactions related to information or informational materials, personal communication, and travel. The exemptions are subject to the same conditions as those named under List-Based Sanctions Programs, and are also fact-specific. Companies must review the broad General Licenses before dealing with Burma and perform name screening and address screening on all contacts.

---

47. *See* OFAC Enforcement Guidelines (2009), *available at* http://www.treasury.gov/resource-center/sanctions/Documents/fr74_57593.pdf.

48. The definition of "U.S. person" under the Burmese Sanctions Regulations ("BSR") includes any U.S. citizen, permanent resident, entity organized under the laws of the United States or any jurisdiction within the United States (including foreign branches), or any person located in the United States at the time of the transaction at issue. 31 C.F.R. §§ 537.321 (2012).

49. Executive Order 13651, § 1(a).

50. 31 C.F.R. §§ 537.202, 537.305.

51. 31 C.F.R. §§ 537.204, 537.311(a).

Comprehensive Sanctions Programs

Comprehensive Sanctions Programs include all the prohibitions of List-Based Programs (*i.e.*, prohibited dealings with SDNs and blocked parties), but also include broader proscriptions on almost all activities involving a particular sanctioned jurisdiction. As of the time of this writing, the four Comprehensive Sanctions Programs include the Cuba, Iran, Sudan, and Syria Sanctions Programs. As with all the United States' sanctions programs, the Comprehensive Sanctions Programs are constantly evolving and their respective prohibitions may change over time. For example, the Syria Sanctions Program originally was a List-Based Program and prohibited only transactions with SDNs and blocked parties. It also included a general order under the EAR. Since 2011, however, the U.S. Government has added more prohibitions to create a near wholesale embargo on transactions with Syria. On the other hand, the Iran Sanctions Program,[52] which started as a Comprehensive Sanctions Program, did not initially have a blocking element but merely required refusal to accept payments from Iran and persons blocked under the OFAC sanctions against Iran. Since 2012, however, the U.S. Government has added many Iranian entities to the SDN List, thereby prohibiting not only transactions with Iran as a whole, but also blocking the property and interests in property of certain individuals and entities.

Example: The Iran Sanctions Program

The OFAC Iranian Transactions and Sanctions Regulations (ITSR) and other regulations and legal authorities of the Iran Sanctions Program apply to U.S. persons.[53] In addition, non-U.S. entities that are owned or controlled by a U.S. person also are prohibited from knowingly engaging in any transaction, directly or indirectly, with the Government of Iran (or any person subject to the jurisdiction of the Government of Iran) that would be prohibited if conducted by a U.S. person or in the United States.[54] As already discussed, the United States imposes controls on non-U.S. persons for reexports of all items subject to the EAR or OFAC rules to countries subject to Comprehensive Sanctions Programs, and to many other countries depending on the classification of the item.

OFAC has not issued comprehensive guidance on its definition of control. However, Section 215(b)(1) of the ITSR provides that an entity is "owned or controlled" by a U.S. person if the U.S. person: (i) holds a 50 percent or greater equity interest by vote or value in the entity; (ii) holds a majority of seats on the board of directors of the entity; or (iii) otherwise controls the actions, policies, or personnel decisions of the entity. OFAC determines on a case-by-case basis whether the type of *de facto* control referenced in clause (iii) exists.

The ITSR prohibit U.S. persons and their owned and controlled subsidiaries from exporting, reexporting, selling, or supplying goods, services, or technology directly or indirectly, to Iran, persons in Iran, and when the benefit of the services is received in Iran.[55] This rule prohibits the provision of goods, services, or technology to any entity

---

52. In this chapter, the "Iran Sanctions Program" includes all the statutes, executive orders, General Licenses, FAQs, advisories, and other guidance at http://www.treasury.gov/resource-center/sanctions/Programs/Pages/iran.aspx (last visited October 15, 2014).

53. The definition of "U.S. person" under the ITSR, like those for list-based programs, includes any U.S. citizen, lawful permanent resident of the United States, entity organized under the laws of the United States (including foreign branches), or any person in the United States. 31 C.F.R. § 560.314 (2012).

54. 31 C.F.R. § 560.215.

55. 31 C.F.R. §§ 560.204 and 560.410.

or individual located in Iran, whether that individual is an Iranian national or not. On the other hand, the ITSR do not prohibit U.S. persons from providing goods, services, or technology to an Iranian citizen or national who is not ordinarily resident in Iran and who is resident in the United States or a third country, so long as the Iranian citizen or national is not acting on behalf of the Government of Iran, an entity organized under the laws of Iran or located in Iran, or an individual located in Iran.[56]

The ITSR also prohibit facilitation and evasion.[57] Accordingly, a U.S. person may not rely on a third party or a non-U.S. affiliate to conduct transactions it otherwise would be prohibited from engaging in on its own. The ITSR prohibit U.S. persons from engaging in any transaction or dealing in, or related to, goods, services, or technology of Iranian origin.[58] The term "services of Iranian origin" includes services performed inside Iran as well as outside Iran by a citizen, national, or permanent resident of Iran if that individual is ordinarily resident in Iran.[59] As OFAC interprets the transfer of funds to be a service, U.S. persons may not accept payments originating from, or transiting through, Iran. As almost all Iranian financial institutions also are blocked, any payment originating from or transiting through Iran would be blocked once it comes under the control of a U.S. person or financial institution.

In addition to the ITSR, other List-Based Sanctions Programs also reach persons located in Iran. For example, the Weapons of Mass Destruction Proliferators ("NPWMD") and Specially Designated Global Terrorists ("SDGT") Programs include several Iranian financial institutions. Because of the designation of most Iranian banks and complex rules related to funds that originate with the Central Bank of Iran, it is difficult to obtain payment even for lawful transactions directly or indirectly to Iran. Many money center banks will not process payments from Iran.

When considering the Iran Sanctions Program, it is also important to analyze the Comprehensive Iran Sanctions, Accountability, and Divestment Act of 2010 ("CISADA"). CISADA authorizes the President to impose restrictions on non-U.S. companies that engage in non-U.S. trade in non-U.S. origin goods and services with Iran and refuse to wind down that trade. The imposition of such controls by an order of the President or the Secretary of State is an example of territorial remedy jurisdiction.[60]

5. Multilateral Export Control Regimes

Four multilateral regimes shape much of the U.S. export control policy: the Wassenaar Arrangement, the Australia Group, the Missile Technology Control Regime, and the Nuclear Supplier Group. The Wassenaar Arrangement on Export Controls for Conventional Arms and Dual-Use Goods and Technologies (the "WA") was established to contribute to international and regional security and stability. It aims to prevent the destabilizing accumulations of arms and dual-use goods and technologies by establishing a process of consultation and, where appropriate, encouraging national policies of restraint and by promoting greater responsibility and accountability in transfers of arms and dual-use

---

56. 31 C.F.R. § 560.306(b)(2) and (d)(3).
57. 31C.F.R. §§ 560.208 and 560.203.
58. 31 C.F.R. § 560.206(a)(1).
59. 31 C.F.R. § 560.306(b)(2). The term "ordinarily resident" is not defined in the ITSR.
60. Comprehensive Iran Sanctions, Accountability, and Divestment Act of 2010, Pub. L. No. 111-195, 124 Stat. 1312 (2010) (signed into law July 1, 2010).

goods and technology. The WA began in 1996 and now includes about 33 members, including Russia but not China. The WA does not publish target countries.[61]

The Australia Group ("AG") was formed in 1985 to prevent the proliferation of chemical and biological weapons. It targets entities that engage in such proliferation in non-member states. It includes about thirty-four members, which do not include Russia or China. The name of the AG stems from Australia's leadership role in forming the organization.[62] The Missile Technology Control Regime ("MTCR") was organized in 1987 to limit the proliferation of missiles capable of delivering weapons of mass destruction. It targets entities that would proliferate missiles in non-member states. It currently has a membership of about 33 countries.[63]

The Nuclear Suppliers Group, established in 1992 to stem the proliferation of nuclear weapons and explosive devices, currently has over 40 members.[64] The above organizations are informal arrangements. They do not rise to the level of an international agreement. Each is a voluntary organization, but is nonetheless important in any diplomatic effort to bring discipline and effectiveness to export control policy. One international treaty relates to export controls—the Chemical Weapons Convention ("CWC"). The EAR implements prohibitions on the export of certain chemicals under the CWC.[65] BIS also plays a role in the verification regime that is a part of the Treaty. The CWC bans the development, production, stockpiling, and use of chemical weapons among its signatories.

6. Enforcement Authority

Civil and criminal penalties exist for violations of U.S. export controls and economic sanctions programs. When the EAA is in lapse and the EAR are extended by IEEPA, the penalties for violations of the EAR are set by the IEEPA Enhancement Act, 50 U.S.C. § 1705 (2013) (enhancing criminal penalties under IEEPA to $1,000,000 and 20 years imprisonment per violation and administrative penalties to $250,000 per violation or twice

---

61. More information about the Wassenaar Arrangement on Export Controls for Conventional Arms and Dual-Use Goods and Technologies is available at <http://www.wassenaar.org>.

62. More information about the Australia Group is available at <http://www.australiagroup.net>.

63. For more information on the Missile Technology Control Regime, see <http://www.mtcr.info/english/index.html>.

64. Additional information about the Nuclear Suppliers Group is available at <http://www.nsg-online.org>.Another informal nuclear export control group, complementing the NSG, called the Zangger Committee (named after its first Chairman) was formed in 1971 and currently consists of 38 member states, including the U.S. The Committee's decisions are not legally binding but its decisions are put into legal effect by unilateral declarations of each member to the other members, with subsequent letters to the Director-General of International Atomic Energy Agency (IAEA) requesting him to publish these unilateral policy declarations. The Committee developed a "trigger list" of (a) source or special fissionable materials, and (b) equipment or materials especially designed or prepared for the processing, use, or production of special fissionable materials. Under Art. III.2 of the Nuclear Non-Proliferation Treaty (NPT), these items should be subject to IAEA safeguards if supplied by NPT parties to any non-nuclear weapon States (NNWS). In 1974, the Committee published the Trigger List, which listed the items that would "trigger" a requirement for safeguards and guidelines governing the export of those items to NNWS not party to the NPT. These guidelines establish three conditions of supply: a non-explosive use assurance, an IAEA safeguards requirement, and a re-transfer provision that requires the receiving state to apply the same conditions when re-exporting these items. Additional information on the Zangger Committee and the Trigger List can be found on the Committee's website at <www.zanggercommittee.org>.

65. 15 C.F.R. § 745 (2002).

the amount of that transaction that is the basis of the violation). Similarly, civil penalties for violation of the ITAR can range into the hundreds of millions of dollars. Under the AECA, criminal conviction for a willful violation of the ITAR can lead to imprisonment for up to 20 years and fines of up to $1,000,000.

OFAC has authority to impose civil penalties for violations under IEEPA (USD $250,000 or twice the amount of the underlying transaction), TWEA and the Libertad Act (USD $65,000), the Iraqi Sanctions Act (USD $325,000), the Antiterrorism Act (USD $55,000 or two times the amount that should have been blocked, whichever is greater), and the Foreign Narcotics Kingpin Designation Act (USD $1,075,000). Generally, Cuba Sanctions Program penalties are assessed under TWEA, and most other OFAC penalties are assessed under IEEPA. Criminal penalties also exist under the IEEPA guidelines described above. Persons convicted of violating TWEA may be imprisoned for up to 10 years and be fined up to the greater of either USD $250,000 for individuals and USD $1,000,000 for organizations, or twice the pecuniary gain or loss from the violation.

7. Limits on the Reach of Certain Reexport Controls and Economic Sanctions

While the above theories demonstrate significant extraterritorial reach, limits nonetheless exist on the extraterritorial reach of U.S. export controls, reexport controls, and economic sanctions. Each of the following limiting theories requires separate consideration and explanation:

1. Limits on the scope of the U.S. regulations based upon the meaning and scope as articulated in the regulations, as opposed to the broad discretion in statutes to implement those regulations;
2. *De minimis* exclusion from the scope of a regulation based upon its own terms;
3. The fact that published technology and source code are outside the scope of certain rules;
4. The U.S. Constitution's requirement for fair notice and clarity in the text of prescriptions;
5. Right to a jury trial and the determination of a mixed question of law and fact on matters such as agency jurisdiction over an item and classification of an item under the ITAR and EAR; and
6. The U.S. Supreme Court's recognition of the rule of reason under the Restatement (Third).

Constitutional Limitations on Export Controls and Economic Sanctions

Three constitutional limits may be imposed on export controls and sanctions: (1) the "void for vagueness" theory related to the substantive due process clause of the Fifth Amendment to the Constitution; (2) the limits on the prescription of behavior of conduct outside of the United States under the rule of reason of the Restatement (Third); and (3) the right to a jury determination on a mixed question of law and fact. These three constitutional limits overcome the constitutional authorities that permit the U.S. Government to regulate foreign commerce.

Void for Vagueness

The U.S. Constitution requires a regulation to have sufficient clarity such that a person of ordinary intelligence can adjust their conduct to avoid liability. The Seventh Circuit Court of Appeals applied this principle in *U.S. v Pulungan*[66] to overrule a jury conviction for a violation of the ITAR. This principle limits the exercise and enforcement of rule-making power whether for extraterritorial application or domestic application.

In *Pulungan*, the Department of Justice charged that Pulungan attempted to export 100 riflescopes to Indonesia via Saudi Arabia to avoid a U.S. embargo against Indonesia (which no longer existed in 2007). A distinguished DDTC Licensing Officer testified that DDTC had concluded the riflescopes had been "manufactured to military specification," per the USML at Category I(f). At the request of the prosecutor, the trial court found as a matter of law that the particular riflescope is a "defense article" and took the issue away from the jury.[67] Pulungan contended that the prosecution did not prove that the particular model of rifle scope was manufactured to a military specification, or that Pulungan knew this (thus resulting in no criminal intent). The Seventh Circuit reversed the criminal conviction in the trial court and observed:

> A regulation is published for all to see. People can adjust their conduct to avoid liability. A designation by an unnamed official, using unspecified criteria, that is put in a desk drawer, taken out only for use at a criminal trial, and immune from any evaluation by the judiciary, is the sort of tactic usually associated with totalitarian régimes.

In an unrelated matter, the U.S. Supreme Court this year held in *Fox v FCC*[68] that, under the Due Process clause of the Fifth Amendment to the U.S. Constitution, a statute or regulation must have sufficient clarity to provide "a person of ordinary intelligence fair notice of what is prohibited . . ." The Court indicated the standard applies for two reasons:

> Even when speech is not at issue, the void for vagueness doctrine addresses at least two connected but discrete due process concerns: first, that regulated parties should know what is required of them so they may act accordingly; second, precision and guidance are necessary so that those enforcing the law do not act in an arbitrary or discriminatory way.

In *Christopher v Smithkline Beecham*,[69] the U.S. Supreme Court declined to defer to the agency's interpretation of certain wage and hour law, because to do so "would seriously undermine the principle that agencies should provide regulated parties "fair warning of the conduct [a regulation] prohibits or requires." The Court further stated that to follow the agency's interpretation in that matter would result in the kind of "unfair surprise" that the Court's decisions have long warned against. In its view, agencies should make

---

66. *United States v. Pulungan*, 569 F3d. 326 (7th Cir. 2009).

67. In fairness to DDTC and the Administration, since 2009 the Administration, DDTC, and BIS have gone to great lengths to make export controls clearer and more objective under ECR, and have provided extensive opportunities for notice and comment. This initiative has included extensive redrafting of control lists such as the USML and CCL, multiple efforts to define "specially designed", and extensive use of notice-and-comment in the rulemaking process.

68. *FCC v. Fox*, 2012 U.S. LEXIS 4661 (June 21, 2012, Decided). The courts have traditionally given considerable deference to the Executive Branch in matters of national security and foreign policy. *See Dames & Moore v. Regan*, 453 U.S. 654 (1981); *Youngstown Sheet & Tube Co. v. Sawyer*, 343 U.S. 579 (1952); *Natural Resources Defense Council v. Nuclear Regulatory Comm'n*, 647 F.2d 1345 (D.C. Cir. 1981).

69. *Christopher v. Smithkline Beecham*, 567 U.S. ___ (June 18, 2012).

changes through notice-and-comment rulemaking, a process under which resulting rules are then unlikely to result in unfair surprise.

Courts have traditionally given considerable deference to the Executive Branch in matters of national security and foreign policy.[70] However, the Supreme Court in *Fox v. FCC* makes clear the void for vagueness standard is not limited to matters when speech is at issue. Moreover, the *Pulungan* decision of the Seventh Circuit stands for the proposition that at least in that Circuit, deference for national security and foreign policy is not absolute in the face of a Constitutional challenge a particular provision is void for vagueness.[71]

Right to Jury Trial and Decision of Mixed Question of Law and Fact

Both the First Circuit and Seventh Circuit have held that a challenge to commodity jurisdiction under the ITAR presents a mixed question of fact for the fact finder, including a jury in a criminal case.[72] In *United States v. Wu*, the First Circuit rejected a void for vagueness challenge but reversed certain counts, because the trial court took away from the jury the mixed question of law and fact as to whether certain electrical devises were described on the USML and therefore subject to the ITAR:

> Here, to convict the defendants of violating the AECA, 22 U. S.C. § 2778(c), the jury had to find not only that the defendants acted with the requisite *mens rea* (willfulness), but also that they actually committed the *actus reus* charged (violation of regulations issued under the statute). Put differently, even if the jury found that Wu and Wei [the defendants] believed that phase shifters fell within the Munitions List restrictions, it would still have to conclude that the phase shifters actually did fall within the Munitions List restrictions (regardless of Wu and Wei's beliefs). And as to whether Wu and Wei violated regulations issued under the AECA, the proper question for the jury was whether Wu and Wei's conduct violated the relevant regulations as those regulations existed at the time the conduct occurred.[73]

Restatement (Third) of Foreign Relations Law

The Restatement (Third)[74] provides factors for courts to consider under a type of rule of reason analysis. The courts have not yet subjected any specific provision of U.S. reexport controls or economic sanctions to analysis under the Restatement (Third). The U.S. Supreme Court has, however, applied the rule of reason of the Restatement (Third) to private antitrust litigation. In two opinions, Justice Breyer and Justice Scalia invoked the rule of reason under the Restatement (Third).[75]

---

70. *See Dames & Moore v. Regan*, 453 U.S. 654 (1981); *Youngstown Sheet & Tube Co. v. Sawyer*, 343 U.S. 579 (1952); *Natural Resources Defense Council v. Nuclear Regulatory Comm'n*, 647 F.2d 1345 (D.C. Cir. 1981).

71. *C.f. United States v. Lackman et. al*, 387 F.3d 42 (1st Cir. 2004) (reviewing constitutionally of the undefined term "specially designed" under the void for vagueness standard); *United States v. Lee*, 183 F.3d 1029, 1031 (9th Cir. 1999) (reviewing constitutionality of the AECA and its implementing regulations), *cert. denied*, 528 U.S. 990, 120 S.Ct. 454, 145 L.Ed.2d 370 (1999), and *cert. denied*, 528 U.S. 1128, 120 S.Ct. 963, 145 L.Ed.2d 835 (2000).

72. *United States v. Wu*, No. 11-1115, No. 11-1141 (1st Cir. Mar. 19, 2014); *United States v. Pulungan*, 569 F.3d 326, 328 (7th Cir. 2009) (Easterbrook, C.J.).

73. *United States v. Wu*, No. 11-1115 at 34.

74. Restatement (Third) of Foreign Relations Law of the United States §§ 402–403 (adopted 1986, published 1987).

75. *See*, F. *Hoffmann-La Roche Ltd. v. Empagran S.A.*, 542 U.S. 155 (2004) and *Hartford Fire Ins. Co. v. California*, 509 U.S. 764 (1993).

Section 403(2) of the Restatement (Third) is entitled "Limitations on Jurisdiction to Prescribe." It requires U.S. courts to evaluate eight factors in determining whether a given exercise of extraterritorial jurisdiction to prescribe the conduct or activity of a person is unreasonable. In connection with a particular extraterritorial provision of U.S. export controls and economic sanctions laws, each of the eight factors should be taken into consideration to determine reasonableness of the extraterritorial reach. In dissent in *Hartford Fire Insurance Co. v. California*, Justice Scalia recognized the Restatement (Third) as a separate limitation on extraterritorial reach that is unreasonable.[76] In the majority, Justice Breyer, citing Justice Scalia, also recognized the Restatement (Third) as a Constitutional limitation on the extraterritorial reach of U.S. laws under a reasonableness standard.[77]

---

76. 509 U.S. 764 at 814–815, 818–819 (1993):

But if the presumption against extraterritoriality has been overcome or is otherwise inapplicable, a second canon of statutory construction becomes relevant: An act of Congress [*815] ought never to be construed to violate the law of nations if any other possible construction remains." *Murray v. Schooner Charming Betsy*, 6 U.S. 64, 2 Cranch 64, 118, 2 L. Ed. 208....

This canon is "wholly independent" of the presumption against extraterritoriality. *Aramco, supra*, at 264 (Marshall, J., dissenting). It is relevant to determining the substantive reach of a statute because "the law of nations," or customary international law, includes limitations on a nation's exercise of its jurisdiction to prescribe. *See* Restatement (Third) §§ 401–416. Though it clearly has constitutional authority to do so, Congress is generally presumed not to have exceeded those customary international law limits on jurisdiction to prescribe.

Consistent with that presumption, this and other courts have frequently recognized that, even where the presumption against extraterritoriality does not apply, statutes should not be interpreted to regulate foreign persons or conduct if that regulation would conflict with principles of international law....

[*818]...

In sum, the practice of using international law to limit the extraterritorial reach of statutes is firmly established in our jurisprudence. In proceeding to apply that practice to the present cases, I shall rely on the Restatement (Third) for the relevant principles of international law. Its standards appear fairly supported in the decisions of this Court construing international choice-of-law principles (*Lauritzen, Romero*, and *McCulloch*) and in the decisions of other federal courts, especially *Timberlane*. Whether the Restatement precisely reflects international law in every detail matters little here, as I believe this litigation would be resolved the same way under virtually any conceivable test that takes account of foreign regulatory interests.

Under the Restatement, a nation having some "basis" for jurisdiction to prescribe law should nonetheless refrain from exercising that jurisdiction "with respect to a person or activity having connections with another state when the exercise of such jurisdiction is unreasonable." Restatement (Third) § 403(1). The "reasonableness" inquiry turns on a number of factors including, but not limited to: "the extent to which the activity takes place within the territory [of the regulating state]," *id.*, § 403(2)(a); "the connections, such as nationality, residence, or economic activity, between the regulating state and the person principally responsible for the [*819] activity to be regulated," *id.*, § 403(2)(b); "the character of the activity to be regulated, the importance of regulation to the regulating state, the extent to which other states regulate such activities, and the degree to which the desirability of such regulation is generally accepted," *id.*, § 403(2)(c); "the extent to which another state may have an interest in regulating the activity," *id.*, § 403(2)(g); and "the likelihood of conflict with regulation by another state," *id.*, § 403(2)(h).

77. "*First*, this Court ordinarily construes ambiguous statutes to avoid unreasonable interference with the sovereign authority of other nations. *See, e.g., McCulloch v. Sociedad Nacional de Marineros de Honduras*, 372 U.S. 10, 20–22, 9 L. Ed. 2d 547, 83 S. Ct. 671 (1963) (application of National Labor Relations Act to foreign-flag vessels); *Romero v. International Terminal Operating Co.*, 358 U.S. 354, 382–383, 3 L. Ed. 2d 368, 79 S. Ct. 468 (1959) (application of Jones Act in maritime case); *Lauritzen v. Larsen*, 345 U.S. 571, 578, 97 L. Ed. 1254, 73 S. Ct. 921 (1953) (same). This rule of construction reflects principles of customary international law—law that (we must assume) Congress ordinarily seeks to follow. *See* Restatement (Third) of Foreign Relations Law of the United States §§ 403(1),

The U.S. export control bar, prosecutors, and courts should now consider seriously whether and under what circumstances the Restatement (Third) imposes limiting principles on the policies, prescriptions, and the degree of nexus between those policies and those prescriptions under U.S. export controls, reexport controls, and sanctions. The regulatory agencies and State should also consider these factors in developing regulations that are enforceable, and in shaping multilateral strategies that will meet the rule of reason. This relates to all regulations issued by all U.S. agencies, including BIS, DDTC, OFAC, DOE and NRC. Justices Breyer and Scalia's support of the Restatement (Third)'s rule of reason is by itself sufficient reason for the export control bar and the U.S. Government to take note of the eight factors. The American Bar Association ("ABA") Section of International Law has recognized the relevance of the rule of reason in the Restatement (Third) in comments regarding a proposed amendment to the ITAR.

Constitutional Limits and the Development of Effective and Enforceable Export Controls and Sanctions Laws

As of this writing, Congress and the President are searching for export controls and economic sanctions that will be effective in addressing concerns regarding nuclear proliferation in Iran, the Russian incursions in the Ukraine, and the evolution of the terrorist group known as the Islamic State of Iraq and Syria ("ISIS" or "ISIL"). Under these circumstances, the Restatement (Third) and its application to reexport controls and sanctions may well provide guidance to shape further multilateral strategies that are both effective and enforceable. The requirement for clarity in rules is more than an argument for effectiveness; it is a substantive due process requirement.

Practitioners and regulators spend the vast majority of their time and effort focusing on the prescriptive rules and statutes. That is as it should be. However, a full understanding of the U.S. export controls and economic sanctions system requires practitioners, prosecutors, regulators, and courts alike to appreciate the various means of jurisdictional reach, the extension of that reach by prosecutorial strategies, and the potential limits that may be imposed by the courts under the Restatement (Third), the void for vagueness doctrine, and the right to allow a jury to decide a mixed question of law and fact.

403(2) (1986) (hereinafter Restatement) (limiting the unreasonable exercise of prescriptive jurisdiction with respect to a person or activity having connections with another State); *Murray v. Schooner Charming Betsy*, 6 U.S. 64, 2 Cranch 64, 2 L. Ed. 208 (1804) ("[A]n act of Congress ought never to be construed to violate the law of nations if any other possible [***237] construction remains"); *Hartford Fire Insurance Co. v. California*, 509 U.S. 764, 817, 125 L. Ed. 2d 612, 113 S. Ct. 2891 (1993) (Scalia, J., dissenting) (identifying rule of construction as derived from the principle of "prescriptive comity")."

Chapter 32

Federal Emergency Preparedness and Response and Homeland Security[1]

Suzanne Spaulding with Michael L. Diakiwski, Michael O. Halas, Kaiya Pontinen Sandler, and Michelle Tonelli

In this chapter:
Introduction
Homeland Security as Protection against Natural Disasters
The Federal Response to 9/11
Key Legal Issues
Homeland Defense — The Role of the Military Within the United States
Critical Infrastructure Protection: A Partnership between the Public and Private Sectors
Chemical Security: Chemical Facility Anti-Terrorism Standards (CFATS)
Cybersecurity
The Future: Effectively Integrating Various Federal Assets into DHS
Selected Bibliography

Introduction

Homeland security is, in its simpiliest form, the art of preparing and responding to manmade and natural disasters. From the birth of the nation to the creation of the Federal Emergency Management Agency (FEMA) and the ultimate formation of the Department of Homeland Security (DHS), the United States has consistently sought to improve and maintain effective federal preparedness for and response to disasters. Regardless of whether the roots of the disaster naturally occur, result from acts of terrorism or are caused by other manmade disasters, there are a number of common elements of civil emergency management that are found in any disaster setting: the need to provide shelter, food, water, and clothing; establish effective communications; ensure the transportation of emergency supplies and equipment; and coordinate the efforts of federal, state, local, and tribal governments. The evolution of the federal response to disasters has consistently included these elements as fundamental to effective preparedness and response — no matter the type of disaster.

---

1. The text on Federal Emergency Preparedness and Response, orginally authored by Mark D. Wallace & H. Crane Miller, is updated and revised from the 2nd edition of this book.

Disclaimer: Any views expressed in this chapter are those solely of the authors and do not represent the position of the U.S. Government.

The realization that homeland security was also a national security issue came in the years following the 1993 attack on the World Trade Center. The foreign terrorist threat had come to the United States. Two years later, a radical group released the chemical agent sarin in a subway in Tokyo, Japan, killing twelve and sending thousands to emergency rooms. The prospect of terrorist attacks involving weapons of mass destruction added to the sense of vulnerability. Over the ensuing years, additional attacks and foiled plots served to highlight this new reality and prompted a series of studies and reports reevaluating our national security structure and policies in light of this changing threat.

Thus, in order to fully discuss homeland security, one must discuss how to protect against and respond to all types of disasters. This chapter will discuss how the United States Government's response to all types of disasters has evolved over the years. It will also discuss the changing nature of the terrorist threat and how this changed the way the federal government is organized to deal with this threat. Lastly, this chapter will look at the legal issues raised by the homeland security imperative.[2]

Homeland Security as Protection against Natural Disasters

Historical Overview, 1789 to 1950

Early in the life of the federal government, Congress received and granted requests for the relief of individual citizens in the wake of a disaster by private bills. Between 1789 and 1801 Congress granted at least sixteen refunds for taxes and duties paid on imported merchandise destroyed or damaged before sale.[3] Beginning in 1794 with the Whiskey Rebellion, Congress began to shift from private bills to more categorical relief for classes of persons. Congress gradually replaced the system of private bills for named individual beneficiaries with general relief bills that appropriated larger sums of money for the benefit of eligible and aggrieved classes of persons.[4] Tax remissions gave way to direct federal relief, to indemnification of property damage and loss, and to food distribution. By 1825, categorical relief surpassed private disaster relief requests.[5] As Congress shifted to categorical forms of relief, it delegated broad administrative authority to commissioners, appointed by the Congress and the President, who were charged with investigating applicants and distributing federal aid.[6]

These earliest examples of federal disaster relief also raised concerns that echo today and remain hallmarks of contemporary legislation, including: the constitutional basis for disaster relief; the primary responsibility of local and state governments for responding to disasters; whether providing certain types of relief constitutes precedent or entitlement for relief from future disasters; eligibility for disaster relief; congressional funding and

---

2. This chapter does not discuss in detail issues of intelligence, terrorism, or other issues that are addressed elsewhere in this volume.

3. Michele L. Landis, *Let Me Next Time be Tried by Fire: Disaster Relief and the Origins of the American Welfare State 1789–1874*, 92 Nw. U.L. Rev. 967, 979 (1998). Ms. Landis argues that the roots of federal welfare programs can be found in the history of disaster relief.

4. *Id.* at 981.

5. *Id.* at 982.

6. *Id.* at 988.

oversight; and delegation of authority to the executive branch to administer, investigate and distribute federal aid.

For more than 160 years Congress exercised the principal authority to provide federal disaster relief. However, short-term and immediately responsive disaster relief remained primarily within the purview of individuals, communities, and the states. Whenever a community or an area of a state was struck by a disaster Congress might appropriate funds or make available assistance from the military, or both. From 1789 until 1950 Congress passed more than 150 separate public and private laws concerning individual floods, tornadoes, fires, epidemics or manmade disasters.[7] Nonetheless, congressional action was not geared to early response, as Congress typically acted long after the occurrence of the disaster. Throughout this period each act of Congress responding to a disaster was an *ad hoc* measure specific to a given event in a particular state or locality. No comprehensive disaster relief legislation existed.

1950: The Shift to the Executive Branch

In 1947 and 1948, Congress began to move from *ad hoc* disaster relief toward general disaster relief legislation.[8] With the advent of the Cold War and the outbreak of the Korean conflict in 1950, Congress recognized the need to plan, prepare for, and respond to civil emergencies. In 1950 Congress enacted three important emergency management statutes that gave executive branch agencies continuing authority to prepare for and respond to disasters: the Federal Civil Defense Act of 1950,[9] the Defense Production Act of 1950,[10] and the first organic legislation authorizing disaster relief, the Disaster Relief Act of 1950,[11] the forerunner of current disaster relief legislation. Under the Disaster Relief Act,[12] for the first time:

(1) The President was given authority to carry out provisions "through such federal agency as he may designate.";

(2) Federal appropriations "supplement the efforts and available resources of State and local governments ...";

(3) The President must find that "any flood, drought, fire, hurricane, earthquake, storm, or other catastrophe in any part of the United States is or threatens to be of sufficient severity and magnitude to warrant disaster assistance by the Federal Government ..."; and

(4) The governor of the state in which "such catastrophe may occur shall certify the need for disaster assistance ..."[13]

The 1950 Act also established a separate "Emergency Fund for the President," the precursor of today's Disaster Relief Fund. With this legislation federal responsibility for preparedness

---

7. 96 CONG. REC. 11899–11902; CHARLES MANNING, LEGIS. HIST. I, pp. 100—110; Landis, *supra* note 3.

8. Pub. L. No. 80-233, 61 Stat. 422 (1947); Second Deficiency Appropriation Act of 1948, Pub. L. No. 80-785, 62 Stat. 1027 (1948).

9. Federal Civil Defense Act of 1950, 50 U.S.C. App. § 2251 (2003). This legislation was repealed in 1994 and most of its authorities were restated as Title VI of the Robert T. Stafford Disaster Relief and Emergency Assistance Act, 42 U.S.C. §§ 5195—5197g (2003).

10. Defense Production Act of 1950, 50 U.S.C. app. § 2061 (2003).

11. Pub. L. No. 81-875, 64 Stat. 1109 (1950).

12. Disaster Relief Act of 1950, Public Law No. 81-875, 64 Stat. 1109, 1110 (1950).

13. *Id.*

and response to civil emergencies shifted from predominate control by Congress to the President.[14]

In the past Congress had acted through authorizations and appropriations acts specific to each disaster. The 1950 Act provided a general authorizing framework for the federal government under which the executive branch could take prompt action to meet the needs of individuals and stricken areas. It established a general government policy for emergency relief for future disasters instead of meeting the needs of response for each individual disaster after it occurs. By creating a general and standardized mechanism to prepare for and respond to disasters, Congress hoped to promote efficiency and economy to the previous *ad hoc* disaster legislation.

1950–1978: Expansion of Disaster Assistance

From 1950 to 1978 Congress enacted laws that expanded the categories of federal assistance and defined parameters for the amount of assistance. Congress' expansion of such authorities recognized that a variety of authorities were necessary to deal with diverse natural and manmade disasters and the unique problems posed by different types of disasters. Those authorities include:

- flood insurance,[15]
- environmental cleanup,[16]
- dam safety,[17]
- earthquake hazards reduction,[18]
- fire prevention and control,[19]
- hazardous materials transportation,[20]
- chemical weapons reduction,[21]
- radiological emergency preparedness,[22] and
- mass care.[23]

National Flood Insurance Program (NFIP). The Flood Control Act of 1936 signaled the federal government's first national involvement in flood hazard management, and established criteria for federal funding for dams, levees, seawalls and other flood control structures. Between 1936 and the mid-1950s the national response to a flood disaster was predominantly through engineered flood control works and disaster relief in the form of

---

14. While Congress granted very broad authority to the President to act, it retained legislative oversight of the programs, spread among many committees of the Congress, and retained its control over the appropriations process.

15. National Flood Insurance Act of 1968, Flood Disaster Protection Act of 1973, 42 U.S.C. §§ 4001–4129 (2001); 44 C.F.R. §§ 59.1–78.14 (2014).

16. Comprehensive Environmental Response, Compensation, and Liability Act of 1980 (CERCLA), 42 U.S.C. §§ 9615–9675 (2010).

17. National Dam Safety Program Act, 33 U.S.C. §§ 467–467n (2006).

18. Earthquake Hazards Reduction Act of 1977, 42 U.S.C. §§ 7701–7709 (2011).; *See also*, Exec. Order No. 12,699, 3 C.F.R., § 269 (1991 Comp.); Executive Order No. 12,941, 3 C.F.R. 955 (1995 Comp.); 44 C.F.R. §§ 361.1–361.8 (2002).

19. Federal Fire Prevention and Control Act of 1974, 15 U.S.C. §§ 2201–2232 (2011). *See also* 44 C.F.R. §§ 151.1–152.9 (2014).

20. Hazardous Materials Transportation Act of 1994, 49 U.S.C. §§ 5115–5116 (2011). *See also* Emergency Planning and Community Right-to-Know Act of 1986, 42 U.S.C. § 11005 (2011).

21. Department of Defense Authorization Act of 1986, 50 U.S.C. § 1521(2011).

22. Atomic Energy Act of 1954, 42 U.S.C. §§ 2011–2297 (2011); 44 C.F.R. §§ 350.1–354.7 (2010).

23. McKinney-Vento Homeless Assistance Act of 1987, 42 U.S.C. §§ 11331–11352 (2010).

emergency housing and distribution of surplus federal commodities. Flood insurance was not available from private insurers because of their concerns that catastrophic flood disasters could lead to insolvency.

Congressional efforts to form a viable flood insurance program began in the late 1940s and led to enactment of the Federal Flood Insurance Act of 1956. The reluctance of private insurers to sell flood insurance, rising flood losses from increased housing and other construction in floodplains, and mounting federal costs for disaster relief and flood control works, inspired passage of the National Flood Insurance Act of 1968 authorizing the National Flood Insurance Program (NFIP).[24] A voluntary program, the NFIP provided subsidized flood insurance in communities that adopted measures to reduce the potentially damaging effects of floods, but it gained acceptance slowly.[25]

Flooding caused by Hurricane Agnes in 1972 in Pennsylvania and other mid-Atlantic states was the catalyst for major changes in the Act. Under the Flood Disaster Protection Act of 1973[26] Congress established mandatory flood insurance purchase requirements, among other changes. Since passage in 1968 Congress has amended the NFIA close to fifty times—broadening and modifying it—attempting to improve its acceptance and compliance.

In 1969 Congress authorized an emergency program that provided limited subsidized flood insurance coverage while communities adopted minimum floodplain management measures and the NFIP completed flood hazard rate maps and studies. In 1977 Congress increased the amount of flood insurance coverage available at actuarial rates.[27] In 1981 Congress prohibited flood insurance for new or substantially improved construction on Department of the Interior-designated undeveloped coastal barriers.[28] The Write-Your-Own program under the Housing and Urban-Rural Recovery Act of 1983[29] allowed private insurers to sell flood insurance and service claims on a non-risk basis, underwritten by the federal government. Congress amended the NFIA again in 1994 to improve compliance, including civil monetary penalties for federally regulated lenders that fail to require flood insurance of borrowers, incentives for communities (such as credits on premium rates) for programs to reduce risks of flood and erosion damage and to reduce flood losses.[30] The 1994 enactment also prohibited disaster relief assistance in a flood disaster area to persons who obtain, but fail to maintain, flood insurance on their property.

Fire Prevention and Control. *America Burning*, the 1973 report of the National Commission on Fire Prevention and Control, was the catalyst for the federal government's expanded role in fire prevention and control.[31] Finding high losses of life and property from fire unacceptable, in 1974 the Congress enacted the Federal Fire Prevention and Control Act,[32]

---

24. National Flood Insurance Act of 1968, 42 U.S.C. §§ 4001–4129 (2010).

25. When Hurricane Camille struck in 1969, only four communities out of a then-estimated 7000 flood prone areas of the country were eligible for flood insurance.

26. Flood Disaster Protection Act of 1973, Pub. L. No. 93-234, 87 Stat. 975 (codified as amended in scattered sections of 42 U.S.C.).

27. Housing and Community Development Act of 1977, Pub. L. No. 95-128, 91 Stat. 1147 (1977).

28. Omnibus Budget Reconciliation Act of 1981, Pub. L. No. 97-35, 95 Stat. 357 (1981). The Secretary of the Interior later designated 188 undeveloped coastal barrier islands on the Atlantic and Gulf coasts as part of the Coastal Barrier Resources System, and further expanded the System under the Coastal Barrier Improvement Act of 1990, Pub. L. No. 101-591, 104 Stat. 2931 (1990).

29. Housing and Urban-Rural Recovery Act of 1983, Pub. L. No. 98-181, 97 Stat. 1155 (1983).

30. National Flood Insurance Reform Act of 1994, 42 U.S.C. §§ 4001–4129 (2010).

31. The report drew attention to fire as a major national problem; the United States led all major industrialized countries in per capita deaths and property loss from fire.

32. Federal Fire Prevention and Control Act, 15 U.S.C. §§ 2201–2234 (2013).

which established a National Fire Prevention and Control Administration in the U.S. Department of Commerce. The Act also established a national fire academy to provide specialized training to the fire services and to assist state and local jurisdictions in their training programs. Congress has amended the Act several times to include arson prevention and control programs,[33] compilation of a national master list of fire-safe hotels and motels,[34] and development of hazardous materials identification, response, and incident data for emergency response personnel.[35] In 1979 Reorganization Plan No. 3 of 1978 and Executive Order No. 12,127 transferred most of the functions and authority vested in the Secretary of Commerce, the Administrator and Deputy Administrator of the National Fire Prevention and Control Administration to the Director of the Federal Emergency Management Agency.[36] In 2002 FEMA brought the National Urban Search and Rescue Response System[37] and the First Responder Grants program under the direction of the U.S. Fire Administrator.

Earthquake Hazards. In 1977 Congress found that all fifty states were vulnerable to earthquake hazards, and that at least thirty-nine states are subject to major or moderate seismic risk. Congress enacted the Earthquake Hazards Reduction Act of 1977[38] to support federal, state, local and private research and planning to reduce the risk of losses in seismic risk areas. This Act made FEMA the lead agency to plan and coordinate the Earthquake Hazards Reduction Program. Under the Act FEMA collaborates with the U.S. Geological Survey, the National Science Foundation, and the National Institute of Science and Technology to conduct and promote research on earthquakes, conduct public education programs, and to disseminate information on building codes and earthquake-resistant new construction and retrofitting of existing buildings.

Radiological Emergency Preparedness. On December 7, 1979, President Carter, acting on the recommendations of the Kemeny Commission on the Accident at Three Mile Island, directed FEMA to take lead responsibility in all offsite planning and response in the vicinity of commercial nuclear power plants. Under a Memorandum of Understanding between the U.S. Nuclear Regulatory Commission (NRC) and FEMA,[39] FEMA coordinates all federal planning for the offsite impact of radiological emergencies. Under the terms of the Memorandum of Understanding, FEMA takes the lead for assessing offsite radiological emergency response plans and preparedness, makes findings and determinations as to the adequacy and capability of implementing offsite plans, and communicates those findings and determinations to the NRC.[40]

---

33. Arson Prevention and Control Act of 1978, 15 U.S.C. §§ 2201–2234 (2013); Arson Prevention Act of 1994, Pub. L. No. 103-254, 108 Stat. 679 (1994).

34. Hotel and Motel Fire Safety Act of 1990, Pub. L. No. 101-391, 104 Stat. 747 (1990).

35. Firefighters' Safety Study Act, Pub. L. No. 101-446, 104 Stat. 1045 (1990).

36. Reorganization Plan No. 3 of 1978, 43 Fed. Reg. 41,943 (Sept. 19, 1978), and Exec. Order No. 12,127, 3 C.F.R. 376 (1979 Comp).

37. The National Urban Search and Rescue Response System currently (2014) consists of twenty-eight task force teams of firefighters, structural engineers, emergency medical personnel, canine search teams, and support personnel, specially trained to locate, rescue and medically stabilize people trapped in confined spaces, such as collapsed buildings, transportation accidents, mines and collapsed trenches. Urban search-and-rescue is a "multi-hazard" discipline, used in a variety of emergencies or disasters, including earthquakes, hurricanes, typhoons, storms and tornadoes, floods, dam failures, technological accidents, terrorist activities, and hazardous materials releases.

38. Earthquake Hazards Reduction Act of 1977, 42 U.S.C. §§ 7701–7709 (2010).

39. Memorandum of Understanding between NRC and FEMA Relating to Radiological Emergency Planning and Preparedness (June 17, 1993) in 44 C.F.R. § 353, app. A (2002). This memorandum superseded previous memoranda dated November 1, 1980, and April 18, 1985.

40. *Id.* at I. (Background and Purposes).

If a disaster damages the area around an operating nuclear power plant such that FEMA concludes that a disaster-initiated review of offsite emergency preparedness is necessary, FEMA will notify the NRC with a schedule for a review. The review is to reaffirm the radiological emergency preparedness capabilities of affected jurisdictions in the ten-mile emergency planning zone, which is around each of America's 103 nuclear power plants. FEMA is to file interim and final reports, and the NRC is to review these and other pertinent information in deciding whether to restart or continue operation of an affected operating reactor.[41]

Chemical Stockpile Emergency Preparedness (CSEP) Program. Congress has directed the Secretary of Defense, acting through the Department of the Army, to destroy lethal chemical agents and munitions stockpiled at eight U.S. Army installations in the continental United States.[42] While chemical stockpiles are located in eight states,[43] owing to the proximity to certain state or local governments that could be affected by accidental releases of the agents, the CSEP program works with ten states, forty counties, three cities, and one Tribal Nation to improve preparedness to protect the people of these communities from any accident at any of the stockpiles. As custodian of the stockpiles, the Department of the Army provides funding, training, guidance and technical support and expertise, and is principally responsible for actions taken within the Chemical Activities/Depot.[44] FEMA is responsible for assisting the surrounding communities and affected states in their preparation, implementation, and exercising of emergency preparedness plans.[45] The planning and stockpile disposal process essentially involves the Department of the Army, Department of Defense, FEMA, and participating state and local governments, with congressional oversight.

Dam Safety. In 1972 a privately owned tailings dam in Buffalo Creek, West Virginia failed, killing 125 people and leaving 3,000 homeless. In response, Congress enacted the National Dam Inspection Act,[46] authorizing the U.S. Army Corps of Engineers to inventory and inspect all non-federal dams. The Teton Dam in Idaho failed in 1976, killing fourteen and causing one billion dollars in damage. In November 1977, Kelly Barnes Dam in Georgia failed, killing thirty-nine. Spurred by dam failures in 1972, 1976, and in 1977, President Carter issued a memorandum on April 23, 1978, directing a review of federal dam safety activities by an *ad hoc* panel of recognized experts. The panel's report in June 1979 contained the first guidelines for federal agency dam owners. In July 1979, Executive Order No. 12,148 gave the director of FEMA responsibility to coordinate efforts to promote dam safety in the federal government.[47]

An October 4, 1979, Presidential Memorandum directed the federal agencies responsible for dams to adopt and implement the Federal Guidelines for Dam Safety. On the recommendation of the National Research Council to create a National Inventory of Dams, Congress authorized the Corps of Engineers in 1986 to maintain and periodically publish updated information on the inventory of dams. Under a memorandum of agreement

---

41. *Id.* at III, I (Recovery from Disasters Affecting Offsite Emergency Preparedness).

42. 50 U.S.C. § 1521 (2012).

43. Anniston Chemical Activity, Alabama; Blue Grass Chemical Activity, Kentucky; Edgewood Chemical Activity, Maryland; Newport Chemical Activity, Indiana and Illinois; Pine Bluff Chemical Activity, Arkansas; Pueblo Chemical Depot, Colorado; Tooele Chemical Activity, Utah; Umatilla Chemical Activity, Oregon and Washington.

44. 50 U.S.C. § 1521(c) (2012).

45. *Id.*

46. National Dam Inspection Act. Pub. L. No. 92-367, 86 Stat. 506 (1972).

47. Exec. Order No. 12,148, 3 C.F.R. 207 (1982 Comp.).

between FEMA and the Corps, FEMA has overseen the maintenance and update of the inventory since 1989. More than sixty-seven states, territories, and federal agencies participate in the update process.

Congress enacted the National Dam Safety Program Act of 1996,[48] which authorizes the National Dam Safety Program. The National Dam Safety Program keeps inventories of dams and develops safety standards for construction, maintenance and repair of the dams.

Activities under the National Dam Safety Program include:

- National Performance of Dams Program—retrieves, archives and distributes information on the U.S. dams performance;
- Training in Emergency Action Planning for dam failures;
- Training Aids for Dam Safety; and
- coordination with the states—working with the American Society of Dam Safety Officials, provides standards for U.S. dam safety programs.

General Disaster Response and Recovery: The Robert T. Stafford Disaster Relief and Emergency Assistance Act

The 1960s and early 1970s brought massive disasters requiring major federal response and recovery operations. Hurricane Carla struck in 1962, Hurricane Betsy in 1965, Hurricane Camille in 1969, and Hurricane Agnes in 1972. The Alaskan Earthquake hit in 1964 and the San Fernando Earthquake rocked Southern California in 1971. These events focused attention on the issue of natural disasters and brought about increased legislation.

When hazards associated with nuclear power plants and the transportation of hazardous substances were added to natural disasters, more than 100 federal agencies were involved in some aspect of preparing for and responding to disasters, hazards, and emergencies. Many parallel programs and policies existed at the state and local level, compounding the complexity of federal disaster relief efforts. The responsibility for implementing these laws shifted several times within the executive branch. A clear lack of federal coordinating authority led to the introduction of four principal bills in the 95th Congress (1977–1978) to consolidate and reorganize federal disaster related functions.[49] The National Governor's Association (NGA) also sought to decrease the many agencies with which state and local governments had to work. The NGA asked President Carter to centralize federal emergency functions.

President Carter presented Reorganization Plan No. 3 of 1978 to the Congress for its approval, using authority enacted to permit the President to organize the executive branch as he saw fit.[50] Reorganization Plan No. 3 established FEMA and transferred fire prevention and control, flood insurance, crime insurance, and emergency broadcast functions from two departments to the new agency.[51] President Carter subsequently ordered the transfer, reassignment, or delegation of civil defense, federal disaster assistance, emergency pre-

---

48. National Dam Safety Program Act of 1996, Pub. L. No. 104-303, 110 Stat. 3658 (1996).
49. H.R. 7222, 95th Congress (1977); H.R. 7649, 95th Congress (1977); S. 526, 95th Congress (1977); S. 1209 95th Congress (1977).
50. Reorganization Act of 1947, 5 U.S.C. §§ 901–912 (2013).
51. *Id.*; Exec. Order No. 12,127, 3 C.F.R. 376 (1979 Comp.).

paredness, defense resource mobilization, earthquake hazards, and certain other functions to FEMA.[52]

Early in its life FEMA was the lead federal agency in such disasters and emergencies including the contamination of Love Canal, the Cuban refugee crisis, and the accident at the Three Mile Island nuclear power plant. Later, the Loma Prieta Earthquake in 1989 and Hurricane Andrew in 1992 focused major national attention on FEMA. FEMA initiated sweeping reforms that streamlined disaster relief and recovery operations and placed new emphasis on preparedness and mitigation. While still maintaining many of its civil defense responsibilities, the end of the Cold War also allowed FEMA to redirect some resources away from civil defense into disaster relief, recovery and mitigation programs.

The basic legal framework for FEMA's response to and recovery from the consequences of major disasters and emergencies is found in the Robert T. Stafford Disaster Relief and Emergency Assistance Act (Stafford Act).[53] It is a flexible authority for responding to a wide variety of hazards, and it provides the legislative basis for coordinating the efforts of more than twenty-seven federal departments and agencies and one non-government organization whose authorities, personnel, resources, and equipment are used as appropriate in any given major disaster or emergency.[54]

First response to a disaster is the job of local government emergency services with help from nearby municipalities, the affected state and related volunteer agencies. If the President declares a major disaster or emergency at the request of a governor, FEMA coordinates federal resources for search and rescue, electrical power, food, water, shelter and other basic human needs. Under the Stafford Act the disaster event must be clearly more than state or local governments can handle alone. A governor's request for a major disaster or emergency declaration could mean an infusion of federal funds, but the governor must also commit significant state funds and resources for recovery efforts. If declared, funding comes from the President's Disaster Relief Fund,[55] which FEMA manages, and other disaster aid programs of other participating federal agencies.

The Stafford Act provides for two major categories of disaster aid:

(1) Federal Assistance to Individuals and Households[56] for damage to residences and businesses or personal property losses. Individual assistance generally falls into:

    (a) Housing Assistance, such as: (1) Temporary Housing; (2) Home Repair Assistance; (3) Replacement; or (4) Permanent Housing Construction.

    (b) Disaster Grants help meet other serious disaster-related needs and necessary expenses not covered by insurance and other aid programs. These may

---

52. Exec. Order No. 12,148, 3 C.F.R. 412 (1979 Comp.).

53. Robert T. Stafford Disaster Relief and Emergency Assistance Act, 42 U.S.C. §§ 5121–5208 (2010).

54. The *National Response Plan (NRP)*, which superseded and incorporated FEMA's *Federal Response Plan (FRP)*, provides the mechanism for coordinating delivery of federal assistance and resources to augment efforts of state and local governments overwhelmed by a major disaster, emergency, or terrorist attack. *See* <http://www.dhs.gov/xlibrary/assets/NRP_Brochure.pdf>; *see also the 2013 National Insfrastructure Protection Plan (NIPP)*. <http://www.dhs.gov/national-infrastructure-protection-plan>.

55. Congress funds the Disaster Relief Fund (DRF) through annual and supplemental appropriations. The annual appropriations typically set a base amount for disaster relief, which can be augmented by supplemental appropriations if a major disaster occurs that requires greater sums than are then available in the DRF.

56. Stafford Act, 42 U.S.C. § 5174 (2010).

include replacement of persona lproperty, transportation, medical, dental, and funeral expenses;

(c) Other Disaster Aid Programs[57] include crisis counseling, disaster-related un-employment assistance, legal aid and assistance with income tax, Social Security and Veteran's benefits. Other state or local help may also be available; and

(2) Public Assistance[58] for repair of infrastructure, public facilities, and debris removal. Public assistance is aid to state or local governments to pay part of the costs of rebuilding a community's damaged infrastructure. Generally, public assistance programs pay for 75 percent of the approved project costs. Public assistance may include debris removal, emergency protective measures and public services, repair of damaged public property, loans needed by communities for essential government functions, and grants for public schools.

Hazard Mitigation. Under the Stafford Act, FEMA encourages disaster victims and public entities to avoid the life and property risks of future disasters. Examples include the elevation or relocation of chronically flood-damaged homes away from flood hazard areas, retrofitting buildings to make them resistant to earthquakes or strong winds, and adoption and en-forcement of adequate codes and standards by local, state and federal government. FEMA encourages and helps fund damage mitigation measures when repairing disaster-damaged structures, funded through a portion of the monies appropriated for disaster relief.[59]

Defense Production Act

For more than fifty years the Defense Production Act (DPA) of 1950[60] has been the primary authority to ensure timely availability of civil resources for military and civil emergency preparedness. The President has delegated much of his authority under the Act to the heads of several agencies, including FEMA, under Executive Order No. 12,919.[61] Under the DPA and Executive Order No. 12,919 the Director of FEMA may use:

- priority orders to require performance under contracts to promote emergency preparedness,[62]
- make determinations for civilian needs supporting national defense,[63]
- voluntary industry agreements normally subject to antitrust restraints,[64]
- standby contractual agreements,[65]
- advisory committees,[66] and

---

57. *See id.* §§ 5177–5183.

58. *Id.* § 5172.

59. 42 U.S.C. § 5170c (2010) authorizes federal contributions for a major disaster not over 15 percent of the estimated total amount of grants to be with respect to the major disaster. If a state has in effect an approved mitigation plan at the time of the declaration of a major disaster FEMA may increase the contribution to 20 percent under 42 U.S.C. 5165(e).

60. Defense Production Act of 1950, 50 U.S.C. app. § 2061 (2012).

61. Exec. Order No. 12,919, 59 Fed. Reg. 29,525 (June 7, 1994).

62. 50 U.S.C. app. §§ 2071(a), 2152(13) (2012). *See also* Stafford Act, 42 U.S.C. § 5195a(b) (2010).

63. Exec. Order No. 12,919 § 202(c), 59 Fed. Reg. 29,525 (June 7, 1994) .

64. 50 U.S.C. app. §§ 2158(a), (c) (2012). Exec. Order No. 12,919, 59 Fed. Reg. 29,525 (June 7, 1994).

65. 50 U.S.C. app. § 2071(a) (2012; 41 U.S.C. § 253(c)(3) (2012), 48 C.F.R. § 6.302–3 (2014).

66. 50 U.S.C. app. § 2158(d) (2012).

- industry executive reserves.[67]

The President has delegated a number of responsibilities to the director of FEMA for the coordination and support of the Act under Executive Order No. 12,919. These responsibilities include the duties to:

- serve as an advisor to the National Security Council (NSC) on DPA authorities and national security resource preparedness issues,[68]
- provide central coordination of the plans and programs incident to the authorities under the order,[69]
- develop guidance and procedures under the DPA that are approved by the NSC,[70]
- attempt to resolve issues on resource priorities and allocations,[71]
- make determinations on the use of priorities and allocations for essential civilian needs supporting the national defense,[72] and
- coordinate the National Defense Executive Reserve (NDER) program activities of departments and agencies in establishing NDER units and provide guidance for recruitment, training and activation.[73]

Initially applicable only to military applications for national defense, Congress amended the Act in 1994 to include "emergency preparedness" in the definition of "national defense."[74] Broadly defined, the term "emergency preparedness" includes preparedness for hazards, and response and recovery from disasters.[75] The definition is derived from the definition of "civil defense" in the now-repealed Federal Civil Defense Act of 1950,[76] merely substituting "emergency preparedness" for "civil defense." This change becomes increasingly important as an instrument for mobilization and priority allocation of resources, services, and facilities not only for the military, but also for the civilian sector in homeland security.[77]

The Departments of Defense, Energy, and FEMA have responsibility under Executive Order No. 12,919 to determine that authority under the DPA is used only to support programs that are necessary or appropriate to promote the national defense (emergency preparedness): the Secretary of Defense with respect to military production, construction and related activities; the Secretary of Energy with respect to energy related activities; and the director of FEMA, with respect to "essential civilian needs supporting national defense, including civil defense and continuity of government and directly related activities."[78]

---

67. *Id.* §2160.
68. Exec. Order No. 12,919, §104(b)(1), Fed. Reg. 29,525 (June 7, 1994).
69. *Id.* §104(b)(2).
70. *Id.*
71. *Id.* §104(b)(3).
72. *Id.* §202(c).
73. *Id.* §601(f).
74. 42 U.S.C. §5195a(b) (2000); 50 U.S.C. app. §2152(13) (2010).
75. 42 U.S.C. §5195a(3) (2010).
76. Federal Civil Defense Act of 1950, 50 U.S.C. app. §2252(d). Pub. L. No. 103-337, 108 Stat. 2663 (1995), repealed the Federal Civil Defense Act of 1950 and restated most of its provisions as Title VI of the Stafford Act, 42 U.S.C. §§5195–5197g (2010).
77. Exec. Order No. 12,919 charges the Department of Commerce to administer the Defense Priorities and Allocations System (DPAS), 15 C.F.R. §700 (2002). The Secretary of Commerce has redelegated to the Secretaries of Defense, Agriculture, Energy, Health and Human Services, and Transportation authority for priority rating of contracts and orders for all materials, services, and facilities needed in support of programs approved under section 202 of Exec. Order No. 12,919.
78. Exec. Order No. 12,919.

Continuity of Operations (COOP) Plans

Under Executive Order No. 12,656 FEMA has the lead responsibility to coordinate the development and implementation of plans for the continuity of operations for essential federal domestic emergency functions.[79] Continuity of operations plans detail procedures and guidance to ensure the continuity of essential functions if normal operations of a government agency are threatened or disrupted. Plans to relocate to alternative sites to continue operations are flexible, tailored to the impact or severity of the threat or disruption. Thus, a terrorist attack, major fire, or natural disaster causing major damage to an agency's facilities could be cause to change the agency's base of operations. Severe weather, power outages, localized fire, or civil disorders could typically cause lower levels of disruption that would not warrant activation of an agency's COOP plan.

Under the National Security Act of 1947[80] the director of FEMA is to advise the President concerning the coordination of the strategic relocation of "government ... the continuous operation of which is essential to the Nation's security." FEMA executes that responsibility under a number of Executive Orders, Presidential Decision Directives, and Federal Preparedness Circulars.[81] Each department and agency is responsible for developing and implementing its COOP plan, with these general objectives:

- ensure the continuous performance of essential functions/operations during an emergency;
- protect essential facilities, equipment, vital records, and other assets;
- reduce or mitigate disruptions to operations;
- reduce loss of life, minimizing damage and losses; and
- achieve a timely and orderly recovery from an emergency and resumption of full service to customers.

The Federal Response to 9/11

A few months before the horrendous 2001 attacks on the World Trade Center and the Pentagon, the United States Commission on National Security/21st Century warned:

> The combination of unconventional weapons proliferation with the persistence of international terrorism will end the relative invulnerability of the U.S. homeland to catastrophic attack. A direct attack against American citizens on *American soil* is likely over the next quarter century. The risk is not only death and destruction but also a demoralization that could undermine U.S. global leadership. In the face of this threat, our nation has no coherent or integrated governmental structures.[82]

Many commentators have noted that the events of September 11, 2001, represented the worst attack on the United States since the bombing of Pearl Harbor in 1941. It is

---

79. Exec. Order No. 12,656 § 1701(2).

80. National Security Act of 1947, 50 U.S.C. § 404(b)(2012).

81. *See e.g.,* Exec. Order No. 12,148 § 2-101, 3 C.F.R. 412 (1979 Comp.); Exec. Order No. 12,472, 3 C.F.R. 193 (1984 Comp.); Exec. Order No. 12,656, 3 C.F.R. 585 (1988 Comp.); Presidential Decision Directive 67, October 21, 1998; Federal Preparedness Circular 65, Federal Executive Branch Continuity of Operations (COOP), July 26, 1999.

82. U.S. COMMISSION ON NATIONAL SECURITY/21ST CENTURY, ROAD MAP FOR NATIONAL SECURITY: IMPERATIVE FOR CHANGE, THE PHASE III REPORT OF THE U.S. COMMISSION ON NATIONAL SECURITY/ 21ST CENTURY, at viii (2001) [hereinafter PHASE III REPORT].

perhaps not surprising, therefore, that the 9/11 attacks prompted the most significant re-organization of our national security apparatus since that undertaken after World War II. Calls for a major reorganization to meet the changing nature of the threat to the American homeland were prevalent prior to the attacks of September 11 but no action had been taken to implement any of the proposals.

It was apparent long before September 11, 2001, that the nature of the terrorism threat had changed from the mid-1970s when it first began to receive international attention. The terrorists of the 70s and early 80s, such as the Palestine Liberation Organization (PLO) and the Irish Republican Army (IRA), were largely political in nature, seeking discrete political objectives. They used terrorism as a way of focusing attention on their cause and forcing governments to negotiate with them. Hostage-taking, traditional airline hijacking, and bomb threats were characteristic tactics and would be accompanied by claims of responsibility and a list of demands. The terrorists hoped that the public would develop some sympathy for the justness of their cause and intolerance for the violence, both of which would result in pressure on the government to bring an end to the terrorism by addressing the terrorists' grievances. Thus, terrorists tended to calibrate the level of violence so that it was sufficient to motivate governments and their constituents, but not so great as to totally alienate the public or make it politically untenable to negotiate with the perpetrators. As terrorism expert Brian Jenkins said in 1974, "[t]errorists want a lot of people watching, not a lot of people dead."[83] This need to calibrate the level of violence contributed to the hierarchical structure that characterized these earlier terrorist groups.[84]

In contrast, the terrorists of greatest concern today are not interested in negotiations and seek to maximize the level of violence. Former Director of Central Intelligence R. James Woolsey noted in 1994 that "[t]oday's terrorists don't want a seat at the table, they want to destroy the table and everyone seated at it."[85] This change in the nature of the threat may have been presaged by the October 1983 attack on the Marine Barracks in Beirut, Lebanon, which killed 241 U.S. service members. The terrorists in that attack had a specific political objective: getting the United States out of Lebanon. Their willingness to inflict significant casualties to achieve that objective appeared to pay off, as the United States withdrew troops from Lebanon shortly thereafter. Some experts believe this is a lesson the terrorists of today took to heart. In December 1988, without warning, a U.S. airliner, Pan Am flight 103, blew up over Lockerbie, Scotland, killing all 270 aboard. There was no claim of responsibility and no list of demands.

In February 1993, this new level of violence reached the American homeland with the bombing of the World Trade Center. This attack killed six people and wounded close to 1,000, but the goal of the terrorists was to topple one of the massive towers into the other. Later that summer, authorities thwarted a plan to bomb other landmarks in New York City, including the Lincoln and Holland Tunnels. This effort at mass casualties was also

---

83. COMMITTEE ON FOREIGN RELATIONS, COUNTERING THE CHANGING THREAT OF INTERNATIONAL TERRORISM: REPORT OF THE NATIONAL COMMISSION ON TERRORISM 2 (2001) [hereinafter NCT REPORT].

84. State sponsorship of terrorists was also a more evident feature of terrorism before the mid-90s. A number of nations used clandestine support for terrorists as an instrument of national security and foreign policy, particularly in the Middle East and the Soviet Bloc. As international attention increasingly focused on terrorism, resulting in 12 United Nations conventions targeting terrorist activity and growing international cooperation, states considering sponsoring terrorists had to consider greater risks of detection and international isolation. Progress on peace talks in the Middle East and the fall of the Soviet Union and movement of Eastern Europe into the Western community of nations also altered the appeal of state sponsorship of terrorism.

85. NCT REPORT, *supra* note 82, at 2.

evident in the discovery in 1995 of a plot by terrorist Ramsi Yousef to bring down eleven U.S. airliners on international flights over the Pacific Ocean. In the following years, attacks on a military barracks in Saudi Arabia in 1996 and on two U.S. Embassies in Africa in 1998 caused 6,059 casualties.[86]

The escalating level of violence, combined with the sarin attack in the Tokyo subway in 1995, also lent greater credence to concerns that terrorists might use weapons of mass destruction. Previously it was thought that the level of destruction and the stigma attached to using chemical, biological, nuclear, or radiological weapons made them unattractive to the terrorist groups of the 70s and 80s. Intelligence reports indicate, however, that the shift in terrorists' motivations and methods has led them to seek the capability to use weapons of mass destruction.[87] Any lingering doubts about the seriousness of the terrorist threat against targets within the United States vanished the morning of September 11, 2001.

In the eighteen months prior to the 9/11 attacks, three congressionally mandated commissions filed reports in which they reviewed various aspects of the terrorism threat and made recommendations for how the U.S. government should organize to combat that threat. All three recommended strengthening the coordination of counterterrorism efforts under a single focal point within the executive branch. They differed, however, on where that focal point should be located, what authorities it should have — particularly with regards to the budget — and whether it should include a Senate-confirmed position. The first commission was the National Commission on Terrorism,[88] the second was the Advisory Panel to Assess Domestic Response Capabilities for Terrorism Involving Weapons of Mass Destruction,[89] and the third was the U.S. Commission on National Security/21st Century.[90] Out of the three commissions the U.S. Commission on National Security/21st Century suggested the most dramatic reorganization. The report called for the creation of an independent National Homeland Security Agency (NHSA) with responsibility for planning, coordinating, and integrating various U.S. government activities involved in homeland security. This new agency would combine the Federal Emergency Management Agency with the three organizations currently responsible for border security — the Coast Guard, the Customs Service, and the Border Patrol. The NHSA would also be responsible for overseeing the protection of the nation's critical infrastructure, including information

---

86. *See id.* at 1–2.

87. *See* George J. Tenet, Testimony before the Senate Select Comm. on Intelligence, *Worldwide Threat — Converging Dangers in a Post 9/11 World* (Feb. 6, 2002).

88. COMMITTEE ON FOREIGN RELATIONS, COUNTERING THE CHANGING THREAT OF INTERNATIONAL TERRORISM: REPORT OF THE NATIONAL COMMISSION ON TERRORISM 2 (2001) [hereinafter NCT REPORT]. This commission noted that the position that was responsible for ensuring that the counterterrorism programs of the various departments and agencies met the President's overall counterterrorism objectives did not have sufficient authority in the budget process. Thus the commission suggested that the Director of the Office of Management and Budget must obtain the concurrence of the National Coordinator for Security, Infrastructure, and Counterterrorism. NCT REPORT at 34.

89. SECOND ANNUAL REPORT OF THE ADVISORY PANEL TO ASSESS DOMESTIC RESPONSE CAPABILITIES FOR TERRORISM INVOLVING WEAPONS OF MASS DESTRUCTION (2000) [hereinafter GILMORE COMMISSION 2ND]. The main recommendation from this commission was to encourage the President to establish a National Office for Combating Terrorism in the Executive Office of the President. The office would be responsible for the full range of deterring, preventing, preparing for, and responding to international as well as domestic terrorism. GILMORE COMMISSION 2ND at v.

90. U.S. COMMISSION ON NATIONAL SECURITY/21ST CENTURY, ROAD MAP FOR NATIONAL SECURITY: IMPERATIVE FOR CHANGE, THE PHASE III REPORT OF THE U.S. COMMISSION ON NATIONAL SECURITY/21ST CENTURY (2001) [hereinafter PHASE III REPORT].

technology. The NHSA director would have cabinet status and would be a statutory advisor to the National Security Council.[91]

After the terrorist attacks of September 11, 2001, President Bush announced a massive federal recovery effort for New York City and began the repair of the Pentagon. Contemporaneous with the recovery effort, Congress and the President began to revisit "homeland security." For the first time since the Cold War the emphasis on emergency preparedness measures shifted from focusing on the response to natural disasters to civil emergency preparedness and the now obvious threat of terrorism.

FEMA's Federal Response to 9/11

Immediately after the September 11, 2001, attacks on the World Trade Center (WTC) and the Pentagon, FEMA led and coordinated the federal response and recovery effort. FEMA's Urban Search and Rescue (US&R) Teams from around the country helped to form the largest search and rescue operation in United States history. In the aftermath of the attacks FEMA deployed twenty of its twenty-eight national US&R Teams to the WTC and five teams to the Pentagon. By October 7, 2001, FEMA had deployed nearly 1,300 US&R members and eighty search and rescue dogs to New York City.[92]

Public Assistance

Much of New York City's transportation system was disrupted because of the WTC attacks. FEMA coordinated state, local and federal resources and established emergency transportation systems including among others ferry service, bus service, train service, and emergency road repairs.[93] The search of the WTC debris and the removal of the debris was a further monumental effort. FEMA coordinated the hiring of a huge cadre of debris removal contractors to haul WTC debris. FEMA gave the Army Corps of Engineers the task of managing WTC debris inspection at the Staten Island (Fresh Kills) Landfill both as a crime scene and as an effort to recover victim remains and personal effects.[94]

At least 2,726 people perished in the WTC attacks; of these 343 were members of the New York Fire Department, twenty-three were members of the New York Police Department, three were state police, and thirty-six were members of the Port Authority. The enormity of the WTC recovery effort greatly taxed local fire and police authorities as the recovery operation continued on a twenty-four-hours-a-day, seven-days-a-week basis. FEMA reimbursed New York for death benefits,[95] overtime,[96] backfill,[97] funeral costs,[98] destroyed vehicles,[99] destroyed communications equipment,[100] and cleaning and

---

91. Phase III Report, *supra* note 90, at 15.

92. FEMA, A Nation Remembers, A Nation Recovers: Responding to September 11, 2001, One Year Later (2002).

93. 42 U.S.C. §5186 (2010); 44 C.F.R. §206.224 (2002); FEMA Disaster Assistance Summary, FEMA-1391-DR-NY, Dec. 9, 2002.

94. 42 U.S.C. §5186 (2010); 44 C.F.R. §224 (2002); FEMA, *supra* note 92, at 17.

95. 42 U.S.C. §5170b(a)(3) (2010); 44 C.F.R. §206.225 (2002); OMB Circular A-87.

96. *Id.*

97. *Id.*

98. *Id.*

99. 42 U.S.C. §5172(a) (2010); 44 C.F.R. §206.226 (2002).

100. *Id.*

decontaminating equipment and facilities.[101] In a strongly symbolic act as well, FEMA delivered a grant to renovate and preserve the Liberty Street Firehouse that was severely damaged in the attacks and that was used as a staging area for much of the recovery.[102]

New York's long-term recovery presented unique challenges. Among other grants for public assistance, FEMA provided grants to help restore the functionality of the New York transportation system including rebuilding subway stations and roads in a joint effort with the Federal Transit Administration.[103] FEMA joined with the Environmental Protection Agency to clean buildings and to monitor air quality in Lower Manhattan. FEMA delivered grants to the New York City Department of Education to pay for instructional make-up time for school days lost because of the attacks.[104] Because the attacks occurred on an election day in New York, FEMA made a grant to pay for the costs of the aborted election.[105]

Individual Assistance

FEMA greatly expanded the use of Stafford Act's individual assistance programs as well in the wake of the September 11, 2001, attacks. FEMA reimbursed for crisis counseling for aggrieved persons in New York, Connecticut, Massachusetts, New Jersey, and Pennsylvania.[106] FEMA processed more than 6,500 claims for Disaster Unemployment Assistance,[107] more than 200,000 Individual and Family Grant applications,[108] and nearly 10,000 Disaster Housing cases.[109] In the largest use of the program to date, FEMA processed more than 16,500 Mortgage and Rental Assistance applications. FEMA's broad Stafford Act authorities were stretched by the WTC attacks but FEMA obligated nearly nine billion dollars to New York's recovery.

The Strategic Response to 9/11

After the terrorist attacks of September 11, 2001, President Bush sought to develop a national strategy to secure the American homeland from further terrorist attacks. On October 8, 2001, President Bush signed Executive Order No. 13,228, establishing the Office of Homeland Security (OHS) within the Executive Office of the President. The President's Executive Order directed the OHS "to coordinate the executive branch's efforts to detect, prepare for, prevent, protect against, respond to, and recover from terrorist attacks within the United States."[110] The order also created a Homeland Security Council, similar to the National Security Council, responsible for "advising and assisting the President with respect to all aspects of homeland security."[111] The members of the council were to include the President, the Vice President, the Secretary of the Treasury, the Secretary of Defense, the Attorney General, the Secretary of Health and Human Services, the Secretary of Transportation, the Director of the Federal Emergency Management Agency, the Director of the Federal Bureau of Investigation, the Director of Central In-

---

101. 42 U.S.C. §§5170(a)(3), 5173 (2010); 44 C.F.R. §§206.225, 206.224 (2002).
102. 42 U.S.C. §5173 (2010); 44 C.F.R. §206.224 (2002); FEMA, *supra* note 92, at 18.
103. FEMA, *supra* note 92, at 30.
104. *Id.* at 33.
105. *Id.*
106. *Id.* at 28.
107. *Id.* at 32.
108. *Id.*
109. *Id.*
110. 66 Fed. Reg. 51,812.
111. *Id.*

telligence, the Assistant to the President for Homeland Security, and "such other officers of the executive branch as the President may from time to time designate."[112] This council was to serve as the mechanism for ensuring coordination of homeland security-related activities of executive departments and agencies and effective development and implementation of homeland security policies.

The next day, October 9, 2001, the White House announced two additional positions: the President's Special Advisor for Cyber Security and the National Director and Deputy National Security Advisor for Combating Terrorism.[113] With regard to the budget, the new Assistant to the President for Homeland Security (AHS) had largely the same authority held by the earlier counterterrorism coordinator on the NSC staff. However, the executive order included a requirement that, prior to the OMB director's forwarding of the proposed annual budget submission to the President for transmittal to the Congress, the AHS "shall certify to the director the funding levels that the Assistant to the President for Homeland Security believes are necessary and appropriate for the homeland security-related activities of the executive branch."[114] It did not make clear, however, what the effect would be of failing to certify an agency's funding levels.

On the anniversary of D-Day, June 6, 2002, the President announced his intention to create a new Department of Homeland Security, in what he described as "the most extensive reorganization of the federal government since the 1940s."[115] This new department would combine FEMA and the key border control agencies, along with the infrastructure protection offices in FBI (NIPC) and Commerce (CIAO). The department would contain four divisions: Border and Transportation Security; Emergency Preparedness and Response; Chemical, Biological, Radiological and Nuclear Countermeasures; and Information Analysis and Infrastructure Protection. Under the President's proposal, there would also continue to be a special advisor for homeland security within the office of the President.

On July 16, 2002, the President delivered the National Strategy for Homeland Security (the "National Strategy") to the American people. The National Strategy identified three strategic objectives: (1) prevent terrorist attacks within the United States, (2) reduce America's vulnerability to terrorism, and (3) minimize the damage from potential attacks and natural disasters.[116] The National Strategy identified various mission areas including, among others, "Defending against Catastrophic Threats" and "Emergency Preparedness and Response" that describe steps to be taken to accomplish the three strategic objectives.

To fulfill the mission area of "Defending against Catastrophic Threats" the National Strategy identified six initiatives:

1. prevent terrorist use of nuclear weapons through better sensors and procedures;
2. detect chemical and biological materials and attacks;
3. improve chemical sensors and decontamination techniques;
4. develop broad spectrum vaccines, antimicrobials, and antidotes;
5. harness scientific knowledge and tools to counter terrorism, and;
6. implement the Select Agent Program.

---

112. *Id.*

113. *See* <http://www.whitehouse.gov/news/releases/2001/10/20011009-4.html>.

114. 66 Fed. Reg. 51,812.

115. President George W. Bush, speech (June 6, 2002) <http://www.whitehouse.gov/news/releases/2002/06/20020606-8.html>.

116. National Strategy for Homeland Security (July 16, 2002), <http://www.gpo.gov/fdsys/pkg/PPP-2002-book2/pdf/PPP-2002-book2-doc-pg1249.pdf >.

To fulfill the mission area of "Emergency Preparedness and Response" the National Strategy identified twelve initiatives:

1. integrate separate federal response plans into a single all-discipline incident management plan;
2. create a national incident management system;
3. improve tactical counterterrorist capabilities;
4. enable seamless communication among all responders;
5. prepare health care providers for catastrophic terrorism;
6. augment America's pharmaceutical and vaccine stockpiles;
7. prepare for chemical, biological, radiological, and nuclear decontamination;
8. plan for military support to civil authorities;
9. build the Citizen Corps;
10. implement the First Responder Initiative of the Fiscal Year 2003 Budget;
11. build a national training and evaluation system; and
12. enhance the victim support system.

In order to implement the initiatives, the National Strategy proposed the creation of a single federal government agency to unite federal resources—the Department of Homeland Security (DHS).[117]

Congress Acts on the President's Proposal

On November 22, 2002, Congress gave final approval to legislation establishing the Department of Homeland Security (DHS). [118] The final bill combined the efforts of the three Commissions, several Congressional proposals, and President Bush's proposal. More than twenty-two agencies from across the federal bureaucracy contributed assets and expertise to establish DHS. As of 2014, DHS has over 240,000 employees and has requested an approximate budget authority of over thirty-eight billion dollars in fiscal year 2015.[119] One of the five established missions of DHS is to "strengthen national preparedness and resilience."[120]

The final bill created four divisions within the Department: Border and Transportation Security; Emergency Preparedness and Response; Chemical, Biological, Radiological and Nuclear Countermeasures, and Information Analysis and Infrastructure Protection. Existing agencies placed under the department's authority included Immigration and Naturalization Service; U.S. Coast Guard; Customs Service; Border Patrol; Federal Emergency Management Agency; Secret Service; Transportation Security Administration; and the border inspection part of Animal and Plant Health Inspection Service. Four distinct offices were transferred to FEMA and contribute to national preparedness and disaster response:[121] the Office of Domestic Preparedness of the Department of Justice; the National Domestic Preparedness office of the FBI; the Domestic Emergency Support Team of the Department of Justice; and the Nuclear Incident Response Team of the Department of Energy.

---

117. *Id.*

118. Homeland Security Act of 2002, Pub. L. No. 107-296, 116 Stat. 2135 (2002).

119. U.S. Department of Homeland Security Press Office, Fiscal Year 2015 Budget Request <http://www.dhs.gov/publication/fy-2015-budget-brief>.

120. Quadrennial Homeland Security Review (QHSR) 2014 (June 18, 2014). <http://www.dhs.gov/publication/2014-quadrennial-homeland-security-review-qhsr>.

121. A full list of components can be found on the DHS webpage. <http://www.dhs.gov/who-joined-dhs>.

A key issue of contention during consideration of this bill was the role of the Department in the analysis of intelligence related to terrorism and homeland security.[122] The legislation establishing the Department of Homeland Security made the Information Analysis and Infrastructure Protection Division (IAIP/DHS) responsible for analyzing all intelligence on terrorist threats to the homeland. After the creation of the Department, however, the President established the Terrorist Threat Integration Center (TTIC), a new entity under the Director of Central Intelligence that was to bring together in one location the analysts from CIA, FBI, NSA, and other intelligence agencies that were looking at the terrorist threat.[123] The objective was to "fuse" information so that all of the analysts had access to information from all of the agencies in order to provide true "all-source" analysis of terrorist threats to the homeland. Over time, the operations officers (*e.g.* CIA case officers and FBI agents) from the various agencies would also move to the same location so that they could continue to get real-time analytical support for operations, although the operators would not be part of the TTIC. IAIP/DHS has representatives in TTIC. In addition, IAIP has a unique role in working with state and local officials, as well as the private sector, to combine threat analysis with vulnerability assessments in order to assess the risk to the nation's critical infrastructure and other key aspects of the homeland. This risk assessment can then be used to develop a strategy for risk management.

The reorganization and consolidation effected by the Act take the "all hazards" approach of the federal government's emergency preparedness and response role a step farther. Now, under one federal agency, the Act combines FEMA's traditional role as the federal agency with the principal responsibility to prepare and respond to natural and manmade disasters with other related federal components. The notion of the "all hazards" emergency preparedness and response approach continues, as DHS is structurally organized for components to defend against both catastrophic terrorist threats as well as the traditional hazards associated with emergency preparedness.

The Department Reorganizes

As with most new endeavors, the first attempt is never perfect. Congress, knowing that some changes would need to be made to the Department, gave DHS the ability to reorganize.[124] Since the passage of the Homeland Security Act of 2002, the Department has reorganized thirteen times. This explains why the Department does not mirror the configuration created by Congress in the 2002 Act. After the last reorganization in 2007, Congress, in each Appropriation Bill to DHS, prohibits the Department from using any appropriated funds to reorganize.[125] Although each of the thirteen "872 Letters" presented to Congress give historical insight into the Department, for the purposes of this chapter, the last two letters which created the current framework of the Department need only be discussed.

Following Hurricane Katrina, Congress passed the Post-Katrina Emergency management Reform Act (PKEMRA) of 2006, Pub. L. No. 109-295, which mandated reorganization of DHS. The Department used the mandate as an opportunity to look at the Department

---

122. Homeland Security Act of 2002, Pub. L. No. 107-296, 116 Stat. 2135, *as amended* (2002).

123. *See* White House Fact Sheet <http://www.whitehouse.gov/news/releases/2003/01/20030128-12.html>.

124. 6 U.S.C. §452

125. *See, e.g.*, Consolidated Appropriations Act, 2008, H.R. 2764, §546 (stating "None of the funds in this Act shall be available to carry out section 872 of Public Law 107-296).

as a whole. Through this analysis DHS, as it stands today, was created.[126] The Department has seven Components[127] and several offices within headquarters.[128] Perhaps the largest change in the 2007 reorganization, besides the strengethening FEMA's role within DHS, was the dismantling of IAIP/DHS into the Office of Intelligence and Analysis (I&A) and the National Protection and Programs Directorate (NPPD). I&A focuses on equipping the operators and decision-makers with timely intelligence information and analysis. It is the heart of the DHS Intelligence Community. NPPD consists of five offices, which collectively, focus on protecting and ensuring the resilience of America's physical and cyber infrastructure.[129]

Questions for Discussion

1. While there was a consensus that homeland security/counterterrorism efforts of the federal government needed to be more centralized, there were different views regarding the structure and authorities of any such focal point. Discuss the advantages and disadvantages of the various proposals, particularly with regard to the issues of whether to create a new department, whether to require Senate confirmation of its leaders, and how to strengthen control over the budget. How are the last two issues related?

2. All of the reports cited agreed that any focal point located within the National Security Council or elsewhere in the Executive Office of the President should not have operational authority. What concerns might underlie that consensus?

3. What considerations may have led to the decision not to place the focal point within the National Security Council structure?

4. The first page of the report of the National Commission on Terrorism contained the following quote from Professor Thomas C. Schelling's foreword to a 1962 book about Pearl Harbor:

> Surprise, when it happens to a government, is likely to be a complicated, diffuse, bureaucratic thing. It includes neglect of responsibility but also responsibility so poorly defined or so ambiguously delegated that action gets lost. It includes gaps in intelligence, but also intelligence that, like a string of pearls too precious to wear, is too sensitive to give to those who need it. It includes the alarm that fails to work, but also the alarm that has gone off so often it has been disconnected. It includes the unalert watchman, but also the one who knows he'll be chewed out by his superior if he gets higher authority out of bed. It includes the contingencies that occur to no one, but also those that everyone assumes somebody else is taking care of. It includes straightforward procrastination, but also decisions protracted by internal disagreement. It includes, in addition, the inability of in-dividual human beings to rise to the occasion until they are sure it *is* the occa-sion — which is usually too late. (Unlike movies, real life provides no musical

---

126. The Department's current organization chart is located at http://www.dhs.gov/xlibrary/assets/dhs-orgchart.pdf.

127. U.S. Customs and Border Protection, U.S. Citizenship and Immigration Services, U.S. Coast Guard, Federal Emergency Management Agency, U.S. Immigration and Customs Enfrocment, U.S. Secret Service, and Transportation and Security Administration.

128. These offices include Science and Techonolgy, National Protection and Programs Directorate, Intelligence and Analysis, the Chief Privacy Officer, and Civil Rights and Civil Liberties.

129. NPPD's five offices are the Office of Cybersecurity and Communication, Office of Infrastructure Protection, Federal Protection Service, Office of Biometric Identity Management (formally US-VISIT), and Office of Cyber and Infrastructure Analysis.

background to tip us off to the climax.) Finally, as at Pearl Harbor, surprise may include some measure of genuine novelty introduced by the enemy, and possibly some sheer bad luck.

The results, at Pearl Harbor, were sudden, concentrated, and dramatic. The failure, however, was cumulative, widespread, and rather drearily familiar. This is why surprise, when it happens to a government, cannot be described just in terms of startled people. Whether at Pearl Harbor or at the Berlin Wall, surprise is everything involved in a government's (or in an alliance's) failure to anticipate effectively.[130]

Does this description apply to the surprise of September 11? To what extent did the re-organization prompted by Pearl Harbor fail to avoid the surprise of 9/11 and why? In what ways did the proposals for reorganization address or fail to address these problems?

5. Do you agree with the current structure of the Department? How might you organize it?

Key Legal Issues

Along with recommendations for a new overarching organizational structure to combat terrorism, there have been calls over the years to re-examine the legal framework for disaster response and preventing and countering terrorism. The National Commission on Terrorism, for example, recommended a review to understand how existing legal authorities apply in responding to the threat of terrorism, particularly catastrophic terrorism,[131] and to identify and remedy gaps in existing authority.[132] This recommendation was echoed in other reports[133] and prompted efforts by non-governmental entities to examine the legal issues that might come into play in response to an imminent threat or attack involving catastrophic terrorism.[134]

No significant action was taken by the federal government to address these legal authorities until after the attacks of September 11, 2001. Legislation introduced within days of those attacks reflected an initial attempt at remedying gaps in existing legal

---

130. Thomas C. Schelling, foreword to Roberta Wohlstetter, Pearl Harbor: Warning and Decision, as quoted in NCT Report, *supra* note 83.

131. "Catastrophic terrorism" as used in this chapter means terrorism that causes mass destruction or mass disruption. It could involve the use of chemical, biological, nuclear, or radiological weapons but could also result from the use of conventional weapons or other means that result in mass destruction or mass disruption through a single attack or a series of smaller attacks. The term is used to refer to attacks that place significant stress on traditional response capabilities.

132. NCT Report, *supra* note 83, at 38.

133. Gilmore Commission 2nd, *supra* note 89, at 20–21.

134. Immediately after the National Commission on Terrorism filed its report, a conference was held on June 22–23, 2000, sponsored by the American Bar Association's Standing Committee on Law and National Security and the McCormick Tribune Foundation, to identify legal issues regarding the role of the military, law enforcement, intelligence, and public health. It produced a conference report. Catastrophic Terrorism: Imminent Threat, Uncertain Response (2001) [hereinafter Catastrophic Terrorism Report]. In addition, the Memorial Institute for the Prevention of Terrorism, in Oklahoma City, Oklahoma, funded a legal review that resulted in a report on January 7, 2002. Barry Kellman, Legal Issues of Catastrophic Terrorism, Consequence Management (2002) [hereinafter "Kellman"].

authority. It resulted in the USA PATRIOT Act,[135] which contains provisions broadening law enforcement, intelligence, and money laundering authorities, among others. The legal review did not stop there; however, as both Congress and the Administration continue to identify changes in the legal environment to meet the changed threat and the need to more effectively defend the homeland.

The sections below will summarize the major legal provisions of the USA PATRIOT Act,[136] as well as other significant changes to federal disaster response that have taken place in more recent years. The following sections also include a brief overview of two key areas not fully covered in other chapters, public health authorities and the role of the military.

The USA PATRIOT Act

On October 26, 2001, the President signed a sweeping antiterrorism bill entitled the Uniting and Strengthening America by Providing Appropriate Tools Required to Intercept and Obstruct Terrorism (USA PATRIOT) Act of 2001.[137] Based on legislation sent to the Congress by the Department of Justice a week after the attacks of September 11, the law includes provisions to expand authorities for criminal investigations and intelligence collection, lower the barriers between these two kinds of activities, disrupt terrorist funding, make it easier to exclude or detain aliens deemed to threaten national security, and authorize funding to improve the capabilities of key federal agencies.

This legislation was passed with unusual speed—though not as quickly as many had predicted—and under unusual circumstances. There were no committee votes so there are no committee reports to provide insight as to legislative intent. It was negotiated and voted on in the aftermath of the most devastating terrorist attack this country has ever suffered, amidst warnings of reprisals for U.S. military action, and a biological attack that forced the offices of the congressional negotiators to close down. In this high-pressure environment, the drafters worked to protect the lives of the people of this nation and preserve their civil liberties. How well the Act accomplishes these objectives depends not only on the compromises reached by the negotiators but also on the way the law is implemented and overseen.

Enhanced Criminal Investigative Authorities

The new law amended the criminal wiretap provisions to provide new criminal statute predicates that would support an application for a wiretap order, permit seizure of voice mail pursuant to a search warrant, and allow victims of computer trespassing (*i.e.* hacking) to invite law enforcement to monitor attacks on their computer networks without needing a court order. The law also allows pen registers and "trap and trace" devices[138] (which have traditionally been used on phones to detect numbers dialed by, and those dialing in to, a target phone) to be used on computer transmissions to obtain "dialing, routing, ad-

---

135. Uniting and Strengthening America by Providing Appropriate Tools Required to Intercept and Obstruct Terrorism (USA PATRIOT) Act of 2001, Pub. L. No. 107-56, 115 Stat. 272 (2001).

136. This summary is based primarily upon summaries and analysis undertaken for the American Bar Association's Standing Committee on Law and National Security by Dale Bosley, Gordon Lederman, Joshua Levy, Steven Kroll, Michael Smith, and Suzanne Spaulding. *See* ABA Nat'l Security L. Rep., Sept. 2001.

137. 115 Stat. 272.

138. These devices are discussed in chapter 26 of this volume.

dressing, and signaling information." Investigators using these devices are prohibited from including the *content* (which is not defined in the law) of those communications. These changes are designed to subject electronic communications to the same rules as telephone communications.

Similar amendments to the Electronic Communications Privacy Act[139] broaden the scope of subpoenas for records of electronic communications to cover Internet sessions (but not the content of those sessions), permit a provider of electronic communications to divulge communications or records to law enforcement to protect life and limb, and permit nationwide service of warrants for electronic surveillance.

With respect to physical searches, an amendment to the Federal Rules of Civil Procedure (FRCP) provides so-called "sneak and peek" authority. An investigator seeking a warrant under this provision must still meet the underlying probable-cause requirement but can delay notifying the target that the warrant has been executed when disclosure may have an adverse result on the investigation. Under such a warrant, investigators can only search; they cannot seize anything.[140]

Enhanced Intelligence Surveillance Authorities Inside the United States

The Act also expanded authorities under the Foreign Intelligence Surveillance Act[141] (FISA) to enable a single application to be applied against targets who attempt to thwart surveillance, for example, by switching phones, without having to go back to the Foreign Surveillance Court (FSC). It lengthens, in certain cases, the duration of initial surveillances and renewals. Furthermore, as in the criminal wiretap provisions, the Act broadens the use of pen registers and trap and trace devices to cover computer transmissions "to protect against international terrorism or clandestine intelligence activities."[142]

A change was also made to the FISA provision that permits access to records and other items. Section 215 of the PATRIOT Act amended FISA to give the FBI the authority to seek an order from a FISA judge or magistrate requiring anyone served with such an order to turn over "any tangible things (including books, records papers, documents, and other items)." Prior to this amendment, this authority was limited to business records held by common carriers, hotels, storage facilities, or car rental companies. The provision as amended is not limited to businesses or business records but would apparently apply to tangible things held by any individual or entity. Its potential application to libraries and bookstores prompted concern about protection of civil liberties.

However, if the information sought involves a U.S. person, the amended provision can only be used if its purpose is to protect against international terrorism or clandestine intelligence activities (espionage) and only if it is not conducted *solely* upon the basis of activities protected by the First Amendment to the Constitution.

Lowering the Barriers between Intelligence and Law Enforcement

The new law permits surveillance under FISA when foreign intelligence is "a significant purpose" rather than "the purpose."[143] This seemingly minor change in the statutory language could significantly lower the wall between criminal investigations and intelligence

---

139. Electronic Communications Privacy Act, 18 U.S.C. §§ 2701–11 (2000).
140. FRCP 41(f)(3)
141. Foreign Intelligence Surveillance Act, 50 U.S.C. §§ 1801–63 (2000).
142. 115 Stat. at 279.
143. 115 Stat. at 291.

collection. Previously, criminal investigators were restricted from providing any guidance or direction to the intelligence collectors within FBI for fear that such collaboration might shift the primary purpose of the FISA collection from intelligence to law enforcement and thereby violate the statute.

After the law was adopted, the Foreign Intelligence Court of Review concluded that there was never any constitutional requirement for distinguishing between a law enforcement and foreign intelligence purpose where the two overlap, as they do with regard to international terrorism. The court tore down the wall that had been erected over a period of twenty-five years between these two communities.[144]

One immediate impact of this is to allow criminal investigators to receive information collected pursuant to FISA. It also allows those investigators to assist in identifying targets.

Provisions in the Act that permit and promote the sharing of foreign intelligence collected by law enforcement officials with the intelligence community further lower the barriers between law enforcement and intelligence collection. This can enhance the ability of the government to prevent future terrorist attacks. However, the potential implications will need to be fully understood and appropriate safeguards put in place to protect civil liberties and avoid undermining public support for the robust foreign intelligence authorities needed overseas.

Money Laundering

Title III of the bill is designed to impede the financing of terrorist activities. It allows the government to confiscate the assets of foreign terrorist organizations, the terrorists themselves, and those who aid them. It permits the government to restrain those assets after indictment but before any final adjudication to ensure those assets are available to satisfy a judgment of forfeiture. Financial institutions are required to have anti-money laundering programs. In addition, the Act expands the scope of predicate money laundering offenses to include providing material support for terrorist organizations.

Immigration Provisions

With respect to border security, the Act expands the grounds for deeming an alien inadmissible or deportable from the United States for terrorist activity, provides for the mandatory detention of aliens whom the Attorney General certifies pose a risk to the national security, and facilitates information sharing within the United States and with foreign governments. The Attorney General is given the authority to detain aliens he certifies are threats to national security, as long as removal proceedings or criminal charges are filed within seven days. In cases where removal is determined appropriate but is not possible, detention may continue upon a review by the Attorney General every six months. The bill also would expand the definition of terrorists for purpose of inadmissibility or removal to include public endorsement of terrorist activity or provision of material support to terrorist organizations.

Natural and Manmade Disaster Response Developments

The Post-Katrina Emergency Management Reform Act of 2006. In 2005, Hurricane Katrina caused catastrophic damage and over 1,800 fatalities in Lousiana and Mississippi.

---

144. *In re* Sealed Case No. 02-001, 310 F.3d 717 (U.S. Foreign Intell. Surveil, Ct. Rev. 2002) <http://www.epic.org/privacy/terrorism/fisa/FISCR_opinion.pdf>.

The Post-Katrina Emergency Management Reform Act of 2006 (PKEMRA) amended the Homeland Security Act of 2002 to make extensive revisions to emergency response provisions while keeping the Federal Emergency Management Agency (FEMA) within the Department of Homeland Security (DHS).[145] PKEMRA set forth provisions amending FEMA's mission, which include:

- leading the nation's efforts to prepare for, respond to, recover from, and mitigate the risks of, any natural and manmade disaster, including catastrophic incidents;
- implementing a risk-based, "all hazards" plus strategy for preparedness; and
- promoting and planning for the protection, security, resiliency, and post-disaster restoration of critical infrastructure and key resources, including cyber and communications assets.[146]

PKEMRA enhanced FEMA's responsibilities and its authority within DHS and transferred many functions of DHS's former Preparedness Directorate to FEMA. FEMA leads and supports the Nation in comprehensive emergency management systems of preparedness, protection, response, recovery, and mitigation.[147]

The Deepwater Horizon Oil Spill. In 2010, forty-five miles off the coast of Louisiana, an explosion and blowout caused the Nation's first declared Spill of National Significance (SONS).[148] From a mile below the surface, oil continuously spewed into the ocean for nearly three months. The United States Coast Guard, which is a DHS component, helped with the emergency response to the Deepwater Horizon oil spill in the Gulf of Mexico.

Following all major oils spills Coast Guard internal regulations call for an Incident Specific Preparedness Review (ISPR) to conduct a thorough investigation and examination of the Coast Guard preparedness and response process. The Deepwater Horizon ISPR conducted evaluations of the process and procedures implemented by the Coast Guard and made recommendations to enhance responses in the future.[149] As a result of the Deepwater Horizon ISPR, the Commandant of the Coast Guard directed that:

- Captains of the Port review Oil Spill Response Plans for offshore (drilling) facilities;
- Area Committees be required to include Worst Case Discharge scenarios for offshore facilities in their respective Area Contingency Plans;
- the National Response Team review large volume and novel dispersant use, and response data management procedures and tools; and
- establish a Coast Guard, FEMA and EPA workgroup to develop recommendations and harmonize the National Contingency Plan and National Response Framework.[150]

The ISPR is one critical method used to evaluate past responses in conjunction with the implementation, integration and effectiveness of national, regional and local oil spill response plans.[151] It takes a case study approach to past disaster responses to allow for enhanced planning and mitigation of future events.

---

145. Department of Homeland Security Appropriations Act, 2007, Title VI, Pub. L. No. 109-295.
146. *Id.*
147. The Federal Emergency Management Agency Publication 1 (November 2010) <http://www.fema.gov/pdf/about/pub1.pdf>.
148. Final Action Memorandum—Incident Specific Preparedness Review (ISPR) Deepwater Horizon Oil Spill (March 18, 2011). <https://www.uscg.mil/foia/docs/DWH/BPDWH.pdf >.
149. *Id.*
150. *Id.*
151. *Id.*

The Sandy Recovery Improvement Act of 2013. In 2012, Hurricane Sandy struck the East Coast of the United States causing over 200 fatalities and billions of dollars in damage. The Sandy Recovery Improvement Act of 2013 (SRIA) was signed into law on January 29, 2013,[152] by President Barack Obama. In many ways, the passage of SRIA represents the most significant legislative change to the Federal Emergency Management Agency's (FEMA) substantive authorities since the enactment of the Robert T. Stafford Disaster Relief and Emergency Assistance Act.[153] The law authorizes several significant changes to the way FEMA may deliver federal disaster assistance to survivors. As of June 2014, 14 of the 17 provisions outlined in this legislation have been completed, implemented as pilot programs, or made otherwise available for immediate use.[154] SRIA's enactment initiated changes to:

- Public Assistance Permanent Work Alternative Procedures,
- Debris Removal Program Alternative Procedures,
- Three-year Nationwide Dispute Resolution Pilot (Arbitration) and Related Changes to Appeals Process,
- Coordination between Federal Transit Administration and FEMA on Public Transportation Infrastructure,
- Analysis of Public Assistance Small Project Threshold ("Simplified Procedures"),
- Reimbursement for Certain Force Account Straight Time,
- Posting Public Assistance Awards and Mission Assignments on the Web,
- De-obligation of Unexpended Sandy Grants,
- Disaster Relief Fund Reporting,
- National Strategy to Reduce Costs on Future Disasters,
- Community Disaster Loans,
- Declarations for Federally Recognized Tribal Governments,
- Individual Assistance Declaration Factors,
- The Lease and Repair Program,
- Other Needs Assistance: Child Care Expenses,
- Changes to the Hazard Mitigation Grant Program (HMGP), and
- The Unified Federal Review Process.[155]

Public Health Authorities

Some of the most challenging legal issues arising from the threat to homeland security involve the legal authorities for protecting public health.

Public health authority is derived almost entirely from the laws of individual states.[156] Most of these laws, however, were written in the 1920s. These laws generally provide very

---

152. Sandy Recovery Improvement Act of 2013, Pub. L. No. 113-2.

153. Sandy Recovery Improvement Act of 2013. <https://www.fema.gov/sandy-recovery-improvement-act-2013>.

154. SRIA Fact Sheet (June 2014) <http://www.fema.gov/media-library-data/1404155047131-873c772998b1e1f9b8962fcb59e42d39/SRIA+Overview+Fact+Sheet+and+Status+Updated+June+30+2014.pdf >.

155. Sandy Recovery Improvement Act of 2013. https://www.fema.gov/sandy-recovery-improvement-act-2013.

156. Terrorism Incident Annex to the Federal Response Plan, Apr. 1999, at TI-1, provides that "[s]tate and local governments exercise primary authority to respond to the consequences of terrorism; the Federal Government provides assistance as required."

broad police powers, have not been used on a wide scale since the first attempt to conquer polio in the United States, and were enacted prior to the expanded notions of individual rights and due process developed in the courts over the last forty years. Thus, it is not clear that the laws would withstand judicial scrutiny under today's standards.[157] Finally, there is a disconnect between the legal authority for responding to a terrorist attack with significant public health implications, which resides primarily at the state level, and the resources and technology required for such a response, which can often be found only at the federal level.

At the Federal level, several statutes, regulations, and Executive Orders offer a broad legal framework for responding to public health emergencies. For example, the Homeland Security Act of 2002[158] and the Robert T. Stafford Disaster Relief and Emergency Assistance Act of 1988[159] each provide general authorities for federal, state, and local and tribal governments to respond to national emergencies. Select sections of the Public Health Service Act[160] address responses to declared public health emergencies. The Federal response to public health emergencies is also governed by regulations and Executive Orders that implement Federal statute.[161]

In the early 2000s, individual states began examining their laws related to public health and considering revisions. One of the first states to respond to this need was Colorado. In May 2000, Denver was the site of a federal government exercise simulating a biological terrorism attack. This was part of a multi-city exercise called TOP OFF, designed to test capabilities for responding to various types of catastrophic terrorism attacks. Stemming largely from preparations for that exercise, Colorado adopted a statute that created an expert emergency epidemic response committee to advise the governor in declaring and handling an emergency epidemic of natural or manmade origin.[162] Colorado chose not to seek to amend or expand existing authorities but, rather, to provide a mechanism for directing their implementation.

Quarantine. Among the most potentially controversial authorities are those for quarantine. In recent decades, the courts have enunciated a variety of constitutional principles to which public health restrictions must conform.[163] Measures that curtail civil liberties, such as

---

157. Catastrophic Terrorism Report, *supra* note 134, at 37.

158. Pub. L. No. 107-296. Section 101(b)(1)(D) of the Homeland Security Act of 2002 (6 U.S.C. 111(b)(1)(D)) directs the Department of Homeland Security to "carry out all functions of entities transferred to the Department, including acting as a focal point regarding natural and manmade crises and emergency planning." *See also* Title V of the Homeland Security Act of 2002, "National Emergency Management" (6 U.S.C. 311–321n).

159. Pub. L. No. 92-388. The Stafford Act authorizes the President to declare an "emergency" or a "major disaster" in response to an event, thereby triggering federal financial assistance to states.

160. *See e.g.,* section 319 (42 U.S.C. 247d), giving the Secretary of Health and Human Services general authority to determine that a public health emergency exists and granting authority to the Secretary to take appropriate action to address the public health emergency; and section 311 (42 U.S.C. 243), giving the Secretary of Health and Human Services general authority to "cooperate with and aid State and local authorities in the enforcement of their quarantine and other health regulations, and [advise] the several States on matters relating to the preservation and improvement of the public health."

161. *See e.g.,* 42 C.F.R. part 70 (interstate quarantine) and 42 C.F.R. part 71 (foreign quarantine). Executive Order 13295 (Revised List of Quarantinable Communicable Diseases), 68 Fed. Reg. 17255 (Apr. 9, 2003), lists eight communicable diseases for which an individual may be apprehended or detained. Executive Orders 13375, 70 Fed. Reg. 17299 (Apr. 1, 2005), and 13674, 79 Fed. Reg. 45671 (August 6, 2014) amended Executive Order 13295 to update and clarify the list further.

162. COL. REV. STAT. § 24-33.5-2104 (2014).

163. *See generally* LAWRENCE O. GOSTIN, PUBLIC HEALTH LAW: POWER, DUTY, RESTRAINT (2000).

quarantine, must be necessary to respond to an imminent public health threat, no more restrictive than needed to protect the public's health, applied in a non-discriminatory manner, and subject to judicial review by persons affected by them.[164] It is not clear that a large-scale quarantine could be implemented in a timely manner and still meet these standards.

In addition to questions about the adequacy and constitutionality of state quarantine authorities, the scope of federal quarantine authority is still being debated. According to statute, "[t]he Surgeon General, with the approval of the Secretary, is authorized to make and enforce such regulations as in his judgment are necessary to prevent the introduction, transmission, or spread of communicable diseases from foreign countries into the States or possessions, or from one State or possession into any other State or possession."[165] However, it is not clear that current regulations would allow restrictions on the movement of people if they have not yet been diagnosed as being infected with a communicable disease.[166]

In light of the significant legal and logistical challenges associated with large-scale quarantine and other coercive responses to a terrorism attack involving an infectious disease, some experts have begun to examine the potential benefits of a greater focus on voluntary measures. One example of such a proposal is a concept called "Shielding," which seeks to break the cycle of a contagious disease attack, ease the distribution of treatment, and mitigate the need for wide-scale quarantine. It would accomplish these objectives through community-based efforts, supported by federal assistance, to encourage and support voluntary decisions by individuals and families to stay at home and self-isolate in response to a bioterrorism attack involving a contagious disease, rather than to flee or gather in public places.[167] It is viewed as "a means of fostering both physical and psychological resistance to and resilience from what many consider our nation's greatest threat in the current war on terrorism."[168] Because it is voluntary, it does not require specific statutory authorization. Similarly, it does not need to meet the rigorous constitutional requirements the courts have set forth in quarantine or other coercive restrictions on freedom of

---

164. In response to the Ebola outbreak in the Fall of 2014, the State of Maine requested that the Maine District Court issue an Order restricting the movements of a nurse who had treated Ebola patients in West Africa. The Court rejected the State's request, and instead, on October 31, 2014, issued an Order requiring the nurse to submit to daily monitoring (i.e. Direct Active Monitoring) of Ebola symptoms, coordinate travel with public health authorities, and provide immediate notification if any Ebola symptoms appear. The Court held that it was "necessary to ensure public safety that [the nurse] comply with Direct Active Monitoring until a hearing can be held on the State's Petition" but that "[t]he State has not met its burden at this time to prove by clear and convincing evidence that limiting [the nurse's] movements to the degree requested is 'necessary to protect other individuals from the dangers of infection' ...". *See* Order Pending Hearing, Mayhew v. Hickox, No. CIV-2014-36 (Me. Dist. Ct. 2014).

165. 42 U.S.C. § 264(a) (2000). *But see* Public Health Security and Bioterrorism Preparedness and Response Act of 2002, Pub. L. No. 107-188, subtit. D, 116 Stat. 594 (2002) (making it easier for the Surgeon General to promulgate quarantine regulations and extend the scope of that authority to cover individuals who are in a "qualifying stage", which is defined as being in a communicable stage or "in a precommunicable stage, if the disease would be likely to cause a public health emergency if transmitted to other individuals." (§ 142, 116 Stat. 594)).

166. 42 C.F.R. § 70.1–.8 (2002).

167. *See* INT'L J. EMERGENCY MENTAL HEALTH, Fall 2002 [hereinafter IJEMH]. *See also* CRITICAL INCIDENT ANALYSIS GROUP, WHAT IS TO BE DONE? EMERGING PERSPECTIVES ON PUBLIC RESPONSES TO BIOTERRORISM (2002).

168. IJEMH, at 231.

movement or association. Moreover, it can be implemented at an early stage in a crisis, before the standards for imposing quarantine may have been met.[169]

Treatment. Questions are also raised regarding the authority to compel individuals to receive treatment or to ration scarce treatment resources. Public health authorities compelled individuals to receive smallpox vaccinations following outbreaks in Muncie, Indiana, in 1893, and in Boston, Massachusetts, in 1901. Four years later, the Supreme Court sided with the state in a case that challenged the Boston policy as unconstitutional.[170] This was decided in 1905, however, so it is not clear that today's Court would reach the same conclusion. In fact, the draft Model State Emergency Health Powers Act[171] provides authority for voluntary, not compulsory, vaccination. Someone may choose not to be vaccinated for reasons of health, religion, or conscience. Public health and medical professionals must decide whether those choosing not to be vaccinated should be isolated or quarantined to prevent the spread of a contagious or possibly contagious disease.

A more likely scenario may be the need to make decisions regarding who will receive scarce supplies of antibiotics or other treatment. The Colorado officials used the authority provided in the recently adopted statute to set up a committee of health experts and others to prioritize the dispensing of vaccines among high-risk groups.[172] Decisions made by health experts, supported by sound medical and public health judgments and set forth in regulation or statue prior to the chaos accompanying an attack, are more likely to withstand judicial scrutiny and ensure an effective public health response.[173]

Information Management. A third major area of potential controversy in the application of public health law to catastrophic terrorism is related to the management of information. Effective detection and mitigation of a bioterrorism attack will require real-time communication of information about patients showing symptoms of disease. Unlike naturally occurring outbreaks, this information, including information identifying individual patients, may need to be shared with emergency management and law enforcement officials in order to mitigate consequences, determine whether it is an intentional act of terrorism, and, if so, attempt to apprehend the perpetrators. However, state and federal privacy requirements may complicate such potentially vital information sharing.[174]

Homeland Defense—The Role of the Military Within the United States

Determining the appropriate role for the military within the borders of the United States is one of the most sensitive challenges arising from the emphasis on homeland

---

169. Richard Bonnie et al., *The Legal Framework for Shielding, in* CRITICAL INCIDENT ANALYSIS GROUP, WHAT IS TO BE DONE? EMERGING PERSPECTIVES ON PUBLIC RESPONSES TO BIOTERRORISM; IJEMH, at 259.

170. Jacobson v. Massachusetts, 197 U.S. 11 (1905).

171. The*Model State Emergency Health Powers Act,*(Proposed Official Draft Dec. 21, 2001), <http://www.publichealthlaw.net/MSEHPA/MSEHPA2.pdf >.

172. Cantigny Conference on State Emergency Health Powers and the Bioterrorism Threat, Apr. 26–27, 2001, sponsored by the Centers for Disease Control and Prevention, American Bar Association Standing Committee on Law and National Security, and the National Strategy Forum <http://www.nationalstrategy.com/april%20conference.htm>.

173. KELLMAN, *supra* note134, at 23.

174. *See, e.g.,* 45 C.F.R. § 164 (2013).

security. In fact, then-Deputy Secretary of Defense John Hamre noted in 1999 that any discussion of homeland defense by the Department of Defense (DOD) elicited a negative reaction from the public and many Americans seemed more fearful of U.S. military intervention inside this country than of an actual terrorist attack.[175] Thus, although the term homeland defense was used as early as 1997 in a report by the National Defense Panel,[176] the department's focus prior to 9/11 was on providing logistical and technical training and support for the consequence management[177] activities of civilian domestic agencies at the federal, state, and local level.[178] In 1999, the Joint Task Force-Civil Support was established for coordinating this support.[179]

On September 11, 2001, the key role of the Department of Defense in homeland defense became immediately apparent. The North American Aerospace Defense Command's (NORAD) Northeast Air Defense Sector (NEADS) in Rome, N.Y., received a call that morning about a possible hijacking. Moments later, as two F-15s were taking off from Massachusetts' Otis Air National Guard (ANG) Base, American Airlines flight 11 crashed into the north tower of the World Trade Center.[180] At the time, NORAD had only twenty fighters on armed alert throughout the North American continent. Only fourteen were in the continental United States at seven bases, the rest were in Alaska and Canada. Within eighteen hours, 300 fighters would be on alert at twenty-six locations.[181]

In recognition of the increasingly important role of the Department in homeland defense, on April 17, 2002, the Secretary of Defense, Donald Rumsfeld and Chairman of the Joint Chiefs of Staff, General Richard B. Myers, announced changes to the Unified Command Plan that established a new combatant command, U.S. Northern Command (NORTHCOM), and assigned it the mission of defending the United States and supporting the full range of military assistance to civil authorities.[182] Specifically, its mission is to "to deter, prevent, and defeat threats and aggression aimed at the United States, its territories, and interests."[183] NORTHCOM's area of operations includes the United States, Canada, Mexico, parts of the Caribbean and the contiguous waters in the Atlantic and Pacific Oceans up to 500 miles off the North American coastline.[184]

---

175. *See* William E. Conner, *Deputy Secretary of Defense Dr. John J. Hamre Challenges Standing Committee to Lead Debate on Homeland Security*, ABA NAT'L SECURITY L. REP., Aug. 1999, at 1.

176. NATIONAL DEFENSE PANEL, TRANSFORMING DEFENSE, NATIONAL SECURITY IN THE 21ST CENTURY, REPORT OF THE NATIONAL DEFENSE PANEL (1997) <http://www.fas.org/man/docs/ndp/front.htm>.

177. "Consequence management" is a term used in the Federal Response Plan, Terrorism Annex, to refer to efforts to manage the consequences after a terrorist incident, which would be led by the Federal Emergency Management Agency (FEMA), as opposed to "crisis management", which refers largely to law enforcement efforts, for which FBI has the lead.

178. *See, e.g.*, Defense Against Weapons of Mass Destruction Act of 1996, Pub. L. No. 104-201, 110 Stat. 2422 (1996); National Defense Authorization Act for Fiscal Year 2001, Pub. L. No. 106-398, §901, 114 Stat. 1654 (2000); GILMORE COMMISSION 2ND, *supra* note 88, at app. M.

179. For additional background on DOD's approach to these issues, see CDR Michael Dobbs, USN, *Homeland Security: New Challenges for an Old Responsibility*, J. HOMELAND SECURITY, Mar. 2001, <http://www.homelandsecurity.org/journal>; Col. Randall J. Larsen, USAF-Ret. & Ruth A. David, *Homeland Defense: State of the Union*, STRATEGIC REV., Spring 2001, at 5.

180. William B. Scott, *Exercise Jump-Starts Response To Attacks*, AVIATION WK. & SPACE TECH., June 3, 2002.

181. *Id.*

182. United States Department of Defense News Release, No. 188-02, Apr. 17, 2002.

183. A Short History of U.S. Northern Command <http://www.northcom.mil/Portals/28/Documents/A%20Short%20History%20of%20USNORTHCOM%20(current%20as%20of%20March%202014).pdf>.

184. *Id.*

DOD distinguishes between homeland security and homeland defense. It defines homeland security as "a concerted national effort to prevent terrorist attacks within the United States, reduce America's vulnerability to terrorism, and minimize the damage and recover from attacks that do occur."[185] Homeland defense, which is one of DOD's homeland security roles, is defined as "the protection of U.S. sovereignty, territory, domestic population and critical defense infrastructure against external threats and aggression."[186]

Legal Authority

While this organizational change attempts to consolidate under a unified command the various military elements involved in homeland security, the legal authority for the military's domestic mission is still somewhat piecemeal and scattered throughout a number of statutes, directives, regulations, and plans.

Recent studies examining issues related to homeland defense have largely supported the conclusion that there is sufficient authority for using the U.S. Armed Forces and the National Guard to assist in preventing or repelling a terrorist attack. While the *Posse Comitatus Act* generally prohibits the use of the Armed Forces "to execute the laws," that language has been narrowly interpreted and is subject to numerous exemptions.[187] Moreover, the Act does not apply to National Guard troops unless they have been federalized, although some state laws impose restrictions on National Guard functions. Finally, given that the President has designated terrorists as "enemy combatants,"[188] military action in response to an attack is likely to be viewed not as "executing the laws" but as defending the nation against attack.

Use of Armed Forces

A report issued by the Center for Strategic and International Studies (CSIS) concluded that "[t]he President unquestionably has the authority to use the armed forces to repel an invasion of or respond to an attack on the United States."[189] The Advisory Panel to Assess Domestic Response Capabilities for Terrorism Involving Weapons of Mass Destruction ("Gilmore Commission") in a report issued December 2001, noted that there is "ample authority for using the military inside our borders for responding to a variety of emergencies."[190]

The constitutional authority for the use of the military domestically rests on three Articles. Article One gives Congress power for "calling forth the militia" to enforce laws and suppress rebellions and insurrections. Article Two sets forth the President's power as Commander-in-Chief of regular federal forces and of the state militias when they are federalized. Finally, Article Four calls on the United States to protect each of the states against invasion and "domestic violence."

---

185. Under Secretary of Defense for Policy, Department of Defense < http://policy.defense.gov/OUSDPOffices/ASDforHomelandDefenseAmericasSecurityAffa.aspx>.

186. *Id.*

187. *See* MAJ Craig T. Trebilcock, USAR, *The Myth of Posse Comitatus*, J. Homeland Security, Oct. 2000.

188. *See, e.g.,* Hamdi v. Rumsfeld, 542 U.S. 507 (2004).

189. Paul Schott Stevens, U.S. Armed Forces and Homeland Defense: The Legal Framework 3 (2001).

190. Third Annual Report of the Advisory Panel to Assess Domestic Response Capabilities for Terrorism Involving Weapons of Mass Destruction 52 (2001) [Gilmore Commission 3rd].

While the use of the military domestically to repel an invasion or put down a rebellion is clearly contemplated in the Constitution, use of the military in more ambiguous situations may require specific statutory authorization, particularly where the duties resemble law enforcement functions. The *Posse Comitatus Act* prohibits the use of the military to execute the laws, "except in cases and under circumstances expressly authorized by the Constitution or Act of Congress."[191] Foremost among the statutes providing express authorization for domestic use of the military are the Insurrection Act[192] and the Stafford Act.[193] In addition, specific statutes provide for the use of the military in situations involving nuclear,[194] biological, or chemical[195] terrorism.

The Insurrection Act was originally designed to authorize the President, at the request of a governor or on his own, to use the armed forces or state militias to put down domestic disturbances that threaten the authority of a state or the federal government. It was cited as authority for the use of troops to enforce desegregation of schools in 1957 and in responding to the riots that followed the Rodney King assault verdict in 1992. Thus, its clearest application would be to disorder that might erupt after a terrorist attack. However, the language of the statute speaks broadly of "any insurrection, *domestic violence, unlawful combination, or conspiracy*"[196] (emphasis added) that significantly hinders the execution of the laws, opposes or obstructs the execution of the laws, or impedes the course of justice under those laws. The determination of whether such circumstances exist is generally within the President's discretion.[197]

The Stafford Act authorizes assistance by the federal government to state and local governments where federal assistance is necessary in carrying out their responsibilities to alleviate the suffering and damage which result from "major disasters." A major disaster is defined as "any natural catastrophe ... or, regardless of cause, any fire, flood, or explosion."[198] The Act also authorizes federal assistance in "emergencies", which is defined as any occasion "for which, in the determination of the President, federal assistance is needed to supplement state and local efforts and capabilities to save lives and to protect property and public health and safety, or to lessen or avert the threat of a catastrophe in any part of the United States."[199] A declaration of emergency can be made when the "situation is of such severity and magnitude that effective response is beyond the capabilities of the State and the affected local governments" or an "emergency exists for which the primary responsibility for response rests with the United States because the emergency involves a subject area for which, under the Constitution or laws of the United States, the United States exercises exclusive or preeminent responsibility and authority."[200] This

---

191. 18 U.S.C. § 1385 (2000). Although the statute refers only to the Army and Air Force, DOD has extended this policy to the Navy and Marine Corps in 32 C.F.R. § 213.10(c) (2002), although some courts have raised questions about the application of the prohibition to those services. *See, e.g.,* KELLMAN, *supra* note 134, at Ch. 2, § 2.1.1, fn. 34 (citing U.S. v. Yunis, 924 F.2d 1086, 1093 (D.C. Cir. 1991)).

192. Insurrection Act, 10 U.S.C. §§ 331–36 (2000).

193. Stafford Act, 42 U.S.C. §§ 5121–5206 (2000).

194. 18 U.S.C. § 831 (2000).

195. Biological and chemical incidents are covered in 10 U.S.C. § 382.

196. 10 U.S.C. § 333.

197. *See, e.g.,* Sterling v. Constantin, 287 U.S. 378, 399–400 (1932); Luther v. Borden, 48 U.S. 1, 42–44 (1849); Marin v. Mott, 25 U.S. 19, 30–31 (1827).

198. 42 U.S.C. § 5122(2) (2000).

199. 42 U.S.C. § 5122(1) (2000).

200. 42 U.S.C. § 5191 (2000). Section 5191 was amended by section 1110 of the Sandy Recovery Improvement Act of 2013 (SRIA) (Pub. L. No. 113-2) to permit the Chief Executive of an Indian tribal government to directly request a disaster or emergency declaration by the President. Prior to

would seem to provide ample authority for deployment of federal troops to prevent a terrorist attack where state and local capabilities are inadequate. However, it does not provide a separate statutory exception to the Posse Comitatus restriction on law enforcement activity.

The Armed Forces can be used to assist in the enforcement of Title 18, section 831, which criminalizes conspiracies or attempts to gain unauthorized access to nuclear material. Pursuant to these provisions, the Secretary of Defense can provide assistance at the request of the Attorney General if the situation poses a serious threat to the interests of the United States and civilian law enforcement personnel are not capable of enforcing the law. The assistance can include use of the military to conduct arrests, searches and seizures, and "such other activity as is incidental to the enforcement of this section, or to the protection of persons or property from conduct that violates this section."[201]

Similarly, there is statutory authority for the military to provide law enforcement assistance in situations involving chemical or biological weapons.[202] The Secretary of Defense and the Attorney General must both determine an emergency exists and the Secretary of Defense must find that such assistance will not adversely affect the military preparedness of the United States. However, arrests, searches and seizures, and direct intelligence collection for law enforcement purposes is not authorized unless necessary for the immediate protection of human life and civilian law enforcement officials are not capable of taking the action.[203]

In addition to the statutory considerations, requests for military assistance are evaluated pursuant to a Department of Defense Directive.[204] There are six criteria: legality, lethality, risk, cost, appropriateness, and readiness. The Department of Justice has cited four types of assistance the military may be called upon to provide in a domestic law enforcement situation involving a threat or an act of terrorism, including WMD terrorism: (1) providing technical support and assistance to law enforcement and other crisis response personnel; (2) interdicting an event and apprehending those responsible; (3) restoring law and order following an incident; and (4) abating the consequences of a terrorist act.[205]

Use of National Guard

The authority and restrictions applicable to the use of the Armed Forces will also apply to the National Guard if they have been called into federal status. However, if the Guard is serving under the control of a state governor, state law controls their activities. Thus, the federal Posse Comitatus Act does not apply to the Guard if they are acting in their state capacity, although some states have their own laws prohibiting the Guard from performing a law enforcement role. Moreover, according the Gilmore Report, some states that do not have such laws have, nevertheless, "specifically prohibited the Guard from performing those functions in their current airport missions."[206]

At the end of 2001, roughly 42,000 Guardsmen had been called to service in response to Operations "Nobel Eagle" and "Enduring Freedom." More than 7,000 Guardsmen were

---

SRIA, tribal groups were treated like local governments and could not directly request disaster declarations.

201. 18 U.S.C. § 831 (2000).

202. 10 U.S.C. § 382.

203. 10 U.S.C. § 382(d).

204. Department of Defense Directive 3025.15, Military Assistance to Civil Authorities, Feb. 18, 1997.

205. Office of the Legal Counsel, U.S. Department of Justice, Federal Legal Authorities for Use in an Incident Involving Weapons of Mass Destruction (2000).

206. Gilmore Commission 3rd, *supra* note 190, at 53.

called by governors, at the President's request, to supplement security at the nation's 420 commercial airports for up to six months.[207] Although these troops were operating under the control of the governors, the federal government was paying the costs.[208] According to a 2012 National Guard Posture Statement, National Guard personnel were deployed around the country to assist with homeland security activities on the Southwest Border (including investigative analyses and counterdrug efforts) and the federal government's response to the Deepwater Horizon Oil Spill.[209]

Despite this extensive deployment of troops for Homeland Security activities, this is not officially a key mission for the National Guard. Thus, the Gilmore Commission has recommended "that the Secretary of Defense direct specific mission areas for the use of the National Guard for providing support to civil authorities for combating terrorism."[210] Similarly, an October 2001 National Emergency Management White Paper on Domestic Preparedness, urges Congress and the Department of Defense to "authorize homeland defense as a key federal defense mission tasking for the National Guard. By providing this authorization and removing restricting language and funding on utilization of National Guard assets and personnel, the civil-military integrated response will be dramatically improved."[211] Of particular concern is the lack of adequate ground and aviation assets to quickly transport the Guardsmen where they are needed. For example, the Adjutant General for the state of California told Congress "in most states the available transportation assets are woefully inadequate to support projected needs."[212]

Thus, legal restrictions do not appear to be a significant factor limiting the potential use of Guard troops for preventing or thwarting a terrorist attack on U.S. soil. Issues related to capability, including resources and training, may present more significant potential obstacles.

Questions for Discussion

1. Are the current exemptions to the Posse Comitatus Act adequate to meet the challenge of preserving homeland security and responding to catastrophic terrorism attacks? If not, what additional authority is needed and how would you structure it?

2. What, if any, federalism issues might be raised by the use of the National Guard in federal status or the commitment of federal troops in a state without consent by the governor? What precedents can you cite, *e.g.*, use of federal troops to enforce integration of public schools? What lessons can we learn from those precedents?

3. Having summarized the legal authority for the domestic use of the military in various roles, it may not always be clear which role applies in a given circumstance. For example, it had always been assumed that if the military were called upon to assist in apprehending the perpetrators of a terrorist attack, it would be acting in support of law enforcement.

---

207. Lt. Gen. Russell C. Davis, USAF, Chief, National Guard Bureau, Statement before the Senate Judiciary Subcomm. on Technology, Terrorism, and Government Information (Dec. 13, 2001).

208. Lt. Gen. Frank G. Libutti, USMC (Ret.), Special Assistant for Homeland Security, Statement before the Senate Judiciary Subcomm. on Technology, Terrorism, and Government Information (Dec. 13, 2001).

209. See 2012 National Guard Bureau Posture Statement, http://www.nationalguard.mil/portals/31/Documents/PostureStatements/2012%20National%20Guard%20Bureau%20Posture%20Statement.pdf.

210. GILMORE COMMISSION 3RD, *supra* note 190, at 52.

211. *See* GILMORE COMMISSION 3RD, *supra* note 190, at app. I.

212. Maj. Gen. Paul D. Monroe, Jr., Adjutant General, State of California, Statement before the Senate Judiciary Subcomm. on Technology, Terrorism, and Government Information (Dec. 13, 2001).

However, given that the Administration has made it clear since the attacks of 9/11 that the war on terrorism is not a rhetorical war, and has designated terrorists as enemy combatants, it may well view the use of the troops to apprehend terrorists in this country as a military operation, not subject to direction from the FBI or to the legal constraints of Posse Comitatus. What kinds of legal authorities should be developed to govern this kind of domestic mission? Should there be rules of engagement for military operations in the continental United States ("CONUS") that differ from those used overseas? If so, in what ways should they differ?

Critical Infrastructure Protection: A Partnership between the Public and Private Sectors

Critical infrastructure is defined in 42 U.S.C. § 5195c(e) as " ... systems and assets, whether physical or virtual, so vital to the United States that the incapacity or destruction of such systems and assets would have a debilitating impact on security, national economic security, national public health or safety, or any combination of those matters." This definition can encompass both federal and state property, and both private and public property. The federal government can take steps to protect its own property and networks, but it is more limited in its actions to protect state and private property.[213] Thus it is necessary for states and the private sector to act to protect their own assets as well. However, it has become clear that in order to fully protect America's critical infrastructure, it is necessary for the federal government, state governments, and private stakeholders to work together.

The first report to acknowledge the necessity of a partnership between the public and private sector was the President's Commission on Critical Infrastructure Protection (PCCIP).[214] Its report, filed on October 13, 1997, addressed both physical and cyber threats to the nation's critical infrastructure, which it defined as "essential services that underpin our society ... energy, banking and finance, transportation, vital human services, and telecommunications."[215] The report highlighted the essential role of the private sector in addressing this security need. "Because the infrastructures are mainly privately owned and operated, we concluded that critical infrastructure assurance is a shared responsibility of the public and private sectors. The only sure path to protected infrastructures in the years ahead is through a real partnership between infrastructure owners and operators and the government."[216] Thus it became clear that a partnership between the private and public sectors was essential to ensuring the resilience of the nation's critical infrastructure.

---

213. The Federal Protective Service is charged to protect federal facitlities and the people thereon. *See* 40 U.S.C. § 1315. The Interagency Security Committee was created to assist federal agencies in developing physical security policies and standards, and promoting best practices in the private and public sector. *See* Executive Order 12,977.

214. CRITICAL FOUNDATIONS: PROTECTING AMERICA'S INFRASTRUCTURES: THE REPORT OF THE PRESIDENT'S COMMISSION ON CRITICAL INFRASTRUCTURE PROTECTION (1997) [hereinafter PCCIP REPORT].

215. *Id.* at ix. *See also* Lee Zeichner, *Critical Infrastructure Assurance, A National Integrated Risk Management Policy*, Feb. 2002, at 2 <http://legalnet.com>, which defines it as "critical services that support national and economic security as well as the public's health and welfare." This definition would include water, police, fire, and emergency management services.

216. PCCIP REPORT, *supra* note 214.

Organizational Efforts

In May 1998, in response to PCCIP recommendations, the President issued Presidential Decision Directive 63 (PDD 63) to address physical and cyber infrastructure vulnerabilities in the federal government and private sector.[217] This directive, along with Combating Terrorism Directive 62 (PDD 62) issued the same day, established a National Coordinator for Security, Infrastructure Protection and Counter-Terrorism to "oversee a broad variety of relevant policies and programs including counter-terrorism, protection of critical infrastructure, preparedness and consequence management for weapons of mass destruction."[218]

PDD 63 also set up the National Infrastructure Protection Center (NIPC) at the FBI to "provide the principal means of facilitating and coordinating the Federal government's response to an incident, mitigating attacks, investigating threats and monitoring reconstitution efforts."[219] It also established the Critical Infrastructure Assurance Office in the Department of Commerce to "work with government agencies and the private sector in developing a national plan" as well as outreach to industry.[220] (Both of these offices were later moved into the new Department of Homeland Security.) Finally, the directive called for the establishment of the National Infrastructure Assurance Council of private sector and state and local officials, and encouraged the private sector to set up Information Sharing and Analysis Centers in cooperation with the government.[221]

A month after the attacks of September 11, 2001, the President announced that the terrorism coordination and information assurance functions were being split into two new positions: Special Advisor to the President for Cyberspace Security and National Director/Deputy National Security Advisor for Combating Terrorism. A week later, the President issued Executive Order No. 13,231, establishing the President's Critical Infrastructure Protection Board, made up of the relevant executive branch departments, agencies, and offices.[222] The mission of the board was to recommend and coordinate programs for protecting information systems for critical infrastructures. This Executive Order also established the National Infrastructure Advisory Council (NIAC), whose members are to be chosen from private sector, academia, and state and local governments.[223] While similar to earlier efforts, these later organizational structures focused more narrowly on information systems for critical infrastructure.

With the establishment of the Department of Homeland Security, the Critical Infrastructure Protection Board was eliminated and the NIAC was put under the new Department.[224] The position of Special Advisor to the President for Cyberspace Security was also eliminated and now falls on DHS. Additionally, the Homeland Security Act

---

217. Office of the Press Secretary, White House, Fact Sheet: Protecting America's Critical Infrastructures: PDD 63, May 22, 1998.

218. Office of the Press Secretary, White House, Fact Sheet: Summary of Presidential Decision Directives 62 and 63, May 22, 1998.

219. Presidential Decision Directive 63, May 22, 1998.

220. *Id.*

221. *Id.*

222. Exe. Order No. 13,231, 66 Fed. Reg. 53,063 (Oct. 16, 2001) <http://www.whitehouse.gov/news/releases/2001/10/20011016-12.html>.

223. *Id.*

224. Office of the Press Secretary, White House, Executive Order Amendment of Executive Orders, and Other Actions, in Connection with the Transfer of Certain Functions to the Secretary of Homeland Security, Feb. 28, 2003 <http://www.whitehouse.gov/news/releases/2003/02/20030228-8.html>.

created the Office of Infrastructure Protection (IP).[225] IP is charged with ensuring the resilience of critical infrastructure through the collaboration with public and private stakeholders. The NIAC, IP, and the cybersecurity mission all fall under the Under Secretary for the National Protection and Programs Directorate (NPPD).

Legal Framework

Since the PCCIP report was written experts have continued to discuss and think about the best means for the private sector and public sector to work together to protect America's critical infrastructure. Currently, the different laws, regulations, executive orders, and presidential policy directives set up a framework with three overarching goals. The first goal is assisting the appropriate entities to prevent an incident and be prepared in case of an incident. The second goal is the timely sharing of accurate information between the public and private sectors. The third goal is the assessment of vulnerabilities of critical infrastructure, including the interdependencies between critical infrastructures. Although the federal government achieves these goals in many different ways, below are three examples that highlight the innovative partnerships that have been created since the PCCIP was written.

One example of the first goal is the National Infrastructure Protection Plan (NIPP).[226] The NIPP was first written in 2006 and then updated in 2009. The most recent update to the NIPP came in 2013 after Presidential Policy Directive 21 (PPD-21) explicitly called for the update.[227] The NIPP seeks to manage the risks from significant threats and hazards to physical and cyber critical infrastructure by informing the many different stakeholders. In order to manage the risks to critical infrastructure the NIPP encourages an integrated approach across the different stakeholders to "[i]dentify, deter, detect, disrupt, and prepare for threats and hazards … ;" "reduce vulnerabilities of critical assets, systems, and networks;" and "mitigate the potential consequences to critical infrastructure of incidents or adverse events that do occur."[228] Thus the NIPP describes "a national unity of effort" in order to assist all levels of government and the private and non-profit sectors to partner together to protect critical infrastructure.[229]

The key framework for permitting private sector entities to share information with the federal government in a timely manner is in the Homeland Security Act, which ensures that critical infrastructure information that the private sector voluntarily shares with the federal government is protected from disclosure.[230] This is commonly known as Protected Critical Infrastructure Information (PCII). The statutory protections overcomes some of the major concerns that private sector has when sharing information with the federal government. Because PCII cannot be disclosed, the private sector does not have to be concerned that the federal government will be required to disclose the information through a Freedom of Information Act request. The statute also prevents the federal government from using the voluntarily given information to regulate industry or in any civil actions.[231]

---

225. Homeland Security Act of 2002, Pub. L. 107-296 § 201, 116 Stat 2135 (2002), *codified at* 6 U.S.C. § 121, as amended.
226. <http://www.dhs.gov/national-infrastructure-protection-plan>.
227. *See* Presidential Policy Directive 21, *hereinafter* PPD-21, *Critical Infrastructure Security and Resilience*, Feb. 2013.
228. *See* The National Infrastructure Protection Plan 2013 (NIPP) p. 3.
229. *Id.* p 2.
230. 6 U.S.C. §§ 131–134.
231. 6 U.S.C. § 133.

These protections have proven crucial to ensure the free flow of information to the federal government regarding critical infrastructure information.

PPD-21 and Executive Order 13,636, issued on the same day in 2013, represent the current strategic thinking regarding how best to protect critical infrastructure. PPD-21 emphasizes the interdependencies between the different sectors. It also recognizes that cybersecurity goes hand-in-hand with protecting critical infrastructure.[232] This focus on the many interdependencies is highlighted by the critical infrastructure centers PPD-21 requires. The two established centers continuously monitor critical infrastructure. One monitors critical cyber infrastructure, the National Cybersecurity and Communications Integration Center (NCCIC—pronounced N-Kick) and the other monitors physical critical infrastructure, the National Infrastructure Coordinating Center (NICC— pronounced Nick). The NCCIC will be discussed below in the cybersecurity section. The NICC maintains situational awareness of the nation's critical infrastructure by information sharing and coordination between DHS and the owners and operators of critical infrastructure. These centers and the focus on the interdependent nature of critical infrastructure sectors open the possibility for greater information sharing between federal agencies as well as the private sector.

Chemical Security: Chemical Facility Anti-Terrorism Standards (CFATS)

On October 4, 2006, President Bush signed into law the Department of Homeland Security Appropriations Act of 2007 (the Act), which authorized the Department of Homeland Security to regulate the security of high-risk chemical facilities.[233] Section 550 of the Act required the Department to issue an interim final rule to provide for the security of certain chemical facilities in the United States, which the Department published on April 9, 2007.[234] The interim final rule codified the Department's Chemical Facility Anti-Terrorism Standards (CFATS) at 6 C.F.R. part 27.

Under CFATS, any chemical facility (except certain facilities expressly exempted by section 550)[235] that possesses a "Chemical of Interest" at or above a specific threshold must submit certain information to the Department so that the Department can determine if the facility is "high risk" and must comply with CFATS. CFATS implements risk-based performance standards so that higher standards will apply to facilities that present the highest level of risk. For example, depending on the level of risk presented by a chemical

---

232. *See* PPD-21. The sectors are Chemical; Commercial Facilities; Communications; Critical Manufacturing; Dams; Defense Industrial Base; Emergency Services; Energy; Financial Services; Food and Agriculture; Government Facilities; Healthcare and Public Health; Information Technology; Nuclear Reactors, Materials, and Waste; Transportation Systems, and Water and Wastewater Systems. The Department of Homeland Security website provides a comprehensive description of each sector. *See* <http://www.dhs.gov/critical-infrastructure-sectors>.

233. *See* Pub. L. No. 109-295, section 550. *See also* The Protecting and Securing Chemical Facilities from Terrorist Attacks Act of 2014, Pub. L. No. 113-254, 128 Stat. 2898 (Dec. 18, 2014). The Act amended the Homeland Security Act of 2002 to reauthorize CFATS and add new provisions to the program.

234. 72 Fed. Reg. 17688 (Apr. 9, 2007).

235. For example, exempted facilities include facilities regulated pursuant to the Maritime Transportation Security Act of 2002 (Pub. L. 107-295) and public water systems (as defined by section 1401 of the Safe Drinking Water Act).

facility, the facility could be required to implement various access control measures and develop and implement an emergency plan to respond to security incidents.

In response to an explosion at a fertilizer distribution facility in West, Texas, in April 2013, President Obama issued Executive Order 13650[236] to enhance the safety and security of chemical facilities and reduce the risk associated with hazardous chemicals to owners, operators, workers, and the surrounding communities. Among other things, Executive Order 13650 established a Federal interagency Working Group, and the President directed the Working Group to seek ways to modernize policies, regulations, and standards related to the safety and security of chemical facilities.[237]

Cybersecurity

Introduction

The nation's cyber infrastructure consists of a decentralized mix of government and private systems. The legal authorities that govern the security of this cyber infrastructure are similarly decentralized: no single authority provides an overarching legal framework for securing the infrastructure. This is not to say there is no legal structure. Broadly, reference to a mix of statutes and executive branch documents reveals three general principles. First, each government agency and private entity has the primary legal responsibility to protect its own systems. Second, despite this generally decentralized structure, the law does impose certain cybersecurity-related procedural and oversight duties on federal entities. Third, the law also seeks to improve the nation's overall cybersecurity posture by mandating or encouraging cooperation and coordination among government and private entities, especially entities that are part of the nation's critical infrastructure. Finally, the law criminalizes certain computer-related conduct. This section focuses on federal cybersecurity law relevant to civilian systems in the homeland security context by discussing highlights of a selection of the authorities that create the just-mentioned, general principles.

The Federal Information Security Management Act of 2002

The Federal Information Security Management Act of 2002 (FISMA), 44 U.S.C. §§ 3541–49, 40 U.S.C. § 11331, includes the statutory codification of the first principle introduced above as applied to the federal government: FISMA assigns primary responsibility for federal information security to agency heads and makes agency chief information officers and senior officials responsible for implementing agency information security measures. *See* 44 U.S.C. §§ 3541–47. FISMA does not impose such a decentralized structure on the private sector. But because the private sector is inherently decentralized, each private entity, like each federal agency, also has the primary responsibility to secure its own systems.

---

236. 78 Fed. Reg. 48029 (Aug. 7, 2013).

237. See section 6(d) of Executive Order 13650. Between submission and printing, the Federal Information Security Modernization Act of 2014, Pub. L. No. 113-283, 128 Stat. 3073 (Dec. 18, 2014) and the National Cybersecurity Protection Act of 2014, Pub. L. No. 113-282, 128 Stat. 3066 (Dec. 18, 2014) were enacted and altered the legal regime discussed in the section of this chapter discussing cybersecurity.

FISMA does not stop at simply placing primary responsibility on each agency for its own systems. It also requires each agency to establish an agency-wide information security program that, among other requirements, mandates notification and consultation with the federal information security incident center in response to security incidents and to coordinate with law enforcement or other agencies as appropriate. *Id.* § 3544. Nor does it leave each agency entirely without supervision over its cybersecurity measures. It requires the Director of OMB to establish a comprehensive framework for ensuring the effectiveness of information security controls over federal information resources, including a general responsibility to supervise information security policies and practices of federal departments and agencies. *Id.* § 3543. To further clarify various roles and responsibilities under FISMA, the Director of OMB has issued a series of memoranda to agency heads, including Office of Mgmt. & Budget, Memorandum M-10-28, *Clarifying Cybersecurity Responsibilities and Activities of the Executive Office of the President and the Department of Homeland Security* (July 6, 2010). That memorandum assigned DHS "primary responsibility within the Executive Branch for the operational aspects of Federal agency cybersecurity with respect to the [f]ederal information systems that fall within FISMA under 44 U.S.C. § 3543." *Id.* Another OMB memorandum, Memorandum M-15-01, *Fiscal Year 2014–2015 Guidance on Improving Federal Information Security and Privacy Management Practices* (October 3, 2014), details requirements for implemenation of a process for DHS to perform regular scans of public facing segments of federal civilian agency networks and streamlines agency reporting of information security incidents to DHS.

The Critical Infrastructures Protection Act of 2001

As noted in sections above, the Critical Infrastructures Protection Act of 2001 (CIPA), 42 U.S.C. § 5195c establishes the basics of federal, critical infrastructure protection measures and defines "critical infrastructure" as any physical or virtual system or asset whose incapacity or destruction "would have a debilitating impact on security, national economic security, national public health or safety, or any combination of those matters." 42 U.S.C. § 5195c(e). Although this definition is not cyber-specific and thus has relevance beyond cybersecurity, many cyber systems fall within its definition. CIPA does not assign specific functions to any federal entity. Instead, it directs the establishment of comprehensive programs to ensure the continuity of essential government functions toward the goal of making any physical or virtual disruption of critical infrastructures "rare, brief, geographically limited in effect, manageable, and minimally detrimental to the economy, human and government services, and national security of the United States." *Id.* § 5195c(c). It also directs federal entities to achieve this goal "in a public-private partnership involving corporate and non-governmental organizations." *Id.* These broad, unassigned goals and responsibilities are — at least in the cybersecurity context — partially assigned and narrowed in other authorities, including the one directly below.

The Homeland Security Act of 2002

The Homeland Security Act of 2002 (HSA), 6 U.S.C. § 101 *et seq.* and scattered sections assigns DHS as the primary leader in critical infrastructure protection activities. In perhaps the most direct statutory statement on DHS's cybersecurity-related authority outside of the federal government, section 223 of the HSA — "Enhancement of Non-Federal Cybersecurity" — requires DHS to have an operational cybersecurity role by directing that DHS's infrastructure protection and information analysis responsibilities be undertaken to provide government entities and private entities that own or operate critical information systems "(A) analysis and warnings related to threats to, and vulnerabilities of, critical information systems; and (B) in coordination with the [Administrator of the Federal Emergency Management Agency], crisis management support in response to threats to, or attacks on, critical information systems." 6 U.S.C. § 143. Section 223 also directs DHS to provide technical assistance to other government entities and the private sector relative to their emergency plans to respond to and recover from major critical information systems failures. *See id.*

The HSA also sets forth DHS's information analysis and infrastructure protection functions, which sets forth the basis for much of DHS's cyber mission. These include, for example, "developing a comprehensive national plan for securing the key resources and critical infrastructure of the United States, including information technology and telecommunications systems (including satellites), emergency preparedness communications systems, and the physical and technological assets that support such systems" and "recommending measures necessary to protect the key resources and critical infrastructure of the United States in coordination with other Federal government agencies and in cooperation with State and local government agencies and authorities, the private sector, and other entities." 6 U.S.C. § 121(d).

PPD-21, "Critical Infrastructure Security and Resilience" and EO 13636, "Improving Critical Infrastructure Cybersecurity"

Presidential Policy Directive 21, "Critical Infrastructure Security and Resilience" (February 2013) (PPD-21) and Executive Order Number 13,636, "Improving Critical Infrastructure Cybersecurity" (February 2013) (EO 13636) comprise some of the most recent cybersecurity-related guidance and authority. These two executive authorities build on statutory infrastructure protection concepts and responsibilities such as those in CIPA and the HSA, primarily by directing DHS and others to take specific actions within their broad statutory powers.

PPD-21 assigns federal agency roles in support of protecting the nation's critical infrastructure. It addresses DHS most extensively, and identifies a wide range of cybersecurity-relayed actions the Secretary of DHS takes to carry out his responsibilities under the HSA. It also directs that DHS maintain and operate critical infrastructure centers, including one known as the National Cybersecurity and Communications Coordination Center (NCCIC). The NCCIC is "a 24x7 cyber situational awareness, incident response, and management center that is a national nexus of cyber and communications integration for the Federal Government, intelligence community, and law enforcement." http://www.dhs.gov/about-national-cybersecurity-communications-integration-center (visited November 3, 2014). It "shares information among the public and private sectors to provide greater understanding of cybersecurity and communications situation awareness of vulnerabilities, intrusions, incidents, mitigation, and recovery actions." *Id.*

Whereas PPD-21 broadly addresses physical and cyber critical infrastructure, EO 13636 focuses on cybersecurity. It does so by addressing many topics, two of which are focused on here: (1) mandatory information sharing by DHS and (2) development of a cybersecurity framework.

EO 13636 imposes two primary cybersecurity information sharing requirements on DHS. First, it requires DHS to ensure the timely production of, as appropriate, unclassified and classified reports of cyber threats that identify specific, targeted, U.S. entities to those targeted entities. Second, it required DHS to expand the voluntary Enhanced Cybersecurity Services Program, which provides classified cyber threat and technical information to certain entities, to all critical infrastructure sectors.

EO 13636 requires the National Institute of Standards and Technology (NIST) to lead the development of a cybersecurity framework consisting of standards, guidelines, and best practices to promote the protection of critical infrastructure. The framework, which has since been developed, provides a prioritized, flexible, repeatable, and cost-effective approach of to help owners and operators of critical infrastructure in managing cyber-security-related risk while protecting business confidentiality, individual privacy and civil liberties. Consistent with the nature of the nation's cyber infrastructure and how it is protected, EO 13636 required NIST to consult with government and private sector entities in developing the framework.

Law Enforcement

The government also seeks to increase the security of the nation's cyber infrastructure by prosecuting, and therefore deterring, computer-related criminal activities. The Computer Fraud and Abuse Act (CFAA), codified at 18 U.S.C. § 1030, is a key computer crime statute. Broadly, the CFAA criminalizes seven areas of conduct commonly referred to as hacking. 18 U.S.C. § 1030(a)(1–7). Perhaps most generically, for example, it criminalizes accessing a computer without or in excess of authorization in certain situations. *Id.* § 1030(a)(2). Another law, the Wiretap Act, 18 U.S.C. § 2511, proscribes any person from illegally intercepting certain communications or disclosing or using illegally intercepted material. Other criminal statutes commonly considered relevant to cyber security include the following sections of 18 U.S.C.: (1) Unlawful Access to Stored Communications, § 2701; (2) Identity Theft, § 1028(a)(7); (3) Aggravated Identity Theft, § 1028A; (4) Access Device Fraud, § 1029; (5) CAN-SPAM Act, § 1037; (6) Wire Fraud, § 1343; and (7) Communication Interference, § 1362. These statutes are enforced to different extents by various federal law enforcement agencies such as the Federal Bureau of Investigations, the Secret Service, and Immigrations and Customs and Enforcement.

Question for Discussion

1. Should there be an amendment to the Freedom of Information Act that would protect all critical infrastructure information, not just that information covered by 6 U.S.C. §§ 131–134? *See* Public Employees for Environmental Responsibility v. United States Section, International Boundary and Water Commission, U.S.-Mexico, 740 F3d 195 (D.C. 2014).

The Future: Effectively Integrating Various Federal Assets into DHS

The evolution of the United States emergency preparedness and response function has emphasized the "all hazards" approach. The events of September 11, 2001, underscored that emergency response to such devastating attacks was programmatically identical and was as effective as if the WTC and Pentagon had suffered from a catastrophic natural disaster. However, the strategic response to 9/11 and the creation of the DHS recognized that the United States had entered into a new age of warfare that could easily be waged in the United States unless there was a new and heightened vigilance. The integration of the many federal components within DHS is intended to accomplish just that—increased American vigilance to prevent terrorist attacks and to ensure the effective response to terrorist attacks, as well as natural and manmade disasters. As DHS enters its second decade of existence, the challenge in this era of emergency preparedness and response is to ensure the continued "all hazards" approach of preparedness and response, while efficiently integrating the various federal components that will prevent and prepare for terrorist threats and other disasters.

Applying the Law: A Hypothetical Biological Terrorism Attack

Using the information contained in this chapter, elsewhere in this book, and gathered from independent research, read the following scenario of a developing bioterrorism attack and answer the questions.[238]

Stage One: Intelligence Reports

CIA analysts are reviewing foreign intelligence reporting that a Russian scientist who worked on the Soviet biological weapons (BW) program has disappeared and may have taken with him stocks of plague bacteria in powder form and aerosol generators.

Independently, an FBI informant reports hearing a rumor that some fringe element of a domestic militia group, not further identified, has been working at a secret compound in a remote desert location somewhere in the United States to develop BW and is now claiming to have the capability to disseminate plague bacteria.

How likely is it that the folks analyzing the FBI info will have seen the FI reporting? How likely that the CIA analysts will see the FBI report? Are there legal barriers to sharing this information?

What can the FBI do at this point to follow up—what investigative techniques can be employed?

If the FBI seeks state and local (S/L) assistance in tracking down this rumor, what are the legal constraints on sharing information with S/L governments?

Suppose the FBI hears the terrorists are about to move the BW in preparation for deployment somewhere in the United States.

Can the FBI request the National Imagery and Mapping Agency (NIMA) to task overhead imagery satellites to target desert areas in the United States in an effort to quickly locate the compound, assuming other methods have failed? Would it make a difference if there were clearer indications of foreign involvement, e.g., stronger indications that the Russian scientist (1) had entered the United States, (2) was working with the U.S. terrorists at the compound?

Does it make any difference that NIMA is a combat support agency? Could DOD request imagery of an area within the United States if no military action was contemplated? What if the terrorists were linked to a foreign nation or an international terrorist group?

Suppose a patient is brought in to a hospital in Santa Fe exhibiting plague-like symptoms. The patient refuses to identify himself or provide any information that might indicate how or when the illness began.

---

238. This scenario borrows heavily from a program sponsored by the American Bar Association's Standing Committee on Law and National Security that was held at the ABA Annual Meeting in August 2002.

Are there legal constraints on the ability of the treating physician or the hospital to share this information, including patient-identifying information, with the CDC? With the FBI? The CIA? State and local law enforcement? If they learned the patient's identity, could they share that information?

If the FBI suspects that the patient may have been exposed to plague bacteria while working on the development of BW, are there legal avenues for attempting to compel the patient to provide information? If the patient provides health care workers with information relevant to an investigation, are there any legal constraints or authorities regarding the ability of the CDC or the FBI to compel these workers to share that information for law enforcement purposes?

Stage Two: The Attack

Some time later, the CDC starts getting additional reports of patients with plague-like symptoms, but these patients are in Minneapolis. Epidemiologists confirm that it is the plague bacteria and the number of patients is growing. It appears that many of the patients attended the same concert.

Does this bolster the FBI's legal authority to use more invasive investigative techniques? What techniques are still not available?

Stage Three: Response

As the number of patients rises, officials at the local, state, and federal levels attempt to assess the situation and determine whether it is appropriate to declare an emergency.

Who has the authority to make such a determination? Under what circumstances? What authority does it trigger?

Before an emergency is declared or any public statements are made, a reporter gets an anonymous tip that there are a growing number of patients at a local hospital who seem to have the plague.

Is there any authority to direct the content of or prohibit a broadcast or other reporting of this information? Any authority to compel media outlets to publish or broadcast government announcements?

As the truly sick and the truly worried flock to overwhelmed emergency rooms, lawyers in the government and in hospital administration offices are asked about the implications of rationing scarce antibiotics, such as denying antibiotics to the sick and dying.

What are the issues that the lawyers should consider?

Federal stockpiles are quickly depleted. Governors in other states are under pressure from their citizens not to allow health facilities to send their supplies of antibiotics to Minneapolis for fear they might be needed in the event of attacks in their own states. Minnesota appeals to the federal government to compel the transfer of antibiotics.

Is there such federal authority? What authority does a governor have to refuse such a federal directive?

Assuming this scenario is likely to last for many weeks and months, there may be time to produce additional vaccines.

Can the President order emergency production of vaccines? Waive liability for that production?

Under what conditions?

Riots occur at hospitals and other treatment distribution centers. The National Guard is mobilized to restore order.

What are the legal issues? Who, besides the governor, can mobilize the Guard? What can they do, what can't they do? What are the pros and cons of federalizing the Guard? Who can call on Guard forces from other states and under what circumstances? Can a neighboring governor prevent his Guard troops from being used in Minnesota?

Meanwhile, the FBI is leading the effort to identify the perpetrators and prevent any future attacks. New reports are coming in that the terrorists intend to strike other cities.

The need to investigate the attack in Minneapolis, as well as to anticipate possible attacks anywhere in the nation, has stretched the Bureau resources. Help from local authorities or even the National Guard is limited since they are already overwhelmed with the need to control public order. There are calls for bringing in military reserves to augment the law enforcement efforts.

What are the legal issues? How do they differ from the issues involved in deploying the National Guard?

Foreign intelligence reports now indicate that the terrorists did indeed have help from the missing Russian scientist.

Does this affect the legal analysis regarding the use of the armed forces within the United States? What if it was an international terrorist group who first put the domestic group in touch with the Russian scientist?

New intelligence indicates that terrorists are hiding somewhere in Cincinnati and are preparing to disperse biological agents in another attack. Investigative and intelligence efforts finally narrow the location to a sixteen-square-block area of apartment buildings. Time is critical.

Does the Bureau or local law enforcement have the legal authority to cordon off the area and conduct a sweep, searching every apartment and every person within the area? If law enforcement lacks the resources to undertake such a search and calls on the military to assist, what are the legal issues? Could it be characterized as a military operation rather than law enforcement? What are the constitutional issues raised by such a characterization?

If information comes in describing the approximate age, gender, and race of one of the terrorists, can law enforcement start rounding up and questioning all those in the general vicinity meeting that description? Would proposed laws banning profiling have any impact on this issue?

Meanwhile, public health authorities are trying to contain the spread of the disease.

Can federal quarantine authority be employed? Do unaffected states have the authority to close their borders to keep the disease from entering? Who can and should enforce any such restrictions and with what level of force?

Who, if anyone, has the authority to shut down airports, trains, and other modes of transportation?

Officials decide to make announcements encouraging people to voluntarily stay at home and avoid contact with potentially exposed individuals.

Do officials need any legal authorization to make such an announcement? What kind of legal authorities might facilitate efforts to support residents who chose that option? (e.g., adequate "good Samaritan" laws; MOUs or contracts with private sector delivery mechanisms that might be drawn upon to deliver food and medicine; legal authority to require "public service announcements").

Is there legal authority to compel people to be vaccinated or immunized in order to control the spread of the disease? Under what conditions? Who has the authority to decide?

Can public employees—health, law enforcement, transportation, etc., be compelled to work even if they might risk exposure to the disease? How about nurses and doctors at private medical facilities?

Final question:

What are the most significant legal issues, if any, that you think should be addressed to more adequately prepare for an effective, constitutional response to a mass casualty or mass disruption terrorist attack?

Selected Bibliography

Forging America's New Normalcy: Securing Our Homeland, Protecting Our Liberty, The Fifth Annual Report to the President and the Congress of the Advisory Panel to Assess Domestic Response Capabilities for Terrorism Involving Weapons of Mass Destruction. December 15, 2003.

Homeland Security: Department Organization and Management—Implementation Phase, CRS Report for Congress, Order Code RL3175, Updated February 4, 2004.

Joint Inquiry Into Intelligence Community Activities Before and After the Terrorist Attacks of September 11, 2001 (Washington, DC: U.S. Senate Select Committee on Intelligence and U.S. House Permanent Select Committee on Intelligence, December 2002).

Protecting America's Freedom in the Information Age: A Report of the Markle Foundation Task Force (New York: The Markle Foundation, October 2002).

Relyea, Harold C., *Homeland Security: Department Organization and Management—Legislative Phase,* CRS Report for Congress, Order Code RL31493.

Chapter 33

Domestic Terrorism

M.E. Bowman

In this chapter:
Defining and Fighting Domestic Terrorism
Policy Constraints
Investigatory Excess?
Post USA PATRIOT Act
Conclusion

Defining and Fighting Domestic Terrorism

The events of September 11, 2001, brought home to Americans a realization that terrorism is not something that happens "over there." That day will be a vestigial memory for generations to come, but for most Americans it likely will remain a perception of mindless violence that originated abroad. It was, by any calculation, a transnational event with origins in Islamic radicalism centered far from American shores. Still, we should not be comforted thinking it was an anomaly of the sort that could arise only from the twisted minds of foreigners. Americans need to be mindful that, before September 11, the most dramatic terrorist event affecting Americans was homegrown destruction. It was April 19, 1995, when the front of the Alfred P. Murrah federal building in Oklahoma City was violently transformed into flying bits of glass, concrete, and twisted metal. That heinous act of terrorism was not perpetrated by foreigners. Timothy McVeigh was an American trained in the military arts not by a foreign terrorist organization, but by the United States Army.

Americans now know that other nations have no monopoly on extremists or extremism and in an age of jihadism we may find homegrown threats of yet a different nature. We know that our open society makes entry into and movement within the United States relatively easy and permits the determined terrorist a degree of freedom greater than in most nations of the world. We also know that terrorism can easily emerge in the United States in a variety of ways. The dilemmas of terrorism are many, but one in particular is fundamental to the American way of life. This, of course, is the dilemma of effectively combating terrorism within the structure of a society predicated on individual liberties. Especially after September 11, we ponder the question of when a devoted student of Islam evolves into a mass murderer. Domestically, we have to consider when legal protest migrates to terrorism.

It is not difficult to investigate and prosecute acts of violence. Law enforcement officers know how to investigate crimes, and terrorist acts are punishable for what they are — murder, arson, and other similar common law crimes. What is difficult is preventing terrorism, and in the United States it is doubly difficult when the threat is domestic. The reason for the difficulty is deeply rooted in our society. Americans guard the right of assembly, speech, and free press perhaps more jealously than any other of our many freedoms. We permit and even protect dissent and unpopular speech. We tolerate assemblies of malcontents who might take delight in witnessing and even perpetrating violence directed at our national institutions or symbols of national strength. Precisely because we protect these freedoms, it is difficult to investigate organized malcontents without chilling their rights of assembly and speech. It is difficult because we choose to make it so. The problem this creates became clear on that April day, when Oklahoma City became the focus of attention in this nation and throughout the world.

Within minutes of the explosion, video of the twisted horror of the Murrah building proved to a horrified public what law enforcement agencies had known for years—there are radical elements of our own society quite prepared to be every bit as destructive as foreign groups. These groups and individuals stretch across the entire political spectrum, but their particular influence ebbs and flows with time. In mid-century we saw a dominance of left-wing terrorism.[1] By the 1990s, right-wing extremism became the more threatening.[2] During the past several years, special interest extremism, such as the Animal Liberation Front (ALF) or the Earth Liberation Front (ELF), has emerged as a serious terrorist threat.[3]

For several decades we viewed international terrorism and domestic terrorism as distinct and separable activities, but it has not always been so and due to radicalized citizens probably will not be so into the future. Indeed, domestic security in the early part of the twentieth century had clear roots in foreign intrigues. In the years following the First World War, the Bolshevik revolution prompted a widespread fear of subversion, which, in turn, generated a primary investigative emphasis for the fledgling FBI. At the direction of the President, FBI director J. Edgar Hoover set the tone for investigation.

> The Bureau desires to obtain from all possible sources information concerning subversive activities being conducted in the United States by Communists, Fascisti, and representatives or advocates of other organizations or groups advocating the overthrow or replacement of the Government of the United States by illegal methods.[4]

---

1. Left-wing groups generally profess revolutionary socialist doctrine. They believe more in change through revolution than through political process. By the 1980s, law enforcement had dismantled most of the infrastructure of these groups. That, coupled with the fall of Communism in Eastern Europe, deprived the larger movement of an ideological foundation and removed any substantial patronage. Some left-wing terrorism still exists, but these are relatively quiescent these days. Even left-wing Puerto Rican separatists have not committed any acts of terrorism since 1999. However, anarchists, operating individually and in groups, caused much of the damage protesting the World Trade Organization in Seattle in 1999.

2. Extremist right-wing groups are particularly difficult to deal with as they tend to engage in activity that is protected by guarantees of free speech and assembly. Law enforcement properly may become involved only when their volatile rhetoric prompts unlawful action.

3. The FBI estimates that the ALF/ELF have committed more than 600 criminal acts in the past five years, causing damage in excess of $43 million. Special Agent James Jarboe, The Threat of Eco-Terrorism, Testimony before the House Resources Comm., Subcomm. on Forests and Forest Health (Feb. 12, 2002) <http://www.fbi.gov/congress/congress02/jarboe021202.htm>.

4. J. Edgar Hoover communication to all FBI field offices, *cited in* 6 *Final Report of the Select Committee to Study Government Operations with Respect to Intelligence Activities*, S. Rep. No. 94-755, at 562 (1976) [hereinafter Church Committee Report].

Although this relates clearly to foreign intrigue, the plan of investigation drawn up by Hoover in 1938 included collection of intelligence information regarding major U.S. industries, labor strikes, the armed forces, educational institutions, Negroes, youth, and the media, among other subjects.[5] This liberal charter for investigation continued into the 1950s and was approved by then Attorney General Herbert Brownell who saw the increased use of the telephone in espionage activity and concluded that, "Surely this nation need not wait until it has been destroyed before learning who its traitors are and bringing them to justice." Much later, the open-ended nature of this charter to investigate was made clear when, in 1981, Brownell testified in the *Socialist Worker's Party* case, that in an intelligence investigation, the subject's citizenship is irrelevant."[6]

Through the years, this charter remained a cornerstone of domestic investigations. In the ebb and flow of history, foreign threats waned but domestic threats remained and there was no perceived need to change the manner of investigation. Measures devoted to thwarting foreign subversion were equally effective for domestic security—assuming there ever was a difference between those undefined terms at all. Where once foreign influence and domestic discontent had been intertwined, the foreign influences slowly faded, but the investigative needs and means remained static. To the policeman, however, this mattered little; the mission was unchanged, only the actors were different. As time passed, the same energies that had been devoted to defeating Communist and Fascist menaces were applied to purely domestic threats. It was a gradual, virtually unnoticed change, but one that soon would lead to considerable angst. Seemingly without conscious thought for the difference between investigating foreign influence and investigating U.S. citizens, law enforcement (and military and intelligence authorities as well) began to apply powers of investigation and information gathering to domestic activities.[7]

Today we have come to understand there is a substantial gulf between the legal regime regulating investigations of international and domestic threats, but it has not always been so and current events threaten to push them more closely together than might be comfortable. Although "subversive activities" was the catchphrase that prompted this slide into investigating Americans, the term was never defined, resulting in a very broad net being cast over activities that were deemed unpopular for whatever reason. As time passed, and the fear of foreign influence waned, it became clear that the real threat was one of violence precipitated for a particular cause. More often than not, the violence was the result of domestic radical political thought. Eventually the terminology would migrate to "domestic terrorism." Today that clarifying terminology helps us to make sense of the issues.

What makes investigation of domestic terrorism especially difficult is that we are a society that tolerates a great deal of unpopular speech. We cherish personal privacy, prefer government to work at a distance, and hold the privileges of the First Amendment preeminent among those rights. Accordingly, it is a fine line that must be trod when law enforcement officials must distinguish between unpopular speech and incitement to

---

5. *See generally* III Church Committee Report, *The Development of FBI Domestic Intelligence Investigations*, at 373–558.

6. American Enterprise Institute for Public Policy Research, "Government and Privacy: Should Greater Controls be Imposed on the Gathering and Utilization of Information About U.S. Citizens by Government Agencies?" at 42.

7. *See, e.g.*, William C. Banks & M.E. Bowman, *Executive Authority for National Security Surveillance*, 50 Am. U. L. Rev. 1, 19–31 (2000).

violence. Moreover, police powers are an awesome force, held in suspicion by Americans who want to be assured that those powers are used only for proper purposes. The perpetual tension between domestic dangers and public security is palpable in our society. The result is that we put restraints on law enforcement to ensure that they use their powers only in accordance with approved standards of conduct. We do this because the American culture distrusts secrecy and centralized authority and because we adhere to a social imperative that protects U.S. citizen privacy.

The difficulty is that the closer terrorism comes to home, the more urgently perceived the problem and the more demanding, and reasonable, the public expectation of protection. Concomitantly, the more immediate and personal the danger, the more compelling the need for a decisive response. Yet, urgency carries with it the possibility, some would claim the probability, of overreaction. Succinctly put, the more urgent the call for public protection, the greater the temptation to ignore or even tread on the freedoms that are the foundations of the American way of life.

We, as a people, have experienced this conundrum before. The post-war years comprised an era of uncertainty, including nuclear threat, which bred a sense of urgency. This gave rise to investigations and intelligence collection activities that would later be scrutinized, found wanting, and eventually regularized by a combination of executive, legislative, and judicial guidance but which, for several decades, were unbounded. Whereas for most of our history Congress had viewed intelligence collection activities with "Nelson's eye,"[8] beginning in the mid-1970s Congress set about to rein in the executive branch. In short order, Congress produced the War Powers Resolution,[9] Hughes-Ryan,[10] the Boland Amendment,[11] and intelligence oversight committees.[12] There are many reasons for the changed attitude of Congress, but the driving force undoubtedly was the 1975 creation of the Senate Select Committee to Study Governmental Operations with Respect to Intelligence Activities, better known as the Church Committee.[13]

---

8. Fighting ashore in Corsica, the future Lord Nelson lost an eye. In later years, when commanding a frigate in battle, he was signaled to break off his attack. When informed of the fact, Nelson put his telescope up to his blind eye and reported that he saw no order to withdraw. He went on to win a historical victory. Only in very recent history has Congress taken an active interest in intelligence matters. Senator Leverett Saltonstall explained congressional inactivity this way: "[I]t is not a question of reluctance on the part of CIA officials to speak to us ... it is a question of our reluctance ... to seek information ... on subjects which I personally, as a member of Congress and as a citizen, would rather not have...." IV Church Committee Report, at 53.

9. Pub. L. No. 93-148, 87 Stat. 555 (1973).

10. Pub. L. No. 93-559, 87 Stat. 1795. The Hughes-Ryan Amendment to the Foreign Assistance Act of 1961 was intended to prohibit the expenditure of funds for covert operations unless and until the President formally made a finding that the proposed operation is important to the national security of the United States.

11. There were actually a series of statutes sponsored by Representative Boland, all designed to limit assistance to anti-Sandinista forces in Nicaragua (known as the Contras). The most restrictive of these, commonly referred to as Boland II, prohibited, absent certain factual showings by the President or express congressional authorization, the use of any funds that would have the effect of supporting military or paramilitary operations in Nicaragua. Pub. L. No. 98-473 § 8066, 98 Stat. 1837, 1935–37 (1984).

12. The Intelligence Oversight Act of 1980 required that the Senate and House Permanent Select Committees on Intelligence be kept "fully and currently informed of all intelligence activities...." Pub. L. No 96-450 § 501(a)(1), 94 Stat. 1975, 1981 (1980).

13. S. Res. 21, 94th Cong., 121 CONG. REC. 1416 (1975). Other committees with similar purposes, notably the Pike and Abzug Committees, also contributed to the change, but the Church Committee stands alone both for far-reaching consequences and for revelations.

For fifteen months the Church Committee, spurred by allegations of wrongdoing within the national intelligence system, conducted the first major inquiry of the intelligence community. The committee, in six volumes of reports, found the intelligence community to be generally unguided, lacking in effective oversight, possessed of a casual disregard of societal values, and occasionally to have engaged in unlawful activity as well.

The committee recognized the need for secret government activities but proclaimed them also to be a threat to democratic society. They found, for example, that covert actions had been excessive, abundant, and lacking in democratic process. They found duplication, waste, and inertia. Most importantly, they alleged constitutional defects, an unbalanced executive process, and a dearth of needed legislation! The correction needed was unclear, but the Church Committee proposed legislation to regulate secrecy in government.[14]

At the same time, the public increasingly was becoming aware of, and demanded, a greater sense of freedom based on individual rights.[15] It was only natural that with a new awareness of personal freedom and an eroding fear of war, the public began to question government intrusion into private life and to seek an openness in government that had not previously been a felt need. The result was a series of efforts by both the executive and legislative branches, supplemented by the occasional judicial pronouncement, to enhance personal liberties and freedoms. The brake was applied to executive branch excesses, primarily in foreign affairs, but also in some domestic situations.[16] One result was that the future investigative procedures of the Federal Bureau of Investigation (FBI) would be structured and carefully managed.

Although most of the impetus for control stemmed from legislative or executive initiatives, perhaps the most poignant illustration of the fundamental issue arose from a judicial decision. The year was 1972 and three individuals had been charged with conspiracy to destroy government property. One was also charged with the dynamite bombing of a CIA office in Ann Arbor, Michigan. The defendants sought information on whether they had been subject to electronic surveillance, hoping to taint the evidence with government misconduct.

The Attorney General conceded warrantless surveillance but defended the action on national security grounds, basing his argument on a string of cases that approved presidential power for warrantless surveillance in national security cases. The district court was un-

---

14. The Church Committee proposed a charter for intelligence agencies, regulation of covert action, and a statutory ban on assassination. Recognizing the inflexibility of legislation, President Ford quickly sought to displace those proposals by issuing Exec. Order No. 11,905, 41 Fed. Reg. 7707 (1976), which imposed process and regulation on intelligence community activities. The Executive Order addressed the primary issues identified by the Committee so most legislative proposals withered at that point. The Ford Executive Order was a template for future executive orders that would regulate the intelligence community. President Carter replaced Exec. Order No. 11,905 with Exec. Order No. 12,036, 43 Fed. Reg. 3678 (1978), and President Reagan replaced that Executive Order with the still current Exec. Order No. 12,333, 46 Fed. Reg. 59,941 (1981).

15. *E.g.*, The Freedom of Information Act, Pub. L. No. 89-554, 80 Stat. 383 (1966), and the Privacy Act, Pub. L. No. 93-579, 88 Stat. 1896 (1974).

16. Technology made it possible to insert names into electronic databases in order to search records, intercept telephone calls, and collate information. The ease with which "watch lists" were created for foreign intelligence purposes translated into domestic activities as well. As Attorney General, Robert Kennedy employed the watch lists against major crime figures to capture their communications. A spin-off called Operation Minaret specifically targeted both cables and telephone calls for information about possible foreign influence on civil disturbances in the United States related to the Vietnam conflict.

persuaded,[17] as was the Sixth Circuit.[18] Still, guidance was lacking even after extensive judicial scrutiny. Finally, in a 1972 Supreme Court decision, Justice Powell set a standard that would hold for the future. In essence, Powell left untouched the presumed executive power to order warrantless surveillance of would-be subversives,[19] but found, as well, a governmental duty to balance "the duty of Government to protect the domestic security, and the potential danger posed by unreasonable surveillance to individual privacy and free expression."[20] Expressing no opinion as to this issue with respect to foreign powers or their agents,[21] Powell made it clear that this was a case of *domestic* security. For domestic situations, protection of constitutional values justified any inconvenience to the government in having to secure a judicial warrant.[22]

Thus the stage was set for what has become a distinction (not always clear, but a distinction nonetheless) between domestic and international terrorism. After the apparent clarity of this opinion, both legislative and executive authorities assumed they had the vision and direction that had been lacking. Because terrorist acts are also criminal acts, and because the FBI has nationwide jurisdiction and investigative authority over nearly all federal crime, that is the law enforcement entity normally responsible for investigating acts of terrorism. To accommodate both investigative and social needs, there soon was created a process for management of FBI investigative techniques that recognized that the American culture will not permit the possibility of terrorism to detract from a jealous guardianship of our personal liberties. It was the unique nature of terrorism, principally domestic terrorism, that generated the fundamental need for the United States to erect control mechanisms for investigative countermeasures to ensure that we will not surrender basic freedoms or endanger democratic principles when investigating terrorist acts and plans.

The beginning point was to define domestic terrorism. The FBI is the agency charged with protecting the American public from terrorism, both foreign and domestic, that occurs on or threatens American soil, so it is natural that the regulatory process was directed at the FBI. To distinguish domestic terrorism from other crime and from international terrorism, the FBI adopted the following definition:

> The unlawful use, or threatened use, of violence by a group or individual based and operating entirely within the United States (or its territories) without foreign direction, committed against persons or property to intimidate or coerce a government, the civilian population, or any segment thereof, in furtherance of political or social objectives.

---

17. "[I]n wholly domestic situations there is no national security exemption from the warrant requirement of the Fourth Amendment." United States v. Sinclair, 321 F. Supp. 1074, 1080 (E.D. Mich. 1971), quoting United States v. Smith, 321 F. Supp. 424, 429 (C.D. Cal. 1971).

18. United States v. Keith, 444 F.2d 652, 669 (6th Cir. 1971). See Chapter 26 for a fuller discussion of the ramifications and importance of Powell's decision in the *Keith* case.

19. United States v. Keith, 407 U.S. 297, 310 (1972) ("We begin the inquiry by noting that the President of the United States has the fundamental duty, under Art. II, § 1, of the Constitution, to 'preserve, protect and defend the Constitution of the United States.' Implicit in that duty is the power to protect our Government against those who would subvert or overthrow it by unlawful means. In the discharge of this duty, the President—through the Attorney General—may find it necessary to employ electronic surveillance to obtain intelligence information on the plans of those who plot unlawful acts against the Government.").

20. *Id.* at 314–315.

21. *Id.* at 321–22.

22. *Id.* at 321.

Because the FBI is also an agency with immense resources and broad police powers, it was felt necessary to ensure that procedures were adopted to guide the manner in which investigations would be conducted. The Attorney General promulgated two sets of guidelines to regulate all FBI investigations. These are (1) the Attorney General's Guidelines on General Crimes, Racketeering Enterprise and Domestic Security/Terrorism Investigations and (2) the Attorney General's Guidelines for FBI Foreign Intelligence Collection and Foreign Counterintelligence Investigations.[23]

It is the first listed set of guidelines that apply to domestic terrorism, since by definition the terrorist activity addressed has no foreign nexus. These procedures stem from an initial promulgation by Attorney General Edward Levi on April 5, 1976. These guidelines were specifically intended to ensure that Americans would not be reluctant to exercise First Amendment rights and that government officials would not be tempted to apply investigative powers to protected activities.[24] Specifically, no investigations may commence based solely on unpopular speech.[25] Moreover, investigations may not be used to disrupt organizations merely engaged in protected First Amendment activity, nor to discredit individuals.

As explained by Attorney General Levi, the guidelines were intended to guide the FBI when conducting domestic security investigations where the activities under investigation "involve or will involve the use of force or violence and the violation of criminal law."[26] He testified at the time that "the main thing in my opinion is that the purpose of the investigation must be the detection of unlawful conduct and not merely the monitoring of disfavored or troublesome activities and surely not of unpopular views."[27]

It is not enough, however, to promulgate guidance. To be effective there must be a means of oversight. Therefore Attorney General Levi also required "compendious reporting" to the Department of Justice by the FBI and established standards for investigative techniques.[28]

In large measure, those guidelines have withstood the test of time. The guidelines were reissued without amendment in 1980 by Attorney General Benjamin Civiletti. However, shortly thereafter it became clear that time and circumstance had rendered some of the guidelines less than optimal. By 1983, the threats of domestic violence against which the Levi Guidelines had been directed were evolving along with technology in general. On

---

23. Attorney General Guidelines are revised from time to time to reflect changes in technology, threats, or legal standards.

24. "In the absence of any information indicating planned violence by a group or enterprise, mere speculation that force or violence might occur during the course of an otherwise peaceable demonstration is not sufficient grounds for initiation of an investigation under this section." § III.B.1.c.

25. For example, "If they ever make me carry a rifle the first man I want to get in my sights is L.B.J." Watts v. United States, 394 U.S. 705, 706 (1969).

26. *FBI Oversight, Hearings Before the Subcomm. on Civil and Constitutional Rights of the House Comm. on the Judiciary*, 94th Cong., 1st & 2d Sess., ser. no. 2, pt. 3, at 258.

27. *Id.*

28. *Id.* For example, to initiate a "full field" domestic security or terrorism investigation, the guidelines require that

> the facts or circumstances reasonably indicate that two or more persons are engaged in an enterprise for the purpose of furthering political or social goals wholly or in part through activities that involve force or violence and a violation of the criminal laws of the United States.... In determining whether an investigation should be conducted, the FBI shall consider all of the circumstances, including: (i) the magnitude of the threatened harm; (ii) the likelihood it will occur; (iii) the immediacy of the threat; and (iv) the danger to privacy and free expression posed by an investigation.

Guidelines, § III.B.1.a.

March 7, 1983, Attorney General William French Smith issued a press release explaining a revision to these guidelines, stating: "The new guidelines are needed to ensure protection of the public from the greater sophistication and changing nature of domestic groups that are prone to violence."[29]

The amendments to the guidelines were specifically intended to make more effective investigative techniques available to the FBI in domestic terrorism cases.[30] The most important change was subtle, but dramatic in effect. The Levi/Civiletti Guidelines had established a predicate investigative standard of specific and articulable facts in order to launch a full investigation.[31] The new version revised the threshold for a full investigation to a reasonable indication.[32] It was also made clear that the authority to conduct these investigations is separate from and "in addition to the general crimes investigative authority...."[33]

To give some balance to the changes, and consistent with public statements of prior Attorneys General, Attorney General Smith personally emphasized that investigations would not be based solely on activities protected by the First Amendment or the lawful exercise of other constitutional rights.[34] One surety built into the system is to require FBI Headquarters approval for any proposal to use an informant to infiltrate a group if there is a possibility that the informant could influence the exercise of First Amendment rights.[35]

Not unexpectedly, the new formulation was quickly tested. In 1984, a consent decree stemming from *Alliance to End Repression v. City of Chicago*[36] had prohibited the FBI from conducting investigations in Chicago solely on the basis of activities protected by the First Amendment. Plaintiffs compared the standards for opening a domestic security investigation[37] with the consent decree and argued that the guidelines should be ineffective in the geographical area of the consent decree as the latter, they claimed, was more stringent.

---

29. Press Release, Department of Justice (Apr. 18, 1983), *reprinted in Attorney General's Guidelines for Domestic Security Investigations (Smith Guidelines), Hearings before the Subcomm. on Security and Terrorism of the House Comm. on the Judiciary*, 98th Cong. 1st Sess. app. A, at 47 (1983).

30. The effect of the Levi Guidelines was dramatic. In March 1978, the FBI conducted 4,868 domestic security investigations per month. By December 1981, the average was reduced to only twenty-six per month. Geoffrey R. Stone, *The Reagan Administration, the First Amendment and FBI Domestic Security Investigations, in* FREEDOM AT RISK: SECRECY, CENSORSHIP, AND REPRESSION IN THE 1980s 272, 276–77 (Richard O. Curry ed., 1988). By 1982, threats of terrorism in the United States prompted changes to the guidelines. The most specific change was to eliminate the specific and articulable facts standard.

31. A preliminary inquiry can be opened on a lower standard, but the scope of a "preliminary" is quite limited. An additional safeguard is built into the full investigation standards, which steers away from using a single actor as a predicate for a lowered threshold for investigation. It requires that "two or more persons are engaged in an enterprise for the purpose of furthering political or social goals wholly or in part through activities that involve force or violence and a violation of the criminal laws of the United States." *Guidelines*, § III.B.1.a.

32. *Id.*

33. *Id.* at § III.B.1.b.

34. By example, "Attorney General Smith said, when persons advocate crime, particularly violent crime—such as blowing up a building or killing a public official—those persons cannot expect law enforcement agencies to refrain from making reasonable further inquiry to ensure protection of the public." Press Release, Department of Justice (Apr. 18, 1983), *supra* note 29, at 47. Assistant Attorney General Jensen further qualified the position when he stated in 1983 that "[i]f it is apparent from the circumstances or context in which the statements are made, that there is no prospect of harm, then further inquiry would not be authorized." *Hearings before the Subcomm. on Security and Terrorism of the Senate Comm. on the Judiciary*, 98th Cong., 1st Sess. 10 (1983).

35. *Guidelines*, § IV.B.3.

36. 742 F.2d 1007 (7th Cir. 1984).

37. "Reasonable indication" for a full investigation and "possibility" for a preliminary.

The Seventh Circuit found no inconsistency between the decree and either the Levi or the Smith Guidelines. A sympathetic Court also noted that the FBI "need not wait till the bombs begin to go off, or even till the bomb factory is found."[38] It "has a right, indeed a duty, to keep itself informed with respect to the possible commission of crimes; it is not obliged to wear blinders until it may be too late for prevention."[39]

Policy Constraints

Implementation of law and regulation always has a heavy underlay of policy and that is especially poignant when addressing the power of law enforcement. Our culture demands that we be assured that the powers of law enforcement, and the label of domestic terrorism, are appropriately focused. Accordingly, to obtain authority for a full domestic terrorism investigation, the Attorney General Guidelines provided that there must be a "reasonable indication" that two or more persons are engaged in an enterprise[40] for the purpose of furthering political or social goals wholly or in part through activities that involve force or violence and a violation of the criminal laws of the United States.[41]

This standard preserved a test of logic. It is somewhat restrictive, but it did not leave the FBI without tools. If the reasonable indication standard is not met, but there is an indication of possible criminal activity, the guidelines recognized that "responsible handling requires some further scrutiny."[42] In that circumstance, an investigation with lesser investigative authority, a preliminary inquiry, may be appropriate. A preliminary inquiry permits limited, nonintrusive checking into initial leads based on the possibility of criminal activity.[43] Additionally, the FBI may engage in a nonintrusive limited checking out of initial leads prior to opening an investigation. However, if it is apparent from the circumstance or context in which the information comes to the FBI that there is no real prospect of harm, then not even a preliminary inquiry would be appropriate.[44]

The most critical element in deciding whether an investigation should be opened is common sense. A supervisory special agent of the FBI must consider the magnitude of the threat, the likelihood that it will occur and the immediacy of the jeopardy. The agent must also consider whether privacy will be denied or free expression inhibited by FBI investigation.[45] For example, demonstrations and protests are ubiquitous in our society, but unless there is reasonable indication that force or violence might occur, initiation of an investigation is not appropriate.[46]

The guidelines also regulate the techniques of investigation, because even if the threshold standards for investigation are met, the manner in which an investigation is conducted

---

38. *Id.* at 1015.

39. *Id.*, citing Socialist Workers Party v. Attorney General, 510 F.2d 253, 256 (2d Cir. 1974) (per curiam).

40. If the focus is not on an enterprise, but rather on an individual, the basis for investigation rests with the general crimes portion of the guidelines.

41. *See supra* note 16.

42. *Guidelines*, § II.B.(1).

43. *Id.* Examples of nonintrusive techniques are examination of FBI indices and files, examination of public records and public sources of information, interview of the complainant, informant, or others knowledgeable of the subject, and physical or photographic surveillance.

44. *Id.* § I.

45. *Id.* § III.B.1.a.

46. *Id.* § III.B.1.c.

is vital to maintain the confidence of a public that jealously guards its privacy. All techniques of investigation must meet constitutional, statutory, regulatory, and policy standards.[47] In addition, the policy to protect individual liberties continues after an investigation has been opened. This is especially important because investigations normally are opened on thresholds of suspicion, not on standards of evidentiary proof. In consequence, it is important to conduct investigations in a manner that does not intrude unacceptably on personal liberties. Additionally, a burden is placed on investigators to investigate promptly; preliminary investigations are only authorized for an initial period of one year. When that sunset provision is tripped, the investigation may be continued only on the authority of senior officials who have reviewed the case and determined that the investigation continues to be warranted.[48] In no case may the investigation be renewed if it does not continue to meet a threshold standard for causation.[49]

Similarly, recognizing the inevitable and legitimate concerns that gathering information on U.S. persons generates, if public source information is collected, it may be retained only after annotating the file with the permissible investigative purpose for which the information was collected. While this is designed to conform to Privacy Act limitations,[50] it is nevertheless an internal safeguard as well, generated by the Department of Justice and the Bureau.

Investigatory Excess?

In recent years, the FBI has been the subject of criticism for a number of matters. Some criticism was probably warranted, for some matters, while other criticisms probably were not. No one should ever expect that investigatory mistakes will not occur, but neither should they be expected. Generally, Americans understand that mistakes make larger headlines than do successes. At any point in time, the Bureau has open investigations, both criminal and national security cases, that easily can reach 60,000. It takes little research to understand that the number of criticisms of FBI investigations, whether warranted or not, are minuscule considering the caseload and the number of agents working the cases.[51] More importantly, however, it is beyond cavil that the Department of Justice has taken steps to ensure the protection of individual liberties when investigating potential crimes. But it is also clear that the Department and the FBI understand that by being overcautious it is all too easy to miss fleeting opportunities to detect and prevent terrorist incidents. Public security lies on both sides of that extremely fine line.

Internally, the FBI takes considerable pride in the unarguable fact that competent investigations have prevented harm to the public on numerous occasions. Many such events remain unpublished, but one specific example was the successful infiltration of the group

---

47. *Id.* § IV. These include, for example, Fourth Amendment and statutory warrant requirements for electronic surveillance and Attorney General Guideline policy compliance for a variety of investigative techniques with the potential to be personally intrusive.

48. *Id.* § III.B.4.b. & c.

49. *Id.* § III.B.4.d.

50. According to 5 U.S.C. § 552a (e) (2003), each agency that maintains a system of records shall— (7) maintain no record describing how any individual exercises rights guaranteed by the First Amendment unless expressly authorized by statute or by the individual about whom the record is maintained or unless pertinent to and within the scope of an authorized law enforcement activity....

51. In 2002, there were approximately 11,000 FBI special agents spread across Headquarters, 56 field offices, 43 embassies, and more than 400 satellite offices called Resident Agencies.

planning to bomb the tunnels into New York City, the United Nations, and 26 Federal Plaza, which led to the successful prosecution of ten terrorists and the prevention of their deadly plans.

More often, the foiling of terrorist plots is accomplished quietly, with the FBI's role concealed from the public. Nevertheless, it is a regular occurrence for some Bureau offices to take successful preventive action against potential violence. These quiet successes do not make headlines and often must, for security reasons, pass entirely unheralded. These are the successes against which the notably few excesses must be balanced.

It stands to reason, of course, that after September 11 it would seem to be a singularly inopportune time to be a terrorist. After all, worldwide revulsion over those attacks led the Irish Republican Army to announce that it would dismantle its weapons arsenal. The ever-strident Basque separatists made peace overtures. Islamic clerics the world over condemned terrorism. Despite the visceral reaction against terrorism, American fringe elements, such as the Environmental Liberation Front remained active. Within five days, ELF ripped up oil-exploration survey markers. Barely a month later ELF firebombed a Bureau of Land Management wild horse corral. Three weeks later police discovered ELF-style firebombs set next to forestry buildings at Michigan Technical University. On January 26, 2002, ELF claimed responsibility for fire damage to a plant-genetics research center under construction at the University of Minnesota. Clearly domestic terrorism has not become quiescent despite public abhorrence of terrorism in general.

Finally, it is important to focus on two facets of the terrorism problem that are under constant scrutiny—authority and resources. With respect to authority, the basic needs of the Bureau generally have been met, although technological advances always means there will be additional authorities that would be useful just to maintain a status quo in investigative ability. It was precisely that sort of consideration that led to the most recent alterations of investigative authority, accompanied by augmented resources.

On October 26, 2001, the President signed into law the USA PATRIOT Act.[52] That act was a sweeping acknowledgment of the fact that law must maintain pace with the threats. With regard to domestic terrorism, the venerable definition used by the FBI (and adopted by many others) was modified significantly. Domestic terrorism now means activities that

   (A) involve violent acts or acts dangerous to human life that are a violation of the criminal laws of the United States or of any State ... ;

   (B) appear to be intended—

      (i)   to intimidate or coerce a civilian population;

      (ii) to influence the policy of a government by intimidation or coercion; or

      (iii) to affect the conduct of a government by mass destruction, assassination, or kidnapping; and

   (C) occur primarily outside the territorial jurisdiction of the United States.[53]

Gone is the requirement that the targeted activity operate "entirely within the United States (or its territories) without foreign direction." Nor is it necessary to find that there is a social or political objective for the terrorist. The focus now is strictly on conduct. Additionally, the USA PATRIOT Act criminalized attacks and other acts of violence against

---

52. Uniting and Strengthening America Act by Providing Appropriate Tools Required to Intercept and Obstruct Terrorism Act of 2001, Pub. L. No. 107-56, 115 Stat. 272.

53. 18 U.S.C.A. § 2331(1) (West 2000 & Supp. 2003).

mass transportation systems,[54] made terrorism a predicate offense for the Racketeer Influenced and Corrupt Organizations statute (RICO),[55] and revised the definitions for Acts of Terrorism[56] to take into account the more recently recognized threats to transportation systems, navigation facilities, pipelines, and other items of critical infrastructure. Similar to espionage and other laws, the USA PATRIOT Act also criminalized harboring or concealing terrorists.[57]

Post-USA PATRIOT Act

In the intervening years, the domestic terrorist threat has evolved and has developed an international flavor, all the while maintaining a domestic quality that requires a new emphasis on prevention. Prior to 9/11 the domestic threat was focused on domestic support for international terrorism, not on terrorism in the homeland. Probably most poignant in those years was the support to HAMAS,[58] characterized in particular by the Holy Land Foundation for Relief and Development (HLFRD).[59] This was generally an arena for fiscal support to HAMAS and not an enterprise for violence in the United States. The counterterrorism focus, prior to 9/11 was general on preventing the support within the United States for terrorism abroad.

Interestingly, under then-Attorney General Janet Reno a domestic terrorism panel was formed to consist of national security lawyers, representatives from the FBI and other agencies. It was scheduled to meet September 11, 2001 but was preempted by the events of that day. It never did meet and the group was disbanded as attention turned to international terrorism. In June of 2014 it was announced that the group would be reconstituted.[60] The reason, of course, is repeated domestic terrorism attempts and ongoing threats.

---

54. 18 U.S.C.A. § 1993 (West Supp. 2003).
55. 18 U.S.C.A. § 1961(1)(G) (West Supp. 2003).
56. 18 U.S.C.A. § 2332b (West 2000 & Supp. 2003).
57. 18 U.S.C.A. § 2339 (West Supp. 2003).
58. "Hamas is a terrorist organization that espouses an extremist Islamic fundamentalist ideology. Hamas was founded in 1987 in the Gaza Strip and is dedicated to the establishment of an Islamic Palestinian State that encompasses Israel, the West Bank and Gaza. Hamas is a militant Palestinian offshoot of the Muslim Brotherhood which was founded in 1928 to replace secular rulers with an Islamic society." Statement of John Pistole, then Deputy Director, FBI Counterterrorism Division, before the House Committee on Financial Service Subcommittee on Oversight and Investigations, September 24, 2003.
59. The Holy Land Foundation was the largest Islamic charity in the United States. Headquartered in Richardson, Texas it was originally known as Occupied Land Fund. In December 2001, the U.S. government designated HLF a terrorist organization, seized its assets, and closed the charity. In 2004, a federal grand jury in Dallas, Texas charged HLF and five former officers and employees with providing material support to Hamas and related offenses. The prosecution did not allege that HLF funded violence; rather, its theory was that HLF distributed charity through local zakat (charity) committees located in the West Bank; that Hamas controlled those zakat committees; and that by distributing charity through Hamas-controlled committees, HLF helped Hamas win the "hearts and minds" of the Palestinian people. The first trial, in 2007, ended in the partial acquittal of one defendant and a hung jury on all other charges. The jury did not return any guilty verdicts. At a retrial in 2008, the jury found all defendants guilty on all counts. The 2008 trial of the charity leaders was dubbed the "largest terrorism financing prosecution in American history." In 2009, the founders of the organization were given sentences of between 15 and 65 years in prison for "funneling $12 million to Hamas."
60. *US to revive panel on domestic terror threats*, Associated Press, June 3, 2014.

The FBI, the primary counterterror agency, defines domestic terrorism as terrorism involving groups based in and operating entirely with, the United States and its territories, without foreign direction. This definition works well for ideological streams such as white supremacy, skinheads, the radical left and the sovereign citizen.[61] One wonders, however, how well it works for the threats we see emerging as this is being written in 2014. The Islamic State of Syria and Iraq (ISIS or ISIL) has successfully recruited hundreds, perhaps thousands of radicalized jihadists from western nations. Some we know to have died in the fighting but there are many who are alive and entitled to return to their native nations—as of this writing the United States estimates some 100 to have left the United States to fight with ISIS. Some of those radicalized westerners could be directed to return to their homelands to carry out terrorist activities, but it is equally possible that they might return to carry out self-directed terrorist acts. In either case they are native citizens.[62]

Homegrown terrorism has attracted significant attention, particularly following the 2004 Madrid and the 2005 London bombings. Domestically we have had numerous poignant examples such as the shoe and underwear bombers.[63] Nevertheless, we may, in the future, face a different domestic threat. In recent years we have witnessed individuals attracted to jihadism arising from ethnic communities within the United States. We can only wait to see what the results may be domestically. Returning citizen jihadists will represent a homegrown threat more closely akin to the international terrorist than to what we have traditionally considered domestic terrorism. It may be that future circumstances will require that we re-visit the definitions of terrorism. One has to question whether we may need to construct separate definitions for homegrown terrorism and domestic terrorism.

Finally, there will always be question marks when a violent act occurs—*i.e., is it really terrorism?* One example occurred in 2005. On October 1, a bomb went off less than 200 yards from the University of Oklahoma Memorial Stadium where more than 80,000 spectators were watching a football game. Joel Henry Hinrichs III died when his back pack exploded. Forensic examination showed that the explosive TATP (the same explosive used by Richard Reid, the shoe bomber). There was little information to go on and terrorism was suspected, but in the final analysis it was concluded he was a loner, it could not be determined that he intended to enter the stadium and since there was no shrapnel in the backpack an accidental discharge was determined to be likely.

Conclusion

The threat of terrorism will be with us for the foreseeable future, both domestically and internationally. While the number of terrorist incidents occurring within the United States actually has declined in recent years, the magnitude and potential lethality we see

---

61. *See, e.g.,* Stewart, Scott, *Domestic Terrorism: A Persistent Threat in the United States*, Security Weekly, August 23, 2012.

62. *See,* Kaplan, Rebecca, *Mike Rogers: US in greater danger now than before 9/11*, The Nation, August 17, 2014.

63. American Airlines Flight 63, carrying 197 people from Paris to Miami was diverted to Boston on December 22, 2001, after passengers and crew saw British citizen Richard Reid trying to light a fuse and subdued him by tying him to his seat. A doctor on board administered a tranquilizer. Umar Farouk Abdulmutallab, tried to bring down Northwest flight 253 over Detroit on Christmas Day 2009 with an underwear bomb. At sentencing he said he was "proud to kill in the name of God."

arising from terrorist acts, both planned and executed, have reached new and frightening proportions. Where once a pipe bomb was left on the street outside a bank, now trucks laden with explosives are driven up to, or under, office buildings where hundreds or thousands of people work. Bio-terrorism is no longer a theoretical danger. Cyber tools threaten both national security information and the critical infrastructure of the United States.[64] Additionally, the destructive nature of terrorism today is more indiscriminate, focused deliberately on mass casualties. We can and must take steps to harden some of the most obvious targets, but there are costs to doing so in a society that prides itself on openness, and there are always alternative potential targets. As we make more obvious targets secure, terrorists will simply seek out more vulnerable targets.[65]

The threats continue to evolve. Where once we feared the Bolsheviks, we evolved to fear ALF and ELF and today are concerned with radical jihadists, both foreign and domestic. Although there are many American malcontents, and groups of malcontents, who may be prepared to do violence and cause harm, most tend to have similar political views that reject big government and are intolerant of nonwhite races and foreign involvement in the United States.

The more traditional groups from whom we feared terrorist activity can mostly be grouped in large, loosely affiliated but recognizable movements. *Christian Identity* (CI) is one such large grouping. CI is comprised of loosely affiliated, often divisive assemblies who share a belief that only Aryans are the children of God and all others are of a different species. CI has grown up through the years with a paramilitary heritage that accepts violence and its members have been responsible for terror campaigns directed at the U.S. federal government and perceived enemies of the white race. They have carried out assassinations, bank robberies, and acts of sabotage directed at the federal government and, in particular, at Jews. As a whole, CI has included groups known as the Aryan Nations, The Covenant, The Sword and the Arm of the Lord, and The Order.

Another similarly amorphous grouping is the *Phineas Priesthood* (PP). More a philosophy than an organization, they are so disunited that it is difficult to ascertain whether the multitudinous criminal acts carried out by PP members are personal or organizational in origin. PP members have carried out numerous bank robberies, murdered abortion doctors, and detonated pipe bombs at abortion clinics and media outlets.

Other domestic terrorist philosophies include:

- *Odinism*, a racist and mutated form of Norse paganism with a neo-Nazi bent;
- *Leaderless Resistance*, a highly decentralized grouping of individuals (to make it hard for law enforcement to infiltrate), which has an actual purpose of conducting terrorist operations and criminal activity;
- *Common Law*, which is comprised of individuals disaffected with a judicial process they believe is corrupt. Common law provides ideological justification to avoid federal and state laws and they routinely engage in pseudo-legalistic activity, such as filing bogus liens and creating fake legal documents; and
- The rise of the *patriot* and *militia* movements represents, in some cases, an even more grass-roots level incarnation of antigovernment, racist, and conspiracy-minded philosophies. These, with their penchant for paramilitary training, weapons

---

64. Dale Watson, Executive Assistant Director, Federal Bureau of Investigation, Counterterrorism and Counterintelligence, The Terrorist Threat Confronting the United States, Statement before the Senate Select Comm. on Intelligence (Feb. 6, 2002) <http://www.fbi.gov/ congress/congress02/ watson020602.htm>.

65. *Id.*

stockpiling, and acceptance only of local authority, are an especially difficult issue for law enforcement officers.[66]

Domestically, prior to 9/11 these made up the bulk of terrorist concerns and still represent the largest numbers for threat. Law enforcement—federal, state, and local—has the unenviable task of dealing with these fellow citizens. The same law enforcement officers who protect our homes and our persons must not only make the fight against terrorism a high priority, but also must make prevention the first priority. In both missions—prevention and law enforcement—investigations should be conducted aggressively, but with scrupulous attention to the expectations of the public they serve. To give that reassurance, and to structure aggressive investigations, the Attorney General Guidelines that supplement the laws and the Constitution of the United States now serve, for the FBI, to permit the aggressiveness needed, but at the same time to temper law enforcement techniques with a respect for the privacy and rights of Americans and visitors to the United States.

The problem today has been greatly exacerbated by the addition of jihadist-type terrorism. Twenty years ago the domestic terrorism problem was fairly well manageable. Today however jihadism has stretched resources thin. First up in the problem area is the necessity of divided attention. No matter that the terrorism threat is enhanced, the other problems assigned to intelligence and law enforcements agencies simply will not go away. Secondly, all governmental resources are needed and relevant to a prevention regime but interconnectivity remains a major problem. Attempts to connect radically different computer systems have so far failed due both to technical issues and substance issues. The means by which the CIA gathers information, and from whom are incredibly sensitive and both the privacy issues and short term sensitivity of FBI investigations often must be protected by law. Additionally, training is largely insufficient across the board, primarily because of the "divided attention" issue. Terrorism is simply one among many threats. We can hope that traditional domestic terrorism will remain the norm, but the events unfolding as this is being written do not augur well for the future. We may well have to take a second look at the neat differentiation between domestic and foreign threats that were so well defined for us in the *Keith* case.

---

66. In September of 1999, a right-wing militia group, the Militia of Montana, posted the following message on their Web site: "I'd like to round up (U.S. Attorney General) Janet Reno, (FBI Director) Louis Freeh (and others)—shoot a few of them and confine them to a 'compound' for seven weeks." Cable News Network, *Militia groups quick to use Waco tapes for own ends* (Sept. 3, 1999) <http://www.cnn.com/US/9909/03/militia.reax>.

Chapter 34

Environmental Law and National Security

John C. Cruden

In this chapter:
Introduction
Part 1: Environmental Policy
Part 2: Pollution Abatement and Wildlife Statutes
Part 3: Specific National Security Issues

Introduction

In the broad sense, all environmental issues are of national security concern. The United States has a vital stake in environmental matters ranging from the long-term impacts of acid rain to the unfettered use of pesticides. War is a special case, however, and fully worth avoiding simply to protect the nation from its environmental effects. During the 1991 Gulf War, for example, Iraqi forces set fire to more than 600 Kuwaiti oil wells, creating toxic smoke that choked the atmosphere for miles. Saddam Hussein's forces released four million barrels of crude oil into the Persian Gulf, killing more than 25,000 birds. Spills of sixty million barrels of oil in the desert formed dangerous oil lakes, which percolated into aquifers. Post-conflict environmental assessments conducted by the United Nations have identified six principal pathways for environmental damage: (1) "Toxic hazards from the bombardment of industrial sites and urban infrastructure," (2) "A legacy of weapons, landmines, unexploded ordnance, and depleted uranium munitions," (3) "Human displacement," (4) "The use of extractive industries to fund conflict," (5) "The loss of water supply, sanitation, and waste disposal infrastructure," and (6) "Direct targeting of natural resources, particularly as part of scorched-earth military tactics."[1]

Why is it, then, that environmental concerns are often thought to be a roadblock to national security, an obstacle in the path of military defense planning? Defense considerations demand that adequate people, resources, and munitions be allocated to deter others from taking adverse actions against us or our vital interests. For our defense

---

1. *Assessing and Restoring Natural Resources in Post-Conflict Peacebuilding*, Edited by David Jensen and Steve Lonergan, at page 414 (EarthScan, 2012, Copyright by Environmental Law Institute and United Nations Environment Programme).

This chapter was written in Mr. Cruden's individual capacity and does not reflect the views of the federal government.

to be fully credible the forces must not only exist, they must practice and be tested. Soldiers must come together on staged battlefields and rehearse their responsibilities; scientists must test their new weaponry; and forces must be stationed where they can quickly respond to any potential threat. Adverse environmental effects flowing from these acts are fairly predictable: supersonic fighter aircraft produce loud noise levels, large M-1 Abrams tanks chew up land surfaces, munitions' residue may affect groundwater, and installations the size of cities can create sewage treatment problems. The consequences of national security preparedness, therefore, create a dynamic tension between legitimate defense planners and thoughtful environmentalists. This tension will be explored in this chapter's discussion of key legislation and leading judicial decisions.

It is important to recognize at the outset that not every environmental lawsuit against a federal agency necessarily involves national security issues. In fact, only a few such cases rise to a level of national security importance. Even for agencies commonly associated with national defense, most environmental suits are similar to those of any major corporation and involve routine activities like dredging, road building, and crop spraying. Yet the impact of those few cases which strike at the heart of national defense concerns, such as suits involving submarine basing, nuclear storage, weapons testing, and chemical demilitarization, make the topic of environmental law and national security of singular importance today.

Because the field of environmental law is now so broad, it is useful to start by setting the conceptual framework for this chapter. First, it is important not to confuse the subject of environmental law with the broader area of environmental concerns. Environmental concerns such as overpopulation and food security are broad, and important, but this chapter addresses only environmental law: the product of legislation, regulations, and judicial decisions. Second, this chapter divides environmental law into two separate parts: (1) environmental policy statutes, and (2) pollution abatement/wildlife statutes. Environmental policy statutes are, roughly speaking more interested in defining the decision-making process than dictating the decision itself. The National Environmental Policy Act (NEPA) is the preeminent example of this type of statute, and it will be analyzed first. Pollution abatement statutes, on the other hand, are "command and control" oriented and establish specific prohibitions and requirements. Examples of pollution abatement statutes are well known, including the Clean Water Act, Clean Air Act, and the Resource Conservation and Recovery Act. This chapter then addresses wildlife statutes, particularly the Endangered Species Act, Marine Mammal Protection Act, and Migratory Bird Treaty Act. These statutes and five real life case studies and extracts from significant court decisions illustrating their application will be explored.

The final part of this chapter will discuss the combined impact of all types of environmental laws on seven specific national security issues: (1) legislation and planning, (2) military basing decisions, (3) training and testing, (4) chemical weapon demilitarization, (5) nuclear shipments, (6) NEPA abroad, and (7) climate change. Leading decisions will be highlighted in each area, with comments covering related issues.

Part 1: Environmental Policy

NEPA: The Cornerstone

One of the seminal events in the history of environmental law was, without question, the enactment of the National Environmental Policy Act (NEPA).[2] Although its drafters may not have fully appreciated the force and effect of its ultimate application, the passage of NEPA, signed into law on January 1, 1970, was a watershed event, the genesis of modern-day environmental activity. NEPA dramatically expanded the scope of judicial review of administrative actions, brought new rules to the agency decision-making process, and gave Congress additional tools and responsibilities to exercise its oversight role. At the forefront of NEPA's concerns are those "major Federal actions significantly affecting the quality of the human environment."[3] From the moment of its enactment, therefore, NEPA has placed federal projects under close scrutiny. Notably, the statute provides no specific exemption for national security matters.

The purpose of NEPA, set forth in Section 2 of the Act, is exceptionally broad in scope. NEPA is designed to:

> [D]eclare a national policy which will encourage productive and enjoyable harmony between man and his environment; to promote efforts which will prevent or eliminate damage to the environment and biosphere and stimulate the health and welfare of man; to enrich the understanding of the ecological systems and natural resources important to the Nation; and to establish a Council on Environmental Quality.[4]

NEPA consists of two separate titles. Title I is by far the more important: its five sections govern both the policy and the procedure of complying with the statute. Title II establishes and describes the Council on Environmental Quality.

It is important to note that NEPA only applies to "major federal actions," a somewhat elastic term that is broader than it might appear. It includes actions with "effects that may be major and which are potentially subject to Federal control and responsibility."[5] In addition, certain indirect federal actions, such as federal financing, federal permits, or federal approval may be determined to be a "major federal action." William H. Rogers, Jr., in his hornbook on environmental law, has a four-part section called "Recurring Issues: Whether, When, Who, What, and Remedies." Although beyond the scope of this chapter, these five issues are the basis of virtually all NEPA litigation today, particularly the questions: "Whether" (Is the action major? Does it have a significant effect?), and "What" (Is the environmental analysis adequate in scope and content?). Because the answers to these questions are often subjective, the nature of the project in question and the quality and quantity of public opposition can be very important factors in the judicial equation.

NEPA law is now a voluminous subject with a thirty-year history. Instead of attempting to summarize its many provisions and judicial interpretations, this chapter will focus on its most important consequences for national security.

---

2. National Environmental Policy Act of 1969 (NEPA), 42 U.S.C. § 4321 et seq. (2003).
3. 42 U.S.C. § 4332(2)(C).
4. *Id.* § 4321.
5. 40 C.F.R. § 1508.18 (2002).

Although there is no question today that NEPA applies to actions by all federal agencies, including those with national defense responsibilities, the manner in which it applies and the degree of deference given to government policymakers is still a frequently litigated topic. The federal judiciary initially led the way in expanding NEPA beyond its general terms to very specific directives. One of the earliest cases interpreting NEPA set the stage for the later litigation explosion:

Calvert Cliffs' Coordinating, Inc. v. U.S. Atomic Energy Commission
449 F.2d 1109 (D.C. Cir. 1971), *cert. denied* 404 U.S. 942 (1972)

J. SKELLY WRIGHT, Circuit Judge:

These cases are only the beginning of what promises to become a flood of new litigation—litigation seeking judicial assistance in protecting our natural environment. Several recently enacted statutes attest to the commitment of the Government to control, at long last, the destructive engine of material "progress." But it remains to be seen whether the promise of this legislation will become a reality. Therein lies the judicial role. In these cases, we must for the first time interpret the broadest and perhaps most important of the recent statutes: the National Environmental Policy Act of 1969 (NEPA). We must assess claims that one of the agencies charged with its administration has failed to live up to the congressional mandate. Our duty, in short, is to see that important legislative purposes, heralded in the halls of Congress, are not lost or misdirected in the vast hallways of the federal bureaucracy.

NEPA, like so much other reform legislation of the last 40 years, is cast in terms of a general mandate and broad delegation of authority to new and old administrative agencies. It takes the major step of requiring all federal agencies to consider values of environmental preservation in their spheres of activity, and it prescribes certain procedural measures to ensure that those values are in fact fully respected. Petitioners argue that rules recently adopted by the Atomic Energy Commission to govern consideration of environmental matters fail to satisfy the rigor demanded by NEPA. The Commission, on the other hand, contends that the vagueness of the NEPA mandate and delegation leaves much room for discretion and that the rules challenged by petitioners fall well within the broad scope of the Act. We find the policies embodied in NEPA to be a good deal clearer and more demanding than does the Commission. We conclude that the Commission's procedural rules do not comply with the congressional policy. Hence we remand these cases for further rule making.

I.

We begin our analysis with an examination of NEPA's structure and approach and of the Atomic Energy Commission rules which are said to conflict with the requirements of the Act. The relevant portion of NEPA is Title I, consisting of five sections. Section 101 sets forth the Act's basic substantive policy: that the federal government "use all practicable means and measures" to protect environmental values. Congress did not establish environmental protection as an exclusive goal; rather, it desired a reordering of priorities, so that environmental costs and benefits will assume their proper place along with other considerations. In Section 101(b), imposing an explicit duty on federal officials, the Act provides that "it is the continuing responsibility of the Federal Government to use all practicable means, consistent with other essential considerations of national policy," to avoid environmental degradation, preserve "historic, cultural, and natural" resources, and promote "the widest range of beneficial uses of the environment without ... undesirable and unintended consequences."

Thus the general substantive policy of the Act is a flexible one. It leaves room for a responsible exercise of discretion and may not require particular substantive results in particular problematic instances. However, the Act also contains very important "procedural" provisions — provisions which are designed to see that all federal agencies do in fact exercise the substantive discretion given them. These provisions are not highly flexible. Indeed, they establish a strict standard of compliance.

NEPA, first of all, makes environmental protection a part of the mandate of every federal agency and department. The Atomic Energy Commission, for example, had continually asserted, that prior to NEPA, that it had no statutory authority to concern itself with the adverse environmental effects of its actions. Now, however, its hands are no longer tied. It is not only permitted, but compelled, to take environmental values into account. Perhaps the greatest importance of NEPA is to require the Atomic Energy Commission and other agencies to *consider* environmental issues just as they consider other matters within their mandates. This compulsion is most plainly stated in Section 102. There, "Congress authorizes and directs that, to the fullest extent possible: (1) the policies, regulations, and public laws of the United States shall be interpreted and administered in accordance with the policies set forth in this Act...." Congress also "authorizes and directs" that "(2) all agencies of the Federal Government shall" follow certain rigorous procedures in considering environmental values. Senator Jackson, NEPA's principal sponsor, stated that "[n]o agency will [now] be able to maintain that it has no mandate or no requirement to consider the environmental consequences of its actions." He characterized the requirements of Section 102 as "action-forcing" and stated that "[o]therwise, these lofty declarations [in Section 101] are nothing more than that."

. . .

To ensure that the balancing analysis is carried out and given full effect, Section 102(2)(C) requires that responsible officials of all agencies prepare a "detailed statement" covering the impact of particular actions on the environment, the environmental costs which might be avoided, and alternative measures which might alter the cost benefit equation. The apparent purpose of the "detailed statement" is to aid in the agencies' own decision making process and to advise other interested agencies and the public of the environmental consequences of planned federal action. Beyond the "detailed statement," Section 102(2)(D) requires all agencies specifically to "study, develop, and describe appropriate alternatives to recommended courses of action in any proposal which involves unresolved conflicts concerning alternative uses of available resources." This requirement, like the "detailed statement" requirement, seeks to ensure that each agency decision maker has before him and takes into proper account all possible approaches to a particular project (including total abandonment of the project) which would alter the environmental impact and the cost-benefit balance. Only in that fashion is it likely that the most intelligent, optimally beneficial decision will ultimately be made. Moreover, by compelling a formal "detailed statement" and a description of alternatives, NEPA provides evidence that the mandated decision making process has in fact taken place and, most importantly, allows those removed from the initial process to evaluate and balance the factors on their own.

Of course, all of these Section 102 duties are qualified by the phrase "to the fullest extent possible." We must stress as forcefully as possible that this language does not provide an escape hatch for footdragging agencies; it does not make NEPA's procedural requirements somehow "discretionary." Congress did not intend the Act to be such a paper tiger. Indeed, the requirement of environmental consideration "to the fullest extent possible" sets a high standard for the agencies, a standard which must be rigorously enforced by the reviewing courts.

. . .

We conclude, then, that Section 102 of NEPA mandates a particular sort of careful and informed decisionmaking process and creates judicially enforceable duties. The reviewing courts probably cannot reverse a substantive decision on its merits, under Section 101, unless it is shown that the actual balance of costs and benefits that was struck was arbitrary or clearly gave insufficient weight to environmental values. But if the decision was reached procedurally without individualized consideration and balancing of environmental factors—conducted fully and in good faith—it is the responsibility of the courts to reverse. As one District Court has said of Section 102 requirements: "It is hard to imagine a clearer or stronger mandate to the Courts."[6]

Comments

1. Judge Skelly Wright's opinion in *Calvert Cliffs'* is the seminal case for a broad, expansive reading of NEPA. It has been extraordinarily influential due to both the force of its language and its scholarly examination of legislative intent. It stands for the proposition that the Act's procedural requirements are not inherently flexible but must be met unless there is a clear conflict with other statutory authority. Further, although a court cannot overturn a substantive decision on NEPA grounds, it can reverse an agency decision for failing to meet the statute's procedural requirements. Judge Wright clearly had an expansive notion of the role of the courts: "Our duty, in short, is to see that the important legislative purposes [of NEPA], heralded in the halls of Congress, are not lost or misdirected in the vast hallways of the federal bureaucracy."[7] In general, courts have followed the charge led by *Calvert Cliffs'* and NEPA, as it operates today, is as much a child of the judiciary as of Congress.[8] The scope of NEPA is often construed broadly. For example, in *Hanley v. Mitchell (I)*,[9] Judge Feinberg wrote that it includes "noise, traffic, over-burdened mass transportation systems, crime, congestion and even availability of drugs."[10]

2. The actual holding of *Calvert Cliffs'* was simply that the Atomic Energy Commission (AEC) (predecessor to the Nuclear Regulatory Commission, or NRC) was required to consider thermal effects in its decisions. This reversed an earlier, pre-NEPA decision by the First Circuit that the Atomic Energy Act of 1954 did not allow the AEC to consider such effects in the licensing process.[11] In fact, even this narrow holding was legislatively overruled by Section 511(c) (2) of the Federal Water Pollution Control Act Amendments of 1972.[12] The author visited Calvert Cliffs in 2014 as it is the first nuclear station to be relicensed by the NRC. It currently provides 30 percent of the power for all of Maryland.

3. At the time *Calvert Cliffs'* was decided, the Council on Environmental Quality (CEQ) had not issued any guidelines to supplement the general requirements of NEPA. The first guidelines, published in April 1971 and revised in 1973, were only advisory in nature.[13]

---

6. *Id.* at 1111–12, 1114–15.

7. *Id.* at 1111.

8. *See, e.g.,* Levanthal, *Environmental Decisionmaking and the Role of the Courts,* 122 U. Pa. L. Rev. 509 (1974).

9. Hanley v. Mitchell (I), 460 F.2d 640 (2d Cir. 1972).

10. *Id.* at 647.

11. *See* New Hampshire v. Atomic Energy Comm'n, 406 F.2d 170 (1st Cir. 1969).

12. Federal Water Pollution Control Act Amendment of 1972, 33 U.S.C. § 1371(c)(2) (1948). *See also* Baltimore Gas & Elec. Co. v. NRDC, 462 U.S. 87 (1983) (upholding NRC rule that a licensing board could assume, for purposes of NEPA review, that permanent storage of some nuclear wastes would not have a significant impact on the environment).

13. *See, e.g.,* Hiram Clark Civic Club, Inc. v. Lynn, 476 F.2d 421, 426 (5th Cir. 1972).

In 1979, CEQ issued regulations which replaced the earlier guidelines and implemented all of the procedural protections of NEPA.[14] Unlike their predecessor guidelines, these regulations are binding and "entitled to substantial deference" by the courts.[15]

4. President Nixon established the Environmental Protection Agency (EPA) in a 1970 executive branch reorganization that brought pollution programs scattered throughout the government into a single agency. EPA was charged with the responsibility to set up, monitor, and enforce federal anti-pollution standards. In addition, EPA has NEPA review authority. Section 309 of the Clean Air Act requires the administrator of EPA to review and comment in writing on the environmental impact of proposed legislation, authorized construction, proposed regulations, or any other major federal agency action.[16] If the administrator determines that the proposal is "unsatisfactory," the matter must be referred to CEQ.[17] EPA has ten regional offices that monitor federal facility compliance with all environmental laws. It has program offices for water, air, solid waste, Superfund, pesticides, and toxic substances. If a federal facility violates any environmental laws or regulations, EPA notifies the facility and action is taken to develop a compliance schedule. Failure to comply could result in adverse administrative action by EPA. However, EPA cannot bring judicial action against another federal agency.

The Environmental Impact Statement: Practice and Controversy

In keeping with NEPA's congressionally mandated concern for the environment, federal agencies are required to "develop procedures to insure the fullest practical provisions of timely public information and understanding of Federal plans and programs with environmental impact in order to obtain the views of interested parties."[18] This requirement for public participation includes a section which has been interpreted as the genesis for the most well-known aspect of NEPA's procedural hurdles: the environmental impact statement or EIS.

Section 102(2) (C) requires that after consulting with, and obtaining the comments of relevant federal and state agencies, each agency which proposes legislation and/or any "other major Federal actions significantly affecting the quality of the human environment" shall prepare a detailed environmental impact statement (EIS).[19] Section 102(2) (C) is the nerve system of NEPA; it provides the energy that runs the entire program. That section is, as many have stated, an "environmental full disclosure act."

The environmental impact statement must be prepared by the responsible official and must include:

(1) the environmental impact of the proposed action,

(2) any adverse environmental effects which cannot be avoided should the proposal be implemented,

---

14. *See* 43 Fed. Reg. 55, 977-56, 007, 40 C.F.R. Pt. 1500 (1983).

15. Andrus v. Sierra Club, 442 U.S. 347, 357–58 (1979). *See also* Melanie Fisher, *The CEQ Regulations: New Stage in the Evolution of NEPA*, 3 Harv. Envtl. L. Rev. 347 (1979).

16. 42 U.S.C. §7609(a).

17. 42 U.S.C. §7609(b).

18. 42 U.S.C. §4321 et seq. (2003).

19. 42 U.S.C. §4332(2)(C).

(3) alternatives to the proposed action,

(4) the relationship between local short-term uses of man's environment and the maintenance and enhancement of long-term productivity, and

(5) any irreversible and irretrievable commitments of resources which would be involved in the proposed action should it be implemented.[20]

NEPA, as implemented by CEQ and agency regulations, creates a systematic, formal process for incorporating environmental considerations into agency decision-making. It mandates an interdisciplinary approach by requiring consultation with other federal agencies which have jurisdiction or special expertise in a particular area. State and local agencies that are involved are to be consulted and their views considered. Finally, there is a specific requirement for public notice and public hearings.[21]

Depending on the nature of the activity being considered, the NEPA process will result in one of the following:

- a finding that the action is exempt by law from NEPA's requirements;[22]

- a finding that the action falls within an existing categorical exclusion;[23]

- an Environmental Assessment followed by a finding of no significant impact or FONSI;[24] or

- an Environmental Assessment leading to an Environmental Impact Statement and, ultimately, a published record of decision.[25]

To achieve some uniformity, agency regulations often include examples of actions normally requiring EISs. An example of such guidance is in Army Regulation 200-2. That regulation gives the following examples of activities that usually require an EIS:

a. Significant expansion of a military facility or installation.

b. Construction of facilities that have a significant effect on wetlands, coastal zones, or other areas of critical environmental concern.

c. The disposal of nuclear materials, munitions, explosives, industrial and material chemicals, and other hazardous or toxic substances which have the potential to cause significant environmental impact.

d. Land acquisition, leasing or other actions which may lead to significant change in land use.

e. Realignment or stationing of a brigade or larger table of organization equipment (TOE) unit during peacetime (except where the only significant impacts are socioeconomic, with no significant biophysical environmental impact).

f. Training exercises conducted outside the boundaries of an existing military reservation where significant environmental damage might occur.

---

20. *Id.*
21. *See* 40 C.F.R. Pt. 1500 (2002).
22. 40 C.F.R. § 1500.6 (2002).
23. 40 C.F.R. § 1508.4 (2002).
24. 40 C.F.R. § 1508.9, § 1508.13 (2002).
25. 40 C.F.R. § 1508.9, § 1508.11 (2002).

g. Major changes in the mission or facilities either affecting environmentally sensitive resources (see Sec. 651.29(c)) or causing significant environmental impact (see Sec. 651.39).[26]

Although each of the above eight examples have potential environmental consequences, they are also areas that are clearly integral parts or products of national security decision-making. Although the EIS process can work well in normal circumstances, it becomes far more complicated in this arena when time is of the essence and classified information exists. Further, the issues are frequently supercharged emotionally, tempting the opponents to sue using the NEPA process to delay, publicize, or prevent particular activity. The following case study presents both the NEPA process and the complications inherent in national security matters.

Case Study I: NEPA and the EIS Requirement

FACTUAL SETTING: The West Loch branch of the Lualualei naval storage area is on the island of Oahu, Hawaii. Since 1959 the West Loch facility has been used for handling and storage of conventional (non-nuclear) ammunition. It is centrally located, only a mile from Honolulu International Airport and two military airports.

In early 1970 the Navy decided to transfer certain unnamed weapons to West Loch. In advance of this decision, an environmental impact assessment (EIA) was prepared in 1975 that concluded that the construction of more than forty earth-covered magazines and other buildings would have no additional significant effects on the environment. While the Navy admitted that the new construction would be capable of storing nuclear weapons, it stated that Navy regulations prohibited them from either admitting or denying plans regarding nuclear weapons.

Although the EIA did not mention the possibility of storing nuclear weapons at West Loch, the Navy did prepare a Candidate EIS covering the storage of nuclear weapons in general (i.e., with no reference to any particular site). The Candidate EIS concluded that such storage did not present significant hazards to the environment.

THE CHALLENGE: Plaintiffs, Catholic Action of Hawaii, sued in 1978 to stop the building of the additional nuclear-capable storage facilities at West Loch. A preliminary injunction was sought and denied. The district court held that although "[t]he construction and use of the storage facilities at West Loch is a major Federal action" under NEPA, the Navy complied "to the fullest extent possible within the restrictions of the security classification guides and the Atomic Energy Act."[27]

DISCUSSION: Before reaching either the Court of Appeals or Supreme Court decisions, the setting and challenge should be analyzed for distinct national security issues. First, does the military have to comply with NEPA in what is clearly a sensitive national security issue? Second, if compliance is necessary, can the courts actually prevent a military decision from being implemented if it fails to meet either substantive environmental law dictates or the procedural requirements of NEPA? If so, are national security concerns taken into account? Finally, what about classified material? Is it protected, or available as part of the record of the decision-making process?

---

26. Environmental Analysis of Army Actions (AR 200-2), 32 C.F.R. §651.42 (2002).
27. Catholic Action of Hawaii v. Brown, 468 F. Supp. 190, 193 (D. Haw. 1979).

Court of Appeals Decision: The Hypothetical EIS

Catholic Action of Hawaii v. Brown
643 F.2d 569, 571 (9th Cir. 1980)

JUDGE MERRILL

...

In the present case it is stipulated that the West Loch facilities are capable of storing nuclear weapons. The public therefore must assume that at least the possibility exists that nuclear weapons, to the extent of the apparent capacity of the facility (assuming that capacity would be apparent to a knowledgeable observer), will be stored at West Loch. Thus, an EIS dealing with the consequences of such possibility would reveal nothing with respect to the likelihood of storage of which the public is not already aware. Such a process of informing the decision maker need not imply that the decision has already been made or what the decision is; the Secretary need never reveal the fact that a decision has been made or what it is. However, the public must receive some assurance, particularly in a situation as potentially catastrophic as this one, that when the decision is made the decision maker will have been adequately informed as to the environmental consequences of each alternative, here including the potential consequences of the storage of nuclear weapons at this particular site. Consideration of the four environmental factors specified by appellants as being critically important is essential if the decision maker is to be adequately prepared when the time for decision respecting nuclear storage arrives.

While we recognize that specific information regarding the number and type of nuclear weapons to be stored at West Loch cannot be revealed to the public, this should not preclude preparation of an EIS, available to the public, generally assessing the impact of such storage. Further, since the EIS in important respects will be hypothetical (hypothesizing, without conceding, that the facility will be put to the use for which it has been made capable), factual information as to the consequences of storage to any specific extent can be based on a series of hypotheses covering the range of options which the facility has openly presented to the Secretary.

...

We conclude that while the district court correctly held that the West Loch project was major federal action, it erred in holding that the Navy has complied with NEPA to the fullest extent possible. We conclude that the EIA and the CEIS provided by the Navy are inadequate and that an EIS is required under the provisions of NEPA.

The Supreme Court Response

Weinberger v. Catholic Action of Hawaii
454 U.S. 139, 143–144, 146–147 (1981)

CHIEF JUSTICE REHNQUIST

We have previously noted "[t]he thrust of § 102(2)(C) is ... that environmental concerns be integrated into the very process of agency decisionmaking. The 'detailed statement' it requires is the outward sign that environmental values and consequences have been considered during the planning stage of agency actions." *Andrus v. Sierra Club*, 442 U.S. 347, 350 (1979). Section 102(2)(C) thus serves twin aims. The first is to inject environmental considerations into the federal agency's decisionmaking process by requiring the agency to prepare an EIS. The second aim is to inform the public that the agency has considered environmental concerns in its decisionmaking process. Through the disclosure of an EIS, the public is made aware that the agency has taken environmental considerations into account. Public disclosure of the EIS is expressly governed by FOIA. 42 USCS § 4332(2)(C).

The decisionmaking and public disclosure goals of § 102(2)(C), though certainly compatible, are not necessarily coextensive. Thus, § 102(2)(C) contemplates that in a given situation a federal agency might have to include environmental considerations in its decisionmaking process, yet withhold public disclosure of any NEPA documents, in whole or in part, under the authority of a FOIA exemption. That the decisionmaking and disclosure requirement of NEPA are not coextensive has been recognized by the Department of Defense regulations, both at the time the West Loch facility was constructed and today. [32 CFR § 214.6 (1980).]

In an apparent attempt to balance what it considered to be the disclosure requirements of NEPA with national security interests, the Court of Appeals concluded that petitioners could prepare and disclose an EIS that would assess the impact of the storage of nuclear weapons at West Loch without revealing specific information regarding the number and type of nuclear weapons to be stored at the facility. 643 F.2d at 572. The EIS could hypothesize, but not concede, that the facility will be used for the purpose for which it has been made capable. *Ibid.* But in inventing the "Hypothetical Environmental Impact Statement," the Court of Appeals departed from the express intent of Congress manifested by the explicit language in § 102(2)(C). That language provides that public disclosure of the EIS shall be governed by FOIA. [5 U.S.C. § 552.] As we concluded in *EPA v. Mink*, 410 U.S. 73, 80 (1973), FOIA was intended by Congress to balance the public's need for access to official information with the Government's need for confidentiality. Of the nine exemptions in Subsection (b) of FOIA, we think two are relevant in determining whether the Navy must release an EIS. Exemption 3, 5 U.S.C. § 552(b)(3), which authorize the withholding of documents "specifically exempted from disclosure by statute," arguably exempts the publication of an EIS under the Atomic Energy Act. [42 U.S.C. § 2011 *et seq.*] But we find it unnecessary to decide this question, because to us it is clear the Exemption 1, 5 U.S.C. § 552(b)(1), is applicable.

...

If the Navy proposes to store nuclear weapons at West Loch, the Department of Defense's regulations can fairly be read to require that an EIS be prepared solely for internal purposes, even though such a document cannot be disclosed to the public. The Navy must consider environmental consequences in its decisionmaking process, even if it is unable to meet NEPA's public disclosure goals by virtue of FOIA Exemption 1.

It does not follow, however, that the Navy is required to prepare an EIS in this case. The Navy is not required to prepare an EIS regarding the hazards of storing nuclear weapons at West Loch simply because the facility is "nuclear capable." As we held in *Kleppe v. Sierra Club*, 427 U.S. 390, 405–406 (1976), an EIS need not be prepared simply because a project is *contemplated*, but only when the project is *proposed*. To say that the West Loch facility is "nuclear capable" is to say little more than that the Navy has contemplated the possibility that nuclear weapons, of whatever variety, may at some time be stored here. It is the proposal to *store* nuclear weapons at West Loch that triggers the Navy's obligation to prepare an EIS. Due to national security reasons, however, the Navy can neither admit nor deny that it proposes to store nuclear weapons at West Loch. In this case, therefore, it has not been and cannot be established that the Navy has proposed the only action that would require the preparation of an EIS dealing with the environmental consequences of nuclear weapons storage at West Loch.

Ultimately, whether or not the Navy has complied with NEPA "to the fullest extent possible" is beyond judicial scrutiny in this case. In other circumstances, we have held that "public policy forbids the maintenance of any suit in a court of justice, the trial of which would inevitably lead to the disclosure of matters which the law itself regards as confidential, and respecting which it will not allow the confidence to be violated." *Totten v. United States*, 92 U.S. 105, 107 (1876). See *United States v. Reynolds*, 345 U.S. 1 (1953). We confront a similar situation in the instant case.

The decision of the Court of Appeals for the Ninth Circuit is reversed, and the case is remanded with instructions to reinstate the judgment of dismissal entered by the District Court.

It is so ordered.

Comments

1. Justice Rehnquist's *Catholic Action* opinion relied heavily on the fact that NEPA provides that public disclosure of an EIS shall be governed by the Freedom of Information Act (FOIA). Since Exemption 1 of FOIA[28] protects classified material dealing with national security, the Court found that the Navy would not have to disclose a report that was exempt from release. This case followed *EPA v. Mink*,[29] which arose out of Congresswoman Patsy Mink's request for documents concerning a proposed underground nuclear test at Amchitka Island, Alaska. At issue was the Court's role: should it inquire into the correctness of the classification or simply rely on the government's assertion? Reading the exemption literally, Justice White held that the Court's inquiry was limited to determining whether the executive had asserted classified matters. The 1974 amendments to FOIA, expressly passed to override *EPA v. Mink*, only exempt documents which are "(A) specifically authorized under criteria established by an Executive order to be kept secret in the interest of national defense or foreign policy and (B) are in fact properly classified pursuant to such Executive order."[30]

2. In his concurring opinion in *Catholic Action*, Justice Blackmun (joined by Justice Brennan) stressed that non-classified data in an EIS would have to be released:

> The Court obviously is quite correct in holding that properly classified materials need not be disclosed under NEPA; even information concerning the existence of an EIS may be withheld when publication would divulge sensitive military information. It remains true, however, that the statute is in part intended to inform the public, *see ante*, at 143, and this informational purpose does not entirely lose its vitality when classified documents are involved. Again, the Defense regulations specifically direct that "[w]hen feasible, [EIS's] shall be organized in such a manner that classified portions are included as annexes so that the un-classified portions can be made available to the public," 46 Fed. Reg. 22902, 22894 (1981); further, the CEQ agrees that EIS's may be organized in such a way "that the unclassified portions can be made available to the public," 40 CFR § 1507.3(C) (1981). In a given case, then, the military must determine whether the information at issue, consistent with the dictates of the relevant Executive Orders, can be released.

---

28. Freedom of Information Act, 5 U.S.C. § 552(b)(1) (2000).
29. EPA v. Mink, 410 U.S. 73 (1973).
30. Freedom of Information Act, 5 U.S.C. § 552(b)(1) (2000).

That principle is applicable in this and in every other case involving classified military material; I must assume that the Court does not hold differently.[31]

3. Army Regulation AR 200-2[32] describes how the military handles classified NEPA documents, requiring that efforts be made to segregate unclassified information and conduct a "meaningful environmental analysis," if the entire document is classified. An interdisciplinary team is then formed "to ensure that the consideration of environmental effects will be consistent with the letter and intent of NEPA, including public participation requirements for those aspects which are not classified."[33]

4. The holding in *Catholic Action* was followed in *Laine v. Weinberger.*[34] In Laine the plaintiffs sought to enjoin an operation at the Seal Beach Naval Weapons Station until such time as the Navy filed an environmental impact statement regarding the Navy's utilization of the facility for the maintenance and storage of nuclear weapons. Unlike *Catholic Action*, there was no new construction undertaken and no major changes in operations. The district court used the same analysis as the Supreme Court in holding that an environmental impact statement was not required.[35]

5. Although NEPA does not have a national security exemption, CEQ regulations do provide for alternative arrangements in emergency situations.[36] One example of such an arrangement is *Valley Citizens for a Safe Environment v. Vest*, in which the court upheld CEQ and the Air Force's determination that an emergency provision in the NEPA regulations "allowed the Air Force to forgo strict compliance" with the statute during Operation Desert Storm.[37] As a result, the Air Force was not required to prepare a supplemental EIS before initiating nighttime flights at a base that previously operated only during daytime hours.[38]

Reviewing Environmental Impact Statements

Having observed NEPA in action in both *Calvert Cliffs'* and *Catholic Action*, there remain a number of other EIS-related issues which consistently affect national security planning. The following is a general discussion of the four most litigated issues.

Standard of Review

An agency's decision not to prepare an EIS, and other claims under NEPA, are subject to judicial review and are governed by the review provisions of the Administrative Procedure Act (APA).[39] In *Marsh v. Oregon Natural Resources Council*,[40] the court expressed the standard as follows: "as long as the [Army Corps of Engineers'] decision not to supplement the FEISS was not 'arbitrary and capricious,' it should not be set aside."[41] Whatever the test,

---

31. Weinberger, 454 U.S. at 149 (1981).

32. AR 200-2, 32 C.F.R. §651.13 (2002).

33. AR 200-2, 32 C.F.R. §651.13(d) (2002).

34. Laine v. Weinberger, 541 F. Supp. 599 (C.D. Cal. 1982).

35. *See also* Citizens for Reid State Park v. Laird, 336 F. Supp. 788 (D. Me. 1982) (upholding Naval and Marine Training exercises without EIS).

36. 40 C.F.R. §1506.11 (2002).

37. Valley Citizens for a Safe Env't v. Vest, 1991 WL 330963 at *2 (D. Mass. May 6, 1991).

38. *Id.* at *5. But see Justice Ginsburg's dissent in Winter v. NRDC, 555 U.S. 7 (2008).

39. Administrative Procedure Act (APA), 5 U.S.C. §701 et seq. *See* Baltimore Gas & Elec. Co. v. NRDC, 462 U.S. 87, 90 (1983).

40. Marsh v. Oregon Natural Res. Council, 490 U.S. 360, 377–78 (1989). *See also* Greenpeace v. Franklin, 14 F.3d 1324 (9th Cir. 1993).

41. Marsh, 490 U.S. at 377.

Judge Skelly Wright's statement that NEPA "sets a high standard for the agencies, a standard which must be rigorously enforced by reviewing courts," accentuates the *Overton Park* requirement that courts take a "hard look" at agency actions affecting the environment.[42]

Substantive Compliance with NEPA

Despite the breadth of NEPA, it is still primarily a procedural statute, as the Supreme Court confirmed in *Vermont Yankee Nuclear Power Corp. v. NRDC*.[43] The Court elaborated in *Strycker's Bay Neighborhood Council v. Karlen*:

> '… NEPA was designed to insure a fully informed and well-considered decision,' but not necessarily a 'decision the judge of the Court of Appeals or of this court would have reached had they been members of the decision-making unit of the agency.' *Vermont Yankee* cuts sharply against the Court of Appeals' conclusion that an agency, in selecting a course of action, must elevate environmental concerns over other appropriate considerations. On the contrary, once an agency has made a decision subject to NEPA's procedural requirements, the only role for a court is to insure that the agency has considered the environmental consequences; it cannot 'interject itself within the area of discretion of the executive as to the choice of the action to be taken.'[44]

Standing

Standing is frequently litigated in NEPA controversies. Under current Supreme Court case law, the plaintiff must demonstrate three requirements to meet Article III standing.[45] First, a plaintiff must have an "injury-in-fact" to a legally protected interest. The injury must be both "concrete and particularized" and "actual or imminent." Second, there must be a causal connection between the injury and the statute. Third, the injury must likely be "redressed by a favorable decision."[46] In *Sierra Club v. Morton*,[47] the Supreme Court also stated that "it is clear that an organization whose members are injured may represent those members in proceedings for judicial review."[48] In *Lujan v. National Wildlife Federation*, an environmental group's challenge to the Department of the Interior's massive land classification program, however, the Supreme Court rejected NWF's claim to "information standing" in its own right, because NWF did not "identify any particular 'agency action' that was the source of [its] injuries," but simply alleged harm from the program as a whole.[49]

The cases are split on whether economic interests alone are sufficient to give a plaintiff standing.[50] This is particularly troublesome for the military's often controversial decisions to close bases or transfer employees to other locations. In some instances, a NEPA challenge has been used to challenge such a proposal even though the central issue was loss of em-

---

42. Citizens to Preserve Overton Park v. Volpe, 401 U.S. 402 (1971).

43. Vermont Yankee Nuclear Power Corp. v. NRDC, 435 U.S. 519 (1978).

44. Strycker's Bay Neighborhood Council v. Karlen, 444 U.S. 223, 227–28 (1980) (quoting *Vermont Yankee*). *See also* Baltimore Gas and Elec. Co. v. NRDC, 462 U.S. 87 (1983) and Kleppe v. Sierra Club, 427 U.S. 390, 420 n.21 (1976).

45. Lujan v. Defenders of Wildlife, 504 U.S. 555, 561 (1992).

46. *Id.* at 561; Friends of the Earth, Inc. v. Laidlaw Envtl. Serv. Inc., 528 U.S. 167, 180–81 (2000).

47. Sierra Club v. Morton, 405 U.S. 727 (1972).

48. *Id.* at 739.

49. Lujan v. Nat'l Wildlife Fed'n, 497 U.S. 871 (1990). *See also* Found. on Econ. Trends v. Lyng, 943 F.2d 79 (D.C. Cir. 1991).

50. *See Annot.*, 61 A.L.R. Fed. §4 (1983).

ployment. In *Breckinridge v. Rumsfeld*,[51] which involved the closing of an Army post in the Lexington-Bluegrass area of Kentucky, the court held that loss of employment was not an interest within the scope of NEPA.[52] In *Jackson County v. Jones*, the EIS was found to be adequate for a relocation plan for approximately 2,000 military personnel and 800 civilian employees from Richard-Gebaur Air Force Base near Kansas City, Missouri to Scott Air Force Base near St. Louis.[53]

Remedies

Because the NEPA procedures are designed to ensure that environmental information is considered by decision-makers and is available to the public before decisions are made, injunctive relief is the usual remedy if an agency is found not to have met the Act's procedural requirements. As the Supreme Court stated in *Amoco Production Co. v. Village of Gambell*:[54]

> [T]he bases for injunctive relief are irreparable injury and inadequacy of legal remedies. In each case, a court must balance the competing claims of injury and must consider the effect on each party of the granting or withholding of the requested relief. Although particular regard should be given to the public interests, 'the grant of jurisdiction to ensure compliance with a statute hardly suggests an absolute duty to do so under any and all circumstances, and a federal judge sitting as chancellor is not mechanically obligated to grant an injunction for every violation of law.'
>
> . . .
>
> Environmental injury, by its nature, can seldom be adequately remedied by money damages and is often permanent or at least of long duration, i.e., irreparable. If such injury is sufficiently likely, therefore, the balance of harm will usually favor the issuance of an injunction to protect the environment.[55]

The issuance of an injunction, temporary or preliminary in nature, preserves the status quo until full consideration can be given to all environmental consequences. Because NEPA is not designed to dictate a particular outcome, permanent injunctions are inappropriate. Further, any injunction may be unnecessary in particular circumstances.[56] The following is a discussion of the leading Supreme Court case on preliminary injunctions for environmental issues that raise significant national security concerns.

Case Study II: NEPA and Preliminary Injunctions

In 2007, several environmental groups filed a lawsuit against the U.S. Navy. The plaintiffs alleged that the Navy violated NEPA by failing to prepare an Environmental Impact Statement (EIS) prior to conducting training exercises off the coast of southern California.

---

51. Breckinridge v. Rumsfeld, 537 F.2d 864 (6th Cir. 1976), *cert. denied*, 429 U.S. 1961 (1977). *See also* Shiffler v. Schlesinger, 548 F.2d 96 (3d Cir. 1979) (consolidation of major portion of Army Signal School with another school).

52. Breckinridge, 537 F.2d at 865.

53. Jackson Cnty., Mo. v. Jones, 571 F.2d 1004 (8th Cir. 1978).

54. Amoco Prod. Co. v. Village of Gambell, 480 U.S. 531 (1987) (Alaskan native village sought injunction claiming that Secretary of Interior had not complied with provisions of statute).

55. *Id.* at 542–45.

56. *See, e.g.*, Weinberger v. Romero-Barcelo, 456 U.S. 305 (1982) (district court's decision not to enjoin operations pending Navy application for Clean Water Act permit reversed by Court of Appeals, but upheld by Supreme Court).

They argued that the Navy's use of mid-frequency active sonar (MFA) during the training exercises harms marine mammals, and an EIS was therefore required. The Navy had prepared an Environmental Assessment (EA) for the training exercises, which concluded that existing mitigation measures were adequate and that a full EIS was not necessary.

The District Court entered a preliminary injunction prohibiting the Navy from using MFA sonar during its training exercises, and the Navy appealed. The Court of Appeals for the Ninth Circuit agreed that an injunction was appropriate, but found that a blanket ban on the use of MFA sonar during training was overbroad, and remanded to the District Court to narrow the injunction. On remand, the District Court entered a new preliminary injunction allowing the Navy to use MFA sonar during its training exercises, provided the Navy implemented six new mitigation measures (beyond the measures already in place).

The Navy agreed to implement four of the mitigation measures, but appealed the other two. At the same time, it sought relief from the Executive Branch. The Council on Environmental Quality (CEQ) authorized the Navy to implement alternative arrangements to NEPA based on "emergency circumstances." The Navy then moved to vacate the District Court's injunction. The District Court refused, and the Court of Appeals affirmed the district court's injunction. An extract of the Court of Appeals decision follows.

Natural Resources Defense Council v. Winter
518 F.3d 658 (9th Cir. 2008)

JUDGE FLETCHER

The [Navy] exercises, which involve the use of multiple surface ships, aircraft and submarines, are part of the "integrated" training phase of the Navy's Fleet Response Training Plan, in which individual naval units—ships, submarines and aviation squadrons—learn and demonstrate skills as members of a strike group.... Upon completion of the integrated training phase the Fleet Commander is able to certify that a strike group is ready for deployment.

. . .

According to the Navy, the ability to execute anti-submarine warfare ("ASW") is critical to a Commander's certification of a strike group. *Id.* Improving ASW is the Pacific Fleet's top "war-fighting" priority because of the proliferation of extremely quiet diesel electric submarines throughout the world. *Id.* ¶ 11; Dec. 14, 2007 Declaration of Rear Admiral John M. Bird ("Bird. Decl") ¶ 16. In turn, an important part of ASW is the use of active sonar, a technology which the Navy deems absolutely necessary to detect today's extremely quiet submarines. The type of active sonar, the use of which NRDC challenges, is mid-frequency active sonar.

. . .

Active sonar involves a vessel or other sonar source emitting a loud noise underwater and then listening for whether the noise comes back to the source, indicating that the noise may have bounced off the hull of a previously undetected submarine.

. . .

The SOCAL exercises are conducted in the Navy's training ranges off the coast of southern California ("the Southern California Operating Area"). This area is located in biologically diverse waters. At least thirty-seven species of marine mammals are found there.

. . .

The Navy acknowledges in its EA that MFA sonar may affect both the physiology and behavior of marine mammals. Exposure to "very high" acoustic energy levels may impair the functioning of marine mammals' visual system, vestibular system and internal organs, and may cause injury to their lungs and intestines. However, the primary physiological effects of MFA sonar are on marine mammals' auditory system: very high sound levels may rupture the eardrum or damage small bones in the middle ear, but even exposure to lower levels of sound may cause permanent or temporary hearing loss.

While we are mindful of the importance of protecting national security, courts have often held, in the face of assertions of potential harm to military readiness, that the armed forces must take precautionary measures to comply with the law during its training ... the district court here carefully balanced the significant interests and hardships at stake to ensure that the Navy could continue to train without causing undue harm to the environment. We review that balance to determine whether it rests on clearly erroneous findings of fact. Having concluded that it does not, we determine that the district court did not abuse its discretion and therefore do not disturb its carefully considered injunction.

The U.S. Supreme Court granted certiorari and reversed the Court of Appeals. An extract of that decision follows.

Winter v. Natural Resources Defense Council

555 U.S. 7 (2008)

CHIEF JUSTICE ROBERTS

"To be prepared for war is one of the most effectual means of preserving peace." 1 *Messages and Papers of the Presidents* 57 (J. Richardson comp. 1897). So said George Washington in his first Annual Address to Congress, 218 years ago. One of the most important ways the Navy prepares for war is through integrated training exercises at sea. These exercises include training in the use of modern sonar to detect and track enemy submarines,something the Navy has done for the past 40 years. The plaintiffs complained that the Navy's sonar training program harmed marine mammals, and that the Navy should have prepared an environmental impact statement before commencing its latest round of training exercises. The Court of Appeals upheld a preliminary injunction imposing restrictions on the Navy's sonar training, even though the court acknowledged that "the record contains no evidence that marine mammals have been harmed" by the Navy's exercises. 518 F. 3d 658, 696 (CA9 2008).

A plaintiff seeking a preliminary injunction must establish that he is likely to succeed on the merits, that he is likely to suffer irreparable harm in the absence of preliminary relief, that the balance of equities tips in his favor, and that an injunction is in the public interest.

...

The District Court and the Ninth Circuit concluded that plaintiffs have shown a likelihood of success on the merits of their NEPA claim. The Navy strongly disputes this determination, arguing that plaintiffs' likelihood of success is low because the CEQ reasonably concluded that "emergency circumstances" justified alternative arrangements to NEPA compliance.

...

[E]ven if plaintiffs have shown irreparable injury from the Navy's training exercises, any such injury is outweighed by the public interest and the Navy's interest in effective, realistic training of its sailors. A proper consideration of these factors alone requires denial of the requested injunctive relief.

...

This case involves "complex, subtle, and professional decisions as to the composition, training, equipping, and control of a military force," which are "essentially professional military judgments." *Gilligan v. Morgan*, 413 U.S. 1, 10 (1973). We "give great deference to the professional judgment of military authorities concerning the relative importance of a particular military interest." *Goldman v. Weinberger*, 475 U. S. 503, 507 (1986).... Here, the record contains declarations from some of the Navy's most senior officers, all of whom underscored the threat posed by enemy submarines and the need for extensive sonar training to counter this threat.

...

These interests must be weighed against the possible harm to the ecological, scientific, and recreational interests that are legitimately before this Court. Plaintiffs have submitted declarations asserting that they take whale watching trips, observe marine mammals underwater, conduct scientific research on marine mammals, and photograph these animals in their natural habitats. Plaintiffs contend that the Navy's use of MFA sonar will injure marine mammals or alter their behavioral patterns, impairing plaintiffs' ability to study and observe the animals.

While we do not question the seriousness of these interests, we conclude that the balance of equities and consideration of the overall public interest in this case tip strongly in favor of the Navy. For the plaintiffs, the most serious possible injury would be harm to an unknown number of the marine mammals that they study and observe. In contrast, forcing the Navy to deploy an inadequately trained antisubmarine force jeopardizes the safety of the fleet. Active sonar is the only reliable technology for detecting and tracking enemy diesel-electric submarines, and the President—the Commander in Chief—has determined that training with active sonar is "essential to national security." Pet. App. 232a.

The public interest in conducting training exercises with active sonar under realistic conditions plainly outweighs the interests advanced by the plaintiffs. Of course, military interests do not always trump other considerations, and we have not held that they do. In this case, however, the proper determination of where the public interest lies does not strike us as a close question.

...

We do not discount the importance of plaintiffs' ecological, scientific, and recreational interests in marine mammals. Those interests, however, are plainly outweighed by the Navy's need to conduct realistic training exercises to ensure that it is able to neutralize the threat posed by enemy submarines. The District Court abused its discretion by imposing a 2,200 yard shutdown zone and by requiring the Navy to power down its MFA sonar during significant surface ducting conditions. The judgment of the Court of Appeals is reversed, and the preliminary injunction is vacated to the extent it has been challenged by the Navy.

It is so ordered.

Comments

1. The majority opinion finds that the balance of interests tips strongly in favor of the Navy. Not all of the Justices agreed, however. Justice Ginsburg, joined by Justice Souter, came to the opposite conclusion: "In light of the likely, substantial harm to the environment, NRDC's almost inevitable success on the merits of its claim that NEPA required the Navy

to prepare an EIS, the history of this litigation, and the public interest, I cannot agree that the mitigation measures the District Court imposed signal an abuse of discretion. For the reasons stated, I would affirm the judgment of the Ninth Circuit."[57]

2. It is important to note that the Navy only challenged two of the six mitigation measures that were imposed in the District Court's second preliminary injunction. Interestingly, the Navy complied with the other four mitigation measures and did not challenge them in court. Therefore, although the Navy ultimately prevailed in the litigation, it also made concessions that resulted in more protections for marine mammals affected by MFA sonar.

3. There is an obvious tension in *Winter* between the U.S. Navy's scientific conclusions and those of the plaintiffs. However, that could change as the Navy gains experience in studying and managing marine resources. For example, Alex Beehler, former Acting Deputy Under Secretary of Defense for Installations and Environment, has stated that "the U.S. Navy is the number one supporter of marine mammal research in the world by far."[58] Such research may facilitate the Navy's ability to balance environmental concerns with its military objectives.

Part 2: Pollution Abatement and Wildlife Statutes

Although NEPA is a well-known environmental statute, it is no longer preeminent. A large number of federal and state pollution abatement statutes have arisen since NEPA's enactment. Air quality, water quality, resource conservation, coastal zones, endangered species, historical sites, toxic substances, and noise concerns are now the dominant environmental catalysts. These state and federal laws include both substantive and procedural requirements. They are frequently linked with NEPA in a single lawsuit, but the substantive requirements they contain increase the impacts of environmental litigation.

The application of these new federal and state laws to defense facilities is of major importance. From the early days of our legal history, the Supreme Court recognized that the power to regulate was the power to destroy.[59] In the past, the Supremacy Clause and the concept of a federal enclave protected military installations from federal and state environmental regulation. Although NEPA presented rather controversial and often burdensome requirements, its principal weapon—the EIS—was only designed to affect the decision-making process; it does not dictate the ultimate decision. The statutes discussed in this section not only affect the process, but also the final result. Therefore, these statutes often penetrate sovereign immunity which would otherwise shield the federal government from state regulations. Accordingly, they are of major importance today to defense planners and deserve careful consideration. This section will first explore pollution abatement statutes and illustrate their application to national security issues in Case Study III (Puerto Rico and Mariel Boatlift) and Case Study IV (Naval Exercises and Vieques Island), then turn to Wildlife Statutes and Case Study V (the Endangered Species Act).

---

57. Winter v. Natural Resources Defense Council, 555 U.S. 7, 54 (2008) (Ginsburg, J., dissenting).

58. *The Local Environment at the U.S. Department of Defense*, 43 ENVTL. L. REP. 11057 (Dec. 2013).

59. McCulloch v. Maryland, 17 U.S. 316 (1819).

Pollution Abatement Statutory Overview

The following is a brief summary of the major federal pollution abatement and wildlife statutes.

Water Pollution

Statutory regulation of water pollution is based on the Federal Water Pollution Control Act (FWPCA),[60] also known as the Clean Water Act (CWA), with amendments in 1972, 1977, and 1987. The Act's major objective is to restore and maintain the "chemical, physical, and biological integrity of the Nation's waters" by regulating the discharge of pollutants into "navigable waters."[61] The Act requires each state to set water quality standards for every significant body of surface water within its borders and Total Maximum Daily Loads (TMDLs), a pollution budget, for each impaired body of water. States must also set effluent limitations, defining the amounts and kinds of pollutants that may be discharged into waterways, and require permits before parties can discharge pollutants under the National Pollutant Discharge Elimination System (NPDES). State or federal NPDES permits are required for any discharge of a pollutant from a point source into navigable water (or waters of the United States). Discharges of dredge and fill material into "waters of the United States" (including wetlands) also require a permit issued by approved states or the Army Corps of Engineers under Section 404 of the Act.

Air Quality

Although some federal legislation dealing with air pollution was enacted in the 1960s, the statutory framework existing today was the product of the Clean Air Act (CAA) of 1970.[62] The Act was amended in 1974, 1977, and 1990. The Clean Air Act establishes the basic legal authority for the nation's air pollution control programs. Air quality standards are attained by regulating air discharges based on federal or state emission limitations. The Act requires the EPA to set primary and secondary national ambient air quality standards (NAAQS) for specific air pollutants such as sulfur dioxide, carbon monoxide, hydrocarbons, ozone, and lead. The various CAA programs, including attainment of the NAAQSs, are generally delegated to the states through implementation in a state implementation plan. Emission limitations are established for specific types of sources such as power plants and cement plants. Hazardous air pollutants like asbestos, mercury, and benzene are limited by national standards. Automotive emissions are also regulated. Federal actions, including financial support, must be in "conformity" with State Implementation Plans and must not unduly delay attainment of the NAAQS.[63] Finally, certain areas with good to pristine air quality, such as wilderness areas and national parks, are closely regulated to prevent significant deterioration.

Drinking Water

The Safe Drinking Water Act of 1974, amended in 1986 and 1996, sets national standards to protect drinking water.[64] States bear primary responsibility for enforcing the standards.

---

60. Federal Water Pollution Control Act (FWPCA), 33 U.S.C. § 1251 et seq. (2000).
61. 33 U.S.C. § 1251.
62. Clean Air Act of 1970, 42 U.S.C. § 7401 et seq. (2000).
63. *See* 42 U.S.C. § 7506(c)(1)(A-B).
64. Safe Drinking Water Act of 1974, 42 U.S.C. §§ 300f-300j-9 (2000).

EPA is responsible for administering the Act, and it issues regulations that set national drinking water standards and rules to protect underground sources of drinking water.

Hazardous and Solid Waste

The Resource Conservation and Recovery Act (RCRA) provides federal guidance and support to states to develop environmentally sound methods of hazardous and solid waste disposal.[65] RCRA requires states to develop and implement municipal waste disposal plans as part of their solid waste plans. Proper disposal of hazardous wastes, such as toxic substances, pesticides, and explosive materials, is carefully controlled. All treatment, storage, and disposal sites must have permits to operate, and their design must be adequate to prevent the waste from moving through the soil and reaching water sources. Active land and disposal sites are monitored constantly for groundwater contamination.

The cornerstone of the RCRA cradle-to-grave hazardous waste management program is the definition and listing of hazardous wastes. EPA identifies a solid waste as hazardous by including it on a list of hazardous substances or by analyzing its characteristics for toxicity, ignitability, corrosivity, and reactivity.[66] Other RCRA sections regulate hazardous waste generators, transporters, and disposal facility owners and operators.

Federal facilities that either produce hazardous waste or have waste disposal sites must comply with all applicable federal, state, and local requirements and obtain permits to treat, store, or dispose of hazardous waste. Federal agencies are also liable for state penalties.

Superfund

The Comprehensive Environmental Response, Compensation, and Liability Act (CER-CLA)[67] created what is frequently referred to as "Superfund." Superfund provides money and authority to direct and oversee the cleanup of old and abandoned waste sites that pose a threat to the public health or environment. A $1.6 billion fund was established by joint federal and industrial financing. Expenditures are reimbursed through civil penalties paid by the responsible polluters. CERCLA requires reporting of contamination by hazardous substances released from facilities or vessels, as well as the existence of old sites. Primary concerns for federal agencies are oil spills and pollution by industrial-type facilities, such as ammunition plants. Increasingly the U.S. is experiencing liability for its wartime activities if the U.S. can be found to have owned or operated a facility in which hazardous substances were disposed.

Other Applicable Environmental Laws

- Coastal Zone Management Act[68] (see discussion below, in Case Study II)
- Noise Control Act of 1972[69]
- Federal Insecticide, Fungicide, and Rodenticide Act[70]

---

65. Resource Conservation and Recovery Act (RCRA), 42 U.S.C. §§ 6901–6987 (2000), *amended by* Pub. L. No. 95-609, 92 Stat. 3079.

66. *See* 40 C.F.R. § 261.

67. Comprehensive Environmental Response, Compensation, and Liability Act (CERCLA), 42 U.S.C. § 9601 et seq. (2000).

68. Coastal Zone Management Act, 16 U.S.C. 1454–1464 (1966).

69. Noise Control Act of 1972, 42 U.S.C. 4901–4918 (1972) (see discussion in Comment 1 following case study IV).

70. Federal Insecticide, Fungicide, and Rodenticide Act, *as amended*, 7 U.S.C. §§ 136–136y.

- Toxic Substances Control Act[71]
- National Historic Preservation Act[72]

Post-Conflict Natural Resource Management

Sound natural resource management can play an important peacebuilding role in post-conflict countries. Competition for scarce natural resources can generate conflict, and war frequently exacerbates such conflicts. For example, a weakened government may be unable to provide the populace with essential resources, such as clean water. In addition, lands, forests, and crops may be damaged, neglected, or intentionally burned and destroyed. Post-conflict societies are often weak or unstable, even after peace has been formally established, and continuing scarcity of natural resources may reignite conflicts and further destabilize the society. It is therefore important for sound, sustainable natural resource management strategies to be established in post-conflict societies.

The Environmental Law Institute, the United Nations Environment Programme (UNEP), the University of Tokyo, and the Specialist Group on Armed Conflict and the Environment of the International Union for Conservation of Nature (IUCN) Commission on Environmental Law have partnered to assess experiences in post-conflict natural resource management and peacebuilding.[73] The project includes case studies on particular issues in specific post-conflict contexts, as well as thematic analyses that examine cross-cutting issues. Practitioners and scholars are working together to identify examples of post-conflict natural resource management issues, looking at both successes and challenges. An Environmental Peacebuilding website has been set up to house the project[74] and several books on post-conflict peacebuilding and natural resource management have been published, addressing such matters as high-value resources, water, land, livelihoods, assessing and restoring resources, and governance.[75]

Federal Compliance with State Environmental Laws

Mandatory federal compliance with some state environmental laws started in 1970. In that year Congress amended the Clean Air Act, requiring federal facilities to meet all state, local, and interstate requirements. In 1972, a similar provision was added to the Federal Water Pollution Control Act. Soon thereafter, President Nixon issued Executive Order No. 11,752, which emphasized that federal facilities should lead the way in abating pollution, but stated that the statute was "not intended, nor should it be interpreted, to require federal facilities to comply with state or local administrative procedures with respect to pollution abatement and control." The executive order limitation was tested in *Hancock v. Train*, a case brought by the state of Kentucky.[76] Using the Clean Air Act's 1970 amendments, state officials attempted to require several military installations, including Fort Knox, to obtain local air pollution permits.

In 1976 the Supreme Court held in *Hancock* and a related case that federal facilities were not bound by state pollution control restrictions in the absence of a "clear and un-

---

71. Toxic Substances Control Act, 16 U.S.C. §§ 1531–1543 (1973).
72. National Historic Preservation Act, 16 U.S.C. § 470 (1966).
73. *Environmental Law Institute,* Improving Natural Resource Management in Post-Conflict Countries, <http://www.eli.org/armed-conflict-environment/post-conflict-natural-resource-management>.
74. Environmental Peacebuilding, http://www.environmentalpeacebuilding.org/.
75. Environmental Peacebuilding, Books, http://www.environmentalpeacebuilding.org/publications/books/.
76. Hancock v. Train, 426 U.S. 167 (1976).

ambiguous" statutory declaration. The Court found that the federal statutes involved did not clearly convey congressional intent to waive federal supremacy, thereby inviting Congress to change the laws.[77] Later in *Department of Energy v. Ohio*,[78] the Supreme Court held that RCRA did not waive government immunity as to punitive fines.

Only a few months after the Supreme Court decided *Hancock v. Train*, Congress accepted the invitation to expressly require federal facility compliance with particular state laws, and enacted the Resource Conservation and Recovery Act of 1976 (RCRA), which required that federal facilities comply with "all Federal, State, interstate, and local requirements, both substantive and procedural...."[79] Subsequently, Congress passed the Federal Facility Compliance Act of 1992, which made the waiver of sovereign immunity explicit.[80] There is no limitation in RCRA concerning the sanctions to which federal agencies and departments may be subjected, and the authority to enforce the pollution abatement requirements in state and local administrative and judicial forums is explicitly provided by statute.

Today, federal facility compliance is a matter of federal policy, dictated by President Carter in Executive Order No. 12,088, "Federal Compliance with Pollution Control Standards."[81] That order requires the head of each executive agency to meet the same substantive, procedural, and other requirements that would apply to a private person. The combination of legislative enactments, like the Federal Facility Compliance Act in RCRA and the federal facilities provisions of the major environmental statutes, mean that the U.S. has waived sovereign immunity for injunctive relief. However, there is a continuing dispute as to whether the U.S. is liable for state penalties after *Department of Energy v. Ohio*.[82] While the U.S. is now liable for state RCRA penalties, courts have held that federal agencies are not liable for Clean Water Act penalties, and the courts are split on Clean Air Act penalties.[83] While national security exemptions from some pollution control standards can be granted, they require presidential action. This escape valve for the President to exempt a specific facility is limited to circumstances when it is necessary (a) "in the interests of national security" or (b) "in the paramount interests of the United States."[84] The President also has one additional national security power in the pollution statutes, the ability to exempt from compliance any "weaponry, equipment, aircraft, ... or other classes ... of property ... which are owned ... by the Armed Forces of the United States ... and which are uniquely military in nature."[85] While this may seem like a potentially broad type of exemption, the President has exercised these powers on only a few occasions. One classic example, illustrating the application of a number of environmental statutes to a particular controversy, as well as the rare use of a presidential exemption, is the 1980 Cuban-Haitian refugee operation.

77. *Id.* (Clean Air Act); EPA v. Cal. ex. rel. State Water Resources Control Bd., 426 U.S. 200 (1976) (Federal Water Pollution Control Act).

78. Dep't of Energy v. Ohio, 503 U.S. 607 (1992).

79. 42 U.S.C. §6911f(a)(2).

80. Federal Facility Compliance Act of 1992, 42 U.S.C. §6961 (2000).

81. Executive Order No. 12,088, Federal Compliance with Pollution Control Standards, 3 C.F.R. §243 (1979).

82. 503 U.S. 607 (1992).

83. *Compare* Cal. ex rel. Sacramento Metro. Air Quality Mgmt. Dist. v. United States, 29 F. Supp. 2d 652 (E.D. Cal 1998), *vacated by* 215 F.3d 1005, *reh'g denied* (9th Cir. 2000) *with* United States v. Tenn. Air Pollution Control Bd., 185 F.3d 529 (6th Cir. 1999). *See also* City of Jacksonville v. U.S. Dep't of the Navy, 348 F.3d 1307, 1317 (11th Cir. 2003) (holding "that the federal facilities section of the CAA unequivocally waives the federal government's sovereign immunity from coercive sanctions, but not from punitive penalties").

84. Exec. Order No. 12,088, *supra* note 74, §§1–7.

85. *See* 33 U.S.C. §1323 (1948); 42 U.S.C. §7418 (1955).

Case Study III: Puerto Rico, Mariel Boatlift, and Federal Exemptions

From late April to October 1980, some 122,000 Cuban and 9,500 Haitian refugees arrived by boat in the United States (sometimes referred to by the point of embarkation in Cuba, Mariel Harbor, as the Mariel boatlift). In May of 1980, President Carter declared that "an emergency exists in the State of Florida," and exercised the provisions of the Disaster Relief Act.[86] He formed an interagency Cuban-Haitian Task Force to handle the day-to-day operation of the refugee resettlement operation. Holding stations were established at Eglin Air Force Base, Florida; Fort Chaffee, Arkansas; Fort Indiantown Gap, Pennsylvania; and Fort McCoy, Wisconsin. Because Forts McCoy and Indiantown Gap did not have winter facilities, a search started for an additional refugee center.

In September, the administration selected Fort Allen, Puerto Rico, as an additional refugee center for approximately 2,000 people and issued a preliminary environmental assessment concluding that there would be no significant environmental impact from expanding Fort Allen to accept the refugees. To provide for immediate relocation, President Carter issued Executive Order No. 12,244 on October 3, 1980, exempting Fort Allen from the restrictions of water, air, noise, and solid waste pollution abatement statutes.

Several lawsuits were initiated to stop the construction on Fort Allen and prevent the transfer of any refugees. An action brought by the Commonwealth of Puerto Rico contended that the decision to place refugees at Fort Allen violated NEPA, the Federal Water Pollution Control Act, the Clean Air Act, the Noise Control Act, the Solid Waste Disposal Act, and the Coastal Zone Management Act.

Although the Refugee Education Assistance Act of 1980[87] specifically exempted the "initial reception and placement in the United States of Cuban and Haitian entrants" from the EIS requirements of NEPA, the U.S. District Court (District of Puerto Rico) on October 8, 1980, enjoined the refugee transfer and related construction based on possible health hazards and the lack of an EIS.[88] That decision was vacated by the First Circuit on October 24, 1980. The Court of Appeals held that "the executive order designation of Fort Allen as a relocation site was not subject to judicial review."[89] Mr. Justice Brennan issued a stay of the Court of Appeal's decision on October 24, but the full Supreme Court vacated the stay on November 3, 1980. This was the posture of the case when hearings commenced again at the district court concerning the motion for a preliminary injunction. The following is the relevant portion of the decision.

Commonwealth of Puerto Rico v. Muskie

507 F. Supp. 1035, 1045–49, 1057–61 (D.P.R. 1981)

On October 3, 1980 approximately nine days after Fort Allen was selected by the Cuban-Haitian Task Force as the relocation site for the refugees, the President issued Executive Order 12,244 (filed in the Federal Register at 10:44 A.M. of October 6, 1980, 45 F.R. 66, 443).

In this Executive Order, the President exercised specific authority conferred by Section 313(a) of the Federal Water Pollution Control Act, supra, Section 118 of the Clean Air Act,

---

86. Disaster Relief Act, 42 U.S.C. § 5121 (2000).
87. Refugee Education Assistance Act of 1980, 8 U.S.C. § 1522 (2000).
88. Colon v. Carter, 507 F. Supp. 1026 (D.P.R. 1980).
89. Colon v. Carter, 633 F.2d 964, 966 (1st Cir. 1980).

supra, Section 4(b) of the Noise Control Act, supra and Section 6001 of the Solid Waste Disposal Act, supra, to Fort Allen. Pursuant to its terms "every effluent source" (water), "each and every particular emission source" (air), "each and every single activity or facility, including noise emission sources or classes thereof", and "each and every solid waste facility" (emphasis supplied), located at Fort Allen were exempt from the respective statutes. The President found that these actions were necessary "in the paramount interest of the United States", and "in order to provide for the immediate relocation and temporary housing of Haitian and Cuban nationals, who [were] located in the State of Florida" to Fort Allen.

. . .

In our opinion of October 8, 1980 we upheld the validity of this order and the exemptions created by it. We reaffirm this decision but upon closer analysis of this order and one of the statutes upon which it is based, we conclude that with respect to the exemption from the Solid Waste Disposal Act, supra, said exemption is limited in scope and does not encompass the full range of the proven consequences of the refugee activities at Fort Allen.

This evidence is uncontradicted to the effect that the refugee operation will generate a large amount of solid waste, which will in turn severely tax the civilian landfill operations of the Municipality of Juana Diaz. The reason for this is that Fort Allen itself has no solid waste management facility. Yet it is only such a facility that can be exempt by the President under Section 6001 of the Solid Waste Disposal Act, supra, and it is only such a facility that is exempt by the Presidential Order. Under this statute, in contrast with the other mentioned Statutes, there is a distinction between "solid waste management facility or disposal site" 42 U.S.C. § 6961(2), which the President has no authority to exempt.

The Fort Allen refugee camp, not having a solid waste disposal facility or site, falls within the purview of 42 U.S.C. § 6961(2), and thus the solid waste producing activity is not exempt. Defendants are thus in violation of 42 U.S.C. § 6961.

. . .

In these circumstances, it is clear that there were violations of NEPA in the selection of Fort Allen. The record demonstrates that there was no careful consideration of environmental factors. Certainly, there was no attempt to study, develop, and describe alternative locations.

Defendants assert that the President, and presumably those to whom he delegates, is not subject to NEPA because he is not an "agency" of the Federal Government. This argument overlooks the delegation previously discussed; and the language of Section 102(1) of NEPA which directs that "the policies, regulations and public laws of the United States shall be interpreted and administered in accordance with the policies" in NEPA, and with no other restrictions than that this be done "to the fullest extent possible." *See Calvert Cliffs' Coord. Com. v. E.E. Com'n.*, supra, at 1114.

The Coastal Zone Management Act ("CZMA"), 16 U.S.C. §§ 1451–1456, has as one of its purposes the encouragement of states to "exercise effectively their responsibilities in the coastal zone through the development and implementation of management programs to achieve wise use of land and water resources of the coastal zone ..." *Id.* Sec. 1452(b). Consequently, once a state has established such a management program and has had it approved by the Secretary of Commerce, see *id.* Sec. 1455, "[e]ach federal agency conducting or supporting activities directly affecting the coastal zone shall conduct or support those activities in a manner which is, to the maximum extent practicable, consistent with approved state management programs," *id.* Sec. 1456 (emphasis added).

. . .

Defendants contend that the CZMA is inapplicable to the activities at Fort Allen. For this proposition they rely upon our decision in *Barcelo v. Brown*, 478 F. Supp. 646 (D.P.R. 1979), and in the definition of the term "coastal zone" contained in the CZMA, 16 U.S.C. § 1453(1).

...

The application of the CZMA to the Fort Allen situation is triggered by the fact that Puerto Rico has an approved coastal zone management program and that the federal activities taking place at Fort Allen will have a direct effect on the designated coastal zone. Pursuant to the regulations promulgated under CZMA, 15 C.F.R. § 930.35(a), Puerto Rico has set out certain activities which in its opinion will presumptively affect the coastal zone. Among those activities are "waste discharge in the coastal watershed" and "waste discharge in the coastal waters." The activities at Fort Allen will result in such discharges. Therefore, even if Defendants ultimately show that the manner in which the activities will be carried out is not inconsistent with Puerto Rico's management plan, they would not be relieved from observing the procedural requirements promulgated pursuant to CZMA. As shown below, these regulations require the filing of a consistent statement at least 90 days prior to undertaking the proposed activity. See C.F.R. § 930.41(a).

In the instant case, however, not only does the evidence show a direct effect on the coastal zone, but there is ample evidence that impact will be adverse. The inevitable result of overloading the capacity of the waste-water treatment facility will be the release of partially treated sewage into the coastal zone. In addition, the thousands of pounds of solid waste that will be dumped into an already severely overloaded landfill that has difficulties with flooding and has been known to permit solid waste to be carried downstream through the coastal zone. Therefore, the activities at Fort Allen will clearly be inconsistent with Puerto Rico's management plan.

These activities are in violation of the CZMA.

Case Study IV: Naval Exercises and Vieques Island

Another time that a request for a national security exemption was actively contemplated was in the context of the next case study, cases involving the Navy's use of the Vieques Island (near Puerto Rico) as a target area. The controversial nature of this bombing has engendered a long series of environmental lawsuits. The first went to the Supreme Court and remains the leading case on the standard for injunctive relief in environmental cases involving national security. For many years, the Navy used Vieques Island, a small island off the Puerto Rico coast, for weapons training. All Atlantic Fleet vessels in the Mediterranean and the Indian Ocean trained at Vieques with exercises simulating combat conditions, including practice bombing operations. During air-to-ground training, however, pilots sometimes missed land-based targets, and bombs accidentally fell into navigable waters governed by the Clean Water Act. The Governor of Puerto Rico sued to enjoin the Navy from training.

Weinberger v. Romero Barcelo

456 U.S. 305 (1982)

In 1978, respondents, who include the Governor of Puerto Rico and residents of the island, sued to enjoin the Navy's operations on the island. Their complaint alleged violations of numerous federal environmental statutes and various other Acts. After an extensive hearing, the District Court found that under the explicit terms of the Act, the Navy had violated the Act by discharging ordnance into the waters surrounding the island without first obtaining a permit from the Environmental Protection Agency (EPA), *Romero-Barcelo v. Brown*, 478 F. Supp. 646 (PR 1979).

. . .

As the District Court construed the FWPCA, the release of ordnance from aircraft or from ships into navigable waters is a discharge of pollutants, even though EPA, which administers the Act, had not promulgated any regulations setting effluent levels or providing for the issuance of a NPDES permit for this category of pollutants. Recognizing that violations of the Act "must be cured," 478 F. Supp., at 707, the District Court ordered the Navy to apply for a permit. It refused, however, to enjoin Navy operations pending consideration of the permit application. It explained that the Navy's "technical violations" were not causing any "appreciable harm" to the environment. *Id.*, at 706. Moreover, because of the importance of the island as a training center, "the granting of the injunctive relief sought would cause grievous, and perhaps irreparable harm, not only to Defendant Navy, but to the general welfare of this Nation." *Id.*, at 707. The District Court concluded that an injunction was not necessary to ensure suitably prompt compliance by the Navy. To support this conclusion it emphasized an equity court's traditionally broad discretion in deciding appropriate relief and quoted from the classic description of injunctive relief in *Hecht Co. v. Bowles*, 321 U.S. 321, 329–330 (1944): "The historic injunctive process was designed to deter, not to punish."

The Court of Appeals for the First Circuit vacated the District Court's order and remanded with instructions that the court order the Navy cease the violation until it obtained a permit. 643 F.2d 835 (1981). Relying on *TVA v. Hill*, 437 U.S. 153 (1978), in which this Court held that an imminent violation of the Endangered Species Act required injunctive relief, the Court of Appeals concluded that the District Court erred in undertaking a traditional balancing of the parties' competing interests. "Whether or not the Navy's activities in fact harm the coastal water, it has an absolute statutory obligation to stop any discharges of pollutants until the permit procedure has been followed and the Administrator of the Environmental Protection Agency, upon review of the evidence, has granted a permit." 643 F.2d at 861. The court suggested that if the order would interfere significantly with military preparedness, the Navy should request that the President grant it an exemption from the requirements in the interest of national security.

Because this case posed an important question regarding the power of the federal courts to grant or withhold equitable relief for violations of the FWPCA, we granted certiorari, 454 U.S. 813 (1981). We now reverse.

. . .

The FWPCA directs the Administrator of the EPA to seek an injunction to restrain immediately discharges of pollutants he finds to be presenting "an imminent and substantial endangerment to the health of person or to the welfare of persons." 33 U.S.C § 1364(a) (1976 ed., Supp. IV). This rule of immediate cessation, however, is limited to the indicated class of violations. For other kinds of violations, the FWPCA authorizes the Administrator of EPA "to commence a civil action for appropriate relief, including a permanent or temporary injunction, for any violation for which he is authorized to issue a compliance order" . . . 33 U.S.C. § 1319(b). The provision makes clear that Congress did not anticipate that all discharges would be immediately enjoined. Consistent with this view, the administrative practice has not been to request immediate cessation orders. "Rather, enforcement actions typically result, by consent or otherwise, in a remedial order setting out a detailed schedule of compliance designed to cure the identified violation of the Act." Brief for

Petitioners 17. *See Milwaukee v. Illinois*, 451 U.S. 304, 320 (1981). Here again, the statutory scheme contemplates equitable consideration.

Both the Court of Appeals and respondents attach particular weight to the provision of the FWPCA permitting the President to exempt federal facilities from compliance with the permit requirements. 33 U.S.C. § 1323(a) (1976 ed., Supp. IV). They suggest that this provision indicates congressional intent to limit the court's discretion. According to respondents, the exemption provision evidences Congress' determination that only paramount national interests justify failure to comply and that only the President should make this judgment.

We do not construe the provision so broadly. We read the FWPCA as permitting the exercise of a court's equitable discretion, whether the source of pollution is a private party or a federal agency, to order relief that will achieve compliance with the Act. The exemption serves a different and complementary purpose, that of permitting noncompliance by federal agencies in extraordinary circumstances. Executive Order No. 12088, 3 CFR 243 (1979), which implements the exemption authority, requires the federal agency requesting such an exemption to certify that it cannot meet the applicable pollution standards. "Exemptions are granted by the President only if the conflict between pollution control standards and crucial federal activities cannot be resolved through the development of a practicable remedial program." Brief for Petitioner 26, n. 30.

Should the Navy receive a permit here, there would be no need to invoke the machinery of the Presidential exemption. If not, this course remains open. The exemption provision would enable the President, believing paramount national interests so require, to authorize discharges which the District Court has enjoined. Reading the statute to permit the exercise of a court's equitable discretion in no way eliminates the role of the exemption provision in the statutory scheme.

    ...

Because Congress, in enacting the FWPCA, has not foreclosed the exercise of equitable discretion, the proper standard for appellate review is whether the District Court abused its discretion in denying an immediate cessation order while the Navy applied for a permit. We reverse and remand to the Court of Appeals for proceedings consistent with this opinion.

Comments

1. The District Court in the Mariel Boatlift/Fort Allen litigation ultimately ordered a permanent injunction based on its finding of violations of NEPA, the Coastal Zone Management Act, the National Historic Preservation Act, the Solid Waste Disposal Act, and the federal common law of nuisance. The Court of Appeals subsequently vacated this decision as moot because the Commonwealth and the federal government agreed that the operation of the facility and disposal of waste would be consistent with local law, including the Puerto Rican coastal management plan.[90] Later President Reagan renewed Executive Order No. 12,327,[91] exempting Fort Allen from compliance with the pollution control statutes, including "each and every solid waste management facility located at Fort Allen."[92]

2. Notwithstanding the district court's finding, the Supreme Court has held that the federal common law of nuisance for interstate and coastal water pollution has been entirely

---

90. Marquez-Colon v. Reagan, 668 F.2d 611 (1st Cir. 1981).
91. Exec. Order No. 12,327, 46 Fed. Reg. 48,893 (1981).
92. *Id.*

preempted by the Federal Water Pollution Control Act.[93] In addition, subsequent courts have held that a presidential decision is not subject to NEPA because that statute exclusively applies to decisions by agencies of the federal government.[94]

3. The Fort Allen case is still the best example of a presidential exemption for federal facilities. At the time he signed Executive Order No. 12,088, President Carter said:

> From now on, all Federal facilities must comply with the same Federal, State, and local environmental standards, procedural requirements, and schedules for cleanup that apply to individual citizens and corporations. I personally will review requests for exemptions, and I will grant them only in cases where I find that national security or the paramount interest of the nation is at stake. I have ordered that the Administrator of the Environmental Protection Agency and the director of the Office of Management and Budget attempt to resolve any conflicts that may arise between Federal agencies and other units of government.[95]

4. Starting in 2002 DOD officials sought exemptions from environmental statutes for military readiness and training exercises as part of their "Readiness and Range Preservation Initiative." The fiscal year 2003 defense authorization law[96] provided a limited exemption for the military from the Migratory Bird Treaty Act following an adverse decision in *Center for Biological Diversity v. Pirie*.[97] Subsequently, in the fiscal year 2004 bill,[98] the Defense Authorization Act included a proposed modification to the Endangered Species Act (ESA) to preclude designation of critical habitat on DOD lands that are subject to an Integrated Natural Resource Management Plan, prepared under Section 101 of the Sikes Act,[99] if the Secretary of the Interior determines that such a plan provides a benefit to the relevant species. In addition, a proposed change to the Marine Mammal Protection Act would have provided a more limited definition of prohibited mammal "harassment" as it applies to military readiness activity. The conference report cited *Natural Resources Defense Council, Inc. v. Evans*,[100] a case in which the Navy was enjoined under the Marine Mammal Protection Act from deploying the SURTASS Low Frequency Active sonar system. DOD continued to seek additional modifications to other environmental statutes in 2004, specifically the Clean Air Act, Resource Conservation and Recovery Act, and the Comprehensive Environmental Response, Compensation, and Liability Act as part of the FY Act; however, these proposals were not enacted.

5. In *Ralls Corp. v. Committee on Foreign Investment in the United States*[101] the D.C. Circuit held in 2014 that an American corporation owned by Chinese nationals was deprived of its due process rights when President Obama issued an order blocking on national security grounds the corporation's wind farm project located near a U.S. Navy facility off Oregon's coast. The Committee on Foreign Investment in the United States (CFIUS) concluded that the corporation's acquisition of the project threatened national

---

93. *See* City of Milwaukee v. Illinois, 451 U.S. 304 (1981).

94. *See, e.g.*, Tulare Cnty. v. Bush, 185 F. Supp. 2d 18, 28 (D.D.C. 2001) (holding that "the President is not a federal agency for the purposes of NEPA").

95. Exec. Order No. 12,088, 43 Fed. Reg. 47,677 (1978).

96. Bob Stump National Defense Authorization Act for Fiscal Year 2003, Pub. L. 107-314; 116 Stat. 2458 (2002).

97. *See* discussion of case and subsequent amendment at Section on Training and Testing, *infra*.

98. National Defense Authorization Act for Fiscal Year 2004, Pub. L. 108-136; 117 Stat. 1392 (2003).

99. Sikes Act, 16 U.S.C. §670a (2004).

100. NRDC v. Evans, 279 F. Supp. 2d 1129 (N.D. Cal. 2003).

101. 758 F.3d 296 (D.C. Cir. 2014), 44 ELR 20156.

security and the President agreed, issuing a presidential order that prohibited the transaction and required the corporation to divest itself of the project. The corporation challenged the order and the Court of Appeals ruled in favor of the corporation.

Wildlife Statutes

The Lacey Act, first enacted in 1900 and most recently amended in 2008,[102] made interstate transportation, import, and sale of wild animals, and other violations of state and foreign game laws, federal offenses. Migratory bird protection came with the passage of the Migratory Bird Act of 1913 and the Migratory Bird Treaty Act of 1918.[103]

The Marine Mammal Protection Act was passed in 1972,[104] followed by the "pit bull" of all environmental statutes, the Endangered Species Act of 1973 (ESA).[105] ESA remains the most stringent and proscriptive of all environmental laws, and it speaks in unequivocal terms. The Act is implemented and the species regulated by two federal agencies: the Fish and Wildlife Service (FWS), a division of the Department of the Interior (terrestrial species) and the National Marine Fisheries Service (NMFS), a division of the Department of Commerce (for most marine species and anadromous fish).

The Purposes Section of the ESA declares that the statute provides protection to both species at risk and the "ecosystems upon which [they] depend."[106] Section 4(a) and (b) provide the criteria and rulemaking procedures for the Services to determine which species are "endangered" or "threatened."[107] The species are then "listed" according to 50 C.F.R. § 17.11 (animals) and § 17.12 (plants), and the critical habitat described in 50 C.F.R. § 17.95 (animals) and § 17.96 (plants). Agency decision-making has firm statutory deadlines, and citizens can sue if any deadline is missed.

Species listed as endangered or threatened under the ESA are afforded certain legal protections. Section 9 establishes specific prohibitions, the most important of which is forbidding the "take" of any protected species by "persons."[108] "Take" is defined broadly in Section 3(19) to include "harass, harm, pursue, hunt, shoot, wound, kill, trap, capture or collect" listed wildlife.[109] In 1982, Congress added a provision authorizing the Services to allow landowners to "take" listed species "incidental" to lawful land uses.[110] To obtain an incidental take permit, the landowner must prepare a conservation plan called a habitat conservation plan (HCP).

Section 7 requires federal agencies to consult with the Services to assure that their "actions" are not likely to jeopardize the continued existence of any listed species "or result in the destruction or adverse modification of [any designated critical] habitat of such species."[111] If the agency cannot conclude that an action is "not likely to adversely affect" a listed species or critical habitat, then "formal" consultation must occur and the

---

102. Lacey Act of 1900, 31 Stat. 187 (1900) (codified as amended at 16 U.S.C. §§ 3371–78 (2000)).
103. Migratory Bird Treaty Act of 1918, 16 U.S.C. §§ 703–12 (2000).
104. Marine Mammal Protection Act, 16 U.S.C. §§ 1361–1421h (2000).
105. Endangered Species Act of 1973, 16 U.S.C. §§ 1531–44 (2000).
106. *Id.* § 1531(b).
107. *Id.* § 1533.
108. *Id.* § 1538.
109. *Id.* § 1532(19).
110. *Id.* § 1539.
111. *Id.* § 1536(a)(2).

Services have to prepare a biological opinion on the impact, identifying, when appropriate, "reasonable and prudent alternatives."[112] If the Service concludes that the taking of a listed species incidental to the proposed agency action will not jeopardize the species, the Service issues an "incidental take statement" along with the biological opinion that authorizes the take.[113] The incidental take statement specifies the amount of take allowed and the terms and conditions to implement reasonable and prudent measures that the Service deems necessary or appropriate to minimize the incidental taking of the species.[114] Any taking of a listed species which is subject to such an incidental take statement and in compliance with the terms and conditions set forth in that statement is not prohibited by the ESA.[115]

Case Study V: The Endangered Species Act

Nineteen years after the Supreme Court dealt with the Clean Water Act in the *Weinberger v. Romero Barcelo* case, a citizen group challenged other Naval exercises at Vieques, this time relying on the Endangered Species Act.

Water Keeper Alliance v. U.S. Department of Defense
271 F.3d 21 (1st Cir. 2001)

Plaintiffs-appellants, Water Keeper Alliance et al. ("Water Keeper"), appeal the denial of their motion for preliminary injunction to stay Department of Navy (the "Navy," one of several defendants-appellees) military exercises on the island of Vieques off Puerto Rico. Water Keeper alleges violations by the Navy of certain procedural requirements under section 7 of the Endangered Species Act ("ESA"), 16 U.S.C. § 1536. The district court found that Water Keeper had failed to show a strong likelihood of success on its ESA theory, that its showing of potential irreparable harm had not been strong, and that the balance of harms, as well as the interest of the public, weighed in favor of denying the motion. Since denial of Water Keeper's motion for a preliminary injunction, the district court has additionally determined that it lacked jurisdiction over the ESA claims because Water Keeper, prior to bringing suit, failed to provide adequate 60-day notice as required by the citizen suit provisions of the ESA. *See* ESA § 11(g)(2)(A), 16 U.S.C. § 1540(g)(2)(A). We hold that notice was adequate for the purposes of the particular ESA claim on appeal here, but affirm on the merits the district court's denial of Water Keeper's motion for a preliminary injunction.

I. STATUTORY FRAMEWORK

The current appeal takes place against the background of a complex statutory framework that we examine at the outset of our opinion. The ESA directs federal agencies to insure that agency action "is not likely to jeopardize the continued existence of any endangered species or threatened species or result in the destruction or adverse modification of habitat of such species." ESA § 7(a)(2), 16 U.S.C. § 1536(a)(2). This substantive requirement that sets up a consultation process between the agency (in this case the Navy) and the National Marine Fisheries Service ("NMFS") and the U.S. Fish and Wildlife Service ("FWS")

---

112. *Id.* § 1536(b), (c), & (d).
113. Id. § 1536(b)(4); 50 C.F.R. § 402.14(i).
114. 50 C.F.R. § 402.14(i)(1).
115. 16 U.S.C. § 1536(o)(2); 50 C.F.R. § 402.14(i)(5).

(jointly, the "Services") to determine whether endangered species or critical habitat are jeopardized by proposed agency action and whether this adverse impact may be avoided or minimized. *See* ESA § 7, 16 U.S.C. § 1536.

Under the ESA, "[e]ach Federal agency shall review its actions at the earliest possible time to determine whether any action may affect listed species or critical habitat." 50 C.F.R. § 402.14(a). Although the determination of possible effects is ultimately the agency's responsibility, see 51 Fed. Reg. 19949, in making this determination, the agency may consult with the Services through "informal consultation." The term simply describes discussions and correspondence between the Services and the agency designed to assist the agency in determining whether its proposed action is likely to impact listed species or critical habitat. *Id.* § 402.13. If, at the conclusion of the informal consultation, the Services issue written concurrences that a "proposed action is not likely to adversely affect any listed species or critical habitat," the agency may proceed with the action without further consultation between the parties. *Id.* § 402.14(b)(1).

However, where the proposed agency action rises to the level of a "major construction activity" the determination as to whether agency action may affect listed species or critical habitat cannot be made through informal consultation alone, but must be based on a "biological assessment." *Id.* § 402.12(b)(1); see also 51 Fed. Reg. 19948 (noting that the biological assessment may be conducted simultaneously with informal consultation or without any informal consultation). A "major construction activity" is "a construction project (or other undertaking having similar physical impacts) which is a major Federal action significantly affecting the quality of the human environment as referred to in the National Environmental Policy Act [NEPA, 42 U.S.C. § 4332(2)(C)]." 50 C.F.R. § 402.02. The biological assessment is a study that "evaluate[s] the potential effects of the action on listed and proposed species ... and determine[s] whether any such species or habitat are likely to be adversely affected by the action ..." 50 C.F.R. § 402.12(a). If, following completion of the biological assessment, the Services issue written concurrences that the "proposed action is not likely to adversely affect any listed species or critical habitat," the consultation is terminated. *Id.* at § 402.14(b).

If, on the other hand, based on either informal consultation or a biological assessment, the Services are unwilling to concur that the agency action is unlikely to impact protected species and habitat, or if the agency independently concludes that its actions may affect listed species or critical habitat, the agency is required to initiate "formal consultation." *See id.,* § 402.14(b) & (b)(1). Formal consultation is initiated by the written request of the agency describing the action and the manner in which it may affect listed species and critical habitat. *Id.* § 402.14(c). Significantly, "formal consultation shall not be initiated by the Federal agency until any required biological assessment has been completed and submitted to the [Services] in accordance with § 402.12." *Id.* § 402.14(c). Nonetheless, formal consultation may take place without a biological assessment if the action is not a major construction activity.

After a period of review and discussion, formal consultation culminates in the Services' issuance of biological opinions advising the agency "whether the action is likely to jeopardize the continued existence of a listed species or result in the destruction or adverse modification of critical habitat," and, if so, whether "reasonable and prudent alternatives" exist to allow the agency to comply with the ESA. 50 C.F.R. § 402.14(h); *see also* ESA § 7(b)(3)(A), 16 U.S.C. § 1536(b)(3)(A). If the Services conclude that the action, or the implementation of any reasonable and prudent alternatives, comply with ESA, the Services must also issue an "incidental take statement" that specifies the amount or extent of the authorized taking of the species. ESA § 7(b)(4), 16 U.S.C. 1536(b)(4); 50 C.F.R. § 402.14(i).

With the basics of the statutory framework in place, we next consider the application of the ESA to the Navy in relation to its training exercises on Vieques.

II. BACKGROUND

The Navy has used the island for military exercises since 1941, including ship-to-shore and aerial bombing with live ammunition. Thirteen endangered and threatened species live on the island of Vieques and in surrounding water, and, as a result, in 1980 and 1981 respectively, pursuant to the ESA and after formal consultation, the NMFS and the FWS issued biological opinions regarding the effects of Navy exercises on the listed species and critical habitat. Both Services found no jeopardy to any listed species or critical habitat from naval exercises on Vieques. Beginning in 1995, the NMFS and the FWS asked the Navy to reinitiate "formal consultations" with the Services to reexamine the effect of the military exercises on the endangered and threatened species of the island. The Services explained that new information regarding the listed species had been obtained since 1981, that the dead or injured species had been found after training exercises (the original biological opinion did not authorize any takings pursuant to ESA section 7(b)(4), 16 U.S.C. § 1536(b)(4)), and that reinitiation was typical after five years. In January 2000, after a period of informal consultation, the Navy agreed to initiate formal consultation with FWS and NMFS. The Navy further indicated its willingness to prepare a biological assessment in anticipation of formal consultation, despite the fact that, in its own determination, it was not required to do so under the regulations. (*See* 50 C.F.R. § 402.12(b)(1); 51 Fed. Reg. 19945, contemplating voluntary preparation of a biological assessment to assist in the determination of whether formal consultation is required.) On January 31, 2000, in the same month that the Navy agreed to reinitiate formal consultation with the Services concerning its use of the Vieques range, the President issued an Executive Order restricting the use of the Vieques training range to no more than 90 days per year and using only non-explosive ordnance. 65 Fed. Reg. 5729 (Feb. 24, 2000). These restrictions were put in place pending a referendum by the citizens of Vieques on the future Navy exercises on the island.

...

After June 2000, the FWS changed its position and informed the Navy that it would require "interim formal consultation" for all exercises during the interim period of August 2000 to December 2001. The Navy agreed and, on July 12, 2000, provided FWS with a "consultation package" covering the planned training exercises through 2001. On July 27, 2000, the FWS issued a biological opinion reviewing the effects of the proposed interim exercises on the endangered and threatened species and finding that the exercises were not likely to jeopardize the continued existence of listed species or result in the destruction of critical habitat. FWS issued an incidental take statement with reasonable and prudent measures to ensure that any take would be minimized.

...

In response to the claimed danger to endangered species asserted by Water Keeper, the Navy argues that the loss of Vieques as a training ground will adversely affect military preparedness. Water Keeper correctly contends that, by enacting the ESA, Congress has already determined that the "'balance of hardships and the public interests tips heavily in favor of protected species.'" *Strahan v. Coxe*, 126 F.3d 155, 171 (1st Cir. 1997) (quoting *National Wildlife Fed'n v. Burlington N. R.R.*, 23 F.3d 1508, 1510 (9th Cir. 1994)). See also *Tennessee Valley Auth.*, 437 U.S. at 184–185, 98 S. Ct. 2279 (finding that the ESA "reveals a conscious decision by Congress to give endangered species priority over the 'primary missions' of federal agencies"). While these precedents direct us to give the endangered species, as alleged by Water Keeper, the utmost consideration, we do not think that they can blindly compel our decision in this case because the harm asserted by the Navy implicates national security and therefore deserves greater weight than the economic harm at issue in *Strahan*.

Water Keeper argues in response that military preparedness will not be affected to the extent that appellees allege. Water Keeper first points out that the Navy statements on which the district court relied in determining the harm to national security assumed that the training exercises utilized live ordnance, whereas the Navy was utilizing inert ordnance, arguably creating a less realistic and thus less instructional simulation of battle. Second, Water Keeper contends that alternative sites can provide the same training opportunities as Vieques. While acknowledging that these arguments could have some merit, the district court determined on the whole that the Navy's evidence in support of its contentions was more reliable and additionally cautioned against substituting judicial judgment for agency judgment in considerations of how and where the Navy should train. The court did not abuse its discretion in coming to this conclusion.

. . .

The effect of a preliminary injunction on the public interest is directly tied to its impact on both military preparedness and the endangered species. For the same reasons laid out above, the district court did not abuse its discretion in finding that the public interest weighed in favor of denying a preliminary injunction. We also note that the two Services charged with protecting the endangered species have not objected to the interim exercises or the process used by the Navy.

For the reason stated above, we find that Water Keeper's request for preliminary injunctive relief was properly denied.

Affirmed.

Comments

1. The third in the series of Vieques litigation arose in 2001 when the Commonwealth of Puerto Rico again challenged planned military exercises. The Commonwealth sought to prohibit the training using the federal Noise Control Act and its own Noise Prohibition Act. The district court dismissed for lack of jurisdiction, holding that the federal Act does not provide a private right of action.[116]

2. Under the ESA, the Department of Defense is generally required to consult with Interior (FWS) or Commerce (NMFS) if its actions are likely to affect listed species. Consultation can be done quickly and may involve classified material. If such a consultation results in a finding of "jeopardy with no reasonable and prudent alternatives," section 7(j) of the ESA directs that "the Committee shall grant an exemption for any agency action if the Secretary of Defense finds that such exemption is necessary for reasons of national security."[117]

3. The leading ESA decision is *Tennessee Valley Authority v. Hill*,[118] written by then Chief Justice Burger. The Court held that the ESA required the issuance of an injunction

---

116. Puerto Rico v. Rumsfeld, 180 F. Supp. 2d 145 (D.D.C. 2002), *vacated*, No. 02-5018, 2003 WL 21384576 (D.C. Cir. June 10, 2003).

117. 16 U.S.C. § 1536(j).

118. Tenn. Valley Auth. v. Hill, 437 U.S. 153 (1978).

to prevent completion of the nearly completed Tellico dam project on the Little Tennessee River. The injunction was based on the threatened destruction of a population of the endangered snail darter and its habitat. The Court's opinion includes reference to national defense considerations:

> It may seem curious to some that the survival of a relatively small number of three-inch fish among all the countless millions of species extant would require the permanent halting of a virtually completed dam for which Congress has expended more than $100 million. The paradox is not minimized by the fact that Congress continued to appropriate large sums of public money for the project, even after congressional Appropriations Committees were appraised of its apparent impact upon the survival of the snail darter. We conclude, however, that the explicit provisions of the Endangered Species Act require precisely that result.
>
> . . .
>
> Furthermore, it is clear Congress foresaw that § 7 [of the ESA] would, on occasion, require agencies to alter ongoing projects in order to fulfill the goals of the Act. Congressman Dingell's discussion of Air Force practice bombings, for instance, obviously pinpoints a particular activity—intimately related to the national defense—which a major federal department would be obliged to alter in deference to the strictures of § 7.[119]

Part 3: Specific National Security Issues

Having described and illustrated with case studies basic environmental law and policy (NEPA) in Part I and pollution-abatement/wildlife statutes in Part II, this part of the chapter addresses specific national security issues. The impact of environmental laws on legislation and planning, military basing decisions, training and testing, chemical weapon demilitarization, and nuclear shipments will each be analyzed by using illustrative cases. Finally, the application of environmental laws to U.S. activities overseas will be reviewed and climate change addressed.

Although it is important to analyze the cases in light of the consistent themes they present, each case also includes unique national security issues with varying degrees of controversy, political attention, time sensitivity, cost, and legislative interest. Those concerns, superimposed on legislation with varying standards, complicate an area that is already extraordinarily complex.

Legislation and Planning

Under CEQ guidelines, an agency must prepare an EIS for every "recommendation or report on proposals for legislation" (including requests for ratification of treaties) submitted to Congress. While this provision was added to ensure early examination of environmental effects, it also provides an opportunity to attack politically controversial projects at their inception. Two examples will suffice: the Atomic Energy Commission's Breeder Reactor Program and President Reagan's MX Missile program.

---

119. *Id.* at 172.

Scientists' Institute v. Atomic Energy Commission

481 F.2d 1079, 1082–83, 1085, 1088, 1091 (D.C. Cir. 1973)

J. SKELLY WRIGHT, Circuit Judge.

Appellant claims that the Atomic Energy Commission's Liquid Metal Fast Breeder Reactor program involves a "recommendation or report on proposals for legislation and other major Federal actions significantly affecting the quality of the human environment ..." under Section 102(C) of the National Environmental Policy Act (NEPA), 42 U.S.C. § 4332(C)(1970), and that the Commission is therefore required to issue a "detailed statement" for the program. The District Court held that no statement was presently required since, in its view, the program was still in the research and development stage and no specific implementing action which would significantly affect the environment had yet been taken. Taking into account the magnitude of the ongoing federal investment in this program, the controversial environmental effects attendant upon future widespread deployment of breeder reactors should the program fulfill present pure scientific research toward creation of a viable, competitive breeder reactor electrical energy industry, and the manner in which investment in this new technology is likely to restrict future alternatives, we hold that the Commission's program comes within both the letter and the spirit of Section 102(C) and that a detailed statement about the program, its environmental impact, and alternatives thereto is presently required. Since the Commission has not yet issued such a statement, we reverse and remand the case to the District Court for entry of appropriate declaratory relief.

I. FACTUAL BACKGROUND: THE LIQUID METAL FAST BREEDER REACTOR PROGRAM

Although more than a superficial understanding of the technology underlying this case is beyond the laymen's ken, a brief summary will prove helpful. Nuclear reactors use nuclear fission — the splitting of the atom — to produce heat which may be used to generate electricity in nuclear power plants. Only a few, relatively rare, naturally occurring substances — primarily Uranium 235 — can maintain the nuclear fission chain reaction necessary for operation of these reactors. There are thus several constraints on the long run potential of nuclear energy for generating electricity unless the new nuclear fuel is "artificially" produced. Such fuel can be produced through the process of "breeding" within a "fast breeder reactor." The fast breeder reactor differs from the now common light water nuclear reactor in that the neutrons which split atoms in the fuel (thereby releasing new neutrons and heat energy) travel much faster than the neutrons in ordinary reactors. The reactor breeds new fuel through what has aptly been termed "a sort of modern alchemy." Some neutrons leave the inner core of the reactor, which is made up of fissionable Uranium-235, and enter a blanket of nonfissionable Uranium-238. When atoms in this blanket are struck by neutrons, they are transmitted into Plutonium-239 not only to refuel itself completely, but also to fuel an additional reactor of comparable size. The Liquid Metal Fast Breeder Reactor (henceforth LMFBR) is simply a fast breeder reactor that uses a liquid metal, sodium, as a coolant and heat transfer agent.

...

II. APPLICATION OF NEPA TO TECHNOLOGY DEVELOPMENT PROGRAMS

NEPA requires federal agencies to include a detailed environmental impact statement "in every recommendation or report on proposals for legislation and other major Federal actions significantly affecting the quality of the human environment...." That the

Commission must issue a detailed statement for each of the major tests facilities and demonstration plants encompassed by the LMFBR program is conceded by the Commission and not at issue in this case. The Commission has already issued an impact statement for its Fast Flux Test Facility to be constructed in Hanford, Washington, and, at the President's request, has completed a statement for the first demonstration plant prior to the time such a statement would normally be issued. Nor is the adequacy of either of these statements as they pertain to their respective individual facilities an issue on this appeal. The question raised, instead, is basically twofold: whether at some point in time the Commission must issue a statement for the research and development program as a whole, rather than simply for individual facilities, and assuming an affirmative answer to this question, whether a statement covering the entire program should be drafted now.

. . .

We think it plain that at some point in time there should be a detailed statement on the overall LMFBR program. The program comes before the Congress as a "proposal for legislation" each year, in the form of appropriations requests by the Commission. And as the Council on Environmental Quality has noted in its NEPA guidelines, the statutory phrase "recommendation or report on proposals for legislation" includes "[r]ecommendations or favorable reports relating to legislation including that for appropriations." In addition, the program constituted "major Federal action" within the meaning of the statute.

We thus tread firm ground in holding that NEPA requires impact statements for major federal research programs, such as the commission's LMFBR program, aimed at development of new technologies which, when applied, will significantly affect the quality of the human environment. To the extent the Commission's "environmental survey" would not be issued in accordance with NEPA's procedures for preparation and distribution, it is not an adequate substitute for a NEPA statement. These procedural requirements are not dispensable technicalities, but are crucial if the statement is to serve its dual functions of informing Congress, the President, other concerned agencies and the public of the environmental effects of agency action, and of ensuring meaningful consideration of environmental factors at all stages of agency decision making.

Comments

1. In the breeder reactor decision, the AEC conceded that it had to do an EIS for each of its major research and development facilities that were part of the Liquid Metal Fast Breeder Reactor (LMFBR) program. In fact, at the time of the litigation the AEC had already prepared two such statements. The issue, then, was whether individual EISs were enough, or whether the AEC had to prepare an EIS for the entire project. Despite the AEC's claim that a consolidated EIS would be premature due to the "remote and speculative nature of the project," the Court of Appeals reversed the District Court and required the more comprehensive EIS.

2. The breeder reactor decision was decided before *Kleppe v. Sierra Club.*[120] In *Kleppe*, the Supreme Court rejected the contention that the Department of Interior had to prepare an EIS for the whole Northern Great Plains Region before taking action to develop coal resources in the area. While the Court recognized that NEPA might require a "programmatic" impact statement in certain situations where the proposed actions are

---

120. Kleppe v. Sierra Club, 427 U.S. 390 (1976).

pending or cumulative in nature, the Court said the issue "is properly left to the discretion of the responsible agencies."[121]

Friends of the Earth, Inc. v. Weinberger

562 F. Supp. 265, 265–70 (D.D.C. 1983), *appeal dismissed*,
725 F.2d 125 (D.C. Cir. 1984)

BARRINGTON D. PARKER, District Judge:

The plaintiffs in this proceeding are several not-for-profit interest groups concerned with the environmental consequences of the MX missile program. The term "MX" is an acronym for "missile experimental", a reference to the new generation of intercontinental ballistic missiles. Several of the organizations have a broad base as to both membership and area of concern. Others have memberships located in the particular geographic areas and regions which are potential sites for the basing and deployment of the MX missile. Each group has a demonstrated commitment to monitor and speak out on environmental issues such as the MX program. They are accordingly involved in a variety of activities including lobbying and publication efforts.

The plaintiffs allege in their complaint that Defense Secretary Caspar Weinberger and Air Force Secretary Verne Orr, the responsible Defense Department officials, have failed to comply with the National Environmental Policy Act of 1969 (NEPA), 42 U.S.C. §4321 et seq. The gravamen of their claims is that the defendants failed to prepare an adequate environmental impact statement (EIS), a NEPA requirement, in connection with the decision in the fall of 1982 to seek congressional approval of the closely spaced basing mode (CSB) as its preferred means of deployment for the MX. The plaintiffs seek judgment from this Court declaring that the defendants have violated NEPA and its implementing regulations. 40 C.F.R. §1508.21. They also seek preliminary relief in the form of an order requiring the Secretaries of Defense and Air Force to prepare an environmental impact statement.

...

While the government's consideration of the MX missile program reaches back to the mid-1970's, the facts which are critical to this proceeding may be briefly stated.

Plaintiffs challenge defendant's efforts to comply with their strict NEPA obligations in connection with the recent CSB basing proposal for the MX missile. The public debate over the basing issue has yielded a variety of options. Among the alternatives considered in recent years are horizontal sheltering in bunkers, vertical sheltering in underground tubes, use of slopesided pools to provide water camouflage over silos, and horizontal concrete tube structures known as hybrid buried trench. A considerable portion of the debate centers upon the survivability of a given basing concept; that is, whether the deployment of the missiles in a particular configuration will insure that a sufficient number of them can survive a nuclear exchange and remain operable to inflict defensive or retaliatory damage upon an aggressor.

Last year, after series of exchanges with Congress over the issue, the Reagan Administration settled upon closely spaced basing as its basing preference for MX missile. This concept contemplated placement of approximately 100 missiles in individual super-hardened silos which would also operate as launchers. The silos would be located close together such that all of the missiles would be placed in an area of approximately one by

---

121. *Id.* at 412.

14 miles. CSB proponents allege that the configuration would result in "fratricide"— phenomenon whereby the explosion of attacking warheads would theoretically disable or destroy other incoming missiles which followed while most of the MX missiles would remain protected through the use of reinforced or superhardened sheltering.

...

The President's CSB proposal was submitted to Congress in November 1982 in response to the congressional directive. That proposal was promptly rejected in an amendment to the Department of Defense Appropriations Act of 1983, passed as part of a continuing resolution statute signed into law on December 21, 1982. P.L 97-377, 96 Stat. 1830(1982). The amendment, named after its sponsor Senator Henry Jackson, adopted a Senate Armed Services Committee recommendation and set forth a detailed response to the President's proposal. Although Congress rejected the CSB proposal, it provided funds for the MX program and hinged their availability upon congressional approval of a basing mode.

The Jackson Amendment established the procedures to be followed by the President in formulating a proposal and by the Congress in evaluating it. Specifically, the President is required to submit a report to the appropriate congressional committees which will then have 45 calendar days to reach a decision. Because of the urgency which apparently accompanies the need for a decision on the missile program, the amendment also imposes a limit on floor debate.

...

Section (7) (C) provides that "the report required under [the Jackson Amendment] shall not be subject to the requirements of section 102(2) (C) of the [NEPA] relating to environmental impact statements." Section (7)(C) speaks only to the President's report as to a basing mode for the MX; once that report is submitted by the President and acted upon by Congress, the NEPA requirements would again apply in connection with the selection of an appropriate site for deployment of the missiles.

For purposes of assessing the alternatives and selecting a preference, the President has established a bipartisan Commission on Strategic Forces chaired by retired General Brent Scowcroft. The Scowcroft Commission presented its report to the President yesterday recommending the use of existing Minuteman silos rather than CSB ... Issuance of the President's proposal to Congress is imminent.

The plaintiffs commenced this action in mid-January seeking relief designed to remedy the defendant's alleged failure to comply with their NEPA obligations in presenting some of the MX basing proposals by requiring preparation of an EIS for use in selecting a basing mode. The plaintiffs propose that the Court direct the defendants to treat the LEIS as a draft statement and then engage in accelerated preparation of a final impact statement.

...

The linchpin of the defendant's argument in support of dismissal on the ground of mootness is the effect of Congress' adoption of the Jackson Amendment. Given the general presumption against repeal by implication, the plaintiffs contend that, insofar as the defendants' NEPA obligations are concerned, the amendment provides a narrow exemption which addresses only the President's report to Congress. Reading the amendment in that fashion and noting the widely accepted policy favoring broad enforcement of NEPA's provisions, the plaintiffs argue that the amendment should not be interpreted as an immunization or erasure of prior NEPA violations. That is, the fact Congress has suspended NEPA as to the President's impending report is not indicative of an intent to allow past infractions to go unremedied.

The defendants assert, and the Court agrees, that the amendment moots any claim as to prior NEPA violations if they indeed occurred and renders this case nonjusticiable. To read the amendment in any other manner would thwart Congress' intent in rejecting the November 1982 CSB proposal as presented and imposing a particular decision-making scheme upon the Executive branch in its selection of a new basing proposal for the MX.

Comments

1. The MX case is an example of Congress specifically legislating a NEPA exemption. The Disaster Relief Act of 1974 exempts a federal agency from compliance with NEPA's EIS requirement if the President declares an emergency.[122] Congress also exempted the trans-Alaskan pipeline from full compliance with NEPA.[123] Another example is the Energy Security Act, which expressly exempted the United States Synthetic Fuels Corporation from compliance with NEPA.[124] Legislation can be prompted by litigation, as in the case that challenged the building of the Memorial to World War II veterans on the Mall in Washington, DC. When NEPA litigation threatened to slow down the project, Congress exempted the property from further NEPA review and made the permit decision not subject to judicial review.[125] This law was subsequently upheld in *National Coalition to Save Our Mall v. Norton*.[126]

2. Many courts have blurred the distinction between legislative proposals and other major federal actions for NEPA purposes, especially regarding congressional appropriations and authorizations. Clearly, if the actions will have a significant effect on the environment, NEPA will still apply.[127] In Section 1508.17 of the CEQ regulations, the term "legislation" is defined to exclude requests for appropriations, in keeping with the Supreme Court's decision in *Andrus v. Sierra Club*.[128]

Military Basing Decisions

The decision to place military installations, weapons systems, or munitions in a particular location is always controversial. In some cases, states compete for the military defense presence because it means more jobs, an infusion of money into the economy, or increased federal government support. In other cases, the state or local citizens actively fight a particular defense project, based on the type of activity involved, projected environmental effects, or desire not to be overcome by federal activity.

There are numerous examples of both sides of this equation. One example, discussed earlier in this chapter, is the Carter Administration's decision to transfer refugees to Fort Allen, Puerto Rico, and the governor's attempt to block the transfer. Similarly, the MX case demonstrates an attack on a basing decision.

---

122. *See* case study concerning Colon v. Carter, 633 F.2d 964, 966 (1st Cir. 1980).
123. *See* Earth Res. Co. of Alaska v. Fed. Energy Regulatory Comm'n, 617 F.2d 775 (D.C. Cir. 1980).
124. Energy Security Act, Pub. L. No. 96-294, 94 Stat. 611 (1980).
125. Pub. L. 107-11, 115 Stat. 19 (2001).
126. Nat'l Coal. to Save Our Mall v. Norton, 269 F.3d 1092 (D.C. Cir. 2002).
127. *See* Aluli v. Brown, 437 F. Supp. 602 (D. Haw. 1977) (annual budget requests for training which involve bombing runs on a Hawaiian island required preparation for an EIS) and Envtl. Def. Fund v. Froehlke, 473 F.2d 346 (8th Cir. 1972) (budget request for a new project is both a proposal for legislation and a major federal action under NEPA).
128. Andrus v. Sierra Club, 442 U.S. 347, 362 (1979).

Four well publicized cases illustrate the application of environmental law to basing decisions. These are the Navy's actions to create a Trident submarine base in Bangor, Washington, to build an Extremely Low Frequency (ELF) communication network for submarines in Wisconsin and Michigan, and to build a carrier battle group homeport in Washington for the aircraft carrier USS Nimitz. Finally, litigation surrounding the Army's decision to transform an existing brigade in Hawaii to a more robust Stryker Brigade Combat team, and the associated environmental considerations. These decisions will be explored using extracts from the relevant court opinions.

Concerned About Trident v. Rumsfeld

555 F.2d 817, 820–23, 826–27, 829–30 (D.C. Cir. 1977)

TAMM, Circuit Judge.

The appellants here, Concerned About Trident, et al. raise questions concerning the adequacy of the environmental impact statement (EIS) prepared under the supervision of the Navy for its newest atomic missile submarine system (Trident), located in Bangor, Washington. In addition, they contend that the Navy failed to follow proper procedures (e.g. failed to weigh the environmental costs of a dedicated site versus its benefits to the public) mandated by the National Environmental Policy Act of 1969 (hereinafter referred to as NEPA). 42 U.S.C. § 4321 et seq. (1970). The district court found that the EIS and Navy procedures fully complied with the mandates of NEPA and therefore dismissed the complaint. After thorough review of the voluminous record in this case, we must agree that the Navy decisionmaking process and the EIS satisfy NEPA in all respects save two. For the reasons set forth, we affirm in part, reverse in part, and remand for a more extended discussion and consideration by the Navy of alternatives to the dedicated site system and their environmental impacts, along with further study by the Navy of the impacts which will be generated by the Trident program after 1981.

The history of Trident (called "ULMS" prior to May 16, 1972) begins in 1966 when the Department of Defense began secret study of alternative systems of nuclear deterrence (Strat-X Study). The Strat-X Study Report recommended in 1967 that a hardened silo-base missile system, when combined with a new submarine-launched ballistic-missile system, was preferable to the other candidate ordered research and development of Trident to begin along the lines of the Strat-X Report. The aim of Trident is to maintain the superiority and survivability of the United States' sea-based nuclear deterrent force in the face of anticipated Soviet anti-submarine warfare improvements over the next few decades. Trident is essentially a further development of the presently deployed Polaris/Poseidon nuclear-powered ballistic-missile submarines which are central to the strategic deterrent force of the United States.

In order to achieve the key survivability prerequisite, the new system incorporated the use of a complete logistical support/refit facility (known as a "dedicated site"). All tasks necessary for the maintenance repair and support of the Trident submarines will be performed at this single dedicated base so that the submarines will spend as little time as possible away from the safety of deep water. The location of this dedicated site was the focus of studies beginning in 1970. Eighty-nine potential sites were initially reviewed. The studies took into consideration the operational requirements of the submarine, the capability of the base to support the Trident missile, the amount of environmental disturbance, and the availability of sufficient land. Meanwhile, the Deputy Secretary of Defense tentatively scheduled the deployment of Trident for 1981. This deployment date was subsequently re-set for various periods ranging from 1975 to sometime in the early 1980's. On December 23, 1971, the Secretary of Defense designated 1978 as the first firm date for the initial deployment of Trident.

By 1972 the first original 89 potential sites had been reduced to 19 nominees. Finding of Fact No. 59; J.A. at 719a-20a. Candidate environmental impact statements were then prepared when it became apparent that four sites were capable of supporting the Trident Program. The district court found that the decisionmakers took into account the environmental assessments laid forth in the candidate EIS's in arriving at their final site selection. Finding of Fact No, 74; J.A. at 728a-20a. The overwhelming strategic and tactical advantages of locating Trident on the Pacific dictated that the Defense Department choose Bangor, Washington, the only one of the four remaining sites located on the Pacific Ocean. Once the site had been tentatively selected, an in-depth environmental assessment of the impacts that Trident would have on the Bangor community commenced. Construction did not begin until the Navy was convinced in August of 1974, after reviewing the final EIS, that the environmental disturbance which would be caused by Trident did not outweigh the military benefits which Trident would achieve for the country.

. . .

The Navy raises several preliminary arguments to the effect that its action is completely free from the strictures of NEPA and court review. The only one which merits any extended discussion is the rather cursory argument that "NEPA cannot possibly apply" to strategic military decisions made by the Department of Defense-Navy. Appellees' Brief at 7–9. We view this as a flagrant attempt to exempt from the mandates of NEPA all such military actions under the overused rubric of a "national defense." This effort to carve out a defense exemption from NEPA flies in the face of the clear language of the statute, Department of Defense and Navy regulations, Council on Environmental Quality ("CEQ") Guidelines, and case law.

. . .

There is no support in either the statute or the cases for implying a "national defense" exemption from NEPA. See *Natural Resources Defense Council, Inc., v. Morton*, 148 U.S. App. D.C. 5, 458 F.2d 827, 836 (1972); *Committee for Nuclear Responsibility, Inc. v. Seaborg*, 149 U.S. App. D.C. 393, 463 F.2d 796, 799 (1971); *People of Enewetak v. Laird*, 353 F. Supp. 811 (D. Hawaii 1973). The Navy, just like any federal agency, must carry out its NEPA mandate "to the fullest extent possible" and this mandate includes weighing the environmental costs of the Trident Program even though the project has serious national security implications.

. . .

Appellants submit that the Final EIS fails to comply with section 102(2)(C) of NEPA in that it: does not adequately analyze and describe the alternatives to the Bangor dedicated site; fails to adequately assess the environmental impacts outside of Kitsap County; fails to discuss the impacts of the possible deployment of more than ten submarines and the early termination of the Trident Program; does not adequately analyze the fiscal impacts of the Program; and finally, is short-sighted in assessing the environmental impacts only up to 1981.

. . .

Although we do not demand the agency "foresee the unforeseeable", make "crystal ball" inquires or prophecies instead of predictions, we do find that the Navy here was too short-sighted in setting forth the environmental impacts of the Trident Program. It need not, and indeed, may not be able to forecast the effects of Trident after 1981 in the same detail or with the same degree of accuracy as it has done for the period prior to 1981, but it is imperative that it make a reasonable effort to discern what the effects of Trident's future operation will be. *See SIPI, supra* at 1092. Thus, we must remand on this point to allow for further Navy analysis.

As the Navy has taken no arbitrary or capricious action here but has attempted to comply in good faith with the mandates of NEPA, failing in only two instances, we do not believe that the issuance of an injunction pending the Navy's revision of the Final EIS is necessary, especially since we have found that the Navy gave proper weight to environmental considerations in deciding to proceed with this strategically important project. *See Committee for Nuclear Responsibility, Inc. v. Seaborg, supra* at 795.

The work on the Trident Support Site at Bangor, Washington may therefore continue. The case is remanded to the district court to afford the Navy an opportunity to correct two deficiencies in the Final EIS mentioned previously. It must supplement its Final EIS to include: 1) an analysis of environmental impacts for a reasonable period after 1981; and, 2) a further discussion of the alternative systems and their environmental consequences which the Navy considered before choosing the dedicated site alternative. This revised Final EIS must be submitted to the district court within 120 days of the issuance of this opinion.

So ordered.

Comments

1. *Trident* is frequently cited as the watershed case for the direct application of NEPA to strategic military decisions. At the outset, the Court recognized that "[t]he overwhelming strategic and tactical advantages of locating Trident on the Pacific dictated that the Defense Department choose Bangor, Washington."[129] Yet, in response to the administration's position that this decision was non-reviewable, the Court responded: "We view this as a flagrant attempt to exempt from the mandates of NEPA all such military actions under the overused rubric of 'national defense.'"[130]

2. What is critical about *Trident* is the extent to which the Navy did consider alternatives and evaluate environmental effects. Eighty-nine alternative sites were initially reviewed, candidate environmental impact statements were prepared for several of the proposed sites, two preliminary EISs were done in 1973, and a complete EIS was done in 1974 for the final site. The draft EIS was sent for comment to all appropriate federal, state, and local agencies, and public hearings were conducted. Nevertheless, the Court found the discussion of alternatives inadequate and held that a consideration of possible effects seven years in the future was not enough. However, the construction was allowed to continue because of the Navy's showing of good faith and the strategic importance of the project.

3. In his concurring opinion, Judge Leventhal agreed that the EIS was defective because it failed to assess the consequences of operating the site after the projected completion date. He also expressed doubt as to whether the Navy met NEPA's requirements when it decided to choose a single new site, as opposed to simply having more submarines on the existing sites. His conclusion is of national security importance:

> It may not be likely that the Defense Department will in the end decide to scrap the Bangor project. But NEPA has been a contributing factor to other governmental

---

129. Trident, 555 F.2d at 821.
130. *Id.* at 823.

decisions to abort projects on which substantial energies and resources had been expended—as in the case of the Trans-Florida canal, or to modify a project even when the central concept is not found to violate the statutory standard—as in the case of the Alaska Pipeline. So it may be here that a fair look at overall environmental aspects will accompany a rethink of strategic concepts.[131]

A second example of a basing decision dramatically affected by environmental laws is the highly political, well-publicized litigation surrounding the Navy's Extremely Low Frequency (ELF) system under construction in Northern Michigan and Wisconsin. ELF is designed to provide a deepwater communication capability for submarines to avoid requiring the submarine to surface completely to communicate, thereby jeopardizing the safety of the crew.

4. Trident issues arose again in *Ground Zero Center for Non-Violent Action v. United States Department of the Navy*, 383 F.3d 1082 (9th Cir. 2004). The plaintiffs challenged the Navy's Trident II missile upgrade program at Bangor Submarine Base in Washington State, arguing that the program violated both NEPA and the ESA. After the district court granted the Navy's motion for summary judgment, the Ninth Circuit affirmed, holding that NEPA does not apply to presidential directives such as President Clinton's decision to upgrade the missiles. The Court also rejected the plaintiff's assertions that the Navy did not adequately consider the risks of an accidental explosion. With regard to the ESA claim, the Court found for the Navy, holding that the Navy had no discretion and that "[w]here there is no agency discretion to act, the ESA does not apply."[132]

Wisconsin v. Weinberger

745 F.2d 412, 414–16, 420, 424–25, 427 (7th Cir. 1974)

HARLINGTON WOOD, Jr. Circuit Judge.

Plaintiff-appellee State of Wisconsin and intervening plaintiff-appellee County of Marquette, Michigan, sued federal appellants seeking the preparation of a supplemental environmental impact statement (SEIS) in connection with Project ELF, an extremely low frequency submarine communications system developed by the Navy, which the Navy undertook to reactivate and expand in 1981. Plaintiffs contended that the Navy's original 1977 environmental impact statement prepared at the time the project first originated should have been supplemented because of new information regarding the biological effects of extremely low frequency electromagnetic radiation. After a trial on the merits, the district court agreed with this contention and enjoined the Navy from proceeding with any additional work on Project ELF in Wisconsin or Michigan and from installing receivers in submarines until a supplemental environmental impact statement had been approved. This expedited appeal followed.

On July 1, 1968, the Navy announced plans to construct an extremely low frequency (ELF) submarine communications test facility within the Chequamegon National Forest near the Town of Clam Lake in northern Wisconsin. This test facility, consisting of two 14-mile strings of overhead antennae mounted on utility poles and a transmitter situated in a fenced compound, became fully operational in 1969. Between 1969 and 1978, while the Navy operated and tested the capability of this facility, two comprehensive ELF projects were formulated. The first, called Project Sanguine, was to include a 6,300 square mile

---

131. *Id.* at 831 (Leventhal, J., concurring).
132. *Id.* at 1092 (quoting Natural Res. Def. Council v. Houston, 146 F. 3d 1118, 1125–26 (9th Cir. 1998)).

grid of buried antenna cable and was to be operational by 1976. Project Sanguine, however, never went into full-scale development. The second system, Project Seafarer, which was proposed in 1977, initially was to consist of two test facilities: the one near Clam Lake, and the other, with a transmitter station and 130 miles of buried antenna cables, to be situated in the upper peninsula of Michigan. In its final, fully-developed form, the system was to have five surface transmitting stations and 2,400 miles of buried antenna cables extending over a 4,000 square-mile area.

In 1978, after initially supporting the allocation of $20.1 million for Project Seafarer research and development, President Carter decided to postpone Project Seafarer indefinitely....

In 1981, however, Congress in its Department of Defense Authorization Act, 94 Stat. 1077, 1081, ordered the Navy to resume research and development for an ELF communications system and directed the President to "submit to the Congress a plan for deployment" of such a system in 1981. In April, 1981, President Reagan advised the Secretary of Defense of his intention to review and decide whether to reactivate Project ELF. The Secretary submitted an ELF proposal to the President on August 13, 1981. On October 8, 1981, President Reagan approved the recommended proposal and advised Congress of his intent to proceed.

For each of the pre-ELF proposals, the Navy provided documentation of the environmental effects of each project by preparing an environmental impact statement (EIS) in accordance with the National Environmental Policy Act of 1969. Of specific concern to the public were the possible effects of continuously exposing human, animals, and plants to extremely low frequency electromagnetic radiation. This concern was acknowledged and addressed by the 1972 EIS and 1975 supplemental EIS prepared in connection with Project Sanguine, and the 1977 EIS prepared in connection with Project Seafarer. The 1977 EIS included a 1977 National Academy of Sciences report commissioned by the Navy studying the biological human health effects of extremely low frequency electromagnetic radiation. This report summarized the state of knowledge concerning these effects and concluded: "On the basis of the evidence available, the Navy believes no adverse effects on human health or performance will be associated with long-term Seafarer exposure."

When the decision to reactivate Project ELF in 1981 was made, no additional environmental impact assessment was made. In June 1983, however, the Navy issued, but did not circulate to the public or to interested federal agencies, an environmental impact assessment of the upgrading of the Wisconsin facility. In that assessment, the Navy observed that the electromagnetic field intensities produced by the ELF system would not increase by upgrading the Wisconsin facility to full operation. This assessment did not reevaluate the conclusions of the 1977 EIS and National Academy of Sciences report that ELF systems would produce no adverse biological effects.

...

We do not believe that NEPA requires the courts to keep watch over an agency's shoulder as a supervisor and direct the agency as to if, when and how it should preliminarily review any new information. Our responsibility is limited to determining whether or not the new information was so significant that for the agency not to act on it was irresponsible, arbitrary, or capricious. It is not enough that the information may be worthy of further inquiry or may be considered important research. Our task is the limited one of determining whether or not the new information presents a seriously different picture of the likely environmental consequences of the proposed action not adequately envisioned by the original EIS, such that the Navy's failure to act on it was arbitrary or capricious. If it was, then the court may order SEIS. To make this determination, however, we do not have to resolve the scientific issue on the merits.

. . .

In short, all of the evidence, viewed in whole or in part, as of 1981 and even the inadmissible evidence accumulated up until the date the complaint was filed, cannot be deemed to have been of such significance as to find that the Navy was arbitrary or capricious in not responding with a SEIS. We have touched only representative samples of the evidence, but as a whole it is generally unimpressive and cannot be deemed sufficiently significant. To elevate the significance of plaintiffs' evidence, in whole or in part, relevant or irrelevant, to the required level of significance could only be deemed to be clearly erroneous.

. . .

We hold that there was no violation of NEPA by the Navy. That being so, the injunction must necessarily be vacated, as we have already done by order, without further consideration. Nevertheless, we proceed to consider the merits of the injunction separately since this panel, although not in unanimous agreement about the underlying NEPA violation is in unanimous agreement that the injunction was warranted.

. . .

The panel is in agreement that even if there had been a NEPA violation, the district court abused its discretion in not undertaking a balancing of the relative harms to the parties before entering the injunction prohibiting the Navy from continuing with Project ELF until SEIS was filed. The district court, in denying the Navy's motion for reconsideration of the injunction, concluded that no balancing was to be undertaken because the point of NEPA is to assure that federal agencies assess the environmental impact of their proposals *before* deciding to proceed with an action. The district court found this case analogous to *TVA v. Hill*, 437 U.S. 153, 98 S.Ct. 2279, 57 L. Ed. 2d 117 (1978), the snail darter case, in which the Supreme Court held that the Endangered Species Act mandated injunctive relief despite countervailing equities. Because in the district court's view allowing the ELF proposal to proceed without first reconsidering its impact except in certain unusual circumstances would frustrate the purposes of the Act, the district court reasoned that there was a presumption that injunctive relief be imposed for a NEPA violation. It ruled that unless the Navy rebutted the presumption by showing that an injunction would not serve the purposes of the Act; the court did not have to undertake a balancing of the relative harms.

. . .

More important, however, is the district court's failure to balance the weight of the alleged NEPA violation against the harm the injunction would cause the Navy and to the country's defense. The Navy has emphasized that an ELF submarine communications system is of the highest priority for national defense. The system will allow our strategic submarine fleet to operate with a greatly reduced chance for exposure and minimize the possibility of detection, thus strengthening the most survivable elements of this nation's nuclear deterrent. President Reagan's directive to deploy Project ELF ordered that it achieve initial operating capability in fiscal year 1985. The Secretary of the Navy also stated in an affidavit that the latest evaluation of Project ELF is that it is essential to the national defense and that any delay in its construction is contrary to national defense interests. We have no basis to ignore those executive representations. At oral argument, counsel for the Navy informed us that preparation of a SEIS, which had already begun, could not be completed before April 1985. Therefore, the delay occasioned by the issuance of an injunction could bring about serious consequences for our national defense. The Soviet

Union allegedly is already advanced in this low frequency submarine communication technique. The district court gave no consideration to these serious circumstances.

...

REVERSED.

Friends of the Earth v. U.S. Navy
841 F.2d 927 (9th Cir. 1988)

LEAVY, Circuit Judge:

...

The Navy plans to build a $272 million permanent "Carrier Battle Group Homeport" at Everett, Washington as part of the Navy's comprehensive defense strategy. The homeport will provide berthing and base facilities for the aircraft carrier USS Nimitz and numerous support ships and service vessels. Establishment of the homeport will entail extensive demolition and construction over several hundred acres. All buildings, piers and wharves currently at the site will be demolished. New buildings, utilities, and parking areas will be constructed. The existing "mole" will be rebuilt and a 1600 foot breakwater will be constructed. Extensive dredging of the harbor to accommodate the Navy's vessels will occur.

The issue of concern to the plaintiffs is the Navy's proposal to dredge approximately 3.4 million cubic yards of sediment from the East Waterway in Everett Harbor and dispose of these spoils in Port Gardner Bay at depths of 310 to 430 feet, using a dredge spoil disposal technique called Confined Aquatic Disposal (CAD). Approximately one-third of the dredge spoils are contaminated with heavy metals and organic compounds. The CAD disposal system involves in-water disposal of contaminated dredge spoils followed by disposal of clean sediment which, theoretically, will cap and isolate the contaminated materials from the marine environment.

...

The Navy has received some required permits and certifications. Under the Rivers and Harbors Act of 1899, 33 U.S.C. § 407 (1986), and section 404 of the Clean Water Act, 33 U.S.C. § 1344 (1986), the Navy must obtain from the Army Corps of Engineers a "404 permit" before it may discharge dredged or fill material into the navigable waters of the United States. The Navy obtained this permit on September 24, 1987. Under section 401 of the Clean Water Act, 33 U.S.C. § 1341 (1986), the state of Washington must certify that the activities authorized by the 404 permit will not adversely affect water quality (Water Quality Certification or 401 certification). The state issued the certification on March 2, 1987.

The permit about which the parties are in dispute comes under the State of Washington's Shoreline Management Act (SMA) and would be obtained from the city of Everett. Wash. Rev. Code §§ 90.58.010–.930 (West Supp. 1987).

...

FOE filed its complaint in district court and moved for a preliminary and permanent injunction barring the Navy from obligating or expending any funds, and from commencing any construction of the homeport, until all shoreline permit review proceedings have terminated. The district court denied the motion for a preliminary injunction.

...

The Navy argues that the SMA permit has been issued. The city of Everett approved, with conditions, the Navy's shoreline permit application. The WDOE then reviewed and approved the permit, imposing some additional conditions. The WDOE's approval constitutes a final order for purposes of either side appealing the decision to the Shorelines Hearings Board. Rev. Wash. Code § 90.58.180.

However, the permit has not been "issued" for purposes of commencing construction pursuant to it. As required by the SMA, the permit expressly states construction pursuant to it may not begin and "is not authorized" until all review proceedings have terminated. This stay extends through the term of the appeal to the Shorelines Hearings Board, but may be lifted by a court asked to review the Board's decision. Wash. Rev. Code § 90.58.140(5). Thus, under Washington law the permit does not allow construction to begin while it is being appealed to the Board. This is consistent with Congress' stated purpose in prohibiting the expenditure of funds for the Everett homeport until all dredging permits are obtained: to ensure that environmental concerns are considered prior to construction.

In summary, the district court abused its discretion by denying the plaintiffs' motion for permanent injunctive relief when it found the plaintiffs had not demonstrated irreparable harm. Under the NDAA and the CWA, the Navy must comply with Washington's SMA, including obtaining a shoreline permit. By commencing construction of the homeport before review of that permit is complete, the Navy violated the NDAA and its shoreline permit. The district court erred in not granting the plaintiffs' request for a permanent injunction.

We reverse the district court's denial of injunctive relief to the plaintiffs. We order that as of the date of the filing of this opinion, the Navy is permanently enjoined from obligating or expending any funds for the construction of the Everett homeport until a Shoreline Management Act permit has been issued. This permit will not be considered issued until it has been approved after review by the Shorelines Hearings Board.

REVERSED.

Ilio'ulaokalani Coalition v. Rumsfeld

464 F.3d 1083 (9th Cir. 2006)

FLETCHER, Circuit Judge:

This appeal requires us to assess whether the Army complied with the National Environmental Policy Act of 1969 ("NEPA"), 42 U.S.C. §§ 4321–4347 (2006), in planning its programs to modernize and streamline its forces, while simultaneously maintaining readiness. While the metamorphosis of the Army and the strategic planning accompanying this transformation is the business of the Army, not the courts, the Army's compliance with NEPA does involve us. As part of its NEPA evaluation of the Army Transformation Campaign Plan, the Army completed a programmatic environmental impact statement ("PEIS"), in which it identified Hawaii as one of the selected sites for transformation. Subsequently, the Army undertook a site-specific environmental impact statement ("SEIS") to detail the impacts on the environment of the Army's expansion, land use, and activities associated with transforming the 2nd Brigade, now stationed on Oahu, Hawaii, into a Stryker Brigade Combat Team ("SBCT") in Hawaii. Plaintiffs, 'Ilio'ulaokalani Coalition, Na 'Imi Pono, and Kipuka ("Hawaiian Groups"), challenged the sufficiency of the Army's NEPA procedure, both at the programmatic and site-specific levels, on two grounds, arguing that (1) the Army failed to comply with NEPA's public notice requirements and (2) both the PEIS and SEIS failed to consider reasonable alternatives. The district court granted summary judgment to the Army, finding that its public notice efforts were compliant with NEPA and that it sufficiently considered reasonable alternatives to transforming the 2nd Brigade in Hawaii. We now reverse the portion of the district court's decision that held that the Army considered all reasonable alternatives to transformation of the 2nd Brigade in Hawaii and remand to require it to prepare a supplemental SEIS to consider all reasonable alternatives, most notably the potential for transforming the 2nd Brigade outside of Hawaii.

. . .

Consideration of Reasonable Alternatives under NEPA

Strategic planning and the Army's metamorphosis are the Army's business, not the courts'. What involves us, however, is NEPA's requirement that the Army prepare an EIS to examine what effects any plans will have on the environment (the extreme example would be a plan for nuclear testing that would require extensive analysis). Here, the Army assumes that it has an obligation to comply with NEPA. That is not at issue. At issue is whether its compliance was adequate.

The Army adopted a "tiered" approach to its compliance with NEPA, preparing a programmatic EIS followed by a site-specific EIS. NEPA regulations encourage agencies to "tier" their environmental impact statements in some situations. *See* 40 C.F.R. § 1502.20.

"Tiering" refers to the coverage of general matters in broader environmental impact statements (such as national program or policy statements) with subsequent narrower statements or environmental analyses (such as regional or basinwide program statements or ultimately site-specific statements) incorporating by reference the general discussions and concentrating solely on the issues specific to statement subsequently prepared.

Tiering is "encouraged ... to eliminate repetitive discussions of the same issues and to focus on the actual issues ripe for decision at each level of environmental review." *Id.* § 1502.20. Here, where the agency is moving from "a program, plan, or policy environmental impact statement to ... a site-specific statement or analysis," *id.* § 1508.28(a), tiering is appropriate.

. . .

An EIS must describe and analyze alternatives to the proposed action. Indeed, the alternatives analysis section is the heart of the environmental impact statement. The agency must look at every reasonable alternative within the range dictated by the nature and scope of the proposal. The existence of reasonable but unexamined alternatives renders an EIS inadequate.

The detail that NEPA requires in an EIS depends upon the nature and scope of the proposed action. The standards normally applied to assess an EIS require further refinement when a largely programmatic EIS is reviewed. The critical inquiry in considering the adequacy of an EIS prepared for a large scale, multi-step project is not whether the project's site-specific impact should be evaluated in detail, but when such detailed evaluation should occur. NEPA requires that the evaluation of a project's environmental consequences take place at an early stage in the project's planning process. This requirement is tempered, though, by the statutory command that we focus upon a proposal's parameters as the agency defines them. The requirement is further tempered by the preference to defer detailed analysis until a concrete development proposal crystallizes the dimensions of a project's probable environmental consequences. When a programmatic EIS has already been prepared, we have held that site-specific impacts need not be fully evaluated until a "critical decision" has been made to act on site development. This threshold is reached when, as a practical matter, the agency proposes to make an "irreversible and irretrievable commitment of the availability of resources" to a project at a particular site.

The agency's challenge and ours is to find the right balance between the efficiency benefits of tiering, described in 40 C.F.R. § 1502.20, deference to the agency's definition of the purpose and need of the proposed action, and the recognition that the PEIS constrains future decision-making and must therefore analyze alternatives in sufficient detail to prevent foreclosure of options with insufficient consideration. *Id.* at 762–63.

. . .

The Army's own experts realized that the Army made site-specific decisions in the PEIS without analysis of their impacts or consideration of reasonable alternatives, as required by NEPA. Despite this, the Army argues that it was appropriate to defer analysis until the SEIS, using the principles of "tiering" as its crutch. The Army settled on transformation of the 2nd Brigade in Hawaii in the PEIS; however, it reached this decision with no analysis of the environmental impacts or of reasonable alternatives to such a transformation. While there is nothing per se improper about reaching these decisions at the programmatic stage, it is improper to do so without undertaking the analysis required by NEPA when those decisions are made.

Comments

1. There was substantial environmental deliberation during the entire period the ELF project was under consideration, including an EIS in 1972 for the original Project Sanguine, a 1975 supplemental EIS, a 1977 National Academy of Sciences Study, and a final EIS in 1977 for Project Seafarer. Because the 1981 ELF proposal was not only similar but smaller than the two previous projects, no new EIS was conducted.

2. The district court held that the Project ELF proposal changed the previous project only incrementally and did not require supplementation of the EIS. The court enjoined the construction; however, on the basis that significant new information on the biological effects of electromagnetic radiation had been discovered since the 1977 EIS. The injunction was vacated by the Seventh Circuit Court of Appeals in *Wisconsin v. Weinberger*.[133]

3. The ELF cases also raise the issue of who is required to prepare an EIS. Technically, only the agencies of the federal government are covered.[134] Thus, an action taken solely by the President or the Executive Office may not require an EIS. This argument was rejected by the court, however, based on the Navy's substantial involvement.

4. The district court in *Wisconsin v. Weinberger* also dealt with a novel argument: that the project would make northern Wisconsin and upper Michigan more likely to be the target of a nuclear attack. The court rejected this position, holding that it was not the type of harm that is cognizable under NEPA.[135]

5. There was a significant dissent by Justice BEA in *Ilio'ulaokalani Coalition v. Rumsfeld*, stating in part:

> This case questions whether a court can second-guess the Army when it decides that modernizing its brigade units as quickly as possible, while maintaining combat readiness, can be done only "in place," i.e., at each brigade's present base location. In the name of environmental "concerns," the majority would require

---

133. Wisconsin v. Weinberger, 736 F.2d 438 (7th Cir. 1984).
134. 42 U.S.C. § 4332(2)(c) (2000).
135. *See also* Metro. Edison Co. v. People Against Nuclear Energy, 460 U.S. 766 (1983).

the Army to consider what it has already reasonably rejected: whether it should consider moving Army units around the country for the new training—regardless it would cause delay in modernizing, lack of combat-readiness and entail prohibitive costs—because of possible environmental impacts training "in place" could cause.

Training and Testing

National defense means more than planning; it requires endless preparation to be credible: soldiers must be trained in simulated combat environments, weapons must be fired, and command and control facilities must be exercised. Many of these activities are noisy, dirty, and even potentially dangerous; yet most would agree that they are an integral part of defense. They are all, however, vulnerable to environmental challenges. One such example was previously discussed concerning litigation surrounding the Navy's bomb testing at Vieques Island, Puerto Rico.

The following cases represent both ends of the spectrum of controversy. The first is a planned test of an underground nuclear warhead in Alaska. The second is a live fire range in Hawaii. The third is a Naval exercise on the Pacific Ocean.

Center for Biological Diversity v. Pirie
191 F. Supp. 2d 161 (D.D.C. 2002)

Plaintiff Center for Biological Diversity (CBD) filed this lawsuit to prevent the use by the United States military of live fire training exercises on the island of Farallon de Medinilla (FDM) because such exercises allegedly kill and otherwise harm several species of migratory birds without a permit, in violation of the Migratory Bird Treaty Act (MBTA), 16 U.S.C. § 703 *et seq.*, and the Administrative Procedures Act (APA), 5 U.S.C. § 701 *et seq.* Defendants, the Secretary of Defense Donald Rumsfeld and the acting Secretary of the Navy, Robert Pirie, have been sued in their official capacity as the heads of the branches of the military that engage in these exercises on FDM.

...

The United States government has used FDM for military training exercises since 1971. Defendants contend that since the 1970's, FDM has represented an important and irreplaceable asset in maintaining the combat readiness of United States military units....

...

An Environmental Impact Statement prepared by defendants and released in June 1999 describes the "ongoing" training exercises on FDM to include the following type of activities. Defendants conduct air-to-surface gunnery exercises, in which aircraft operating from aircraft carriers deliver 500-pound bombs and air-to-ground missiles to the surface of FDM. Aircraft fire machine guns, cannons, and missiles at the surface of FDM. According to the EIS, annual training consists of four 5-day Navy exercises, three 3-week Marine Corps exercises and five 14-day combined force exercises. During the approximately 320 sorties flown each quarter, Air Force bombers drop 500, 750 and 2000 pound bombs, precision-guided munitions and mines on FDM. In addition, Navy ships fire 5-inch deck-mounted guns, using highly explosive, point-detonating rounds at the surface of FDM. These Navy activities may occur monthly during Pacific transits, with a ship remaining at FDM for approximately two days, and as part of joint exercises for approximately 12 days every two years. The Navy fires approximately 1,040 5-inch shells and 400 76mm shells annually. Finally, Navy SEALs use rigid hull inflatable boats to fire grenades, missiles, rifles and machine guns at the surface of FDM approximately four times a year. *See* Achitoff Dec., Ex. 7 (June 1999 EIS).

...

It is uncontested that defendants' military training activities on FDM will kill birds covered by the MBTA. "Defendants' live-fire training exercises occasionally kill migratory birds protected by the MBTA." Defs' Combined Statement of Material Facts, at P 2. After a survey of FDM conducted in 1996, the FWS concluded:

> There is no question that bombing of this island will result in the death of seabirds, migratory shorebirds, and possibly even the endangered Micronesian megapode. On several occasions we observed boobies nesting very close to unexploded ordinance [sic]. While the unexploded ordinance [sic] may not provide an immediate threat to the birds, it does indicate that bombs do fall in active nesting areas. Although there may be peaks in the seabird breeding season, our observation indicate that breeding probably occurs year-round.

...

On April 15, 1996 the Navy applied to FWS for a permit pursuant to MBTA regulations that would allow them to incidentally "take" migratory birds on FDM as a result of the military exercises there.

...

The MBTA was enacted in 1918 to implement a convention between the United States and Great Britain (on behalf of Canada) for the protection of migratory birds. It has since been amended to cover conventions with Mexico, Japan, and the former Soviet Union. 16 U.S.C. §§ 703, 712. The MBTA prohibits, among other things, any killing of designated migratory birds. The language of the MBTA is unequivocal:

> Unless and except as permitted by regulations made as hereinafter provided in this subchapter, it shall be unlawful at any time, by any means or in any manner, to pursue, hunt, take, capture, kill, attempt to take, capture, or kill.... any migratory bird ... included in the terms of the [conventions between the United States and Great Britain, Mexico, Japan, and Russia.].

16 U.S.C. § 703. This prohibition applies with equal force to federal agencies. *Humane Society v. Glickman*, 217 F.3d 882 (D.C. Cir. 2000).

...

Defendants do not dispute that several species of birds found on FDM are protected by the MBTA. Nor do defendants deny that some of these birds have been killed and will be killed as a result of defendants activity....

Thus, defendants [*sic*] activities are unlawful unless they are in some way authorized by the regulations promulgated pursuant to the authority granted in the MBTA. Defendants can find no such authorization in the regulations. The MBTA authorizes the Secretary of the Interior to promulgate regulations permitting taking of migratory birds as long as the regulations are consistent with the Convention. 16 U.S.C. § 704; 712(2). The regulations prohibit the taking, possessing, importation, exportation, transportation, selling, or purchasing of any migratory birds except as allowed by a valid permit. 50 C.F.R. § 21.11. "Take" is further defined in the regulations to include "pursue, hunt, shoot, wound, kill, capture, or collect," or attempt to do so. 50 C.F.R. § 10.12.

As discussed above, defendants applied to FWS for a permit allowing them to take birds in connection with their activities on FDM and that application was denied on August 5, 1996. Despite that permit denial, defendants have continued to kill migratory birds. Because they continue to kill these birds without complying with the statutory and regulatory provisions for a permit, defendants are violating the MBTA.

Committee for Nuclear Responsibility, Inc. v. Seaborg
463 F.2d 796, 796–98 (D.C. Cir. 1971)

PER CURIAM:

Plaintiffs, conservation groups seeking to enjoin an underground nuclear explosion (code-named Cannikin) on Amchitka Island, Alaska, appeal from the District Court's denial of a preliminary injunction, and seek leave to appeal under 28 U.S.C. § 1292(b) from the District Court's order resolving certain questions as the proposed detonation becomes ever more imminent. On October 28, 1971, we denied plaintiff's motion to stay the test, but affirmed the District Court's order requiring the Government to produce for *in camera* inspection certain documents which plaintiffs had been attempting to discover for months. Following *in camera* inspection on October 30, the District Court entered an order on November 1, which directed that some of these documents be released to plaintiffs (per Schedule A), but upheld the Government's objection to the release of other documents (in Schedule B). The Government does not seek to appeal, under § 1292(b), the rulings requiring disclosure.

Plaintiffs immediately appealed from the denial of a preliminary injunction. They move for summary reversal and stay. We deny that motion.

With regard to the discovery order, we have concluded that it would be inappropriate to entertain an appeal on this interlocutory matter at this time. The application for leave to appeal is denied.

The denial of a preliminary injunction was accompanied by findings of fact and conclusions of law in which the District Court indicated, *inter alia*, (1) that the Impact Statement issued by the Atomic Energy Commission (AEC) satisfied all the requirements of the National Environmental Policy Act (NEPA), 42 U.S.C. § 4331 *et seq.* (1970); (2) that none of the documents examined *in camera* by the District Court contained discussions of environmental hazards of substance not "alluded to" in the AEC's Impact Statement; (3) that defendants have complied with NEPA and all applicable law and are not threatening to engage in illegal action; and (4) that the courts lack jurisdiction to enjoin this "presidential decision."

While we do not modify the order of the District Court, we do not accept the propositions upon which it relied. In our view the case does present a substantial question as to the legality of the proposed test. But it does not necessarily follow that plaintiffs are entitled to an injunction against the test.

. . .

Our failure to enjoin the test is not predicated on a conviction that the AEC has complied with NEPA in setting forth the dangers of environmental harm. The NEPA process— which is designed to minimize the likelihood of harm—has not run its course in their courts. We are in no position to calculate the dangers from the Cannikin test.

As to the harms which will accrue if the test is enjoined, they were presented to us by the Government in a paper filed October 26, 1971. The Government indicated that the process of stemming the test hole was scheduled to begin that day, and it did apparently begin on schedule. The Government's paper stated:

> Stemming involves putting gravel and other materials down the test hole on top of the nuclear device. This prevents release of radioactive materials into the atmosphere. Stemming makes it impractical to recover the test device. If the device were not detonated at full yield, it would probably be destroyed with a non-nuclear charge.
>
> If we were to start stemming and then discover we could not conduct the full-yield test, we would be prevented from another test for at least a year since there is not another device or test hole readily available. Such a delay would prevent the deployment of the Spartan interceptor in the Safeguard system by at least a year or force us to enter into production of the Spartan warhead when it has not been fully tested. Moreover, the costs of preparation for this test, which are not recoverable if the test does not proceed, would be at least 118 million dollars. Moreover, an additional 70 to 120 million dollars would be required to prepare again for another test.
>
> The risks increase substantially each day because the weather deteriorates in the Amchitka area from this time on; reasonably good weather is necessary for proper observation of the test by ground stations and for other supporting operations. Also, the device is already at the bottom of the test hole and any delay increases the risk of mechanical problems. For instance, the devise is protected from the environment at 6,000 feet depth by a life-support system which has a limited life. In short, a period of bad weather combined with technical problems, both of which are unpredictable, could prevent the test. Each day of delay substantially increases these risks.

The Government also indicated that an injunction, and the resulting disruption of the Safeguard-ABM missile system, could well jeopardize the Strategic Arms Limitation Talks.

While the Government's assertion of monetary damage from an injunction is not minimal, it does not weigh as heavily with us as its assertions of potential harm to national security and foreign policy—assertions which we obviously can not appraise—and given the meager state of the record before us, we are constrained to refuse an injunction. *Cf.* Reynolds v. Sims, 377 U.S. 533, 585, 84 S.Ct. 1362, 12 L. Ed. 2d 506(1964); Note, Developments in the Law—Injunctions 78 Harv. L. Rev. 994, 1005–1008 (1965). While we deny preventive relief, it should be clear that plaintiffs may yet prevail in their claim that the AEC failed to comply with NEPA in approving the Cannikin test.

...

The plaintiffs' motion for summary reversal of the order of the District Court denying the motion for a preliminary injunction is denied. We also deny plaintiffs' application for leave to appeal the order of the District Court withholding certain documents from plaintiffs on the grounds of privilege.

So ordered.

Comments

1. In *Malama Makua v. Rumsfeld*,[136] the District Court for Hawaii granted an injunction stopping military training in the Makua Valley. The case subsequently settled when the

---

136. 163 F. Supp. 2d 1202 (D. Haw. 2001).

Army agreed to conduct an EIS and the plaintiffs agreed to a schedule allowing the Army to conduct its training.

2. *Committee for Nuclear Responsibility* is the most important case involving nuclear testing and NEPA. The case went through seven judicial hearings, including three each in the U.S. District Court and the U.S. Court of Appeals for the District of Columbia and one in the U.S. Supreme Court. Although the test was not enjoined, the various courts made it clear that the decision was reviewable. It is important to note that the AEC never questioned its responsibility to prepare an EIS; the dispute was the adequacy of the EIS based on both public and secret studies. Ultimately, the Court stated that it was "in no position at this juncture to enter a stay order that would interject the Court into national security matters that lie outside its province."[137] Appeal for injunction to the Supreme Court in this case was denied on November 6, 1971, and the test was conducted that same day.[138] Justices Douglas, Brennan, and Marshall voted for a temporary restraining order. Justice Douglas, in his opinion, relied on a secret memo prepared by the Chairman of the CEQ, Russell Train, to raise two substantive dangers with the proposed test: seismic problems (the explosion could trigger earthquakes or tidal waves) and venting (radioactive material from the explosion might escape to the surface).

3. Nuclear testing has been the subject of enormous amounts of litigation. For example, military service members who participated in Cold War era tests in Nevada and the Pacific have sued the responsible agencies, alleging that exposure to the radioactivity was the proximate cause of their present illness (usually cancer).[139]

4. Shortly after the Alaskan litigation, another district court allowed an AEC underground test in Nevada to take place.[140] In 1981, the Public Lands Legal Foundation filed a suit in the District of Columbia to enjoin the Air Force from testing a non-nuclear device in the Nevada desert. Although no EIS was prepared, an EA was completed. The test was to "provide and confirm ground motion data regarding soil compaction, which data would be used in the engineering design of the proposed MX missile system shelter, wherever they may be built. The data will also be available for any underground strategic system the Government may need to develop in the future." The court denied the injunction.[141]

5. In a training and testing case, *Westside Property Owners v. Schlesinger*,[142] the owners of land near Luke Air Force Base in Phoenix, Arizona, brought suit challenging the training of German pilots and the presence of F-15 jet aircraft. The plaintiffs based their case on NEPA and the Noise Pollution Control Act of 1972. The district court dismissed and the court of appeals affirmed, holding that the EIS was adequate and that the Noise Control Act did not authorize the Federal Aviation Administration to control noise pollution resulting from military flights. Litigation was later brought challenging military pilot training exercises as an unlawful "taking" within the proscription of the Fifth Amendment, alleging that high noise levels lower property values.[143]

---

137. Comm. for Nuclear Responsibility v. Seaborg, 463 F.2d 788, 795 (D.C. Cir. 1971).

138. *See* Comm. for Nuclear Responsibility v. Schlesinger, 404 U.S. 917 (1971).

139. *See, e.g.,* Gaspard v. United States, 713 F.2d 1097 (5th Cir. 1983); Lombard v. United States, 690 F.2d 215 (D.C. Cir. 1982); Jaffe v. United States, 663 F.2d 1226 (3d Cir. 1981), *cert. denied*, 456 U.S. 972 (1982).

140. Nielson v. Seaborg, 348 F. Supp. 1369 (C.D. Utah 1972).

141. Pub. Lands Legal Found. v. United States, Civil No. L. 81-187, April 16, 1981 (D.C.D.C.).

142. Westside Property Owners v. Schlesinger, 597 F.2d 1214 (9th Cir. 1979).

143. Testwuide v. United States, 56 Fed. Cl. 755, 757 (2003).

6. Following the District Court opinion in *Center for Biological Diversity v. Pirie*,[144] the Navy appealed. While the appeal was pending, Congress amended the MBTA to provide an exemption for the military from prohibitions concerning "incidental taking of migratory birds during military readiness activities."[145] That Section specifically exempts military exercises from MBTA restrictions until the Secretary of Interior publishes a new regulation exempting "the Armed Forces for the incidental taking of migratory birds during military readiness activities ..." Military readiness activities are defined to include "all training and operations of the Armed Forces that related to combat" but does not include "the routine operation of installation operating support functions, industrial activities," or the construction and demolition of such facilities.

7. EPA has in only one instance taken an enforcement action which resulted in the cessation of live-fire training at a military base—at the Massachusetts Military Reservation on Cape Cod, Massachusetts. EPA issued several administrative orders under the Safe Drinking Water Act after determining that the groundwater aquifer underlying the reservation, the sole source of drinking water for Cape Cod residents, was threatened with contamination. The Department of Defense is currently conducting cleanup work under the orders with most live-fire activities now halted.[146]

8. In *Lee v. United States Air Force*,[147] the Tenth Circuit considered a challenge by ranchers and livestock raising associations to the Air Force plans to permit the German Air Force to station, for training purposes, thirty fighter aircraft at Holloman Air Force Base. The court rejected claims that the Air Force failed to consider reasonable environmental alternatives, failed to adequately assess the potential impact of the property on property values in surrounding areas, used a flawed methodology to analyze noise impacts, used outdated studies to assess livestock impacts, and failed to consider the impact of aerial refueling or the potential secondary effects of aircraft accidents.

Chemical Weapon Demilitarization

In 1985, Congress directed the Department of Defense to destroy the nation's stockpile of chemical agents and munitions ("chemical demilitarization") then located at Johnson Atoll in the Pacific Ocean and a number of sites in the United States.[148] The original stockpile consisted of 30,000 tons of chemical warfare agents contained in obsolete or unserviceable weapons that were manufactured during and after World War II. To rid the United States of these weapons and any potential threat they might pose, the Defense Department, through the Department of the Army, chose several sites throughout the county at which to implement the weapons-destruction mandate. One of these sites is the Tooele Chemical Agent Disposal Facility in Tooele, Utah, a hazardous waste storage, treatment, and disposal facility that is permitted under RCRA.

Three types of chemical agent were stored at the Tooele Facility: two nerve agents, referred to as "GB" and "VX," and a blistering agent referred to as "mustard." The liquid agents are contained in separate containers that fall into one of three categories: (1) projectiles, bombs, and rockets which contain propellant or explosives (referred to generally as "energetics"), (2) other projectiles that do not contain energetics, and (3) large steel

---

144. 191 F. Supp. 2d 161 (D.C. Cir. 2002).
145. FY 2003 Defense Authorization Act, § 315.
146. U.S. EPA, *Massachusetts Military Reservation*, http://www.epa.gov/region1/mmr/.
147. Lee v. U.S. Air Force, 354 F.3d 1229 (10th Cir. 2004).
148. *See* 50 U.S.C. § 1521(a).

bulk storage containers known as "ton containers."[149] After completing an evaluation and risk assessment of the nation's stockpile of chemical weapons, the Army completed an Environmental Impact Statement and Record of Decision, selecting on-site incineration as the means by which the nation's weapons would be destroyed. This action was challenged by several citizen groups in a request for a preliminary injunction. The court denied the citizen groups' request and they appealed to the Tenth Circuit. The following is an extract of that decision.

Chemical Weapons Working Group v. U.S. Department of the Army
111 F.3d 1485 (10th Cir. 1997)

In this appeal, Appellants Chemical Weapons Working Group, Inc., Sierra Club, and Vietnam Veterans of America Foundation (Plaintiffs) argue that the district court erred in denying their request for a preliminary injunction and in dismissing their claims under the Clean Water Act, Resource Conservation and Recovery Act, 1986 Department of Defense Authorization Act, and Administrative Procedures Act. Finding none of their arguments persuasive, we affirm.

. . .

Before allowing the Army to proceed with its incineration plan, Congress required it to conduct Operational Verification Testing of the Johnston Atoll Chemical Agent Disposal System, a full-scale, operational chemical weapons incineration plant of Johnston Island that was designed to prototype for incinerators at other stockpile sites such as Tooele . . .

. . .

Presently, the Army has all permits necessary to operate Tooele. The Utah Department of Environmental Quality has issued both Clean Air Act and Resource Conservation and Recovery Act permits under its delegated authority from the Environmental Protection Agency. The Army has thus far conducted two trial burns at Tooele without chemical agent to determine whether the facility can destroy agent and other materials without releasing a significant amount of toxins into the environment. The Utah Department of Environmental Quality has approved the results of both tests. . . .

After extensive hearings, the district court denied Plaintiffs' request for a preliminary injunction of the Army's scheduled incineration operations at Tooele because none of the requirements for injunctive relief had been met. First, the court found Plaintiffs had failed to establish irreparable harm because the health risks associated with the Army incineration operations were too speculative, while Plaintiff's allegation of a National Environmental Policy Act violation was, without more, insufficient to meet the irreparable harm requirement. Next, the court found Plaintiffs had failed to meet the balance of harms requirement for injunctive relief, relying principally on the Army's 1987 and 1995 quantitative risk assessment results. Finally, the district court held Plaintiffs were unlikely to prevail on the merits of their claim under the National Environmental Policy Act because the Army's 1996 Record of Environmental Consideration was entitled to rely on its own experts in determining whether Supplemental Environmental Impact Statement was warranted.

. . .

On appeal, Plaintiffs argue that the district court's balance of harms finding is clearly erroneous because it overestimates the accident-related risk of continued storage, while

---

149. Chem. Weapons Working Group v. U.S. Army, 935 F. Supp. 1206, 1209 (D. Utah 1996).

underestimating the chronic health-related risks of routine incineration operations. We disagree. Although Plaintiffs' evidence on the health-related risks of short-term dioxin exposure is significant, we cannot conclude that the district court's finding on this issue is without any rational basis. To the contrary, the court's conclusion is amply supported by the results of the Army's 1987 and 1995 quantitative risk assessments as well as the Stockpile Committee's 1994 report which specifically considered the health-related risks associated with routine incineration operations. We therefore affirm the district court's denial of Plaintiffs' other arguments justifying a preliminary injunction in this instance. Because we conclude the district court properly denied injunctive relief, we also do not address Plaintiffs' claim that a remand is necessary to consider the effect a preliminary injunction would have on the public interests.

Comments

1. The Army's chemical demilitarization has been the subject of extensive litigation. In the highlighted case, plaintiff CWWG filed a second motion for a preliminary injunction. After a six-day hearing, the district court entered findings of fact and conclusions of law denying CWWG's motion.[150] In July 1997, CWWG filed a second amended complaint, asserting two new claims and resurrecting four old claims that had been dismissed previously because the facility had not yet begun operations. In September 1997, the district court granted the Army's motion to dismiss four of CWWG's counts. The court of appeals affirmed in *Chemical Weapons Working Group v. U.S. Department of Defense*.[151]

2. Although this case was in federal court because the challenge was brought directly against the military, many of the cases are in state court. As previously discussed, the Federal Facility Compliance Act of 1992 was a complete waiver of sovereign immunity, requiring Department of Defense facilities to get state RCRA permits when treating, storing, or disposing of hazardous waste. If the state does not grant a permit, the Army can appeal in state appellate courts.[152] However, even when the state grants a permit, citizen groups can challenge the state's administrative action. The Army frequently intervenes in those state actions to protect its national security interests.[153]

3. The United States' stockpile of unitary chemical weapons is at 8 sites in the continental United States: Umatilla, Oregon; Pueblo Colorado; Tooele, Utah; Anniston, Alabama; Pine Bluff, Arkansas; Newport, Indiana; Kentucky Blue Grass, Kentucky; and Aberdeen, Maryland. In addition, litigation has arisen challenging shipment of a stockpile from Germany to Johnston Atoll. *See, Colorado Department of Public Health and the Environment v. U.S.*, 693 F.3d 1214, (10th Cir. 2012) (affirming district court dismissal on preemption grounds of action under state RCRA provisions to bar the storage/destruction of chemical weapons); *Sierra Club v. Gates*, 499 F.Supp.2d 1101 (S.D. Ind., 2007) (denying PI motion under state RCRA provisions to enjoin shipments of the product of VX from Newport, Indiana to incineration facility in Port Arthur, Texas, and to enjoin incinerating in Port Arthur; *Chemical Weapons Working Group v. U.S. Department of Defense*, 655 F. Supp. 2d 18 (D.D.C. 2009) (NEPA challenge to Army's plan to incinerate chemical weapons at located at Anniston, Alabama, and three other facilities; court granted defendant's cross-

---

150. *CWWG II*, 963 F. Supp. 1083 (D. Utah 1997).

151. Chem. Weapons Working Group v. U.S. Dep't of Defense, No. 00-4110, 2003 WL 1232579 (10th Cir. Mar. 18, 2003).

152. *See* Pine Bluff for Safe Disposal v. Ark. Pollution Control & Ecology Comm'n, 127 S.W.3d 509 (Ark. 2003).

153. *See, e.g.*, Sierra Club v. Utah Solid Waste & Hazardous Waste Control Bd., 964 P.2d 335 (Utah Ct. App. 1998).

motion for summary judgment); *Families Concerned About Nerve Gas Incineration* v. Dept. of the Army, 380 F. Supp. 2d 1233 (N.D. Ala. 2005) (granting defendants' motions for summary judgment of plaintiff's state RCRA claims); and *Greenpeace v. Stone*, 748 F. Supp 749 (D. Hawaii 1990) (denying PI in NEPA challenge to moving chemical weapons from Germany to Johnston Atoll).

4. Other federal agencies, such as the Department of Energy, also face state challenges for their cleanup responsibilities. A classic example concerning the shipment of nuclear waste, which was challenged on environmental grounds, occurred in the following case study.

Nuclear Shipments

Hodges v. Abraham

300 F.3d 432 (4th Cir. 2002), *cert. denied* 123 S. Ct. 871 (2003)

In 1995, the DOE began to consider the issues of whether and how to close its Rocky Flats Environmental Technology Site near Denver, Colorado ("Rocky Flats"). In order to carry out such a closing, the DOE must transfer the plutonium at Rocky Flats to other DOE sites for storage and eventual disposition. As such, the DOE considered utilizing its Savannah River Site (the "SR"), located near Aiken, South Carolina, for the storage and disposition of Rocky Flats Plutonium. It prepared various NEPA compliance documents and materials analyzing and explaining the potential use of SR for these purposes. After nearly seven years of study, the DOE announced, in its April 19, 2002, Amended Record Decision (the "April 19 ROD"), that six metric tons of surplus plutonium will be transferred from Rocky Flats to SR for long-term storage.

On May 1, 2002, Governor Hodges initiated this lawsuit, seeking to enjoin the DOE from shipping the Rocky Flats plutonium into the Palmetto State. He maintained that the DOE violated NEPA in failing to properly consider the environmental consequences of its April 19 ROD, and that it had failed to comply with NEPA procedures prior to issuance of the ROD. On cross-motion for summary judgment, the district court rejected the positions of Governor Hodges in their entirety, and it declined to award injunctive relief against the DOE. *Hodges v. Abraham*, CA No. 1:02-1426-22, Memorandum Opinion and Order (D.S.C. June 17, 2002).

. . .

A.

The events giving rise to this dispute began over fifty years ago, with the advent of nuclear technology and nuclear weapons. During the Cold War—from the late 1940's to the late 1980's—the United States and the Soviet Union engaged in a nuclear arms race, and they produced thousands of nuclear weapons powered by tons of plutonium. Following the demise of the Soviet Union and the end of the Cold War, our country and the post-Soviet government of Russia acted both bilaterally and unilaterally to reduce their nuclear weapons stockpiles. In January 1994, they issued a *Joint Statement Between the United States and Russia on NonProliferation [sic] of Weapons of Mass Destruction and Means of their Delivery*, which established the mutual goal of "safe, secure, long-term storage and disposition of surplus fissile materials." In order to demonstrate our nation's commitment to this goal, President Clinton, on March 1, 1995, unilaterally announced that a total of 38.2 metric tons of our plutonium was no longer necessary for defense purposes, and that it therefore constituted "surplus plutonium." In September 2000, the United States and Russia formally pledged in writing that each would dispose of thirty-four metric tons of surplus plutonium. *Agreement Between the Government of the United States of America and the Government of the Russian Federation Concerning the Management and Disposition of Plutonium Designated as No Longer Required for Defense Purposes and Related Cooperation.* Pursuant to this Agreement, each country committed to "seek to begin operation of facilities [to dispose of the surplus plutonium] ... not later than December 31, 2007."

B.

In this country, the responsibility for monitoring, storing, and disposing of nuclear materials, including plutonium, necessarily rests with the federal Government, specifically the DOE. 42 U.S.C. §§ 7112(10), 7133(a)(8). Since the President's 1995 pledge, the DOE has studied and explored several options aimed at determining the most effective way to fulfill its responsibility to store and dispose of our nation's surplus plutonium. Throughout this effort, the DOE has been subject to the requirements of NEPA, a statute enacted in 1969 to ensure that environmental concerns play a role in government decisionmaking.

...

Before proceeding to address the specific contentions of Governor Hodges, it bears emphasizing that NEPA is an "action-forcing" statute. It requires federal agencies to identify and evaluate the environmental consequences of their proposed actions. *Robertson*, 490 U.S. at 350; *Hughes River*, 81 F.3d at 443. Under NEPA, an agency is obliged to take a "hard look" at a proposal's environmental consequences before deciding to proceed; however, once it has taken such a look, the agency is not obligated to choose any particular course of action. *Robertson*, 490 U.S. at 350. Moreover, if the agency has taken the required "hard look," we must defer to it unless its decisions were arbitrary or capricious. *Hughes River*, 81 F.3d at 443. Therefore, in assessing the merits of Governor Hodges's contentions, we must consider whether the DOE adequately identified and evaluated, prior to its April 19 ROD, the environmental consequences of storing the Rocky Flats plutonium at SR-KAMS. If we conclude that the DOE acted properly in that connection, we must then determine whether the decisions it premised on that analysis were arbitrary or capricious.

...

Governor Hodges's final contention on appeal is that, even if the DOE substantively examined the environmental effects of its proposed action, it failed to comply with NEPA's procedures in connection with its April 19 ROD. As the district court properly observed, "the April 19 ROD decouples storage and disposition, taking away a precondition to storage of Rocky Flats plutonium at SR which had been found in all prior RODs (approval of SR for the immobilization facility)." *Id.* at 23 The Governor asserts that this change in the DOE's proposal—from storage at SR-KAMS pending disposition to storage at SR-KAMS without regard to disposition—required the DOE to prepare and file another NEPA compliance document, such as an SA. He maintains that the DOE was required to examine whether this change in its proposal created any significant environmental impacts not previously studied, and that it had therefore failed to take a "hard look" at the environmental consequences of its April 19 ROD.

In fact, however, the DOE properly explored, prior to issuance of the April 19 ROD, whether the decoupling of plutonium storage from plutonium disposition created any new environmental concerns. The April 19 ROD specifically referenced those earlier NEPA compliance materials, and it explained the analyses they had made. After noting that the 1998 SA had analyzed the impact of storage of the Rocky Flats plutonium at SR-KAMS for a period of ten years, the April 19 ROD made the following pertinent observation:

[T]he storage of surplus plutonium in the KAMS facility could extend beyond the 10-year period estimated in [the 1998 SA]. Therefore, DOE prepared [the 2002 ASA].... which evaluated the potential for storage beyond 10 years at the KAMS facility. That SA concluded that potential impacts from the continued storage of surplus plutonium in the KAMS facility at SR for this additional period are not substantially different from those addressed in the original analysis of storage in APSF contained in [the 1996 PEIS].

67 Fed. Reg. 19,434 (April 19, 2002). As this provision makes clear, the DOE prior to issuing its April 19 ROD, conducted a preliminary inquiry by examining its previous NEPA documents, and it concluded that its decision to decouple the storage of surplus plutonium from the disposition clearly did not create any significant environmental impacts. *Idaho Sporting Congress*, 222 F.3d at 566; *Piedmont Envtl. Council*, 159 F. Supp. 2d at 270–71. As such, because it was apparent that the proposed change did not create a new environmental picture from that previously studied, the DOE decided that no further NEPA documentation was necessary. In these circumstances, we are satisfied that the DOE took a "hard look" at the environmental consequences of its proposed course of action prior to promulgating its April 19 ROD. *Idaho Sporting Congress*, 222 F.3d at 566 (recognizing limited role for non-NEPA environmental evaluation procedures to determine whether supplemental EA or EIS is required). Therefore, because the DOE has complied with the requirements of NEPA, and because its decision to place the Rocky Flats plutonium in long-term storage at SR-KAMS was neither arbitrary nor capricious, we will not disturb it.

Comments

1. This 2002 incident created significant press when Governor Hodges threatened to call out the South Carolina National Guard to stop the movement of DOE trucks. In fact, the governor issued an executive order after losing in District Court.[154] The United States then returned to the district court and obtained an injunction against the governor. In the election following this case, Governor Hodges lost.

2. Although a *parens patriae* action cannot be the basis for standing,[155] the Fourth Circuit has held that a state governor may establish standing in a NEPA suit against the Department of Energy by establishing proprietary interests in the land, streams, and drinking water of the state.[156]

NEPA Abroad

Like many other U.S. statutes, the application of NEPA to matters outside the United States was not specifically addressed in the statute or its legislative history. Section 102(2)(F) of NEPA contains the only specific reference to environmental considerations in international activities. It directs federal agencies to:

recognize the worldwide and long-range character of environmental problems and, where consistent with the foreign policy of the United States, lend appropriate support to initiatives, resolutions, and programs designed to maximize

---

154. S.C. Exec. Order No. 2002-14 (2002).
155. Massachusetts v. Mellon, 262 U.S. 447, 485–486 (1923).
156. Hodges v. Abraham, 300 F.3d 432, 448 (4th Cir. 2002).

international cooperation in anticipating and preventing a decline in the quality of mankind's world environment.[157]

Early CEQ guidelines also required federal agencies to assess the environmental effects of a proposed action "as it affects both the national and international environment."[158] Despite this broad language, there was no indication that NEPA's procedural requirements were intended to reach beyond the United States. This question of extraterritorial application has been the subject of several major cases and a number of scholarly articles.

One of the earliest cases involving the application of NEPA abroad was *Wilderness Society v. Morton*.[159] In *Wilderness Society*, the D.C. Circuit Court of Appeals held that a nonresident Canadian citizen and a Canadian environmental group had sufficient interests to justify intervention in an action challenging the adequacy of an EIS prepared for the proposed Trans-Alaskan oil pipeline. In a later case, the issue involved construction of the Darien Gap Highway in Panama and Columbia. Although the government's EIS was ultimately held adequate, that occurred after the district court enjoined construction of the highway, initially because there was no EIS and later because the first EIS was inadequate.[160] On appeal, the court largely sidestepped the issue of the extraterritoriality of NEPA by gaining the agreement of both parties that there would be potential adverse effects from the highway construction inside the United States (spread of cattle disease along the highway into the U.S.). The court expressly declined to rule on extraterritoriality, leaving "resolution of this important issue to another day."[161] Similarly, in *National Organization for Reform of Marijuana Laws (NORML) v. United States*, the Department of State agreed to prepare an EIS on the effect of U.S. support of poisonous herbicide spraying of marijuana and poppy plants in Mexico. Again, the court concluded that "the extraterritoriality of NEPA remains an open question in this circuit."[162] Direct confrontation of extraterritoriality occurred in following cases.

In a suit to enjoin a simulated nuclear test in the Pacific Trust Territory of Enewetak Atoll, the hereditary and elected leaders of the Atoll argued that NEPA is applicable everywhere in the world where a U.S. agency takes action that would significantly affect the quality of the human environment. The court avoided the issue by finding that NEPA applies to U.S. trust territories and enjoined the test.[163]

In *Gemeinschaft Zum Schutz des Berliner Baumbestandes v. Marienthal*,[164] a group of plaintiffs, including U.S. citizens residing in Berlin and a German environmental group, sought to enjoin a nine million dollar housing construction project by the Defense Department in West Berlin. The plaintiffs alleged that the project would adversely affect the scenic use and habitat of endangered birds, animals, and plants. The Court declined to issue a preliminary injunction because the plaintiffs had failed to present a substantial case on the merits of a NEPA violation. A portion of that decision follows.

---

157. 42 U.S.C. § 4332(2)(F).

158. 38 Fed. Reg. 20,553 (1973).

159. Wilderness Soc'y v. Morton, 495 F.2d 1026 (D.C. Cir. 1972) (per curiam).

160. *See* Sierra Club v. Coleman, 405 F. Supp 53 (D.D.C. 1975) and 421 F. Supp. 63 (D.D.C. 1976).

161. Sierra Club v. Adams, 578 F.2d 389, 392 n.14 (D.C. Cir. 1978).

162. Nat'l Org. for Reform of Marijuana Laws (NORML) v. U.S., 452 F. Supp. 1226, 1232 (D.D.C. 1978).

163. People of Enewetak v. Laird, 353 F. Supp. 811 (D. Haw. 1973).

164. Gemeinschaft Zum Schutz des Berliner Baumbestandes v. Marienthal, Civil No. 78-1839, 9 E.L.R. 20011 (Oct. 20, 1978).

Gemeinschaft zum Schutz des Berliner Baumbestandes v. Marienthal
Civil No. 78-1839, 9 E.L.R. 20011 (Oct 20, 1978)

RICHEY, J.:

Presently before the court is a motion by the plaintiffs to enjoin the United States Army from constructing an apartment complex in West Berlin for violations of the National Environmental Policy Act (NEPA), 42 U.S.C. §4321 et seq., and Defense Department environmental regulations, 40 C.F.R. part 214. For the reasons that follow, the court declines to issue a preliminary injunction.

In order to invoke NEPA and the environmental regulations of the Department of Defense, "federal action" must be involved, 42 U.S.C. §4332; 32 C.F.R. §214.2 ("Defense action"). In this case, the housing project which is being challenged was initiated by the German government, is being constructed by the German government, is being paid for by the German government, and, if the building is completed, title will be in the German government. The plaintiffs contend that federal action is involved because of a land swap arrangement the federal government participated in, the ordering of a temporary halt in construction by the American Commandant, the refusal of the Army to allow a local Berlin court to hear a challenge to the project, and the pervasive American influence on the project.

The court finds that the plaintiff has yet to demonstrate this may add up to federal action. In order to qualify as federal action there must be some affirmative conduct on the part of the government, not simply a failure to prevent what the government has the power to prevent. *NAACP v. Wilmington Medical Center*, 436 F. Supp. 1194, [8 ELR 20012] (D. Del. 1977); *State of Alaska v. Andrus*, 429 F. Supp. 958, 963 [7 ELR 20505] (D. Alas. 1977). Intervening to temporarily halt construction and failing to consent to a German court's challenge to the construction cannot qualify as such action. Merely swapping the land to preserve buildings of historic interest at the German government's request does not amount to federal action under the circumstances in this case. Merely because the Army has declined to intervene and exercise its authority to halt construction is insufficient to transform action by the German government into federal action. If the court were to accept the plaintiffs' argument that a failure to intervene is sufficient to constitute federal action, all major actions by the German government would be subject to review by the American courts because technically, the United States Army has the ultimate authority in the American sector to modify local law. Plainly, such a rule of law would be unacceptable.

Moreover, in balancing the hardship to the parties, the court recognizes that at this time, judicial interference in the German government's actions in West Berlin raises serious foreign policy considerations. Since the plaintiffs have failed to present a "substantial case on the merits" and the balance of hardship is not in the plaintiffs' favor, the plaintiffs' request for injunctive relief is denied. Accordingly, it is, by the court, this ninth day of November 1978,

ORDERED, that the plaintiffs' motion for a preliminary injunction be, and the same hereby is, denied.

Another area in which the overseas applicability of environmental laws is relevant is in the continuing effort of the United States to centralize its holdings of plutonium, hazardous waste, and chemical munitions. In *Hodges v. Abraham*, the challenge to the Department of Energy's transfer of nuclear materials was discussed. In that case, however, there was no question of NEPA's applicability, but rather whether the statutory requirements were met. This next case raises the question of whether NEPA is applicable at all. As a prelude to the case extract, it is important to know that during the 1986 Tokyo Economic Summit President Reagan and German Chancellor Kohl reached an agreement that U.S. chemical munitions would be removed from Germany by the end of 1992. Subsequently, President George H. W. Bush accelerated that schedule. Environmental groups then sought an injunction prohibiting the movement of chemical munitions to Johnston Atoll for destruction. The following is an extract of the court's opinion.

Greenpeace USA v. Stone
748 F. Supp. 749 (D. Haw. 1990)

...

Having found for purposes of this motion that there exists a presidential commitment in the form of an agreement with Chancellor Kohl and the people of the FRG to remove the European stockpile from Germany by the end of 1990, the court next turns to whether NEPA requires the defendants to prepare a comprehensive EIS which evaluates the environmental impacts of the movement of those munitions within West Germany.

First, absent evidence of Congressional intent to the contrary, a federal statute should be construed as applying only within the territorial jurisdiction of the United States. *Foley Bros. v. Filardo*, 336 U.S. 281, 285, 69 S. Ct. 575, 93 L.Ed. 680 (1949); *McKeel v. Islamic Republic of Iran*, 722 F.2d 582 (9th Cir. 1983); *Meredith v. U.S.*, 330 F.2d 9, 11 (9th Cir. 1964); *Commodity Futures Trading Comm'n v. Nahas*, 738 F.2d 487, 493 (D.C. 1984).

Although the language of NEPA indicates that Congress was concerned with the global environment and the worldwide character of environmental problems, it does not explicitly provide that its requirements are to apply extraterritorially. The purpose of NEPA is to "declare a national policy which will encourage productive and enjoyable harmony between man and his environment...." 42 U.S.C. §4321 (emphasis added). The Act provides that all agencies of the federal government shall prepare EIS's for major federal actions "affecting the quality of human environment." 42 U.S.C. §4332. NEPA, however, also requires federal agencies to "recognize the worldwide and long-range character of environmental problems." 42 U.S.C. §4332(F). The Act clearly recognizes, however, that actions should be taken "consistent with the foreign policy of the United States." *Id.*

Plaintiffs cite to portions of the Congressional Record in an effort to persuade this court that Congress' intent was that NEPA be applied to environmental impacts abroad. This court is convinced that Congress intended to encourage federal agencies to consider the global impact of domestic actions and may have intended under certain circumstances for NEPA to apply extraterritorially. However, as Judge Wilkey of the D.C. Circuit noted, "NEPA's legislative history illuminates nothing in regard to extraterritorial application." *NRDC v. NRC*, 647 F.2d at 1367.

Hence, the court must determine whether Congress intended NEPA to apply under circumstances such as these and whether under the unique facts presented, defendants have violated NEPA by failing to prepare a comprehensive EIS for actions taken outside of the United States and within a foreign country pursuant to an executive commitment and in furtherance of a Congressional mandate.

The court recognizes its ability and duty to interpret federal statutes and executive agreements. *Japan Whaling Ass'n v. American Cetacean Soc.*, 478 U.S. 221, 106 S. Ct. 2860, 2866, 92 L.Ed.2d 166 (1986). Similarly, the court acknowledges that the political question doctrine does not bar this court from addressing questions which may implicate national security issues. *See No GWEN Alliance v. Aldridge*, 855 F.2d 1380 (9th Cir. 1988); *Romer v. Carlucci*, 847 F.2d 445 (8th Cir. 1988). In deciding whether Congress intended NEPA to reach extraterritorially, however, the court must take into consideration the foreign policy implications of applying NEPA within a foreign nation's borders to affect decisions made by the President in a purely foreign policy matter. *See, e.g., Tel-Oren v. Libyan Arab Republic*, 726 F.2d 774, 804 (D.C. Cir. 194), *cert. denied*, 470 U.S. 1003, 105 S. Ct. 1354, 84 L. Ed. 2d 377(1985); *see also McCulloch v. Socidad Nacional*, 372 U.S. 10, 83 S. Ct. 671, 677–678, 9 L. Ed. 2d 547(1963).

The removal of the stockpile from the FRG is an action undertaken by the United States Army and Department of Defense with the encouragement, cooperation and approval of the West German government. As noted in *NRDC v. NRC*, 647 F.2d at 1356, "[t]his is not a case of the United States imperiously imposing its will on [a foreign county]." These obsolete munitions have been stored on West German soil since 1968 at the sufferance of the West German people and the President's commitment to the FRC to remove these munitions by the end of 1990 undoubtedly stemmed from diplomatic concerns which are clearly beyond the purview of this court's review.

. . .

An extraterritorial application of NEPA to the Army's action in the FRG with the approval and cooperation of the FRG would result in a lack of respect for the FRG's sovereignty, authority and control over actions taken within its borders. Although there is no question that the movement of the weapons is being effectuated in large measure by the United States Army personnel to eliminate United States weapons, the removal operation takes place entirely within the FRG and the environmental impacts of the actual overland transportation of the stockpile are felt solely within that country. The West German government has reviewed and approved the operation. A West German court has denied a request for injunctive relief brought by West German citizens to halt the movement of the weapons, finding that the operation comported with and did not violate West German law. *See* Translation of the Decision of the Administrative Court of Cologne, July 20, 1990. Imposition of NEPA requirements to that operation would encroach on the jurisdiction of the FRG to implement a political decision which necessarily involved a delicate balancing of risks to the environment and the public and the ultimate goal of expeditiously ridding West Germany of obsolete unitary chemical munitions.

. . .

Based on existing precedent, the legislative history and the facts presented here, this court must conclude, absent a clear congressional intent to the contrary, that NEPA does not apply to the movement of munitions through and within West Germany. *See Commodity Futures Trading Comm'n*, 738 F.2d at 493. Such an application of NEPA to actions on foreign soil would result in grave foreign policy implications and would substantively interfere with a decision of the President and a foreign sovereign in a manner not intended or anticipated by Congress.

The court must emphasize that the decision is limited to the specific and unique facts which are presented here. In other circumstances, NEPA may require a federal agency to prepare an EIS for action taken abroad, especially where United States agency's action abroad has direct environmental impacts within this country, or where there has clearly been a total lack of environmental assessment by the federal agency or foreign country involved. *See Sierra Club v. Adams*, 578 F.2d 389, *NORML*, 452 F.Supp. At 1233. That is not the case here.

Application of NEPA to the Global Commons

The foreign policy considerations which were critical to the preceding analysis of extraterritorial NEPA application are not implicated to the same extent by the transoceanic shipment of the European stockpile from West Germany to Johnston Atoll. The global commons portion of the Army's action does not take place within the sovereign borders of a foreign nation or in concert with that foreign nation. Accordingly, the question of NEPA application to the transoceanic shipment of the chemical munitions presents a different question.

In addition and in contrast to the intra-German portion of the operation, the Army did in fact prepare a written evaluation of the environmental impacts of the transoceanic shipment of the European stockpile, albeit in a separate document from the SSEIS. Defendants prepared a 142-page environmental assessment, the GCEA, dated March 1990.

. . .

The conclusion reached in the GCEA is that "normal operations of all routes would cause no significant impact on the environment of the global commons, assuming that none of the low probability accidents examined actually occur." Finding of No Significant Impact (FONSI), April 30, 1990. The FONSI also states that "only a complete loss of a vessel, uncontrollable ship fire, or large terrorist attack could result in some release of contaminants but the probability of these events is very low."

Defendants contend that Executive Order 12114 is the exclusive law governing evaluation of the environmental impacts of the global commons portion of the movement of the European stockpile. Executive Order 12114 provides, in part, as follows:

> 1-1. Purpose and Scope. The purpose of this Executive Order is to enable responsible officials of Federal agencies having ultimate responsibility for authorizing and approving actions encompassed by this Order to be informed of pertinent environmental considerations and to take such considerations into account, with other pertinent considerations of national policy, in making decisions regarding such actions. While based on independent authority, this Order furthers the purpose of the National Environmental Policy Act ... consistent with the foreign policy and national security policy of the United States, and *represents the United States government's exclusive and complete determination of the procedural and other actions to be taken by Federal agencies to further the purpose of the National Environmental Policy Act, with respect to the environment outside the United States, its territories and possessions.* (Emphasis added.)

The order requires the preparation of an EIS for major federal actions significantly affecting the environment of the global commons outside the jurisdiction of any nation (e.g., the oceans or Antarctica)." Executive Order 12114, section 2-3(a).

The court cannot conclude, as defendants would suggest, that Executive Order 12114 preempts application of NEPA to *all* federal agency actions taken outside the United States. Such an application of an Executive Order would be inappropriate and not supported by law. *See, e.g., Independent Meat Packers Assn'n v. Butz,* 526 F.2d 228, 236 (8th Cir. 19756), *cert. denied, Nat'l Ass'n of Meat Purveyors v. Butz,* 424 U.S. 966, 96 S.Ct. 1461, 47 L. Ed. 2d 733 (1976). Nevertheless, the court is persuaded under the specific facts of this case that the Army's compliance with Executive Order 12114 is to be given weight in determining whether NEPA requires defendants to consider the global commons portion of the removal of the European stockpile in the same EIS which covers the JACADS project.

. . .

Plaintiffs make much of CEQ comments on the application of NEPA to federal actions abroad. The comments relieved upon, however, preceded the issuance of Executive Order 12114 in 1979. Since that date, the CEQ's Tenth Annual Report indicates that the CEQ consulted extensively with the Department of State to assist the Carter administration in drafting an order which would approach the issue "in a way sensitive both to environmental and foreign policy concerns." "Environmental Quality–1979, The Tenth Annual Report of the Council on Environmental Quality" (December 1979) at 582 (footnotes omitted). The CEQ has also taken steps to implement that order. *See* CEQ, Environmental Effects Abroad of Major Federal Actions, Executive Order 12114, Implementing and Explanatory Documents, Memorandum for Heads of Agencies with International Activities, 44 Fed. Reg. 18722 (March 23, 1979).

The transoceanic movement of the munitions is a necessary consequence of the stockpile's removal from West Germany. In that sense, it is a "connected activity" to both the removal of the weapons from West Germany *and* the ultimate disposal of the weapons at Johnson Atoll. *See* 40 C.F.R. § 1502. Nevertheless, the court finds the transoceanic shipment's relationship to the removal of the weapons from West Germany is compelling and hence, implicates many of the same foreign policy concerns which affect the movement of the weapons through West Germany and distinguish it from the actual incineration of the weapons at the JACADS facility.

These considerations, together with the Army's preparation of the GCEA pursuant to Executive Order 12114, compel this court to hold that defendants have not violated NEPA by failing to consider the transoceanic shipment of chemical munitions to Johnston Atoll in the same comprehensive EIS as the incineration of those munitions.

Mayaguezanos por la Salud y el Ambiente v. United States

198 F.3d 297 (1st Cir. 1999)

On February 3, 1998, the Pacific Swan, a British-flag freighter carrying a cargo of vitrified high-level nuclear waste, passed through the Mona Passage, a stretch of seas between the islands of Puerto Rico and Hispaniola. It was bound for Japan by way of the Panama Canal, from France. A day earlier, a group of fisherman and environmental organizations from western Puerto Rico, fearing an accident or maritime disaster, brought this action for an injunction to stop the shipment until the United States filed an Environmental Impact Statement (EIS) in accordance with the National Environmental Policy Act (NEPA), 42 U.S.C. § 4321 *et seq.* After the parties filed cross-motions for summary judgment, the district court denied the claim for injunctive relief and dismissed the action. *See Mayaguezanos por la Salud y el Ambiente v. United States*, 38 F. Supp. 2d 168, 178 (D.P.R. 1999). We affirm on different reasoning.

. . .

The voyage of the Pacific Swan is part of a modern circumferential trade. Uranium from the United States is sent to Japan to fuel nuclear energy reactors. Japan ships the reactors' spent fuel to COGEMA, a French nuclear power company, for recycling at its La Hague plant. This process recovers a substantial portion of reusable fissionable material, which is turned into nuclear fuel (either RepU fuel, comprising uranium, or MOX fuel, comprising plutonium and uranium). It also generates high-level nuclear waste, which includes trace amounts of uranium and plutonium. The waste is vitrified according to specifications that have been approved by French and Japanese governments and placed in casks that meet criteria set forth by the International Atomic Energy Agency in its Regulations for the Safe Transport of Radioactive Material. Both the waste and the fuel are returned to Japan on board specifically designed ships that meet the standards of the International Maritime Organization's Code for the Safe Carriage of Irradiated Nuclear Fuel, Plutonium and High-Level Radioactive Wastes in Flasks on Board Ships, IMO Resolution A 18/Res. 748, Annex (1993). The private shippers choose the return route to Japan from three options: the Cape of Good Hope, Cape Horn, or the Panama Canal.

The U.S. connection to this trade occurs in two ways. First, the United States supplies the uranium to Japan under a 1988 agreement between the two countries. *See* Agreement for Cooperation Between the Government of the United States and the Government of Japan Concerning Peaceful Uses of Nuclear Energy, Nov. 4, 1987, H.R. Doc. No. 100-128 (1987) (entered into force July 17, 1988), *available at* 1988 WL 582501 at *3. ("*U.S.-Japan Agreement*"). Second, the transport of the nuclear waste shipments through the Mona Passage means that the ship traverses waters in which the United States has some interests, even if they are not territorial waters.

...

On appeal, Mayaguezanos has refined its argument to a single attack: the federal courts have jurisdiction to consider this action under NEPA and the United States's failure to regulate the passage of such nuclear waste through its Exclusive Economic Zone (EEZ) waters is a "major federal action" within the meaning of NEPA. Mayaguezanos argues that there is a major federal action because the United States is required to play some role in the transport of this waste under various international agreements and customary international law. This complex of interests and responsibilities, they contend, suffices to establish "major federal action" under NEPA. The United States rejoins that the shipment of waste is the "action," it is not being carried out by a federal agency but by private parties, and the facts do not meet the tests to determine if there is federal action where the primary action is carried out by private players.

...

Mayaguezanos's core argument is that the United States granted or was required to grant specific authorization for the shipments of this nuclear waste from France to Japan under the provisions of the U.S.-EURATOM Agreement.

...

Here, the appropriate authority, which was not the United States, made the determination that the waste at issue was "practically irrecoverable," and, as a result, no longer governed by the [U.S.-EURATOM] Agreement. In addition, the International Atomic Energy Agency terminated its safeguards because the reprocessed waste was "practically irrecoverable." As such, the Agreement does not cover such waste materials and so there is no U.S. federal action involved.

...

Mayaguezanos maintains as well that the Pacific Swan's passage through U.S. EEZ waters in the Mona Passage activates NEPA's major federal action requirement. The boundaries of the United States extend, by a 1989 Presidential Proclamation, to twelve nautical miles off-shore, an area called the territorial sea. *See* United States v. Ramirez-Ferrer, 82 F.3d 1131, 133 (1st cir. 1996) (en banc). Since the distance between Mona Island and the island of Puerto Rico is about thirty-nine miles, there are at least fifteen miles of international waters and twenty-four miles of territorial sea in that part of the Mona Passage that runs between the two islands. *See id.* Under customary international law, the United States has sovereignty and jurisdiction over its territorial seas, subject to the right of innocent passage. *See* United States v. Louisiana, 363 U.S. 1, 34, 80 S.Ct. 961, 4 L.Ed.2d 1025 (1960).

In addition to the territorial seas, the United States has an interest in the two-hundred-mile EEZ. *See* 1 Schoenbaum, *Admiralty and Maritime Law* §2-16, at 33–36 (2d ed. 1994). This case concerns the EEZ, as it is undisputed that the Pacific Swan did not enter U.S. territorial waters. The interests of a coastal state in its EEZ largely have to do with development of natural resources and the availability of scientific research. A coastal state has limited powers in the EEZ under customary international law....

Whatever the scope of the United States's potential powers, either multilaterally or unilaterally, over the EEZ, it is clear that the United States has not exercised any such powers with respect to the transport of nuclear waste. Simply stated, the United States has chosen not to regulate shipments of nuclear waste through its EEZ—there is no requirement that it do so, nor is it immediately evident that it would have that authority if it so chose. Under these circumstances, there is no major federal action.

Where this country's multilateral relationships are involved there is a particularly heavy burden on Mayaguezanos to demonstrate a "major federal action" for NEPA purposes, and thus to involve the courts. It has not come close. That is not to say that Mayaguezanos's concerns about the safety of the shipments are frivolous, a matter that we do not judge, only that such concerns should be presented elsewhere.

ARC Ecology v. U. S. Dep't of Air Force

411 F.3d 1092 (9th Cir. 2004)

CALLAHAN, Circuit Judge:

A decade after the United States vacated its occupation of Clark Air Force Base ("Clark") and Subic Naval Base ("Subic") in the Philippines, the plaintiffs-appellants ("the appellants") seek to invoke specialized statutory procedures under the Comprehensive Environmental Response, Compensation, and Liability Act ("CERCLA"), 42 U.S.C. §§9601 *et seq.*, to compel the U.S. government to perform a preliminary assessment and cleanup of the alleged contamination thereon. As citizens and residents of the Philippines, the appellants argue that CERCLA applies extraterritorially to afford them relief. The district court dismissed the appellants' complaint for failure to state a claim. We affirm because CERCLA does not provide for the extraterritorial application sought by the appellants.

. . .

The United States began its operation of Clark and Subic in the early Twentieth Century when it had control of the Philippines. In 1947, after the Philippines attained independence, the United States and the Philippine government entered into an agreement that allowed the United States to continue operating Clark and Subic ("Bases Agreement"). 61 Stat. 4019, T.I.A.S. No. 1775, 1947 U.S.T. LEXIS 393 (1947). The United States maintained the bases until 1992, when it withdrew its military personnel and turned the bases over to the Philippine government.

The appellants are two non-profit environmental organizations and 36 individual Philippine residents "who live and/or travel ... and/or have family members that live and/or travel on or near the Clark and/or Subic properties[.]" The defendants-appellees ("the appellees") are the Department of the Air Force, Department of the Navy, Department of Defense, and the Secretary in his official capacity. In June 2000, the appellants petitioned appellees Air Force and Navy to conduct preliminary assessments at Clark and Subic. The appellees declined, stating that "CERCLA does not apply to … property [ ] located outside the territorial boundaries of the United States" and that "the Philippine government has relinquished any right to demand environmental restoration of the [ ] property by executing a[n] amendment to the [ ] Bases Agreement."

In December 2002, the appellants commenced this CERCLA citizens' suit, alleging that they have been or are likely to be exposed to contamination at Clark and Subic created during the prior American occupation of those facilities. They sought an order compelling the defendants to conduct preliminary assessments at Clark and Subic and a declaratory judgment that CERCLA applies to those bases. The appellees responded by filing a motion to dismiss, contending, *inter alia*, that the complaint failed to state a claim pursuant to Federal Rule of Civil Procedure 12(b)(6). The district court granted the motion to dismiss, concluding that the relevant provisions of CERCLA do not apply extraterritorially.

The court relied on the statutory presumption that "'legislation of Congress, unless a contrary intent appears, is meant to apply only within the territorial jurisdiction of the United *States.*'" *ARC Ecology v. United States Dep't of the Air Force*, 294 F. Supp. 2d 1152, 1157 (N.D. Cal. 2003) (quoting *EEOC v. Arabian Am. Oil Co.*, 499 U.S. 244, 248 (1991) ("*Aramco*")). The appellants timely appealed from the final judgment of dismissal. FED. R. APP. P. 4(a).

… The appellants cannot state a claim under CERCLA due to the statutory presumption against extraterritoriality. The Supreme Court and this court have adhered to the longstanding principle of American law that legislation is presumed to apply only within the territorial jurisdiction of the United States unless the contrary affirmative intention of Congress is clearly expressed. *Aramco*, 499 U.S. at 248 (quoting *Foley Bros. v. Fliardo, 336 U.S. 281, 285 (1949)); Subafilms, Ltd. v. MGM-Pathe Communications Co., 24 F.3d 1088, 1095 (9th* Cir. 1994). Courts must assume that Congress legislates with knowledge of the presumption that a statute "is primarily concerned with domestic conditions." *Aramco*, 499 U.S. at 248 (quotations omitted); *see also Small v. United States*, 125 S. Ct. 1752, 1755 (2005) ("In determining the scope of [a] statutory phrase we find help in the commonsense notion that Congress generally legislates with domestic concerns in mind." (quotation omitted)). In essence, then, courts must resolve restrictively any doubts concerning the extraterritorial application of a statute. *Smith v. United States*, 507 U.S. 197, 204 (1993).

Comments

1. Considerable initial disagreement arose among various federal agencies concerning their obligations to comply with NEPA when taking actions overseas. Based on the Act's uncertain language, the Department of Defense took the position that there was no overseas EIS requirement, thereby limiting the extraterritorial effect of NEPA.[165] The DOD proposed a number of policy reasons for limiting NEPA's extraterritorial effect, including interference with the President's ability to conduct foreign policy by causing delays in overseas projects, creating disruptive litigation, and requiring breaches of confidentiality in gather information.

2. *Gemeinschaft* was later the subject of an appeal and an unusual collateral suit in West Berlin. Following the dismissal of the preliminary injunction in the District of

---

165. *See* 124 CONG. REC. 37773–37803 (daily ed. Oct. 14, 1983) (Office of the General Counsel, Department of Defense, *The Application of the National Environmental Policy Act to Major Federal Actions with Environmental Impacts Outside the United States*).

Columbia, the plaintiffs brought the same suit before a temporary U.S. court in Berlin which was hearing the case of an East German who had hijacked a Polish plane and landed in the U.S. Sector of Berlin. The judge, who was also a federal district court judge in New Jersey, agreed to hear the case notwithstanding the Berlin court's limited jurisdiction and the fact that *Gemeinschaft* was still pending in the District of Columbia. However, the judge did not ultimately rule on the case. Instead, following his decision in the hijacking case, the U.S. Ambassador terminated the judge's employment.[166]

3. In 1979 President Carter issued Executive Order No. 12,114, "Environmental Effects Abroad of Major Federal Actions,"[167] in an effort to resolve this dispute. Under the executive order, an environmental impact statement is required for several actions, including "major Federal actions significantly affecting the environment of the global commons outside the jurisdiction of any nation (e.g., the oceans or Antarctica)." In some circumstances, two other documents may be required: "bilateral or multilateral environmental studies" and "concise reviews of the environmental issues involved." The Executive Order exempts certain actions from these requirements, including intelligence activities and arms transfers, certain actions taken when national security interests are involved, and disaster and emergency relief action. Over the years there has been much scholarly attention to this issue.[168]

4. Although NEPA does not apply abroad, there is uncertainty concerning application of environmental laws in the Exclusive Economic Zone (EEZ). Under the 1992 Law of the Sea Convention, a nation bordering the ocean may establish a territorial sea of up to 12 nautical miles from its shore and exercise full sovereignty. Beyond the territorial sea, a coastal nation may also establish an EEZ of up to 200 miles. The Marine Mammal Protection Act (MMPA) prohibits any person or vessel from taking marine mammals "on the high seas."[169] Similarly, the ESA prohibits a take of endangered species "upon the high seas."[170] The MMPA does not, however, prohibit such taking in foreign territorial waters.[171] Accordingly, it is important to determine whether a foreign EEZ constitutes high seas or territorial waters. In one case, *Natural Resources Defense Council v. U.S. Department of the Navy*,[172] an environmental group challenged the Navy's Littoral Warfare Advanced (LWAD) effort. LWAD is a logistical support function of the Office of Naval Research that provides support services to experimental anti-submarine warfare technologies, including sonar, for at-sea testing. Plaintiffs claimed that LWAD requires programmatic analysis under NEPA and programmatic consultation under the ESA. The court rejected

---

166. *See* United States v. Tiede, 86 F.R.D. 227 (1979) (hijacking case) and Dostal v. Haig, 652 F.2d 173 (D.C. Cir. 1981) (appeal of NEPA decision).

167. Exec. Order No. 12,114, "Environmental Effects Abroad of Major Federal Actions," 44 Fed. Reg. 1957 (1979).

168. *See, e.g., Comment: NEPA's Role in Protecting World Environment*, 131 U. Pa. L. Rev. 353 (1982); Note, *The Extraterritorial Scope of NEPA's Environmental Impact Statement Requirement*, 74 Mich. L. Rev. 349 (1975); Note, *The Extraterritorial Application of NEPA under Executive Order 12,114*, 13 Vand. J. Transnat'l L. 173 (1980); and Harry Almond, *The Extraterritorial Reach of United States Regulatory Authority Over the Environmental Impact of Its Activities*, 44 Alb. L. Rev. 789 (1980). *See also* CEQ Guidance, Memorandum to Heads of Agencies on the Application of the National Environmental Policy Act to proposed federal actions in the United States with transboundary effects (July 1, 1997).

169. 16 U.S.C. § 1372(a)(1).

170. 16 U.S.C. § 1538(a)(1)(C).

171. United States v. Mitchell, 553 F.2d 996 (5th Cir. 1977) (capture of dolphins within three mile limit of Commonwealth of the Bahamas not subject to MMPA).

172. NRDC v. U.S. Dep't of the Navy, 2002 U.S. Dist. LEXIS 26360 (C.D. Cal. Sept. 17, 2002).

both of these arguments, holding that the Navy's test-by-test approach is appropriate. However, in so doing, the court also rejected defendants' argument that NEPA does not apply to sea tests with impacts outside U.S. territory and denied defendants' motion for summary judgment on this issue, adopting the reasoning of the D.C. Circuit's *Massey* decision. The court held: "Because the United States exercises substantial legislative control on the EEZ in the area of the environment stemming from its 'sovereign rights' for the purpose of conserving and managing natural resources, the Court finds that NEPA applies to federal actions which may affect the environment in the EEZ." The court did not directly address the applicability of NEPA to sea tests in foreign EEZs.

5. Although Fifth Amendment "takings" cases are not strictly environmental, the underlying allegations can be based on environmental statutes or regulations. In *El-Shifa Pharmaceutical Industries Co. v. United States*,[173] the Court of Federal Claims addressed the Fifth Amendment takings claim that arose out of the 1998 terrorist attacks that destroyed the American Embassies in Kenya and Tanzania, killing 300 people and injuring 3,000. In response, by presidential order the United States launched Tomahawk cruise missiles against terrorist targets in Afghanistan and Sudan. The Sudan target was a factory associated with the terrorist figure Osama Bin Laden and involved in the production of materials for chemical weapons. The El-Shifa Pharmaceutical Company sued, seeking fifty million dollars for the destruction of their facility. In dismissing the case, the court ruled that the Fifth Amendment "Takings Clause does not extend to claims arising out of military operations against enemy war-making instrumentalities."[174]

6. In *Arc Ecology* the Court also addressed the argument that international law supported the appellants' position. The court disagreed stating, in part, "The appellants offer no authority for the proposition that international law recognizes a current claim for a preliminary assessment or cleanup of Philippine territory based on actions taken over a decade ago. Furthermore, assuming that the United States "injured" the Philippines during its operation of Clark and Subic, compensation presumably was or should have been negotiated between the two nations when the United States turned the bases over to the Philippines. Thus, we do not find that the appellants have presented an actual conflict between domestic and international law."

Climate Change and National Security

Massachusetts v. EPA

549 U.S. 497 (2007)

JUSTICE STEVENS

A well-documented rise in global temperatures has coincided with a significant increase in the concentration of carbon dioxide in the atmosphere. Respected scientists believe the two trends are related. For when carbon dioxide is released into the atmosphere, it acts like the ceiling of a greenhouse, trapping solar energy and retarding the escape of reflected heat. It is therefore a species—the most important species—of a "greenhouse gas."

Calling global warming "the most pressing environmental challenge of our time," a group of States, local governments, and private organizations alleged in a petition for certiorari that the Environmental Protection Agency (EPA) has abdicated its responsibility

---

173. El-Shifa Pharm. Indus. Co. v. United States, 55 Fed. Cl. 751 (2003).
174. *Id.* at 755–56.

under the Clean Air Act to regulate the emissions of four greenhouse gases, including carbon dioxide.

Specifically, petitioners asked us to answer two questions concerning the meaning of §202(a)(1) of the Act: whether EPA has the statutory authority to regulate greenhouse gas emissions from new motor vehicles; and if so, whether its stated reasons for refusing to do so are consistent with the statute.

. . .

The Act defines "air pollutant" to include "any air pollution agent or combination of such agents, including any physical, chemical, biological, radioactive ... substance or matter which is emitted into or otherwise enters the ambient air." §7602(g). "Welfare" is also defined broadly: among other things, it includes "effects on ... weather ... and climate." §7602(h).

. . .

On the merits, the first question is whether §202(a)(1) of the Clean Air Act authorizes EPA to regulate greenhouse gas emissions from new motor vehicles in the event that it forms a "judgment" that such emissions contribute to climate change. We have little trouble concluding that it does. In relevant part, §202(a)(1) provides that EPA "shall by regulation prescribe ... standards applicable to the emission of any air pollutant from any class or classes of new motor vehicles or new motor vehicle engines, which in [the Administrator's] judgment cause, or contribute to, air pollution which may reasonably be anticipated to endanger public health or welfare." 42 U.S.C. §7521(a)(1). Because EPA believes that Congress did not intend it to regulate substances that contribute to climate change, the agency maintains that carbon dioxide is not an "air pollutant" within the meaning of the provision.

The statutory text forecloses EPA's reading. The Clean Air Act's sweeping definition of "air pollutant" includes "*any* air pollution agent or combination of such agents, including *any* physical, chemical ... substance or matter which is emitted into or otherwise enters the ambient air...." §7602(g) (emphasis added). On its face, the definition embraces all airborne compounds of whatever stripe, and underscores that intent through the repeated use of the word "any." Carbon dioxide, methane, nitrous oxide, and hydrofluorocarbons are without a doubt "physical [and] chemical ... substance[s] which [are] emitted into ... the ambient air." The statute is unambiguous.

. . .

In short, EPA has offered no reasoned explanation for its refusal to decide whether greenhouse gases cause or contribute to climate change. Its action was therefore "arbitrary, capricious ... or otherwise not in accordance with law." 42 U.S.C. §7607(d)(9)(A). We need not and do not reach the question whether on remand EPA must make an endangerment finding, or whether policy concerns can inform EPA's actions in the event that it makes such a finding. Cf. Chevron U.S.A. Inc. v. NRDC, 467 U.S. 837, at 843-844, 104 S. Ct. 2778, 81 L. Ed. 2d 694 (1984). We hold only that EPA must ground its reasons for action or inaction in the statute.

The judgment of the Court of Appeals is reversed, and the case is remanded for further proceedings consistent with this opinion. It is so ordered.

Comments

1. *Massachusetts v. EPA* is widely regarded as a landmark case. Although the holding of the case is narrow, the decision triggered a series of events that led to federal regulation

of GHG emissions. After the case was decided, EPA issued an endangerment finding for GHG emissions from new motor vehicles, finding that such emissions "cause, or contribute to, air pollution which may reasonably be anticipated to endanger public health or welfare." EPA then promulgated GHG emissions standards for new motor vehicles and certain stationary sources. Since *Massachusetts v. EPA*, the Supreme Court has decided two other significant cases involving greenhouse gases. In *American Electric Power v. Connecticut*,[175] the Court unanimously reversed the court of appeals and held that states and private parties could not seek judicially-imposed reductions in greenhouse gas emissions against electric utilities under a federal common-law nuisance theory. In *Utility Air Regulatory Group v. EPA*,[176] the Court rejected part of EPA's stationary source rule, while upholding the agency's ability to regulate stationary sources that were already required to get a permit for other reasons.

2. Climate change raises serious national security concerns. In 2012, then Secretary of Defense Leon Panetta stated that "climate change has a dramatic impact on national security: rising sea levels, to severe droughts, to the melting of the polar caps, to more frequent and devastating natural disasters all raise demand for humanitarian assistance and disaster relief."[177]

3. The U.S. Navy has been particularly proactive in developing sources of renewable fuel. As of 2014, the Navy produced twelve percent of its annual energy from renewable sources.[178] Examples of these sources include solar voltaic, wind energy, ocean energy, geothermal energy, renewable thermal energy, and biomass and methane. The Navy also plans to deploy a "Great Green Fleet" carrier strike group, which will be fueled by alternative sources of energy, in 2016. A demonstration of the Great Green Fleet took place during the 2012 Rim of the Pacific exercise.[179]

4. In March 2014, the Department of Defense released its Quadrennial Defense Review,[180] the every four year report articulating the current doctrine of the US military. The opening sentence in Secretary Hagel's introduction notes: "The 2014 Quadrennial Defense Review (QDR) seeks to adapt, reshape and rebalance our military to prepare for the strategic challenges and opportunities we face in the years ahead." This QDR clearly addresses the national security implications of climate change—highlighting the significant degree to which the climate change threat is taken seriously by the U.S. military. The Executive Summary on page VI points to the impact of climate change on both missions and installations:

> The impacts of climate change may increase the frequency, scale, and complexity of future missions, including defense support to civil authorities, while at the same time undermining the capacity of our domestic installations to support training activities. Our actions to increase energy and water security, including

---

175. 131 S. Ct. 2527 (2011).

176. No. 12-1146 (June 23, 2014).

177. U.S. DEPT. OF DEFENSE, Secretary of Defense Speech, Environmental Defense Fund Reception (Energy, Security, and the Environment), as Delivered by Secretary of Defense Leon E. Panetta, Renwick Gallery, Washington D.C., Wednesday, May 2, 2012, *available at* <http://www.defense.gov/speeches/speech.aspx?speechid=1667>.

178. U.S. NAVY, *Energy, Environment and Climate Change: Renewable Energy and Sustainability*, <http://greenfleet.dodlive.mil/energy/shore/renewable/>.

179. U.S. NAVY, *Energy, Environment and Climate Change: Great Green Fleet*, http://greenfleet.dodlive.mil/energy/great-green-fleet/.

180. The 2014 Quadrennial Defense Review (QDR) is mandated by Congress at 10 U.S.C. §11 8(a). The report can be found at <http://www.defense.gov/pubs>.

investments in energy efficiency, new technologies, and renewable energy sources, will increase the resiliency of our installations and help mitigate these effects.

On page 8 of the introduction, under the heading "Global Trends," the document identifies the "threat multiplier" nature of climate change. It states:

Climate change poses another significant challenge for the United States and the world at large. As greenhouse gas emissions increase, sea levels are rising, average global temperatures are increasing, and severe weather patterns are accelerating. These changes, coupled with other global dynamics, including growing, urbanizing, more affluent populations, and substantial economic growth in India, China, Brazil, and other nations, will devastate homes, land, and infrastructure. Climate change may exacerbate water scarcity and lead to sharp increases in food costs. The pressures caused by climate change will influence resource competition while placing additional burdens on economies, societies, and governance institutions around the world. These effects are threat multipliers that will aggravate stressors abroad such as poverty, environmental degradation, political instability, and social tensions—conditions that can enable terrorist activity and other forms of violence.

And finally, in the chapter on "Defense Strategy," beginning on page 25:

Finally, the Department will employ creative ways to address the impact of climate change, which will continue to affect the operating environment and the roles and missions that U.S. Armed Forces undertake. The Department will remain ready to operate in a changing environment amid the challenges of climate change and environmental damage. We have increased our preparedness for the consequences of environmental damage and continue to seek to mitigate these risks while taking advantage of opportunities. The Department's operational readiness hinges on unimpeded access to land, air, and sea training and test space. Consequently, we will complete a comprehensive assessment of all installations to assess the potential impacts of climate change on our missions and operational resiliency, and develop and implement plans to adapt as required.

Climate change also creates both a need and an opportunity for nations to work together, which the Department will seize through a range of initiatives. We are developing new policies, strategies, and plans, including the Department's Arctic Strategy and our work in building humanitarian assistance and disaster response capabilities, both within the Department and with our allies and partners.

Index